TILEY'S
REVENUE LAW

Tiley's
Revenue Law

8th Edition

Glen Loutzenhiser DPHIL
Associate Professor of Tax Law, University of Oxford
and Tutorial Fellow in Law, St Hugh's College, Oxford

·HART·
PUBLISHING
OXFORD AND PORTLAND, OREGON
2016

Hart Publishing
An imprint of Bloomsbury Publishing Plc

Hart Publishing Ltd
Kemp House
Chawley Park
Cumnor Hill
Oxford OX2 9PH
UK

Bloomsbury Publishing Plc
50 Bedford Square
London
WC1B 3DP
UK

www.hartpub.co.uk
www.bloomsbury.com

Published in North America (US and Canada) by
Hart Publishing
c/o International Specialized Book Services
920 NE 58th Avenue, Suite 300
Portland, OR 97213-3786
USA

www.isbs.com

HART PUBLISHING, the Hart/Stag logo, BLOOMSBURY and the
Diana logo are trademarks of Bloomsbury Publishing Plc

First published 2016

© Glen Loutzenhiser 2016

Glen Loutzenhiser has asserted his right under the Copyright, Designs and Patents
Act 1988 to be identified as Author of this work.

British Library Cataloguing-in-Publication Data
A catalogue record for this book is available from the British Library.

ISBN: PB: 978-1-50991-145-5
ePub: 978-1-50991-147-9

Typeset by Compuscript Ltd, Shannon
Printed and bound in Great Britain by TJ International Ltd, Padstow, Cornwall

To find out more about our authors and books visit www.hartpublishing.co.uk. Here you will find extracts,
author information, details of forthcoming events and the option to sign up for our newsletters.

Preface

This eighth edition of *Revenue Law* is the first edition not written by John Tiley CBE, QC (Hon), FBA, LLD. John's death in June 2013 was a tremendous loss to his family, friends, colleagues and former students. He made a major contribution to the study, teaching and practice of tax law, both in the UK and internationally. He was a giant in his field, and a valued mentor and friend to me. He is greatly missed.

I am sure it will come as no surprise to readers that John was immensely proud of *Revenue Law*. Preparing the new editions and supplements was a labour of love for him, and a central fixture of his working life. His boundless energy and unique sense of humour, as well as his deep understanding and passion for tax law, clearly shine through in its pages. I first started working with John on the fourth edition of *Revenue Law* and was very pleased when he asked me to co-author the seventh edition. I've devoted considerable time and effort to updating this new version with the overall aim of keeping as much of the structure, tone and content intact as possible, whilst reflecting current developments and, of course, occasionally, slipping in my own views. It is perhaps of some small comfort that future students, teachers, practitioners and others interested in tax law will be able to benefit from John's insights and wisdom, and get to know something of the man himself, through this book for (hopefully) many years to come.

I am very grateful to my academic colleagues around the UK who responded to the publisher's survey with their ideas for improving this edition and I've taken much of their feedback on board. Most obviously, the two books of the last edition (*Revenue Law* and *Advanced Topics in Revenue Law*) have been merged back into one volume. I am also grateful to have colleagues in Oxford who have kept me up-to-date on developments in their areas of expertise, including John Vella, Anzhela Cédelle (née Yevgenyeva) and Michael Devereux from the Oxford University Centre for Business Taxation, and my Oxford law faculty colleagues Edwin Simpson, Roger Smith, and, of course, Judith Freedman. I must also extend my thanks to my colleagues at St Hugh's College, and in particular Mike Macnair and Joshua Getzler, for allowing me extra time this past year to help launch the new part-time Oxford MSc in Taxation and work on this new edition. I did not use any research assistants on this edition, and so any errors or omissions in the text are mine. I have endeavoured to ensure the law is correct as of June 2016, but I think it goes without saying that a textbook of this nature is not meant to be relied upon as tax advice in anyone's particular circumstances.

My thanks also go out to the team at Hart Publishing, now an imprint of Bloomsbury Publishing plc, and in particular Sinéad Moloney for commissioning the new version, and Tom Adams for seeing it through to publication. I am also grateful to Pinsent Masons LLP for supporting the teaching of tax law in Oxford. The unexpected death of PM partner James Bullock, who died before his time in 2015 and who did so much to support tax teaching and research in Oxford, was another tremendous loss to the tax community. Finally, I am grateful for the love and support of my wife Eleanor, son Toby, and my family back in my native Canada. On the colour for the new edition, John's long-standing tradition was to have his young grandchildren choose it; this version's colour scheme is Toby's suggestion. GL

Contents

List of Abbreviations

AAP	annuity and annual payment
ACE	allowance for corporate equity
ACT	advance corporation tax
AESS 2000	all-employee share scheme
AFR	alternative financial return
AIM	Alternative Investment Market
APSS	approved profit-sharing scheme
AR	applicable rate
ASB	Accounting Standards Board
ASP	alternatively secured pension
BES	business expansion scheme
CAA	Capital Allowances Act
CBA	chargeable business assets
CCCTB	common consolidated corporate tax base
CD	certificate of deposit
CDFI	community development finance institution
CDT	capital disposals tax
CEN	capital export neutrality
CFC	controlled foreign company
CfD	contract for differences
CGT	capital gains tax
CGTA 1979	Capital Gains Taxes Act 1979
CIN	capital import neutrality
CIOT	Chartered Institute of Taxation
CIT	comprehensive income tax
CPM	comparable profits method
CPS	Crown Prosecution Service
CTA	Corporation Tax Act
CTC	child tax credit
CTT	capital transfer tax
CUP	comparable uncontrolled price
DDS	deeply discounted security
DLT	development land tax
DLTA 1976	Development Land Tax Act 1976
DPTC	disabled person's tax credit
DTR	Department for Transport and the Regions
ECHR	European Convention on Human Rights and Fundamental Freedoms 1950
ECJ	European Court of Justice
EEA	European Economic Area
EEIG	European Economic Interest Grouping

EFTA	European Free Trade Association
EIS	enterprise investment scheme
EMI	enterprise management incentive
EMU	European Monetary Union
ER	entrepreneurs' relief
ESC	extra-statutory concession
ESOP	employee share ownership plan
ET	expenditure tax
F(No 2)A	Finance (No 2) Act
FA	Finance Act
FB	Finance Bill
FII	franked investment income
FOREX	foreign exchange
FRS	financial reporting standard
GAAP	generally-accepted accounting practice
GAAR	general anti-avoidance rule
GDP	gross domestic product
GNP	gross national product
GWR	gift with reservation
HMRC	HM Revenue and Customs
IAS	International Accounting Standard
IASB	International Accounting Standards Board
ICAEW	Institute of Chartered Accountants in England and Wales
IFS	Institute for Fiscal Studies
IHT	inheritance tax
IHTA 1984	Inheritance Tax Act 1984
ISA	individual savings account
ITA 2007	Income Tax Act 2007
ITEPA 2003	Income Tax (Earnings and Pensions) Act 2003
ITTOIA 2005	Income Tax (Trading and Other Income) Act 2005
LLP	limited liability partnership
MNI	modified net income
MPS	money purchase scheme
MSC	managed service company
NAFTA	North American Free Trade Agreement
NICs	National Insurance Contributions
NR	non resident
OECD	Organisation for Economic Co-operation and Development
OEIC	open-ended investment company
OTS	Office of Tax Simplification
PA 1989	Pensions Act 1989
PACE 1984	Police and Criminal Evidence Act 1984
PAYE	pay as you earn
PB	principal beneficiary
PCTA 1968	Provisional Collection of Taxes Act 1968
PEP	personal equity plan
PET	potentially exempt transfer
PRP	profit-related pay
PRs	personal representatives
PSC	personal service company

QCB	qualifying corporate bonds
QUEST	qualifying employee share trust
RDS	relevant discounted security
RR	retirement relief
RRA	rate of return allowance
SIS	share incentive scheme
SIT	settlor interested trust
SORP	Statement of Recommended Accounting Practice
SP	Statement of Practice
SSAP	Statement of Standard Accounting Practice
SUB	subsidiary company
TA 1988	Taxes Act 1988
TCA 2002	Tax Credits Act 2002
TCEA 2007	Tribunals, Courts and Enforcement Act 2007
TCGA 1992	Taxation of Capital Gains Act 1992
TEC	Treaty Establishing the European Community
TEU	Treaty on European Union
TFEU	Treaty on the Functioning of the European Union
TIOPA 2010	Taxation (International and Other Provisions) Act 2010
TMA 1970	Taxes Management Act 1970
TSI	transitional serial interest
TSS	terminal salary scheme
UET	universal expenditure tax
UITF	Urgent Issue Task Force
UKP	UK parent company
UnASOS	unapproved share option scheme
USM	Unlisted Securities Market
VAT	value added tax
VATA 1993	Value Added Tax Act 1993
VCT	venture capital trust
VRS	variable rate security
WFTC	working families tax credit
WTC	working tax credit

Table of Cases

PART I

Introduction to UK Tax Law

1

Definitions and Theories

1.1   A Tax

1.1.1 Definitions

A useful place to begin a textbook on taxation is with the meaning of 'tax'.[1] The *Oxford English Dictionary* defines a tax as 'a compulsory contribution to the support of government levied on persons, property, income, commodities, transactions etc, now at a fixed rate mostly proportionate to the amount on which the contribution is levied'. This, when stripped of its limited view as to the purpose of taxation, its irrelevant description of the tax base and its undue stress on proportionate as opposed to progressive taxation, tells us very little, beyond the fact that taxes are compulsory. To this criterion one may add that taxes are imposed under the authority of the legislature levied by a public body and that they are

---

[1] There is much of comparative interest in Peters (ed), *The Concept of Tax*, EATLP International Tax Series, vol 3 (IBFD, 2005). For a useful and concise introduction to taxation generally, including the question of what is a tax, see Smith, *Taxation: A Very Short Introduction* (OUP, 2015).

intended for public purposes.[2] In the UK payments for chancel repairs have been held not to be payable to a public authority and so, by inference, are not taxes.[3]

1.1.2 Charging for Services

These criteria become clearer when distinguishing a tax from a charge for a government service.[4] First, some service must be provided directly to the individual if the payment is to be a charge for a government service.[5] There is a substantial difference between paying a road toll and paying a tax to be used for the defence of one's country. Secondly, the charge must be related to the service given, and not varied according to the person's ability to pay or to some other criterion such as the value of that person's property.[6] Therefore, the Canadian courts have held that provincial probate fees which varied with the size of the estate were taxes; they were intended to raise money for the court administration in general, not just to offset the actual costs of probate.[7] Plans announced in February 2016 to substantially increase probate fees in the UK from a flat fee of £215 to a charge of up to £20,000 on estates worth more than £2 million makes this issue a topical one. Thirdly, it is no objection that a charge may result in a profit, provided only that the profit is a reasonable one.[8] On this basis a steep increase in charges for services provided by the Government, as used to be the case in pre-privatisation days with water rates, energy prices or in Post Office charges, had some of the characteristics of a tax when intended as a fiscal device to restrain domestic consumption.[9] In the Government's own statistics, items treated as taxes include National Insurance Contributions (NICs). In the UK we have the phenomenon of local councils imposing conditions on the grant of planning permission, eg that the developer will provide a swimming pool for the residents. This form of extortion is thought not to be a tax, but it is not really a payment for services either.[10] Whether the Central London congestion charge is a tax or a service charge is the subject of a long-running dispute between Transport for London and some foreign governments.[11] The US Embassy in London takes

---

[2] Major J, in *Re Eurig's Estate* (1998) 165 DLR (4th) 1, 10, citing Duff J in *Lawson v Interior Tree, Fruit and Vegetable Committee of Direction* [1931] SCR 357 (Can). See also Latham CJ in *Matthews v Chicory Marketing Board* (1938) 60 CLR 263, 276 (Vic).

[3] *Aston Cantlow PCC v Wallbank* [2003] UKHL 37; [2003] 3 WLR 283, reversing the CA [2001] EWCA Civ, [2002] STC 313 but saying nothing on the tax point. On the tax aspect, see Morritt V-C [2002] STC 313 at paras 43 and 44. The history of chancel repairs is explained by Lord Scott in para 97 *et seq* in the HL.

[4] *Air Caledonie v Commonwealth* (1988) 165 CLR 462, esp 467: immigration legislation including airport passenger fee for immigration clearance charged on all passengers arriving in Australia on an overseas flight; fee was a tax and so Act invalid.

[5] Duff CJ, in *Re Tax on Foreign Legations and High Comrs' Residence* [1943] SCR 208 (Can). Note the refusal of Lord Cairns to use the presumption of a strict interpretation of tax law when considering tolls: *Pryce v Monmouthshire Canal and Rly Companies* [1879] 4 App Cas 197, 202.

[6] Montgomery J in *Société Centrale D'Hypothèques v Cité de Quebec* [1961] QLR 661; see also water rates and *Daymond v South West Water Authority* [1976] AC 609; [1976] 1 All ER 39.

[7] *Re Eurig's Estate* (1998) 165 DLR (4th) 1, 11; see Bowman (1998) 46 *Canadian Tax J* 1278.

[8] Minister of Justice in *Dominion of Canada v Levis City* [1919] AC 505 (PC).

[9] See Sabine, *British Budgets in Peace and War* (Allen & Unwin, 1970) 163, and Carter (chair), Canada Royal Commission on Taxation, *Study No. 24* (Queen's Printer, 1966) 1–10.

[10] It is an 'exaction'; for a general discussion from the US perspective, see *Law and Contemporary Problems*, vol 50.

[11] Considered in Bowler Smith and Ostik, 'Towards a classification of the Central London congestion charge as a tax' [2011] BTR 487. The authors argue it is a tax because it is effectively compulsory for diplomats and disproportionate to the service (if any) provided them.

the position that the congestion charge is a tax and refuses to pay it on the basis of the 1960 Vienna Convention on Diplomatic Relations, which prohibits the direct taxation of diplomatic missions. Transport for London, on the other hand, views it as a service charge, which is outside the scope of the Convention.

1.1.3 Other Issues

A number of more subtle points have arisen in Australia:

(1)   The fact that raising money is not the Government's primary purpose in imposing a levy does not prevent it from being a tax.[12]

(2)   The element that the collection be compulsory was held to be satisfied where the state compulsorily acquired an asset (flour) and then allowed the former owner to reacquire it at a higher price, requiring him to store it at his own risk in the meantime.[13] The difference between the two prices was held to be an excise tax even though there was no legal obligation, as opposed to commercial necessity, to buy back the flour.

(3)   An arbitrary exaction is not a tax; it must be possible to point to the criteria by reference to which the liability to pay the tax is imposed, and to show that the way in which the criteria are applied does not involve the imposition of a liability in an arbitrary or capricious manner.[14] The Australian High Court upheld a provision under which tax was to apply unless the Commissioner was 'of the opinion that it was unreasonable that the section should apply'.[15] In this vein some judges have also stated that compulsory acquisition by the Government cannot be a tax.[16] In the UK it has been held that a tax which operates entirely arbitrarily breaches the right in Article 1 of the First Protocol to the Human Rights Convention.[17]

(4)   The requirement that the money should be paid to the Government was called into question when a levy was imposed on blank recording tapes, with the levy to be paid to a body set up by the music industry to compensate artistes. This was held to be a tax even though it was not levied by a public authority; what mattered was that there was a compulsory acquisition of money under statutory powers which was not a payment for services.[18]

---

[12]   *Northern Suburbs Cemetery Reserve Trust v Commonwealth* (1993) 24 ATR 1, 7 (primary purpose to encourage employers to provide training); see also *Osborne v Commonwealth* (1911) 12 CLR 321; and the discussion in Zines, *The High Court and the Constitution*, 4th edn (Butterworths, 1997) 29–31.

[13]   *A-G (NSW) v Homebush Flour Mills Ltd* (1937) 56 CLR 390.

[14]   *DFC of T v Brown* (1958) 100 CLR 32, 40; discussed in *MacCormick v FCT* (1984) 15 ATR 437; 'bottom-of-the-harbour' scheme legislation imposing liability on shareholders who had ceased to hold shares in the company held not to be arbitrary.

[15]   *Giris Pty Lt v FCT* [1969] 1 ATR 3; however the reasoning is confused—Zines, *op cit*, 159.

[16]   *MacCormick v FCT* (1984) 158 CLR 622, 640.

[17]   Per Morritt V-C in *Aston Cantlow PCC v Wallbank* [2001] EWCA Civ; [2002] STC 313, para 45; decision reversed on different grounds.

[18]   *Australian Tape Manufacturers Association v Commonwealth* (1993) 176 CLR 480 (Copyright Act including levy on blank tapes with proceeds paid to copyright owners whose works might be copied; Act held invalid as the levy was a tax).

1.1.4 European Union Law

At the time of writing the status of the UK in the EU is up-in-the-air following the result of the June 2016 referendum in which a slim majority of the public voted in favour of the UK leaving the EU. The implications of Brexit for UK tax law are discussed further in chapter seventy-seven, but for now at least the EU remains a Member State of the EU. Article 30 of the Treaty on the Functioning of the European Union (TFEU) (ex Art 25 TEC) directs Member States to refrain from introducing between themselves any new customs duties on imports or exports, or any charges having equivalent effect. In applying this provision the Court of Justice of the European Union (CJEU) looks at the effect of the tax and not its purpose. It struck down an Italian tax on the export of art treasures, so getting around the Italian Government's argument that the purpose of the levy was to keep national art treasures within Italy.[19] It also held that a country could not invoke what is now Article 36 TFEU (ex Art 30 TEC) to justify a tax; Article 36 could only be used to justify non-fiscal barriers falling within Article 34 TFEU (ex Art 28 TEC).[20]

Article 30 TFEU does not apply to charges for services. The CJEU, like the Canadian courts before it, has insisted that for a charge to escape Article 30 TFEU on this basis, the trader must receive a separate identifiable benefit in return for the sum paid and that the sum must be proportionate to the benefit. As such, a charge levied at a frontier as part of a general system of quality control has been struck down.[21] A fee for an inspection where the inspection is mandatory under EU law may be justified and so escape Article 30 TFEU.

1.1.5 Social Security Contributions

Provided these could be regarded simply as compulsory insurance payments, they may be considered as the price of a benefit purchased directly but compulsorily from the state, although the compulsory element might have turned such payments into taxes. However, now that such payments in the UK are graduated in a way which does not relate directly to the graduation in benefit, they ought to be treated as taxes.[22] This is particularly true when the payer has earned enough to be entitled to maximum benefits and so can derive no benefit from the exactions which still have to be paid,[23] or, conversely, is entitled to a benefit without having to contribute.[24] Despite this, many in the UK cling lovingly (but misguidedly) to the principle that social security levies are a contribution towards funding state pensions and the National Health Service not a tax.

---

[19] Case 7/68 *Commission v Italy* [1968] ECR 423; [1969] CMLR 1.

[20] See discussion by Weatherill and Beaumont, *EU Law*, 3rd edn (Penguin, 1999) ch 13.

[21] Case 63/74 W *Cadsky SpA v Instituto nazionale per il Commercio Estero* [1975] ECR 281; see also Case 170/88 *Ford Espana SA v Spain* [1989] ECR 2305, esp on proportionality. A different conclusion was reached where the inspection was merely authorised by Union law.

[22] See, eg, Mirrlees *et al* (eds), *Tax by Design: The Mirrlees Review* (OUP, 2011) 126–32. *Metal Industries (Salvage) Ltd v S T Harle (Owners)* [1962] SLT 114 held employer's contribution to be taxes.

[23] For example, continuing to pay NICs on earnings above the upper earnings limit.

[24] See Johnson and Stears (1996) 17(1) *Fiscal Studies* 105, discussing the basic state retirement pension.

1.1.6 Fines

A more subtle problem is the difference between a fine and a tax, particularly when government motives on such matters as cigarette smoking are, to say the least, ambiguous.[25] At first sight it might appear that there is no difference between a fixed rate of fine and a tax, but the power of the court to vary the normal fine and to enjoin against continued breach[26] marks off the breach of the criminal law from the carrying on of a taxable activity. Fines or penalties imposed to regulate an activity are more complex; penalties imposed to encourage prompt compliance with filing or other requirements are really more in the nature of late filing charges or interest charges than fines.[27] The distinction matters because traders may not deduct fines in computing their taxable profits,[28] but may be able to deduct taxes. The status of property seized by the state is not explored in the case law,[29] although it has been suggested that the effect of the statutes such as the Proceeds of Crimes Act 2002 is to treat forfeiture as a fine in specie.[30]

1.2 Objectives and Functions of Tax

Much of the material which follows is economic in formulation. However, this is because there has been too little participation by UK legal scholars in the debates. The tax system expresses many political and social values; critics and defenders of those values will therefore have much to say about aspects of current and proposed tax rules, just as they have about any other aspects of legal rules. One can find much of interest in the contributions from critical legal theory and from feminist jurisprudence.[31]

1.2.1 Raising Revenue

The classical function of the tax system is to raise revenue to meet government expenditure. As an alternative to taxation, the Government might commandeer resources or print money, or even borrow it, but taxation is either more efficient or more just than any of

---

[25] For sustained denunciation of such taxes, see the essays collected in Shughart (ed), *Taxing Choice* (The Independent Institute, 1997). For a comparison of regulatory fines and taxation as ways of encouraging behaviour, see Ogus (1998) 61 *MLR* 767. See also Poddar, *Taxation to 2000 and Beyond*, Canadian Tax Foundation Paper No 93, ch 3. *The Economist*, 27 July 1996, 19–21, cites Hopkins of Rochester Institute of Technology (US); and see R Hahn, (ed), *Risks Costs and Lives Saved* (OUP, 1996); Viscusi of Duke University is quoted as reporting a cost–benefit analysis showing that a regulation saved 13 lives at a cost of $4m a piece.

[26] *A-G v Harris* [1961] 1 QB 74; [1960] 3 All ER 207; but see also Menzies J in *Fairfax v FCT* (1965) 114 CLR 1, 17.

[27] US Senate Report No 92–437, 92 Cong 1st Sess 74 (1971).

[28] *McKnight v Sheppard* [1999] STC 669.

[29] See Boudreaux and Pritchard in Shughart, *op cit*, ch 15.

[30] See Mumford and Aldridge [2002] BTR 458 at 467.

[31] A valuable starting point is the sceptical article by Zelanak (1998) 76 *North Carolina L Rev* 1521, and the footnote-laden responses at 1581–88. For a brief introduction to feminist issues and a valuable bibliography, see Young in Krever (ed), *Tax Conversations* (Kluwer, 1997) 261. See also (1999) *Sydney L Rev* 487; Mumford, *Tax Policy, Women and the Law* (CUP, 2010); and Phillips *et al* (eds), *Challenging Gender Inequality in Tax Policy Making: Comparative Perspectives* (Hart Publishing, 2011).

these.[32] The government expenditure that requires to be met is either the provision of services which the free market cannot provide, such as defence, law and order and parks, or the provision of services which the state feels are better provided by itself, such as health services and education—often called public goods.[33] Views as to which services should be provided by the state have changed over the years—as privatisation shows. Whether, in practice, taxes were raised to meet expenditure, or vice versa, was a question which caused great worries in the 1970s.[34] As Levi shows in her classic study,[35] while rulers maximise revenue to the state, they cannot do just as they please; they are subject to the constraints of relative bargaining power *vis à vis* constituents, their transaction costs and discount rates. These constraints determine the choice of revenue system.

1.2.2 Redistribution

In the past, great emphasis was placed on the objective of redistribution of wealth. This had two quite distinct forms. The first was the doctrine that taxation should be based on ability to pay; it could also be based on the idea that the tax system should correct the outcome of pure market forces. The second form presupposed that the existing distribution[36] was unjust and concluded that this should therefore be undone. This second principle sees confiscation as a legitimate objective of taxation. These views were very influential from 1945 until the election of Mrs Thatcher in 1979.

From 1979 to 1997 wealth became socially acceptable, and it was seen that productive wealth, providing, for example, increased employment, was positively desirable. During this period the poor were helped by welfare payments rather than by the tax system. Important changes to the structure helping the poor were made but were general in nature—lowering the rate of tax, including NICs, and raising the tax threshold.

The Blair Government elected in 1997 kept to this creed, but having committed itself not to raise the basic or higher rates of income tax, it used the language of fairness rather than redistribution. There are various forms of redistribution; for example, any change in the tax burden is redistribution. The 1999 working families' tax credit cost £5bn, the same as the amount raised by the abolition in 1997 of pension funds' right to the repayment of a dividend tax credit—few saw this as a redistribution from tomorrow's pensioners to today's working families.[37] Methods of redistribution through the tax system include not only increasing the rate of tax but also abolishing allowances or reducing their value—perhaps to be replaced by tax credits. One can also look to the tax transfer system, whereby progressive taxes on income are used to fund subsidies to low-income households and

---

[32] Carter (chair), Canadian Royal Commission on Taxation, *Report, Vol 2* (Queen's Printer, 1966), 2–7.

[33] On user charges as alternatives for certain goods, see Bird in Krever (ed), *op cit*, 513–46.

[34] See Diamond, *Public Expenditure in Practice* (Allen & Unwin, 1975) 66; cited by Morgan, *Over Taxation by Inflation* (IEA, 1977) 59.

[35] Levi, *Of Rule and Revenue* (University of California Press, 1988); in addition to Levi's own examples, see those from 1688 to 1783 in Brewer, *The Sinews of Power* (Unwin, 1989).

[36] For a Labour view on the present distribution while in opposition, see *Social Justice: A Report of the Commission on Social Justice* (1994); but see also the critique by The Adam Smith Institute. In the 1970s the Royal Commission on Distribution of Income and Wealth published much data. For figures, see Mirrlees Review, *op cit*, ch 2 (income) and ch 15 (wealth).

[37] Perhaps because some of the money was used to finance an immediate cut in the corporation tax rate.

the use of progressive taxes to fund public services which particularly benefit the poor, eg public housing. One might also consider, subject to the realities of the EU's VAT system,[38] adjusting indirect taxes so that taxes on goods purchased largely by high-income consumers are combined with subsidies to other services which are used chiefly by low-income consumers.[39]

1.2.3 Management of the Economy

The role of tax changes in altering the level of demand is now accepted, although mechanisms such as credit control and the raising of welfare payments are other useful devices in stabilising the economy.[40] Governments let their borrowings rise as economies slow down, provided this reflects the cyclical effects of automatic stabilisers, lower tax revenue and higher unemployment pay, and not a sudden rush into long-term commitments for extra spending or reduced tax rates. Since the late 20th century, greater emphasis has been placed on monetary measures such as interest rates and exchange rates,[41] though interest rates have been stuck at historic lows in the UK and elsewhere in recent years, leaving less room for monetary policy. If the UK were to join the Economic and Monetary Union (EMU) of the EU, it would lose its right to set interest and exchange rates; one might then expect fiscal policy to become more prominent (unless that were also pooled). The possible effects of joining the EMU were examined by the Treasury in an important study published in 2003;[42] recent economic troubles in Continental Europe, not to mention the June 2016 referendum in favour of Brexit, will be seen by some as evidence that the UK decision to remain outside the EMU was a good one. It has also been suggested that tax can play a role in curbing financial volatility, with variants of the so-called Tobin tax being floated by the European Commission and others as a form of 'international solidarity levy'.[43]

1.2.4 Affecting Behaviour

The tax system is more than a matter of economics. It may be used for specific purposes, such as discouraging the use of alcohol, cigarettes or sugary drinks, and so impact on individual forms of pleasure. Where subsidies are provided, short-term ones may be more effective than long-term.[44] The UK predilection for tea rather than coffee, which lasted for many generations, was the result of a price difference driven by fiscal policy.[45] The tax system can

---

[38] See *R v Customs and Excise Commrs, ex parte Lunn Poly Ltd* [1998] STC 649.

[39] Musgrave and Musgrave, *Public Finance in Theory and Practice* (McGraw-Hill, 1989) 11.

[40] On use of tax to cope with financial volatility, see Haq Kaul and Grunberg (eds), *The Tobin Tax Essays* (OUP, 1996).

[41] See Sandford, *Public Finance*, 4th edn (Pergamon, 1992) ch 12. Other useful sources include Dell, *The Chancellors* (HarperCollins, 1997) and Davies, *A History of Money* (University of Wales Press, 1996) esp ch 8.

[42] *Fiscal Stabilisation and EMU* available on line from https://www.gov.uk/government/organisations/hm-treasury.

[43] See Haq Kaul and Grunberg (eds), *op cit*. On revival, see the European Commission's 2011 proposal for a financial transaction tax [COM(2011) 594 final], and analysis in Vella, Fuest and Schmidt-Eisenlohr [2011] BTR 607 and Englisch, Vella and Yevgenyeva [2013] BTR 223.

[44] Goldberg (1994) 49 *Tax L Rev* 305; see also Ogus, *op cit*.

[45] Niall Ferguson, *Empire* (Penguin Books, 2004) 16.

also affect much more important issues, such as how to deal with climate change and global warming.[46]

1.2.5 The Power of Tax

It is misleading to regard taxes simply as a means of obtaining revenue. Tax is the most pervasive and privileged exercise of the police power of the state. It determines the directions in which people may become wealthy by determining the directions in which they may not.[47] By using its taxing power, a government may make some people rich and other people poor without falling foul of charges of corruption or favouritism, unless, of course, their reliefs are targeted too narrowly. With the Proceeds of Crimes Act 2002 the UK added the extraction of the proceeds of crime to its list of goals to be achieved through the tax system.[48]

1.3   Criteria Used in Tax Design[49]

1.3.1 Adam Smith's Canons of Taxation and the Meade Committee List

According to the Meade Committee Report (1978),[50] a good tax structure must take into account many factors: the effects on economic incentives; its fairness as between persons of similar taxable capacity; its effects upon distribution between rich and poor; whether it is compatible with desirable international economic relations; and its simplicity, ease of understanding and absence of excessive administration costs. This list is of great importance since it shows how matters have developed since Adam Smith listed his famous 'Canons of Taxation', 200 years ago in *The Wealth of Nations*,[51] ie that tax should be charged in proportion to ability, that it should be certain not arbitrary, that it should be charged at a time which was most convenient to the taxpayer and that the costs of collection should be as low as possible. The Meade Committee list, with its emphasis on matters of efficiency and international relations, reflects the influence of what economists know as the optimal theory of taxation.[52] An altogether different approach uses benefit theory; tax should be

[46] For a good starting point see Duff, [2003] *Canadian Tax J* 2063–118.
[47] Groves (1948) 1 *National Tax J* 23; on tax system as legal maid-of-all-work, see Fuller, *Morality of Law*, revised edn (Yale University Press, 1969) 166.
[48] See Mumford and Aldridge [2002] BTR 458.
[49] For tax design itself, see Michielse and Thuronyi (eds), *Tax Design Issues Worldwide* (Kluwer Law, 2015), and Thuronyi *et al, Tax Law Design and Drafting* (IMF, 1996) vol 1 and (1997) vol 2. On the balance between ad valorem and specific taxation, an issue in indirect design, see Keen (1998) 19 *Fiscal Studies* 1.
[50] Meade, *The Structure and Reform of Direct Taxation* (Allen & Unwin, 1978), 20. The Mirrlees Review's economic approach to tax design—with its emphasis on the 'rules of thumb' of neutrality, simplicity and stability—is explained in Mirrlees Review, *op cit*, ch 2. For a briefer but useful discussion see Smith, *Taxation: A Very Short Introduction, op cit*, ch 6.
[51] (OUP, 1976) Book 5, ch 2, 825–28; for some necessary correctives, see Lynn (1976) 29 *National Tax J* 369.
[52] Among other books, see Atkinson and Stiglitz, *Lectures on Public Economics* (McGraw-Hill, 1980); Prest and Barr, *Public Finance*, 7th edn (Weidenfeld, 1985); Sandford, *Public Finance*, 4th edn (Pergamon, 1992); Shoup, *Public Finance* (Weidenfeld and Nicolson, 1969); Musgrave and Musgrave, *op cit*; Rosen, *Public Finance*, 5th edn (McGraw-Hill, 1999); and Stiglitz, *Economics of the Public Sector*, 2nd edn (Norton, 1988).

charged and payers pay because they receive benefits from the state. This is an old and generally unfashionable approach and is not considered further here.[53]

Whichever list is chosen, some way must be found of overcoming the conflict between these different criteria. The extent and nature of that conflict depend upon to which school of economic thought one belongs—reconciliation is more difficult for older views of economics than for the optimal tax theory. A third school of economic thought, public choice theory, must also be examined. We first consider the criteria in the light of the older approach which has dominated both Royal Commissions and so much government thinking and rhetoric. See further §1.4 below.

1.3.2 Equity[54]

Equity is traditionally divided into two types: horizontal equity, which means that those in equal circumstances should pay an equal amount of tax; and vertical equity, which means that those in unequal circumstances should pay different amounts of tax. The reason why equity is regarded as important is partly the moral view that it is right and proper, in the same way that equality before the law is right and proper, and partly a pragmatic view that if a system is believed to be fair and equal, taxpayers will be more willing to co-operate with it. However, the statement that equity is important does nothing to help one determine which circumstances are equal and which are unequal.[55] Thus, does equity demand that allowance be made for regional differences with regard to amenities and living costs?[56] Equity may be satisfied by a proportional system of taxation, just as much as by a progressive system of taxation. In assessing how equitable a system is, attention must be paid to the whole range of taxes and benefits. Setting the top rate of income tax to 40% in 1988 recognised that equity does not demand confiscation. It is evident that tax systems can affect the level of inequality in a society. A novel and interesting question, which has been investigated by American scholars, is whether different types of inequality lead to different types of tax systems.[57] Equity issues may also arise between countries and between generations.[58]

1.3.3 Neutrality[59]

This became the most important canon in the 1980s. A tax is neutral if it avoids distortions of the market. A selective tax, such as the now defunct motor vehicle tax, is not neutral, since it encourages consumers to spend their money on another item rather than on a car.

---

[53] For a good account, see Cooper, (1994) 11 *Australian Tax Forum* 397.

[54] On tax fairness, see Murphy and Nagel, *The Myth of Ownership* (OUP, 2002) and Murphy, *The Joy of Tax: How a Fair Tax System Can Create a Better Society* (Bantam Press, 2015).

[55] 'Vertical equity means graduated or disproportional taxation... and the moment you abandon... the cardinal principle of exacting from all individuals the same proportion of their income or their property, you are at sea without rudder or compass, and there is no amount of injustice or folly you may not commit': McCulloch, *A Treatise on the Principles and Practical Influence of Taxation and the Funding System* (Adam and Charles Black, 1863) 145.

[56] See Knoll and Griffith 'Taxing Sunny Days' (2003) 116 *Harvard L Rev* 987–1025.

[57] Sokoloff and Zolt (University of California, Los Angeles).

[58] See Robinson (1998) 19 *Fiscal Studies* 447.

[59] Groves (1948) 1 *National Tax J* 18; and Bracewell Milnes [1976] BTR 110.

A tax such as insurance premium duty or airport passenger duty may, however, be seen as neutral because it strives to impose a duty on something which is outside the value added tax (VAT) net and so reduces the disparity. Other areas where neutrality is much invoked are the taxation of a company as compared with that of a partnership, and the taxation of profits earned within, compared with those earned outside, the UK.

The UK tax system has many rules which break the principle of neutrality. Worse, there are many technical rules which make significant tax differences according to which of two or more methods is adopted to achieve a given result. The effect is harmful since it encourages the expenditure of money on expert tax advice (expenditure which is, in economic terms, unproductive) and on schemes which may make a trade less efficient. The assimilation of tax rates, both in the corporate and personal sectors, so far as they apply to income and capital gains, was a major advance in the direction of neutrality. The New Labour administration abandoned this assimilation of rates and reopened this area for tax planning. This state of affairs remains unchanged under the present Conservative government.

Of course, a system may consciously choose to distort the market. Thus, the oft-mooted tax on those who drive their cars into city centres is an attempt to keep many such users off the road, so clearing the way for improved public transport—and less congestion. The principle of neutrality simply asserts that all distortions should be conscious and so subject to justification through the political process.

1.3.4 Certainty

Certainty means first that the scope of the tax should be clear. Penumbral areas cause resentment among taxpayers cast into the darkness and undermine the principle of equity, besides increasing the cost of the system. The canon of certainty entails both that the tax can be enforced and that enforcement will actually occur. A tax that is easily evaded causes resentment and often a decline in taxpayer morality. Certainty means also that the Treasury will be able correctly to predict how much tax is gathered in[60] and, perhaps, the effects of the tax.

1.3.5 Administrative Efficiency

Only those who regard the duty of the tax system as being to confiscate wealth in order to provide employment would be happy with a tax the administration costs of which exceeded the tax yield. Capital gains tax (CGT) is a prime example of a situation where, because of the grant of exemptions, the yield from the tax may decline while the costs of collection as a percentage of the tax collected may increase sharply. In 2014–15 the cost yield ratio for income tax was 0.83%; NICs 0.27%; and corporation tax, 0.71%.[61] The cost to the Revenue in pence per pound paid came to 1.42p for personal tax credits and 0.51p for child benefit.[62]

---

[60] However, see Nigel Lawson on the risks of 'seduction by apparently precise fine tuning' in his memoirs, Lawson, *The View from No 11* (Bantam Press, 1992) 376.

[61] HMRC Annual Report and Accounts 2014–15 (HC 18), 25. These percentages tend to rise when economic activity is slack and fall when it picks up.

[62] *Ibid.*

In line with other departments HMRC has had to make efficiency savings. They claim to have done so and reject any suggestions that service standards have slipped.[63]

These figures take no account of compliance costs, which comprise: money costs, such as fees paid to legal advisers; time costs, such as time spent on preparing tax returns; and psychological costs, such as the stress and anxiety often caused by incomprehension of tax returns and obligations. Surveys have shown that even by ignoring the psychological elements, the costs of compliance were several times the administrative costs.[64] These costs are large, they are particularly inequitable in their incidence and they create resentment. Reduction of such costs should therefore be, and continue to be, an object of tax policy. UK compliance costs have tended to be lower than the average for OECD countries. This is partly because of the absence (until 1997) of a self-assessment system, and partly because of the presence of what is believed to be an efficient PAYE system. However, a 1999 UK study showed that for 1995–96 compliance costs came to £1bn, with smaller businesses the hardest hit since they were unable to enjoy economies of scale or cash-flow advantages of deducting sums from employees' pay before paying the Government; a 2010 study for the Mirrlees Review arrived at a similar conclusion.[65] Where these conditions do not apply, for example in relation to CGT, compliance costs can be very high. Of course, statistics can prove anything—if one employs an accountant to prove to the Revenue that no CGT is due, should one be glad to have a nil tax liability, or cross because one has had to pay to establish it?

1.3.6 Symmetry

Although this is not an economic criterion, it was much in demand in the 1980s and 1990s. In essence, symmetry demands that when a transaction is entered into by two taxpayers, the tax treatment of the two should, in certain circumstances, be symmetrical. An absence of symmetry may create opportunities for arbitrage. Symmetry is not a natural state of affairs. If A sells an asset to B there may be many tax factors governing A which are quite irrelevant to B. Thus, the transaction may be on capital account by A and on revenue account by B; A may have to pay tax on the proceeds in one year and B be entitled to a deduction in another; or the UK tax system may govern A, but a foreign tax system may govern B. Symmetry has been a feature of recent tax reform in quite distinct ways. There have been efforts to stop A and B from exploiting differences of timing where they are closely related, while leaving the situation as it is for unrelated taxpayers. Equally, for example in the corporation tax rules for loan relationships in the Corporation Tax Act (CTA) 2009, Parts 5–7, there have been efforts to ensure the same treatment for A and B regardless of whether they are

---

[63] *Ibid*, 18–23.

[64] The principal UK scholar here is the late Cedric Sandford. For an introduction, see *More Key Issues in Tax Reform* (Fiscal Publications, 1995) ch 6; Sandford (ed), *Tax Compliance Costs Measurement and Policy* (Fiscal Publications, 1995); and Sandford, Godwin and Hardwick, *Administrative and Compliance Costs of Taxation* (Fiscal Publications, 1989). See also Evans, Pope and Hassledine, *Tax Compliance Cost, a Festschrift for Cedric Sandford* (Prospect Publications, 2001). On particular difficulties, eg those experienced by widows and divorced women, see James, Lewis and Allison, *The Comprehensibility of Taxation* (Avebury, 1987).

[65] Collar and Godwin, (1999) 20 *Fiscal Studies* 423 and Shaw, Slemrod and Whiting, 'Administration and Compliance' in Mirrlees *et al* (eds), *Dimensions of Tax Design: The Mirrlees Review* (OUP, 2010) 1100 *et seq*.

related; in that area, therefore, the legislation has got rid of the distinction between capital and income and differences of timing.

1.4   Three Schools of Economic Thought

When the first edition of this book was written, the prevailing school was the 'equity' school. Since then, two other views—the optimal theory of tax and public choice theory—have joined equity in the foreground of the debate over tax policy. The views are well summarised by Hettich and Winer in a 1985 article on which the following text draws heavily.[66] They conclude that a new synthesis is needed since the three schools clash sharply.

1.4.1 The Comprehensive Income or Equity School

The comprehensive income tax is most associated with Simons[67] and Haig; its objective was to create an equitable tax system to be achieved by having a comprehensive tax base as best representing a person's ability to pay (see below at §1.6.1). Normally this is achieved by an income tax, but it might also be achieved by an expenditure tax or a mixture of the two. Simons considered that other taxes should be abolished, except property tax and petrol tax. This approach naturally gave rise to much debate on the ideal tax base. It rejects special provisions or 'preferences'. It is the approach most favoured by law students because it is relatively easy to understand. It was worked out most fully by the Canadian Royal Commission in 1966. Its theoretical strength—the single idea of equity—is also its weakness, however. A single idea could not accommodate ideas such as economic efficiency as part of its base. Strong on horizontal equity, it can, of itself, provide no structure for vertical equity.

1.4.2 The Optimal Taxation School[68]

Whereas Haig-Simons' scholars want a tax base which is broad, optimal tax theorists want a base which is inelastic;[69] they favour utilitarianism over equity.[70] This school goes back to sacrifice theory and stresses that all taxpayers should suffer an equal sacrifice, while also saying that the least sacrifice should be occasioned to the whole. Sacrifice may also be explained in terms of loss of utility or loss of social welfare as a whole. Stripped of this intimidating terminology the doctrine is simply utilitarian in nature. Tax designers must take account of the effects of the tax rules so as to achieve the best trade-off between the

---

[66] Hettich and Winer (1985) 38 *National Tax J* 423–45.

[67] Simons, *Personal Income Taxation* (University of Chicago Press, 1938).

[68] Mirrlees, *Tax by Design, op cit*, 35–39. For a tough introduction, see Heady (1993) 14 *Fiscal Studies* 15; see also Durlauf and Blume (eds), *The New Palgrave Dictionary of Economics* 2nd edn (Palgrave Macmillan, 2008). The seminal article is Ramsey (1927) 37 *Economic Journal* 47. For examples of optimal tax theory, see Cooper (1994) *Federal Tax L Rev* 414, and Zolt (1996) 16 *Virginia Tax Rev* 39.

[69] Head, in Head and Krever (eds) *Tax Units and the Tax Rate Scale* (Australian Tax Research Foundation, 1996), 210.

[70] Kaplow (1995) 48 *National Tax J* 497.

inevitable costs of the tax and the goals of equity; this is done by looking for and at the effects of changes on the welfare of households. This means that one must be able to model the effects of tax. Tax A will be better than tax B if it produces the same amount of revenue for the Government but involves less loss of satisfaction to the taxpayer.

As an example of this approach one may look at the deduction of expenses. The equity school looks on these as matters which are deductible because they are part of the costs of earning income; the optimal theory looks at the consequences, both distributional and economic, invites one to decide which consequences one wants and then shapes the tax system accordingly.[71] Since governments rarely seem to do anything optimally, these findings have not been fully exploited by them; they have been much better exploited by insurance companies.[72] The theory has no formal counterpart to the Canadian 1966 Royal Commission (see §1.4.1), but Hettich and Winer point out that the Meade Committee Report in 1978 placed great emphasis on the role of economic efficiency; the Committee also stated that it is an important guide for tax design rather than a practical basis for tax reform. It is optimal taxation, understandably, that guided the work of the Mirrlees Review.

Optimal taxation differs from equity in several ways. Perhaps most significantly, it does not claim universality but simply to be a useful way of looking at things. It provides a basis on which the degree of vertical equity in the tax may be determined; that basis is the trade-off. It is also open to persuasion on the question whether the marginal tax rate should rise progressively, accepting, for example, that there might be much to be said for having low marginal rates of tax at the bottom and top of the income scale. It also has no problem with the idea of many taxes rather than one—as long as each is optimal. Optimal tax is a highly sophisticated approach which depends on the quality of the information it gets on what people do.

While equity taxation tends to disregard such matters as the imputed income arising from household services (when considering family taxation), or leisure as an alternative to income (usually on the ground that these are immeasurable), optimal taxation regards these as important. Optimal tax accepts that it may not be possible to tax such items, since they are hard to quantify, but insists that they be taken into account as part of the assessment of the efficiency of the tax.[73]

The point is well made by Apps in language typical of this school:[74]

> Modern public finance theory recognizes that information asymmetries constrain the government to taxing indicators of what it would like to tax. Observed money income is such an indicator and gives rise to complications because among other things, it omits the value of non-market time. Ideally the government would like to impose lump sum taxes of varying amounts on given characteristics of individuals, such as endowments and tastes, that determine their opportunity sets and levels of well being, but these cannot be observed. The consequent constraint on the choice of tax base gives rise to two important problems (i) horizontal and vertical inequities due to 'errors'; the indicators are not perfectly correlated with the opportunities and well being of the individual and (ii) efficiency losses due to incentive effects; the indicators are usually under the control of the individual and so taxing them is distortion.

---

[71] Griffith (1994) 41 *UCLA L Rev* 1769; discussed by Edgar, in Krever (ed), *Tax Conversations* (Kluwer, 1997).
[72] *The Economist*, 12 October 1996, 120, celebrating the award of the Nobel Prize for Economics to Vickrey and Mirrlees.
[73] For example, Apps, in Head and Krever, *op cit*, ch 3; and Jones and Savage, *op cit*, ch 4.
[74] Apps, *ibid*, 83.

1.4.3 Public Choice Theory

This school, associated with the names of Brennan and Buchanan,[75] rejects the assumption made by other schools that government is inherently benevolent. Its insight is that while everyone accepts that those in business act in their own interest rather than the public good, the same is also true of government officials, who will be concerned to provide advice which appeals to their superiors and so enhances their chances of promotion.[76] Government is capable of malevolence, or at least is at risk of being taken over by malevolent interest groups. Public affairs should be analysed on the basis that the voter is the consumer and the officials are the company. A top official cannot always know what every junior official does—hence the unbreakable coffee pot.[77] Moreover, a bureaucracy can be a budget max-imiser.[78] It follows that taxpayers need constitutional protection against taxation. Ideally, taxes should be imposed (and designed) by a special convention of taxpayers. If taxes to be imposed by existing political institutions, they should operate behind a Rawlsian 'veil of ignorance'.[79] Naturally, such an approach, with its emphasis on the acceptability of the process rather than the result, tells us relatively little about the ideal tax structure; loopholes are acceptable if the process is acceptable.

Whereas the Haig-Simons school wants a base which is broad and optimal theorists want one which is inelastic, public choice theorists compromise by wanting a base which is nar-rower than that of the first group and more elastic than that of the second; the object is always to reduce revenue potential and to control the size of the public sector.

1.4.4 Partial Tax Reform

While these ideas may be used as the basis of complete redesign of a tax system, as in the Canadian Royal Commission of 1966 (see §1.4.1), they are also of importance as arguments used in the course of partial tax reform.[80] Four lessons must be learned, however. First, any fundamental reform of the tax law over a brief period will generate windfall gains and losses on a wide scale, and in a capricious and inequitable pattern.[81] Secondly, the period of transition may be difficult politically; undoing a piece of economic folly can be difficult.[82] Thirdly, as a survey of the voter reaction to the Canadian goods and services tax shows,

---

[75] *The Power to Tax* (CUP, 1980); see also Brennan, in Krever (ed), *op cit*, 87–106; Buchanan (1976) 6 *Journal of Public Economics* 17; and Brennan and Buchanan (1977) 8 *Journal of Public Economics* 255. See also Symposium (1998) 51 *National Tax J* 359. Among critics, see Shaviro (1990) 139 *University of Pennsylvania L Rev* 1, esp 64. For a good textbook based on public choice theory, see Hillman, *Public Finance and Public Policy* (CUP, 2003).

[76] See Tullock, *The New Palgrave Dictionary of Economics* (Macmillan, 1987) vol 3, 1040.

[77] The US Department of Defense is supposed to have designed a coffee pot which was so strong that it would not break up in a crash that would kill all the crew members and destroy the plane itself.

[78] On the famous Proposition 13 designed to curb budget maximisers in California, see Conference Supple-ment to (1979) *National Tax J*.

[79] Rawls, *A Theory of Justice* (OUP, 1972). For a starting point, see Solomon and Murphy (eds), *What is Justice?* (OUP, 1990) Pt 2.

[80] On partial tax reform, see Feldstein [1976] 6 *Journal of Public Economics* 71; on reform more generally, see Sandford, (ed), *Successful Tax Reform* (Fiscal Publications, 1993).

[81] See Vickrey (1968) *University of Florida L Rev* 437, reprinted in (1996) *Public Economics* 171, 179.

[82] *Ibid*. Vickrey chooses the classical system of corporate taxation and points to the high nominal rates of tax during a transition to an integration model.

'political parties would do well to avoid a detailed programme of tax reform as a platform to contest elections. Voter misconceptions and ignorance combined with scare tactics from other parties, can be a recipe for disaster'.[83] The fourth lesson comes from the Meade Committee Report in 1978, which not only stressed the problem of transition but also underlined the point that tax systems have to operate in an international world; one's own dreams may be impractical if not implemented by trading partners.[84]

1.5 Classification of Taxes[85]

1.5.1 Proportional, Progressive and Regressive

A proportional or neutral tax is one which takes a constant proportion of income; a progressive tax takes an increasing proportion as income rises;[86] a regressive tax takes a declining proportion of income as income rises. A progressive tax system may be more or less steep; the UK income tax system has become much less steep since 1979, developing into the two-rate structure (25% and 40%) introduced in 1988. Despite some adventures in between, 2008 saw a return to simplicity, with 20% and 40% for non-savings income and a pattern of 10%, 20% and 40% for savings income. This was short-lived, with the introduction of third 45% top rate and a clawback of personal allowances further muddying the rate schedule.

The case for a progressive tax system rests on vertical equity and, perhaps more basically, on assumptions about the obligation of citizens to the community in which they live, assumptions which give rise to issues much wider than mere economic analysis. Feminist theory suggests that women may be more supportive of redistribution than men.[87] If state expenditure is to be financed, it is thought proper that those with the most should contribute the most, ie that they should pay not just more (which would be the case under a proportional tax) but 'more more'. At one time this was explained in terms of benefit, ie that those with the most got the most benefit from the protection of their wealth which the state afforded;[88] but this reasoning was plainly insufficient once the state entered the field of social security. Modern optimal explanation tends to be in terms of sacrifice theory, or of marginal or discretionary income,[89] the point here being that the provision of the essentials

---

[83] Wallschutsky and Lewis, *More Key Issues in Tax Reform* (Fiscal Publications, 1995) ch 10; see also Steinmo in Sandford (ed), *op cit*, ch 11.

[84] Meade Report, *op cit*, ch 21.

[85] On fluidity of terminology, see Hicks (1946) 56(221) *Economic J* 38.

[86] If there is a flat rate of tax but an initial exemption or threshold, there will, as income above that threshold rises, be a constant rate of tax but a higher average tax rate. This is a mutation of progressive tax, sometimes called a degressive tax.

[87] See Kornhauser (1987) 86 *Michigan L Rev* 465. See also Kornhauser (1997) 76 *North Carolina L Rev* 1609–28 and Kornhauser (1997) 47 *American University L Rev* 151, maintaining her view by criticising certain empirical research.

[88] See Blum and Kalven, *The Uneasy Case for Progressive Taxation* (University of Chicago Press, 1953); and Galvin and Bittker, *Income Tax: How Progressive Should It Be?* (American Enterprise Institute for Public Policy Research, 1969).

[89] See Fagan (1938) 46 *J Pol & Econ* 457; and Carter (chair), Canadian Royal Commission on Taxation, *Report*, *Vol 2* (Queen's Printer, 1966).

of life takes a certain amount of income, and that above this level individuals have discretion over how they will spend it. It is more legitimate to tax the discretionary income than the essential income. Economic advantages are also claimed in that a progressive tax system diminishes oscillations in the trade cycle (by taking money out of the economy as incomes rise) and assists demand management (by shifting money into the hands of those liable to spend it). Today's arguments also come from 'personal well being'.[90]

The argument against a progressive tax turns largely on incentives. It is thought that high rates of tax discourage that spirit of enterprise which ought to be a mainspring of human activity. A high marginal tax rate, on one view, should encourage individuals to work even harder to achieve an increase in net income—the 'income effect'—or to take more leisure instead of working—the 'substitution effect'.[91] Surveys provide little cogent support for either view. A study by Brown and Sandford on the effect of the 1988 income tax rate changes on 300 accountants concluded that there was a negligible effect on work effort and enterprise, and no discernible effect on emigration or immigration and no increase in revenue.[92] This is in line with earlier experience which suggested that at rates of 40% or less, income tax has a slight incentive effect, and at 70%, a net disincentive effect.[93] The same survey, however, suggested one possible and, if so, very significant benefit—the rates may have reduced tax avoidance and improved the quality of investment. A variant of these views suggests that if the rich are taxed less they will invest more, so generating wealth for others—the so-called 'trickle-down effect'. JK Galbraith is supposed to have described this theory as being that if the horse is fed enough oats, some will pass through to the road for the sparrows.[94]

The problem of progression must also be examined in the light of deductions. A high marginal rate of tax may provide an incentive to spend more money on an item of deductible expense, eg to decide to fly across the Atlantic by first class rather than economy class. If I have a marginal rate of 80%, then 80% of the fare is paid by the government. If I choose to fly first class because I will be paying only 20% of the fare, the tax system encourages inefficiency. Another factor against progressive taxation is that it can lead to a separation of political power from financial responsibility; this view also lays behind the replacement of domestic rates with the community charge, or poll tax as it came to be known.[95] A further problem is that while there may be little elasticity about working for a wage, there may be a much greater elasticity when one comes to the effect of taxes on capital.[96]

[90] See valuable articles in [2004] *Boston College Law Review*, especially Grifiths at 1363; see also comment by Kornhauser (2005) 106 *Tax Notes* 1069.

[91] Break [1957] BTR 101; Working Group on Migration Cmnd 3417 (1967); and Taxation and Incentives (IFS, 1976). See also Carter (chair), Canadian Royal Commission on Taxation, *Study No. 4* (Queen's Printer, 1966); and Chatterjee and Robinson (1969) 17 *Canadian Tax J* 211–20. Bracewell-Milnes has pointed out that a comparison of a real with a hypothetical situation is something which cannot be done empirically, but he also points out that incentives are none the less real for being empirically immeasurable: *Is Capital Taxation Fair?* (Institute of Directors, 1974) 9.

[92] Brown and Sandford [1991] BTR 414; also in *Key Issues in Tax Reform* (Fiscal Publications, 1993) ch 9.

[93] See Sandford, *Economics of Public Finance* (Butterworth-Heinemann, 1992) 158–60.

[94] Cited by Molloy (1994) *National Business Rev* (New Zealand).

[95] On the story of this tax, see Butler, Adonis and Travers, *Failure in British Government: The Politics of the Poll Tax* (OUP, 1994). On Scottish experience, see Scobbir, Reid and Barker [1990] BTR 343.

[96] McLure (1980) 33 *National Tax J* 311; and Boskin (1978) 86 *Journal of Political Economy* S3.

These various points must, however, be judged from the general viewpoint and not merely from that of income tax. First, if proportional taxation is accepted as preferable to regressive taxation then some taxes, of which income tax is a prime example, must be made progressive in order to offset the regressive effects of other taxes—always assuming that social security benefits are not sufficient to offset these taxes.[97] The Mirrlees Review emphasised the importance of considering the progressivity of the tax system *as a whole*—making the system as a whole progressive does not require every individual tax to be progressive.[98] Secondly, society must decide how much of its social expenditure is to be financed out of taxes and how much by direct payment, for example the provision of retirement benefits and education; if these are to be financed by direct payment, the case for a progressive tax becomes stronger, since the level at which income becomes discretionary is raised. Thirdly, a tax system with a tax base which fails to catch many types of income must, given a certain sum of government expenditure, have a higher rate than one which catches all. Lastly, it by no means follows that a progressive tax need be a penal tax.

1.5.2 Direct and Indirect Taxes[99]

This distinction is not important for UK tax law, but is for some Commonwealth and European countries with federal structures. According to Mill:[100]

> A direct tax is one which is demanded from the very persons who, it is intended or desired, should pay it. Indirect taxes are those which are demanded from one person in the expectation and intention that he shall indemnify himself at the expense of the other: such as the excise or customs. The producer or importer of a commodity is called upon to pay a tax on it, not with the intention to levy a peculiar contribution upon him, but to tax through him the consumers of the commodity, from whom it is supposed that he will recover the amount by means of an advance in price.

On this definition certain taxes on expenditure, eg motor vehicle licence duty, are direct taxes. The distinction has become less clear as the real incidence of taxation has been explored by economists. Thus, economic research suggests that the taxation of profits of companies in an open economy may result in the shifting of that tax, in the long term, to the employees of the company.[101] Such a tax has, however, been classified as direct because courts, such as the Privy Council on appeals from Canada, have paid attention to that part of Mill's formulation which emphasised the intention and expectation that the tax would be shifted. There is thus a fundamental distinction between the economic recoupment of a direct tax and the simple passing on (often in the form of a straight percentage of the price) which is the hallmark of an indirect tax, ie between the recovery of a direct tax by a more-or-less circuitous operation of economic forces and the passing on of a tax in recognisable form. In applying this distinction the courts will treat a tax as direct notwithstanding that actual payment may be enforced against some intermediary, so that income tax

---

[97] The argument is disputed by Bracewell-Milnes [1974] BTR 378.
[98] Mirrlees Review, *Tax by Design, op cit*, 26.
[99] Hicks [1946] *Economic J* 38.
[100] Principles of Political Economy, Book V, ch 3.
[101] See eg Arulampalam, Devereux and Maffini, (2009) 'The direct incidence of corporate income tax on wages', Oxford University Centre for Business Taxation Working Paper CBTWP09/17.

on employment income is not less direct because the employer must deduct tax. Canadian provincial probate fees were held to be direct taxes because although the personal representatives were liable for the tax, they were liable only in their representative capacity and not liable personally. The tax was thus a direct tax on the estate, not an indirect tax levied on the personal representatives.[102]

In Canada direct taxes may be levied by the federal or provincial governments; indirect taxes are imposed by the Federal Government alone. The courts have classified as direct taxes not only such taxes as income tax and capital duty,[103] but also a tax on department store catalogues distributed without charge.[104] On the other hand, they have classified as indirect taxes not only such obvious items as customs and excise duties and sales tax, but also stamp duty,[105] a succession duty which could be collected from someone other than the beneficiary (eg, a personal representative)[106] and gross revenue taxes.[107] Every tax must be judged on its own. By rejecting—inevitably—the test of economic incidence which would mean that almost every tax was at risk of being classified as indirect,[108] the courts have been forced back on to a test of whether or not the general tendency of a tax can be passed on, and this must lead to borderline cases. This has, in turn, led to the use of direct taxes only marginally different from indirect taxes, for example the use of consumer taxes rather than excise taxes and of succession duty rather than estate duty. Combining tax reductions with pay restraint—as attempted in the UK the mid-1970s[109]—threatened to turn employment income tax into a charge on the employer as a form of grossing-up the net wage.

The balance between direct and indirect taxation has long been a problem in the UK, owing to the contrasting philosophies of different governments which, believing that direct taxation was progressive and indirect taxation regressive,[110] acted accordingly. In 1979 Geoffrey Howe reduced the rate of income tax, paying for it by increasing VAT. Despite the contemporary uproar, he was merely restoring the balance to what it had been earlier—a point he himself never made. The divide between the two types of tax is not absolute. Indirect taxes may affect the cost of living and so be taken into account when fixing tax threshold and social security levels. A state may, when introducing a sales or value added tax, also introduce credits against income taxes for the amount of the new tax—with refunds made to those who did not pay income taxes.[111]

Indirect taxes are also of interest for the light they shed on social attitudes. It has been observed that it is generally a feature of the civilised world that the most unacceptable vices are punished by imprisonment; or worse, the somewhat less serious vices are punished

---

[102] *Re Eurig's Estate* (1998) 165 DLR (4th) 1, 12–13.

[103] *Bank of Toronto v Lambe* (1887) 12 App Cas 575; Lord Greene in *A-G for British Columbia v Esquimault and Nanaimo Rly Co* [1950] AC 87, 113. La Forest, *Allocation of Taxing Power under the Canadian Constitution*, 2nd edn (Canadian Tax Foundation, 1981) ch 4.

[104] *Minister of Finance of New Brunswick v Simpson Sears Ltd* (1982) 130 DLR (3rd) 385.

[105] *A-G for Quebec v Reed* (1884) 10 App Cas 141.

[106] *Cotton v R* [1914] AC 176; distinguishing *R v Lovitt* [1912] AC 212.

[107] *R v Caledonian Colleries Ltd* [1928] AC 358.

[108] La Forest, *op cit*, 74.

[109] See Healey, *The Time of My Life* (Penguin, 1990) 397.

[110] Eg, Snowden, cited in Mallet and George, *British Budgets 1913–1921* (Macmillan, 1933) 10: 'These taxes violate every canon of taxation, because they tax a man not in proportion to his ability to pay nor according to those benefits he receives but according to his personal tastes.'

[111] Pechman, IFS Lecture (1973), 8.

by fines and the most venial by heavy taxes. It is impossible to dismiss the idea that an Erewhon-like reversal of attitudes might take place, so that, for example, sales of tobacco and alcohol will render the vendor liable to imprisonment, whilst excise will be imposed on soft drugs and the use of brothels—as well as income tax on the proceeds of both.[112]

1.6 Tax Base and Income: Theory

The UK tax system contains a series of separate but sometimes overlapping direct taxes. Of these, traditionally the most important has been income tax.[113] Such a tax has many advantages. The evidence suggests that, at least in the absence of very high rates, it has a smaller disincentive effect than other taxes, that it is the most effective tax in redistributing income, that it serves as a strong, built-in stabiliser by collecting more money as incomes rise, and that through it the Government can influence the savings ratio and so the growth rate.[114] There are two principal theoretical models for direct taxation. The first is the comprehensive income tax (CIT) or net accretion principle; the second is the expenditure tax (ET).

1.6.1 Comprehensive Income Tax: Haig-Simons

Under this principle income is:[115]

> [T]he algebraic sum of (1) the market value of rights exercised in consumption and (2) the change in the value of the store of property rights between the beginning and end of the period in question. In other words, it is merely the result obtained by adding consumption during the period to 'wealth' at the end of the period and then subtracting 'wealth' at the beginning.

For those frightened by the word 'algebraic', the concept means simply that income is the net sum of consumption and saving.[116] On this definition income would include not merely income as conventionally defined but also all capital gains[117] and even gifts, inheritances and lottery winnings. Moreover, because assets would be valued at the end of each year, all increases in wealth would be brought in—whether or not realised. The principle would apply equally to losses.

---

[112] Messere, IFS Lecture Series No 2 (1974) 18. Note also Menzies J in *Fairfax v FCT* (1965) 114 CLR 1, 17, suggesting that a special prohibitive tax on income derived from the sale of heroin may not be a law 'with respect to taxation' but rather a law made for the suppression of the trade by imposing penalties described as tax for participation in it.

[113] For a survey of different views of income, see Wüller (1938) 53 *Political Science Quarterly* 83, 557, and (1939) 54 *Political Science Quarterly* 555. See also Holmes, *Concept of Income* (IBFD, 2000).

[114] Due and Friedlander, *Government Finance*, 251; Jay [1957] BTR 16.

[115] Simons, *Personal Income Taxation* (University of Chicago Press, 1938) 50. The Canadian Royal Commission in 1966, *op cit*, famously attempted to build a system on this principle: see esp *Report Vol 3*, 22–25, 39–53, 461–531, and resulting literature, esp Bittker 80 *HL Rev* 925, 81 *HL Rev* 1032; Musgrove 81 *HL Rev* 44; Pechman 81 *HL Rev* 63; Galvin 81 *HL Rev* 1016. For reflections after 20 years, see Sandford [1987] BTR 148; Brooks *et al, The Quest for Tax Reform* (Carswell, 1988); and *Osgoode Hall LJ*, vol 26 (1988).

[116] Bradford, *Untangling the Income Tax* (Harvard University Press, 1986) 17.

[117] Simons, *op cit*, 81 was not worried that tax might be deferred until realisation but his followers were: Surrey, *Pathways to Tax Reform*, (Harvard University Press, 1973) 120.

1.6.2 The Imputed Income Problem

Few ideas cause law students from common law countries more difficulty than this: grasping the idea gives a view of life akin to that gained by Alice going down the rabbit hole. Imputed income arises where 'an individual who owns productive assets, or who supplies production services, uses them directly to produce goods or services that he consumes himself'.[118] For example, if farmer Alf supplies himself with his own produce, he is, in effect, bartering his time and the use of his capital for the food he eats. Although he does not turn his goods or services into cash income, he should be taxed on the value of the profits from the goods or services he receives. Few would doubt that if Alf exchanges his produce with produce from farmer Ben, each has income—even though it is received in kind. Self-sufficiency and exchange should, in economic theory, be treated alike.[119] Under present UK law the exchange situation is clearly taxable (if not often reported) and self-sufficiency may give rise to income tax if it comes within *Sharkey v Wernher* (see below at §23.5.1).

Students have even more difficulty with the next example—the imputed rent that arises from owner occupation of property. Yet in 1989 this basis of taxation was used in 12 of the 23 OECD countries;[120] it had been in force in the UK as the original Schedule A until 1963[121] and was the basis of the rating system of local taxation until 1989.[122] The rating system was replaced by the community charge, to be replaced, in turn, by the council tax.[123] There is much to be said for a property tax as a proxy for imputed income.[124] Under the old Schedule A, occupiers of property were charged on the annual value of the property, in theory the amount of rent that could be charged. If they were the owners, this value was added to their income from other sources to compute total income. If they were not the owners but paid rent to someone else, they were entitled, when paying that rent, to deduct income tax and set that off against their own liability.[125]

The theory of this charge to tax was upheld by the Royal Commission in 1955[126] on grounds of equity. Suppose Alf and Beryl each have a capital sum. Alf invests the money in income-producing assets and has to pay rent for his living accommodation; Beryl buys a house. Alf will pay income tax on investment income but is not allowed to deduct the rent paid; Beryl will pay no tax since she receives no taxable benefit under current UK law. This is inequitable; their taxable capacities are the same, but their tax liabilities differ.

---

[118] Carter (chair), Canadian Royal Commission on Taxation, *Report, Vol 3* (Queen's Printer, 1966), 47. For discussion of the theory, see Marsh (1943) 58 *Political Science Quarterly* 514–36; Goode (1960) 15 *J Finance* 504; and Merz (1977) 30 *National Tax J* No 4.

[119] For discussion, see (1988) 43 *Tax L Rev* 447. However, see Goode, *The Individual Income Tax* (Brookings, 1976) 150–51, arguing that the performance of these services competes with leisure, which is another form of consumption which escapes tax, so that imputed income should not be taxed.

[120] Messere, *Tax Policy in OECD Countries* (IBFD, 1993) 281, Table 10.13; for an earlier survey, see Merz (1977) 30 *National Tax J* 435–38. For distributional consequences of alternative solutions in the UK, see Callan (1992) 13(1) *Fiscal Studies* 58. On taxation of housing, see below §32.3.5.

[121] Eg, ITA 1952, ss 82–116, repealed by FA 1993, s 14.

[122] See Local Government Finance, Cmnd 6543 (1976), 169–71.

[123] For review of the community charge, see Butler, Adonis and Travers, *Failure in British Government: The Politics of the Poll Tax* (OUP, 1994). On Scottish experience, see, Scobbir, Reid and Barker [1990] BTR 343.

[124] See Bradley [1996] BTR 168.

[125] Royal Commission Final Report, Cmnd 9474 (1955), §§811–15.

[126] *Ibid*, §§824–35; see also Schreibe (1978) 31 *National Tax J* 10.

This argument has often proved misleading for lawyers. First, equity may equally be satisfied by proving that rent should be deductible in computing income rather than that the owner-occupier should be taxed on the value of the notional benefit. However, few would wish to see such an erosion of the tax base, and the problems of housing finance are far too deep to be treated in such a way.[127] Secondly, using the rent forgone as the measure of liability suggests that the basis of liability is income forgone, eg, that a person would be taxed who deliberately chooses to invest in shares with a lower than average return. However, this is to misunderstand the doctrine—the owner-occupier is being taxed on a benefit received, not one forgone.

A critic of imputed income may also try to kill it off by pointing to its potential application. The classic 19th-century example concerned the drastic tax changes which occurred when a man married his housekeeper, so that she no longer received a taxable salary for her services. Further, if the tax system decides to tax those who, for example, grow their own vegetables as a hobby, it must then decide whether to allow them to deduct the costs incurred in that and, perhaps, other, less-productive hobbies. Most tax systems reject any idea that personal expenditure should be deductible. The housekeeper problem can be put in a form more acceptable to some 21st-century readers in the form of the proposal that housework should be regarded as taxable income; this might be accompanied by a refundable tax credit for low-income individuals.[128]

The UK system of taxing owner-occupiers fell into disrepute and complexity because of the difficulty of carrying out the five-yearly valuation and the many restrictions on housing after the Second World War. There was also constant pressure for deductions for repairs in computing taxable income, which came close to making the tax voluntary; today, an insistence that such deductions would be allowed only against a valid receipt bearing the relevant VAT registration would have interesting effects on the black economy. Further, when the overdue valuation was carried out it was realised that this would lead to a sudden jump in tax liabilities, and so be deflationary. The ultimate decision to abolish the charge rested just as much on a political desire to help owner-occupiers and others, as on any doctrinal view.

1.6.3 *Expenditure Tax*

Dissatisfaction with the comprehensive income tax base (CIT) has led to the periodic revival of interest in a direct tax based on expenditure (ET), such as by the Meade Committee Report published in 1978.[129] Similar schemes have been put forward in Australia,[130] Ireland, Sweden[131] and the United States.[132] It is fair to say that in the UK the idea took much

---

[127] For a model of how to write a book on housing finance, see Hills, *Unravelling Housing Finance* (OUP, 1992).
[128] Staudt (1996) 84 *Georgetown L Rev* 1571–647.
[129] See also Kaldor, *An Expenditure Tax* (Allen & Unwin, 1955).
[130] Parsons, (1986) 3 *Australian Tax Forum* 233.
[131] First Report of the Commission on Taxation Dublin (July 1982) and Lodin, *Progressive Expenditure Tax: An Alternative* (LiberFörlag, 1978).
[132] For more modern pleas for a consumption tax, see Goldberg, *The Death of the Income Tax* (OUP, 2013) and Graetz, (2002) 112 *Yale LJ* 261–99. There is useful survey by Toder, in Krever, (ed), *Tax Conversations, op cit*, p 159; US Treasury Blueprints for Basic Tax Reform, 1st edn (1979), 2nd edn (1984); see also Bradford, *op cit*; Andrews 87 *HL Rev* 1113; Warren 88 *HL Rev* 947; Andrews 88 *HL Rev* 981; and Pechman, (ed), *What Should be Taxed* (Brookings Institution, 1980). For criticism, see Gunn (1979) 46 *University of Chicago L Rev* 370; and Musgrave in Thirsk and Whalley (eds), *Tax Policy Options in the 1980s*, Canadian Tax Paper no. 66 (Canadian Tax Foundation, 1982), 20.

of it strength from the very high rate structure then prevalent and the effect of those rates on the costs of capital to business. The reduction in rates has reduced—but not removed—these objections, enabling one to see things more calmly.

   Although this idea has gone underground in recent years, it is still very much alive, and will be due for resurrection as economies develop an increasing thirst for investment and so seek ways of encouraging savings. This idea is distinct from the familiar indirect taxes on expenditure such as VAT; it would apply progressive rates of tax to a taxpayer's total expenditure over the year. The UK has a number of tax rules designed to encourage saving, such as the rules governing pensions and individual savings accounts (ISAs), and the introduction of the tax-free Personal Savings Allowance in 2016. One interesting side-effect has been that because people are encouraged to save, they often end up with a larger estate when they die. The tax rules are designed to give relief from income tax and/or CGT—not IHT. So the Chancellor may end up taking three times as much in IHT as he gives away in the other taxes—but later.

1.6.3.1 An Ideal ET

In its purest form, an ideal tax would start with something close to a CIT by requiring a composite return of a person's receipts during the year. From this would be deducted sums spent on saving, and to the resulting figure would be added sums spent from capital on consumption-dissaving. There would thus be two key differences from the present tax base: it would not tax income saved but would tax capital dissaved. The chances of such a tax being achieved in its purest form are as remote as achieving a pure CIT.

1.6.3.2 Half-way Houses

Some of the objectives of an ET could be achieved in less pure forms by:

(1)   not taxing income from saving—as has been the trend in the UK with ever-increasing ISA limits, combined with the Dividend Allowance and the Personal Savings Allowance—or, as the Mirrlees Review recommended, exempting the 'normal' return to savings;[133]
(2)   giving remission from tax on sums spent on savings during the year; or
(3)   replacing basic rate income tax with a VAT and then having a pure ET for higher-rate taxpayers—the extra sums gathered by the VAT presumably being used to increase welfare payments for those below the present tax threshold.

Of these, (1) does not tax dissaving from capital, (2) does so only erratically and (3) would preserve the present divide between basic and higher-rate taxpayers and between proportionate and progressive taxes, and has become more difficult to apply in light of the new income tax rate structure and the increase in VAT rates from 8% in 1978 to 20% today.

---

[133] Mirrlees Review, *Tax by Design, op cit*, ch 14. This would be accomplished by making interest on ordinary bank and building society accounts free from tax, and by providing a 'rate-of-return allowance' (RRA) for substantial holdings of risky assets such as equities, which can provide higher returns. For simplicity, the Review recommended retaining tax-free treatment of the returns from smaller holdings of equities and mutual funds, as with the present equity ISAs (*ibid* at 488).

1.6.3.3 Arguments for ET

The first argument for an ET is that while, like a CIT, it claims to be based on ability to pay, ET also claims to be based on a moral principle that one should be taxed on what one takes out of the common pool of production. The disadvantage of this, apart from doubts over the notion of a common pool, is that it completely ignores contributions made to society otherwise than through saving. Moreover, Keynesian economics suggests that there can be a moral virtue in spending on consumption when the economy is slack.

Secondly, some arguments are based on those things which an ET tries to do but which a CIT does not: in particular, that an ET will encourage saving by providing a higher rate of return than would be the case under a CIT. This arises because in calculating the total return one would take account of the fact that one puts into the investment an amount which has not been taxed. To this there are a number of counter arguments. If there is a constant total demand for saving within the economy, the effect may be a fall in interest rates, so that the true net yield will be as before. Moreover, what would be the effect of the tax on dissaving? Would it diminish the incentive to save? Further, while the tax seems to encourage a person who can save—for example an entrepreneur building up his business—it says nothing about a person who inherits wealth. There may be a distinction between the two in that the latter may be subject to a heavy capital accessions tax; yet will not such a tax also have a strong effect on the initial incentive to save? Lastly, is it really desirable to allow the accumulation of wealth through saving without limit? In other words, would an ET be a miser's charter?[134]

Thirdly, a negative argument is that an ET will avoid some of the complexities of the conventional income tax. In 1978 the list of rules to be abolished was:

(1)   the distinction between income receipts and capital receipts;
(2)   close company apportionment rules;
(3)   special rules for trusts;
(4)   averaging rules; and
(5)   inflation relief for capital gains.

Of these, (1) is also aimed at by a CIT and appears unattainable, although various anti-avoidance rules have helped; (2) has been achieved, though a good argument could be made that as corporate tax rates continue to fall something like these rules may be necessary to prevent the use of a company as a money box; (3) may be conceded, but (4) and (5) are more controversial. Point (4) has been made less acute by the reductions in rates. As to (5), one should note that while a CIT may accept the desirability of indexing capital gains which an ET does not, ET does this only at the price of taxing all such gains whether or not due to inflation; the only question for an ET is whether the proceeds are spent or saved. Indexation relief for capital gains was introduced in 1982 and still survives for corporation tax.

Fourthly, problems arose from the distortions of the capital market, which distortions would not arise under an ET since all investment would be tax free. Distortions arose because different tax rates meant different tax returns for different individuals; moreover,

---

[134] See O'Kelley (1981) 16 *Georgia L Rev* 1.

these distortions were compounded by the fact that some assets received capital allowances while others did not. There was therefore a substantial lack of fiscal neutrality in the capital market, which was illustrated dramatically by the Meade Committee. Added irrationality arose from the different systems of taxation applied to incorporated and unincorporated businesses, and by the different treatment accorded as a business uses loan capital or equity capital, and whether a company retains or distributes its profits. After 1978 some of the distortions were reduced—particularly by the 1984 changes to capital allowances and the 1987 and 1988 assimilation of capital gains and income tax rates (since abandoned except for corporation tax). If distortions persist, those changes still show an alternative way of dealing with them—remove the incentives to invest and reduce general tax rates, ie a full-blown CIT combined with a flat-rate tax.

1.6.3.4 Problems with a Pure ET[135]

Most problems were raised in 1978; the intervening years have not solved them. First, some old problems will remain, for example how one determines the income to be adjusted for saving and dissaving, and what the distinction is between a business expense incurred in producing income (and so deductible) and a (chargeable) consumption expense. Secondly, there are problems common to both a CIT and an ET, such as the selection of the appropriate tax unit. Thirdly, there is the central problem of defining expenditure, particularly problems of loans, gifts, housing and education, the last being tied up with the appropriate treatment of human capital.[136] Again, what of contributions to charities? A good argument can be made that consumption should be confined to divisible private goods and services, consumption of which by one household precludes enjoyment by others; it follows that this would not cover collective goods the enjoyment of which is not preclusive. Whether to accept this and, if so, where to draw the line, are matters of policy and judgement choice rather than logical demonstration.[137]

Some problems may be resolved by having a scheme of registered assets (saving) and unregistered assets (consumption). This enables taxpayers to invest their money in order to be taxed immediately or subsequently. However, this solution is questionable; acute problems of theory underlying a tax based on both moral and economic principles should not be resolved by taxpayer choice based on treasury *fiat*. Further, such a scheme causes problems. First, it presupposes a nation of avid readers who will know, at the end of each tax year, just what their expenditure is to date, and who will therefore spend the last Sunday of the tax year arranging purchases of registered or unregistered assets to determine their final tax liabilities to their best advantage. Secondly, an ET bears harshly on a person who faces a heavy and unexpected item of expense, unless he has had the foresight to build up a stock of unregistered assets which can be realised without tax liability and the good fortune to ensure that their value has not been ravaged by inflation. Thirdly, the scheme may impact

---

[135] This section draws heavily on the principal response to the Meade Report: Prest [1978] BTR 176. For a defence, see Kay (1980) 1(3) *Fiscal Studies* 47. On criticism of proposals for taxation of capital, see Bracewell-Milnes [1979] BTR 25, 42 (Kay), 43. On use of direct consumption taxes in developing countries, see Zodrow and McClure (1990) 46 *Tax L Rev* 405.

[136] On which, see Zelanak (1996) 50 *Tax L Rev* 1; and Kaplow, *op cit*, 35.

[137] On charitable deductions, see Andrews 86 *HL Rev* 309, 344–75; and Bittker (1972) 28 *Tax L Rev* 37.

harshly on the elderly, since it is usual for a person to retire on a pension and with some capital. Such people use capital in retirement; at present they pay tax only on their income, whereas under an ET they would have a greater tax liability. It is true that they may have been able to save more thanks to an ET, but they are still left with a higher final liability at a time when they cannot increase income.

Lastly, three other areas of difficulty may be noted. The first concerns the rate of tax, which will clearly have to be higher than the current rates of income tax in force to pay for the relief of savings and which, as just seen, will cause particular problems for the old since they tend to dissave. However, empirical research into the German system suggests that the revenue loss may not be as great as feared; this is because the tax yield from income from capital is dropping.[138] The second difficulty is transitional: how would the system deal with assets acquired before an ET was introduced?[139] The third difficulty is one of scope: how would such a system work internationally,[140] particularly in countries which retained an income tax base; and how would one deal with an individual who saved up money in the UK but who then spends it overseas?

The Meade Committee Report produced solutions to all these problems. It may be concluded that a system of ET is indeed workable, but that the adjustments needed to make the scheme workable also reduce its attractions.

1.6.3.5 ET and the Current UK Income Tax

Income tax in its present form may be seen, like many around the world, as a compromise between the two principles,[141] except that the term 'compromise' suggests a degree of 'conscious' thought. Something close to an ET applies to pension arrangements under which there is full deduction for payments into a scheme, non-taxability while the assets are held in the fund and eventual tax liability on the pension. Yet this favours the person who can plan long term—it suits the savings patterns of civil servants rather than entrepreneurs. Some degree of compromise (or inconsistency) may actually be justifiable.[142]

The current UK income tax law is limited by four principal factors. First, for income tax there is the 'Schedular' system, which makes no attempt to tax matters not falling within the various Schedules; this system remains in place despite the rewrite legislation. Secondly, in applying the terms used by the legislators, the courts have adopted a view that capital gain should and can be distinguished from income—a view reinforced by the doctrine that income must have a source. Although the UK has had a tax on capital gains since 1965, it is a limited and unsatisfactory tax. Thirdly, there are numerous exceptions to the bases for the various taxes, based on a mixture of practicality and expediency. This problem is not unique to the UK tax system, and it has become common to refer to many of the reliefs and

---

[138] Becker and Fuest (2005) 26 *Fiscal Studies* 491; this article contains much mathematical data.
[139] See Zodrow in Krever (ed), *op cit*, p 187.
[140] See Musgrave in Krever (ed), *op cit*, p 447–69.
[141] Thus the final note of Gunn's article in (1979) 46 *University of Chicago L Rev* 370, referring to the Meade Committee Report, states that the UK has so many special rules for savings that it employs an ET in any case. On US compromise, see McNulty 88 *California L Rev* 2098–182.
[142] For example, McCaffery 70 *Texas L Rev* 1145.

exemptions as shelters or tax expenditures.[143] The virtue of this analysis is that by dramatising the cost of a relief, it may cause the relief to be re-examined, not least to see whether the same objective might be achieved another way. There are, however, difficulties, particularly over definition. Tax shelters have been succeeded by other problems stemming from the financial world, with its development of new financial instruments[144] undermining traditional principles of the tax system, such as the distinction between capital and income, or rules about timing, and by the real or virtual world of electronics where the principles most at risk are those relating to the location of income. Lastly, there is the problem of the attitude of the courts towards avoidance schemes, a story in its own right and with its own chapter (chapter five below). In 1978, when the Meade Committee reported, it was fair to say that UK courts had not yet shown much willingness to protect the tax base against flagrantly artificial schemes.

1.7 Tax Expenditures

A tax expenditure is a concept radically distinct from an expenditure tax. It has been defined as 'an exemption or relief which is not part of the essential structure of the tax in question but has been introduced into the tax code for extraneous reason'.[145] An example is mortgage interest relief from income tax; this is thought to be a tax expenditure because it is not an essential feature of an income tax and because the Government has forgone tax on the amount of the interest paid. Such a relief is the functional equivalent of a public expenditure. The concept is useful in that it dramatises the cost of reliefs and so may cause a re-examination of the reliefs. If the relief can be justified as a public expense, it may still have to be justified in terms of efficiency, ie that the tax system is the most appropriate way of providing the expenditure. A list of the current UK reliefs is set out in chapter seven. It may be argued that subsidies through the tax system do not have to be by deduction as opposed to credit.[146]

The concept is not, however, without difficulties. First, there is the problem of determining what reliefs are part of 'the essential structure' of the tax.[147] This problem is more acute in the UK, where there seems to be little agreement on what the essential

---

[143] The United States has experienced special problems which were settled temporarily in the Tax Reform Act 1986 (TRA 1986): see Birnbaum and Murray, *Showdown at Gucci Gulch* (Vintage, 1987); Chirelstein [1986] *Florida State L Rev* 207; and Graetz (1988) 40 *UFla L Rev* 617. On the TRA 1986, see comment by Auerbach and Slemrod (1997) 35 *J Economic Literature* 589, 628: 'A decade of analysis had not taught us much about whether the TRA 1986 was a good idea (which is not the same as saying that it was not a good idea).'

[144] See Schenk in 'Foreword to Colloquium on Financial Instruments' (1995) 50 *Tax L Rev* 487.

[145] Willis and Hardwick, *Tax Expenditure in the United Kingdom* (Heinemann, 1978) 1. The concept was developed by Stanley Surrey: see, generally, Surrey and McDaniel, *Tax Expenditures* (Harvard University Press, 1985); Bradford, *op cit*, ch 11; and summary by Brooks (1986) 34 *Canadian Tax J* 681. For a more recent analysis see Burton and Sadiq, *Tax Expenditure Management: A Critical Assessment* (CUP, 2013).

[146] Saez (2004) 88 *Journal of Public Economics* 503.

[147] See Bittker (1969) 22 *National Tax J* 244; and Bittker, *Taxation of Income, Estates and Gifts* (Warren Gorham & Lamont, 1993) §3.6. Bittker also asks why a tax expenditure budget is not mirrored by an 'expenditure tax budget', based on the theory that excluding a group of citizens from a subsidy granted to other similarly situated citizens is equivalent to taxing the excluded persons: *ibid* at 368 and §3.6.

structure is. Thus, a revenue expense incurred by a businessman in generating profit, eg paying employees a proper wage, is an expense incurred in achieving what is to be taxed and so a part of the essential structure. However, one may have more difficulty with the proper treatment of losses and their relief against either general income or trading income from the current or later years. Another example is mortgage interest (finally repealed in 2000). In 1799 relief was available for all types of interest, since these payments were regarded as charges on income and so part of the essential structure of the tax; viewed in this light, mortgage interest relief might be considered one of the last embodiments of true principle rather than an anomaly. One might try to avoid these difficulties by reducing the object of the exercise to that of indicating 'the cost of special tax provisions which can be considered as alternatives to direct expenditure and loan programmes'.[148] However, this not only reduces an important exercise in theory to the level of a political game over departmental budgets, but begs the question of how costs are estimated.[149] Supporters of an expenditure or consumption tax have to face similar problems in distinguishing what is an essential part of the tax, ie an item which should be deductible as an item of saving or investment, from what is an item of consumption and so not deductible; consumption is not a self-defining term.

---

[148] Surrey and Hellmuth (1969) 22 *National Tax J* 530.

[149] The process usually assumes that the taxpayer would spend his money in exactly the same way and be subject to his marginal rate of tax; it thus ignores the effect of taxing the income.

2

Jurisdiction: The Taxing Power

2.1 The Power to Tax: The UK, the Tax Year and the Annual Tax

The power to levy taxes is only one manifestation of the sovereignty of Parliament. The Bill of Rights provides that no charge on the subject shall be levied by pretence of prerogative without the consent of Parliament.[1] The Bill of Rights is not pure history; in the 1992 decision in the *Woolwich Building Society* case, it was invoked by Lord Goff as one reason for granting restitution.[2] By contrast, the Court of Appeal said it would make a mockery of the law to suggest that a fraudster can escape with impunity by piously invoking the benefit of the Bill of Rights.[3] Although the power to tax has been at the very centre of some of our major constitutional law disputes, including the execution of a King, until relatively recent times there has been a lack of engagement with public law issues by UK tax academics. To some civilian lawyers this seems quite impossible. There is a presumption that express statutory authority is needed before a tax can be imposed;[4] however, this does not apply to a charge levied for services.[5] Taxation bills begin in the House of Commons, the powers of the House of Lords being limited.[6] Each year a Finance Bill begins in March or April.

---

[1] 2 Will and Mar (c 2) Art 4; on tax provisions of the Bill of Rights, see Williams [1989] BTR 370.
[2] [1992] STC 657, 677.
[3] *C and E Commissioners v Total Network* [2007] EWCA Civ 39, [2007] STC 1005 at para 31.
[4] *A-G v Wiltshire United Dairies* (1921) 37 TLR 884. Cf Emergency Powers (Defence) Act 1939, ss 1(3) and 2. On (non-) limitation by international law, see *Cheney v Conn* [1968] 1 All ER 779; 44 TC 217. The same presumption applies to requisitioning a person's property without paying for it: *A-G v De Keyser's Royal Hotel* [1920] AC 508; on which, see Scott and Hildesley, *The Case of Requisition* (OUP, 1920).
[5] *China Navigation Co Ltd v A-G* [1932] 2 KB 197.
[6] Parliament Act 1911, s 1. See, generally, Bradley and Ewing, *Constitutional and Administrative Law*, 13th edn (Longman, 2002) ch 17 and Erskine May, *Parliamentary Practice*, 23rd edn (Butterworths, 2004) chs 29–33.

Currently this is preceded by a pre-Budget report ('Autumn Statement') in November or early December of the previous year announcing proposed changes in the tax system, when spending decisions are also announced.[7]

2.1.1 The United Kingdom

The legislation applies to the United Kingdom, ie England, Wales, Scotland and Northern Ireland, and the Scilly Isles,[8] but not to the Channel Islands or the Isle of Man.

2.1.2 Tax Year

For income tax and CGT, the tax year runs from 6 April to 5 April, so that the year from 6 April 2016 to 5 April 2017 is known as the tax year 2016–17.[9] Different rules apply to corporation tax.[10] The reason for these dates is that the financial year originally began on Lady Day, 25 March; this was changed in 1752 when the calendars were altered.[11] Almost any dating is arbitrary and change now would, if we still lived in a world in which Britain traded with its imperial (date-sharing) partners, merely substitute the apparently rational for the attractively picturesque. Today, however, there may well be compliance-cost advantages in moving to a tax year beginning on 1 January, this being the most common in other trading partner countries.[12] The date 31 March still marks the end of the Government's financial year.

2.1.3 Annual Taxes

Income tax and corporation tax, but not CGT, IHT, VAT or stamp duties, are annual taxes, and the charge is reimposed by Parliament each year in the Finance Act (FA).[13] The result is that the income and corporation tax acts are really in the nature of clauses suspended in the legal ether, waiting to come into effect whenever any Act imposes a tax.[14] The fact that the tax is enacted annually means that special rules are needed to enable certain reliefs to be rolled forward.[15] The Finance Act also amends the rules for the other taxes.[16] The resulting combination of measures of great economic importance and matters of great technical

---

[7] A unified Budget (ie, one covering both spending and taxing) was tried from November 1993 to November 1996. It had been proposed in *Budgetary Reform*, Cm 1867 (March 1992); it was criticised in *The Economist*, 27 November 1993, but supported by many worthies including the Armstrong Report for IFS (1980) and Treasury and Civil Service Committee of HC 1982. See also Symposium Fiscal Studies, vol 14, No 1, 77.

[8] TA 1988, Sch 30, paras 6(2)(b), 21. See also FA 1986, s 108 on the definition of the UK relating to oil taxation.

[9] ITA 2007, s 4.

[10] And, before its abolition, to development land tax (DLT): see DLTA 1976, s 13.

[11] Royal Commission (1920), App 7(o).

[12] The case for the change was argued more than 20 years ago by Johnson (1980) 1(3) *Fiscal Studies* 29.

[13] Income Tax Act 2007, s 4. The term Finance Act was first used in 1894: see Cook [1994] BTR 365.

[14] Per Atkin LJ in *Martin v Lowry* (1926) 11 TC 297, 317.

[15] Per Lord Hoffmann in *Taylor v MEPC* [2004] STC 123, para 12.

[16] The practice of having a single bill dealing with all taxes stems from Gladstone's battles with the House of Lords: see Magnus, *Gladstone* (John Murray, 1954), 151. There is nothing inevitable about this; the Australian Constitution, s 55, requires law imposing tax to deal with one subject of taxation only; this is to prevent earmarking of unrelated matters which the Senate cannot amend because of s 53.

subtlety, discussed against the background of the hurly burly of Parliamentary procedure, is, not surprisingly, capable of error. In recent years major pieces of legislation on tax have been enacted outside this Bill process, eg the Tax Credits Act 2002 and the Child Trust Funds Act 2004. There have also been the Acts emanating from the Tax Law Rewrite process—the Capital Allowances Act 2001, the three Income Tax Acts, two Corporation Tax Acts and one Act concerned primarily with international matters (see further §3.1.2 below).

The notion of income tax as an annual tax is rooted in history, with the need to ensure that the Crown did not try to tax its subjects without having to recall Parliament. It is also an optimistic reminder that income tax was originally a temporary tax; the tax has remained in force every year since 1842. The notion of an annual tax is, however, more modern. Parliament granted the tax for three years in 1842, 1845 and 1848, and for seven years in 1853.

2.1.4 Qualifications

These statements must now be qualified in four ways. First, since 1913 there has been statutory authority for collecting taxes on the authority of a resolution of the House of Commons notwithstanding that the Finance Bill itself has not yet been passed. Secondly, the legislation passed by the UK Parliament will be of no effect to the extent that it breaches European Union law; legislation which breaches discrimination rules will have no effect against a citizen of another Member State, and an appropriate directive not enacted by the UK Parliament will be of direct effect and so can be used by a qualifying taxpayer. Thirdly, we have the European Convention on Human Rights incorporated into UK domestic law to some extent by the Human Rights Act 1998. Fourthly, we now have an increasing delegation of the taxing power to the Scottish and Welsh Assemblies. These are discussed at §§2.2–2.5.

2.2   Qualification (1): The Provisional Collection of Taxes

Since income tax is an annual tax and is imposed by a charge in each year's Finance Act, difficulties have arisen where the Finance Act has not become law by the start of the tax year (6 April). Until 1913 tax could not lawfully be collected simply on the basis of a resolution of the House of Commons.[17] The Provisional Collection of Taxes Act (PCTA) 1913 (now PCTA 1968) gave temporary statutory effect to resolutions of the House of Commons.[18] Resolutions, if passed in March or April, expire on 5 August next, and if passed in any other month, expire after four months.[19] New taxes are expressly excluded. In the days of the unified budget, Royal Assent was required by 5 May.[20]

---

[17] *Bowles v Bank of England* [1913] 1 Ch 57. The Finance Acts of 1909, 1910 and 1911 reached the statute book 13, seven and seven months respectively after the start of the financial year. Mr Bowles was an opposition backbencher; the dilatory Chancellor was Lloyd George.

[18] On temporary effect of resolution for stamp duty, see FA 1973, s 50.

[19] PCTA 1968, s 1. The background is explained in the Government White Paper, Budgetary Reform, Cm 1867 and, more specifically in HM Treasury press release, 31 December 1992, [1993] *Simon's Tax Intelligence* 160.

[20] FA 1993, s 205.

2.3 Qualification (2): The European Union

2.3.1 *EU's Own Resources*[21]

Since 1975 the financial basis of the EU has been provided entirely out of the revenues of the Union. It consists of (a) agricultural levies, (b) customs duties and (c) a proportion of VAT. Discussions on sources and amounts of EU revenue, including recent moves to raise funds through an EU-wide financial transactions tax, appear never-ending.

2.3.2 *Restraints on Fiscal Sovereignty: The Basic Position*

EU law limits the rights of member governments to levy taxes by taking precedence over Acts of Parliament.[22] This supremacy does not apply to those areas in which sovereignty has not been ceded.

Supremacy issues first arise in connection with UK legislation. The UK Parliament may find that its legislation conflicts with principles of EU law,[23] or that it has not followed the proper procedure, eg by not consulting the Commission,[24] so that in either case its legislation is of no effect. However, issues also arise when an individual taxpayer is accorded rights under EU law through the doctrine of direct effect.[25] A provision giving rise to direct effect must be clear and concise; it must be unconditional and unqualified, and not subject to the taking of any further measures on the part of a Union or national authority; and it must leave no substantial discretion in its implementation to a Union or national authority.[26] Several Treaty provisions have been given direct effect in taxation. The CJEU has asserted a pre-emptive jurisdiction to forestall divergent interpretations of a directive by allowing a reference by a national court on what is actually a domestic tax issue but which arises from legislation based on an EU law.[27]

A failure to implement directives properly and in time will enable a taxpayer to assert the rights set out in the directive against the Member State[28] if the conditions for direct effect apply. In addition, the citizen may be able to recover damages from the state under the principle in *Francovitch*[29] for failure to implement the directive—this right may arise even though the principle required for direct effect is not satisfied.[30]

At the time of writing the status of the UK in the EU is up-in-the-air following the result of the June 2016 advisory referendum in which a slim majority of the public voted in favour of the UK leaving the EU. The implications of Brexit for UK tax law are discussed further in chapter seventy-seven.

---

[21] The broadest, technical, overall account of EU tax harmonisation policy is Terra and Wattel, *European Tax Law*, 6th edn (Kluwer, 2012).

[22] *Stoke-on-Trent City Council v B & Q plc* [1991] 4 All ER 221, 223.

[23] As in the famous *Factortame* case: *R v Secretary of State for Transport, ex parte Factortame* [1991] 1 AC 603.

[24] As in *R v Customs and Excise Commrs, ex parte Lunn Poly Ltd* [1999] STC 350.

[25] Case 26/62 *Van Gend en Loos v Nederlandse Tariefcomissie* [1963] ECR 1.

[26] Edward and Lane, *European Community Law*, (Butterworths, 1995) para 133.

[27] Case C–28/95 *Leur Bloem* [1997] STC 1205; see Betten [1999] *CMLR* 165.

[28] The so-called 'vertical' direct effect of directives allows the enforcement of rights against the Member State but not against other citizens.

[29] Edward and Lane, *op cit*, para 148.

[30] Case C–91/9 *Faccinni Dori v Recreb* [1994] ECR I–3325.

34 _Introduction to UK Tax Law_

2.3.2.1 State Aid

Another EU law restriction on Member States taxation powers, which has risen in prominence in recent years, is the prohibition on state aid in Article 107 TFEU (ex Art 87 TEC). Pursuant to Article 107 TFEU, save as otherwise provided in the EU Treaties, any aid granted by a Member State or through State resources in any form whatsoever which distorts or threatens to distort competition by favouring certain undertakings or the production of certain goods shall, in so far as it affects trade between Member States, be incompatible with the internal market. Under Article 108 TFEU (ex Art 88 TEC), the Commission can require States to abolish or alter aid that is not compatible with the internal market having regard to Article 107, or where the aid is being misused. Case law establishes clearly that tax provisions which are in substance state aid fall foul of these provisions unless clearance has been obtained for them from the Commission under Article 108 TFEU.[31] In recent years the European Commission has challenged the tax affairs of high-profile multinationals, arguing that key tax rulings and comfort letters issued by Member States to the multinationals violated the prohibition on state aid. This is discussed more fully in chapter seventy-seven.

2.3.2.2 Indirect Taxes and Similar Charges

Article 110 TFEU (ex Art 90 TEC) prohibits discrimination against imports from other Member States by the levying of charges higher than those imposed on domestic products. Article 111 TFEU (ex Art 91 TEC) prohibits refunds on exports exceeding the actual taxation imposed on the goods. Article 113 TFEU (ex Art 93 TEC) addresses how the legislation of turnover taxes can be harmonised, a process which has given us the famous Sixth Directive imposing a common tax base to VAT throughout the Union, enacted in the UK as the VATA 1984, now consolidated as the VATA 1994. This surrender of sovereignty in relation to turnover taxes does not extend to taxes which are not turnover taxes, eg insurance premium tax.

2.3.2.3 Direct Taxes—No Compensation for Effects on Trade

Article 112 TFEU (ex Art 92 TEC) extends the principle of Article 111 TFEU (ex Art 91 TEC) to direct taxation and prohibits Member States from operating systems of compensation for the effects of direct taxation on trade within the EU. However, this is subject to a right of derogation, provided the Government obtains authorisation from the Commission.

2.3.2.4 Harmonisation

Article 115 TFEU (ex Art 94 TEC) provides for the approximation of laws by directives, and it is on this basis that the Commission has tried to achieve harmonisation of company taxes. No article _requires_ harmonisation of direct taxes in the way that Article 113 TFEU does for indirect taxes. Directives under Article 115 TFEU require unanimity in the Council. There has been regular UK legislation to implement directives, as in 1990 when the Revenue were placed under a duty to provide information about liabilities to tax in another Member State.[32]

---

[31] See also the Commission, Notice of 11 November 1998, 98/C384/03 and an EC Commission Report C (2004) 434.
[32] FA 1990, s 125.

Into this area the Court of Justice of the European Union (CJEU) has made what some see as erratic, narrow and often destructive contributions to harmonisation on the basis of the non-discrimination principle. The non-discrimination principle is embodied for tax purposes in four fundamental freedoms: the free cross-border movement of employees (Article 45 TFEU; ex Art 39 TEC); freedom of establishment for businesses (Article 49 TFEU; ex Art 43 TEC); freedom to provide services (Article 56 TFEU; ex Art 49 TEC); and free movement of capital (Article 63 TFEU; ex Art 56 TEC). It is thought that these specific powers prevent the CJEU from relying on the more general anti-discrimination rule in Article 18 TFEU (ex Art 12 TEC).[33] More and more frequently, tax provisions which infringe, or may infringe, these freedoms are being challenged in court actions brought by taxpayers in the national courts, with a reference made to the CJEU for advice under the procedure in Article 267 TFEU (ex Art 234 TEC). The impugned rules are also often the subject of investigation by the Commission, which may bring its own court proceedings against a Member State. The Commission also exercises its right to make submissions to the CJEU in cases brought by taxpayers.[34] For more see chapter seventy-seven below.

2.4 Qualification (3): Human Rights Law

2.4.1 *Human Rights Convention*[35]

The UK signed the European Convention on Human Rights and Fundamental Freedoms in 1950, but saw no need to incorporate it into domestic law—no doubt because it was thought that rights were sufficiently well protected through existing judicial and political procedures. Eventually, in 1998, the Convention was given some effect in domestic law by the Human Rights Act 1998. Since 2 October 2000[36] the UK courts have been under a duty to interpret legislation in a way which is compatible with the Convention rights; and if this is impossible, they have a power to declare that legislation is incompatible with the Convention.[37] However, the Act is not retrospective.[38] The fact that the courts (High Court and above) have the power to make this declaration explains how Convention rights are to be reconciled with the sovereignty of Parliament. If Parliament decides it does not want to amend the law, even by the fast-track process suggested in the Act, there is nothing a litigant

---

[33] See Richardson [1998] BTR 281, 291, citing Case C–112/91 *Werner v FZA Aachen-Innenstadt* [1993] ECR I-429, para 20. While the case law has been concerned to make sure that a non-national is treated at least as favourably as a national, attention is now being paid (but not yet by the Court) to the opposite problem—where the non-resident is treated more favourably, and the Member States compete unfairly for business. The EU has an (unenforceable) code of conduct for Member States in such matters: see Schön (ed), *Tax Competition in Europe* (EATLP/IBFD, 2003).

[34] Usually these are in support of the taxpayers, but in *Bosal Holding BV* [2003] ECR I-9409 the Commission made some submissions in support to the Member State—to no effect.

[35] See generally Baker [2000] BTR 211; also printed in *European Taxation and Comparative Perspectives on Revenue Law* (CUP, 2008) ch 10.

[36] Certain matters concerning the Scottish Parliament and Executive were already subject to the Act and the Scottish courts.

[37] Human Rights Act 1998, ss 3 and 4.

[38] *R v Allen (No 2)* [2001] UKHL 45; [2001] 4 All ER 768; [2001] STC 1537, Lord Hutton at para 23; and *Al Fayed v Advocate General for Scotland* [2002] STC 910. See Lord Rodger (2005) 121 *LQR* 57.

can do but follow the familiar path to Strasbourg.[39] Equally, there is nothing to stop the Westminster Parliament from repealing the Act itself, or withdrawing from the Convention altogether—and in the current political climate fundamental reform along these lines is a distinct possibility.

Section 6(1) of the Human Rights Act 1998 makes it unlawful for a 'public authority'— an expression covering not only a court or tribunal, but also any person whose functions are, even in part, of a public nature eg revenue departments—to act in way which is incompatible with Convention rights; judicial remedies are governed by section 8. The court or tribunal must have regarded to, but is not bound by, the jurisprudence of the 'Strasbourg Organs'.[40]

Also, to reconcile the 1998 Act with sovereignty of Parliament, the duty imposed by section 6(1) is qualified. Thanks to section 6(2)(a), the duty does not apply to an act if as a result of one or more provisions of primary legislation the authority could not have acted differently. Under section 6(2)(b), the duty in section 6(1) does not apply where there are one or more provisions of, or made under, primary legislation which cannot be read or given effect to in a way which is compatible with Convention rights, and the authority was acting so as to give effect to or enforce those provisions. So when the UK tax legislation gave a relief for widows but not for widowers, the Revenue were entitled to rely on section 6(2)(b) as a complete defence to an action based on a breach of the Convention rights against discrimination on grounds of sex. As the House of Lords held, the Revenue were simply acting under provisions which were incompatible with that Convention right. Their Lordships also held that the Revenue could not be compelled to grant an extra statutory concession to cover the case; what would have happened if the Revenue's power to grant concessions had been wider was a matter for speculation.[41] The Strasbourg Court found no reason to compensate the widowers by levelling up.[42]

Retroactive legislation does not conform easily to human rights doctrines but has been a standard feature of a system, such as that in the UK, which is still dominated by Diceyan views of parliamentary sovereignty. Thus, what is now CTA 2010, section 52 and ITA 2007, section 81, banning loss relief on dealings in commodity futures, was introduced in 1978 but was retrospective to 6 April 1976.[43] Another problem arises from the practice of reversing court decisions with retrospective effect save for those litigants who had actually won their cases *vis à vis* the Revenue: the reversal of *IRC v Padmore*[44] and the famous *Woolwich Building Society v IRC* case[45] are examples here. However, it has to be noted that no challenge to retrospective legislation has yet been successful in Strasbourg.[46]

---

[39] *R v IRC, ex parte Wilkinson* [2005] UKHL 30.

[40] Human Rights Act 1998, s 2.

[41] *R v IRC, ex parte Wilkinson* [2005] UKHL 30; compare Lord Hoffmann at para 23 with Lord Brown at para 43.

[42] *Hobbs v UK* [2008] STC 1469 App 63684/00.

[43] In *R (on the application of Huitson) v Revenue & Customs Commissioners* [2010] EWHC 97 (Admin), retrospective UK legislation to counter tax avoidance by artificial arrangements was held not to breach human rights as it was proportionate.

[44] [1988] 62 TC 352.

[45] [1993] AC 90.

[46] See Baker [2000] BTR 225.

In *National Provincial Building Society v UK*,[47] the European Court of Human Rights declined to interfere with the UK legislature's reversal of the *Woolwich* case with retroactive effect in relation to building societies other than the Woolwich. However, while at first sight it appears to leave a high 'margin of appreciation' to the signatory states in fiscal matters, the decision is narrow in scope. First, it proceeds on an interpretation of the facts distinctly favourable to the Revenue. Secondly, it deals with a situation in which Parliament had tried to amend the law and where the subordinate law-making process had got it wrong first time; as such, the UK system was allowed a second chance to do by primary legislation what it had certainly wanted to do at the start, because this was obviously consistent with the legislature's intent (one cannot pretend that the building societies had much in the way of legitimate expectations). Thirdly, the case tells us nothing about the attitude of the Court if the UK legislation had tried to remove the fruits of victory from the Woolwich Building Society itself.

Yet human rights doctrines are clearly having an influence on the Revenue.[48] Possibly because the Minister introducing legislation has to certify to the House that the legislation is compatible with the 1998 Act.[49]

2.4.2 Other Sources

The second way in which the Human Rights Convention is important is the influence it has had on the development of UK law, especially in administrative law matters.[50] With the incorporation of the Convention into UK law, one might expect the process to continue and even accelerate, although the form in which it has been incorporated may discourage the courts from challenging parliamentary sovereignty too directly.

Lastly, the Convention is influential in the development of fundamental principles of EU law, principles said to emerge in part from the common traditions of the Member States.[51] In addition, post-Lisbon, the EU's own Charter of Fundamental Rights of the European Union now has the same legal force as the Treaties (Article 6(1) TEU). The importance here is that fundamental principles and the Charter are capable of direct effect, and therefore, thanks to the supremacy of EU law, will override Diceyan parliamentary sovereignty.[52]

2.4.3 Issues

The various Convention rights recognised by the Human Rights Act 1998 are those listed in the Convention and the First and Sixth Protocols.[53] There is no doubt that tax legislation may be declared incompatible with the European Convention.[54] The Commission

---

[47] [1997] STC 1466; see Baker, *op cit*, 225.

[48] See the cautious FA 2004 legislation amending an unexpected decision on the Limitation Act: FA 2004, ss 320 and 321. Readers are also directed to Williamson [2014] BTR 119 for a current note on HMRC's digital policy and human rights, and a follow up note [2014] BTR 347.

[49] Human Rights Act 1998, s 19(1)(a).

[50] See, eg, Klug and Starmer [1997] *Public Law* 223.

[51] Hartley, *The Foundations of European Union Law*, 7th edn (OUP, 2010) ch 5.

[52] See, eg, *Hodgson v Commrs of Customs and Excise* [1996] V&DR 200: right of appeal conferred when none available under domestic law.

[53] Human Rights Act 1998, s 1 and Sch 1.

[54] *R (Wilkinson) v IRC* [2002] STC 347 (first instance); not in issue on appeal [2003] EWCA Civ 814; [2003] STC 1113.

on Human Rights and the European Court of Human Rights have indicated a willingness in principle to use Article 1 of the First Protocol in an appropriate case, and this has
been accepted in principle by the Court of Appeal when dealing with an 'irrational' tax.[55]
The Convention bans confiscation, and there must come a point at which excessive taxation becomes confiscation.[56] The 1997 privatisation windfall tax charged on the difference
between the flotation price and a multiple of average profits for the first four years was a
tax on shareholders who had not necessarily benefited from these profits in those years, and
was clearly vulnerable to challenge; but no challenge was mounted.[57] Both the Commission
and the European Court of Human Rights have also indicated a willingness to use Articles
1 and 14 of the Convention, the non-discrimination articles. A complaint was made that
a UK rule which gave a relief to a married man whose wife was incapacitated but not to
a married woman whose husband was incapacitated, breached the Convention. This was
ruled admissible, but a friendly settlement was reached.[58] TA 1988, section 259 was immediately changed.[59] Litigation on the UK widow's bereavement allowance under TA 1988,
section 262 was at first ended by a friendly settlement, but the Revenue refused to grant
relief to Mr Wilkinson.[60] However, discrimination may be cured by withdrawing relief from
those previously entitled to it just as much as by extending it to the applicant, and this
duly happened. The Convention may also become relevant when considering procedures
adopted by the Revenue in administering tax law (see chapter four below). The question
has been raised whether an Act excluding legal professional privilege would be a breach of
Convention rights. Lord Hoffmann thought it would require exceptional circumstances to
justify such a provision, and that the public interest in collecting revenue would not be sufficient justification.[61]

Issues of discrimination on grounds of gender and through lack of respect for family
life, a combination of pleas based on Article 14 (linked to Article 1 of the First Protocol)
and Article 8 of the Human Rights Convention, are likely to be particularly difficult.[62] In
Burden v UK,[63] an IHT privilege available only to married couples had been withheld from
one party in a couple who had cohabited for 30 years. The reason why they could not use a
civil partnership was that they were sisters. If this had been held to breach the Convention,

---

[55] See Court of Appeal in *Aston Cantlow PCC v Wallbank* [2001] EWCA Civ 713; [2002] STC 313; reversed by
HL on other grounds. See also Burton J in *R (on application of Professional Contractors Group Ltd) v IRC* [2001]
STC 629 (no breach of Art 1 of the First Protocol). The human rights argument was not pursued in the CA [2002]
STC 165.

[56] *Svenska Managementgruppen AB v Sweden* (1985) Application No 11036/84 45 DR 211, Commission.

[57] On this windfall tax, see Chennells (1997) 18 *Fiscal Studies* 279. *The Economist*, 5 July 1997, speculated that
the costs of a lengthy legal battle were thought to be too high; it is more likely that the companies did not wish to
challenge a government with such a large popular mandate so soon after the election, especially since companies
subject to greater competitive pressure would, under the formula, pay less tax than other companies. On earlier
windfall taxes, see Unwin [1984] BTR 343.

[58] *McGregor v UK*, Application 30548/96.

[59] FA 1998, s 26.

[60] The House of Lords would not have given any monetary compensation. *R v CIR, ex parte Wilkinson* [2005]
UKHL 30, esp Lord Hoffmann at paras 24–28.

[61] *R (on application of Morgan Grenfell) v Spec Comm of Income Tax* [2002] UKHL 21; [2002] STC 786, para 39.

[62] See Baker, *op cit.*

[63] [2008] STC 1305, App 13378/05; see below at §53.1.1.1.

one can see quickly that there would be similar pleas by other couples, heterosexual or homosexual, who had cohabited for lesser periods. However, there will be other problems. Just as cohabitees will be demanding privileges given to married couples, so married couples will be wondering whether assessments made under anti-avoidance rules applicable to spouses should be overturned because they do not apply also to cohabitees. Thus while cohabitees might seek the protection of the exemption for interspousal transfers in IHTA 1984, section 18, a married woman might wonder why she has to suffer from section 203, which makes her liable for certain IHT when a cohabitee is not liable. If such 'counter-claims' by spouses succeed, many provisions of the tax code will have to be revisited; if they fail, we shall end with a pick-and-mix approach in which cohabitees can choose which rules they want, scarcely a dignified conclusion to arguments alleged to be based on respect for family life. One halfway house would be to allow cohabitees to have the protection of the rule for spouses and civil partners in IHTA 1984, section 18, but on condition that they abide by all other tax rules relating to spouses; however, such a mealy-mouthed approach has been rejected by the Court of Justice in its anti-discrimination jurisprudence. The Treasury can by regulation remove inequality of treatment based on gender or, only in the case of a parent, marital status.[64]

2.5   Qualification (4): Federalism

The UK Parliament at Westminster, as the sovereign body in tax matters, has allowed other organs of government to levy taxes. The council tax is levied by local authorities under the Local Government Finance Act 1992. The Scottish Parliament was given a limited tax-varying power under the terms of the Scotland Act 1998. However, both of these measures are Acts of the Westminster Parliament, and so may be amended or repealed by that Parliament. If federalism is to develop within the UK, financial matters will have to be addressed, since the taxing power is central to any division of powers in a federal system—just as it was the key power in the struggle between the Crown and the English Parliament in the 17th century.[65] One judicial observer has gone so far as to assert that the importance of tax in a federal system is that, more than any other power, it has the capacity to destroy federalism.[66] No doubt this is one of the many reasons why Member States are so reluctant to transfer significant revenue-raising powers to the institutions of the EU.

The Scotland Act 2012 began a new chapter of devolution of taxing powers from Westminster to Holyrood. The Act introduced the Scottish rate of income tax, which gives the Scottish Parliament the power to set an annual rate of income tax for Scottish taxpayers from April 2016, and to keep all the money raised in Scotland (see also §7.1.3 below). Scottish Ministers used their newly devolved powers to introduce two new taxes, replacing

---

[64] The power is contained in FA 2005, s 103, and the Treasury has made regulations under the Civil Partnerships Act 2004.

[65] For illustrations of the issues, see *Fiscal Design Surveys across Levels of Government*, OECD Tax Policy Study No 7 (OECD, 2002) and Messere *et al*, *Tax Policy: Theory and Practice in OECD Countries* (OUP, 2003) ch 5.

[66] See the discussion in Zines, *The High Court and the Constitution*, 4th edn (Butterworths, 1997) pp 34–36, citing for this belief Latham CJ in the *Banks Nationalisation* case *Bank of New South Wales v Commonwealth* (1948) 76 CLR 1, 183–84 (Zines goes on to express some scepticism).

the UK Landfill Tax with a Scottish Landfill tax (SLfT) and the UK Stamp Duty Land Tax with a Scottish Land and Buildings Transaction Tax (LBTT). Revenue Scotland was established as the new tax authority for Scotland's devolved taxes.[67]

Following the 'No' vote against Scottish independence in the September 2014 referendum, the pace for further devolution of taxing powers to Scotland—and to a lesser degree Wales and Northern Ireland—has increased. The Scotland Act 2016 provides measures enabling Holyrood to set income tax rates (from April 2016) and thresholds (from April 2017) on earnings in Scotland, and assigns a portion of VAT revenues to Scotland beginning in 2019–20.[68] HMRC has undertaken consultations on some of the technical aspects of implementing the Scottish rate of income tax, including the meaning of 'Scottish taxpayer'. Finally, the Tax Collection and Management (Wales) Act 2016 established the Welsh Revenue Authority and the legal framework for the administration of the proposed new devolved taxes—also a land transaction tax and landfill disposals tax—from April 2018.

---

[67] For more details see St Clair, *Scottish Tax Yearbook* (Thomson Reuters, 1st ed 2015).
[68] For a comprehensive analysis of the Scotland Act 2016 see Eden [2016] BTR 134.

3

Sources

3.1   Statutes

3.1.1 The Shape of the Statute Book

The statute law for a particular tax can be found in the statute which introduced that tax, as amended subsequently. Amendments may take the form of an amendment to the text of the original Act, or may involve the creation of a new provision in the new Act and so exist alongside the original Act. A tax Bill is usually certified as a Money Bill, which means that although the House of Lords may amend it, the House of Commons is not bound by the amendment and the Bill may take effect in its unamended form within one month of being sent from the Commons to the Lords.[1] A bill on a particular matter may contain extensive tax provisions and yet not be a Money Bill.[2] In recent years the House of Lords Select Committee on Economic Affairs has had hearings on the Finance Bill and has made valuable reports. Its membership includes former Treasury Ministers. The issues chosen for report tend to be administrative or procedural in nature; politically sensitive issues tend to be avoided. HMRC Officials give evidence to the Committee by consent of their ministers.

If a Bill contains an exemption for a specific person or entity, it is a hybrid bill, and so has its own very long procedure (enabling other entities to object).[3] It has therefore been known for certain, apparently general, alterations to be drawn in such a way as to have the specific effect sought. As Nigel Lawson put in relation to one such clause, '[f]ortunately in this context, the language in which Finance Bills are drafted is so arcane as to bear little resemblance to the English language and no-one spotted what this particular clause was really about'.[4]

---

[1] A Money Bill is defined under Parliament Act 1911, s 1(2) as one dealing only with matters of national (as opposed to local) taxation, public money or loans, or their management; the Speaker's certificate is conclusive. See Erskine May, *Parliamentary Practice*, 22nd edn, 806–08.

[2] Eg, Limited Liability Partnerships Act 2000.

[3] May, *op cit*, 483–84.

[4] Lawson, *The View from No 11* (Bantam Press, 1992) 354–55.

Consolidation is a regular feature of UK tax legislation; it has its own streamlined procedure since no changes in the law are being made.[5] The Rewrite legislation had its own procedure under which the legislation was presented in the House of Commons but then referred to a joint committee of both Houses on which the Commons have a majority. This legislation did sometimes change the law, but in ways too small to cause difficulty.[6] The quite distinct concept of codification is regarded as an impossible task; but an invaluable attempt was made in 1936.[7]

3.1.1.1 Corporation Tax

This legislative process is well illustrated by the history of corporation tax. Corporation tax was introduced not in a separate Corporation Tax Act but as part of FA 1965, namely Part IV (sections 46–89). Consolidation followed in the Income and Corporation Taxes Act of 1970 and again in the Act of the same title in 1988. Important provisions are to be found in later Acts, such as the Capital Allowances Act 2001 and the Taxation of Chargeable Gains Act 1992. The final stages of the Rewrite project saw the main corporation tax provisions rewritten into the Corporation Tax Act 2009 and Corporation Tax Act 2010, and the international rules into the Taxation (International and Other Provisions) Act 2010.

3.1.1.2 Income Tax

Most of the legislation now is to be found in the three income tax acts known as the Income Tax (Earnings and Pensions) Act (ITEPA) 2003, Income Tax (Trading and Other Income) Act (ITTOIA) 2005 and the Income Tax Act (ITA) 2007. The reader will have noted the weasel word 'most'. As the 2007 Act states in section 3, there are other rules not contained in these three Acts. Some of the other locations are mentioned in section 3, others are not. There is therefore no statute which provides a reader with a list of all the relevant provisions. This is clearly contrary to the policy behind Parliament's decision to grant the money for the Rewrite programme. It is also little short of a national disgrace and shows that responsibility for the statute book should be removed from HMRC.

Present government policy is that when later changes are made to rules in the three Income Tax Acts, they should take effect as changes to those Acts and not as free-standing separate bodies of legislation. We shall have to wait and see. One may then hope for consolidation of the income tax legislation, and possibly the corporation tax provisions as well.

3.1.1.3 Capital Gains

The UK has a capital gains tax (CGT) which is separate from the income tax. This was first enacted by FA 1965, namely Part III (ss 19–45). It was consolidated in 1979 as the Capital

---

[5] On parliamentary procedures for consolidation, see Tax Law Review Committee, *Final Report on Legislation* (IFS, 1996), [Pt 2.]

[6] Standing Order No 60. See Annual Report and Plans for 2008/09, paras 2.20 *et seq*. Interested readers are advised to consult the archived reports of the Tax Law Rewrite project, available on http://webarchive.nationalarchives.gov.uk/20140109143644/http://www.hmrc.gov.uk/rewrite/. ITA 2007, s 1029 gives the Treasury an important statutory power to undo—with retrospective effect—rewrite provisions in ITA 2007 which accidentally change the law. Section 1028 gives the Treasury power to make consequential provisions. There is no such power in ITEPA 2003 or ITTOIA 2005.

[7] Cmnd 5123.

Gains Tax Act (CGTA) 1979. That Act was followed by the Taxation of Chargeable Gains Act (TCGA) 1992. The difference in wording is because, while CGT is imposed on individuals, equivalent gains accruing to companies are usually charged to corporation tax. So even now, with the new rewritten Corporation Tax Acts it is still necessary to refer to the 1992 Act. At the very least, the capital gains rules should be consolidated.

3.1.1.4 Other Taxes and Acts

The IHT legislation was the last to be consolidated, in 1984. The Taxes Management Act (TMA) 1970 has not been rewritten. Changes to the law introducing self-assessment for income tax have mostly been fitted into the TMA structure; the result is not especially elegant. An example of free-standing administrative provisions is the Disclosure of Tax Avoidance Schemes rules found in FA 2004, sections 306–319.

3.1.2 Reform

The Rewrite programme mentioned above was driven by dissatisfaction with the state of tax statute law, which is nothing new but has become more intense;[8] neither is it confined to the UK. The first problem (a) is the sheer quantity of legislation. Vann claims that Australia has the longest tax statute in the world, though some UK experts say that the UK's is longer because of the Rewrite.[9] The second problem (b) is that the quality of the legislation is poor: again, Vann claims that Australia has the most unreadable tax statute in the world. This generates a desire to make statutes more intelligible and so more accessible. However, (c) judges, faced with a mass of complexity, have tended to play it safe and give a literal interpretation.[10] This causes draftsmen also to play it safe, enacting yet more detailed, and therefore over-long and incomprehensible, provisions. Draftsmen also take great care over transitional matters.[11] These criticisms could be applied with equal force in the UK, at least until recently.

The UK legislation, particularly as first seen by a new student, has two more specific flaws: (d) unless the relevant legislation has been rewritten, it is often hard to find the right part of the statute, especially if one has to comb through many amending Finance Acts; further, (e) the legislation is so lacking in structure that one can, say, look at provision or part of a provision inserted into an existing section and have little, if any, clue as to what it is trying to do—until one goes to secondary sources such as Hansard, or the Revenue background materials where these are available.

As already seen, some of these criticisms have been addressed slowly and, in the opinion of some, none too well by the UK's Tax Law Rewrite project, which ran from 1997

---

[8] For example, Tax Law Review Committee, *op cit*; for important earlier work, see Special Committee of Tax Law Consultative Bodies (September 1993 and 15 March 1990); and Gammie, *The Process of Tax Reform in the UK*, (Law Society, 15 March 1990).

[9] Ault *et al*, *Comparative Income Taxation*, 2nd edn (Kluwer, 2004)[10.]

[10] For example Deane J in *Hepples v FCT* (1991) 91 ATC, esp 4818–19. The Court of Appeal decision in *Mayes v Revenue & Customs Commissioners* [2011] EWCA Civ 407 is a good UK example.

[11] There is much interesting US debate on transitional rules: see Logue (1996) 94 *Michigan L Rev* 1129; Graetz (1977) 126 *University of Pennsylvania L Rev* 47; and Kaplow (1986) 99 HLR 506.

until 2010. This stemmed from a backbench amendment to the Finance Bill in 1995,[12] but with Australian and New Zealand precursors.[13] Although originally seen as a simplification measure, that proper and welcome—though probably impossible—task was abandoned. The outcome, nothing more (or less) than a rewrite of the existing law in up-to-date language with even the ambiguities of the old law proudly preserved. In so far as the legislation tries to provide a better structure and arrangement, it addresses flaws (d) and (e) above. How far it succeeds with problem (b) is a matter which John Tiley decided to address at greater length in the permissibly less neutral atmosphere of his Preface to the 6th edition of this book. One should, however, record that many efforts have been made in recent years outside the area of the Rewrite to improve the general intelligibility of new tax legislation. It is a matter of some regret that the long-winded, dispersed and narrative style of the Rewrite ignores those efforts, and forces on us a style which is hard to use—and that nothing seems capable of stopping the present perverse process.

Other, more substantial anxieties have been expressed. Thus, the new legislation makes the historical thread more difficult to follow. In turn this raises the fundamental question how far the courts are going to allow lawyers to go back to the original legislation to interpret the new version; if the courts say that they can, one has gained little except extra words to read; if they say that they cannot, they will undermine the no-change premise of the process. Further, by its refusal to be anything more than a rewrite, the process preserves and highlights the underlying incoherence of the law.[14] The (independent) Budd Committee's proposal that there should be a Tax Structure Review Project has died a silent death.[15] The younger generation, who will have learned only from the new legislation, may find some of these doubts misplaced. They may even be convinced that the legislation really is easier to use and that there are consequent savings of time and so of costs for taxpayers. The HMRC Rewrite estimate of savings to the profession is £70m if each tax professional saves one hour per month.[16] There is also evidence from Australia about whether simplified drafting reduces the psychological costs of compliance.[17] Overall, therefore, it can be seen that the Rewrite did not solve many of our problems, and may even have made some of them worse. These things matter not just because of the needs of students, but also because of the needs of other members of the community; tax legislation which is hard to understand increases compliance costs.[18]

A very different proposal might address all three problems—to move to a more explicitly principle-based tax system. A statement of principles would make it easier for judges (and others) to interpret the statutes and might also make for a shorter statute book. Judges would

[12] FA 1995, s 160; the Revenue report and background paper written under s 160 is entitled 'The Path to Tax Simplification' (1995); for reservations, see Beighton [1996] BTR 1 and Kerridge [2003] BTR 257.
[13] In Australia, The Tax Law Improvement Project (TULIP); on New Zealand, see Sawyer [2007] BTR 405 and Prebble 54 *IBFD Jnl* at 290; for empirical evidence of degree of enhanced readability, see Smith and Richardson (1999) 20 *Fiscal Studies* 321.
[14] Kerridge [2003] BTR 257.
[15] IFS Tax Law Review Committee, Parliamentary Procedures for the Enactment of Rewritten Tax Law, para 7.6 (Nov 1996).
[16] See Annual Report and Plans for 2008/09, para 2.26.
[17] Woellner *et al* [2007] BTR 717; see also Evans, *Taxing Personal Capital Gains* (Australian Tax Research Foundation, Research Study 40, 2003) Table 5.22.
[18] Eg, Evans, *op cit*, Table 5.22.

have to interpret such statutes purposively. In New Zealand the traditional approaches to interpretation have been abolished in favour of an Interpretation Act, under which judges are to accord to every Act and statutory provision such fair, large and literal interpretation as will best ensure the attainment of the object of the legislation according to it true intent, meaning and spirit.[19] Another hope is that tax law can be made more purposive in form, and the Tax Law Rewrite Project produced some early essays in this direction;[20] purposive legislation, purposively construed is the goal. The boundary between principle and purpose is obscure, however. Without going down any of these routes, it might be better to insist that tax legislation should be recognised as having a structure and ensuring that the structure is adhered to.[21]

One model for a principle-based approach may be seen in EU law, whether through the Treaties themselves or through directives, as with VAT.[22] Another model is the Dutch Tax Code. Van Raad, after noting that in the 1960s the Dutch code for personal income tax covered less than 20 pages in print, complained that by 2001 it had grown to more than four times its original size and that three decades of additions (often dealing with avoidance) had obfuscated the Act's original, well-balanced structure. He also noted that tax Acts and decrees now amounted to some 500 pages of print.[23] In comparison, the number of pages of UK tax legislation in 2010 alone amounted to over 8,000.[24]

As always, one must not try to build too great hopes on new approaches to statutory drafting. Simpler words mean little without a simpler policy behind them. Principles and purposes clearly have a role, but there seems little escape from highly-detailed information at some stage in the process.[25] In the common law world this may take the form of regulations, as in the United States, statutory instruments or binding rulings, as in Australia, New Zealand and Canada, or Revenue practice, as in the UK. It may also take the form of 'safe harbour' provisions in the statute itself. Prebble suggests that one reason why Continental systems may have less detailed legislation is his possibly chauvinistic view that they have not yet reached the levels of sophistication of Anglophone systems and tolerate more breaches of neutrality in their tax bases.[26] Whether sophistication is a good or bad thing is not explored. Prebble's other argument is more fundamental and goes to the nature of tax law. 'Income tax law,' he writes,[27]

> is different in kind from law in general and from tax laws (such as VAT) which depend on transactions or states of fact. Unlike other laws, income tax law does not relate to its subject matter, which is the facts and legal relations in business activity. Income tax law ignores some facts and transactions and it recharacterises others. In other words it is dislocated from its subject matter.

The use of the word 'dislocated' suggests a degree of unnaturalness and difficulty. An easier way of making the point is to say that the facts with which the income tax system has to

---

[19] This goes back to 1888. Richardson (1986) 12 *Monash L Rev* 35, 36.
[20] Eg, *The Relief for Trading Losses of Companies* (February 1998).
[21] Pagan [1993] 4 *Fiscal Studies* 90.
[22] Avery Jones (1996) 17(3) *Fiscal Studies* 63; for comments, see Prebble [1998] BTR 112.
[23] Ault, *op cit*, 94. The same lament was made by the UK's 1936 Codification Committee comparing the Acts of 1842 and 1853 with the law in 1936.
[24] Mirrlees et al (eds), *Tax by Design: The Mirrlees Review* (OUP, 2011) 2.
[25] See also McCaffery [1990] *Wisconsin L Rev* 1267.
[26] [1998] BTR 112, 123.
[27] [1998] BTR 112 (see comment on VAT at 123); and [1994] BTR 380.

wrestle include not only the raw primary facts (including legal facts), but also the characterisation of those primary facts established by other branches of law—a process entirely familiar to students of the conflict of laws.[28] Tax law must frequently draw lines between activities which are legally distinct but economically similar; legislators may drawn these lines where they wish, but efficiency arguments suggest that lines should be drawn so that a transaction or item is taxed in the same way as its closest substitutes.[29]

There are also parliamentary problems. If new statutes are to be made more purposive in nature, what happens to the old statutes? It might also raise other issues, such as the role of the House of Lords in fiscal matters.[30]

3.1.3 Current Rules of Interpretation: Approaches and Rules

UK tax law recognises several approaches to issues of construction. The best traditional summary was set out by Lord Donovan in *IRC v Mangin*:[31]

(1)   The words are to be given their ordinary meaning. They are not to be given some other meaning simply because their object is to frustrate legitimate tax avoidance devices. ... [M]oral precepts are not applicable to the interpretation of revenue statutes.

(2)   ... [O]ne has to look merely at what is clearly said. There is no room for any intendment. There is no equity about a tax. There is no presumption as to tax. Nothing is to be read in, nothing is to be implied. One can only look fairly at the language used.

(3)   ... [T]he object of the construction of a statute being to ascertain the will of the legislature it may be presumed that neither injustice nor absurdity was intended. If therefore a literal interpretation would produce such a result, and the language admits of an interpretation which would avoid it, then such an interpretation may be adopted.

(4)   ... [T]he history of an enactment and the reasons which led to its being passed may be used as an aid to construction.

Today, and especially since the decisions of the House of Lords (and from 2009 the Supreme Court) in the avoidance cases discussed in chapter five, the ordinary meaning has to be weighed more explicitly against context and purpose. As usual, the more variables there are, the more difficult it is to tell what weight to place on one variable rather than another. In the past judges have had to wrestle with legislation of great complexity, and from time to time have warned that it is possible that the obscurity of an enactment or the uncontrollable width of its language—or of the discretion needed to implement it—may compel a court to find that no reasonable construction is available and that the taxpayer is therefore not to be charged.[32] In the same vein, Lord Walker has said that a Crown argument which would entail a perpetual liability (to pay interest on a tax liability) subject only

---

[28] [1997] BTR 180, 191.

[29] Weisbach (2000) 29(1) *J Legal Studies*, Pt 1; arguing that the benefits of keeping the substitutes together outweighs the negative effects of raising an inefficient tax.

[30] See IFS Tax Law Review Committee, Parliamentary Procedures for the Enactment of Rewritten Tax Law (Nov 1996).

[31] [1971] AC 739, 746; [1971] 1 All ER 179, 182. However see Robertson, *Judicial Discretion in the House of Lords* (OUP, 1999) ch 3.

[32] *Customs and Excise Commrs v Top Ten Promotions Ltd* [1969] 3 All ER 39 (HL) at 93 per Lord Donovan, and at 95 per Lord Wilberforce; *Vestey v IRC* [1980] AC 1148; [1980] STC 10.

to a discretionary (and possibly dubious) official power of remission, should be rejected as being so disproportionate a remedy as to raise a real doubt whether Parliament could have intended it.[33] The House of Lords has shown itself capable, on the one hand, of depriving a provision of any effect[34] and, on the other, of imposing double taxation.[35] Whether the same results would be achieved today is unclear.

Where a flaw in the legislation is detected, modern judges tend to favour a statutory analysis under which the taxable results corresponded with the actual results, ie, the commercial (or economic) consequences.[36] Another strand is to say that the court has to do its best to make sense of the statute, and that means not only making grammatical sense of the text but also finding a rational scheme in the legislation—if possible.[37]

3.1.3.1 Establishing Parliamentary Purpose—*Pepper v Hart*

The court may look at the purpose and history of the relevant legislation, and to this end reference may be made to the state of the law, and to the material facts and events with which it is apparent that Parliament was dealing.[38] In *Pepper v Hart*,[39] the House of Lords, reversing centuries of case law, held that the court could consult Hansard in order to interpret the words of the legislation where that legislation was ambiguous or obscure, or led to an absurdity. The courts would rely on statements made by ministers or other promoters of the Bill and any other parliamentary material needed to understand those statements and their effects—provided the statements relied on were clear.[40] In this case the House concluded that a reading of Hansard showed that in 1976 a particular statement by the minister in charge of the Bill meant that in determining the measure of cost incurred by an employer in providing an in-house benefit in kind, it was necessary to look at marginal cost not overall cost. It followed that that was how the provision should be construed.

This approach to interpretation is controversial,[41] and one authoritative source suggested that its main beneficiary would, through the emphasis on ministers' statements, be the executive.[42] Such fears have been reduced to some extent by the decision of the House of Lords in *Wilson v First County Trust*,[43] where Lord Nicholls treated the rule simply as a source of background information and thought that one could not equate ministerial statements with the will of the legislature.[44] There is a quite separate argument that such

---

[33] *Melham Ltd v Burton* [2006] UKHL, 6 [2006] STC 908, para 19.

[34] *IRC v Ayrshire Employers Mutual Insurance Association Ltd* [1946] 1 All ER 637; 27 TC 331 (HL).

[35] *Cleary v IRC* [1967] 2 All ER 48; 44 TC 399.

[36] Lord Walker in *Jerome v Kelly* [2004] UKHL 25; [2004] STC 887, para 28.

[37] *Billingham v Cooper* [2001] EWCA Civ 1041; [2001] STC 1177; see also Viscount Simon LC in *Nokes v Doncaster Amalgamated Collieries Ltd* [1940] AC 1014 at 1022.

[38] See Lord Macdermott in *IRC v Rennell* [1964] AC 173, 198; and Lord Macdermott in *Madras Electric Supply Corp Ltd v Boarland* [1955] AC 667, 686; 35 TC 612, 640; [1955] 1 All ER 753, 760.

[39] [1992] STC 898.

[40] [1992] STC 898, 922, 923.

[41] For review, see Kavanagh (2005) 121 *LQR* 98; for criticism, see Baker [1993] *CLJ* 353; Bennion [1995] BTR 325 and Lord Steyn (2001) *OJLS* 59 and 24 *Sydney L Rev* 5 at 13–16. For history and comparisons, see Rawlinson [1983] BTR 274; articles cited by Arnold in (1984) 32 *Canadian Tax J* 400; and Bale (1995) 74 *Canadian Bar Rev* 1. For a case which should have been decided differently, see *Leedale v Lewis* [1982] BTR 835 as discussed at [1983] BTR 70 (JFAJ). See also Robertson, *op cit*, ch 5.

[42] Davies [1993] BTR 172.

[43] [2003] 3 WLR 568.

[44] *Ibid*, paras 59 and 67.

statements give rise to some sort of estoppel or legitimate expectation as to how the executive will apply the legislation, but this is as yet still unsettled.[45]

Hansard has been cited to the court in subsequent cases, but with no decisive effect.[46] Usually, judges either refer to Hansard under this rule, or state that the *Pepper v Hart* criteria are not met (but referring to Hansard in any case and stating that it makes no difference). Unsurprisingly, there has been no case in which judges have said that the provision is clear and so no reference may be made, but that if they had looked at Hansard it would have made a difference.

Finally, it should be noted that the statutory general anti-abuse rule in FA 2013, Part 5 contains a novel and unusually broad evidentiary rule in section 211 that goes well beyond the *Pepper v Hart* approach: 'in determining any issue in connection with the general anti-abuse rule, a court or tribunal may take into account—

(a) guidance, statements or other material (whether of HMRC, a Minister of the Crown or anyone else) that was in the public domain at the time the arrangements were entered into, and
(b) evidence of established practice at that time.'

3.1.3.2 Other UK Statutory Interpretation Rules

While the courts will try to avoid highly inequitable or manifestly unfair results,[47] where the words are wholly unambiguous the court is bound by their literal interpretation, however unreasonable.[48] Arguments based on competing anomalies do not find favour.[49] Where a statutory provision is enacted but is based upon a misconception of what the law then was, the law remains as it was and does not share the misconception of the legislature.[50]

There is a presumption that provisions dealing with the machinery of taxation do not impose a charge.[51] The courts will not construe a machinery provision so as to defeat the charge;[52] however, the absence of machinery has been used to qualify a charge.[53] There is a presumption that words used in the same contexts in different statutes are used in the same sense.[54] Where a particular interpretation would give HMRC the power to distribute the burden of tax between taxpayers, the courts will reject it.[55] The courts may lean against a construction which HMRC is unwilling to apply in its full rigour.[56] When interpreting a consolidated enactment, the court should not, in general, refer to the earlier Acts. However,

---

[45] See Kavanagh, *op cit*, 115 *et seq*.
[46] Eg, *Massmould Holdings Ltd v Payne* [1993] STC 62.
[47] *Coutts & Co v IRC* [1953] AC 267, 281; [1953] 1 All ER 418, 421, per Lord Reid.
[48] *Plumbly v Spencer* [1999] STC 677, 684, per Robert Walker LJ; see also Lord Reid in *IRC v Hinchy* [1960] 1 All ER 505, 512; 38 TC 625, 652.
[49] *Dale v IRC* [1953] 2 All ER 671, 676; 34 TC 468, 488 (HL), per Lord Normand.
[50] *Davies, Jenkins & Co Ltd v Davies* [1967] 1 All ER 913, 915, 922; 44 TC 273, 287, (HL).
[51] *Straits Settlements Commr of Stamps v Oei Tjong Swan* [1933] AC 378, 389, per Lord Macmillan.
[52] *IRC v Longmans Green & Co Ltd* (1932) 17 TC 272, 282.
[53] *Colquhoun v Brooks* (1889) 14 App Cas 493, 506; 2 TC 490, 500.
[54] *Gartside v IRC* [1968] AC 553, 602; [1968] 1 All ER 121, 131, per Lord Reid. But this is only a presumption: see Atkin LJ in *Martin v Lowry* [1926] 1 KB 550, 561; 11 TC 297, 315.
[55] *Vestey v IRC* [1980] AC 1148; [1980] STC 10; 54 TC 503.
[56] *Wicks v Firth* [1983] 2 AC 214, 231; [1983] STC 25, 29, per Lord Bridge; quoted by Chadwick LJ in *Dunlop International v Pardoe* [1999] STC 909, 916.

the court is entitled to have regard to the fact that a subsection was later added to the original section.[57]

The Taxes Acts[58] are applicable in England and Wales, Scotland[59] and, for most of them, Northern Ireland. It follows that the language they employ should be construed so as to have, as far as possible, uniform effect in all four countries alike.[60] Some provisions speak the language of the English lawyer, perhaps with some Scots legal phrases casually thrown in; here, the courts must take the meanings of the legal expression from the law of the country to which they properly belong and must then apply that meaning by analogy, even if such a construction does violence to some of the best-established doctrines of Scots law.[61] Lord Walker has said that the fact that the legislation has to apply in Scotland is a good reason for not being swayed by highly technical arguments from English land law. He also said that when asked to deal with a flaw in the legislation, he would always tend to favour a statutory analysis under which the taxable results corresponded with the actual results, ie the commercial (or economic) consequences.[62]

When provisions are ambiguous, the court may consider the effect of subsequent legislation only when the two views of the original statute are equally tenable and there are no indications favouring one rather than the other. The argument advanced in favour of this rule is that the new provision could only have been required if one view was held by Parliament rather than the other.[63]

Where statutes deem certain things to be as they are not, the court must consider for what purposes and between what persons the statutory fiction is to be resorted to.[64] However, this does not require the court to abandon the golden rule of construction, ie that the grammatical and ordinary sense of the words should be adhered to unless that would lead to absurdity or inconsistency, in which case the grammatical and ordinary sense of the words may be modified to avoid that absurdity and inconsistency but no further.[65]

3.1.4 The Literal versus Purposive Debate

The blend of approaches in Lord Donovan's words (see §3.1.3 above) is not only about the most coherent explanation of what judges actually do; it also avoids 'schools' of thought.[66]

---

[57] *IRC v Joiner* [1975] 3 All ER 1050; [1975] STC 657; 50 TC 449, but note the more restrictive approach of Lord Diplock and see the discussion by Baxter in [1976] *Conveyancer* 336, 343. See also Bramwell [1992] BTR 69.

[58] Defined in TA 1988, s 831.

[59] On construction and Scots law, see the positive suggestions by Jones [1986] BTR 75; as far as one can see, these suggestions have been completely ignored.

[60] Viscount Simon in *IT Commrs for General Purposes (City of London) v Gibbs* [1942] 1 All ER 415, 422; 24 TC 221, 236, 244, (HL). Hence, English courts will follow Scottish decisions: *Wiseburgh v Domville* [1956] 1 All ER 754, 758; 36 TC 527, 538–39 (CA), per Lord Evershed MR.

[61] *Lord Advocate v Countess of Moray* [1905] AC 531, 540 (HL) per Lord Macnaghten.

[62] Lord Walker in *Jerome v Kelly* [2004] UKHL 25; [2004] STC 887, para 28.

[63] *Finch v IRC* [1985] Ch 1, 15; [1984] STC 261, 272 (CA) per Oliver LJ; and *Westcott v Woolcombers Ltd* [1986] STC 182, 191; 60 TC 575, 586, per Hoffman J.

[64] Eg *RC v Metrolands (Property Finance) Ltd* [1981] STC 193, 208; 54 TC 679, 697, per Nourse J.

[65] In *Jerome v Kelly* [2004] UKHL 25, [2004] STC 887 at para 43, Lord Walker followed 'the general guidance' of Peter Gibson J in *Marshall v Kerr* [1993] STC 360, 365; 67 TC 56, 79 (CA) and noted that although the House of Lords (1994 STC 638) allowed the appeal on other grounds, Lord Browne Wilkinson expressly approved these words (at 649).

[66] The well-known antipathy between Lord Simonds and Lord Denning on these issues is a warning precedent.

For completeness, however, mention should be made of two of these schools or approaches. It is no longer appropriate to spend much time on the first, though it should be noted for historical purposes, eg when reading old cases.

3.1.4.1 The Literal Approach

The literal approach was, for a long time, the favoured UK approach to tax interpretation. People were not to be taxed unless they were designated in clear terms by the taxing Act as taxpayers and the amount of their liability was clearly defined.[67] One reason for this is that, apart from statute, there is no liability to pay any tax and no antecedent relationship between the taxing authority and the taxpayer, so that no reasoning founded on any such *a priori* liability or relationship may be used in the construction of the Act.[68] Other reasons may include the need to protect the individual from the state, the analogy of criminal offences and some sort of *contra proferentem* rule, but these do not explain the strictness with which other tax provisions are construed against the taxpayer.

Strict interpretation was applied to the taxpayer just as much as to the Revenue. If a literal interpretation produced a construction whereby hardship fell on innocent beneficiaries by the rights, monstrous or otherwise, conferred on the Revenue, that interpretation must be adhered to and the hardship produced was not a relevant consideration.[69]

3.1.4.2 The Purposive Approach

The purposive approach is intended to stand in complete contrast to the literal approach. Such contrasts are usually unfair. Literalists accuse purposivists of wanting to ignore the plain words of the statute; purposivists accuse literalists of 'legalism' and of wanting to be bound by the plain words of a statute even though the purpose of the statue is clear. However, as Sir Owen Dixon said on becoming Chief Justice of Australia, speaking, admittedly, of constitutional matters, '[t]here is no other safe guide to judicial decisions in great conflicts than a strict and complete legalism'.[70] This, of course, ignores the problems of what is meant by 'legalism'.

The first modern tax case where a majority of the House of Lords came out in favour of the purposive approach was *McGuckian v IRC* in 1997.[71] For Lord Steyn the 1981 decision in *WT Ramsay Ltd v IRC*[72] marked an intellectual breakthrough, in that tax law could catch up with the rest of the legal system and move from a literal interpretation to one based on context, designed to identify the purpose of a statute and give effect to it.[73] This has been repeated again and again since 1997, eg by the House of Lords in *Barclays Mercantile Busi-*

---

[67] *Vestey v IRC* [1980] STC 10, 18; 54 TC 503, 581, per Lord Wilberforce; but contrast *Floor v Davis* [1979] 2 All ER 677; [1979] STC 379 (in which Lord Wilberforce dissented).

[68] *Pryce v Monmouthshire Canal and Railway Companies* (1879) 4 App Cas 197, 202, 203, per Lord Cairns LC.

[69] *Re Joynson's WTs* [1954] Ch 567, 573, per Danckwerts J; and see *IRC v Hinchy* [1960] 1 All ER 505; 38 TC 625.

[70] (1952) 85 CLR xiv. For reaction against formalism (as opposed to legalism), see Zines, *The High Court and the Constitution*, 4th edn (Butterworths, 1997), 444–49.

[71] [1997] STC 918. Canadian courts have apparently reverted from purposive to plain meaning: see *Corporation Notre Dame de Bon Secours v The Queen* (1995) 95 DTC 5017 and *Friesen v The Queen* (1995) 95 DTC 5551.

[72] [1982] AC 300, [1981] STC 174.

[73] For an example of tax law being regarded as different, see Evans LJ in *Ingram v IRC* [1997] STC 1234, 1251, where, after outlining the argument, he says, 'I would be prepared to hold in any other context that this produces a result which is so clearly at variance with the apparent object of [the section] that it cannot be regarded as a proper interpretation of the section'.

ness Finance in 2005[74] and the Supreme Court in *UBS AG and DB Group Services (UK)* in 2016.[75] The effects of adopting this approach remain uncertain. It can certainly make a change to the ways in which cases are argued and judgments written; it may also make a difference to the ways in which statutes are drafted. What is unclear is whether it will make any difference to the results of cases—though in the avoidance area in recent years it does appear to be aiding HMRC.[76] Courts must have a clear idea as to the purpose to be achieved, which raises the issue of which extrinsic aids may be used.[77]

3.1.5 US Developments

The UK's legal history has been marked by a tendency for American ideas to filter into the system many years after they have become current in the United States; often the period is related to the gap between a judge being a student in the US and becoming a judge in the UK. The purposive approach (§3.1.4.2 above) was promulgated with particular vigour by Hart and Sacks in their seminal but cyclostyled work *The Legal Process*.[78] However, just as the UK courts started moving towards purpose, some US courts were re-emphasising the role of textual formalism in the interpretation of statutes, a move associated especially with Justice Scalia.[79] The approach was set out by Justice Scalia in the following terms in *Green v Bock Laundry Machine Co*:[80]

> The meaning of terms in statute books ought to be determined, not on the basis of which meaning can be shown to have been understood by a larger handful of the members of Congress; but rather on the basis of which meaning is (1) most in accord with context and ordinary usage, and thus most likely to have been understood by the whole Congress which voted on the words of the statute (not to mention the citizens subject to it), and (2) most compatible with the surrounding body of law into which the provision must be integrated—a compatibility which, by a benign fiction, we assume Congress always has in mind.

There are many reasons why it may be inappropriate for the UK to model its approach to interpretation on that of the US. The systems are too dissimilar for an instinctive adoption of US practices, and these differences show themselves not only in words used when approaching legislation but, more fundamentally, in the role of the court, the drafting of legislation and the attitude to rule-formality.[81]

---

[74] *Barclays Mercantile Business Finance v Mawson* [2004] UKHL 51; [2005] STC 1. See below §5.6.

[75] *UBS AG v R&C Comrs; Deutsche Bank Group v R&C Comrs* [2016] UKSC 13. See below §5.6.6.

[76] See below §5.6. See also Arnold (2001) 49 *Canadian Tax J* 1, saying that Canadian judges pay only lip service to purposive construction in the avoidance area.

[77] On (lax) Canadian practice, see Bowman TCCJ in *Glaxo Wellcome Inc v The Queen* (1996) 96 DTC 1159; and Bowman (1995) 43 *Canadian Tax J* 1167, 1186. On extrinsic aids and the UK GAAR see above §3.1.3.1 and below §5.5.3.

[78] Finally published by Foundation Press in 1995.

[79] (1990) 37 *UCLA L Rev* 621; see also Eskridge, *Dynamic Statutory Interpretation* (Harvard University Press, 1994) ch 1, n 64 for some later literature. For a discussion of US tax law in the light of the new approaches, see Popkin (1988) 61 *Southern California L Rev* 541; and Livingston (1996) 51 *Tax L Rev* 677. For UK comments, see Cross, Bell and Engle (eds), *Statutory Interpretation*, 3rd edn (Butterworths, 1995). See also MacCormick and Summers, *Interpreting Statutes* (Dartmouth, 1991).

[80] 490 US 504, 528.

[81] See, generally, Atiyah and Summers, *Form and Substance in Anglo-American Law* (OUP, 1987) chs 1, 4, 11; there is a summary of some of the points by Popkin [1991] BTR 284–86.

3.2 Cases

Cases are authorities in the usual way according to the rule of precedent, save that tax is a UK law and so English courts will accept Scottish decisions as binding, and vice versa. However, in assessing the value of a precedent in tax law, special complications arise from the fact that the appeal structure in the UK allows the courts to reverse a decision of the Tribunals (formerly Commissioners) only for error of law or because it cannot be supported on the evidence.

3.3 Revenue Practice—Information

Although not directly binding, statements of Revenue practice are of great importance in the practical administration of the system. Major changes of policy in recent years have led to a great increase in the amount of information being made available, especially on the HMRC website. One of the purposes of the Rewrite legislation was to take account of current HMRC practice and to make the legislation reflect what is done. So provisions were rewritten to take account not only of extra-statutory concessions but also of everyday practice. These informal arrangements sometimes defer a charge. Naturally, the Revenue assumes that taxpayers taking the benefit of the deferral will pay the deferred tax in due course; however, the fact that the basis was concessionary used to mean that there was no legal obligation to do so. Such an obligation was imposed in 1999;[82] it is a reserve power in that it is imposed only if the taxpayer fails to observe the terms of the concession. The charge cannot be for less than the amount deferred by way of concession.

3.3.1 Extra-statutory Concessions and Statements of Practice

Extra-statutory concessions (ESCs) are few, tightly-written and almost legislative in form. A booklet gathering these concessions together (IR 1) is published periodically and available online.[83] One crucial difference between an ESC and a statutory provision is that the Revenue can withhold the benefit of the concession if it is so minded without direct legal— as distinct from political or administrative—consequences.[84] However, the development of administrative law remedies[85] suggests that an assessment made on the basis of withholding a concession could be quashed on the basis of breach of the duty to act fairly as between

---

[82] FA 1999, s 76. For an example of the problem, see *Fallon v Fellow* [2001] STC 1409 concerning now-withdrawn ESC D14, but note that at para 46 Park J explains why the taxpayer should not be criticised. The notes to the Finance Bill 1999 refer specifically to Concessions D15 (now withdrawn), D16 and D22. See also Revenue Interpretation, Tax Bulletin No 43, October 1999, and Revenue CGT Manual, paras 13650–62.

[83] See current list of ESCs (updated April 2015) online at: https://www.gov.uk/government/publications/extra-statutory-concessions-ex-inland-revenue. More than 30 ESCs were removed from the list in the latest update because they were 'obsolete' or had been legislated.

[84] *R v CIR, ex parte Wilkinson* [2003] EWCA Civ 814; [2003] STC 1113—not even to give effect to Convention rights under the Human Rights Act 2000 (eg para 46), approved [2005] UKHL 30, para 20; see also *Al Fayed v Adv General for Scotland* [2004] STC 1703, para 55.

[85] Rowland [1995] BTR 115 argues that these judicial review remedies are not enough.

different taxpayers.[86] Such a situation would arise only where the taxpayers could bring themselves within the scope of the concession.

In this connection, it is important to note that the list of concessions is prefaced with a general statement that a concession will not be given where an attempt is made to use it for tax avoidance.[87] In a note to one concession the Revenue stated that concessions are used 'to deal with what are, on the whole, minor or transitory anomalies ... and to reduce cases of hardship at the margins of the code when a statutory remedy would be difficult to devise or would run to a length out of proportion to the intrinsic importance of the matter'.[88] Some concessions may not be concessions at all.[89]

New ESCs have become much less common in recent years, following the House of Lords decision in *R v IRC, ex parte Wilkinson*.[90] In that case Lord Hoffmann accepted that HMRC have a wide managerial discretion under TMA 1970, section 1, which, in his Lordship's view, 'enables the commissioners to formulate policy in the interstices of the tax legislation, dealing pragmatically with minor or transitory anomalies, cases of hardship at the margins or cases in which a statutory rule is difficult to formulate or its enactment would take up a disproportionate amount of Parliamentary time.' However, Lord Hoffmann also emphasised the limits of this discretion, holding that the discretion was not so wide 'as to enable the commissioners to concede, by extra-statutory concession, an allowance which Parliament could have granted but did not grant, and on grounds not of pragmatism in the collection of tax but of general equity between men and women.' On legality of concessions and new procedure post-*Wilkinson* to give some ESCs statutory force, see below §4.2.3.

Statements of practice (SPs) are published on a regular basis; these are only slightly less formal than the concessions.

3.3.2 Revenue Interpretations and Decisions

Statements of Practice are supplemented by published Revenue interpretations; these interpretations are heavily qualified and HMRC will not necessarily regard itself as bound by them. Revenue Decisions are notes of decisions in individual cases. No new decisions have been released since 1994.

3.3.3 Manuals

The most interesting source of information (from an academic point of view) is the internal manuals which have now been published and are on available on the HMRC website. Certain passages are held back for operational reasons. Some of the contents are essays of the highest quality and interest and they often contain worked examples. Until recently these were confidential to the Revenue, although of course their contents were well known

---

[86] Eg the unsuccessful application in *R v IRC, ex parte J Rothschild Holdings* [1987] STC 163; *R v Inspector of Taxes, ex parte Brumfield* [1989] STC 151; *R v IRC, ex parte Kaye* [1992] STC 581.

[87] This general anti-avoidance statement was used by the Revenue to defeat a move to quash an assessment for breach of natural justice in *R v IRC, ex parte Fulford-Dobson* [1987] STC 344.

[88] Inland Revenue Press Release, 16 February 1989, [1989] *Simon's Tax Intelligence* 74.

[89] In *Steibelt v Paling* [1999] STC 594, 604, Sir Richard Scott V-C refused to regard ESC D24 as a concession so much as an interpretation.

[90] [2005] UKHL 30, per Lord Hoffmann at paras 20–23.

to those highly-trained inspectors who left the service for private practice. In proceedings for judicial review a court ordered discovery of such documents, but only because the taxpayer's argument relied on having been informed that there was a Revenue view of the correct construction of a provision and that that construction was in his favour.[91]

3.3.4 Rulings

There is no general scheme whereby taxpayers can obtain advance rulings on the tax consequences of a particular transaction. However, in practice advice is often available provided there is a detailed scheme; the Revenue usually insist on knowing the identity of the taxpayer concerned.[92] In November 2006 the Varney Committee reviewed links with large businesses. The Chancellor announced that he would implement the review in full; hence HMRC has now agreed to bring in advance rulings.[93] However, it is not a general system of rulings; its purpose is to give business certainty about the tax consequences of significant investments and corporate reorganisations. It is not aimed to pass judgment on avoidance schemes but to help those who provide clear plans for investment, reconstructions and reorganisation.[94]

   Generally, one can say that HMRC does not provide a free legal aid clinic, but it is in its interests to be helpful. Where an application for judicial review is made on the basis of a ruling, the Revenue will be bound by the ruling only if the taxpayer gave full details of the specific transaction on which he sought the Revenue's ruling, indicated the ruling sought and made it plain that a fully-considered ruling was sought, and indicated the use he intended to make of any ruling given, and the ruling or statement made was clear, unambiguous and devoid of qualification.[95] A breach of a representation by the Revenue will not amount to an abuse of power if the taxpayer knows that clearance at local level is not to be treated as binding on the Revenue, or he has not fully disclosed all relevant material to the inspectors.[96] Full disclosure is not necessarily made merely because sufficient information has been disclosed to enable inferences to be drawn. In principle a clearance may be withdrawn; however, the consequent transaction may have gone too far for the Revenue to do this without administrative law consequences.[97] It is not yet clear whether obtaining a ruling on the status of a taxpayer will necessarily protect the taxpayer from assessment to tax on a transaction if that transaction was not disclosed.[98] In certain circumstances the legislation

---

[91] *R v IRC, ex parte J Rothschild Holdings plc* [1986] STC 410; upheld [1987] STC 163; 61 TC 178 (CA).

[92] The terms on which advice is available in Inland Revenue Code of Practice 10.

[93] HM Treasury Press Release 92/06, 17 November 2006, Proposal 4.6.

[94] One may contrast the treatment of big business with that meted out to two taxpayers in what is known as the Arctic Systems case, more formally *Jones v Garnett* [2005] EWCA Civ 1553, [2006] STC 283, CA.

[95] *R v IRC, ex parte MFK Underwriting Agencies Ltd* [1989] STC 873; 62 TC 607; see also *R v IRC, ex p Camacq Corp* [1989] STC 785; 62 TC 651; Tidball [1991] BTR 48; and, more generally, Hinds [1991] BTR 191.

[96] *Matrix-Securities Ltd v IRC* [1994] STC 272; 66 TC 587 (HL). For a full account of the facts, see *Matrix Securities Ltd v Theodore Goddard* [1998] STC 1. See also text of letter from the Inland Revenue dated 3 June 1994 and reprinted in [1994] *Simon's Tax Intelligence* 729. Among notes on this case, see Eden [1994] BTR 254; and Sandler [1994] *CLJ* 273.

[97] *Matrix-Securities Ltd v IRC* [1994] STC 272; 66 TC 587 (HL); the taxpayer may have a claim for damages: [1992] STC 272, 284, per Lord Griffiths; see below at §4.2.

[98] *R v IRC ex p Howmet Corp* [1994] STC 413 (QBD).

will prescribe a clearance procedure, usually as part of broad anti-avoidance legislation.[99] A right of appeal against a refusal of clearance is not always available; whether the refusal to give a right of appeal breaches human rights legislation awaits resolution.[100]

3.3.5 Legitimate Expectation

With the exception of rulings, HMRC are not generally bound by their guidance. However, in the joined cases of *Davies and another* and *Gaines-Cooper*,[101] the taxpayers argued that HMRC's guidance on residency in booklet IR20 contained a more benevolent interpretation of the circumstances in which an individual becomes non-resident and not ordinarily resident in the UK than did the ordinary law, or, alternatively, that prior to 2005 it was the settled practice of HMRC to adopt such a benevolent interpretation of IR20, either of which gave rise to a legitimate expectation that the benevolent interpretation would be applied to determinations of their residency status. In dismissing the taxpayers' appeals, the Supreme Court held (4:1) that the proper construction of IR20 did not support the taxpayers' contention and that there was insufficient evidence of any settled practice on the part of the HMRC by way of departure from the IR20 guidance. Of more general interest, however, is that by the time the case reached the Court of Appeal, HMRC had accepted that their published guidance and their practice could give rise to legitimate expectations on the part of taxpayers such as to become binding. In the case of practice in particular, however, the evidential hurdle will be difficult for taxpayers to overcome.

In *Samarkand Film Partnership No. 3, Proteus Film Partnership and three partners v HMRC*,[102] the Upper Tribunal rejected the taxpayer's claim of legitimate expectations in a tax avoidance situation. The UT concluded (quite rightly) that if the Revenue has qualified its guidance by stating it will not necessarily be applied in a tax avoidance case, it would not be unfair, let alone conspicuously or outrageously so, for HMRC in such a case to do exactly what they have said they might do, which is not to apply the guidance.

---

[99] Eg ITA 2007, s 701 and CTA 2010, s 749 (ex TA 1988, s 707), but not TCGA 1992, s 30. For an example of difficulties that arise in practice, see ICAEW memorandum TR 657, reprinted in [1987] *Simon's Tax Intelligence* 321.

[100] See views of professional bodies reported in [1991] *Simon's Tax Intelligence* 453, para 19. In addition, the Revenue also publishes their views on some points of interpretation, eg in correspondence with professional bodies and, increasingly, in their quarterly Bulletins. In the past, information has also been gleaned from the reports of the Parliamentary Commissioner for Administration and the Revenue's own Adjudicator.

[101] [2011] UKSC 47, and see case note by Welsh and Eden [2011] BTR 643.

[102] [2015] UKUT 211 (TCC). At time of writing the case was under appeal to the CA.

4

The Setting of the Tax System

4.1   Introduction

Making the fiscal system work is, said the two Musgraves, a large part of making democracy function.[1] The setting of the UK tax system is important for a variety of reasons. Clearly, one has to know the basic rules governing the reporting of income, the calculation of tax and the enforcement of liability to tax. Secondly, one ought to be aware of Revenue powers to ensure that the basic structure works, including the imposition of interest or penalties under the tax legislation or the criminal law, and the role of other agencies where tax fraud and other fraud overlap. However, it is also important to put this structure into a wider context. One part of that wider context is concerned with the balance of power between

---

[1] Musgrave and Musgrave, *Public Finance in Theory and Practice*, 1st edn, 1958 preface (reprinted in 5th edn, McGraw-Hill, 1989) xvii.

taxpayers and the executive.[2] Tax is, after all, probably the branch of law through which most citizens come into contact with the state. Another part of that context is the need to be able to assess the efficacy of the rules in the same way as a criminologist looks at the efficacy of the criminal law.[3] In the administration of the tax system one has to ask what the rules are for. Research in some, though not all, areas of government regulation suggest that a flexible approach to enforcement may be much better than a top-down, legalistic, going-by-the-book version.[4] However, this assumes that the regulator's purpose is to try to educate and to secure co-operation. Whether this is the right model for the tax system is precisely the question at issue.

Tax enforcement is an area where the effects of deterrence and compliance approaches have for some time been largely unknown.[5] However, in response to academic research, the Australian Taxation Office adopted an enforcement pyramid approach under which the staff first adopt the low-cost option of persuasion and then move on to more deterrence-oriented options.[6] One needs to know when the demands of equity may have to reduce in the name of effective compliance. One has to know about the extent to which the professions are to be seen as enforcers of the system through codes of ethics imposed on qualified practitioners (and the extent to which knowledge of the code forms part of the qualification process). In order to form some assessment of the system it is also desirable to know how efficient are the services provided by tax professionals. However, the tax system should also be seen as a system which has to work. Finality is an important virtue, and yet this can mean that Revenue practice is upheld even though it is not consistent with the law. Administrative efficiency is a value greatly prized by HMRC, but experience shows that the Government is anxious to use the Revenue to carry out non-tax programmes, such as the repayment of student loans and the working families tax credit;[7] even the change to self-assessment in 1997, which was clearly a tax matter, was not handled satisfactorily. These—and many other—reasons suggest that the material to be sketched in this chapter is important; however, there is much room for more research.

4.2   The Board of Revenue and Customs

For many years responsibility for the administration[8] of income tax, CGT, corporation tax, IHT and stamp duty was entrusted to the Board of Inland Revenue. The Board consisted of the Commissioners, and it is because of this collective group that the term 'the Revenue' (as opposed to the Board) is usually treated by tax folk as taking the plural form of verbs. Although the legislation used to talk of inspectors and collectors, recent legislation consistently refers to an 'officer of the Board' rather than 'an Inspector'. The collection function has

---

[2] See, eg, Goldberg [1996] BTR 9.

[3] See, eg, the outstanding work by Braithwaite and Braithwaite (eds), *Taxing Democracy* (Ashgate, 2005).

[4] Eg Bardach and Kagan, *Going by the Book: The Problem of Regulatory Unreasonableness* (Temple University Press, 1982); Braithwaite, *To Punish or Persuade: The Enforcement of Coal Mining Laws* (SUNY, 1985). See also Hillman, *Public Finance and Public Policy* §7.3.

[5] Adreoni *et al* (1998) 36 J *Economic Literature* 818.

[6] See Braithwaite and Braithwaite, in N Shover and JP Wright (eds), *Crimes of Privilege* (OUP, 2001) 405–19.

[7] For comments of CIOT Low Incomes Tax Reform Group, see CIOT Press Release, 4 October 1999.

[8] On the role of tax policy during the 1980s, see Beighton [1987] *Fiscal Studies* 1.

ceased to be separate from the rest of revenue work. In 2005 the Board of Inland Revenue was merged with that for Customs and Excise to form the Board of Revenue and Customs.[9]

4.2.1 The Department

The combined Board is one of the three departments—along with the Treasury and the Bank of England (now independent in some matters)—which report to the Chancellor of the Exchequer. Denis Healey wrote that other departments considered themselves to be at least as independent of the Treasury as the three armed services were of the Ministry of Defence.[10] He also said that the Inland Revenue considered itself as laying down the law to a nation of natural tax dodgers, while Customs and Excise were more down to earth, believing that human frailty is often rooted in a lack of understanding rather than in deliberate dishonesty.

The years 1997–2004 were characterised by a stream of ideas coming from the Treasury—some good, some not—and the Revenue seeming to be always on the back foot, resisting ideas in order to try to make them workable. Many people outside the government machine also spent a lot of time participating in the consultation processes to try to sort out matters that should have been dealt with earlier. These and other shortcomings were highlighted by the O'Donnell *Review of the Revenue Departments*.[11] In response, 2004 saw a reorganisation, with the Revenue's top policy people being moved into the Treasury's Budget and Public Finance Directorate and the launch of a new Tax Policy Partnership. Whether this even sharper separation of policy from delivery has been a success is an open question. Rather more unease has been expressed over the decision to merge the Inland Revenue with Customs and Excise. In principle, the idea of combining VAT administration with that for income and corporation taxes ought to bring reduced costs for and better service from the government and reduced compliance costs for taxpayers.

At one time the Inland Revenue worked in local offices at which taxpayers could discuss their tax affairs with the relevant officer. The 1980s saw a change of practice, with business dispersed to regional offices;[12] the trend has continued with further HMRC office closures and the change in social practices resulting in greater willingness to use the telephone, the Internet and electronic communication. All this is now justified in Departmental Reports as reducing the costs of running the tax system, albeit at the cost of losing the more personal touch of the former structure.

4.2.2 Scrutiny

The Board is scrutinised by various persons or bodies, including the Parliamentary Commissioner for Administration (or Ombudsman), the Revenue's own Adjudicator[13] and the

---

[9] CRCA 2005. For more see: https://www.gov.uk/government/organisations/hm-revenue-customs/groups/hmrc-board

[10] Healey, *The Time of My Life* (Penguin, 1990) 373.

[11] Cm 6163 March 2004; see especially ch 5 'Coordinating tax policy making'; for comment. see Wales [2004] BTR 543–65.

[12] See the interesting letter by Battishall [1988] BTR 155.

[13] See Beighton (1998) 16 *Tax Notes International* 1439–45. For a comparison of the UK Adjudicator with the US taxpayer advocate (to the advantage of the UK), see Kornhauser (1998) 16 *Tax Notes International* 537. See also Stebbings [1993] BTR 301 and comments on the First Report [1994] BTR 545.

National Audit Office. Within Parliament it is scrutinised by the Public Accounts Committee and by the Select Committee on the Treasury and the Civil Service.[14] The Revenue make Reports to the Treasury which are laid before Parliament. Rather worryingly the Adjudicator's Report for 2015 shows that in 2014–15 the Adjudicator received a record high 1,102 new complaints and resolved 1,850, upholding 85% either partially or substantially.[15] The comparable figure in 2010 was only 52%. More worryingly, a 2011 Commons Treasury Select Committee report into the administration and effectiveness of HMRC found there is 'considerable dissatisfaction among the public and tax professionals with the service provided by the Department'.[16] The Committee identified serious concerns in a number of areas, including unacceptable difficulties contacting HMRC by phone, 'endemic delays' in responding to post, and an increasing focus on online communication that may exclude those without reliable Internet connection.[17]

In 2012, in response to criticism from the Public Accounts Committee (chaired by the Rt Hon Dame Margaret Hodge MP) and others over HMRC's alleged 'sweetheart deals' to settle several large tax disputes—deals later reviewed by Sir Andrew Park for the National Audit Office and found to be reasonable (see §4.2.3)—HMRC made several important changes to its internal governance structure. First, a new post of Tax Assurance Commissioner was created. Second, HMRC released its new code of governance for tax dispute resolution. A new tax disputes resolution board was created, comprised of senior HMRC officials and the Tax Assurance Commissioner, and guided by HMRC's litigation and settlement strategy. The board is charged with resolving all cases where the tax in dispute is at least £100 million, along with a sample of cases involving tax of between £10 million and £100 million. The board is also empowered to make recommendations in sensitive cases, cases involving novel or unusual features, and cases with a potential adjustment of £500 million or more. In addition, the Tax Assurance Commissioner has oversight of settled cases with a view to improving the process for future settlements.[18]

In recent years the Public Accounts Committee's hearings scrutinising HMRC has become high profile, headline-grabbing media events (some would say media circuses). In 2013, PAC held hearings on the much lower than expected tax receipts from an agreement between the UK and Switzerland targeting tax evasion by UK residents. The Committee also focused on HMRC's reporting of its operational performance. Central to those discussion was a report from the National Audit Office that concluded that errors in setting past performance targets too low had led to HMRC overstating its performance in recent years. In 2014, PAC's spotlight turned to HMRC's slow response to tax avoidance, with the Committee encouraging HMRC to 'do more, faster'. Further PAC hearings in 2015 saw then HMRC chief executive Lin Homer grilled by the Committee over HMRC's 'pathetic' response (to quote Margaret Hodge) to information it received about clients of HSBC's Swiss division alleging evading tax.

---

[14] See, eg, the very critical report on the administration of tax credits, HC Select Committee, Tenth HC Paper 2002–03 No 834. On the early work of this Committee, see Robinson in *The New Select Committees* (1989); and on Treasury response, see Hills [1981] 4(1) *Fiscal Studies* 1.

[15] Adjudicator's Report (2015), available at http://www.adjudicatorsoffice.gov.uk/pdf/report2015.pdf.

[16] Treasury Select Committee Report (2011), available at http://www.parliament.uk/business/committees/committees-a-z/commons-select/treasury-committee/news/hmrc-publication/.

[17] *Ibid.*

[18] The annual report of the Tax Assurance Commissioner (for 2014/15) is available at https://www.gov.uk/government/uploads/system/uploads/attachment_data/file/444911/How_we_resolve_tax_disputes.pdf.

In September 2015, Meg Hellier MP replaced the outspoken Margaret Hodge as its chair, and HMRC provided the Committee with an update of their investigation into the HSBC Swiss leaks. According to HMRC, over two-thirds of taxpayers on the list were reported to have paid the correct amount of tax, a further 1100 taxpayers settled tax owed and just one taxpayer was prosecuted (out of 150 potential targets identified). HMRC's attempts to improve its poor record in answering taxpayer telephone calls in a timely fashion was also the subject of discussion. According to a Citizens Advice study, taxpayers spend an average of 47 minutes on the phone waiting to speak to someone at HMRC; HMRC countered that its own figures are an average waiting time of 10 minutes. A May 2016 NAO report also was highly critical of HMRC's service standards for personal customers in 2014–15 and the first half of 2015–16.[19] At Budget 2016, the Government announced it was investing £71 million to make it quicker and easier for individuals and small businesses to deal with HMRC. The new measures include a secure email service, and phone lines and Webchat open 7 days a week from April 2017, plus a dedicated phone service and online forum for new businesses and self-employed individuals.

In 2016, the PAC hearings focused on a new alleged sweetheart deal between HMRC and Google over back taxes.[20] PAC was especially critical of the lack of transparency about tax settlements, which made it impossible to judge whether HMRC has settled the Google dispute for the right amount of tax, particularly in light of reports that other tax authorities including France were pursuing Google for larger sums. The Committee also called for HMRC to devote more resources to settle tax investigations more quickly. Most worrying for HMRC, the public furore over the Google settlement called into question the efficacy of HMRC's 2012 governance reforms including the role of HMRC's Tax Assurance Commissioner. As Freedman commented in the *Financial Times*, 'however robust the procedures established in 2012 are, it is clear from the debate about Google that they have not met the concerns of either commentators or the public'. Freedman further argued, correctly, that it is vital that HMRC be allowed to administer the tax law, and be trusted by the public to do a good job of it: the media and politicians cannot be ultimate arbiters of the tax that is due. Freedman suggested that it might be necessary to consider a different approach to HMRC oversight, possibly with a new, specialised and independent branch of the National Audit Office.[21]

Margaret Hodge had her critics during her time chairing PAC, especially amongst practitioners who objected to her brash manner of questioning HMRC officials and others, and thought her generally uninformed on tax. But it is undeniable that in turning the PAC spotlight on HMRC and the operation of the international tax regime in particular, she put tax on the front pages of newspapers and grabbed the public's and politicians' attention in a way heretofore not seen. Her contributions will no doubt continue in her next role as chair of a new all-party parliamentary group on responsible tax.

---

[19] See https://www.nao.org.uk/wp-content/uploads/2016/05/The-quality-of-service-for-personal-taxpayers.pdf, and see HMRC's response at https://www.gov.uk/government/news/hmrc-service-standards-for-personal-customers.

[20] See PAC 'Corporate Tax Settlements' report at http://www.publications.parliament.uk/pa/cm201516/cmselect/cmpubacc/788/788.pdf.

[21] Freedman, 'We should create a tax system that reassures the public' *Financial Times* (9 Feb 2016). See also Freedman [2016] BTR 7 and Freedman's 2016 CIOT Address on 'Restoring Trust' at http://www.taxadvisermagazine.com/node/8483.

4.2.3 Commuting Liability

The Board is under a duty to collect taxes, but is not guilty of an abuse of power in entering into special arrangements absolving taxpayers from liability to tax. The scope of the power to make such arrangements does not extend to an agreement under which the Revenue renounced their right and duty to investigate the true financial circumstances of a taxpayer for a certain number of years in return for a fixed sum amount each year.[22] The Revenue were therefore entitled to resile from that agreement.

One taxpayer has no sufficient interest to ask a court to investigate the tax affairs of another;[23] however, this must be distinguished from a situation in which the Revenue's approach to a question of interpretation of law is wrong.[24] In carrying out the duty laid on it the Board must act with administrative common sense.[25] However, this discretion does not justify a court in construing a section of an Act so as to give the Board discretion over how to allocate a tax liability between different taxpayers, neither does it provide a legal basis for the practice of extra-statutory concessions.[26] Unlike the Revenue, the former Customs and Excise had statutory authority to grant certain reliefs.[27] Judges remain critical of the Revenue claim to have a power to make extra-statutory concessions.[28] They have decided that they have no power to order the department to give the taxpayer the benefit of a concession, ie, to make an assessment which is not in accordance with the law.[29] However, they have in effect ordered the Revenue to give the taxpayer beneficial tax treatment under the benefit of an existing practice which had applied to the particular taxpayer over many earlier years; this was because the change of practice was an irrational exercise of Revenue discretion and breach of the doctrine of legitimate expectations.[30]

The power to make concessions is usually based on HMRC's responsibility, now under TMA 1970, section 1, for the collection and management of the various taxes. The 2005 decision of the House of Lords in *R v IRC, ex parte Wilkinson*[31] suggested that the power was not as wide as previously thought (by HMRC). By FA 2008, the Treasury may make statutory instruments to give concessions and practices statutory effect, presumably where there is a doubt whether the concession etc comes within TMA 1970, section 1.[32]

---

[22] *Al Fayed v Advocate General for Scotland* [2002] STC 910, and, more generally, *Fletcher v Thomson* [2002] EWHC Admin 1552; [2002] STC 1149, in which the taxpayer failed to provide any proof of unfairness or breach of legitimate expectations. See also *R (On the Application of Bamber) v HMRC* [2006] EWHC 3221 (Admin), [2006] STC 1035.

[23] *IRC v National Federation of Self-Employed and Small Businesses Ltd* [1981] 2 All ER 93; [1981] STC 260 (Fleet Street amnesty not illegal).

[24] *R v A-G, ex parte ICI* (1986) 60 TC 1; [1987] 1 CMLR 72.

[25] *Vestey v IRC* [1980] STC 10, 19; 54 TC 503, 582, per Lord Wilberforce. The Board remits tax in certain cases when the failure to collect was due to official error; the extent of this practice is governed by the taxpayer's circumstances: ESC A19.

[26] *Vestey v IRC* [1980] STC 10, 35; 54 TC 503, 599, per Lord Edmund Davies, citing Williams [1979] BTR 137.

[27] Customs and Excise (General Reliefs) Act 1979, s 13.

[28] See also Wade and Forsyth, *Administrative Law* (OUP, 2004) 410.

[29] *R v IRC, ex parte Wilkinson* [2005] UKHL 30.

[30] *R v IRC, ex parte Unilever* [1996] STC 681. On legitimate expectations see Wade and Forsyth, *op cit*, 372 et seq. See also *R (On the Application of Bamber) v HMRC* [2006] EWHC 3221 (Admin), [2006] STC 1035.

[31] [2005] UKHL 30.

[32] FA 2008, s 160.

As briefly mentioned earlier, in 2011, the Common's Public Accounts Committee held hearings to investigate reports that HMRC officials had agreed 'sweetheart deals' settling tax disputes with large companies that cost the Treasury millions of pounds in tax and interest. The Committee's report criticised HMRC for systemic governance failures in the way its senior officials handle tax disputes with large companies, and expressed concern that the department treats large companies more favourably than other taxpayers.[33] A 2012 National Audit Office follow-up review of 5 settlements with large companies concluded that the settlements reached were all 'reasonable', but expressed concern over the processes by which the settlements were reached.[34] In response, HMRC accepted that its governance arrangements had not provided sufficient assurance and that independent scrutiny of large settlements was needed—see §4.2.2 for a description of the changes made.

4.2.4 Confidentiality/Secrecy

Information received in the execution of duty may not be disclosed to other bodies, including other government departments, without statutory authority.[35] Release of information relating to the tax affairs of 'an identifiable person' without such authority or consent may be a criminal offence.[36] The modern mantra that we need 'joined-up government' can undermine this confidentiality. Release to the Revenue departments of other countries may be authorised under treaty provisions[37] or under EU law.[38] In the Public Accounts Committee's 2011 report into HMRC's 'sweetheart' settlement deals with large companies (see §4.2.3), the Committee expressed frustration with top HMRC officials using taxpayer confidentiality as an excuse to try to avoid the Committee's scrutiny.[39]

In *R (on the application of Ingenious Media Holdings Plc) v Revenue and Customs Commissioners*,[40] a company that had promoted film investment tax avoidance schemes and the company's chief executive officer alleged that the Revenue and Customs Commissioners had breached the Commissioners for Revenue and Customs Act 2005, section 18 by disclosing information about them to journalists in an off-the-record briefing which led to the publication of their names in articles about tax avoidance. The Court of Appeal dismissed the appellants' claims, holding that a factually correct disclosure not involving the private affairs of a taxpayer and which had the effect of raising the total tax revenue or reducing the effect of tax avoidance schemes which the commissioners genuinely considered ineffective was a disclosure which a reasonable citizen would expect them to be free to make. Leave to appeal to the Supreme Court was granted and the decision was pending at the time of writing.

---

[33] Public Accounts Committee Report (2011), available at http://www.publications.parliament.uk/pa/cm201012/cmselect/cmpubacc/1531/153102.htm. The Committee found, eg, that in some cases the same officials negotiated and approved the settlements.

[34] National Audit Office, *HM Revenue & Customs: Settling large tax disputes*, HC 188 (14 June 2012).

[35] CRCA 2005, s 18 *et seq*; ex TMA 1970, s 6 and FA 1989, ss 182, 182A. See also public interest immunity in *Lonrho v Fayed (No 4)* [1994] STC 153.

[36] FA 1989, s 182, replacing the Official Secrets Act 1911, s 2.

[37] See chapter seventy below.

[38] FA 2002, Sch 39; FA 1990, s 125.

[39] Public Accounts Committee Report (2011), *op cit*.

[40] [2015] EWCA Civ 173.

4.2.5 Reliance on Revenue Statements

Conventional wisdom is that there are no estoppels against the Crown; hence, no legal reliance may generally be placed on statements by officers of the Board so as to make the court determine a tax appeal in the way stated by those officers.[41] However, compensation has been obtained through the Parliamentary Commissioners for Administration or the Adjudicator, and may be available in tort.[42] In addition, such statements may furnish the very basis for an application for judicial review of a Revenue decision, eg based on legitimate expectations.[43]

4.2.6 Citizens' Charter

Like other government departments, the Inland Revenue was party to the (now superseded) Citizens' Charter.[44] A taxpayer relied on it in court to argue that no reasonable inspector who had the Charter in mind would have issued a notice seeking information from the taxpayer in such terms; the taxpayer failed on the facts.[45] Since 2009, HMRC has a new duty to prepare a Charter including standards of behaviour and values. The Charter was revised in 2016 and is available on the HMRC website.[46] HMRC must report at least once a year, showing how far they have demonstrated these values.

4.3 Establishing Liability to Tax—Self-Assessment and Revenue Assessment

A liability to tax arises when taxpayers are assessed to tax; today, the assessment will usually be made by the taxpayers themselves (self-assessment), but may sometimes be made by HMRC, ie where the self-assessment provisions do not apply. Where a taxpayer falls within the self-assessment regime but the Revenue make an assessment, eg because the taxpayer has not made a return, the theoretical position is that the assessment is indeed made on the taxpayer's behalf and so is a self-assessment which remains valid until vacated by the delivery of the proper return.[47] Penalties, interest and surcharges may also be due; the role of the

---

[41] Southend on Sea Corp v Hodgson (Wickford) Ltd [1962] 1 QB 416; [1961] 2 All ER 46; see, however R v IRC, ex parte J Rothschild Holdings plc [1987] STC 163; 61 TC 178, where an estoppel issue was raised in judicial review proceedings but failed on the facts.

[42] Wade and Forsyth, op cit, 336–42; and, for a critical view Craig 93 LQR 398; see also comments of Lord Griffiths in Matrix Securities Ltd v IRC [1994] STC 272, 284 (HL), on possible compensation claim if the Revenue withdraws clearance after expense incurred in reliance on the clearance; see also Eden [1994] BTR 263. On wider issues, see the fascinating book by Farnsworth, Changing Your Mind: The Law of Regretted Decisions (Yale University Press, 1999).

[43] See §3.3.5 above and §4.4.5 below; see also Hinds [1991] BTR 191.

[44] Inland Revenue Press Release, 13 August 1991, [1991] Simon's Tax Intelligence 771; see also Inland Revenue Press Release, 11 February 1992, [1992] Simon's Tax Intelligence 178. The Citizens' Charter has been superseded; on which see Brodie, Taxation, 13 April 2000, 40.

[45] Kempton v Special Commrs and IRC [1992] STC 823; 66 TC 249.

[46] CRCA 2005, s 16A, added by FA 2009, s 92; and see https://www.gov.uk/government/publications/your-charter.

[47] TMA 1970, s 9(3). See Collison, Income Tax Under Self Assessment (Acco).

surcharge is confined to self-assessment. The rules for assessment outside self-assessment are not discussed here. If the taxpayer has not received a return, there is an obligation to give notice of any liability to tax within six months of the end of the year.[48]

At Budget 2015 the Chancellor announced plans to move towards eliminating the need to file annual tax returns, as part of HMRC's development of a system of online digital accounts. The plan aims to see more than 50 million individuals and small businesses have a secure, personalised digital tax account by 2020.[49] According to HMRC, taxpayers with their own digital tax account will be able to self-serve instead of having to phone or write HMRC, eg to notify of a change of address. The digital account will provide pre-populated information about savings and employment income, obviating the need for taxpayers to give HMRC information they already have. This promises to be a major development in taxpayer-HMRC relations with the potential for significant reductions in compliance and administration costs. It is also a major implementation challenge for a department with legacy IT systems and a dubious record on undertaking major IT projects, and for that reason practitioners have urged HMRC to move more carefully and cautiously in the transition to digital accounts. For now, self-assessment remains and is discussed next.

4.3.1 Self-assessment

The self-assessment regime applies whenever a taxpayer is sent a notice by an officer of the Board.[50] At present the Revenue send these forms only to individual taxpayers who are self-employed or whose tax affairs are complicated; there is no legislative reason (as opposed to practical reason) for them to stop there. The regime applies to income tax, CGT and some classes of NICs. It applies to partnerships[51]—even though the primary liability is on the partners to make their own returns—and to trustees.[52] In 2016, HMRC were given a 'simple assessment' power to make an assessment of income tax or CGT liability on the basis of information in its possession, without the individual first being required to complete a self assessment tax return.[53]

4.3.1.1 Filing Date

The return must be delivered by the filing date—generally either 31 October (if filing by paper) or 31 January (if filing electronically) following the tax year, ie filing by 31 January 2017 for the tax year ending 5 April 2016. The taxpayer must file the return[54] and calculate and pay the tax.[55] Failure to make the assessment means that the Revenue may do this for the taxpayer.[56] Getting more people to file online is a major HMRC goal. As an

---

[48] TMA 1970, s 7(1).
[49] See 'Making Tax Easier' at https://www.gov.uk/government/publications/making-tax-easier.
[50] TMA 1970, s 8.
[51] TMA 1970, ss 12AA, 12AB—see ch 19 below.
[52] TMA 1970, s 8A—see ch 29 below.
[53] See https://www.gov.uk/government/publications/income-tax-simple-assessment/income-tax-simple-assessment.
[54] TMA 1970, s 8; on dates see s 8(1D) added by FA 2007. If notice is given after 31 October, the return is due three months after the date notice was given.
[55] TMA 1970, s 9.
[56] TMA 1970, s 9(3).

encouragement to early filing, the period during which HMRC must start an enquiry now runs from the date of delivering the return, whether or not this is done electronically.[57] As from 2010, HMRC has the power to compel people to file online; the ether thus becomes 'a mandatory medium for the exercise of the power of the state over the citizen'.[58] The question whether we want this to happen is one which attracts little discussion—unlike in the United States.[59] The apparent disappearance of data disks in 2007 raised genuine doubts as to whether HMRC can be trusted to look after such information.

For many taxpayers a more significant date is 31 October. If a taxpayer delivers the return by 31 October, the Revenue must do the arithmetic on the basis of the figures supplied and calculate the tax due.[60] This is not the same as Revenue assessment—it is self-assessment with the aid of Revenue calculation. Tax is due on the same date—31 January. There are penalties for late and incorrect returns,[61] which may be fixed or tax-related and may be reduced or waived by the Revenue.[62] In May 2015 a newspaper investigation revealed that HMRC had adopted a policy of waiving the £100 penalty for late filing tax returns in the vast majority of cases where taxpayers had appealed and offered an excuse for being late. In HMRC's view, 'expediting' the appeals process in this way allowed the department to focus more resources on targeting evasion and avoidance rather than penalising ordinary people who are trying to do the right thing. On receiving the form the Revenue check it for arithmetical errors before making the assessment on the basis of these figures. Questions of substance are left till later. If the Revenue check reveals even the most trivial of errors, the effort is returned to the taxpayer. If this happens after 31 October, the Revenue do not guarantee to do the calculation in time. The taxpayer may amend the return within 12 months of the filing date and the Revenue may revise the assessment to correct 'obvious' errors or mistakes within nine months.[63] If a return has been made negligently or fraudulently and the return is then amended, this does not prevent the Revenue taking action, including penalties in respect of the earlier error.[64]

In *Cotter v HMRC*,[65] the Supreme Court considered the fundamental question of what constitutes a 'return' under the self-assessment regime. The decision has important ramifications for those claiming loss relief in particular because it affects whether tax needs to be paid upfront pending the satisfaction of an HMRC enquiry into the validity of the claim. The Supreme Court chose a narrow interpretation, holding that in the context of TMA 1970, section 9A a 'return' refers to the information in the tax return which is submitted for the 'purpose of establishing the amounts in which a person is chargeable to income tax' for the relevant year of assessment. The Court recognised that this conclusion left some uncertainty as to its application in particular circumstances, but suggested that

---

[57] See TMA 1970, s 9A(2), as amended by FA 2007.
[58] FA 2002 s 135; the quotation is from Troup [2002] BTR 352.
[59] See Slemrod (2006) 27 *Fiscal Studies* 1–16.
[60] TMA 1970, s 9(2).
[61] On self-assessment and status of incomplete returns and use or provisional figures, see RI 191.
[62] TMA 1970, 102.
[63] TMA 1970, ss 9(4), 9ZA, 9ZB.
[64] RI 196.
[65] [2013] UKSC 69.

HMRC amend the design of the return form so as to make it clear which parts of it request information relevant to the calculation of tax for the relevant year (and are therefore part of the return form proper) and which parts merely provide information in respect of free-standing claims.

4.3.1.2 Underpayment Surcharges

Surcharges apply where the tax is not paid at all or is underpaid. A surcharge of 5% of the unpaid tax due applies after 30 days, and a similar amount after a further six months and also 12 months.[66] Again, the Revenue may waive or reduce the surcharge.[67] A right of appeal exists on the basis of a reasonable excuse for not paying the tax;[68] inability to pay the tax is not a reasonable excuse.[69] Surcharges will not be imposed if a taxpayer finds a bona fide mistake and volunteers the information to the Revenue at once and pays the tax.[70]

4.3.1.3 The 12-Month Enquiry Window

Under TMA 1970, section 9A, the Revenue may investigate the return within 12 months after the day on which the return was delivered—the 'enquiry window';[71] this is to recover tax underpaid under the self-assessment process. Thereafter, tax may be recovered only under the discovery powers in TMA 1970, section 29. This is begun by a formal written notice; no reason need be given. There is no need to complete the enquiry within the 12-month period. The notice of enquiry triggers various information powers[72] which may only be used to get information reasonably required for the purpose, a matter on which an appeal may be made to the Tribunals.[73] Documents not in the taxpayer's power or possession may not be called for under this power. These enquiry powers are separate from other information powers. There are parallel provisions where an officer investigates a claim made outside a tax return.[74] The taxpayer must be told when the enquiries are completed;[75] this prevents any further enquiry under this rule,[76] but not under the discovery power in section 29. It is likely that certain criteria will be evolved by the Revenue in selecting returns for attention, but the recent reports do not say how many are conducted.[77] There is also a random selection of a very small proportion of returns.[78]

---

[66] FA 2009, Sch 56, para 3.
[67] FA 2009, Sch 56, para 9.
[68] FA 2009, Sch 56, paras 13–16.
[69] FA 2009, Sch 56, para 16(2); and Collison, *op cit*, para 22.1.
[70] Collison, *op cit*, para 22.1.
[71] TMA 1970, s 9A; on similar provisions for partnership returns, see s 12AC. On late returns, see s 9A(2).
[72] FA 2008, Sch 36, para 1.
[73] FA 2008, Sch 36, para 29.
[74] TMA 1970, Sch 1A, para 5.
[75] TMA 1970, s 28A(5). In *Tower MCashback LLP 1 and another v Revenue & Customs Commissioners* [2011] UKSC 19 the Supreme Court held that the particular closure notice did not limit the Special Commissioners' jurisdiction to hear any evidence or any legal argument, subject only to an obligation to ensure a fair hearing.
[76] TMA 1970, s 9A(3).
[77] See HMRC *Enquiry Manual*, available at http://www.hmrc.gov.uk/manuals/emmanual/Index.htm; needless to say, many of the principles are quite rightly kept secret.
[78] HMRC *Enquiry Manual*, para EM0093. Collison, *op cit*, relying on the then *Handbook*, para 370, suggested 1 in 1,000.

4.3.2 Discovery Assessments

If an officer discovers that income or capital gains which should have been assessed have not been, or that an assessment is or has become insufficient or that any relief is or has become excessive, that officer may make an assessment to recover the loss of tax. The notion of discovery is interpreted widely in relation to Revenue assessments, but the circumstances in which discovery assessments may be made is narrowed for self-assessment.

The self-assessment rules restrict the power to make a discovery assessment. The taxpayer is safe if the return was made in accordance with normally-accepted practice at the time it was made.[79] Secondly, if the return was not in accordance with such practice, the discovery assessment may be made only if the situation was brought about carelessly or deliberately by either the taxpayer or agent,[80] or if the officer could not reasonably be expected to be aware, on the basis of the information then available to him, that additional tax was due under TMA 1970, section 29.[81] Information is made available if it is contained in the taxpayer's return or other forms, eg a claim, or is produced in the course of the enquiry. It is also treated as made available if it can reasonably be expected to be inferred by the officer, or is notified in writing by the taxpayer.[82]

The question whether information was 'made available' to the Revenue was considered by the Court of Appeal in *Langham v Veltema*.[83] A transaction had been reported by the taxpayer to his Inland Revenue office (KL) but without mentioning any value. In fact a valuation had been obtained by the taxpayer, which is why the taxpayer was held not to have been negligent. Another form, containing further information, was supplied by the taxpayer's employer (form P11D), which contained the valuation figure of £100,000 and was sent to the employer's (quite different) tax office (E). An enquiry by the E office eventually led to an agreed valuation of £145,000, by which time it was too late for the KL office to use that figure—if the taxpayer had come within the protection of section 29(5). The Court of Appeal held that the list of information specified in section 29(6) was exhaustive so that the taxpayer could not use the information supplied by his employer to the other office. It also held that the fact of reporting the transaction without any figures and without providing the valuation did not protect the taxpayer from the out-of-time assessment. Professional opinion on this decision was mostly hostile.[84] Some may agree with the Court of Appeal and think not only that the taxpayer should not have been able to use the information supplied by the employer, but also that the taxpayer should have done more to draw the Revenue's attention to the need to go further.[85] Others will feel that the whole point of the self-assessment enquiry window has been weakened and that the Revenue department, which prides itself on its electronic databases, should have been able to link the employer's return with that of the taxpayer. At issue is the nature of the self-assessment process. The

---

[79] TMA 1970, s 29(2)—the concept is borrowed from TMA 1970, s 33 for claims by the taxpayer.
[80] TMA 1970, s 29(4).
[81] TMA 1970, s 29(5).
[82] TMA 1970, s 29(6).
[83] [2004] STC 544.
[84] Eg, 'staggering': Martin, *Simons Tax Briefing* Issue 128 p 7.
[85] Contrast Park J [2002] STC 1557, paras 24 and 29, for the taxpayer with Auld LJ in CA at paras 33 and 34 for the Revenue.

Court of Appeal seems to have regarded it as little different from what had gone before. This seems doubtful; the new system was a compromise between the Revenue, whose costs were greatly reduced, and taxpayers, whose costs were increased in return for greater and earlier finality. This decision unbalances that compromise. There is no doubt that the KL inspector had failed to follow the Revenue Manual's instructions. There was much discussion as to what precisely the taxpayer should have done, but this is now addressed in Revenue guidance.[86]

In the old assessment rules the word 'discover' covered a variety of circumstances; the word was apt to cover any case in which, for any reason, it newly appeared that the taxpayer has been undercharged.[87] Therefore, an assessment could be made where the Revenue decided that a company should be treated as a dealing company rather than an investment company,[88] where a new inspector took a different view of the law from his predecessor,[89] or to correct an arithmetical error in the computation. Under the pre-1996 law it was held that a new assessment might not be made under section 29 if there had been an agreement between the Inspector and and the taxpayer on the point within TMA 1970, section 54.[90] The effect of settling the appeal is to create a contract; it follows that if the document recording the contract does not do so accurately, it may be rectified.[91] Where a taxpayer made a claim which was erroneously agreed by an inspector, a later inspector was not entitled to make a 'discovery' assessment on finding the error.[92] The test is whether a reasonable man would conclude that the inspector had agreed the claim. Since the agreement rule remains in place, this must still be good law. The normal time limit for a section 29 assessment, duly applied in *Langham v Veltema*, is four years after the end of the year of assessment to which it relates.[93] The case of *The Queen (on the application of Andrew Michael Higgs) v HMRC*[94] cast some doubt on whether the four-year period applied to self-assessment, but legislation was quickly introduced to confirm the four-year period.[95] The period is extended to six years and 20 years, respectively, for loss of tax brought about carelessly or deliberately.[96]

The scope of HMRC's discovery powers is an area of ongoing development in the courts. In *HMRC v Lansdowne Partners Ltd Partnership*,[97] the Court of Appeal restricted the scope of the powers in situations where the taxpayer's liability turned on a question of law. In *HMRC v Charlton, Corfield & another*,[98] a case on an assessment issued outside the

---

[86] IR guidance, 24 December 2004, [2005] *Simon's Weekly Tax Intelligence* 12–19 and SP 1/06. Note also Arden LJ's views at para 51. For a recent case in which HMRC were not allowed to reopen the assessment, see *Revenue & Customs Commissioners v Lansdowne Partners* [2010] EWHC 2582 (Ch).

[87] *Cenlon Finance Co Ltd v Ellwood* [1962] 1 All ER 854, 859; 40 TC 176, 204, per Viscount Simonds.

[88] *Jones v Mason Investments (Luton) Ltd* (1966) 43 TC 570; Monroe [1967] BTR 75.

[89] *Parkin v Cattell* (1971) 48 TC 462.

[90] The taxpayer is protected only on the particular point agreed: *Kidston v Aspinall* (1963) 41 TC 371.

[91] *R v Inspector of Taxes, ex parte Bass Holdings Ltd* [1993] STC 122; 65 TC 495 (group relief to be allowed once, not twice). Silence in face of an offer does not make an agreement: *Schuldenfrei v Hilton* [1999] STC 821 (CA), eschewing language of offer and acceptance.

[92] *Scorer v Olin Energy Systems Ltd* [1985] STC 218; 58 TC 592 (HL); see Williams [1992] BTR 323; on Revenue practice, see Statement of Practice SP 8/91.

[93] TMA 1970, s 34 as amended by FA 2008, s 113 and Sch 39.

[94] [2015] UKUT 92.

[95] TMA 1970, s 34A.

[96] TMA 1970, s 36 as amended by FA 2008, s 113 and Sch 39.

[97] [2011] EWCA Civ 1578

[98] [2012] UKFTT 77.

statutory time limit, the Upper Tribunal upheld the First-tier Tribunal's decision in favour of the taxpayer on the basis that an officer would have been reasonably expected to have been aware of the insufficiency of tax such as to justify an assessment with the information provided by the taxpayer's return before the closure of the enquiry window. Of more general interest, the Upper Tribunal provided some broad comments on the extent of HMRC's powers of discovery: discovery can be based on (1) a change in the interpretation of the law; (2) new facts coming to light; (3) new awareness of the relevance of facts not previously considered; and (4) simply the realisation that HMRC had failed to act on a timely basis before. Importantly, the Upper Tribunal stated that HMRC needs to show that it was not in possession of adequate information, or could not reasonably have inferred the relevance of the information they were in possession of, from an honest taxpayer's timely returns, accounts and accompanying documentation and correspondence, in order to make a valid discovery assessment.[99] In *Freeman v HMRC*,[100] the First-tier Tribunal held that a discovery assessment was invalid because HMRC could have been reasonably expected, on the basis of information available to it at the relevant time, to have been aware of the loss of tax. The tribunal concluded that a document provided to HMRC in April 2000, in the context of an enquiry into the taxpayer's 1997–98 return, was 'information available' in relation to the 2002–03 tax year, and, further, TMA 1970, section 29(6)(d)(ii) had no temporal restriction.[101]

4.3.3 Payments and Record Keeping

A central part of the self-assessment system requires the taxpayer to make payments on account in advance of 31 January following the end of the year. These are due, in two equal instalments, by 31 January *in* the tax year and 31 July *following* that year. Normally these are calculated on the income for the previous year.[102] There is a *de minimis* limit for this obligation: no payment is due if the sum is less than £1,000. Likewise no payment is due if more than 80% of the preceding year's liability will be collected by deduction at source.[103]

The payment on account settles the liability to pay on account. There is no liability to pay either interest or any surcharge if the year's income turns out to be higher than estimated. However, if the year's income is lower, taxpayers will receive interest (although this usually is deducted from their eventual overall liability to tax).[104] The liability to pay on account may be avoided if the liability will be covered by deduction at source[105] or there will be no liability to tax at all; claims may be made at any time before 31 January following the tax

---

[99] For further commentary on these cases see Whitehouse and Stricklin-Coutinho, Tax Journal (12 Oct 2012).

[100] [2013] UKFTT 496 (TC).

[101] For further commentary see Craggs and Brook, Tax Journal (1 Nov 2013). Interested readers should also see Vaines, Tax Journal (11 Sept 2015), for a review of other developments in this area. Notwithstanding the taxpayer wins just discussed, Vaines is quite critical of the state of the law, ultimately concluding: 'The law and practice on discovery assessments has lost its balance and, along with it, any realistic protection for the taxpayer'.

[102] Special rules apply if the assessment is late or is amended, etc: TMA 1970, s 59A, esp subs (4)–(4B).

[103] TMA 1970, s 59A(1)(d); on deduction at source, see s 59A(8).

[104] TMA 1970, s 30(1).

[105] Elaborately defined in TMA 1970, s 59A(8).

year.[106] A Revenue officer may waive the liability by notice.[107] Penalties arise if a claim to reduce the liability is made fraudulently or negligently.[108]

At one time a payment by cheque was treated as received when the cheque was received by the Revenue—provided it was paid on first presentation. This rule has been overridden by regulations which now provide that the payment is made only when the funds have been cleared into HMRC's account. The purpose of the change is to remove the cash-flow advantage of payment by cheque as opposed to an electronic transfer.[109] If the taxpayer sends a cheque to the Revenue 'in full and final settlement' of existing liabilities, and the accompanying letter states that if the cheque is cashed the Revenue will be taken to have accepted it in full settlement, the Revenue may cash the cheque and still proceed for any disputed balance. This is the product of the contract doctrine of offer and acceptance.[110] There is case law authority that the doctrine of set off may also be invoked in suitable cases of liquidated cross-claims,[111] and FA 2008, sections 130–134 provide a statutory regime for set off by HMRC of sums payable to a taxpayer against amounts owed to HMRC. HMRC may charge a fee for payments by specified methods, eg credit cards. Payment by electronic transfer is now required of employers with 250 or more people on their payroll.[112]

If the taxpayer is carrying on a trade, profession or business (including the letting of property), all necessary records must be kept until the fifth anniversary of the due date for payment.[113] Therefore, records for 2016–17 must be kept until 31 January 2023. There are also rules as to the form in which records of a business must be kept.[114] A shorter period applies if there is no trading, etc income. Taxpayers potentially are liable for a penalty of up to £3,000 for failure to keep records, though such penalties are likely to apply only in more serious cases.[115]

4.3.4 Subsequent Events

Once an assessment has been made, it cannot be changed except under the TMA 1970 rules,[116] which broadly means Revenue enquiry (section 29), appeal (see below at §4.4)[117] and agreement (above §4.3.2).[118] It may be open to the Revenue to issue a second (additional) assessment rather than to seek an increase in the first on appeal.[119] Provided the assessment is not to make good a loss brought about carelessly or deliberately, a taxpayer may also reopen matters by making a claim for any further relief for that year within one

---

[106] TMA 1970, s 59A(3).
[107] TMA 1970, s 59A(9).
[108] TMA 1970, s 59A(6).
[109] TMA 1970, s 70A(3), added by FA 2007, s 95.
[110] *IRC v Fry* [2001] STC 1715.
[111] *Melham Ltd v Burton* [2006] UKHL 908, [2006] STC 908, esp para 22.
[112] FA 2003, ss 204 and 205.
[113] TMA 1970, s 12B(1), (6).
[114] TMA 1970, s 12B(3); on penalties see *ibid*, s 12B(5).
[115] TMA 1970, Sch 1A, para 2A.
[116] TMA 1970, s 30A.
[117] TMA 1970, s 50(6)–(9); the right of appeal is given by s 31.
[118] TMA 1970, s 54.
[119] *Duchy Maternity Ltd v Hodgson* [1985] STC 764.

year from the end of the chargeable period in which an assessment is made.[120] The validity of the assessment is unlikely to arise under self-assessment, but may do so in the few remaining cases of Revenue assessment. An assessment is valid even though it refers to an incorrect provision.[121] An assessment may be saved from invalidity by TMA 1970, section 114,[122] which lists various errors which may not invalidate the assessment. However, an assessment issued for the wrong year cannot be saved by section 114 even though the taxpayer was not and could not have been misled.[123]

Taxpayers may claim that too much tax has been paid by reason of their own error or mistake, in which case the Revenue will grant relief.[124] The overpayment may arise under the self-assessment regime or otherwise. Tax legislation includes many reliefs, elections, etc, which have to be claimed by the taxpayer.[125] Frequently this will now be done in the course of the self-assessment process.[126] A taxpayer who has forgotten to make a claim may be able to amend the self-assessment return—the residual error mistake claim applies to all assessments, including self-assessments. Amendments of claims are also allowed.[127] Where an assessment is made under section 29, and is not to make good to the Crown any loss of tax brought about carelessly or deliberately, the taxpayer may make any claim for further relief for that year within one year from the end of the chargeable period in which an assessment is made.[128]

Unless statute prescribes otherwise, claims must be made within four years after the end of the year of assessment to which they relate.[129] If an assessment is made late, the consequential claim may be made up to any time after the end of the fiscal year following that in which the assessment is made.[130] There are further rules for appeals following the refusal of a claim.

4.3.5 Assessment of Self-Assessment

At first sight the shift of costs from the Revenue to the general taxpayer seems a rather perverse form of privatisation. There is, however, more to the problem than that. Clearly, a desire to reduce government expenditure is one of the aims of the change; another is a sincere wish to reduce some taxpayers' compliance costs. Under the old system of assessment, the Revenue had to make assessments within certain, and often quite unrealistic, time limits, not least because only when the assessment had been made could a liability to pay tax

---

[120] TMA 1970, ss 43A, 43B, added by FA 1989, s 150: it appears that this does not apply when the assessment is an original (but late) assessment, as distinct from an additional assessment.

[121] *Vickerman v Personal Representatives of Mason* [1984] STC 231.

[122] On s 114, see *Fleming v London Produce Co Ltd* [1968] 2 All ER 975; 44 TC 582.

[123] *Baylis v Gregory* [1987] STC 297; 62 TC 1 (CA). See also *IRC v McGuckian* [1994] STC 888; 69 TC 1 (CA NI), where the court refused to allow the alteration of an assessment where the inspector had been under a misapprehension but had not made a mistake, since he had intended to do what he had done.

[124] TMA 1970, s 33 and Sch 1AB; however, see Stopforth [1989] BTR 151 for limitations on this relief.

[125] The procedure is laid down in TMA 1970, s 42. It applies also to elections: s 42(10).

[126] TMA 1970, s 42(2), subject to subs (3) which refers to PAYE computations.

[127] TMA 1970, s 42(9).

[128] TMA 1970, ss 43A, 43B. It appears that this does not apply when the assessment is an original (but late) assessment as distinct from an additional assessment.

[129] TMA 1970, s 43 as amended by FA 2008, s 113 and Sch 39.

[130] TMA 1970, s, 43(2); for further assessments, see ss 43A, 43B.

actually arise. If, often for very good reasons, accounts were not ready, the inspector would make an estimated or provisional assessment. This would be followed by amended or additional assessments, which represented a very real compliance cost to major taxpayers. The self-assessment system avoids such unnecessary 'ping-pong' by making the taxpayer submit his return by 31 January, and ensures government cash flow by the system of payment of accounts. There are, however, others, eg older taxpayers,[131] for whom the change represented a new and significant expense—but a great opportunity for tax advisers. It may be that the real world with which the tax system has to grapple can no longer be adequately policed without this shift in practice, and that older people's interests have to be sacrificed.

Another major benefit has been a reform of some of the less-intelligible substantive rules, notably the abolition of the preceding year basis of assessment and the rewriting of the Schedule A rules (now ITTOIA 2005, Part 3). Forms have had to be rewritten to enable taxpayers to calculate their own tax, instead of supplying information required by the Revenue. The rules for deduction at source (below at §27.5) were amended to bring them into line with the forms. The rule under which the Revenue can be required to do the calculations is also beneficial and bridges the old system with the new. There are also philosophical (or even constitutional) aspects in the rights of citizens to take charge of their part in the process. Rights, however, also come with obligations. Under the old regime taxpayers could disclose the nature of any transaction without being obliged to indicate to the Revenue that certain anti-avoidance provisions might apply. Under self-assessment, taxpayers must apply the relevant provision to themselves; failure to do so may lead to interest, surcharges and, of course, penalties. They cannot rely, as in the old days, on the Revenue deciding not to apply the provision.

Overall, the change has been completed successfully in that the self-assessment system is firmly in place and delivering tax payments.[132] The reader is referred to the latest HMRC Annual Reports for figures and percentages. Apart from some teething troubles,[133] notably over the boundary between partnership tax and individual partner tax, and between PAYE and self-assessment, things seem to be going better. One improvement was the shortened form for certain taxpayers. It remains to be seen when the Revenue will achieve their target of 95% accuracy in administering these matters. Just how the Revenue strikes a balance between deterrence and forgiveness in administering the system, and how willing they are and should be to use the reasonable excuse provisions remain open questions. American experience, which the Chancellor invoked as a good precedent when introducing the system in 1993, later turned very sour, with Revenue agents confessing to malpractices used to terrorise or mislead taxpayers.[134] This led to a new and weaker structure for the US Internal Revenue Service (IRS); as with so many things in the US, matters did not stay this way for long, especially after the Enron Scandal.

Furthermore, how will the nation divide between those who think they can cheat on a system which has so relatively few checks and those honest or even fearful people who will

---

[131] For special problems, see CIOT Low income Tax Reform Group.

[132] See Sixth Report of the House of Commons Select Committee on the Treasury 1998–99; and comments by Chamberlain [1999] BTR 445.

[133] See [1998] *Simon's Weekly Tax Intelligence* 58, 741.

[134] On US legislative response, see Mumford [1997] BTR 481; see also the experience of Professor Graetz in Graetz (1977) 126 *University of Pennsylvania L Rev* 47, 92.

not claim all the reliefs to which they might be entitled? The present UK self-assessment system has two major mitigating features as compared with more general systems. One is the rule requiring the Revenue to do the actual calculations if the return is submitted by 31 October. The second is the exclusion of most employees. If the system required all employees to file returns—or all taxpayers to monitor their digital accounts regularly as appears to be the plan for the future—we might read of proposals to substitute expenditure tax for an income tax and read articles about how many unnecessary returns/digital accounts could be got rid of.[135]

4.4 Appeals

The structure of tax appeals changed fundamentally when Part 1 of the Tribunals, Courts and Enforcement Act (TCEA) 2007 took effect from 1 April 2009. The new system is outlined at §4.4.3 below, after an explanation of the former regime—which applied to nearly all of the cases discussed in this book.[136]

Those outside HMRC sometimes wonder how particular cases are picked for trial and then for any further appeal. As part of a modernisation exercise and building on experience in other countries, FA 2008, section 119 provided framework legislation for a right to a preliminary review of appealable decisions. The review is necessarily within HMRC, but will be independent of those who made the original decision to litigate.

4.4.1 Appeals to Commissioners Against Assessment

A taxpayer might wish to appeal against an officer's amendment to his self-assessment,[137] or against the refusal of a claim or election.[138] Similarly, a taxpayer, aggrieved with an assessment which is not a self-assessment, might want to appeal. The taxpayer had to give notice in writing to the Revenue within 30 days of its issue.[139] By contrast, notice of a VAT appeal was sent to the tribunal itself.[140] Other methods of 'appeal' included seeking the opinion of the court[141] and an originating summons,[142] but not arbitration.[143] Other avenues are discussed in §4.4.5 below.

---

[135] Like Graetz (2002) 112 *Yale LJ* 261–99.

[136] Readers are directed to an interesting empirical study by Blackwell on variation in the outcomes of tax appeals between Special Commissioners in [2013] BTR 154. The author uses a dataset of 746 reported cases from 1995 to 2009 to identify substantial variation between Special Commissioners and to examine whether such variation can be attributable to the professional background of tribunal members.

[137] Ie, under TMA 1970, s 28A(2) or (4); on partnerships, see ss 28B(3) and 30B(1).

[138] Ie, under TMA 1970, s 28(4A).

[139] TMA 1970, s 31.

[140] See, generally, Avery Jones [1994] BTR 3.

[141] As in *A-G v National Provincial Bank Ltd* (1928) 14 TC 111.

[142] As in *Buxton v Public Trustee* (1962) 41 TC 235 (charitable nature of trusts), but not in *Argosam Finance Co Ltd v Oxby* [1964] 3 All ER 561; 42 TC 86 (vexatious).

[143] See Sheridan [1978] BTR 243. The US Tax Court (rule 124) allows binding arbitration on questions of fact; usually, these are questions of valuation: see Sansing (1997) 50 *National Tax J* 279.

The appeal could be made either to the General Commissioners, a body of lay persons assisted by a qualified clerk,[144] or to the Special Commissioners, who were highly, qualified persons. The Commissioners' role was to adjudicate rather than to assess.[145] The final rules on Special Commissioners restricted eligibility for future appointments to persons who were legally qualified and made it usual for a Commissioner to sit singly. Legislation reserved particular appeals to one or other body; otherwise the choice was with the taxpayer. Appeals also lay to the Lands Tribunal and the special tribunal appointed under TA 1988, section 706, now ITA 2007, section 704.

The choice of tribunal as between the two sets of Commissioners was governed by certain factors: for example, the General Commissioners sat locally[146] and were cheaper and quicker; however, the Special Commissioners were a more professional body with more time to give to a complex case and, perhaps, had a reputation for insisting on more proof from the Revenue in cases of alleged omitted profits. Costs could be awarded by the Special Commissioners against a party who had behaved 'wholly unreasonably' and had so behaved 'in connection with the hearing'.[147] Merely adhering to an untenable argument was not such behaviour unless the argument was known to be untenable.[148] The question whether reasonableness was to be determined objectively or subjectively was never conclusively decided.[149] The Special Commissioners could sit in public.[150] Legal aid was not available in either tribunal, but there was no reason why a taxpayer could not use a *McKenzie* friend in appropriate circumstances.[151] The taxpayer could elect which body to appeal to, but this election could be overridden by a direction of the General Commissioners.[152] The General Commissioners were empowered to transfer a case to the Special Commissioners if the latter body consented and the case involved either complex matters or would take too much time.[153]

Each party was allowed to produce evidence.[154] The onus was (and still is) on the taxpayer to disprove the assessment,[155] a rule which may be rationalised on the basis that the taxpayer knows all the facts and therefore should have to prove them. Once an appeal was launched, it could be withdrawn only with the consent of the Revenue.[156] An appeal could be made out of time if a reasonable excuse was provided.[157] Procedure at hearings was

---

[144] On clerks see Stebbings [1994] BTR 61; on history, see Stebbings [1992] BTR 398.

[145] *Wicker v Fraser* [1983] STC 505; see also Stebbings [1993] BTR 52.

[146] On choice, see TMA 1970, s 44(2) *et seq.*

[147] Special Commissioners (Jurisdiction and Procedure) Regulations 1994 (SI 1994/1811), para 21. See Vollans [2003] BTR 15–24.

[148] *Carter v Hunt* [2000] STC (SCD) 17.

[149] In *Salt v Young* [1999] STC (SCD) 249, the Commissioner suggested that the test may be subjective.

[150] Special Commissioners (Jurisdiction and Procedure) Regulations 1994, para 15. On human rights problems, see Baker [2000] BTR 211, 243.

[151] On *McKenzie* friends, see *McKenzie v McKenzie* [1970] Ch 33. However, *R v Leicester City Justices* [1991] 3 All ER 935 shows that there is no right to such a friend; on use in proceedings not held in public, see *R v Bow County Court, ex parte Pelling* (1999) NLJ 1369.

[152] TMA 1970, s 31(5A)–(5E).

[153] TMA 1970, s 44(3A).

[154] See Regulations for Special and General Commissioners 1994 (SIs 1994/1711 and 1994/1812), paras 17 and 15, respectively; on expert evidence, see paras 12 and 9 respectively.

[155] *Norman v Golder* [1945] 1 All ER 352; 26 TC 293.

[156] TMA 1970, s 54.

[157] TMA 1970, s 49; see *A-G for Scotland v General Commissioners for Aberdeen* [2005] CSOH 135, [2006] STC 1218 and *R on application of Cook v General Commissioners* [2007] EWHC 167 (Admin), [2007] STC 499.

governed by regulations.[158] Both sets of Commissioners could review their decisions on an application by a party or of their own motion,[159] but only for administrative error, the failure of one party to appear (for good and sufficient reason), or the failure of accounts to reach the tribunal even though they had been delivered to the Revenue. The procedures were different from VAT appeals. *Inter alia*, the Commissioners normally sat in private, whereas the VAT tribunal sat in public. Appeal lay from the Commissioners to the Chancery Division and, in the case of the General Commissioners, by case stated; an appeal from the VAT Tribunal went to the Queen's Bench Division.

4.4.2 Further Appeals and Reversing the Commissioners

In England and Wales, a further appeal lay to the High Court from a decision of the General Commissioners by the ancient (but procedurally improved) process of case stated.[160] In Scotland, appeal lay to the Court of Session and in Northern Ireland to the Court of Appeal (Northern Ireland). Appeals lay only on questions of law.[161] A party must have applied within 30 days after the Commissioners made their determination, declared dissatisfaction with that determination and asked for a case to be stated for the opinion of the High Court.[162] Failure to apply in the right 30-day period meant that no appeal could be made.[163] The clerk had 56 days in which to state the case and there were procedures for commenting on the case.[164] The Commissioners had the power to require the would-be appellant to identify the question of law to be addressed in the case stated.[165] The case-stated procedure was enduring rather than endearing.[166] General Commissioners were entitled to refuse to state a case where the taxpayer appellant did not identify the issue of law to be appealed.[167]

Appeals could go from the Special Commissioners by simple appeal,[168] without the complexity of the case stated. However, the appeal still lay only on questions of law and, moreover, any tax found by the Special Commissioners to be due must have been paid.[169] Appeals could go from the Special Commissioners direct to the Court of Appeal,[170] but only on questions of law.

---

[158] Made under TMA 1970, ss 56B, 56C; on information powers of Special Commissioners, see SI 1994/1811, regs 4, 9, 18.

[159] SIs 1994/1811 and 1994/1812, paras 17, 17; see, generally, Stebbings [1995] BTR 395.

[160] Chancery Division Civil Procedure Rules Order 29. A case stated does not 'disclose a cause of action' and so proceedings to strike out a case stated under the old RSC Ord 18 were inappropriate; *Petch v Gurney* [1994] STC 689 (CA).

[161] TMA 1970, s 56.

[162] See SI 1994/1812, paras 20–23.

[163] *Haven Healthcare (Southern) Ltd v York* [2005] EWHC 2212 (Ch), [2005] STC 1662.

[164] For an example of problems facing the parties, see *Fitzpatrick v IRC* [1991] STC 34.

[165] SI 1994/1812, reg 20(3).

[166] For history and criticism, see Stebbings [1996] BTR 611.

[167] *R (on the application of Jesner) v General Commissioners of Income Tax for the Division of Upper Renfrew Ward* [2010] STC 1045, [2010] CSOH 23.

[168] TMA 1970, s 56A.

[169] TMA 1970, s 56A(8), (9).

[170] TMA 1970, s 56A(2); see also Civil Procedure Rules 1999, r 52.

4.4.3 Appeals from 1 April 2009: The New Tribunal System

The TCEA 2007 came into effect from 1 April 2009. Under the new regime, the House of Lords (from September 2009, the Supreme Court), the Court of Appeal, the Court of Session and the Northern Ireland Court of Appeal have the same roles as before.[171] Below this, all has changed. The previous High Court jurisdiction with its split between appeals (Chancery Division) and review (Admin) was replaced by one single jurisdiction exercised by the Upper Tribunal.[172] The new Upper Tribunal sits in chambers, and one of the upper chambers is devoted to tax and finance.

Below this is the First-tier Tribunal, which replaced the Special and General Commissioners, the VAT Appeal Tribunals and a host of other tribunals, including that in ITA 2007, section 704 (transactions in securities). The main point is that all administrative tribunals, not just tax ones, have been brought into one structure.[173] The majority of appeals are meant to commence in the First-tier Tribunal generally on a no-costs basis. Both tiers have the power to review their decisions. Appeal from the First-tier to the Upper Tribunal is, as before, on points of law only, with permission of either Tribunal.[174] The Upper Tribunal can hear first-instance appeals in more legally (as opposed to factually) complex cases, and has full costs jurisdiction. It is a superior court of record and its decisions are binding on the First-tier Tribunal. Appeals from an Upper Tribunal decision lie to the Court of Appeal, with permission. The appeal must be on a point of law and must either (a) raise an important point of principle or practice, or (b) have some other compelling reason to be heard. Appeals from the Court of Appeal lie to the Supreme Court, again with permission.

4.4.4 When Can the Court Reverse the Tribunals?

Decisions of the First-tier and Upper Tribunals (formerly the Commissioners) can be reversed only for error of law, and so not simply on the basis that the appellant judge would have reached a different conclusion.[175] The facts may be such that the court assumes there has been some error of law. In *Edwards v Bairstow and Harrison*,[176] Lord Radcliffe said it did not much matter whether this state of affairs was described as one in which there was no evidence to support the determination, the evidence was inconsistent with and contradictory of the determination, or the true and only reasonable conclusion contradicted the determination. Rightly understood, each phrase propounded the same test. He preferred the last of the three.

The question whether an issue is one of fact or law is not always easy.[177] Dickinson wrote memorably of 'matters of law which grow downwards into the roots of fact while matters of

---

[171] TCEA 2007, ss 13 and 14.

[172] TCEA 2007, ss 15–21.

[173] TCEA 2007, ss 30–38 contain the powers for making the transfers; see also Sch 6.

[174] TCEA 2007, ss 9–11.

[175] For an interesting example, see Park J in *Usetch v Young* [2004] EWHC Ch 2248; [2004] STC 1671.

[176] [1955] 3 All ER 48, 57; 36 TC 20, 229; see application by Megarry J in *Redditch Electro-Plating Co Ltd v Ferrebe* (1973) 48 TC 635, 645; and qualification by Lord Diplock in *CCSU v Minister for Civil Service* [1985] AC 384, 410.

[177] See Lord Simon in *Ransom v Higgs* [1974] STC 539, 561. Among much literature, see Endicott (1998) 114 LQR 292. For similar US position issues, see *Dobson v Commissioner* 320 US 489 (1943), the inside story of which is told by Stark 54 *Tax L Rev* 171, 223 *et seq*.

fact reached upwards without a break into matters of law'.[178] Some see the whole exercise as legalism rather than realism, and treat the distinction between law and fact as a legal fiction on the basis of which judges determine jurisdiction.[179] Nevertheless, some matters, like the construction of documents or statutes, are clearly questions of law; others, such as whether a document was executed on a particular date, are clearly questions of fact. Difficulties arise where the Tribunal of first instance, having decided the true meaning of the statute in issue, have to apply that meaning to the facts. The difficulties are of two sorts.

The first difficulty is the familiar problem of finding the right approach[180] to primary and secondary facts, the latter being inferences drawn from the former. In general such inferences are matters of fact and the courts are reluctant to substitute their own views, the more so since the Tribunal members, at first instance, unlike the court, have seen the witnesses. These secondary facts are still findings of fact.[181] Thus the question whether a trade is being carried on is one of fact. The Tribunal Members must not only decide the primary facts, such as what transactions were carried on and when, but also form their own conclusion as to whether or not these activities amounted to a trade, a conclusion which must depend on a whole range of circumstances and impressions.[182] However, the question of the meaning of trade is one of law. Therefore, the question whether an isolated transaction can come within the meaning of trade is one of law; whether the particular transaction comes within the meaning of trade is one of fact. The legal system ought to accept that if a particular issue is one of fact, cases on almost identical facts may fall either side of the line. Some judges have been tempted extricate themselves from the mess by characterising the issue as one which is of mixed law and fact.[183] Such judges are incorrect in their premise and so in their conclusion. Other judges show greater humility.[184] The second difficulty is that the law can be formulated in such a way as to leave it more or less to the Tribunal members to decide the case, depending on the level of abstraction employed. Thus, in employment cases the issue may be: is a payment a reward for services or, more simply, is it an emolument? Clearly, the latter leaves more to the Tribunal members and reduces the court's power to intervene. Some judges have tried to solve this problem by suggesting that some questions of law should be dealt with on an *Edwards v Bairstow and Harrison* approach (below at §21.1.3).

When the court has heard an appeal it may make such order as it may see fit.[185] This has been interpreted widely so as to enable the court to uphold an assessment as if it had been made under a different section, or to remit the matter to the Tribunals with a direction to uphold it as if it had been made under a different section. The court is confined by the facts determined and the issues raised by the case stated, and is neither expected nor permitted to wander further afield.[186] The court may sometimes remit the case to the Tribunals for

---

[178] *Administrative Justice and the Supremacy of Law* (1927), 51; quoted by Beatson [1984] 4 *OJLS* 22, 31.

[179] Laws [1999] BTR 159.

[180] See, eg, Beatson [1984] 4 *OJLS* 22, 39–45.

[181] Lord Brightman in *Furniss v Dawson* [1984] STC 153, 167.

[182] Lord Sands in *IRC v Hyndland Investment Co Ltd* (1929) 14 TC 694, 700.

[183] Lord Templeman in *Fitzpatrick v IRC (No 2)* [1994] STC 237, 242e, 246g (HL). See Olowofoyeku [1996] BTR 28 and Tiley [2010] BTR 55 at 78–81.

[184] Lord Jauncey and Lord Mustill in *Fitzpatrick v IRC (No 2)* [1994] STC 237, 248, 255 (HL).

[185] TMA 1970, s 56(6).

[186] *McKnight v Sheppard* [1997] STC 846 (CA); reproving Lightman J for his approach in [1996] STC 627.

additional findings of fact. However, this will be done only if such findings are material to some tenable argument, at least reasonable upon the evidence adduced and not inconsistent with findings already made.[187]

A new, more liberal approach to the question of an appellate court's scope for review has emerged in recent years, championed by Lord Carnwath.[188] In *Jones v First-tier Tribunal (Social Entitlement Chamber)*,[189] Lord Carnwath suggested that an expert appellate tribunal 'should be permitted to venture more freely into the "grey area" separating fact from law, than an ordinary court.' Further, Lord Carnwath stated that 'issues of law' in this context should be interpreted as 'extending to any issues of general principle affecting the specialist jurisdiction'. Lord Carnwath repeated his view on this subject in *HMRC v Pendragon plc.*[190]

Arguments based on Lord Carnwath's approach are starting to appear with some regularity in tax cases before the Upper Tribunal, with the judges urged to take a more expansive approach, eg on assessing whether the LLP was trading in the *Eclipse 35* case discussed below at §19.3. To date, however, those arguments have yet to make much impact on the Upper Tribunal judges, who so far have been reluctant to depart from the traditional approach of appellate courts to the law-fact dividing line. This has been the case even in the handful of cases where an Upper Tribunal judge has accepted, in theory, that he or she has the power to take a more expansive approach.[191] Perhaps this reflects an appreciation that the lower tax tribunal brings expertise to its case load and thus may not be an 'ordinary court' in the sense used by Lord Carnwath.

4.4.5 Other Possible Routes to Challenge Tribunals' or Officers' Decisions

4.4.5.1 Judicial Review

This remedy is equally applicable to the decision of the Tribunals or to the original assessment; it is also applicable, quite separately from the assessment process, to any situation in which officers of the Revenue exercise a power committed to them by the state. An application may be made only if the court has granted leave. It is subject to a time limit of three months from the date the ground first arose (although the court may extend the limit) and requires an applicant to have sufficient interest or *locus standi*.[192] The Upper Tribunal has judicial review powers and is subject to judicial review by the High Court only when acting clearly beyond its statutory remit.

The court will not allow an applicant to use judicial review where the point should be dealt with by appeal.[193] Conversely, allegations of unfairness in the conduct of the appeal are matters for judicial review and not for appeal.[194] When judicial review is sought, applicants

---

[187] *Consolidated Goldfields plc v IRC* [1990] STC 357, 361, Scott J; applied in *Carvill v IRC* [1996] STC 126; but distinguished in *Bradley v London Electricity plc* [1996] STC 231.

[188] Carnwath, 'Tribunal justice—a new start' [2009] Public Law 48.

[189] [2013] UKSC 19.

[190] [2015] UKSC 37; for commentary see Brinsmead-Stockham, Tax Journal (25 Sept 2015).

[191] See eg *HMRC v Arkeley Ltd (in liquidation)* [2013] UKUT 0393 (TCC).

[192] RSC Ord 53, rr 3, 4.

[193] See discussion by Dyson J in *R v IRC, ex parte Bishopp* [1999] STC 531.

[194] *Mellor v Gurney* [1994] STC 1025.

must ensure that they do not act too early or too late.[195] The grounds for judicial review of the exercise of a power are, of course, the same as in other areas of law, and were set out in 1985 by Lord Diplock[196] as comprising illegality, irrationality and procedural impropriety. Illegality covers errors of law; irrationality covers *Wednesbury* unreasonableness, ie a decision which is so outrageous in its defiance of logic or accepted moral standards that no sensible persons who applied their minds to the question could have arrived at it; procedural impropriety covers not only the failure to observe the rules of natural justice but also errors in the tribunal's own procedures. Today this formulation must also be interpreted to embrace the emerging doctrines of legitimate expectations and proportionality.[197] One of the more high-profile judicial review cases in tax in recent years was UK Uncut Legal Action's unsuccessful application to the High Court seeking a declaration that the tax settlement between HMRC and Goldman Sachs was unlawful.[198]

4.4.5.2 Public Law Defence

The second remedy is to establish a public law defence to a Revenue enforcement action,[199] eg by arguing that the original assessment is *ultra vires* and therefore void. In *IRC v Aken*[200] this line of argument was used—unsuccessfully—to argue that the profits of prostitution could not be taxable since, as a matter of law, the profits of an illegal activity cannot be subject to tax. The Court of Appeal rejected this argument. Judges will no doubt keep this use of the *ultra vires* doctrine under very tight control to prevent it from becoming another avenue of appeal. Inspectors do not act *ultra vires* merely by making a mistake of law. Since *IRC v Aken* was decided, the courts have developed the law on collateral challenge. The House of Lords held that it is open to citizens charged with a criminal offence to argue that the law under which they are charged is invalid.[201] That case concerned a prosecution for breach of a byelaw against smoking. The House had to distinguish a recent case[202] which had not allowed a person to challenge the validity of an enforcement notice in the planning notice enforcement proceedings, and did so by treating the matter as one of statutory construction. In planning law Parliament had provided a complex system of appeal and the decision was addressed to the defendant; the exercise of the right of appeal and judicial review was enough. These cases might have had weight in tax matters but were swept aside by the Court of Appeal in *Pawlowski v Dunnington*.[203]

---

[195] See, eg, *R v IRC, ex parte Ulster Bank* [1997] STC 832 (CA), (too early); *R v IRC, ex parte Allen* [1997] STC 1141 (too late).

[196] *Council of Civil Service Union v Minister for Civil Service* [1985] AC 374, 410.

[197] Wade and Forsyth, *op cit*, ch 11; on unreasonableness see Hickman [2004] *CLJ* 166–98.

[198] *R (oao) UK Uncut Legal Action Ltd v HMRC* [2013] EWHC 1283, and see case note by de Cogan [2013] BTR 552. The Goldman Sachs settlement was one of the alleged 'sweetheart deals' discussed above at §4.2.2. Interested readers should also see Sandit, Tax Journal (11 Sept 2015) for a useful 'review' of this area, and also the material on legitimate expectations above at §3.3.5.

[199] Wade and Forsyth, *op cit*, ch 9; *Pawlowski v Dunnington* [1999] STC 550 (taxpayer allowed to argue legality of condition for Revenue action under PAYE regulations allowing action against employee for recovery of tax following deduction by employer). On differences between public law defence and judicial review, see *ibid*, 557, per Simon Brown LJ.

[200] *IRC v Aken* [1990] STC 497 (CA).

[201] *Boddington v British Transport Police* [1999] 2 AC 143; see Elliott 3 *Judicial Review* 144; Forsyth [1998] *Public Law* 364; and Hare [1998] *CLJ* 429.

[202] *R v Wicks* [1998] AC 92.

[203] *Pawlowski v Dunnington* [1999] STC 550.

4.4.5.3 Damages

The third remedy is the altogether more ingenious suggestion that a cause of action lies against the Crown for damages, perhaps even exemplary damages, on the unlawful collection of or demand for tax.[204] This argument may gain credibility as a result of the incorporation of the Human Rights Convention in October 2000. However, a credible argument is not necessarily a successful one. On the very different question whether HMRC owe the taxpayer a duty of care in administering the tax system, see below at §4.9.

4.4.5.4 Restitution

The law on restitution in tax matters continues to evolve. The courts have recognised claims for restitution of tax unlawfully demanded, on the basis of *Woolwich Equitable Building Society v IRC*.[205] In addition, in *Deutsche Morgan Grenfell v IRC*, the House of Lords held that money paid under a mistake of law may be recovered in an action for restitution.[206] These restitutionary claims are commonly known, respectively, as *Woolwich* claims and *DMG* claims. *Deutsche Morgan Grenfell v IRC* was one of a stream of cases which have entered the lists; many stem from decisions of the European Court of Justice (ECJ now CJEU), since these have given rise to decisions which were unexpected. Some might think that saying that the tax was paid under a 'mistake' was a rather odd use of language, but it enables the court to hold that the taxpayer has a ground for a remedy in restitution without having to decide the big question whether the claimant needs to show a ground or can instead rely on some general overarching principle of unjust enrichment. The House held that there was no special exemption for tax, and it made no difference that the payments had been made under a settled understanding of the law (a matter very relevant to TMA 1970, section 33 but not here). Their Lordships held that sums were paid under a mistake because they had been paid in the belief that a group income election was not open to the taxpayers. That became clear only when the ECJ gave its decision in the *Metalgesellschaft* case in 2001,[207] and so the limitation period began to run only as from that date.

FA 2004, section 320 amended the limitation period for claims based on mistake of law brought on or after 8 September 2003, by directing that the period ran for six years from the date of payment and not from the date the mistake was discovered. FA 2007, section 107 imposed this rule for claims brought before that date unless there was a House of Lords decision before 6 December 2006 or the action was part of a group litigation order. The aim of these provisions was to significantly limit the ability of taxpayers to bring *DMG* claims, which were more worrying for the UK tax authorities because the six year limitation period commences only on discovery of the mistake rather than, in the case of *Woolwich* claims, at the time of the tax overpayment. In *NEC Semi-Conductors v IRC*, also known as *Boake Allen*, the House of Lords held that there was no relevant discrimination and expressly declined

---

[204] Wilde [1995] BTR 137, relating Art 4 of the Bill of Rights to the Crown Proceedings Act 1947. The argument may be weakened (but not destroyed) by the decision of the House of Lords in *O'Rourke v Camden BC* [1998] AC 188; on which see Carnwath [1998] *Public Law* 407.

[205] [1993] AC 70.

[206] [2006] UKHL 49 [2007], STC 1 [2003] STC 1017. For comments see Virgo [2007] BTR 27; and more generally in *Comparative Perspectives on Revenue Law* (CUP, 2008) ch 6.

[207] [2001] STC 452. See also, in relation to a claim for interest arising out of a claim for restitution, *Sempra Metals (formerly Metallgesellschaft) v IRC* [2004] STC 1178.

to consider hypothetical remedies.[208] The question of the relationship between a claim in restitution for recovery of a payment made under a mistake of law and the regime in TMA 1970, section 33 for error and mistake claims was not considered in *Deutsche Morgan Grenfell*. It did, however, reach the Court of Appeal in *Monro v HMRC*.[209] The Court held that where a claim under section 33 was barred by the defence in subsection (3)—viz that HMRC could rely on the fact that the payment was in accordance with the general practice prevailing at the time—there could be no claim in restitution either. In *Test Claimants in the Franked Investment Income Group Litigation*,[210] the Supreme Court held that on the facts TMA 1970, section 33 did not exclude either *Woolwich* claims or *DMG* claims as HMRC had argued. Importantly, the Supreme Court also held that FA 2007, section 107 did not block the taxpayers' *DMG* claims because that provision infringed the EU law principle of effectiveness. The judges disagreed, however, on whether FA 2004, section 320 was effective, and referred the question to the ECJ. This decision is an extremely important one for taxpayers seeking tax repayments as a result of UK tax rules being found to be in breach of EU law. It is also potentially very damaging for the Exchequer.

The Supreme Court's decision in *FII GLO* seems to suggest that the UK is moving towards the position reached long ago in the US. In the US an aggrieved taxpayer may either challenge the assessment using the Tax Court and then appeal to the Federal Court of Appeals, or can pay the tax and then sue to recover it in the Tax Court or Federal Court of Claims, from which appeal lies to the Federal Court of Appeals. Such developments are best achieved by sound legislative consideration rather than by a restitution side wind. In another ECJ-inspired piece of litigation, various taxpayer companies gathered together to litigate a point of law not on the basis of the normal appeal to the Special Commissioners but by seeking a group litigation order which would be litigated in the High Court. Happily this claim failed in the House of Lords—but only by a bare majority.[211] FA 2013, sections 231 and 232 introduced yet more rules concerning overpayment relief, particularly in relation to tax charged contrary to EU law. As Lyons describes in his BTR note,[212] section 231 is inspired by the different approaches of the Court of Appeal[213] and the Supreme Court[214] in the ongoing *FII Group Litigation* concerning the legislation governing error or mistake claims in section 33 of the Taxes Management Act 1970 (TMA). That legislation now has been repealed and is replaced by amendments to the provisions on recovery of overpaid tax in Schedule 1AB to the Taxes Management Act 1970. Section 232 ensures a consistent definition of 'relevant year' for the purposes of the four year limitation period applicable to claims under Schedule 1AB.

Furthermore, as just noted, the Supreme Court in *FII GLO* had unanimously held that FA 2007, section 107 was incompatible with EU law. That provision attempted retrospectively to take away the right of action for claims that had already been brought under the extended time limit in the Limitations Act 1980, section 32(1)(c). In a somewhat delayed response

[208] [2007] UKHL 25, [2007] STC 1265.
[209] [2008] EWCA Civ 306, [2008] STC 1815, upholding [2007] EWHC 114 (Ch), [2007] STC 1182
[210] [2012] UKSC 19.
[211] *Re Claimants under Loss Relief Group Litigation Order* [2004] STC 1054 (CA). See also Williams, *Unjust Enrichment and Public Law* (Hart Publishing, 2010).
[212] Lyons [2013] BTR 548.
[213] [2010] EWCA Civ 103.
[214] [2012] UKSC 19.

to that decision, FA 2014, section 299 attempted to make FA 2007, section 107 compliant by adding a new exclusion to the rules in subsection (5A) providing that the restriction in subsection (1) does not have effect in relation to an action relating to a mistake of law and charging of tax contrary to EU law.[215]

In addition to legislative action and reaction, the case law itself in this complex area continues to develop as cases painstakingly wind their way through the European and UK courts. Specifically at issue in the third instalment of *FII GLO* in the CJEU[216] was the lawfulness of FA 2004, section 320. That provision retrospectively removed the Limitation Act 1980, section 32(1)(c) right to make common law mistake of law claims within six years of when the taxpayer knew or with reasonable diligence should have known that they had been mistaken in their view of the relevant law. In considering the reference from the Supreme Court, which was divided on the lawfulness of section 320, the CJEU decided that the requirement on a member state to give adequate prospective notice, including a reasonable period for relevant claims to be made, when that state shortens the claims time period, applies equally where there are two (or more) alternative claims routes. The *FII GLO litigation* was returned to the High Court. Henderson J found for the taxpayers on their substantive claims,[217] but an appeal by HMRC is pending at the time of writing.[218]

In another important case *Littlewoods Retail Ltd & Others v HMRC*,[219] the taxpayer was successful in the Court of Appeal in its claim for the recovery of compound interest in respect of wrongly-paid VAT. A statutory scheme had provided for recovery of principal and simple interest, which the taxpayer argued was insufficient. The CJEU had decided that in accordance with the principle of effectiveness, the recovery afforded to the taxpayer must represent an 'adequate indemnity' for its loss,[220] but the implementation of this guidance was left for the national court. In a decision of legal principle with potentially broad implications, the Court of Appeal concluded that 'adequate indemnity' was not a rigid 'straitjacket' requiring compound interest in every case, but that in the CA's view the relevant legislation (VATA 1994, section 78) did deprive the taxpayer of an adequate indemnity. Further, this provision (and section 80) were incapable of interpretation in conformity with EU law and were therefore disapplied. HMRC's appeal to the Supreme Court was pending at the time of writing.[221]

Finally, in an interesting new approach to limit the damage to the Exchequer from restitutionary claims, in F(No 2)A 2015 the Government imposed a special 45% corporate tax rate on restitutionary interest.[222] According to the explanatory note, the Government was concerned that the interest element of restitutionary awards would be taxed at an historically

---

[215] See commentary by Baker [2014] BTR 474, raising concerns with the efficacy and desirability of this approach.

[216] Case C-362/12.

[217] [2014] EWHC 4302 (Ch).

[218] For more see Cussons, *Tax Journal* (10 Jan 2014) and note that Baker in his commentary on the FA 2014 changes to FA 2007, section 107 is critical that no modifications were made to section 320–see [2014] BTR 474.

[219] [2015] EWCA Civ 515.

[220] Case C-591/10 *Littlewoods Retail and Others v HMRC* [2012] STC 1714.

[221] In the meantime, the taxpayer's cross-appeal against the levying of corporation tax on the VAT repayment was denied by the Supreme Court: see [2016] UKSC 7. Interested readers are directed to a current note by Schote [2014] BTR 103 on the San Giorgio 'cause of action' for restitution of tax.

[222] CTA 2010, ss 357YA–357YW.

low rate of tax. The 45% rate is thought to better reflect the corporation tax rates in effect over the periods to which typical awards related as well as the effect of compounding interest not taxed in the year to which it relates. It remains to be seen if Brexit may offer further damage-limiting opportunities.

4.5 Encouraging Payment of Tax

HMRC has sometimes been criticised for not doing all they might to collect tax that is due. FA 2009 added two powers to help. First, section 97 of and Schedule 49 to the Act allow HMRC to obtain contact details on their debtors. Secondly, section 110 and Schedule 58 allow HMRC to use the PAYE system for the recovery of debts from employees. In addition, FA 2009, section 111 provided a statutory basis for allowing taxpayers to enter into a managed payments plan, ie payment by instalments. Compliance with the plan is treated as payment of the debt. Section 108 deals with the suspension of penalties during the currency of any agreement for deferred payments.

HMRC's powers to levy interest on unpaid taxes, collect unpaid taxes through the courts, and pursue non-compliant taxpayers for civil penalties and criminal sanctions are discussed next.

4.5.1 Late Payment—Problems of Interest

Interest runs from the date on which tax is payable to the date of actual payment.[223] This applies to tax due on an assessment, payments on account, the balancing charge to tax, an amendment to a self-assessment, unpaid PAYE and any surcharge. Interest is now calculated on a compound basis.[224] Concessionary relief is available if the taxpayer dies before the payment date.[225] If an enquiry results in an increase in tax liability, the taxpayer will be liable for the increase in the amount due under a balancing payment and the following year's payment on account, as well as interest on the increased balancing payment and on any extra payments on account. Payment of the following year's balance in full and at the right time will prevent interest liability arising on the payments on account for that year.[226] Although the taxpayer may agree with the Revenue to postpone the payment of tax where a liability is in dispute,[227] this will have no effect on the remorseless application of the rules where tax is eventually held to be due. Interest is charged at a rate set by statutory instrument and is presently 3%;[228] it is not deductible in computing income.[229]

---

[223] TMA 1970, s 86—the due date is set out in the self-assessment process.

[224] For details on calculation of late payment interest see FA 2009, s 101 and Sch 53. On interest see Collison, *op cit*, §§22.6–22.10.

[225] FA 2009, Sch 53, Pt 2, s 12 ex ESC A17.

[226] Collison, *op cit*, §22.6.

[227] Under TMA 1970, s 55.

[228] FA 2009 ss 102–103. On definitions, administration and commencement, see ss 104 and 105 and related schedules. For current and historical rates see https://www.gov.uk/government/publications/rates-and-allowances-hmrc-interest-rates-for-late-and-early-payments/rates-and-allowances-hmrc-interest-rates.

[229] TMA 1970, s 90.

Taxpayers intending to appeal against the amendment or assessment may apply to post-pone the payment of tax in dispute; any tax not in dispute is due at the normal time. If the taxpayer and the Revenue cannot agree (in writing) on the amount in dispute, the Tribunal may determine the matter.[230] If the taxpayer pays the tax but later wins the appeal, the tax will be refunded together with a repayment supplement; if the appeal is lost, tax is due as from the original proper date with any interest consequences. Where tax has been overpaid, repayments will carry interest as from 31 January following the end of the fiscal year.[231] The payments are tax free.[232] This mirrors the liability to pay interest on unpaid tax. A repay-ment supplement may arise if payments on account of tax or balancing liability are found to be excessive, there is a reduction in any surcharge or penalty, or there is a repayment on any other income tax paid by or on behalf of the taxpayer. The rate of interest is less than that used for interest due to the Revenue and also is set by statutory instrument.[233]

4.5.2 Court Action

HMRC has a formidable battery of powers to collect tax.[234] HMRC may sue in the mag-istrates' court (for amounts up to £2,000),[235] the county court (without limit)[236] or the High Court.[237] There is no limit on the jurisdiction of the sheriff court in Scotland.[238] The Crown's status as preferential creditor on insolvency has been abolished.[239] In a simplifica-tion move, F(No 2)Act 2015 set the rate of interest which applies on taxation-related debts payable under a court judgment or order by HMRC to Bank of England base rate plus 2%. In addition, the late payment interest rate of 3% applies to taxation-related debts owed to HMRC under a court judgment or order.[240] In the past, the Revenue could also, after obtaining a warrant from a justice of the peace, levy distraint on the goods and chattels (but not perishable food)[241] of the person liable, and could obtain a warrant to enter premises during the daytime.[242] This power did not amount to an execution within the Insolvency Act 1986, section 183.[243] Under FA 2008, the power to distrain was confined to Northern Ireland, and HMRC's powers to take control of goods were brought together and modern-ised. For England and Wales the procedure used now is that in TCEA 2007, Schedule 12; in

---

[230] TMA 1970, s 55; on time limit, see s 55(3).

[231] TA 1988, s 824.

[232] TA 1988, s 824(8).

[233] FA 2009, s 103. For current and historical rates see https://www.gov.uk/government/publications/rates-and-allowances-hmrc-interest-rates-for-late-and-early-payments/rates-and-allowances-hmrc-interest-rates.

[234] The Revenue's powers to sue in court were simplified and widened by changes to ss 66, 67 and 70 and by a new TMA 1970, s 69, added by FA 2001, s 89. The Revenue also have powers to direct withholding tax at source, eg from visiting entertainers and sportsmen.

[235] Summary Proceedings (Financial Limits) Order 1991 (SI 1991/1625).

[236] County court proceedings involving HMRC were rationalised and improved by FA 2008, ss 135–138.

[237] See the County Courts Act 1984, ss 40(2) and 41(1) for power to transfer proceedings, and SI 1991/724 amending TMA 1970, s 66.

[238] TMA 1970, s 67.

[239] Insolvency Act 1986, Sch 6, repealed by the Enterprise Act, 2002.

[240] F(No 2)A 2015, s 52. The new rules take effect from 8 July 2015 on new and pre-existing judgments/orders.

[241] *Morley v Pincombe* (1848) 2 Exch 101.

[242] TMA 1970, s 61.

[243] *Re Modern Jet Centre Ltd* [2006] EWHC 1611 (Ch), [2006] STC 808.

Scotland there is a single application for a summary warrant.[244] In general, a bankruptcy court will not go behind an assessment to tax.[245]

F(No 2)A 2015 also introduced a controversial new HMRC power to recover debts due to it directly from the debtor's bank or building society accounts (including ISAs).[246] The stated aim of the 'enforcement by deduction from accounts' power is to target those who have the means to pay what they owe but deliberately choose not to do so, despite repeated contact from HMRC. A number of taxpayer protections are in place. The debt must be an established debt in excess of £1,000, and HMRC must be satisfied that the person is aware that the sum is due and payable. Debtors targeted for the use of this power must receive a face-to-face visit, and must be left with a minimum 'safeguarded amount' of £5,000 across all accounts. Debtors will have 30 days to object to HMRC's 'hold notice' before any money is transferred to HMRC and can make an appeal to the county court.[247] Commentators have expressed concern over the efficacy of the taxpayer safeguards and have questioned whether HMRC should be given a power that effectively gives them a priority over a taxpayer's other creditors—'a stealthy reintroduction of Crown preference'.[248]

4.5.3 Penalties and Criminal Offences

4.5.3.1 Penalties

The old penalties regime which dealt with fraudulent or negligent conduct was discarded by FA 2007.[249] The 2007 legislation introduced a consistent set of penalty rules across most of the taxes administered by HMRC.[250] The regime applies where a document in a prescribed list (eg the tax return) is inaccurate and this leads to:

(1)   an understatement of a liability to tax;
(2)   a false or inflated loss; or
(3)   a false or inflated repayment claim.

For the regime to apply it is necessary that the behaviour should be either 'careless' or 'deliberate'. 'Deliberate' may be either deliberate but not concealed (where the person makes no arrangements to conceal it), or deliberate but concealed (eg false evidence in support of an inaccurate figure). The category of 'careless' is widened to cover a situation in which the document, although inaccurate, was neither carelessly nor deliberately inaccurate and the person later discovers the inaccuracy but fails to take reasonable steps to tell HMRC.[251]

---

[244]   FA 2008, ss 127–129.
[245]   In *Lam v IRC* [2005] EWHC 592 (Ch), [2006] STC 893, an appeal against a bankruptcy order on the ground that the tax was not due was dismissed.
[246]   F(No 2)A 2015, s 51 and Sch 8.
[247]   For commentary see Gordon [2015] BTR 646. See also Adams and Goldberg, Tax Journal (20 Feb 2015).
[248]   Gordon [2015] BTR 646.
[249]   FA 2007, s 97 and Sch 24.
[250]   FA 2008 extended the treatment to other taxes, including IHT, as from a date no earlier than 1 April 2009: see FA 2008, s 122 and Sch 40; HMRC Technical Note BN 96, 12 March 2008.
[251]   FA 2007, Sch 24, Pt 1, paras 1–3.

The amount of error-related penalty is calculated according to 'potential lost revenue', and is mitigable by prompted or unprompted disclosure:[252]

(1)   for conduct that is careless the penalty is up to 30% of the extra tax owing;
(2)   for deliberate but not concealed conduct it is 20%-70%; and
(3)   for deliberate and concealed conduct it is 30%-100%.

There is much important detail here which is beyond the scope of an account such as this. One rule allows for a complete waiver of penalty where there has been an unprompted disclosure of a failure to take reasonable care.[253] There are also rules bringing in overstatements of income as well as understatements, and dealing with different types of disclosure (which, as just seen, may mitigate liability). Special circumstances may also justify HMRC in reducing the penalty: for example, an understatement by one person is balanced by an overstatement by another.[254] FA 2007 Schedule 24, Part 3 (paras 13–17) governs procedure; it contains clear rights of appeal (paras 15–17). Part 4 (paras 18–21) deals with errors committed by an agent; for example, it makes a taxpayer liable for careless errors of an agent. Part 5 contains definitions and miscellaneous consequential changes. Since the penalty is geared to the tax lost, no penalty can arise if any tax would be time-barred; a simple 20-year period now applies.[255] Anyone who assists in preparing the return or account may be fined up to £3,000. In the absence of co-operation the Revenue will press for maximum penalties.

FA 2009, section 106 and Schedule 55 introduced an additional code of penalties for failure to make returns:

(1)   A £100 penalty is imposed immediately after the filing due date. On this point it should be noted that in May 2015 a newspaper investigation revealed that HMRC had adopted a policy of waiving the £100 penalty for late filing tax returns in the vast majority of cases where taxpayers had appealed and offered an excuse for being late;
(2)   After three months late, a daily fine of £10 is imposed up to a 90 day maximum of £900. This is in addition to the fixed penalty above;
(3)   After six months late, a penalty of 5% of tax due or £300 (whichever is higher) is imposed;
(4)   After twelve months late, a further penalty of 5% of tax due or £300 (whichever is higher) is imposed, with the potential for higher fines of up to 100% if the taxpayer has deliberately withheld and concealed information needed by HMRC to assses the tax owing.

FA 2009, section 107 and Schedule 56 impose penalties relating to the failure to pay tax due and are additional to the interest regime described above in §4.5.1. For example, for income tax due on 31 January and unpaid by the end of February, the penalty is 5% of the tax owing. If the tax is still unpaid by the end of July, a further 5% penalty applies. Another

---

[252] FA 2007, Sch 24, Pt 2, paras 4–11; lost revenue is defined in paras 5–8.
[253] FA 2007, Sch 24, para 10.
[254] FA 2007, Sch 24, para 11.
[255] TMA 1970, s 36.

5% penalty is imposed if tax is unpaid more than twelve months later. Schedule 56, paragraph 10 provides for the suspension of penalties while an agreement for deferred payment is current; section 108 provides for penalties if the agreement is broken. Section 109 and Schedule 57 complete the work begun in 2007, principally by making some amendments to earlier rules. These penalties (FA 2007, Schedule 24; FA 2008, Schedule 40 and FA 2009, Schedule 55) apply to income, etc in the UK or from jurisdictions with which the UK automatically exchanges information. For other jurisdictions FA 2010, section 35 and Schedule 10 apply higher penalties. Finally, FA 2008, section 123 and Schedule 41 impose penalties on persons for failure to notify HMRC that they are chargeable to tax.

In severe cases the Revenue may opt to press charges in the criminal courts;[256] a criminal prosecution does not exclude penalties.[257] The thinking behind penalties and criminal prosecutions ought to be quite distinct. A criminal conviction is for proven wrongdoing and invites severe sanctions, whether imprisonment, or a fine or both, and all the other consequences of a conviction, such as the almost complete impossibility of obtaining a visa to countries like the United States. Penalties, by contrast, may be seen as compensating the Revenue for the extra time and effort they have had to expend on correcting the errors in the original return. The Revenue prefer the penalty procedure to criminal prosecution, since prosecution is a drastic step which ought to be reserved for really serious cases, and because of the practical difficulties involved in preparing criminal cases.[258] The decision to prosecute in a particular case is amenable to judicial review; however, the present policy of selective prosecution has been upheld, there being no obligation on the Revenue to prosecute all such cases.[259] If, however, a criminal prosecution succeeds, the imposition of a custodial sentence of up to three years is very likely; short-term prison sentences are often accompanied by a swingeing fine.[260] Whether this private prosecution cum plea bargaining service is consistent with the proper goals of the criminal law (as opposed to the convenience of tax administrators) is another matter.[261]

The peculiar nature of these penalty powers in TMA may be illustrated by a number of special rules:

(1) Proceedings may be before the First-tier Tribunal—and so heard in private.[262]
(2) The death of the taxpayer does not end the proceedings.[263]
(3) The Board has power to mitigate penalties even after the courts have pronounced.[264]

---

[256] For example, Theft Act 1968, s 32(1)(a); *R v Hudson* [1956] 1 All ER 814; 36 TC 561; see also Keith Committee, *Enforcement Powers of Revenue Departments*, Cmnd 8822 (1983), chs 9, 13, 22.
[257] Statement of Practice SP 2/88.
[258] Evidence submitted to the Royal Commission on Criminal Procedure.
[259] *R v IRC, ex parte Mead and Cook* [1992] STC 482; 65 TC 1.
[260] See Ahmad and Hingun [1995] BTR 581 who suggest that sentencing guidelines from the Court of Appeal are more flexible than in the 1960s.
[261] See Roording [1996] *Crim L Rev* 240. For an early article contrasting the treatment of social security fraud and tax fraud, see McEwan [1981] *Conveyancer* 114. On plea bargaining see Ashworth, *Sentencing and Criminal Justice*, 3rd edn (Butterworths, 2004) 23–25.
[262] TMA 1970, s 100C.
[263] TMA 1970, s 100A.
[264] TMA 1970, s 102.

(4)   There is a special right of appeal to the courts against the summary award of penalties by the First-tier Tribunal.[265]

(5)   There are time limits for the recovery of penalties.[266]

Prior to 2005 there was an important statutory rule of evidence, known as the Hansard procedure, which applied to any criminal or civil proceedings as well as to those for penalties, under which the Revenue could inform the taxpayer (by reading an extract from Hansard) that they had the power to accept a pecuniary settlement and that the Board had a practice of being influenced by a full confession of all tax irregularities, or that the extent to which the taxpayer was helpful and volunteered information was a factor which was taken into account when assessing penalties. This statutory wording, found in TMA 1970, section 105 (as amended in 2003), was designed to permit what was undoubtedly coercive behaviour, but its effects were not altogether clear, eg how this wording might be reconciled with the Human Rights Convention right to remain silent and not to incriminate oneself.[267]

In 2005, the Hansard procedure was replaced by a new Code of Practice 9 (COP 9) in respect of the civil investigation of tax fraud.[268] One aim of the new procedures was to try to make sure that human rights were not accidentally breached.[269] The COP 9 procedures were modified in 2012 by the introduction of the Contractual Disclosure Facilty (CDF). The main features of the CDF are the absence of an absolute guarantee at the outset of a COP 9 investigation that the taxpayer will not be investigated with a view to criminal prosecution for tax fraud. Instead, such a guarantee is provided only where the taxpayer enters into a contractual disclosure arrangement and has made an outline disclosure under that arrangement. In addition, HMRC has offered specially-targeted arrangements whereby groups of taxpayers suspected of non-compliance are offered reduced penalties and immunity from criminal prosecution in return for full disclosure and payment of tax due, eg on undeclared offshore income. An example is the Liechenstein Disclosure Facility (LDF), which operated from 2009 to 2015.

A decision by the Revenue to offer immunity from prosecution as part of a settlement involving the payment of tax, interest and penalties in respect of tax offences, normally prevents criminal prosecution by the Revenue. However, where there are offences other than offences under the tax legislation, the Crown Prosecution Service (CPS) may still launch a prosecution of its own; the doctrine of the indivisibility of the Crown does not prevent this.[270] It may be that the CPS will be allowed to do this only where the taxpayer did not expect the settlement to terminate the CPS prosecution;[271] if the case is not so confined,

---

[265]   TMA 1970, s 53.

[266]   TMA 1970, s 103.

[267]   *R v Allen* [2001] STC 1537 at 35; see Hilliard [2003] BTR 6.

[268]   For details see the Code of Practice 9 leaflet, available at https://www.gov.uk/government/publications/code-of-practice-9-where-hm-revenue-and-customs-suspect-fraud-cop-9-2012.

[269]   Code of Practice 9. On post *Gill* changes to Code of Practice 9, see Hill and Cam, *Taxation*, 13 January 2005.

[270]   *R v W* [1998] STC 550; for criticism, see Elwes and Clutterbuck [1999] *Crim L Rev* 138.

[271]   Rhodes *et al* (1998) 148 *NLJ* 747; the article contains a useful explanation of the different modes of Revenue investigation and suggests that it was important in this case that the Revenue proceeded in the 'neutral' mode. The authors were involved as counsel on the case—is it desirable for them to be allowed to comment in this way?

the decision will seriously have weakened the Revenue's negotiating hand. Conversely, as already seen, where a criminal prosecution has been brought for fraud, the Revenue may still seek to exact penalties under the tax legislation.[272]

The Revenue may begin these cases following a tip-off about a likely suspect (ex-spouses and ex-employees are common sources), or they may simply disbelieve the taxpayer's return.[273] Once alerted the Revenue may require a complete statement of means and a satisfactory explanation of all sums appearing in bank accounts or supporting a luxurious lifestyle. To this end the Revenue are reported to keep records of all horse-racing results. An exhaustive back duty inquiry may lead to the exoneration of the taxpayer, in which case the Revenue may reimburse the taxpayer's costs, but only if there was a serious error on the Revenue's part.

4.5.3.2 Tax Law and Criminal Law

There is something of a cultural gap between the precise technical world of the tax lawyer and the broad brush of the criminal lawyer; however, over-confidence about an avoidance scheme can become evasion and lead to a prison sentence,[274] for the taxpayer and adviser alike. The common law offence of cheating the public revenue still exists, being expressly preserved by the Theft Act 1968,[275] with no maximum penalty and with uncertain and wide ambit.[276] As ATH Smith writes:

> Like many of the ill defined common law offences, cheating is one whose boundaries are indistinct, and the courts have not resisted the temptation recently to extend the law (or take an extensive view of its scope) when the issue has arisen.[277]

Ormerod suggests that the *actus reus* of the offence has become so wide that it can best be stated in negative terms:[278]

> There is no need for a dishonest act; an omission will suffice.[279] The act or omission must be intended to prejudice the Inland Revenue, Customs and Excise or the DSS—and not a local authority. There is no requirement of operative deception, or of a need to prove actual loss to the revenue or to any other. It is not necessary to prove that the conduct resulted in any gain to [the taxpayer]. The type of behaviour caught includes failing to account for VAT, withholding PAYE and national insurance contributions, failing to register for VAT and simply failing to disclose income.

Self-assessment has imposed new obligations on taxpayers to report and assess their liabilities accurately. The breadth of the offence means that the only live issue at the trial will be

---

[272] On practice, see Statement of Practice SP 2/88 and IR 131.

[273] Other sources include government contracts, a customer being suspicious when asked for a bearer cheque (*Rosette Franks (King Street) Ltd v Dick* (1955) 36 TC 100) and even a reported robbery (*Crole v Lloyd* (1950) 31 TC 338). Informers may be rewarded, on which see *R (Churchouse) v IRC* [2003] EWHC 681 Admin; [2003] STC 629.

[274] A court may also make a confiscation order under the Criminal Justice Act 1988, s 71.

[275] Theft Act 1968, s 32(1)(a).

[276] For criticism (and references to relevant literature), see Ormerod (ed), *Smith and Hogan, Criminal Law*, 11th edn (OUP, 2005) 793 *et seq*; and ATH Smith, *Property Offences* (Sweet & Maxwell, 1994), paras 20–106 *et seq.*

[277] Smith, *op cit*, para 20–106.

[278] Ormerod, *op cit*, 626.

[279] The appellant's submission (that there was no duty to disclose) would, if accepted, 'provide nothing but a licence for cynical and deliberate tax evasion': *R v Dimsey* [1999] STC 846, 859, per Laws LJ.

dishonesty.[280] Criminal lawyers dislike the width of the common law offence, particularly as expressed in *R v Mavji*,[281] that is, the fact that the decision creates a liability for omissions as opposed to acts and that it removes any requirement of deception[282] (making something akin to fraud suffice). There are also wider objections to the role of criminal law and judicial activism, and unease over the central element of dishonesty.[283] The test used asks whether the defendant's act was dishonest by the standards of reasonable and honest people, and whether the defendant realised that his act would be regarded as dishonest by such people. The former question is really one of law and not appropriate for a jury.[284] This, of course, leads to another and more fundamental question, ie whether it is appropriate to have trial by jury at all where the facts are complex.[285]

Other potentially relevant statutory provisions include:

(1)   *Fraudulent evasion of income tax.* FA 2000, section 144 created a new offence of being knowingly concerned in the fraudulent evasion of income tax, which is now found in TMA 1970, section 106A. This applies to acts or omissions occurring on or after 1 January 2001. Curiously, it applies only to income tax and not to other taxes under the supervision of HMRC. It was a last-minute addition to the Finance Bill 2000 and was in response to the Grabiner Report on the Informal Economy.[286]

(2)   *The Proceeds of Crime Act 2002.* The 2002 Act is of great importance to the tax system.[287] The Act created a new Assets Recovery Agency, which has powers to recover the proceeds of crime by civil rather than criminal process. It has many other powers, including one over the functions of the Revenue in relation to a taxpayer where there are reasonable grounds to suspect that a person's income or gains are derived from crime—although not the prosecution of tax offences.[288] There are now obligations on advisers to pass information to the authorities where they know or suspect that another is engaged in money laundering, or have reasonable grounds for such suspicion; there is also a related obligation not to tip off the person about whom disclosure has been made. These obligations apply to tax advisers, but section 233 of the Act expressly preserves the scope of legal professional privilege, which makes the

---

[280] Ormerod, *op cit*, 626–27.
[281] [1987] 1 WLR 1388.
[282] Smith, above, para 20–111.
[283] Griew [1985] *Crim L Rev* 341; and other literature cited by Ormerod, *op cit*.
[284] See Ormerod, *op cit*, 632 *et seq*.
[285] See, in a different context, Wright, *Complex Trials and Financial Regulation*, LSE Financial Markets Group Special Paper No 104 (August 1998). Rosalind Wright, Director of the Serious Fraud Office, drew attention to the decision of the Court of Appeal quashing the conviction in the County Natwest trial (*R v Cohen and others* (1992) 142 NLJ 1267 (CA)) because the trial took too long and the issues were too complex. In *Revenue and Customs Prosecutions Office v May and others* [2010] STC 1507, [2010] EWCA Civ 521, a flat was held not to be realisable property of the defendant and so not subject to a confiscation order.
[286] See Ormerod [2002] *Crim LR* 3 and Salter [2002] BTR 489–505; the Grabiner Report March 2000 is available from The Public Enquiry Unit, HM Treasury.
[287] On the Act see Mumford and Alldridge [2002] BTR 458–69 and on a few year's experience Cory [2007] BTR 356; see also contributions to *The Tax Journal* by Bullock and Collins, eg 11 September 2006, 6–8. The act repealed the former confiscation powers under the Criminal Justice Act 1988, s 71.
[288] Proceeds of Crime Act 2002, s 323(3)(b).

broad approach taken by the courts to this privilege all the more important.[289] Other obligations include those to keep records and identification of clients. The Revenue and professional bodies have tried to provide guidance.[290] In an earlier case the Court of Appeal rejected a Crown argument the confiscation order should have extended to all of the defendant's undeclared profits.[291]

(3) *Money Laundering Regulations.* These are made not under the Proceeds of Crime Act 2002 but under the EU Money Laundering Directives.[292] The UK Regulations also refer to the Financial Services and Markets Act 2000 and the Money Laundering Regulations 2007, pursuant to which HMRC supervises money service businesses, high value dealers, trust or company service providers, and accountancy service providers.

(4) *Insolvency Act, 1986, section 212.* HMRC sometimes use this action for misfeasance and breach of duty, eg by alleging directors of insolvent companies have breached their fiduciary duties by misapplying company funds.[293]

(5) *Companies Act 2006, section 993.*[294] HMRC can pursue cases of criminal tax fraud under the company law fraudulent trading rules.

Finally, at Summer Budget 2015 the Government announced further measures aimed at cracking down on criminal activity, the hidden economy and serious non-compliance. First, HMRC will be given £60 million of increased funding by 2020–21 in order to triple the number of criminal investigations into serious and complex tax crime, particularly by wealthy individuals and corporations. The Government aims to increase the number of prosecutions for tax crime to over 100 a year by the end of the current parliament. Second, the government is extending HMRC's powers to acquire data from online intermediaries and electronic payment providers to identify those operating in the hidden economy. Third, around £300 million over 5 years from 2016 will be directed towards tackling non-compliance by small and mid-sized businesses, public bodies and affluent individuals with an aim to bring in an additional £2 billion over that period. Fourth, an additional £36 million will be invested over 5 years from 2016 to tackle serious non-compliance by trusts, pension schemes and non-domiciled individuals. Budget 2016 had further measures to address the hidden economy, including a new criminal offence that removes the need to

[289] *R (Morgan Grenfell & Co Ltd) v Special Comr of Income Tax* [2003] AC 563 and *Three Rivers District Council and Others v Governor and Company of the Bank of England (No 6)* [2004] UKHL 48. In *R (on the application of Prudential plc and another) v Special Commissioner of Income Tax and another* [2013] UKSC 1, the Supreme Court declined to extend the common law legal advice privilege to clients of non-legally qualified tax advisers, even where the advice in question was legal advice. The Court's ruling confirms the status quo.

[290] HMRC Departmental Committee, Cm 7107, 53.

[291] A-G's reference (No 25 of 2001) [2001] EWCA Crim 1770; [2001] STC 1309, concerning Criminal Justice Act 1988, s 71.

[292] For details see https://www.gov.uk/topic/business-tax/money-laundering-regulations.

[293] *In Re Pay Check Services 3 Ltd and others* [2009] STC 1639, [2009] EWCA Civ 625 the scheme sought to make use of the lower rate of company tax for 'small' companies was flawed because companies became associated. The Court of Appeal held however that H, an individual, was not a de facto director of the relevant company (see eg Elias LJ at para 115), and that conclusion was upheld by the Supreme Court: see *Holland v HMRC* [2010] UKSC 51. For use by HMRC of intentional economic torts (intentionally inducing breach of contract, causing loss by unlawful means, and conspiracy), see two House of Lords decisions, *OBG Ltd v Allan* [2007] UKHL 21 and *Total Network SL v Revenue & Customs Commissioners* [2008] UKHL 19. For comment, see O'Sullivan (2008) *CLJ* 459.

[294] Ex Companies Act 1985, s 458. See Barry, *Tax Journal*, 9 January 2006, 9.

prove intent for the most serious cases of failing to declare offshore income and gains, and civil penalties for offshore tax evaders (and those who 'enable' such evasion).

4.5.3.3 Criminal Law and Tax Avoidance

The courts have examined the question of when tax avoidance becomes cheating the public revenue. First, it may be assumed that if the scheme is successful at the technical tax level, there can be no criminal offence; the public revenue cannot be cheated if it has lost no tax.[295] This means that the transactions must be genuine (as opposed to shams—on which distinction see below at §5.6.3). If the scheme succeeds as technical tax law, it does not matter that there was no initial full disclosure of all the facts, provided the Revenue eventually agree, or a court eventually holds, that no tax has been lost. However, a prosecution for attempting to cheat the public revenue raises particular difficulties in the light of the changes made by Criminal Attempts Act 1981, as a result of which attempting the impossible may still be a criminal offence.[296] The practical problem for the defence in such cases is to establish that the scheme works; the device of a trial within a trial without the jury, however appropriate, is unavailable since the issues are often of mixed fact and law. The theoretically correct solution would be to adjourn the criminal case until the tax answer has been reached by the tax tribunal.[297]

Secondly, it may be assumed that in the converse situation where the scheme is a sham, there is potential criminal liability, especially if there has been suppression of relevant facts. This leaves a middle situation where the scheme is not a sham but still fails at the technical level, so that a tax liability does arise but the taxpayer fails to report it.[298] In *R v Dimsey*,[299] the Court of Appeal had no hesitation in upholding a conviction. It was held that an individual who had *de facto* control of a company and so arranged its affairs that the company made profits but did not declare them to the Revenue, was cheating the Revenue; the position would be even stronger if the company was set up to operate in such a way. The case also shows that the words used in a judge's summing-up, like some cases stated, must be viewed in context; errors of tax law will not, of themselves, invalidate the conviction. There is something wrong here; simply leaving such matters to the jury seems perverse, the more so when one reads statements of judges who have no experience of tax law trying to explain some of the doctrines in terms a jury are meant to understand. At least this decision is an improvement on the earlier and most unsatisfactory[300] case of *R v Charlton*,[301] even if it does nothing for those convicted in that case. Tax lawyers find this 'robust' attitude inappropriate and wonder whether criminal law will find it possible to cope with the concept of innocent evasion.[302] This is not to say that the criminal law has no role to play here, just that the accused has a right to have his state of mind properly put in evidence.

---

[295] It is not, however, necessary for the prosecution to prove a loss to the Revenue: see *R v Hunt* [1994] STC 819, 827.

[296] Smith and Hogan, *op cit*, 419–26.

[297] And this is believed to have happened in one or two cases.

[298] And see Lord Walker (2004) 120 *LQR* 412, 420.

[299] [1999] STC 846.

[300] Thus, at no point did the judges in charge of the case address (or, apparently, understand) the distinction between a sham transaction and a transaction entered into for tax avoidance purposes: see generally Venables (1997) 7 *Offshore Taxation Rev* 1; and Brandon (1998) 8 *Offshore Taxation Rev* 9.

[301] [1996] STC 1417; for comment by one of those convicted, see Cunningham, *Taxation*, 4 January 1996, p 329.

[302] On problems of scope of evasion, etc, see Sawyer [1996] BTR 483.

4.5.4 Compliance—Effectiveness of Sanctions?

Work has been carried out in the United States to investigate the effects of sanctions under tax law on taxpayer behaviour. Although the conclusions reached are tentative, they do not make encouraging reading for the Revenue. By looking at the extent to which taxpayers think they will be audited (perceived certainty) and the severity of any sanction imposed (perceived severity), Long and Schwartz,[303] after examining later returns by people who had been audited, concluded that audits appeared to be marginally effective in reducing the frequency of reporting errors but not their size, and that there were almost as many people who were initially compliant who became non-compliant, as taxpayers who had been non-compliant but who became compliant. The conclusion that the presence of audits did not decrease non-compliance naturally raises the question why this should be so. Answers tend to focus on the negative effects of the blanket enforcement of complex laws. These included the IRS tendency to treat violators the same whether they acted inadvertently or intentionally, the lack of relative risk to the determined violator who would usually get away with paying tax and interest, so avoiding penalties, and the lack of judicial review. Needless to say, other surveys suggest different results.[304]

The UK rules normally include penalties as well as interest, and also provide for appeals against penalties. However, while it is a matter for debate whether the Revenue are able to distinguish sufficiently between deliberate and inadvertent loss, there can be no doubting that the UK tax rules are now about as complex as the US rules were then. The complexity is not helped by the fact that the relevant UK rules are scattered across a multitude of statutes. Another study suggests that audit may be better at deterring the overstatement of deductions as opposed to the under-reporting of income.[305] As a fascinating footnote, one should record the (again US) survey on the effects of status in income tax audits. Using occupational status as a measure of status, Kinsey and Stalans conclude that taxpayers of higher status tended to get more advantageous settlements than those of lower income status—but only as long as they represented themselves. Once tax practitioners were involved, status advantages disappeared—'tax practitioners level the playing field by disrupting social influence and deference processes'.[306] An altogether different line of work suggests ways in which one should behave when being audited, in order to get the best result. The provision of 'soft lighting, alcohol, videos and more' is not recommended, since this suggests that the company has something to hide.[307]

4.6   Revenue Information Powers

4.6.1 Gathering Information from Third Parties

TMA 1970 gave the Revenue power to issue notices to gather various details, including the names of lodgers resident in a person's dwelling house,[308] any interest payments made by

---

[303] Long and Schwartz, paper presented to *Annual Meeting of Law and Society Association* (Washington, DC, June 1987) on work carried out in 1986.

[304] Eg Witte and Woodbury (1985) 38 *National Tax J* 1.

[305] Kinsey, *Criminal Justice Abstracts*, September 1986, 403–25.

[306] Kinsey and Stalans, September 1996, looking at state as opposed to federal audits.

[307] See (1998) 46 *Canadian Tax J* 733, describing some of the advice given in a piece under review as 'somewhat Machievellian and borderline unethical'.

[308] TMA 1970, s 14; see also s 15 (employers), s 16 (fees, etc, paid to traders, etc) and s 16A (agency workers).

banks or other persons without deducting tax,[309] and payments from lessees, etc, in relation to Schedule A.[310] In addition, there was a rule requiring persons in receipt of taxable
income belonging to another to provide information;[311] these words were interpreted by
the court at face value and so could be used to require an auctioneer to provide details of
the sums paid to a seller.[312] There was a separate power for stock jobbers transactions[313] and
certain information about securities,[314] and separate rules for capital gains.[315]

New rules to replace these powers were introduced by FA 2008, Schedule 36, and amended
and extended by FA 2009. In the case of direct taxes, HMRC now have an express power
to inspect records required under record-keeping legislation, a power to require supplementary information relevant to establishing the taxpayer's correct position and a separate
power to require third parties to provide information. Also added were powers to obtain
information from persons liable to counteraction of a tax advantage under TA 1988, section
703 (ITA 2007, section 684). HMRC also were given new powers to enter (softened to 'visit')
business premises to inspect records, assets and premises. New penalties were provided in
relation to these powers, along with rules for appeals against penalties and notices demanding information—save where there has been judicial approval in advance. Lastly, a new
criminal offence of destroying or concealing records requested under a notice authorised
by a tribunal also was introduced.[316]

4.6.2 *Powers to Obtain Information and Documents*

Under FA 2008, Schedule 36, Part 1, HMRC now have wide powers to obtain information
and documents for the purpose of checking a taxpayer's tax position, including by issuing taxpayer notices, third-party notices and (with the approval of the Tribunal) 'identity
unknown' notices. A taxpayer who receives a notice to provide information or documents
must do so within the time specified in the notice and in the manner specified therein.
An HMRC officer may by written notice to a third party require that person to provide
information or produce documents reasonably required for checking the tax position of
a known person, or in relation to taxpayers unknown. HMRC has used this power already
to obtain information from financial institutions in relation to UK residents with overseas
bank accounts. FA 2011 expanded HMRC's data-gathering powers to include obtaining
information from other 'data holders'.

4.6.3 *Powers to Inspect Businesses*

FA 2008, Schedule 36, Part 2 introduced new HMRC powers to inspect businesses—but
not the power to force entry or to search. An HMRC officer may enter a person's business

---

[309] TMA 1970, s 17 (banks, etc) and s 19 (others); if tax is deducted, other reporting provisions apply which
do not depend on notice.
[310] TMA 1970, s 19.
[311] TMA 1970, s 13.
[312] *Fawcett v Special Commissioners and Lancaster Farmers Auction Mart Co Ltd* [1997] STC 171; 69 TC 279
(CA); reversing Rattee J at [1995] STC 61. For criticism of the decision of Rattee J, see [1995] BTR 181.
[313] TMA 1970, s 21.
[314] TMA 1970, ss 23, 24.
[315] TMA 1970, ss 25–28.
[316] FA 2008, Sch 36, s 53.

premises and inspect the premises, including assets and documents of the business, where reasonably required for the purpose of checking the person's tax position.

4.6.4 Criminal Tax Fraud Powers

Pursuant to FA 2007, HMRC's powers of investigation in criminal matters in England, Wales and Northern Ireland now are governed in accordance with PACE 1984. For a description of the pre-2007 regime, see the fifth edition of this book. The current rules govern powers of search and seizure (including search warrants), production orders and arrest powers. For search warrants, a magistrate may issue a warrant for HMRC officers to enter and search premises if the magistrate has reasonable grounds for believing that an indictable tax offence has been committed, and that there is material on the premises that is likely to have substantial value in the investigation and be admissible at trial. This is a higher threshold than under the old TMA 1970, section 20C procedure, which required only reasonable grounds for suspecting an offence. In *R (Mercury Tax Group) v Revenue & Customs Commissioners*,[317] Underhill J quashed a warrant obtained on the basis that HMRC had reasonable cause to suspect an offence had been committed. The case concerned an avoidance scheme which would have been perfectly valid if operations had been genuine and carried out in the right order. What seems to have undone HMRC was the failure to disclose all the relevant information, but HMRC's case also was not strong. Under the seizure powers, it is lawful for HMRC to seize items, including items where it is not practicable to determine on-site if they are subject to lawful seizure (or, for example, subject to legal professional privilege). HMRC officers also are bound by the PACE Codes of Practice. Finally, the Serious Organised Crime and Police Act 2005 (SOCPA 2005) sections 60–70 provide further investigatory powers in respect of tax crimes where the potential loss to the Treasury from relevant offences—including cheating the public revenue—is at least £5,000.

4.7   The Professional's Role: Ethics

The role of the tax adviser has emerged in a typically English, pragmatic way. Work is carried out not only by lawyers (whether barristers or solicitors) and accountants (in one or other professional body of accountants), but also by the increasingly influential Chartered Institute of Taxation (CIOT) which attained chartered status in 1994. There are also advisers who have no professional qualification as such, ranging from retired and highly-skilled members of the Revenue to complete freelancers with less impressive achievements.

Professional tax advisers face a range of problems concerning professional ethics.[318] Clearly, they are under a duty to their clients, but they also owe a duty to observe the

---

[317] [2009] STC 743, [2008] EWHC 2721.

[318] See *Professional Conduct in Relation to Taxation*, jointly issued by ICAEW AAT, ACCA, ATT, CIOT, ICAS and STEP (1 May 2015), available at http://www.ion.icaew.com/ClientFiles/c1db2be4-7bd5-41f3-996a-764f237080bb/TAXGUIDE%2001-15%20-%20PCRT.pdf; see also New Zealand guidelines, printed at [1996] BTR 502–4; and Ross, *Ethics for Tax Practitioners* (Australian Tax Research Foundation, Study No 18).

profession's standards. They must not make a tax return they know to be false (or they will face not only disciplinary procedures but also criminal prosecution). However, there are many more difficult or grey areas where professionals may disagree on whether the Revenue should be informed of something, eg where the client takes a particular view which is different from the published Revenue view (here, the decision whether or not to inform must rest with the client). While there is no need to provide the Revenue with gratuitous information, relevant facts should never be concealed; further allegations of disclosure now arise under the Money Laundering Regulations.[319] In this connection, the revised (2007) rules on penalties where the taxpayer fails to tell HMRC of an under-assessment should be noted.[320] This area of professional ethics is much studied in the United States and awaits proper study in the UK.[321] The question whether it is professional to engage in aggressive tax planning remains to be explored in the UK.[322] FA 2012, Schedule 38, provided HMRC with new powers to obtain working papers from tax agents engaged in dishonest conduct, and impose penalties of up to £50,000. The new rules also introduced the possibility of publishing details of such dishonest agents. Budget 2016 announced further measures aimed at those who 'enable' tax avoidance schemes and offshore tax evasion.

4.8   Administration and Human Rights

Although the European Convention on Human Rights says little directly on tax matters, the courts and the Commission have used the Convention indirectly.[323] The Convention gives various procedural rights in civil cases, including the rights to a fair trial and appeal to an independent tribunal (Article 6(1)), and, in criminal cases, more substantial rights such as a presumption of innocence, a right to be informed promptly of the nature and cause of the accusation, adequate and reasonable time and facilities to prepare a defence, a right to legal aid if insufficient means are available and a right to examine prosecution witnesses (Article 6(2)). Phrases such as 'civil rights and obligations' and 'criminal charge' have autonomous meanings. So a tax dispute is not regarded as giving rise to 'a civil obligation'—and so is not within Article 6(1) which guarantees the right to a fair trial.[324] However a civil claim which originates in tax, eg a claim in restitution for wrongly-paid tax, may give rise to such a right.[325] Similarly, although tax law is not the same as criminal law, the court has held

---

[319]   *Professional Conduct in Relation to Taxation, op cit,* and especially Chapter 5 on irregularities.
[320]   FA 2007, Sch 24, para 2.
[321]   See papers given at the ABA Conference (London, July 1985), including one on UK aspects by Avery Jones.
[322]   See Infanti (2003) 22 *Virginia Tax Rev* 589, criticising aggressive tax planning by tax professionals. In the same vein, see David Cay Johnston, *Perfectly Legal* (Penguin Publishing, 2004) and Braithwaite, *Markets in Vice, Markets in Virtue* (OUP, 2005). Alternative dispute resolution has not been explored in the fiscal context in the UK, but Braithwaite, a leading advocate, has a salutary message: 'Silencing lawyers in ADR is a more productive path than reforming them.' See Braithwaite, *Restorative Justice and Responsive Regulation* (OUP, 2002) 249.
[323]   See Baker [2000] BTR 211.
[324]   *Ferrazini v Italy* Application 44759/98 [2001] STC 1314. Of the 18 judges, six dissented. The majority decision had been anticipated by the Court of Appeal in *Eagerpath Ltd v Edwards* [2001] STC 26.
[325]   *National and Provincial Building Society v UK* [1997] STC 1466 and dicta in *Eagerpath Ltd v Edwards* [2001] STC 26.

that an action for a tax penalty may be a 'criminal charge' within Article 6(2).[326] Other issues which have been held to be capable of coming within Article 6(2) include a 100% tax penalty,[327] an unjustifiably prolonged Revenue investigation[328] and a penalty imposed for fraud committed by someone else.[329] The classification of an automatic, tax-geared penalty in *Bendenoun v France*[330] as a criminal matter depended on the co-existence of several features: that the surcharge covered all citizens as taxpayers, that it was intended to deter, that it was substantial and that imprisonment could be imposed if it were not paid. How a penalty would be regarded if it lacked some of these features is unclear.[331] Article 8, guaranteeing respect for private and family life, has also been invoked to counter Revenue searches without a warrant[332] and, at Commission level only, a Revenue request for information about detailed personal expenditure.[333]

4.9   Tort: HMRC's Duty of Care

Mishaps occur in any administrative system, and the question arises whether a taxpayer may recover damages for breach of a statutory duty of care arising either out of the statute itself or under a common law duty of care under which the HMRC as employer are liable for the negligence of its employees. These matters were explored in *Neil Martin Ltd v HMRC*.[334] The case itself arose out an application for a certificate giving exemption from certain rules. The rules required the taxpayer to deduct income tax at source when making payments, provided that the company had been given a certificate. Chadwick LJ first held that no private law action for damages could arise under the relevant legislation. The legislation did not expressly give any right to compensation, but did provide a system of appeals to the Commissioners in the event of an unjustified refusal of a certificate. He held that the appeal system was sufficient protection for taxpayers and there was no room to imply a duty of care.[335] Similar reasoning meant that there was no common law duty on the Revenue to process the application with reasonable expedition.

Turning to the question of vicarious liability for the alleged negligence, Chadwick LJ made three points. First, the primary responsibility for making the application in the correct form was on the taxpayer. Secondly, there could be no liability for any failure on the

---

[326] *C and E Commrs v Han* [2001] EWCA Civ 1041; [2001] STC 1188; see also the ECtHR decision in *Georgiou v UK* [2001] STC 80 and cases there cited. See also *King v UK (No 2)* [2004] STC 911, formerly *King v Walden* [2001] STC 822.

[327] *JJ v Netherlands* Application 21351/93 (1998) 28 EHRR 168.

[328] *Hozee v Netherlands* (1998)—much would depend on the degree of co-operation of the taxpayer.

[329] *AP, MP and TP v Switzerland* (1997) 26 EHRR 541.

[330] (1994) 18 EHRR 544.

[331] See Persson-Osterman, *Cambridge Yearbook of European Legal Studies* (Hart Publishing, 1999).

[332] *Funke v France* (1993) 16 EHRR 297, 332, 357 (no warrant was needed under French law at that time).

[333] *X (Hardy-Spirlet) v Belgium* (1982) 31 DR 231.

[334] [2007] EWCA Civ1041, [2007] STC 1802.

[335] *Ibid*, para 53.

part of the Revenue where merely 'administrative' mistakes had been made in processing the application. So no common law duty of care was owed to the claimant company by either the unidentified employee at the office who inserted the incorrect taxpayer reference number on the form, or by the unidentified employee who posted the CIS6 certificate to the wrong address.[336] Thirdly, he held that there would be liability where an officer had offered to fill in the form for the taxpayer and had done so incorrectly.[337]

---

[336] *Ibid*, para 72, relying on Mummery LJ in *Carty v Croydon London BC* [2005] 1 WLR 2312 at para 83, that a court should not impose a liability for which the employer would be vicariously liable if it would 'introduce by the back door an action for breach of statutory duty in a case where ... no cause of action for breach of statutory duty was created by the relevant legislation.'

[337] *Ibid*, para 73.

5

Tax Avoidance

5.1 Language—Avoidance, Evasion, Mitigation and Planning

Politicians, tax officials and practitioners spend a lot of time and energy on the problem of tax avoidance. From the perspective of government, tax avoidance is a problem because it nibbles away at the edges of the tax base, so reducing government revenue and, in extreme cases, making government policy look foolish. However, the precise nature of the problem depends on the precise definition of 'avoidance' to be adopted. So those who do not regard avoidance as a problem but simply as part of a battle of wits would agree with Orow, who has written:

> [T]ax avoidance has more to do with what the legislature did not impose rather than what it actually imposed by way of taxation. It covers cases where legislative intention and policy miscarried and failed to anticipate and reach the transaction under consideration. Reduced to its bare essentials, tax avoidance is a conceptual anomaly that exists in the minds of those whose sense of morality is violated by certain tax effective practices.[1]

While no one seems to have a very precise idea of what is meant by the term,[2] conventional discussion distinguishes avoidance from evasion, the latter being illegal. If two people marry in order to reduce their tax burden they are practising tax avoidance; if they tell the Revenue that they are married when they are not, they are guilty of tax evasion, and may well be prosecuted. There is also an important distinction between a scheme under

---

[1] [2004] BTR 410, 415.
[2] See IFS Tax Law Review Committee (TLRC), *Report on Avoidance* (November 1997) 2.

which no liability to tax arises (tax avoidance) and one under which a charge arises but the tax cannot be collected.[3] The latter may be evasion and subject to penalty, and even to a criminal charge. Other terms used in discussion—and in case law—are tax mitigation and tax planning, which may be seen as subsets of tax avoidance or as independent categories, depending on the context; they are all to be distinguished from tax evasion. Unfortunately, tax evasion itself has developed a number of 'frayed edges'. Thus, it is sometimes used to cover all case of non-compliance, even though non-compliance may be deliberate or accidental and may give rise to penalties under tax legislation, prosecution under criminal law or both.[4] Evasion may even result from taking a position on tax legislation which is later shown to be incorrect, and even though that position was reasonably based since it relied on a decision of a Special Commissioner.[5] If these are all examples of evasion, its greatest cause may be not fraud or greed but the complexity of the tax legislation; the category, instead of being one of undoubted opprobrium, may become a matter of judicial hindsight. It is such considerations which encourage those who believe in a low rate, broad-based tax system, with few opportunities for tax saving.

Tax mitigation[6] is distinguished from tax avoidance because judges, when dealing with a provision turning on the presence of tax avoidance, invented the term 'mitigation' in order to mark off transactions which would not be caught by the provision.[7] In this context, therefore, tax mitigation and tax avoidance are mutually exclusive. Tax avoidance arises where the taxpayer reduces a liability to tax without incurring the economic consequences that Parliament intended to be suffered by any taxpayer qualifying for such reduction in that liability.[8] Tax mitigation arises where the taxpayer takes advantage of a fiscally attractive option afforded by the tax legislation, and genuinely suffers the economic consequences that Parliament intended to be suffered by those taking advantage of the option. There are therefore two elements: economic consequences and parliamentary intent. The first element asserts that there should be some genuine economic consequences, while the second enables the court, on a case-by-case basis, to control which consequences will qualify. Today, a couple marrying to reduce tax would be treated as examples of tax mitigation.

The problem with tax mitigation is that, as the House of Lords have agreed, while it provides a coherent reason for saying, in a particular case, that the facts do not amount to avoidance, and so do not trigger the application of some rule, it does not provide a clear way of telling whether those particular facts fall one side of the line or the other. Thus, it can be a conclusion, not a test, and so restates the problem rather than solves it.[9] So why

---

[3] See comments of Brightman J in *Roome v Edwards* [1979] STC 546, 561–65 (removed from bound volume—see [1979] BTR 261). See also the comments of Templeman LJ in *IRC v Stype Investments Ltd* [1982] STC 625, 637.

[4] Cooper (1994) 50 *Tax L Rev* 35.

[5] Eg, the scope of ITEPA, Pt 3, Ch 5 (ex TA 1988, s 145) in relation to shadow directors in *R v Allen* [2001] STC 1537.

[6] See, eg, Lord Templeman in *Ensign Tankers (Leasing) Ltd v Stokes (Inspector of Taxes)* [1992] 1 AC 655, 676–77; [1992] STC 226, 240–41; 64 TC 617, 741–42, and Lord Goff at 681, 244–45 and 746–47 respectively.

[7] Eg, Lord Templeman in *Commr of Inland Revenue v Challenge Corp* [1987] AC 155, 167–68; [1986] STC 548, 554–55 (PC, New Zealand).

[8] *IRC v Willoughby* [1997] STC 995, 1003–4.

[9] See Lord Hoffmann in *MacNiven v Westmoreland Investments Ltd* [2001] STC 237, para 62. For a rare attempt to take matters further, see Rosenberg (1988) 87 *Michigan L Rev* 365–497, arguing that avoidance arises because the tax system uses a transactional rather than economic basis to determine income. As such, avoidance arises if a taxpayer's tax return under-states income when computed on an economic basis, unless the taxpayer's behaviour corresponds with statutory policy goals of statutory provision underlying that under-statement.

is it that there were no 'genuine economic consequences' in the leading avoidance case of *Furniss v Dawson*?[10]

Tax planning is what all sensible people do in order to reduce their tax liabilities. The boundary between tax avoidance and tax planning is shadowy at best; what matters is the boundary between successful and unsuccessful tax planning. Tax planning is best understood by reference to 'who', 'what', 'when' and 'where':[11]

— *Who'* Tax planning may involve the careful selection of the particular taxpayer who will, for example, receive the income or realise a loss; thus, it may be another member of the family with little other income or relief, or a subsidiary of a company.

— *What'* With care, it may also be possible to influence the type of receipt, whether capital or income, or one type of income rather than another, eg employment income or business income. While there has been much legislative (and occasional judicial) activity to prevent a person from converting income into capital, there has been none to stop conversion in the opposite direction.

— *When'* Timing is also important; and paying attention to timing may enable the taxpayer to postpone a liability to tax, for example by taking advantage of a deferral rule, or to avoid being caught by an artificial tax rule which forbids, for example, the carrying back of an unused capital loss.

— *Where'* Location is important, since placing income or assets outside the taxing jurisdiction may mean no liability to UK tax, or no liability until income is remitted to the UK. The downside of this is that liability may be incurred under the foreign tax system. However, the foreign tax system may be different from the UK system, and the exploitation of gaps between tax systems is the forte of the international tax specialist.

5.2 Importance

The importance of tax avoidance for present purposes is fourfold. First, from the wider perspective it is not possible to assess the effectiveness of a tax system unless it can be seen what degree of avoidance is practised and permitted by the system. Thus, to have a rule that trading profits of charities are not exempt from tax is one thing; to learn that this is routinely avoided by having a separate trading company which assigns its profits to its charitable owners makes the rule look less fierce. Secondly, while legislation to counter avoidance may be among the most complex in our tax code, it may also be among the simplest and shortest in terms of formulation. Thirdly, from the law student's perspective, the case law on avoidance tell us much about the problems posed by legislation and statutory purpose. Lastly, and perhaps most obviously, it means that the Government does not get as much money as it hoped to get. HMRC's estimate of this 'tax gap' for 2012–13 was £34 billion per year, which represents about 6.8% of the total theoretical tax liabilities for that year.[12]

---

[10] See below at §5.6.4.

[11] For a more sophisticated (US) account, see Stiglitz, *Economics of the Public Sector*, 4th edn (Norton, 2004) ch 24; see also Cooper's analysis of tax shelters in (1985) 85 *Columbia L Rev* 657.

[12] HMRC, *Measuring Tax Gaps* (October 2014), available at https://www.gov.uk/government/uploads/system/uploads/attachment_data/file/364009/4382_Measuring_Tax_Gaps_2014_IW_v4B_accessible_20141014.pdf.

5.3 Methods of Legislative Control

5.3.1 Ten Methods of Legislative Control—Plus One

No legislature can allow taxpayers to continue to arrange their affairs in such a way that the tax system becomes voluntary (pay the Revenue or pay an adviser),[13] or that government revenue falls short of what is needed. Various solutions have been suggested or adopted. Of the list which follows, the 1966 Canadian Royal Commission gave us (1)–(3) and (5);[14] it is not pretended that the boundaries are always precise. A recurring issue is the appropriate mental element.[15]

(1)   The 'sniper approach' contemplates the enactment of specific provisions identifying, with precision, the type of transaction to be dealt with and prescribing, with precision, the tax consequences of such a transaction. This has been the traditional pattern of UK legislation. One example is the rule for business entertainment expenses.[16]

(2)   The targeted anti-avoidance rule. This is a rule formulated in terms of countering 'avoidance' and which forms an integral part of the code. It is wider than (1) but not as general as (3) or (6). It has become a very common feature of legislation when a new set of rules is introduced. Examples include TCGA 1992, section 16A.

(3)   The 'shotgun approach' contemplates the enactment of some general provision imposing tax on transactions which are defined in a general way. The difference between this and the sniper approach lies in its conscious rejection of certainty. Examples may be found in ITA 2007, Part 13 (sections 682 *et seq*). These sections create penumbral areas, although such areas are circumscribed.

(4)   The 'transaction not at arm's length approach' provides that the tax consequences will be different from what they would normally be, by treating the transaction as if it had taken place between parties at arm's length.[17] Typical examples are the rules substituting market value for the price, if any, actually received for disposal of capital assets, and sales between associated persons for business profits purposes for income tax. Technically, this is a means of carrying out one of the other approaches, rather being than a separate approach, since the circumstances in which the technique is applied can be described with more or less precision.

(5)   The 'administrative threshold approach' grants wide powers to an official in order to counteract specified tax avoidance transactions and states what is to happen if the official wishes to invoke the rule. An example is the Australian legislation dealing with 'bottom of the harbour' schemes.[18] UK examples are TCGA 1992, sections

---

[13] For contrasting views of the 1970s and the *Rossminster* saga, see Gillard, *In the Name of Charity* (Chatto & Windus, 1987); and Tutt, *The Tax Raiders* (Financial Training Publications, 1985), reviewed by Davies [1988] BTR 311.

[14] Carter (chair), Canadian Royal Commission on Taxation, *Report, Vol 3* (Queen's Printer, 1966), App A, 552.

[15] On which, see Avery Jones [1983] BTR 9, 113.

[16] ITTOIA ss 45–47; CTA 2009, s 1298–1300 (ex TA 1988, s 577).

[17] There is almost no UK authority on when people are dealing at arm's length—see a discussion of Canadian material in Owen (1992) 40 *Canadian Tax J* 829.

[18] Constitutionality was considered in *MacCormick* (1984) 15 ATR 437.

30–33 and 137. To what extent these are powers and to what extent they impose duties on the tax authorities has not yet been explored. These powers are specific. The UK tax system has also known more general powers. There is no such provision in UK law at present.[19]

(6)   The general anti-avoidance rule or general anti-abuse rule (GAAR). This is close to (5), but the difference is that it purports to have justiciable boundaries determined by court process rather than by administrative discretion. It is a recent addition to UK tax law (in 2013); older examples can be found in Canada, South Africa, Australia and New Zealand.

(7)   Retrospective legislation. In some ways the easiest and most effective method, retrospective legislation was used famously in 1978 to stop relief for losses arising from commodity straddles.[20] Today, the possibility of challenge under the human rights legislation has been a restraint rather than a complete bar on such legislation.[21] There is the immediate political problem of getting a provision through Parliament. It has for many years been common for an announcement to be made in Parliament that a particular scheme will be dealt with in the next Finance Bill and that the legislation will be retrospective to the date of the announcement; this is unlikely to attract human rights problems and has encountered no parliamentary problems. It has become even more common as a result of the FA 2004 disclosure rules.

More controversial is the announcement on 2 December 2004 that legislation to stop avoidance of the rules applicable to reward for employment would apply not only to the schemes to be set out in the FA 2005 but also any other schemes designed to frustrate the intentions of Parliament, where necessary from 2 December 2004.[22] A second is the pre-owned assets income tax charge designed to counteract avoidance of IHT. This charge arises where schemes have been carried out since 1986 but the person by reference to whose circumstances IHT is charged is still alive (below §47.6). Changing the IHT rules would be retrospective; changing the income tax rules is not but is simply retroactive. As Dickson J, the great Canadian judge, said, 'no one has a vested right to continuance of the law as it stood in the past'.[23] FA 2008, section 58 went further than these. In countering an avoidance scheme, the 2008 Act changed the test of when a person is treated as a member of a partnership and declared it to have been the law before FA 2008 (below at §20.10.7). As the scheme has not yet been tested in court, it is not yet clear whether this provision is retroactive—it certainly has the capacity to be so. In the Committee stage of the Bill the Financial Secretary said, 'I am satisfied that in these unusual circumstances, retrospective clarification of the law is fair, proportionate and in the public interest. This is the human rights test that we must apply'.[24] People do not seem to mind

---

[19] On excess profits tax during the Second World War, see below at §5.5.

[20] FA 1978, s 31; now ITA 2007, s 81 and CTA 2010, s 52(1)–(3), ex TA 1988, s 399(2). For details of the scheme see Gillard, *op cit*, 182–92.

[21] This was held compatible with the European Convention on Human Rights: see *A v United Kingdom* (Application 8531/79) and comment by Baker [2005] BTR 1.

[22] http://www.hm-treasury.gov.uk/media/938/F0/pbr04_PMGstatement.pdf.

[23] *Gustafson Drilling (1964) Ltd v MNR* [1971] 1 SCR 271, 282–83, cited by Loomer [2006] BTR 64, 67.

[24] Public Bill Committee, 22 May 2008, col 372.

retrospective legislation which is in favour of the taxpayer. FA 2008 contains such a provision and the only explanation appears to be that otherwise many people would have been liable to penalties. This explanation lacks intellectual rigour and could be spread very wide if taken seriously. More controversially, in February 2012, the Government announced new legislation would be introduced to close down two tax avoidance schemes that were disclosed to HMRC by a high-street bank.[25] Elements of the new legislation have retrospective effect, changing the law from 1 December 2011 before the disclosed schemes (and similar schemes used by other banks) had been implemented. The Government justified the retrospective legislation on the basis that the schemes were highly aggressive and had the potential to cost the Treasury billions of pounds. Others, including the chairman of the Commons Treasury Select Committee, raised concerns that the retrospective elements damaged the certainty of the UK tax system and were harmful to investment and job creation.[26]

(8)   Penalties.[27] At present, tax avoidance is lawful whether or not it is successful. This means that if an avoidance scheme is attempted but fails, the taxpayer must simply pay the tax with any interest or surcharges. By contrast, in New Zealand a special tax penalty of 100% of the shortfall is incurred where 'abusive tax avoidance' leads to a shortfall of NZ $10,000 or more in the self-assessment system. The penalty is reduced to 25% if there is adequate disclosure when the return is filed—a very important practical matter since so much turns on whether the Revenue can discover what was going on.[28] There are also penalties of 20% for taking an incorrect tax position. These have been criticised for blurring the distinction between evasion and avoidance.[29] The UK GAAR did not have a tax-geared penalty when enacted in 2013, but one was added in 2016.

(9)   Criminal law. The principal differences between this approach and (8) above are that penalties may include imprisonment and disqualification from offices. Criminal law also exposes the advisers to liability. A particularly interesting idea would be to create a criminal offence of recklessly submitting a tax return.

(10)   The alternative minimum tax (AMT) on gross income. This is attractive to governments because much planning involves using deductions. Such a tax is in force in Canada and the United States,[30] but can all too quickly become a lazy way for the government to gather revenue. In the US it was estimated that one effect of the 2001 tax cuts was that one-third of all US taxpayers would ultimately be subject to the AMT.[31]

---

[25] See amendments and ministerial statement at http://www.hm-treasury.gov.uk/finance_bill_2012_consultation.htm.

[26] See http://www.parliament.uk/business/committees/committees-a-z/commons-select/treasury-committee/news/hhhh/.

[27] See TLRC report, *op cit*, ch 6.

[28] See Keith Committee, *Enforcement Powers of Revenue Departments*, Cmnd 8822 (1983) ch 7; and the facts of *IRC v McGuckian* [1997] STC 908.

[29] On the New Zealand experience, see Sawyer [1996] BTR 483 and, more broadly, *Tax Compliance, Report to the Treasurer by a Committee of Experts* (Wellington, NZ, December 1998) esp ch 6.

[30] ITA, ss 127.5–127.55 (Canada) and IRC §55 (US). On US, see Bittker, *Taxation of Income, Estates and Gifts* (Warren Gorham & Lamont, 1993) §111.4. The tax receives characteristically trenchant criticism by Bittker (1966) 21 *Tax L Rev* 1.

[31] See Burman *et al*, *The Individual AMT; Problems and Potential Solutions*, Brookings Tax Policy Discussion Paper No 5; on consequent expensive repeal of AMT, see Burman (2002) 96 *Tax Notes* 1641.

(11)   Lastly, legal rule may be abandoned in favour of social pressure. If one considers how drinking and driving has become socially unacceptable, the same could be achieved in relation to tax avoidance, by proclaiming the virtues of the honest taxpayer.[32] Perhaps the nebulous nature of such pressure will match the nebulous nature of the concept. One should not hope for too much—it is easy to tell whether a person has been drinking alcohol, but much less easy to tell when a person has indulged in tax avoidance. Yet social pressure has developed a particular subset of rules—those of corporate governance.[33] These may yet prove useful to the Revenue. Meanwhile it remains true that many companies are conscious of their public reputation and have no wish to be pilloried in the newspapers for indulging in curious practices. A notable example is Starbucks, which in 2014 reacted to a public outcry over its UK tax affairs by committing to pay £20 million in corporation tax over two years through forgoing tax deductions on royalties, capital allowances and other expenses. The Australian Tax Office has encouraged company boards to think about their responsibilities and the risks they may run if too adventurous.[34]

5.3.2 Disclosure, High-Risk Promoters, Follower Notices and Accelerated Payments

5.3.2.1 Disclosure of Tax Avoidance Schemes (DOTAS)

As will have been seen, when the Government decides to act, much depends on the speed with which it is able to introduce legislation, and that will depend on how effective government systems are for detecting avoidance schemes. During the 1970s it was often a condition of buying a scheme that claims for the relevant relief should be delayed until the last possible moment. By 2004 it was apparent that the Revenue needed to know about schemes more quickly, and so FA 2004 introduced a duty on those involved in implementing avoidance schemes to disclose details to the Revenue.[35]

The Disclosure of Tax Avoidance Schemes (DOTAS) rules require a promoter to provide the Revenue with information about notifiable arrangements and proposals for notifiable arrangements within a specified time.[36] Arrangements are notifiable if they come within any description prescribed by Treasury regulations and enable, or might be expected to enable, any person to obtain a tax advantage in relation to any tax so prescribed in relation to the arrangements. It is also necessary that the main benefit or one of the main benefits that might be expected to arise from the arrangements is the obtaining of that advantage. There are extensive regulation-making powers, and extensive regulations have been made.[37] The provision applies to a wide range of taxes under the jurisdiction of HMRC—income tax, CGT, corporation tax, IHT, petroleum revenue tax, ATED, stamp duty land tax and stamp duty reserve tax;[38] separate disclosure regimes apply for VAT and NICs.

---

[32] See Schiemann LJ in *Schuldenfrei v Hilton* [1999] STC 821, 832.
[33] Freedman [2004] BTR 332, 339–42.
[34] Freedman, *op cit*, at 342; the process includes a list of 10 points—see https://www.ato.gov.au/.
[35] FA 2004, ss 306–19; for comment see Fraser [2004] BTR 282–96 and 451–59.
[36] FA 2004, ss 306–308.
[37] FA 2004, s 317.
[38] FA 2004, s 318(1) 'tax'.

The promoter must provide the Revenue with information on a notifiable proposal within a prescribed period of the earliest of these dates: (a) the date on which the promoter first makes a firm approach to another person in relation to a notifiable proposal, (b) when the promotor makes the notifiable proposal available for implementation or (c) when the promoter first becomes aware of any transaction forming part of the proposed arrangements.[39] He does not have to notify the Revenue if someone else has already done so.[40] Where a promoter is resident outside the UK and no promoter is resident within the UK, the obligation to report falls on the client.[41] Where there is no promoter, the duty to notify falls on those entering into any transaction which is part of the notifiable arrangements.[42] Once the Board has been informed, it may give the arrangements a reference number; further provisions deal with the obligations of promoters and parties to pass the number to the relevant taxpayers.[43]

Nothing requires any person to disclose to the Board any privileged information, ie anything to which a claim to legal privilege or its Scottish counterpart could be maintained in legal proceedings.[44] Where a person fails without reasonable excuse to disclose a scheme as required, that person is subject to penalties of up to £600 per day, or up to £5,000 per day if a Tribunal has issued a disclosure notice.[45] A separate provision authorises the Revenue to direct how the information is to be provided.[46]

In 2006 the House of Lords Select Committee was pleased to note a broad consensus among witnesses from the private sector that the rules were working well, in particular by excluding unnecessary disclosures: 'Setting up the necessary reviewing machinery has created more work for tax professionals and the burden is ultimately passed on to their clients in costs. However, judged by the results described to us by HMT and HMRC, we concluded that this compliance burden was proportionate and justified by the outcome in terms of reducing the tax gap.'[47] Proportionate does not mean completely successful. The ensuing years have seen a continuous stream of amendments to plug gaps and broaden the reach of DOTAS. In 2006 the regulations were amended so that they no longer defined transactions but made greater use of particular features of transactions called hallmarks; the hallmarks include tests, such as whether there is confidentiality, a premium fee, the presence of off-market terms or being a standardised tax product.[48] Further changes were made in 2007 to try to ensure greater compliance with the intentions of the legislation and to prevent

---

[39] FA 2004, s 308. On multiple promoters and multiple proposals, see FA 2004, s 308(4),(5).
[40] FA 2004, s 308(3).
[41] FA 2004, s 309.
[42] FA 2004, s 310.
[43] FA 2004, ss 311–313.
[44] FA 2004, s 314; on scope of legal advice privilege, see *Three Rivers District Council v Bank of England* [2005] UKHL 48.
[45] FA 2004, s 315 and TMA 1970, s 98C.
[46] FA 2004, s 316.
[47] House of Lords Select Committee on Economic Affairs Sub Committee on the Finance Bill 2006, Bill Report, para 24.
[48] Tax Avoidance Schemes (Promoters and Prescribed Circumstances) Regulations 2006 SI 2006/1543, on which see Bland [2006] BTR 653. Further amendments were made in Tax Avoidance Schemes (Prescribed Descriptions of Arrangements) (Amendment) Regulations, SI 2013/2595 to clarify certain aspects of the confidentiality hallmarks and replace the pensions hallmark with a new hallmark relating to employment income provided through third parties.

it becoming simply a self-regulating area.[49] FA 2008 also made changes, principally to the system under which a scheme is allocated a scheme reference number; these changes are important for the practical working of the scheme rather than of theoretical interest.[50] The disclosure rules were tightened further by FA 2010, section 56 and Schedule 17, which provided a new definition of and rules for promoters, extension to 'introducers', and raised the penalties for failure to disclose. In 2012 the Government launched a new consultation on extending the hallmarks to capture avoidance schemes not presently notifiable; additional amendments and regulations to broaden and strengthen the DOTAS rules subsequently followed. FA 2015 Schedule 17 changed the DOTAS regime to give HMRC the power to obtain prescribed information on the users of undisclosed avoidance schemes. The penalties for users who fail to comply with DOTAS reporting requirements were increased, and protections for 'whistle-blowers' on failures to comply were introduced. Draft regulations were issued in July 2015 aimed at greatly extending DOTAS as it applies to IHT—some say excessively as the proposal's intention is to encompass any arrangements that aim to avoid IHT on death or on lifetime transfers.

It is clear that the DOTAS rules are effective in other ways—the volume of new provisions each year making mention of them gets greater each year. However, this does consequential damage to the statute book by making more and more rules. Finally, it should be noted that reporting regimes such as DOTAS are viewed as an important part of the G20/OECD Base Erosion and Profit Shifting (BEPS) project, and were the focus of Action 12 (see below §69.11).[51] In the 2016 Business Tax Road Map, the Government stated that the UK will be monitoring international developments in respect of such regimes.[52]

5.3.2.2 High-Risk Promoters, Follower Notices and Accelerated Payments

In August 2013 HMRC launched a consultation 'Raising the stakes on tax avoidance', which caused some concerns amongst tax professionals. The HMRC proposals included new statutory powers targeting 'high-risk' tax promoters, requiring disclosure of all information provided to prospective users of notifiable schemes and permitting HMRC to publicly identify high-risk promoters. The proposals also included steep fines for non-compliant promoters and users who failed to settle with HMRC once a similar scheme has been defeated in the courts. The promoters of tax avoidance schemes rules were introduced in FA 2014.[53] FA 2014 also introduced the latter 'follower notice' powers into force, along with a new 'accelerated payment' power, which requires users of tax avoidance schemes that have been notified under DOTAS or that are counteracted by the new GAAR to pay the disputed tax up front.[54]

While HMRC sees these new powers as important new fronts in its war on tax avoidance—by eg reducing the financial benefits for taxpayers from dragging on 'no-hoper' litigation—many in the profession view them as excessive and potentially a significant deterrent to those considering pursuing legitimate disputes in the tribunals. According to

---

[49] FA 2004, ss 308A, 313A, 306A and 314A, added by FA 2007, s 108, on which see Bland [2007] BTR 584.
[50] FA 2008, s 111 and Sch 38.
[51] OECD, *BEPS Action 12 'Mandatory Disclosure Rules' Final Report* (Oct 2015).
[52] HM Treasury, *Business Tax Road Map*, (March 2016), 23.
[53] FA 2014, ss 234–283.
[54] FA 2014, ss 199–233.

figures released at Budget 2015, HMRC predicts that by the end of 2016 over 64,000 users of avoidance schemes will have been required to pay tax upfront, and by the end of 2019–20 the measure will have brought forward over £5.5 billion in payments. Much will depend on HMRC's implementation. Taxpayers have already gone to the courts seeking judicial review over follower notices and accelerated payment notices (APNs) received, and HMRC has withdrawn hundreds of APNs in response to taxpayer challenges.[55] Could this be another example of HMRC taking powers intended for a few and applying them too widely?[56]

The Revenue's development of tools to further combat the economics of tax avoidance continued in 2015. FA 2015 Schedule 18 extended the accelerated payment regime to group relief surrenders. From 12 April 2015, the accelerated payments regime also applies to NICs. FA 2015 Schedule 19 imposed obligations on high-risk promoters to notify HMRC of relevant changes to notified schemes. HMRC were also given the power to publish information about high-risk promoters and notified schemes, and to issue conduct notices to promoters and connected persons.

Finally, HMT and HMRC released a joint paper in March 2015 entitled 'Tackling Tax Avoidance and Evasion', which summarises recent steps taken as well as future plans.[57] The planned next steps include:

— further measures to toughen the consequences for tax evaders and those who help them, including publically naming evaders and 'enablers' of evasion
— continued focus on onshore and offshore evaders, by analysing data including Merchant Acquirer data on credit/debit card sales and supporting investigative bodies in criminal prosecutions (confirmed at Budget 2016)
— introducing a new strict liability criminal offence for those who have not paid the tax due on offshore income (confirmed at Budget 2016 and fast tracked into FA 2016, section 166, partly in response to the publication of the Panama Papers)
— introducing new civil penalties for enablers of tax evasion (confirmed at Budget 2016 and also fast tracked into FA 2016, section 162)
— creating a new offence of corporate failure to prevent tax evasion or the facilitation of tax evasion (presently under consultation)
— further toughening of the range of penalties available to HMRC, including attaching a tax-geared penalty to the GAAR (confirmed at Budget 2016 and a penalty of 60% of the counteracted tax was introduced in FA 2016, section 158 amending FA 2013)
— a new surcharge on serial avoiders whose latest tax return is incorrect as a result of a further failed avoidance scheme (introduced in FA 2016, section 159 and Schedule 18)
— naming and shaming serial avoiders, and those that abuse tax credits could have their access to reliefs restricted. Restricting reliefs in this way is quite novel, highly controversial, and (it would seem) difficult to target in an effective and proportionate way. Nevertheless, the government confirmed at Budget 2016 it will proceed along these lines and legislation was introduced in FA 2016, Schedule 18, Part 4).

---

[55] See eg *Rowe and Others v HMRC* [2015] EWHC 2293, decided in HMRC's favour. HMRC has withdrawn hundreds of APNs previously issued in relation to IR35 and employee benefit trusts.

[56] For commentary see Gething [2014] BTR 445 (on follower notices and accelerated payment notices) and Salter & Oats [2014] BTR 454 (on high-risk promoters).

[57] See paper at https://www.gov.uk/government/publications/tackling-tax-evasion-and-avoidance.

— asking the regulatory bodies who police professional standards to take on a greater lead and responsibility in setting and enforcing clear professional standards around the facilitation and promotion of avoidance.

In summary, the Revenue has acquired a raft of innovative anti-avoidance powers since the introduction of DOTAS in 2004—and intends to acquire even more in the near future. These powers principally have targeted the economics of promoting and undertaking tax avoidance schemes. The next section delves further into the merits of an over-arching statutory response to tax avoidance in the form of a general anti-avoidance (or anti-abuse) rule. This is followed by an examination of the judiciary's approach to tax avoidance.

5.4 Is Avoidance a Problem?

The case for legislation to outlaw avoidance may be put in a number of ways:

(1) The result would be a simplification of the tax laws. However, simplification in the code would simply produce uncertainty at the administration level and thus destroy the real advantage of simplification.

(2) It would act as a deterrent to other tax avoidance projects.[58] This would be an advantage, since prevention is better than the resentment that arises when taxpayers, who are unable to take advantage of these schemes, see others using them until such time as the legislature catches up. However, deterrence must not impede genuine business transactions. One solution to this problem is a clearance procedure that is provided sufficient resources.

(3) It would prevent so much skill and so many human resources being devoted to rather dubious activities.[59] Ignoring the mere rhetoric in the word 'dubious', and not pausing to question the premise of the criticism that those possessing these skills could be put to more productive uses, it may be concluded that such skills would be used simply in corresponding with the Revenue to determine whether a scheme would fall within the discretion, instead of challenging such a scheme in court. Being able to express an argument is not as important as understanding how the Revenue exercise a particular discretion and so having the information which governs the argument. The best way of lowering the costs of tax advice lies in the publication of information; the Revenue manuals tend to fall silent when avoidance looms.

(4) If recent judicial attempts to develop doctrines to counter tax avoidance have passed their zenith (see below §5.6), a statutory anti-avoidance device may be necessary to maintain the integrity of the tax base. Moreover, a statutory provision can run from a certain date and, although not strictly necessary, could include provision for a clearance procedure, neither of which is true for judicial doctrine.[60]

---

[58] The present tax code has *in terrorem* provisions, eg TIOPA 2010, Pt 4 (ex TA 1988, s 770A); ITA 2007, Pt 13, Ch 4 (ex TA 1988, s 775); and TCGA 1992, s 30.

[59] The price of legal expertise is high.

[60] For criticisms of judicial solution, see TLRC report, *op cit*, ch 4.

Other arguments are more questionable. Thus, it is not known how much tax is lost by 'artificial' as opposed to 'legitimate' tax avoidance schemes.[61] There is little direct evidence that avoidance leads to evasion, although the resentment that comes from watching others save tax may cause a decline in taxpayer morality—a proposition which leads to an examination of the tax base and of those items of income which escape tax altogether, just as much as those which escape tax through artificial devices. Lastly, there is no evidence that artificial devices cause any increase in the burden on other taxpayers.

If the case for a general anti-avoidance rule is rejected, and the case for a sniper as distinct from the shotgun approach is accepted, it is necessary also to accept all the consequences of that approach. If the argument is based on the rule of law, the concept of certainty and the rejection of official discretion, then one must also reject any discretion of the Revenue to soften the application of a particular rule in hard circumstances. All too often critics of the Revenue really want the best of both worlds—Revenue bound hand and foot by red tape in their efforts to get taxes, but with unfettered power to waive tax due. It would be unwise to leave this problem without noting the comment of the 1955 Royal Commission that the existence of widespread tax avoidance is evidence that the system, not the taxpayer, is in need of radical reform.[62]

5.5   Precedents, Proposals and the GAAR

A general anti-avoidance provision was included in the UK's excess profits tax during the Second World War.[63] However, that scheme was less than fully effective: (a) because the Revenue needed to have access to information, and parliamentary feeling on this was extremely sensitive and unwilling; and (b) because the test of counter-avoidance was the motive of avoiding tax, and the Revenue found it extremely difficult to provide evidence to rebut alleged motives.[64] It is largely due to the experience of that tax that later anti-avoidance provisions have tended to refer to matters such as the main benefit rather than motive; this change was made in the excess profits tax in 1944.[65] Similar powers were part of profits tax[66] and the special charge in 1967.[67] They were not part of the retrospective increase in surtax rates for 1972–73 imposed in 1974, presumably because it was too late for taxpayers to rearrange their affairs.[68] An interesting general rule in the tax credits legislation is aimed at those who deprive themselves of income for the purpose of securing entitlement to tax credits.[69]

[61] See Sandford, *Hidden Costs*, (Institute for Fiscal Studies, 1973) ch 8.

[62] Cmnd 9474 (1955) §33; cited by Kay [1979] BTR 354, 365.

[63] FA 1941, s 35; for an example of its application, see *Crown Bedding Co Ltd v IRC* [1946] 1 All ER 452; 34 TC 107 (CA).

[64] Sir Leonard Barford, IFS Conference, 22; see also Sabine, *British Budgets in Peace and War (1936–1945)* 197, 200, 260.

[65] FA 1944, s 33.

[66] FA 1951, s 32; see [1964] BTR 129.

[67] FA 1968, s 50.

[68] FA 1974, s 8.

[69] Tax Credits (Definition and Calculation of Income) Regs SI 2002/2006 para 15.

Examples of the administrative control approach may be found in Germany,[70] the Netherlands,[71] Canada,[72] Australia[73] and New Zealand.[74] The United States partially codified its judicial economic substance doctrine, but the situation there is different from that in the UK.[75] Many Continental countries have a doctrine of abuse of rights—in addition to, or in place of, a general anti-avoidance provision.[76] No country seems to be at ease with its system, but this is largely because of the elusive nature of the distinction between acceptable and unacceptable tax avoidance and shifts in judicial perceptions, which are every bit as difficult as those in the UK. Thus, in Australia, the first general provision was subsequently replaced because it had suffered too much at the hands of the judges. Later case law not only weakened the new provision but reinvigorated the old.[77] The CJEU also has developed a doctrine of abuse. Under this approach, a state can justify its discriminatory provision as necessary to prevent avoidance and provided it meets the tests of proportionality. The choice between these various approaches is not an easy one, since equity and certainty are in conflict. Tax equity demands that artificial tax avoidance schemes should be of no effect, yet certainty demands that the tax laws should be such that an individual can arrange his affairs in the expectation that he will or will not have to pay tax.

5.5.1 *IFS Tax Law Review Committee's Proposal 1997*

In 1997 The IFS Tax Law Review Committee (TLRC) produced a report with a number of conclusions. First, the report recommended that specific avoidance provisions should continue to be used. Secondly, without actually recommending a GAAR, it suggested that a GAAR with proper safeguards might well be preferable to the (then) present uncertain state of case law. The report went on to recommend safeguards which it regarded as proper. The TLRC GAAR had several elements:

— A purpose clause to deter or counteract transactions which are designed to avoid tax in a way which conflicts with or defeats the evident intention of Parliament.
— The basic rule, which contrasts a 'tax-driven' transaction with a normal transaction; a person is to be taxed in accordance with the normal transaction. Where the tax-driven

---

[70] See TLRC report, *op cit*, 29.
[71] See Van der Stok [1998] BTR 150.
[72] See Arnold [1995] BTR 541; Roxan [1998] BTR 140; and TLRC report, *op cit*, 17–21. For an early detailed analysis, see Arnold and Wilson (1988) *Canadian Tax J* 829, 1123, 1369.
[73] See Harris [1998] BTR 124; and TLRC report, *op cit*, 21–24; on the *Spotless* case, see also Krever (1997) 45 *Canadian Tax J* 122.
[74] For an excellent and comprehensive comparative study of GAARs around the world see Lang et al (eds), *GAARs: A Key Element of Tax Systems in the Post-BEPS World* (IBFD, 2016). See also TLRC report, *op cit*, 24–26.
[75] Internal Revenue Code § 7701(o). See also Tiley [2004] BTR 304, 325; Tiley and Jensen [1998] BTR 161; and TLRC report, *op cit*, 26–28. On US experience, see also Symposium on Corporate Tax Shelters in (2002) 55 *Tax Law Review* 125–464; another symposium in (2001) 54 *Southern Methodist Law Review* 3–238; and McMahon *Southern Methodist L Rev* 195; McMahon (2002) 94 *Tax Notes* 1017 (25 February 2002); and McMahon (2003) 98 *Tax Notes* 1721 (17 March 2003).
[76] See Ward *et al* [1985] BTR 68; and Ward and Cullity [1981] *Canadian Tax J* 451; see also Frommel (1991) *Intertax* 54 (France).
[77] See Harris [1998] BTR 124; see also [1996] BTR 453, 656. On old Australian law, see Lehmann in Krever (ed), *Australian Taxation Principles and Practice* (Longman, 1987).

transaction does not have a non-tax objective and so there is no normal transaction, tax is to be charged as if it had not taken place.
— Protected transactions. The rule is not applied to a protected transaction. If there is a multiple step transaction the rule will not apply if the transaction, taken as a whole, is entirely or mainly a protected transaction.
— Burden of proof. It is to be assumed that a transaction is not a tax-driven transaction; but, equally, it is to be assumed that it is not a protected transaction.
— The procedure to be followed by the tax authority would be spelt out. The authority would issue written notice specifying the tax-driven transaction and the normal transaction, stating that it was not a protected transaction and giving details of every other person to whom it had given written notice relating to the same transaction.
— The taxpayer could invite the authority to review its decision, giving reasons why it should do so.
— Appeal would then lie to the Special Commissioners or VAT Tribunal.
— All this would be backed up by a prior clearance procedure, with provision being made for publication of advance rulings.
— Finally, an annual report would be made to Parliament, giving full details of the operation of the rule.

UK tax authorities flirted with the idea of a GAAR in 1998, building on, but departing from, the TLRC model. The TLRC was severely critical of the Revenue's proposal.[78]

While the work of the IFS Committee represented a particular viewpoint, it was not one which was generally shared at that time by the profession, so the proposal was killed by a combination of Revenue anxiety and professional indifference. The indifference of the profession has reaped its own reward as each major amendment to the tax base, usually corporation tax, has contained its own mini-GAAR in the form of unallowable purpose test—and without the protection of a statutory advance rulings system.[79]

5.5.2 The Aaronson Report 2011

In December 2010, the Exchequer Secretary asked Graham Aaronson QC to lead a new study into a possible UK GAAR. In 2011 the committee (of which the late John Tiley was a member) recommended that a narrowly-focused general anti-abuse rule, rather than a sweeping anti-avoidance rule, should be introduced.[80] The committee set out in detail how it should function, and included illustrative draft provisions and guidance. The committee's GAAR would apply to the main direct taxes—income tax, CGT, corporation tax and petroleum revenue tax, as well as NICs. It was aimed only at egregious, contrived and abusive tax schemes, and included a number of safeguards, including explicit protection for reasonable

---

[78] TLRC Response to IR's Consultative Document (IFS, February 1999).
[79] CTA 2009, s 441, ex FA 1996, Sch 9, para 13 (Loan Relationships and since 2002 foreign exchange); FA 2002, Sch 26, para 23 (Derivatives), Sch 29, para 111 (Intellectual Property); FA 2004, s 137, adding TA 1988, Sch 23A, para 7A (Manufactured Overseas Dividends); and FA 2004, s 38, inserting a new TA 1988, s 75 (Management Expenses), noting especially s 75(5); see also the reasons for removing annual payments from the category of charges on income in Finance Bill 2005, cl 132 and Revenue Notes on Clauses.
[80] See http://www.hm-treasury.gov.uk/tax_avoidance_gaar.htm.

tax planning and for arrangements entered into without any intent to reduce tax. The burden of proof that the planning was not 'reasonable' would be on HMRC. As a further safeguard, an Advisory Panel constituted with a majority of non-HMRC members would be established to advise whether HMRC would be justified in applying the GAAR. The Panel's advice (anonymised) would be published. At Budget 2012, the Government announced a consultation on new draft GAAR legislation based on the illustrative clauses in the Aaronson Report, along with other aspects, including the establishment of the Advisory Panel and appropriate guidance, with a view to legislating a GAAR in FA 2013.

5.5.3 The GAAR

FA 2013, sections 206–215 and Schedule 43 introduced the long-awaited general anti-abuse rule. The GAAR applies to counteract tax advantages arising from abusive tax arrangements involving the income tax, corporation tax, CGT, IHT, petroleum revenue tax, stamp duty land tax, and ATED.[81] Separate legislation in 2014 extended its reach to NICs. Arrangements will be 'tax arrangements' if it would be reasonable to conclude, having regard to all the circumstances, that their main purpose, or one of their main purposes, was obtaining a tax advantage.[82] Thus, the purpose is determined on an objective, not subjective, basis. A tax advantage includes tax reliefs, repayments, avoidance and deferral.[83]

Once a 'tax arrangement' is found to exist, the next step is to assess whether the arrangement is 'abusive'. This takes us to the crucial double reasonableness test in FA 2013, section 207(2)—arrangements are abusive if the entering or carrying out of the arrangements 'cannot reasonably be regarded as a reasonable course of action' in relation to the relevant tax provisions, having regard to all the circumstances and in particular to

(a) the consistency of the substantive results of the arrangements with the principles and policy underlying the tax provisions,
(b) whether the means used in achieving those results involve the use of contrived or abnormal steps, and
(c) whether the arrangements are intended to exploit any shortcoming in the tax provisions.

A further indication that an arrangement might not be reasonable is if it results in profits or losses which diverge from economic reality and it is reasonable to assume that such a result was not the anticipated result when the relevant tax provisions were enacted.[84] In the event that the GAAR does apply to the arrangement, the counteraction of the tax advantages under the GAAR is on a 'just and reasonable' basis.[85] This might involve ignoring a circular transaction, or applying the tax effect of the most likely alternative form of transaction. Importantly, section 211 contains a novel and unusually broad evidentiary rule that goes well beyond the normal *Pepper v Hart* approach to extrinsic materials: 'in determining

[81] FA 2013, s 206.
[82] FA 2013, s 207(1).
[83] FA 2013, s 208.
[84] FA 2013, s 207(4).
[85] FA 2013, s 209.

any issue in connection with the general anti-abuse rule, a court or tribunal may take into account—

(a)   guidance, statements or other material (whether of HMRC, a Minister of the Crown or anyone else) that was in the public domain at the time the arrangements were entered into, and
(b)   evidence of established practice at that time.'

FA 2013, Schedule 43 sets out further procedural requirements, including those related to the creation and operation of the GAAR advisory panel. The panel is meant to be act as a reality check on HMRC's view that the GAAR should be applied to a given arrangement. Although HMRC initially insisted on representation on the panel (as envisioned by the Aaronson Report), this position was subsequently abandoned in the face of calls for the 'independence' of the panel. The first chairperson of the panel—appointed by HMRC, what does say this say about 'independence'?—is Patrick Mears, formerly a senior tax partner at a large firm. Importantly, the GAAR legislation provides that a court or tribunal 'must take into account' the GAAR panel's opinion about the arrangements giving rise to the GAAR assessment.[86] The precise nature of the relationship between the GAAR advisory panel and the courts, however, and many other details are still to be worked out. Freedman (another member of the Aaronson committee) has expressed some concerns over the panel's role, describing it as a 'strange animal, with an odd role constitutionally'.[87] It is also noteworthy that one member of the GAAR advisory panel has already stepped down after being filmed by the BBC's Panorama programme offering participants at a tax conference advice on how to 'keep money out of the Chancellor's grubby mitts'. As of June 2016 no cases have yet been referred to the GAAR advisory panel.

   HMRC has issued guidance on the GAAR, which has been approved by the GAAR advisory panel.[88] Importantly, pursuant to FA 2013, section 211(2)(a), a court or tribunal faced with a GAAR issue 'must take into account' HMRC guidance approved by the panel. The guidance begins in paragraph B2.2 by citing Lord Tomlin's famous dictum from the *Duke of Westminster* (§see 5.6.1 below) but goes on to state that legal entitlement to minimise taxes does not make all tax avoidance reasonable. The guidance further states that the view that taxation is legalised theft is an 'extreme view' that cannot be reasonably held. The examples provided in Part B have come under some criticism on the basis that they appear to be clearly egregious schemes, which could be defeated by technical argument or the *Ramsay* principle (see §5.6.4 below), with the result that the examples add little in the way of understanding as to what the GAAR will add.[89]

   In 2016 the government attached a penalty of 60% of tax due to all cases successfully tackled by the GAAR.[90] It should be noted that the possibility of applying special penalty or rates of interest regimes to tax recovered under the GAAR was considered and rejected in the 2011 Aaronson report. According to Graham Aaronson QC:

---

[86] FA 2013, s 211(2)(b) and Sch 43, para 11.
[87] [2013] BTR 373.
[88] See https://www.gov.uk/government/publications/tax-avoidance-general-anti-abuse-rules.
[89] Readers are directed to the note by Greenbank in [2013] BTR 505, and the article in the same issue by Gammie at 577.
[90] FA 2013, s 212A and Sch 43C.

[I]ncluding such provisions would be seen as presenting an irresistible temptation to HMRC to wield the GAAR as a weapon rather than to use it, as intended, as a shield. For this reason I do not consider that it would be appropriate to include any provisions for applying special rates of interest or penalties to tax recovered by use of the GAAR.[91]

5.6   UK Judicial Approaches to Tax Avoidance[92]

The questions facing the courts in avoidance cases arise because the taxpayers have arranged their affairs so as to come within the words of the statute—in their view. The Revenue authorities argue that the facts do not come within the words of the statute, whether because of a different view of the law or a different view of the facts. This is the world of statutory construction and, as seen in §3.1 above, the current view is that the words of the statute must be interpreted in their context and with an eye to the purpose of the provision.[93] This is of course no different from any other branch of statute-based law. The history of the case law of the last 30 or so years shows that the law has been much more turbulent than the anodyne statement just set forth would suggest; that statement does, however, represent the basic principle to be applied. That turbulence has surrounded the concept of the 'composite transaction', a concept that has been regarded as a rule or an approach and now simply as one example of the modern approach to the construction of statutes. So the question whether the concept applies is itself now a question of construction.[94] There was at one time a strand of criticism which regarded the early line of cases as unconstitutional;[95] the final approach just described resolves that issue.

Two major cases in the new millennium have established the new basis for the new approach, although the first caused chaos of its own which was corrected in the second. The first is *MacNiven v Westmoreland Investments Ltd*.[96] Westmoreland (WIL) was a property company that owed £70m, including £40m arrears of interest on loans from a pension fund, the members of which were also its only shareholders. If the interest could be paid, WIL would be able at that time to use that payment as a charge on income, so creating a loss which could be set against profits the company might earn in later years, even, subject to then TA 1988, section 768, profits earned following a change of ownership. The scheme enabled this payment to be made.[97] The pension fund shareholders lent the money to WIL, which passed it back as a payment of interest. The facts thus disclosed a preordained series of transactions carried out in order to secure a payment of interest and a tax advantage in that WIL now had an allowable loss. In the Court of Appeal, Peter Gibson LJ placed the

---

[91] Aaronson Report, *op cit*, para 5.47.

[92] Among many important articles, see Freedman (2007) 123 *LQR* 53; Gammie [2006] BTR 294; Templeman (2001) 117 *LQR* 565; Walker (2005) 121 *LQR* 121; Hoffmann [2005] BTR 197; and [2004] BTR Issue No 4.

[93] *Barclays Mercantile Business Finance Ltd v Mawson (Inspector of Taxes)* [2004] UKHL 51; [2005] STC 1; and *IRC v McGuckian* [1997] STC 908; 69 TC 1; [1997] NI 157.

[94] *Barclays* (above); and *MacNiven v Westmoreland Investments Ltd* [2001] UKHL 6; [2001] STC 237; 73 TC 1.

[95] See eg, Bartlett [1985] BTR 338.

[96] Above; see Tiley [2001] BTR 153.

[97] It is a nice question whether the problem could still arise under the loan relationship rules in CTA 2009, Pts 5–7. If the connected party rules apply, the deduction would be given only if, as in the present case, the interest was actually paid.

transaction on the tax mitigation side of the line as distinct from tax avoidance,[98] not least because what upset the Revenue here was not the fact of the payment of interest but rather the fact that the payment was made to a tax exempt body. This reason, although not its formulation, also appealed to Lord Nicholls in the House of Lords.[99]

Lord Hoffmann, giving the major speech with which all members of the House concurred, held:

(1) that construing the relevant legislation in its context, the question to be decided was whether there had been a payment;
(2) that in the present context one had to distinguish terms which should be construed legally from those which should be interpreted commercially;
(3) that the term 'payment' was to be construed legally as opposed to commercially; and
(4) in this case, the legal meaning was that there was a payment if the legal obligation to pay interest had been discharged.

It followed that there was no room for the Revenue's broadly formulated principle.

This major narrowing of the earlier case law led to an article by Lord Templeman in which he outlined the dissent he would have given if he had not retired.[100] Lord Hoffmann's point (2) became treated as holy writ. The courts, however, had great difficulty in deciding which concepts were legal and which were commercial, and even in deciding the precise concepts to be categorised in this way.[101] Its status as a rule was repudiated in the next case as being the very negation of purposive construction.[102]

The second case is *Barclays Mercantile Business Finance Ltd v Mawson (Inspector of Taxes)*.[103] Here, an Irish company, BGE, had built a pipeline. It sold the pipeline to the taxpayers, BMBF, for £91.3m. BMBF leased the assets back to BGE, which granted a sublease onwards to its UK subsidiary. The question was whether BMBF was entitled to a capital allowance in respect of the £91.3m spent, as BMBF argued, to acquire an asset used in its business of finance leasing. The simple finance deal was then hedged around with many complex money flows; BMBF argued that purpose of these arrangements was to ensure that the sums due from BGE under the lease arrangements would actually come through. The Barclays team thought their primary concern in drawing up arrangements was to ensure the bank met the capital adequacy rules laid down by the UK banking regulatory authorities. The Revenue saw things differently; they argued that if one looked at the scheme as a whole, its terms did not amount to security arrangements. They so protected the position of BMBF as to prevent BMBF from incurring any expense at all, and so took it outside the scope of the relevant provision.[104] On this view the expense was incurred neither (a) on the

---

[98] [1998] STC 1138, 1144g.
[99] Para 13.
[100] (2001) 117 *LQR* 575.
[101] Eg, *Barclays Mercantile Business Finance Ltd v Mawson (Inspector of Taxes)* [2002] EWCA Civ 66; [2003] STC 66.
[102] HL, para 38, referring to Ribeiro PJ in *Arrowtown* [2003] HKFCA 46, paras 37 and 39, and the 'perceptive judgment' of the Special Commissioners (Theodore Wallace and Julian Ghosh) in *Campbell v IRC* [2004] STC (SCD) 396. Only the politically curious will wonder why they did not also refer to the criticisms by Lord Millett in *Arrowtown*.
[103] [2004] UKHL 51; [2005] STC 1; Tiley [2005] BTR 273.
[104] Contrast Park J's analysis in *Barclays Mercantile Business Finance v Mawson* [2002] EWHC Civ 1527 at paras 14–34 with the Court of Appeal's reasoning, [2002] EWCA Civ 1853 at paras 26–36.

provision of machinery and plant, nor (b) for the purposes of BMBF's trade or (c) at all.[105] The crux of the decision of the House of Lords was that the only party on whom the court should concentrate was the finance lessor (BMBF), not the finance lessee (BGE). The statutory requirements were concerned entirely with the acts and purposes of the lessor. The Act said nothing about what the lessee should do with the purchase price, how he should find the money to pay the rent or how he should use the plant. For their Lordships there was nothing in the statute to suggest that 'up-front finance' for the lessee was an essential feature of the right to allowances. The statutory test was based on the purpose of the lessor's expenditure, not the benefit of the finance to the lessee.[106]

It is not—and probably never will be—possible to state the true doctrine of tax avoidance conclusively. This is partly because of the changing membership of the judiciary, partly because of the nature of the judicial process, partly because of the variety of the situations and partly because questions of statutory construction are matters of opinion on which views may differ.[107]

5.6.1 Respect for Legal Facts Created by the Parties (Westminster)

That the courts must have respect for the legal facts created by the parties was laid down by Lord Tomlin in *IRC v Duke of Westminster*[108] when he said:

> Every man is entitled if he can to arrange his affairs so that the tax attaching under the appropriate Acts is less than it otherwise would be. If he succeeds in ordering them so as to secure that result, then, however unappreciative the Commissioners of Inland Revenue or his fellow taxpayers may be of his ingenuity, he cannot be compelled to pay an increased tax.

It followed that a transaction which, on its true construction, was of a kind that would escape tax, was not taxable on the ground that the same result could have been achieved by a transaction in another form which would have attracted tax.

In *IRC v Duke of Westminster*, the Duke covenanted to pay an employee a sum of £1.90 per week; the covenant was to last seven years, whether or not the employee remained in the Duke's service. The employee already had a wage of £3 a week, and he was told that while he would be legally entitled to the full £3, it was expected that, in practice, he would take only the balance of £1.10 to bring his total up to £3. The purpose of the scheme was to enable the Duke to deduct the payment in computing his total income for surtax.[109] The scheme succeeded; the true construction of the document showed that these sums were not income of an employee under Schedule E (now ITEPA 2003) but income from an annuity under Schedule D, Case III (now ITTOIA 2005, Part 5, Chapter 7). As Lord Tomlin said, there could be no collateral contract to serve the Duke, ie collateral to the bond. Even if there had been, it could not have affected the nature of the rights arising under the bond.[110]

[105] [2002] EWCA Civ 1853 at para 25.
[106] [2004] UKHL 51 at para 42.
[107] For a helpful attempt to summarise the present state of the law on the *Ramsay* principle, see Lewison J in *Berry v Revenue & Customs Commissioners* [2011] UKUT 81, [2011] STC 1057 at para 31.
[108] [1936] AC 1; [1919] TC 490, 520.
[109] The scheme was stopped in 1936. See now ITTOIA 2005, s 727, ex TA 1988, s 347A.
[110] [1936] AC 1, 18–19; 19 TC 490, 519–20.

In reaching this conclusion the court was entitled to look at all the circumstances of the case, including the fact that the taxpayer had received a letter containing the expectations of the Duke already referred to. However, the court was also entitled to look at the fact that the legal right to payment would continue even though the employment ceased. In this connection the Commissioners' conclusion that the payments would start as employment income but would cease to be such income if the employee ceased to be employed by the Duke, looks very odd.

This decision is a shibboleth for modern judicial attitudes. Lord Atkin, dissenting, thought that the covenant was a term of the contract of employment and not just an expectation.[111] Some expressly or implicitly take the simple contractual line expressed by Lord Atkin; others take a more apocalyptic line.[112] In *Barclays Mercantile Business Finance* there are references to courts having been blinkered in their approach to the facts, but the *Westminster* case is not mentioned. The *Westminster* starting point was accepted by Lord Wilberforce in *Ramsay* (see below at §5.6.4). While it is fashionable in some quarters to treat the *Westminster* case as a political rather than doctrinal decision, this seems superficial.[113] One should distinguish the *Westminster* doctrine outlined above from a *Westminster* approach which tended to look kindly on attempts to avoid tax. This approach no longer represents the law.

Lastly, although the courts have long recognised that tax avoidance is lawful, it is not yet a virtue. In *Re Weston's Settlement*,[114] the Court of Appeal declined to approve a variation of trust where the only advantages accruing to the beneficiaries on whose behalf they were being asked to approve the variation were financial, stemming almost exclusively from the saving of tax. Similarly, in *Sherdley v Sherdley*,[115] the Court of Appeal declined to make an order for financial provision of a child when the only reason for that order would have been the tax saving; this was reversed by the House of Lords, but it is an indication of a certain judicial attitude.

5.6.2 Courts Looks to Facts not Labels

The *Westminster* doctrine was sometimes expressed as being that the court must look to the form of the transaction and not its substance. This formulation is misleading, however, in that it tends to suggest that the form of a transaction, a matter which may be within the control of the taxpayer, will be conclusive for tax purposes. Often, though, the legal form used by the parties is not conclusive, and here it is accepted that the court must look at the substance of the matter in order to determine the true tax consequences of the transaction in the legal form adopted by the parties. Thus, by looking at the substance, the court might conclude that this form attracted tax just as much as another. In these instances the court is not putting upon the transaction a legal character which it does not possess, but is trying to discover the true character in tax law of the transaction entered into.[116] As such, the court

---

[111] [1936] AC 1, 14–15; 19 TC 490, 516–17.
[112] Lord Steyn in *IRC v McGuckian* [1997] STC 907; 69 TC 1.
[113] Likhovski (2004) 25 *Cardozo L Rev* 953–1018.
[114] [1969] 1 Ch 223; [1968] 1 All ER 720. For comment, see Bretten [1968] *Conveyancer* 194; Harris [1969] *Conveyancer* 183, 191 *et seq.*
[115] [1987] STC 217; see [1987] BTR 337.
[116] *IRC v Mallaby-Deeley* [1938] 4 All ER 818, 825; 23 TC 153, 167, per Sir Wilfrid Greene MR.

may hold that a trade is carried on by a partnership even though the only document states that there was none,[117] that a trader is still trading even though he says he is not,[118] or that the person claiming to trade is simply the means through which the trade is carried on by someone else.[119] In such contexts the documents cannot be used to deny proven facts.

Where, however, both the facts and the legal arrangements point in the same direction, the court may not disregard them.[120] It follows that the name given to a transaction by the parties concerned does not necessarily decide the nature of the transaction.[121] A description of a series of payments as an annuity or a rent charge does not determine its character.[122] It goes without saying that this rule applies whether it is invoked by the taxpayer or by the Revenue. All the cases in which the Revenue succeeded under the *Ramsay* composite transaction rule (see below at §5.6.4) may be seen as examples of this rule.

5.6.3 The Court is not Bound to Respect Sham Transactions

The court is not bound to respect a sham transaction because its sham nature prevents the parties from creating the legal facts hoped for. In the 'canonical' words of the then Diplock LJ in *Snook v London and West Riding Investments Ltd*, a transaction is a sham if the acts done were intended to give the appearance of creating legal rights different from those which were actually created.[123] Such schemes fail for the simple reason that the tax falls to be levied on the basis of the actual legal rights created. This argument, although frequently advanced by the Revenue, does not meet with great success. The new approach, based on the decision of the House of Lords in *Furniss v Dawson*,[124] encouraged the courts to give the Revenue occasional glimpses of success. In *Sherdley v Sherdley*,[125] Sir John Donaldson MR thought that an order to pay school fees to a school on behalf of a child, and made at the suit of the parent against whom the order would have been made, would be a sham. This use of the sham argument is highly questionable and probably erroneous. The decision was later reversed by the House of Lords, but without discussion of this point.[126] Since then the orthodox narrow definition of a sham transaction has prevailed.[127] Anxieties about the precise relationship between the sham transaction and questions of construction have lain behind articles of the law of trusts and beyond.[128] Thus Conaglen points out that the sham

---

[117] *Fenston v Johnstone* (1940) 23 TC 29.
[118] *J and R O'Kane & Co Ltd v IRC* (1922) 12 TC 303.
[119] *Firestone Tyre and Rubber Co Ltd v Lewellin* [1957] 1 All ER 561; 37 TC 111.
[120] *Ransom v Higgs* [1974] 3 All ER 949; [1974] STC 539.
[121] Secretary of State in *Council of India v Scoble* [1903] AC 299; 4 TC 618.
[122] *IRC v Land Securities Investment Trust* [1969] 2 All ER 430; 45 TC 495.
[123] See Diplock LJ in *Snook v London and West Riding Investments Ltd* [1967] 1 All ER 518, 520, [1967] 2 QB 686, 702; and Lord Devlin in *Campbell Discount Ltd v Bridge* [1962] 1 All ER 385, 402. 'Canonical' status was conferred in *A v A* 2007 EWHC 99, 32 (where the arrangement was held not to be a sham). See also Lee [1996] *NILQR* 377; and McCutcheon [1978] BTR 196 on Revenue arguments in *Frost v Newstead* [1978] STC 239; 53 TC 525.
[124] [1984] STC 153; [1984] 1 All ER 530.
[125] [1986] STC 266, 273. Balcombe LJ disagreed (at 278) and Neill LJ made no comment.
[126] [1987] STC 217.
[127] See, eg, Lord Goff in *Ensign Tankers (Leasing) Ltd v Stokes* [1992] 1 AC 655, 681; [1992] STC 226, 244–45; 64 TC 617, 746–47.
[128] Simpson and Stewart (eds), *Sham Transactions* (OUP, 2013), including chapters by Macnair (early uses), Simpson (sham and purposive construction), Davies (employment), Conaglen (trusts and intention), Vella (UK tax), Gammie (UK tax), Kirby (Australian tax) and Loutzenhiser (Canadian tax); McFarlane and Simpson in

doctrine is different from questions of construction because of the wider types of evidence that may be admitted in a sham case.[129] It is not completely clear how the *Ramsay* approach fits in with the doctrine of the sham.[130]

In the important employment law case *Autoclenz v Belcher*,[131] the Supreme Court repeated Diplock LJ's classic formulation of the sham doctrine in *Snook*. The Court did not overrule *Snook* but nor did it expand the doctrine, holding instead that written terms in contracts between parties with unequal bargaining power could be disregarded for reasons other than sham. The most important recent tax case on sham transactions is *Hitch v Stone*,[132] where the Court of Appeal, reversing the High Court, upheld the original finding by the Commissioners that a transaction was a sham. Emphasising that the test of the common intention of the parties was subjective, the Court asked whether the parties had intended to create different rights and obligations from those appearing from the relevant document and, in addition, whether they had intended to give a false impression of those rights and obligations to third parties. The fact that the act or document was uncommercial, or even artificial, did not mean that it was a sham. One must distinguish a situation where parties make an agreement which is unfavourable to one of them or artificial, from one where they intend some other arrangement to bind them. In the former situation, they intended the agreement to take effect according to its tenor. In the latter situation, the agreement was not to bind their relationship and so was a sham. The Court also said that the fact that parties subsequently departed from an agreement did not necessarily mean that they never intended the agreement to be effective and binding. However the Court further held that it was not necessary that every party to the act or document should be a party to the sham; so that a document might, in unusual circumstances, be held to be a sham in part only.[133]

5.6.4 *Transactions: Courts Will Look at End Results Whether the Transaction is (a) Circular and Self-cancelling* (Ramsay *and* Burmah*) or (b) Linear* (Furniss v Dawson)

Although the facts of the *Ramsay* case are complicated, the actual decision is easy to grasp: the court used the composite transaction approach to decide that a series of self-cancelling, preordained transactions, effected solely to generate an allowable loss for CGT purposes, was not to be given that effect.[134] *WT Ramsay Ltd v IRC*[135] concerned CGT. A company (R) had a large gain (£187,977) and wished to create an allowable loss which could be set against the gain and so remove its liability for tax. Under the scheme, R bought shares in a company and proceeded to make it two loans (L1 and L2), each of £218,750 at 11%; the loans were

---

Getzler (ed), *Rationalising Property Equity and Trusts, Essays in Honour of Edward Burn* (Butterworths, 2003) ch 8; Vella [2007] *JCLS* 243; Conaglen [2008] *CLJ* 176.

[129] Conaglen, *CLJ*, op cit, 182.
[130] See Gammie [2006] BTR 294.
[131] [2011] UKSC 41, and for commentary see Davies, 'Employment Law' in Simpson and Stewart, *Sham Transactions, op cit*, 185.
[132] [2001] STC 214, reversing the High Court [1999] STC 431.
[133] [1999] STC 431, paras 64 *et seq*; and see Conaglen, *CLJ, op cit*, 202 *et seq*.
[134] See also *Campbell v IRC* [2004] SpC 421; [2004] STC (SCD) 396, especially paras 70 *et seq*.
[135] [1982] AC 300; [1981] STC 174; 54 TC 101. The scheme was countered (in 1978) by what is now TCGA 1992, s 30.

made with the aid of the funds borrowed from a bank associated with the vendors of the scheme. R had the right to decrease the rate of interest on one loan, on one occasion only, provided there was a corresponding increase on the other loan. R reduced the rate on L1 to nil and so had to increase the rate on L2 to 22%; it sold L2 for £391,481, its market value, so realising a gain of £172,731. In due course L1 was repaid at par by the company, but the shares in the company were sold at a large consequential loss (£175,731). The narrow *ratio* of the House of Lords' decision was that the gain on the sale of the debt was a chargeable gain because the debt was a debt on a security (a chargeable asset) and not a simple debt (a non-chargeable asset). However, the wider and more important *ratio* was that the court was entitled to look at the whole transaction and so to conclude that the taxpayer had suffered a loss of only some £3,000. As Lord Wilberforce said:[136]

> [The approach for which the Crown contends] does not introduce a new principle; it would apply to new and sophisticated legal devices, the undoubted power and duty of the courts to determine their nature in law and to relate them to existing legislation. While the techniques of tax avoidance progress are technically improved, the courts are not obliged to stand still.

Although *WT Ramsay v IRC* dealt with artificial circular self-cancelling transactions,[137] mainstream commercial transactions by major companies were soon brought within the new approach by the decision of the House of Lords in *IRC v Burmah Oil Co Ltd*.[138] In this case the company, B, had transferred property to a subsidiary, S, but had left the money outstanding. As the property had declined in value and was the only substantial asset held by S, it was clear that the debt was worthless. By means of a loan from a fellow subsidiary bank, SB, S was enabled to repay the original loan to B and, by means of a rights issue, attracted further money from B with which to pay off SB. S was then liquidated. The effect was to substitute equity (a chargeable asset) for simple debt (a non-chargeable asset).[139] The scheme failed. The House of Lords, applying the *Ramsay* doctrine, refused to allow B to deduct the payments made under the rights issue in computing its loss on the shares of S when S was liquidated. There were superficial differences between the facts in this case and those in *Ramsay* in that the scheme was designed only for B, instead of being bought 'off the shelf', and that B used its own money in making the various payments instead of borrowing it—but these differences were of no real importance. In *Barclays Mercantile Business Finance*, *Burmah* was treated as a case where a series of circular payments which left the taxpayer company in exactly the same financial position as before was not regarded as giving rise to a 'loss' within the meaning of the legislation.[140]

Any remaining doubts were blown away by the decision of the House of Lords in *Furniss v Dawson*.[141] Here, a shareholder wished to sell his stake in company A to company C (Wood Bastow). He followed what Lord Brightman called 'a simple and honest scheme which merely seeks to defer payment of tax until the taxpayer has received into his hands the gain which he has made'. The shares in company A were exchanged for shares in company B (Greenjacket), and company B then sold the shares in company A to company C.

---

[136] [1982] AC 300, 326; 54 TC 101, 187.
[137] As had been argued in the case itself, 54 TC 101, 182; see Berg [1984] BTR 128.
[138] [1982] STC 30; 54 TC 200. See Goldberg [1982] BTR 13; and Ashton [1983] BTR 221.
[139] The Commissioners had found that the steps would, almost inevitably, have been carried through.
[140] *Barclays Mercantile Business Finance v Mawson* [2004] UKHL 51 at para 35.
[141] [1984] AC 474; [1984] STC 153; 55 TC 324.

The House of Lords held that although there was an express finding that all the steps were genuine, nonetheless the effect of the transactions for tax purposes was that the shareholder had disposed of his shares in company A to company C in return for consideration paid to company B.

Lord Brightman, after stressing that no distinction was to be drawn in fact (because none existed in reality) between a series of steps carried through under a non-binding arrangement and those carried through under a contract, stated that the preconditions for the applicability of the *Ramsay* principle were:[142]

> First, there must be a pre-ordained series of transactions; or, if one likes, a single composite transaction. This composite transaction may or may not include the achievement of a legitimate commercial (ie, business) end ... Secondly, there must be steps inserted which have no commercial (business) purpose apart from the avoidance of a liability to tax—not 'no business effect'. If those two ingredients exist, the inserted steps are to be disregarded for fiscal purposes.

Therefore, the preordained series of transactions began with the sale by the taxpayer to company B and ended with the sale by company B to company C. This led to the excision of the intervening steps; therefore the whole scheme fell to be treated as a sale by the taxpayer direct to company C in return for money paid to company B, thereby excising company B from this affair until the very end. This formulation must be treated with caution, since if company B is ignored, the result is nonsensical in that the taxpayers end up holding shares in company B, the very existence of which, it seems, should be ignored. The analysis in *Barclays Mercantile Business Finance* was that the composite transaction approach is used to ascertain the true parties (the taxpayer and company C) and to ascertain the true dealing in a transaction which was a non-exempt disposal to C and so not a tax exempt disposal to B.[143] In *Furniss v Dawson* Lord Bridge took a wider approach:[144]

> When one moves from a single transaction to a series of interdependent transactions designed to produce a given result, it is, in my opinion, perfectly legitimate to draw a distinction between the substance and the form of the composite transaction without in any way suggesting that any of the single transactions which make up the whole are other than genuine ...

The importance of this approach is, first, that it enables one to explain the existence of company B and, secondly, that it is much wider and more flexible than the simple—almost mechanistic—excision approach of Lord Brightman. The consequences of Lord Bridge's approach would be extremely wide. Even the US tax system, which Lord Bridge mentions, although not with unqualified enthusiasm, and which accepts the doctrine that the court must tax by reference to substance rather than form, finds it extremely hard to determine when the legal form of a transaction is to prevail.[145] Today it is likely that Lord Bridge's substance over form approach would be rejected since it is unnecessary.

---

[142] [1984] AC 474, 527; [1984] STC 153, 166g; 55 TC 324, 401.

[143] *Barclays Mercantile Business Finance v Mawson* [2004] UKHL 51 at para 35.

[144] [1984] AC 474, 517; [1984] STC 153, 158; 55 TC 324, 392.

[145] For a general account of US doctrine, see Bittker, *Federal Taxation of Income Estates and Gifts*, op cit, esp ch 4. For an example of scepticism, see Rice, 51 *Michigan L Rev* 1021. See also Millett [1986] BTR 327; and Tiley [1987] BTR 180, 220; Tiley [1988] BTR 63, 108. For examinations of the UK cases from a US perspective, see Popkin [1991] BTR 283; and Brown, 15 *Hastings Intel & Comparative L Rev* 169.

Furniss v Dawson was unsatisfactory in that the House had deliberately refrained from explaining the juridical basis for what they were doing. Thus it was unclear whether this new approach was meant to override the *Westminster* doctrine. On one view, which the Revenue proceeded quite properly to argue, the court had created a judicial anti-avoidance doctrine which was to be applied by the courts either on the analogy of one other of the American models, such as substance over form, business purpose, step transaction or the very different American doctrine of the sham transaction, or on the analogy of EU law as some external and overriding doctrine to be applied in all circumstances. The American model did not survive *Craven v White*[146] (see below). The EU-like approach was demolished by the House of Lords in *MacNiven v Westmoreland Investments Ltd.*[147] The idea that tax law was different from other parts of the legal system was demolished in *Barclays Mercantile Business Finance Ltd.*[148] The initial uncertainty as to what the courts were doing explained why the new approach was rejected in Ireland,[149] Canada[150] and Australia.[151]

The later history and current state of the composite transaction doctrine has been told in past editions and articles.[152] It will now be considered more briefly:

(1)   In determining whether there is a composite transaction the court asks whether, at the time of the first transaction, it was 'practically certain' that the second would follow.

In *Craven v White* (and joined appeals *IRC v Bowater Property Developments Ltd* and *Baylis v Gregory*)[153] the House of Lords had to consider the status of *Furniss v Dawson* and its application to three sets of facts. The House was in determined mood and anxious to limit the uncertain effects of *Furniss v Dawson* (above); this their Lordships did by limiting the earlier case in spectacular style. In *IRC v Bowater Property Developments Ltd* the court was dealing with a development land tax (DLT) fragmentation scheme. A sister company to the taxpayer company was contemplating a sale to X. The sale did not materialise and the land was sold to the taxpayer for 97.5% of its market value. Subsequently, in order to take advantage of the rule that allowed each disponer, for DLT purposes, to claim an exemption on the first slice of realised development value (at that time £50,000), the taxpayer transferred the land in question to five companies in the same group. This transfer had corporation tax consequences for the taxpayer company. A year later X reopened negotiations, and 19 months after the disposal by the taxpayer to the five companies, contracts were exchanged between the five companies and X. This deal was for a different price and on different terms from the original deal. Could this be treated as a single disposal by the taxpayer company to X, thus giving the companies only one exemption rather than five? A unanimous House of Lords said 'No'.

---

[146] [1989] AC 398; [1988] STC 476; 62 TC 1. See Ashton [1988] BTR 482; Mansfield [1989] BTR 5; and Tiley [1989] BTR 20.

[147] [2001] UKHL 6; [2001] STC 237; 73 TC 1.

[148] [2004] UKHL 51; [2005] STC 1.

[149] *McGrath v McDermott* [1988] IR 258.

[150] *Stubart Investments Ltd v The Queen* [1984] CTC 294; 84 DTC 6305.

[151] *John v FCT* (1989) 166 CLR 417, 435; see Harris [1998] BTR 124, 127.

[152] Eg [2004] BTR 297.

[153] *Craven and White; IRC v Bowater Property Developments Ltd; Baylis v Gregory* [1989] AC 398.

In *Baylis v Gregory* the taxpayer was contemplating the sale of his company to Y. He went through a *Furniss v Dawson* operation and transferred the shares in his company to an Isle of Man company in exchange for shares in that company. However, Y, unlike Wood Bastow in *Furniss v Dawson*, did not complete the sale. A year or so later a new and independent purchaser, Z, appeared, and after a further eight months, the sale to Z went through. Since the taxpayer had an intention to use the same provision as that which the taxpayers were trying to use in a *Furniss v Dawson* scheme, did it follow that the eventual sale to Z was by the taxpayer rather than by the Isle of Man company? A unanimous House of Lords said 'No' and the taxpayer got his deferral.

In *Craven v White* the taxpayer owned all the shares in company, Q, and was advised that it should seek either a merger or a sale. As a first step the taxpayer carried through a *Furniss v Dawson* style share for share exchange with an Isle of Man company. At that time there was the prospect of either a merger with company C or a sale to company O. If the merger had gone through there would have been a deferral of liability under the reorganisation provisions in any case. If, however, the sale to O took place, the facts were close to *Furniss v Dawson*. At the time of the share exchange (11 July) the prospects for the sale to O did not look promising, but on the same day O asked for a further meeting. Following further negotiations, including one 'stormy meeting', the sale to O finally went through on 9 August of the same year. The Commissioners rejected the taxpayer's evidence that its sole intention in carrying through the exchange was to merge with C, and said that the primary objective was the sale to O and that the taxpayer was keeping its options open. This time the House of Lords held—but by a bare majority—that the taxpayer was not to be taxed as if it had sold its shares direct to O; the entity making the disposal to O was the Isle of Man Company.

Having quickly and decisively rejected the view that *Furniss v Dawson* should be taken as the beginning of the development of a general anti-tax avoidance jurisprudence,[154] the House of Lords considered the degree of certainty that had to exist before the steps could be said, to use Lord Brightman's word, to be 'preordained'. Lord Keith said that steps could be said to be preordained if, and only if, at the time the first step was entered into the taxpayer was in a position, for all practical purposes, to secure that the second step was also entered into. Lord Jauncey was tempted by a formulation in terms of whether there was no real likelihood that the second step would not go through, but felt that this might be too rigid; the temptation to be a parliamentary draftsman was resisted. Lord Oliver's full formulation was:[155]

> (1) That the series of transactions was, at the time when the intermediate transaction was entered into, preordained in order to produce a given result; (2) that that transaction had no other purpose than tax mitigation; (3) that there was at that time no practical likelihood that the pre planned events would not take place in the order ordained, so that the intermediate transaction was not even contemplated practically as having an independent life; and (4) that the preordained events did in fact take place. In these circumstances the court can be justified in linking the beginning with the end so as to make a single composite whole to which the fiscal results of the single composite whole are to be applied.

---

[154] Among many matters which troubled the House, as they had troubled the Court of Appeal, was what the legal status of the first transaction would be while one waited to see what might ensue, and, in particular, the status of any assessments to tax which might have been made on the basis of that first transaction (as might have occurred in the *Bowater* case).

[155] [1989] AC 398 at 514.

The two dissentients in *Craven v White* were Lord Templeman and Lord Goff.[156] Lord Goff considered that the matter could not be dealt with on the practical certainty test. While the interruption in *Bowater* and the unformed plan in *Baylis v Gregory* obviously dictated the conclusion in those cases, *Craven v White* was different since the sale to O was a primary purpose of the share exchange. Lord Templeman felt that the three majority speeches went too far in narrowing *Furniss v Dawson* and would revive a surprised tax avoidance industry. He said that *Craven v White* was indistinguishable from *Furniss v Dawson*.[157] He protested that the House had not laboured in *Furniss v Dawson* to bring forth a mouse, and that the limitations placed upon that case by the majority were based neither on principle nor on the speeches in that case.

Cases since *Craven v White* have reiterated the test there laid down.[158] In 2004 the House of Lords put a gloss on *Craven v White* to prevent planners being too clever. The court will look at the commercial reality of the transaction and not ignore the composite effect of transactions simply because the parties had deliberately included a commercially irrelevant contingency, creating an acceptable risk that the scheme might not work as planned. This was *IRC v Scottish Provident Institution* in 2004, a case in which the House does not give the legislation the close purposive analysis required by *Barclays Mercantile Business Finance*—decided by the same panel on the same day as *Scottish Provident*.[159] In *Scottish Provident*, the company was trying to take advantage of an apparent gap in the transitional rules when the loan relationship rules came into force in 1996. In the simplified form as set out in the House of Lords, it bought a right, not an obligation, to buy five-year gilts at 90% of their par value—in return for a premium; it sold a right, not an obligation, to buy five-year gilts at 70% of their par value. The company's idea was that the premium would not be taxable because it was a mutual company and the deal would be carried out before the new rules came into force in 1996, while the related (but netted out) loss of £20m would be allowable because it was timed so as to fall under the new rules. The House pointed out that the scheme could just as well have fixed it at £80 and achieved the same tax saving by reducing the Citibank strike price to £60. It would all have come out in the wash. Thus the contingency upon which SPI relied for saying that there was no composite transaction was a part of that composite transaction, chosen not for any commercial reason but solely to enable SPI to claim that there was no composite transaction. It is true that it created a real commercial risk, but the odds were favourable enough to make it a risk which the parties were willing to accept in the interests of the scheme. To give effect to that contingency would take everyone back to the world of artificial tax schemes, now equipped with anti-*Ramsay* devices. In *Scottish Provident* the House found itself able to conclude that the Special Commissioners had committed an error of law by concluding that there was a realistic possibility of the options not being exercised simultaneously, which meant, *without more*,[160] that the scheme could not be regarded as a single composite transaction.

---

[156] See also Lord Cooke in *IRC v McGuckian* describing *Craven v White* as a 'difficult case': [1997] STC 908, 920g; 69 TC 1, 85.

[157] However, his test is very close to that of Lord Oliver.

[158] For example, *Fitzwilliam v IRC* [1993] STC 502; 67 TC 614 (HL); and *Hatton v IRC* [1992] STC 140; 67 TC 759, both dealing with *IHT*; and *Shepherd v Lyntress* [1989] STC 617; 62 TC 495.

[159] [2004] UKHL 52; [2005] STC 15 reversing [2003] STC 1035, possible because of the concessions made. see Gammie in *Comparative Perpectives on Revenue Law* (CUP, 2008), 25 at 36.

[160] Emphasis added.

(2)   Where the composite transaction is commercial in nature the end result must reflect
      the commercial reality.

Lord Templeman delivered the unanimous opinion of the House of Lords in *Ensign Tankers (Leasing) Ltd v Stokes*: the correct approach is to look at the commercial reality of the
situation.[161] What may matter just as much is the emphasis placed by Lord Templeman on
the obligation of the courts to ensure that the taxpayer does not pay too much tax, not just
too little. Neither the taxpayer nor the Crown should be deprived of the fiscal consequences
of the taxpayer's activities properly analysed. In the *Ensign* case, the question was whether
the taxpayer was entitled to capital allowances for expenditure incurred on the production
of a film. The taxpayer company, E, which, as may be surmised from its full name, had little
to do with the world of films, formed a limited partnership, V, with some other companies
to provide finance for a film, called 'Escape to Victory', to star Michael Caine and featuring
such soccer legends as Bobby Moore and Pele. V put up 25% of the estimated cost of the
film ($3.25m out of $13m), the balance being provided by a non-recourse loan made to
the general partner by the film company, L, a part of the Lorimar group with whom the
partnership had no other connection. The partners, including E, had no personal liability.
The film company was also to be responsible (on similar terms) for any cost overrun. The
receipts from the film would be divided 25% to the limited partnership and 75% to the film
company until the loan was paid off, and then to paying off the loan to cover the costs of
the overrun of costs ($1m) and any interest on such loans.
    What V, and therefore E, hoped to achieve was that in return for putting up less than
25% of the cost,[162] they would be able to receive capital allowances on the total cost of
production; this was because the rate of corporation tax was then 50% and the rate of the
relevant allowances 100% of the expenditure. The Crown's attack was no less extreme; this
was not a trading transaction, and therefore E was not entitled to any allowance at all, not
even the expenditure of $3.25m which had been incurred. The House of Lords held that
this was a trading transaction; V, and therefore E, were entitled to capital allowance on the
expenditure actually incurred. However, the expenditure incurred was $3.25m, not $14m.
This conclusion involved a close analysis of the facts to determine their true legal effect. The
scheme would not be allowed to have the apparently magical effect of creating expenditure
for tax purposes of $14m while incurring real expenditure of only $3.25m. The expenditure
of the remaining $10.75m was really incurred by L.[163]
    There is a Privy Council case from New Zealand on their GAAR and its application to a
scheme involving non-recourse film finance. Unfortunately the case, *Peterson v CIR*,[164] is
unsatisfactory. First, the Privy Council were split 3:2, and one is left wondering how a different constituted panel would have decided. Secondly, many will find the minority view
very cogent.[165] Thirdly, the majority stress the very unsatisfactory way in which the Revenue
authorities had handled the appeal process and the way in which the matters for decisions

---

[161] *Ensign Tankers (Leasing) Ltd v Stokes* [1992] 1 AC 655, 671; [1992] STC 226, 236; 64 TC 617, 736; see
Shrubsall [1992] BTR 279.
[162] After taking account of the cost overrun which was also financed by non-recourse loan.
[163] On present Revenue treatment of 'security' arrangements in relation to films, see Statement of Practice SP
1/98, paras 66–68, continuing pre-*McGuckian* practice.
[164] [2005] UKPC 5; [2005] STC 448.
[165] *Ibid* para 91.

had been defined.[166] Fourthly, the majority go out of their way to suggest a way in which the Revenue might have won.[167]

(3)   The result of the application of the composite transaction doctrine must be intellectually sustainable; the court's job is to identify the composite transaction; it may not alter the character of the transaction or pick bits out of it (*Fitzwilliam v IRC*).[168] The details are set out below at §45.7.4.

(4)   The essence of the new approach is to give the statutory provision a purposive construction in order to determine the nature of the transaction to which it is intended to apply and then to decide whether the actual transaction (which might involve considering the overall effect of a number of elements intended to operate together) answers to the statutory description.

The courts do not have to put their reasoning into the straitjacket of first construing the statute in the abstract and then looking at the facts. It might be more convenient to analyse the facts and then ask whether they satisfy the requirements of the statute. But however one approaches the matter, the question is always whether the relevant provision of statute, upon its true construction, applies to the facts as found.[169] The composite transaction doctrine is thus to be seen as a rule of statutory application as much as interpretation.

(5)   The correct characterisation of a composite transaction is a question of law, although Lord Brightman suggested otherwise in *Furniss v Dawson*. The views of Lord Keith in *Fitzwilliam v IRC*[170] are to be preferred.

(6)   The composite transaction doctrine, as formulated in *Furniss v Dawson*, applies where steps are inserted which have no business purpose other than the avoidance of tax.

It is not, however, necessary that the attempt to save tax would have succeeded.[171] It is not clear whether this concentration on avoidance is helpful or even correct any more; all commercial transactions should be viewed the same way, whether they are avoidance transactions or not.[172]

(7)   Where a particular step has been inserted in a composite transaction, the composite transaction doctrine will not apply if the taxpayer can show that there is a commercial purpose, however slight, behind the inserted step.

(8)   The composite transaction approach is not confined to income tax or CGT; whether it applies to another tax depends on the nature of that tax.

---

[166] *Ibid* paras 21–28.
[167] *Ibid* paras 48–53.
[168] *Fitzwilliam v IRC* [1993] STC 502, 515; 67 TC 614, 731 (HL); see also *Renaud v IRC* [1999] STC (SCD) Sp Com.
[169] *Barclays Mercantile Business Finance v Mawson* [2004] UKHL 51 at [32].
[170] [1993] STC 502, 515; 67 TC 614, 731 (HL).
[171] *IRC v McGuckian* [1997] STC 907, 914; 69 TC 1, 77, per Lord Browne Wilkinson.
[172] Thus in *Barclays*, Park J did not regard it as an avoidance transaction but still applied the doctrine, [2002] EWHC Ch 1421; [2002] STC 1068, at para 38.

So far the cases have involved CGT, income tax (or their corporate equivalent) and stamp duties. The doctrine has even made a surprise appearance in landlord and tenant law.[173] It has been held that IHT is affected despite having its own anti-avoidance provision in the associated operations rule.[174] The doctrine has not been applied to VAT, perhaps because VAT is a European tax on individual supplies which cannot be looked through.[175] The ECJ jurisprudence on VAT and avoidance may prove to be more favourable to the Revenue authorities thanks to the EU doctrine of abuse of rights.[176] However, that doctrine is not a general anti-avoidance doctrine.[177] As stated by the court in *Halifax*, although Community (now Union) law must not be used for abusive ends, it must also value the principle of certainty.[178] Where the taxable person chooses one of two transactions, the Sixth (VAT) Directive does not require him to choose the one which involves paying the highest amount of VAT. If the doctrine is to apply, it must be on the basis that there are sufficient objective factors. It is hard to resist the conclusion that this approach can be made to look very like the approach of the House of Lords in the *Barclays Mercantile Business Finance* decision.

The new approach is ideally designed to counter stamp duty avoidance schemes because it requires a broad view of the transaction which is being carried out by the instrument. This approach was adopted by the Privy Council in *Carreras Group Ltd v Stamp Comr*[179] and by the Hong Kong Final Court of Appeal in *Collector of Stamp Revenue v Arrowtown Assets Ltd*.[180] The Special Commissioners have pointed out that this is simply a matter of determining the correct nature of the instrument and that the composite transaction doctrine is not needed for this purpose.[181] Now that the doctrine is one of characterisation of the facts, all taxes are potentially open to its application. In *Arrowtown*, a company had issued shares which were regarded as being shares for Hong Kong company law purposes and carried the valuable right to appoint a director. Otherwise the shares carried only deferred rights, there was no right to a winding up and a right to a dividend only if the issuing company made profits greater than the Gross National Product of the United States. The court held that these shares were not 'issued share capital' for the purposes of the Hong Kong stamp duty legislation, which exempted from stamp duty transactions between companies which had a 90% shareholding relationship. The shares were issued solely to create an artificial relationship between companies in order to obtain stamp duty relief. The relief was not given.

In *Carreras Group Ltd v Stamp Comr*,[182] the Jamaican stamp duty legislation granted an exemption for shares transferred as part of a reorganisation of share capital. On 27 April,

---

[173] *Gisborne v Burton* [1988] 3 All ER 760 (CA); see comment by Martin [1988] *NLJ* 792.

[174] *Fitzwilliam v IRC* [1993] STC 502; 67 TC 614 (HL).

[175] *Customs and Excise Commrs v Faith Construction Ltd* [1989] STC 539, upholding [1988] STC 35; for a note on the 1988 decision, see Sinfield [1988] BTR 200.

[176] On abuse of rights and European tax law, see Schön in *Comparative Perpectives on Revenue Law* (CUP, 2008) ch 4. See also de la Feria and Vogenauer, *Prohibition of Abuse of Law: A New General Principle of EU Law?* (Hart, 2011).

[177] See AG Maduro in the related cases of *Halifax* (Case C255/02), *BUPA* (Case C419/02) and *University of Huddersfield* (Case C223/03), reproduced in [2006] STC 919; and comments by Doumas and Engelen [2006] BTR 429 and by TL [2006] BTR 399, 407–08.

[178] [2006] STC 919 at para 72.

[179] [2004] UKPC 16; [2004] STC 1377, approved by HL in *Barclays Mercantile Business Finance v Mawson* [2004] UKHL 51 at para 38.

[180] [2003] HKCFA 46; (2004) 6 ITLR 45.

[181] *Campbell v IRC* [2004] STC (SCD) 396 at para 76.

[182] [2004] UKPC 16; [2004] STC 1377.

shares were exchanged for debentures which were to be redeemed on 7 May (actually redeemed 11 May). The Privy Council treated the exchange and the redemption as one transaction and so held to be not within the exemption. Lord Hoffmann dealt with one question of uncertainty as follows:[183]

> Counsel argued that if the representative of Carrerras had handed the share certificates over the desk in exchange for the debenture and the representative of Caribbean had then handed it back in exchange for a cheque, it would be hard to say that the relevant transaction should not be characterised as an exchange of shares for money. But what if the debenture had been redeemed a year later? Why should a fortnight be insufficient to separate the exchange from the redemption? One answer is that it is plain from the terms of the debenture and the timetable that the redemption was not merely contemplated (the redemption of any debenture may be said to be contemplated) but intended by the parties as an integral part of the transaction, separated from the exchange by as short a time as was thought to be decent in the circumstances.

(9)   Both the taxpayer and the Revenue may invoke the composite transaction approach.

If the doctrine is truly a matter of applying the tax legislation to the facts before the court then there is no logical reason why the taxpayer should not seek to characterise the facts in issue as one composite transaction.[184] The obstacle is the decision of the Court of Appeal in *Whittles v Uniholdings Ltd (No 3)*,[185] where the Court rejected an invitation to treat the two parts of a foreign currency arrangement as one. The decision of the Court of Appeal should no longer be treated as binding on this point.

(10) Where the taxpayer can bring itself clearly within (the purpose of) a specific relieving
      provision of the tax legislation, the court will not withhold that relief.

This issue is at the heart of the distinction between tax avoidance and tax mitigation; the *Ramsay* approach did not apply to tax mitigation. However, it is also central to the purposive construction approach as worked out in *Barclays Mercantile Business Finance*. Following precedents in other countries which have had to wrestle with general anti-avoidance provisions, it may be argued that the courts should not allow the use of the *Ramsay* principle if the taxpayer has simply carried out a straightforward transaction falling exactly within the purpose and ambit of a provision of the tax legislation.[186] In *Shepherd v Lyntress Ltd*, Vinelott J rejected a 'frontal assault on the ability of a group to hive down losses into a subsidiary and to sell the subsidiary to another group willing to purchase it so that it can set its own gains against the losses'.[187] The problem is how to mark this off from the use of the share-for-share exchange rule in *Furniss v Dawson* itself. Presumably, what marks *Furniss v Dawson* off from this scenario is the fact that the share exchange was followed immediately

---

[183] [2004] UKPC 16; [2004] STC 1377, at para 15.
[184] There are early but conflicting *dicta* in *Pattison v Marine Midland Ltd* allowing the taxpayer to invoke the argument against the Crown's effort to 'invent an artificial accounting scheme which serves no purpose and is designed solely to create a liability to tax': [1983] STC 269, 276 (CA). In *Ewart v Taylor* [1983] STC 721, Vinelott J gave the taxpayer 'only very limited chances of success'. See also Vinelott J in *Bird v IRC* [1985] STC 584, 647.
[185] [1996] STC 914; 68 TC 528, 594.
[186] As was stated by Walton J in *Reed v Nova Securities Ltd* [1982] STC 724 at first instance.
[187] [1989] STC 617, 650; 62 TC 543.

by the sale. The inclusion of the words 'the purpose of' in brackets in the italic heading above, would make the test more restrictive by contemplating the need for a person to show that he comes within the purpose and spirit of the relief. This is envisaged in the TLRC formulation of the protected transaction, and it may not be correct as current UK case law since *Barclays Mercantile Business Finance*.

5.6.5 *Avoidance Other than in Composite Transactions; Traditional Judicial Functions*

The composite transaction approach is only one of the techniques used by the courts to control avoidance; it does not supersede the application of other, and usually more traditional, methods of applying tax law. An avoidance transaction which escapes the composite transaction doctrine may still fail, as happened in one judicial view in *IRC v McGuckian* (below). Lord Hoffmann had put the general point clearly in a non-tax case, when he said:

> [I]f the question is whether a given transaction is such as to attract a statutory benefit … or burden, such as income tax, I do not think it promotes clarity of thought to use terms like stratagem or device. The question is simply whether upon its true construction the statute applies to the transaction. Tax avoidance schemes are perhaps the best example. They either work … or they do not work. If they do not work, the reason is simply that, upon the true construction of the statute, the transaction which was designed to avoid the charge to tax actually comes within it. It is not that the statute has a penumbral spirit which strikes down devices or stratagems designed to avoid its terms or exploit its loopholes. There is no need for such spooky jurisprudence.[188]

What *Barclays Mercantile Business Finance* does is to blend the composite transaction approach into the general rules. There is, however, one House of Lords case requiring mention. In *IRC v McGuckian*,[189] the facts of the case were relatively simple. The taxpayer (M) wanted to avoid exposure to wealth tax and so implemented a scheme to reduce the value of shares in an Irish company (B) which he owned with his wife. The scheme involved (a) the payment of large sums by way of dividend by B, (b) the establishment of a non-resident trust of which M and his wife would be beneficiaries, although only his wife was an income beneficiary, and (c) the sale by the trust of the rights to the dividends—the sale was to a company resident in the UK (MA). If the scheme succeeded, it would not only avoid wealth tax but also extract the profits from the company in tax-free form as far as M was concerned. Although all five speeches in the House of Lords concur in the result, there are in fact two strands of thought. The speeches of Lord Browne-Wilkinson and Lord Clyde are highly analytical and straightforward applications of the composite transaction doctrine; those of Lord Steyn and Lord Cooke are more wide-ranging; Lord Lloyd agreed with all of them and gave no reasons of his own. *McGuckian* is mentioned in *Barclays Mercantile Business Finance* only for the citation of Lord Steyn's approach, which was the same as that of the House in *Barclays Mercantile Business Finance*. In *McGuckian* the inspector made the assessment two weeks before the six-year deadline,[190] not under TA 1988 section 730

---

[188] *Norglen Ltd v Reeds Rains Prudential Ltd* [1997] 3 WLR 1177, 1186.
[189] [1997] STC 908.
[190] On subsequent litigation on whether the inspector had a duty to make an assessment within the time allowed rather than seeking leave to make it outside, see *Re McGuckian* [1999] STC 578.

(a bond washing rule) but under section 739, a provision dealing with transfers of assets abroad by virtue of which M had power to enjoy the income of a non-resident (the trust). M's counsel argued that the assessment was wrong in law, because what M could enjoy from the trust was not income but capital. The House held that the effect of applying the composite transaction doctrine was that the trust was treated as receiving not capital but income, ie not the proceeds of sale of the right to the dividend but the dividend itself. The only reason for the assignment of the right of the dividend was to gain a tax advantage. It was then necessary to apply the tax legislation by disregarding the assignment and applying section 739 to the real transaction.

However, both Lord Steyn and Lord Cooke would have held the payment to the trust for the right to the dividend to be income not capital, without reference to the *Ramsay* principle at all.[191] Thus the cases are part of a wider formulation in which the courts will develop a purposive approach to questions of interpretation. This is precisely what they did in *Barclays Mercantile Business Finance*. The scope of the actual decision in *McGuckian* may be narrow, and certainly does not justify a general view that a sum received in return for a right to income is necessarily income.[192] One view of the case is that it was one where a taxpayer, entitled to a dividend which has been declared, sells the right to that dividend to a third party for a sum which is funded by the very dividend payment itself.[193]

5.6.6 *The Cases Since* Barclays Mercantile Business Finance

HMRC has had a quite a run of success in challenging tax avoidance in the courts since *Barclays Mercantile Business Finance*. Victories include *Macdonald v Dextra Accessories*[194] on deductions (below at §22.4.3.1) and the CGT case of *West v Trennery* (below at §40.2.2).[195] They may also have been surprised by their success in *Scottish Provident*.[196]

In *Prudential v Revenue & Customs Commissioners*,[197] Morritt C dismissed the taxpayer's appeal from the Special Commissioners. The principal question was whether a 'front end' payment was a 'qualifying' payment for the purpose of the foreign exchange rules then in force (FA 1994); if it were, it would be deductible, so giving rise to the advantage sought by the taxpayer company. Morritt C held that a payment could be a qualifying payment only if made 'to secure the making of the contract'; here the payment was made not by way of inducement to enter into the contract, but in fulfilment of it (para 54) and no amount of mislabelling could alter the facts (para 55). The result, and Morritt C's reasons, were affirmed by the Court of Appeal. Readers are also directed to the com-

---

[191] This implicit repudiation of the decision in *IRC v Paget* (1938) 21 TC 667 is in accordance with a decision of the Australian High Court (*FCT v Myer Emporium Ltd* (1987) 18 ATR 693), a case not cited in *McGuckian* but undoubtedly well known to Lord Cooke. On *Myer*, see Wainemeyer (1994) 19 *Melbourne U L Rev* 977. *Paget* was the reason for the introduction of what was TA 1988, s 730; if Lords Steyn and Cooke are right, s 730 was redundant. Once again, Lord Lloyd agreed with all the reasoned speeches so we may take it that this proposition had the backing of a majority of the House of Lords.

[192] *IRC v John Lewis Properties plc* [2002] EWCA Civ 1869; [2003] STC 117, see Macdonald [2003] BTR 203.

[193] *Campbell v IRC* [2004] STC (SCD) 396, para 74, referring to Lord Hoffmann in *Westmoreland*, [2001] STC 237, at paras 51–57, esp paras 54 and 55, and by Lord Millett in *Arrowtown*, (2004) 6 ITLR 454 at para 147.

[194] [2005] STC 1111.

[195] [2005] STC 214.

[196] [2005] STC 15.

[197] [2008] STC 2820, [2008] EWHC 1839 (Ch), aff'd [2009] EWCA Civ 622.

ments of Lord Hoffmann in the Hong Kong case of *CIR v HIT Finance Ltd.*[198] In the first part of the case the court held that scheme would succeed, as it had in *Westmoreland* and *Barclays Mercantile Business Finance*. However, the general anti-avoidance provision[199] was a different matter. Lord Hoffmann concluded that the borrowing and repayment had been introduced into the transaction for the sole or dominant purpose of avoiding tax. There was little evidence to suppose there was some other purpose (para 20).

The same is true of *Astall v Revenue & Customs Commissioners*, where the Court of Appeal dismissed the taxpayer's appeal.[200] Mary Arden LJ (at para 42) could see no reason to hold that the new approach to statutory interpretation applied only if there was a composite transaction consisting of several elements destined to lead to a particular result. It could also apply where, as here, there was a single multi-faceted transaction which on its face operated in a particular way but which when examined against the facts of the case did not operate as a transaction to which the statute was intended to apply. The Revenue were also successful in *Revenue & Customs Commissioners v Limitgood; Revenue & Customs Commissioners v Prizedome.*[201]

The Supreme Court decision in *Tower MCashback LLP 1 and another v Revenue & Customs Commissioners* was an important win for the Revenue.[202] At issue was a software development financing scheme involving the sale of software licensing rights to four newly-created limited liability partnerships (LLPs). The LLPs obtained the funds required to pay the consideration under the software licensing agreements from investor members of the LLPs. The investors contributed 25% from their own funds and obtained the remaining 75% from bank borrowing, on non-recourse, uncommercial terms. The LLPs claimed the full amount of the consideration paid under the software licensing agreements as first year capital allowances. The Supreme Court unanimously found for the Revenue, and disallowed 75% of the claimed allowances. The Court held that entitlement to capital allowances requires there to have been real expenditure for the real purpose of acquiring plant or machinery for use in a trade. On the facts, money passed around in a loop did not so qualify. The Court emphasised that in the context of a complex preordained transaction, the court's task is to test the facts, realistically viewed, against the statutory test, purposively construed—adopting Ribeiro PJ's formulation of the *modern Ramsay* approach in *Arrowtown,* which had been cited with approval in *Barclays Mercantile Business Finance* (at para 36). Lord Walker, writing the lead judgment, also defended the Court's somewhat surprising reliance on *Ensign Tankers,* in apparent preference to *Barclays Mercantile Business Finance,* stating (at para 80):

> [I]t is to be expected that commentators will complain that this Court has abandoned the clarity of *BMBF* and returned to the uncertainty of *Ensign*. I would disagree. Both are decisions of the House of Lords and both are good law. The composite transactions in this case, like that in *Ensign* (and unlike that in *BMBF*) did not, on a realistic appraisal of the facts, meet the test laid down by the CAA, which requires real expenditure for the real purpose of acquiring plant for use in a trade. Any uncertainty that there may be will arise from the unremitting ingenuity of tax consultants and investment bankers determined to test the limits of the capital allowances legislation.

---

[198] (2007) 10 HKCFAR 717.
[199] Inland Revenue Ordinance Cap 112, s 61A.
[200] [2010] STC 137, [2009] EWCA Civ 1010.
[201] [2009] STC 980, [2009] EWCA Civ 177.
[202] [2011] UKSC 19, [2011] STC 1143.

Two further examples of HMRC successes are *Chappell v Revenue and Customs Comrs*,[203] involving a manufactured overseas dividend scheme, and *Blumenthal v Revenue and Customs Comrs*,[204] involving a qualifying corporate bonds scheme. Both cases were wins on the modern approach to *Ramsay*—purposive construction of the statute combined with a realistic view of the facts. *Schofield v Revenue and Customs Comrs*[205] is another *Ramsay* win for HMRC. The case concerned a CGT avoidance scheme using options in an attempt to create an allowable loss to wipe out a pre-existing gain combined with a matching but non-taxable gain (as the taxpayer was then non-resident). This case is very much a composite transaction, particles in a gas chamber type-case, in the vein of *WT Ramsay* itself and *Scottish Provident*. In *William Ferguson v HMRC*,[206] the First-tier Tribunal followed Lewison J's summary of the present state of play on *Ramsay* in *Berry v HMRC*[207] to defeat a highly artificial scheme attempting to exploit tax relief on gifts to charity.

Another very significant HMRC win came in the joined cases of *UBS AG* and *DB Group Services (UK)*.[208] The Supreme Court reversed the Court of Appeal and applied the *Ramsay* approach to defeat two banker bonus schemes designed to exploit the 'restricted securities' rules (see below §17.3.1). Lord Reed (the other judges agreeing) began with some opening remarks about 'Houdini' attempts by taxpayers to escape tax and the amount of intellectual effort devoted to tax avoidance and then cited *Barclays Mercantile Business Finance* for the proposition that 'the modern approach to statutory construction is to have regard to the purpose of a particular provision and interpret its language, so far as possible, in the way which best gives effect to that purpose' (at para 61). He then proceeded to review many of the authorities on *Ramsay* discussed in this chapter, from which he extracted two key factors in applying the modern approach to tax legislation. First, that tax is generally (but not always) imposed by reference to economic activities or transactions which exist 'in the real world', quoting Lord Wilberforce in *WT Ramsay*. Second, and more controversially, if the legislation at issue is operating in the real world, and a tax avoidance scheme has elements which have been inserted without any business or commercial purpose but are intended to have the effect of removing the transaction from the scope of the charge, '… it is quite likely that a purposive interpretation will result in such steps being disregarded for fiscal purposes' (at para 65). This language is very reminiscent of the no-business purpose rule in *Furniss v Dawson*. Lord Reed then acknowledged elements without commercial purpose should not always be disregarded, as some legislative provisions 'confer relief from taxation even where the transaction in question forms part of a wider arrangement undertaken solely for the purpose of obtaining the relief', citing *MacNiven v Westmoreland Investments Ltd* and *Barclays Mercantile Business Finance* as examples.

After citing Ribeiro PJ's now famous formulation of the *Ramsay* approach from *Arrowtown*, Lord Reed then turned from purposive interpretation to considering what it meant to view facts 'realistically' (at para 68):

> The point is that the facts must be analysed in the light of the statutory provision being applied. If a fact is of no relevance to the application of the statute, then it can be disregarded for that

[203] [2013] UKFTT 98 (TC).
[204] [2012] UKFTT 497 (TC).
[205] [2012] EWCA Civ 927.
[206] [2014] UKFTT 433 (TC).
[207] [2011] UKUT 81 TCC.
[208] *UBS AG v R&C Comrs; Deutsche Bank Group v R&C Comrs* [2016] UKSC 13, analysed in [2016] BTR 3.

purpose. If, as in *Ramsay*, the relevant fact is the overall economic outcome of a series of commercially linked transactions, then that is the fact upon which it is necessary to focus. If, on the other hand, the legislation requires the court to focus on a specific transaction, as in *MacNiven* and *Barclays Mercantile*, then other transactions, although related, are unlikely to have any bearing on its application

Other high-profile wins for HMRC in cases involving marketed tax avoidance schemes have been decided on more conventional legal grounds (ie without recourse to *Ramsay*), and particularly on the basis that the taxpayer was not carrying on a trade with a reasonable prospect of profit and/or did not incur deductible trading expenses. Such cases include the *Eclipse Film Partners (35) LLP* case (discussed below at §19.3),[209] *Samarkand Film Partnership No. 3, Proteus Film Partnership and three partners v HMRC*,[210] *Brain Disorders Research Limited Partnership v HMRC*,[211] *Patrick Degorce v HMRC*[212] and *Acornwood LLP and others v HMRC*,[213] which is another in the line of Icebreaker promoter cases. In *Acornwood*, five Icebreaker LLPs acted as lead case for about 50 Icebreaker LLPs involving approximately 1,000 individual taxpayers. The First-tier Tribunal accepted HMRC's view that the fees allegedly paid for the exploitation of IP rights were not wholly & exclusively incurred for trading purposes and that the tax reliefs would otherwise be denied by specific anti-avoidance rules in any event. The First-tier Tribunal decided that it was not necessary to invoke the *Ramsay* principle, but opined in obiter that had it been so necessary, the Tribunal would have defeated the scheme on *Ramsay* grounds. As Doran notes, the approach taken by the First-tier Tribunal to the 'reality' of the use of the largely borrowed funds in *Acornwood* appears similar to that adopted by the Supreme Court in *Tower MCashback*.[214]

Taxpayers have had some successes, however. In the next two cases the Revenue failed because the taxpayer took advantage of gaps between different sets of rules. *Revenue & Customs Commissioners v Bank of Ireland Britain Holdings Ltd*[215] involved an interest repo scheme and TA 1988, section 730A. Section 730A was one of a number of provisions attacking schemes under which taxpayers turn taxable income into a capital sum; the legislation turns it back into taxable income. Here, however, the scheme did not turn income into capital but arranged matters so that the income accrued to a non-resident company outside the charge to corporation tax (para 41). Counsel did not claim that there was any fiscal or economic merit in the result for which they contended; they simply submitted that the relevant legislation admitted of only one construction, and if the result was not to the Revenue's liking then the Revenue had only themselves to blame for procuring the enactment of such complex deeming provisions without giving enough thought to the consequences. The Court of Appeal agreed.

Another taxpayer success was *Revenue & Customs Commissioners v D'Arcy*,[216] which concerned the accrued income scheme.[217] Under a scheme the taxpayer (DA) had made a

---

[209] [2015] UKFTT 325 (TC).
[210] [2015] UKUT 211. At time of writing the case was under appeal to the CA.
[211] [2015] UKFTT 325.
[212] [2015] UKUT 447 TCC.
[213] [2014] UKFTT 416 (TC). At time of writing the case was under appeal to the UT.
[214] Doran, *Tax Journal* (23 May 2014).
[215] [2008] STC 253, [2007] EWHC 941 (Ch); [2008] STC 398, [2008] EWCA Civ 58.
[216] [2008] STC 1329, [2007] EWHC 163 (Ch).
[217] TA 1988 s 710, now ITA 2007, Pt 12 (ss 615 *et seq*).

sale and repurchase of gilts—a repo transaction. Henderson J dismissed the Crown's appeal from the Special Commissioner. The taxpayer had taken advantage of an unintended gap left by the interaction between two different sets of statutory provisions—TA 1988, section 710 and section 737A—which allowed DA to claim a deduction. In Henderson J's view, what the Revenue were really complaining about was that the accrued income scheme and the manufactured payment scheme were not one coherent set of rules; the accrued income scheme did not give rise to a charge which counterbalanced DA's deduction under section 737A. This did not entitle Henderson J to construe section 710 differently to fill the gap.

In a third case, *Mayes v Revenue & Customs Commissioners*,[218] the Revenue failed more dramatically. The case involved a marketed tax scheme called SHIPS 2, which sought to take advantage of the complex and highly artificial regime governing the taxation of life assurance bonds in order to manufacture a tax loss. In essence, this regime is a perfect example of tax legislation not operating 'in the real world'. Proudman J held that HMRC had completely failed to establish the purpose for which they argued (see eg para 25). The Court of Appeal agreed with Proudman J, and leave to appeal the decision to the Supreme Court was denied. Mummery LJ described the scheme as commercially 'pointless', but found for the taxpayer, stating (at para 64): 'The *Ramsay* principle does not allow legal events to be deprived of their legal or fiscal effects simply because they are inserted for a tax saving purpose or can be described as "unreal" or "artificial".' Toulson LJ concurred, albeit reluctantly, noting (at para 100) that 'it instinctively seems wrong, because it bears no relation to commercial reality and results in a windfall which Parliament cannot have foreseen or intended'. It appears that the 'unreal' and 'artificial' nature of the statutory provisions at issue effectively deprived the judges of any opportunity to undertake a *BMBF* or *Tower MCashback* purposive analysis. Even if the judges had the benefit of Lord Reed's analysis in *UBS AG and DB Group Services (UK)*, most likely the result would not have been any different. The *Mayes* case is discussed in the Aaronson Committee's report on a GAAR for the UK, with Graham Aaronson QC concluding: 'SHIPS 2 shows the inadequacy of the existing means of combating highly artificial tax avoidance schemes. It, and other schemes like it, provide the answer to the question "does the UK need a GAAR?". The answer is that it does.'[219]

5.6.7 Conclusions

The period beginning in 1979 saw sharp variations in judicial attitudes towards tax avoidance, particularly in the House of Lords. The period began with two decisions upholding avoidance schemes and adopting a strict construction: *IRC v Plummer*[220] and *Vestey v IRC*.[221] There followed a more radical era, beginning with *WT Ramsay v IRC* in 1981 and culminating in *Furniss v Dawson* in 1984. That more radical approach was restricted by the 1988 decision in *Craven v White*, but restriction is not abolition and did not prevent the House of Lords from overruling *IRC v Plummer* as being inconsistent with the new approach in *Moodie v IRC*.[222] After that, the narrowing of the possibilities for the Revenue

[218] [2008] STC 1329, [2007] EWHC 163 (Ch), aff'd [2011] EWCA Civ 407, [2011] STC 1269.
[219] Aaronson Report, *op cit*, para 3.23.
[220] [1979] STC 793; 54 TC 1.
[221] [1980] STC 10; 54 TC 503.
[222] [1993] STC 188; 65 TC 610 (HL).

in *Fitzwilliam v IRC*[223] was followed by their reopening in *McGuckian*. Today, since *Mac-Niven* and *Barclays Mercantile Business Finance*, all is a matter of statutory construction, so that the basic principle is clear. However, while the basis may be clear, this simply opens the door to the real issue, which is how the statutes should be interpreted; this is not easy, as Canadian discussions show all too well.[224] Following, *UBS AG* and *DB Group Services (UK)*, the key question will be whether the legislation operates 'in the real world'; if so, there will be considerable scope for judges to interpret the statute in a way that justifies disregarding non-commercial steps in tax schemes. This no doubt means that tax planners will need to be more creative in ensuring some commercial reason, even a limited one, underlies all the elements. Those representing the taxpayer in court will also be unwise to concede a step has no commercial purpose. The matter is well summarised in the old newspaper headline, 'Less chaos, more uncertainty'. It is no longer necessary, as was done at this point in earlier editions of this book, to try to make sense of the case law using the distinction between tax avoidance and tax mitigation.[225] It is now necessary, however, to consider whether the GAAR will be an improvement on the case law. The simplification of the basis of the case law removes many of the difficulties but still leaves open the question whether the addition of a GAAR without a statutory clearance procedure will be better than the pre-GAAR system. What is clear is that, even though a GAAR has been introduced, the players (government and taxpayers alike) are still at the mercy of the courts. In the meantime we await with interest the first application of the GAAR.

Two strands need to be added to the GAAR debate. The first is to recognise that having a GAAR, and especially an apparently narrowly targeted one, does not mean that it can replace the plethora of targeted and mini anti-avoidance rules. In 2009 the IFS Tax Law Review Committee examined recently enacted legislation and identified 195 provisions or groups of provisions, of which 35 were targeted anti-avoidance rules (TAARs).[226] Replacing these TAARs with a GAAR would not necessarily help, since some were very carefully drafted. The Committee identified a further 30 or so provisions which could have been dealt with by a GAAR. However, this still leaves 120 or so provisions or sets of provisions where a GAAR would not achieve what the actual provision achieved. The second strand is that current thinking is no longer so keen on having a rulings procedure. The Aaronson Committee report is an example, and the enacted GAAR has no such procedure. An interesting comment on this came from Mr Dave Hartnett before the House of Lords Select Committee in 2006:

> I think there is a very significant issue that arises there: how sensible would it be to offer pre-transaction clearances for what were very clearly tax avoidance arrangements? Again, how sensible is it to offer arrangements like that which then enable planners to refine their product again and again and again, as we have seen with some of our existing clearance measures, until they have got something that they think works?[227]

It is easy to criticise the courts for caution. However, one might say that the judges may be wise to proceed cautiously and not just reach a conclusion in favour of the Revenue out of a

---

[223] [1993] STC 502; 67 TC 614 (HL).
[224] See the debate started by Arnold (2006) 54 *Canadian Tax Journal* 167 and continued at 674 *et seq*.
[225] See above at §5.1; and especially Lord Nolan in *IRC v Willoughby* [1997] STC 995, 1003–04.
[226] Bowler, *Countering Tax Avoidance in the UK: Which Way Forward?*, TLRC Discussion Paper No. 7 (2009).
[227] Mr Hartnett (Q 283), quoted in Report on Finance Bill 2006, para 62.

perceived need to prevent avoidance. One reason for this is that a decision sought by HMRC may have unpredictable consequences; the result may be turned round so that while this scheme fails, a reverse scheme, not before the court, will then be set up.[228] In other cases it may be that the taxpayer is arguing for a point of view which challenges the prevailing orthodoxy and which, while good for that person or scheme, will cause substantial difficulties for others if it succeeds.[229] These points mean that tax cases fall into that category of legal dispute known as polycentric disputes. Fuller famously argued that such disputes were unsuitable for adjudication.[230] King has argued—correctly, of course—that Fuller is wrong on this point, and that tax disputes show this.[231]

---

[228] Eg the famous 'reverse *Harrison v Nairn Williamson*' scheme first described by Park [1977] BTR 110, 113.
[229] Eg Lightman J in *Melville v IRC* [2000] STC 1271, para 22; Revenue appeal dismissed [2001] STC 1271 CA.
[230] (1978–79) 92 *Harvard Law Review* 353.
[231] [2008] *Public Law* 101; he discusses the tax cases at 111 *et seq.*

PART II

Income Tax

6

Historical Introduction[1]

6.1   The Introduction of Income Tax

6.2   Later 19th Century

6.3   Modern Times

6.1   The Introduction of Income Tax

It is customary to date the introduction of income tax to Pitt's need to finance the war against France. So in 1798 Pitt took an existing tax base using property and expenditure, the so-called 'assessed taxes', and multiplied the levels at which the sums were to be paid; although the act is known as the Triple Assessment, there were actually varying rates of increase.[2] In doing so Pitt took the figures already returned for 1797 as the basis.[3] The apparent novelty was that the legislation also provided exemption for those on incomes below £60, abatement for those with incomes below £200 and, for the remaining taxpayers, a rule limiting their total liability to not more than 10% of total income. In effect the tax bill was the lower of the tax on income as computed or the Triple Assessment. Income thus became important as a relief from tax as much as an alternative basis for tax. There was a parallel Voluntary Contribution for those who did not want to pay the tax. In 1799 the Triple Assessment was replaced by Pitt's Income Tax proper.[4] Again, Pitt's machinery provisions were developed from the 1797 Act which had been copied from the Land Tax Act. The tax was based on a general return by the taxpayer of income for the year; a return could be challenged by the Surveyors, who could ask for details under 19 different heads. The tax was charged at 10s in the £ on all incomes over £200, with, in effect, a graduated rate between £60 and £100 and exemption below £60. Among permissible deductions were allowances for children, interest and life assurance. The tax was not a success and was repealed when peace came.[5]

Before looking to see how Pitt's first use of income developed, one must note that the idea of a direct tax on income was not new. Pitt did not take his inspiration from the economists but possibly from France, where a tax of 10% (the *dixieme*) had been imposed on

---

[1] The history of the modern UK tax system is told in two magisterial volumes by Martin Daunton: *Trusting Leviathan 1799–1914* (CUP, 2001) and *Just Taxes 1914–1979* (CUP, 2002), with immense scholarly apparatus. A more limited and more technical history of the period since 1799 is to be found in *Simons Direct Tax Service: Division A1.4*. For a short account but from a longer view, see Sabine, *A Short History of Taxation* (Butterworths, 1980).

[2] *Simons* A1.403.

[3] 38 Geo III, c 16.

[4] 39 Geo III, c 13.

[5] Those wanting a broader political background will find one in Hague, *William Pitt the Younger* (Harper Collins, 2004); on the Triple Assessment itself, see *ibid*, pp 417–18.

income from land, salaries, securities and businesses[6]—sources we have known until very recently as Schedules A, E, C, F and D of the UK income tax. Scholars have also shown that there are precedents for taxes on income in England in the Middle Ages.[7] Apart from the assessed taxes (£2m in 1792), the main other sources of government revenue were the land tax (probably also £2m) and the customs and excise duties (£17m in 1792). The start of the assessed taxes may be seen as going back to 1696 and the introduction of the window tax. The idea was that tax should be charged on luxury items, so sparing the poor, and such assessed taxes came to be charged on carriages, horses, female servants, dogs, gamekeepers and many other items.

Income tax returned in 1803 following the breakdown of the Peace of Amiens. The 1803 statute for which Addington's name is preserved in history contained a number of features different from the 1799 Act.[8] First, instead of a mere general statement of income agreed with the Surveyor, taxpayers now had to return their income under different headings called Schedules. These had, however, been used already where Surveyors decided to challenge the general return. Secondly, there was the system of deduction at source;[9] this was so effective that although the rate of income tax in 1803 was one half of that of 1798, the yield was the same. The effectiveness of the scheme of deduction is also because it was already in place, going back not just to the land tax of 1688 but to many earlier provisions.[10] The 1803 Act was followed by further Acts in 1805 and 1806. Significantly, the 1806 Act was called the Property and Income Tax Act, showing that contemporaries did not necessarily regard it as an income tax in the way one would today.[11] The 1806 Act was repealed in 1816, but the version revived by Peel in 1842 is the 1806 Act with a few amendments.[12] The 1806 version of the income tax was well described in a later Inland Revenue report:[13]

> As the former duty was imposed on a general account of income from all sources, the present duty is imposed on each source by itself, in the hands of the first possessor, at the same time permitting its diffusion through every natural channel in its course to the hands of the ultimate proprietor. Instead of the landlord and various claimants upon him in succession it looks to the occupier only.[14] Instead of the creditor it looks to the fund from which the debt is answered.[15] In place of a complicated account collected from various sources from which the income of an individual is derived it applies to the source itself to answer for its increase. By these means its objective is attained with more facility and celerity, and with less intricacy and disclosure, diminishing the occasion of evasion by means of exaction; thus the charge is gradually diffused from the first possessor to the ultimate proprietor, the private transactions of life are protected from the public eye and the Revenue is more effectually guarded.

---

[6] Sabine, *op cit*, 118.

[7] Eg, tax on the annual value of land 1404 Rot Parl III, p 522, cited by Jurkowski, Smith and Crook, *Lay Taxes in England and Wales 1188–1688* (Public Record Handbook No 31). See also the case for 1166 argued by Phillips [1964] BTR 225, 227.

[8] 43 Geo III ch 122, virtually re-enacted as 45 Geo 3, c 49 (1805) and 46 Geo 3, c 65 (1806). On the genesis of the legislation from 1799 to 1806, see Farnsworth Addington, *Author of the Modern Income Tax* (Stevens, 1951).

[9] 43 Geo III, c 122, s 102.

[10] See Soos, *The Origins of Taxation at Source in England* (IBFD, 1997).

[11] See Tiley, *Studies in the History of Tax Law* (Hart Publishing, 2004) 81 *et seq*.

[12] *Simons* A1.410.

[13] 28th Report C 474 (1885) p 30.

[14] This refers to the old Sch A, above §1.6.2.

[15] This refers to TA 1988 ss 348 and 349, now greatly reduced; see below §27.5.

Behind the elegant rhetoric are some important points. The tax was for most people a flat rate tax, and for most people there was therefore no need for a general return of income and so no need for government intrusion into their private financial affairs. The tax was not only easy to administer but gained general public support for that reason. This administrative success made it harder for later governments to introduce changes such as graduation and differentiation. It also explains: (a) why there was no provision in TA 1988 imposing tax on a person's income—instead TA 1988, section 1 levied tax on the various heads of income listed in the rest of section 1(1); and (b) why provisions allow assessment to tax on the persons 'receiving or entitled' to the income (as in TA 1988, section 21(1), Schedule A and section 59(1) Schedule D, now scattered throughout ITTOIA 2005).

6.2   Later 19th Century

Income tax has remained in force since 1842. Although today income tax is, as ITA 2007, section 4 tells us, an annual tax, and so is levied one year a time, it was not always so—the 1842 Act established the tax for five years, and that of 1853 for seven years. The prevailing debates in the 19th century revolved around progression (then called graduation), and the taxation of earned versus unearned income (or differentiation).[16]

Some of the ideas put forward in the cause of differentiation were dismissed as quite unworkable. An 1862 Committee considered Hubbard's idea that one could get the right balance between taxing income from property as differentiated from income from labour, by capitalising property and profits and charging duty on a rate of interest in relation to the nature of the capital. The tax could be adjusted according to capital value of the property or income, the tenure and the age of its owner. The idea was savaged by the 1862 Committee:

> [We] have arrived at the conclusion that the plan proposed by their chairman does not afford a basis for a practicable and equitable readjustment of the income tax and they feel so strongly the dangers and ill consequences to be apprehended from an attempt to unsettle the present basis of the tax without a clear perception of the mode in which it is to be reconstructed that they are not prepared to offer any suggestion for its amendment.[17]

An equally clear and elegantly insulting rejection had come 10 years earlier by the Board of Inland Revenue commenting on a 1851 proposal. Having said that it was perhaps not within its province to make any observations on the evidence, nonetheless the Board might be permitted to observe that '[the idea] cannot be ... reduced by its proposers to any intelligible detail so as to enable a judgment to be formed of the advantages or the possibility of carrying it into practical effect.'[18] This general attitude on the part of the Inland Revenue of hostility to change—especially to anything which would unsettle the way in which the tax was administered and perceived—is a recurring theme of the time, as Daunton's works so clearly show.[19] The 1862 Committee's reasons are similar to those which were, in 1976, regarded as making a wealth tax unworkable in the UK.

[16] Daunton, *Trusting Leviathan*, ch 6.
[17] Cited 28th Annual Report C 4474, p 75.
[18] First Report, p 33.
[19] Eg, in *Trusting Leviathan*, above n 1, at 5.

6.3 Modern Times

The history of the different parts of the tax system, such as CGT, corporation tax, capital allowances and IHT, is woven into the text which follows. However, some features may be mentioned now. First, at one time those wanting fundamental reform of the tax system would ask for a Royal Commission.[20] Today such a commission would take too long and almost certainly outlive the life of the Government which set it up. Incoming governments, such as those of 1979 and 1997, often have their own agendas worked out before coming into office and see no need to delay. We therefore have committees or consultations with working parties, and green papers. The last UK Royal Commission on tax reported in 1955, and there was also a Royal Commission in 1920. Before then there had been a somewhat complacent Departmental Committee Report in 1905, followed by a Select Committee of the House of Commons set up in 1906 to look into the twin problems of graduation and differentiation, and the report of the 1936 Committee on Codification. Canada had the famous Carter Report, the 1966 report of a Royal Commission. There have also been major official reports in Australia, New Zealand and other countries. Most recently we have the IFS-led Mirrlees Review in the UK, which built upon the Meade Report of 1978. Although the IFS is a private foundation fiercely proud of its independence, its works have acquired a strong reputation for the depth and sharpness of their analysis.

Secondly, there is the tax structure—rates of tax and the tax base. For just over a hundred years from its introduction the income tax was a flat rate tax. This did not mean that the actual burden was flat, since there were exemptions and abatements for people by reference to their income, and it was possible to have different rates of tax for the different schedules. However, it meant that for Victorian England, the rich did not pay as much as they might. This led to much debate over graduation, ie a progressive income tax, and differentiation, ie having different rates of tax for earned and unearned income. Lloyd George finally succeeded in introducing these features into the UK tax system in his famous budgets of 1910 and 1911.[21] Graduation was achieved by introducing a separate new tax on higher incomes—the super tax later to be replaced by surtax. The super tax followed the recommendations of the 1906 Departmental Committee, as did the relief for earned incomes (earned income relief) which enabled the tax burden on earned income to be reduced. This meant that the 'standard' rate of income tax was actually the rate charged on investment income, so that the effective rate charged on earned incomes would usually be appreciably lower. Moreover, the effective burden on lower incomes earned or investment was often reduced through abatements and reliefs for people with low total incomes.

This structure remained until 1973, when surtax was merged with income tax to make one tax; at the same time the basic rate of tax replaced the standard rate. This was more than a matter of words, since the basic rate was that charged on earned income, differentiation being achieved by the levying of an additional rate of tax once investment income had passed a certain point. The mechanisms by which a lower effective rate of tax had been levied on lower incomes had been phased out, and so for most of the years since 1973 the basic rate of tax has been the starting rate of tax for most taxpayers. Lower rates (under

---

[20] Sandford (ed), *Successful Tax Reform* (Fiscal Publications, 1993).
[21] Daunton, *Trusting Leviathan*, above n 1, ch 11.

various names) have been charged from 1991 to 2008—and also from 1977 to 1979. Higher tax rates were a major feature of post-war Britain. In 1979 the top tax rate on earned income was 83%, which with an additional rate for investment income gave a marginal rate of 98%. The 83% was reduced to 60% in 1979; the additional rate, which had been gently reduced in scope since 1979, was abolished in 1984 and the higher rate reduced in 1988 to 40%. By that time the basic rate had been reduced to 25% so that the UK then had just two rates of income tax. Complexity has followed since then.

Why did people put up with such high rates for so long? One answer is the stoicism of the British people. However, a more likely explanation lies in the gaps in the tax base. In the early 1960s, reliefs were available for almost all interest payments—not only mortgage interest (without restrictions) but also any other interest, even an overdraft at a bank (but not for the interest element in hire purchase). There was also a flat rate relief for life assurance premiums (removed 1984). The income tax on the imputed income of owner-occupiers was abolished in 1963. There was no CGT (until a short-term one in 1962 and the present long-term one in 1965), so that converting income into capital gain by schemes such as dividend stripping (stopped in 1960) or selling gilts (bond washing—stopped in 1985) was profitable. The attitude of the courts towards avoidance schemes is probably best described as bewilderment rather than benevolence; and the tradition of literal interpretation, combined with a slow legislative system which took each clause of a Finance Bill on the floor of the House of Commons, meant that catching up was slow. Even so, tax avoidance had not reached the aggressive pitch prevalent in the 1970s, when high rates of tax combined with inflation made many taxpayers feel the system was unfair. Reductions in rates have been paid for in two ways.[22] One is the increase in the burden of other taxes (especially VAT) and the other is the reduction in the value of other reliefs.[23] The 1988 cut in income tax was combined with an increase in the rate of CGT (so as to align it with income tax).

---

[22] For the story down to 1997, see Tiley [1998] BTR 317.

[23] Reliefs which have been abolished include mortgage interest. The married couple's allowance which was introduced in 1990 has also been abolished except for those born before 6 April 1935.

7

Income Tax: Basic Concepts

7.1   Introduction

Under the doctrine that income tax is an annual tax, each year's Finance Act begins by charging income tax for that year. In most countries one would then be referred to a piece of primary legislation setting out in comprehensive, if exhausting, terms what income is taxed. Because of the weakness of the Tax Law Rewrite process, this is not possible in the UK. Instead we have an avowedly non-exhaustive list, which first sets out the heads of charge spread over three separate Income Tax Acts and then acknowledges that there are other heads of charge to be found outside those three Acts. ITA 2007, section 1(1) directs that income is taxable if it falls within one or other of the heads of charge listed. ITA 2007, Part 2, Chapter 1 (sections 3–5) deals with the charge to income tax; Chapter 2 (sections 6–21) deals with the different rates of tax and the different types of income to which those rates apply; this material is covered in the present chapter of this book. ITA 2007, Chapter 3 (sections 22–32) deals with the way in which the person's liability to income tax is determined; this material is covered in chapters ten to twelve of this book. Chapter eight below examines rules, to be found in different parts of the tax legislation, on how the family and its members are taxed. Chapter nine deals with NICs and their relationship to the tax system, along with some aspects of the social security system, and gives an outline of the tax credit system.

Income tax is charged at the rates in force for the particular tax year on the income attributed by the tax system to that year. The tax system therefore sets the rates of tax (which may vary according to the type of income), defines what is meant by income, and defines when and to whom it arises and, because of international rules, where it arises. This chapter looks at the definition of 'income' in relation to the various Acts.

7.1.1 What is 'Income'?[1]

For most foreign tax systems, other than those based on the UK model, a book such as this would now launch into a discussion, possibly deep but certainly theoretical, of the nature of income. We would invoke theories such as those discussed at §1.6 above. The UK tax system's concept of income is quite different; it raises many deep and interesting issues, but ducks this particular problem of the nature of income itself. The UK view of income is based on two simple ideas, to which the Rewrite adds a third. The first is that, as we have just seen, the receipt must fall within one of the heads of charge in the non-exhaustive statutory list. If the receipt does not fall within one of these heads, it is not taxable income—even if some economist or other theoretician says it is. Because of this approach, the UK system is described as a 'schedular' system—the term 'schedule' meaning here a type of list. The second idea, which is simpler to state than to apply, is that the receipt must not be capital. The third idea, which is much clearer to see as a result of the rewritten legislation in 2003, 2005 and 2007, is that the receipt should not be taken out of that list by a statutory exemption.

In deciding which items to put into its list of taxable transactions, the UK has traditionally adopted the pragmatic approach of taxing those things with which the tax administration can deal. Given this pragmatic approach in the legislation, it is unsurprising that UK courts have not been adventurous in recognising new types of taxable income. While the words of Lord Steyn and Lord Cooke in *IRC v McGuckian*[2] in 1997 could have been the start of a wider view, subsequent history and successive editions of this book have suggested that theirs were going to be lone voices. Australian courts seem to have already taken a similar course, with wider views being reined back in the light of the judicial experience.[3]

American courts, with no schedular system to restrain them but, rather, a *global* view of income,[4] have been vigorous in finding many different types of income. So gambling winnings, which are not taxable as income in the UK, are taxable in the US. In *Zarin v Commissioner*,[5] the

---

[1] See Daunton in Tiley (ed), *Studies in the History of Tax Law* (Hart Publishing, 2004) chs 1 and 4; and Thuronyi, *Comparative Tax Law* (Kluwer, 2003) chs 2 and 7.

[2] [1997] STC 907, 69 TC 1. In separate speeches the two Lords adopted a broad, purposive interpretation of the relevant tax provisions (relying on the *Ramsay* approach to construction) in holding that a tax avoidance scheme aimed at converting income into capital was ineffective.

[3] *FCT v Myer Emporium Ltd* (1987) 18 ATR 693, a case not cited in *McGuckian* but undoubtedly well known to Lord Cooke. On *Myer*, see Waincmyer (1994) 19 *Melbourne U L Rev* 997 and, 12 years later, Justice Young, *The Second Annual Melbourne Tax Lecture*, 2006. Later judicial discussions at Full Federal Court level include *Stone v FCT* (2003) 53 ATR 214; 198 ALR 541; *FCT v Cooling* (1990) 21 ATR 13; and *FCT v Montgomery* (1999) 42 ATR 475; see the discussion by Coleman and McKerchar, paper given at the *2nd Tax Law History Conference* (Cambridge, July 2004).

[4] See discussion by Bittker and Lokken, *Federal Taxation of Income, Estates and Gifts* (Warren, Gorman & Lamont, 1989) §5.1; on lessons to be learned from US tax policy, see articles in (1998) 184 *Fiscal Studies*.

[5] 916 F 2d 110 (1990). This case generated much literature, among the best of which are Shaviro 45 *Tax L Rev* 215; Newman 50 *Tax Notes* 667; and Gunn 50 *Tax Notes* 893. See also Dodge, Johnson and Shaviro 45 *Tax L Rev* 677, 697, 707 respectively.

taxpayer had borrowed $3.4m of gambling chips, lost them all at the tables and then agreed to settle with the gambling house for $500,000. The court's decision that the taxpayer was not liable to tax on the $2.9m debt forgiven is very controversial. Such intellectual vigour with which the US courts find income is matched by the vigour with which they explore related issues in deductions—as the debates on the concept of 'human capital' and the possible deduction of educational expenses show.[6] These discussions are equally relevant to debates on general tax policy in the UK, but have no part to play in the court process in our country.

In recent years the distinction between some global and schedular systems has become less sharp as some global systems have adopted schedular features, such as the different rates of tax for different types of income or restrictions on relief for losses so that they cannot be set off against all types of income.[7] Thus, the Nordic countries have moved from a global system based on progressive rates to a schedular system with a progressive tax applying to most types of income, but with investment income and capital gains taxed at low uniform rates with restrictions on deductibility of passive losses.[8]

7.1.2 Who Pays Income Tax?

ITA 2007 makes it clear that income tax is paid by individuals at certain rates. However, basic rate tax is not confined to individuals, which indicates, correctly, that income tax is also paid by persons or entities other than individuals. The principal other 'persons' are trusts and estates in administration, and ITA 2007 has separate provisions for these other persons (sections 11 and 14).

Partnerships are now taxed on a transparent basis, with each partner responsible for his own tax affairs. A partner who is an individual will pay income tax. Companies resident in the UK usually pay corporation tax rather than income tax; however, non-resident companies may occasionally find themselves liable to income tax (section 5). Income tax also applies to shadowy entities called 'bodies of persons'; these are defined in ITA 2007, section 989, but the definition rarely applies.[9]

7.1.3 Rate Structure for Income Tax

7.1.3.1 Individuals

The income tax structure in ITA 2007, Part 2, Chapter 2 contains four main rates: the basic rate (20%), the higher rate (40%), and the additional rate (45%). Savings income (other than dividends) is as above, except that there is a 0% starting rate for savings income only, with a limit of £5,000. If an individual's taxable non-savings income is above this limit then

---

[6] On human capital, see Beer [1987] BTR 392; on the US debate on human capital see, *inter alia*, Zelanak (1996) 51 *Tax L Rev* 1, discussing views of Kaplow (1994) 80 *Virginia L Rev* 1477; and response by Kaplow to Zelanak (1996) 51 *Tax L Rev* 35. The Kaplow–Zelanak debate is part of a wider debate over a consumption tax. See also Stephan (1984) 70 *Virginia L Rev* 1357. For UK work in relation to certain training costs, see Blundell, Dearden, Maghir and Sianesi (1999) 20 *Fiscal Studies* 1.

[7] See Ault *et al*, *Comparative Income Taxation*, 2nd edn (Kluwer, 2004), 167–69, 237–43.

[8] See, eg OECD Tax Policy Report No 9, *Trends and Reforms in OECD Countries* (2004) ch 1 and 92–98.

[9] The concept should therefore be repealed. See Avery Jones [1991] BTR 453.

the starting rate for savings will not apply. For 2016–17, the income tax rate structure is as follows:

Taxable Income (£)	Rate
0–32,000 (basic rate)	20%
32,001–150,000 (higher rate)	40%
Over 150,000 (additional rate)	45%

In Summer Budget 2015, the Government announced a ceiling (or 'lock') for the main rates of income tax, the standard/reduced rate of VAT and employer and employee Class 1 NICs at 2015–16 levels. Another lock to prevent the rates of class 1 NICs (for employers and employees) from being increased is contained in the National Insurance Contributions (Rate Ceilings) Act 2015.

From 6 April 2016, in a major shake-up to the taxation of savings income (and moving closer to the Mirrlees Review suggestion to tax only excess returns to capital) taxpayers have a tax-free Personal Savings Allowance on up to £1,000 of savings income (eg interest earned on bank accounts) for basic rate taxpayers and up to £500 for higher rate taxpayers. Additional rate taxpayers are not eligible for the allowance. The Summer Budget 2015 also announced a radical new regime for taxing dividends, partly to address the long-standing tax 'imbalance' in favour of conducting business through a company rather than in unincorporated form. Under the new rules, with effect from 6 April 2016, the former dividend tax credit system was abolished and replaced by a £5,000 tax-free amount of dividends for all individuals (the 'Dividend Allowance') and new dividend tax rates:

— 7.5% on dividend income within the basic rate band
— 32.5% on dividend income within the higher rate band
— 38.1% on dividend income within the additional rate band

FA 2014, section 296 and Schedule 38 provide for a new income tax rate structure for Scottish taxpayers, which is designed to take effect from 6 April 2016. The non-savings income of a Scottish taxpayer will be subject to the 'Scottish' basic, higher or additional rate, as appropriate. The applicable rates are found by taking the corresponding UK rate, less 10 percentage points, plus any rate set by the Scottish Government ('the Scottish rate'). The new rate structure is just the beginning of what promises to be much more extensive devolution of taxing powers from Westminster following the 'No' vote in the 2014 Scottish independence referendum (see also §2.1.1 above).[10]

7.1.3.2 Other 'Persons'

Trusts are not 'individuals'. So far as trustees are concerned, most trusts are taxed under one of two regimes. Under one regime the trust is taxed at the basic rate of tax (20%); neither the starting savings, nor the higher rate, or the additional rate applies. Under the other

---

[10] For commentary see Eden [2014] BTR 472 and an earlier current note on this subject by Barr [2013] BTR 262.

regime, which applies in broad terms where income is 'accumulated or discretionary' (ITA 2007, sections 479 and 480), there is a special rate of tax that is now called, confusingly, 'the trust rate'. This is 45% for most income, but 38.1% for dividend income. See further chapter twenty-nine below, where the quite separate issue of the taxation of the beneficiaries is also considered. For treatment of estates in administration and dividends/savings income accruing to them, see chapter thirty below.

7.1.3.3 The Short-lived 50% Additional Rate of Income Tax

In March 2012 the Treasury released the results of its study on the Exchequer effect of the 50% additional rate of income tax. The Treasury found 'a considerable behavioural response' following its introduction in 2010, particularly in terms of income brought forward to 2009–10 to avoid the new rate. The Treasury's best estimate is that the yield from the new 50% rate was less than £1 billion and possibly negative—well below the original £2.5 billion estimated yield. The Treasury cautioned that these conclusions were based on only one year of data and were thus applicable only to the very short term; the longer-term impact might be different, one way or the other. It was partly on the basis of these findings that the additional rate was reduced to its present 45%, beginning in the 2013–14 tax year.

7.2   The Schedular or Category System

7.2.1 The Schedules and Categories

The UK has a schedular system of income for both income tax and corporation tax. Income tax has been rewritten in the form outlined in §7.2.2 below. The legislation for corporation tax in TA 1988 has been rewritten primarily in the Corporation Tax Acts (CTAs) 2009 and 2010. A knowledge of the old form of the schedular system is needed (see §7.2.3 below) because virtually all the case law which the student will have to read is based on the old form of the legislation. We now put more flesh on the bones of the new list and then set out the traditional schedular definition of income.

7.2.2 The Modern Form

ITA 2007, section 3 lists various heads of income:

(1)   Amounts charged to tax under ITEPA 2003, Part 2—employment income (chapters thirteen to eighteen of this book);
(2)   Amounts charged to tax under ITEPA, Part 9—pension income (below, chapter eighty);
(3)   Amounts charged to tax under ITEPA, Part 10—social security income (below, chapter nine);
(4)   Amounts charged to income tax under ITTOIA 2005, Part 2—trading income (below, chapters nineteen to twenty-three): this covers both trades and professions;
(5)   Amounts charged to income tax under ITTOIA 2005, Part 3—property income (below, chapter twenty-five): this is primarily income from land, but covers not only

receipts such as rent but also certain premium payments which would otherwise be regarded as capital;

(6) Amounts charged to income tax under ITTOIA 2005, Part 4—savings and investment income (below, chapters twenty-six and twenty-seven): among the receipts covered here are dividends and other receipts from companies (including non-resident companies), interest and related receipts, gains from life policies, gains from certain transactions in deposits and gains from sales of foreign dividend coupons;

(7) Amounts charged to income tax under ITTOIA 2005, Part 5—miscellaneous income (below, chapter twenty-eight): here we find not only the old residual charge to income tax Schedule D, Case VI, but also some other items, including annual payments (which featured in the *Duke of Westminster* case, above §5.6.1), income arising under settlements treated as belonging to the settlor (below, chapter thirty-one) and beneficiary's income from an estate in administration; and

(8) Other heads, *including* ITA 2007, Part 10 (Charities), Part 12, Chapter 2 (Accrued income profits) and Part 13 (Tax Avoidance), as well as FA 2004, Part 4, Chapter 5 (Pensions) and F(No 2)A 2005 (Social security pension lump sums).

Although the explanatory notes accompanying the text are extremely good in explaining in micro terms what the Acts do—and do not—there is no list of the other occasions of charge.

7.2.2.1 Priorities

With so many heads and possible overlaps, rules are needed to determine which provision applies. The treatment begins in ITTOIA 2005, section 2, which contains an overview and list of these provisions. The first Chapter of each Part of ITTOIA 2005 and ITEPA 2003 begins with rules as to priority between this and other Parts and between Chapters of Parts. To take just the first of these, section 4 lists a few provisions in ITTOIA 2005, Part 3 and ITEPA 2003 which have priority over Part 2. However, the priority rules do not cover everything, and ITTOIA 2005, section 2(3) then says ominously that the rules in the various sections 'need to be read with other rules of law (whether in this Act or otherwise) about the scope of particular provisions or the order of priority to be given to them'. So the priority rules apply unless they do not. This represents a considerable effort at systematisation when compared with older rules in §7.2.3; it is, however, very necessary given the proliferation of the heads of charge.

7.2.2.2 Territorial Scope

Another feature of the rewritten legislation is the treatment of territorial scope. ITTOIA 2005 lists the income under the different categories in Parts 2, 3, 4 and 5, and each Part has some rules for UK source income and some for foreign income; so ITTOIA 2005, Part 3 applies to income from land in the UK (section 264) and from land outside the UK (section 265). Further rules on territorial scope appear, usually early on in each Part. There is an important provision in ITTOIA 2005 on the territorial scope of various charges.[11] This may seem elementary, but the pattern in the older law was different; finding the territorial rules

---

[11] ITTOIA 2005, Sch 1 adding now ITA 2007, ss 1015–1016, ex TA 1988, s 827A, which defined the scope, and s 833, which listed 39 provisions under ITTOIA 2005 and added nine from other Acts.

in the older statutes was anything but straightforward, and those coming from the old law to the new should be pleasantly surprised. Yet it must also be remembered that the Rewrite does not change the *substance* of the law. If income from a foreign property (old Schedule D, Case V) is treated differently from that from UK land (old Schedule A), those differences remain and have to be—and are—expressed in the new rules.

7.2.2.3 Deduction at Source

ITA 2007, Part 15 requires express mention at this point, especially for older readers. This is a major change of form. It takes a category of payments and makes them simply deductible in computing net income. This dismantles for income tax an intricate and arcane set of rules which, in effect, allowed the payer a deduction for these items, but did so in a way which was far more complex and subtle and was based on the notion of a charge on income.[12] The change removes many irrational points and traps beloved of examiners. Its abolition may be likened to the removal of a bad tooth; the relief is immense, but one can feel the gap.

7.2.3 The 'Old' Schedules

Indicating the very different relative importance of different sources of income in 1803, the first head of the old schedular system, **Schedule A** (TA 1988, section 15), taxed the annual profits or gains arising in respect of rent and similar payments from land in the UK. Rent from property outside the UK forms a second but separate aggregate and was taxed under Schedule D, Case V. **Schedule B** (section 16) was repealed in 1988.[13] This Schedule taxed the occupation of certain woodlands in the UK on a special value (a form of imputed income). **Schedule C** (section 17) was repealed in 1996 as part of the simplification of the tax treatment of interest; interest formerly within Schedule C then came within Schedule D, Case III. **Schedule D** (section 18) taxed annual profits or gains which fall into one or other of its six Cases:

— Case I, which is now ITTOIA 2005, Part 2 for income tax, taxes profits or gains arising from any trade;
— Case II, which is also in ITTOIA 2005, Part 2 for income tax, taxes the profits or gains arising from a profession or vocation;
— Case III taxes interest, annuities and other annual payments, together with discounts and those dividends from public revenue which previously fell within Schedule C; these receipts are now found in ITTOIA 2005, Parts 4 and 5 for income tax;
— Case IV, which was repealed in 1996 as far as corporation tax was concerned, taxes residents on the profits or gains arising from securities outside the UK; these are now in ITTOIA 2005 for income tax;
— Case V taxes residents on the profits or gains arising from possessions out of the UK; these are now scattered through ITTOIA 2005; and
— Case VI taxes 'any annual profits or gains not falling under any other Case or Schedule'; this is now part of ITTOIA 2005, Part 5 for income tax.

---

[12] See, eg Tiley [1981] BTR 263.
[13] The charge to tax under this Schedule was abolished with effect from 6 April 1988 subject to transitional provisions in FA 1988, s 65, Sch 6.

Schedule E (TA 1988, section 19) taxed emoluments from an office or employment; the tax was usually collected by PAYE. This Schedule had three Cases according to international factors, and the rules are now all in ITEPA 2003. **Schedule F** (section 20) taxed distributions by companies resident in the UK; the tax was due on the dividends of the year of assessment and, for most taxpayers was, in effect, levied at source. Schedule F was repealed by ITTOIA 2005 and all such income is now taxed under Part 4, Chapter 3.

Buried in these provisions are rules on the territorial scope of the income tax. Schedule D, Cases IV and V (and parts of Schedule E) charged residents on their worldwide income; the other parts of Schedule E, as well as Schedule A and D, Cases I–III and VI, charged non-residents on their income arising within the UK.

7.2.4 The UK's Schedular System

Although each category or Schedule has its own rules for computation of income, and at one time the Schedules had different dates for payment, different rates and different administrations, it remains true that the income tax is one tax. It was in this context that Lord MacNaghten uttered his famous aphorism that income tax, if he might be pardoned for saying so, was a tax on income.[14]

A schedular system like that of the UK has four features which differentiate it from a pure global system:

(1) *Income*. If an income receipt does not fall within any Part or Schedule, it is not taxable; there is no need to seek a general definition of 'income'.[15]

(2) *Rules exclusive*. Where income falls within a Part/Schedule, it falls to be computed in accordance with the rules in that Part/Schedule and no other. As Lord Radcliffe has said:[16]

Before you can assess a profit to tax you must be sure that you have properly identified its source or other description according to the correct Schedule; but once you have done that, it is obligatory that it should be charged, if at all, under that Schedule and strictly in accordance with the Rules that are there laid down for assessments under it.

It is a necessary consequence of this conception that the sources of profit in the different Schedules are mutually exclusive; it is this idea which is now enacted in the various priority rules mentioned above.

In *Fry v Salisbury House Estate Ltd*,[17] a company received rents from unfurnished offices in a building. The company also provided services for the offices, such as heating and cleaning, at an additional charge. The rents were chargeable under Schedule A, although the basis of assessment at that time was not simply the rents minus costs of maintenance which we have today but the annual value of the premises, which were revalued every five years, minus a statutory allowance for running costs—an example of imputed income. The

---

[14] *LCC v A-G* [10901] AC 26, 35; 4 TC 265, 293.
[15] *Graham v Green* [1925] 2 KB 37; 9 TC 309.
[16] *Mitchell and Edon v Ross* [1961] 3 All ER 49, 55; 40 TC 11, 61. However, see Kerridge [1980] BTR 233.
[17] [1930] AC 432; 15 TC 266. Decision reversed by FA 1940, ss 13–18.

company agreed that its profits from the ancillary services fell within Schedule D, Case I, but resisted the Revenue's argument that the company was liable to tax on the actual rent received under Schedule D, Case I rather than just on the notional imputed rent charged under Schedule A. The Revenue conceded that they would have to make an allowance in computing tax under Schedule D, Case I for the tax due under Schedule A.[18] The House of Lords found for the company. Although the company could be said to be carrying on a trade, and therefore fell within Schedule D, Case I, the Schedules were mutually exclusive and each Schedule was dominant over its own subject matter. The charge under Schedule A therefore excluded the charge on the excess rent under Schedule D, Case I.

In *HMRC v PA Holdings*,[19] the Court of Appeal held that dividends paid on restricted shares given to employees as part of a contrived scheme to avoid NICs and income tax on annual bonuses were taxable as employment income. Lord Justice Moses (Lady Justice Arden and Lord Justice Kay agreeing) overturned the conclusion of the lower tribunals that the dividends fell under both Schedule E (applying *Hochstrasser v Mayes*) and Schedule F, but that the operation of Schedule F and section 20(2) of ICTA 1988 precluded Schedule E taxation. Moses LJ instead held that the factual conclusion by the First-tier Tribunal that the income fell within Schedule E precluded any finding that the income also falls within Schedule F. He stated [at para 60]:

> Once that conclusion had been reached, there was no room whatever for any further consideration of a different Schedule. If the payments were emoluments in the hands of PA's employees, they could not be dividends or distributions in the hands of those employees. Any other conclusion offends the basic principle expressed in *Fry [v Salisbury House Estate Ltd]* that if income falls within one Schedule it cannot be taxed under another.

The CA's decision in *PA Holdings* raised concerns amongst tax professionals that dividends paid in other circumstances, particularly involving small owner-manager companies, risked being subject to employment income treatment as well. To mitigate these concerns, and following the taxpayer's decision to drop its appeal to the Supreme Court, HMRC announced it intend to limit the application of the ratio in *PA Holdings* to similarly contrived avoidance schemes. HMRC emphasised that the scheme in *PA Holdings* sought to combine dividend treatment with a corporation tax deduction, a situation that was not likely to arise with standard owner-manager remuneration arrangements.[20]

Although the Schedules were mutually exclusive, the Cases within each Schedule were not; the Revenue could choose the Case to apply. Therefore an insurance company might be taxed under Schedule D, Case I either on its profit, or on its investment income minus management expenses.[21] Such choices will not often arise, and ITTOIA 2005 has produced its own express rules on priorities, which make much of this learning redundant.

---

[18] See *Russell v Aberdeen Town and County Bank* [1888] 2 TC 321.

[19] [2011] EWCA Civ 1414.

[20] Schemes involving the use of alphabet shares, which allow different levels of dividends to be paid on different classes of ordinary shares, are at risk, though HMRC has acknowledged that it will be difficult to argue a properly-declared dividend where a corporation tax deduction is not also sought is anything other than a true dividend. See note by John Stokdyk, quoting David Heaton, on Accounting Web at http://www.accountingweb.co.uk/article/pa-holdings-drops-appeal-dividends-case/540484.

[21] *Simpson v Grange Trust Ltd* [1935] AC 422, 427; 19 TC 231, 251 (HL per Lord Wright).

(3) *Losses*. Losses arising under one Part/Schedule may not necessarily be set against a profit under another; losses attract only such relief as each set of rules allows. Some types of loss may be set off against general income of the same or preceding (but not later) year, notably losses from trades or professions within ITTOIA 2005, Part 2 (ex Schedule D, Cases I and II).[22] However, losses under ITTOIA 2005, Part 3 (ex Schedule A) and Part 5, Chapter 8 (ex Schedule D, Case VI) are given relief only by being rolled forward to be set off against the income of later years taxed under the same Part/Schedule or Case.[23] Losses under ITTOIA 2005, Part 2 that have not been used up by being set off against general income of the same and following year, may then be rolled forward indefinitely, but only against profits of that trade.[24]

(4) *Choice of Schedule*. Businesses in the financial sector often had their profits taxed under ITTOIA 2005, Part 2 (ex Schedule D, Case I). However, as with insurance companies, it was, in theory, open to the Revenue, for example, to insist on interest received being taxed under Part 4 (ex Schedule D, Case III) instead. This could have significant effects if the business was trying to use trading losses from past years or a foreign tax credit, which could be set only against income of the trade and so not against the Part 4 income. The segregation of interest income to Part 4 led to the loss or foreign tax credit not being available until a later period, or being lost completely. Today, these consequences do not apply for corporation tax, and ITTOIA 2005 has its own priority rules which supersede these now historical points. The Revenue's right to choose in relation to insurance companies was abolished by FA 2008, section 43.

7.3   The UK Concept of Income

Apart from the schedular system, which, as already seen, excludes any receipt not coming within one of the Schedules, the UK has two important principles limiting the scope of the tax: 'capital' (§7.3.1) and 'source' (§7.3.2). There is also an unresolved issue relating to beneficial entitlement (§7.3.3).

7.3.1 Capital is not Income

The original Schedules included the wide phrase 'annual profits' and contained, in Schedule D, Case VI, a residuary case to cover receipts not caught by the other Schedules and Cases. However, the courts construed that phrase in a limited way—generally, profits are income only if they possess a (rather notional) quality of recurrence[25]—and confined Case VI to profits similar to those caught by the other Schedules and Cases (see below at §28.1).

---

[22] ITA 2007, ss 64 and 72, ex TA 1988, ss 380 and 381.
[23] ITA 2007 ss 118 and 152, ex TA 1988, ss 379A and 392.
[24] ITA 2007, s 83, ex TA 1988, s 385.
[25] *Moss Empires Ltd v IRC* [1937] AC 785; 21 TC 264. This does not prevent single payments from being caught, eg the single commission paid in *Ryall v Hoare* [1923] 8 TC 521 and taxed under Sch D, Case VI, now ITTOIA 2005, Pt 5.

The courts' decision to exclude capital is entirely understandable. When income tax was first introduced in 1799, not only were various existing forms of capital already subject to other taxes, but there was also a substantial area of law, that of trusts, where a very sharp distinction between income and capital receipts had been drawn.[26] The fundamental nature of the distinction between income and capital does not mean that it is easy to apply.[27] Today, the UK income tax is supplemented by a quite separate CGT—a separation that causes people used to a single tax (eg Australians) much linguistic difficulty.

Although the legislature has occasionally intervened to tax capital receipts, eg certain premiums on leases, the proceeds of certain life assurance policies and golden handshakes, the basic distinction between income and capital is central to the system. The reason for this acceptance by the legislature is probably the high value placed by the legislature on the requirement of certainty in the sense of enforceability or practicality, even at the expense of equity—it is part of the pragmatic quality of the UK tax system. It also explains the great insistence on the system of deduction of tax at source, a system which has, at one time or another, covered almost all payments other than the profits of a trade or profession, and short interest. The legislature was, for a long time, reluctant to tax payments which could not conveniently be taxed at source.[28] As a consequence of these rules, non-taxable receipts include not only capital gains, but also gambling winnings,[29] instalments of capital and most gifts, and including the remission of a debt and loans.[30]

7.3.2 The Source

Interpretation of the Schedules is governed by the doctrine of the source. As was seen in the long quotation in §6.1, the idea of taxing income not globally but source-by-source was at the heart of the 1803 Act. This idea has bitten deeper and the courts have held that every piece of income must have a source,[31] and reports abound with references to 'fruit and tree'.[32] ITTOIA 2005 reinforces this notion by identifying the source of the particular head of income.

---

[26] See, eg, Daunton, 'What is Income?' in Tiley (ed), *Studies in the History of Tax Law*, (Oxford 2004), 3; and Tiley, 'Aspects of Schedule A' in Tiley (ed), *Studies in the History of Tax Law*, (Oxford 2004), 81. Financial markets had not yet reached a point at which to stretch the credibility of the distinction.

[27] For example, Lord Macdonald in *California Copper Syndicate Ltd v Harris* [1904] 5 TC 159, 165.

[28] See, eg RC 1920, §156; both graduation and differentiation were (rightly) regarded as inconsistent with deduction at source: Mallet, *British Budgets 1887–1913* (BiblioBazaar, 2009), 278.

[29] *Graham v Green* (1925) 9 TC 309. The gambling industry pays many taxes, but the exemption for an individual winner is a remarkable exception to the principle of taxing according to ability to pay. For treatment in some other countries, see Ault *et al*, *Comparative Income Taxation*, 2nd edn (Kluwer, 2004), 185. The present position was defended by the Royal Commission on Gambling, Cmnd 6643(1976), esp 31. On taxation of gambling more generally, see IFS Green Budget 2000, §7.3.

[30] A genuine loan is not income. It could, in theory, be treated as a receipt when received, and as a deduction when repaid, but this would be administratively burdensome and would give rise to opportunities for income averaging or splitting. Loans may be taxed if made by a close company to a participator. See also *Jacobs v IRC* (1925) 10 TC 1; *Clayton v Gothorp* [1971] 2 All ER 1311, 47 TC 168; *Esdaile v IRC* (1936) 20 TC 700; and *Stoneleigh Products Ltd v Didd* (1948) 30 TC 1. For a conceptual analysis of below-market loans, see Hadari [1995] BTR 557.

[31] Eg, *Brown v National Provident Institution* [1921] 2 AC 222, 246; 8 TC 57, 89 (per Lord Atkinson); and *Leeming v Jones* [1930] 1 KB 279, 297; 15 TC 333, 349–50 (per Lord Hanworth). See also, eg, *Stainer's Executors v Purchase* [1951] 2 All ER 1071; 32 TC 367; and *Carson v Cheyney's Executors* [1958] 3 All ER 573; 38 TC 240.

[32] For comparative treatment, see Krever (1990) 7 *Australian Tax Forum* 191.

The doctrine, however, developed some curious by-products in the form of decisions exempting certain types of income which clearly ought to have been taxed; these by-products are of course not affected by ITEPA 2003 and ITTOIA 2005. These payments escaped tax because, as income tax was an annual tax, it followed that not only must the income arise within the tax year, but the source must also exist in that tax year. Hence, it was decided that:

(1) post-cessation receipts of a trade were not taxable;
(2) where a person was taxed on a remittance basis and money was brought into this country in a year in which its source did not exist, no tax was payable; and
(3) payments made after an employment had ceased but for services rendered as an employee could not be attributed retrospectively to the years of service.[33]

All of these examples have since been reversed by statute.

7.3.3 Beneficial Entitlement?

A question discussed in other jurisdictions, but not yet in proper detail in the UK, is whether a receipt can be income if it does not 'belong' to the person receiving it. The situation arises when X receives a payment from Y and is not simply under a personal obligation to repay it but is not the owner of the property in law, or where X holds the property on trust for Y. This may be considered on a Part by Part or Schedule by Schedule basis on the question what amounts to a *receipt* of income. So in Schedule A, the landlord's obligation to keep service charge contributions separate under the Landlord and Tenant Act 1987, section 42(3)(b) prevented it from being a receipt by the landlord.[34]

However, there are deeper issues.[35] In the pensions case of *Hillsdown Holdings v IRC*,[36] Arden J, dealing with a provision imposing a special charge to tax on an employer receiving a payment from an approved pensions scheme, said that the fact that the person (the employer) receiving a payment from a pension fund held it on resulting trust for the trustees meant that the payment had not been 'received' at all and so was not caught by the relevant provision. *Hillsdown* was distinguished by the Court of Appeal in *Venables v Hardy*[37] on the basis that its case concerned different provisions. The Revenue reserved their right to argue that *Hillsdown* was wrongly decided on another occasion. These matters did not arise in the House of Lords.[38]

In the UK context matters are muddied slightly by the fact that trustees are liable to income tax as trustees. Trustees who receive trading or property income for their beneficiaries cannot generally avoid tax on the ground that they hold the income for their beneficiaries (see chapter twenty-nine). However, there may be a distinction between the trust situation, in which the trustee is entitled to the property as a matter of law but holds it for

---

[33] *Bray v Best* [1989] 1 All ER 969; [1989] STC 159 (HL).
[34] De Souza [1998] *Private Client Business* 267, 270.
[35] Discussed in the New Zealand context by Chan and Simester (2000) 6 *New Zealand J Tax L & Policy* 24–39.
[36] [1999] STC 561; 71 TC 356.
[37] [2002] EWCA Civ 1277; [2002] SC 1248.
[38] [2003] UKHL 65; [2004] STC 84.

the beneficiary, and that in which the taxpayer received property from X but X still owns it. This may perhaps be squared with the statute by saying that personal entitlement matters when one is being taxed as an individual, but not when being taxed as a trustee.

7.4 Timing

7.4.1 *Importance of Timing*

The issue of timing is important for several obvious reasons:

(1)   Income tax is charged as income of a year of assessment, ie income from 6 April 2016 to 5 April 2017 is brought into the taxpayer's self-assessment for 2016–2017, which has to be done by 31 January 2018. The taxpayer must therefore include all such income, omitting income attributable to other years, and will be liable to interest surcharge and penalties for incorrect submission.

(2)   The law may be changed so that the tax treatment will differ according to whether the payment is income of year 1 or year 2.[39]

(3)   Pension contribution relief is subject to a maximum amount which is related to the person's relevant earnings for that year.

(4)   The Revenue must generally issue any discovery assessments within six years of the end of the chargeable period to which they relate.[40]

(5)   The effective rate of tax may vary according to the time it becomes chargeable. This is because the taxpayer's marginal rate of tax may vary from one year to the next, and because UK tax law contains no general averaging provision.

(6)   In general, the value at the time the income arises is relevant for tax purposes; subsequent changes in value are usually ignored.[41]

(7)   Reliefs may be available against the income of a particular year.[42]

The issue of timing is relevant to a more subtle matter, namely, the non-correlation of the rules with regard to receipts with those for expenses. Once a profit has been earned, the Crown's right to be paid the tax does not depend on what the taxpayer chooses to do with it. In *Mersey Docks and Harbour Board v Lucas*, the harbour board was allowed to levy dock dues and to apply these first to maintaining the docks and paying interest on sums borrowed, and then to apply the surplus to a sinking fund to pay off the debt. The fact that it was obliged to treat the surplus in this way did not prevent it from being taxable profit.[43] Clearly, planning opportunities may arise, but as usual they have to be planned carefully

---

[39]   As in *Strick v Longsdon* (1953) 34 TC 528 (special contribution for 1947–48).

[40]   TMA 1970, s 34; income tax seems to have been avoided in *Heasman v Jordan* [1954] 3 All ER 101; 35 TC 518. This leads to obvious avoidance, whereby a special bonus would be declared for one year, more than six years before the declaration. As a result legislation was introduced; this became TMA 1970, s 35 (now superseded).

[41]   This is of crucial importance when dealing with payments in kind or payments in foreign currency. For authority in the latter instance, see *Payne v Deputy Federal Commr of Taxation* [1936] AC 497; [1936] 2 All ER 793; and *Greig v Ashton* [1956] 3 All ER 123; 36 TC 581.

[42]   As in *Parkside Leasing Ltd v Smith* [1985] STC 63; 58 TC 282.

[43]   (1883) 2 TC 25, see esp Lord Blackburn at 33.

in advance. In *Way v Underdown (No 2)*,[44] an insurance agent gathered in a premium, say £1,000, and subsequently paid back to the client an amount equal to his commission on the premium, say £100. It was held that since the agent was under no obligation to repay, he could not deduct the £100 in computing his taxable profits; he was therefore taxable on the commission, just as the Mersey Docks and Harbour Board had been. However, had the agent simply agreed to collect only £900 in the first place, he might well not have been taxed on the £100. One cannot be taxed on income one does not acquire; however, once income has been acquired, a deduction for paying it back will be allowed only if it is permitted by the deduction rules appropriate to the Schedule. Therefore, preventing the income from arising will avoid tax, whereas a receipt followed by a disposal may not.

7.4.2 General Timing Rules

Timing questions depend first on whether accounting principles are adopted. If they are, as in ITTOIA 2005, Parts 2 (trading income) and 3 (income from property), then those principles must be considered. Where accounting principles are not relevant, a two-stage process is adopted. The first stage is to ask whether tax law treats the income as arising when it falls due or only when it is paid. The general answer given by UK cases is that an assessment cannot generally be made until the payment has been received. The second stage asks whether the payment, once received, may be backdated or, to use the customary terminology, 'related back' and be treated as income of the period when it became due.[45] However, this backdating does not occur very often. Usually, the payment is taxable only when paid, and is then treated as income of the year of receipt, summarised in the much-abused dictum that 'receivability without receipt is nothing'.[46] This has been applied to the payment of arrears of interest, causing payments for six years to be treated as the taxable income of one year.[47] Precise rules cannot be stated owing to the dearth of authority. Statute now provides that there can be no relating back for earnings falling within ITEPA 2003; the income is taxed when received or when due for payment, whichever is the earlier.[48]

7.4.2.1 Receipt?

Various parts of the legislation insist that income must have been received before it can be taxed.[49] What amounts to receipt? Where trustees or personal representatives receive income, that receipt may be treated as receipt by the beneficiaries, as may receipt of income by an agent for a principal or by one partner for the other.[50] It has been held, however, that the mere receipt of a cheque is not a receipt of income, even if drawn on

---

[44] [1975] 2 All ER 1064; [1975] STC 425; 49 TC 648 (CA).

[45] This applies to payments falling within TA 1988, s 835; see *Whitworth Park Coal Co Ltd v IRC* [1959] 3 All ER 703; 38 TC 531. It used to apply to payments falling within Sch E, but see now below at §14.2.

[46] Rowlatt J in *Leigh v IRC* [1928] 1 KB 73, 77; 11 TC 590, 595.

[47] *Leigh v IRC, ibid* (Sch D, Case IV). Concessionary relief was available for retrospective increases in such foreign pensions (ESC A55, now withdrawn), but relief was enacted as ITEPA 2003, ss 575(2)(c), 613(3). A completely different approach is adopted for interest payments for corporation tax: see FA 1996.

[48] ITEPA 2003, s 30, ex TA 1988, s 202A.

[49] Eg, ITTOIA 2005, s 240 (post cessation receipts).

[50] *IRC v Lebus' Executors* (1946) 27 TC 136, 147.

the Bank of England.[51] Where a taxpayer directs payment to a third party, so that the taxpayer never actually receives payment, the economic control shown by the direction is still sufficient to amount to receipt.[52] The crediting of an account, which act endures to the benefit of the account-owner, will also be a receipt,[53] as will a payment made direct to a third party to discharge the taxpayer's obligations to that third party.[54] Where a payer is under a duty to deduct the recipient's tax on that income, the sum withheld is treated as having been received by the taxpayer.[55]

7.4.2.2 Remittances

Certain foreign income is taxable not because it has accrued but because—and so only when—it is remitted to the UK.

7.4.2.3 Preceding Year and Current Year (Historical Explanation)

The preceding year basis of assessment, now happily obsolete, survived until 1996–97. It may therefore be necessary to consider it in order to understand a case relating to those years. It did not apply to corporation tax. Some may see a very faint echo of the old system in the rules directing payment of tax on account in two instalments by reference to the previous year's income.[56] Similarly, one should note the crude tax credit rules (see below at §9.4), which in some cases use the previous year's income as the basis for the current year's entitlement.

Usually, the income for the year of assessment is that arising, in the sense just discussed, within the year from 6 April to 5 April next—the current year basis. Therefore income arising in, say, 1992–93 was taxed as income of 1992–93. Under the preceding year system, however, the income for 1992–93 would have been taxable as income of 1993–94. The theory was that the source was taxed on its statutory income for the year of assessment, the preceding year's income being simply the measure of that income. As Rowlatt J once put it: 'You do not tax the years by which you measure; you tax the year in which you tax and you measure by the years to which you refer.'[57]

Under the preceding year basis the income was taxed according to the rates in force in the year of assessment, and not those in the year when the income actually arose. It followed that the amount taken as income for the year of assessment might bear no relation to the income actually arising during that period; if there was a sharp drop in income from the source, the tax payable during the year might even exceed the income from that source. The system gave rise to many problems and caused many complexities in the tax legislation.[58] The biggest objection to the old system was that when it was applied to a business, the total

---

[51] *Parkside Leasing Ltd v Smith* [1985] STC 63; 58 TC 282. By contrast, a payment in respect of tax to the Revenue is treated as occurring when the cheque was received by the Revenue, provided the cheque is paid on first presentation (TMA 1970, s 70A).

[52] Lord Hansworth MR in *Dewar v IRC* [1935] 2 KB 351, 367; 19 TC 561, 577.

[53] *Dunmore v McGowan* [1978] 2 All ER 85; [1978] STC 217; discussed at [1982] BTR 23, the point there taken being approved in *Macpherson v Bond* [1985] STC 678. *Dunmore v McGowan* was followed in *Peracha v Miley* [1990] STC 512 (CA) (see below at §26.1.2), but distinguished in *Girvan v Orange Personal Communication Services Ltd* [1998] STC 567.

[54] *Cf Salter v Minister of National Revenue* (1947) 2 DTC 918.

[55] ITA 2007, s 848, ex TA 1988, s 349(1).

[56] TMA 1970, s 59A; see ch 4 above.

[57] *Fry v Burma Corp Ltd* (1930) 15 TC 113, 120, followed in *Moore v Austin* [1985] STC 673.

[58] See the 3rd edn of this book, paras 5.12 and 5.13, and Revenue Consultation Document on a Simpler System for the Self Employed, discussed by Shipwright [1992] BTR 12.

profit taxed was not the total profit made.[59] The repeal was beneficial and overdue (but not particularly well executed).

7.5 Exemptions

Certain types of payment or persons are specifically exempt from liability to income tax by legislation or concession. The legislation and concessions are gathered together in statutory form in ITEPA 2003, Part 4 in so far as they relate to ITEPA income—see further below chapter fifteen—and in ITTOIA 2005, Part 6 in so far as they relate to other types of income. ITA 2007 contains some heads of charge and deals with exemptions in the context of each charge, eg Part 12 (Accrued Income Profits and Losses) and its exemptions in Chapter 3. The following list is not exhaustive, but indicates the types of exemption made:

(1) *Welfare payments.* ITEPA 2003, Part 10, Chapters 4 and 5 exclude certain social security benefits, eg invalidity benefit and analogous payments by foreign countries to UK residents. On housing grants paid by local authorities, see section 644. Exemptions apply to adoption allowances (ITTOIA 2005, section 744) and certain pensions for disabled employees. Interest on damages payable for personal injuries and annuities (including the assignment of such annuities) payable under structured settlements of claims for such injuries are exempt under ITTOIA 2005, sections 731 and 751. Also exempt are New Deal payments to the over-50s, etc (ITTOIA 2005, section 781).

(2) *Employment-related payments.* ITEPA 2003 exempts many payments under this category, eg redundancy payments (section 309), the first £30,000 of compensation for loss of employment (section 403), long service awards, luncheon vouchers, and miners' coal. See, principally, ITEPA 2003, Part 4.

(3) *State service.* ITEPA 2003, section 297A exempts the Operational Allowance for members of the armed forces; the allowance has to be designated as such and currently applies to Iraq and Afghanistan. ITEPA 2003 exempts from income tax war widows' pensions, wounds and disability pensions, allowances, bounties and gratuities paid for additional service in the armed forces, and annuities and additional pensions to holders of gallantry awards (sections 638–641). Other state service exemptions include Foreign Service allowances for civil servants (section 299), and certain payments for Ministers and MPs (sections 291 and 294).

(4) *Savings.* The tax system grants special tax privileges to savings, including savings income falling within the tax-free Personal Savings Allowance and savings income earned in an ISA. Special rules also apply to compensation for mis-sold pensions (FA 1996, section 148, amended by FA 2004), annuities under certain policies (ITTOIA 2005, Part 8, Chapter 8, ex TA 1988, sections 580A and 580B) and certain bonds when held by non-residents (FA 1996, section 154, ITTOIA 2005, Part 8, Chapter 6).

(5) *Education and training.* Scholarship income arising from a scholarship held by a person receiving full-time instruction at a university, college, school or other educational establishment is exempt from income tax (ITTOIA 2005, section 776; see also SP 4/86,

---

[59] This was largely because of special rules governing the beginning and ending of the business or other source.

revised in 1992 on sandwich courses, the need for revision arising as a result of *Walters v Tickner* [1992] STC 343). Interest attached to certain repayments of student loans to the student attracts a special rule (ITTOIA 2005, section 787, added by FA 1999).

(6) *Exempt persons.* TA 1988, sections 505–514, partly rewritten, provide reliefs for, among others, charities (see now ITA 2007, Part 10), the British Museum and Natural History Museums, scientific research organisations, agricultural societies and the Atomic Energy Authority.

(7) *Exempt people—international.* There are exemptions for various foreign consuls and other foreign representatives (ITEPA 2003, sections 300–302 and ITTOIA 2005, section 771),[60] various payments to members of visiting forces (ITEPA 2003, section 303) and certain other international organisations (ITA 2007, section 979). There is a 2006 exemption (ITTOIA 2005, s 756A) for certain payments for victims of Nazi persecution; there is also a CGT exemption (TCGA 1992, section 268A).

(8) *Government.* There are exemptions for local authorities and health service bodies. The Crown is not liable to tax unless statute provides otherwise;[61] therefore, the private estates of the Crown are subject to tax.[62]

(9) *Major Sporting Events.* For example, various exemptions for persons, whether athletes or organisers, were provided in FA 2006, sections 65–68 in respect of the London 2012 Olympic Games.

(10) *The environment.* FA 2007 added an exemption for income from the sale of small amounts of electricity generated by a microgeneration system or from the receipt of a renewable obligation certificate (ITTOIA 2005, sections 782A–782B); it also added an exemption from CGT (see TCGA 1992, section 263ZA).

7.6 Prohibited Deductions

The legislation may provide that certain sums are not to be deductible in computing income under various heads. There are now just two such provisions. ITTOIA 2005, section 56 (ex TA 1988, section 577A) provides very succinctly that, in computing the profits of a trade, no deduction shall be made for any expenditure incurred in making a payment which amounts to the commission of a criminal offence. This is extended by ITTOIA 2005, section 867 to all other types of income under the 2005 Act. Perhaps oddly, section 56 does not apply to either ITEPA 2003 or CGT. Official examples are bribes contrary to the Prevention of Corruption Acts and payments contrary to the Prevention of Terrorism Acts.[63] These examples are much narrower than the potential ambit of the section, which seems to encompass any act amounting to the offence of aiding and abetting the commission of an offence by another. Presumably, a criminal offence means an act or omission which is an offence under

---

[60] See Morris [1991] BTR 207; and exchange of views by Adderley and Morris on a stamp duty point at [1992] BTR 122. The government must be recognised by the UK: *Caglar v Billingham* [1996] STC (SCD) 150.

[61] On royal taxation, see Pearce and Crump [1994] BTR 635; and Bartlett [1983] BTR 99.

[62] Crown Private Estates Act 1862, s 8. There is much background material in Hall, *Royal Fortune* (Bloomsbury, 1992), summarised in *The Economist*, 25 January 1992, 35.

[63] Inland Revenue Press Release, 11 June 1993; [1993] *Simon's Weekly Tax Intelligence* 957.

the criminal law of some relevant part of the UK rather than under some foreign jurisdiction. Expenditure incurred in making a payment induced by blackmail is also barred.[64] The other provision deals with business entertainment expenses under ITEPA 2003 and ITTOIA 2005, where the prohibition covers trades, property business and other income arising under ITTOIA 2005 (see below at §18.3.4.1).[65]

7.7 Classification of Income (I): Savings, Dividends, etc and Ordinary Income

7.7.1 Types of Income: What is Savings Income?

7.7.1.1 Savings Income

As seen above at §7.1.3, 'savings income' may attract a special rate of tax or be tax-free if it falls within the Personal Savings Allowance. Savings income is defined in ITA 2007, section 18 as consisting of income chargeable under ITTOIA 2005, Part 4, Chapter 2 (interest), Chapter 7 (purchased life annuities) and Chapter 8 (profits from deep gain securities), and under Part 12, Chapter 2 of ITA 2007 (accrued income profits). There is no continuing need for mention of any equivalent foreign income as this now falls within the relevant chapters. Income taxed on a remittance basis cannot be savings income for purposes of any savings rates.

7.7.1.2 Dividend Income

ITA 2007, section 19 defines dividend income as any income falling into ITTOIA 2005, Part 4, Chapters 3, 4, 5 or 6 (dividends, etc). Also included is any foreign relevant foreign distribution brought in by ITTOIA 2005, Part 5, Chapter 8, which means a payment which manages to escape Chapter 4 but would be within Chapter 3 if the company had been resident in the UK.

7.7.1.3 Specific Exclusions

Certain types of income are specifically excluded. These include: (a) any annuity other than a purchased life annuity; (b) any other annual payment that is not interest; and (c) as indicated above, any overseas income that is assessed on a remittance basis.[66] In addition, it is provided that income treated as arising on a 'chargeable event' when a withdrawal is made from a non-qualifying life assurance policy[67] is not within the definition of 'savings income'.

7.7.1.4 Policy: and Exclusion of Land

Rent from land charged under ITTOIA 2005, Part 3 is not savings income because it is mentioned in the list. In a tax system that prides itself on being friendly to savings, this is surprising. However, it may be justified either on the basis that interest relief is available where

---

[64] ITTOIA 2005, ss 56(2) and 890(3) and CTA 2009, s 1304, ex TA 1988, s 577A(1A).
[65] ITTOIA 2005, ss 47–49 and 889; CTA 2009, ss 1298–1200 (ex TA 1988, s 577).
[66] ITA 2007, ss 19–20, ex TA 1988, s 1A(2)(a).
[67] ITTOIA 2005, s 465.

loans are used to buy land, but not when they are to buy shares or bonds, or on the basis that it would be impolitic to tax earnings more heavily than rent. This still leaves the puzzle as to why the general savings rate was introduced. It dates back to 1996, the last year before the New Labour administration. It may have had little to do with helping 'small' savers and a great deal to do with reducing the sums paid back to pension funds and charities—from the then basic rate of 23% to 20%. This process was carried to its (illogical) conclusion in 1997, when the Government abolished the repayment of tax credits on dividends to these bodies while leaving them free to recover tax withheld at source on interest.

7.7.2 Rates for Taxing Savings and Dividend Income

In determining whether savings income above the Personal Savings Allowance and/or dividend income above the Dividend Allowance falls within the basic rate band, ITA 2007 provides that savings and dividend income are to be treated as the highest part of an individual's income (other than termination payments and income arising on certain chargeable events).[68] Suppose that the taxpayer has property income equivalent to any reliefs, employment income of £16,000 and interest income of £4,000 gross. His interest income will be taxed at 20%. If the employment income rises, say to the point at which higher rate liability arises, the interest income is treated as the top slice of the taxpayer's income and so liable to tax at 40%. If a taxpayer has both savings income and dividend income, ITA 2007, section 16 provides that (a) the savings income and dividend income are together treated as the highest part of the person's total income, and (b) the dividend income is treated as the higher part of that part of the person's total income.

7.7.2.1 Boundary Problems

Where a taxpayer's other income is less than the upper limit of the basic rate band, but the addition of savings income takes the taxpayer above that band, tax is charged at the lower rate on the amount of income required to bring the rate up to the upper limit of the basic rate band, and tax at the higher rate is charged on the excess.

7.8 Classification of Income (II): Earned and Investment Income

7.8.1 Importance (Historical)

The categories of earned income and investment income were abolished by ITA 2007. Much of the learning on the distinction survives for calculating relevant earnings for pension relief. Until 2007 it was important for identifying certain income of husband and wife, but ITA 2007 rewrote the rule in a new form.[69] The distinction is *not* the same as that in §7.7 above, ie between savings and other income for tax rate purposes; thus, income from land will be investment income, but is not savings income.

---

[68] ITA 2007, s 16, ex TA 1988, s 1A(5), (6), inserted by FA 1996, s 73.
[69] ITA 2007, s 836—and see interesting explanatory notes to the section.

The UK system has made greater use of the distinction in the past, as three examples show:

(1)   Until 1984, investment income was taxed more heavily than earned income.[70] From 1973 to 1984 this was achieved by a device known as the additional rate;[71] in 1983–84 this was charged on that part of an individual's total income which consisted of investment income in excess of £7,100.[72]

(2)   From 1973 to 1990, when joint taxation of spouses was the rule, a wife could elect to be taxed separately from her husband in respect of her earned income but not her investment income.

(3)   For a far longer period, also ending in 1990, the distinction was also important for the wife's earned income relief.[73]

7.8.2 Policy: Differentiation

Differentiation, ie a higher tax on investment income as opposed to earned income, was abolished in 1984. This higher rate of tax had been part of the system since 1907, when it was introduced as an alternative to a wealth tax.[74] Clearly, investment income is heavily concentrated in the upper income groups,[75] but many retired people derive a substantial percentage of their income from investments. Today, the chaotic rate structure and the refusal to allow those exempt from income tax to recover the tax credit on dividends make for a very unclear picture when one tries to discover the extent to which differentiation is part of the system. In other countries, eg Sweden, the tax system has moved in a different direction, with normal progressive rates charged on earned income and a flat rate tax on investment income.[76] Several reasons have been advanced for differentiation:[77]

(1)   The basis on which the argument for differentiation was eventually put was the precariousness of industrial incomes. This would be more obvious at a time when family settlements were still the rule and wealth was expressed in terms of income rather than capital.

---

[70]   FA 1971, s 32(1) (repealed by TA 1988, s 844, Sch 31); see *Ang v Parrish* [1980] 2 All ER 790; [1980] STC 341 and see below at §31.1).

[71]   Before 1970, the 'standard rate' of income tax applied to all 'income' while 'earned income' attracted a special relief.

[72]   F (No 2) A 1983, s 1.

[73]   TA 1988, s 257(6) as originally enacted.

[74]   FA 1907, s 19. Originally, differentiation was achieved by a special relief for earned income, but after 1973 the basic rate applied to earned income and an additional rate to investment income. See also Meade, *The Structure and Reform of Direct Taxation* (Allen & Unwin, 1978), 317–18; Sandford, Willis and Ironside, *An Annual Wealth Tax*, esp 17:29.

[75]   Inland Revenue Statistics (2007), Table 3.4; see also *Royal Commission on Distribution of Income and Wealth*, 7th Report, Cmnd 7595 (1979) 2:51.

[76]   Stevens (1996) *EC Tax Rev* 6; Messere et al (2003) *Tax Policy: Theory and Practice in OECD Countries* (OUP, 2003), 79, Table 6.4.

[77]   For history and Inland Revenue obstacles to attempts to introduce differentiation, see Daunton, *Trusting Leviathan* (CUP, 2001) *passim*, but esp at 91 *et seq*, and Daunton, *Comparative Perspectives on Revenue Law* (CUP, 2008) ch 8.

(2) The cost of obtaining investment income is less than the expense incurred in earning a living, or even in terms of effort, irksomeness or merely sacrifice of leisure. The generous principles of deductions in computing profits under ITTOIA 2005, Part 2 reduce the force of this argument just as the rules under ITEPA 2003 increase it.

(3) A more diffuse argument asserts that the possession of capital gives power and other advantages over and above those arising in the form of investment income.[78] However, the adoption of a wealth tax or, where wealth is acquired by succession, an inheritance tax may be preferable to a surcharge on income; if power is the criterion, one should consider those aspects of society which give power without capital, especially through lending or giving money to political parties, or through being an unelected/unaccountable government adviser.

(4) A lower rate of tax on earned income offers some incentive to taxpayers to stimulate personal effort. Estate duty, when introduced in 1894, was presented as a form of differentiation and as a deferred income tax; of course estate duty was not repealed when the relief for earned income was introduced.

(5) A surcharge would be a tax on leisure; this carries more conviction when the threshold is higher.

It may be noted that a political party (or government) wishing to charge all earned income to NICs may see little wrong in attaching a similar level of tax to investment income.

---

[78] The same point may be used against an expenditure tax: see, eg, Jones (1985) 29 *St Louis L Rev* 1155, 1170.

8

The Tax Unit

8.1 Introduction

The choice of tax unit—individual or family—is a battleground. As Apps points out:[1]

> The taxation of the family is arguably the central issue in the analysis of reforms of the tax system. Families form by far the largest group of taxpayers, they earn the greatest share of income, and direct and indirect taxes on their income are the largest source of government revenue ... All too often the debate is motivated by ideological commitment to reinforcing traditional gender roles within the family and to extending the gap between rich and poor. Much of the controversy surrounding reforms widely debated in recent years can be traced to the fact that they imply major changes of distribution of tax burden within and across families which are inconsistent with conventional equity and efficiency criteria for tax design. So, one may conclude that tax law provides us with a sharp instance of what some think life is all about—money, sex and power.

Much of the debate has an air of grand theory about it. A different approach may be to break the debate down into different issues, some requiring an individual basis, others a family unit basis.[2] However, even this approach has problems of defining the unit, where the unit rather than the individual is to be taken into account. It is important to note that the question whether the tax system should look to the family unit is separate from the question whether that unit should be based on the legal status of marriage. This chapter concentrates on income tax. Income tax, CGT and IHT all start from the premise that spouses are to be treated as separate taxpayers. Capital taxes still favour marriage: IHT gives exemptions for inter-spousal transfers, even when the parties are living apart; CGT directs that inter-spousal transfers shall be at such figure that neither gain nor loss accrues. However, this is confined to spouses living together and is not necessarily an advantage.

---

[1] Apps in Head and Krever (eds) *Tax Units and the Tax Rate Scale* (Australian Tax Research Foundation, 1996), 81.
[2] Eg, Maloney (1989) 3 *Canadian J Women & L* 182.

Many taxes use the concept of connected or associated persons, with marriage always coming within these links.

Putting all these rules together shows that 'separate taxation' does not entail that married persons are treated in the same way as unrelated individuals throughout the UK tax system. In very broad terms, current UK law is a pragmatic compromise in an area where compromise is unavoidable. The compromise arises because the current law tries to do three things, viz: (a) give certain tax advantages to those who are married or civil partners; (b) provide that certain transactions within the very close family should not give rise to tax effects, which may be either advantageous or not, depending on the circumstances; and (c) prevent that same very close family from taking undue advantage of the tax rules. Many of the rules currently formulated in terms of marriage have been amended by regulations as a result of the Civil Partnerships Act 2004, which recognises relationships between persons of the same sex who register as civil partners as from 5 December 2005.[3] A survey of the 205 rules amended under the regulations made when the status of civil partnerships was recognised showed that while the calculation called for some matters of judgement, just over 100 come within group (a) above and just over 50 come within group (c).[4] In what follows the term 'spouse' must be also taken to cover civil partner and 'marriage' to cover civil partnership as well. The Marriage (Same Sex Couples) Act 2013 made the marriage of same sex couples lawful in England and Wales, and thus 'spouse' below now encompasses a spouse of the same or opposite sex. The UK legislation also allows the Treasury to remove any inequality of treatment based on gender or (only in the case of parents) marital status. Why different taxes should treat the family unit differently is unclear. Pragmatism may be preferred to theory, but more likely it is simple muddle.

8.2 UK History[5]

8.2.1 Spouses

Under the law prevailing up to 1973, a wife's income was simply treated as that of her husband. This meant that her income was added to his and so taxed at the cumulative rate appropriate to their joint income. However, in practice the provision of an additional personal relief for married women (the wife's earned income relief) and the practice of having a long band of income taxed at what we now call the basic rate reduced this financial injustice. The first major change came in 1973 when spouses were allowed to elect that the wife should be taxed separately on her earned income.[6] This change was only of advantage to those whose combined incomes took them significantly into higher rate liability, since one effect of the election was for the husband to lose a right to the married man's allowance

---

[3] FA 2005, s 103, giving the Treasury a power to act by statutory instrument.

[4] Tiley [2006] *CLJ* 289.

[5] See Salter in R Probert (ed), *Family Life and the Law under One Roof* (Ashgate, 2007) ch 8; and the 3rd edn of this work, ch 6. For an account of challenges under the European Convention of Human Rights, see Baker [2000] BTR 211 at 252.

[6] On 'earned income', see above at §7.8.2.

and have to make do with an ordinary personal allowance instead.[7] The 1973 change did not affect the wife's investment income, which was not taxed separately until the general change to separate taxation which came into effect in 1990. The basic old rule of aggregation had one other effect: all the wife's tax affairs were handled by her husband, while she had no right or duty to see his. This demeaning state of affairs could be avoided only if the wife opted to be assessed separately (as very few chose to do).[8]

It must be recalled that the older law made some sense under the previous social and fiscal conditions to which it applied. Social conditions were based on the norm of a single-earner household (in which the earner was nearly always the husband), the extreme rarity of people cohabiting unless they were married, and a tax system which had a long band of income taxed at a single rate which would be the family's marginal rate whether one or both spouses worked.

8.2.2 Children

From time to time the UK system has treated all unearned income of an unmarried child under the age of majority as that of the parents, eg, 1968–72. Previously parental child allowances, ie allowances claimed by parents because they had children, formed part of the UK income tax system until 1979–80, before being abolished as a result of the introduction of the child benefit scheme. Before 1979–80 the tax system provided child allowances, while the social security system provided family allowances. Tax allowances would be given to the father in calculating his tax liability, while family allowances were usually paid in cash to the mother each week. There were also rules which phased out the benefit of the family allowances for the relatively well-off. In 1979–80 child tax reliefs were abolished; the money saved was used to increase family allowances, which were recast as child benefit and still payable to the mother.

In response to the cold winds of austerity, the Government sought to save money by changing costly child benefit from a universal benefit to one that is means-tested (and in a novel way). From 7 Jan 2013, a high-income child benefit income tax charge effectively claws back child benefit where the recipient or his/her partner has adjusted net income in excess of £50,000.[9] The claw back takes the form of an income tax charge under ITEPA 2003, Part 10, Chapter 8. The charge applies on a tapering basis on income over £50,000 and will completely offset any child benefit paid once income exceeds £60,000. Interestingly, the income tax charge may well apply to a different individual than the recipient of the child benefit—for example, a husband can be subject to income tax on child benefit paid to the wife/mother). Those who will be subject to the charge must have registered for self-assessment or risk a penalty (adding injury to injury!). Individuals can avoid the income tax charge if the recipient opts out of receiving child benefit in the first place, eg if it is clear that at least one of the partners will have income in excess of £60,000.

---

[7] TA 1988, s 287.
[8] TA 1988, s 283 (repealed as from 1990 by FA 1988).
[9] For commentary see Loutzenhiser [2012] BTR 370.

8.3   Current UK Income Tax Law

8.3.1 *The Tax Unit*

8.3.1.1 Individuals not Spouses[10]

The present UK income tax reflects the conflicting values of the recent age of extreme individualism and the new wish to use the tax system to alleviate child poverty through tax credits. The basic income tax unit in the UK is the individual. Individual taxation took effect in 1990. From 1990 to 2000, marital status had one significant income tax advantage—the married couple's allowance. However, that was removed with effect from 2000 as part of a shift in fiscal concern from marriage to children.[11]

The reasons for the 1990 change to individual taxation are mostly self-evident. The changing role of women and an overdue recognition of their rights came to be combined with unease about defining the family unit to which any tax regime, whether favourable or unfavourable, should be applied.[12] The 1990 married couple's allowance was a some-what dubious device to ensure that there were no losers as a result of the change; its value was steadily eroded by Chancellors of both Conservative and Labour governments.[13] The increasing emphasis on the individual[14] and on doctrines of neutrality also played a part. Among the strands of these doctrines was the desirability of allowing spouses to act as independent persons when looking after their tax affairs, so affording a degree of privacy. Because a husband had been accountable under joint taxation for his wife's income, it had been necessary for the wife to disclose information about her income to her husband—but not vice versa. The need for a wife to disclose even a small 'nest egg' saved up for a special purpose of which her husband may not have approved was reported to have led to much distress for wives.[15] Some married men were also uncomfortable with the tax regime imposing upon them a duty to declare and pay tax on their wives' income—income of which they might not even have been aware.[16] The fact that all correspondence concerning a wife's income tax was sent to her husband also was very unpopular with wives.[17]

As a consequence, the present system permits a degree of income-splitting between spouses. The introduction of the new credits for children reopened the issue of individual taxation. From the point of view of a policy geared to fairness and helping the lower-paid, the needs of the family unit should determine entitlement to credits, and this is the basis

---

[10] On Swedish abolition of joint taxation, see Lindencrona (2002) 30 *Intertax* 474–76.

[11] See similar but later debate in Canada, Kershaw (2002) 50 *Canadian Tax J* 1949–78.

[12] The change to the individual as the basis of tax was made by Nigel Lawson, who was Chancellor in Mrs Thatcher's third administration. His predecessor, Sir Geoffrey Howe, had wished to make the change (and had published a Green Paper on this in 1980—Cmnd 8093) but seems to have encountered resistance from Mrs Thatcher, perhaps because she thought that the idea came from Sir Geoffrey's wife, Elspeth: see Lawson, *The View from No 11* (Bantam, 1992) 881.

[13] On the period 1990–97, see [1998] BTR 317, 339–40.

[14] Symbolic of these values is the change of terminology in certain CGT reliefs from 'family' company, to 'personal' company, eg, TCGA 1992, ss 157, 163, as amended by FA 1993.

[15] Freedman and others, *Property and Marriage: An Integrated Approach* (The Institute for Fiscal Studies, London 1988) 114; Equal Opportunities Commission, *Income Tax & Sex Discrimination* (Manchester 1979) 21–22.

[16] *Ibid.*

[17] Equal Opportunities Commission, *op cit*, 19–20.

for the tax credit regime currently in force.[18] The debate resurfaced to some extent when the high-income child benefit income tax was introduced, with comparisons drawn in the media between two-earner couples each earning below the threshold and able to keep all the benefit as against a single-earner couple with income over the threshold.[19]

8.3.1.2 Children as Individuals

The current system also treats parents and children as separate. Permissible income-splitting between parents and minor children, however, is much more restricted than between spouses. Parents with children may claim the working tax credit. Previously, tax reliefs for children were available, but these were abolished as a corollary of the introduction of the tax-free child benefit. Child-care expenses have not usually been deductible in the UK. However, they form a major element of the Tax Credit System. Recent changes to employment taxation rules have been designed to avoid unnecessary charges on such benefits provided by employers for their employees. Relief has been available under American and Canadian laws, which allow deduction of actual costs on childcare when a parent goes out to work.[20] Such deductions are limited by maximum figures and by the age of the children. These limits are an attempt to distinguish the expense of going out to work from mere personal expenses—the relief is designed to meet the needs of working parents and not simply to subsidise domestic service. The precedent of the relief is important, because the expense is incurred for a mixture of business and personal reasons. If the expense is allowed, why should relief not be given to handicapped persons who incur expenses in riding to work by taxi, to professional people who incur expenses in obtaining qualifications, or to wage earners who incur expenses in moving from job to job?[21]

While much has been done to help families with young children, the focus has been quite deliberately on encouraging going out to work rather than encouraging the having of children.[22] Recent evidence suggests that older mothers and migrants are boosting the number of births in the UK.[23] Given the way in which society currently expects younger women to behave—have a career and buy a house—it is no wonder that they are postponing motherhood.[24] Here what matters is to think about whether the UK should move to the French model, which gives major income tax advantages to families with young children. France is said to have the highest birth rate in the EU. Between 1988 and 1997, Quebec gave a tax incentive to people to have children; birth rates amongst those eligible for the full subsidy rose by 25%.[25]

---

[18] See ch 9.

[19] FA 2012, s 8 and Sch 1. For further commentary see Loutzenhiser [2012] BTR 370.

[20] On Canadian childcare expense deduction and a justification by reference to potential income, see Gagne (2001) 49 *Canadian Tax J* 636.

[21] See Pechman, (1955) 8 *National Tax J* 120; and Arnold (1973) *Canadian Tax J* 176.

[22] The Government's case was well set out in *Tax credits; reforming financial support for families*, No 11, March 2005, http://webarchive.nationalarchives.gov.uk/20091222074811/http://www.hm-treasury.gov.uk/bud05_adtaxcredits.htm.

[23] See the discussion of national statistics in *Guardian*, 8 June 2007, 13.

[24] For the impact of children on women's paid work, see Paull (2006) 27 *Fiscal Studies* 473; see also Kornstad and Thoresen (2006) 27 *Fiscal Studies* 330 on Norwegian changes.

[25] Mulligan (2005) 87 *The Review of Economics and Statistics* 539.

8.3.2 *Whose Income is it and Treatment of Joint Income*

UK legislation begins by assuming that an individual's income is income which accrues to that individual in accordance with the rules appropriate to each head of income (or Schedule). Income-splitting between spouses may be practised if, for example, the wife runs a business and employs her husband. The money paid to the husband will be deductible in computing the profits of the wife's business, and will be taxable to the husband as employment income. Such arrangements must, of course, be genuine and are closely scrutinised by the Revenue to ensure that they do not fall foul of the settlements provisions considered in chapter thirty-one.[26] Capital-splitting is also permitted. Since the UK knows no system of community of property, spouses may put assets into joint names or divide assets between them as they wish. There is a system of potential community of property, in that the courts have very extensive powers to reallocate the assets on divorce, including pension rights, but this does not affect the spouses' right initially to divide their wealth as they see fit.

Where income is joint income, it is normally divided according to the owner's interests in it.[27] For spouses and civil partners living together, this result is modified in two ways:

(1) *Income from property in joint names—the equal division rule.* Where property is held in the names of a husband and wife who are living together, the starting point is that income from that property is divided equally between the spouses unless the spouses make a declaration[28] that they wish to be taxed according to their actual entitlements.[29] A declaration once made remains in force. There is no provision for revocation of a declaration. If the spouses cease to live together, both the statutory presumption of equality and any declaration cease to apply, and thereafter income will be attributed according to their entitlements. It is expressly provided that the declaration ceases to be effective automatically if the beneficial interests in the income or the property cease to accord with the declaration.[30]

This equal division rule does not apply if the property is held in the name of one spouse only. Here any income legally belonging to both of them should be divided between them for tax purposes too—in accordance with their correct legal rights. The equal division rule is expressly excluded in certain situations. These are: (a) where a valid declaration is in force; (b) where the income consists of partnership income or arises from a UK property business consisting of the commercial letting of furnished holiday accommodation; (c) where neither of the spouses is beneficially entitled, eg because they are trustees; and (d) where the income to which one spouse is entitled beneficially is treated as the income of the other

---

[26] They must also conform to the minimum wage legislation as will usually be the case if the purpose is to use up the husband's personal reliefs.

[27] TA 1988, s 277 was repealed by ITA 2007 as being 'unnecessary' so that the rule now rests on general principle.

[28] The form of the declaration is governed by ITA 2007, s 837, ex TA 1988, s 282B. Notice of election must be given to the inspector within 60 days beginning with the date of the declaration and declarations do not have retroactive effect.

[29] ITA 2007, s 836, ex TA 1988, s 282A.

[30] ITA 2007, s 837(5), ex TA 1988, s 282B(5).

or of a third party by some other tax provision. The rule of equal division is also excluded where the income in question is a distribution from shares in a close company to which their actual beneficial entitlements are not equal.[31] The Revenue have used the settlement provisions in ITTOIA 2005, section 624 (ex TA 1988, section 660A) to counteract a number of income-splitting arrangements between spouses involving shares in family companies. One way of beating the Revenue argument was to place the shares in both names so that the equal division rule would direct that the income of the spouses be shared equally, hence the exclusion of the equal division rule.

(2) *Inter-spousal transfers.* The settlement rules in ITTOIA 2005, Part 5, Chapter 5 may apply where income arises under a 'settlement'. A settlement is defined as including any disposition, trust, covenant, agreement, arrangement or transfer of assets.[32] Conventional case law limits the scope of these rules by stating that a settlement occurs only if there is some element of 'bounty' about the transaction.[33] The Revenue view is that bringing a spouse into partnership is an arrangement. Therefore, if a wife brings her husband into partnership and he does not truly earn his share of the profits, the income accruing to him will be treated as accruing to her; bounty is shown by the fact that he did not earn his share. The Revenue take a similar view where the business is run by a company. The question whether the Revenue view is right was settled in HMRC's favour by the House of Lords in *Jones v Garnett*.[34] In a series of obiter remarks, a majority held that the arrangement, which consisted of the issue of shares, was a settlement. In this case only two shares were issued, one to H and one to W—and W was not a director.

In broad terms, where one spouse has carried out a transaction falling within this definition of settlement, and income later arises to the other spouse as a result of that transaction, the income is treated as that of the settlor-spouse and not of the other spouse. The actual wording of the provision covers situations wider than this. This rule therefore appears to prevent income-splitting between the spouses by devices or stratagems for transferring either assets or income between them. There are three exceptions or groups of exceptions to the rule:

(i)   First, there are exceptions from the term 'spouse'. These are:
- (a) a person to whom the settlor is not for the time being married but may later marry;
- (b) a spouse from whom the settlor is separated under an order of a court, or under a separation agreement or in such circumstances that the separation is likely to be permanent; or
- (c) the widow or widower of the settlor.[35]

The rules are adapted to cover civil partner equivalents.

---

[31] ITA 2007, s 836, exc E, ex TA 1988, s 282(1A), added FA 2004.
[32] ITTOIA 2005, s 620, ex TA 1988, s 660G. The settlement provisions are discussed in more detail in ch 31.
[33] Below §31.2.2.
[34] [2007] UKHL 35; for comment see further below at §31.2.2.
[35] ITTOIA 2005, s 625(4), ex TA 1988, s 660A(3).

(ii)   The rule does not deprive an 'outright gift' between the spouses from having that
       effect for tax purposes. The legislation does not wish to inhibit such generosity but
       is anxious to prevent the exploitation of the separate taxation of spouses. It therefore
       provides that an outright gift of property by one spouse to the other is to be treated as
       outside these settlement rules unless either:
       (a)   the gift does not carry a right to the whole of that income; or
       (b)   the property given is wholly or substantially a right to income.[36]

In addition, a gift is not an outright gift if it is subject to conditions, or if the property given
or any derived property is, or will or may become, in any circumstances whatsoever, payable
to or applicable for the benefit of the donor.[37]

   Point (b) was considered in *Young v Pearce*,[38] where Sir John Vinelott held that where
two taxpayers arranged for their trading company to issue preference shares to their wives,
dividends later declared in respect of the preference shares were within (b) and so fell to be
treated as income of the husbands. Although there was an outright gift of the preference
shares, the fact that the shares carried no rights other than a right to income, eg they carried no rights on a winding up of the company, showed that they were substantially a gift of
income. In *Jones v Garnett* the House of Lords held that the property given consisted of the
(single) share and that there was an outright gift of that share by the husband to the wife.
As it was a straightforward ordinary share, there was nothing in the transaction to bring
it anywhere near *Young v Pearce* and point (b). In December 2007, HMRC began consulting on how to undo this result.[39] Draft legislation was withdrawn soon after its release in
2008, but was soon abandoned and no new legislative proposals have been issued.[40] In two
post-*Jones v Garnett* husband and wife income-splitting cases involving family companies
and dividend waivers, the Special Commissioners/First-tier Tribunal found income had
arisen under a settlement in *Buck v Revenue & Customs Commissioners*[41] and in *Donovan and McLaren v HMRC*.[42] In both cases the dividend waivers did not fall within the
spousal 'outright gifts' exemption because they were simply a right to income. The First-tier
Tribunal relied in part, controversially, on constructive trust principles in finding that no
element of bounty was present and thus no settlement existed in *Patmore v Commissioners
for HMRC*.[43]

(iii)   Payments on family breakdown generally are also outside the rule.

---

[36]   ITTOIA 2005, s 626, ex TA 1988, s 660A(6).
[37]   ITTOIA 2005, s 626, ex TA 1988, s 660A(6).
[38]   [1996] STC 743; 70 TC 331.
[39]   See HMRC, *Income Shifting: a Consultation on Draft Legislation* (December 2007).
[40]   For comment on the proposal, see especially Redston [2007] BTR 717. For the history of companies and
families, see Oliver and Harris, *Comparative Perspectives on Revenue Law* (CUP, 2008) ch 11.
[41]   [2009] STC (SCD) 6.
[42]   [2014] UKFTT 048 (TC).
[43]   [2010] UKFTT 334 (TC). In the judge's view, as the company purchase was funded partly with a mortgage
on the family home—jointly-owned by the taxpayer and his wife—the arrangement lacked the necessary element
of bounty.

8.3.3 *Children*

The presence of children affects tax liability in a number of ways but, at least at present, less so than in most other systems.[44] The current tax credits explicitly support child-care expenses quite high up the income scale. Children of whatever age are independent persons as far as the tax system is concerned. Their income is in principle therefore taxed separately from that of their parents. Their personal reliefs are available to be set against their own income only. There is no quotient system in the UK. As with spouses, income-splitting through employment is possible for children. However, here too the taxpayer must be able to establish the genuineness of the payment. In one case a parent sought to deduct payments to a child, but the court concluded that they were really pocket money and so not genuine income of the child—and so not deductible.[45]

Income arising in favour of an unmarried child aged under 18 is treated as that of the parent if the income arises under a settlement made by the parent.[46] The term 'settlement' used in ITTOIA 2005, Part 5, Chapter 5 is widely defined to include any transfer of assets (see further chapter thirty-one below). Therefore if S opens a bank account in the name of her child, M, and puts £10,000 in it, the interest arising from that £10,000 will be treated as income of S and not of M.[47] There is a *de minimis* exception of £100 from all sources under ITTOIA 2005, s 629. There is also an exception if the money was placed in an accumulation trust and the money is not paid out to M or used for M's benefit while a minor.[48] Such income is taxed at ordinary trust rates—and not those of the settlor.

8.4 The Policy Debate on Choice of Tax Unit

The correct tax treatment of the family is one of the most contentious issues in tax policy. The traditional starting point is that there are two broad choices of tax units between which the tax system must choose. One option is to adopt the individual as the tax unit. This is the model used in the UK and the majority of OECD countries. The other option is to use a joint spousal or even a family tax unit, aggregating the incomes of couples (and possibly their children) before applying tax rates—probably using a different rate schedule from that used for single individuals. The US permits joint taxation of married couples by election for federal income tax purposes, and France is a rare example of a family tax unit system. Once the choice of primary tax unit has been made, some refinements to the system may then be introduced, eg individual tax unit but allowing unused personal allowances to be transferred between spouses.

This section begins with a brief overview of approaches internationally to the choice of tax unit, and then outlines the primary theoretical and policy arguments raised in the tax

---

[44] For details of tax thresholds for different family units, see Inland Revenue Statistics 2004, para 2.7; see earlier volumes for earlier years. For comparisons, see Messere, *Tax Policies in OECD Countries* (IBFD, 1993) Tables 10.5 and 10.6; Messere *et al*, *Tax Policy: Theory and Practice* (OUP, 2003) Table 2.5; and below at §8.4.1.

[45] *Dollar v Lyon* [1981] STC 333; 54 TC 459.

[46] ITTOIA 2005, s 629, ex TA 1988, s 660B.

[47] *Thomas v Marshall* [1953] 1 All ER 1102; 34 TC 178.

[48] ITTOIA 2005, s 631, ex TA 1988, s 660B(2).

unit debate. This debate sometimes leads to the listing of criteria to consider, individual items being not only disputable but also conflicting. The following list is from the Meade Report, chapter 18:[49]

(1)   The decision to marry or not to marry should not be affected by tax considerations.[50]
(2)   Families with the same joint resources should be taxed equally.
(3)   The incentive for a member of the family to earn should not be blunted by tax considerations which depend upon the economic position of other members of the family.
(4)   Economic and financial arrangements within the family (eg, as regards the ownership of property) should not be dominated by sophisticated tax considerations.
(5)   The tax system should be fair between families which rely upon earnings and families which enjoy investment income.
(6)   Two persons living together and sharing household expenditures can live more cheaply and therefore have a greater taxable capacity than two single persons living separately.
(7)   The choice of tax unit should not be excessively costly in loss of tax revenue.
(8)   The arrangements involved should be reasonably simple for the taxpayer to understand and for the tax authorities to administer.

Such lists are of dubious value since the criteria are of different orders and often rest on a prejudgement of one fundamental question, ie whether the basic unit is to be the family household or the individual. Consider, for example, criterion 3. Although presented as a truth, it is in fact a consequence, perhaps a desirable one, of taking the individual as a unit. If the family is taken as the unit, this criterion cannot be met, for the reasons discussed in §8.4.5 below. However, if this criterion were reshaped, a different criterion would be produced which the family unit could satisfy, ie 'if it is desirable that the family should earn more money, should the tax system encourage a member to start work rather than an existing earner to earn more?'[51]

   These arguments show that there is little chance of agreement over the criteria. The position is further complicated by the fact that even if the criteria were agreed, there is a fundamental and inevitable conflict between criterion 1 (referred to in the literature as 'marriage neutrality') and criterion 2 ('couples neutrality') if the tax system is progressive. This can be illustrated with a simple example. Suppose that H1 earns £20,000, and H2 earns £40,000. In a progressive tax system the total tax paid by H2 almost certainly will be more than double that paid by H1, owing eg to increasing marginal tax rates. Suppose that H1 marries W1 who also earns £20,000, so that their combined income is £40,000. In order for criterion 1 to be satisfied, this means that the combined tax on their income of £20,000 each would need to be the same as two single individuals—but this would be less than that paid by H2 on his £40,000. Suppose further that H2 marries W2, who earns nothing, so that their combined income is £40,000. If we say that the tax burden on H1 and W1 should not alter when they

[49]   Meade Report, *op cit*.
[50]   For effects of change in tax law on timing of marriage in UK and Canada, see Gelardi (1996) 49 *National Tax J* 17.
[51]   For scepticism of empirical studies on how families allocate the extra tax burden when one member returns to work, see McIntyre in Head and Krever (eds), *op cit*, 9–11; for evidence of reluctance to return to work if tax rates high, see Gann (1980) 59 *Texas L Rev* 25.

marry (criterion 1), we are faced with the fact that the tax burden on H1W1 is less than the burden on H2W2 and, thus, couples neutrality (criterion 2) will not be met.

Although much has been written in the academic literature on choice of tax unit, the optimal tax policy literature on this subject is relatively sparse.[52] Choice of tax unit was not addressed as a separate topic in the Mirrlees Review, though Brewer, Saez and Shephard in their paper consider how the design of taxes and benefits affecting an individual should be affected by the presence of a co-resident partner or dependent children. The authors conclude that deriving optimal tax results for couples is extremely complicated and the limited studies to date make it difficult to reach definitive conclusions.[53] Nevertheless, the economic literature has much to add to the analysis of incentives/disincentives to marry and for secondary earners (primarily women) to work outside the home, as will be seen below.

8.4.1 International approaches[54]

A 2008 study found that the individual was the most commonly used basic tax unit in the OECD, adopted by over two-thirds of the member countries. Amongst other OECD countries, Germany, the Czech Republic, Ireland, Luxembourg, Poland, Switzerland and the US either allowed or required joint spousal taxation; only France and Portugal taxed on a family unit basis that includes dependent children. Under the French quotient system,[55] the family income—including that of the children—is first aggregated, whether it comes from spouse or child, and is then divided according to the number of people in the family, a child counting as a half, save for single parent families, where the first child counts as a whole. Thus, a married couple with two children would have their income divided into three parts. The general rates of tax are then applied to each part separately and the tax due is the aggregate. The system lowers the average tax rate and, by sharply mitigating the theoretically progressive tax system, discriminates heavily against the single person. The French approach, which is of long standing, may be seen historically as part of that country's need to address the loss of manpower in two world wars, but there is also an important cultural aspect in the value placed by French society on the family as such. Other systems may apply different schedules to families and individuals, with the premises behind the schedules varying widely.[56]

---

[52] Notable exceptions include Boskin and Sheshinski, 'Optimal Tax Treatment of the Family: Married Couples' (1983) 20 J of Public Econ 281; Brett, 'Optimal Nonlinear Taxes for Families' (2006) International Tax and Public Finance 225; Kleven, Kreiner and Saez, 'The Optimal Income Taxation Of Couples' (2006) NBER Working Paper 12685; Cremer, Lozachmeur and Pestieau, 'Income Taxation of Couples and the Tax Unit Choice, (2007) Core Discussion Paper No 2007/13; Kleven, Kreiner and Saez (2009), 'Supplement To "The Optimal Income Taxation Of Couples"' Econometrica Supplementary Material 77.

[53] Brewer, Saez and Shephard, 'Means-testing and Tax Rates on Earnings' in Mirrlees et al (eds), *Dimensions of Tax Design: The Mirrlees Review* (OUP, 2010) 121 et seq.

[54] For a 1998 European survey, see Soler Roch (ed), *Family Taxation in Europe* (Kluwer, 1999). For general literature, see the citations by Brooks in Head and Krever (eds), *op cit*; see also Messere (1993), *op cit*, esp the tables at 10.2–10.6; and the contributions by McIntyre (on the United States) and Sommerhalder (on Europe) in Head and Krever (eds), *op cit*. Also on marriage penalties in the US, see Zelanak (2000) 54 *Tax Law Review*, 1. For older analyses, see Oldman and Temple (1959) 12 *Stanford LR* 585; Bittker (1974) 27 *Stanford LR* 1389; and Carter (chair), Canadian Royal Commission on Taxation, *Study No. 10* (Queen's Printer, 1966).

[55] For a comparison of the French quotient system and units of consumption, see *Impôts et Réforme Fiscale* (Cahiers Francais No 274, January 1996), 28.

[56] See also above §8.2.3 and Messere *et al* (2003), *op cit*, §6.6.

8.4.2 Definitional Issues

If the tax unit is anything other than the individual, this immediately raises definitional issues—first and foremost, who counts as a 'spouse'? Should a joint spousal tax unit apply only to married couples or should it also include same-sex couples who have entered into some form of legally-recognised registered partnership? Can cohabiting but unmarried/unregistered couples qualify as spouses? If so, for how long must they have cohabited before qualifying for spousal treatment—one year, three years? Should it matter for this purpose whether the couple have a sexual relationship or not? Could economically interdependent siblings or friends ever qualify for tax treatment as a 'couple'?

From a definitional point of view, the individual as tax unit has the great advantage of being a bright-line test and easy to administer. As Bittker notes, sociologists may find it useful to study groups that engage in joint decision-making or that manifest a common interest in the economic well-being of their members, but it is difficult if not impossible to administer a tax law that employed 'such squishy phrases'.[57] In defining a spousal tax unit, the easiest and less 'squishy' option is to use a formal test such as marriage and civil registration. Formal tests, however, will inevitably exclude groups that are only marginally different, so far as relevant economic or social relationships are concerned, from those within the definition.[58] If married couples are taxed more favourably on their combined income than two individuals, for example, is it not horizontally equitable to extend similar treatment to couples cohabiting together on a long-term basis in a 'common law marriage'?

An even more problematic question is what constitutes a 'family'? Choosing the family as the tax unit raises all the difficulties associated with defining a spousal unit, and then some. Obviously a decision has to be made on who to include in the family unit—spouses (however defined) and minor children, of course, but what about stepchildren, children spending time in two homes, adult children living with their parents or attending university, and elderly relatives living with their children? Oliver and Harris go so far as to suggest a family company could be considered part of a family tax unit.[59] Once the family unit has been determined, the difficult challenge of setting an appropriate rate schedule/quotient system remains.

Whilst the UK tax system frequently distinguishes between married couples/civil partners and unmarried couples—most notably in the capital gains and inheritance tax contexts but also for transferrable personal allowances—for purposes of determining eligibility for tax credits (see §9.4 below) certain unmarried cohabitants are treated in the same way as married couples and registered civil partners. Tax credits are calculated by reference to the circumstances of the 'family' and 'couple', where 'couple' is defined to include spouses and registered civil partners as well as unmarried/unregistered couples 'living together as husband and wife or civil partners'.[60] Similarly, the term 'partner' in ITEPA 2003, section 681G—relevant to the post-2012 means-testing of Child Benefit—includes married

---

[57] Bittker (1975) 27 *Stanford L R* 1389, 1399. See also Brooks, *op cit*, 63.
[58] *Ibid.*
[59] Oliver and Harris, *op cit*, 246.
[60] TCA 2002, s 3(5A), and see HMRC, Tax Credits Technical Manual TCTM09320, available at http://www.hmrc.gov.uk/manuals/tctmanual/TCTM09320.htm.

spouses, civil partners, and those living together as husband and wife or civil partners. Tax credit-like wording also has crept into the 'managed service company' rules in ITEPA 2003, Part 2, Chapter 9, which are aimed at addressing tax-motivated attempts to disguise employment through the use of intermediaries: 'a man and a woman living together as husband and wife are treated as if they were married to each other' and 'two people of the same sex living together as if they were civil partners of each other are treated as if they were civil partners of each other'.

The HMRC technical manual on tax credits lists the following 'signposts' they consider relevant in determining whether an unmarried couple is living together as husband and wife: (i) living in the same household, (ii) stability of the relationship, (iii) financial support, (iv) sexual relationship, (v) dependent children, and (vi) public acknowledgement (ie representing themselves to others as a couple).[61] Interestingly the manual states that couples should not be asked about their sexual relationship though any information disclosed should be considered. The manual also notes that some marriages lack a sexual component and sexual relationships occur outside marriage without any indication that the parties wish to live together as husband and wife.[62] Obviously the HMRC guidelines will not always be easy to apply; one needs to know quite a bit about the couple in order to weigh up all these factors, which inevitably requires a significant intrusion into the couple's lives.

One might conclude that the tax credit definition including couples 'living together as husband and wife' could also be used more broadly in the tax system. At first glance it appears inconsistent to use an individual unit for income tax and a joint unit for tax credits. There is no normative inconsistency, however, in using an individual tax unit for income tax purposes and basing welfare payments (including those delivered in the form of a tax credit) on household income. As Brooks argues, government payments aimed at relieving poverty in working families and families with children are 'quite sensibly' based upon some function of consumption instead of control of income.[63] Moreover, calculating need-based welfare payments by reference to family income does not imply full sharing of family resources, only that the low-earning partner in a one-earner family is not likely 'in need' if the other partner earns a high income.[64] Finally, social welfare programs require a high level of expensive and intrusive auditing, particularly around the economics of a claimant's living arrangements. Social support is by its nature intrusive, as the State has to understand the claimant's situation and needs in order to arrive at an appropriate response that addresses those needs. In contrast, none of this is inherently necessary for a tax, even one levied on ability to pay. Tax is a burden the State is imposing on a large percentage of the population as opposed to needs-based assistance the State is providing to a much smaller group; to attempt to apply a social support structure to the income tax would be very difficult and extremely costly to administer.[65]

---

[61] HMRC, Tax Credits Technical Manual TCTM09340, available at http://www.hmrc.gov.uk/manuals/tctmanual/TCTM09340.htm.

[62] HMRC, Tax Credits Technical Manual TCTM09345, available at http://www.hmrc.gov.uk/manuals/tctmanual/TCTM09345.htm.

[63] Brooks, *op cit*, 78.

[64] *Ibid.*

[65] *Ibid.*

8.4.3 Couples Neutrality and Marriage Neutrality

One of the main arguments offered in support of a joint spousal tax unit is that couples with equal total income should pay the same tax no matter how the income is distributed between them—criteria 2 in Meade's list. This 'couples neutrality' argument can also justify allowing couples to transfer unused personal allowances between them—why should a couple where one spouse earns £20,000 and the other nothing pay income tax when a couple with both spouses earning £10,000 will pay no tax after the application of the personal allowances? Critics of the 2012 Child Benefit changes similarly complained that a family with two people each earning £49,000 (total income £98,000) will keep their entire Child Benefit while a one-earner family with income of £60,000 will lose it completely.[66]

The 1920 and 1954 Royal Commissions supported continuing the aggregation of a wife's income with that of her husband's partly on the basis of couples neutrality.[67] Prominent defenders of the US system of joint spousal income tax returns on the basis of couples neutrality include Surrey, Bittker and also McIntyre and Oldman. They argue that the principle of horizontal equity—that like taxpayers pay like taxes—requires that equal-income couples pay equal taxes.[68] In the UK, Oliver and Harris have taken a similar stance.[69] Aggregating spousal incomes has the added advantage of eliminating incentives for couples to undertake tax-motivated income-splitting arrangements, ie to move income from a higher-rate spouse to a lower-rate spouse in order to reduce the couple's combined tax. Interestingly, some commentators argue that this is not a concern and actually could be a positive feature if the arrangement involves genuinely transferring ownership of income-producing assets to lower-income spouses who are predominantly women.[70]

Another common justification for joint taxation is that each member of the couple/family will *benefit* more or less equally from the total available income without regard to the source distribution.[71] The Canadian Royal Commission in 1966, in arguing for a family tax unit, expressed the point thusly:[72]

> We believe firmly that the family is today, as it has been for many centuries, the basic economic unit in society. Although few marriages are entered into for purely financial reasons, as soon as a marriage is contracted it is the continued income and financial position of the family which is ordinarily of primary concern, not the income and financial position of the individual members. Thus, the married couple itself adopts the economic concept of the family as the income unit from the outset. In Western society the wife's direct financial contribution to the family income through employment is frequently substantial. It is probably even truer that the newly formed family acts as a financial unit in making its expenditures. Family income is normally budgeted

[66] See eg Ramesh and Osbourne, 'Budget 2012: pulling back from child benefit cliff edge still leaves dangers', *The Guardian*, (21 March 2012).
[67] 1920 Royal Commission, paras 252–53; 1954 Royal Commission, para 119.
[68] See eg McIntyre and Oldman, 90 *Harv L Rev* 1573, 1575–1579. The material in §8.4.3 is an abridged version of a more extensive discussion in Loutzenhiser [2015] BTR 110.
[69] Oliver and Harris, *op cit*, 285.
[70] Brice, *The Tax Treatment of the Family Unit* (PhD thesis, University of London, 1982), 7, 357, 369, 592–593 and 627.
[71] McIntyre and Oldman, *op cit*, 1590.
[72] Carter (chair), Canadian Royal Commission on Taxation, *Report*, Vol 3 (Queen's Printer, 1966), 123. For criticism, see McIntyre in Brooks (ed), *The Quest for Tax Reform: The Royal Commission on Taxation 20 Years Later* (Carswell, 1988).

between current and capital outlays, and major decisions involving the latter are usually made jointly by the spouses.

Support for this position can be found in the Haig-Simons definition of income.[73] This takes as its starting point the income actually received by the taxpayer and asserts the irrelevance of the particular source of the sums spent on consumption or added to the store of wealth; it thus focuses on benefit. Individual taxation focuses not on benefit but on *control*. It asserts that the tax system should tax the person who controls the source and/or disposition of that income. Behind these two normative propositions are two empirical propositions. Joint taxation asserts that spouses usually share the material benefits generated by their income. Individual taxation, however, asserts that the person who controls the source decides the disposition.[74]

Critics of couples neutrality, however, contend that one- and two-earner couples with equal taxable incomes are generally not equal in taxpaying ability—the one-earner couple is significantly better off because it has greater imputed income from self-performed services and fewer non-deductible work-related expenses (such as clothing and commuting).[75] Other commentators have criticised the 'intuitive' assumption that married couples pool their resources, arguing either that there is not enough economic data on the extent to which married couples share income[76] or that the evidence that does exist points to a move towards individualisation in couples' finances in recent years that may be indicative of a long-term change in norms and values.[77]

For yet other commentators the question is not simply whether people think equal taxation of equal-income couples is desirable, but whether it is a more important equity concern than the incompatible goal of 'marriage neutrality', that is, that the tax system should not provide incentives either to marry or not to marry.[78] For example, in Zelenak's view, marriage neutrality is more important than couples neutrality because people are more aware of marriage penalties and bonuses than they are of whether or not equal-income couples are paying equal taxes: marriage penalties and bonuses can be determined without reference to any other taxpayers and it is simple to calculate the effect of prospective marriage and post-marriage yearly differences.[79]

---

[73] See, generally, Head and Krever (eds), *op cit*. For an utilitarian argument in favour of the family tax unit, see Steuerle, 'Tax Treatment of Households of Different Size' in Penner (ed), *Taxing the Family* (1983).

[74] UK research suggests that there is little pooling: see Lundberg, Pollok and Wales (1997) *J Human Resources* 463, showing that the 1977 change from tax allowance to child benefit resulted in much more expenditure on children. For discussions of foreign family-sharing practices, see McIntyre (1985) 49 *Albany L Rev* 275 and Kornhauser (1993) 45 *Hastings L Rev* 63. McCaffery 40 *UCLA L Rev* 983 uses the game theory to argue that actual sharing is irrelevant; Zelenak 67 *Southern California L Rev* 339 argues that couples share, but that the control principle is still valid.

[75] Meade Report, 382; Zelenak, (1994) 67 *S Cal L Rev* 339, 361; Kesselman, 'Income Splitting and Joint Taxation of Couples: What's Fair?' (2008) 14 IRPP Choices 1, 26–27; McCaffery, *Taxing Women* (Chicago: University of Chicago Press, 1997), 120–126.

[76] Vogler, Brockmann and Wiggins, (2006) 57 *British J of Sociology* 455; Kornhauser, (1993) 45 *Hastings L J* 63; Kornhauser, (1996) 69 *Temple L Rev* 1413.

[77] Pahl, (2005) 4 Social Policy & Society 381 and Pahl, (2008) 37 *J of Socio-Economics* 577.

[78] Zelenak, (1994) 67 *S Cal L Rev* 339, 361.

[79] *Ibid*. For more on marriage neutrality see 1920 Royal Commission, para.254; 1954 Royal Commission-para.117; *The Taxation of Husband and Wife*, 1980 Green Paper, para 4(b); Meade Report, 377, criteria 1; Brice, *op cit*, 592.

8.4.4 *Privacy*

As noted above in the brief history of the UK move to independent taxation, one of the Government's main objectives in adopting independent taxation in 1988 was to give married women the same privacy and independence in their tax affairs as everyone else.[80] These privacy concerns resurfaced again, albeit to a lesser degree, with the 2012 introduction of means-testing for Child Benefit and the 2014 introduction of partially-transferable personal allowance between spouses. For example, in order for a married couple to determine whether the benefits of the transferable allowances are available to them, the couple will need to know if one spouse has insufficient income to use his or her allowance, if that person's spouse is a basic-rate taxpayer and potentially eligible to receive a transfer of the unused allowance, and if transferring some or all of the permitted amount of allowance might tip the recipient spouse into the higher-rate band. Some taxpayers may well decide that privacy is more important than pursuing the modest financial benefit which results from transferring allowances.

8.4.5 *Work incentives*

As previously discussed (above at §1.5.1) high marginal tax rates lead to the substitution effect—as progressively more tax is levied on a taxpayer's employment earnings, so that each hour worked generates less and less additional take-home pay, the taxpayer will have a greater incentive to forgo labour for leisure or untaxed domestic work. In a joint tax unit system, the incentive for one spouse to earn can be blunted by tax considerations which depend on the economic position of the other spouse.[81] Furthermore, a joint tax unit with one rate schedule applicable to couples invariably encourages families to think in terms of a primary and secondary earner. This in turn gives rise to strong disincentives against second earners working in the paid workforce because they enter it at the high marginal tax rate of the primary earner—what McCaffery and Apps refer to as the 'secondary-earner bias.'[82] In contrast, under an individual tax unit system, the fact that one's spouse is a higher-rate taxpayer and paying tax at a marginal rate of 40% will as a general matter have little or no impact on the other's spouse marginal tax rate or work incentives.

McCaffery and Apps, amongst others, are strong critics of joint taxation because of the negative incentive effects it has on women and their participation in paid labour outside the home.[83] Although McCaffery acknowledges that the second earner could in some cases be the husband, he maintains (as do Apps and Brooks) that historically it is far more likely to

---

[80] See §8.3.1.1 above.

[81] Meade Report, 377, criteria 3; Hoynes, 'Commentary on Brewer, Saez and Shephard, "Optimal Household Labor Income Tax and Transfer Programs: An Application to the UK"' in Mirrlees et al (eds), *Dimensions of Tax Design: The Mirrlees Review* (OUP, 2010), 176. The material in §8.4.5 is an abridged version of a more extensive discussion in Loutzenhiser [2015] BTR 110.

[82] The Meade Report expressed similar concerns (at 387) when considering the advantages and disadvantages of an unrestricted quotient system under which a couple's earned and investment income is combined and then one-half of the total is allocated to, and taxed in the hands of, each partner.

[83] McCaffery, *Taxing Women, op cit*, 19; Apps, *op cit*, 84–90.

be the wife because women earn less than men (the well-known 'gender gap') and because of the realities of childbirth, which will mean that a wife will need to leave the workforce temporarily and the family will then be faced with the decision as to whether or not she should go back to work.[84] Finally, research in Australia suggests that secondary-earner participation in the labour market also has significant implications for the level of savings in the household, and for the broader economy overall.[85]

8.4.6 Supporting Marriage through the Tax System

Whilst marriage remains the main form of partnership between women and men in the UK, because the marriage rate has been declining and marriage is being deferred until later in life, the number of unmarried cohabiting couples has increased dramatically. In the early 1960s in Britain fewer than one in 100 adults under 50 are estimated to have been cohabiting at any one time, compared with one in six currently.[86] Moreover, unmarried cohabitation is expected to become increasingly common in the UK and to spread across a wider range of the population in terms of age. The UK Government Actuary's Department has predicted that by 2031 the number of cohabiting couples in England and Wales will have increased to 3.8 million—over one in four couples.[87]

Such statistics might well suggest to some that the institution of marriage is in need of government support. But is this a worthwhile objective for the Government to pursue through the tax system? Many participants in the debate about the legal and fiscal support provided for families, and the ways in which welfare benefit and tax policy might be used to encourage or discourage particular family forms, take the position that marriage should be supported on the basis that research studies have shown that marriage is often associated with the best outcomes for children.[88]

Research by the IFS provides a valuable assessment of the strength of the claims that marriage should be supported by the tax system because of the positive effects marriage has on children's outcomes in comparison to other relationships. Whilst previous research has shown that, on average, 'married couples tend to have more stable relationships, and raise children with higher cognitive and socio-emotional development, than cohabiting couples',[89] it is widely recognised that marital status may not be the *cause* of these differences. Crawford and Greaves have stressed the importance of using good evidence to

---

[84] McCaffery, *Taxing Women, op cit*, 19–26; Apps, *op cit*, 81; Zelenak, (1994) 67 S Cal L Rev 339, 343, 365–378; Brooks, *op cit*, 84–68.

[85] Rees, 'A New Perspective on Capital Income Taxation' in Evans, Krever and Mellor (eds), *Australia's Future Tax System: The Prospects After Henry* (Sydney: Thomson Reuters, 2010), Ch.6, 132. See also Apps and Rees, *Public Economics and the Household* (CUP, 2009).

[86] Law Commission, *Cohabitation: The Financial Consequences of Relationship Breakdown* (Law Com No 307, 2007), Cm.7182, para.1.10, citing the principal projections of the Government Actuary's Department, Marital Status Projections for England and Wales (2005). The material in §8.4.6 is an abridged version of a more extensive discussion in Loutzenhiser [2015] BTR 110.

[87] Law Commission, *op cit*, para.1.10.

[88] *Ibid*, para 2.36.

[89] Crawford, Goodman and Greaves, *Cohabitation, marriage, relationship stability and child outcomes: final report*, IFS Report R87 (October 2013), 5.

inform policymaking and cautioned, in particular, against drawing conclusions from the link between parents' marital status and relationship stability and children's outcomes:[90]

> There is a strong correlation between parents being married and children who are more successful academically and in other ways. But there is not good evidence of a causal link—though we can't say for sure that such a link does not exist. Researchers must be careful not to interpret or present statistically significant associations as evidence of causation. In turn, policymakers must be cautious about using such associations as a basis for policymaking.

Even if one accepted that marriage should be supported for its positive outcome on children, are tax measures likely to have any impact on an individual's decision to marry or remain married? In a commentary for the Mirrlees Review, Hoynes concluded that marriage is sensitive to the financial incentives inherent in welfare systems, but that 'the estimated elasticities with respect to the tax-induced financial incentives to marry (and divorce) are small'.[91] It should also be noted that other research has found that some cohabitants think that it is wrong to take on what they view as the serious commitment of marriage for legal or financial reasons.[92] The media does occasionally report on long-term cohabiting taxpayers deciding to get married to 'avoid' inheritance tax, however.[93] Perhaps the spectre of a substantial IHT charge of up to 40% on gifts between unmarried cohabitants but not married spouses/civil partners makes this tax a sensible exception to the general rule.

8.5 Conclusion

One reads such literature with a shaking head. Altruism ('love' seems an overloaded and intrusive expression) seems to be absent from the debate. Of course the debate goes far wider than just the taxation of the family, and the tax unit issue provides an important instance of another dispute, ie the role of gender in society.

---

[90] Crawford and Greaves, *The crucial role of good evidence in evidence-based policymaking*, IFS Observations (October 25, 2013).

[91] Hoynes, *op cit*, 182.

[92] Law Commission, *op cit*, para 2.42.

[93] See eg 'Wayne Sleep: "I got married to avoid paying inheritance tax"' *Sunday Telegraph* (11 October 2015).

9

Taxation and Social Security

9.1   Introduction[1]

The social security system is relevant for tax lawyers for three immediate reasons. First, some social security benefits are taxable, while others are not; secondly, the progressivity of the tax system cannot be assessed without taking account both of the effect of the reduction in benefits as income rises and of the impact of National Insurance contributions (NICs); thirdly, NICs are particularly important when considering benefits in kind. However, behind all these is awareness that tax and social security are two systems within which an individual's rights depend on the answer to one question: What is my income? Since two systems turn on one question, it is tempting for an interfering or ambitious Chancellor to think that the systems should and could be merged. The material in this chapter is important, because nothing better illustrates personal tax policy since 1997 than the extensive use of tax credits.

In 2010 the Coalition Government announced its intention to reform the tax credits and benefit system in a fundamental way.[2] A new universal credit was to be introduced to provide a basic allowance with additional elements for children, disability, housing and caring. The roll-out has been delayed and it is now up to the present Conservative government to implement. The Universal Credit is intended to support people both in and out of work, and eventually will replace the working tax credit, child tax credit, housing benefit, income support, income-based jobseeker's allowance and income-related employment and support allowance. The Government intends to adopt a phased approach to the introduction of

---

[1] The history of the issues may be seen in the reports and Green Budgets produced by the Institute for Fiscal Studies (IFS), starting with eg *Tax Reform: Options for the Third Term* (1987) 13–29; on welfare reform under the Labour Government, see IFS Symposium 2002 (2002) 23 *Fiscal Studies* 503 and (2003) 24 *Fiscal Studies* 119.

[2] See https://www.gov.uk/universal-credit/overview. For the consultation documents see http://www.dwp.gov.uk/policy/welfare-reform/legislation-and-key-documents/universal-credit/.

universal credit, followed by the gradual closure of existing benefits and tax credits claims. As a result, the discussion below on working tax credit and child tax credits is brief. Readers interested in the details of the operation of these tax credits are directed to the 6th edition of this book.

9.2   Taxation of Benefits[3]

Payments under the present social security system fall into two main categories: contributory benefits, which depend on certain contribution requirements being met; and non-contributory benefits. The taxation of benefits is governed by ITEPA 2003.[4] The longer-term contributory benefits are usually taxable. These include social security pensions such as the state retirement pension, graduated retirement benefit, industrial death benefit, widow's pension, widowed parent's allowance and widowed mother's allowance (both the basic flat-rate allowance and any earnings-related increase—ITEPA 2003, section 577). Under ITEPA 2003, section 660, the taxable benefits include the bereavement allowance (a lump sum), statutory maternity, paternity or adoption pay, statutory sick pay and incapacity benefit. Of the short-term contributory benefits, the state maternity allowance is exempt from tax. The jobseekers' allowance is taxable up to a certain maximum; any child maintenance bonus is always exempt.[5]

Non-contributory benefits are generally exempt from income tax.[6] These include various war disablement benefits and industrial injury benefits. Others are means-tested and the system does not usually charge income tax as well because the means-testing itself is regarded as a sufficient 'tax'. Among the non-taxable but means-tested benefits are income support (but see below), social fund benefits, council tax benefit and housing benefit. Also exempt are the child tax credit and the working tax credit; the state pension credit is also exempt. The non-taxable, non means-tested benefits include child benefit, attendance allowance and the Christmas bonus for pensioners. New Deal payments to employees by employers are taxable once the subsidy level is passed (ITEPA 2003, section 655(3)). FA 2008 added in-work credit, return to work credit, in-work emergency discretion fund payments and in-work emergency fund payments.

Although generally exempt from tax, income support is taxable in two situations.[7] The first is where the payment is made in respect of a period where the right to income support is conditional on the claimant being available for employment. The second is where the payment is for a period in which the claimant is one of a married or unmarried couple

---

[3] For a comprehensive list, see 'Social Security' in Tolley's *Income Tax*, latest edition. On social security law generally, see Wikeley, Ogus and Barendt, *Law of Social Security*, 5th edn (Butterworths, 2005) and Wikeley's chapter in Probert (ed), *Family Life and the Law under One Roof* (Ashgate, 2007) ch 7. The widow's pension and widowed mothers' allowance apply only where the relevant person died before 9 April 2001 (they were superseded by the gender-neutral bereavement and widowed parent's allowances).

[4] ITEPA 2003, s 655 et seq charges all social security benefits unless specifically exempted, on which see s 677. ITEPA 2003, s 577 et seq charges pensions.

[5] ITEPA 2003, ss 670–675.

[6] ITEPA 2003, s 677.

[7] *Ibid*, ss 665–669.

and the claimant, but not the other partner, is involved in a trade dispute as a result of which reduced income support is payable. However, in these cases tax is not charged on any income support in excess of the 'taxable maximum'.

9.3   Impact of NICs

NICs are important because they affect the tax burden on the employer, the employee and sometimes the self-employed.[8] Governments hemmed in by political constraints, and so unable to raise the explicit rate of income taxes, have sometimes regarded NICs as a useful alternative source of revenue.[9] For employees, the normal Class 1 rate in 2016–17 is 12% of earnings between the primary threshold set at £155 a week and the upper earnings limit, set at £827 a week. There is a charge at 2% on sums above £827 a week. The rate of employer's NICs for 2016–17 is 13.8% on all earnings over £156 a week, with no upper limit. These rates are reduced for both employer and employee if the employee is contracted out of the state earnings-related pension scheme. Confusingly, there is also the 'lower earnings limit', which is £112 a week. This figure is not relevant for NIC purposes but is the minimum which must be reached if the year is to count for contribution purposes and so give entitlement to contributory benefits—a matter relevant to planning how much to take out of an owner-managed company. The self-employed pay Class 2 NICs of £2.80 a week, subject to a small earnings threshold of £5,965 pa. Class 2 NICs are to be abolished entirely from April 2018. The self-employed also pay 9% on earnings between the lower profits limit of £8,060 pa and the upper profits limit of £43,000 pa (all figures for 2016–17). Earnings above the upper profits limit are charged at 2%. The sums raised are large—NICs raised £107.3bn in 2013–14, second only to £157.7bn from income tax and slightly higher than the £106.5bn from VAT.[10]

NICS have been the subject of several recent reform measures. At Budget 2013 the Government announced a new 'employment allowance' giving businesses, charities and community sports club up to £2,000 annually towards their employer Class 1 secondary NICs bill from April 2014. The Government expected up to 1.25 million businesses would benefit, and around 450,000 of these businesses would pay no employer NICs at all. In 2015 the allowance was bumped up to £3,000 and new anti-avoidance measures to prevent companies with a sole director/employee from claiming the allowance were introduced; both are effective from April 2016. The Government also abolished employer NICs in relation to earners under 21 from 6 April 2015. This exemption does not apply to those under 21s earning more than the upper earnings limit.

From April 2016 employers of apprentices under the age of 25 are longer be required to pay employer Class 1 NICs on earnings up to the upper earnings limit.

The most dramatic reform was revealed at Budget 2016. The government announced it will abolish Class 2 NICs from April 2018—quite soon after moving to having these paid

---

[8]   See IFS Green Budget 2004, ch 4.

[9]   See [1998] BTR 317, 334–35.

[10]   For review of changes to the NIC regime since 1997, see IFS Green Budget 2008, 283 *et seq*; and Mirrlees *et al* (eds), *Tax by Design: The Mirrlees Review* (OUP, 2011) ch 5.

through self-assessment—and will reform Class 4 NICs to introduce a new contributory benefit test.

9.3.1 History

These rates represent a considerable rationalisation on what had previously been in force. Earlier systems had been progressive, in that the tax rate rose as income rose. However, at first these were applied not just to the 'slice' above the critical threshold figure but to all earnings. This system, known as the 'slab' system, meant that the marginal effects of £1 of extra income could be to cause a very severe tax burden. It is no wonder, therefore, that it was not in the interests of either employer or employee to raise wages in certain situations, unless by a very great amount—hence, the bunching of wage rates at certain levels. NICs provided the last example of the UK's use of the slab system; the slab system was also used for super tax from 1911 to 1926, and for estate duty until 1968.

'Poverty traps' and 'unemployment traps', or, more generally, the 'surtax on the poor', have been addressed in stages, though inevitably have not been completely eradicated.[11] Before the Social Security Act 1986 came into force, the reduction in benefits combined with the start of income tax and NICs led to the net rate of 'tax' exceeding 100%. This was because the social security claw-back rules were applied to gross income, ie before income tax or NICs. After the Social Security Act 1986 the amount of benefit was related to income net of tax and NICs.[12] Writing in 1993, Hills suggested that while the 1986 reforms largely removed the problem of people losing more than 100% of any extra income, and so ending up worse off, substantially more people faced rates above 70%. These figures applied to families in work; those out of work and receiving income support could still lose 100% of additional part-time earnings.[13] Further work was carried out by Nigel Lawson in 1989,[14] but it fell to Gordon Brown to complete the process by (temporarily) aligning the earnings threshold for NICs to that of the personal relief for income tax, paid for by an extra charge on employer's contributions for higher-paid employees.[15] The introduction of tax credits, beginning with the working families' tax credit, has been another major reform, but the proud boast that the credits would help many relatively well-off families meant a major increase in the number of people facing high marginal effective rates of tax.[16]

9.3.2 Integration?

A full integration of NICs with income tax would mean major administrative and compliance gains, but also major distributional changes. First, the base would be enlarged. NICs are not charged on the same basis as ordinary income.[17] They apply to ITEPA 2003 earnings

---

[11] See HM Treasury, *Budget 2012*, HC 1853 (21 March 2012), Table D.3: Current Receipts, OBR forecast.
[12] See Cmnd 9691.
[13] Hills, *The Future of Welfare* (Joseph Rowntree Foundation, 1993) 25, who pointed out that in 1992–93, 1.9m unemployed non-pensioners were receiving income support and in this position.
[14] For assessment, see Dilnot and Webb (1989) 10(2) *Fiscal Studies* 38.
[15] Achieved by 2000–01.
[16] Written Answer (see Hansard, 23 May 2000).
[17] See Sandler, *Harmonising the Fringes of National Insurance and Income Tax* (IFS Commentary 36).

and, sometimes, ITTOIA 2005, Part 2 profits. Class 1A rates apply to all benefits in kind taxable under ITEPA 2003; however, this is usually a charge on the employer and not on the employee.[18] There is no charge on bank interest, dividends, pensions—or capital gains. Secondly, the group of those paying would be enlarged, since NICs are not payable by those aged under 16 or above state pension age. It will be seen that, if these two enlargements were adopted, the elderly would be hit by a proverbial double whammy. Thirdly, many of the rights arising as a result of paying NICs are directly related to the number of years of contribution, so that the contributory principle itself has to be considered. For a cogent review of the literature and history, see Adam and Loutzenhiser—they conclude that integration is to be desired on economic grounds of transparency and administrative efficiency but, rightly, that the barrier is primarily political.[19] The Mirrlees Review arrived at similar conclusions.[20]

At Summer Budget 2015, the Government announced that it has asked the Office of Tax Simplification (OTS) to review closer alignment of income tax and NICs. This follows earlier consultations aimed solely at operational integration.[21] In its 2016 report, the OTS recommended a seven-stage programme for bringing the two taxes closer together.[22] The steps include moving to an annual, cumulative and aggregate basis for NICs, aligning the definition of earnings and expenses under both taxes, and bringing taxable benefits in kind into Class 1 NICs. At Budget 2016, the Government announced it will commission the OTS to review the impacts of moving employee NICs to an annual, cumulative and aggregated basis and moving employer NICs to a payroll basis. It remains to be seen, however, whether the practical difficulties and political inertia hampering integration can be overcome.

9.4   Tax Credits: Tax Credits Act 2002 and Later

9.4.1 Introduction

One of New Labour's major ideas was the use of tax credits to solve problems of poverty through redistribution. The first effort, embodied in the Tax Credits Act of 1999, was considered in the 4th edition of this work at §9.4 and, as there explained, provided for two existing social security benefits, called family credit and disability working allowance, to be turned into two brand new tax credits—the working families tax credit (WFTC) and the disabled person's tax credit (DPTC). These represented the latest efforts to provide support for families, but were driven by a desire to do so without creating too many disincentives to work. These were really welfare payments masquerading as tax credits.

The Tax Credits Act (TCA) 2002, which came into force on 6 April 2003, repealed the 1999 Act and created two new credits—the child tax credit (CTC) and the working tax

---

[18] See generally Tiley and Collison, *UK Tax Guide*, Pt IX.

[19] Adam and Loutzenhiser, *Integrating Income Tax and National Insurance: an interim report* (Institute for Fiscal Studies, 2007) available at http://www.ifs.org.uk/publications/4101.

[20] Mirrlees *et al* (eds), *op cit*, 126–32.

[21] The Office of Tax Simplification has also recommended integration of income tax and NICs. At Budget 2011 and again at Budget 2012, the Government announced its intention to consult on the integration of the 'operation' of the income tax and NICs systems. For the limitations of this approach, see commentary in Loutzenhiser [2011] BTR 363.

[22] OTS, *The closer alignment of income tax and national insurance*, (March 2016).

credit (WTC).[23] On an annual basis, and using maximum figures for 2015–16, CTC is worth £2,780 per child, plus the basic family element of £545; WTC is worth a maximum of £1,960, with a further £2,010 for certain couples and lone parents.[24] The rules for these credits are closer to tax than to social security. Each credit contains rules enhancing the value of the credits where there is a person who is severely disabled; in this way the DPTC ceased to exist as a separate allowance but has been absorbed into the rest of the system. The two credits must be kept distinct.

The introduction of these two credits meant the repeal of the children's tax credit, but the formerly universal welfare benefit known as child benefit remains in existence. This leaves couples with children and single parents with three possible sources of support: (a) the child benefit, which from 2013 ceased to be universal as it will not be paid to households with at least one partner earning more than £60,000; (b) CTC; and (c) WTC. However, WTC is significantly wider than the old rules; it is also available to households consisting of single people and couples without children, provided they are aged 25 or over. In broad terms, lone parents and couples with children must work 16 hours a week; households with no children must work 30 hours a week. As with WFTC and DPTC, the value of benefits is reduced as incomes rise. Income is determined on a household basis, a move which has rekindled old debates over the value of taxing the family rather than the individual.

Sadly, the introduction of the 2003 credits was not well handled by the Government. The tax profession also took some time to realise that there might be problems. In the meantime, the people who really suffered were families, who struggled to understand how the absurdly complicated claims form were to be filled in. It is curious that a tax system which decided not to apply self-assessment to those with simple tax affairs whose tax burdens fell mostly under ITEPA 2003 and PAYE, imposed heavy compliance burdens on those least able to afford professional help. Those families then had to wait while the administration failed to respond in keeping with its own timetable. Whether an extra year was needed or whether the scheme was too complex even for the Revenue to administer are matters to be examined by PhD students in the years to come, though one hopes that the Government will learn the necessary lessons more quickly. The matter was considered—and the Revenue severely criticised—by the House of Commons Public Accounts Committee 2003–04 Session 14th Report.[25] The problems were stated by the Committee to be due in large part to deficiencies in IT systems, although this seems to place excessive faith in systems as opposed to skilled personnel. Later years bring later criticisms, but also a confidence on the part of HMRC, expressed in their Annual Reports, that things are getting better.

One feature of the system is of great practical importance: the provisional nature of all awards. This means that when the Revenue carry out their checks and find, for example, that too much credit has been paid out, there is no legal obstacle to the Revenue recovering the excess from the overpaid person. These clawbacks were at first handled very badly.[26]

---

[23] For a detailed account of the Act, the regulations and the various policy considerations, see Lee (2003) 10 *Journal of Social Security Law* 7.

[24] For more details on the 2015–16 annual amounts for child tax credit and working tax credit, along with income thresholds, see https://www.gov.uk/browse/benefits/tax-credits.

[25] See also complaints of the CIOT's Low Income Tax Reform Group and other bodies, 29 September 2004, and the Ombudsman: Tax Credits Putting Things Right 2005–06 Session, 21 June 2005.

[26] *Money with your Name on it* (Citizens Advice Bureau, June 2005).

As described in the introduction to this chapter, as the Universal Credit is replacing the CTC and WTC, the description of the details of the credits below is much shorter than in previous editions of this book.

9.4.2 Child Tax Credit

The CTC is paid to a person who has responsibility for the child; it is paid direct rather than through the wage packet. A person may claim the credit if responsible for one or more children (ie below age 16) or qualifying young persons (ie under 20 if in full-time secondary education).[27] It is available whether or not the claimant is in work. Entitlement runs until 31 August following the child's sixteenth birthday. The regulations supply rules for determining when a person has responsibility; these rules begin with a test based on with whom the child normally lives, provide for competing claims and for an election to choose which is the main carer—but not to split the sum.

9.4.3 Working Tax Credit

This credit arises if the claimant is in qualifying remunerative work. The person must work for not less than 16 hours a week if there is a child or if the person has a disability, and for not less than 30 hours if the claimant is 25 or older and has no child and no disability. Special rules are made for maternity leave, for sick pay periods, for seasonal workers, for workers or on strike or under suspension and for gaps between jobs; a person receiving a sum in lieu of notice is not treated as being in employment for that period.

A non-working household will not be entitled to WTC but will instead receive income support and the jobseeker's allowance.

9.4.4 Issues and Problems with the CTC and WTC Regimes

The basing of the CTC and WTC on household income was quite correct in terms of targeting, but meant that the advantages of keeping one's tax affairs secret from one's partner, not to mention the freedom to go out and work knowing that one's marginal rate of tax will not depend on one's partner's income, disappeared not only for spouses but also for any situation in which there was a relevant partnership.

More worrying was the effect of the credits—and of loss of credits—on families and family formation; did the credits encourage single parent families; was a regular income from the state preferred to the income earned by a new partner? Did couples decide to be 'an item' without actually living together? Much of this debate was carried through with a possibly exaggerated view of the benefits of some families and a reluctance to face up to the ever-expanding costs of ever-expanding systems. What was more worrying was the minefield created for parents. If they claimed credits to which they were not entitled, there was the risk of prosecution by a zealous departmental officer whose department has been set a

---

[27] TCA 2002, s 8(3) and the Child Tax Credit Regulations 2002 (SI 2002/2007), reg 5; on overlap with grants to encourage young people to stay on at school, see Lee, *op cit*, n 77.

performance target. If so, the Act created a form of entrapment of which a civilised society should feel ashamed.[28]

9.4.5 The New Universal Credit

With a phased introduction underway, the universal credit is replacing the WTC, CTC, housing benefit, income support, income-based jobseeker's allowance and income-related employment and support allowance.[29] Contributory benefits will not be replaced. The universal credit is an integrated working-age credit that will provide a basic allowance, with additional elements for children, disability, housing and caring. One stated aim of the new universal credit is to improve financial work incentives by ensuring that support is not reduced in as abrupt a manner as under the WTC and CTC systems as people return to work and increase their working hours and earnings. It is expected that claimants will lose about 65 pence in universal credit for every pound they earn after tax from additional work. The Department of Work and Pensions (and not HMRC!) will be responsible for managing overall administration of the credit. For those in employment, universal credit is to be calculated and delivered electronically, with credit payments automatically adjusted according to PAYE monthly income. The Government hopes that the universal credit system will be simpler and will respond more quickly to changes in earnings than the tax credits system it is replacing.

9.5 Relationship: Other Aspects of Social Security and Tax[30]

The tax system is better at taking from people according to their ability to pay than at giving to them according to their need; the latter has been the peculiar job of the social security system.[31] The money for the social security system comes, in part, from NICs. Before 1965 these contributions were generally deductible in computing taxable income;[32] when these ceased to be deductible the personal allowance was increased by an equivalent amount, but since that time, contributions have increased at a faster rate than personal allowances. To the extent that NICs do not provide sufficient finance, the Exchequer provides funds out of general taxation.[33]

---

[28] Among much new literature, see in particular (i) Lee (2003) 10 *Journal of Social Security Law* 7 (cited above); (ii) Brewer, Goodman, Shaw and Sibieta, *Poverty and Inequality in Britain 2006* (IFS, 2006); (iii) Whiteford, Mendelson and Millar, *Timing it Right? Tax Credits and How to Respond to Income Changes* (Joseph Rowntree Foundation); and (iv) Brewer, *The IFS Green Budget 2006*, ch 12 and *Green Budget 2007*, ch 12.

[29] See the documents provided on the Department of Work and Pensions website at http://www.dwp.gov.uk/policy/welfare-reform/legislation-and-key-documents/universal-credit/.

[30] See Parker, *Instead of the Dole* (Routledge, 1989). On differences between attitudes to income tax evasion and to social security fraud, see Walker (1978) 18 *British J Criminology* 348; Deane (1981) 21 *British J Criminology* 47; and Cook, *Rich Law Poor Law: Different Responses to Tax and Supplementary Benefit Fraud* (Open University Press, 1989).

[31] That the social security system is more significant in the reduction of inequality is clear from Hills, *op cit*, ch 1.

[32] The employer's contribution is deductible in computing business profits as part of labour costs.

[33] On governments' inconsistent approaches to the need to balance the books, see [1998] BTR 317, 344.

Further ideas for reform should be mentioned. This is the abolition of the ceiling on NIC contributions. This could be seen as a simple measure of equity, particularly following the reductions in higher rates of income tax in 1988, but, of course, the effect would be to undermine the economic policy considerations behind those reductions. The Labour Government made a first step towards this by imposing a 1% increase in contributions on all relevant income in 2002, and the rate for 2011–12 increased to its present level of 2%. Another reform would be to recognise that one class of income, ie investment income, is not subject to NICs. This is not surprising in historical terms since no benefits could arise by virtue of such income either. However, in order to compensate for not being subject to NICs, all such income could now be subject to income tax at the higher rate; this would be part of a flat rate of tax on investment income. The Meade Committee[34] recommended a return to the Beveridge Scheme, whereby benefits could be made at a generous level (above the poverty line) and supplementary benefit would be needed only for the few who fell through that net for some reason. Among its suggestions for financing this scheme were permitting allowances to be set only against earned income. Instead the Government is once again considering further alignment in the operation of NICs and income tax—but not yet full integration.

---

[34] Meade, *The Structure and Reform of Direct Taxation* (Allen & Unwin, 1978), ch 13.

10

Deductions and Credits
for Taxpayer Expenditure and Losses

10.1 Introduction

The deductions discussed in this chapter are for sums spent by taxpayers or losses incurred by them; the overall level is therefore beyond the immediate control of the Revenue. Some are deductions from income, some are partial deductions, and some are credits. Rules for credits tend to be more complicated to draft, especially if any unused credits can be carried to another year.[1] It is sometimes suggested that the deduction by reference to actual expenditure should be replaced by standardised fixed-sum deductions with or without the right to deduct actual expenditure if higher.[2] The argument for a standardised sum is that it sacrifices equity but reduces administrative and compliance costs.

These deductions are also important as part of the discussion of the nature of income, ie what deductions should be allowed and why. The answers to these questions depend on the model of the relevant tax base. Advocates of tax expenditure find deductions for charitable contributions (and, in the United States, medical expenses) objectionable. Andrews, however, defines the tax base in terms of personal consumption and accumulation of real

---

[1] Sunley, (1977) 30 *National Tax J* 243.
[2] Kaplow, (1994) 50 *Tax L Rev* 1 considers whether an individual with qualifying expenditure just below the threshold should be treated less favourably.

goods and services, rather than net income, and so approves of these deductions.[3] Sections §§10.2–10.7 below deal with allowable deductions in full, but with occasional restrictions as to the type of income against which they may be set. Section §10.8 *et seq* below deal with partial deductions. Step 6[4] contains a number of general rules for deductions for individuals. So the reliefs and allowances must be given effect in such a way as will result in the greatest reduction in the taxpayer's liability to tax. However, a relief may be given effect only in so far as there is sufficient income from which to deduct it, and cannot be given more than once. ITA 2007, section 26 deals with taxpayers other than individuals. ITA 2007, sections 27 and 28 contain equivalent general rules for sums which may be deducted in a different way—as tax reductions.

The reliefs and allowance and tax reductions mentioned in this chapter fit into the statutory calculation scheme discussed below at §12.2 at steps 2, 3 or 6. The reader is advised (a) to revisit this chapter after looking at §12.2, and (b) to wonder at the hideous complexity of the system clearly exposed by the rewritten legislation.

10.2   Interest Payment Relief

This section deals with certain interest payments which are deductible in computing income; for payment after 5 April 2007, the rules are in ITA 2007, Part 8, Chapter 1, sections 383–412.[5] Interest may also be deductible from a particular source falling within a particular Schedule, eg payments in connection with a trade falling within ITTOIA 2005, Part 2. For many years the concept of interest was defined simply by reference to common law notions. FA 2005 recognised new concepts called the alternative financial return and the profits share return; FA 2007 added the alternative finance investment bond and profit share agency; these returns are treated as interest for tax purposes including the present reliefs; see further §26.2.3.[6]

From 1799 until 1969, the UK system took the view that interest was deductible because the tax was levied on income and, in computing income, all charges on that income, including interest, should be deducted. Unfortunately, this gave rise to great complexity, not least due to the machinery by which it was implemented. Today, interest payments are deductible only if the interest is on a loan to defray money applied for certain defined purposes.[7] The most significant deduction of interest, which was abolished as from 6 April 2000, was where money was used to purchase a private residence; this was usually given at source and so was called MIRAS or 'mortgage interest relief at source'.[8]

---

[3] Andrews, 86 *Harvard LR* 309; on tax expenditures, generally see above at §1.8. These and other ideas are discussed by Griffith (1980) 40 *Hastings L J* 343.

[4] ITA 2007, s 25.

[5] Ex TA 1988, s 353. The reason why these are deductible in computing 'income' as opposed to 'total income' is that they apply to certain entities (eg, estate in administration) for which total income is not relevant.

[6] FA 2005, ss 46 *et seq*, as amended.

[7] The purposes are set out in ITA 2007, ss 388–403, ex TA 1988, ss 354–365; there are supplementary provisions in ss 404–412, ex 366–368. The further rules for MIRAS are contained in ss 369–379; these MIRAS rules remain in force for loans within TA 1988, s 365, a provision left untouched by ITA 2007.

[8] Hence MIRAS: TA 1988, s 354.

Seven purposes for deducting interest are relevant today under ITA 2007, Part 8, Chapter 1:[9]

(1) for a partner to buy machinery or plant;
(2) for an employee to buy machinery and plant;
(3) to acquire an interest in a close non-investment holding company;
(4) to acquire an interest in an employee-controlled company;
(5) to acquire an interest in a partnership;
(6) to invest in a co-operative; and
(7) to enable personal representatives to pay certain IHT.

Purposes (1)–(6) take effect as normal deductions at the taxpayer's marginal rate.[10] Since the last purpose is available only to personal representatives, it takes effect at their rate as personal representatives.

10.2.1 General Rules

Relief is not available if the interest is incurred in overdrawing an account or debiting the holder of a credit card.[11] The interest paid must be in respect of a loan to the taxpayer; sums paid in respect of a guarantee of a loan to another do not qualify.[12] Where a loan account is created by the consolidation of and transfer from overdrawn accounts, nothing is actually paid to defray money applied for a particular purpose and so no relief is due.[13] The loan must not have been used for other non-qualifying purposes first; some reliefs have time limits.[14] Where the rate of interest exceeds a reasonable commercial rate, no relief is given for the excess.[15] A loan for mixed purposes may be apportioned.[16]

10.2.2 Anti-avoidance

CTA 2010, sections 777–779, ex TA 1988, s 786 (not rewritten for income tax), are designed to prevent the conversion of non-deductible interest into a deductible annuity or other income stream; section 778 treats the payment of such an annuity as a payment of yearly interest. Similarly, the transfer of such an income-earning asset with a duty to sell back may result in the income of the asset being treated as that of the transferor, as will the assignment, surrender or waiver of any income. This is of much less importance for income tax now that the scope of the annual payments (ex Schedule D, Case III) has been reduced in scope, but it remains relevant where Case III applies, eg for business purposes.

---

[9] ITA 2007, s 386.
[10] ITA 2007, s 386(4).
[11] ITA 2007, s 384; on what is an overdraft, see *Walcot Bather v Golding* [1979] STC 707; 52 TC 64.
[12] *Hendy v Hadley* [1980] 2 All ER 554; [1980] STC 292.
[13] *Lawson v Brooks* [1992] STC 76.
[14] ITA 2007, s 385(2)–(4), ex TA 1988, s 367(2).
[15] ITA 2007, s 384(2), ex TA 1988, s 353(3)(b); on commercial rate of interest see anti-avoidance rule in s 384(3)–(5), added by FA 2008, Sch 22, para 17.
[16] ITA 2007, s 386(2), ex TA 1988, s 367(4)—see explanatory notes on changes.

More broadly, ITA 2007, section 809ZG and CTA 2009, section 443 (ex TA 1988, section 787) deny relief under any provision of the Tax Acts, including therefore ITA 2007, section 383 in respect of interest when a scheme has been created the sole or main benefit of which is the obtaining of a reduction in tax liability by means of the relief. This was particularly designed to deal with schemes whereby an individual pays a substantial sum by way of (allowable) interest in advance and then sells the right to the capital; as a result the court looks at the scheme as a whole and not at each separate payment.[17] An example of this sort of scheme is *Cairns v MacDiarmid*,[18] where the Court of Appeal, applied the *Ramsay* doctrine and held that interest payable under a scheme was not interest for these purposes.

10.2.3 *Qualifying Purposes*

(1) and (2) *Purchase of Machinery or Plant Eligible for Capital Allowances By Partner or Employer (sections 388–391).*
    While the partnership itself may claim the capital allowance on the plant acquired with the loan, only the individual partner can deduct the interest paid by that partner under this rule. This relief is available only in the year the advance is made and the next three years of assessment. Analogous relief is given where the capital allowance is claimed by the employer but the employee pays the interest.

(3) and (4) *Acquisition of an interest in a close company or an employee-controlled company (sections 392–397).*
    Relief for interest is allowable if the loan is used to acquire ordinary share capital in a close company, or is acquired by the company for use in its trade (or to repay an eligible loan). The company must not be a close investment holding company[19] and must exist wholly or mainly for the purpose of carrying on a trade.[20] Interest relief is not usually available if the business consists of the occupation of commercial woodlands.[21] Relief is due if the holding is a material interest or if the taxpayer works for the greater part of the time in the actual management or conduct of the company. Relief is still available if the company was close when the interest in the company was acquired, but is no longer close when the interest is paid. Relief will continue after shares in one company are exchanged for shares in another, provided a new loan would have satisfied all these conditions.[22] Relief is not available for shares if the person acquiring them (or that person's spouse) claims relief under the enterprise investment scheme.[23] Similar relief is available to buy ordinary share capital of an employee-controlled company.[24] The receipt of sums from

---

[17] *Westmoreland Investments Ltd v Macniven* [1998] STC 1131 (CA), (s 787 not applicable).
[18] [1983] STC 178; 56 TC 556; see Gillard, *In the Name of Charity* (Chatto & Windus, 1987), 64, 264.
[19] ITA 2007, s 392(2), ex TA 1988, s 360(1A).
[20] See *Lord v Tustain* [1993] STC 755; 65 TC 761; for discussion of the case and later amendments to s 360, see Watson [1994] BTR 527.
[21] ITA 2007, s 411, ex FA 1988, Sch 6, para. 3(3), se
[22] ITA 2007, s 410, formerly ESC A43.
[23] ITA 2007, s 392(3), ex TA 1988, s 360(3A); semble relief is withheld even if the claim for BES relief subsequently fails (eg, because the trade is not a qualifying trade): ICAEW Memorandum TR 759, [1989] *Simon's Tax Intelligence* 718.
[24] ITA 2007, s 396, ex TA 1988, s 361.

the company may be treated as a repayment of the loan, so bringing about a reduction or extinction of the claim.[25]

(5) and (6) *Buying into a partnership or co-operative (sections 398–402).*

Relief is also given on loans used to buy an interest in a partnership, or to contribute capital or a premium, or to lend money to the partnership for use in its trade; the partnership must not be limited or an LLP.[26] The purchaser must still be a partner in the period for which the relief is claimed (and not a limited partner) and must not have recovered capital from the partnership—unless it has been taken into account.[27] The loan must still be for use in the partnership business: where A, a partnership, took out a loan for the purposes of partnership B, of which A itself was a member, A was held entitled to the relief.[28] At one time relief under these rules could be restricted for partners under some forms of partnership with limited liability or where the partner was not active.[29] These restrictions on relief for interest were removed by FA 2005 but other anti-avoidance rules were added (see below §20.10.7). Similar relief is available for interest on a loan to buy an interest in a co-operative or to lend money to such a body.[30] The relief is restricted for a film partnership by section 400.

(7) *Enabling personal representatives to pay certain IHT.*

See ITA 2007, sections 403-405 for the IHT-related qualifying purposes.

10.3   Income Losses[31]

Where a source of income generates a loss, the amount of income is zero (not a negative sum). However, the legislation allows certain losses to be deducted by being set against income. As will be seen below, some losses may be set against general income, while others may be set only against income of a certain type.

10.3.1 Trading Losses

Four basic rules apply (for more details see further §20.10 below):

(1)   A trading loss in one year may be set off against the general income of that and the previous year of assessment, a relief known as a sideways relief.[32] More formally, the relief is from tax on an amount of income for that year equal to the amount of the loss; where the income exceeds the loss, the taxpayer is relieved of all liability to tax.[33]

---

[25] ITA 2007, s 402, ex TA 1988, s 363(2); on which see Inland Revenue Interpretation RI 12.
[26] ITA 2007, s 399(2), (3), ex TA 1988, s 362(2).
[27] As set out in ITA 2007, ss 406–408, ex TA 1988, s 363.
[28] *Major v Brodie* [1998] STC 491.
[29] ITA 2007, ss 104–107, ex TA 1988, s 117.
[30] ITA 2007, ss 401–402.
[31] For general discussion, see RC Cmnd 9474 (1955) ch 19; and for trading losses, see Cmnd 8189, 77–83.
[32] ITA 2007, s 64, ex TA 1988, s 380.
[33] *Ibid.*

(2)   The legislation allows a carry-back of a trading loss where the loss arises in the year of assessment in which the trade is first carried on or the next three years of assessment.[34]

(3)   The loss may be rolled forward (indefinitely), but can only be set against later trading income *of that trade*—relief downwards.[35] See further below §20.10.3.

(4)   Terminal losses may be carried back and set against earlier profits of the same trade within a set period.[36] A terminal loss is one sustained in the year of assessment in which the trade is permanently discontinued and in that part of the preceding year of assessment beginning 12 months before the date of discontinuance.

Note that FA 2008 added a £25,000 cap for sideways reliefs from non-active losses: see ITA 2007, section 74A and further below §20.10.6.

10.3.2 Other Types of Loss

10.3.2.1 Property Businesses

The mid-1990s reconstruction of Schedule A (now ITTOIA 2005, Part 2) for income tax has meant a new provision governing related losses.[37] The general rule is that the rents from all properties in the UK are aggregated and expenditure is deducted from the aggregate. This automatically provides loss relief for a deficit on a single property, where there is other property let to provide a surplus. Any surplus losses may be rolled forward indefinitely and set off against any profit of a property business carried on in a subsequent year.[38] In one situation, however, the loss may be relieved against general income of the same year of assessment. Broadly, this arises where there are net capital allowances arising from plant and machinery used in an agricultural estate.[39] Special rules allow certain unused losses from before 1995–96 to be treated as Schedule A losses: these are losses under the old Schedule A, under Schedule D, Case VI for furnished lettings, and excess interest.[40]

10.3.2.2 Furnished Holiday Lettings

Loss relief is available when a letting is within the definition of furnished holiday lettings (below at §25.3.2).[41] In *Brown v Richardson*,[42] the Special Commissioners considered a claim for loss relief on the basis that property had been acquired to be 'let on a commercial basis and with a view to the realisation of profits'.[43] An accountant and his wife had purchased a property in Cornwall, the entire purchase being funded by a mortgage secured on the couple's main residence. A partnership agreement was drawn up between the husband

---

[34]   ITA 2007, s 72, ex TA 1988, s 381. It is the loss that arises in the fiscal year that is relievable: see *Gascoine v Wharton* [1996] STC 1481; 69 TC 147, in which a taxpayer argued unsuccessfully that reliefs should be given for a loss arising in an accounting period, part of which was not during the year of assessment.

[35]   ITA 2007, s 89, ex TA 1988, s 388.

[36]   *Ibid.*

[37]   ITA 2007, s 117, ex TA 1988, s 379A, added by FA 1995, Sch 6, para 19.

[38]   ITA 2007, s 118, ex TA 1988, s 379A(1); on calculation of loss, see s 379A(7).

[39]   ITA 2007, ss 120–124, ex TA 1988, s 379A(5).

[40]   ITA 2007, s 122, ex FA 1995, Sch 6, para 19(2), (3), referring to TA 1988, ss 392, 355(4).

[41]   ITA 2007, s 127, ex TA 1988, s 503(1).

[42]   [1997] STC (SCD) 233.

[43]   TA 1988, s 504.

and wife, so that profits arising on the letting of the Cornish property were split equally between them but any losses were allocated wholly to the husband. Losses arose, primarily because of significant finance charges. The Special Commissioners held that account had to be taken of the deduction of charges on income in considering whether the letting was with a view to profit, even though they were not technically part of the calculation of profit; 'profits' meant commercial profits and not tax-adjusted profit.

10.3.2.3 Employment Income

Relief for employment losses may be claimed under ITA 2007, Part 4, Chapter 5 (sections 128–130). However, although section 128 refers to employments (but not to offices), the Revenue's position has been that a claim can never arise, even when expenses exceed emoluments. This is because expenses are deductible only if they are defrayed out of the emoluments, and are deductible only from those emoluments. This is made clear by ITEPA 2003, section 329. However, employees can claim capital allowances for certain expenditure, and these are given effect as deductions and so potentially give rise to losses. Section 128 of the 2007 Act revives the allowance by disapplying another rule. This change is quite beneficial to the few who will take advantage of it, but one wonders why this was done through the Rewrite. *J Martin v HMRC*[44] provides a notable example of how an employee can incur a loss from employment. It is apparently the first reported case on the concepts of negative taxable income and negative earnings under ITEPA 2003, section 11(3)(a), which provides for relief under ITA 2007, section 128. Upon leaving his employment, the taxpayer was required to repay a bonus received in a prior year. In allowing relief for the taxpayer's repayment of bonus, the First-tier Tribunal held that the full amount of the original bonus had been correctly treated as income in the year payment was received, and that the repayment in a later year was negative taxable income in that year. The First-tier Tribunal's sensible conclusion was upheld by the Upper Tribunal.[45]

10.3.2.4 ITTOIA 2005, Part 5, Chapter 8

Relief for what used to be Schedule D, Case VI losses may be claimed under ITA 2007, section 152 against other miscellaneous income of that year and then rolled forward and set against other Case VI income of later years. However, statutes which place certain types of income in Case VI often restrict their use to absorb losses.

10.3.2.5 ITTOIA 2005, Parts 2 and 3

A loss arising from a trade or profession carried on wholly overseas may be entitled to relief in full under ITA 2007, sections 64, 72, 83 or 89.[46] With effect from 1998–99, losses from the letting of foreign property have been relieved in the same way as losses from the letting of property within the UK.[47] Thus, all rental income arising from overseas property is pooled, and expenses incurred in generating that income are deducted therefrom. This has the effect that loss relief is given immediately for a deficit of income on a particular property

---

[44] [2013] UKFTT 040 (TC). For commentary see Watson [2013] BTR 132.
[45] [2014] UKUT 0429 (TCC).
[46] ITA 2007, s 95(2,) ex TA 1988, s 391(2).
[47] Originally added by FA 1995, s 41(8).

where another property has produced a surplus. An overall deficit is carried forward to a subsequent year.[48]

10.3.2.6 ITTOIA 2005, Part 4—Schedule D, Cases III and IV and Schedule F

No relief is possible under these Schedules (applicable to savings and investment income) since the income tax legislation does not permit any deductions.

10.4 Loss on Shares in Unquoted Trading Companies

Although capital losses are the province of CGT and may not be set off against income, an exception is made where the loss arises from the disposal of unquoted shares in a trading company or member of a trading group; the rules are now in ITA 2007, Part 4, Chapter 3 (sections 131–151). The 2007 Act makes no fewer than 16 changes, which indicates how necessary some form of review was. The purpose is to allow entrepreneurs to escape the restrictive CGT rules. The loss is computed on CGT principles. The relief is available only in respect of shares for which T, the individual, or T's spouse or civil partner, subscribed[49]—as distinct from those acquired through gift, inheritance or purchase. Shares held by another as nominee for the individual also count.[50] The couple need not be living together when the shares are subscribed for, but must be so when the shares are transferred.[51] The term 'subscribed' is amplified to cover other situations, eg corresponding bonus shares.[52] The shares must be ordinary share capital.[53] The company must be a 'qualifying trading company'; a company qualifies only if it satisfies complex criteria as to what it has been doing (eg trading—but not in items such as shares or land)[54] and for how long (six years if previously an investment company or a dealer in forbidden items). In addition, the company must not have its shares quoted on a recognised stock exchange and must be resident in the UK.

The disposal must be an arm's-length sale, a distribution on winding up, or the deemed disposal which arises when shares have become of negligible value.[55] Relief is denied even for those disposals if there is a share exchange for non-commercial reasons or value-shifting has occurred. The relief may be claimed for the year in which the loss is realised or the preceding year.[56] Any unused loss may be set only against capital gains. Where the taxpayer also has a loss entitled to relief under ITA 2007, sections 64 and 72, the present loss is absorbed first.

Further rules apply where there are mixed holdings, eg where some shares were acquired by subscription and others by inheritance. The rules restrict the loss to what would have been the deductible cost if mixing had not occurred. The mixing rules may be avoided by

---

[48] ITA 2007, s 120, ex TA 1988, s 379A(1)(a).
[49] ITA 2007, s 135, ex TA 1988, s 574(3).
[50] Section 149, change 32.
[51] Section 135 (and see explanatory notes, change 22).
[52] ITA 2007, 135(4).
[53] ITA 2007, s 151, ex TA 1988, ss 576(5), 832(1).
[54] ITA 2007, ss 134 and 137, ex TA 1988, s 576(4), (5), as amended by FA 1989, Sch 12, para 4.
[55] ITA 2007, s 131(3), ex TA 1988, s 575(1).Words 'for full consideration' removed. On timing of disposal, see ITA 2007, s 151, change 35.
[56] ITA 2007, s 133(3), (4), ex TA 1988, s 574(1), (2).

issuing different types of shares.[57] There are also rules on part disposals.[58] Special rules apply also to shares acquired on reorganisations and similar events.[59] Legislation now affirms 'beyond doubt' the Revenue view that the withdrawal of funds from share accounts with building societies or industrial and provident societies cannot give rise to this relief.[60]

10.5   Annual Payments and Royalties: Sums Within ITA 2007, Chapter 8, Part 4

ITA 2007, sections 448 and 449 in effect allow the assignment of income in certain defined situations. These are payments made for bona fide commercial reasons in connection with the individual's trade, profession or vocation, eg partnership retirement annuities and certain earn-out arrangements and payments: see further chapters twenty-seven and thirty-one below. For many years relief was given by means of the device of a charge on income (ex TA 1988, section 348). ITA 2007 abolishes that device for income tax and gives relief in a simpler way—as a deduction in computing net income.[61]

10.6   Qualifying Gifts to Charity Under Gift Aid and Other Schemes

The gift aid scheme allows a person an income tax deduction for a contribution of (a) money; (b) qualifying securities; or (c) land.[62] Two different techniques are used to give effect to these deductible items. For land and securities the value is allowed as a deduction at step 2—in moving from total income to net income.[63]

For gifts of money, the tax system treats the taxpayer as having made a net payment which must therefore be 'grossed up' to reflect the relevant basic rate of income tax.[64] As far as the donor is concerned, the overall effect of a gift of £800 is the same as if he had paid £1,000 to the charity and then claimed the deduction at 20% when settling his tax affairs for the year. As the majority of taxpayers do not go through the self-assessment system, this system is, for them, more efficient. In any event, the charity claims the £200 back from HMRC. If the donor is a higher-rate taxpayer (40%), the charity still recovers £200 and the donor recovers the tax relief on the difference between the higher rate and the basic rate—a further £200—from HMRC. There is now a process by which the £200 can be transferred from the taxpayer to the charity if the taxpayer so wishes. On payroll giving see §18.3.4.3.

---

[57] ITA 2007, s 148, ex TA 1988, s 576. On mixed holdings, see ITA 2007, changes 27–29.
[58] ITA 2007, s 147, change 26.
[59] ITA 2007, changes 23–25.
[60] ITA 2007, s 135, ex TA 1988, s 576(5).
[61] ITA 2007, s 24(2) and ss 447–452, and changes 81 *et seq*.
[62] ITA 2007, Pt 8, Chs 2 (ss 413–430) and 3 (ss 431–446), ex FA 1990, s 25, TA 1988, ss 505, 587B and 587C.
[63] ITA 2007, s 23, step (2) and s 24(1)(a).
[64] For statutory guidance on how to gross up, see ITA 2007, s 998.

10.7   'Full' Deductions for Certain Items Restricted as to Types of Income

Apart from losses, other sums are deductible in full, but only against certain classes of income. Examples may be found in the rules in FA 2004, section 190, so that relief for pension contributions is usually available against relevant earnings, and in ITTOIA 2005 post-cessation expenditure (see below at §23.4).

10.8   Tax Reductions and Deductions at Specified Rates

ITA 2007, section 26 sets out a list of available 'tax reductions', which take effect at step 6 of the calculation rules (and not as deductions in computing total income at step 3). One such reduction is for transferable tax allowances for married couples and civil partners. Many of these reductions are tax incentives to undertake particular forms of investment. Under the Enterprise Investment Scheme (EIS), relief is permitted at a current rate of 30% (not the taxpayer's marginal rate).[65] For 2015–16 the maximum investment is £1,000,000 pa. A similar regime applies to Seed Enterprise Investment Scheme (SEIS) relief[66] at a 50% rate on maximum investment of £100,000 pa and social investments ('SI') relief at a 30% rate on maximum investment of £1,000,000 pa.[67] Venture capital trust relief is another form of relief by way of tax reduction (with a limit of £ 200,000 pa) and is permitted for contributions to collective investment schemes.[68] The rate of deduction has varied between 20% and 40%, and is currently 30%.[69]

The year 2000 saw the introduction of a relief for investment by individual or companies[70] (but not trusts) in an accredited community development finance institution (CDFI). Again, it is not a simple deduction from income but a reduction in the investor's income tax liability at step 6—in this case equal to 5% of the invested amount.[71] There is no limit on the amount that may be invested. The relief may be claimed for five years, so making a maximum relief of 25% of the investment. The relief cannot give rise to a repayment. The investment must be of the right type (a loan or issue of shares or securities) and various general conditions must be met, eg that the investor must not control the CDFI and must be the sole beneficial owner of the investment. Further rules provide for the withdrawal of relief, eg if the investor disposes of the investment in a non-permitted way during the five-year period.

A person making qualifying maintenance payments[72] could claim a reduction in tax in respect of those payments subject to a maximum of a sum equal to 10% of the minimum

---

[65] ITA 2007, Pt 5.
[66] ITA 2007, Pt 5A.
[67] ITA 2007, Pt 5B.
[68] ITA 2007, Pt 6.
[69] ITA 2007, s 263.
[70] ITA 2007, Pt 7, ss 333–382, FA 2002, s 57 and Schs 16 and 17.
[71] ITA 2007, s 335(2).
[72] ITA 2007, s 453, ex TA 1988, s 347B.

married couple's allowance (£3,220 for 2015–16). Its practical repeal was a surprise, and probably an unintended casualty of the decision to abolish the married couple's allowance (see §11.4.2); it is available today only if either the payer or the recipient was born before 6 April 1935.[73]

Other examples of tax reductions at specified rates are to be found in the reliefs considered in chapter eleven; these are not dealt with in this chapter because they are fixed deductions given by reference to the circumstances of the taxpayer rather than to sum spent by the taxpayer.

10.9   Benefits Whether or Not Taxpayer Liable to Tax

These categories must be noted since they cause sums to be paid by the Revenue even though the person making the original payment is not subject to tax. They include WTC and CTC (see §9.4).

---

[73] ITA 2007, s 454, ex TA 1988, s 347B (1A).

11

Personal Reliefs and Tax Reductions

11.1   General Structure

We now turn to the rules for deductions allowed by the tax system on account of personal circumstances.[1] There are now very few of these, since the adjustment of tax burden according to personal circumstances is also the province of the tax credit system. Under ITA 2007, section 23, two deductions can be made from net income at step 3: the basic personal allowance, and the blind person's relief. The others take the form of tax 'reductions' at step 6. In many ways a tax reduction is like a credit against one's tax liability, but the introduction of the tax credits considered in chapter nine means that it would be very confusing to use the term 'credit' here. Since tax reliefs reduce the amount of income that is taxable, they are more valuable to those paying at higher rates than to those paying at lower rate.[2] Tax reductions, by contrast, are worth the same amount to all taxpayers and so may be seen as 'fairer'.

Tax reductions are of use only if one has a tax liability. The logic behind the tax credit system is to provide benefit of value to taxpayers and non-taxpayers alike. What lies behind all three sets of rules is a wish to allocate the tax burden according to ability to pay. These allowances may be claimed only by individuals as opposed to, for example, trusts, and therefore are distinguishable from other deductions such as loss relief. Further, they may generally be claimed only by residents. Allowances are available only for the year of assessment; allowances which are not used in one tax year cannot be rolled forward (or backwards) to another year. Similarly, they are personal in the sense that they cannot normally be assigned directly.[3] Some may be assigned indirectly if one person can provide income for another to

---

[1] For an economic analysis of take up of (old age) means-tested benefits, see Hancock *et al* (2004) 25 *Fiscal Studies* 279, and on taxation of pensioners see the 15-country survey by Keenay and Whitehouse (2003) 24 *Fiscal Studies* 1.

[2] For a defence of reliefs as opposed to credits, see Brannon and Morse (1976) 26 *National Tax Jo* 599, 659; and Gottschalk (1976) 29 *National Tax Jo* 221.

[3] On assignment of the married couple's allowance for those born before 6 April 1935, see ITA 2007, ss 51–53, ex TA 1988, s 257BB.

absorb that other's allowance. The sums are index-linked but may be overridden by express legislation.[4]

The basic rate limit, ie the point at which higher-rate liability begins, is set for 2016–17 at £32,000, a drop from earlier years to offset the benefit to higher-rate taxpayers from successive increases in the basic personal allowance.[5] Personal allowances for individuals are phased out as their 'adjusted net income' rises above £100,000 by £1 for every £2, resulting in a marginal rate of 60% as opposed to the otherwise relevant rate of 40%.[6] The concept of adjusted net income is also used where a taper is applied to old people's reliefs. From 2010–11 another rate of income tax, called the 'additional rate', applies on income in excess of £150,000; presently the rate is 45%. As a corollary, the 'additional dividend rate' was introduced, which is now 38.1%. The trust rate and dividend trust rate also rose to match these rates—45% and 38.1%, respectively.

11.1.1 Non-residents

Individuals who are not resident are entitled to personal reliefs under ITA 2007 only if they fall within certain categories, and then only on a special basis. The categories are:[7]

(1)   nationals of an EEA state;[8]
(2)   persons who are or have been employed in the service of the Crown, any missionary society or in the service of any territory under Her Majesty's protection;
(3)   persons resident in the Channel Islands or the Isle of Man;
(4)   persons who have previously resided within the UK but who are compelled to live abroad for reasons of health, or the health of members of their families resident with them; and
(5)   widows whose late husbands (or widowers whose late wives) were in the service of the Crown.

In addition, some double taxation treaties may provide for relief of non-residents as if they were British subjects. The category of non-resident national of an EEA state as shown in (1) above was added by FA 2008. One effect of the change was to ensure that the rules referred to the current list of EEA members. Another was to ensure that all UK nationals qualified for personal allowances—the UK being a member of the EEA.[9] These qualifying non-residents receive their allowances in full. The 'married couple's' allowances under sections 45 and 46 are transferable if the transferee is resident or a qualifying non-resident.[10] However, the special transitional rules in section 257D (repealed in 2000) did not apply if the husband was not resident in the UK.[11] A separate category for Commonwealth citizens was removed effective for 2010–11.

---

[4] ITA 2007, s 57, ex TA 1988, s 257C.
[5] ITA 2007, s 10(5).
[6] ITA 2007, s 35.
[7] ITA 2007, s 56, ex TA 1988, s 278(2).
[8] ITA 2007, s 56(3)(za), ex TA 1988, s 278(9).
[9] ITA 2007, s 56, as amended by FA 2008, s 70.
[10] ITA 2007, s 47(2).
[11] TA 1988, s 278(2A).

11.1.2 Reductions

The effect of an income tax reduction at this step is to take a deduction in the individual's tax liability. The list of reductions is in ITA 2007, section 26 and includes the partially transferable tax allowance for married couples and civil partners. The amount of the reduction is limited and is currently set at 10% of a specified amount. The reduction may be taken only if there is sufficient tax from which to deduct it,[12] ie there cannot be any repayment. However, in calculating whether there is sufficient tax the income in respect of which a foreign tax credit is claimed *is treated* as available—in effect the credit is ignored, a rule favourable to the taxpayer.[13]

11.2 The Reliefs

11.2.1 The Basic Personal Relief

Under ITA 2007, section 35, all individuals resident in the UK—and, as just noted at §11.1.1, some non-residents—are entitled to a deduction from net income by way of personal relief. For 2016–17 the figure is £11,000. So, if a taxpayer has employment income of £11,010, the personal relief will reduce his taxable income to £10 and the tax bill will be £2 (since the 20% basic rate will apply). As a deduction in computing taxable income, its effect is to reduce the top slice of total income—it will therefore be more valuable to a 40% taxpayer (£4,400) than to a 20% taxpayer (£2,200). The personal relief will be no use to a nil rate taxpayer. The personal relief is reduced by £1 for every £2 of adjusted net income over £100,000, so is no use to a taxpayer with income in excess of £122,000.

It should be noted that the personal allowance has increased substantially in recent years as the Government has aimed to take lower income taxpayers out of the income tax net entirely; in 2010–11 the personal allowance was a mere £6,475. At Budget 2016 the Government said it intended to raise the personal allowance further still, to £11,500 in 2017–18, with a view to reaching a personal allowance of £12,500 and a higher-rate threshold of £50,000 by the end of the current parliament. Further, when the personal allowance reaches £12,500, it will then increase in line with the annual equivalent of an individual working 30 hours per week at the national minimum wage adult rate.

FA 2014, section 11 added new sections 55A–E to ITA 2007 introducing the ability for one spouse to transfer a limited amount of his or her unused personal allowance to his or her spouse. Unused personal allowance of up to 10% of the standard personal allowance is transferrable but only to a basic-rate paying spouse or registered civil partner. Roughly 4 million married couples and civil partnerships—about 1/3 of such families and about 1/6 of families with children—are eligible. Although the benefit to each spousal unit is relatively small (about £200), the expected cost of this measure to the Exchequer is not small—£515m in 2015-16 rising to £820m in 2018-19.[14] Early indications are, however,

---

[12] ITA 2007, s 29(2), ex TA 1988, s 256(2).
[13] ITA 2007, s 27, esp sub-ss (5) and (6), ex TA 1988, s 256(3)(c).
[14] Budget 2014 estimates. For commentary see Ball [2014] BTR 356 and Loutzenhiser [2015] BTR 110.

that take up has been very low, in the region of only 8 per cent of eligible couples; this is hardly surprising given the relatively small benefit on offer and the need to make a separate application for it.

11.2.2 Blind Person's Relief

Under ITA 2007, section 38, a registered blind person is entitled to a deduction from net income—of £2,290 for 2016–17.[15] The person must be registered with a local authority for at least a part of the year; this excludes non-residents. If the eye condition develops in one year but registration is not completed until the next, the relief may (no longer simply by concession) be given for the first year.[16] If the claimant is married or in a registered civil partnership, any unusable part of the allowance may be transferred to the spouse or partner.[17] In determining the extent of the blind person's allowance which cannot be used, and so is available for transfer, no account is taken of the couple's tax reduction under section 45 or section 46; similarly, where the blind person is a married woman who is entitled to the whole or part of the married couple's reduction, that married couple's reduction is also ignored.

11.3   Personal Tax Reduction for Those Attaining 65 by 6 April 2000

There is additional principal 'tax reduction' available to certain married couples and civil partners, but only if either the taxpayer or the taxpayer's spouse/partner was aged over 65 on 6 April 2000 (see §11.4.2).

11.4   Older Taxpayers

Three rules have applied special treatment for older taxpayers. The personal relief may be higher—for now—and the tax reduction for married persons and civil partners may be available. The third rule is the retention of the qualifying maintenance deduction (see §10.11 above). The problem of poverty among older people is very severe; as far as those owning their homes are concerned, releasing the value of that capital could be a significant help.[18] However, the issues presented by the very fact of an ageing population are also significant, as this leads to lower savings, slower investment growth and a reduced rate of national economic growth.[19]

---

[15] On rules for calculating net adjusted income from which this relief is to be deducted, see ITA 2007, s 58, ex TA 1988, s 265(3).

[16] ITA 2007, s 38(4), ex ESC A86.

[17] ITA 2007, s 39.

[18] See Symposium (1998) 19 *Fiscal Studies* 141; and Hancock (1998) 19 *Fiscal Studies* 249.

[19] Disney (1996) 17(2) *Fiscal Studies* 83.

11.4.1 Increased Level of Personal Allowance[20]

The higher personal allowance for those born between 6 April 1938 and 5 April 1948 has recently been repealed. The higher personal allowance for those born before 6 April 1938 is repealed from April 2016, but for 2015–16 was £10,660. The allowance was reduced by £1 for every £2 of adjusted net income in excess of £27,700. If the taxpayer died during the fiscal year, the test was applied in respect of the age that individual would have attained by the end of that fiscal year.[21] The relief depended exclusively on the age of the claimant. With a basic rate of tax of 20%, the effect of the restriction in age allowance was to give a marginal rate of tax of 30% when clawing back the extra personal relief.

11.4.2 Couple's Reduction

This is available to married couples and registered same-sex couples who are living together, provided either the taxpayer or the taxpayer's partner was born before 6 April 1935, ie had reached age 65 by 6 April 2000 and so has reached age 81 by 5 April 2016.[22] It takes the form of a reduction in tax, currently calculated at 10%, by reference to a set sum. For 2016–17, the set sum is £8,355. The maximum sums are reduced as total income rises but cannot be pulled down below the minimum amount in section 43 of £3,220. The formula for phasing out is the same as was formerly used for the increased personal allowance, and so begins at £27,700.

11.4.2.1 Allocating and Sharing of Reliefs

For marriages on or after 5 December 2005 and civil partnerships (which only became possible on that date) the rules are relatively simple.[23] Section 46 allows an initial claim by the spouse or civil partner with the higher net income; equality of incomes requires a joint election.[24] These rules may also apply to spouses who married before 5 December 2005 but who elect to come within them.[25]

First there is the sharing rule, by which half of the minimum amount of the relief may be transferred unilaterally by the individual wholly entitled to the relief or by a joint election (sections 47 and 48). Then there is the retransfer rule; if an election has been made and one taxpayer is entitled to the whole relief, one half may be transferred back.[26] The overall effect is that spouses and partners who do things in the right way and at the right time can allocate the entire relief to whichever of them they wish, or can share it equally.

The only provision allowing for unequal sharing or for a complete transfer back is where one of them is *unable* to use the relief because of a lack of income.[27] Being unable to use the income is quite distinct from being unable to use the deduction as advantageously as one's spouse or civil partner.

[20] For history and criticism, see Morris (1981) 2(3) *Fiscal Studies* 29.
[21] ITA 2007, s 41 and FA 2005, s 9 provide an increase above that for normal indexation.
[22] ITA 2007, s 45, ex TA 1988, s 257A.
[23] ITA 2007, s 46, ex TA 1988, s 257Ab, added by Tax and Civil Partnership Regulations 2005 (SI 2005/3229).
[24] ITA 2007, s 46(2)(e) and (6).
[25] ITA 2007, s 46(2)(b).
[26] ITA 2007, ss 48 and 49; on procedure elections, see s 50.
[27] ITA 2007, ss 51–53, ex TA 1988, s 257BB.

For marriages before 5 December 2005, the formal starting point of the legislation is still that the husband is the person entitled to this reduction.[28] The wife may then claim her half of the allowance as of right and they may jointly elect that she should get all of it; the husband can then claim his half back.[29] As with the more modern marriage rule above, the outcome is that each has a right to claim half of the allowance, but entitlement to the whole allowance is possible only with the consent (tacit or express) of the other.

11.4.2.2 Married and Living Together?

The question whether the parties are married is governed by the law of marriage and by the private international law rules for the recognition of marriages in other states. The term 'wife' means 'lawful wife', ie a woman with whom the taxpayer has entered into a relationship of marriage recognised by the civil law of the appropriate part of the UK.[30] Under the pre-1990 rules it was held that when a husband was separated from his wife but then contracted a valid (polygamous) second marriage to a second wife, he was entitled to the allowance, as the phrase 'his wife' could be construed as meaning 'a person being his wife'.[31] Spouses/partners living under the same roof but in separate households are not living together.[32]

---

[28] ITA 2007, s 45, ex TA 1988, s 257A(1).

[29] ITA 2007, s 47, ex TA 1988, s 257BA.

[30] *Rignell v Andrews* [1990] STC 410; 63 TC 312.

[31] *Nabi v Heaton* [1983] STC 344; 57 TC 292 (CA).

[32] *Holmes v Mitchell* [1991] STC 25; 63 TC 718, applying the divorce test formulated in *Hopes v Hopes* [1949] Probate 227; [1948] 2 All ER 920 (CA). If the married couple live apart and one maintains the other wholly and voluntarily, they are still taken as living apart.

12

Calculations

12.1   Introduction

ITA 2007, Part 2, Chapter 3 (sections 22–32) sets out, for the first time in a UK statute, the way in which income tax is to be calculated. Section 23 introduces new concepts of 'total income' (step 1) and 'net income' (step 2). It does not use the expression 'taxable income' but instead takes the taxpayer/reader through seven steps, at the end of which one has reached the taxpayer's liability for the year. Except that one has not quite reached the end, since section 32, signposted from section 22(2), goes on to list 19 liabilities which have not been dealt with in the calculation.

This chapter considers these rules, before turning to a discussion of some problems of progressions (§12.8). In §12.6 we examine the different structures and rates which have applied at various times since the Second World War.

12.2   Calculation (ITA 2007, Section 23)

12.2.1 Step 1 Items Included in Total Income

The taxpayer's total income consists of those amounts on which the taxpayer is chargeable to income tax for the year. This involves finding the appropriate category (or part of the income tax legislation) after taking account of the various priority rules, and then applying the rules of the category including any rules as to location and timing. Capital allowances given as deductions in computing business income thus are deductible at this point. If the figures show a loss, the amount to be included is nil.

ITA 2007, section 31 sets out a particular timing rule which applies where the income has been subject to deduction at source. This rule applies even though the income accrues under other tax rules in a different year. ITA 2007, Part 15 (sections 847–997) contains rules as to the duty to deduct tax from different types income and how the deduction affects the calculation of taxable income (sections 848 and 968).

Example (Martin and Penny)

The following example, involving Martin (M) and Penny (P), a married couple living together, will be used as the basis for the explanation which follows.

Let us begin with Martin, as his circumstances are less complicated, and just do the calculation. M is a separate taxpayer for income tax purposes; his income as a general matter is not relevant to P's tax liability—or vice versa. Their combined income may be relevant when we come to tax credits, but in their circumstances they have no entitlement to tax credits. Suppose M simply earns £20,000 as earnings falling with ITEPA 2003 in 2016–17. M is entitled to a personal allowance under ITA 2007, section 35. He will also deduct the payment of £1,000 to his retirement benefits scheme; this relief is now usually given by deduction at source:

ITEPA income	£20,000
Less pension contribution	(1,000)
Total income	£19,000
Less basic personal relief	(11,000)
Taxable income	£ 8,000
Tax at 20% on £8,000	£1,600

Let us now turn to Penny. Facts (a)–(h) will be considered first.

In the tax year 2016–17: (a) P is married, with children aged 19 and 15; (b) P has trading profits of £43,000 taxable under ITTOIA 2005, Part 2; (c) P received £6,000 as director of a company; (d) P received payments of £4,500 by way of dividend from UK resident companies, (e) interest of £4,000 gross from a building society and (f) £500 gross interest from a bank; (g) P also received £4,800 by way of rent and has allowable rental expenses of £650. (h) Two years ago P created a revocable trust in favour of P's children; in 2016–17, £5,500 of income arose in the trust.

Taking each fact in turn:

(a)   The presence of P's children does not give rise to any personal relief and P has too much income to qualify for CTC or WTC. P is also eligible to receive Child Benefit of £20.70 per week, as she has one child under the age of 16. However, to the extent that the higher of her and her partner's income exceeds £50,000, the higher earner (in this case Penny) is subject to an income tax charge. Once her income exceeds £60,000, the income tax charge will equal the Child Benefit she receives (see §8.2.2)

(b)   The trading profits: these are ITTOIA 2005, Part 2 income of £43,000.

(c)   The payment as director is ITEPA 2003, Part 2 income of £6,000.

(d)   The dividends from UK resident companies are income under ITTOIA 2005, Part 4, Chapter 3; however, the entire £4,500 of dividends are covered by her £5,000 Dividend Allowance and are tax-free.

(e)   The building society interest of £4,000 is ITTOIA 2005, Part 4, Chapter 2 income.

(f)   The bank interest of £500 is also ITTOIA 2005, Part 4, Chapter 2. From 6 April 2016, as a higher-rate taxpayer P has a Personal Savings Allowance that exempts from tax the first £500 of saving income, including bank and building society interest.

(g)   Rent gives ITTOIA 2005, Part 3 income of £4,150.

(h)   This is a settlement within ITTOIA 2005, Part 5, Chapter 5. Since one child is over 17, only one half of the income will be treated as P's (£2,250).

This makes P's total income of £59,400, after giving effect to the Personal Savings Allowance and Dividend Allowance. As both spouses are using their full personal allowances, the ability to transfer a limited amount of unused personal allowances between married couples does not apply. Even if M's income was below his personal allowance, as P is a higher-rate taxpayer the transfer would not be available.

12.2.2 *Step 2 from Total Income to Net Income—Deductions and Reliefs*

The move from total income to net income is made by deducting any sum allowable under the legislation. Section 23 of ITA 2007 refers to the list in section 24; section 24(1)(a) sets out six sums available only to individuals, and section 24 (1)(b) set out 20 available both to individuals and others subject to income tax. The explanatory notes remind one that the section does not list reliefs available under ex TA 1988, section 811 (now TIOPA 2010, section 112, concerning deduction for foreign tax) or TA 1988, section 798C (now TIOPA 2010, section 35, concerning deduction for disallowed foreign tax credits). They also say that each deduction rule may have its own special rules about the treatment of unused reliefs. The list in section 24(1)(b) includes capital allowances in certain unusual situations, eg special leasing arrangements within CAA 2001, section 258.

ITA 2007, section 25 contains general rules for deductions for individuals. So the reliefs and allowances must be given effect in such a way as will result in the greatest reduction in the taxpayer's liability to tax. However, a relief can be given effect only in so far as there is sufficient income from which to deduct it, and cannot be given more than once.

From 6 April 2013, a cap applies to a number of income tax reliefs that are deductible in calculating income tax liability under Step 2 of ITA 2007, section 23, including trade and property loss reliefs and qualifying loan interest. The cap is the greater of £50,000 or 25% of adjusted total income: see new section 24A and the list of reliefs subject to the cap in section 24A(6).[1]

---

[1] For commentary see Oates and Salter [2013] BTR 398.

12.2.3 Step 3 Personal Reliefs

Any personal relief allowable under Part 3, Chapter 2 of ITA 2007 (eg the blind person's allowance) is deductible at this stage. ITA 2007, sections 27 and 28, containing the general rules for deductions for individuals and others, apply here too, so the reliefs and allowances must be given effect in such a way as will result in the greatest reduction in the taxpayer's liability to tax. However, a relief can be given effect only in so far as there is sufficient income from which to deduct it, and cannot be given more than once.

12.2.4 Steps 4 and 5 from Income to Tax

It is now time to calculate the tax due on the various items remaining. This involves first (step 4) deciding which items are subject to the basic and higher rate, which to the savings rate and which to the rates for dividend.

The various amounts of tax are then added together (step 5).

12.2.5 Steps 6, 7 and X

At step 6 we give effect to the various items given relief by a reduction in tax (see above at §10.8).

At step 7 we add in various accidental charges, such as six charges arising from breaches of the pension scheme rules in FA 2004. Also at this point we meet the charge on a social security pension lump sum and the charge to tax on a gift aid payment when it transpires that the donor who made the grossed-up payment (see §10.6 above) did not have enough liability to income tax or CGT to cover the tax on the sum deducted (ITA 2007, section 424).

At step X we turn to section 32, which lists 15 occasions of charge, including some situations where a relief is withdrawn. Also in the list is any liability under ITA 2007, Part 13, Chapter 1 (transactions in securities).

Example (P Continued) (Facts (I)–(N))

During the year, P paid: (i) mortgage interest of £10,000, (j) interest of £2,200 on a loan to acquire an interest in the close company for which P works, and (k) £4,000 to an ex-spouse under a court order made in 1986. (l) P paid £800 net (£1,000) gross to a charity under the gift aid scheme (on grossing up at 20%, see §12.2.6 below). (m) P also paid £875 in life assurance premiums (on a contract made before 14 March 1984) and (n) £8,500 under a personal pension plan

P is unable to deduct the mortgage interest (i), the payment to the ex-spouse (k) or (m); until relatively recently all three items would have been deductible. P's permitted deductions are: (j) £2,200 (loan interest), (n) £8,500 (pension—but only from relevant earnings) and (l) £1,000 to charity: a total of £11,700. P's net income is therefore £59,400—£11,700 = £47,700.

Step 3 Personal Reliefs

P is entitled to her own personal relief of £11,000, leaving taxable income of £36,700. Tax is calculated as follows:

£32,000 at 20%	£6,400
£4,700 at 40%	£1,880
Total tax	£8,280

12.2.6 From Taxable Income to Tax

Total tax due from P is £8,280. The sum is quite distinct from the amount of cash she is called on now to pay; this is because some amounts of the tax have already been paid, eg the tax withheld at source under PAYE.

P has two further tax complications. First, P is also entitled to relief on tax of £125 in respect of her life assurance premium of £1,000; this is given effect by the payment of a net premium of £875,[2] and so is ignored for present purposes. If the contract had been made after 12 March 1984, however, no relief would be given.

Secondly, there is P's £800 contribution to charity. So far it has been deducted from P's total income. Under the gift aid rules (above §10.6), this is grossed up at 20% to £1,000; no basic rate tax is due on this £1,000, but P can deduct the £1,000 in computing the extra tax owing from her by reason of her being liable to the higher rate. This means that she gets tax relief of £180.

12.2.7 Allocation of Rates and Reliefs

This is done by ITA 2007, section 27 for individuals and section 28 for others. The general principle (section 27(2)) is that reliefs are given in the order which gives the greatest reduction of tax. This general principle is subject to a number of exceptions dealing with Venture Capital, Enterprise Investment and Community Investment reliefs, interest on loan to buy an annuity within TA 1988, section 353(1A), qualifying maintenance payments and certain life insurance payments. There is also a special exclusion for credits for foreign taxes. However, it is expressly provided that interest and dividends are to be treated as the highest part of a taxpayer's income, with dividends being the highest part of that part.[3] Before self-assessment it was Revenue practice to allocate tax rates so that the earliest tax due was charged at the first and lowest rates. Now that there is a single combined date for reporting income and paying tax, this is no longer necessary.

---

[2] TA 1988, s 266(5) has not yet been not rewritten.
[3] ITA 2007, s 16, ex TA 1988, s 1A(5).

12.3   Averaging: Spreading and Top-Slicing

There is no general averaging procedure in the UK tax system whereby income is averaged out over a number of years. Instead, the system takes the view that income tax is an annual tax and therefore relates only to income arising in that year. Averaging is thus allowed over the year—but not beyond it.

12.3.1 Mitigating Unfairness

This is unjust in a number of ways:

(1)   It is inequitable for those with fluctuating incomes.[4]
(2)   It is inequitable for individuals whose income fluctuates around the bottom of the tax scale, since unused personal allowances may not be rolled forward to subsequent years. The arguments against allowing such rolling forward are largely administrative; it would also make the yield from taxes more difficult to predict.
(3)   The absence of an averaging clause causes injustice to the individual who suddenly receives an exceptional sum which the tax system treats as income. These abnormal receipts are different from the problem of fluctuating incomes from one source, not least in that the receipt may be isolated and subjected to special treatment by the tax system.

The UK tax system has some features which permit mitigation of the single-year approach to income:

(1)   *Top-slicing.* This now applies to certain dealings with life policies.[5] The technique involves taking a certain fraction of the taxable sum and then calculating the tax payable on that slice as if it were the top slice of the income of the relevant year. That rate is then applied to the whole sum. Thus, if the sum were £15,000, the slice £1,000 and the rate of tax on that slice 20%, 20% would be applied to the whole £15,000. This technique differs from (3) below in that the payment is taxed only by reference to one year.
(2)   *Averaging: farmers and creative artists.* There is a system of averaging for farmers.[6] The profits of two years are compared. If the profits of either year are nil or less than 75% of the other, the profits may be equalised.[7] Tapering relief is available where the level

---

[4] Royal Commission, Cmnd 9474 (1955), §205. On reform, see *ibid*, §202; Carter (chair), Canadian Royal Commission on Taxation, *Report, Vol 2* (Queen's Printer, 1966), 253; Steuerle, McHugh and Sunley, (1978) 31 *National Tax J* 19.

[5] ITTOIA 2005, ss 535–537, replacing the repealed TA 1988, s 550. The rules for premiums on leases (TA 1988, s 39(3), Sch 2) were repealed by FA 1988, s 73, and those for government stock (s 52) by FA 1996.

[6] ITTOIA 2005, Pt 2, Ch 16 (ss 221–224); one definition of farming is given in s 221(2), which takes in the old concession that farming includes intensive livestock rearing for human consumption (ex ESC A29).

[7] ITTOIA 2005, s 222.

of profit change is between 70% and 75%.[8] Averaging is not permitted in the first or last years of assessment, or if the cash basis is used to calculate profits. From April 2016 the two year averaging period can be increased to five years if certain volatility conditions are met.[9] The model of the averaging system for farmers was applied in 2001 to certain other types of income.[10] The relevant profits are those accruing from qualifying creative works; the works may be literary, dramatic, musical or artistic or designs.[11]

(3) *Spreading: patents.* ITTOIA 2005, section 590 allows spreading forward; a sum received in return for patent rights is taxable as income but may be spread over the year of receipt and the next five years.

12.3.2 Reform

Among the ideas for dealing with fluctuating incomes, two stand out. One is a tax adjustment account in which taxpayers could 'park' their income but without interest until drawing it down (when tax would be paid). One problem with this is how to prevent a taxpayer from deriving benefit from the income before it is drawn down.[12] The idea was recommended by the Canadian Royal Commission (1966), provided it was accompanied by a block averaging system.[13] The consequent Canadian legislation permitted a taxpayer to buy an income-averaging annuity.[14] A very different solution has been proposed by Vickery.[15] The object is lifetime averaging—an attempt to build year by year what the PAYE system achieves week by week. The disadvantages of the proposal are that long-run changes in the value of money would produce new inequities, and the system cannot cope with problems of family reorganisations. There would also be undesirably long lags in changing effective tax rates if the ability to pay increases (or decreases) sharply.

12.4 Extra/Excess Liability

Extra liability, which before ITTOIA 2005 was known as 'excess' liability, is a relic from the days of surtax. It is a liability to higher rate tax (40%) when there is no liability to basic (or lower) rate tax. Thus, the liability arises to the extent that the tax liability exceeds the basic or lower rate liability, so making the 'excess' or 'extra' 18% or 20%. In its strict sense, excess liability arises when gains arise on non-qualifying life policies (ITTOIA 2005, section 530) and when relief arises for IHT on accrued income (ITTOIA 2005, section 669).

---

[8] ITTOIA 2005, s 223.
[9] ITTOIA 2005, s 222A.
[10] TA 1988, s 95A and Sch 4A, added by FA 2001, s 71.
[11] ITTOIA 2005, s 221(3). For criticism of the original version, see Parry Wingfield [2001] BTR 319.
[12] As with the remittance basis: see below at §71.4.
[13] Vol 3, 261–80.
[14] Income Tax Act 1972 (Canada), s 61.
[15] Vickrey, *Agenda for Progressive Taxation* (Ronald Press, 1947) 164 (also in Vickrey, *Public Economics* (CUP, 1996) 105–19); and Bird and Head, *Modern Fiscal Issues* (Toronto University of Press, 1973) 117.

12.5   Progression and the UK Tax System

The rate structure set out above represents the present UK pattern of progression.[16] Details of the actual distribution of the tax burden are recorded in annual HMRC statistics. The estimates for 2015–16 suggested that, of the 29.7 million taxpayers, 24.7 million will have a marginal tax rate of 20% (the basic rate) or nil, 4.6 million will have 40% (ie higher-rate taxpayers), and 332,000 will have 45% (additional rate).[17] In the same year, 27.5% of the income tax will be attributable to the top 1% of taxpayers, the top 10% will have contributed 58.9%, and the lowest 50% will have contributed just 9.5%.[18] A comparison with the figures for 1998–99, used in the 4th edition of this book, showed that then there were only 2.3m taxpayers paying at more than the basic rate. This illustrates the phenomenon known as fiscal drag; so long as the rate brackets increase in line with inflation—and not the much higher rate of earnings—more people are dragged into the higher brackets.

Certain features of the UK income tax structure call for comment. The first is the number of bands in existence. In 1978–79 bands consisted not only of reduced and basic rates, but also nine slices taxed at higher rates—to which could be added the additional rate. From 1988 to 1992 the system survived with just two bands—basic rate and higher rate. The UK reduction in the number of rates is typical of many OECD countries:[19] the biggest reductions occurred in Italy, which, between 1975 and 1989, cut its bands from 32 to seven, and the US, which cut the bands from 25 to three. The second feature of the UK income tax structure is the long band of income taxed at basic rate. The explanation for this is largely administrative; it facilitates deduction at source and reduces the number of additional assessments the Revenue need to make and the number of calculations taxpayers must undertake if they are subject to self-assessment. It has the further advantage of taxing entities like trusts at reasonable rates. Since, however, the changes in the bands are tied to the cost of living and not average earnings, these advantages have been reduced. The third feature of the UK income tax structure is the presence of the starting rate band. Lower rate bands existed until 1970, when the last was abolished in the cause of administrative simplicity. The reduced rate was revived in 1978[20] but repealed in 1980 for administrative reasons. The reduced rate did not help the lower-paid, it did not significantly increase incentives and it had little effect on the poverty trap. Research has suggested that raising tax allowances may be a better way of helping the poor.[21]

Despite these practical objections, the idea of a reduced rate band retained a central place in the hearts of many tax reformers, including Gordon Brown, Chancellor of the Exchequer from 1997 to 2007. Yet Mr Brown made the 2007 change which abolished the reduced rate

---

[16] See also Slemrod and Bakija, *Taxing Ourselves* (MIT, 1996) ch 3.

[17] See https://www.gov.uk/government/uploads/system/uploads/attachment_data/file/428961/Income_Tax_Liabilities_Statistics_May_2015.pdf.

[18] *Ibid*.

[19] Dilnot, in Sandford (ed), *Key Issues in Tax Reform* (Fiscal Publications, 1993), ch 1; and Messere (1993), *op cit*, ch 3 and (2003), Table 2.3. See also Vanistendael (1988) 5 *Australian Tax Forum* 133. On New Zealand experience, which makes the UK seem very timid, see Stephens (1993) 14(3) *Fiscal Studies* 45.

[20] It was responsible for an increase in the cost/yield ratio from 1.87% to 2%: Board of Inland Revenue, 122nd Report.

[21] Morris and Warren (1980) 3 *Fiscal Studies* 34–43. See also IFS, Tax Options for 1991 (Commentary No 25) 64, 65.

band. Arguments based on administrative considerations are much less cogent now that we have self-assessment and computers. Personal reliefs may be seen as a form of zero-rate band for those entitled to them. The level of that personal relief is relatively high in comparative terms and has increased substantially in recent times—well in excess of inflation.[22] It can be seen that the profile of the system is high–low–high (or not-so-high). The effect of this is to give most play to economic forces, such as incentives, in the middle of the income band. This has the advantage that it establishes a floor to poverty and a ceiling to riches. Optimal tax theory might suggest a profile that is low–high–low in terms of marginal rates, but this would probably be opposed on distributional grounds and certainly rejected on political grounds.[23] A possible compromise is constant marginal rates.[24]

12.6 Retrospective Historical Introduction: Rates and Structures

The structure of rates meant to apply as from 2008–09 showed a clear wish to have fewer income tax rates, 20% and 40%—the 10% rate being retained only for savings income and for certain capital gains from business assets. From 2010 we had the 50% rate as well, which dropped in 2013 to 45%. Capital gains tax had two rates—18% and 28% until 6 April 2016, when the old rates continued to apply only to carried interest and residential property and the general rates dropped to 10% and 20%.

From 2000–01 until 2008–09, the rates were 10%, 22% and 40%. In the 1990s, the starting rate was 20% and the basic rate ranged from 23 to 25%. In 1989–90 the system was much simpler; just two rates of income tax applied to individuals—the basic rate of 25% and the higher rate of 40%—which applied to all types of income.[25] There was no starting rate and no lower rate. Certain trusts might have to pay an additional rate on certain types of income. Capital gains tax was charged at the same rates as ordinary income. Going back further to 1978–79,[26] the basic rate was 33%, with a lower rate of 25% applying to the first £750. Basic rate liability expired at £8,000, after which no fewer than nine higher rates applied, reaching the top rate of 83% at £24,000. If the taxpayer had investment income over £1,700, a surcharge or 'additional rate' applied: 10% on the first £550 and 15% thereafter. Therefore, a taxpayer with over £24,000 of taxable income which included more than £2,700 of investment income had a marginal rate of 98% on such income. The normal rate for CGT was 30%; it was not tied to the income tax rate until 1988.

In 1967–68 a 'standard' rate applied, which was set at just over 41%.[27] Three lower rate bands took the form of alleviations of income tax (credits) rather than of taxable income. In addition to income tax (at 41%), surtax[28] was charged retrospectively by FA 1968,

---

[22] Carter (chair), Canadian Royal Commission on Taxation, *Report, Vol 3* (Queen's Printer, 1966) 261–80.

[23] Meade, *The Structure and Reform of Direct Taxation* (Allen & Unwin, 1978), ch 14. But see Slemrod (1983) 36 *National Tax J* 361–69.

[24] Meade Report, *op cit*, 316, 'the administrative advantages would be incalculable'.

[25] FA 1989, s 30.

[26] FA 1978, s 13.

[27] FA 1967, s 13.

[28] Introduced by FA 1926; the previous tax, super tax, which had been the subject of Lloyd George's battles with the House of Lords, was introduced in 1911. The reasons for the change from supertax to surtax can be found in the 1920 Royal Commission, 28–40, esp para 131; supertax was based on a slab system, ie one in which the total

at 10 rising rates, reaching 50% and so a combined top rate of 91%. The fusing of the two taxes into one occurred in 1973 as a result of FA 1971. In 1967–68 there was no additional rate on investment income because earned income attracted a special relief—earned income relief. Personal reliefs took effect not as deductions in computing income but as reliefs from income tax on a set sum (ie credits); moreover, credits might not have been available against surtax as opposed to income tax. FA 1968 had another surprise for taxpayers—a special charge of 45% on investment income over £3,000, making a theoretical top rate of 136%. This was quite deliberate; the Chancellor intended the tax to be paid out of capital as an alternative to increasing CGT or introducing a wealth tax.[29] Capital gains tax was charged at 30%. Going back still further to 1957,[30] the same basic structure of income tax with its reduced rates, surtax with its many bands, and earned income relief (extended to surtax for the first time that year) all existed, but there was one important difference: there was no CGT.

As one rehearses these snapshots, a number of historical features must be understood. The first is the ferocity of the income tax rates for much of the period.[31] The second is the move towards, then away from, and then towards alignment of rates of CGT (introduced in 1965) with income tax rates. Aligned in 1988, CGT taper relief reintroduced the non-alignment, and this was made even clearer by the 2008 change to the single 18% rate. From 2010 there had been a small move back towards alignment with the new 28% rate applicable to those earning above the basic-rate income threshold, but the CGT rates dropped again to generally 20% from 6 April 2016. The third is the separate structure of income tax and surtax (until 1973). The fourth is the pre-1970 proliferation of lower rates of income tax below the standard rate. The fifth is the difference between having a basic rate charged on income with an additional rate charged on investment income, and a standard rate on all income with earned income relief. The obvious lessons to be learned are:

(1)   that tax climates can change and, with the UK's electoral system, can do so very quickly;

(2)   that there are many fiscal mechanisms for achieving what the Government wants; and

(3)   that almost any proposal for change means reviving what has been tried before.

The less obvious lesson is that one should perhaps refrain from condemning too quickly all those who, faced with such punitive rates, sought ways of reducing its burden, especially by converting income into capital gain. As Wheatcroft reportedly said, a tax system breathes through its loopholes. It is also pertinent to recall the comment of the 1955 Royal Commission that the existence of widespread tax avoidance was evidence that the system, not the taxpayer, stood in need of radical reform.[32]

---

income was treated as one slab and taxed at the relevant rate—eg 20% and 40%. Surtax was based on the familiar slice system under which each slice of the total income had its own rate; the slab system led to anomalies when abatements ceased, allowances ended or higher brackets were reached.

[29]   Butterworths, *Annotated Legislation*: Finance Act 1968, 79.

[30]   FA 1957, s 13.

[31]   FA 1988, ss 23, 24.

[32]   Cmnd 9474, §33; cited by Kay [1979] BTR 354, 365.

13

Employment Income: Scope and PAYE

13.1 Introduction

The taxation of employment income is governed by the Income Tax (Earnings and Pensions Act) 2003. ITEPA 2003 replaced those parts of TA 1988 and later statutes governing the old Schedule E with a separate Act of 725 sections and eight schedules. The structure and content of the Act require one to refer to its subdivisions, not least because the draftsman often makes cross-references to these rather than to sections, so one must get used to the Act being divided into Parts which are subdivided into Chapters. Like the previous Schedule E, the Act covers earnings from employment (Part 3, Chapter 1). Also like the previous Schedule E, it covers certain amounts which are treated as earnings, not only benefits in kind (also in Part 3) but also balancing charges under the capital allowance legislation and sums arising where agency workers or intermediate personal service companies are concerned.[1] These receipts are known compendiously as 'general earnings'.

Parts 1 and 2 of ITEPA 2003 are introductory. Part 3, as just noted, covers employment earnings and amounts treated as earnings. Part 4 is a most welcome feature as it gathers together most of the exemptions which were previously scattered around the Act; unfortunately, not all of them are to be found here and the system of cross-referencing from the charging parts of the Act is sometimes poor. Part 5 governs deductions. ITEPA 2003 has its own jargon and in addition to using 'general earnings' it also at times uses 'specific employment income', which are amounts that 'count as' employment income.[2] These amounts

---

[1] ITEPA 2003, s 7(2), (3) and (5).
[2] For explanation see ITEPA Technical Notes 2 and 3.

include income from certain golden handshakes and some benefits from and payments to unapproved pension schemes (Part 6)[3] and from securities (Part 7).[4] Like the old Schedule E, the new Act also covers the taxation of pension payments (Part 9)[5] and certain social security payments (Part 10).[6] The PAYE scheme is to be found in Part 11 and payroll giving in Part 12.

References to statutory provisions in chapters thirteen to eighteen of this book are to ITEPA 2003, unless otherwise noted.

13.1.1 Scope

Income tax is now charged on employment income, ie the earnings from an employment or office.[7] The basic definition of earnings in Part 3, Chapter 1 (section 62), having referred to salaries, wages, fees, certain gratuities and benefits in kind, then uses the old and continuing words 'emoluments of the employment'. Since ITEPA 2003 rewrites, but does not generally reform, the law, all the old case law built on the word 'emolument' still applies. So payments for services are taxed as emoluments; however, a payment from an employer to an employee for some other reason than the employment may escape tax. Further, and less obviously, a payment from a non-employer may be taxable as employment income—if it is for services rendered under a contract of employment.[8] The test in these cases is one of causation; an emolument is a payment in return for acting as or being an employee.[9] A running issue is the extent to which these are matters of form as opposed to substance, ie the question is to be answered by reference to what the parties said in their arrangements.[10] Income taxable as employment income is earned income.[11]

Unlike the old Schedule E, ITEPA 2003 expressly provides guidance as to how one moves from the various items of income—and allowable expenditure—to sums which are to be taxed. Where general earnings are concerned, the amount charged is the net taxable earnings from the employment in that year. These are taxable earnings less allowable deductions; only very rarely can a loss arise.[12] The amount of the taxable earnings may be

---

[3] ITEPA Explanatory Notes Changes 104–6.

[4] ITEPA 2003, s 7(2), (4) and (6).

[5] ITEPA Explanatory Notes Changes 135–42.

[6] See ITEPA Explanatory Notes Changes 135 and 143–46.

[7] Previously TA 1988, s 19(1) as recast, for 1989–90 and later years by FA 1989, s 36(2). Until 1922, Sch E was confined to income from a public office (including the director of a company) or public employment; other employments were in Sch D. In 1922 employments were moved to Sch E unless they came with Sch D, Case V; overseas remuneration from non-public office or employment remained in Sch D, Case V until FA 1956, s 101, when a three-Case structure (Cases I, II and III) was introduced.

[8] *Blakiston v Cooper* [1901] AC 104, 5 TC 347, HL; however, the fact that the payment is not by the employer may be a factor in helping a court conclude that such a payment is not an emolument (*Pritchard v Arundale* [1972] Ch 229, 47 TC 680).

[9] *Shilton v Wilmshurst* [1991] STC 88, 64 TC 78; see also Lord Radcliffe in *Hochstrasser v Mayes* [1960] AC 376, 389, 392, who said that the test goes beyond one of simple reward for services but must still be referable to the performance of duties under the contract.

[10] See Ward [1992] BTR 139 and the employment law case of *Autoclenz Limited v Belcher and Others* (at §13.2.2).

[11] TA 1988, s 833(4), as amended by ITEPA 2003.

[12] ITEPA 2003, ss 9(2), (3) and (6) and 11. For an example see *J Martin v HMRC* [2013] UKFTT 040 (TC), which involved the repayment of a bonus received and taxed in a previous year. The case is discussed above at §10.3.2.3.

governed by international factors.[13] Where what the Act calls 'specific income' is concerned, ie income within Parts 5 and 6, one has to calculate the 'net taxable specific' income, which again depends on amounts of specific income and relevant deductions; no loss relief is possible.[14] ITEPA 2003 goes on to define the person liable for tax or 'taxable person', which is largely a function of what had gone before, though it adds that the person's personal representatives are liable in respect of sums received after the death—as a debt from the estate (section 13). One might say that the effort made by ITEPA 2003 is unmemorably phrased.[15]

The term 'earnings' is defined in section 62(2) to include not only gratuities and incidental benefits, but also 'emoluments', a term defined under the previous legislation as including 'all salaries, fees, wages, perquisites and profits whatsoever'.[16] This was enough to tax many benefits in kind. However, as section 62 makes clear, a payment in kind is taxable as earnings only if, in addition to being an emolument, it is convertible into money. For this reason a wider test (now to be found in Part 3, Chapter 10) applies for many benefits in kind, whether or not convertible into money. These benefit in kind rules are all lumped together in Part 3, Chapters 3–11 to make the 'benefits code'.

13.1.2 Expenses

The rules on expenses are found in Part 5 of the Act. By section 336, expenses are deductible in calculating taxable earnings if they are incurred wholly, exclusively and necessarily in the performance of the duties of the office or employment. Travelling expenses have their own rules (sections 337 and 338)—they must be either: (a) 'necessarily incurred in the performance of the duties of' the office or employment, a long-established and interestingly litigated expression, or (b) come within a relatively new category, first established in 1998, relating to travel for necessary attendance at a temporary workplace. The holder of the office or employment must, for sections 336–338, have been obliged to incur and pay the expense as holder of the employment. Normally the amount of a deduction under Part 5 may not exceed the earnings from which it is deductible. Capital allowances may be claimed by the employee in respect of machinery and plant if incurred necessarily.[17] Most earnings paid by the employer are subject to a system of deduction of tax at source—the PAYE system.[18] Whether or not subject to that system, income is assessed on a current year basis. It is taxed when it is received or becomes due for payment, whichever is the earlier; the old case law rule which backdated payments to the year in which the service was performed was abolished in 1989.[19]

---

[13] ITEPA 2003, s 10(2), referring to Chs 4 and 5 of Pt 1.

[14] ITEPA 2003, ss 9(4)–(6) and 12.

[15] For explanation see ITEPA Technical Notes 4–7.

[16] ITEPA 2003, s 62(2), ex TA 1988, s 131. A perquisite is merely a casual emolument additional to regular salary or wages (*Owen v Pook* [1970] AC 244, 225, [1969] 2 All ER 1, 5, per Lord Guest).

[17] CAA 2001, s 15; but not for cars, *ibid*, s 36.

[18] ITEPA 2003, Pt 11 (ss 682–712), ex TA 1988, s 203 (see below at §13.4).

[19] FA 1989, s 36, see below §14.2.3.

13.2   Office or Employment

13.2.1 *Office*

ITEPA 2003 taxes employment income from employments and offices.[20] It goes on to define an office as 'including in particular' any position which has an existence independent of the person who holds it and may be filled by successive holders.[21] Examples include a director of a company (even if under a contract of employment and owning all the shares),[22] a trustee or executor,[23] a company auditor,[24] a National Health Service consultant[25] and a local land charges registrar.[26] By contrast, a person appointed to act as an inspector at a public inquiry does not hold an office since the post has no existence independent of the holder; there is neither continuity nor permanence.[27] The Court of Appeal has said that an office and an employment are not mutually exclusive.[28] It is not necessary that an office should be constituted by some enactment or other instrument, nor that it should have any public relevance; however, an office is more than just a job description.[29] It thus seems that the essence of an office is the independence of its existence from the identity of the present holder.[30] It is from this element of independence that the element of continuity may be said to derive.[31]

13.2.2 *Employment*[32]

The definition of employment in ITEPA 2003 provides a good example of one of the worst features of its drafting style.[33] By section 4, 'employment'

> includes in particular (a) any employment under a contract of service (b) any employment under a contract of apprenticeship and (c) any employment in the service of the Crown.

[20] ITEPA 2003, Pt 2, Ch 1 (ss 3–5).

[21] ITEPA 2003, s 5(3). These words are taken from the judgment of Rowlatt J in *Great Western Railway Co v Bater* [1920] 3 KB 266, 274; 8 TC 231, 235, although Rowlatt J added the longer accepted words 'subsisting, permanent and substantive'. See, generally Napier [1981] *Industrial Law Journal* 52; and Ward [1989] BTR 281, 283–95. This is not a 'complete' definition (*McMillan v Guest* [1942] AC 561, 564; 24 TC 190, 201 per Lord Atkin). When *Great Western Railway v Bater* was decided, Sch E covered only public offices or employments of a public nature; other offices or employments fell within Sch D. *Bater* concerned a railway clerk, and the House of Lords, undoing the accepted practice of decades, placed him in Sch D. The legislative response, anticipated by the 1920 Royal Commission, was to move all the offices or employments to Sch E (see Monroe, *Intolerable Inquisition* (Sweet & Maxwell, 1981) 25 *et seq.*)

[22] *Lee v Lee's Air Farming Ltd* [1961] AC 12, [1960] 3 All ER 420, PC. The posts of director and managing director may be separate offices (*Goodwin v Brewster* (1951) 32 TC 80).

[23] *Dale v IRC* [1951] 2 All ER 517, 34 TC 468; *A-G v Eyres* [1909] 1 KB 723.

[24] *Ellis v Lucas* [1966] 2 All ER 935, 43 TC 276.

[25] *Mitchell and Edon (Inspectors of Taxes) v Ross* [1961] 3 All ER 49, 40 TC 11.

[26] *Ministry of Housing and Local Government v Sharp* [1970] 2 QB 223, [1969] 3 All ER 225.

[27] *Edwards v Clinch* [1981] STC 617, 56 TC 367: duties of a public nature did not necessarily make the post an office.

[28] See Buckley and Oliver LJJ [1980] STC 438, 445d, 455d.

[29] *McMenamin v Diggles* [1991] STC 419, 430, 431; 64 TC 286, 302, per Scott J.

[30] Ward [1989] BTR 281, 287.

[31] *Ibid*, 294.

[32] See generally Freedman, IFS Tax Law Review Committee Discussion Paper No 1, February 2001; and Crawford and Freedman, 'Small Business Taxation' in Mirrlees *et al* (eds), *Dimensions of Tax Design* (OUP, 2010) 1044.

[33] For explanation, see ITEPA Technical Note 1.

The use of the words 'includes in particular' rather than 'means' is unnecessary caution in an age when judges interpret the words of statutes purposively and in their context. The definition should not include the words to be interpreted. To make matters worse 'employment under a contract of apprenticeship' is a legal nonsense since an apprenticeship is not an employment.

An employment was once described as a post and as something 'more or less analogous to an office',[34] but modern cases generally take a different tack and equate employment with a contract of service. In this way tax law uses a concept familiar in other parts of UK domestic law such as tort and employment law, and this is now to be found in section 4(1)(a). In EU law the boundary between Articles 45 and 49 TFEU (ex Arts 39 and 43 TEC) builds on the same foundations by characterising the essence of employment (as opposed to self-employment) status as being the relationship of subordination; in the absence of subordination, an activity carried out for the benefit of other economic operators or consumers is regarded as self-employment.[35] If the arrangement under which sums are paid to a taxpayer is one for services, it falls outside the ITEPA 2003.

13.2.2.1 Case Law Tests for Employment

The common law courts have used different tests at different times.[36] It is not possible to gain much assistance by comparing the facts of previous cases to see which facts are common, which are different and what weight was given to the common facts; the evidence must be weighed separately in each case.[37] At one time the courts' approach was based on control.[38] Where subjection to a person (the master) was inappropriate, the courts looked at subjection to the rules of an organisation—the integration test.[39] Another test was based on 'economic reality' and took into account methods of payment, the freedom to hire others, whether the workers provided their own equipment, whether they had investments in their own business, arrangements for sick pay and holiday pay, and how the worker was treated for income tax and National Insurance.[40] This last point is particularly unhelpful when the very point in issue is one of classification for tax and NICs. A relatively recent development has produced a test based on mutuality of obligation[41] and looks at the duration of employment, regularity of employment, whether the workers have the right to refuse work and trade custom. Under this test there is no contract of service if the worker can say 'No'—ie there is no obligation on the worker to accept an invitation to provide services. This last test has been used as the basis of much planning by employers anxious to get an arrangement treated as one for services and not of service. In labour law some workers rendering services

---

[34] *Davies v Braithwaite* [1931] 2 KB 628, 635, per Rowlatt J; see Ward, *op cit*, 295–300.

[35] Eg, the opinion of the Advocate-General in *Asscher v Staatsecretarius* [1996] STC 1025, 1031, para 28.

[36] Deakin and Morris, *Labour Law*, 2nd edn (Butterworths, 1998), §3.4. On the Canadian enterprise control test, see Flannigan (1988) 36 *Can Tax Jo* 145.

[37] *Walls v Sinnett* [1987] STC 236, 245, per Vinelott J.

[38] Deakin and Morris, *op cit*, §3.4.5; *Yewen v Noakes* (1880) 6 QBD 530, 538; 1 TC 260, 263, per Bramwell LJ.

[39] Deakin and Morris, *op cit*, §3.4.6; *Beloff v Presdram* [1973] 1 All ER 241, 250. See also the copyright case of *Stevenson, Jordan and Harrison Ltd v Macdonald and Evans* [1952] 1 TLR 101, 111, per Lord Denning.

[40] Deakin and Morris, *op cit*, §3.4.7, citing *Hall v Lorimer* [1994] STC 23, CA, and *Market Investigations Ltd v Minister of Social Security* [1969] 2 QB 173.

[41] Deakin and Morris, *op cit*, §3.4.8, citing *O'Kelly v Trusthouse Forte plc* [1984] QB 90, [1983] 3 All ER 456.

under a contract for services are brought within the employment protection category by legislative redefinition.[42] Some cases have mixed all the elements in these different tests.[43]

Another test asks whether those performing the services are in business on their own account.[44] It is open to a fact-finding tribunal to conclude that a person is in business on his own account when all that he provides are personal services.[45] This involves looking at the person's overall activities rather than just one contract at a time—see further below §13.2.3.1. It is equally open to a fact-finding tribunal to conclude that a person is in business on his own account even though there is what purports to be a written contract of employment.[46] In *Autoclenz Limited v Belcher and Others*,[47] an important employment law case that also is relevant to the question whether an individual is an 'employee' for tax purposes, the Supreme Court held that the Employment Tribunal had been entitled to disregard terms included in the written agreement between the parties describing the workers as independent contractors on the basis that the documents did not reflect what was actually agreed between the parties. According to Lord Clarke (Lords Hope, Walker, Collins and Wilson agreeing), the focus must be to discover the actual legal obligations of the parties. To carry out that exercise the tribunal will have to examine all the relevant evidence, including the written terms themselves, read in the context of the whole agreement, as well as evidence of how the parties conducted themselves in practice and what their expectations of each other were. Lord Clarke cautioned that the circumstances in which contracts relating to work or services are concluded are often very different from those in which commercial contracts between parties of equal bargaining power are agreed; this must be taken into account in deciding whether terms of any written agreement in truth represent what was agreed. By contrast, a person under contract to provide clerking services to a set of barristers' chambers was held to be an independent contractor on the particular facts.[48]

Lastly, some miscellaneous points. If no services are to be performed, the contract is not one of employment.[49] North Sea divers are expressly excluded from ITEPA 2003 if taxed under special provisions in ITTOIA 2005.[50] A person employed by a company is an employee of the company. Where a man held himself out to be an employee of a company which he controlled and created, the question whether he was such an employee or a self-employed person was treated as a question of fact.[51] The fact that the contract is illegal cannot, of itself, convert an employee into a self-employed person. The status of contracts of employment which are illegal has not been explored in the tax context.[52]

In a 2015 report reviewing the state of the law on employment status, the Office of Tax Simplification concluded (unsurprisingly) that employment status is indeed an area

---

[42] Eg, the Employment Rights Act 1996, s 230(3).
[43] Deakin and Morris, *op cit*, §3.4.9; *Ready-Mixed Concrete (South East) Ltd v Ministry of Pensions* [1968] 2 QB 497, [1968] 1 All ER 433.
[44] *Andrews v King* [1991] STC 481.
[45] *Hall v Lorimer* [1994] STC 23, 66 TC 349, CA; followed in *Barnett v Brabyn* [1996] STC 716.
[46] *McManus v Griffiths* [1997] STC 1089, 70 TC 218.
[47] [2011] UKSC 41.
[48] *McMenamin v Diggles* [1991] STC 419, 64 TC 286.
[49] *Clayton v Lavender* (1965) 42 TC 607.
[50] ITEPA 2003, s 6(5), referring to ITTOIA 2005, s 15, ex TA 1988, s 314.
[51] *Cooke v Blacklaws* [1985] STC 1 (the illegality of the arrangement was a factor, but not a conclusive one).
[52] For general problems, see Deakin and Morris, *op cit*, §3.4.4.

in need of attention.[53] The OTS highlighted a number of pressing issues and outlined a number of possible reforms, including the option of a statutory employment test.

13.2.2.2 Secondment

Problems may arise where an employee is seconded to work for another firm.[54] Thus, where E, the employee, earns fees from the second company but is required to account to the first company for those fees, there is authority to suggest that the payments to E should be treated as E's taxable income and so subject to PAYE; however, by concession, this is not required.[55] Where the employee is seconded to work for a charity on a temporary basis, an express provision allows the employer to deduct the costs as if the employee had remained working for the employer.[56] This provision assumes (perhaps wrongly) that the payments to the seconded employee are taxable as employment income.

13.2.3 *Several Employments or One Profession?*

A taxpayer may have more than one source of income. The existence of a daytime employment is compatible with the co-existence of a trade or profession,[57] and the activity or skill used in the employment may be the same as that used in the trade or profession. Therefore, doctors may be part-time employees of a hospital trust and carry on a part-time private practice; their pay under the former source will be taxed under ITEPA 2003, while that from the latter will be taxed under ITTOIA 2005, Part 2. Similarly, a barrister with a daytime income under ITTOIA 2005, Part 2 may also have evening employment as a lecturer within ITEPA 2003.[58] The premise of the case law is that, in accordance with the schedular system of income taxation, a source cannot fall into two Schedules or one Schedule and ITEPA 2003 at the same time. Kerridge has argued, challengingly, that this premise is incorrect, but the argument has not been made in any reported case since his views were published.[59]

13.2.3.1 *Davies v Braithwaite, Fall v Hitchen, Hall v Lorimer*

A person may hold several offices and so be taxed under ITEPA 2003 (not ITTOIA 2005, Part 2 as a profession).[60] However, in relation to a series of employments, two quite distinct approaches may be seen. In *Davies v Braithwaite*,[61] Lilian Braithwaite acted in the UK in a number of plays, films and wireless programmes. She had separate contracts for each play

---

[53] Office of Tax Simplification, *Employment status report*, at https://www.gov.uk/government/publications/employment-status-review.

[54] In *Caldicott v Varty* [1976] STC 418, [1976] 3 All ER 329, 51 TC 403, a civil servant seconded to work for the Fiji Government was held to be still employed by the Crown in the UK.

[55] ESC A37, para 2. If it is E's taxable income, it is hard to see how E can then deduct the sums when they are paid over to his employer since this is a disposition of income not the cost of earning it. It appears more correct to say that the obligation to account prevented the payment from having the quality of income in E's hands.

[56] ITTOIA 2005, s 70 and CTA 2009, s 70, ex TA 1988, s 86.

[57] *Davies v Braithwaite* [1931] 2 KB 628, 635; 18 TC 198, 203, per Rowlatt J.

[58] *Sidey v Phillips* [1987] STC 87, 59 TC 458.

[59] [1980] BTR 233.

[60] *IRC v Brander and Cruickshank* [1971] 1 All ER 36, 46 TC 574. Compare *Marsh v IRC* [1943] 1 All ER 199, 29 TC 120; Nock [1973] BTR 260.

[61] [1931] 2 KB 628, 18 TC 198. For a slightly more modern example, see *Household v Grimshaw* [1953] 2 All ER 12, 34 TC 366.

and wireless appearance. She also recorded for the gramophone and had appeared in a play on Broadway, New York. Since the performance in New York was completely outside the UK, she argued that it was an employment and, as such, that she would be taxable at that time only on such sums, if any, as she remitted to the UK. The Revenue argued that this was merely one engagement in her profession as an actress, a profession carried on inside and outside the UK, so that she was taxable on an arising basis under Schedule D, Case II. The Revenue won. Rowlatt J said:[62]

> Where one finds a method of earning a livelihood which does not contemplate the obtaining of a post and staying in it, but essentially contemplates a series of engagements and moving from one to the other … then each of those engagements could not be considered an employment, but is a mere engagement in the course of exercising a profession, and every profession and every trade does involve the making of successive engagements and successive contracts and, in one sense of the word, employments.

The second approach is totally different. In *Fall v Hitchen*,[63] a professional ballet dancer was held to be liable to tax under Schedule E in respect of a contract with one particular company because that contract, looked at in isolation, was one of service and not one for services. Pennycuick V-C held that this concluded the matter.[64] This is quite different from Rowlatt J, who had started with the general scheme of the taxpayer's earnings and then asked where the particular contract fitted in. In *Davies v Braithwaite* no one seems to have asked whether the particular contract was one of service or one for services.[65]

Davies v Braithwaite was resurrected in *Hall v Lorimer*.[66] Here the Court of Appeal held that while the distinction between a contract of service and one for services was critical, this did not, of itself, determine whether the particular contract should be classified as one or the other. In deciding upon that classification the court may look at whether the taxpayer is in business and so see how the contract fits in with the taxpayer's overall activities. Therefore, a vision mixer who worked for 80 days over a four-year period, all on one- or two-day contracts, was held to be taxable under Schedule D, rather than Schedule E, Nolan LJ citing both *Davies v Braithwaite* and *Fall v Hitchen*. Meanwhile, it should be noted the decision in *Fall v Hitchen* (where the one contract in issue was for rehearsal time plus 22 weeks) is consistent with *Hall v Lorimer*. The approach of the Court of Appeal does not sit easily with that of the House of Lords in *IRC v Brander and Cruickshank* and *Mitchell and Edon v Ross* (see §13.2.3.3 below).

There is no infallible criterion[67] and there are many borderline cases. Aspects to be considered now are whether those involved provide their own equipment or hire their own helpers, what degree of financial risk they run, what degree of responsibility they have and

---

[62] [1931] 2 KB 628, 635; 18 TC 198, 203.

[63] [1973] STC 66, [1973] 1 All ER 368; no appeal was made. See [1990] *Simon's Tax Intelligence* 173.

[64] [1973] 1 All ER 368, 374. The taxpayer had no other contracts at that time (unlike Miss Braithwaite); indeed, his was a full-time contract and one which prohibited him from taking on outside activities without his employer's consent.

[65] In *Mitchell and Edon v Ross* [1960] Ch 498, 521; 40 TC 11, 43, in the Court of Appeal, Lord Evershed distinguished *Davies v Braithwaite* as not involving a contract of service. See also *Bennett v Marshall* [1938] 1 KB 591, [1938] 1 All ER 93, 22 TC 73.

[66] [1994] STC 23, CA.

[67] See, eg, Nolan LJ in *Hall v Lorimer* [1994] STC 23, 30e.

how far they can profit from sound management.[68] The Revenue find the task as difficult as anyone else,[69] as was shown by the evidence in the unsuccessful challenge to personal service company legislation on EU and human rights law grounds in *R (on application of Professional Contractors Group Ltd) v IRC*.[70]

Whether a contract is one of service or for services appears to be a question of law, so far as the identification of the relevant criteria is concerned, but the balancing process of applying those criteria seems to be left to the Tribunals (formerly Commissioners) as a question of fact.[71] Over the years, the Revenue have waged campaigns to bring many people within Schedule E and ITEPA by threatening to make the payer responsible for the payment of income tax under the PAYE system. The payer usually submits to this pressure since there is nothing to gain by resisting.[72] The Revenue have issued guidance in Factsheets ES/FS1 and ES/FS2, replacing the previous booklet IR 56.[73] One may contrast the delegated power of the former DSS to categorise workers by statutory instrument for NIC purposes.[74]

13.2.3.2 Arrangements Made by Intermediaries: The IR35 Legislation

The famous IR35 legislation,[75] now in ITEPA 2003, Part 2, Chapter 8,[76] was designed to enlarge the scope of the employment tax and NIC regimes where personal service companies (PSCs) and other intermediaries are used to try to avoid liability under section 62. Introduced in 2000, the IR35 rules apply in situations where:

(1)   an individual worker personally performs services for the ultimate client;
(2)   the worker has a material interest in the intermediary;
(3)   the intermediary receives a payment for the services performed by the worker; and
(4)   the worker would otherwise be regarded—absent the intermediary—as an employee of the ultimate client under the usual case law tests for contract of service.

If these conditions are satisfied then the worker is deemed by the legislation to receive a payment from the intermediary of an amount determined by reference to the payments received by the intermediary. This deemed payment to the worker is treated as his or her employment income and is subject to PAYE and NICs; it is also deductible in computing the profits of the PSC for corporation tax purposes.[77]

---

[68]   *Ready Mixed Concrete (South East) Ltd v Minister of Pensions* [1968] 2 QB 497, [1968] 1 All ER 433; *Sidey v Phillips* [1987] STC 87, 59 TC 458.

[69]   See Revenue Tax Bulletin, February 2000.

[70]   See *R (on application of Professional Contractors Group Ltd) v IRC* [2001] STC 629 at paras 44–49, commenting on the current law on the boundary between employment and self-employment and the role of the Revenue in administering this legislation.

[71]   *O'Kelly v Trusthouse Forte plc* [1984] QB 90, [1983] 3 All ER 456, CA. *Cf* Lord Widgery CJ, in *Global Plant Ltd v Secretary of State for Social Services* [1972] 1 QB 139, 154, 155. See criticism by Pitt [1985] *LQR* 217.

[72]   See HC Official Report, Vol 45, cols 384–85, 13 July 1983, [1983] *Simon's Tax Intelligence* 309.

[73]   See *Simon's Direct Tax Service*, E4.211 for practice on particular occupations.

[74]   Social Security (Categorisation of Earners) Regulations 1978 (SI 1978/1689).

[75]   The debate became known as the 'IR35' issue because this was the number of the original press release issued in the run-up to Budget 1999. Details of the revised proposals were contained in a press release, 23 September 1999, [1999] *Simon's Weekly Tax Intelligence* 1587.

[76]   Previously FA 2000, Sch 12.

[77]   ITEPA 2003, s 49. The deemed employment payment amount is calculated under ITEPA 2003, s 54.

Despite the amount of effort that went into drafting, the IR35 rules proved to be less than entirely successful in deterring the use of PSCs to avoid the employment tax regime. The explanation given by the Government in 2007[78] was that IR35 did not operate effectively in situations where either the person had many contracts during the year, or there were large numbers of individuals working through a particular, mass-marketed intermediary, because the IR35 legislation involves looking at each contract separately to see whether Chapter 8 applies. In 2007, ITEPA 2003, Part 2, Chapter 9 (sections 61A–61J) was therefore inserted in an attempt to address these deficiencies, and especially the problem of mass-marketed intermediaries (and other intermediaries) collectively referred to as managed service companies (MSCs). The PSC legislation was not repealed; where both apply, the MSC rules prevail.

Chapter 9 took effect from 6 April 2007 and charges payments made through MSCs. Where the MSC has an MSC provider, Chapter 9 applies to all the service companies made available by that person (sections 61B and 61D). The MSC provider is someone 'involved with the MSC': where the person is involved only in certain limited ways, eg as legal adviser or a normal independent employment agency, that person is not a 'provider' and so the MSC legislation is excluded (section 61B(2)–(4)). The list of persons who are 'involved' covers providers or associates of providers who control or influence the provision of the services, or anyone giving or promoting an undertaking to make good any tax loss. The Treasury may exclude categories of persons from being providers (section 61C). There are rules for calculating the deemed employment income and a rule excluding distributions by the MSC from being taxed as dividends (sections 61E and 61H). The PAYE regulations apply to the MSC as amended, as do the various ITEPA 2003 rules set out in section 61F.[79] The MSC may deduct the deemed employment payments in computing its income.[80] The rules do not affect the operation of the separate rules on workers supplied by agencies.[81]

In 2011 the Office of Tax Simplification conducted a review of the operation of the IR35 rules and found general agreement that the legislation was little used and largely 'managed round' by those within its ambit, though often at some expense.[82] On the other hand, the OTS noted that IR35 still was viewed by HMRC as 'an important deterrent'. The OTS recommended pursuing structural reforms along the lines suggested by the Mirrlees Review that would result in more neutral taxation of economic activity carried on in different legal forms.[83] Such reform, the OTS concluded, had the potential to make the IR35 rules obsolete. As an alternative to major structural reform, the OTS made several recommendations for improving the administration of the IR35 rules. In 2014 the House of Lords Select Committee on Personal Service Companies issued a report calling on HMRC to do more to show that the revenue protection claims underlying their support for IR35 outweighs its complexity and the costs it imposes. The Committee also suggested HMRC should improve their guidance on IR35 and the basic differences between employment and self-employment.[84]

---

[78] See Budget 2007 Press Release BN46.

[79] ITEPA 2003, s 688A and s 717(4) as amended.

[80] ITTOIA 2005, s 164A (for income tax) and FA 2007, Sch 3, para 10 (for corporation tax).

[81] ITEPA 2003, s 48(2), ex FA 2000, Sch 12, para 24.

[82] Office of Tax Simplification, *Small Business Tax Review* (March 2011) and *Small Business Tax Review: Final Report* (February 2012).

[83] Mirrlees *et al* (eds), *Tax by Design: The Mirrlees Review* (OUP, 2011) ch 19.

[84] See http://www.parliament.uk/business/committees/committees-a-z/lords-select/personal-service-companies/.

At Budget 2016, the Government launched yet another consultation, this one aimed at reforming the IR35 rules as they apply in the public sector only.[85] The intention is that responsibility for determining whether IR35 applies will move from the personal service company to the public sector employer, agency, or third party from April 2017. If IR35 does apply, that party will be responsible to account for income tax and NICs. HMRC plan on introducing clear objective tests to assist public sector engagers in determining whether these new rules will apply to a particular engagement.

13.2.3.3 Consequences

The consequences of coming within ITEPA 2003 as opposed to ITTOIA 2005, Part 2 are extensive, and rest on the doctrine that the Schedules are mutually exclusive. In *IRC v Brander and Cruickshank*,[86] Lord Donovan said that this doctrine was unreal and served no useful purpose; indeed, its application in that case would cause administrative chaos.

(1) Expenses incurred for an office or employment under ITEPA 2003 will be deductible only if they conform to the strict test laid down in ITEPA 2003, Part 5, sections 336 *et seq*; expenses incurred for a trade or profession will be deductible on a different and more generous test. By concession, travelling expenses of directorships held as part of a professional practice are allowed as deductions under ITTOIA 2005, Part 2.[87]

In *Mitchell and Edon v Ross*,[88] the taxpayer, Ross, held an appointment as a consultant radiologist under the Birmingham Regional Hospital Board, and served at a number of hospitals under that authority. He was also in private practice as a consultant radiologist, which practice he carried on at his home in Rugby. The Revenue admitted that Ross was correctly assessed under what is now ITTOIA 2005, Part 2 in respect of his private practice, but argued that income accruing from the hospital board should be assessed—and so calculated—as employment income. At first instance and in the Court of Appeal,[89] the taxpayer argued unsuccessfully that the positions with the hospital board were not offices. He further argued that if the income was correctly assessable as employment income, the employment should nonetheless also be seen as part of his profession within ITTOIA 2005, Part 2, so that the ITTOIA rules for deduction of expenses should apply to permit the deduction of those expenses which were not deductible from employment income. This rested, in part, on a finding by the Commissioners that these employments were a necessary part of his profession as consultant radiologist and merely incidental to that profession.[90] Only the second point was argued in the House of Lords, and the taxpayer lost. The House held that if the profits were assessable as employment income then expenses in respect of that employment could be allowed only if they conformed to the requirements of what is now ITEPA

[85] See https://www.gov.uk/government/publications/off-payroll-working-in-the-public-sector-reforming-the-intermediaries-legislation.
[86] [1971] 1 All ER 36, 46; 46 TC 574, 595. The concessionary relief at ESC A37 should also be noted—tax treatment of directors' fees received by partnerships and other companies.
[87] ESC A4; and Inland Revenue interpretation RI 105.
[88] [1961] 3 All ER 49, 40 TC 11.
[89] [1959] 3 All ER 341, 40 TC 11 (first instance); and [1960] 2 All ER 218, 40 TC 11, CA.
[90] 40 TC 11, 32.

2003; the appointment could not be treated for tax purposes as part within and part outside the Schedule.[91]

(2)   Terminal payments in connection with the ending of an office or employment may escape tax in whole or in part.[92] Compensation for the loss of a trading asset will usually be a trading receipt.[93] In *IRC v Brander and Cruickshank*,[94] the House of Lords held that where a firm of Scottish advocates with a substantial general legal business also acted as secretaries and/or registrars for some 30 to 40 companies, each appointment was a separate office. Therefore, sums received on the termination of two such appointments escaped tax.[95] The status of the earlier decision in *Blackburn v Close Bros Ltd*,[96] where sums were held to be trading receipts, is uncertain. It was doubted by Lord Guest,[97] with whom Lord Upjohn agreed, but Lord Morris regarded the facts of the earlier case as being quite different[98] and considered that the offices were not trading assets. Lord Donovan would have followed the earlier case if there had been a finding of fact that the taxpayer had sought the office as part and parcel of his trade or profession.[99] On such a finding Lord Donovan would have been prepared to hold that income payments fell within what is now ITEPA 2003 and terminal payments within what is now ITTOIA 2005, Part 2. Lord Reid dismissed the appeal 'for the reasons given by your Lordships'.[100]

Given the logic of *Mitchell and Edon v Ross*, it is hard to understand any conclusion other than that of Lord Guest.[101] If an office falls exclusively within ITEPA 2003, it does not cease to be an office simply because it was sought; while if different payments from the same source can fall under two Schedules, as Lord Donovan suggested, the selection of the applicable rules from the range offered by the two Schedules seems arbitrary. *Hall v Lorimer* may be reconciled with this on the basis either that it is still possible for a person carrying on a profession to hold an office taxable under ITEPA 2003, or, if the boundary between office and employment is too difficult to accept, that it is still possible for such a person to enter into a contract of service or an office. The matter then becomes one of the facts—and one is back to the distinctions drawn by Lord Donovan.

(3)   The costs of acquiring the office will not be deductible under ITEPA 2003 but will usually be deductible under ITTOIA 2005.[102]

---

[91] On the concordat reached between the Revenue and the medical profession, see *Simon's Direct Tax Service* E4.211; and for former concession on treatment of retirement benefit provision, see ESC A9 (now withdrawn).

[92] Under ITEPA 2003, Pt 6, Ch 3 (ss 401 *et seq*), ex TA 1988, ss 148, 188(4).

[93] But it may still escape tax as a gift or a capital payment and not a trading receipt (see below at §21.7).

[94] [1971] 1 All ER 36, 46 TC 574.

[95] ITEPA 2003, s 403, ex TA 1988, s 148, applies when the payment is not otherwise chargeable to tax. The finding that the post was an office and so within Sch E meant that the payment was not chargeable to tax under some other Schedule, thus enabling s 403 to operate.

[96] (1960) 39 TC 164.

[97] [1971] 1 All ER 36, 45; 46 TC 574, 593.

[98] *Ibid*, 42, 590.

[99] *Ibid*, 47, 595.

[100] *Ibid*, 40, 588.

[101] If the taxpayer was not carrying on a profession, the payment might have fallen within Sch D, Case VI, but this seems to be excluded by the conclusion that the post was an office and so within ITEPA 2003. One consequence of Lord Guest's view is that a company can hold an office and so have that income computed under ITEPA 2003.

[102] *Cf* Pennycuick J in *Blackburn v Close Bros Ltd* (1960) 39 TC 164, 173.

(4)   Solicitor trustees receiving annuities from the trust fund for acting as trustees have tra-
       ditionally been taxed on the receipt under ITTOIA 2005, Part 4 and with tax deducted
       at source. However, as an office, the post of trustee ought to fall within ITEPA 2003,
       and therefore cannot fall within ITTOIA 2005.

(5)   ITEPA 2003 and its predecessor, Schedule E, have operated for over 60 years under the
       PAYE system and on a current year basis. Until 1996, ITTOIA 2005, Part 2 taxpayers
       were taxed on a preceding year basis and are still not subject to PAYE.

(6)   The capital allowances structure is much wider for trades than for employments.

13.2.3.4 Commentary

The income tax system draws a sharp distinction between the employed and self-employed.
Yet income tax is not alone in doing this; the distinction is also fundamental (confining
oneself to tax law) to social security contributions and benefits, and to VAT. In statistical
terms the distinction is probably more significant than that between capital and income. As
will be appreciated, the advantages and disadvantages of classification are mixed. However,
there has been little effort until recently to quantify them. What makes matters worse is that
although the distinction may be easy to state, it can be extremely difficult to apply. Recent
developments such as casualisation and home-working make it harder still. An important
but now dated comparative survey showed that other countries have the same problems
and that this is a very fraught area, with the self-employed arguing keenly to protect their
interests.[103] The 2015 OTS report on employment status confirms this is still the case.

One solution would be to align the different tax rules so as to reduce the significance of the
distinction—this is the approach recommended by the Mirrlees Review.[104] Another would
be to make status easier to determine, for example by de-linking the tax status from other
rules and stating that tax classification can be different from labour law or tort. Perhaps
Rowlatt J was right after all in looking at the overall situation and not just the particular
contract. A more troubling aspect concerns the role of HMRC. It is obviously in the interest
of that department, and so for government revenue, that people who belong under ITEPA
2003 should not escape some of that burden by claiming to be self-employed. The Revenue
Manual, which is what inspectors use for guidance in their discussions on this subject with
taxpayers, was heavily criticised by the court in *R (on application of Professional Contractors
Group Ltd) v IRC*,[105] and has been rewritten—with algorithms. HMRC has also designed
an Employment Status Indicator (ESI) computer program (accessible via its website) to aid
those who engage workers in determining whether a worker is employed or self-employed.
The ESI determination is presumably based on similar algorithms. The ESI outcome can
relied upon as evidence of a worker's status for tax/NICs/VAT purposes only if the answers
to the ESI questions accurately reflect the terms and conditions under which the worker
provides their services, and the ESI has been completed by an engager or their authorised
representative; if the tool has been completed by or on behalf of a worker the result is only
indicative.[106]

---

[103] Chamberlain and Freedman (1997) *Fiscal Studies* 87; and see Freedman, *op cit*.
[104] Mirrlees *et al* (eds), *op cit*, ch 19.
[105] *R (on application of Professional Contractors Group Ltd) v IRC* [2001] STC 629.
[106] See http://tools.hmrc.gov.uk/esi/screen/ESI/en-GB/summary?user=guest.

13.3   International Aspects

13.3.1 Scope

ITEPA 2003 charges tax by reference to a number of international factors.[107] The consequence of this division will be that while payments for services in the UK will always be
taxed here, payments for services outside the UK will be taxed either (a) in full as they arise,
or (b) not at all, or (c) only when they are remitted to the UK.

   If the employee is resident in the UK, ITEPA 2003 starts by charging tax on the earnings
in full.[108] If the employee is UK resident but domiciled elsewhere, the remittance basis may
apply to the foreign earnings (section 22). Exactly how the remittance basis applies has
been greatly changed by fundamental changes in FA 2013. Essentially, the remittance basis
applies differently depending upon whether the employee satisfies a 3-year period of non-
residency test in section 26A. This test is satisfied if the employee was:

(1)   non-UK resident for the previous 3 tax years, or
(2)   UK resident for the previous tax year but non-UK resident for the 3 tax years before
      that, or
(3)   UK resident for the previous 2 tax years but non-UK resident for the 3 tax years before
      that, or
(4)   non-UK resident for the previous tax year, UK resident for the tax year before that and
      non-UK resident for the 3 tax years before that.

If the remittance basis applies but the employee fails to satisfy the test in section 26A, then
pursuant to section 22 the employee is taxable on the full amount of general earnings remitted to the UK to the extent that they are 'chargeable overseas earnings'. Under section 23, an
employee's general earnings are chargeable overseas earnings if the test in section 26A is not
satisfied and (a) the person is not domiciled in the UK, (b) the employment is with a foreign
employer and (c) the duties are performed wholly outside the UK.[109] Sums permitted to be
deducted in calculating the chargeable overseas earnings include certain expenses, contributions to pension schemes and capital allowances; these amount cannot also be deducted
under section 11 and its satellite rules (section 22(5)). Where the employee has not only this
employment but also an associated employment the duties of which are performed wholly
or partly inside the UK, a restriction may apply to prevent avoidance (section 24). None of
earnings will be chargeable overseas earnings to the exent that another anti-avoidance rule
in respect of related employments with a UK employer in section 24A applies.

   If the remittance basis applies and the employee does satisfy the test in section 26A, then
the rules in section 26 apply instead. Pursuant to section 26, the employee will be taxed on

---

[107] ITEPA 2003 finally abolished the three Cases of Sch E—but as a matter of form rather than substance; on
history of the Cases down to 1991, see Sheridan [1991] BTR 214.
[108] ITEPA 2003, s 15.
[109] ITEPA 2003, s 23(2). On allocation of earnings where duties are performed partly in the UK and partly
outside, see Statement of Practice SP 5/84. The Rewrite explanatory notes for the change in ss 23 and 24 (change 3)
are an interesting challenge.

the remittance basis on foreign general earnings in respect of duties performed outside the UK; thus, the employee will be taxed in the UK only to the extent that those foreign general earnings are remitted to the UK.

Liability arises on sums received in the UK whether or not the office or employment is still held when the earnings are received in the UK,[110] the earnings being treated as belonging to the last year in which the employment was held.[111] In determining whether duties are performed wholly outside the UK,[112] duties performed in the UK but which are purely incidental to the performance of duties abroad are ignored.[113] Some duties are declared to be performed in the UK, such as certain duties on board ships and aircraft.[114] These rules are varied for seafarers and their 100% reduction (section 40). There are also rules for the Continental shelf; general earnings from employment in the UK sector of the Continental shelf are treated as being in respect of duties performed in the UK (section 41).

A separate charge in Chapter 5B (sections 41F-41L) deals with the taxation of specific income from employment-related securities for internationally mobile employees, and replaces rules formerly in Chapter 5A (section 41A-E).[115]

13.3.2 Deductions for Travel Costs

This section covers the rules allowing the taxpayer to deduct certain travel costs. The term 'travel' is to be construed narrowly and does not extend to the costs of accommodation or subsistence which attract their own—and more—restrictive rules, set out in §13.3.3.

13.3.2.1 Initial and Final Travel Expenses

Initial and final travel expenses are not incurred 'in the performance of the duties' but to enable a person to carry out those duties (or return from having carried them out) and so cannot come within the normal deduction rule in ITEPA 2003, section 337. Particular legislation (section 341) therefore applies where (a) the employee is UK resident, (b) the duties of the employment are performed wholly outside the UK and (c) if the employer is a foreign employer, the employee is domiciled in the UK (section 341(2)–(4)); these are of course the circumstances in which the employee is taxable in full on general earnings and cannot use the remittance basis. The employee may deduct the costs of travel from a place in the UK to take up the employment, and of travel to a place in the UK on its termination (section 341(8)). The reference to 'a place in'[116] the UK is presumably to ensure that where,

---

[110] ITEPA 2003, ss 22(3) and 26(3), ex TA 1988, s 202A(2)(b), reversing *Bray v Best* [1989] STC 159, HL. On finding the right year, see ITEPA 2003, s 30, ex TA 1988, s 19, para 4A and s 202A(3).

[111] ITEPA 2003, s 30(3); this rule applies to general earnings but not to amounts treated as earnings under the benefits code (s 30(4)).

[112] See *Taylor v Provan* [1974] STC 168, 175; [1974] 1 All ER 1201, 1208; *Barson v Airey* (1925) 10 TC 609.

[113] ITEPA 2003, s 39, ex TA 1988, s 132(2). *Cf* TA 1988, s 335; *Robson v Dixon* [1972] 3 All ER 671; 48 TC 527; *Taylor v Provan* [1973] 2 All ER 65, 74.

[114] ITEPA 2003, s 40, ex TA 1988, s 132(4); *Graham v White* [1972] 1 All ER 1159, 48 TC 163. The concessionary relief for the daily subsistence allowances paid to detached national experts seconded to the European Commission has now been made statutory and classed as an exemption so featuring in Pt 4 of the Act—see ITEPA 2003, s 304 (for concession, see Inland Revenue Press Release, 29 March 1994, [1994] *Simon's Tax Intelligence* 458).

[115] Substitution by FA 2014, s 52 and Sch 9.

[116] Added by TA 1988, s 193(3).

for example, an employee flies from Glasgow to the United States via Heathrow, the costs of the flight from Glasgow to London are deductible and not just the costs of travel from the airport of departure from the UK. Section 341(5) allows apportionment if the travel is only partly attributable to this purpose.

13.3.2.2 Travel Between Employments

Travel costs are deductible under section 342 where the UK resident employee has more than one employment the duties of at least one of which are performed wholly or partly outside the UK. The other conditions are (a) that the travel is to carry out the duties of the employment at the destination, (b) that the employee has performed duties of another employment at the place of departure, and (c) that the place of departure or destination or both are outside the UK. The reason for the provision is, once again, the limitations of section 337; travel from one employment to another could not be said to be 'in the performance of the duties' of either, so a special rule is needed. This rule applies to journeys both from and to the UK, but the employment (section 342(5)) must not be such as to give rise to earnings taxed on a remittance basis (section 342(6) and (7)). Again, apportionment is authorised if there is more than one purpose (section 342(8)).

13.3.3 *Other Deductions; Reimbursed Expenses and Corresponding Payments*

It is important to appreciate the nature of the rules in this area of law, sections 370–376. They are not concerned to allow an employee to deduct certain costs of travel, accommodation and subsistence. Rather, they apply where an employer has provided such facilities, so that the sum concerned is brought into charge as a benefit, eg under Part 3, Chapter 10; the rules then allow the employee to deduct the amount of the included benefit. The same analysis and result apply where the employee pays the amount and is then reimbursed by the employer; here the reimbursement would otherwise come within Part 3, Chapter 3. So while the sections appear to be—and are—framed in terms of deductions, they are limited to deductions of amounts that first have to be 'included'. These rules also mean that where these costs are borne by the employee and not by the employer, no deduction can be obtained. This makes the employer the effective regulator of what is and what is not allowed. Other systems do not have such restrictions and find them bizarre.

13.3.3.1 Employee's Travel Duties Performed Abroad

The scope of section 370 is similar to—though not identical with—sections 340 and 341. In broad terms, section 370 allows for the non-taxation of sums 'included' for employees' travel in three situations, the last of which is confined to vessels. These rules are confined to tax under ITEPA 2003, section 15, ie not the remittance basis. The sums may be included because the employer provides the facilities, eg pays for the ticket or reimburses the employee.

(1)   Where the employee is absent from the UK wholly and exclusively for the purpose of performing the duties of one or more employments, the duties must be performed outside the UK and the journey must either be from a place outside the UK where duties are performed or a return journey back (section 370(3)).

(2)   Where the duties are performed partly in and partly out of the UK, they must be such that duties being performed overseas may only be performed there, and the journey must be wholly and exclusively[117] for the purpose of performing those duties (in the case of an outward journey) or (in the case of an inbound journey) returning after performing such duties (section 370(4)).

(3)   The condition that the duties may be performed only outside the UK is relaxed for seafarers.[118]

13.3.3.2 Family Travel and Travel for Family Reasons

Return journeys by the employee during the performance of the duties of employment and the costs of travel by the employee's family are matters regulated separately by section 371, a more restrictive rule than section 370.[119] First, the cost must be either provided (ie paid for by the employer) or reimbursed by the employer (section 371(1)(a)), as in the accommodation and subsistence rule (see §13.3.3.3 below).[120] Secondly, the employee must be absent from the UK for a continuous period of at least 60 days,[121] whether or not in the year of assessment, for the purpose of performing the duties of the employment. Thirdly, the journey must be between a place in the UK and a place outside the UK where such duties are performed (section 371(4)). So if the employee is working in New York and the family want to join up in Florida, the cost of a UK–Florida flight is not given the relief under section 371 unless, possibly, they fly through New York first. Fourthly, the spouse or child must be accompanying the employee at the start of the absence, visiting the employee during that period or returning to a place in the UK after visiting the employee (section 371(5)). The deduction is limited to two outwards and two inwards journeys in any year of assessment (section 371(6)). Children must not be aged over 17[122] at the beginning of the outwards journey.

13.3.3.3 Accommodation and Subsistence

Expenses of accommodation and subsistence, previous known as board and lodging, to enable employees to carry out the duties of their employment, are deductible (a) if met directly by the employer, or (b) having been incurred by the employee, are then reimbursed by the employer (section 376(1)). Therefore, no deduction is allowed where employees meet the expenses but are not reimbursed; this is presumably because in situations in which deduction is permitted, the employer will claim to deduct these sums in computing his profits and so the Revenue can check the sums claimed by the employer against the sums claimed by the employee. Where the expense is incurred partly for a non-employment purpose, section 376(3) permits apportionment of those costs attributable to the employee, but will allow nothing for the spouse or family.

---

[117] On 'wholly and exclusively' in a slightly different context, see *Mallalieu v Drummond* below at §22.2.1.

[118] ITEPA 2003, s 370(5); on location of duties, see s 372, excluding s 40(2), ex TA 1988, s 194(7)–(9).

[119] ITEPA 2003, s 371. The travel may be from or to 'any place in' the UK (ex TA 1988, s 194(3)).

[120] ITEPA 2003, s 371(1), ex TA 1988, s 194(2).

[121] ITEPA 2003, s 371(3), ex TA 1988, s 194(2). On costs of travel by a wife to accompany a director or an employee in precarious health, see ESC A4(d) (the phraseology of this concession is flagrantly sexist).

[122] ITEPA 2003, s 371(7): a person reaches the age of 18 at the start of the day which is his 18th birthday (Family Law Reform Act 1969, s 9).

13.3.3.4 Travel by Employees Not Domiciled in the UK

Employees who are not domiciled in the UK but who are paid for duties performed in the UK are also governed by special rules (sections 373–375). Such employees must not have been resident in the UK for either of the two years preceding the year of assessment in which they arrived, or must not have been in the UK for any purpose during the two years ending with the 'qualifying arrival date' (section 375). The special rule permits the deduction of costs of travel to and from the country in which the employee normally lives,[123] provided the travel is to a place in the UK in order to perform the duties of the employment here—or to return at the end.[124] If the employee is present in the UK for a continuous period of at least 60 days for the purpose of carrying out the duties of the employment, the family travel rules are as for UK domiciled employees (section 374). Once here the employee is entitled to the benefit of these rules for a period of five years beginning with the date of arrival.[125] This means that the relevant journey must be begun within the five-year period.[126]

13.3.3.5 Certain Foreign Earnings—Corresponding Payments

Certain foreign earnings may attract further deductions for 'corresponding payments' (section 355). The earnings qualify if the employee is not domiciled in the UK and the employment is with a foreign employer. The payment must have been made out of those earnings. In addition, it must not reduce the employee's liability to UK tax but be made in circumstances corresponding to those that would so apply if all the relevant elements were in the UK. The most common example is an employee's contributions to a foreign pension fund which corresponds to a UK pension fund for which relief could be given. Such payments are allowable only if they are made out of the foreign earnings and, save for pension contributions, Revenue practice may require proof that there is not sufficient overseas income (on which UK tax is not payable) to enable the payments to be made without having recourse to the foreign earnings.[127]

13.3.4 Double Tax Treaties

The effect of double tax treaties on a person who is not resident in the UK may be to grant exemption from ITEPA 2003.

13.3.5 Note for Seafarers and History

From 1974 until 1998 it was possible for an employee who had earnings for services rendered abroad (whether for a foreign or UK-based employer) to claim a 100% deduction for

---

[123] ITEPA 2003, s 373(4), avoiding the old-fashioned 'place of abode'.
[124] ITEPA 2003, s 373(4); apportionment is permitted by s 373(6).
[125] ITEPA 2003, ss 373(3) and 375, ex TA 1988, s 195(2), (3). The journey must be undertaken within the five-year period.
[126] ITEPA Explanatory Notes Change 102.
[127] *Schedule E Manual*, para SE32665. The more recent *Employment Income Manual* is silent on this point (see EIM32660 *et seq*).

payments for those services.[128] Since 1998 this has been possible only for seafarers.[129] The rule remains of general importance for past years and for certain termination payments attributable to past years.[130] From 1974 until 1992 it was even possible to claim pension contribution deductions.[131] To qualify for the 100% deduction the earnings had to be for a 'qualifying period' of at least 365 days of absence from the UK. Complicated rules related to the number of days the employee was allowed back in the UK during this period. This was repealed in 1998 because it was being 'exploited' by 'a few' high-earning individuals who were able to arrange their affairs so that they did not pay tax in the other country either.[132] If these words are to be taken at face value, the sensible thing would have been to tie the 100% deduction to non-taxable status of the payment in the other country. It is therefore more likely that the Treasury had its eye on the £250m it hoped to recoup. It is also likely that some of those high-earning individuals rearranged their affairs so as to achieve non-resident status.

13.4 PAYE[133]

13.4.1 Introduction

PAYE is the UK system of cumulative withholding of tax at source. It has become a mark of good manners to praise the UK's PAYE system, but there is little cogent evidence to support such an assessment in unqualified form.[134] While the system works well, it is only as good as the quality of the information supplied. A withholding system, it has been said:[135]

> Combines the expedient and the objectionable. It is a rough and ready system which virtually garnishes taxpayers' incomes, sometimes for debts they do not owe but subject in this event to refund. ... It is surprising that this withholding system, to which strong objections may be raised on grounds of principle, has aroused so little comment. It has probably done more to increase the tax collecting power of central governments than any other one tax measure of any time in history.

In 2010 the introduction of a new HMRC computer system led to the scandalous revelation of widespread errors in the PAYE codes of millions of UK taxpayers. Approximately 6 million UK taxpayers had the wrong amount of tax deducted under PAYE in the previous two tax years, of which 1.4 million received letters informing them that they owed more

---

[128] TA 1988, Sch 12.

[129] TA 1988, s 192A, added by FA 1998. On definitions of oil rigs and offshore installations, see FA 2004, s 146 and Sch 27. On the meaning of days of absence in TA 1988, Sch 12, para 3(1), see *Carstairs v Sykes* [2000] STC 1103.

[130] TA 1988, s 188(3) and Sch 11, para 10.

[131] TA 1988, Sch 12, para 1A, added by F(No 2)A 1992, s 54.

[132] Inland Revenue Press Release, 17 March 1998, [1998] *Simon's Tax Intelligence* 453.

[133] For accounts of the system, see RC (UK) 2nd Report, §§16–26, and 118th Report of the Board of Inland Revenue, Cmnd 6302 (1976), §§93–125. See now ITEPA 2003, Pt 11 (ss 682–712), ex TA 1988, ss 203, 205–207, 828, and the Income Tax (Pay as You Earn) Regulations 2003 (SI 2003/2682) which came into force 6 April 2004 and superseded Income Tax (Employments) Regulations 1993 (SI 1993/744). For some very dated comparisons with the United States, see Murray [1962] BTR 173.

[134] See Brodie (1998) 145 *Taxation* 271 at 272.

[135] MacGregor [1956] 4 *Can Tax Jo* 171, 173; Carter (chair), Canadian Royal Commission on Taxation, *Study No. 16* (Queen's Printer, 1966) 17.

than £300. Those owing less than £300 eventually had their tax debt waived by HMRC. Yet more errors were uncovered in millions of PAYE codes in 2011 and again in 2012. In 2010 the Government launched a consultation on improving the operation of PAYE, which has led to a move towards the collection of real-time information (RTI) in order to simplify taxation and reduce burdens on business. Described by HMRC as 'the biggest change in PAYE in 70 years', from 6 April 2013, all employers operating PAYE are required to make RTI returns to HMRC providing pay and deduction information on or before the day payments are made to employees. Those employers with fewer than 50 employees were given a longer transitional period to allow them time to adapt their systems for RTI. If RTI returns are not made on time then penalties will apply, with the amount of the penalty based on the number of employees.[136] The OTS has recommended that HMRC should conduct a post-implementation review into RTI, to investigate whether full 'on or before' reporting is necessary in all circumstances and what further scope there is to extend/harmonise easements for small employers.[137]

The PAYE system imposes a duty on the employer[138] to account once a month (but quarterly for certain employers)[139] for the tax that he has deducted or ought to have deducted. PAYE is distinct from provisions which direct that basic rate tax is to be deducted at source, eg under the scheme for payments to sub-contractors.[140] The language of the scheme is that it applies to 'relevant payments', which are payments of 'net PAYE income'. PAYE income includes PAYE employment income, PAYE pension income and PAYE social security income.[141] 'Net' income indicates that some deductions—pension contributions and gift aid—are allowable.[142] Certain payments are then excluded from the PAYE system and are left to be taxed under self-assessment, eg most social security payments, social security pensions, relocation expenses, and certain other expenses and liabilities.[143] The rules on the scope of PAYE have been subtly rewritten and theoretically expanded by ITEPA 2003.[144] By widening the scope of PAYE the legislation does not alter the total amount of tax reaching the Revenue but may alter the liability as between employer and employee. Rules requiring electronic communication are in force for specific employers who are large employers, and came into force for medium-sized employers for the year beginning 6 April 2005.[145] Where the system does not apply, eg in the case of a non-resident employer, the employee must use the self-assessment system.

In view of its effectiveness PAYE has been expanded in various ways. It also provides ample encouragement to the Revenue to argue that a contract is one of employment, and so within the PAYE system, and not self-employment. In certain situations, eg of casual employments, the Revenue may direct employees to operate the PAYE system themselves.[146] The PAYE

Regulations were rewritten in 2003 as part of the Tax Law Rewrite programme. The Commentary sets out 125 changes, nearly all of which are of 'no practical effect' or which 'bring the law into line with practice'. One change allows the code to be adjusted for overpayments or underpayments under the self-assessment system.[147] The Regulations were amended to define how PAYE was to apply when the employment income tax rules were changed retrospectively. The technique is to create 'notional payments'.[148]

The question whether the Revenue could make a PAYE coding taking account of a relief to which the taxpayer was not yet entitled was decided in the negative in a case involving relief for Lloyds losses against pension income.[149] The Revenue wanted to delay giving the relief since the loss could not be determined until the end of the year, but the court saw no reason why a coding could not be made on a provisional basis. Everyone accepted that loss would wipe out tax liability so that it was a simple cash-flow exercise. The decision has now been partly reversed in the PAYE regulations; the Revenue are given the power to do so but the taxpayer may not insist.[150]

In *IRC v Herd*,[151] the House of Lords held that the PAYE regulations should not apply unless there was a clear direction that they should. The Revenue argued for the narrow construction, while the employee argued for a wide construction so that the burden would fall on the employer and not on himself. The charge had arisen under what became TA 1988, section 138 (later repealed), on the unrealised gain on shares acquired as an employee. A specific provision now applies the PAYE rules to certain benefits from share options, etc, but did not do so then.[152] Lord Mackay said that the Schedule E charge was not on the amount paid but on the net gain, and this involved questions of the market value of shares which are not publicly quoted and so could involve considerable calculation and, perhaps even more importantly, substantial judgements on matters of opinion.[153] He went on to emphasise that his view applied only where a particular payment was treated only in part as assessable to income tax under Schedule E; it would not prevent a payer being under an obligation to deduct tax where it was clear that there were two or more payments made together, some of which were emoluments under Schedule E while others were not.[154]

The Special Commissioners have held that a payment in kind which could be converted into money was a payment for PAYE.[155] The Court of Appeal has held that, in the context of the PAYE system, payment generally means actual payment, ie the transfer of cash or its equivalent.[156] However, following the development of the *Ramsay*[157] judicial anti-avoidance doctrine discussed in chapter five, in terms of the *MacNiven*[158] approach, it was a commercial rather than a legalistic concept, and so the *Ramsay* doctrine or approach

---

[147] Commentary: Change No 121.

[148] FA 2006, s 94.

[149] *Blackburn (IoT) v Keeling* [2003] EWCA Civ 1221, [2003] STC 1162.

[150] Income Tax (Pay as You Earn) Regulations 2003, regs 13–14.

[151] [1993] STC 436, 66 TC 29.

[152] ITEPA 2003, s 700, ex TA 1988, s 203FB; TA 1988, s 138 was repealed before s 203FB came into force. On s 700, see ITEPA explanatory notes change 152.

[153] [1993] STC 436, 442e.

[154] *Ibid*, 443d.

[155] *Paul Dunstall Organisaton Ltd v Hedges* [1999] STC (SCD) 26.

[156] *DTE Financial Services v Wilson* [2001] STC 776 at para 42, per Jonathan Parker LJ.

[157] *WT Ramsay Inc v IRC* [1982] AC 300.

[158] *MacNiven v Westmoreland* [2001] STC 237.

could be used to turn the steps of a composite transaction into a payment. Since *Barclays Mercantile Business Finance*[159] the same result will follow, but with different reasoning. The Court rejected counsel's submission that to apply the *Ramsay* principle to the PAYE system would inevitably introduce confusion and uncertainty into the statutory code:

> The true position, as I see it, is that for those employers who operate the PAYE system in a straightforward manner, and who do not resort to the complexities of tax avoidance schemes, there will be neither confusion nor uncertainty; whereas for those employers who choose to operate such schemes the effect of applying the *Ramsay* principle is to restore the certainty which the legislature intended.[160]

The legislation addresses the timing of payments for PAYE (ITEPA 2003, section 686).

13.4.2 Widening the Ambit by Legislation

13.4.2.1 Benefits

Although PAYE was originally applied only to money payments, it has since been extended to certain benefits in kind, notably cash vouchers (ITEPA 2003, section 693), non-cash vouchers (section 694), credit tokens (section 695) and convertible assets (section 696),[161] but also enhancing the value of an asset (section 697) and share options etc (sections 698–700). Apart from these extensions, PAYE applies to almost all income within ITEPA 2003, including, therefore, pensions income and certain welfare payments (section 683(3)–(5)); it therefore applies, for example, to payments of expenses and expense allowances within ITEPA 2003, Part 3, Chapter 3, and to any securities related income within Part 7.[162] FA 2015, section 17 provided the authority for HMRC to amend the PAYE regulations to collect income tax on specified benefits through PAYE from 6 April 2016. For now, the specified benefits include cars, fuel, private medical insurance and gym memberships. On the use of coding to collect tax on benefits outside the PAYE system, see §13.4.4 below.

13.4.2.2 Payments by Others

PAYE applies to certain payments by third parties. Where earnings are paid by a third party, a deduction of tax under PAYE may still be required.[163] There is also an express provision to allow the PAYE system to operate when there are organised arrangements for sharing tips and the person running the scheme is not the principal employer.[164] Tips paid by customers, eg in a restaurant, are employment incomes of the workers but are not paid by the employer and so fall outside the PAYE system as far as the employer is concerned. The PAYE obligations can be applied to the administrator of a tip-sharing scheme (sometimes referred to as the 'tronc master'), and since 6 April 2004 there is an obligation on an

---

[159] *Barclays Mercantile Business Finance v Mawson* [2004] UKHL 51.

[160] *Ibid*, para 43.

[161] In *DTE Financial Services Ltd v Wilson* (above) the Court of Appeal held that the payment fell within ex TA 1988, s 203(1) and so did not have to consider s 203F.

[162] ITEPA 2003, s 683(2), referring to ss 10(2) and (3) which embrace Pts 4–7 inclusive.

[163] See also *Booth v Mirror Group Newspapers plc* [1992] STC 615.

[164] ITEPA 2003, s 692; ITEPA explanatory notes change 150.

employer who is aware that a tip-sharing system is in operation to provide the Revenue with details of the administrator.[165]

PAYE may also apply to payments by an intermediary (section 687). The concept of a payment by an intermediary is widely defined. PAYE also applies where a contractor hires employees of another person (the mobile UK workforce provision). This applies where the employee works for someone other than the employer and that someone, known as the relevant person, pays the employer; one or other of these will operate the PAYE system. The Revenue have the power to direct the relevant person to apply the system if it appears to the Revenue that tax will not be deducted or accounted for as usual (section 691). Whenever ITEPA 2003 is extended to workers, the PAYE regulations will follow—so workers supplied by agencies are brought within the Act by section 44 and so, potentially, within PAYE.[166] The PAYE regulations also apply where intermediaries such as PSCs and MSCs are involved.[167]

13.4.2.3 International

The obligation on an employer to operate the PAYE system arises if he has a sufficient tax presence in the UK. For this purpose, a non-resident company carrying on business in the UK through a branch or an agency has a sufficient presence.[168] This obligation is widened by two provisions. First, where an employee works for a person based in the UK but the actual employer is based overseas (and so outside the PAYE regulations), the person for whom the employee is working can be made to apply the PAYE system on behalf of the employer. The same burden falls on the person for whom the work is done where someone other than the employer makes the payment and is also outside the UK.[169] Special rules in section 689A apply to oil and gas workers on the Continental shelf. The second situation arises where an employee is not resident in the UK or meets the 3-year non-residency test in section 26A; the PAYE system is designed to apply only to those earnings which are for work done in the UK.[170] The practical problem is that when the payments are actually made, it may be unclear how much of the remuneration will be taxable. Employers may ask for a direction as to the proportion to be subject to PAYE; if no direction is sought, the whole payment is subject to the system. Provision is also made for accommodating split-years.

13.4.3 Liabilities Under PAYE

13.4.3.1 Employers

The employer is liable to deduct PAYE in accordance with software and/or tables supplied by the Revenue and taking account of the PAYE coding of the employee, which is based

---

[165] Income Tax (Pay as you Earn) Regulations 2003, reg 100; ex 1993, reg 84B and Rewrite commentary, para 567; on scope of tronc arrangements, see *Figael v Fox* [1992] STC 83.

[166] ITEPA 2003, s 688. On practice, see RD4 (February 1992); see also FA 1998, s 55 for another example.

[167] ITEPA 2003, ss 56, 61G.

[168] *Clark v Oceanic Contractors Inc* [1983] STC 35 (where the branch was deemed to be in the UK by what is now TCGA 1992, s 276(7)).

[169] ITEPA 2003, s 689, ex TA 1988, s 203C; see also Inland Revenue Press Release, 11 April 1994, [1994] *Simon's Tax Intelligence* 490.

[170] ITEPA 2003, s 690, ex TA 1988, s 203D; see also Inland Revenue Press Release, 11 April 1994, [1994] *Simon's Tax Intelligence* 490. ITEPA explanatory notes changes 148 and 149.

on the individual's reliefs for the year.[171] If the employer fails to deduct, the Revenue may demand the money from the employer.[172] If the Revenue proceeds against the employer, the employer cannot, in turn, recover from the employee on the authority of *Bernard and Shaw Ltd v Shaw*.[173] In the *Shaw* case, the court so held because the employee was not a trustee for the employer and because the action for money had and received would not lie; the employer could only retain the sums from later payments to the employee[174] (which would be of no value if the employment had ceased). Today, it is unclear whether a different result would be reached on the basis that the principle of restitution has superseded the old action for money had and received. In so far as the result turned on the construction of the appropriate legislation, it may well be that the same result would be reached. When the PAYE system has been applied to income, the Crown may make an assessment as regards income in the light of the practice generally prevailing (section 709), provided it does so within 12 months following the year for which the assessment was made—a rule which binds the Revenue and does not affect the taxpayer's right of appeal.[175] Separate provisions apply where an employer makes a lump sum settlement of PAYE which, it is estimated, should have been deducted on wages paid.[176]

13.4.3.2 Employees

If there has been an under-deduction of tax by the employer, the Revenue may recover the tax from the employee in two very different situations. First, the Revenue may recover tax not deducted by the employer from the employee if they are satisfied that the employer took reasonable care to comply with the regulations and that the failure was due to an error made in good faith.[177] Secondly, the Revenue may recover from the employee where they are of the opinion that the employee received the sum knowing that the employer had wilfully failed to deduct the tax.[178] The same applies to sums which have been assessed on the employer under these rules and not paid within 30 days of the notice. Again, the Board is involved and the employee must receive the sum knowing that the employer had wilfully failed to deduct the tax.[179] It has been held that where the Revenue seek to use this power in county court collection proceedings, it is open to the defendant-employee to raise the public law defence that on no view of the evidence could the Board reach that conclusion.[180]

---

[171] Made under ITEPA 2003, s 685. On coding, see the Income Tax (Pay as You Earn) Regulations 2003, regs 13 and 14, ex 1993, regs 6–13.

[172] Income Tax (Pay as You Earn) Regulations 2003, regs 68–72.

[173] [1951] 2 All ER 267 (KB); see the discussion by Weisbard (1996) NLJ 1124.

[174] Note also the very special case of *Philson & Partners Ltd v Moore* (1956) 167 EG 92 where there had been an express term in a severance agreement between employer and employee that the employee should settle outstanding matters with the Revenue.

[175] *Walters v Tickner* [1993] STC 624, 66 TC 174, CA.

[176] ITEPA 2003, ss 703–707, ex TA 1988, s 206A; and Income Tax (Pay as You Earn) Regulations 2003, regs 94–106, ex 1993, regs 80A–80N.

[177] Income Tax (Pay as You Earn) Regulations 2003, reg 72(3), ex 1993, reg 42(2).

[178] *Ibid*, reg 72(3), ex reg 42(3); as in *R v IRC, ex parte Sims* [1987] STC 211, 60 TC 398; and *R v IRC, ex parte Cook* [1987] STC 434, 60 TC 405.

[179] Income Tax (Pay as You Earn) Regulations 2003, reg 81, ex 1993, reg 46A; for an unsuccessful challenge by the employee under an older version, see *R v IRC, ex parte McVeigh* [1996] STC 91, 68 TC 121.

[180] *Pawlowski v Dunnington* [1999] STC 551, CA.

13.4.4 The Cumulative Withholding System

The system is one of cumulative withholding over the year. Full account is taken of the employee's income from this source and of such personal allowances as each may be entitled to. In essence, each is allowed 1/52nd of the relevant allowances each week, or 1/12th each month. At the end of any week taxable income is calculated by subtracting the accumulated 1/52nd shares of the allowances from the taxable pay to date. If the income rises over the year the tax will rise with it; if it falls, eg because of a change of job or a strike, a repayment may be made by the employer, or lower tax paid for the rest of the year. In the 1970s it was realised that if an employee went on strike late in the tax year, the tax repayment due would help supplement any strike pay and so prolong the strike. Repayments to people directly involved in a strike are therefore not made until the employee returns to work or finds other employment.[181]

Although the system applies to ITEPA 2003 income only, it may, in effect, be used to collect tax in respect of other sources. This is achieved by directing that the taxpayer's allowances shall be attributed to those other sources of income, thus reducing the allowances to be set against the ITEPA 2003 income and so gathering the tax from the employment. The system may also be used to collect underpayments of tax from that or a previous year, as well as to refund overpayments. At one time, benefits in kind were not subject to PAYE directly; they could, however, be taxed indirectly by reducing the value of the reliefs which might be set against PAYE income through the coding system. Where the value of these benefits exceeds the available allowances there is provision for 'negative coding', which applied whenever non-PAYE pay exceeded the allowances. Negative coding creates 'additional pay' which may be taxed at source.[182] The tax to be deducted from a particular cash payment is not to exceed 50% of the payment.[183]

13.4.5 PAYE and Self-assessment

In principle, the primary charge to income tax is the charge under self-assessment. PAYE is simply a method of withholding tax, which is brought into the calculation of the balancing payment. However, the Revenue do not issue self-assessment forms to most of those whose incomes fall predominantly under the PAYE system. Moreover, where the underpayment in the year amounts to £1,000 or less and arises solely in respect of earnings to which PAYE is applied, the underpayment may be collected by adjustment of the PAYE code. A particular problem under self-assessment is that a director or an employee who receives benefits in kind and to whom a self-assessment tax return is not issued, is not in a position to know whether the Revenue are proposing to collect tax on the benefits in kind through amendment of the PAYE code for the following year, or whether he should notify chargeability in order to make his own self-assessment. Penalties may be imposed if the employee does not notify chargeability. The Revenue accept that employees who receive such a copy of the information on a P11D may assume that any items on it which are not already taken into

---

[181] Income Tax (Pay as You Earn) Regulations 2003, reg 57, ex 1993, reg 36.
[182] *Ibid*, reg 7(2), ex 1993, reg 7(2)(b)(ii).
[183] *Ibid*, reg 23(5), ex 1993, reg 2(1).

account for PAYE 'will be' taken into account, so that there is no need to notify chargeability because of them. This does not, however, apply where the particular employee knows that the P11D return has not, in fact, been submitted to Revenue.[184]

13.4.6 Commentary

There are disadvantages in the PAYE system. First, there is the trouble and expense to employers of finding and paying staff to operate the system. In fact, many of these staff are ex-employees of the Revenue who leave for better pay after having been trained by the Revenue. The expense of these employees will be deductible by the employer in computing his profit for the year, but this still leaves a substantial burden of the operating costs of the system to fall on the employer.[185] One wonders whether a tax credit rather than a tax deduction might not be more appropriate. Secondly, there is the fact, less pronounced in the PAYE system than in other cruder withholding systems, that tax may be withheld incorrectly and that a repayment may take some time to take effect. Thirdly, it is sometimes alleged that the PAYE system, while providing refunds if income drops, also taxes more steeply if income goes up, and thus directs the taxpayer's attention to the fact that the increase is taxed at the marginal rather than the average rate. This may have a disincentive effect in that the repayments side of the PAYE system could encourage absenteeism later in the tax year when the tax refunds may be greater. A fourth disadvantage lies in the very perfection of the structure. Its complexity meant that it could become something of a straitjacket in the days before computerisation.[186] The absence of PAYE from incentive payments such as that in *Glantre Engineering Ltd v Goodhand*[187] meant that an employer could leave the employee to pay the tax if the employer so chose, especially if the employee had left the employment.

---

[184] Statement of Practice SP 1/96.
[185] On compliance costs, see above at §1.3.5.
[186] It was regarded as responsible for such pre-1990 anomalies as a wife's earned income allowance being the same as a single person's, and not interfering with the husband's claim to the married man's allowance.
[187] [1983] STC 1, 56 TC 165.

14

Employment Income: Emoluments/Earnings

14.1 Earnings

ITEPA 2003 is intended to rewrite rather than reform the law. In Taxes Act 1988, section 19 was the main charging provision taxing 'emoluments' from employment. In ITEPA 2003, section 6 charges income tax on general earnings as well as specific employment income, and then defines general earnings in a way which covers not only emoluments within section 62(1) but also others matters, principally benefits in kind, which are treated as income. In what follows, section 62 will be taken as the modern equivalent of the emoluments previously charged under section 19.

Two House of Lords cases provide the key to the test of taxable emoluments (now earnings). The first, *Hochstrasser v Mayes* (1959) talks about rewards for services. While some refinement of some of the words used in that case may now be needed, it still represents a starting point. The second, *Shilton v Wilmshurst* (1991), uses more flexible words, holding that an emolument 'from employment' means an emolument 'from being or becoming an employee', but in the particular context of a payment to undertake employment with someone else. The precise relation between the two tests is unsettled. When reading the cases in this chapter, and in particular those cases when the courts find that a payment was not taxable, one must be aware that many cases would now fall within the benefits code in Part 3, Chapter 10. The cases in this chapter apply a legal test to decide whether a payment is an emolument. Part 3, Chapter 10 has an (almost) irrebuttable presumption that a payment made to the employee by or at the expense of the employer is chargeable.[1]

14.1.1 Tests

In *Hochstrasser v Mayes*,[2] a sum of money paid to compensate an employee for a loss incurred on selling his home was held not to be taxable. Upjohn J said that the payment would be an emolument if it was made in reference to the services rendered by the employee by virtue of the office, and if it was something in the nature of a reward for services past, present or future. In the House of Lords Viscount Simonds accepted this as entirely accurate, subject only to the observation that the word 'past' might be open to question. In *Laidler v Perry*,[3] Lord Reid added that sums might be taxable even though they are not rewards, eg sums given to employees in the hope that they will produce good service in the future. These comments suggest, as does the *Oxford English Dictionary*, that a reward is a recompense for something past (whether good or evil). In *Bray v Best*[4] in 1989, Lord Oliver could not read the expression 'a reward for services' as anything more than a conventional expression of the notion that a particular payment arises from the existence of the employer–employee relationship and not from something else. In *Shilton v Wilmshurst*,[5] the House of Lords held that there was no reason to limit the scope of emoluments to those situations in which the payer has an interest in the performance of the duties.

Lord Reid's words in *Laidler v Perry* were applied in two decisions of the House of Lords before *Shilton v Wilmshurst*. In *Brumby v Milner*,[6] sums of money held in a profit-sharing scheme were distributed when the scheme was wound up. The House held that this payment, like the previous income payments, arose from the employment and from no other source; it was therefore taxable. The employees were and continued to be in employment. In *Tyrer v Smart*,[7] the taxpayer applied for shares in his employing company, having preferential right of application as an employee. The House held that he was taxable on the advantage gained.

Hamblett v Godfrey[8] is a decision of the Court of Appeal which may be read as suggesting that a payment can taxable under section 62 as an emolument even though not a reward for services if it is 'connected with' the employment. Both of the preceding House of Lords cases impose a test based on causation, rejecting a 'but for' and sine qua non test under which any payment is an emolument if it would not have been paid but for the employment. If the Court of Appeal meant to impose a 'but for' causation test, the decision is obviously wrong, but it is clear that the Court of Appeal would not have attempted any such thing. What the Court of Appeal was trying to do was to resolve an issue in a particularly difficult part of

---

[1] Eg, after the bomb attacks on London in July 2005, employers wishing to make ex gratia payments to their staff caught up in these events found that the staff were taxable under Pt 3, Ch 10 even though they were quite clearly not taxable under s 62.

[2] [1959] Ch 22; see further §14.1.2 below.

[3] [1966] AC 16, 30; 42 TC 351, 363. See also Browne-Wilkinson VC in *Shilton v Wilmshurst* [1990] STC 55, 59 and 61; 64 TC 78, 95, 99, CA.

[4] [1989] STC 159, 167.

[5] 64 TC 78 at 109 per Lord Templeman.

[6] [1976] STC 534, [1976] 3 All ER 636.

[7] [1979] STC 34, [1979] 1 All ER 321 (HL).

[8] [1987] STC 60, [1987] 1 All ER 916 (CA).

the law dealing with payments for surrenders of rights. The case law had already established that payments for giving up some rights were taxable earnings and payments for giving up other rights were not. The case is therefore discussed in that context—see §14.4.4.4.

14.1.2 Hochstrasser v Mayes[9]

The taxpayer worked for ICI Ltd, a large concern with factories in different parts of the UK. To encourage its employees to remain in the service of the company if asked to move to a different part of the country, the company promised to make good any loss incurred by the employee through a fall in the value of a house which the employee owned. On being moved from Hillhouse to Wilton, the taxpayer sold his house in Fleetwood for £1,500; it had originally cost £1,850. ICI reimbursed him this loss of £350 and the Revenue sought to assess him on the £350. These payments were not enough at that time to trigger the application of what is now Part 3, Chapter 10. The Revenue claim failed; they argued that all payments by employers to their employees 'as such' were taxable, unless they were payments in return for full consideration in money or money's worth other than for services under the employment. The House of Lords rejected this approach unanimously. It was not disputed that the company would not have made this payment if the taxpayer had not been an employee. It also was clear that the company thought that it was going to benefit by having a more settled workforce if a scheme like this were in operation. Moreover, because the taxpayer had a perfectly standard wage, it could not be said that this was disguised remuneration. The House[10] held that the payment was not in respect of his services to the company but rather to compensate him for the loss which he had sustained, and was, therefore, not taxable. It may be noted that the company was getting the best of both worlds: the sum was not taxable in the hands of its employee but was deductible by the company in computing its profits.

What about other possible payments? As the Revenue's counsel put it, to be recouped a loss by someone else is plainly a profit. If these profits escaped tax, which profits would not? It was agreed that if the employee had suffered bereavement and the company had seen fit to grant him something from its benevolent fund, such payment would not have been taxable.[11] However, if the employee had been compensated for a loss on an investment on the Stock Exchange, it is not obvious that he would have escaped tax in respect of such a payment, although this has since been held to be so.[12] Only Lord Denning gave reasons why an indemnity of the last type would be taxable.[13] Unfortunately, this example was premised on the view that the indemnity would be by way of reward for services, a premise which automatically makes the sum taxable. Lord Denning went on to say that the sum would be taxable because the losses were 'his own affair' and nothing to do with his employment, but this would be no less true of the hypothetical bereavement.

---

[9] [1960] AC 376, 38 TC 673. Kerridge [1982] BTR 272 argues that the case should have been decided on the basis that the housing arrangements were the subject of a collateral contract. On slightly different Canadian legislation, see the equivalent case of *Ransom v MNR* [1967] CTC 346, discussed by Arnold and Li (1996) 44 *Can Tax Jo* 1; and *R v Phillips* [1994] 1 CTC 383.

[10] [1960] AC 376.

[11] *Ibid*, 392, per Lord Radcliffe. So the House would not have charged the July 2005 payments under s 62.

[12] *Wilcock v Eve* [1995] STC 18, 67 TC 223.

[13] [1960] AC 376, 396.

14.1.3 Shilton v Wilmshurst[14]

This case concerned the transfer of Peter Shilton, then and for a long time thereafter the England football team's goalkeeper, from Nottingham Forest to Southampton in 1982. Nottingham Forest paid Shilton a fee of £75,000 as an inducement to leave the club—and so go off its payroll. The Court of Appeal and Morritt J held that the sum was not taxable under what is now section 62. The emolument had to be referable to the performance of services by the employee under the contract of employment. The House of Lords took a different view. Lord Templeman said:[15]

> Section [62] is not confined to 'emoluments from the employer' but embraces all 'emoluments from employment'; the section must therefore comprehend an emolument provided by a third party, a person who is not the employer. Section [62] is not limited to emoluments provided in the course of the employment; the section must therefore apply first to an emolument which is paid as a reward for past services and as an inducement to continue to perform services and, second, to an emolument which is paid as an inducement to enter into a contract of employment and to perform services in the future. The result is that an emolument 'from employment' means an emolument 'from being or becoming an employee'. The authorities are consistent with this analysis and are concerned to distinguish in each case between an emolument which is derived from being or becoming an employee on the one hand and an emolument which is attributable to something else on the other hand, for example from a desire on the part of the provider of the emolument to relieve distress or provide assistance to a home buyer. If an emolument is not paid as a reward for past services or as an inducement to enter into employment and to provide future service but is paid for some other reason, then the emolument is not received 'from the employment'.

It is not clear to what extent this formulation is meant to be a summary of existing case law and to what extent it is meant to mark a new point of departure, but it shows how far the law had developed since 1959. This was made all the clearer by Ward's summary in 1992:[16] a sum is taxable if it is received in respect of:

(1) having acted as or having been an employee;
(2) acting as or being an employee;
(3) continuing to act as or continuing to be an employee;
(4) becoming an employee; or
(5) undertaking to do anything within (2)–(4).

In applying these tests the courts take a realistic view of the facts. In *O'Leary v McKinlay*,[17] a football club made a long loan to trustees who held the money for a player. The income from the resulting investments was held to be income from the employment and not income from a loan, which would now come within ITTOIA 2005, Part 4.

One remaining issue concerns the question of whether a payment is an emolument: is this a question of law or of fact? In *Hochstrasser v Mayes* (§14.1.2 above), Upjohn J took the question to be one of inference from primary fact and of legal inference, thus making the

---

[14] [1991] STC 88, 64 TC 78; see Kerridge [1991] BTR 311.
[15] [1991] STC 88, 91; 64 TC 78, 105.
[16] Ward [1992] BTR 139 (written before *Mairs v Haughey* [1993] STC 569); on which see [1994] BTR 77.
[17] [1991] STC 42, 63 TC 729.

question one of law. In *Tyrer v Smart*,[18] however, the inference seems to have been treated as one of the fact and so within the sole jurisdiction of the Commissioners. The position is as confused as it is unfortunate; the earlier view seems preferable.[19]

14.1.4 Consequences of the Causation Test

In so far as the question is one of causation it is clearly not one of consideration, and the court is not confined to any expressions of consideration in any service contract. In *Pritchard v Arundale*,[20] a payment expressed in the contract of service to be in consideration of that service escaped tax. Conversely, in *IRC v Duke of Westminster*,[21] Lord Atkin would have held the payment to be an emolument notwithstanding that the service was expressed not to be the consideration.

In *Bridges v Bearsley*,[22] property (shares in the employer company) was transferred by other shareholders (X and Y) to an employee, B, under a deed which said that the transfer was in consideration of B remaining a director of the company. When the court looked at the circumstances surrounding the transfer, it was clearly due to a wish to honour a promise made to B by the father of X and Y that the father would leave the shares to B by will and thus was not a taxable emolument for B. Since the test was one of causation, the court could look at all the circumstances. As seen above, a payment caused by something other than services must escape tax. Moreover, the onus is on the Revenue to show that the payment is an emolument.[23] Where a payment is caused both by service and by something else, principle would suggest an apportionment of the payment, at least where this is practicable.[24] Whether there will be an apportionment if the sum is paid for two causes, neither of which can be valued, remains unclear.[25] Just as a payment by an employer may not be an emolument, so a payment by someone other than the other party to the contract of employment may be an emolument.[26]

14.1.5 Services Past

The state of the case law on this point is not very secure. The issue of the liability to income tax of payments for services past was expressly left open by Viscount Simonds in *Hochstrasser v Mayes* in 1960 (see §14.1.2 above). In *Shilton v Wilmshurst* in 1991 (see §14.1.3 above), Lord Templeman said that such payments will be taxable if they are also intended as an inducement to continue to perform future services, and so by implication

---

[18] [1979] STC 34.
[19] Macdonald [1979] BTR 112.
[20] [1971] 3 All ER 1011, 47 TC 680.
[21] [1936] AC 1.
[22] (1957) 37 TC 289, CA.
[23] *Hochstrasser v Mayes* [1959] Ch 22, per Viscount Simonds.
[24] *Mairs v Haughey* [1993] STC 569; *Carter v Wadman* (1946) 28 TC 41. In *Tilley v Wales* [1943] AC 386, 25 TC 137, the House of Lords was relieved of the task of deciding whether an apportionment should be made since this was agreed between the parties.
[25] The Court of Appeal left this open in *Shilton v Wilmshurst* [1990] STC 55, 64 TC 78.
[26] The person making the payment may be required to deduct tax under the PAYE system (*Booth v Mirror Group Newspapers* [1992] STC 615).

not taxable where there was no such inducement. In between there had been *Brumby v Milner* in 1975 and *Bray v Best* in 1989 (see §14.1.1 above), where in each case the sum at issue had been held to be an emolument of—and so now earnings from—the employment. It has been held that a tip to a taxi driver is taxable even though given only at the end of the service.[27] A bonus payment to an employee[28] and a payment on completion of, say, 25 years' service with the company[29] are taxable, although in these cases, since the employment had not yet terminated, the payments may be seen as incitements to even greater service and loyalty in the future. By ITEPA 2003, section 323, replacing a previous concession,[30] an award in the form of a tangible article or shares in the employing company is tax free if the cost is reasonable, ie it does not exceed £50 per year of service. This limit does not appear to apply when the employee is leaving the employment.

None of these cases appears actually to turn on the question of payment for past services, but the payments must have escaped tax had the point not been accepted.[31] The fact that past consideration is no consideration is irrelevant since the test is one of causation and not of consideration. The true line seems to be drawn not between services future and services past, but between a transfer caused by services and one caused by something else, eg a gift for personal reasons. The fact that the service is past is only one factor in enabling this line to be drawn.[32] In *Moore v Griffiths*,[33] the fact that the payment was not known about until after the services had been rendered tended to show that it was a testimonial, and so not taxable.

14.1.6 *Capital Payments*

A few dicta suggest that payments may escape section 62 if they are capital payments.[34] These dicta are unsound if they mean that a payment made in return for services may escape section 62 because of its capital nature. In no case has the classification of a payment as capital been the prime reason for holding that the payment is not taxable; in a few cases a payment which has escaped tax because it was not made in return for services has been conveniently but irrelevantly (or even inaccurately) described as capital sum.[35] The description 'capital' is therefore best regarded simply as a convenient label for certain types of non-emoluments.[36]

---

[27] *Calvert v Wainwright* [1947] 1 All ER 282, 27 TC 475.

[28] *Radcliffe v Holt* (1927) 11 TC 621. However, will the emphasis on inducement as to future service mean that ordinary tips paid to a taxi driver who, to the knowledge of the payer, is about to retire, escape tax?

[29] *Weston v Hearn* (1943) 25 TC 425.

[30] See ex ESC A22.

[31] See *Henley v Murray* [1950] 1 All ER 908, 31 TC 351, 366, per Evershed MR: 'nor was it a reward for his past service' (not taxable); similarly, Lord Warrington in *Hunter v Dewhurst* (1932) 16 TC 605, 643.

[32] As in *Cowan v Seymour* [1920] 1 KB 500, 7 TC 372; *Denny v Reed* (1933) 18 TC 254.

[33] [1972] 3 All ER 399, 48 TC 338.

[34] Eg, Lord Denning MR in *Jarrold v Boustead* [1964] 3 All ER 76, 81; and Lord Simon in *Tilley v Wales* [1943] AC 386, 393, 25 TC 136, 149.

[35] *Prendergast v Cameron* (1939) 23 TC 122, 138, Finlay LJ.

[36] For authority against such usage, see Walton J in *Brumby v Milner* [1975] STC 215, 227, 51 TC 583, 598; and Lord Coulsfield in *IRC v Herd* [1992] STC 264, 286, 66 TC 29, 55; however, see Goldberg [1971] BTR 341, 345.

14.2　Timing

14.2.1　Normal Basis

ITEPA 2003 has its own terminology, bordering on the theological. Where the employee is resident in the UK, section 15(1) taxes the full amount of any general earnings 'for' the tax year, while section 15(2) refers to the full amount received in a tax year as being an amount of taxable earnings from the employment in that year. This is supplemented by section 16, which states that general earnings are 'for' a particular year if they are earned in or otherwise in respect of, a particular period. Section 18 then tells us when money earnings are received and section 19 deals with the receipt of non-money earnings. Section 18 applies to all money payment including sums caught by Part 3, Chapter 10. The old law referred, more simply, to the full amount of emoluments received in the year in respect of the office or employment concerned.[37]

Under section 18, earnings in money are to be treated as received at the earlier of (a) when the payment is made of, or on account of, the earnings; and (b) when the person becomes entitled to payment of, or on account of, earnings.[38] The meaning of the expression 'on account of' is not amplified. Where the person becomes entitled to payment but does not receive the payment, eg through the insolvency of the company, there is no provision giving relief.[39] Similar rules also apply to PAYE.[40] Since this test uses entitlement to payment as well as actual payment as tests of liability, it is not really a receipts basis at all but a mixture of receipts and earnings bases. Its importance is that it rejects decisively the old law, under which the payment would be treated as income of the period during which the services were rendered, and a payment made in later year would be backdated.

Section 19, dealing with non-money earnings, directs that if the amount is treated as earnings for a particular year then it is income of that year. Section 19 gives no further rules as to when in the year it is so treated. If that does not provide the answer, the benefit is treated as received in the year in which it is provided.[41]

14.2.2　Directors

Because directors can control how they are paid, three special timing rules apply:

(1)　If the person is a director at any time during the year of assessment and the earnings relate to an office or employment with that company,[42] the date on which sums on account of earnings are credited in the company's accounts or records is used. This applies whether or not there is any fetter on the right to draw the sum.

---

[37] TA 1988, s 202A(1)(a); see also ICAEW Memorandum TR759, [1989] *Simon's Tax Intelligence* 716.

[38] ITEPA 2003, s 18(1) Rules 1 and 2, ex TA 1988, s 202B(1), added by FA 1989, s 37(1); for origins, see Keith Committee, *Report on Enforcement of Revenue Powers*, Cmnd 8822 (1983), 141–45.

[39] Contrast the position in Sch D, Cases I and II (TA 1988, s 74(j)).

[40] ITEPA 2003, s 686, ex TA 1988, s 203A.

[41] ITEPA 2003, s 19(4).

[42] ITEPA 2003, s 18(1) Rule 3, ex s 202B(1)(c)–(e), (2), (3); the term 'director' is defined in ITEPA 2003, s 18(3) (ex TA 1988, 202B(1)(5), (6)) (whether or not that office or employment is the directorship).

(2)   If the amount to be paid for a period is determined before the period ends, the payment is treated as chargeable when that period ends, even though no payment has yet been made.

(3)   Where the amount for the period is not known until later, eg when the bonus is finalised, the date of that determination will be taken. Where more than one of these rules, including the general rules in §14.2.1, applies, the earliest date will be taken.

14.2.3 Ceased Office

It is not necessary that the office or employment should exist in the year in which the receipt arises.[43] If, in the year concerned, the office has never been held, the emoluments are to be treated as earnings for the first year in which the office is held (section 17(2)). Conversely, if the office or employment is no longer held, the earnings are to be treated as earnings of the last such year (section 17(3)). To this extent the legislation retains the doctrine of the source. Section 17 does not address the problem arising where a person holds an office, resigns it, and then resumes and receives a payment between the two periods of tenure. In such circumstances the answer presumably turns on the question, 'which period of tenure is the payment for?'

14.2.4 Other Rules; Non-money Earnings and International

The timing rules for money do not override specific statutory timing rules for cash or non-cash vouchers, credit tokens and payments of compensation on retirement or removal from office.[44] They are also excluded for certain taxable benefits including the beneficial occupation rules; cars, vans and related benefits; loans; and the residual liability to charge. If no specific rule applies, the earnings are treated as received when they are provided. Where Part 2, Chapter 5 (non-UK international factors) comes into play, the legislation repeats the notions of earnings for a tax year and then repeats the rules on the timing of money earnings and non-money earnings.[45] However the sections go on to provide the details of the remittance basis.

14.3   Money's Worth—Discharge of Employee's Obligation: The Rule in *Nicoll v Austin*

ITEPA 2003, section 62(2)(b) refers specifically to 'any gratuity or other profit or incidental benefit of any kind … if it is money or money's worth', and section 62(3) goes on to define 'money's worth' as being something of direct monetary value to the employee, or capable of being converted into money or something of direct monetary value to the employee.

---

[43] ITEPA 2003, s 17, ex TA 1988, s 202A(2).
[44] ITEPA 2003, s 19; ex TA 1988, s 202B(6).
[45] ITEPA 2003, ss 29–32 largely repeat ss 15–19.

Section 62(1)(c) refers to anything else that constitutes an emolument of the employment. It is quite immaterial whether the matters to be discussed should be treated as belonging under one head rather than another, but long-established case law clearly brings them into (c).

Payments applied for the benefit of the taxpayer are just as much income as moneys paid directly.[46] Where an employer discharges an existing pecuniary obligation of the employee, E, the sum paid is treated as E's income, even if it is income tax as in *Hartland v Diggines*.[47] In *Hartland v Diggines*, a promise to pay a salary 'without any deductions and taxes which will be borne by' the employer was interpreted as an agreement to pay such sums as after deduction of tax gives the net salary after deduction of tax.[48] This has been applied equally where employer and E are jointly liable.[49] The fact that the employer is under no obligation to make the payments is irrelevant.

In *Nicoll v Austin*,[50] the principle was applied to future obligations. The taxpayer was life director of, and had a controlling interest in, his employing company. Under his contract of service he was to continue to reside in his own house but the company would pay all outgoings in respect of his house, including rates, taxes and insurance, and the costs of gas, electric light, telephone, and of maintaining the house and gardens[51] in proper condition; however, the house remained the taxpayer's. Finlay J held that the payments made by the company constituted money's worth to the taxpayer, who was therefore taxable.[52] However, *Nicoll v Austin* does not apply if, after leaving the employer and before being used to discharge the liability of the employee, the payment has become the income of someone else. In *Barclays Bank Ltd v Naylor*[53] payments were made into the bank account of a child of the employee out of a discretionary trust set up by the employer to help with employees' school fees. Cross J held that the payments had become the income of the child, and the fact that income had been used to discharge the father's legal obligation to pay the school fees was insufficient to turn the income of the child into the income of the parent. The rule in *Nicoll v Austin* must be taken as subject to all the categories of exempt income gathered together in ITEPA 2003, Part 4; so a payment of an expense in connection with the provision of a parking place does not give rise to tax.[54]

---

[46] Eg, *Drummond v Collins* [1915] AC 1011, 6 TC 525.

[47] [1926] AC 289, 10 TC 247. See also *IRC v Miller* [1930] AC 222, 15 TC 25; *IRC v Leckie* (1940) 23 TC 471. An under-deduction of a director's PAYE which is accounted for to the Revenue by the employer is taxed under ITEPA 2003, s 223, ex TA 1988, s 164 (on which, see Revenue, Schedule E Manual, paras 3230 *et seq*).

[48] *Jaworski v Institution of Polish Engineers in Great Britain Ltd* [1951] 1 KB 768, [1950] 2 All ER 1191. But, Cf *Jennings v Westwood Engineering Ltd* [1975] IRLR 245. Tax-free remuneration for directors was prohibited by Companies Act 1985, s 311, but was thought to have little impact in practice and was repealed when Companies Act 2006 was introduced. On definition of 'director', see Companies Act 2006, ss 250–251, and compare ITEPA 2003, s 67, ex TA 1988, s 168.

[49] *Richardson v Worrall* [1985] STC 693, 58 TC 642 (quaere whether this will not be so if the primary liability and the primary benefit are the employer's).

[50] (1935) 19 TC 531.

[51] For a doubt about the gardens, see Lord Evershed MR, in *Wilkins v Rogerson* (1961) 39 TC 344, 353.

[52] By concession this rule does not apply to the heating, lighting, cleaning and gardening costs of certain clergymen (ESC A61).

[53] [1960] 3 All ER 173, 39 TC 256. Today the scheme will not succeed if E comes within ITEPA 2003, Pt 3, Ch 10 (ex TA 1988, s 154); the payment will be taxable under s 212 and cannot be treated as exempt under s 331 as scholarship income. See also *Constable v FCT* (1952) 86 CLR 402.

[54] ITEPA 2003, s 237, ex TA 1988, s 197A.

14.4 Examples of General Principles

The question whether a particular receipt arises from the employer–employee relationship or from something else has been much explored in the case law. Clearly, the more cogent the 'something else' is, the more chance a taxpayer has of arguing that the payment falls outside section 62.

14.4.1 General

Payments for services include not only ordinary wages and salaries, but also less obvious payments, such as those to mark a period of service with the employer[55] and bonus payments whether or not contracted for[56] and even if paid at Christmas.[57] A sum paid 'to preserve an employer's good name and good staff relations' was held to be taxable even though it was designed to compensate staff for the withdrawal of a benefit in kind.[58]

A payment for services may arise even if the service is not within the scope of duty. In *Mudd v Collins*,[59] a director who negotiated the sale of a branch of the company's business was held taxable on the sum of £1,000 granted him by the company as commission. However, if the taxpayer can show that the payment is not for services but a testimonial, as in *Cowan v Seymour*,[60] tax will not be due. As the source of the payment was the decision of the shareholders of the (now liquidated) company, the payment would not fall within Part 3, Chapter 10. Today, this decision must be considered borderline.[61]

14.4.2 Reimbursements

A payment by an employer to reimburse an expense incurred by the employee in the employment is not an emolument[62] (but this situation is not without its critics).[63] This is so even if the employee would not have been able to deduct the expense himself under section 336. However, it is assumed that this applies only to expenses incurred in connection with the employment.[64] The reimbursement of an expense must be distinguished from

---

[55] *Weston v Hearn* [1943] 2 All ER 421, 25 TC 425.

[56] *Denny v Reed* (1933) 18 TC 254. See ITEPA 2003, s 323, ex ESC A22.

[57] *Laidler v Perry* [1965] 2 All ER 121, 42 TC 351. On Christmas parties, see ITEPA 2003, s 264, ex ESC A70; the limit is now £150 per head (increased by statutory instrument).

[58] *Bird v Martland* [1982] STC 603, 56 TC 89. ITEPA 2003, ss 321 and 322 (ex ESC A57) now govern payments for suggestion schemes.

[59] (1925) 9 TC 297, Rowlatt J. See also *Radcliffe v Holt* (1927) 11 TC 621.

[60] [1920] 1 KB 500, 7 TC 372.

[61] *Cowan v Seymour* was distinguished in *Shipway v Skidmore* (1932) 16 TC 748 and in *Patrick v Burrows* (1954) 35 TC 138; but was, surprisingly, followed in *IRC v Morris* (1967) 44 TC 685, where the Court of Session held that there was evidence to support the Commissioners' findings. ITEPA 2003, s 403, ex TA 1988, s 148, applies only to payments 'in consequence of the termination of the office' and so not here.

[62] *Owen v Pook* [1969] 2 All ER 1, 45 TC 571; see also *Donnelly v Williamson* [1982] STC 88, 54 TC 636. Reimbursement of car parking expenses when the parking space is at or near the place of work is not taxable: ITEPA 2003, s 237 (ex TA 1988, s 197A, added by FA 1988, s 46(4), (5)).

[63] See Lord Simon (dissenting) in *Taylor v Provan* [1975] AC 194, 218, 49 TC 579, 615; and Evans [1988] BTR 362.

[64] Thus, in *Richardson v Worrall* [1985] STC 693, 58 TC 642, a reimbursement of the cost of petrol obtained for private use was taxable; but in *Donnelly v Williamson* [1982] STC 88, 54 TC 636, a reimbursement of a teacher's costs for doing something outside the contract of service (attending a parents' evening) was not taxable.

an expense allowance, which is treated as an emolument.[65] ITEPA 2003 pays much closer attention than previous legislation to the treatment of reimbursements and when they are included and when excluded (see below §16.2); however nothing in the 2003 Act alters the position with regard to the first sentence of this paragraph, which is based on a decision of the House of Lords.

14.4.3 Gifts, Including Those for Sporting Achievements

Payments which have escaped section 62 include those made to relieve poverty,[66] as a mark of personal esteem, or to mark some particular occasion, such as the passing of an examination.[67] Today they are unlikely to escape Part 3, Chapter 10 if made by or at the expense of the employer.

14.4.3.1 Taxable Gifts

The mere fact the donor is not the employer does not prevent the gift from being an emolument; the question is whether the payment is made because of the services rendered by the employee in the course of his employment. On this basis, Atkinson J held, long ago in 1947,[68] that a tip to a taxi driver was taxable, but added that a tip of £10 would not be taxable if it was paid at Christmas or when the driver was going on holiday and was intended to acknowledge the driver's qualities and faithfulness rather than as a reward for regular service; today's equivalent of £10 in 1947 is over £300.[69] As the customer was not the employer but a third party, the presumption in Part 3, Chapter 10 would not apply. However, as always, the question is one of fact and degree. Christmas presents will be taxable if they are customary or indiscriminate.[70] There is an exemption from tax, now statutory, for gifts from third parties which are earnings up to £250 pa (section 324).

14.4.3.2 Tests

In *Moorhouse v Dooland*,[71] Jenkins LJ stated four principles:

(1)   The test of liability to tax on a voluntary payment made to the holder of an office or employment is whether, from the standpoint of the person who receives it, it accrues to him by virtue of his office or employment or, in other words, by way of remuneration for his services.

---

[65] *Perrons v Spackman* [1981] STC 739, 55 TC 403.

[66] *Turton v Cooper* (1905) 5 TC 138.

[67] *Ball v Johnson* (1971) 47 TC 155 (not taxable even though the bank required the employee to take a bankers examination); however, the payment is viewed by the Revenue as coming within ITEPA 2003, s 201, ex TA 1988, s 154, if the employee is paid at a rate of £8,500 pa or higher (ICAEW Memorandum TR786, [1990] *Simon's Tax Intelligence* 205).

[68] *Calvert v Wainwright* [1947] 1 All ER 282, 27 TC 475; on Revenue practice, see [1984] *Simon's Tax Intelligence* 187 and [1985] *Simon's Tax Intelligence* 187.

[69] [1947] 1 All ER 282, 283, 27 TC 475, 478. See also *McBride v Blackburn* [2003] STC (SCD) 139 SpC 356.

[70] *Wright v Boyce* [1958] 2 All ER 703, 38 TC 167, CA; and *Laidler v Perry* [1966] AC 16, [1965] 2 All ER 121, 42 TC 351. In the latter case a company gave each of its employees a £10 voucher at Christmas, regardless of their rate of remuneration or personal circumstances; this replaced the traditional Christmas turkey which, for some reason, could not be obtained. A senior employee earning more than £2,000 a year thought the payment a charming Christmas gesture rather than as a payment for services, but this did not prevent the vouchers from being taxable under what is now s 62.

[71] *Moorhouse v Dooland* [1955] Ch 284, 304, 36 TC 1, 22.

(2)   If the recipient's contract of employment entitled him to receive the voluntary pay-
      ment, that is a strong ground for holding that it accrues by virtue of the office or, in
      other words, is remuneration for his services.
(3)   The fact that the voluntary payment is of a periodic or recurrent character affords a
      further, though less cogent, ground for the same conclusion.
(4)   On the other hand, a voluntary payment may be made in circumstances which show
      that it is given by way of present or testimonial on grounds personal to the recipient,
      as, for example, a collection made for the particular individual who is at the time vicar
      of a given parish because he is in straitened circumstances, or a benefit held for a pro-
      fessional cricketer in recognition of his long and successful career in first-class cricket.
      In such cases the proper conclusion is likely to be that the voluntary payment is not a
      profit accruing to the recipient by virtue of his office or employment, but a gift to him
      as an individual, paid and received by reason of his personal needs or by reason of his
      personal qualities or attainments.

These principles were stated in a case concerning a payment by a third party; where the
payer is the employer, the intentions of the payer should also be considered.[72] The amount
of the payment is also relevant.[73]

14.4.3.3 Clergy Cases

It was decided early on that grants from a fund to supplement the incomes of clergy in
poorly-endowed parishes were emoluments.[74] Although these grants were not from the
employers, they were paid for services and paid to the clergy by virtue of their offices. The
reason for the payments was to augment stipends—not to make grants to clergy because
they were poor. In *Blakiston v Cooper*,[75] the House of Lords held that Easter offerings which,
by custom and episcopal prompting, were given to the vicar, were also taxable.[76] The giving may be voluntary but it is not spontaneous, and there is an element of recurrence.[77]
However, if the gift had been of an exceptional kind, such as a golden wedding present,[78] a
testimonial or a contribution for a particular purpose (ie to provide a holiday or a subscription due to the personal qualities of the particular clergyman), it might be a mere present.[79]
The Church of England now pools the Easter offerings for redistribution at diocesan level;
one listens to episcopal denunciations of the greed of tax planners with interest. However,
the technicalities of the employment status of the clergy are also interesting.

---

[72]   *Laidler v Perry* [1966] AC 16, 35, 42 TC 351, 366, per Lord Hodson; and see Brightman J in *Moore v Griffiths*
[1972] 3 All ER 399, 411 (employer's gift; third party's gift). If the company had, in return for its payment, used the
footballer's name to advertise its products, that payment would have been taxable under Sch D, Case VI. Quaere
whether allowing one's receipt of a gift to be used for advertisement will not also fall within Sch D, Case VI.
[73]   Hence, the difference between the wage and the benefit in *Seymour v Reed* and the £10 tip in *Calvert v Wainwright*. See also Lord Denning MR in *Laidler v Perry* [1965] Ch 192, 199, 42 TC 351, 361.
[74]   *Herbert v McQuade* [1902] 2 KB 631, 4 TC 489.
[75]   [1909] AC 104, 5 TC 347.
[76]   'It may appear startling that those who on a particular Sunday—and that one of the most significant in the
Christian year—contribute to the collection in their church, should be rendering unto Caesar nearly half their
contributions, but so undoubtedly it is' (per Lord Evershed in *Moorhouse v Dooland* [1955] Ch 284, 299); Whitsun
gifts to the curate are also taxable (*Slaney v Starkey* [1931] 2 KB 148, 16 TC 45).
[77]   *Seymour v Reed* [1927] AC 554, 569, 11 TC 625, 653, per Lord Phillimore.
[78]   *Corbett v Duff* [1941] 1 KB 730, 740, 23 TC 763, 779, per Lawrence J.
[79]   *Blakiston v Cooper* [1909] AC 104, 107, per Lord Loreburn.

14.4.3.4 Sporting Achievements—Bonus or Appreciation?

Seymour v Reed,[80] concerns the world of 1920s cricket. Seymour, the taxpayer, was a professional cricketer employed by Kent. In 1920 he was awarded a benefit season. Members of the club subscribed money to a fund for him, and he was allowed to receive the gate money at one of the home matches of that season.[81] The gate money of £939.80 was held by trustees, together with the subscriptions, until Seymour had found a farm. The money was then paid over to him and used by him for the payment of the farm. The Revenue attempted to tax the £939.80 for the year when it was paid over. The attempt failed. The payment was a personal gift and not employment income. Seymour had no right to a benefit season—the benefit would usually be towards the close of a man's career and was intended to provide an endowment on retirement—it was intended as an appreciation for services past rather than an encouragement for services to be rendered.[82] Today the question how far the payments would fall within Part 3, Chapter 10 may turn on the subtleties of whether the members of the club were also the employers.

By contrast, in *Moorhouse v Dooland*[83] the Revenue succeeded. Dooland was a professional cricketer employed by East Lancashire. Under club rules he was entitled to talent money of one guinea every time he scored 50 runs or more, took six wickets or scored a hat-trick. In the 1950 and 1951 seasons Dooland qualified for talent money, and the resulting public collection, six and 11 times respectively. The Revenue successfully claimed tax in respect of the public collections. *Seymour v Reed* was distinguishable on almost every point. Dooland had a contractual right to a collection; Seymour had no such right to his benefit. Dooland had a collection whenever he performed well; Seymour had only one benefit. Dooland's payments were small compared with his salary; Seymour's payment was very great. On similar reasoning, footballers' benefits after only five years have been held to be taxable.[84]

It does not follow that all collections for special feats would fall within the definition of emoluments. Thus, if Dooland had no contractual right to a collection but had scored 50 runs and then taken all 10 wickets in a match so that the achievement was exceptional,[85] such a collection might not be taxable. In so far as the sums were contributed by members of the public, they would not fall within Part 3, Chapter 10. In *Moore v Griffiths*,[86] payments made by the Football Association to mark England's victory in the World Cup in 1966 were held not to be taxable. The payment was intended to mark the Football Association's pride in a great achievement, and it would be more in keeping with the character and function of the Association to construe the payment as a testimonial or mark of esteem. Brightman J added darkly, but presciently, that the payment had no foreseeable element of recurrence.[87]

Following an announcement at Autumn Statement 2015, a statutory scheme was introduced to place a limit on the favourable income tax treatment afforded income from

[80] [1927] AC 554, 11 TC 625.
[81] For his performance, see John Wisden's *Cricketer's Almanack* 1920.
[82] This is a question of fact and proof: see esp Lord Phillimore at [1927] AC 554, 572, 11 TC 625, 655.
[83] [1955] Ch 284, [1955] 1 All ER 93, 36 TC 12.
[84] *Corbett v Duff* [1941] 1 All ER 512, 23 TC 763.
[85] [1955] Ch 284, 298, per Lord Evershed MR.
[86] [1972] 3 All ER 399.
[87] *Ibid*, 411; quaere whether this meant that recurrence was not foreseeable for these players.

sporting testimonials and benefit matches for employed sportspersons.[88] Testimonials that are non-contractual or non-customary—eg of the kind in *Seymour and Reed*—and granted or awarded on or after 25 November 2015 for income from events taking place on or after 6 April 2017 are now subject to income tax. This is irrespective of whether they are arranged by the sportsperson's employer or by an independent testimonial committee. The first £100,000 of a one-off testimonial is granted exemption.[89]

14.4.4 Compensation for Surrender of Advantage—Not Taxable

A payment by way of compensation for giving up some advantage rather than by way of reward for services is not taxable as an emolument.[90] This principle is applied even though the surrender of the advantage is a necessary consequence of taking the employment, save where the advantage or right being surrendered is inseparable from, or is closely connected with, the employment. The decision whether a particular payment is for services or by way of compensation is judged according to the reality and not mere words—the tests looks at causation and not consideration.

14.4.4.1 Starting the Job—'Golden Hellos'

Where an employer makes a payment to an employee at the commencement of service, it is a question of fact whether this is a taxable payment for future services or non-taxable compensation for some loss. Remuneration for services is still remuneration for services even if it is paid in a lump sum in advance.[91] Whereas it would be very difficult to demonstrate that periodical payments are anything but taxable under ITEPA 2003, the fact that the payment is a lump sum is a factor that may be taken into account.[92]

In *Pritchard v Arundale*,[93] the taxpayer, A, was in practice as a senior chartered accountant when a business friend, F, persuaded him to leave the practice and join him in business, as joint managing director of a company. A received a full salary at the commercial rate but insisted upon a stake in the business. F, who owned all but three of the 51,000 shares in the company, transferred 4,000 to A. A was held not taxable on the value of the shares transferred. Although the contract of service stated that the friend agreed to transfer the shares in consideration of A undertaking to serve the company, a contractual expression of consideration was not conclusively determinative of causation, and in any case that expression did not mean that that was the sole consideration.[94] Other factors[95] were the date of the transfer

---

[88] ITEPA 2003, s 226E *et seq*. See also https://www.gov.uk/government/publications/income-tax-update-to-treatment-of-income-from-sporting-testimonials/income-tax-update-to-treatment-of-income-from-sporting-testimonials.

[89] ITEPA 2003, s 306B.

[90] Where the payment is made in return for an undertaking the effect of which is to restrict the employee as to his conduct or activities, the payment may be taxable under ITEPA 2003, s 225, ex TA 1988, s 313 (see §14.4.5 below).

[91] See, eg, Lord Greene MR in *Wales v Tilley* (1942) 25 TC 136, 142. See also *Teward v IRC* [2001] STC (SCD) 36.

[92] *Pritchard v Arundale* [1971] 3 All ER 1011, 1022, 47 TC 680; followed in *Vaughan-Neil v IRC* [1979] STC 644, [1979] 3 All ER 481, 54 TC 223.

[93] [1971] 3 All ER 1011, 47 TC 680.

[94] [1971] 3 All ER 1011, 1022, 47 TC 680, 687.

[95] Quaere how substantial these really are.

being six months before service started, the nature of the transfer, that the transferor was not technically the employer but only the principal shareholder of the employer, and that the taxpayer's surrender of his existing livelihood was expressed elsewhere in the contract. These points were emphasised by Walton J in *Glantre Engineering Ltd v Goodhand*[96] when holding that a payment to an employee who had given up an employment elsewhere was taxable. This leaves open the question of whether the distinction is between employment and self-employment, or is simply one of fact; the latter is to be preferred. Where the payment is to induce the person to leave an employment, the sum may be taxable under ITEPA 2003, section 403, but this must be distinguished from a payment to take up a different employment as in *Shilton v Wilmshurst* (§14.1.3 above). Where the payment is by the employer, Part 3, Chapter 10 may come into play.

14.4.4.2 Loss of Amateur Status—Rugby League

At one time a person who joined a rugby league club was barred from ever again playing for, or even visiting, a rugby union club. If discovered on a rugby union ground as a spectator, he would be asked to leave. If he signed as a professional he would be barred from competing as an amateur in, for example, athletics.[97] Compensation for loss of these privileges was held non-taxable in *Jarrold v Boustead*.[98] By contrast, in *Riley v Coglan*,[99] the sum involved was £500, of which £100 was to be paid on signing the professional forms and the balance on taking up residence in York. The player agreed to serve for the remainder of his playing career, or for 12 years if longer. If he failed to serve the whole stipulated period, a proportionate part of the £500 was to be repaid by way of ascertained and liquidated damages. The Commissioners followed *Jarrold v Boustead*, but on appeal that case was distinguished by Ungoed-Thomas J, who concluded that the £500 was to be a running payment for making the player available to serve the club when required to do so.[100] The distinction was one of fact. Coglan's contract nowhere mentioned the abandonment of amateur status, but neither did Boustead's, which provided for the payment of £3,000 on signing professional forms, from which the court inferred that the payment was for loss. Coglan's £500 was coupled with the proviso that £400 was to become payable only when he took up residence in York, a factor suggesting that the payment was for services to the club. These, however, are minor differences. The principal distinction is that in Boustead's case no part of the £3,000 was returnable, whereas Coglan might have had to return some of his £500. In *Pritchard v Arundale* (see §14.4.4.1) the transfer was out and out.

14.4.4.3 Reality and the Sunday Organist

It is significant that in *Jarrold v Boustead* (above) the disqualification of the player from rugby union or amateur athletics was for life. On parity of reasoning, if C, a church organist, were required to give up Sunday golf as one of the conditions of employment and was paid £500 compensation, that sum would not be taxable under section 62.[101] If, however,

[96] [1983] STC 1, 56 TC 165; see also *Curran v MNR* [1959] CTC 416.
[97] *Jarrold v Boustead* [1964] 3 All ER 76, 781; 41 TC 701, 704.
[98] [1964] 3 All ER 76, 41 TC 701.
[99] [1968] 1 All ER 314, 44 TC 481.
[100] *Cf* the signing on payment in *Cameron v Prendergast* [1940] AC 549, [1940] 2 All ER 35.
[101] Lord Denning MR in *Jarrold v Boustead* [1964] 3 All ER 76, 80; 41 TC 701, 729.

the condition was against playing golf at those times when C ought to be playing the organ, the payment would only be a thinly-disguised remuneration. More difficult is the question whether such a sum would be taxable if the disqualification against Sunday golf or against playing rugby union were binding only so long as C was church organist or played rugby league. It may be significant that in *Pritchard v Arundale* (see §14.4.4.1), where there was nothing to prevent the taxpayer from resuming his practice as a chartered accountant on leaving his employment, Megarry J stressed the difficulties which a person of the taxpayer's age would find in building up his practice again.[102]

14.4.4.4 Payment as Part of Employer–Employee Relationship—Taxable

A payment for loss of a right which is part of the employer–employee relationship is taxable following *Hamblett v Godfrey*.[103] The question posed by this decision is whether and, if so, how far this widens the traditional test based on reward for services. A payment in return for the surrender of a right which is part of the employer–employee relationship, as opposed to mere social advantages, falls within section 62. Therefore compensation for loss of the right to join a trade union was held taxable in *Hamblett v Godfrey*. In *Shilton v Wilmshurst*,[104] Lord Templeman said that the rights lost in *Hamblett v Godfrey* were not personal rights but were directly connected with the employment; it followed that the source of the payment was the employment. *Shilton v Wilmshurst* leaves intact the tax-free status of the payment in *Pritchard v Arundale*. *Jarrold v Boustead* was not cited, but presumably remains in place for the same reason. Purchase LJ used the test of direct connection in *Hamblett v Godfrey* itself.[105]

A payment made to compensate for the loss of a contingent right (eg to a non-statutory redundancy payment) takes its character from the right it replaces. Since the non-statutory redundancy payment would have been tax free, compensation for its loss is also tax free.[106] In *Mairs v Haughey*, the Court of Appeal in Northern Ireland[107] made the point more sharply by holding that the payment was made in order to compensate for loss of those rights and not as an inducement to enter into the new contract of employment. Lord Hutton LCJ (NI) thought that *Hamblett v Godfrey* had not widened the law, saying that the payment was made for continuing to be an employee at GCHQ.[108] In *Mairs v Haughey*, the business of the employer, R1, was being bought out by a new company, R2. E, the taxpayer employee, was offered an employment by the new employer, R2, on condition that he did not take the redundancy payments due to him from R1 under a non-statutory redundancy scheme; instead, in the event of the buy-out being successful, he would receive an ex gratia sum from R1 the company, which was the sole shareholder in R2. Part of that sum was equal to a fraction of what would have been received for redundancy under the old scheme. The part which was for becoming an employee with the new company was taxable by reason

---

[102] [1971] 3 All ER 1011, 1023c. Curiously, this point was not emphasised in *Glantre Engineering Ltd v Goodhand* [1983] STC 1.
[103] [1987] STC 60, [1987] 1 All ER 916 (CA).
[104] [1991] STC 88, 95, 64 TC 78, 111.
[105] [1987] STC 60 at 69.
[106] *Mairs v Haughey* [1993] STC 569, 66 TC 273, 347 HL; for critical comment, see Ward [1994] BTR 77.
[107] [1992] STC 495, CA NI.
[108] *Ibid* at 521.

of *Shilton v Wilmshurst* but the other was not.[109] In *Mairs v Haughey*, Lord Woolf also said that prima facie a payment made after the termination of employment is not an emolument from the employment unless, for example, it is simply deferred remuneration.[110]

Despite Lord Hutton's remarks, the wider view of *Hamblett v Godfrey* was repeated by Carnwath J in *Wilcock v Eve*.[111] Carnwath J held that an ex gratia payment to an employee for loss of rights under a share option scheme fell on the *Hochstrasser v Mayes* side of the line rather than the *Hamblett v Godfrey* side, and so was not taxable under what is now section 62. This was because this was what the House of Lords had decided in the pre-*Hamblett v Godfrey* case of *Abbott v Philbin*.[112] The House had held that the value of a grant of the right to a share option could be a taxable emolument but the value realised on its exercise could not.

14.4.4.5 Payment for Giving up Right Already Lost—Taxable

If the right being compensated for no longer exists, it is hard to establish that a payment is made to compensate for its loss. In *Holland v Geoghegan*,[113] refuse collectors had had their right to sell salvaged property lawfully terminated; they went on strike, but returned to work on payment of £450 compensation for loss of earnings due to the termination of the scheme. Foster J, reversing the Special Commissioners, held that since the right to sell salvaged property had been lawfully terminated, the payment was not one of compensation for loss of a right but an inducement to return to work, and so taxable.

14.4.5 Restrictive Undertakings; Statute Intervenes

ITEPA 2003, section 225 is one of a group of provisions to be found in Part 3, Chapter 12. It treats a payment in respect of an employment-related restrictive undertaking as earnings under section 7(5). Its predecessor was originally introduced[114] to reverse the decision of the House of Lords in *Beak v Robson*.[115] In that case a director agreed to continue serving the company at a salary of £2,000 a year, and received £7,000 in return for an agreement not to compete with the business within a radius of 50 miles for five years. The £7,000 was held not taxable.

Section 225 applies wherever consideration is provided by the employer, whether to the employees or to others, in return for an undertaking, whether or not binding, the tenor and effect of which is to restrict employees as to their activities. The undertaking may be given before, during or after the employment. For the section to apply it must also be shown that the payment was made 'in respect of' the undertaking. This requirement is not satisfied where the undertaking involves taking on the very duties inherent in and inseparable from

---

[109] [1993] STC 569, 66 TC 273, HL.
[110] [1993] STC 569, 579j, 66 TC 273, 346.
[111] [1995] STC 18, 67 TC 223; the Revenue claim based on what is now ITEPA 2003, Pt 3 Ch 10 (ex TA 1988, s 154) also failed.
[112] [1961] AC 352, 39 TC 82.
[113] [1972] 3 All ER 333, 48 TC 482.
[114] Ex TA 1988, s 313, originally FA 1950, s 16. The purpose of backdating the section for some of the payments was to catch payments made to the managing directors of Austin and Morris Motor Companies; see Sabine, *A History of Income Tax* (Allen & Unwin, 1966), 116. For a case in which s 313 might have applied but the facts were held to fall within s 401, see *Appellant v Inspector of Taxes* [2001] STC (SCD) 21.
[115] [1943] 1 All ER 46, 25 TC 33.

the office or employment itself. So, in *Vaughan-Neil v IRC*,[116] a barrister who undertook to cease to practice at the planning bar on taking up his employment with a building contractor was held not taxable on the payment in return for the undertaking under what is now section 225.

Valuable consideration other than a payment given in return for a restrictive undertaking is now the subject of a separate provision—section 226. The whole sum is subject to income tax in the usual way.[117] Before 1988 the whole was taxed in an unusual way in that it was subject only to excess liability.[118] The payment is deductible by the payer—whether or not it would be deductible under normal principles and even if it is a capital payment.[119] This is achieved by directing any sum to which (the substituted) section 225 applies and which is paid or treated as paid by a person carrying on a trade, profession or vocation, may be deducted as an expense. This wide authorisation apparently applies not only to payments which would otherwise be non-deductible by reason of being capital, but also to payments for dual purposes or even those where the sole motivation of the payer was not for the purposes of trade.

14.4.6 The Redirection Principle

In *The Advocate General for Scotland v Murray Group Holdings Ltd and Others*,[120] an employee benefits trust (EBT) case involving sub-trusts established for the benefit of the families of executives and footballers employed by Rangers FC and related companies, the Scottish Court of Session accepted HMRC's argument that the EBT arrangements amounted to 'a mere redirection of emoluments or earnings' and were accordingly subject to income tax. In the Tribunals, the judges had spent considerable time and intellectual effort analysing technical questions about the operation of the sub-trusts, including what level of control was exercised by the employee over the sub-trusts and whether the trustees had general discretion as to what happened to the funds. The Court of Session, however, held that the funds 'redirected' to the trusts were ultimately derived as consideration for the employee's services and, further, took the view that what happened to the funds once redirected to the trusts was essentially irrelevant. In articulating this new redirection principle, the Court adopted a 'realistic' view of the facts (relying on the modern articulation of the *Ramsay* principle: see above §5.6), with Lord Drummond Young stating (at para 56): 'if income is derived from an employee's services *qua* employee, it is an emolument or earnings, and is thus assessable to income tax, even if the employee requests or agrees that it be redirected to a third party. That accords with common sense.' Leave to appeal to the Supreme Court was

[116] [1979] STC 644, [1979] 3 All ER 481.
[117] ITEPA 2003, s 225(3), ex TA 1988, s 313(1), as substituted by FA 1988.
[118] TA 1988, s 313(2), as originally enacted.
[119] ITTOIA 2005, s 69 and CTA 2009, s 69, ex FA 1988, s 73. Before 1988 the payment was often non-deductible because of the decision of the Court of Appeal in *Associated Portland Cement Manufacturers Ltd v Kerr* [1946] 1 All ER 68, 27 TC 103.
[120] [2015] CSIH 77. For a critical commentary of the decision see Small and Macleod [2016] BTR 27. The commentators argue that the Court of Session's 'wide approach to the interpretation of "earnings" seems to contrast with the approach recently taken by the Supreme Court in *HMRC v Forde and McHugh Ltd* [2014] UKSC 14, where it was held that funds contributed by a company to an unapproved pension scheme for the benefit of a director were not "earnings" for the purposes of NICs.'

granted in March 2016, and at the time of writing the case had not yet been heard. The payments at issue would most likely now be caught by the 'disguised remuneration' legislation in ITEPA 2003, Part 7A, which has effect from 6 April 2011.

14.5 Termination of Contracts: Compensation Payments

Payments on the termination of an office or employment are governed by an untidy mixture of statute and case law. The case law turns on the scope of what is now section 62. A payment which would fall within section 62 may be excluded by statute. A payment which escapes section 62 may be subject to the favourable tax regime in section 403 (see §14.5.4 below). The following is, in part, an illustration of the principles in §14.4 above, but the case law is best treated separately. Following an OTS review of the income tax and NIC treatment of termination payments, the Government launched a consultation in 2015 aimed at reforming and simplifying the rules.[121]

The OTS identified a number of problems with the rules on termination payments. Most significantly, the OTS concluded that while most people assume that any 'payoff' is tax free up to £30,000, in practice this is far from the case. In general the well-advised can obtain the exemption; others too often miss out. One OTS reform suggestion was to tie the exemption to statutory redundancy and to allow any payment, to a multiple of the statutory redundancy amount, to be tax free.

The Government consultation document agrees with the OTS that simplification is required, and that the first step should be to remove the present distinction between the tax/NIC treatment of contractual and non-contractual termination payments. By removing these distinctions the government intends that all payments made in connection with termination of an employment will be earnings and subject to income tax and employer/ employee NICs. To mitigate perceived harshness, it also intends to introduce some form of new exemption from income tax and NICs.

At Budget 2016, the Government announced that, from April 2018, it will tighten the scope of the £30,000 exemption and align the income tax and NICs rules so employer NICs (but not employee NICs) are due on those payments above £30,000 that are already subject to income tax.

14.5.1 Rules

Payments will come within section 62 only if made in return for services. If an employee owns property adjoining his employer's factory, sums paid by way of compensation under a claim for nuisance will not be taxable since they are not made in return for services. The matter does potentially give rise to a charge under Part 3, Chapter 10 if the payment is by an employer which is a company, but the chargeable amount is nil as the employee gave full value in settling the claim. Problems arise where the claim arises out of the contract of

---

[121] HMT and HMRC, *Simplification of the Tax and National Insurance Treatment of Termination Payments* (Consultation, 24 July 2015).

employment. The courts might have followed the line taken under ITTOIA 2005, Part 2 (Business Income) and held that sums paid in lieu of income are themselves income. However, under ITEPA 2003 a different approach prevails; sums paid to settle genuine compensation claims will escape tax under section 62[122]—although, as has been seen, such sums will usually come within section 403. The cases considered below are full of fine distinctions, and some important issues are still unresolved. The cases therefore turn on their own facts and, in particular, on the construction of the particular contractual arrangements.

Statutory redundancy payments are excluded from section 62 (but not from section 403) by statute.[123] Non-statutory redundancy payments are similarly excluded in practice if they are genuinely made on account of redundancy—whether the scheme is a standing one or an ad hoc arrangement to deal with a specific situation.[124] Payments incurred by an employer in providing counselling and other outplacement services to an employee in connection with the ending of the office or employment are excluded from ITEPA 2003 altogether.[125] Otherwise they would give rise to a taxable benefit under section 201; the exclusion therefore also applies to the reimbursement of expenses incurred by the employee. There is a similar exemption for retraining courses in section 331. These exclusions were extended to part-time employees in 2005.[126]

14.5.2 *Case Law on Compensation Claims by Employees Against Employers*

In 1950, Sir Raymond Evershed MR memorably described the line drawn by the cases in this area as 'a little wobbly'.[127] Nothing much has changed. He added that the taxpayer could not make the payment one by way of compensation for loss of office simply by using a formula; that is also still good law, indicating that the matter is to be treated as one of substance and not of words or labels.[128] The following principles are relevant in this area (in (1)–(4) the payment escapes section 62; in (6)–(9) the payment falls within section 62; (5) is a grey area):

(1)   A sum paid by way of commutation of pension rights does not fall within section 62.[129] This is not technically a matter which involves the compromise of a right arising under the contract of employment since, while the right may have its sources in such a contract, the pension itself is a taxable entity distinct from the office or employment.[130]

---

[122] If the compensation takes the form of annual payments it will be taxable as income under Sch D, Case III (*Asher v London Film Productions Ltd* [1944] KB 133, [1944] 1 All ER 77). See also *Taxation Commr (Victoria) v Phillips* (1937) 55 CLR 144.

[123] ITEPA 2003, s 309, ex TA 1988, s 579; the authority for being taken into account under s 403, ex s 148, is s 309(3), ex s 580.

[124] Statement of Practice SP 1/94 (revised to take account of *Mairs v Haughey* [1993] STC 569).

[125] ITEPA 2003, s 310, ex TA 1988, s 589A.

[126] FA 2005, s 18.

[127] In *Dale v De Soissons* 32 TC 118, 126.

[128] *Ibid*, 127.

[129] *Tilley v Wales* [1943] AC 386, [1943] 1 All ER 280, 25 TC 136; see discussion in Report of the Committee on the Taxation Treatment of Provisions for Retirement, Cmnd 9063 (1954) (the Tucker Report), paras 265–69. See also Woodhouse and Goode in *Tolley's Tax Planning 2003–04*, ch 60.

[130] *Tilley v Wales* [1943] AC 386, 392, 25 TC 136, 149.

(2) A payment to compensate for loss of rights under a non-statutory redundancy scheme is not taxable because it simply compensates for the loss of payments that would themselves be non-taxable.[131] Compensation for loss of rights under a voluntary redundancy scheme has escaped tax under section 62,[132] but payments made to all employees, whether or not they were made redundant, have not.[133] In the same vein, a protective award made under the Trade Union and Labour Relations (Consolidation) Act 1992, section 189, where the employer had failed to follow the right procedures on redundancy, was held to be not taxable under section 62 though it was under section 403; the right arose from the Act and not from the contract of employment.[134] The same is likely to follow from an award of compensation for unfair dismissal under the Employment Rights Act 1996.[135]

(3) A payment by way of compensation on the wrongful termination of the contract of employment, whether following judgment or by settlement, does not fall within section 62.[136]

(4) A payment made under a compromise agreement to settle a potential race discrimination claim is not earnings from employment under section 62, even if the amount is calculated by reference to alleged underpayments of salary and bonuses.[137]

(5) It is unclear whether a payment will escape section 62 if it consists of a sum stipulated in the contract as being paid by way of liquidated damages in the event of termination.[138] In theory, such payments should be treated the same as (3) since they have the same purpose. The boundary between (4) and (5)–(6) below would therefore be one of construction of the agreement. If this is correct, the sums will have to be a genuine pre-estimate of loss. One technical distinction is that in (5) and (6) the contract is not broken, whereas in (4) it is; however, this does not help to answer the question on which side of the line the arrangement falls. One might argue in favour of bringing (4) within section 62 that, since such a sum is part of the contract and therefore capable of inspiring the employee to greater effort, it must be a payment for services. However, the same inspiration may be derived from knowing that in the event of breach, a party can sue for unliquidated damages. At present it seems as though the combination of there being no breach of contract and the sum being paid in line with the contract is enough to bring the payment within section 62.

(6) A payment for continuing to work falls within section 62.[139] Where it is agreed between employer and employee that the contract shall cease with effect from a future

---

[131] *Mairs v Haughey* [1993] STC 569; for critical comment, see Ward [1994] BTR 77.

[132] *Mairs v Haughey* [1993] STC 569, HL (see above §14.4.4.4).

[133] *Allan v IRC* [1994] STC 943.

[134] *Mimtec Ltd v IRC* [2001] STC (SPD) 63.

[135] See *Wilson v Clayton* [2004] EWHC ChD 898; [2004] STC 1022, aff'd [2004] EWCA Civ 1657, where the payment was not in fact made under that Act but purported to be so; Patten J still held that the payment fell outside s 62 for other reasons. Gibson LJ agreed in the Court of Appeal.

[136] See *Henley v Murray* [1950] 1 All ER 908, 909, 31 TC 351, 363.

[137] In *Mr A v HMRC* [2015] UKFTT 0189 (TC), the FTT focused on the bank's reasons for making the payment. For commentary see Cooper and Granville-George, *Tax Journal* (19 June 2015).

[138] It is hard to find clear authority for this, but it may be implicit in *Henley v Murray*; it is certainly inconsistent with the words used by Vinelott J in *Williams v Simmonds* [1981] STC 715. See also Inland Revenue Bulletin February 2003 explaining how the Revenue will analyse payments in lieu of notice.

[139] See discussion of *Hofman v Wadman* (1946) 27 TC 192 in *Henley v Murray* 31 TC 351; and comments by Stamp J in *Clayton v Lavender* (1965) 42 TC 607. See also *Ibe v McNally* [2005] EWHC 1551 (Ch), [2005] STC 1426.

date, and the contract is allowed to run its natural course until that date, all sums paid under the contract come within section 62. Payments made while serving out a period of notice remain taxable under section 62.

(7)   A payment in lieu of notice is taxable—at least where the right to make such payment is reserved to the employer in the contract of employment; whether this is so is a question of construction.[140] This is because the employer is not breaking the contract by giving notice and then making a payment in lieu of notice.[141]

(8)   Where the contract of employment stipulates the sum to be paid in the event that the contract does not run its full course, the payment of that sum in accordance with the contract comes within section 62. In *Dale v De Soissons*,[142] a three-year service agreement was terminable by the company at the end of one or two years; the company exercised its right to terminate the agreement after one year and paid the stipulated sum of £10,000. The payment was held to be taxable. As Lord Evershed put it:[143]

> The contract provided that he should serve either for three years at an annual sum or, if the company so elected, for a shorter period of two years or one year at an annual sum in respect of the two years or one year, as the case might be, plus a further sum, that is to say it was something to which he became entitled as part of the terms upon which he promised to serve.

The taxpayer was also caught in *Williams v Simmonds*.[144] Here the contract was expressed to be ended in certain events and a sum then became payable under the contract. The taxpayer had the option, under the contract, of treating the contract as not ended, but did not do so. Vinelott J pointed out that if he had taken that option and then reached a settlement, the sum would have been outside section 62. If (7) is right, and especially if (4) above is determined in favour of the Revenue, a clear, but perhaps unfortunate, distinction arises between those who have the forethought to stipulate in advance what sums shall be due in the event of early termination of the contract, and those who are content to await events. Others therefore prefer not to ask 'what is the formal source from which the sum emerges?' but to ask 'for what is the sum designed to be paid?' On this view, a genuine pre-estimate of loss should escape section 62 even though it is stipulated for in the contract and (4) is decided in favour of the taxpayer.

(9)   A payment which is not to compensate for the termination of one employment but to encourage the start of another, will be treated as a taxable emolument under section 62 arising from the new employment. *Shilton v Wilmshurst*[145] highlights the unsatisfactory gap between payments taxable under section 62 and compensation claims. A payment by an employer for breach of a contract of employment (eg a golden handshake) is not taxable under section 62 because it is not paid under the contract but for breach

---

[140] *EMI Group Electronics Ltd v Coldicott* [1999] STC 803; *SCA Packaging Ltd v HMRC* [2007] EWHC 270 (Ch), 2007 STC 1640, on which see Watson [2007] BTR 370.

[141] *Richardson v Delaney* [2001] STC 1328.

[142] [1950] 2 All ER 460, 32 TC 118, CA.

[143] [1950] 2 All ER 460, 462, 32 TC 118, 127. See also *Henry v Foster* (1931) 16 TC 605.

[144] [1981] STC 715, 719, 55 TC 17, 22; for criticism, see Wosner [1982] BTR 121.

[145] [1991] STC 88, 64 TC 78; on the Court of Appeal decision, see Macdonald and Kerridge [1990] BTR 313 and 315, respectively.

of it. Therefore, if an employer, R, breaks the contract and pays compensation, the payment will fall outside section 62. However, if R acts as a good employer and finds a new employment for the employee before the dismissal, the payment, which is made to the employee for taking up the new employment, will be taxable under section 62. All turns on the reason for the payment (and the evidence needed to establish it). There is much sense in the argument in *Shilton* that the payment was made to end his employment with Nottingham Forest; however, this was not so on the facts as found. There may be good sense in abolishing the special treatment for golden handshakes altogether. Lord Templeman's speech in *Shilton* (see §14.1.3 above) may be seen as a step towards achieving this objective by reducing the credibility of the distinctions in this area. Meanwhile, employees and their advisers know that if they want to bring the payment within section 403, they must be extremely careful.

(10) Multiple causes—apportionment. Where a payment is made for two causes, one for future services and the other for compensation for loss of office or some other right, the courts will apportion the payment where possible.[146] Whether there will be an apportionment if the sum is paid for two causes, neither of which can be valued, remains unclear.[147]

14.5.3 Compensation for Modifying Contracts of Employment—Hunter v Dewhurst

A payment for the modification of the contract of employment ought, in principle, to be capable of escaping section 62 in the same way as a payment for termination.[148] The case law on giving up employment-related rights considered at §14.4.4 above shows that the courts have not found this area easy. However, in practice, where the contract of employment continues, it can be very difficult to persuade the courts that the payment is one for giving up a right under the contract as distinct from a payment for the services still to be rendered. In *Hunter v Dewhurst*,[149] the taxpayer wished to retire and live in Scotland, but the company wanted him to continue as a director, although undertaking less work for less pay. This rearrangement would have meant a reduction in a sum payable under a clause in the company's articles prescribing compensation of a sum equal to five years' earnings. The taxpayer agreed to continue as a director but received a lump sum of £10,000 under an agreement in which he renounced all rights to the compensation payment. The House of Lords held that this payment escaped tax, largely on the ground that it was compensation for the surrender of his contingent rights under the clause in the articles.[150] By contrast, in

---

[146] *Mairs v Haughey* [1993] STC 569; *Carter v Wadman* (1946) 28 TC 41. In *Tilley v Wales* [1943] 1 All ER 280, 25 TC 136, the House of Lords was relieved of the task of deciding whether an apportionment should be made since this had been agreed between the parties.

[147] This was left open by the Court of Appeal in *Shilton v Wilmshurst* [1990] STC 55, 64 TC 78.

[148] In *Henley v Murray* [1950] 1 All ER 908, 31 TC 351, however, Lord Evershed had distinguished the abrogation of an agreement from its modification.

[149] (1932) 16 TC 605. The Special Commissioners decided in favour of the taxpayer, as did Rowlatt J and three members of the House of Lords; all three members of the Court of Appeal and two members of the House of Lords decided in favour of the Revenue.

[150] This is emphasised in the explanation of *Hunter v Dewhurst* in *Cameron v Prendergast* [1940] 2 All ER 35, 23 TC 122.

Tilley v Wales[151] the taxpayer agreed to take a reduced salary of £2,000 a year in return for a payment of £20,000.[152] It was held that this was referable to the agreement to continue to serve as managing director at a reduced salary. As such, it was advance remuneration and fell within what is now section 62.

Hunter v Dewhurst is a decision which has been distinguished[153] more often than it has been followed,[154] and is probably best confined to its special facts.[155] However, there does appear to be a clear distinction in principle between the surrender of rights under the contract, which may be taken as analogous to the surrender of pension rights in *Tilley v Wales*, and a payment in consideration of refraining from resigning. In *McGregor v Randall*,[156] the taxpayer had been entitled to commission on profits; he received compensation in return for the loss of this right. In all other respects the employment continued. Scott J held that section 62 applied; he confined *Hunter v Dewhurst* to its special facts and distinguished *Tilley v Wales* and *Du Cros v Ryall*[157] on the basis that the rights lost there would not or could not be enjoyed while the employment was current. Neither *Hunter v Dewhurst* nor *McGregor v Randall* was cited in *Hamblett v Godfrey*, discussed above at §14.4.4.

14.5.4 *Itepa 2003, Section 403: The Special Regime for Payments and Benefits Outside Section 62*[158]

ITEPA 2003, Part 6, Chapter 3 contains rules on payments and benefits on termination of employment in so far as these are not caught by some other part of income tax. In the language of ITEPA 2003, these are examples of 'specific employment income' and deal with amounts which are 'treated as earnings'. Payments or benefits[159] received on retirement or removal from office or employment and which are not otherwise chargeable to income tax are taxed under section 403 if they exceed £30,000.[160] Section 403 is a separate charging provision and may therefore apply even though the taxpayer left the UK and was neither resident nor ordinarily resident in the UK in the year in which the employment ended and the payment was made.[161] The payments or benefits must be received directly or indirectly

---

[151] [1943] 1 All ER 280, 25 TC 136.

[152] The sum paid was £40,000, but this was apportioned between the loss of pension rights and the reduction in salary.

[153] *Cameron v Prendergast* [1940] 2 All ER 35, 23 TC 122; *Tilley v Wales* [1943] 1 All ER 280, 25 TC 136; *Leeland v Boarland* [1946] 1 All ER 13, 27 TC 71; *Bolam v Muller* (1947) 28 TC 471; *Holland v Geoghegan* [1972] 3 All ER 333, 48 TC 482.

[154] *Duff v Barlow* (1941) 23 TC 633 and *Tilley v Wales* (above) appear to be the only reported cases in which *Hunter v Dewhurst* has been applied, but in the former *Cameron v Prendergast* (above) was not cited. Lord Woolf refused to express any opinion in *Mairs v Haughey* 66 TC 273, 348.

[155] Eg, Sir Raymond Evershed MR in *Henley v Murray* [1950] 1 All ER 908, 911, 31 TC 351, 366.

[156] [1984] STC 223, [1984] 1 All ER 1092, 58 TC 110.

[157] (1935) 19 TC 444.

[158] For 1998 reformulation, see [1998] BTR 420; on reporting requirements, see SI 1999/70.

[159] Defined in s 402 as anything that would be a taxable emolument of the employment if received for the employment, or would have been chargeable but for an earnings only exemption; this is subject to s 402(2)–(4) which exclude various items, eg a sum for removal expenses that would be exempt under s 271—on s 402(4) see ITEPA Explanatory Notes Change 107. On why TA 1988, s 148(5) has disappeared see ITEPA Technical Note 42. For pre-1988 law on provision of a car as part of the package, see *George v Ward* [1995] STC (SCD) 230.

[160] ITEPA 2003, s 403, ex TA 1988, s 148, Sch 11, as rewritten by FA 1998 and replacing former ss 148, 188.

[161] *Nichols v Gibson* [1994] STC 1029, 68 TC 611.

in consideration of, or in consequence of, or otherwise in connection with the termination or change.[162] Where a sum is paid to an unapproved retirement benefits scheme and section 386 applies, the charge under section 401 does not apply.[163]

If the package includes a continuing benefit, such as the use of a car, the benefit is taxable in the year in which it is enjoyed. The benefit is charged at the same rate as the individual's rate for the year of enjoyment.[164] A payment is caught even if it is made to the personal representatives of the holder or past holder of the office or employment, and even if it is paid to the spouse or any relative or dependant of his, as is a payment on his behalf or to his order.[165] The employee is also taxable even where the benefit is received by another.[166] Cash receipts are treated as received when the payment is made or the recipient is entitled to call for it. A non-cash benefit is treated as received when it is actually used or enjoyed.[167]

14.5.4.1 Exclusions

Exclusions exist for payments on death, disability or injury,[168] for certain pension benefits or indemnity insurance liabilities and for certain payments in relation to services for a foreign government of an overseas territory within the Commonwealth.[169] 'Injury' does not include injury to feelings; the injury has to be a medical condition that has led to the termination of employment or to a change in duties or level of earnings.[170] A payment which is not a retirement benefit but is made for wrongful dismissal may come within section 403, but Revenue practice requires a close examination of the facts to determine the genuineness or otherwise of the claim.[171] This is in order to separate payments coming within section 403 from those coming within section 394 which imposes a charge in full (ie no £30,000 exemption) on any benefit received from an unapproved retirement benefits scheme. Certain payments in respect of other types of foreign service are treated on a special basis according to the length of service.[172]

14.5.4.2 £30,000 Threshold

In calculating the £30,000 threshold, any redundancy payment or ex gratia payment must be included, but not certain supplementary contributions to retirement schemes.[173] There are also valuation rules for valuing benefits (cash and non-cash).[174] Two payments for the

---

[162] ITEPA 2003, s 401(1), ex TA 1988, Sch 11, para 2.

[163] ITEPA 2003, s 386(4), original added by FA 2002, Sch 6 para 6.

[164] ITEPA 2003, s 401(4), ex TA 1988, s 148(4); at one time it was tied to the year on termination.

[165] ITEPA 2003, s 401(1), ex TA 1988, Sch 11, para 2.

[166] ITEPA 2003, s 401(4), ex TA 1988, Sch 11, para 14(1). On liability of personal representatives of employee, see ITEPA 2003, s 403(5), ex TA 1988, Sch 11, para 14(2).

[167] ITEPA 2003, s 403(3), ex TA 1988, s 148(4).

[168] ITEPA 2003, s 406, ex TA 1988, Sch 11, para 3; see *Horner v Hasted* [1995] STC 766, 67 TC 439.

[169] ITEPA 2003, ss 407, 409–412, ex TA 1988, Sch 11, paras 4–6.

[170] *Moorthy v Revenue and Customs Commissioners* [2016] UKUT 13 (TCC) and see commentary by Firth [2016] BTR 152.

[171] Statement of Practice SP 13/91, as amplified by a note from the Law Society, 7 October 1992, [1992] *Simon's Tax Intelligence* 869.

[172] ITEPA 2003, s 413 and 414, ex TA 1988, Sch 11, paras 9–11. On the need to define a place of service, see *Wienand v Anderton* [1977] STC 12, 51 TC 570. ITEPA explanatory notes change 109.

[173] ITEPA 2003, s 408. See also Statement of Practice SP 2/81 and ITEPA explanatory notes change 108.

[174] ITEPA 2003, s 415, ex TA 1988, Sch 11, para 12; ITEPA explanatory notes change 110. On loans, see ITEPA 2003, s 416, ex TA 1988, Sch 11, para 13.

same employment, or two payments for different employments with the same or associated employers,[175] are aggregated, but payments for distinct employments with unassociated employers are not. Where payments are aggregated, the aggregation is cumulative from year to year, the £30,000 exemption being applied to earlier payments before later ones.

14.6 Disguised Remuneration

The seemingly endless cat-and-mouse game between HMRC and taxpayers engaged in schemes to avoid employment taxes and NICs gave rise to yet more new legislative manoeuvres in 2011 and 2014. FA 2011 added 69 pages of complex 'disguised remuneration' legislation principally aimed at putting a stop to the use of employment benefit trusts of the kind at issue in the Rangers case discussed above at §14.4.6. Where a third party makes provision for what is in substance a reward or recognition or loan in connection with the employee's employment, the rules in Part 7A of ITEPA 2003 are intended to ensure that income tax and NIC charges arise. On measures to combat disguised employment in limited liability partnerships (LLPs) see §20.9 below. In FA 2014 the government introduced a new TAAR into ITEPA 2003, section 46A that seeks to counter false self-employment arrangements. A matching rule for NICs is effective from 6 April 2014. The rules were further tightened in 2016, eg to catch loans made to an employee by a third party before the disguised remuneration legislation came into effect. If the loan is not repaid on or before 5 April 2019, a disguised remuneration charge will arise unless a settlement has been agreed with HMRC. The details of these rules are outside the scope of this book.[176]

---

[175] ITEPA 2003, s 404, ex TA 1988, Sch 11, paras 7, 8.
[176] See David Cohen's FA 2011 note in [2011] BTR 381.

15

Benefits in Kind and the Convertibility Principle

15.1   Earnings and Benefits in Kind

The taxation of benefits in kind raises (at least) three separate tax issues:[1]

(1)   Is the benefit taxable under ITEPA 2003?
(2)   Is it subject to PAYE?
(3)   Is it liable to NICs?[2]

Today, many benefits in kind chargeable under ITEPA 2003 are also subject to PAYE[3] and attract Class 1A NICs; formerly, PAYE and NICs would often not be payable at all. Class 1A NICs differ from the normal Class 1 in that there is no charge on the employee but only on the employer. This may be rationalised on the basis that many of the employees concerned are well-off and above the point at which their Class 1 contribution rate drops to only 2%.

15.1.1 Policy

Benefits in kind also raise questions of policy. Such benefits may tie employees to employers unduly, especially if the tax regime taxes such benefits lightly in comparison with a simple cash payment. In principle, all benefits in kind should be taxed, partly in order to satisfy requirements of equity and partly because failing to tax them properly leads to distortions.

---

[1] Other issues include whether, when and how the employer may deduct the associated costs. For a good modern critique, see Brooks (2004) 49 *McGill LJ* 255–308. For other and older material, see *Taxation of Fringe Benefits* (OECD, 1988) and Scott, on Australia and New Zealand, in Sandford (ed), *Key Issues in Tax Reform* (Fiscal Publications, 1993), 22.

[2] See *Tolleys Tax Planning* 2007–08, ch 16.

[3] ITEPA 2003, ss 7(2) and 683(1).

The Government's freezes on pay, prices and dividends in the 1970s led to the increase in benefits in kind as a way of getting round those restrictions.

Benefits in kind are much loved by UK employers as motivational devices to recruit and, perhaps more importantly, to retain good staff. Incentives are used to reward high flyers or to provide incentives to improve performance. One employee received a demand for £1,200 tax, plus interest and penalties, for an all-expenses- paid trip to a sunshine paradise. Employers may pay the tax themselves, but they may simply fold arms and provide the Revenue with details of the benefit supplied—especially if the employee has subsequently left. In such circumstances, any exemption from PAYE and NIC becomes very important. The Revenue has an Incentive Valuation Unit to tax such benefits. Recent figures[4] show that cars were responsible for 50% of the total tax raised by the rules on benefits in kind. Other significant benefits in kind are car fuel (10%) and private medical and dental insurance (23%). The total tax raised was £2.53bn, with an additional £1.04bn in NICs.

Valuation difficulties may, however, prove too great. The current rules, introduced in 1988, systematically exclude any tax charge for the provision of a parking space (now ITEPA 2003, section 237). This was done in return for doubling the tax charge for the car itself. Valuing parking spaces had proved to be an administrative nightmare, eg where a company uses space in its otherwise unused basement. Fixed scales also gave rise to problems, since a farmer parking in an empty field in Lanarkshire would pay as much as a city commuter.[5]

15.1.2 Tax Rule Choices

The general principle in ITEPA 2003, section 62 that money's worth is income, also applies to benefits in kind—but with difficulty.[6] Where an employer, R, provides an employee, E, with a benefit in kind, any tax system encounters two sets of problems. The first is to define the benefits to be taxed; the second is to value them. On the first point, rules are needed to prevent a tax charge arising simply because an employer provides an office or staff support—or a better office or better support. The system, if it is of a puritanical disposition, may also have to consider at what point an office becomes so luxurious that it should be treated as a chargeable benefit. On the second point, the system provides three principal choices:

(1)   The most obvious choice, but also the most impractical, is to tax E on the value of the benefit to E. The impracticality arises from the subjective nature of the assessment. In Simons' famous example, how does one tax an employee who is given tickets to a Wagner opera, preferably a long one, and who hates any form of opera?[7]

(2)   The second choice, convertibility, taxes the employee by reference to the sums which could be derived by converting the benefit into cash.

(3)   The third choice is to use the cost incurred by the employer in providing the benefit.

---

[4] Revenue Statistics August 2015 (for 2012–13), available at https://www.gov.uk/government/collections/taxable-benefits-in-kind-and-expenses-payments-statistics.

[5] *The Economist*, 8 August 1992; the doubling of the car charge raised £1.4bn for the Exchequer.

[6] For explanation see ITEPA Technical Note 13.

[7] Simons, *Personal Income Taxation* (University of Chicago, 1938), 53.

The UK currently uses choices (2) and (3)—with extensive statutory glosses. Choice (2), convertibility, was developed by the courts and applies to all employees, subject, of course, to any statutory exclusions or modifications. Choice (3), the cost to R, was introduced by legislation in 1948. For many years, this legislation applied only to employees earning £8,500 a year or more and to all directors. From 6 April 2016, however, the legislation applies to all employees but some special exemptions were introduced to mitigate the impact of this change on low-paid ministers of religion and also for live-in caregivers in respect of board and lodging (see chapter sixteen below). Choice (3) applies to a widely defined—but not universal—group of benefits. It has its own set of statutory exclusions or modifications and elaborate rules for determining the cost to the employer. The cost basis is supplementary to convertibility in that it applies only when the latter does not. Convertibility is still important, because it must be applied before the cost basis. It is not used for NICs.[8] A 1997 review concluded that while the advantage distorted the market, it was not right simply to value benefits in kind for NICs at least on anything like the income tax rules, given that the current NICs use a different pay period basis (ie weekly or monthly, not annually).[9]

15.1.3 The Benefits Code and Its Role in ITEPA 2003

ITEPA 2003, Part 3, Chapter 1 (section 62) defines earnings. Then Part 3, Chapter 2, which refers to 'the benefits code' stretching over Chapters 3–11, explains how the benefits code relates to earnings, contains some general rules and provides some definitions. Chapter 12 is not part of the benefits code at all but provides six types of 'earnings', one of which (section 223) concerns only directors and so used to be in the rules for directors and employees earning at least £8,500.

A nice example of the need to keep these heads apart is provided by FA 2004, section 79. ITEPA 2003, section 320 had provided an exception from tax under the benefits code for loaned computer equipment but not from the charge under section 62 if, for example, the employee had an option to take cash instead. Section 79 made the exception apply for section 62 as well as for the benefits code. The exception was then removed entirely for computer equipment loaned after 6 April 2006, in part because the Government decided it was being abused by, for example, the provision of video game consoles.

ITEPA 2003, section 64 usefully explains the relationship between the earnings code and the benefits code. If the same benefit comes under both codes, it is taxable under the earnings code and any excess under the benefits code. This rule is an improvement on the older and less clear rule. Formerly, under section 65 the Revenue had a long-standing and administratively important power to give a clearance—known as a dispensation—satisfied that no tax would be due under these rules.[10] This power was repealed with effect from 6 April 2016 with the introduction of Part 4, Ch 7A providing for a general exemption from income for paid or reimbursed expenses. Sections 66–69 contains definitions of employment, directors, full-time working director and material interests in a company.

---

[8] On liability to NIC, see Tiley and Collison, *UK Tax Guide*, §§52.15 *et seq* and §53.08 *et seq*.

[9] Taylor, *The Modernisation of Britain's Tax and Benefit System Report No 2* (1997), para 2.16.

[10] The dispensation power was repealed by FA 2015, s 12. ITEPA 2003, s 96 formerly contained a separate dispensation power relating to vouchers or credit-tokens; this also was repealed by FA 2015, s 12 with effect from 6 April 2016. ITEPA 2003, ss 65(6) to (9) and 96(5) to (8) continue to have effect in relation to a pre-commencement dispensation, however.

15.2   The Convertibility Principle—Section 62 and *Tennant v Smith*

The convertibility principle forms part of the definition of earnings in section 62, ie Part 3, Chapter 1; as such it is not part of the 'benefits code', which means Part 3, Chapters 3–11 (discussed in chapter sixteen). Section 62(3) states that money's worth means something that is (a) of direct monetary value to the employee, or (b) capable of being converted into money or something of direct monetary value to the employee.

In *Tennant v Smith*,[11] the taxpayer was agent for the Bank of Scotland at Montrose. He had to occupy the bank house as custodian for the whole premises belonging to the Bank, and also to transact any special bank business after bank hours. He was not allowed to vacate the house even for a temporary period unless he had the special consent of the directors, who sanctioned the occupation of the house by another official of the bank during the agent's absence. The agent had to lock up the bank and attend to the security of the safe. There was a night bolt from the agent's bedroom to the bank's premises. The agent was not allowed to sublet the bank house, nor to use it for any purpose other than the bank's business. The bank house was suitable accommodation for him but, as Lord Macnaghten observed, 'his occupation is that of a servant and not the less so because the bank thinks proper to provide for gentlemen in his position in their service accommodation on a liberal scale'.[12] His total income from other sources came to £375 and the value of his occupation of these premises was placed at £50. Where a taxpayer's income was below £400 he was entitled to abatement.[13] The House of Lords held that the agent was not assessable under Schedules D or E[14] in respect of his occupation of the premises and so was entitled to the abatement. Lord Halsbury stated that the thing sought to be taxed 'is not income unless it can be turned to money'.[15] The agent's occupation of the premises was not capable of being converted into money since he could not let it.[16]

15.2.1   Types of Convertibility

A benefit may be converted in ways other than simple sale. In *Abbott v Philbin*,[17] an option to acquire shares was non-assignable, but the employee was taxable on its value because money could have been realised in other ways—by raising money on the right to call for the shares. A Special Commissioner has held that where a taxpayer received rights under a

---

[11] [1892] AC 150, 3 TC 158, HL.

[12] *Ibid*, 162, 169.

[13] 5 & 6 Vict (c 35), s 163.

[14] Neither was he assessable under Sch A, since it was not he but the bank which was the occupier: [1892] AC 150, 158, 3 TC 158, 166, per Lord Watson; and 162, 169 per Lord Macnaghten.

[15] *Ibid*, 156, 164; to the same effect see Lord Watson at 159, 167; Lord Macnaghten at 163, 170; Lord Field at 164, 171; and Lord Hannen at 165, 172. Lord Morris concurred.

[16] With the bank's tacit consent he used the premises for an insurance business, but this was ignored. At one time it was thought that where a person was in beneficial occupation but that occupation was not convertible (into money or money's worth), then if the employer paid the Sch A tax in respect of that occupation, the employee was not taxable in respect of that payment under Sch E (*M'Dougall v Sutherland* (1894) 3 TC 261; overruled in *IRC v Miller* [1930] AC 222, 15 TC 25).

[17] [1961] AC 352, 378–79, 39 TC 82, 125, per Lord Radcliffe.

contract of employment and those rights could be converted only at a price well below their intrinsic value, the right was not taxable at all.[18]

15.2.2 Restricting Convertibility

In *Tennant v Smith*, Lord Halsbury said that a thing could be treated as money's worth where the thing was capable of being turned into money 'from its own nature'.[19] However, in that case the only reason why the agent could not turn his occupation of the house into money was the fiat of his employer. Clearly, the loopholes in the tax net will be greatly widened if it is left to the employer to decide whether a benefit is convertible and so assessable. The courts have indicated that while restrictions imposed by employers may be treated as an effective restriction,[20] this will only be so if the conditions are genuine.[21] In *Heaton v Bell*,[22] Lord Diplock went further and said that limitations on use arising from a contract collateral to the contract of employment into which the employee entered of his own volition would not escape tax.[23]

15.2.3 Salary Sacrifice

A benefit may also be turned into money by being surrendered, or by not being accepted.[24] In *Heaton v Bell*,[25] an employee was loaned a car by his employers and went on to what was called an amended wage basis. If the true effect had been that the employee took a lower wage and received the free use of a car, a majority of the House would have held that the employee was taxable in respect of the use of the car on the amount he would have received if he had surrendered that use.[26] Such statements are obiter since the House preferred a different construction.[27] It has since been held that where employees could, and did, use a non-chargeable method of obtaining a benefit, the fact that they could have chosen a different method which could have resulted in a tax liability was itself enough to give rise to

---

[18] *Bootle v Bye* [1996] STC (SCD) 58; it was also relevant that the event which would have made the intrinsic value realisable was outside the taxpayer's control.

[19] [1892] AC 150, 156, 3 TC 158, 164.

[20] For example, *Ede v Wilson and Cornwall* [1945] 1 All ER 367, 26 TC 381 shares were issued subject to a condition that they would not be sold without employer's permission; it was held that valuation must take account of the restriction on the effect of a term forbidding assignment of a debt. On effectiveness of a prohibition on assignment of a chose in action, see *Helstan Securities Ltd v Hertfordshire County Council* [1978] 3 All ER 262.

[21] Lord Reid in *Heaton v Bell* [1969] 2 All ER 70, 79, 46 TC 211, 247.

[22] [1969] 2 All ER 70, 95, 46 TC 211, 264.

[23] *Cf* the test that in order to be deductible, an expense must be required by the job and not simply by the employer (see below at §18.3.2).

[24] See also former ESC A60 (agricultural workers outside those chapters of the benefits code applicable to directors and employees earning at least £8,500), now withdrawn.

[25] [1969] 2 All ER 70, 46 TC 211.

[26] *Ibid*, 84, 263, per Lord Morris of Borth-y-Gest, and 96, 265, per Lord Diplock. To the same effect, but by a different route, see Lord Reid, dissenting (at 79, 247). While Lord Morris and Lord Diplock would have quantified the benefit as the sum subtracted each week × 52 (the number of weeks in the year), Lord Reid would have taken the same sum × 50, since two weeks' notice had to be given before returning to the scheme. Therefore, while Lord Morris and Lord Diplock appear to tax the benefit forgone, Lord Reid would appear to tax the benefit that could be obtained. Lord Reid seems more correct.

[27] The correct construction of the agreement was that there was no change in the wage but the employers were entitled to deduct a sum each week in respect of the use of the car. It followed that tax was due on the gross wage each week, with no deduction for tax purposes for the sum withheld on account of the car.

such a liability.[28] They used their company's credit card to pay for petrol, but could instead have paid in cash and obtained a refund; although they used the card, they were taxed on the basis that they could have paid cash and so turned the benefit to pecuniary account. Today, the fuel charge applies generally to such facts, but this does not disturb the principle.

Where a car is made available to the employee under Part 3, Chapter 6 and an alternative to that benefit is offered, the mere fact that the alternative is offered does not make the benefit of the car chargeable to tax under these general principles.[29] The effect is that the employee will be taxed on the benefit chosen. The reason behind this apparently anodyne piece of legislation is to ensure that NICs are not avoided.[30] On accommodation, see §16.4.6.

Limited forms of statutory salary sacrifice arrangements are now permitted; however, at Budget 2016 the Government announced its intention to review such arrangements generally, with a view to limiting tax and NIC benefits to eg pensions, childcare, and health-related benefits such as Cycle to Work.

15.2.4 *Extent of Liability*

Convertibility provides the test not only of liability but also of its extent. In *Weight v Salmon*,[31] the employee was given the right to apply for shares at less than market price and was held assessable on the difference between the market price and the price he paid. In *Wilkins v Rogerson*,[32] the employee was provided with a suit; he was held assessable on the second-hand value of the suit, which was only one-third of the purchase price, a fact which involved 'no reflection on the tailor' because 'it is notorious that the value of clothing is very much reduced the moment that it can be called second hand'. The value is ascertained at the date when the asset comes into charge, usually on receipt.[33] Although a special rule now applies to certain share options, other options are subject to the general rule. If an asset is received in non-convertible form but later becomes convertible, there is little reason why a charge should not arise at the later time.

15.2.5 *Anomalies and Distinctions*

The test of convertibility gives rise to distinctions which mean significant variations in tax liability according to fiscal skill or simple luck:

(1)   Whereas the provision of a benefit such as a board and lodging escapes tax, the payment of an allowance in lieu of providing that benefit does not. In *Fergusson v Noble*,[34] the taxpayer, a plain-clothes policeman, was allowed to buy his own clothes suitable

---

[28] *Westall v McDonald* [1985] STC 693, 721, 58 TC 642, 679.
[29] On ITEPA 2003, s 120, ex TA 1988, s 157, see below §16.4.1.
[30] ITEPA 2003, s 119, ex TA 1988, s 157A, original provision added by FA 1995, s 43; see Inland Revenue press release, 21 July 1994, [1994] *Simon's Tax Intelligence* 888.
[31] (1935) 19 TC 174.
[32] [1961] 1 All ER 358, 39 TC 344.
[33] *Abbott v Philbin* [1961] AC 352, [1960] 2 All ER 763, 39 TC 82.
[34] [1919] SC 534, 7 TC 176. See, to same effect, *Sanderson v Durbridge* [1955] 3 All ER 154, 36 TC 239; *Evans v Richardson* (1957) 37 TC 178.

for duty and was given an allowance of £11.71. Uniformed members of the police force were provided with a uniform free of charge. It was held that the allowance was liable to tax. On similar reasoning, an employee who is provided with an official house may not be taxable (but for special legislation) whereas one who is provided with an allowance is taxable,[35] a matter of great importance when the special legislation does not apply.

(2) Contrast the employee who receives a salary and, in addition, some non-convertible benefit, such as necessaries, in respect of which extra benefit there is no tax, with another employee who receives a salary and has to pay out of that salary a counter amount to secure the same necessaries.[36] The latter is assessable on the total salary and not entitled to deduct the cost of those necessaries unless they come within the strict test laid down by ITEPA 2003, section 336 (below, chapter eighteen).[37]

(3) Consider the borderline between the rule in *Tennant v Smith* and that in *Nicoll v Austin*.[38] If an employer buys each employee a new suit at Christmas, all the employees are taxable, but only on the second-hand value of the suit[39] (*Tennant v Smith*). If, however, the employees have already bought their suits but not yet paid for them, and the employer settles the debts for them, they are taxable on the amount paid to the tailor (*Nicoll v Austin*). The question of whose is the liability to be discharged, rather than what right the employees acquired, explains what a very technical area of law remains. However, its clarity leads to further anomalies. When employees drive into a garage and pump petrol into their cars, they may be agents for the employer or acting on their own account.[40] If the employer is an undisclosed principal, the employee is personally liable on the contract, which may be enough to make the employee liable to income tax on the full sum.[41]

---

[35] *Corry v Robinson* [1934] 1 KB 240, 18 TC 411. The tax paid on a rent allowance was reimbursed by police authorities in the following financial year by means of a compensatory grant. In principle, the grant itself was taxable: see HC Written Answer, 31 January 1986, [1986] *Simon's Tax Intelligence* 40; the grant was abolished in 1995 under the Police Regulations 1995 (SI 1995/215).

[36] However, see ITEPA 2003, s 316 enacting ESC A1 (flat rate allowances for clothes and tools), and the even more extraordinary s 306 enacting ESC A6 (no tax on allowances paid to miners in lieu of their free coal).

[37] In *Cordy v Gordon* [1925] 2 KB 276, 9 TC 304, the taxpayer was employed at an asylum and received a salary together with board, lodging, washing and uniform, for which he was required to pay sums which varied according to the cost of living: he was held assessable on the gross salary. See also *Machon v McLoughlin* (1926) 11 TC 83; *Bruce v Hatton* [1921] 2 KB 206, 8 TC 180. Cf *Edwards v Roberts* (1935) 19 TC 618.

[38] (1935) 19 TC 531.

[39] See *Wilkins v Rogerson* [1961] 1 All ER 358, 39 TC 344, per Donovan LJ.

[40] *Richardson v Worrall* [1985] STC 693, 58 TC 642.

[41] The presence of joint liability on the part of employer and employee does not necessarily mean that discharge by the employer will be a taxable emolument (see *Richardson v Worrall* [1985] STC 693, 718, 58 TC 642, 675.

16

The Benefits Code and Exemptions

16.1   Introduction

16.1.1 The Rationale for a Legislative Scheme for Employment Benefits[1]

One product of *Tennant v Smith*[2] was a substantial amount of tax avoidance. What would otherwise have been remuneration was dressed up as an expense allowance, or paid in the form of benefits in kind. Expense allowances were taxable in so far as they exceeded the sums actually spent by the recipient on behalf of his employer,[3] but difficult to trace. Benefits in kind, in so far as they could be traced, were taxable only if convertible into money or money's worth, and then only on the second-hand value. On the other hand, the full cost of providing employee benefits or allowances were deductible by the employer in computing

---

[1] HMRC practice is explained in Booklet 480.
[2] [1892] AC 150, 3 TC 158. See above §15.2.
[3] Such sums escaped tax only if they were deductible under the rules in ITEPA 2003, Part 5, Chapter 2, ex TA 1988, ss 198 or 201.

the profits of the business. To prevent such avoidance special legislation was introduced in 1948 and is now to be found in revised form in ITEPA 2003, Part 3.[4] The rules also apply to payments to participators in close companies.

16.1.2 To Whom Does the Legislation Apply?

Prior to 6 April 2016, the legislation on benefits applied to directors,[5] whatever their salary (since they can fix their own income), and to employees whose earnings amounted to £8,500 or more.[6] Section 216 expressed this rule negatively—the provisions did not apply to someone who is not a director and who earns less than £8,500. The figure of £8,500 was set in 1978.[7] In 1989 it was, correctly, decided that employees earning over £8,500 were no longer to be described as 'higher-paid'. In 2016 a full-time worker on the minimum wage of £7.20 per hour has an annual income of over £14,000.

In an important and long overdue simplification of the benefits tax rules, FA 2015, sections 13–14 and Schedule 1 abolished the £8,500 threshold for 'higher-paid employment', with effect from 6 April 2016. This is a fundamental structural change, which responds to a recommendation made by the Office of Tax Simplification (OTS), and means that from that date all employees are subject to one general statutory regime for the taxation of their benefits and expenses. Some special exemptions were introduced to mitigate the impact of this change on low-paid ministers of religion and also for live-in caregivers in respect of board and lodging. Readers interested in the operation of the £8,500 threshold should consult *Revenue Law, 7th edition.*

Finally, in a long overdue simplification measure recommended by the OTS, FA 2016, section 13 adds a new trivial benefits in kind exemption (cost less than £50) in ITEPA 2003, sections 323A-C with effect from 6 April 2016.

16.2 Payments for Expenses and Expense Allowances

Under sections 70–72, the general rules is that any sum paid to an employee[8] and paid by reason of the employment[9] 'in respect of expenses' is, unless otherwise chargeable to tax, to be treated as income of the director or employee.[10] These concepts are the same as for

---

[4] Ex TA 1988, ss 153–168. Before 1976 certain employments were exempt, notably charities and non-trading bodies such as the civil service and trade unions. The present legislation draws no such distinctions The abolition of these exemptions had been recommended by the Royal Commission, Cmnd 9474 (1955), §221; charities and non profit-making bodies are still distinct in that a director of such a body may be treated as an employee and not a director (ITEPA 2003, s 216(3), ex TA 1988, s 167(5); the same rule applies to living accommodation ITEPA 2003, s 99(3), ex TA 1988, s 145(5) (above §15.4)).

[5] ITEPA 2003, s 216, ex TA 1988, s 167(1). On travelling expenses note ESC A4 (not yet codified or repealed).

[6] The use of a fixed sum was criticised as arbitrary by the Royal Commission, *op cit*, §220; however, the combination of a fixed sum and the passage of time has worked wonders for the Revenue.

[7] FA 1978, s 23, with effect from 1979–80.

[8] ITEPA 2003, s 70, ex TA 1988, s 153; see *Jennings v Kinder* [1958] 1 All ER 369, 38 TC 673.

[9] ITEPA 2003, s 71; all sums paid by the employer are treated as paid by reason of the employment unless the employer is an individual and the payment is made in the normal course of the employer's domestic, family or personal relationships.

[10] ITEPA 2003, s 72—unless another head of charge applies, s 70(5).

Part 3, Chapter 10 and will be considered further in §16.3. The sections apply not only to expense allowances, but also to reimbursement of expenses actually incurred, since here too there is payment in respect of expenses.[11] The only expenses not caught are those which the employer meets directly. The recipient may, however, deduct sums actually expended if they satisfy the tests laid down in Part 5, Chapter 2.[12] ITEPA 2003 applies to all sums paid in a tax year, including sums paid before or after the period of actual employment (section 70(3) and (4)). Section 72 also applies to sums put at the employee's disposal and paid away by him (section 70(2)). Thus, sums are caught even though the money at no time becomes the property of the employee.[13] The employer must report all such payments. In order to avoid too much paperwork, a notice of nil liability was often issued, but such notices were not usually given for 'round sum allowances'.[14]

The operation of these rules has been greatly simplified, however, by the introduction of a new exemption regime for expense payments and benefits provided to employees where the employee would have been eligible for a deduction under the expenses rules had the employee paid the equivalent amount herself.[15] The exemption regime in ITEPA 2003 Part 4 Chapter 7A, which was implemented following yet more recommendations made by the Office of Tax Simplification, has effect from 6 April 2016. The regime comes with (the obligatory) anti-avoidance rules. The payment or reimbursement by the employer cannot be provided as part of a relevant salary sacrifice arrangement. The exemption also is not available where the expenses or benefits are provided as part of an arrangements to reduce the employee's earnings subject to tax/NICs and one of the main purposes of the arrangement is to avoid tax/NICs.[16]

16.3 Benefits in Kind: General or Residual Charge on Employment-Related Benefits

16.3.1 Outline of the Benefits Code

The ITEPA 2003 benefits code deals with rules for specific benefits (Part 3, Chapters 6–9) before the general rules (Part 3, Chapters 10 and 11), and then tries to justify this by downgrading the general charge to a 'residual' charge. Those who have been teaching this material for years will not find the change helpful or sensible. The only thing to be said for it is that in terms of benefits actually provided, the rules on cars affect more people than these general rules. However it is the general rules which remain to catch any unlisted benefit and in relation to which there has been most case law. They are therefore treated first here.

---

[11] ITEPA Pt 3 Ch 3 thus sweeps in reimbursements of expenses actually incurred even though, under *Owen v Pook* [1969] 2 All ER 1, 45 TC 571 (above at §14.4.2) they are not technically emoluments (see Royal Commission, *op cit*, §226).

[12] ITEPA 2003, s 72(3). The burden of proof rests on the taxpayer to show that the expense comes within these provisions (*McLeish v IRC* (1958) 38 TC 1). On reimbursement of fees for solicitors practising certificates, see a statement by the Law Society, 24 February 1993, [1993] *Simon's Tax Intelligence* 341.

[13] The effect of this extension on s 218(1), step (b), ex TA 1988, s 167(2)(b) (see §16.1.3 above) is to make almost any employee with financial responsibility subject to these rules.

[14] HMRC Booklet IR 480, §2.

[15] ITEPA 2003, s 289A.

[16] ITEPA 2003, ss 289D–E.

Section 201 states that Chapter 10 applies to employment-related benefits, ie a benefit or facility of any kind provided by reason of the employment. Repeating the concepts used in Chapter 3, Chapter 10 applies to all benefits provided in a tax year, including benefits provided before or after the period of actual employment. Benefits provided by the employer are treated as paid by reason of the employment—unless the employer is an individual and the payment made in the normal course of the employer's domestic, family or personal relationship (see further below). The previous wording (TA 1988, section 154) covered accommodation (other than living accommodation), entertainment, domestic or other services, or other benefits or facilities of whatsoever nature. This wide-ranging provision even taxed prizes for passing examinations.[17] This will still be so. There is no reason in principle why the section should be confined to benefits in kind; it has been held to apply to cash.[18]

Tax is charged on the 'cash equivalent' of the benefit (section 203), usually the cost of the benefit to the person providing it (section 204). Chapter 10 does not apply if (or to the extent that) E, the employee, has 'made good' the expense to R, the employer.[19] An expense may be made good by E by the payment of cash, or by providing some other consideration (but not by providing services under the contract of employment).[20] Chapter 10 does not apply if one of the other provisions of the benefits code applies, or would do so but for an exception, or if the benefit comes within section 221 (sickness or disability payments); these are called excluded benefits.[21] Importantly, the relationship with the 'earnings' rule in section 62 is governed by section 64. If the same benefit gives rise to a charge under the benefits code (amount B) and also under section 62 (amount A) then section 62 applies to the extent of amount A, leaving the benefits code to pick up the pieces by taxing the amount, if any, by which B exceeds A.[22] If the benefit could be converted into cash but only for less than its cost, section 64 makes it clear that the excess comes within Chapter 10. If, however, the resale value is higher than cost, it appears that the Revenue can insist on tax on the balance of the higher amount under *Tennant v Smith*.[23]

Chapter 10 (like Chapter 3) applies only where the benefit is provided 'by reason of the employment'. However, as already seen, all provision for E, or for members of E's family or household, by the employer, R, is treated as made by reason of the employment—unless it can be shown that R is an individual and that the provision was made in the normal course of R's domestic, family or personal relationship.[24] So if the family business is incorporated, the benefit of this rule is lost. A benefit is treated as provided by the employer if

---

[17] ICAEW Memorandum TR 786, [1990] *Simon's Tax Intelligence* 205.

[18] See *Mairs v Haughey* [1992] STC 495.

[19] ITEPA 2003, s 203(2), ex TA 1988, s 156(1). If the employee pays a sum equal to the cost of providing the benefit he escapes Chapter 10 even though the market value is higher. Quaere whether a tenant paying a full market rent thereby 'makes good' to the lessor any sums spent by the lessor even though those sums exceed the rent. See *Luke v IRC* [1963] 1 All ER 655, 578, 40 TC 630, per Lord Reid; but contrast Lord Guest at 586, 652.

[20] *Mairs v Haughey* [1992] STC 495, 66 TC 273, CA NI.

[21] ITEPA 2003, ss 201(2) and 202. In *Wicks v Firth* [1983] STC 25, 56 TC 318, the House of Lords held that although a scholarship awarded to the taxpayer's child by his employer was a benefit provided to the taxpayer by reason of his employment, it was exempt under TA 1988, s 331 as scholarship income. However, the effect of this decision has been reversed by what is now ITEPA 2003, s 212, ex TA 1988, s 165 (see below at §16.4.7).

[22] ITEPA 2003, s 6(1) and (2); living accommodation in Chapter 5 has its own rule in s 109.

[23] [1892] AC 150, 3 TC 158. See above §15.2.

[24] ITEPA 2003, s 201(3), ex TA 1988, s 168(3); quaere whether this can apply if the business is owned by a trust so that the trustees are the employer and a benefit is provided under the trust. This provision did not apply in

it is provided at his cost (section 209). In *Wicks v Firth*,[25] scholarships awarded by trustees were held to be provided at the cost of the employer since the trustees used money supplied by the employer and were only performing duties imposed on them by the employer. If, as in *Wicks v Firth*, the benefit is provided by someone other than the employer,[26] so that the deeming provision does not apply, Chapter 10 will apply only if the benefit is provided 'by reason of the employment'. According to Lord Oliver in that case, this test may be satisfied if the employment is not the sole or even the main cause but only an operative cause (ie a condition of benefit). The problem with this is that the test for Chapter 10 is then different from the general test of causation for section 62.[27] Any such difference was decried by Carnwath J in *Wilcock v Eve*, but that was on the basis that the test for section 62 was wider than the test of simple reward.[28]

16.3.2 Case Law Limits on Chapter 10

Although section 201 talks simply in terms of the provision of certain benefits, case law imposes some limits:

(1) E, the director or employee, must accept or acquiesce in the provision of the benefit. Therefore, Lord Reid in *Rendell v Went*[29] considered that it was important that the director knew and accepted what was being done on his behalf, even though he may not have realised how much it was costing. Lord Reid would express no opinion on the case of a company spending a large sum of money without the director's knowledge to procure an unwanted benefit. E will usually be aware of the benefit and may avoid tax by a disclaimer.[30] However, the legislation also applies to benefits conferred on members of E's family or household, an expression replacing 'servants, dependants or guests'.[31] It would seem unjustifiable to charge E with tax on sums spent in the provision of a benefit to some member of E's family of which E knew nothing, whether or not E would have been pleased if he had known—even worse if E had known but disapproved of it—yet it seems to be taxable.

(2) Chapter 10 does not require that E should receive the exclusive benefit. Therefore, it can apply when the service benefits both the employer and E. It is immaterial that E would have spent less on the service if he had had the sole choice. In *Rendell v Went*[32] a company incurred expenses of £641 in the (successful) defence of one of its directors on a charge of causing death by dangerous driving. That sum was held to fall within

Mairs v Haughey [1992] STC 495, 66 TC 273, CA NI (where the Court said that a payment which was not caused by the employment could not have been paid by reason of the employment) because the payment was not made by the employer.

[25] [1983] STC 25, 31, 56 TC 318, 363, per Lord Templeman; see Shipwright [1983] BTR 254.
[26] As in *Mairs v Haughey* [1992] STC 495, 66 TC 273.
[27] [1982] STC 76, 80, 56 TC 318, 338, per Lord Denning MR in the Court of Appeal. This point was left open by the House of Lords: see Lord Templeman [1983] STC 25, 32, 56 TC 318, 364.
[28] [1995] STC 17, 30.
[29] [1964] 2 All ER 464, 466, 41 TC 641, 655.
[30] If E can escape tax by not using the Cup Final ticket (unless caught by convertibility), R might, of course, choose to dismiss E for such ingratitude.
[31] ITEPA 2003, s 201(2); on old law, see TA 1988, s 168(4). E will be chargeable if the gift is to E's child.
[32] [1964] 2 All ER 464, 41 TC 641; on apportionment, see below at §16.3.7.

what is now Chapter 10. The expense had been incurred 'in the provision of a benefit to' the director, regardless of the fact that there might be good commercial reason for the expenditure and regardless of the fact that the director, left to himself, would have spent no more than £60 and no one suggested that he could have received free legal aid.

(3)   Subject to (4) below, the question whether there must be some benefit to E is a fine one. The courts have said that the receipt of a sum which was a fair valuation for loss of rights is not a benefit.[33] However, it may well be that the director in *Rendell v Went* would be chargeable because a service had been provided, even if he had been found guilty and given the maximum sentence, so that no advantage had been gained. Similarly, where a facility is provided, it is presumably irrelevant that the employee would rather not have the benefit. Thus the cost of providing a seat in a party for the FA Cup Final would be taxable to E even though he detests football and would prefer to be at Covent Garden to attend a performance of *Götterdämmerung*—or vice versa.[34]

(4)   Employees are not liable to tax under Chapter 10 if they have given full value for what is received. In *Mairs v Haughey*,[35] the Court of Appeal for Northern Ireland held that there was no liability under what is now Chapter 10 where the employee received money in return for surrendering rights. Chapter 10 could apply to payments of money, but the employee had given full value by surrendering the rights. It follows that if there is some, but not full, value, a charge may arise on the undervalue.

16.3.3 Statutory Exceptions

Another feature of ITEPA 2003 is the decision to treat exceptions from a charge not in provisions adjacent to the charging rules but miles away.[36] So the exceptions from Part 3, Chapter 10 which used to be found in TA 1988, sections 155 etc, next to the old head of charge, are now to be found in Part 4 of the Act in sections 227–326. The point of making a benefit exempt from Chapter 10 only is either that there is a wish to charge it under some other head, or that the only charge that can arise under ITEPA 2003 is one under Chapter 10. The following are among those excepted from the remit of Chapter 10 by rules in Part 4:

(1)   The provision of accommodation, supplies or services used in premises occupied by the employer,[37] provided any use for non-work purposes is insignificant.[38] Thus, a director is not chargeable on sums spent on an expensive secretary or on luxurious office furniture. This test was softened in 2000 to extend the exemption to benefits used outside the workplace where they are provided solely for the purpose of the employment and used primarily for this purpose, and are not expensive assets like yachts or planes (section 326(5)).

---

[33] *Mairs v Haughey* [1992] STC 495, 66 TC 273, CA NI. This point was not argued before the House of Lords.
[34] Such discrimination is ruled out by Donovan LJ in *Butter v Bennett* (1962) 40 TC 402, 414.
[35] *Mairs v Haughey* [1992] STC 495, 66 TC 273, CA NI.
[36] For explanation, see ITEPA Technical Notes 26 and 28.
[37] Presumably the test of occupation is that under the pre-1977 law and not that in TA 1988, s 145 (see above at §15.4).
[38] ITEPA 2003, s 316; ex TA 1988, s 155ZA, added by FA 2000, Sch 27, para 10 and superseding TA 1988, s 155(2). Non-work use includes family use.

(2)   Any pension, annuity, lump sum, gratuity or other like benefit to be given to the director or employee or his spouse, children or dependants on his death or retirement (section 307(1)).

(3)   Annual health screening and medical check-up. Also, medical insurance for foreign visits and medical treatment, the need for which arises while the director or employee is abroad (section 325).

(4)   Entertainment by someone unconnected with E's employment (section 265).

(5)   Benefits provided in connection with overnight absences from home (sections 240(2) and 241).

(6)   Living accommodation (and any other benefits which are subject to other parts of the benefits code).[39]

(7)   The loan of computer equipment made available before 6 April 2006 up to £500 in benefit (see §16.3.3.2 below).

(8)   Certain childcare expenses (see §16.3.3.1 below).

(9)   The loan of a bicycle or bicycle safety equipment for use on qualifying journeys.[40]

(10) A works bus service, or of support for public transport bus service for use for qualifying journeys.[41]

(11) Mobile phones. At one time there was a scale charge of £200 whenever a mobile telephone was provided and that phone was available for the private use of the employee or members of his family or household.[42] This was repealed in 1999 such that no charge arose under the general rule in Chapter 10 or under section 62.[43] FA 2006, section 60 inserted a new section 319, which limits the exclusion of the loan of a mobile phone to one per employee; a loan to a member of the employee's household is not exempt. The new rule does not apply to loans which began before 6 April 2006. HMRC's policy had been that this exemption did not apply to smartphones (such as Blackberrys and iPhones), but from March 2012 those devices are considered to qualify so long as their primary function is to make and receive phone calls. When the benefit is exempt, the use of a voucher or credit token is also exempt: see sections 266 and 267, as amended by FA 2006, section 60(1) and (2).

(12) Certain meals supplied in canteens. The exemption for free or subsidised meals applies only if the same standard of food or subsidy is applied for all employees.[44]

The Treasury has power to exclude minor benefits by statutory instrument; this power has been used to exempt welfare counselling.[45] Legislation rendering a payment non-taxable as income also exempts the employee from liability under Chapter 10, whether the payment is

[39] ITEPA 2003, s 202(1)(a) (note also (b) and (c)), ex TA 1988, s 154(2).
[40] ITEPA 2003, s 244, ex TA 1988, s 197AC, added by FA 1999, s 50 (see below at §18.2.4.4).
[41] ITEPA ss 242 and 243, ex TA 1988, ss 197AA, 197AB, added by FA 1999, s 48 (see below at §18.2.4.2).
[42] TA 1988, s 159A; on apportionment, see s 159(4)–(6); for definitions, see s 159(8).
[43] ITEPA 2003, s 319, ex TA 1988, s 155A(a). On irrelevance of whether it is provided in a car, see ITEPA Technical Note 35.
[44] ITEPA 2003, s 317, as amended by FA 2004.
[45] The power is now in ITEPA 2003, s 210, ex TA 1988, s 155ZB, added by FA 2000, s 57. On welfare counselling, see SI 2002/20280.

made to the employee or a member of his family.[46] Provisions which exclude benefits from ITEPA 2003 exclude any charge under Chapter 10 (eg the provision of in-house sporting or other recreational facilities)—but each rule has to be read with care (section 261). Of those listed above, (1), (2), (3) and (5) are true exceptions from Chapter 10 in that they are exceptions only from Chapter 10. Others, eg (7) and (11), are exceptions from Chapter 10 and other heads. Some in the original version of this Chapter were complete exemptions from income tax, eg (4) and (10), while others were later amended to become completely exempt, eg (9) and (12). The decision to include in ITEPA 2003 many reliefs previously to be found in the concessions adds to the list of exemptions from tax and so from Chapter 10. There is a list of the reliefs in Part 4 of the Act at the end of chapter fifteen of this book.

16.3.3.1 Childcare

No liability to tax arises with respect to a benefit consisting of the provision of certain childcare facilities.[47] This is subject to many conditions, for example:

(1) the child must be one for whom the employee has parental responsibility,[48] or must reside with the employee or be a child (including a step-child) of the employee and be maintained at his expense (section 318);
(2) the care must be provided on premises which are not used mainly as a private dwelling;
(3) if the premises are not made available by the employer alone, the care must be provided under an arrangement made by persons who include the employer, the care must be provided on premises made available by one or more of those persons and, under the arrangement, the employer must be wholly or partly responsible for financing and managing the provision of care; and
(4) the care is provided under a scheme open to employees generally, or generally to those employees at a particular location (section 318(4)–(7)).

There is also a registration requirement for the premises (section 318(4) and (5)).

FA 2004 added a new limited exemption for other childcare provided by an employer or the provision of childcare vouchers (see below §16.5). If the relevant conditions are satisfied, tax applies only to the amount of the cash equivalent of the benefit in excess of the 'exempt amount' of qualifying childcare provided by a registered or approved caregiver (other than the partner of the employee or a relative of the child where the care is provided in the child or parent's home) (sections 318A–318D). The child must be a child or stepchild of the employee who is maintained (wholly or partly) at the employee's expense, or be a person for whom the employee has parental responsibility and who is resident with the employee. The care must be provided under a scheme that is open to employees generally or to those at a particular location. FA 2005, section 16 extended this exemption to the administrative costs of providing any relevant voucher.

---

[46] See *Wicks v Firth* [1983] STC 25, 56 TC 318, HL; see Shipwright [1983] BTR 254. The particular exemption in that case (TA 1988, s 331) has now been the subject of special legislation (see below at §16.4.7) but the principle remains, unless the Supreme Court follows its own (bad) precedent in the House of Lords decision in *Thomson v Moyse* (1958) 39 TC 291.

[47] ITEPA 2003, s 318, ex TA 1988, s 155A; a 'child' is a person aged under 18, and 'care' is defined as including supervised activities (ITEPA 2003, s 318(8), ex TA 1988, s 155A(7)). See generally RI 181.

[48] ITEPA 2003, s 318(3), defined by reference to the Children Act 1989, s 3(1) (ex TA 1988, s 155A(8)).

FA 2011 reduced the limit on the exempt amount of qualifying childcare for higher-rate and basic-rate taxpayers from £55 per week to £22 and £28, respectively; the new limits do not apply to existing members of schemes who joined before 6 April 2011. It also slightly eased the requirement that the scheme be open to employees generally under a relevant salary sacrifice arrangements, or relevant flexible remuneration arrangements. At Budget 2016, the Government confirmed it was introducing a new childcare scheme in 2017 to benefit employees and also the self-employed. Parents, employers and other family members will be able to pay into an online account to cover cost of childcare paid to a registered provider. For every 80p contributed, the government will add 20p, up to a cap of £10,000 of costs. Transitional relief under the existing employer-supported childcare scheme will be available

16.3.3.2 Computer Equipment

As a matter of principle, Chapter 10 applies where an employee borrows computing equipment from his employer and could use it outside the employer's premises or for non-business purposes. FA 1999 introduced a limited exception by excluding a charge on the first £500 of benefit as determined under those rules (section 320). Therefore, if R, the employer, bought a computer for £2,500 and lent it to E, the employee, the 20% charge (see §16.3.5) of £500 was exactly covered by the exception; however, if R then paid for and installed a software upgrade, a charge applied to that excess since the threshold was exceeded. Computing equipment was defined so as to include not only the computer itself (including software), but also such peripherals as modems, printers, scanners, disks and similar items designed to be connected to or inserted into the computer. Telephones were not, however, included (section 320(7)). The loan must not have been confined to employees who were directors, nor may the terms offered to directors have been more beneficial than those to other employees (section 320(3)). This partial exclusion rule applied only to loans (section 320(2)). FA 2004 extended this exception to liability under section 62 as well.[49] FA 2006, section 61 then removed the exception for equipment made available on or after 6 April 2006, on the grounds that computer equipment had become generally more affordable and also because the exception was being abused, eg by the provision of music players and video game consoles. The repeal of section 320 leaves matters to the general rule in section 316, excluding a benefit charge on assets provided for business use where the private use is not significant.

16.3.4 *Extent of Charge: Cash Equivalent*

16.3.4.1 Cost—The Basic Rule

Section 203 treats the 'cash equivalent' of the employment-related benefit as earnings from the employment for the tax year in which it is provided, and then defines 'cash equivalent' as the cost of a benefit. The cost of the benefit is then defined as 'the expense incurred in or in connection with the provision of the benefit less any part of the costs made good by the employee' (section 204). The practical effect is that if the cost of the benefit is £100, and the

---

[49] FA 2004, s 79.

employee's, E's, marginal rate is 40%, E will acquire the benefit (£100) but pay tax of £40. However, if E had paid for the benefit out of his own pocket, the salary would have had to be increased by £167 to give £100 net of tax with which to acquire an equivalent benefit. The reason why section 203 uses this technique is to ensure consistency with Chapter 3, section 72; the amount charged is the same whether E receives £100 under an expense allowance which is then spent on the object, or receives the object as a benefit in kind. This example may be criticised for failing to compare like with like, since the comparison is between tax of £40, leaving E with the benefit in kind, and tax of £67, leaving a benefit worth £100.

16.3.4.2 Cost—Marginal or Average?

In the famous case of *Pepper v Hart*[50] the House of Lords held that cost meant marginal cost, not average cost. *Pepper v Hart* concerned the provision of education at a private school (Malvern College) for a child of a member of the teaching staff. The member of staff paid a fee equal to one-fifth of the normal fee, which was more than enough to cover the marginal cost to the school but was substantially less than the average cost paid by other pupils. The House held that marginal cost should be used; since this had all been 'made good' by the employee, no charge arose.[51]

The decision of the House was in accordance with what was thought to be general Revenue practice and, famously, what had been said to the House of Commons in 1975 (on which see chapter three above). However, the issue is not easy to resolve. Suppose that an airline provides an employee with a free seat on a flight from London to New York. One view, not canvassed in *Pepper v Hart*, is that cost means opportunity cost, ie that if the airline could have sold the seat to an ordinary passenger at £500, it would have had an opportunity cost of £500, but it forwent the opportunity of making that sum. It is generally thought that such a cost is not 'incurred'. The second view, marginal cost, means the extra cost of carrying this passenger, ie the cost of providing another meal together with the amount of fuel needed to carry the extra weight. Of course, it might also entail a very large sum, eg if regulations required that another member of the cabin staff had to be hired. Matters are unclear if two employees were given the free flight but the extra member of staff was triggered by only one of them. The third view, the average cost, would mean that the airline must average the entire cost of the journey over all the passengers. However, this cost would itself be a matter of dispute since it is necessary to consider how much of the overhead cost should be included, ie should it be (a) the marginal cost to the airline of running the flight, so spreading the cost over the number of passengers on the flight (a matter of some interest if, for example, the employee were the only passenger on the flight); or (b) the appropriate proportion of the cost of the entire operations of that month (or year), so treating the employee as receiving a benefit far higher than the normal fare? At present, the matter would be resolved in favour of marginal cost, so that if no expense is incurred in providing the benefit, no charge can arise under Chapter 10.

---

[50] [1992] STC 898, 65 TC 421; criticised by Bennion [1995] BTR 325. For wider criticisms see §3.1.3.1 above.
[51] On practical consequences, see Inland Revenue Press Release, 21 January 1993, [1993] *Simon's Tax Intelligence* 196.

16.3.4.3 Incidental Expenses—Sale of an Asset by Employee to Employer

A charge under section 203 may arise where an employee sells an asset to the employer and the right or opportunity to do so arises by reason of the employment, memorably referred to as an employment-related asset transfer. Where this occurs, no liability to tax arises by virtue of a payment or reimbursement of expenses incurred on the transfer. The expenses must be incurred wholly and exclusively as a result of the transfer, and the expenses must not be of a kind normally met by the transferor. This rule began life as a concession.[52]

16.3.4.4 Asset Used Before Transfer to Employee

Section 206(2) states that if the benefit consists of an asset, and that asset has been used or has depreciated since it was bought, the market value is to be used instead of the price. However, there are exceptions to section 206, notably where the asset is not an 'excluded asset' and has already been provided as a relevant employment-related benefit (section 206(3)). Excluded assets are cars, computers, cycles and cyclists' safety equipment (section 206(6)).

16.3.5 Asset Lent by Employer

Under section 205, where the asset remains the property of the employer, the employer is deemed to incur a cost equal to the sum of (a) the annual value of the asset, and (b) any other expense incurred in providing the asset other than the cost of producing or acquiring the asset.[53] The figure at (a) will be increased if the employer pays a sum by way of rent or hire which exceeds the annual value, the higher figure being taken instead. The annual value of the asset varies according to the benefit. In the case of land, one looks to the annual rental value of the land, assuming that the tenant pays all the taxes usually paid by a tenant and the landlord pays for things like repairs and insurance[54] (see above at §15.4). For other assets, the figure is 20% of its market value at the time it was first applied by the employer for the employee.[55] So if an employer lends an employee a cat, the cash equivalent will be the sum of (a) 20% of the cost of the cat, plus (b) the full cost of food and any veterinary services paid for by the employer. The costs of acquisition or production of the asset are excluded from (b), presumably because they are taken into account under (a). Acquisition and production have been construed widely. Expenditure resulting in the replacement or renewal of the asset as distinct from its maintenance is excluded; on this basis, sums spent on supplying a house with a new water main were not part of (b) and so escaped tax.[56]

---

[52] ITEPA 2003, s 326. On previous concession, see Inland Revenue Press Release, 27 April 1994, [1994] *Simon's Tax Intelligence* 581.

[53] ITEPA 2003, s 205, ex TA 1988, s 156(4), eg repair and insurance.

[54] ITEPA 2003, ss 205(3) and 207.

[55] ITEPA 2003, s 205(3), ex TA 1988, s 156(5); the percentage was 10% where the asset was first provided before 6 April 1980.

[56] *Luke v IRC* [1963] 1 All ER 655, 40 TC 630.

16.3.6 Transfer of an Asset After Employment-Related Use by Employee

If an asset is subsequently transferred to the employee, E, section 206 normally charges E on the market value of the asset when it is so transferred.[57] However, a different rule applies if it would give rise to a higher charge (section 206(3)). The problem arises when an asset, eg a hi-fi, is lent to E who uses it by reason of the employment so as to come within section 205. When the asset has depreciated significantly in value, the employer transfers it to E. The cash equivalent for the first two years will have been calculated on the basis of the rules already considered. Under section 206(3) the cash equivalent on the transfer to E is the greater of (a) the asset's market value at that time less any price paid for it by the employee, and (b) the market value when it was first provided, but with a deduction for amounts already taxed and any sum paid for it (section 206(5)). This alternative does not apply to cars, bicycles, etc or computers.

Example

R provides E with a hi-fi costing £600. After two years R sells the system to E for £150, its market value being £250. E is liable on the higher of: (a) £250—£150 = £100; and (b) £600—(2 × 20% × £600)—£150 = £210. E is therefore liable on (b).

16.3.7 Apportionment of Expenditure

If the expense is incurred by the employer partly to provide a benefit for the employee and partly for other purposes, section 204 states that only a proper proportion of the expense so incurred will be caught by section 203. In *Westcott v Bryan*,[58] a managing director wished to live in London but the company insisted that he live in a large rambling house set in two acres of garden close to the factory in a rural area of North Staffordshire. He paid the company a rent of £140 pa and £500 pa for services, and also paid the rates. In the tax year the company spent £1,017 on gas, electricity, water, insurance of contents, telephone, cleaning, window cleaning, gardener's wages and maintenance. The house was bigger than the taxpayer either needed or desired, but no specific area was set aside for the entertainment of the company's guests. The Court of Appeal held that an apportionment under what is now ITEPA 2003, section 204 should be made even though the expenses could not clearly be severed on either a temporal or a spatial basis. The method of apportionment was not canvassed in the Court of Appeal,[59] but at first instance Pennycuick J had said that apportionment could be calculated only on a rough-and-ready basis, to determine what proportion of the total expense was fairly attributable to the use or availability for use of the house by the company.[60]

Where a particular expense benefits both employer and employee, and no part of the expenditure is on something which benefits the employer exclusively, no apportionment can be made. In *Rendell v Went*[61] (the driving case) the employer had spent a sum of money

---

[57] ITEPA 2003, s 206(2), ex TA 1988, s 156(3); transaction costs incurred by the transferor are ignored (*ibid*).
[58] [1969] 3 All ER 564, 45 TC 467.
[59] But see *ibid*, Sachs LJ, 571, 493.
[60] 45 TC 487.
[61] [1964] 2 All ER 464, 467, 41 TC 641, 659; this distinction is criticised by Kerridge [1986] BTR 36.

in the provision of a benefit when the employee, E, would have spent less, and no part of the sum was spent on something which did not benefit E. In *Westcott v Bryan* the expenditure was made for two distinct purposes, only one of which was of benefit to the director. Where section 204 directs an apportionment, section 203(2) limits its charge to so much of the expense as is not made good by the employee, E. Where, therefore, a sum is to be apportioned and E receives a payment for the benefit, the question arises whether the expense is apportioned first and then the payment is set off against that apportioned figure, or whether the set-off occurs first and the apportionment is then applied to that reduced figure. The former would seem more correct, but the latter view appears to have been accepted in *Westcott v Bryan*.

16.4   Particular Rules for Certain Benefits

16.4.1 *Cars, Classic Cars, Pooled Cars and Vans*

In the UK company cars are much sought after. Tax treatment of company cars, however, has become more unfavourable over the years. Today the taxable benefit arising from having a company car available for private use is significant. In addition, both employer's NIC (Class 1A) and PAYE may be chargeable. Nevertheless, company cars account for about half the new car registrations in Britain, and surveys routinely show that employees would keep their company cars even if all the tax advantages were abolished.

16.4.1.1 Car Available for Private Use

Where a car is available for private use by reason of the employment, the employee is chargeable under ITEPA 2003, Part 3, Chapter 6, section 120 on the cash equivalent of the benefit of the car being available for private use.[62] The Court of Appeal held that this provision did not apply where an employee leased a car from the employer and paid market value lease charges,[63] but this result was overturned by statute except where the employer's business is vehicle hire.[64] Section 120 applies only if the car has been made available without any transfer of the property in it. In *Christiensen v Vasili*, the employer bought a car, the employee acquired a 5% share and then the car was made available for the employee's use. Allowing the Revenue's appeal, Pumfrey J held that the car had been made available to the employee without a transfer of property and so came within what is now ITEPA 2003, section 120.[65]

Current rules, which have applied as from April 2002, base that cash equivalent on a mixture of the price of the car and a level of CO_2 emissions. The level of CO_2 emissions is set by ITEPA 2003, section 239 and contains lower figures year by year. Where two members of the same family are provided with cars by their common employer, relief ensures that each is subject to a single charge rather than double charge.[66] Where two or more employees are

---

[62] ITEPA 2003, ss 114–120, ex TA 1988, s 157(1).
[63] *HMRC v Apollo Fuels Ltd and others* [2016] EWCA Civ 157.
[64] ITEPA 2003, ss 114(1A) and 117(3).
[65] [2004] EWHC ChD 476; [2004] STC 935.
[66] ITEPA 2003, s 169, enacting ESC A71.

chargeable in respect of the same car, the benefit is apportioned between them.[67] There are special rules for temporary replacements.[68] Section 119 provides that where the employee is offered a benefit which is an alternative to the use of a car, eg a payment of £20 a year, the mere fact that this alternative is offered does not make the benefit chargeable as general earnings under section 62. The point is that the offer of £20 may make the benefit taxable under section 62 and so make NIC chargeable only on £20. Section 119 prevents this avoidance.[69]

The appropriate percentage

Until 2002 the taxable benefit varied according to the amount of business-related mileage done. While this was compatible with feelings of fairness, it also encouraged high business-related mileage. Current rules for cars registered on or after 1 January 1998[70] are based on a mixture of the price of the car and a level of CO_2 emissions.[71] However, other variables are whether the car is a diesel or a car without an emissions figure at all (eg an electric car) and the date of first registration. The CO_2 figure is then used to find the appropriate percentage for that car for that year on a table (minimum 5% and maximum 37%); the taxable benefit is that percentage of the price of the car (section 139). A special appropriate percentage of 0 per cent applies to cars with CO_2 emissions of zero. An expensive car with high CO_2 emissions and high business mileage will have a higher tax charge than under the old rules; an expensive car with low emissions and a low business mileage may well be cheaper. A cheap car with low CO_2 emissions will certainly be cheaper. 'Mondeo man' may well find little difference. If a disabled employee has to have an automatic rather than a manual transmission, the extra emission is excluded (section 138).

Offsetting payments

Sums paid by the employee to the employer for the year may be set against the cash equivalent of a company car, but only if the employee is required to pay the sums as a condition of the car being available for his private use, including use by members of his family or household (section 144). Sums paid for other purposes cannot be offset. A sum paid to obtain a more expensive car does not reduce the benefit.[72] An insurance premium paid for a company car was held to be payable to insure the car and not for its use; since the scale charge covers the costs of insuring the vehicle, this seems to be an unimaginative (and certainly non-purposive) construction of the statute.[73] A capital contribution by the employee on the provision of the car or an accessory can be take into account in determining the price of the car—see discussion below under 'Price' (section 132).

---

[67] ITEPA 2003, s 148, ex ESC A71; on which, see *Taxation* (1998), Vol 142, No 3676. see ITEPA explanatory note change 267.

[68] ITEPA 2003, s 145; see ITEPA explanatory note change 25.

[69] See discussion of the convertibility principle above at §15.2.

[70] ITEPA 2003, ss 135 and 136.

[71] ITEPA 2003, s 121, introduced by FA 2000, Sch 11. The Revenue notes to the legislation suggested that some 300 million extra business-related miles were driven.

[72] *Brown v Ware* [1995] STC (SCD) 155; E cannot deduct tax paid under s 120 as a travelling expense under ITEPA 2003, s 338, ex TA 1988, s 198 (*Clark v Bye* [1997] STC 311).

[73] *IRC v Quigley* [1995] STC 931.

Scope

The benefits covered by the charge are all those concerned with the provision of the car, ie capital cost, insurance, maintenance, etc, and no charge can arise under Chapter 10 (section 239). However, the charge under section 120 does not cover the costs of a chauffeur (section 239(4)), petrol (section 157) or car phones (unless installed and used only for business calls).[74]

Price

The appropriate percentage is applied to the price of the car, a concept which is itself elaborately defined but which is basically the list price plus accessories, delivery charge, VAT and car tax.[75] Any price actually paid by the employer is ignored. An imported car is priced according to its UK list price, notwithstanding that the level of prices in the UK is notoriously high. If the car has no list price, a notional price is taken.[76]

Initial accessories. The cost of standard accessories[77] included in the list price of the car will already have been brought into account. Special rules apply to other accessories, eg those made available as an option by the manufacturer (section 125(2)). The price of the car will have to be increased to take account of the list price of fitted accessories as set by the manufacturer or distributor where this is available—including VAT, delivery and fitting charges (sections 127–129). Where a list price is not available a notional price is used (section 131). Accessories for conversion for use by a chronically sick or disabled person are ignored.[78]

Later accessories. Where an accessory is made available to E after the car is first made available,[79] the list price of accessories over £100 (including VAT, fitting and delivery) and fitted after 31 July 1993 will be included in the price of the car as regards the year in which they are fitted and all subsequent years. The removal of the accessory does not seem to have been contemplated by the legislation, although the replacement of an accessory is to be covered by Treasury regulations; one wonders whether a removal can be equated with replacement by nothing. The £100 figure may be raised by Treasury regulation.

Capital contribution by E. If E makes a capital contribution to the provision of the car or accessory, the sum reduces the price of the car—not the cash equivalent. A maximum of £5,000 may be taken into account, although this sum may be raised by Treasury regulation (section 132).

Classic cars. Special rules apply where the value of the car exceeds £15,000 and is higher than the manufacturer's list price when it was first registered, ie its price for the year. The car must be more than 15 years old at the end of the tax year (section 147). In such circumstances

---

[74] Statement of Practice SP 5/88.

[75] ITEPA 2003 ss 122–124, ex TA 1988, s 168A(1), (2), (9); on timing of availability, see ex s 168A(12); on date of first registration, see ex s 168(5)(d).

[76] ITEPA 2003, s 124, ex TA 1988, s 168A(8).

[77] The rules on accessories are set out in ITEPA 2003, ss 125–131, ex TA 1988, s 168A(11); see HC Official Report, Standing Committee D, cols 197–202, [1995] *Simon's Tax Intelligence* 267. Note s 125(2), ex TA 1988, s 168A(11), defining accessories (but excluding a mobile phone, equipment for a disabled person to drive a car and conversion to LPG); s 125(1), ex TA 1988, s 168A(10), defining qualifying accessories; and s 125(4), ex TA 1988, 168A(9)(c), (d), distinguishing standard accessories from optional accessories.

[78] ITEPA 2003, ss 125(2)(c) and 172, ex TA 1988, s 168AA.

[79] ITEPA 2003, s 126(3), ex TA 1988, s 168C.

the cash equivalent is calculated by applying the relevant percentage to the open market value of the car (and accessories) at the end of the tax year or, if different, the last day on which it was available to the employee (section 147(2)). As with other cars, contributions towards the cost of the car or accessories may be deducted up to a limit of £5,000 (section 147(5)–(7)).

Exception—pooled cars

If the car is one of a pool (a concept which is elaborately defined and which broadly means that the car must be genuinely available to more than one employee and not regularly garaged at an employee's house) and any private use is purely incidental to its business use, the car is not treated as being available for the employee's use and is not a taxable benefit (section 167).

16.4.1.2 Vans Available for Private Use

A special basis of charge exists for certain commercial vehicles, statutorily referred to as vans.[80] A van is defined as a vehicle built primarily to carry goods or burdens of any description (a phrase which the Revenue clearly believe excludes the carriage of people), with a gross vehicle weight of 3.5 tonnes or less.[81] Where the gross vehicle weight exceeds this figure, any benefit from heavier vehicles is to be exempt from any charge, provided the employee's use is not wholly or mainly private use; since this is an exemption it appears in Part 4 not Part 3 (section 238). The rules for vans changed at the start of 2005–06 in a number of ways which are indicated in what follows. The overall effect was to simplify the law, to make the van rules much closer to those for cars and, as from 2007–08, to increase the charge substantially. In addition, also as from 2007–08, there is a separate charge for the provision of fuel for private use in vans.[82]

The benefit from the private use of vans was previously exempt from the scale charge for cars, and the cash equivalent was therefore calculated on the basis of the general rules for assets made available for the use of employees. This changed in 1993 when new rules were introduced, with a cash equivalent, unchanged since 1993, of £500 if the van was less than four years old at the end of the year concerned, or £350 if it was older.[83] Beginning with the tax year 2007–08 the cash equivalent increased significantly to £3,000, and for 2016–17 it is £3,170.[84] However, if the 'restricted private use condition' is met the cash equivalent is nil.[85] This condition, which began in 2005–06, is satisfied if:

(1) the terms on which the van is available to the employee prohibit its private use otherwise than for the purposes of ordinary commuting, and neither the employee nor a member of the employee's family or household makes private use of the van otherwise than for that purpose; and

(2) the van is available to the employee mainly for use for the purposes of the employee's business travel.

---

[80] ITEPA 2003, ss 114(3A) and 154–159, ex TA 1988, s 159AA.

[81] ITEPA 2003, s 115(1), ex TA 1988, s 168(5A); see Inland Revenue Press Release, 16 March 1993, para 3, [1993] *Simon's Tax Intelligence* 437.

[82] FA 2004, s 80 and Sch 14. Inland Revenue Press Release BN42.

[83] ITEPA 2003, s 157(1), step 2 and s 166, ex TA 1988, Sch 6A, para 1.

[84] ITEPA 2003, s 155.

[85] ITEPA 2003, s 155, modified by FA 2004, s 80 and Sch 14, para 5.

The usual reductions are applicable for periods where the van is unavailable,[86] shared,[87] pooled[88] or where payment is made as a condition of its being available for private use (section 159). For 2015–16, the cash equivalent is 20% of the usual amount for a van which does not produce CO_2 emissions, with the percentage due to increase each year until it becomes 90% of the usual amount in 2019–20.

16.4.2 Car Fuel for Company Cars and Vans

Under section 149, a special scale charge applies where the employer provides free petrol for private motoring in company cars. The charge takes the form of using the appropriate percentage used for the car charge and then applying that to a set figure, which for 2016–17 is £22,200 (section 150). A nil figures is taken if the fuel is made available only for business use, or if the employee is required to make good all the expense incurred in connection with private use and does pay the sums involved (section 151). There are apportionments for when the car or the free fuel facility are unavailable or the fuel is made available only for business travel, or the employee makes good the entire sum spent on private travel[89] or the car is shared (section 153). Perhaps anomalously, there is no reduction in charge if the employee reimburses the employer only a part of the cost. This charge does not apply where an employer provides fuel for a car which is not a company car, in which case the general rules of sections 72 (Chapter 3) and 203 (Chapter 10) apply. Previously the fuel charge applied to company cars but not to company vans. Beginning in 2007–08, similar fuel charge rules apply to company vans.[90] The default cash equivalent amount of the benefit for vans is set at £598 for 2016–17, subject to reduction in the same manner as for cars.

16.4.3 Low Interest Loans

Under ITEPA 2003, Part 3, Chapter 7, section 175, employees are taxable on a cash equivalent of the benefit of taxable but cheap loans, provided the loans are employment-related.[91] A cash equivalent arises if the employee pays no interest on the loan or pays at a rate below the official rate (section 181). Section 188, which deals with writing off such loans, is discussed at §16.4.4 below. A loan is made when it is advanced and not when its terms are varied.[92] A loan is caught whether the employer grants, guarantees or merely facilitates the loan.[93] In determining whether a loan is an employment-related loan it is immaterial whether or not the terms on which the loan is provided constitute a fair bargain.[94]

---

[86] FA 1993 introduced TA 1988, s 159A and Sch 6A. See now ITEPA 2003, s 158, ex TA 1988, Sch 6A, para 2.
[87] ITEPA 2003, s 157; for explanation, see ITEPA Technical Note 17.
[88] For explanation, see ITEPA Technical Note 18.
[89] ITEPA 2003, s 152; the difference between s 152(2)(c) and s 151 is subtle and may be even illusory.
[90] ITEPA 2003, ss 160–164, added by FA 2004, s 80 and Sch 14, para 5.
[91] Ex TA 1988, s 160(1). On practical problems, see ICAEW Memorandum TR 738, [1998] *Simon's Tax Intelligence* 738. On advances to meet necessary expenses, see ITEPA 2003, s 179, replacing SP 7/79; see ITEPA explanatory note change 29.
[92] *West v Crosland* [1999] STC (SCD) 147.
[93] ITEPA 2003, s 173(2)(b), ex TA 1988, s 160(5)(c).
[94] ITEPA 2003, s 173(1A).

A loan includes any form of credit; as such, an advance of salary is caught.[95] It has been held that an interest-free equity loan, under which the borrower is to repay not the exact sum received but a proportion of the proceeds of sale of a property bought with the aid of the loan, is still a loan.[96] In *Grant v Watton*,[97] G, an estate agent, formed a service company to provide services to the business in return for fees from G's business. G was a director of the company. The court held that when the business failed to pay the fees to the company on time, the company was providing G with a form of credit; as G was a director of the company, tax was due under what is now section 175. In another tax context it has been held that a loan requires consensus, so that a misappropriation by a director did not give rise to a loan.[98] The loan must be employment-related, but may be made to the employee or to his relatives.[99] 'Relative' is defined differently from 'family' and means spouse, lineal ascendant or descendant, brother or sister of the employee or the spouse, and the spouses of those people (section 174(6)). It is, however, open to employees to show that they derived no benefit from the loan (section 174(5)(b)).

16.4.3.1 Exclusions

(1) *De minimis.* The charge does not apply if the total of all such loans does not exceed £10,000.[100] At one time the exclusion was by reference to the amount of the cash equivalent of the loan, but this entailed all the expense of calculating the cash equivalents.

(2) *Commercial terms.* Loans made on commercial terms by an employer whose business includes the making of loans, where a substantial proportion of those loans are made to members of the public at large, and at arm's length, are excluded from liability to tax. The terms on which the loans are made to the employee must be comparable to the loans to the public.[101]

(3) *Fixed-term loans originally at the official rate.* The charge is aimed at loans below the official (market) rate of interest. If the loan is a fixed-interest loan and was not below that rate when it was made, the subsequent increase in the official market rate in a later year does not cause the loan to become chargeable.[102]

(4) *Death.* An employee's loan ceases to be outstanding on his death (section 190(1)(a)); as such, no cash equivalents can arise for later periods.

(5) *Other termination of employment.* Although the legislation does not in terms address the issue of the ending of employment, section 175 applies only for those periods during which the person is in employment.[103]

---

[95] ITEPA 2003, s 173(2)(a); *Williams v Todd* [1988] STC 676, 60 TC 727.

[96] *Harvey v Williams* [1995] STC (SCD) 329; and *Gold v Inspector of Taxes* [1998] STC (SCD) 215 (the loan was secured on the house). The facts as reported assume that the house would go up in value; whether the lender would bear a share of any loss if the house had gone down in value is not clear.

[97] [1999] STC 330.

[98] *Stephens v T Pittas Ltd* [1983] STC 576.

[99] ITEPA 2003, s 174; note especially in the present context s 174(5)–(6).

[100] ITEPA 2003, s 180, ex TA 1988, s 161(1); see ITEPA explanatory note change 30. FA 2014, section 22 raised the de minimas limit from £5,000 to £10,000 effective from 6 April 2014.

[101] ITEPA 2003, s 176, ex TA 1988, s 161(1A), (1B). On Revenue practice, see Revenue interpretation RI85.

[102] ITEPA 2003, s 177, ex TA 1988, s 161(2); on pre-1978 loans, see s 161(3).

[103] Ex TA 1988, s 160(1). This point is the stronger because ITEPA 2003, s 188 (ex TA 1988, s 160(2)) is expressly made to apply after the employment has ceased.

(6) *Qualifying loans.* Qualifying loans are loans in respect of which the borrower may claim a deduction for the interest as a trading expense or as being for eligible for relief under TA 1988, section 353 or ITA 2007, section 383 (section 178). Qualifying loans are not taken into account in calculating the *de minimis* limit (section 180(1)).

(7) *Bridging loans.* Section 173(3) carefully makes a cross-reference to the exemption in sections 288 and 289 for certain bridging loans connected with employment moves; those exemptions mean that section 175 is excluded too. No liability can arise under section 188 because the loan must be discharged before the end of the period.

16.4.3.2 Relation to Other Tax Rules

Although the tax system provides relief for such interest under these rules, it first treats the cash equivalent of the benefit as arising, and then allows the deemed amount to be deducted under the other rules.[104] Where there is a taxable cheap loan and so the cash equivalent is treated as earnings from the employment for the year, the employee is treated as having paid interest on a loan equal to the cash equivalent (section 184(2)). The deemed payment accrues during the year but is treated as paid at the end (section 184(4)). The interest is not treated as income of the lender, neither is it relevant loan interest (section 184(5)). Not surprisingly, E is not allowed to say that he has paid the interest and so there should be no tax liability (section 184(3)). Where an amount treated as an emolument is also a distribution under ITTOIA 2005, Part 4, Chapter 3, section 366(3) of the 2005 Act directs that ITEPA 2003 is to prevail.

16.4.3.3 Pre-employment Loans

Sections 173 and 174 refer to 'employment-related loans', a term which refers to a loan made by the employee's employer and certain other similar situations. Where a loan was not made during employment and, some time later, the employment begins and the rate of interest is reduced, it is uncertain whether a charge arises.[105] It is clear that section 186 replacement loans do not apply since that provision refers only to one such loan replacing another.

16.4.3.4 Calculating the Cash Equivalent: The Official Rate

Section 175 applies whether the employee pays no interest or pays at a rate below the official rate. If the employee pays no interest, the cash equivalent will be the notional interest calculated at the official rate; if, however, he does pay interest, only the difference between what is actually paid for the year and what would be due at the official rate is brought in.[106] If there

---

[104] ITEPA 2003, s 184(2)–(5), ex TA 1988, s 160(1A); they are treated as paid at the end of the year or trading period, or, if earlier, the end of the employment.
[105] Quaere the position of a fixed-interest loan if the interest was paid at the official rate when the loan was made but not when E becomes the employee.
[106] ITEPA 2003, s 175(3), ex TA 1988, s 160(1). The payment is 'for' the year and so does not have to be paid during the year.

are two or more employment-related loans they are treated separately (section 175(4)), a matter of importance where different rates of interest are paid on different loans. It will be seen that the reduction in the cash equivalent is due only if the interest is paid; where an assessment is made on the basis that interest has not been paid and it later is, there is a right to claim relief.[107]

The amount of interest due at the official rate is calculated first by taking a simple average of the loan outstanding at the beginning and end of the tax year, multiplying this by the number of months of the loan in the year and divided by 12, and then applying the official rate (section 182). However, either the taxpayer or the Revenue may elect that the interest be calculated on a day-to-day basis—a matter of importance where the amount of the loan fluctuates during the year.[108] The official rate is determined by reference to commercial mortgage rates.[109] The rate may be found on the HMRC website; for 2015–16 the rate was 3%.[110]

16.4.3.5 Replacement Loans

Further provisions deal with the calculation of the interest where an employment-related loan is replaced, directly or indirectly, (a) by a further employment-related loan, or (b) by a non-employment-related loan which, in turn, is, in the same year of assessment or within 40 days thereafter, replaced, directly or indirectly, by a further employment-related loan. In these circumstances the rules are applied as if the replacement loan or loans were the same as the first employment-related loan.[111]

Example

A has borrowed £10,000 from his employer just before the start of the year of assessment. On 30 June he repays £3,000, but on 3 September he borrows another £4,000. The amount outstanding at the end of the year of assessment is £11,000. A pays £450 in interest; assume that the official rate is 5%.

(1) Simple calculation:

Average amount outstanding during the year (£11,000 − £10,000) / 2 = £10,500
Official rate at 5% would give £525, and thus a cash equivalent of (£525 − 450) = £75.

---

[107] ITEPA 2003, s 191; see ITEPA explanatory note change 35.

[108] ITEPA 2003, s 183, ex TA 1988, Sch 7, para 5; on Revenue practice, see HMRC booklet 480 (2012), para 17.30 *et seq.* On time limits see ITEPA 2003, s 183(2); see ITEPA explanatory note change 32.

[109] SI 1989/1297, as amended by SI 1991/889; [1989] *Simon's Tax Intelligence* 695, [1991] *Simon's Tax Intelligence* 434.

[110] See https://www.gov.uk/government/publications/rates-and-allowances-beneficial-loan-arrangements-hmrc-official-rates.

[111] ITEPA 2003, s 186, ex TA 1988, Sch 7, para 4(2)–(4), added by FA 1995, s 45. See ITEPA explanatory note change 33.

(2)   More precise calculation:

First period £10,000 × 85/365 × 5%	£116.43
Second period £7,000 × 65/365 × 5%	£62.32
Third period £11,000 × 215/365 × 5%	£323.97
Total	£502.72

Thus, cash equivalent is £502.72—£450 = £52.72

16.4.3.6 Foreign Currencies

Special rules provide for the calculation of the official rate of interest where the loan is made in the currency of a foreign country. For this rule to apply, the employee must normally live in that country and have done so at some time within the period of six years ending with the year of assessment.[112] Regulations have been made for loans in Japanese yen and Swiss francs.[113]

16.4.4 Loans Written Off

Where the whole or part of an employment-related loan is released or written off, ITEPA 2003, section 188 imposes a charge on the amount so released or written off (section 188(2)). The release of a loan to a relative comes within this rule, unless the employee can show that he derived no benefit from the loan.[114] Any charge under ITTOIA 2005, Part 4, Chapter 6 (ex TA 1988, section 421) has priority.[115]

16.4.4.1 Exceptions

(1)   *Other provisions*: section 188 does not apply if the amount written off is otherwise chargeable to tax (eg under ITTOIA 2005, Part 4, Chapter 6, ex TA 1988, section 421);[116] however, section 188 will apply if the other provision is ITEPA 2003, Part 6, Chapter 3 (termination benefits), or ITTOIA 2005, section 633—because the charge under those rules may be less.
(2)   *Death*: no charge arises on a release which takes effect after the death of the employee (section 190(2)).

16.4.4.2 Non-exceptions

Section 188 is quite distinct from section 175 and applies whether or not the loan was chargeable under section 175. The charge will therefore arise even though the loan released carried a full commercial rate of interest or was used for a qualifying purpose. Similarly,

---

[112] ITEPA 2003, s 181(2), ex TA 1988, s 160(5), words added by FA 1994, s 88(2).
[113] Taxes (Interest Rate) Regulations 1989 (SI 1989/1297, as amended), reg 5.
[114] ITEPA 2003, s 174(5)(b); in this case the loan is not employment related.
[115] ITEPA 2003, s 189(1)(b); see ITEPA explanatory note change 34.
[116] ITEPA 2003, s 189, ex TA 1988, s 161(5). See also ITEPA Technical Note 19.

the charge will arise even though the loan was released or written off after the employment ceased (section 188(2)). Where the employment later terminates or ceases to be within these rules, but the loan continues, any subsequent replacement loan will also be subject to these rules—unless it is itself under these rules regarded as having been obtained by reason of another employment (section 188(3)).

16.4.5 Living Accommodation

Where living accommodation is provided for E by reason of E's employment (or for E's family or household), E is chargeable under ITEPA 2003, Part 3, Chapter 5 on the cash equivalent of the benefit.[117] It is immaterial whether or not the terms on which the accommodation is provided constitute a fair bargain.[118] There is now a statutory rule which applies where the accommodation is provided for more than one employee.[119]

16.4.5.1 Otherwise Chargeable

Section 102 does not apply where the accommodation is chargeable to E as income under some other provision. One way[120] in which E would be 'otherwise chargeable' is by coming within the general principle of convertibility (see §15.2 above); E would be chargeable on the profit which could have been made by sub-letting the property or granting licences. However, E would also be chargeable under the general principle if the employer offered E £20 as an alternative to the accommodation, ie a salary sacrifice. This proved tempting for taxpayers and was stopped by legislation in 1996. Section 109 states that the provision of a cash alternative does not prevent section 102 from applying.[121] This makes section 102 the prior but not exclusive charge; any excess may be taxed under section 62.

16.4.5.2 Provided by Reason of Employment?

Whether living accommodation is provided by reason of the employment is a question of fact; however, it is deemed to be so provided if it is provided by the employer. This assumption may be avoided if it is shown that (a) the employer is an individual and provides the accommodation in the normal course of domestic, family or personal relationships (section 97(2)); or (b) the accommodation is provided by a local authority for its employee on terms which are no more favourable than those for non-employees similarly circumstanced (section 98), a rule which means that a council house tenant cannot be charged extra rent simply because of working for the council. Rule (a) applies only where the employer is an individual, presumably because only an individual can have domestic family or personal relationships; this leaves open the case of a family business run by a trust where, for example, the owner of the business has died and the estate has not yet been

---

[117] ITEPA 2003, ss 97, 102 *et seq;* and see definition of 'annual value' in s 110; see ITEPA explanatory note changes 23 and 24. On period for which benefit accrues, see ITEPA Technical Note 16.
[118] ITEPA 2003, s 97(1A).
[119] ITEPA 2003, s 108; see ITEPA explanatory note change 22.
[120] E is not chargeable under ITEPA 2003, s 203 (ex TA 1988, s 154) because s 202 (ex s 154(2)) excludes s 203 if any of Chs 3 to 7 apply.
[121] The predecessor of s 109 (TA 1988, s 146A) was added by FA 1996, s 106; it also applies to s 105 (ex TA 1988, s 146).

administered. If the accommodation is provided by someone other than the employer and so escapes the deeming provision, it may still give rise to tax if it can be shown that the accommodation was in fact provided by reason of the employment (as may be the case if the accommodation is provided by an associated company or trust).

16.4.5.3 Scope of Charge

Section 102 applies to living accommodation;[122] it does not apply to ancillary services, which are usually incapable of being turned into money and so will not give rise to any charge, except, perhaps, under ITEPA 2003, section 203. Such liability under section 203 may be capped by section 315.[123]

16.4.5.4 Exceptions from Section 102: Non-beneficial Occupation

If the accommodation is provided by reason of the employment, the cost will still not be chargeable if the taxpayer comes within any of three situations which correspond broadly with non-beneficial occupation which may be derived from the old cases of representative occupation:[124]

(1)   Where it is necessary for the proper performance of the employee's duties that E should reside in the accommodation.
(2)   Where the employment is of a type where it is customary to provide living accommodation, and the accommodation is provided for the better performance of the duties of the employment.
(3)   Where, there being a special threat to E's security, special security arrangements are in force and E resides in the accommodation as part of those arrangements.

Exceptions (1) and (2) are themselves excluded (so that a charge to income tax will arise under section 102 after all) if the taxpayer is a director of the company providing the accommodation; however, this is softened by excluding a director who works full time and does not have a material interest in the company (section 99(3)–(5)).

A further exception exists as regards a home outside UK owned through a company. ITEPA 2003, section 100A, added by FA 2008, is a retrospective provision but wholly in the taxpayer's favour, and therefore does not disturb people. It applies to living accommodation outside the UK provided for a director (D) or a member of the director's family. The company must be wholly owned by D, or by D and other individuals. The company must be the holding company for that property at the relevant time. Section 100B provides exceptions, eg if the property was acquired at an undervalue or to avoid tax. It affects a UK resident individual who decided to put a foreign holiday home into a company and who did not appreciate that a charge might arise. Quite why this group should be absolved from tax and not, say, those who had accommodation within the UK or who were well aware of

---

[122] ITEPA 2003, s 97, ex TA 1988, s 145(7).
[123] If the occupation comes within the categories of non-beneficial occupation (see §15.4.1.4), the charge under s 203 (ex TA 1988, s 154) must not exceed 10% of the total emoluments (ITEPA 2003, s 313, ex TA 1988, s 163); see below §15.4.7.
[124] ITEPA 2003, ss 99(1) and (2) and 100; on Chevening House, see s 101 and note that s 315 does not apply.

the liability and therefore did not put their property into a company, is not at all clear. The HMRC explanatory notes suggests that otherwise many people would have been liable to penalties. This seems insufficient.

16.4.5.5 Exceptions—Examples

Employees coming within exception (1) in §15.4.1.4 above will include caretakers, hotel managers, and other staff who are compelled to live in hotels, and the bank manager in *Tennant v Smith*.[125] For this group the necessity to be in occupation must be due to the relationship between the duties and the accommodation, and not to the personal exigencies of the taxpayer.[126] Exception (2) covers farm workers, miners and even some university teachers. The requirement that it should be 'customary' to provide the accommodation in that kind of employment is an interesting one; customs may change and may, presumably, be satisfied even though occupation is not required by the employer. The rule that the provision must be for the better performance of the duties is presumably a question of fact and is to be determined objectively, paying attention to—but without being bound by—the terms of the employment and the views of the employer. In *Vertigan v Brady*[127] the taxpayer failed to come within exception (2) because the provision of accommodation was not sufficiently common to be 'customary'. Among the issues considered by the court were (a) how many employers in this industry provided accommodation, (b) for how long the practice had continued, and (c) whether it had achieved general acceptance.

16.4.5.6 The Charge

Assuming for the moment that the cost of providing the accommodation does not exceed £75,000, the charge is on the rental value to the employee of the accommodation for that period. A deduction may be made for any sum made good by E to the person at whose cost the accommodation is provided (section 105). Rent paid by the employee is therefore deductible. Benefits in kind provided in return may also, in principle, be taken into account, but only if they relate clearly to the accommodation.[128] The rental value is calculated by reference to the annual value under section 110. If those at whose cost the accommodation is provided pay rent which is higher than the annual value, that higher figure is to be taken (section 105(4)). In the absence of any provision directing otherwise, it is to be assumed that in calculating the annual rent hypothetically payable, account is taken of all the terms of the occupation, even those imposed in connection with the office or employment. The employee may deduct from the value as ascertained any sums allowable under ITEPA 2003, Part 5, Chapters 2 and 5 (section 364).

In 2009, ITEPA 2003, section 105 was amended, and new sections 105A and 105B introduced, to stop attempts to avoid tax through the payment of a lease premium rather than a full market rent for the use of the accommodation. The new rules require the value of the lease premium to be taken into account when computing the benefit charge where the lease is for less than 10 years. The charge related to the premium is computed using a formula allocating the lease premium to the relevant period based on the length of the relevant

---

[125] [1892] AC 150, 3 TC 158, HL.
[126] *Vertigan v Brady* [1988] STC 91, 60 TC 624.
[127] *Ibid.*
[128] *Stones v Hall* [1989] STC 138, 60 TC 738.

period as a proportion of the total lease period, and also takes into account the effect of break clauses (if any).

16.4.5.7 Addition to the Charge Using Calculation Under ITEPA 2003, Section 106

If E is taxable under ITEPA 2003, Part 3, Chapter 5 and the accommodation cost more than £75,000 to provide, the charge is increased. The excess over £75,000 is calculated under section 106 and E is treated as receiving a loan of the amount by which the cost exceeds £75,000, and a percentage of that loan is treated as income in that year. The figure of £75,000 has not been changed since the section was introduced in 1983.[129] One of the (sensible) Rewrite changes is to make this extra liability part of the overall liability in respect of the living accommodation.

For sections 105 and 106 the cost of providing the accommodation is the purchase price plus improvement expenditure, less any amount paid by E as reimbursement for the expenditure or as consideration for the tenancy (section 104). If, when E first occupies the accommodation, the person providing the accommodation has held an estate or interest in the property for the previous six years, the market value at the date on which E first occupies the property is substituted for the purchase price.[130] Payments to reimburse expenditure incurred in acquiring the accommodation are deductible; market value is defined in section 107(3).[131] Employees are taxed on the additional value to them of the accommodation, which is:

[**(Cost of providing accommodation—£75,000)** × **appropriate %**]—**excess rent**

'Excess rent' is the amount by which any rent paid by the employee exceeds the value to the employee of the accommodation. The percentage is the official rate of interest set for the purpose of calculating the benefit of beneficial loans to employees in force on 6 April beginning the year of assessment.[132]

Example

On 6 April 2006, E begins to occupy a house provided by X, E's employer. The house had been purchased by X on 9 November 2002[133] for £196,000; X then spent £8,000 on improvements. E reimbursed X £1,000 of the expenditure and pays a rent which exceeds the value to him of the property by £2,000. The official rate of interest on 6 April 2006 was 5%.

The cost to the employer of providing the property is (£196,000 + £8,000)—£1,000 = £203,000. The additional value of the property to E is [(£203,000—£75,000) × 5%]—£2,000 = £4,400. E is therefore taxed on an additional benefit of £4,400 in 2006–07.

---

[129] FA 1977, s 33A added by FA 1983.

[130] ITEPA 2003, s 107, ex TA 1988, s 146(6), but this does not apply if the employee's first occupation began before 31 March 1983 (s 146(8)).

[131] ITEPA 2003, s 107(3), ex TA 1988, s 146(11).

[132] The rate was 4% for 2010–11: see http://www.hmrc.gov.uk/rates/interest.htm.

[133] If X had purchased the property in 1997, the market value of the property on 6 April 2006 would have been substituted for the purchase price.

16.4.6 Living Accommodation: 10% Cap for Certain Ancillary Services in Certain Cases

As we have seen, the provision of living accommodation is specifically excluded from ITEPA 2003, Part 3, Chapter 10 and is governed by Part 3, Chapter 5. As we have also seen, the exception in section 99(1) and (2) for the first two cases of non-beneficial occupation does not apply if the employee is a director of the company providing the accommodation, or of an associated company, unless (a) the employee has no material interest, and (b) the employment is either as a full-time working director, or the company is a charity or is non profit-making.[134] These rules have to be recalled when considering section 315.

The provision of certain ancillary services such as maintenance is different and does fall within Chapter 10. However, where the occupation is excluded by sections 99(1), (2) or 100, the taxable amount is subject to a cap under (the far-away) section 315 in ITEPA 2003, Part 4, Chapter 11. The rule applies to sums in respect of:

(1) heating, lighting or cleaning the premises;
(2) repairs (other than structural repairs),[135] maintenance or decoration; and
(3) the provision of furniture or other appurtenances or effects which are normal for domestic occupation.

Where these exceed 10% of the net amount of the earnings from the employment, the excess is not taxed.[136] Where the accommodation is provided for part of the year but the employment is for a longer (or shorter) period, the percentage is applied to the net amount of the earnings from the employment attributable to the period of occupation. Any sums made good by the employee are deducted from the 10% cap. The 10% limit does not apply where the director has a stake of more than 5% or is a part-time director of a profit-seeking concern (because such a person is not exempt from Part 3, Chapter 5). The 10% limit does not apply where the ancillary services are other than those listed; liability in respect of such services is without limit. The specific exception of structural repairs is presumably because the Revenue accept the view expressed in *Luke v IRC*[137] that these are part of the cost of acquiring or producing the asset.[138] Costs to the owner as owner, such as insurance and fuel duty, are likely part of the cost of providing the living accommodation and so fall within Part 3, Chapter 5.[139]

---

[134] ITEPA 2003, s 99(3)–(5); ESC A61 does not apply to clergymen not in lower-paid employment.

[135] Including repairs which would be the landlord's responsibility under a lease within the Landlord and Tenant Act 1985, ss 11, 16, 36.

[136] ITEPA 2003, s 315, especially calculation rules in s 315(5).

[137] [1963] 1 All ER 655, 40 TC 630; FA 1976, s 62(5).

[138] See former TA 1988, s 156(5)(b). This was the line taken by Lord Guest, Lord Pearce and by Lord Reid ('this is a case of any port in a storm', [1963] 1 All ER 655, 665, 40 TC 630, 646) and by Lord Dilhorne, *ibid*, 661, 643. The consequence of the repair will be an increase in the annual value of the premises. To hold that the expense of repair did not fall within s 156(5) and then to increase the annual value would be a flagrant case of double taxation.

[139] See, however, *Luke v IRC*, above, on the forerunner of s 154.

16.4.7 Scholarships

ITTOIA 2005, section 776, which is unaffected by ITEPA 2003, provides a general exemption from income tax for scholarship income. ITEPA 2003, section 215 restricts this exemption from Part 3, Chapter 10 to the person holding the scholarship—reversing the decision of the House of Lords in *Wicks v Firth*.[140] As a result of sections 212 and 215, a director or employee receives a taxable benefit if a scholarship is provided to a member of his family or household under arrangements made by his employer or a person connected with E. The charge is on the amount of the payment from the fund to the person holding the scholarship.[141] The charge does not apply if the award is by an individual employer in the course of the normal domestic family or personal relationships (section 212). No taxable benefit arises if the scholarship is awarded under a trust or scheme to a person receiving full-time education, and not more than 25% of the payments made under the trust in that year would have been taxable were it not for this provision (section 213), ie the payments would have been exempt under ITTOIA 2005, section 776 but for ITEPA 2003, section 212.

16.4.8 Director's Tax Paid by Employer

If an employer fails to deduct tax from a director's earnings under PAYE, but that tax is accounted for to the Revenue by someone other than the director, a chargeable benefit arises equal to the tax accounted for (section 223). The benefit is reduced by the amount of any reimbursement made by the director. An amount accounted for after the employment ends is treated as a benefit of the last year of assessment in which the director was employed by the company, unless it was accounted for after the director's death (section 223(6)). The provision applies only to directors, and then only if they have no material interest in the company (ie not more than 5% interest) and they are full-time working directors, or the company is non profit-making or a charity (section 223(7)).

16.5 Vouchers and Credit Tokens

The legislation concerning vouchers (cash and non-cash) and credit tokens is one area where the format of the legislation has been greatly improved by the ITEPA 2003.[142] Part 3, Chapter 4 begins with cash vouchers. A voucher provided to an employee by reason of his employment that may be exchanged for cash is taxed in full on that exchange amount and subject to the PAYE system.[143] Cash vouchers do not give rise to a charge if they are available to the public generally or issued under a Revenue-approved scheme, or if the sums themselves would be exempt from tax, eg because would not be employment income of the employee if paid directly.[144] Where the voucher is attached to a card, the income arises

---

[140] [1983] STC 25, 56 TC 318.

[141] ITEPA 2003, s 214; see ITEPA explanatory note change 40; this rule avoids very complex calculations.

[142] See ITEPA explanatory notes changes 18–20.

[143] ITEPA 2003, s 81; on presumptions and families see, ss 73(2) and 74.

[144] ITEPA 2003, ss 78–80; the Revenue must be sure of being able to collect the tax to be charged for the sums on money received and sure that the tax can be collected under the PAYE scheme, s 79(2).

at the time of attachment (section 73(3)). For the voucher to be a cash voucher it must be exchangeable for a sum of money not substantially less than the expense incurred by the person providing the voucher; this rule is disregarded where the money is substantially less but the difference is due to the provision of sickness benefit (sections 75(1) and 76).

A non-cash voucher, including a 'cheque voucher',[145] is one that may be exchanged for money, goods or services—including childcare and transport. It gives rise to liability if it is provided to the employee or family by reason of employment (sections 82 and 83). The liability is on an amount equal to the cost to the person at whose cost the voucher and the money, goods or services for which it may be exchanged are provided;[146] the value of the benefit is ignored (section 95). The liability normally arises when the expense is incurred[147] or, if later, when the voucher is received, although the appropriation of the voucher (eg by sticking it on a card held for the employee) is treated as receipt by the employee.[148] There are exemptions for certain non-cash vouchers, which include (a) vouchers available to the public generally, and (b) travel concessions for certain employees of passenger transport undertakings under a scheme approved before 26 March 1982 (sections 85 and 86). Similar rules apply to credit tokens and credit cards (sections 90–94). When employees use a credit token to obtain money, goods or services, they are charged to income tax on earnings from employment equal to the expense involved; the costs of providing the token and of any interest charges are ignored.[149]

Relief is given when the vouchers or credit tokens are used to meet proper employment expenses, or where the employee makes good the cost involved (sections 362 and 363). In addition, Part 4, Chapter 6 provides 14 exemptions for non-cash vouchers and six for credit tokens which are used to provide benefits which are exempt when given directly (sections 266 and 267), and then provides further exemptions for incidental overnight expenses, certain benefits from cars, vans and lorries, and also small gifts of vouchers and tokens from third parties.[150] Gifts are small so long as they do not exceed £250 per employee each year (section 324(6)). For the practice where incentive award schemes are provided by way of voucher, see Statement of Practice SP 6/85. Section 96A also provides that the Treasury may make regulations to exempt the use of vouchers and tokens to obtain benefits which are exempt under Part 4 of ITEPA 2003.

ITEPA 2003, section 270A allows a limited exemption for 'qualifying childcare vouchers' provided for an employee to enable the employee to obtain the provision of care for a child.[151] If the relevant conditions in section 270A are satisfied, liability to tax under Part 3, Chapter 4 arises only in respect of so much of the cash equivalent of the benefit as exceeds the 'exempt amount' of per employee for each week of qualifying childcare provided by a registered or approved caregiver (other than the partner of the employee or a relative

---

[145] Defined in ITEPA 2003, s 84; the charging provision is s 87, ex TA 1988, s 141.

[146] ITEPA 2003, s 87(2), ex TA 1988, s 141. The formula is slightly modified for transport vouchers (s 87(4)) and cheque vouchers (s 87(5)).

[147] ITEPA 2003, s 88(1). For cheque vouchers, the year is that in which the voucher is handed over in exchange for the goods, etc, ITEPA 2003, s 86(2).

[148] FA 1988, ss 47, 48.

[149] ITEPA 2003, s 94. These interest charges were originally created to give rise to liability under FA 1981, s 71, but this was removed by FA 1982, s 45.

[150] ITEPA 2003, ss 268–270, 270, making a cross reference to s 324.

[151] ITEPA 2003, s 270A, added by FA 2004, s 78 and Sch 13, para 2. 'Childcare voucher' is defined in s 84(2A).

of the child where the care is provided in the child or parent's home).[152] More than one person may be entitled to an exempt amount in respect of the same child, but an employee is not entitled to an exempt amount under both section 270A and section 318A (Part 4, Chapter 11 exemption for childcare provision for an employee: see §16.3.3.1). The child must be a child or stepchild of the employee who is maintained (wholly or partly) at the employee's expense, or be a person for whom the employee has parental responsibility and who is resident with the employee. The care must be provided under a scheme that is open to employees generally, or to those at a particular location. FA 2005 widened this exemption by excluding the administration costs of providing the voucher for the year.[153]

FA 2011 reduced the limit on the exempt amount of qualifying childcare vouchers for higher-rate and basic-rate taxpayers from £55 per week to £22 and £28, respectively; the new limits do not apply to existing members of schemes who joined before 6 April 2011. It also slightly eased the requirement that the scheme be open to employees generally where the vouchers are offered under a relevant salary sacrifice arrangements, or relevant flexible remuneration arrangements. At Budget 2016, the Government confirmed it was introducing a new childcare scheme in 2017 to benefit employees and also the self-employed. Parents, employers and other family members will be able to pay into an online account to cover cost of childcare paid to a registered provider. For every 80p contributed, the government will add 20p, up to a cap of £10,000 of costs. Transitional relief under the existing employer-supported childcare scheme will be available.

16.6 Minor Receipts

Part 3 of ITEPA 2003 began with Chapter 1 which contained just one provision—section 62 on earnings—which, as we have seen, is the counterpart to the old section 19 of the Taxes Act 1988. Chapters 2–11 have dealt with taxable benefits and done so in a way which is not always comfortable. The final chapter of Part 3—Chapter 12, entitled 'Payments Treated as Earnings'—deals with a variety of provisions, some of which are sometimes referred to elsewhere in this text. These are:

(1) Section 221—sickness benefits. Qualifying sickness benefit payments are treated as income for the period of absence to which they relate. If the payment come from a fund to which both employer and employees have contributed, the charge is restricted to that part attributable to the employer's contribution. This is not discussed elsewhere.

(2) Section 222—payments by employer on account of tax where deduction not possible (see §13.4.2.2 above). These refer to 'notional' payments under various PAYE rules, viz, ss 687, 689, and 693–700 if the employee does not make good the tax to the employer. The tax element is treated as earned 30 days after that of the notional payment.

(3) Section 223—payments on account of director's tax other than by director—see §16.4.8.

---

[152] ITEPA 2003, s 270A, cross-referencing ss 318A–318D.
[153] FA 2005, s 15 amending ITEPA s 270A.

(4)   Section 224—payments to non-approved pension arrangements under TA 1988, section 648 (not rewritten at present). See ITEPA explanatory notes changes 104–106.

(5)   Sections 225 and 226—payments and other valuable consideration given for undertakings—see §14.4.5.

16.7   Exemptions and Exclusions

This section brings together a number of distinct but related rules dealing with earnings. To follow the language of ITEPA 2003, it brings together (a) some income falling within Part 3, Chapter 1; (b) two types of income that come within some of Part 3, Chapters 2–11 (the benefits code); and (c) other income that comes within Part 3, Chapter 12. In the rather mystifying language of ITEPA 2003, section 7, (a) are 'general earnings' while (b) and (c) are 'treated as earnings'. For completeness, section 7(6) mentions the receipts in ITEPA 2003, Part 6. Sums within Part 6 are not 'earnings', neither are they 'treated as earnings'; rather, they 'count as employment income'. Certain earnings from securities and securities also 'count as employment income' and are discussed in overview in chapter seventeen of this book.

Lastly, this section also draws together some of the exemptions in Part 4 of the Act. Here again the ITEPA 2003 has some peculiarities all of its own, with some rules which qualify or limit particular types of charge in Part 3 being treated as exemptions, and so in Part 4, many sections away from the charge they are limiting. A list of the headings in Part 4 concludes the chapter. One of the more striking features of the ITEPA 2003 is the decision to place exemptions from income tax in a separate part, Part 4 (sections 227–326). The advantage of this is that it gathers exemptions together whether they are from all parts of the charge or only from some of the heads. One disadvantage is the same as the advantage; gathering these things together when the charge is only from one head makes little sense except to emphasise the diverse or chaotic nature of the current UK employment income tax. Unfortunately it is also true that there are exemptions which are not in Part 4. The structure of Part 4 has one other advantage, in that it highlights the distinction between an exemption and a deduction. Part 4 begins with some new terminology. Earnings-only exemptions are defined by section 227(2) as an exemption which prevents liability to tax arising in respect of *earnings* but does not prevent liability from arising in respect of other employment income. Employment income exemption means an exemption which prevents liability to tax in respect of employment income at all. Perhaps the legislation could have said particular exemption and general exemption.[154]

On timing, ITEPA 2003, section 19, dealing with non-money earnings, directs that if the amount is treated as earnings for a particular year then it is income of that year. Section 19 gives no further rules as to when in the year it is so treated. If that does not provide the answer, the benefit is treated as received in the year in which it is provided.[155]

---

[154] For explanation of the ITEPA approach, see ITEPA Technical Note 28.
[155] ITEPA explanatory note change 2 and ITEPA Technical Note 14.

16.7.1 Relocation Benefits and Expenses

Part 4, Chapter 7 (sections 271–289) was introduced in 1993 to replace earlier concession-ary reliefs,[156] and grants relief for certain sums paid, whether to the employees or another on their behalf (eg the removal company) in respect of various benefits and expenses. The present limit or ceiling of £8,000[157] may be increased by Treasury Order;[158] this figure has not been increased since 1993. Payments must be made or benefits provided before the end of the year following the year in which the employment is changed or moved, or a new job started; this day is now called the 'limitation day'.[159] The exemption does not apply if the earnings come within sections 22 or 26.

Eligible removal benefits[160] and expenses are those made on: disposal of the old resi-dence; acquisition of the new residence; abortive acquisition; transporting belongings; travelling and subsistence; and bridging loans, including a beneficial bridging loan.[161] Also allowed are expenses incurred by the employee as a result of the change of residence, on the purchase of domestic goods intended to replace goods used at the first residence but not suitable for use in the new one—subject to offset for sums received on the sale of the goods from the first home, which must be brought into account.[162] Vouchers for such expenses are also included.[163]

The expenses must be reasonably incurred by the employee in connection with a change of sole or main residence.[164] Therefore:

(1) the change of residence must result from the employee starting a new employment, or from an alteration in the employee's duties (without a change of employer) or an alteration in the place at which those duties are carried out;

(2) the change must be made wholly or mainly to allow the employee to have his resi-dence within a reasonable daily travelling distance of the place where the duties are to be performed; and

(3) the employee's former home must not be within a reasonable daily travelling distance from the place where the new duties are to be performed.[165]

If the claim is based on a change in the duties of the employment or the place of employ-ment (as opposed to a change of employer), no relief is available if the former home was

[156] Inland Revenue Press Release, 16 March 1993, para 2; [1993] *Simon's Tax Intelligence* 439. The concessions superseded were A5 and A64 based on *Hochstrasser v Mayes*.

[157] ITEPA 2003, s 287.

[158] ITEPA 2003, s 716.

[159] ITEPA 2003, s 274, ex TA 1988, Sch 11A, para 3(3).

[160] ITEPA 2003, ss 272(1) benefits and 272(3) (expenses). Both eligible expenses and eligible benefits may be amended by Treasury Order (ITEPA 2003, s 286, ex TA 1988, Sch 11A, paras 15, 23); this applies to ITEPA 2003, ss 277–285 and not just ss 279–285 (FA 2004, Sch 17, para 9).

[161] ITEPA 2003, s 272, referring to ss 277–281, ex TA 1988, Sch 11A, paras 7–13; see also Inland Revenue Press Release, 14 April 1993, [1993] *Simons Tax Intelligence* 626. On express inclusion of costs for children, see ITEPA explanatory note change 62.

[162] ITEPA 2003, ss 272 and 284; on loans, see ITEPA explanatory note change 61; and on the ending of the deduction of sale proceeds where goods are sold, see ITEPA explanatory note change 65.

[163] ITEPA 2003, s 272(2); see ITEPA explanatory note change 60.

[164] ITEPA 2003, ss 272(1) and 273, ex TA 1988, Sch 11A, paras 3, 25.

[165] ITEPA 2003, s 273, ex TA 1988, Sch 11A, para 5.

beyond reasonable daily travelling distance from the former place of employment.[166] There is no need actually to sell the old residence to qualify for this relief—it is sufficient that it is no longer the only or main residence, eg where the old house is rented out or used only at weekends. The Revenue view seems to be that the family must also use the new home as their main residence, but that this is not required of employees coming to work from abroad.[167]

In determining whether the limit of £8,000 has been reached, the rules in the benefits code (Part 3, Chapter 10) are applied to bring in the cash equivalent of the benefits. Any sums which would otherwise fall within Part 3, Chapter 5 (living accommodation) are also brought in—less sums made good by the employee.[168] If the relocation package includes a beneficial loan on which tax is chargeable and the employee has not used up the £8,000 exemption on the other costs of moving house, the bridging loan, or part of it, may be included to use up the total relief available by removing days from the period for which tax is chargeable in respect of the loan.[169] In the case of foreign removals, sums allowed under other rules are not counted against the £8,000 limit.[170] A further rule excludes taxable car and van facilities.[171] These are left to be taxed under the relevant part of the benefits code (Part 6) and so do not affect the £8,000 total here.

16.7.2 Training, Scholarship and Apprenticeship Schemes

ITEPA 2003, section 311 is concerned with helping an employee get new skills with a view to changing employment, hence its appearance in Part 4, Chapter 10. The section provides an exemption in respect of expenditure incurred by an employer in connection with training schemes; the exemption allows the employer to deduct the expenditure, while exempting the employee from any liability to tax.[172]

The exemption is given for expenditure reimbursed or incurred by the employer in connection with a qualifying course of training. The employee must have been employed for two years and the opportunity to take the course must be available either generally to employees and former employees or to a particular class of such persons.[173] The course must be designed to impart or improve skills or knowledge relevant to and intended to be used in the course of gainful employment (including self-employment) of any description, and the course must be entirely devoted to the teaching and/or practical application of such skills or knowledge.[174] In addition, the course must not last more

---

[166] ITEPA 2003, s 273(4), ex TA 1988, Sch 11A, para 5(4).

[167] Inland Revenue Press Release, 14 April 1993, [1993] *Simon's Tax Intelligence* 626.

[168] ITEPA 2003, s 287, ex TA 1988, Sch 11A, para 24. On calculation rules to prevent double counting, see ITEPA explanatory note change 66.

[169] ITEPA 2003, s 288, ex TA 1988, s 191B.

[170] ITEPA 2003, s 282, ex TA 1988, Sch 11A, paras 12(4), 21A(7), (8).

[171] ITEPA 2003, s 283; see ITEPA explanatory note change 63.

[172] ITEPA 2003, s 311, ex TA 1988, s 588(1) (Sch E); see also CTA 2009, s 74, ex TA 1988, s 588(3) for deduction in computing profits and CTA 2009, s 1221, ex TA 1988, s 588(4) for treatment as expense of management of investment company.

[173] ITEPA 2003, s 311(4), ex TA 1988, s 589(3)—the two-year employment condition means two years before he starts the course or ends the employment, whichever is the earlier.

[174] ITEPA 2003, s 311(3), ex TA 1988, s 589(3).

than two years; the old condition that all the teaching and practical application must take place in the UK has been removed, presumably because of EU freedom of establishment considerations.

The course must be undertaken by an employee (or former employee) with a view to retraining. The course cannot be regarded as undertaken with a view to retraining unless it is begun while employed by the employer or within one year of ceasing to be so; it is also necessary that the employee should in any event cease to be so employed within two years of the end of the course.[175] This underlines the purpose of the provision—to encourage employers and employees to get retrained and then re-employed or self-employed elsewhere. Where the employee attends a full-time course at a university or technical college, payments by the employer may qualify as scholarship income; a Statement of Practice sets out the relevant conditions.[176]

16.7.3 Work-related Training

Part 4, Chapter 4[177] prevents any tax liability arising from the provision of certain benefits, or the payment or reimbursement of expenses connected with such benefits. The benefits are work-related training (section 250) and the individual learning account (section 255).

Section 250 provides an exemption for the expenditure incurred by the employer and the benefit received by the employee for work-related training. This differs from section 311 in that the training is for an employee who is to be kept on the books of the employer and who is on the books when the expense is incurred.[178] This legislation replaced a previous concession.[179] The course must be 'work related' and not be within a prohibited list of activities.[180] Where the employee has to bear the expenses they are deductible.[181]

16.8   Other Exemptions

Part 4, Chapter 2 Mileage allowances and passenger payments

— Mileage payments (sections 229–232)—no liability for approved mileage payments.
— Passenger payments (sections 233–234) applies to exclude the charge arising under the rules for cars (section 120) or vans (section 154).

---

[175] ITEPA 2003, s 311(4)(b), ex TA 1988, s 589(4); re-employment within two years is a breach of the conditions and this triggers a charge under s 312; any breach of these conditions has to be reported within 60 days of the employer coming to know of it and the normal six-year time-limit for assessments runs from the end of the year in which the breach occurred; there are also Revenue information-gathering powers in s 312.
[176] Statement of Practice SP 4/86.
[177] ITEPA 2003, ss 250–260, ex TA 1988, s 200B–200H, added by FA 1998 and FA 2000. See ITEPA explanatory note changes 51–54. See also ITEPA Technical Notes 30 and 31.
[178] *Silva v Charnock* [2002] STC 425.
[179] ESC A63.
[180] ITEPA 2003, s 253, ex TA 1988, s 200C.
[181] ESC A64 (now listed as obsolete).

Part 4, Chapter 3 Other transport, travel and subsistence. See also §18.2

— Parking (section 237) (see ITEPA Technical Note 29).
— Modest use of heavy goods vehicle (section 238).
— Discharging liability of employee—no tax liability apart from fuel charge (section 149)—where charge arises under cars or van rules or would do but for section 239.
— Incidental overnight expenses and benefits (sections 240 (on which see ITEPA explanatory note change 44) and 241).
— Travel by unpaid directors of non-for-profit companies (section 241A) and travel where directorship held as part of trade or profession (section 241B)
— Works transport services (section 242).
— Support for public bus services (section 243).
— Cycles and cyclist's safety equipment (section 244).
— Travelling and subsistence during public transport strikes (section 245).
— Transport between work and home for disabled employees: general (sections 246 and 247).
— Transport home: late night working and failure of car-sharing arrangements (section 248—see ITEPA explanatory note changes 47–50).
— Emergency vehicles for employees of certain emergency services (section 248A).

Part 4, Chapter 4 Exemptions: education and training

— Work-related training (sections 250–254—see §16.7.2).
— Individual learning account training (sections 255–260—see §16.7.3).

Part 4, Chapter 5 Exemptions: recreational benefits

— Recreational facilities (sections 261–263).
— Annual parties and functions (s 264).
— Third party entertainment (section 265, and was confined to Part 3, Chapter 10 but is now general—see ITEPA explanatory note changes 56–58).

Part 4, Chapter 6 Exemptions: non-cash vouchers and credit tokens

— See §16.5 above.

Part 4, Chapter 7 Exemptions: removal benefits and expenses

— See §16.7.1 above.

Part 4, Chapter 7A Exemption for paid or reimbursed expenses

— See §16.2 above.

Part 4, Chapter 8 Exemptions: special kinds of employees

— Accommodation benefits, outgoings and allowances of ministers of religion (sections 290, 290A and 290B) and exemption from certain provisions of the benefits code for low-paid ministers of religion (sections 290C-290G).
— MPs, government ministers etc, Termination payments to MPs and others who are ceasing to hold office, including, thanks to FA 2008, the Greater London authority; Overnight expenses allowances of MPs; Overnight expenses of other elected representatives; UK and European travel expenses of MPs and other representatives; and Transport and subsistence for Government ministers, etc. (sections 291–295).
— MEPs—FA 2009, section 56 extends the equivalent of double-tax relief to salary payments made by the EU to MEPs now subject to Union tax. Payments of transitional allowance will also be treated as termination payments, bringing the tax treatment into line with similar payments to MPs.
— Armed forces (sections 296–298): Armed forces' leave travel facilities; Armed forces' food, drink and mess allowances; Reserve and auxiliary forces' training allowances. Members of the armed forces of the Crown who receive the designated 'Operational Allowance' are not liable to tax on it; Council tax relief for HM forces; Continuity of Education Allowances for HM forces.
— Crown employees foreign service allowances (section 299).
— Consuls, foreign agents etc (sections 300–302).
— Visiting forces and staff of designated allied headquarters (section 303).
— Experts seconded to European Commission and other EU bodies (section 304 and 304A).
— Offshore oil and gas workers; mainland transfers (section 305).
— Miners, etc coal and allowances in lieu of coal (section 306); see ITEPA explanatory note change 69.
— Carers board and lodging (section 306A).
— Sporting testimonials (section 306B)

Part 4, Chapter 9 Exemptions: pension provision

— Death or retirement benefit provision (section 307); see ITEPA explanatory note change 70.
— Exemption of contributions to approved personal pension arrangements (section 308) and overseas pension schemes (section 308A), plus independent advice on conversions and transfers of benefits (section 308B).

Part 4, Chapter 10 Exemptions: termination of employment

— Limited exemptions for statutory redundancy payments (section 309).
— Outplacement benefits; sections 310–312 covering counselling and other outplacement services and retraining courses. See ITEPA explanatory note changes 71–74.

Part 4, Chapter 10 Bonus payments by certain employers (sections 312A-312I)
    Part 4, Chapter 11 Miscellaneous exemptions

— Living accommodation (sections 313–315), covering repairs and alterations to living accommodation (section 313); payment of council tax, etc paid for certain living accommodation (section 314—see ITEPA explanatory note change 75) and limited exemption for expenses connected with certain living accommodation (section 315—see ITEPA explanatory note change 76), ie non-beneficial occupations including those necessary for the proper performance of duties.

— Work accommodation, supplies and services used in employment duties (section 316); Home workers additional household expenses (section 316A); Workplace meals (section 317) (see ITEPA explanatory note change 77) and note that FA 2010, section 60 amended ITEPA 2003, section 317 to deny the exemption for the benefit of free or subsidised workplace meals where an employee gives up the right to earnings or other benefits in return for such meals; Childcare (section 318); Limited exemption for other childcare (section 318A); Mobile telephones (section 319); Eye tests and special corrective appliances required by health and safety regulations (section 320A); Health screening and medical check-up, one per year (section 320B); Recommended medical treatment up to £500 (section 320C). Note that of these sections, section 316 is only relevant to Part 3, Chapter 10. Sections 317, 318, 318A, and 319, which used to be confined to Chapter 10, are now general sections, as are sections 316A, 320A, 320B and 320C.

— Awards and gifts (sections 321–324), covering suggestion awards (see ITEPA explanatory note change 78), long service awards (see ITEPA explanatory note change 79) and small gifts from third parties (see ITEPA explanatory note change 59).

— Overseas medical treatment (section 325) and health and employment insurance payments (section 325A).

— Expenses incidental to sale, etc of asset of a kind not normally met by transferor (section 326—see ITEPA explanatory note change 80).

— Fees related to monitoring schemes for vulnerable persons (section 326A).

— Advice relating to proposed employee shareholder agreements (section 326B).

17

Employee Share Schemes

17.1   Introduction

17.1.1 Legislative History: The Statute Outlined

Special rules applicable to certain employee share schemes are found in Part 7 of ITEPA 2003, which is entitled 'Employment income; income and exemptions relating to securities'.[1] Despite its length and complexity, Part 7 is not all-embracing; it begins (section 418)

---

[1] On FA 2003 changes, see Stratton [2003] BTR 374.

by warning the reader that these provisions are not the only ones that may be relevant, and specifically mentions section 62 and Part 3, Chapter 10.

Part 7 has two main purposes. First, it wants to restrict the use of securities, interests in securities and options to avoid tax, whether on employment income under ITEPA 2003, NICs or PAYE. The use of the term 'securities' is deliberately wider than shares. The tax treatments of options in relation to assets which are not on the list of securities, eg land, remain subject to general principles of the Act. Secondly, Part 7 wants to recognise the use of shares as an acceptable method of remuneration and so provide appropriate tax exemptions. The twin aims make for complicated rules. Part 7 relates to the structure of ITEPA 2003 through section 7(2), which classifies Part 7 income as an amount which 'counts as' employment income. Those chapters of Part 7 (Chapters 6–10) which provide rules for the use of securities (usually shares) as remuneration do not apply to office holders.[2] There are also special rules narrowing the normal international scope of ITEPA 2003.[3] These rules cannot generate a negative amount; such an amount is treated as nil.[4]

FA 2003 was enacted after ITEPA 2003 had come into force and provided a major overhaul of the legislation in this area. One may regret that the overhaul was not done earlier, since the resulting scarring of the statute book is not attractive. There were three principal changes. The first was the overdue extension of the rules to cover all securities and not just shares. The second was a new set of Chapters, 3A–3D, dealing with acquisitions above or below market value and the manipulation of values; this enabled the repeal of a number of other rules in ITEPA 2003, including two entire chapters of the benefits code—Part 3, Chapters 8 and 9. The third was the extension of PAYE and NICs to produce a uniform application across the rules.

The chapters of Part 7 are as follows: Chapter 1 deals with introductory matters; Chapter 2 with restricted securities, which may be seen as a wider version of the previous conditional interests in shares; Chapter 3 with convertible securities; Chapter 4 with post-acquisition benefits from securities; and Chapter 5 with securities options. Into this scheme FA 2003 planted Chapters 3A–3D, all concerned with potential avoidance through the manipulation of values, so Chapter 3A deals with securities with artificially depressed market value; Chapter 3B with securities acquired with artificially enhanced market value; Chapter 3C with securities acquired for less than market value; and Chapter 3D with securities disposed of for more than market value. Chapters 3A to 3D contain their own heads of charge. However, they do not radically alter the situations giving rise to charge—rather they have their own rules imposing tax on the acquisition of securities (Chapter 5) or the removal of restrictions on securities (Chapter 2), or the conversion of convertible securities (Chapter 3) and so on. Sometimes they adjust the value to be used for the other provision; more usually they apply their own head of charge.

As a result of these rules there are many opportunities for the Revenue to tax. It is a welcome feature of these rules that taxpayers may often elect that they do not apply. This usually means that taxpayers are given the chance to pay tax at once by reference to the

---

[2] ITEPA 2003, s 417(6).
[3] Eg ITEPA 2003, ss 421E and 474.
[4] ITEPA 2003, s 419; for explanation, see ITEPA Technical Note 43.

unmanipulated value rather than in stages. This is presumably in response to points made in the long period of consultation. Special rules apply to research institution spin out companies.

ITEPA 2003, Part 7, Chapter 6 on Share Incentive Plans, originally introduced by FA 2000, applies to all employees and has three distinct elements: free shares (maximum £3,600 pa), partnership shares (bought by the employee up to £1,800 pa) and matching shares (given on a 2-for-1 basis by the employer to match the partnership shares). Chapter 7 (sections 516–520) covers SAYE option schemes, while Chapter 8 (sections 521–526) addresses Company Share Option Schemes. Chapter 9 (sections 527–541) deals with Enterprise Management Incentives, also dating from FA 2000. This is a very generous share option scheme which is available only to a relatively few employees. Chapter 10 (sections 542–548) deals with priority share allocations.

Because these rules are often complex and restrictive, it is still common for employers to offer employees (usually only key employees) benefit schemes which fall outside the rules. Unapproved share option schemes became more popular after 1996 when the then approved schemes were limited to £30,000, but suffer from the rules also introduced in 1996 which make them subject not only to income tax but also NICs and PAYE.[5] Any discount on the grant of non-approved options is subject to NICs. 'Phantom schemes' exist under which a tax bonus is tied to the company's share price. Neither actual shares nor options are involved here. Other, intermediate schemes may be set up in which the company buys shares for an employee but holds them in trust.

The ability to earn profits in approved employee share schemes eligible for CGT treatment rather than income tax, and thus subject to the comparatively low 10%/20% rates of tax (plus large annual allowance) rather than the top 45% rate of income tax, makes these forms of compensation potentially very attractive. The schemes can be somewhat burdensome to operate, although some of administrative burdens were reduced in FA 2013 following a review of employee share schemes by the Office of Tax Simplification.[6] These changes included expanding the 'good leaver' rules, removing the 'material interest' rules in relation to SIPs and SAYEs, and removing the limitation on restrictions for SIPs, SAYEs and CSOPs.[7] FA 2014 then made a further especially significant change—removing the previous requirement for HMRC approval of schemes and replacing it with a system of online self-certification for new schemes.[8] As a consequence the word 'approved' was removed from the names of the relevant schemes in ITEPA 2003. Thus, the formerly 'approved' schemes are now referred to in this book generally as 'tax advantaged'. Particular schemes, following the wording of the amended legislation, technically are now referred to by reference to the relevant schedule of ITEPA 2003 where the details of their operation can be found—eg 'Schedule 2 SIP schemes'—but in this book the relevant schedule typically is omitted for convenience.

---

[5] ITEPA 2003, s 698, rewritten by FA 2003; originally TA 1988, s 203FB.
[6] See https://www.gov.uk/government/publications/employee-share-schemes-review.
[7] FA 2013, s 14 and Sch 2. For commentary see Ball [2013] BTR 394.
[8] FA 2014, ss 49–52 and Schs 8 and 9. For commentary see Fry and Cohen [2014] BTR 386.

17.1.2 Tax and Non-tax Factors Affecting Choice of Scheme[9]

In studying the rules the following points must be noted which affect the willingness of the employer and employee to choose a particular benefit, bearing in mind always that their interests may not be the same:

— Does the employer incur an expense—if so, is it deductible in computing profits?
— If the employee receives a benefit, when will it be taxable?
— If the employee receives a benefit, will it be taxable to income tax under ITEPA 2003, or to CGT under TCGA 1992?
— If the employee receives a benefit, will it be subject to PAYE?
— If the employee receives a benefit, will it be subject to NICs?
— Will the employee incur a charge to tax if shares are sold within a certain period?
— What are the risks of unexpected tax charges (usually called 'chargeable events')?

From a wider perspective:

— Must the scheme be available to all employees?
— Is there any limit on the amount that can be put into the scheme?
— What does the scheme do to the share structure of the company? Is there a risk of dilution? Does the company receive any money from the employee—a potentially valuable source of funding?
— Will the scheme give rise to employee participation in the company to a degree which 'management' may find unacceptable?
— How free are employees to sell the shares and thus rid themselves of the links with the company which these schemes are meant to foster?
— How flexible are the schemes? Clearly, tax-advantaged schemes will be less flexible than non tax-advantaged schemes since they have to conform to statutory conditions.
— What financial risks are inherent in the scheme (share values may go down as well as up)?
— From the employee's viewpoint, share options have attractions over other share plans in that no money has to be invested, there is no risk of loss since options do not have to be exercised and success may lead to a very high rate of return owing to the element of gearing involved.

The battery of sets of rules and factors makes this area complicated. In this book it is not appropriate to cover every detail; as such only the principal points will be considered in relation to each scheme. However, some other general points must be grasped.

First, this is a political minefield. Some believe in the value of share schemes as ways of encouraging better performance by executives and general loyalty of the workforce as a whole. A profit-sharer tends to take a longer-term view of company, is less inclined to leave and is probably more sympathetic to the introduction of new machinery or work practices. However, a company does not benefit if it simply uses such schemes as a way of warding

---

[9] See, generally, Scott and Savage, *Tolley's Tax Planning 1999–2000*, ch 56, 1622–69, esp at 1643–55; and Williams, *Taxation of Employee Share Schemes* (Butterworths, 1995), ch 1. Company law aspects are well covered by Whitewright, McMichael and Lawson, *Tolley's Tax Planning 2003–04*, 56.24 *et seq*.

off takeovers. Loyalty is important not only for the company itself but also more widely, since a company with a loyal workforce is far more likely to spend money in its training and development, a matter seen as a real problem when the UK is compared with other countries. When the logic of such reward systems became too obvious, as in the case of the newly-privatised companies which made substantial profits in cutting expenses by making staff redundant, the populist streak of Conservatism meant that benefits were restricted (eg the £30,000 limit imposed in 1996). By contrast (Old) Labour governments have traditionally been hostile to schemes attracting tax privileges, and have usually sought to impose tax penalties. Profit-sharing schemes have been anathema both to the hard left (collaborationist) and the right-to-manage right, but one may oppose them on other grounds. Some critics emphasise that options may become valueless due to a change in the general market conditions even though the company itself has been successful in comparison with other companies in the sector in which it competes. Such critics prefer long-term incentive plans using such comparisons.[10] The Liberal Democrats[11] were responsible for the introduction of savings-related option schemes and approved profit-sharing schemes in the period of minority government from 1977–79. At Budget 2012, the Coalition Government announced that a review into the role of employee ownership in supporting growth, and consider options for removing barriers to take-up. The ensuing Nuttal Review concluded that there is a substantial body of evidence demonstrating the benefits of employee ownership in terms of business performance and employee well-being, and made a series of recommendations aimed at promoting employee ownership.[12]

Secondly, much of the practical effect of the different schemes must be assessed against a changing background of the relationship between income tax and CGT. The alignment of the rates of tax in 1988 reduced the advantage of having capital gains rather than income; however, the advantage was widened first by the introduction in 1998 of increasingly generous taper relief, and remained after the move to the 18% flat rate of CGT (combined with the repeal of taper relief) in 2008. The advantage narrowed somewhat with the 2010 addition of the 28% top rate of CGT, but grew again when the top CGT rate dropped generally to 20% from 6 April 2016; compared to income tax rates of 40% or 45% the advantage clearly remains. The question whether it is better for a particular taxpayer to have capital gain or ordinary income does depend, however, on the taxpayer's circumstances.

Thirdly, it is open to any employer to arrange a mix of these benefits, so taking full advantage of the statutory reliefs while adding non tax-advantaged schemes on top.

17.1.3 Emoluments in form of Shares and Share Options—Basic Rules

ITEPA 2003, section 7(2) introduces a distinct type of income, being an amount which 'counts as' employment income; this type includes[13] income falling with Part 7 of the Act or 'income ... relating to securities'.

---

[10] For example, Goobey, *The Times*, 25 November 1995, Business letters.
[11] Technically, their predecessor parties.
[12] *Sharing Success: The Nuttall Review of Employee Ownership* (July 2012), available at https://www.gov.uk/government/uploads/system/uploads/attachment_data/file/31706/12-933-sharing-success-nuttall-review-employee-ownership.pdf
[13] ITEPA 2003, s 7(6). The other (Pt 6) is a ragbag of rules.

17.1.3.1 Remuneration in Shares

If, in return for services, an employee, E, receives shares in the employing company, tax is chargeable on the value of those shares.[14] Since the charge does not arise under any of the special rules in Part 7, this will be ordinary earnings within section 62. If the shares are ordinary shares, the market value on the date of receipt will be taken as the taxable amount since they could be sold at that price. If, however, they are received subject to conditions which reduce their value, the reduction will usually be reflected in a reduced taxable amount.[15] This was used as the basis of much planning in share incentive schemes.

17.1.3.2 Priority Allocations and ITEPA 2003, Part 7, Chapter 10

Income may also arise within ITEPA 2003, section 62 if employees are given priority in a public offer and so end up with more shares than they would have got as members of the public—assuming that the values at allocation exceeded the price paid.

Special rules in ITEPA 2003 may exclude the charge in such cases.[16] Chapter 10 first deals with offers to the public and employees, and provides an exemption where there is a genuine offer to the public at a fixed price or tender.[17] The exemption applies even though the employees are given priority, provided:

(1)   the number of priority shares is limited and no more than 10% of the shares are offered to the employees in priority;[18]
(2)   all persons entitled to the priority allocation receive it on similar terms; and
(3)   the offer is not restricted wholly or mainly to directors or employees above a certain level of remuneration.[19]

The exemption does not apply to any discount.[20]

Secondly Chapter 10 provides separate but similar rules granting exemption where there is both an offer to the public and a separate offer to employees at the same time.[21] The rules are aligned so that one looks at both issues together to apply the limits as to the number of employee shares.[22] Again the exemption does not extend to discounts, although the enactment of this statutory purpose is more complicated and uses the device of a 'registrant discount'.[23]

In practice, many flotations are made by placement and not by public offer, and so technically fall outside these protective rules.[24] These rules had to be modified to take account of privatisations involving two or more companies.[25]

---

[14] *Weight v Salmon* (1935) 19 TC 174.
[15] *Ede v Wilson and Cornwall* [1945] 1 All ER 367, 26 TC 381.
[16] ITEPA 2003, Pt 7, Ch 10, ss 542–548, ex FA 1988, s 68; see [1987] *Simon's Tax Intelligence* 716, 866.
[17] ITEPA 2003, s 542.
[18] ITEPA 2003, s 542(3) and (4). For explanation, see ITEPA 2003 Technical Note 52. Ex FA 1988, s 68(1A)(a), added by FA 1989, s 66 and FA 1991, s 44(4); see [1988] *Simon's Tax Intelligence* 748, and [1989] *Simon's Tax Intelligence* 106.
[19] ITEPA 2003, s 542(5)–(6); on 'similar terms' see s 546.
[20] ITEPA 2003, s 543.
[21] ITEPA 2003, s 544.
[22] ITEPA 2003, s 544(3) and (4).
[23] ITEPA 2003, s 545; the discount is defined further in s 547.
[24] Cohen [1997] *Business Law Review* 131.
[25] ITEPA 2003, s 544, ex FA 1988, s 68 (1ZA), (1ZB), added as from 16 January 1991 by FA 1991, s 44(3).

17.1.3.3 Options to Acquire Shares

Acquisition of option. If E receives an option to buy shares, income arises under section 62 equal to the value of the option, ie the difference between the price payable under the option and the market value of the shares on the date of receipt of the option.[26] If, therefore, the price payable under the option is the market value at the time of the grant, no tax is due under section 62.

Exercise of option. If the shares rise in value before the exercise of the option, a charge to tax will not arise under section 62 when the option is exercised. However, a charge may arise under Part 7 thanks to section 476 (which does not apply, however, to the various favoured schemes). The reason why no charge arises under section 62 was explained by the House of Lords in *Abbott v Philbin.*[27] There, E received an option to buy shares at £3.42 each, the market value at the date of the option, and exercised it in a subsequent tax year when the market value of the shares was £4.10. The House of Lords held that the emolument arose in the year the option was acquired, and at that time E received no benefit from it since he was merely given an option to buy at what was then full market value. The fact that the emolument subsequently increased in value did not mean that that increase in value was an emolument. Although this case has been reversed for options over shares—and now securities—it remains good law for options over other types of property.

Disposal of shares. Disposal will usually trigger a charge to CGT rather than income tax; any income tax could arise only under ITTOIA 2005, Part 2. Since the asset disposed of is the shareholding, CGT will be charged on the gain realised after the acquisition of the shares.

Loans to acquire shares. ITEPA 2003, Part 3, Chapter 7 may apply if the loan is on advantageous terms or is written off (see §16.4.3 and §16.4.4).[28]

17.2   FA 2003—Scope and Background

FA 2003 provided a major overhaul of the legislation in this area, the only regret being that the overhaul was not done in time to be taken into account properly in ITEPA 2003. As already seen, there were three principal changes. The first was the extension of the rules to cover all securities and not just shares. The second was a new set of chapters, Chapters 3A–3D, dealing with acquisitions above or below market value, and with the manipulation of values. The third was the extension of PAYE and NICs to produce a uniform application across the rules.

17.2.1 Securities

Securities are defined in ITEPA 2003, section 420 to cover not only shares and debentures but also warrants, certificates, futures rights under certain insurance policies and rights

---

[26] *Weight v Salmon* (1935) 19 TC 173.
[27] [1961] AC 352, [1960] 2 All ER 763, 39 TC 82.
[28] ITEPA 2003, Pt 3, Ch 8, which created a notional loan in certain situations, and Ch 9, which applied where shares were disposed of for more than market value, were repealed by FA 2003, their scope having been absorbed into the new rules.

under contracts for differences.[29] FA 2006, section 92 first brought options within the concept of security in section 420(1)(f); it then amended section 420(5)(e) by excluding options to acquire securities (unless they fail a purpose test) from Part 3, Chapters 1–5. These changes were backdated to 2 December 2004. The application of PAYE to such retrospective charges, both in the context of section 92 and generally, is governed by changes made by FA 2006, section 94. The Treasury is given power to amend this Part of the Act by statutory instrument.[30] Market value is defined by reference to the CGT rules and envisages consideration in non-monetary form.[31]

Sections 421B–421L provide some overarching rules for ITEPA 2003, Part 7, Chapters 2–4A (see §17.3), now including Chapters 3A–3D (see §17.4). So the rules apply where the securities are employment-related securities, ie securities acquired by a person by reason of the employment of that (or some other) person;[32] employment includes former or prospective employment. Acquisition is determined by reference to beneficial entitlement.[33] The expression 'by reason of employment' is elaborated upon in the same way as for other provisions of the Act, eg section 201, so a security is not acquired by reason of employment if made available to the person by an individual in the normal course of the individual's domestic, family or personal relationships.[34]

The rules cease to apply in three situations.[35] They cease to apply immediately after the securities are disposed of—unless to an associated person—or immediately before the death of the employee. They also cease to apply seven years from the ending of the employment. However, this rule has to be widened to cover situations in which the person was employed by one company but had shares in another, or obtains employment with a person connected with the employer or company. The start of the seven-year period must be after the acquisition of the securities.

17.2.2 Associated Persons

Section 421C defines associated persons in relation to employment-related securities. This concept is important and potentially misleading. Other parts of the tax legislation use expressions such as 'the employee and any associates of the employee'. Section 421C uses a different technique by lumping together the employee and the associates and describing them all as 'associated persons'. So the definition covers both the person acquiring the shares and, if different, the employee. It also includes 'any relevant linked person', ie someone who is a connected person or member of the same household. This too is interesting; the more old-fashioned 'connected person' is defined in terms of legal relationships.[36] The 'household' refers to less formal relationships but is not further defined.

---

[29] ITEPA 2003, s 420 as amended F(No2)A 2005, Sch 2. For example, see Notes to Finance Bill.
[30] ITEPA 2003, s 420(6).
[31] ITEPA 2003, ss 421 and 421A.
[32] ITEPA 2003, s 421B(1).
[33] ITEPA 2003, s 421B(2).
[34] ITEPA 2003, s 421B(3).
[35] ITEPA 2003, s 421B(4)–(7).
[36] ITEPA 2003, s 718 refers to ITA 2007, s 993 (ex TA 1988, s 839).

Rules are provided for situations in which shares or other securities are replaced or added to, or where there is a change in the person's interest.[37] These rules give us expressions such as 'additional securities' and 'replacement securities'.

17.2.3 Exclusions

Originally, the rules in Chapters 2–4 did not apply to shares acquired under an offer made to the public.[38] However, the scope of this exception was reduced as part of the FA 2004 anti-avoidance drive; it now applies only to Chapters 2, 3 and 3C, but there is an anti-avoidance main purpose test.[39] Previously the rules did not apply to matters within Chapters 6–8, but these exceptions were repealed.[40] There are definitions of employee-controlled companies and associated company, the CTA 2010, section 449 definition being used.[41] Further, since some rules (Chapters 2, 3 and 3A) refer to the acquisition of employment-related securities, rules are needed to determine the consideration given for such acquisitions.[42] These rules take account of options and replacement options, and contain a rule linking certain transactions to form one transaction.[43]

Lastly, there is an elaborate duty to provide information, backed up by a list of reportable events, and of persons obliged to report.[44]

17.3   Securities Schemes

The first type of security scheme relevant here was the share purchase incentive scheme. This was introduced to avoid ITEPA 2003, section 476.[45] Instead of being given an option to buy a share for £1—the current market value of the share which might in due course be worth £3—E would be issued with a share which ordinarily would have had a current market value of £3 but which was subject to restrictions making it worth only £1. At a later date the restrictions would be removed. The increase in value could not be subject to tax under what is now section 476, since the employee did not realise a gain by exercising a right to acquire shares—the shares were already owned. If the company capitalised its profits to pay them up, there would be a charge under the residual charge for the director, etc in section 203 (ex TA 1988, section 154) on the employee on the amount so spent, but this would usually be much less than the gain realised.

Faced with such schemes the legislature provided two sets of rules. Set one (see §17.3.1 and §17.3.2 below) introduced in 1998, clarified the treatment of conditional acquisitions

---

[37] ITEPA 2003, s 421D.
[38] ITEPA 2003, s 421F.
[39] ITEPA 2003, s 421F(1A).
[40] ITEPA 2003, s 421G, repealed by FA 2004, s 88.
[41] ITEPA 2003, s 421H.
[42] ITEPA 2003, s 421I.
[43] ITEPA 2003, s 421I(5)-(7), especially s 421I((7), which takes 'release' of a right to include agreeing to the restriction of its exercise.
[44] ITEPA 2003, ss 421J-421L.
[45] Ex TA 1988, s 135.

of shares and the conversion of convertible shares. Set two (see §17.3.3), introduced—and amended—much earlier, provided a separate charge on the growth in the value of shares in certain circumstances. FA 2003 rewrote these rules, extending them to securities as opposed to just shares, but also, sometimes, simplifying them. Some of the simplification is achieved by the addition of Chapters 3A–3D (§17.4 below) and the consequent relocation of provisions.

Here we follow the order in the 2003 Act rather than the historical order.

17.3.1 Restricted Securities (Previously Conditional Interest in Shares)[46]

The legislative restrictions on the use of share options (see §17.5 below) led in practice to greater use of long-term share incentive schemes in which benefits accrued only if performance conditions attached to the shares were satisfied. However, the assumption that there was no charge on the grant of such shares, but only when the conditions were satisfied and benefits received, rested, until 1998, on general principle rather than express provision. It could, contrary to the general assumption, be argued, on the basis of *Abbott v Philbin*,[47] that there should be a charge on the grant of the shares based on a prediction, ie a guess, as to the chance that the particular employee would derive a benefit in the fullness of time thanks to the success of the company or the stock market's assessment of the company. If this was correct, the charge based on guesswork at the time of the grant would exclude any charge when the conditions were removed. Therefore, in 1998 the Revenue moved to enact rules validating the general assumption.

The rules to be considered apply to what were at first termed 'conditional acquisitions of shares'; ITEPA 2003, Part 7 originally changed the heading to Chapter 2, 'Conditional Interest in Shares', but FA 2003 renamed it 'Restricted Securities'. In any event, the securities must be employment-related securities (see §17.2.1 above).[48] FA 2003 made the whole application of Chapter 2 a matter of election, but usually in the interest of paying the tax up front (see below). There are elaborate rules as to when securities are restricted by 'any contract, agreement, arrangement or condition'.[49] Included are provisions concerning the transfer, reversion or forfeiture of the employment-related securities if certain conditions arise or do not arise, as well as restrictions concerning the freedom of the security holder to dispose of the security. There are also exceptions where the securities are subject to forfeiture for misconduct or for other permitted reasons; these exceptions are subject to a tax-avoidance main purpose test, but redeemable securities are caught anyway.[50] If the condition attached to the securities must be satisfied (or not) within five years, there will be no charge on the acquisition of the securities.[51] The exclusion from charge on acquisition does not prevent any liability arising under Chapters 3 (acquisition by conversion), 3C (the rule on

---

[46] On pre-ITEPA 2003 changes see Richards [1999] BTR 340.

[47] [1961] AC 354, (1961) 39 TC 382.

[48] ITEPA 2003, s 422–432.

[49] ITEPA 2003, s 423, ex TA 1988, s 140C; for parallel NIC treatment, see [1998] *Simon's Tax Intelligence* 729, 1358.

[50] ITEPA 2003, s 424 amended by F(No 2)A 2005, Sch 2, ex TA 1988, s 140C(1A), (3A), added by FA 1999, s 43.

[51] ITEPA 2003, s 425, ex TA 1988, s 140A(3) is subject to s 476, ex 135 (charge on exercise of non tax-advantaged share options).

acquisition for less than market value) or 5 (acquisition by exercise of a share option), but the employer and employee may jointly elect irrevocably that the charges under Chapters 3, 3C and 5 do not apply.[52]

There will, however, be a charge on the occurrence of a chargeable event if and when the holding becomes unrestricted, or on any earlier sale of the securities or any interest in them.[53] The charge is on a portion of the market value of the shares (when the holding becomes unconditional or on prior disposal), less allowable deductions[54] and relief for employer's Class 1 NICs paid by the employee.[55] Any liability on the grant of the shares will be taken into account to prevent a double charge.[56] There is an exclusion from this charge if the employment-related securities are shares in a class, the restriction applies to all the shares in the class and the non employment-related shares in that class are also affected by a similar event.[57] This exception was used as the basis for tax avoidance schemes, and so FA 2004 added a rule that the exception is available only if the avoidance of tax or NICs was not the main purpose, or one of the main purposes, of the arrangements under which the right or opportunity to acquire employment-related securities was made available.[58]

If the market value has been manipulated in the ways envisaged under Chapters 3A–3D, charges may arise under those Chapters. There are consequential rules for CGT and relief from corporation tax for the contributions.[59] FA 2003 provided an election that all outstanding restrictions should be ignored, so enabling the tax to be finalised—on the basis of the full unmanipulated value—instead of having to drag on until another chargeable event just because of some trivial condition.[60]

However section 431 goes even further and makes the application of the rules in Chapter 2 a matter of election. Employer and employee may jointly elect that either all the restrictions or any specified restrictions should not apply.[61] The effect of this is to open up the entire value to possible charges under the general principle in section 62, or under the rule for conversions in section 439(3)(a) or under Chapters 3C, 5 or Part 7A—unless an exception applies. So a full charge arises at once if the right was acquired as part of an avoidance scheme.[62] However, the election is beneficial if the shares are acquired under a tax-advantaged scheme or research institution spin-out.[63] At one time, if the condition could be satisfied beyond the five-year period there was an immediate charge when the shares were obtained. The charge has now been abolished for shares issued after the relevant date.[64]

These rules have been the focus of much tax planning. The ensuing litigation, concerning banker bonus schemes in particular, has added to the canon of cases on the modern

[52] ITEPA 2003, s 425(3)–(5); on forms and time limits, see s 425(5).
[53] ITEPA 2003, ss 426 and 427, ex TA 1988, s 140A(4).
[54] ITEPA 2003, s 428, ex TA 1988, s 140A(5); market value is defined in s 421, ex s 145A(6) and allowable deductions in s 428(7), ex ss 140A(7), 140B.
[55] ITEPA 2003, s 428A, added by FA 2004, s 85 and Sch 16, para 1.
[56] ITEPA 2003, s 428, ex TA 1988, s 140A(7).
[57] ITEPA 2003, s 429 test modified by F(No 2)A 2005, Sch 2.
[58] ITEPA 2003, s 429(1A) added by FA 2004, s 86.
[59] See TCGA 1992, ss 119A and 149AA and FA 2003, Sch 23.
[60] ITEPA 2003, s 430. See also s 430A concerning exchange of securities.
[61] ITEPA 2003, s 431(1) and (2).
[62] ITEPA 2003, s 431B.
[63] ITEPA 2003, ss 431A (added 2004) and 454 (added 2005).
[64] FA 1999, s 42(2).

approach to the *Ramsay* principle. In the joined cases of *UBS AG* and *DB Group Services (UK)*,[65] the Supreme Court applied the modern *Ramsay* purposive interpretation approach to defeat two such schemes executed before the tax avoidance purpose test was added in 2004. Lord Reed (the other judges agreeing) concluded that the reference in ITEPA 2003, section 423(1) to 'any contract, agreement, arrangement or condition which makes provision to which any of subsections (2) to (4) applies' is to be purposively construed 'as being limited to provision having a business or commercial purpose, and not to commercially irrelevant conditions whose only purpose is the obtaining of the exemption' (at para 85). On the facts of those cases, once the commercially irrelevant conditions were ignored, the shares at issue did not qualify as 'restricted securities' and *Abbott v Philbin* applied. Thus, income tax was payable on the value of the shares as at the date of their acquisition, account being taken of any effect which the commercially irrelevant conditions may have had on the value.

17.3.2 Convertible Securities: Charge on Conversion, etc

Rules creating a charge on the conversion of securities were originally introduced—in 1998[66]—to supplement another charge, known as the growth-in-value charge[67] (FA 1988, section 78), which did not apply when one class of shares was converted into another. The charge on conversion survives in Part 7, Chapter 3 even though the growth-in-value charge does not.

The condition for the charge to arise is that the person has acquired employment-related securities,[68] and the securities carry a right or a possible entitlement to convert them into securities of a different description.[69] The charge no longer arises simply on conversion. Instead it arises first—under section 439(3)(a)—where on the conversion the beneficial entitlement to the new securities accrues to an associated person. Other parts of section 439 apply to the disposal of the securities by an associated person otherwise than to another associated person, the release of the right to convert, or the receipt by an associated person of any benefit in money or money's worth other than the new securities. Remembering the definition of 'associated person' in section 421C, one can see that the charge arises whether the person is the person who acquired the employment-related securities in the first place, the employee or any relevant linked person.[70]

The charge is on the market value of the new securities following conversion, less any deductible amounts[71] and relief for employer's NICs paid by the employee.[72] There is, however, an exception for the entire conversion of shares of one class if the conversion affects any other shares similarly.[73] In order to take advantage of this exception, the com-

---

[65] *UBS AG v R&C Comrs; Deutsche Bank Group v R&C Comrs* [2016] UKSC 13 and see above §5.6.6.
[66] TA 1988, ss 140D–140F, inserted by FA 1998, s 51.
[67] FA 1988, s 78.
[68] ITEPA 2003, s 435. On employment-related securities, see ITEPA 2003, s 421B(8), ex TA 1988, s 140H.
[69] ITEPA 2003, s 436, ex TA 1988, s 140D(2); definition tightened by F(No 2)A 2005, Sch 2. For parallel NIC treatment, see [1998] *Simon's Tax Intelligence* 729, 1358.
[70] ITEPA 2003, s 421C; the definition was tightened by FA 2004, s 90.
[71] ITEPA 2003, ss 440–442, ex TA 1988, s 140D and 140E.
[72] ITEPA 2003, s 442A added by FA 2004, s 85.
[73] ITEPA 2003, s 443(1)–(3), ex TA 1988, s 140D(8), (9), modified by F(No 2)A 2005, Sch 2.

pany must be employee-controlled by virtue of these shares immediately before the conversion. Alternatively, the majority of the company's shares of the original class must at that time not be employment-related securities.[74] If the market value has been manipulated in the ways envisaged under Chapters 3A–3D, charges may arise under those Chapters. Here too the exception was used as the basis for avoidance, and so FA 2004 added a rule that the exception is available only if the avoidance of tax or NICs was not the main purpose, or one of the main purposes, of the arrangements under which the right or opportunity to acquire employment-related securities was made available.[75]

Again there are consequential rules for CGT and corporation tax rules on relief for contributions.[76]

17.3.3 Post-acquisition Benefits

ITEPA 2003, Part 7, Chapter 4 originally stretched from section 447 to section 470; as a result of FA 2003 it now runs from section 447 to section 450. As compared with the rules described in *Revenue Law*, 4th edition, §16.4.3, the major change is the removal of any mention of dependent subsidiaries, which was only made possible by the introduction of Chapters 3A–3D (see §17.4 below).

The charge in section 447 applies where the securities are employment-related securities and a benefit is received by an associated person in connection with the securities. Remembering the definition of 'associated person', one can see that the charge arises whether the person is the person who acquired the employment-related securities in the first place, the employee or any relevant linked person.[77] The charge arises in the year in which the benefit is received and is on the full market value of the benefit. There is the usual exception where the securities are shares of a class, the benefit is received by all the share owners in that class and either the company is employee-controlled by virtue of that holding or the majority of the shares of that class are not employment-related securities.[78] The usual exception was used as the basis for avoidance, and so here too FA 2004 added a rule that the exception is available only if the avoidance of tax or NICs was not the main purpose, or one of the main purposes, of the arrangements under which the right or opportunity to acquire employment-related securities was made available.[79] On research institution spin-out companies, see §17.11.

17.4   Anti-avoidance: Manipulation of Values

Into this legislative scheme FA 2003 planted Chapters 3A–3D, sections 446A–446Z,[80] all concerned with avoidance through the manipulation of values: Chapter 3A deals with

---

[74] ITEPA 2003, s 443(3) and (4).
[75] ITEPA 2003, s 443(1A), added by FA 2004, s 86.
[76] TCGA 1992, ss 119A and 149AA, and FA 2003, Sch 23.
[77] ITEPA 2003, s 421C.
[78] ITEPA 2003, s 449.
[79] ITEPA 2003, s 449(1A), added by FA 2004, s 86, strengthened by F(No 2)A 2005, Sch 2.
[80] IRPR BN 29, April 2003, [2003] *Simon's Tax Intelligence* 741.

securities with artificially depressed market value; Chapter 3B with securities with artificially enhanced market value; Chapter 3C with securities acquired for less than market value; and Chapter 3D with securities disposed of for more than market value.

17.4.1 Securities with Artificially Depressed Market Value

Chapter 3A applies where the market value of employment-related securities is reduced by things done 'otherwise than for genuine commercial purposes', a phrase defined as including situations where tax avoidance is a main purpose.[81] There is also an arm's-length test for group transactions, but with an exception for a payment for group relief under CTA 2010, section 183(1).[82]

17.4.1.1 Acquisition[83]

There is a charge where the market value of the employment-related securities at the time of acquisition has been reduced by at least 10% by transactions over the previous seven years. The charge is not to affect various other charges—section 62, section 203, Chapters 3, 3C or 5 of Part 7, and Chapter 2 of Part 7A.[84] However, a charge under section 425(2) excludes a charge here.

The amount taxed is usually that by which the fair market value of the securities has been reduced, judging the facts as at the time of acquisition. If that reduction is less than the consideration actually paid for the employment-related securities, the acute consideration is taken instead.[85] Where a charge under Chapter 2 would arise (post-acquisition charges on restricted securities), it is excluded in favour of the charge under Chapter 3A.[86] If the securities are convertible and so come within Chapter 3, the value for Chapter 3A is to be determined as if they were not convertible, so leaving the convertibility increase to be dealt with under Chapter 3.[87]

17.4.1.2 Other Tax Charges

The section 426 charge on restricted securities applies if the market value of the employment-related securities has been reduced by 10% within the period of seven years ending with the chargeable event.[88] It also imposes a charge if the value is artificially low on 5 April of any year.[89]

17.4.1.3 Conditional Interests

The legislative technique used here is different. Where the employee has a conditional interest in the securities and a chargeable event occurs but the market value of the securities has been artificially reduced, the necessary adjustments are made to the post-chargeable event

[81] ITEPA 2003, s 446A.
[82] ITEPA 2003, s 446A(2)(b).
[83] ITEPA 2003, s 446B.
[84] ITEPA 2003, s 446B(3) and (4).
[85] ITEPA 2003, s 446C.
[86] ITEPA 2003, s 446D(1).
[87] ITEPA 2003, s 446D(2).
[88] ITEPA 2003, s 446E(1)(a).
[89] ITEPA 2003, s 446E(1)(b).

market value. This means that the charge still arises under sections 427 or 428 by reference to the adjusted value.

Convertible securities under Chapter 3 receive similar treatment. The charge under section 439(3)(a) is based on the fair not depressed value;[90] there are consequential changes to the value of the consideration or benefit received.[91] FA 2004 made changes in consequence of its new anti-avoidance rule.[92]

17.4.2 Securities with Artificially Enhanced Market Value

Chapter 3B, section 446L imposes a charge on the amount by which the market value of securities has been increased by artificial, ie non-commercial, means, provided the increase is at least 10%.[93] Artificiality is determined using the same tests as for Chapter 3A. Where the securities are 'relevant' restricted securities, the amount charged under section 446L is adjusted.[94] Section 446N deals with the situation in which the securities have been relevant restricted securities during the relevant period, and makes further deductions/adjustments to reflect the earlier charge on the occurrence of the chargeable event under section 428. FA 2004 added an anti-avoidance rule.[95]

17.4.3 Securities Acquired for Less Than Market Value

Chapter 3C deals with employment-related securities acquired either for no payment at all, or for a payment which is less than the market value. The rule is framed in terms of payment as opposed to consideration and expressly states that any obligation to make a payment after the acquisition is to be ignored—only actual payments will do. 'Payment' is not further defined, so the position of consideration in non-monetary form is unclear.[96]

The effect is to create a notional loan of the underpayment by the employer to the employee and then make the relevant parts of the low-interest loan rule in Part 3, Chapter 7 apply.[97] Further rules determine the amount of the loan.[98] A further charge arises if the loan is treated as discharged where the employment-related securities are disposed of to an associated person or there is a release of the obligation to pay.[99] Release is then supplemented by 'transferred or adjusted so as no longer to bind any associated person'. However, the notional loan is also treated as ended if the employee dies or payment of any of the amounts outstanding is made by an associated person. It seems that payments by a person about to become an associated person are not caught. FA 2005 added an anti-avoidance rule.[100]

---

[90] ITEPA 2003, s 446H.
[91] ITEPA 2003, s 446I.
[92] ITEPA 2003, s 446IA.
[93] ITEPA 2003, s 446L.
[94] ITEPA 2003, ss 446M and 446N; relevance determined under s 446M(4).
[95] ITEPA 2003, s 446NA.
[96] There is no cross-reference to s 197(3).
[97] ITEPA 2003, s 446S(3).
[98] ITEPA 2003, s 446T.
[99] ITEPA 2003, s 446U.
[100] ITEPA 2003, s 446UA added by F(No 2)A 2005, Sch 2.

Chapter 3C is excluded in certain situations.[101] These are where the shares are in one class and all the shares in that class have been acquired at less than market value and either the company is employee controlled by virtue of that class or, going in the opposite direction, less than half the securities are employment-related securities.[102] Here too the exception was used as the basis for avoidance and so FA 2004 added a rule that the exception is available only if the avoidance of tax or national insurance contributions was not the main purpose, or one of the main purposes, of the arrangements under which the right or opportunity to acquire employment-related securities was made available.[103]

Where Chapter 3C applies, the charge is additional to any other head—section 62, section 203, Chapters 3, 3A and 5 of Part 7, or Chapter 2 of Part 7A.[104]

17.4.4 Securities Disposed of for More Than Market Value

The final anti-avoidance measure is Chapter 3D dealing with securities disposed of for a consideration which exceeds market value. It applies where the employment-related securities are disposed of by an associated person so that no associated person is any longer beneficially entitled to them.[105] The amount of the consideration less the market value of the securities and any allowable expense in connection with the disposal counts as employment income of the employee.[106] The Scottish case *Gray's Timber Products v Revenue & Customs Commissioners*[107] sheds some light on the determination of market value of shares under these rules. At issue was whether rights under a subscription agreement requiring the purchase of the taxpayer's shares along with an extra payment to him in the event that more than 50% of the company's shares were sold, were to be taken into account in determining the market value of his shares for purposes of ITEPA 2003, section 446X(b) when such a sale occurred. The majority (Lord Osbourne dissenting) held that the rights were personal to the taxpayer and were not to be so taken into account; the taxpayer's shares had the same value as the other ordinary shares. The extra payment was subject to income tax under ITEPA 2003, section 446Y. The result, and the majority's reasoning, was confirmed on appeal by a unanimous Supreme Court, with Lord Walker expressing the hope 'that Parliament may find time to review the complex and obscure provisions of Part 7 of ITEPA 2003'.[108]

17.5   Special Tax Rules for Securities Options

17.5.1 Introduction

FA 2003 rewrote the original ITEPA 2003, Part 7, Chapter 5, with sections 471–484 replacing the original sections 471–487. Securities option schemes cause problems in any tax

---

[101] ITEPA 2003, s 446R.
[102] ITEPA 2003, s 446R(1)–(4).
[103] ITEPA 2003, s 446R(1A) added by FA 2004, s 86.
[104] ITEPA 2003, s 446V.
[105] *Ibid.*
[106] ITEPA 2003, s 446Y(3).
[107] [2009] STC 889, [2009] CSIH 11.
[108] [2010] UKSC 4, at para 45.

system. Most tax systems agree that the grant of an option to buy, for example, shares at a figure below the market value is taxable earnings, and that the gain accruing between the time of acquisition of the shares, ie the exercise of the option, and the date of disposal should be charged as a capital gain. Problems arise over how to tax the change in value between the date of the grant of the option and the date of its exercise.

The rules in Chapter 5 apply where the option has been acquired by reason of employment of that person—or any other person;[109] such an option is called an 'employment-related securities option'. The Chapter has its own definition of associated persons.[110]

17.5.2 *Acquisition of Option and Later Chargeable Events*

ITEPA 2003, section 473 emphasises that section 475 excludes any liability under s 62 or under Part 3, Chapter 10 where an employment-related securities option is acquired. A slight but necessary qualification is made for the situation in which a CSOP option is acquired at a discount.[111] However, it then provides[112] that a charge may arise under section 446B (Chapter 3A) where the market value has been artificially depressed, Chapter 3C where the securities are acquired for less than market value or section 476 where the securities are acquired as the result of the exercise of an option already within Chapter 5. Liability under section 476 may also arise on the assignment or release of the option, and so that liability has to be preserved.[113] Any liability under these rules may be excluded if the option comes within Chapters 7, 8 or 9—ie SAYE option schemes, CSOP schemes or Enterprise Management Incentives, discussed below at §§17.7–17.9.

It will be seen that section 475 excludes liability whether the option can only be exercised within 10 years or not; the previous law made a valuation distinction here, but that is not part of the final 2003 scheme.[114] ITEPA 2003, section 476 on chargeable events also applies where the option is an employment-related securities option.[115] The list of chargeable events[116] is:

(1) the acquisition of securities 'pursuant to' the option, ie the exercise of the option;
(2) assigning or releasing of the option where the assignment is for consideration and not to another associated person;
(3) the receipt of a benefit in money or money's worth in connection with the option, apart of course from the securities acquired under (1) or the consideration received under (2).

17.5.3 *Amount Charged*[117]

The taxable amount as determined under the legislation counts as employment income under Part 7 of ITEPA 2003. Normally the amount will be the difference between the price

---

[109] ITEPA 2003, s 471.
[110] ITEPA 2003, s 472—it is similar in content to s 421C but framed for options; hence this definition also was tightened by FA 2004, s 90.
[111] ITEPA 2003, s 475(2), referring to s 526.
[112] ITEPA 2003, s 473(2).
[113] ITEPA 2003, s 473(3).
[114] Contrast ITEPA 2003, s 475.
[115] ITEPA 2003, ss 471 and 476, ex TA 1988, s 135.
[116] ITEPA 2003, s 477; the definition was tightened by FA 2004, s 90.
[117] ITEPA 2003, ss 478, 479 (especially sub-ss (1)–(4)) and 480.

paid under the option (including the price of the option) and the market value of the shares acquired under the option—ie the gain less any deductible amounts.[118] Analogous rules apply to the assignment or release of the option,[119] and in all cases there are further special relief rules, eg for Class 1 NICs or any special social security contributions paid by the employee.[120] Further rules apply where one option is exchanged for another; a form of rollover is applied.[121]

These rules do not prevent substantial gains being made when options are given in the run-up to the flotation of a private company, since the value of the share will rise following flotation as there is now a market for the shares.[122] In the light of this, companies often allow employees to have options tied to the post-flotation price.

The predecessor of section 476 (ex TA 1988, section 135) was held to be an independent charging section and therefore applied whether or not the benefit of the option could be converted into cash.[123] It was also applied to the exclusion of what is now section 62.[124] Section 476 does not apply in certain international situations.[125]

The effect of section 476 has been to make share option schemes unattractive in tax terms outside the tax-advantaged schemes. The company receives money when the option is exercised, but not as much as on a sale to the public at that time. Although E will not normally have to pay tax until the exercise of the option, the gain on exercise is treated as E's employment income. Moreover, E may have to sell some of the shares to raise the money to pay the tax. The scheme also involves some dilution of equity. One variant scheme addresses these issues: on the exercise of the option, the company pays money to a trust, which then buys shares for E and transfers them to E. This does not avoid section 476, but since only the net-of-tax sum is invested, it avoids any need to sell shares and reduces equity dilution. As has already been stressed, the better way of avoiding section 476 is to take advantage of the statutorily-approved exceptions to that section (see ITEPA 2003, Part 7, Chapters 7, 8 and 9).

17.6   Share Incentive Plans

17.6.1 Introduction to SIPs

FA 2000 introduced yet another scheme, then called an 'all employee share plan' and now a Schedule 2 'share incentive plan' or SIP (ITEPA 2003, Part 7, Chapter 6 and Schedule 2). The plan was expected eventually to cost around £400 million a year, with around 625,000 employees owning shares in their companies for the first time.[126] In 2013–14, 520 plans appropriated shares at a tax cost of £300 million and NIC cost of £220 million.[127]

---

[118] ITEPA 2003, s 478.
[119] ITEPA 2003, ss 478, 479(5)–(8) and 480.
[120] ITEPA 2003, ss 481 and 482.
[121] ITEPA 2003, s 483.
[122] Cohen [1997] *Business Law Review* 132, stating that the average discount given for option grants between 6 and 12 months before flotation worked out at 84.4%.
[123] *Ball v Phillips* [1990] STC 675, 63 TC 529.
[124] *Wilcock v Eve* [1995] STC 18, 67 TC 223.
[125] ITEPA 2003, s 474.
[126] See Inland Revenue Press Release, 10 November 1999, [1999] *Simon's Tax Intelligence* 1803.
[127] HMRC Share Scheme Statistics available at https://www.gov.uk/government/statistics/share-incentive-plan.

If the conditions are observed, all shares in the SIP, held for five years, are completely free of income tax and CGT while so held.[128] The plan may contain three elements, each with its own rules.[129] These are called free shares, partnership shares and matching shares; there is also a fourth category comprising dividend shares. The plan may be on a group basis.[130] Notice of the SIP must be given to HMRC and annual returns filed.[131] The plan must have a purpose, as defined by the legislation, to provide benefits to employees in the form of shares which give them a continuing stake in the company.[132]

The plan must be available to all employees resident in the UK who meet certain conditions of eligibility.[133] There must be no preferential treatment of directors, no further conditions and no loan arrangements.[134] The employee may not also have any options held under another SIP;[135] however, where the employee participates in more than one SIP run by the same company or a connected company, the several plans are treated as one.[136]

There are also conditions as to equal treatment to ensure that all are eligible to participate and that those who do so participate on similar terms.[137] However, this does not prevent discrimination on the basis of hours worked, remuneration or length of service; neither does it prevent plans from being performance-related (see §17.6.2 below). The shares must be ordinary shares which are fully paid-up and not redeemable.[138] The shares must either be listed or be shares of a company which is not under the control of another company, save where that other company is a listed company.[139]

17.6.2 The Free Share Plan

Employers may give up to £3,600 pa of shares to employees.[140] Employers do not have to treat all employees alike but may discriminate among them, eg for reaching performance targets and so rewarding 'personal, team or divisional performance'. These plans resemble APSSs; however, unlike those schemes, the award of free shares may be linked to performance provided the criteria are objective and are fair to all employees, ie the targets set are broadly comparable.[141] Comparable does not mean identical and, under one variant, up to 80% of shares may be awarded on the basis of performance, as long as the highest performance award is not more than four times greater than the highest non-performance award

---

[128] On income tax advantages, see ITEPA 2003, ss 488–499 as amended by FA 2003; on s 499, see ITEPA 2003 Explanatory Notes, Change 127. On CGT, see TCGA 1992, Sch 7D, paras 1–8, added by ITEPA 2003, Sch 6, para 221, referring to 'Schedule 2' SIPs.

[129] See generally ITEPA 2003, s 488 and Sch 2, and specifically Sch 2, para 2, ex FA 2000, Sch 8, para 1.

[130] ITEPA 2003, Sch 2, para 4, ex FA 2000, Sch 8, para 2.

[131] ITEPA 2003, Sch 2, paras 81A and 81B, ex FA 2000, Sch 8, paras 4, 5.

[132] ITEPA 2003, Sch 2, para 7, ex FA 2000, Sch 8, para 7.

[133] ITEPA 2003, Sch 2, paras 8, 14–17, ex FA 2000, Sch 8, paras 7, 13–14.

[134] ITEPA 2003, Sch 2, paras 10–12, ex FA 2000, Sch 8, paras 10–12.

[135] ITEPA 2003, Sch 2, para 18, ex FA 2000, Sch 8, para 16.

[136] ITEPA 2003, Sch 2, para 18A added by FA 2003.

[137] ITEPA 2003, Sch 2, paras 8 and 9, ex FA 2000, Sch 8, paras 8, 9.

[138] ITEPA 2003, Sch 2, paras 25–28, ex FA 2000, Sch 8, paras 59–62.

[139] ITEPA 2003, Sch 2, para 27, ex FA 2000, Sch 8, para 67.

[140] ITEPA 2003, Sch 2, para 35.

[141] ITEPA 2003, Sch 2, paras 38–42, ex FA 2000, Sch 8, paras 27–30.

to an employee on similar terms.[142] There are also rules about the information to be given to employees.[143]

Free shares are held by trustees and appropriated to the participant.[144] The shares must remain with the trustee for a period of at least three years and not more than five years.[145] If the shares leave the plan before three years, there is a charge on the market value of the shares on leaving.[146] The shares may be withdrawn tax-free within the three-year period if the employment ends because of redundancy or disability, or for other accepted cause.[147] If the shares are withdrawn between years three and five, there is a charge on the lesser of the value of the shares when awarded and the value of the shares when leaving.[148]

17.6.3 Reinvestment of Cash Dividends (Dividend Shares)

Dividends accruing on the plans shares may either be distributed in the usual (taxable) way, or be reinvested in 'dividend shares'.[149] The shares have their own three-year holding period.[150] Once the three years have passed there is no income tax charge on these shares. The share may be left in the plan or transferred, as the employee wishes. If the holding period rules are broken, the dividend used to pay for the shares becomes taxable.[151] Certain amounts which are not reinvested may be retained by the trustees and then paid out if not used.[152]

17.6.4 CGT Liability

A CGT liability may accrue if the employee, having had the shares transferred, then sells them. No liability arises on the appropriation or on withdrawal[153] as the shares are treated as having been disposed of without giving rise to a chargeable gain and immediately reacquired at market value; neither is there any liability on disposal of rights under a rights issue.[154] Since the base cost of the shares will be the value when they are transferred to the employee, little if any liability will arise if the employee sells them immediately. So long as the shares remain in the plan the employee is treated as beneficially entitled to them as against the trustee.[155] Once the shares have been withdrawn by the employee—something

---

[142] ITEPA 2003, Sch 2, para 41(2)(c), ex FA 2000, Sch 8, para 29(1)(c).
[143] ITEPA 2003, Sch 2, para 40, ex FA 2000, Sch 8, para 28. ITEPA 2003 Explanatory Notes, Change 161. On para 42, see ITEPA 2003 Technical Note 64.
[144] On powers and duties see ITEPA 2003, Sch 2, paras 70–80 ex FA 2000, Sch 8, paras 68–86.
[145] ITEPA 2003, Sch 2, para 36, ex FA 2000, Sch 8, para 31; the participant may direct the trustees to do various things, including accepting certain offers in relation to the shares—see ITEPA 2003, Sch 2, para 37, ex FA 2000, Sch 8, para 32.
[146] ITEPA 2003, s 505(2), ex FA 2000, Sch 8, para 81(2).
[147] ITEPA 2003, s 498, ex FA 2000, Sch 8, para 87.
[148] ITEPA 2003, s 505(3) ex FA 2000, Sch 8, para 81(3).
[149] ITEPA 2003, Sch 2, paras 62–69, ex FA 2000, Sch 8, paras 53–58. See also ITEPA 2003 Technical Note 66.
[150] ITEPA 2003, Sch 2, para 67, ex FA 2000, Sch 8, para 57.
[151] ITEPA 2003, Sch 2, para 67, ex FA 2000, Sch 8, para 57.
[152] ITEPA 2003, Sch 2, para 68, ex FA 2000, Sch 8, para 58.
[153] TCGA 1992, Sch 7D, para 5, ex FA 2000, Sch 8, para 101.
[154] TCGA 1992, Sch 7D, para 8, ITEPA 2003, Sch 6, para 55, ex FA 2000, Sch 8, para 104.
[155] TCGA 1992, Sch 7D, para 3, ITEPA 2003, Sch 6, para 55, ch 8, para 99.

required after five years anyway—they become chargeable assets and potentially liable to CGT. The shares are pooled separately.[156] Gains realised by the trustees are not normally liable to CGT.[157]

17.6.5 *The Partnership Share Plan*[158]

Employees may buy shares out of their pre-tax monthly salary or weekly wages up to a maximum of £1,800 a year or £150 a month.[159] There is also a maximum limit of 10% of salary.[160] Partnership shares can be purchased by the participant at one of three values—the present basis, market value at the beginning of the accumulation period, or market value at the acquisition date of the shares by the employee.[161] Another rule requires the employee to be informed about the possible effect of these rights on benefit entitlement.[162] The rules give the employee a tax deduction for the sums spent on the purchase of the shares. The payments must be deducted from the employee's salary.[163] The plan may allow for money to be accumulated; if it does not, the sum must be invested within 30 days.[164] Sums may not be accumulated beyond 12 months.

As the employee has paid for the shares, there is no minimum period during which the shares must be retained and the employee will face no charge if the shares are left in the plan for five years. If shares are removed before three years have passed, the employee must pay income tax on the value of the shares when they are removed.[165] There is no deduction for the original price since it was tax free. If shares are removed between years three and five, the employee must pay income tax on the lesser of the sums used to buy the shares and the value when removed.[166] Charges may also arise if share money is paid over to the employee or on cancellation payments to E.[167] Sums set aside by the employee in this way are tax free yet are not deductible from salary in computing relevant earnings for pension's limits.

Dividend shares may arise under a partnership share scheme. The rules are the same as for free shares (see §17.6.2 above).

17.6.6 *Matching (Partnership) Shares*

Employers may match partnership shares by giving employees up to two free shares for each partnership share they buy. The matching shares must be on the same terms and

---

[156] TCGA 1992, Sch 7D, para 4, ITEPA 2003, Sch 6, para 55, ex FA 2000, Sch 8, para 100.

[157] TCGA 1992, Sch 7D, para 2.

[158] ITEPA 2003, Sch 2, paras 43–57, ex FA 2000, Sch 8, paras 33–48.

[159] ITEPA 2003, Sch 2, para 46, ex FA 2000, Sch 8, para 36; there is also a minimum of £10 a month, ITEPA 2003, Sch 2 para 47, ex FA 2000, Sch 8, para 37.

[160] ITEPA 2003, Sch 2, para 46(2), ex FA 2000, Sch 8, para 36(2); on salary, see ITEPA 2003, Sch 2, para 43, ex FA 2000, Sch 8, para 48.

[161] ITEPA 2003, Sch 2, para 52.

[162] ITEPA 2003, Sch 2, para 48, ex FA 2000, Sch 8, para 38.

[163] ITEPA 2003, Sch 2, para 45(1), ex FA 2000, Sch 8, para 35(1).

[164] ITEPA 2003, Sch 2, para 50, ex FA 2000, Sch 8, para 40; on plans with accumulation powers, see ITEPA 2003, Sch 2, para 52(2), ex FA 2000, Sch 8, para 42(2).

[165] ITEPA 2003, s 506(2), ex FA 2000, Sch 8, para 86(2).

[166] ITEPA 2003, s 506(3), ex FA 2000, Sch 8, para 86(3).

[167] ITEPA 2003, ss 503 and 504, ex FA 2000, Sch 8, paras 84, 86.

carry the same rights as the partnership shares; the matching shares must be appropriated at the same time and to all employees on the same basis.[168] There are rules about giving employees information. The holding period rules are the same as for free shares (§17.6.2 above); further rules allow the company to require forfeiture of the matching shares when the employee leaves the employment.[169]

Income tax and CGT rules are the same as for free shares. The rules for dividend shares apply here too (§17.6.3 above).

11.6.7 Miscellaneous

Employers may deduct the costs of setting up and running the plan, and the market value of any free and matching shares used in the plan.[170] CTA 2009, section 989(1)(aa) denies a corporation tax deduction, however, where a payment to a SIP trust is made as part of a tax avoidance scheme, where the main purpose or one of the main purposes of the paying company is to obtain the deduction. The trustees are given a power to borrow money to buy the shares or subscribe for rights issues.[171] HMRC has powers to enquire into a SIP's compliance with the requirements of Schedule 2, decide that a SIP is not a Schedule 2 SIP where those requirements are not met, and impose penalties on the company for failure to comply.[172]

17.7   Save As Your Earn Share Option Schemes

Since 1980 it has been possible to combine a share option scheme with a savings scheme so as to take advantage of the tax efficiency of the savings scheme to provide the funds to finance the exercise of the option.[173] HMRC statistics show that in 2013–14, 270 companies granted Save As You Earn (SAYE) share options to 450,000 employees; the initial market value of shares over which options had been granted that year totalled £1.71 billion and the average value per employee of the shares over which options had been granted was £3,810. In that same year 310 companies had options exercised by a total of 170,000 employees with a total gain on the options of £650 million; the cost of the tax relief was £180 million and NIC relief was £140 million.

17.7.1   General Overview of SAYEs

17.7.1.1   The Scheme

The tax treatment of SAYE option schemes is governed by ITEPA 2003, Part 7, Chapter 7 and Schedule 3. The tax treatment of linked savings arrangements is determined in accordance

---

[168] ITEPA 2003, Sch 2, paras 58–61, ex FA 2000, Sch 8, paras 49–52.
[169] ITEPA 2003, s 505, ex FA 2000, Sch 8, para 81.
[170] CTA 2009, Pt 11, Ch 1, ex TA 1988, Sch 4AA.
[171] ITEPA 2003, Sch 2, para 76, ex FA 2000, Sch 8, para 69.
[172] ITEPA 2003, Sch 2, paras 81E-81K.
[173] TA 1988, s 185, Sch 9, Pts I–III, VI. On amendments relating to the retirement age and to ensure equality of treatment for men and women, see FA 1991, s 38.

with ITTOIA 2005, sections 702–708.[174] The employee's savings contribution must not exceed £500 a month.[175] The option is not normally exercisable for three or five years (ie the period needed to attract the bonus on maturity of the savings scheme) and the price for the shares must not exceed the proceeds of the contract. Notice of the scheme must be given to HMRC and annual returns filed.[176]

17.7.1.2 Who May Participate?

The participants in the scheme, ie those eligible to participate, must include all UK-resident employees (whether full-time or part-time) or full-time directors with, in each case, a qualifying period of no more than five years' service.[177]

17.7.1.3 Shares

The shares must be ordinary share capital and must be quoted, shares in a company not controlled by another company, shares in a company which is subject to an employee-ownership trust, or shares in a company under the control of a non-close quoted company.[178] The shares must be fully paid up and not redeemable.[179] The price at which the shares may be acquired must not be manifestly less than 80% of the market value at the time the option is acquired[180] (oddly the 80% figure was not changed in 1996). Schemes may contain provisions allowing for the transfer of rights following a takeover so as to give rights to acquire shares in the new company.[181] This must be agreed by the new company, and the value of the new option must be the same as that of the old option.

17.7.2 Tax Treatment

If these conditions are met, no income tax charge (or NICs) arises on the grant of the option.[182] No income tax charge (or NICs) arises on the exercise of the option unless it is exercised within three years of the grant.[183] Following exercise, capital gains tax rules will apply as usual, with the exercise price used as the cost of the shares in computing the gain or loss on disposal. Certain exercises within that period, eg when that scheme ends, are also exempt.[184] Special rules may apply if the company is taken over or some similar event occurs.[185] Any bonus or interest received under the linked savings arrangement is tax-free.[186] The employer may deduct the costs of introducing such schemes and corporation

---

[174] ITEPA 2003, s 516 and Sch 3, para 24, ex TA 1988, Sch 9, para 16A.
[175] ITEPA 2003, Sch 3, para 25(3)(a), ex TA 1988, Sch 9, para 24(2)(a).
[176] ITEPA 2003, Sch 3, paras 40A-40E.
[177] ITEPA 2003, Sch 3, paras 6–10, ex TA 1988, Sch 9, para 26, as amended by FA 1995, s 137.
[178] ITEPA 2003, Sch 3, para 19, ex TA 1988, Sch 9, para 11.
[179] ITEPA 2003, Sch 3, para 20, ex TA 1988, Sch 9, paras 12, 13; ITEPA 2003, Explanatory Notes Change 168.
[180] ITEPA 2003, Sch 3, para 28, ex TA 1988, Sch 9, para 25 as amended by FA 1989, s 62(3); see also cases on Sch 9, para 29. On para 28, see ITEPA 2003, Explanatory Notes Change 169.
[181] ITEPA 2003, Sch 3, paras 38 and 39, ex TA 1988, Sch 9, para 15; on capital gains consequences, see TCGA 1992, s 238.
[182] ITEPA 2003, s 475.
[183] ITEPA 2003, s 519.
[184] ITEPA 2003, s 519(3).
[185] ITEPA 2003, Sch 3, paras 34–38, ex TA 1988, Sch 9, para 21.
[186] ITTOIA 2005, s 702.

tax relief will normally be available when options are exercised on the amount of the benefit received by the employee.[187] HMRC has powers to enquire into compliance with the requirements of Schedule 3, decide that a SAYE option scheme is not a Schedule 3 SAYE option scheme where those requirements are not met, and impose penalties on the company for failure to comply.[188]

17.8 Company Share Option Plan Schemes

17.8.1 General Overview of CSOPs

A survey showed that whereas in 1987, 90% of companies had approved schemes compared with 10% that had unapproved schemes, by 1996, 80% of companies had approved schemes compared with 85% unapproved.[189] Explanations included the 1988 equalisation of tax rates for CGT and income tax, and the 1996 reduction in the limit for approved schemes to options over shares with a market value of £30,000. Another explanation was the 1996 rule that schemes had to be open to all employees, which applied as from 1996 and did not affect existing options. Symbolically—and accurately—the 1996 rule changes meant that schemes which had previously been called 'discretionary' schemes were instead called 'company' share schemes.

In 1993–94, 70,000 employees received options over shares with an initial value totalling £1,750 million; the average per employee was £25,000 and the cost of the tax relief was £70 million. In 2013–14 the comparable figures were 25,000, £200 million, £8,200 and £70 million (plus NIC relief of another £40 million).[190] There is a decided downward trend in the employee participation figures, particularly in recent years. In its March 2012 report on approved share schemes, the OTS questioned whether the CSOP scheme was still relevant and recommended that the Government consider phasing it out or, in the alternative, merging it with the EMI scheme. For now at least, CSOPs remain and the relevant rules are in ITEPA 2003, Part 7, Chapter 8 and Schedule 4. As with other tax-advantaged schemes, self-certification notices must be given to HMRC, options must be notified electronically to HMRC and annual returns filed.[191]

17.8.2 Tax Treatment

17.8.2.1 Benefits

Where an option is granted under a Schedule 4 CSOP scheme, no charge arises on the exercise of the option provided it is exercised not less than three nor more than 10 years

---

[187] CTA 2009, Pt 12 and see s 1221 referring to s 999, ex TA 1988, s 84A added by FA 1991, s 42.
[188] ITEPA 2003, Sch 3, paras 40F-40K.
[189] Cohen [1997] *Business Law Review* 131.
[190] HMRC Share Schemes Statistics, available at https://www.gov.uk/government/statistics/company-share-option-plans.
[191] ITEPA 2003, Sch 4, paras 28A-28E.

after the grant.[192] Instead, a charge to CGT arises on the disposal of the shares on the difference between the full cost of the option shares and the disposal proceeds. This is all subject
to the anti-avoidance provision in ITEPA 2003, section 524(1)(c).

Under ITEPA 2003, section 475, no tax charge arises on the grant of the option.
However, section 475 is subject to section 526. Under section 526, where the amount or
value of the consideration given for the option and the price payable under it is less than
the market value of the shares at that time, the difference is treated as share-related employment income in the year of the grant.[193] The right under an option to acquire shares at
a discount of up to 15% of market value was abolished by FA 1996 as part of the reaction against gains being made by certain executives following privatisation.[194] The amount
chargeable to income tax is treated as consideration given on the acquisition of the shares
when one comes to calculate the gain on the disposal of the shares.[195]

Any capital gain is calculated by reference to the actual consideration received rather
than market value;[196] the value of services or past services rendered by the employee is
excluded,[197] so that virtually the only consideration to be brought in will be pecuniary.
Finally, the employer can deduct the costs of introducing such schemes and corporation tax
relief will normally be available when options are exercised on the amount of the benefit
received by the employee.[198]

17.8.2.2 Conditions

Unlike 'all employee' plans such as SIPs and SAYEs, CSOP schemes are discretionary—a
company can choose to offer options to certain employees and not others. Any full-time
director or qualifying employee (whether full-time or part-time) of the company establishing the scheme (the grantor company), or of another company covered by the group
scheme, is eligible to participate.[199] Anyone with a material interest in a company must be
excluded, as must a part-time director.[200]

The value of the shares (at the time the option is granted) over which each participator
may hold unexercised options is restricted to £30,000. For earlier schemes the limit was

---

[192] ITEPA 2003, s 524, ex TA 1988, s 185(3), (5).

[193] ITEPA 2003, s 526, ex TA 1988, s 185(4).

[194] TA 1988, s 185(6B), added by FA 1991, s 39(5), which also amended s 185(6) and added s 185(6A) on
interaction with CGT and amendment of TCGA 1992, s 120 to avoid double charge (see FA 1993, s 105). Not in
ITEPA 2003 because spent.

[195] TCGA 1992, Sch 7D, para 12, ex TA 1988, s 185(7).

[196] TCGA 1992, Sch 7D, para 13, added by ITEPA 2003, Sch 6, paras 207 and 221.

[197] TCGA 1992, s 149A(3).

[198] CTA 2009, Pt 12 and see s 1221, referring to s 999, ex TA 1988, s 84A, added by FA 1991, s 42.

[199] ITEPA 2003, Sch 4, paras 7 and 8, ex TA 1988, Sch 9, para 27, as amended by FA 1995, s 137; previously only
full-time directors and full-time employees qualified, although they might exercise the rights after the employment ended. HMRC accept that the exercise of a CSOP option can be made subject to the attainment of objective
targets (by the company or option-holder): see HMRC Employee Share Schemes User Manual ESSUM44250,
based on principles established in *IRC v Burton Group plc* [1990] STC 242, 63 TC 191.

[200] ITEPA 2003, Sch 4, para 8(1) and 9, ex TA 1988, Sch 9, para 8; on definition of material interest, see ITEPA
2003, Sch 4, paras 10–14, ex TA 1988, s 187(3), Sch 9, paras 37–40; ITEPA 2003, Sch 4, para 13, ex TA 1988, Sch
9, para 40, was originally added by FA 1989, s 65 and excludes shares held in an employee benefit trust in the
calculation of a person's holding, unless caught by ITEPA 2003, Sch 4, para 15(2), ex TA 1988, Sch 9, para 40(3).
See also FA 1989, Sch 12, para 9. On para 11, see ITEPA 2003 Explanatory Notes Change 174.

the greater of (a) £100,000, and (b) four times the emoluments (for PAYE purposes, less benefits) in the year of assessment or the preceding year (or the 12 months beginning on the first day in the year of assessment for which there are such emoluments).[201] Within these limits the size of the option is at the company's discretion. FA 2010 responded to so-called 'geared growth' arrangements designed to circumvent the £30,000 maximum limit on the value of CSOP shares. The avoidance schemes involved share options granted over shares in companies which were under the control of a listed company. FA 2010, section 39 removed ITEPA 2003, Schedule 4, paragraph 17(1)(c), so that from 24 March 2010 shares in a company which is under the control of a listed company are no longer shares to which a CSOP scheme might apply.

The shares must be part of the fully paid-up ordinary share capital of the grantor company (or certain controlling companies)[202] and must be quoted on a recognised stock exchange, shares in a company not under the control of another company unless the controlling company is quoted (and is not a close company), or shares in a company which is subject to an employee-ownership trust.[203] There are further rules relating to the other shareholdings. The majority must be 'employee control' shares or 'open market' shares.[204]

The rights must be non-transferable. However, the PRs of deceased participants may exercise rights within one year of death (and subject to the 10-year rule—see §17.8.2.1 above).[205]

The company must be, or be controlled by, a single company.[206] The scheme may contain provisions allowing for the exercise of options or exchange of rights on certain company events, eg following a takeover; rights to acquire shares in the new company may be acquired.[207] This has to be agreed by the new company and the value of the new option must be the same as that of the old option.

The material terms of the option must be set out in a written agreement at the time the option is granted.[208] HMRC has powers to enquire into compliance with the requirements of Schedule 4, decide that a CSOP scheme is not a Schedule 4 CSOP scheme where those requirements are not met, and impose penalties on the company for failure to comply.[209]

---

[201] ITEPA 2003, Sch 4, para 6, ex TA 1988, Sch 9, para 28.

[202] ITEPA 2003, Sch 4, paras 16–19, ex, TA 1988, Sch 9, paras 10–12. TA 1988, Sch 9, para 10(c)(i), relating to shares in a consortium company, was repealed by FA 1989, s 64. The effect is to reduce the stake to be held by a member company of the consortium from 15 to five, making it easier for the consortium members shares to be used in this way. On paras 18 and 19, see ITEPA 2003, Explanatory Notes Changes 175 and 168 respectively.

[203] ITEPA 2003, Sch 4, para 17(2), ex TA 1988, Sch 9, paras 11, 12.

[204] ITEPA 2003, Sch 4, para 20, ex TA 1988, Sch 9, para 14.

[205] ITEPA 2003, Sch 4, paras 23–25, ex TA 1988, Sch 9, para 27(2), (3). On para 26, see ITEPA 2003 Explanatory Notes Change 176.

[206] ITEPA 2003, Sch 4, para 2, ex TA 1988, Sch 9, para 1(3); on relief for jointly-owned companies, see Sch 4, para 34, previously ESC B27. See ITEPA 2003 Explanatory Notes Change 173.

[207] ITEPA 2003, Sch 4, paras 25A- 27, ex TA 1988, Sch 9, para 15(7); on capital gains consequences, see TCGA 1992, s 238.

[208] ITEPA 2003, Sch 4, para 21A.

[209] ITEPA 2003, Sch 4, paras 28F-28K.

17.9   Enterprise Management Incentives

17.9.1   General Overview of EMIs

17.9.1.1   Overview

Enterprise management incentives (EMIs) are share option schemes designed to help small companies attract and retain the key people they need, and to reward employees for taking a risk by investing their time and skills in helping small companies achieve their potential. The rules introduced in 2000 were widened in 2001,[210] EMIs bear testimony to New Labour's striking willingness to grant great favours to small groups of people, and are found in ITEPA 2003, Part 7, Chapter 9 and Schedule 5. In 2009–10, a mere 2,190 companies had granted these options in favour of 16,900 employees; the average value per employee was £9,000. The annual tax cost was estimated to be £9 million and a NIC cost of £40 million.[211] In 2013–14, nearly 3,000 companies had granted these options in favour of 20,000 employees; the average value per employee was £15,400. The annual tax cost was estimated to be £70 million and a NIC cost of £40 million.

An option qualifies as an EMI option only if granted for commercial reasons in order to recruit or retain an employee (originally, ie in FA 2000, a 'key' employee) to or in a company;[212] it must not be part of a scheme or arrangement the main purpose of which is the avoidance of tax. There is presently a limit of £250,000 per employee and the company may grant up to £3 million (originally £1.5 million) of these EMI share options.[213] The £250,000 limit is calculated by reference to the value of the option shares at the time the option was granted. Where an employee holds options over £250,000, EMI treatment will apply to the first £250,000. Unexercised options granted to the employee under a CSOP scheme count towards this limit. The £250,000 limit applies to a three-year period beginning with the date of the grant; so if an employee is given £250,000 of share options in the first year and exercises them in the third year, no new options may be taken out until year four when the third anniversary of the grant comes round. Although EMI schemes previously did not require formal HMRC approval, FA 2014 introduced an online self-certification procedure along the same lines as that used for SIPs, SAYEs and CSOPs. Grants of EMI options must be notified electronically to HMRC and annual returns need to be filed with HMRC.

This scheme is meant to apply to small, high-risk companies. The company must be a qualifying company,[214] ie one which is an independent[215] trading[216] company with fewer than 250 full-time employees and gross assets not exceeding £30 million.[217] The company may be listed or unlisted, but must meet qualifying conditions and in particular must not

---

[210] FA 2001, ss 61 and 62, See Cohen [2001] BTR 309.
[211] HMRC Share Schemes Statistics available at https://www.gov.uk/government/statistics/enterprise-management-incentives-share-option-schemes.
[212] ITEPA 2003, Sch 5, para 4, ex FA 2000, Sch 14, para 9.
[213] ITEPA 2003, Sch 5, paras 5–7, ex FA 2000, Sch 14, paras 10, 11. At Budget 2008, the employee limit was raised from £100,000 to £120,000 in respect of options granted on or after 6 April 2008.
[214] ITEPA 2003, Sch 5, paras 8–23, ex FA 2000, Sch 14, paras 12–17.
[215] ITEPA 2003, Sch 5, para 9, ex FA 2000, Sch 14, para 13.
[216] ITEPA 2003, Sch 5, paras 13 and 14, ex FA 2000, Sch 14, para 17.
[217] ITEPA 2003, Sch 5, paras 12–12A, ex FA 2000, Sch 14, para 16.

be involved in certain prohibited types of trade.[218] The receipt of substantial sums by way of royalty or licence fee will disqualify a company, unless the IP rights were created by the company or another group company.[219] To ensure that the EMI scheme complies with EU state aid guidelines, F(No 3)A 2010 removed the need for a company granting EMI options to operate wholly or mainly in the UK. Instead, the company will only need to have a PE in the UK. In the case of a parent company, at least one company in the group that is carrying on a qualifying trade must have a PE in the UK.[220] Only qualifying companies may form a group; only the parent may grant EMI options. Subsidiaries will prevent the parent from granting EMI options unless each subsidiary meets certain control and holding requirements.[221] These requirements were amended by FA 2004, making it easier for a subsidiary to satisfy the tests; for a trading subsidiary the threshold is reduced to 51% subsidiaries. The provisions also permit certain property management subsidiaries to qualify, so long as they meet the higher, 90% subsidiary threshold.[222] The relief also applies to a company carrying on activities of R&D from which it is intended that a qualifying trade will emerge.[223]

There is no provision expressly allowing the company to deduct the costs of setting up these schemes.

17.9.1.2 The Employee[224]

Eligible employees must work for the company for a substantial amount of their time, ie 25 hours per week or, if less, 75% of their working time;[225] they may be inventors, scientists or experts in raising finance. The idea is that company may offer up to £3 million worth of share options to help it recruit and retain the people that they need to make their company successful and grow. There are rules on the relationship between this and other share schemes.[226] The employee must not have a material interest, ie control of 30% or more of the ordinary share capital.[227]

The option must be capable of being exercised within 10 years;[228] a charge arises if it is not exercised within the period.[229] The option may be conditional, provided the condition can occur within the period. The option must be over the ordinary share capital of the company and must be fully paid-up and not redeemable.[230]

---

[218] ITEPA 2003, Sch 5, paras 15–23, ex FA 2000, Sch 14, paras 18–26.

[219] ITEPA 2003, Sch 5, para 19, ex FA 2000, Sch 14, para 22. Pursuant to Sch 5, para 19, receipt of royalties is an excluded activity except where from 'relevant intangible asset' (RIA). The RIA category was widened by FA 2007, s 61 to allow assets to be transferred to new subsidiaries without losing RIA status.

[220] ITEPA 2003, Sch 5, paras 14A and 15, ex FA 2000, Sch 14, para 18.

[221] ITEPA 2003, Sch 5, paras 10 and 11, ex FA 2000, Sch 14, paras 14, 15.

[222] Amending ITEPA 2003, Sch 5, para 11 and adding paras 11A and 11B.

[223] ITEPA 2003, Sch 5, para 15(2), ex FA 2000, Sch 14, para 18(2).

[224] ITEPA 2003, Sch 5, paras 24–33, ex FA 2000, Sch 14, paras 27–36.

[225] ITEPA 2003, Sch 5, paras 26 and 27, ex FA 2000, Sch 14, para 29.

[226] ITEPA 2003, Sch 5, para 5(4), ex FA 2000, Sch 14, para 10(6). Options under para 5(4) count towards the limit.

[227] ITEPA 2003, Sch 5, paras 28–33; on employee trust see ITEPA 2003, ss 550–554, ex FA 2000, Sch 14, paras 30–36.

[228] ITEPA 2003, Sch 5, para 36, ex FA 2000, Sch 14, para 39.

[229] ITEPA 2003, s 529(2)(3), ex FA 2000, Sch 14, para 42(2).

[230] ITEPA 2003, Sch 5, para 35, ex FA 2000, Sch 14, para 38(1)(a).

The option must be non-assignable[231] and the terms must be agreed in writing.[232] However, there are no rules directing the conditions under which the share may be issued; so the shares may be non-voting or subject to pre-emption rights on the part of the company. This is to allow the company to protect its independence.[233]

17.9.2 Tax Treatment

If the option is granted at current market value, there is no income tax (or NIC) liability on either the grant[234] or the exercise of the option.[235] However, if the option price is below market value, the value of the discount counts as employment income of the year of the grant.[236] The company may grant options at a price above market value if it wishes. Corporation tax relief will normally be available when options are exercised equal to the difference between the market value when the shares are acquired and the amount that the employee pays for them. Where EMI options were granted at a discount, relief is given for both the amount of the discount and the amount that would have been charged to tax but for the EMI relief.[237] The rules giving the company a deduction for corporation tax were widened by FA 2006 where the qualifying EMI option is over restricted shares and is at a discount. Previously the deduction was limited to the amount of the discount; it now extends to the amount that would have been taxable but for the income tax relief under the EMI rules. Another change widened the corporation tax relief where the EMI option is over convertible shares.[238] Capital gains tax will apply on the disposal of the shares received. Where the shares are sold more than a year after the option was granted, entrepreneurs' relief will generally be available to reduce the CGT rate to 10% on the first £10 million of lifetime gains (see below §32.7).

17.9.2.1 Disqualifying Events[239]

The precise effect of such an event depends on its nature. The events are:

(1) loss of independence, ie becoming a 51% subsidiary of another company or otherwise coming under the control of another company;[240]
(2) ceasing to meet the correct trading activities requirements;
(3) ceasing to meet the eligible employee requirements, eg the 75% working time conditions;[241]

---

[231] ITEPA 2003, Sch 5, para 38, ex FA 2000, Sch 14, para 41.
[232] ITEPA 2003, Sch 5, para 37, ex FA 2000, Sch 14, para 40.
[233] Inland Revenue Memorandum, 4.7 and 4.9.
[234] ITEPA 2003, s 475, ex ITEPA 2003, s 528.
[235] ITEPA 2003, s 530, ex FA 2000, Sch 14, para 45.
[236] ITEPA 2003, s 531, ex FA 2000, Sch 14, para 45.
[237] HMRC manual ESSUM57900, available at http://www.hmrc.gov.uk/manuals/essum/essum57900.htm.
[238] The rules for restricted and also convertible shares were rewritten into CTA 2009, s 1012, ex FA 2003, Sch 23, paras 21–22C. See HMRC Notes on clauses for examples.
[239] ITEPA 2003, ss 533–539, ex FA 2000, Sch 14, paras 47–53.
[240] On control, see ITEPA 2003 Technical Note 51.
[241] ITEPA 2003, s 535, ex FA 2000, Sch 14, para 52.

(4) alterations in the terms of the option, the effect of which is to increase the value of the shares or to break the rules as to qualifying options;[242]
(5) any relevant alteration in the share capital of the company;[243]
(6) any relevant conversion of the shares;[244]
(7) granting the employee an option under another scheme if this would take the employee over the £120,000 maximum level.[245]

The shares must be valued at the date of the disqualifying event.[246] Relief on the value down to that event continues to be available, but any later increase in value is subject to a charge under Part 5.[247]

17.9.2.2 Other Employment Income Share Option Rules

ITEPA 2003, Part 7, Chapter 3C, which would otherwise deem a loan if the option price were below market value, is excluded.[248] However, the legislation makes it clear that nothing in the EMI code affects the operation of various provisions in Part 7 which are listed as Chapters 2–4, subject to what has just been said about Chapters 3C and 5 (§17.9.2.1 above). So nothing in the new rules will prevent a charge from arising under section 476 on the release of rights attached to shares acquired under a qualifying option or where conditions on securities are removed and the charge arises under Chapter 2, section 427 (ex TA 1988, section 140A) or, if there is a conversion coming within Chapter 3, section 438 (ex TA 1988, section 140D).[249] There will also be a charge under section 476 (ex TA 1988, section 135) if a sum is received for the release of rights under the option itself.[250]

Capital gains tax[251] will be payable when the shares are sold. Where there is a rights issue in respect of shares acquired under these options, there is no amalgamation of the two holdings for CGT purposes.[252]

Further rules apply to the effect of a company reorganisation, as where the company in which the employee had the relevant options is taken over and new replacement options are given by the new company.[253]

17.10 Employee Shareholder Scheme

Under a scheme created in 2013 a person with 'employee shareholder' status is entitled to certain income tax, NICs and capital gains benefits on employee shares.[254] An employee

---

[242] ITEPA 2003, s 536(1)(a).
[243] ITEPA 2003, s 536(1)(b) and (c) and 537, ex FA 2000, Sch 14, para 49.
[244] ITEPA 2003, ss 536(1)(d) and 538, ex FA 2000, Sch 14, para 50.
[245] ITEPA 2003, ss 536(1)(e) and 539.
[246] ITEPA 2003, s 532, ex FA 2000, Sch 14, para 53; ITEPA 2003 Explanatory Notes Change 130.
[247] ITEPA 2003, s 541, ex FA 2000, Sch 14, para 55.
[248] ITEPA 2003, s 540(1), ex FA 2000, Sch 14, para 54.
[249] ITEPA 2003, s 541(1), ex FA 2000, Sch 14, para 55(1)(b) or (c); note s 541(2) on valuation.
[250] ITEPA 2003, s 541(2), ex FA 2000, Sch 14, para 55(1)(a).
[251] TCGA 1992, Sch 7D, paras 14–15, added by ITEPA 2003, Sch 6, para 221, ex FA 2000, Sch 14, paras 56–57.
[252] TCGA 1992, Sch 7D, para 16, added by ITEPA 2003, Sch 6, para 221. The rules in TCGA 1992, Sch 7D, para 16 disappy the usual reorganisation or reduction of share capital rules in TCGA 1992, ss 127–130.
[253] ITEPA 2003, Sch 5, paras 39–43, ex Sch 14, paras 59–63; note also s 534 para 42(2). On replacement options, see ITEPA 2003 Explanatory Notes Change 177.
[254] See https://www.gov.uk/guidance/employee-shareholders.

shareholder is someone who works under an employment contract and owns at least £2,000 worth of shares in the employer's company or parent company. Such a person is generally exempt from income tax and NICs on the first £2,000 worth of employee shareholder shares received.[255] An employee shareholder is also eligible for a lifetime exemption from CGT of £100,000 (formerly £50,000) on the disposal of employee shares. This applies to employee shareholder shares acquired in consideration of an employee shareholder agreement entered into from midnight at the end of 16 March 2016.[256] The quid pro quo is that employee shareholders are not entitled to certain statutory employment rights, including in relation to unfair dismissal and redundancy payments.

17.11   Research Institution Spin-out Companies

One class of shares—those in research institution spin-out companies—receive specially favourable treatment in ITEPA 2003, Part 7, Chapter 4A.[257] The treatment arises where there is a transfer of intellectual property (IP) to or from one or more research institutions to a spin-out company. The shares in the spin-out company must be acquired before the IP transfer agreement or within 183 days afterwards, and the opportunity to acquire the shares must arise by reason of the employment by the research institutions or company. In addition, the person acquiring the shares must be involved in the research. Tax avoidance must not be a main purpose of the arrangement under which the opportunity to acquire the shares arose.[258]

If the conditions are satisfied, the taxable amount under Chapter 4 (post-acquisition benefit) in respect of the benefits from IP transfer is nil (section 453). In addition, there is a deemed election under section 431 to disapply Chapter 2 (section 454) and Chapter 3B (section 455). The overall effect is to prevent charges from arising at a time when the researcher will have acquired the shares but, being an academic, may not have funds with which to pay the tax.

---

[255] ITEPA 2003, ss 226A-226D.
[256] TCGA 1992, ss 236B-236G.
[257] Added by FA 2005, s 20. FA 2005 made other consequential changes to various parts of the legislation.
[258] ITEPA 2003, ss 451 and 456–460.

18

Employment Income: Deductions and Expenses

18.1 Introduction

ITEPA 2003, Part 5 contains six chapters and provides two main sets of rules for deductions—in Chapters 2 (sections 333–360A) and 5 (sections 369–377). Chapter 2 re-enacts well-known and mostly long-established rules for deductions for expenses paid by employees. Chapter 5 brings together rules on deductions for earnings representing benefits under certain provisions of the benefits code, eg Part 3, Chapter 10. These have been 'included' under Chapter 3 and now have to be excluded if they meet the conditions for Part 5, Chapter 5. Of the remaining chapters of Part 5, Chapter 1 provides some general rules for deductions; Chapter 3 deals with deductions from benefits code earnings; Chapter 4 authorises fixed-sum allowances for repairing and maintaining work equipment[1] or payable out of the public revenue; and Chapter 6 covers deductions for seafarers' earnings.

For Chapter 2, three principal provisions must be kept in mind when considering the deductibility of expenses paid by the employee. First, the general rule in ITEPA 2003, section 336 allows a deduction from earnings if

(a) the employee is obliged to incur and pay the expense as holder of the employment, and

(b) the amount is incurred wholly, exclusively and necessarily in the performance of the duties of the office or employment.[2]

---

[1] Previously Concession A1, see ITEPA explanatory notes change 100.
[2] Ex TA 1988, section 198, as rewritten in FA 1998, s 61, superseding an earlier effort in FA 1997, s 62.

Secondly and thirdly, sections 337 and 338 enact two travel expense rules. In each case the first element is the same as that for section 336, part (a)—ie the employee must be obliged to incur the expense[3] and must pay it as holder of the employment.[4] Section 337 after repeating part (a) echoes 19th-century law by requiring that the expenses be necessarily incurred on travelling in the performance of the duties of the employment. Section 338, which dates back to only 1998, requires (b) that the expenses must be attributable to the employee's necessary attendance at any place in the performance of the duties of the employment. These words preserve many of the old concepts. One minor presentational change, made in 1998, was the removal of a reference to the costs of keeping a horse to enable employees to perform their duties.[5] Although most of the established case law concern travel expenses, we shall consider the general rule in section 336 (below §18.2) first before the specific travelling expense rules in sections 337 and 338 (§18.3).

While sections 336–338 are usually quite adequate for expenses paid by the employee, some consistency of treatment is needed when, say, a higher-paid employee buys a train ticket and the expense is borne by the employer (a) through a round sum allowance (taxed as earnings under what is now section 62), (b) by a specific expense payment (now Part 3, Chapter 3), (c) via a credit card (a credit token) or (d) the employer actually buys the ticket and hands it over (a non-cash voucher). So ITEPA 2003, Part 5 not only deals with these rules where the expense is paid by the employee, but also provides further rules in the other chapters—see further below §18.4.

Before turning to the detail of ITEPA 2003, Part 5, Chapter 2, we must note some general rules in Chapter 1. First, section 328(1) provides that the deduction is allowed only against earnings from *the* employment, and not any other employment. This rule is widened for ministers of religion, refined for earnings out of the public revenue and then restricted by a number of rules which require that the expense be set against particular receipts specified (section 328(2)–(5)). Section 329 provides that a deduction for expenses is not to exceed the earnings; so the expenses may reduce the tax to nil but cannot give rise to a net loss. Again this rule is widened for ministers of religion and disregarded for certain statutory hypotheses in making other calculations (sections 329 and 332). Section 329 looks odd when ITA 2007, sections 23 and 128 expressly allow the loss arising *in an employment* to be set off.[6] The Notes to the Bill suggest that a loss may arise in three situations: (a) for ministers of religion; (b) where capital allowances exceed the earnings income; and (c) where the loss arises because the employee's contract makes him liable for losses as well as entitled to profits.[7] *J Martin v HMRC* is an example of an employee incurring negative employment

---

[3] In *Bevins v McLeish* [1995] STC (SCD) 342, the taxpayer unsuccessfully argued for relief for expenditure that had not actually been made.

[4] In *Harrop v Gilroy* [1995] STC (SCD) 294, a taxpayer unsuccessfully argued for expenses to be relieved against unemployment benefit.

[5] The horse was introduced in 1853 (see 16 and 17 Vict c 34, s 51); on its Trojan characteristics, see Lord Reid in *Taylor v Provan* [1974] STC 168, 175, [1974] 1 All ER 1201, 1206, 49 TC 579, 605. For another view of the horse, see Pollock MR in *Ricketts v Colquhoun* [1925] 1 KB 725, 732. See also *Elderkin v Hindmarsh* [1988] STC 267, 60 TC 651.

[6] Ex TA 1988, section 380 allowed the loss *arising from an employment* to be set off.

[7] See ITEPA explanatory note change 81. The rule in section 329 replaces the old and very long-established requirement that the expense had to be paid 'out of' the earnings; it was these words which the Revenue took to justify their position that there could be no loss.

income in a year, in this case as a result of having to repay a bonus received and taxed in a prior year upon leaving his employment.[8]

Section 330 forbids double deductions, eg where the employee has incurred an expense but may also claim a fixed-sum allowance,[9] and section 331 provides an order in which deductions are to be made by referring to the relevant provisions elsewhere. For the rules where a foreign element is involved, see above at §13.3.

18.2 The General Rule for Deducting Employment Expenses

As already noted, under the general deductibility rule in ITEPA 2003, section 336, expenses must be incurred in the performance of the duties of the office or employment and necessarily be so incurred. In addition, these expenses must also be incurred wholly and exclusively in the performance of those duties. The words of the general rule were described by Vaisey J[10] as being 'stringent and exacting; compliance with each and every one of them is obligatory if the benefit of the rule is to be claimed successfully. They are to my mind, deceptive words in the sense that when examined they are found to come to nearly nothing at all'.

18.2.1 In The Performance of Duties

The cases draw a sharp distinction between expenditure incurred in the performance of the duties of an employment, and expenditure incurred in order either to enable the employee to do the job initially[11] or to enable him to perform the duties of that employment more efficiently. Thus, the cost of engaging a housekeeper to look after one's family and so enable one to go out to work is not deductible,[12] a situation which is radically changed in effect (but not in theory) by the system of tax credits (see §9.4)—for those who qualify. Many of the cases on the 'in the performance of duties' test relate to travel expenses, which uses the same test. Those cases are discussed under §18.3.1 below.

18.2.1.1 Subscriptions and Agent's Fees

In a case brought under what is now section 336, subscriptions to professional bodies paid by a county medical officer of health were disallowed,[13] even though the journals received from those societies enabled him to keep himself properly qualified. This rule was reversed by statute and subscriptions are now deductible—but only for a relatively limited list of

---

[8] [2013] UKFTT 040 (TCC), discussed above at §10.3.2.3.
[9] See ITEPA explanatory note change 82.
[10] *Lomax v Newton* (1953) 34 TC 558, 561–62.
[11] *Lupton v Potts* [1969] 3 All ER 1083, 45 TC 643; *Elderkin v Hindmarsh* [1988] STC 267, 60 TC 651.
[12] *Bowers v Harding* [1891] 1 QB 560, 3 TC 22; *Halstead v Condon* (1970) 46 TC 289.
[13] *Simpson v Tate* [1925] 2 KB 214, 9 TC 314, Rowlatt J.

professional membership fees[14] (the list does not cover trade unions) and for annual subscriptions to approved societies (sections 343 and 344). This does not usually extend to
allow professional people to claim tax relief on their membership subscriptions to professional bodies while employed.[15] A specific provision now allows an actor to deduct agent's
fees, including payments to bona fide co-operatives;[16] another deals with the housing costs
of clergymen; here we have one of the few ITEPA 2003 changes adverse to the taxpayer.[17]
Other specific provisions are considered in §18.2.4 below.

18.2.1.2 Improvement Not Enough

A schoolteacher who attended a series of weekend lectures in history at a college for adult
education for the purposes of improving his background knowledge could not deduct
those expenses.[18] There is a distinction between qualifying to teach and getting background
material, on the one hand, and preparing lectures for delivery, on the other hand.[19] Similarly, a clerk who was obliged to attend late meetings of the council and who bought himself a meal before the meeting was not allowed to deduct the cost of the meal; he had been
instructed to work late, not to eat.[20] On similar grounds, an employee was not allowed to
deduct the costs of a record player and gramophone records which he had purchased for
the purpose of providing a stimulus of good music while he worked especially late at night.
As Cross J drily observed, 'it may well be that [he] was stimulated to work better by hearing good music, just as other people may be stimulated to work better by drink'.[21] More
recent examples offer little comfort for hopeful or ingenious taxpayers. So the court denied
a deduction where the taxpayer sought to deduct legal expenses incurred to be registered
with the Securities Association.[22] The same conclusion was reached when a professional
rugby player sought to deduct the costs of various dietary supplements to boost body mass
and muscles,[23] and where a psychotherapist incurred expenses on a personal psychotherapy
course, even though this was a condition of employment.[24] In *Revenue and Customs Comrs v
Banerjee*,[25] however, the Court of Appeal allowed a claim by a trainee medical registrar

---

[14] ITEPA 2003, s 343(1), ex TA 1988, s 201; on changes in ss 343–45, see ITEPA explanatory note changes
84–89. The list of professions in s 343(2) now includes health professionals, legal professionals (ie licensed convey-
ancers) and driving instructors, but not lawyers or accountants; this does not prevent people in self-employment
from deducting these costs. A list of approved societies is available on the HMRC website; see [1998] *Simon's Tax
Intelligence* 986. On fees for solicitor's practising certificates, see notice by The Law Society, 24 February 1993,
[1993] *Simon's Tax Intelligence* 341.
[15] HC Written Answer, 30 March 1990, [1990] *Simon's Tax Intelligence* 317.
[16] ITEPA 2003, s 352; see ITEPA explanatory note change 90, ex TA 1988, s 201A, added by FA 1990, s 77, as
amended by FA 1991, s 69.
[17] ITEPA 2003, s 351, ex TA 1988, s 332; see ITEPA explanatory note change 91.
[18] *Humbles v Brooks* (1962) 40 TC 500; ESC A64 was described as obsolete following the launch of Individual
Learning Accounts (now repealed).
[19] (1962) 40 TC 500, 504. Even if this distinction had been ignored, the expenditure might have failed on the
ground of necessity since it was possible that a properly qualified history teacher could have been appointed who
would not have needed to attend the course.
[20] *Sanderson v Durbidge* [1955] 3 All ER 154, 36 TC 239; neither could the recorder in *Ricketts v Colquhoun*
[1926] AC 1, 10 TC 118.
[21] *Newlin v Woods* (1966) 42 TC 649, 658.
[22] *Ben Nevis v IRC* [2001] *Simon's Weekly Tax Intelligence* 1109.
[23] *Ansell v Brown* [2001] STC 1166.
[24] *Snowdon v Charnock* [2001] *Simon's Weekly Tax Intelligence* 1111.
[25] [2010] EWCA Civ 843, [2010] STC 2318.

to deduct certain training expenses. As it was a training contract, the expenses had been incurred 'in the course of performing the duties' of that contract. The judges also agreed that it was necessary to look at the whole training course rather than individual pieces of it.

18.2.1.3 Newspapers

The House of Lords demands uniformity between Scotland and England. The distinction between expenditure incurred in the performance of the duties of the employment and that which is incurred simply to prepare oneself to carry out those duties has been explored in *Smith v Abbott*.[26] Four journalists claimed in respect of expenditure on newspapers and periodicals.[27] The Commissioners held in relation to each of them that the reading of the material was a necessary part of their duties as staff photographer, sports reporter, news sub-editor and picture editor; it was inherent in their jobs. They therefore concluded that the expenses were deductible. This was upheld by Warner J and by the Court of Appeal, but reversed (by a majority) by the House of Lords. Lord Templeman pointed out that the reading was not done at their place of work but at home, while travelling to and from work and in the employees' own time;[28] the fact that there was no contractual obligation to buy and read these papers was irrelevant.[29] Under such circumstances the journalists did not purchase and read the newspapers in the performance of their duties but for the purpose of ensuring that they would carry out their duties efficiently.[30]

The first two reasons for Lord Templeman's conclusions are non-controversial: (a) that any other decision would enable journalists to claim for a wide range of items entirely on their own discretion, including wining and dining;[31] and (b) that the work of the journalists did not begin until they reached the office.[32] The third reason is different: (c) that on the almost identical facts in *Fitzpatrick v IRC (No 2)*, which was heard by their Lordships jointly with *Smith v Abbott*, a Special Commissioner sitting in Scotland had reached a different decision from that of the English General Commissioners in *Smith v Abbott*, and they could not both be right.[33] This is fallacious since all depends upon the evidence, and two other members of the majority, Lord Jauncey and Lord Mustill, were much more circumspect in concluding that while there were differences in evidence, they were not in the end sufficient to justify a different decision.[34] The dissentient, Lord Browne-Wilkinson, concluded that the court had no power to overrule the findings of the Commissioners.[35] His points were dissected by Lord Templeman in a manner which was fraternal only in the sense that the best rows are within the family.[36]

---

[26] *Fitzpatrick v IRC (No 2)*; *Smith v Abbott* [1994] STC 237, 66 TC 407, HL.

[27] Technically, like the taxpayer in *Taylor v Provan* (see §18.2.1.2), they were claiming under s 336 (ex s 198) in order to escape from a charge under Pt, 3 Ch 3 (ex TA 1988, s 153) in respect of an allowance to cover these items.

[28] [1994] STC 237, 245b, 244a, 247d; 66 TC 407, 524, 522, 527 respectively.

[29] *Ibid*, 245j, 524.

[30] *Ibid*, 243b, 521.

[31] *Ibid*, 247a, 526.

[32] *Ibid*, 244a, 522.

[33] *Ibid*, 242e, 520.

[34] *Ibid*, 248, 255, 528, 536; the fifth member of the Committee, Lord Keith, agreed with Lord Templeman.

[35] *Ibid*, 254, 535.

[36] *Ibid*, 247–48, 527.

18.2.2 Necessarily so Incurred

The cases often fail to distinguish the requirement that the expense be incurred in the performance of the duties of the employment from the requirement that it be necessarily so
incurred. It is, however, clear from the cases that the test of necessity is objective. Hence an
employee with defective eyesight cannot recover the cost of his glasses.[37] Many of the cases
on the 'necessarily' test relate to travel expenses under section 337, which uses the same test.
Those cases are discussed under §18.3.1 below.[38]

The fact that the employer requires the particular expenditure is not decisive.[39] As
Donovan LJ put it:

> The test is not whether the employer imposes the expense but whether the duties do, in the sense
> that irrespective of what the employer may prescribe, the duties cannot be performed without
> incurring the particular outlay.[40]

Therefore, a student assistant in the research laboratories of a company, who was required
to attend classes in preparation for an external degree from the University of London, was
not allowed to deduct his expenses,[41] any more than a soldier was obliged to share in the
costs of the mess.[42] In *Brown v Bullock*,[43] a bank manager was not allowed to deduct the
cost of his subscription to a London club even though it was 'virtually a condition of his
employment'. However, in *Elwood v Utitz*,[44] a director of a company in Northern Ireland
who was obliged to travel to and stay in London frequently was allowed to deduct the costs
of his subscription to a London club since he was buying accommodation, and the fact that
he chose to buy it at a club rather than a hotel was immaterial.

18.2.3 Wholly and Exclusively

Many of these cases could as easily be explained on the ground that the expenditure was
not incurred wholly and exclusively for the employment. Thus, in the mess cases there was
some element of personal benefit,[45] while in *Brown v Bullock* (above) the bank manager
derived personal benefit from the membership of the club. Unlike the test of necessity, the

---

[37] *Roskams v Bennett* (1950) 32 TC 129. FA 2006, s 62 added ITEPA 2003, s 320A, which excludes from liability
for income tax the provision for employees of eye tests and special corrective appliances shown to be necessary by
the test. The exemption does not apply to glasses generally but where provision is required by health and safety
regulations; see Budget 2006 note BN31 (March 2006).

[38] See eg *Ricketts v Colquhoun* [1926] AC 1, 10 (seen below at §18.3.1.2). But if the taxpayer is the only person
capable of doing the job, different questions arise (*Taylor v Provan* [1974] STC 168, [1974] 1 All ER 1201, 49 TC
579; also see below at §18.3.1.2).

[39] But the fact that an employer has not sanctioned it greatly weakens the taxpayer's case; see *Owen v Burden*
[1972] 1 All ER 356, 358, 47 TC 476, 481 (county surveyor unable to deduct cost of journey to Japan to attend
world road congress) and *Maclean v Trembath* (1956) 36 TC 653, 666.

[40] *Brown v Bullock* (1961) 40 TC 1, 10.

[41] *Blackwell v Mills* [1945] 2 All ER 655, 26 TC 468. He was not performing his duties as a laboratory assistant
when he was listening to the lecture (26 TC 468, 470).

[42] *Lomax v Newton* [1953] 2 All ER 801, 34 TC 558; *Griffiths v Mockler* [1953] 2 All ER 805, 35 TC 135. A major
in the Royal Army Pay Corps would have been subject to disciplinary action if he had not paid, but mess membership was not necessarily in the performance of his duties as an officer.

[43] [1961] 1 All ER 206, 40 TC 1. Counsel for the bank manager conceded that his client could still perform the
duties of a bank manager even though he had not been a member of the club.

[44] (1965) 42 TC 482.

[45] *Griffiths v Mockler* (1953) 35 TC 135 at 137.

requirement of 'wholly and exclusively' is not wholly objective.[46] Thus, the expenditure may satisfy this test if its sole object is the performance of duties, regardless of the fact that it may bring about some other incidental result or effect.[47] In *Revenue and Customs Comrs v Banerjee*,[48] the Court of Appeal allowed a claim by a trainee medical registrar to deduct certain training expenses. They agreed that the expenses had been incurred 'in the course of performing the duties' of that contract, but disagreed on whether the payment was so incurred 'exclusively'. Pitchford LJ, dissenting, held that the taxpayer was not only seeking to be trained but also to obtain professional advancement, ie become a consultant, and this was the basis of his decision ([60] and [62]). The majority, however, thought the matter was settled by looking at the training course *as a whole* rather than at individual pieces of it (Rimer LJ at [38]–[39] and Hooper LJ at [68]).

Where a person wears ordinary clothes but of a standard required by the employer, no part of the cost is deductible.[49] However, where a car is being used sometimes for business purposes and sometimes for personal purposes, part of the costs is allowable. The distinction between the two cases is that when the car is being used for business purposes it is being used only for those purposes, whereas when the clothes are worn at work they have a dual purpose, part-business, part-personal.[50] Therefore, where a telephone is used partly for business calls, the taxpayer may deduct the business calls but not the others; in theory, there is no deduction for any part of the telephone rental.[51]

18.2.4 Miscellaneous Non-travel Provisions

18.2.4.1 Entertainment Expenses

CTA 2009, section 1298 and ITTOIA 2005, sections 45–47 prohibit the deduction of relevant business entertainment expenses. Deduction of these expenses is also disallowed by ITEPA 2003, section 356, which extends to business-related gifts. This could lead to a double non-deduction if the employee incurs an expense which the employer reimburses, or where the employee is given an allowance for the purpose. Not only is the employee taxable in respect of the reimbursement or allowance, but the employer also is unable to deduct the expense of reimbursement or allowance. In order to avoid such a result, ITEPA 2003, section 357 provides that in these circumstances the prohibition in section 356 does not apply, and so the employee is not taxable on the reimbursement or allowance.[52]

18.2.4.2 Home Working

Although section 316A exempts from tax a payment by an employer for certain expenses incurred through working at home, it is limited to that circumstance. It does not allow the

---

[46] *Elwood v Utitz* (1965) 42 TC 482, 498, per Lord MacDermott CJ.
[47] 42 TC 482, 497, relying on cases decided under schedule D, Case II—but before *Mallalieu v Drumond* [1983] STC 665, 57 TC 330.
[48] [2010] EWCA Civ 843, [2010] STC 2318.
[49] By analogy with *Mallalieu v Drummond* [1983] STC 665, HL (see §22.2 below), and subject to the same exceptions.
[50] *Hillyer v Leaks* [1976] STC 490, 51 TC 590; *Woodcock v IRC* [1977] STC 405, 51 TC 698; and *Ward v Dunn* [1979] STC 178, 52 TC 517.
[51] *Lucas v Cattell* (1972) 48 TC 353.
[52] ITTOIA 2005, s 46(3)(b); CTA 2009, s 1299(3)(b). On ITEPA 2003, s 357, see ITEPA Technical Note 38.

employee to deduct such costs which are barred by section 336.[53] Payments to pension schemes are deductible under the relevant legislation.

18.2.4.3 Payroll Giving

In a major departure from orthodox tax theory, an employee is allowed to deduct from his pre-tax earnings contributions to charity under an approved payroll deduction scheme. There is now no maximum amount. The scheme has effect both for employment income (ITEPA 2003) and for PAYE.[54]

18.2.4.4 Liability Insurance Premiums and Uninsured Liabilities; Employment and Post-Employment

Sections 346–350 allow a deduction for money spent either on discharging a liability related to the employment together with associated costs and expenses, or on a premium for a qualifying contract of insurance relating to an indemnity against a liability related to the employment. The effect is to remove liability on the employee where these costs are met by the employer and to give relief for the employee's own expenditure—including expenditure up to six years after the year in which the employment ends.[55] Post-employment deductions may be set against net income (sections 555–564). The relief may, like post-cessation business expenses, be set against CGT.[56] The burden must fall on the employee rather than the employer. Pursuant to ITEPA 2003, sections 346(2A) and 556A, employee liabilities will be deductible only where they are not derived from arrangements the main purpose, or one of the main purposes, of which is the avoidance of tax.

18.3 Qualifying Travelling Expenses Paid by Employee[57]

The discussion below analyses qualifying travelling expenses under two categories:

Category (a). Section 337(1)(b) refers to amounts necessarily incurred on travelling in the performance of the duties of the employment. The problem of two employments within one group is addressed by section 340, which provides expressly that expenses of travel by an employee between two places at which the employee performs duties of different offices or employments under or with companies in the same group, are treated as necessarily expended in the performance of the duties which the employee is to perform at the destination and so are deductible.[58] A 51% subsidiary test is used to determine when companies are members of the same group.[59]

---

[53] *Kirkwood v Evans* [2002] EWHC ChD 30; [2002] STC 231, Patten J reversing General Commissioners.

[54] ITEPA 2003, Pt 12, ss 713 *et seq*, ex TA 1988, s 202, as amended by FA 1996, s 100 and FA 2000, s 38. Payment may be made through an agency charity approved by the Revenue (ITEPA 2003, s 714(2), ex TA 1988, s 202(7)).

[55] ITEPA 2003, s 347(2), referring to the deduction in s 555, ex TA 1988, s 201AA, added by FA 1995, s 91. See also Revenue Interpretation RI 131.

[56] FA 1995, s 92(6)–(8).

[57] ITEPA 2003, s 337, ex TA 1988, s 198(1B). See also Inland Revenue Guide 490 (2002).

[58] ITEPA 2003, s 340; on ss 340–342, see ITEPA explanatory note change 83.

[59] ITEPA 2003, s 340(6); one may be a 51% subsidiary of the other, or both may be 51% subsidiaries of a third company.

Category (b). Section 338 allows the expenses of travelling which (i) are attributable to the employee's necessary attendance at any place in the performance of the duties of the employment, but (ii) which are not expenses of ordinary commuting or private travel.[60] Of these, (i) is designed to clarify the law concerning the costs of travel to or from home or a temporary workplace, while (ii) is designed to prevent (i) from opening the door too wide. These changes were intended to clarify the law; the explanation of the original clarifications was rumoured to be 50 pages long.

In September 2015 the Government published a discussion document aimed at 'modernising' the rules on travel and subsistence expenses. Following a review, the Government decided these rules were more or less operating satisfactorily and were generally well understood by taxpayers and thus changes were not required; however, some restrictions were imposed on tax relief for home to work travel and subsistence expenses for workers engaged through an employment intermediary.[61]

18.3.1 Category (A): S 337—Established Law

The case law behind section 337 provides much of the background to section 338. The two sections are alternatives; it is enough for the sum to come within one of them to be deductible. Under section 337, an employee may deduct amounts necessarily expended on travelling in the performance of the duties of the employment. This rule is very strict and concessions were made for particularly hard cases, the most interesting being the exemption of extra travel and subsistence allowances when public transport was disrupted by strikes or other industrial action; where the employee had to work late or was severely disabled; or where car-sharing arrangements had broken down.[62] Such concessions are now made statutory by ITEPA 2003, sections 245 *et seq* (see below at §18.3.5). Other concessions have been superseded by section 338.[63]

18.3.1.1 Necessarily Incurred in the Performance of the Duties of the Employment

To be deductible the cost must be 'incurred in the performance of the duties of the employment'—and necessarily so incurred. The Revenue view is that it is not necessary to take the shortest possible route, provided there were good business reasons for the route chosen.[64] The costs of travelling to work from home are not, in general, deductible[65] under this head, because the costs are incurred not in the course of performing the duties but in order to get to the place where the duties are to be performed. Therefore, an employee cannot deduct the extra costs of having to travel to work by car even though the car is needed for work once he gets there.[66]

---

[60] Ordinary commuting or private travel is defined in ITEPA 2003, s 338, ex TA 1988, Sch 12A.

[61] ITEPA 2003, s 339A. See https://www.gov.uk/government/publications/income-tax-employment-intermediaries-and-relief-for-travel-and-subsistence.

[62] Former ESCs A58, A59, A66 (revised 1999).

[63] Former ESC A65 and RI 73.

[64] RI 99.

[65] *Cook v Knott* (1887) 2 TC 246; *Revell v Elsworthy Bros & Co Ltd* (1890) 3 TC 12; *Andrews v Astley* (1924) 8 TC 589; *Ricketts v Colquhoun* [1926] AC 1, 10 TC 118.

[66] *Burton v Rednall* (1954) 35 TC 435. It is interesting to compare the position in tort when the question is whether an employee is acting in the course of his employment—see *Smith v Stages* [1989] AC 928, [1989] 1 All ER 833 (HL).

In deciding whether an expense is incurred 'necessarily' the courts began with an objective test. In *Ricketts v Colquhoun*,[67] Lord Blanesburgh said that the expense had to be one which each and every occupant of the particular office was necessarily obliged to incur. Thus, the necessity must emerge from the job rather than from the personal circumstances of the employee; as such, a Recorder travelling from home to court might deduct the expenses only if they would be incurred by any other person fulfilling the duties of that office, which was not so. This view, although making some sense in the context of a long-established statutory office with very particular duties (such as a Recorder), is inconsistent with the modern bargaining process under which the goals of an employment contract may be coloured by the interests of both employer and employee. This inevitably demands that more attention be paid to the needs of the employees, particularly when individual contracts are being negotiated with senior employees.[68] As two later decisions of the House of Lords show, in determining whether the expense would be incurred by each and every occupant of the office, it is now necessary to consider who might be appointed to hold the office. If the range of reasonable appointees is restricted, the test must be applied in relation to such potential appointees, and it is then necessary to ask whether each of these persons, if appointed, would have to incur the expense; if the answer is 'yes', then the expense is deductible notwithstanding that some other person, who would not be a suitable appointee, might not have to incur it (*Owen v Pook*).[69] In an extreme case it may be possible to show that the taxpayer is the only person in the world who can carry out the duties (*Taylor v Provan*).[70]

18.3.1.2 Three House of Lords Cases[71]

(1) *Ricketts v Colquhoun*[72]

The taxpayer (Ricketts) lived in London and was a practising member of the London Bar. He was taxable under Schedule D, Case II in respect of his earnings at the Bar. He was also Recorder of Portsmouth and was taxable under Schedule E in respect of his earnings from this source. He sought to deduct the costs of travelling from his home to Portsmouth. The House of Lords rejected his appeal on two main grounds. First, when travelling to his place of work he was travelling not in the course of those duties but in order to enable him to perform them;[73] his duties only began at Portsmouth. Secondly, the expenses could not be said to have been incurred necessarily;[74] since a Recorder could have lived in Portsmouth, the costs of travel from London were not necessary. A further point was that his choice of abode in London was a personal matter and the expenses consequent on that choice were therefore personal expenses.

---

[67] [1926] AC 1, 7, 10 TC 118, 135 (*cf* Lord Salmon in *Taylor v Provan* [1975] AC 194, 227, 49 TC 579, 622).
[68] Ward [1988] BTR 6.
[69] (1969) 45 TC 571.
[70] [1974] STC 168, [1974] 1 All ER 1201, 49 TC 579.
[71] See Ward [1988] BTR 6.
[72] [1926] AC 1, 10 TC 118.
[73] *Ibid*, 4, 133, per Lord Cave LC.
[74] *Ibid*, 7, 135, per Lord Blanesburgh. *Cf* Lord Salmon in *Taylor v Provan* [1974] STC 168, 190, [1974] 1 All ER 1201, 1223, 49 TC 579.

(2) *Owen v Pook*[75]

The taxpayer (O) was a medical practitioner who resided at Fishguard. He also held part-time appointments as obstetrician and anaesthetist at Haverfordwest 15 miles away. Under these appointments O was on 'standby duty' two weekends a month and on Monday and Friday nights, at which times he was required to be accessible by telephone. If he was called at home, O would give advice by phone, sometimes set out at once and at other times await further reports. He was responsible for his patient as soon as he received the telephone call. Although he received a payment for travelling expenses, this was only for the last 10 of his 15 miles. O was assessed in respect of the payments received for the 10 miles and denied his claim for deduction in respect of the five miles. His appeal to the courts against this assessment was successful. Since he had two places where his duties were performed, the hospital and his residence with the telephone, the expenses of travel between the two places were deductible.[76] Lord Wilberforce said that the job as actually constituted and the purpose for which he incurred the expenses differed greatly from Ricketts' case.[77]

(3) *Taylor v Provan*[78]

This case suggests that the personal qualifications of the taxpayer may sometimes supply the material to satisfy the objective test of necessity. The taxpayer (T) was a Canadian citizen living in Toronto. He was the acknowledged expert in the brewing world on successful expansion by means of amalgamation and merger. T did most of his work in connection with the English amalgamations in Canada and The Bahamas, but he made frequent visits to England. He had extensive Canadian interests for which he worked from his offices in Toronto and The Bahamas. He agreed to serve as director of brewing companies 'for reasons of prestige', although this had the unfortunate effect of bringing him within what are now ITEPA 2003, Part 3, Chapters 3 and 10 (ex TA 1988, sections 153, 154). T received no fees for his services since he regarded it as a business recreation, but his travelling expenses were reimbursed. The House of Lords held unanimously that the reimbursements were sums spent on behalf of the company and so came within what is now ITEPA 2003, Part 3, Chapter 3. This is accepted by those who drafted ITEPA 2003.[79] The House then held (by 3:2) that the expenses were deductible, and so the taxpayer escaped from the effect of being brought within Part 3, Chapter 3. Of the majority, Lord Morris[80] and Lord Salmon[81] held that the taxpayer's duties were performed both in the UK and in Canada so that there were at least two places of work, as in *Owen v Pook*. Travel to England could not therefore be dismissed as travel from home to a place of work.

The other member of the majority, Lord Reid, gave a rather different account of *Owen v Pook*.[82] He considered that the distinguishing fact in *Owen* was that O had been in part-time

---

[75] [1969] 2 All ER 1, 45 TC 571. *Owen v Pook* was distinguished in *Bhadra v Ellam* [1988] STC 239, *Parikh v Sleeman* [1988] STC 580 (upheld on narrower grounds, [1990] STC 233, CA) and *Knapp v Martin* [1999] STC (SCD) 13 (all cases concerning the medical profession).

[76] See Lord Guest, 45 TC 571, 590, Lord Pearce, 591 and Lord Wilberforce, 596.

[77] *Ibid*; see Ward [1988] BTR 6, 14, 15.

[78] [1974] STC 168, [1974] 1 All ER 1201, 49 TC 579.

[79] For explanation, see ITEPA Technical Note 36.

[80] *Taylor v Provan*, 177, 1210, 609.

[81] *Ibid*, 191, 1224, 623.

[82] *Ibid*, 174, 1207.

employment, and that it had been impossible for the employer to fill the post otherwise than by appointing someone with commitments that could not be given up. It was therefore necessary that whoever was appointed should incur travelling expenses. This approach goes much wider than any pronouncement in recent years, and undermines both the decision of the House of Lords in *Ricketts v Colquhoun* and much of the practice of the Revenue. It followed that the expenses in *Taylor v Provan* were deductible because T was the only person who could do this job which he was only willing to do from Canada, and that he did some of the work in Canada. The question arises how far Lord Reid's approach undermines the earlier decision in *Ricketts v Colquhoun*. No member of the majority in *Taylor v Provan* wished to question the result of that earlier decision, but Ricketts' post as Recorder of Portsmouth was part-time and anyone appointed would, at that time, have had to be a member of the Bar. However, Ricketts was not the only member of the Bar who could have been appointed, and it was possible that another appointee would have lived in Portsmouth. Another explanation supporting the older case could be that Ricketts' home was not a place of work. This would conclude the matter, if, as may well be the case,[83] Lord Reid's explanation of *Owen v Pook* rested on the assumption that there were two places of work.

18.3.1.3 An Alternative Explanation—Itinerants

The explanation of *Owen v Pook* and *Taylor v Provan* may not be that home was one of the places of work, but that in each case their employment was, in a sense, itinerant. In *Owen v Pook* there was no reason why the employment should have been located in O's home. What mattered was that he assumed responsibility for the patient when he received the telephone message. If he was out with friends for the evening and had given their telephone number instead of his own, that should not make his friends' house one of his places of work. The point was *when* his duties commenced rather than where. In the same way, in *Taylor v Provan* the House of Lords seemed to be concerned with the question 'Was he travelling in the performance of his duties?' rather than 'Was his office a home and, if not, did he travel from his office or from his home?'. On this approach one can reconcile the earlier decision of *Nolder v Walters*,[84] where an airline pilot sought unsuccessfully to deduct the cost of travelling from his home to the airport. The fact that he was summoned by his employer made no difference. While travelling to the airport he was not under his employer's command. He was travelling to his office, not from one office to another. If this approach is right, far more attention is being paid to the subjective circumstances of the parties to the contract than was apparent from the approach of Lord Blanesburgh in *Ricketts v Colquhoun*.[85]

18.3.1.4 Amount

It is unclear whether the objective rule that the expenses must have been necessarily incurred limits the amount of expenditure that may be deducted. In *Marsden v IRC*,[86] the

---

[83] This emerges from *ibid*, 174, 1207, 605.

[84] (1930) 15 TC 380.

[85] See, generally, Ward [1988] BTR 6.

[86] [1965] 2 All ER 364, 42 TC 326; see also *Perrons v Spackman* [1981] STC 739, where it was held that a mileage allowance was an emolument of the taxpayer's employment, since it included a significant contribution to the overhead costs of putting a car, which was maintained for both private and official use, on the road and could not therefore be a mere reimbursement of expenses actually incurred.

taxpayer, who was an investigator in the Audit Division of the Inland Revenue, used his car for travelling on official business. There was no evidence that he could not have travelled by public transport. His claim to deduct the difference between the allowance he received, which was based on car mileage, and what he actually spent, was rejected by his employers and by the courts. Pennycuick J said that the scale of expenses must be a question of fact and degree, and that the answer must turn not only on the price of transport but also on such considerations as speed, convenience, the purpose of the journey, and the status of the officer, etc.[87] In *Owen v Pook*,[88] Lord Wilberforce rejected the idea that an expense was deductible only if precisely those expenses had to be incurred by each and every employee.

18.3.2 Category (B): S 338—Travel to or from a Temporary Workplace

Section 338 establishes that expenses may be deducted where, in addition to satisfying part (a) and so being such that the employee is obliged to incur them as holder of the employment, the expenses must also satisfy (b) and be attributable to the necessary attendance at any place of the holder of the employment in the performance of the duties of the office or employment, provided these expenses are not expenses of (i) ordinary commuting, or (ii) private travel.

The first words retain the elements both of necessity and of the performance of duties, and seem to be inspired by (and fit the facts of) the decisions in *Owen v Pook* and *Taylor v Provan*; however, the words also fit *Ricketts v Colquhoun* (see above, §18.3.1.2). Their purpose is, subject to exclusions (i) and (ii), to allow the costs of travel from home or from a permanent workplace to a temporary workplace—and of the return travel. The rule allows the deduction of all costs so incurred and not, as was first enacted, only the additional costs. In computing additional costs it was initially proposed that there would be a deduction for any saving realised by not having to incur ordinary commuting costs; however, this proved unworkable.[89]

A workplace is permanent if it is one which the employee regularly attends in the performance of the duties of the employment, provided it is not a temporary workplace (section 339(2), (3)). The concept of the permanent workplace has to be extended for depots and bases and for area-based employees (section 339(4), (7)). The key to the new rule is the temporary (non-permanent) workplace, defined as a place which the employee attends in the performance of the duties of the employment for the purpose of performing a task of limited duration or for some other temporary purpose. This clearly fits *Owen v Pook* and *Taylor v Provan*, but again, it also fits *Ricketts v Colquhoun*; Haverfordwest, London and Portsmouth were all temporary. The concept of a temporary workplace is narrowed by the exclusion of a place where the employee is to work for 24 months or for all of a fixed term (section 339(2), (3), (5)).

---

[87] [1965] 2 All ER 364, 367, 42 TC 326, 331. One may add that of these the status of the officer looks extremely odd and the Revenue's own scale of allowances made to Marsden, which gave, depending upon the type of business on which he was engaged, two quite distinct allowances, makes a nonsense of some of the arguments used by the Revenue in these cases.

[88] [1969] 2 All ER 1, 12, 45 TC 571, 596.

[89] TA 1988, s 198A, proposed to be added by FA 1997, s 62 but repealed by FA 1998, s 61 without having ever coming into effect. See Inland Revenue Press Release, 8 April 1998, [1998] *Simon's Tax Intelligence* 602.

18.3.2.1 Exclusion of Ordinary Commuting Travel

Ordinary commuting travel means travel between the employee's home and permanent workplace; it also covers travel from a place that is not a workplace in relation to the employment, to that permanent workplace (section 338(3)). Commuting expenditure is therefore non-deductible whether it is on travel from home, or from a friend's home or an hotel. Travel between any two places which is for practical purposes substantially ordinary commuting travel is treated as ordinary commuting travel (section 338(2)). Where an employee worked mostly at home but, as required by the employer, travelled once a week to the employer's offices for business purposes, the court held that the travel was ordinary commuting.[90]

18.3.2.2 Exclusion of Private Travel

There can be no deduction for costs of travel between the employee's home and a place that is not a workplace[91] in relation to the employment (E1). If the place is one where the employee, E, works, but for a different employer (E2) or on E's own account, the costs are not deductible from the earnings of E1. In addition, there can be no deduction for the costs of travel between two places if neither is a workplace in relation to the employment. The Recorder's travel to Portsmouth in *Ricketts v Colquhoun* (see §18.3.1.2) was private so far as the Lord Chancellor's Department was concerned. Travel between any two places which is, for practical purposes, substantially private travel is treated as private travel (section 338(4)).

18.3.2.3 Application of Rule

The words requiring that the travel be required by the employment are presumably to be applied objectively. The Revenue have stated that they will not seek to disallow first-class rail travel on the ground that only standard class was necessary.[92] However, this does not allow relief where the mode of transport is a form of reward as opposed to being attributable to business travel.[93]

18.3.2.4 Examples[94]

(1) Clive lives and works in Dagenham but goes to Devon for the weekend to stay with friends. He remains in Devon on the Monday, working on papers he has brought with him from the office. He is not entitled to relief for the cost of the journey from Dagenham to Devon as it is private travel.

(2) Derek normally works at his employer's offices in Edinburgh, travelling each day from his home in East Kilbride. One day he has to visit Perth to undertake some work in Perth for his employer. The cost of the return journey from East Kilbride to Perth is £34. Derek is entitled to relief for £34, being the full cost of the business travel.

---

[90] *Kirkwood v Evans* [2002] EWHC 30 (Ch), [2002] STC 231, Patten J reversing General Commissioners.

[91] Ie a place at which the employee's attendance is necessary in the performance of the duties of the employment (ITEPA 2003, s 339(1), ex TA 1988, Sch 12A, para 2(3)).

[92] HMRC booklet IR 490, para 5.14.

[93] *Ibid*, para 5.15.

[94] Based on IR 490, para 1.9. A host of other interesting examples can be found in that guide as well: see https://www.gov.uk/government/publications/490-employee-travel-a-tax-and-nics-guide.

(3) Emma is an engineer who works on installing machines at the premises of her employer's various clients throughout the UK. Emma has no permanent workplace and attends each temporary workplace for a short period only. One week she travels from her home in Folkestone to work at an employer's client's premises in Falkirk, where she stays in a hotel for four nights before returning to Folkestone. The cost of the Folkestone to Falkirk return journey is £130. The cost of four nights in the hotel plus meals is £300. Emma is entitled to relief for £430, being the full cost of her business travel.

18.3.3 Other Travel Rules: Exemptions from Benefits Code, etc

18.3.3.1 Incidental Overnight Expenses

Sections 240 and 241 provide a statutory exemption from liability to income tax for certain incidental overnight expenses. The broad effect is to exclude any charge on the expenses[95] or reimbursements where the overnight accommodation costs associated with them would be allowable deductions under the various travel rules. A maximum of £5 per night is available for expenses in the UK and £10 elsewhere, but these limits may be varied by statutory instrument.[96] The limits are spread over the period of absence rather than being applied to each night separately, but the effect of exceeding the maximum is that the whole sum becomes taxable.

An allowable, incidental, overnight expense is one paid wholly and exclusively for the purpose of paying or reimbursing any expense which is incidental to being away from the usual place of abode during a qualifying absence from home (section 240(4)–(6)). An absence from home qualifies if it is a continuous period throughout which the employee is obliged to stay away from his usual place of abode—now incisively rewritten as 'the place where the employee normally lives throughout the period'—and during which he has at least one overnight stay away from that place. In addition, there must be no overnight stay at a place other than a place the expenses of travelling to which would be deductible if they had been incurred.

18.3.3.2 Car Parking

The provision of car parking facilities is also excluded from an income tax charge (section 237). The reason for this apparently strict rule is that an earlier attempt to charge such benefits was found to be unworkable.

18.3.3.3 Miscellaneous—Official Travel

The legislation contains exceptions for leave travel facilities for the armed forces (section 296) and for incidental benefits to holders of certain public offices (section 295). Special rules apply to allowances for MPs,[97] which have been extended once to the costs of visits to

---

[95] Ex TA 1988, s 200A, added by FA 1995, s 93. The exclusion is effective for ITEPA 2003, Pt 3, Chs 3, 4 and 10.

[96] ITEPA 2003, s 241, ex TA 1998, s 200A(1)–(3). However, some provisions allowing the deduction of travel expenses do not open the door to s 241—these are listed in s 240(7) as excepted foreign travel provisions, referring to ss 371, 374 and 376.

[97] ITEPA 2003, s 291 (termination payments) and s 292 (overnight expenses).

EU institutions in Brussels, Luxembourg or Strasbourg and now, further, to EU candidate countries and EFTA countries.[98] The rules have also now been extended to members of the Scottish Parliament and Welsh Assembly (sections 293 and 294).

18.3.4 *Employer Assistance with Travel to and During Work*

FA 1999 introduced five provisions to prevent the tax system interfering with environmentally sensible ideas on the part of employers. By giving relief for the costs of travel to work as well as during work, these rules represent a major change of theory.

18.3.4.1 Works Bus Service

Section 242 removes any charge to income tax if an employer provides a works bus service.[99] The bus must have a seating capacity of 12 or more, or be a minibus with a seating capacity of 9, 10 or 11.[100] The service must be one for conveying employees on qualifying journeys; the employees may belong to one or more employers (section 243(2)). Journeys qualify not only if they are between one workplace and another, but also, and in complete contrast to the rules in section 338, if they are between home and workplace (section 249). In either case, the journey must be in connection with the performance of the duties of the employment, and the service must be available to employees generally.[101] ITEPA 2003 also requires that the service must be used only, or substantially only, by employees or their children.[102] This means that the exemption will not be lost just because the bus is used for some other occasional purpose. It is necessary, however, to distinguish the service from the bus itself. If the bus is used for qualifying journeys and for separate non-qualifying journeys, there will be a charge for the latter; if, however, there are non-qualifying aspects to a single journey, there will be a charge unless the substantial compliance condition is satisfied. The reference to children allows the bus to be used for getting children to school, but is not confined to that.[103]

18.3.4.2 Support for Public Transport

Section 243 removes any income tax charge where an employer provides financial or other support for a public transport bus service. Again, the employees may belong to one or more employers and the service must be for qualifying journeys. The support must be provided directly to the operator; if the service is not a local bus service as defined, the terms on which the employees travel must not be more favourable than those that apply to other passengers.[104] In any case the service must be available to employees generally (section 243(3)).

---

[98] ITEPA 2003, 294, amended by FA 2004. Ex TA 1988, s 200, amended by FA 1993, s 124 and FA 2002.

[99] See ITEPA explanatory note change 45, originally TA 1988, s 197AA(1), (2), added by FA 1999, s 48.

[100] ITEPA 2003, s 242(3), ex TA 1988, s 197AA(3), (8). See ITEPA explanatory note change 46.

[101] ITEPA 2003, ss 242(1) and 249, referring to s 339, ex TA 1988, s 197AA(4), (7).

[102] ITEPA 2003, s 242(1)(c) replacing the hideously-worded TA 1988, s 197AB(4).

[103] Children are defined in ITEPA 2003, s 242(2), ex TA 1988, s 197AA(5); they must not be aged over 17.

[104] ITEPA 2003, s 243(1). This rule, introduced by FA 2002, s 33, supersedes the original more stringent condition that they had to pay the same fares as other passengers.

18.3.4.3 Motorbikes and Cycles

The various exemptions from tax for car parking spaces are extended to spaces for parking motorcycles and facilities for parking cycles.[105] Why cycles need 'facilities' and motorcycles need only 'spaces' is unclear. Presumably this wording is intended to cover facilities for locking up bicycles.

18.3.4.4 Bicycles

Section 244 removes any charge to income tax where an employer lends an employee a cycle or a cyclist's safety equipment.[106] The benefit or facility must be available to employees generally. The employee must use it mainly for qualifying journeys.[107] Safety equipment is not defined, but presumably includes lights, reflective strips and coats, and safety helmets; it is unlikely to cover fancy gears (which will be part of the cycle), or a rain-cape or lock. Some softening of these boundaries may occur in practice.

18.3.4.5 Bicycle Mileage

ITEPA 2003 now exempts a business allowance of 20p per business mile cycled (below §18.3.6). This allows an employer to pay an employee such a sum, and for the employee to claim that allowance to the extent that the employer does not pay it. The original notice stated that the employee could not claim both this allowance and the capital allowance; however, the capital allowance is no longer available.[108] The Revenue's original intention to allow costs of travel to and from work under this head was contrary to the capital allowance legislation.

18.3.5 Other Exemptions

ITEPA 2003 brings together yet further exemptions. These are the modest private use of a heavy goods vehicle (section 238), the limits of the scope of the charge in respect of cars and vans (section 239), travelling and subsistence during public transports strikes (section 245, ex ESC A58), transport between work and home for disabled employees (section 246, ex ESC A59) and the provision of certain types of car for disabled employees (section 247, ex ESC A59), and transport home after late-night working or the failure of car-sharing arrangements (section 248, ex ESC A66).[109] FA 2004 adds section 248A, which creates an exception from liability for emergency vehicles for employees of certain emergency services and who are obliged to be able to respond to emergencies as part of their normal duties. The vehicle must not be available for private travel other than when on call and must usually carry a flashing light.

---

[105] ITEPA 2003, s 237(3), ex FA 1999, s 50; 'cycle' and 'motorcycle' are defined by reference to the Road Traffic legislation (s 244(5), ex s 46(3)) and include tricycles as well as bicycles.

[106] Originally TA 1988, s 197AC(1), (5), added by FA 1999, s 47(1).

[107] ITEPA 2003, s 244(3), a great improvement on the original drafting in TA 1988, s 197AC(4). See original text.

[108] CAA 2001, s 36, as amended by FA 2001, s 59; Inland Revenue Notes to Finance Bill 1999, cl 47 (which became FA 1999, s 50).

[109] See ITEPA explanatory notes changes 47–50.

18.3.6 *Mileage Allowances*

This exemption was put on a statutory basis in 2001 and re-enacted in ITEPA 2003.[110] If R, the employer, pays E, the employee, a mileage allowance, any profit made by E is taxable under general principles. There is, however, a voluntary administrative arrangement known as the fixed-profit car scheme. The scheme is a safe harbour scheme; sums paid within the limits are safe. The scheme covers only sums paid for business travel, not sums paid for private travel. The scheme now applies to motorcycles and cycles as well as to cars and vans.

Current mileage rates, unchanged from 2011–12, are as follows (section 230):

	Up to 10,000 miles	After 10,000 miles
Car or van	45p	25p
Motorcycle	24p	24p
Cycle	20p	20p

These figures apply only to exempt qualifying payments, not to allow a deduction. In addition, up to 5p per mile may be paid free of tax for each employee travelling as a passenger on a business journey.

Mileage allowances—the difference between these rates and the higher figures paid by companies—are considered to be remuneration and, as such, taxable. Figures published by motoring organisations often include the costs of breakdown recovery and of interest forgone on the value of the car—which are clearly liable to tax.

18.4   Other Expenses

ITEPA 2003, Part 5, Chapter 3 deals with deductions from three types of benefits code earnings, and in particular those relating to (a) vouchers etc, (b) living accommodation, and (c) the general or residual charge in the benefits code, ie Chapters 3, 4 and 10. A deduction may well also be claimed under Part 5, Chapter 5, but these are alternatives (section 369(3)). Section 362 allows a deduction where a non-cash voucher within section 87 is provided, and if the employee had incurred and paid the costs there would have been a deduction under Part 5, Chapter 2 or Chapter 5 (section 362(1)). The deduction is not to exceed the amount treated as earnings (section 362(2)). Similar rules are enacted for credit tokens within section 92, or where living accommodation is provided and falls under Part 3, Chapter 3, or the benefit comes within the general charge under Part 3, Chapter 10 (sections 363–365). Where the benefit code deductions arise, the legislation appears to be being generous by allowing them to be set against all earnings from this source and not just the benefits code earnings; however, the rules go on to limit the deductions to the amount of the benefit code earnings or an appropriate proportion. Not only is the policy of this restriction hard to fathom, it is also hard for an ordinary reader to draw out of the words used.[111] Part 5, Chapter 4 (sections 366–368) authorises fixed-sum allowances for repairing

---

[110] ITEPA 2003, s 229, replacing TA 1988, ss 197AD–197AG.
[111] ITEPA explanatory notes changes 98 and 99.

and maintaining work equipment or payable out of the public revenue; the allowances are set down by the Treasury. Part 5, Chapter 5 (sections 369–377) contains four rules of which three are international (see above §13.3 and the fourth concerns expenses on personal security assets and services.[112] Chapter 6 covers the special 100% deduction for seafarers' earnings (see above §13.3.5).

18.5   Reflections

The test of deductibility under these rules is strict, even severe. A particularly strong example of this is *Eagles v Levy*,[113] where the employee had to sue his employer to recover wages due to him and was not allowed to deduct the costs of the action because such costs were not incurred in the course of the performance of his duties. The self-employed could presumably deduct the costs of pursuing a trade debtor. The restrictive nature of the test of deductibility has often been commented upon, usually adversely,[114] and it remains true that the test appears to be much stricter than that laid down for businesses, where the requirement is that the expenditure be wholly and exclusively for the purposes of the business.[115] A good example of the discrepancy is *Hamerton v Overy*,[116] where a full-time anaesthetist sought to deduct the cost of maintaining a telephone, a maid to take messages, a subscription to the Medical Defence Union and the excess of his car running expenses over the allowance received from his employers. All these items would have been deductible if he had been in private practice; none was deductible under Schedule E. Had he succeeded in establishing two places of work, as the taxpayer did in *Owen v Pook* (see §18.3.1.2), the first and last expenses might well have been deductible.

The discrepancy creates tax-planning problems. If Tom, a trader, incorporates his business, his allowable expenses will fall under ITEPA 2003. Some who fall within ITEPA 2003 try to avoid the problem by forming a management company which employs them: their own expenses remain under the 2003 Act, but the company may, in computing its profits, deduct expenses not deductible by an individual employee. The essence of this distinction is that ITEPA 2003 requires that the expense be necessarily incurred in the performance of the duties, while ITTOIA 2005, Part 2 is satisfied with a purpose test. However, the discrepancy may be exaggerated. First, many expenses disallowed under ITTOIA 2005, Part 2 are similarly disallowed under ITEPA 2003. Thus, travelling expenses from home to

---

[112] See ITEPA explanatory notes change 101 and Technical Note 39. Previously FA 1989, ss 50–52; apportionment is directed where there is dual purpose (s 51); for the Revenue view on scope, see ICAEW Memorandum TR 759, [1989] *Simon's Tax Intelligence* 719. For a rare case see *Hanson v Molesworth* [2004] STC (SCD) 288, Sp Com 410.

[113] (1934) 19 TC 23.

[114] Rowlatt J in *Ricketts v Colquhoun* (1924) 10 TC 118, 121; Croom Johnson J in *Bolam v Barlow* (1949) 31 TC 136, 129; Danckwerts J in *Roskams v Bennett* (1950) 32 TC 129, 132; Harman LJ in *Mitchell and Edon v Ross* [1960] Ch 498, 532; [1960] 2 All ER 218, 232; 40 TC 11, 51. But *cf* Lord Radcliffe in *Mitchell and Edon v Ross* [1962] AC 814, 841; [1961] 3 All ER 49, 56; 40 TC 11, 62; and Rowlatt J in *Nolder v Walters* (1930) 15 TC 380, 389.

[115] See Lord Evershed MR in *Brown v Bullock* (1960) 40 TC 1, 9. However, note also Brodie, *Tax Line* (May 1995), 7 citing an instance where the ITEPA taxpayer could deduct an expense where the Sch D taxpayer could not, because the former came within a Revenue agreement.

[116] (1954) 35 TC 73.

work are generally disallowed under both Schedules,[117] as are other expenses of a personal nature, such as living expenses. Secondly, it must be noted that some expenses allowed under ITTOIA 2005, Part 2 may subsequently be recouped by the Revenue, as, for example, where trading stock is bought and later sold or valued at market value on discontinuance. The cost of a home/office which is allowed under Schedule E will not affect the exemption of the principal private residence from CGT, whereas the same allowance under ITTOIA 2005, Part 2 will result in a partial loss of that exemption. Thirdly, there remains the crucial difference between an employment and a profession or trade, and between being an employee and being an owner. If E, an employee, incurs expense for his employer, E's employer may reimburse the expense, whereas a trader has to bear the expense itself. Unfortunately, the ITEPA 2003 reimbursement may well be taxable, as in *Smith v Abbott*.[118] The parties have two solutions. One is for the employer to incur the expense, so excluding Part 3, Chapter 3; the other is to increase the employee's wages sufficiently to cover the taxable reimbursement—and to pay the associated NICs.

One legislative approach to the problem is to keep the present strict rule and provide exceptions for particular situations, such as the child-minding expenses disallowed in *Halstead v Condon*[119] or the fees payable in *Lupton v Potts*.[120] In practice the Revenue seem to allow[121] some expenses, such as the non-taxation of allowances for teachers or judges in respect of books, or the home study allowance.[122]

---

[117] See MacDonald [1978] BTR 75, commenting on *Sargent v Barnes*. See also the discussion below at §22.2.4.6.

[118] [1998] STC 267.

[119] (1970) 46 TC 289.

[120] [1969] 3 All ER 1083, 45 TC 643.

[121] Some reliefs depend on agreements between the Revenue and various trades unions, the results being made available to their members.

[122] This was thought to be outside ITEPA 2003, s 336 (ex TA 1988, s 198) in *Roskams v Bennett* (1950) 32 TC 129, but inside in *Elwood v Utitz* (1965) 42 TC 482, 495.

19

Business Income—Part I: Scope

19.1 Introduction

19.1.1 Trade

ITTOIA 2005, section 5 charges income tax on the profits of a 'trade, profession or vocation'. For present purposes, the word 'trade' may be taken to cover the other two terms as well. Section 6 imposes a charge on a UK resident in respect of the trade wherever it is carried on, but on a non-resident only in respect of trading activities within the UK. Section 7 charges the full amount of the profits but it is not a capital gains tax,[1] although the width of the definition of 'trade' may make it appear like one at times.

---

[1] On Revenue power to make alternative assessments, see eg *IRC v Wilkinson* [1992] STC 454, 65 TC 28, CA. Presumably a taxpayer cannot make alternative self-assessments.

Trade is defined statutorily for income tax and corporation tax as including 'any venture in the nature of trade'. Thus, even a one-off transaction can be a trade.[2] The pre-Rewrite definition in TA 1988, section 832 was trade included 'any trade, manufacture, adventure or concern' in the nature of trade. Nothing appears to turn on the change from 'adventure' to 'venture', and the older term is still used in this book occasionally when referring to older decisions. Judicial definitions of 'trade' have been given sparingly. In *Ransom v Higgs*,[3] Lord Reid said that the word 'is commonly used to denote operations of a commercial character by which the trader provides to customers for reward some kind of goods or services'; and in the same case, Lord Wilberforce said 'trade normally involves the exchange of goods or services for reward ... there must be something which the trade offers to provide by way of business. Trade moreover presupposes a customer.' Therefore, where the British Olympic Association set about raising fund by sponsorship and donations, a Special Commissioner held that the activities were not commercial and so did not amount to a trade.[4] The question whether there is a trade, as defined, is one of fact. This means that it is for the Commissioners/Tribunals not only to determine the primary facts, such as what transactions were carried out, when, by whom and with what purpose, but also to conclude that the transaction was or was not a trade as defined.[5] Although this conclusion is an inference, it is usually treated as one of fact.[6] Where the findings are inconsistent, it is for the court to judge.[7]

It is not always to the advantage of the Revenue to argue that a particular transaction is a venture in the nature of trade, since losses resulting from a venture will be eligible for loss relief.[8] In this connection one may note the old Australian rule which allowed a taxpayer to claim a loss only if the taxpayer reported that the asset was acquired for profit when making the first return after the acquisition.[9] UK tax advisers take the view that self-assessment requires the reporting of income only and not of a loss.

19.1.2 Who is Trading?

19.1.2.1 Not Me But My Partner

If T is trading then T, and only T, is liable to tax on the profits. Tax is levied on the traders and not on the transactions. Hence, if T carries out three transactions each with a different partner, it is possible to conclude that in view of the frequency of the transactions, T was

---

[2] ITA 2007, s 989– 'trade' includes any venture in the nature of trade. The same definition applies for corporation tax purposes and is in CTA 2010, s 1119. Prior to the Rewrite, the definition of trade included any 'trade, manufacture, adventure or concern' in the nature of trade: TA 1988, ss 831, 832. On the relations between the last words and the nouns, see *Johnston v Heath* [1970] 3 All ER 915, 46 TC 463.

[3] [1974] 3 All ER 949, 955 (per Lord Reid), 964 (per Lord Wilberforce). An external Name at Lloyd's does not trade at all: *Koenigsberger v Mellor* [1995] STC 547, 67 TC 280.

[4] *British Olympic Association v Winter* [1995] STC (SCD) 85.

[5] *Leeming v Jones* [1930] 1 KB 279, 15 TC 333, CA; aff'd sub nom *Jones v Leeming* [1930] AC 415, 15 TC 333, HL; *Hillerns and Fowler v Murray* (1932) 17 TC 77.

[6] See, eg Endicott (1998) 114 *LQR* 292 and above §4.4.2.

[7] *Simmons v IRC* [1980] STC 350, [1980] 2 All ER 798, 53 TC 461; see Preece [1981] BTR 124 and Walters [1981] BTR 379.

[8] *Stott v Hoddinott* (1916) 7 TC 85; but *cf Lewis Emanuel & Son Ltd v White* (1965) 42 TC 369.

[9] Income Tax Act (Australia), s 52, although the Commissioner had the power to grant relief if this was not observed (applies only to pre-1985 property because of the introduction of CGT in Australia in 1985).

carrying on a trade but that T's partners were not.[10] The boundary between enabling someone else to carry on a business and carrying it on oneself is a fine one.[11]

19.1.2.2 Not Me But My Company or Trust

T does not trade merely by procuring that another person or entity does so. In *Ransom v Higgs*,[12] land was owned by a company owned by H and his wife. H agreed to a scheme by which the company developed the land and paid the profits to a discretionary trust. It was held that the trade of developing the land was not carried on by H. As Lord Reid put it: 'He did not deal with any person. He did not buy or sell anything. He did not provide anyone with goods or service for reward. He had no profits or gains.'[13] There was no evidence that the trade carried on by the company was in fact carried on by H. H had not compelled but merely persuaded the company to conduct a trading operation and so could not be said to be the trader. In deciding who is trading, the court looks to the facts. In *Smart v Lowndes*,[14] a half share in land owned by T's wife was held to be T's trading stock.

19.1.2.3 A Rogue Case

Where a trading operation is carried out by a company, there is some authority for the view that the gain realised on the sale of shares in the company may be a trading receipt (*Associated London Properties Ltd v Henriksen.*)[15] Although the Court of Appeal was clear that the decision turned on its facts, it is not completely clear what these facts were. If the facts had been that the new company was simply the agent of its owners, so that in fact the trade was carried on by them and not by the company, the case could be treated as just a useful illustration of a general principle; however, the case appears to disregard the separate legal personality of the company. The decision has not been much used by the Revenue, despite its potentialities to counter tax avoidance.

19.1.3 *Where is the Trade Carried on?*

ITTOIA 2005, Part 2 removes the old Case I and Case V distinction for income tax[16] and brings within the charge to income tax a trade carried on by a UK resident, wherever that trade is carried on. It also provides for an ending (or discontinuance) of one trade and the start (or commencement) of another when a change of residence occurs,[17] although it adds, beneficially, that this is not to affect the ability to roll losses forward under ITA 2007, section 83.[18] Where a non-resident carries on a trade or profession in the UK, liability arises under

---

[10] *Pickford v Quirke* (1927) 13 TC 251; *Marshall's Executors v Joly* [1936] 1 All ER 851, 20 TC 256.

[11] *Alongi v IRC* [1991] STC 517.

[12] [1974] STC 539, [1974] 3 All ER 949, 50 TC 1; see Twitley [1974] BTR 335.

[13] [1974] STC 539, 545; [1974] 3 All ER 949, 955; 50 TC 1, 79.

[14] [1978] STC 607, 52 TC 436, narrowing still further *Williams v Davies* [1945] 1 All ER 304, 26 TC 371.

[15] (1944) 26 TC 46; distinguished in *Fundfarms Development Ltd v Parsons* [1969] 3 All ER 1161, 45 TC 707.

[16] Formerly TA 1988, s 18 (1)(a)(ii), and see *Colquhoun v Brooks* (1889) 14 Ap Cas 493, 2 TC 490, which provides that a trade carried on wholly outside the UK was within Sch D, Case V and not Case I.

[17] ITTOIA 2005, s 17 (individuals) and s 18 (companies).

[18] ITTOIA 2005, s 17(3); on loss relief under s 83 (ex TA 1988, s 385) see below §20.10.3.

Part 2, but the person is only chargeable on the profits arising in the UK.[19] The question of where a person is carrying on a trade turns on the question where the activities take place from which the profits truly arise. This issue may be decided by looking at the place the contract is made. Budget 2016 announced new rules to make it clear that profits from trading in UK land are always taxable, whether made by UK residents or overseas property developers.

19.1.4 *Profession or Vocation*

ITTOIA 2005, section 5 also charges income tax on the profits of any profession or vocation. One has to look at the start of each chapter of ITTOIA 2005, Part 2 to see whether it applies to professions and vocations as well as to trades. Neither 'profession' nor 'vocation' is defined by statute. Case law establishes that a profession involves the idea of an occupation requiring either purely intellectual skill or manual skill, controlled, as in painting and sculpture or surgery, by the intellectual skill of the operator. Such occupations are distinct from those which are substantially the production or sale, or arrangements for the production or sale, of commodities. Therefore a journalist and editor carry on a profession, but a newspaper reporter carries on a trade.[20] The question is one of fact and degree, and the crux is the degree of intellectual skill involved. Where the Commissioners held that a person who ran a service for taxpayers seeking to recover overpaid tax or to reduce assessments was carrying on a trade, the Court of Appeal considered that there was no error of law.[21] 'Vocation' is a word which has fallen out of fashion—today one probably thinks of an actor as carrying on a profession rather than a vocation.[22] Tax case law treats a vocation as analogous to a calling, a word of great signification meaning the way in which one passes one's life.[23] A dramatist,[24] racing tipster[25] and jockey[26] have all been held to be carrying on a vocation, but not a perennial gambler,[27] nor a film producer.[28]

Where an individual is carrying on a profession, the assessment on the profits of that profession will encompass profits on transactions closely linked with that professional activity even though they would, if taken on their own, amount to carrying on a trade. In *Wain v Cameron*,[29] Professor Wain had carried on his profession of writer for at least 30 years. He then sold his manuscripts and working papers to his university library, but retained the copyright. The court held that the gains made on the sale were chargeable as part of the profits of his profession.

---

[19] ITTOIA 2005, s 6(2), TA 1988, s 18(1)(a)(iii).

[20] *IRC v Maxse* [1919] 1 KB 647 at 656; 12 TC 41 at 61.

[21] *Currie v IRC* [1921] 2 KB 332, 12 TC 245. Other traders include a stockbroker (*Christopher Barker & Sons v IRC* [1919] 2 KB 222) and a photographer (*Cecil v IRC* (1919) 36 TLR 164).

[22] Laurence Olivier was held to be carrying on a vocation in *Higgs v Olivier* (1952) 33 TC 133.

[23] *Partridge v Mallandaine* (1886) 18 QBD 276, 278, 2 TC 179, 180, per Denman J.

[24] *Billam v Griffith* (1941) 23 TC 757.

[25] *Graham v Arnott* (1941) 24 TC 157.

[26] *Wing v O'Connell* [1927] IR 84.

[27] *Graham v Green* [1925] 2 KB 37, 9 TC 309.

[28] *Asher v London Film Productions Ltd* [1944] KB 133, [1944] 1 All ER 77.

[29] [1995] STC 555, 67 TC 324. Contrast *Satt v Fernandez* [1997] STC (SCD) 271, where a Special Commissioner held that the profession of an author carried on by S was separate from a trade of publishing (also carried on by S); at that time cash accounts were acceptable for the profession but not for the trade.

A profession must be distinguished from a trade because:

(1)   certain capital allowances, eg those for research and development, are available only to traders;[30]
(2)   whereas an isolated transaction may be an adventure in the nature of trade, an isolated service cannot fall within Part 2 but only within Part 5, Chapter 8 (old Case VI);
(3)   the rule in *Sharkey v Wernher* (see below at §23.5.1.3) may not apply to professions;
(4)   exemption from CGT for certain damages is confined to professions and vocations;[31]
(5)   there is some suggestion that the deduction rules are less fair for professions than for trades;[32]
(6)   a company may not be able to carry on a profession[33] (although there are dicta to this effect, the fact remains that many professions are now carried on under the protection of an entity such as an LLP);
(7)   at one time,[34] special rules allowed cash basis accounting for certain professions.

For some critics these seven are but slight reasons for maintaining the distinction between a trade and profession.[35] Nevertheless, the distinction remains and is clearly embodied in ITTOIA 2005.

19.1.5 Property Income

Income from property is not trading income. Therefore, income from the exploitation of property rights by letting out residential property[36] or granting licences to use intellectual property is not within ITTOIA 2005, Part 2. (See further below at §19.7.)

19.2   Illegal Trading

The question whether the profits of an illegal trade are taxable has produced conflicting dicta, but the answer clearly ought to be, and on balance of authority now is, 'Yes'.[37] The difficulty with UK case law is finding decisions dealing with trading which is criminal, as opposed to contracts which are unenforceable for illegality.[38] However, in *Minister of*

---

[30] The other allowances not available to professions are those for industrial buildings (obsolescent), mineral extraction, agricultural buildings (obsolescent) and dredging.
[31] TCGA 1992, s 55.
[32] *Norman v Golder* (1944) 26 TC 293, 297, per Lord Greene MR.
[33] *William Esplen, Son and Swainston Ltd v IRC* [1919] 2 KB 731; but the point was left open by Browne Wilkinson J in *Newstead v Frost* [1978] STC 239, 249, 53 TC 525, 537.
[34] Statement of Practice SP A27; the change was made by FA 1998, s 42.
[35] Kerridge [2005] BTR 287, 303.
[36] *Webb v Conelee Properties Ltd* [1982] STC 913.
[37] See *Mulholland and Cockfield* [1995] BTR 572; and *Day* [1971] BTR 104.
[38] Eg, *IRC v Aken* [1990] STC 497, CA (prostitution is a trade but not criminal). See also *Partridge v Mallandaine* (1886) 18 QBD 276, 2 TC 179 (bookmaker's profits were taxable even though wagering contracts were unlawful) and *Lindsay, Woodward and Hiscox v IRC* (1933) 18 TC 43.

Finance v Smith,[39] the Privy Council held that the profits of illegal brewing during the prohibition era were taxable. Today, the true principle may be that taxpayers cannot set up the
unlawful character of their acts against the Revenue.[40] There have been some suggestions
that the profits of burglary would not be taxable, because crime is not a trade.[41] It is, however, suggested that these cases should not be followed; any other conclusion may lead to
distinctions between acts illegal per se and acts which are merely incidental to the carrying-
on of a trade. There may be difficulty in calculating profits in such cases, since there is a civil
obligation to restore the goods to their owner, and it should be remembered that a consistently unprofitable trade may not be a trade at all. Fines are not deductible in computing
trading profits.[42] On the rule barring the deduction of certain payments which amount to
criminal offences, see above at §7.6.

19.3   Trade and Ventures in the Nature of Trade—Scope

19.3.1 Principles, Facts and Examples

The question whether there is a trade or a venture in the nature of trade is one of fact.
What follows is an attempt to synthesise the many cases in this area and to indicate not
only what factors the courts take into account but also the frail nature of those factors.
However, it is hard not to agree with the following comments of Sir Nicolas Browne
Wilkinson V-C in 1986.[43]

> Like the Commissioners I have been treated to an extensive survey of the authorities. But as far
> as I can see there is only one point which as a matter of law is clear, namely that a single one-off
> transaction can be an adventure in the nature of trade. Beyond that I have found it impossible
> to find any single statement of law which is applicable to all the cases in circumstances. I have
> been taken through the facts of the cases....I fear that the General Commissioners may become
> as confused by that process as I did. The purpose of authority is to find principle not to seek
> analogies to facts.

In 1904 the Lord Justice Clerk said that the question was whether the sum or gain which
has been made was a mere enhancement of value by realising a security, or a gain made in

---

[39] [1927] AC 193.

[40] *Southern v AB* [1933] 1 KB 713, 18 TC 59 (profits of bookmaker's street and postal betting were taxable);
Mann v Nash [1932] 1 KB 752, 16 TC 523 (profits of 'fruit' and 'diddler' automatic machines were taxable); contrast *Hayes v Duggan* [1929] IR 406 (profits of illegal sweepstake were not taxable; the court should uphold the
policy of a statute passed to prevent corruption of the public). It may need emphasising today that such activities
were then actually criminal.

[41] Eg, *Lindsay v IRC* (1932) 18 TC 43, 56, per Lord Sands.

[42] Fines are not deductible expenses (*McKnight v Sheppard* (1999) STC 669, 674, discussing *IRC v Alexander
von Glehn & Co Ltd* [1920] 2 KB 553, 12 TC 232); fines for excess axle loads on lorries were held deductible in
Day and Ross Ltd v R [1976] CTC 707, but these would not now be followed in the UK. See discussion by Brooks
(1977) 25 *Can Tax Jo* 16.

[43] *Marson v Morton* [1986] STC 466, 470.

an operation of business in carrying out a scheme for profit-making.[44] In 1955 the Royal Commission listed six 'badges of trade':[45]

(1) the subject matter of the realisation;
(2) the length of period of ownership;
(3) the frequency or number of similar transactions by the same person;
(4) supplementary work on or in connection with the property realised;
(5) the circumstances responsible for the realisation; and
(6) motive.

A slightly different list of badges is used in this text.[46]

Two examples

(1) In *Wisdom v Chamberlain*,[47] the taxpayer (W) had assets worth between £150,000 and £200,000. Fearing that sterling might be devalued, W's accountant concluded that silver bullion would be a suitable hedge and tried to buy £200,000 worth for W. However, the brokers would sell only £100,000 worth, which was financed on a loan from the brokers of £90,000 at 3% above bank rate. Five months later the accountant managed to get £200,000 worth of bullion from the brokers on the basis that the original purchase would be repurchased by the brokers, at a loss to the taxpayer of £3,000. The new deal was financed by loans of £160,000 from a bank and £40,000 from the brokers, both for a maximum period of one year and at high rates of interest. The brokers were under an obligation to buy back the bullion for £210,000 within a certain period. Between October 1962 and January 1963 the bullion was disposed of at a profit of £48,000 after deducting interest of £7,000. The Commissioners held that this was a transaction in the nature of trade, and the Court of Appeal held that they were amply justified in reaching that conclusion. For Harman LJ, this was 'a transaction entered into on a short term basis for the purpose of making a profit out of the purchase and sale of a commodity and if that is not an adventure in the nature of trade I do not really know what it is'.[48] Salmon LJ observed that if the taxpayer had realised his other assets and used the proceeds to finance the purchase of the bullion the case might have been different. The facts of the case, however, presented a trading adventure—'and a very sensible and successful one. I for my part cannot see that it is any the less a trading adventure because [it is described] as something to offset the loss incurred by a fall in the value of sterling or as a hedge or insurance against devaluation'.[49]

---

[44] Lord Macdonald in *California Copper Syndicate Ltd v Harris* (1904) 5 TC 159, 165.
[45] Cmnd 9474 (1955), para 116.
[46] For another list, see *Marson v Morton* [1986] STC 46, 59 TC 381, discussed below.
[47] [1969] 1 All ER 332, 45 TC 92.
[48] *Ibid*, 336, 106.
[49] *Ibid*, 339, 108.

(2)   By contrast, in *Marson v Morton*,[50] T, who owned a company which traded as whole-
      sale potato merchants, bought three or four acres of land, on the advice of an estate
      agent (L). He had no plan to use the land. He intended to make a capital profit and
      perhaps sell it in two years (L said to T that T might double his money). T had no
      idea as to the cost of the land, and it was only when he was asked to sign documents
      that he realised that a third party was involved in lending the money. His trust in L
      was based on the fact that L had appeared in good company at a weekend gathering.
      Three months later L advised T to sell the land. L did not tell T that the purchaser was
      a company with which L was connected. T had not sought independent advice on
      the value or potential of the land. L had, correctly, told T that the land had planning
      permission. T had intended to keep the land as a medium-term investment, but by
      the time he had acquired it he was feeling 'edgy' about L and was glad of the chance to
      sell. L did not quote any selling price and T did not seek independent advice. At that
      time the difference between income tax and CGT rates was very high. The General
      Commissioners held that as L had not been instructed to sell at any particular price or
      time, the transaction was like an investment in stocks and shares. Sir Nicolas Browne
      Wilkinson V-C described the facts as highly unusual and the procedures adopted as
      'extremely unconventional, to say the least', and the case as one of those which fell into
      'the no man's land'. He refused to interfere with the decision of the Commissioners
      that T was not trading.

19.3.2 Purpose of Profit

An intention to make a profit is not a necessary ingredient of a trade, but its presence helps
to establish a trading transaction.[51] Operations of the same kind and carried out in the
same way as those which characterise ordinary trading are not the less trading operations
because they make a loss or there is no intention to make a profit.[52] However, a scheme
which inevitably involves a loss may not be a trading transaction;[53] so losses on loan transactions with no commercial element in them have been disallowed.[54]

Looking beyond cases which have no commercial purpose, it is important to pay atten-
tion to actions rather than to words. In *Ensign Tankers (Leasing) Ltd v Stokes*,[55] the House of
Lords held that the investment of funds in the production of a film was a trading transac-
tion even though much of the motivation was to obtain a tax advantage. According to Lord
Templeman (at TC 677) '[t]he production and exploitation of a film is a trading activity'.
The transaction was not a sham and could have resulted in either a profit or a loss; there

---

[50] [1986] STC 46, 59 TC 381.
[51] *Torbell Investments Ltd v Williams* [1986] STC 397, 59 TC 357.
[52] See Lord Reid in *JP Harrison (Watford) Ltd v Griffiths* [1962] 1 All ER 909, (1960) 40 TC 281, and cases there
cited. See also *Building and Civil Engineering Holidays Scheme Management Ltd v Clark* (1960) 39 TC 12 (profit
but not trading). A related issue is whether a particular transaction carried out by a person who is clearly trading
forms part of the trade, even though a loss must result.
[53] *FA and AB Ltd v Lupton* [1971] 3 All ER 948, 47 TC 580.
[54] *Overseas Containers Finance Ltd v Stoker* [1989] STC 364, 61 TC 473, CA.
[55] [1992] STC 226, 243j, 64 TC 617, 749.

was real expenditure of real money. In the Court of Appeal it had been held that there was an intention to gain a fiscal advantage. In such circumstances the Court of Appeal remitted the case to the Commissioners to weigh the fiscal elements against the non-fiscal elements to decide whether the transaction was entered into (a) for essentially commercial purposes but in a fiscally advantageous form, or (b) essentially for the purpose of obtaining a fiscal advantage under the guise of a commercial transaction.[56] However, in the House of Lords Lord Templeman said, surely correctly, that neither the Commissioners nor the courts were competent or obliged to decide such issues.[57] In that case Lord Templeman said of *FA and AB Ltd v Lupton*[58] that, on the true analysis of the transaction, the consequence of the tax avoidance scheme in *Lupton* was that the trader did not trade at all; there was neither profit nor loss. The House in that case had not addressed the problem of what was to happen where, as in *Ensign* itself, there was actual expenditure.

The use of the trading concept in the fight against tax avoidance has reappeared in recent cases. An important example is the film partnership cases, most notably *Eclipse Film Partners No 35 LLP v HMRC*.[59] The Eclipse 35 partnership and its members entered into a complex series of transactions in relation to the acquisition, distribution and marketing of film rights for two films produced by the Disney group of companies ('Enchanted' and 'Underdog'). The individual members of the Eclipse 35 partnership, including some well-known football managers, borrowed money to contribute to its capital and paid interest of approximately £293 million on the money borrowed. The members claimed tax relief in respect of that interest, but such relief was available only if Eclipse 35 was carrying on a trade and only if the borrowed money was used wholly for the purpose of that trade. Unfortunately for the members of the partnership, the Upper Tribunal agreed with the First-tier Tribunal's finding that Eclipse 35 was not trading and that its involvement lacked commercial substance. Somewhat controversially, the UT also agreed with the FTT that speculation was a characteristic of trading and that it was not present in this case. Unlike the FTT, however, the UT did not go so far as to conclude that speculation is a necessary requirement of trading in all cases. The UT's decision was upheld on further appeal. According to Sir Terence Etherton, delivering the judgement of the unanimous Court of Appeal, when the FTT described Eclipse 35's involvement as lacking commercial substance, the FTT was really doing little more than stating a conclusion already reached that, essentially, 'the relationship between Disney and all its related entities, on the one hand, and Eclipse 35, on the other hand, was one in which Eclipse 35 acquired an investment rather than carried on a trade.'[60] The CA distinguished this case from *Ensign Tankers* on the basis that 'Eclipse 35 did not pay for the production of the Films and the FTT concluded that the reality was that it did not make a significant contribution towards their exploitation.'[61] The Supreme Court refused leave to

---

[56] [1991] STC 136, 147–49, 64 TC 617, 720–22, per Browne-Wilkinson V-C. The Court of Appeal had reversed Millett J.
[57] [1992] STC 226, 241, 64 TC 617, 742.
[58] [1971] 3 All ER 948, 47 TC 580.
[59] [2012] UKFTT 270 TC upheld by the UT on appeal on the trading issue [2013] UKUT 0639 (TCC) and [2015] EWCA Civ 95. For commentary see notes by Bates, *Tax Journal* (18 May 2012 and 17 January 2014) and Vella [2012] BTR 252.
[60] [2015] EWCA Civ 95, para 146.
[61] [2015] EWCA Civ 95, para 151.

appeal, after a short hearing.[62] The case is a good example of the difficulty in convincing appellate courts to overturn a lower court decision that a person is not trading.

Another example of the use of the trading concept to defeat tax avoidance schemes is *Flanagan and Others v HMRC*.[63] This case concerned the 'Working Wheels' tax avoidance scheme marketed to 450 high net worth individuals, including fund managers and a former Radio 1 DJ. The taxpayers claimed to be used car salespeople who had incurred substantial borrowings generating losses of tens of millions of pounds, which were applied to reduce their taxable income from other sources. The tax tribunal quite rightly decided that this highly artificial scheme was ineffective, partly on that basis that the taxpayers were not trading. Judge Bishop concluded that the fiscal drivers for the so-called trade were so great that the 'shape and character of the transaction is no longer that of a trading transaction'— quoting Lord Morris in *FA and AB Ltd v Lupton*—and, further, that the appellants 'were instead engaged in an arrangement designed only to give the illusion of trading…'.[64] The use of trading as a weapon against tax avoidance, however, does raise a concern that the interpretation ascribed to this very important concept in tax avoidance cases will have unintended and undesirable effects on its interpretation in non-avoidance contexts as well.[65]

If there is an intention to make a profit but then to apply it in some worthy way, there is a trading activity. The tax system is concerned with the acquisition, not with the distribution, of profit.[66] However, it is necessary to distinguish a trade from a merely charitable endeavour. In *Religious Tract and Book Society of Scotland v Forbes*[67] the question was whether colportage, ie the sending out of colporteurs to sell Bibles and to act as cottage missionaries, was a trade. The Court of Exchequer (Scotland) ruled that the activity, which could not possibly be carried on at a profit, could not be a trade, with the result that the losses on colportage could not be set off against what were undoubtedly trading profits from the Society's book shops. It would therefore appear that while the impossibility of profit will prevent the activity from being a trade, the absence of a profit motive will not.

19.3.3 Motive for Acquisition

The motive attending the acquisition of an asset is a factor which, when there is doubt, is to be thrown into the balance.[68] An acquisition under a relative's last will and testament is clearly different from a purchase with a view to speedy resale.[69] If T embarks on a venture which has the characteristics of trade, T's purpose or object cannot prevail over it. But if the acts are equivocal, T's purpose or object may be very material.[70] If a bank acquires the

---

[62] [2016] UKSC 24.

[63] [2014] UKFTT 175 (TC).

[64] [2014] UKFTT 175 (TC), para 86.

[65] For commentary on these developments see Crosley [2014] BTR 256, Peacock [2014] BTR 509 and Bates and Harrison, *Tax Journal* (13 March 2015).

[66] *Mersey Docks and Harbour Board v Lucas* (1883) 8 App Cas 891, 2 TC 25.

[67] (1896) 3 TC 415. On the need to take a broad view when many activities are intertwined, see *British Olympic Association v Winter* [1995] STC (SCD) 85.

[68] As in *Lucy and Sunderland Ltd v Hunt* [1961] 3 All ER 1062, 40 TC 132 (Commissioners finding that there was a trade reversed) and *West v Phillips* (1958) 38 TC 203 (houses built to let were investments); see Bates [1958] BTR 76.

[69] But distinguish *Pilkington v Randall* (1965) 42 TC 662, where one beneficiary bought the interest of another and was held to be within what is now ITTOIA 2005, Pt 2 (Sch D, Case I).

[70] *Iswera v IRC* [1965] 1 WLR 663, 668, per Lord Reid.

shares of a customer who was in difficulties, but not intending to hold the shares as circulating assets, the transaction will be on capital account.[71] The acquisition of an asset with the hope of making a profit on the resale does not inevitably signify a venture in the nature of trade, since a good investment should generate some capital appreciation.[72] The time at which resale is foreseen is of greater importance.[73]

However, if taxpayers argue that it was not their intention to make a profit through resale, the onus is on them to produce some plausible explanation for the purchase, such as an intention to enjoy the income before reselling.[74] Further, taxpayers' assertions that they intended to buy an asset for investment purposes, whether as an investment fund for old age or as a hedge against devaluation,[75] have not been allowed to stand against other facts. The Revenue thus seems to get the best of both worlds: the taxpayer's state of mind can make up for equivocal acts, while unequivocal acts cannot be distorted by intent.[76] In assessing these matters the case stated must be examined in the round.[77] A finding that the taxpayer had no predetermined intention to sell one property when buying another is only one finding.[78] If there is no prospect of immediate profit through resale, this may suggest that the acquisition is not a venture in the nature of trade. However, whatever the taxpayer's original intention may have been, that may change.

19.3.3.1 Companies

A separate question concerns companies which, as legal persons, have their capacity limited by their objects. The court, in deciding whether or not there is a venture, may look at the objects of the company,[79] but a statement therein limiting the company's powers to investment is not conclusive against liability to tax on its income.[80] On the other hand, if a company is set up which has the power to purchase land and to turn it to account, such operations are likely to be regarded as trading operations,[81] and it has been suggested that the mere setting up of a company points to a trading intention because of the implied continuity of the company.[82]

19.3.3.2 Pension Fund Trustees

The question of motive reappears in the important case of *Clarke v British Telecom Pension Scheme Trustees*,[83] a major case on the taxation of pension schemes. The taxpayers were

[71] *Waylee Investment Ltd v Commrs of Inland Revenue* [1990] STC 780, PC; see also *Beautiland v Commrs of Inland Revenue* [1991] STC 467, PC.
[72] *IRC v Reinhold* (1953) 34 TC 389.
[73] With the emphasis on 'foreseen' as opposed to when it actually took place (*Marson v Morton* [1986] STC 46, 59 TC 381).
[74] *Reynold's Executors v Bennett* (1943) 25 TC 401.
[75] *Wisdom v Chamberlain* [1969] 1 All ER 332, 45 TC 92.
[76] Eg, *Mitchell Bros v Tomlinson* (1957) 37 TC 224.
[77] For a good example, see *Kirkham v Williams* [1991] STC 343, 64 TC 253.
[78] *Kirkby v Hughes* [1993] STC 76.
[79] *Cooksey and Bibbey v Rednall* (1949) 30 TC 514, 521.
[80] *Eames v Stepnell Properties Ltd* (1966) 43 TC 678, CA; *Emro Investments Ltd v Aller* (1954) 35 TC 305.
[81] *IRC v Reinhold* (1953) 34 TC 389; and see *IRC v Korean Syndicate Ltd* [1921] 3 KB 258, 12 TC 181, and *Ruhamuh Property Co Ltd v FCT* (1928) 41 CLR 1648; see also *Lewis Emanuel & Son Ltd v White* (1965) 42 TC 369.
[82] *IRC v Reinhold* (1953) 34 TC 389, per Lord Carmont.
[83] [2000] STC 222; see Kerridge [2000] BTR 397.

trustees administering pension schemes and, as such, were exempt from tax on various forms of investment income, including underwriting commissions charged at that time under Case VI, but not if charged under Case I.[84] The Revenue made assessments on the basis that the commissions were chargeable under Schedule D, Case I. On the evidence, transactions were frequent and with relative lack of risk that the sub-underwriters would be left with the shares.[85] The Commissioners had described the trustees' entry into these arrangements as 'habitual, organised, for reward, extensive and business-like' but that they came within Case VI. The Court of Appeal, reversing Lightman J and restoring the decision of the Commissioners, held that the transactions fell outside Case I and so were not taxable under Case I. It is likely that if these transactions had been carried out by an ordinary individual, liability would have arisen under Case I. However, ordinary individuals do not have the same overall investment responsibilities as trustees, and it is therefore necessary to wait and see what, if anything, the courts may do in another case.

19.3.4 The Individual

Where a single transaction is involved and is of a nature close to, but separate from, what is undoubtedly a trade carried on by an individual, it is likely that the courts will conclude that the transaction is a venture in the nature of a trade.[86] In *T Beynon & Co Ltd v Ogg*,[87] where the company acted as agents for the purchase of wagons and bought some on their own account, the profits on the resale of those wagons were held taxable, as were the profits in *Cape Brandy Syndicate v IRC*,[88] where South African brandy was acquired for blending and resale in the UK by three persons who were members of firms engaged in the wine trade. In these cases, T was held assessable on the profits of the adventure in the nature of trade; however, the profits did not form part of the other trading activities but did have a distinct taxable source. There is some authority to suggest that if a person has a skill and makes money by it, the profit is more likely to be taxable;[89] however, today the absence of a skill appears to be neutral.[90]

19.3.5 The Subject Matter

The courts take the view that certain commodities are more likely to be acquired as investments than as the subject of a deal. There are two main groups of examples. Objects recommended for investment in the light of these cases include wine, gold coins and reversionary interests. Antiques and works of art are similarly recommended, provided they are retained for some time and not sold by commercial methods.

---

[84] Ex TA 1988, s 592(3)(c).

[85] It is true that the underwriting commissions all related to companies in which the trustees held shares, but the opportunity to earn those commissions did not appear to have come to them because they owned the shares, which may afford only a slender basis of distinction.

[86] *Cayzer and Irvine & Co v IRC* (1942) 24 TC 491, 496, per Lord Normand.

[87] (1918) 7 TC 125.

[88] [1921] 2 KB 403, 12 TC 358.

[89] *Smith Barry v Cordy* (1946) 28 TC 250, 260, per Scott LJ; but doubts as to the correctness of this decision were raised in *Ransom v Higgs* [1974] STC 539, [1974] 3 All ER 949.

[90] *Johnston v Heath* [1970] 3 All ER 915, 921, per Goff J.

19.3.5.1 Not Income-yielding?

If the object yields income, whether in the form of rent or dividends, that object was at one time more likely to be an investment than an object which yields no income.[91] Where the court can see some fruit, the source of the fruit is likely to be a tree. A subtle case is *Snell v Rosser Thomas & Co Ltd*,[92] where the taxpayer, a developer, bought a house and 51 acres of land. The house produced rent from tenants, but the land produced no income and was therefore stock in trade. In determining whether or not there is income the courts have looked not simply at the flow of money to the taxpayer, but also at any outflow. In *Wisdom v Chamberlain*,[93] the interest payments were of importance, while in *Cooke v Haddock*,[94] rent of £167 a year had to be set against the £320-a-year interest.

However, *Marson v Morton*[95] stressed that it was no longer self-evident that land could not be an investment unless it produced income. While the legal principle could not change, life itself could: 'Since the arrival of inflation and high rates of tax on income new approaches to investment have emerged putting the emphasis on the making of capital profits at the expense of income yield.'[96] Tribunals should not treat new investments as falling within ITTOIA 2005, Part 2 just because those interests did not generate income (as conventionally understood), nor endeavour to put old types of investments into Part 2 for the same reason when other factors point in the other direction.

Profits on a sale of property which produces income may nonetheless be taxable as trading profits all depends on the individual circumstances of the case. Thus, stocks and shares bought by a bank in order to make good use of funds in hand and subsequently disposed of in order to finance repayments to depositors, were treated as trading stock of the banking business.[97] Moreover, a company which, in addition to building ships, ran a passenger service and bought and sold four ships for that service in rapid succession, was held taxable on the profits from the resales of the passenger ships as part of their general trading profits.[98]

19.3.5.2 Aesthetics, Etc

If the object does not yield income but can be enjoyed in kind, so that there is pleasure or even pride in its possession,[99] as where a person buys a picture for purposes of aesthetic enjoyment, any profit on resale will escape income tax. Conversely, the purchase of a commodity which gives no such pleasure and which cannot be turned to account except by a process of realisation, may well give rise to a taxable profit.[100] Examples of this turn not only

---

[91] *Salt v Chamberlain* [1979] STC 750.

[92] [1968] 1 All ER 600, 44 TC 343; and consider the factory in *WM Robb Ltd v Page* (1971) 47 TC 465 (factory built to let or to sell; Commissioners' finding that there was a trade not disturbed).

[93] [1969] 1 All ER 332, 45 TC 92.

[94] (1960) 39 TC 64.

[95] [1986] STC 463, 59 TC 381.

[96] *Ibid*, 472, 393, per Browne-Wilkinson V-C.

[97] *Punjab Co-operative Bank Ltd v Amritsar IT Comr Lahore* [1940] AC 1055, [1940] 4 All ER 87; a similar rule applies to insurance companies (*General Reinsurance Co Ltd v Tomlinson* [1970] 2 All ER 436, 48 TC 81, discussed in *General Motors Acceptance Corpn v IRC* [1985] STC 408, 59 TC 651).

[98] *J Bolson & Son Ltd v Farrelly* (1953) 34 TC 161.

[99] See Lord Normand in *IRC v Fraser* (1942) 24 TC 498; quaere how a trust can enjoy such an object—in which case one should consider the liability of pension funds which purchase works of art.

[100] Consider the tax position of unit holders in trusts whose purpose is to make investments in commodities, as distinct from unit holders in companies producing commodities.

on the nature of the commodity, such as the railway wagons in *Gloucester Railway Carriage and Wagon Co Ltd v IRC*,[101] but also on the quantity, as in *Rutledge v IRC*[102] which involved the resale of one million rolls of lavatory paper; however, as always, these are questions of fact, and it was also important in *Rutledge* that T had no intention other than to resell the property at a profit.[103]

19.3.5.3 Land

Land is another asset which can easily yield taxable profits.[104] If the owner of a house actually lives in it, the house is unlikely to be trading stock. However, occupation is not conclusive, and courts have been reluctant to disturb a finding by the Commissioners that there was an adventure in the nature of trade. In *Page v Pogson*,[105] T built a house for himself and his wife, and then sold it six months after completion. He then built another house nearby, but had to sell it when his job was moved from the south to the east of England. He was held taxable on the profits of the sale of the second house, and Upjohn J felt himself unable to reverse that finding, although doubting whether he would have reached that decision himself.

19.3.6 Processing—Supplementary Work

The alteration of the asset by the taxpayer may suggest that there is a venture in the nature of trade. If a purchaser carried through a manufacturing process which changed the character of the article, eg converting pig-iron into steel, there is likely to be a trade. However, merely to put the asset into a condition suitable for a favourable sale, such as cleaning a picture or giving a boat a general overhaul, would not suggest a trade. In *IRC v Livingston*,[106] the taxpayer, a ship repairer, together with a blacksmith and a fish salesman's employee, purchased a cargo vessel which they converted into a steam drifter and then sold without using it for fishing. The alterations took nearly four months and were carried out by two of the three for wages. The Court of Session held that the profit was taxable. The mere enhancement of value, as by obtaining planning permission,[107] is not sufficient to create a trade, neither is the normal use of the asset. So whereas the planting of rubber trees did not indicate a trade in *Tebrau (Johore) Rubber Syndicate Ltd v Farmer*,[108] the blending of brandy in the *Cape Brandy Syndicate* case did.[109] *Jenkinson v Freedland*[110] must be regarded as a most unusual case. There, the taxpayer bought two stills which were coated with a resinous substances, and succeeded in removing it by a process of his own devising. It was held that

---

[101] [1925] AC 469, 12 TC 720; see Ziegel [1961] BTR 155, 164.
[102] (1929) 14 TC 490; and see also *Martin v Lowry* [1927] AC 312, 11 TC 297 (44 million yards of aeroplane linen).
[103] *Mamor Sdn Bhd v Director General of Inland Revenue* [1985] STC 801, 806, PC.
[104] See Crump [1961] BTR 95; Pearce [1962] BTR 144.
[105] (1954) 35 TC 545; *cf Sharpless v Rees* (1940) 23 TC 361; and *Shadford v H Fairweather & Co Ltd* (1966) 43 TC 291.
[106] [1927] SC 251, 11 TC 538.
[107] *Taylor v Good* [1974] STC 148, [1974] 1 All ER 1137, 29 TC 277; see Nock [1974] BTR 184.
[108] (1910) 5 TC 658.
[109] [1921] 2 KB 403, 18 TC 358.
[110] (1961) 39 TC 636.

there was no trade on these particular facts, but this turned largely on the eventual sale of the stills by the taxpayer to his own company.

19.3.7 Realisation

'Some explanation, such as a sudden emergency or opportunity calling for ready money, negatives the idea that any plan of dealing prompted the original purchase.'[111] There are few reported cases in which this point has been made successfully. *In Stott v Hoddinott*,[112] an architect was obliged, as a term of a contract, to take up shares in the company granting him the contract. He subsequently sold those shares in order to provide funds to take up shares under later contracts with other companies. It was held that this was a capital transaction and, as such, he was not entitled to relief in respect of the loss he sustained.

The presence of an organisation through which the disposal of the asset is carried out is one of the hallmarks of a trade, not least because the expenses of such an organisation will be deductible in computing the net profit on the deal.[113] Equally, another factor in deciding whether or not a trade has been discontinued is whether the trade organisation has ceased to exist in an identifiable form.[114] However, the presence or absence of an organisation is not conclusive in deciding whether or not there has been a venture in the nature of trade. As Lord Wilberforce said in *Ransom v Higgs*, '[o]rganisation as such is not a principle of taxation, or many estimable ladies throughout this country would be imperilled'.[115]

The number of steps taken to dispose of the asset is a fragile indicator of a trade.[116] The purchase of goods in bulk and their resale in smaller quantities is the essence of a wholesale–retail trading operation. In *Cape Brandy Syndicate v IRC*,[117] one of the factors in favour of a trade was that the brandy was disposed of in some 100 transactions spread over 18 months. On the other hand, the fact that a large number of disposals of land occurred did not make them trading transactions in *Hudsons Bay Co Ltd v Stevens*.[118] Conversely, a single disposal may nonetheless amount to an adventure in the nature of trade.[119]

19.3.8 Frequency of Transactions

The frequency of transactions is only one factor in determining whether a trade exists; an investor is still an investor even though the investments are switched. As Harman J once said: 'A deal done once is probably not an activity in the nature of trade, though it may be. Done three or four times it usually is. Each case must depend on its own facts.'[120] However,

---

[111] Royal Commission 1955, Cmnd 9474 (1955), §115.
[112] (1916) 7 TC 85; see also *Mitchell Bros v Tomlinson* (1957) 37 TC 224; and *Page v Pogson* (1954) 35 TC 545.
[113] Lord Radcliffe in *Edwards v Bairstow and Harrison* [1955] 3 All ER 48, 58, 36 TC 207, 230.
[114] *Andrew v Taylor* (1965) 42 TC 557.
[115] [1974] 3 All ER 949, 966; note ESC C4.
[116] *IRC v Reinhold* (1953) 34 TC 389, 395, per Lord Russell.
[117] [1921] 2 KB 403, 417, 12 TC 368, 376. For another example, see *Martin v Lowry* (1926) 11 TC 297, 320.
[118] (1909) 5 TC 424.
[119] Eg, *T Beynon & Co Ltd v Ogg* (1918) 7 TC 125.
[120] *Bolson v Farrelly* (1953) 34 TC 161, 167; see also *Foulds v Clayton* (1953) 34 TC 382, 388; *Pickford v Quirke* (1927) 13 TC 251.

while it is clear that repeated transactions may support the inference of a trade, and that an isolated transaction may nonetheless be a venture in the nature of trade, there is also authority that where a transaction is repeated the court may use that fact to place the label of trade on the original transaction. In *Leach v Pogson*,[121] T was a serial driving school incorporator. It was agreed that he was liable to income tax on the profits from subsequent transactions, but T argued that he was not liable in respect of the profit on the first. It was held that he was so liable and that the subsequent transactions could be used to support that conclusion. It is probably of great importance that in that case, while he had no intention of embarking upon the business of establishing and selling motoring schools when the first one was set up, T did have that intention before he sold it. The case would thus appear to be correctly decided, although perhaps more appropriately dealt with as a case of a change in the character of the transaction.

19.3.9 Duration of Ownership

A 'fast buck' is the essence of a deal. A long period between the acquisition of an asset and its disposal may corroborate an intention to hold it as an investment.[122] Conversely, a quick sale invites a scrutiny of the evidence to see whether the acquisition was made with that intent.[123] One element of an investment is that the acquirer intends to hold it for some time, with a view either to obtaining some benefit in the way of income in the meantime or obtaining some profit, but not an immediate profit by resale.[124] Where the asset can be turned into profit only by resale, the court adopts a realistic approach.[125]

However, while an asset acquired on a short-term basis, as in *Wisdom v Chamberlain* (see §19.3.1 above), will often be the subject of a venture, it does not follow that a disposal within a short period amounts to a trade, as *Marson v Morton* (again see §19.3.1 above) shows. In *IRC v Reinhold*,[126] the taxpayer admitted that he acquired the property with the intention of reselling it and that he had instructed his agents to sell whenever a suitable opportunity arose. The land was sold after three years. This isolated transaction escaped income tax. Much more doubtful, however, is the decision of Danckwerts J in *McLellan, Rawson & Co Ltd v Newall*,[127] in which the Commissioners' decision that there was a taxable profit was reversed, even though the taxpayer had entered into an arrangement to sell the woodlands while he was still negotiating for their purchase.

19.3.10 Timing

It is a question of fact not only whether there is a venture in the nature of trade, but also when it begins—and ends. It is also important to separate the question whether a trade

---

[121] (1962) 40 TC 585.
[122] *Harvey v Caulcott* (1952) 33 TC 159, 164, per Donovan J.
[123] *Turner v Last* (1965) 42 TC 517, 522–23, per Cross J.
[124] *Eames v Stepnell Properties Ltd* (1966) 43 TC 678, 692, per Buckley J.
[125] *Eames v Stepnell Properties Ltd* [1967] 1 All ER 785, (1966) 43 TC 678 (Commissioners' finding there was no trade reversed); see Harman LJ, 794, 701.
[126] (1953) 34 TC 389.
[127] (1955) 36 TC 117.

has begun from the question whether any income has arisen from it.[128] Where an asset is acquired and subsequently disposed of, it is open to the court to conclude from the evidence that the whole transaction was a venture in the nature of trade. It is, however, open to the court to conclude that an asset was acquired with the intention of retaining it as an investment but that trading subsequently commenced, so that the profit accruing on resale is taxable.[129] What is clear is that at any one time the asset must either be trading stock or a capital asset; it cannot be both at the same time.[130]

In computing the profit where the trade is begun after the asset is acquired, the asset must be brought into account at its market value at that time.[131]

19.4 Sales by Personal Representatives and Liquidators

19.4.1 *The Rule*

Personal representatives (PRs) may be empowered to carry on the deceased's (D's) business by the terms of the will; however, their acts may amount to carrying on a trade for the purposes of income tax whether or not there is such power.[132] If they are held to be trading, the liability to tax is theirs personally—not qua executors.[133] The job of PRs is to realise the assets of the estate and distribute them among the beneficiaries. There is therefore a presumption that they were not carrying on a trade if all they did was realise the asset in a way advantageous to the estate.[134]

19.4.2 *Farming*

Whether the acts amount to carrying on a trade is a matter of degree and must depend on the nature of the trade, as two cases concerning farming show. In *Pattullo's Trustees v IRC*,[135] the taxpayers were the representatives of a tenant farmer (D) who also carried on the trades of cattle dealer and feeder. The farm and the cattle dealing business were bequeathed specifically, so that the only asset to be realised was the feeding business. D died in November, when the cattle were already on the land of other farms feeding from and manuring that land. The PRs considered they had to complete the contracts for economic reasons. They also bought more cattle in order to consume the remaining feedstuffs on the farms. The

---

[128] See *Eckel v Board of Inland Revenue* [1989] STC 305, PC.

[129] *Taylor v Good* [1973] 2 All ER 785, [1973] STC 383, 49 TC 277.

[130] *Simmons v IRC* [1980] STC 350, [1980] 2 All ER 798, 53 TC 461; see Preece [1981] BTR 124; Walters [1981] BTR 379. It is also clear that a case stated must be examined in the round (*Kirkby v Hughes* [1993] STC 76, 65 TC 532).

[131] *Simmons v IRC* [1980] STC 350, [1980] 2 All ER 798, 53 TC 461. This is the converse of *Sharkey v Wernher* (see below at §23.5.1). See also TCGA 1992, s 161 (and below at §42.2.1). Cases in which this rule should have been applied include *Leach v Pogson* (1962) 40 TC 585 and *Mitchell Bros v Tomlinson* (1957) 37 TC 224.

[132] *Weisberg's Executrices v IRC* (1933) 17 TC 696.

[133] *Cohan's Executors v IRC* (1924) 12 TC 602. Note Romer LJ in *Hillerns and Fowler v Murray* (1932) 17 TC 77, 92.

[134] *Cohan's Executors v IRC* (1924) 12 TC 602, 620, per Sargant LJ; approved by Greene MR in *Newbarns Syndicate v Hay* (1939) 22 TC 461, 472.

[135] (1955) 36 TC 87.

cattle were all sold by the following June. The Commissioners held that the PRs were carrying on the business of cattle feeding and were not simply preparing the estate assets for sale, even though this was their motive. The Court of Session held that there was evidence to support the Commissioners' finding of liability to tax through trading.

However, in *IRC v Donaldson's Trustees*,[136] the Commissioners held there was no trading; again, their conclusion was not reversed by the Court of Session. In this case, D was a farmer whose sole interest was a pedigree herd of Aberdeen Angus cattle. D died in March 1955. The trustees were advised to sell the heifer calves in September 1955 and the bull calves in February 1956. They did this, but had to keep the cattle alive and well in the meantime. The manager was told that the cattle were to be sold, and the farm was rearranged for preparing them for sale instead of grazing and breeding. It was held that the occupation of the farm was simply for the termination of husbandry and there was no trade.

It is thus a question of fact and degree whether the acts amount to the realisation of the asset or to trade.[137] However, if the acts are equally consistent both with the carrying on of a trade and with mere realisation, the act will be mere realisation, since to hold otherwise would deprive the executors of their right *vis-à-vis* the Revenue to realise their testator's assets in the ordinary way.[138] In *Donaldson's Trustees*, the PRs were able to show a positive change from the normal pattern of farming. In *Pattullo's Trustees*, the Revenue could show, by the purchase of extra cattle, a continuation or development of the trade.

19.4.3 Insisting Against Partners

Where D was carrying on a trade in partnership with others, the executors may insist that the assets should be realised on D's death so that they may administer the estate. Where assets are realised, the court may hold that, as far as the estate is concerned, the process is one of mere realisation.[139] In the absence of a finding that the executors did not consent to the continuation of the trade but insisted upon their share of the assets, the court will uphold a finding by the Commissioners that there was a continuation of the trade.[140]

19.4.4 Liquidation

The duty of a liquidator (L) is like that of the PRs—to realise the assets.[141] The courts may ask the question: What reason is there to suppose that the winding up was done for any

---

[136] (1963) 41 TC 161.

[137] *Wood v Black's Executor* (1952) 33 TC 172.

[138] *Newbarns Syndicate v Hay* (1939) 22 TC 461, 476, per Greene MR.

[139] As in *Marshall's Executors, Hood's Executors and Rogers v Joly* [1936] 1 All ER 851, 20 TC 256, where it was proved.

[140] As in *Newbarns Syndicate v Hay* (1939) 22 TC 461, where the process of realisation took 10 years and the executor attended all partnership meetings as a voting participant, something he was not entitled to do as the mere executor of a deceased member.

[141] *IRC v Burrell* [1924] 2 KB 52, 73, 9 TC 27, 42, per Atkin LJ. In these cases it is irrelevant that the assets were the trading stock of the company or represented undivided profit. The same principles apply to trustees holding on an assignment for the benefit of creditors (*Armitage v Moore* [1900] 2 QB 363, 4 TC 199, supplying steam power is trading, not realising an asset) and to a receiver for debenture holders (*IRC v Thompson* [1936] 2 All ER 651, 20 TC 422).

purpose other than the normal carrying out of the duties of a liquidator?[142] There is a presumption that a mere disposal is not a trading operation.[143] On the other hand, sums paid to the liquidator in respect of trading contracts made before the date of liquidation will be trading receipts.[144]

19.5 Retirement—When Does Trading End?

19.5.1 Selling Trading Stock

To dispose of trading stock following retirement may well be trading, since the moment when trade ceases is a question of fact. Declarations by the trader are not, of themselves, decisive. In *J and R O'Kane Ltd v IRC*,[145] the taxpayers had carried on the business of wine and spirit merchants. They announced their intention to retire in early 1916 but did not complete the disposal of their stock until late 1917, an operation which was carried out mostly in 1917 and which took the form of many small sales. The only purchases made for the business after the announcement of their retirement were under continuing contracts with distillers. The Special Commissioners held that the trade did not end in early 1916 and that the proceeds of the disposal sales were therefore taxable as the profits of the trade. The House of Lords held that there was abundant evidence for the Commissioners' findings. On the other hand, in *IRC v Nelson*[146] there was only a 12-day gap between the decision to retire and the disposal of the stock, and the whole stock was sold together with the rest of the business (the casks, the trade name, and office furniture and fittings) in one sale to one customer. The Commissioners held that the disposal was not by way of trade and the Court of Session held that there was evidence to support the conclusion.

19.5.2 Completing Contracts

Problems arise on the completion of executory contracts entered into before retirement. In *Hillerns and Fowler v Murray*,[147] the trade was run by a partnership which was dissolved by lapse of time under the terms of the partnership deed. At that time the partners held trading stock and subsequently acquired other stock under contracts entered into before the dissolution. The trading stock was used to fulfil orders placed by customers before the dissolution; no new contracts, whether for purchase or sale, were entered into after dissolution. The Commissioners held that there was evidence of trading after dissolution. Although Rowlatt J reversed their decision, the Court of Appeal held that there was evidence to support the Commissioners' conclusion; the (alleged) presumption that a sale by an executor or a liquidator was a realisation of an asset and not a trading activity, did not apply. Where,

---

[142] *Wilson Box (Foreign Rights) Ltd v Brice* [1936] 3 All ER 728, 20 TC 736, esp at 742 per Lawrence J, and 747, per Slesser LJ; and *John Mills Production Ltd v Mathias* (1964) 44 TC 441, 456, per Ungoed Thomas J.

[143] *Wilson Box (Foreign Rights) Ltd v Brice* [1936] 3 All ER 728, 20 TC 736.

[144] *IRC v Oban Distillery Co Ltd* (1932) 18 TC 33.

[145] (1922) 12 TC 303.

[146] [1939] SC 689, 22 TC 716.

[147] (1932) 17 TC 77.

however, it is clear that trading has ceased, subsequent disposals will escape income tax.[148] Therefore, a sale of slag heaps 18 years after a company's iron works had shut down was not a part of their trade; it was not argued that this was a new trade.

19.5.3 Is Purchaser Trading?

Where T sells a trade to another (P), T ceases to trade. Whether P, in selling T's former trading stock, commences to trade or simply realises assets is a matter of fact.[149] If P is a company which is under some obligation to hand over the whole or part of the profits of the trade to T, it may be concluded that P is simply T's agent, so that T does not cease to trade.[150] An alternative conclusion on the facts may be that the old trade has ceased but that T has commenced a new trade through the agency of P.[151] The choice between these two outcomes is not merely academic since, apart from the commencement and cessation provisions, there are such questions as unused loss relief, which will be lost under the second outcome.

19.6   Mutual Business

19.6.1 The Idea

It is necessary to distinguish a profit from a trade, from an excess of contribution over expenditure. If a person allows himself £60 a week for housekeeping, but spends only £50, no one would contend that the £10 saved was taxable profit. The immunity of the £10 from tax rests on two principles, either of which is sufficient: one is that a person cannot trade with himself; the other is that the sum does not represent a profit.

Example—clubs

This immunity has been applied to groups of people who combine for a purpose and contribute towards expenses, as in the case of a golf club whose members pay a club subscription. Here, any excess of income from subscriptions over expenses is free from tax.[152] Each member is entitled to a share of the surplus, and it is irrelevant that there is only a limited liability to contribute to any deficiency.[153] Wherever, therefore, the contributors to, and the recipients from, the fund are the same people,[154] it is impossible to say that the contributors derive profits from the contributions made by themselves to a fund which could only

---

[148] *Beams v Weardale Steel Coal and Coke Co Ltd* (1937) 21 TC 204.
[149] *Lucy and Sunderland Ltd v Hunt* [1961] 3 All ER 1062, 1066, 40 TC 132, 139.
[150] *Baker v Cook* [1937] 3 All ER 509, 21 TC 337.
[151] *Southern v Watson* [1940] 3 All ER 439, 23 TC 566; see also *Parker v Batty* (1941) 23 TC 739.
[152] *Carlisle and Silloth Golf Club v Smith* [1913] 3 KB 75, 6 TC 48 and 198; distinguished in *Carnoustie Golf Course Committee v IRC* [1929] SC 419, 14 TC 498.
[153] *Faulconbridge v National Employers Mutual General Insurance Association Ltd* (1952) 33 TC 103.
[154] But identity does not mean absolute equality (*Municipal Mutual Insurance Ltd v Hills* (1932) 16 TC 430, 448, per Lord Macmillan); as long as the relationship is reasonable.

be expended or returned to themselves.[155] Even if the club had a bar at which drinks were served at prices which yielded a profit, there is no liability to tax since the bar is merely a part of the club, and is open only to members, who thus make certain additional contributions to the fund. The situation is different where the bar is open to the public,[156] since the contributors to the fund are no longer the same as the recipients from it; profits from the bar would be taxable even if the rest of the club ran at a loss. Liability would also arise if the facts showed that the bar was a distinct trading venture separate from the rest of the club. The mutuality principle extends to mutual insurance companies and to institutions like the BBC[157] and members' clubs. It has no role to play in property income (ITTOIA 2005, Part 3, section 321).

19.6.2 Mutual Companies

The principle of mutuality applies even though the contributions are made to a separate legal entity[158]—such as a company—provided the company exists simply for the convenience of its members and as an instrument obedient to their mandate (eg a mutual insurance company).[159] Income from investments is taxable in the usual way. Any excess of premium income over liabilities will also be the income of the company. However, provided such income is returnable to the members either in the form of bonuses or by way of reduction of premiums, that income is exempt from tax since, although the company is trading,[160] this sum is not a profit to its members.[161] A member who surrenders a policy loses any entitlement to future bonuses despite having contributed to them. Conversely, a person who becomes a member of the company by taking out a policy may become entitled to a portion of the surplus contributed by someone else. Such possibilities do not prevent there being mutuality, since the excess of contributions must go back to the policy holders as a class even if not precisely in the proportions in which they have contributed to them.[162]

It is, however, essential that such companies should be mutual companies, ie where only the policy holders are the members of the company. If the company has shareholders who do not hold life policies but who are entitled to the profits of this business, the company is not a mutual company.[163] Today, a body corporate and an unincorporated association are subject to corporation tax.

---

[155] See *English and Scottish Joint Co-operative Wholesale Society Ltd v Assam Agricultural IT Comr* [1948] AC 405, 419, [1948] 2 All ER 395, 400, per Lord Normand; *IRC v Eccentric Club Ltd* [1924] 1 KB 390, 12 TC 657; and Finlay J in *National Association of Local Government Officers v Watkins* (1934) 18 TC 499, 506.

[156] *Grove v Young Men's Christian Association* (1903) 4 TC 613.

[157] *BBC v Johns* [1964] 1 All ER 923, 41 TC 471.

[158] See Rowlatt J in *Thomas v Richard Evans & Co Ltd* [1927] 1 KB 33, 47, 11 TC 790, 823.

[159] For criticism, see Royal Commission, Cmnd 9474 (1955), §22; and Monroe [1961] BTR 398.

[160] See Lord Cave in *IRC v Cornish Mutual Assurance Co Ltd* [1926] AC 281, 286–87, 12 TC 841, 866–67, criticising Lord Watson in *New York Life Insurance Co v Styles* (1889) 14 App Cas 381, 2 TC 460.

[161] See, eg, Lord Macmillan in *Municipal Mutual Insurance Ltd v Hills* (1932) 16 TC 430, 448.

[162] On position of newcomers, see Upjohn J in *Faulconbridge v National Employers Mutual General Insurance Association Ltd* (1952) 33 TC 103, 121, 124–25.

[163] *Last v London Assurance Group Coprn* (1885) 10 App Cas 438, 2 TC 100.

19.6.3 *Limits of Mutuality*

19.6.3.1 Dealings with Non-members

The principle of immunity applies only to profits from mutual dealings between contributors. Mutual insurance companies are taxable on the ordinary income accruing from transactions with non-members. Thus, in *New York Life Insurance Co v Styles*,[164] the House of Lords held that the company was not taxable on its profits from premium income from members' participating policies. It was agreed that the company was taxable on its profits from policies for fixed sums without profits and from its general annuity business with strangers, since they were not members of the company, just as it was taxable on its investment income. Exemption is afforded not to the profits from members, but to the non-profit of mutual dealings.

19.6.3.2 Lack of Genuine Mutuality

In *Fletcher v IT Comr*,[165] a members' club owned a bathing beach in Jamaica. It permitted guests at certain hotels to use the beach on payment of an entrance fee. The club was clearly taxable on the profits of these fees since it was carrying on a trade with non-members. The club then altered its arrangements, abolishing the payment of a fee by the hotel guests and making the hotels voting members of the club.[166] However, each hotel member, like each individual, held only one share. The hotels, like the individual members, paid a sum by way of subscription and, in addition, a sum which was based on the number of its guests using the beach. Gross receipts were £1,750. The Revenue sought to tax the club on the profit element in the relevant proportion of the hotel membership subscription. Lord Wilberforce said that although a uniform fee was not essential, nevertheless, if mutuality were to have any meaning.[167]

> There must be a reasonable relationship, contemplated or in result, between what a member contributed and what, with due allowance for interim benefits of enjoyment, he may expect or be entitled to draw from the fund; between his liabilities and his rights.

The great use of the beach made by hotel guests was not sufficient allowance, and so the mutuality principle did not apply. This decision provides the (uncited) basis for a Revenue interpretation on profits arising from green fees at a golf club. Clearly, the profit arising from fees paid by a member is not taxable, whereas profit from fees paid by a non-member is taxable. However, temporary membership will be enough to create mutuality only if the rights of temporary members are similar to those of full members.[168]

---

[164] (1889) 14 App Cas 381, 2 TC 460; see also *Municipal Mutual Insurance Ltd v Hills* (1932) 16 TC 430, HL.

[165] [1972] AC 414, [1971] 3 All ER 1185; distinguished in *Westbourne Supporters of Glentoran Club v Brennan* [1995] STC (SCD) 137.

[166] An earlier scheme had made the hotels members but without voting rights, and it had been held that this scheme failed because the hotels were not truly members.

[167] [1971] 3 All ER 1185, 1191.

[168] RI 84; see Harris [1998] BTR 24.

19.6.3.3 Non-mutual Business with Members[169]

Not all business between a company and its members is mutual business. A business cannot escape tax on its profits for a year simply because, at the end of the year, it discovers that all its business has been with its members. In *English and Scottish Joint Co-operative Wholesale Society Ltd v Assam Agricultural IT Comr*,[170] a company was set up to own and manage a tea estate, with the bulk of its produce going to its two shareholders who advanced money by way of loan to be set off against the price due for the tea supplied by the company to its shareholders. It was held that the company had earned profits from dealings with its shareholders and so was taxable. This conclusion could not have been avoided by restricting the company's business to sales to its members.[171] A different result might have been reached if the business had not been incorporated; a different practical result would have been reached if the price paid for the tea had been fixed so that no profit would have been earned.[172]

19.6.4 Emasculated Legislation

An attempt was made in 1933[173] to tax the profits of mutual companies from dealings with members, by directing that such profits or surplus should be treated as if those transactions were transactions with non-members. Since it was the mutuality of the transaction rather than the fact that it was with a member which gave immunity from taxation, the House of Lords, in a somewhat unimaginative construction of the statute, ruled that even if the transactions had been with non-members they would have been exempt from tax, thus depriving the statute of any force.[174] Whether the Supreme Court would reach the same conclusion today is unclear. When such companies became the subject of profits tax, the legislature was more direct and simply taxed the profits of the trade of mutual companies. This more direct approach succeeded.[175]

19.6.5 Claw Back of Tax-deductible Contribution

The exemption from tax afforded by mutual dealings does not operate to prevent certain contributions being claimed as deductions in computing the taxable income of the contributor.[176] Thus, a payment to a fire insurance scheme is deductible whether or not the scheme is mutual. If the mutual business then ceases, there will be a repayment to the contributor (C) of any surplus—but without any charge to tax. C may recover more than has been paid.[177] If C made a contribution of £100 and has a marginal tax rate of 40%, the

---

[169] *Municipal Mutual Insurance v Hills* (1932) 16 TC 430.

[170] [1948] AC 405, [1948] 2 All ER 395.

[171] *Ibid*, 417, 399.

[172] *Ibid*, 421, 401 (perhaps by treating the application of profit as a discount reducing the price); see *Pope v Beaumont* [1941] 3 All ER 9, 24 TC 78.

[173] FA 1933, s 31.

[174] *Ayrshire Employers Mutual Insurance Association Ltd v IRC* [1946] 1 All ER 637, 640, 27 TC 331, 347; note the comments in *Fothergill v Monarch Airlines Ltd* [1981] AC 251. The section remained on the statute book unamended until the pre-consolidation changes of 1987.

[175] See also Royal Commission, Cmnd 9474 (1955), §593.

[176] *Thomas v Richard Evans & Co Ltd* [1927] 1 KB 33, 11 TC 790.

[177] *Stafford Coal and Iron Co Ltd v Brogan* [1963] 3 All ER 227, 41 TC 305, HL; see Monroe [1963] BTR 370.

after-tax cost of the contribution would be £60; if, however, the business is wound up, there will be a repayment of £100 free of tax. Without special legislation this device could be used to build up tax-free reserves. Hence, under corporation tax, where a body corporate is being wound up or dissolved, and a non-taxable sum was paid to a person who was then allowed to deduct that payment in computing the profits, gains or losses of a trade, profession or vocation, the receipt is treated as a trading receipt of the trade or, if the trade has ceased, as a post-cessation receipt. This applies only where the receipt is not otherwise taxable and where the receipt does not represent capital.

19.7   Occupation of Land or Trade

ITTOIA 2005, like its predecessors, draws a line between the exploitation of land (Part 3) and income derived from occupying land (which can be within Part 2).[178] As seen above (§19.1.5), income derived from the exploitation of property is property income under Part 3 (for land), rather than trading income under Part 2.[179] Income arising under Part 3 is determined in many ways as if it was from a trade, but is nonetheless not trading income and remains taxable under Part 3. A good example is income from furnished lettings.[180] See also below at §§25.3 and 25.7.

19.7.1 *Farms*

All farming and market gardening in the UK is taxed under Part 2,[181] and all farming carried on by any particular person or partnership or body of persons is treated as one trade.[182]

19.7.2 *Other Land*

The occupation of land for purposes other than farming or market gardening managed on a commercial basis and with a view to realisation of profits is similarly within Part 2.[183] Actual occupation is required; granting a licence to someone else to occupy is not enough.[184]

---

[178] ITTOIA 2005, s 9, ex TA 1988, s 15, and Sch A, para 2.
[179] *Webb v Conelee Properties Ltd* [1982] STC 913.
[180] *Gittos v Barclay* [1982] STC 390, 55 TC 633.
[181] ITTOIA 2005, s 9(1), ex TA 1988, s 53(1). On the scope of market gardening, see *Bomford v Osborne* (1940) 23 TC 642, 660, esp per Scott LJ. Originally, farmers came within Sch B, and remained there partly because of the difficulty farmers had in keeping accounts. When they were moved to Sch A, the Chancellor, announcing the proposed change, was misreported as saying that farmers should be treated like other 'traitors' rather than 'traders' (Sabine, *History of Income Tax* (Allen & Unwin, 1966), 118).
[182] ITTOIA 2005, s 9(2) and, on partnerships, s 859(2), ex TA 1988, s 53(2); hence, if X has farm A, with accrued losses and unused capital allowances, and buys farm B, he may set those losses and allowances against the profits of farm B even if subsequently he sells farm A (*Bispham v Eardiston Farming Co (1919) Ltd* [1962] 2 All ER 376, 40 TC 322; noted at [1962] BTR 255. This provision does not appear to apply to market gardening; see, generally, de Souza [1991] BTR 15.
[183] ITTOIA 2005, s 10(1), ex TA 1988, s 53(3). See *Sywell Aerodrome Ltd v Croft* [1942] 1 All ER 110, 24 TC 126. If the land is not managed on a commercial basis, a charge may arise under the miscellaneous income head under Pt 5, Ch 8 (Sch D, Case VI—see below at §28.5).
[184] *Webb v Conelee Properties Ltd* [1982] STC 913, 56 TC 149.

19.7.3 Woods

Until 1988, woodlands managed on a commercial basis were subject to a separate regime under Schedule B; the repeal of Schedule B means that such profits are now not taxed as income at all.[185] Conversely, no allowable losses can arise under Part 2 from the occupation of commercial woodlands in the UK.[186] Actual occupation was required under this rule; simply having a licence to fell and remove timber or clear the land for replanting was not enough.[187] By statute, the cultivation of short rotation coppice is regarded as farming not forestry.[188] See further below at §25.6.

19.7.4 Mines, Etc

Profits from mines, quarries and other specified concerns, including ferries and canals, also fall within Part 2.[189]

19.7.5 Statutory Softening

ITTOIA 2005, sections 18–21 contain four rules which mitigate the severity of the boundary between trade income and property income.[190] Section 18 concerns tied premises and, in broad terms, applies where the person owning the tied premises provides trade supplies to the person in occupation. The owner is allowed to treat the payment for the premises as part of the trading income instead of being distinct property income. Section 19 provides a similar blending rule for a person owning a caravan site but also involved in running it. Section 20 allows a person with surplus business accommodation to treat the income from letting as part of the trade profits. Section 21 applies where a person who uses land for a trade also receives a payment for UK electric lines and wayleaves on that land; this may be taxed under Part 2 instead of Part 3, Chapter 9. Sections 20 and 21 apply to professions and vocations as well as to trades.

---

[185] TA 1988, s 54, repealed 1988.

[186] ITTOIA 2005, s 254.

[187] TA 1988, s 16(6), repealed in 1988.

[188] ITA 2007, s 996 for income tax and FA 1995, s 154 for corporation tax and CGT, but not IHT.

[189] ITTOIA 2005, s 10, ex TA 1988, s 55.

[190] Section 18 was TA 1988, s 98; ss 19–21 represent developments from existing concessions or practices—see explanatory notes.

20

Business Income—Part II: Basis of Assessment and Loss Relief

20.1   Current Year Basis

For many years, and for most of the years over which the case law relevant to ITTOIA 2005, Part 2 (Schedule D, Cases I and II) has developed,[1] the profits of a trade or profession were charged to income tax on a 'preceding year' basis (see below at §20.5). After a transitional year in 1996–97, the 'current year' basis was applied to all such profits as from 1997–98. The charge is now on the profits of the tax year,[2] which are defined as the profits for the basis period for the year.[3] This is subject to special rules in ITTOIA 2005, Part 8 for certain types of foreign income.

---

[1] The preceding basis has never been part of corporation tax (which was introduced in 1965).
[2] ITTOIA 2005, s 7.
[3] ITTOIA 2005, s 7(2): on basis period see Pt 2, Ch 15 (ss 196–220).

As announced at Budget 2016, the Government is introducing a new £1,000 allowance for trading income from 6 April 2017. Individuals with trading income below £1,000 will no longer need to declare or pay tax on that income. Individuals with trading income above the allowance will be able to calculate their taxable profit either by deducting their expenses in the usual way or by deducting the allowance.

In chapters twenty to twenty-three of this book, statutory references are to ITTOIA 2005 unless otherwise noted.

20.1.1 Basis Periods: Summary

The present system is designed to ensure that over the lifetime of the business the profits brought into tax are the same as the profits actually earned by that business—by the use of 'basis periods'. Usually the basis period will be the 12-month period used by the business for its own accounting process. After ITTOIA 2005 the income tax system does not have a single formal fall-back position to tax by reference to the profits accruing from 6 April to 5 April, although this is sometimes the effect. Special rules apply when a business starts, when there is a change of accounting date and when the business ends. When a business starts it is possible that some profits will be used in each of the two years; such doubly brought-in profits are called 'overlap profits'. The taxpayer will be given credit, called 'overlap relief', for the doubly-charged profits by being allowed to deduct an equivalent sum later on—either at the end (or 'discontinuance') of the business, when all things can be brought into line, or on a prior change of accounting date ('change of basis'). The amount of overlap profit is not index linked and the tax on those profits is little better than a forced loan to the Government.

20.1.2 The General Rule

Generally, the basis period is the period of 12 months ending with the accounting date in that year (section 198). The accounting date is normally the date in the tax year to which accounts are drawn up or, if there are two or more such dates, the latest of them.[4] Therefore, if T's business has been running for some years using a calendar year basis and T makes £200,000 profit in the year ending 31 December 2015 and £300,000 in the year ending 31 December 2016, this rule will give £200,000 as the figure for tax year 2015–16 and £300,000 for tax year 2016–17. This general rule applies unless any of eight other rules applies. Experience suggests that it is helpful to list these eight rules now and so avoid unnecessary fear. These rules (discussed below) are those for:

(1)   the first tax year;
(2)   the second tax year;
(3)   a year in which there is no accounting date;
(4)   the final tax year;
(5)   where the first accounting date is shortly before the end of a tax year;

---

[4] ITTOIA 2005, s 197, for qualifications, see s 197(2).

(6)   a tax year in which the middle date is treated as the accounting date;
(7)   a change in accounting date in the third year; and
(8)   change of accounting date in a later year.

Of these, (5) and (6) are changes made by ITTOIA 2005 but based on previous Revenue practice; they are designed to avoid some of the complexities of the other rules.

20.1.3 The Starting Years

20.1.3.1 Year of Commencement—Tax Year 1

When a trade begins, a charge arises in that first year and extends to the profits arising in the year, ie from 1 January to 5 April (section 199). Therefore, if T starts to trade on 1 January 2016 and makes up the first set of accounts to the period ending 5 April 2016, the accounting period and the basis period both run from 1 January 2016 to 5 April 2016; the profit of that period is taken for the tax year 2015–16. If the first set of accounts is made up to 31 December 2016, the basis period is still that from 1 January 2016 to 5 April 2016 and so the profit of the accounting period will be apportioned to 2015–16 on a daily basis (95/365ths) (section 203). So, if the profit for the calendar year shown by the accounts is £365,000, the amount apportioned to 2015–16 will be £95,000.

20.1.3.2 Second Tax Year of Business and the Overlap Profit

Section 200 is more complicated than section 199 but its effect is usually to tax the trade on the profits of a first 12 months—even though these will have been used already to measure the profits for the first year. The treatment of the second year depends on how the accounts are made up, as follows:

(1)   *12-month accounting period ending in second tax year and first accounts.* The 12-month period ending with T's accounting date is taken as the basis period if the tax year is the first year of assessment in which the accounting date falls 12 months or more after the commencement date (section 200(2)). This is because the relevant provision directs that the general rule applies (see §20.1.2). So, if T begins the business on 1 January 2016 and makes up the first accounts to 31 December 2016, the profits of that first period are taken for tax year 2016–17; if those profits come to £365,000, tax is due on £365,000. The self-assessment must be made by 31 January 2018 and tax paid by then. Note that of that £365,000, £95,000 was also taken for tax year 2015–16; this sum is treated as 'overlap profit', ie the profit of the period overlapping the two tax years.

(2)   *Not the first accounts.* It is not actually necessary that these should be T's first set of accounts. However, here again ITTOIA 2005 directs that the general rule is to apply, and one takes the period of 12 months ending with the accounting date. Suppose that T starts to trade on 1 January 2016 but makes up the first set of accounts to 29 February 2016 and the second set to 28 February 2017. The second set will be used, since what is required by the general rule is a 12-month set of accounts ending in year 2. This time it will be the profits from 1 March 2016 to 5 April 2016 which will provide the overlap profit.

(3) *Accounting period ending in year 2 less than 12 months.* If, as before, T starts business on 1 January 2016 but makes up the first accounts to 30 September 2016, the general rule is not satisfied and another rule must apply—and so ITTOIA 2005, section 199(2) directs that the period of the first 12 months is the basis period for 2016–17. So, if T's second set of accounts run to 30 September 2017, this rule will apply to make the accounting profits of the period ending 30 September 2017 the profits for 2017–18, ie the third tax year. The self-assessment for 2017–18 must be made by 31 January 2019.

(4) *No accounting period ending in second year.* Here, the actual profits of year 2 are used, apportioning as necessary (section 200(4)).

20.1.4 Minor Rules

ITTOIA 2005, section 201 directs that where there is no accounting date in the tax year, the basis period is the period of 12 months beginning immediately after the end of the basis period for the previous tax year. For years ending 31 March to 4 April, ITTOIA 2005 contains rules which are a matter of taxpayer choice[5] and apply where the first accounting date is just before the end of tax year. These rules prevent overly-fine apportionment of taxable profits—and of overlap profits (section 208(1)). Where there are slight variations in accounting dates, the rules are intended to avoid the application of the change of accounting date rules, and are therefore discussed below at §20.4.

20.2 Treatment of Overlap Profits

Because of these complicated rules, the same accounting profits may appear in the taxable profits for both years 1 and 2. This is because the profit period for the second year overlaps that period for the first year; hence the expressions 'overlap period' and 'overlap profits'. These rules fall short of the scheme adopted by most other countries and which the UK tax system was able to adopt for corporation tax in 1965—a simple current year basis. Quite what rational reason there is for having to wait until the end of one's trading life before being given credit for the double taxation, with no indexation for inflation and with no regard for the different rates of tax which may be in force in the different years, is hard to imagine. Overlap profits may also arise if there is a change of accounting date and the gap between the start and end of the period is less than 12 months.[6] Taking the first three years together, it may be seen that the present system brings about an alignment of the basis period with the annual accounting period in either the second or the third year. Once this has been done, the basis period will change only if there is discontinuance or an effective change of accounting date.

The simplest way to avoid the double charge is to have no taxable profits for the opening period. Another way is to have no overlap period, ie to have the business year end on 5 April.

---

[5] ITTOIA 2005, ss 208–10; on election, see s 208(3) and (4).
[6] ITTOIA 2005, ss 214–16, ex TA 1988, s 62.

It may be that the real purpose of the overlap rules is to encourage taxpayers to take such a date. The effect of sections 208–210 is to allow the taxpayer to avoid having overlap profits if the date chosen is not 5 April but 31 March, or 1, 2, 3 or 4 April. In general, the earlier in the year the business starts, the greater the amount of overlap period and so potential overlap profit. If the business begins on 7 April 2016 and ends on 6 April 2017, the first year profit will virtually all be charged in year 2017–18 and again in 2018–19. By contrast, the business beginning on 5 April will have only one day of overlap profit.[7] Relief for the double tax is given when the business ceases (see below at §20.3) or there is a change of accounting date to a date later in the year (see below at §20.4).

Although a 31 March or 5 April year end will avoid an overlap profit, it does not follow that this must be the date to choose. If a business will have a modest or very low profit in the first year and thereafter a significant rise, it may be worth having a 7 April or 30 April year end: the amount of overlap profit will be modest and the deferral of tax liability significant.[8] However, whatever date is chosen, the more the tax is deferred, the greater is the need to ensure that there is enough money with which to pay the tax which eventually accrues.

20.3 Cessation/Discontinuance—The Final Year

The basis period for the year of discontinuance will generally be the period beginning immediately after the end of the basis period for the preceding tax year and ending with the date of discontinuance (section 202(1)). While this means that the basis period may be longer than 12 months, it also ensures that there will be no gap between the basis periods and that, over the life of the business, all the profits will have been brought into charge to tax.

Example

T has been making up his accounts on a yearly basis ending on 30 June. T ceases to trade on 31 December 2015. The last accounts that will have been taxed as the measure of taxable profits are those for the year ending 30 June 2014, the figures being used for tax year 2014–15. For 2015–16, the year of 'discontinuance', the basis period covers all the remaining days, ie 1 July 2014 to 31 December 2015 (549 days).

The only exceptions to this rule are where the trade ceases in the first or second years, but this is a matter of formulation not of policy (section 202(2)). Here, too, there is no gap between periods; neither, incidentally, is there any overlap. The significance of discontinuance is that it may bring about a claim for overlap relief and the deduction from the final profits of any remaining overlap profits figure. Assuming no changes of accounting date and a constant 12-month cycle, the overlap profit will be that which arose for the 279 days from 1 July to 5 April of the business's first year. Subtracting 279 from 549 leaves 270, which

---

[7] FA 1994, Sch 20, para 2(4), as amended (1995); for details, see Tiley and Collison, *UK Tax Guide* (Butterworths, 1998–99), para 7.44. Overlap profits may also occur if they arose in 1996–97 from a business begun before 6 April 1994.

[8] Hill in *Tolley's Tax Planning 2003–04*, §9.2.

is precisely the number of days from 6 April to 31 December 2015. If the overlap relief causes a loss, the excess is given loss relief in the usual way against general income of that year and the previous year under ITA 2007, section 64 or section 72. However, it may also be treated as a terminal loss and carried back three years under ITA 2007, section 89 (see below §20.10).

Terminal loss relief which cannot be absorbed within this three-year period is lost, so that the profits which will have been assessed to the business will be greater than the profits actually earned.[9] Where this is a risk, the presence of overlap profits from the opening year may exacerbate the problem, since the relief for overlap profits takes the form of a simple deduction from trading profits; at the very least, taxpayers ought to have the right to repayment of the tax on the overlap profit regardless of the loss position. The present position encourages taxpayers to close their business before they might otherwise do; the presence of overlap profits increases that risk.

20.4   Change of Basis Period

Sections 215 and 216 deal with changes of accounting periods. This must be distinguished from changes of accounting basis which have their own rules (ITTOIA 2005, Part 2, Chapter 17; see below §21.11). Taxpayers may change their accounting dates, whether because accounts are not made up to the old date, or are made up to a new date or both. This freedom is unlimited during the first three years (sections 214 and 215). However, later changes must meet three conditions:[10]

(1)   that the first accounting period ending with the new date must not exceed 18 months;
(2)   that notice is given to the inspector no later than 31 January following the year of assessment; and
(3)   that either—
    (a)   no accounting change has been made in any of the preceding five years of assessment, or
    (b)   T can satisfy the Revenue that the change is being made for bona fide commercial reasons—an expression which does not extend to the obtaining of a tax advantage (section 217(4)). A Revenue officer who is not satisfied of this must give notice within 60 days; an appeal lies to the Tribunals.[11]

Where the conditions are not satisfied, the basis period is 12 months ending with the old accounting date (section 216(5)). If the trade reverts to the original accounting date in the following year, all is well. If not, it is treated as a new change of accounting date and examined afresh (section 219). If the conditions are satisfied, it is obvious that the new accounting date will not be the same. If the period ending with the new accounting date is

---

[9]   Fuller, *Simons* (2000) 7 *Tax Briefing* Issue 5.
[10]   ITTOIA 2005, ss 217 and 218, ex TA 1988, s 62A.
[11]   If T's application fails, a new attempt may be made the following year—or T may revert to the original date.

less than 12 months the basis period is given by section 198, ie 12 months ending with the new accounting date and so generating new overlap profits (section 216(3)).

Thus, suppose that T has operated on a year basis from 1 July 2014 to 30 June 2015 but subsequently changes to a calendar year ending on 31 December 2015. The profit from 1 January to 31 December 2015 will be taken for tax year 2015–16, even though part of that period has already been taken for the 2014–15 six-month accounting period. This will, in turn, give rise to immediate overlap relief for any overlap profits remaining unrelieved. So, if the accounting period is 18 months, overlap relief will be available for six months. If the overlap period was nine months, this will means that approximately[12] two-thirds of the original overlap profit will now be available for deduction. It will be seen that the two-thirds fraction is applied to the original, unindexed overlap profit, not to the equivalent proportion of the current profits.

Where the new accounting date is more than 12 months, the relevant period begins immediately after the end of the previous accounting period and ends on the new accounting date (section 216(4))—which is more than 12 months. It may be worth making a change of accounting date earlier rather than later, especially if this means reducing profits below the higher rate threshold. Perhaps it is for such reasons that changes of accounting date are permitted without preconditions in the first three years.

ITTOIA 2005, section 220 contains detailed rules, including two trivial points about periods ending on 31 March to 4 April and the correct treatment of 29 February, but also a more important rule allowing profits to be apportioned on a reasonable basis rather than a strict daily basis, provided it is used consistently. The essence of the formula in TA 1988, section 63A previously used to determine the amount of overlap profits which can be used on a change of accounting date is: (B − C)/D where B is the number of days in the basis period and C is the number of days in the year of assessment (365 or 366). D is more complex, being the aggregate of the number of days in the period (or periods) which have been taken into account twice but with a deduction for the number of days given by the variable B − C in any previous applications of the section. This fraction is then applied to the overlap profit less any amount already relieved in this way; this is referred to as A in the section.

Example

X started business on 1 July 2002. The first year's profits came to £12,000. The effect of the rules for the starting year is that X's taxable profits for 2002–03 were 279/365 × £12,000, or £9,172, and for the second year £12,000. X's overlap profits from this are agreed at £9,172. In 2006, X decides to change the accounting date to 31 December 2006. The basis period for 2006–07 is 1 July 2005 to 31 December 2006 (549 days).

Applying the above formula, B will be 549 days; C will be 365; and D will be 279. The resulting fraction is applied to the amount of available overlap profit (£9,172), and means that £6,048 will be available for set-off against the profits for the 18-month period for 2004–05 and that only £3,124 will be left for relief on a subsequent change of accounting date or on cessation of the business.

---

[12] Because the sums are calculated on a daily, not a monthly, basis.

The result would be the same under ITTOIA 2005, section 220 if the facts arose in 2005–06 or later.

20.5 Historical Note: The Preceding Year Basis

Before 1997–98, income tax was levied on the profits and gains of the trade, profession or vocation on a preceding year basis, ie on the profits of the year preceding the year of assessment. As has been seen, if a business makes up its accounts on a calendar year basis, the profits for the year from 1 January to 31 December 2000 will—under present rules—be the profits or gains to be charged in the tax year 2000–01. Under the preceding year basis, the tax year 2000–01 would take the profits of the business period ending in the year *before* 2000–01, ie the profits of the period 1 January to 31 December 1999. This enabled the precise liability for the tax year 1999–2000 to be fixed before 1 January 2000, the date on which one half of the tax fell due, the second half being due on 1 July. The present system achieves the same objective by making the tax payable on 31 January 2001, and echoes the old system by demanding payments on account on 1 January and 1 July 2000.

There were two main problems with the preceding year basis. The first was that the Revenue thought, correctly, that ordinary taxpayers could not understand it and so could not be expected to apply it properly under the new self-assessment system. The second problem was that the system contained overlaps in the early years of assessment (on a scale much greater than under the current year system) and compensated for this by having gaps at the end of the life of the business. Therefore, while the profits of some periods were taxed more than once at the beginning of the business, there were periods at the end of the business where the profits were not taxed at all. This meant not only that the total profits subjected to tax were not the same as those earned by the business over the lifetimes of that business, but also that taxpayers could exploit these gaps.[13]

20.6 Starting (Commencement)

20.6.1 When Does Trading Begin?

It is important to determine when a trade commenced in order to apply ITTOIA 2005, sections 199 and 200 correctly, and to fulfil the obligations arising from self-assessment. At one time this was important because pre-commencement expenditure was deductible only as a result of specific statutory provisions.[14] Today, an expense incurred in the seven years before trading is treated simply as an expense incurred on the day of commencement (section 57). This relief is not, however, without its traps. A pre-commencement expense is deductible only if incurred by the trader, not by someone else; therefore, the benefit of

---

[13] Eg, *Reed v Clark* [1986] Ch 1, [1985] STC 323, 58 TC 528; and legislative counter in TA 1988, s 110A (now ITTOIA 2005, s 17) treating a change of residence as a cessation and commencement.

[14] *City of London Contract Corpn Ltd v Styles* (1887) 2 TC 239.

the expense will be lost if the business is incorporated when trading begins. Similarly, if company A in a group incurs the expense, while company B, in the same group, carries on the trade, neither can deduct—A never trades, while B does not incur the expense.[15]

Neither the formation of an intention to commence trading nor the incurring of capital expenditure for the purpose of preparing to trade proves that the trade has begun. In *Birmingham and District Cattle By-Products Co Ltd v IRC*,[16] the appellant company was incorporated on 20 June 1913. Its directors then arranged for the installation of plant and machinery, and entered into agreements for the purchase of raw materials and the sale of its products. The raw materials were received on 6 October. The company's trade was held to begin on 6 October, when it started to use the raw materials to manufacture its product.

However, in *Cannop Coal Co Ltd v IRC*,[17] where the trade was to be the mining of coal by sinking pits in the Forest of Dean, the company had, since 1909, extracted a certain amount of coal from a drift nearby for use in its machines and, finding that it had extracted more than it needed, sold the excess to the public. The company was held to have commenced trading when it sold the excess coal to the public, and not in 1912 when coal began to emerge from the pits. That the coal company was engaged in a trade in those three years seems beyond argument, and it was too fine a point to say that the trade was different from the mining of coal from the pits.

A difficult question concerns the use of small-scale pilot projects involving resale to the public in deciding precisely what product to make. It was important in *Cannop Coal Co Ltd v IRC* that the sales were substantial,[18] and it may therefore be that pilot projects are not trading.

20.6.2 Developing Existing Trade or Starting New Trade?[19]

If A carries on a trade and starts a new line of activity, it is a question of fact and degree[20] whether A is developing an existing activity or starting a second (parallel) trade. There is no rule of law that a person, whether or not a company, cannot carry on more than one trade, and it is immaterial that there is one consolidated balance sheet. As Rowlatt J put it in a case where the two activities had both been bought from another company, 'the real question is, was there any inter-connection, any interlacing, any interdependence, any unity at all embracing those two businesses?'[21] Therefore, if a trader commences a new trade alongside his established trade, the two trades are treated separately,[22] even for purposes of loss relief and capital allowances; the sources are distinct. Conversely, the amalgamation of two trades may be treated as the cessation of both and the commencement of one new trade.[23]

---

[15] RI 32.
[16] (1919) 12 TC 92 (an excess profits duty case).
[17] (1918) 12 TC 31 (another excess profits duty case). In both instances the Revenue won.
[18] In one year 68% of the coal was resold, and in another, 84%.
[19] See also Revenue Bulletin (February 1996), 285.
[20] *Howden Boiler and Armaments Co Ltd v Stewart* (1924) 9 TC 205; *Cannon Industries Ltd v Edwards* (1965) 42 TC 151.
[21] *Scales v George Thompson & Co Ltd* (1927) 13 TC 83, 89.
[22] *Fullwood Foundry Ltd v IRC* (1924) 9 TC 101.
[23] *George Humphries & Co v Cook* (1934) 19 TC 121.

A relatively modern example is *Seaman v Tucketts Ltd.*[24] A new group acquired control of the company in 1956. The company carried on the trade of manufacture and sale of confectionery; this included the purchase and resale of such goods from other manufacturers, which ended early in 1958. In September 1958 the two retail shops were closed, and in November 1958 manufacture ceased. By April 1959 the existing stocks and the factory had been sold. The company, which had previously bought sugar and cellophane for its own business, now bought these for resale to the new parent company at cost plus 10%. Two years later it began to supply confectionery again. Reversing the Commissioners, Pennycuick J held that the only true and reasonable conclusion was that, at the end of 1958 when the manufacture had ceased, a new trade of sugar merchants, including the buying and selling of cellophane paper, had been commenced. The case was remitted to the Commissioners to determine whether the confectionery trade had been discontinued or had been merely quiescent. *Seaman v Tucketts Ltd* shows that not only may there be a termination of one trade and the commencement of another, but there may also be a contraction of one trade and the commencement of another, even though the second trade deals with a commodity employed in the original trade. There is also authority that a substantial change in management policy can lead to discontinuance and a new commencement.[25] However, a barrister does not, on taking silk, start a new profession.[26]

The current rules on partnerships and ITTOIA 2005 are set out below at §20.9. Under a now repealed rule, there was a discontinuance and a commencement where there was a change in the people carrying on the trade—unless one person continued from the old group to the new. However, this 'unless' assumed that the trade carried on by the previous owners was continued under the new partnership, ie there was no actual discontinuance. So, if the new owners did not carry on the existing business but started a new one, there would be discontinuance. In *Maidment v Kibby*,[27] the taxpayer partners ran a fish and chip shop in P; they then bought a shop in Q and ran the new shop in their own style, under their own name, with a single system for buying materials and with one set of accounts. The Revenue argued that although the Q shop had retained its identity, there had been a change of persons running the trade and so a discontinuance. The Commissioners rejected the argument; the High Court held that it was open to the Commissioners to do so. Today the partnership tax rules are different (§20.9.2) but the case remains an interesting example of trade identification.

20.7 Stopping (Discontinuance)

20.7.1 Is There Discontinuance?

Discontinuance occurs where T, a trader, ceases to carry on the trade or, in appropriate circumstances, changes the manner of trading. It is a question of fact whether the particular

---

[24] (1963) 41 TC 422.
[25] See Rowlatt J in *Kirk and Randall Ltd v Dunn* (1924) 8 TC 663, 670.
[26] *Seldon v Croom-Johnson* [1932] 1 KB 759, 16 TC 740.
[27] [1993] STC 494, 66 TC 137.

change is the ceasing of one trade and the commencement of another, or is simply a normal development of the previous trade.

For example, where a taxpayer has two offices and closes one, the question is whether the continuing office is continuing the trade. Clearly, this will be so if the original business was not one but two separate businesses, each run from its own office, in which case the continuing office continues its trade as before.[28] As with commencement, these are matters of fact and degree. In *Rolls Royce Motors Ltd v Bamford*,[29] the original Rolls Royce Ltd, RRL, had developed and built motorcars since 1906; since 1915 it had also been involved in the manufacture of aero engines. In 1971 a large project, the RB211 engine, went seriously wrong; the aero engine business was put into the hands of a new company, and the motor company business was put into the hands of the (separate) taxpayer company, RRM. The Commissioners decided that RRM had not been carrying on the same trade as RRL; the court held that this was the only rational conclusion, and so RRM could not use the losses incurred by RRL on the RB211 project.

A trade does not cease if it is merely in abeyance. There is therefore no discontinuance just because of a mere interruption in production[30] or disposal of assets,[31] or even the appointment of a receiver.[32] Business is not the same as 'being busy' and long periods of inactivity may occur.[33] It is, however, a question of fact whether a particular trade has lapsed into a period of quiescence or has ceased. A trade may be treated as permanently discontinued, notwithstanding that the former trader later commences a new trade which is in all respects identical with the previous ceased trade.

In *Kirk and Randall Ltd v Dunn*,[34] the new owners of a trading company obtained no new contracts and tried to sell the premises; they then had their works and plant requisitioned during the First World War. However, the managing director tried to obtain contracts overseas. Rowlatt J, reversing the Commissioners, held that the company was still trading since there was evidence of business activity resulting in expenditure and loss. However, in *JG Ingram & Son Ltd v Callaghan*,[35] where the period was much shorter, the Court of Appeal upheld the Commissioners' finding that there was not just unprofitability but inactivity, and so a discontinuance. In this case the company had, by May 1961, ceased to produce rubber goods, sold off its stock and dismissed its staff, the plan being to switch to plastics. From September 1961 to June 1962 products were manufactured by another subsidiary of the owner and sold over the owner-company's name. In this way the goodwill was kept alive, but the operations of the company were confined to little more than bookkeeping and debt collecting. It was held that the trade was not kept alive between those dates.

---

[28]   *C Connelly & Co v Wilbey* [1992] STC 783, 65 TC 208.

[29]   [1976] STC 162, 51 TC 319.

[30]   *Merchiston Steamship Co Ltd v Turner* [1910] 2 KB 923, 5 TC 520.

[31]   *Aviation and Shipping Co Ltd v Murray* [1961] 2 All ER 805, 39 TC 595; see also *Watts v Hart* [1984] STC 548, 58 TC 209.

[32]   *Wadsworth Morton Ltd v Jenkinson* [1966] 3 All ER 702, 43 TC 479.

[33]   *South Behar Rly Co Ltd v IRC* [1925] AC 476, 12 TC 657; Cf *Morning Post Ltd v George* (1941) 23 TC 514.

[34]   (1924) 8 TC 663. See also *Robroyston Brickworks Ltd v IRC* (1976) 51 TC 230.

[35]   [1969] 1 All ER 433, 45 TC 151, CA. The same conclusion was reached in *Tryka Ltd v Newall* (1963) 41 TC 146, ChD, noted in [1964] BTR 286, and *Goff v Osborne & Co (Sheffield) Ltd* (1953) 34 TC 441.

20.7.2 Effects of Discontinuance

When a trade, profession or vocation is permanently discontinued, the basis of assessment is determined by ITTOIA 2005, section 202. However, special rules apply relating to relief for losses and capital allowances which may, contrary to the usual rule, be carried back on discontinuance. In so far as these losses or capital allowances exceed the income of the period over which they are taken back, they are lost (save for post-cessation receipts) and cannot be used by anyone else, even a successor to the trade. Sections 173 and 182 direct the valuation of trading stock and work in progress on a permanent ending of the trade. At one time sums paid just before discontinuance would be non-deductible because they were not spent in order to keep the business alive.[36] A statutory exception was made for certain redundancy payments,[37] but the principle itself is now doubtful as it has been held that a sum paid in order to close down a business is still incurred for the purpose of producing profits.[38]

20.8　Succession or Buying Assets

20.8.1 The Concept

A succession arises where a business which was owned by A is transferred to B, who carries it on.[39] The question whether the trade has been transferred by A to B, or whether A has disposed of the business, is relevant in various parts of the tax legislation.[40] Thus, the corporation tax rules allow a loss to be transferred from company P to company S if S takes over the trade from which the loss has arisen (and S is P's subsidiary). This also has implications for commencement and discontinuance, since if B simply buys assets, the matter can be treated as yet another activity of B's existing trade; if, however, B succeeds to A's trade, A will cease to carry on the trade (discontinuance) and B will start the trade (commencement) alongside B's existing trade. Where a succession to a trade occurs, neither losses nor unused capital allowances incurred by A may be used by B[41]—unless express authority can be found.

The origin of the concept of succession lay in the application of the rule that profits were measured not on the preceding year basis but on the average of three previous years' business. The original concept of succession allowed B to continue to use the three years' average which A had started. It was necessary, therefore, that there existed a 'very close identity' between the business in A's ownership and the business in B's. The reform of Schedule D in 1926 ended the three-year moving average and directed that there was discontinuance by A and a commencement by B even though there was a succession.

---

[36]　*Gooden v A Wilson's Stores Holdings Ltd* (1961) 40 TC 161.

[37]　ITTOIA 2005, s 79, ex TA 1988, s 90, and see RI 103.

[38]　*IRC v Cosmotron Manufacturing Co Ltd* [1997] STC 1134; see also Lord Clyde in *IRC v Patrick Thomson Ltd* (1956) 37 TC 145, 157; noted in Baker [1958] BTR 89.

[39]　See Graham [1959] BTR 193.

[40]　See also CAA 2001, ss 259 and 559.

[41]　Eg, *Rolls Royce Motors Ltd v Bamford* [1976] STC 162.

If B succeeds to A's trade, B will be taxed in the opening years in accordance with the rules for commencement,[42] even though B absorbs the acquired trade into an existing one and that it is, in reality, one business.[43] However, once the opening-year rules are spent, the figures for the trade acquired will form part of the general profit of the trade into which it has merged. Again, these sections are applicable whether in their new or old form. If the new trade is not absorbed into the old one but is a distinct entity, the commencement provisions will apply and there will be no merging once those provisions are spent.

20.8.2 Rules on Whether There Has Been a Succession

The question for the Commissioners (now Tribunals) is 'whether it is true and fair to say that the business in respect of which the successor is said to be making profits is the business to which [the successor] succeeded'.[44]

20.8.2.1 Purchase of Assets of Trade is Not a Succession

Where a company which ran a tramp shipping business bought a ship second-hand from another trader, there was no succession to that person's trade but only the purchase of a ship.[45] This is, however, a question of fact, and it was important in that case that the purchaser acquired no list of customers along with the ship, that the ship had no special route along which only she plied her trade, and that no goodwill came with the ship. Since the origin of the concept of succession lay in the application of the rule that profits were measured by the average of three previous years' business, there had to be a 'very close identity' between the business in the former proprietorship and the business in the new proprietorship.[46] A very close identity is, however, not the same as a complete identity. Thus, a successor to a business with, say, 50 shops, may choose to close some of them in order to make alterations in the goods sold, to change suppliers, or to cut out a particular class of customer or a particular area.[47] The question whether such changes prevent there being a succession to the business is one of fact.

There may be a succession even though there is no purchase of the entire assets.[48] In one case a circular was distributed to the former trader's customers that the new owners had acquired the 'trading connection' of the former traders. The Commissioners held that there was no succession, and the courts felt unable to reverse that conclusion. Conversely, in another case, a circular distributed to the public described the new firm as 'successors', even though the new firm took over no merchandise, no lists of customers and none of the staff, except a few work people. However, they were held to be successors by the Commissioners, and the courts, again, declined to intervene.[49]

---

[42] ITTOIA 2005, ss 199 and 200.
[43] *Bell v National Provincial Bank* [1904] 1 KB 149, 5 TC 1; *Briton Ferry Steel Co Ltd v Barry* [1939] 4 All ER 541, 23 TC 414; if it is a separate trade it must be treated separately (*Scales v George Thomson & Co Ltd* (1927) 13 TC 83).
[44] *Laycock v Freeman, Hardy and Willis Ltd* [1938] 4 All ER 609, 614, 22 TC 288, 298, per Sir Wilfrid Greene MR.
[45] *Watson Bros v Lothian* (1902) 4 TC 441. Compare *Bell v National Provincial Bank of England* [1904] 1 KB 149, 5 TC 1.
[46] *Reynolds, Sons & Co Ltd v Ogston* (1930) 15 TC 501, 524, per Rowlatt J; approved by Lord Hanworth MR at 527.
[47] *Laycock v Freeman, Hardy and Willis Ltd* (1938) 22 TC 288, 297, per Sir Wilfrid Greene MR.
[48] *Reynolds, Sons & Co Ltd v Ogston* (1930) 15 TC, 524.
[49] *Thomson and Balfour v Le Page* (1923) 8 TC 541.

20.8.2.2 No Succession to a Part of a Trade

In *James Shipstone & Son Ltd v Morris*,[50] Rowlatt J held that there can be no succession to part of a trade: 'There must be two businesses, one left and the other taken.'

20.8.2.3 No Succession by Accident

No succession occurs through the accidental acquisition by B, who continues in business, of custom left by A, who goes out of business. For there to be a succession, there must be a transfer by one trader to another of the right to that benefit which arises from connection and reputation.[51]

20.8.2.4 Succession Only to Existing Trade

No succession occurs where the trade has ceased before being acquired by B, its new owner, nor where B closes down the business immediately after acquiring it. Thus, if a business went bankrupt and remained in the hands of the trustee in bankruptcy for 12 months before the assets were sold, it is likely that such a sale would be treated as a sale of assets rather than of the business.[52] Indeed, there is authority that where a business has had to sell to recoup heavy losses, it is likely that there is no succession.[53] However, where a business suffered extensive fire damage and ceased to trade with the public, but kept together its employees and various pieces of equipment, a delay of 17 months between the fire and the acquisition of the business by a new owner did not prevent there being a succession.[54]

20.8.3 *Applying the Rules*

The leading modern case on the transfer of losses to a new company in the same ownership is *Falmer Jeans v Rodin*.[55] A manufactured jeans for B, which B sold. B supplied the materials to A and B paid for A's services on a cost plus basis. When A began making losses, it stopped trading and transferred its trade and assets to B. Thereafter, manufacturing appeared as a separate cost-centre in B's accounts. Millett J, allowing B's appeal from the Commissioners, held that B was carrying on A's trade, ie there was a succession, so section 343 applied and B could use A's losses.

Apart from *Falmer Jeans*, the case law is dominated by two old cases. In *Laycock v Freeman, Hardy and Willis Ltd*,[56] the respondent company (B) bought shoes from wholesalers and resold them to the public. Some 20% to 30% of its supplies came from two subsidiary companies which it controlled. In 1935 the subsidiary companies went into voluntary liquidation and the liquidator assigned all the assets and goodwill to B, which also took on all the staff. B then sold all the products of the factories previously owned by the subsidiary companies in its shops. The Court of Appeal held that there was no succession. The business

---

[50] *James Shipstone & Son Ltd v Morris* (1929) 14 TC 413, 421; and see *Stockham v Wallasey Urban District Council* (1906) 95 LT 834.

[51] *Thomson and Balfour v Le Page* (1923) 8 TC 541, 548.

[52] *Reynolds, Sons & Co Ltd v Ogston* (1930) 15 TC 501 at 528, per Greer LJ.

[53] *Wilson and Barlow v Chibbett* (1929) 14 TC 407 at 413, per Rowlatt J.

[54] *Wild v Madam Tussauds (1926) Ltd* (1932) 17 TC 127.

[55] [1990] STC 270, 63 TC 55.

[56] *Laycock v Freeman, Hardy and Willis Ltd* [1938] 4 All ER 609, 614, 22 TC 288, 298, per Sir Wilfrid Greene MR.

of the subsidiary companies was that of wholesale manufacturing concerns; that business had ceased. Manufacturing was still carried on, but the business of wholesale manufacturing was not. There was no provision allowing the profits realised by the retail sales to be dissected and split up into a wholesaler's profit and a retailer's profit, and then deeming the wholesale part to have been taken over by B.

This is inconsistent with *Falmer Jeans*, and it is therefore not surprising that Millett J criticised the older case's distinction, between manufacturing for sale wholesale and manufacturing goods for sale retail, as false:

> It is impossible to discern any sensible fiscal policy for differentiating, for the purpose of applying the opening year provisions, between the acquisition of a manufacturing business by a wholesaler and the acquisition of a similar business by a retailer. They are both examples of vertical integration.[57]

Laycock v Freeman, Hardy and Willis was distinguished in *Briton Ferry Steel Co Ltd v Barry*,[58] where the appellant company produced steel bars which were then supplied to six wholly-owned subsidiary companies. These companies, in turn, converted the bars into black plate and tinplate. Sales were handled by another wholly-owned subsidiary. In 1934 the six subsidiary companies were wound up, and the conversion of the bars into black plate and tinplate was carried on by the appellant company using the plant and workforce of the former companies. The Commissioners held that there was a succession to the trades carried on by the subsidiaries. The fact that the company, through its shares, already controlled them was irrelevant, as was the fact that another subsidiary company controlled their sales.[59] The Court of Appeal refused to interfere with that decision.

In *Laycock v Freeman, Hardy and Willis* the business of the subsidiaries—making profits by wholesale sales—had ceased, and the business of retail manufacturing had begun. In *Briton Ferry* the business of the subsidiary companies—making profits by the conversion of steel bars into black plate and tinplate and resale—still existed, but was being carried on by someone else,[60] with the retail side being handled by a separate legal entity. The fact that someone had previously supplied the steel bars was irrelevant.

The approach of Millett J in the later case of *Falmer Jeans* is based on a more flexible view of business. Suppose that the old cases were taken at face value and there was a manufacturing concern with five distinct stages involved in the manufacturing process, each stage carried out by a separate company. The old cases would suggest that if one company takes over its neighbour, there would be a succession if the acquiring company was at an earlier stage in the process but not if it was at a later stage. As Millet J said, any vertical integration should suffice. A further problem concerns the calculation of the profit of the trade acquired. In *Laycock v Freeman, Hardy and Willis*, the Court of Appeal held that it was 'wholly illegitimate' to invent a notional sale from the wholesale stage of the enterprise to the retail stage at a price which would yield a notional 'wholesale profit'.[61] But in *Briton Ferry* the same Court, having again rejected a notional sale, directed that the transfer of the

[57] [1990] STC 270, 279–80, 63 TC 55, 68.
[58] [1939] 4 All ER 541, 23 TC 414; applied *IRC v Spirax Manufacturing Co Ltd* (1946) 29 TC 187.
[59] [1938] 4 All ER 429, 434–35, 23 TC 414, 431–32, per Macnaghten J.
[60] [1939] 4 All ER 541, 547, 23 TC 414, 431, per Sir Wilfrid Greene MR.
[61] [1938] 4 All ER 609, 616, 22 TC 288, 300, per Sir Wilfrid Greene MR.

steel bars from one artificial side of the trade to the other should be treated as carried out at the actual cost of production. This ensured that the profit from the whole operation would be attributable to the newly acquired sector of the trade.[62] It is suggested that the Court was perhaps being a little ingenuous.

20.9 Partnerships

20.9.1 Is There a Partnership?

It is a question of fact whether a particular person (P) is a partner in an enterprise or merely a senior employee. However, in so far as this involves construing a document, it will raise questions of law. Although the receipt by P of a share of the profits is prima facie evidence that P is a partner, further evidence may be needed to establish exactly when the partnership begins to trade.[63] In *Fenston v Johnstone*,[64] the appellant wished to buy some land but lacked finance. He therefore agreed with another person to share the profits and losses, and to assist in the development of the land. The written agreement stated that there was no partnership, and described the appellant's share of the profits as a fee for introducing the other person to the vendor. The court held that there was a partnership. However, in *Pratt v Strick*[65] the court held that there was no partnership where a doctor sold his practice to another but agreed, as part of the sale, to stay in his house with the purchaser for some three months, introducing the purchaser to the patients and sharing receipts and expenses over that period. In both the above cases the courts reversed the Commissioners.

20.9.2 Taxation of Partnerships

A partnership is not treated for income tax purposes as an entity which is separate and distinct from its partners. Instead, profits are computed as if the partnership was an individual, and a partner's share in the profits for a period is to be determined according to the interests of the partners during that period.[66]

ITTOIA 2005, Part 9 (sections 846–863) governs partnerships. As just seen, the premise of the legislation is that the existence of the firm is ignored. It is not treated as an entity separate from the partners but each partner's share accrues to the partner and is taxed directly to the partner (sections 852, 854). Section 852 deems each partner (P) to carry on a separate own trade commenced on becoming a partner or, if later, when the trade itself begins.[67] If the actual trade was previously carried on by the partner alone, the deemed trade is taken to begin so far as that person is concerned when the actual trade began (section 852(3)). Proceeding symmetrically, the law states that the deemed trade ends when P ceases to be a partner or, where the actual trade is subsequently carried on by P alone, at the time when

---

[62] [1939] 4 All ER 541, 550, 23 TC 414, 434, per Sir Wilfrid Greene MR.
[63] *Saywell v Pope* [1979] STC 824, 53 TC 40.
[64] (1940) 23 TC 29.
[65] (1932) 17 TC 459; see also *Bulloch v IRC* [1976] STC 514, 51 TC 563.
[66] ITTOIA 2005, Part 9, ex TA 1988, s 111(1), (2), (3).
[67] ITTOIA 2005, s 852(2), ex TA 1988, s 111(3)(a). On effect of residence of partner, see s 848(2) and (3).

the actual trade or profession ceases permanently (section 852(4)). If the partner continues to carry on the trade alone after other partners have left, there is a deemed ceasing when the last partner leaves. A separate provision contains ancillary rules on basis periods (section 853). These rules apply to trades, professions and businesses (section 847(3)), and to claims for losses (section 849(2)). They also apply where the partnership has mixed income, ie trading profits and other 'untaxed' non-trading income—broadly, income from which tax has not been deducted at source.[68]

These rules mean that partners are individually liable for tax on their own shares of the profits, and that the taxable share is related to the actual share and not the profit-sharing ratio in force in a subsequent year.[69] Moreover, once the trade has begun there will be no deemed discontinuance by reason of a change in the partners as far as the continuing partners are concerned (since the deemed separate trade has not ended). In the days of the old regime, when there was only one trade carried on by all the partners, a change of partners led to a discontinuance with a commencement of the same trade by different people. The consequences of this rule (including an opt-out election from some of the rules) were laid down by the rule which became the original TA 1988, section 113. This section has been rewritten for the new regime. There is now no discontinuance for the person continuing to carry on the business; of course, there is discontinuance for those who leave. There is also a discontinuance if the partners change the trade: see *Maidment v Kibbey* at §20.6.2 above.

In its January 2014 Interim Report on the taxation of partnerships, the Office of Tax Simplification (OTS) described the current look-through system of not taxing the partnership itself but rather taxing each partner on his or her share of the partnership's profits and losses as working 'but like a comfortable old shoe it is a little worn at the edges and may have a couple of holes coming through'. The OTS was particularly keen for HMRC and the tax system to take a more systematic and coordinated approach to partnerships.[70] To that end HMRC agreed to update some of its guidance and publish a new consolidated partnership tax manual. FA 2014 also implemented a number of short-term fixes to taxing partnerships recommended by the OTS along with two more substantial changes aimed at curbing tax avoidance with limited liability partnerships (LLPs) and other partnerships.[71] The first big change concerned disguised salary. An interesting tax feature of LLPs in place since 2000 was that all members of the LLP were deemed by the tax legislation to be partners for all the activities of the LLP and thus taxed under the ITTOIA 2005 rules. This rule applied even where the member would have been treated as an employee if the LLP had been a traditional or general partnership. Perhaps unsurprisingly, this deeming feature was abused to minimise employment tax liability on persons who were in substance employees of the LLP but who were made 'members' in order to take advantage of the more generous NIC regime applicable to the self-employed. Testimony before the House of Lords Finance Bill Sub Committee revealed examples including 'one so-called LLP partnership that had

---

[68] ITTOIA 2005, s 854, ex TA 1988, s 111(4). Untaxed is defined in s 855(5).
[69] On allocation, see ss 850 and 851.
[70] See https://www.gov.uk/government/publications/partnerships-review.
[71] For commentary on the FA 2014 Schedule 17 changes see Baldwin [2014] BTR 416. That Baldwin has some concerns with the legislation is obvious from the first sentence of his comment when he calls the Schedule 17 partnership package: 'as good an example as you will ever find in the world of tax of going the wrong way to the wrong destination'.

20,000 partners in it' and 'occasional fruit pickers being officially partners in an LLP.'[72] FA 2014, Schedule 17, Part 1 introduced new rules into ITTOIA 2005, sections 863A *et seq* seeking to counter this abuse in the form of conditions which if not satisfied results in the LLP member paying income tax and NICs as an employee and also the LLP paying employer NICs. There is some controversy as to whether the rules are too widely drafted, and if a better approach would have been to rely on the usual case law tests for employment as is the case for partners in a general partnership.

The second major component of the FA 2014 partnership package concerned mixed member partnerships. Under the previous rules, a common practice apparently had developed whereby a disproportionate share of profits was allocated to corporate members of partnerships (including LLPs and general partnerships) in order to minimise or defer the total amount of tax borne by the partners. In particular, such an arrangement could be used to reduce the tax charge on profits intended for reinvestment in the partnership's business—a form of self-help remedy to address one of the significant tax disadvantages of adopting the partnership form instead of a company. ITTOIA 2005, sections 850A *et seq* now allow partnership allocations to be adjusted where (1) profits represent deferred profit of an individual or (2) profits allocated to a non-individual member exceeds the appropriate notional profit and an individual partner has the 'power to enjoy all or any part of the non-individual's profit share.

At Budget 2016 the Government announced a new consultation on how partnerships calculate their tax liabilities. This consultation will include a number of areas where the Government considers the taxation of partnerships could be seen as uncertain, including issues highlighted by the Office of Tax Simplification's partnerships review.

20.10 Relief for Trading Losses

20.10.1 *Sideways Relief: General Income of that and Previous Year of Assessment*

If a trade, profession or vocation sustains a loss, the correct figure for the profits chargeable to income tax for the year is nil. Under ITA 2007, section 64, a person who sustains trading losses may claim relief from tax[73] by making a deduction in calculating net income under the rules in ITA 2007, section 25; hence, where the loss exceeds the income from the trade, the taxpayer is relieved of all liability to tax.[74] As the loss may be set against other income, ITA 2007 refers to it as a 'sideways' relief.[75] This formula means that loss relief is computed on an accounts basis, ie by reference to the same basis periods as income from the same source. It also means that the income may be from any source and of any type, whether earned or unearned, or savings. These sideways reliefs are of great value and have therefore been the subject of planning and avoidance, especially, but not only, through partnerships. When the legislation counters abuse of sideways reliefs, it usually does so in relation to the

[72] House of Lords Finance Bill Sub Committee 2014 report, testimony of John Whiting, OTS, para 47.
[73] On relief for a Lloyd's name, see *Holliday v De Brunner* [1996] STC (SCD) 85.
[74] ITA 2007, s 64, ex TA 1988, s 380(1)(a).
[75] Eg ITA 2007, s 103.

reliefs described at §§20.10.1 and 20.10.2, and the CGT relief in TCGA 1992, sections 261B and 261C, to which ITA 2007, section 71 refers.

The deadline for the notice is 31 January following the year when the loss arises—the normal self-assessment date.[76] The claim must be for the whole of the loss which can be set against the income—one cannot make a claim just a part, eg for such part of the income as reduces one's income to the amount of one's personal reliefs.[77] So if one has income of £15,000, the personal relief of £10,600 and a loss of £5,000, one has to use the whole loss of £5,000, so 'wasting' £600 of the personal relief. Alternatively, one may choose not to use the relief at all and hope to get better value for it under another rule in another year. Unused loss relief may be carried back one year and set off against general income of that year.[78] If one has losses for more than one year, relief claimed on the current year basis will be given priority over relief carried back one year,[79] but there is no obligation to claim relief on the current year if one prefers instead to carry it back. Needless to say, the relief cannot be claimed twice.[80]

In the unusual case of *English Holdings v HMRC*,[81] a non-resident company carrying on a trade in UK land through a permanent establishment (PE) in the UK incurred a loss for corporation tax purposes. The same company carried on a letting business in the UK but not through a PE, with the result that the profits from the lettings were subject to income tax (and not corporation tax). The First-tier Tribunal agreed with the taxpayer that the corporation tax loss from trading could be set off against the income tax profit from the lettings under ITA 2007, section 64.

20.10.2 Sideways Relief for Losses in Early Years of Trading

A carry-back of a trading loss is permitted under ITA 2007, section 72 where the loss arises in the year of assessment in which the trade is first carried on, or the next three years of assessment;[82] it thus applies to losses arising in the first four years of business. The loss may be carried back and set off against general income for the three years before that in which the loss is sustained.[83] Income of an earlier year is taken first, so a loss incurred in 2016–17 may be carried back to 2013–14. When the accounting period of the business goes past the end of the year of assessment in which the trade begins, the loss in that period is apportioned. Partial claims for loss relief are not permitted. It should also be noted that since relief is given by reference to the basis period and not to the fiscal period, the choice of accounting date will determine how far back one can go.

---

[76] ITA 2007, s 64(5), ex TA 1988, s 380(1).

[77] ITA 2007, s 65, making explicit what was implicit before.

[78] ITA 2007, s 64(2), ex TA 1988, s 380(l)(b). Temporary measures introduced in FA 2009 (section 23 and Schedule 26) allowed a business to carry a trading loss of up to £50,000 arising in 2008–09 and 2009–10 back three years instead of just one, to help businesses through the recession.

[79] ITA 2007, s 65, ex TA 1988, s 380(2).

[80] ITTOIA 2005, s 206 and ITA 2007, ss 63 and 100.

[81] [2016] UKFTT 436.

[82] Ex TA 1988, s 381. It is the loss that arises in the fiscal year which is relievable (see *Gascoine v Wharton* [1996] STC 1481, 69 TC 147, where a taxpayer unsuccessfully argued that reliefs should be given for a loss arising in an accounting period, part of which was not incurred during the year of assessment).

[83] Eg ITA 2007, s 103.

Although section 72 applies both to trades and professions, it applies only to individuals. If a trade is acquired from a spouse or civil partner, the four tax years run from the date the spouse/civil partner began to trade.[84] However, this restriction applies only when T, the claimant, and the spouse/civil partner were living together; it follows that this restriction does not apply where T succeeds to a trade on the death of the other spouse/civil partner. Although relief may be claimed under both ITA 2007, sections 64 and 72, and the claimant may decide in which order to apply the reliefs, the loss cannot be apportioned between them.[85]

20.10.3 Downwards Relief; Set-off against Future Profits of that Trade

To the extent that relief for the allowable loss has not been given against general income—whether under ITA 2007, section 64 or some other provision—ITA 2007, section 83 allows the loss to be carried forward and set off against the future profits (if any) of *the* trade.[86] Note the emphasis on *the* trade—if the taxpayer carries on multiple trades the carryforwarded loss is streamed and can be applied against future profits only from the same trade that had generated the loss. The carryforward period is not limited to any particular number of years.[87] The relief must be given against the earliest profits available,[88] and a claim must be made.[89]

Where the trade has received income taxed by deduction at source, such as interest or dividends, the loss carried forward under section 83 may be set off against that taxed income and a repayment claim made in the case of interest.[90] However, this applies only when the payment would have been treated as trading profits but for the fact that tax had already been deducted.[91] The right to roll losses forward is available provided only that the taxpayer carries on the particular trade; it is lost, therefore, on discontinuance of the trade.

If the business is transferred to a company, and the sole or main consideration is the transfer of shares of the company to an individual (or nominees), an accumulated loss may be carried forward by the previous owner.[92] This provision applies whether the business is incorporated or taken over by an existing company. ITA 2007, section 86 does not allow the company to claim relief against the future profits of the trade, but instead allows T, the individual, to claim relief against income derived by T from the company, whether by dividend or otherwise, for example under a service agreement.[93] Making a change, section 86 lays down no rule as to the order in which the loss is set against particular heads of income. As the explanatory notes point out, the pre-2007 rules which provide such an order rule date back to 1927, when earned income was taxed differently from investment income. This may not convince as a reason for making the change, since ITA 2007 still provides for the

---

[84] ITA 2007, s 74(4), (5), ex TA 1988, s 381(5).
[85] *Butt v Haxby* [1983] STC 239, 56 TC 547.
[86] Ex TA 1988, s 385(1); see *Gordon and Blair Ltd v IRC* (1962) 40 TC 358.
[87] For comparative (corporation tax) limits, see OECD Report (1991), Table 3, 81–88. On policy and comparisons, see Donnelly and Young (2002) 50 *Can Tax Jo* 429 and [2005] BTR 432.
[88] ITA 2007, s 84, ex TA 1988, s 385(1)(b).
[89] ITA 2007, s 83(1). On importance of claim, see *Richardson v Jenkins* [1995] STC 95, 67 TC 246.
[90] ITA 2007, s 85, ex TA 1988, s 385(4).
[91] On which, see *Nuclear Electric plc v Bradley* [1996] STC 405, 68 TC 670, HL.
[92] ITA 2007, s 86, ex TA 1988, s 386.
[93] ITA 2007, s 86(5).

possibility of different rates for savings income. More convincingly, the notes suggest that
a restriction would not fit with self-assessment. Moreover, it had no practical effect, since
HMRC practice allowed taxpayers to make the set-off in the order which provided maximum benefit.

It will also be noted that the trading loss may be set against income from the company no
matter how the company makes its profits, eg from other trades. It is not necessary that T or
T's nominees own all the shares in the company. The relief may be claimed provided only
that the company carries on the business transferred by the individual and that individual
pays tax. In addition, T, the individual, must be beneficially entitled to the shares throughout the tax year for which relief is claimed;[94] in the year of the incorporation this means
from the date of the transfer until the end of the tax year (not, if different, the basis period).
Curiously, there seems to be no requirement that the beneficial ownership be unbroken,
only that it last throughout the year of assessment in question. If, therefore, T sells the
shares in January 2014 but then buys them back in March 2014, T should be able to resume
the loss claim in 2015–16.

20.10.4 Vertical Relief for Terminal Losses

A terminal loss is a loss sustained in the year of assessment in which the trade is permanently
discontinued and in that part of the preceding year of assessment beginning 12 months
before the date of discontinuance.[95] Once a trade, profession or vocation has been permanently discontinued, there can *ex hypothesi* be no carryforward of a loss under ITA 2007,
section 72. A terminal loss may, however, be carried back and set off against the profits taxed
under ITTOIA 2005, Part 2 from that trade for the year in which the trade ends and the
three preceding years of assessment. The calculation of the terminal loss brings any overlap
profit into account.[96] Relief is given as far as possible from the assessment of a later rather
than earlier year.[97] Assessments may thus have to be reopened. The reference to the year of
discontinuance is needed for the following situation. If the trading year ends in June 2016
and discontinuance occurs in December 2016, a loss in the final period of trading may be
set against the income until June under section 89 as well as against general income under
ITA 2007, section 64.

As with the other loss rules, dividends or interest on investments arising during any relevant period but which are excluded from the computation of profits may be used as profits
against which the terminal loss may be set.[98] Where a partner (P) retires, discontinuance
occurs under ITTOIA 2005, Part 9 and a terminal loss is calculated for the retiring partner
only. This loss is set off against that part of the partnership income which was included in
P's total income for each relevant year. P's share of the loss is governed by his share of the
profits at the date of discontinuance. If a continuance election is made, no terminal loss
relief is permitted for any of the partners.[99]

---

[94] ITA 2007, s 86(3), ex TA 1988, s 386(3).
[95] ITA 2007, s 90(1), ex TA 1988, s 388(6).
[96] ITA 2007, s 90(5).
[97] ITA 2007, s 91, ex TA 1988, s 388(3).
[98] ITA 2007, s 92, ex TA 1988, s 388(4).
[99] ITA 2007, ss 62(3) and 89(1), ex TA 1988, s 389(4).

20.10.5 *When is a Trading Loss Allowable?*

Loss relief is important not only to the genuine trader, but also to others who have used it as the basis of schemes. To claim relief the trader must have been carrying on a trade and allowable expenses must exceed trading receipts.[100] ITA 2007, sections 66 and 74 provide that a trading loss qualifies for relief under sections 64 and 72 if the trade was carried on a commercial basis and with a view to the realisation of profit.[101] Sections 64 and 72 (the two sideways relief rules—see §§20.10.1 and 20.10.2 above) are the rules which allow set-off against general income and so need protection; there is no need for such rules under sections 83 and 89, where the set-off is only against the profits of the trade. Further, the trade must have been carried on in a commercial way for the whole of the basis period, whether or not there has been a change in the manner in which the trade was being carried on and whether or not there has been a change in the persons running the trade, if at least one person was running it for the year. Before ITA 2007 this rule was applied by reference to the year of assessment as opposed to the basis period. Hence for those pre-2007 years, a further rule applied if the trade was set up or discontinued (or both) in the year of assessment; the test was applied to those parts of the year in which the trade was in being. The concessionary relief for maintenance expenses of owner-occupied farms not carried on a commercial basis is now classified as obsolete.[102]

Under ITA 2007, sections 66 and 74, the loss is not relievable unless the trade was being carried on a commercial basis and with a view to the realisation of profits. In *Walls v Livesey*,[103] the Special Commissioner considered that relief under section 72 was available where profits may have been expected a reasonable time after the four-year period provided for claims. The Revenue seem to take a narrower view.[104] In *S Kitching v HMRC*,[105] the First-tier Tribunal dismissed the taxpayer's claim for sideways relief against employment income for losses from operating a part-time running kit business, applying the uncommercial trade restriction in ITA 2007, section 66. The taxpayer's business, although run on an apparently commercial basis with retail premises, had suffered losses every year for ten years since its inception. In the tribunal's view, the taxpayer was unable to satisfy the requirement in section 66 that the trade be carried on with a (subjective) view to the realisation of profits.

Certain other losses may also be given restricted sideways reliefs; these include ring fence trades (eg certain films), and certain first year or trade leasing allowances (sections 75–82). Where a loss attracts only restricted sideways relief, it is not usually able to obtain the CGT relief under TCGA 1992, section 261B either.

---

[100] See *Ensign Tankers Leasing Ltd v Stokes* [1992] STC 226, 64 TC 617, HL; and *FA and AB Ltd v Lupton* [1971] 3 All ER 948, 47 TC 580; see above at §19.3.1 as to what is a trading transaction.

[101] Ex TA 1988, s 384; *Walls v Livesey* [1995] STC (SCD) 12; *Wannell v Rothwell* [1996] STC 450, 68 TC 519; and *Delian Enterprises v Ellis* [1999] STC (SCD) 103. On genesis of the legislation, see Stopforth [1999] BTR 106.

[102] Former ESC B5.

[103] [1995] STC (SCD) 12.

[104] HMRC, Business Income Manual BIM85705 *et seq.*

[105] [2013] UKFTT 384 (TC).

20.10.6 Capping the Losses: £25,000 Cap for Sideways Reliefs Where Person Not Active

Even if the activity satisfies the tests at §20.10.5, the UK rules now have a cap of £25,000 where the person is non-active. The cap was introduced by FA 2008 and builds on a similar cap where partners are involved (see §20.10.7 below). In 2008, HMRC came to learn of schemes, much like those involving partners, where an individual other than as a partner carried on trade in a non-active capacity. The new rules deny full sideways relief, including CGT relief, where the person spends fewer than 10 hours a week personally engaged in the trade.[106] If the loss arises from tax avoidance arrangements, there is no relief at all. Where there are no such arrangements, the sideways relief is capped at £25,000 pa.[107] These rules do not apply where the loss is from qualifying film expenditure, because films already have their own restrictions.[108] As HMRC still come across avoidance exploiting this loss relief, in 2010 an anti-avoidance provision banning relief for tax-generated losses was added (ITA 2007, section 74ZA) and section 81 repealed.

20.10.7 Restrictions on Reliefs for Certain Trading Losses: Partnerships[109]

Loss relief is always granted to a 'person'. Thus, where a partnership produces a loss, the loss is apportioned among the partners and each individual partner may choose to make whatever claim is appropriate for his individual circumstances. This treatment is afforded to Scottish partnerships as well as English partnerships.[110] Thus, partner A may wish to set his share of the trading loss against his investment income; partner B may choose to carry forward his loss against trading profits of a later year. While apportionment among the members was clearly enacted as the basic principle, tax planners decided to play games with the question of membership itself. Schemes emerged which involved offshore, ie foreign, trusts and partnerships. The members of the partnership were also beneficiaries of a trust and were entitled to the income as beneficiaries of the trust. The planners argued that thanks to double tax treaties, the UK had no right to tax the partnership income of the foreign trustees. The scheme was counteracted by Parliament enacting that the members of a firm include any person entitled to a share of income of the partnership. This rule applies for income tax, corporation tax and CGT; unusually, the provisions are declared always to have had effect.[111]

   The rules in ITA 2007, Part 4, Chapter 3 apply further restrictions to a limited partner, a member of a limited liability partnership (LLP) and a non-active partner.

20.10.7.1 Limited Partnerships Under the Limited Partnerships Act 1907

In a limited partnership, the limited partner's capital contribution (and so the amount of risk borne) is limited. The agreement may nonetheless provide that the trading loss of

---

[106] ITA 2007, s 74A, ss 74A–74D, all added by FA 2008, s 60 and Sch 21.
[107] ITA 2007, s 74B.
[108] ITA 2007, ss 74A(7) and 74B(5); terms defined in s 74D.
[109] For the legislative history, see the successive notes by Shipwright in British Tax Review Finance Act Issues.
[110] ITTOIA 2005, Pt 9, ex TA 1988, s 111(1).
[111] ITTOIA 2005, s 858(4), ex TA 1988, s 115(5C) and TCGA 1992, s 59(4), all added by FA 2008, s 58.

the partnership should be attributed to the limited partners in full. In *Reed v Young*,[112] the House of Lords held that relief could be claimed under TA 1988, section 380, even where the loss so attributed exceeded the amount of capital at risk. ITA 2007, section 104 now limits the relief given for this 'sideways relief' under section 64 or section 72. The restrictions apply both to limited partnerships registered as such and to similar arrangements limiting liability.[113] Relief is limited to 'the individual's contribution to the firm at 'the appropriate time' (broadly, the end of the basis period and not, as before 2007, the end of relevant year of assessment). ITA 2007 makes a change by making the rules refer to the contribution to the firm as distinct from one to the trade with consequential changes if the firm carries on more than one trade.[114] In essence, these reliefs are available only to the extent that the taxpayers' capital is actually at risk. As the mischief at which these rules are aimed concerns sideways reliefs, losses caught by these rules may still be carried forward for relief under ITA 2007, section 83. Similar restrictions apply to a member of an LLP: see ITA 2007, section 107. There are separate rules for corporation tax; ITA 2007 provides amended versions of the rules which remain and apply for certain reliefs.

20.10.7.2 Non-active Partners

These rules also apply to non-active partners if the loss arises from the relevant trade in an early year (ITA 2007, sections 104(5)(b) and 107(6)(b)). The details are contained in sections 110–113. The rules are particularly aimed at situations in which the person makes a contribution but then reduces it (section 111(4)). HMRC is percentage allowed to recover loss relief which has become excess loss relief because the partner's claim has been followed by a 'relevant reduction' in his contribution to the trade. The restricted but unrelieved losses may be revived if the individual does after all get involved in the trade (section 113). FA 2008, section 61 aligned the definition of non-active partner with that for ITA 2007, section 74A (above §20.10.6).

20.10.7.3 HMRC Regulation-making Power

ITA 2007, section 114 gives HMRC power to make regulations excluding contributions for the purposes of sections 104, 107 and 110. These may have retrospective effect and must be approved by a resolution of the House of Commons.

20.10.7.4 Films

FA 2004 added special rules on partnerships exploiting films, which are now in ITA 2007, section 115. These rules were intended to block schemes under which individuals used accounting principles (not the special film reliefs) to generate large losses followed by a guaranteed income stream, so deferring the income tax liability; ITA 2007 refers to it as a 'relevant agreement'. Certain expenditures are excluded from section 115 by section 116. On film reliefs, see below at §24.2.14.

---

[112] [1986] STC 285, 59 TC 196.
[113] Ex TA 1988, s 117(2); the Budget Press Release refers to persons participating in joint venture arrangements when liability is limited: see [1985] *Simon's Tax Intelligence* 147; the phraseology covers, eg, non-recourse loans.
[114] See explanatory notes change 16; see also changes 15 and 17.

20.10.8 *Other Restrictions on Losses*

Losses on dealings in commodity futures are restricted where partnerships are involved.[115] Restrictions also apply to hobby farming. Where losses are sustained in a trade of farming or market gardening, relief is not available under section 64 if, despite satisfying the test in section 66, a loss was incurred in each of the five prior years.[116] It should be remembered that all farming, but not market gardening, is treated as one trade, so that a loss on one farm may be set off against the profits of another. Special provision is made for the genuine farmer who has a reasonable expectation of profit but whose business will take longer than six years to come right.

20.10.9 *Cross-references: Other Trading Loss Rules*

On set-off of trading losses against capital gains under TCGA 1992, sections 261B and 261C (inserted by ITA 2007), see ITA 2007, section 71 and below at §33.10.6. On restrictions for 'sideways' relief under sections 64 or 72 for losses from wholly foreign trades, see ITA 2007, section 95. On relief for qualifying payments made after the trade has ceased (post-cessation trade relief), see below at §23.4.

---

[115] ITA 2007, s 81.
[116] ITA 2007, ss 67–70, ex TA 1988, s 397.

21

Business Income—Part III:
Principles and Receipts

21.1 Measure of Income: The Role of Accounting Practice in Income Tax

21.1.1 Legislative Framework and Current Principles

ITTOIA 2005, section 5 charges tax on the profits of the trade, profession or vocation, while section 7 charges the full amount of the profits of the basis period for that year.[1] ITTOIA 2005, Part 2, Chapter 3 contains basic rules for calculating profits covering both receipts and expenses; Chapter 6 contains further rules on receipts, while later chapters deal with a range of specific issues. Two matters which previously were dealt with under Schedule D, Case VI have their own charging provisions under ITTOIA 2005, Part 2; these are Chapter 17 for amounts chargeable to income tax on a change of accounting basis (below §21.11) and

---

[1] TA 1988, ss 18 and 60. The 1988 version of TA 1988, s 18 referred to 'profits or gains', but this was changed to annual profits or gains by FA 1998.

Chapter 18 for post-cessation receipts (below §23.4). FA 2013, section 17 and Schedule 4 introduced the option of cash basis accounting for tax for small, unincorporated businesses.[2] The new regime in ITTOIA 2005, Chapter 3A, sections 31A-31F follows on from a recommendation made by the Office of Tax Simplification (OTS) to offer the possibility of a simplified form of accounting to the smallest of businesses. However, as Gravestock states in his BTR note, '[i]t is quite extraordinary that such a good idea can go so very wrong with major unintended consequences.' The cash-based accounting scheme is in fact quite complex, stretching to over 28 pages of legislation in FA 2013. While the original OTS proposals called for a £30,000 receipts threshold, ITTOIA 2005, section 31B ultimately provides for a much higher threshold generally aligned with the VAT registration threshold (turnover of £83,000 p.a. for 2016–17). While this greatly increased the number of businesses potentially able to benefit from the new regime, it also led to concerns about avoidance—and hence to a very detailed and complicated set of rules that seem far removed from the original aim of simplification.

21.1.1.1 Law and Accounting[3]

In order to determine the profits or gains of a trade, profession, or vocation, ITTOIA 2005, section 25[4] (ex FA 1998, section 42) requires consideration of generally-accepted accounting practice (GAAP). The introduction of this requirement was controversial, and the application of it today remains so. In the UK the relevant accounting practice will be set either by the UK's own Financial Reporting Council (FRC),[5] or by the International Accounting Standards Board (IASB) (see further §21.1.2).[6] For the purposes of ITTOIA 2005, Part 2, the profits of the trade or profession must be computed in accordance with GAAP. However, section 25 also contains the important limitation that this is *subject to any adjustment required or authorised by law*. The question when an adjustment is required or authorised by law will have to be addressed by the courts in due course. An underlying but very important issue is whether the courts are going to treat the actual application of GAAP in individual cases as a matter of fact or as a matter of law.[7]

As an example of an adjustment required by law one may take depreciation of certain capital expenditure. As was said by the House of Lords in *Barclays Mercantile Business Finance*:

> A trader computing his profits or losses will ordinarily make some deduction for depreciation in the value of the machinery or plant which he uses. Otherwise the computation will take no account of the need for the eventual replacement of wasting assets and the true profits will be overstated. But the computation required by Schedule D (whether for the purpose of income or corporation

---

[2] For commentary see Gravestock [2013] BTR 401.

[3] On role of accounting principles, but going wider, see the important Discussion Papers by Macdonald and Martin, published by the IFS Tax Law Review Committee.

[4] For companies the analogous provision is CTA 2009, s 46.

[5] For more information on the FRC see https://www.frc.org.uk/Our-Work/Codes-Standards/Corporate-reporting/Standards-in-Issue.aspx, and especially the Forward to Accounting Standards. The standard-settting function of the FRC was formerly the responsibility of the Accounting Standards Board (ASB).

[6] On the narrowing gap between the then ASB and IASB, see Wild and Hill, Tax Journal (24 January 2005) and also Pacter IFRS Pocket Guide 2016 at http://www.ifrs.org/Use-around-the-world/Documents/2016-pocket-guide.pdf.

[7] Freedman (2004) 2 *eJournal of Tax Research* 71 *et seq.*

tax) has always excluded such a deduction. Parliament therefore makes separate provision for depreciation by means of capital allowances against what would otherwise be taxable income.[8]

In an important House of Lords decision on the relationship between accounting and tax law, the 2007 combined appeals in *HMRC v William Grant & Sons Distillers Ltd* and *Small (Inspector of Taxes) v Mars UK Ltd*, the accounting treatment sought by the taxpayers was upheld for tax purposes.[9] These concerned the correct treatment of depreciation embedded in the cost of unsold trading stock. The House said that the taxpayers' accounting treatment was in accordance with the best practice as embodied in accounting standards. Further, they rejected the Revenue's argument that this treatment was inconsistent with the rule denying the deduction capital of expenditure (ITTOIA 2005, section 33 and CTA 2009, section 53, ex TA 1988, section 74(1)(f)).[10] Lord Hoffmann, making a different point, observed at para 15 that the courts have always rejected submissions that accounts which comply with the best practice of accountants as embodied in the accounting standards must go further and comply with some further fundamental principles of accounting.

A move to harmonise accounting standards internationally began in the 1970s under the auspices of the International Accounting Standards Committee (IASC). From 1973 until 2001 the IASC issued a number of influential International Accounting Standards (IAS). After a reorganization in 2001, the International Accounting Standards Board (IASB) took over from the IASC;[11] new standards issued by the IASB are referred to as International Financial Reporting Standards (IFRS). Many IASs issued by the predecessor authority are still in use today. In the discussion that follows references to IAS include IFRS. The issue of the status of international accounting standards became urgent because EC Regulation 1606/2002, dealing with company law, stated that consolidated group accounts of companies listed on a stock exchange had to be drawn up in accordance with IAS as from 1 January 2005, provided that those standards have been approved by the European Commission under Article 3 of the Regulation.[12]

For accounting periods beginning on or after 1 January 2005, GAAP in ITTOIA 2005, section 25 refers either to IAS or to UK GAAP, depending on the choice made by the company or other entity preparing the accounts.[13] The UK accounting standards have become more closely aligned with IAS over the years, but some difference remain. This is evident from the introduction to FRS 100, which states that the FRC aims to provide financial reporting standards that have consistency with international accounting standards 'unless an alternative clearly better meets the overriding objective'. Details of the various

---

[8] *Barclays Mercantile Business Finance v Mawson* [2004] UKHL 51, para 3; see also *Mars UK Ltd v Small* [2004] STC (SCD) 253 Sp C 408. On Parliament's provision for depreciation of certain plant and machinery in the CAA 2001, see ch 24 of this book.

[9] [2007] UKHL 15, [2007] STC 680; see Parry Wingfield (2007) *Tax Journal*, 28 May, 13–15. On history, note also RI 242, now due for review.

[10] [2007] UKHL 15, and especially Lord Hope at [38].

[11] For details on the IASB organisation structure, see http://www.ifrs.org/About-us/IASB/Pages/Home.aspx and also Pacter, IFRS Pocket Guide 2016 at http://www.ifrs.org/Use-around-the-world/Documents/2016-pocket-guide.pdf.

[12] The new standards may apply from an earlier date if the company has been so directed.

[13] FA 2004, s 50 and now see the definition of 'generally accepted accounting practice' in ITA 2007, s 997 and CTA 2010, s1127. On FA 2004 sections see Mainwaring [2004] BTR 473. On the narrowing gap between ASB and IASB see Wild and Hill (2005) *The Tax Journal* 24 January, 13.

accounting standards are available on the IASB website and, for UK standards, on the FRC website.[14] A (very) full account is provided by the annual volume of GAAP written by Ernst and Young and published by Lexis Nexis. The annual *Pocket Guide to IFRS Standards* is also very useful.

The introduction of IASs and IFRS has done nothing to reduce the debate about whether the tax system should be tied to these things.[15] Meanwhile the question has been raised by the European Commission whether these standards might be used as the basis for a common EU tax base.[16] A project by the Centre for European Policy Studies divided the accounting standards into three categories: (a) those where the standards definition would be acceptable; (b) those where they needed adjustment because of giving the taxpayer too much discretion; and (c) those where adjustments would be needed for other reasons.[17] Examples discussed in each category were: (a) long-term construction contracts (now IFRS 15) and leases (now IFRS 16); (b) depreciation of tangible assets, research and development costs, and goodwill (IAS 16) and contingent liabilities (IAS 37); and (c) financial assets and liabilities (now IFRS 9), investment property (IAS 40), post-employment benefits (IAS 19) and the whole problem of the treatment of losses.

In 2011, the European Commission issued a proposal for a Council Directive on a common consolidated corporate tax base (CCCTB), which would allow companies to opt for a single set of rules when calculating their taxable income throughout EU countries.[18] The CCCTB aims to offer companies one single set of corporate tax base rules to follow, and the possibility of filing a single, consolidated tax return with one tax administration for their entire activity within the EU. The company's tax base would then be shared out amongst the Member States in which it is active, according to a specific formula taking into account three factors: assets, labour and sales. After the tax base has been apportioned, each Member State concerned can tax its apportioned share at its own corporate tax rate. The theory behind the CCCTB sounds straightforward, but the political and technical difficulties encountered proved difficult to surmount and the project lapsed in recent years. It was revived in 2015 with an announcement by the Commission that it intends to issue a new proposal in 2016. The proposal will be for a mandatory CCCTB and the primary focus will be on securing the common corporate tax base (a CCTB) before moving on to address consolidation.[19] Certain Member States, including the UK, at least for now, are decidedly against the CCCTB proposal. As a result, if the CCCTB project manages to proceed, it very likely will be implemented initially by only a subset of Member States under the enhanced cooperation procedures in Art 20 TEU and Art 326 TFEU *et seq.*

[14] See http://www.ifrs.org/Pages/default.aspx and https://www.frc.org.uk/Our-Work/Codes-Standards/Accounting-and-Reporting-Policy/Accounting-Standards-and-Statements-issued-by-the.aspx.

[15] See eg Schoen (2005) 58 *Tax L Rev* 111 (The Tillinghast lecture for 2004); Freedman (2004) 2 *eJournal of Tax Research* 71 *et seq*; and chapters by Harris and by Hrdinkova in Michielse & Thuronyi (eds), *Tax Design Issues Worldwide* (Kluwer, 2015).

[16] EC COM (2001) 582 (final) and SEC (2001) 1681. See also For discussion and much citation of literature see Schoen [2004] *European Taxation* 426 *et seq*. The citations include [2003] *European Taxation* 269 *et seq*; and, from the US, Manzon and Plesko (2002) 55 *Tax Law Review* 175 *et seq*.

[17] Gammie, *Achieving a Common Consolidated Corporate Tax Base in the EU* (CEPS, 2005) esp ch 4.

[18] COM(2011) 121/4 'Proposal for a Council Directive on a Common Consolidated Corporate Tax Base (CCCTB)'.

[19] For the status and background information on the European Commission's CCCTB project, see the Commission's website at http://ec.europa.eu/taxation_customs/taxation/company_tax/common_tax_base/index_en.htm.

21.1.1.2 Case Law

Before FA 1998 there were two distinct approaches to the relationship between questions of law and principles of accountancy: one asserted that the court should first look to see what accountancy prescribed, and then see whether any rule of law contradicted it;[20] the other asserted that the court should first determine the question as a matter of law, see whether accountancy gave a different answer, and then determine which should prevail. It will be appreciated that the first approach gives much greater weight to accountancy practice than the second. The former approach has, in effect, been enshrined by legislation, but it had already been reached by case law.

The first approach was accepted by the Court of Appeal in *Gallagher v Jones*[21] when it doubted whether any judge-made rule could override a generally-accepted rule of commercial accountancy which (a) applied to the situation in question, (b) was not one of two or more rules applicable to that situation, and (c) was not shown to be inconsistent with the true facts or otherwise inapt to determine the true profits or losses of the business. This formula, whilst on its face quite deferential to commercial accounting, leaves considerable scope for judicial intervention in practice, ie because many accounting standards do allow more than one permitted method for applying the standard.[22] This new approach was followed in later cases.[23] However, the decision has not been universally welcomed; as Freedman scathingly noted:

> The arguments for the taxpayer were too stark and left important issues unexplored. These issues were not explored because of the weight given to SSAP 21. To accept a standard without investigation of its objectives and effects is ... an abdication of responsibility by the court.[24]

As just noted, in *Gallagher v Jones*, the Court of Appeal considered that no judge-made rule could override generally-accepted principles of commercial accountancy where, inter alia, there was not one of two or more rules applicable to that situation. This issue arose in *Willingale v International Commercial Bank Ltd*[25] where the House of Lords, upholding all the lower tribunals, held that the bank, although having made up its accounts on one basis, was entitled to insist that, for tax purposes, another basis should be taken. The decision was by a bare majority and has been heavily criticised. Today these profits would be taxed under the loan relationship rules in CTA 2009, Parts 5–7, discussed below in chapter sixty-three.[26]

---

[20] Eg, Salmon J in *Odeon Associated Theatres Ltd v Jones* [1972] 1 All ER 681, 689, 48 TC 257, 283A; Lord Haldane in *Sun Insurance Office Ltd v Clark* [1912] AC 443, 455, 6 TC 59, 78; and Lord Clyde in *Lothian Chemical Co Ltd v Rogers* (1926) 11 TC 508, 520; see also Report of the Committee on the Taxation of Trading Profits, Cmnd 8189 (1951), §135 (the Tucker Report).

[21] [1993] STC 537, esp 555–56, per Sir Thomas Bingham MR.

[22] Freedman [1993] BTR 468, 477.

[23] *Johnston v Britannia Airways Ltd* [1994] STC 763; on which, see Park, Cook and Oliver [1995] BTR 499. Following this case, ICAEW wrote to the Inland Revenue for clarification of the Revenue's interpretation of this decision. The correspondence is published in ICAEW Press Release, 12 April 1995, Guidance Note TAX 10/95, [1995] *Simon's Weekly Tax Intelligence* 703. See also *Sycamore plc and Maple Ltd v Fir* [1997] STC (SCD) 1.

[24] Freedman [1993] BTR 468, 477.

[25] [1978] 1 All ER 754, [1978] STC 75, 52 TC 242; on which, see Pagan [1992] BTR 75; see also Vinelott J in *Pattison v Marine Midland Ltd* [1981] STC 540.

[26] See also [1978] STC 75, 80, 52 TC 242, 272; and White [1987] BTR 292, 295.

21.1.2 Generally-Accepted Accounting Practice (GAAP)

21.1.2.1 Possible Relationships

It is clear that the aim of accountants is in some senses the same as that of the Revenue: both seek to measure the income of a precise, and so artificial, period.[27] The balance of the relationship may take several forms, among which the system might be said (a) simply to accept the accounting treatment at face value, (b) to follow the accounting treatment while reserving to itself a power to depart from it for some good reason of its own, (c) explicitly to adopt the accounting treatment for certain items only[28] or (d) to refuse to follow the accounting treatment at all. In the US there has long been great resistance to equating financial accounting with tax accounting. The typical US view is that it is much easier to conclude that a certain rule of tax law is contrary to generally-accepted accounting principles, than it is to define such principles.[29]

21.1.2.2 What is Generally-Accepted Accounting Practice?

For many years TA 1988, section 836A defined GAAP as meaning 'such generally accepted accounting practices with respect to accounts for UK companies that are intended to give a true and fair view'. This was repealed by FA 2005, presumably for obsolescence. Since 1947 the Companies Act has required that limited companies prepare annual accounts that give a 'true and fair view'. The Accounting Standards Committee (ASC), which issued approximately 25 Statements of Standard Accounting Practice (or SSAPs), was established in 1970 in response to the need for accounts to have a 'true and fair view.'[30] The ASC was superseded by the Accounting Standards Board (ASB) in 1990, which was set up under powers in the Companies Act 1989. Comments by judges, and even academic criticisms relating to years before 1970, should not be given much weight.[31] The Financial Reporting Council (FRC), a body on which the professional accounting bodies are joined by other city institutions, formerly guided the ASB and acted as a proactive voice in public debate on these matters.[32] In 2012, the FRC assumed responsibility under the Companies Act 2006 for accounting standards from the ASB.[33] With effect from 1 January 2015, the FRC fundamentally revised reporting standards for the UK (and Republic of Ireland), replacing the existing standards with five new Financial Reporting Standards (FRS 100, 101, 102, 103, and 104), along with a new standard for micro-entities (FRS 105).

The accounting standards that were first developed by the ASC were designed to provide authoritative—but not mandatory—guidance on what constituted a 'true and fair view'. Thus accounting standards provide principles, rather than a prescriptive and exhaustive body of rules, to determine what constitutes a 'true and fair view'. This approach continued in the Financial Reporting Standards (FRSs) issued by the ASB and now FRC. FRSs are

---

[27] See Walton J in *Willingale v International Commercial Bank Ltd* [1976] STC 188, 194–95.

[28] Eg, pre-2004 corporation tax rules for loan relationships.

[29] Seghers (1948) *National Tax J* 341.

[30] See White [1987] BTR 292.

[31] Eg, Lord Denning's dismissive reference in *Heather v PE Consulting Group* (1972) 48 TC 293, 322F.

[32] Thomas, *Introduction to Financial Accounting*, 5th edn (McGraw-Hill, 2005), 14.

[33] Statutory Auditors (Amendment of Companies Act 2006 and Delegation of Functions etc) Order 2012 (SI 2012/1741).

intended to be authoritative statements on how certain transactions and events should be treated in a reporting entity's financial statements; however, the standards also recognise that the application of FRS requires judgement. For example, FRS 102, section 10, replacing former FRS 18 (which had replaced the older SSAP 2 referred to in many of the cases), sets out the principles to be followed by an entity in selecting accounting policies. Under FRS 102, paragraph 8.6, an entity is required to disclose, in the summary of significant accounting policies or other notes, the judgements, apart from those involving estimations, that management has made in the process of applying the entity's accounting policies and that have the most significant effect on the amounts recognised in the financial statements.

The SSAPs and now FRSs are clearly relevant to establishing a true and fair view. They are also within the approach adopted by the courts in *Gallagher v Jones* (1993). In *Herbert Smith v Honour*,[34] by contrast, there was no SSAP available to the court. Although the court in *Symons v Weeks*[35] had adopted the timing treatment in SSAP 9 for receipts, the Revenue at first refused to accept claims made under SSAP 9 for losses on long-term contracts. SSAP 9 states that these losses must be recognised as soon as they can reasonably be foreseen. The High Court, agreeing with the Special Commissioner, rejected the Revenue's argument. The Revenue conceded defeat.[36]

21.1.2.3 General Principles

Traditionally, accounting practice has relied on a number of general principles, either where there is no accounting standard or where there is a conflict within and between accounting standards. Historically, these more general principles include prudence, materiality and economic effect.

FRS 102, paragraph 2.9 defines prudence as 'the inclusion of a degree of caution in the exercise of the judgements needed in making the estimates required under conditions of uncertainty, such that assets or income are not overstated and liabilities or expenses are not understated'. Prudence thus demands that losses be written off as soon as they are recognised.[37] This is inconsistent with a principle of tax law, which states that neither profit nor loss should be anticipated.[38] However, as just seen, that principle was rejected in *Symons v Weeks*.[39] The concept of prudence is consistent with the historical cost method of accounting but is at odds with the more recent shift towards fair value accounting, which considers income and expenditure in terms of balance sheet movement and is thought to provide more relevant information to users.

FRS 102, paragraph 10.3 also provides that an entity need not follow a requirement in an FRS if the effect of doing so would not be material. According to FRS 102, paragraph 2.9, information is material if its omission or misstatement, individually or collectively, could influence the economic decisions of users taken on the basis of the financial statements. This unquantifiable approach approves broad-brush treatment at a level which may be

---

[34] [1997] STC (SCD) 293; noted by Freedman [1998] BTR 186 *et seq*. On appeal [1999] STC 173, see below §23.3.1.

[35] [1983] STC 195.

[36] Inland Revenue Press Release, 20 July 1999, [1999] *Simon's Weekly Tax Intelligence* 1302.

[37] Available from the Financial Reporting Council website at https://www.frc.org.uk/.

[38] Freedman [1998] BTR 186.

[39] Inland Revenue Press Release, *op cit*.

regarded as highly material by the Revenue. Moreover, accountants may take a broad view where the same economic effect may be achieved by different forms of legal relationships.[40] In FRS 102, paragraph 2.9 this is described as 'substance over form'—transactions and other events and conditions should be accounted for and presented in accordance with their substance and not merely their legal form. A good example is the treatment of 'finance leases' in FRS 102, section 20. A lease is classified as a finance lease if it transfers substantially all the risks and rewards incidental to ownership. Under the substance over form approach, a finance lease is treated for accounting purposes as if the lessee had purchased the asset from the lessor and financed the purchase with a loan from the lessor. Various examples of relevant factors in deciding if a lease is a finance lease are provided in paragraph 20.5, including if the lease term is for the major part of the economic life of the asset even if title is not transferred, or if at the inception of the lease the present value of the minimum lease payments amounts to at least substantially all of the fair value of the leased asset. Thus, legal differences that are not relevant for financial reporting purposes may be ignored for financial reporting; whether they should be ignored for tax purposes depends on what the tax rule is. Legal differences which are not relevant for financial reporting may still be relevant for tax purposes.[41] Tax officials may instead insist that each transaction be analysed strictly; they will certainly insist that each of the two parties to a transaction treats it the same way.

Finally it is worth highlighting that accounting principles, even fundamental general principles, change over time. A good example is the concept of prudence, which had fallen out of favour as old-fashioned and was conspicuously absent from FRS 18 but resurfaced in FRS 102 in 2015—after the global financial crisis.

21.1.2.4 For Whom are Accounts Prepared?

Accounts are written for those who want to use accounts; tax computations are prepared for the tax officers. Accounts are used by managers for purposes of internal management, and by those outside a company when deciding whether to invest in that company through share equity or to make a loan to the company. The interests of such groups are not the same as those of HMRC. For example, French supermarket companies are owned by families or other large shareholders and use accelerated depreciation to minimise taxes on profits; most British supermarkets, on the other hand, depend on the stock market for capital and depreciate their assets slowly in order to boost profits.[42]

21.1.2.5 Why Not Let Accounting Practice Rule?[43]

In some countries, and particularly in Continental Europe, the starting point is the set of accounts prepared by the firm's accountants.[44] Despite ITTOIA 2005, section 25, this approach remains controversial. Although, at first sight, accepting accounting treatment at

---

[40] See Macdonald (1991) 54 *MLR* 830, 837–46.
[41] See *Klockner Ina v Bryan* (1990) 63 TC 1, 26–27.
[42] Cortejns, Cortejns and Lal, INSEAD paper, cited in *The Economist*, 29 April 1995.
[43] For articles by Freedman and by Schoen, see *op cit*.
[44] See, eg, material in Ault *et al*, Part 1; *Fiscal Versus Commercial Profit Accounting in Netherlands, France and Germany* (IBFD, 1998). See also McCourt and Radcliffe [1995] BTR 461.

face value would avoid the need for a second set of accounts for tax purposes, this is very naive, as Continental experience shows:

(1)   In countries where accounts are used as the tax base, one result has been very conservative accounting policies. Revaluations of assets in balance sheets may trigger a disposal for CGT, and so a charge to tax; to avoid this, revaluations do not take place. This strictness is not what financial markets need, and some countries have developed a pattern by which individual companies adopt the strict approach, while group accounts are constructed on a less conservative and more subjective approach. Once the company wants to be quoted on the New York Stock Exchange, the need for more transparent accounts can cause unpleasant tax liabilities.

(2)   GAAP should be seen as a developing body of principles rather than a precise set of rules; to make tax follow GAAP may inhibit the development of those principles. In Continental Europe very strict accounting rules have developed (to reduce subjectivity).

(3)   There is no reason to assume that accounting practice should necessarily adapt to the Revenue's view, and it may develop differently over time. Rejecting the idea that legislation may require the tax system to follow whatever system of Current Cost Accounting was in force at that time, the Revenue's 1982 Green Paper on Corporation Tax stated: 'If this were the case, the effect would be that the ultimate decision about the level of taxation for business profits would to a significant degree be delegated to the accounting profession. It is difficult to see that this would be acceptable to Parliament.'[45] Yet this was done to a large extent in 1998.

(4)   Many practices are now applied only to certain taxpayers. UK GAAP has been developed by and for the UK corporate sector; small businesses are meant to have administrative costs alleviated and are not expected to adopt all of them. For example, SSAP 9, which was used in *Symons v Weeks* (§21.1.2.2 above), was not meant to apply to small businesses.

21.1.3   *Remaining Differences between UK Tax Law and Accounting*

Given the qualifications in section 25 and in *Gallagher v Jones* (§21.1.1.2 above), ordinary principles of commercial accounting must sometimes yield to tax law.[46] Examples are as follows:

(1)   The courts have consistently held that the question whether an expenditure is on capital or revenue account is one of law—whatever the accounting view.[47] By treating these issues as questions of law, the courts have enabled themselves to keep complete residual control. There are signs that the some judges do not want this to be treated

[45]   Cmnd 8456, para 10.26.

[46]   Viscount Simonds in *Ostime v Duple Motor Bodies Ltd* [1961] 2 All ER 167, 169, 39 TC 537, 566.

[47]   *Beauchamp v FW Woolworth plc* [1989] STC 510, 61 TC 542, where the tax treatment coincided with the accountancy treatment. See also *Associated Portland Cement Manufacturers Ltd v Kerr* [1946] 1 All ER 68, 27 TC 103 (decision against accounting evidence); and *Heather v PE Consulting Group* [1973] 1 All ER 8, 48 TC 320 (decision consistent with accounting evidence).

as matter of heavy jurisprudence but rather as one to be determined from a practical and business point of view—and so pre-eminently for the specialist tribunal of fact, especially in borderline cases.[48] Yet accounting practice has to face the same issues and deals with them in a different way. So where accountants deal with expenses, they have to decide which expenses are to be written off in full and at once, and which are to be deferred, say, until the asset acquired is disposed of. The former is analogous to a trust lawyer's income expense and the latter to a capital one.

(2)   It is an elementary accountancy principle that capital expenditure on a depreciating asset is not written off in full and at once, but neither is it simply deferred until the asset is disposed of. Accountants write this expenditure off against profits over the lifetime of the asset, adopting one of several accepted methods to calculate how much depreciation should be taken in a given year and based on judgment on matters such as the expected useful life of an asset. However, as seen at the start of this chapter, tax law allows the deduction of capital expenditure only if that expenditure falls within the capital allowances system (see chapter twenty-four below). The UK capital allowance system is generally more restrictive than accounting depreciation, eg providing little or no capital allowances for buildings notwithstanding that buildings typically are depreciated in the accounts.

(3)   Consistent with the principle under (1) above, accountancy practice may write off abortive expenditure as a revenue expense, but there is tax law authority that abortive capital expenditure is not deductible in calculating income for tax purposes.[49]

(4)   Certain expenditure, which is clearly revenue rather than capital, is nonetheless not deductible because barred by other rules, eg as not incurred 'wholly and exclusively' for the purpose of earning a profit or because it is not directed to the earning of profits.

(5)   Similarly, certain items of expenditure will be deducted by the accountants in ascertaining the income for the year, but disallowed by some other express provision, such as business entertainment expenses.[50]

(6)   The courts have not confined their decisions on points of accountancy to those situations where an express statutory provision is in point. In the past, the courts have also ruled on such questions as the correct method of assessing work in progress,[51] and of valuing stock in trade[52]—matters where there is no express provision, and, in the last case, the courts have ruled that there is such a thing as the 'correct' method even though accountancy knows of many methods. The extent to which the courts will treat these as valid legal principles circumscribing ITTOIA 2005, section 25 is unclear, as is the Revenue's willingness to stand by some of them. One should note that previously the Revenue were not swayed by arguments based on consistency from year to year, nor inhibited about seeking to change the basis from year to year, eg

---

[48] Eg Buxton LJ in *Able UK Ltd v HMRC* [2008] STC 139, [2007] EWCA Civ 1207, para 28, citing Dyson LJ in *IRC v John Lewis Properties plc* [2002] EWCA Civ 1869, [2003] STC 117. See also Lawrence Collins LJ in the *Able* case at para 22.

[49] *Southwell v Savill* [1901] 2 KB 349, 4 TC 430.

[50] ITTOIA 2005, ss 45–47, ex TA 1988, s 577 (see below at §22.6.3).

[51] *Ostime v Duple Motor Bodies Ltd* (see below at §23.5.3).

[52] Eg, the prohibition of LIFO (see below at §23.5.2.2).

cash-to-earnings basis. The Revenue have also challenged accounts on bases which they previously had accepted over a period of many years.[53]

(7) Bona fide commercial payments and receipts sometimes fall outside the tax system, whereas they cannot fall outside the accounting system, eg exchange differences on a liability, as in *Beauchamp v Woolworth*.[54] Although the issue of such exchange differences has been remedied for corporation tax, it has not been for income tax.

21.1.4 The Concept of Revenue

Rather surprisingly, there has been limited specific guidance on revenue recognition under UK GAAP. Until FRS 102 was issued in 2015, there was no comprehensive UK standard on the topic of revenue; however, there were a number of standards that dealt with issues surrounding revenue (see eg SSAP 9, already referred to). Accountants relied on the general GAAP framework, and therefore on the concepts discussed above, to determine the appropriate treatment of an item of revenue. FRS 102, section 23 now provides specific guidance on accounting for revenue arising from the following transactions and events in particular:

(a) the sale of goods (whether produced by the entity for the purpose of sale or purchased for resale);
(b) the rendering of services;
(c) construction contracts in which the entity is the contractor; and
(d) the use by others of entity assets yielding interest, royalties or dividends.

For example, under FRS 102, paragraph 23.10, an entity shall recognise revenue from the sale of goods when all the following conditions are satisfied:

(a) the entity has transferred to the buyer the significant risks and rewards of ownership of the goods;
(b) the entity retains neither continuing managerial involvement to the degree usually associated with ownership nor effective control over the goods sold;
(c) the amount of revenue can be measured reliably;
(d) it is probable that the economic benefits associated with the transaction will flow to the entity; and
(e) the costs incurred or to be incurred in respect of the transaction can be measured reliably.

Tax law, as we shall discuss next, provides an even more prescriptive approach to determining business income and therefore profits.

---

[53] Eg, *BSC Footwear Ltd v Ridgway* [1970] 1 All ER 932, 47 TC 511 (practice accepted for 30 years); and *Ostime v Duple Motor Bodies Ltd* [1961] 2 All ER 167, 39 TC 537 (practice accepted for 28 years).
[54] [1989] STC 510, 61 TC 542.

21.2 Trading Stock

A payment arising from the disposal of trading stock in the normal course of business is normally a trading receipt. Traditionally 'trading stock' means (a) raw materials, (b) finished products, and (c) work in progress. It does not extend to plant, mere utensils (as distinct from raw materials) or a source of trading stock.[55] ITTOIA 2005, section 174 now provides a longer definition of 'trading stock'; among the points it makes is the need to include services provided in the course of the trade as well as goods.

The question whether an item is trading stock must depend on the nature of the trade. In *Abbott v Albion Greyhounds (Salford) Ltd*,[56] a greyhound racing company argued that the dogs used in their races were trading stock and so should be valued at the end of each year. This was rejected by Wrottesly J on the ground that the saleable value of the kennel was at no time a commercial picture of the company's success or failure. Had the company bought and sold dogs by way of trade, the answer would have been different. Similarly, working sheepdogs would not be regarded as trading stock of a farm. This is separate from the question whether a profit on sale would be a capital or an income receipt. Special rules relating to farm animals are contained in ITTOIA 2005, Part 2, Chapter 8. Further rules on the treatment of trading stock are considered in §21.10 and in chapter twenty-three below.

21.3 Capital Receipts

ITTOIA 2005, section 96 specifically excludes capital receipts. A sum arising from the disposal of the business itself or of a business asset of a capital nature is normally a capital receipt. In *British Borneo Petroleum Syndicate Ltd v Cropper*,[57] a sum received in return for the surrender of a royalty agreement was held to be a capital receipt. The terms on which an asset is sold may, however, give rise to a revenue profit. In *Lamport and Holt Line Ltd v Langwell*,[58] A, a shipowner, sold shares in B, a company trading as fuel suppliers, to C, another company of fuel suppliers. The contract provided that A should receive part of the commission which C received for supplying oil to A. These part-commissions were held to be trading receipts of A. A sum received in return for a right to income may be income or capital depending on the circumstances (see §22.4.3.11).

21.4 Receipts for Non-Trade Purposes

While a payment in return for goods or services supplied in the course of trade will be a trading receipt, a payment made for reasons other than trade will not. This is because a sum

[55] In *Willingale v International Commercial Bank Ltd* [1978] STC 88, an argument that the bills of exchange were trading stock was not pursued.
[56] [1945] 1 All ER 308, 26 TC 390; see also *General Motors Acceptance Corpn v IRC* [1985] STC 408.
[57] [1969] 1 All ER 104, 45 TC 201.
[58] (1958) 38 TC 193; see also *Orchard Wine and Spirit Co v Loynes* (1952) 33 TC 97.

received otherwise than in return for trading activities is simply a windfall in the nature of a gift; it is a by-product of a trade rather than an operation in the carrying-out of the trade.[59] Therefore, a solicitor or doctor does not have to bring into professional accounts a legacy from a grateful client, even though the legacy is expressed to be in gratitude for professional services to the testator or the testator's late spouse.[60]

The courts look at the reason for the payment—not whether there was an obligation to pay it. However, the payment of an extra sum for work already paid for will usually be a trading receipt even though the payment was voluntary.[61] A testimonial or solatium after the trading connection has ceased will escape tax because the payment is made in recognition of past services, not in respect of past services (eg settling an unpaid bill) or for future services.[62] The question turns on the nature of the payment rather than the motive of the payer. The fact that the payer chooses a measure related to previous services, eg a sum equivalent to five years' commission, is similarly irrelevant. In *Murray v Goodhews*,[63] a brewing company terminated a number of tenancy agreements with the taxpayer and chose to make voluntary payments of some £81,000 over two years. These payments were held not to be trading receipts of the tenants. Three factors pointing to this were: (a) that although an ex gratia payment had been mentioned early in the negotiations, there was no disclosure of the basis on which the payment was calculated, (b) there had been no subsequent negotiations between the parties on this point, and (c) the amount had not been calculated by reference to profit earned.

Payments escaping tax on this basis have included a payment to a firm of accountants on not being reappointed to act as auditors to a company which had changed ownership, the sum being equivalent to one year's salary,[64] and a payment to an insurance broker on the ending of a relationship with a client when that client was taken over by another company.[65] In practice, a prize awarded to an author for his literary work is not treated as taxable.[66] On the other hand, a payment to assist a taxpayer club to improve its curling facilities was held to be a trading receipt since the purpose of the payment was to enable the club to remain in business.[67] Similarly, in *McGowan v Brown and Cousins*,[68] a payment to compensate an estate agent for the loss of a fee-earning opportunity was held to be a trading receipt. The issue is one of fact. In *Murray v Goodhews*, the payment escaped tax despite the continued trading relationship between the parties; whereas in *McGowan v Brown and Cousins*, the payment was taxable even though the trading relationship had ended. The latter point is

[59] *Simpson v John Reynolds & Co (Insurances) Ltd* [1974] STC 271, 290, 49 TC 693, per Pennycuick V-C.
[60] *Simpson v John Reynolds* [1975] STC 271, 273 per Russell LJ.
[61] *Temperley v Smith* [1956] 3 All ER 92, 37 TC 18; *Isaac Holden & Sons Ltd v IRC* (1924) 12 TC 768, (see below at §23.2.2); *Australia (Commonwealth) Taxation Commr v Squatting Investment Co Ltd* [1954] AC 182, [1954] 1 All ER 349.
[62] *Murray v Goodhews* [1978] STC 207, 213, [1978] 2 All ER 40, 46, 52 TC 86, 109, per Buckley LJ. See Eyre [1978] BTR 65; and Davies [1979] BTR 212.
[63] [1978] STC 207, [1978] 2 All ER 40, 52 TC 86. On deduction by the brewers, see *Watney Combe Reid & Co Ltd v Pike* [1982] STC 733, 57 TC 372.
[64] *Walker v Carnaby, Harrower, Barham and Pykett* [1970] 1 All ER 502, 46 TC 461.
[65] *Simpson v John Reynolds & Co (Insurances) Ltd* [1975] STC 271, 49 TC 693, CA.
[66] [1979] *Simon's Tax Intelligence* 76.
[67] *IRC v Falkirk Ice Rink Ltd* [1977] STC 342, [1977] 3 All ER 844, 51 TC 42.
[68] [1975] STC 434, 52 TC 8.

reinforced by the decision in *Rolfe v Nagel*.[69] Here a payment made by one diamond broker to another, because a client had transferred his business, was held taxable. The facts were unusual in that the broker was unable to earn commission from a client until the client had been accepted as 'an active client', a process taking a number of years. Other facts supported this conclusion; thus, the two brokers agreed to accept whatever a third broker would think suitable and the sum, £15,000, was not paid until the client became 'active'.

The fact that these testimonial payments escape tax is consistent with the case law under ITEPA 2005/Schedule E. The payment may give rise to a capital receipt, however, and so be liable to CGT if it can be related to an asset.

21.5   Incidental Payments

A payment arising incidentally in the course of a trade may be a trading receipt even though it is not for the supply of the particular stock in which the trader actually trades; the recurrence of such transactions will make this conclusion more likely. The cases concern items which are used (or used up) in the running of the trade without being clearly either capital or trading stock. They arise in the course of the conduct of the business and, by and large, from that business being carried on in the ordinary way. Cases where payments for compensation have been treated as trading receipts (see §21.7) may be seen as further examples.

21.5.1 Investments of Spare Cash

Where a bank or insurance company invests spare cash in securities or shares on a short-term basis, profits on resale may be trading receipts of the bank or company.[70] However, such profits were held to be part of a separate trade when realised by another type of company.[71]

21.5.2 Foreign Exchange

Today, the special loan relationship regime applies to foreign exchange transactions by most companies subject to corporation tax;[72] this regime does not apply to the remaining companies or to those subject to income tax. This special regime ignores the distinction between income and capital but still asks whether a foreign exchange transaction is made in the course of trade. Most of the income tax case law concerns the distinction between income and capital.

Suppose that a trader (T) invests in foreign exchange which is later realised at a gain (or loss). Foreign exchange profits arising on capital account are capital and so not trading

---

[69] [1982] STC 53, 55 TC 585.
[70] *General Reinsurance Co Ltd v Tomlinson* (1970) 48 TC 81; see also *Nuclear Electric plc v Bradley* [1996] STC 405, 68 TC 670.
[71] *Cooper v C and J Clark Ltd* [1982] STC 335, 54 TC 670.
[72] CTA 2009, Pts 5–7. On swaps and 'non-corporates', see RI 263.

receipts.[73] However, in *Imperial Tobacco Co Ltd v Kelly*,[74] the company bought tobacco leaf in America and, to this end, bought dollars over the year. With the outbreak of the Second World War the company, at the request of the Treasury, stopped buying American leaf, and thereafter its dollars were acquired by the Treasury at a profit to the company. The Court of Appeal held this to be profit of the trade. It did not matter that the company did not carry on the trade of dealing in foreign exchange; what mattered was that the dollars had been bought as the first step in an intended commercial transaction. One can thus view the dollars as equivalent to raw materials. The Court left open the correctness of the earlier case of *McKinlay v HT Jenkins & Son Ltd*.[75] A firm of builders that intended to buy marble in Italy had bought lire for £16,500. The lira then rose in value against the pound and the holding was sold in order that a profit might be realised on the exchange. The sale price was £21,870, a net profit of approximately £6,700. The value of the lira then fell and the firm bought the required currency needed (£19,386), which sum was allowed as a deduction in computing the profits. Rowlatt J upheld the Commissioners' decision that the £6,700 was not taxable as a profit of the trade. Today, it seems likely that the profit would be taxable, either because the case cannot stand with the later decision of the Court of Appeal in *Imperial Tobacco*, or because the decision to withdraw the lire holding from the ambit of the trade may cause the rule in *Sharkey v Wernher*[76] to operate.

A trading profit is taxable only if it has arisen; in foreign exchange transactions the courts have distinguished conversion, which may cause a profit to arise, from mere translation, which does not. In *Pattison v Marine Midland Ltd*,[77] a bank raised a fund of dollars by way of loan and proceeded to lend dollars in the course of its banking business. When the original funding loan was repaid, the dollar had strengthened against sterling. The House of Lords held that the bank was not taxable on the sterling profit that arose on the withdrawal of the money from the bank's lending fund since the fund had never been converted into sterling and had been translated into sterling only for balance sheet (as distinct from profit and loss account) purposes. As the fund had never been converted into sterling, the money was like an asset held by the company, generating income by being hired out. The asset might be specific or, as in *Pattison v Marine Midland Ltd*, fungible. *Pattison v Marine Midland* and a revised Statement of Practice on matching transactions remain applicable for income tax.[78]

21.5.3 Contracts for Supply of Trading Stock

A profit arising on the disposal of a contract for supply of trading stock may be a trading receipt—provided it takes revenue form. In *George Thompson & Co Ltd v IRC*,[79] certain ships belonging to a shipping company had been requisitioned by the Australian Government.

---

[73] *Davies v Shell Co of China Ltd* (1951) 32 TC 133.

[74] [1943] 2 All ER 119, 25 TC 292; see also *Landes Bros v Simpson* (1934) 19 TC 62; and *O'Sullivan v O'Connor* [1947] IR 416.

[75] (1926) 10 TC 372.

[76] See below at §23.5.1.

[77] [1984] STC 10, 57 TC 219, HL; see Pagan [1984] BTR 161.

[78] SP 2/02 superseding SP1/87; for criticism of SP1/87, see Henbrey [1986] BTR 1.

[79] (1927) 12 TC 1091.

The company was left with contracts for the supply of coal in excess of its needs. It therefore transferred the benefit of the contract to another company—not by assignment, but by a transfer of the right to take delivery at a premium first of 6s (30p) a ton and then of 10s (50p) a ton. Although the company had only rarely sold coal previously, Rowlatt J had no difficulty in holding that this was a revenue receipt of the trade. The coal had not been bought as capital on capital account, but as a thing which the company needed to buy and use as consumable stores. The purchase of the coal had been arranged as a part of the company's business, so that it could not be treated as a separate business.

21.5.4 Know-how

The old cases on know-how distinguished payment for the use of know-how[80] from payment for disposing of know-how (eg when the know-how was disposed of along with other assets of the trade in a foreign country).[81] Where, however, the company had to supply know-how as a condition of entering into a trading arrangement in a country with which there had been no previous trade, the receipt was one on revenue account since the transaction did not materially affect the company's profit-making structure.[82] Statute (ITTOIA 2005, Part 2, Chapter 14) now provides that all payments in return for know-how are trading receipts if the know-how has been used in the trade and the trade is still carried on.[83] Where a person disposes of a trade or part of a trade, any consideration for know-how is generally dealt with as a payment for goodwill. However, this does not apply where the parties jointly elect otherwise, or if the trade was carried on wholly outside the UK (in which circumstances the old case law will apply).[84] Corporation tax has its own code in relation to intangibles.

21.6   Payments for Restriction of Activities or Sterilisation of Assets

A payment received as the price for a substantial restriction on a business or as compensation for the sterilisation of a capital asset is either not a trading receipt at all or is a capital receipt. However (as will be seen below at §21.7), a payment received as a surrogatum for trading profit is itself a trading receipt. The boundary between the two is easier to state than to apply.

In applying the two principles the court's task is complicated by the fact that a payment may come within this head even though the measure used by the parties to determine the level of payment is loss of profit—the measure does not determine the quality of the

---

[80] *Rolls Royce Ltd v Jeffrey* [1962] 1 All ER 801, 40 TC 443 (noted at [1961] BTR 263); *Musker v English Electric Co Ltd* (1964) 41 TC 556 (noted at [1963] BTR 306); and *IRC v Desoutter Bros Ltd* (1945) 29 TC 155, 162; but *cf IRC v Iles* (1945) 29 TC 225.

[81] *Evans Medical Supplies Ltd v Moriarty* [1957] 3 All ER 718, 37 TC 540.

[82] *Coalite and Chemical Products Ltd v Treeby* (1971) 48 TC 171; followed in *John and E Sturge Ltd v Hessel* [1975] STC 127 at 148, Walton J upheld [1975] STC 573 (CA); 51 TC 183, 208.

[83] ITTOIA 2005, s 193, ex TA 1988, s 531(1).

[84] ITTOIA 2005, ss 194 and 195(2), ex TA 1988, s 531(3).

payment. The leading modern authority is *Higgs v Olivier*.[85] Laurence Olivier, a well-known actor, had entered into a covenant that he would not, for a period of 18 months, appear as an actor in, or produce or direct, any film to be made anywhere by any other company. In return he received £15,000 from the company which had just made the film *Henry V*, in which he had starred. The reason for this deal appears from the case stated: 'He was quite a popular film actor, appearing in quite the ordinary kind of films, and the company thought that if he made a more ordinary film than *Henry V*, the public would go to that instead.' The covenant was made after the film had been completed and released in England, where it did not make much money; the film was hailed a success only after its release in New York. Thus, the covenant was separate from the original contract to make the film. The Special Commissioners held that the sum was paid to Olivier for refraining from carrying on his vocation, and was therefore a capital receipt. The Court of Appeal held that the payment was for a restriction extending to a substantial portion of professional activities open to him, and so was not a trading receipt; it may thus be seen as analogous to the capital receipt cases discussed above at §21.3. The Court also stressed that the covenant could not possibly be regarded as being in the ordinary run of the vocation of actors. By contrast, in *White v G and M Davies (a firm)*,[86] the receipt of a premium payment by a farmer under an EEC scheme was held to be a trading receipt. In return for the payment the farmer undertook not to sell milk products for four years and to ensure that dairy cattle accounted for no more than 20% of his herd. Browne-Wilkinson J distinguished *Higgs v Olivier* on the basis that the current restrictions controlled the way in which the taxpayer carried on his business, whereas this had not been so in the earlier case. A similar result was reached in *IRC v Biggar*.[87] Another way of distinguishing these cases is to stress that the covenant in *Higgs v Olivier* was most unusual.

The rule excluding such payments was applied in *Murray v Imperial Chemical Industries Ltd*,[88] where the company received a sum in return for agreeing not to trade in a certain country; this 'keep-out' payment was made under an agreement whereby the company allowed another firm to use its patent in that country. The payment was therefore held to be a capital receipt. However, the rule was not applied in *Thompson v Magnesium Elektron Ltd*,[89] where a company producing magnesium, and therefore needing chlorine, agreed to buy chlorine from another company and agreed not to manufacture chlorine or caustic soda (a by-product of the manufacture of chlorine) beyond its own needs. The company was to receive payments calculated on the amount of caustic soda it would have produced. It was held that the payments simply affected the price the company was paying for its chlorine. The payment was therefore held to be a revenue receipt. It would appear that if the

---

[85] [1952] 1 Ch 311, 33 TC 136. *The Times*, 23 November 1944, wrote: 'A great play has been made into a great film ... his white horse and his armour become him wonderfully ... [the film] is a test case to see whether there is a future in the cinema for Shakespeare and others of his cast and mould.'

[86] [1979] STC 415, 52 TC 597; the judge noted the unfairness of treating the payment as income of one year. Today, the farmer would be able to use the averaging regime (explained above at §12. 3) and would also benefit from the reduced rates of income tax in 1988.

[87] [1982] STC 677, 56 TC 254; another case in which *Higgs v Olivier* has been distinguished is *Tapemaze Ltd v Melluish* [2000] STC 189.

[88] [1967] 2 All ER 980, 44 TC 175. For Revenue practice, see note RI 52.

[89] [1944] 1 All ER 126, 26 TC 1.

payment had been a lump sum it would not have been a trading receipt,[90] since the form of the payment would have suggested that it was made for not making caustic soda, rather than for receiving chlorine.

21.7   Surrogata for Trading Profits—Compensation Payments

21.7.1 *Basic Rule; Holes*

A sum received in respect of trading stock is income whether it is the proceeds of sale, damages for breach of contract or for tort, or compensation on compulsory acquisition. The occasion for the receipt is immaterial. Lord Clyde illustrated this in *Burmah Steamship Co Ltd v IRC:*[91]

> Suppose someone who chartered one of the Appellant's vessels breached the charter and exposed himself to a claim of damages ... there could, I imagine, be no doubt that the damages recovered would properly enter the Appellant's profit and loss account for the year. The reason would be that the breach of the charter was an injury inflicted on the Appellant's trading, making (so to speak) a hole in the Appellant's profits, and damages recovered could not be reasonably or appropriately put ... to any other purpose than to fill that hole. Suppose on the other hand, that one of the taxpayer's vessels was negligently run down and sunk by a vessel belonging to some other ship owner, and the Appellant recovered as damages the value of the sunken vessel, I imagine that there could be no doubt that the damages so recovered could not enter the Appellant's profit and loss account because the destruction of the vessel would be an injury inflicted, not on the Appellant's trading, but on the capital assets of the Appellant's trade, making (so to speak) a hole in them, and the damages could therefore ... only be used to fill that hole.

The appellants had bought a ship which required extensive repairs before it could put to sea. The repairer was in breach of contract in that he did not complete the repairs until some five months after the due date. The appellant recovered £1,500 damages for late delivery, the sum being an estimate of the loss of profit. The sum was held to be income. The purchase price of the ship would, however, have been a capital item; it should follow, therefore, that had the purchaser arranged for a reduction in price, that reduction would have meant a lower capital price, and so would have been a taxable income receipt.[92] A payment for the use of a capital asset is a revenue receipt, but one for its realisation is a capital receipt.[93]

21.7.2 *Examples*

The rule that a surrogatum for loss of profit is an income receipt has been applied consistently in the following circumstances: where a company which had acquired a licence to take

---

[90] As in *Margerison v Tyresoles Ltd* (1942) 25 TC 59; see Hannan and Farnsworth, *The Principles of Income Taxation* (Stevens, 1952), 138.

[91] (1930) 16 TC 67, 71, 72.

[92] *Ibid*, 73, per Lord Sands. See also *Crabb v Blue Star Line Ltd* [1961] 2 All ER 424, 39 TC 482 (proceeds of insurance policy against late delivery held to be capital). On treatment of compensation payments for compulsory slaughter of farm animals, see ESC B11 and RI 235.

[93] *Greyhound Racing Association (Liverpool) Ltd v Cooper* [1936] 2 All ER 742, 20 TC 373.

Noel Coward's *Cavalcade* on tour in the UK received damages because a film of that show was released to the detriment of the profits of the tour;[94] where a firm that made steamships received damages from a purchaser in return for the cancellation of an agreement to buy ships;[95] where timber which was the trading stock of a company was destroyed by fire and sums were received from an insurance company equal to the replacement value of the timber;[96] and, similarly, where sums were payable under an insurance policy against loss of profit.[97] Payments by the state for loss of profit to an individual while serving on a jury or local authority are considered to be taxable receipts.[98]

Slightly less obviously, the rule has been applied where a company received a large sum under a life policy it held on one of its key employees,[99] the services of the employees being regarded as being as much part of the trading activities of the business as the goods which were its trading stock. The court noted that sums paid to induce the resignation of a director had been held to be income expenditure.[100]

A company whose jetty was damaged by the negligent navigation of a tanker was held taxable on the damages received in so far as they represented damages for loss of the use of the jetty during repairs, but not on the much larger sum needed to repair the jetty.[101] It is unclear what would have happened had there been no clear apportionment of the damages.

When the payment is a capital receipt, it may well give rise to CGT.[102] The rule that a surrogatum for loss of profit is an income receipt has also been applied to compensation for increased revenue expenditure.[103] Where both the lost profits and the damages are taxable, no account is taken of the tax situation in assessing the damages, save for the exceptional case where justice demands it.[104] Where damages are received for loss of profit, the fact that the damages are used to write down certain capital expenditure incurred during the contract is irrelevant; the payment is nonetheless an income receipt.[105]

21.7.3 Basis of Measure Does Not Determine Quality of Payment

There is no necessary relation between the measure used for the purpose of calculating a particular result and the nature of the figure arrived at by means of the application of

---

[94] *Vaughan v Archie Parnell and Alfred Zeitlin Ltd* (1940) 23 TC 505; criticised by Hannan and Farnsworth, *op cit*, 263–64. It follows that no deduction for tax may be made in assessing the damages (*Diamond v Campbell-Jones* [1961] Ch 22, [1960] 1 All ER 583).

[95] *Short Bros Ltd v IRC* (1927) 12 TC 955.

[96] *J Gliksten & Son Ltd v Green* [1929] AC 381, 14 TC 364.

[97] *R v British Columbia Fir and Cedar Lumber Co Ltd* [1932] AC 441; see also *Mallandain Investments Ltd v Shadbolt* (1940) 23 TC 367.

[98] RI 18.

[99] *Williams Executors v IRC* [1942] 2 All ER 266, 26 TC 23, distinguished in *Greycon Ltc v Klaentschi* [2003] STC (SCD) 360. It appears that in general it is Revenue practice not to treat lump sum proceeds as trading receipts if no claim was made to deduct the premiums as trading expenses. But it does not follow that the company can opt to have the proceeds treated as capital by not claiming relief for the premiums; the proper tax treatment of the proceeds must be considered on its own merits.

[100] *BW Noble Ltd v Mitchell* (1926) 11 TC 372.

[101] *London and Thames Haven Oil Wharves Ltd v Attwooll* [1967] 2 All ER 124, 43 TC 491.

[102] Under TCGA 1992, s 22; see *Lang v Rice* [1984] STC 172, CA.

[103] *Donald Fisher (Ealing) Ltd v Spencer* [1989] STC 256, 63 TC 168, CA.

[104] *Deeny v Gooda Walker Ltd* [1995] STC 439, 453; Potter J aff'd in the House of Lords on other grounds at [1996] STC 299.

[105] *IRC v Northfleet Coal and Ballast Co Ltd* (1927) 12 TC 1102.

that test. It is clear from the cases that a payment determined on the basis of loss of profit can be capital payment. In *Glenboig Union Fireclay Co Ltd v IRC*,[106] the taxpayer company (G) held leasehold rights in certain fireclay seams with the right to remove minerals. The seam at issue ran under the railway track of the Caledonian Railway Company (CalR). CalR obtained an interdict to prevent G from removing fireclay from the seam pending the hearing of its case against G, in which it claimed that although the lease granted the right to remove minerals, fireclay was not a mineral. CalR lost its case and then exercised its powers compulsorily to prevent G from exercising its rights. Eventually it was agreed that a large sum should be paid to G for loss of the fireclay. The House of Lords held that the sum was a capital receipt. The case concerned excess profits duty and it was the Revenue who argued that the receipt was capital.[107] The company argued that as that seam would have been fully worked out in two-and-a-half years, the sum paid was nothing but a surrogatum for profits lost. Lord Buckmaster regarded that argument as fallacious:[108]

> In truth the sum of money is the sum paid to prevent the Fireclay Company obtaining the full benefit of the capital value of that part of the mines which they are prevented from working by the railway company. It appears to me to make no difference whether it be regarded as the sale of the asset out and out, or whether it be treated merely as a means of preventing the acquisition of profit which would otherwise be gained. In either case the capital asset of the company to that extent has been sterilised and destroyed, and it is in respect of that action that the sum ... was paid.... It is now well settled that the compensation payable in such circumstances is the full value of the minerals that are left unworked, less the cost of working, and that is of course the profit that would have been obtained were they in fact worked. But there is no relation between the measure that is used for the purpose of calculating a particular result and the quality of the figure that is arrived at by means of the application of that test.

The payment was therefore held to be a capital receipt. Thus, compensation for the sterilisation of a capital asset is a capital payment; but this leaves the question, what is a capital asset?[109] In *Glenboig*, an item of fixed capital was sterilised. This must be distinguished from the prevention of the acquisition of profit.[110] Extraction industries have always been odd for tax purposes since the process of their trade turns fixed capital into circulating capital.[111] Thus, in *Glenboig*, had CalR accidentally destroyed the fireclay after it had been extracted, it would appear that the sums payable by way of damages would have been a trading receipt.

The House of Lords did not have to consider the correct tax treatment of the damages for wrongful interdict.[112] The Court of Session held that the sum was a capital receipt on the ground that it was the reimbursement of expenditure of a capital nature because it proved to be totally fruitless owing to the expropriation proceedings.[113] The parties settled this

---

[106] (1922) 12 TC 427, 464, HL, per Lord Buckmaster.

[107] The higher the company's profits before 1914, the lower the excess profits duty.

[108] (1922) 12 TC 427, 464.

[109] On goodwill as capital asset, see Lord Evershed MR in *Wiseburgh v Domville* [1956] 1 All ER 754, 758, 36 TC 527, 539.

[110] Eg, *Waterloo Main Colliery Co Ltd v IRC* (1947) 29 TC 235.

[111] *Taxes Commr v Nchanga Consolidated Copper Mines Ltd* [1964] AC 948, 964, [1964] 1 All ER 208, 212, per Lord Radcliffe.

[112] The amount payable to the fireclay company in respect of expenses of keeping the seam open but unused while the interdict prevented the company from working it.

[113] *British Insulated and Helsby Cables Ltd v Atherton* [1926] AC 205, 211, per Viscount Cave LC; *Southern v Borax Consolidated Ltd* [1940] 4 All ER 412, 23 TC 597.

aspect of their liability before going to the House of Lords. If this payment had been held to be a revenue receipt[114] the droll result would have been that: (a) the payment computed by reference to loss of profit was a capital payment, while the payment in this case, not so computed, but which was for loss of profit, was a trading receipt; and (b) a payment relating to a period of three years would be an income payment, whereas the payment in this case, relating to the two-and-a-half years it would have taken to exhaust the fireclay, was a capital payment. *Glenboig* was discussed in the 2007 case of *Able (UK) Ltd v HMRC*.[115] Here the taxpayer (A) received compensation for being excluded from the use of part of its land for three years. The land was first used for landfill tipping. W, a water company, sought to acquire part of the site compulsorily. A countered by seeking permission to use the site for the disposal of hazardous waste. Eventually this was granted and W withdrew its application. Compensation of just over £2m was agreed. The Court of Appeal held that the payment was neither for the realisation of the site nor its exhaustion, but was simply for the temporary loss of use—and therefore was income.

21.7.4 Contracts Relating to Structure of Business

Damages paid for breach of a contract to make good the loss of profit from that contract will usually be treated as income. It makes no difference what the importance of the contract is to the trade. However, it is necessary to distinguish profit-earning contracts from those relating to the whole structure of the profit-earning apparatus of the trade. In *Van den Berghs Ltd v Clark*,[116] the appellant company entered into an agreement with a competing Dutch company in 1912. The agreement provided for the sharing of profits, the bringing-in of any other margarine concerns they might acquire, and the setting-up of a joint committee to make arrangements with outside firms as to prices and limitation of areas of supply of margarine. The agreement was intended to last until 1926 at the earliest, with later variations extending that to 1940. The outbreak of the First World War upset the arrangements of the Dutch company, and eventually that company agreed to pay the appellant company £450,000 for cancelling the agreement. The House of Lords held that the sum was paid for loss of future rights under the agreement, which was a capital asset and therefore was a capital receipt. Lord Macmillan said:[117]

> The ... agreements which the Appellants consented to cancel were not ordinary commercial contracts made in the course of carrying on their trade; they were not contracts for the disposal of their products or for the engagement of agents or other employees necessary for the conduct of their business; nor were they merely agreements as to how their trading profits when earned should be distributed between the contracting parties. On the contrary the cancelled agreements related to the whole structure of the Appellants' profit making apparatus. They regulated the Appellants' activities, defined what they might and what they might not do, and affected the whole conduct of their business. The agreements formed part of the fixed framework within which their circulating capital operated; they were not incidental to the working of their profit making

---

[114] As suggested by Lord Clyde in *Burmah Steamship Co Ltd v IRC* (1930) 16 TC 67, 72; although in the *Glenboig* case Lord Clyde had thought it a capital receipt (1922) 12 TC 427, 450.
[115] [2007] EWCA Civ 1207, [2008] STC 134.
[116] (1935) 19 TC 390, HL.
[117] *Ibid*, 431, 432.

machine but were essential parts of the mechanism itself. They provided the means of making profits, but they themselves did not yield profits.

Sums paid on the variation of an agreement which relates to the whole structure of the profit-making apparatus are capital. In *Sabine v Lockers Ltd*,[118] the taxpayers held the main distributorship for the Austin motor company in the Manchester area; they were not allowed to enter into any agreement with any other manufacturer. Sums paid for variation of that contract were held to be capital receipts. The distributorship lasted only for one year, with a right of renewal for a further year, but there was reasonable prospect of further yearly renewals.

In both *Van den Bergh's Ltd v Clark* and *Sabine v Lockers Ltd* the agreements related to the framework of the company's business, rather than to the disposal of the company's products. It is less easy, but apparently not impossible,[119] for a contract of the latter type to be treated as a capital asset. However, the mere fact that traders arrange their work on the basis of a particular contract is insufficient to make that contract one relating to the structure of their business. Thus, a shipbuilding company may make only a few ships a year, but an order for a ship is a profit-yielding contract; damages for breach will therefore be an income receipt.[120]

21.7.5 Agency Contracts

The restriction, even though temporary, of profit-making apparatus is very different from the mere loss of trading opportunity which occurs when an agency contract on commission ends and a lump sum is received for the cancellation. At first sight it would seem that such contracts, producing income, must be capital assets,[121] but they are usually treated as revenue assets since their acquisition and replacement are normal incidents of the business. They are disposal contracts in that the company is disposing of services. Such contracts are not a capital assets, and the sums received will be taxed as mere trading receipts. In *Shove v Dura Manufacturing Co Ltd*,[122] Lawrence J gave three reasons why there was nothing of a capital nature about these contracts: 'No money was spent to secure it; no capital asset was acquired to carry it out; its cancellation was only an ordinary method of modifying and realising the profit to be derived from it.'

In *Kelsall Parsons & Co v IRC*,[123] the appellants commenced business in Scotland as manufacturer's agents and engineers in 1914, when one of their two agencies was for a firm in Birmingham making electric switch gear. A series of agency agreements was made with the firm, the last of which was for three years from 30 September 1932, but this was terminated by agreement on 30 September 1934, the firm agreeing to pay £1,500 compensation to the appellants. The Court of Session held that the sum was a trading receipt. It was true that

---

[118] (1958) 38 TC 120.
[119] Note Ungoed Thomas J in *John Mills Productions Ltd v Mathias* (1964) 44 TC 441, 453.
[120] *Short Bros Ltd v IRC* (1927) 12 TC 955; for a similar result for a film star, see *John Mills Productions Ltd v Mathias* (1964) 44 TC 441.
[121] *Anglo-French Exploration Co Ltd v Clayson* [1956] 1 All ER 762, 766, 36 TC 545, 557, per Lord Evershed MR.
[122] (1941) 23 TC 779, 783.
[123] (1938) 21 TC 608; applied in *Creed v H and M Levinson Ltd* [1981] STC 486, 54 TC 477; see also *Croydon Hotel and Lesure v Bowen* [1996] STC (SCD) 466.

the appellants had built up a considerable technical organisation to handle this particular agency agreement,[124] but that was insufficient to bring the facts within the principle in *Van den Berghs Ltd v Clark*. In reaching this conclusion it was important to Lord Normand and Lord Fleming that the agreement had only one year to run. As Lord Normand put it, this was not a case where 'a benefit extending over a tract of future years is renounced for a payment made once and for all'.[125]

In *Barr Crombie & Co Ltd v IRC*,[126] the appellants managed ships; 98% of their business came from an agreement with another company for a period of 15 years from 1936, which was terminated in 1942 when the shipping company went into liquidation. A large sum paid in respect of the eight years left of the agreement was held to be a capital receipt. Taking all the facts into account, Lord Normand considered that the effect on the company's structure and character was such as to bring the facts within *Van den Berghs Ltd v Clark*. Although the effect of the cancellation was to leave the company with practically nothing left of its business, the difficulty remains that *Barr Crombie* illustrates that the distinction between a contract which is merely one created in the ordinary life of the business and one which relates to its profit-making structure, may be a matter of degree rather than kind. It is possible to use dramatic language to show the importance of that degree, as Lord Russell did in *IRC v Fleming & Co (Machinery) Ltd*,[127] where he distinguished the situation in which the rights and advantages surrendered on cancellation were such as to destroy or materially cripple the whole structure of the recipient's profit-making apparatus, involving the serious dislocation of the normal commercial organisation and resulting, perhaps, in the cutting-down of staff previously required, from that in which the benefit surrendered was not an enduring asset and where the structure of the recipient's business was so fashioned as to absorb the shock as one of the normal incidents to be expected and where it appears that the compensation received is no more than a surrogatum for future profits surrendered.[128] These are, however, only explanations and illustrations. There was no reduction in the staff employed as a result of the cancellation of the agreement in *Van den Berghs Ltd v Clark*; but the fact that the workforce had to be reduced after the cancellation was insufficient to turn the compensation into a capital receipt in *Elson v James G Johnston Ltd*[129] In *Barr Crombie* itself, Lord Normand stressed that none of the factors which distinguished the case from *Kelsall, Parsons & Co v IRC* was conclusive of itself, but that the combination of such factors was.[130]

What *Barr Crombie* establishes is that compensation may be a capital receipt even though the contract is a disposal contract. However, there is also authority for the proposition that a pure disposal contract will not be a capital asset, no matter how big it is.[131] Therefore, it must be concluded that in *Barr Crombie* the contract was a capital asset primarily by

---

[124] 21 TC 608, 615.

[125] *Ibid*, 620.

[126] (1945) 26 TC 406. See also *California Oil Products Ltd v FCT* (1934) 52 CLR 28 (company formed to operate one agency and liquidated following its cancellation; compensation on cancellation was held to be a capital receipt).

[127] (1951) 33 TC 57, 63.

[128] *Ibid*, per Lord Russell.

[129] (1965) 42 TC 545.

[130] (1945) 26 TC 406, 412.

[131] *John Mills Productions Ltd v Mathias* (1964) 44 TC 441, 456, per Ungoed Thomas J.

reason of its duration and, because the business had been built around that contract, it was not a mere disposal contract.[132] The agency had been the company's principal asset since the trade commenced, so that it could not be said that its loss was a normal incident of the business. Further, the loss of the agency necessitated the complete reorganisation of the taxpayer's business, a reduction in staff and the taking of newer and smaller premises. Such a case must be distinguished from one in which the taxpayer is able to continue in exactly the same line of business as before, notwithstanding that his one source of income has ceased.[133]

21.7.6 Subsidies

Subsidies are treated on the same principles as compensation payments. The court looks to the business nature of the payments, and treats them as trading receipts at the time of payment if they were intended to be used in the business. Where a subsidy is paid in advance and may therefore have to be repaid, in whole or in part, the question is whether the payment is a loan or a receipt. Payments in the nature of a subsidy from public funds made to an entrepreneur to assist in the carrying on of the trade or business are trading receipts.[134] A subsidy which takes the form of a payment to bring the receipt for an item of trading stock product up to a certain level is clearly a trading receipt.[135] Similarly, payments to enable the trader to meet trading obligations are trading receipts when made; however, payments of unemployment grants to assist with a specific project of a capital nature have been held not to be trading receipts.[136] In general, a payment to maintain employment is neither clearly capital nor revenue.[137] The subsidy may come from another company. In *British Commonwealth International News Film Agency Ltd v Mahany*,[138] a payment to a subsidiary company as a supplement to its trading revenue and in order to preserve its trading stability was held to be a trading receipt.

21.8   Money Not Yet Belonging to Trader

At present, case law suggests that where a trader receives sums of money from customers on their behalf, the receipt is not a trading receipt and so is not to be brought into account.

---

[132] *Cf ibid*, 455, per Ungoed Thomas J.

[133] *A Consultant v Inspector of Taxes* [1999] STC (SCD) 64.

[134] *Pontypridd and Rhondda Joint Water Board v Ostime* [1946] AC 477, 489, 28 TC 261, 278, per Viscount Simon; see also *Poulter v Gayjon Processes Ltd* [1985] STC 174. ITTOIA 2005, s 107 (ex TA 1988, s 93) expressly makes grants under the Industrial and Development Act 1984 and similar Acts trading receipts unless clearly capital.

[135] *Lincolnshire Sugar Co Ltd v Smart* (1935) 20 TC 643, 667. See also *Higgs v Wrightson* (1944) 26 TC 73 (ploughing subsidies held to be trading receipts); *Burman v Thorn Domestic Appliances (Electrical) Ltd* [1982] STC 179, 55 TC 493.

[136] *Seaham Harbour Dock Co v Crook* (1930) 16 TC 333; as explained in *Poulter v Gayjon Processes Ltd* [1985] STC 174, 58 TC 350.

[137] *Ryan v Crabtree Denims Ltd* [1987] STC 402, 60 TC 183; although the judgment in this case focuses on the purpose for which the payment is applied, it is to be assumed that one looks first at the purpose for which the payment was made.

[138] [1963] 1 All ER 88, 40 TC 550, HL. *Cf Moss' Empires Ltd v IRC* [1973] AC 785, 21 TC 264.

This is the case even though the trade is carried on by a partnership and the sums held for the customers are allocated to the partners as a domestic arrangement for book-keeping purposes.[139] If, however, the sums originally repayable to the customers cease to be so by reason of the Limitation Act 1980, they become trading receipts of the period when the claims are barred.[140] In such cases the quality and nature of the receipt are fixed when the money is received, but the timing issue is different.[141] It remains to be seen whether accounting standards will be developed to change these rules, and whether the courts will accept such standards as overriding these legal principles.

The question whether the money belongs to the customers or to the trader must depend on the facts. Where a sum is paid to a trader by way of part payment, it is still the customer's money; whereas if the money is paid by way of deposit, it is irrecoverable by a purchaser in default and so becomes the property of the trader immediately on payment. A deposit is therefore a trading receipt.[142] In *Pertemps Recruitment Partnership v R and CCC*,[143] customers had mistakenly overpaid the taxpayer who had transferred the sums to the balance sheet and then released them to the profit and loss account. Arnold J held (para 83) that the sums were trading receipts of the taxpayer; they were property of the taxpayer even though the customers had a claim for restitution, and so distinguished *Morley v Tattersall*.

21.9 Payment Falling Within Different Part/Schedule or Case

In the days of the Schedules, income correctly taxed under another Schedule could not be taxed under Schedule D, Case I, and so could not enter into the computation. Thus, rental income in respect of land in the UK was assessable under Schedule A,[144] and employment income, pension income and social security income were taxed under Schedule E. This effect is preserved by ITTOIA 2005, Part 2, Chapter 1 (section 4), which gives priority to ITTOIA 2005, Part 3 and ITEPA 2003 in these cases.

A line must also be drawn between trading receipts and annual payments falling within ITTOIA 2005, Part 5, Chapter 7; a payment which forms part of the trading activities of the recipient cannot be pure income profit in his hands and so cannot fall within Part 5, Chapter 7. A payment incorrectly received under deduction of tax must form part of the profits,[145] while one that was correctly so received cannot be a trading receipt.[146] ITTOIA 2005 does not need to say anything about this. If, however, a particular receipt could be taxed under both Case I and another Case, it could not be assessed to tax twice. The

[139] *Morley v Tattersall* [1938] 3 All ER 296, 22 TC 51 (the limitation period did not begin to run in this case in respect of any of the payments: 29 TC 274, 284); applied in *Anise Ltd v Hammond* [2003] STC (SCD) 258.
[140] *IRC v Jay's the Jewellers Ltd* [1947] 2 All ER 762, 29 TC 274.
[141] *Tapemaze Ltd v Melluish* [1999] STC (SCD) 260.
[142] *Elson v Price's Tailors Ltd* [1963] 1 All ER 231, 40 TC 671.
[143] [2011] STC 1346.
[144] See below at §25.1; see also *Lowe v JW Ashmore Ltd* [1971] 1 All ER 1057, 46 TC 597 (sales of turf by farmer taxable under Case I not Sch A); noted at [1970] BTR 416.
[145] See below at §27.5.
[146] *British Commonwealth International Newsfilm Agency Ltd v Mahany* [1963] 1 All ER 88, 40 TC 550.

Revenue could override the taxpayer's choice.[147] ITTOIA 2005 provides its own priority rules for the other parts of the Act—Part 3 (section 258), Part 4 (sections 359 and 360) and Part 5 (section 619)—which should resolve most problems. But one should not forget the warning in section 2(3) about the relevance of 'other rules of law'. Where dividends or other distributions are received by a trader dealing in investments, those should be taxable under Part 4, Chapter 3 and only under that Part. However, since 1997 statute has provided that they are to be taxed only under Part 2—this was introduced so as to prevent any right to claim repayment, or make any other use, of any tax credit.[148]

21.10 Valuing the Receipt: Market Value

In deciding the amount to be included as a trading receipt, regard must be had to the rules substituting market value for any price agreed between the parties, especially the transfer pricing provisions[149] and the rule in *Sharkey v Wernher* (see below at §23.5.1). Under the transfer pricing rules, an arm's length value must be substituted for the price agreed between the parties. These rules were extended to purely domestic transactions in 2004—in response to ECJ decisions that these broke the non-discrimination articles of what is now the TFEU.[150] The general view is that these rules do not apply to income tax but only to corporation tax, and it is for this reason that they are discussed below at §72.4. In any event they do not usually apply to small or medium-size enterprises.[151] Such enterprises may elect irrevocably to be subject to these rules, and the Revenue may direct that a medium-size enterprise apply them.[152]

21.11 Adjustment Income

Adjustment income arises under ITTOIA 2005, Part 2, Chapter 17 when there is a change in the accounting basis on which the profits of the trade or profession are calculated. This must be distinguished from a change in accounting date (above §20.4). The change must be either a relevant change of accounting approach, or a change in the tax adjustment applied (section 227(4)–(6)). Both the old basis and the new must be in accordance with the law

---

[147] *Liverpool and London and Globe Insurance Co v Bennett* [1913] AC 610, 6 TC 327; for Revenue powers under self-assessment, see TMA 1970, s 28A(7A) and FA 1998, Sch 18, para 84.

[148] ITTOIA 2005, s 366(1), ex TA 1988, s 95, as amended in 1997. On previous law, see speech of Viscount Simonds in *Cenlon Finance Ltd v Ellwood* [1962] 1 All ER 854, 40 TC 176; criticised at [1962] BTR 320 and [1963] BTR 133; and *FS Securities Ltd v IRC* [1964] 2 All ER 691, 41 TC 666, HL; noted at [1964] BTR 53 and [1964] BTR 281.

[149] Taxation (International and Other Provisions) Act (TIOPA) 2010, Pt 4, ex TA 1988, s 770A and Sch 28AA.

[150] The case was *Lankhorst-Hohorst* (C-324/00) [2002] ECR I-11779, in which German thin capitalisation rules were held to be a restriction on the free movement of capital (now Art 63 TFEU), and the freedom to provide services (now Art 56 TFEU).

[151] TIOPA 2010, s 167, ex TA 1988, Sch 28A, para 5B. See also FA 2004, ss 30–33; and Vander Wolk [2004] BTR 465–68.

[152] TIOPA 2010, s 168, ex TA 1988, Sch 28AA, para 5C.

and practice of that period (section 227(1)). Any adjustment income, as calculated under the rules, is treated as arising on the last day of the first period to which the new basis applies. The rules do not apply to income subject to the remittance basis.

A negative amount is called an adjustment expense; in making the calculation certain expenses previously brought into account are excluded (section 234). The adjustment expense is treated as arising on the last day of the first period to which the new basis applies. The general timing rule does not apply to all assets. If the asset is stock, work in progress or depreciation, the change of basis will be deferred until the asset is realised or written off (section 235). Further special rules apply if there is a change from a realisation basis to mark to market; here there is also an election to spread the adjustment income over six years. Similarly, a barrister or advocate is given a right to spread when making an election under ITTOIA 2005, section 160 (below §23.1.3). As seen at §21.1.2.2 above, the adoption of UITF 40 on the recognition of revenue from service contracts and SSAP 9 gives rise to such 'adjustment income', which may thus be spread over six years.[153]

21.12   Reverse Premiums

Reverse premiums,[154] known in Canada by the more appropriate name of 'lease induce-ment payments',[155] were held to be capital receipts, and so non-taxable, in the 1998 Privy Council's decision in *CIR v Wattie*.[156] This decision produced a lack of symmetry, in that such payments would often be made by property developers so that the sums paid would be deductible, while the sum received would not be taxable. However, there were many instances in which this lack of symmetry did not arise.[157] The decision was superseded by FA 1999, Schedule 6 (now, for income tax purposes, ITTOIA 2005, Part 2, Chapter 6, sections 99–102). Such payments are now taxable—regardless of their treatment in the hands of the person making the payment. The rule catches payments and other benefits. Examples of other benefits, which must be paid to X, are contributions to X's costs in fitting out the building or relocating a business, and taking over X's liabilities under an old lease of the premises.[158] The payment must be made by way of inducement in connection with a property transaction, ie one under which X, or a person connected to X, becomes entitled to an estate or interest in, or a right in or over, land.[159] The payment must come from G, the grantor of the estate, interest or right, or other persons connected with G. The purpose is to catch the reverse premium paid when the lease is granted; it is not intended to catch a payment by a lessee to someone to persuade that person to take over a lease when the lease

---

[153] FA 2006, Sch 15.
[154] See Challoner [1999] BTR 350.
[155] See, generally, Carr (1998) 46 *Can Tax Jo* 953.
[156] [1998] STC 1160. The decision is equally applicable to UK tax (see *ibid*, 1169j, 1170e, per Lord Nolan). See Coull [1999] BTR 117.
[157] Eg, *Southern Counties Agricultural Society v Blackler* [1999] STC (SCD) 200.
[158] Inland Revenue Notes to Finance Bill 1999, para 31. ITTOIA 2005, s 99, Conditions A and C, ex FA 1999, Sch 6, para 1. On connected person status, see ITTOIA 2005, s 103, referring to ITTOIA 2005, s 878(5), ex TA 1988, s 839.
[159] ITTOIA 2005, s 99, Condition B.

subsequently becomes onerous.[160] However, the Revenue view is that Schedule 6 catches a premium payable to an assignee where it is, in substance, an inducement to take a grant of a lease dressed up as an assignment.[161]

The tax treatment of X depends on X's tax status. If a trading purpose exists, the reverse premium enters the profits of that trade, profession or vocation.[162] In any other circumstances, it may be treated as a property business receipt under ITTOIA 2005, Part 3.[163] In any event, the sum is treated as a revenue receipt.[164] Under the principles of commercial accounting, the receipt will be spread over the period of the lease or, if shorter, until the first rent review.[165] However, if the arrangements are not at arm's length, ie some or all of the parties to the relevant arrangements are connected persons and the terms of those arrangements are not such as would reasonably have been expected if those persons had been dealing at arm's length,[166] the whole sum must be taxed at once or, as the statute more precisely puts it, in the first relevant period of account.[167] Therefore, if the trade has not yet begun, it will be treated as taxable in the first period of account of that trade. Where the premium has been taken into account in calculating the allowable expenditure for capital allowance purposes, by reducing the allowable expenditure, it is not chargeable under these rules. This is to prevent what would, in effect, be a double charge.[168] Taxability is excluded if the transaction relates to an individual's only or main residence,[169] or if the matter already falls within the regime governing sale and leaseback.[170]

---

[160] Inland Revenue Notes to Finance Bill 1999, para 33. The Revenue view is that a rent-free period is another reverse premium, but that no notional charge arises.

[161] *Ibid.*

[162] ITTOIA 2005, s 101(1), ex FA 1999, Sch 6, para 2(2).

[163] ITTOIA 2005, s 101(3) referring to s 311, ex FA 1999, Sch 6, para 2(3).

[164] ITTOIA 2005, s 101(1), ex FA 1999, Sch 6, para 2(2).

[165] Inland Revenue Notes to Finance Bill 1999, para 32.

[166] ITTOIA 2005, s 102, ex FA 1999, Sch 6, para 4.

[167] ITTOIA 2005, s 102(3), ex FA 1999, Sch 6, para 3.

[168] ITTOIA 2005, s 100(1), ex FA 1999, Sch 6, para 5; see also Inland Revenue Press Release 19 May 1999, [1999] *Simon's Weekly Tax Intelligence* 934.

[169] ITTOIA 2005, s 100(2), ex FA 1999, Sch 6, para 6.

[170] ITTOIA 2005, s 100(3) and (4), ex FA 1999, Sch 6, para 7 (and below at §22.7).

22

Business Income—Part IV: Trading Expenses

22.1 Introduction

The right to deduct expenses in computing taxable profit rests not on any express statutory provision but on the absence of any express prohibition; the right to deduct is inferred from the fact that it is the *profit* of a trade that is taxed, not the receipts.[1] UK tax law has proceeded on its usual pragmatic basis.[2] ITTOIA 2005 carries on this process by gathering together the various restrictions (Chapter 4) and special reliefs (Chapter 5) and preceding them with basic rules (Chapter 3), which include some rules on deductions. Section 31 invents two categories of rules and says that any 'relevant permissive rule', ie a rule expressly giving a right to deduct, has priority over any 'relevant prohibitive rule', ie a rule expressly prohibiting a deduction; however, each category is refined. The first category refers to

---

[1] For corporation tax, TA 1988, s 817 formerly prohibited all deductions save those expressly authorised. This provision was repealed by CTA 2009, on the grounds that it was unnecessary and no longer required. According to the explanatory notes, change 101 '[t]his change is in taxpayers' favour in principle. But it is expected to have no practical effect as it is in line with generally accepted practice.' Note also that ex TA 1988, s 74 (now ITTOIA 2005, s 34 and CTA 2009 s 54) does not authorise deductions but forbids them. On the difficulties in this formulation, see Romer LJ in *Anglo Persian Oil Co Ltd v Dale* [1932] 1 KB 124, 144, 16 TC 253, 272.

[2] For a discussion of the relationship between the deductibility of expenses and consumption, see Edgar in Krever (ed), *Tax Conversations* (Kluwer, 1997) 309–27.

Chapter 5 (except sections 60–67), Chapter 11 (specific trades) and Chapter 13 (unremittable income). So a rule for a specific trade in Chapter 11 will allow a deduction even though it is capital. The 'second' category is defined in abstract terms, but there is also express exclusion of sections 48 (car hire) and 55 (crime-related payments). So the crime-related payment rule in section 55 will override a rule expressly granting a deduction. The rules on rent-a-room relief and foster care relief, which can apply to trading income but not only to such income, are found in Part 7, Chapters 1 and 2.[3]

As ITTOIA 2005 states in section 27, there is no requirement that an amount must actually have been paid. However, case law shows the expense must have been incurred. An expense cannot be deducted if it may be recalled at will or recouped from another person.[4] In *Rutter v Charles Sharpe & Co Ltd*,[5] the company made payments to trustees of a fund held for the benefit of its employees. It was held that the company could not deduct these payments since it could, at any time, wind up the scheme and then enforce the return of the payments. The mutuality principle may lead to the same conclusion where a payment is made to a trade association—as opposed to a company.[6] Another problem arises where the trader purchases supplies from a subsidiary or related company and a part of the profit accruing to the other company will be returned to the trader. In *IRC v Europe Oil (NZ) Ltd*,[7] the profit accruing would return to the trader as tax-free dividend and the price was fixed in advance to ensure the exact return to the trader. The Privy Council held that the expenditure was not incurred exclusively in the purchase of trading stock and, under the (sensible) tax system prevailing in that country, an apportionment was allowed. However, all depends on the facts. In a later case[8] the Privy Council held that the relations between the trader and the supplier were such that the former had no legal right to the profit, and so the whole sum was allowed to be deducted.

The right to deduct is limited by a number of case law rules developed from the statute and/or the courts' notion of the meaning of profit:

(1)   the expense must have been incurred for business purposes—the principle of remoteness (§22.2);
(2)   it must have been incurred only for business purposes—the principle of duality (§22.2);
(3)   it must have been incurred for the purpose of earning profit—the rule in *Strong & Co of Romsey Ltd v Woodifield* (§22.3);
(4)   it must be an expense of earning profit and not a division of profit (§22.3.2);
(5)   it must be of an income nature as opposed to a capital nature, ie it must be a revenue expense (§22.4);
(6)   it must not be barred on grounds of public policy (§22.5); and
(7)   it must not be expressly barred by some statutory provision (§22.6).

---

[3]   ITTOIA 2005, ss 23, 792 and 813.
[4]   *Bolton v Halpern and Woolf* [1979] STC 761, 770; reversed for other reasons at [1981] STC 1453, 53 TC 445.
[5]   [1979] STC 711, 53 TC 163.
[6]   The Revenue will grant a complete deduction in return for taxing the association; see *Simons Taxes*, B.3.1441.
[7]   [1971] AC 760.
[8]   *IRC v Europa Oil (NZ) Ltd* [1976] STC 37.

Previously, the courts stated that, in satisfying all these rules, regard must be had to established commercial accounting principles.[9] Today, the role of accounting practice is less clear since many of these rules are now treated as matters of law rather than of fact, and so potentially outside section 25 and Lord Bingham's dictum in *Gallagher v Jones* (above §21.1). However, evidence of accounting practice is no doubt admissible.

Finally, it should also be noted that FA 2013, section 18 and Schedule 5 introduced new Chapter 5A into Part 2 of ITTOIA 2005 permitting individuals and partnerships of individuals the option of choosing to use fixed expenses when calculating their business profits.[10] The rules in ITTOIA 2005, sections 94B to 94I cover mileage claims, use of home for business and where premises are used as both a home and as business premises. The rates for mileage claims mirror the rates already used for employees, ie 45p for the first 10,000 miles and 25p after that for a car. The allowable expenses for use of home for business are quite low, ranging from between £10 and £26 per month depending upon the number of hours worked. As a result this is unlikely to be a popular option with taxpayers. The relatively high fixed sum non-business use amounts where premises are used as both a home and as business premises would seem to make this option similarly unpopular.

22.2   Wholly and Exclusively—Remoteness and Duality

Some 30 years ago, one leading writer argued that the rules on deducting expenses were obscure, inconsistent and generally inequitable, while the other thought that the law was clear-cut, uniform and generally inequitable.[11] Case law before (or since) has not improved matters. Rules (1) and (2) listed in §22.1 above are derived from the general rule in ITTOIA 2005, section 34(1) (ex TA 1988, section 74(1)(a)), which prohibits the deduction of expenses not being money wholly and exclusively laid out for the purposes of the trade. Rule (1) states that an expense which is not for the purposes of the trade is not deductible; rule (2) states that an expense which is partly for the purposes of the trade and partly for other purposes similarly is not deductible. Rule (2) is thus little more than an *a fortiori* example of rule (1). Where the liability is non-deductible for duality, a payment to be rid of the liability will be similarly non-deductible. In *Alexander Howard & Co Ltd v Bentley*,[12] the taxpayer company paid a lump sum to be rid of a contingent liability to pay an annuity to the widow of its governing director; the annuity payments would not have been deductible since not paid wholly and exclusively for trade purposes but rather as an adjunct to shares; it followed that the lump sum payment was similarly not deductible.

A dictum based on a concession in a case suggests that the word 'wholly' may refer to the quantum of the money expended, while the word 'exclusively' refers to the motive or

---

[9] For commentary see Gravestock [2013] BTR 401.

[10] *Usher's Wiltshire Brewery Ltd v Bruce* [1915] AC 433, 468, 6 TC 399, 436, per Lord Sumner.

[11] See the exchange between Kerridge [1986] BTR 36 and Ward [1987] BTR 141. See also Klein (1966) 18 *Stanford Law Review* and Halperin (1973) 122 *University of Pennsylvania LR* 859 for traditional perspectives; and Griffith (1994) 41 *UCLA LR* 1769 for quasi-optimal analysis. For a discussion of Griffith and similar authors, see Edgar in Krever (ed), *op cit*, 293 at 351–57.

[12] (1948) 30 TC 334.

object accompanying it.[13] However, taken literally, this would mean that the purchase of two different items at one time and by one payment would not be deductible at all even though the bill clearly listed the two items and gave separate prices. This cannot be (and is not) correct, and it is doubtful, therefore, whether the concession should have been given such credence.[14]

22.2.1 Four Rules from Three Cases

The case law is dominated by three decisions: *Mallalieu v Drummond*,[15] *Vodafone Cellular Ltd v Shaw*[16] and *McKnight v Sheppard*.[17] *Mallalieu v Drummond*, a House of Lords decision, is the leading authority in this area, the main speech being by Lord Brightman; it suggests three rules. *Vodafone Cellular Ltd v Shaw*,[18] a Court of Appeal decision with the main judgment by Millett LJ, glosses all three rules and adds a fourth. *McKnight v Sheppard*, a House of Lords decision, appears, like *Vodafone*, to confine some of the possibilities aroused by *Mallalieu v Drummond*. The rules which emerge seem to be as follows, with (a) those laid down by the House of Lords in *Mallalieu v Drummond* and (b) the *Vodafone* glosses:

(1) (a) Whether the expenditure was incurred exclusively to serve the purposes of the trade is a question of fact; (b) the purpose must be to benefit the trade rather than the trader.

(2) (a) In deciding the taxpayer's purpose, the court is not confined to conscious purposes; (b) save in obvious cases which speak for themselves, the court must determine the taxpayer's subjective intentions at the time of the payment, but the court must also have regard to those consequences which are so inevitably and inextricably involved in the payment that, unless merely incidental, they must be taken to be a purpose for which the payment was made.[19] It is clear that (b) places significant limits round the potential scope of (a); these limits were reinforced in *McKnight v Sheppard*.

(3) (a) One must distinguish a second 'purpose' behind the expenditure, which will disqualify the deduction, from an 'effect' of that expenditure, which will not disqualify the expenditure even though some benefit accrues to the taxpayer, T; (b) the benefit to T will be an 'effect' rather than a purpose if it is 'a consequential and incidental effect'.

(4) *Vodafone* only: the question does not involve an inquiry of T whether T consciously intended to benefit a trade or personal advantage by the payment. The primary

---

[13] Romer LJ in *Bentleys, Stokes and Lowless v Beeson* [1952] 2 All ER 82, 85, (1952) 33 TC 491, 503. Romer LJ pointed out that this was conceded, not argued.

[14] See Kerridge [1986] BTR 36.

[15] [1983] 2 AC 861, [1983] STC 665, HL. For Australian development, see *Magna Alloys and Research Pty Ltd* (1980) 80 ATC 4542; and Parsons, *Income Taxation in Australia* (Lawbook Co, 1985), 6.2–6.16.

[16] [1997] STC 734, CA.

[17] [1999] STC 669.

[18] [1997] STC 734, CA.

[19] Some of these phrases derive from the speech by Lord Oliver in *MacKinlay v Arthur Young* [1986] STC 491, 504, 62 TC 704, 757.

inquiry is to ascertain what was the particular object of T in making the payment; it is then for the Commissioners to classify that purpose as business or personal.

The following text will relate these rules to the facts of the cases.

Mallalieu v Drummond

In this case a barrister sought to deduct revenue expenses incurred in connection with dark clothes she had bought for wearing in court, such clothes being required by court etiquette. The undisputed evidence was that her expenditure was motivated solely by thoughts of court etiquette and not at all by mere human thoughts of warmth and decency. Counsel for the taxpayer disclaimed any reliance on his client's dislike of black clothing, so the question was reduced to this: if clothing is purchased for use only on business occasions and such clothes are only so used (or for proceeding to and from work), is the expense deductible? The House of Lords said 'No'.

Rule (1) and (2). In addition to the business purpose there were the other purposes of warmth and decency. As Lord Brightman said, 'I reject that notion that the object of a taxpayer is inevitably limited to the particular conscious motive in mind at the moment of expenditure'.[20]

Rule (3). Earlier cases had decided that the courts could ignore an incidental benefit to the taxpayer. This was, in effect, reformulated by Lord Brightman in his distinction between the object of the taxpayer in incurring the expenditure and the effect of the expenditure:[21] 'Expenditure may be made exclusively to serve the purposes of the business, but it may have a private advantage. The existence of that private advantage does not necessarily preclude the exclusivity of the business purpose.'[22] His Lordship gave an example of a medical consultant flying to the south of France to see a patient; if a stay in the south of France was a reason, however subordinate, no deduction could be claimed; whereas if it were not a reason but an unavoidable effect, the deduction could be made.

While there may be substance in what the House of Lords said, there are uncomfortable questions of degree to be resolved. Thus, Lord Brightman would have allowed expenditure by a self-employed nurse on clothing dictated by the practical requirements of the act of nursing and the maintenance of hygiene, and even that by a self-employed waiter on the provision of 'tails', this being the particular design of clothing required in order to obtain engagements.[23] For similar reasons, presumably, the Revenue were disposed to concede expenditure on wig, gown and bands in the instant case. While the borderline nature of these cases may be clear, the reasoning behind that status is not. Lord Brightman could not have meant that the nurse's uniform has no purpose of warmth or, at least, decency. What he probably meant was that the warmth/decency purpose is so incidental as to qualify as an effect rather than a purpose.

---

[20] [1983] STC 665, 673b, 57 TC 330, 370.
[21] For early worries, see [1983] BTR 199.
[22] [1983] STC 665, 669f, 57 TC 330, 366.
[23] *Ibid*, 673e, 370.

Vodafone Cellular Ltd v Shaw [24]

In Vodafone, the taxpayer company, T, was part of a group of companies. An expense was incurred by T which benefited two other companies in the group. The Commissioners decided that the directors wanted to benefit the trading entity which the three companies represented, and had given no thought to the position of the two subsidiaries. However, the purpose of the directors was to benefit the trading position of the whole group; the interests of all three companies were considered together. Under the absurd and unjust rules stemming from the duality principle, an expense incurred by one group company to benefit its own trade only is deductible in full; by contrast, an expense incurred for the trade of itself and of two sibling companies is not deductible at all. The Commissioners, and Jacob J, concluded that the purpose was to benefit all three companies and not just T, so that none of the expenditure was deductible. This was reversed by the Court of Appeal on the ground that the real purpose was to benefit only the taxpayer company's own trade, and that the Commissioners had drawn the wrong conclusions from their own findings.

McKnight v Sheppard

The most recent decision, *McKnight v Sheppard*,[25] accepts the *Vodafone* approach to *Mallalieu v Drummond*. A taxpayer, S, incurred legal expenditure in proceedings before his professional body (the Stock Exchange). If found guilty he could have been suspended from carrying on his profession, or expelled altogether. The Commissioner found that the sole purpose was the preservation of his trade, and that considerations of personal reputation were effects rather than purposes. The House of Lords agreed and held that the legal expenditure was deductible because the expenditure was for the purpose of enabling S to carry on business. The question whether there was secondary purpose of protecting S's name and reputation was classified by Lord Hoffmann as an effect and not as a purpose, the basis for which was the finding by the Commissioner. As Lord Hoffmann put it, after referring to Lord Brightman's example of the medical consultant:[26]

> If Lord Brightman's consultant had said that he had given no thought at all to the pleasures of sitting on the terrace with his friend and a bottle of Côtes de Provence, his evidence might well not have been credited. But that would not be inconsistent with a finding that the only object of the journey was to attend upon his patient and that personal pleasures, however welcome, were only the effects of a journey made for an exclusively professional purpose. This is the distinction which the commissioner was making and in my opinion there is no inconsistency between his conclusion of law and his findings of fact.

The case depends crucially on the findings of fact. Had the Commissioner found that concern for personal reputation had been a purpose and not an effect, it is unlikely that the appeal would have succeeded. Why decency and clothing should be subconscious purposes in *Mallalieu v Drummond*, while personal reputation was here only an effect is unclear; this lack of clarity is institutionalised by treating it as a matter of fact.[27]

---

[24] [1997] STC 734 (CA).
[25] [1999] STC 669 agreeing with CA [1997] STC 684.
[26] [1999] STC 669, 673f.
[27] See also *Taylor v Clatworthy* [1996] STC (SCD) 506 (lending money on terms which were very attractive to the lender, eg 33.3% interest, not just to secure appointment but also to make good investment) and *Executive*

22.2.2 Dissection (Permissible) Contrasted with Apportionment (Not Permissible)

The duality rule does not permit the apportionment of expenses incurred for dual purposes. However, it does not prevent the dissection of expenditure to discover parts which are wholly and exclusively for business purposes and so which are deductible; this is now recognised by ITTOIA 2005, section 34(2). If a professional person uses a room at home as an office, the expenses of that office are deductible, and this will be so even though the electricity, council tax and other bills apply to the house as a whole and have to be dissected in order to discover the part attributable to the office.[28] In these cases, the sum is dissected in order to discover that part which is wholly for business purposes, wholly being a matter of quantum; the test of exclusive business purpose is then applied to that part. Therefore, a telephone bill may be dissected to see which calls were business; however, the limits of the dissection rule were shown by a Schedule E case in which the courts refused to allow the deduction of part of the three-month rental payment.[29] Dissection received its most generous application in *Copeman v William J Flood & Sons Ltd.*[30] An unreasonable amount of remuneration had been paid to two employees—both children of the firm's managing director—but the court allowed the employer firm to deduct that part which would have been reasonable. There could have been no dissection in *Bowden v Russell and Russell,*[31] where T had a dual purpose in crossing the Atlantic, since the precise point in mid-Atlantic at which the solicitor ceased to be travelling for personal reasons and began to travel for business reasons could not be identified.

22.2.3 Commentary

The present position is unsatisfactory, since there is clear evidence from the 1950s that the Revenue did, in practice, allow an apportionment in a situation similar to *Bowden v Russell and Russell* (above), provided there was a genuine business element, as would be the case with the running and garage expenses of a car used partly for personal and partly for business purposes.[32] Whether the Revenue practice, backed by the courts, has become more severe since then is unclear.[33] The problem of devising an acceptable way to distinguish business expense from other expenditure is not unique to the UK.[34] Moreover, the literature

---

Network v O'Connor [1996] STC (SCD) 29, 35 (even if not a conscious motive, it was inescapably an object for incurring the expense—dictum not ratio).

[28] *Gazelle v Servini* [1995] STC (SCD) 324.

[29] *Lucas v Cattell* (1972) 48 TC 353.

[30] [1941] 1 KB 202, 24 TC 53. Other excessive remuneration case include *Stott and Ingham v Treharne* (1924) 9 TC 69 and *Horton v Young* (1971) 47 TC 60; but contrast *Earlspring Properties Ltd v Guest* [1993] STC 473. On whether tax systems can/should police levels of remuneration by limiting deductions, see Stabile (1998) 72 *St John's Law Review* 81.

[31] [1965] 2 All ER 258, 42 TC 301.

[32] See Report of the Committee on the Taxation of Trading Profits, Cmnd 8189 (1951), 157 and 161 and Royal Commission Cmnd 9474 (1955), paras 123, 129, 133.

[33] See Kerridge [1986] BTR 36, 43. See also the discussion of *McLaren v Mumford* [1996] STC 1134 by Grierson [1996] BTR 627 and Freedman [1996] BTR 634.

[34] On the United States, see Andrews (1972) 86 *Harvard Law Review* 309; Halperin, *op cit*; Klein (1966) 18 *Stanford Law Review* 1099; and the immensely enjoyable 'Life is a Beech' by Newman (1988) 38 *Tax Notes* 501; see also Ault *et al*, *Comparative Income Taxation*, 2nd edn (Kluwer, 2004), 204–19.

shows that the problem is a difficult one.[35] The harshness of the UK rule may be softened by allowing apportionment, but this still leaves the decision on which basis the apportionment should be made.[36] Another problem is devising a system of rules which are efficient in the economic sense, ie rules which encourage efficient mixed expenditures, and discourage those which are inefficient.[37]

A solution may be to separate personal benefit from work benefit. However, Kerridge shows that benefit is a slippery concept. Thus, lunch with a client may yield three types of benefit to the taxpayer: a work benefit (how much they would have spent if they had only professional purposes in mind); a pleasure benefit (how much they would have been willing to spend if they had only been looking after themselves); and a necessity benefit (how much extra they had to spend over the normal cost of sandwiches). Adding these together may give a total figure greater than the actual cost. Thus, if the lunch cost £20, the three benefits might be worth £24, £4 and £2 respectively. Of these, the necessity benefit is the easiest to measure, the others being significantly more subjective. Rules might be devised which allowed T to deduct the amount by which the expenditure (£20) exceeded the non-work benefit (£4 + £2), ie £20—£6 = £14, sums up to the equivalent of the work benefit (£20) or a proportion which the work benefit (£20) bore to the total benefit (£30), ie £13.33.

These three rules allow apportionment. However, Kerridge suggests other possible rules. Thus, (a) any deduction of spending with mixed purposes could be forbidden (the UK rule), (b) the deduction of the entire expense if the work benefit alone (£24) would justify the expense (£20) could be permitted, or (c) a deduction in full could be allowed whenever the work benefit (£24) exceeded the non-work benefit (£6). These rules avoid apportionment problems at the expense of sharp distinctions at the margins.

Efficient taxation analysis begins by stating that a mixed expenditure is efficient if, in a non-tax world, the cost of the expenditure is less than the sums of its business and personal values. In a world with taxes, it is necessary to examine after-tax costs and after-tax values. Under an ideal tax structure, only expenditures which are efficient under a pre-tax basis would be made. Inefficient expenditures could be made unless the system taxes the elements of personal consumption. This approach has been explored by Griffith[38] in ways which are initially similar to Kerridge. Under this approach, full deductibility of the expense is permitted, but tax is then charged on the basis of personal consumption, or the excess, if any, of cost (£20) over business value (£24) or proportion which the business (£24) bears to personal values (£6). Griffith then looks at the differences between the methods with regard to (a) information requirements and (b) distribution effects, before turning, in a highly sophisticated analysis, to ask which may be the most efficient. The Griffith solutions make better sense in the context of the US tax system, with its global concept of income.

---

[35] Kerridge [1986] BTR 36 and Ward [1987] BTR 141.
[36] Eg, *Fletcher v FCT* (1991) 22 ATR 613.
[37] Griffith (1994) 41 *UCLA LR* 1769.
[38] *Ibid.*

22.2.4 Examples

22.2.4.1 Food, Drink and Conferences

The subconscious purpose test causes problems with residential conference expenses. The costs of food and lodging must be incurred at least partly because one has to eat and sleep[39] (or are these just unavoidable effects of the initial decision to attend the conference?). *Watkis v Ashford Sparkes & Harwood*[40] was the first case on this issue after *Mallalieu v Drummond*. Nourse J held that the cost of overnight accommodation at the annual conference of a firm was deductible, and that no distinction could be drawn between the costs of accommodation and the costs of food and drink consumed. This was despite the fact that in the same case expenditure on meals taken at a time when the taxpayers would normally have eaten was held to be incapable of being incurred exclusively for business purposes. The moral seems to be that if a taxpayer wishes to secure deduction of meal expenditure, he must also have accommodation expenses. The test in such cases is whether the expense is incurred as a business person or as a human being. In reliance on this approach, Nourse J also held that the cost of modest lunches eaten by solicitors during office meetings was not deductible. He specifically held that certain older cases (*Edwards v Warmsley, Henshall & Co*[41] and *Bowden v Russell and Russell*)[42] were unaffected by *Mallalieu v Drummond*. In *Edwards*, a partner in a firm of chartered accountants was allowed to deduct costs of travel, accommodation and a conference fee when representing the firm at the International Congress of Accountants in New York. In *Bowden*, the sole partner of a firm of solicitors was not allowed to deduct the cost of attending meetings of the American Bar Association in Washington and the Empire Law Conference in Ottawa. The evidence against him was so overwhelming that the Revenue argued it both on the basis of remoteness and on duality.[43]

22.2.4.2 Groups of Companies

As the *Vodafone* case above shows, the duality rule has been invoked by the Revenue not only to prevent a deduction incurred for a personal purpose, but also where the other purpose is the trading purpose of another trade, even where the trade is carried on by another group member.[44] This means that a company will be unable to deduct expenditure incurred partly for its own purposes and partly for the trading purposes of another group

---

[39] See also *Caillebotte v Quinn* [1975] STC 265, [1975] 2 All ER 412, 50 TC 222 (the extra cost incurred because the taxpayer had to eat while on business away from home was not deductible). See also Shaller 24 *Duqesne LR* 1129.

[40] [1985] STC 451, 58 TC 468; followed in *Prior v Saunders* [1993] STC 562, 66 TC 210. On acceptance of this decision and practice for lorry drivers, see RI 51.

[41] [1968] 1 All ER 1089, 44 TC 431.

[42] [1965] 2 All ER 258, 42 TC 301.

[43] He went in an unofficial capacity and was accompanied by his wife, although no claim was made in respect of those expenses attributable to her. He admitted that there were also holiday and social purposes for the trip. He argued that his attendance was in order to maintain the firm's efficiency, to obtain new clients and to improve the office organisation. See, further, Kerridge [1986] BTR at 52.

[44] [1995] STC 353; see also *Garforth v Tankard Carpets Ltd* [1980] STC 251, 53 TC 342; the same point arose in *Lawson v Johson Matthey plc* [1990] STC 149, 158–59, 65 TC 39, 52–53, but was not argued on appeal; see also *Watney Combe Reid and Co v Pike* [1982] STC 733, 57 TC 372. For an exceptional case the other way, see *Robinson v Scott Bader Co Ltd* [1980] STC 241, [1980] 2 All ER 780, 54 TC 757.

member. This unfortunate result may be avoided by establishing that while the expenditure benefits both companies, nonetheless the purpose was to benefit only one.[45] This was achieved in *Vodafone*, where the expense was incurred for the trading entity as a whole without giving conscious thought to the position of individual companies.[46] It may also be avoided by sharing the costs with the other companies so that each pays its own share; however, the basis on which that division should be made is not clear. Expenditure for the purpose of two separate trades of one person is, in theory, deductible from neither,[47] but it is unlikely that this absurd result would be applied by the Revenue or by the courts. Where one company in a group takes over trading stock from another company in the group, the costs of the acquisition are deductible even though the group or the other company may have motives of its own; the motive of the expenditure-making company is determinative.[48]

In *Interfish v HMRC*,[49] the Court of Appeal upheld the decisions of the Upper and First-tier Tribunals that sponsorship payments made by a fishing business to a rugby club were not wholly & exclusively for the purpose of the fishing business's trade. Although this case is not strictly a 'group of companies' case, the central issue is reminiscent of the central issue in *Vodafone*. In *Interfish*, the CA and both Tribunals concluded that the payments made by the fishing business were intended to benefit another entity, namely the rugby club. It was this finding of duality of purpose that justified denying the deduction under the wholly & exclusively test. The decision of Moses LJ is well worth reading, as a cogent (and entertaining) review of the authorities on purpose.

22.2.4.3 Charity Not Business

Expenditure in the form of subscriptions to charity is the generous act of good citizens. There is, therefore, a duality of capacity about the payment—part as trader, part as citizen.[50] However, whether the explanation is remoteness or duality, such expenditure is rarely deductible.[51] The same reasoning bars payments for political purposes.[52] Business gifts other than to charity have their own non-deduction rules under ITTOIA 2005, sections 45 and 47 (see below at §22.6.3).

22.2.4.4 Trade Associations

Subscriptions to trade associations are, according to case law, deductible to the extent that the expenditure by the association would have been deductible if incurred directly by the

---

[45] As in *Robinson v Scott Bader Co Ltd*, above.

[46] For a perhaps optimistic view of the case, see Saunders [1997] BTR 404.

[47] See Walton J in *Olin Energy Systems Ltd v Scorer* [1982] STC 800 at 820, 58 TC 592 at 612.

[48] *Torbell Investments Ltd v Williams* [1986] STC 397.

[49] [2014] EWCA Civ 876. Permission to appeal to the SC was refused.

[50] See Romer LJ in *Bentleys, Stokes and Lowless v Beeson* [1952] 2 All ER 82, 85, 33 TC 491, 505. For another possible reason, see discussion on division of profits below at §22.3.2.

[51] *Bourne and Hollingsworth Ltd v Ogden* (1929) 14 TC 349 (annual subscription to hospital used by employees deductible in practice, but two, special, large subscriptions not deductible); *Hutchinson & Co (Publishers) Ltd v Turner* [1950] 2 All ER 633, 31 TC 495. See former ESC B7 (1994) *Simon's Direct Tax Service*, Division H4.2 and former ESC B32 (1994) on expenses of running a payroll-giving scheme.

[52] *Joseph L Thompson Ltd v Chamberlain* (1962) 40 TC 657; cf *Morgan v Tate and Lyle Ltd* [1954] 2 All ER 413, 35 TC 368 (discussed below at §22.4.3).

subscriber.[53] In practice, however, the Revenue grant complete deduction for the subscription in return for the taxability of the association.[54] Contributions to approved local enterprise agencies are deductible by express provision.[55]

22.2.4.5 Medical Expenditure

At first sight medical expenditure is incurred to put right that which is medically wrong, and so not for business purposes; the subconscious medical purpose cannot be ignored. In *Murgatroyd v Evans-Jackson*,[56] the taxpayer, a trademark agent, fell ill and was treated in a private nursing home for five weeks, his reason for selecting private care being that he required a separate room from which to conduct his business, a facility not available under the National Health Service. He claimed only 60% of the cost, a matter which admitted duality of expenditure; but Plowman J also held that had the taxpayer claimed the whole of his costs, he would still not have been able to deduct the expense, since one reason for going into the nursing home was to receive treatment. However, it might be argued that since the choice was not between a greater and a lesser expense but between no expense at all under the National Health Service and this expense as a private patient, the whole expense was in fact for business purposes. Moreover, the decision does cause some fine distinctions. Thus, if the agent had had a bed in a room with other patients but had also rented another room as an office, the rent of that other room would have been deductible. *Murgatroyd v Evans-Jackson* must be distinguished from a case where the operation itself is for business purposes.[57] In the unusual case of *Parsons v Revenue and Customs Commissioners*,[58] a stunt performer in the entertainment industry was allowed to deduct certain medical expenses related to a knee and back injury, but not expenses related to his general health and fitness.

22.2.4.6 Travelling and Commuting Expenses

Travelling expenses provide further examples of the general rule.[59] Travel from home to one's main place of work is not deductible, even though one works at home. In *Newsom v Robertson*, expenses incurred by a barrister in travelling from home to chambers were not deductible, even though the Revenue had granted a 'study allowance'.[60] The reason for the distinction is that, although the barrister works in both places, it is clear that the profession is carried on in chambers; chambers, not home, provide the base of operations, and so travel from chambers to home in the evening is not motivated wholly and exclusively by the desire to do more work. The expense is thus, at least in part, a personal living expense and not a

---

[53] *Lochgelly Iron and Coal Co Ltd v Crawford* (1913) 6 TC 267.

[54] See *Simon's Direct Tax Service*, B3.1441. On the non-taxability of the association, see *Joseph Adamson & Co v Collins* [1938] 1 KB 477, 21 TC 400.

[55] ITTOIA 2005, s 82, ex TA 1988, s 79.

[56] [1967] 1 All ER 881, 43 TC 581; noted by Wallace [1967] 285; and see *Norman v Golder* [1945] 1 All ER 352, 26 TC 293; see also Kerridge [1986] BTR 41.

[57] See Pennycuick J in *Prince v Mapp* [1970] 1 All ER 519, 525, 46 TC 169, 176.

[58] [2010] UKFTT 110 (TC).

[59] *Sargent v Eayrs* [1973] STC 50, [1973] 1 All ER 277, 48 TC 573; see Macdonald [1978] BTR 75, 83. The matter is also discussed by Smith [1977] BTR 290, [1978] BTR 203 and [1981] BTR 211.

[60] *Newsom v Robertson* [1952] 2 All ER 728, 33 TC 452; the allowance would have been granted under TA 1988, s 74(c).

business expense.⁶¹ Similarly, solicitors are not able to deduct the cost of travelling from home to office. However, if a solicitor had two offices, and went to the nearer office first, then to the further office and then back to the nearer office, he would be allowed to deduct both journeys between the offices.⁶² Such a conclusion rests on the fact that the office is a place where the profession is carried on. Where a dental surgeon visited his laboratory (L) on his way through from his home (H) to his surgery (S), he was not allowed to deduct the cost of travel from L to S.⁶³ The purpose of the expenditure was to get from H to S; the fact that it also enabled him to stop at L could not affect that purpose.

A person's home may be a 'base of operations'. If so the costs of travel from the base of operations to places of work are deductible, as in the case of *Horton v Young* involving an independent contracting bricklayer.⁶⁴ However, when the occupation is itinerant only within a certain area but the taxpayer lives outside that area, the costs of travel, at least as far as the border of that area, would not be deductible.⁶⁵ The use of phrases such as 'base of operations' is attractive but must not get in the way of applying the actual words of the statute. A milkman's 'base of operations' would be the roads along which he had to deliver his products and would not include the home from which he had to travel to the depot to pick up his stock; in any event, it was easier to say that his travel from home to the depot was not wholly and exclusively for business purposes.⁶⁶

An important recent case is *Samad Samadian v Revenue & Customs*.⁶⁷ The First-tier Tribunal denied the taxpayer, a self-employed consultant geriatrician, his claim for business travel between his home (accepted as a place of business) and two hospitals where he saw patients (other places of business). In the Tribunal's view, this case could be distinguished from *Horton v Young* because '[p]art of his object in making those journeys must, inescapably in our view, be in order to maintain a private place of residence which is geographically separate from the two hospitals. It follows that even though we find he has a place of business also at his home, his travel between his home and those two locations cannot be deductible, on the basis of the reasoning in *Mallalieu [v Drummond]*.' The decision was upheld by the Upper Tribunal, with Sales J. agreeing with the FTT's analysis and, in so doing, relying heavily on *Newsom v Robertson*. This case suggests it will be more difficult for self-employed professionals and traders who use their home as a place of business to deduct travel expenses on journeys between their home and other fixed and predictable places of business. There is some evidence that this marks a tightening of HMRC practice, though it may be that the older case law can justify the stance in *Samadian* and that nothing has really changed: it has merely been explained. The case also has the effect of more closely aligning the rules on travel for the self-employed with the statutory scheme applicable to employees.⁶⁸

---

⁶¹ [1952] 2 All ER 728, 730, 33 TC 452, 462, per Somervell LJ.
⁶² *Ibid*, 731, 464, per Denning LJ.
⁶³ *Sargent v Barnes* [1978] STC 322, [1978] 2 All ER 737, 52 TC 335.
⁶⁴ *Horton v Young* [1971] 3 All ER 412, 47 TC 60; see Paterson [1971] BTR 376.
⁶⁵ [1971] 2 All ER 351, 356, per Brightman J.
⁶⁶ *Jackman v Powell* [2004] EWHC ChD; [2004] STC 645.
⁶⁷ [2014] UKUT 13 (TCC).
⁶⁸ For more commentary see the case note by Freedman & Loutzenhiser [2014] BTR 248.

The case of *Huhtala v HMRC* [69] is a rare example where the taxpayer incurred travel expenses with a private aspect but was able to successfully clear the wholly & exclusively threshold, in part at least. In *Huhtala* a freelance journalist decided to write a book about living on a boat, and sought to deduct some of his expenses of transporting and mooring his boat in France (where he lived with his wife) in computing his income from self-employment. He was unsuccessful before the First-tier Tribunal, but the Upper Tribunal directed a re-hearing in light of some confusion over the evidence supporting the expenses. Before a new panel, the First-tier Tribunal accepted that the expenses of transporting the boat to France and craning it into place were allowable expenses of his self-employment as a writer, but that expenses relating to ownership of the boat more generally had a dual purpose and were not allowable. In finding that the sole purpose of moving the boat was to write the book, 'even if it might be said that the effect of so doing had the incidental effect of conferring some benefit on the Appellant', the tribunal was influenced by the fact that he could otherwise have remained living in his London flat and kept the boat moored in Southampton. This led the tribunal to conclude that an analogy could be drawn with hotel and travel expenses incurred on short business trips. As he would have owned a boat for professional and personal use (this one or his former, smaller one) irrespective of the move to France, however, ownership costs such as ongoing mooring and insurance charges were not allowable.

22.2.4.7 Miscellaneous Personal (Non-deductible) Expenses

These include, for example, the revenue costs of a pied à terre over the office[70] and sums paid to children in the nature of pocket money rather than payments for services on the taxpayer's farm.[71] Expenditure on a child's nanny is not deductible; expenditure for secretarial services is deductible. Payments to a nanny for secretarial services are therefore deductible, where the facts are established.[72] There have, as yet, been no cases on the deduction of educational expenses.[73] Cases have been decided primarily under TA 1988, section 74(1)(a) (now ITTOIA 2005, section 34(1)(a)), although many were argued under the now repealed section 74(1)(b) in the alternative. There is no reported case of an expense being deductible under section 74(1)(a) but not under section 74(1)(b).

22.2.5 *Purposes and Partnerships*

Since, in English tax law, a partnership is not a taxable entity, it follows that the purposes to be investigated are those of the partners. This can seem unreal where a firm has, for example, 98 partners, and it is therefore tempting to equate such partnerships with companies, which have separate legal personality. Provided that temptation is resisted, it will follow that expenditure incurred to reimburse a partner for the costs of removing personal belongings, when moving the place of work from one part of the country to another at the request of

---

[69] [2012] UKFTT 79 (TC).

[70] *Mason v Tyson* [1980] STC 284, 53 TC 333.

[71] *Dollar v Lyon* [1981] STC 333, 54 TC 549; see also *Earlspring Properties Ltd v Guest* [1993] STC 473, 67 TC 259.

[72] RI 82. On childcare costs, see also Heen (1995) 13 *Yale Law and Policy Review* 173.

[73] See Davenport (1992) 42 *Case W Res LR* 793 and McNulty (1973) 61 *California LR* 1.

the other partners, will not be deductible. The House of Lords so held in *MacKinlay v Arthur Young McClelland Moores & Co.*[74] Logic does not require the non-deductibility of payments in return for goods or services supplied by the partner to the partnership. So, where P, the partner, has granted the partnership a lease of property owned by P, there is no reason why the rental payments should not be incurred wholly and exclusively for business purposes;[75] they will, of course, be taxed in the hands of landlord P under ITTOIA 2005, Part 3.

22.3   Expenditure Must be Incurred for Purpose of Earning Profits (The Davey Dictum)

In *Strong & Co of Romsey Ltd v Woodifield*,[76] Lord Davey said that '[i]t is not enough that the disbursement is made in the course of or arises out of or is connected with the trade or is made out of the profits of the trade. It must be made for the purpose of earning profits.' This famous gloss on the statute seems to have little effect in the practice of the Revenue, but enables the Revenue to grant, by concession, that which ought to be deducted as of right. The taxpayer company's business included both brewing and inn-keeping. A chimney at one of its inns fell and injured a guest. The guest sued and recovered damages of £1,490, which the company sought to deduct in computing its profits. Today the case is remembered principally for Lord Davey's dictum. However, for Lord Loreburn and the other members of the House (but not for Lord Davey) the critical provision was what is now ITTOIA 2005, section 34(1)(b) (ex TA 1988, section 74(1)(e)) which prohibits the deduction of any loss not connected with the trade, profession or vocation. Whether the expense is barred by section 34(1)(a) or (b) is, in one sense, immaterial: the expense may not be deducted. It has been pointed out that there is no case in which it has been distinctly held that an expenditure which satisfies (a) has not passed (b).[77]

In an unhappily apt phrase, Lord Loreburn said that losses could not be deducted 'if they fall on the trader in some character other than that of trader'. He considered that the loss fell on the trader in its character as householder, not as trader. It may be supposed that one reason why this decision has not been reversed is that businesses now insure their premises, such premiums being deductible.[78] The fineness of the distinction inherent in the House of Lords' approach may be seen from two examples given by Lord Loreburn:[79]

Losses sustained by a railway company in compensating passengers for accident in travelling might be deducted. On the other hand if a man kept a grocer's shop, for keeping which a house is

---

[74] [1989] STC 898, HL; reversing [1988] STC 116, 62 TC 704, CA.

[75] *Heastie v Veitch & Co Ltd* [1934] 1 KB 535, 18 TC 305; see also Lord Oliver in *MacKinlay v Arthur Young* [1989] STC 898, 905, 62 TC 704, 755.

[76] [1906] AC 448, 453, 5 TC 215, 220. This decision was based largely on what is now TA 1988, s 74(e) (see below at §22.6.1), but is generally treated as an authority on TA 1988, s 74(a) (eg *Morgan v Tate and Lyle Ltd* [1954] 2 All ER 413, 35 TC 367; see below at §22.4.3). For another case exploring the relationship between s 34(1) (a) and (b), see the judgment of Lightman J in *McKnight v Sheppard* [1996] STC 627, but note reversal for other reasons in [1997] STC 846 and [1999] STC 669.

[77] *McKnight v Sheppard* [1997] STC 846, 851, per Nourse LJ.

[78] *Usher's Wiltshire Brewery Ltd v Bruce* [1915] AC 433, 6 TC 399.

[79] *Ibid*, 452, 419.

necessary, and one of the window shutters fell upon and injured a man walking in the street the loss arising thereby ought not to be deducted.

Not only were these examples unclear, but they could be made to suggest that deduction should have been allowed in that case. First, it is not clear what point was being made. On the one hand, the example of the grocer's house was reasonably clear: if the house was separate from the shop then there is a distinction between trading expenses and personal expenses, and the same might be true if the premises were all in one and the shutter fell off the residential part of the premises. If, however, the point was the distinction between trading and personal expenses, then surely the expense should have been deductible in the instant case.

However, if the distinction was between trading and house holding (between, at that time, Schedule D, Case I and Schedule A), that suggests a very restricted scope to be given to the example of the railway company, and could mean that the company could deduct expenditure for damages where the engine was driven negligently with a resulting accident, but not if injury occurred by a piece of station platform giving way. What would happen if there were a defect in a piece of static equipment, such as a signal, is, again, unclear. Lord James expressed doubts about the application of the principle to the inn customer, but would have had no doubts about the non-deductibility of an injury to a stranger walking down the street outside the inn. Such a distinction seems quite incredible today. In *Icebreaker 1 LLP v Revenue and Customs Commissioners*,[80] the taxpayers were seeking to deduct sums as trading expenses on the basis that they were incurred for the purposes of their trade of film distribution. Vos J held that a large part was not so spent because it was actually used for investment and security; some of the balance, however, was deductible. The case has interesting things to say on when one can look at the uses to which the money was put to answer the question of original purpose.

22.3.1 Examples of Sums Satisfying Test

The test is relatively easy to satisfy: sums spent for the purpose of earning profit will be deductible even though no profit is expected that year;[81] moreover, since the test is one of purpose, the sums will be deductible even though no profits accrue at all.[82] Losses incurred which are incidental to the carrying-out of the business are similarly deductible.[83] Damages for libel may be deductible when the libel is published in the course of a newspaper business; such damages must be distinguished from those payable for a libel not incidental to the business[84] and from penalties imposed by a court or professional tribunal.[85] Penalties,

---

[80] [2010] UKUT 477 (TCC), [2011] STC 1078.
[81] *Vallambrosa Rubber Co Ltd v Farmer* (1910) 5 TC 529; *James Snook & Co Ltd v Blasdale* (1952) 33 TC 244. On timing, see below at §23.3.2.
[82] *Lunt v Wellesley* (1945) 27 TC 78.
[83] *Golder v Great Boulder Proprietary Gold Mines Ltd* (1951) 33 TC 75. A sum paid in settlement of a civil claim in connection with the formation of a company was held to be deductible because it was not paid for any proven infraction of the law. On losses resulting from the collapse of BCCI, see Inland Revenue interpretation RI 57.
[84] *Fairrie v Hall* (1947) 28 TC 200.
[85] *IRC v Von Glehn & Co Ltd* [1920] 2 KB 553, 12 TC 232. *McKnight v Sheppard* [1999] STC 6769; the taxpayer did not appeal against this part of the judgment of Lightman J ([1996] STC 627). On Canadian experience, see Krasa (1990) 38 *Can Tax Jo* 1399; see also below at §22.6.

fines and interest charges in respect of the VAT legislation are expressly non-deductible (section 54). In Australia, sums lost in an armed robbery were deductible because the banking of takings was part of the operations of the business.[86] Damages for wrongful dismissal of employees are, in practice, allowed, although this is hard to reconcile with Lord Davey's dictum. Legal expenses are also deductible even though not for the direct purpose of earning profits, provided they are incurred in the running of the business.[87] Advertising expenses, although originally in doubt,[88] are now clearly deductible,[89] as are sponsorship costs, provided, in practice, that the sole purpose is to provide the sponsor with a benefit commensurate with the expenditure.[90] In *Knight v Parry*,[91] a solicitor was not allowed to deduct the costs of defending (successfully) an action in which professional misconduct and breach of a former contract of employment were alleged. The court held that the sums were spent, at least in part, to ensure that the solicitor was not precluded from carrying on his practice, and this was not the same as expenditure referable to the carrying-on of that practice. This was criticised by Lightman J in *McKnight v Sheppard*.[92]

The principle of deductibility has become so wide that the dictum in *Strong & Co of Romsey Ltd v Woodifield* should either be repealed or be regarded as having force only in the light of the frequently-quoted statement of Viscount Cave LC:

> [A] sum of money expended, not of necessity and with a view to a direct and immediate benefit to the trade, but voluntarily and on the grounds of commercial expediency, and in order indirectly to facilitate the carrying on of the business, may yet be expended wholly and exclusively for the purposes of the trade.[93]

The Davey gloss on the statute seems to have relatively little overall effect, but is still capable of biting at times. Its repeal was recommended by the Tucker Committee and the Royal Commission.[94] ITTOIA 2005 says nothing about it. However, Lord Radcliffe once said that he did not know of a wider criterion that would not be vulnerable in other ways and that the phrase had become part of our income tax language;[95] he might have added that it had also become part of some Commonwealth statutes.[96]

---

[86] *Charles Moore and Co (WA) Pty v FCT* (1956) 95 CLR 344.

[87] See *Spofforth and Prince v Golder* [1945] 1 All ER 363, 26 TC 310; see also the judgment of Lightman J in *McKnight v Sheppard* [1996] STC 627, but note reversal for other reasons at [1997] STC 846 and [1999] STC 669.

[88] See Kelly CB in *Watney & Co v Musgrave* (1880) 1 TC 272, 277.

[89] *Morley v Lawford & Co* (1928) 14 TC 229.

[90] HL Written Answer, 26 October 1987, vol 489, col 405. If the taxpayer enjoys ballooning, does this enable his company to deduct the sponsorship costs of a balloon journey across the Atlantic? What if he is a sole trader?

[91] [1973] STC 56, 48 TC 580.

[92] [1996] STC 627, 675. This issue was not addressed by the Court of Appeal [1997] STC 846 or House of Lords [1999] STC 665.

[93] *British Insulated and Helsby Cables Ltd v Atherton* [1926] AC 205, 211.

[94] Report of the Committee on the Taxation of Trading Profits, Cmnd 8189 (1951), §§151–154; and *Royal Commission on the Taxation of Profits and Income*, Final Report, Cmnd 9474 (1955), §128, the latter stating that 'it is extremely difficult to give it any concrete meaning'.

[95] *IRC v Dowdall O'Mahoney and Co Ltd* [1952] 1 All ER 531, 542 and 33 TC 259, 285.

[96] Eg, Canada: see *Royal Trust v MNR* [1957] DTC 1055; and Australia: *Charles Moore and Co (WA) Pty v FCT* (1956) 95 CLR 344.

22.3.2 *Expenditure Not Division of Profits*

A sum paid in the course of earning a profit is clearly distinct from a distribution of the profit made. A dividend by a company or a payment under a profit-sharing arrangement is a distribution of profit made and not an expense of earning it;[97] by contrast, a payment of interest will usually be a deductible expense. The question whether a payment is one of interest or a distribution of profits is one of substance.[98]

The rule has been applied to render non-deductible certain payments by a company purporting to be by way of remuneration to directors or employees. Therefore, remuneration based on a percentage of profits (deductible) must be distinguished from a distribution of profits (non-deductible). While a resolution at an annual meeting to pay a bonus as an appropriation of profit will be conclusive that it is just that (and so no-deductible),[99] the absence of such a resolution does not make it deductible.[100] Excessive remuneration has generally been dealt with under the 'wholly and exclusively' rule, but this rule could have been applied instead. This rule also bars a deduction for reserves for future expenditure.[101]

22.3.2.1 Partnerships

Payments by a partnership to its employees will be treated as deductions, but the division of profits between partners must be just that, and no payment to a partner in return for services can qualify as a deductible emolument.[102] A partnership may deduct the cost of the salary of an employee, but not the share of profits accruing to a partner. However, rent paid by the partnership to a partner is deductible, unless excessive.[103] A payment towards a partner's personal removal costs, being personal in nature, cannot be deducted.[104]

22.3.2.2 The TOTE

The present rule was applied to prevent the deduction of sums paid out of the totalisator fund (TOTE) to racecourse owners to assist in improving amenities at racecourses, and to provide subsidies to owners and trainers.[105] The distinction inherent in the rule is a fine one, but turns on the precise definition of the trade. The trade was that of running totalisators at racecourses and the expenditure in question was not incurred for the purpose of that trade.

---

[97] See *Eyres v Finnieston Engineering Co Ltd* (1916) 7 TC 74; *Utol Ltd v IRC* [1944] 1 All ER 190.

[98] *Walker v IRC* [1920] 3 KB 648.

[99] As in *Pegg and Ellam Jones Ltd v IRC* (1919) 12 TC 82.

[100] See Lord Maughan in *Indian Radio and Cable Communications Co Ltd v IT Commr Bombay* [1937] 3 All ER 709, 713–14; and *British Sugar Manufacturers Ltd v Harris* [1938] 2 KB 220, 21 TC 528. See also *Union Cold Storage Co Ltd v Adamson* (1931) 16 TC 293; *Overy v Ashford Dunn & Co Ltd* (1933) 17 TC 497.

[101] *Edward Collins & Sons Ltd v IRC* (1925) 12 TC 773.

[102] Salaried partners are, in practice, treated as employees, not partners.

[103] *Heastie v Veitch & Co* [1934] 1 KB 535, 18 TC 305.

[104] *MacKinlay v Arthur Young McClelland Moores & Co* [1989] STC 898, 62 TC 704.

[105] *Young v Racecourse Betting Control Board* [1959] 3 All ER 215, 38 TC 426.

22.3.2.3 Taxes

The rule has also been applied to prevent the deduction of taxes on profits, whether imposed by the UK[106] or by some foreign government.[107] However, other taxes may be deductible. Thus, business rates[108] may be deductible, as may road licences and stamp duty,[109] in all instances depending upon the actual circumstance of the case. In *Harrods (Buenos Aires) Ltd v Taylor-Gooby*,[110] the taxpayer company operated in Argentina and was liable to an annual local tax levied on the capital of the company. The court held that the tax was deductible, since it was not a tax that depended upon the company having earned any profits but was simply an essential cost of trading in that country. The actual circumstances may show that the particular tax is a capital expense, in which case it will not be deductible.[111]

22.3.2.4 Costs of Tax Appeals

More controversially, the rule has been applied to prevent the deduction of expenses incurred by a company in appealing, successfully, against an assessment to tax on profits. The expense of preparing the documents needed to be filed under the Companies Acts would clearly be deductible, as would the preparation of accounts for internal management.[112] However, as Lord Simonds put it in *Smith's Potato Estates Ltd v Bolland*:[113]

> What profit he has earned he has earned before ever the voice of the tax-gatherer is heard. He would have earned no more and no less if there was no such thing as Income Tax. His profit is no more affected by the exigibility of tax than is a man's temperature altered by the price of a thermometer, even though he starts by haggling about the price of it.

As a matter of practice, the Revenue do allow the costs of preparing the income tax return, but not additional accountancy expenses incurred as a result of an investigation revealing discrepancies where negligent or fraudulent conduct is involved.[114] In *McKnight v Sheppard*, Lord Hoffmann gave a resounding defence of *Smith's Potato Estates*.[115] The costs were not an element in the computation of profit but were logically and temporarily subsequent to the profits being earned.

---

[106] Lord Halsbury in *Ashton Gas Co v A-G* [1906] AC 10, 12.

[107] *IRC v Dowdall O'Mahoney & Co Ltd* [1952] 1 All ER 531, 33 TC 259. On deduction of overseas tax, see ex TA 1988, s 811 (TA 1970, s 516).

[108] *Smith v Lion Brewery Co Ltd* [1911] AC 150, 5 TC 568.

[109] *Harrods (Buenos Aires) Ltd v Taylor-Gooby* (1963) 41 TC 450, per Buckley J.

[110] (1963) 41 TC 450.

[111] Eg, stamp duty on conveyance of land forming part of the fixed capital of the trade or if the payment in *Harrods (Buenos Aires) Ltd v Taylor-Gooby* had been a once-only payment for the right to trade in Argentina.

[112] *Worsley Brewery Co Ltd v IRC* (1932) 17 TC 349, esp 360, per Romer LJ.

[113] [1948] 2 All ER 367, 374, 30 TC 267, 293. One criticism is that expenditure in order to preserve the company's assets is deductible (see *Morgan v Tate and Lyle*, below at §22.4.3). However, the expense must still be expenditure and not division of profit (see §22.3.2) on the authority of *Smiths Potato Estates*; the motive for the payment cannot turn profit into an expense. This reasoning seems to be contrary to that of the Court of Appeal in *Heather v PE Consulting Group Ltd* [1973] 1 All ER 8, 48 TC 320. The position cannot therefore be clearly stated.

[114] Statement of Practice SP 16/91 and amended for self-assessment by RI 192.

[115] [1999] STC 669, 674e.

22.4 Expenditure Must be Revenue, Not Capital

22.4.1 Introduction

Capital expenditure is not deductible in computing profits even though incurred wholly and exclusively for business purposes.[116] This proposition is made statutory by ITTOIA 2005, section 33. Certain capital expenditure may qualify for relief under the capital allowance system, however.[117] The task of distinguishing revenue from capital expenditure is not easy, and the problem has been made difficult by the inevitable fact that words or formulae that have been found useful in one set of facts may be neither relevant nor significant in another.[118] No test is paramount.[119] There is no rule whereby the treatment of the expenditure in the hands of the payer predetermines its character in the hands of the payee; so an item may be a revenue expense for the payer and a capital receipt for the recipient, or, conversely, a capital expense and a revenue receipt.[120]

In deciding these difficult questions, the court's task is to determine the true profits of the business. However, the court is hampered by the fact that a deductible expense must be entered when the expense is incurred and therefore cannot be spread over a number of years. It follows that to allow a major item of expenditure as a deduction in one year, when its benefits will be spread over many, will necessarily give a distorted picture of the profitability of the company.[121] This accounting-based approach suggests that accounting principles could have a role to play in deciding whether a particular expense is capital or revenue in nature; however, such principles cannot make any part of a capital expense deductible.

22.4.2 Concepts/Tests

22.4.2.1 Fixed and Circulating Capital[122]

Expenditure on the fixed capital of a business is capital expenditure, not revenue. Fixed capital is retained in the shape of assets which either produce income without further action, eg shares held by an investment company, or are made use of to produce income, eg machinery in a factory. Circulating capital is that which the company intends should be used by being temporarily parted with and circulated in the business, only to

---

[116] On history, see Edwards [1976] BTR 300.

[117] ITTOIA 2005, s 28, referring to receipts and expenses under the Capital Allowances Act 2001.

[118] *Taxes Commr v Nchanga Consolidated Copper Mines Ltd* [1964] AC 948, 959, [1964] 1 All ER 202, 212, per Lord Radcliffe.

[119] *Caledonian Paper plc v IRC* [1998] STC (SCD)129, 134; citing *Regent Oil Co Ltd v Strick* [1966] AC 295, 43 TC 1.

[120] *Regent Oil Co Ltd v Strick* [1966] AC 295, 43 TC 1.

[121] See Lord Reid in *Regent Oil, ibid,* at 316, 31.

[122] The dual reference to capital is unfortunate, but it refers to the capital of the company and so the source from which the expenditure is funded. Relatively recent instances of judges using the concept include *Pattison v Marine Midland* [1981] STC 540, 555 (Vinelott J) and [1984] STC 10, 11 (Lord Fraser); see also Reynolds [1982] BTR 238. See also the sharp differences of view expressed by Dyson LJ and Arden LJ in *IRC v John Lewis Properties plc* [2003] STC 117, [2002] EWCA Civ 1869.

return with—it is hoped—profit, eg money spent on trading stock.[123] The difficulty with this test is that it sometimes begs the very question at issue.[124]

22.4.2.2 Enduring Asset or Advantage: the *Atherton* Test

The second test was enunciated by Viscount Cave in *Atherton v British Insulated and Helsby Cables Ltd*[125] and became known as the 'enduring benefit test'. Viscount Cave stated:

> When an expenditure is made not only once for all, but with a view to bringing into existence an asset or advantage for the enduring benefit of a trade, I think there is very good reason (in the absence of special circumstances leading to an opposite conclusion) for treating such an expenditure as properly attributable not to revenue but to capital.

The principal difficulty with this test is that many types of expenditure have an enduring effect, and not all of them are of a capital nature. Thus, a payment to be rid of an unsatisfactory employee or agent is a revenue expense,[126] but one to be rid of a term of a lease is a capital expense.[127] A payment to a trust for the benefit of certain employees where the amount and duration of the fund were uncertain and the whole fund could have been distributed at any time was held to be a revenue expense.[128] A payment to persuade an institution to buy the worthless shares of a subsidiary was similarly held to be revenue since the expenditure did not bring any asset into existence or procure any advantage for the enduring benefit of the trade but was, instead, to remove the threat to the taxpayer's whole trade resulting from the subsidiary's insolvency.[129] It may therefore be as well to remember that the purpose of Viscount Cave's remarks was not to provide an infallible guide in all circumstances, but to explain how to approach one-off payments.

22.4.2.3 Identifiable Asset

In *Tucker v Granada Motorway Services Ltd*,[130] it was held that it is necessary first to identify the asset on which the sum has been spent, and then classify the sum spent. Sums spent on an asset of a non-capital nature cannot be capital; sums spent on capital assets may be. If the asset is of a capital nature, the nature of the particular expense must be considered. Therefore, sums spent on acquiring the capital asset will be capital, while sums spent maintaining or repairing it will be revenue.[131]

---

[123] See Swinfen Eady LJ in *Ammonia Soda Co v Chamberlain* [1918] 1 Ch 266; Romer LJ in *Golden Horseshoe (New) Ltd v Thurgood* [1934] 1 KB 548, 18 TC 280; and *Pattison v Marine Midland Ltd* [1981] STC 540. This is not a question of pure fact *(Pyrah v Annis & Co Ltd* (1956) 37 TC 163, 173 per Lord Evershed MR).

[124] See Lord Macmillan in *Van den Berghs Ltd v Clark* (1934) 19 TC 390, 432.

[125] [1926] AC 205, 213, 10 TC 155, 192.

[126] See *Anglo Persian Oil Co Ltd v Dale* (1931) 16 TC 253.

[127] *Tucker v Granada Motorway Services Ltd* [1979] STC 393, [1979] 2 All ER 801.

[128] *Jeffs v Ringtons Ltd* [1985] STC 809, [1986] 1 All ER 144.

[129] *Lawson v Johnson Matthey plc* [1992] STC 466, 470, HL; distinguished in *Stone & Temple Ltd v Waters* [1995] STC 1.

[130] [1979] STC 393, [1979] 2 All ER 801.

[131] In *Walker v Joint Credit Card Co Ltd* [1982] STC 427, Walton J. had to decide whether a payment to a business rival to close its business was made to secure an enduring benefit to trade or was made in relation to short-term advantages. The court held the payment to be capital (in the absence of evidence that the rival's trade was withering away within a reasonable space of time). In *Whitehead v Tubbs (Elastics) Ltd.* [1984] STC 1, the Court of Appeal held that a payment for release from terms of a loan agreement lasting nine years was a capital payment for a capital asset.

This test has been used in connection with liabilities. If the liability is on capital account, a loss, eg an exchange loss, incurred on repayment of the loan will be a capital loss, whereas it would have been a revenue loss if the loan had been a revenue transaction.[132] The test is not without difficulties. The place of the asset within the business is not usually too difficult to determine; indeed, it is similar to the old distinction between fixed and circulating capital. However, problems arise where the asset is not discernible as part of the assets of the business, as with trading arrangements with other traders or the modification of a company's charter or articles of association. Money spent in removing restrictions on a company's business has been held to be a revenue expense.[133] Care must also be taken in defining the asset accurately.[134] Thus, if T borrows money for a period, does T simply receive cash or a furtherance of the trade for the period of the loan?[135] It would, however, be foolish to reject the asset test simply because it does not provide an answer to all cases; the danger is that it will be applied, as have its predecessors, without regard to the variety of facts or the disclaimer of universality uttered by its formulators.

22.4.2.4 Once for All

In *Vallambrosa Rubber Co Ltd v Farmer*,[136] Lord Dunedin said that capital expenditure was something which would be spent once and for all, and income expenditure was something which would recur every year. In *Ounsworth v Vickers Ltd*,[137] Rowlatt J refined the point by saying that the distinction was between expenditure to meet a continuous demand and expenditure made once and for all. The case law shows that one-off expenditure can be revenue, as in *IRC v Carron*,[138] and regular payments can be capital, as in *Ramsay v IRC*.[139]

22.4.2.5 Capital Structures

In *Taxes Comrs v N'Changa Consolidated Copper Mines Ltd*,[140] Lord Radcliffe said that there was a demarcation between the cost of creating, acquiring or enlarging the permanent (which does not mean perpetual) structure of which the income is to be the produce or fruit, and the cost of earning that income itself or performing the income-earning operations. He added that this was probably as illuminating a line of distinction as the law by itself is likely to achieve. This approach is used in the explanation which follows.

---

[132] *Beauchamp v FW Woolworth plc* [1988] STC 714, 721c; reversed on appeal at [1989] STC 510, 61 TC 542, HL.

[133] Held to be a revenue expense in *IRC v Carron Co* [1968] SC 47, 45 TC 18, HL.

[134] *Bolton v International Drilling Co Ltd* [1983] STC 70, 56 TC 949.

[135] See *Beauchamp v FW Woolworth plc* [1989] STC 510, 61 TC 542.

[136] (1910) 5 TC 529, 536.

[137] (1915) 6 TC 671, 675.

[138] [1968] STC 47, 45 TC 18, HL.

[139] (1938) 23 TC 153 (see below at §27.4.5).

[140] [1964] AC 948, 960, [1964] 1 All ER 208.

22.4.3 *Examples*

22.4.3.1 Acquisition of a Business (Capital) or Running a Business (Revenue)

The costs of acquiring a business are capital expenses. Expenses incurred shortly after acquiring a business may be treated as part of the acquisition cost and so be non-deductible.[141] The matter is, however, one of fact.[142] The costs of running a business are clearly revenue expenses and, as such, payments to employees for their services are deductible.[143] To allow such payments to be taxable in the hands of the employee but not deductible by the employer, would amount to double taxation. There is, however, no correlation between the two, and it is possible for a payment to be deductible by the employer and not taxable to the employee,[144] as in the case of certain benefits in kind. Deductible sums include not only salaries proper, but also pensions[145] and retirement gratuities. There is no rule that to be deductible the payment must relate to services rendered in that year.[146] However, lump sum payments to fund future payments tend to be capital payments.[147]

FA 1989, section 42 (now ITTOIA 2005, section 36) introduced an important timing rule for the deduction of emoluments which was, broadly, that these are not to be deductible if provision is made for a sum in the accounts but the sum is not paid (or otherwise becomes the employee's remuneration) within nine months of the end of the employer's period of account.[148] This rule also applies to sums for which provision is made in the accounts 'with a view to their becoming emoluments'. It was held that the question whether the amounts were so held had to be decided as at the end of the nine-month period.[149] In *Macdonald v Dextra Accessories*,[150] the House of Lords, agreeing with the Court of Appeal, held that the words 'with a view to' did not mean 'for the sole purpose of' and amounted to an unspecific and flexible expression which should be interpreted to embrace the whole range of possibilities open to the trustees. The judges were not worried by the fact that there would be no deduction for sums which actually ended up nowhere near an employee; this tough but realistic view is to be commended. The legislation was rewritten by ITEPA 2003 and

---

[141] *Royal Insurance Co v Watson* [1897] AC 1, 3 TC 500; *Bassett Enterprises Ltd v Petty* (1938) 21 TC 730.

[142] *IRC v Patrick Thomson Ltd* (1956) 37 TC 145.

[143] But not sums paid to the Revenue in respect of tax not deducted under the PAYE scheme (*Bamford v ATA Advertising Ltd* [1972] 3 All ER 535, 48 TC 359). Incentive payments are deductible even if they are to enable the workforce to buy control of the employer (*Heather v PE Consulting Group Ltd* [1973] 1 All ER 8, 48 TC 320; see the discussion of this case in *E Bott Ltd v Price* [1987] STC 100, 106).

[144] See above at §14.1.2. Conversely, employers cannot deduct the costs of share options (since there is no 'cost' this does not prevent the employee from being taxable in appropriate circumstances, as in *Weight v Salmon* (1935) 19 TC 174—see above at §15.2.4).

[145] *Smith v Incorporated Council of Law Reporting for England and Wales* (1914) 6 TC 477.

[146] *Hancock v General Reversionary Society and Investment Co Ltd* [1919] 1 KB 25, 7 TC 358.

[147] *Rowntree & Co Ltd v Curtis* (1924) 8 TC 678; *British Insulated and Helsby Cables Ltd v Atherton* [1926] AC 205, 10 TC 155. But see TA 1988, s 592(4) (FA 1970, s 21(3)). See also *Hancock v General Reversionary Society and Investment Co Ltd* [1919] 1 KB 25, 7 TC 358; and *Jeffs v Ringtons Ltd* [1985] STC 809, [1986] 1 All ER 144, 58 TC 680.

[148] This rule applies also to property income (see ITTOIA 2005, s 272) and to other income (see ITTOIA 2005, s 865).

[149] *Macdonald v Dextra Accessories* [2003] STC 749 (HC).

[150] *Macdonald v Dextra Accessories* [2005] UKHL 47, [2005] STC 1111.

is now part of ITTOIA 2005; the earlier law used the expression 'potential emoluments'; no change of substance was intended by the Rewrite.

In the early 2000s employee benefit schemes proliferated; these were mostly schemes for highly-paid employees. While it was likely that such schemes fell foul of section 36 and other rules, Parliament enacted further rules in FA 2003 (now ITTOIA 2005, sections 39–46). Like section 36, these restrict the deductions for contributions to third parties for the benefit of employees where contributions are paid to a third party but no qualifying benefits or expenses emerge in the same period or the next nine months.[151] As with section 36, this was seen as a better—and certainly an earlier—way of tackling this form of avoidance than trying to tax the benefits. The rules do not apply to the provision of retirement benefits.[152] These rules were circumvented by the employer not making a new payment to an intermediary but by itself declaring a trust over its existing assets, until this was countered by FA 2007, section 34.

22.4.3.2 Facilities for and Reorganisation of the Business (Capital)

Facilities for the reorganisation of the business are clearly capital of the business, so expenditure on them may be capital. Thus, building a factory is a capital expense, as is ancillary work, such as the provision of a water supply, drainage and roads.[153] Similarly, the cost of sinking a mine shaft is a capital expense,[154] as is the cost of reconverting an oil rig at the end of its lease period[155] or the cost of acquiring a waste tipping site,[156] although legislation now permits the deduction of both restoration payments and preparation expenditure in closely defined circumstances.[157] Capital allowances may be available for such expenditure, but the availability of capital allowances excludes the revenue deduction for restoration payments and preparation expenditure on waste disposal projects.

The expense of moving from one set of business premises to another is a capital expense,[158] although the costs of removing trading stock are not so regarded. In practice, removal costs which are forced on the trader, as on the expiration of a lease, are allowed. Where, however, the general rule applies, it prevents the deduction of ancillary costs such as conveyance expenses. Once-for-all expenditure on a reorganisation may be capital. This was so in *Watney Combe Reid & Co Ltd v Pike*,[159] where a brewery made ex gratia payments to tenants under a scheme by which separate management companies were substituted for tenants. The purpose was to make the assets more profitable, but it was important that the scheme involved a new corporate structure and a new way of doing business. Facilities

---

[151] The rules apply to accounting periods ending on or after 27 November 2002—FA 2003 Sch 24, para 11. See generally Inland Revenue Press Release 27 November 2002, [2002] *Simons Tax Intelligence* 1612.

[152] ITTOIA 2005, s 39(4); see also s 272 (property income) and s 866 (other income). The original list of exemptions in FA 2003, Sch 23, para 8 is longer than that in s 39(4).

[153] *Boyce v Whitwick Colliery Co Ltd* (1934) 18 TC 655; *Bean v Doncaster Amalgamated Collieries Ltd* [1944] 1 All ER 621, 27 TC 296; *Pitt v Castle Hill Warehousing Co Ltd* [1974] STC 420, [1974] 3 All ER 146. See also *Ounsworth v Vickers Ltd* [1915] 3 KB 267, 6 TC 671.

[154] *Bonner v Basset Mines Ltd* (1912) 6 TC 146.

[155] *RTZ Oil and Gas Ltd v Elliss* [1987] STC 512, 61 TC 132.

[156] *Rolfe v Wimpey Waste Management Ltd* [1989] STC 454, CA (Special Commissioner reversed, 62 TC 399).

[157] ITTOIA 2005, ss 165–168, ex TA 1988, ss 91A, 91B.

[158] *Granite Supply Association Ltd v Kitton* (1905) 5 TC 168.

[159] [1982] STC 733.

may be financial as well as physical. In *Whitehead v Tubbs (Elastics) Ltd*,[160] a payment was made to secure the release of a term in a loan agreement which had significantly limited the company's power to borrow money. This payment was held to be capital. By contrast, in the earlier case of *IRC v Carron*,[161] the court held that a payment to secure the alteration of a company's constitution was a revenue expense. *Carron* was distinguished in *Whitehead*, inter alia on the ground that in *Carron* no asset was brought into existence, neither was there any expenditure on any asset or liability of the company.

The distinction between income and capital for the purposes of loan relationships (including foreign exchange transactions) has been abolished for corporation tax. The distinction, however, remains central for income tax.[162] Statute permits the deduction of incidental costs of loan finance,[163] and interest is the subject of a special set of rules (see below at §22.6.2). In *Beauchamp v FW Woolworth plc*,[164] the taxpayer, with an annual turn-over of some £300m, borrowed 50m Swiss francs for a five-year period; the loan was imme-diately converted into sterling. The following year the taxpayer incurred a second such loan, which was also converted. In due course the loans were repaid but, owing to the decline of sterling against the Swiss franc, at a large loss. The House of Lords held that the loan was an accretion to capital and not a revenue transaction, and therefore the loss was not allowable. The precise ratio is not easy to determine. At one point Lord Templeman spoke of the loan having to be temporary and fluctuating, and incurred in meeting the ordinary running expenses of the business if it was to be on revenue account and so deductible.[165] However, this was said in the context of distinguishing *Regent Oil Co Ltd v Strick*,[166] and stress was laid on the question whether the petrol tie or loan could be said to be an ordinary incident of marketing. A more abstract statement by Lord Templeman was that the loan would be on revenue account only if it were part of the ordinary day-to-day incidence of carrying on a business.[167] This seems to be the more promising starting point.

22.4.3.3 Expansion of a Business (Capital) or Maintenance of a Business (Revenue)

The expense of an application for planning permission over land is generally capital, since the land is a capital asset and this expense is more than mere maintenance.[168] Similarly, the premises are capital assets, so that, for example, where a brewer applies for a licence for new premises, the legal cost of applying for the new licence is not deductible.[169] In *Pyrah v Annis*,[170] it was held that the costs of an unsuccessful application to vary an

---

[160] [1984] STC 1; 57 TC 472, CA.
[161] (1968) 45 TC 18, HL.
[162] For discussion of Canadian and UK cases, see Friedlander (2005) 53 *Can Tax Jo* 897; the UK cases are at 904–19.
[163] ITTOIA 2005, s 58, timing issue decided in *Cadbury Schweppes v Williams* [2002] STC (SCD) 114.
[164] [1988] STC 714; this marks the case off from *Pattison v Marine Midland Ltd* [1984] STC 10, 57 TC 219.
[165] [1989] STC 510, 518; 61 TC 542, 581.
[166] [1966] AC 295, 43 TC 1. This test was also applied in *Tanfield Ltd v Carr* [1999] STC (SCD) 213.
[167] [1989] STC 510, 517; 61 TC 542, 581.
[168] *ECC Quarries Ltd v Watkis* [1975] STC 578, [1975] 3 All ER 843, 51 TC 153. A land developer may deduct such expenses since the land is not capital for such a trader.
[169] *Morse v Stedeford* (1934) 18 TC 457.
[170] [1956] 2 All ER 858, 37 TC 163.

existing public carrier's licence by increasing the number of vehicles from four to seven was capital expenditure because the licence was an asset retained by the trader which produced income. This must be distinguished from *IRC v Carron*,[171] where the company was entitled to deduct the legal costs of altering its charter so as to remove restrictions on ordinary business operations. Sums spent on software to ensure that an existing computer system could cope with the millennium were regarded as revenue expenditure. However, such sums will be capital expenditure if they are part of a major new project instituting other changes, and that project is itself capital in nature.[172] In *Markets South West (Holdings) Ltd v Revenue and Customs Commissioners*,[173] the taxpayer operated market premises and incurred expenses on a planning appeal. Avery-Jones J ruled that in so far as the expenses were to enlarge the terms of the planning permission by removing restrictions retrospectively, they were capital; in so far as they were incurred to argue that there had been no breach of existing planning controls and that the taxpayer had an existing right to trade in the way sought, however, they were revenue.

22.4.3.4 Preservation of Capital (Revenue)

Sums paid to preserve the capital or capital assets of the business are revenue expenses. The capital preserved may include the goodwill and the ability to trade. In *Cooke v Quick Shoe Repair Service*,[174] the firm had bought a business and arranged for the vendor (V) to settle outstanding liabilities to suppliers and employees. When V failed to do so, the firm paid off the creditors and was held entitled to deduct the sums so paid because they were paid to preserve the goodwill of the business, not to buy it.

Sums paid to protect title to capital assets have been held to be revenue expenses. The reason for this is that the expenses are incurred in maintaining the company's capital, and so are just as deductible as expenses of repair and maintenance on the fixed assets of the company.[175] Such expenditure does not result in either the improvement or the acquisition of a fixed capital asset.[176] Sums spent to protect the good name of the business by resisting an unfounded allegation of misrepresentation have been held deductible, as have sums paid by way of settlement of a civil claim against the trade.[177] The importance of correctly identifying the asset being protected was shown in *Bolton v International Drilling Co Ltd*.[178] Here, a company's sole income-earning asset was originally acquired subject to another person's option to reacquire it. A sum paid for release of the option was held to be capital

---

[171] (1968) 45 TC 18.

[172] RI 180.

[173] [2011] STC 1469, [2011] UKUT 257 (UT).

[174] (1949) 30 TC 460; described as 'an odd case' by Walton J in *Garforth v Tankard Carpets Ltd* [1980] STC 251, 259, 260, 53 TC 342, 351. See also *Walker v Cater Securities Ltd* [1974] STC 390, [1974] 3 All ER 63, 49 TC 625, where the taxpayer owned shares in a customer-company. X had an option to buy these shares. The sum paid by taxpayer to X for release of the option was held to be a revenue expense. This conclusion is supported by Revenue evidence. In *Bolton v International Drilling Co* [1983] STC 70, 92, 56 TC 449, 475, a payment was considered in substance to be to keep an important customer, not just to acquire a capital asset.

[175] Distinguish *Pitt v Castle Hill Warehousing Co Ltd* [1974] STC 420, [1974] 3 All ER 146, where a sum paid to exchange one capital asset (a strip of land) for another (an easement over another strip) was held to be capital.

[176] *Southern v Borax Consolidated Ltd* [1940] 4 All ER 412, 23 TC 597.

[177] *IT Comr Bihar and Orissa v Singh* [1942] 1 All ER 362.

[178] [1983] STC 70, 56 TC 449. In *Walker v Joint Credit Card Co Ltd* [1982] STC 427, 55 TC 617, sums paid not just to preserve goodwill but to improve it, were held to be capital expenditure.

expenditure because until that time the trade's right in the asset was not one of complete ownership; the payment did not preserve the original title but improved it.

A controversial application of the above principle occurred in *Morgan v Tate and Lyle Ltd*,[179] where the company successfully claimed to be entitled to deduct expenses incurred in a publicity campaign to defeat the proposed nationalisation of the company which was to take the form not of the compulsory acquisition of its shares, but of the compulsory acquisition of its assets. On this basis the House of Lords held that the costs of the campaign were deductible. If the company had been faced with a takeover of its business by a group of persons anxious to acquire control through the purchase of its shares, it was clear that the costs of resisting such a takeover would not have been deductible, the threat in such a case being to the existing management rather than to the assets or trade of the company. In *Lawson v Johnson Matthey plc*,[180] it was held that where an expense had been incurred to preserve the company's trade, the court could ignore the means by which it was done (by the disposal of worthless shares in a subsidiary company). The House of Lords held that, on the facts, that money was paid, and paid solely, to enable the taxpayer company to continue in business; the test was objective.[181]

22.4.3.5 Ending Onerous Contractual Obligations and Restrictions (Either)

A payment for disposing of a permanent disadvantage or onerous burden may be an enduring benefit and so a capital expense. This will usually be the case where the expenditure replaces the source of disadvantage with a new asset. One starting point is to ask whether the payments made under the liability being disposed of would themselves be revenue expenses.[182] A payment to settle a capital liability is clearly a capital payment. Therefore, where a company had agreed to buy a ship to use in its trade, a payment made on cancellation of the contract was a capital expense.[183] Conversely, an expense incurred to dispose of a revenue expense ought to be deductible; if a surrogatum for loss of profit is a trading receipt, a commutation of deductible outlay should be a revenue expense. In *Mitchell v Noble*,[184] a payment to be rid of a director whose continuance in office would have been detrimental to the company was held to be a revenue expense because: (a) the company received no enduring advantage; (b) no asset of the company was enhanced; (c) an employee is not a permanency; and (d) the satisfactory state of the workforce is not regarded as part of the capital of the business. In *Anglo-Persian Oil Co Ltd v Dale*,[185] this was extended to allow the deduction of substantial payments to agents to terminate an agency agreement which still had 11 years to run. This decision equated an agency with a contract of employment and rested on the statement by Lawrence LJ in the Court of Appeal that the cancellation 'merely effected a change in the company business methods and internal organisation leaving its fixed capital untouched'.

---

[179] [1954] 2 All ER 413, 35 TC 367. *Cf Hammond Engineering Co Ltd v IRC* [1975] STC 334. On deductibility of expenditure on the 1975 Common Market Referendum, see Lustgarten [1976] BTR 337.
[180] [1992] STC 466, HL; reversing [1991] STC 259, 65 TC 39, CA.
[181] See Saunders [1992] BTR 150.
[182] *Bean v Doncaster Amalgamated Collieries Ltd* (1944) 27 TC 296, 312, per Simon LJ.
[183] *Countess Warwick Steamship Co Ltd v Ogg* [1924] 2 KB 292, 8 TC 652.
[184] *Mitchell v BW Noble Ltd* [1927] 1 KB 719, 11 TC 372.
[185] [1932] 1 KB 124, 141, 16 TC 253, 272.

However, while it appears that payments to dispose of liabilities which are capital in nature will not be deductible, it does not follow that payments to dispose of or replace revenue expenses are necessarily deductible. It is necessary to distinguish disposing of a charge on revenue from acquiring a capital asset which enables disposal of such a charge. The purchase of labour-saving machinery is a capital expense and cannot be converted into a revenue expense simply because it can be shown to reduce the wage bill.[186] In addition, if a channel is continually being silted up and the trader decides to replace the silting channel with a concrete one, that is capital expenditure even though the costs of clearing the silt would have been a revenue expense.[187]

Where a lease is a capital asset of the business, a payment for the surrender of the lease in commutation of the liability to pay rent is a capital expense and not deductible.[188] Similarly, a payment to vary the terms of the lease will be a capital expense because the payment rendering the lease either more advantageous or less disadvantageous improves the lease. In *Tucker v Granada Motorway Services Ltd*, the landlord (the Minister of Transport) was entitled to rent from the lessees of a motorway service station together with an additional rent based on takings, the latter to include an element for tobacco duty. As tobacco duty rose, the lessees found it difficult to make a profit, and so it was agreed to exclude the tobacco duty from the calculation in return for a lump sum. The House of Lords held that the lump sum was a capital expense; it was irrelevant that the purpose of the expenditure was to increase profit.[189]

Payments of rent under the lease are revenue expenses, whereas the payment of a premium is capital[190]—even if paid by instalments—provided the lease itself formed part of the capital structure of the business.[191] Therefore, where a company had a lease of a shop for five years and the company ceased to use that shop after two years, the rent was deductible in computing its profits assuming, as was the case, that the trade itself was still conducted from other premises.[192]

22.4.3.6 Repairs (Revenue) or Improvements (Capital)[193]

TA 1988, section 74(1)(d) expressly disqualified 'any sums expended for repairs of premises occupied ... for the purposes of the trade beyond the sum actually expended for the purpose', a provision which restricts deductions to sums actually spent and therefore prohibits the deduction of sums set aside by way of reserve for future expenditure. Section 74(1)(g) prohibited the deduction of any capital employed in improvements of premises occupied for the purposes of the trade, profession or vocation. ITTOIA 2005 repealed both paragraphs (d) and (g) for income tax. At first sight, paragraph (g) seems to be directed to the

---

[186] *Anglo-Persian Oil Co Ltd v Dale* (1931) 16 TC 253, 261, per Rowlatt J.

[187] *Mitchell v BW Noble Ltd* [1927] 1 KB 719, 728, 11 TC 372, 415, per Rowlatt J.

[188] *Cowcher v Richard Mills & Co Ltd* (1927) 13 TC 216; *Mallett v Staveley Coal and Iron Co Ltd* [1928] 2 KB 405, 13 TC 772; see also *IRC v William Sharp & Son* (1959) 38 TC 341.

[189] [1979] STC 393, [1979] 2 All ER 801, 53 TC 92. See also *Southern Counties Agricultural Society v Blackler* [1999] STC (SCD) 200 (payment of reverse premium capital).

[190] On adjustment where part of premium is treated as income, see ITTOIA 2005, ss 60–67, ex TA 1988, s 87.

[191] *IRC v Adam* (1928) 14 TC 34; see Report of the Committee on the Taxation of Trading Profits, Cmnd 8189 (1951), §247.

[192] *IRC v Falkirk Iron Co Ltd* (1933) 17 TC 625.

[193] There is much comparative interest to be derived from Durnford (1997) 45 *Can Tax Jo* 395.

source from which the trader chooses to finance the improvements; however, it is generally taken to mean that sums spent on improvements are capital payments and therefore not deductible, while sums spent on the repair of capital assets are deductible. The question whether work is a repair or an improvement is one of fact.[194]

Money spent on the replacement of one kind of rail by a superior kind is not deductible, since it increases the value of the railway line.[195] Expense incurred in increasing the number of sleepers under each rail was admitted to be capital expense in *Rhodesia Railways Ltd v Bechuanaland Protectorate IT Collector*,[196] but the railway company was allowed to deduct as repairs the cost of works in renewing 74 miles of railway track by replacing rails and sleepers. This was not an improvement since it only restored the worn track to its normal condition and did not increase the capacity of the line in any way. Money spent on pulling down a chimney and building a new, bigger and better chimney,[197] or on renovating a factory with a higher roof line and so more space, is not deductible.[198] No deduction may be claimed for such part of the expenditure on improvements as would have been needed to pay for mere repair.[199] As Danckwerts J commented, 'it seems ... to be a hardship and something which is calculated to discourage manufacturers from making the best use of their property'.[200] On the other hand, if the work consists of a number of separate jobs, it may be possible to distinguish between the different items, thus allowing some of the expense. In *Conn v Robins Bros Ltd*,[201] the construction of a lavatory was held to be an improvement, but the insertion of steel joists was held to be a repair.

These rules are not confined to physical assets. Sums spent on training courses for proprietors are regarded as capital if they are intended to provide new expertise, knowledge or skill, as distinct from mere updating.[202]

22.4.3.7 Renewals (Capital) or Repairs (Revenue)?[203]

This is another version of the issue discussed at §22.4.3.6 above. The replacement of a slate on a roof would be a repair, but the rebuilding of a retort house in a gas works would be a renewal.[204] As Buckley LJ said in *Lurcott v Wakely and Wheeler*[205] (not a revenue case),

'repair' and 'renew' are not words expressive of clear contrast ... repair is restoration by renewal or replacement of subsidiary parts of a whole. Renewal, as distinguished from repair, is reconstruction

[194] *Conn v Robins Bros Ltd* (1966) 43 TC 266, 274.
[195] *Highland Rly Co v Balderston* (1889) 2 TC 485; and see *LCC v Edwards* (1909) 5 TC 383.
[196] [1933] AC 368, 372; but see Lord Cooper in *Lawrie v IRC* (1952) 34 TC 20. 25.
[197] *O'Grady v Bullcroft Main Collieries Ltd* (1932) 17 TC 93.
[198] *Thomas Wilson (Keighley) Ltd v Emmerson* (1960) 39 TC 360; *Lawrie v IRC* (1952) 34 TC 20; *Mann Crossman and Paulin Ltd v IRC* [1947] 1 All ER 742, 28 TC 410.
[199] For reasons which were no longer rational, a different rule applied to Sch A until April 2001 thanks to ESC B4. This was withdrawn in 2001: for ESC B4 rule, see IR 150, paras 147 *et seq*.
[200] *Thomas Wilson (Keighley) Ltd v Emmerson* (1960) 39 TC 360, 366.
[201] (1966) 43 TC 266.
[202] Inland Revenue interpretation RI 1.
[203] See Smith [1982] BTR 360, 366 *et seq*.
[204] See Rowlatt J in *O'Grady v Bullcroft Main Collieries Ltd* (1932) 17 TC 93, 101 and Donovan J in *Phillips v Whieldon Sanitary Potteries Ltd* (1952) 33 TC 213.
[205] [1911] 1 KB 905, 923, 924; cited, eg, by Lord MacMillan in *Rhodesia Railways Ltd v Bechuanaland Protectorate IT Collector* [1933] AC 368, 374. The case concerned the construction of a lessee's covenant to keep in thorough repair and good condition.

of the entirety, meaning by the entirety not necessarily the whole but substantially the whole subject matter under discussion.

Baxter has suggested that 'repairs' are the opposite of 'improvements', but that some expenditure on repairs can be on capital account.[206] Using this approach, expenditure on reinstating the capital value of business assets is capital expenditure. It is clear that the scope of repairs is treated as a question of law—and so within the court's jurisdiction. This test presupposes a satisfactory definition of the unit repaired or renewed. In *O'Grady v Bullcroft Main Collieries Ltd*,[207] a chimney used to carry away fumes from a furnace had become unsafe, and so the company built a new one. Rowlatt J said that in his view the chimney was not a part of the factory but an entirety, and so capital. Similarly, in *Wynne-Jones v Bedale Auction Ltd*,[208] it was held that the relevant unit was the cattle ring, not the whole auction complex, so that the expenditure was capital. On the other hand, in *Samuel Jones & Co (Devonvale) Ltd v IRC*,[209] the costs of replacing an unsafe chimney at a factory were held deductible. In the Court of Session, which reversed the Special Commissioners, Lord Cooper said that the factory was the entirety; the chimney, therefore, was only part of the entirety. The court also stressed the low cost of the replacement of the chimney relative to the insured value of the factory, a point not taken in *O'Grady v Bullcroft Main Collieries Ltd*. The distinction between 'a part' and 'the entirety' appears to be a convenient method of describing a conclusion rather than a helpful test, but it contains the words by reference to which the evidence is assembled and assessed.

Auckland Gas Co Ltd v CIR[210] is a nice case. The taxpayer company supplied a gas network of underground cast iron and steel pipes. In order to reduce the losses due to leaks, it inserted polyethylene piping into the existing metal pipes; the old pipes were left in the ground to act as supports for the polyethylene pipes. This technique was better than trying to track down and repair individual gas leaks in the original. The Privy Council agreed with the New Zealand Court of Appeal that the expenditure was capital and so non-deductible. The insertion programme did not restore the gas distribution system to its original state but provided something new, and the fact that the motive was to reduce maintenance expenditure could not alter that conclusion.

The question seems to be one of the size and importance of the work. One big job may be capital, whereas a combination of small jobs may be revenue. In *Phillips v Whieldon Sanitary Potteries Ltd*,[211] the replacement of a barrier protecting a factory from water in a canal was held to be a renewal and so capital expenditure, the court taking into account the extent of the work, the permanent nature of the new barrier and the enduring benefit it would confer on the business by preserving a part of the fixed capital. In that case Donovan J followed the *Bullcroft* case and reversed the Commissioners.

---

[206] [1977] BTR 184.

[207] (1932) 17 TC 93; the ratio was that the chimney was an addition, there being no evidence that the old one was pulled down.

[208] [1977] STC 50, 51 TC 426; the whole case is severely criticised by Baxter [1977] BTR 184. See also *Margrett v Lowestoft Water and Gas Co* (1935) 19 TC 481 (replacement of reservoir capital).

[209] (1951) 32 TC 513.

[210] [2000] STC 527; Maples [2001] BTR 92.

[211] (1952) 33 TC 213; contrast *Conn v Robins Bros Ltd* (1966) 43 TC 266.

Expenditure may be in respect of a repair as opposed to a renewal, even though it is carried out some time after the need for the repair first arose. Thus, the costs of keeping a channel dredged would be income expenditure even though the dredging was done only once every three years or so.[212]

22.4.3.8 The Initial Repair Problem[213]

Where a trader acquires an asset which requires extensive repairs before it is in a usable condition, the expenses of those repairs are not deductible since they are as much capital expenditure as the costs of acquiring the asset itself. Were the rule otherwise, a trader could convert at least a part of the prospective capital expense into a revenue item by buying the asset in an incomplete state and finishing the work himself, perhaps by employing the person who had worked on it before its acquisition. In *Law Shipping Co Ltd v IRC*,[214] a shipping company bought a ship which was at that date ready to sail with freight booked. The Lloyd's survey was then overdue but, with the consent of the insurers, the ship was allowed to complete the voyage. The ship cost £97,000 and the company had to spend an extra £51,558 on repairs in order for the vessel to pass the survey. Of that sum, some £12,000 was in respect of repairs caused by deterioration during the voyage and was allowed by the Revenue; the balance of £39,500 was not. The Court agreed with the Revenue.

In *Law Shipping* the expenditure was required to make the asset commercially viable; a different rule applies where the asset is already so viable. In *Odeon Associated Theatres Ltd v Jones*,[215] the company bought a cinema in 1945. Only small sums had been permitted to be spent in the previous five years, and restrictions on repair work lasted for some time after the war. The cinema was open to the public and was a profit-earning asset. The Court of Appeal held that sums spent subsequently to the acquisition in respect of the deferred repairs were deductible. The primary reason was that such would be in accordance with the normal principles of commercial accountancy, as the Commissioners had made a finding not made in the *Law Shipping* case. However, there were other differences. Although in the *Law Shipping* case the ship had been permitted to complete one voyage, it was clear that subsequently a full insurance survey would be needed, and the price showed that substantial expenditure would be needed before the ship would again be a profit-earning asset. By contrast, the cinema was an immediate income-earning asset and it appeared that the price had not been affected by the fact of disrepair. Two other facts are material. First, even if the vendors had wished to carry out the repair work before the sale, they would have been unable to do so because of the restrictions. Secondly, there was no indication that the taxpayer had in fact been put to greater expense by reason of the deferred repairs.

22.4.3.9 Allowable Capital Expenditure—The Renewals Basis

The distinction between repair and renewal is blurred by the Revenue practice of allowing the cost of replacing machinery and plant as a revenue expense. This practice is distinct

---

[212] *Ounsworth v Vickers Ltd* (1915) 6 TC 671, per Rowlatt J.
[213] See Smith [1982] BTR 360, 361.
[214] [1924] SC 74, 12 TC 621; see also *IRC v Granite City Steamship Co Ltd* [1927] SC 705, 13 TC 1, and the expenditure on the branch line in *Highland Rly Co v Balderston* (1889) 2 TC 485.
[215] [1972] 1 All ER 681, 48 TC 257, CA. This decision must cast doubt on *Jackson v Laskers Home Furnishers Ltd* [1956] 3 All ER 891, 37 TC 69; on which see Silberrad [1957] BTR 73.

from the capital allowances system. There appear to be two distinct legal bases for this practice (which, confusingly, is called a renewals allowance). One is the general theory of profit, which would equate a renewal with a repair and would regard both as maintaining intact the capital originally invested in the physical assets of the business.[216] The other regards the deduction for the replacement asset as broadly relieving the deprecation suffered on the original asset.[217] The disadvantage of this basis is that it is inconsistent with the cases considered above and would presumably apply to a range of expenditures other than those on machinery and plant. The renewals allowance applies only to deductions for expenditure on the replacement of implements, utensils or articles such as loose tools and similar assets, and thus would not necessarily cover all types of machinery and plant.[218] It seems best to regard this as an extra-statutory concession dating from the days when there were no capital allowances. This not only avoids the above problems, but also justifies the Revenue's insistence that some renewals allowances are to be made only over a period of two or three years.

Where the renewals basis is adopted, the allowance given is the cost of the new article (excluding additions or improvements), less the scrap or realised value of the replaced article. The cost of the new article may be greater or less than that of the old. Claiming the renewals allowance when the replacement is bought does not prevent a later switch to the capital allowance system. The two systems of relief are alternatives, although since the renewals allowance usually gives an immediate write off of all the expenditure, it is usually advantageous.[219]

At Budget 2016, the Government announced its intention to eliminate the renewals allowance for traders from 6 April 2016.

22.4.3.10 Trading Stock—the Tree (Capital) or the Fruit (Revenue)

The purchase of trading stock is generally a deductible revenue expense. However, care is needed to distinguish the purchase of trading stock from the purchase of an asset bearing trading stock. Thus, the purchase of a mine for extraction purposes is an item of capital expenditure and not the purchase of trading stock.[220] In *IRC v Pilcher*,[221] a fruit grower was not allowed to deduct the cost of purchasing a cherry orchard, not even that part which represented the value of the nearly ripe crop. The contract had expressly included 'this year's crop', but that meant only that the vendor was not to be entitled to pick the crop ripening between contract and completion. The grower had purchased an income-earning asset and not two separate items, namely the trees and the crop. In these cases, trading stock is distinguished from capital. As such, considerable care is needed in defining the trade. In one case sums spent by a timber merchant on the purchase of standing timber were not

---

[216] See 114th Report of Commissioners of Inland Revenue, §40.

[217] See HMRC Business Income Manual BIM46935.

[218] See *IRC v Great Wigston Gas Co* (1946) 29 TC 197. An item may be capital expenditure even though on utensils: see *Hinton v Maden and Ireland Ltd* [1959] 3 All ER 356, 38 TC 391.

[219] See ESC B1.

[220] *Alianza Co Ltd v Bell* [1906] AC 18, 5 TC 172; *Stratford v Mole and Lea* (1941) 24 TC 20.

[221] [1949] 2 All ER 1097, 31 TC 314. It is unclear how far the case turns on the distinction between *fructus naturales* and *fructus industriales* (see Report of the Committee on the Taxation Treatment of Provisions for Retirement, Cmnd 9063 (1954) (the Tucker Report) and criticism by Crump [1960] BTR 366).

deductible,[222] whereas in another case the costs of standing timber bought by a dealer in standing timber were deductible.[223]

The purchase of a business and the purchase of trading stock as part of that business are both capital expenditure. Normally, separate entries will take care of trading stock *stricto sensu*, but this will not cover incidental profit-making sources. In *John Smith & Son v Moore*,[224] the taxpayer had inherited his father's business in return for a sum which included a figure of £30,000 for specific unexpired contracts for the supply of coal. The son was not allowed to deduct the £30,000. Viscount Haldane held that the contracts formed part of his fixed capital, so that it was the coal which was the circulating capital; Lord Sumner held that the business was not that of buying and selling contracts but buying and selling coal, and that the price paid was the price of acquiring the business.[225] The decision clearly needs some explanation, since contracts for the supply of trading stock can lead to trading profits in ways other than taking delivery of trading stock.[226] In *Taxes Comr v N'Changa Consolidated Copper Mines Ltd*,[227] Viscount Radcliffe explained the decision as resting on two important elements in the facts of the case: one element was that an aggregate price had been paid for the entire business as it stood; the other was that the son did not acquire stock in trade. However, the facts suggest that the son was not carrying on business on his own account before his father's death, in which case it was a simple case of pre-trading expenses. This leaves the court free to dissect the price paid where the business is taken over by a person already trading.

22.4.3.11 Trading Arrangements

General sums paid to regulate the structure of a business tend to be capital, although the duration of the arrangement is of importance.[228] A sum paid in instalments to secure a customer for 10 years was held to be capital,[229] as was a payment to a trade association to prevent the sale of the business of a member of the association to a non-member.[230] A payment to a retiring employee for a covenant not to compete was held to be capital and so not deductible.[231] It may be argued both that such payment was made in order to preserve the business and so was deductible, but that a significant advantage was also gained, and so the payment was of capital.[232] On balance, it would seem that since the expense of buying up a rival business in order to suppress it is capital, the same should apply to a long-term agreement to the same effect. Such arrangements relate to the commercial structure of the business. The question is, however, one of fact and degree.

---

[222] *Hood Barrs v IRC (No. 2)* [1957] 1 All ER 832, 37 TC 188; noted by Silberrad [1957] BTR 174; see also *Kauri Timber Co Ltd v IT Commr* [1913] AC 771.

[223] *Murray v IRC* (1951) 32 TC 238.

[224] [1921] 2 AC 13, 12 TC 266.

[225] *Ibid*, 20, 282, 283.

[226] *Thompson v IRC* (1927) 12 TC 1091.

[227] [1964] 1 All ER 208, [1964] AC 948. See also *Whimster & Co v IRC* (1925) 12 TC 813; and Lord Reid in *Regent Oil Co Ltd v Strick* [1965] 3 All ER 174, 185, 43 TC 1, 36.

[228] See *Taxes Commr v N'Changa Consolidated Copper Mines Ltd* [1964] AC 948, [1964] 1 All ER 208 (one year—revenue expense).

[229] *United Steel Companies Ltd v Cullington* (1939) 23 TC 71.

[230] *Collins v Joseph Adamson & Co* [1937] 4 All ER 236, 21 TC 400.

[231] *Associated Portland Cement Manufacturers Ltd v Kerr* [1946] 1 All ER 68, 27 TC 103.

[232] Note Lord Reid in *Regent Oil Co Ltd v Strick* [1965] 3 All ER 174, 183; 43 TC 1, 35.

Petrol ties[233]

After 1945, the petrol trade was arranged at retail level on the basis that a garage would sell several brands of petrol. However, after 1950, oil companies began to secure exclusive agreements with garage owners under which X Co would provide the owners with benefits if the owners agreed, through contractual ties, to sell only X Co's petrol.[234] Some payments were held to be revenue expenditure of the oil companies, even in cases of contractual ties which were to last five years.[235] The garage owner's tax liability was different. In so far as the payments were for reimbursement of capital expenditure, they were capital receipts,[236] as where the petrol company paid for substantial new buildings. However, in so far as the payments were reimbursements of revenue expenditure, for example sales promotion, they were revenue receipts.[237] Further, if the amounts were related to gallonage they were treated as rebates on trading stock and so as revenue payments.[238] On the other hand, the garage owner could successfully invoke the principle in *Glenboig Union Fireclay Co Ltd v IRC* (above §21.7.3) by arguing that the payment was in return for the restriction of his trading opportunities, an argument that succeeded in a case involving a 10-year tie.[239] The exclusivity war was not confined to the UK. In *BP (Australia) Ltd v Taxation Commr*,[240] the Privy Council considered sums paid by an oil company by way of a 'development allowance' to garage owners in return for a five-year tie (the amount being related to the estimated gallonage) to be revenue expenditure.

Lease and leaseback

In order to ensure that the sums received were capital receipts, a system of the lease and leaseback was adopted. The garage owner would grant a lease to the oil company, which would promise to pay a nominal rent and a large premium. The company would then sub-lease the garage to the owner, who would covenant to sell only the company's products, on breach of which the sub-lease would end. The premium would be a capital receipt by the garage owner.[241] This scheme was considered by the House of Lords in *Regent Oil Co v Strick*,[242] its judgment being given on the same day as that of the Privy Council in *BP (Australia) Ltd v Taxation Commr*, with identical judges but no mention of the one case in the other. Payments under the scheme by Regent Oil were based upon estimated gallonage, and the period ranged from five years to 21 years. It was stated that the company had 5,000 agreements in the UK, mostly of the older variety without a lease. The House of Lords unanimously held that the payments in respect of the lease arrangements were capital expenditure and so not deductible. The distinction between a five-year tie of the old type, the expenditure on which was a revenue item, and a five-year lease, the premium on

---

[233] For a general discussion of the cases, see Whiteman [1966] BTR 115; the leading cases were cited in *Rolfe v Wimpey Waste Management Ltd* [1988] STC 329, 62 TC 399.

[234] *BP (Australia) Ltd v Taxation Commr* [1966] AC 224, [1965] 3 All ER 209.

[235] *Bolam v Regent Oil Co* (1956) 37 TC 56.

[236] *IRC v Coia* (1959) 38 TC 334.

[237] *Evans v Wheatley* (1958) 38 TC 216; *Tanfield Ltd v Carr* [1999] STC (SCD) 213.

[238] In *Regent Oil v Strick* [1965] 3 All ER 174, 191, 43 TC 1, 43 Lord Morris approved *Bolam v Regent Oil* only on this ground.

[239] *IRC v Coia* (1959) 38 TC 334.

[240] [1965] 3 All ER 209, [1966] AC 224.

[241] Now subject to tax in part by CTA 2009, s 217, ex TA 1988, s 34.

[242] [1965] 3 All ER 174, 43 TC 1.

which was a capital item, meant that the distinction had to be sought in the nature of the asset acquired by the company. Under the lease scheme the company acquired not only an interest in the land but also a better security, since if the owner broke the covenant it could terminate the sub-lease and take possession under the lease. The commercial needs of the company in a changing market, which had affected the Privy Council, were ignored by the House of Lords. An argument that the ties were payable out of circulating capital because they were to secure orders and would therefore come circulating back, which had impressed the Privy Council, was rejected.

The present position is, perhaps inevitably, uncertain. A tie accompanied by a lease would seem to be capital; but Lord Reid in *Regent Oil Co v Strick* considered that payments for very short leases, eg two or three years, might be revenue.[243] A tie unaccompanied by a lease will usually be a revenue expense, even if it lasts for five years. There is authority that such a tie for 20 years will not be a revenue expense since it lacks the element of recurrence, but where the line is to be drawn between five and 20 years remains to be seen (although in *Bolam v Regent Oil* a six-year tie was classified as revenue). The stress in the House of Lords on the nature of the asset acquired suggested that a premium payment in respect of a lease would be a capital item. One reason for this was that the payment would be capital in the hands of the recipient, an erroneous reason made the more absurd by the subsequent decision by the legislature to tax part of the premium as income of the recipient. Whether a premium in respect of a short lease would be treated as a revenue receipt of the trade rather than being dealt with under the ITTOIA 2005, Part 3 rules remains to be seen.[244] In *IRC v John Lewis Properties plc*, the Court of Appeal held, by a majority, that a sum received for the sale of a right to rent for five years and a day was a capital receipt.[245] For the majority Dyson LJ, after emphasising that he was dealing only with the context in which a sum was received in return for a right to income, identified five factors for consideration, though explaining that none was decisive—the duration of the right, the value of the asset assigned, the reduction in the value of the assignor's interest, whether the payment was a capital sum and whether there was a transfer of risk.

In *Beauchamp v FW Woolworth plc*,[246] Lord Templeman, in explaining these cases, stated that where the expenditure had been held to be a revenue account it was because the petrol tie had become an integral method of trading and an ordinary incident of marketing. These cases were therefore immaterial in considering the status of a five-year loan. Attempts to turn taxable streams of income into something different through sales were countered by FA 2008.

22.5 Public Policy

The court may refuse to allow the deduction of expenses on grounds of public policy. This is the basis for the view of the House of Lords in *McKnight v Sheppard*,[247] disallowing the

---

[243] *Ibid*, 187, 38.
[244] ITTOIA 2005, s 261 gives primacy to Pt 2 rules.
[245] [2003] STC 117, [2002] EWCA Civ 1869.
[246] [1989] STC 510, 518, 61 TC 542, 581.
[247] [1999] STC 669, esp 674f, 675c, per Lord Hoffmann.

deduction of a fine imposed by a professional body. The purpose of the fine was to punish the taxpayer, and that purpose would be diluted if he were allowed to share the cost with the rest of the community by being allowed to deduct it for tax purposes. However, legal fees incurred in connection with the hearing were deductible since the rule of public policy did not extend this far.[248] In *McLaren Racing Ltd v HMRC*,[249] the taxpayer sought to deduct in computing its trading profits a £32 million fine imposed by Formula One racing for spying on rival team Ferrari. The two First-tier Tribunal judges fundamentally disagreed on the result, and by casting vote the taxpayer won. Hellier J, presiding, concluded that the fine was distinguishable from statutory fines as well as the type of fine at issue in *McKnight v Sheppard*, and was 'wholly and exclusively' incurred for purposes of the taxpayer's trade. Hellier J rejected HMRC's arguments that public policy dictated that the fine should not be deductible, holding that 'it was not levied for the protection of the public but mainly for the regulation of commercial activity'. On appeal, the Upper Tribunal reversed Hellier J's decision, holding that the fine was penal in nature and there was a sufficient degree of public interest to conclude that for public policy reasons it should not be deductible.[250] Going forward this decision leaves several questions unresolved, such as where the boundary lies in determining whether a fine is penal or not, and what level of public interest needs to be involved to justify denying a deduction.

22.6 Statutory Prohibitions

22.6.1 General

It was once customary to begin with TA 1988, section 74, which listed prohibited deductions. When section 74 was rewritten by ITTOIA 2005, Chapter 4, many of its prohibitions were removed. Sections 74(1)(a) and (e) were rewritten as ITTOIA 2005, s 34,[251] and paragraphs (b) and (o) were repealed for corporation tax. Many of these deductions are clearly not allowable on normal accountancy principles. The list antedates those principles; in 1951 its retention was recommended in order that Inspectors of Taxes might have something in black and white to show small shopkeepers who are 'among the class of persons most apt to suppose that they might charge some of their domestic expenses against their business receipts.'[252] Its rewriting is long overdue and welcome. The following account is designed partly for historical purposes and partly to assist people reading the cases.

Section 74(1)(b) of TA 1988 prohibited the deduction of sums for the maintenance of the parties or their families in establishments or any sum expended for other domestic or private purposes distinct from the trade, profession or vocation. Whether the first limb prescribes a purely objective test was not settled. It has been held that the expression

[248] On Similar US rule, see Tyler (1965) 20 *Tax Law Review* 665.
[249] [2012] UKFTT 601 (TC).
[250] [2014] UKUT 0269 (TCC).
[251] Only (b) and (o) are repealed completely; the rest continue for corporation tax.
[252] Report of the Committee on the Taxation of Trading Profits, Cmnd 8189 (1951), §137.

'maintenance', while not restricted to domestic maintenance, is confined to the ordinary necessities of life.[253]

Section 74(1)(c) prohibited the deduction of certain payments of rent of domestic office and dwelling houses.

Section 74(1)(d) concerned the repair of premises and the supply, repair and alteration of articles and utensils, and limits the deductions to sums actually so expended[254] (see above at §22.4.3).

Section 74(1)(e) (now ITTOIA 2005, section 33(1)(b)) prevents the deduction of any loss not connected with or arising out of the trade, profession or vocation. This provision provided the ratio for the majority of the House of Lords in *Strong v Woodifield* (see above at §22.3). A loss is different from an expense in that it comes from outside the trader's pocket, not within. Thus, petty pilfering by an employee is a loss, but money spent on legal advice is an expense or disbursement.[255] The provision also means that a loss sustained in a transaction not forming part of the trade cannot be deducted.[256] Section 74(1)(e) has been said to involve substantially the same test as section 74(1)(a);[257] however, the boundary is not yet finally settled and may never be.[258]

Section 74(1)(f) prohibited the deduction of any capital withdrawn from, or any sum employed or intended to be employed as, capital in the trade, but with an express allowance for interest.[259] ITTOIA 2005, section 33 prohibits the deduction of capital and section 28 now governs the deduction of interest; the opening words of paragraph (f) are repealed. The opening words of (f) were held to refer particularly to capital losses in connection with loans and guarantees financing the trade. There is, however, a distinction between a capital loss and a revenue loss. Losses on money advanced by a consortium to a colliery company were held to be capital,[260] but losses incurred when a solicitor guaranteed a client's overdraft were held to be revenue, the distinction being that the guarantee was a normal incident of the profession.[261] Later, the section operated to prohibit the deduction of a premium due on the redemption of preference shares or the repayment of loan capital. The section did not appear to apply to an exchange loss incurred on repayment of a loan in foreign currency as it applied only to the loans themselves.[262]

---

[253] *Watkis v Ashford Sparkes & Harwood* [1985] STC 451; s 74(1)(b) was also considered briefly in *Prince v Mapp* (1970) 46 TC 169.

[254] In *Jenners Princes Street Edinburgh Ltd v IRC* [1998] STC (SCD) 166 this was held to mean expended in an accounting sense, and so permitted the deduction of the full cost of repairs when the contract had been put out to tender. The effect of the change from 'premises occupied for the purposes of a trade' to 'premises occupied for a Schedule A business' is unclear: see Gammie and de Souza, *Land Taxation* (Sweet & Maxwell, 1986), vol 1, para A.5.107; and now withdrawn Revenue leaflet Taxation of Rents (IR 150), para 157.

[255] *Allen v Farquharson Bros & Co* (1932) 17 TC 59, 64, per Finlay J. See also *Roebank Printing Co Ltd v IRC* (1928) 13 TC 864; and *Bamford v ATA Advertising Ltd* [1972] 3 All ER 535, 48 TC 359.

[256] Eg, *FA and AB Ltd v Lupton* (see above at §19.3.2).

[257] *McKnight v Sheppard* [1997] STC 846, 851, per Nourse LJ; however, see above at §22.3.

[258] See the interesting discussion in *Sycamore and Maple v Fir* 1997 STC (SCD) 1, 91 *et seq.*

[259] This reverses *European Investment Trust Co Ltd v Jackson* (1932) 18 TC 1.

[260] *James Waldie & Sons v IRC* (1919) 12 TC 113; for a fuller example, see *Beauchamp v FW Woolworth plc* [1987] STC 279.

[261] *Hagart and Burn-Murdoch v IRC* [1929] AC 386, 14 TC 433, HL; *Jennings v Barfield and Barfield* [1962] 2 All ER 957, 40 TC 365.

[262] *Beauchamp v FW Woolworth plc* [1988] STC 714, 718c, 61 TC 542, 568; it follows from this decision that the earlier decision in *European Investment Trust Co Ltd v Jackson* (1932) 18 TC 1, which disallowed interest under

Section 74(1)(g) prohibited the deduction of capital employed on improvements of business premises (see above at §22.4).

Section 74(1)(h) prohibited any deduction for interest which might have been made if any of the sums mentioned in section 74(f) and (g) had been laid out as interest. This bars notional interest, but not actual interest. The new rules on interest are at §22.6.2.

Section 74(1)(j) concerned debts not shown to be bad (see below at §23.2.3). It continues in ITTOIA 2005, section 35 but has been amended.

Section 74(1)(k) barred any average loss beyond the actual amount of loss after adjustment, and concerns insurers.

Section 74(1)(l) prohibited the deduction of any sums recoverable under an insurance or indemnity. This is surprisingly limited and does not prohibit the deduction of sums recoverable, for example, in tort, although any sums actually recovered will be taken into account.

Section 74(1)(m) barred a deduction for corporation tax for annuities or other annual payments payable out of the profits, and section 74(1)((p) did the same for any royalty or other sum paid in respect of the use of a patent. These payments fall within the system of deduction at source as it survived ITA 2007, which repealed TA 1988, sections 348 and 349. ITTOIA 2005, section 51, which mirrored TA 1988, section 74(1)(p), has also been repealed by ITA 2007. It will be noted that annual payments for bona fide commercial reasons in connection with an individual's trade, profession or vocation are subject to the system of deduction at source and relief in ITA 2007, sections 448 and 900 (below at §27.5). Sections 74(1)(n) and (o) prohibited certain interest deductions, eg interest paid to a person not resident in the UK that exceeded a reasonable commercial rate.

TA 1988, section 74 had provisions dealing with the interaction of business deductions with the system of deduction at source contained in TA 1988, sections 348 and 349. Those provisions were largely repealed by ITA 2007.

22.6.2 Interest

A person carrying on a trade may, in computing the profits, deduct the interest payments incurred in that trade. Such payments will be deductible on general accounting principles, so that deductibility is distinct from the special rules discussed above at §22.1. Section 74(1)(f) of the TA 1988 was interpreted to mean that the prohibition on the deduction in respect of capital was not to mean the disallowance of interest. This effect is preserved by ITTOIA 2005, section 29, which thus states that interest is of a revenue nature but still leaves the actual deductibility to general principles, eg as to the business purpose of the loan.[263] Double relief for interest is excluded by ITTOIA 2005, section 52.

this provision, was to be explained solely on the ground that a concession as to the meaning of the statute was disregarded (see [1988] STC 714, 718a, 61 TC 542, 568). In other words, the decision should be disregarded. This issue was not touched on by Lord Templeman in the House of Lords ([1989] STC 510, 61 TC 542).

[263] Notes to Clauses.

22.6.3 *Business Gifts and Entertainment Expenses*

The general rule that expenses incurred wholly and exclusively for the business were deductible led to particular problems in the area of business entertainment expenses, such expenses being deductible even though paid on a lavish scale. A famous example was the modest firm which, in the 1960s, deducted £3,600 in computing its profits, of which £1,700 was on account of the purchase of a grouse moor. While such expenditure may have been justified by a business purpose, there was also the chance that the hospitality was offered purely in the hope that it would be reciprocated, which meant that the leisure activities of senior businessmen were being subsidised by the Revenue. There is no reason why the taxpayer should subsidise such things.

ITTOIA 2005, section 45 now prohibits the deduction of expenses—including incidental expenses—incurred in providing 'business entertainment', a phrase defined to include hospitality of any kind (section 45(3)(a)). Section 47 extends to the provision of gifts. The disallowance turns on the facts, not the purpose of the trader.[264] The same rule applies to Part 3. The policy behind section 45 extends to employment income, and ITEPA 2003, section 356 prevents the employee from deducting such expenses.[265] However, this does not cover all the possibilities. If the employer pays an employee an allowance purely for entertainment purposes, the employer may not deduct the allowance in computing his profits; the employee is taxable on the allowance but may deduct any expenditure satisfying the rule in ITEPA 2003, Part 5, whether or not it would satisfy ITEPA 2003, section 356. If, however, the employer pays the employee a general allowance to cover terms which include entertainment, the position is reversed. The employer may deduct the cost of the allowance (section 48(2)), assuming that it also satisfies the other rules (eg section 33), but the employee may deduct only such entertainment costs as satisfy both provisions in ITEPA 2003 and ITTOIA 2005.[266] The same two-pronged pattern applies to expenses incurred in providing an employee with a gift.

Some entertainment expenses are permitted:

(1) Expenses incurred in the entertainment of bona fide members of staff are deductible. Curiously, the requirement of reasonableness is absent here (section 46(3)). The exception does not apply when the entertainment is incidental to the provision of entertainment for outsiders.

(2) Expenses are deductible if they are—
  (a) incurred in the provision of that which it is a person's trade to provide, and
  (b) the entertainment is provided by him in the course of his trade either for payment or gratuitously if it is provided with the object of advertising to the public generally (section 46(2)).

---

[264] *Fleming v Associated Newspapers Ltd* [1972] 2 All ER 574, 46 TC 401 (see below).
[265] ITEPA 2003, ss 356–58.
[266] Ex TA 1988, s 577(3). This reverses the normal process under ITEPA 2003, Pt 3, Ch 3 s 153, which charges the employee but allows the employer to deduct (see above §18.3.4.1).

Examples of expenses within group (a) would be the provision of food by a restaurateur or of theatre tickets by a theatre owner, and examples of those within group (b) are free samples of products or complimentary theatre tickets for the press, although not for friends.

The exception is limited to the provision of 'anything which it is his trade to provide'. 'Anything' has been construed to mean business entertainment, so that it must be a person's trade to supply such entertainment. Hence, a journalist providing drinks for potential sources of information, or meals for the softening-up of contributors, does not fall within the exception.[267] It was that person's trade to produce newspapers, not refreshment; it would follow that if that person offered not drinks but a copy of his paper, that expense might be deductible. Another problem is whether the person must supply the entertainment himself. Thus, if the owner of a fried chicken shop provides business entertainment in his own shop, with his own fried chicken, he can clearly deduct his costs, but it is not clear whether he could deduct the costs of entertaining the same people at the Ritz. In this latter instance he is supplying that which it is his trade to supply, but the sums would probably not be deductible merely because of the coincidence of the entertainment provided with his own trade. It is probable that the expense is deductible only if his trade supplies the entertainment.

Permitted gift rules are set out in section 47 and are mostly analogous to the exceptions for entertainment. They include:

(1) sums paid to employees provided they are not (exclusively) to enable the employee to provide gifts in connection with the trade;
(2) the cost of items which it is the trader's trade to provide if given away in the ordinary course of trade and to advertise the trade to the public generally;
(3) the costs of small gifts (up to £50 pa per donee)) if they carry conspicuous advertisements, such as calendars and diaries;[268]
(4) the cost of gift for employees;
(5) gifts to a charity, including the Historic Buildings Commission and the National Heritage Memorial Fund.[269] This leaves the taxpayer with the task of ensuring that the gift also escapes section 33.

22.7 Sale and Leaseback; Disallowance of Excess Rent

22.7.1 Leasebacks of Land

Where rents in excess of the commercial rent are paid under a leaseback arrangement, the excess is not deductible.[270]

---

[267] *Fleming v Associated Newspapers Ltd* [1972] 2 All ER 574, 46 TC 401.
[268] ITTOIA 2005, s 47(3). The figure was increased from £10 by FA 2001, s 73. The limit may now be varied by statutory instrument.
[269] ITTOIA 2005, s 47(5).
[270] ITA 2007, Pt, 12A Chs 1–2, ex TA 1988, s 779. Top-slicing relief was repealed for 1989–90 and subsequent years.

22.7.2 *Leased Assets Other than Land*

Where, before the sale and leaseback, the asset was used in the trade, the allowable deduction is limited to the commercial rent.[271] Disallowed rental payments may, however, be rolled forward and used in later periods when the rent paid is below the commercial rent. Where the asset was not so used, and the payer, having received a tax deduction for his rent, then receives a capital sum under the lease, the deduction is clawed back to the extent of that sum;[272] the claw back is reduced when part of the rent has been disallowed. This rule also applies where the lessor's interest belongs to an associate of the payer and the associate receives a capital sum, in which case the charge is on the associate. Further rules apply to leased assets subject to hire purchase agreements.[273]

22.8 Expressly Permitted Expenditure

Certain types of expenditure are made deductible by statute. These are mostly items which would otherwise be non-deductible under ITTOIA 2005, section 34 or are capital expenditure (section 33). In ITTOIA 2005 they are grouped under Chapter 5, sections 56–94A (rules permitting deductions) and Chapter 11, sections 149–172 (on particular trades). They include:

(1)   incidental costs of loan finance (section 58);
(2)   contributions to approved local enterprise agencies (sections 82 *et seq*), local enterprise companies, training and enterprise councils, and business-link organisations and urban regeneration companies;
(3)   applications for patents, designs or trade marks (sections 89–90);
(4)   gifts of trading stock to charities and educational establishments (sections 108–110);
(5)   the costs of seconding employees to charities and educational establishments (sections 70–71);
(6)   contributions to agent's expenses paid in connection with the payroll deduction scheme for charitable gifts by employees (section 72);
(7)   premiums in connection with leases payable in respect of business premises when the landlord is chargeable under ITTOIA 2005, Part 3, Chapter 4 (sections 60–67);
(8)   certain capital expenditure by a cemetery or cremation authority (sections 169–172);
(9)   rents paid for tied premises (section 19);
(10)   certain sums in connection with post-cessation receipts (sections 254–255);
(11)   payments, etc to an employee for restrictive undertakings taxable under ITEPA 2003, sections 225 and 226 (section 69);
(12)   employer's redundancy payments (section 76) and costs of providing counselling and retraining services to employees in connection with the termination of their employment (sections 73–75);

---

[271] ITA 2007, Pt 12A, Ch 3, ex TA 1988, s 782.
[272] ITA 2007, Pt 12A, Ch 4, ex TA 1988, s 781; 'capital sum' includes insurance proceeds.
[273] ITA 2007, s 681DE, ex TA 1988, s 784.

(13)   most sums permitted under the capital allowance system (CAA 2001);

(14)   Revenue expenditure on scientific research (section 87);

(15)   replacement and alteration of trade tools (section 68, repealed from 6 April 2016);

(16)   personal security expenses (section 81);

(17)   payments of export credit guarantee department (section 91);

(18)   certain travelling expenses connected with foreign trades (sections 92–94).

ITTOIA 2005, Part 2, Chapter 11, which contains rules making some expenditure expressly allowable for particular trades, also covers dealers in securities, persons authorised under the Financial and Investment Services Management Act 2000, dealers in land, ministers of religion, barristers, mineral exploration and access, persons liable to pool betting duty, intermediaries treated as making employment payments, managed service companies and waste disposal. Of the above, (1) on loan finance is worth additional mention. It does not apply for corporation tax as the loan relationship rules in CTA 2009, Parts 5–7 allow such expenses. The expenditure must be incurred wholly and exclusively for the purpose of obtaining finance or repaying it. It has been held that expenses incurred in repaying a loan, the effect of which will be to enable the business to borrow new money for expansion, is not within section 58 since the expansion purpose prevents it.[274]

22.9   Enhanced Expenditure; Tax Credits for Revenue Expenditure by Companies

The concept of a tax credit for revenue expenditure is in some ways similar to the old investment allowance. It is nonetheless interesting, especially as the company may claim a tax credit even where there are insufficient profits. As it is confined to companies, it is considered below at §62.2.5.

---

[274] *Focus Dynamics v Turner* [1999] STC (SCD) 1.

23

Business Income—Part V: Timing and Trading Stock (Inventory)

23.1   Accounting Bases, Earnings Basis and Cash Basis

23.1.1 Current Status

The tax system measures the profits of a business for a particular period. Today, ITTOIA 2005, section 25 provides that the profit must be measured in accordance with GAAP—subject to any adjustment required or authorised by law. The 1993 decision of the Court of Appeal in *Gallagher v Jones* (above at §21.1.1.2) also refers to the role of accounting practice in measuring profits, unless it is 'otherwise inapt to determine the true profits or losses of the business'. These two formulae give courts considerable flexibility in preferring a rule of law to accounting practice, but so far the courts have shown few signs of wanting to do so, and the Revenue have shown little enthusiasm in inviting the courts to do so.

It is essential first to distinguish what may for convenience be called the 'earnings' basis from the cash basis. The cash basis was abolished in 1998 subject to an exception for new barristers and advocates. Following a recommendation of the Office of Tax Simplification (OTS) the cash basis was reinstated in 2013 in a limited form for small, unincorporated businesses; the exception for barristers and advocates was withdrawn (see above §21.1.1). Under the earnings basis the actual dates of payment are ignored; sums due but not yet paid, whether debits or credits, are brought into account. This is now subject to special statutory rules, eg those for the payment of remuneration chargeable in the hands of the payee under ITEPA 2003.[1] By contrast, the cash basis took into account only sums of money actually spent or received, regardless of when they became due. One consequence of the cash basis was that post-cessation receipts escaped all income tax. Therefore, if a barrister retired from practice because he was appointed to the Bench or to government office (such as Lord Chancellor), all sums paid after the day of retirement would be tax free. There was no obligation to enter the unpaid sums as a debt due to the barrister, since this obligation arose only when an earnings basis was used. This immunity from taxation arose from the doctrine of the source; when the sums were paid there was no source and so they could not be taxable income. This anomaly was criticised by the Royal Commission in 1955,[2] and was changed by FA 1960 (now ITTOIA 2005, Part 2, Chapter 18). It is reasonable to suppose that Lord Simon, who served as Lord Chancellor in two administrations, took advantage of this pre-1960 gap in the law on each occasion it arose before him; his remarks in some of the tax avoidance cases should, perhaps, be read in the light of this good fortune.

23.1.2 Finality of Accounts; Reopening

A recurring issue is whether the tax system will allow an account to be reopened. The two UK rules, grounded in case law, are as follows:

(1)   An account may be reopened to include figures which do not appear in the accounts at all or are shown to be wrong.

(2)   However, the account cannot be reopened if the amount of the liability stated in the accounts was correctly stated as the finally agreed amount of the liability.

The leading case on (2) is *British Mexican Petroleum Co Ltd v Jackson*.[3] The taxpayer company had incurred a large liability in year 1; in year 3 the creditor released part of that liability. The House of Lords held, first, that the release could not alter the amount of the liability entered for the year 1 and, secondly, that the sum released could not be treated as a trading receipt in year 3.[4]

Legislation reversed the second part of the *British Mexican* decision. The release is now to be treated as a trading receipt in the period of release.[5] This suggests that the legislature accepted the first part of the decision in *British Mexican*. The Revenue view is that a release is a release, whether it is gratuitous or for value; however, the extent of any value received would have to be brought into account to reduce the sum taxable.[6] Statute provides that a release forming part of a voluntary arrangement under the Insolvency Act 1986 does not

---

[1]   ITTOIA 2005, ss 36 *et seq*, FA 1989, s 43 as amended and FA 2003, Sch 24.

[2]   Royal Commission on the Taxation of Profits and Income, Final Report, Cmnd 9474 (1955), 12.

[3]   (1932) 16 TC 570; and see Atkinson J in *Jays the Jewellers Ltd v IRC* [1947] 2 All ER 762, 768, 29 TC 274, 284.

[4]   The UK has no 'recapture of tax benefit' doctrine, as does the United States—see the *Kirby Lumber* case ((1931) 284 US 1); on cancellation of debt in the United States, see Bittker and Thompson (1978) 66 *California LR* 1159.

[5]   ITTOIA 2005, s 99, ex TA 1988, ss 94, 87(4); *Wildin v Jowett* [2002] STC (SCD) 389.

[6]   Inland Revenue interpretation RI 50. The Revenue view is based on cases decided under TA 1988, s 421.

give rise to a trading receipt.[7] FA 2005 widened the statutory rule to cover impairment losses and debts to be settled otherwise than in money.[8] The Revenue view is that *British Mexican* has no application to the different question of the taxability of a trade debt which is not released but simply written off or not pursued, and is later written back into the accounts.[9]

Illustration—*Symons v Weeks*

Under rule (1) above, the figure originally entered may be adjusted if it has not yet been finally agreed between the Revenue and the taxpayer as a final figure,[10] and *a fortiori* where no figure appeared in the accounts at all.[11] In such instances the courts favour the use of hindsight. However, in the particular circumstances of *Symons v Weeks*,[12] Warner J reasserted the authority of rule (2) above. Staged payments to architects involved a substantial element of payment in advance, but the exact whole fee would not be known until the work was completed. In accordance with accounts which had been properly drawn up, only a portion of the sum received in a year was shown as a trading receipt. Warner J said that *Simpson v Jones*,[13] which had given us rule (1), could not apply to a case where accounts had been drawn up correctly, and therefore the Revenue could not amend the figures retrospectively. The taxpayer was right in seeking to be taxed on the figures in the accounts.

23.1.3 *Former Relief for Barristers and Advocates*

ITTOIA 2005, section 160 formerly gave special relief to barristers and advocates who were in actual practice, for a period of account ending no more than seven years after starting to practice, ie when they first hold themselves out as available for fee-earning work. The rules allowed barristers and advocates to compute profits: (a) on the old cash basis, or (b) by reference to fees earned, the amount of which has been agreed and in respect of which a fee note has been delivered. This special regime was withdrawn with effect from the 2013–14 tax year, coinciding with the introduction of a limited cash basis regime for small unincorporated businesses.

23.1.4 *Adjustment Income*

On spreading of adjustment income when a basis changes, see sections 238–239 above at §21.11.

---

[7] ITTOIA 2005, s 99(2), ex TA 1988, s 94 as amended by FA 1994, s 144(2).
[8] FA 2005, Sch 4, para 3.
[9] RI 238.
[10] *Bernhard v Gahan* (1928) 13 TC 723.
[11] *Simpson v Jones* [1968] 2 All ER 929, 44 TC 599.
[12] [1983] STC 195, 56 TC 630 (Warner J pointed out that if the Revenue had not insisted on a change from cash basis to earnings basis, they could have got what they wanted).
[13] [1968] 2 All ER 929, 44 TC 599.

23.2 Receipts

Three general principles have been developed by the courts (but, as always, these are now subject to accounting principles). The first is a realisation principle based on the time when the profits are ascertained or realised. The second is a matching principle, which will override the first principle when it is appropriate to do so and shift the receipt back to the period when the receipt was earned.[14] The third principle is that the courts will give effect to accounting evidence to move a payment which has been received forward to a later accounting period. The three principles are now discussed in turn.

23.2.1 Profits Ascertained or Realised

This principle is a rule against anticipation of profits.[15] The accounting principle of prudence is another basis for the rule. Sums due, whether to or from the trade, must be entered when, and only when, all the conditions precedent to earning or paying them have been fulfilled; this is a question of construction of the particular contract.[16] The leading case is *JP Hall & Co Ltd v IRC*.[17] In March 1914, the company made a contract to supply certain electric motors, deliveries to begin in June 1914 and end in September 1915, with payment within one month of delivery. The final delivery did not take place until July 1916. The company argued that the receipts should have been taken as earned when the contract was made—in March 1914. Lord Sterndale MR put the matter simply: 'These profits were neither ascertained nor made at the time these two contracts were concluded.'[18] The profits therefore could not have been anticipated.

As Baxter showed years ago,[19] such an analysis is on the simple side. In the real world of commerce:

(1)   the trader (T) glimpses the far-off possibility of gain;
(2)   T starts to deploy assets, eg by buying raw materials;
(3)   the assets mature, eg become finished goods;
(4)   the trader becomes entitled to payment;
(5)   T receives payment; and
(6)   any risk of claims in respect of the contract, eg for faulty goods, passes away.

In such cases everything turns on the construction of the agreement or statute giving rise to the payment. In *Johnson v W Section Try Ltd*,[20] a payment for compensation for refusal

---

[14] See the speeches of Lord Fraser and Lord Keith in *Willingale v International Commercial Bank* [1978] STC 75, 52 TC 242. See also Freedman [1987] BTR 61 and 104; and White [1987] BTR 292.

[15] For example Lord Reid in *Duple Motor Bodies v Ostime* (1961) 39 TC 537, 569. For an efficiency analysis of rules from a US perspective see Shaiviro (1992) 48 *Tax Law Review* 1.

[16] *Johnson v WS Try Ltd* (1946) 27 TC 167 at 185, per Lord Greene MR.

[17] [1921] 3 KB 152, 12 TC 382.

[18] *Ibid*, 155, 389. The company's case was not strengthened by the fact that its accounts showed the receipts as brought in only after delivery.

[19] [1978] BTR 65, 67.

[20] [1946] 1 All ER 532, 27 TC 167.

of planning consent was held to date from the date of the final agreement with the council, it being open to the council until that time to change its mind and grant the consent. FRS 12 dictates a similar result. In *Willingale v International Commercial Bank Ltd*,[21] the House of Lords held that bills of exchange owned by the bank gave rise to profit only when they were realised, whether by sale or on maturity. FRS 12 does not dictate this result, which was probably wrong in 1977 and is certainly wrong now.[22]

23.2.2 Matching Principle: Relating Back to Time Profit Earned

Under this principle, legal rules and accounting principles also converge—both wish to match the receipts with the relevant expenditure. Payments have been related back to the moment of the service even though there was no legal right to payment at the time of that service, as in *Isaac Holden & Sons Ltd v IRC* (see below); moreover, payments have been related back even though the trade has since been discontinued.[23] The general principle was stated by Viscount Simon LC in *IRC v Gardner, Mountain and D'Ambrumenil Ltd*:[24]

> [S]ervices completely rendered or goods supplied, which are not to be paid for till a subsequent year, cannot generally be dealt with by treating the taxpayer's outlay as pure loss in the year in which it was incurred and bringing in the remuneration as pure profit in the subsequent year in which it is paid or due to be paid. In making an assessment ... the net result of the transaction, setting expenses on the one side and a figure for remuneration on the other side, ought to appear ... in the same year's profit and loss account and that year will be the year when the service was rendered or the goods delivered ... This may involve ... an estimate of what the future remuneration will amount to ... [but this provisional estimate] could be corrected when the precise figure was known, by additional assessment ...

The matching principle matches receipts with the moment the services are rendered or the goods supplied, not with the moment a legally enforceable right to payment arose. This has three consequences:

(1)   Where the goods have been delivered, so that the contract has been executed, but payment will not become due until some later time, that payment must be related back to the time of the delivery; in the meantime a provisional figure may have to be put into the accounts. In *IRC v Gardner, Mountain and D'Ambrumenil Ltd*, sums due to be paid and so paid only in 1938 in respect of underwriting services performed in 1936 were attributed to 1936.[25]

(2)   A payment cannot be related back to a time before the services were completed or the goods delivered.[26]

---

[21] [1978] STC 75, [1978] 1 All ER 754, 52 TC 242.
[22] For guidance on the timing of the receipt of income in the form of agricultural subsidies, see Inland Revenue interpretation RI 94.
[23] *Severne v Dadswell* [1954] 3 All ER 243, 35 TC 649.
[24] (1947) 29 TC 69, 93.
[25] For modern law of taxation of Lloyd's underwriters, see FA 1993, ss 171–184.
[26] *John and E Sturge Ltd v Hessel* [1975] STC 127, 51 TC 183; *JP Hall & Co Ltd v IRC* [1921] 3 KB 152, 12 TC 382 (see above at §23.2.1).

(3)   A payment cannot be related back if it is not directly in return for goods supplied or services rendered.[27] So in *Gray v Lord Penrhyn*,[28] a firm of auditors had been negligent in failing to spot defalcations by the taxpayer's employees. The firm subsequently made good the loss but the sums were not related back to the years of the defalcations or the negligence. Instead, the sums were treated as trading receipts in the year of payment which was also the year in which the liability was agreed. This may also be one of the factors behind the decision of the House of Lords in *Willingale* (§23.2.1 above).[29]

Apart from *Gardner, Mountain*, the leading case is *Isaac Holden & Sons Ltd v IRC*.[30] The company was a member of a federation of companies engaged in combing wool for the Government. In July 1918, a provisional price increase of 10% was agreed between the federation and the Government, to operate from 1 January 1918; and in 1919 a total increase of 20% was agreed, with effect from 1 January 1918. The company's trading account ending 30 June 1918 had included the 10% increase, but Rowlatt J directed that it should take account of the 20% increase. The accounts were reopened because no provision for this possibility had been made in the original accounts.

Receipts have been adjusted to take account of subsequent payments not only where services have been rendered, as in the previous cases, but also where the Government requisitioned trading stock[31] and a ship,[32] where payments wrongfully extracted by a government official were reimbursed,[33] and where a ministry agreed to modify an agreement so as to make good a loss sustained by the taxpayer but took a long time paying the sum.[34] In *Harrison v John Cronk & Sons Ltd*,[35] the House of Lords held that there could be no relating back where, at the end of the trading period, only a guess could be made as to the correct measure of the eventual receipts. The case has since been described in the House of Lords as exceptional and as laying down no such general principle.[36] The decision may also be per incuriam since none of the cases on relating back was cited.

23.2.3 Special Rules for Default of Debtor

An adjustment for the default of a debtor is made when the default occurs, and is not related back. This was implemented by ITTOIA 2005, section 35, the predecessor of which (TA 1988, section 74(1)(j)) had been rewritten in 1994 to take account of developments in insolvency law.[37] Under section 35, no deduction may be made for any debts except so far

---

[27]   *Severne v Dadswell* [1954] 3 All ER 243, 248; 35 TC 649, 659, per Roxburgh J.
[28]   [1937] 3 All ER 468, 21 TC 252.
[29]   [1978] STC 75, 87, per Lord Keith.
[30]   (1924) 12 TC 768.
[31]   *IRC v Newcastle Breweries Ltd* (1927) 12 TC 927.
[32]   *Ensign Shipping Co Ltd v IRC* (1928) 12 TC 1169.
[33]   *English Dairies Ltd v Phillips* (1927) 11 TC 597.
[34]   *Rownson, Drew and Clydesdale Ltd v IRC* (1931) 16 TC 595. In each of the above four cases the effect was to increase the taxpayers' liability to excess profits duty.
[35]   [1936] 3 All ER 747, 20 TC 612.
[36]   *IRC v Gardner, Mountain and D'Ambrumenil Ltd* (1947) 29 TC 69, 106 (per Lord Porter), 94 (per Viscount Simon); see also at 111 (per Lord Simonds).
[37]   Insolvency Act 1986; or the Insolvency (Northern Ireland) Order 1989 (SI 1989/000). See RI 81.

as: (a) the debt is bad, (b) the debt is estimated to be bad[38] or (c) the debt is released wholly and exclusively for the purposes of the trade, profession or vocation as part of a statutory insolvency arrangement.[39] In the case of the bankruptcy or insolvency of the debtor, (b) is satisfied as to the whole debt, except to the extent that any amount may reasonably be expected to be received on the debt (section 35(2)). The reason for the introduction of (c) was that the previous version allowed debts to be deducted only when and to the extent that they were proved to be bad, ie irrecoverable. This did not allow the deduction of debts released as part of the new insolvency practice. For similar reasons (b) now provides that a deduction may be taken where the debt is a doubtful debt to the extent that it is estimated bad.[40] This should enable creditors to obtain relief even though they might be expected to have recovered more of the debt by putting the debtor into liquidation or bankruptcy.

Corporation tax has its own rules as part of the loan relationship regime.[41] The old corporation tax rule, section 74(1)(j) and (2), was repealed, and TA 1988, section 88D (now CTA 2009, sections 55 and 970) substituted to reflect the new international accounting terminology of 'impairment loss'. The test for (a) can be severe. A distant prospect that a company's debt may have been paid by the former chairman under a personal guarantee prevented a claim for relief from being established.[42] Meanwhile the value of the potential right to deduct declines year by year.

ITTOIA 2005, section 35 also has the effect of disallowing a tax deduction for a general reserve set up for bad debts. Each debt must be considered separately; the technical accounting term for recognising that a debt has declined in value is that the debt is 'impaired'. If a debt is impaired, the drop in value must be recognised in the income statement—when the 'carrying amount' of the debt exceeds its 'recoverable value'. The practice of the Revenue is that if a debt becomes bad in a year after it first accrues, an allowance may be made in that later year with no relating back.[43] *A fortiori* where a debt is brought in, no allowance may be made for the expense of collecting it in a later year, such expenses belonging to the later year.[44] Accounting practice may allow for general reserves; section 35 overrides such practice unless *Absalom v Talbot*[45] applies.

A debt which has been received or is owed in a foreign country but in circumstances in which foreign exchange restrictions in that country do not allow the debt to be remitted, is not, technically, a bad debt. However, by ITTOIA 2005, Part 2, Chapter 13, replacing and expanding a concession, the debt will be given relief by being treated as a bad debt.

---

[38] For an example, see *Sycamore and Maple v Fir* [1997] STC (SCD) 1, 67 *et seq.*

[39] Defined ITTOIA 2005, s 256.

[40] ITTOIA 2005, s 35, ex TA 1988, s 74(1)(j) and FA 1994, s 144(1); see also Inland Revenue Press Release, 30 November 1993, [1993] *Simon's Tax Intelligence* 1514, and RI 81.

[41] CTA 2009, Pts 5–7, ex FA 1996, Sch 9, paras 5 *et seq.*

[42] *Taylor v Clatworthy* [1996] STC (SCD) 506.

[43] This Revenue practice was approved by Lord Atkin and by the two dissentients, Lord Simon and Lord Porter, in *Absalom v Talbot* [1944] 1 All ER 642, 26 TC 166. Lord Russell of Killowen and Lord Thankerton expressed no opinion. The practice was accepted by Macnaghten J and the Court of Appeal in *Bristow v William Dickinson & Co Ltd* [1946] KB 321, 27 TC 157.

[44] *Monthly Salaries Loan Co Ltd v Furlong* (1962) 40 TC 313. In 1961, the Revenue made special arrangements for credit traders: see *Simon's Direct Tax Service*, Pt B3, 1151ff.

[45] [1944] 1 All ER 642, 26 TC 1669. On accounting practice, see Thomas, *An Introduction for Financial Accounting*, 4th edn (McGraw-Hill, 2002), ch 12.

Relief is not available if the amount is used to finance the foreign business or is applied any other way, has been given relief under some other rule or if the debt is covered by insurance (section 190). The rewriting is designed to make the rule better adapted for the era of self-assessment.[46] The relief may be withdrawn in appropriate circumstances, eg where the amount ceases to be unremittable or is used in the overseas business (section 191).

ITTOIA 2005, section 34 deals only with deductions and does not state what debts are to be brought into account, nor at what value. The value of a debt is a matter of fact and is not necessarily its face value, even if it is not proved to be a bad debt. In *Absalom v Talbot* (above), the taxpayer was a speculative builder. His purchasers had the option, after payment of a deposit and a sum borrowed from a building society, of leaving the balance outstanding on granting the taxpayer a second mortgage on the house, the sum to be repaid with interest over a period of 20 years. The Revenue insisted on the face value of the debts being incorporated into the accounts until such time as it was proved to be bad, seeing no difference between the present circumstances and those in which the builder, having received the amount outstanding, chose to lend it out at interest. This was rejected by a bare majority in the House of Lords. Once it was accepted that the value of debts was not their face value, considerable problems of implementation arise. One solution would have been to bring in the payments as they were made. The objection to that in 1944 was that payments after discontinuance would have escaped tax even though the earnings basis was employed, an objection no longer valid.[47] Another solution would have been to value the debts, but here it would not have been possible to make adjustments to take account of actual returns. Therefore, Lord Atkin, in *Absalom v Talbot*, preferred the inclusion of the debts at their face value on one side of the account, and a reserve on the other which would be calculated on the ordinary risk of bad debts, but adjusted annually to take account of actual payments made or not made. Such a reserve would not be prohibited by section 35 because that section applies only to debts correctly brought in at face value.

23.2.4 Payment in Advance—Relating Forward?[48]

It ought to follow from the matching principle that where a payment is received in advance, that sum should enter the account only when the service has been rendered or the goods supplied. In the case of sale of goods, accounting practice generally takes as the relevant date that when the goods are transferred, and so there is a transfer of significant risks (see now IFRS 15). A case supporting relating forward is *Symons v Weeks*,[49] but that decision may best be seen as one based on strong accounting evidence in the case of a long-term construction contract. Such contracts used to have their own separate international standards (SSAP, IAS 11) but are now also in IFRS 15. Case law on expenses[50] also recognises spreading forward

---

[46] Inland Revenue Press Release, 11 April 1991, [1991] *Simon's Tax Intelligence* 395.
[47] Because of TA 1988, s 103.
[48] See Thomas, *op cit*, ch 13; and Francovich (2002) 50 *Can Tax Jo* 1239–1306.
[49] [1983] STC 195, 56 TC 630; see also *Arthur Murray (NSW) Pty Ltd v FCT* (1965) 114 CLR 314. For history of the Murray Dance Studios, see *The Economist*, 14 August 1999, 76.
[50] Eg, *Johnston v Britannia Airways* [1994] STC 763, 67 TC 99.

on the basis of a possible accounting method. In the United States this spreading forward of a prepayment has been denounced as bad economics, bad accounting and bad tax.[51]

Older authority[52] holds that money belonging to the trader will be treated as a trading receipt when received (or due); this might be seen as overriding the matching principle, at least where the sum received is final and is a trading receipt, and may be taken as applying in the absence of accounting evidence as in *Symons v Weeks*. In *Elson v Price's Tailors Ltd*,[53] customers ordering a made-to-measure garment would be asked for a deposit. These deposits were, as a matter of practice, returned to any customers who did not like the finished goods, but some clients did not return to claim their deposits. Before the Commissioners the taxpayer argued that the deposits should have become trading receipts only when the customers took delivery. The Crown argued for the date the deposits became forfeitable or, alternatively, when they were transferred to head office. Ungoed-Thomas J held that the payments were truly deposits and not part-payments, and so were security for the completion of the purchase; the money therefore belonged to the taxpayer and the payments were trading receipts when received. However, the judge went on to reject the argument that the relating-back doctrine applied where the payment preceded the performance of the contract. This seems illogical. In *Elson v Price's Tailors* the Crown did not apparently argue for the year of receipt but only for the date the deposits were forfeitable. In *Sun Insurance Office v Clark*,[54] insurance premiums paid in advance for a year were not treated as income only of the year of receipt, but a proportion was to be carried forward to the following year.

23.2.5 Receipts in Kind: Timing Governs Quantum

The only difference between a payment in money and a payment in kind is that the value of the former is more obvious. Where, therefore, a trading receipt is received otherwise than in sterling, whether in foreign currency or in kind, a value must be put on the receipt at the time it becomes a trading receipt, ie when it is delivered or, if earlier, when it is due. Subsequent changes in value should be ignored.[55] It is no objection to such valuation that the benefit in kind cannot, in fact, be converted into cash. In *Gold Coast Selection Trusts Ltd v Humphrey*,[56] the trust had sold certain rights in a gold mine concession in exchange for shares in a company and was held taxable on the value of the shares so received, even though it would have been impossible to obtain a reasonable price for them if they had all been sold in one go on the Stock Exchange.

Where a dealing company receives shares, such shares will be valued as trading receipts only when they represent the end of a trading transaction, as opposed to a step in the course of a transaction.[57] There must, however, be some sort of realisation. In *Varty v British South*

---

[51] Johnson (1995) 50 *Tax Law Review* 373; note also Halperin (1985) 95 *Yale Law Journal* 516, arguing that the customer making the prepayment should be taxable on the interest that could be attributed to such a prepayment; and Klein (1994) 41 *UCLA LR* 1686.

[52] *Elson v Price's Tailors Ltd* [1963] 1 All ER 231, 40 TC 671.

[53] See above §21.8.

[54] [1912] AC 443, 6 TC 59.

[55] *Greig v Ashton* [1956] 3 All ER 123, 36 TC 581.

[56] [1948] 2 All ER 379, 30 TC 209. See [1970] BTR 150.

[57] In *Royal Insurance Co Ltd v Stephen* (1928) 14 TC 22, 28.

Africa Co,[58] by contrast, a company had an option to subscribe for shares in company C at par and decided to exercise that option. The court held that there was no realisation and so no taxable profit at the time. The question in all cases is one of fact and substance, but the *Varty* case appears to be the only reported instance involving securities where the court has held that there was no realisation. Therefore, even an exchange of shares under a company amalgamation scheme has constituted a realisation, as has the exchange of mortgage bonds against one company for debenture stock in a new one when the first company's finances were being restructured.[59] Even the exercise of an option in a government savings scheme to convert the holding into a new government stock was held to be a realisation.[60]

On this basis, where securities—the original holding—are held as circulating capital, trading receipts arise when they are disposed of and are an allowable expense on their reinvestment in the new holding. If, however, they are held as fixed capital, a form of rollover relief may apply, so postponing liability in respect of the resulting capital gain (see below at §42.4). To further the policy behind CGT relief, ITTOIA 2005, section 150 provides that where that relief would apply if the assets were such that the proceeds of sale would not be trading receipts, the original holding is not treated as disposed of and the new holding is treated as the same asset.

23.3 Deductions for Revenue Expenses

In relation to expenses, two particular sets of issues arise and are considered here: the first is what to do with a liability which is not yet certain; the second is how to deal with a liability which has arisen but which may need to be entered into the accounts over more than one period of account (ie spread).

23.3.1 Contingent Liabilities[61]

The question whether a deduction may be made for a contingent liability must be answered first by reference to GAAP. No such evidence was forthcoming in *Peter Merchant Ltd v Stedeford*.[62] The taxpayer ran a canteen for a factory owner and was under a contractual obligation to replace utensils. Owing to wartime scarcities, however, it was not possible to replace the utensils. The accountant recommended that the amounts owing under the liability to replace be deducted each year. However, he had committed an error of law by construing the contract to mean that there was a liability to replace the stock each year rather than at the end of the contract; it followed that deduction could not be allowed each year.

Accounting practice, as set out in FRS 102 (formerly FRS 12) and, in almost identical terms, in IAS 37, and therefore applicable to tax law, distinguishes liabilities for which

---

[58] [1965] 2 All ER 395, 42 TC 406.
[59] *Royal Insurance Co Ltd v Stephen* (1928) 14 TC 22; *Scottish and Canadian General Investment Co Ltd v Easson* (1922) 8 TC 265.
[60] *Westminster Bank Ltd v Osler* [1933] AC 139, 17 TC 381.
[61] See Thomas, *op cit*, ch 27, 395–98.
[62] (1948) 30 TC 496.

provision must be made in the accounts (so giving rise to the deduction for tax purposes) from liabilities for which a note to the account suffices (for which no deduction will be made).[63] So, under FRS 102, paragraph 2.38 a business is not to recognise a contingent asset in its accounts. An asset is contingent if it is simply a 'possible' asset, ie one where the inflow of economic benefits is probable but not 'virtually certain'. Under FRS 102, paragraph 2.39 provision must be made for liabilities if: (a) the entity has a present obligation as a result of a past event, (b) it is probable that a transfer or economic benefit will be required to settle the obligation and (c) a reliable estimate can be made of the amount of the obligation. More detail is provided in FRS 102, section 21, 'Provisions and Contingencies'. Contingent liabilities, for which a mere note suffices and so have no tax consequences (as yet), are possible obligations arising from past events the existence of which will be confirmed only by the occurrence of one or more uncertain future events not wholly within the entity's control, or present obligations arising from past events which are not recognised because it is not probable that a transfer of economic benefit will be required to settle them or the amounts cannot be measured with sufficient reliability. Common examples of contingent liabilities are warranties and refunds, environmental costs, health and safety, onerous leases and court cases. So a pending court case against the taxpayer does not need a provision; if the likelihood of loss is remote, a note in the accounts will do.[64] No provision should be made for merely contingent assets, ie a possible asset where the inflow of economic benefit is probable but not virtually certain. The position in FRS 102 follows the position in FRS 12, which was a change in accounting practice. Consequently, certain cases in which evidence of old accounting practices led the courts to allow a deduction would now be decided differently.

23.3.1.1 Pre-1998 Case Where the Court Ruled Against the Deduction of a Future Liability—No Change

Expenses are not deductible simply because the events giving rise to the need for that work have occurred. In *Naval Colliery Co Ltd v IRC*,[65] a company's mines were damaged during a strike which ended on 2 July 1921; no element for the costs of reconditioning the mine could be included for the period ending 30 June 1921. The same decision would be reached under FRS 102.

23.3.1.2 Pre-1998 Cases Where the Court Allowed a Deduction and Where the Same Result Follows Under FRS 12

In *Herbert Smith v Honour*,[66] a firm of solicitors moved to a new office block which it leased. The firm was still liable to pay rent in respect of premises it no longer occupied, but the market was weak. The firm sought to deduct a sum in the year of the move to cover the expected shortfall between the sums it was still liable to pay and the sums it was liable to get back in rent on subleases. The 1990 forecast proved to be over-optimistic and further provisions had to be made in later years. The Revenue disputed the company's right to deduct the sum in 1990, insisting instead that only the actual shortfall accruing in 1990 should be

---

[63] On FRS 12 see also Collins, 754 *The Tax Journal*, 16 August 2004, p 13.
[64] Collins above.
[65] (1928) 12 TC 1017.
[66] [1999] STC 173.

deducted, on the basis that liabilities could not be anticipated. The Commissioners agreed with the Revenue, noting that the firm's method was not the only one which accountants could use. In the High Court the firm's appeal was allowed. The court held that the commercial principle of accounting should be accepted, and there was no rule of law against anticipating liabilities which prevented the court from accepting it. The Revenue accepted the decision and announced their acceptance of FRS 12 for future years.[67] The facts fall within FRS 12 (now FRS 102, paragraph 2.39) since the liability to pay the rent on the lease of the vacated premises had accrued.

23.3.1.3 Pre-1998 Cases Where the Court Allowed a Deduction, but Where FRS 102 May Prohibit it

In *IRC v Titaghur Jute Factory Co Ltd*,[68] a foreign statute imposed an obligation on employers to pay gratuities to employees on leaving the company service. The amount depended on the final salary and the length of service, including years of service before the statute came into force. However, the statute did not require the company to set aside sums to meet this obligation. Taken literally, FRS 102 would disallow this deduction in that there was no present obligation arising out of a past event. Such an interpretation of FRS 102 would seem unduly restrictive. Similar problems arose in *Johnston v Britannia Airways Ltd*.[69] Here the court allowed a company's major overhaul costs in respect of aero engines to be spread over the period of three or four years leading up to the overhaul. This decision depended on the recognition of the treatment as being in accordance with the then accepted principles of commercial accountancy, and followed the general approach to such questions taken in *Gallagher v Jones*.[70] However, it is hard to see that there was any present obligation to overhaul the engines until the four-year period had expired.[71] *Jenners Princes Street Edinburgh Ltd v IRC*[72] was a decision before FRS 102 (and its predecessor FRS 12) but following *Gallagher v Jones*. The company was faced with a large repair expense. It had completed a feasibility study in year 1, and in year 2 had entered into a contract for the works to be carried out over a period covering years 2 and 3. The company sought to deduct the entire expenditure costs in year 1 on the basis of established accounting principles. Surprisingly, the appeal succeeded; even more surprisingly, the Revenue acquiesced in this. The decision is inconsistent with old case law, such as the *Naval Colliery* case (above). FRS 102, paragraph 2.39 seems to prevent the company in such circumstances from any right to deduct the sum until year 2.

A case which may be relevant to condition (c) of FRS 102, paragraph 2.39 (above) is *Southern Railway of Peru Ltd v Owen*.[73] This case also involved setting aside sums for future

---

[67] Inland Revenue Press Release, 20 July 1999, [1999] *Simon's Weekly Tax Intelligence* 1302.

[68] [1978] STC 166, 53 TC 675; see Edey [1956] BTR 1172, Phillips [1957] BTR 351, and the decision of Lush J, allowing the deduction of future expenses of maintaining graves, in *London Cemetery Co v Barnes* [1917] 2 KB 496, 7 TC 92.

[69] [1994] STC 763, 66 TC 77; for view that the case was explicable under the matching principle, see Macdonald [1995] BTR 484, dissented from by McMahon and Wheetman [1997] BTR 6.

[70] [1993] STC 537, 67 TC 99, CA; discussed in Macdonald, *op cit*, and McMahon and Wheetman, *op cit*.

[71] Collins, 754 *The Tax Journal Issue*, 16 August 2004, p 13 agrees.

[72] [1997] STC (SCD) 196. On Revenue acceptance, see Inland Revenue Press Release, 20 July 1999, [1999] *Simon's Weekly Tax Intelligence* 1302.

[73] [1956] 2 All ER 728, 36 TC 602; see [1986] BTR 4; and the decision of Lush J, allowing the deduction of future expenses of maintaining graves in *London Cemetery Co v Barnes* [1917] 2 KB 496, 7 TC 92.

payments to employees on redundancy, retirement or death. The payments were to be of one month's salary for each completed year of service, the salary being computed according to the rates in force at the time of redundancy or other cause, with certain protection for employees whose salaries declined. No payments were due, however, if an employee on a fixed-term contract resigned before the term had expired, or where an employee was dismissed for just cause. The company argued that it should charge against each year's receipts the cost of making provision for the retirement benefits that it would ultimately have to pay, and conceded that, as a corollary, it would not be able to deduct the actual payments made each year. These figures were rejected by the House of Lords. It held, first, that the figures failed to take account of the length of time that would pass before the payments would become due (a factor which could be met by a discounting process), secondly that the company failed to recognise that the legislation which had created the present pension system could also vary it and, thirdly, that there was the possibility that a certain number of employees would forfeit their rights to payments. For these reasons the figure which the company was trying to deduct, although correctly deducted in order to give a 'true and fair' view of the profits, and necessarily so for the purposes of the Companies Acts, was not sufficiently precise for the Income Tax Acts and probably would not be allowed by FRS 102.

Many cases involve provisions under foreign legislation. Payments to UK-approved pension schemes are deductible under FA 2004 when they are made, ie when paid by the company to the pension scheme managers or trustees.[74] This is an example of a rule of law overriding an accounting principle.

23.3.2 *Payments Attributable to More than One Year: Spreading*

In relation to payments attributable to more than one year, the question is the opposite of that governing contingent liability. The question is whether a payment which has been made can be taken as a deduction, or whether it must be spread forward. In 1993 the Court of Appeal, in *Gallagher v Jones*,[75] held that the expenses must indeed be spread forward if accounting practice required it, and concluded that SSAP 21 did so require it. It followed that no rule of law could prevent the application of SSAP 21. The same result would now follow under ITTOIA 2005, s 25. Before the introduction of FRS 12 (now FRS 102), SSAP 21 applied to finance leases, which were to be contrasted with operating leases. Under an operating lease the non-cancellable period was usually much less than the economic life of the asset and the lessor was at risk with regard to the market value of the asset at the end of the lease. Under a finance lease these risks are shifted to the lessee; payment under the lease are much more closely related to the economic life of the asset.[76] Under FRS 102, section 20, a lease is classified as a finance lease if it transfers 'substantially all the risks and rewards incidental to ownership'. Under the substance over form approach, a finance lease is treated for accounting purposes as if the lessee had purchased the asset from the lessor and financed the purchase with a loan from the lessor. Thus, for financial reporting purposes, the lessee recognises the associated finance costs over the term of the lease, and depreciates the 'asset'.

---

[74] FA 2004, s 196, ex TA 1988, s 592(4).
[75] [1993] STC 537, 66 TC 77, CA. For criticism see §21.1.1.2.
[76] On taxation of leasing, see Mainwaring, *Tolley's Leasing in the UK*.

Finance leases now have their own capital allowance rules. These developments left the earlier decision in *Vallambrosa Rubber Co Ltd v Farmer*[77] in an uncertain state. In that case the company sought to deduct the costs of superintendence, weeding, and control of pests and similar expenditure on a rubber estate, even though rubber trees take seven years to start producing rubber and so only one in seven of the rubber trees was actually in production. The claim succeeded. The case itself was concerned mainly with the distinction between capital and revenue. It does not appear that the Crown argued that the expenses should have been allowed only when the trees began to produce. In *Gallagher v Jones* the Court of Appeal said that the case did not lay down a broad principle.[78] Today it would seem that the accounting would depend on whether the sums satisfied the definition of 'asset' in FRS 102, paragraph 2.15 *et seq*, and especially if future economic benefits are expected to flow to the entity from the work performed.[79] Otherwise, the principle of prudence would seem to require the deduction of such sums when they are incurred.

In *Gallagher v Jones*, the position concerned a finance lease and SSAP 21 (the relevant standard now is FRS 102, section 20). The Revenue had indicated in 1991 that they accepted SSAP 21, and that payments under finance leases were deductible for tax purposes as they were allocated under SSAP 21 and not simply by reference to the date they fell due.[80] The company failed in its claim to deduct sums paid under a finance lease as they were made. The lease provided for payment, during an initial period of 24 months, of a large initial payment, followed by 17 monthly instalments; in the secondary period which began after 24 months a nominal rent was due. The Revenue argued that the initial payment and the 17 monthly instalments should be spread evenly over the 24-month period as, they argued, was suggested in SSAP 21. Reversing Harman J, the Court of Appeal held that SSAP 21 should be followed, though it appears not in its entirety. The uncontradicted evidence before the Commissioner and given by an accountant who was the advisor to the Revenue was that the taxpayers' simple approach would give a completely misleading picture of their trading results. In a case note on *Gallagher v Jones*, Freedman highlights that no expert accountancy evidence was brought on behalf of the taxpayers, which Freedman argues contributed to a failure by the courts to properly analyse SSAP 21, including its objectives and effects, and a failure to consider other potentially relevant standards.[81]

23.4   Post-Cessation Receipts and Expenses

23.4.1 Receipts[82]

This is a particularly tiresome area since the income tax rules on post-cessation receipts are in ITTOIA 2005, Part 2, Chapter 18 (sections 241–259), whilst those on post-cessation expenses are in ITA 2007, sections 96–101. At one time sums received after discontinuance

---

[77] (1910) 5 TC 529.
[78] [1993] STC 537, 547f, 66 TC, 113, CA.
[79] FRS 102, section 34 also contains reporting requirements for specialised activities, including agriculture.
[80] Statement of Practice SP 3/91 (for leases entered into on or after 11 April 1991).
[81] Freedman, 'Ordinary Principles of Commercial Accounting—Clear Guidance or a Mystery Tour?' [1993] BTR 468 (on *Gallagher v Jones*).
[82] See Heaton [1960] BTR 268; Monroe [1961] BTR 284.

by a person who had previously carried on a trade, profession or vocation and relating to that trade were not taxable. This was because they were received when the source no longer existed. Such (tax-free) sums could arise even when the earnings basis had been properly applied at the discontinuance. Under the earnings basis, any sum due appeared as a credit item in the final account, so that at first sight no loss to the Revenue accrued. However, two problems arose. The first problem related to certain types of earnings which, because of their uncertain nature, could not be included in the profits figures until they took the shape of payments. One case concerned a percentage of film receipts paid to a film actor; and another a royalty payment in respect of books.[83] The court held that the Revenue could not reopen the accounts since a best estimate of earnings had been made. The second problem related to debts. A sum owed to a trader could, in the final account, have been written off as irrecoverable; a subsequent, unexpected payment would therefore escape tax.[84] Conversely, the final account might have included a debt the trader owed in respect of the trade, but the creditor might have released the debt after the discontinuance. These matters could not lead to the reopening of the accounts since the accounts were correct when submitted.

A third problem was more general and related to cash basis taxpayers who were immune from taxation on those sums received after ceasing to do business. It followed that there was no relief for post-cessation expenses either. The first two problems were addressed by rules in 1960, and the third in a separate set of rules in 1968.[85]

23.4.1.1 The Legislative Solution

ITTOIA 2005 brings the 1960 and 1968 rules together in one statutory scheme (Part 2, Chapter 18). First, all sums received *after*[86] the discontinuance and arising from the carrying-on of the trade are chargeable provided their value was not brought into computing the profits of any period before the discontinuance. The charge now arises under ITTOIA 2005, section 242.[87] This did not of itself deal with the general exemption of post-cessation receipts, which was tackled by what became TA 1988, section 104. ITTOIA 2005 simply brings them together in the definition of post-cessation receipts in section 246 as a sum received after a person permanently ceases to carry on a trade and which arises from the carrying on of the trade before the cessation.[88]

The second change made in 1960 and now in ITTOIA 2005, section 249 concerns the release of a debt after cessation. Where a debt has been allowed in the computation of the profits of a trade before it was discontinued, and the whole or any part of the debt is later released, the amount released is treated as a sum received.[89] A covenant by the creditor

---

[83] *Stainers Executors v Purchase* [1951] 2 All ER 1071, 32 TC 367; and *Carson v Cheyney's Executors* [1958] 3 All ER 573, 38 TC 240; noted by Stanford [1959] BTR 72. If not originally received in the course of trade, the receipts would be, and would continue to be, taxable under Case III: *Mitchell v Rosay* (1954) 35 TC 496, 502; the source would be the obligation, not the trade.

[84] The UK has no general doctrine that the cancellation of a debt gives rise to income; this is in part due to the schedular system.

[85] FA 1960, s 32 and FA 1968, s 18.

[86] Contrast *Symons v Weeks* [1983] STC 195, 56 TC 630, where the sum was received before the discontinuance but was not recognised as a trading receipt for accounting purposes until after the discontinuance.

[87] Ex TA 1988, s 103(1), (2)(a).

[88] ITTOIA 2005, s 246(1); on partners see s 246(2) and (3).

[89] ITTOIA 2005, s 249, ex TA 1988, s 103(4). ITTOIA 2005 takes account of the comments of Megarry J in *Simpson v Jones* [1968] 2 All ER 929, 936, 44 TC 599, 609.

not to sue, being analytically distinct from a release, might not cause a charge to tax, but decisions such as *McGuckian*[90] suggest that too much reliance should not be placed on this. A release forming part of a voluntary arrangement under the Insolvency Act 1986 does not give rise to a trading receipt (section 249(3)). Section 248 deals with bad debts which turn out not to be bad debts after cessation. Where a deduction has been allowed for a debt under ITTOIA 2005, section 35 and is then paid after all, but after the cessation, the payment is treated as a post-cessation receipt (section 248). Some other types of post-cessation receipts will be referred to below.

23.4.1.2 Exclusions

Chapter 18 does not apply to sums received by a person beneficially entitled to them who is not resident in the UK, provided the sums represent income arising from a country or territory outside the UK (section 242(3)). Also excluded are lump sums paid to the PRs of an author—but not the author himself—of a work as consideration for the assignment by them of the copyright or public lending rights, wholly or in part.[91] Lastly, sums received on the transfer of trading stock or work in progress are excluded to prevent an overlap with ITTOIA 2005, Chapter 12 (sections 173–186) and to avoid depriving the exceptions in those sections from any income tax effect (section 252). Other exclusions arise where the sums are chargeable as other income or as part of the profits under normal rules, or where they arise from a trade carried on wholly outside the UK (section 243(1)–(3)).

23.4.1.3 Tax Treatment

The charge is on the person receiving or entitled to the receipts, which may or may not be the former trader, and is on an actual receipts basis (sections 244–245). The receipt is treated as earned income.[92] The sum will usually be taxed by reference to the year of receipt, but it may, at the option of the taxpayer or T's personal representative, be carried back to the date on which the discontinuance occurred (section 257). The price for backdating is the loss of the right to claim any post-cessation allowance or loss under section 254 (sections 245–256).

23.4.1.4 Further Rules

Where a trade is transferred and the transferee acquires the right to collect what would otherwise be post-cessation receipts of the former trader, the sums paid to the transferee are treated as the receipts of his trade as they are received (section 251(2)). Where the right to receive the payments is given away, it would appear that no tax can be charged even if the payments are then made to a person connected with the former trader. Since the tax system has charged the sums paid for the right to receive the sums involved, there is no need for liability in respect of any actual receipts later, and the legislation expressly so provides.[93]

---

[90] *IRC v McGuckian* [1997] STC 908, HL.

[91] ITTOIA 2005, s 253, thus preserving the immunity from tax in the *Haig* case (see below at §28.4).

[92] ITTOIA 2005, s 256—and as relevant earnings for pension contribution purposes, FA 2004, s 189(2)(b).

[93] ITTOIA 2005, s 251(4), ex TA 1988, s 106(2). An unsuccessful attempt to bring facts within s 106(2) was made in *Brewin v McVittie* [1999] STC (SCD) 5, where the Revenue successfully invoked the *Ramsay* principle to argue that there had been no real change in the person carrying on the business.

23.4.2 Expenses

In calculating the sum to be charged, any expenses that could have been claimed if the trade had continued are deductible; capital allowances to which T was entitled immediately before the discontinuance no longer receive separate mention (section 254). The above rules were limited to the extent that relief could be given only if provision had been made for expenses in the final accounts or there were chargeable post-cessation receipts against which they could be set.[94] The rules were therefore relaxed by the addition of section 109A by FA 1995:[95] the payment must be made within seven years of the discontinuance; relief is given not by being taken back to the final year of trading or by being set against post-cessation receipts only, but by being set against income of that year equal to the amount of the payment.[96] This relief relates only to certain types of expenditure called qualifying payments. The payments must have been made wholly and exclusively for the purposes specified. ITA 2007, section 97 lists the qualifying expenditures as:

(1)   expenditure to remedy defective work done in the course of the former trade or profession, or paid by way of damages (whether awarded by a court or agreed in negotiation on a claim);
(2)   legal or other professional expenses incurred in connection with claims for such expenditure;
(3)   insurance against the risk; or
(4)   collecting an unpaid debt already taken into account in computing the profits of the trade.

These deductions will be reversed, by rules which are in ITTOIA 2005, if sums are received for insurance or otherwise to meet (1) or (2); similar rules apply to (3) and (4) (section 246).

   Any sum received in meeting the costs incurred in collecting a debt already taken into account in computing the profits or gains of the former trade or profession must be set off.[97] These rules also deal with the converse case of business debts due at the time of the discontinuance but which subsequently prove to be uncollectible.[98]

23.5 Trading Stock (or Inventory) and Work in Progress

23.5.1 Disposal of Trading Stock: Substitution of Market Value

23.5.1.1 Background

In general, where trading stock is disposed of, the sum to be entered into the accounts will be the actual price realised on the disposal. If the goods have been given away, perhaps for

---

[94] See Inland Revenue interpretation RI 25.
[95] For expenses incurred after 29 November 1994 (FA 1995, s 90).
[96] ITA 2007, ss 86 and 125, ex TA 1988, s 109A(1).
[97] ITA 2007, s 99.
[98] ITA 2007, s 98.

reasons of advertisement, there will be no sum to be entered. Neither the Revenue nor the taxpayer are, in general, allowed to substitute a fair market price for that in fact obtained.[99] There are three exceptions to this rule: transfer pricing; *Watson v Hornby*; and *Sharkey v Wernher*. The third may simply be a development of the second. The three exceptions are examined further below.

23.5.1.2 Exceptions

(1) Transfer-pricing; Large Businesses

The first exception arises where one of the parties to a transaction was directly or indirectly participating in the management and control of capital of the other party, and the terms of the contract or other provision are not those which would have been made between independent persons.[100] This provision is discussed further at §21.10 above. This rule applies only if the 'provision' would generate an advantage in relation to UK tax.[101] This rule used not to apply where both parties were subject to UK tax, but this restriction was removed in order to meet the requirements of the ECJ in Luxembourg. However, the new rules generally apply only where the business is large.

(2) *Watson Bros v Hornby*[102]

Where one trader has two distinct trades and transfers goods from one trade to the other, the transfer must be treated as a sale and purchase, not at cost but at a reasonable price.[103] In *Watson Bros v Hornby*, the trader transferred stock from a trade taxed under Schedule D, Case I—that of chicken breeder and hatcher—to a farm which at that time was taxed under Schedule B. The court held that the sale should be at a reasonable price; as the market value was less than the cost of production, the taxpayer succeeded in establishing a trading loss.

(3) *Sharkey v Wernher*[104]

The same principle of transfer at a reasonable price applies more broadly, ie when a trader disposes of trading stock otherwise than in the course of trade, for example when trading stock is appropriated for other purposes such as by being withdrawn for personal consumption or use by the trader or any other person, unless the disposal is a genuine commercial transaction. The value entered in the books of the transferor is also entered in the books of any trader acquiring the stock.[105] A system which provided for no figure to be entered into the accounts by way of credit on the occasion of a self-supply would give the

---

[99] *Craddock v Zevo Finance Co Ltd* [1946] 1 All ER 523, 27 TC 267, 288.

[100] TIOPA 2010, s 147, ex TA 1988, Sch 28AA, para 1. This superseded TA 1988, s 770, which had originally appeared as FA 1951, s 37, replacing General Rule 7 of ITA 1918 which had been confined to dealings between a resident and non-resident. See White [1979] BTR 35.

[101] TIOPA 2010 s 147(2), ex TA 1988, Sch 28AA, para 1(2)(b).

[102] [1942] 2 All ER 506, 24 TC 506; see also *Long v Belfield Poultry Products Ltd* (1937) 21 TC 221. See discussion by Kerridge [2005] BTR 287, 288–289.

[103] Sale of Goods Act 1979, s 8.

[104] [1955] 3 All ER 493, 36 TC 275. See Kerridge [2005] BTR 287.

[105] *Ridge Securities Ltd v IRC* [1964] 1 All ER 275, 44 TC 373. See Crump [1964] BTR 168. This means that the transferee gets the whole profit free of tax, but a double charge to tax is avoided; contrast *Skinner v Berry Head Lands Ltd* [1971] 1 All ER 222, 46 TC 377 when the transferee was fixed with the whole gain; noted by Nock [1971] BTR 189.

self-supplier a great tax advantage. In *Sharkey v Wernher*, Lady Zia Wernher carried on the business of a stud farm; she also rode horses for pleasure. She transferred a horse reared at the farm to her personal use and entered the costs incurred in respect of the horse until the date of its transfer as a credit item in the accounts of the stud farm; there was therefore no attempt to take tax advantage of the deductions she had already been allowed. The House of Lords held that market value should be entered.

The draft bill which became ITTOIA 2005 was going to enact *Sharkey v Wernher* as a statutory principle, but at the time wiser heads prevailed.[106] As GAAP developed it was decided that the correct figure for accounting purposes should now be the cost of the stock rather than market value. Looking at ITTOIA 2005, section 25, one had to ask whether the old decision of the House of Lords was an adjustment to GAAP 'required or authorised' by law. FA 2008, section 34 ultimately reinstated the market value rule in statutory form for appropriations on or after 12 March 2008. It applies both for income tax (ITTOIA 2005, Part 2, Chapter 11A, sections 172A *et seq*) and corporation tax (CTA 2009, sections 156–116).[107]

In reading the cases it should be recalled that most of these transactions took place when there was no CGT. In *Sharkey v Wernher*, the Revenue thus turned its defeat in *Watson Bros v Hornby* to good use; Lady Zia Wernher had to enter the horse at market value.[108] Viewed as case law, the decision in *Sharkey v Wernher* is subject to three possible technical objections:

(1)   The profit alleged to be made comes from a course of dealing with oneself; it is precisely because this is alleged to be impossible that no charge to tax arises from mutual dealings. In reply, Viscount Simonds said that 'the true proposition is not that a man cannot make a profit out of himself but that he cannot trade with himself',[109] a principle which was not to apply where trading stock was removed from the trade for a man's own use and enjoyment. However, this is not consistent with other formulations of the mutuality principle.

(2)   The decision appears to conflict with the fundamental principle that a person is taxed on what is actually earned and not on what he might have earned. However, in *Sharkey v Wernher* the taxpayer received value; the question therefore is the figure to be entered in the accounts. Lord Radcliffe rejected the idea of taking the cost figure on the grounds that market value 'gives a fairer measure of assessable trading profit' and was 'better economics'.[110] A trader concerned with the profitability of the trade would find that 'better book-keeping' would use market value. However, the issue is not what constitutes good book-keeping but the correct basis for taxation. In this regard it may be noted that the cost figure was in conformity with then accepted accountancy practice[111] and the views of the Royal Commission.[112]

(3)   It is said that if *Sharkey v Wernher* was correctly decided, there is no need for the transfer pricing regime now in TIOPA 2010, Part 4. There is little substance to this objection. It is now clear that *Sharkey v Wernher* applies to transactions between

---

[106] March 2004 draft bill clauses 110 *et seq*.
[107] For background to changes and discussion see Kerridge [2008] BTR 439 and Gordon, (2008) *Taxation*, vol 161, 449–53.
[108] See the analysis of speeches by Kerridge [2005] BTR 287, 290–93.
[109] [1955] 3 All ER 493, 496, 36 TC 275, 296.
[110] *Ibid*, 506, 307.
[111] See Lord Oaksey (dissenting); and Edey [1956] BTR 23, 34.
[112] Royal Commission, *op cit*, §§489–90.

different persons whether or not one controls the other, so that its ambit is wider than these sections; further, it is also clear that a transaction may be at an undervalue and still outside *Sharkey v Wernher*, so that the transfer pricing rules may apply. In addition, the transfer pricing rules apply to assets other than trading stock; it is not yet clear whether *Sharkey v Wernher* does. To make matters better still for the Revenue, it appears that *Sharkey v Wernher* may be used even though the transfer pricing rules are excluded.

23.5.1.3 The limits of the Rule in *Sharkey v Wernher*

The most serious criticism of the decision of the House of Lords is simply that of the uncertainty as to the scope of the notional income. The Revenue issued SP A32, which remains in force; Kerridge wonders whether it is actually consistent with the decision.[113] The FA 2008 legislation is based on the Statement of Practice.

(1) It would appear first that the rule is confined to ITTOIA 2005, Part 2. Thus, landlords who allow themselves to occupy one of their houses would not be treated as owing themselves an economic rent for the property chargeable under Part 3. At one time this could be stated with some confidence. Since the reformulation of Schedule A, and its use of Schedule D principles in determining profit, this may be less certain.

(2) It is not clear whether the rule applies to professions. In *Mason v Innes*,[114] the author, Hammond Innes, wrote a book called *The Doomed Oasis*. Shortly before completing the manuscript he assigned the copyright to his father by way of gift. It was agreed that the market value of the copyright at that date was £15,425. The rule in *Sharkey v Wernher* was not applied. The effect in *Mason v Innes* was that not only did the Revenue see their share of the copyright vanish, but it was still left bearing the loss of tax resulting from the deduction of expenses incurred by the author in the creation of the copyright. Lord Denning MR said that a professional man was different from a trader, and suggested that a picture painted by an artist was different from a horse produced on a stud farm. His Lordship's second reason was that this professional man was taxed on a cash basis, whereas a trader was taxed on an earnings basis, a distinction which ought to be irrelevant since it goes to calculating liability to tax rather than deciding what items should be taxable.[115] His Lordship's third reason was the set of anomalies that would result, notably in contrast with the rules which permitted spreading of copyright income and the taxation of post-cessation receipts, both of which provisions must have been passed on the basis that notional sales could not arise from the transfer of the copyright.[116] On the other hand, the area is full of anomalies anyway. A more convincing reason for the decision of the Court of Appeal is given by Potter:[117]

[T]he whole point of *Sharkey v Wernher* was that some figure had to be entered in the trading account because an item of trading stock that stood in that account at cost was taken out. An

---

[113] Kerridge [2005] BTR, 287, 295–96.

[114] [1967] 2 All ER 926, 44 TC 326; criticised by Pickering [1967] BTR 76 and 209. Assignments of copyright may fall within ITA 2007, Pt 13, Ch 4 (s 776), ex TA 1988, s 775, and may also be subject to CGT and IHT. See Kerridge, loc cit, 299.

[115] See, however, Russell LJ in *Mason v Innes* 44 TC 326, 341.

[116] TA 1988, ss 534, 104.

[117] [1964] BTR 438, 442.

author does not however enter his copyrights in his professional account. He does not deal in copyrights. His earnings are in essence fees for services, not proceeds of sale of assets. He pays tax on what he receives or is entitled to receive, no account being taken of opening or closing stock.'

On this basis *Mason v Innes* was correctly decided, but it may mean a closer examination of the boundary between a profession and a trade. Thus, an artist who sells his own pictures might be regarded as carrying on the profession of an artist and the trade of a picture dealer. In this event the value of the paintings will be entered into his trading account at their then market value. However, while Potter's suggestion is convincing, it may also be obsolete. As a result of ITTOIA 2005, section 25, professional persons are required to bring the value of work in progress into their accounts; work in progress leads to copyrights.

(3)   *Mason v Innes* may mean that the rule applies only to dispositions of trading stock[118] and so does not extend to other items in the trade. Thus, the disposal of an agency at an undervalue would not be a disposal of trading stock, neither would the private papers transferred in *Wain v Cameron*.[119] If this is correct, there will be analogous exclusions for the assets of a profession.

(4)   The rule does not apply to a sale at a fairly negotiated price. In *Jacgilden (Weston Hall) Ltd v Castle*,[120] a property developer acquired the right to buy a hotel for £72,000. He later transferred that right to a company for £72,000, although at the time the hotel was worth £150,000. The company then sold the hotel for £155,000. The company sought to have the hotel entered into the books of the company at its market price as opposed to the actual cost price—and failed. There was no question of the contract for sale being an illusory, colourable or fraudulent transaction; it was a straightforward and honest bargain between the developer and the company.

(5)   The rule may not apply to a transfer on discontinuance to one carrying on a trade in the UK and in whose accounts the cost of the stock transferred will appear as a revenue deduction.[121] The statutory rules in ITTOIA 2005, Part 2, Chapter 12 may here exclude *Sharkey v Wernher*.

23.5.2 End of Year Valuations

The value of trading stock unsold at the end of one period is carried forward on the balance sheet as an asset for accounting periods, to be recognised as a cost when the stock is sold and in the period in which the related revenue is recognised: see FRS 102, section 13 and especially paragraph 13.20. Case law established long ago that the figure entered is cost or market value—whichever is the lower.[122] The effect is that losses may be anticipated, but not profit—an example of the sound conservative accounting principle of prudence. The

---

[118] See Russell LJ in *Mason v Innes* 44 TC 326, 341.

[119] [1995] STC 555. See above §19.1.4.

[120] [1969] 3 All ER 1110, 45 TC 685. In *Julius Bendit Ltd v IRC* (1945) 27 TC 44, the test seems to have been whether the deal was a bona fide trading transaction (which it was); the same result was reached in *Craddock v Zevo Finance Co Ltd* [1944] 1 All ER 566, 27 TC 267. These cases might be decided differently today, but the principle which they represent is probably sound.

[121] *Moore v RJ MacKenzie & Sons Ltd* [1972] 2 All ER 549, 48 TC 196; noted by Nelson [1972] BTR 118.

[122] *Whimster & Co v IRC* (1926) 12 TC 813.

lower of cost and market value principle is part of the accounting standards on trading stock (also referred to as 'inventory')—see IAS 2 and FRS 102, paragraphs 13.4 and 13.19.

Income tax is charged on the profit of the trade over a particular period, usually the accounting year of the business. The true profit for the period—ignoring overheads—is not simply sums for goods sold received minus sums spent, but sums received for goods sold minus sums spent on those goods. Thus, suppose that R, a retailer, sells shoes. In the first year R spends £100,000 on shoes, and sells half of them for £100,000. In the second year R sells the other half for £100,000, but buys no more stock. On a naive view, the profit for the first year was nil but for the second year £100,000; this would give a much distorted view of the profitability of R's business. Hence, the rule records £50,000 (the cost of the unsold trading stock) as an asset of the business at the end of the first year and recognises it as an expense of the second when the goods are sold. Over the two-year period the naive view and the correct view produce the same total profit. They differ in the methods of determining the profit of a particular artificial period during the life of the business. This rule may also be seen in the context of matching; it ensures that the receipts from the second year sales are matched with the purchase costs of the shoes then sold.

In valuing stock the taxpayer may use any method which gives a true and fair view on an accounting basis, subject to any adjustment required or authorised by law. The usual methods for valuing stock include specific identification, weighted-average and first-in, first-out (FIFO): see FRS 102, paragraphs 13.17–13.18. Earlier Revenue practice was similar.[123] On correct accounting practice the cost of stock incorporates an element of production overheads including depreciation, see FRS 102, paragraph 13.8 and the *Mars* and *Grant* cases (2007), discussed above at §21.1.1.1.

23.5.2.1 Trading Stock

The first problem is to decide the range of assets to which the valuation should apply. In the case of manufacturing, the term 'trading stock' covers raw materials, finished stock and work in progress (on which see below at §23.5.3); therefore it does not cover capital assets. Stock not yet delivered is not yet trading stock.[124] Similarly, a loss on the hiring of ships on time charter could not be anticipated by the invocation of this rule,[125] since such charters are not trading stock. Whether losses other than on trading stock can be anticipated is another matter; today, the new reliance on FRS 102, paragraph 2.39 may allow the deduction of some such losses.

23.5.2.2 Which Stock is it?

The next problem is to determine what trading stock is to be valued. While a small shoe shop may be able to determine precisely which shoes were sold at the end of the year, it is less practicable to expect an oil distributor to be able to say how many litres of oil it has in

---

[123] Statement of Practice SP 3/90 (now been superseded by Inland Revenue Press Release, 20 July 1999, [1999] *Simon's Weekly Tax Intelligence* 1302). On current accounting practice see Thomas, *op cit*, ch 15.

[124] *Edwards Collins & Sons Ltd v IRC* (1925) 12 TC 773. In *Willingale v International Commercial Bank Ltd* there was no suggestion that the bills were trading stock; otherwise, the Revenue would have won.

[125] *Whimster & Co v IRC* (1926) 12 TC 813; and see *Scottish Investment Trust Co v Forbes* (1893) 3 TC 231; and *Lions Ltd v Gosford Furnishing Co and IRC* (1961) 40 TC 256 (future hiring receipts not stock in trade); on which, see Silberrad [1962] BTR 119.

stock at the end of work on the last day of the accounting period, and there is in fact no obligation on it to measure the stock at the end of that day before resuming business. The Revenue appears content to rely on an annual stocktaking, with any necessary adjustments. Modern computerized tracking systems make identifying which items of stock have been sold and which remain at year end more straightforward and more common than in the past.

Nevertheless, determining the cost of goods is complicated if the goods are fungibles, and prices alter in the course of the trading period. Three principal types of formulae are used by accountants: see FRS 102, paragraph 13.17. The first, which is the one generally accepted for tax purposes, is 'first-in, first-out' (FIFO), ie last in, still there. If prices are rising, this means using the cheaper stock first, so that the cost of the goods sold is low. The stock remaining at the end of the year, an asset in the accounts, will therefore be the more expensive items. The FIFO system has the advantage that the closing stock will be valued at the more recent prices so that, depending on the rapidity of turnover and the rate of price change, it will be valued at a figure more or less close to replacement cost. FIFO has, however, the converse disadvantage that it matches past costs with current receipts, and thus, in an era of inflation, may give an over-optimistic picture of profitability. This led to the introduction of stock relief, which applied from 1975 to 1984. The second formula, which was rejected for tax purposes by the Privy Council in *Minister of National Revenue v Anaconda American Brass Ltd*,[126] is the opposite of the first—ie last-in, first-out (LIFO). Today LIFO is expressly not permitted for accounting purposes under FRS 102, paragraph 13.18 and also is not permitted by the Revenue. The third formula—the weighted average—is a compromise. This looks at the different prices paid for the stock over the period, and weights the price according to the quantity of stock bought at each price.

The different methods of determining the stock to be valued yield different results and so different profit figures for each accounting period. However, over the lifetime of the business all three methods will give the same figure of profits if applied consistently, since the same total amount will have been spent on stock and received on sales, and any remaining stock is valued on cessation under ITTOIA 2005, Part 2, Chapter 12. For tax purposes, even if the same total profit is taxed, different tax rates and, for individuals, the complexities of overlap profits and overlap relief may mean that the total tax charged may vary according to the method chosen.

23.5.2.3 Lower of Cost and Market Value

The cost is that at the original acquisition. Expenses incurred in keeping the goods in good condition are ignored;[127] these expenses properly belong to the time they were incurred since their value will not be recouped subsequently. Market value means net realisable value, and not replacement cost. Thus, where a retail shoe shop values trading stock, the correct figure for market value should be the normal retail price, rather than the price the

---

[126] [1956] AC 85, [1956] 1 All ER 20; see criticism by Edey [1956] BTR 23 and Harris, April Conference of Canadian Tax Foundation (1967), 93, 95. See also Eldridge (1953) 6 *National Tax Jo* 52; Barron (1959) 12 *National Tax Jo* 367; and Phillips (1960) 13 *National Tax Jo* 383. The company made cogent, if self-interested, submissions to the Canadian Royal Commission (on file at the Canadian Tax Foundation in Toronto).

[127] *Ryan v Asia Mill Ltd* (1951) 32 TC 275, 298, per Lord Reid.

shop would have to pay wholesale to replace that stock. On the other hand, if the trade were that of a wholesale supplier of shoes, the figure would be that which the trader would receive on a wholesale disposal. In *BSC Footwear Ltd v Ridgway*,[128] the House of Lords held that a retail shoe shop should value unsold stock by reference to the value to be expected in a sale and with a deduction for the salesperson's commission, but without any allowance for the general expenses of the business for later periods of account. Therefore, no deduction could be made for the normal retail mark-up. As Lord Pearson put it:[129]

> The correct principle is that goods should not be written down below cost price unless there really is a loss actual or prospective. So long as the fall in prevailing prices is only such as to reduce the prospective profit the initial valuation at cost should be retained.

In applying the formula—cost or market value, whichever is the lower—each item may be treated separately, so that one may be valued at cost and another at market value.[130] This is consistent with the idea of anticipating losses but not profits. Where stock is acquired by gift, the receipt is treated as being at market value.[131] When the transfer falls within the rule in *Sharkey v Wernher* (see §23.5.1 above), the value at which the transferor is taken to dispose of it is taken as the acquisition cost to the transferee.

23.5.2.4 Change of Method

The same method must be used at the end of the year as was used at the beginning.[132] However, the method used at the opening of the second period need not be the same as that used at the closing of the first period. Where such change occurs, there will be either a double charge or no charge at all on the difference between the closing stock of the first period and the opening stock of the second.[133]

23.5.2.5 Land Developer: Ground Rents and Rent Charges

Where a builder (X) grants a house purchaser a long lease but charges both a premium and a ground rent, there is no outright disposal of X's interest in the land.[134] X's previous freehold interest is now subject to the lease. It follows that the reversion is still part of X's stock and must be entered at cost or market value, whichever is the lower.[135] The cost of the reversion must include that part of the cost which is the building cost. The formula to ascertain that part is $A/(A+B)$, where A is the market value of the reversion (traditionally a multiple of the rental) and B is the premium.[136]

---

[128] [1971] 2 All ER 534, 47 TC 511; noted by Clarke [1970] BTR 65 (CA) and [1971] BTR 318 (HL) See also criticism by Cope 4 *Journal of Business Finance* 98.

[129] [1971] 2 All ER 534, 550, 47 TC 511, 540.

[130] *IRC v Cock Russell & Co Ltd* [1949] 2 All ER 889, 29 TC 387.

[131] See per Lord Greene MR in *Craddock v Zevo Finance Co Ltd* [1944] 1 All ER 566, 27 TC 267.

[132] *Steel Barrel Co Ltd v Osborne No 2* (1948) 30 TC 387.

[133] Although the Revenue will not agree to a change without good reason, they do not seem to insist upon consistency in their own conduct: see, eg, *Duple Motor Bodies Ltd v Ostime*, below, and *BSC Footwear Ltd v Ridgway* [1971] 2 All ER 534, 47 TC 511.

[134] *BG Utting & Co Ltd v Hughes* [1940] 2 All ER 76, 23 TC 174.

[135] *Heather v G and A Redfern and Sons* (1944) 26 TC 119.

[136] See case stated in *J Emery & Sons Ltd v IRC* [1937] AC 91, 20 TC 213, 219.

A very different situation arises if X reserves a rent charge,[137] chief rent or, in Scotland, a ground annual.[138] The House of Lords has held that there is a realisation of the interest in land for money (the price) and money's worth (the rent). The market value of the rent charge must therefore be entered as a trading receipt in the year of sale; the rent is also treated as a trading receipt when it falls due. On the other hand, the eventual disposal of the land will not give rise to a trading receipt unless the court holds that there is a trade of dealing in rent charges.

23.5.3 Work in Progress

Where the trader is a manufacturer and there is work in progress at the end of the accounting period, the value of that work in progress must be brought into account. Under previous accounting practice, SSAP 9 directed that the costs should cover the employees' time up to the balance sheet date, plus attributable overheads. If the contract is a long-term contract, the provisions of SSAP 22, which was applied in *Symons v Weeks*,[139] or any superseding accounting principles should be observed. In 2004 the ASB added Application Note G to SSAP 9, which provided that a professional firm which has work in progress relating to a contract which is not a long-term contract should recognise value arising from that contract as soon as a right to consideration has arisen. This change in accounting practice caused much debate and even anxiety. The eventual outcome was a ruling by the ASB's UITF (UITF 40) providing interpretative guidance on Note G and legislation in FA 2006, section 102 and Schedule 15 to mitigate the tax consequences arising from a change in accounting practice made to conform with Note G. Taxpayers caught by the change in practice could claim adjustment income treatment and spread the effects over six years under now ITTOIA 2005, Part 2, Chapter 17 for income tax (below at §23.5.4). The relevant accounting standards for recognising revenue on service contracts and construction contracts are now found in FRS 102, section 23. According to FRS 102, paragraph 23.14, in general, when the outcome of a transaction involving the rendering of services can be estimated reliably, an entity shall recognise revenue associated with the transaction by reference to the stage of completion of the transaction at the end of the reporting period (sometimes referred to as the percentage of completion method).

It is often difficult to determine cost. In *Duple Motor Bodies v Ostime*,[140] the company made motor bodies and had, since 1924, used the 'direct cost' of ascertaining the cost of the work in progress, meaning that only the cost of materials used and labour directly employed in the manufacture were included. This gave a loss of £2,000. The Revenue argued that the cost should have been computed on the 'on-cost basis', meaning that there should also have been included the proportion of overhead expenditure, with the effect that the profits for the year would have increased, since the deductible expenses would have been offset by the extra item on the credit side of the balance sheet. This gave an extra profit figure of £14,000. This would have the odd result that if work were slack, so that the same quantity of

---

[137] *Broadbridge v Beattie* (1944) 26 TC 63.
[138] *J Emery & Sons Ltd v IRC* [1937] AC 91, 20 TC 213.
[139] [1983] STC 195, HC (see §21.1.2.2 above).
[140] [1961] 2 All ER 167, 39 TC 537.

overheads would have to be spread over fewer items, the 'cost' of the work in progress would be increased, so that while the company's receipts dropped, its taxable profits in respect of work in progress would be increased. The accountancy profession was divided on the issue of which method should be adopted. The House of Lords held that the Revenue had failed to show that the 'direct cost' was wrong, especially in this case where it had been used for so long, and dismissed the Revenue's appeal. Their Lordships declined to lay down any general principle—the real question was what method best fitted the circumstances of the particular business. FRS 102, paragraph 13.8, now provides that the cost of inventory should include direct costs and 'a systematic allocation of fixed and variable production overheads that are incurred in converting materials into finished goods'.

A question the courts have found difficult is whether the trader can anticipate a loss in respect of work in progress. The market value of work in progress is difficult to assess since the work, as such, is unsaleable, a point agreed on the facts in *Duple Motor*. Where, however, it is clear that a loss will be incurred when the work is completed, there seems to be no way in which that loss can be anticipated, although in *Duple Motor* Lord Reid said that there must be some way of doing it.[141] For financial reporting purposes, if the work in question is a construction contact, FRS 102, paragraph 23.26 provides that when it is probable that total contract costs will exceed total contract revenue, the expected loss shall be recognised as an expense immediately.

23.5.4 *Change of Valuation Basis*

The rules governing the tax consequences of a change in the basis on which profits of a trade are calculated for tax purposes are now found in ITTOIA 2005, Part 2, Chapter 17. A change in basis may trigger a tax adjustment in the form of adjustment income or expense (ITTOIA 2005, section 228). Where a firm changes its basis of valuation, the strict position is that this may result in an extra profit which would have accrued during earlier years if the new system had been in operation. Such extra profits are taxable in the year in which they accrue, which is the year in which they are revealed, and are not backdated.[142] However, Revenue practice now distinguishes valid bases of valuation, ie bases accepted by the accountancy profession, from invalid bases. Where a change is made from one valid basis to another, the opening stock figure must remain the same as the closing figure for the previous period. Therefore, whether the change results in a higher or lower opening figure, the Revenue will neither allow a tax-free uplift nor seek to tax the business, arguing that the opening and closing figures in the year of change must be on the same basis.[143] A change from a non-valid basis to a valid basis is also likely to receive indulgent treatment—provided there is no question of fraud or negligence.

---

[141] *Ibid*, 572. This valuation would have avoided the problem in the case since the market value of a half-finished coach is probably less than the cost.

[142] *Pearce v Woodall-Durkhon Ltd* [1978] STC 372, [1978] 2 All ER 793; criticised by Chopin [1978] BTR 313. See also Statement of Practice SP 3/91, para 3; see also paras 7–9 on long-term contracts.

[143] Statement of Practice SP 3/91, para 4.

23.5.5 *Valuation of Trading Stock on Cessation*

When a trade has been discontinued the residual rule under ITTOIA 2005, rule (a), is that stock is entered at its open market value (section 175(4)). However, under rule (b), the actual sale price is preferred where the stock is sold, etc, to a person who carries on, or intends to carry on, a trade in the UK, provided the cost will enter that person's trading income.[144] However, rule (b) could lead to manipulation, so that if the parties are connected, the price to be taken is that which would have been obtained in a transaction between independent persons dealing at arm's length; this is rule (c).[145] Rule (b) is preferred to rule (c) if the stock consists of parts of a production herd (section 180). Probably of greater importance is an election under which rule (b) may also still apply, by election of the parties, if the figure given under rule (c) exceeds both the price paid by the purchaser and the 'acquisition value' of the stock (section 178). The acquisition value is the most that would be taken into account for the purposes of assessing its cost if there had been an open market sale (section 178(5)). The point of this exception is to allow the parties to avoid the charge on unrealised profits which would otherwise arise.[146] Whatever figure emerges from these rules is then taken as the cost of the stock to the purchaser (section 180).

The purpose of these rules is to prevent a person from discontinuing business, bringing trading stock into account at cost value and then reselling it at the higher market value, so securing a large gain free of income tax, as nearly happened in *J & R O'Kane & Co Ltd v IRC*.[147] They apply whenever a trade is discontinued, except where a trade carried on by a single individual is discontinued by reason of death (section 173(3)). The market value will, however, be taken for IHT purposes.

Similar rules apply to work in progress at the discontinuance of a profession (sections 182–185). The phrase 'the amount that would have been paid for a transfer of the work in progress at the time of the cessation as between parties at arm's length' is substituted for 'market value'. Where this amount exceeds the actual cost of the work, the taxpayer may elect to pay no tax now but have any sums actually received later taxed as post-cessation receipts under Part 2, Chapter 18.[148]

---

[144] ITTOIA 2005, s 176, ex TA 1988, s 100(IA), added by FA 1995, s 140; see [1995] BTR 254. See *Moore v RJ Mackenzie & Sons Ltd* [1972] 2 All ER 549, 48 TC 196. Trading stock is defined in s 137(4).

[145] ITTOIA 2005, s 177, ex TA 1988, s 100(IA)(b), added by FA 1995, s 140; for definition of 'connected persons', see ITTOIA 2005, s 179, ex TA 1988, s 100(IF).

[146] Inland Revenue Press Release, 29 November 1994, [1994] *Simon's Tax Intelligence* 1479.

[147] (1922) 12 TC 303.

[148] ITTOIA 2005, ss 185(1) and 247, ex TA 1988, s 101(2); on post-cessation receipts, see above §23.4.

24

Capital Allowances

24.1   Introduction

The legislation on this subject is contained within the Capital Allowances Act (CAA) 2001, as later amended.[1] The 2001 Act was the first major product of the Tax Law Rewrite Project. It sensibly begins with general provisions affecting all allowances, before passing on to the individual allowances. Allowances for Plant And Machinery (Part 2 of the Act, sections 10–270) are followed by those for Industrial Buildings (Part 3, sections 271–360, but from 2011 no longer available); Converting Unused Business Premises in Disadvantaged Areas (Part 3A, sections 360A–360Z4) (added by FA 2005); Agricultural Buildings (Part 4, sections 361–393, but from 2011 no longer available); Flat Conversions (Part 4A, sections 393A–393W, added by FA 2001 and abolished by FA 2012); Mineral Extraction (Part 5, sections 394–436); Research and Development (Part 6, sections 437–451); Know

---

[1] See Pearce [2001] BTR 359.

How (Part 7, sections 452–463); Patents (Part 8, sections 464–483); Dredging (Part 9, sections 484–489); and Assured Tenancy (Part 10, sections 490–531). Part 10 has expired, in that claims cannot be made for new expenditure but existing allowances still run; thus CAA 2001, section 570A, the anti-avoidance rule introduced by FA 2003, applies here too. This statutory order of Parts 2 and 3 is a reversal of previous practice in legislation on capital allowances and reflects, at last, the change in the economic importance of the different allowances since 1945.

24.1.1 Policy Considerations

24.1.1.1 The Problem

Expenses incurred in the acquisition of a capital asset are not deductible in computing the profits of a trade.[2] If the asset has a limited life, its value to the business will decline. The causes of this decline may be physical, such as wear and tear on plant and machinery, or economic, such as obsolescence or a change in trading policy. The decline causes the cost of the asset to become an expense to the company for accounting purposes; the capital has been consumed. Accounting principles recognise this cost by allowing a deduction for depreciation for accounting purposes,[3] but no provision was originally made for tax purposes, perhaps because income tax was thought to be only temporary.

The UK tax system has relaxed this strict approach by making allowances for certain capital expenditure, including the capital allowance system. The structure of the present system goes back to the Income Tax Act 1945, which defined certain types of capital expenditure qualifying for allowances and specified different rates of allowance. Broadly speaking, the list is the same today, although there have been changes in the way in which the allowances are made and in recent times allowances for most buildings have been withdrawn. The legislation was consolidated in the Capital Allowances Acts of 1968 and 1990, now superseded by CAA 2001.

24.1.1.2 Grander Theories

Depreciation rules would also be needed under a comprehensive income tax, unless an accounting definition of income was adopted so that full depreciation was made over an appropriate period. Depreciation rules would not be needed under an expenditure tax since all investment would be deductible immediately.

A price is paid if such alternatives are rejected. Theorists complain that systems such as the UK's begin by discriminating against capital spending and in favour of employment costs; these systems then adjust by giving allowances, and overcompensate by also allowing a deduction for interest on the money used to buy the asset. Theorists have further enjoyment with the idea of an economic rent which would take capital expenditure into account.[4] The big question whether allowances can affect investment decisions must be

---

[2] See above §22.5 and *Coltness Iron Co v Black* (1881) 6 App Cas 315, 1 TC 311.

[3] See eg Financial Reporting Council, *FRS 102: The Financial Reporting Standard applicable in the UK and Republic of Ireland*, para 17.16 *et seq.*

[4] The idea of rent is associated particularly with the great economist Ricardo; see Sraffa (ed), *The Works and Correspondence of David Ricardo* (CUP, 1981). A rent resource tax for oil and gas is discussed by Garnaut and Ross, (1975) 85 *Economic Journal* 272; on North Sea Oil taxation, see Devereux and Morris, *IFS Report Series No 6* (Institute for Fiscal Studies,1983).

seen as part of a wider view of the effects of taxes on business behaviour.[5] Those who believe that adjusting allowances affects the overall level of investment, point to the fact that capital investment by businesses is a lower percentage of GNP than spending by either consumers or governments; also, it is much more volatile.[6]

24.1.1.3 The UK System—Scope and Rates

As has been seen, the UK tax system of allowances is as haphazard and history-driven as other parts of the system.[7] The UK system is unusually strict (ie mean) in relation to assets for which it allows deductions, notably by the exclusion for many years of non-industrial buildings, from 2008–2011 the phasing out of building allowances entirely even for industrial and agricultural buildings and, at least until 2000, the shamefully slow refusal to do much more than the minimum to adapt the system to take account of the development of IP rights. A 2016 ranking of the UK's competitiveness internationally by the Oxford University Centre for Business Taxation concluded that the UK is very competitive on statutory corporate tax rate relative to other OECD countries, but is higher than the OECD average on Effective Marginal Tax Rate (EMTR), which takes into account both tax rate and tax base. According to the report's authors, the comparatively high UK EMTR is attributable primarily to capital allowances that are low by international standards.[8]

The UK's policy on the actual rate of depreciation has shifted dramatically over the years. This is because, although the current view is that the tax system should recognise the need to write off the cost of depreciating assets, another view would argue that the stimulation of investment demands tax incentives (which view dominated in the period before 1984).[9] This older idea may be traced back to 1932—the middle of the Depression—when allowances were first made available at a rate faster than the commercial rate of depreciation. The decision to revive, even if on a temporary basis, the first-year allowance, in 1992,[10] was also attributable to the need to give relief for the recession.[11] In 1954 investment allowances were added to the rights under the writing-off process. The weakening of the depreciation basis was also seen in the rules for plant and machinery, which, apart from the first-year allowance, applied a single rate of depreciation (25%) whatever the life of the asset, to any remaining expenditure and to a general pool of such expenditure. Today, special rules for short- or long-life assets modify this criticism in part. However, the palliatives

---

[5] See Mintz (1996) 16(4) *Fiscal Studies* 23, 46–49.

[6] Eg, Ford and Poret, *OECD Economic Studies No 16* (OECD, 1990).

[7] HM Treasury, *Corporation Tax*, Cmnd 8456 (1982), ch 15. For comparative material, see *Taxing Profits in a Global Economy* (OECD, 1991), ch 3, Tables 3.5, 3.9–3.12.

[8] Devereux, Habu, Lepoev, and Maffini, *G20 Corporation Tax Ranking* (March 2016). See also Maffini (ed), *Business Taxation under the Coalition Government*, Oxford University Centre for Business Taxation (Feb 2015), 24–25. The EMTR is 'the tax component of the user cost of capital and identifies the percentage rise in the cost of capital for an investment project due to taxation. Conditional on locating in the UK, it affects the scale of investment: a higher cost of capital is associated with lower investment.'

[9] See Prest and Barr, *Public Finance in Theory and Practice* (Weidenfeld & Nicolson, 1985), 16.4; and Hendershott and Cheng, *How Taxes Affect Economic Behaviour* (Brookings Institute, 1981), 85, both stressing other factors affecting investment decisions such as interest rates and inflation. See also the review of older literature by Sumner, *IFS Lecture Series No 4* (Institute for Fiscal Studies, 1976).

[10] Accountancy depreciation can consider the individual asset; a tax system must accommodate many kinds of assets in one rate, unless it opts for free depreciation.

[11] On effects, see Bond, Denney and Devereux (1993) 14(2) *Fiscal Studies* 1. Other alleviating rules, eg extending relief for corporate losses, were introduced at the same time by FA 1992.

for SMEs may be seen as some crude offset for other regulatory burdens imposed upon them. Meanwhile, the combination of the rules on rates and scope means that very different rates of return may be made from different investments. Those who like the present system argue that there is little evidence of underinvestment. There is a significant need for helpful empirical work here.[12]

It was perhaps ironic that the tax system abandoned depreciation as the rational basis of its allowances system just as such evidence as there was suggested that the incentive effects of the allowances were limited and related more to the timing of investment than to its volume. When 100% allowances were given, the question could be asked what further incentives remained, other than outright cash grants,[13] and where it would all stop. Was the effect of the system simply to maintain marginally profitable businesses and to exempt manufacturing industries from liability to corporation tax?

In 2008, as in 1984, the taxpayers paid for reduced corporation tax rates by having reduced capital allowances; the overall result in 1984 was to reduce the incentives to invest but with very marked, short-term opportunities as the new rates came in.[14] This was coupled with the further irony of a rapidly contracting manufacturing base, the very area of the economy most favoured by the 1970s' approach.[15]

24.1.1.4 Further Problems

Other issues remain.[16] Why should the allowances be on an historic cost basis with no allowance for inflation?[17] In a period without inflation there is no problem, since the replacement cost will equal the allowed cost—for an exactly equivalent asset. The issue is whether the purpose is to find the correct balance if the trade were to cease that day, or is to tackle the problem of financing a continuing trade. However, such a rise in cost base would also require adjustments to the balancing charges,[18] which is at present levied on purely paper gains. Again, why should the balancing charge be limited to recapturing the allowance already made? Why not extend it to the capital gain arising on disposal? Why should there be such different allowances for such different assets? At present, pooling is confined to plant and machinery, and its effect is close to permitting rollover relief, as in CGT. Why should there be no allowance for the depreciation of what, for many, is their most important capital asset—their own earning power?[19] Why should one not be able to write off the

---

[12] Some work in this area is being undertaken by the Oxford University Centre for Business Taxation: see eg Maffini, Xing and Devereux, 'The impact of investment incentives: evidence from UK corporation tax returns' (WP16/01) and Liu and Harper, 'Temporary Increase in Annual Investment Allowance: A 2013 Finance Act Note' (WP13/12) also published in [2013] BTR 385.
[13] Allowances are also given in the form of relief for interest payments. Grants were introduced between 1966 and 1970; see, *inter alia*, Lazar [1966] BTR 179; White Paper, *Investment Incentives*, Cmnd 4516 (HMSO, 1970), §2; and, in a wider context, Sharpe (1979) 95 *LQR* 206. On discretionary element, see *British Oxygen Co Ltd v Minister of Technology* [1971] AC 610, [1970] 3 All ER 165.
[14] Devereux (1988) 9(1) *Fiscal Studies* 62.
[15] Feldstein and Summers (1979) 32 *National Tax Jo* 4.
[16] See ideas discussed in HM Treasury, *Corporation Tax, op cit*, chs 11, 15.
[17] For a comparison of accelerated depreciation with inflation adjustments, see Feldstein (1981) 34 *National Tax Jo* 29.
[18] See Tucker Committee Report, Cmnd 8189 (1951) §§102–115; Royal Commission on the Taxation of Profits and Income, *Final Report*, Cmnd 9474 (1955), paras 350–62, and Morley, *Fiscal Implications of Inflation Accounting* (Institute for Fiscal Studies, 1974), ch 1.
[19] In 1915 excess profits duty was applied to trades but not to professions. McKenna, the Chancellor of the Exchequer, justified this on the ground that it would be impossible to devise a satisfactory datum line in the case

costs of one's training for a profession?[20] Again, why should the system take the form of a deferral of tax? In such form it is a long-term credit and therefore has no effect on reported profits; an immediate tax credit might be preferable.[21] To all these proposals there is one short reply, namely, that they make the mistake of supposing that the system has something to do with justice, equity and depreciation; it has not. Such proposals are best seen as (possibly expensive) tools of economic planning.

24.1.2 History[22]

The first statutory allowance was granted in 1878, 'as representing the diminished value by reason of wear and tear during the year' of plant and machinery used in a trade. This allowance was held not to extend to obsolescence, a matter changed by concession in 1897 and by statute in 1918. Also in 1918, special depreciation allowances were made to mills, factories and other similar premises,[23] on the basis that the vibrations from the machinery might weaken the building. The Royal Commission of 1920 considered, but rejected, any general scheme of capital allowances.

The Income Tax Act 1945 took a wider view; its basic structure remains in place today even though the material was substantially rearranged, as well as being rewritten, by CAA 2001. It defined those types of capital expenditure which qualified for allowances; many did not—and still do not—qualify. Apart from allowances for plant and machinery, all allowances were confined to income taxable under Schedule D, Case I (some clearly to particular trades) and did not extend to professions (old Schedule D, Case II) or employment income (old Schedule E). A few allowances applied to property income (old Schedule A); these were widened and brought closer to trading income by FA 1997.[24]

24.1.3 Accelerated Allowances

For many years the tax system enshrined the belief that tax allowances encouraged investment. Hence, elaborate allowances were given to allow the writing off of capital expenditure far ahead of any real depreciation or obsolescence—either by first-year allowances or by generous writing-down allowances. However, legislation in 1984 and 1985 reduced the rates of allowances, making them closer to actual depreciation, and compensated for this by reducing the rate of corporation tax. This has not prevented Parliament from reviving specially enhanced allowances from time to time. Since 1997 we have got used to a battery of much-targeted allowances for plant and machinery of particular types and particular

---

of members of a profession who made their profits by the excessive expenditure of their capital, that is their energy, brain power and health.

[20] On human capital, see Beer [1987] BTR 392; and other articles cited in above at §7.1.1.

[21] See discussions by Lindholm (1951) 4 *National Tax Jo* 180; Wiseman (1963) 16 *National Tax Jo* 36; and Bird (1963) 16 *National Tax Jo* 41.

[22] On the history, see *Royal Commission on the Taxation of Profits and Income, Final Report*, Cmnd 9474 (1955), §§308–26; *Richardson Committee on Turnover Taxation*, Cmnd 2300 (1964) ch 6; and Edwards [1976] BTR 300.

[23] To be found in CAA 1990, s 18(1)(a), now superseded by CAA 2001, s 274.

[24] See below at §24.2.3 (CAA 2001, s 248); see also *ibid*, ss 249 (furnished holiday lettings) and 250 (overseas property business).

taxpayers. Those who believe that adjusting allowance affects the overall level of investment point to the fact that capital investment by UK businesses is a lower percentage of GNP than spending by either consumers or governments; it is also much more volatile.[25]

Although the idea of using real depreciation as measured by accounting standards was mentioned as part of the Review of Corporation Tax in August 2002, there was never any chance of its being adopted. The use of accounting principles for tax depreciation is frequently to be found in Continental European tax systems. Such systems had previously had very conservative accounting principles—in marked contrast to the present accounting principles, with their increased emphasis on relevance and fair value accounting.

24.1.4 Types of Allowance

The UK system uses three principal types of allowance, with another two types added in 2008:[26]

(1)   initial or first-year allowances[27] of a substantial percentage of the capital expenditure, only a few of which are currently available;

(2)   writing-down allowances during the life of the asset, which clearly does not apply if a 100% initial allowance has been used;

(3)   balancing adjustments, which may take the form of either an allowance or a charge on the occurrence of an appropriate event, such as the end of the trade or the disposal of the asset;

(4)   tax credits or enhanced tax allowances (added in 2008). As this is available only for companies which have spent money on green technologies qualifying for first-year allowances but also have a loss (and so no profits against which to set the allowance), it is discussed below at §62.2.5;

(5)   Annual Investment Allowance of £200,000 for business investment in most types of plant and machinery (added in 2008 and originally £50,000). Where the business spends more than £200,000, the excess is governed by the normal allowance rules; it is therefore best seen as a form of initial 100% allowance tied to the amount spent.

Of these, the first is self-explanatory. However, the second and third are not. Writing-down allowances are given on a reducing balance basis, so that the same percentage, eg 18%, is given each year but applied to a reducing balance of expenditure. So £100,000 of expenditure attracting an allowance at 18% will give rise to an allowance of £18,000 the first year, leaving £82,000 as the balance of expenditure not yet written off. The allowance for the second year will be £14,760 (ie 18% of £82,000), leaving a balance of £67,240. For the third year, the allowance is 18% of £67,240 or £12,103, and so on. The reducing balance achieves total write off only after an infinite number of years.

---

[25] See below at §24.12.2.

[26] In 1954 an investment allowance was introduced, which was, in effect, a tax-free subsidy. It did not reduce the depreciable cost of the asset for other allowances, neither was it taken into account for the purpose of any balancing allowance or charge. See, further, Cmnd 9667. It was abolished in 1966 (FA 1966, s 35).

[27] The difference is that an initial allowance and a writing-down allowance may be claimed in the first year; but a first-year allowance and a writing-down allowance cannot both be claimed in the first year.

The balancing allowance or charge is designed to bring the allowances into line with actual expense. If the amount so far allowed is less than the amount spent, an extra or 'balancing' allowance is permitted. A balancing allowance may be denied where the sale proceeds have been reduced by a tax avoidance scheme.[28] If, however, the allowance exceeds the expense, a sum is imposed by way of 'balancing charge' to recapture that part of the allowance which was not needed. The charge recovers only the amount that has been allowed; thus, if the resale value of an asset exceeds its original cost the excess is a matter for CGT. There is no provision whereby the balancing charge may be spread over the number of years for which the allowance was claimed. Today, a balancing charge is treated as a receipt of the trade or other type of qualifying activity or business.[29]

24.1.5 Incurring Capital Expenditure

Perhaps oddly, capital expenditure is defined by exclusion, and is any sum spent on the acquisition of the asset, etc, provided the sum is not allowable as a deduction in computing the profits or gains of the qualifying activity carried on, which may be a trade, profession or vocation, property business or employment carried on by the person incurring the expense.[30] Sums falling within ITA 2007, Part 15, Chapter 6 are also excluded.[31]

As the material in chapter twenty-two on the distinction between capital and revenue shows, these boundaries are not precise.[32] In general, allowances cannot be claimed for sums met directly or indirectly by others; however, an allowance may be claimed if the other person is not a public body and is not eligible for tax relief in respect of the payment.[33] In relation to public bodies, there is special exemption for certain grants for Northern Ireland under the Industrial Development Act 1982.[34] Provision is made, however, for allowances for contributions to the capital expenditure of others.[35]

Further rules exclude double relief claims.[36]

24.1.5.1 Not for Finance

Sums spent merely on the provision of finance do not qualify for allowances. In *Ben-Odeco Ltd v Powlson*,[37] the taxpayer was going to carry on a trade of hiring out an oil rig. In order to finance the construction of the rig, it had to borrow money, and for this had to pay commitment fees (£59,002) and interest (£435,988). These sums were charged to capital

---

[28] CAA 2001, s 570A, added by FA 2003, s 164.

[29] Eg for plant and machinery, CAA 2001, ss 55(3) and 247–252. For other types of allowance, see ss 352, 391, 432, 450, 463, 478 and 489. In *IRC v Wood Bros (Birkenhead) Ltd* [1959] AC 487, 38 TC 275, the House of Lords held that the balancing charge was not income of the company for the purpose of the surtax direction. This was reversed for the apportionment of the income of close companies under the 1965 scheme.

[30] CAA 2001, s 4(2).

[31] CAA 2001, s 4(4).

[32] Eg *Rose & Co (Wallpaper and Paints) v Campbell* [1968] 1 All ER 405, 44 TC 500 (pattern books of current wallpaper stock not capital expenditure).

[33] CAA 2001, ss 532 *et seq.*

[34] CAA 2001, s 534; and see *Birmingham Corpn v Barnes* [1935] AC 292, 19 TC 195. See also ESC B49 for allowances where the grant to the taxpayer is revoked.

[35] CAA 2001, ss 537–541; see also s 155.

[36] CAA 2001, ss 7–10.

[37] [1978] STC 460, [1978] 2 All ER 1111.

(correctly) in the company's accounts. However, the House of Lords held that the sums did not qualify for capital allowance treatment; they had been spent not on the provision of plant and machinery but on the provision of money. This case was distinguished in *Van Arkadie v Sterling Coated Materials Ltd*,[38] where the extra (sterling) cost of a price to be paid by instalments but in foreign currency was treated as allowable expenditure. It was critical in this case that the contract provided for payment to be made by instalments; a different conclusion would have been reached if the contract had provided for a single payment made with the aid of a loan from a bank which the purchaser then paid off in instalments.

The question whether expenditure incurred for tax avoidance purposes comes within the Act is considered below and in relation to the *Barclays Mercantile Business Finance* case.[39]

24.1.5.2 When Incurred?

CAA 2001, section 5 provides two rules, but these do not apply to plant and machinery. The first looks at the date on which there is an unconditional obligation to pay, ie in the case of a conditional obligation, the moment when the obligation to pay becomes unconditional.[40] Where the purchaser acquires title before the obligation becomes unconditional, the expenditure will be treated as incurred in the period in which title passed, provided the obligation becomes unconditional not more than one month after the end of that period.[41] The second rule applies to the date on which the expenditure became payable.[42] It applies where the due date for payment is more than four months after the obligation to pay has become unconditional.

Originally, only the second rule applied. The reason behind this change adding the first rule was to bring the capital allowance rules into line with accountancy practice (which takes this date as the one on which title normally passes). The difference is that an obligation to pay may have become unconditional even though the sum does not have to be paid until a later date;[43] here the due date for payment is taken. The rules on timing also include an anti-avoidance rule which applies where the obligation to pay becomes unconditional on a date earlier than that which accords with normal commercial usage and the sole or main benefit to be derived is the obtaining of the allowance.[44]

24.1.5.3 A Special Case—Non-recourse Finance

Under a non-recourse finance arrangement the lender does not seek repayment from the borrower personally but is content with some other source, eg the stream of income from the asset. Such loans are common in extraction industries, where the bank is content to be repaid from the stream of money flowing from the ore extracted. However, such arrangements have also been used in tax avoidance schemes. The status of expenditure financed by non-recourse loans was unclear following the opaque speech of Lord Templeman in *Ensign Tankers (Leasing) Ltd v Stokes*.[45] In principle, as Millett J had held at first instance,

---

[38] [1983] STC 95.
[39] *Barclays Mercantile Business Finance Ltd v Mawson* [2005] STC 1 (HL) and see above §5.6.
[40] CAA 2001, s 5(1); see also Inland Revenue interpretation RI 54.
[41] CAA 2001, s 5(4).
[42] CAA 2001, s 5(5).
[43] CAA 2001, s 5(5).
[44] CAA 2001, s 5(6).
[45] [1992] STC 226, 64 TC 617, HL (see above at §5.6.4); on US experience, see Shaviro (1989) 43 *Tax Law Review* 401.

the fact that a borrower who obtains a non-recourse loan incurs no personal liability to repay the lender ought to be irrelevant; the capital allowance legislation is concerned with the taxpayer's ability to spend capital in acquiring the asset, not with the taxpayer's liability to repay the lender.[46] In the House of Lords, Lord Goff explained that the non-recourse nature of the loan was only one of the elements which enabled him to conclude that this expenditure had not been incurred by the taxpayer: other factors included the fact that the lender (L) was also the (US) company producing the film; that the money was paid into a special bank account opened at a bank nominated by L; and that when the money was paid in by L, an identical sum was repaid by the taxpayer to L out of the same account on the same day. On such facts Lord Goff found it impossible to conclude that the money paid into the account by L was in any meaningful sense a loan; the payment was simply money paid in as the first step in a tax avoidance scheme.[47] Lord Templeman, however, with whom all the other judges agreed, stated:[48]

> By reason of the non-recourse provision of the loan agreement the loan was not repayable by [the taxpayer] or anyone else. A creditor who receives a participation in profits in addition to the repayment of his loan is of course a creditor. But a creditor who receives a participation in profits instead of the repayment of his loan is not a creditor. The language of the document in the latter case does not accurately describe the true legal effect of the transaction which is a capital investment by the 'creditor' in return for a participation in profits.

After mentioning the views of Millett J, Lord Templeman went on to set out the type of facts which Lord Goff had stressed. The result was that it was unclear whether non-recourse finance never works, or whether it fails only in circumstances such as those in *Ensign Tankers*.[49] This issue arose again when *Ensign Tankers* was applied in the 2011 case of *Tower MCashback LLP 1 and another v Revenue & Customs Commissioners*.[50] It now appears that judges will take into consideration the non-recourse nature of financing as one factor in interpreting the facts before them 'realistically' (under Ribeiro PJ's much-cited, modern formulation of the *Ramsay*[51] principle in *Arrowtown*)[52] in arriving at a conclusion as to the amount of qualifying expenditure incurred for capital allowances purposes. In *Tower MCashback*, the Supreme Court held that the taxpayer LLPs were not entitled to their full claim for 100% first-year capital allowances in respect of certain software licences partly purchased with investor funds (25%) and partly financed through uncommercial, non-recourse loans (75%), because the LLPs had not 'incurred', in any meaningful sense, qualifying expenditure of the amount claimed. The claim instead was restricted to 25% of the consideration payable under the software licence agreement as that, in the Court's view, was the amount actually incurred on acquiring the rights under the agreement. Lord Walker, giving the lead judgment, also addressed

---

[46] [1989] STC 705, 769, 64 TC 617, 705.

[47] [1992] STC 226, 246, 64 TC 617, 747–8.

[48] *Ibid*, 233, 733.

[49] For Revenue treatment of 'security' arrangements in relation to the special allowances for films, see Statement of Practice SP 1/98, paras 66–68.

[50] [2011] UKSC 19, [2011] STC 1143.

[51] *WT Ramsay Ltd v IRC* [1982] AC 300, giving rise to the composite transactions doctrine under which intermediate steps inserted into a transaction entirely for tax purposes could be ignored. For a detailed discussion of the evolution of the *Ramsay* doctrine see above at §5.6.4.

[52] *Collector of Stamp Revenue v Arrowtown Assets Ltd* [2003] HKCFA 26.

arguments as to the 'uncertain' application of the CAA 2001 provisions, and the relationship between *Ensign Tankers* and the more recent, and apparently conflicting, result in favour of the taxpayer in *Barclays Mercantile Business Finance Ltd v Mawson (Inspector of Taxes)*,[53] stating (at para 80):

> The composite transactions in this case, like that in *Ensign* (and unlike that in *BMBF*) did not, on a realistic appraisal of the facts, meet the test laid down by the CAA, which requires real expenditure for the real purpose of acquiring plant for use in a trade. Any uncertainty that there may be will arise from the unremitting ingenuity of tax consultants and investment bankers determined to test the limits of the capital allowances legislation.

24.1.6 Giving Effect to Allowances

The rules as to giving effect to capital allowances are set out in relation to each allowance. They are normally given effect in taxing the trade or other qualifying activity,[54] and so are claimed in the return of income from that source. Sometimes, where there is no relevant source, the allowance must be claimed in another way.[55]

24.1.6.1 The Qualifying Activity: ITTOIA 2005, Parts 2 and 3

Where the allowance is given effect in taxing the trade or other qualifying activity, it is treated as a deductible expense for the period of account to which it relates; similarly, a balancing charge is treated as a trading receipt.[56] Therefore, the correct profits figure will be profit less capital allowances, and any excess allowances will automatically generate a trading loss. Claims for allowances are normally made in the tax return.[57]

The widest allowance, for plant and machinery, is given for any qualifying activity, of which trade is the first example. Other activities include any ordinary UK property business, furnished holiday lettings, overseas property business, profession or vocation, mining, etc concerns listed in ITTOIA 2005, section 12/CTA 2009, section 39(4), the management of an investment company, special leasing of plant or machinery, and an employment or office. Each such source treats the capital allowance in the same way.[58]

The allowance is 'treated as' an expense rather than being an expense. Hence, a taxpayer is under no obligation to take allowances available but has discretion whether to take them or not.[59] In relation to non-resident companies, rules direct the separation of sources subject to income tax from those subject to corporation tax.[60] Allowances are computed by reference to qualifying expenditure and disposals in each chargeable period.[61] Since allowances are given on an annual basis, they will be increased or reduced if the chargeable period is

---

[53] [2004] UKHL 51, [2005] STC 1; Tiley [2005] BTR 273. See also above at §5.6.
[54] See, for plant and machinery, CAA 2001, ss 15 and 247; and for other allowances, ss 352, 360Z, 391, 392, 393T, 432, 450, 463, 478, 489 and 529.
[55] CAA 2001, s 3(4) and (5); on partnership returns, see ss 3(6) and 258.
[56] CAA 2001, s 247(b); the list of ss is the same as in n 38.
[57] CAA 2001, s 3(2); a very few are made under TMA 1970, s 42—see s 3(4). For treatment under self-assessment under corporation tax, see FA 1998, Sch 18, Pt IX.
[58] CAA 2001, ss 248–262.
[59] CAA 2001, s 3(1), confirming *Elliss v BP Oil Northern Ireland Refinery Ltd* [1987] STC 52, 59 TC 474, CA.
[60] CAA 2001, s 566.
[61] Defined in CAA 2001, s 6.

greater or less than 12 months. The concept of the chargeable period replaced the old concept of the basis period in 1994.[62]

The 'chargeable period' is the accounting period of a company or the period of account of someone liable to income tax.[63] Where the allowance is made in taxing the trade, profession or vocation, the period of account is usually any period for which accounts are made up for the purposes of the trade.[64] Where, as in the opening two years, two periods of account overlap, the period common to both is deemed to fall in the first period of account only. If there is an interval between two periods of account, the interval is deemed to be part of the first period of account.[65] In this way the allowance—or charge—is given only once. Any period of account greater than 18 months is subdivided; the first subdivision begins with the commencement date of the original period, and later subdivisions are set at 12-month intervals.[66] Any net loss is, in the case of a trade, given effect for income tax as an ordinary trading loss and so set off against general income under ITA 2007, section 64 or 72, or rolled forward against future profits under section 83.

For sources other than trades professions or vocations, eg a property business, the period taken is the tax year.[67] For UK and overseas property businesses, see above at §10.3.2.1.

24.1.6.2 Other Allowances Given by Repayment

Other allowances where there is no available trade must be claimed and are given effect by discharge or repayment of tax on the appropriate income.[68] Examples are allowances for investment and insurance companies.[69] Any excess is carried forward to the income of the same class in succeeding years. The period of account is the year of assessment.[70]

24.1.7 Amounts: Price or Market Value?

24.1.7.1 Sales Between Connected Persons

The amount of a charge or an allowance due on a sale clearly depends upon the amount received. Normally, the actual sale price is taken. However, CAA 2001 contains a number of rules directing that market value is taken instead. The first, the 'control' test, is an elective rule designed at least in part to help business.[71] For allowances under Parts 3 (industrial buildings), 4 (agricultural buildings), 5 (mining), 6 (research and development) and 10 (assured tenancies), market value is taken in two situations. The first situation uses the control test and applies where (a) the buyer is a body of persons[72] over whom the seller has control,[73] or (b) vice versa, or (c) both buyer and seller are under the control of some other

---

[62] See CAA 1990, s 160 for the original version.
[63] CAA 2001, s 161(2), as amended by FA 1994.
[64] CAA 2001, s 6(4), s 160(2), substituted by FA 1994, s 212.
[65] CAA 2001, s 6(5).
[66] CAA 2001, s 6(6).
[67] CAA 2001, s 6(2)(b).
[68] CAA 2001, s 3 and, for leasing businesses, ss 258–261.
[69] See CAA 2001, ss 253–257, referring to CTA 2009, s 1233 and TA 1988, s 76 (not rewritten).
[70] CAA 2001, s 6(2).
[71] CAA 2001, s 567. Plant and machinery have their own rules, *ibid*, s 214.
[72] Defined in TA 1988, s 832(1), ITA 2007, s 995.
[73] Defined in CAA 2001, s 574.

person,[74] or (d) they are connected persons. The sale will be treated as being at market value unless the parties elect for it to be at the alternative amount of the written-down value of the assets. The purpose behind the main rule may be to prevent avoidance, at least for those situations in which the alternative test does not apply; the purpose behind the alternative is to allow the transfer of the property between such persons in such a way that no balancing adjustment is necessary. Hence this election is available only when capital allowances and charges can be made on both parties.[75] The election must be made within two years of the sale.[76] The election is not open to a dual resident investment company.[77]

The second situation, the 'tax advantage' test, in which market value is taken, is whenever it appears that the sole or main benefit which might have been expected to accrue was the obtaining of a tax advantage, ie any allowance under CAA 2001 other than plant and machinery, which once more has its own rules.[78] No election is possible here.[79] A separate rule applies to the transfer of a UK trade carried on by a company resident in another EU Member State.[80] The transfer is treated as giving rise to neither allowances nor charges, provided the transferee is within the charge to UK tax.[81]

This tax advantage test is quite distinct from the rule denying a balancing allowance where sale proceeds have been reduced by tax avoidance scheme.[82]

As already indicated, plant and machinery has its own, more complex, regime.[83] Know-how also its own provision.[84]

24.1.7.2 Apportionment of Proceeds When Sold Together

Special rules apply when the sale involves both an asset in respect of which allowances have been claimed and another asset.[85] The net proceeds of sale must be apportioned on a just and reasonable basis; the Commissioners are not bound by any apportionment made by the parties.[86]

24.1.7.3 Discontinuance and Deferrals: Succession to Trades

In general, where a person carrying on an activity which qualifies for capital allowances, eg a trader (T1), discontinues a trade, a balancing charge or allowance is made. Any capital allowances still unused cannot be carried forward if one trade ends and another one

---

[74] Defined in CAA 2001, ss 574 and 575, modelled on ex TA 1988, s 839. Allowances under CAA 2001, Pts 3A, 4 or 4A are excluded (s 570(1)).

[75] CAA 2001, s 570(2)(a).

[76] CAA 2001, s 570(5).

[77] CAA 2001, s 570(2)(b). See below at §69.6.

[78] CAA 2001, s 567(4); see *Barclays Mercantile Industrial Finance Ltd v Melluish* [1990] STC 314, 63 TC 95.

[79] CAA 2001, s 569(1)(b).

[80] CAA 2001, s 567(5) excludes ss 568–570; s 561(2) applies instead.

[81] CAA 2001, s 561, esp s 561(1)(c).

[82] CAA 2001, s 570A, added by FA 2003, s 164. This rules applies to the allowance for industrial buildings in Pt 3 of the Act but also to those for agricultural land (§24.5), flat conversions (§24.6), mining (§24.7) and assured tenancies (§24.3.7.2).

[83] CAA 2001, ss 214 *et seq* (see below at §24.4.7); and for successions, etc see s 567(1).

[84] CAA 2001, s 455; this has the 'control' test without an election but has no 'avoidance' test.

[85] CAA 2001, ss 562 and 572(1)–(3).

[86] CAA 2001, s 562; eg *Fitton v Gilders and Heaton* (1955) 36 TC 233; *A Wood & Co Ltd v Provan* (1968) 44 TC 701.

begins.[87] If property—as opposed to the trade—is acquired by another person (T2), T2 may be able to claim allowances in respect of its own capital expenditure, including that in respect of items bought from T1; that expenditure may in turn give rise to balancing charges or allowances to T1.

A special rule applies where there is the transfer of a UK trade to a company resident in another EU Member State and TCGA 1992, section 140A applies to capital assets. Since the effect of section 140A is to apply a no gain, no loss rule to the capital asset for capital gains purposes, the same result is achieved for capital allowance purposes, provided the transferee is within the charge to UK tax.[88] The effect is that the transfer itself does not give rise to any allowances or charges, and that the new owner's allowances are calculated on the same basis as the old owner's allowances. The same tax-neutral effect applies when an asset is transferred under a merger within TCGA 1992, section 140E—the formation of a European Company where the asset remains within the UK tax charge (see §60.14).[89]

Where the trade is acquired by T2 so that there is succession to the trade, market value is used. The new traders are entitled to allowances as if they had acquired the assets at market price,[90] although they are not entitled to initial, as opposed to writing-down and first-year, allowances. Market value is also used when companies cease to trade under section 337(1).[91] Curiously, perhaps, these rules do not apply to allowances under Part 2 (plant and machinery has its own rules), Part 6 (research and development) or Part 10 (assured tenancy).[92]

24.1.8 Choice of Allowances

A capital expense may fall within more than one category of allowance. In the absence of any express provision the taxpayer may choose the most favourable category, subject to general rules designed to prevent double allowances.[93]

24.1.9 Capital Allowance and Revenue Expense Compared

It is worth setting out the ways in which a capital allowance differs from a deductible expense, as follows:

(1) The allowance must be an item of capital expenditure as distinct from revenue.
(2) Whereas a revenue expense is deductible unless statute directs otherwise, a capital allowance is made only if the statute so permits.
(3) Whereas an allowance may be claimed in respect of expenditure incurred before a trade or other qualifying activity commences (although only when the activity begins),[94] an expense so incurred is deductible only if it is incurred within seven years of the trade beginning.

---

[87] See above at §20.8 and below at §62.2.
[88] CAA 2001, s 561, esp s 561(1)(c).
[89] CAA 2001, s 561A added by F(No 2)A 2005, s 56.
[90] CAA 2001, s 559.
[91] CAA 2001, s 558; see FA 2001, Sch 21, para 4, correcting CAA 2001, s 558.
[92] CAA 2001, s 557.
[93] CAA 2001, s 7(1).
[94] CAA 2001, s 6(2).

(4)   A revenue expense incurred partly for trade and partly for other purposes is not deductible, whereas such duality results in an apportionment of capital expenditure.[95]

(5)   A revenue expense is deductible at once and in full, whereas allowances are made only at specified rates and often over several years.

(6)   A revenue expense must be taken into account at the proper time, whereas there is no obligation to claim a capital allowance.

24.2   Plant and Machinery

24.2.1 Elements

24.2.1.1 First-year Allowances and Writing-down Allowances

The present scheme of capital allowances for plant and machinery was first enacted by FA 1971; the scheme has been much amended. The basic structure consists of first-year allowances[96] and annual writing-down allowances.[97] For some time up to 1984, first-year allowances were given at a rate of 100%. These were abolished by FA 1984 but were revived for particular purposes subsequently, such as the lower rate temporary allowance because the economy was in recession (1992–93),[98] or out of a wish to help SMEs (each year since 1997)[99] or to encourage investment by small enterprises in plant or machinery which is either to do with information and communication technology (ICT)[100] or (by an enterprise of any size) energy saving.[101] The rate—and scope—of these revived first-year allowances has varied. First-year allowances were at one time also available under transitional relief for certain regional projects in development areas.[102] FA 2008 repealed some provisions which are spent (CAA 2001, sections 40–43 and 45)

As from April 2012, writing-down allowances are given at a rate of 18% on the value of qualifying expenditure; expenditure on (and receipts on the disposal of) different items of plant and machinery is usually pooled. Special rules apply to certain assets. The plant and machinery must be used for a qualifying activity (see further §24.1.6.1).[103] Where the asset is provided or used only partly for a qualifying activity, any first-year allowance

---

[95]   Eg *GH Chambers (Northiam Farms) Ltd v Watmough* [1956] 3 All ER 485, 36 TC 711, where an extravagant choice of motor car for personal reasons led to a reduction in the allowance. ITTOIA 2005, s 34(2) and CTA 2009, s 54(2) now provide for apportionment where dual purpose expenses can be dissected into permissible and impermissible portions.

[96]   CAA 2001, ss 39–52. It was not possible to claim both the first-year allowance and the writing-down allowance for the same period—which is why the allowance is called a first-year allowance rather than an initial allowance.

[97]   CAA 2001, ss 52 and 56.

[98]   CAA 2001, ss 47–49.

[99]   On the current scope of first-year allowances, see CAA 2001, ss 39–51 and §24.3.5 below.

[100]   CAA 2001, s 45, repealed in 2008 and replaced by the AIA.

[101]   CAA 2001, s 45A.

[102]   CAA 1990, s 22(2); for history and avoiding Hybrid Bill status, see Lawson, *The View from No 11: Memoirs of a Tory Radical* (Bantam Press, 1992) 354.

[103]   CAA 2001, ss 15–20.

must be reduced and any writing-down allowance must be calculated on the basis that the asset is the subject of a single asset pool.[104] These rules represent a sharp contrast to the rules for deductible revenue expenditure, where of course there is no deduction for expenditure which is incurred for dual purposes.[105] Expenditure on a share in plant or machinery qualifies for an allowance.[106] Further rules restrict both first-year and writing-down allowances if there is what CAA 2001 calls a 'partial depreciation subsidy', ie a contribution.[107]

24.2.1.2 Successions

The plant and machinery provisions in CAA 2001 include special rules allowing the transfer of assets without balancing adjustments on successions to businesses, so that the result is tax neutral.[108] However, acquisitions by sales and other relevant transactions between connected persons may also attract certain anti-avoidance rules, some of which insist on market value being used (below §24.2.15).[109]

24.2.1.3 Unusual Acquisitions: Change of Use and Gifts—Market Value?

The amount of expenditure for which the taxpayer, T, is entitled to claim is not usually a problem where the asset is bought outright. If T brings plant or machinery into use in the trade and had originally bought the asset for other purposes, or if the asset is acquired by way of gift, it used to be the market value of the asset when it was brought into the use of the trade which was taken as the amount of expenditure incurred.[110]

However, the allowance will be based on the lower of that market value and the (unindexed) original cost.[111] So if a world-class violinist buys a Stradivarius for his collection and later decides to use it for public performance, the allowance will be given by reference to the original cost; of course the term 'cost' has to be taken in its CAA 2001 context, so that if the violinist inherited the violin, the market value at the time of the inheritance would be used rather than cost.

The precise treatment of non-residents with taxable activities in the UK through a permanent establishment has been clarified.[112] Entitlement to the allowance depends on liability to UK tax. So where only a part of the trade is subject to UK tax, only an equivalent part of the allowance may be claimed; to achieve this, the UK part of the trade is treated as a separate trade. Consequential rules have to apply to changes in the amount of UK trade, so that there is a reduction in the allowance if the portion of the trade attributable to the UK part declines.[113]

---

[104] CAA 2001, ss 205–208.
[105] CAA 2001, ss 11(4), 205–207.
[106] CAA 2001, s 270.
[107] CAA 2001, ss 209–212.
[108] CAA 2001, s 265.
[109] CAA 2001, ss 213 *et seq*.
[110] CAA 1990, s 81; the gift is treated as a purchase from the donor for this amount for the purposes of s 75.
[111] CAA 2001, ss 13 (change of purpose) and 14 (acquisition as gift); original versions added by FA 2000, s 75.
[112] CAA 2001, s 15(1), originally added by FA 2000, s 75; naturally this does not apply to those parts of the CAA 2001 which already refer to activities outside the UK.
[113] CAA 2001, s 208, original version added by FA 2000, s 75.

24.2.1.4 Similar Reliefs

Equivalent but distinct relief is given under CAA 2001 for expenditure on thermal insula-tion (section 28) and on personal security measures (section 33).[114] While these expendi-tures attract capital allowances, they do not give rise to balancing charges.

24.2.1.5 Partners

Where the plant is used by a partnership for a trade carried on by the partnership, allow-ances will be given to the partners in the usual way. Special provision is made where a partner owns the asset but allows the partnership to use it for its trade. Here, the allowance will be given to the partnership, and any sale or gift by the partner to the partners will be ignored. This provision does not apply where the plant is leased to the partnership for payment.[115]

24.2.1.6 Qualifying Activities: General

Plant and machinery allowances can apply only if the taxpayer is carrying on a qualify-ing activity.[116] Such activities cover not only trades, professions and vocations,[117] but also ordinary UK property businesses,[118] UK and EEA furnished holiday lettings,[119] ordi-nary overseas property businesses,[120] mines and similar concerns listed in ITTOIA 2005, section 12 or CTA 2009, section 39(4),[121] the management of investment companies[122] and special leasing arrangements.[123] These activities all have their own rules for giving effect to the allowances. These activities qualify only to the extent that any profits or gains would be chargeable to UK tax.[124]

24.2.1.7 Qualifying Activities: Employment

An employment or office is also a qualifying activity, and so an employee or office holder may obtain capital allowances to set against employment income in respect of 'plant and machinery necessarily provided by the employee for use in his employment'.[125] The term 'necessarily' means that a finding that another holder of the office could have performed the duties without incurring the expense is fatal to the claim.[126] For most employments, it is not possible for E, the employee, to claim a capital allowance for a computer/word pro-cessor purchased by E for use in E's employment, since it is usually possible to perform the duties of that employment equally by pen, paper and brain.[127] Moreover, the Revenue often

---

[114] CAA 2001, ss 28 and 30–33; s 28 widened to all qualifying activities by FA 2008, s 71.
[115] CAA 1990, s 65.
[116] CAA 2001, s 15.
[117] CAA 2001, ss 15 and 247.
[118] CAA 2001, ss 16 and 248.
[119] CAA 2001, ss 17, 17B and 249.
[120] CAA 2001, ss 17A and 250.
[121] CAA 2001, ss 15 and 251.
[122] CAA 2001, ss 18 and 253; on life assurance businesses, see ss 254–257.
[123] CAA 2001, ss 19 and 258–261.
[124] CAA 2001, s 15(1).
[125] CAA 2001, ss 15 and 36; see also ss 20 (excluding certain offices, etc) and 262.
[126] *White v Higginbotham* [1983] STC 143, 57 TC 2839 (no allowance for audio visual aids for clergyman).
[127] On the now-repealed absence of a tax charge where a computer was provided by the employer, see above at §16.3.3.2.

argue that the very fact that E rather than his employer purchases the equipment is proof that the purchase is not 'necessary' for the employment.

However, an employee may not claim any allowances for purchases of motor vehicles or bicycles. Instead the employee must claim under the Revenue's fixed-profit car scheme, which includes an allowance for the capital cost of the vehicle (see above §18.2.6).[128]

24.2.2 'Belong to'/'Owned by'

24.2.2.1 Overview

Under CAA 1990, the asset had to 'belong to' the person incurring the expense in consequence of the payment. This was changed by CA 2001 to the more understandable rule that the asset must be 'owned by' that person; the change is meant to be simply stylistic.[129] In *Stokes v Costain Property Investments Ltd*,[130] a tenant had installed a lift in a leased building. Since the lifts immediately became the property of the landlord under general land law principles, they could not be said to 'belong to' the tenant, and so it was held that the tenant was not entitled to the allowance.[131] Further, in *Melluish v BMI (No 3)*,[132] the House of Lords held that a lessee has no right to an allowance if he has a right to remove the fixture at some future time, eg at the end of the lease, but which fixture has become the property of the landlord in the meantime. This is because the concept of a fixture which remains personal property is a contradiction in terms and an impossibility in law;[133] and because the argument would make it uncertain whether an asset belonged to—or ceased to belong to—the lessee according to whether he had or had not got a right to remove the asset (eg where the landlord committed a breach of the lease which the tenant then forgave). It follows that a contractual right to remove the fixture cannot prevent its becoming part of the land and so ceasing to belong to the installer.

In *Melluish*, the words 'in consequence of' in the 1990 Act were held to be satisfied where a payment was made by the taxpayer to induce the holder of an option to reacquire the property to release that option.[134] These words form no part of CAA 2001, which refers simply to capital expenditure incurred on the provision of plant of machinery.[135]

In *Melluish*, the taxpayer leased central heating, boilers, lifts and similar equipment to local authorities. The items were installed in buildings owned by the local authorities. In so far as *Melluish* decided that equipment-lessors could obtain allowances under the special rules introduced to reverse *Costain* where plant was leased to non-taxpayers such as charities or local authorities, the decision was reversed—save where the *lessor* had an interest in the land.[136]

---

[128] FA 2001, s 59 amending CAA 2001, s 36; on ministerial statement, see Standing Committee A, 1 May 2001.

[129] CAA 2001, ss 11(4)(b) and 52(1)(b); for earlier rules, see CAA 1990, ss 22(1)(b), 24(1)(b).

[130] [1984] STC 204, [1984] 1 All ER 849, CA; see Scott [1985] BTR 46. Contrast the 'relevant interest' rules for industrial buildings (below at §6.3.3). See also *Melluish v BMI (No 3) Ltd* [1995] STC 964, 68 TC 1.

[131] The landlord (to whom the lifts did belong) could not claim an allowance because it had not incurred the expenditure.

[132] [1995] STC 964, 68 TC 1.

[133] *Ibid*, 971, 974, 71–72, 75, *per* Lord Browne-Wilkinson.

[134] *Bolton v International Drilling Ltd* [1983] STC 70, 56 TC 449.

[135] CAA 2001, s 11(4)(a).

[136] CAA 1990, s 53(1A)–(1C) added by FA 1997, Sch 16, para 3, now superseded by CAA 2001, ss 177(3).

24.2.2.2 Reversing *Costain*: The Fixtures Rules

The situation resulting from *Stokes v Costain* was unjust, and a new scheme was introduced for expenditure incurred in 1984.[137] A fixture is treated as owned by the lessee (L) (or similar person) who incurred the expenditure in providing the plant or machinery for the purposes of a trade carried on by L (or for leasing otherwise than in the course of a trade) if (a) the plant or machinery becomes in law a part of the land, and (b) at that time L has an interest in the relevant land.[138] The rules also apply where the plant becomes a fixture before the capital expenditure is incurred. The lessee's allowance excludes the lessor's allowance, but a lessor who contributes to the expenditure is not excluded.[139] Naturally, (a) and (b) above turn on land law principles. Tax courts have had to consider whether automatic public conveniences (APCs) and bus shelters were part of the land (they were), and whether a right to enter to clean, maintain and repair was enough to satisfy (b) (it was not).[140]

FA 2000 widened the definition for qualifying expenditure by an equipment lessor to cover leased assets under the Affordable Warmth Programme.[141] The same Act amended the definition of 'fixture' so as to include boilers and radiators, even though these are (relatively) easy to remove; as this was always thought to be the law, the change had retroactive effect.[142] A later Act governs fixtures supplied by energy service providers.[143] The effect is to treat the equipment lessor or provider as being the owner, but only for CAA 2001 purposes.

Special provisions govern disputes over whether the item is a fixture,[144] expenditure (and disposals) by equipment lessors[145] and the transfer to a lessee of the right to an allowance.[146] Rules also apply where an interest in the land is sold and the price is referable to the fixture,[147] and when the fixture ceases to belong to a particular person.[148] These rules are to be taken at face value; the allowances are not confined to cases where the user is liable to tax.[149] Other rules limit the amount qualifying for allowances to the original cost of the fixtures and prevent multiple claims.[150] Rules also prevent the acceleration of allowances.[151] The 1997 legislation allowed the vendor and purchaser of property to allocate part of the purchase price to fixtures.[152]

There are also rules imposing obligations on taxpayers to amend their returns to report relevant changes of circumstances in relation to these rules.[153]

---

[137] Now CAA 2001, ss 172–204. Before 1984 matters were dealt with by concession; the taxpayers in *Stokes v Costain* were apparently not willing to agree to one of the conditions in that concession.

[138] Defined in CAA 2001, ss 173–175 and 202.

[139] Under CAA 2001, ss 172(5) and 537.

[140] *Decaux v Francis* [1996] STC (SCD) 281.

[141] CAA 2001, ss 180 and 203, original amendments made by FA 2000, s 79.

[142] CAA 2001, ss 172(1) and 173(1) and (2), original amendments made by FA 2000, s 78.

[143] CAA 2001, s 180A added by FA 2001 s 66.

[144] CAA 2001, s 204.

[145] CAA 2001, ss 177–180 and 192–196.

[146] CAA 2001, s 183; and where the lessee would be entitled to the allowance, but the lessor would not (s 184).

[147] CAA 2001, s 181.

[148] CAA 2001, ss 188–191.

[149] *Melluish v BMI (No 3) Ltd* [1995] STC 964, 980b, 68 TC 1, 82I, HL, *per* Lord Browne-Wilkinson.

[150] CAA 2001, ss 9 and 182–184, original version added by FA 1997, Sch 16, para 4.

[151] CAA 2001, s 197, original version added by FA 1997, Sch 16, para 5.

[152] CAA 2001, s 198, original version added by FA 1997, Sch 16, para 6.

[153] CAA 2001, s 203.

24.2.3 *What is Plant and Machinery?*

24.2.3.1 General

Neither 'plant' nor 'machinery' is defined in CAA 2001, and the question whether an item is plant or machinery depends on the facts of the case. Where an item qualified both for plant and machinery allowance and industrial buildings allowance (withdrawn from April 2011),[154] it was likely that the former, usually more generous, relief was claimed.[155] In 1994 Parliament provided some clarification on the boundary between plant and its setting, but difficult cases still appear (see below at §24.2.4).

Different definitions have been suggested for specific instances. In *Yarmouth v France*, a claim was brought by a workman under the Employers' Liability Act 1880 for damages for injuries sustained due to a defect in his employer's plant, in that case a vicious horse. Lindley LJ stated:[156]

> …[I]n its ordinary sense [plant] includes whatever apparatus is used by a business man for carrying on his business—not his stock-in-trade which he buys or makes for sale; but all goods and chattels, fixed or moveable, live or dead, which he keeps for permanent employment in his business.…

This test has been helpful but not exclusive[157] in capital allowance cases. The test clearly covers fixtures and fittings of a durable nature. Therefore, railway locomotives and carriages[158] and tramway rails[159] have been held to be plant, as have knives and lasts used in the manufacture of shoes,[160] but not the bed of a harbour,[161] nor stallions for stud purposes.[162]

It is now clear that plant and machinery is not confined to things used physically[163] but extends to the intellectual storehouse of the trade or profession, eg the purchase of law books by a barrister.[164] However, rights to exploit plant are not 'plant'—a matter of great concern in the area of IP.[165] It is not necessary that the object be active, although a passive object may be less obviously plant.[166]

It has been suggested, eg by the Revenue, that a thing which lacks physical manifestation cannot be 'plant'. If this is true, it leads to a substantial and regrettable lack of clarity with regard to many items of IP. The piecemeal income tax provisions for copyright, know-how and certain types of scientific research are no substitute for modern and coherent law. Special legislation now applies to computer software.

---

[154] *IRC v Barclay Curle & Co Ltd* [1969] 1 All ER 732, 45 TC 221 (see below at §24.2.4); the area of overlap has been reduced by statutory rules on when setting is plant.

[155] Double allowances are excluded by CAA 2001, s 7.

[156] (1887) 19 QBD 647 at 658.

[157] Lord Donovan in *IRC v Barclay Curle & Co Ltd* [1969] 1 All ER 732, 751, 45 TC 221, 249.

[158] *Caledonian Rly Co v Banks* (1880) 1 TC 487.

[159] *LCC v Edwards* (1909) 5 TC 383.

[160] *Hinton v Maden and Ireland Ltd* [1959] 3 All ER 356, 38 TC 391 (expected to last only three years); noted at [1959] BTR 454.

[161] *Dumbarton Harbour Board v Cox* (1918) 7 TC 147.

[162] *Earl of Derby v Aylmer* [1915] 3 KB 374, 6 TC 665.

[163] *McVeigh v Arthur Sanderson & Sons Ltd* [1969] 2 All ER 771, 775, *per* Cross J; noted at [1969] BTR 130.

[164] *Munby v Furlong* [1977] STC 232, [1977] 2 All ER 953.

[165] *Barclays Mercantile Industrial Finance Ltd v Melluish* [1990] STC 314, 63 TC 93, 122.

[166] *Jarrold v John Good & Sons Ltd* [1963] 1 All ER 141, 40 TC 681.

24.2.3.2 Computer Software

Where capital expenditure is incurred on the outright acquisition of computer software, the normal plant and machinery allowance is available.[167] However, problems arise where a capital sum is paid for a licence to use the software or for the provision of software by electronic means. In the first instance, it cannot be said that the software is owned by the taxpayer, while in the second, it may lack the degree of tangibility necessary for plant to exist.[168] Today, software acquired under a licence is treated as owned by the person carrying on the qualifying activity (T) as long as T is entitled to the right, while computer software is treated as being plant or machinery.[169] The disposal values depend on the circumstances of the grant of the licence.[170]

24.2.4 *Plant or Setting*

24.2.4.1 Statutory Prescription of Settings[171]

Since 1994, statute has in part governed the boundary between plant and machinery and settings; originally CAA 1990, Schedule AA1, now CAA 2001, sections 21–25. It must be said, however, that the way this is done is neither intuitive nor straightforward.

By way of overview, Section 21 begins by providing List A, which are assets which must be treated as *buildings* and not as plant. Section 22 then provides List B, which are certain *structures* which must be treated in the same way. Section 23 gives us List C, which is a long list of exceptions to Lists A and B. One might at first glance think that List C is a list of expenditure qualifying as plant or machinery—but that is not the case! In fact, section 23(3) states, somewhat cryptically, that whether expenditure on List C is expenditure on the provision of plant or machinery is 'unaffected by sections 21 and 22'. The implication is that the question of whether expenditure on List C is plant or machinery must be answered by the courts on the particular facts, but bearing in mind that the assets on List C are ones that had previously satisfied the test of plant.[172] Examples include expenditure on the provision of a dry dock, decorative assets provided for the enjoyment of the public in hotels and restuarants and a glasshouse which is constructed so that the required environment (ie air, heat, light, irrigation and temperature) for growing plants is provided automatically by means of devices which are an integral part of its structure. List C does not affect a number of special provisions which treat specified expenditure as if it were on plant or machinery—eg thermal insulation, sports grounds and security.[173] Lastly, to give taxpayers some comfort in these rules, section 25 provides that expenditure on building alterations connected with the installation of plant and machinery is to be treated as being incurred on the plant and machinery.

---

[167] On boundary between capital and revenue, note Inland Revenue interpretation RI 56.

[168] *Barclays Mercantile Industrial Finance Ltd v Melluish* [1990] STC 314, 63 TC 93, 122.

[169] CAA 2001, s 71, predecessor originally added by F(No 2)A 1992, s 68.

[170] CAA 2001, s 72; on limits, see s 73.

[171] Originally added by FA 1994, s 117.

[172] CAA 2001, s 23, List C, paras 23 and 17.

[173] CAA 2001, ss 27–33; on application of thermal insulation on industrial buildings to overseas property business, see FA 2001, Sch 21, para 1, amending CAA 2001, s 28.

The premise behind the post-1994 statutory framework is that buildings and structures cannot qualify as plant (although it is also stated that the broad aim is that expenditure on buildings and structures which already qualify as plant should continue to do so).[174] However, for the most part the lists reflect what the courts have achieved. The effect of the change is partly to provide detailed guidance and partly to prevent judges from changing the law themselves. We now turn to consider these sections in more detail.

(a) *Buildings.* CAA 2001, section 21 begins with buildings, and excludes from the category of 'plant or machinery' any expenditure on the provision of a building. It defines 'building' as including any asset in the building which is incorporated into the building, or which, by reason of being movable or otherwise, is not so incorporated but is of a kind normally incorporated into buildings.[175] This abstract statement is supplemented by Lists A (section 21) and C (section 23). List A sets out six categories of assets which *cannot* be plant or machinery,[176] including walls, floors, ceilings, doors, gates, shutters, windows and stairs, mains services, waste disposal, sewerage and drainage, shafts, etc for lifts, and moving walkways and fire safety systems. Examples of the 33 items in List C, and so which *may* be 'plant' under case law principles, are electrical, cold water, gas and sewerage systems provided mainly to meet the particular requirements of the trade, or provided mainly to serve particular plant or machinery used for the purposes of the trade. Cold stores, caravans provided mainly for holiday lettings and any movable building intended to be moved in the course of the trade are also in List C and so may also be plant. The legislation leaves it to the taxpayer to establish that these items are plant under existing case law. To make things clearer, it is provided that an asset cannot come within any of the first 16 items in List C if its principal purpose is to insulate or enclose the interior of the building, or to provide an interior wall, a floor or a ceiling which (in each case) is intended to remain permanently in place.[177] FA 2008 adds to List C expenditure on the installation or replacement of specified 'integral features' under section 33A. The features are electrical and cold-water systems, heating and air-conditioning systems, lifts escalators and moving walkways, and external solar shading (being thought to be environmentally beneficial).[178]

(b) *Structures, assets and works.* Again, the legislation (CAA 2001, section 22) begins with a prohibition—expenditure on the provision of plant or machinery does not include any expenditure on the provision of structures or other specified assets in List B, or any works involving the alteration of land.[179] Section 22 defines a 'structure' as a fixed structure of any kind, other than a building. List B contains seven categories which cannot qualify. It includes not only tunnels, bridges, railways and airstrips, but also any dam, reservoir or barrage (including any sluices, gates, generators and other equipment associated with it), any dock and any dike, sea wall, weir or drainage ditch; the list ends ominously with any structure not within any other item in this list

---

[174] Inland Revenue Press Release, 30 November 1993, [1993] *Simon's Tax Intelligence* 1539.
[175] CAA 2001, s 21(3).
[176] CAA 2001, s 23 List C, para 2.
[177] CAA 2001, s 23(4).
[178] CAA 2001, ss 33A and 33B added by FA 2008, s 73; the list is in s 33A(5).
[179] On which, see *Family Golf Centres Ltd v Thorne* [1998] STC (SCD) 106.

(a statement that is then qualified with a few exceptions, including telecommunication and gas structures).

List C includes expenditure on the provision of towers used to support floodlights, of any reservoir incorporated into a water treatment works, of silos used for temporary storage or on the provision of storage tanks, of swimming pools, including diving boards, slides and any structure supporting them and of fish tanks or fish ponds. List C was substantially widened in the course of the Parliamentary debate.[180]

(c) *Land.* Lastly, CAA 2001, section 24 provides that expenditure on the acquisition of any interest in land cannot qualify as expenditure on plant. This bar also extends to any asset which is so installed or otherwise fixed in or to any description of land as to become, in law, part of that land.[181]

24.2.4.2 Plant or Setting: Case Law Principles

As already noted, List C in section 23 provides a list of expenditure which *may* qualify a plant, with the question to be determined by reference to the case law. Plant does not include the place where the business is carried on; 'plant' is that *with which* the trade is carried on as opposed to the 'setting or premises' *in which* it is carried on.[182] Plant carries with it a connotation of equipment or apparatus, either fixed or unfixed. It does not convey a meaning wide enough to cover buildings in general. It may cover equipment of any size. Equipment does not cease to be plant merely because it discharges an additional function, such as providing the place in which the business is carried on, eg a dry dock,[183] but these categories are not necessarily mutually exclusive and the different scope of the allowances makes correct classification of great practical importance. It has been held that special partitioning used by shipping agents to subdivide floor space to accommodate fluctuating office accommodation requirements was plant, some stress being laid on the fact that office flexibility was needed.[184] Something which becomes part of the premises, as opposed to merely embellishing them, is not plant, save where the premises are themselves plant,[185] as in *IRC v Barclay, Curle & Co Ltd* (see §24.2.4.3 next).

24.2.4.3 Defining the Unit

It is often a crucial question whether various items are taken separately or treated as one installation. This is a question of fact and so for the Tribunals (formerly Commissioners) to decide, subject only to the tests in *Edwards v Bairstow and Harrison*, namely where the appellant judge concludes that the only true and reasonable conclusion contradicts the Tribunal's determination.[186] In *Cole Brothers Ltd v Phillips*,[187] the taxpayer, T, had spent money on electrical installations in a large department store (John Lewis at the Brent

---

[180] See Inland Revenue Press Release, 9 March 1994, [1994] *Simon's Tax Intelligence* 339.

[181] CAA 2001, s 24; rule added to CAA 1990 by FA 1994, s 117; the definition of 'land' in the Interpretation Act 1978 is modified, CAA 2001, s 24(2).

[182] *Jarrold v John Good & Sons Ltd* [1963] 1 All ER 141, 40 TC 681, 696, *per* Pearson LJ.

[183] See Sir Donald Nicholls V-C in *Carr v Sayer* [1992] STC 396, 402, 65 TC 15, 22.

[184] *Jarrold v John Good & Sons Ltd* [1963] 1 All ER 141, 40 TC 681. The decision of the Commissioners was left intact.

[185] *Wimpy International Ltd v Warland* [1989] STC 273, 279e, 61 TC 51, 96, CA, *per* Fox LJ.

[186] [1955] 3 All ER 48. See above at §4.4.4.

[187] [1982] STC 307 HL; [1981] STC 671, 55 TC 188, CA.

Cross shopping centre, London). One argument advanced by T was that the whole electrical installation was one item. This was rejected by the Commissioners; the appellate courts treated the issue as a matter of fact for the Commissioners, but the discomfort shown by the speeches in the House of Lords is marked.[188] The issue arose later in *Attwood v Anduff Carwash Ltd*,[189] where the question was whether a car-wash site was a single plant. The Commissioners held that it was, but the appellate courts held that neither the whole site nor the wash hall alone could be treated as a single unit.

(a) *Dry dock—IRC v Barclay, Curle & Co Ltd.* While there is a clear distinction between the shell of a building and the machinery currently used in it, there are considerable difficulties where a large and durable structure is created for a specific purpose. This occurred in the leading case of *IRC v Barclay, Curle & Co Ltd*.[190] The taxpayer had constructed a dry dock, a process requiring the excavation of the site and the construction of a concrete lining. The Revenue agreed that such expenditure incurred on the dock gate and operating gear, the cast-iron keel blocks and the electrical and pumping installations related to plant, but argued that, while the expenses of excavation and concreting might relate to industrial building, they did not relate to plant and machinery. The Revenue lost.

It will be noted that while a dock is now classified as a structure, and so not capable of qualifying for allowances as plant, a dry dock is classified differently. The expenditure on the concrete lining was held to be in respect of plant, because it could not be regarded as the mere setting in which the trade was carried on but was an integral part of the means required for the trading operation. Lord Reid said that a structure which fulfils the function of plant was, prima facie, plant.[191] However, later cases show that this 'business' or 'function' test must yield to the 'premises' test (see *(b)* below). CAA 2001 expressly provides that where capital expenditure is incurred on alterations to an existing building incidental to the installation of plant or machinery for the purposes of trade, allowances may be claimed in respect of such expenditure just as if the works formed part of the plant or machinery.[192]

(b) *Fast food restaurant—Wimpy v Warland.* The fact that an item has a business use (the business test) is not enough to make it plant; an item cannot be plant if its use is as the premises or place on which the business is conducted (the premises test).[193] In *Wimpy v Warland*,[194] the taxpayer sought (unsuccessfully) to claim allowances for expenditure on shop fronts, wall panels, suspended ceilings, mezzanine floor, decorative brickwork, wall finishes, a trapdoor and ladder. As Fox LJ stated:

> There is a well established distinction, in general terms, between the premises in which the business is carried on and the plant with which the business is carried on. The premises are not plant. In its simplest form that is illustrated by [the] example of the creation of atmosphere in a hotel by beautiful buildings and gardens on the one hand and fine china, glass

---

[188] See [1982] STC 307, 312–13, *per* Lord Hailsham, 314f, *per* Lord Wilberforce, and 316a, *per* Lord Edmund-Davies

[189] [1997] STC 1167, CA.

[190] [1969] 1 All ER 732, 45 TC 221.

[191] *Ibid*, 740, 239.

[192] CAA 2001, s 25.

[193] *Wimpy International v Warland* [1988] STC 149, 171b; 61 TC 51, 82d, *per* Hoffmann J.

[194] [1989] STC 273, 279; 61 TC 51, 96, CA.

and other tableware on the other. The latter are plant; the former are not. The former are simply the premises in which the business is conducted.

(c)   *Planteria—Gray v Seymour's.* The case of *Gray v Seymour's*[195] involved what might loosely be called a high-tech glasshouse used in a garden centre. As Nourse LJ stated:

> While the cold frames which formerly provided a similar function to that of the planteria might well have been plant, the same cannot be said of the planteria itself. It is a structure to which plants are brought already in a saleable condition, albeit that some of them tend to be in there for quite considerable periods and others require special treatment ... The fact that the planteria provides the function of nurturing and preserving the plants while they are there cannot transform it into something other than part of the premises in which the business is carried on. The highest it can be put is that it functions as a purpose-built structure. But ... that is not enough to make the structure plant.

24.2.4.4 Defining Setting

The distinction between setting and plant depends in part upon the degree of sophistication to be employed in the concept of a setting.[196] The problem is acute when electrical apparatus and wiring are concerned.[197] The matter must be resolved by the use of the functional test, so that, for example, while lighting will not usually be plant, it will become so if it is of a specialised nature, as where it is designed to provide a particular atmosphere in a hotel; this must be judged by reference to the intended market.[198] The Revenue have consistently refused to treat wiring leading to such apparatus as plant. Under section 21, List A places mains services and systems of electricity generally in the category of assets which cannot qualify as plant, while List C *allows* electrical systems to be plant if provided mainly to meet the particular requirements of the trade, or to serve particular plant or machinery used for the purposes of the trade.[199]

24.2.4.5 Case Law Survey

The case law distinction between buildings and apparatus is, perhaps inevitably, indistinct. The cases have shown that items which cannot be plant under the case law test include a prefabricated building at a school used to accommodate a chemical laboratory,[200] a canopy

---

[195] [1995] STC 706, 711b; 67 TC 401, 413. For a general Revenue view on glasshouses, see Inland Revenue interpretation RI 33, updated by RI 185.

[196] *Imperial Chemical Industries of Australia and New Zealand v Taxation Commr of the Commonwealth of Australia* (1970) 120 CLR 396.

[197] In *Cole Bros Ltd v Phillips* [1982] STC 307, HL; [1981] STC 671, 55 TC 188, CA, the Revenue agreed that wiring to certain items such as alarms and clocks was plant, but said that (a) transformers, switchgear and the main switchboard, and (b) specially designed lighting fittings were not plant. The Commissioners held that the transformers were plant, but not the other items under (a) or any of (b). The Court of Appeal held that the switchboard was plant because of the fact that some of the wiring had been agreed to be plant. The House of Lords agreed with the Court of Appeal in treating the remaining items as matters for the Commissioners' decision as matters of fact.

[198] *Cole Bros Ltd v Phillips* [1982] STC 307, 55 TC 188, HL; *Hunt v Henry Quick Ltd* [1992] STC 633, 65 TC 108; *IRC v Scottish and Newcastle Breweries Ltd* [1982] STC 296, 55 TC 252 (note that the light fitting was allowed in *Wimpy International Ltd v Warland* [1988] STC 149, 176; 61 TC 51, 88). On the 1982 House of Lords decisions, see [1983] BTR 54.

[199] The Revenue rely strongly on *J Lyons & Co Ltd v A-G* [1944] Ch 281, [1944] 1 All ER 477.

[200] *St John's School v Ward* [1975] STC 7, 49 TC 524 (note the astonishingly harsh refusal by Templeman J to allow an apportionment between the building and the equipment).

over a petrol station[201] (although this has since been doubted),[202] an inflatable cover over a tennis court[203] and a floating ship used as a restaurant.[204] These failed the business test since they performed no function in the trade. Many of these cases now appear in the statutory list of assets which cannot qualify as plant. Permanent quarantine kennels,[205] putting greens at a nine-hole golf course,[206] a car-washing facility operated on a conveyor belt system[207] and an all-weather race track for horse racing[208] probably met the business test, but certainly failed the premises test. On the other hand, it has been held that a silo used in the trade of grain importing was not simply part of the setting and had to be considered together with the machinery and other equipment within it.[209] Similarly, a swimming pool at a caravan site was held to be plant since it was part of the apparatus of the business.[210] Also held to be plant were decorative screens placed in the windows of a building society's offices (since the screens were not the structure within which the business was carried on)[211] and, perhaps surprisingly, mezzanine platforms installed by a wholesale merchant to increase storage space.[212] In the celebrated House of Lords case of *IRC v Scottish and Newcastle Breweries Ltd*,[213] murals designed to attract customers were held to be plant, as was a metal seagull sculpture and other items designed to create 'ambience'.

These cases prove the old adage that an ounce of evidence (before the Commissioners) is worth a ton of law. Of the 13 High Court cases reported between 1975 and 2004, eight were cases in which the Revenue successfully appealed against a Commissioner's determination that the items were plant, one was a successful appeal by a taxpayer against a Commissioner's decision in favour of the Revenue, in two the court agreed with the Commissioners that the items were plant, and in two the Commissioners had originally decided that *some* items were plant, but the court subsequently decided that *more* items were plant. Of the items which the courts have decided are plant, one or two have now been set out in the non-plant category by the statutory list.[214]

24.2.5 First-year Allowances and the Annual Investment Allowance

24.2.5.1 First-year Allowances

The expenditure on plant and machinery qualifying for first-year allowances is set out in CAA 2001, Part 2, Chapter 4 (sections 39–51); the rules for calculating the allowances are

---

[201] *Dixon v Fitch's Garage Ltd* [1975] STC 480, [1975] 3 All ER 455, 50 TC 509.
[202] *Cole Bros Ltd v Phillips* [1982] STC 307, 311; 55 TC, 223, *per* Lord Hailsham; but see the pointed comment of Walton J in *Thomas v Reynolds* [1987] STC 135, 140; 59 TC 502, 508.
[203] *Thomas v Reynolds* [1987] STC 135, 59 TC 502.
[204] *Benson v Yard Arm Club Ltd* [1979] STC 266, [1979] 2 All ER 336, 53 TC 607.
[205] *Carr v Sayer* [1992] STC 396, 65 TC 15.
[206] *Family Golf Centres Ltd v Thorne* [1998] STC (SCD) 106.
[207] *Attwood v Anduff Car Wash Ltd* [1997] STC 1167, CA.
[208] *Shove v Lingfield Park (1991) Ltd* [2004] EWCA Civ 391; [2004] STC 805; in a similar vein the Special Commissioners refused to treat a five-a-side football pitch as plant in *Anchor International v IRC* [2003] STC (SCD) 115.
[209] *Schofield v R and H Hall Ltd* [1975] STC 353, 49 TC 538.
[210] *Cooke v Beach Station Caravans Ltd* [1974] STC 402, [1974] 3 All ER 159, 49 TC 514.
[211] *Leeds Permanent Building Society v Procter* [1982] STC 821, 56 TC 293.
[212] *Hunt v Henry Quick Ltd* [1992] STC 633, 643–44; 65 TC 108, 124 (note the doubts of Vinelott J).
[213] [1982] STC 296, 55 TC 252, HL.
[214] Eg the windows in *Leeds Permanent Building Society v Procter* [1982] STC 821.

in section 52, which includes a helpful table. Although general first-year allowances were abolished by FA 1984, as part of Nigel Lawson's corporation tax reform, Chancellors have been unable to resist bringing them back for specific purposes, but there are fewer after the changes of 2008.[215] First-year allowances of 100% are given for expenditure on plant and machinery that is energy-saving or environmentally beneficial, cars with low carbon dioxide emissions and electric cars, gas refuelling stations, and plant and machinery for use in designated assisted areas. The table in CAA 2001, section 52 also lists a first-year allowance for expenditure for use wholly in a special ring-fenced trade—mostly to do with North Sea Oil.[216]

24.2.5.2 The Annual Investment Allowance

The annual investment allowance (AIA) is, in effect, a 100% first-year allowance for up to £200,000 of capital expenditure per year. The principal legislation is in CAA 2001, Part 2, Chapter 3A (sections 38A and 38B, and sections 51A–51N). AIA is available if the expenditure is incurred by a qualifying person and is not caught by the general exclusions listed in section 38B.[217] Section 38B excludes expenditure: (1) in the period during which permanent discontinuance takes place; (2) on cars; (3) by ring-fence trades; (4) by a person in connection with a change in the nature or conduct of the trade of another person where one of the main benefits of the change is to obtain AIA; and (5) certain deemed expenditures—real expenditures are needed. As with the other allowances, T must incur the expenditure in the chargeable period and own the asset at some point during that period.[218] T may choose part only of the allowance. If the chargeable period is less than 12 months the allowance is reduced proportionately. The legislation lists provisions restricting allowances which restrict the AIA as well. These apply where the asset is used only partly for the qualifying activity, there is a partial subsidy and where the asset is acquired in certain listed circumstances, eg from a connected person; further, no allowance may be claimed for an additional VAT liability.[219] FA 2008 added section 218A to deal expressly with the AIA; thus the allowance is not available if there is an arrangement entered into wholly and/or mainly to enable a person to obtain an AIA to which that person would not otherwise be entitled.

As it is a single capped allowance, the AIA rules go on to provide many detailed restrictions to prevent people getting too much relief. So a company can only have one AIA, no matter how many qualifying activities it carries on. If the company forms part of a group, there is only one AIA per group—though the group may allocate the AIA to any company with right amount of qualifying expenditure. There are further rules on companies under common control though not technically part of a group (section 51E). Section 51D covers two or more groups under common control. Terms such as 'control' and 'related' are defined in sections 51F and 51G. Companies are related if they share premises or have similar activities, ie more than 50% of turnover is derived from qualifying activities of the same type—an EU classification system is used.

---

[215] CAA 1990, s 22(2); for history and avoiding hybrid Bill status, see Lawson, *op cit*, 354. It was not possible to claim both the first-year allowance and the writing-down allowance for the same period, which is why the allowance is called a first-year allowance rather than an initial allowance.

[216] CAA 2001, ss 45F and 45G added by FA 2002, Sch 21, para 10.

[217] CAA 2001, s 38A; the amount is given by s 51A.

[218] CAA 2001, s 51A(1)(2).

[219] CAA 2001, ss 205, 210, 214–217 and 241.

With sections 51H–51K we move beyond the corporation tax sector to individuals and partnerships consisting only of individuals. We find rules analogous to the company rules. A restriction applies where there are two or more qualifying activities carried on by a qualifying person and they are both (a) controlled by the same person and (b) related to each other. The restriction is that only AIA may be used—though it may be allocated as the taxpayer wishes. For some reason the legislation does not include any provisions on how the AIA may be used by trusts.

There are special rules for short periods (section 51L). Each chargeable period must be looked at separately. The problem of periods longer than 12 months is taken care of for companies by the corporation tax rule that an accounting period cannot exceed 12 months (see above §2.4.2). For other businesses, equivalent rules are provided by section 51M. Section 51N modifies the rule in section 51M to deal with the situation in which a person controls two or more related activities in a tax year and more than one of the related activities has a chargeable period of more than one year. There is a bar on double allowances where the expenditure also qualifies for a first-year allowance. The taxpayer has a free choice but must choose.[220] The concept of pooling has no part to play in the treatment of AIA or first-year allowances.[221]

24.2.6 *Writing-down Allowances, Balances and the Pool*

The 'main' writing-down allowance, which is now given on an 18% reducing balance basis, applies where the taxpayer, T, incurs capital expenditure on the provision of plant and machinery wholly or partly for the purposes of the trade.[222] In addition, as we have seen, the asset must be owned by T.[223] For many years the percentage was 25% then 20%, but this was changed to 18% as from 1 April 2012 for corporation tax and 6 April 2012 for income tax.[224] The 25% figure remains for 'ring-fence' trades.[225]

It is not necessary that the asset should have been brought into use in the trade. If the chargeable period is greater or less than 12 months, the figure of 18% is increased or reduced accordingly.[226]

Whether T is entitled to writing-down allowance, a balancing allowance or a balancing charge depends on the amount of available qualifying expenditure (AQE), the total value of any disposal receipts (TDR) and what has happened. If the AQE exceeds the TDR, T is entitled to the writing-down allowance. If T ceases to carry on the qualifying activity, the amount by which AQE exceeds TDR becomes a balancing allowance in the final chargeable period of the qualifying activity.[227] If TDR exceeds AQE, there is a balancing charge in that period—even if the qualifying activity continues.

---

[220] CAA 2001, s 52A.
[221] CAA 2001, s 53.
[222] CAA 2001, s 11(4)(a).
[223] CAA 2001, s 11 (4)(b).
[224] CAA 2001, s 56, as amended by FA 2008, s 80.
[225] CAA 2001, s 56(1A), added by FA 2008.T
[226] CAA 2001, s 56(2).
[227] CAA 2001, s 54(4).

24.2.6.1 Pooling

Although practitioners had talked for years of pools and pooling, these terms did not become part of the statutory language until CAA 2001. Today there are three main pools to talk about; in addition, some assets form pools on their own—single asset pools.

The main pool Generally, all plant and machinery used in the trade is placed in one pool—the main pool—and the 18% main writing-down allowance is applied to the value of that pool as a whole.[228]

The special rate pool[229] Here the rate of writing-down allowance is generally 8%.[230] Expenditure in this pool is that on:

(a) thermal insulation;
(b) integral features (see §24.2.4.1 above);
(c) long-life assets acquired on or after 1 or 6 April 2008;
(d) long-life assets acquired before those dates and now transferred to the pool. For (d) the transfer means an increase in the rate from 6%;[231]
(e) cars acquired after April 2009 with high carbon dioxide emissions (see §24.2.10.2 below); and
(f) the provision of cushion gas incurred on or after 1 April 2010; and
(g) solar panels acquired on or after 1 or 6 April 2012.

The small pool.[232] This rule applies only to the main pool and special rate pool. Where the unrelieved expenditure is £1,000 or less, the whole balance may be written off at once (a 100% writing-down allowance). This writing off applies where the unrelieved expenditure is in the main pool or the special pool, or both. The taxpayer does not have to do this and may elect to take part only. The thinking behind the pool is that with the introduction of the AIA, businesses are likely to have small pockets of pre-2008 expenditures which are unlikely to grow. Businesses should not be made to keep track of these.

Separate pooling. Certain items *must* be pooled separately. The first group forms single asset pools, which naturally means that only expenditure on the particular asset is relevant.[233] The rate of 18% applies as from April 2012. The relevant assets are:

(1) short-life assets;[234]
(2) ships (here the law allows deferments of writing-down allowances at will);[235]
(3) assets used partly for non-qualifying purposes;[236]
(4) assets the wear and tear on which is subsidised.[237]

---

[228] CAA 2001, s 54.
[229] CAA 2001, Ch 10A (ss 104A–104E).
[230] CAA 2001, s 104D.
[231] On long-life assets, see CAA 2001, ss 54(4) and (5), referring to s 101.
[232] CAA 2001, s 56A, added by FA 2008, s 81.
[233] CAA 2001, s 54(6).
[234] CAA 2001, s 83 *et seq.*
[235] CAA 2001, s 127.
[236] CAA 2001, s 206.
[237] CAA 2001, ss 211 and 538.

Other separate pooling rules. Assets used in overseas leasing attract a 10% rate of write off.[238]

Separate pooling used to come about under the 1990 Act if the statute deemed a separate trade to be carried on, eg each lease otherwise than in the course of the trade of leasing.[239] As we have seen, CAA 2001 rejects the paradigm case of trading in favour of the abstract phrase 'qualifying activity', so this particular example is redesignated as the qualifying activity of special leasing of plant and machinery.[240]

Certain short-life assets *may* be pooled separately if the taxpayer so elects.[241] As we have seen no writing-down allowance may be claimed for the period during which permanent discontinuance takes place; only a balancing allowance (or charge) is made.[242] A balancing adjustment may be made where a non-resident trades through a permanent establishment in the UK and the proportion of the total trade represented by the UK branch or agency changes—downwards (ie is reduced).[243]

Examples

(1) If an asset cost £1,000 and it was the only asset in the pool, the AQE is £1,000 and the TDR is zero; the writing-down allowance for that year would be £180 (18% of £1,000). In the second year the WDA would be 18% of £820, ie £148.

(2) Suppose that an asset was bought in the first year for £1,000 so that a £180 allowance was claimed in the first year, and that a second asset was bought in the second year for £9,200. There are still no disposals. The pool of AQE for the second year is £820 left unrelieved from the first year plus £9,200 for the new asset, making a total AQE of £10,020. The maximum WDA would be 18% of £10,020, ie £1,804.

(3) Continuing on from (2), suppose that the first asset was sold in the third year for £1,000. Assuming that all allowances have been claimed, the AQE at the start of the third year would be £8,216 (£10,020–1,804). This must now be reduced by the £1,000 TDR, so that in the third year the allowance will be 18% of £7,216, or £1,299.

24.2.7 Disposal Value[244]

Disposal value is relevant when a disposal event occurs.[245] In the account that follows, T is the person who has incurred the qualifying expenditure.[246] Disposal events arise when:

(1) the asset ceases to belong to T, eg it is sold;

(2) T loses possession of the asset in circumstances in which it is reasonable to assume that the loss is permanent;

---

[238] CAA 2001, s 54(4) and (5), referring to s 107.
[239] CAA 1990, s 61(1), not needed as part of CAA 2001 and so not re-enacted.
[240] CAA 2001, s 15(1), 19 and 258–261.
[241] CAA 2001, s 86, below §24.3.3.
[242] CAA 2001, ss 55(4) and (5), and 65.
[243] CAA 2001, s 208.
[244] Defined in CAA 2001, s 61(1) (see above at §24.2.4). See also s 66 helpfully listing provisions about disposal values in other parts of the Act.
[245] See CAA 2001, s 61(2) and, in relation to computer software, ss 72, 281A, s 55(4).
[246] On hire purchase, note CAA 2001, s 67(4).

(3)   the asset has been used in mineral exploration and access, and has been abandoned on site;
(4)   the asset ceases to exist as such (as a result of destruction, dismantling or otherwise);
(5)   the asset begins to be used wholly or partly for purposes other than those of the trade;[247]
(6)   the asset begins to be leased under a long funding lease (Chapter 6A); or
(7)   the trade is permanently discontinued.

When a disposal event occurs, the relevant disposal value must be brought into account.[248]

In the final chargeable period of the activity there may be a balancing charge—if the cumulative allowances exceed the expenditure. Alternatively, there may be a balancing allowance if the allowances are less than the expenditure.[249] There cannot be writing-down allowance in this final period.[250]

24.2.7.1 Amounts

The disposal value to be brought into account depends upon the event by reason of which it is taken into account,[251] but it cannot exceed the capital expenditure incurred on that item, any excess being subject to capital gains legislation. Thus, if an asset was purchased for £1,000 and sold five years later for £1,600, the disposal value to be brought into account for capital allowances purposes will be the original cost of £1,000 with the gain of £600 potentially subject to CGT. Also, the disposal value to be deducted from the pool must not exceed the cost of the plant to the person disposing of it.

Market value. Where the plant was acquired as a result of a transaction or series of transactions between connected persons, the greatest acquisition expenditure incurred in any of the transactions concerned is the maximum disposal value.[252] This rule not only applies on a disposal to a connected person or to an acquisition from a connected person, but also extends to an acquisition as a result of a transaction between connected persons with whom the disposer need not be connected.[253] If the asset has been sold, the proceeds of sale are taken;[254] and if that sale has been affected by some event, for example if the asset has been damaged, account is also taken of any insurance or compensation money received.

Where the market value is greater than the proceeds of sale, market value will be taken unless there is a charge to tax under ITEPA 2003 or the buyer can, in turn, claim a capital allowance in respect of plant or machinery or an R&D allowance.[255] The reason for this is presumably because the low sale price will give rise, in turn, to low allowances. There is also a bar on taking an undervalue if the buyer is a dual resident investment company connected with the seller—introduced as part of the general drive against such companies.[256]

---

[247] On assets used partly for qualifying activity, see CAA 2001, ss 11(4) and 205–207.
[248] CAA 2001, s 60.
[249] For general rules, see CAA 2001, ss 55–56.
[250] CAA 2001, s 55(4) and (5).
[251] CAA 2001, s 61(2).
[252] CAA 2001, s 62(2) and (3).
[253] *Ibid.*
[254] See *IRC v West* (1950) 31 TC 402.
[255] CAA 2001, s 61(2) and (4)(a).
[256] CAA 2001, s 61(2) and (4)(b).

End of asset. If the event is the demolition or destruction of the asset, the disposal value is the sum received for the remains, together with any insurance or compensation. In other instances of permanent loss, eg theft, the disposal value is simply any insurance or compensation. In all other cases, market value is taken.[257]

End of trade—and successions. If the event is the permanent discontinuance of the trade, which is followed by the sale, demolition, destruction or permanent loss of the asset, the disposal value on discontinuance is that specified for the event.[258] A special election may apply if there is a succession to a trade by a connected person,[259] in which case the predecessor's written-down value will override other provisions referring to market value.[260] These rules apply for the writing-down allowances; first-year allowances—and the AIAs—are not available where one person succeeds to a qualifying activity carried on by another person.[261]

No election may be made if the buyer is a dual resident investment company.[262] The right to elect is restricted to cases where both parties are within the charge to UK tax on the profits of the trade, and is subject to a time limit of two years starting with the date of the transaction.[263] The election may be made by a partnership.[264] In all other cases market value is taken.[265] For the period in which permanent discontinuance occurs, neither a first-year nor a writing-down allowance is given, everything being settled by the balancing allowance or charge.

Where two items are sold together, as will often be the case when the trade ends, the disposal proceeds will be apportioned on a just and reasonable basis.[266]

Where the disposal comprises certain qualifying gifts, eg to an educational establishment within ITTOIA 2005, section 108 or CTA 2009, section 105, there is a nil disposal value.[267]

24.2.8 Short-life Assets—The Non-pooling Option

The effect of the 18% writing-down allowance is that, thanks to its reducing balance basis, approximately 90% of the cost will be written off over 12 years. Because some assets have a shorter life expectancy, rules allow such assets to be kept out of the general pool.[268] If the asset is disposed of, any balancing allowance is given immediately instead of waiting for the overall effect on a pool—but only if it is disposed of within eight years. The asset will be kept in a pool of its own and the normal 18% writing-down allowance applied on a reducing basis.[269] The (irrevocable) election to treat the asset as a short-life asset must be made

---

[257] CAA 2001, s 61(2), items 3 and 4.
[258] CAA 2001, s 61(2), item 6.
[259] CAA 2001, s 266.
[260] CAA 2001, ss 266 and 267. The provisions overridden are ss 104 (long life assets), 108 (overseas leasing pool) and 265 (normal succession rule).
[261] CAA 2001, s 265, as amended by FA 2008, Sch 24, para 14.
[262] CAA 2001, s 266(1)(c).
[263] CAA 2001, s 266(1)(b); see FA 2001, Sch 21, para 4, amending CAA 2001, s 266.
[264] CAA 2001, s 574.
[265] CAA 2001, s 265; on succession on death, note s 268(5)–(7), added by FA 1990.
[266] CAA 2001, ss 562—on procedure, see s 563.
[267] CAA 2001, s 63.
[268] CAA 2001, ss 83–89. On practice, see Statement of Practice SP 1/86.
[269] CAA 2001, s 86(1).

within two years of the year of acquisition.[270] The election is not available in relation to assets which seem to have in common the fact that they are required to be pooled separately in any case.[271]

In practice, assets which have an expected useful life of less than two years are depreciated over the life span, and are not pooled.[272] Further rules apply where short-life assets are provided for leasing, there is a sale at an under value or a disposal to connected persons.[273]

24.2.9 Long-life Assets

Before 2008 the writing-down allowance for plant and machinery was set at 6% per annum, calculated on a reducing balance, where it was reasonable to expect that the plant and machinery would have an economic life of at least 25 years.[274] FA 2008 moved long-life assets to the special rate pool at first a 10% and now an 8% writing-down allowance. The original rate of 6% was set because of the substantial disparity between the rapid rate at which capital allowances are given and the slow rate at which plant, such as reservoirs and power stations, is written down in the financial accounts of newly-privatised companies. Assets excluded from this rule include fixtures in a dwelling house, retail shop, showroom, hotel or office, ships, railways assets and any mechanically-propelled road vehicle.[275] This reduced rate of allowance is not meant to hurt small businesses and so does not apply where the total expenditure is £100,000 or less; an individual or partnership must satisfy further conditions about active involvement in the business.[276] Where this treatment is applied, the long-life asset is treated as creating a pool separate from other assets. Other provisions apportion composite expenditure between a long-life asset and an asset with a shorter life.[277]

An anti-avoidance rule applies where a claim has been made on a long-life asset and a later claim (by that claimant or another person) in respect of any qualifying expenditure incurred on the same asset is made—here the long-life rules are to continue to apply even though, eg the new owner otherwise might be within the £100,000 exemption.[278]

24.2.10 Motor Vehicles

Since 2009, capital allowances in respect of expenditure on a car are determined according to the car's carbon dioxide emissions.[279] Under this regime, cars with CO_2 emissions of less than 130g per kilometre qualify for the main rate of WDAs.[280] The threshold will drop to

---

[270] CAA 2001, s 85(1)–(4).
[271] The list is in CAA 2001, s 84.
[272] *Tax Bulletin* (November 1993).
[273] CAA 2001, ss 87–89.
[274] CAA 2001, ss 90–104; on definition, see s 91, added by FA 1997; on problems of definition, see Gammie [1997] BTR 241. The 6% limit is applied by s 102.
[275] CAA 2001, ss 93–96, added by FA 1997.
[276] CAA 2001, ss 97–100.
[277] CAA 2001, s 92(1).
[278] CAA 2001, s 103.
[279] FA 2009, Sch 11, para 26.
[280] CAA 2001, s 104AA, added by FA 2009, Sch 11, para 8.

110g/km in April 2018. Cars with higher CO_2 emissions are allocated to the special pool and qualify for 8% WDAs.[281] Electric cars and cars with CO_2 emissions below 75g per kilometre qualify for 100% FYAs.[282] That threshold will drop to 50g/km in April 2018.

24.2.11 Hire Purchase

Where plant or machinery is purchased by the taxpayer, T, on hire purchase or conditional sale contracts, first-year and writing-down allowances may be claimed in respect of the capital element.[283] The plant or machinery is treated as belonging to T and to no one else, provided T is entitled to the benefit of the contract. Capital expenditure to be incurred by T under the contract after the plant or machinery has been brought into use in the trade is treated as incurred at that time. T is thus treated as incurring the full capital cost at that time. Special provisions apply where the option under the contract is not exercised.[284] The actual words of this provision go wider than merely hire purchase. The Revenue have pointed out that the words of the provision are apt to cover situations in which capital expenditure is incurred on goods which are never owned, eg a deposit paid for goods which are then not supplied.[285]

Where this rule deems the asset to belong to X but the special rules for fixtures deemed it to belong to Y, the fixtures rule prevails;[286] although this was introduced by FA 2000, it is deemed always to have had effect. Where the hire-purchase rule deems the asset to be X's and it then becomes a fixture and so is deemed as belonging to Y, X is treated as selling the asset to Y.

24.2.12 Leasing—Special Rules

The capital allowance rules governing leasing are quite detailed; what follows is a brief overview of the key elements.

24.2.12.1 Trade of Leasing Qualifies

If T leases out an asset—ie is the lessor—in the course of a trade, capital allowances will be available in the usual way.[287] The use to which the lessee puts the asset is not relevant in determining the lessor's rights. T is entitled, as owner of the goods leased, to the allowances, whether these are first-year or writing-down allowances. There may be difficulties in showing that the asset 'is owned by' T if the lessee has been given an option to purchase the asset, but this issue remains unexplored.[288] The particular trade of finance leasing attracts special rules (see §24.2.15 below).

---

[281] CAA 2001, s 104A, amended by FA 2009, Sch 11, para 7.
[282] CAA 2001, s 45D.
[283] CAA 2001, ss 67–69. A hirer under such an agreement is very different from a mere lessee; see Inland Revenue Press Release, 27 October 1986, [1986] *Simon's Tax Intelligence* 680.
[284] CAA 2001, s 67(4); on disposal value, see s 68.
[285] Inland Revenue interpretation RI 10.
[286] CAA 2001, s 69, added by FA 2000, s 80.
[287] *Barclay Mercantile Business Finance Ltd v Mawson* [2004] UKHL 51, [2005] STC 1, and see above §5.6.
[288] The effect of an option needs close attention; in practice, the lessee can be given much the same economic benefit by reducing the leasing charge or extending the period of the lease. This is all subject to the post-2006 rules on long-funded leases: see below at §24.2.12.6.

24.2.12.2 Not in Course of Trade—Separate Qualifying Activity

Where T leases out an asset otherwise than in the course of trade, CAA 2001 directs that it is to be treated as the separate qualifying activity of special leasing.[289] Any charge is treated as arising for corporation tax in accordance with section 259.[290] Capital allowances may still be available but cannot be set against general income of the lessor—only against other income from special leasing.[291] However, if the asset is not used for the purpose of a qualifying activity carried on by the lessee, the lessor may only set the allowance off against other income from that particular special leasing activity.[292] Unused allowances may be rolled forward indefinitely.[293] There are separate rules for corporation tax.[294] The effect of this is to make equipment leasing an unattractive proposition, except when it is a full-time business. The right to allowances does not apply where the plant or machinery is let for use in a domestic house.[295] The 1992 restriction on first-year allowances, which applied where the lessor carried on a trade of leasing, also applies here.[296]

24.2.12.3 Overseas Leasing

A number of special rules apply to overseas leasing. First, it may attract rates of 18%, 10% or 0%. Overseas leasing is defined as meaning a lease under which the lessee is not resident in the UK and does not use the asset exclusively for earning profits chargeable to tax.[297] So, if a person is resident in the UK and the asset is exclusively for the purposes of earning profits which are chargeable to tax in the UK, the normal 18% rate will apply. However, 'profits or gains chargeable to UK tax' do not include those arising to a person who can claim relief under a double taxation agreement, eg the UK branch of a foreign company.[298] The full rate of 18% may also be claimed if the asset comes within what the Act calls 'protected leasing', a term which covers both short-term leasing of plant or machinery and certain arrangements for ships, aircraft or transport containers.[299]

If the overseas leasing does not come within the notion of protected leasing, the rate of writing-down allowance is restricted to 10%, unless the long-life asset rate would apply anyway.[300] The restriction to 10% is to apply only for the designated period, which means broadly 10 years from the time the person brought the asset into use.[301] However, even that reduced rate of allowance is not available if the asset is used for a non-qualifying purpose and certain other conditions are satisfied, eg the lease is for more than 13 years.[302]

In applying the 10% rate a separate overseas leasing pool must be established; a long-life asset must be the subject of a separate asset pool, as must any other asset required to be

---

[289] CAA 2001, ss 15 and 19 and superseding CAA 1990, s 65; s 19 contains rules on the cessation of leasing.
[290] The income tax charge arises under s 258.
[291] CAA 2001, s 258.
[292] CAA 2001, s 258(3).
[293] CAA 2001, s 258(5).
[294] CAA 2001, ss 259 and 260; group relief is excluded by s 260(7). On life assurance companies, see s 261.
[295] CAA 2001, s 15(3), referring to s 35.
[296] CAA 2001, Sch 3, para 47(5).
[297] CAA 2001, s 105.
[298] CAA 2001, s 110.
[299] CAA 2001, s 105(5) and ss 121, 123 and 124.
[300] CAA 2001, s 109.
[301] CAA 2001, ss 109(2)(a) and 106.
[302] CAA 2001, s 110.

placed in a separate pool by other rules.[303] A disposal from the overseas pool to a connected person may attract a restriction, in that allowances on the disposal and the new acquisition must be calculated by reference to disposal value if that is lower than the market value.[304]

24.2.12.4 Administration, Qualifying Purpose, Partnerships

CAA 2001 includes rules on the recovery of excess allowance and of allowances which should not have been claimed at all, for joint lessees and on duties to supply information.[305]

The concept of 'qualifying purpose' is relevant to whether or not the taxpayer's allowance is reduced to 0%; some of the concepts are also used in the definition of a protected transaction. The qualifying situations are those in which:

(1)   the buyer uses the asset for short-term leasing;
(2)   the lessee uses the asset for short-term leasing and either is resident in the UK or uses it in a trade carried on here; or
(3)   the buyer uses the asset for the purposes of a trade other than leasing.[306]

The purpose of these rules is to exclude the situation in which the lessee uses the asset for personal consumption. The other qualifying purpose rules relate to ships and aircraft transport; these rules all require that the asset is leased to lessees who use it for purposes other than leasing, and the lessees would have been entitled to capital allowances in respect of the asset if they had incurred the expenditure themselves[307]—this provides a fiscal connection between the lessee and the UK.

Restrictions apply to leasing partnerships. For example, X, Y and Z Ltd are partners who buy plant and claim allowances. X and Y then withdraw from the partnership, leaving Z to face the balancing charge, but Z is a non-resident company. Relief under TA 1988, sections 380 and 381 is denied where the scheme has been entered into with a company partner in prospect.[308]

24.2.12.5 Lessee's Expenditure

Where the lessee (L) incurs capital expenditure on the provision of plant or machinery for the purposes of L's trade under the terms of L's lease, the asset is treated as belonging to L provided the trade continues.[309] The asset in fact belongs to the owner-lessor (O). When the lease ends the rules as to disposal value and balancing charges are applied as if the original expenditure had been incurred by O. Thus, the allowance is given to L, but any balancing charge may be levied on O. As a result of the rules reversing *Stokes v Costain Property Investments Ltd*,[310] this does not now apply to plant and machinery which becomes part of a building on other land.

---

[303]   CAA 2001, s 107.
[304]   CAA 2001, s 108.
[305]   CAA 2001, ss 111–120.
[306]   CAA 2001, ss 121 and 122. Interpreted by the Court of Appeal in *BMBF (No 24) v IRC* [2004] STC 97.
[307]   CAA 2001, ss 123–125.
[308]   TA 1988, s 384A moved out of the CAA by Sch 2, para 30—previously CAA 1990, s 142.
[309]   TA 1988, s 61(4).
[310]   [1984] STC 204, [1984] 1 All ER 849, CA; CAA 1990, s 61(4)(b) (see above at §24.2.2.1).

24.2.12.6 Long Funding Leases

Reversing the *Barclays Mercantile Business Finance* case,[311] under CAA 2001, sections 70A *et seq*,[312] expenditure incurred on provision of plant or machinery for leasing under a long funding lease is not allowable expenditure for the lessor. The lessee may claim allowances under the rules in sections 70A–70E; these provide different amounts according to whether the lease is a long funding operating lease or a long funding finance lease.[313] A lease is a long lease only if it exceeds five years; further rules exclude it if it does not exceed seven years.[314]

A funding lease is defined as a plant or machinery lease which meets one or of more of three tests: the finance lease test, the lease payments test (section 70O) and the useful economic life test (section 70P).[315] The lessee's right to claim an allowance may be excluded if the lessor may claim it.[316] There are also exclusions for certain allowances relating to buildings where the lessor may still claim.[317] There is an anti-avoidance rule (section 70V) and many rules on transfer variations, etc.[318]

There are also related CGT rules on a deemed disposal by the lessor, with special values, when plant or machinery is used under a long funding lease, and on the relationship between capital allowances and CGT.[319]

FA 2009, section 64 and Schedule 32 introduced a number of changes to the taxation of long funding leases in response to taxpayers' disclosure of schemes to avoid tax. The first change was to the value to be brought into account where a long funding lease commences;[320] it is now the greater of (a) the market value of the plant and (b) the qualifying lease payments.[321] The second change makes sure that the definition of 'disposal receipts' in section 60 includes a disposal on the determination of a long funding lease under section 70E. The third is favourable to taxpayers and makes sure that an initial payment brought in as a disposal value is not also taxed as income.[322] Lastly, the rules make it clear that the AIA is not available to the lessee under (a) a transfer and long funding leaseback arrangement, or (b) a hire-purchase and long funding leaseback arrangement.[323] FA 2011, section 33 closed down a scheme involving long funding leases that sought to benefit more than once from the tax relief for the residual value payment.

24.2.13 Ships

For many years, ships have been treated specially for capital allowance purposes. In effect, free depreciation is allowed.[324] Expenditure on ships is not pooled. There is no statutory

---

[311] *Barclays Mercantile Business Finance Ltd v Mawson* [2005] STC 1 (HL).
[312] Added by FA 2006, s 81 and Sch 8; note CAA 2001, ss 70YE–70YJ for definitions.
[313] CAA 2001, ss 70B and 70C.
[314] CAA 2001, s 70I; note modification by FA 2008 as a result of other changes.
[315] CAA 2001, ss 70K, and 70N–70P.
[316] CAA 2001, s 70Q.
[317] CAA 2001, ss 70G and 70R –70U.
[318] CAA 2001, ss 70V–70YD.
[319] TCGA 1992, ss 26A and 41A.
[320] CAA 2001, s 61, Table 1, item 5A.
[321] Defined in CAA 2001, s 61(5A).
[322] CTA 2010, s 890, ex TA 1988, s 785B.
[323] Amended CAA 2001, s 51A (10)).
[324] CAA 2001, ss 127–158.

definition of a 'ship', but there have been many decisions on its meaning under the Merchant Shipping Acts. A hopper barge without engine or sail was held to be a ship,[325] but a floating gas container without power and not fitted for navigation was not.[326] A statutory definition of qualifying ships is, however, provided for the purpose of the 1995 rules on deferment of balancing charges.[327]

Balancing charges arising on the disposal of qualifying ships[328] may be rolled over for a period of up to three years to be set off against subsequent expenditure[329] on new ships within that period. The ship may have been owned by the taxpayer previously, but there must be a six-year gap between ownerships.[330]

FA 2000 introduced an alternative basis of taxation of shipping under which corporation tax would be based, in part, on tonnage.[331]

24.2.14 *Films and Sound Recordings; Master Versions*

The story of the tax treatment of the film and sound recording industries is convoluted and highly political.[332] For present purposes only a few brief points need be made. When a film is made, many of the production costs will be deductible as ordinary revenue expenditure. Some items will be capital and so open to relief through the capital allowance system. These capital items would include the costs of acquisition of a film tape or disk. In the days of 100% first-year capital allowances, much less turned on the distinction than previously. CAA 1990, section 68 allowed taxpayers to take such expenditures as revenue expenditure. Revenue treatment was required unless the taxpayers elected for capital allowance treatment. More detailed rules followed, eg F(No 2)A 1992, sections 40A *et seq*. After this, the Revenue became worried about 'abuse' of the allowances they had so carefully created. Special legislation was therefore passed in F(No 2)A 2002, section 99, which restricted the 1992 reliefs. For example, these were to be withheld unless the film was 'genuinely intended for theatrical release', as defined in section 99.[333]

Since then further rules followed. As far as income tax was concerned, these were gathered together in ITTOIA 2005, Part 2, Chapter 9 (sections 130–144, mostly now repealed). However, they were immediately strengthened—from a Revenue perspective—by FA 2005.[334] FA 2006 produced a completely new system of rules for films, but left the ITTOIA 2005 rules, in a very reduced form, to apply to sound recordings.

---

[325] *The Mac* (1882) 7 PD 126, CA.

[326] *Wells v Gas Float Whitton No 2 (Owners)* [1897] AC 337, HL; see also *Wirth Ltd v SS Acadia Forest* [1974] 2 Lloyd's Rep 563.

[327] This limit does not apply if the ship is lost at sea or is irreparably damaged: CAA 2001, s 151.

[328] Defined by CAA 2001, ss 151–154, added by FA 1995. See Inland Revenue Press Release, 20 July 1994, [1994] *Simon's Tax Intelligence* 882.

[329] Defined by CAA 2001, ss 146–150.

[330] CAA 2001, s 147.

[331] FA 2000, s 82 and Sch 22. There is much useful background in HM Treasury, *Independent Inquiry into a Tonnage Tax* (12 August 1999).

[332] Those wanting to follow the twists and turn of the last several years should read the excellent notes by Shipwright in the various Finance Act issues of the BTR.

[333] Later ITTOIA 2005, s 144.

[334] ITTOIA 2005, ss 140A–140E, repealed by FA 2006, s 178 and Sch 26 Pt 3(4).

A quite different set of rules has been concerned with ensuring that if the various qualifying expenditures gave rise to losses, only the right sort of losses accruing to the right sorts of people would qualify, a matter of particular moment to partnerships (see above §20.10 and below §24.2.14.2).

24.2.14.1 Basic Rules

As far as sound recordings are concerned, expenditure incurred on the production or acquisition of the original master version of a sound recording is revenue in nature.[335] There are also rules for the allocation of that expenditure.[336] However, the option to elect back into the capital allowance system was removed. ITTOIA 2005 applies only for income tax; there are separate rules for corporation tax.[337]

FA 2006 removed films from the ambit of ITTOIA 2005, and in section 42 and Schedule 5 gave a tax credit to film production companies instead. Special loss rules are contained in FA 2006, sections 43–45.

24.2.14.2 Avoidance

The tax treatment of films shows the UK tax system at its most typical. Reliefs are given to humour a particularly vociferous or influential group. The reliefs are limited so as to benefit only that group. The group or their advisers then seek to undermine the spirit of reliefs and the Government retaliates by restricting the relief. For example, FA 2002 introduced rules to restrict the 1992 reliefs unless the film was genuinely intended for release, and to deal with successive acquisitions of the same film. It did so by limiting the relief to sums paid for the first acquisition from the producer.[338] In turn, these rules were superseded by wider rules in FA 2005.

FA 2004[339] was directed at schemes which had, in the Government's view, exploited these film reliefs. The purpose behind the original rules was to grant accelerated recognition of costs, so giving rise to loss relief. When or, more often, if the film proved to be profitable, the loss relief would be recaptured by a charge to tax. Schemes had been devised which turned the intended deferral relief into a permanent relief, so that no charge arose when later profits accrued from the film. The 2004 rules (now ITA 2007, sections 797 *et seq*) were designed to ensure that a charge would arise after all. The charge applies where there is a disposal of the individual's right to profits from the trade. FA 2005 added rules specific to film reliefs in connection with partnership losses and the at-risk rules were amended.[340] These are now ITA 2007, sections 790 *et seq*.

Lastly, FA 2009, section 65 and Schedule 33 introduced yet more anti-avoidance rules in response to taxpayers' disclosures, this time concerning long funding leases of films.[341] The schemes disclosed involved partnerships ending existing leases and replacing them with

---

[335] ITTOIA 2005, s 134.
[336] ITTOIA 2005, s 135.
[337] FA 2006, ss 48–50.
[338] ITTOIA 2005, s 140(2), FA 2002, s 101.
[339] FA 2004, ss 119–123. See also Inland Revenue Press Release 10 December 2003, [2003] *Simon's Tax Intelligence* 2321; and Revenue examples 10 February 2004, [2004] *Simon's Tax Intelligence* 332.
[340] FA 2005, s 79.
[341] CTA 2010, s 376, ex TA 1988, s 502GD. See also ITTOIA 2005, s 148FD.

new leases intended to qualify as long funding leases for plant. The blocking legislation is not confined to partnerships.

24.2.15 Anti-avoidance: Relevant Transactions, Finance Leases and Leasebacks

The provisions on plant and machinery contain additional rules to deal with other avoidance situations. What follows is a brief overview of the key elements. The rules generally remove any right to any AIA or first-year allowance and restrict the right to writing-down allowances.[342]

The first restrictions are aimed at 'relevant transactions', broadly sales, hire purchase and assignments of right under contracts.[343] The restrictions apply if there is a relevant transaction:

(1) between connected persons;
(2) that has an "avoidance purpose", ie where the main purpose, or one of the main purposes, of a party entering into the transaction was to obtain a tax advantage; or
(3) which falls within the description of sale and leaseback, ie if the asset which has been used in the seller's business continues to be so used despite the sale.[344]

The next restrictions are aimed at situations in which the asset is used by a connected person or there is no continuity in the seller's business. The restrictions are that the buyer cannot obtain an AIA or first-year allowance[345] and writing-down allowances are given to the buyer by reference to the disposal value brought into account by the seller.[346] These restrictions do not apply if the plant and machinery is the subject of a sale and finance leaseback.[347]

In relation to the AIA, there is a further restriction which denies the allowance where there are arrangements designed to obtain the allowance to which the person would not otherwise be entitled.[348] This is a free-standing provision and not confined to related transactions.

Further and similar restrictions apply if the transaction is a finance lease.[349] A finance lease is a lease which is treated in the accounts of the lessor (or a person connected with the lessor) as a finance lease or loan under properly drawn-up accounts. No writing-down allowance is to be given for that part of the chargeable period which falls before the expenditure was incurred; the effect of this is to delay, not prohibit, the entitlement to the allowance for the expenditure incurred.[350] The rule does not apply if there is also a disposal of the asset in the same period.[351]

---

[342] CAA 2001, ss 213–230.
[343] CAA 2001, s 213.
[344] CAA 2001, ss 214–216. On predecessor of s 215, see *Barclays Mercantile Industrial Finance Ltd v Melluish* [1990] STC 314, 63 TC 95. See also s 218ZA governing restrictions on writing-down allowances under s 215.
[345] CAA 2001, s 217.
[346] CAA 2001, s 218.
[347] CAA 2001, ss 217 and 218, as amended by FA 2008, Sch 20.
[348] CAA 2001, s 218A.
[349] CAA 2001, ss 219–220.
[350] CAA 2001, ss 219 and 220.
[351] CAA 2001, s 220(3).

Where there is a sale and finance leaseback, meaning a sale and leaseback where a finance lease is involved, several provisions in this part of the Act used to apply, but these were greatly reduced in 2008. CAA 2001, section 225 removes any entitlement to any allowances if the lessor does not bear the greater part of the risk of non-payment;[352] for this purpose, guarantees by the persons connected with the lessee are ignored.

Finance leasebacks received further legislative attention in 2004.[353] The 2004 rules apply only where the disposal value has already been restricted under the preceding rules, and are designed to prevent taxpayers from obtaining not only the benefit of the capital allowances but also deductions for lease rentals. The amount of rental that may be deducted is restricted to a 'permitted maximum', ie the total of the finance charge shown in the accounts and depreciation, but using the value after applying the restriction.[354] Other provisions deal with early terminations of leases and other events that 'crystallise' the future benefits. These increase the profits of the lessee and are to prevent the taxpayer from 'sidestepping' the new rule.[355] There are consequential adjustments to the rules for lessors; some of these rules no longer apply to lease and finance leasebacks but only to sale and leasebacks.[356] These rules are subject to some degree of mitigation. There is a special election for both sale and lease-back and sale and finance leaseback where the transaction involves assets which are both new and unused.[357] There is a provision to explain how these rules apply to hire-purchase contracts; this does not involve new and unused assets.[358] Lastly, there is an exception, once more involving new and used assets, sold by manufacturer or suppliers in the ordinary course of their business.[359]

FA 2010, section 27 and Schedule 5 dealt with two more schemes, restricting qualifying expenditure to the present value of the lessor's income from the asset plus the present value of the asset after any rental rebate.[360] The Schedule also restricts the deduction for the rental rebate.[361] A disallowed loss may still be allowable for chargeable gains purposes (paragraph 2(6)). Additional rules, applicable only for corporation tax, are designed to counter avoidance arising from the transfer of entitlement to benefit from a capital allowance on plant and machinery used for the purpose of a trade.[362] The problem arises where tax written-down value is greater than its balance sheet value. The Revenue have seen transactions where companies with large pools of unclaimed capital allowances have been sold into a new group principally to enable the new group to get at the allowances through group relief.[363] The legislation uses an 'unallowable purpose rule'.[364]

---

[352] CAA 2001, s 225.
[353] CAA 2001, ss 228A–228J added by FA 2004, s 134 and Sch 23, providing transitional rules. Sections amended by FA 2007, Sch 5, para 16 to prevent avoidance; s 228A amended by FA 2008.
[354] CAA 2001, s 228B.
[355] CAA 2001, s 228C; 'sidestepping' comes from para 91 of the Revenue Note on the clause.
[356] CAA 2001, s 228D, as amended by FA 2007, Sch 5, and s 228E.
[357] CAA 2001, ss 227 and 228.
[358] CAA 2001, s 229.
[359] CAA 2001, s 230.
[360] CAA 2001, s 228MA and see definitions in s 228MC.
[361] See CTA 2009, s 60A and ITTOIA 2005, s 55B.
[362] CAA 2001, ss 212A–212S, added by FA 2010, s 26 and Sch 4.
[363] HMRC Explanatory Notes on FA 2010, para 76.
[364] CAA 2001, s 212M.

24.3   Industrial Buildings

CAA 2001, Part 3 (sections 271–360) governs allowances for industrial buildings. These rules used to permit capital allowances to be claimed where capital expenditure has been incurred on the construction of an industrial building or structure which is to be occupied, principally, for the purposes of a trade.[365] To qualify, the building must have been an industrial building or structure, which was elaborately defined in CAA 2001, section 274, Tables A and B. This area has been much litigated. It is fair to say that the courts, taking their lead from some narrow legislation, have taken a consistently restrictive view of what can come within this category. The general effect of the definition is to confine allowances to productive, as opposed to distributive, industries. Industrial building allowances were abolished completely after 1 April 2011 (for corporation tax) or 6 April 2011 (for income tax),[366] though a purchaser of an industrial property will want to know to what extent allowances have been claimed in respect of the property's fixtures by the previous owner as it may affect future claims due to section 186. Readers interested in these allowances should refer to earlier versions of this book.

24.4   Renovation or Conversion of Unused Business Premises in Disadvantaged Area

CAA 2001, Part 3A (sections 360A–360Z4)[367] concerns qualifying expenditure incurred after 10 April 2007 and before April 2017 on converting a qualifying building into qualifying business premises, or renovating a qualifying building which is or will be qualifying business premises.[368] This regime is unaffected by the withdrawal of industrial building allowances from April 2011. Expenditure does not qualify if it is the cost of the land itself, of extending a qualifying building, of developing adjacent land and most machinery and plant. The building must be in a designated disadvantaged area. The premises must not be available for use as a dwelling house—or be so used. The person claiming the allowance must have a relevant interest in the building. The building must not have been used for a year or more.

The initial allowance is 100%; there is also a 25% writing-down allowance.[369] There are rules on the effect of grants, on balancing allowances and charges adjustments, on how expenditure is to be written off and on VAT liabilities and rebates.[370] Further supplementary rules include important provisions on how the allowances and charges are to be given effect for trades, lessors and licensees.[371]

At Budget 2016 the Government confirmed that this allowance will expire on 31 March 2017 for corporation tax and 5 April 2017 for income tax.

---

[365]   CAA 2001, s 305.
[366]   FA 2008, s 81 and Sch 27.
[367]   Added by FA 2005, s 92 and Sch 6, para 1 with effect for expenditure on or after 11 April 2007.
[368]   CAA 2001, ss 360B–360D.
[369]   CAA 2001, ss 360G–360K.
[370]   CAA 2001, ss 360L–360S.
[371]   CAA 2001, ss 360T–360Z4.

24.5 Agricultural Buildings

Part 4 (sections 361–393) governs the allowances for expenditure on agricultural land. These allowances could be claimed by a person with a relevant interest in agricultural land who incurred capital expenditure on the construction of a building such as a farmhouse, farm building or cottage, fences and other works, eg drainage.[372] Before 2008 the allowance was a writing-down allowance over 25 years, ie 4% pa.[373] As with the industrial buildings allowance, this allowance was abolished as from April 2011 after a period of phasing out,[374] though a purchaser of an agricultural building will want to know to what extent allowances have been claimed in respect of the fixtures by the previous owner as it may give rise to a restriction on future claims due to section 9. Readers interested in these allowances should refer to earlier versions of this book.

24.6 A Conversion of Parts of Business Premises into Residential Flats

Part 4A (sections 393A–393W) was added by FA 2001 to give capital allowances for expenditure on converting or renovating qualifying business premises into flats. The scheme must be seen in the context of other fiscal incentives to assist urban regeneration—brown land. This regime applied in respect of expenditure incurred prior to April 2013 and is no longer available. Readers interested in these allowances should refer to earlier versions of this book.

24.7 Mineral Extraction

Part 5 (sections 394–436) governs mineral extraction allowances. UK companies operating abroad or in the North Sea usually derive their money from mining metals and/or oil and gas. Companies operating within the UK mine mostly building materials, notably sand and gravel, china clay and slate. The history of these allowances has been erratic to say the least, and different rules applied according to the place being mined. The current rules were introduced by FA 1986.[375] They apply where the taxpayer carries on a mineral extraction trade, ie working of a source of mineral deposits, the last phrase being extended to cover geothermal energy.[376]

---

[372] CAA 2001, s 361. A person with a 'relevant interest' is defined in s 364 and includes an owner in fee simple, a lessee and the Scottish equivalents; allowances for forestry land were abolished for chargeable periods beginning on or after 20 June 1989 (FA 1989, s 120).

[373] CAA 2001, ss 364–368, with further definitions, eg in relation to Scotland, in s 393s; the mortgagor holds the relevant interest rather than the mortgagee: s 366.

[374] FA 2008, s 82.

[375] On transition, see CAA 1990, s 119.

[376] CAA 2001, s 394.

'Qualifying expenditure' is defined by both inclusion[377] and exclusion.[378] Thus, the expense incurred in an abortive application for planning permission is allowed,[379] but expense incurred on the acquisition of a site on which further expense will be incurred which will qualify for relief is not.[380] Expenditure on plant and machinery is usually left to the plant and machinery system of allowances (see §24.2 above), but this will not apply where the expense is a pre-trading expense and the asset is disposed of before the trade begins; such expense may, therefore, be qualifying expenditure.[381] A similar rule applies to pre-trading exploration expenditure.[382] Also included are certain payments by mining concerns for site comfort and development outside the UK.[383] Expenditure on restoring a site at the end of the operation also qualifies.[384]

When qualifying expenditure is incurred for the purposes of mineral extraction, writing-down allowance is given by reference to the amount by which the qualifying expenditure exceeds any disposal proceeds received during the period. The scheme is a simple reducing balance, so that previous allowances reduce the qualifying expenditure. For pre-trading expenditure on plant and machinery disposed of before the trade begins, and pre-trading exploration expenditure, the figure is 10%; for other qualifying expenditure, the figure is 25%.[385] The allowance is given in taxing the mineral extraction trade.[386] The cost of the land is not qualifying expenditure; a valuation is carried out by assuming that there is no source of mineral deposits and that only existing or authorised use is allowed.[387] Further rules apply to qualifying expenditure on second hand assets.[388] CAA 2001, section 570A, the anti-avoidance rule explained at §24.3.6.2, applies here too.

FA 2002 imposed a corporation tax surcharge on certain ring-fenced trades. As if in compensation, it added a first-year allowance to the mineral extraction allowance.[389] The allowance is 100% of the expenditure, and there is an express provision to deal with artificially-inflated claims for first-year allowances.

24.8 Research and Development Allowances

Part 6 (sections 437–451) governs R&D allowances. FA 2000 made two important changes in this area. First, it provided some new definitions and procedures for the long-established scientific research allowance, now renamed 'research and development allowances'.

---

[377] CAA 2001, s 395.
[378] CAA 2001, s 399.
[379] CAA 2001, s 396(2).
[380] CAA 2001, s 414(2).
[381] CAA 2001, s 402; otherwise the plant and machinery rules apply (s 399(1)).
[382] CAA 2001, s 401.
[383] CAA 2001, s 415.
[384] CAA 2001, s 416 (but only if the work is carried out within three years of the termination; the cost is treated as incurred when the trade ends).
[385] CAA 2001, s 418.
[386] CAA 2001, s 432.
[387] CAA 2001, s 404; a similar valuation is used for calculating the disposal proceeds (s 400(2)).
[388] CAA 2001, ss 407–413.
[389] CAA 2001, ss 416A–416E, added by FA 2002, Sch 21, paras 8–13. The surcharge was added by TA 1988, s 501A, inserted by FA 2002 s 91.

Secondly, it provided a new tax credit for expenditure on R&D by companies; the credit is not available if the expenditure is capital in nature and so is not considered here,[390] but see below at §§62.2.2 and 62.2.5.

Research and development allowances are available for capital expenditure on R&D, provided it is related to the trade carried on (or to be carried on).[391] The research may be carried on by someone other than the trader, provided it is on behalf of the trader, an expression which requires something close to agency.[392] Whether activities are R&D is now decided by reference to accounting concepts.[393] Costs in acquiring rights in scientific research are not allowed.[394] There are also exclusions for expenditure on dwellings and on land, but with exceptions and qualifications.[395] Apportionment of expenditure is permitted.[396]

The allowance is 100% of the cost, less any sums received for disposal values. Disposal values arise if the taxpayer ceases to own the asset, or it is demolished or destroyed while in his ownership.[397] Allowances are given as receipts of the trade and charges as expenses.[398] The relevant chargeable period is that in which the expenditure was incurred, save that for pre-trading expenditure the chargeable period beginning with the commencement is taken.[399]

The taxpayer may reduce the amount of the allowance claimed in any one period; unclaimed allowances are taken into account in calculating balancing charges.[400] Sums paid to approved research associations, universities and institutions may be deductible as if they were revenue expenditure.[401]

24.9 Know-how

Part 7 (sections 452–463) governs know how. Know–how means any industrial information or techniques likely to assist in the manufacture or processing of goods or materials.[402] The phrase is then widened to cover working mineral deposits and operations in agriculture, fishery or forestry.

[390] FA 2000, Sch 21, para 3(2); appeals on whether expenditure was on R&D were brought within the ordinary tax appeal structure and not, as previously, decided by the Secretary of State for Trade and Industry; CAA 1990, s 82A as added by FA 2000, Sch 19.

[391] CAA 2001, ss 437 and 439. On 'relating to', see *Salt v Young* [1999] STC (SCD) 213, where the Special Commissioner said that one should not trace causality back too far. T's trade was in publishing books, but that did not mean that expenditure on a computer used in carrying out research in writing the book was deductible under this head. On meaning of 'research and development', see ITA 2007, s 1006(1)–(5) and CTA 2010, s 1138(1)–(5), ex TA 1988, s 837A (referred to by CAA 2001, s 437(2)).

[392] CAA 2001, s 439(1); *Gaspet Ltd v Elliss* [1985] STC 572.

[393] ITA 2007, s 1006(1)–(5) and CTA 2010, s 1138(1)–(5), ex TA 1988, s 837A(2)–(5); this brings in SSAP 13.

[394] CAA 2001, s 438(2).

[395] CAA 2001, ss 438 and 440.

[396] CAA 2001, s 439(4).

[397] CAA 2001, s 443.

[398] CAA 2001, s 450.

[399] CAA 2001, s 441(2).

[400] CAA 2001, ss 442–443; on timing see s 444, and on costs of demolition s 445.

[401] Under ITTOIA 2005, s 88, CTA 2009, s 88 (ex TA1988, s 82B), very correctly relocating CAA 1990, s 136. On accounting treatment, see SSAP 13.

[402] CAA 2001, s 452.

Qualifying expenditure is then given relief if the person acquiring the know–how uses it in his trade, or subsequently uses it in a trade set up later. There are also rules allowing relief when goodwill has been acquired, or the trade was acquired and was previously carried on wholly outside the UK, ie outside the charge to UK tax.[403] Certain expenditure is excluded, ie where the know-how is acquired in circumstances where there is control, or if the expenditure would be given relief under some other rule.[404]

The form of relief follows the familiar pattern of a separate pooling and asking whether the AQE exceeds the TDV.[405] Unlike expenditure on patents (below), the allowance is given only for 25% of the excess of AQE over TDV.[406]

24.10 Patents

Part 8 (sections 464–483) governs patents. CAA 2001 introduces a new regime for patents. Allowances are now given when a person incurs qualifying expenditure on 'the purchase of patent rights', a phrase which extends to the acquisition of a licence.[407] Expenditure is subdivided into trading and non-trading; such expenditure 'qualifies' if the trade is within the charge to UK tax or the non-trading income is liable to UK tax.[408]

The expenditure is then pooled, each trade being a separate pool and all the non-trading expenditure a separate pool.[409] One then calculates the AQE, ie expenditure for the current period plus any unrelieved from a previous period.[410] Where the AQE exceeds the TDR, a 25% writing-down allowance is given;[411] if TDR exceeds the AQE, the whole excess is charged to tax. There are rules for allocated expenditure to pools[412] and for calculating the TDR; it is provided that the TDR may not exceed the original capital expenditure,[413] showing once more that the purpose of the balance is to recapture the allowance, not to charge any gain.

The allowance or charge is given effect in taxing the trade. If there is no trade, the allowance is set off against patent income[414] and a charge is made; there is a separate rule for corporation tax.[415]

There is the usual anti-avoidance rule where buyer and seller are connected or the sole or main benefit for the sale or other transaction is to obtain an allowance under this part of the Act (Part 8).[416]

---

[403] CAA 2001, s 454.
[404] CAA 2001, s 455 also referring to CTA 2009, s 178(1)–(3), ex TA 1988, s 531(2).
[405] CAA 2001, ss 456–463.
[406] CAA 2001, ss 400D, 458(1).
[407] CAA 2001, ss 464–466.
[408] CAA 2001, ss 467–469.
[409] CAA 2001, s 470.
[410] CAA 2001, ss 473–475.
[411] CAA 2001, ss 471–472.
[412] CAA 2001, s 474.
[413] CAA 2001, s 476.
[414] Defined CAA 2001, s 483.
[415] CAA 2001, ss 479 and 480.
[416] CAA 2001, s 481.

Capital payments received for the disposal of patent rights are taxed as income and spread over six years.[417] If the individual dies before the six-year period ends, any remaining instalments may be spread back; similar rules apply on discontinuance or on the winding up of a company.[418]

The rule allowing certain receipts from royalties to be spread over several years remains in force.[419]

24.11   Dredging

Part 9 (sections 484–489) deals with dredging. Allowances are given for capital expenditure incurred in dredging. The trade must consist of maintaining or improving the navigation of a harbour, estuary or waterway; alternatively, the dredging must be for the benefit of vessels using a dock occupied for the purpose of the trade, as where a trader incurs its own expense for its own dock.[420] Dredging refers only to acts done in the interests of navigation.[421] In general, the allowance is similar to that for industrial buildings. The straight-line writing-down allowance is 4%.[422] If the trade is permanently discontinued before the expenditure has been written off, there is an immediate write off of the balance.[423] There is no balancing charge.

---

[417]   CTA 2009, ss 912–920, ex TA 1988, s 524.
[418]   CTA 2009, ss 918 and 1272, ex TA 1988, s 525.
[419]   CTA 2009, ss 924–925, ex TA 1988, s 528.
[420]   CAA 2001, s 484, undoing *Dumbarton Harbour Board v Cox* (1918) 7 TC 147.
[421]   CAA 2001, s 484(3).
[422]   CAA 2001, s 487.
[423]   CAA 2001, s 488.

25

Income from Land in the United Kingdom

25.1   Introduction

Income from land arising under the old Schedule A was rationalised for income tax in 1995[1] and for corporation tax in 1998;[2] the income tax rules were amended in 1998. The rationalisation was needed because of the advent of self-assessment. The income tax rules then were rewritten by ITTOIA 2005, Part 3, and the corresponding rules for corporation tax by CTA 2009, Part 4.

ITTOIA 2005, Part 3 income from property is taxed on a current basis using most of the Part 2 rules for the calculation of income, including the requirement of an acceptable accounting basis subject to any adjustments required or authorised by law. However, the Parts remain distinct.[3] Income under ITTOIA 2005, Part 3 is not trading income, therefore it cannot be relevant earnings for pension contribution rules. Moreover, separate legislative provision must be made for losses and capital allowances. Similarly, CGT reliefs applicable to trading do not apply automatically.

In this chapter statutory references are to ITTOIA 2005 unless otherwise noted.

---

[1] FA 1995, s 39, Sch 6; on transition, see HC Official Report, Standing Committee D (Sixth sitting), col 166, 9 February 1995, and Inland Revenue Press Release, 20 February 1995, [1995] *Simon's Weekly Tax Intelligence* 250.

[2] FA 1998, s 38, Sch 5.

[3] On priority under ITTOIA 2005, see s 2 (general) and the very specific ss 261 and 262. The boundary between trade and property is explored generally in the Canadian context by Durnford (1991) 39 *Can Tax Jo* 1131.

25.2   Basis of Charge and Calculation of Income

25.2.1 Elements of Part 3

Under ITTOIA 2005, tax is charged on the annual profits or gains arising from 'a property business' carried on for the generating of income from land.[4] The idea of estate or interest in land in the UK is widened to cover the right to use a caravan or houseboat at a single location in the UK.[5] Income from land outside the UK is also taxed under Part 3.[6] Part 3 does not apply to profits arising from the occupation of land (see below at §25.7). Lest the term 'business' be considered too restrictive, ITTOIA 2005 has a second limb, which covers transactions entered into for such exploitation, the transaction being deemed to have been entered into in the course of such a business.[7]

As announced at Budget 2016, the Government is introducing a new £1,000 allowance for property income from 6 April 2017. Individuals with property income below £1,000 will no longer need to declare or pay tax on that income. Individuals with property income above the allowance will be able to calculate their taxable profit either by deducting their expenses in the usual way or by deducting the allowance.

25.2.1.1 Annual Profits

The use of the words 'annual profits' underlines the point that capital sums are not caught by this head—unless some other provision so provides. Payments for wayleaves are brought in where they are for an easement over land within a Part 3 business.[8]

25.2.1.2 Rent and Furniture

Rent under a lease, which includes the use of furniture, was at one time chargeable wholly under Schedule D, Case VI, unless the landlord elected to be taxed in part under Schedule A. Such rent is now taxed entirely under ITTOIA 2005, Part 3—unless it has already been taxed under Part 2 as the profits of a trade which makes the furniture available for use in premises.[9] See further §25.3.

25.2.1.3 Liability

The income tax charge applies to the person receiving, or entitled to, the income, a formula which is the same as for ITTOIA 2005, Part 2.[10] The income is charged on the full amount of the profits or gains arising in the year of assessment—a current year basis (section 270). The tax is due, like all other parts of income tax under the self-assessment regime, on

---

[4] ITTOIA 2005, ss 264 and 266(a), ex TA 1988, s 15 and Sch A, para 1(1). The previous wording in TA 1988 referred to 'exploitation'—as a source of rents or other receipts—of any estate, interest or rights in or over any land in the UK.

[5] ITTOIA 2005, s 266(4), ex TA 1988, s 15 and Sch A para 3. Rental income from caravan sites may be amalgamated with associated trading income—ITTOIA 2005, s 20, ex ESC B29.

[6] ITTOIA 2005, s 265; note s 269(3) on Ireland.

[7] ITTOIA 2005, ss 264(b) and 265(b), ex TA 1988, s 15, and Sch A, para 1(2).

[8] ITTOIA 2005, Pt 3, Ch 9, ss 344–348; ex FA 1997, s 60. On wayleaves as, sometimes, Pt 2 income, see also s 22.

[9] ITTOIA 2005, s 308, ex TA 1988, s 15, and Sch A, para 4 as amended.

[10] ITTOIA 2005, s 271, ex TA 1988, s 21(1); old rules in s 23 for collecting tax from agents and lessees were abolished in 1995.

31 January after the end of the year of assessment. The payment on account rules in TMA 1970, section 59A apply to this as to other types of income.

25.2.1.4 Rent

Rent is not defined for tax purposes. Its general meaning is a payment due from tenant to (land)lord by reason of tenure; it must be reserved as rent.[11] However, it has been held that a payment may be rent even though there is no right to distrain for it.[12] The rent is a sum payable for the lease, and the obligation to pay passes to an assignee. The payment of a premium in instalments is not rent.[13]

25.2.1.5 Other Receipts

'Other receipts' which may arise from the exploitation of land are stated to include payments in respect of a licence to occupy or otherwise use land, or exercise any other right over land (section 266(3)). Examples include such items as licence fees for advertisement hoardings, parking fees and service charges which are not reserved as rent, provided they are not in respect of services constituting a trade. Thus, a separate charge for meals would fall within ITTOIA 2005, Part 2, whereas if a lease provides for the provision of a service for which no separate payment is made, eg heating, the whole rent comes within Part 3 and the cost of heating is an allowable expense. In *Beecham Group Ltd v Fair*,[14] payments made by an employer to an employee for the use of the employee's garage to store samples and stock for use in the employee's work were held to be employment income within ITEPA 2003 and so not Schedule A. Where a trader lets a part of the building in which the trader carries on a business, the rents are treated as trading income under Part 2.[15] Certain income in the form of dividends from Real Estate Investment Trusts is treated as income under Part 3. Some situations are impossible to classify. Where a farmer sold turf from his land he was held taxable under Schedule A but also, in the alternative, under Schedule D, Case I.[16] It is unclear what effect this breach of the schedular system has.[17]

25.2.1.6 Damages

Damages for trespass to land and loss of rent are not liable to income tax as rent.[18] However, damages to a landlord in respect of a tenant overstaying the end of a lease were held to be income in a later Privy Council case,[19] so the matter may be less clear. If the payments are not taxable at all, it follows that in assessing damages the court should take account of the

---

[11] On general meaning, see Gray and Gray, *Elements of Land Law*, 3rd edn (Butterworths, 2000) 329–34.

[12] *T and E Homes Ltd v Robinson* [1979] STC 351, 52 TC 267.

[13] *Toronto Dominion Bank v Oberoi* [2004] STC 1197 [2002] EWHC 3216. But a premium may sometimes be taxed as if it were rent (ITTOIA Pt 3 Ch 4, s 276 *et seq*, ex TA 1988, s 35).

[14] [1984] STC 15, 65 TC 219.

[15] ITTOIA 20, s 21, codifying Revenue practice, eg in Inland Revenue Printed Booklet 150, *Taxation of Rents*, §§501 *et seq*. On apportionment between Sch A and Sch D, Case I when the election is not made, see *ibid*, §522.

[16] *Lowe v Ashmore Ltd* (1970) 46 TC 597; see also above at §19.7.

[17] The very enigmatic ITTOIA 2005, s 2(3) suggests that the draftsman of that Act does not know either; see above, §7.2.2.

[18] *Hall & Co v Pearlberg* [1956] 1 All ER 297n, [1956] 1 WLR 244.

[19] *Raja's Commercial College v Gian Singh & Co Ltd* [1976] STC 282, [1976] 2 All ER 801, PC (damages for almost six years; occupation after end of lease; damages equal to excess of market rent over rent under former lease).

tax which the claimant has not had to pay and grant only the net sum under the rule in *British Transport Commission v Gourley*.[20] This situation must be distinguished from that where a claim is brought for arrears of rent, since such sums are clearly within Part 3.

25.2.2 Exclusions from Part 3

Specifically excluded from ITTOIA 2005, Part 3 are:[21]

(1) profits arising from the occupation of land (see ITTOIA 2005, sections 9 and 11);
(2) any profits or gains charged to tax under Part 2 by ITTOIA 2005, sections 9, 10 and 12 (eg farming and market gardening, mines, quarries, sand and gravel);
(3) any sums charged to tax under ITTOIA 2005, Part 3, Chapters 8 and 9 (mining and other royalties);[22]
(4) in the case of a company, any debits and credits brought into account under the loan relationship rules.

Tax under ITTOIA 2005, Part 3 is still a tax on income and not on capital gains.[23] A premium accruing on the grant of a lease giving possession of premises would, but for special legislation in ITTOIA 2005, Part 3, Chapter 4, fall outside these rules. However, a gain accruing from the assignment, as distinct from the grant, of a lease,[24] or the grant of a lease of shooting rights, is still a matter for CGT, not income tax. Similarly a sum payable in return for the grant or release of an easement would normally escape income tax, as would a one-off payment for allowing a motorway contractor to tip sub-soil onto a taxpayer's land.[25]

25.2.3 Basis of Charge and Calculation of Income

In computing Part 3 income the principles and various computational rules of Part 2 apply.[26] These include rules relating to business entertainment expenses, expenditure involving crime and redundancy payments,[27] and the business income timing rules for deducting emoluments, etc.[28] More crucially, they include the 'generally accepted accounting practice' rule in ITTOIA 2005, section 25. Other non-computational rules applying to Part 2[29] are

[20] [1956] AC 185, [1955] 3 All ER 796. In *Hall v Pearlberg*, above, the rate of tax used was that at the time of the judgment, but this appears to be wrong since the rates of tax for the years in issue were known.
[21] ITTOIA 2005, s 267, ex TA 1988, s 15, and Sch A, para 2.
[22] The paper trail is through ITTOIA 2005, ss 261 and 262, remembering that s 261(a) makes Pt 2 apply in case of an overlap.
[23] See, eg, the arguments raised (unsuccessfully) in *Jeffries v Stevens* [1982] STC 639 and *Lowe v JW Ashmore Ltd* (1970) 46 TC 597.
[24] Unless the original lease is granted at an undervalue (ITTOIA 2005, s 282, ex TA 1988, s 35; see below at §25.5.4).
[25] *McClure v Petre* [1988] STC 749, 61 TC 226.
[26] See list in ITTOIA 2005, s 272, ex TA 1988, Sch 21A(2); ITTOIA 2005, s 69, ex FA 1988, s 73(2) (consideration for restrictive undertakings); FA 1989, ss 112, 113 (expenditure in connection with the provision of a security asset or service).
[27] ITTOIA 2005, ss 45–47, 55, 76–80, ex TA 1988, ss 577, 577A, 579, 580; others are ss 588–589B.
[28] ITTOIA 2005, ss 36–44, ex FA 1989, s 43.
[29] Ex TA 1988, Sch 21B.

most of the post-cessation rules,[30] ie ITTOIA 2005, Part 10 (effect for income tax purposes of change in the persons engaged on trade), section 18 (effect of company beginning or ceasing to carry on trade) and section 57 (pre-trading expenditure). In addition, the FA 1998 rules on change of accounting basis in section 44 and Schedule 6, as replaced by FA 2002, Schedule 22, apply, but in an adapted form for ITTOIA 2005.[31]

25.2.3.1 Timing—Receipts

Given the application of ITTOIA 2005, section 25, tax computations must be prepared on an acceptable accounting basis—subject to any adjustment required or authorised by law. This generally means that incomings are recognised on a matching basis and not simply by reference to when they were due or, still less, to when they were received. Therefore, rent payable in advance or arrears must be attributed to the use of the property for the period for which the tenant is paying, making such apportionments as may be needed. However, sums which cannot be attributed to a period should probably be taxed by reference to the time they were received; this receives indirect support from the 1998 rule that a receipts basis is applied to the various sums caught under Part 3, Chapter 4.

Receipts will also include service charge contributions from tenants. However, if the property is residential, the landlord's duty to keep the money in a separate account may prevent this.[32] Whether a stand-alone maintenance trust is a good planning idea is uncertain.[33]

25.2.3.2 Expenses

The correct treatment of expenditure also depends on accounting principles. A premium on an insurance policy may properly be split between tax years and related to the period for which the insurance cover was provided. In *Jenners Princes Street Edinburgh Ltd v IRC*,[34] the Special Commissioners held that in accordance with accounting practice it was permissible for the company to make provision for the full cost of repairs when the contract was put out to tender and that this was not barred by TA 1988, section 74(d) (now ITTOIA 2005, section 68).

25.2.3.3 Pooling

Since the source is the business of exploiting land, it is no longer necessary, as it was under the 1963 law, to treat different properties as different sources; expenses incurred on different properties will be pooled, regardless of whether they are still owned. However, it should not be forgotten that expenditure incurred in whole or in part for non-commercial reasons should not now be allowable at all. It is likely that the use of ITTOIA 2005, Part 2 tax principles for Part 3 will further highlight problems with the duality principle.

---

[30] ITTOIA 2005, Pt 3, Ch 10. The exceptions are *ibid*, s 107, which treats the post-cessation receipt as earned income, and s 109, which provides a special relief for persons born before 6 April 1917. Note also that the deduction parts of TA 1988, s 109A have not been rewritten by ITTOIA 2005.

[31] ITTOIA 2005, Pt 3, Ch 7 (adjustment income).

[32] Landlord and Tenant Act 1987, s 43(2)(b); see de Souza (1998) *Private Client Business* 267, 270.

[33] See de Souza, *op cit*, 271.

[34] (1998) STC (SCD) 166; s 74(d) restricts certain deductions to sums actually expended, but this was held to mean expended in an accounting sense. On Revenue acceptance of this decision, see Inland Revenue Press Release, 20 July 1999, [1999] *Simon's Weekly Tax Intelligence* 1302. Section 74d is not re-enacted for income tax by ITTOIA 2005.

25.2.3.4 Losses

Losses incurred in a property business generally may be used to offset future profits of the property business only.[35] This general rule is subject to two exceptions:

(1)   losses resulting from claims for capital allowances; and
(2)   agricultural expenses in connection with the management of an agricultural estate.

In these two cases, the losses may be applied against other income.[36]

25.2.4 Partnerships

Where a trading partnership receives income from various sources, the basis period for determining income which accrues to the partnership, and which is then treated as income of the individual partners, is the Part 2 basis period for the relevant year of assessment.[37] This applies overlap profits rules for all income—including Part 3 income. Overlap relief is given under those rules at a subsequent change of accounting date or on the early retirement of the partner. However, joint ownership of property does not, of itself, create a partnership. Where there is no partnership, the partnership return is not required and there is no overlap problem. It is very important therefore to be able to determine whether income is from partnership property or joint property.[38]

25.2.5 Deductions including Finance Costs

Certain situations attract special rules for deductions, including expenditure on sea walls (section 315) and expenditure on energy-saving items incurred before April 2015 (section 312). Capital allowances are given for machinery and plant used in the business as if it had been set up on or after 6 April 1995.[39] Expenditure on plant to be used in a dwelling house is excluded.[40] The calculation of income by reference to business income rules means that interest will be deductible, or not, according to the rules in ITTOIA 2005, Part 2. The change may also means that interest will be deductible by reference to the date on which it falls due rather than the date of payment. This also means not only that there is a duty to withhold lower rate income tax in the circumstances prescribed, but also that the duality rules in ITTOIA 2005, section 34 will become relevant—a matter of particular importance if the property is not let at a commercial rent. If property is let at a commercial rent for part of the year, and at a non-commercial rent for the rest of the year, apportionment of the interest would seem to be possible.

Starting from April 2017, the amount of relief available to individual landlords of residential property for mortgage interest and other finance costs is restricted to the basic rate

---

[35] ITA 2007, s 118. There is no right to carry back unrelieved losses of a property business.
[36] ITA 2007, s 120.
[37] ITTOIA 2005, ss 854–856, ex TA 1988, s 111(4), (7), (8).
[38] For a discussion of five different situations, see Tiley and Collison, *UK Tax Guide* 2007–08 (Butterworths, 2007), paras 9.06, 10.08.
[39] CAA 2001, s 16, ex CAA 1990, s 28A, added by FA 1997.
[40] CAA 2001, s 35; apportionment for part use is directed by s 35(3).

of income tax.[41] The broad policy aim behind the restriction is to prevent higher rate and additional rate taxpayers from benefiting from a higher 40% or 45% taxpayer 'subsidy' on their finance costs, which was thought to give individual landlords an unfair advantage over owner-occupier homebuyers in a challenging housing market. The restrictions do not apply to furnished holiday lettings and will be phased in over four years. Beginning in 2017–18, an individual landlord can deduct 75% of finance costs in the usual way, with the remaining 25% given instead as a basic rate tax reduction. The respective figures are 50% and 50% for 2018–19, and 25% and 75% for 2019–20. In 2020–21, relief for all such finance costs will be by way of basic rate tax deduction. The restrictions clearly will make renting residential property less attractive for some individual landlords, especially combined with higher stamp duty land tax rates on the purchase of additional residential properties.[42] Whether owner-occupiers will benefit from the government's intervention in the housing market in this way is less clear.[43]

25.2.6 Payments to Non-residents

Where the property income accrues to a person whose 'usual place of abode' is outside the UK (the 'non-resident'),[44] there has long been an obligation on the person making the payment, and on a person who is the agent of a non-resident agent, to deduct tax at basic rate.[45] The tax must be accounted for quarterly;[46] there is an obligation to make an annual return.[47] The present rules give the Revenue power to allow the payment to be made gross if they approve an application by the non-resident;[48] that approval may be withdrawn.[49] The withholding rule does not apply where the income is paid to the UK branch of a non-resident company and which is chargeable to corporation tax.[50] This procedure does not require notice by either the landlord or the Revenue to the tenant, on whom is cast therefore a duty to know the landlord's usual place of abode. Under established case law, the right to deduct tax is lost as soon as the payment is made gross.[51] There is no right to make good the failure to deduct by making a deduction from a subsequent payment, even one falling within the same tax year.[52] The cases may have to be reconsidered in the light of the restitution decision of the House of Lords in *Deutsche Morgan Grenfell v IRC*.[53]

---

[41] ITTOIA 2005, ss 272A and 272B, 274A and 274B as well as ITA 2007, ss 399A and 399B, all added by F(No 2)A 2015, s 24.

[42] For more on the stamp duty charges see https://www.gov.uk/government/consultations/consultation-on-higher-rates-of-stamp-duty-land-tax-sdlt-on-purchases-of-additional-residential-properties/higher-rates-of-stamp-duty-land-tax-sdlt-on-purchases-of-additional-residential-properties.

[43] For commentary see Herring and Hutton [2015] BTR 609.

[44] There may be subtle differences between place of abode and residence.

[45] ITA 2007, s 971, ex TA 1988, s 42A (added by FA 1995), and SI 1995/2902, regs 8(2) and 9(1). The earlier rule, TA 1988, s 43, used the machinery in ss 349, 350. Section 42A is not rewritten by ITTOIA 2005.

[46] SI 1995/2902, reg 10.

[47] *Ibid*, reg 11.

[48] The conditions are set out in SI 1995/2902, reg 17; among other things, the non-resident must show that he has complied with any requirements of the Tax Acts or Management Acts, or that he does not expect to be liable to pay any UK tax.

[49] SI 1995/2902, reg 19.

[50] *Ibid*, reg 8(3).

[51] *Tenbry Investments Ltd v Peugeot Talbot Motor Co Ltd* [1992] STC 791.

[52] *Ibid*.

[53] [2006] UKHL 49, [2007] STC 1; see below at §27.5.5.

25.3   Furnished Lettings

25.3.1 *General Rules*

Rent for the occupation of the property charged under these rules now also extends to situations where the rent includes the use of furniture.[54] Further rules apply if the rent fulfils the conditions for furnished holiday lettings. The capital allowance rules applicable where machinery and plant are let by a person do not apply where the letting is for use as a dwelling house.[55] Prior to April 2016, concessionary relief was given for wear and tear on furniture in furnished lettings. Broadly, a taxpayer could elect to choose between the actual costs of replacement on the 'renewals' basis, or taking a 10% deduction from the rent received less any council tax or water rates which the landlord pays.[56] Taking the 10% deduction did not prevent a taxpayer from claiming renewals allowance for renewing fixtures which were an integral part of the building. However, no deduction has been permitted for the landlords' costs of obtaining alternative accommodation for themselves, since these are in the nature of personal expenditure.[57] The wear and tear relief was abolished from April 2016 and residential landlords are instead permitted to deduct the actual costs of replacing furnishings. Example: Furnished Lettings Assessment 2016–17 (not furnished holiday lettings)

Year ended 5 April 2017		
Rent received		£3,500
Less: allowable expenses:		
Council tax	£560	
Water rates	80	
Actual cost of replacing furnishings	286	
Insurance	300	
Repairs to property	500	
Accountancy fees	600	2,326
Profit		£1,174

25.3.2 *Furnished Holiday Lettings*

ITTOIA 2005, Part 3, Chapter 6 treats income from the commercial letting of furnished holiday accommodation as arising under a property business. The following beneficial rules otherwise applicable only to trades also apply:[58]

(1)   The income is to be treated as relevant earnings for personal pension arrangements.

---

[54] ITTOIA 2005, s 308, ex TA 1988, s 15, para 4. The Law Commission rejected a proposal to move rent from furnished lettings into Sch A, partly because the variable amounts from such furnished lettings make the Sch A machinery less appropriate (Cmnd 4654 (1971) §61). The advent of self-assessment removed this problem.
[55] CAA 2001, s 35; on apportionment, see s 35(3).
[56] ESC B47; T must also deduct any payments for services normally borne by a tenant.
[57] *Wylie v Eccott* (1913) 6 TC 128.
[58] ITTOIA 2005, ss 322(2), 327–328, ex TA 1988, s 503.

(2) Loss relief rules as for trades (see above at §10.3.1).
(3) Capital allowances, including rules introduced in FA 2011 applicable to plant and machinery used in both furnished and unfurnished lettings.
(4) Rollover relief for CGT (see below at §42.4).
(5) Entrepreneur relief for CGT (see below at §42.5).
(6) CGT relief for gifts of business assets (see below at §36.3).
(7) Bad debt CGT relief for loans to traders (see below at §34.4).
(8) Relief for pre-trading expenditure (see above at §20.6).

The three-year carry back rule for losses in the first three years of a trade is adapted.[59] However, the relief allowing trading losses to be set against capital gains does not extend to losses from furnished holiday lettings. In addition, from April 2011, sideways relief against other income, terminal loss relief and corporation tax relief for losses against total profits are no longer available.

Expenditure is deductible as if the letting were a trade. The CGT rules in (4)–(7) above apply as if the 'trade' were carried on throughout the year and the property used only for such purposes, save where the accommodation is neither let commercially nor available to be so let (unless prevented by works of construction or repair).[60] The purpose of this rule is to withhold the relief if there is any period of owner-occupation. Provision is also made where the house being replaced was eligible for exemption as an only or main residence.[61] The rules are intended to bring a measure of certainty to these areas. Where the taxpayer does not fulfil the stringent conditions laid down, it may still be possible to argue that a trade is being carried on and so to come within Part 2 rather than Part 3. The rules may be seen as recognition of the artificial nature of the division between property income and trading income; it remains to be seen whether other instances of this artificiality will also be amended.

Stringent conditions must be satisfied before a letting is treated as a furnished holiday letting. The property must be in the UK or, from April 2011, the EEA. The letting must be on a commercial basis and with a view to the realisation of profit, the tenant must be entitled to the use of the furniture and the property must be qualifying holiday accommodation (sections 323–325). The property must be available for letting to the general public during the season and available for not less than 210 days, and it must be let for at least 105 days. For a period of at least seven months, it must not normally be in the same occupation for continuous periods exceeding 31 days. Where these conditions are fulfilled in relation to one property but not another, the taxpayer may elect to have the properties averaged (section 326). Thus, if property 1 is let for 120 days and property 2 for 100 days, an averaging election will make both properties let for 110 days, so that both qualify. Separate elections must be made in respect of property in the UK and property in the EEA. These conditions must be satisfied by reference to periods of 12 months, being the year of assessment for an individual and the accounting period of a company (section 324). Special rules apply where the accommodation was not within these rules in the previous year: the

[59] ITA 2007, s 127, ex TA 1988, s 503(2)–(4).
[60] TCGA 1992, s 241(4), (5).
[61] TCGA 1992, s 241(6).

12-month period runs from the date of the first letting; in the converse situation, the period begins on the last date of letting. FA 2011 also introduced a 'grace period' election that may be made where properties meet the qualifying period rules for one year but not the next.

25.4   Individual's Rent a Room Exemption

The purpose behind this complicated relief is to provide an incentive to those who have spare rooms in their homes and wish to let them out.[62] A 'qualifying individual' who receives relevant sums in respect of a 'qualifying residence' may elect to be exempt from income tax on the relevant sums up to a limit—currently a gross rent of £7,500.[63] Sums are relevant rent a room receipts if they are in respect of the use of furnished accommodation in the residence (or residences), or any relevant goods or services.[64] Goods and services are relevant if they are, or are similar in nature to, meals, cleaning and laundry (section 786(2)). If the individual has any non-relevant sums from the same residences, relief is not available (section 790). ITTOIA 2005 makes explicit that the relief applies to non-residents in respect of UK property and to UK residents wherever the property may be.[65] The Revenue view is that this relief does not extend to income from uses other than as furnished living accommodation.[66] A residence is a qualifying residence if it is the individual's only or main residence at any time in the basis period (section 784(1)).[67] Technically the relief is from Part 2 or Part 5, Chapter 8, and so reference must be made to the basis period, ie a period in which profits or gains income tax falls finally to be computed in respect of the source.[68]

The exemption is given in respect of relevant sums, which are, as already seen, defined in terms of sums accruing and so do not take account of any allowable deductions. The exemption is given up to a basic amount, currently £7,500 (section 789(4)). This applies to the basis period and subsequent 12-month periods (section 790(2)). This amount is reduced by 50% (to £3,750) if, at any time during the year, sums accrue to any other person (or persons) in respect of the residential accommodation or relevant goods or services, and at that time the residence is the individual's only or main residence (section 789(3)).[69] This rule applies where, for example, A and B share a house and jointly let a room to C, or A lets a room to D and B lets a room to E. However, this rule applies only where A and B receive money; if A and B arrange affairs so that all the income accrues to A or to B, the limit will be £7,500; if the money is shared, the limit will be £3,750. Pursuant to section 788,

---

[62] Inland Revenue Press Release, 18 June 1992, (1992) *Simon's Tax Intelligence* 617.
[63] ITTOIA 2005, Pt 7 Ch 1, ex F (No. 2) A 1992, s 59, Sch 10, paras 1, 6, 9; and SI 1996/2953 and SI 2015/1539. The limit in s 789 be varied by Treasury Order.
[64] ITTOIA 2005, s 786, note explanatory notes change 139 in respect of F(No 2)A 1992, s 59, Sch 10, para 2(2).
[65] ITTOIA 2005, s 786, explanatory notes change 140.
[66] RI 80.
[67] ITTOIA 2005, s 787(1), ex TA 1988, s 59, Sch 10, para 7; there is no relief for job-related accommodation. In this, and in the definition of a residence, the rules are similar to those for the old deduction of mortgage interest.
[68] ITTOIA 2005, s 786(3) and (4), ex TA 1988, s 59, Sch 10, para 3.
[69] ITTOIA 2005, ss 789(3) and 790(3), (4), ex TA 1988, s 59, Sch 10, para 5(4).

in determining the gross sums received, account must be taken of any balancing charge falling due in respect of machinery and plant by including that amount as part of the gross receipt.[70]

The relief is in respect of sums accruing, and account is not generally taken of any capital allowances or balancing charges (other than that required for section 788 purposes), or of any other expenses (section 793(3)). Two sets of elections flow from this. First, the taxpayer may elect that the relief should not apply (section 799); this will be valuable if, for example, the allowable expenses and other deductions give rise to a loss. Secondly, the taxpayer may choose between being taxed on the whole profit in the usual way, or elect to be taxed on the gross receipts so far as they exceed £7,500,[71] provided receipts exceed that amount only by a small amount.

25.5 Taxation of Premiums, etc as Income

25.5.1 Elements

Since ITTOIA 2005, Part 3 taxes only the annual profits and not the capital gains arising from land, the payment of a premium by a tenant to his landlord would escape income tax,[72] even though it results in a lower rent and so a lower income for the landlord. The obvious scope for tax avoidance was particularly an issue in the years before CGT was introduced; the incentive remains today, given the lower rates of CGT as compared to income tax. For this reason, premiums on leases for 50 years or less are taxed, but in a special way, by ITTOIA 2005, Part 3, Chapter 4.

25.5.1.1 Premium

A premium is defined as including 'any like sum whether payable to the immediate or superior landlord or to a person connected with such landlord'.[73] Thus, a payment required by a landlord on the grant of a lease to a tenant, and a payment exacted by the tenant on the grant of a sub-lease would both fall within this rule; a payment required by the tenant on the assignment of the lease, however, would not. Case law provides a further definition of 'premium' as any sum of money paid by the tenant to the landlord in consideration of the grant of a lease.[74] It is unclear whether a payment of the lessor's costs by the lessee will be a premium.[75] The sum need not be mentioned in the lease document. A sum paid in or in

---

[70] ITTOIA 2005, ss 788(1), (2) and 802, ex TA 1988, s 59, Sch 10, para 9(4)–(6). On s 788, see explanatory notes change 141.

[71] ITTOIA 2005, ss 796 and 797. On form of election, see ITTOIA 2005, s 800, ex TA 1988, s 59, Sch 10, para 12.

[72] *O'Connor v Hume* [1954] 2 All ER 301, [1954] 1 WLR 824. Conversely, payment of the premium by the lessee was held to be a capital expense in *Green v Favourite Cinemas Ltd* (1930) 15 TC 390.

[73] ITTOIA 2005, s 307(1). A payment to a third party other than a connected person is a probably a premium; such a payment is a premium for the purposes of Landlord and Tenant (Rent Control) Act 1949 (*Elmdene Estates Ltd v White* [1960] AC 528, [1960] 1 All ER 306). A premium in non-monetary form is caught (CTA 2009, ss 246(4) and 247(2), ex TA 1988, s 24(4)).

[74] *Clarke v United Real (Moorgate) Ltd* [1988] STC 273, 299, 61 TC 353, 387, per Walton J (a CGT case).

[75] See Beattie [1963] BTR 245.

connection with the granting of a lease, eg key money, is presumed to be a premium, unless either it is rent or sufficient consideration is given for it (section 306(3)).

25.5.1.2 Duration of Lease

The rules apply only to what ITTOIA 2005 calls a short-term lease, ie one the effective duration of which is 50 years or less (section 303). The definition of a 50-year lease takes full account of the commercial realities. Thus, if a tenant has a 40-year lease with an option to extend it for a further 20 years, account may be taken of the circumstances making it likely that the lease will be so extended. Similarly, if a tenant, or a person connected with him, has the right to a further lease of the same premises or part of them, rather than a right to extend the existing lease, the term may be treated as not expiring before the end of the further lease. Both these provisions, by lengthening the lease, favour the landlord. However, if any of the terms of the lease (whether relating to forfeiture or to any other matter) or any other circumstances render it unlikely that the lease will continue beyond a date falling short of the expiry of the term of the lease, the lease will be treated as if it ended not later than that date, provided the premium would not have been substantially greater had the lease been expected to run its full term. Thus, a 51-year lease with an option to the landlord to terminate it after five years would be treated as a five-year lease, as would one which provided that after five years the rent, originally a full commercial rent, should be quintupled. The question of what is 'unlikely' is judged at the time the lease is granted (section 304). The rule, by focusing on what is likely or unlikely, means that a lease for lives may fall within these rules if the life is unlikely to last more than 50 years despite the imposition of a 99-year lease under the Law of Property Act 1925, section 149.

25.5.2 Taxing the Premium

A premium payable in respect of a lease of 50 or less years is treated as payable by way of rent and falls within ITTOIA 2005, Part 2, Chapter 4 (section 277(2)). The charge is on the person to whom the payment is due, and so may be on someone other than the landlord. The landlord or other person is treated as becoming entitled when the lease is granted.[76] Without modification, this rule could cause two problems. The first is a sharp distinction between a 49-year lease and a 51-year lease. The second is that it could result in a substantial sum—which is really attributable to the number of years the lease is expected to run—being treated as the income of one year.

The first problem is solved by the fractional reduction of the premium, that fraction being related to the duration of the lease, as defined; the longer the lease, the less the chargeable sum. The premium is reduced by 1/50 for each complete period of 12 months (other than the first) comprised in the duration of the lease (section 277(5)). Only complete years are taken into account, so that a premium on a lease for two years less a day would be chargeable in full. The sum by which the premium is reduced is not taxable in any

---

[76] ITTOIA 2005, s 277(4), ex TA 1988, s 34(1) and (7A). Quaere how one 'grants' an agreement for a lease; see further *City Permanent Building Society v Miller* [1952] Ch 840, 853, [1952] 2 All ER 621, 628.

subsequent year.[77] The second problem is regarded as no longer causing any difficulty in view of the sharp reduction in income tax rates in 1988; the earlier top-slicing relief provisions were therefore repealed.[78] If the premium is payable by instalments, the taxpayer can spread the taxable fraction of the premiums over a period permitted by the Revenue; this period must not exceed eight years (section 299).

25.5.3 Widening the Net

25.5.3.1 Improvements—Payments in Kind

ITTOIA 2005, section 278 provides that if the terms subject to which the lease is granted impose on the tenant an obligation to carry out any work on the premises,[79] the amount by which the value of the landlord's estate immediately after the commencement of the lease exceeds the value which it would have had if no such obligation had been imposed on the tenant, is treated as a premium. The measure of liability is the benefit received by the landlord, not the cost incurred. Since the provision applies whenever there is an obligation to carry out work, there is a specific exclusion where the works are such that the costs would be deductible by the landlord as an expense of his property business if he had to carry out those works, eg works of maintenance (section 278(4), (5)).

Section 279 extends the scope of these provisions to sums payable instead of rent. Section 277 deals with premiums on the grant of a lease and section 278 with work carried out under an obligation imposed by the lease. Section 279 applies where the lease imposes on the tenant an obligation to pay a sum of money in lieu of the rent.[80] The need for section 279 is subtler than appears at first sight. Section 279 (and also section 281, discussed below) applies to any lease and not just to leases with less than 50 years to run. It applies where the lease imposes the obligation to pay the sums of money in lieu of rent for a period and that period is 50 years or less. So what matters is not the length of the lease but the length of the period for which the obligation arises.

25.5.3.2 Commutation of Rent or Surrender of Lease

Section 280 treats as a premium any sums which become payable by the tenant in lieu of rent or as consideration for the surrender of the lease, but only if those sums are payable under the terms of the lease. A payment in lieu of rent is attributed to the period covered by the payment. Therefore, if, under a 10-year lease, the tenant pays rent of £7,000 pa, but with the right at any time after the first year to pay £50,000 and a rent of only £2,000 pa, and that right is exercised, the £50,000 is treated as a premium. In calculating the charge to tax on sums in lieu of rent, the duration of the lease is the period for which the payment is being made. Thus, if the right in the above example is exercised when there are eight years of the lease remaining, the calculations assume an eight-year lease.

---

[77] The part not taxed as a premium may nonetheless be liable to income tax under Pt 2, if the lessor deals in land, or to CGT.

[78] FA 1988, s 75, repealing TA 1988, Sch 2.

[79] This premium does not extend to work on other property belonging to the landlord; neither does it apply when the tenant does work under an obligation outside the lease.

[80] This was all part of the original TA 1988, s 34(1), as was s 280.

25.5.3.3 Variations and Waivers

The next rule does not, in terms, apply only to leases originally granted for less than 50 years; however, it causes a charge to arise only if the variation or waiver occurs when the lease has less than 50 years to run (section 276(3)). A sum payable by a tenant on the surrender of a lease, where that sum is not stipulated in the original lease, does not fall within section 280.[81] However, such sum may come within section 281, which catches payments payable by the tenant as consideration for the variation or waiver of any terms of the lease. A 'waiver' means the abandonment of a right in such a way that the other party is entitled to plead the abandonment by way of confession and avoidance if the right is later asserted; it is not confined to total abandonment of the right. Therefore where a tenant's option to renew a lease had lapsed, a sum paid to the landlord for the reinstatement of the option was a payment for the variation or waiver of a term of the lease,[82] whether or not such sum was stipulated in the lease. Payments within section 281 are treated as becoming due when the contract of variation is entered into (section 281(4)). Payments within section 281, if paid to someone other than the landlord, are chargeable only if paid to a person connected with the landlord, there being no such restriction for payments within section 280. Pre-1963 leases are also caught.

25.5.4 Assignment of Lease Granted at an Undervalue

Although, in general, payments by an assignee of the lease to the assignor escape tax, this will not be the case if the lease was granted to the assignor or some predecessor in title at an undervalue.[83] If A grants a lease to B at a rent plus a premium, the provisions discussed above will charge the premium to income tax. If A grants the lease to X, who assigns it to B, and X is obliged to pay A money for the privilege of assignment, the sum will be taxed to A under sections 280 or 281. If X is not obliged to pay A money for the privilege, the economic benefit may still accrue to A if, for example, X is a connected person or a family company. Section 282 therefore provides that: (a) if the original[84] grant of the lease was at an undervalue, so that a sum could have been charged by way of premium—'the amount forgone'—that sum shall be computed, and (b) if the lessee subsequently assigns the lease, any consideration payable on the assignment can be taxed to X the assignor under Part 3 as if it had been a premium[85] under the lease, but only to the extent of the amount forgone.[86] This rule cannot be avoided by X assigning to Y without permission, who then assigns to B at a premium, since section 282 applies to any assignment of the lease. Therefore Y would be liable to tax under Part 3 on the excess of the premium paid to him by B over any pre-

---

[81] Neither does s 278, ex TA 1988 s 34(4) apply to payments due on expiration of the term of forfeiture. Quaere a clause which allows the tenant to break the lease on payment.

[82] *Banning v Wright* [1972] 2 All ER 987, 48 TC 421, HL, where the option lapsed owing to a breach of covenant by the lessee.

[83] Nor if the landlord takes a short lease back.

[84] If the original grant was for full value, the fact that a subsequent assignment was not for full value does not create a potential charge under this rule.

[85] Fractional reduction rules apply under s 282(5).

[86] Any excess may be liable to CGT.

mium paid by him to X. This process continues until the amount that has been rendered chargeable equals the amount forgone.

The amount chargeable is that before the percentage reduction; the reduction is calculated by reference to the initial duration of the lease and so remains constant. The charge is on the assignor, not the grantor, and it applies whenever the original grant was at an undervalue; it is not confined to situations where the lessee is a person connected with the grantor.

25.5.5 *Sale with Right of Reconveyance*

Despite all these rules, it was still possible to exact the equivalent of a premium from a 'tenant' by conveying to him the entire interest of the vendor while reserving to the vendor a right to reacquire the property at some future date. Thus, instead of giving B a seven-year lease for £40,000, A could convey the land to B for £60,000 and reserve a right to buy it back from B for £20,000 after seven years. ITTOIA 2005, section 284 is designed to correct such a situation. It applies when the terms subject to which an estate or interest is sold provide that it will or may be required to be reconveyed to the grantor (A) or to a person connected with A. The amount by which the sale price exceeds the repurchase price is charged to the vendor—not the connected person—as receipts of the property business under these rules,[87] the amount being assessed at the time of the sale and not of the repurchase. The sum so charged is not described as a premium, but the fractional reduction for the length of the 'lease' will apply, thus reducing the amount chargeable by 1/50 for each complete year after the first year between the sale and the reconveyance.[88] If the sale does not fix the date of the reconveyance but fixes the price, it is assumed that the reconveyance will occur at the earliest possible date.[89] If the sale does not fix the date of the reconveyance and the price varies with the date, the sum to be taxed will be computed on the assumption that the price on reconveyance will be the lowest obtainable.[90] The sum is treated as received when the estate of interest is 'sold' and further rules specify when the estate or interest is 'sold'.

A notional premium may also arise, but under section 285, if the terms of the sale provide that the purchaser is to lease, rather than reconvey, the property back to the vendor. If the lease is to be later than that, the grant of the lease back is treated as a conveyance of the property at a price equivalent to the sum of (a) the amount of the premium (if any) for the lease back, and (b) the value, at the date of the sale, of the right to receive a conveyance of the reversion immediately after the lease begins to run. Thus, the value of the reversion on the lease and any premium paid are deducted from the original sale price.[91]

No notional premium arises if the lease is granted and begins to run within one month after the sale; this protects the normal commercial transactions of lease and lease back.

---

[87] ITTOIA 2005, s 276(1), ex TA 1988, s 15 and Sch Apara 1(2).
[88] ITTOIA 2005, s 284(1), ex TA 1988, s 36(1). This provision causes difficulty in the common case where a landowner sells mineral rights but with an option to buy back at the land's agricultural value.
[89] ITTOIA 2005, s 286(6), ex TA 1988, s 36(1).
[90] ITTOIA 2005, s 286(5), ex TA 1988, s 36(2)(a).
[91] ITTOIA 2005, s 285(6), ex TA 1988, s 36(3).

25.5.6 *Reliefs*

25.5.6.1 Franking the Premium on a Sub-lease; the Additional Calculation Rule

If a charge to tax has arisen on a payment under ITTOIA 2005, sections 277, 279, 280 or 282 (ie not sections 284 or 285), that payment may be used to frank, in whole or in part, a similar charge arising from a dealing with the interest granted. As the provision deals with payments it cannot apply to section 278. What ITTOIA 2005 calls 'the additional calculation' is designed to prevent a double charge to tax. Thus, if A grants a lease for 46 years to X, and X pays a premium of, say, £100,000, that premium will be subject to tax under section 281, the amount chargeable being £10,000. If X assigns the lease to Y, normally[92] no charge will arise, but if X grants Y a sub-lease for, say, nine years and exacts a premium of, say, £12,000, he is liable to be taxed on £10,080 under section 281. Relief is given for the sub-lease premium (section 282). Using the language of TA 1988, the amount chargeable on the grant by A to X (£10,000) is 'the amount chargeable on the superior interest', and the amount chargeable on the grant by X to Y (£10,080) is 'the later chargeable amount'. The amount to be charged to X on the grant of the sub-lease is the excess, if any, of 'the later chargeable amount' over the appropriate fraction of the amount chargeable on the superior interest. The numerator of the appropriate fraction is the period in respect of which the later chargeable amount arose (nine years), and the denominator is the period in respect of which the earlier amount arose (46 years), so that the fraction will be 9/46 of £10,000 or £1,960. The excess of the later chargeable amount is therefore £10,080–1,960 = £8,120 and X's chargeable amount is reduced to £8,120. The language of ITTOIA 2005 is fuller and longer, but not necessarily lovelier; the essence is the same.

If the second sum, ie that payable by Y to X, is payable by instalments, X's relief will be to treat those instalments as rent.

The purpose of the relief is not only to avoid a double charge to tax, but also preserve the tax neutrality between an assignment of a lease and the grant of a sub-lease. Thus, the longer the sub-lease is, the greater the appropriate fraction of the first sum chargeable which may be set off against the new charge. Relief is not available for sums charged under section 284. Previously, schemes were entered into specifically so as to create large sums deductible under section 287 or sections 60–67. An interest in land would be sold off with a provision for reconveyance at a reduced price. Today, where a vendor is assessed under section 284 on the notional extra rent, the purchaser can no longer set that rent off against any tax due on the grant of a sub-lease under section 287, neither may the notional rent be deducted under section 60.

25.5.6.2 Set-off of Premium Against Rent

If a tenant grants a sub-lease, the rent received under that sub-lease is taxable, but the tenant may deduct the rent paid under his own lease. Similarly, if the tenant pays a premium charged under these rules other than section 284, there is a deduction of part of that

---

[92] Unless s 282 (lease at undervalue, see above at §25.5.4) applies.

premium from the rent derived from the sub-lease.[93] These rules are elaborately set out in ITTOIA 2005, sections 291–295.[94]

Example

If A grants B a lease for 25 years, B paying a premium of £100,000, and B sublets to C for £6,000 a year, B is allowed to deduct from his receipts the sum of $1/25 \times £100,000 \times (50-24)/50 = £52,000/25$ or £2,080 plus any rent paid to A. The set-off is thus limited to that part which is taxable in A's hands. If B assigns the lease to X, X may also set off the £2,080 each year. Where the sub-lease is also at a premium, B may deduct the taxable element of the premium paid to A from the taxable element of the premium he receives from C. Where the sub-lease is at a premium and a rent, the part of the premium paid to A is set off against the taxable element of the premium in priority to the rent.

25.5.7 Interaction of Part 3 Premium Rules with Part 2

Where the tenant is able to deduct the rent paid in computing the profits of a business, whether because the lease is of business premises or trading stock, he may similarly deduct the proportion of any premium charged under these rules.[95] That proportion is spread over the duration of the lease. Rental income accruing to a dealer in land should be charged under Part 3. However, if the income is small in relation to other income, it is treated as part of the computation under Part 2.[96] Where a dealer in land receives a payment which is taxable as a premium under these rules and a part of that payment is chargeable under those sections,[97] that part is so charged and only the excess is treated as trading income.

25.6 Occupation of Woodlands

Woodlands occupied on a commercial basis are not taxed either under ITTOIA 2005, Part 3 (which specifically excludes profits arising from the occupation of land), or under Part 2.[98] The purpose is to ensure that losses arising from the occupation of commercial woodlands are not regarded as losses for Parts 2 or 3. Profits from the trees as distinct from the land are taxable, and so relief is also given for losses. Previously, woodlands were taxed under Schedule B, but this was abolished in 1988.[99] The transitional rules expired in 1993. Schedule B is of interest as an example of imputed income. The charge was on the value of land used for commercial forestry, which worked out at about 15p per acre. The basis was applied throughout the period of occupation of the land by the taxpayer.

---

[93] TA 1988, s 37(4); adapted for ITTOIA 2005 by s 37A.

[94] Sections 296–298 preserve the same relief to the extent that they arise before 2005–06 and so under TA 1988, s 37.

[95] ITTOIA 2005, ss 60–67, ex TA 1988, s 87.

[96] Law Commission, Cmnd 4654 (1971), §69.

[97] ITTOIA 2005, s 158, ex TA 1988, s 99(2), (3); but note the qualification of s 36(2)(b) in s 99(3).

[98] ITTOIA 2005, Pt 2, s 11, FA 1988, Sch 6, para 3.

[99] For history, see *Simon's Direct Tax Service*, A5.101; and Scott LJ in *Bamford v Osborne* [1940] 1 All ER 91, 94, 23 TC 642, 651.

25.7 Exclusion—Occupation of Land

There is no liability to tax under ITTOIA 2005, Part 3[100] (or, previously, Schedule B) on an occupier in respect of the value of his occupation of land; only the generation of income from the land counts for Part 3. Profits arising otherwise may be taxable under some other Schedule.[101] It follows that the case law on Schedule B is of interest here. If the occupier cuts the timber and turns it into furniture, profits from the furniture trade will be taxed under Part 2.[102] In *Collins v Fraser*,[103] it was held that the payment under Schedule B satisfied the income tax liability provided all that was done to the timber was in order to make the produce of the soil marketable in some shape or form. This may go as far as turning timber into planks, at which point trade would take over and the timber would be entered into the accounts of the trade at the then market value, thus ensuring that all 'profits' up to that time would be outside the charge to income tax. Profits derived after that point from the making of crates were held to be taxable. Parliament has declared that short rotation coppice is an activity of farming and not woodlands.[104]

25.8 Rent Factoring

TA 1988, sections 43A–43G, originally added in 2000, were repealed in 2006.[105] They were designed to stop schemes such as that which succeeded in *IRC v John Lewis Properties plc*[106] (above at §22.4.3.1). They are superseded by the 'structured finance arrangement' legislation, now in CTA 2010, Part 16. A discussion of the operation of that complex regime is beyond the scope of this book.

---

[100] ITTOIA 2005, ss 267 and 768, ex TA 1988, s 15 and Sch A, para 2(1).
[101] For example Pt 2/Sch D, Case I, as in *Jaggers v Ellis* [1996] STC (SCD) 440 (profits from Christmas tree operations were held taxable under Sch D, Case I since the source was a Christmas tree plantation not a woodland).
[102] *IRC v Williamson Bros* (1949) 31 TC 370, 377. The boundary between trade and property is explored in the Canadian context by Durnford (1991) 39 *Can Tax Jo* 1131.
[103] [1969] 3 All ER 524, 46 TC 143, Megarry J. Similar problems arose over the extent of farming when that fell within Sch B: see, eg, *Back v Daniels* [1925] 1 KB 526, 544, 9 TC 183, 203, per Scrutton LJ (a cheese factory would be outside Sch B); *Long v Belfield Poultry Products Ltd* (1937) 21 TC 221 (profits from hatching out eggs were not profits from the occupation of land, so falling outside Sch B).
[104] ITTOIA 2005, s 876, ex FA 1995, s 154.
[105] FA 2000, s 110.
[106] [2003] STC 117.

26

Savings Income: Interest and Premium, Bond and Discount

26.1   Introduction

ITTOIA 2005, Part 4 contains most of the rewritten rules on the taxation of savings.[1] Chapter 1 is the customary introductory chapter and contains rules as to territorial scope and priorities. Chapter 2 deals with interest, whether UK source (ex Schedule D, Case III) or foreign (ex Schedule D, Case IV). Chapter 2A concerns 'disguised interest'. Chapter 3 deals with dividends and other distributions from UK resident companies (ex Schedule F), while Chapter 4 deals with dividends from non-resident companies (ex Schedule D, Case V). One reason why Chapters 3 and 4 are distinct is that the chargeable income is

---

[1] For comparative treatment, see *IFA Cahiers* 1994 Conference, vol LXXIXa, especially the general report by Arnold at 491–540 (and Bibliography). While this Cahier concentrates on interest as a deduction, there is much of importance on the definition of interest. On the Canadian definition of interest, see Edgar (1996) 40 *Can Tax Jo* 277, which also discusses reform on the lines of the accruals system adopted in New Zealand (subsequently also adopted for corporation tax in the UK). For an account of the very interesting New Zealand Accrual rules, see Smith (1998) 46 *Can Tax Jo* 819. For theoretical discussions of ways of tackling the time value of money, see Halperin (1986) 95 *Yale LJ* 506; and Lokken (1986) 42 *Tax Law Review* 1.

defined quite differently for the two bases. Chapters 5 and 6 deal with two other rules relating to payments by companies resident in the UK.

The rules on the accrued income profits from securities (see §26.4) were originally going to be rewritten in ITTOIA 2005 but are now to be found in ITA 2007, Part 12 instead.

ITTOIA 2005, Part 4, Chapter 7 is on purchased life annuities; Chapter 8 returns to interest-type payments from bonds, ie profits from deeply discounted securities; Chapter 9 is on gains from life policies; Chapter 10 formerly concerned distributions from unauthorised unit trusts but has been repealed; Chapter 11 is dealt with below at §26.7.

Each of these Chapters of Part 4 has its own charging provision and so there are also rules as to priorities within Part 4 (section 367) and between Part 4 and other Parts (section 366). Section 366 lists provisions having priority over Part 4 in case of overlap; these are, principally, ITEPA 2003 and ITTOIA 2005, Parts 2 and 3. Part 4 is not quite the residual head of charge, as Part 5 contains further heads which yield priority to Part 4 in case of overlap: section 575. The corporation tax rules on interest and similar payments in CTA 2009, Parts 5–7, known as loan relationships, are discussed in chapter sixty-three below.

The taxation of income on savings held outside tax-preferred structures such as ISAs and pensions was fundamentally changed with the introduction of the Personal Savings Allowance (PSA). From 6 April 2016, basic-rate taxpayers do not pay tax on the first £1,000 of savings income such as interest earned on bank current accounts. Higher-rate taxpayers can earn up to £500 of savings income tax-free but additional rate taxpayers have no tax-free allowance. In an important structural change to the way tax is collected on such income, from that date banks and building societies are no longer required to automatically withhold 20% in income tax from the interest earned on non-ISA savings. Instead, financial institutions will report directly to HMRC on taxpayer savings income so that the amount earned by each taxpayer can be automatically reflected in the taxpayer's digital account with HMRC. The PSA has greatly simplified the taxation of such income, with the result that the rules discussed below will apply to only a relatively small number of taxpayers with non-ISA savings income in excess of the PSA.

26.1.1 The Scope of ITTOIA 2005, Part 4, Chapter 2

ITTOIA 2005, Part 4, Chapter 2 charges income tax on the full amount of interest arising in the tax year, and the charge is on the person receiving or entitled to the interest.[2] Further provisions of Chapter 2 bring in not only discounts (other than from deep gain securities) but also building society dividends, open-ended investment company distributions, authorised unit trust distributions, industrial and provident society payments, and funding bonds.[3] Unlike ex TA 1988, Schedule D, Case III, the charge extends to interest whatever its source. There is no charge on foreign interest accruing to a non-resident.[4]

With the single exception of a 'deeply discounted security' (see below at §26.6.3), no deductions may be made—a rule which applies with equal ferocity to UK source dividends (Part 4, Chapter 2).[5] This non-deduction rule is achieved in ITTOIA 2005 by saying that

---

[2] ITTOIA 2005, ss 369–71.
[3] ITTOIA 2005, ss 372–81.
[4] ITTOIA 2005, Pt 4, Ch 1, s 368.
[5] The 'full amount wording' is in ITTOIA 2005, Pt 4, Chs 2 and 3, ex TA 1988, s 64; and see *Soul v Caillebotte* (1964) 43 TC 657.

the charge is on the full amount of the interest arising. In turn this means that interest paid on a loan to buy securities cannot be set directly against the interest received.[6] Before 1969 a general relief was available against income for interest paid on loans so that, while it could not be set directly against the interest received, it could, nonetheless, benefit from the relief in a different and broader way. Since 1969, relief for interest paid has been restricted (see above at §10.2). The rule against deduction of expenses associated with the receipt of interest and dividends gives this charge something of the air of a gross receipts tax, a matter of importance when other countries are considering whether to grant credit relief for the UK tax paid. Other costs incurred, eg legal fees on making the loan, are matters for CGT, if at all.[7] These non-deduction rules apply for ITTOIA 2005, Part 4; different rules apply if the debt is held as part of a trade and the rules in Part 2 apply.[8]

The recipients of these income payments are liable to income tax, generally by self-assessment. Deduction at source rules are to be found in ITA 2007, Part 15 (see below at §26.5.2); certain types of interest attract an obligation on the payer to withhold at the 20% savings rate (with varying degrees of sanction).

26.1.2 Basis of Assessment

Since 1996–97, assessments to income tax have been made on a strict current year basis.[9] This means that a person is taxed on the full amount of interest arising in the period 6 April to 5 April. An exception arises where a trading partnership receives income outside ITTOIA 2005, Part 2, eg interest, where the income of the basis period for the partnership is taken instead to determine the income of the partnership. That income is then apportioned to the individual partners. For periods before 1996 the preceding year basis was used unless statute provided otherwise (as it did for bank and building society interest).[10]

26.1.3 When Does Income Arise?

Generally, income arises only when it is received or enures to a person's benefit.[11] For this purpose it has been held that payment by cheque is not income when the cheque is received but, probably, only when the proceeds of the cheque are received, whether as cash or on being credited to the account of the payee.[12] The question when a payment enures to the

---

[6] A right to deduct may arise under the corporation tax loan relationship rules in CTA 2009, Pts 5–7 where the taxpayer is carrying on an investment trading business and so can deduct under CTA 2009, Pt 3 (trading income), or where the interest, while falling outside the loan relationship rules, qualifies as a management expense of an investment or insurance company.

[7] Most debts are not assets for the purposes of CGT anyway (TCGA 1992, s 251).

[8] On priority of Pt 2, see s 359(1).

[9] ITTOIA 2005, s 363, ex TA 1988, s 64, added by FA 1994, s 206.

[10] TA 1988, s 64 (original version). Under the preceding year basis special rules applied for opening and closing years: TA 1988, ss 66, 67 (repealed with effect from 1996 by FA 1994).

[11] *Dunmore v McGowan* [1978] STC 217, [1978] 2 All ER 85, 52 TC 307; see also *Whitworth Park Coal Co Ltd v IRC* [1961] AC 31, [1959] 3 All ER 703, 38 TC 531.

[12] *Parkside Leasing Ltd v Smith* [1985] STC 63, 69d (if the crediting is conditional, it is assumed that income is not received until the crediting has become unconditional). Contrast the rule for the payment of tax in TMA 1970, s 70A; and for PAYE payments, SI 2003/2682, reg 219, originally added by SI in 1996.

advantage of a taxpayer has been explored in cases concerning banks, where the payment of interest is deferred or diverted. Simple deferral of the bank's liability to pay interest to the lender means that the interest has not been received and so is not yet taxable; it does not matter whether this deferral is forced, voluntary or by agreement. This must be contrasted with cases where the lender, L, has done something in respect of the interest and the interest has been appropriated to L's use in some way, if deposited at L's directions or if lying under L's name at the bank.[13]

In *Dunmore v McGowan*,[14] the interest not paid to L was held by the bank in accordance with an agreement under which neither interest nor the balance of the account could be withdrawn while the taxpayer was under a liability to the bank in respect of a guarantee. The Court of Appeal held that the interest income was taxable to the taxpayer as it arose each year. This case, which at first sight seems to be wrong, in that a promise by a debtor to pay is not usually regarded as a receipt of income, may be justified on the basis that it was not a case of non-receipt by the taxpayer but of positive appropriation by him. This was followed in *Peracha v Miley*,[15] where interest credited to the taxpayer, but retained by the bank as security under a guarantee, was held taxable when so credited, even though it was highly unlikely in that case that the taxpayer would ever see any of his interest.

Earlier, *Dunmore v McGowan* had been distinguished in *Macpherson v Bond*.[16] Here the taxpayer had charged money in a bank account to a bank to secure the debts of a third party. Vinelott J held that on the facts, the crediting of the money to the taxpayer's account did not reduce any personal liability on the part of the taxpayer to the bank under a guarantee to the bank, because no guarantee had been given.

26.2   Meaning of Interest

There is no statutory definition of 'interest'.[17] Case law, however, provides four elements in establishing 'interest'. First, as Rowlatt J put it in *Bennett v Ogston*,[18] interest is 'payment by time for the use of money'. Therefore, a payment on a loan may be interest, but a dividend on a share is not. Secondly, the payment must not be excessive, a rule which may be based on Scots, ie civil, law origins.[19] Thirdly, the use of the word 'interest' is not conclusive.

---

[13] Neuberger J in *Girvan v Orange Personal Communication Services Ltd* [1998] STC 567, 588e.
[14] [1978] STC 217, [1978] 2 All ER 85, 52 TC 307. The court rejected an argument that the arrangement amounted to a trust since there was no evidence to support it. Had a trust been established, the income could not have been said to have accrued to the taxpayer even though he would have gained some incidental advantage from it.
[15] [1990] STC 512, 63 TC 444, CA. *Macpherson v Bond* [1985] STC 678, 58 TC 579 (see below) was, in turn, distinguished on the basis that in *Peracha v Miley* there was an immediate reduction in the amount of the taxpayer's personal liability.
[16] [1985] STC 678, 58 TC 579; whether Vinelott J was right to distinguish *Dunmore v McGowan* in this way was deliberately not commented upon by Dillon LJ in *Peracha v Miley* [1990] STC 512, 518 63 TC 444, 464.
[17] See Beer [1986] BTR 271.
[18] (1930) 15 TC 374, 379.
[19] *Cairns v MacDiarmid* [1982] STC 226; but on appeal Sir John Donaldson MR thought that, on the facts, the payment might be just ([1983] STC 178).

Therefore, where the 'interest' was due shortly after the loan and exceeded the principal sum, the court had little difficulty in holding that the payment was not interest.[20] Fourthly, in the UK, unlike some other countries, there has to be some underlying debt or other obligation to pay money to which the interest relates. These four basic principles have been embroidered in the cases.

Compensation for delay in payment must be distinguished from compensation for delay in performing some other obligation. Payments by time for the use of money are distinct from payments by time for non-performance of obligations; the fact that time is used to measure a payment is not enough to make the payment interest when there is no principal debt.[21] Suppose that A has just bought a lot of whisky and then gives B an option to buy that whisky at any time within six months at a price of £100, plus 'interest' at the rate of 12% per annum from the time A bought the whisky until B exercises the option. If B exercises the option after three months and pays £103, this would be a simple purchase for £103 and not a purchase for £100 plus £3 interest.[22] This is because until B exercises the option there is no underlying contract for purchase in respect of which the interest can accrue. The situation is therefore distinct from that in which B had agreed to buy in the first month and had also agreed to pay an extra 1% a month for each month until the payment was made. In such cases one must not assume that a sum which is an ingredient in determining an interest payment is itself a payment of interest; the question is whether it is payment by time for the use of money.[23]

It is unclear whether a payment by a guarantor in respect of interest due from the principal debtor is itself interest.[24] However, a payment under a contract of indemnity has been held to be interest where the guarantor expressly guaranteed payment of this interest by being party to a promissory note 'as primary obligor', as distinct from accepting a general obligation to make good the general contractual defaults of the principal.[25]

26.2.1 Premiums and Discounts

If A lends B money for a fixed period, A may insist not only on the current general rate of interest, but also on some extra payment. A may charge extra interest or ask for a larger sum to be paid back than was lent, ie a premium. A premium will be treated as an interest payment unless it can be shown that it is a payment on some other account, eg to cover the risk of foreign exchange fluctuation or the risk of non-payment. If it is a payment on some other account, it may be income under ITTOIA 2005, Part 5, Chapter 8, or even a capital receipt.

---

[20] *Ridge Securities Ltd v IRC* [1964] 1 All ER 275, 44 TC 373; *cf Chevron Petroleum (UK) Ltd v BP Development Ltd* [1981] STC 689.

[21] *Re Euro Hotel (Belgravia) Ltd* [1975] STC 682, [1975] 3 All ER 1075. See discussion by Edgar (1996) 44 *Can Tax Jo* 327.

[22] Sir Robert Megarry VC in *Chevron Petroleum (UK) Ltd v BP Development Ltd* [1981] STC 689, 695j.

[23] See also *Cooker v Foss* [1998] STC (SCD) 189.

[24] See *Westminster Bank Executor and Trustee Co (Channel Islands) Ltd v National Bank of Greece SA* (1970) 46 TC 472, 485 (Court of Appeal saying that it was); but *cf* 494 (point left open by the House of Lords). This is different from the question whether the guarantee payment is interest 'on a loan', a matter of importance for deduction under TA 1988, s 353 (see ch 10 above).

[25] *Re Hawkins, Hawkins v Hawkins* [1972] Ch 714, [1972] 3 All ER 386.

Under ITTOIA 2005, discounts are treated as interest within Part 4, Chapter 2 unless they are profits from deeply discounted securities.[26]

26.2.1.1 Premium and Interest

Where A borrows £90 from B on the basis that A will not only pay a reasonable commercial rate of interest for the loan for the year, but will also repay £100 in 12 months, the extra £10 is a premium and is not treated as interest for tax purposes.[27] A different result would be reached if A had not agreed to pay any interest at all; here the £10 would be treated as interest since it was clearly a payment by time for the use of money. Similarly, if interest is charged at an unreasonably low rate and the extra sum is geared to the length of the loan, the courts have held the extra sum to be interest, even though the parties called it a premium.[28] This does not breach the 'form versus substance' rule, since the description given by the parties is not conclusive of its legal form and the test is whether £10 or the extra sum represents payment by time for the use of money. Extrinsic evidence is admissible.

26.2.1.2 Discount, Interest and Premium

A may issue promissory notes at £90 with a promise to redeem at £100 in one year's time. Despite the economic similarity with the premium, the legal position here is different; the £10 is treated as a discount, not as a premium. Profits arising from discounts are not interest (see below at §26.6),[29] although they are taxed as income under Part 4, Chapter 2. Although these distinctions are easy to put into words and, once grasped, generate a certain satisfaction, they are unreal in economic or commercial terms.[30] Both discounts and premiums are payments by time for the use of money and should be treated alike—as they are now for corporation tax and generally for income tax. However, whereas corporation tax has created a whole, new statutory scheme and language under which income (and expenses) accrue year by year, so that distinctions between income and capital have (almost) been abolished, income tax has continued to be considered under the old concepts.

26.2.1.3 Cases

In *Davies v Premier Investment Co Ltd*,[31] a company issued unsecured promissory notes at par without interest, but offered to redeem them at a premium of 30% after six years, with the alternative of a premium calculated at 5% pa should the company redeem the notes or go into voluntary liquidation before six years. The premium was held to be interest. This conclusion might not have been reached had the premium been 30% regardless of when the notes were redeemed.

Where normal commercial rates of interest are charged, the question whether any 'premium' or discount is taxed as interest is determined according to the following rules laid down in *Lomax v Peter Dixon*:[32]

---

[26] ITTOIA 2005, s 381.
[27] *Lomax v Peter Dixon* [1943] 2 All ER 255, 259, 25 TC 353, 363.
[28] *IRC v Thomas Nelson & Sons Ltd* (1938) 22 TC 175.
[29] See also *Lomax v Peter Dixon* [1943] 2 All ER 255, 259, 25 TC 353, 363, per Lord Greene MR.
[30] See Warren (1993) 107 HLR 460.
[31] [1945] 2 All ER 681, 27 TC 27.
[32] [1943] 2 All ER 255, 262, 25 TC 353, 367.

(1) If interest is charged at a rate that would be reasonably commercial on a reasonably sound security, there is no presumption that a 'discount' or a 'premium' is interest.
(2) The true nature of the payment is a matter of fact rather than of law.
(3) Among the factors relevant will be the contract itself, the term of the loan, the rate of interest expressly stipulated for, the nature of the capital risk and the extent to which, if at all, the parties expressly took or may reasonably be expected to have taken the capital risk into account in fixing the terms of the contract.

It should also be noted that in *Lomax* the payments were made by a foreign company, and under the foreign law the payments probably were interest (and so deductible under that law).

26.2.2 Interest and Damages

The notion that interest is a type of service charge for the use of money may explain the initial reluctance of judges to treat as interest for income tax purposes sums awarded as interest when calculating damages—such sums originally being treated as extra damages.[33] In *Riches v Westminster Bank Ltd*,[34] however, this approach was held to be wrong. The taxpayer successfully sued a business partner for his share of the profit on a transaction (£36,255) which the partner had concealed. The judge also awarded him £10,028 as interest at 4% since the original deception, exercising his discretion under the Law Reform (Miscellaneous Provisions) Act 1934, section 3. It was held by the House of Lords that the £10,028 was interest. As Lord Simon put it: 'It is not capital. It is rather the accumulated fruit of a tree which the tree produces regularly until payment.'[35]

26.2.3 Alternative Financial Arrangements and Disguised Interest

Certain payments under alternative financial arrangements are equated with interest for income tax and with the loan relationship legislation for corporation tax.[36] One example of such a payment is an alternative financial return (AFR). These arrangements are known as parts of legal systems where religion does not permit the payment of interest, such as Islam. An AFR arises where a person, X, buys an asset and sells it to Y, leaving the price unpaid until a later date; the price paid by Y is greater than that paid by X—the difference in the prices is the AFR.[37] The AFR is not treated as relevant consideration for CGT purposes.[38] Other alternative financial arrangements involve diminishing share ownership, investment bonds, and profits share agency. The rules governing alternative financial arrangements formerly in FA 2005 were rewritten into ITA 2007, Part 10A in 2010.[39] Space precludes further discussion of these rules.

---

[33] Eg, *IRC v Ballantine* (1924) 8 TC 595.
[34] [1947] 1 All ER 469, (1947) 28 TC 159.
[35] *Ibid*, 471, 188.
[36] For income tax, ITA 2007, Pt 10A; ex FA 2005, ss 50 and 51.
[37] ITA 2007, s 564C, ex FA 2005, s 47.
[38] ITA 2007, s 564V, ex FA 2005, s 53.
[39] Taxation (International and Other Provisions) Act 2010, s 365, Sch 2.

The disguised interest rules in ITTOIA 2005, Part 4, Chapter 2A also apply to interest-like returns. Interested readers are directed to the HMRC manual.[40]

26.3   Yearly Interest

It is sometimes necessary (usually when considering deductions rather than receipts) to distinguish yearly or annual interest from other interest.[41] The basic rule is that interest payable on loans or other sums which are expressed or intended to last 12 months or longer is yearly interest, while interest on loans both expressed and intended to last less than 12 months is not. In applying this test the courts have regard to the business realities of the situation.[42] Yearly interest, which presumably means the same as annual interest, is not defined by statute. The distinction between yearly and short interest depends on the intention of the parties.[43] If a banker makes a loan to a customer, to be repaid at the end of three months, the interest payable is not annual.[44] If, on the other hand, a mortgagor executes the usual form of mortgage, under which he becomes liable at law to pay the amount borrowed at the end of six months, the interest payable is, nonetheless, annual.[45] A technical explanation for this distinction is that in the case of a bank loan, the contract specifies that the repayment of capital with interest is to be on a fixed day, and there is no law, without a new contract by the parties, which states that interest is payable thereafter as a matter of right.[46] A simpler explanation is commercial reality: mortgages are not usually repaid at the end of six months; both parties envisage that the mortgage may last longer than 12 months and thus the loan is in the nature of an investment, as opposed to a short loan on moneys presently payable but held over.[47]

In determining whether interest is yearly, the courts have regard to substance, so that a three-month loan does not carry yearly interest merely because the rate is expressed in annual terms.[48] A loan of no fixed term carries yearly interest even though that interest is payable half yearly, quarterly or weekly.[49] Following the same approach, interest may be yearly even though the principal is payable after less than a year[50] or even on demand.[51] Interest may be yearly even though the amount borrowed and the rate of interest both fluctuate.[52] Interest will also be yearly if the period of the loan is expressed and intended to be one year only.[53]

---

[40] Taxation (International and Other Provisions) Act 2010, s 365, Sch 2.
[41] See http://www.hmrc.gov.uk/MANUALS/saimmanual/saim2710.htm.
[42] *Minsham Properties Ltd v Price* [1990] STC 718, where a loan replacing a short-term overdraft was held to be a long-term loan generating yearly interest.
[43] *Cairns v MacDiarmid* [1983] STC 178, 181, CA.
[44] *Goslings and Sharpe v Blake* (1889) 23 QBD 324, 2 TC 450.
[45] *Re Craven's Mortgage, Davies v Craven* [1907] 2 Ch 448.
[46] *Goslings and Sharpe v Blake* (1889) 23 QBD 324, 328, 2 TC 450, 454, per Lord Esher.
[47] *Garston Overseers v Carlisle* [1915] 3 KB 381, 6 TC 659, per Rowlatt J.
[48] *Goslings and Sharpe v Blake* (above). See also *Cairns v MacDiarmid* [1982] STC 226.
[49] *Re Janes' Settlement, Wasmuth v Janes* [1918] 2 Ch 54.
[50] As in a mortgage.
[51] *Corinthian Securities Ltd v Cato* [1969] 3 All ER 1168, 46 TC 93; noted at [1970] BTR 144.
[52] *IRC v Hay* (1924) 8 TC 636.
[53] *Ward v Anglo-American Oil Co Ltd* (1934) 19 TC 94 (quaere if repayable in 365 days).

It is hard to see why, given the above approach, interest awarded on damages[54] or interest payable by a purchaser on an outstanding contract[55] should be yearly, at least in the absence of some positive intention on the part of the vendor to treat the outstanding amount as an investment rather than a nuisance. These are both, however, situations in which the courts have held the interest to be yearly interest.

26.4   Accrued Income Profits ex Accrued Interest

26.4.1   *General Position*

Few areas better show the difficulties encountered by the UK tax system in clinging to the distinction between income and capital than this.[56] The loan relationship rules for corporation tax have enabled these rules to be abolished—but only for corporation tax. ITTOIA 2005 was going to rewrite the TA 1988 rules for income tax, but in the end this was done by ITA 2007, Part 12, Chapter 2.

As a matter of general law, interest accrues from day to day even if it is payable only at intervals, and is therefore apportionable in point of time between persons entitled in succession to the principal.[57] However, if a person owning a security sells that security with the right to any accrued interest, the price received for the security is just that, and cannot be dissected into one element representing the principal and another representing the unpaid but accrued interest.[58] It follows that the purchaser is liable to tax on the whole of the interest paid.[59] This starting point may still apply (for income tax) when the accrued interest scheme (see below at §26.4.2) does not apply; the starting point cannot apply for corporation tax since the loan relationship rules supersede it.

These general rules gave rise to the sale of gilts before the stocks went ex-div (ie no longer carrying the right to the most recently declared dividend) and the consequent conversion of income into capital gain for the seller. Of course, the buyer would be subject to tax on the whole of the income of the period, even though ownership had persisted only for a part of it, but the difficulties inherent in this could be avoided if the buyer was a charity or pension fund, or some other entity exempt from tax. One risk for the buyer would be greed; if the sales occurred sufficiently often, they could attract a Revenue argument that this was an adventure in the nature of trade. If the seller were held liable under ITTOIA 2005, Part 2, this could not affect the tax position of the buyer if that person was subject to tax under ITTOIA 2005, Part 4, Chapter 2.

The theoretical analysis devised by the courts was carried further when the courts held that the right to the interest could be sold separately from the securities themselves, and the

---

[54] *Jefford v Gee* [1970] 2 QB 130, 149, [1970] 1 All ER 1202, 1210; the facts were unusual in that the sale was deferred for more than 12 months.

[55] *Bebb v Bunny* (1854) 1 K & J 216. On practical problems, eg under TA 1988, s 349(2)(c), see [1971] BTR 333.

[56] For a view that the trouble stemmed from an unsophisticated view of ownership, see Cunningham and Schenk (1992) 47 *Tax Law Review* 725.

[57] *Halsbury's Laws of England* (4th edn), vol 32, para 106.

[58] *Wigmore v Thomas Summerson & Sons Ltd* [1926] 1 KB 131, 9 TC 577.

[59] *Schaffer v Cattermole* [1980] STC 650.

purchase price would be for the sale of a right and not an interest payment, even though the date for payment had arrived before the sale.[60] Legislation to counter these decisions in certain tax-saving situations is considered in chapter sixty-three. On recent avoidance cases, see §5.6 above.

26.4.2 Accrued Income Profits Scheme

For a long time the Treasury, presumably anxious to do nothing to inhibit the sale of gilts, was content with the large revenue loss which stemmed from the freedom to convert accrued income into capital gain, even though the purchaser might have been a tax-free pension fund and the vendor safe from CGT by reason of the annual exemption or holding the securities for at least 12 months. This changed in 1986: presumably the Treasury was then confident about its ability to sell gilts and therefore more able to proclaim its belief in tax neutrality. When the scheme is excluded, the rules described at §26.4.1 above still apply.

In essence, the scheme is simple. Where securities bearing interest (ie cum-div) are disposed of, the tax system will treat the interest as accruing from day to day. Therefore, on the sale of such securities cum-div, the vendor (V) must pay tax on the interest accruing to that date, and the purchaser (P) will deduct that amount from the interest payment V receives, so that only the interest accruing after the purchase will be charged to tax. When the purchase is made ex-div, the converse rules apply. Since the scheme, in effect, treats what had been capital gain as income, it is interesting to note the convergence of rules under this scheme and CGT rules.[61]

26.4.2.1 Assets

'Securities' are defined[62] widely and include any loan stock at a fixed or variable rate of interest,[63] whether issued by a public body, company or any other body. Specific exclusions apply to ordinary or preference shares, national and war savings certificates, bills of exchange and other bills, and certificates of deposit.

26.4.2.2 Transfer with Accrued Interest

On a transfer[64] with accrued interest the transferor is treated as entitled to a sum equal to the 'accrued income profit', which is a time-apportioned part of the later interest payment, although this will be overridden by the actual payment when the transferee accounts separately for the interest and capital.[65] For the purposes of the time apportionment, the

---

[60] *IRC v Paget* [1938] 1 All ER 392, 21 TC 677.

[61] Eg, ITA 2007, s 653, ex TA 1988, s 727 on stock lending explicitly referring to CGT rules, and the final amendment of the provisions dealing with death (s 636, ex s 721) to bring it into line with a CGT change made 25 years earlier.

[62] ITA 2007, s 619, ex TA 1988, s 710.

[63] The term 'interest' is defined in ITA 2007, s 671, ex TA 1988, s 711(9).

[64] Defined in ITA 2007, s 620(1), ex TA 1988, s 710(5) as including sale, exchange and gift. Where a person exchanges a gilt for a gilt strip there is a deemed transfer (ITA 2007, s 648, ex TA 1988, s 722A).

[65] ITA 2007, 632(3), ex TA 1988, s 713(4).

transferor (V) is treated as entitled to interest accruing for the number of days up to and including the date of settlement.[66] An interest period must not exceed 12 months.[67]

26.4.2.3 Sums

The accrued proportion of the interest on the securities payable for the period is A ÷ B, where A is the number of days in the interest period up to and including settlement day and B is the number of days in the interest period.[68]

Example

A security has interest payment dates of 15 January and 15 July. It is quoted ex-div on 28 December and 27 June. The six-monthly interest payment is £500. If V sells the security cum-div in a period ending with settlement day on 15 December, V will not actually receive the interest payment due on 15 January, but, for tax purposes, is treated as receiving (153/184) of £500 = £415.76.

The figures conform to the words of the legislation, but not to Stock Exchange practice which is to take the number of days from the last interest payment to the date of the settlement date and divide it by 365 (366 in a leap year). This factor is then applied to the year as a whole. It is understood that these figures, which are shown on contract notes, are accepted by the Revenue.

If, in the example above, V had sold ex-div with a settlement day on 2 January, he would have received the whole interest payment on 15 January but would be entitled to treat a fraction of it as capital; the fraction would have been (184 − 171)/184 which, applied to £500, gives a rebate of £35.33.

26.4.2.4 Converse—Without Accrued Interest

On a transfer without accrued interest, V is treated as entitled to relief on the accrued income loss and the transferee is treated as entitled to that amount. The loss is calculated in a similar way to the accrued amount but is, of course, the converse figure.

26.4.2.5 Tranches

Where securities are issued in tranches, the rules, as originally framed, failed to catch a device in which the size of an existing issue was increased by the issue of further securities of the same stock without distinguishing between the original issue and the new issue. The price of the new securities would include a sum representing interest on the existing securities. That sum is now subject to the apportionment system.[69]

26.4.2.6 Timing

Where, under these rules, V is treated as entitled to a sum, the sum is treated as received on the last day of the interest period.[70] The charge is under ITA 2007, Part 12, Chapter 2.[71]

---

[66] Defined in ITA 2007, s 674, ex TA 1988, s 712.
[67] See ITA 2007, s 673(1), ex TA 1988, s 711(4).
[68] ITA 2007, s 662, originally added by FA 1991.
[69] *Ibid.*
[70] ITA 2007, s 714(1).
[71] ITA 2007, s 714(2). Formerly the charge was under Sch D, Case VI.

An interest period is a period ending with an interest payment day,[72] but any period in excess of 12 months is divided, so that no period can exceed 12 months;[73] in this way an interest period can end without an interest payment day.

26.4.2.7 Relief for P

It is central to the scheme that P, the party not treated as receiving income, is granted relief. The relief is set against any sums P is treated as receiving under these rules, and is then set against the sums actually received by way of interest during the interest period. Where the interest period does not end with an interest payment day and there is no deemed income under these rules, the relief may be rolled forward to the next interest period.[74]

26.4.2.8 Excluded Transferors, Transferees and Transfers

The above rules are excluded in a number of situations, in which case there will be no deemed income for one party. The exceptions are:[75]

(1) where V (the transferor) is trading and the transfer is taken into account in computing V's profits;[76]
(2) where V is an individual[77] and on no day in the year of assessment in which the interest period ends (or the previous year) does the nominal[78] value of securities held by V exceed £5,000 (when income from the securities is deemed to be the income of another person, the securities are treated as belonging to both).[79] The figure of £5,000 has not been changed for many years.
(3) a *de minimis* provision similar to (2) for an estate in administration;[80]
(4) a *de minimis* provision similar to (2) for a trust for a disabled person;[81]
(5) where V is not resident in the UK for any part of the chargeable period or ordinarily resident for that period and is not a non-resident UK trader;[82]
(6) where the interest arises from stock lending transactions;[83]
(7) where the interest arises from on-cash collateral provided in connection with approved stock lending arrangements;[84]
(8) securities which are exempt while held by non-residents.[85]

---

[72] ITA 2007, s 711(3).
[73] ITA 2007, s 711(4); the tax treatment is governed by s 711(8).
[74] ITA 2007, s 714(6).
[75] ITA 2007, s 638, ex TA 1988, s 715.
[76] ITA 2007, s 642.
[77] ITA 2007, s 639.
[78] Defined in ITA 2007, ss 676 and 677, ex TA 1988, s 710(11) as the value by reference to which the interest is calculated, or the original issue price.
[79] ITA 2007, s 639(5), ex TA 1988, s 710(9). See *HMRC v Darcy* [2008] STC 1329.
[80] ITA 2007, s 640, ex TA 1988, s 715(1)(c).
[81] ITA 2007, s 641, defined by reference to TCGA 1992, Sch 1.
[82] ITA 2007, s 643, ex TA 1988, s 715(4), (5).
[83] ITA 2007, s 653, ex TA 1988, s 129 (as much amended).
[84] ITA 2007, s 654, ex TA 1988, s 129A, Sch 5A, added by FA 1995.
[85] ITTOIA 2005, s 714.

26.4.2.9 Special Transactions

Special rules apply to nominees and trusts,[86] situations where foreign currency is involved,[87] delayed remittances,[88] appropriations to and from trading stock,[89] conversion of securities,[90] transfers which carry a right to receive the interest on a payment day falling before the settlement day (such interest is called 'unrealised interest'),[91] variable rate securities[92] and situations in which the interest is in default.[93]

The meaning of variable rate security (VRS) in section 627 came before the courts in *Cadbury Schweppes plc v Williams*.[94] The case relates to the 1994 tax year and so before the loan relationship regime (now in CTA 2009, Part 5) applied. The loan notes specified a fixed rate of interest, but the amounts of interest were paid on irregular days and in irregular amounts. The Court of Appeal held, though only by a majority, that notes were not VRSs and so the inspector could determine the amount treated as accruing in the period, ie such amount (if any) as the inspector decided was just and reasonable.

26.4.2.10 Companies

The accrued income profits scheme was repealed for corporation tax when the loan relationships regime came in.

26.4.2.11 Exempt Entities

Transfers by charities are exempt, but special rules apply if the property ceases to be held for charitable trusts.[95] Transfers by retirement schemes are also exempt if the interest would have been exempt.[96]

26.4.2.12 Options

The accrued income profits scheme does not apply to a transfer of securities if there is an obligation in that or some related agreement to buy back the same or similar securities, or if there is an option to reacquire the securities and that option is subsequently exercised.[97]

---

[86] ITA 2007, s 666, ex TA 1988, ss 711(6), 720.

[87] Eg, in calculating the amount of interest or the nominal value under ITA 2007, ss 664 and 665, ex TA 1988, s 713.

[88] ITA 2007, ss 668–670, ex TA 1988, s 723.

[89] ITA 2007, s 650, ex TA 1988, s 722.

[90] ITA 2007, ss 620(1)(b) and 624, ex TA 1988, ss 710(13) and 711(6).

[91] ITA 2007, s 625, ex TA 1988, s 716.

[92] ITA 2007, ss 626 and 635, ex TA 1988, s 717; for an ingenious but unsuccessful argument by a taxpayer on the scope of variable rate securities, see *Cadbury Schweppes plc v Williams (Inspector of Taxes)* [2005] EWHC 1610 (Ch), [2006] STC 210.

[93] ITA 2007, ss 659–661, ex TA 1988, ss 718 and 719.

[94] [2006] EWCA Civ 657, [2007] STC 106.

[95] ITA 2007, ss 645 and 652, ex TA 1988, s 715(1)(d)–(3).

[96] ITA 2007, s 646, ex TA 1988, s 715(1)(k), (2).

[97] ITA 2007, ss 653 and 654, ex TA 1988, s 727A, added by FA 1995, s 79. On Treasury power to modify by regulation following the introduction of a gilt repo market, see ITA 2007, s 656, ex TA 1988, s 737E, added by FA 1995, s 83. On the scope of s 727A, note HC Official Report, Standing Committee D (Twelfth Sitting), cols 365, 366; (1995) *Simon's Weekly Tax Intelligence* 359.

26.4.2.13 Other Tax Rules

Certain rules concern the effect of charges on CGT and double taxation relief. On a sale cum-div where an accrued amount is treated as a person's income, the disposal consideration is reduced by an equal amount to avoid a dual charge. Similarly, the effect of a relief is to increase the consideration to avoid a double loss. If the accrued income profits scheme is excluded (eg by reason of exemption), there is no adjustment for that party for CGT purposes. Double tax relief for any foreign tax may be available. When an actual payment of interest is reduced for tax purposes by a relief under these rules, any foreign tax credit may also be reduced.[98] Provision is made for the interaction of this scheme with ITA 2007, Part 13, Chapter 2, section 720.[99]

26.4.2.14 Death

At one time there was a deemed transfer of securities, with accrued interest, to the PRs.[100] However, since 1996 no such transfer takes place if the securities are passed on to a legatee.[101] In this way the accrued income profits scheme finally took the CGT approach adopted in 1971. Where the securities are not transferred to a legatee but disposed of by the PRs, the scheme will apply in the usual way. If the securities were disposed of by V (the now deceased) in V's lifetime, the scheme will apply in the usual way, but the PRs may have to settle V's tax liability in respect of the transfer.

26.5   Deduction of Tax at Source

26.5.1 Deposits Which are Relevant Investments

Prior to the introduction of the Personal Savings Allowance from 6 April 2016, rules in ITA 2007, Part 15, Chapter 2 ensured that deduction of tax at the basic rate (20%) applied to interest on investments which are 'relevant investments' made with a 'deposit-taker'.[102] The main obligation under section 851 was repealed in 2016, but some of the key definitions are relevant for other rules in Part 15. 'Deposit-taker' is, broadly, any bank, but may also be a local authority.[103] An investment is 'relevant' if the person beneficially entitled to it is an individual (provision is made for concurrent interests), a personal representative as such, or trustees of a discretionary or accumulation trust.[104] Thus, the scheme does not apply to payments to companies or trusts (at least when no individual is entitled to the current income; see below at §29.2. The current year basis applies.[105] Among investments not

---

[98] TIOPA 2010, s 10, ex TA 1988, s 807.

[99] ITA 2007, s 747, ex TA 1988, s 742(4)–(7).

[100] TA 1988, s 716, repealed in 1996.

[101] ITA 2007, s 636, ex TA 1988, s 721(2).

[102] ITA 2007, s 851, ex TA 1988, s 480A.

[103] The list is set out in ITA 2007, s 853, ex TA 1988, s 481(2), but s 854, ex s 482(6), contains exceptionally wide powers enabling the Treasury to designate persons as deposit-takers.

[104] ITA 2007, s 856, ex TA 1988, s 481(4), (4A); on Scottish partnerships, see s 856(4), ex s 481(4)).

[105] TA 1988, s 480C, added in 1990 but now superfluous (repealed by ITTOIA 2005).

considered 'relevant'[106] are qualifying certificates of deposit, general client account deposits, premium trust funds of Lloyd's underwriters, debts on securities listed on a recognised stock exchange, debentures, foreign accounts for non-residents and certain large deposits (£50,000) for a minimum period of 28 days. Also excluded are certain payments on the disposal or exercise of certain rights connected with deposits.[107] A targeted anti-avoidance rule in section 917A applies to tax avoidance arrangements involving intellectual property royalty payments made on or after 17 March 2016.

26.5.2 Other Payments of Interest

Payments of *yearly* interest falling within ITA 2007, section 874 are made subject to withholding at the basic rate.[108] The scope of this rule has been greatly altered in recent years, usually by being narrowed, with that narrowing usually applying to companies. Part 15, Chapter 3 also applies to many payments by or between companies, so that the recipient may pay corporation tax rather than income tax. This is pursuant to section 977. Because the tax deducted is income tax, the deduction rules in Part 15, Chapter 15 apply. Payments of yearly interest fall within section 874 if they are made (a) by a company[109] or local authority otherwise than in a fiduciary or representative capacity, or (b) by or on behalf of a partnership of which a company is a member. Further, tax must be deducted by any person if yearly interest is paid to another person whose usual place of abode is outside the UK (a form of withholding tax).[110] The section 874 duty to withhold does not apply to a payment of interest on an investment if (a) the payment is made by a deposit-taker, and (b) when the payment is made, the investment is a relevant investment (see §26.5.1).

Even if the payment satisfies the criteria for deduction, it must be paid gross if it comes within the list in sections 875–888. That list includes (a) interest payable on an advance from a bank where the person beneficially entitled to the interest is within the charge to corporation tax with respect to that interest (section 879), and (b) interest paid by such a bank in the ordinary course of its business (section 878), a question answered by reference to ordinary UK banking practice at the time. Yearly interest paid by a bank where the borrowings related to the capital structure of the bank were not made 'in the ordinary course of business'.[111] The list also includes interest paid on a deposit with the National Savings Bank, interest on a quoted Eurobond, interest paid in the ordinary course of business by a person authorised under the Financial Services and Markets Act 2000, and certain other payments by recognised clearing houses and investment exchanges.

Where the interest payment is subject to deduction, the payer must account for the tax to the Revenue and provide a statement of deduction.

---

[106] ITA 2007, ss 863–870, ex TA 1988, s 481(5).

[107] That is, payments within ITTOIA 2005, s 552(1)(c), ex TA 1988, s 56A—see s 481(5A).

[108] ITA 2007, s 874, ex TA 1988, s 349(2); until 1968 payments of yearly interest, as opposed to short interest, came within the full scheme of deduction at source (later ss 348, 349). Short (ie not yearly) interest payments have always been free of withholding—and were not deductible in computing total income (*IRC v Frere* [1964] 1 All ER 73, 42 TC 125). On early history, see Stebbings [1989] BTR 348.

[109] On how the company is defined and what it does with the tax deducted, see below chapter fifty-nine.

[110] ITA 2007, s 874(1)(d), ex TA 1988 s 349(2).

[111] See *Royal Bank of Canada v IRC* (1971) 47 TC 565; and Statement of Practice SP 12/91.

26.6   Discounts

26.6.1 What are Discounts?

When the Government (or a company) borrows money for a certain period, eg seven years, by means of a bond or bill, the bill is issued at, say, £60 with a promise that the Government or company will pay a larger sum, say £100, at the end of the period. The bond may—or may not—also carry interest. The £40 profit made by the holder, X, at the end of seven years is a profit from a discount and was taxable under TA 1988, Schedule D, Case III on receipt.[112] In the UK[113] it was distinct from—and not taxable as—interest.[114] If a regular business of discounting exists, the assessment is made instead under ITTOIA 2005, Part 2. Under TA 1988, the Revenue had the choice in the matter; under ITTOIA 2005, Part 2 treatment is obligatory.[115] The £40 discount looks very like an interest payment. The distinction between a debt of £100 with a discount of £40, and a debt of £60 with a premium of £40, is a fine one; in each case the total sum eventually paid is £100. However, the distinction is real in law:

> In the interest account, interest upon the amount is charged upon each bill until it is actually paid; but when a bill is discounted, the interest to be deducted is calculated up to the time when it becomes due and for no longer period.[116]

26.6.2 Traditional UK Viewpoint—Liability on Maturity

Liability arises when the income promised by the issuer is realised, ie when the bill reaches maturity.[117] In *Ditchfield v Sharp*,[118] trustees bought an interest-free promissory note with a guarantee from the vendor that they would receive not less than 75% of the face value. The profit accruing on maturity was held liable to tax under Schedule D, Case III as this was an income receipt from a discounting transaction. The Court of Appeal also held that if the whole gain could be liable to tax as arising from a discount then the whole gain should be so taxed, notwithstanding that, on another analysis, at least part of the gain could be said to be interest. Today the charge to income tax will arise under ITTOIA 2005, Part 4, either under Chapter 2 because discounts are equated with interest, or under Chapter 8 (§26.6.3 below) if the discount is 'deep' and securities are equated with 'deeply discounted securities'.[119]

---

[112] ITTOIA 2005, s 381, old law: *Brown v National Provident Institution* [1921] 2 AC 222, 232, 8 TC 80, 83, per Lord Haldane; and *Lomax v Peter Dixon* [1943] 1 KB 671, 27 TC 353, 364, per Lord Greene MR.

[113] These give rise to problems in many tax systems; see Ault *et al*, *Comparative Income Taxation*, 2nd edn (Kluwer, 2004), 260.

[114] *Ditchfield v Sharp* [1983] STC 590, 57 TC 555, CA.

[115] As in *Willingale v International Commercial Bank Ltd* [1978] STC 75, 52 TC 242.

[116] *Thompson v Giles* (1824) 2 B & C 422, 432, per Holroyd J; and see *Torrens v IRC* (1933) 18 TC 262.

[117] See Hembrey [1982] BTR 74.

[118] [1983] STC 590, 57 TC 555, CA; the taxpayers were not allowed to argue that, since the notes were long-term, the profit could be capital; such a point should have been taken before the Commissioners.

[119] ITTOIA 2005, ss 381 and 427.

26.6.2.1 Companies

The traditional way in which discounts are taxed is not immediately obvious. Where a company, for example, issued bonds at £60 and promised to redeem them in seven years' time at £100, there was a loss to the company of £40. The tax system, while allowing the company to claim that loss, did so only when the loss was realised—ie when the bonds were redeemed for £100. However, since 1996 the loan relationship rules for companies (now in CTA 2009, Parts 5–7) mean that the loss will now be spread over the years on an accrual basis.

26.6.2.2 Bond Holders

Bond holders were treated symmetrically. Therefore, if X bought the bond on issue at £60 and received £100 on maturity seven years later, there would be liability of the profit of £40 on maturity—and not before. However, what if towards the end of year 5 X sold the bond to Y for, say, £92? On the traditional analysis, X's gain of £32 was not treated as an income profit of £32 but as a capital gain of that amount. When at the end of the seventh year, Y received £100, there would be an income receipt not of £8 but of the whole £40 profit which was due to the holder on maturity. Whether Y would also be treated as suffering a capital loss of £32 would depend on other rules. Needless to say, Y would either be a complete idiot to enter into such a transaction, or would have reliefs available to absorb the income of £40 or be exempt from tax. Such a system lasted until 1984 only because the structure of the tax system ensured that there were always knowledgeable vendors and purchasers with widely differing tax circumstances. Since 1984 there have been special rules for deep discount bonds, but the older rules remain for what one might call 'shallow' discount bonds. The rules from 1984 to 1996 are now obsolete—except for transitional effects; as just explained, the traditional analysis is not obsolete.[120]

26.6.3 1996 Onwards—'Deeply Discounted Security'

26.6.3.1 Definition

When the corporation tax rules for loan relationships in CTA 2009, Parts 5–7 were introduced by FA 1996, the income tax rules were simplified; these were rewritten by ITTOIA 2005 and are now Part 4, Chapter 8. There is now only one category which receives special treatment—the deeply discounted security, previously the relevant discounted security (RDS). To see whether a security comes within this category, the amount paid on issue must be compared with the amount payable on maturity or redemption (the result is the discount).[121] The amount paid on issue excludes certain allowable costs. The amount payable on redemption excludes any payment by way of interest on that occasion.[122] The discount is relevant if it represents more than 15% of the amount payable on redemption, or if it is 15% or less but exceeds 1/2Y%, when Y is the number of years between issue and redemption; months and part months may be taken into account as 1/12 fractions of years.[123] Therefore a discount of 5% is deep if the life of this security is less than 10 years.

---

[120] On the effect of the 1984 changes, see Hills (1984) 5(3) *Fiscal Studies* 62.
[121] ITTOIA 2005, s 430, ex FA 1996, Sch 13, para 3(4), referring to para 1(4).
[122] ITTOIA 2005, s 430(4), ex FA 1996, Sch 13, para 3(6).
[123] ITTOIA 2005, s 430(1), ex FA 1996, Sch 13, para 3(4).

Gilt strips and, since F(No 2)A 2005, strips of non-government (eg corporate) bonds are specifically included—in each case with special rules.[124]

The 1996 rules did not, initially, cover circumstances where the holder became entitled to payment on redemption.[125] In seeing whether the gain was 'deep', the amount payable on redemption was compared with the amount payable on the earliest possible redemption date. If the holder had an option to redeem at par or at a very small discount, the security would not be 'relevant' since it would not be deep enough. In turn, this enabled the holder to defer any tax until redemption as opposed to intermediate transfer (ie under the old, pre-1984 rules), while the issuing company could get a deduction year by year because of the corporation tax loan relationship rules.

To correct this lack of symmetry, FA 1999 provided that every possible occasion must be examined, not just the earliest; if the gain is, would or might be deep on any one of those occasions, the security is 'relevant'[126] and so comes within the rules. An exception is made where the holder's option to redeem arises because of a default by the issuer—provided redemption is unlikely.[127] This applies only to redemptions which were at the option of the holder. In ITTOIA 2005 this is achieved by referring to a commercial protection condition or a third party condition, either of which must be satisfied if the sum paid on redemption is to be outside Chapter 8.[128]

26.6.3.2 Issue

There are no special rules to determine the date of issue. Case law suggests that shares are issued when an application has been followed by allotment and notification—and completed by entry on the register. In the case of securities, allotment and notification should suffice.[129] The presence of an enforceable contract to issue is not enough. Special rules apply to issues in tranches.[130]

26.6.3.3 Redemption

The date of redemption is important under these rules. The redemption date is the earliest date on which the holder has an absolute right to require redemption. The concept of redemption is also important as an occasion on which a charge arises under the rules. Conversion is equated with redemption—whether the conversion is into share capital or any other securities—provided the conversion is made under rights conferred by the securities.[131]

---

[124] ITTOIA 2005, s 443 *et seq* and ss 425A–425G added by F(No 2)A 2005, Sch 7; ex FA 1996, Sch 13, paras 13, 13A, 13B and 14.

[125] FA 1996, Sch 13, para 3, as rewritten by FA 1999, s 65; see Lindsay [1999] BTR 351; see also Inland Revenue Press Release 15 February 1999, (1999) *Simons Weekly Tax Intelligence* 253. On timing, see FA 1996, Sch 13, para 3(3).

[126] ITTOIA 2005, s 430(1), ex FA 1996, Sch 13, para 3(1) (1999 version).

[127] ITTOIA 2005, s 431, ex FA 1996, Sch 13, para 3(1A) (1999 version).

[128] ITTOIA 2005, s 431.

[129] This was the conclusion reached by the House of Lords in connection with BESs, see *National Westminster Bank v IRC* [1994] STC 580, 67 TC 1; contrast TA 1988, Sch 4, para 1(3) (old law), where shares were contained in letters of allotment.

[130] ITTOIA 2005, ss 434–36, ex FA 1996, Sch 13, para 10.

[131] ITTOIA 2005, s 437 and 440, ex FA 1996, Sch 13, para 5.

26.6.3.4 Exclusions

The following securities cannot be deeply discounted securities (DDSs):[132]

(1) shares in a company;
(2) gilt-edged securities which are not strips;[133]
(3) excluded indexed securities, ie where the amount payable on redemption is linked to the value of a chargeable asset;[134]
(4) life assurance policies;
(5) capital redemption policies;[135] and
(6) subject to special rules, securities issued under the same prospectus as other securities which have been issued previously and which are not themselves DDSs.

26.6.3.5 Charge on Disposal of a DDS

ITTOIA 2005, Part 4, Chapter 8 charges the profits arising on the disposal of a DDS. Unlike the traditional approach and the rules from 1984 to 1996, these rules allow the taxpayer (T) to set certain expenses against gains and even, at one time, to end up with a loss, a provision that had to be restricted in 2003. This is of great importance in theory since the income tax charge under Part 4, Chapter 8 is aligning itself with CGT rules and so reducing the difference between the two taxes; any difference would be unreal in this area. ITTOIA 2005 makes this even more apparent by talking of 'disposal' instead of 'transfer'.

A profit may arise where T disposes of the DDS or becomes entitled, as the person holding the security, to a sum on its redemption. To see whether there is a profit, the amount payable to T on the disposal or redemption is compared with the amount T paid to acquire the DDS. The excess (the statute does not use the simple word 'gain') is reduced by allowable costs to give the profit. The profit arises in the year of the transfer or redemption and not when the sum is received. Allowable costs are broadly the costs incurred by T in connection with the acquisition, transfer or redemption. The sum paid for the asset itself is not a cost incurred in connection with the acquisition—and vice versa.[136] Where these rules apply, the normal interest charge under Part 4, Chapter 2 is excluded.[137] ITA 2007, Part 13, Chapter 2 (dealing with the transfer of assets abroad) is expressly applicable.[138]

26.6.3.6 Losses

Originally, if these calculations yielded a loss, relief was claimed by setting the loss against general income of the year of the disposal or redemption.[139] This remains in force but

---

[132] ITTOIA 2005, s 432 *et seq*, ex FA 1996, Sch 13, para 3(2).
[133] On application to strips of government securities, see ITTOIA 2005, ss 443–452; on treatment of non-government strips, see ss 425A–425G, added by F(No 2)A 2005, Sch 7.
[134] ITTOIA 2005, ss 432, 433, ex FA 1996, Sch 13, para 13. See also *Investor v IRC* [1998] STC (SCD) 244.
[135] Within the meaning of ITTOIA 2005, s 473(2), ex TA 1988, Pt XIII, Ch II (ie ss 539–554).
[136] ITTOIA 2005, s 439(1), ex FA 1996, Sch 13, para 1(4).
[137] ITTOIA 2005, s 367.
[138] ITTOIA 2005, s 459, ex FA 1996, Sch 13, para 12.
[139] Ex FA 1996, Sch 13, para 2—the claim must have been made within a period ending 12 months after 31 January following the end of the year of assessment.

only where the security has been held continuously since before 27 March 2003 and the security was listed on a recognised stock exchange at some time before 27 March 2003. There is a special rule to bar a loss arising on the disposal of such a security after 27 March 2003 where the issue was at an excessive price and the holder had a relevant connection with the issuer.[140] Losses realised before 27 March 2003 were given effect.

26.6.3.7 Market Value

Echoing CGT rules, a transfer is treated as made at market value if it is between connected persons for a consideration which is not in money or money's worth, or otherwise than by way of bargain at arm's length.[141]

26.6.3.8 Disposal

'Disposal' includes any transfer of the security by way of sale, exchange, gift or otherwise.[142] Like the CGT rules, there are express provisions[143] for conditional agreements—which become transfers only when they become unconditional—and for treating a transfer under an agreement as taking place when the agreement is made, provided the transferee becomes entitled to the security at that time. However, unlike the CGT rules, there is no express provision for mortgages, bankruptcy or hire purchase.

26.6.3.9 Death

Where the taxpayer (T) dies, there is a deemed transfer of the security immediately before death at market value. His PRs are treated as acquiring the security for that amount on T's death.[144] On a transfer of the DDS by PRs to a legatee, the PRs are treated as obtaining, in respect of the transfer, an amount equal to the market value of the security at the time of the transfer. There is nothing akin to the CGT rules which treat the legatee's succession as dating back to the death.[145] It appears that basic rate income tax will apply to any profits realised by the PRs in the course of administering the estate; the oddity is that since 1998, capital gains realised by the PRs are charged at the 'rate applicable to trusts', which is higher.

26.6.3.10 Trustees

Where the security is held by trustees, the profit is calculated in accordance with the rules already outlined.[146] If income arising from the trust would be treated as that of the settlor, the same treatment applies to this profit. The trustees pay at 'the rate applicable to trusts'.[147] The rules do not usually apply to non-resident trustees or to unauthorised unit trusts.[148]

---

[140] ITTOIA 2005, ss 453–456.
[141] ITTOIA 2005, ss 448 (acquisitions) and 449 (disposals), ex FA 1996, Sch 13, paras 8, 9; on connected persons, see TA 1988, s 839.
[142] ITTOIA 2005, s 437(1), ex FA 1996, Sch 13, para 4(1).
[143] ITTOIA 2005, s 438, ex FA 1996, Sch 13, para 4(3), (4).
[144] ITTOIA 2005, ss 437(3) and 440, ex FA 1996, Sch 13, para 4(2).
[145] ITTOIA 2005, s 440, ex FA 1996, Sch 13, para 6(7), (8).
[146] ITTOIA 2005, s 457.
[147] ITTOIA 2005, s 457(4).
[148] ITTOIA 2005, s 458 with consequent barring of any allowable losses.

26.6.4 History: 1984–1996

From 1984 to 1996 much more complicated rules applied. In 1984 special rules for 'deep discount securities' were introduced.[149] The rules were amended in 1989 to include a new category of 'relevant deep discount securities'. FA 1989 also introduced rules for a new category of asset, 'deep gain securities'. The purpose of the 1989 changes was to extend the 1984 rules to new types of security, which became possible following the abolition of the new issues queue.[150] The 1984 rules for deep discount securities meant that if, as in our previous example (see above at §26.6.2), X sold the bond in the course of its life, the income tax liability would be shared between X and Y instead of all falling on Y. However, the income accruing to X was calculated not on the basis of the actual price received from Y, but on an even attribution of the income over the life of the bond under a mathematical formula.[151] If that formula gave X income of £91 rather than £92, the extra £1 was dealt with under the CGT regime. In its turn, Y was treated as acquiring at £91 and so as having an income of £9 on maturity, not £8. The 1989 rules for deep gain securities were simpler, in that there was no mathematical formula. In consequence, X would be treated as realising income of £22, while Y would be treated a receiving income of £8.[152]

26.6.5 Free of Tax for Non-Residents

The Treasury has power to issue securities on condition that they would be free of tax in the hands of non-residents.[153] In *Hughes v Bank of New Zealand*,[154] it was held that the Revenue could not get round this rule by charging tax under Schedule D, Case I. The case also held that the non-resident could deduct the cost of obtaining capital invested in this way; but, by FA 1940, s 60, the Treasury was given power to issue securities on terms which overrode that aspect of the decision.

26.7 Disposal of Certificate of Deposit Rights

The tax treatment of profit arising from the disposals of a certificate of deposit (CD) is an example of the statutory use of Schedule D, Case VI, still current for corporation tax, to catch certain profits which fall through the tax net. Under general tax law, any profit from the sale of a certificate was previously exempt from CGT,[155] while no income tax charge could arise unless the holder was a dealer and so liable under Schedule D, Case I. There was no liability under Schedule D, Case III since the gain was not in the nature of interest, and

---

[149] Consolidated as TA 1988, Sch 4.

[150] Inland Revenue Press Release, 14 March 1989, (1989) *Simon's Tax Intelligence* 193.

[151] TA 1988, Sch 4, para 4 (repealed 1996); the fraction attributable to each year was deductible by the company year by year as a charge on income—*ibid*, Sch 4, para 5 (also repealed 1996).

[152] FA 1989, Sch 11, para 5—the company was unable to deduct anything until maturity. FA 1989, Sch 11 was repealed by FA 1996.

[153] See now ITTOIA 2005, Pt 6, Ch 6; ex FA 1996, s 154 and FA 1998, s 161.

[154] [1938] 1 All ER 778, 21 TC 472.

[155] By TCGA 1992, s 251.

the profit on a discount was charged to the person holding the certificate on maturity.[156] Statute therefore intervened and provided that the profit should be charged to income or corporation tax under Schedule D, Case VI,[157] now rewritten for income tax as ITTOIA 2005, Part 4, Chapter 11. The effect is that all profit will now be charged to tax, whether it is interest or capital gain on disposal or maturity. CDs are excluded from the accrued income regime.[158] This was later supplemented to bring in a right under an arrangement to receive an amount (with or without interest) in pursuance of a deposit of money. When the right comes into existence there is no CD in respect of that right, but the person for the time being entitled to the right is entitled to call for a CD.[159] This is presented as a kindness to enable paperless CDs to be treated in the same way as paper CDs, to the benefit of the Central Money Markets Office of the Bank of England.[160]

ITTOIA 2005 brings the charge into Part 4 as Chapter 11, which therefore has its own charging provision and expressly makes the person receiving or entitled to the profits or gains liable for tax on the full amounts of the profits or gains arising.[161] The addition of 'rights' is taken care of by making the charge one on the disposal of deposit rights, and defining 'rights' to cover both the certificate and the rights.

26.8   Dividends and Other Distributions by UK Resident Companies

26.8.1 Part 4, Chapter 3

This short section is designed to alert the reader to some outline points in the taxation of dividends, which is described in more detail in chapter sixty-one below. The old Schedule F rules can now be found in ITTOIA 2005, with the calculations contained in ITA 2007. When a person subject to income tax receives a dividend from a company resident in the UK, the recipient is liable to tax under ITTOIA 2005, Part 4, Chapter 3.[162] Basically, from 6 April 2016, the dividend will be liable to tax at the following rates:

— 0%, if the dividend falls within the £5,000 Dividend Allowance;
— 7.5% on dividend income falling within the basic rate band;
— 32.5% on dividend income falling within the higher rate band; or
— 38.1% on dividend income falling within the additional rate band.

---

[156] See above at §26.2.
[157] TA 1988, s 56; 'certificate of deposit' has a wide definition under ITTOIA 2005, s 1019, ex TA 1988, s 56(5).
[158] ITA 2007, s 619(3), ex TA 1988, s 710(3)(da).
[159] ITTOIA 2005, s 552(1)(c), ex TA 1988, s 56A, added by F(No 2)A 1992, Sch 8.
[160] Inland Revenue Press Release, 10 March 1992, [1992] *Simon's Tax Intelligence* 322.
[161] ITTOIA 2005, s 551–554; for Sch D, Case VI these are taken care of by TA 1988, ss 59 and 69.
[162] ITTOIA 2005, s 383.

26.8.2 *Part 4, Chapter 5*

ITTOA 2005, Part 4, Chapter 5 on the taxation of stock dividends is an interesting topic.[163] The taxation of stock dividend income is governed by a mixture of Part 4, Chapter 5 for income tax and CTA 2010, sections 1049–1050 (ex TA 1988, sections 249–251) for corporation tax. It is considered in its dividend context below at §61.4.

26.8.3 *Part 4, Chapter 6*

ITTOIA 2005, Part 4, Chapter 6 touches on the taxation of certain receipts from close companies, a topic considered in chapter sixty-seven below. Part 4, Chapter 6 covers a small part of this area of law, rewriting TA 1988, section 421 (taxation of borrower on release of special type of loan). This deals with the taxable income treated as arising when certain types of loan made by a close company or by a company controlled by a close company are released.[164] The loan must have been made to an individual who is a participator in the company, or to an associate of the participator. The charge is on the person to whom the loan was made and is on the gross amount of the debt written off or released.[165] Separate sections now deal with the situations in which the borrower is liable as settlor under ITTOIA 2005, section 633, where the borrower has died or where the loans were made to trustees and the trusts have ended.[166]

26.9 Dividends from Foreign Companies

Dividends from foreign companies are covered by ITTOIA 2005, Part 4, Chapter 4. They are discussed in chapter sixty-one below.

---

[163] For some comparative information, see Ault *et al, op cit*, 297–99.
[164] ITTOIA 2005, s 415.
[165] ITTOIA 2005, ss 416 and 417, replacing TA 1988, s 421.
[166] ITTOIA 2005, ss 418–420, replacing TA 1988, ss 421(2) and (3) respectively.

27

Miscellaneous Income Including
Annual Payments

27.1 Introduction

ITTOIA 2005, Part 5, entitled 'Miscellaneous Income', covers a range of receipts. The principal one covered in this chapter of the book is annual payments (ITTOIA 2005, Part 5, Chapter 7). Others are receipts from intellectual property (Part 5, Chapter 2), films as non-trade business (Chapter 3) and telecommunication rights (Chapter 4). For Part 5, Chapter 5 on income from settlements, see below chapter thirty-one; for Part 5, Chapter 6 on beneficiaries income for estates in administration, see below chapter thirty; and for Part 5, Chapter 8 on income not otherwise charged, see below chapter twenty-eight.

ITTOIA 2005 contains its priority rules for Part 5 in Chapter 1, and section 575 lists the many situations in which priority is given to other parts of the tax legislation. No provision makes anything in Part 5 have priority over any other part of the legislation. Section 576 deals with priority between different Chapters in Part 5. Territorial aspects are covered in section 577, which sets out the usual rules that UK tax arises if the person is resident in the UK or the source is in the UK.[1] ITA 2007, Part 15 is also relevant; the rules therein relate to deduction of tax at source, and collection of tax, from a variety of types of payments.

Annuities and annual payments (AAPs) used to be of great importance in personal tax planning since they provided the basic means of transferring income between taxpayers. They also made use of a system of deduction at source, which was not only an elegant

---

[1] There is one slight qualification in s 587 which makes a non-resident liable to UK tax on the disposal of patent rights only if the patent is a UK Patent; in effect this area has its own notion of source.

device in the 19th-century system that used a single rate of tax, but also the product of a great deal of history.[2] The system of deduction at source did not fit with the system as easily once higher rates of tax were introduced. Nonetheless, the system of assigning income (and income tax liability) survived[3] until well into the 1980s, when it was used by grandparents to pay grandchildren's school fees and by parents to support their adult children at university;[4] such covenants were examples of tax mitigation rather than avoidance.[5] Finally, in 1988 the scope of the system of deduction at source was greatly reduced by excluding from Schedule D, Case III all but a few types of income paid by individuals. The concept remains important, however, for the taxation of trusts and companies.[6] The 1988 reforms, while succeeding in reducing its scope, failed to reduce the in-built conceptual problems.

One positive development was the reversal of the decision in *Ang v Parrish* by ITTOIA 2005—below §31.1. Further important changes were made by ITA 2007, which rewrote and improved the rules on deduction at source (Part 15, Chapter 6, section 900), and the mechanism for giving relief to the payer when these payments are made (Part 8, Chapter 4, sections 448 and 449). These two functions—of deduction of tax from the annuities, etc and relief for the payer of the annuity, etc—were previously carried out by one set of rules granting a deduction, as advocated in previous editions of this book.[7] The new rules give the person making a payment falling within ITA 2007, Part 8, Chapter 4 (sections 447–452) on whom a duty to deduct is imposed by sections 900, 901 or 903, a right to deduct those sums in computing net income (ITA 2007, sections 23 and 25(b)). However, a deduction is allowed only to the extent that there is taxable income or, more correctly, modified net income (MNI) available; the concept of MNI is unique to this part of ITA 2007 and is considered below (§27.5). Under ITTOIA 2005,[8] tax deducted under either section 900 or section 901 is treated as paid by the recipient. If tax is not deducted when it should be, the recipient is nonetheless liable to income tax on the full amount.

In this chapter, §§27.2–27.4 deal with the scope of ITTOIA 2005, Part 5, Chapter 7 in relation to AAPs, while §27.5 deals with the machinery for deduction at source. The definition of annual payments covered in §§27.2–27.4 is also important for corporation tax, where they have a much wider scope.

27.2 ITTOIA 2005, Part 5, Chapter 7

27.2.1 Today's Scope; Qualifying Annual Payment

Today, as far as individuals are concerned, the scope of ITTOIA 2005, Part 5, Chapter 7 has been greatly reduced. However, it still applies to certain situations in which AAPs made

[2] See, generally, Soos, *The Origins of Taxation at Source* (IBFD, 1998); the early part of the story is also told in [1995] BTR 49. For 1980s criticism, see [1982] BTR 263.
[3] The practice was also defended in Royal Commission on the Taxation of Profits and Income, Final Report, Cmnd 9474 (1955) §§144–61 (esp §§149 *et seq*).
[4] The Inland Revenue supplied a do-it-yourself kit in *IR 74*.
[5] Lord Templeman in *IRC v Challenge Corporation* [1986] STC 548, 554.
[6] The scheme for the taxation of annual payments is used for distributions by unauthorised unit trusts (ITA 2007, s 941, ex TA 1988, s 469(3), (4)).
[7] Eg 5th edn at §27.5.7, and see generally [1981] BTR 263.
[8] ITTOIA 2005, s 686; ITTOIA 2005 repeals TA 1988, 348(1)(d), and also puts the previous case law into statutory form (eg *Stokes v Bennett* [1953] 2 All ER 313, 34 TC 337).

by individuals are income of the recipient; in turn, such AAPs are also deductible by the assignor. Naturally, these rules do not apply if the special settlement rules discussed in chapter thirty-one below decree the income to be that of the assignor after all.

ITTOIA 2005, section 683 begins by charging all annual payments in Part 5, Chapter 7 and then, so far as individuals are concerned, exempting everything under section 727, except for a few categories in Part 6, Chapter 8.[9] The principal category of annual payments by individuals which remain chargeable under Part 5, Chapter 7 comprises commercial payments, ie made for bona fide commercial reasons in connection with the individual's trade, profession or vocation,[10] eg partnership retirement annuities[11] and certain earn-out arrangements.[12] Annual payments outside Part 5, Chapter 7 are neither deductible as an allowable charge on the income of the payer, nor taxable income of the payee.[13]

ITTOIA 2005 makes a formal difference when we come to international matters. All AAPS are dealt with under Part 5, Chapter 7 wherever they arise, subject to the international scope rules in Part 5, Chapter 1 (section 577). As a result, ITTOIA 2005 gives us an express provision excluding foreign maintenance payments if an equivalent UK payment would be excluded.[14] The system of deduction at source and relief for the payment in §27.5 applies *only* to UK source AAPs and cannot apply to foreign source payments. TA 1988 made it clear that no deductions for expenses could be claimed, so that, as with interest and dividends, this charge had something of the air of a gross receipts tax.[15] ITTOIA 2005 regards this rule as unnecessary since it has already taxed the full amount of income arising.

Over the years a number of exemptions from tax have been made. ITTOIA 2005, Part 6, Chapter 8 also gathers these together. They include periodical payments of personal injury damages, payments under qualifying health and insurance policies, payments to adopters, and certain payments to be spent on safety measures at sports grounds and paid by persons liable to pool betting duty.[16]

27.2.2 Basis of Assessment

Since 1996–97, almost all assessments have been made on a strict current year basis,[17] ie the full amount of income arising in the period 6 April to 5 April.[18] Before 1996 the preceding year basis was used unless statute provided otherwise.[19] The meaning of when

---

[9] ITTOIA 2005, Pt 6, Ch 8, ss 727–730.

[10] ITA 2007, s 900; ITTOIA 2005, s 728.

[11] On Scottish partnerships, see ITA 2007, s 905, ex TA 1988, s 347(6).

[12] *IRC v Hogarth* (1940) 23 TC 491; distinguishing *Ramsay v IRC* (1935) 20 TC 79. Another exempt category is a payment within ITA 2007, s 904 (ex TA 1988, s 125(1))—but this apparent latitude is to enable the anti-avoidance aspect of the provisions to work. Covenanted payments to charity were moved to gift aid in 2000: FA 2000, s 41, ITA 2007, s 899(5). Payments of interest are not exempted from being income; the deduction rules outlined above at §26.5 apply: see ITTOIA 2005, ss 728–729, ex TA 1988, s 347A(2)(a).

[13] ITTOIA 2005, s 727, ex TA 1988, s 347A(1).

[14] ITTOIA 2005, s 730.

[15] A matter of importance when other countries are wondering whether to grant credit relief for the UK tax paid.

[16] Ex TA 1988, ss 329AA, 329AB, s 580A, FA 1991, s 121.

[17] ITTOIA 2005, ss 684 and 685; TA 1988, s 64, as replaced by FA 1994, s 206.

[18] If a trading partnership receives income outside Sch D, Case I, the basis period for the partnership is taken instead.

[19] TA 1988, ss 66, 67 (repealed with effect from 1996 by FA 1994).

income arises was discussed in the context of the pre-1996 rules. Generally, income under AAPs arises only when it is received, not when it is due. The concept of 'enuring to one's advantage'[20] developed in the interest cases, has not been explored in the context of AAPs; this may be because of the dominating influence of the system of deduction at source which naturally highlights actual payment. Following the interest treatment, it is likely that a payment by cheque will not be income when the cheque is received but probably only when the proceeds of the cheque are received, whether as cash or credited to the payee's account.[21]

27.3 Annuity

Unlike TA 1988, ITTOIA 2005 mentions 'annual payments' but not 'annuities'. This is because nowadays most annuities will be taxed either under Part 4 as savings income, or under ITEPA 2003, as with retirement annuities. It is useful, however, to begin by looking at an annuity so that one knows what it is, and because the idea of an annuity has helped to shape the courts' attitude in determining what constitutes an annual payment. An annuity arises 'where an income is purchased with a sum of money and the capital has gone and has ceased to exist, the principal having been converted into an annuity'.[22] An annuity must be distinguished from the payments of a debt by instalments.[23] In an annuity the capital has gone, and in a normal life annuity contract, payments will continue provided the annuitant lives; an annuity is thus an insurance against outliving capital. On the other hand, where a debt is paid by instalments, the debt remains, and liability is not usually affected by the death of either party.

If a taxpayer buys an annuity from an annuity provider with cash, it is clear that what is received is an annuity, and tax is due on the payments received. Several cases have been concerned with attempts to get payments of the same economic value as an annuity out of an annuity company, while making sure that the payments are not themselves annuities. The two principal cases[24] have been described as very special, and the reasoning of one as hard to follow.[25] Another decision treating sums borrowed as loans not annuities[26] was reversed by narrow legislation.[27] ITTOIA 2005 repeals that repealing provision as being 'unnecessary'. All that can be said is that every case must be determined on its own facts. Many advances by insurance companies are now taxed under rules in Part 4.

---

[20] *Dunmore v McGowan* [1978] STC 217, [1978] 2 All ER 85 (see above at §26.1.3); see also *Whitworth Park Coal Co Ltd v IRC* [1959] 3 All ER 703.

[21] *Parkside Leasing Ltd v Smith* [1985] STC 63, 69d (if the crediting is conditional it is assumed that income is not received until the crediting has become unconditional).

[22] *Foley v Fletcher and Rose* (1858) 3 H & N 769, 784, per Watson B. Qualifying purchased annuities are now dissected (ITTOIA 2005, Pt 6, Ch 7, ex TA 1988, s 656).

[23] See below at §27.4.5.

[24] Principally, *Perrin v Dickson* [1930] 1 KB 107, 14 TC 608 (deposit not annuity); distinguished in *Sothern-Smith v Clancy* [1941] 1 All ER 111, 24 TC 1 (annuity), but applied in *Sugden v Kent* [2001] STC (SCD) 158.

[25] By Lord Greene MR in *IRC v Wesleyan and General Assurance Society* [1948] 1 All ER 555, 30 TC 11. Lord Greene's speech was cited in *MacNiven v Westmoreland Investments* [2001] STC 237, para 60, by Lord Hoffmann.

[26] *IRC v Wesleyan and General Assurance Society* [1948] 1 All ER 555, 30 TC 11.

[27] Ex TA 1988, s 554.

27.4   Other Annual Payments

'Annual payment' is construed *eiusdem generis* with annuities[28] or yearly interest of money;[29] a rent of land is not an annual payment.[30] Although the legislation talks of 'payments', payments in kind fall within this head of charge.[31] Case law establishes that a payment is an annual payment if:

(1)   there is some legal obligation to pay the sum;
(2)   it possesses the essential quality of recurrence implied by the description 'annual';
(3)   it is 'pure income profit' in the payee's hands;
(4)   it belongs to the payee; and
(5)   it is part of the payee's income as opposed to being a capital payment.

There may be a sixth rule, ie that the payment must be a 'division of the profits of the payer'. An annual payment may be removed from this category by statute, as has been done with personal injury damages in the form of periodical payments and similar compensation under statutory or other schemes (ITTOIA 2005, sections 731–734).

27.4.1   The Obligation

The question whether there is an obligation to pay an annual payment is distinct from whether the obligation is created for valuable and sufficient consideration,[32] and has been satisfied on relatively flimsy facts.[33] The obligation may be involuntary, eg under a court order or a statute.[34] A series of voluntary gifts or ultra vires payments by a company cannot be annual payments.[35] Dividend payments by companies are not annual payments since a company is under no obligation to pay a dividend.[36]

Where trustees have an express discretion to make payments to an object of the trust,[37] sums paid under that discretion are not regarded as voluntary[38] (see below at §29.3.3). Payments by trusts were not affected by FA 1988 and so remain Part 5, Chapter 7 income of the recipient.[39] The income tax rules for trusts have now been rewritten by ITA 2007; the duty to deduct arises under section 901, not section 900.

---

[28]   The 1988 legislation assumed that an annuity payable by an individual was an annual payment, and ITA 2007 acts on that assumption.

[29]   *IRC v Whitworth Park Coal Co Ltd* [1958] 2 All ER 91, 102, 38 TC 531, 548, per Jenkins LJ.

[30]   *Hill v Gregory* [1912] 2 KB 61, 6 TC 39; see ex TA 1988, s 18.

[31]   Presumably the machinery in §27.5 does not apply.

[32]   *Smith v Smith* [1923] P 191, 197, per Lord Sterndale, and 202, per Warrington LJ.

[33]   Eg, *Dealler v Bruce* (1934) 19 TC 1.

[34]   *Foley v Fletcher and Rose*, (1858) 3 H & N 769.

[35]   *Ridge Securities Ltd v IRC* [1964] 1 All ER 275, 44 TC 373.

[36]   *Canadian Eagle Oil Co Ltd v R* [1945] 2 All ER 499, 504, (1945) 27 TC 205, 245.

[37]   A payment by a charitable trust would, however, be regarded as voluntary since the beneficiary under the trusts is a charity and not the person benefited (*Stedeford v Beloe* [1931] 2 KB 610, 626, per Romer LJ).

[38]   *Drummond v Collins* [1915] AC 1011, 6 TC 525 (a decision on foreign source income within Schedule D, Case V).

[39]   ITTOIA ss 728–729 (ex TA 1988, s 347A(2)) are confined to individuals.

27.4.2 Recurrence

It is the word 'annual' which indicates that a payment falling within this head of charge must, like interest on money or an annuity, have the quality of being recurrent or capable of recurrence.[40] For this reason an obligation which cannot last longer than 12 months cannot create an annual payment.[41] On the other hand, if the obligation can endure that long, the actual frequency of the payment, eg whether it is payable weekly[42] or monthly, is irrelevant. It is also irrelevant that the sum paid may vary; so payment of a sum such that, after tax at the basic rate in force in the year of payment, equals £50 is an 'annual payment'. It is also irrelevant that the obligation is contingent, so that no sum may be payable under the obligation at all, as under a guarantee. The purpose of the rule seems to be to exclude payments which are casual and temporary and therefore fall more easily into ITTOIA 2005, Part 5, Chapter 8 (which has no requirement of recurrence) than this head.[43] Weekly payments are 'annual'. The annual payment in such cases is the weekly sum multiplied by the number of weeks in the year, which may be 52 or 53 depending upon the day of the week on which the obligation falls.

27.4.3 Pure Income Profit[44]

It is inconsistent with the scheme of deduction at source that ITTOIA 2005, Part 5, Chapter 7 should contain payments which are likely to be gross receipts of the payee against which expenses may be set, and so not pure income.[45] Hence, a trading receipt cannot be an annual payment. Scrutton LJ provided a famous example in *Howe v IRC*:[46]

> If a man agrees to pay a motor garage £500 a year for five years for the hire and upkeep of a car, no one suggests the person paying can deduct income tax from each yearly payment. So if he contracted with a butcher for an annual sum to supply all his meat for a year, the annual instalment would not be subject to tax as a whole in the hands of the payee, but only that part of it which was profits.

The same principle applies to receipts of the payee's profession. Where a solicitor trustee was entitled to charge for his services under a charging clause, such payments were not within this head of charge even though, by agreement with the beneficiaries and other trustees, they took the form of a percentage of the trust income.[47]

27.4.3.1 Other Payments; The Non-fatal Effect of Counter-Stipulations

The presence of some counter-stipulation may deprive payment to a non-trading body of its character of pure income benefit. The difficulty is to know where precisely this line is to be drawn. At one time it was thought that the presence of any counter-stipulation

---

[40] *Moss Empires Ltd v IRC* [1937] AC 785, 795, 21 TC 264, 299, per Lord Maugham.
[41] *Smith v Smith* [1923] P 191, 196, per Lord Sterndale.
[42] ITTOIA 2005, Pt 5, Ch 7, s 683(2), ex TA 1988, s 18; see also *Re Jane's Settlement* [1918] 2 Ch 54.
[43] *Whitworth Park Coal Co Ltd v IRC* [1959] 3 All ER 703, 716, 38 TC 531, 575, per Lord Radcliffe.
[44] In *IRC v London Corpn (as Conservators of Epping Forest)* [1953] 1 All ER 1075, 1081, 34 TC 293 at 320, Lord Normand said that the formula would lose nothing by the omissions of the words 'pure' and 'profit'.
[45] *Whitworth Park Coal Co Ltd v IRC* [1959] 3 All ER 703, 715, 38 TC 531, 575, per Lord Radcliffe.
[46] [1919] 2 KB 336, 352, 7 TC 296, 303; see also *Re Hanbury, Comiskey v Hanbury* (1939) 38 TC 588.
[47] *Jones v Wright* (1927) 13 TC 221.

or condition would be fatal,[48] but this view was rejected by the House of Lords in *Campbell v IRC*.[49] Today, a counter-stipulation will deprive the payment of the quality of pure bounty, but not necessarily of its character as pure income profit. In *Campbell*, Lord Donovan pointed out that in *Westminster v IRC*[50] Lord Macmillan said that if, in return for the annuity, the employee had promised to work for lower wages, the payments would still be within this head of charge, a view with which Lord Wright agreed.

27.4.3.2 Charities and Pure Income Profit

The above problems were discussed in connection with covenants in favour of charities, which may offer inducements in order to obtain those covenants. In *IRC v National Book League*,[51] the charity provided a central lending library, arranged exhibitions, ran a book information service and made available to members various rooms at its headquarters, such as sitting rooms, a restaurant and a cocktail bar. Payments under covenants in its favour were held not to be pure income profit. The correct basis of the decision is that the covenants were simply a club subscription in return for the annual provisions of goods and services.[52] The question of what inducements can be offered remains, therefore, a matter of doubt.

The provision of such facilities for private viewing days for friends of a particular museum, or priority booking for certain performances by a theatre or opera company, is probably not sufficient to prevent payments from being the pure income profit of the charity. The offer of seats at reduced prices was fatal in one first instance decision[53] decided before, and not commented upon in, *Campbell v IRC*. The effect of the very common practice of third parties offering discounts has not been determined; since these have no cost for the charity, it is hard to see why they affect the question whether a payment is pure income profit.

For the status of covenanted payments to charity from 1988 to 2000, see the 4th edition of *Revenue Law*, page 537.

27.4.4 Income of the Payee

The payment must be income of the payee and not that of someone else; it will not be the payee's income if there is a legally enforceable obligation requiring him to hand it on to someone else. This is another explanation of *Campbell v IRC*.[54]

27.4.5 Capital or Income? The Dissection Problem

27.4.5.1 The Issue

An annual payment is taxable under this head only if it is income. Where, therefore, a series of payments is made, the law must decide whether the payments are the income of the

---

[48] Eg, the judgments of the Court of Appeal in *IRC v National Book League* [1957] 2 All ER 644, 37 TC 455; and *Campbell v IRC* [1967] 2 All ER 625, 45 TC 427.
[49] *Ibid.*
[50] [1968] 3 All ER 588, 606, 45 TC 427, 474.
[51] [1957] 2 All ER 644, 37 TC 455.
[52] *Campbell v IRC* [1968] 3 All ER 588, 594, 45 TC 427, 462; and *IRC v National Book League* [1957] 2 All ER 644, 652, 37 TC 455, 475, per Morris LJ.
[53] *Taw and Torridge Festival Society Ltd v IRC* (1959) 38 TC 603, [1960] BTR 61.
[54] Eg [1970] AC 77, 108, [1968] 3 All ER 588, 603, 45 TC 427, 472, per Lord Upjohn.

recipient or merely a payment of capital by instalments: if the former, each payment is an annual payment; if the latter, each is capital and so not an annual payment. The answer may be that the payment is partly income and partly capital. However, in this instance the income element is not an annual payment but instead one of interest. The question for the court is the true legal nature of the transaction into which the parties have entered.[55] In answering this question, extrinsic evidence is admissible.[56] As Lord Hoffmann has observed, such distinctions allow taxpayers to structure their transactions so as to come within one concept or the other.[57]

27.4.5.2 The Test

The test is whether, as a matter of substance, the payments are instalments of the purchase price or pure income payments.[58] This is not regarded as destroying the principle laid down in *Duke of Westminster v IRC* (above §5.6.1), because the test does not involve putting upon a transaction between parties a character which in law it does not possess, but instead involves discovering what is the true character in law of the transaction entered into.[59]

27.4.5.3 Four Preliminary Points

Four matters are clear, although they tend to add to the confusion. First, the fact that a payment is made out of capital in no way affects the question whether the payment is income of the recipient. Therefore, annuity payments are taxable even though under the terms of the will or settlement giving rise to them the trustees are empowered to have recourse to capital in order to pay the sum, and the trustees exercise that power.[60] Secondly, the label which the parties choose to give to the payment is not conclusive; thus, an 'annuity' payment has been held to be capital.[61] Thirdly, the courts have stressed that the question in every case is one of the true legal nature of the transaction[62] and that every case is to be decided on its own facts. A particular fact may have been the dominating factor in a case, but that is not the same as a conclusive test.[63] Fourthly, the courts have stated that they cannot regard the conduct of the parties as conclusive, but that they may draw comfort from the fact that the decision of the court corresponds with that conduct.[64]

27.4.5.4 Four Principles

(1)   Where a definite sum of money is due and the payment of that sum in one lump would be a capital receipt of the payee, as where it is made in return for an asset, the

---

[55] *IRC v Church Commrs for England* [1976] STC 339, [1976] 2 All ER 1037. An agreement may contain two different types of payment, as in *IRC v British Salmson Aero Engines Ltd* [1938] 3 All ER 283, 22 TC 29.

[56] *IRC v Church Commrs for England* [1976] 2 All ER 1037, 1044, per Lord Wilberforce.

[57] *MacNiven v Westmoreland Investments Ltd* [2001] STC 237, para 60; the concepts of income and capital were business concepts.

[58] *Brodie's Will Trustees v IRC* (1933) 17 TC 432, 440.

[59] *Mallaby-Deeley v IRC* [1938] 4 All ER 818, 825, 23 TC 153, 167, per Sir Wilfrid Greene MR.

[60] See below at §29.3.4.

[61] *Secretary of State in Council of India v Scoble* [1903] AC 299, 4 TC 618.

[62] *IRC v Church Commrs for England* [1976] STC 339, [1976] 2 All ER 1037.

[63] *Dott v Brown* [1936] 1 All ER 543.

[64] *IRC v Hogarth* (1940) 23 TC 491, 500, per Lord Normand.

same quality attaches to the payment even though it is paid by instalments. Such payments will not be annual payments.[65]

This principle is best illustrated by a case on the sale of a business. In *Ramsay v IRC*,[66] T agreed to buy a dental practice. A primary price of £15,000 was agreed, but T agreed to pay it in the form of £5,000 immediately and subsequently to pay each year for 10 years a sum equal to 25% of the net profits of that year. These were described as capital payments and no interest was payable. It was held that the payments were not annual payments but capital instalments, so that the taxpayer could not deduct income tax when making each payment; this conclusion coincided with what the parties had actually done.

(2)   However, where a bargain was always considered to be in income terms, and was concluded in income terms, and there was nothing in the documents to give the transaction a capital character, the payments will be pure income. This is even more likely if the payments are expressed in terms strongly suggestive of income, such as a rent charge.

IRC v Church Commrs for England,[67] a charity sold a reversion on a lease to the tenant in consideration of rent charges, payable annually for 10 years and amounting in aggregate to £96,000 each year. It was clear that at no time was the purchaser willing to purchase for a single lump sum. The House of Lords held that these payments were pure income and could not be dissected into capital and interest payments.

(3)   Where despite principle (1) above, a series of payments is made in exchange for a right to income payments, the payments are likely to be pure income. This is the basis of the decision in *Chadwick v Pearl Life Insurance Co*.[68] The plaintiff (P) owned a lease which had 10 years to run. The total income from the sublease was £1,925 pa and the rent payable under the lease was £300, leaving a rental income of £1,625. P sold his interest to the defendant (D) for £1,000 and a covenant by D to pay £1,625 pa for 10 years. No sum was fixed as the total amount due on the sale, although that total sum could clearly have been ascertained (£17,250). Since the intention of the transaction was that P should continue to receive as income to the end of the term the same amount he had previously received as rent, Walton J concluded that the payments were income, although he observed that the distinction was a fine one.

(4)   If the payment is not pure income, it may be dissected into capital and interest where the parties, who are buying and selling a capital asset, having agreed on a price, then make provision for payment of that price by instalments, the amount of which is so calculated, and shown to be so calculated, as to include an interest element.[69] In *Secretary of State in Council of India v Scoble*,[70] the East India Company bought a railway from a company and was empowered to pay outright or in instalments over a period of 46 years; the instalments, although called an annuity, were dissected.

---

[65] There is very little to be gleaned from *Foley v Fletcher and Rose* (1853) 3 H and N 769, other than an inconclusive survey of a wide variety of solutions.

[66] (1935) 20 TC 79; see also *Mallaby-Deeley v IRC* [1938] 4 All ER 818, 23 TC 153. Compare *IRC v Hogarth* (1940) 23 TC 491.

[67] [1976] STC 339, [1976] 2 All ER 1037. This case may be taken as an *a fortiori* example of principle (3), since the calculation of the sum involved a wish to maintain an income equivalent to the rent for the remainder of the lease and to establish a fund which could then yield that sum in perpetuity.

[68] [1905] 2 KB 507.

[69] *IRC v Church Commrs for England* [1976] STC 339, 345, [1976] 2 All ER 1037, 1043, per Lord Wilberforce.

[70] [1903] AC 299, 4 TC 623.

Where no lump sum purchase price has been agreed, the question is decided after considering the transaction as a whole. This may explain the most extreme example of dissection: *Vestey v IRC*.[71] The taxpayer sold shares worth £2m for £5.5m, the sum to be paid in 125 yearly instalments of £44,000. The agreement stated that the price of £5.5m was to be without interest. The Revenue sought to charge the taxpayer surtax either on the whole payment as an annuity, or on a part of it as interest. Cross J upheld the second claim.

The enthusiasm with which Cross J preferred the second approach to the first is not to be found in the later decision of the House of Lords in *IRC v Church Commrs for England*.[72] The facts of that case fell on the other side of the line, principally because the transaction was thought of throughout in income tax terms (see principle (2)), and because there was no evidence that the parties had ever settled on a firm lump sum price. Lord Wilberforce accepted the *Vestey* decision as correct despite the fact that the only figure agreed on by the parties was the overall price of £5.5m.[73] Today it is likely that when the parties have agreed on a fixed sum, the sum will be dissected and will not be pure capital unless the period is short and the contract is in a common form. Dissection into interest and principal was directed in *Vestey* where the period was 125 years, but not in *Ramsay* where the period was 10 years and the contract was for the disposal of a business, the price being ascertained on a common and reasonable basis.

27.4.6 Doubtful Rule: Division of Profits

This unilluminating rule, which asserts that the payment must be a division of profits as opposed to spending profits, concentrates on the payer; assignments of income must be distinguished from a mere spending of profits.[74] This concentration on the payer seems out of place when the issue is whether certain payments are income of the payee, and gives a disproportionate effect to the system of deduction at source in the now repealed TA 1988, section 348.

27.5 Machinery: Deduction at Source

27.5.1 Individuals: The Deduction

The deduction under ITA 2007, section 900 is where P, an individual, makes a qualifying annual payment to T and the payment is a commercial annuity or an annual payment. Within section 899, P has a duty to deduct basic rate tax. Therefore, if P is due to pay T £1,000, P will deduct £200 and pay only £800. The tax is collected through P's self-assessment form, whether or not P is liable to the self-assessment process otherwise (section 900(3)). In effect, the band of income on which P is liable to tax at basic rate is extended. Failure to deduct does not relieve the payer of the obligation. For payment by

---

[71] [1961] 3 All ER 978, (1961) 40 TC 112; Phillips [1962] BTR 32.

[72] [1976] STC 339, 345, [1976] 2 All ER 1037, 1043, per Lord Wilberforce.

[73] Actuarial report made to the trustees referred to in the case stated in *Vestey v IRC* (1961) 40 TC 112, 115.

[74] *Jones v Wright* (1927) 13 TC 221, 226, per Rowlatt J; and see Lord Hanworth MR in *Westminster v IRC* (1935) 19 TC 490, 505.

individuals, the basic rate is prescribed by section 900. It is the rate in force for the year in which the payment is made.

27.5.2 Individuals: The Relief and Modified Net Income

Under ITA 2007, section 448(2), P is entitled to relief from income tax for a sum equal to the gross amount of the payment. It seems that the sum must actually have been deducted from the payment. It follows from this structure that the relief cannot be greater than the amount of P's liability to tax. If the sum due from P is £1,000 and P's taxable income against which he can set the payment is £600, he will obtain relief only on £600—at whatever rate is due on that income. However, it is also true that if there is enough 'modified net income' (MNI) then P is entitled to the relief—the old learning about whether relief could be given when the payment was actually made out of capital is swept away.[75] As Lord Wilberforce said in *IRC v Plummer*:[76]

> What is significant … is not the actual source out of which the money is paid, nor even the way in which the taxpayer for his own purposes keeps his accounts, if indeed he keeps any, but the status of a notional account between himself and the Revenue. He is entitled, in respect of any tax year, to set down on one side his taxed income and on the other the amount of the annual payments he has made and if the latter is equal to or less than the former, to claim the benefit of the section.

The rules also state that the total relief open to P must not exceed the amount of P's MNI. MNI is defined in sections 1025 and 1026 and contains two sets of rules. One directs that certain types of income cannot give rise to a deduction. These are called 'non-qualifying income' and are listed in section 1026—they are particularly unusual types of income, including (non-qualifying) dividends for which there is no tax credit under sections 399 and 400, and stock dividends (section 413). The other set consists of special rules which are to be ignored and mostly have to do with reliefs which make things apply for a different year, eg loss relief carried forward to a later year.

27.5.3 Payers Other Than Individuals

27.5.3.1 The Duty

Here the duty to deduct is imposed by ITA 2007, section 901 and the right to relief by sections 449 *et seq*. There is no requirement that the qualifying annual payment should be for P's commercial purposes. For obvious reasons a special restriction, imposing the commercial requirement, applies to a PR inheriting an annual payment obligation entered into by the deceased (section 901(2)). If the person has MNI, there is an obligation to deduct tax at the basic rate. If there is no MNI, the 'applicable rate' (AR) is used (section 902). The AR will be the basic rate, though the savings rate (currently the same) is used for an annuity payment under the purchase life annuity. Once again, the sum will be collected through the self-assessment process.

---

[75] Explanatory notes, change 82.
[76] [1979] STC 793, esp 799, per Lord Wilberforce. See also Lord Morris in *Chancery Lane Safe Deposit Co Ltd v IRC* [1966] 1 All ER 1, 12, 43 TC 83, 112. This is the ratio of the case (*Moodie v IRC* [1990] STC 475, 496, per Hoffmann J; see also [1991] STC 433, CA).

27.5.3.2 The Relief

Under section 449(2), P is entitled to relief from income tax for a sum equal to the gross amount of the payment (defined in section 452); the relief is given at step 2 of the calculation in section 23 (see §12.2.2 above). Once more it seems that the sum must actually have been deducted from the payment and it is the rate in force at that time which applies. Further, the relief cannot be greater than the amount of P's liability to tax. These rules too state that the total relief open to P must not exceed the amount of P's MNI. MNI is defined in sections 1025 and 1026.

27.5.4 Ineligible Payments Old Case Law Preserved

It is not true that if there is enough MNI then P will necessarily be entitled to the relief. The old learning about whether relief could be given when the payment was actually made out of capital is preserved by the concept of the payment 'ineligible for relief' set out in section 450.

Four rules must be borne in mind:

(1) A payment is ineligible for relief if, or so far as, it can lawfully be made only out of capital or income that is exempt from income tax.
(2) A payment is ineligible for relief if the payment or any part of it is charged to capital. This is derived from the famous (or notorious) decision in *Chancery Lane Safe Deposit Co Ltd v IRC*.[77] Here the House of Lords barred the deduction where a particular payment had been charged to capital, not as a matter of mere domestic accounting but as the result of a deliberate decision, even though the company had ample funds out of which to meet both the interest payments and dividends. The practical effect of creating a fund out of which larger or later dividends could be paid was sufficient to exclude the right. However, some may feel that there is much to be said for the dissenting views trenchantly expressed by Lord Reid and Lord Upjohn in *Chancery Lane*. First, there was no previous authority compelling the House to that conclusion. One early case had been found to be similar on the facts but, as Lord Upjohn memorably observed: 'We are not bound to follow a case merely because it is indistinguishable upon the facts. A decision even in your Lordships' House is binding on your Lordships only because it lays down some principle of law or for reasoning on some particular facts.'[78] Secondly, it would not be easy to distinguish mere domestic accounting from a deliberate decision. Thirdly, in this case the decision led to effective double taxation.[79]
(3) A payment is ineligible for relief if the person who makes the payment treats it or any part of it as made out of income that is exempt from income tax, and the rights or obligations of any person are or may in the future be different from what they would

---

[77] [1966] 1 All ER 1, 43 TC 83. The decision was reaffirmed in *Fitzleet Estates Ltd v Cherry* [1977] STC 397, [1977] 3 All ER 996, 51 TC 708, HL, showing that if the (now) Supreme Court is to be persuaded that it has made a mistake, it is best to show that the erroneous case is not recent.
[78] [1966] 1 All ER 1, 128; 43 TC 83, 122.
[79] The company paid tax on its profits but could not recoup that tax by withholding under s 348.

have been if the payment or part had not been so treated. *Birmingham Corpn v IRC*[80] provides an example. Here the taxpayer's decision to charge the payment to capital had the practical effect that it entitled the taxpayer to a larger subsidy.

(4)   Relief is denied if the payment or a part of it is not ultimately borne by the person who makes it. However, there is an exception: rule (4) does not apply if the person making the payment is liable to income tax on an amount, and it is because the person receives that amount or benefits from it in some other way that the payment or the part concerned is not ultimately borne by that person.

27.5.5   *Miscellaneous Points*

(1)   Tax deducted—T's immunity from basic rate liability. Under ITTOIA 2005,[81] tax deducted under Part 15, Chapter 6 and ITA 2007, section 848 is treated as paid by the recipient. T, the payee, is safe from direct assessment, whether or not P, the payer, accounts for the tax to the Revenue.

(2)   There are still issues about the effects of a failure to deduct. Under the old law P had a direct interest in deducting if he had a right to do so, since he was allowed to keep the payment for himself—and so was punished for failing to deduct by being out of pocket. It followed that in general no action would lie against the overpaid T for recovery of the sum, and P had no right to withhold later payments to secure reimbursement.[82] This rule was subject to a number of exceptions.[83] Today the effect of a failure to deduct is simply that one has failed to deduct. T is unable to claim the benefit of the deduction as none has been made.

If P fails to deduct tax and so pays more than necessary, he may be able to recover the overpayment from T in restitution, whether the mistake is one of fact or law (see above §4.4.5.4).

27.6   'Free of Tax'

27.6.1   *Effect of Agreements*

TMA 1970, section 106(2) provides that any agreement for the payment of interest, rent or other annual payment in full, without allowing the deduction of income tax, is void; in other words, the part relating to non-deduction is of no effect.[84] If P agrees to pay T £100 a year without deduction, P is nonetheless entitled to deduct tax under section 348, or bound

---

[80] [1930] AC 307, 15 TC 172; see also *BW Nobes and Co Ltd v IRC* [1964] 2 All ER 140, 43 TC 133.
[81] ITTOIA 2005, s 686; ITTOIA 2005 repeals s 348(1)(d) and also puts the previous case law into statutory form (eg *Stokes v Bennett* [1953] 2 All ER 313, 34 TC 337.
[82] *Re Hatch* [1919] 1 Ch 351.
[83] Tiley, *Revenue Law*, 3rd edn (Butterworths, 1991), §13.63.
[84] *Booth v Booth* [1922] 1 KB 66.

to do so under section 349. Section 106(2) applies only to agreements,[85] and not to wills or orders of the court.[86] In appropriate cases the court will rectify an agreement to avoid section 106(2).[87]

Where there is an agreement that P shall pay T £100 'free of tax', the House of Lords held in *Ferguson v IRC*,[88] overriding a long line of authority, that such agreement does not fall foul of section 106(2), by construing the agreement to mean that P must pay T such sum as, after deduction of income tax, leaves £100. On the facts, T's relevant marginal rate was basic rate; it is unclear what would happen if T's marginal rate were 40% or 0%.

27.6.2 The Rule in Re Pettit

Where P is to pay T £100 'free of tax', P will make a payment of £100; if T's marginal rate is 20%, this is equivalent to £125 gross and T's income is therefore taken to include not £100 but £125. If T has no other income, he may reclaim £25 from the Revenue on account of his personal reliefs. If T were allowed to keep the sum, he would benefit by £125, and not £100 as undertaken by P. T is therefore directed by the rule in *Re Pettit*[89] to hold the sum recovered from the Revenue on trust for P—and T is under an obligation to make the repayment claim.[90] If T has other income, the value of the personal reliefs must be shared between the annuity and the other income; the rule in *Re Pettit* will apply to that proportion of the reliefs which the gross amount of the annuity bears to T's total income. It should be noted that in every reported case T has been entitled to a repayment of tax. However, the principle should apply wherever T is entitled to set a relief from tax against annuity income in whole or in part—and not simply when a repayment claim is made to the Revenue. T is obliged to account for relief from tax not only in respect of personal allowances but also for loss relief claimed under ITA 2007, Part 4, Chapter 2.[91] The obligation to account causes problems in adjusting the total income of P and T. Revenue practice is to treat P as entitled to additional income equivalent to the grossed-up sum repaid.

In practice there is a clear distinction between £100 'free of tax', to which the rule in *Re Pettit* applies, and 'such sum as after deducting tax at the current rate shall leave £100'— known as a formula deduction covenant—to which the rule does not apply; the former indicates the extent to which T is to benefit, while the latter does not. Where the annuity is 'free of tax', the annuitant is assured of a constant net sum and the payer of a constantly

---

[85] *Re Goodson's Settlement, Goodson v Goodson* [1943] Ch 101, [1943] 1 All ER 201.

[86] An agreement to carry out an order of the court is subject to s 106(2) (*Blount v Blount* [1916] 1 KB 230).

[87] *Burroughes v Abbott* [1922] 1 Ch 86; distinguished in *Whiteside v Whiteside* [1950] Ch 65, [1949] 2 All ER 913.

[88] [1969] 1 All ER 1025, 46 TC 15.

[89] [1922] 2 Ch 765.

[90] *Re Kingcome, Hickley v Kingcome* [1936] Ch 566, [1936] 1 All ER 173. On the position of non-residents, see *Re Jubb, Neilson* (1941) 20 ATC 297. In *Re Batty, Public Trustee v Bell* [1952] Ch 280, [1952] All ER 425. Vaisey J held that a wife could be made to elect for separate assessment so as to be compelled to make the repayment claim. On appeal it was held that the rule in *Re Pettit* did not apply, so this issue was not discussed. However, if the husband holds any repayment on trust for the wife (*Re Cameron, Kingsley v IRC* [1965] 3 All ER 474, 42 TC 539), it ought to follow that the payer can compel the wife to compel the husband to make the claim. See also *Re Tatham, National Bank Ltd and Mathews v Mackenzie* [1945] Ch 34, [1945] 1 All ER 29.

[91] Ex TA 1988, s 380; see *Re Lyons, Barclays Bank Ltd v Jones* [1952] Ch 129, [1952] 1 All ER 34. Although T is under a duty to make the claim for a repayment when it is due, it did not appear that T is obliged to claim relief under s 380 rather than under s 385.

fluctuating liability; where the deduction formula applies, the payer is assured of a constant net outflow and the payee of constantly fluctuating net receipts. In addition, where the annuity is 'free of tax', the liability of the payer will vary according to the financial position of the payee; where the deduction formula is used, the benefit to the payee varies with his financial position. The rule in *Re Pettit* does not apply to a deduction formula covenant. The rule in *Re Pettit* applies to agreements, estates and trusts. However, its status in Scotland is unclear. Illogically, the rule does not apply to court orders,[92] with the result that the same words will have one effect in an agreement and a different effect in an order.

27.6.3 *Construction of Court Orders*

Since TMA 1970, section 106(2) does not apply to court orders, the courts have long felt able to construe an order to pay £x 'free of tax' as an order to pay such sum as, after deduction of income tax at the basic rate, leaves £x.[93] If the order is to pay '£x less tax', it is construed as an order to deduct basic rate tax on £x under the relevant provisions and to pay the balance. The words 'less tax' are taken simply to show that tax must be deducted by the payer from the amount specified.

[92] *Jefferson v Jefferson* [1956] 1 All ER 31, [1956] P 136.
[93] *Spilsbury v Spofforth* [1937] 4 All ER 487, 21 TC 247.

28

Income Not Otherwise Charged

28.1 Introduction

ITTOIA 2005, Part 5, Chapter 8 is entitled 'Income not otherwise charged' and is part of the modern form of Schedule D, Case VI for income tax purposes. By the time the Rewrite began, Schedule D, Case VI had two functions. The first—now in Part 5, Chapter 8—was as the residual head of charge, catching income which was properly subject to income tax but not otherwise caught. The second, less intellectually glamorous, was to act as a receptacle into which Parliament placed the various receipts it wished to add to the tax system but which did not belong easily elsewhere. Examples of this second use are now to be found not only elsewhere in Part 5 but also in other parts of the legislation and now the ITA 2007.

ITTOIA 2005, section 687 charges income tax on income from any source that is not charged to income tax under any other provision of ITTOIA 2005 or any other Act. The wording of section 687 suggests that it will not be necessary to refer to section 575 on priority between Part 5 and other pieces of legislation.[1] Previously, income tax was charged under Schedule D, Case VI on any annual profits or gains not falling under any other Case of Schedule D and not charged by virtue of Schedules A, E and F. It was thus the residual Case in the residual Schedule. Section 687 rejects 'annual profits' in favour of 'income' and articulates in legislative form the need for a source, which had been developed by case law. No change in the scope of the charge is intended.[2]

The established case law suggested four principles: (a) the profit must be annual; (b) it must be of an income nature; (c) it must not be gratuitous; and (d) it must be analogous to some other head of Schedule D. The removal of (a) is justified in that the term had

---

[1] However, the opening chapter of Pt 5 is needed when considering the territorial scope of Ch 8: see ITTOIA 2005, ss 574(4) and 577, and Explanatory Notes to Bill, paras 801–16.

[2] Explanatory Notes to Bill, para 1196.

come to add nothing; however, it was part of the old wording and so part of the argument in the cases. In relation to (a), it was held that 'annual' did not mean recurrent.[3] Casual profits might therefore be caught—but only if of an income, as opposed to a capital, nature.[4] As Rowlatt J observed: 'Annual can only mean calculated in any one year and … "annual profits or gains" means "profits or gains in any year as the succession of years comes round."'[5]

A profit derived from the sale of an asset will either be income from an adventure in the nature of trade, and so taxable under ITTOIA 2005, Part 2, or be of a capital nature, and so outside both Part 2 and the present rule.[6] The receipt must have a source and be distinct from that source. Hence, a mere gift, the finding of a thing or mere gambling winnings (see below at §28.2) do not fall to be taxed as income under section 687[7] any more than does a capital gain. On the other hand, a receipt in return for services rendered will be caught by section 687 if not by some other head. In such circumstances, the effort made in rendering the service is regarded as the source.

28.2 Gambling and Distinguishable Transactions

28.2.1 Punter and Bookmaker

Profits arising from gambling transactions do not fall within Part 5, Chapter 8;[8] such transactions are merely irrational agreements. The events which entitle gamblers to their winnings do not, of themselves, produce the profit; there is no increment and no service, only an acquisition.[9] This must be distinguished from an organised seeking of profits, which may create a trade and so give rise to profits or gains. Even where, as in *Graham v Green*, gambling is the taxpayer's sole means of livelihood, it is neither a trade nor a profession, and so any winnings escape tax under ITTOIA 2005, Part 2[10] as well as under Part 5, Chapter 8. However, this does not prevent courts from holding that a bookmaker is carrying on a vocation and is therefore taxable under ITTOIA 2005, Part 2, the distinction being that a bookmaker has an organisation.[11]

---

[3] *Jones v Leeming* [1930] AC 415, 422, (1930) 15 TC 333, 359, per Viscount Dunedin; see also Rowlatt J in *Townsend v Grundy* (1933) 18 TC 140, 148.

[4] *Jones v Leeming* [1930] AC 415, (1930) STC 333; for a complex example, see *Black Nominees Ltd v Nicol* [1975] STC 372.

[5] In *Ryall v Hoare* [1923] 2 KB 447, 455; see also 'the plant is not annual—it is the sowing that is annual' (*ibid* at 454). The word 'annual' did not therefore add very much by way of definition, which was not surprising since all the other Cases of Sch D also taxed annual profits or gains, and Case VI was analogous to them. See also Lord Inglis in *Scottish Provident Institution v Farmer* (1912) 6 TC 34, 38: 'There is nothing said in the Act about a gain being necessarily within the year of assessment.'

[6] *Jones v Leeming* [1930] AC 415, (1930) 15 TC 333.

[7] See *Graham v Green* [1925] 2 KB 37, 39 and 9 TC 309, 312, per Rowlatt J.

[8] Ibid.

[9] See *Graham v Green, ibid*, 139, 312, per Rowlatt J, who draws a parallel with finding and gift.

[10] The Revenue argued in favour of liability under Sch D, Case II in *Graham v Green, ibid*.

[11] *Partridge v Mallandaine* (1886) 18 QBD 276; and *Graham v Green* [1925] 2 KB 37, 42, (1925) 7 TC 309, 314.

28.2.2 Gambling Incidental to Other Activities

Mere gambling winnings are distinct from winnings incidental to a taxable activity. Thus, in *Norman v Evans*,[12] the taxpayer leased horses bred at his stud to other persons to be raced by them, and received half of all of the horses' winnings. The sums paid were held to be taxable under Schedule D, Case VI as being sums due under the lease. However, where a bet is made on professional skill, it is still only a bet and therefore not taxable. In *Down v Compston*,[13] a golf professional, taxable under what is now ITEPA 2003, was held not taxable in respect of money won on bets with other persons with whom he played golf. This decision should be contrasted with certain Commonwealth cases where gains from betting associated with other taxable horse racing activity have been subjected to income tax as part of that other activity—by a horse owner,[14] horse trainer,[15] registered bookmaker[16] and even by a horse owner who leased racehorses from his stud farm.[17] The question must be one of fact. *Down v Compston* (above) was distinguished in *Burdge v Pyne*[18] when the proprietor of a gambling club was held taxable on the profits of his own gambling at the club as trading income.

28.2.3 Futures, etc

Also to be distinguished from mere gambling is speculation. A person who, for example, buys rights on the stock exchange for cotton futures[19] in the hope of an increase in capital value, is a speculator and not a gambler. The distinction is that the contract to buy or sell the cotton is a very real one from the point of view of the vendor and gives rise to very real contractual rights, whereas in a gambling transaction both parties regard the matter as a mere wager. The profits of speculation in commodity futures will be taxable as trading income if there is a sufficient substratum of activity to give rise to the finding that there is a trade.[20]

28.2.4 Services

Also to be distinguished from mere gambling are payments for the provision of services. So a professional tipster is taxed under ITTOIA 2005, Part 2.[21] However, an occasional tipster may fall into the present rule since the definition of a vocation contains no concept analogous to an adventure in the nature of trade (see below §28.4).

---

[12] [1965] 1 All ER 372, (1965) 42 TC 188, per Buckley J.
[13] [1937] 2 All ER 475, (1937) 21 TC 60, per Lawrence J.
[14] *Knight v Taxation Commr* (1928) 28 SR NSW 523.
[15] *Holt v Federal Taxation Commr* (1929) 3 ALJ 68.
[16] *Vandenberg v Taxation Commr New South Wales* (1933) 2 ATD 343.
[17] *Trautwein v Federal Taxation Commr* (1936) 56 CLR 196.
[18] [1969] 1 All ER, (1969) 45 TC 320.
[19] *Cooper v Stubbs* [1925] 2 KB 753, (1925) 10 TC 29; followed in *Townsend v Grundy* (1933) 18 TC 140.
[20] See Pollock MR in *Cooper v Stubbs* [1925] 2 KB 753, 765, (1925) 10 RC 29, 48.
[21] *Graham v Arnott* (1941) 24 TC 157.

28.3   Profits Analogous to Trading Profits

Given the width of the judicial definition of 'trade' and the statutory notion of an adventure in the nature of trade, it might appear that there is little scope for Part 5, Chapter 8. Indeed, as already seen,[22] it is clear that in relation to an isolated transaction where a profit arises on resale of an object, there is no scope for section 687. Where, however, there are regular as opposed to isolated transactions,[23] there is some authority for a charge. Case law shows that profits from stud fees for serving mares of other owners were taxed under Case VI rather than under Case I,[24] provided the matter was simply incidental to the business. The legislative decision to charge farmers as traders rather than under Schedule B removed most, but not all, of the tax advantages derived by the taxpayer from not being charged under Case VI. It seems likely, in the light of the cases on income derived from property and services, that even very occasional fees will be taxable.

Liability under ITTOIA 2005, Part 2 differs from that under section 687 in a number of respects:

(1)   Generally, liability under Part 2 is on a business year basis, with the problems of the profits of any overlap period, while liability under section 687 is simply on a current year basis.[25]

(2)   Capital allowances may be available under Part 2 but not under section 687.

(3)   Income under Part 2 may be earned and so be relevant earnings for pension provision; not all income under section 687 will be so treated.[26]

(4)   Losses suffered under Part 2 may be set off against general income of that and the next year, but only against later profits of the same trade; losses under section 687 may be set off only against other section 687 income, but may be rolled forward against all such income of later years.[27]

(5)   Profits under Part 2 are computed on an approved accounting basis; those under section 687 are computed on a receipts basis.[28]

(6)   The income of a charity under Part 2 is exempt from tax if certain conditions are met; there is no exemption for the income of a charity under section 687.[29]

(7)   While income from investments is exempt in the hands of the trustee of a pension fund, there is also an express exemption for income from underwriting commissions taxable under what was Case VI now section 687; the exemption does not extend to trading income.[30]

---

[22] *Jones v Leeming* [1930] AC 415, 420, (1930) 15 TC 333, 357, per Lord Buckmaster.

[23] *Earl of Derby v Bassom* (1926) 10 TC 357, 371, per Rowlatt J.

[24] At that time farming was taxed under Sch B and not, as now, Sch D, Case I (TA 1988, s 53(1)). Assessments in stud fees under Case VI were upheld in *Malcolm v Lockhart* [1919] AC 463, (1919) 7 TC 99.

[25] ITTOIA 2005, ss 198 and 688, ex TA 1988, ss 60, 69.

[26] See FA 2004, s 189(2), ex TA 1988, s 833(4)(c); and see above at §7.8.1. In *Hale v Shea* [1965] 1 All ER 155, (1965) 42 TC 260, Buckley J appears to have thought that the question of whether income was earned was independent of the question of whether liability arose under Case VI.

[27] TA 1988, ss 380, 383, 392; so s 392 was rewritten by ITTOIA 2005.

[28] ITTOIA 2005, ss 25 and 688. *Pearn v Miller* (1927) 11 TC 610, 614; *Grey v Tiley* (1932) 16 TC 414.

[29] ITA 2007, s 524 and CTA 2010, s 478, ex TA 1988, s 505. However, another provison may provide an exemption for charities.

[30] FA 2004, s 186(1), ex, s 592(3); considered in *Clarke v British Telecom Pension Fund Trustee Ltd* [2000] STC 222 CA.

The differences may be illustrated by the plight of owners of stately homes who open their homes to visitors. If this is done on a commercial basis, liability arises under Part 2; if it is not, liability arises under section 687. Under section 687, the only costs allowable will be those involved in showing the house, such as wages of guides, additional cleaning, advertising and the purchase of souvenirs. If, however, the matter comes within Part 2, also deductible are the costs of upkeep of the building and its gardens, wages of caretakers and gardeners, heating, lighting and insurance. Allowances may also be claimed for expenditure on car parks, plumbing, refreshment rooms and access roads.

28.4   Activities Analogous to a Profession or Vocation

The definition of a profession or vocation does not include a concept equivalent to an adventure in the nature of trade. Therefore, a taxpayer receiving profits in return for services which are not sufficiently regular to amount to a vocation will not be taxed under Part 2 but only under section 687. Again, however, the case law shows that care must be taken to distinguish income in return for services from capital receipts for the disposal of property.

28.4.1 Casual Authorship

In *Hobbs v Hussey*,[31] T, a solicitor's clerk, who had not previously carried on the profession of author, agreed to write his memoirs and assign the copyright in return for payment. T was held taxable on the proceeds under Case VI (now section 687). In *Earl Haig's Trustees v IRC*,[32] however, trustees who held the copyright in certain diaries and who allowed an author to use the materials in those diaries 'so far as the public interest permitted' in return for a half share in the profits of the book, were held not taxable. The Court of Session held that the sums were capital payments in return for the partial realisation of assets and so escaped income tax, and not, as the Special Commissioner had held, remuneration for the use of and access to the diaries by the author (and so taxable under Case VI as being income derived from property).

The question is whether the transaction is really a sale of property, or whether it amounts to the performance of services. A transaction may be one for the performance of services even though it involves some subsidiary sale of property, eg dentures supplied by a dentist. Therefore, in *Hobbs v Hussey*, the payments were held to be income even though, as part of the contract, the taxpayer transferred his copyright in the articles.[33] In *Alloway v Phillips*,[34] where memoirs were ghosted, the fact that the author promised not to write for any other publisher was not sufficient to fall outside Case VI since this restriction was simply an adjunct of the main contract.

---

[31] [1942] 1 All ER 445, (1942) 24 TC 153.
[32] [1939] SC 656, (1939) 22 TC 725.
[33] See Lawrence J in *Hobbs v Hussey* [1942] 1 All ER 445, 446, (1942) 24 TC 153, 156. For the converse case where the court disregarded a trifling service, see *Bradbury v Arnold* (1957) 37 TC 665; and the *Earl Haig* case (1939) 22 TC 725.
[34] [1980] STC 490, [1980] 3 All ER 138, (1980) 53 TC 372 (see below at §28.6).

It has not been easy for taxpayers to place themselves on the *Haig* side of the line, which is of course inherently vague. Thus, in *Housden v Marshall*,[35] where a jockey agreed to make available to a reporter his reminiscences and supporting documents together with the right to use a facsimile of his signature, payments to the jockey were held taxable. The situation is complicated by two further factors. First, the test of what is income as opposed to capital seems to be different under this rule from that applying under Part 2, where sums received for the sale of copyright have been held to be income receipts.[36] Secondly, the Solicitor-General commented in *Hobbs v Hussey* that he was not to be taken as admitting that the *Haig* case was rightly decided.[37] However, it would appear to follow from the present authorities that had Hobbs and Marshall written their reminiscences first and then allowed them to be published, sums received in return for the sale would have escaped tax under section 687 but would, in such circumstances, now be liable to CGT. What was fatal to their case was that under the contract they agreed to perform services, in the one case to write memoirs and in the other to supply information. Thus, where there has been a discontinuance of a profession so that Part 2 is inapplicable, a subsequent sale will not be caught by section 687 if there have been no activities analogous to a profession after discontinuance.[38]

28.4.2 Introduction Fees

A person who introduces a potential purchaser to a vendor may expect some appreciation in pecuniary form. An introducer having a right to sue for these sums is taxable under section 687.[39] In the absence of such a right there is no such liability;[40] such sums escape tax just like any other gifts, the law not concerning itself with the motive of a donor. An introducer content to rely on faith rather than law will escape tax. This principle was extended in *Scott v Ricketts*,[41] where an estate agent was paid £39,000 in consideration of withdrawing any claim he might have to participate in a development scheme. The Court of Appeal held that although the payment was made under a contract, there was no liability under this head: (a) because the original scheme was not a legally enforceable agreement; and (b) because the payment was made in settlement of a moral claim or for the sale of an asset, and neither gave rise to a profit under this head. It is highly questionable whether the sum was paid under a contract since a moral claim does not amount to good consideration.

28.4.3 Miscellaneous

Commission payments received by a director for guaranteeing the company's bank overdraft were taxable under this head because they were received by virtue of services which

---

[35] *Howson v Monsell* [1950] 2 All ER 1239, (1950) 31 TC.

[36] *Ibid*, (SchD, Case II). *Cf Beare v Carter* [1940] 2 KB 187, (1940) 23 TC 353 (Sch D, Case VI).

[37] [1942] 1 KB 491, 495, (1942) 24 TC 153, 155.

[38] *Withers v Nethersole* (1948) 28 TC 501, HL. See also *Beare v Carter* [1940] 2 KB 187, (1940) 23 TC 353, where the advance to an author for a new edition of a work published many years previously was held to be a capital sum which was not assessable.

[39] *Brocklesby v Merricks* (1934) 18 TC 576. The possibility of a charge as income of a profession was reserved by the Crown. See also *Bloom v Kinder* (1958) 38 TC 77.

[40] *Dickinson v Abel* [1969] 1 All ER 484, (1969) 45 TC 353.

[41] [1967] 2 All ER 1009, (1967) 44 TC 303.

had been rendered.[42] The same result followed when a solicitor guaranteed an overdraft of a third party, since the commission was earned by the pledging of credit.[43] In each case there was a contractual right to the payment. Whether such sums should be taxed under Part 2 as a receipt of a profession or under this head is one of fact. Such receipts are held taxable and are not treated as capital payments, because the source from which the income flows is not the service but the individual's efforts, and those efforts are capable of recurring.[44] There was some doubt whether a prostitute was taxable under Part 2, or this head or not at all. It appears that where the Revenue are aware of the source of income, a charge has been made under this head. However, a charge as trading income under Part 2 has now been upheld.[45]

28.5   Analogy of Income from Property

Schedule D, in addition to taxing the annual profits of a trade, profession or vocation, also taxed 'the annual profits or gains arising or accruing from any type of property whatsoever'.[46] Although the cases under Schedule D, Case VI were not always decided expressly on this analogy, it would appear that many of them may be so rationalised and, indeed, that much of the talk of a 'source', now part of ITTOIA 2005 itself, is an implicit recognition of the analogy. Thus, stud fees received for the services of a stallion[47] could be caught using this analogy. However, where sums derived from the sale of a right to nominate a particular dam for whom the stallion should stand were taxed, the analogy of the sale of property was specifically rejected.[48] Again, sums received for the use, as distinct from the disposal, of information,[49] for the display of property such as Earl Haig's diaries,[50] for the pledging of credit[51] or for the leasing of a horse[52] could all fall intelligibly within this analogy, which has the further advantage of focusing attention on the sums earned by the property, which would be income, as distinct from the sums received on the disposal of the property, which would be capital.

Where the property is land, income received is usually taxable under ITTOIA 2005, Part 3 (ex Schedule A), especially following changes made to Schedule A in the mid-1990s. Previously, income outside Schedule A and so caught by Schedule D, Case VI included sums received for car parking, or visitors' green fees at a golf club.[53] Income derived from the

---

[42]   *Ryall v Hoare* [1923] 2 KB 447, (1923) 8 TC 521.
[43]   *Sherwin v Barnes* (1931) 16 TC 278; but *cf Trenchard v Bennet* (1933) 17 TC 420, where in reality shares received were not for the guarantee but in order to gain control of a company—a capital asset—and so were not taxable.
[44]   *Whyte v Clancy* [1936] 2 All ER 735, (1936) 20 TC 679.
[45]   *IRC v Aken* [1990] 1 WLR 1374, [1990] STC 497, (1990) 63 TC 395, CA.
[46]   Ex TA 1988, s 18.
[47]   As in *Earl of Derby v Bassom* (1926) 10 TC 357.
[48]   *Benson v Counsell* [1942] 1 All ER 435, (1942) 24 TC 178.
[49]   As in *Housden v Marshall* [1958] 3 All ER 639, (1958) 38 TC 233.
[50]   See Lord Normand in *Earl Haig's Trustees v IRC* [1939] SC 676, 682, (1939) 22 TC 725, 732.
[51]   Eg, *Wilson v Mannooch* [1937] 3 All ER 120, (1937) 21 TC 178.
[52]   Eg, *Norman v Evans* [1965] 1 All ER 372, TC 188, 42.
[53]   *Coman v Rotunda Hospital (Governor) Dublin* [1921] 1 AC 1, esp 12–14, (1921) 7 TC 517, 559, 560. See also *Forth Conservancy Board v IRC* [1931] AC 540, (1931) 16 TC 103.

furnished letting of a house,[54] being in return for the use of the furniture as well as for the use of the land, previously fell within Schedule D, Case VI but is now all within Part 3.[55]

Income derived from commodity and financial futures and traded options were removed from the scope of this rule to CGT by FA 1985.[56] This change does not affect income arising from dealing in assets in such a way as to give rise to liability as trading income under Part 2.

28.6   Foreign Questions

In accordance with the general principles of the tax system, but now made expressly so by statute, gains accruing to non-residents which would be taxable under section 687 are taxable where the source of income is in the UK.[57] In *Alloway v Phillips*,[58] a person resident in Canada who agreed to provide information in Canada about her life as the wife of one of the Great Train Robbers, was held taxable under this head because the contract was made, enforceable and provided for payment in England, by a company resident in England. On this basis a different result would have been reached if the contract had been with the company's Canadian subsidiary.

Where the source of income is outside the UK but the income arises in favour of a UK resident, the better view was that the charge arose under Case V rather than under Case VI.[59] Any other conclusion would have removed the remittance basis from any income under this head, while leaving it intact for income within other Cases. ITTOIA 2005, Part 8 solves the problem the other way round by making the remittance basis—and other relevant foreign income rules—available to qualifying foreign income within Part 5, Chapter 8 (section 830(2)(o)).

28.7   Computation

Tax is chargeable under section 687 in respect of income, and not simply on receipts. Sums spent in earning the income may therefore be deducted in computing the taxable profits or losses.[60] Tax is charged on a current year basis.[61] Repeating the old language, the

---

[54] Furnished letting is not usually a trade: see *Gittos v Barclay* [1982] STC 390; on the boundary between trade and property in the Canadian context, see Durnford (1991) 39 *Can Tax Jo* 1131.

[55] ITTOIA 2005, s 308, ex TA 1988, s 15(4). ITTOIA 2005, s 309 makes a cross-reference to 'rent a room' relief in Pt 7, Ch 1 (see §25.4).

[56] ITTOIA 2005, s 779, ex TA 1988, s 128.

[57] As in *Curtis-Brown Ltd v Jarvis* (1929) 14 TC 744.

[58] [1980] STC 490, [1980] 3 All ER 138, (1980) 53 TC 372.

[59] *Colquhoun v Brooks* (1889) 14 App Cas 493, (1889) 2 TC 490 (HL), and note *Lilley v Harrison* (1952) 33 TC 344, CA. See also ITTOIA Explanatory Notes, para 1190.

[60] See *Curtis Brown Ltd v Jarvis* (1929) 14 TC 744. See also Explanatory Notes, para 3262 and ITTOIA 2005, Sch 2, Pt 12 preserving old rules despite addition of deductions in other parts of Ch 5. On foreign income, see Pt 8, Ch 3.

[61] ITTOIA 2005, s 688(1), ex TA 1988, s 69. Before 1996–97 an inspector could direct that another period be taken.

charge is on the person receiving or entitled to the income.[62] Any loss under a transaction[63] falling within Part 5, Chapter 8 (now called 'miscellaneous transactions') may be set off against income from any other miscellaneous transaction within that year or any later year,[64] subject, however, to express statutory direction. Such losses may not be set off against income under any another type of income of the same year. Income is chargeable on the full amount of income arising in the tax year. This probably means when it is received. This emerges from the unsatisfactory case of *Grey v Tiley*,[65] where counsel for the Crown conceded, probably contrary to the wishes of the inspector involved, that the taxpayer could not be taxed in respect of the year when the money became due to him.

---

[62] ITTOIA 2005, s 689, ex TA 1988, s 59(1).

[63] On meaning of transaction, see *Barron v Littman* [1951] 2 All ER 393, (1951) 33 TC 373.

[64] ITA 2007, Pt 4, Ch 7, ex TA 1988, s 392.

[65] (1932) 16 TC 414, where the court felt bound by *Leigh v IRC* [1928] 1 KB 73, (1928) 11 TC 590 (decided in relation to foreign income within the old Case IV).

29

Trusts

29.1   General Scheme

UK rules on the taxation of trusts are a mixture of judge-made law and statutes. The judge-made rules are sensible efforts to adapt the tax system to the trust;[1] the statutory additions are concerned generally to prevent taxpayers taking advantage of the trust regime through discretionary trusts. These rules were largely rewritten in ITA 2007. In this chapter, references to statutory provisions are to ITA 2007 unless otherwise noted.

The problem of the relationship between the taxation of trustees and the taxation of beneficiaries resembles that of companies. One can devise various models. What we shall call Model 1 would levy no tax at trustee level but simply allow income to flow through to the beneficiary; this could be supplemented by a rule collecting provisional tax at trustee level on behalf of the beneficiary (Model 1A). Model 2, the opposite of Model 1, would treat the trustees as the sole legitimate object of taxation and not tax the beneficiary at all. Models 3 and 4 would mitigate the severity of Model 2. Model 3 would tax the trustees first, but then allow the beneficiary a credit for the tax paid at trustee level. Model 4 would tax the trustees but would first allow them to deduct those parts of income passed on to the beneficiary; the beneficiary would then be taxed on what was received. If the income tax were a flat rate tax with no personal deductions, it might not make much difference which model was adopted. Given the existence of a progressive tax, however, choices must be made.

The UK system makes a sharp distinction between different types of trust, and does so by using no fewer than three of the models just outlined. It uses Model 3 for many type of trusts; here the basic rate of income tax will normally apply to the trust income. It uses

---

[1] This chapter deals with express trusts. On constructive trusts and the tax system, see Glover in Oakley (ed), *Trends in Contemporary Trust Law* (OUP, 1996) 315–31; and Brown and Rajan (1997) 45 *Can Tax Jo* 659.

Model 4 for certain trusts where discretionary or accumulated income arises; here the rate of income tax is not the basic rate but what section 9 refers to as 'the trust rate'. This is currently 45% (38.1% for dividends). It is unfortunate that ITA 2007 uses the term 'the trust rate' since the wording suggests that it applies universally; it does not apply universally, but principally to those trusts set out in ITA 2007, Part 9, Chapter 3. The UK system also uses Model 1 for trusts for vulnerable persons (§29.3.5).

The need for separate rules for discretionary trusts was to prevent a trust being used as a device in which income is taxed at rates below the individual top rate and then accumulated; this point was all the more relevant in the days (as late as 1978–79) when the top rate of income tax for individuals was 98%. The trust rate became 40% in 2004 and 50% in 2010 and is now aligned with the additional rate of tax of 45%. In recognition of the fact that these rates were perhaps fiscal overkill, the trust rate does not apply to the first tranche of such income; initially £500, the first tranche is now £1,000 and this is taxed at the basic rate. In the UK, where trustees act on behalf of an incapacitated person, they are treated as the agents of the beneficiary and tax is assessed on the trustees on behalf of (and by reference to the circumstances of) the beneficiary.[2] This is quite distinct from the rules at §29.3.5 on trusts for vulnerable persons.

A consultative document on the reform of this area of income tax was issued in 1991. It included a proposal to integrate income tax and CGT treatments. But this was abandoned for reasons which were not made clear.[3] Further consultations were begun in 2004. Following these consultations, FA 2006, sections 89 and 88 and Schedules 13 and 12 made major amendments, some definitional, to the income tax and CGT rules on trusts as described in Budget Note BN 35. Apart from clearing up a number of points, the main purpose was to align the tax rules for both income tax and CGT. The changes include an election that a sub-fund may be treated as a separate settlement; for the CGT consequence see §40.5 below. On the rules on the residence of trustees, see now sections 475–76.

29.1.1 Settled Property

Section 466 directs that any property held in trust, other than property held by a person as nominee for another or as trustee for another who is absolutely entitled as against the trustee or would be but for being an infant or otherwise under disability, is property comprised in a settlement and, however expressed, settled property. This builds on the previous CGT definition; for the meaning of some of these terms and as explored in case law, see §40.1.2.4 below.

29.1.2 Settlor

Section 467 defines 'settlor' and introduces the concept of 'settlor of property'. The definition first covers the person who makes a settlement, whether directly or indirectly, eg someone who provides property directly or indirectly for the purpose of the settlement or

---

[2] TMA 1970, s 72; *IRC v McIntosh* (1955) 36 TC 334.
[3] See Inland Revenue Press Release, 18 March 1993, [1993] *Simon's Tax Intelligence* 516. For reviews, see Kerridge (1994) 110 *LQR* 84; Venables (1992) 13 *Fiscal Studies* 106; and Venables, *Comments on the Trusts Consultative Document* (Key Haven, 1991).

has made reciprocal arrangements (see further section 465(7) and (8)); these rules have obvious overtones of the rules discussed in chapter thirty-one.

29.1.3 Death

ITA 2007, sections 467 and 468 deal with death and provide that D is a settlor if, on D's death, settled property is, or is derived from, property of which he was competent to dispose immediately before his death, which is defined in section 468 in terms analogous to the CGT rule. Section 469 provides that D ceases to be a settlor if there is no property comprised in the settlement which is derived from him if: (a) he has not made any undertaking to provide property in the future, and (b) he is not party to any relevant reciprocal arrangements.

29.1.4 Certain Transfers

Sections 470 and 471 deal with how to identify the settlor when there has been a transfer between settlements otherwise than by way of bargain at arm's length; the settlor of the first trust is treated as a settlor of the transferee as well. This does not apply (section 470(2)) if the transfer is by reason of an assignment, etc by a beneficiary under the first settlement or under the exercise of a general power of appointment, or where the deceased is treated as the settlor under section 473(4).

29.1.5 Variation

Section 472 provides further rules to identify the settlor where a will or intestacy is treated as varied for CGT purposes, ie TCGA 1992, section 62(6) applies. So, if the property was not settled property immediately before the settlement, it is those who would otherwise have taken the property who are the settlors—and not the deceased (section 472(2)–(5)). Section 473 directs when the deceased is to be treated as the settlor. The first is where property would have become comprised in a settlement on D's death and the variation makes it go to another settlement. The other is where D was already the settlor. In each case the settlement is treated as made immediately before D's death (section 472(5)) unless it is already so treated (section 472(6)).

29.1.6 Sub-fund Election

The tax system has faced a number of problems in deciding when a disposition by trustees created a new trust and when it remained part of the existing trust. FA 2006 added a CGT election to treat a sub-fund as a separate trust (TCGA 1992, Schedule 4ZA). The income tax consequences of such an election are spelt out in ITA 2007, section 477. These indicate who are to be the relevant trustees for income tax purposes. The basic rule is that at the moment the election takes effect, the trustees of the sub-trust become absolutely entitled to the trust property as against the trustees of the principal settlement. The income tax rules apply accordingly.

29.1.7 *The Principle (or Rule) in Re Hastings-Bass*

Lastly, the basis and scope of the principle or rule in *Re Hastings Bass* has been a matter of particular interest in the realm of taxation and administration of trusts. Although the principle derives its name from the 1975 decision of the Court of Appeal in *Re Hastings-Bass, decd. Hastings-Bass and others v Inland Revenue Commissioners*,[4] recent cases have adopted the formulation by Lloyd LJ, sitting as a judge of the High Court, in *Sieff v Fox*,[5] that

> where trustees act under a discretion given to them by the terms of the trust, in circumstances in which they are free to decide whether or not to exercise that discretion, but the effect of the exercise is different from that which they intended, the court will interfere with their action if it is clear that they would not have acted as they did had they not failed to take into account considerations which they ought to have taken into account, or taken into account considerations which they ought not to have taken into account.

Whilst the principle appears related to the general law of mistake, its origin—as noted by Norris J in *Futter and another v Futter and others*[6]—is instead to be found in cases on the validity of the exercise of trustees' powers. It is also clear from *Sieff* and *Futter* that tax consequences are among the matters which may be relevant for the purposes of the principle. The effect of application of the principle in *Re Hastings-Bass* is to render void the act to which it applies. In *Futter*, Norris J applied the principle to void a transaction in which trustees acting on incorrect tax advice from their solicitors advanced funds in a manner that triggered an unexpected CGT liability. The principle therefore seemed particularly helpful to negligent tax advisers (and their professional indemnity insurers).

As HMRC were reluctant to intervene in these cases, and since both the trustees and the beneficiaries normally wanted the principle to apply, there was little opposition to an order being made; consequently, the scope of the principle widened over time.[7] This development was not without controversy—in the opening paragraphs of Norris J's judgment in *Futter* he suggested the development of the principle had strayed from its original course, but nevertheless went on to apply it. Eventually HMRC changed its policy and decided to take a more active interest in such cases, including becoming joined as a party.[8] When *Futter* and its companion case *Pitt v Holt* reached the Court of Appeal, the judges refused to apply the principle.[9] Lloyd LJ, giving the lead judgment, said that the principle should be available only where the trustees have acted in breach of duty. Where trustees have acted both within their powers and in compliance with their duties, Lloyd LJ held there was no basis upon which to set aside the transaction.

On further appeal to the Supreme Court,[10] Lord Walker (the other six judges agreeing) adopted a position similar to that of Lloyd LJ, holding in *Futter* that a court should intervene when trustees had acted in such a way as to amount to a breach of their fiduciary duty. In Lord Walker's view, it was not sufficient to show that the trustees' deliberations had

---

[4] [1975] Ch 25.
[5] [2005] EWHC 1312 (Ch) at [119].
[6] [2010] EWHC 449 (Ch), [2010] STC 982.
[7] Bhandari [2011] BTR 288. See also Nolan, 'Controlling fiduciary power' (2009) *CLJ* 293.
[8] Bhandari [2011] BTR 288.
[9] *Pitt v Holt, Futter v Futter* [2011] STC 809, [2011] EWCA Civ 197. See Bhandari [2011] BTR 288.
[10] *Futter & Cuthill v HMRC; Pitt & Others v HMRC* [2013] UKSC 26. See commentary see Ng [2013] BTR 566.

fallen short of the highest possible standards or that the court would, on a surrender of discretion by the trustees, have acted in a different way. On the facts in *Futter*, the trustees' exercise of the power of advancement had been valid and there were no grounds for the court to interfere. The implications of this decision is that it will be much more difficult for trustees to convince the courts to step in and set aside their misguided decisions. In *Pitt*, however, the Supreme Court allowed the appeal and set aside a settlement of damages for personal injury. Rather than relying on *Re Hastings Bass*, the Court instead held that a voluntary disposition could be set aside on the grounds of equity where there had been a mistake which was sufficiently serious to satisfy the conditions set down in *Ogilvie v Little-boy*.[11] On the facts in *Pitt* the Court decided that would it be unconscionable or unjust to leave the mistake uncorrected, as the settlement could have been made to comply with the relevant statutory scheme without any artificiality or abuse of that relief. While the result in *Pitt* is understandable, the wider implications of the application of the doctrine of mistake to unwind poor tax planning are very uncertain, and will be highly dependent on the specific facts.[12]

29.2   Trustee

29.2.1   The Trustee's Liability

Whether the trust has discretionary or accumulated income within ITA 2007, Part 9, Chapter 3 (section 480) or not, the basis for the trustee's liability to income tax follows lines which have been in place since the start of income tax itself. The person liable to income tax on income arising under ITTOIA 2005, Parts 2 and 3 is the person 'receiving or entitled to' the income charged.[13] So the trustee is liable to income tax on these sorts of income even though holding it for the beneficiary and not beneficially. Under ITTOIA 2005, Part 4, Chapter 3, a tax credit is available to a person 'receiving' a distribution,[14] who pays tax at the appropriate rate, with the amount of tax credit reflecting that fact.[15] Trustees come within each of these rules even though they are not entitled to the income beneficially; they are 'entitled' to the income in that they can sue for it and they may be said to receive it.

29.2.1.1   As Trustees

Trustees are assessable to income tax regardless of the personal tax circumstances of the beneficiary or of themselves. They are assessable and chargeable not as agents for the beneficiary, nor as trustees per se, but simply because they receive income.[16] This is so even if

---

[11] (1897) 13 TLR 399 (HL).

[12] Post-*Pitt v Holt* examples of the court setting aside transactions on the grounds of mistake include *Bainbridge v Bainbridge* [2016] EWHC 898 (Ch) and *Van Der Merwe v Goldman and HMRC* [2016] EWHC 926 (Ch).

[13] ITTOIA 2005, ss 8 and 271, ex TA 1988, ss 21(1), 59, Schs A and D; see also *Dawson v IRC* [1989] STC 473, (1989) 62 TC 301, HL; and *Reid's Trustees v IRC* [1929] SC 439, (1929) 14 TC 512. TA 1988, s 21(1) is now ITTOIA 2005, s 271; TA 1988, s 59 has been re-enacted in 19 sections, eg s 8.

[14] ITTOIA 2005, s 397, ex TA 1988, s 231.

[15] ITA 2007, Pt 2, Ch 2, ex TA 1988, ss 1A, 1B.

[16] *Williams v Singer* [1921] 1 AC 65, 71, 7 TC 387, 411, per Viscount Cave.

there is only one beneficiary who is of full legal capacity.[17] Trustees cannot be taxed if their circumstances (or the circumstances of those of them whom it is sought to tax) are such as to prevent them from being within the charge to tax. In *Dawson v IRC*[18] there was a discretionary trust and no beneficiary was entitled to the income. The administration of the trust was carried on outside the UK, the principal beneficiaries were resident outside the UK, and no income was remitted to the UK. There were three trustees, only one of whom was resident in the UK. The Revenue's attempt to tax the single UK resident trustee failed since they could not show that the trustee had sufficient control[19] over the income so that the income had accrued to him. This decision rejected an established Revenue practice and was reversed by legislation.[20] In calculating the total income of trustees for the purposes of tax liability, the trust income is not added to their personal incomes; conversely, trustees' personal incomes are ignored in computing their liability as trustees.

29.2.1.2 Reliefs

A trust may not claim any personal reliefs of the trustees, nor, since it is not an 'individual',[21] may the trust claim any personal reliefs for itself. On the other hand, a trust may be entitled to various reliefs which are available to 'persons', such as loss relief or deductions on account of interest. Similarly, a trust may deduct and retain income tax on making a payment falling within section 449. The trustees may be guilty of a breach of trust if they fail to so deduct.[22]

29.2.1.3 Expenses

In computing the taxable income of a trust outside ITA 2007, Part 9, Chapter 3,[23] no deduction may be made for trust expenses incurred in the administration of the trust, any more than individuals with investment income can deduct associated expenses.[24] If a trustee has £1,000 net rental income, and £100 trust expenses, income tax for 2016–17 will be 20% of £1,000, ie £200. This bar is directed at trust expenses, not expenses which are deductible in computing particular income from a particular source. Where a trust carries on a trade, it is taxable only on the profits of that trade; any expenses incurred in earning those profits may be deducted according to normal principles. Such profits are not earned income of the trust.[25]

Most trust income will be investment income arising under ITTOIA 2005, Part 5, Chapter 7, or Part 4, Chapter 3, and so is usually subject to taxation by deduction at source. In other instances, for example where the trustees receive rent or carry on a trade, they must make a self-assessment.[26]

---

[17] *Hamilton Russell's Executors v IRC* (1943) 25 TC 200.

[18] [1989] STC 473, (1989) 62 TC 301, HL; in the Court of Appeal ([1988] STC 684) considerable emphasis was placed on the joint nature of the title and responsibility of trustees; see [1989] BTR 249.

[19] There was negative control in that the trustee's consent was needed before the discretions could be exercised, but this was held not to be sufficient.

[20] FA 1989, s 110. It should be noted that none of the income accrued to trustees in that case from sources in the UK; the decision insists on finding a basis for liability in the words of the taxing statutes (ie TA 1988, ss 18, 59) rather than on established practice.

[21] It is very difficult to find authority for this rule, but it is generally accepted: see Farrand [1977] *Conv (NS)* 5.

[22] *Re Sharp* [1906] 1 Ch 793.

[23] Ex TA 1988, s 686. On s 686, see below at §29.2.3.2.

[24] *Aikin v Macdonald's Trustees* (1894) 3 TC 306.

[25] *Fry v Shiels Trustees* [1915] SC 159, (1915) 6 TC 583 (see above at §7.8.2).

[26] TMA 1970, ss 8A, 9. On HMRC practice, see *Tax Bulletin*, August 2005.

29.2.2 Exceptions to General Liability

29.2.2.1 Income Accruing to Beneficiary Not to Trustees

Since trustees are liable to tax simply because income accrues to them, it follows that they are not liable where income accrues only to the beneficiary. In *Williams v Singer*,[27] income from investments held in the United States was, at the direction of the trustees, who were resident in the UK, paid directly to the beneficiary, who was domiciled and resident outside the UK. The beneficiary, if taxable at all, would only have been taxed on a remittance basis, and since no income was remitted to this country, no tax was due from her. The Revenue's attempt to charge tax on the trustees failed.[28] The trustees had not been 'in actual receipt and control' themselves and so were not liable.

Under TMA 1970, section 76, a trustee who has authorised the receipt of profits by the person entitled thereto, or his agent, is only required to make a return of the name, address and the profits of that person, ie the beneficiary. This was relied on in the House of Lords in *Williams v Singer* as negativing any further liability on the trustees,[29] but is completely immaterial since it is concerned only with the trustee's duty to supply information with regard to the assessment of the beneficiary.

29.2.2.2 Beneficiary Not Liable to Income Tax

Where trustees receive income, they may not be assessed if the income accrues to a beneficiary in whose hands it is not liable to income tax.[30] This is a second explanation of *Williams v Singer*.[31] This applies only where the link between the income and the beneficiary is established; it cannot apply to absolve trustees when, for example, income is accumulated contingently for a beneficiary.[32]

This exception cannot be said to be firmly grounded since it blurs the nature of the trustees' liability with that of the beneficiary.[33] It comes close to saying that the trustee is not liable to income tax when there is a beneficiary with a vested life interest[34] (see §29.3 below). If the exception is sound, it is very limited, applying only where the income is not liable to income tax in the hands of the beneficiary (as where he is non-resident), and not applying where the income is liable to tax but no income tax will be due (eg by reason of personal allowances due to the beneficiary).

---

[27] [1921] 1 AC 65, (1921) 7 TC 387. See also *Dawson v IRC* [1988] STC 684, (1988) 62 TC 301 CA. On Singer family's tax and trust litigation, see Parrott and Avery Jones [2008] BTR 56.

[28] Conversely, in *Drummond v Collins* [1915] AC 1011, (1915) 6 TC 525, where foreign income accrued to a non-resident trustee, by whom it was accumulated, there was no liability on a resident beneficiary who was chargeable only on a remittance basis, since it was not his income.

[29] [1921] 1 AC 65, 71, (1921) 7 TC 387, 411.

[30] Lord Clyde in Reid's *Trustees v IRC* [1929] SC 439, 449, (1929) 14 TC 512, 525.

[31] [1921] 1 AC 65, 71, (1921) 7 TC 387, 412.

[32] Such income does not 'belong to' the beneficiary (*Stanley v IRC* [1944] 1 All ER 230, (1944) 26 TC 12). *Sed quaere* if the beneficiaries are non-resident; see *Kelly v Rogers* [1935] 2 KB 446, 468, (1935) 19 TC 692, 714.

[33] The position is further complicated by the rule that a trustee may be liable for tax due from a non-resident beneficiary under TMA 1970, s 78 (non-residents).

[34] It is clear that the beneficiary is liable (*IRC v Hamilton Russell's Executors* [1943] 1 All ER 474, (1943) 25 TC 200), as are the trustees.

29.2.3 Rates of Tax

29.2.3.1 Non-discretionary Trusts

Generally, neither the starting rate[35] nor the higher rate of tax applies to trustees since they are not 'an individual'; income tax is therefore charged at the rate appropriate to the type of income. Generally, the basic rate of 20% applies. Prior to 6 April 2016, dividend income was usually taxed at the dividend ordinary rate of 10%, but with a 10% credit. Post 6 April 2016, the new Dividend Allowance is restricted to individual recipients only; it is not available to trustees. Trustees subject to the 20% basic rate will pay tax on dividend type-income at 7.5%.[36]

29.2.3.2 Discretionary and Similar Trusts

Trustees are liable to tax at a special rate—'the rate applicable to trusts'—where the income is to be accumulated, or is payable at the discretion of the trustees or any other person (whether or not there is a power to accumulate).[37] This definition focuses on the trust definition of income, not the tax definition. If trustees develop land and the proceeds are treated as capital for trust purposes, a charge to basic rate income tax may nonetheless arise under ITA 2007, Part 13, Chapter 3. However, no charge will arise under section 479, since this section applies only to sums which are income 'to be accumulated or payable at' the trustee's discretion; as the sums are trust capital, they do not come within this definition.[38]

The rate of tax was set at 34% in 1997,[39] thus falling between corporation tax and the higher income tax rate. It was raised to the higher income tax rate of 40% in 2004 and to 50% in 2010, but dropped to 45% from April 2013. As slight compensation for these increases, these rates for trusts do not apply for the first £1,000 of such income.[40] However, the increase in the band was backed up by a new provision which reduces the £1,000 if the settlor has made more than one settlement and these exist in that tax year; the £1,000 is to be shared equally between the settlements, but with a minimum of £200 each.[41] From 6 April 2016, the tax rate on dividend income falling within the first £1,000 of income is 7.5%; on income above £1,000 the dividend trust rate is 38.1%.[42] The tax is due under a self-assessment on 31 January following the end of the year of assessment in which it arose.[43]

As noted, certain types of dividend income are taxed at 'the dividend trust rate',[44] usually applicable only to trusts within ITA 2007, Part 9, Chapter 3. These are the distributions listed in section 482 and are the purchase or redemption by the company of its own shares

---

[35] ITA 2007, ss 6(1)(a), 10(1), 20(1), ex TA 1988, s 1(2)(aa), added by FA 1992, s 9.

[36] The treatment of trustees under the post-6 April 2016 dividend tax rules was finally confirmed by HMRC in April 2016: see https://www.gov.uk/trusts-taxes/trusts-and-income-tax.

[37] ITA 2007, ss 479(1), (2) and 481(2), ex TA 1988, s 686(1).

[38] Potter and Monroe, *Tax Planning* (Sweet & Maxwell, 1982), §3-07; for a similar problem where sums are paid to trustees by a company buying its own shares in circumstances not coming within TA 1988, s 219, see *ibid*, §3-08.

[39] ITA 2007, s 9(1), (2), ex TA 1988, s 686(1A). The increase to 34% was made by F(No 2)A 1997.

[40] Ex TA 1988, s 686D, added by FA 2005, s 14.

[41] ITA 2007, s 492. There is an obvious analogy with TCGA 1992, Sch 1 (see below at §40.1.2.1).

[42] See https://www.gov.uk/trusts-taxes/trusts-and-income-tax.

[43] TMA 1970, s 59B(4).

[44] ITA 2007, s 9(2), ex TA 1988, s 686(1A). See, generally, Revenue Interpretation, February 1999, [1999] *Simon's Weekly Tax Intelligence* 254.

or rights to acquire shares.[45] This rate does not apply to certain types of trust (eg unit trusts, pensions and charities), to income treated as the settlor's[46] or to purchases falling within CTA 2010, section 1033 (subject to capital gains treatment). The scope also has been widened to cover a range of gains arising on a certain event, eg gains on life insurance contracts (ITTOIA 2005, section 467) and certain options (ITTOIA 2005, section 557). Those provisions previously made the person receiving the profits the person liable to tax; section 482 makes it clear that the trustees are liable when the asset is held as settled property. Income arising from service charges held in trust by certain social landlords is not to be taxed at more than the basic rate (section 480(3)). The rules in ITA 2007, Part 9, Chapter 3 are not confined to discretionary trusts as such, but also apply where beneficiaries have contingent interests and the Trustee Act 1925, section 31 empowers the trustees to apply income for their maintenance. The rules also apply to income which the trustees have power to withhold, eg when they exercise a power to accumulate under a protective trust where the discretionary trust has arisen.[47]

Non-resident trustees may be liable to additional rates even though they are not liable to basic rate tax on that income.[48]

Exceptions

Section 479 does not apply to sums which, before being distributed, are income of any person other than the trustees, eg a beneficiary with a vested interest in the income, or of an annuitant; sums which are treated as income of the settlor are also excluded.[49] Exceptions also exist for charities and pension funds.[50]

Expenses

In relation to expenses, a two-pronged rule applies. First, income spent on expenses properly chargeable to income is excluded from section 479. The question whether an expense is properly chargeable to income is determined according to general trust law, any express provision in the instrument permitting the charge of the expense against income being ignored.[51] Secondly, however, such expenses are to be charged at the rate that would have applied if they had not been subject to section 479.[52] This formula continues the effect of the old rule under TA 1988, section 686, which took the form of an additional rate. Where the discretionary trust is not resident in the UK, the expenses which may be relieved in this way are limited to the fraction equivalent to the proportion of the trust's total income

---

[45] ITA 2007, ss 481(3) and 482 'Type 1', ex TA 1988, s 686A(1), (2).

[46] ITA 2007, ss 481(1)–(4) and 482, ex TA 1988, s 686A(1).

[47] *IRC v Berrill* [1981] STC 784, (1981) 55 TC 429.

[48] *IRC v Regent Trust Co Ltd* [1980] STC 140; this is despite the fact that the credit for s 479 (ex s 686) tax against s 496 (ex s 687) liability is not available on a literal interpretation of s 498 (ex s 687(3)(a)).

[49] ITA 2007, s 480(3), ex TA 1988, s 686(2)(b).

[50] ITA 2007, ss 479(1)(b) and 480(4)(a), ex TA 1988, s 686(2)(c).

[51] In *Carver v Duncan* [1985] AC 1082, [1985] STC 356, (1985) 59 TC 125, HL, life insurance premiums and fees for investment advice were held to be non-deductible; it was not clear whether they were 'expenses' anyway. On general trust law, see also *HMRC v Trustees of Peter Clay* [2008] STC 928, [2007] EWHC 2661 (Ch). In *Revenue & Customs Commissioners v Peter Clay Discretionary Trust* [2009] STC 469, [2008] EWCA (Civ) 1441, the Court of Appeal, reversing the Chancery Division judge ([2008] STC 928) in part, held that a wider range of fees could be apportioned between income and capital: see especially paras 40–46. Whether the fees of an investment adviser could be deducted might depend on when the decision to accumulate was made.

[52] ITA 2007, ss 484(1), (2), (4), (5), 486(1), Sch 2, para 102, ex TA 1988, s 686(2AA).

which is subject to UK tax. For this purpose, trust income which escapes UK tax because the trustees are non-resident or are able to use double taxation relief is not 'subject to UK tax'.[53] Expenses are disallowed if the income is payable to a non-resident beneficiary in whose hands it is not liable to UK tax.[54]

Rate order

Since there are now so many different rates of tax applicable to different types of income, rules are needed to direct the order in which deductions are made.[55] The order is: (a) ITTOIA 2005, Part 4, Chapter 3 income, widened to cover some related corporate distributions; (b) foreign savings income; (c) other savings income; and (d) income chargeable at basic rate.

29.3 Beneficiary

29.3.1 Beneficiary's Credit for Tax Paid by Trustees

Where trustees have paid the tax and administration expenses and the balance belongs to a beneficiary (B) as income, as where B has a vested life interest in the income, that balance is liable to income tax as B's income. The amount received is grossed up at the relevant rate to take account of the basic or lower rate tax paid by the trustees; in turn, B can use that tax as a credit. Therefore, a net receipt of rental income of £720 will be grossed up at 20% to £900. If B's rate of tax is nil, he will recover £180 from the Revenue. A receipt of interest of £720 also will be grossed up 20% and B will recover £180. If B is liable to tax on the interest at 40%, he must pay an extra £180 to make a total of £360.

ITTOIA 2005, Part 4, Chapter 3 income of £810 is grossed up to £900 by adding back the credit of £90 at 10%. In accordance with the new regime for dividend taxation, however, the £90 cannot be recovered from the Revenue. If B is liable to tax at the ITTOIA 2005, Part 4, Chapter 3 dividend upper rate of 32.5%, tax of £292.50 will be due, against which the £90 credit can be set, making a net payment of £202.50.

While the credit process is clear, the underlying theory is not. Where B is currently entitled to the income under the trust, the result of the decision of the House of Lords in *Baker v Archer-Shee*[56] is that B is entitled to—and so taxable on—the income as and when it arises in the hands of the trustee.[57] This means that B will be taxable under the Schedule and Case appropriate to the income as it arises. Different principles apply where there is an annuity

---

[53] ITA 2007, s 487, ex TA 1988, s 686(2A), (2B).

[54] ITA 2007, ss 487(1)–(4), 499(1), 501(1)–(4), 502(1)–(3), 1023, ex TA 1988, ss 686(2A), 689A (non-residence).

[55] ITTOIA 2005, s 486, ex TA 1988, s 689B.

[56] [1927] AC 844, (1927) 11 TC 749. The facts of this case were favourable to the Revenue's contentions. Not only was the beneficiary sole life tenant, she had also been given the power to nominate trustees and was herself involved with the management of the fund to the extent that her consent was needed for any change of investments. The majority decision may be criticised for failing to distinguish between an active and a passive trust; it may be argued that the decision does not apply to an active trust. See also the explanations in *Reid's Trustees v IRC* [1929] SC 439, (1929) 14 TC 512.

[57] However, in determining whether the income is earned or investment income, the question is whether it was earned by the beneficiary and not whether it was earned by the trustees (see above at §7.9).

under the trust, since the annuitant is liable under ITTOIA 2005, Part 5, Chapter 7 and the new rules in ITA 2007, sections 449 and 901.

29.3.2 Vested Rights in Income

29.3.2.1 When Do Vested Rights Exist?

A beneficiary is currently entitled to the trust income if the trustees are under a duty to pay the income to the beneficiary who is then absolutely entitled to it—or to have it applied at his direction.[58] Benefits in kind are caught; the question whether the benefit is convertible into money is irrelevant.[59] If the beneficiary's title to the income is contingent, or vested subject to being divested,[60] it is not taxable as his income. Where a trustee receives income from investments held for a tenant for life, each sum received is the income of the tenant for life as soon as it is received and regardless of the date on which it is paid over to the beneficiary. This is because the income is immediately under the beneficiary's control.[61]

Rights arising under a Scottish interest in possession trust are technically annual payments under ITTOIA 2005, Part 5, Chapter 7; but it is provided that where English law would treat the beneficiary as having an equitable right in possession, the rights of the beneficiary are to be treated in the same way—despite the general Scottish position.[62] This decree does not apply if the trustees are not resident in the UK.

29.3.2.2 Expenses

Sums received by the beneficiary are grossed up to reflect the tax rate paid by the trustees. However, this grossed-up income will not necessarily be the same as the trustees' income. *Macfarlane v IRC*[63] decided that trust expenses, although non-deductible in computing the trustees' income, are deductible in computing the income of the beneficiary. Suppose that a trust has gross rental income of £1,000, and expenses of £100. For 2016–17 income tax on the trustees will be £200, ie 20% of £1,000. The beneficiary will receive £700; £700 grossed up at 20% gives income of £875 (not £900). The beneficiary thus gets credit only for the 20% tax paid by the trustees on £875 (£175), and not the whole £200 tax paid by them.

Is this rule correct? Certainly its basis is suspect. *Macfarlane v IRC* rests on an earlier case[64] in 1926 in which the Court of Session held further that the beneficiary's income was the sum received net of tax paid by the trustees and then minus expenses, making a sum of £580 in the above example. The reasoning on this point was destroyed by the decision of the House of Lords in *Baker v Archer-Shee* but was reaffirmed on the main point by *Macfarlane v IRC*.[65] The reason given for the deduction was that the expenses were

---

[58] *Tollemache v IRC* (1926) 11 TC 277; *Miller v IRC* [1930] AC 222, (1930) 15 TC 25.
[59] *Lindus and Hortin v IRC* (1933) 17 TC 442.
[60] *Stanley v IRC* [1944] 1 All ER 230, (1944) 26 TC 12; *Brotherton v IRC* [1977] STC 73, (1977) 52 TC 137.
[61] *Spens v IRC* [1970] 3 All ER 295, 299, 46 TC 276, 285, per Megarry J.
[62] ITA 2007, s 464. This is because of the intricacies of the taxation of dividends and is probably obsolete (FA 1993, s 118); for explanation, see Inland Revenue Press Release, 9 July 1993, [1993] *Simon's Tax Intelligence* 1048.
[63] [1929] SC 453, (1929) 14 TC 532.
[64] *Murray v IRC* (1926) 11 TC 133.
[65] Cited with approval by Lord Blanesburgh in *Baker v Archer-Shee* (1926) 11 TC 749, 786.

incurred before the beneficiary received the money, not by anyone she employed but by the trustees appointed by the settlor.[66] This is inconsistent with the notion that the income is the beneficiary's as soon as it is received by the trustees.[67] The anomaly may be the prohibition on allowing the trustees to deduct their expenses.[68]

29.3.2.3 Other Deductions and Reliefs

Other concerns arise over the difference between trust income under trust law and the beneficiary's income for tax purposes. Thus trust law is not concerned with capital allowances (or balancing charges), nor with relief for losses from earlier years, still less with the now obsolete preceding year basis. A trust may be able to charge depreciation or other expenses expressly prohibited for tax purposes in its trust accounts. These do not usually cause a difference between the income of the trustees and the income of the beneficiary for tax purposes, except in relation to expenses. The position with regard to capital allowances is not clear.[69]

29.3.2.4 Stock Dividends

An enhanced stock dividend may be income or capital of the trust, or may give rise to an obligation on the trustees to take the payment as capital but to compensate the life tenant for the loss of the dividend. Revenue practice is to accept the treatment decided upon by the trustees—provided it is supportable on the facts.[70] In *Sinclair v Lee*,[71] an allocation of shares to a trust on a demerger gave rise to no tax liability on the trustee because of an express provision; it was prevented from being taxable income of the income-beneficiary only by being classified by the court as capital. This decision has been criticised for creating a wholly unsatisfactory distinction between shares received (as in this case) on an indirect demerger, and those received in a direct demerger (which would belong to the tenant for life).[72] Others view the decision as a welcome limitation on the rights of the income beneficiary in a modern commercial context.

29.3.3 No Vested Right in Income

29.3.3.1 Accumulations

A beneficiary may have a vested and indefeasible interest in income but a different set of rights in capital. In *Stanley v IRC*,[73] the appellant had a vested life interest in certain property, but the trustees had a power under the Trustee Act 1925, section 31 to accumulate the

[66] (1926) 11 TC 133, 138, per Lord Sands.
[67] *Cf* Lord Sands, *ibid*, 540.
[68] These expenses are deductible in computing the trust's liability to the applicable rate for discretionary and accumulation trusts (ITA 2007, s 487(1), ex TA 1988, s 686(2A)).
[69] On the question of whether the tenant for life is entitled to capital allowances, see Venables, *Tax Planning Through Trusts* (Chatto & Windus, 1987), §20:20 and Venables, *Comments on the Consultative Document, op cit*, App C. On allocation of tax burdens more generally, see Goodman (1983) 31 *Can Tax J* 169–82.
[70] See Statement of Practice SP 4/94; and discussion by Hutton in *Tolley's Tax Planning 1999–2000*, 1707, 1715–21.
[71] [1993] Ch 497, [1993] 3 All ER 926.
[72] Hitchmough [1993] BTR 406, 408.
[73] [1944] 1 All ER 230, (1944) 26 TC 12.

income during his minority. This power was exercised until the appellant reached the age of majority, when he became entitled to the accumulated income. When the appellant reached that age, the Revenue sought to levy additional assessments to cover the years in which the income had been accumulated. The Trustee Act 1925, section 31 provided that when a person died before reaching the age of majority, the accumulated income was not to be paid to that person's estate, as would be the case if his title to that income were absolute, but instead added to capital. It followed that although the infant beneficiary had a vested life interest, he had only a contingent right to the income or, at best, a right that was vested subject to being divested if he failed to reach the age of majority. It could not be said that the income was his in the years as it arose, since there would be no guarantee that he would reach that age and so no certainty that he would be entitled to the income. The case also illustrates that when the beneficiary under an accumulation trust reaches the age of majority, or whatever event is specified in the trust, and so becomes entitled to the accumulated income, that income cannot be taxed as his in the year of receipt because it is then a capital payment to him and not the income of that year.

Today, the tax liability of the beneficiary under an accumulation trust depends on the nature of the right in the income. If B's interest is vested, B will be taxed like any other beneficiary with such an interest. The income—less trust expenses—is taxed as B's income, even though it is, in fact, accumulating in the hands of the trustees. Moreover, the fact that B has such a right will mean that the trustees do not have to pay at the special rate applicable to trusts.[74] This will occur when a contingent beneficiary reaches the age of majority, since the Trustee Act 1925, section 31 gives him a right to subsequent income even though his interest in capital remains contingent. If, however, B's interest is contingent, as when he is still under 18, the income cannot be treated as B's unless and until it is actually made his, eg under a power.[75]

29.3.3.2 ITA 2007, Section 494

Basic rule

Where trustees make any payment to the beneficiary in the exercise of discretion[76] and the payment is income of the person to whom it is paid,[77] section 494 requires the trustees to gross up the payment at the applicable rate.[78] Therefore, if the trustees make a payment of £1,650 in 2016–17, this will be grossed up at 45% to £3,000 (ie £1,650 + tax of £1,350). This is so whether or not there is trust income available in that year. The tax of £1,350 can be collected from the trustees.[79] This tax is due on 31 January following the end of the year in which it arose.[80] It follows that the beneficiary, B, is then treated as receiving £3,000 which

---

[74] Because it belongs to the beneficiary before it is distributed (ITA 2007, ss 479(1), 480(1)–(4), ex TA 1988, s 686(2)(b)).

[75] *Drummond v Collins* [1915] AC 1011, (1915) 6 TC 525.

[76] ITA 2007, s 493. The same words were found in TA 1988, s 686.

[77] Or is treated as income of the settlor.

[78] ITA 2007, s 494, ex TA 1988, s 687(1), (2).

[79] ITA 2007, ss 23, 30(2), 494(1)–(4), 496(1)–(5), ex TA 1988, s 687(2). Note ESC B18, where income would escape UK tax if paid direct to the beneficiary instead of through a trust. On former concession for employee trusts, see ex ESC A68.

[80] TMA 1970, s 8A(1A).

has been taxed at 45%; if B is not a higher-rate taxpayer, any repayment will be calculated on that basis.

Is it income? Pursuant to section 493, section 494 applies only if B receives income. Once income has been accumulated it becomes capital for trust purposes, so that any later payment will be capital and outside section 494. No part of sections 493 or 494 treats a payment of capital as income if it could have been paid out of income if it had not been accumulated; such a device is part of the anti-avoidance rules in ITTOIA 2005, sections 624 *et seq.*

Credit for taxes paid

The trustees' liability to the Revenue under section 494 can be reduced by various payments. The first and principal deduction will be any tax under section 479 reflected in the trustees' tax pool: see sections 496–98. This set off is available even if the section 479 tax was paid in a previous year of assessment.

Complications arise when the rates change. Thus, if the trust accumulates income in year 1 when the rate is, say, 34%, but makes the distribution in year 2 when the rate is 50%, the trust will have to pay at 34% in year 1 under section 479, which will then form part of the trustees' tax pool, but can use that tax only against the tax due at 50% under section 494 in year 2, so causing an extra 16% to be due. The beneficiary's income is grossed up at the rates for year 2. If, on the other hand, the rate drops from 50% to 34%, it appears that the extra 16% already paid is lost as the trustees' pool cannot fall below nil. Further, if the liability under section 494 is in a year previous to that in which the liability arises under section 479, it may be that no relief can be given. This is where Model 4 (§29.1) is not applied precisely.

Credit for tax on dividend income

The second deduction comprises a group of taxes paid on types of dividend income.[81] These are listed separately because the rate of credit which can be used has been reduced following the 1999 changes to the tax credit on dividends and, more recently, the abolition of the dividend tax credit from 6 April 2016. The full effect of the 1999 changes was not appreciated since it was assumed that trusts would fund most of this payment out of accumulated pre-1999 income; however, it has become a real problem for new trusts and for those which have exhausted pre-1999 income.

The effect of the changes is that the tax available for credit against section 494 liability is restricted to the difference between the dividend trust rate and the ordinary dividend rate. This restriction increases the tax cost of a distribution out of such income over costs out of other income, such as interest or rent. Thus, trustees may be advised not to invest in equities, a classic breach of the principle of neutrality. One solution to this problem is to prevent the income from being trust income in the first place (see above §29.2.2). However, the Revenue do not regard a mere dividend mandate directing payment to the beneficiary instead of to the trust as sufficient for this purpose. Where income now distributed to a beneficiary has already been treated as income of the settlor—under the rules in chapter thirty-one—it comes with a non-repayable notional credit.[82] FA 2008 made a minor adjustment to the

---

[81] ITA 2007, ss 497 and 498(1), ex TA 1988, s 687(3)(a1)–(bc).
[82] ITTOIA 2005, s 685A.

provision's ordering rule to ensure that this does not push the beneficiary's non-trust savings and dividend income into a higher bracket.[83]

Credit for other taxes

Further rules apply to allow credit for tax paid on (a) undistributed income on hand when the new regime was introduced in 1973,[84] and, subsequently,[85] (b) a stream of receipts which show how complicated the tax system has become. The list includes sums charged under overseas bonds, the accrued income scheme, development gains and the old and new rules for discounted securities.

29.3.4 Discretionary Trust and Annual Payments

Section 493 refers to payments[86] of income, thereby excluding payments of capital. Section 493 thus assumes that such payments fit into the general scheme of income as annual payments taxable to the beneficiary under ITTOIA 2005, Part 5, Chapter 7. The assumption that the place of payments under discretionary trusts is to be found in ITTOIA 2005, Part 5, Chapter 7 is reinforced by ITTOIA 2005, section 685A: see chapter thirty-one below.

Three points arise:

(1) *Capital or income—loans.* The rules apply only where the receipt by the beneficiary properly falls to be treated as his income, and so not where it is a capital payment. Where, therefore, trustees make a loan to the beneficiary eligible for the receipt of income, the receipt cannot be treated as his income, and no tax will be due. However, the courts have treated such payments as income where the trustees have no power to make the loan.[87] Further, whether a payment is a loan or income is a question of fact.[88]

(2) *Non-resident beneficiary.* A non-resident beneficiary receiving income under a discretionary trust is not generally entitled to repayment of the tax borne by the trustees. However, in practice the Revenue 'look through' to the underlying income and may grant any relief, including double taxation relief under the applicable agreement, which might have been available if the income had been paid direct.[89] The question whether the Revenue should 'look through' more frequently is an interesting one.

(3) *Capital as income.* Where trustees hold property on trust but have to pay an annuity or other annual payment, the annuitant's liability falls to be determined under ITTOIA 2005, Part 5, Chapter 7. This liability survives the 1988 changes to Case III since those changes apply only to annual payments made by individuals.[90]

---

[83] ITTOIA 2005, s 685A(5A), (5B), added by FA 2008, s 64.
[84] FA 1973, s 17(3) (proviso).
[85] ITA 2007, ss 497 and 498, ex TA 1988, s 687(3)(d)–(k).
[86] Widened by ITA 2007, s 493(5), ex TA 1988, s 687(5) to cover payments in money or money's worth.
[87] *Esdaile v IRC* (1936) 20 TC 700; the lack of power could not be cured by agreement between the trustees and only some of the beneficiaries.
[88] *Williamson v Ough* [1936] AC 384, (1936) 20 TC 194. *Cf Peirse-Duncombe Trustees v IRC* (1940) 23 TC 199.
[89] Statement of Practice SP 3/86; for Revenue practice where there is a discretionary trust of the residue of an estate of a deceased person, see below at §30.5.
[90] ITTOIA 2005, ss 728–729, ex TA 1988, s 347A(2).

Whether the payments are to be regarded as an annuity or as a series of payments of capital depends upon the rights of the recipient, and not on the source of the payments. In *Brodie's Will Trustees v IRC*,[91] the annuity was charged on both income and capital so that the trustees were under a duty to have recourse to capital. The payments were held to be annuities and as wholly taxable as income of the recipient. In *Lindus and Hortin v IRC*,[92] trustees had discretion to use capital to make good any shortfall in the trust income; the payments were held to be annuities. This principle was applied in *Cunard's Trustees v IRC*,[93] where the trustees had power to use capital to supplement the income of the tenant for life.

In all the above cases there was a series of recurrent payments over a substantial period of time. The cases were taken by the Revenue to justify the position that any payment out of the capital of a trust fund which was intended to be used by a beneficiary for an income purpose (eg payment of school fees) was income of the beneficiary.[94] However, this approach was rejected by the Court of Appeal in *Stevenson v Wishart*,[95] where payments made in exercise of a power over capital[96] were not payments of income and could not be turned into income simply because they were applied to an income purpose. Where trustees have a discretion to resort to capital, the effect of exercising that discretion may be to cause the payment to fall within ITA 2007, section 479, since the sum is received by A, the annuitant, as income even though it was not A's income before the discretion was exercised.

The Revenue approach was also rejected in the earlier case of *Lawson v Rolfe*,[97] where a tenant for life was entitled, under the law applicable to the settlement, to all bonus shares issued by corporations in which the trust held shares. Issues of such shares were frequent, and the Revenue argued that the frequency of the payments meant that they should be treated as income payments and so as taxable in the hands of the beneficiary. This argument was rejected. There was all the difference in the world between a series of payment by the trustees under the terms of the will and the distributions by the companies in this case, which, as far as the trust was concerned, were purely fortuitous and unplanned.

Whether it is advantageous to convert capital into income depends on the tax circumstances of those concerned.[98] If the beneficiary is not an additional-rate taxpayer and the trust has surplus section 686 income accumulated from previous years, creating ITTOIA 2005, Part 5, Chapter 7 (ex Schedule D, Case III) income will enable the difference between the trust rate and the beneficiary's actual marginal rate to be repaid. It should not be forgotten either that income payments are excluded when considering exit charges for IHT, thanks to section 65(5)(b) (see below §50.4.1).

---

[91] (1933) 17 TC 432.
[92] (1933) 17 TC 442.
[93] [1946] 1 All ER 159, (1946) 27 TC 122.
[94] See Venables, *Tax Planning Through Trusts* (Chatto & Windus, 1987), §20:19.
[95] [1987] STC 266, [1987] 2 All ER 428; on which, see Wiggin and Rawlinson [1986] BTR 124; and Potter and Monroe, *op cit*, §3-09.
[96] This is an important case since the beneficiary was also an income beneficiary.
[97] [1970] 1 All ER 761, (1970) 46 TC 199; see [1970] 1970 BTR 142.
[98] Potter and Monroe, *op cit*, §3–10.

29.3.5 *Trusts for Vulnerable Persons*

This is an area in which the two-tier approach, under which both trustees and beneficiaries are liable, may be softened. Where these rules apply, and the appropriate election is made, the trustees are to be liable for no more income tax than would have been due if the income had accrued directly to the vulnerable beneficiary. There are equivalent rules for CGT (below §40.1.3). The broad effect for income tax will often be a substantial saving in income tax as compared with the normal charge at the trust rate, since the trust will be able to take advantage of the vulnerable beneficiary's personal reliefs and basic rate band. The legislation has not been rewritten, but ITA 2007, section 462(12) provides a cross-reference.

The rules on trusts for vulnerable persons are contained in FA 2005 but apply as from 6 April 2004. They are a consequence of the decision, which also took effect from 6 April 2004 but under FA 2004, to increase the special trust rate of income tax—and, until 2008, for CGT—from 34% to 40%.[99] The legislation does not apply if the property falls within ITTOIA 2005, sections 624 *et seq* so that the income is treated as that of the settlor.[100] The vulnerable persons who qualify are disabled persons and 'relevant minors'. Disabled persons are defined at length, and the definition was extended in FA 2013 and FA 2014;[101] minors are relevant if aged under 18 and at least one of their parents has died.[102] Their trust rights arise under (a) the statutory trusts on intestacy, (b) the will of a deceased parent of the minor or (c) the criminal injuries compensation scheme.[103] Trusts under (b) and (c) must meet various conditions and basically must be accumulation trusts for that beneficiary; no income may be applied for the benefit of any other person. A trust will not fail to meet these conditions just because of the statutory power of advancement.[104] Scots law is taken into account.[105] Dissection of assets between qualifying and non-qualifying persons is allowed.[106] For trusts created on or after 8 April 2013, the trustees may apply the 'annual limit'—the lesser of £3,000 and 3% of the settled property—for the benefit of another person in any tax year.[107]

Where trustees hold property on qualifying trusts for a vulnerable person, the trustees are first to determine their total income tax liability in respect of the income of the qualifying trust (TQTI); this process takes full account of any trust expenses properly chargeable to income or so chargeable but for any express provision of the trust.[108] They are then to calculate the extra tax on which the vulnerable person would be liable if the trust income were his—so treating it as the top slice of his income (VQT1). For this purpose reliefs given

---

[99] Notes to original Finance Bill, cls 39–61, para 120. In 2010 the rate became 50%, dropping to 45% in 2013.
[100] FA 2005, s 25(3). ITTOIA 2005, s 624 was previously TA 1988, s 660A.
[101] FA 2013, section 216 and Schedule 44 implemented an alignment of the definition of 'disabled person' for all tax purposes. The definition is to be found in new Schedule 1A to FA 2005. For commentary see Lemos [2013] BTR 511.
[102] FA 2005, ss 38 and 39.
[103] FA 2005, ss 34 and 35.
[104] *Ibid*.
[105] FA 2005, s 42.
[106] FA 2005, s 36.
[107] FA 2005, s 34.
[108] FA 2005, s 27.

by reduction, such as the married couple's allowance or EIS, are ignored, but general reliefs such as the basic personal allowance are taken into account. The amount by which TQTI exceeds VQT1 is not charged to the trustees.[109] The election must be made by the vulnerable person and the trustees jointly. Such an election is irrevocable.[110] There are separate enquiry powers and interpretation rules.[111]

---

[109] FA 2005, s 26.
[110] FA 2005, s 37.
[111] FA 2005, ss 40 and 41.

30

Death and Estates

30.1 Introduction

Estates must settle the liability of a deceased person (D) to income tax on the income that accrued during D's lifetime.[1] From 13 October 2014 any outstanding income tax liabilities or repayments for PAYE taxpayers are worked out by HMRC automatically; alternatively, HMRC will notify the personal representatives (PRs) if a self-assessment return needs to be filed.[2] The time limit for making assessments is four years after the year of assessment in which the death occurred.[3] The Revenue may, within that period, go back six years to collect tax lost due to D's fraud or negligence, or where the loss of tax is due to the deceased's careless or deliberate conduct. So if D dies in July 2017, HMRC has until 5 April 2022 to recover any tax found to be lost due by reasons of D's carelessness, ie back to the year 2011–12.[4] In computing this liability the personal reliefs of D in the year of death are permitted in full; there is no reduction where D died before 5 April. If the deceased was carrying on a trade, his death will involve a discontinuance and so possible use of overlap relief.

Income becoming due after, but in respect of a period before, the death of D is treated as that of the estate, not of D, for the purposes of income tax.[5] However, for the purposes of IHT, income is apportioned. This means that a part of the payment may be charged both to IHT as the D's asset and to income tax as the income of the estate (and so perhaps of

---

[1] TMA 1970, s 74, and note s 40(1).
[2] See https://www.gov.uk/after-a-death/tax-and-benefits.
[3] TMA 1970, s 40(1).
[4] TMA 1970, s 40(2).
[5] *IRC v Henderson's Executors* (1931) 16 TC 282; the situation may be distinguished from that in which the dividend becomes due before, but is paid after, the death (*Potel v IRC* [1971] 2 All ER 504, (1971) 46 TC 658).

the beneficiary). In computing the beneficiary's income for excess liability, the residuary income of the estate is therefore reduced by the amount of IHT payable in respect of that income.[6]

30.2   Liability of the Personal Representatives

Like trustees, PRs are assessable to income tax on the income of the estate at the lower (savings) rate on savings income, the ordinary ITTOIA 2005, Part 4, Chapter 3 rate on dividend income and the basic rate on other income. Gains accruing on certain life policies are treated as income of the PRs.[7] Like trustees, PRs are not liable to tax at the higher rate, nor may they use the starting rate.[8] They are not liable to the trust rate. They may not use any of D's personal allowances remaining unabsorbed by D's income. They may, however, claim relief in respect of interest payments, or in respect of any loss which they incur in running a business. Interest in respect of unpaid IHT is not deductible,[9] but interest on a loan to pay IHT is deductible if the loan is made to the PRs and relates to tax payable personally before the grant of representation. Only interest on the first year of the loan is deductible; excess interest may be carried back and then forward.[10] On liability to tax on trading income, see above at §19.4.

30.3   Liability of the Beneficiary

30.3.1   General

ITTOIA 2005, Part 5, Chapter 6 contains a specific head of charge (section 649) on income arising to a beneficiary from an estate; such income is called 'estate income'. Until the administration is complete, no beneficiary has any rights in the property of the estate or to the income from it.[11] It follows that no beneficiary is liable to income tax on the income of the estate as such;[12] liability may arise when an income distribution is made to a beneficiary. The question whether administration is complete is a matter of fact, the issue being whether the residue has been ascertained.[13] A prolonged administration may mean a fund administered with expertise and not taxed at higher rates of income tax; conversely, if the prospective beneficiaries have low incomes and so unused personal allowances, the administration might be expedited.

---

[6] ITTOIA 2005, s 669, ex TA 1988, s 699; what ITTOIA 2005 insists on calling 'extra' as opposed to the old 'excess' liability is defined in s 669(3), ex s 699(2).

[7] ITTOIA 2005, s 511, ex TA 1988, ss 547(1)(c), (7A), 553(7A).

[8] *IRC v Countess of Longford* [1927] 1 KB 594, (1927) 13 TC 573.

[9] *Lord Inverclyde's Trustees v Millar* (1924) 9 TC 14.

[10] ITA 2007, ss 403–405, ex TA 1988, s 364.

[11] *Stamp Duties Comr (Queensland) v Livingston* [1965] AC 694, [1964] 3 All ER 692.

[12] *R v IT Special Purposes Comrs, ex parte Dr Barnardo's Homes National Incorporated Association* [1920] 1 KB 26, (1920) 7 TC 646; *Corbett v IRC* [1937] 4 All ER 700, (1937) 21 TC 449; see also *Prest v Bettinson* [1980] STC 607, (1980) 53 TC 437.

[13] *George Attenborough & Son v Solomon* [1913] AC 76.

30.3.1.1 UK and Foreign Estates

The rules for taxing the beneficiaries vary according to whether the estate is a UK estate or a foreign estate. A UK estate is defined as one the income of which comprises only income which has borne UK tax or for which the PRs are directly assessable. However, an estate is not a UK estate if the PRs are exempt from UK tax by reason of residence outside the UK.[14] It follows that if a foreign estate only has income which is neither taxed by deduction nor assessable on the PRs, there is no liability to UK income tax.[15] An estate which is not a UK estate is a foreign estate.[16] In applying these rules certain amounts are ignored, ie stock dividends, the release of a loan from a close company and certain gains on life policies.[17]

30.3.1.2 Specific Legacies

Where the PRs vest a specific legacy in the legatee (L), intermediate income accruing during the administration is related back and so assessed on L at the time income accrued to the property.[18]

30.3.1.3 Interest on a Legacy

Where a legacy carries interest, L is liable to tax on that interest under ITTOIA 2005, Part 4, Chapter 2 if it has become L's income. An attempt to disclaim the interest failed where a sum had been set aside to pay the legacy.[19] From this it should follow that where no sums have been set aside, L may have a right to interest but will not be taxable in respect of it yet. Where L receives the legacy with interest, it is an open question whether the payment relates back.

30.3.2 Residue

In comparison with TA 1988, ITTOIA 2005 contains a great number of sections. One has to disentangle the aggregate income of the estate, defined in section 664, from the residuary income of the estate, defined in section 666. The aggregate income includes the various heads of income accruing to the PRs, but it also encompasses deductions. In addition to permitting any deductions allowable in computing the different types of income, there is also an exclusion of two types of 'exempt income'. The first is income to which a beneficiary is entitled under a specific disposition. The second is any income devolving on the PRs otherwise than as assets available for the payment of debts. Both these changes are due to ITTOIA 2005. The residuary income of the estate is the income of the estate less further deductions. These are interest payments, annual payments properly payable out of residue, management expenses (if properly charged to income) and any excess deductions from a previous year. The rules surrounding interest have been relaxed by ITTOIA 2005, but still exclude any deduction for interest on unpaid IHT within section 233.

---

[14] The two types are defined in ITTOIA 2005, s 651, ex TA 1988, s 701(9).
[15] *Simons Taxes*, §C.4.104.
[16] ITTOIA 2005, s 651(1).
[17] ITTOIA 2005, s 651(4) referring to s 680, ex TA 1988, s 701(10) and (10A).
[18] *IRC v Hawley* [1928] 1 KB 578, (1928) 13 TC 327.
[19] *Spens v IRC* [1970] 3 All ER 295, (1970) 46 TC 276; cf. *Dewar v IRC* [1935] 2 KB 351, (1935) 19 TC 561.

30.3.2.1 Grossing Up at the Applicable Rate

Any sums which are actually paid[20] during the administration period, whether in respect of a limited or an absolute interest, are grossed up[21] at the applicable rate. They are then treated as the beneficiary's income for the year of assessment in which the sum was paid or, if the interest has ceased, as income for the year of assessment in which it ceased.[22] Income from a foreign estate is not subject to UK tax; if UK tax has nonetheless been charged, eg by deduction at source, the gross income is apportioned, so that the income must be grossed up to reflect the UK tax paid.[23] The applicable rate does not mean the rate applicable to trusts under ITA 2007, section 479; it means the rate applicable to the type of income in the residuary estate out of which the amount is paid, eg income subject to the basic rate (20%).[24] Where dividend income is treated as having borne tax at the special rate for dividends, the normal dividend rules apply. The beneficiaries may then use the tax charged at the applicable rate as a credit against their own tax liability. The beneficiary cannot make a repayment claim in respect of any ITTOIA 2005, Part 4, Chapter 3 income,[25] but may use such income to frank payments falling within ITA 2007, sections 449 and 901.

30.3.2.2 Income Treated as Bearing Tax in Hands of PRs

Special rules apply to certain types of income which are not directly assessable to UK tax in the hands of the PRs. These are stock dividends, release of loans made to a participator in a close company, certain gains on life policies[26] and, since 1999, all Part 4, Chapter 3 income (dividends).[27] When amounts of such income are allocated to individual beneficiaries, these types of income are allocated last.[28] Income is treated as having borne tax at the dividend ordinary rate, except life policy gains which are treated as having borne tax at the lower rate.[29] No repayment of tax may be made.[30] The tax is available as a credit against the beneficiary's own tax liability in respect of the limited interest arising from a foreign estate; it is this credit which represents the change from earlier rules. The rules also specify the rate of UK tax, which is the applicable rate for such payments out of UK estates. Dividend income was brought into the list of relevant amounts in 1999 so as to prevent any right to repayment of tax.

---

[20] ITTOIA 2005, ss 667 and 671; payment is widely defined in ITTOIA 2005, s 681, ex TA 1988, s 701(12).

[21] Grossing up is directed by ITTOIA 2005, ss 656 (UK estate) and 657 (foreign estate); on rate, see s 663. These provisions were formerly TA 1988, ss 695(2), (4), 696(3), (4). Benefits in kind must be grossed up (*IRC v Mardon* (1956) 36 TC 565).

[22] On final year of limited interest, see ITTOIA 2005, s 674(4), ex TA 1988, s 695(2).

[23] On grossing up of foreign estate income, see ITTOIA 2005, ss 657 *et seq*. For relief for foreign tax, see s 678, ex TA 1988, s 695(5).

[24] ITTOIA 2005, s 679, ex TA 1988, s 698A (referring to TA 1988, ss 1A and 1B), TA 1988, s 701(3A).

[25] ITTOIA 2005, s 680(6); the ban on repayment applies also to the gains from a life policy.

[26] ITTOIA 2005, s 680(3)(b), referring to ITTOIA 2005, ss 403(5), 409(3) and 511(5); ex TA 1988, s 699A(1)(a).

[27] ITTOIA 2005, s 680(3)(a), ex TA 1988, s 699A(1)(b), (1A), refer to Sch F and a distribution within s 233(1).

[28] ITTOIA 2005, s 679(5), ex TA 1988, s 699A(2)(b).

[29] ITTOIA 2005, s 680(4), ex TA 1988, s 699A(3), (4).

[30] ITTOIA 2005, s 680(5), ex TA 1988, s 699A(5).

30.4   Residuary Beneficiary

30.4.1 *Limited Interest*

Beneficiaries have a limited interest if they do not have an absolute interest but would have a right to income if administration were complete.[31] It is an open question whether a person whose interest is vested subject to being divested is entitled to the income.[32] Any sums which are actually paid[33] during the administration period in respect of a limited interest are grossed up at the applicable rate under the rules explained at §30.3.2 above. They are then treated as the beneficiary's income for the year of assessment in which the sum was paid or, if the interest has ceased, as income for the year of assessment in which it ceased.[34] Income from a foreign estate is grossed up to reflect the UK tax paid.[35] Rules are needed to determine the source of any income distributed. Therefore, payments are treated as coming first from income taxed at basic rate, and then from certain types of income treated as bearing tax.[36]

30.4.1.1 Completion of Administration

Where the administration of an estate is complete, the beneficiaries bring in income that has accrued to the PRs during the administration as and when it is received by them,[37] as part of their self-assessment. Any sums in the estate remaining payable to the beneficiaries are income of the year in which the administration is completed. This is subject to one minor qualification; if a beneficiary's interest ended before the year in which administration was completed, eg where he dies, it is instead treated as income of the year in which the interest ceased.[38] For estates where the administration was completed before 6 April 1995, a more complex system required a spreading-back of the remaining sums over the period of administration.[39] The current rule is simpler to apply (and more appropriate to self-assessment), but means that income will be concentrated in one year.

The income on which the beneficiary is taxed will almost certainly bear little relation to the actual income of the estate in respect of which the PRs are chargeable. This is partly because administration expenses are deductible in computing the beneficiary's income, not in computing the estate income, but also because the fluctuation in rates of tax and the variation in the estate income mean that the estate income may arise at times different from the dates of payment.

---

[31] ITTOIA 2005, s 650(2), ex TA 1988, s 701(3).
[32] The doubts stem from *Stanley v IRC* (see above at §29.3.3.1).
[33] On transfers of assets as payments, see ITTOIA 2005, s 681, ex TA 1988, s 701(12).
[34] ITTOIA 2005, s 674, ex TA 1988, s 695(2).
[35] ITTOIA 2005, s 678, ex TA 1988, s 695(5). TA 1988, s 695(6) has been removed by ITTOIA 2005; see Explanatory Notes.
[36] ITTOIA 2005, s 679, ex TA 1988, s 701(3A)(b), as amended.
[37] FA 1995, Sch 18. On adjustments after the administration period, see ITTOIA 2005, s 682.
[38] ITTOIA 2005, s 674(4), TA 1988, s 695(3) (1995 version).
[39] TA 1988, s 695(3) (original version).

30.4.1.2 Source

Income of a legatee who was not resident or not ordinarily resident in the UK was formerly treated, by concession, as if it arose directly from the various sources, even though the estate was a UK estate (eg where the sole assets were UK government securities).[40] This was a famous example of 'looking through' to the underlying income.

30.4.1.3 Information

The PRs have a duty to provide the beneficiary with information on the amount of tax at the applicable rate which the income is deemed to have borne.[41]

30.4.2 Absolute Interest

A beneficiary (B) has an absolute interest in residue if, on the hypothesis that the administration were then complete, he would be entitled to the capital or part of it in his own right.[42] It is unclear whether a person entitled to capital but subject to the payment of an annuity is entitled to it 'in his own right'.[43]

30.4.2.1 Sums Actually Paid

Payments during the administration period are grossed up at the applicable rate and treated as B's income of the year of payment.[44] The various rules as to applicable rates and sources of payments are explained above at §30.3.[45]

30.4.2.2 Payments in Excess of Aggregate Income Entitlement

Since B is also entitled to the capital, rules separate income payments from capital payments. Income treatment applies only to the extent of what ITTOIA 2005 calls B's 'assumed income entitlement' for that year; any excess is treated as capital. 'Assumed income entitlement' is the amount which would be the aggregate of the amounts received for that year of assessment and all previous years of assessment in respect of the interest if that person had a right in each year to receive those amounts, and had received the amounts in the case of a UK estate; these sums must be grossed up to reflect income tax at the applicable rate for that year.[46] In the case of a foreign estate, this calculation assumes that B has received only the residuary income for that year, without grossing up.[47]

30.4.2.3 Residuary Income

This was discussed at §30.3.2 above; if deductions exceed the sums paid as income, the deficit may be carried forward.[48]

---

[40] Former ESC A14.

[41] ITTOIA 2005, s 682A, ex TA 1988, s 700(5), (6), added by FA 1995.

[42] ITTOIA 2005, s 650(1), ex TA 1988, s 701(2).

[43] See *Simon's Direct Tax Service*, Pt C4.107.

[44] ITTOIA 2005, ss 652(2), 656, 657 and 660(2) ex TA 1988, s 696(3), as replaced by FA 1995.

[45] On transfers of assets, see ITTOIA 2005, s 681, ex TA 1988, s 701(12).

[46] ITTOIA 2005, s 665, ex TA 1988, s 696 added by FA 1995.

[47] ITTOIA 2005, s 665(1) (step 2), ex TA 1988, s 696(3B).

[48] ITTOIA 2005, s 666(2), ex TA 1988, s 697(1A), added by FA 1995, Sch 18, para 4(1) and see also ex ESC A13 (1994).

30.4.2.4 Completion of Administration

When the administration is completed, the amount paid out during administration is compared with the aggregate income entitlement down to and including that year. If the amount paid is less than the entitlement, the balance is treated as income paid immediately before the end of the period of administration.[49] This balance must be grossed up as necessary. Adjustments are also necessary if the benefits received are less than the aggregate residuary income, for example if debts payable out of residue are discovered late in the administration period. Any reduction is carried out first against the income of the year of the completion of administration, with any remaining reductions taking effect against the income of earlier years.[50] ITTOIA 2005 makes a small change in the taxpayer's favour by allowing any excess allowable estate deductions in the final year to be set against the amounts on which the beneficiaries are taxable.[51]

30.4.2.5 Exempt Beneficiary

If the residuary beneficiary is exempt from income tax, a repayment may be due. In the long-lost days of composite rates of tax on building society interest, a repayment could be obtained if the residuary income included building society income since the Revenue did not look through to the underlying source.[52] However, look-through was permitted by concession, and to the taxpayer's advantage, in certain instances, eg where B was a non-resident.[53] These matters of look-through are still of occasional importance.

30.4.2.6 Information

The PRs are under an obligation, enforceable at the suit of the person making the request, to respond to a request in writing for details of the deemed income.[54]

30.5 Residue Held on Discretionary Trusts

If the residue is held on discretionary trusts, the provisions so far considered do not apply, since there exist neither absolute nor limited interests. ITTOIA 2005 provides that income is treated as arising from a person's discretionary interest in residue if a payment is made in that person's favour.[55] Where income is paid indirectly through a trustee, any payment to the trustee is treated, for the purpose of the rules, as income paid to the trustee.

---

[49] ITTOIA 2005, s 652(3), 660(2) and 665, ex TA 1988, s 696(5) substituted version; a different rule applied before 1995.

[50] ITTOIA 2005, ss 666 and 668, ex TA 1988, s 697 (1995, Sch 18, para 4(2)). On power to make assessments, see ITTOIA 2005, s 682, ex TA 1988, s 700(2).

[51] ITTOIA 2005, s 667 (Explanatory Notes).

[52] Statement of Practice, SP 7/80 (obsolete).

[53] ESC A14.

[54] ITTOIA 2005, s 682A, ex TA 1988, s 700(5), (6).

[55] ITTOIA 2005, s 650(3) and also s 662, which defines the basic amount of estate income; The previous version of this rule in ex TA 1988, s 698(3) applied also to payments made via discretionary trusts (Statement of Practice, SP 4/93).

30.6   Successive Interests in Residue

ITTOIA 2005 makes extensive provision for the treatment of successive interests in residue.[56] It includes a section allowing apportionment where the other parts of the residuary estate in which successive interests subsist do not quite correspond.[57]

30.6.1 Death of Beneficiary before Administration Complete

Provision is made for the possibility that the beneficiary might die before administration is complete. If the beneficiary had an absolute interest, that interest passes to his PRs and the income of the first estate will form part of the beneficiary's estate. The PRs are treated as succeeding to the absolute interest despite their representative status.[58]

30.6.2 Successive Limited Interests

Where successive interests in the residue arise for some other cause, such as assignment or disclaimer, different rules apply.[59] Where successive limited interests follow each other, they are treated as being one and the same.[60] While this means that the whole residuary income will be divided between successive holders, allowance will be made for sums due to the first holder which are paid to that holder after the assignment, such sums being treated as income of the first holder.

30.6.3 Limited then Absolute

If a limited interest is followed by an absolute interest, the absolute interest is treated as having always existed. The rules in ITTOIA 2005 are then applied as if the payment made to the holder of the limited interest had been made to the holder of the absolute interest.[61] This does not undo the liability of the holder of the limited interest, but ensures that all the income is properly taxed to one or other of them and that each is taxed on what he actually receives.

30.6.4 Successive Absolute Interests

Successive absolute interests may arise as by assignment. Here, the change in beneficiary is ignored. The aggregate income entitlement is calculated in the usual way. The effect is that

---

[56] ITTOIA 2005, ss 671–76.
[57] ITTOIA 2005, s 676 (Explanatory Notes).
[58] ITTOIA 2005, s 650(5), ex TA 1988, s 698(1).
[59] ITTOIA 2005, ss 673–75, ex TA 1988, s 698(1A), added by FA 1995.
[60] *Ibid.*
[61] ITTOIA 2005, ss 673 and 674.

each beneficiary is taxed on what he received. If any adjustment has to be made at the end of the administration period, this will fall primarily on the second holder of the interest.[62] ITTOIA 2005 goes to some lengths, in comparison with the previous law, to explain how the reduction is to be calculated; the change reflects the current practice, but represents a worse legal position for some and a better one for others.[63]

---

[62] ITTOIA 2005, s 659(3) and 671, ex TA 1988, s 698(2), substituted by FA 1995.
[63] Explanatory notes change 119.

31

Income Splitting:
Arrangements and Settlements

31.1 Introduction

ITTOIA 2005, Part 5, Chapter 5, for which the charging section is section 619, is the modern form of the settlements provisions previously in TA 1988, Part XV.[1] ITTOIA 2005, Part 5, Chapter 5 contains a series of provisions designed for two principal purposes. The first is to restrict the use of other taxable entities (such as trusts) as piggy banks, in which income may be taxed at the rates appropriate to that entity, rather than at the settlor's (S's) marginal rates, and so grow more rapidly before being passed back for S or S's spouse to enjoy. The second purpose is to restrict the income-splitting opportunities within the family, ie between spouses and between parents and minor children. A third purpose, and now almost peripheral, was to restrict the income assignment possibilities created by the system for taxing covenants (see above at §27.5), which system remains in place despite the abolition of the general right of individuals to deduct sums paid under covenants.

---

[1] On early history, see articles by Stopforth [1987] BTR 417, [1990] BTR 225, [1991] BTR 86, [1992] BTR 88, [1994] BTR 234, [1997] BTR 276 and, on charitable covenants, [1986] BTR 101.

These provisions were comprehensively rewritten and simplified with effect from the beginning of 1995–96, a reform which was most welcome. Unfortunately most of the (quite voluminous) case law is on the pre-1995 law, and so care is needed when reading it; great efforts were made by the draftsman to try and make the provisions intelligible. Separate rules apply to funds for the maintenance of heritage property.[2] The 1995 reforms originally contained two provisions which would have recast the treatment of capital sums to do with loans between settlors and settlements. These were later withdrawn for reconsideration, but with the consequence that some old provisions dealing with such capital sums (ITTOIA 2005, sections 633 *et seq*) linger on (see below at §31.6). With effect from December 2005, the Civil Partnership Act extended the treatment of married couples under the UK personal income tax to include registered same-sex couples. References to 'spouses' in this chapter should be read as also applying to civil partners from that date.

Under the current rules, the offending income is treated as that of the settlor for income tax purposes;[3] The settlor is given a right to recover the tax from the entity concerned.[4] The previous rules had a halfway stage—treating the income as income of the settlor for excess liability only. The distinction between income which is accumulated and that which arises is sometimes important (see below at §31.6). When income is treated as that of the settlor under one of these rules, prior to amendments introduced by FA 2006, the correct legal analysis was that the income arose first in the hands of the settlement and then was transferred to, or back to, the settlor by parliamentary transfer. At one time this could have surprising results as the, happily now obsolete, decision in *Ang v Parrish*[5] showed. In that case what had begun as the settlor's earned income was returned to him as investment income, which was at that time subject to a higher rate of tax. Meantime it has been held, at Special Commissioner level, that the effect of these rules was to transfer back to the settlor only that which had accrued as taxable income in the hands of the other person.[6]

The mechanics for the application of section 619 were amended by FA 2006, Schedule 13, paragraph 5, and the rule in *Ang v Parrish* was finally laid to rest after 26 years. Income arising under a settlement but treated as the settlor's is now to be treated as if it arose directly to the settlor and so at the rates that would have applied had the income arisen directly to him. So income from a trade is taxed under ITTOIA 2005, Part 2, and interest under ITTOIA 2005, Part 4. However, the legislature could not resist one restriction. If the trade run by the trustees sustains a loss, the settlor is not allowed to use it; it is not crystal clear whether the trustees may. When a charge is made on the settlor under these rules, the question arose whether the beneficiary under a discretionary trust was safe from charge. For years immunity was conferred by a discretion, but FA 2006 made this statutory (ITTOIA 2005, section 685A).

A study of these rules might leave one with the impression that a trust is never effective for tax purposes. This is untrue. Provided one avoids settlements in favour of a spouse,

---

[2] ITA 2007, ss 507–510, ex TA 1988, s 691.

[3] ITTOIA 2005, s 619, referring to ss 624, 629, 633 and 641, ex TA 1988, s 660A.

[4] ITTOIA 2005, s 646, ex TA 1988, s 660D.

[5] [1980] STC 341, [1980] 2 All ER 790, (1980) 53 TC 304. See 4th edn of this book, §31.1.

[6] *Jones v Garnett* [2004] SpC 432; [2005] STC (SCD) 9, para 71; for facts see below §31.2.2. This issue was not raised on appeal—[2005] EWHC 849 (Ch).

registered same-sex partner or unmarried minor children, and has taken all steps to exclude oneself, income may be accumulated or distributed without any adverse income tax consequences under these rules. Even settlements in favour of unmarried minor children may work, provided the income is accumulated while they have that status. One may even be a trustee and thus control the selection of beneficiaries, again other than one's spouse or unmarried minor children, under a discretionary trust or a power of appointment. The judicial approach to tax avoidance that has developed from *WT Ramsay v IRC*[7] can apply in this area,[8] and has been applied to reverse one earlier House of Lords decision.[9]

31.2   Arrangements and Settlements

It is odd that ITTOIA 2005, which was part of the Rewrite process and so was meant to make the statute law accessible and intelligible, here repeats the established wording of TA 1988, Part XV and is formally entitled 'Settlements' rather than some longer but more accurate title such as 'Ineffective dispositions of income'. The law does not take the view that income splitting should be countered only where it takes place behind devices akin to the strict settlement. The term 'settlement' includes any 'disposition, trust, covenant, agreement, arrangement or transfer of assets'.[10] The essence of a settlor is as the source of the funds from which the income derives. ITTOIA 2005 achieves this by treating a person as if he has made or entered into a settlement directly or indirectly, and then by saying that a person is treated as having made a settlement if he has provided funds for the settlement.[11]

The word 'settlement' is not a dominating word which colours the others; the word 'arrangement' is not a term of art.[12] Acts which have been held to be settlements include the setting-up of corporate structures (arrangement) and the disclaimer of an interest by a beneficiary (disposition). The limiting factor is that a transaction can be a settlement only if it contains an element of bounty (see below at §31.2.2). The Revenue view, upheld by the House of Lords in *Jones v Garnett*,[13] is that bringing a spouse into partnership may be an arrangement. Therefore, if a wife brings her husband into partnership and he does not truly earn his share of the profits, the income accruing to him may be treated as accruing to her (absent a statutory exception: see below at §34.4.2.2). Bounty is shown by the fact that he did not earn his share, and it would not have been an arrangement that his wife would have entered into with someone with whom she was dealing at arms' length.[14]

---

[7] [1982] AC 300. See discussion at §5.6 above.

[8] *Ewart v Taylor* [1983] STC 721.

[9] *Moodie v IRC* [1993] STC 188; reversing *IRC v Plummer* [1979] STC 793, [1979] 3 All ER 775, (1979) 54 TC 1.

[10] ITTOIA 2005, s 620, repeating TA 1988, s 660I(1).

[11] ITTOIA 2005, s 620(2) and (3).

[12] Greene MR in *IRC v Payne* (1940) 23 TC 610, 626. *Cf Shop and Store Developments Ltd v IRC* [1967] 1 AC 472, [1967] 1 All ER 42 (stamp duty).

[13] [2007] UKHL 35.

[14] *Jones v Garnett, ibid*, paras 22–24 per Lord Hoffmann; and see RI 268.

31.2.1 Cases

In *IRC v Mills*,[15] the taxpayer was Hayley Mills (H) who, as a child film star, appeared in many films. In order to make sure that her earnings were 'legally protected', her father, John Mills, formed a company and settled the shares of that company on trust for H with various contingent remainders over. H then signed a service contract with the company, giving the company the right to her exclusive services for a period of five years at a salary of £400 a year. The company received large sums for the films H made (including *Polyanna* and *Tiger Bay*), and distributed those sums in the form of dividend to the trustees. Since the trustees did not distribute the income, the question arose whether the income accumulated by the trust could be treated as H's. The House of Lords held that there was a settlement, that H was the settlor and that the source of the dividends was the money paid for her work, so that she had by her work provided the settlement with income indirectly. The result at that time was that income accumulated by the trustees was deemed to be H's; today all the income, accumulated or not, would be treated as H's.[16]

In *IRC v Buchanan*,[17] property was settled by X on A for life, with remainder to B for life on protective trusts and remainder to B's children. The settlement also provided that if B should disclaim her life interest, the property should be administered at the moment when B's interest would have fallen into possession as if B were dead, thus avoiding the discretionary trusts that would otherwise have arisen on A's death following the disclaimer. B disclaimed her interest and the next day A released his interest. The Court of Appeal held that the destruction of an interest was a disposition. B had a disposable interest in that she had the right to income after A's death and could end that entitlement or not as she chose. The result was that the disclaimer was a settlement, and so income arising in favour of B's infant children was deemed to be B's.[18]

31.2.2 No Bounty, No Settlement

In *Jones v Garnett*[19] members of the House of Lords, especially Lord Hoffmann and Baroness Hale, felt that the term 'bounteous' was distinctly old fashioned or even patronising. Despite these very cogent observations, we retain the term to reflect its use in the established case law. If there is no element of bounty, the transaction is not a settlement; this follows even if the transaction is not carried out for commercial reasons. In *IRC v Levy*,[20] an interest-free loan by a taxpayer to a company wholly owned by him—a transaction which the Commissioners had found to contain no element of bounty—was not a settlement.

---

[15] [1974] 1 All ER 722, [1974] STC 130. Note TA 1988, s 775. Where a stranger provides trustees with advice as a result of which the income of the fund is increased, it appears that this section cannot apply since the stranger provides advice not funds (see *Mills v IRC* 49 TC 367, 408, per Viscount Dilhorne).

[16] The actual case involved what was then TA 1988, s 673; the income would now be caught by ITTOIA 2005, s 624.

[17] [1957] 2 All ER 400, (1957) 37 TC 365.

[18] Under what was then TA 1988, s 663; the income would now be caught by ITTOIA 2005, s 629, ex TA 1988, s 660B.

[19] [2007] UKHL 35.

[20] [1982] STC 442, (1982) 56 TC 68.

In *IRC v Plummer*,[21] a charity paid £2,480 to the taxpayer (T) who covenanted to pay the charity a sum which, net of tax at basic rate, would amount to £500 each year for five years. The purpose of the scheme was to enable T to reduce his liability to surtax. The payments were annual payments, being income of the charity under Schedule D, Case III and, in consequence, deductible under TA 1988, section 835. The difference between £500 grossed up at basic rate and £500 was thus relieved from surtax, enabling T to keep the benefit of the tax relief himself. Despite the fact that the arrangement was made solely to obtain the tax advantage, the House of Lords held that, as there was no bounty between the parties, it was not a settlement. Today the scheme would fail either because their Lordships have since held that the payments were not 'annual payments' after all,[22] or because such schemes were stopped (prospectively) by statute in 1977 (see below at §31.7.3). However, this still leaves *Plummer* as an example of the no-bounty test. The validity of the bounty test has been questioned. Suppose that X settles property for two years upon trust for X absolutely if X survives the period and, if not, for Y, and that Y provides full consideration for his interest. *Plummer* seems to say that there is no settlement, and yet this is the very type of avoidance at which provisions like the old TA 1988, section 673 were aimed.[23]

In applying the test the courts look at the transaction as a whole. In *Chinn v Collins*,[24] trustees exercised a power of appointment in favour of a beneficiary who later assigned his contingent interest under that exercise as part of a scheme to avoid tax. The House of Lords held that there was a settlement. The settlor's bounty in creating the settlement remained incomplete until the appointment was made and the trustees then conferred bounty on the beneficiary. The test of bounty was applied in *Butler v Wildin*.[25] Parents, who were architects, had worked for a company without fee. They had arranged for shares to be held by their infant children. It was held that there was a settlement—the parents were being bounteous to their children.

The problems of applying the bounty test are shown by what is widely known as the *Arctic Systems* case, more correctly *Jones v Garnett*,[26] a case in which the two Special Commissioners were divided[27] but which ultimately the House of Lords decided in favour of the taxpayer. In doing so, their Lordships confirmed that an arrangement must be bounteous in order to be a settlement. In *Jones v Garnett*, H the taxpayer was a skilled IT specialist who had been made redundant and decided to set up in business on his own. H and W (his wife who had good office skills) bought Arctic Systems, an off-the-shelf company. There were good commercial reasons for using a company rather than H trading on his own account. The shares were divided equally between H and W; H was the sole director and W was company secretary. H provided the company's technical and money-making skills as an IT consultant, while W provided her administrative skills which were extensive. W was not

---

[21] [1979] STC 793, [1979] 3 All ER 775. For an interesting analysis of the speeches, see Murphy and Rawlings (1981) 44 *MLR* 617, 643 *et seq.*

[22] *Moodie v IRC* [1993] STC 188; see, generally, Gillard, *In the Name of Charity* (Chatto & Windus, 1987).

[23] Venables, *Tax Planning Through Trusts* (Chatto & Windus, 1987), §20:26.

[24] [1981] STC 1, [1981] 1 All ER 189, (1981) 54 TC 311; see discussion in *IRC v Levy* [1982] STC 442, (1982) 56 TC 68.

[25] [1989] STC 22, (1989) 61 TC 666.

[26] For commentary on the case see Robson [2005] BTR 15–21, Loutzenhiser [2005] BTR 401 and [2006] BTR 140, Kerridge [2007] BTR 591, Tiley [2006] *CLJ* 289, and Gammie, Redston and Loutzenhiser in [2007] BTR no 6.

[27] [2005] STC (SCD) 9. As the Special Commissioners were divided, the senior prevailed.

made a director; she had no right to dividends, and as these were decided upon by H, she received them at his discretion. Each received a small salary with dividends in the £20,000+ range. The company paid corporation tax. The Revenue invoked TA 1988, section 660A (now ITTOIA 2005, section 624). This was on the basis that there was a settlement, and that the property comprised in the settlement consisted of the shares and so the dividend income from the shares to W was to be treated as H's instead.

Both Special Commissioners held that there was an arrangement.[28] The senior Special Commissioner said that this was because the shares were allocated with the intention of declaring dividends in the future.[29] The other Special Commissioner held that there was no element of bounty *when the shares were acquired*; for her, an intention to provide bounty (dividends) later on was not the same as the provision of bounty itself. She pointed to the fact that the appellant was not under any obligation to provide services to the company at that time, ie when the shares were allocated;[30] this shows how very narrow the divide is between the two Special Commissioners and how easily a very slightly different set of facts might give rise to different results. The House of Lords ultimately decided in HMRC's favour on the question whether the arrangement was bounteous and constituted a settlement, but in the taxpayer's favour on the application of the rule excluding outright gifts between spouses from the settlement rules—on which see chapter eight above.

31.2.3 Property Comprised in Settlement

The term 'settlement' is so widely defined that the more crucial question[31] is to determine what property is comprised in the settlement. The key statutory concept in TA 1988 was that property is settled by the settlor if it originated from him or her. This is rendered in ITTOIA 2005 as saying that a person is treated as settlor if he has made or entered into a settlement directly or indirectly, and then by saying that a person is, in particular, treated as having made a settlement if he has provided funds directly or indirectly for the purposes of the settlement.[32]

It may be that there is more than one settlor (see further below §31.3.2), in which case references to property comprised in the settlement refer only to property originating from the settlor;[33] references to income arising include only income originating from the settlor.[34] References to property originating from a settlor refer to: (a) property which the settlor has supplied directly or indirectly for the purposes of the settlement, (b) property representing that property and (c) so much of any property as represents both property so provided and other property as, on a just apportionment, represents the property so provided.[35] It is expressly provided that property representing accumulated income is caught.[36] In *Chamberlain v IRC*,[37] S transferred assets to a company which he

---

[28] [2005] STC (SCD) 9, at paras 57 and 118.
[29] *Ibid* at para 61.
[30] [2005] EWHC 849 (Ch) at [127].
[31] *Chamberlain v IRC* [1943] 2 All ER 200, 203, (1943) 25 TC 317, 329, per Lord Thankerton.
[32] ITTOIA 2005, s 620(2) and (3).
[33] ITTOIA 2005, s 644(3), ex TA 1988, s 660E(2)(a).
[34] ITTOIA 2005, s 644(3)(b), ex TA 1988, s 660E (2)(b).
[35] ITTOIA 2005, s 645(1), ex TA 1988, s 660E(5).
[36] ITTOIA 2005, s 645(4), ex TA 1988, s 660E(7)(b).
[37] *Chamberlain v IRC* [1943] 2 All ER 200, (1943) 25 TC 317.

controlled, and trustees acquired ordinary shares issued by the company. The trustees paid for the shares with money given to them by S. S later gave them more money with which to buy further shares. It was held that the property comprised in the settlement was the money given by S and the shares purchased with that money—but not the assets of the company itself.

31.3 Settlor

31.3.1 Settling Property

The term 'settlor' covers not only any person by whom the settlement was made or entered into,[38] but also a person who has done so directly or indirectly. This phrase is then made the subject of a non-exclusive example, by 'having provided (or having undertaken to provide) funds, directly or indirectly for the purposes of the settlement'.[39] In *IRC v Buchanan*,[40] B made the settlement, and was therefore a settlor, when she disclaimed her interest. Similarly, there was an indirect provision of funds in the case of the film star in *IRC v Mills*,[41] where it was said that purpose connotes neither a mental element nor a motivating intention.

A settlor makes a settlement by carrying out any steps of that settlement. Where the taxpayer had carried out one step, and later a scheme was devised and carried out by his solicitors and accountants, the scheme was held to be part of his settlement even though he was not consulted or present at any meetings.[42] An infant can make a settlement—as in *IRC v Mills*.[43]

The notion of a settlor is widened to include one who has made a reciprocal arrangement with another person for that other person to make or enter into the settlement.[44] The purpose here is to catch the obvious device whereby A makes a settlement on B's children and, in return, B makes a settlement on A's children; however, there must be a reciprocal arrangement.[45] If X gives property to Y who transfers it to a settlement, Y is the settlor and X is not—unless there is some conscious association between X and the proposed settlement.[46]

Case law establishes that where funds are provided for a settlement, a very strong inference is drawn that those funds are provided for the purpose of the settlement,[47] an inference which will be rebutted if it is established that they were provided for another purpose. In *IRC v Mills*, the infant provided funds for the purposes of a settlement, even if unconsciously.

---

[38] ITTOIA 2005, s 620(2), ex TA 1988, ss 660G(1), 682A(1).
[39] ITTOIA 2005, ss 620(3)(a) and (b), ex TA 1988, s 660G(2).
[40] [1957] 2 All ER 400, (1957) 37 TC 365.
[41] [1974] 1 All ER 722, 727, [1974] STC 130, 135, per Viscount Dilhorne.
[42] *Crossland v Hawkins* [1961] 2 All ER 812, (1961) 39 TC 493; discussed by Park J in [2005] EWHC 849 (Ch) at [37]–[41].
[43] No argument was raised that Hayley Mills could have the arrangement set aside on the grounds of its invalidity by reason of her infancy.
[44] ITTOIA 2005, s 620(3)(c), ex TA 1988, ss 660G(2) and 682A(1).
[45] Eg, *Hood Barrs v IRC* [1946] 2 All ER 768, (1946) 27 TC 385.
[46] *Fitzwilliam v IRC* [1993] STC 502, 516, per Lord Keith.
[47] *IRC v Mills* [1974] 1 All ER 722, 727, [1974] STC 130, 135.

31.3.2 *Multiple Settlors: Whose Income?*

As we have already seen, the breadth of the definitions of 'settlement' and 'settlor' means that more than one person may be a settlor in relation to a particular settlement.[48] Two issues arise: (a) Are there two settlors? (b) If so, what are the consequences?

Where there is more than one settlor, the rules apply to each settlor as if each were the only settlor.[49] Given the definition of 'settlement', it follows that there are two or more settlors if income arising under the settlement originates from two or more persons. References to property comprised in the settlement refer only to property originating from that settlor, and references to income arising include only income originating from that settlor.[50] Where the property originating from the settlor is not the only property in the settlement, an apportionment is made.[51]

In *IRC v Mills* (above) it was held that while the father was clearly a settlor, so was his daughter, H; and since it was H's services which supplied the company with funds from which to pay dividends to the trust, she indirectly provided the income for the settlement; hence, all the income originated from her. The problem of the two settlors did not therefore arise in relation to the taxpayer and her father, and what would happen in such a case was left undecided by the House of Lords.[52] In *IRC v Buchanan* (see §31.2.1) the Revenue argued that the income accrued to B's children in consequence of her disposition. Yet if A had not released his interest, no income would actually have accrued to the children. The Revenue won but did not make any assessment for any year before that in which A died. In the Court of Appeal, X was regarded as not being a settlor for this purpose, a conclusion difficult to reconcile with *Chinn v Collins*.[53]

In *D'Abreu v IRC*,[54] in simplified terms, property had been settled by P on his daughters J and A: each half was held for life, with remainders over to children in default of appointment; and in default of children, the half of one was to pass to the other. In 1959, J, who never married, released her power to appoint in favour of any husband she might marry; A then released and assigned her contingent interest in J's half to the trustees of her half and then exercised the power of appointment in favour of her children. The result was that when J died in 1963, the income from her half accrued to A's children who were still infants. Oliver J held that, as in *Buchanan*, the whole of the income accruing to A's children did so in consequence of A's acts and so fell within what is now ITTOIA 2005, section 629. However, he went on to say that even if J were also a settlor, the provisions directed that the section was to apply to each settlor as if each were the only settlor; all the income therefore originated from A and apportionment could not be made on the basis of an actuarial valuation of their interests in 1959.

Two comments may be made. First, the decision draws a sharp and unfortunate distinction between successive and other interests. Thus, if A and J had, under the Variation of

---

[48] ITTOIA 2005, s 620, ex TA 1988, s 660G.

[49] ITTOIA 2005, s 644(1), ex TA 1988, s 660E(1).

[50] ITTOIA 2005, s 644(3), ex TA 1988, s 660E(2).

[51] ITTOIA 2005, s 645(1)(c), ex TA 1988, s 660E(5).

[52] In the Court of Appeal, Orr L.J. suggested that this was simply a case in which it is left to the Revenue authorities to act reasonably ([1973] STC 1, 22, [1972] 3 All ER 977, 998).

[53] [1981] STC 1, [1981] 1 All ER 189; see §31.2.2.

[54] [1978] STC 538.

Trusts Act 1958, extracted capital sums which they had then jointly settled on A's children, it is at least arguable that the income from J's fund would not have fallen within the section. Secondly, difficulties remain. Suppose that there are successive life interests for H and W, and they both release their interests in favour of their infant children; it seems unlikely that a court would say that they were both settlors and so tax the income twice. The appropriate answer would be to apportion on the basis of actuarial valuation of their interests, but this was rejected in *D'Abreu v IRC* (above). To treat the matter as turning on the reasonableness of the Revenue is to make liability turn on administrative discretion, the very view rejected by the House of Lords in *Vestey v IRC*.[55] It is therefore to be hoped that *D'Abreu v IRC* is not the last word.[56]

31.4 First Charging Provision: Charge on Income Arising

31.4.1 *What is Income Arising?*

ITTOIA 2005, section 624 charges the settlor on income arising under the settlement. Income arising under a settlement includes any income chargeable to income tax, whether by deduction or otherwise; it thus makes no allowance for any trust management expenses.[57] It also includes any income which would have been so chargeable if it had been received in the UK by a person domiciled and resident in the UK. This creates a hypothetical remittance to a hypothetical resident and so catches all income wherever it arises.[58] An exception must therefore be made to deal with a settlor who is not domiciled or resident in the UK and so would not be chargeable to UK tax on that income.[59] This exception is then qualified to deal with the situation in which the income is remitted. Such remitted income is treated as arising in the year of remittance if the settlor would have been taxable in the UK by reason of his residence.[60]

31.4.2 *Settlor Retaining Interest*

ITTOIA 2005, section 624(1) (ex TA 1988, section 660A) begins by deeming income arising under a settlement to be income of the settlor for all purposes of the Income Tax Acts and not as the income of any other person. Section 625 refines the rules as to when a person is treated as retaining an interest. Section 626 excludes outright gifts between spouses, while section 628 excludes certain gifts to charities. Section 627 lists income to which section 624 does not apply. These provisions make the material much easier to understand, although the draft bill of March 2004 was in some way even more comprehensible. Under section

---

[55] [1980] AC 1148, [1980] STC 10.

[56] However, the approach of Chadwick J in the IHT case of *Hatton v IRC* [1992] STC 140 (see below at §48.4.1) clearly contemplates two persons being settlors of the same property.

[57] ITTOIA 2005, s 648(1), ex TA 1988, s 660G(3).

[58] Reversing *Astor v Perry* [1935] AC 398, (1935) 19 TC 255.

[59] ITTOIA 2005, s 648(2), ex TA 1988, s 660G(4).

[60] ITTOIA 2005, ss 648(3)–(5), ex TA 1988, s 660G(4).

625, the settlor has an interest in property if there are any circumstances in which that property or any related property is, or will or become, payable to or applicable for the benefit of the settlor or the settlor's spouse.[61] 'Related property' means income from that property or any other property directly or indirectly representing proceeds of, or of income from, that property or income.[62]

The types of income which are specifically charged or excluded will be considered after looking further at the far-reaching scope of section 624.

Illustration of the first general provision—revocable settlements

If a settlement can be revoked and, on that revocation, the property reverts to the settlor or the settlor's spouse, the terms of section 625(1) will be satisfied and income arising is treated as that of the settlor.[63] If, on revocation, only a part of the property will so revert, only that part of the trust income arising is treated as the settlor's income. Powers caught include a power to advance the whole of the settled capital to the settlor,[64] and a power to diminish the property comprised in the settlement or the income which people other than the settlor or the settlor's spouse might receive from it.[65] If, in such circumstances, the rights of the settlor or the settlor's spouse are increased, section 624 will apply. These illustrations come from decisions on the pre-1995 rules.

Other examples of these provisions applying include the failure to transfer the settlor's entire beneficial interest with a consequent resulting trust,[66] or the settlor retaining a general power of appointment or a special power of which he was one of the objects. This was carried further in *Glyn v IRC*,[67] where the power was to be exercised jointly by S and his son. Although the Revenue admitted that the relevant provision would not have applied if the power had been vested in the son alone, the court held that S was caught by the section. This conclusion seems surprising in view of the fact that the son's concurrence was needed for the exercise of the power, but it may be regarded as having been realistic since the relevant provision was concerned only to charge income which was accumulated. If no appointment could be made without S's consent, he could thereby determine whether or not the income was accumulated. It is unclear whether the fact that the settlement itself was brought about by a joint arrangement with the son forms part of the ratio of the case; it certainly provides a means of distinction.

It is not every chance of the reduction in the trust assets that gave rise to an application of the old provision—only a power to be found in the settlement and derived directly there from. In *IRC v Wolfson*,[68] the settlement was of shares in a company which was controlled by S. S was thus in a position to deprive the trust of its income. This was held not to amount to a power of revocation. However, a different result might have followed if the company

---

[61] ITTOIA 2005, s 625(1), ex TA 1988, s 660A(2).

[62] ITTOIA 2005, s 625(5), ex TA 1988, s 660A(10).

[63] A supplemental deed is not retroactive (*Taylor v IRC* [1946] 1 All ER 488n, (1946) 27 TC 93).

[64] *Kenmare v IRC* [1957] 3 All ER 33, (1957) 37 TC 383.

[65] Legislation overruling *IRC v Saunders* [1957] 3 All ER 43, (1957) 37 TC 416; see [1957] BTR 392.

[66] *Hannay's Executors v IRC* (1956) 37 TC 217; as nearly happened in *IRC v Bernstein* [1961] 1 All ER 320, (1961) 39 TC 391; and *Pilkington v IRC* [1962] 3 All ER 622, (1962) 40 TC 416.

[67] [1948] 2 All ER 419, (1948) 30 TC 321.

[68] [1949] 1 All ER 865, (1949) 31 TC 158.

had been set up as part of the scheme of settlement; it would then have been permissible to look at the structure of the company to determine whether there was a power of revocation.[69] Therefore, if a settlement is expressed to endure only as long as the company exists, and S has the power to cause the company to go into liquidation, section 624 may apply.[70]

31.4.2.1 Case Law Limits of 'in Any Circumstances'—Case Law from Earlier Provisions

The language of section 625(1) is based on that found in the now repealed TA 1988, section 673.[71] Limits placed on the scope of the phrase 'in any circumstances' in the old case law are as follows:

(a) No interest is retained if the settlor's power over the assets is fiduciary rather than beneficial. In *Lord Vestey's Executors v IRC*,[72] a power to direct investments granted to S and another and not to the trustees did not cause the section to operate. Similarly, the possibility that the settlor might become a trustee of another settlement to which the first settlement transfers funds should not have that effect.

(b) The section did not apply if the property might come back to the settlor only through the independent act of a third party.[73] In *Muir v IRC*,[74] Pennycuick J stated that the section must be confined to cases where income or property will or might become payable to or applicable for the benefit of the settlor either under the trusts of the settlement itself or under some collateral arrangement having legal force. Therefore, the possibility that a beneficiary to whom funds are properly paid might then decide to make a gift to the settlor should not be taken into account. The same would hold good if a beneficiary chose to leave his property to the settlor by will. However, where the settlor's position as heir gave him the right to succeed not as beneficiary under the beneficiary's will or intestacy but because the remainder was given by the settlement to those falling within the class, the section applied.[75]

(c) The possibility that the property will come back to the settlor's estate after death and not during the settlor's lifetime is too remote.[76]

(d) The mere fact that there is some doubt about the validity of the trust does not cause the section to apply.[77] Eventually the doubt would be resolved one way or another and then the issue could be determined. Unfortunately, this could have caused a problem for the Revenue, since by the time the doubt was resolved it might be too late to make an assessment. Under the self-assessment regime this problem is shifted

---

[69] *Ibid*, 868, 169, per Lord Simonds.
[70] By analogy with *IRC v Payne* (1940) 23 TC 610. Cf *Chamberlain v IRC* [1943] 2 All ER 200, (1943) 25 TC 317.
[71] This provision also stated that S retained an interest if, 'in any circumstances whatsoever, any income or property which may at any time arise under or be comprised in that settlement is, or will or may become, payable to or applicable for the benefit of [S] or [the spouse] of [S]'.
[72] [1949] 1 All ER 1108, (1949) 31 TC 1.
[73] *Fitzwilliam v IRC* [1993] STC 502, 516, per Lord Keith, on an analogous provision.
[74] [1966] 1 All ER 295, 305, (1966) 43 TC 367, 381.
[75] *Barr's Trustees v IRC* (1943) 25 TC 72.
[76] *IRC v Gaunt* [1941] 2 All ER 82, (1941) 24 TC 69. It is unclear whether S's spouse must also predecease the return of the asset to his estate; since the spouse will benefit, if at all, only through S's generosity in leaving her an interest in his estate, it seems that the section should not apply.
[77] *Muir v IRC* [1949] 1 All ER 1108, (1949) 31 TC 1; *Barr's Trustees v IRC* (1943) 25 TC 72.

to taxpayers. A different problem might arise under the wait-and-see rule for perpetuities, since the validity of the remainder will not be resolved until some future date. It is presumed that the statutory direction[78] that the gift will fail only when it becomes clear that vesting cannot occur within the perpetuity period, and that the gift is to be treated as valid until that time, is effective for tax purposes, thus excluding the section.

(e)   The possibility that the settlor may derive some incidental benefit in the course of a commercial transaction should be ignored.[79] This gives rise to many difficulties, not the least of which is distinguishing circumstances where the benefit of the interest is incidental to the commercial transaction of the loan from those where the commercial rate of interest is incidental to the benefit of obtaining a loan.

(f)   Presumably, the possibility of subsequent legislation or the migration of the trust to a country which would regard the trust (or part of it) as invalid should be ignored.[80]

The Revenue originally took the view that the settlor retained an interest if the trustees could, or had the power to, pay the capital transfer tax (now IHT) due on the transfer since the property in the settlement could be used to meet a liability that was the settlor's—even though jointly with the trustees. This view was later abandoned.[81]

31.4.2.2 Statutory Limits

ITTOIA 2005 contains a number of statutory exclusions. First, section 625(4) states that a 'spouse' of the settlor does not include: (a) a person to whom the settlor is not for the time being married but may later marry; or (b) a spouse from whom the settlor is separated under an order of a court, or under a separation agreement or in such circumstances that the separation is likely to be permanent; or (c) the settlor's widow or widower. Of these, (a) is an enactment of previous Revenue practice; (b) is recognition of the fact that the marriage is at an end; and (c) is in line with earlier case law, since an ex-spouse is not a spouse.[82]

Permitted Interests

No charge arises if the settlor only has rights or a hope in the event of:

(1)   the bankruptcy of someone who is or may become beneficially entitled to the property or any related property; or

(2)   an assignment of or a charge on the property or any related property being made or given by some such person; or

---

[78] Perpetuities and Accumulations Act 1964, s 3(1).

[79] See *Wachtel v IRC* [1971] 1 All ER 271, 280, (1971) 46 TC 367, 381; see Burgess [1971] BTR 278 and note Lord Morton in *Lord Vestey's Executors v IRC* (1949) 31 TC 1, 114, who said that while a loan at a commercial rate of interest might benefit a person by tiding him over a difficult period, it was not money lent 'for the benefit of the debtor within TA 1970, s 447.

[80] Quaere whether the trust contained an express power to migrate to a country with such a rule.

[81] Statement of Practice SP 1/82 (for years 1981–1982 *et seq*).

[82] Point (c) comes from *Lord Vestey's Executors v IRC* [1949] 1 All ER 1108, (1949) 31 TC 1.

(3)   in the case of a marriage or civil partnership settlement, the death of both the parties to the marriage or civil partnership and of all or any of the children of the marriage or civil partnership; or

(4)   the death at any age of a child of the settlor who had become beneficially entitled to the property or any related property at any age not exceeding 25.[83]

It will be seen that (4) refers to death at any age, whereas the earlier law had referred to death under the age of 25.

It will be seen that these conditions are alternatives, so that section 624 is excluded if any one of them is satisfied. However, the legislation goes on to say that section 624 is also excluded if and so long as some person is alive and under the age of 25, during whose life that property, or any related property, cannot become payable or applicable as mentioned in that subsection except in the event of that person becoming bankrupt, or assigning or charging his interest in the property or any related property.[84]

The difference between the first group of provisions and the second provision is that the four events listed in the first paragraph above are alternatives, but those in the second paragraph are not. Thus, a settlement on trust to accumulate the income until X reaches the age of 25 and then for X for life determinable on X's bankruptcy and then to revert to the settlor, will not satisfy the conditions in the first paragraph, but will satisfy the conditions in the second. Had the accumulations been directed to end at age 28, not 25, the accumulated income would have been treated as that of the settlor only in the years after X reached 25.

Outright Inter-spousal Gifts

The general rule as stated in ITTOIA 2005, section 625(1) would deprive gifts between spouses of any effect for income tax. Not wishing to inhibit such generosity, but anxious to prevent the undue exploitation of the separate taxation of spouses, the legislation directs that an outright gift of property by one spouse to the other will not be treated as a settlement unless either (a) the gift does not carry a right to the whole of that income, or (b) the property is wholly or substantially a right to income.[85] A gift is stated not to be an outright gift if it is subject to conditions, or if the property given or any related property is, or will or may become, in any circumstances whatsoever, payable to or applicable for the benefit of the donor.[86] These words have been the subject of much attention; see chapter eight and §31.3.2 above. This rule was extended by regulations made under FA 2005 to outright gifts by registered civil partners.

Permitted Income

Section 627 prevents section 624 from applying to various types of income. First, it excludes income stemming from family breakdown arrangements. More formally, it excludes income arising under a settlement made by one party to a marriage by way of provision for the other after the dissolution or annulment of the marriage, or while they are separated under

---

[83]   ITTOIA s 625(2), ex TA 1988, s 660A(4).
[84]   ITTOIA 2005, s 625(3), ex TA 1988, s 660A(5).
[85]   ITTOIA 2005, s 626(2) and (3), ex TA 1988, s 660A(6).
[86]   ITTOIA 2005, s 626(4), ex TA 1988, s 660A(6).

an order of a court; under a separation agreement; or in such circumstances that the separation is likely to be permanent.[87] This applies only to the extent that the income arising is payable to or applicable for the benefit of that other party.

Charitable Gifts and Loans by Individuals

Section 627(2)(b) excludes any qualifying donation by an individual to a charity within the terms of FA 1990, section 25. In addition, section 620(1) specifically excludes the settlement rules where an individual makes a charitable loan arrangement, ie interest-free or low interest loans of money to a charity.[88] But for the new rule, ITTOIA 2005, sections 624 or 629 would apply to the income from such a loan since the loan capital will come back to S, ie the lender, when the loan is repaid. It appears that not only had charities found ways round this problem, but the Revenue had been generous (or lax) in deciding whether or not to apply the letter of the rules to such loans. The purpose of the change is to encourage the making of such loans.

Income Benefits Under Pension Funds and Trading Annual Payments

ITTOIA 2005, section 627(2)(c), which may be traced back to FA 2001, provides that income consisting of benefits under various approved pension schemes is not income to which section 671 can apply.[89] Next, section 627 excludes annual payments which are made by an individual for commercial reasons in connection with the individual's trade, profession or vocation.[90]

Gifts to Charity by Certain Trusts

FA 2000 provided new rules allowing a trust to make gifts to charity without triggering any liability under the provisions discussed in this chapter.[91] These are the trust counterpart of the rules for individuals just explained. These rules have been rewritten as ITTOIA 2005, section 628. The rules apply to 'qualifying income'; income qualifies if it is to be accumulated, is payable at the discretion of the trustees or any other person (whether or not there is a power to accumulate), or which before being distributed belongs to any person other than the trustees (eg an interest in possession trust).[92] In the case of a discretionary trust, the charity is an object of the discretion and in the case of an interest in possession trust it is entitled to income under the terms of the trust. The trustees must be resident in the UK and this condition must be satisfied when the income arises.[93] The effect of these rules is that the settlement rules are excluded if the income belongs to the charity under the trust or is given by the trustees to the charity during the year. However, this does not mean that there are no income tax issues. What it means is that the qualifying income is treated as that of the trust as opposed to the settlor. This opens the way for the liability of the trustee and beneficiary to be determined in the normal way under the rules in chapter twenty-nine above.

---

[87] ITTOIA 2005, s 627(1), ex TA 1988, s 660A(8).
[88] ITTOIA 2005, s 620(5), FA 2000, s 45.
[89] Previously TA 1988, 660A(9)(c), added 2001—which replaced a narrower rule, TA 1988, s 660A(7).
[90] ITTOIA 2005, s 627(2)(a).
[91] FA 2000, s 44; only s 44(4) does not reappear in ITTOIA 2005, ss 626, 676.
[92] ITTOIA 2005, s 628(5).
[93] ITTOIA 2005, s 628(1).

If the trust is bare trust, the rules in the present chapter do not apply anyway; any gift by the trust in these circumstances is treated as a gift by the individual beneficiary under the normal gift aid rules. Where the trust is an interest in possession trust and the charity is entitled to the income, the trustees pay the income tax in the usual way *qua* trustees and then hand the sum net of income tax to the charity. The charity can then reclaim the tax already paid by the trustee under the rules in chapter twenty-nine—and so not if the source is a dividend. Where the trust is not an interest in possession trust but, say, a discretionary trust, the trustee will have to settle the trust liability under section 686.

A source problem may arise if the qualifying income given away to charity is less than the total trust income arising that year. Where this occurs, the charity's income is to be taken as drawn rateably from the different types of income, eg dividend income taxed at 10% and savings income or rental income taxed at 20%.[94] Naturally this yields to any express provision in the settlement.[95] It will be interesting to see whether it will become normal practice to include clauses directing whence charitable payments should be made—and how quickly the fiscal assumptions underlying those clauses will change.[96]

31.4.2.3 Mechanics of Charge

Under ITTOIA 2005, Part 5, Chapter 5, the tax due from the settlor as a result of the application of section 624 is charged under section 619.[97] The deductions and reliefs allowed are the same as would have been allowed if the income had actually been received by the settlor.[98] A rule which is not re-enacted for income tax is that income is deemed to be the highest part of the settlor's income.[99] This may be because a new and separate rule lists the items of income which are to be treated as dividend income and so is treated as the top part of the settlor's income under other rules.[100] The settlor is given a right of indemnity for the amount of the tax paid against any trustee, or any other person to whom the income is payable by virtue of or in consequence of the settlement.[101] The settlor may obtain a certificate with relevant details from the Revenue.[102] Nothing in these rules excludes a charge to tax on the trustees as persons by whom any income is received.[103] The settlor can make a claim for any personal reliefs that would otherwise be unused; any repayment of a sum which could not have been claimed back had the trust income not been deemed to be the settlor's must be handed over to the trust.[104]

Although the settlor will, usually, have a marginal rate higher than that of the beneficiary, it may happen that the reverse is the case, and in that event, the settlement rules, which treat the income as the settlor's, may actually reduce the amount of tax otherwise payable. However, there are limits. In *Becker v Wright*,[105] the payee was resident in the UK but her

---

[94] ITTOIA 2005, s 628(2).
[95] ITTOIA 2005, s 628(3).
[96] ITTOIA 2005, s 628(2), FA 2000, s 44(3).
[97] ITTOIA 2005, ss 619, 666, ex TA 1988, s 660C(1).
[98] ITTOIA 2005, ss 623, 670, ex TA 1988, s 660C(2).
[99] TA 1988, s 660C(3).
[100] ITTOIA 2005, s 619.
[101] ITTOIA 2005, s 646, replacing TA 1988, s 660D.
[102] ITTOIA 2005, s 646(2), ex TA 1988, s 660D.
[103] ITTOIA 2005, s 646(8), ex TA 1988, s 660D(3).
[104] ITTOIA 2005, s 646(3), ex TA 1988, s 660D(2).
[105] [1966] 1 All ER 565, (1966) 42 TC 591.

father-in-law, the payer, was resident in Trinidad. A covenant was to last only three years and the payee's husband was assessed to tax under Schedule D, Case V (now part of ITTOIA 2005, Part 5, Chapter 7). He argued that the effect of the relevant settlement rule was to deem the income to belong to the payer (ie the payee's father-in-law) 'for all the purposes of the Income Tax Acts' and so was not his. Stamp J, however, held that this would mean a charge on income of a non-resident arising outside the UK, which was contrary to the general principles of the UK tax system.

31.5   Second Charging Provision: Income Arising Under an Accumulation Settlement—Parental Settlements on Unmarried Minor Children[106]

31.5.1 *General*

The UK income tax system does not aggregate the income of a child with that of the parent. Since 1936 an exception has been made to prevent income splitting when the income is derived from the parent. Such income is attributed to the parent, but only provided the child has not entered into marriage or civil partnership and is under the age of majority, ie 18. Thus, income arising in favour of adult children escapes this rule.[107]

The rule contained in ITTOIA 2005, section 629 is that any income arising under a settlement as previously defined, and which does not fall within the general rule in section 624 but which is paid during the life of the settlor to or for the benefit of the settlor's unmarried or 'non civil-partnered' minor child, is treated as that of the settlor.[108] There is a *de minimis* exception where the child's 'relevant settlement income', ie income caught, does not exceed £100 from all sources within section 629.[109] (The rule applies whenever the settlement was made—whether before or after 1995.) The definition of settlement is the same as for section 624; however section 629 is wider than section 624 in that it catches payments even though the settlor does not retain an interest. So an outright gift of money by a father where money was paid into a savings bank account was held to be a settlement.[110] It is important to remember that in such circumstances it is only the income derived from the gift which is treated as the father's income, not the sum given by him.

Section 629 also applies whether the income arises under an ordinary trust or a bare trust created by the parent for the child under which the income is treated as that of the child.[111] This change was made by FA 1999. Before then the rule did not apply where income arose under a bare trust created by the parent for the child, ie where the capital and income were

---

[106] See Kerridge (1994) 110 *LQR* 84, 97 *et seq.*

[107] For definitions, see ITTOIA 2005, s 629(7).

[108] ITTOIA 2005, s 629(1); references to payments include payments in money or money's worth (TA 1988, s 660B(6)(c)).

[109] ITTOIA 2005, s 629(3).

[110] *Thomas v Marshall* [1953] 1 All ER 1102, (1953) 34 TC 178.

[111] ITTOIA 2005, s 629(3), ex TA 1988, s 660B(1)(b), added by FA 1999, s 64; Inland Revenue Press Release, 9 March 1999, [1999] *Simon's Weekly Tax Intelligence* 459.

held on trust for the child absolutely, and the income arising was simply retained by the trustee, ie not formally accumulated. Since 1999 bare trusts may still have some role to play in tax planning, eg to take advantage of capital gains exemptions, where the trust is made by a relative other than the parent, or where the trust takes effect under the parent's will.[112]

'Child' is defined as 'including' a stepchild, but ITTOIA 2005 has, at last, removed the reference to an 'illegitimate child'.[113] The 1995 definition, unlike its predecessor, does not mention an adopted child, presumably because an adopted child is to be treated as the child of the adoptive parents.[114] Whether this includes a foster child remains to be seen, although this seems unlikely since the two examples in the statutory definition are precise legal relationships. If payments are made to or for a child who has, since the date of the settlement, been adopted by someone else, the correct construction of section 629 would suggest that the beneficiary must be a child of the settlor in the year of assessment; being a child of the settlor at the date of the settlement is not enough.

Where the settlor is assessable to tax under section 629, any tax paid by the trustees at the rate applicable to trusts in respect of income distributed is available to the settlor as a credit.[115] By concession, this extends to non-resident trusts.[116]

31.5.2 Accumulations and Section 629

No charge arises under section 629 if income arising under a settlement is retained or accumulated by the trustees.[117] Similarly, no charge arises if income has not been retained or accumulated and a capital payment is made.[118] However, once income has been retained or accumulated, any subsequent payment made by virtue or in consequence of the settlement (or any relevant enactment) to or for the benefit of an unmarried or non civil-partnered minor child of the settlor falls within section 629 income if, or to the extent that, there is available retained or accumulated income.[119] In deciding whether there is retained or accumulated income available, it is necessary first to calculate the aggregate income which has arisen under the settlement since it was begun, and then disregard four categories of payment:

(1) income which has already been treated as income of the settlor or of a beneficiary other than an unmarried or non civil-partnered minor child;
(2) income which has been paid (whether as income or capital) to or for the benefit of a beneficiary other than an unmarried or non civil-partnered minor child of the settlor; it will be seen that only actual payments are taken into account—and only payments out of income;
(3) income arising under a bare trust in 1995–96 and the next two years, and which has slipped through the tax net, but only to the extent that the income was subject to tax

---

[112] See Miller [1999] BTR 350.
[113] ITTOIA 2005, s 629(7), ex TA 1988, s 660B(6)(a).
[114] Adoption and Children Act 2002, s 67.
[115] ITA 2007, s 494, ex TA 1988, s 687.
[116] ESC A93.
[117] ITTOIA 2005, s 631(1).
[118] ITTOIA 2005, s 629 does not apply to a payment of capital.
[119] ITTOIA 2005, s 631(1), ex TA 1988, s 660B(2).

(ie not exempt by reason of allowances to be set against total income—eg personal allowances).[120] The effect of this change is that where income has arisen in favour of the child before 9 March 1999 and has escaped tax at that time because of the child's personal allowances, it will be caught if it is distributed on or after that date;

(4)   income properly spent on trust expenses or, more formally, income applied in defraying trust expenses of the trustees which were properly chargeable to income (or would have been so chargeable but for any express provisions of the trust). The definition of this category is the same as for old TA 1988, section 686 (on which, see above at §29.2.4).

The legislation also makes express provision for an offshore income gain[121] accruing in respect of a disposal of assets made by a trustee holding them for a person who would be absolutely entitled as against the trustee but for being minor. In such circumstances the income treated as arising by reference to that gain is deemed to be paid to that person.[122] The absence of the previous requirement of irrevocability is illusory since revocability will cause the settlement to fall within section 624. The exclusions in sections 624, 625, 626 have no role to play in section 629. However, there is a rule excluding any qualifying income given to trustees of a charity, or which is income to which a charity in entitled under the terms of the trust.[123]

31.6   Third and Fourth Charging Provision: Capital Sums Paid to the Settlor and Sums from Connected Bodies

The third and fourth charging provisions were to have been comprehensively reformed in 1995 but in the end were retained. They have been rewritten by ITTOIA 2005, which has created two charging provisions rather than the previous one; this is a great improvement. The rules have two advantages. The first is that they are tolerably well known; the second is that they are significantly better than the rules proposed in the Finance Bill. However, while these rules are well known, they are still riddled with traps: as Potter and Monroe put it when writing of what is now the fourth charging provision, 'loans and repayments of loans between settlor and settlement should be avoided at all costs'.[124]

31.6.1 Basics—Capital Sums

If income has been accumulated and a capital sum is paid by the trustees directly or indirectly[125] to the settlor, ITTOIA 2005, section 633 treats that sum as the settlor's

---

[120] ITTOIA 2005, s 631(5), ex TA 1988, s 660B(3)(bb), (3A) added by FA 1999, s 64(2), (3).
[121] ITTOIA 2005, s 632, ex TA 1988, s 660B(4), ie a gain within Pt XVIII, Ch 5.
[122] The reference to income is to that arising under TA 1988, s 761(1).
[123] ITTOIA 2005, s 630.
[124] Potter and Monroe, *Tax Planning* (Sweet & Maxwell, 1982), §3–05.
[125] ITTOIA 2005, s 633(1), ex TA 1988, s 677(1); it is unclear whether these words add anything (*IRC v Wachtel* [1971] 1 All ER 271, (1971) 46 TC 543).

income unless it was not paid for full consideration in money or money's worth.[126] This applies whenever there is 'available income'[127] in the trust, ie both where accumulated income exists in the fund when the sum is paid and, subject to limits, even when the accumulation arises subsequently. In one instance, however, even sums paid for full consideration cause a charge. If the trustees lend money to the settlor or the settlor's spouse, there is a promise to repay—and so full consideration—and yet also the risk that the repayment terms might not be enforced, at least as long as the settlor is alive. In this way the settlor could create a fund which would be taxed only at trust rates and yet enjoys what was once the settlor's own money at the same time. Section 634 therefore defines 'capital sum' as any sum paid by way of a loan, and goes on to extend this to any sum paid (by the trustees to the settlor or the settlor's spouse) by way of repayment of a loan.[128] A capital sum does not cause section 634 to apply if it could be payable to the settlor only in one of the events specified in section 625(2) or on the death specified in section 625(3).[129]

At first, TA 1988, section 677 did not catch payments to third parties to whom the settlor owed money.[130] However, this and other loopholes are now sealed; the term 'capital sum' for purposes of ITTOIA 2005, section 633 extends to:

(1)   any sum paid to the settlor (or to the settlor's spouse) jointly with another person;
(2)   any sum paid to a third party at the settlor's direction;
(3)   any sum paid to a third party by virtue of the assignment by the settlor of the right to receive it; and
(4)   any sum otherwise paid or applied by the trustees for the benefit of the settlor.[131]

31.6.2 Loans and Repayments

The concept of 'loan' is central to these provisions, yet the term is not further defined. Case law shows that the term is not confined to the common law relationship of debtor and creditor, and applies equally where there is an equitable right to reimbursement.[132] A loan need not be in cash, and a secured loan is still a loan. A loan is a loan even though the person giving it may view the transaction as an investment.[133]

Once the loan is repaid it ceases to be subject to these rules for the years subsequent to that in which the repayment takes place.[134] Therefore, if a loan was made in 2016–17, was repaid in 2018–19 and income is accumulated for the first time in 2020–21, section 633 will have no effect. Furthermore, if S receives a loan of £5,000 which is then repaid, and a new loan of £5,000 is taken out, S will be liable to a charge on £5,000, not £10,000.

---

[126] ITTOIA 2005, s 634(1), ex TA 1988, s 677(9).
[127] Defined in ITTOIA 2005, s 635(3), ex TA 1988, s 677(2).
[128] ITTOIA 2005, ss 634(1)(a), 679(1), ex TA 1988, s 677(9), as amended in 1995.
[129] ITTOIA 2005, s 634(3)(a). See above at §31.6.1.
[130] *IRC v Potts* [1951] 1 All ER 76, (1951) 32 TC 211.
[131] ITTOIA 2005, ss 634(4)–(6), ex TA 1988, s 677(10).
[132] *De Vigier v IRC* [1964] 2 All ER 907, (1964) 42 TC 24.
[133] *McCrone v IRC* (1967) 44 TC 142.
[134] ITTOIA 2005, s 638(1), ex TA 1988, s 677(4).

Section 633 also applies where a loan by the settlor to the trustees is repaid.[135] Analogous mitigating rules apply. Where the loan has been repaid but the settlor then makes a further loan of an amount not less than the original loan, section 633 does not apply.[136] This provision is curious in that it applies only where the original loan has been completely repaid; there is no proportionate relief for a partial repayment. However, while the rule requires complete repayment, this does not necessarily mean repayment in full; an agreement by the settlor to accept a lesser sum in complete discharge of the original loan may suffice.

The capricious nature of these rules has caused much adverse comment, especially when innocent transactions are caught. In *De Vigier v IRC*,[137] trustees held property for two infant children contingently upon their attaining the age of 25, with a power to accumulate and maintain. The trustees had wished to take advantage of a rights issue by a company whose shares they held, but they had no money and no power to borrow. The trustees were S's wife and a solicitor. S's wife therefore paid £7,000 into the trust bank account to pay for the shares, and within nine months, that sum had been repaid in two equal instalments. S was held taxable on the grossed-up equivalent of £7,000 (£12,174 at that time). The sum was paid by way of repayment of a loan. The fact that S's wife right to the repayment arose from the equitable right of an indemnity given to a trustee who incurs expenses on behalf of the trust, rather than the common law claim on a contract of loan, made no difference. Yet had the trust had the power to borrow, and had S's wife merely guaranteed that loan, no charge would have arisen.[138] In *De Vigier* an advance of money was made to the trust upon the terms that it was to be repaid out of the trust fund. This was held to be a loan.

31.6.3 The Charge from Income

The whole purpose of the legislation is to prevent settlors deriving benefit for themselves from property, the income of which may be taxed at a lower rate than if it were still theirs. ITTOIA 2005, section 633 therefore applies only to the extent that the payment could have been made from 'available income', ie to the extent that the income arising under the trust since it was created[139] is greater than the sums distributed or which, although not distributed, have already been treated as the settlor's, together with the tax on these payments.[140] Perhaps because the payment is made to the settlor, he is given no statutory right to be reimbursed out of the trust funds in respect of the tax; for the same reason, any repayment of tax by reason of the settlor's personal reliefs may be retained by the settlor.[141] These acts of apparent generosity are, however, more than offset by the fact that there is no way of refunding the tax when the settlor, or the settlor's estate, repays the loan.[142] ITTOIA 2005 includes a rule preventing a double charge under these rules and the close company loan rules.[143]

---

[135] See *Piratin v IRC* [1981] STC 441.
[136] ITTOIA 2005, ss 638(4) and (5), ex TA 1988, s 677(5).
[137] (1964) 42 TC 24.
[138] *Ibid*, 33, per Russell LJ.
[139] Or since the year 1937–38 if shorter!
[140] ITTOIA 2005, ss 633 and 635, ex TA 1988, s 677(1), (2).
[141] ITTOIA 2005, s 646 does not apply to s 633.
[142] *Cf* TA 1988, s 419(4).
[143] ITTOIA 2005, ss 639(1), (2), ex TA 1988, s 677(3).

31.6.3.1 Eleven-Year Rule

Where the capital sum paid exceeds the undistributed income, the excess is carried forward and charged to the settlor in the next year to the extent that there is undistributed income available up to the end of that year, and so on for succeeding years subject to a maximum of 11 years.[144] There is no 11-year maximum to the carry-back rule where the income has been accumulated before the capital sum is paid. An allowance is made for sums already charged under section 633.[145] Once the 11-year limit has passed it falls out of account for section 633, but it cannot then reduce the amount of available income which may be matched against a subsequent capital payment.

31.6.3.2 The Charge

The sum is charged on the settlor under ITTOIA 2005, section 619 and not as previously under Schedule D, Case VI. The charge is on the undistributed income grossed up at the rate applicable to trusts.[146] Credit is given for such tax as has been charged on the trust.[147] Trustees who have made payments to the settlor, and which fall within section 633, must therefore distribute all the trust income each year until the settlor dies or the 11-year period expires. If S emigrates, it would appear that, the source being within the UK, the charge to tax remains, although if S has little other UK income the tax bill may be reduced.

31.6.3.3 Risks

A further problem is that the sum is treated as the settlor's income in the year of payment, notwithstanding that it may have been accumulated over many years. It is small wonder that most trusts now contain a clause making it a breach of trust to pay any capital sum to the settlor or the settlor's spouse. Such clauses are simply a reminder to trustees, since payments actually made can fall within section 633 even though in breach of trust.

31.6.4 Sums from Connected Bodies

Section 641 causes section 633 to apply with equal vigour to capital sums received by the settlor from a body corporate connected with the settlement, eg a loan from the company.[148] A body corporate is connected with a settlement if it is at any time in the year either (a) a close company (or not a close company only because it is not resident in the UK) and the participators then include the trustees of the settlement, or (b) controlled by such a company.[149]

Partly because of the habit of using accumulation trusts to receive dividend income from private companies, which income was not needed by the family owners, this provision was a lethal trap whenever the settlor considered making a loan to the company, or vice versa.

---

[144] ITTOIA 2005, ss 633(4), (5).

[145] On previous law, see Lord Reid in *Bates v IRC* [1967] 1 All ER 84, 90, (1967) 44 TC 225, 261.

[146] ITTOIA 2005, s 640, ex TA 1988, s 677(6), (7).

[147] ITTOIA 2005, s 640(2), ex TA 1988, s 677(7).

[148] ITTOIA 2005, s 641(2), ex TA 1988, s 678. For reason, see Lord Reid in *Bates v IRC* [1967] 1 All ER 84, 90, (1967) 44 TC 225, 261.

[149] ITTOIA 2005, s 643(4); originally added by FA 1995, Sch 17, para 11. This means that whenever a trust has shares in a family company, S must beware whenever he takes or makes a loan.

In order, therefore, to limit the operation of section 633 to those situations in which it could fairly be said that the settlor was deriving some benefit from the accumulation, section 641 goes on to provide that section 633 shall apply only where there has been an 'associated payment', ie a payment by the trustees to the company in a period of five years ending or beginning with the date on which the payment is made to the settlor.[150] Further, section 633 does not apply where the loan is repaid within 12 months and the period for which loans are outstanding in any five-year period does not exceed 12 months.[151]

When a capital payment is made by the company to the settlor, and that payment precedes the making of an associated payment from the trustees to the company, the settlor is not taxed until that associated payment is made.[152]

31.7 Settlements of Income—Covenants and Other Annual Payments

31.7.1 *General*

Covenants and other obligations under which annual payments arise are clearly settlements and so potentially within these rules. ITA 2007, sections 900–901 deprive most annuities or other annual payments by individuals of any income tax effect. Such payments are neither deductible as a charge on the income of the payer, nor income of the payee arising under ITTOIA 2005, Part 5, Chapter 2.[153] The effect of this is that since no income arises under the disposition giving rise to the legal obligation to make the payments, there is nothing for the settlement rules to bite on. However, some payments fall within Part 5, Chapter 2 and are not removed by sections 900–901 of the 2007 Act. For these, the income arising will be treated as that of the settlor under the settlement rules, unless the settlor can show that the income arises from property in which he has no interest, or a statutory exclusion applies. The statutory exclusions in ITTOIA 2005, sections 627 and 628 have been considered above at §31.4.2. Of particular importance here are the exclusions of maintenance payments and of annual payments made by an individual for bona fide commercial reasons in connection with his trade, profession or vocation.[154]

31.7.2 *Qualifying Donations for Charity/Covenanted Payments to Charity*

At one time, qualifying donations to charity were usually made by covenant and such covenants were excluded from the scope of the settlement rules. More recently, simple gifts to charity have also qualified for tax relief and so, since the start of 2000–01, any income arising under a qualifying donation to charity is outside the settlement rules.[155]

---

[150] ITTOIA 2005, s 641(1)(b), term defined s 643(3).
[151] ITTOIA 2005, s 642, ex TA 1988, s 678(6).
[152] ITTOIA 2005, s 641(4).
[153] ITTOIA 2005, s 727, ex TA 1988, s 347A(1).
[154] ITTOIA 2005, ss 627(2)(b), 673(1) and (2), ex TA 1988, ss 660A(8) and (9).
[155] ITTOIA 2005, s 627(2)(b), ex TA 1988, s 660A(9)(b) as amended by FA 2000, s 41. See further the 4th edn of this book.

31.7.3 *Reverse Annuities, etc*

ITA 2007, sections 900–901 do not affect the operation of section 904,[156] which was first introduced in 1977 to deal with 'reverse annuities'.[157] Section 904 applies where the annuity or annual payment charged under ITTOIA 2005, Part 5, Chapter 2 is made under a liability incurred for money or money's worth, and all or any of the consideration is not required to be brought into account in computing the income of the person. The effect is that the payment is not deductible in computing total income. The deduction at source rules under ITA 2007, sections 900–901 are excluded. FA 2005 amended the former TA 1988, section 125 so that it also applied to prevent the deduction when the consideration consists of a dividend or of the right to receive one.[158] The purpose behind this change was to prevent avoidance schemes aiming to create tax deductions from central arrangements whereby annual payments were given in return for the right to receive foreign dividends.[159] The rule applies whenever the payment is made under a liability incurred for money or money's worth. It does not therefore affect purely voluntary covenants; neither does it affect the purchase of annuities from insurance companies, since the sums paid by the individual will enter into the profits of the company. There are a number of other exceptions.[160]

---

[156] ITTOA 2005, ss 728–729, ex TA 1988, s 347A(2)(d).
[157] TA 1988, s 125, reversing *IRC v Plummer* [1979] STC 793, [1979] 3 All ER 775 (see above at §31.2.2). On history see Stopforth [2007] BTR 557.
[158] ITA 2007, s 904, ex TA 1988, s 125(1)(b)(i) as amended by FA 2005.
[159] Inland Revenue Press Release March 2005; the FA 2005 provision also repeals TA 1988, ss 801(4A)–(4D).
[160] ITA 2007, s 904, ex TA 1988, s 125(3).

PART III

Capital Gains Tax

32

Introduction and Policy

32.1 Introduction

In the UK, tax is charged on capital gains realised—or deemed to be realised—when assets are disposed of and the resulting computation shows a net gain. The key concepts are asset, disposal and gain. Where gains are realised by individuals, trusts or estates, it is capital gains tax (CGT). Where the gains are realised by companies, it is corporation tax which is due, although the computation of the gains is determined in accordance with the CGT rules. In recent years, wide differences have emerged between the CGT and corporation tax treatment of gains. The major difference is the rate of tax. The rate of CGT on gains realised by individuals on or after 6 April 2016 generally is 10% and 20%. The pre-2016 rates of 18% and 28% still apply for carried interest and for chargeable gains on residential property. Corporation tax generally is levied at one rate of 20% from April: the rate is set to drop to 17% by 2020. The CGT rate is different from that on income; the corporation tax rate is the same on gains as on income, but with many unique reliefs and rules.

The UK tax on realised gains, whether CGT or corporation tax, is complicated because practical and policy reasons make it fall short of the Haig-Simons theoretical ideal concept of income discussed in chapter one above. These reasons will emerge as the chapters in Part III of this book unfold, but practical reasons largely explain the decision to exclude most motor cars and political reasons explain the decision to exclude the private residence. In 1966 Muteen observed that the idea behind the tax was not to collect money for the fisc—that could be done more simply—but to bring more equity into the system.[1] In 1995 Muteen concluded that a CGT simple enough to be easily administered may tolerate inequities of a degree many experts would find intolerable.[2]

---

[1] [1966] BTR 138, 139.

[2] In Sandford (ed), *More Key Issues in Tax Reform*, (Fiscal Publications, 1995), 34, 47. See also Evans and Sandford [1999] BTR 387.

32.2   Why Tax Capital Gains?

The main reason for taxing capital gains is that capital gains, whether or not realised, are just as much relevant to ability to pay as income liable to income tax, and therefore should be taxed on grounds of equity, both vertical and horizontal.[3] Indeed, for most economists,[4] capital gains are just as much income as profits of a trade or a salary. Thus, an increase in wealth due to the sale of shares in a company, the increase being due to the retention and reinvestment of profits by the company, is hard to distinguish from an increase due to the receipt of a dividend. And, for theoreticians, there is no need for a realisation either; there is an increase in wealth whether or not that increase is realised. The same is true where the increase in share value is due to the market deciding to capitalise an expected increase in company income.[5] The development of new financial instruments has made this simple truth even clearer.

If capital gains were taxed as income, this would avoid the problems of distinguishing between income and capital receipts[6] and reduce the erosion of the tax base through taking income benefits in capital form. However, while everyone (or nearly everyone) in the world of theory agrees with such an approach, no tax system taxes capital gains in this way.[7] Most countries, including the UK, tax on a realisation basis, although they may also use the accrual basis (so taxing some gains—and relieving some losses—which have accrued but not been realised); some examples may be found in the UK corporation tax rules. However, many systems that tax realised gains do not do so on the same basis as income, and many tax gains only partially. There seems to be an atavistic impulse which prevents the full taxation of gains; this leads to a lack of principle, with gaps in the tax base, such as the exemption for private residences and inconsistent changes in legislation.[8]

---

[3] The majority report of the UK Royal Commission of 1955 was against capital gains taxation—see Royal Commission on the Taxation of Profits and Income, Final Report, Cmnd 9474 (1955), 94–108. Its views are dissected and rejected in the Minority Report (pp 34–84). The case for CGT is also considered (enthusiastically) in Krever and Brooks, *A Capital Gains Tax for New Zealand* (Institute of Policy Studies, Wellington, 1990), where a valuable bibliography is buried in the footnotes. A CGT was advocated for New Zealand in a consultative document issued in 1989, but was not implemented partly for practical and partly for political reasons; this did not stop many other provisions being introduced into the New Zealand law. For a wide-ranging survey of US literature, see the 'Report of a Colloquium on Capital Gains' (1993) 48 *Tax L Rev* 315. Among older sources, see David, *Alternative Approaches to Capital Gains Taxation* (Brookings, 1968); Carter (chair), Canada Royal Commission on Taxation, *Report, Vol 3* (Queen's Printer, 1966), 325–87; Seltzer, *The Nature and Tax Treatment of Capital Gains and Losses* (New York, National Bureau of Economic Research, 1951); Simons, *Personal Income Taxation* (University of Chicago Press, 1938), ch 7; Ilersic, *The Taxation of Capital Gains* (Staples Press, 1962); Australian Taxation Review Committee Preliminary Report, ch 9; *Australian Tax Forum,* (1989) vol 1, issue no 2; Blum (1957) 35 *Taxes* 247; and Kaldor, *An Expenditure Tax* (Unwin, 1955), 54–87. On history see Daunton, *Just Taxes 1914–1979* (CUP, 2002) and Stopforth, in Tiley (ed), *Studies in the History of Tax Law* (Hart, 2004), ch 6 and [2005] BTR 584.

[4] Eg, Simons, *op cit*, 9; Miller (1950) 59 *Yale Law Jo* 837, 1057; and Sandford, *Taxing Personal Wealth* (George Allen & Unwin, 1971), ch 7.

[5] But see 1955 Royal Commission Minority Report, *op cit*, §110.

[6] See especially Break (1952) 7 *Journal of Finance* 214.

[7] For the position in OECD countries in 1990, see *Taxing Profits in a Global Economy* (OECD, 1991), Table 3.4 (corporate gains) and Table 3.21 (investors in shares); and Messere, *Tax Policy in OECD Countries* (IBFD, 1993), 312–22.

[8] See Evans and Sandford [1999] BTR 387.

Whether that impulse is soundly based, and whether capital gains should, in the jargon, enjoy some 'preference', is still unresolved.[9] Some regard the whole idea of a CGT as flawed, as an unwarranted restriction on the use of capital and as a deterrent to risk taking (see further §32.4.1).[10]

32.3 Design Problems

32.3.1 Accruals or Realisation[11]

In most tax systems, including the UK, capital gains are taxed primarily or exclusively on a realisation basis. This means that although tax is deferred until such time as the gain is realised, by the same token no relief is given for the sum invested in the purchase of the asset until realisation either. To tax accrued but unrealised gains would require periodic valuations, a matter of particular difficulty for non-financial assets.[12] Taxing accruals also raises the question whether it is desirable to compel a person to sell in order to raise the money needed to pay the tax. Further, such a system requires equitable relief for losses.

However, to tax gains only as they are realised gives rise to the so-called 'lock-in effect'[13]— the taxpayer is reluctant to realise the gain for fear of the consequent tax liability, a prospect rendered even less attractive by the fact that the system may provide, as in the UK, that gains accrued but unrealised on death escape CGT altogether.[14] The incentive to defer disposal of an asset arises because of the costs of switching investments rather than retaining them. Thus, suppose I have an asset with £100 base cost; the current value is £160. If I sell it and pay CGT of £12.00 (20% of the gain) I shall only have £148.00 to reinvest.

There are two contrary legislative solutions to this. One is to allow a deferral of tax whenever there is a change of investment. This is axiomatic under an expenditure tax (ET, below §32.5) and also achieved under a capital disposals tax (CDT, below §32.6). Its adoption, using either an ET or a CDT, would drive a big wedge between the treatment of capital gains and ordinary income. An alternative solution is sporadically to direct deemed realisations— such as on death. Actual tax systems tend to be compromises between the two principles.[15]

---

[9] See Cunningham and Schenk,'Tax Law Review Symposium' (1993) 48 *Tax L Rev* 319, and comments by Halperin (*ibid* at 381) and Shaviro (*ibid* at 393).

[10] For a vigorous denunciation of the tax, see Sutherland *et al, A Discredited Tax: The CGT Problem and its Solution* (IEA, 1992).

[11] For an analysis in efficiency terms, see Zodrow (1993) 48 *Tax L Rev* 419, 467 *et seq.*

[12] See Sandford, Willis and Ironside, *Wealth Tax* (Heinemann, 1975), ch 10. The taxation of unrealised gains was dismissed as 'incapable of satisfactory solution' by Carter (chair), Canada Royal Commission on Taxation, *Report, Vol 3* (Queen's Printer, 1966), 50. Today an accruals basis of taxation is used in the UK for foreign exchange transactions and various financial instruments, but only for corporation tax and for certain assets held by insurance companies (TCGA 1992, s 212). An accruals basis is also used in New Zealand for many financial assets.

[13] A variant form of lock-in arises if the rate of tax fluctuates—as where a part of the gain is treated as income.

[14] However the UK's IHT may well tax the whole value of the property and not just the gain.

[15] See Avi Yonah (2004) 57 *Tax Law Review* 483–502. For an analysis of where to draw the line on efficiency grounds, see Schenk (2004) 57 *Tax L Rev* 503–48.

32.3.2 Losses

The issue of losses probably most restrains tax designers. Full adoption of a CGT should mean full relief for losses—including not only setting capital losses off against ordinary income, but even rolling losses back.[16] Under an ET or a CDT this problem would not arise, since relief for the purchase price is given earlier.

32.3.3 Inflation

To make no allowance for inflation and so simply to tax on a paper gain is to turn CGT into a form of wealth tax,[17] and to provide a further disincentive to investment or saving. It also gives government a vested interest in inflation. Yet to make an allowance for inflation in CGT while making no such allowance for those living on fixed incomes is to create an inequity.[18] One answer is to align the rate of tax on capital gains with that on income, as was done in the UK from 1988 to 1998 for CGT and still is the case for corporation tax. The raising of the income tax threshold in approximate line with inflation may then be seen as a sufficient protection for those living on fixed incomes and those living on capital gains. The UK was, comparatively, very generous in granting both a large annual exemption and an inflationary indexation relief. If inflation is taken into account, various techniques are available. One would be simply to raise the acquisition and allowable deductions each year by a certain amount—the solution adopted in the UK from 1982–98 in the form of indexation relief for CGT and still in place for corporation tax.[19] Another technique would be to lower the rate of tax according to the number of years over which the asset had been held.[20] This was done in the UK, but only in part, through a system of 'tapering relief' from 1998 to 2008.

32.3.4 Attribution to a Particular Year

One of the objections to a CGT is the inherent unfairness of taxing very occasional gains as income of one year, a matter of greater moment in the 1960s and 1970s when the rates of income tax were more progressive than now. Systems which, unlike the UK, have a general averaging scheme can integrate the gains tax with the income tax by treating the whole or part of the gains as income.[21]

32.3.5 Private Residence

Typical of the holes in the tax base for CGT is the exemption for residences (see below §34.7). This exemption is very expensive and must be seen primarily as a political

[16] As was done in the United States until the 1930s; see Ilersic, *op cit.*
[17] See Sandford, *op cit*, 4, 238–40; Carter (chair), Canadian Royal Commission on Taxation, *Study No. 19* (Queen's Printer, 1966), 73–82. On computation issues, see Morley, *Fiscal Implications of Inflation Accounting* (IFS, 1974), 24–27.
[18] Ilersic, *op cit*, 22–25.
[19] On complicated calculation where many different items of expenditure have occurred, eg in assembling a holding of shares in a company at different times and at different prices, see ch 41 below.
[20] See Sandford, *op cit*, 240.
[21] In the UK between 1962 and 1971, gains realised within six months (subsequently one year) were treated as income under Sch D, Case VII.

decision.[22] There are no technical reasons for the exemption, which could be viewed as further encouragement for individuals to invest their wealth into that privileged asset, the family home. Until 1997 the US used a rollover rule, which allowed owners to postpone their liability to tax until death or until they bought a lower-cost house, combined with a limited exemption ($125,000) for people aged over 55.[23] In 1998 the US moved to a cash limited exemption of $500,000 for joint filers; the amount is still $500,000 as of 2015.[24] Gains above those thresholds are taxed at rates of 15–20%.

However, any discussion of this issue, or of the related issue of the non-taxation of imputed income (§1.6.2 above) must take account of other taxes. A 2014 study by the OECD using statistics from 2012 showed that when one included council tax, stamp duty, business rates, IHT and VAT on repairs, tax on residential housing and commercial property in the UK as a percentage of total taxation was the highest in the developed world at 11.9%, more than double the OECD average of 5.5%.[25] Any change widening the tax base would create problems if it applied to those who already owned their homes, as well as labour mobility problems. (One might add that the opposition parties might promise to repeal the tax and so win the next election.)

32.4   Criticisms of a CGT[26]

32.4.1 Economic Risks

A CGT is not necessarily free of economic risks. It might, in the absence of generous rollover relief, reduce saving.[27] This is of concern in the corporate sector, where such an effect would run counter to the policy of encouraging firms to retain profits to finance investment. However, this raises issues not only of the relationship between the taxation of company profits and the taxation of dividends, but also of the use by government of capital allowances and investment grants. Further, a CGT may discourage risky investments.[28] These fears do not appear to have been borne out,[29] and in any case must be set against the distortions which result from a system which exempts capital gains completely.

[22] See McGregor (1973) 21 *Can Tax Jo* 116; Clayton (1974) 22 *Can Tax Jo* 295, Ilersic, *op cit*, 44; the rule is defended by Willis and Hardwick, *Tax Expenditure in the United Kingdom* (Heinemann, 1978), 49–51.

[23] IRC §§1031 (the rollover) and 121 (for the over-55s); see Bittker, *Taxation of Income, Estates and Gifts*, (Warren Gorham & Lamont, 1993), §44.5.

[24] Non-joint filers were allowed $250,000 (which is still $250,000 in 2015); the exemption was not meant to be used more than once every two years: Auten and Seschovsky (1997) *National Tax Journal Conference Proceedings* 223. Carter (chair), Canada Royal Commission on Taxation, *Report, Vol 3* (Queen's Printer, 1966), 358, recommended an exemption for gains on the sale of a private residence up to a limit ($25,000) but the Canadian Income Tax Act simply exempted (and still exempts) such gains.

[25] OECD, *Revenue Statistics 2014* (December 10, 2014), Tax Structures, Table 22.

[26] See, eg Sutherland *et al, op cit*.

[27] Quaere whether this has led to the huge increase in the percentage of savings channelled through privileged savings media. For an analysis, see Zodrow (1993) 48 *Tax L Rev* 419, 469 *et seq*.

[28] On risk, see Bankman and Griffith (1992) 47 *Tax L Rev* 377; (1992) 48 *Tax L Rev* 163; Zodrow, *op cit*, 478 suggests that a cut in the CGT rate would make business people less risk-averse.

[29] 'The taxation of property gains has had very little effect on the level of investment in the United States': Carter (chair), Canada Royal Commission on Taxation, *Report, Vol 3* (Queen's Printer, 1966), 339 and *Report, Vol 6*, ch 37; but contrast Wallich (1965) 18 *National Tax Jo* 133, 437; see Blum, (1965) 18 *National Tax Jo* 430: Zodrow, *op cit*, 466, notes the decline in the importance of the individual as a source of investment funds.

32.4.2 Yield

The yield from CGT is not substantial, and may fluctuate unpredictably; the legislation is necessarily complicated, and the extent of avoidance and evasion is uncertain.[30] According to HMRC's statistics,[31] in 2013–14 approximately 191,000 individuals paid £4.95bn in CGT on gains of £30bn, and 20,000 trusts paid £535m in CGT on gains of £2.12bn. The CGT yield is tiny compared to the £158 billion paid in income tax. Much of CGT is paid by a very small number of taxpayers—over one-half of the CGT collected in 2013–14 came from a mere 5,000 taxpayers, each with gains of at least £1 million. A further one-third of CGT was paid by those with taxable incomes below £32,010 (then the start of the income tax higher rate band). In 2012–13, 69% of the total gains realised came from financial assets including quoted and unquoted shares. Residential property accounted for 14% of gains and other non-financial assets 17%.

Administration costs to the Revenue, for whom CGT is expensive to collect, and compliance costs incurred by taxpayers are substantial.[32] HMRC statistics for 2012–13 shows that CGT is the most expensive tax which the department collects, at 1.22% of the tax assessed. This was more than income tax (1.00%). Cost issues have been highlighted by comparative work in Australia showing that these costs are increasing—and are a source of even greater concern in the UK than they are in Australia.[33]

The UK tax, with its exclusion of pre-1982 gains realised after March 1988, its generous annual exemption and its many other exemptions, whether on grounds of practicality (such as chattels disposed of for less than £6,000) or expediency (such as gambling winnings and the principal private residence), shows all the characteristics of the compromise needed to provide a tax that is politically acceptable while being neither too inequitable nor too unworkable. It may be concluded that the present position reflects the view that the justification for a CGT is simply that the inequities of having one are less than the inequities of not having one.[34]

32.5   Capital Gains and an Expenditure Tax

Although part of the attraction of an expenditure tax (ET) is the proper and consistent treatment of capital expenditure and receipts, the Meade Committee thought it necessary to retain a CGT for some assets.[35] Under its main ET proposals, the purchase price of a

---

[30] Substantial avoidance was checked by *WT Ramsay v IRC* [1982] AC 300, [1981] STC 174, (1981) 54 TC 101 (see above at §5.6.4) and various pieces of legislation, especially TCGA 1992, ss 30, 137.

[31] HMRC, *Capital Gains Tax Statistics*, October 2015, available at https://www.gov.uk/government/statistics/capital-gains-tax-statistics.

[32] See, generally, Sandford, *Hidden Costs and Tax Compliance Costs* (Fiscal Publications, 1995), ch 7.

[33] Evans, *Taxing Personal Capital Gains* (Australian Tax Research Foundation, 2003) 40. On causes of compliance costs, see *ibid*, Table 5.23. On compliance costs generally, see Sandford, *Hidden Costs and Tax Compliance Costs, op cit*, ch 7, and the bibliography to Evans's book.

[34] Sandford, *Hidden Costs and Tax Compliance Costs, op cit*, 24.

[35] Meade, *The Structure and Reform of Direct Taxation* (Allen & Unwin, 1978), 179–80.

registered asset would be a deductible expense in the year of purchase, and the proceeds would be a taxable receipt in the year of receipt. There would thus be no difference in the tax treatment of the proceeds of the asset and the income from it. Conversely, sums spent on an unregistered asset would be ignored—as would the proceeds on disposal. The Committee classified most durable goods used for personal consumption, eg clothes and furniture, as unregistered assets. Problems would arise, however, if potentially valuable assets, for example a painting by Rembrandt, could be treated as being unregistered assets. The Committee therefore favoured the retention of a CGT for such assets, such a tax being properly indexed and containing generous rollover provisions.

The Mirrlees Review considered an ET but opted instead to recommend the introduction of a rate of return allowance (RRA) on investments in capital assets.[36] The RRA would be determined by applying a risk-free nominal interest rate to a cumulated stock of savings held in particular assets. Under this approach, nominal gains less the RRA are taxed, resulting in only the 'excess' gain above the normal rate of return being subject to tax. If capital gains are not realised until a future period, the unused RRA is carried forward, and uprated at the normal rate of return. Although this may at first glance appear complicated, the mechanics are similar to the computation of indexation relief. The excess return is taxed at the same rate schedule as earned income (including employee and employer NICs), but with reduced rates for capital gains on shares to reflect corporation tax already paid. In common with an ET, the RRA approach, it is argued, can achieve more neutral tax treatment of capital gains and cash income, and does not require indexation for inflation.

32.6 Capital Disposals Tax

Under a capital disposals tax (CDT), tax would be levied on the difference between the amount received on the disposal of qualifying assets (broadly the same assets as are now subject to CGT) and the amount spent on the acquisition of such assets in each tax year. The similarity to the ET is obvious, ie tax would be payable on the amount by which dissaving exceeds saving in any one year. CDT reduces the fiscal discrimination between savings in different forms and financed in different ways. For example, under CDT it makes no difference whether a given investment is reinvestment or is financed out of income. Since tax crystallises only when the disposal proceeds are spent, there is no lock-in problem and there would be no tax discrimination in switching investments. Lastly, by abandoning the matching concept, CDT eliminates many of the complexities of CGT at a stroke—complex indexation provisions become superfluous, as do rules for matching share transactions, part disposals and so forth.[37]

---

[36] Mirrlees *et al* (eds), *Tax by Design: The Mirrlees Review* (OUP, 2011) ch 14.
[37] IFS Commentary No 8, *Reforming Capital Gains Tax*, §1.24.

32.7   Brief History of CGT

Not one year has gone by without some tinkering or more drastic reform of CGT. What follows is a brief outline of the key dates:

1965–70: CGT is and always has been a highly political tax. It was introduced into the UK by the Labour Government in 1965 as tax separate from income tax and with a rate at 30%; this was not a flat rate as various reliefs, whether related to total income or total gains, could lower it. Before then a number of capital receipts had been drawn into the income tax net, eg premiums on leases and certain bond washing proceeds. In 1962 a more general tax on capital gains was introduced by the Conservative Government in partial response to a boom in land and share prices, but only for short-term gains ('short-term' initially meant six months, but this was extended to 12 months in 1965). The short-term tax took the form of Schedule D, Case VII and, naturally, charged income tax rates. Case VII continued in 1965 alongside the CGT which was charged at much lower rates—for most taxpayers. The 1965 Act was in some ways a purist's dream, with countless deemed disposals (especially for settled property) and a pure system for taxing gains on death, under which death gave rise to a disposal at market value by the deceased. Unfortunately, the Act was not well drafted.

1970–74: The return of the Conservative Government in 1970 meant extensive revision of the legislation. The deemed disposal on death was replaced by the present rule, under which there is an acquisition by the PRs at market value but no disposal by the deceased. This meant that estate duty (later to be superseded by CTT and IHT) became the sole tax on death, and the concept of charging all gains during an individual's lifetime was dropped. Other changes included the abolition of Schedule D, Case VII and several of the deemed disposals for settled property.

1974–79: Under another Labour Government, various experiments were tried out in relation to the tax threshold. Anti-avoidance provisions were introduced, the most spectacular of which dealt with the facts of *WT Ramsay*[38] before that case reached the courts (see now TCGA 1992, section 30).

1979–97: This was a period of Conservative Government. The two most notable dates were 1982, which saw the introduction of indexation relief for inflation (but only for periods after 1982, so requiring much valuation of assets by reference to 1982) and 1988, when the rate of CGT was aligned with that of income tax by treating the gain as being the top slice of income. This increase in the effective rate of tax from 30% to 40% was offset by the removal of any, still unrealised, pre-1982 gains from any liability to CGT. Reliefs were introduced or expanded, eg reinvestment relief (1993), but there were also many anti-avoidance provisions.

---

[38] *WT Ramsay v IRC* [1982] AC 300, [1981] STC 174, (1981) 54 TC 101. The particular scheme at issue in *Ramsay* involved the adjustment of interest rates on matching loans in order to create a gain that was non-taxable and a corresponding loss that, the promoters hoped, would be allowable and could be applied against other, taxable gains.

1997–2008: The year 1997 saw the advent of a Labour Government, which led to tapering relief in place of indexation relief but only for periods after March 1998. Tapering relief is a common feature of other systems, but most such systems allow the taper to continue until no charge is levied once an asset has been held for more than a certain number of years. Spain moved away from this taper system to the system the UK was abandoning. Other changes included the phasing-out of retirement relief (no longer needed in view of the general tapering relief for business assets, but now revived in the form of entrepreneurs' relief) and the abolition of the reinvestment relief (largely replaced by new rules for VCTs, etc). If the Government wished to reduce substantially the rate of tax on business assets, it is a nice question whether that would have been better done by retaining indexation for all assets and then applying a 10% rate for such assets. The endless tinkering with taper relief shows that it was not well thought through. In 1999 the rate structure was changed yet again and the UK had only two rates of CGT for individuals—20% and 40%—by analogy with income from savings. FA 2000 made the 10% rate available for capital gains, but did not back-date it.[39] Over the years, the gap between corporate taxation of gain and CGT has widened. Typical of this is the fact that tapering relief was not applied to corporate gains in 1998 and has not been extended to them since.

2008: In an ill-managed attempt to simplify the system, the Chancellor of the Exchequer announced in October 2007 that, as from the following April, the rate of CGT would be 18%. Both taper relief and indexation relief were abolished. One effect was to increase the rate of CGT on business assets from, in many cases, 10% to 18% for disposals after 5 April 2008. The rate on non-business assets (eg second homes) came down. To placate the business lobby, entrepreneurs' relief was introduced to preserve the effect of the 10% rate of the first £1m of otherwise chargeable gains (see below at §42.5). This uses concepts derived from the old retirement relief, abolished in 1998. Entrepreneurs were not the only people to lose out on the change. The House of Commons Treasury Committee report on Budget 2008 noted that the Association of British Insurers thought the change would have severe effects on the sale of insurance bonds. The Chancellor was unmoved.[40] One may note that FA 2008 gave a six-month extension to certain IHT changes in trusts; it is surprising that no similar extension was given in this area, especially as many of the details were not known until quite late in the day.

2010–2014: A new 28% rate of CGT was introduced, alongside the existing 18% rate, for gains realised on or after 23 June 2010. The 28% rate applies to gains accruing to the trustees of a settlement, the PRs of a deceased persons, and individuals if income tax is chargeable at the higher rate or the dividend upper rate in respect of any part of an individual's income for a tax year. In addition, the limit on entrepreneur's relief was raised, in stages, to £10m. 2013 saw a new CGT charge on UK resident and non-resident non-natural persons (eg companies and collective investment schemes) disposing of UK residential property.

2015–present: In 2015, the CGT regime was extended to levy a charge on non-resident individuals disposing of UK residential property. In 2016, the main CGT rates were decreased

[39] FA 2000, s 37.
[40] House of Commons Treasury Committee, *2008 Budget*, HC 430 (7 April 2008), paras 79–85.

to 10% and 20% for disposals on or after 6 April 2016. The previous rates of 18% and 28% continue to apply for carried interest and for chargeable gains on residential property.

The future of CGT is unclear. It is a major problem for certain types of taxpayer, but the combination of the large annual exempt amount and tax rates below that levied on income means that there is not a very large constituency of voters demanding reliefs. There is probably less political will to make further substantial structural changes. What is clear is the importance attached by the Government to issues of international competitiveness; such thinking led to the corporation tax exemption from liability arising on the disposal of substantial shareholdings if the proceeds are reinvested in appropriate companies or assets in 2002. Similarly, a Canadian Study in 2000,[41] while making many interesting theoretical points in favour of a tax preference for capital gains, also emphasises the need to be competitive with the US, which also has a large tax preference for capital gains. In 2004, Jersey rejected taxing capital gains for fear of scaring away capital.[42]

---

[41] Mintz and Wilson CD Howe Institute Commentary No 137, February 2000 (available on https://www.cdhowe.org/sites/default/files/attachments/research_papers/mixed/mintz-2.pdf.
[42] For review of Jersey taxation, see https://www.gov.je/LifeEvents/MovingToJersey/Pages/Tax.aspx.

33

Structure and Elements

33.1   The CGT Legislative Framework

Capital gains tax (CGT) is paid by individuals, partners, trusts and estates. The CGT legislation was first introduced in 1965, and was then consolidated in the Capital Gains Tax Act 1979. Because companies pay corporation tax on their capital gains rather than CGT, some of the legislation dealing with companies formed part of TA 1970 and thus part of the next consolidation of income and corporation taxes in 1988. These parts were united with the rest of the capital gains legislation in the 1992 consolidation; because it covers both CGT and corporation tax, the Act is entitled the Taxation of Chargeable Gains Act 1992 (TCGA 1992).

Gains realised on or after 6 April 2016 generally are subject to a 10% or 20% rate, depending on the taxpayer's taxable income. The rates are 18% and 28% for carried interest and for chargeable gains on residential property. For individuals there is no specific relief for inflation, which had been given from 1982 to 1998 through indexation relief. Neither is there any taper relief according to which the gain is reduced by reference to the length of time the asset has been owned, which had given from 1998 to 2008. CGT does not apply to gains accruing before 1965. The rebasing of the tax to 1982 provides further reliefs for assets acquired before 1982, but subject to restrictions which may involve the pre-1988 law. See further below §§43.5 and 43.6.

References to statutory provisions in chapters thirty-three to forty-three of this book are to TCGA 1992 unless otherwise noted.

33.1.1 Concessions

The CGT legislation is backed up by the usual array of concessions, statements of practice, Revenue interpretations and a very detailed Revenue Manual. These informal arrangements sometimes allow taxpayers to defer a charge. Naturally, the Revenue assumes that the tax-payer will declare and pay the deferred tax in due course, but the fact that the deferral was given on the basis of a concession rather than strict law meant that there was often no legal obligation on the taxpayer to do so. It says much for UK taxpayers that most made their proper returns in due course. However, some did not, and so rules provide that where a person has taken advantage of such a concession, there is now a legal obligation to pay the deferred tax in due course; a charge is imposed on the amount of the gain relieved for the earlier period. The charge is a reserve power in that it is imposed only if the taxpayer fails to observe the terms of the concession. The charge cannot be for less than the gain deferred by way of concession. Some have argued that when the now repealed tapering relief rules applied, the charge might have been for more than the gain deferred.[1]

33.1.2 Interpretation

The capital gains legislation is interpreted in the same way as other tax legislation; a number of the leading tax avoidance cases have been CGT cases, including *WT Ramsay*.[2] However, CGT is still a relatively new tax and the courts have not yet decided whether 'gain' is to develop the same degree of nuance as the term 'income', which has quite clearly developed a meaning of its own. While the courts have mixed imaginative constructions in cases like *Marren v Ingles*[3] and principled arguments rooted in a clear view of the structure of the Act in cases like *Kirby v Thorn EMI*,[4] they have also given us the notorious case of *Smith v Scho-field*,[5] where the judges were sharply divided over whether the word 'gain' took its meaning from its context or whether it has a meaning independent of the context, the latter view prevailing in the House of Lords.

In *Aberdeen Construction Group v IRC*,[6] Lord Wilberforce stated that any interpretation of the statutory provisions must have a 'guiding principle', and that the purpose of the leg-islation is to tax capital gains and make allowance for capital losses, 'each of which ought to

---

[1] TCGA 1992, ss 284A, 284B, added by FA 1999, s 76; see Shipwright [1999] BTR 357; see also Inland Revenue Bulletin No 43 and CGT Manual, paras 13650–62.
[2] For an important analysis of the views of the judges, and especially of Lord Hoffmann, see Stavely [2005] BTR 609.
[3] [1980] 1 WLR 93, [1980] STC 500, (1980) 54 TC 76.
[4] [1987] STC 621, (1987) 60 TC 519, CA.
[5] 65 TC 669. Here Charles Potter QC and a unanimous Court of Appeal ([1992] STC 249) disagreed with Hoffman J ([1990] STC 602) and a unanimous House of Lords ([1993] STC 268 [1993] 1 WLR 398).
[6] [1978] AC 885, 893, [1978] STC 127, 131, (1978) 52 TC 281, 296F.

be arrived at on normal business principles. To paraphrase a famous cliché, the capital gains tax is a tax upon gains: it is not a tax upon arithmetical differences'. In so far as this statement is intended to mean that a court should hesitate before accepting results which are paradoxical and contrary to business sense (as Lord Wilberforce also stated), the statement is welcome, but courts have not always heeded this advice. Fortunately, Lord Wilberforce's approach was echoed by Lord Walker in 2004 in *Jerome v Kelly*,[7] when Lord Walker said that when asked to deal with a flaw in the legislation he would always tend to favour a statutory analysis under which the taxable results corresponded with the actual results, ie the commercial (or economic) consequences.[8]

33.1.3 Scheme of the Act

The scheme of the CGT legislation is that for there to be a charge to tax there must be:

(1)   a 'disposal'—of a type relevant to CGT (which may be real or deemed);
(2)   of an 'asset' of a type relevant to CGT;
(3)   by a person chargeable to the tax;
(4)   on which a chargeable gain computed under the Act arises.

As is clear from (4), only 'chargeable' gains are subject to tax. Tax is charged on chargeable gains accruing to (ie realised by) a person during a year of assessment (section 2(1)). TCGA 1992 does not specify how a gain should be computed but simply directs that one must first determine the consideration, ie the value, whether real or market value, received from the disposal of the asset, and then deduct the allowable costs associated with the asset. As just mentioned this may encourage judges to see CGT as a simple tax on arithmetical differences rather than as one with its own principles.[9] The allowable costs may, in turn, attract an indexation allowance (if a company), or the gain may attract other relief. Accountancy practice has nothing to contribute in identifying what constitutes a 'disposal' and, unfortunately, little to say when measuring the sum charged. The rules contained in the legislation can be far removed from sums which might be identified as a gain in constructing financial accounts.

33.1.4 CGT and Income Tax

CGT is a tax separate from income tax, although a number of the machinery provisions relating to assessments, appeals, etc are common. Importantly, any gain liable to income tax is excluded from CGT (section 37). Losses available for set-off against income are not allowable losses for CGT, although some relief has been provided for trading losses and certain post-cessation losses to be set against capital gains.[10] Conversely, an excess

---

[7]   [2004] UKHL 25.
[8]   *Ibid*, at [34].
[9]   However, the arithmetical differences must relate to the particular assets in issue (*Whittles v Uniholdings (No 3)* [1996] STC 914, 924, per Nourse LJ).
[10]   TCGA 1992, ss 261A–261E, inserted by ITA 2007, ex FA 1991, s 72, note signposting by ITA 2007, s 101. See below §33.10.6.

of capital losses cannot be set off against income liable to income tax. Further, deductions that are or would be allowable for income tax are not generally allowable for CGT (section 39).

Although sound theory would try to reduce the differences between the taxation of ordinary income and that of capital gains, the UK tax system still contains many substantial differences in addition to those described above. Whereas income tax requires that income should have arisen from a source within the schedular system, CGT requires the presence of a particular asset; whereas income tax requires a receipt or an accrual, CGT requires a disposal; CGT has two main rates of tax (10% and 20%), while income tax has three primary and different rates (20%, 40% and 45%); the income tax personal reliefs have at best a distant counterpart in the annual exempt amount for CGT; exemption of particular items from income tax or CGT sometimes overlap but usually diverge; lastly, the rules on international scope are much wider for income tax than for CGT, since a non-resident individual is rarely subject to CGT but is potentially liable to income tax on income from any UK source. These differences usually stem from the fact that the UK's CGT is little more than a pragmatically-constrained tax bolted on to the income tax system to catch gains from particular assets.

Much tax legislation is premised on a wish to prevent people converting income into capital gains. In view of the many differences which have now arisen, although typically it is better to be subject to CGT rather than income tax there are also situations in which it is better to come within income tax rather than within CGT. The CGT legislation has not yet countered such planning devices. This reinforces the view of CGT as a device designed primarily to protect the income tax base.

33.1.5 *Deferral of CGT*

TCGA 1992 contains a number of rules deferring liability to tax. These rules are of two types. One type is sometimes called 'rollover' relief and applies where the gain is rolled over from one asset to another by being removed from the sale figure for the first asset and added to the purchase price of the second. For example, A buys at 40 and disposes to B at 100; B later sells the asset at 150. A has a gain of 60 and B a gain of 50. If the tax system imposes a rollover, A is treated as selling to B at 40; B will have to pay tax on the whole 110. This result is achieved where the A–B disposal is directed to be at such figure that neither gain nor loss accrues to A. Sometimes these deferrals are a matter of election; other reliefs such as entrepreneurs' relief can make the election decision less obvious. The same reduction in the value of the asset may be directed where A disposes of one asset and acquires another.

The second type of deferral rule is called 'holdover' relief and arises, strictly speaking, where the tax system allows A to defer liability to pay tax on the 60 gain until some later event. The gain is not rolled into the base cost of another asset and here only one taxpayer is involved. Although these two techniques are used extensively in the legislation, readers should be warned that they are not always consistently referred to as 'rollover' and 'holdover', and the terms sometimes are used more or less interchangeably.

33.2 Persons Chargeable

CGT is charged on chargeable gains accruing to a person in a year of assessment during any part of which he is resident in the UK, or during which he is ordinarily resident in the UK.[11] Partners are each liable for the tax on their share of gains realised by the partnership.[12] Trustees and PRs are chargeable in respect of gains realised on a disposal, whether actual or deemed, in the course of administration. PRs may also be liable for tax due in respect of gains realised by the deceased in his lifetime.

A body subject to corporation tax has its gains charged to that tax and not to CGT. Shareholders are liable to CGT on the disposal of their shares, assuming that they are not corporations. Corporation tax paid by a corporation is not imputed to the shareholder even though it may be shown that the latter's gain is attributable entirely to the gain already taxed in the company. This can lead to double taxation of gains—and double relief for losses. However, if a capital gain is distributed by the company to the shareholder, the corporation tax paid may be partially imputed by virtue of a lower rate of tax on the dividend. Undistributed capital gains of a non-resident close company may be attributed to the participators (section 13). Authorised unit trusts, VCTs and investment trusts are exempt from tax on capital gains (section 100(1)).

Prior to 6 April 2013, a non-resident was subject to CGT only in respect of UK assets used for the purposes of a trade carried on in the UK through a branch, or UK assets held for the purposes of the branch (section 10). FA 2013, section 66 and Schedule 25 introduced a new CGT charge on UK resident and non-resident non-natural persons (eg companies and collective investment schemes) disposing of UK residential property initially worth more than £2m but this was subsequently lowered to £1 million (from 1 April 2015) and then to £500,000 (from 1 April 2016). This CGT charge applies to dispositions of properties that are subject to a separate new Annual Tax on Enveloped Dwellings (ATED). The CGT charge applies to disposals with effect from 6 April 2013. For companies, corporation tax applies to any part of the gain built up before 6 April 2013, with a CGT charge at 28% applying to any part of the gain attributable from 6 April 2013 onwards. ATED-related losses are ring-fenced and are allowed to be set-off only against ATED-related gains. The policy rationale for the ATED and ATED-related CGT charge is to discourage 'enveloping' of homes in non-natural vehicles, which had become a common structure for minimising stamp duty land tax on the purchase of London property in particular. It should be noted that some non-tax benefits remain for holding property in this way, eg anonymity.[13]

FA 2015, Schedule 7 extended the CGT regime to levy a charge on non-residents—including individuals—disposing of UK residential property. The charge applies on gains arising on or after 6 April 2015, and there are rebasing rules for property owned prior to that date. Tax is levied at the usual rates applicable to UK residents of 18% or 28% for individuals, 28% for trustees and 20% for companies. If the property gives rise to

---

[11] TCGA 1992, s 2(1). In *R v IRC, ex parte Fulford-Dobson* [1987] STC 344, an attempt by a taxpayer to get round this rule by a scheme using ESC D2 failed (see above at §3.3.1).

[12] A European Economic Interest Grouping (EEIG) is treated in broadly the same way as a partnership for the purpose of charging tax on capital gains: TCGA 1992, s 510A(6), see below at §42.7.5.

[13] For commentary see Soares [2013] BTR 459.

an ATED-related chargeable gain that charge will take priority over this CGT charge. However, this charge will take priority over other provisions, including those attributing gains to settlors and beneficiaries non-resident trusts and to UK participators in non-resident companies. CGT reliefs such as holdover and rollover relief are available in certain circumstances. The non-resident making the disposal is required to file a tax return (NRCGT return) within 30 days following completion of the disposal.

33.3   Rates of Tax

Section 4, as amended by FA 2008, section 8, read quite simply: 'The rate of capital gains tax is 18%.' One of the points of fiscal contention between the Coalition parties forming the government in 2010 was the Liberal Democrats' desire to align CGT rates with income tax rates, as had been achieved in 1988. The Conservative party, on the other hand, did not wish to impose sharply-increased rates of tax. The compromise reached—and enacted by amending TCGA 1992, section 4 and adding section 4A (and section 4B on losses, see §33.10 below)—applies to gains accruing on or after 6 April 2016. The rate of CGT in respect of gains accruing to a person in a tax year is 10% (section 4(2)). However, the rate is 20% in respect of gains accruing to the trustees of a settlement, or to the PRs of a deceased person (section 4(3)). It is also 20% for an individual if income tax is chargeable at the higher rate in respect of any part of that individual's income for a tax year (section 4(4)). Those wondering why the rate is 20% and not 40%, as in 1988, should recall that in 1988 indexation relief was available. Higher rates of 18% and 28% apply for carried interest and for chargeable gains on residential property. Readers will also note that there has been no re-enactment of the former rules in sections 77–79, repealed in 2008, which treated gains arising under a settlement as gains of the settlor where the settlor retained an interest. As before, personal reliefs (or other income tax deductions, except trading losses) may not be used to offset chargeable gains.[14]

   If no income tax is chargeable at the higher rate or the dividend upper rate in respect of the income of that individual for a tax year, but the amount on which the individual is chargeable to CGT exceeds the unused part of the individual's basic rate band (defined in section 4(7) and (8)), the rate of CGT is 20% on the excess (section 4(5)). For the purposes of section 4(5), gains attracting entrepreneurs' relief (section 169N(3), below §42.5) are treated as forming the lowest part of the amount on which an individual is chargeable to CGT.

33.4   Annual Exempt Amount

There is a simple annual exemption for gains accruing to individuals (section 3). For 2016–17, the figure is £11,100, which is slightly more than the £11,000 basic personal

---

[14] Although by reducing the rate of tax on income they may reduce the rate of tax on the gains.

allowance for income tax.[15] Where gains are taxed at different rates in the tax year, the exempt amount under section 3 is applied to any allowable losses in such way as is most beneficial to the person (section 4B(3)).This annual exemption is meant to be index linked to changes in the Consumer Price Index, unless Parliament decides otherwise—as has generally been the case in recent years. Husband and wife are each entitled to the annual exemption. On annual exemptions for trusts and estates, see §40.1.2.1 and §39.6.1. Under the FA 2008 reforms for gains taxed on the remittance basis, the annual exempt amount is not generally available (section 3(1A)).

Example

In 2016–17, T has taxable income after personal allowance of £29,600 and also a capital gain on the disposition of quoted shares of £21,100. The first £11,100 of the capital gain is exempt, leaving a taxable gain of £10,000. £2,400 of the gain (£32,000–£29,600) will be taxed at 10% and the remaining £7,600 at 20%.

33.5 Payment of CGT

CGT generally is due on the same day as income tax, ie 31 January following the end of the year of assessment in which the gain is realised. No payment on account is required and capital gains do not affect the calculation of the sum required on account for income tax. The problems of valuation inherent in the CGT regime are relevant to surcharges and penalties, but not to interest.[16] Note that where the chargeable gains accruing to the taxpayer do not exceed the annual exempt amount and the relevant consideration does not exceed four times that amount, the taxpayer need only make a statement to that effect (section 3A). At Autumn Statement 2015, as part of a recent series of tax changes aimed at reducing the attractiveness of buy-to-let investments, the Chancellor announced that the CGT on the sale of certain residential property (let properties and also second homes) is to be paid within 30 days of sale.

33.6 Payment by Instalments

CGT may be paid by instalments in three situations:

(1) Where the consideration is payable in instalments and the taxpayer, T, so chooses (section 280). Payments must be spread over a period starting on (or after) the date of disposal and extending at least 18 months. CGT may then be paid in instalments extending over a maximum period of eight years; instalment relief also ends once the last instalment of consideration is received if this is earlier. Before self-assessment

---

[15] CGT (Annual Exempt Amount) Order 2005 (SI 2005/721). See also below §33.11.
[16] A 'best estimate' of figures must be marked as such and will then not prevent the return from being a completed return: see Revenue Booklet SAT2 (1995).

this relief was available only if T could satisfy the Board that 'he would otherwise suffer undue hardship'; today, this restrictive condition no longer applies. Payment by instalments does not apply where the sale agreement operates so that the full sum is paid at the time of the sale but some or all of the sale consideration is then lent back to the purchaser. In *Coren v Keighley*,[17] land was sold for £3,750 with a loan back to the purchaser of £2,250 repayable by monthly instalments; CGT was due on the entire £3,750 at the normal due date. A separate rule provides an adjustment where the consideration is later shown to be irrecoverable (section 48).

(2)   For gifts of certain assets (section 281). The asset must be land, shares or securities giving the donor a controlling interest, or unquoted shares or securities.[18] This relief is not available if there is a holdover election available under section 165 (gift of business asset) or section 260 (gift subject to IHT); these gave rise to certain avoidance schemes stopped by FA 2004 (see below §36.4.2).

(3)   Under TCGA 1992, Schedule 7, paragraphs 4–7. The instalment option is also available where an election to hold over the gain arising on a gift of a business asset under section 165 is available, but the gain that can be held over (under the terms of that election) is less than the chargeable gain that arises overall. This may arise if only a fraction of the gain qualifies for relief, eg where shares are given away and the company whose shares are transferred has *chargeable* assets that are not *chargeable business* assets.[19]

Under (2) and (3), if the donee sells the asset, all instalments of tax that have not been paid at that date become immediately payable, with interest (section 281(7)(b)).

33.7   Tax Base Exemptions and Reliefs

The following assets are exempt assets in that no chargeable gain arises on the disposal of them—and so no relief is given for any loss arising:

(1)   debts other than the debt on a security (section 251);
(2)   covenants (section 237);
(3)   certain wasting assets (section 45);
(4)   private residence (section 222);
(5)   government stock (section 115);
(6)   qualifying corporate bonds (section 115);
(7)   EIS shares and certain BES shares (sections 150 and 150A);
(8)   woodlands (section 250);
(9)   passenger vehicles (section 263);
(10) certain chattels (section 262).

[17] (1972) 48 TC 370.
[18] TCGA 1992, s 281; see below §41.3.2.
[19] TCGA 1992, s 281(1)(b)(ii) and Sch 7, para 7.

Certain events or disposals are treated as not giving rise to a chargeable gain, as follows:

(1)   death (section 62);
(2)   gifts to charity (section 256);
(3)   share for share exchanges (section 135) or other company reconstructions (section 127);
(4)   inter-spouse/civil partner transfers (section 58);
(5)   transfers of assets within a group (section 171);
(6)   transfers by certain special taxpayers (sections 215–221 and 264–267);
(7)   transfers of shares to an employee share ownership trust (section 229);
(8)   transfer to the Treasury in settlement of an IHT liability of a work of art (section 257);
(9)   shares within a personal equity plan or ISA (section 151);
(10) decorations for valorous conduct (section 268);
(11) foreign currency for personal use (section 269);
(12) the disposal of a right to a payment of compensation for Nazi persecution (section 268A);
(13) FA 2006 added various powers to make regulations to exempt persons connected with the Olympic Games in 2012, eg competitors and staff (FA 2006, sections 65 and 66).

Of these (3)–(5) may in effect simply defer tax but the others are genuine exemptions. We shall come across other deferrals of tax in the course of Part III of this book.

33.8   The Market Value Rule

Under section 17, an acquisition or a disposal of an asset is treated as taking place at market value if it takes place otherwise than by way of a bargain made at arm's length. The legislation states that this applies in particular where the acquisition or disposal is by way of gift or on a transfer into settlement by a settlor, or by way of distribution from a company in respect of shares in the company.

Section 17 also states that the market value rule applies where

the acquisition or disposal is wholly or partly (a) for a consideration that cannot be valued, or (b) in connection with an individual's own or another's loss of office or employment or diminution of emoluments, or otherwise in consideration for or recognition of his or another's services[20] or past services in any office or employment or of any other service rendered or to be rendered by him or another.

Section 17 is excluded if there is an acquisition of an asset without a disposal and the consideration is either non-existent or is less than the market value (section 17(2)). In these circumstances the acquisition consideration will be nil, or the actual value, as appropriate. The purpose of this rule is to defeat schemes known as 'reverse *Nairn Williamson*[21] schemes', under which shares were issued to shareholders (so being acquired by them with-

---

[20] Eg, *Director v Inspector of Taxes* [1998] STC (SCD) 172.
[21] *Harrison v Nairn Williamson Ltd* [1978] STC 67.

out being disposed of by the issuing company). Although a relatively small amount might be subscribed (especially if the issued share capital was not substantial), the shares acquired were valued at market value, thus giving the shareholders a substantial uplift in the base cost of their holding.

33.9 Connected Persons

Many CGT rules turn on connected person status,[22] eg the market value rule.[23] In *Kellogg Brown and Root Holdings (UK) Ltd v Revenue & Customs Commissioners*,[24] Sir Andrew Morritt C dismissed HMRC's appeal, holding that section 28 applied to determine the time of connection for purpose of section 18. Connected persons for the purposes of CGT are those within the five categories set out next.

33.9.1 Relatives

A taxpayer is connected with his/her spouse/civil partner, brother, sister, ancestor or lineal descendant. A taxpayer is also connected with the spouse/civil partner of any one of those individuals and with those relations of the spouse/civil partner.[25] An individual's uncle, aunt, nephew and niece are not connected persons for CGT purposes, although they are for IHT purposes.[26] These connections turn on status, not on whether they are living together. A spouse thus ceases to be a connected person, and the spouse's relatives cease to be connected, only at decree absolute.

33.9.2 Trusts

A trustee (X) is connected with the settlor (S) of the settlement of which X is trustee and with any person who is connected with S—so long as S is alive (section 286(3)). The income tax meaning of the word 'settlor' applies,[27] thus including any person who has provided or undertaken to provide funds directly or indirectly for the purpose of the settlement, or who has made with any other person a reciprocal arrangement for that other person to make or enter into the settlement. X is also connected with any close company of which the trustees of the settlement are participators, with any company controlled by such a company and with any company that fulfils this definition but is not close solely by virtue of not being resident in the UK (section 286(3A)).

A person's network of connections as trustee is separate from that as himself. X, as trustee, will be treated as connected with S's daughter, P, so far as trust matters are

---

[22] Eg, restriction of loss relief (s 18(3)) and loans (s 251(4)).
[23] TCGA 1992, s 18(2) deems transfer to be not by way of bargain at arm's length.
[24] [2009] STC 1359, [2009] EWHC 584 (Ch), upheld [2010] STC 925, [2010] EWCA Civ 118.
[25] TCGA 1992, s 286(2); on regulatory powers re civil partnerships, see FA 2005, s 103.
[26] IHTA 1984, s 272.
[27] ITTOIA 2005, s 620, ex TA 1988, s 660G.

concerned; but if X sells his personal property to P, this is not necessarily a transaction between connected persons. A connection can be made only through an individual while still living. Thus, after the death of S, X is not connected with any individuals under these provisions.

33.9.3 Partners

Partners are connected with persons with whom they are in partnership, with the spouse or civil partner of any partner and with the brother, sister, ancestor or lineal descendant of any partner. However, this connection does not apply 'in relation to acquisitions or disposals of partnership assets pursuant to bona fide commercial arrangements'.[28] Any transaction between an incoming partner and the existing partners is in practice treated as a bona fide commercial arrangement made otherwise than between connected persons.[29] The scope of the bona fide arrangement rule is uncertain.[30] Where the partnership contracts with an individual partner to sell to that partner, for a commercial consideration, an asset that has previously been on the partnership balance sheet, it is clear that the subsection operates so that the transaction is not treated as being made between connected persons. However, it is less clear where the asset in question has not been on the partnership balance sheet, as is commonly the case with goodwill.

33.9.4 Companies and Other Companies

A company is connected with another company if the same person has control of both, or a person has control of one and persons connected with him, or he and persons connected with him, have control of the other. The same applies if a group of two or more persons has control of each company, and the groups either consist of the same persons or could be regarded as consisting of the same persons by treating (in one or more cases) a member of either group as replaced by a person with whom he is connected (section 286(5)).

33.9.5 Companies and Controlling Individuals

A company is connected with an individual if that individual has control of it, or where a group of individuals who are connected persons have control of the company (section 286(2)). Further, any two or more persons acting together to secure and exercise control of a company are treated in relation to that company as connected with each other.[31]

---

[28] TCGA 1992, s 286(4); see Goldberg [1975] BTR 91 and Ray [1975] BTR 198.
[29] Statement of Practice SP D12.
[30] See Tiley and Collison, *UK Tax Guide 2011–12* (Lexis Nexis, 2011), §16.51. Probably the better view of such a transaction is that a distinction has to be drawn between: (i) an asset owned by the partnership, which is a 'partnership asset' within the meaning of s 286(4); and (ii) an individual's interest in the partnership, which is not a 'partnership asset' within the meaning of s 286(4).
[31] TCGA 1992, s 286(3); on the meaning of a similar income tax expression, note *Steele v European Vinyls Group* [1996] STC 785.

33.10   Losses

Allowable losses can be valuable since they can be used to reduce liability to tax. The point of the scheme in the famous *WT Ramsay* case (see §5.6.4 above) was to create such losses artificially. CGT is charged on the balance of chargeable gains less allowable losses realised in a year of assessment (section 2(2)(a)). Allowable losses[32] thus attract automatic relief by set-off against total chargeable gains for that year. This is not a matter of election, and so applies whether or not the effect is to waste the annual exempt amount. Thus if A has £7,000 of chargeable gains and £7,000 of allowable losses in the same year, A has no liability to CGT but also no losses to use in another year. With the ending of the single rate of CGT, rules were needed to deal with the attribution of losses. Section 4B (added by F(No2)A 2010 for disposals on or after 23 June 2010) states that where gains accruing to a person in a tax year are chargeable to CGT at different rates, any allowable losses may be deducted from those gains in such way as is most beneficial to that person. This applies also to the exempt amount under section 3. Naturally this rule is subject to any enactment containing a limitation on the gains from which allowable losses may be deducted.

33.10.1 Computation

Losses are computed in the same way as gains. If the disposal may give rise to a chargeable gain, it may also give rise to an allowable loss; whereas if it gives rise to a non-chargeable gain, it cannot give rise to an allowable loss (section 16(2)). Any allowable loss not relieved by offset against other gains in the year in which it arises is carried forward and set against chargeable gains accruing in the next subsequent year in which they arise (section 2(2) (b)). Whereas the automatic offset of an available loss against gains of the same year is made *before* considering the annual exempt amount, losses brought forward from a previous year are relieved only in so far as they bring the net gains down to the amount specified as the annual exempt amount (section 3(5)(b)). Where the loss brought forward exceeds the amount by which the gain exceeds the annual exempt amount, the still unrelieved loss is carried forward to a later year. So if A has £7,000 of allowable losses in year 1 and £7,000 of chargeable gains in year 2, A is not obliged to put the losses against the gain in year 2 but can roll them forward to a later year.

It will be seen that the loss is carried forward, not back. If B has £7,000 of chargeable gains in year 1 after taking account of the annual exemption (ie £18,100 of gains altogether) and £7,000 of allowable losses in year 2, B is not allowed to carry the loss back to year 1—but may still carry the loss forward to year 3 and later years. The refusal of the system to allow losses to be carried back encourages taxpayers to dispose of assets in good time so as to use a loss.

---

[32] For an example of the difficulties some taxpayers have in understanding how losses may (and may not) arise, see *Neely v Ward* [1991] STC 656.

33.10.2 Carry Back

Where the deceased (D) made disposals prior to his death and has losses arising from disposals in the fiscal year in which D dies, the losses are set first against chargeable gains for that year and then against any chargeable gains in the previous three years, later years being counted before earlier years (section 62(1)(b)). Where, at death, the market value of an asset is less than the deceased's acquisition cost, no allowable loss arises. This is because the asset is deemed to have been acquired by the PRs without the deceased having made a disposal. This is the disadvantage of the rule that also excludes unrealised capital gains from CGT on D's death.

Where a taxpayer (T) sells an asset in the first year for an unascertainable deferred consideration, T must pay CGT in the first year and must include the very speculative market value of the unascertainable right (see *Marren v Ingles* below §35.4.1). When T sells the right in the third year and incurs a loss as compared with the original market value, the normal CGT rules would not allow a carry back. Rules now allow T to elect to carry the loss back in the circumstances specified.[33]

33.10.3 Disallowed Losses

Section 16A, added by FA 2007 but applying to disposals on or after 6 December 2006, is best described as a targeted general anti-avoidance rule aimed at stopping the creation of capital losses.[34] It applies to both corporation tax and CGT.[35] The section disallows the capital loss if the loss arises from or in connection with 'arrangements' and a main purpose of the arrangement is to secure a tax advantage; these terms are defined widely (section 16A(2)). A further rule adds that in deciding whether the loss is disallowed, it makes no difference that there were no gains against which to set the loss or that the tax advantage that would be secured would be secured by another person. This is a typical modern clause. HMRC, tired of chasing planners with specific rules, have gone for a more general provision, although section 16A is wider than most such rules.

33.10.4 Restrictions on Loss Relief

The tax system is very suspicious of losses arising on a disposal of an asset to a connected person. Relief is permitted only against a chargeable gain arising from a disposal to that same connected person. The gain may arise in that or in some later year (as long as connected person status continues) but not an earlier year.[36]

No relief is permitted for a non-resident on assets outside charge. A person who is non-resident in the year of assessment is subject to CGT only on assets used for the carrying-on of a trade of a branch in the UK (section 10(1)) and on UK residential property. It follows

---

[33] TCGA 1992, ss 279A–279D, added by FA 2003 s 162; see Parry-Wingfield [2003] BTR 392–96.

[34] TCGA 1992, s 16A, added by FA 2007, s 27; see Shipwright [2007] BTR 456.

[35] TCGA 1992, s 8(2A)–(2C), added by FA 2006, s 69; see DF Williams [2006] BTR 550. Section 16A builds on a provision introduced in 2006 that applied for corporation tax only. The corporation tax rule was repealed when the present rule came into effect.

[36] TCGA 1992, s 18(2), but with an exception in s 18(3) for certain trusts for the public good.

that relief for losses is available only in respect of such assets.[37] In principle relief was not permitted for losses of a non-domiciled person. Separate loss rules now apply if the remittance basis is involved.[38]

33.10.5 Assets of Negligible Value[39]

Where A invests money in an asset which later becomes valueless, it is clear that A has suffered a commercial loss. Since there is no actual disposal, relief is provided by allowing A to make a claim the effect of which is to treat the claim as a disposal (section 24). A must be able to show that there has been an 'entire loss, destruction, dissipation or extinction of an asset'. A claim may be made whether or not any capital sum has been received by way of compensation or otherwise. The claim may be part of the self-assessment, or free-standing. The effect of a claim is that the asset is treated as having been sold and immediately reacquired at the date of the claim for an amount equal to the value specified in the claim.

33.10.5.1 Backdating

A claim may be made so that the date of disposal is treated as having been any date specified during the period from 24 months before the beginning of the fiscal year in which the claim is actually made.[40] Thus, a claim made on 31 January 2016 may be backdated to 6 April 2013. In order to backdate in this manner, the asset must be of negligible value both at the date of claim and at the earlier date. Indexation may be claimed only in accordance with the legislation in force at the date of claim.

33.10.5.2 Negligible

'Negligible' is less than 'small' and so should be considerably less than the 5% Revenue yardstick used for the word 'small'.[41] The Revenue usually accept that such a claim arises where the loss is less than £10,000, where the company is registered in the UK, is not a plc and is in liquidation or has ceased trading.[42] If an asset has been stolen, the Revenue will accept a claim despite the fact that the asset still exists with its value unchanged.

33.10.5.3 Indexation Allowance and Negligible Value Claim

Since one is dealing with a loss, there is no room for indexation relief after April 1995[43] (but see §33.10.7 below).

33.10.5.4 Land and Buildings: Separate Assets

For the purpose of a negligible value claim, a building may be treated as a separate asset from the land on which it is situated (section 24(3)). Where there is a claim that a building

---

[37] TCGA 1992, ss 10, 16(3) and note special provisions for temporary non-residents in ss 10A and 10AA.
[38] TCGA 1992, ss 16ZA–16ZD, added by FA 2008.
[39] On partnership interests becoming of negligible value, see Eastaway [1984] BTR 207.
[40] TCGA 1992, s 24(2)(b), ex FA 1996, Sch 35, para 4.
[41] The Revenue maintain lists of quoted securities which they accept have become of negligible value for the purposes of TCGA 1992, s 24: see http://www.hmrc.gov.uk/cgt/negligible_list.htm.
[42] Revenue Internal Guidance, Capital Gains Manual, CG 13139–46.
[43] FA 1994, s 93.

has become of negligible value, the effect of the claim is to establish a loss on the building but, at the same time, to treat the site as having been sold and immediately reacquired for an amount equal to its market value. If this yields a gain on the land, that gain will automatically offset (and so reduce) the loss.

33.10.5.5 Recovery

An asset may have a negligible value at one date and then regain value. Such an outcome does not undo the negligible value claim—it simply lands one with a potential CGT liability based on the gain as compared with the value accepted at the time of the claim.[44]

33.10.6 Set-off of Trading Losses

Income losses are not, in general, a permitted deduction from chargeable gains in the case of persons other than companies. However, trading losses under ITTOIA 2005, Part 2 may be set off against chargeable gains.[45] The amount of the loss for which relief may be claimed is the balance after set-off against income for the year of loss or any other year. The loss is treated as an allowable capital loss for that year, and is therefore set off against chargeable gains before taking account of the annual exemption. Therefore, if D has £20,100 of chargeable gains and £9,000 of trading loss, the relief will reduce the chargeable gains to £11,100 which will be covered by the annual exemption. There is no provision for claiming only part of the trading loss which would otherwise be available. If the trading loss exceeds the chargeable gains for the year, the excess is not treated as an allowable capital loss but is carried forward as a trading loss.[46] Because a claim for set-off of trading losses against general income may be made for the year following the year of loss (ITA 2007, section 64), a CGT claim may also be made for that year—provided the trade continues in that year. Only trading losses may be used in this way. It follows that the £25,000 cap on certain non-active losses and the ban on tax-generated losses in ITA 2007, sections 74A and 74B (see §20.10.6 above) apply here where a taxpayer tries to set a loss against a capital gain.

33.10.7 Losses and Indexation Relief

Indexation relief still applies for corporation tax and so some discussion of the principle involved is important. Indexation as reformed in 1995 does not allow the creation of a loss but only the reduction of a gain to zero. This restriction is contrary to principle (see below §43.4). It may also have an unfortunate effect where an asset is split into two parts which are disposed of separately. Whereas indexation relief would apply in the normal way to an outright disposal of the asset in one transaction, the splitting of the asset may give rise to a gain on one part of the asset, reduced to a lower level by indexation, and a gain on another part which is more than offset by indexation relief. The amount by which the gain is more than offset is lost to the taxpayer. The situation is worse if the net result of the sale of the second part is a loss before any indexation relief is applied.

---

[44] TCGA 1992, s 24(2)(a).
[45] ITA 2007, s 71, referring to TCGA 1992, ss 261B and 261C, ex FA 1991, s 72; see Stopforth [1992] BTR 384, emphasising reasons for procedural complexities.
[46] TCGA 1992, s 261B(5), (6).

33.11   Spouses and Civil Partners

33.11.1 Separate Taxation

Spouses and civil partners pay their own CGT arising on the disposal of their own assets (section 279(7)). As individual taxpayers, each is entitled to claim a full annual exempt amount each year. It has always been the case that the gains and losses arising to one party to a marriage have been computed separately from those arising to the other party. Prior to 1990–91, however, CGT was levied on the husband for gains made both by him and by his wife, unless they were living apart.[47]

Where there is a disposal of property which has been held jointly by the spouses or civil partners, the split of proceeds and acquisition costs follow the division of the equitable interest between them. Where no division is specified, Revenue practice is to regard the split as being into two equal halves.[48] The special income tax treatment is not applied, except that where the couple declare an unequal split of income, the Revenue will presume that this also holds for CGT.[49] Neither the annual exempt amount nor any allowable losses are transferable between them.

33.11.2 Transfers Between Spouses and Civil Partners Living Together

Transfers between spouses and civil partners who are living together are treated as taking effect at such value that neither gain nor loss accrues to the disposing person (section 58).[50] This gives the couple an advantage, in that it enables one person to switch the potential liability on an as yet unrealised gain (or entitlement to an allowable loss) to the other, so that the other can dispose of the asset and so realise the gain or loss.[51] However, it prevents them further manipulating their entitlements to reliefs, etc, by passing the asset back and forth at current market values. Section 58 applies if they are living together at any point in the year of assessment; it probably follows that it applies if they separate during the year and the transfer is made after the separation but before the end of the year.[52] The no gain/no loss rule in section 58 does not apply to appropriations to or from trading stock; in such circumstances market value is instead taken, to preserve the integrity of the rules on the interaction of income and CGT. Neither does the rule apply to *donationes mortis causa*, the purpose here being consistency with the exception from CGT of assets passing on death.

---

[47] CGTA 1979, s 45; see *Aspden v Hildersley* [1982] STC 206 (an election was available to charge tax on the wife for her gains; the tax was calculated by splitting the single annual exempt amount between the spouses; for discussion of Revenue view that *Aspden* was wrong, see Potter and Monroe *Tax Planning* (Sweet & Maxwell, 1982), §2.25).

[48] Inland Revenue Press Release, 21 November 1990, [1990] *Simon's Tax Intelligence* 985.

[49] On joint holdings, see Thexton, (2000) 143 *Taxation* 170.

[50] On use of this to avoid tax, see *Gubay v Kington* [1984] STC 99 and notes by Goodhart and Dolby at [1984] BTR 117 and 124, the latter arguing whether Lord Templeman failed to spot a case of tax avoidance.

[51] Potter and Monroe, *op cit*, §2-21, suggest that if the recipient spouse sells the asset on, the transfer to that spouse should take place before finding a purchaser to avoid an argument that the later transfer was pre-ordained, as in *Furniss v Dawson* [1984] AC 474 (see above §5.6.4).

[52] Potter and Monroe, *op cit*, §2.25.

Indexation relief had special rules for transfers between spouses and civil partners but these are now obsolete.[53] There was also a rule for tapering relief.[54]

33.11.3 Separation

If the spouses separate, the no gain/no loss rule continues to apply until the end of the tax year in which they separate. However, they are still connected persons until decree absolute of divorce (and may continue to be connected persons under some other rule, eg business partners). A transfer which takes place as part of the financial settlement on divorce is normally regarded as being for a consideration which cannot be valued, and so takes place at market value.[55] The choice of assets to be transferred is naturally a matter to which much thought must be given. In *Aspden v Hildesley*,[56] a husband transferred property to his wife; the property comprised a house which was not his only or main residence. The husband was held taxable on the increase in value of the house since he had acquired it. The precise timing on transfers is thus a matter of some importance. Where the parties reach agreement on the terms of their settlement and the agreement then becomes part of a court order, the usual view is that the transfer takes place at the time of the consent order—and not that of the prior agreement—or, if different, the decree absolute.[57]

Once the spouses are no longer living together they may each have an exempt private residence. However, this exemption is tied to ownership. If, therefore, H owns the property but W occupies it, the relief may be lost; in practice this is not a problem if the transfer is made within three years of the parties separating (not divorcing).[58] While there was a Revenue concession[59] allowing the exemption if W was occupying the property, the concession did not apply if H was living in another property and claiming that as his only or main residence. The concession applied only where H transferred the house to W—and not if the house was sold to a third party. Since the concession encouraged the spouses to rearrange their interests before separation, it may have precipitated hostile acts; this ran counter to recent family law legislation and contrasted with the IHT exemption for transfers between spouses (see §53.1.1 below). The concession was enacted, without significant change, in 2009 as TCGA 1992, section 225B.

The courts may order that one spouse be allowed to occupy the property with the children while they are growing up, and then order a sale when the property is no longer needed, with the proceeds being then divided between the spouses (the *Mesher* order).[60] The effect of this order is to retain the exemption while the arrangement lasts. There is some uncertainty about the effect of a clause that the occupying spouse should pay 'rent' to the

---

[53] Any indexation allowance available to the disposer was taken into account in computing the acquirer's cost of acquisition, subject to the general rule since 1993 that its effect is only to reduce a gain. TCGA 1992, s 56(2), (3); on pre-1993 indexation, see *ibid*, s 55(7); on preservation of pre-1982 basing, see *ibid*, Sch 3, para 1.

[54] Any period of ownership by the transferor was available to the transferee. *Ibid*, Sch A1, para 15.

[55] TCGA 1992, s 17(1)(b) and Inland Revenue CGT Manual, para 22509. Timing transfers so that they take place after connected party status ceases may be advantageous if TCGA 1992, ss 29 and 30 (value shifting) provisions are potentially applicable.

[56] [1982] STC 206.

[57] See discussion in (1996) 138 *Taxation* 324.

[58] The three-year rule is in TCGA 1992, s 223.

[59] Former ESC D6.

[60] See *Mesher v Mesher* [1980] 2 All ER 126.

other; if it is truly rent then it will be chargeable income of the recipient (and not deductible by the payer) and will endanger the entitlement to the CGT exemption. There is also some uncertainty as to whether the order creates a settlement for CGT purposes.[61] Another form of order creates a deferred charge, under which H will receive either a specified sum of money or a specified proportion of the proceeds when the property is sold. Unfortunately, because of the CGT rules on debts, the above two orders may produce different results. If H is entitled to a specified proportion of the proceeds, he may be treated as realising a gain when the charge is realised.[62]

CGT problems also arise if the spouses have joint interests in separate plots of land and exchange those interests on separating. There is some relief if the value of the interests exchanged is identical, but this will rarely be achieved.[63] The court may order secured maintenance. This may involve the transfer of property by one spouse (H) to trustees; W then looks to the trustees and not to H for payment. When W ceases to be entitled to payments the trust ends and the property is transferred back to H. The transfer to the trustees will be a disposal for CGT purposes at current market value (since the trustees and the spouses are connected persons). If the trustees dispose of the assets during the trust, a CGT charge on those assets will arise (for which H may be made accountable).[64]

[61] See Wylie, *ICAEW Digest* No 229 (May 2002), para 1.8.
[62] *Ibid*, para 1.9.
[63] *Ibid*, para 1.10, using s 152 (assets qualifying for business relief) and former ESC D26, now TCGA 1992, ss 248A–248E.
[64] *Ibid*, para 1.11.

34

Assets

34.1   What is an Asset?

CGT applies only to a gain realised on the disposal of an asset. This has two major consequences: first, if there is no asset, there can be no chargeable gain—or allowable loss;[1] and secondly, qualifying expenditure may be deducted only when the asset to which it relates is disposed of.

TCGA 1992, section 21(1) states that all forms of property are assets, whether or not situated in the UK. Property is not further defined. However, assets are stated to include: (a) options, debts and incorporeal property generally; (b) any currency other than sterling;[2] and (c) any form of property created by the person disposing of it, or otherwise coming to be owned without being acquired. Property 'owned without being acquired' covers items such as goodwill and property which is simply found. Property 'created' includes items such as paintings, copyrights, patents and crops.

This definition leaves uncertain the scope of many shadowy rights which might be called incorporeal property. The statutory words do not confine the definition to interests in or over other property. Hence, rights under contractual licences may equally be 'property', and sums received on the redemption of a rent-charge, the release of a covenant and the release

---

[1] Eg, a loss arising on a liability (*Beauchamp v Woolworth* [1989] STC 510, (1989) 61 TC 510).

[2] Distinguish a holding of foreign currency from a debt expressed in foreign currency which will generally be an exempt asset—below §34.4.1 (for a limited exception, see TCGA 1992, Sch 11, paras 13, 14).

of a right to occupy the matrimonial home may all give rise to CGT (section 22). These are, however, actual or potential legal rights of action and capable of being owned in the normal legal sense. 'Rights' which may underlay such rights of action but which cannot be owned in this sense are not assets. In *Kirby v Thorn EMI*,[3] the Court of Appeal held that a company's right to trade and compete in the market place was not an 'asset', but that a payment which could be related to the goodwill of the company, as distinct from the goodwill of one of its subsidiaries, was taxable.

The meaning of 'asset' had been considered in the earlier House of Lords decision in *O'Brien v Benson's Hosiery (Holdings) Ltd*.[4] There, the House held that the bundle of rights of an employer under a service agreement was an asset for CGT purposes, so that a sum received by the employer to secure the release of the employee was derived from that asset and thus liable to CGT. The fact that the rights could not be assigned by the employer was irrelevant; it was sufficient that they could be 'turned to account'. *Kirby v Thorn EMI* provided a necessary check on some of the arguments in *O'Brien* which had come close to saying that if a sum was received then it must have been derived from property. It must also be remembered that in *O'Brien* the right was, like the others already mentioned, legally enforceable in some way or other. However, in view of the approach in *O'Brien*, it would follow that an unenforceable promise could be an asset; this because of an old estate duty case[5] in which the proceeds of a void insurance policy which had been paid over were held to be part of the deceased's estate; this may be because the contract was illegal for want of insurable interest and the sum was irrecoverable. If liability turns on irrecoverability, attention will now have to be paid to the effects of the doctrine of restitution. The same applies to other rights barred by statute, especially as such rights may be enforced indirectly and the acknowledgement of a claim can revive a right that would otherwise be statute barred.

34.2   Identifying the Asset

CGT is charged on a gain; the gain is the consideration received for the asset less the cost (or deemed cost) of the asset. The correct identification of the asset is therefore important. Further, where CGT is charged under section 22 on a capital sum derived from an asset, the gain is computed by taking from the capital sum received the cost (in whole or in part) of the asset that has directly caused the receipt of the capital sum. It is critical, therefore, to identify correctly the asset from which the consideration or capital sum is derived.[6] This causes particular problems where a compensation claim arises in connection with a contract relating to an asset and that asset receives special treatment under the CGT rules.

---

[3] [1987] STC 621, (1987) 60 TC 519; on this basis amateur status is not an asset and so the sum received in *Jarrold v Boustead* (see above at §14.4.4) would not be subject to CGT. Quaere the sums received in *Higgs v Olivier* (1952) 33 TC 136 (above §21.6).

[4] [1980] AC 562, [1979] STC 735, [1979] 3 All ER 652, but *cf Cleveleys Investment Trust Co v IRC* [1975] STC 457, (1975) 51 TC 26 (rights acquired by a guarantor against the debtor company on discharge of a debt to a third party were not assets for CGT).

[5] *A-G v Murray* [1904] 1 KB 165.

[6] See, eg Sparkes [1987] BTR 323; and [1988] BTR 29.

A precise and almost unworkable view of the matching process was taken in *Zim Proper-ties Ltd v Procter*;[7] the law is made less rigid in practice by a long-standing concession—ESC D33. In *Zim*, Warner J held that a right of action for damages relating to a conveyance of property was an asset separate from the property conveyed. The taxpayer (T) had contracted to sell property, but the purchaser repudiated the contract alleging that T's solicitors had failed to demonstrate good title to the property. T then sued its solicitors for negligence; the action was settled out of court by the solicitors paying T damages of £69,000. T claimed that the £69,000 was compensation for the depreciation in value of the property caused by the solicitors' action (or inaction). Warner J rejected this view:[8]

> Assuming ... that it was proper to describe the £69,000 as 'compensation' for something, it could only be described as compensation for the consequences of the firm's alleged negligence. The depreciation in the value of the properties was not a consequence of that negligence. It was something which, if it happened, happened as a result of the forces affecting the property market in Manchester, independently of that negligence.

The effect of this decision would be to deny a deductible acquisition cost in many circumstances. In relation to underlying assets, ESC D33 provides, with respect to capital sums derived from rights of action (but not for capital sums derived from statutory or contractual rights), the following concession (at para 9):

> Where the right of action arises by reason of the total or partial loss or destruction of or damage to a form of property which is an asset for capital gains tax purposes, or because the claimant suffered some loss or disadvantage in connection with such a form of property, any gain or loss on the disposal of the right of action may by concession be computed as if the compensation derived from that asset, and not from the right of action. As a result a proportion of the cost of the asset, determined in accordance with normal part-disposal rules ... may be deducted in computing the gain. For example, if compensation is paid by an estate agent because his negligence led to the sale of a building falling through, an appropriate part of the cost of the building may be deducted in computing any gain on the disposal of the right of action ...

If a relief or exemption was or would have been available on the disposal of the relevant underlying asset, it will be available on the disposal of the right of action. For example, if compensation is derived from a cause of action in respect of damage to a building suffered by reason of professional negligence, and the compensation is applied in restoring the building, deferment relief under section 23 will be available as if the compensation derives from the building itself. Other reliefs which may become available in this way include private residence relief, entrepreneurs' relief and roll-over relief. The Revenue are prepared to consider extending time limits in cases where because of a delay in obtaining a capital sum in compensation, the normal time limit allowed for a relief has elapsed. If the right of action relates to an asset which is specifically exempt from CGT, such as a motor car, any gain on the disposal of the right of action may be treated as exempt.

ESC D33 was revised in 2014 and a consultation launched on legislating it. From 27 January 2014, only the first £500,000 of chargeable gains not linked to an asset is exempt from tax. Taxpayers receiving compensation of more than £500,000 that they believe to be exempt can ask HMRC to consider whether further relief can be given. The consultation

---

[7] [1985] STC 90.
[8] *Ibid*, at 109.

proposed a cap on the exemption of £1 million instead. Controversially, in the consultation document a suggestion was made that legislating paragraphs 9–10 of ESC D33 (relief where there is an underlying asset) was not necessary because these paragraphs were not really concessionary, on the authority of *Pennine Raceway Ltd v Kirklees Metropolitan Council (No 2)*.[9] This case held that compensation received from a council following the revocation of planning permission was derived from the company's licence to conduct drag racing rather than right to sue the council. Readers may be surprised to see such reliance placed on this case, and may rightly question the consultation interpretation, especially as *Zim Properties* was unchallenged in *Pennine Raceway*. At the time of writing, the consultation had concluded, but the Government had not yet determined its response.[10]

34.3 Pooled Assets—Securities

In general, each asset is treated as a distinct item, so that tax arises only on the disposal of that asset and is then computed in the light of the expenditure on that asset. Shares or securities of a company being of the same class and held by one person in one capacity are regarded as indistinguishable parts of a single asset—a holding—so that the sale of a part of the holding is treated as a part disposal (section 104, see further below at §41.2). At one time this applied to any fungible assets but this is no longer the case.[11] The final sentence re fungible assets is incorrect and should instead read that the rule continues to apply to fungible assets, with former CTGA 1979, s 65(7)(b) re-enacted in TCGA 1992, s 104(3)(ii).

34.4 Loans, Debts and Covenants

Loans and debts give rise to several problems. The basic rule is that neither chargeable gain nor allowable loss arises from a debt. This is subject to exceptions for: (a) a debt on a security; (b) certain foreign bank accounts for private use; and (c) the assignee of the debt. Relief is given for losses on certain loans to traders and for guarantors of such loans. Special rules apply for covenants, government stock and qualifying corporate bonds.

34.4.1 *Exclusion for Debts*

No chargeable gain arises on the disposal of a debt or an interest in a debt, other than a debt on a security (section 251(1)). The assumption behind the exemption from CGT is, no doubt, that an ordinary commercial debt does not normally produce a gain but only the risk of a loss, and so it would be inappropriate to provide tax relief for losses arising from such risks. This assumption must give ground in a number of circumstances. From 1985 until 1993, when a fixed-sum debt would always create a loss by virtue of indexation being available, there was considerable activity in attempting to identify a debt as a debt on security[12] and, hence, able to trigger an allowable loss. The general exemption rule applies to debts in foreign currencies. Thus, if $100,000 is lent when the exchange rate is $1.50 to the pound and then repaid some years later when the exchange rate is $2 to the pound, the gain is not subjected to CGT. This contrasts with the treatment of a bank deposit (section 252). If £50,000 is converted at £1–$2 and put on the dollar denominated bank deposit, and then the $100,000 is withdrawn once the exchange rate has moved to £1–$1.50, the gain of £16,667 is subject to CGT (unless the deposit is for personal expenditure outside the UK of the taxpayer or his family or dependants).

34.4.1.1 Loss and Connected Person

A further restriction on allowable losses is imposed when a debt is assigned to a connected person. No allowable loss can arise on the disposal of a debt (whether or not it is a debt on a security) by a person connected with the original creditor (or with his PR or legatee) where that person acquired the debt directly from the creditor, or indirectly through other connected persons (section 251(4)).

34.4.1.2 Satisfaction as Disposal

The satisfaction of a debt is treated as a disposal of the debt by the creditor (section 251(2)). This rule is subject to exceptions for certain company reconstructions and amalgamations.[13] It applies to all debts, including debts on a security. The disposal occurs when the debt is satisfied. Satisfaction of part of the debt means a part disposal. Provision is made for the situation in which the debt is satisfied not by a payment but by the transfer of an asset (section 251(3)). Assuming that the satisfaction is not a chargeable disposal within section 251(1), rules are needed to protect the creditor should the asset be later disposed of. In calculating the gain on such a disposal the creditor's acquisition cost is the higher of (a) the market value of the asset and (b) the amount of the debt.[14] So if an asset worth £8,000 is transferred in satisfaction of a debt for £10,000, and later sold by the creditor for £13,000, there is a gain of £3,000 not £5,000. In this way the creditor does not have to pay tax on the first £2,000 gain of the gain which is actually his loss on the debt. Any indexation allowance is to be calculated on the £8,000 not the £10,000. Naturally if the value of the property acquired is greater than the amount of the debt the higher value is taken; so if the asset is worth £11,000 and is later sold for £13,000, the gain is only £2,000 not £3,000.

Where property is sold, but the price is left outstanding by way of a loan and the purchaser defaults so that the vendor takes back the property, ESC D18 may enable the erstwhile vendor to choose to treat the transaction, for CGT purposes, as if it had not occurred.

34.4.2 Loans to Traders

Relief is available for losses on certain loans to traders. The money must be used by the borrower (B) wholly for the purposes of a trade carried on by B, not being a trade which consists of or includes the lending of money. B must be resident in the UK. The debt must

---

[12] As in *Taylor Clark International v Lewis* [1998] STC 1259.
[13] TCGA 1992, s 251(2), subject to ss 132, 135.
[14] On which see *Stanton v Drayton Commercial Investments Ltd* [1982] STC 585, 55 TC 286.

not be a debt on a security.[15] Where a person makes one loan (L1) then another (L2) to refinance the first, the court looks to the purpose behind L1 to decide whether the relief applies. Otherwise a company which had incurred borrowings for a non-qualifying purpose could bring the matter within the relief by simply rescheduling its debt.[16]

34.4.2.1 Conditions for Relief

The loan must be wholly or partially irrecoverable[17] and the lender (L) must not have assigned the right to recover the irrecoverable amount. L and B must not be either spouses or civil partners living together, or group companies when the loan was made or at any subsequent time (section 253(1)). The 'subsequent time' is up to the time at which the claim for relief is made. As originally enacted, the relief was given on a claim being made, and the loss accrued at the date of making the claim, even though the loan may have been irrecoverable at an earlier date. However, there is now legislative provision for backdating the claim to the time it became irrecoverable, subject to a maximum of two years.[18]

34.4.2.2 Claw Back

The relief is clawed back if L later receives any repayment of the loan, or other consideration in respect of it. L is treated as having made a gain equal to 'so much of the allowable loss as corresponds to the amount recovered' (section 253(5)).

34.4.2.3 Guarantors

Where a payment is made by a guarantor (G) guaranteeing a qualifying loan to a trader, G may claim a loss equal to the amount he pays under the guarantee.[19] G may not claim relief if L and B were companies in the same group either when the loan was made or at any subsequent time. Relief is also denied where the guarantor and lender are both companies in the same group at the time the guarantee was given, or at a subsequent time (section 253(4)(d)). Relief is available where the guarantor and the borrower are companies in the same group.

34.4.3 *Debt on a Security*

34.4.3.1 Debt

The traditional meaning of a 'debt' is a liability to pay a certain sum of money. In *Marren v Ingles*,[20] the taxpayer argued that an obligation to pay a sum of money in the future, the sum to be related to the future profits of the business being sold, was a debt and so outside CGT. The House of Lords rejected this plea. The meaning of the word 'debt' depended very much on its context. It was capable of including a contingent debt which might never be payable. It was also capable of including a sum of which the amount was not ascertained. However, it did not apply to 'a possible liability to pay an unidentifiable sum at an unascertainable date'.

---

[15] TCGA 1992, s 253(1); debt on a security is defined in s 132.
[16] *Robson v Mitchell* [2005] EWCA Civ 585, [2005] STC 893, Neuberger LJ at [23].
[17] Defined by TCGA 1992, s 253(9); see also *Cann v Woods* [1999] STC (SCD) 77.
[18] TCGA 1992, s 253(3A), added in 1996 enacting previous ESC D36.
[19] TCGA 1992, s 253(4); on timing see s 253(4A) added by FA 1996.
[20] [1980] STC 500, 506, (1980) 54 TC 76, 100, per Lord Fraser.

This conclusion did not prevent the contract from creating an asset within the scope of the CGT legislation, and a gain arose. Planning measures often involve ensuring that a debt is created so that no CGT liability can arise.[21]

34.4.3.2 'On a Security'

The expression 'a debt on a security' is not defined in the legislation. Lord Wilberforce, in *Ramsay v IRC*,[22] said that many learned judges have found it baffling both on the statutory wording and as to the underlying policy. It should be noted that the taxpayer lost in all five cases mentioned in this section.

Section 132(2)(b) defines 'security' as 'includ[ing] any loan stock or similar security whether of the Government of the United Kingdom or any other government, or of any public or local authority in the United Kingdom or elsewhere, or of any company, whether secured or unsecured'. The term is made expressly applicable in other parts of the Act, including section 251. The Revenue view is that the reference to 'loan stock' implies a class of debt the holdings in which are transferable by purchase and sale, and the words 'whether secured or unsecured' in the definition make the existence of a charge immaterial.[23]

34.4.3.3 Judicial View—Investment and Market

The principal judicial view is that such a debt must be something in the nature of an investment, and refers to those securities which are or may be subject to a conversion.[24] Stress has also been laid on embodiment of the obligation in a certificate which is evidence of the ownership of the share or stock and of the right to receive payment. A debt on a security is a debt evidenced in a document as a security. As such it is different from a letter of acceptance, or a bill of exchange or an unsecured debenture.[25] The same emphasis on a document or certificate creating a marketable security may be seen in *Aberdeen Construction Group Ltd v IRC*,[26] where the taxpayer company had contracted to sell a loss-making subsidiary in the days before relief for losses to qualifying traders was available. The terms of sale allowed the sale of the share capital for £250,000 on condition that the company wrote off loans totalling £500,000 made to its subsidiary. The parent tried to get relief for the loans thus written as being a 'debt on a security'. The claim failed.

34.4.3.4 Unusual Debts

Different considerations apply to unusual debts. T's claim failed in *Ramsay v IRC*,[27] where T tried to establish that the debt was not a debt on a security and so not subject to any chargeable gain. Lord Wilberforce stressed that the debt was very different from ordinary debts. In his opinion, Parliament had been trying to distinguish mere debts, which normally (although there were exceptions) did not increase but could decrease in value, from debts with added characteristics such as could enable them to be realised or dealt with at a profit. It was important to contrast debts simpliciter, which might arise from trading and a

---

[21] See [1984] BTR 259.
[22] [1982] AC 300, 329 [1981] STC 174, 184, (1981) 54 TC 101, 189.
[23] Statement of Practice SP D25.
[24] *Cleveleys Investment Trust Co v IRC* (1971) 47 TC 300, 315, per Lord Cameron.
[25] *Ibid*, 315, per Lord Migdale (dissenting).
[26] [1978] AC 755, [1978] STC 127, (1978) 52 TC 281.
[27] [1982] AC 300, [1981] STC 174, (1981) 54 TC 101.

multitude of other situations, commercial or private, and loans, which were certainly a narrower class and which presupposed some kind of contractual structure. Lord Wilberforce considered that this debt was a debt on a security. It was created by contract, the terms of which were recorded in writing; it was designed, from the beginning, to be capable of being sold and, indeed, to be sold at a profit.[28]

In a later case, *Taylor Clark International Ltd v Lewis*,[29] a loss arose on a promissory note. Holding that the debt was not a debt on a security, the court stressed the lack of a 'structure of permanence'; the debt had no fixed term and repayment could have been demanded by the creditor, or effected (without penalty) by the debtor, at any time. The key to that case was that a debt on a security had to be marketable in a realistic sense.[30]

34.4.4 Covenants

No chargeable gain accrues on the disposal of a right to, or to a part of, annual payments due under a covenant made by any person and which was not secured on any property (section 237(c)). This is presumably because the annual payments are themselves taxable in full as income (see §27.2 above). In *Rank Xerox Ltd v Lane*,[31] the House of Lords held that this rule was confined to situations where there was a gratuitous promise to make the payments and the promise was enforceable only because of its form. In that case the taxpayer was held liable on the gain arising from the disposal to its shareholders of a right to receive royalty payments.

34.5   Tangible Movable Property

The appropriate treatment of movable property[32] gives rise to some difficulty. For example, the tax system would tax an individual on gains realised if he sold his Louis XV bed at a gain, while not allowing him any relief if he threw away his worn-out sheets and duvets. Some systems segregate assets into different classes, eg into 'personal use' assets and others, and allow losses on personal use assets to be set only against gains on such assets. The UK adopts a more Draconian approach. Some assets simply do not give rise to chargeable gains and so do not give rise to allowable losses. This occurs if the movable property is (a) a wasting asset, or (b) sold for £6,000 or less, or (c) a road vehicle.

34.5.1 Wasting Assets

No chargeable gain accrues on the disposal of tangible movable property, or an interest in such property, where the property is also a wasting asset (section 45(1)). A wasting asset is

---

[28] *Ibid*, 329, 184, 189.
[29] [1997] STC 499, 522d, per Robert Walker J at first instance.
[30] [1998] STC 1259, 1272, per Peter Gibson LJ; see also *Tarmac Roadstone Holdings Ltd v Williams* [1996] STC (SCD) 409.
[31] [1979] STC 740, (1979) 53 TC 185. For an interesting analysis of the speeches, see Murphy and Rawlings (1981) 44 *MLR* 617, 632 *et seq.*
[32] Rules which apply only to tangible movable property will not cover fixtures before severance.

defined as an asset having a predictable life of 50 years or less.[33] Plant and machinery are always assumed to have a life of less than 50 years.[34] The exemption is extended to disposals of wasting assets that are tangible movable property used in a trade where expenditure attributed to the asset was deducted in computing profits of a trader under the cash basis.[35] However, the exemption for wasting assets does not apply to assets in respect of which capital allowances were or could have been claimed, or to commodities dealt with on a terminal market.[36] See further below §42.1. In the remarkable case of *HMRC v The executors of Lord Howard of Henderskelfe*,[37] the Court of Appeal held that a substantial gain on the sale of a painting by the executors of the late Lord Howard was not chargeable to CGT. The CA accepted that the portrait by the 18th Century painter Sir Joshua Reynold that had been sold for £9.4 million had become a wasting asset because it had been included for exhibition in a part of Castle Howard open to the public for business. In so doing the painting constituted 'plant' of that business and, by the operation of TCGA 1992, section 44, a wasting asset. Permission to appeal to the Supreme Court was refused. In response, FA 2015, section 40 amended TCGA 1992, section 45 so that from April 2015 the wasting asset exemption will apply only if the person selling the asset has used it as plant in her own business.

34.5.2 Disposal for £6,000 or Less

If an asset which is tangible movable property is disposed of and the amount or value of the consideration does not exceed £6,000, there is no chargeable gain.[38] The consideration taken into account is the gross amount, before any expenses of disposal, although full effect must be given to any indexation relief. Therefore, the sale of an asset bought for £800 in 1999 but sold for £6,000 in 2015 attracts no CGT. If the asset is sold for more than £6,000, any gain is computed in full in the normal way. This could lead to ludicrous differences in treatment once the consideration passes £6,000. Marginal relief therefore applies under which the gain is limited to five-thirds of the difference between the consideration and £6,000 if this would give a lower figure (section 262(2)). If the asset is sold for £6,400, the gain would have been £5,600 but this is restricted to £400 × 5/3 (ie £667).

Where a chattel is disposed of for less than £6,000, the allowable loss is computed on the assumption that the consideration was £6,000. If A acquires an antique object for £7,000 but sells it, in a falling market, for £5,200, the loss will be limited to £1,000. The system rightly sees no need for marginal rules for losses.

There are a number of anti-avoidance provisions:

(1) *Part disposal.* Provisions exist to counter exploitation of the chattel exemption by successive disposals of part-interests in a chattel worth more than £6,000. Where there is a disposal of a right or interest in or over tangible movable property, the

---

[33] TCGA 1992, s 44, applied by s 45(5).
[34] TCGA 1992, s 44(1)(c). The Revenue consider that the definition of 'machinery' includes antique clocks and watches, as well as custom-made vehicles such as racing cars, commercial vehicles and locomotives, etc (Inland Revenue interpretation RI 88). Such items are consequently exempt if used for private purposes.
[35] TCGA 1992, s 47A.
[36] TCGA 1992, s 45(2)–(4).
[37] [2014] EWCA Civ 278.
[38] TCGA 1992, s 262(1). For disposals before 6 April 1989 the limit was £3,000.

consideration for the disposal is treated as the aggregate of the sum received for the interest disposed of and the market value of the remainder (section 262(5)). Any marginal relief is calculated as already described by reference to the deemed consideration for the disposal, and the relief is then allocated pro rata to the actual disposal consideration. Suppose that Q sells a one-third share in a watercolour for £2,500. He had bought the water colour two years before for £900. The value of his remaining two-thirds interest is £5,000. The disposal consideration is deemed to be £7,500 and so the chattel exemption is not available. The gain is then calculated under the normal part disposal rules: Q is allowed to deduct one-third of the acquisition costs (£300) from the receipt of £2,500, giving a gain of £2,200. The five-thirds marginal relief alternative gives a figure of 5/3 × (£7,500–£6,000) or £2,500 as opposed to £6,400 (£7,500–£900), and so is applicable. When the £2,500 is allocated pro rata, the gain of £2,500 on the one-third interest is reduced by £833 to £1,667.

This principle is also applied to the loss restriction. If, in the above example, Q had purchased the picture for £8,400, and had sold a share for £1,500 (value of remainder £3,000), the position would be as follows. The allowable loss without restriction is £1,300, ie £1,500 (proceeds) less allowable costs (£2,800). However, if the proceeds are deemed to be £6,000 against allowable costs of £8,400 there is a loss of £2,400 of which Q's share will be one-third, or £800. These rules do not require that several part disposals are treated as taking place at one time. It follows that there may still be an advantage in making a series of part disposals in order to take advantage of the annual exemption or some other personal circumstance.

(2) *Sets*. Different provisions apply to a set of articles where the owner can make a disposition of one of the items in the set rather than, in the case of a single object, making a part disposal of it. The disposal of one item of the set is not treated as a part disposal of the set. However, special rules apply if there is a disposal of more than one item (a) to the same person, (b) to persons who are acting in concert, or (c) to persons who are connected with each other (but not necessarily connected with the disposer).

Whether the disposals take place on the same or different occasions, the two or more transactions are treated as a single transaction disposing of a single asset with any necessary apportionments of marginal relief and in restriction of losses.[39] The apportionment is made by reference to the consideration received for each of the items concerned. If disposals of parts of a set are made over a period of years, it appears that marginal relief or loss restriction for earlier years may be affected, although there is no extension of the normal six-year time limit for assessment or repayment claims. The following example illustrates the use of these rules to deny section 262 relief.

Example

Geoff purchases a set of six antique dining chairs for £5,400 (£900 each) in October 1998. In December 2010, he sells three of the chairs to a dealer for £4,200 (£1,400 each). He sells

---

[39] TCGA 1992, s 262(4). Quaere when the recipients must be acting in concert or connected persons; is it the time of the first disposal, or the subsequent one or both?

the remaining three chairs to the same dealer also for £4,200 a year later in September 2011. Disposal proceeds per chair come to £1,400, with allowable cost of £900, so G has a chargeable gain of £500. Applying section 262(4), the consideration (£8,400) exceeds £6,000, so the only question is whether marginal relief applies. The effect of marginal relief would be to limit the chargeable gain limited to 5/3 × (£8,400−£6,000) = £4,000, or £667 per chair. As this sum exceeds the actual gain of £500 it is ignored.

There is no definition of a set, although the Revenue used to take the view that only two items cannot constitute a set.[40] The statute requires that items of a set should all have been owned at one time by one person and that they are disposed of by that person. The provisions do not apply where the set is owned by connected persons.

34.5.3 *Motor Vehicles*

Motor vehicles are not chargeable assets if adapted or constructed for the carriage of passengers; the exemption does not apply to a vehicle of a type not commonly used as a private vehicle and unsuitable to be so used (section 263). The Revenue will not agree to exemption for single-seater sports cars or motorcycles[41]—presumably because they consider that a driver is not a passenger. This unimaginative construction is probably wrong, but a literal-minded court might uphold the Revenue. One consequence of the Revenue's position is that an expensive motorcycle bought for £10,000 and sold for £6,000 will give rise to a loss claim for £4,000—unless regarded as a wasting asset.

34.6 Land

34.6.1 *General*

Land is responsible for a substantial portion of the yield from CGT. Land also attracts a number of special rules modifying or illustrating the basic principles of CGT. Because of its capacity to generate substantial increases in wealth through development, land has attracted special legislation in the past. TA 1988, section 776, introduced in 1969 when CGT rates were lower than income tax rates, is still in force, though it has been rewritten into ITA 2007, section 752 and CTA 2010, section 815; since these rules charge certain profits to income or corporation tax, this will exclude any charge to CGT. Development land tax was in force from 1976–85,[42] and existed alongside both CGT and the section 776 charge.

34.4.6.1 Definition of Land

The definition of land includes 'messuages, tenements, and hereditaments, houses and buildings of any tenure' (section 288(1)). The CGT rules do not usually refer to 'land' but

---

[40] However, in RI 214 (January 2000), the Revenue discuss whether a pair of shotguns may be treated as a set.
[41] Manual CG, para 76907.
[42] For a general review, see Grant [1986] *JPL* 453. On abolition, see Lawson, *The View from No 11* (Bantam Press, 1992) 363.

to 'an interest in land'; this includes an interest in a building, even though the land beneath may be in separate ownership. As a result of the wide definition of 'land', the Revenue consider that rollover relief is potentially available on the grant of an option over land, despite the treatment in section 144 where an option is regarded as separate from the asset to which it relates.[43]

34.4.6.2 Location

In determining whether an asset is located in the UK or elsewhere, any interest in land will be treated as situated where the land is situated, except where the interest is solely in the land acting as security (section 275(1)). A debt secured on land is located where the creditor is resident (section 275(1), (2)).

34.4.6.3 Wasting Asset

Freehold land is never a wasting asset, whatever its nature and whatever the nature of the buildings and works on it. A lease with 50 or fewer years to run is a wasting asset (section 44(1)(a)).

34.4.6.4 Effect of Exchange of Joint Interests

If A and B are joint beneficial owners of a piece of land and they exchange their interests so that each becomes sole owner of part, a strict analysis says that A has made a disposal of A's interest in the part now owned solely by B—and vice versa—so giving rise to a disposal by each of them.[44] To avoid this result, rollover relief applies.[45] Where the property is a dwelling house, so that the only or main residence exemption may apply (see §34.7 below), the relief will be given only if all individuals accept that they acquire the other person's interest at its original base cost and on the original date of acquisition.

34.6.2 *Furnished Holiday Lettings*

Furnished holiday lettings are treated as a trade for CGT; all individual lettings made by one person (or one partnership) are treated as one single trade (section 241(3)). CGT reliefs are available in respect of:

(1)   rollover relief under sections 152–157;
(2)   entrepreneurs' relief under section 169(1);
(3)   holdover relief under section 165; and
(4)   relief for loans to traders under section 253.

The effect of treating the lettings as one single trade is to allow these reliefs to apply to the various properties as one mass instead of only on an individual, and so much more restricted, basis. The property must have been let commercially, or have been available to

---

[43] Revenue interpretation RI 11.
[44] Doubt may have been cast on this analysis by the judgment in *Jenkins v Brown* [1989] STC 577, where a disposal was held not to have occurred on a distribution of land holdings out of a pool held by trustees. It was held that the measure of the beneficial interests of the settlors was unaffected by the trust.
[45] TCGA 1992, ss 248A–248E, ex ESC D26; the concession was based on the analogy of TCGA 1992, ss 247, 248.

have been so let or prevented from being let commercially by works of construction or repair. At least one of these conditions must have been satisfied at some time during the chargeable period.[46] The treatment afforded to furnished holiday accommodation is not dependent on profits being made.[47]

34.7 Exemption for Only or Main Residence

34.7.1 Basic Rules

A gain is wholly or partly exempt if it is attributable to the disposal of, or of an interest in,[48] a dwelling house which is or has been the owner's only or main residence. The house does not have to be such a residence at the time of disposal, provided it was such at some time during the period of ownership (section 222).

Because the exemption is confined to interests in the house, disposals of assets other than such interests are not exempt. The Revenue, rightly, treated a pre-1996 interest in the proceeds of sale of land as an interest in land, but do not grant relief where the house is owned through a housing association; this view is certainly harsh and possibly wrong. Since a leasehold interest is an interest in land, a sum paid by a landlord to the lessee of an only or main residence to secure the surrender of the lease is exempt.[49] Formerly by concession but now enacted as TCGA 1992, section 225C, relief extends to profits realised by employees who, under relocation arrangements set up by their employer, sell their house to a relocation company (or to the employer) at market value and share in any subsequent profits on the sale of the house.[50] There is no requirement that the residence should be in the UK.

The residence must be a dwelling house; this is a question of fact. The term 'dwelling house' is not defined; the equivalent income tax relief for mortgage interest was extended to caravans and houseboats,[51] and a caravan has qualified for CGT.[52] The courts also look at the degree of residence—temporary residence does not suffice, as was made clear when a taxpayer unsuccessfully argued that one month's stay while purchasing a permanent home should qualify.[53] The exemption is not available if the acquisition of the house was wholly or partly for the purpose of making a gain from its disposal.[54] Similarly, where expenditure is incurred in carrying out improvements or in acquiring additional land with the purpose of gain, there will be a charge on the proportion of the gain attributable to

---

[46] TCGA 1992, s 245(1). For an individual, the chargeable period is the fiscal year; for a company the chargeable period is the accounting period.

[47] *Walls v Livesey* [1995] STC (SCD) 12.

[48] TCGA 1992, s 222. The Revenue accept that an 'interest' does not extend to a residence occupied under licence: see Inland Revenue interpretation RI 89.

[49] Quaere, however, if he receives compensation for agreeing not to seek a new lease since the interest is disposed of.

[50] TCGA 1992, s 225C, ex ESC D37.

[51] TA 1988, s 354(7) (now repealed).

[52] See *Makins v Elson* [1977] STC 46, (1977) 51 TC 437 on the degree of residence required.

[53] *Goodwin v Curtis* [1998] STC 475; see also *Moore v Thompson* [1986] STC 170, (1986) 61 TC 15.

[54] TCGA 1992, s 224(3); see *Jones v Wilcock* [1996] STC (SCD) 389 (taxpayer argued unsuccessfully that he was caught by s 224(3) so as to be able to claim loss relief; those who believe that property values always go up should study the figures in this case).

that expenditure. A mere hope of making a gain is probably insufficient to lose the exemption. Sections 222A–C set out how the relief applies to non-resident owners. Under section 222B, which applies to both residents and non-residents, the relief can be claimed for a tax year only if the individual (or spouse) is resident in the country where the property is located or spends at least 90 days living in the property (or other property in that country).

34.7.2 Residence[55]

Several relatively recent tribunal decisions have considered the meaning of 'residence' for purposes of the private residence CGT relief—sometimes with surprising results. In *Morgan (David) v HMRC*,[56] the taxpayer had intended to purchase and move into a property with his girlfriend. Their relationship ended, but he decided to proceed with the purchase, moved in for about two months to get the house ready to let, and then moved back in with his parents. He let the property for about five years before selling it for a gain. Despite the short period of occupancy, the First-tier Tribunal ruled that the house qualified as his residence and he was eligible for the CGT relief. By contrast, in *Moore (Piers) v HMRC*,[57] the taxpayer's marriage broke down and he moved out of the matrimonial home into another property he owned. He lived there for about eight months before selling it and purchasing another home with a new partner. The First-tier Tribunal held that the property did not qualify as his residence because he intended to live there only temporarily. From these two decisions it appears that a taxpayer's subjective motive for occupation has become the deciding factor in determining whether a property is a 'residence'. Given that it is not uncommon for homeowners, especially first-time buyers, to view a house as a temporary step on the ladder towards their 'forever home', the Tribunals' recent approach is perhaps overly restrictive and uncertain.

34.7.2.1 Associated Buildings

The courts have had much difficulty with buildings related to the home. In one case it was held that a separate bungalow adjacent to but within the curtilage of a dwelling house was part of the dwelling house even though the bungalow was occupied by a part-time caretaker.[58] However, this approach was rejected by the Court of Appeal in *Lewis v Lady Rook*.[59] Adopting an 'entity' approach, with the dwelling house as the 'entity', the Court was not concerned by the fact that the other building was separate from the main building, but asked whether it was part of the dwelling house. This was to be answered by asking whether it was 'within the curtilage of and appurtenant to' the main house. Applying that test, the Court held that the exemption did not apply to a gain realised on the sale by the owner of the main house, Lady Rook, of a cottage occupied by one of her gardeners, even though she

[55] See Lee [1988] *Conveyancer* 143; and Wilde [1993] *Conveyancer* 222.
[56] [2013] UKFTT 181 (TC).
[57] [2013] UKFTT 433 (TC). See also note by Vaines in Tax Journal (20 Sept 2013).
[58] *Batey v Wakefield* [1981] STC 521, (1981) 55 TC 550; distinguished on its facts in *Green v IRC* [1982] STC 485, (1982) 56 TC 10. See also *Markey v Sanders* [1987] STC 256, (1987) 60 TC 245 (staff bungalow within grounds and separated by ha-ha was taxable—Commissioners reversed); and *Williams v Merrylees* [1987] STC 445, (1987) 60 TC 297 (staff lodge exempt—Commissioners not reversed but doubted).
[59] [1992] STC 171, (1992) 64 TC 567. As to the Revenue interpretation of 'curtilage', see HMRC Capital Gains Manual CG64245.

could summon help from the gardener by ringing a large ship's bell or flashing a flashlight; the cottage was not within the curtilage. She was also held chargeable for an earlier period during which the cottage had been occupied rent free by the widow of a previous gardener; the effect of this was to penalise a person for acting in a benevolent capacity towards a person to whom she felt a moral obligation.[60]

34.7.2.2 Grounds of the Main Residence

As well as the actual site of the dwelling house, land is included in the exemption if the owner has it as the garden or grounds of the dwelling house, for his own occupation and enjoyment. If the garden or grounds exceed 0.5 hectare, the exemption applies only if the larger area was, having regard to the size and character of the house, required for the reasonable enjoyment as a residence. The sale of a garden separate from the rest of the house causes difficulties. To be exempt the garden must be occupied as such, with the house, at the time of the disposal. Where the house is sold with part of the garden and the remainder of the garden is sold later, the subsequent sale is not entitled to the exemption.[61] If the order of sales were reversed, both sales would qualify.[62] The point is taken by the Revenue only where the garden has development value.[63] A separate sale of the garden may, where the garden is in excess of 0.5 hectare, weaken the plea that the garden was required for the reasonable enjoyment of the house. The garden does not have to be adjacent to the house. In *Wakeling v Pearce*,[64] the Special Commissioners applied the exemption on the sale of a plot physically separate from the taxpayer's residence by a distance of some 25–30 feet. The Commissioners found, as a fact, that the land in question had been used as the garden or grounds of the house by the taxpayer for many years, and this use continued up to the time of sale.[65]

34.7.2.3 Several Flats or One Home?

A no less intriguing problem arose in *Honour v Norris*,[66] where five flats in separate buildings in a London square were used to create a single home. If outhouses or separated gardens can be part of a residence, arguably accommodation could be spread across adjacent buildings. However, Vinelott J rejected out of hand a submission that these flats could form one residence; declining to lay down any general principles he described the submission as 'an affront to common sense'.[67]

---

[60] Sparkes [1990] BTR 260, commenting on the decision of the Chancery Division at [1990] STC 23.

[61] *Varty v Lynes* [1976] STC 508, (1976) 51 TC 419.

[62] The position where the sales are simultaneous is unclear.

[63] HMRC, 'Private Residence Relief' Helpsheet 283 (2012), 5.

[64] [1995] STC (SCD) 96.

[65] For Revenue practice, see RI 119, which treats gains as taxable if they arise from land used for agriculture, commercial woodlands, trade or business, or which has been fenced off from the residence to be sold for development. The exemption will apply, however, to land which has traditionally been part of the grounds of the residence but which, at the date of sale, is unused or overgrown, and to paddocks or orchards—provided there is no significant business use.

[66] [1992] STC 304.

[67] See angry criticisms by Norris (the taxpayer) in [1993] BTR 24, 40: 'It may reasonably be expected that a High Court judge will have a greater knowledge of the law than a body of lay Commissioners but it is by no means necessarily to be expected that he has been blessed with a greater ration of common sense. If the courts are to abandon law in favour of common sense then different sources will have to be found for the selection of judges.' See also Pearce Crump [1993] BTR 12.

34.7.3 *Periods When Not Used as the Main Residence*

Full exemption applies where the dwelling house has been occupied throughout the period of ownership as the owner's main residence.[68] Where the period of ownership contains other periods, the starting point is to apportion—on a simple fractional bases. If a house has been sold realising a gain of £100,000 and was used for letting for the first seven years and as a residence for the last seven years, one half of the gain will be exempt under section 222. A similar result may be reached if the division was by space and not by time (section 222(10)). The legislation contain several rules designed to provide further relief.

34.7.3.1 Last 18 Months

The last 18 months of ownership are treated as a period of owner-occupation, whether or not so occupied, provided the house has at some time been the only or main residence.[69] This period was formerly 36 months, and the 36 month period still applies for individuals where they or their spouses/civil partners are disabled or are long-term residents in a care home

34.7.3.2 Apportionment—Time

As already seen, where the house was used as the person's main residence for only part of the period of ownership, partial exemption applies, and is given by apportionment of the overall gain rateably to the period of owner-occupation as a main residence.[70] Where the individual has held different interests in the property, the period of ownership is treated as commencing with the acquisition of the first interest in respect of which allowable expenditure was incurred (section 222(7)). The apportionment rule is mandatory; there are no rules directing a deemed disposal at fair market value at the time of the change of use.

Example (a)—disposal 2016

Jim purchased a house as his main residence for £150,000 on 1 March 2008 and occupied it as such until 31 May 2008. From then until its sale on 1 September 2016, the house was occupied rent-free by J's son and daughter-in-law. The net proceeds of sale are £250,000.

Disposal consideration	£250,000
Acquisition cost	£150,000
Chargeable gain	£100,000

The exempt period consists of the first two months of ownership plus the last 18 months = 20 months. Total period of ownership since March 2008 was 102 months, so the exempt

---

[68] TCGA 1992, s 222. The legislation does not say that the ownership must be of the land, and it is therefore arguable that the period of ownership is that of the dwelling house, a matter of importance where land is bought and a house is subsequently built on it.

[69] TCGA 1992, s 223(1), (2). The period was extended to 36 months in relation to disposals on or after 19 March 1991 (previously 24 months), and then reduced to 18 months for disposals on or after 6 April 2014. The length of the period is intended to take account of the prevailing level of activity in the housing market. For commentary see Loutzenhiser [2014] BTR 406.

[70] TCGA 1992, s 223(2); only periods of ownership after 31 March 1982 are relevant in making the time apportionment (s 223(7)).

part of the gain was 20/102 of £100,000 (£19,608) and the chargeable part was 82/102 of £100,000 (£80,392). Tax at 28% (assumed) CGT is £22,510.

Example (b)—disposal 2019

Assume instead the sale took place in September 2019 and the gain is still £100,000. The total period of ownership would be three years longer (138 months). The exempt part of the gain would be 20/138 (£14,493) and the chargeable part (118/138) £85,507. This is taxed at 28% (assumed), making CGT of £23,942.

34.7.3.3 Apportionment—Space

Apportionment will also take place if a part of the house has been used exclusively for business purposes, eg a surgery attached to a doctor's residence.[71]

34.7.3.4 Letting—£40,000 Exemption

Gains attributable to a period of letting as residential accommodation are partially or wholly exempt; this additional relief is available on a letting either of the whole dwelling house or of part of it.[72] In *Owen v Elliott*,[73] the Court of Appeal gave a generous interpretation of this exemption, holding that accommodation could be regarded as let 'as residential accommodation' even though the occupants did not use it as residential accommodation. The case involved a family-run hotel partially occupied by the family as their home; the hotel was held to have been let as residential accommodation. The gain which becomes chargeable as a result of the letting is reduced by the smaller of (a) the gain attributable to owner-occupation, and (b) £40,000 (section 223(4)(b)). It seems that in a case where chargeable gains arise as a result of letting and also for some other reason, eg the house is left unoccupied or is used partially for business, the gain resulting from the letting must be identified separately. However, there are no provisions setting out how this is to be done.

Suppose that T sells his house at a net gain of £51,000, and that one-third of the gain comes within this rule. The rule states that the chargeable gain (£17,000) attributable to this one-third is to be chargeable only to the extent that it exceeds (a) £34,000 and (b) £40,000; it is therefore exempt from tax. If the gain is increased by 50% to £76,500, the chargeable gain goes up to £25,500; the figure for (a) is now £51,000 and (b) 40,000; (b) ensures that the gain is still exempt. However, if the gain is increased by 75%—to £133,875—the chargeable gain is now £44,625, (a) is now £89,250 and (b) is still £40,000; (b) is the critical lower figure and T has a potential CGT liability on £4,625 (potential in that it may be covered by T's annual exemption).

34.7.4 Periods of Deemed Residence

The rules deem periods of non-occupation as periods of residence. First, as already seen, the period of 18 months immediately before disposal is treated as a period of

---

[71] TCGA 1992, s 224(1); no relief is lost if a room is used exclusively for employment purposes or partly for business purposes and partly for personal use (RI 80).

[72] TCGA 1992, s 223(4). Distinguish a lodger living as a member of the owner's family (see Statement of Practice SP 14/80). The letting must be as residential occupation, ie the persons to whom the accommodation is let must use it as their home.

[73] [1990] STC 469, (1990) 63 TC 319 CA; see Sparkes [1990] BTR 385.

owner-occupation (section 223(1)). In practice, a 12-month period before occupation is also treated as owner-occupation if the owner cannot take up residence because the house is being built or repaired.[74] Only the excess is then treated as a chargeable gain.[75]

Secondly, certain other periods are treated as periods of residence, provided they are both preceded and followed by periods of occupation[76] and no other residence is eligible for relief during the period of absence. These periods, which may all be claimed in aggregate and are subject to certain conditions in section 223(3A) and (3B), are:

(1)   any period of up to three years;

(2)   any period of overseas employment;[77] and

(3)   any period not exceeding four years during which the owner could not occupy the house by reason of place of work or a reasonable condition imposed by an employer that he should reside elsewhere (section 223(3), (7)).

Where the period of absence under (1) or (2) is exceeded, only the excess (not the whole period) is treated as giving rise to a chargeable gain.[78]

Thirdly, job-related accommodation. The insistence on actual occupation of the dwelling house was harsh on those who had to live in accommodation provided by their employers. The legislation therefore treats the period of ownership as a period of occupation (section 222(8)) where a person, E, resides elsewhere in accommodation which is job-related. That other accommodation is job-related if it fulfils criteria identical with those for exemption from ITEPA 2003, Part 3, Chapter 5 (taxable benefits: living accommodation—see §15.4 above).[79] The exemption applies to the ownership of a dwelling house, provided E intends to use it in due course as E's only or main residence; it is not clear whether the land must be in the UK or the Republic of Ireland.[80] Similar relief is provided in the case of self-employed persons where they are required to occupy the dwelling house for the purposes of carrying on their trade under the terms of a contract entered into at arm's length.[81] The reliefs are withheld if E has a material interest in the company, unless the employment is as a full-time working director or the company is non profit-making or established for charitable purposes only;[82] there is an analogous restriction for the self-employed.[83]

---

[74] ESC D49.

[75] [1983] *Simon's Tax Intelligence* 116.

[76] Periods of occupation need not immediately precede and follow the period of absence, but they must be periods of actual occupation, not other qualifying periods of absence. Where, on a person's return, he is not able to resume occupation because the terms of his employment require him to live elsewhere, this condition is treated as satisfied (TCGA 1992, s 223, ex ESC D4).

[77] Where the house belongs to one spouse or civil partner and the other is required to go overseas, the condition is treated as satisfied (TCGA 1992, s 223, ex ESC D3).

[78] [1983] *Simon's Tax Intelligence* 116, para 13; and confirmed by the Inland Revenue Technical Division.

[79] Ex TA 1988, s 356(3)(a), applied by TCGA 1992, s 222(8)(a), with the criteria now repeated in s 222(8A)(a).

[80] As was required by the equivalent relief for mortgage interest (former TA 1988, s 354(1)).

[81] TCGA 1992, s 222(8A)(b), ex TA 1988, s 356(3)(b), (5).

[82] TCGA 1992, s 222(8B), ex TA 1988, s 356(4); on definitions see s 222(8D), ex s 356(6).

[83] TCGA 1992, s 222(8C), ex TA 1988, s 356(5).

34.7.5 Election for Main Residence

An individual may have only one exempt residence. If T has more than one residence, there must be an election to decide which is to be exempt.[84] An individual may only elect between dwelling houses. T could not select a house which was always let to tenants, although an occasional letting is probably not inconsistent with residence. Any such election can take effect for a period beginning up to two years before the election is made (section 222(5)(a)). However, it appears, on somewhat shaky authority, that the election must be made within two years of the taxpayer having more than one residence, even though it may be varied thereafter.[85] Thus, suppose that X buys house 1 in January 2015; he then buys house 2 in May 2016, so giving rise to a right to elect between houses 1 and 2 until May 2018. X then disposes of house 1 in June 2017 and buys house 3 in November 2017, so having two houses once more. X can elect, but can an election in favour of house 2 be backdated to May 2016 or only from November 2017? The official answer is that it can be backdated only to November 2017. This decision has been criticised as being odd in practical terms.[86] The case law authority on which it rests is also suspect, owing to the repeal of part of the legislation.[87]

If a taxpayer has more than one residence then, if his interest in each of them, except one, is such as to have no more than a negligible capital value on the open market (eg a weekly rented flat or accommodation provided by an employer), the two-year time limit for nominating one of those residences as the individual's main residence for capital gains purposes will be extended where the individual was unaware that such a nomination could be made.[88] The late election will be deemed effective from the date on which the individual first had more than one residence. Where a husband and wife or civil partners live together, they are entitled to only one private residence exemption between them and they must make any election jointly.[89] Whether or not the spouses or civil partners have more than one house, one may take advantage of any period during which the house was the main residence of the other (section 222(7)). So, if a man dies and leaves the main residence to his wife or civil partner, who does not occupy the house but sells it four years later, the wife or civil partner will not be taxed in full on the whole gain since the death, but only on a proportion which takes account of the deceased's period of occupation—whether or not the wife or civil partner was also in occupation.

When stories of property flipping MPs abusing this election for private residence relief hit the newspapers in 2009 in the context of the wider Parliamentary expenses scandal, it seemed it would just be a matter of time before the relief was tightened up.[90] The reduction of the deemed owner-occupier period from 36 months to 18 months went

---

[84] Under TCGA 1992, s 222(5).

[85] *Griffin v Craig-Harvey* [1994] STC 54, 66 TC 396.

[86] See Norris [1994] BTR 534, drawing attention to the difficulties a taxpayer would have faced if the court had looked at Hansard; for another comment, see Hutton (1994) *Private Client Business* 146.

[87] Maurice Parry-Wingfield (personal communication); TCGA 1992 s 225(5)(b) was repealed as part of the self-assessment regime.

[88] ESC D21.

[89] TCGA 1992, s 222(6). As to the position where one spouse or civil partner has interests in more than one residence and the other has none, see RI 75. The position is unaffected by the independent taxation of such couples. On separated couples, see TCGA 1992, s 225B, ex ESC D6 (1994), and above at §33.11.3.

[90] For commentary see Loutzenhiser [2014] BTR 406.

part of the way (see above §34.7.3.1), but attention then turned to restricting abuse of the main residence election. In March 2014 HM Treasury and HMRC launched a consultation on implementing CGT on non-residents owning residential property in the UK. The consultation contained some proposals that would impact on UK residents as well. One such proposal concerns the ability of those with more than one property to elect which one will be covered by the relief. The consultation paper requested comments on two potential alternatives to the present system. Under the first option the determination is made instead by taking into account all relevant evidence—as is presently the case where an election has not been made—including factors such as the address where the taxpayer's spouse or family lives, post is sent, and that is on the electoral roll. The second option replaces the election with a fixed rule that identifies a person's main residence—for example, the one in which the person has been present the most in any given tax year. At the time of writing it remain to be seen what, if any, changes will be made to the existing election system.

34.7.6 Dwelling House Held by Trustees

An exemption may be claimed by trustees if the dwelling house is owned by them and has been the main private residence of someone entitled to occupy it under the terms of the trust, or who is allowed by the trustees to occupy it and would be entitled to the income from the house or from the proceeds of sale (section 225). When trustees of a discretionary trust in exercise of their discretion allow an object of the trust to occupy the house, the object is entitled to occupy the house under the terms of the trust since there is a right to remain in occupation until asked to leave by the trustees.[91] The relief is also available where the residence is held by PRs. One or more individuals must have occupied the property as their only or main residence immediately before and immediately after the death, and they must be entitled as legatees to at least 75% of the net proceeds of the disposal by the PRs. The PRs must make a claim.[92]

34.7.7 Residence of Dependent Relative—5 April 1988 Position Preserved

Before 1988 an individual, or a married couple living together, could also claim exemption in respect of one private residence which was provided for a dependent relative rent-free and without any consideration of any sort (section 226). Although this relief has been withdrawn, it may still apply if the property is disposed of today but was the sole residence of a qualifying dependent relative on 5 April 1988 or at some earlier time. Occupation after April 1988 may qualify if it has been continuous and existed on that date. However, a break in occupation after 1988 followed by a resumed occupation is not enough for later periods to qualify for the exemption.

---

[91] *Sansom v Peay* [1976] STC 494, [1976] 3 All ER 375.
[92] TCGA 1992, s 225A, added by FA 2004, s 117 and Sch 22; this provision enacts ESC D5—but with differences which are explained in Revenue Notes to Clause 112, paras 90–93.

34.8   Works of Art

Three special rules apply to works of art: (a) exemption for disposals to the right people; (b) conditional exemption for CGT by analogy with the IHT treatment; and (c) holdover relief.

34.8.1 *Exempt Disposals*

A gain is exempt from CGT if the disposal is (a) of property accepted by the Treasury in satisfaction of a liability to IHT;[93] or (b) to a museum, etc listed in Schedule 3 to IHTA 1984.[94]

34.8.2 *Conditional Exemption*

Where IHTA 1984, section 30 gives conditional exemption from IHT on a transfer (see §54.4 below), there is an equivalent exemption from CGT (TCGA 1992, section 258(3)). However, this exemption is confined to gifts and certain deemed disposals by trustees. The conditional exemption takes the form of holdover relief; the disposal is treated as having been made for a consideration such that it is made at no gain/no loss. CGT may arise on a later sale if IHT also becomes chargeable (section 258(5)).

34.8.3 *Holdover Relief*

There is also a holdover relief when assets are transferred to a fund established for the maintenance of historic buildings, etc.[95]

34.9   Woodlands: Timber

No CGT charge arises on the disposal of trees or saleable underwood in respect of woodlands managed by the occupier on a commercial basis and with a view to the realisation of profits.[96] Land on which short rotation coppice is cultivated is treated as agricultural land, not woodland.[97] On a disposal of any woodland, such part of the acquisition cost—or the disposal consideration—as is attributable to the trees and underwood is disregarded for CGT. This exclusion prevents a taxpayer from buying land, cutting the timber and then claiming a loss for the decline in value due to the felling.

---

[93] TCGA 1992, s 258(2)(b); IHTA 1984, s 230.
[94] TCGA 1992, s 258(2)(a); IHTA 1984, Sch 3.
[95] TCGA 1992, s 260(2)(b)–(f).
[96] TCGA 1992, s 250. Before 6 April 1988 the exemption for the disposal of standing timber was applied to woodlands within Sch B for income tax purposes.
[97] FA 1995, s 154. The provision is deemed to have come into force on 29 November 1994.

35

Disposals: (1) General

35.1 Meaning of Disposal

In the world of tax planning, disposals may be made either to realise a gain or to trigger a loss; in the real world they are made because owners want to rearrange their assets or simply need some cash. The central concept of disposal is not defined,[1] but neither has it yet caused much reported litigation. It seems to cover any form of transfer or alienation of the beneficial title to an asset (whether legal or equitable) from one person to another, involving a disposal by one and an acquisition by the other. A disposal by trustees of shares in the course of administration is clearly a disposal on this definition since beneficial title passes to the purchaser; the fact that the disposers are not beneficially entitled is irrelevant. An exchange of assets is a disposal of each asset involved. An involuntary disposal may still be a disposal;[2] however, a disclaimer does not constitute a disposal.[3]

TCGA 1992 extends the concept of disposal by treating certain shifts of economic value as disposals even though no asset is disposed of (see below at §35.5). In looking at these and other deemed disposals, the courts have been reluctant to interpret the legislation in such a way as to find that a disposal occurs at a moment of which the alleged disposer might not have been aware. A poignant example of this is the refusal of the court to find that a beneficiary had become absolutely entitled as against trustees, in a case in which a

---

[1] Definitions are available in other Acts, eg ITA 2007, Pt 13, Ch 3, ex TA 1988, ss 776(4), 777(2), (3). In *Turner v Follet* [1973] STC 148, (1973) 48 TC 614, the Court of Appeal made extremely heavy weather of the point whether the definition in the text is right. A loan is not a disposal, but a loan must be distinguished from a gift: see *Dewar v Dewar* [1975] 2 All ER 728. On switching between different unit trusts in a multi-portfolio, see TCGA 1992, s 102.

[2] But this effect may be undone by legislation (TCGA 1992, s 66 (bankruptcy), ss 245, 246 (compulsory purchase)).

[3] TCGA 1992, s 62(6)(a) and see *Re Paradise Motor Co Ltd* [1968] 2 All ER 625.

deemed disposal would have occurred when a person lost the capacity to have children (below §40.7.1.2).[4]

The person liable to tax is the person who makes the disposal. The fact that that person feels morally obliged to hand a percentage of the proceeds over to other family members who had lent him the money to buy the asset is irrelevant.[5]

35.2 Timing of Disposal

Just as there is no general definition of a disposal, so there is no general rule for the timing of a disposal (or acquisition). While there are some specific rules, general matters are left as questions of general law. Therefore, the gift of a chattel takes effect when there has been delivery of the chattel with the requisite intention. Similarly, the transfer of shares other than bearer shares requires the registration of the transfer by the company. Transfers of other types of property, such as land or copyright, require certain formalities, such as a deed or writing.[6]

A transfer which falls short of these formalities may nonetheless be an effective transfer in equity and so qualify as a disposal for CGT. Thus, in *Re Rose*,[7] a gift of shares was held to be effective in equity for estate duty purposes when the transferor/settlor had done all in his power to complete the transfer and all that remained was registration by the company; this would have continued even if the directors had refused to register the transfer. By contrast, in *Re Fry*,[8] the transferor still had to complete certain exchange control forms and so equity could not intervene to make the gift effective. *Re Rose* had distinguished the earlier decision in *Macedo v Stroud*,[9] where it was held that a gift of shares became effective only when registration took place because the registration was undertaken by the donor himself and not some third party.

35.2.1 Disposal Under Contract: When the Contract is Made

Where an asset is disposed of and acquired under a contract, the time at which the disposal and acquisition take place is the time the contract is made and not, if different, the date of conveyance (section 28(1)).[10] Thus, the usual time will be that at which the acceptance reaches the offeror, subject to the rules on postal acceptance.

In *Jerome v Kelly*,[11] the House of Lords held that the function of this rule is simply to decide when the disposal takes place; it does not also change the identity of the person making the disposal. In (very) simplified form, A owned land and made a contract of sale to C in

---

[4] *Figg v Clark* [1997] STC 247; for an example of similar reluctance in the less personal context of capital allowances, see Lord Browne Wilkinson in *Melhuish v BMI (No 3)* [1995] STC 964, 974b, (1995) 68 TC 1, 75.

[5] *Burca v Parkinson* [2001] STC 1298.

[6] Eg, the Law of Property Act 1925, s 52, or the Copyright Designs and Patents Act 1988, s 90(3).

[7] [1949] Ch 78.

[8] [1946] Ch 312.

[9] [1922] 2 AC 330.

[10] On application of TCGA 1992, s 28 in context of determining connected party status, see §33.9 above.

[11] [2004] UKHL 25, [2004] STC 887; see Staveley [2004] BTR 439.

April 1987; the contract was unconditional as far as this rule was concerned, but contained various alternative scenarios. A assigned the benefit of the contract to B. In December 1989 the sale was completed. The House of Lords held that the rule did not introduce further statutory fictions as to the parties. It followed that the disposal was under the conveyance to the purchaser and so was made by B and not by A. As B was not resident at that time, there was no charge to tax. The decision of the Court of Appeal in *Underwood v HMRC* confirmed that section 28 does not define the disposal to be a contract, but only deems when a disposal (once established) has been made.[12]

35.2.1.1 Variations: is there a Disposal 'Under the Contract'?

The general rule applies only when the disposal takes place 'under the contract'; whether this is so is a question of fact. The question can be particularly difficult if a contract is later varied and the issue arises whether the disposal is under the original contract as varied, or under a completely new contract. In *Magnavox Electronics Co Ltd v Hall*,[13] X, the taxpayer, made a contract to sell property to A in 1978; X went into liquidation and A later defaulted. A new purchaser, B, was found by X's liquidator; B was willing to buy, but at a lower price. In July 1979 the liquidator arranged for X to acquire a company, S; A assigned its contractual rights to S, and S then varied the original contract so as to reflect the new lower price agreed with B; S then made a separate contract to sell the property to B. The Court of Appeal held that these arrangements did not enable X to argue that the disposal took place under the 1978 contract—and so in 1978. The agreement between X and S did not vary the 1978 contract since A was not a party to it. The court invoked *Furniss v Dawson*[14] to disregard the interposition of S.

35.2.1.2 Contract Unenforceable

If the disposal is under the contract, it nevertheless will be treated as made when the contract is made even though the contract itself is unenforceable.[15]

35.2.1.3 Conditional Contract

If the contract is conditional, the disposal occurs when the condition is satisfied; 'condition' here means something on which the existence of the contract depends, rather than a major contractual term.[16] The courts have taken a pragmatic rather than legalistic line.[17]

35.2.1.4 Condition Precedent

An example of a condition which will defer the time of the disposal is a condition precedent. In *Pym v Campbell*,[18] a sale of a patent was subject to the invention being approved by a

---

[12] [2009] STC 239, [2008] EWCA Civ 1423, particularly Lawrence Collins LJ at [49] and [50] and the elegant judgment of Lord Neuberger, esp at [63] and [68]. See also McKie (2008) 162 *Taxation* 58–61 and 82–84. *Underwood* also calls into question the viability of the well-established practice known as 'bed and breakfasting', under which assets are regarded as being disposed of under a sales contract.

[13] [1986] STC 561, (1986) 59 TC 610.

[14] [1984] AC 474, [1984] STC 153, (1984) 55 TC 324.

[15] *Thompson v Salah* (1972) 47 TC 559 (a case concerning Sch D, Case VII).

[16] *Hatt v Newman* [2000] STC 113.

[17] *Eastham v Leigh London and Provincial Properties Ltd* (1971) 46 TC 687, CA.

[18] (1856) 6 E&B 370.

third party; the third party did not approve and so the purchaser was not liable for refusing to complete the purchase. Another example would be an agreement to sell land subject to the grant of planning permission for the construction of a building on the land; this would be conditional until planning permission was obtained.[19]

35.2.1.5 Condition Subsequent

As is clear from *Pym v Campbell*, a contract which is subject to a condition precedent to its formation, eg a contract if X marries in April, is not strictly a conditional contract since there can be no contract at all until the condition is satisfied. By contrast, in the case of a condition subsequent there is a contract but it may fail. Hence, it is considered that a contract with a condition subsequent, eg a contract unless X marries by the end of April, would give rise to a disposal only when it was clear that the condition could not occur, ie the end of April.

35.2.1.6 Contractual Conditions

The fact that a contract to dispose of an asset is expressed to be subject to performance by X, the transferee, of obligations imposed on X by the contract (promissory conditions precedent to performance) does not make the contract a conditional contract. Thus, an agreement to grant a lease of land subject to the construction of a building on the land by the intending lessee was held to be unconditional in *Eastham v Leigh London and Provincial Properties Ltd*.[20] Similarly, a condition under which the contract terminates on the failure by one of the parties to perform his obligations under the contract (a promissory condition subsequent) would not make the contract a conditional contract.

35.2.1.7 Disposals Under a Consent Order

Normally, the terms of a consent order made by agreement between the parties to court proceedings derive their force and effect from the parties' agreement and so take effect when the agreement is made. In matrimonial proceedings, however, the terms embodied in the order derive their effect from the order itself and not from the agreement.[21] In *Aspden v Hildesley*,[22] the agreed terms were embodied in an order made before decree absolute. This was not a full consent order but an order that the agreed terms be filed 'and made a rule of court'. Nevertheless, it was argued that the terms had effect only by virtue of the order and that, as the order was made before decree absolute, it was conditional upon the decree nisi being made absolute in due course; this was to make the disposal under the terms in the order take effect on decree absolute.[23] However, the court held that this was not made out on the facts; the agreement provided for the immediate transfer of the taxpayer's interest in the property and could not have been set aside if the decree had not been made absolute.

---

[19] As in *Hatt v Newman* above; distinguish Lord Walker's observations in *Jerome v Kelly* [2004] UKHL 25; [2004] STC 887, para 36.
[20] (1971) 46 TC 687, CA.
[21] *De Lasala v De Lasala* [1979] 2 All ER 1146, PC.
[22] [1982] STC 206, (1982) 55 TC 608.
[23] Matrimonial Causes Act 1973, ss 23(5), 24(3).

35.2.2 *Is a Contract a Disposal?*

Section 28 deals with the timing of the disposal when an asset is transferred under a contract and does not answer the question whether the contract itself is the disposal. This question is or has been of importance for several reasons. First there is the basic obligation on a taxpayer under the self-assessment regime to report a disposal; if the disposal has not yet occurred, there is no obligation to report it. Secondly, there is a more sophisticated problem: section 28 applies only when the asset is conveyed or transferred, and so does not expressly deal with a contract which is not completed. Where a deposit is forfeited, the forfeiture is not treated as the disposal of an asset (section 144(7)), but the contract itself will be treated as a part disposal of the asset if it creates an interest in or right over the asset (section 21(2)), a matter which presumably turns on whether equity could order specific performance of the contract. If, however, the specifically enforceable contract is itself the disposal then the Revenue may be able to ignore the subsequent ending of the contract and so charge CGT both on the original part disposal and the subsequent ending of the equitable interest. The approach of the House of Lords in *Jerome v Kelly*[24] to prefer makeshift answers to strict logic would not encourage the Revenue to take such a view.[25]

In view of the practical difficulties raised, it seems preferable to reject the notion that the contract is itself a disposal, and to do so whether or not the contract is specifically enforceable. It follows that when property is disposed of under an unconditional contract of sale, the disposition takes place under the contract; and that when the contract is not followed by a disposal, it is not open to anyone to treat the contract itself as a part disposal.[26]

35.2.3 *Asset Lost or Destroyed*

Where an asset is deemed to be disposed of by reason of its entire loss or destruction, the time of the deemed disposal is the time at which the loss or destruction occurs (section 24(1)). Where the owner of the asset later receives compensation for the loss, the date of receipt is the time of disposal (section 22(2)). These statements may be reconciled by treating the right to receive compensation as a separate asset arising at the time of the loss, or at the time the claim is proved, so that the receipt of compensation is the disposal of that right, not the disposal of the original asset. However, this conclusion is inelegant.

35.3 Disposals Which are Not Disposals: Mortgages, Bankruptcy and Hire Purchase

Certain disposals such as mortgage and bankruptcy are removed from giving rise to a potential CGT charge because the reality of the situation persuaded the legislature that there was no underlying disposal. This reality is all the clearer because while in mortgages

---

[24] [2004] UKHL 25; [2004] STC 887.
[25] Eg Lord Hoffmann at paras 12 and 13; and Lord Walker at paras 44–46.
[26] By analogy with the forfeiture of deposit rule in TCGA 1992, s 144(7).

everyone expects the property to pass back to the mortgagor at the end of the period, exactly the opposite is the case for hire purchase. Hence under hire purchase transactions the disposal is at the beginning of the period of use and not at the end. If, for any reason, the property does not pass to the hirer, the tax is 'adjusted' (section 27).

35.3.1 Mortgages

A mortgage is, in essence, a security for a debt; as such, neither a conveyance or transfer by way of security nor a retransfer on redemption of the security is treated as involving any acquisition or disposal.[27] Any dealing with the asset by the mortgagee for the purpose of giving effect to the security is treated as an act by a nominee of the mortgagor. So a sale will be a disposal by the mortgagor (section 26(2)). An asset is treated as passing free of the security. When an asset is acquired subject to a security, the value of any liability taken over by the acquirer is treated as part of the consideration; a converse rule applies on disposal.[28] If an asset is bought for £3,000, subject to a mortgage of £7,000, the buyer is treated as buying it for £10,000; and if the asset is then sold for £5,000, still subject to mortgage of the same amount, there will be a gain of £2,000 since the consideration on disposal will be £12,000. When a vendor disposes of land, grants a mortgage to the purchaser and later recovers possession on default by the purchaser, the original disposal is, by concession, undone.[29]

35.3.2 Insolvency

Just as the mortgagee's acts are treated as those of the mortgagor, so the acts of a trustee in bankruptcy are treated as those of the bankrupt (section 66). However, the trustee in bankruptcy is assessable for the tax.[30]

35.3.3 Hire Purchase

Where a person, P, acquires an asset under a contract of hire purchase, the transaction is treated as if it amounted to an entire disposal of the asset to P at the beginning (section 27). If the period terminates, but the property in the asset does not pass to P, all necessary adjustments are made. The implication appears to be that the disposal and acquisition deemed to have occurred at the outset are then treated as not having taken place, so that the hirer is not treated as disposing of the asset when the interest terminates. However, P may be treated as having disposed of his rights under the contract, depending upon the circumstances.

---

[27] TCGA 1992, s 26(1). On what is a mortgage, see *Beattie v Jenkinson* [1971] 3 All ER 495, (1971) 47 TC 121 (a decision on Sch D, Case VII). Since 1925 a mortgage of freehold land does not end by retransfer but by cesser of the mortgagee's leasehold interest. One must presume that the draftsman's apparent oversight would be corrected by any court.

[28] TCGA 1992, s 26(3). This rule is stated to apply where the liability is assumed by the acquirer; however, an assignee of a mortgagor does not assume the liability (*Waring v Ward* (1802) 7 Ves 332); technical arguments have not found great favour with the courts.

[29] ESC D18.

[30] *Re McMeekin* [1974] STC 429, (1974) 48 TC 725, QBD (NI).

The legislation does not state how the disposal consideration is to be valued. However, the Revenue practice in hire purchase cases is to divide the total of the rent and purchase price into capital and interest elements, and to tax only the latter as income. If this is followed, the capital element will be the purchase price rather than the sum payable under the option. In practice the asset will probably be a car (as in *Lyon v Pettigrew*,[31] where the vehicle was a taxi but a chargeable gain arose in respect of consideration paid for the licence), a wasting asset or an asset the cost of which is less than £6,000 (see §34.5 above), so that the problem may not arise often.

35.4   Disposal Without Acquisition

35.4.1 Capital Sums Derived from Assets

A disposal of assets by their owner may occur even though no asset is acquired by anyone else, for example if the owner of the assets receives a capital sum which is derived from the assets (section 22). This last, simple-looking phrase has caused many problems.[32] Section 22 applies only to a capital sum; if a receipt is held to be income rather than capital, it cannot apply.[33] Section 22 applies 'in particular' to four types (see below at §35.4.2) of capital sum. It follows that facts may come within the general words even if not within the four categories. However, facts apparently within one or other of the four categories cannot be brought within the section if they do not come within the general words;[34] moreover, the four categories can be looked at as aids to the interpretation of the general words. The rule requires that the asset should have been owned by the person treated as disposing of them. A mere hope or expectation cannot be owned, and so, presumably, cannot be an asset. However, the wide scope of the term and the willingness of the courts to infer the existence of an asset from the receipt of a sum should not be overlooked.

In *Marren v Ingles*,[35] shares were sold for a cash sum plus the right to receive a further sum, to be computed by reference to future, unpredictable events. The right to receive the future sum was held to be an asset.[36] When the events occurred and the further sum was paid, that sum was 'derived from' the right to receive the sum and so there was a disposal of that asset. This is the case whether or not the person paying the capital sum acquires any asset.[37] Where the further event brings about a loss, a special carry back rule now applies (above §33.10.2).

---

[31] [1985] STC 369, (1985) 58 TC 452.
[32] See *Sparkes* [1987] BTR 323.
[33] *Lang v Rice* [1984] STC 172, where a sum paid as compensation for loss of trading profit was held to be an income receipt and so outside s 22.
[34] *Zim Properties Ltd v Procter* [1985] STC 90, 106, (1985) 58 TC 371, 390, relying on what, in effect, Lord Wilberforce and Lord Fraser both said in *Marren (Inspector of Taxes) v Ingles* [1980] 3 All ER 95, [1980] STC 500, (1980) 54 TC 76, to overrule the contrary view expressed by Nourse J in *Davenport (Inspector of Taxes) v Chilver* [1983] STC 426, 439, (1983) 57 TC 661, 677.
[35] [1980] 3 All ER 95, [1980] STC 500, (1980) 54 TC 76.
[36] *Ibid.*
[37] Reversing *IRC v Montgomery* [1975] STC 182, 189, (1975) 49 TC 679. As to 'earn-out' sales, where the deferred consideration takes the form of shares and the value of the shares is unascertainable when the right is conferred but will become clear only when the profits have been earned and so are available to pay for the shares, see TCGA 1992, s 138A.

The requirement that the capital sum must be derived from an asset applies to each of the four categories; a sum derived from some other source is not caught by these rules. Sums payable under the Agricultural Holdings Act 1986 to an agricultural tenant for disturbance on the surrender of his tenancy,[38] or under the Landlord and Tenant Act 1954 to a business tenant for like loss, are not subject to CGT. The sums are payable under these Acts by way of compensation for various types of loss and expense, and so are not sums derived from the lease.[39] Compensation under an Order in Council for expropriation of an asset by a foreign government has been held liable to CGT because, inter alia, the right to compensation in that case was an independent property right.[40]

Where a person received a capital sum in settlement of an action for negligence against solicitors in relation to a conveyance matter concerning particular properties, it was held that the charge to CGT stemmed from the right to sue and not from the properties concerned, and thus was not a part disposal of those properties.[41] A sum received for entering into a restrictive covenant, in connection with the sale of shares in subsidiary companies, has been held not to be a capital sum derived from an asset, because the freedom to engage in the activities concerned was not an asset. However, the sums were held to have been received in part for agreeing not to exploit the goodwill attaching to the group and so were taxable anyway.[42]

Compensation for the release of an option to participate in a development has been held taxable under this head.[43] The fact that another provision stated that the abandonment of an option was not the disposal of an asset was irrelevant.[44]

35.4.2 The Four Categories

35.4.2.1 Categories (1) and (2)—Compensation and Insurance Payments

If capital sums are received by way of compensation for any kind of damage or injury to or loss of or depreciation of assets, there is a disposal of those assets, and a consequent gain or loss by reference to the acquisition cost of those assets. These words are of wide effect and are not limited to physical damage. A similar rule applies to sums received under a policy of insurance against the risk of any kind of damage or injury to, or the loss or depreciation of, assets. Thus, if a trader loses a capital asset by fire and recovers under his insurance policy, there is a disposal of the asset even though the insurance company does not acquire it.

---

[38] *Davies v Powell* [1977] 1 All ER 471, [1977] STC 32, (1977) 51 TC 492. One must distinguish the statutory exclusion in TCGA 1992, s 249 for certain grants to vacate uncommercial agricultural land under the Agriculture Act 1967, s 27.

[39] *Drummond v Austin Brown* [1984] STC 321, 325, (1984) 58 TC 67, 86, which distinguished a sum paid by a landlord in return for the surrender of the 'fag end' of a lease. It was also important that the landlord was entitled to possession. On the distinction between surrender and notice to quit, see *Barrett v Morgan* [2000] 1 All ER 481.

[40] *Davenport v Chilver* [1983] STC 426, (1983) 57 TC 661, although in this case liability was virtually removed because the new right was deemed to have been acquired for market value. The position would now be different as a result of TCGA 1992, s 17(2).

[41] *Zim Properties Ltd v Procter* [1985] STC 90, (1985) 58 TC 371; but see ESC D33. For a more fundamental argument that CGT is not payable on damages at all, see Wilde [1991] BTR 5.

[42] *Kirby v Thorn EMI* [1987] STC 621, (1987) 60 TC 519.

[43] *Powlson v Welbeck Securities Ltd* [1987] STC 468, CA, (1987) 60 TC 268.

[44] TCGA 1992, s 144(4); see below §38.3.1.

Compensation or damages received as the result of a court action, or by negotiated settlement of such an action, is a disposal of the right of action and is subject to CGT. In most cases, the base cost of the rights will be nil where they came into being on or after 10 March 1981. This is so even if the compensation or damages relate to an underlying asset. However, ESC D33 may relate the damages to the underlying asset where the right of action arises because of total or partial loss of, or damage to, the asset. Thus, the base cost of the asset will be available to compute any chargeable gain, and the various replacement and reinstatement reliefs may be claimed. Where there is no underlying asset, eg in a case involving damages for professional negligence resulting in expense to the plaintiff,[45] the gain up to £500,000 is, by ESC D33, treated as exempt. Gains in excess of this amount may be exempt subject to notification to, and review by, HMRC. Payments made under a contractual warranty or indemnity are not regarded as affected by the *Zim Properties* case and will reduce the purchaser's acquisition cost. Sums obtained by way of compensation or damages for any wrong or injury suffered by an individual on his person or in his profession or vocation are not chargeable gains.

Reliefs

Restoration. In the absence of special provisions, compensation or insurance payments for damage to assets would be treated for CGT as part disposals. However, under section 23(1), if the sum is wholly (or all but a small sum which is not needed for the purpose) applied in restoring the asset, the receipt is not to be treated as a disposal. If the restored asset is later disposed of, the sums received are deducted from the allowable expenditure. If only a part of the sum is so used, that part will be deducted from allowable expenditure on a subsequent disposal, but the remainder will be treated as consideration for a part disposal of the asset (section 23(3)).

Example

Alf's picture cost £90,000 in 2014. In 2016 the picture, then worth £120,000, was damaged in a fire. Alf incurred £20,000 in restoration costs but received £20,000 under his insurance policy. This receipt may be treated as a disposal under section 22 for £20,000. However, Alf may instead claim that it should not be so treated, in which case the allowable expenditure on the picture (which includes the cost of restoration) will be reduced by £20,000 if he later sells the picture or otherwise disposes of it. If, however, he recovers £25,000, the part spent in restoration (£20,000) will be treated as outlined above, while the balance of £5,000 will be taxed immediately.

Replacement. If the asset is damaged, lost or destroyed, there is relief from CGT on replacement. The compensation or insurance payment received must be applied in acquiring a replacement asset within one year of the receipt, or such longer period as the inspector may allow (section 23(4)). The consideration for the disposal is then treated as such that neither gain nor loss accrues. The acquisition cost of the new asset is reduced by the excess of the compensation (plus scrap value, if any) over the deemed consideration for disposal of the old asset (section 23(5)). The reduction may be greater than the chargeable gain where not all of the gain would have been chargeable.

---

[45] *Zim Properties Ltd v Procter* [1985] STC 90, (1985) 58 TC 371.

Example

A acquired an asset for £10,000, spending a further £2,000 on it. In July 2016 the asset was destroyed in an accident caused by B's negligence and has a scrap value of £500. B pays £15,000 damages. The replacement asset costs £16,000. The disposal is treated as taking place at £12,000. The new asset is treated as being acquired at £16,000 less £15,000–(£10,000 + £2,000), ie £3,000 and less the scrap value of £500, giving a revised cost of £12,500, not £16,000.

If the asset is lost and only part of the sum is used to replace it, there is some relief, provided the part unspent is less than the amount of the gain. In other words, postponement of tax liability is available only to the extent that it is necessary to make use of the gain in the replacement. There are three limitations under this rule. First, this relief, in effect, allows taxpayers to postpone their tax liability, not escape it, unless perhaps they can later take advantage of an exemption such as that on death. Secondly, these rules do not apply to wasting assets (section 23(6)). Thirdly, the relief is expressed to be limited to an owner of property.[46]

35.4.2.2 Category (3)—Forfeiture or Surrender of Rights

Capital sums received by a person in return for forfeiture or surrender of rights, eg the surrender of a lease, or for refraining from exercising rights, are taxable. Thus, a sum received for the release of a restrictive covenant or for an agreement not to sue on a contract would be chargeable events. As has been seen, it is not possible to use section 22 to widen the scope of the term 'assets'.[47] So no charge arises when a sum is received for the surrender of something which is not an asset (eg the right to play amateur rugby, as in *Jarrold v Boustead*).[48] A charge does not arise either when the asset surrendered is an exempt asset (eg a life interest under a settlement) or a debt. If the owner of a right over an asset releases it, there is a disposal even though no consideration is received.[49]

35.4.2.3 Category (4)—Use of Assets

Capital sums received for the use or exploitation of assets are also caught. Thus, a sum received in return for the right to exploit a copyright or to use the goodwill created by that person would be caught, including, perhaps, the part disposal resulting from a restriction on trading activities, as in *Higgs v Olivier* (see above at §21.6).

35.5 Gratuitous Value Shifting: Disposals of Value Without Disposal of Asset

TCGA 1992 contains unusual and sometimes complex rules relating to value shifting, the principal example of which is section 29 (see below at §36.6).

---

[46] Insurance proceeds received by the lessee of land are, by concession, exempt if accepted by the lessee in discharging an obligation to restore damage to property (TCGA 1992, s 23(8), replacing ESC D1).

[47] *O'Brien v Benson's Hosiery (Holdings) Ltd* [1978] 3 All ER 1057, [1978] STC 549, CA.

[48] (1964) 41 TC 701 above §14.4.4.2.

[49] The disposal will be treated as taking place at market value if done gratuitously (TCGA 1992, s 17(2)).

35.6   Part Disposals

35.6.1 *The A/(A + B) Formula*

Where there is a part disposal, the proportion of the acquisition cost attributable to the part disposal is $A/(A + B)$, where A is the consideration for the disposal and B is the market value of the remainder (section 42).[50] Assume that 15 years ago X bought a house and grounds asset for £90,000. In September 2016 part of the grounds is sold for development, for which X receives £100,000. The market value of the house and land following the sale is £250,000. The proportion of the £90,000 that may be deducted is £100,000/(£100,000 + 250,000) (or 2/7), which gives £25,714. The resulting gain for CGT purposes is £74,286.

This apportionment process applies only to the costs common to the part disposed of and the part retained. There is no apportionment of expenditure which, on the facts, is wholly attributable to either the part disposed of or that retained (section 42(4)). The incidental costs of the part disposal therefore are attributable solely to the part disposed and are not apportioned. In practice the formula is not strictly applied on the disposal of quoted shares in a pool, the costs being apportioned simply pro rata to the number of shares disposed of.

The cost of the part of the land disposed of may be calculated on an alternative basis, under which the part disposed of will be treated as a separate asset and any fair and reasonable method of apportioning part of the total cost to it will be accepted, eg a reasonable valuation of that part at the acquisition date.[51]

35.6.2 *What is a Part Disposal?*

Under section 21, a part disposal arises where

> an interest or right in or over the asset is created by the disposal, as well as where it subsists before the disposal, and generally, there is a part disposal of an asset where, on a person making a disposal, any description of property derived from the asset remains undisposed of.[52]

This very wide definition presumably refers only to beneficial property, so that a declaration of trust over an asset gives rise to a total rather than a part disposal. There is therefore a part disposal when either (a) there is a disposal of a physical part of an asset, as in the example in §35.6.1 above of selling a part of grounds, or (b) rights are created out of an asset, as where a lease is granted by the freeholder or an easement over land. From (b), it follows that an agreement which has purely contractual effect is not of itself a part disposal.[53]

The boundary between the disposal of an entire asset and a part disposal of a larger asset is difficult to draw and is best seen as a question of fact. It is, however, of great importance because of the different methods of calculation. In relation to a piece of land with

---

[50] For provisions where there was a part disposal before 6 April 1988 of an asset owned on 31 March 1982, see TCGA 1992, Sch 3, para 4.

[51] Statement of Practice SP D1.

[52] TCGA 1992, s 21(2)(a). See generally Whiteman, *Whiteman on Capital Gains Tax*, 4th edn (Sweet & Maxwell, 2008) §§7.21 *et seq.*

[53] *Anders Utkilens Rederi A/S v OIY Lovisa Stevedoring Co A/B and Keller Bryan: Transport Co Ltd* [1985] STC 301.

distinguishable elements, such as a house, garden and farm buildings, etc, the Revenue approach is that a single acquisition bought in one go is best treated as a single asset. The approach of the Revenue is different, however, if the correspondence surrounding the acquisition shows that different units were looked at separately, or if it is otherwise possible to make a satisfactory apportionment of the price.

There is some direct authority. In *Cottle v Coldicott*,[54] the Revenue successfully argued that the sale of a milk quota without any land was the sale of a separate asset and not a part disposal of the land—a conclusion which may have turned on matters of EU law rather than traditional English law. *Anders Utkilens Rederi A/S v OIY Lovisa Stevedoring Co A/B and Keller Bryan: Transport Co Ltd*[55] was a more complex case. The taxpayer (T) was a defendant in litigation. The plaintiff and T settled an appeal. Under the terms of the compromise, T agreed to sell its premises, plant and machinery (the property) and to divide the proceeds with the plaintiff. T subsequently went into creditor's voluntary liquidation; the property was sold a year later. In a dispute between the plaintiff and T as to the burden of tax, the court held that the compromise was a part disposal by T to the plaintiff—and so T had to pay the tax then arising. T argued unsuccessfully that the terms were merely contractual and that the plaintiff received no proprietary interest until the proceeds were received. In *Berry v Warnett*,[56] S transferred shares to a nominee trustee and a few weeks later assigned his beneficial interest to a Jersey company in return for money and a life interest. The House of Lords held that the sale was a disposal of S's entire beneficial interest in the shares and not a part disposal of the holding. The life interest could not be said to be property 'derived from' an asset which remained undisposed of. In the *Zim* case (see §35.4.1 above) the court held that a sum received on the settlement of a negligence action against solicitors arose from the right to sue, which was an asset separate from the property to which the claim related.

In order to solve these issues it is worth remembering that the actual question is whether section 42 applies, and that both section 21(1)(b) and section 42(2) refer to 'property remaining undisposed of'. Whiteman points out that there can be an entire disposal even though the person disposing of the asset is left with a chargeable asset related in some way to the original. He cites situations in which an asset is transferred to a company in return for new shares issued by the company and where there is a sale of a business for unascertained consideration.[57] These must be contrasted with other situations which are unquestionably examples of part disposals, such as the grant of a lease out of a freehold and the sale of shares forming part of a pool. A possible test is that in the first two cases the person making the disposal is left with an item of property which did not exist before the disposal; whereas in the last two there is an asset which can be identified as being undisposed of throughout. However, the legislation talks of there being a part disposal when T holds 'any description of property derived from the asset [remaining] undisposed of' (section 22(1)(b)). This suggests that some disposals are part disposals even where there is not an asset remaining in the vendor's ownership throughout the transaction. Thus, a sale of land subject to a leaseback is generally treated as a part disposal, even though there is an instant

---

[54] [1995] STC (SCD) 239.
[55] [1985] STC 301.
[56] [1982] STC 396, (1982) 55 TC 92.
[57] Whiteman, *op cit*, §§7-27 and 7-28.

during the transaction at which the person making the disposal has no interest in the land at all.[58] Whiteman concludes that this may leave *Berry v Warnett* as an isolated case.

35.6.3 Relief from A/(A + B) for Certain 'Small' Part Disposals

The practical disadvantage of the A/(A + B) formula is the need to calculate B, the market value of the part remaining—a process which may be expensive. To solve this, TCGA 1992 provides a different treatment in four circumstances. There is no immediate charge to tax, but the consideration received is treated as reducing the acquisition cost which is set against the ultimate disposal of the asset concerned. This treatment is not available if the consideration received for the part disposed of exceeds the expenditure allowable in respect of the entire asset; here, there is an immediate charge to CGT.[59] The four circumstances are:

(1)   a capital distribution (section 122(2));
(2)   cash received on a share reorganisation (section 116(13));
(3)   a premium on conversion of securities (section 133(2)); and
(4)   cash received on compulsory acquisition of land (section 243(1)(a)).

In addition, the sum received must be 'small'. It was not immediately clear whether 'small' meant small in absolute terms or only in proportion to the purchase price. In *O'Rourke v Binks*[60] the latter view was rejected. T received £246,000 on a reorganisation. This amounted to 15.58% of the acquisition cost of the original holding, but less than 5% of the value of the original holding immediately before reorganisation. The Court of Appeal held that this was not 'small', holding that what was 'small' was a question of fact and degree and had to be considered in the light of the circumstances in any particular case. The Court stated that the purpose behind the legislation was the need to avoid assessments in trivial cases; this was not such a case. However, there is no evidence for the Court's view that this was the purpose of the legislation. Subsequently the Revenue stated that it would continue its long-standing approach of accepting as 'small' 5% or less of the value of the shares/land, but would also accept as 'small' any receipt of £3,000 or less. A taxpayer may, however, argue that the particular circumstances of a case justify an amount in excess of these limits to be regarded as 'small', or, alternatively, that an amount below these limits should not be so regarded.[61]

Where there is a part disposal of land, the consideration received is treated as reducing the base cost, in the same way, if the consideration does not exceed the lower of £20,000 or one-fifth of the market value of the land holding immediately prior to the part disposal.[62]

---

[58] On dangers of such arguments, see Lord Hoffmann in *Ingram v IRC* [1999] STC 37, at 44.
[59] For example TCGA 1992, s 244.
[60] [1992] STC 703, 65 TC 165.
[61] RI 164.
[62] TCGA 1992, s 242(1)(a), (3)(a).

36

Disposals: (2) Gifts, Bargains Not at Arm's Length and Other Gratuitous Transactions

36.1   Gift as Disposal

Some jurisdictions think it inappropriate to charge tax where no value is being realised. Others, like the UK, treat the passing of an asset from one person's tax regime to another's as an occasion of charge. Under FA 1981 the donor could have elected for a deferral of tax on a gift, but this was repealed by FA 1989.[1] Under the market value rule (above §33.8), the gain is computed on the basis that the asset is disposed of at its market value at the time it is given (TCGA 1992, section 17(1)). In *Turner v Follett*,[2] the taxpayer argued that in giving the shares away he had suffered a capital loss and it was contrary to natural justice to treat him as having made a gain. The Court of Appeal rejected his appeal.

A gift may be exempt under one of the general exempt disposal rules. In addition, there are express exemptions for a *donatio mortis causa* (section 62(5)) and a gift of land to a housing association (section 259).

36.1.1 When Does a Gift Take Place?

There are no special CGT rules to determine when a gift takes place. Under the general property law rules,[3] a gift becomes effective when the donor either makes an effective

---

[1] See, generally, Venables [1989] BTR 333.
[2] [1973] STC 148.
[3] *Milroy v Lord* (1862) 4 De GF & J 264.

transfer of the asset to the donee with the intention of making a gift, or makes an effective declaration of trust. An example of the latter is *Berry v Warnett*.[4] The taxpayer, T, settled shares on trust on 4 April 1972 giving himself a life interest, and sold the life interest two days later for £130,753. The House of Lords held that the settlement on 4 April 1972 constituted a disposal of the shares for CGT purposes; T was assessed by reference to the market value of the shares on that date.

36.1.2 Donee's CGT Liability

Although the primary CGT liability is with the donor, D, if D fails to pay the tax within 12 months of the date from which it becomes payable, the Revenue may assess the donee, E (section 282(1)). The liability is still D's; as such, if D is a higher-rate taxpayer and has used his annual exempt amount on other disposals, the Revenue can collect tax equal to 20%/28% of the gain from E, even though E may be impecunious. E is given a right of reimbursement from D (section 282(2)). The assessment must be raised within two years of the tax having been due and payable by the donor. Thus, for a gift made in 2016–17, the Revenue are able to collect tax from the donee only by raising an assessment between 1 February 2018 and 31 January 2019.

36.2 Connected Persons

Many CGT rules turn on connected person status.[5] For definition of 'connected person', see above at §33.9. Section 18(2) applies the market value rules in section 17 to any disposal between connected persons.[6] This treatment applies irrespective of the motive of the parties or the price paid. It also entails that holdover relief under section 165 may be available.[7] However, section 18(2) is excluded if section 17 is also excluded; it will not apply, therefore, where there is an acquisition but no disposal, eg an issue of shares by a company to a controlling shareholder, or a disposal but no acquisition, eg on the repurchase or redemption of shares by a company (section 17(2)). Loss relief is restricted where a loss arises on a disposal to a connected person (see above at §33.9).

36.2.1 Market Value Where Assets Disposed of in a Series
of Transactions: Connected Persons

In estimating the market value of an asset for CGT, regard is normally had only to that asset in isolation. However, the value may be increased by section 19 where a disposal forms one

---

[4] [1982] STC 396, 55 TC 92, [1982] 2 All ER 630.
[5] Eg, loans (s 251(4)).
[6] TCGA 1992, s 18(2) deems the transfer not to be by way of bargain at arm's length.
[7] This may be useful where a commercial bargain is entered into but the parties cannot be certain that the value placed on the asset by the Revenue will equate to their own view of the value. The availability of a holdover election is also potentially of assistance where there are a number of transactions and one of the transactions, viewed alone, could be held to trigger a gain in excess of the gain computed by reference to the consideration actually passed.

of a series of linked transactions. Section 19 applies where, by two or more transactions, A disposes of assets to another person, B, with whom A is connected—or to two or more persons with each of whom A is connected. Connected person status is vital and there must be connection with a common disponor (not necessarily between each disponee). Section 19 is an anti-avoidance rule, and applies only if the original market value (section 20(3)) of the assets transferred is less than the appropriate portion of the aggregate market value of the assets disposed of by all the transactions in the series (section 20(4), (6)–(9)). The original market value is simply the market value determined without regard to the linked transactions rule. The aggregate market value used to determine the uplifted transaction value is the value of the transferred assets in aggregate, determined as at the time of the transaction in question. However, it is in some ways a weak anti-avoidance rule, since it applies to linked transactions (transactions which take place within a six-year period) (section 20(3)).

Suppose that A has a 60% holding in A Co. On 1 January 2015 A transfers 20% holdings to B. This is repeated on 1 January 2016 and 2017. The years 2016 and 2017 transactions are linked with the 2015 transaction and with each other. Assuming (as is usually the case) that the value of the 60% holding is greater than the value of three 20% holdings, section 19 makes each subject to CGT on the basis that the value given away is one-third of a 60% holding. If the value of a 40% holding is greater than that of two 20% holdings, section 19 will apply in 2016 to adjust the figures for the first two transfers. The figures will then be adjusted again in 2017. The linked transactions rule does not override the normal rule as to valuation on a disposal between spouses or civil partners living together (section 19(2)). Special provisions apply to assets passed down chains, which include intra-group transfers (section 19(5)–(6)). In contrast to the House of Lords decision in *Furniss v Dawson*,[8] it is generally considered that this rule is solely a valuation rule and does not change the timing of the disposal.

36.3   Holdover Relief: Disposal of Asset Within Specified Categories

36.3.1   *How Holdover Relief Operates*[9]

Holdover relief is available on gifts and whenever there is 'a disposal otherwise than under a bargain at arm's length'.[10] The gain that would otherwise be chargeable to tax is held over so that the gain crystallised by the donor, D, is reduced to nil. The donee's, E's, acquisition cost is also reduced. A partial holdover claim is not permitted; the claim must be for the whole of the gain (subject only to the statutory reduction given by virtue of actual consideration or by chargeable non-business assets). Suppose that D's acquisition cost of the business asset was £40,000 and that D gives the asset to E when it is worth £100,000 after four years' ownership. The gain is £60,000. Assuming they elect to hold over, the chargeable gain is reduced from £60,000 to nil. Now assume that E sells the asset for £150,000 after a further five years. The sale proceeds (£150,000) are reduced by the base cost; this is £100,000, but

---

[8] [1984] AC 474, 517; [1984] STC 153, 158; 55 TC 324, 392 (see §5.6.4 above).
[9] On holdover relief and 1982 rebasing, see TCGA 1992, Sch 4, para 5.
[10] TCGA 1992, s 1651(1)(a). It also extends to settled property, see *ibid* Sch 7, para 2. See generally Whiteman, *Whiteman on Capital Gains Tax*, 4th edn (Sweet & Maxwell, 2008) §§18.51A *et seq.*

has to be reduced by £60,000 on account of the gain held over. This makes deductible costs of £40,000 and the gain £110,000. The whole £110,000 gain becomes taxable, but all on E's disposal—not part on D's and part on E's.

36.3.1.1 Non-residence and Emigration

The relief is available only if E is resident in the UK, so as to ensure that the deferred tax will eventually be paid. If E is a UK resident company, it must not be controlled by a person or persons who are not resident in the UK, and the person who controls the company must not be connected with the donor (sections 166 and 167). Gifts to dual resident trusts are also outside the relief (section 169). Where the donee becomes non-resident, the gain held over becomes subject to CGT, and the deferral ends (section 168). Further provisions address the operation of the relief on gifts of UK residential property interests to non-residents (section 167A and 168A).

36.3.1.2 Restrictions

The right to hold over is subject to various restrictions where the gain is otherwise chargeable or wholly relieved.[11] However, in addition, holdover is not permitted for disposals on or after 9 November 1999 where the transfer is of shares and securities and the transferee is a company.[12] The reason for this change was that the holdover was being widely abused.[13] This abuse arose where the purpose was not to defer the liability on a bona fide gift but to avoid a CGT liability on an anticipated sale. This might be achieved if the company was able to use some tax exemption or other tax shelter. Other changes with effect from the same date prevent holdover relief on a disposal to a dual resident trust.[14] Further restrictions were added in 2004—see §36.4.2.

36.3.1.3 Forms

Unless the gain is made on a disposal to a trustee, both D and E must sign the claim (section 165(1)), which must be made within six years of the end of the fiscal year in which the disposal is made.[15] Procedures exist under which the election for relief may be made without a valuation of the asset being agreed with the Revenue.[16]

36.3.2 Qualifying Assets

The asset must be:

(1)   an asset used for the purposes of a trade carried on by the transferor, by his personal company or by a member of a trading group of which the holding company is his personal company;[17] or

---

[11] TCGA 1992, s 165(3), referring to Sch 6, esp paras 7(2) or 8(2), but also to s 116(10b) and s 260(3).
[12] TCGA 1992, s 165(3)(b), as amended by FA 2000, s 90.
[13] IR Notes to Finance Bill 2000, s 90.
[14] By adding s 169 to list in s 165(1).
[15] TMA 1970, s 43.
[16] Statement of Practice SP 8/92.
[17] TCGA 1992, s 165(2)(a). Before 1993 the test was whether it was D's family company. For definitions, see s 165A, added by FA 2008 and superseding the definitions inserted in 1998 for the now repealed taper relief.

(2)   unquoted shares or securities in a trading company (section 165(2)(b)(i)); or
(3)   shares or securities in a trading company or holding company which is the transferor's
       personal company (section 165(2)(b)(ii)); or
(4)   property that qualifies for agricultural property relief for IHT purposes.[18]

Category (1) includes an asset used for the purpose of a trade carried on by D in partnership; the size of D's interest in the partnership is not relevant. For category (3), an individual's personal company is one in which the individual is able to exercise not less than 5%
of the voting rights in the company (section 165(8)(a)). The legislation takes a relaxed view
of category (4), which applies whether D is entitled to relief at 50% or at 100%. The claim
is not limited to the value on which agricultural property relief is available. If farmland is
given away and the majority of the value of the land is a reflection of its potential development value, rather than its agricultural value, holdover relief may nevertheless be claimed
on the entire gain.

36.3.2.1 Sale at Undervalue

Where consideration passes on a transfer, but the consideration is less than the market
value of the asset transferred, holdover relief may be claimed provided the other conditions
for relief are fulfilled. In such a case, the gain held over is reduced by the amount by which
the sale consideration exceeds the sums allowable as acquisition costs (section 165(7)). Suppose that the land cost £50,000 and is worth £110,000 when it is sold for £65,000. The
£60,000 gain which would otherwise be held over must be reduced by £15,000 to £45,000.

36.3.2.2 Partial Reliefs

Apart from sales at undervalue, relief is available on an apportioned basis if:

(1)   the asset was not used for the purpose of a trade throughout the period of ownership;[19]
(2)   the disposal is of a building and part of the building was not used for the purpose of
       the trade;[20]
(3)   the disposal is of shares in a company and the company has non-business chargeable
       assets at the time when a disposal is made of its shares.[21]

An asset used for the purpose of trade, etc, must be so used at the time of disposal.[22] Point
(1) applies if the asset was so used at the time of disposal, but there were periods of other
use earlier; a time apportionment takes place.[23] For (2) a 'just and reasonable' apportionment is made.[24] No apportionment is necessary, however, in the case of land and buildings
qualifying for agricultural property relief.[25]

---

[18] TCGA 1992, Sch 7, para 1(1).
[19] TCGA 1992, Sch 7, para 5.
[20] TCGA 1992, Sch 7, para 6.
[21] TCGA 1992, Sch 7, para 7.
[22] The Revenue take a strict view of this rule (See Capital Gains Manual CG66952).
[23] TCGA 1992, Sch 7, para 5(1).
[24] TCGA 1992, Sch 7, para 6(1).
[25] TCGA 1992, Sch 7, paras 5(2), 6(2).

36.3.3 Anti-avoidance Rule—Settlor Interested Trusts

Holdover relief is denied where disposal is to a settlor interested trust (SIT).[26] This rule is not affected by the repeal of section 77 in 2008.[27] Assume A has shares purchased for £10 and gives the shares to B when they are worth £25; B then sells them for £30. A realises a gain of £15 thanks to section 17 and B realises a gain of £5. The consequence of the election in section 165 is that A realises no gain but B realises a gain of £20. The worry for the Revenue arose when B was a settlement in which A, the settlor, had an interest and so had access to the proceeds from the trust.[28] The trust might have allowable losses which would offset the gain of £20 or might exploit reliefs to achieve the same end. In this way A would escape CGT on the whole or part of the gain. Under this rule, A's right to claim holdover relief is barred; and there is a claw back of the relief [29] if the trust is not an SIT at the time of the disposal by A but becomes one later.

The claw back works by means of a charge on A at the time the trust becomes an SIT, with consequential increases to the base cost for the trustees to prevent double charging. The claw back charge applies even where the asset has been disposed of before the trust becomes an SIT. This will lead to a charge on A and a recomputation of any charge on the trustees. The claw back period runs from the relevant disposal (ie that by A to the trustees of the SIT) and ends immediately before the sixth anniversary of the start of the tax year next following that in which the relevant disposal was made. So if the disposal is made in October 2014, the relevant period ends immediately before 6 April 2021.

36.4 Holdover Relief: Gains Subject to Inheritance Tax

36.4.1 General

There is no restriction on the type of asset for which a claim may be made under section 260, which allows a holding over of a gain arising on any transfer which is chargeable to IHT. 'Chargeable' means immediately chargeable (as opposed to a potentially exempt transfer (PET)—see §45.1.2 below). It is not necessary for IHT actually to be payable, as the requirement is satisfied where the transfer is covered by the IHT annual exempt amount or by the IHT nil rate band. Relief is not available for a PET, even if it becomes chargeable by virtue of the death of the donor within the seven-year period (section 260(2)(a)). However, the relief may be claimed in respect of certain transfers which are exempt from IHT.[30] A claim for holdover relief under section 260 cannot be made in respect of a transfer between spouses or civil partners living together. Hence, where they have separated, the transfer of an asset from one party to the other after the end of the fiscal year in which they separate crystallises

---

[26] TCGA 1992, ss 169B–169G, added by FA 2004 and Sch 21, para 4.

[27] Settlement, settlor and interest are defined by ss 169E–1689G in ways similar to those for ITTOIA, s 619, ex TA 1988, s 660A (see §31.1–31.3 above); s 169G contains a similar information power. The exceptions are in s 169D.

[28] Recorded in the Notes to Clause 111 of Finance Bill 2004.

[29] Under s 169C.

[30] IHTA 1984, s 30 or s 78(1) (designated property or work of art); ss 27, 57A or Sch 4 (maintenance funds for historic buildings), s 24 (transfer to a political party) and s 71 (accumulation and maintenance trust).

a capital gain on which tax is potentially payable, unless the conditions of section 165 are fulfilled. It is also excluded if the transfer is to a dual resident trust.[31]

There is some uncertainty over the scope of the holdover relief where the IHT transfer relates to property subject to an accumulation and maintenance trust settled before 22nd March 2006. Holdover relief is available where the disposal is an occasion on which IHT tax would be chargeable but for IHTA 1984, section 71(4). Section 71(4) is a relief from IHT where the beneficiary of such a trust acquires an interest in possession (see §49.2.1 below). However, the beneficiary will usually be treated as having already acquired an interest in possession at age 18,[32] even if the property remains in the settlement. Section 71 will apply only if that normal rule is excluded. Where, as often happens, the vesting of capital has been preceded by the vesting of the interest in possession, the conditions for holdover relief do not, strictly, apply. This is because the occasion on which the IHT relief has applied is not the occasion on which the asset 'passes to' the beneficiary. It is not clear what happens if the trustees exercise a power of advancement on the beneficiary's 18th birthday, so that the CGT disposal occurs on the same day but not from the same cause.

36.4.2 Anti-avoidance

The rule on SITs discussed above in §36.3.3 also applies to holdover relief under section 260. However, a further rule applies only where section 260 and private residence relief (above §34.7) would apply; the rule bars dual relief.[33] The Revenue worry is the exploitation of the private residence relief and the deferral relief in section 260. Under this rule, when the house is transferred, either the *transferor* may elect to benefit from gift relief under section 260, or the *recipient* may elect for private residence relief (section 226A(2), (3)). Taking a Revenue example,[34] Jill has a house which does not qualify as her only or main residence and she wishes to give it to Paul. The base cost is £100,000 and the current value £250,000. She transfers it to a trust in which she has no interest but under which the trustees may allow named persons, including Paul, to occupy the property. The trustees allow Paul to occupy the property as his only or main residence. Paul moves out after a few months and the trustees sell for £270,000. The trustees come within the residence exemption in section 225 (above at §34.7.6). Because of the nature of the trust, the transfer by Jill to the trustees is a chargeable disposal for IHT purposes and so comes within section 260. Jill would claim the holdover relief, so reducing the figure at which the disposal to the trustees takes place to £150,000. This removes Jill's liability, while section 225 removes the trustees' liability to CGT. Under the 2004 rules, either Jill can claim the holdover relief or the trustees can claim the private residence relief.

There is an exception for certain trusts for the maintenance of historic buildings where there is an election under ITA 2007, section 508.[35] There is no need for an exception for disabled persons, as IHTA 1984, section 89 makes the person a beneficiary with an interest in possession, so making the transfer a PET as opposed to a chargeable transfer—and so

---

[31] As from 9 November 1999; TCGA 1992, s 260(1). as amended by FA 2000, s 90.
[32] As in *Begg-MacBrearty v Stilwell* [1996] STC 413.
[33] TCGA s 226A, added by FA 2004, s 117, Sch 22.
[34] Note to Finance Bill 2004, cl 112, para 73.
[35] TCGA 1992, s 226B(1). The ITA 2007 election was formerly in TA 1988, s 691(2).

outside section 260 altogether. These rules apply to disposals by the trustees or individuals on or after 10 December 2003 and there are detailed transitional rules.[36]

36.5 Holdover Relief and Property in Trust

The vesting of property in a beneficiary is a disposal by trustees and is made 'otherwise than under a contract at arm's length' (section 165(1)(a)). Hence, an election for holdover relief may be made where either section 260 is satisfied or the transfer is chargeable to IHT (which will always be the case where there is a transfer in or out of a discretionary settlement), or section 165 applies because the asset is a qualifying asset. The settling of property and the passing of an asset to a beneficiary by virtue of the exercise of the trustees' discretion are also 'otherwise than under a contract at arm's length' and so holdover relief may be available.

An election to hold over a gain arising on the transfer into trust is made unilaterally by the settler (section 165(1)(b)). An election on the transfer of an asset out of trust is made by the trustees and the recipient beneficiary jointly. Holdover relief may be claimed by trustees where an asset is used for the purposes of a trade carried on by a beneficiary who has an interest in possession in the settled property.[37] Where trustees transfer shares to a beneficiary and wish to claim holdover relief under section 165, it is necessary either for the shares to be unquoted shares in a trading company, or for the trustees to be entitled to exercise 25% or more of the voting rights in the company immediately prior to the disposal.[38]

36.5.1 Death Crystallises Charge

Where an election for holdover relief is made on the transfer of an asset into trust, whether under section 165 or under section 260, the gain held over may be brought into charge on the death of certain life tenants of the trust (sections 72–74). The gain brought into charge is normally the gain which was held over; however, the gain brought into charge cannot exceed the gain measured by reference to the market value of the asset at the time of the death of the life tenant. This gain may, in turn, be held over under section 260, where the death of the life tenant is an occasion of charge to IHT, eg for an interest in possession trust settled before 22 March 2006. There is an exception to the availability of the further claim to holdover relief where, at the death, the property passes to the surviving spouse of the deceased life tenant or into trust in which the surviving spouse has a life interest.[39] Where the gain is crystallised, an immediate charge to CGT arises, unless a deferral may be claimed because the asset comes within section 165(2).

---

[36] FA 2004, Sch 22, para 8.
[37] TCGA 1992, Sch 7, para 2(2)(a)(ii).
[38] TCGA 1992, Sch 7, para 2(2)(b).
[39] IHTA 1984, s 18(1) then operates so that the transfer is not chargeable to IHT; hence, the condition for a holdover relief claim under TCGA 1992, s 260 is not satisfied.

36.6   Gratuitous Value Shifting: Disposal of Value Without Disposal of Asset

The term 'disposal' is widened to catch three types of transaction. In all three, the market value which would be payable by the acquirer under a bargain at arm's length is taken as the consideration; any consideration given for the disposal is taken into account. Section 29 of the 1992 Act is discussed here because it is an unusual provision. A charge arises whether or not there is any consideration, so that potentially it applies whether the disposal is gratuitous or for value.[40] However, it follows from this that, unlike normal disposals, there is no charge to CGT where the consideration given equals (or exceeds) that full market value.

The first type of transaction is where 'a person' has control of a company and exercises that control so that value passes out of shares in the company owned by him, or by a person with whom he is connected, and passes into other shares in, or rights over, the company (section 29(2)). A controlling shareholder using his voting power to pass a resolution increasing the rights of a particular type of share at the expense of his own is clearly shifting value to the other shareholders, although no particular piece of property has been disposed of.[41] The controlling shareholder cannot claim holdover relief on the deemed disposal since no shares have actually been transferred—even though holdover relief could have been claimed on a gift of the shares themselves. Despite the fact that the singular 'person' is referred to, it has been held that the section applies where two or more persons control the company.[42] It has also been held that control was exercised when, under a pre-arranged scheme, a winding-up resolution was passed, even though the taxpayer himself did not vote on the motion.[43] Outside the context of a scheme, the taxpayer must presumably vote in order to 'exercise' control. The unusual nature of this rule is mirrored by the rule for losses (section 29(3)); where value has passed out of shares in this way, loss relief may not be claimed. A literal reading would suggest that this no-loss rule applies only to shares and not to the second or third type of transaction discussed next.

The second type of transaction is where, after a transaction whereby the owner of any property has become the lessee of the property, there is an adjustment of the rights and liabilities of the lease which is as a whole more favourable to the lessor (section 29(4)).

The third type of transaction is where an asset is subject to a right or restriction, and a transaction takes place whereby that right or restriction is extinguished or abrogated in whole or in part. The figure taken is the value accruing to the owner of the property from which the restriction falls (section 29(5)).

---

[40] TCGA 1992, s 29(1)(a).

[41] The legislation does not, however, limit itself to value shifting into shares held by others, and could apply where value is shifted between different classes of shares held by the same person. This is understood to be the Revenue view.

[42] *Floor v Davis* [1979] STC 379,52 TC 609 [1979] 2 All ER 677.

[43] In the light of the decision in *WT Ramsay Ltd v IRC*, see above §5.6.4, it would appear that the same result would have been reached if, as part of the scheme, they had voted against the resolution.

37

Leases

37.1 Introduction

The CGT rules governing leases are complex and the discussion that follows focuses on the key elements. In part, the complexity of the CGT rules simply reflects the complexity of the transactions with which the law is dealing; however, it also reflects the complexity of neighbouring areas of tax law, especially income tax. The provisions deal with two main issues: (a) the determination of gains or losses on the disposal of the lease by the lessee; (b) the circumstances in which the grant of a lease is a disposal or part disposal by the landlord—and how any gains should be computed. These rules apply generally to leases of movable and immovable property.

37.2 Wasting Asset Rules

Special computational rules apply on the disposal of a lease which has 50 years or less to run at the time of the disposal. Such a lease is a wasting asset (TCGA 1992, section 44). The wasting asset writing-down rules apply as soon as the lease becomes a wasting asset;[1] once the lease has less than 50 years to run, the writing-down rules apply regardless of the original length of the lease.

Three rules apply to determine the duration of a lease; these are to prevent short leases appearing as long leases.[2] The rules are applied by reference to the facts which were known or ascertainable at the time when the lease was created (or acquired by the disposer)[3] and are as follows:

(1) *Notice.* Where the lease can be ended by notice given by the landlord, it is treated as ending at the earliest date on which it could be ended.[4] A lease for 50 years which the

---

[1] TCGA 1992, Sch 8, para 1(5).
[2] They are similar, but not identical, to the old Sch A rules in TA 1988, s 38.
[3] TCGA 1992, Sch 8, para 8(6).
[4] TCGA 1992, Sch 8, para 8(2).

landlord may terminate by notice after five years is treated as a five-year lease—even
after the five-year period has passed.

(2) *Commercial reality.* Where any of the terms of the lease render it unlikely that the lease
will continue beyond a certain date, the lease is treated as ending on that date.[5] A lease
which specifies a date on which it is to become more onerous, eg because the rent is
to be increased, is treated as a lease expiring on that date.[6] A simple rent review clause
should not have this effect if the review is simply to bring rent into line with market
values so that it may go down as well as up.

(3) *Extension.* Where the terms of the lease include provision for the extension of the lease
beyond a given date by notice given by the tenant, these provisions apply as if the term
of the lease extended for as long as it could be extended by the tenant, but subject to
any right of the landlord by notice to determine the lease.[7]

A lease of movable property which is a wasting asset is deemed to terminate not later than
the end of the life of the wasting asset.[8]

A lease with less than 50 years to run is not treated as a wasting asset in two situations.
The first is where, at the beginning of the ownership of a lease, it is subject to a sub-lease not
at a rack rent, and it is estimated at that time that the value of the lease, when the sub-lease
falls in, will exceed the lessee's acquisition cost; such a lease is not a wasting asset until the
sub-lease falls in.[9] The second exception is where the lease qualifies for capital allowances,
eg on a lease of an industrial building; this is the normal rule for all assets qualifying for
capital allowances.[10]

37.3 Writing Down the Expenditure

A lease of land becomes a wasting asset only when it has less than 50 years to run.[11] When
a lease has no more than 50 years to run, the expenditure attributable to its acquisition is
deemed to waste away over the balance of its duration. Section 46, directing a straight-line
basis, does not apply. Instead, a special curved basis applies to a lease of land, with less depreciation in the early years of the lease and more depreciation towards its end. This curved
basis was thought to give the true commercial measure. Despite this, the straight-line basis
was selected for other parts of CGT, notably pre-1965 assets and wasting assets other than
land. Any applicable indexation relief (section 53(3)) is given only on the expenditure not
yet written off.

---

[5] TCGA 1992, Sch 8, para 8(3).
[6] TCGA 1992, Sch 8, para 8(4).
[7] TCGA 1992, Sch 8, para 8(5).
[8] TCGA 1992, Sch 8, para 9(3).
[9] TCGA 1992 contains various formulae; it is not clear whether, when the lease does become a wasting asset,
the amount P(l) in TCGA 1992, Sch 8, para 1(4)(a) is 100.00 (the normal rule for leases which become wasting
assets by passing the 50-year point), or the percentage applicable to the actual duration left. The latter seems
more sensible.
[10] TCGA 1992, Sch 8, para 1(6).
[11] TCGA 1992, Sch 8, para 8(1).

So suppose that a block of flats was leased for 99 years from 1 January 1936, and that the leasehold interest was acquired by A Ltd on 31 May 1997 for £105,000 and sold on 1 March 2005 for £500,000. The unexpired term on acquisition in 1997 was 37 years and 7 months, and on disposal was 29 years and 10 months. The table in TCGA 1992, Schedule 8, para 1 gives the relevant percentages as 93.497 (P1) and 86.226 (P3). The statute directs that A Ltd may not take account of a fraction of the expenditure of £105,000; that fraction is (P1—P3)/P1. The fraction works out at 0.078, so 7.8% of the acquisition cost (£8,190) is disallowed. This reduces the allowable acquisition cost from £105,000 to £96,810 and increases the gain (before indexation or other reliefs) from £395,000 to £403,190.

The reason why the fraction refers to P3 rather than P2 is that P2 is reserved for any allowable costs of improvement, etc, since the asset was acquired.

37.3.1 Situations Attracting Special Treatment

37.3.1.1 Landlord and Tenant Act 1954

A new lease granted as the result of an application under the Landlord and Tenant Act 1954 is a new asset, separate from the original lease and so not derived from it.[12] None of the expenditure in respect of the original lease is available to be taken into account in relation to a disposal of the new lease.

37.3.1.2 Leasehold Reform Act 1967

A new lease under the Leasehold Reform Act 1967 is not an extension of the old lease.[13] This is because the CGT legislation requires the extension to be included in the terms of the lease; the statutory right arises under the Act, not under the lease.

37.3.1.3 Surrender and Re-grant

By concession ESC D39, no CGT charge is treated as arising if the old lease is surrendered in return for the grant of a new, longer lease of the same property to the same lessee. The transaction must be between unconnected parties bargaining at arm's length, and not connected with a larger scheme or series of transactions. The lessee must not receive a capital sum, and the terms of the new lease must not differ from those of the old lease in any respect other than its duration and the amount of rent payable.

37.3.1.4 Merger

Where the lessee acquires a superior lease or the freehold reversion, the interests in the two assets are merged and the original lease is extinguished (section 43). By concession ESC D42, the expenditure allowable on a disposal of the merged interest will include the costs of the superior interest and of the first lease (written down if the duration was less than 50 years) to the date of the acquisition of the superior interest. If the superior interest is itself a lease with duration of less than 50 years, the total of these amounts is written down to the date of disposal of the merged lease.

---

[12] *Bayley v Rogers* [1980] STC 544, (1980) 53 TC 420.
[13] *Lewis v Walters* [1992] STC 97, (1992) 64 TC 489.

37.4   Granting a Lease: Premium

The CGT rules on the grant of a lease refer frequently to the concept of a 'premium'. A 'premium' is defined as including any sum (other than rent) paid on or in connection with the grant of a tenancy, except in so far as other sufficient consideration for the payment is shown to have been given. A premium also includes 'any like sum, whether payable to an intermediate or a superior landlord'[14]—presumably meaning a sum paid by the tenant to the landlord for the lease. See also §25.5.1 above on the taxation of premiums under ITTOIA 2005, Part 3, Chapter 4. There is judicial authority that a premium is a sum of money paid to a landlord in consideration of the grant of a lease.[15] In *Clarke v United Real (Moorgate) Ltd*, counsel tried to gloss these words by arguing that the sum also had to be paid to the landlord 'as landlord'.[16] The judge agreed that sums paid for plumbing work were not a premium, partly because, on counsel's definition, they were not paid to the landlord as landlord, and partly because, as the judge pointed out, they were not paid to the landlord in consideration for the grant of the lease. However, any sums which were agreed to be paid to the landlord in consideration of the grant of the lease (and so under the terms of the construction lease) would amount to a premium, even though the sums were equal to the costs of construction or plumbing. Statute treats certain sums as lease premiums, eg payment in lieu of rent, consideration for the surrender of a lease and consideration for the variation of a lease.[17] In relation to Scotland, a premium includes, in particular, a grassum payable to any landlord or intermediate landlord on the creation of a sub-lease.[18]

Gifts and connected persons. Where there is a variation or waiver of any of the terms of a lease and, had the transaction been at arm's length, a sum would have been expected to have been paid as consideration for the variation or waiver, this sum is treated as a lease premium if the landlord and tenant are connected persons, or the transaction was entered into gratuitously.[19]

When does the premium arise? The time at which the lease premium is deemed to have arisen depends on the event. Where an actual premium is paid, the time is the date of the grant of the lease.[20] A payment in lieu of rent or a variation or waiver is treated as arising when the sum is payable.[21] Where the premium is imputed by the relationship between the parties, the operative date is the date on which the sum would have been payable had the parties acted at arm's length.[22]

---

[14] TCGA 1992, Sch 8, para 10(2).
[15] Lord Goddard in *R v Birmingham (West) Rent Tribunal* [1951] 2 KB 54, 57; [1951] 1 All ER 198, 201: 'The whole conception of the term is a sum of money paid to a landlord as consideration for the grant of a lease.' See also *Toronto Dominion Bank v Oberoi* [2004] STC 1197 on whether a payment was rent or a premium.
[16] [1988] STC 273, 299; (1988) 61 TC 353, 387.
[17] TCGA 1992, Sch 8, para 3, amended by FA 1996.
[18] TCGA 1992, Sch 8, para 10(3).
[19] TCGA 1992, Sch 8, para 3(7).
[20] TCGA 1992, s 28(1) and Sch 8, para 3.
[21] TCGA 1992, Sch 8, para 3(2)(a), (3)(a).
[22] TCGA 1992, Sch 8, para 3(4).

37.5   Granting a Lease as a Part Disposal: Computational Problems

Where the payment of a premium is required under a lease, there is a part disposal of the freehold or other asset out of which the lease is granted.[23] This is in accordance with general principles, but is expressly articulated. Where a lease is granted for a full rent but without a premium, there is a part disposal but no chargeable gain will arise; this is because the only consideration received is the right to the rent, and that is not relevant consideration (section 37(1)). Where the lease granted is a bargain at arm's length, or if the lessee is a person connected with the lessor, the amount of the premium deemed to have been given is the market value of the lease (section 17(1)).

Where there is a part disposal, the A/(A + B) formula in section 42 is applied (see §35.6.1). In valuing B (the property remaining undisposed of), it should be noted that B includes the right to the rent or other payment.[24]

Example

T Ltd bought a freehold factory for £180,000 in May 1998. After occupying it for the purposes of its own business, it grants a 15-year lease to a company for £50,000 with effect from 1 December 2005. The capitalised value of rentals under the lease is £150,000 and the freehold reversion is worth £200,000. This means that A = 50,000 and B = (200,000 + 150,000); so A/A + B = 50,000/(50,000 + 350,000), or 1/8. This means that the allowable expenditure is restricted to 1/8 × £180,000, ie £22,500. The relevant indexation allowance, available to T Ltd because it is subject to corporation tax, is applied to £22,250 giving, hypothetically, £2,633. Total allowable expenditure of £25,133 is set against the disposal consideration of £50,000 to give a net gain of £24,867.

Sublease out of short lease. The A/(A + B) formula in section 42 does not apply in the case of a lease granted out of a lease which is a wasting asset under the rules just described.[25] Rules restrict the part of the expenditure on the short head lease which may be deducted. That part is the part that may be written off, using the curved-line basis for land and the straight-line basis for other assets.[26] These rules apply not only to acquisition costs, but also to expenditure on improvements.[27]

Low premium. If the premium is less than the sums which would be obtainable if the rent receivable under the sub-lease were the same as the rent payable under the head lease (eg, if the rent charged on the sub-lease is double that charged under the lease out of which the sub-lease is created), a further adjustment takes place. If the premium is one half of the amount so obtainable, only one half of the expenditure attributable to the sub-lease is taken.[28]

---

[23] TCGA 1992, Sch 8, para 2(1).
[24] TCGA 1992, Sch 8, para 2(2), applying s 42.
[25] TCGA 1992, Sch 8, para 4.
[26] TCGA 1992, Sch 8, para 4(2)(a). If the lease is granted out of a short lease, the allowable expenditure is the amount which will have wasted over the term of the sub-lease, given by the fraction P(4)—P(5)/P(l)I, where: P(l) = the percentage applicable to the unexpired term of the head lease at the date of acquisition; P(4) = the percentage applicable to the unexpired term of the head lease at the date the sub-lease is granted; P(5) = the percentage applicable to the unexpired term of the head lease at the date the sub-lease expires.
[27] TCGA 1992, Sch 8, para 4(2).
[28] TCGA 1992, Sch 8, para 4(2)(b).

Sub-lease of part. Further provisions deal with the grant of a sub-lease of part of the land comprised in the head lease.[29] The proportion of the expenditure is taken by comparing the value of the property covered by the sub-lease with the value of all the property comprised in the head lease; the remainder of the expenditure is apportioned to the part not disposed of.[30]

Income tax. Where income tax has been paid in respect of the premium by the sub-lessor, rules exist to prevent double charging. If the lease has been granted out of a freehold or long lease, the premium subject to CGT is reduced by the amount subject to income tax.[31] However, the reduced premium is substituted only in the numerator, not in the denominator, of the A/(A + B) formula for apportioning allowable expenditure. In the case of a short lease granted out of a short lease, the CGT computation follows the normal format and the amount of the premium subject to income tax is then deducted from the chargeable gain.[32] This deduction may reduce a gain but may not create an allowable loss.[33]

37.6 Reverse Premiums

Reverse premiums, better described as lease inducement payments, are paid by the landlord to the tenant to persuade the tenant to take up the lease on the terms offered. Such premiums are now treated as revenue receipts,[34] and so cannot give rise to CGT for the tenant; even before 1999 there were no CGT implications for the tenant since the tenant was not disposing of an asset. The landlord is usually carrying on a trade so that these expenses would be deductible under ITTOIA 2005, Part 2; where the landlord in not carrying on a trade, the statutory hypothesis of the trade will prevent any CGT deduction. Further, any expenditure would at best be to enhance the value of the landlord's interest, and since this will cease to be reflected in the state of the asset[35] once the lease has expired, it is yet again not deductible.

37.7 Mineral Royalties

Where mineral royalties are received under a mineral lease or agreement, one half of the royalties received are treated as income and one half as capital (section 201(1)). The capital element is then a capital sum derived from an asset.[36] Where the royalty relates not only to the winning and working of the minerals but also to other matters, an apportionment may be needed.[37]

---

[29] TCGA 1992, Sch 8, para 4(3).
[30] For worked example, see *Simon's Direct Tax Service* C 12.1217.
[31] TCGA 1992, Sch 8, para 5(1).
[32] TCGA 1992, Sch 8, para 5(2).
[33] For a worked example, see *Simon's Direct Tax Service* C 12.1218.
[34] FA 1999, s 54, Sch 6 (see above at §21.12).
[35] As required by TCGA 1992, s 38(l)(b).
[36] TCGA 1992, s 22(l)(d). See Inland Revenue, Capital Gains Manual, CG 12960–6.
[37] The Mineral Royalties (Tax) Regulations 1971 (SI 1971/1035).

38

Options

38.1 Introduction

The real world provides many instances of options, ranging from an agreement to buy a specific piece of property, to contracts bought and sold on international exchanges. CGT begins by stating that an option is an asset for CGT purposes,[1] but then provides many other rules. Special rules are required to charge any sums paid on the grant of an option (by treating the grant of an option as a self-standing disposal) and to deal with the effects of both the exercise and abandonment of an option. In addition, there are a number of special computation rules and rules for special types of option. These provisions deal with 'call' options, ie options under which the grantee (X) has a right to *buy* an asset, and 'put' options, where X has a right to *sell*. It is not necessary that the intended vendor in either of these options should already be the owner of the property; this means that the commercial background to these rules on options is complicated and so the option rules are similarly difficult. What follows below is a description of the key elements.

Quoted options are those which are quoted on a recognised stock exchange at the time of the disposal.[2] Traded options are those which are quoted on a recognised stock exchange or a recognised futures exchange at the time of the disposal.[3] Financial options are those other than traded options, relating to financial matters such as currency, shares, securities or interest rates.[4]

---

[1] TCGA 1992, s 21(1)(a); see Baxter [1975] *Conv* 240.
[2] See definition in TCGA 1992, s 288(1), referring to ITA 2007, s 1005.
[3] For 'recognised stock exchange' and 'recognised futures exchange', see TCGA 1992, s 288(1), (6).
[4] Defined TCGA 1992, s 144(8); the Treasury may expand the financial option category by order (s 144(9)).

38.2   Grant of Option

The grant of an option is treated as the disposal of an asset, namely the option (section 144(1)). This treatment is provisional; later events may cause the grant to be charged as part of a larger transaction, eg where the option is exercised. The Revenue often wait to see whether the option is exercised before making an assessment under this rule, particularly where the sum paid for the option is small and the option period is short. This treatment is specified as to apply in particular, but not (by inference) exclusively, where grantors bind themselves to sell what they do not own and, because the option is abandoned, never have occasion to own, and where grantors bind themselves to buy what, because the option is abandoned, they do not acquire (section 144(1)). In *Randall v Plumb*,[5] the taxpayer received £25,000 for the grant of the option, but this sum was repayable in certain circumstances; the court decided that, in the circumstances, the contingent obligation to repay had to be taken into account notwithstanding the option rules. So the Revenue could not simply charge the whole £25,000.

Any part disposal, which might otherwise arise if the option were granted over property in which the grantor had an interest and the option were specifically enforceable, is excluded.[6] The exclusion of the part disposal appears to be applied by the Revenue only for the purpose of computing gains on the grant of the options. If, on general principles, the option is an interest in the underlying asset (as in the case of an option to acquire an estate in land), the gain may qualify for reliefs such as replacement of business assets, provided the requisite conditions are satisfied in relation to the underlying asset.[7] Since the grant of an option is considered to be a disposal of a separate asset, and not a part disposal of the grantor's interest in the asset, there is no allowable expenditure other than incidental costs of disposal, and the full net amount of any consideration received for the grant of the option is taxable. Indexation relief does not apply for corporation tax. The grant of an option to acquire an asset may be a disposal even though the grantor will not dispose of any asset when the option is exercised; for example, if a company issues options to subscribe for its own shares, the exercise of the options would not involve any disposal by the company.

38.3   Simple Disposal of Option

Where a person entitled to exercise an option disposes of it, eg by sale, exchange or gift, the gain or loss is computed according to normal CGT principles, including, where appropriate, the wasting asset rules. Special rules apply only where the disposal is by the abandonment of the option or by its exercise. The disposal of a traded option by the grantor is disregarded for CGT if it arises because the option is closed out by acquisition of a second

---

[5] [1975] STC 191, (1975) 50 TC 392; criticised by Baxter, *op cit*, 243, 247. See also above at §37.5.
[6] *Randall v Plumb* [1975] STC 191, (1975) 50 TC 392; and *Strange v Openshaw* [1983] STC 416, (1983) 57 TC 544.
[7] Revenue interpretation RI 11.

traded option of the same description. The costs of closing out, including the cost of the second option plus incidental costs of acquisition, are deducted in computing the gain on grant of the original option (section 148).

38.3.1 *Abandonment of Option*

The abandonment of the option by the person entitled to exercise is not normally a disposal (section 144(4)). The effect is to prevent any argument that any money lost by the grantee should give rise to an allowable loss. Case law holds that there will be a disposal by the grantee, however, if a capital sum is received for abandoning the option. This disposal is taken to arise under section 22 as the receipt of a capital sum derived from an asset.[8] The receipt of a sum for the 'release and abandonment' of an option was treated in the same way;[9] it follows that a mere agreement to release the option may also amount to an abandonment and the sum received be taxed in full. It is more than likely that the draftsmen did not consider abandonment for consideration.[10]

An allowable loss may be treated as arising if the option is a quoted option to subscribe for shares, a traded option, a financial option, or an option to acquire business assets. This is because in relation to these assets, section 144(4) directs that there is to be a disposal on abandonment. In computing the losses the wasting asset rules in section 46 do not apply (section 146). The forfeiture of a deposit paid in contemplation of a proposed purchase or in respect of any other transaction is treated as if it were the abandonment of an option binding the grantor to sell (section 144(7)). Hence, there is no loss relief for the person losing the deposit. However, there is a disposal of an asset (the option) by the party who received the deposit; the amount forfeited is treated as the consideration received. Since the 'option' is a chargeable asset in its own right, these consequences ensue even though the asset to which it relates may have been exempt, eg a private residence.

38.4   Exercise of Option

On exercise of the option, the grant and the exercise are treated as one transaction (section 144(2)); the disposal is treated as taking place when the option is exercised (section 28(2)). One effect of this rule is to prevent a sale from being carried out in two stages by option and exercise so as to take double advantage of the annual exemption. However, for the purposes of the indexation allowance for corporation tax, the cost of the option is treated as an expense separate from the price paid for the option.

---

[8] *Golding v Kaufman* [1985] STC 152, (1985) 58 TC 296. The decision of Vinelott J has been criticised for giving an unduly wide meaning to the term 'abandonment' when the same result could have been reached by a simpler route: see Marsh [1985] BTR 124. On this basis, 'abandonment' should be narrowly construed, so leaving releases and surrenders of options within the CGT net.
[9] *Welbeck Securities Ltd v Powlson* [1987] STC 468, (1987) 60 TC 269, CA; criticised by Avery Jones [1987] BTR 304.
[10] Avery Jones [1987] BTR 304, 307, arguing that such sums are not within CGT.

38.4.1 Treatment of Grantor

38.4.1.1 Call Options

In the case of a 'call' option, ie one binding the grantor to sell an asset, the consideration received for grant of the option is treated as part of the consideration for the sale (section 144(2)(a)). From this, it may be inferred that the single transaction referred to is the sale of the asset. Hence, there is no longer any liability under section 144(1) on the grant of the option.

38.4.1.2 Non-chargeable Gains

Where the exercise of the option involves a transaction which is not a disposal, eg an option followed by the issue of shares by a company, no chargeable gain arises either under section 144(1) on grant of the option or under section 144(2) on the subsequent transaction. A similar non-chargeable result would occur if the option were one to purchase an asset where the disposal of the asset would be exempt, eg the grantor's principal private residence.

38.4.1.3 Cash Settlements

A special rule applies where the grantor pays the option holder cash in full settlement of all obligations under the option. The grant and exercise are treated as a single transaction in which the money paid for the option is the consideration for the option and the sum paid in settlement is an item of incidental expenditure incurred (section 144A). Apportionments are applied where a payment is made in partial settlement.

38.4.1.4 Put Options

In the case of a 'put' option, ie one binding the grantor to buy, the consideration for the option is deducted from the grantor's allowable costs in respect of the asset when that asset is subsequently disposed of (section 144(2)(b)).

38.4.1.5 Indexation (Corporation Tax)

Although the allowable costs are reduced, it does not follow that indexation relief will be available only in respect of the expenditure as reduced. This relief continues to be available in respect of the sum paid for the option as from the time it was paid (section 57(2), (3)).

38.4.2 Treatment of Grantee

The exercise of an option is not a disposal of any asset by the grantee (section 144(3)). Whether the option is exercised as between the original parties or assignees, the acquisition and the exercise of the option are treated as a single transaction.

38.4.2.1 Call Options

Where the option binds the grantor to sell, the grantee's costs in acquiring the option are added to the costs of acquiring the asset. Although the option would have been a wasting asset in relation to a disposal of the option, there is no reduction in the cost of the option. When applicable, indexation relief is applied to the two sums separately (section 145).

38.4.2.2 Connected Persons

Different rules apply on disposal of an asset acquired by the exercise of an option in situations involving connected persons. Where the grantor and the grantee are connected persons, a loss accruing to the grantee will be an allowable loss only if it accrues on the disposal of the option at arm's length to a person not connected with him (section 18(5)). It follows that in the case of a call option, the disposal of any asset acquired by exercise of the option cannot give rise to an allowable loss.

38.4.2.3 Cash Settlements

Where the grantor pays the option holder cash in full settlement of all obligations under the option, the grant and exercise are treated as a single transaction in which the sum paid is the consideration for the disposal of the option and the settlement money is treated as an item of incidental expenditure incurred (section 144A). Apportionments are made where a payment is made in partial settlement.

38.4.2.4 Put Options

Where the option binds the grantor to buy, the cost of the option to the grantee (or to his assignees) is treated as an incidental cost in relation to the grantee's disposal of an asset on exercising the option (section 144(3)(b)). It follows that there will be no indexation relief in respect of the cost of the option. If the grantor and the grantee are connected persons, no allowable loss can arise to the grantee on exercise of the option (section 18(4)).

38.4.3 Calculation: The Market Value Rule

The legislation includes rules on the interaction of the option rules with section 17. In *Mansworth v Jelley*,[11] the taxpayer, J, was given an option to buy shares in his employer company. He exercised the option and immediately sold the shares. He argued that his base cost in the shares was the market value at the date the option was exercised—since section 17 applied the market value rules and section 144(3) treated the grant of the option and the exercise as one transaction. The Revenue argued that where there was a grant and exercise, the base value should be the sum of the price paid for the shares and the market value of the options when given (nil). Lightman J found in favour of the taxpayer, but the Revenue enacted their view as section 144ZA.[12]

This legislation had to be reinforced two years later as it was used as the basis for schemes to reintroduce unlimited deferral of CGT on gifts which were meant to have been stopped in 1989.[13] These schemes used uncommercial prices, so section 144ZB creates an exception to section 144ZA and applies where section 144ZA would apply but the exercise is non-commercial, as determined under section 144ZC; section 144ZD excludes certain

---

[11] [2002] EWHC ChD 442; 2002 STC 1013 and note by GR [2003] BTR 12–14.
[12] TCGA 1992, s 144ZA, added by FA 2003, s 158; see Inland Revenue Press Release Rev BN 31, [2003] *Simon's Tax Intelligence*.
[13] TCGA 1992 ss 144ZB–144ZD added by F(No 2)A 2005, s 35 and Sch 5; background explained in pre-Budget Report Press Release. There is a worked example in paras 36 and 40.

arrangements from section 144ZB so that section 144ZA applies after all. The schemes under attack were designed to use options to get round the normal charge that would apply under section 17 on a gift, as the following Revenue example shows:

Example

C and D are connected persons. C gives D an option, allowing D to sell an asset worth £90,000 to C for £30,000 in two months' time. D pays nothing for the option which has no value when granted. D exercises the option and sells the asset to C. Under section 144ZA in its original form, D's disposal proceeds came to just £30,000, and as this sum is the same as the acquisition cost, there is no net gain. C acquires the asset for £30,000. D has transferred an asset worth £90,000 for £30,000 and has reintroduced deferral. The deferral is undone by section 144ZB.

38.5   Options Binding Grantor to Transactions Other Than Sale or Purchase

References to options include options binding the grantor to grant a lease for a premium or to enter into any other transaction which is not a sale; references to buying and selling in pursuance of an option are construed accordingly (section 144(6)). If X grants Y a binding option to grant a lease and the option is exercised, the grant of the option plus the grant of the lease for a premium are treated as a single transaction. The consideration received by X for the option will be added to the premium on the lease; the sum will be treated as received by X for the grant of the lease. If the option is not exercised, X is treated as having disposed of the option (section 144(1)) and so is chargeable.

Since neither the abandonment nor the exercise of the option by Y is a disposal of any asset by Y, a forfeited deposit is not an allowable loss (section 144(7)). Where Y exercises the option, the acquisition of the option and the transaction resulting from its exercise are treated as a single transaction. Y's acquisition costs for the lease will be the sum paid for the option and the premium. Just as with an option to buy or sell, so the option may relate to a transaction which is not a disposal for CGT, eg an option binding a company to issue shares to the holder of the option. Where, on the exercise of the option, the grant of the option and the issue of the shares are treated as a single transaction (section 144(2), no chargeable gain arises. Chargeable gains might arise, however, if the option was abandoned and never exercised, as the grant of the option is treated as a disposal.

38.6   Application of Wasting Asset Rules

An option having a predictable life of 50 years or less is a wasting asset; the rules restricting the deduction of expenditure therefore apply (section 46). The costs are written off over the life of the option on a straight-line basis. If there is a transfer of an option to buy or sell quoted shares or securities, the option is regarded as a wasting asset, the life of which ends when the right to exercise it ends or, if earlier, when it becomes valueless.[14] If the option is exercised, the full amount paid for the grant is added to (or deducted from) the amount payable on exercise, without writing off any amount up to the date of exercise. These wasting rules do not, however, apply to options to acquire assets to be used for the purposes of a trade carried on by the person acquiring the assets. The rules also do not apply to a quoted option to subscribe for shares in a company, traded options or financial options.

38.7 Further Rules

Gains accruing on the disposal by any person of any option or contract to acquire or dispose of gilt-edged securities or qualifying corporate bonds are not chargeable gains.[15] This is because chargeable gains do not arise on the disposal of either of these assets. Further rules apply to options over rights to acquire qualifying shares in a building society, various employee share option and incentive schemes (sections 149–149B).

---

[14] TCGA 1992, s 146(2), (4)(b).
[15] TCGA 1992, s 115. The concept of disposing of the contract is widened by s 115(3) to cover the closing-out of the contract by entering into a contract with reciprocal obligations, ie a matched transaction.

39

Death

39.1   Introduction

From 1965 to 1971, both estate duty and CGT were charged at death. Since 1971, the principle underlying the legislation is that the only potential charge at death is the succession tax in force at the time, ie inheritance tax. As a result, under the present system, transfers of chargeable assets during lifetime give rise to potential CGT, but transfers on death escape the charge. This is accomplished in TCGA 1992, section 62 by providing that death is not a disposal for CGT purposes and the personal representatives (PRs) acquire the assets for a consideration equal to the market value at the date of death. Because there is no disposal by the deceased, D, there is no CGT on any gain remaining unrealised at D's death (or any relief for losses). The rule applies whether or not any IHT is actually due, eg because the value of the estate is below the IHT nil-rate band threshold. This system has been heavily criticised by tax policy commentators for its generosity and especially for encouraging people to hold on to assets that have risen in value even if, absent tax considerations, they would prefer to sell and put the proceeds to a different, perhaps more productive use.[1]

Where the PRs sell an asset of the estate, CGT is charged on the sale, taking the market value at the date of death as the base cost. However, if the PRs dispose of an asset by passing it to a beneficiary, B, under the will or on intestacy, there is no CGT; B is treated as acquiring the asset as at the death of D and at its value at that time (section 62(4)). Similar but not identical[2] rules may apply to settled property where a beneficiary dies (sections 72, 73).

---

[1] See Chamberlain, 'Capital Taxes—Time for a Fresh Look?' [2015] BTR 679; Lee, 'Inheritance Tax—An Equitable Tax No Longer: Time for Abolition' (2007) 7 *Legal Studies* 678; and Mirrlees *et al* (eds), *Tax by Design: The Mirrlees Review* (OUP, 2011) ch 15. The Mirrlees Review editors are particularly critical, concluding (at 15.3): 'Whatever kind of wealth transfer tax one does (or does not) want, there is no case for forgiveness of CGT on death.'

[2] TCGA 1992, s 74, under which a charge crystallises on settled property when it would not crystallise on unsettled property.

Death may be treated as giving rise to taxable events in other parts of the tax system on the basis of a deemed disposal.[3]

39.2 Settling the Deceased's Lifetime CGT Liabilities

Where, in the year of assessment in which he dies, an individual has allowable losses, in excess of chargeable gains, such losses may be rolled backwards for the preceding three years of assessment, taking later years first.[4] This applies only from 6 April to the date of the death, ie not 12 months from the date of death. The relief does not apply to an excess of allowable losses in the year before that of death, since such losses are set off against gains after allowable losses for the year (section 62(2)). Any liability in respect of CGT due from the deceased is deductible in computing the value of the estate for IHT purposes.

39.3 Acquisition by PRs at Market Value on Death

39.3.1 Acquisition

The PRs (or others on whom the property devolves) are deemed to acquire property of which the deceased, D, was competent to dispose. The acquisition is at market value at the date of death (section 62(1)(a)). However, there is no deemed disposal by D; hence, any potential liability in respect of unrealised gains is extinguished—any potential allowable losses are also lost. This means that a person with large, unrealised gains can make deathbed gifts to another and avoid CGT—but not IHT. If one spouse or civil partner, H, with large unrealised gains, gives property to the other spouse or civil partner, W, there will be neither CGT nor IHT liability, as transfers between spouses or civil partners generally are exempt for IHT purposes (see §53.1 below).

D is competent to dispose[5] of any assets which D might, if of full age and capacity, have disposed of by will. This includes any severable beneficial share in joint property, but not property over which D had a power of appointment.

39.3.2 Relationship between CGT and IHT

39.3.2.1 Values

Where IHT has been paid, the value taken at the date of death is the value on which IHT was charged. This applies even where a valuation of related property is required, which would not be brought into account under the normal rules for valuing an asset for CGT

---

[3] Eg, taxing offshore income gains, relevant discounted securities and the accrued income scheme.
[4] See also above §33.10.2.
[5] TCGA 1992, s 62(10). In order to apply this test all the assets which could have passed under the will of an adult domiciled in England and Wales are taken into account. Where the asset is overseas, the effect of the foreign law is excluded by deeming the asset to be in England—but only for this purpose.

(section 274). Because of the different IHT reliefs, eg those which reduce the value of the land for IHT purposes, the IHT value of the property may not be the same as the value on which IHT is eventually charged. Therefore, if farm land is valued at £200,000, the value transferred for IHT purposes may be reduced to £100,000 by reason of agricultural relief; the value for the CGT acquisition remains at £200,000. This rule is the subject of statutory clarification when the nil rate band applies for IHT purposes. If the valuation of an asset does not take place for IHT until the death of the surviving spouse, nothing in this rule requires the value at the second death to be taken for CGT.

39.3.2.2 Lifetime Gifts

On a gift with reservation, which is treated as the remaining part of the donor's estate on death for IHT, the market value for CGT is undisturbed and remains that of the date of the gift (assuming the gift is a disposal for CGT); unlike IHT, CGT does not take the value at death. Similarly, in the case of a PET, which becomes a chargeable transfer for IHT because the donor dies within seven years of the date of the transfer, the CGT treatment of the gift is undisturbed since the gift is not treated as included in the transferor's estate on death.

39.3.2.3 *Donatio Mortis Causa*

A *donatio mortis causa* is not subject to CGT when made;[6] as such, the donee takes at the market value at the date of death.[7]

39.3.2.4 Planning

If H is on his deathbed and W has assets which have large unrealised gains, it appears that if W gives the asset to H, who then dies having made a will in W's favour, the transfer by W to H will be tax neutral under section 58, the gift back to W will be free of IHT since they are spouses or civil partners, and the capital gains liability will be removed by section 62 since they are spouses or civil partners and they are living together.[8]

39.3.2.5 Held-Over Gain

On death crystallising held-over gains in relation to settled property, see above §36.5.1.

39.4 Variations

39.4.1 *Disclaimer or Variation*

As with IHT, CGT gives effect to a variation[9] by an instrument in writing or a disclaimer[10] made within a two-year period from the date of death. The variation or disclaimer is not a

---

[6] TCGA 1992, s 17 is excluded by s 62(5).

[7] TCGA 1992, s 62(5), 64(2).

[8] Potter and Monroe, *Tax Planning* (Sweet & Maxwell, 1982), §2–27, advising that the arrangement should be safe from *Furniss v Dawson* [1984] AC 474 (see above §5.6.4), at least if the will has been made first.

[9] On construing variation, see *Schnieder v Mills* [1993] STC 430.

[10] The disclaimer does not have to be by an instrument in writing; as with IHT, the formalities in TCGA 1992, s 62(7) were amended by FA 2002, s 52. The analogous treatment of variations and disclaimers for IHT is discussed at §46.5.1 below.

disposal (so there can be no CGT), and for the purposes of section 62, the CGT rules apply as if the new scheme had been made by the deceased (section 62(6)). The rule is confined to property of which the deceased was competent to dispose (section 62(10)). It does not apply where the variation or disclaimer is in return for extraneous consideration (section 62(8)). As with IHT, the Revenue pay great attention to the distinction between a disclaimer and surrender; once a gift has been accepted, it can only be surrendered. Although the rule deems the variation to be by the deceased, this is not for each and every purpose. In *Marshall v Kerr*,[11] the Court of Appeal held that the deeming process did not deem a settlement actually made by a non-resident beneficiary to have been made by the resident deceased. The House of Lords reached its decision on different grounds, but approved the reasoning of the Court of Appeal.[12] The later decision of the House of Lords in *Jerome v Kelly*[13] is consistent with this approach. A variation may be made within the two-year period whether or not the administration has been completed or the property has been distributed in accordance with the original dispositions (section 62(9)).

39.4.2 Inheritance (Provision for Family and Dependants) Act 1975

Exactly as with IHT, any order made under the Inheritance (Provision for Family and Dependants) Act 1975 directing the PRs to pass assets or make payments to D's dependants has effect as from the date of D's death.[14] The dependant in whose favour an order is made is treated as a legatee. This procedure differs from disclaimers and variations, discussed above at §39.4.1, eg in that there is no two-year time limit and there must be a court order.

39.5   Disposal to 'Legatee'

When the estate is administered, the PRs will dispose of the property to the specific and residuary legatees. Where B acquires an asset 'as legatee', B is taxed as having acquired the asset when the PRs acquired it (section 62(4)). Thus, if there is a specific legacy of a piece of furniture which cost D £1,500 and which was worth £6,500 when he died, leaving the piece specifically to A, A will be taken to have acquired it at £6,500, even though when she eventually receives it, it could be worth £8,000 or £5,000. This has the consequence that where some of the assets have accrued gains and other losses, and there are two legatees, one resident in the UK and the other non-resident, it will be advantageous to transfer the assets with the losses to the UK resident (so that he may take advantage of them in due course) and the other assets to the non-resident, so that they will escape UK CGT.

There are two other important effects of this statutory treatment. First, until its repeal in 2008, taper relief was applied by reference to the total period from the date of death to the

---

[11] [1993] STC 360, (1993) 67 TC 56.
[12] [1994] STC 638, 649f, (1994) 67 TC 56, 92H, per Lord Browne-Wilkinson.
[13] [2004] UKHL 25, [2004] STC 887.
[14] Inheritance (Provision for Family and Dependants) Act 1975, s 19(1). The analogous treatment for IHT is discussed at §46.5.4 below.

beneficiary's disposal of the asset. Secondly, tax on the beneficiary's disposal is determined according to the circumstances of the beneficiary alone. Where beneficiaries of an estate are not subject to tax owing to the availability of allowable losses or unused annual exemption, it would normally be appropriate for the PRs to make a declaration that they pass beneficial interest in an asset to one or more beneficiaries in advance of the sale of the asset. Such a sale is then made by the PRs acting as trustees of each of the beneficiaries. The gain is then subject to tax as a gain made by the beneficiary.

An asset is acquired by a person 'as legatee' if it is taken under a testamentary disposition or on an intestacy; the phrase is defined as including any asset appropriated by the PRs in or towards satisfaction of a pecuniary legacy or any other interest or share in the property devolving under the disposition or on intestacy (section 64(2)). The effect is that a pecuniary legatee takes as legatee, as does a residuary or a specific legatee, but a creditor does not.[15] The position of a person entitled to part of the estate and who buys from the PRs an asset in satisfaction of that claim but for a price greater than the value of that claim, by paying the difference, is obscure.[16] It is presumably irrelevant that the asset was acquired by the PRs after the death. It is also likely that a person acquiring an asset by exercising an option to buy that asset granted to him by the will also takes as a legatee, but this question cannot be regarded as settled. Technically, once a clear residue has been ascertained, the PRs become trustees. Where an asset is transferred to B, the beneficiary, before administration is complete, B takes 'as legatee'. However, where a transfer is made after such completion, the disposal may take place at the time of that completion and not on the transfer, since B will usually have been absolutely entitled as against the PRs when they became trustees. There can, therefore, be no later disposal by the trustees to B. If the trustees are not the same as the PRs, they presumably take 'as legatees'.

39.6 Disposals by PRs during Administration

39.6.1 Basic Rules

The PRs will have acquired assets at the date of death in the manner outlined at §39.3. Any disposal during administration otherwise than to a person 'as legatee' may give rise to CGT in the usual way, even if the purpose of the disposal is to raise money to pay tax or to pay the proceeds to the beneficiaries—unless they are already absolutely entitled (see below at §40.3) as against the PRs, in which case any liability falls on the beneficiaries.[17] On the FA 2004 statutory relief for private residences held by PRs, see §34.7.6 above. The PRs are treated as a single body of persons but having the same residence and domicile as the deceased, D, at the time of his death.[18] If D was non-resident, there will be no CGT liability on the PRs even if they are resident.

---

[15] Quaere whether the equitable doctrines of performance and satisfaction apply.
[16] In *Passant v Jackson* [1985] STC 133, (1985) 59 TC 230, the reasoning of Vinelott J suggests that such an acquisition is not 'as legatee'; appeal dismissed [1986] STC 164, CA.
[17] *Prest v Bettinson* [1980] STC 607, (1980) 53 TC 437.
[18] TCGA 1992, s 62(3); on liability, see also s 65(1).

39.6.1.1 Rate

The PRs are not to be treated as 'an individual' (section 65(2)), and CGT on any chargeable gains accruing to them is assessed at 20%/28% (section 4(3)). Prior to 2008, CGT was assessed at the special rate for trusts—40%.[19] This has the result that capital gains realised by PRs generally will be taxed less heavily than income accruing to them. In the years before 1998–99, PRs had to pay only at the basic rate of income tax.[20]

39.6.1.2 Annual Exemption

Unlike trustees, PRs are entitled to the full annual exemption (currently £11,100) for the year in which the deceased died (in addition to the same exemption for the deceased himself) and for the next two years of assessment (section 3(7)). Despite this relief, the selection of which assets to sell and which to retain for transmission in specie to the legatees is of great practical importance.

39.6.2 *Computation of Gain*

The gain arising on a disposal by the PRs is measured by comparing the sale proceeds with the value of the asset at death (section 62(1)(a)). The House of Lords has held that the deductible expenditure may include a suitable part of the costs of obtaining probate,[21] as incidental expenses suffered by the executors on their acquisition of the assets at the death of the deceased. Where actual expenditure has been incurred on the granting of probate in respect of a specific asset, the amount of that actual expenditure is treated as the incidental cost of acquisition. In most cases, however, expenditure will have been incurred on the granting of probate for the whole estate and not specific to an asset. The Revenue will accept a computation with an allowance in accordance with a published table under which percentage of costs allowed declines as the gross value of the estate rises.[22]

---

[19] TCGA 1992, s 4(1AA)(b), added by FA 1998; basic rate applied from 1988–98. The rate was increased from 34% to 40% by FA 2004, s 29.

[20] D also could have paid at the basic rate, depending on the circumstances.

[21] *IRC v Richards' Executors* [1971] 1 All ER 785, (1971) 46 TC 626; see below §43.2.1.

[22] Statement of Practice SP 2/04 superseding SP 8/94.

40

Trusts

40.1   General Structure

40.1.1 Trusts and CGT

Trusts give rise to various problems for a CGT. The principal one is the familiar one of finding a way of preventing double taxation. In CGT this is achieved by charging the trustee but not the beneficiary, ie charging the trustees on gains realised in the course of administration and treating the disposal of a beneficial interest as one which has no CGT consequences.

A charge to CGT may arise: (a) on the creation of the settlement; (b) where gains accrue to trustees during the settlement; and (c) on the occurrence of certain events which are deemed to be disposals of the trust assets. In (b) and (c) the general principle is to charge the tax on the trustees, who are treated as a single and continuing body of persons (section 69(1)). This is so even if the property is held by different sets of trustees.[1] The trustees are not liable where: (a) they are bare trustees (see below at §40.3); (b) a trust gain accruing to a non-resident trustee is attributed to a beneficiary under section 87; or (c) a trust gain is attributed to the settlor (under section 76 or 86). Trustees are liable to the usual 20%/28% rate of tax and an annual exempt amount which differs from that applying to individuals.

---

[1] TCGA 1992, s 69(3). An example is where part of the land held under the Settled Land Act has been sold so that the proceeds of the sale will be in the hands of the trustees, while the remaining land will be in the hands of the tenant for life.

Trustees who have not been properly appointed are not trustees of the settlement for section 69. Although they may, as trustees de son tort, be liable for various breaches, they have no authority to exercise powers in the trust deed itself.[2]

The disposal of a beneficial interest in settled property is normally exempt, thereby preventing the effective double taxation of trust gains. The exemption does not apply if the disposal is by a person who has acquired the interest for a consideration in money or money's worth (section 76) or if the trustees are not resident in the UK (section 85(1)). For this and other exceptions, see below §40.8.2.

40.1.2 Trustees' Liability—Exemptions and Rates

CGT is charged on the gains of persons (section 1(1)) and so on the gains of trusts. However, as in other areas of tax law, a trust is not an individual and so rules unique to individuals do not apply to trusts.

40.1.2.1 Annual Exempt Amount

Trustees are entitled to an annual exemption, which is one half of the exempt amount for an individual. Therefore, for 2016–17, the exemption applies to the first £5,550 of gains.[3] The full individual amount (£11,100) applies for trusts for certain types of disability.[4] If the settlor has made more than one settlement since 6 June 1978, the exempt amount must be split between them—although there is a minimum exempt amount of one-tenth of the amount available to an individual. Therefore if there were two settlements, each would get an exemption of £2,775; if there were 12 settlements, each would have the minimum exemption of £1110. The identity of the settlor is important; the identity of the trustees is irrelevant. If one individual is trustee of several settlements then each has its own annual exempt amount in full.

40.1.2.2 Rate of Tax

CGT is charged on trusts at 20%/28% on any chargeable gains accruing from 6 April 2016 onwards (section 4(3)). From 1965–88 trustees paid CGT at the flat rate of 30%, like everyone else. From 1988–97 trusts paid at the basic rate of income tax, unless they were accumulation or discretionary trusts, in which case the rate was increased by 10%.[5] In 1997 a special rate for trusts was introduced at 34% for these discretionary trusts; this was extended to all trusts in 1998. The rate increased from 34% to 40% in 2004, and dropped to 18% in 2008 before increasing to 28% in 2010 and dropping to 20% generally (but remaining at 28% for residential property and carried interest) from 6 April 2016.

40.1.2.3 Incidence

The CGT legislation says nothing about the incidence of the tax as between the beneficiaries; this is therefore left to trust law. Where the property disposed of forms part

---

[2] *Jasmine Trustees Ltd and others v Wells & Hind (a firm) and another* [2007] EWHC 38 (Ch), [2007] STC 660.
[3] TCGA 1992, Sch 1, s 3(3).
[4] TCGA 1992, Sch 1, para, 1; for definitions, see Sch 1, para 1(6).
[5] *TCGA 1992*, s 5, repealed in 1992; discretionary trust was defined by reference to TA 1998, s 686.

of the capital of the trust, any CGT accruing will fall on the capital. If, however, the trust document or some right were to provide that all the produce of a particular source, even a capital gain, were to be paid to a life tenant, it would seem that the tax should fall on that life tenant rather than on the general capital.

40.1.2.4 Settled Property

Following extensive consultation, FA 2006, section 88 and Schedule 12 made major amendments, some definitional, to the CGT rules on trusts.[6] These changes are mirrored by FA 2006, section 89 and Schedule 13. For the background and purpose, see chapter twenty-nine above. Unlike income tax, CGT did have a rudimentary framework for trusts (see TCGA 1992, sections 60 and 68 *et seq*). Property is declared to be settled if it is held in trust and it is not a bare trust.[7] Property being administered as part of a deceased's estate is not settled property; neither is property vested in a trustee in bankruptcy (section 66). FA 2006 rewrote section 68 in the same form as the income tax provision, with the result that section 68 now makes it clear that any property comprised in a settlement, however expressed, is settled property.

Section 68A defines 'settlor' and introduces the concept of 'settlor of property'; the definition first covers the person who makes a settlement, whether directly or indirectly, eg someone who provides property directly or indirectly for the purpose of the settlement or has made reciprocal arrangements (see further section 68A(3) and (4)). This approach has obvious overtones of the income tax settlement provisions rules discussed in §31.3. Like the income tax rule, section 68A also deals with death, and provides rules for when the deceased is treated as the settlor and for when the person ceases to be treated as the settlor (section 68A(2) and (6)). Section 68A(2)(b) provides that D is a settlor if, on D's death, settled property is, or is derived from, property of which he was competent to dispose immediately before his death; this last phrase is already part of CGT law—section 62(10))—and there is cross-reference in section 68A(5). Section 68A(6) provides that D ceases to be a settlor if there is no property comprised in the settlement which is derived from him and (a) he has not made any undertaking to provide property in the future, and (b) he is not party to any relevant reciprocal arrangements.

Like the income tax rule, section 68B deals with transfers between settlements otherwise than by way of bargain at arm's length; the settlor of the first trust is treated as a settlor of the transferee as well. This does not apply (section 68B(6)) if the transfer is by reason of an assignment, etc by a beneficiary under the first settlement or under the exercise of a general power of appointment, or where the deceased is treated as the settlor under section 68C(6). A nice point is the exclusion of section 18(2) by section 68B(7), which would otherwise have brought a bargain at arm's length back in. Section 68C provides further rules to identify the settlor where a will or intestacy is varied and the terms of section 62(6) are satisfied. If the property was not settled property immediately before the settlement, it is those who would otherwise have taken the property who are the settlor—and not the deceased (section 68C(2) and (3)). Section 68C(5) and (6) direct when the deceased is to be treated as the settlor. The first instance is where property would have become comprised in a settlement

---

[6] See Budget 2006, note BN 35.
[7] TCGA 1992, s 68, subject also to s 99(1) (unit trusts).

on D's death and the variation makes it go to another settlement. The other instance is where D was already the settlor. In each case the settlement is treated as made immediately before D's death (section 68C(7)), unless it is already so treated (section 68C(8)).

40.1.2.5 Scope of Settlement

Since various events cause a deemed disposal of the settled property, it is important to know exactly what property is subject to the settlement concerned.[8] If there is one settlement and the property is in the hands of different trustees, statute provides that they are treated as a single body of trustees (section 69(3)). See below at §40.5.

Three situations must be distinguished:

(1)   A single disposition may create more than one settlement. The creation of distinct but undivided shares in one asset gives rise to one settlement even though the shares are held on different trusts.[9] However, a different answer may be reached if there are distinct assets as well as different trusts; this will be the case especially where more than one settlor is involved.

(2)   Where property is added to an existing settlement, the presumption is that no new settlement is created, although special factors, such as distinct trustees or an independent trust instrument, may lead to a different conclusion.

(3)   Where trustees exercise a power to subject property to further trusts, it is a question of fact whether the new trusts are part of the main settlement or a new one. This is to be decided by invoking practical common sense in the light of established legal doctrine.

40.1.3 *Trusts for Vulnerable Persons*

As with income tax (above §29.3.5) so with CGT, special rules concerning trusts for vulnerable persons were introduced as from 6 April 2004. The trustees must be otherwise liable for the tax and be resident in the UK during any part of the tax year.[10] The rules do not apply if the vulnerable person dies during the year.[11] Where these rules apply, and the appropriate election is made, the trustees are to be liable for no more CGT than would have been due if the gain had accrued directly to the vulnerable beneficiary. These rules are a consequence of the decision, which also took effect from April 2004 but under FA 2004, to increase the special trust rate of income tax—and so for CGT—from 34% to 40%.[12] The introduction in 2008 of a flat rate of tax simplified the operation of these rules considerably; the addi-

---

[8] It is also important for other reasons, eg the annual exemption, the residence of trustees and whether trustees of one fund are liable for tax arising as a gain from another part.

[9] *Crowe v Appleby* [1976] STC 301, (1976) 51 TC 457.

[10] FA 2005, s 30(1); gain accruing to the trustee include any arising under TCGA 1992, s 13.

[11] FA 2005, s 30.

[12] Notes to original Finance Bill, cls 39–61, para 120.

tion of the 28% rate in 2010 (now generally 20%) reintroduced some complication. For the definition of 'vulnerable persons' and the qualifying trusts, see §29.3.5 above. As for income tax, an election must be made by the vulnerable person and trustees jointly. Such an election is irrevocable.[13] There are separate enquiry powers and interpretation rules.[14] FA 2013, section 216 and Schedule 44 implemented an alignment of the definition of 'disabled person' for all tax purposes, now found in new Schedule 1A to FA 2005.

40.2   Settlor Retaining Interest

40.2.1   General

Prior to 2008, where the settlor (S) or S's spouse retained an interest in the settled property, chargeable gains of the trust arising in that year[15] were treated as accruing to S and taxed at S's marginal rate of income tax.[16] This applied only if both S and the trustees were either resident in the UK during any part of the year, or ordinarily so resident during the year.

S was entitled to recover from the trustees any CGT paid on trust gains.[17] However, if the trustees had net allowable losses for the year, the benefit of the losses did not pass to S in that year but was carried forward to be set off against trust gains of the following year.[18] S was specifically barred from using tapering relief.[19] When the flat rate of tax was introduced in 2008, this regime was no longer required and the rules in sections 77–79 were repealed. On settlor-interested trusts and the barring of the holdover election by FA 2004, see above §36.3.3.

40.2.2   Protecting Former Section 77, the Flip-Flop Device and the Meaning of Derived Property

Much legislative effort has been spent in trying to stop the so-called 'flip-flop scheme'. Section 76B and Schedule 4B, considered in more detail in the 4th edition of this book, were added in 2000 to address transfers of value by trustees linked with trustee borrowing. These rules were supplemented by Schedule 4C dealing with international aspects. Here a settlor would be facing liability to CGT on trust gains through having retained an interest and so being within section 76, and so with a gain to be taxed at 40% as opposed to, at that time, 34%. While all these provisions were being introduced, the validity of the scheme was subject to a judicial flip-flop in *Trennery v West*,[20] with each tier of appeal reversing

[13] FA 2005, s 37.
[14] FA 2005, ss 40 and 41.
[15] For a scheme avoiding former TCGA 1992, s 77 by using a different trust, see Potter and Monroe, *Tax Planning* (Sweet & Maxwell, 1982), §3-19A; for a 'more provocative' scheme see *ibid*, §3-19C.
[16] Formerly TCGA 1992, ss 77–79. For an unmeritorious and unsuccessful attempt to defeat the rules on non-resident trusts by the use of these provisions, see *de Rothschild v Lawrenson* [1994] STC 8, (1994) 67 TC 300.
[17] Formerly TCGA 1992, s 78.
[18] Formerly TCGA 1992, s 2(4), (5).
[19] Formerly TCGA 1992, s 77(6A).
[20] [2005] UKHL 5.

the court below. At the time of the facts in this case the trust rate was only 25%, so that the potential saving was even greater.

The scheme was relatively simple—in hindsight. The story begins with the creation of trust 1 by the settlor taxpayer (T) and his wife. Step 2 sees him transfer business assets to the trust with, at that time, a right to holdover relief. Step 3 sees T create a second trust. Step 4 sees the trustees first borrow money on the security of assets in the trust (this, being a mortgage, is not a disposal of the assets) and then secondly advance the money to the trustees of the trust created at step 3 in which the settlor of the first trust has an interest. At step 5, T and his wife are excluded from the first settlement. In the following tax year the trustees of the first trust sell the assets and use the proceeds to repay the debt. The settlor receives his or her money from the second trust. If the device is successful, the gains cannot be charged on the settlor because, in the tax year that they are realised, the settlor no longer has an interest in the first trust. In the case of a UK trust, the trustees are charged at the rate applicable to trusts (then 34%) on the gains, instead of the settlor being charged at his or her marginal rate of tax of (then) 40%. Former section 77 said that the settlor was regarded as having an interest in the settled property if any property comprised in the settlement—*or any derived property*—was or might become payable, etc to or for the benefit of himself or his wife. Derived property was defined as income from that property or any other property directly or indirectly representing proceeds of, or of income from, that property or income therefrom. The House of Lords held that the loan was income derived and so the scheme failed. The speech of Lord Walker in particular shows that the House was going to avoid giving a narrow construction to this anti-avoidance provision.[21]

To counter this, Schedule 4B directs a deemed disposal at market value; the disposal is by the trustees of trust 1 and applies to assets in trust 1 at that time.[22] These rules remain in force; they apply only if the trust falls within section 86 or section 87. Schedule 4A is another provision designed to protect the policy behind former section 77. As it concerns the disposal of a beneficial interest, it is discussed below at §40.8.

40.3   Bare Trust

Where assets are held by a trustee for another person who is absolutely entitled as against the trustee, or for two or more persons who are so entitled, the property is not settled and the acts of the trustee are treated as the acts of the beneficiary, and disposals between them are disregarded (section 60(1)).[23] All gains and losses and consequent liability are the concern of the beneficiary, B, and not the trustee.

---

[21] Eg, *ibid*, paras 40, 44 and 45.

[22] *Ibid*, paras 1(2) and 10.

[23] The same also applies to Lloyd's Underwriters (section 206). Therefore, if A transfers property to T to hold on trust for A absolutely, there is no chargeable disposal.

40.3.1 *Beneficiary's Absolute Entitlement*

B is absolutely entitled if he has the exclusive right, subject only to satisfying any outstanding charge, lien or other right[24] of the trustee to resort to the asset for the payment of duty, taxes, costs or other outgoings,[25] to direct how that asset shall be dealt with. 'Other outgoings' are construed *eiusdem generis* with rates and taxes, and so do not include an annuity.[26] This definition sits oddly with the trust doctrine that a beneficiary who is absolutely entitled has the right to end the trust but no power to direct the trustee on how the latter's discretion shall be exercised. It appears that a right to call for the conveyance of the trust asset to the beneficiary meets this test even though the beneficiary cannot control the trustee in other ways. If the test is whether the beneficiary can call upon the trustees for the transfer of the trust property, the answer may turn on the nature of the trust property. Thus, a co-owner of land has no right to call for the land itself because of the trust of the land.[27] Similar problems arise with certain shares in a private company and to mortgage debts.[28] However, it appears likely that such technical points will not be accepted by the courts and that therefore such property is not settled property for CGT.[29]

A residuary legatee does not hold absolutely as against the PRs during the administration of the estate.[30] Disposals by PRs to pay debts and pecuniary legacies cannot therefore be attributed to the legatee, since those assets never formed part of the residue to which the legatee was entitled.

40.3.2 *Pooling Owners as Co-owners; Contrast Interest in Succession*

Another area of difficulty concerns the extension of the bare trust concept to co-owners. In cases where there is more than one beneficiary, the rule applies where the beneficiaries are entitled against the trustees absolutely and 'jointly'. The word 'jointly', although not a term of art,[31] is not the same as 'joint tenants'. Therefore, there is a bare trust whether the owners hold as joint tenants or as tenants in common. In *Booth v Ellard*,[32] 12 members of a

---

[24] This is mentioned because otherwise a very small right could lead to the postponement of tax otherwise payable under TCGA 1992, s 71 (*Stephenson v Barclays Bank Trust Co Ltd* [1975] 1 All ER 625, 638, per Walton J).

[25] These words refer to some personal right of indemnity and are not apt to cover another beneficial interest arising under the same instrument (*Stephenson v Barclays Bank Trust Co Ltd* [1975] 1 All ER 625, 636, per Walton J). Charges are included in this list because of the estate and powers of the mortgagee (*Crowe v Appleby* [1975] STC 502, 510, per Goff J).

[26] *Stephenson v Barclays Bank Trust Co Ltd* [1975] 1 All ER 625 (the property ceased to be settled property when specific assets were appropriated to satisfy the annuity, that appropriation causing a deemed disposal under TCGA 1992, s 71).

[27] On effects of Trusts of Land and Appointment of Trustees Act 1996, see Gray and Gray, *Elements of Land Law*, 4th edn ch 11, esp at 11.227 *et seq*.

[28] See comments of Walton J in *Stephenson v Barclays Bank Trust Co Ltd* [1975] 1 All ER 625, 637, who said that one of several co-owners would, in these circumstances, have to wait until the property was sold before being entitled to call for the transfer of his or her share. In relation to shares, note the special circumstances in *Booth v Ellard* [1980] STC 555.

[29] See *Jenkins v Brown* [1989] STC 577, where land comprised in a pool held by trustees was conveyed to beneficiaries according to their interests prior to the trust being created.

[30] *Cochrane v IRC* [1974] STC 335, (1974) 49 TC 299; see also *Prest v Bettinson* [1980] STC 607, (1980) 53 TC 437.

[31] *Kidson v Macdonald* [1974] STC 54, [1974] 1 All ER 849, (1974) 49 TC 503.

[32] [1980] STC 555, 572, (1980) 53 TC 393.

family held 72% of the shares in a family company. They pooled their holdings by transferring them to a trust. They gave the trustees elaborate instructions as to how various matters should be dealt with, including voting rights. The court held that the arrangement gave rise to co-ownership, not settled property. The interests were concurrent not successive, and the interests of the co-owners were the same. This was followed in *Jenkins v Brown*,[33] where members of a family put various pieces of land into a trust with the idea of maintaining the continuity of the family farming unit. The beneficial interests were expressed as a percentage of the value of the property as a whole, calculated by reference to the values of what was originally put in. When one member of the family, F, withdrew the same piece of land that he had put in, the Revenue claimed CGT on the basis that that this was a disposal by trustees and chargeable to CGT. The court held that there was no disposal. It was wrong to treat each of the family members as having disposed of their interests in that piece of land. The court looked at the interests in the mass and not at the individual case. From this it appears to follow that there would have been no disposal if F had taken out a different piece of land from that put in.

Where two persons are entitled to succession, eg to A for life, remainder to B, there is not a bare trust, even though together they are entitled, if of full age, to terminate the trust.[34] This is sensible, since if there were a bare trust, it is unclear how those gains would be apportioned. Under the trust only B is entitled to the capital and yet A would not normally consent to the ending of the trust unless the capital were divided between them. The Revenue would therefore either attribute the whole gain to B, or divide it between A and B in accordance with some arbitrary assumptions of life expectancy and willingness, thus making A chargeable with a gains liability in respect of capital which may never be his.

40.3.3 Absolutely Entitled Because Might Be

A bare trust exists not only where persons are absolutely entitled as against the trustee, but also where they would be so entitled but for being infants or under a disability. However, this must be the only reason for not being absolutely entitled. In *Tomlinson v Glyn's Executor and Trustee Co*,[35] where property was held 'for such of the beneficiaries as shall attain the age of 21 years or marry under that age' (21 was then the age of majority), the beneficiary, even if he had not been an infant, would not have been absolutely entitled since his interest was contingent upon attaining his majority (or marrying before that time). A further reason was that the interests of the beneficiaries might have been defeasible *pro tanto* if other children were born, so that it could not be said that these infants had 'vested indefeasible interests in possession'. The result was that a gain realised by the trustees during the administration was a disposal by the trustees and so chargeable at their rate

[33] [1989] STC 577.
[34] Under the rule in *Saunders v Vautier* (1841) Cr & Ph 240. 'It is clearly settled property' (*Kidson v Macdonald* [1974] 1 All ER 849, 858, (1974) 49 TC 503, per Foster J).
[35] [1970] 1 All ER 381, (1970) 45 TC 607. What would have happened if the beneficiary had married and so satisfied the condition precedent while still an infant? *Semble* that there is a disposal by the trustees under TCGA 1992, s 71 (see below at §40.7; but see Wheatcroft [1969] BTR 63.)

(then at 30%), and could not be attributed to the beneficiaries (in which case the rate would have been nil).

40.4   Transfer Into Settlement

A transfer into settlement, whether revocable or irrevocable, is a disposal of the entire property thereby becoming settled property.[36] The provision directs that the disposal shall be total and not partial, even though the settlor has some interest under the settlement. This rule is different from that for IHT (see below at §48.5). The rule directing a total disposal applies even where there is consideration. These rules assume that one knows when one is making a transfer. Under modern trust law, rights in land may be created quite informally thanks to doctrines such as proprietary estoppel, or constructive or resulting trusts. Davis has argued, convincingly, that most of the problems, here as in IHT, may be solved by a flexible interpretation of the tax provisions.[37] Clearly something has to be done. However, the disposal is only of the property settled. If, therefore, the settlor has a piece of property but settles only a part of that property, there will be a part disposal of the property. If Simon declares himself trustee of shares for Angela for life, but does not expressly grant a remainder, the question whether there is a settlement of the shares or of a life interest in the shares must be answered by studying the wording and intention of the settlement.[38] This provision is probably superfluous to the extent that it states that there is to be a total disposal even though the settlor is a trustee or the sole trustee of the settlement, since, if this is the only link remaining between settlor and the property settled, it would appear that there has in fact been a total disposal. Any gain or loss on the disposal is computed by taking the consideration to be the market value of the assets concerned, since the gift is a transaction other than by way of a bargain at arm's length. Since the settlor is connected with the trustees, any allowable loss arising on the gift into settlement will be capable of set-off only against chargeable gains arising on subsequent disposals to the trustees.

40.4.1   Holdover Relief

If the transfer is an immediately chargeable transfer as opposed to a PET for IHT (section 260), or if the assets transferred are defined business assets (section 165), the settlor, S, may elect that any gain accruing on the transfer should be held over.[39] Prior to the 2006 changes to the IHT treatment of trusts, the main opportunity for making a holdover claim where business assets were not involved was likely to be on the transfer of assets to trustees of a discretionary settlement. As most *inter vivos* transfers to a trust now are immediately chargeable for IHT purposes, the availability of this holdover relief has taken on greater importance. When discretionary trusts paid CGT at 34% and individuals at 40%, there

---

[36] TCGA 1992, s 70.
[37] [2006] BTR 458.
[38] *Berry v Warnett* [1982] STC 396 (a decision concerned with the earlier formulation of s 70 which spoke of a gift in settlement where the settlor argued that he had settled the remainder but not the life interest).
[39] On holdover relief see §§36.3 and 36.4. On restriction of loss relief, see below at §40.6.2.

were advantages in S settling the asset on trusts from which S and S's spouse were excluded. Holdover relief was claimed under section 260 so that, when the trustees sold the asset, the gain would be taxed at 34% instead of 40%. This was clearly better than S selling the asset and then settling the proceeds. This was countered in 2004 by reshaping the holdover rule and increasing the rate of tax to 40%. It was less of a concern following the introduction in 2008 of the flat 18% tax rate, but has increased in importance following the introduction in 2010 of the 28% rate (now generally 20%).

40.5   Transfer by Trustees—Creation of Two Trusts or Continuation of One?

If trustees appoint property on trust on terms under which it is still settled property, it is necessary to determine whether the asset is still within the old trust or has migrated to a new trust. In broad terms it is a question of fact to be decided after examining the trust documents. Practical common sense must be used in the light of established legal doctrine.

The distinction between the two situations is important for the following reasons:

(1)   If assets are moved from one fund to another within the settlement, there is no disposal. However, if assets are transferred from one settlement to another, the transfer constitutes a disposal for CGT purposes and will take place at current market value.

(2)   Each trust has its own annual exempt amount.

(3)   Losses of one settlement cannot be set against the gains of another.

(4)   For the purpose of valuing unquoted shares, the blocks of shares held by trustees of separate settlements are valued separately.

(5)   The CGT self-assessment is made by the trustees of the settlement. This remains true provided the property remains in the main settlement. Therefore, if there are separate trustees of the sub-trust, the trustees of the main settlement, not the trustees of the sub-trust, must make that assessment. This is simply a self-assessment rule and does not affect the liability of all trustees for the tax due on a disposal of any part of the trust property.

The question whether a new trust has been created is answered by asking what a person with knowledge of the legal context of the word 'settlement' under established doctrine and applying that knowledge in a common sense way to the facts would conclude. In *Roome v Edwards*,[40] a settlement was created in 1944. In 1955, in exercise of the power in the original deed, a power of appointment was exercised and funds were set aside on trusts for two of the beneficiaries; the life tenant surrendered her life interest in respect of the asset set aside. The case concerned a capital gain arising in 1972–73, by which time the separate

---

[40] [1981] STC 96, [1981] 1 All ER 736, (1981) 54 TC 359; see also *Ewart v Taylor* [1983] STC 721, (1983) 57 TC 401.

fund had trustees, TS, who were resident in the UK, whereas the trustees for the main fund, TM, were resident outside the UK. The House of Lords held that the actions of the trustees fell short of creating two settlements out of a single settlement. Applying the common sense test, Lord Wilberforce said that the critical distinction between a single trust and two trusts turned on the question whether the trusts of the 1955 fund were exhaustive of the beneficial interests. Whereas the exercise of a special power of appointment would probably keep a single settlement in being, the exercise of a power to appoint and appropriate property to the beneficiaries and to settle it for their benefit would create a separate settlement. This conclusion meant TS were accountable for tax on a disposal by TM, even though TM were non-resident and could not be controlled by TS in any way.[41] In *Ewart v Taylor*,[42] this principle was applied to identify a separate trust arising from a particular exercise of a power of appointment.

In *Bond v Pickford*,[43] the Court of Appeal held that property remained part of the first settlement even though appointed on exhaustive trusts, because the power under which the appointment was made did not authorise the trustees to remove the property from the trusts altogether. Slade LJ distinguished powers in the wider form, the exercise of which would have created a separate settlement, and powers in the narrower form, the exercise of which did not have such an effect, before adding that it would be surprising if the CGT rules were different from the general legal rules applying to trusts.[44] In *Swires v Renton*,[45] the language of the original deed did not place the power in one or other category, but the language used in the deed of appointment rebutted the inference that a separate trust was intended.

The Revenue look suspiciously on arguments that an appointment has created a separate settlement, and advise officers to resist any attempt by the trustees to start by analysing the position at the present time.[46] The problems arising from the subtleties of when a disposition by trustees creates a new trust and when it remains part of the existing trust are to some extent resolved by an election to treat a sub-fund as a separate trust. The extensive procedural rules are contained in TCGA 1992, Schedule 4ZA, added by FA 2006, Schedule 12. The trustees may make the election—the fund is known as a sub-fund settlement. The consequences are spelt out in Schedule 4ZA, paragraphs 17–22. These matters include:

(1) timing—the sub-fund settlement is treated as having been created at the time when the sub-fund election is treated as having taken effect. Such an election cannot be treated as having taken effect before 6 April 2006 (paragraph 17);

(2) trusteeship (paragraph 18)—a person (T) holding the property in the sub-fund will normally cease to be a trustee of the principal settlement. A trustee of the principal settlement is not normally a trustee of the sub-fund settlement;

[41] The solution seems to be either to ensure that the appointed fund is truly separate and to pay the tax resulting from the deemed disposal of the assets appointed, or to retain control of the subsidiary part by having joint trustees. See also Statement of Practice SP 7/84.
[42] [1983] STC 721, (1983) 57 TC 401.
[43] [1983] STC 517, (1983) 57 TC 301; see Ive [1984] BTR 55.
[44] [1983] STC 517, 527, (1983) 57 TC 301, 321.
[45] [1991] STC 490, (1991) 64 TC 315.
[46] Capital Gains Manual, paras 33296 and 33301.

(3)   absolute entitlement (paragraph 19)—when the sub-fund election takes effect, trustees of the sub-fund settlement are treated as having become absolutely entitled to the property comprised in that settlement as against the trustees of the principal settlement; and

(4)   interaction (paragraphs 20–22)—there are further rules on the interaction of the sub-fund election with the rules in section 71 and on migration and the timing and valuation of the property (sections 87–91).

40.5.1 Variation of Trust: Transfer to Another Settlement[47]

When a trust is varied under the Variation of Trusts Act 1958 the variation itself is probably not a disposal; but if the terms of the variation provide for any actual or deemed disposal, then there is a disposal.[48] Since the better view is that it is the order of the court, rather than the arrangement, which is the variation, the date of the disposal will be that of the order.[49] Where some of the beneficiaries are *sui juris* and the court's consent is sought on behalf of those who are not *sui juris*, the agreement among the former group is presumably in the nature of a conditional contract. Where the property reverts to the settlor on the death of a life tenant, the disposal and reacquisition take place not at the value on the death but at the trustee's adjusted base cost (section 73(1)(b)).

40.6   Disposals During Trust Period

Gains or losses will accrue to the trustees on the disposal of assets in the course of administration, as where the trustees sell some of the trust investments to buy new ones. The trustees are chargeable on their chargeable gains, less allowable losses for the year of assessment, in much the same way as individuals. For more on the annual exempt amount and rate, see §40.1.2 above.

40.6.1 Reliefs[50]

Where the asset to be disposed of is a dwelling house, an exemption may be claimed by trustees if the dwelling house is owned by them and has been the main private residence of a person entitled to occupy it under the terms of the trust, or who is allowed by the trustees to occupy it and would be entitled to the income from the house or from the proceeds of sale (section 225). Where trustees of a discretionary trust in exercise of their discretion allow a beneficiary of the trust to occupy the house, the beneficiary is entitled to occupy the house under the terms of the trust since he has a right to remain in occupation until asked

---

[47] See also McCutcheon [1980] BTR 174; and Underhill and Hayton, *Law of Trusts and Trustees*, 16th edn (Butterworths, 2002) at 501.
[48] But note TCGA 1992, s 76(2); and *Hoare Trustees v Gardner* [1978] STC 89, (1978) 52 TC 53.
[49] Lord Reid and Lord Wilberforce in *IRC v Holmden* [1968] AC 685, 701–02, 710–13.
[50] Reinvestment relief was available before 1998: TCGA 1992, s 164B.

to leave by the trustees.[51] The relief applies also to property held by PRs but occupied both before and after the death by an individual entitled to an absolute or limited interest in the proceeds of sale.[52] On restrictions introduced in 2004, see above §34.7.6.

40.6.2 Losses

In general, trustees may use their losses in much the same way as individuals, ie by setting them off against gains of the same year or carrying them forward. As we shall see below (at §40.7.1), further rules allow trust gains to be carried over to a beneficiary who becomes absolutely entitled as against the trustee. TCGA 1992, section 79A restricts this relief where the following conditions apply:

(1) there has been a transfer to the trustees and allowable expenditure has been reduced because of a claim to holdover relief (see §§36.3 and 36.4 above) in relation to that earlier disposal to the trustees;
(2) the transferor (or any connected person) on that earlier disposal has at any time acquired an interest in the settled property, or entered into an arrangement to acquire such an interest; and
(3) any person has become entitled to receive consideration in connection with that acquisition or arrangement.

These three conditions show that the legislation is concerned with situations in which the trust has losses, but the gains come from assets previously held outside the trust but passed into the trust at a low value using the holdover relief.

The effect of section 79A is that when the trustees dispose of that asset, or of any other asset on which the gain has been deferred, the trustees may not use any of their available losses against the resulting gain; for this purpose the gain means the whole of the gain and not just the part deferred (section 79A(2)). Without some such rule, individuals with large potential capital gains would be able to buy their way into trusts with actual or potential losses and then use the trust losses to offset the gains arising on the subsequent disposal of the assets. Section 79A does not prevent the holdover of the gain but does prevent the use of trust losses. So whereas the rule in §40.7.1 (discussed below) is designed to restrict relief for losses brought into the trust, this rule deals with the opposite device of gains being brought in.

40.7 Deemed Disposals

In addition to the actual disposals that arise in the course of the administration of the trust, there are two principal[53] deemed disposals. These are the vesting of trust property in

---

[51] *Sansom v Peay* [1976] STC 494.
[52] TCGA 1992, s 225A, ex ESC D5.
[53] There is also a deemed disposal where property subject to charitable trusts ceases to be so (TCGA 1992, s 256(2)).

a beneficiary (section 71) and the termination of a life interest in possession on death (section 72). Although these are deemed disposals, any tax due will be charged on the trustees in the usual way, ie after taking account of any losses or annual exempt amount that may be available to them. It is Revenue practice usually to allow holdover relief on deemed disposals where a gain would arise, although strictly it is unclear whether such an election is competent. Rollover is, in any case, currently limited to:

(1)   transfers of business assets (section 165); or
(2)   transfers chargeable to IHT (section 260);[54] or
(3)   certain exempt transfers by trustees of accumulation and maintenance settlements.

The value at which the deemed disposal takes place is the market value of the trust assets on the date of disposal. Hypothetical costs of such a disposal and acquisition are excluded, but actual costs are not.[55]

40.7.1 Person Becoming Absolutely Entitled Against the Trustee: Section 71

40.7.1.1 Deemed Disposal by Trustees

When a person becomes absolutely entitled to any settled property as against the trustees, whether because the trust itself ends or the property leaves the settlement through the exercise of a power of advancement, the trustees are deemed to dispose of all the assets forming part of the settled property to which the beneficiary becomes entitled at their market value, and immediately to reacquire them at the same value.[56] The deemed disposal, in effect, ends the capital gains regime of the trust and commences that of the recipient under a bare trust, even though the assets themselves remain with the trustees. It follows that any gains or losses arising on the deemed disposal will be those of the trust, whilst any subsequent gains or losses arising on the assets concerned will be those of the beneficiary. The deemed disposal also occurs if the person would be absolutely entitled as against the trustee but for being an infant or other person under disability (section 71(3)).

40.7.1.2 Impossibility of Having Children

If a trust deed vests property in the children of a settlor on the attainment of a specified age by the last child to be born to the settlor, there is a CGT disposal when the last child reaches the specified age. For CGT purposes, the test is applied on the assumption that a person is capable of having a child so long as that person is alive. In *Figg v Clarke*,[57] this was held to occur when the father died in 1990. The trustees had argued that the impossibility of having more children had occurred in 1977, being the date on which the last

---

[54]   Eg transfers of assets to trustees of discretionary settlements.
[55]   *Allison v Murray* [1975] STC 524, [1975] 3 All ER 561, (1975) 51 TC 57. One term in a variation of a trust required A to take out a life insurance policy and pay a premium; the court held that the actual expenditure of the premium was not deductible since it was incurred for the purchase of trust assets of another beneficiary's interest.
[56]   TCGA 1992, s 71; on deductible expenditure, note s 64(1).
[57]   [1996] STC 247, (1996) 68 TC 645; for an earlier discussion of hysterectomy and castration as events causing the disposal, see [1968] BTR 56.

child attained the age of 21, it being impossible for the father to have any further children (on 17 November 1964 he had suffered an accident as a result of which he was paralysed from the chest down). Thus, the fertile octogenarian who has been removed from the scenario in the rule against perpetuities lives on here. One reason is that if it were otherwise, there would be a deemed disposal whenever a person became infertile, an event of which taxpayer and trustees might or might not be aware.[58] The trustees pointed out that a court may order that assets be passed to beneficiaries on the basis of evidence of the impossibility of there being any future members of the class of beneficiaries. If the beneficiaries go to court and seek the administrative jurisdiction of the court, and obtain an order for distribution, there would seem to be a deemed disposal thanks to the order.

40.7.1.3 Ceasing to Be Settled Property on Death of Life Tenant

Where the property ceases to be settled on the death of certain life tenants—principally in relation to an interest in possession trust settled before 22 March 2006—there is a deemed disposal, but neither chargeable gain nor allowable loss accrues (section 73). Where such a life tenant dies but that person's interest extends to only part of the property, a chargeable gain or allowable loss will arise in respect of the part not represented by the deceased's interest (sections 73(2), 74(3)).

40.7.1.4 Crystallisation of Deferred Charge

If, however, a chargeable gain were held over when the settlement was created, the death of the life tenant may crystallise the gain. The gain will be computed by applying the normal rules or, if lower, the held-over gain (section 74). The gain will be crystallised only in respect of assets that continue to be held at the date of death. This gain may itself be held over, since there is also a transfer of value subject to IHT (section 260). However, if an asset passes to the surviving spouse of the deceased beneficiary (or the surviving spouse becomes the life tenant), the exemption from IHT prevents there being a chargeable transfer and so section 260 cannot apply.

40.7.1.5 Tracing

The disposal is of those assets to which the person becomes entitled. In *Chinn v Collins*,[59] where a beneficiary assigned his interest to X, who became entitled to a holding in a company but who was then obliged to sell a similar holding to the beneficiary, it was held that the beneficiary became entitled to the shares received from X.

40.7.1.6 Transfer of Net Losses to Beneficiary

Where a person become absolutely entitled to settled property as against the trustees, any allowable loss which has accrued to the trustees in respect of that property, or is represented by the property to which the person has become entitled, is transferred to the beneficiary, in so far as it has not been used by the trustees against gains accruing to the trustees on that disposal, ie what the statue calls 'pre-entitlement gains' (section 71(2), (2A)). In addition,

---

[58] [1996] STC 247, 262, per Blackburne J.
[59] [1981] STC 1, [1981] 1 All ER 189, (1981) 54 TC 311; on the Court of Appeal judgment, see Blom-Cooper [1979] BTR 301.

expenditure incurred by the trustees in transferring assets to a beneficiary who has become entitled to those assets is treated as expenditure by the beneficiary and may be put against the consideration received on the subsequent disposal of the asset by that beneficiary (section 64(1)(b)). The transfer of losses from the trustees to a beneficiary is mandatory. The trustees cannot set the losses off against their own later gains.

Pre-entitlement gains are those arising to the trustees on the deemed disposal itself, or at any time earlier during the same year of assessment.[60] If the trustees cannot use the loss in this way it is transferred to the beneficiary, but subject to the very substantial restriction that it may be set off only against a gain arising on the disposal of the same asset. To avoid some problems, the loss may be set off against gains arising from an asset derived from that very asset, but this applies only where the asset is land.[61] Rules prescribe when the beneficiary may roll the loss forward (section 71(2D)(c)). For transfers to beneficiaries before 16 June 1999, a more generous rule applied.[62] Where cash is distributed to a beneficiary, a strict reading of the statute suggests that the beneficiary takes over the loss only where the cash represents the proceeds of the sale of an asset sold at a loss.

40.7.1.7 Allocation

The apportionment of losses amongst beneficiaries is not addressed by statute. Revenue practice suggests that officers should accept any reasonable basis of apportionment adopted by the trustees.[63]

40.7.2 *Termination of a Life Interest in Possession on Death but Settlement Continues: Section 72*

The second deemed disposal and reacquisition by the trustees is when a life interest in possession terminates on the death of the person beneficially entitled to the interest (section 72(1)(1)). This deemed disposal will relate to property remaining subject to the settlement; property leaving the settlement will fall within the first deemed disposal. If, for example, property is settled on A for life or until marriage, with remainder to B for life, with remainder to C absolutely, then on A's death there will be a deemed disposal of the settled property at market value. However, consistent with the general principle that no chargeable gains should arise on death where the life tenant is subject to IHT on the value of the trust property (principally in the case of an interest in possession trust settled before 22 March 2006), no chargeable gain or allowable loss arises (section 72(1)(b))—except where a chargeable gain was held over on the disposal of the assets to the trustees. Since 5 April 1982 there has been no deemed disposal where the life interest terminates otherwise than on the death of the life tenant; thus the trustees' acquisition cost is unchanged. Since this CGT 'uplift' applies only on death, it is debatable whether any IHT advantages of an earlier termination are outweighed by the CGT disadvantages.[64]

---

[60] TCGA 1992, s 71(2A), added in 1999.
[61] TCGA 1992, s 71(2)(b)(ii); the rules are elaborated in subs 71(2B).
[62] TCGA 1992, s 71(2), original version.
[63] CG Manual, para 37205.
[64] Potter and Monroe, *op cit*, §6-20.

40.7.2.1 Life Interest in Possession

'Life interest', as such, is not defined, so that it must be taken to bear its usual technical meaning; the distinctions between a lease and a life estate must be observed. However, statute declares that 'life interest' includes a right under the settlement to the income of, or to the use or occupation of, settled property for the life of a person other than the person entitled to the right; as such, a life interest *pur autre vie* is included (section 72(3)). The term also includes a right to income under the settlement for lives. A lease for lives does not fall within the provision, since settled property is defined as any property held in trust, and a lease for lives does not operate behind a trust.[65] There is excluded from the definition of a life interest any right which is contingent on the exercise of the discretion of the trustee or the discretion of some other person. In view of the further requirement that the life interest be in possession, and of the principle that the objects of a discretionary trust do not have any interest in the trust property,[66] this provision may appear superfluous.

An interest in possession is not further defined. Generally, an interest is in possession if it gives an immediate entitlement to the income as it arises. A duty or power to withhold the income negatives possession. Thus a power to accumulate the income negatives possession, save where the accumulation is for the person with the interest. A power to revoke the entitlement or to appoint another does not affect the immediate entitlement to the income since, until the power is exercised, the income belongs to the beneficiary.[67] On the termination of a life interest on an occasion other than death of the life tenant, there is now no disposal under these rules. At one time other events gave rise to deemed disposals.

40.7.2.2 Discretionary Trusts

There is no deemed disposal on the termination of a beneficiary's rights under a discretionary trust since the beneficiary has no life interest in possession. Gains or losses will, however, arise when the trustees dispose of trust property in the course of administration, or when they exercise their powers over capital to cause settled property to cease to be settled. In the early days of CGT a deemed disposal took place every 15 years.[68]

40.7.2.3 Life Interest in Part of Settled Property

There is deemed disposal on the death of the life tenant whether the life interest in possession is all or any part of settled property.[69] Where the interest relates only to part of the property, there is a deemed disposal only of that part. A life interest which is a right to part of the income of settled property is treated as an interest in a corresponding part of the property.[70] Thus, if property is held on trust for A and B for their lives with remainders over, A's death will cause a deemed disposal of one half of each of the assets forming part of the settled property. If, however, two settlements had been created, one with life interest

---

[65] Law of Property Act 1925, s 149.

[66] *Gartside v IRC* [1968] AC 553, [1968] 1 All ER 121.

[67] Quaere whether trustees can make a binding decision to appoint income to someone before it has arisen.

[68] FA 1965, s 25(7).

[69] See Statement of Practice SP D10—practice where part can be identified with specific assets or assets appropriated within three months.

[70] See *Pexton v Bell* [1976] STC 301, [1976] 2 All ER 914, (1976) 51 TC 457; noted by Milne [1976] BTR 257.

to A and the other with life interest to B, there would be a deemed disposal of all the assets forming part of A's settlement. If there is a life interest in income from part of the settled property and no right of recourse to, or to the income of, the remainder of the settled property, that part is treated as a separate settlement. 'Part', in this context, means fraction and not necessarily a separated piece, so that four one-quarter shares of the income for life[71] create four separate settlements.[72] Normally, an annuity is not treated as a life interest, notwithstanding that it is payable out of or charged on settled property or the income of settled property (section 72(3)). However, it will be so treated if it is created by the settlement and some or all of the settled property is appropriated by the trustees as the exclusive fund out of which the annuity is payable (section 72(4)). The fund so appropriated is treated as a separate settlement.

40.8   Disposal of a Beneficial Interest

40.8.1 General

The beneficiary's interest in a settlement is an asset for CGT purposes. Therefore, if property is held on trust for A for life with remainder to B, and A sells or gives away the life interest, A has made a disposal of an asset under general principles. The same is true of a gift or sale by B of B's interest. However, under section 76, any gain arising on the disposal of an interest under a settlement is exempt from a charge to CGT.[73] The way in which section 76 operates is to recognise the disposal but deem it not to be a chargeable gain. For this purpose, 'an interest under a settlement' includes an annuity, life interest or reversionary interest. The disposal of an interest under a bare trust is the disposal not of an interest under a settlement but of the underlying asset.[74]

Exemption from liability does not apply in the following five circumstances:

(1)   The person disposing of the interest acquired it by purchase and is not the person for whose benefit the interest was created (section 76(2)).
(2)   The interest on which the disposal is made was acquired by purchase by a previous holder (section 76(2)).
(3)   The trustees of the settlement concerned are neither resident nor ordinarily resident in the UK (section 85(1)).

---

[71] Assuming they are not joint tenants, yet the wording of s 72(4) stresses that there must be no right of recourse to the income. Quaere the future right of recourse by virtue of survivorship.

[72] *Pexton v Bell* [1976] STC 301, [1976] 2 All ER 914, (1976) 51 TC 457; *Allison v Murray* [1975] STC 524, [1975] 3 All ER 561, (1975) 51 TC 57; hence, the termination of one share causes a deemed disposal of that quarter share only, and not of the whole settled property.

[73] TCGA 1992, s 76(1); on release of power to revoke, see Peacock (1998) *Private Client Business* 16 (concluding that this comes within s 76(1) and so is safe from CGT).

[74] TCGA 1992, ss 60 and 68; see also *Harthan v Mason* [1980] STC 94, (1980) 53 TC 272.

(4) The disposal took place at a time when the trustees were resident or ordinarily resident in the UK, but the trustees subsequently cease to be so resident.[75]

(5) A deemed disposal on sale of trust interest: see §40.8.2.

If the predictable life of the person by reference to whose life the duration of the interest is measured is 50 years or less at the date the interest was acquired, the asset will be a wasting asset and special computational rules apply (section 44). The form of the charging provision in section 76(2) is that a charge arises when a person becomes 'absolutely entitled as against the trustee to any settled property'. Thus, a CGT charge arises when assets pass to a beneficiary out of a trust, the interest in which was purchased by the beneficiary. The consideration for such a deemed disposal is the market value of the property received by the beneficiary, less any CGT charge on the trustees under section 71(1).

Variation of trusts involving the transfer of beneficial interests will not cause a disposal of those interests, provided they are all interests under the same settlement and none was acquired for money or money's worth. If, however, an interest under one settlement is used as consideration for the acquisition of a beneficial interest under another, very different results may follow. There may, moreover, be a deemed disposal by the trustees.

40.8.2 *Deemed Disposal on Sale of Trust Interest*

FA 2000 tackled schemes which exploited section 76 by creating TCGA 1992, section 76A and Schedule 4A. Schedule 4A applies where there is a disposal for consideration of an interest in settled property (defined broadly in paragraphs 2 and 3) and the trust is a 'settlor-interested settlement', ie satisfies conditions analogous to those in former section 77 (see paragraph 7(4)). Other conditions are that the trustees are UK resident for the year in which the interest is disposed of (paragraph 5) and that any 'settlor' has been resident or ordinarily resident in the UK in that or the previous five years. In such circumstances there is a deemed disposal and reacquisition by the trustees of the relevant underlying asset (on which see paragraph 8) when the interest is disposed of. A double charge under this and section 76A is prevented by paragraph 10.

There were two schemes at which this rule is aimed. Under the first, settlors would settle assets pregnant with gain and retain an interest themselves, thereby preventing any charge when the trust was created. The settlors would then sell the beneficial interest and so realise the value of the assets tax free. The deemed disposal at market value prevents this by charging the gains to the settlors.

The other scheme involved the 1999 rules (above §40.2.2) restricting the right of the trust to use its losses. As the Inland Revenue Notes to the Finance Bill 2000 (paragraph 20) put it:

> Valuable assets are placed in trust, a contingent interest in the settled property is created in favour of the settlor, entitling him or her to acquire the trust property after a short period of time. The interest is then sold to the trustees of another trust which has unused losses. The trustees of the

---

[75] TCGA 1992, s 80; where an interest in a resident settlement has been disposed of subject to the exemption, the trustees may be deemed to realise chargeable gains if the settlement subsequently becomes non-resident (s 85(1)).

second trust subsequently acquire the assets from the first trust, using holdover relief. The assets are then sold by the trustees of the second trust who offset the losses against the gains.

Because the gains deemed to be realised are now charged to the settlor, holdover relief (see §§36.3 and 36.4 above) will not be available and a central part of the scheme collapses. There are rules for dealing with long-drawn-out disposals (paragraph 13).

41

Shares, Securities and Other Fungible Assets

41.1 Introduction

Shares give rise to a number of distinct issues in capital gains legislation. First, there is the boundary between capital gain and ordinary income. The UK tax system, like many others, treats a number of situations in which profits arise when shares (or other assets) are sold as giving rise to ordinary income. This is because of the ease with which the market can create different ways of achieving the same economic result.[1] Secondly, although CGT usually requires a disposal, computation problems arise when there is a disposal of part of a holding of shares acquired at different times (a composite holding). This problem extends to all fungible assets. Thirdly, there are a number of ways in which value may be extracted from shares without an actual disposal, and so the system creates a deemed disposal (see above at §36.6). Fourthly, the opposite problem occurs where there is a disposal but the tax system does not want there to be a charge to tax just then and so grants a deferral. Many of these issues also arise in connection with securities. In this chapter it will be assumed that the term 'share' includes securities, unless otherwise stated. One should note for corporation tax purposes that the loan relationship regime applies to securities but not to shares; where that regime applies, there is no room for the CGT rules about to be considered.

Shares and other financial assets are very significant as a source of CGT. According to HMRC's statistics,[2] in 2012–13, 69% of the total gains realised came from financial assets

---

[1] Eg Warren (1993) 107 *Harvard LR* 460 (financial contract innovation).

[2] HMRC, *Capital Gains Tax Statistics*, October 2015, available at https://www.gov.uk/government/statistics/capital-gains-tax-statistics.

including quoted and unquoted shares. UK and foreign shares not listed on the London stock exchange accounted for 52% of total chargeable gains.

41.2   Identification Rules for Shares, Securities and Other Fungible Assets

If T buys 100 shares in BP and later sells them, the CGT system has no difficulty in seeing that T has bought and sold 100 BP shares; the problem arises if T has built up the holding over the years, eg by buying 10 shares each year, and decides to sell only 50—what is the correct base cost? The purpose of the identification rules is to find the appropriate cost base for the shares being disposed of; this will enable the correct initial cost to be determined. Such rules are also needed to apply indexation relief for corporation tax. Unfortunately, the history of CGT has been so turbulent that different identification rules have applied at different times. One result of the 2008 simplification for CGT has been a major simplification of these rules for CGT but not for corporation tax.

These rules apply to 'securities', ie shares or securities of a company, with the important exemption of qualifying corporate bonds (which are exempt from CGT under section 115) and securities caught by the income tax accrued income or offshore fund rules (sections 103(3), 108). They also apply to any other assets where they are of a nature to be dealt in without identifying the particular asset disposed of or acquired, eg commodities or foreign currency. Where such assets are disposed of today, it may be necessary to apply different identification rules for different issues.

41.2.1 Range of Choice

A tax system has a range of such rules to choose from. It may simply take a first in, first out (FIFO) approach or a last in, first out (LIFO) approach, or it may mix the rules by applying LIFO for a certain period and then FIFO for another. Alternatively, it may treat the whole as a pool, growing or contracting as shares are acquired or disposed of; anything short of a complete disposal of the holding will then be a part disposal of the pool. It may also decide to permit the identification of actual shares actually disposed of. Today, the FIFO and LIFO approaches apply to acquisitions since 5 April 1998; the pool approach applies to shares acquired between 1982 and 1998; and identification of the actual shares applies to shares held on 6 April 1965.

41.2.2 Current Rules

41.2.2.1 Basic Rules

The current CGT rules are different from those for corporation tax. CGT uses one basic rule: that all the shares, etc of the same class acquired by the same person in the same capacity are indistinguishable parts of a single asset growing or diminishing on the occasions on which additional securities are acquired or some securities of the class are disposed of. So if A acquired 2,000 shares at £5 a share (cost £10,000) and then acquired another

1,000 shares at £15 a share (cost £15,000), A now has a holding of 3,000 shares at a cost of £25,000. If A now sells half of them, the relevant acquisition cost is half of the total cost, making £12,500. The net gain will be taxed at 10%/20%. This applies even though the transfer is of particular identifiable securities. Securities which are issued on terms restricting the holder's right to dispose, eg to an employee, are pooled separately, provided the restrictions remain (section 104(4)).

This basic rule is subject to two timing rules:

(1) *Disposals on or before acquisitions made the same day* (section 105). These are treated as a single transaction. If Anne has 100 BP shares, and then goes into the market on Tuesday and buys a further 100 on Tuesday morning, and then sells 100 on Tuesday afternoon, she is treated as selling the ones she bought in the morning.

(2) *Disposals and acquisitions made within the following 30 days* (section 106A(5)). Within the 30-day period a FIFO system applies (section 106A(4)). This is aimed at the time-honoured device of 'bed and breakfasting' for shares. Under this device, shares could be sold on Tuesday and repurchased on Wednesday. This might trigger a gain or a loss. One reason to trigger a gain might be to make full use of the annual exempt amount, or to set a gain off against a loss already realised; a reason to realise a loss is to avoid the CGT ban on carrying losses backward to another year.[3] Under rule (2), if John has 100 BP shares and sells them on 31 March, his disposal will be treated as effective unless he buys 100 BP shares at any time during April.

Rules (1) and (2) apply only if the sale and the acquisition are of the same class of share in the same company and held by the person in the same capacity;[4] so the acquisition of a different class of share or of shares in a different company will not trigger either rule. While a person who holds some shares beneficially and others as trustee is clearly holding in separate capacities, some questions arises where eg a husband and wife hold some shares beneficially and others jointly. On balance, the Revenue view that the joint holding belonging partly to one spouse and partly to the other is treated in each case in the same capacity seems sensible, but some have raised technical difficulties.[5] The rules apply only to shares or other securities and so not to land or chattels. Since it is essential for beneficial ownership to pass on the initial sale, it may be difficult to persuade the Revenue of the genuineness of a bed and breakfast transaction for other assets; shares have a genuine market with genuine prices in which to operate.

The normal rule in section 105(1) is that where two holdings of shares are acquired on the same day, they are treated as a single acquisition and so have an average acquisition cost. If T later makes a part disposal of the shares, T may now elect that the non-share scheme shares be treated as sold first. The point is that these non-scheme shares are likely to have a higher acquisition costs and so give rise to a lower charge to CGT. A scheme to get round the bed and breakfast rules succeeded in *Davies v Hicks*.[6] It—and several simi-

---

[3] For discussion see Butler [2002] BTR 21.
[4] On employee shares subject to restrictions, see TCGA 1992, s 104(4).
[5] Thexton (1999) 143 *Taxation* 170.
[6] [2005] EWHC 847 (Ch), [2005] STC 850.

lar schemes notified to HMRC—was reversed by excluding one rule (section 106A(5)) in certain international situations. Shares within this category form a pool on their own.

These rules have made bed and breakfasting ineffective as a way of realising losses. An alternative plan is to sell the shares but have the immediate reacquisition carried by one's spouse or civil partner (with whom one is living). If necessary, one can use the proceeds of the sale to fund the purchase after having first given them to one's spouse or civil partner. This has become known as 'bed and spousing'. We wait to see whether this is caught by TCGA 1992, section 16A (above §33.10.3).

41.2.2.2 Election

Special rules apply where T acquires some of the shares in the open market and others under the EIS (see §41.8) or a tax-advantaged share option scheme.[7] These are designed to help employees.

41.2.2.3 Corporation Tax

Corporation tax retains some of these reliefs and therefore the position is more complex. It has the general pooling rule in section 104. It then uses the same or earlier day rule in section 105 (CGT timing rule (1)). The general rules are in section 107: instead of CGT's 30-day timing rule (2), it has a 10-day rule (section 107(3)); but in section 108, its own definition of 'relevant securities', we read that securities are to be identified with securities acquired within the previous 12 months and, subject to this, with securities acquired at a later date rather than an earlier date—so reducing the effect of indexation reliefs. Sections 110 *et seq* explain how the indexation allowance works for corporation tax; the value of the pool must be adjusted for inflation on each occasion there is a disposal or acquisition (section 110). The rules expressly cover calls on shares (section 113) and payment for options (section 114). Section 109 deals with pre-April 1982 share pools. Pre-1965 acquisitions may also have to be considered (below §43.6). From 1983 to 1987 a system of parallel pooling existed, but only for companies. This was a matter of election and was intended to help companies with computerised records of large holdings. This too is dealt with in the corporation tax rules (section 112). The lesson to be learnt from the corporation tax rules is that the UK tax system tries very hard to adapt to keep track of the changes it makes—and probably makes too many changes.

41.3   Capital Reorganisations and Distributions

41.3.1 Summary

A company makes a capital distribution if it makes any distribution in money or money's worth which would not be treated as income in the hands of the recipient for purposes of income tax (section 122(5)(b)). A capital distribution is a disposal or part disposal of the shares held, the consideration being the amount received by the shareholder

---

[7] TCGA 1992, ss 105A and 105B, added by FA 2002, s 50. See also discussion above in chapter seventeen.

(section 122(1)). Taxable capital distributions commonly include distributions in liquidation, repayment of share capital, repurchase by a company of its own share capital and certain capital distributions by foreign companies of a type unknown to UK company law.[8] There will be no disposal if the capital distribution consists of shares or securities issued as part of capital reorganisation (such as scrip or rights issue) or, on election, where the capital distribution is 'small'.

41.3.2 Reorganisations

Reorganisation is not treated as a disposal of a shareholding (section 127). Reorganisation occurs if there is a 'reorganisation or reduction of share capital'; this is stated to include (a) the allotment of shares or debentures in proportion to shareholdings, and (b) any alteration of share rights—assuming that there are at least two classes.[9] As the word 'include' implies, (a) and (b) are simply illustrations; the guiding principle appears to be that there is continued identity of the shareholders, holding their shares in the same proportions.[10] Although a reduction in share capital is reorganisation, both the paying-off of redeemable share capital[11] and the redemption of shares other than by the issue of new shares or debentures are specifically excluded, since in both cases income rules apply (section 126(3)). The reorganisation rules do not apply to the extent that the shareholder receives consideration other than the new holding (such as a cash payment) from the company, or any consideration from the other shareholders (section 128(3)).

41.3.2.1 Bonus (Scrip) Issues

Where new shares or securities are allotted to shareholders without consideration, the new shares or debentures are treated as forming one combined asset with the shares previously held, and make a new holding, but with the old date of acquisition and acquisition cost (but see scrip dividends, below).[12] There is neither acquisition of the new shares or debentures, nor disposal of the original shares. Therefore, on a bonus issue of shares of the same class as the original holding, the bonus shares are simply added to those already held. On any subsequent disposal of part of the holding, gains or losses are computed by taking the appropriate proportion of the cost of the original shares. Suppose that A holds 100 shares in X Co, bought at £2 each. If X Co issues bonus shares on a one-for-two basis, A will now have 150 shares; the 50 new shares are simply added to A's holding and A's base cost of £200 is unchanged.

---

[8] See chapter sixty-one below for more detail.

[9] TCGA 1992, s 126; an allotment to debenture holders does not qualify.

[10] *Dunstan v Young Austen Young Ltd* [1989] STC 69; 61 TC 448. On US approach to reorganisation, see Bittker and Lokken, *Federal Taxation of Income, Estates and Gifts* (Warren, Gorman & Lamont, 1989) ch 94; and Tiley [1988] BTR 124 *et seq*.

[11] It is unclear whether shares must be expressly redeemable, or whether the general company law power to buy back shares in certain circumstances makes all shares redeemable.

[12] TCGA 1992, s 127. Shares issued as stock dividends (and so taxable as income) are treated as acquired for the appropriate amount in cash pursuant to TCGA 1992, ss 141, 142. Special rules also apply to certain shares acquired as an employee.

41.3.2.2 Rights Issues

If the person provides consideration for the new shares or debentures, as on a rights issue, again the holding forms a single asset but the consideration paid is added to the expenditure incurred on the holding (section 128(1)). Thus, if B holds 1,000 shares in Y Co, bought at £3 each, B's base cost is £3,000. Y Co allows shareholders to buy one new share for every 10 at the special price of £5 a share. If B exercises the rights and pays £500 for the extra 100 shares, B will have a holding of 1,100 shares with a combined base cost of £3,500. For the purposes of the indexation allowance, still relevant for corporation tax, the consideration paid is treated as a separate item of relevant expenditure incurred when it is actually incurred and not as having been incurred on the acquisition date of the original shares.[13]

Scrip dividends are treated as separate acquisitions. FA 1998 changed the pooling rules in TCGA 1992, section 142 so that the shares received are treated as separate assets in their own right acquired at the appropriate amount in cash. If the shareholder elects to take the stock dividend and the market value of the scrip exceeds the market value of the original shares, value will flow from the original shares into the scrip shares. It is a nice question whether a CGT liability can arise.[14] Indexation relief for corporation tax may arise.

41.3.2.3 Anti-avoidance Rules

(1) *Consideration not new.* The consideration will not be 'new'—and will not be added to the base cost of the holding—if it originates from the shares themselves rather than from the shareholder, for example if it consists of the surrender, cancellation or alteration of the original shares, or if the new shares are paid up out of the assets of the company or out of a dividend or any other distribution declared—but not made— out of the company's assets. This is to prevent uplift in the base cost by the use of the company's assets.

(2) *Need for increase in value of holding.* Any new consideration, eg that payable under a rights issue, forms part of the allowable cost of the shares only to the extent that the reorganised shareholding is more valuable than the original.[15] This restriction counters schemes intended to secure relief for losses on loans.[16] There could be difficulties for a minority shareholder in an unquoted company subscribing for a rights issue, since the value of his minority holding is unlikely to increase by as much as the amount subscribed.

---

[13] TCGA 1992, ss 126, 131, 132.
[14] Ie under TCGA 1990, s 29; see Conway, (1998) 142 *Taxation* 270, and Ghosh (1999) 143 *Taxation* 64 (for liability arising); and Southern, (1998) 142 *Taxation* 347 (against liability arising).
[15] TCGA 1992, s 128(2) proviso.
[16] See *IRC v Burmah Oil Co Ltd* [1980] STC 731; although this decision was reversed by the House of Lords at [1982] STC 30, the legislation was not removed.

41.3.3 Computation

41.3.3.1 Part Disposal of the New Holding

The basic rule is that the apportionment of costs is made pro rata to market values at the date of disposal.[17] However, this does not apply if the holding consists of more than one class of share or debenture and one or more of the elements of the new holding is quoted. If any of the classes are listed on a recognised stock exchange, the allowable costs are apportioned pro rata to the market values of each element on the first day of market quotation (section 130).

41.3.3.2 Unpaid Calls

Where there are unpaid calls in respect of any of the shares or securities in the new holding, adjustments may be required when apportioning allowable costs. The amounts unpaid are treated as part of the allowable costs to be apportioned, but the market values used in the apportionment are similarly increased.[18] For indexation purposes, calls paid are treated as expenditure incurred when the shares are acquired, unless payable more than 12 months after that date (section 131).

41.3.3.3 Rights Issue—Sale of Rights

A sale of rights under a rights issue is an example of a taxable capital distribution. The distribution is not a new holding; instead, the shareholder is treated as having disposed of an interest in the holding (section 122) and as having received consideration equal to the market value of the distribution (section 17(1)(a)). The sale of rights under a rights issue will be treated as a part disposal.[19] There will similarly be a part disposal if, on a bonus or rights issue, the company sells fractional entitlements on the market and allocates the cash to shareholders.

41.3.3.4 Exception for Small Distributions

The amount of the distribution is compared with the value of the shares in respect of which the distribution is made (section 122(2), (5)). In practice, the distribution is treated as small if it amounts to less than 5% of the value of the shares, valued after the distribution is made. If the recipient so elects, the amount received is deducted from the allowable expenditure. There is no need for the *amount* of the distribution to be small.[20]

41.3.3.5 Liquidation

Where a liquidator makes a distribution of the entire assets of the company to the shareholders, there is a disposal of their shares for a consideration equal to the value of the assets so distributed.[21] Usually, however, the liquidator will make a number of successive

---

[17] TCGA 1992, s 129(1). This provision relates only to the cost of the original shares, not to the cost of the rights issue; this is difficult to reconcile with the 'one asset' principle of the reorganisation rules.

[18] TCGA 1992, ss 129(2), 130(2).

[19] TCGA 1992, s 123 (whether or not company has made a provisional allotment; a relaxed valuation rule applies to disposal of rights).

[20] *O'Rourke v Binks* [1991] STC 455, (1991) 65 TC 165; size is a relative concept not an absolute one.

[21] This is also a disposal by the liquidator on behalf of the company.

distributions to the shareholders. Since each distribution is a part disposal of the shares, great practical difficulties arise because of the need to find the market value of the shareholding after each such distribution.

41.3.3.6 Winding Up

A more fundamental problem is whether there is a notional disposal by the company when winding up commences. The company ceases to be beneficially entitled at that point, and a trust arises in favour of creditors and contributors; accordingly, it is unclear whether beneficial ownership is in suspense[22] or passes to the shareholders.[23] If the latter is correct, the holders become entitled to receive the assets, so that there is a disposal by the company to the shareholders when winding up commences. In practice the Revenue treat the shareholders as making a part disposal as and when cash or other property is received. Since the 'in suspense' view is to be preferred,[24] the Revenue practice is correct.

41.4   Conversion of Securities: Section 132 Deferral

The technique of treating the original and the new holding as the same asset is applied to the conversion of securities. These transactions are dealt with separately in the legislation since securities are distinct from share capital. Under section 132, there is no disposal where debentures are converted into shares or into other securities, whether or not the taxpayer could have those securities redeemed for cash as an alternative to conversion.[25] There is, however, a part disposal where the person also receives a premium in addition to new securities—unless the consideration is small, ie, in practice, less than 5% of the value of the securities.[26]

41.5   Company Reconstructions and Section 135 Deferrals

In certain situations the tax system decides that there should not be a disposal for CGT purposes even though assets, shares or securities are disposed of. Today these rules apply only where there are bona fide commercial reasons for the transactions (section 137); there is a statutory clearance procedure (section 138, see below at §41.5.3).

---

[22] *IRC v Olive Mill Ltd* [1963] 2 All ER 130, (1963) 41 TC 77.
[23] See Court of Appeal in *Ayerst v C and K (Construction) Ltd* [1975] STC 1, [1975] 1 All ER 162; aff'd by the House of Lords on other grounds at [1975] STC 345, [1975] 2 All ER 537.
[24] Lloyd LJ in *Sainsbury v O'Connor* [1991] STC 318, 325–26, (1991) 64 TC 208, 244.
[25] TCGA 1992, s 132(1). On the meaning of 'securities', s 132(3)(b); *Cleveleys Investment Trust Co. v IRC* (1971) 47 TC 300 and *Taylor Clark International Ltd v Lewis* [1998] STC 1259].
[26] TCGA 1992, s 133; s 134 deals with the (temporarily) obsolete problem of government stock acquired as compensation on nationalisation. For disposals after 5 April 1988 of government securities acquired as compensation stock before 1 April 1982, no gain or loss crystallises (TCGA 1992, Sch 4, para 4(5)).

41.5.1 Exchange of Securities for Those in Another Company

The issue of shares or debentures in exchange for shares or debentures in another company is treated as if the two companies were the same and the exchange was a reorganisation of the share capital.[27] In this way the reorganisation treatment already described is invoked. If cash forms part of the consideration received by the shareholder, there is a part disposal to that extent. An example is *Furniss v Dawson*,[28] where the Dawson family exchanged the shares in their operating company for shares in Green Jacket (GJ). They hoped to be treated as having exchanged shares in the operating company for shares in GJ, and that the shares in GJ would be treated as having been acquired by them at the same time and for the same consideration as the shares in the operating company. The application of the composite transaction doctrine (above §5.6.4) prevented this.

41.5.1.1 Circumstances

TCGA 1992, section 135 treatment is available in the following three circumstances. First, the acquiring company holds (or in consequence of the exchange will hold) more than 25% of the ordinary share capital of the other company. Second, the exchange is part of a general offer seeking control (ie 51%) of that capital (notwithstanding that the offer may subsequently be made unconditional). Third, the acquiring company holds (or in consequence of the exchange will hold) the greater part of the voting power in the other company. Notwithstanding the reference to share capital, section 135 can apply to an exchange involving a unit trust or a company with no share capital.[29]

41.5.1.2 Exchanges Involving Qualifying Corporate Bonds

Rules are needed where the exchanges involve receiving qualifying bonds since these are exempt from CGT. Where the exchange is in consideration of debentures which are qualifying corporate bonds,[30] any gain (or loss) on the old holding is merely frozen and comes back into charge on the disposal of the bonds (section 116). This may result in a considerable burden in cases where the company issuing the bonds becomes insolvent and the bond holders do not recover their investment, since any loss on the bonds themselves is not an allowable loss.[31]

41.5.1.3 Change of Status of Security

Where a security changes from a chargeable asset to a qualifying corporate bond other than by means of reorganisation, the change in status of the security is treated as a conversion of securities within TCGA 1992, section 132.[32] Such a situation may arise, for example, where a security is issued and the holder has a right to convert the security into a foreign currency. Provided the foreign currency option is in existence, the security is not a qualifying

---

[27] TCGA 1992, s 135. On pre-1982 exchanges (with no relief for pre-1982 gains), see *ibid*, s 35.

[28] [1984] AC 474; [1984] STC 153; 55 TC 324.

[29] TCGA 1992, s 135(4) and (5); on FA 2002 changes, see Nolan [2002] BTR 266.

[30] Certain debentures which are not securities are treated as corporate bonds when issued in exchange for shares or debentures in another company on a merger (TCGA 1992, s 117(6A)).

[31] A certain relief formerly was available for older bonds (ex ESC D38).

[32] Ex FA 1997, s 88.

corporate bond. This security may, however, become a qualifying corporate bond merely by the holder failing to exercise the option to convert to the foreign currency and, thereby, cause the proceeds paid at maturity to be payable in sterling.

41.5.1.4 Using Earn-out Rights for Exchange of Securities

It is not uncommon for a company acquisition to involve the payment of deferred consideration, the quantum of which is related to future results of the target company. Where the deferred consideration takes the form of shares in or debentures of the acquiring company, shares in the acquiring company can be identified with the shares in the target company, so that no gain arises until there is a disposal of the shares acquired on the earn-out;[33] this is a matter of election, but since 2003 it has been assumed that the election will be exercised, ie the election must be exercised if one wants not to defer matters but to crystallise the gain or loss immediately.[34]

41.5.2 *Schemes of Reconstruction Involving the Issue of Securities*

The rules relating to reorganisations of capital are also adapted to cover schemes of reconstruction where securities are issued by a company (B) to holders of shares or debentures in another company (A). In this situation no exchange of securities takes place; the original securities are either retained, perhaps with altered rights, or cancelled. In this case, section 136 treats the original securities as having been exchanged for the new ones, so that the provisions in section 135 apply. The shares or debentures in B must be issued to these persons in respect of and in proportion to (or as nearly as may be in proportion to) their relevant holdings in A. This provision also makes express mention of companies with no share capital (section 136(5)). In addition, the arrangement must be entered into for the purposes of, or in connection with, a scheme of reconstruction, a concept explained in Schedule 5AA.[35] 'Scheme of reconstruction' means a scheme of merger, division or other restructuring that meets the first and second, and either the third or the fourth, of the following conditions:

(1)   The issue of ordinary share capital of a company or companies to the right people (ie those with interest in the original company) and not to anyone else.

(2)   Equal entitlement to new shares among all those with rights in the original company.
      In looking at (1) and (2) one must disregard any preliminary reorganisation and any subsequent issue of shares or debentures.[36]

(3)   Continuity of business: the effect of the restructuring must be that where there is one original company, the business—or substantially the whole of the business carried

---

[33] TCGA 1992, s 138A, added by FA 1997, s 89. This treatment was previously given by ESC D27.

[34] TCGA 1992, s 138A, as amended by FA 2003 s 161 applying to rights conferred on or after 10 April 2003; see Parry-Wingfield [2003] BTR 391.

[35] The rules were rewritten as a result of *Fallon v Fellows* [2001] STC 1409, which held that a partition was not a reconstruction. See commentary in Ball [2001] BTR 409 and see *Unilever UK Holdings v Smith* [2002] STC 113 where the company failed in its argument that there had been a reorganisation. Burton J held that the cancellation of an entire class of shares was neither a reduction in share capital nor a variation or alteration of the rights attached to ordinary shares.

[36] Sch 5AA, paras 6 and 7.

on by the company—must be carried on by a successor company which is not the original company.

This condition is then adapted so as to apply where there is more than one original company or more than one successor company, so making provision for the partition of a business.[37] The legislation makes express provision for what is in reality a single business carried on by two or more companies, and for the situation in which the company carrying on the business is controlled by another—the business goes with control. There is also an express exclusion where assets are held for the purpose of making a capital distribution under TCGA 1992, section 122 in respect of shares in the company.

(4)   If condition (3) is not satisfied, the issue must be in pursuance of a compromise or arrangement with members under Part 26 of the Companies Act 2006 or analogous legislation; for this condition, no part of the business of the original company may be transferred under the scheme to any other person.

41.5.3 Anti-avoidance

The reliefs in section 135 (and so section 138A) and section 136 are available only if two conditions are satisfied:[38] (a) the transaction must be effected for bona fide commercial reasons; and (b) it must not form part of a scheme or arrangement of which the main purpose, or one of the main purposes, is avoidance of liability to CGT or corporation tax.[39] In *Snell v HMRC*, Sir Andrew Morritt held that the 'liability' to CGT must include a contingent or prospective liability. He added that while the context in which the phrase was used could limit its ambit in relation to prospective liabilities, in a context such as this, where liability may be deferred on certain conditions, there was no reason to exclude it. These conditions do not apply—so relief is always available—to a shareholder holding not more than 5% of, or 5% of any class of, the shares in or debentures of the original company. In calculating this 5%, shares or debentures held by connected persons are treated as held by the shareholder.

A clearance procedure makes it possible to establish in advance whether or not the two conditions are regarded by the Revenue as satisfied (section 138). There is also provision for the recovery of tax remaining unpaid after six months; tax is recovered from the person holding the shares unless there has been an intervening disposal.[40] The second condition ((b) above) does not state which of the parties must have the purpose of the scheme in mind. Common sense suggests that the purpose should be that of the disposer, since he is the person otherwise liable to an immediate charge to CGT; however, caution suggests that the purpose is to be found in the scheme, and so the minds of all or any of the parties to it. In *Coll and another v Revenue & Customs Commissioners*,[41] the Upper Tribunal held that

---

[37]   The very point at issue in *Fallon v Fellows* [2001] STC 1409 on which see Ball [2001] BTR 409.

[38]   TCGA 1992, ss 135(6), 136(6) and 137. The facts in *Furniss v Dawson* (see §5.6.4 above) occurred before this provision was introduced.

[39]   *Snell v HMRC*, [2006] EWHC 3350 (Ch), [2007] STC 1279.

[40]   Other than a disposal between spouses or civil partners living together (s 58) or between members of a group of companies (s 171).

[41]   [2010] STC 1849, [2010] UKUT 114 (TCC).

section 137 was an all-or-nothing provision applicable to a particular transaction and so to all relevant shareholders (rather than being applied to each such shareholder separately); on the facts section 137 applied to prevent the deferral under section 135.

41.6   Miscellaneous

Strips of deeply discounted securities. F(No 2)A 2005, having brought such strips within the income tax rules (see §26.6.3 above), also provides that no capital loss can be claimed (TCGA 1992, section 151D).

Issue of shares. A company does not own its shares; as such, the issue of shares is not a chargeable disposal by the company. The figure at which the shares are issued, a matter of importance in calculating acquisition cost, is governed by TCGA 1992, section 17 (see above at §33.8).

Changing share rights. Alterations in share rights may be chargeable disposals (see above at §36.6).

Offshore funds. The gain arising on the disposal of a material interest in an offshore fund (an offshore income gain) is charged to income tax or corporation tax: for details see discussion below at §79.9.

41.7   Venture Capital Trusts

Various reliefs apply to venture capital trusts (VCTs).[42] Briefly, for chargeable gains purposes, these are (a) exemption for the VCT itself from tax on its chargeable gains[43] and (b) exemption from CGT for an individual on gains on a disposal of ordinary shares in the VCT provided the shares disposed of were acquired within the permitted maximum acquisition limit of £200,000 per tax year.[44] Losses on disposal are not allowable for CGT purposes. For further details on VCTs see below at §78.4.

41.8   Enterprise Investment Scheme

On the disposal of shares which have qualified for relief under the Enterprise Investment Scheme (EIS), there is, for once, a one-way street for the taxpayer: any gain is exempt from CGT, but any loss is allowable.[45] There are also rules to continue the exemption following mergers and reconstruction.[46] In the case of a merger, the other company must be one that has qualified for relief under either the EIS or the former Business Expansion Scheme that

---

[42] For a more detailed discussion of these rule see Stratton, *Tolley's Tax Planning*, ch 62.
[43] TCGA 1992, s 100(1); the trust is liable to tax on its income.
[44] TCGA 1992, s 151A; the exemption is subject to the rules in s 151A(2).
[45] TCGA 1992, s 150A(2), (2A).
[46] TCGA 1992, s 150A(8A), (8B).

was in effect from 1984 to 1993. Reinvestment relief is also available.[47] This relief defers the CGT charge on a gain arising from the disposal of any asset where the gain is reinvested in a qualifying EIS investment within the period beginning one year before the realisation of the gain and ending three years after the realisation. For further details on the EIS see below at §78.5.

41.9   Government Stock and Qualifying Corporate Bonds

Any gain or loss on the disposal of gilt-edged securities is exempt from CGT.[48] This may be seen as taking a depressingly prescient view of the value of such securities, or as a subsidy to the gilt market. However, there is a similar exemption for qualifying corporate bonds (QCBs).[49] This exemption was introduced in 1984 as part of the new rules on deep discount bonds; with gains on such bonds subject to income tax, there was no need for a CGT charge in addition. This was reinforced by the fact that with the introduction of indexation relief in 1982 and its extension in 1985 to give relief for losses (an extension which lasted until FA 1994), charging QCBs to CGT would actually have meant many potential allowable losses rather than chargeable gains.

---

[47] TCGA 1992, Sch 5B.
[48] TCGA 1992, s 115(1), Sch 9.
[49] TCGA 1992, s 115(1)(b); on meaning, see *Harding v HMRC* [2008] STC 1965, [2008] EWHC 99 (Ch).

42

Capital Gains Tax and Business

42.1   Capital Allowances

42.1.1 Introduction

Rules are needed to govern the interaction of the capital allowance system and CGT. As described in chapter twenty-four above, where a capital allowance is given, the trader, T, is allowed to write off the cost of an asset against the profits of his trade; if T sells the asset at more than the written-down value, there will be a balancing charge. However, the balancing charge does no more than recover income or corporation tax allowances already given, and does not tax any profit (or allow any loss) which T makes by selling the asset for more (or less) than was paid for it. Consequently, any balancing charge is brought into account when computing the consideration for disposal, notwithstanding the general exclusion for sums chargeable to income tax or corporation tax as income.[1] Although most of the assets will be wasting assets, the CGT wasting asset rules do not apply where the asset qualifies for capital allowances[2] (see further below at §42.1.2). Suppose an asset is bought for £8,000; it has capital allowances of £3,000, giving a written-down value of £5,000. It is then sold for £8,000. There will be a balancing charge of £3,000. For CGT purposes the asset is treated as bought

---

[1] TCGA 1992, s 37(2). See *Hirsch v Crowthers Cloth Ltd* [1990] STC 174, (1990) 62 TC 759.
[2] TCGA 1992, s 47 excludes s 46; s 45(2)(b) excludes s 45(1).

for £8,000 and sold for £8,000, so giving no gain. If the asset had been sold for £10,000, the balancing charge would still be £3,000 and there would be a gain for CGT of £2,000.

Where assets are sold and a net gain accrues, the fact that capital allowances have been claimed does not prevent the historic cost from being claimed as allowable expenditure[3] since such allowances will have been recaptured by the balancing charge. Where, however, a loss arises on disposal of an asset on which allowances have been granted, the expenditure allowable for CGT is reduced by the amount of the capital allowance.[4] Capital allowances include any balancing allowance on disposal; one must of course also take account of any balancing charge on the disposal. In some periods of the indexation allowance it was possible for an allowable CGT loss to arise. If the asset such as an industrial building had been deemed, for capital allowances purposes, to have been acquired by the disposer at its written-down value, account must have been taken of any allowances made to the previous person entitled to them.[5]

42.1.2 Capital Allowances and CGT Movable Property Rules

Three rules are relevant here. Section 262 will exclude any CGT if the assets on which capital allowances have been claimed are tangible movable property sold for £6,000 or less. However section 45, which normally excludes from CGT any asset which is tangible movable property and a wasting asset, does not apply if, since the beginning of the period of ownership, that asset has been used solely for the purposes of a trade, profession or vocation and T was entitled to claim capital allowance in respect of the expenditure on the asset.[6] T cannot come within the CGT exemption by electing not to claim the capital allowance—the test is whether the allowance could have been claimed under statute; neither is it necessary that the asset should have been brought into use.[7] Lastly, section 46, which directs a straight-line scaling-down of deductible expenditure costs for a wasting asset before the gain is calculated, does not apply to a wasting asset that qualified for capital allowances.[8]

42.2 Appropriations to and from Stock in trade

Rules are needed to govern situations in which assets move between the ITTOIA 2005, Part 2 income tax regime and CGT, and between the different parts of corporation tax. Although FA 2008, section 34 and Schedule 15 put the income tax treatment of an appropriation on a statutory footing (above §23.5), the CGT rules are untouched.

---

[3] TCGA 1992, s 41(1). On 1988 rebasing to 1982, see *ibid*, Sch 3, para 3; on pre-1965 assets, see Sch 2, para 20.
[4] TCGA 1992, s 41; allowances include the renewals allowance (s 41(4)), whether or not the allowance is claimed.
[5] TCGA 1992, s 41(3), and see s 41A, added to deal with the interaction of these rules and the new long funding lease rules.
[6] TCGA 1992, s 45(2). Capital allowances are capable of being claimed if the expenditure concerned is of a qualifying kind. Expenditure is not of a qualifying kind if the asset is sold before being brought into use so that no allowances are due (*Burman v Westminster Press Ltd* [1987] STC 669, (1987) 60 TC 418).
[7] *Burman v Westminster Press Ltd* [1987] STC 669, (1987) 60 TC 418.
[8] TCGA 1992, s 47(1); presumably, *Burman v Westminster Press Ltd* [1987] STC 669, (1987) 60 TC 418 applies here too.

42.2.1 *Appropriation to Trade*

On the appropriation of capital assets to trading stock of a trade, section 161(1) directs that there is a deemed disposal at market value, unless the nature of the asset is such that the disposal would be exempt from CGT. Since this disposal does not apply if there would be no chargeable gain, the exemptions for wasting chattels (subject to the capital allowance restriction) and chattels where the consideration does not exceed £6,000 are of particular importance here. Where a trader, T, is assessable to income tax under ITTOIA 2005, Part 2, T may elect that the figure at which the trading stock is entered is reduced by the amount of any gain or increased by the amount of any loss.[9] Where such an election is made, no chargeable gain or allowable loss arises on the appropriation to trading stock. Instead, the market value of the asset to be included in the computation of trading profit is reduced by the amount of the chargeable gain which would otherwise have arisen (or increased by the amount of the allowable loss which would otherwise have arisen). The effect of this election is to leave income tax to be levied in due course on the profit derived from the disposal in the course of trade. Suppose X has an asset with base cost of £10 and current value of £25. On appropriation to X's trade, X may either enter it at £25 and pay CGT on the gain of £15, or enter it in the books of the business at £10 and defer all tax until later.

In order to qualify as an appropriation to trading stock there must be a genuine trading purpose in mind.[10] Thus, the asset must be not only of a kind sold in the ordinary course of the trade, but also acquired with a view to resale at a profit.[11] While fiscal considerations must be put to one side when considering whether an asset was acquired 'as trading stock', they may be very relevant when considering the purpose of the transfer and whether it was for the company's trade.[12]

42.2.2 *Appropriation from Trade*

Where an asset which has been trading stock is appropriated by the trader for any other purpose, or is retained on the ending of the trade, it is deemed to be acquired for CGT at the figure entered in the accounts of the trade (section 161(2)). The figure at which the asset is entered in the accounts of the trade will presumably be the amount relevant for income tax purposes. whether under the rule in *Sharkey v Wernher*[13] or, on discontinuance, under ITTOIA 2005, section 173. On a death, section 173 will not apply, but market value will be imposed by section 62. Therefore, if the asset went in at £25 and came out at £36 on the death, it must exit the company books at £36.

---

[9] TCGA 1992, s 161(3). Where the trade is carried on in partnership, all partners must join in the election (s 161(4)).

[10] *Coates v Arndale Properties Ltd* [1984] STC 637, (1984) 59 TC 516; *Reed v Nova Securities* [1985] STC 124, (1985) 59 TC 516; see also *N Ltd v Inspector of Taxes* 1996 STC (SCD) 348.

[11] *Reed v Nova Securities Ltd* [1985] STC 124, 130F, (1985) 59 TC 516, 563, per Lord Templeman.

[12] Per Jonathan Parker LJ in *New Angel Court Ltd v Adam* [2004] EWCA Civ 242; [2004] STC 779 at paras 93–95; for discussion see Shiers [2004] BTR 297–303.

[13] [1956] AC 58.

42.2.3 *Spouses/Civil Partners and Trading Stock*

Section 58 directs that there is no chargeable gain or allowable loss on a disposal between spouses or civil partners living together; the asset is treated as disposed of and acquired for a consideration of such amount that neither gain nor loss accrues. However, this treatment does not apply if, until the disposal, the asset has formed part of the trading stock of a trade carried on by the person making the disposal, or if the asset is acquired as trading stock for the purposes of a trade carried on by the person acquiring the asset. Instead, the transfer is treated as being made at market value, but with an election available (section 58(2)(a)).

42.3 Incorporation: Transfer of a Business to a Company

The transfer of a business to a company is a disposal of the assets of the business by the owner, and so may give rise to chargeable gains and allowable losses. However, a rollover relief applies where shares are received in exchange for the business (section 162), where the business,[14] and not merely the assets of the business, is transferred to a company as a going concern;[15] all the business assets (other than cash) must be transferred. In practice, the assumption of liabilities by the company is not required. The gain is computed and then allocated to the shares and any other consideration received in return. The assumption of liabilities by the company is not in practice treated as consideration for the transfer.[16] The gain allocated to the other consideration is chargeable immediately. When the shares are themselves disposed of, the amount by which the gain has been reduced and which escaped tax before must be deducted from the cost of the shares and so becomes chargeable.[17]

The deferral on incorporation was made elective in 2002.[18] Although one would like to think this was a matter of overdue equity, it appears that the reason for the change was to correct yet another anomaly to do with taper relief. A wants to get the maximum benefit of business asset taper relief. Without the election the asset would cease to be within the CGT and taper relief regime, and would be subject to corporation tax and indexation. A would therefore gain by being able to elect.[19] Previously A would have had to structure the transaction so as to fall outside section 162. The meaning of a 'business' for TCGA 1992, section 162 purposes was considered in *Elizabeth Ramsay v HMRC*.[20] The Upper Tribunal overturned the decision of the First-tier Tribunal and held that the extensive services Mrs Ramsay provided the tenants letting her five flats constituted a serious undertaking earnestly pursued and thus qualified as a business for CGT purposes.

---

[14] The meaning of 'business' (as distinct from trade or profession) is uncertain: see *American Leaf Blending Co Sdn Bhd v Director-General of Inland Revenue* [1978] STC 561, [1978] 3 All ER 1185.

[15] Whether there is a continuing business is a question of fact, to be decided on the circumstances at the time of transfer: see *Gordon v IRC* [1991] STC 174, (1991) 64 TC 173.

[16] ESC D32.

[17] On rebasing, see TCGA 1992, Sch 4, para 2; on pre-1965 control, see *ibid*, Sch 2, para 21.

[18] TCGA 1992, s 162A inserted by FA 2002, s 49.

[19] The Revenue Notes to the Finance Bill.

[20] [2013] UKUT 0266 (TCC).

For those incorporated businesses that for one reason or another no longer require limited liability and the other benefits incorporation offers, FA 2013, sections 58–61 introduced a limited form of disincorporation relief from 1 April 2013. The relief is discussed below at §60.8. Briefly, the temporary new relief allows a company to transfer certain types of assets to its shareholders who continue to operate the business in an unincorporated form, without the company incurring a corporation tax charge on the disposal of the assets. The qualifying transfer must occur between 1 April 2013 and 31 March 2018 for the relief to apply. Although the relief is available to a wide range of businesses, a number of conditions must be satisfied. Most notably, pursuant to section 59, Condition C the total market value of the qualifying assets of the business (including land and goodwill) included in the transfer must not exceed £100,000.[21] Early indications suggest that disincorporation relief has had a low take-up. This is hardly surprising given the conditions attached to it, particularly the £100,000 cap on total market value. Recent changes to the taxation of dividends may stoke more interest.

42.4   Replacement Asset Rollover Relief

42.4.1   *Outline*

CGT could become a serious obstacle to the operation of business if CGT had to be paid every time a business asset was realised at a profit. Rollover relief is one of the methods by which CGT addresses the lock-in problem when dealing with business assets, and allows CGT to be deferred until the new asset is disposed of (section 152). Whether the gain will then be chargeable will depend on the taxpayer's circumstances—and the law—at that time. Rollover relief may be complete or partial. Rollover relief is available only where the taxpayer carries on a trade and both the old and new assets are used in a trade carried on by the taxpayer. The new asset must be acquired within specified time limits, which may be extended by the exercise of Revenue discretion.[22] The relief operates only within the context of CGT. If, therefore, the transaction is characterised as an income transaction, these rules cannot apply.[23] Where the new investment is a depreciating asset, rollover relief acts instead as a deferral (section 154). Rollover relief may also be available to an individual in respect of an asset used in the trade of a company, in the course of employment or by a partnership. Where the new asset is property which later becomes the taxpayer's principal private residence, the change of use does not, of itself, cause the deferred tax to become payable. Under self-assessment, T may choose not to pay CGT on a disposal where a claim for rollover relief on that disposal is expected (section 153A). The effect of failing to get relief can be dramatic. In *Re Loquitur*,[24] the court held that the taxpayer was not entitled to relief,

---

[21] For commentary see Gotch [2013] BTR 446 and for detailed guidance on the new regime see HMRC CGT manual para CG65800 et seq.

[22] TCGA 1992, s 152(3); in *R on application of Barnett v IRC* [2003] EWHC Admin 2581, [2004] STC 763, Davis J held that the General Commissioners had no business making findings of fact which might compel the Revenue to grant the extension.

[23] See Harper [1990] *Conveyancer* 115.

[24] [2003] EWHC ChD 999; [2003] STC 1394.

with the result that accounts prepared on the basis that the claim was good were incorrect, with the further consequence that the payment of a dividend was unlawful—since there were insufficient profits available. There was also a consequential liability on the directors to repay the money under the Insolvency Act 1986, section 212.

42.4.2 Operation of the Rollover Relief

A trader, T, who disposes of assets used for the purposes of the trade throughout the period of ownership, may elect to defer any liability to CGT by means of rollover relief (section 152). Other qualifying assets must be acquired within a prescribed period before or after the date of the disposal. The deferral is until such time as T disposes of the new assets or interest in the new assets; however, because the deferral simply takes the form of an adjustment of the cost of the new assets, the deferred charge does not crystallise merely because the trade is discontinued or the asset ceases to be used for trade purposes. Alternatively, the new assets may be disposed of at a loss, or some other relief (such as entrepreneurs' relief) may be available.

If rollover relief is claimed, the disposal is treated as made for a consideration such that neither gain nor loss accrues. The buyer of the old asset is, however, unaffected by the claim. The chargeable gain that would otherwise have arisen to T is deducted from the base cost of the new assets. Full rollover relief is available, provided the acquisition cost of the new assets equals or exceeds the actual disposal proceeds of the old asset. If T sells an asset for £100,000 which originally cost £60,000, T has a gain of £40,000. If the new asset costs £120,000, T may elect to defer liability to pay CGT on the £40,000 gain now, but the base cost of the new asset will be lowered from £120,000 to £80,000 (section 152(1)). If, therefore, the new asset is later sold for £150,000, T will have a gain of £70,000 on the new asset, instead of £40,000 on the old asset and £30,000 on the new.

Where a gain is rolled over against more than one item of qualifying expenditure, there is no prescribed method of apportioning the gain. Relief is available where a person sells a business, or a business asset, and for purely commercial reasons subsequently repurchases the same asset.[25] However, this does not extend to improvement expenditure on an asset following a part disposal of that asset.[26]

Where the trade use was for only part of the period of ownership, an apportionment is made (section 152(7)). An asset used only partly for trade purposes does not qualify at all, although this rule is relaxed for buildings (section 152(6)). A person carrying on two trades, whether successively or concurrently, is treated as carrying on one trade (section 152(8)). Hence, relief may be claimed where the old asset belonged to trade A and the new asset belonged to trade B. Too long a gap between trade A and the start of trade B will prevent them from being carried on successively.[27] For disposals before 6 April 1988, the whole period of ownership, including periods before 6 April 1965, is relevant in computing the restriction.[28] For disposals after 5 April 1988, only periods made following the new base date of 31 March 1982 are relevant in the time apportionment calculation (section 152(9)).

---

[25] ESC D16.
[26] *Watton v Tippett* [1997] STC 893, 69 TC 491, CA. See also below at §42.4.9.
[27] *Steibelt v Paling* [1999] STC 594.
[28] *Richart v J Lyons & Co Ltd* [1989] STC 665, (1989) 62 TC 261, CA.

Rollover relief is available to any person (whether an individual, a company or trustees), provided that person is carrying on a trade. The court has held that the trade must be genuine, and the acquisition of the replacement asset must be a genuine trading transaction.[29] 'Trade' for this purpose includes not only an adventure in the nature of trade but also a profession, vocation, office or employment (section 158(1)(c)). The term also covers public authorities, the occupation of woodlands on a commercial basis, the leasing of premises (eg by a brewer) and various non profit-making activities,[30] as well as furnished holiday lettings (section 241). However, letting property is not a trade.[31]

42.4.3 Partial Rollover: No Full Reinvestment of Proceeds

To the extent that the gain does not have to be used in the purchase of the new asset, it cannot be deferred. In such a case the chargeable gain is limited to the difference between the disposal proceeds of the old asset and the acquisition cost of the new asset (section 153). The balance of the chargeable gain is rolled over against the cost of the new asset. Where the gain is only partly chargeable, eg because of time apportionment, the gain rolled over is scaled down rateably. Therefore, if T sells an asset for £100,000 which originally cost £60,000, T has a gain of £40,000. If the new asset costs £92,000, T may elect that the base cost of the new asset be lowered from £92,000 to £60,000, leaving T liable to pay CGT on the £8,000 gain not needed for the new asset. If there is full reinvestment of the proceeds but a subsidy from a third party, full rollover relief may be available. In one case, T sold part of a piece of land, so giving rise to a potential liability to CGT, and used the proceeds to build a new structure on the remaining land. The court held that the amount of the rollover was not affected by the fact that T had received a grant to help with the new building.[32]

42.4.4 Assets

Relief is available only if the assets sold and acquired come within a defined (but wide) list (sections 152, 155). There is no need for the two assets to be in the same category. The list includes: (a) any building or part of a building and any permanent or semi-permanent structure in the nature of a building, occupied (as well as used) only for the purposes of the trade;[33] (b) any land occupied (as well as used) only for the purposes of the trade; and (c) fixed plant or machinery which does not form part of a building or of a permanent or semi-permanent structure in the nature of a building—the term 'fixed' applies both to plant and machinery.[34] The list also includes some specific items: (d) ships, aircraft and hovercraft; (e) goodwill; (f) satellites, space stations and space vehicles (including launch vehicles); and (g) quotas for milk, potatoes, ewe-and-suckler-cow-premiums and fish.[35]

[29] *Re Loquitur* [2003] EWHC ChD 999; [2003] STC 1394.
[30] TCGA 1992, ss 156, 158(a)–(e); and see ex ESC D15. On the boundary between woodlands and agriculture, see above §19.7; note that short rotation coppice is now treated as agriculture (FA 1995, s 154).
[31] *Hatt v Newman* [1999] STC (SCD) 171.
[32] *Wardhaugh v Penrith Rugby Union Football Club* [2002] STC 776.
[33] For an illustration, see *Carter v Baird* [1999] STC 120.
[34] *Williams v Evans* [1982] STC 498, (1982) 59 TC 509.
[35] Fish were added by FA 1999, s 84; on the history of problems presented by milk quotas, see Cardwell and Lane [1994] BTR 501.

Items (a) and (b) above require occupation by the taxpayer. The test of occupation developed in the old case law on Schedule E and the pre-1963 Schedule A still applies here.[36] The issue was often whether employees occupied property on behalf of their employer (representative occupation) or themselves (beneficial occupation). The test is whether the occupation is essential to the performance of the duties of the occupying servant. Occupation of a farmhouse is rarely representative occupation. In *Anderton v Lamb*,[37] rollover relief was claimed—on the facts unsuccessfully—for houses occupied by junior partners of a partnership. Statute provides that land does not qualify under (b) if it is occupied for the purposes of a trade of dealing in or developing land, unless the profit on sale of such land would not be a profit of the trade (section 156). In *Mertrux Ltd v HMRC*,[38] the taxpayer sold its Mercedes car dealership business to a purchaser for consideration by way of a transfer agreement, along with a separate undertaking that the purchaser would make a territory release payment (TRP) to the vendor. In order to increase its claim for rollover relief, the taxpayer argued that the TRP was a capital sum derived from goodwill (a qualifying asset for relief purposes). The CA did not accept this argument, partly because the dealership's goodwill was dealt with in the separate transfer agreement and partly because the CA concluded that the goodwill associated with the Mercedes name did not belong to the taxpayer.

42.4.5 Further Rules

42.4.5.1 Acquisition of a New Asset—Relaxations

The requirement that a new asset be acquired is substantially relaxed in practice. Thus, rollover relief applies (a) where a partnership asset is partitioned on the dissolution of the partnership,[39] and (b) where the disposal proceeds are used to improve an existing asset used for the purposes of the trade rather than acquiring a new asset,[40] or acquiring a further interest in an asset already used for the trade.[41] The rules are also relaxed where the new asset is not brought immediately into use but work is done on it and it is then brought into use, for example where land is bought and a building is built or reconstructed. The land must not be used for any non-trade purpose or let during this period of work.[42]

42.4.5.2 Timing

The new acquisition must take place within a period beginning 12 months before, and ending three years after, the date of disposal, or such other time as the Board may, by notice in writing, allow (section 152(3), (4)). However, if an unconditional contract for the acquisition has been entered into, provisional rollover relief may be given at once and any adjustments made later such as would be necessary if, for example, the contract were

---

[36] *Northern Ireland Commr of Valuation v Fermanagh Protestant Board of Education* [1969] 1 WLR 1708, 1772, per Lord Upjohn.

[37] [1981] STC 43, 55 TC 1.

[38] [2013] EWCA Civ 821.

[39] ESC D23.

[40] ESC D22.

[41] ESC D25.

[42] ESC D24. In *Steibelt v Paling* [1999] STC 594, the judge said that this view was a correct interpretation, not a concession.

cancelled. The discretion to extend belongs to the Board and not the Commissioners (now Tribunals).[43]

42.4.5.3 Application of Proceeds

Although the legislation requires that the proceeds be applied in acquiring the new asset, this does not appear to carry too literal an interpretation. In practice, it is sufficient to match disposal proceeds with one or more items of qualifying expenditure, regardless of how that expenditure was, in fact, financed.

42.4.5.4 Use by Personal Company

Where the trade is carried on by a personal company but the person owning and replacing the asset is an individual (I), relief may be claimed by I, provided the company is I's personal company (section 157). The old and new assets must both be used either for a trade of the individual, or for a trade of the company. The relief is not available if the assets are held by another company, or if the company owns the asset and the individual carries on the trade. It is not possible to roll over gains realised by I against expenditure incurred by the company, or vice versa. The term 'personal company' replaced the previous 'family company' in 1993—yet another mark of the age of individualism.

42.4.6 New Asset—Use in Trade

The new asset[44] must be 'taken into use, and used only, for the purposes of the trade' (section 152(1)). This encompasses expenditure on an asset which is required for the trade of a subsidiary.[45] The new asset must actually be taken into use on the acquisition; intention is not sufficient.[46] While the phrase 'on the acquisition' in section 152(1) does not imply immediacy, it does exclude dilatoriness; the taking into use and the acquisition must be reasonably proximate to one another.[47] ESC D24 applies here also and allows relief where the new asset is not brought immediately into use but work is done on it and it is then brought into use, for example where land is bought and a building is built or reconstructed. The land must not be used for any non-trade purpose or let during this period of work.

42.4.7 Investment in a Depreciating Asset[48]

Rollover relief is modified where the new asset is a depreciating asset, ie a wasting asset or one which will become a wasting asset within 10 years.[49] The gain is not deductible from the cost of the new asset but is instead held over until the new asset is disposed of or ceases to be used for the purposes of the trade, or, if neither has happened, 10 years have expired.

---

[43] *R on application of Barnett v IRC* [2003] EWHC Admin 2581; [2004] STC 763.
[44] On ownership, see *Carter v Baird* [1999] STC 120.
[45] *Robinson v Scott Bader Co Ltd* [1981] STC 436, 54 TC 757.
[46] *Temperley v Visibell* [1974] STC 64, 49 TC 129; *Campbell Connelly & Co Ltd v Barnett* [1994] STC 50, 66 TC 380.
[47] *Milton v Chivers* [1996] STC (SC) 36, 40.
[48] On rebasing, see TCGA 1992, Sch 4.
[49] TCGA 1992, s 154. On merger with a Societas Europaea (SE), see s 152(2A) and (2B), added by F(No 2)A 2005, s 64.

The rules provide for the possibility of a further asset being acquired which is not a depreciating asset (section 154(6)). Although the further acquisition need not occur within the usual period beginning on the disposal of the first asset, it must occur when the new asset is disposed of or ceases to be used for the purposes of the trade, or, if neither has happened, 10 years have expired. Part of the held-over gain may be rolled over if the expenditure on the non-depreciating asset is insufficient for full rollover.[50]

42.4.8 Partnerships

Rollover relief is available to an individual (I) who owns an asset which has been used in the trade carried on by I in partnership with others. Where an asset is held by a partnership, I, as a partner, is treated on the basis that he owns a fractional part of the asset (section 59). Hence, I can claim rollover relief in respect of a gain arising on I's part of an asset sold by the partnership. He can then roll the gain into an acquisition by the partnership or, alternatively, an acquisition made by I personally (ie outside the partnership), whether for the purposes of the partnership trade or for some other trade. One partner can claim the relief whether or not the others do.

42.4.9 Reinvestment in the Same Asset

The fact that the disposal can occur before or after the acquisition raises the question whether rollover relief is available where T acquires an asset and then sells part of it, ie T claims rollover relief on the basis that the gain arising on the part disposal of an asset be rolled into the previous acquisition of the same asset. The judicial answer is that T is not entitled to the relief in these circumstances. In *Watton v Tippett*,[51] T purchased freehold land and buildings (unit 1) for £295,560 with the laudable aim of running an indoor cricket facility (a trade). T incurred further expenditure on unit 1 of £131,464 for the (possibly less laudable but more profitable) purpose of using it as a 10-pin bowling alley. Facing financial difficulties, T sold part of the premises (unit 1A) for £292,407. T tried to roll over the gain on the part disposal into the expenditure of £131,464 incurred less than 12 months before the part disposal and, also, into the original £295,560. The Court of Appeal strongly criticised the statutory language used for the rollover relief provisions but ruled, '[w]hat is crucial … is that there must be an acquisition of assets other than the assets disposed of.'[52] So the taxpayer lost.

42.5   Entrepreneurs' Relief

One of the great purposes (and effects) behind taper relief was to give business assets a better deal. By the time taper relief had settled in, the effective rate of CGT on assets held for two years was 10%. This was to be compared with a 40% rate, subject to indexation relief

---

[50] On death, see ESC D45.
[51] [1997] STC 893, 69 TC 491, CA.
[52] *Ibid*, STC 899b, 507H, per Peter Gibson LJ.

under the pre-1998 rules. When the Chancellor announced his intention to have a flat rate CGT of 18% without taper relief, the business community complained at being asked to pay tax at 18% rather than 10%. After much discussion, the Government came up with entrepreneurs' relief (ER).[53] ER is a lifetime relief and may therefore require the taxpayer to keep records for far longer than the normal six years.

ER is based on the old retirement relief (RR), repealed in 1998.[54] Under ER, the person making the right sort of disposal of a business pays tax at a special rate of tax of 10% on the first £10m of realised gains—and the usual 20% rate thereafter (section 169N). Under RR, the person had to have reached the age of 55 or be retiring early on grounds of ill health. RR gave exemption on the first £250,000 of realised gains and half tax on the next £750,000.[55] Although RR described itself in the statute as retirement relief, it was not necessary that the person should go into retirement, save when aged under 55. It sufficed that he was disposing of the business or part of it, or of business assets in the way defined. Although the relief was abolished in 1998, it continued on a sliding scale for disposals up to 5 April 2003.

ER, which must be claimed,[56] comes in three separate types: (a) for individuals, (b) for trusts, and (c) for partnerships. In each case there must be a 'material disposal' of business assets.[57] The rules talk of 'relevant business assets'. Take first the case of a business carried on by an individual (or by a partnership of which the individual is a member). Here assets comprised in the disposal of the business are relevant if they are assets used for the purposes of the business. The statute expressly includes goodwill, other than disposals of goodwill on or after 3 December 2014 to close companies in which the seller is related.[58] This change, in combination with a related change on amortisation of goodwill, greatly reduces the tax advantages previously available from incorporating a trade by selling the trade including goodwill to a new company in return for debt. Previously, the gain on the sale of the trade would have been taxable at a low 10% rate of CGT after ER and the company would benefit from tax relief on amortisation of the purchased goodwill. In addition, the company's repayment of the debt out of future profits represented a way to extract money from the company free of income tax and NICs.[59] The combination of restricting ER on the disposal of goodwill from 3 December 2014 and abolishing corporation tax relief for the amortisation of purchased goodwill from 8 July 2015 (see below §63.4.1) may well tip the balance in favour of using the reliefs in TCGA 1992 section 162 or 165 when incorporating a trade. It will also reduce the number of disputes between taxpayers and HMRC over the value attributed to goodwill in the incorporation. At Budget 2016, however, the Government announced it was relaxing somewhat the restriction on claiming ER on gains related to goodwill. For disposals made on or after 3 December 2014, ER will be able to be claimed, subject to certain conditions, on gains on the goodwill of a business when that business is transferred to a company controlled by five or fewer persons or by its directors.[60]

---

[53] TCGA 1992, Pt 3, ss 169H–169S.
[54] TCGA 1992, ss 163–163A.
[55] TCGA 1992, Sch 6, para 13, as amended in 1994.
[56] For procedure, see TCGA 1992, s 169M.
[57] Defined in TCGA 1992, s 169L.
[58] TCGA 1992, s 169LA.
[59] For more commentary on this point see Miller [2015] BTR 489.
[60] Amended TCGA 1992, s 169LA.

The statute also expressly excludes shares, securities or other assets held as investments. The relief is given for relevant gains and losses, ie gains and losses computed in accordance with the relevant CGT rules. ER is simpler than RR—it does not need the concept of the chargeable business asset. Finally, sections 169T–V allow claims for ER in relation to previously held-over gains on investments in enterprise investment schemes or in social enterprises.

The amount in respect of which this relief may be claimed (TCGA 1992, section 169N) was increased from £1 million to £2 million by FA 2010, section 4 for disposals on or after 6 April 2010, and to £5 million for qualifying business disposals on or after 23 June 2010 by F(No 2)A 2010, section 2. From 6 April 2011, the amount of relief increased again, to £10 million. By TCGA 1992, section 4(6), added by F(No 2)A 2010, Schedule 1 and applying to disposals on or after 23 June 2010, where the new higher rates of CGT tax apply (since 6 April 2016 generally 20%), gains attracting ER are treated as the lowest part of the gains on which the individual is subject to tax.

At Budget 2016, the Government announced further changes to ER. First, it will extend ER to external investors in unlisted trading companies. This 'investors' relief' applies to newly issued shares purchased on or after 17 March 2016 and held for a minimum of 3 years from 6 April 2016. Gains will be subject to a separate lifetime limit of £10 million.[61] In addition, for disposals made on or after 18 March 2015, ER will be permitted on a disposal of a privately-held asset when the accompanying disposal of business assets is to a family member. ER will also be permitted in some cases involving joint ventures and partnerships, where the disposal of business assets does not meet the existing 5% minimum holding conditions. These changes will also take effect for disposals made on or after 18 March 2015.

42.5.1 *Material Disposal by Individual*

In the case of a business owned by an individual, three situations are covered:

(1) *Where the disposal is of the whole or part of a business.* Here the disposal is 'material' if the business has been owned by an individual throughout the period of one year ending with the date of the disposal.

(2) *Where the particular disposal is not of the business itself but of one or more assets which, at the time at which the business ceased to be carried on, were in use for the purposes of the business.* Here, as in (1), the business must have been owned by the individual throughout the period of one year ending with the date of the cessation, and the disposal of the assets must be within three years of that cessation. On this reading, which is based on the Revenue Notes, this category is concerned with post-cessation disposals and gives our former business person three years to dispose of trade-related assets. It is necessary to distinguish the sale of a part of a business from the sale of an asset used in the business. This was the subject of case law discussion in the old RR rules. In *McGregor v Adcock*,[62] relief was refused where there was a sale of 5 acres of a 35-acre

---

[61] TCGA 1992, s 169VA *et seq.*
[62] [1977] STC 206, [1977] 3 All ER 65.

farm and nothing to suggest that the scale of the business was significantly altered by the sale. Other cases suggest that if an argument is based on a change in the scale of activities following a sale of assets, one has to establish a direct link between the change in scale and the sale.[63] Both RR and ER refer to 'a business'. The ER legislation states that there must be a trade, profession or vocation carried out on a commercial basis and with a view to the realisation of profit; the question whether an activity amounts to the carrying on of a business is one of fact (section 169S(1)). A finding by the Commissioners that the management of property was not a business was not disturbed by the courts.[64] The IHT case law on business property relief may also be relevant (see below at §54.2.2). ER is also available for furnished holiday lettings (section 241(3A)).

(3)   *Where the business is incorporated and the individual sells shares or securities.* Relief is also available when the disposal is of shares or securities in a company owning the business, and the company is a trading company which is either that individual's personal company or a member of a trading group of which the holding company is that individual's personal company (section 169I). This category also covers the disposal of an interest in shares or securities, including a disposal within section 122 (capital distribution in respect of shares). For the company to be the personal company of the individual (D), D must satisfy two sets of rules. First, D must be entitled to at least 5% of the ordinary share capitals and to exercise 5% or more of the voting rights (section 169S(3)). Shareholdings held in common must be attributed in proportion. It has been held that a voting right which a person chooses not to exercise is still a voting right.[65] Secondly, D must also be a full-time working officer or employee of the company, or, if the company is a member of a group of companies, a full-time working officer or employee of one or more companies in that group (section 169I(6)). 'Full-time' is not otherwise defined. Relief also applies where the company ceases to be a trading company without becoming a member of a trading group, or ceases to be a member of a trading group without continuing to be (or becoming) a trading company (section 169I(7)). Here the disposal must be within one year of the cessation. (RR used the concept of a commercial association in addition to that of a group, but this is not part of ER.) At Budget 2016, the Government announced it was reviewing the definition of 'trading company' for ER purposes to ensure it is operating effectively.

42.5.2 Trusts

Section 169J deals with the disposal of 'settlement business assets' and gives analogous relief where there is a qualifying beneficiary. An individual is a qualifying beneficiary if having an interest in possession either in the whole of the settled property, or in the part which consists of the business or business assets. There are analogous rules and conditions for the disposal of the assets of the business or of shares in the business (situations (2) and (3) in §42.5.1 above).

---

[63] *Atkinson v Dancer; Mannion v Johnston* [1988] STC 758. See also similar issue in *Pepper v Daffurn* [1993] STC 466.
[64] *Harthan v Mason* [1980] STC 94.
[65] *Hepworth v William Smith Group* [1981] STC 354.

42.5.3 Partnership/Personal Company

Section 169I(8) extends the rules in section 169I to cover an individual who carries on business as a member of a partnership, and deals with joining or leaving the partnership. Section 169K deals with the situation in which the trade is carried on by the partnership but the asset disposed of is owned by the individual outside the partnership or by a company which is that individual's personal company. Analogous relief is given as to the assets and periods for disposal.

42.5.4 Calculation of Relevant Gains and Losses

The relevant gains and losses arising from the material disposals must be calculated. If the disposal of the business results in disposals under both section 169I and section 169J, the relief is given to the individual first and to the trust second (section 169N(3) and (8)). If a gain or loss is taken into account and given the special rate of tax under ER, it cannot be given any other effect (section 169N(9)). Further rules provide for reorganisations of shareholdings. Normally the shares are treated as continuing and not disposed of (TCGA 1992, section 127), but parties may elect to treat the reorganisation as if it involved a disposal (sections 169Q and 169R), eg where QCBs are involved and a gain would arise under section 116(10). There are elaborate rules on transition and interaction with EIS and VCT (Schedule 3, paragraphs 6 and 7).

42.6 Reinvestment Reliefs (Obsolete)

Reinvestment relief applied from November 1993 to April 1998. It is of theoretical interest as an example of a relief designed to encourage investment in unquoted companies; it is also interesting as an example of the need for complex legislation to protect a relief from exploitation. Reinvestment relief remained of current practical interest because of the risk that reliefs given before April 1998 would be clawed back; the claw-back period was three years from the time of the acquisition of the new investment (section 164F(12)). The relief was replaced in April 1998 by rules allowing gains to be deferred if the proceeds were invested in companies qualifying under the EIS (see §41.8).

42.7 Partnerships[66]

TCGA 1992 states simply that where two or more persons carry on a trade or business in partnership, any partnership dealings shall be treated as dealings by the partners and not by the firm as such (section 59). To make matters workable, the Revenue issued Statement

---

[66] The classic analysis by Lawton, Goldberg and Fraser, *The Law of Partnership Taxation*, 2nd edn (Oyez Pub, 1979), ch 9, still holds good in large measure; see also Whiteman, *Whiteman on Capital Gains Tax*, 4th edn (Sweet & Maxwell, 2008) ch 29.

of Practice D12, supplemented by Statement of Practice SP 1/89. This is clearly inconsistent with the true legal position in a number of respects, and it is open to any partnership to apply the correct legal position—consistently. The Revenue starting point is that the firm as such owns nothing; instead, each partner owns a share in each of the partnership assets without any discount for the size of that share.[67]

Assets held as partner—distinguish other capacities. As a matter of general CGT law, if a partner, P, is both the beneficial owner of property and a trustee of a settlement, P acts in two totally separate capacities. An election made by P in respect of the property owned beneficially does not affect the property held by P as trustee of the settlement.

Partner and personal (private). This principle applies also, in the Revenue view, to property held by P as a partner in a partnership. For example, the Revenue has insisted that a rebasing election made in respect of partnership assets does not affect assets which P holds privately.[68] Following on from an OTS review of partnerships, in 2015 HMRC revised Statement of Practice D12 on the CGT treatment of partnerships. The changes are mostly presentational rather than changes to HMRC's approach, which was thought by the OTS to work reasonably well.

42.7.1 Disposal of Assets by a Partnership

Where an asset is disposed of by a partnership to a third party, each partner is treated as disposing of a fractional share of the asset. So if there are three partners and their shares are 50%, 30% and 20%, the relevant gains and losses will be attributed to them in these proportions. The Revenue view is that one should allocate the gain amongst the partners in accordance with 'the ratio of their shares in asset surpluses at the time of the disposal'.[69] This is, in general, in accordance with the entitlement of the partners to capital profits. However, if the gain on a particular disposal of a particular asset is allocated differently from that applied to capital profits generally, the specific allocation is followed in assessing the gain. The partners are taken to have agreed a change to their capital sharing ratios in relation to that particular disposal and the agreement is evidenced by the actual allocation of proceeds. If the surplus is not allocated, but for example is put to a common reserve, one looks to the specified asset surplus-sharing ratio, failing which the ordinary profit-sharing ratio. Where the partnership agreement does not specify a particular division of capital profits, entitlement to capital profits is in the same proportions as the entitlement to income profits. Such entitlement may be shown in a partnership deed, or may be inferred from the action of partners.[70]

Where an asset which has previously been held as 'partnership property' is passed to one or more partner(s), eg on dissolution, the partner who receives the asset is not regarded simply as disposing of a fractional share in it; in such circumstances it is important to see which partners receive the asset. Statement of Practice D12, paragraph 3 says that the start-

---

[67] SP D12, para 1. See also Capital Gains Manual CG27150.
[68] Inland Revenue interpretation RI 9.
[69] SP D12, para 2.
[70] See, eg, the willingness of the court to identify terms of a purely oral partnership agreement in *Munro v Stamp Duties Commr* [1934] AC 61, [1933] All ER Rep 185, PC.

ing point is to compute the gains which would be chargeable on the individual partners if the asset had been disposed of to a third party at its current market value. Gains attributed to partners who do not receive a share in the asset are then chargeable on those partners. Where the gain is allocated to a partner, P, who has received the asset (or a share therein), there is no charge on the distribution. Instead, P's allowable cost to be put against a subsequent disposal is the market value of the asset received, reduced by the amount of the gain which would have been charged on P.

42.7.2 Changes in Profit-sharing Ratios

42.7.2.1 Revenue Practice—No Gain, No Loss

A change in profit-sharing ratios may arise where a new partner is admitted to the partnership or an old partner retires; it may also arise if the partners make such a change among themselves. It is at this point that Revenue practice and strict legal analysis seem to diverge. The basic rule in Statement of Practice D12, paragraph 4 is that the disposals which arise are treated as taking place at a consideration giving rise to neither a gain nor a loss. Statement of Practice SP 1/89 adds that the no gain, no loss provision is computed after taking account of indexation allowance.[71] The no gain, no loss treatment is excluded in three situations (listed below). The effect of the no gain, no loss treatment is a reduction in the base cost for a partner whose share in the asset is reduced and an increase for one whose share is increased. The normal rules for part disposal apportionments are not applied; instead, a fractional basis is used. The consistent use of this approach means that partners who leave a partnership lose their share of the acquisition costs.

Suppose that there are three partners—Mother, Daughter and Son—with equal shares and that the firm's only asset was bought some time ago for £300,000. Suppose that Mother wishes to reduce her input and so agrees a drop to a 10% interest, leaving the others with 45% each, and that these arrangements are in line with an arm's length transaction. Mother's base cost in the asset drops from £100,000 to £30,000, while Daughter's and Son's rises from £100,000 to £135,000.

42.7.2.2 Exceptions

(1) *Adjustment through the accounts.*[72] A revaluation does not give rise to CGT since it is not a disposal; however, any revaluation will be reflected in an increase (or decrease) in the partner's current or capital account. Where the revaluation of one or more partnership assets coincides or is followed by a change of profit share, the change of profit share is treated as a part disposal of the partner's interest in that asset. The consideration for the disposal is the fractional difference between the partners' old and new share applied to the value placed on the revalued asset. This treatment applies whether there is an increase or a reduction in the value of an asset shown on the balance sheet. Thus, in a falling property market, a partnership may recognise that the

---

[71] It may also be treated for the purposes of TCGA 1992, Sch 3 as if it were in para 1 of that Schedule.
[72] SP D12, para 5.

value of its freehold property has reduced, and the reduction is shown in the fixed assets on the partnership balance sheet. Any change in profit shares following this reduction gives an allowable loss for partners.

Suppose that J and K trade as equal partners, having bought the goodwill of their business for £100,000, and that the goodwill is later revalued to £160,000. Shortly after the revaluation they take in a new partner, L, on an unequal split of 40% each for themselves and 20% for L. J and K are treated as disposing of a fractional share in the goodwill; the fraction for each of them is the change from a 50% stake to a 40% stake in an asset which has been revalued to £160,000, so is £16,000 with an equivalent cost of £10,000, leaving each of them with a pre-indexation relief gain of £6,000. L's acquisition cost of the 20% share in the goodwill is £32,000.

(2) *Payment outside the account.*[73] Where there is a change in profit-sharing ratios, any payment between partners outside the partnership account is relevant consideration. An example in Statement of Practice D12 is a payment for the goodwill where the goodwill is not included in the balance sheet. This commonly arises where a new partner is admitted and buys a share from existing partners. However, consideration has passed and so there is a disposal by the other partners to the new partner.

(3) *Bargains not at arm's length and connected persons.*[74] Partners are connected persons 'except in relation to acquisitions or disposals of partnership assets pursuant to bona fide commercial arrangements' (section 286(4)). It follows that since an interest in the partnership is not a 'partnership asset', partners are, strictly, connected persons in relationship to a disposal of an interest in the partnership.[75] Nonetheless, Statement of Practice D12 states that the no gain, no loss treatment will also be applied to transactions between an incoming partner and existing partners unless the partners are connected other than by partnership (eg mother, daughter and son) or are otherwise not at arm's length (eg uncle and nephew). In these circumstances the transfer of a share in the partnership assets may fall to be treated as having been made at market value. Even here, market value will not be substituted if nothing would have been paid had the parties been at arm's length.

42.7.2.3 Changes in Profit-sharing Ratio—The Legal Analysis[76]

A change in profit-sharing ratios normally means a change in the relative interests which different partners have in the assets of the firm. Where an asset is potentially chargeable to CGT, there can be little doubt that such a change is a disposal by any partners whose shares are reduced; however, is the consideration the actual consideration which passes (which is frequently nothing) or the market value of the asset at that time? Two arguments may be advanced in favour of market value. The first is to invoke section 17 on the basis that the disposal is for a consideration which cannot be valued (section 17(1)(b)). This may

[73] SP D12, para 6.
[74] SP D12, para 7.
[75] See, eg, the discussions on the nature of an interest in partnership in *Hadlee v Commissioner of Inland Revenue* [1993] STC 294, PC.
[76] See the discussion in Whiteman, *op cit*, §§29.19 *et seq*, and Lawton, Goldberg and Fraser, *op cit*, at §§9.016 *et seq*.

be particularly apt in partnership situations, eg where a partner's share is decreased by his giving up responsibility for an aspect of the partnership's affairs. The second is to rely on the clear statutory inference that partners are connected persons in relation to these assets. Section 286(4) states that partners are connected persons, 'except in relation to acquisitions or disposals of partnership assets pursuant to bona fide commercial arrangements'. The exception for partnership assets seems to apply only to transactions between those persons who are already partners. Thus, if two individuals are in partnership and decide to admit into partnership a third, the transaction that causes the admission of the third individual is not a transaction between partners and, hence, the first two individuals are not connected with the third, unless there is a totally separate family connection.

Most partnership arrangements ought to qualify as bona fide commercial arrangements since the only reason for a commercial partnership to be in existence is for bona fide commercial reasons. Thus, an increase in P's share because of P's greater value to the partnership should be a bona fide commercial transaction. In *A-G v Boden*[77] it was established for estate duty purposes that there was a bona fide commercial transaction when younger partners took part of the profit share of the older partner at the time when he was relieved of an appropriate part of the burden of work. By contrast, there was no bona fide commercial transaction where the reduction in profit share was, in reality, an act of bounty by the older partner.[78]

42.7.3 Annuity Purchased for Retiring Partner

Where an annuity is provided, the capitalised value of that annuity is treated as consideration subject to CGT (section 37(3)). Statement of Practice D12, paragraph 8 directs that the sum subject to CGT in the hands of the retiring partner is treated as allowable expenditure by the remaining partners on the acquisition of the additional fractional shares in partnership assets. However, this does not apply if a partnership makes annual payments to a retired partner out of its own funds and not by purchase of a life annuity. Here, the capitalised value of the annuity is treated as assessable consideration if it is no more than may be regarded as a reasonable recognition of the past contribution of work and effort by the partner to the partnership. Where P had been in the partnership for at least 10 years, an annuity is regarded by the Revenue as reasonable recognition if it is no more than 40/60 (two-thirds) of P's average share of the profits for the best three of the last seven years whilst a full-time partner. A sliding scale applies to periods of less than 10 years. If P has been a partner for a shorter period, the following fractions are applied: 1/60 for each of the first five years; 8/60 for six years, 16/60 for 7; 24/60 for eight years; and 32/60 for nine years.

42.7.4 Mergers and Demergers of Partnerships

In principle, a merger or a demerger is treated in the same way as a change of profit-sharing ratio. However, it should be noted that the connected person status for dealings with partnership assets in section 286(4) cannot cause a partner in one partnership to be connected

---

[77] [1912] 1 KB 539—a case concerning the estate duty provisions of FA 1894, s 3(1).
[78] *Re Clark* (1906) 40 ILTR 117.

with a partner in another partnership simply because the partnerships are about to merge. Where Statement of Practice D12 is followed and there is no revaluation in the partnership balance sheets, a merger or demerger is treated as no gain, no loss. In the more usual situation where the firm is about to merge or the firm is about to demerge and revalue chargeable assets in its balance sheet, rollover relief under sections 152–158 may be claimed by a partner in so far as he disposes of part of his share of the assets in the old firm and acquires a share in other assets in the merged firm.[79] Similarly, on a demerger, rollover relief may be claimed, subject to satisfying the normal requirements, where there is a disposal of assets passing to the other part of the demerged firm from that in which the individual remains a partner but, in return, that individual acquires an increased share in the assets of the part of the firm in which he remains.

42.7.5 *European Economic Interest Grouping*

The CGT treatment of European Economic Interest Groupings (EEIGs)[80] largely follows that of partnerships. Thus, members of an EEIG are taxed separately on chargeable gains,[81] and disposals are deemed to occur where a person joins or leaves an EEIG, or where there is a change in the person's share in the EEIG.[82]

---

[79] SP D12, para 9.

[80] TCGA 1992, s 285A(5), ie a grouping formed in pursuance of Council Regulation (EEC) No 2137/85 of 25 July 1985.

[81] TCGA 1992, s 285A(1), ex TA 1988, s 510A(6), applying TCGA 1992, s 59.

[82] TCGA 1992, s 285A(1), ex TA 1988, s 510A(3)(b). The Revenue consider that Statement of Practice D12 does not apply to non-trading EEIGs (Inland Revenue Press Release, 19 April 1990, [1990] *Simon's Tax Intelligence* 382).

43

Computation of Gains

TCGA 1992 does not contain a section setting out a structure for determining gains.[1] Instead, it directs the adjustments to be made to the 'consideration' and lists the allowance or prohibited expenses. Gains (and losses) are computed simply by deducting the allowable costs of an asset from the adjusted consideration arising from the disposal.

43.1 Consideration

43.1.1 The Concept

The concept of consideration is relevant to calculating both the proceeds of a disposal and the costs of acquisition. The consideration for the disposal is the actual amount due, in

---

[1] Unlike, eg, the Canadian Income Tax Act, s 40(1)(a) of which defines a 'gain' as the proceeds of disposition minus the adjusted cost base and selling expenses. The US system has many rules to deal with the cost 'basis' of an asset, and judges have been adventurous in making adjustments to basis where this is required. Of course, this approach of the TCGA 1992 resembles that used to define income and business profits in TA 1988.

money or money's worth. This sum will be taken as the acquisition consideration for the new owner.[2]

Valuing the sum due may depend on a close analysis of the contract. In *Stanton v Drayton Commercial Investment Co Ltd*,[3] investments had been bought by the taxpayer, T, from an insurance company. The case concerned a later disposal by T, but the issue turned on the consideration paid for the shares by T. T paid for the shares by issuing some of its ordinary shares to the insurance company at an agreed price of 160p per share. The agreement was conditional on permission being obtained for the shares to be dealt with on the Stock Exchange. That agreement was later obtained and so the agreement became unconditional. The following day the shares were first quoted on the Stock Exchange at the price of 125p per share. The House of Lords held that the consideration was to be assessed at 160p per share, as T argued, and not the 125p for which the Revenue contended. The agreement had been made at arm's length; there was no reason for going behind this agreed value. Although the market value was lower, this would be relevant only when no proper agreed value was available. Where the consideration received includes an asset (eg a right), the asset will be valued when acquired—as in *Marren v Ingles*.[4] The later disposal of that right may also give rise to CGT.

In a computation of the gain, consideration for the disposal should be brought into account without any discount for the delay in the receipt of the disposal consideration, or for the risk of any part of the consideration being irrecoverable.[5] Consideration does not become partly 'irrecoverable' merely because it is expressed in a foreign currency which declines in value against sterling.[6] Adjustments are made if, in the event, part of the irrecoverable consideration proves to be recoverable (TCGA 1992, section 48).

43.1.2 Consideration in Foreign Currency

A gain must be computed in sterling. Where the consideration is in a foreign currency, both acquisition and disposal consideration must be converted into sterling at the rate of exchange applying at the time. This is applied separately to acquisition and disposal.[7] Whether the sums should be converted using the rate on the day on which the payments falls due or the day of actual payment is not settled; in practice, the latter date is usually taken. The rule means that there may be a gain in sterling terms even though there is none in the foreign currency. Thus, suppose an asset is bought for 100,000 Swiss francs (SF) when the rate is £1 = SF4, and resold for SF100,000 when the rate is £1 = SF2. In SF terms there is no gain, but in sterling terms the asset has doubled in value from £25,000 to £50,000 and so there will be a gain. Conversely, there may be a loss in the foreign currency and no gain in UK terms—as would have happened if the asset had been sold for SF50,000.

---

[2] TCGA 1992, s 38(1)(a). On finding the consideration, see also *Revenue & Customs Commissioners v Collins* [2009] STC 1077, [2009] EWHC 284 (Ch) per Henderson J.

[3] [1982] STC 585, 55 TC 286; see also *Spectros International plc v Madeen* [1997] STC 114, 138b.

[4] [1980] STC 500, 54 TC 76; distinguished in *Fielder v Vedlynn Ltd* [1992] STC 553, 65 TC 145, where certain undertakings giving rise to further consideration were held to be of no additional value.

[5] TCGA 1992, s 48; s 48 was amended by F(No 2)A 2005, Sch 7, para 7, so that it does not apply to consideration consisting of rights under a creditor relationship within FA 1996, Pt 4, Ch 2.

[6] *Loffland Bros North Sea v Goodbrand* [1998] STC 930, CA.

[7] *Bentley v Pike* [1981] STC 360, 53 TC 590; followed in *Capcount Trading v Evans* [1993] STC 11, 65 TC 545.

It is tempting to argue that because there is no gain in terms of the foreign currency, there should be none under UK tax law. However, this ignores the asset-based nature of the CGT and the need to tie receipts and expenditure to the asset. This becomes all the clearer if one considers an asset where the price is in one foreign currency and the sale is in another foreign currency.[8] Income tax is different; the no gain result will be reached under the matching principle used for ITTOIA 2005, Part 2 outside the corporation tax area.[9] Where consideration received in a foreign currency is kept in a foreign bank account, there may be a further gain or loss when the currency is converted into sterling. Foreign currency is usually an asset for CGT purposes.[10]

43.1.3 Consideration Consisting of a Right—Valuation and Identification Problems

A contract may provide for the seller to be paid a further sum on the occurrence of a defined event. This is common where shares in a private company are sold and the seller is to receive a further sum if the profits exceed a certain sum in the next few years. This right to receive the further consideration is part of the consideration for the first disposal; it must be valued and incorporated in that CGT computation along with other sale consideration.[11] If it cannot be valued, a nil valuation may have to be taken. The value determined for this first computation is then the acquisition cost of the asset and used when it is disposed of, ie when the further money is obtained. In *Marren v Ingles*,[12] the taxpayer, T, sold shares in a private company for £750 per ordinary share, plus the right to receive a further cash payment in certain circumstances. This cash payment was to be calculated by reference to the market value of shares following the flotation of the company. In the event, the taxpayer received a further £2,825 per share as a result of the flotation. The House of Lords held that the original disposal was for consideration consisting of two parts—the cash sum of £750 per ordinary share and the right. Tax was due in respect of *x*, the gain on the right when the £2,585 was received. The extent of the gain, ie what, if any, acquisition cost could be put against the £2,825, was not decided. It is not clear whether the right is a wasting asset; however, it is not movable property.

43.1.4 Consideration Which Cannot be Valued—Market Value Rule

Where there is a disposal of an asset wholly or partly for a consideration which cannot be valued, the market value of the asset disposed of is treated as the consideration (section 17(1)(b)). The market value of the consideration is not relevant since that cannot be valued. The same rule, using the market value of the asset disposed of, is used where the disposal is 'in connection with [the taxpayer's] own or another's loss of office or employment or diminution of emoluments, or otherwise in consideration or recognition of his or another's services or past services in any office or employment or of any other service rendered or to be rendered by him or another.'

[8] See *Capcount Trading v Evans* [1993] STC 11, 23, 65 TC 545, 560.
[9] *Pattison v Marine Midland* [1984] STC 10, 57 TC 219.
[10] See TCGA 1992, s 252.
[11] *Fielder v Vedlynn* [1992] STC 553, 64 TC 145.
[12] [1980] STC 500, 54 TC 76; see also *Marson v Marriage* [1980] STC 177, 54 TC 59.

43.1.5 *Apportionment of Consideration*

Consideration may have to be apportioned between disposals or between income and capital. Unless there is a specific direction in statute, any 'necessary' apportionment adopted is to be by such method as is 'just and reasonable'.[13] It is not clear what is meant by the word 'necessary'. If the parties have apportioned the consideration themselves, the Revenue insist that they may still apportion on a different basis—even though the parties' own basis is reasonable. The opposite argument, that the apportionment is not 'necessary' in these circumstances, has not yet been put before the courts.

In *EV Booth (Holdings) Ltd v Buckwell*,[14] the parties had agreed to sell shares and to settle a debt; the agreement specified separate considerations for the two elements of the agreement. The court held that the agreement ruled and it was not open to the taxpayer to reallocate the consideration in a different way. In *Aberdeen Construction Group Ltd v IRC*,[15] shares were sold in return for a sum of money and the waiver of a loan of £250,000. A majority in the House of Lords held that the matter should be remitted to the Commissioners for an appropriate apportionment. The distinction is between paying one sum for two items (*Aberdeen*), in which event apportionment follows, and two separate sums one for each of two items (*Booth v Buckwell*), where it does not.[16] The actual effect in *Booth v Buckwell* was to leave the taxpayer with a CGT liability where, in a business sense and taking the two assets together, it had barely broken even;[17] correct planning would no doubt have avoided this conclusion. The problem arises yet again from having a CGT based on assets instead of more general capital receipts tax.

43.1.6 *Consideration Liable to Income Tax—Excluded*

In valuing the consideration, any money or money's worth which is chargeable as income of the disposer, whether to income tax or corporation tax, or which enters into the computation of profits for those taxes is excluded.[18] An exception is made where the payment is taken into account for the purposes of a balancing charge (section 37(2)). However, the capitalised value of a rentcharge or a right to any other income is expressly included as consideration, notwithstanding that the income receipts will themselves be subject to income tax or corporation tax.[19] In practice, it will sometimes be necessary to determine whether the receipts are, in fact, income, or instalments of a capital sum.[20] Where there is a disposal for a consideration which includes a right to receive rent, the capitalised value of the rent is excluded as consideration by this rule; however, it may still be relevant in other areas, eg in applying the part disposal formula (see above §37.5).

---

[13] TCGA 1992, s 52(4); references to 'appearing to the inspector or on appeal the Commissioners concerned' were removed to facilitate self-assessment.

[14] [1980] STC 578, 53 TC 425.

[15] [1978] AC 885, [1978] STC 127, 52 TC 281.

[16] [1980] STC 578, 584, 53 TC 425, 432.

[17] Wosner [1981] BTR 58 at 61.

[18] TCGA 1992, s 37(1). This also prevents any CGT liability on payments falling within ITEPA 2003, ss 401–403, ex TA 1988, s 148.

[19] TCGA 1992, s 37(3). Note that in such cases the capital element in the annuity which was exempt from income tax under ex TA 1988, ss 656, 657 is not the same as the capitalised value.

[20] See, eg, *IRC v Adam* (1928) 14 TC 34.

43.1.7 *Allowance for Liabilities*

43.1.7.1 General Rule

Where the vendor assumes an actual liability on the disposal of an asset, it seems clear that the liability must be deducted from any consideration received, although the position, in practice, will depend upon the terms agreed between the parties. If the transferee assumes any liability of the transferor as part of the transaction, the value of the liability is to be added to any other consideration given. However, any liability in respect of the asset disposed of which remains with the transferor is not deductible from the consideration received.[21]

43.1.7.2 Certain Contingent Liabilities

Where an agreement incorporates a contingent liability, section 49 directs that in this situation no account is taken of the contingent liability in the initial computation of the gain arising. This treatment ends when the contingency ends (section 49(2)). The three situations in which no account is taken of the contingent liability are the assignment of a lease, the sale of land or of an interest in land, and the sale of property other than land. The contingent liabilities are: (a) those arising on default by the assignee in relation to his obligations under the lease; (b) any liability in relation to a covenant for quiet enjoyment or any other obligation assumed as a vendor of land or of any estate or interest in land, or as lesser; and (c) those in respect of a warranty or representation made on a disposal by sale or lease of property other than land.

The purpose of section 49 is probably to insist on the immediate calculation of any CGT in full without having to take account of the obligations normally (or abnormally) undertaken by a vendor. Such obligations are quite different from a condition—precedent or subsequent. Section 49 was not therefore applied in *Randall v Plumb*.[22] There, T granted a company an option to buy land which he farmed. The company deposited £25,000 with him in consideration for the grant of an option. In the event that the company exercised the option, this sum was to be treated as part of the purchase price; if planning permission was not obtained by the company for the extraction of sand, etc, the £25,000 was repayable. The court held that the contingent liability to repay £25,000 was not an obligation assumed by T 'as the vendor' of land but 'in the event of his not being the vendor' and so section 49 did not apply. There was therefore no obligation on T to pay tax on the £25,000 on receipt. It did not follow that no CGT was due—T would have to pay tax on the £25,000 less an allowance for the contingent obligation to repay. This decision has been criticised as requiring much guesswork in valuing the consideration and because it is difficult to find a statutory basis on which to adjust the figures should T have to repay the money. Further, the test is not whether T was a vendor of land, but whether he was the vendor of an interest in land and the option was an interest in land.[23]

In *Sir Fraser Morrison v HMRC*,[24] the taxpayer had sold shares in a company in return for shares of the purchaser, and later was sued by the purchaser for misrepresentation.

---

[21] This seems to follow from the judgment in *Coren v Keighley* [1972] 1 WLR 1556, 48 TC 370.
[22] [1975] STC 191, 50 TC 392, discussed and distinguished in *Garner v Pounds* [2000] STC 420 (HL).
[23] Baxter (1975) 39 *Conv* NS 240.
[24] [2014] CSIH 113.

An out-of-court settlement was reached and the taxpayer paid the purchaser £12 million without accepting liability. When the taxpayer disposed of his shares in the purchaser, he claimed the £12 million as a reduction in the capital gain under section 49 on that basis that is was the enforcement of a contingent liability in respect of representations he had made on the disposal of his original shareholding. The Scottish Court of Session, reversing the decision of the Upper Tribunal, agreed with the taxpayer that his contingent liability was the representations made to the purchaser, the ultimate consequence of which was to lead to the settlement that reduced the value of the gain realised by the taxpayer on the disposal of his shares. The Court of Session remitted the case to the First-tier Tribunal to decide whether the whole, or if not what part, of the settlement payment made by the appellant was attributable to representations made by the appellant giving rise to the contingent liability falling within section 49(1)(c).[25]

43.2   Allowable Expenditure

43.2.1 Seven Categories of Allowable Expenditure

TCGA 1992, section 38 provides that costs which may be deducted from consideration are limited to certain categories. These are acquisition costs ((1)–(3))[26] and improvement costs ((4)–(6)),[27] plus the costs of disposal ((7)).[28] In view of the complex language of the section, these are best broken open into the following categories:

(1)   Consideration, in money or money's worth, given by the taxpayer, T, or on T's behalf, wholly and exclusively for the acquisition of the asset (eg the purchase price).

(2)   Any incidental costs to T of the acquisition. Incidental costs must have been incurred by the person making the disposal, wholly and exclusively for the purposes of the acquisition. This includes the costs of establishing title. Such costs are expressly limited to fees, commission or remuneration paid for the professional services of any surveyor, valuer, auctioneer, accountant, agent or legal adviser, and the costs of transfer or conveyance (including stamp duty), together with the costs of advertising to find a seller (section 38(2)). Fees for the services on acquisition must be distinguished from the fees payable for investment advice, which are not allowable. Expenses of travel to inspect property with a view to purchase are not allowable, even if the property is, in fact, acquired.

(3)   If the asset was not acquired by T, any expenditure wholly and exclusively incurred by T in providing the asset; these words must be read in the context of the rest of the section. So where the asset is an option to buy land within a specified period, the land being subject to an existing obligation, it could not be said that the costs of implementing the obligation were incurred 'in providing' the option; this was because implementing the obligation was not a prerequisite to exercising the option.[29]

[25] For commentary see Eden [2015] BTR 180.
[26] TCGA 1992, s 38(1)(a).
[27] TCGA 1992, s 38(1)(b).
[28] TCGA 1992, s 38(1)(c).
[29] *Garner v Pounds* [2000] STC 420 (HL).

(4) Expenditure wholly and exclusively incurred by T for the purpose of enhancing the value of the asset, being expenditure reflected in the asset at the time of disposal, eg the costs of building a warehouse on a piece of land—provided the warehouse is still standing at the time of the disposal (see below).
(5) Expenditure incurred in establishing title to the asset, eg a Land Registry fee on registering land that has been acquired (see further below).
(6) Expenditure on preserving or defending the title to the asset. This will include, for example, the cost of a court action to stop the loss of the asset, or damage to an asset, by another person. Such costs are allowable even where the decision of the court is against the taxpayer (section 38(1)(b), see below).
(7) Incidental costs of disposal (see (2) above).

Rule (4): improvement expenditure

Expenditure wholly and exclusively incurred on the asset by the person making the disposal or on his behalf is allowable if it is for the purpose of enhancing the value of the asset (section 38(1)(b)). Such expenditure must still be reflected in the state or nature of the asset at the time of the disposal. If the expenditure is so reflected, no matter in how small a way, it is allowable in full. So if a new bathroom were fitted in a house and then, before disposal, that bathroom were gutted and completely replaced by an even shinier new bathroom, the cost of the first renewal would not be allowed; clever tax planning might have led to a less satisfactory new bathroom.

It appears that the expenditure must make an identifiable change in the state or nature of the asset. In *Aberdeen Construction Group Ltd v IR C*,[30] expenditure on the waiver of a loan could not be deducted since it did not make an identifiable change in the particular assets sold, ie shares. It follows that a payment to a valuer to determine the authenticity of a painting or other work of art is, strictly, not deductible—whatever the verdict. This rule also excludes an advance payment to a builder who goes bankrupt before beginning work. When the disposal is by contract followed by conveyance it is unclear how far, if at all, the improvements must be reflected in the state or nature of the asset at the time of the conveyance as opposed to the contract.[31]

A payment may be required in order to make a disposal, but this does not, of itself, permit a deduction for this payment unless the payment makes a change to the asset or its value. In *Emmerson v Computer Time International Ltd*,[32] rent was owed to a landlord. The landlord agreed to consent to an assignment of the lease on condition that the rent arrears were paid. The rent arrears were not deductible in the CGT computation. Any initial repairs to property which is to be let and which are not allowable under ITTOIA 2005, Part 3 may fall to be treated as improvement expenditure allowable in computing a capital gain—when the property is disposed of.[33] The application of the former taper relief in the context of improvement expenditure was quite generous. Relief was given simply on the basis of the

---

[30] [1978] AC 885, [1978] STC 127, 52 TC 281.
[31] *Chaney v Watkis* [1986] STC 89, 58 TC 707.
[32] [1977] STC 170, [1977] 2 All ER 545, 50 TC 628.
[33] Statement of Practice SP D24. Quaere how this interacts with the rule in TCGA 1992, s 39(2), discussed at §43.2.2 below.

period of ownership of the asset; it was not necessary, as it still is for indexation relief for corporation tax, to treat the improvement expenditure as a separate item with its own time period.

HMRC v Julian Blackwell,[34] is an interesting and rare case on the scope of allowable expenditure under TCGA 1992, section 38(1)(b). In 2003 following an unsuccessful takeover attempt, the taxpayer undertook certain obligations to Taylor & Francis in relation to his shares in a publishing company (BP) in return for £1m. In 2006, he paid £17.5m to Taylor & Francis to be released from the obligations and enable him to sell his BP shares to John Wiley & Sons. The taxpayer claimed the £17.5m as allowable expenditure in computing the capital gains on the subsequent disposal of the shares. Reversing the First-tier Tribunal, the Upper Tribunal found that the relevant asset for the purposes of section 38(1)(b) comprised the bundle of rights and obligations which would pass to the purchaser rather than those which exclusively affected the vendor. As the obligations to Taylor & Francis were personal to the taxpayer and could not affect a buyer, the UT held that the payment 'was not reflected in the state or nature of the shares' sold, and so was not allowable expenditure. The UT also held that under the 2006 agreement Mr Blackwell did not 'establish, preserve or defend any right over his asset'. Consequently, the £17.5 million did not qualify as allowable expenditure. The case was well argued for the Revenue and the language of section 38(1)(b) is clearly restrictive (perhaps unnecessarily so); however, one could be justified for viewing the result as overly technical given how detached it appears from the underlying economics.

Categories (5) and (6): title

Costs are allowable if incurred wholly and exclusively by the owner (but not on his behalf) in establishing, preserving or defending his title to, or to a right over, the asset. This category must be distinguished from acquisition costs and operates narrowly. The word 'establishing' is limited by the words 'preserving' and 'defending'. In a case involving a settlement, a beneficiary secured the agreement of the trustees to vest the trust funds in her absolutely.[35] She was, however, required to take out a single premium policy on her life, written in favour of the trustees, to indemnify them against her predeceasing another beneficiary having a contingent interest. It was held that the payment of the premium was not to establish the beneficiary's defeasible interest in the fund, since that was not in dispute, but to acquire something greater, ie the absolute interest. Hence, the costs could be deducted only if they came within the category of acquisition costs.

Despite this, the main obstacles to claiming allowable expenditure under this heading are the exclusion of expenditure which would be deductible as a revenue expense if the asset were a fixed asset in a trade, and the income tax rule that money spent on defending title to a capital asset is a revenue expense (above §22.4.3.4). For example, a sum paid by a liquidator in respect of arrears of rent, even if it had been spent in preserving the asset (a leasehold interest), would not have been deductible.[36] However, the incidental cost of

---

[34] [2015] UKUT 0418 (TCC).
[35] *Allison v Murray* [1975] STC 524, [1975] 3 All ER 561, 51 TC 57. The expense did not come within category (1) since it was not consideration for the acquisition of absolute title but was to acquire the other beneficiary's contingent interest.
[36] *Emmerson v Computer Time International Ltd* [1976] STC 111, [1976] 2 All ER 131.

valuing shares and securities for estate duty purposes has been held to be allowable for CGT under this category, on the grounds that the main purpose is to obtain probate of the will, which establishes the title of the executors to the assets.[37] The Revenue allow such expenses in practice on the basis of a fixed scale according to the value of the estate. Of course, if the sum would have been deductible as a trading receipt, eg as in *Morgan v Tate & Lyle*,[38] it is not allowable as a CGT deduction.

43.2.2 Restrictions

43.2.2.1 Revenue (Actual and Hypothetical) Expenditure

(1) *Actual.* Just as sums taken into account in computing income are excluded from the consideration for CGT, so revenue expenditure is disallowed in computing chargeable gains. A sum is not allowable expenditure for CGT if it is allowable as a deduction in computing the profits or losses of a trade, profession or vocation for purposes of income tax, or as a deduction in computing any other income for the purposes of the Income Tax Acts (section 39(1)). This exclusion is extended to sums which would be deductible in computing losses but for the fact that there are insufficient profits against which the losses may be offset.

(2) *Hypothetical.* There is a second, more stringent, limitation on the deduction of expenses. Expenditure is not deductible for CGT if, on the hypothesis that the asset was employed as a fixed asset of a trade, the expenditure would be deductible in computing the profits of that trade for income tax purposes (section 39(2)). For assets such as land and buildings, this restriction denies relief for maintenance expenditure, even where the property is not let. It is important to bear in mind that even extensive expenditure on rehabilitating an asset may be deductible for income tax, unless it can be shown that the dilapidations requiring attention depressed the price paid for the asset.[39]

43.2.2.2 Market Value

Where market value is taken as 'acquisition cost', rather than expenditure incurred, no deduction may be claimed for incidental expenditure that *might* have been incurred on an actual acquisition (section 38(4). It does not follow that there can be no deductible expenditure on a deemed disposal—actual costs are deductible. Thus, legal and other fees were held deductible when incurred on the preparation of a deed of variation, under which funds would be divided between a tenant for life and the remainderman, the variation being a deemed disposal.[40]

---

[37] *IRC v Richards' Executors* [1971] 1 All ER 785, 46 TC 626; but see also *Passant v Jackson* [1986] STC 164, 59 TC 230.

[38] [1955] AC 21, 35 TC 367.

[39] *Odeon Associated Theatres Ltd v Jones* [1973] Ch 288, [1972] 1 All ER 681, 48 TC 257 (see above at §22.4.3.8).

[40] *IRC v Chubb's Settlement Trustees* (1971) 47 TC 353.

43.2.2.3 Miscellaneous

Where expenditure is allowable, T must be able to show that it has been incurred; no allowance may be made for the value of the purely notional cost of work carried out by the owner
himself.[41] No deduction may be made more than once (section 52(1)). No deduction may
be made if it has been or is to be met out of public money, whether of the Crown, or
any government or local authority anywhere (section 50). No deduction may be made for
insurance premiums, etc, under a policy of insurance of the risk of any kind of damage or
injury to or loss or depreciation of, the asset (section 205). No deduction may be made for
payments of interest (section 39(3)).

43.2.3 *Expenditure by Someone Other than Taxpayer*

Categories (1), (3) and (4) above allow expenditure incurred on behalf of the disposer. This
is apt to cover expenditure incurred by a person, such as a trustee or mortgagee, whose acts
are treated as those of the owner. The position is less clear if any other person pays for the
improvements, eg by way of gift to the owner. It is not necessary that the owner should
ultimately bear the cost, but it may be necessary that there should be some sort of contractual relationship of the nature of an agency between the owner and the person incurring
the expenditure.[42] Particular problems arise in the case of joint tenancies, where one joint
tenant incurs expenditure on the asset but the other subsequently becomes solely entitled.
Property law suggests that the whole should be allowable since each joint tenant has an
interest in the whole property. However, it is not clear that one joint tenant 'necessarily'
incurs the expenditure on behalf of the other, in the absence of any additional agreement
between them. On a death of one of the joint tenants, that tenant's severable share will
be deemed acquired by the other at its market value (section 62(10)); it follows that any
expenditure incurred by the deceased prior to death will no longer be relevant.

43.2.4 *Apportionment of Expenditure*

The categories of allowable expenditure all require that the costs be incurred 'wholly and
exclusively' for the acquisition or improvement, etc. It seems that in practice this phrase is
interpreted by the Revenue less restrictively than is ITTOIA 2005, section 34 for income tax.
There is some judicial authority for this; the House of Lords held that expenditure incurred
on valuing stocks and shares both for probate and estate duty was allowable notwithstanding the apparent dual purpose.[43] This may, however, simply have been because the estate
duty payment was incidental to the main purpose of obtaining probate. It is clear that where
the main purpose is allowable, expenditure is deductible in full even though there is some

---

[41] *Oram v Johnson* [1980] STC 222, 53 TC 319.

[42] *Gaspet Ltd v Ellis* [1985] STC 572, [1985] 1 WLR 1214, a case concerning scientific research allowances under
CAA 1990, s 137.

[43] *IRC v Richards' Executors* [1971] 1 All ER 785, 46 TC 626: Lord Reid (*ibid*, 790, 635) construing it 'so as to
give a reasonable result'; Lords Upjohn and Morris dissented. See also *IRC v Chubb's Trustees* (1971) 47 TC 353,
where legal fees were held to be deductible because they were paid on variation, causing a deemed disposal; the
Revenue argument that the fees were paid in order to divide up the settled property was dismissed.

subsidiary or incidental purpose which is not allowable. Conversely, no sum is deductible at all if the allowable purpose is purely incidental.[44] This leaves open the question whether an apportionment may be made where there are two main purposes, only one of which is allowable.[45] Where a taxpayer carried out a scheme designed to avoid CGT, the expenses of the scheme were deductible even though it might be argued that one of the purposes of the expenditure was to avoid tax.[46] There is no authority on this point since the House of Lords' Schedule D decision in *Mallalieu v Drummond* (see above §22.2.1); it may one day be necessary to speak of effects and not of incidental purposes.

Where a sum has been spent on two or more assets the expenditure must be apportioned (section 52(4)). The issue in such cases is the correct construction of the agreement, and is the same as for apportionment of consideration (see above at §43.1.5). Issues under both apportionment and restriction (see §43.2.2) arose in *Drummond v Revenue & Customs Commissioners*.[47] The taxpayer (D) carried out a CGT loss avoidance scheme. D had bought a second-hand life policy in 2001 for £1.962m. He then surrendered the policy and obtained its surrender value of £1.75m (based on the premiums paid); the surrender cost him £210,000. He claimed, invoking section 37, that in calculating his gain he could exclude the £1.75m of surrender value from the proceeds of sale because this was liable to income tax under special rules (then TA 1988, section 541, now ITTOIA 2005, Part 4, Chapter 9). This would leave him with the large loss now claimed. Today this would be countered by TCGA 1992, section 16A, added in 2007. The Court of Appeal held that this was not a correct application of section 37. Rimer LJ was not going to be party to any 'black letter literalism'; the purpose of these rules was to avoid double taxation and not to avoid any tax altogether.

43.2.5 Reduction of Expenditure on Wasting Assets

On the disposal of a wasting asset the allowable expenditure is written off on a straight-line basis, calculated day by day (section 46(1)). In making these calculations the residual or scrap value is not written off. For example, if an asset cost £370,000, and has £5,000 residual or scrap value, the remaining £365,000 will be written off over its predictable life; if that life is 10,000 days (ie just over 27 years), the £365,000 will be reduced by £36.50 a day. So a sale after 5,000 days will mean that of the £370,000, only £5,000 plus £182,500 will be deductible as acquisition expenditure.

A wasting asset is one with a predictable life not exceeding 50 years (section 44(1)). It should be assumed that the life will end when the asset is of no further use; normal usage is to be expected. Freehold land cannot be a wasting asset, whatever its nature and whatever the nature of the buildings or works on it. Neither antique furniture nor precious stones will be wasting assets. Whether some recent works of art will be wasting assets depends on

---

[44] *Cleveleys Investment Trust v IRC* [1975] STC 457.

[45] The point was not directly tackled in *IRC v Richards' Executors* [1971] 1 All ER 785, 46 TC 626, since the cost of valuing the stocks and shares were essential to obtaining probate (see eg Lord Guest at 46 TC 626, 644).

[46] *Eilbeck v Rawling* [1980] STC 192, [1980] 2 All ER 12, CA; not commented upon by the House of Lords at [1982] AC 300, [1981] STC 174, [1981] 1 All ER 865, 54 TC 101. See generally the discussion in Whiteman, *Whiteman on Capital Gains Tax*, 4th edn (Sweet & Maxwell, 2008) §8.37.

[47] [2009] EWCA Civ 608, [2009] STC 2206.

the application of the 50-year test. The vulnerability of certain works of art to strong sunlight should not make them wasting assets since 'normal' use would presumably provide enough protection. Wine presents other problems, since most wine is undrinkable after 50 years and very few people can afford the facilities to look after it sufficiently well; whether proper storage is 'normal' use, and so enough to prevent some wine from being wasting assets, is another matter.

43.2.6 Deduction of IHT

Where IHT is chargeable on a transfer which is also a disposal for CGT, holdover relief may be claimed under section 260 or section 165. If the transferee, E, pays IHT on such a transfer and the transferor claims the relief, the IHT is deductible by E as part of the acquisition cost to be put against the ultimate disposal of the asset by E.[48] On the converse case of deducting CGT in computing IHT, see below at §55.5.4.1.

43.3 Taper Relief

43.3.1 Introduction[49]

One of the key features of the 1998 reform of CGT was the substitution of taper relief for indexation relief—for CGT but not for corporation tax.[50] Its major effect was to introduce a low rate of tax on most business assets; as was suggested in the discussion of the history of CGT in §32.7 above, this effect might have been better achieved by retaining the old indexation system and simply applying a lower rate of tax on business assets. One of the key features of the 2008 reform of CGT was the abolition of taper relief for disposals on or after 6 April 2008.[51] This change had no effect for corporation tax as taper relief did not apply to corporation tax. One major effect of the abolition of taper relief was an increase in the rate of tax on business assets. Protests from those who lost by the change led to the entrepreneurs' relief considered above at §42.5.

43.4 Indexation Allowance

43.4.1 Introduction

Where a company makes a disposal, indexation allowance is computed up to the month of disposal. For a disposal after 5 April 1998 and before 6 April 2008 by an individual,

---

[48] TCGA 1992, ss 67(1), (3), 165(10), (11), 260(7), (8); on valuation for one tax being conclusive for the other, see s 274.

[49] See, on original legislation, Jamieson [1999] *Private Client Business* 66, 140; and on later changes Mackie [2001] *Private Client Business* 10 and 62. For an outline of taper relief, seethe fifth edition of this book at §43.3.

[50] TCGA 1992, s 53(1A), added by FA 1998, s 121.

[51] FA 2008, s 6 and Sch 2.

trustees or PRs, indexation allowance is calculated to 5 April 1998 only.[52] Taper relief was then applied to the computed gain,[53] ie after taking account of indexation. The move to the single rate of 18% for CGT by FA 2008 enabled Parliament to abolish the pre-1998 effect of indexation for CGT. Some of the benefits of this trade-off have since disappeared for higher-income taxpayers, trustees and PRs with the 2010 introduction of the 28% rate (now generally 20%).[54] Indexation still applies for corporation tax, however, and this is achieved by inserting section 52A.

43.4.1.1 Calculation of Allowance

The indexation allowance is a fraction of the allowable expenditure. The fraction is given by the formula (RD—RI) × RI, where RD is the retail prices index figure for the month in which the disposal occurs and RI that for the month in which the expenditure is incurred (section 54(2)). If RI exceeds RD, the indexation allowance is nil (section 54(8)). The fraction is to be expressed as a decimal, taken to the nearest three decimal places (section 54(4)). Where there are several items of allowable expenditure incurred at different times, the indexed rise is calculated separately for each, and the aggregate is then the indexation allowance.

Indexation applies only to items of relevant allowable expenditure, broadly the cost of acquisition and any expenditure on enhancement or preservation of title (section 53(2)(b), see above at §43.2.1). It does not apply to deductions such as foreign tax which is not taken as a credit. Where an element of expenditure falls to be reduced (the most obvious example is the reduction of expenditure on leased property), increased or excluded, the indexed rise applies only to the expenditure as reduced, increased or excluded.[55] The delights of applying the indexation rules where unit trusts have been subscribed to on a monthly basis since 1964 may be imagined; a Revenue Statement of Practice allows the 12 purchases made during a year to be treated as if there were one purchase halfway through the year.[56] The indexation allowance is treated as a deduction from the gain computed under general chargeable gains rules. It may reduce the gain to produce either a smaller gain or neither a gain nor a loss, but cannot, at present, turn the gain into a loss or increase a loss. From 1985–95 indexation could turn a gain into a loss or increase a loss; the logic of the relief was seen to clash with Revenue concerns about avoidance but, in truth, the Revenue seem never to have liked indexation.

43.4.1.2 Pre-1982 Expenditure

Indexation was introduced in 1982 and applies only as from 1 April 1982; a gain for a prior period is termed 'unindexed gain'. Where an asset was acquired before 1 April 1982 and disposed of after 5 April 1988, the allowance is calculated by reference to the market value on 31 March 1982 rather than the various items of expenditure incurred before that date,

---

[52] TCGA 1992, s 53(lA).

[53] TCGA 1992, s 2A(2).

[54] FA 2008, Sch 2.

[55] TCGA 1992, s 53(3). On a merger of a lease into a superior interest, the indexation allowance on disposal of the merged interest will be based on the expenditure on the original lease, wasted down to the date of the merger where appropriate (ESC D42).

[56] Statement of Practice SP 2/97. The method of computation in the statement applies to approved investment trusts and open-ended investment companies, as well as authorised unit trusts.

if this gives a result favourable to the taxpayer (section 55(1), (2)). However, the 31 March 1982 value must be used to compute the indexation allowance if the taxpayer has made an election under TCGA 1992, section 35(5). The rules provide for changes in the state of the asset since 31 March 1982.[57] Readers should note that the election under section 35(5) now applies only for corporation tax.

43.4.1.3 Part Disposal and Indexation

On a part disposal, the deductible expenditure in respect of the whole asset must be apportioned before the indexation allowance is calculated. The indexation allowance on the part disposal applies only to that part of each item of expenditure which is to be taken into account on the disposal (section 56(1)).

43.4.2 *Special Situations*

43.4.2.1 Indexation Losses—Transitional Relief

A very limited transitional relief for indexation losses arose for disposals made on or after 30 November 1993, but before 6 April 1995, by individuals or by certain trustees.[58]

43.4.2.2 No Gain, No Loss

Certain CGT provisions apply a no gain, no loss rule to certain types of disposal, for example on a transfer of an asset between member companies in groups. For a disposal of this kind after 5 April 1985, the consideration for the disposal takes account of any indexation allowance due to the transferor, by treating the disposal as giving rise to an indexation allowance equal to the indexed gain.[59] Other detailed rules apply to more complex situations arising from the frequency with which CGT rules changed.[60]

43.4.2.3 Relevant Receipts

Receipts do not give rise to a disposal but reduce the amount of relevant expenditure; indexation takes account of the reduction in allowable expenditure, but only from the date of the receipt (section 57). For example, if a shareholder sells 'rights' on a rights issue, the amount received is not treated as a chargeable disposal if the proceeds amount to less than 5% of the value of the shareholding ex-rights.

43.4.2.4 Reorganisations, etc

Where, on a reorganisation of a company or an amalgamation, new shares are acquired, they are generally treated as if the original acquisition were still in existence. If new consideration is provided, it is treated as new relevant allowable expenditure (section 131). The indexed rise on the expenditure is therefore calculated by reference to the date the new

---

[57] TCGA 1992, s 55(4). For disposals before 6 April 1988, but after 5 April 1985, the use of the 31 March 1982 value for indexation purposes was elective.
[58] FA 1994, s 93.
[59] TCGA 1992, s 56(2); for earlier periods, see FA 1982, Sch 13, para 3.
[60] Eg, TCGA 1992, s 55(6) (more than one such transfer); s 56(3) effect of losses and s 55(8) (base cost enhanced by pre-1993 indexed loss).

consideration was provided, not by reference to the date the allowable expenditure on the original shareholding was incurred.

43.4.2.5 Calls on Shares, etc

Unpaid calls due in respect of the shares are treated as having been paid when the shares were acquired, provided they are paid within 12 months of that date (section 113(1)(b)). Calls paid outside the 12-month period are treated as separate items of expenditure incurred when paid, and the indexation allowance on disposal of shares is calculated accordingly. In a number of so-called 'privatisation issues', the 12-month rule did not apply since there was no issue of shares, merely a transfer of existing shares by the Secretary of State.

43.4.2.6 Options

Lastly, special rules also apply to options. The acquisition of property under an option is treated as an acquisition when the option is exercised, but in computing the indexed rise, the sums paid for the option are treated as separate items of expenditure incurred when the option was acquired (section 145).

43.5 Rebasing to 31 March 1982

43.5.1 Introduction

Although CGT was introduced in 1965, it was 'rebased' to 1982 by FA 1988. Rebasing meant that, in general, only gains arising after 31 March 1982 would be taxed. This involved revaluing assets as at 31 March 1982, but the practical problems arising were reduced by the fact that a similar exercise had already been carried out for indexation relief. Thus, if an asset had been bought in 1976 and sold in 1990, only the post-1982 gains would be taxed. If the asset had been sold in 1986, tax would have been paid on the full gain realised since 1976; there was no reopening of the tax paid. This apparent generosity was reduced by the fact that the tax rates were increased in 1988, by being aligned with income tax rates.

43.5.1.1 CGT: Mandatory Rebasing to 31 March 1982 Asset Values for Individuals, Trustees and PR

As part of its simplification reform, FA 2008 required all assets disposed of by individuals, trustees and PRs to take their values as at 31 March 1982 (unless an election for a different value had already been made before 6 April 2008). A person subject to CGT also lost the right to (re)elect back into the 31 March 1982 value. This was accomplished by adding section 35(2A), which makes most of the other rebasing rules and exceptions in section 35 apply only to corporation tax.

43.5.1.2 Corporation Tax: Rebase Unless Elect

This simplification process did not apply to corporation tax because corporation tax did not have a low flat rate of tax applied. Section 35, introduced in 1988, provides that where an asset was held on 31 March 1982, the tax is calculated by reference to the value as at 31 March 1982 by deeming a sale and repurchase at market value at that time (section 35(2)). T might, however, prefer that there be no rebasing—as where the base cost of the asset is higher than the value as at 31 March 1982. Section 35 not only contains a number of rules for such situations (section 35(3)), but also gives T the right to elect that rebasing should apply after all (section 35(5)), provided this is done in relation to all T's assets and not on a pick-and-mix basis; this still applies for corporation tax. The election to take the 31 March 1982 value must be made within two years of the end of the year of assessment in which the first disposal to which it applies was made. In strictness, the first relevant disposal would be a disposal of any asset, even if the asset or the gain was exempt. In practice the Revenue will exercise their discretion[61] and ignore disposals on which the gain would not be a chargeable gain by virtue of a statutory provision (eg the sale of a passenger vehicle such as a car). The election, which is irrevocable, applies to all disposals, including those made before the election, to which rebasing applies.[62] The election is, in turn, prevented from applying to certain disposals;[63] as such, it does not cover plant or machinery (and similar assets) where capital allowances were or could have been claimed.

43.5.2 Election on No Gain, No Loss Disposal

If A Ltd disposes of an asset acquired after 31 March 1982 but on a no gain, no loss disposal, A Ltd is treated as acquiring it on 31 March 1982, so making the asset eligible for the rebasing election.[64] For disposals on or after 6 April 2008 this applies only for corporation tax. A further provision applies to an intra-group transfer. This applies where B Ltd acquired assets under a post-5 April 1988 disposal from A Ltd (another member of a group of companies) to B Ltd, and B Ltd later makes a disposal to C Ltd. If A Ltd has already made the election, B Ltd's disposal of the asset is also covered by that election, whether or not B Ltd has made such an election—and so B Ltd may not make an election.[65]

43.5.3 Rolled-over Gain

Although the rebasing of CGT to 31 March 1982 affects only disposals made after 5 April 1988, it does have important implications for certain prior transactions. This is because while rebasing effectively eliminates pre-1982 gains, it does so only for disposals after 1988.[66]

43.5.4 Gains Deducted from Acquisition Costs

The first problem[67] concerns gains realised before 1 April 1982, but which were deducted from acquisition expenditure on a new asset acquired after 31 March 1982 but before 6 April 1988 and where the asset is then disposed of after 5 April 1988. Examples include

---

[61] Statement of Practice SP 4/92.

[62] For partnerships, see Revenue Interpretation RI 19. An election made in respect of partnership assets is made by a person in the capacity of partner; thus a separate election is required for assets held privately. In the same way, an election for assets held privately will not apply to assets held in the capacity of partner.

[63] TCGA 1992, Sch 3, para 7.

[64] TCGA 1992, Sch 3, para 1.

[65] TCGA 1992, Sch 3, para 2.

[66] TCGA 1992, Sch 3, para 1, 2.

[67] TCGA 1992, s 36 and Sch 4, para 2.

rollover relief where insurance money is spent on a replacement asset (section 23) and replacement of business assets (section 152).[68] Here, the amount of deducted gain to be brought into charge is reduced by one half; though for disposals on or after 6 April 2008 this applies only for corporation tax.[69] This was a rough-and-ready measure of equity. Thus, if A bought an asset in 1980 and gave it away to B in 1985 in circumstances qualifying for holdover, and B then disposed of the asset in 2000, one half of the gain held over in 1985 would be removed from charge. If A had given the asset away to B in 1981, not 1985, it appears that the gain would be washed away completely, ie lost to the tax system.

43.5.5 Deferred Gains

A similar 50% relief applies to deferred gains, The relief does not affect the basis of the new asset but simply takes the form of a postponed charge.[70] Again, for disposals on or after 6 April 2008, this applies only for corporation tax. The list includes section 140 (securities acquired in transfer of business of overseas branch to non-resident company), section 179 (company leaving group after section 171 acquisition), section 134 (compulsory acquisition of shares), section 248 (land compulsorily acquired and proceeds invested in depreciating assets), section 154(2) (business asset disposed of but proceeds invested in depreciating asset), section 168 (crystallisation of charge when donee emigrates) and section 116 (reorganisation involving acquisition of qualifying corporate bonds). The 50% relief applies where the original asset was acquired before 31 March 1982, the deferring event occurred between 1 April and 5 April 1988 (inclusive), and the disposal occurs any time after 5 April 1988. Where certain postponing events occurred before 1 April 1982 the charge is simply lost.[71]

43.5.6 Reorganisations

Capital reorganisations in respect of shares, mergers and reconstructions before 1 April 1982 result in a rebasing to the value of the new shareholding at 31 March 1982.

43.5.7 Miscellaneous

Separate rules apply where the asset was not owned at 31 March 1982 but was acquired by means of a defined no gain, no loss transaction, and either the transferor held it at 31 March 1982 or it was acquired through one or more disposals after that date which came within the list of no gain, no loss transactions.[72] The list is now in the interpretation provision TCGA 1992, section 288. Where an asset is derived from another asset held on 31 March 1982, for example an undivided interest in land formerly held as joint tenant, simple rebasing to 1982 applies.[73]

---

[68] Another example is s 247 (compulsory acquisition of land).
[69] TCGA 1992, s 36 and Sch 4, paras A1, 1, 2; on the situation where the asset acquired between 1982 and 1988 was a depreciating asset, see Sch 4, para 3.
[70] TCGA 1992, Sch 4, paras 1, 4(2).
[71] TCGA 1992, Sch 4, para 4(5), listing ss 134, 140(4), 154(2), 248 (3).
[72] TCGA 1992, Sch 3, para 1; adjustments are made if losses arise on the disposal.
[73] TCGA 1992, Sch 3, para 5.

43.5.8 Part Disposal

Where an asset was held at 31 March 1982 and there was then a part disposal before 6 April 1988, the allowable expenditure attributable to the part remaining is the amount relating to the whole asset less the fraction allocated to the part disposed of.[74] The effect of rebasing is not to value the retained part separately at 31 March 1982, but to recompute the allowable expenditure taking the cost of the whole asset as its value at that date.[75]

43.5.9 Claim

Relief for pre-6 April 1988 charges is due only if claimed within two years of the end of the accounting period in which the asset concerned is disposed of after 5 April 1988.[76] Claims must be supported by all necessary particulars, which presumably includes a computation of the gain arising on the earlier disposal, where this has not already been produced.

43.6   Time Apportionment—Assets Held at 6 April 1965

CGT was introduced by FA 1965 and was designed to apply to all gains arising on or after 6 April 1965, even, unlike the Australian legislation in 1985, to gains realised after 6 April 1965 on assets acquired before the tax was introduced. Rules now found in TCGA 1992, Schedule 2, and since 2008 applicable only for corporation tax and not for CGT in respect of individuals, trusts or PR, carry out this policy in two ways. For certain assets which are easy to value, or where the taxpayer elects, one takes the value as at 6 April 1965 and calculates the gain as if the taxpayer had acquired the asset at that date for market value (subject, of course, to rebasing to 31 March 1982). The second technique is to apportion the gain on a straight-line basis over the length of the period the asset has been owned and exclude that part attributable to the pre-CGT era.

Time apportionment does not apply to certain assets where a market value can readily be ascertained, ie shares and securities which were quoted on a recognised stock exchange,[77] or units in a unit trust where the unit trust managers regularly publish prices.[78] It is also excluded for two special situations—land reflecting development value[79] and unquoted shares that were subject to reorganisation before 6 April 1965. It is also excluded if the taxpayer elected[80] to value the asset at 6 April 1965. For quoted shares and securities and unit trusts a further rule applies. The amount of gain or loss is restricted by reference to historic cost without any time apportionment.[81] Thus if the actual historic cost is greater than the value on 6 April 1965, the historic cost is taken—which will mean a smaller gain, or even a loss. If the 6 April value gives a loss and the historic costs a gain then neither gain nor loss arises (the same applies in the converse situation).

---

[74] TCGA 1992, s 42; see above at §35.6.
[75] TCGA 1992, Sch 3, para 4.
[76] TCGA 1992, Sch 4, para 9.
[77] TCGA 1992, Sch 2, para 1(1)(a).
[78] TCGA 1992, Sch 2, para 1(1)(b).
[79] TCGA 1992, Sch 2, para 9.
[80] Under TCGA 1992, Sch 2, para 17(1).
[81] TCGA 1992, Sch 2, para 2.

43.6.1 *Method of Calculation*

The gain is presumed to grow evenly from the date of acquisition or 6 April 1965, which-ever is later.[82] However, expenditure incurred before 6 April 1965 is taken into account in computing the gain. Where expenditure is incurred after the asset is acquired (but before 6 April 1965), the gain attributable to that expenditure is treated as accruing at an even rate from the date when the expenditure was first reflected in the value of the asset, and not from the date of acquisition. The total gain is allocated between the original acquisition expendi-ture and the subsequent expenditure according to the amounts of each.[83] Each element is then time apportioned as appropriate, but gains attributable to expenditure incurred after 5 April 1965 are not adjusted. However, the gain will be divided according to the value actually attributable to each and not the costs incurred if there is no expenditure on acqui-sition, or if that initial expenditure was disproportionately small compared with any item of subsequent expenditure, having regard to the value of the asset immediately before that subsequent expenditure.[84] Special provisions apply to part disposals; in essence, the whole of the remainder is deemed disposed of at open market value.[85] On a part disposal before 6 April 1965, the effect is that time apportionment on subsequent disposals on or after that date runs from the date of the earlier part disposal. On a part disposal after 5 April 1965, the time apportionment ends on the date of the part disposal, and subsequent gains on the remainder are brought in without reduction.

Where part of a gain arising from a dwelling house acquired before 6 April 1965 is charge-able, the time apportionment rule is applied first, followed by the appropriate fraction.[86] Where one asset is derived from another, the new asset is treated as if it had been acquired at the same time as the other.[87]

43.6.2 *Indexation Allowance in the House of Lords*

In *Smith v Schofield*,[88] the House of Lords held that any indexation allowance is deducted from the gain before the time apportionment fraction is applied. The effect of this is, of course, that part of the allowance for inflation after 1982 is allocated against the gain which arose prior to April 1965. Lord Jauncey commented:

> My Lords, I reach this decision with regret because its effect is that an allowance which was given to offset the effect of inflation on gains accruing from and after 1982 is in part being attributed to notional non-chargeable gains accruing prior to 6th April 1965, a situation which cannot occur where an election of valuation on that date is made. In the present case the effective value of the indexation allowance will be reduced by more than one-third. The decision will have the same effect on losses. I should be surprised if Parliament had intended such a result.

---

[82] TCGA 1992, Sch 2, para 16(6).
[83] TCGA 1992, Sch 2, para 16(4).
[84] TCGA 1992, Sch 2, para 16(5).
[85] TCGA 1992, Sch 2, para 16(7).
[86] TCGA 1992, Sch 2, para 16(10).
[87] TCGA 1992, Sch 2, para 16(9).
[88] [1993] STC 268, 277, (1993) 65 TC 669, 708; on mathematics and first instance decision, see Robson [1991] BTR 38; on Court of Appeal decision, see Robson [1992] BTR 106.

43.7   Valuation

In a number of circumstances the market value of the assets is required to be substituted for any actual consideration passing. The rules for determining market value are generally the same as for IHT (see chapter fifty-five below). Some other rules should, however, be mentioned. Where the value of an asset has been ascertained[89] for IHT, that valuation is also taken for CGT purposes (section 274). Unless 'special circumstances' exist, the value to be taken for quoted shares and securities is taken from the *Stock Exchange Official Daily List* (section 272(3)). The value is either the lower of the two prices shown in the quotations plus one-quarter of the difference between the two figures, or halfway between the highest and lowest prices at which bargains, other than bargains made at special prices, were recorded for the relevant date. Where both figures are available, the lower figure is used. (Prices in *The Times*, for example, are at the halfway mark, not quarter-up.)

Special circumstances are limited. In *Crabtree v Hinchcliff*,[90] the stock market figure was taken even though price-sensitive information was known to the directors but not to the Stock Exchange. Lord Dilhorne suggested that the exclusion would come into play if price-sensitive information was known to the directors but had not been made public, although the nature of the information was such that company law required it to have been placed in the public domain.[91] Special rules are needed if the asset is a shareholding and there have been disposals after 1982.[92] 'Costs reasonably incurred in making a valuation … required for the purposes of the computation of the gain' are allowed, by statute, as a deduction in computing the gain (section 38(2)). While this permits the deduction of costs incurred in making the valuation so as to be able to comply with the obligation to submit a tax return, it does not extend to costs incurred in negotiating over or contesting the liability to CGT arising out of that disposal; conducting a tax controversy with the Revenue; or litigating the matter before any tribunal or in the courts.[93]

---

[89] See Revenue Interpretation RI 110, stating the Revenue view that a value is not 'ascertained' if no IHT is payable on a transfer and the Revenue simply accepts the taxpayer's figures.

[90] (1971) 47 TC 419.

[91] *Ibid*, 450.

[92] Inland Revenue Manual CG, paras 50874, 50902.

[93] *Caton's Administrators v Couch* [1996] STC 201, 229, per Morritt LJ; see also Revenue Interpretation RI 63.

PART IV

Inheritance Tax

44

Inheritance Tax: Introduction

44.1   Introduction

'We have never got taxes on inheritance right,' wrote one commentator immediately after the present structure was enacted.[1] This chapter summarises the structure and then turns to policy, before returning to a more detailed outline. Inheritance tax (IHT), introduced in 1986, is a direct tax on transfers of property. Unlike the capital transfer tax (CTT) which preceded it, IHT is designed to operate primarily as a tax on transfers which occur on death. In order to prevent too obvious avoidance, the tax also charges retrospectively certain gifts made within the previous seven years. Gifts which are potentially liable to IHT if the transferor should die within this period are known as 'potentially exempt transfers' (PETs). There is no tax on such transfers when they are made, but if the donor dies within seven years the potential exemption is lost.

The scheme of the tax is further strengthened by the inclusion of gifts made outside the seven-year period but from which the deceased has not been entirely excluded for the past seven years. Some transfers are chargeable immediately—whether or not the trans-

---

[1] Goodhart [1988] BTR 473. See also Chamberlain, 'Capital Taxes—Time for a Fresh Look?' [2015] BTR 679, recommending abolition of IHT; Lee, 'Inheritance Tax—An Equitable Tax No Longer: Time for Abolition' (2007) 7 *Legal Studies* 678; Mirrlees *et al* (eds), *Tax by Design: The Mirrlees Review* (OUP, 2011) ch 15 and Tiley, *Parsons Lecture 2007*, available on the University of Sydney website at http://sydney.edu.au/law/parsons/pdfs/johntiley-lecture_290307.pdf. On harmonisation within the European Community (now Union), see (1995) 5 *EC Tax Law Review* 88.

feror dies within seven years. The primary example is a transfer to a trust. A transfer is immediately chargeable rather than potentially exempt unless express authority can be found for making it a PET. In this book the term 'immediately chargeable transfers' refers to those which are immediately chargeable; the term 'chargeable transfers' will cover both those which are immediately chargeable and PETs which have become chargeable. The legislation takes the form of extensive amendment of the CTT legislation which had been consolidated in 1984; this explains why the principal legislation is called the Inheritance Tax Act 1984 (IHTA 1984).

IHT is thus a direct tax on transfers of capital. It is a cumulative charge on chargeable transfers made over any seven-year period during the transferor's lifetime and on death. Unlike succession duty, and despite its name, it is charged by reference to the circumstances of the transferor and not those of the transferee. Unlike CGT, it is a charge on the whole of the value transferred; some transfers will give rise to both taxes, with the liability to the IHT becoming clear only on the deceased's death. Unlike a wealth tax, it is charged on moving and not on stationary wealth. The tax's title is a complete misnomer designed to camouflage a return to the old estate duty of 1974.[2]

IHT is an unpopular tax, and yet the yield from it is relatively low. In 2014–15, receipts from IHT came to £3.8 billion, or a mere 0.6% of total tax receipts. Of this, £3,659 m was attributable to the charge on death, £132 m to charges on trusts and £13 m on lifetime transfers. In total, only 17,917 estates were charged IHT—approximately 3.1% of all deaths.[3] Approximately 70% of total IHT was paid by a mere 4,500 estates, with net assets of at least £1 million each. Looking just at the estates on death, in 2012–13 various exemptions (discussed in more detail below) reduced the value otherwise taxable by £15,681 m, comprising: surviving spouse, £10,318 m; charities, £2,107 m; agriculture, £1,285 m; business property other than unquoted shares, £408 m; unquoted shares, £1,246 m; relief on sale of assets, £71 m; and others, £247 m.

In the remaining chapters of Part IV of this book, references to statutory provisions are to IHTA 1984 unless otherwise noted.

44.2   Policy[4]

44.2.1 *Why Tax on Death?*

The attractions and advantages of taxing a transfer on death are that the property generally has to be valued on death anyway for purposes of administration, that a legacy is something

---

    [2] Sandford [1986] BTR 140, 141.
    [3] HMRC inheritance tax statistics, available at https://www.gov.uk/government/collections/inheritance-tax-statistics.
    [4] Sandford, *More Key Issues in Tax Reform* (Fiscal Publications, 1995), 49–69; Aaron and Munnell (1992) 45 *National Tax Jo* 119; Graetz (2002)112 *Yale LJ* 261. In the United States much anguish was caused by an article by McCaffery (1994) 104 *Yale LJ* 283 arguing that a progressive consumption tax was better than a wealth transfer tax in advancing liberal egalitarian ideas; for subsequent (very theoretical) discussion, see Colloquium (1996) 51 *Tax Law Review* 357. There is much useful comparative material in (1994) 34 *European Taxation* 335. On UK history up to 1984, see Dobris [1984] BTR 363.

of a windfall to the legatee and that the burden of tax will thus not seem as great as it might have done. However, there are significant problems of policy and design.[5] Assuming that it has been decided why any tax should be levied and what constitute desirable criteria, there are still policy issues specific to the area of capital transfers, issues the resolution of which may well affect the choice of tax. Such transfer taxes are not inevitable—neither Australia nor Canada has such taxes, having instead opted for levying a CGT charge on death. The US provided a temporary repeal of its estate tax in 2001, but the tax was reinstated with effect from 1 January 2010.[6]

If the tax is viewed as part of the redistribution of wealth to other sectors of society, a system of confiscation on death, or its modern equivalent of high rates of tax on death levied by reference to the circumstances of the deceased, may sometimes be the result.[7] If, on the other hand, a system of family protection is opted for, a system may result under which transfers within the family are exempt or taxed only at low rates while charging transfers outside the family net at high rates. This basis lends itself to some sort of compromise if it is felt that the purpose of family protection is to exempt transfers within the same generation, eg to a spouse, rather than to allow the passing of fortunes to one's children. While an integrated gift and estate tax looks like the logical answer, there are social facts to observe; people are much less inclined to give away money during their lifetimes and lifetime-giving has a different pattern from death-giving—the former tends to be unequal, the latter almost always equal.[8] The failure to give away more in life is not tax driven; indeed, people would give away far more if that were their object.[9]

If a transferor-based system is opted for, further choices are available. Thus, should one system apply to both lifetime and death transfers, should there be separate taxes or should there be just tax on death? IHT, with its limit of lifetime cumulation to a period of seven years, seems to make the tax on lifetime transfers voluntary. Thus, a married couple could, by using the £3,000 exemption each year (total £21,000) and the £325,000 threshold for 2016–17 (and frozen until April 2021), transfer £346,000 each, ie £692,000 between them, each seven years and pay no IHT. Those who are caught are the foolish or the unlucky— or perhaps simply parents who do not sufficiently trust (or like) their children—or those whose assets are not easily transferable. It is also highly questionable whether there should be such a marked absence of tax neutrality as to the timing of gifts. An ingenious compromise is to use different rates of tax on life and death but, instead of a zero rate threshold, to apply a fixed amount of credit.

---

[5] For commentary see Chamberlain, 'Capital Taxes—Time for a Fresh Look?', *op cit*; Lee, 'Inheritance Tax—An Equitable Tax No Longer: Time for Abolition', *op cit*; *Mirrlees Review, op cit*, ch 15.

[6] *Unemployment Insurance Reauthorization and Job Creation Act of 2010*. For the background story see Graetz and Shapiro, *Death by a Thousand Cuts* (University of Princeton Press, 2001).

[7] On the US estate and gift tax as a redistributive tool, despite its low rates, see Fennell (2003) 81 *North Carolina Law Rev* 567.

[8] See NBER Research Papers No 6345 by McGarry and No 6337 by Poterba; reviewed in *The Economist*, 28 February 1998, 101. Horsman (1975) *The Economic Journal* 516 estimated the amount of duty avoided in the late 1960s to be 10% of the net capital value of all estates assessed for duty; some may see this as a retaliation against increasingly severe rates of taxation in general.

[9] For an explanation of why people do not give more away, written in terms of cognition theory, see Fennell (2003) 81 *North Carolina Law Rev* 567.

A further problem is how to cope with business assets, farms and timber. To go for true tax neutrality by ignoring the special status of these types of property is to impose a heavy burden on those whose wealth is invested in them; while to give special privileges encourages people to put their money into these assets, thus increasing their market price and so making them perhaps unattainable by those true farmers or foresters who would make the best use of the land.

A major argument for taxing capital is that a tax based on income, particularly as defined in the UK, is inequitable in that it fails to tax many receipts, but taxes those it does catch at high rates. Further, an income tax does not catch the person with large capital who chooses to live off that capital.

44.2.2 How to Tax on Death—Donor or Donee?

44.2.2.1 Donor

The main advantage of a donor-based tax like IHT is that the tax is comparatively simple both for the Revenue and for executors.[10] It is easily collectible and certain as soon as the total value of property passing on death has been ascertained. HMRC estimated the cost of collection of IHT in 2012–13 at 0.88% of revenue raised—below the 1% cost of collecting income tax and 1.22% cost of CGT. IHT is less affected than alternative taxes by the intricacies of wills and settlements. It also makes an advantage of something its critics think wrong—by not shaping the tax according to the circumstances of the beneficiary, the tax enables the person to distribute property on death free of any pressures from the taxman, an example of fiscal neutrality.

44.2.2.2 Donee

A donee-based tax is different; it charges by reference to the circumstances of the donee. This may be called an accessions tax or an inheritance tax; it is quite different from the UK's current IHT (old UK taxes, such as succession duty and legacy duty, are examples). Donee-based taxes may be progressive or flat rate. They may charge different rates according to the relationship between the deceased and the legatee, as in many Continental European countries.[11] Such taxes may even take account of the existing wealth of the legatee, other legacies or gifts already received by the legatee. Ireland has had an interesting lifetime cumulative accessions tax.

Some say that a donee based-tax encourages the wider distribution of wealth, since a lower amount of tax will be payable if wealth is dispersed among a number of beneficiaries than if it is given only to one. To this, two answers may be given. First, it is not necessarily the case, since all will depend on the form the IHT takes. Secondly, talk of the distribution of wealth as one of the objectives of a tax system generally means redistribution from the very rich to the very poor rather than the distribution of wealth among four children of a wealthy person—such a distribution is likely to occur in any case.

---

[10] See *Taxation of Capital on Death*, Cmnd 4930 (1972); and Sandford, Willis and Ironside, *An Accessions Tax* (IFS, 1973). On American Law Institute proposals, see Andrews (1967) 22 *Tax Law Review* 589.

[11] Messere, *Tax Policy in OECD Countries* (IBFD, 1993), table 11.6, listed 17 such OECD countries.

44.2.3 *Fundamental Alternatives*

Among alternatives that have been canvassed are the following:

(1) *Taxing gifts as income.*[12] Certain gifts are taxed as income already, but if the rates of tax on income were higher than those on capital this would not be well received. There is the further problem that the UK has no averaging provision, although this is not much of a problem given the current rate structure of IHT. Almost every argument usually put forward for taxing income may be used to justify the taxing of gifts as income; of course, this may merely underline the weakness of those arguments.

(2) *Wealth taxes.* Wealth taxes would tax static wealth. This was last suggested officially in the UK in the 1970s; a Select Committee examined the question in 1976 but was unable to agree.[13]

(3) *Wealth tax plus differentiation.* This would charge inherited wealth at a higher rate than earned wealth; moreover, the more distant the relative from whom the wealth was inherited, the higher the rate charged, so a transmission of property inherited from one's parents might be taxed at 20%, while that of property from one's grand-parents might attract a tax of 50%.

(4) *The Meade Committee.*[14] The Meade Committee proposed an ingenious set of ideas based ultimately on a merger of wealth and accessions taxes. The core element was called AWAT (an annual wealth and transfer tax). This spawned variants, one being known as PAWAT (a progressive annual wealth and transfer tax). As with the normal accession tax, there would be cumulation over the lifetime of the individual who would suffer tax at progressive rates as total accessions increased. However, the rate of tax would depend also on age—the younger the donee, the greater the tax. The higher rate would be justified by being a single lump-sum payment on account of wealth tax; after all, the younger the donee, the greater the number of years one might expect to retain and enjoy the (taxable) wealth. This backdoor wealth tax meant that if the donee then gave the property away, there should be a refund to the donor (for the years of ownership not enjoyed) and a charge due on the new donee.

Another version was a linear AWAT (LAWAT); the rate was not progressive and so would not rise with the total accessions to the donee. This would involve simply a payment on

---

[12] Carter (chair), Canadian Royal Commission on Taxation, *Report, Vol 3* (Queen's Printer, 1966), 465; see Bradford, *Untangling the Income Tax* (Harvard, 1986), 21.

[13] Select Committee on a Wealth Tax, Cmnd 5704; Prest [1976] BTR 7–15. For problems of defining wealth, see Bradford, *op cit*, 21–24. The Chancellor of the Exchequer of the time, Denis Healey, wrote in his memoirs: 'Another lesson was that you should never commit yourself in Opposition to new taxes unless you had a very good idea how they will operate in practice. We had committed ourselves to a Wealth Tax; but in five years I found it impossible to draft one which would yield enough revenue to be worth the administrative cost and the political hassle … I suspect the Conservative Party is even more unhappy that Mrs Thatcher promised to abolish the rates without having the slightest idea what to put in their place' (*The Time of My Life* (Penguin, 1990), (404)). Much useful material on wealth taxes was gathered in Smith, *Personal Wealth Taxation* (Canadian Tax Foundation Tax Paper, 1993); see also the symposium reported at (2000) 53 *Tax Law Rev* 257–695.

[14] Meade, *The Structure and Reform of Direct Taxation* (London, Allen & Unwin, 1978), ch 13; see review by Bracewell Milnes [1979] BTR 25 and see Avery Jones in *Comparative Perspectives on Revenue Law* (CUP, 2008), ch 9.

account of wealth tax based on the difference between the ages of the donor and the donee. It follows that where the donee is older than the donor, there would necessarily be a refund of tax. In an attempt to reinstate the progressive principle, the Meade Committee came up with a third proposal—age gap AWAT (AGAWAT). This would be a gross cumulation of all gifts received and be combined with a wealth tax based on a multiple which would not be the number of years that the donee might be expected to retain the property, as with PAWAT, but simply the age difference between the two parties. This would involve the arbitrary assumption that the donee would pass his wealth on at the same age at which he had received it. The tax rate could rise with the total of accessions to wealth, giving the tax its progressive element. One may probably admire the ingenuity of the proposals rather than their effect.

(5) *The Mirrlees Review.* The final report of the Mirrlees Review editors was highly critical of the existing IHT. The editors argued that it is unfair because the richest can organise their affairs to avoid paying IHT, and it is inefficient because certain classes of assets (notably agricultural property and business assets) can escape charge. The Review editors recommended reform rather than abolition, but concluded that there was a stronger case for a tax on lifetime receipts—taxing donees on transfers received on an ongoing and cumulative basis—than for a tax on estates at death, notwithstanding the administrative and transitional difficulties involved. In addition, they recommended abolishing CGT forgiveness at death on the basis that it is poorly targeted.[15]

In summary, history suggests that in this area in particular, no tax system stays in place long enough to affect the generation for whom it was originally designed.

44.2.4 Dangers of Comparisons

As always, absence of thought is hazardous. It has been pointed out by Bracewell-Milnes that the case in favour of capital taxation is part of the general climate of opinion. He goes on to say that the case is not a logical construction and so cannot be destroyed by logic; but it may, perhaps, be weakened:[16]

> To give a historical perspective, one may imagine the objections that might have been brought against a reformer arguing a few years ago that the practice of burning witches was pointless and undesirable and should be brought to an end. The burning of witches is a long-established custom and is the general practice abroad. It is strongly supported by public opinion and its discontinuance would be ill received. Many thoughtful persons find it hard to believe that witches render any positive service to society; it might be thought more reasonable to regard some of their services as a positive disservice. Witchcraft represents a sinister and ominous concentration of power. Witches are only a small minority of the population and their punishment is richly deserved. Besides, they feel no pain.

---

[15] Mirrlees *et al* (eds), *op cit*, ch 15.
[16] Bracewell Milnes, *Is Capital Taxation Fair?* (Institute of Directors, 1974) 69. The case for abolishing CTT is considered by Dobris in [1984] BTR 363.

44.3   An Outline of IHT

44.3.1   Occasions of Charge

IHT is charged whenever there is a chargeable transfer of value, ie a disposition causing loss to a person's estate which is not an exempt transfer[17] (see §44.3.1.1 below). In addition, IHT is charged in certain other situations (see §§44.3.1.2–.6 below), where transfers are treated as transfers of value but are not deemed to be dispositions.

44.3.1.1   IHT Payable on Transfer of Value

A transfer of value is any disposition by which the value of a person's estate is reduced. The tax is levied at one of two rates on the transferor, either 0% or 20% in the case of a lifetime transfer (section 7(2), Schedule 1). The effect is a mixture of proportional and progressive features, ie the more transfers of value made, the higher the average tax liability is likely to be. It is cumulated with chargeable transfers made in the previous seven years. A lifetime transfer (eg a gift) will be a transfer of value unless the transfer is exempt. Where the transfer is for consideration, the consideration received will enter into the computation of the value transferred, with only the balance being chargeable. However, commercial transactions are not treated as transfers of value, neither are certain other dispositions.

The legislation divides transfers of value into those which are immediately chargeable and those which are only potentially chargeable, which the Act chooses to call potentially exempt transfers (PETs). Immediately chargeable transfers enter the transferor's cumulative total of transfers at once; as soon as the total goes over the nil rate bands, tax becomes due. By contrast, PETs do not give rise to tax straight away and do not enter the transferor's cumulative total of transfers unless and until the donor dies within a period of seven years from the date of the transfer, whereupon they become chargeable as lifetime transfers but at death rates, with reductions if the donor dies more than three years after the gift. Most types of gift are PETs; however, the system now draws a distinction between outright gifts, which may often be PETs, and many gifts through trusts which are not. It will usually be advantageous to create a PET rather than an immediately chargeable transfer.[18] In contrast with some other tax systems, the donor remains liable for the tax if death occurs within seven years; the same applies to any additional tax due if the transfer is immediately chargeable and the donor dies within seven years and so death rates are charged at death (section 204(6)). This is usually funded by a seven-year term assurance policy taken out by the donor at the time of the gift.[19]

44.3.1.2   Death

On D's death there is a transfer of all the property to which D was beneficially entitled immediately before death; the transfer on death is cumulated with lifetime transfers made up to seven years before, whether chargeable immediately or having become so by reason of

---

[17]   IHTA 1984, s 3(4).

[18]   However, this will not be the case if, eg, holdover relief is claimed for CGT under TCGA 1992, s 260; Potter and Monroe, *Tax Planning* (Sweet & Maxwell, 1982), §3–22.

[19]   Potter and Monroe, *op cit*, §5–13 and, on CGT aspects, §5–17.

the loss of their potentially exempt status. Certain gifts from which D reserved a benefit are treated as still belonging to D on death (see chapter forty-seven below).

The death charge differs from the lifetime charge in four ways:

(a) The tax rate on death is 0% or 40%; that on immediately chargeable lifetime transfers is 0% or 20%.
(b) Some of the exclusions are confined to lifetime transfers and others to transfers on death.
(c) While immediately chargeable lifetime transfers must be grossed up to ascertain the loss to the transferor's estate where the burden of IHT falls on the transferor, there is usually no need to gross up on death for the simple reason that the benefits eventually distributed out of the estate will necessarily be net of IHT; for similar reasons there is no grossing up of PETs should tax become payable.
(d) Events after death may sometimes affect IHT charged on the death, but these do not affect lifetime transfers.

44.3.1.3 Settled Property—Interest in Possession

There is a transfer of value not only where the transferor makes a chargeable transfer, but also where he is treated as making one. This may occur if a person is beneficially entitled to a relevant interest in possession in settled property. Such entitlement is treated for IHT purposes as extending not to the value of the life interest but to the value of the settled property underlying it. If X is entitled to the whole of the income of a fund worth £50,000, X is taken to be beneficially entitled to £50,000. X is, therefore, treated as making a transfer of value of £50,000 if he dies, disposes of the interest or if the interest ends. This is cumulated and, where appropriate, aggregated with X's own property (see chapter forty-nine below). The scope of this rule was greatly reduced in 2006 (see below at §49.1); briefly, an interest in possession which arises after 21 March 2006 is included only if it is an 'immediate post-death interest', a 'disabled person's interest' or a 'transitional serial interest'.

44.3.1.4 Settled Property—No Relevant Interest in Possession

Where there is no relevant interest in possession in settled property qualifying for the treatment just outlined, eg a discretionary trust or most interest in possession trusts settled after 21 March 2006, different rules apply. In general there is a periodic charge every 10 years at a special rate on the property held in the settlement on such trusts. There is also a partial charge if property ceases to be subject to the trusts between such anniversaries or before the first one (see chapter fifty). Some settlements receive favoured treatment (see chapter fifty-one).

44.3.1.5 Companies

A company is not liable to IHT when it makes a disposition reducing the value of its estate since that charge is restricted to dispositions by individuals.[20] A company may, in certain

---

[20] On application to limited liability partnerships under Limited Liability Partnerships Act 2000, see IHTA 1984, s 267A.

circumstances, be entitled to a beneficial interest in possession in settled property, but unless the company's business consists of the acquisition of interests in settled property, the settlement will be taxed as if there were no interest in possession. (See below, §50.2.1.)

Where a close company makes a transfer of value, the transfer of value may, however, be attributed to its individual participators and be treated as having been made by them. There may also be a charge on the trustee participators, depending upon the type of trust. There is also a deemed transfer of value when a person's rights in the company are reduced in value as a result of an alteration in the rights of his shares.

44.3.1.6 Life Policy

A special charge applies to life policies under section 263.

44.3.2 *Exemptions and Reliefs*

Exemptions and reliefs take various forms. Some direct that a particular transfer shall be exempt up to a certain limit, eg gifts in consideration of marriage of up to £5,000 (section 22); others direct that a transfer shall be exempt in full (transfer to any UK-domiciled spouse or civil partner). Others give relief by a special basis for valuation, by a reduction in the value transferred (eg business property) or by omission from the estate until some later event occurs (eg the conditional exemption for works of art and, but only on death, timber). The effects of these reliefs are not as dramatic today with the present rate structure as it was 20 years ago. Other exemptions and reliefs take the form of a reduction in the tax otherwise payable, eg quick succession relief or double taxation credit relief, so that the value transferred must still be cumulated in full and the tax normally payable ascertained before relief can be given. Reliefs may also take the form of an exemption in whole or in part from aggregation. In addition, some dispositions are not 'transfers of value' (see below at §45.5). This means that they have no effect for IHT if made during a lifetime; the same transfer may, however, be chargeable if made on death, etc, ie when the charge does not depend on there being a disposition.

44.4   Calculation of Tax

The amount of tax chargeable depends on four principles: progression, grossing up, aggregation and cumulation. The accurate administration of the tax also rests on transfers being reported (and taxed) in the right order. Rules are needed for special cases where transfers are reported late (§44.5) or where an asset is transferred in stages (§44.6).

44.4.1 *Progression*

For transfers after 5 April 2015 there are three rates: a long zero rate band (£325,000), a single rate of 40%, and a rate of 20% which is applied to transfers chargeable during lifetime (section 7 and Schedule 1). The fact that a single rate of tax, whether 20% or 40%, will apply once the zero rate band has been used up is extremely important from a planning point of view. In the days of multiple rates, which applied before 1988, it was often necessary to decide who should make a transfer when, and in whose favour.[21] Rate bands are normally index linked.[22] However, the threshold for tax has been frozen until the end of the 2020–21 tax year at £325,000, and the indexation rules in section 8 have been suspended. For deaths on or after 6 April 2012 estates will be able to reduce their IHT rate by 10% (to 36%, ie 40% less 4%) when they leave a charitable legacy of 10% or more of their net estate.

In addition, F(No 2)A 2015, section 9, introduced a new extra nil rate band solely for residential property. The policy behind this extra nil rate band was 'to reduce the burden of IHT for most families by making it easier to pass on the family home to direct descendants without a tax charge'.[23] The simplicity of this aim has proved to be complex to implement, particularly as the government also does not want to discourage the older generation from downsizing. Working through the new rules one cannot help but wonder if a simple increase in the nil rate band would have been a much better, albeit less targeted, option.

Turning now to those rules, the 'residence nil rate amount' in IHTA 1984, sections 8D-8M will apply where an individual's estate includes an interest in residential property, which is then inherited by one or more direct descendants, namely the individual's child, step-child or foster-child or their lineal descendants. The property must have been the individual's residence (ie not a buy-to-let property) at some point when it formed part of their estate. The value of the residence nil-rate band for an estate will be the lower of the net value of the interest in the residential property (after deducting any liabilities such a mortgage) and the maximum amount of the band. The maximum amount starts at £100,000 for 2017–18 and will increase by £25,000 p.a. until reaching £175,000 for 2020–21. After that it will be indexed to consumer price inflation. The residence nil rate band starts to be withdrawn once an individual's estate is valued at £2m, with £1 being withdrawn for every £2 of value over that amount. So as not to discourage downsizers, further (complicated) tracing legislation is included in the FA 2016, Schedule 15 to ensure individuals do not lose the residence nil rate amount when they dispose of a property and buy a less valuable one (or do not buy another property).[24] The new band will take effect for relevant transfers on death on or after 6 April 2017. It will be transferable where the second spouse or civil partner of a couple dies on or after 6 April 2017 irrespective of when the first of the couple died.

44.4.2 Grossing Up

A feature of IHT is the need sometime to gross up the value of a gift, ie to treat the value given as the sum after tax has been paid on it. Thus, where a donor makes a gift of £80,000 and the donor is to pay the tax, the gift of £80,000 will be grossed up at 20% (ie multiplied by 100/(100–20)) to make £100,000. There is much sense in this rule, as discussed below at §45.3.3. Normally, grossing up is relevant only on lifetime transfers, but there are some situations where it is necessary to gross up a net transfer on death (see below at §53.3).

---

[21] Potter and Monroe, *op cit*, §1.02.

[22] IHTA 1984, s 8; on transition see s 9 and Sch 2.

[23] HMRC, *Inheritance Tax: main residence nil-rate band and the existing nil-rate band*, available at https://www.gov.uk/government/publications/inheritance-tax-main-residence-nil-rate-band-and-the-existing-nil-rate-band/inheritance-tax-main-residence-nil-rate-band-and-the-existing-nil-rate-band.

[24] IHTA 1984, ss 8FA-8FE.

44.4.3 Aggregation

Where more than one piece of property is the subject of one chargeable transfer, the tax chargeable on the total or aggregate value transferred is attributed to the properties in the proportion which they bear to the aggregate (section 265). The most obvious example is a transfer on death, where there is a transfer of all the pieces of property which form part of D's estate, as defined. The principle of aggregation may, however, also be relevant to lifetime transfers. Thus, if S settles property which includes land and shares, the burden of the tax will be shared rateably between the different pieces of property transferred, and thus affect the extent of the Revenue charge on each piece.

When different funds pass in different directions, the amount of tax borne by each fund is increased by reason of the existence of other funds passing elsewhere. Thus, if D had made no chargeable transfers during life but, immediately before death, had free estate of £205,000 and a relevant life interest in a fund worth £200,000, the tax due on a transfer of £405,000 would be divided between the free estate (205/405ths) and the settled property (200/405ths).

44.4.3.1 Exemptions from Aggregation

Transfers which are exempt from liability are also exempt from aggregation. For the same reason, transfers which are conditionally exempt, such as works of art and, but only on death, timber (see below at §46.3), are also exempt from aggregation and so do not affect the tax paid by the rest of the property transferred. The effect of undoing the conditional exemption is that the property must be added back to the estate; however, it must be taxed at the highest marginal rate and not the average estate rate. The payment of premiums in respect of certain life policies issued before 29 March 1968 formerly gave rise to an exemption from aggregation.

44.4.3.2 Transfers on Same Day—Most Advantageous Treatment Rule

All chargeable transfers made on the same day are aggregated regardless of the actual order in which they are made, save that a lifetime gift made on the day of death is treated as taking place before that on death (section 266(1)). However, in calculating the amount of tax, the transfers are assumed to be made in the order which results in the lowest value chargeable, a matter of importance where one gift bears its own tax while another does not; the lower the figure at which grossing up is to be carried out, the less the tax. As PETs always bear their own tax, this rule has little importance for them.

For example, suppose A, whose cumulative total stands at £50,000 short of the nil rate band threshold, makes two gifts in settlement, each of £50,000 and each on discretionary trusts on the same day, 4 July 2015. The gift to trust X is to bear its own tax; tax on the gift for trust Y is to be borne by A.

If the gift to trust X is made first, the tax on it will be nil; this will exhaust the zero lifetime rate band, so that trust Y will have its tax assessed on the basis that £50,000 is grossed up at 20%, making tax of £12,500. Total tax on the two trusts will be £12,500 and A's cumulative total will now be £387,500 (£275,000, £50,000, £50,000 and £12,500). If, however, the gift to trust Y is made first, tax on it will be nil and tax on trust X will be £10,000, making total tax of £10,000 and leaving A's cumulative total at £385,000. It follows that the second method will be used. The total tax of £10,000 is divided between the trusts in the proportion £50,000:£60,000, making the tax on trust X £4,545.50, and that on trust Y £5,454.50.

44.4.4 Cumulation—But only over Previous Seven Years

44.4.4.1 Principle

Cumulation requires that the tax on the present transfer must take account of chargeable transfers already made by the transferor. A properly integrated lifetime and death tax would cumulate all chargeable gifts whenever made (as the old CTT tried to do). However, under current UK rules, chargeable transfers made more than seven years previously cease to be cumulated.[25] Of course, when a transfer ceases to be cumulated that is all that happens; there is no question of repaying the tax charged.

44.4.4.2 Which Transfers?

Transfers which are cumulated are those which are the chargeable transfers of this transferor.[26] Not cumulated are exempt transfers, conditionally exempt transfers until a chargeable event has occurred, PETs, unless and until the donor dies within the neither seven-year period,[27] or transfers which are made by others. Transfers of settled property treated as made by this transferor, for example the termination of this person's beneficial life interest in possession, must be cumulated if death follows within seven years, since they are treated as PETs.

44.4.4.3 Which Values?

The values to be cumulated are those transferred by chargeable transfers. Where a particular relief takes the form of a reduction in the value of the property and so in the value transferred, such as agricultural relief or relief for business assets, it is the value so reduced which is cumulated. Where, however, the relief takes the form of a reduction in tax, such as quick succession relief or double taxation relief by credit, the whole value transferred must be cumulated both to ascertain the amount of tax which is to be reduced and to ascertain the value transferred for subsequent transfers.

44.4.4.4 PET Rules

A PET remains potentially exempt until the passage of seven years, in which point it becomes exempt (section 3A(4)), or the death of A, the transferor, in that period, in which case it becomes chargeable; tax is due six months after the month in which A dies (section 226(3A)). It is assumed that the transfer will reach total exemption by the passing of seven years until this is disproved (section 3A(5)); so no tax will therefore become due at the time of the gift. If A dies within that period, the transfer loses its potentially exempt status retrospectively and is taxed as if it had been a chargeable transfer when it was made. It is not treated as taking place immediately before the death, which means it not only avoids

---

[25] IHTA 1984, s 7(1); FA 1986, s 101, Sch 19.
[26] For a modest exception where transfer of value is charged but not cumulated, see s 94(4).
[27] IHTA 1984, s 3A(5), but then with retroactive effect.

being part of the general transfer on death but also has a further advantage over leaving things till death if the asset rises in value in the meantime. There may be disadvantages if a chargeable transfer had been made in the seven years before the PET, since the tax on that transfer must be taken into account when calculating the tax on the PET, even though it is more than seven years before the death.

There are further consequences where A makes a PET within the seven-year period, but later makes an immediately chargeable transfer; here, the tax on the immediately chargeable transfer will have been calculated on the basis that the previous transfer was exempt. This must be corrected. The removal of the exempt status is not completely retrospective, however, since the rates to be applied will be those in force at the date of death. There is a reduction if the transfer was made more than three years before the death; the rate of tax will be tapered if the donor dies more than three years after making the PET (see below §46.1.2).

Example:

(a) In May 1994 Alf made a chargeable transfer of £170,000 to a discretionary trust. (b) In June 1995 he married, as a result of which his life interest in a fund worth £500,000 ceased. (c) In May 2002 he made a chargeable transfer to another discretionary trust of £50,000. (d) In June 2004 he made a chargeable transfer of £175,000. (e) In July 2013 Alf died, having assets worth £250,000.

1994 and 1995: The 1994 transfer in trust was a chargeable transfer of £170,000; it was the gross amount and took account of any tax due under the 1994–95 lifetime rates. In 1995, Alf's marriage triggered a transfer of £500,000, but this was, under rules then in force, a PET and so no tax was due and his total remained at £170,000.

2001: In 2001 the 1994 transfer ceased to be cumulated and his total dropped back to nil.

2002 and 2004: The 2002 transfer made Alf's total £50,000, but with no tax due because of the nil rate band. The 2004 transfer of £175,000 made his total rise to £225,000 but, again, with no tax due because of the nil rate band.

2009 and 2011: In 2009 the £50,000 transfer made in 2002 ceases to be cumulated and Alf's total drops back to £175,000. In 2011 the £175,000 transfer made in 2004 ceases to be cumulated and his total drops back to nil.

Death: When Alf dies in 2013, he can leave an estate of £325,000 which falls to be taxed only by reference to a cumulative lifetime total of nil and so will bear no tax.

On these facts, Alf will have left/given away a lot of money and paid little tax apart from that in the early days. The trusts will have to pay their own tax periodically (see chapter fifty), but this will not affect Alf's own IHT liability.

It may seem that where a transferor has made no previous transfers but proposes to dispose of a large amount of wealth, it would usually be advantageous for the chargeable transfer to precede the potentially exempt one so as to enable the former to use the transferor's nil rate band. However, whereas the tax payable on the death in respect of a PET is always determined *de novo*, this is not true of the chargeable transfer. So, where the tax paid in respect of the chargeable transfer on that occasion is higher than that which would be payable on such a transfer on death, there is no refund of the tax already paid, and this gives rise to a greater total burden of tax.[28]

44.5   Taxation of Transfers Reported Late

The cumulation principle requires that transfers be reported correctly and promptly. Where a transfer (A) is reported late and in the meantime a later transfer (B) has been taxed, that tax may not have been calculated correctly. Section 264 is designed to remedy this. It was introduced in 1981 when CTT moved to a system of 10-year cumulation.[29] Section 264 applies only where payment has been accepted in respect of the later transfer by the Revenue.[30] Where B is more than seven years after A, there is no real difficulty. Owing to the seven-year cumulation rule, tax (plus interest) will be due on A at the rates prevailing at the date of that transfer and not at the later (and, most probably, lower) rates. Liabilities in respect of A do not affect B.[31] When a limited exemption, now principally the £325,000 exemption for transfers to a non-domiciled spouse or civil partner applies (see §53.1 below), the benefit of the exemption is given to B rather than A, even though A was made first (section 264(7)). So if each is of £325,000, the B transfer gets the exemption and the A transfer is wholly liable.

Where the gap is less than seven years, tax on A is, of course, charged at the rates appropriate to its actual date. However, no attempt is made to reopen the tax on B. A is charged not only to the tax that should have been charged when it was made, calculated at the rates then in force, but also to an amount equal to the difference between the tax that would have been charged on B if it had been included in the transferor's cumulative total at the right time. Thus the burden of the extra tax falls on A, not B. The rules in section 264 apply when the A transfer is 'discovered'. The transfer is discovered if it is notified under the relevant reporting rules or, if it is not notified, on the date on which the Board give notice of a determination under section 221.[32] Interest is charged on the tax which should have been paid on the earlier transfer in the normal way, but interest on the additional tax relating to B (but, as just seen, charged on A) runs only from six months from discovery of A (section 264(6)).

More complex situations can arise. When there are two unreported transfers, the extra tax is apportioned by reference to the values transferred (section 264(3)). This rule is modified if tax has been settled in respect of one of the earlier transfers; no further tax is due in respect of the settled transfer, but this does not reduce the liability of the unsettled transfer (section 264(4)). Provision is also made for the situation in which the transfer is itself an earlier transfer in relation to another later transfer (section 264(5)).

---

[28] See, generally, *Tolley's Estate Planning 2003–04*, ch 4.

[29] Although the period of cumulation for IHT is seven years, s 264 still refers to earlier transfers effected within 10 years of a later one (IHTA 1984, s 264(2)).

[30] In full satisfaction of the tax due: IHTA 1984, s 264(1)(b), (2)(b).

[31] IHTA 1984, s 264(2) specifically states that the difference is not chargeable on the value transferred by the later transfer.

[32] IHTA 1984, s 264(9). An account of a PET is needed only if it becomes chargeable by reason of the death of the transferor within seven years; the time limit for doing so is 12 months from the end of the month in which the death occurred (s 216(1)(bb), (6)(aa)).

44.5.1 Acceptance in Full Satisfaction

Section 264 applies only where payment has been accepted in respect of the later transfer by the Revenue in full satisfaction of the tax due. If no tax has been paid in respect of the transfer because it attracts a nil rate of tax, it is treated as having been accepted by the Board on the date of the delivery of the account as required by section 216 (section 264(8)). It is unclear whether a payment by instalments can have this effect, or whether it is necessary to wait until all the instalments have been paid; if the policy is to protect the transfer, section 264 should apply in full.

44.6 Transfer of Asset in Stages—Future Payments

Section 262 applies where a disposition for money or money's worth is a transfer of value *and* money is paid, or assets are transferred, more than one year after the disposition. This provision is more complex than at first appears since it applies only where the assets are transferred by the transferor more than one year after the disposition. It is dealing with delayed transfers of value. Thus, it does not apply simply because A sells an asset to B at a figure below market value and B is to pay by instalments. In such a case B may be paying by instalments but B is not making a transfer of value—A is. For example, suppose A agrees to sell B 10,000 shares worth £60,000, for £18,000,[33] the shares to be transferred in tranches of 2,000 shares over five years. Tax will be charged on a fraction $(60,000–18,000)/60,000 = 7/10\text{ths})$ making the transfer in the first year $7/10 \times £12,000$, or £8,400. The importance of this fraction is considerable. By spreading the value over the five years, section 262 may enable A to use the annual £3,000 exemption. On the other hand, there may have been intervening transfers having the effect of increasing the rates of tax. However, the important point is that this fraction is applied to the value of the shares at the time each transfer is made. Thus, if the shares double in value, the chargeable transfer of the next tranche will be $7/10 \times £24,000$, or £16,800.[34]

Section 262 applies only where the disposition is for a consideration in money or money's worth. It would therefore not apply if A simply made a covenant to transfer the shares over five years.

44.7 Definitions

44.7.1 Estate

The notion of an estate is important because: (a) a disposition gives rise to IHT only if it causes a reduction in the value of the transferor's estate (section 3(1)); and (b) on death D

---

[33] It is assumed that the £18,000 is a single cash payment. However, if B agreed to pay £25,000 over five years, it would be necessary to discount this figure of £25,000 and, again, £18,000 is taken to be the present value of the sums to be paid.

[34] Note that the fraction does not increase to 8.5/10.

is treated as having made a transfer of value equal to the value of D's estate immediately before death.[35] D's estate is reduced by allowable liabilities. Thanks to section 49(1), D's estate will include settled property in which D had a beneficial interest in possession. As part of the 2006 reforms, the definition of 'estate' now excludes an interest in possession in settled property where the rules for bereaved minors or age 18 to 25 trusts apply (ie sections 71A and 71D, see below at §51.3). Because of the narrowing of section 49, an interest in possession which arises after 21 March 2006 is included only if it is an immediate post-death interest, a disabled person's interest or a transitional serial interest. For new rules making certain purchased interests part of a person's estate, see section 5(1B) (below §49.2.1).

44.7.1.1 Beneficially Entitled

An estate is the aggregate of all the property to which D is beneficially entitled. Property held in a fiduciary capacity is not included. Property is widely defined in section 272 as 'including except where the context otherwise requires rights and interests of any description'. It will therefore cover not only tangible property, but also equitable rights, debts and other choses in action, and, indeed, any rights capable of being reduced to a money value. Thus, D's estate will include a share of property held in common and a severable share of property held on joint tenancy. It would not include damages obtainable under the Fatal Accidents Acts in respect of a wrongful act causing death since these belong to D's dependants. Winnings on a football pool accruing to the members of a syndicate accrue to the members even though the winnings are initially received by a person as stakeholder for the syndicate.[36]

Legislation passed in 2002 directs that, for transfers of value on or after 17 April 2002, settlement powers are not to be treated as 'property' for IHT purposes.[37] This reversed a court decision where a settlor created a discretionary trust, reserving a right to require the trustees, among other things, to transfer the property back to him. The right was held to be property.[38] The effect of the court decision was to enable the taxpayer to succeed in a CGT avoidance scheme which involved the creation of the trust as a chargeable transfer and a huge reduction in the value transferred for IHT purposes by the use of the power.[39] The 2002 legislation applies to estates of people who died before 17 April 2002, showing that the success of the CGT scheme brought dangers to other taxpayers.[40]

A mere hope is presumably not a 'right' even 'of any description'; however, a completed payment stemming from such a hope is not a mere hope.[41] Sums paid by trustees of a superannuation scheme in the exercise of a discretion to pay a lump-sum death benefit to a member's dependant do not form part of the member's estate but will, of course, become part of the estate of the dependant. Property to which a person is entitled as a corporation

---

[35] IHTA 1984, s 4(1). For analysis of rights on uninfeft proprietor under Scots law and analysis of IHTA 1984, s 5(2), see *Linlithgow (Marquess) v Revenue & Customs Commissioners* [2010] STC 1563, [2010] CSIH 19.
[36] Statement of Practice E14.
[37] FA 2002, s 119, amending the definition of 'property' in IHTA 1984, s 272 and adding ss 47A and 55A; see Whitehouse [2002] *Private Client Business* 265; and Campbell [2002] BTR 341–43.
[38] *Melville v IRC* [2001] EWCA Civ 1247; [2001] STC 1271.
[39] *Simons Finance Act 2002 Handbook* suggests that some CGT schemes using variations of that used in *Melville* may still work.
[40] See also Lightman J in *Melville and others v IRC* [2000] STC 628, para 22.
[41] *A-G v Quixley* (1929) 98 LJKB 652, CA (gratuities part of estate).

is not included (section 271). 'Excluded property' does not form part of a person's estate immediately before death (see below at §45.4.1). A person beneficially entitled to an interest in possession in settled property is treated as beneficially entitled to the property in which the interest subsists, and not to the interest itself (section 49(1)). Thus the tenant for life of a fund worth £100,000 whose free estate is worth £50,000, will on death make a chargeable transfer of £150,000.

44.7.1.2 General Power

D's estate will also include property (other than settled property) over which D has a general power, ie one enabling D, assuming D has full legal capacity, to dispose of it. A general power to charge money on such unsettled property is treated as giving beneficial entitlement to the money. A 'general power' is defined as 'a power or authority enabling the person by whom it is exercisable to appoint or dispose of property as he thinks fit' (section 5(2)). This definition has been used to treat the entire sum in a joint account as part of the estate of one of the holders.[42] A power to nominate a beneficiary under a life policy has also been held to be a general power.[43]

44.7.1.3 Two Estates at One Time?

There is no rule which prevents an asset from being in two estates at the same time. This is likely to be more common as a result of the rules in FA 1986, section 102 treating a gift subject to reservation as remaining chargeable on the donor's death (see chapter forty-seven below). Where A makes a revocable gift of personalty to B, the property appears to form part of the estate of both of them. It forms part of the estate of A since there are no restrictions on the right to revoke; A can therefore revoke the gift and dispose of the property as he thinks fit. It forms part of the estate of B since B gets good title subject to A's right to revoke.[44]

The issue does not arise if D makes an incomplete gift: there will be no disposition since the title has not passed and so there is no reduction in the value of the transferor's estate. This will still be the case even though the title is eventually perfected under the rule in *Strong v Bird*,[45] since here the title is not perfected until death and the transfer on death is treated as taking place immediately before death.

The issue might arise if D has a general but fiduciary[46] power over property, for example an agent duly authorised to sell on behalf of the owner. It would appear that the property ought not to form part of D's estate. It is, however, arguable that it may come within the definition of a general power, since that is not expressly confined to a power which gives D the beneficial right to the proceeds of sale. Such a conclusion would have the odd result that the property will at once form part of the estate of the vendor and of the agent, and so is most unlikely.[47] One answer to this is to say that the agent has a power to sell, not a power

---

[42] *O'Neill v IRC* [1998] STC (SCD) 10; however, only this person had operated the account. See also *Anand v IRC* [1997] STC (SCD) 58.

[43] *Kempe v IRC* [2004] STC (SCD) 462.

[44] Presumably A's right to revoke will be taken into account in valuing B's right.

[45] (1874) LR 18 Eq 315.

[46] IHTA 1984, s 5(2) declares that the person with a general power is to be treated as beneficially entitled to it so that the fiduciary quality of the power is irrelevant.

[47] See Standing Committee A, cols 629, 630, 4 February 1975.

to give, and so no power to dispose as he thinks fit; this leaves open the case of a power of attorney.

44.7.2 Connected Persons

Persons are connected with each other in the same way as for CGT (see above at §33.9, but with the addition of uncles, aunts, nephews and nieces.[48]

44.7.3 Excluded Property[49]

The following are excluded property:

(1) property, other than settled property, situated outside the UK, provided the person beneficially entitled to it is an individual domiciled outside the UK.[50] The law has been clarified by a provision extending excluded property status to a holding in an authorised unit trust and a share in an open-ended investment company if the individual beneficially entitled is domiciled outside the UK;[51]

(2) settled property situated outside the UK, provided the settlor was domiciled outside the UK when the settlement was made;[52]

(3) a reversionary interest in settled property, provided the person beneficially entitled to it is not domiciled in the UK;[53]

(4) certain other reversionary interests in settled property;[54]

(5) certain types of property situated in the UK owned by persons domiciled elsewhere (see below at §58.4) and by visiting forces (section 155);

(6) securities issued by certain international organisations.

44.8 Exempt Persons

Exemptions for certain kinds of property are given to:

(1) foreign diplomats and consular officers;[55]

(2) senior staff of international organisations;[56]

(3) visiting forces[57] (these reliefs may not be used by British citizens, British Dependent Territories citizens or British Overseas citizens);

---

[48] TCGA 1992, s 286 (see above at §33.9); incorporated and adapted by IHTA 1984, s 270.
[49] On effects, see IHTA 1984, ss 3(2), 5(1) (see below at §45.4.1) and ss 53(1), 82 (see below at §50.2.4).
[50] IHTA 1984, s 6(1) (see below at §58.4.1).
[51] IHTA 1984, s 6(1)(1A), added by FA 2003, s 186.
[52] IHTA 1984, s 48(3) (see below at §58.5).
[53] IHTA 1984, s 6(1) (see below at §58.5.2).
[54] IHTA 1984, s 48(1), as amended (see below at §49.9.2).
[55] Diplomatic Privileges Act 1964, s 34; and Consular Relations Act 1968.
[56] Orders made under International Organisations Act 1968.
[57] IHTA 1984, s 155.

(4)   EU officials. For death duty (and wealth tax) purposes and in the application of double
      taxation agreements, officials and other servants of the EU and of the European
      Investment Bank who, solely by reason of the performance of their duties, establish
      their residence in a member country other than that of their domicile, are considered
      as having maintained their domicile in the country in which they were domiciled
      for tax purposes at the time of entering the service of the EU (if a member of the
      EU).[58] Similarly, movable property is treated as situated in the country of domicile.[59]
      These provisions apply equally to the spouses of such persons (to the extent that they
      are not separately engaged in a gainful occupation) and to their dependent children.
      A survivor's pension to the widow of an official constitutes emoluments and, hence, is
      exempt from national taxation.[60]

---

[58] Protocol on the Privileges and Immunities of the European Communities, Art 21 (see Cmnd 5179).
[59] *Ibid*, Art 14.
[60] Case 7/74 *Van Nidek (Widow Von Geldern) v Inspector of Registration and Succession at Rijswick* [1975]
1 CMLR 192, ECJ.

45

Transfers of Value by Disposition

45.1 Transfers Chargeable and Potentially Exempt

45.1.1 Transfer of Value

IHT is charged on the value transferred by a chargeable transfer (IHTA 1984, section 1). A transfer of value is any disposition made by a person (A, the transferor) as a result of which the value of A's estate immediately after the disposition is less than it would be but for the disposition (section 3). However, the statute may direct otherwise; thus, if it is shown that the transfer was not intended to confer any gratuitous benefit on any person and either it was made in a transaction at arm's length between persons not connected with each other or was such as might be expected to be made in such a transaction, no charge arises, it being declared not to be a transfer of value.[1]

---

[1] IHTA 1984, s 10 (see below at §45.5.1).

A transfer is a chargeable transfer if it is a transfer of value made by an individual after 26 March 1974 other than an exempt transfer[2] or a potentially exempt transfer (PET) made after 17 March 1986.[3] At a technical level it is necessary to distinguish (a) the value transferred by a transfer of value from (b) the value transferred by a chargeable transfer. This is because (a) is calculated ignoring the exempt transfer rules and without regard to grossing up (on which see below at §45.3.3). The technical niceties are important when considering the application of reliefs, such as business relief.

A strategy for giving[4] must take account not only of the distinction between PETs and immediately chargeable transfers and other IHT aspects, but also the CGT aspects. The two key CGT aspects are the uplift on death under TCGA 1992, section 62 (above §39.3) and the possibility of holding over under section 260 (above §36.4).

45.1.2 Potentially Exempt Transfers

45.1.2.1 Definition

The potentially exempt transfer (PET) was introduced in 1986 on the change from CTT to IHT. Most lifetime transfers are PETs. A PET has three elements:[5]

(1) The transfer must be a transfer of value made by an individual.[6]
(2) It must otherwise be a chargeable transfer (in whole or in part). So, if the transfer is exempt under other rules it remains fully exempt and is not made potentially chargeable.
(3) It must, in broad terms, be either a gift to another individual (including, where appropriate, a settled gift under which the individual has an interest in possession) or a gift into an appropriate form of trust. Where the 2006 rules apply, this means a gift into a disabled trust or a gift into a bereaved minor's trust on the coming to an end of an immediate post-death interest. A gift into an accumulation and maintenance trust is a PET only if made before 22 March 2006; the same cut-off date means PET treatment is not available on the creation of most interests in possession.[7]

45.1.2.2 Condition (3) Elaborated: Two Initial Issues

The third condition is the subject of statutory elaboration. One initial difficulty is that it is not clear whether the definition is intended to be exhaustive; it is thought that this is so, but the conclusion is not crystal-clear.[8] Another difficulty is that probably a wide view of the term 'gift' is meant to be taken. Since one is only talking about transfers of value, the

---

[2] IHTA 1984, s 2(1). On partly exempt transfers, see *ibid*, s 2(2); see also below at §53.3 for rules on allocation of reliefs.
[3] IHTA 1984, s 3A(1), added by FA 1986, Sch 19.
[4] Potter and Monroe, *Tax Planning* (Sweet & Maxwell, 1982), §3-36 *et seq*.
[5] IHTA 1984, s 3A(1), added by FA 1986, Sch 9, para 1 and amended to apply to interest in possession settled property after 16 March 1987 by F(No 2)A 1987, s 96.
[6] On or after 18 March 1986; for earlier transfers, see FA 1986, Sch 19, para 1.
[7] As defined in IHTA 1984, s 71 (see below at §49.2).
[8] Venables, *Inheritance Tax Planning* (Key Haven, 1988), §2.1.2.8.

term cannot widen the scope of the tax, but the question is whether it narrows it—taken literally so that a sale at an undervalue might not count as a PET since it is not necessarily a gift. However, the solution is to treat a sale at an undervalue as a gift of the part of the price forgone.

45.1.2.3 Section 3A(2)(a)

A gift is to an individual, and so potentially exempt to the extent that the value is attributable to property which, by virtue of the transfer, becomes comprised in the estate of the other individual; it does not matter whether it becomes so comprised as settled or unsettled property. This form of words would seem to ensure that where the disposition causes a loss to the estate of the transferor, A, greater than the benefit to the estate of the transferee, B, the whole transfer is potentially exempt, and not just to the extent of the value of the property disposed of by A. Thus, to take the usual example, if A has 60 of the 100 shares in a company and gives B 20, the loss of A's estate reflects the loss of control. If this is all to be treated as a gift to B, it will be potentially exempt. In turn, this means that if A wishes to give B 20 shares but to settle the other 40 on discretionary trusts, A will be well-advised to make the gift to B first, so ensuring that the loss of control will be the subject of a PET and not an immediately chargeable transfer.[9]

45.1.2.4 Section 3A(2)(b)

Where the value is not attributable to property becoming comprised in the estate of B, the other person, it is treated as being 'to an individual' to the extent that, by virtue of the transfer, B's estate is increased; again, it does not matter that the increase is in the value of settled property comprised in B's estate. This rule is designed to cover indirect transfers, ie situations in which there is a transfer of value but no property becomes part of B's estate, as where A, the donor, pays off some of B's debts, pays a premium on a life policy belonging to B or allows an option to buy on advantageous terms to lapse. However, it contains something of a trap since the opening words refer to the situation where the value is not attributable to property becoming comprised in the estate of another person (not individual). Thus, a gift to a company which has the incidental effect of increasing the value of the estates of its participators cannot be a PET and may be immediately chargeable.[10]

What both rules have in common is a requirement that there should be an increase in the value of the estate of an individual; from this it follows that if there is no such increase, the transfer cannot be a PET. One situation in which this would seem to occur is where a grandparent pays the school fees of a grandchild; here, there is no increase in the value of the grandchild's estate. The result is that there may be an immediate transfer, not a PET. This unfortunate result may be avoided by making the gift directly to the child or, if the parents are the contracting parties, to the parents. Similar problems (and solutions) arise if A buys B a holiday.

---

[9] Ibid, §2.1.2.11.

[10] Ibid, §2.1.4 who, however, points out that where the donor simply allows an option to lapse, which has the effect of increasing the value of the company's assets and so the estates of the participators, the gift can be a PET since the words at the beginning of this rule exclude it only where no property becomes part of the estate of another person.

For transfers before 22 March 2006 to an accumulation and maintenance trust or a trust for a disabled person the rule in s 3A(2)(a) is followed, but there is no room for s 3A(2)(b).[11] It follows that the payment of a premium on a life assurance policy kept up for the benefit of such a trust is not a PET. A similar rule applies where, on or after that date, the transfer was a gift into a bereaved minor's trust on the coming to an end of an immediate post-death interest.

45.1.2.5 Scope of PETs; Exclusions and Inclusions

Where tax is charged 'as if' a transfer of value had been made, the transfer cannot be a PET (section 3A(6)). Thus, a transfer of value by a close company is not a PET.[12] However, by special provision, the termination of an interest in possession in settled property can be.[13] The scheme of charging settled property in which there is no interest in possession does not use the concept of a transfer of value and thus remains outside the scheme of PETs. PET treatment is applied to certain gifts with reservation and the discharge of a non-deductible liability.[14] In addition, various situations have been specifically excluded from being PETs. Where there is an alteration in the rights in a close company falling within section 98, the transfer of value cannot be potentially exempt.[15] Certain deferred charges on timber stemming from the days of estate duty cannot be PETs.[16]

45.2   Disposition

45.2.1 General

The word 'disposition' is not defined in the legislation,[17] although it is stated to include a disposition effected by associated operations. Disposition is not the same as 'disposal' used in CGT or in the definition of a gift with reservation for IHT. A disposition need not be of any existing property,[18] so that distinctions between the creation and the disposition of interests are immaterial; all that is required is some act or, in some situations, an omission, which results in a loss in value to a person's estate.

45.2.1.1 Destruction

From this it may appear to follow that deliberately to destroy an asset, for example a picture or stamp, would be a disposition, as would an accidental destruction, although the absence of an intent to confer a benefit will usually prevent a charge arising.[19] The notion of a transfer, however, suggests the need for a transferee, so that it might be argued that

---

[11] IHTA 1984, s 3A(3).

[12] However, see discussion by Gordon [2004] *Private Client Business* 274–82.

[13] IHTA 1984, s 3A(7), added by F(No 2)A 1987, s 96.

[14] FA 1986, ss 102(4), 103(5).

[15] IHTA 1984, s 98(3), added by FA 1986, Sch 19, para 20 (see below at §52.2).

[16] IHTA 1984, Sch 19, para 46.

[17] Contrast estate duty (FA 1939, s 30(3)).

[18] It must, however, be of property as defined above at §44.7, so that a disposition of services would not cause a charge to tax, whereas the disposition of a right to be paid for services would.

[19] See also Watson [1993] *Private Client Business* 334.

even deliberate destruction could not be a disposition.[20] Against this, it might be pointed out that the word 'transferee' was almost completely removed in the 1984 consolidation[21] and the word to be construed is 'disposition', not 'transfer'. Moreover, to suggest that the destruction of an interest, as where a lessee surrenders his lease to his landlord, is not a transfer of value would open the door to avoidance. The position is obscure.

If the destruction of a picture is not a transfer of value,[22] whereas the surrender of a lease is, there are several ways of justifying this distinction. The first is to say that in the case of a surrender there may be a *scintilla temporis*[23] during which the landlord holds the tenant's interest before it is destroyed by merger; the picture case is therefore distinguishable. The second is to say that the loss must be to the transferor's estate and an estate consists of rights; the surrender of the lease is a transfer of the rights to the landlord, whereas the destruction of the asset is not. A third is to say that whether or not the estate consists of rights, there is a transfer of property by an act of the lessee in surrendering the lease; one difficulty here is that an act whereby the lessee forfeits the lease cannot be treated in the same way.[24]

45.2.1.2 Liabilities

The incurring of a liability will result in a reduction of a person's estate and so be a disposition, provided the liability is deductible in computing the value of the estate under the relevant rules (see below at §55.3). Where the liability is not deductible, there is no reduction in the transferor's estate and so no value is transferred. Thus, if I agree to guarantee my son's overdraft, there will be no reduction in the value of my estate since a liability incurred otherwise than for consideration is deductible only if, and to the extent that, it is incurred for consideration in money or money's worth.[25] Should I have to pay sums under the guarantee, such payments will be transfers of value at that time. On the discharge of a non-deductible liability in respect of a loan as a transfer of value, see below at §55.3. The voluntary waiver of a loan is a transfer of value by the creditor: in practice the Revenue insist upon a deed in such cases.[26]

45.2.2 Timing

The use of a concept of a disposition causing loss to an estate rather than a transfer of property means that where a mother transfers shares to her son by way of gift, there will be a

---

[20] Destruction of an asset by disclaimer was held to be a disposition in *IRC v Buchanan* [1957] 2 All ER 400, (1957) 37 TC 365 (TA 1988, s 660B); see above at §31.2.1. See also Venables, *Tax Planning Through Trusts* (Chatto & Windus, 1987), §11.03.

[21] Removed from, eg, IHTA 1984, s 199(1)(a).

[22] But suppose that A has a valuable stamp, his son B has another copy of the same stamp and that these are the only two copies known to exist in private hands; each stamp is worth £20,000, but if A destroys his stamp, B's will be worth £60,000.

[23] However, note Lord Hoffmann in *Ingram v IRC* [1999] STC 35, 44g: 'I do not think that a theory based on the notion of a scintilla temporis can have a very powerful grasp of reality.'

[24] The forfeiture probably does not count as an omission under IHTA 1984, s 3(3) (see below at §45.2.3).

[25] A liability must be distinguished from a contract with proprietary effect. Thus, if A contracts to sell land to B, B acquires an estate contract—an incumbrance against that land; the loss to A's estate therefore arises at the time of the contract.

[26] *Law Society's Gazette*, 18 December 1991, [1992] *Simon's Tax Intelligence* 30. The Revenue rely on *Pinnel's Case* (1602) 5 Co Rep 117a; and *Edwards v Walters* [1896] 2 Ch 157, CA.

transfer of value as soon as the estate suffers loss, ie when the transferor has done all in her power to effect the transfer, rather than the time when the transfer is entered in the books of the company.[27] Similarly, where there is a sale at an undervalue, the transfer of value will take place when the contract is made. It also follows that subsequent changes in the value of the thing disposed of are ignored. Thus, it is advantageous—for IHT—to retain things the value of which will remain static or even fall, and to give away things the value of which will appreciate.

45.2.3 Omission to Exercise a Right

Section 3(3) states that where the value of a person's estate is diminished and that of another person's estate is increased by the first-mentioned person's omission to exercise a right he shall be treated as having made a disposition at the time, or the latest time, when he could have exercised the right, unless it is shown that the omission was not deliberate. This is one of the rare instances in which an increase in the other person's estate is relevant; however, the measure of value is still the loss to the transferor, not the benefit to the transferee. It follows that if the omission does not increase another person's estate, no tax is due. Where a benefit to the other person's estate occurs, the transfer may be potentially exempt, since section 3(3) treats the omission as a disposition and not simply as an event to be taxed as if it were a transfer of value. The 2006 changes to interests in possession in settled property have to be taken into account here too; only interests which have the effect of increasing the person's estate are relevant.

The failure of a landlord to exercise a rent review clause, thus increasing the value of the lessee's interest, would fall within this provision, as would the failure on the part of a shareholder to exercise rights under a rights issue, a course of action which might increase the value of shares taken up, especially where control of a company is involved, or allowing an option to purchase a property at a favourable price to lapse. At one time the Revenue invoked section 3(3) where a settlor, chargeable to income tax on income of a settlement under the rules considered in chapter thirty-one above, failed to exercise his right of indemnity against the trust (see now below §48.5.3).

The omission is treated as a disposition. It is open to the person to bring the transaction within one of the rules excluding liability, particularly that for bona fide deals without donative's intent in section 10 (see §45.5.1 below). Section 3(3) applies only on the omission to exercise a right. 'Right' is not defined but presumably means a legal right. Thus, if a tenant commits an act as a result of which his lease is forfeited, the section may not be used to charge him on the ground that he omitted to exercise his 'right' not to commit the act.[28] On omission to seek larger pension when life expectancy declines, see §45.5.3.2.

---

[27] *Re Rose* [1949] Ch 78, [1948] 2 All ER 971.

[28] Normally, it would be hard to argue that such an act is a disposition. Quaere, however, where the forfeiture results not from an act, but from a failure to act.

45.3   Value Transferred

The value transferred is not simply the amount which B, the transferee, receives, but rather is the amount by which the value of the estate of A, the transferor, is reduced (section 3). This has three major consequences for calculating the value transferred.

45.3.1   Determining the Loss

The estate concerned is that of the transferor; the estate of the transferee is not relevant in determining whether there is a transfer of value, although it is relevant in determining whether the transfer is potentially exempt. Thus, if a particular disposition results in a greater loss to the transferor than benefit to the transferee, it is that greater loss which is taken into account for tax. For example, if A has 60% of the shares in a company[29] and B has 40%, the transfer by A to C of one-third of A's holding (20% of the shares of the company) will give C simply a minority holding in the company. On the other hand A will have lost control of the company, so that the loss sustained will be greater than the value of the benefit received by C; it is A's loss which is used to measure the value of the transfer for tax. Again, suppose that G pays the school fees of her grandson J; the value transferred is the loss to G, the amount spent by her, and the issue of how to value the benefit received by J does not arise.[30] On whether this may be potentially exempt, see above at §45.1.2.

The converse of this consequence is equally true. Where a particular disposition results in a greater benefit to the transferee than loss to the transferor, only that loss is taxed.[31] Thus, to revert to the earlier example, if B now gives the 40% holding to C, it is the loss of a 40% holding which will be taxed even though the benefit to C, through now having a 60% holding, is much greater.

The loss to the transferor's estate will depend on the extent of his estate. Where A gives B a fur coat or a painting, it is clear that there is a transfer of the coat or the painting, and the value of that object, grossed up as necessary, will be the measure of the transferor's loss and so the chargeable amount. More complicated questions may arise, however, where A buys the object for B. Suppose that A sees a picture for sale in an antique shop for £50, but knows that it is really by a famous artist and worth £50,000. If A buys the picture and takes it home, and there gives it to B, that will be a net chargeable transfer by A of £50,000. If, however, A is in the shop with B and pays £50 to B with which to buy the picture, or perhaps pays the £50, instructing the antique dealer to deliver the picture to B, then, provided neither the picture nor any right to the picture becomes part of A's estate, there will be a net chargeable transfer of only £50.[32] The question of the precise subject matter of the gift is also relevant to gifts with reservation, since the rules as to tracing property do not apply if the property given is a sum of money in sterling or any other currency (see §47.5.3 below).

---

[29] If A had 80% and gave 20% to C, A would still have voting control of the company, but would have lost the power to wind up the company (which requires 75%).

[30] Under the estate duty rules it was Revenue practice that education could not be valued and so its value was nil.

[31] IHTA 1984, s 3(3).

[32] *Cf* Goff J in *Ralli Bros Trustee Co Ltd v IRC* [1967] 3 All ER 811, 820.

Where A's transfer to B is void, there is no loss to A's estate and so no chargeable transfer. Where the transfer is voidable, the same result should follow, since A's right to rescind the transfer and recover the property is part of his estate; there may be a transfer when the right to rescind is lost. However, section 150 is premised on the assumption that a voidable transfer is effective despite the existence of the right to rescind (see below at §45.4.4). Similarly, a gift subject to a condition precedent causes no loss to the estate until the condition occurs; a gift subject to a condition subsequent is analogous to a voidable transfer when the right to rescind has not yet become exercisable.

45.3.2 Sale at Undervalue

Any consideration provided in return for the property is automatically taken into account. Thus, if A sells a piece of property worth £1,000 to B for £400, there will be a transfer of value of £600. Where the consideration provided in return is full but is paid to someone other than the vendor, there will also be a transfer of value. When A sells the property worth £1,000 to dealers and directs them to pay the price to B, there will be a transfer of value by A to B of £1,000, and the subject matter of the transfer is £1,000 not the property.

45.3.3 Grossing Up

Suppose that A, whose chargeable transfers exceed the nil rate band, makes an immediately chargeable transfer of £10,000 to a discretionary trust. If A bears the burden of the tax the amount of the gift must be grossed up at 20% to take account of the tax due; the loss sustained by A will be the amount transferred plus the tax due (a total of £12,500). Since this is the total amount of the loss to the estate, £12,500 will enter A's cumulative total. If, on the other hand, the trust bears the burden of the tax, there is no grossing up and the total loss to A's estate is only £10,000 (see above at §44.4.2). Grossing up has no role in a PET since the primary liability rests on the donee.

This strengthens rather than weakens the logical structure of the tax as IHT charges the reduction in the value of the estate. The grossing-up rule has the further strength that it avoids differences of principle between lifetime chargeable transfers and those on death. On death there is a transfer of all the property to which the transferor was beneficially entitled, whether actually or notionally. On transfers on death only the sums net of tax will reach the beneficiaries. One is used to thinking of transfers on death in gross terms. There is no reason why this should not also apply to transfers inter vivos.

The grossing-up principle applies to the value transferred, ie the loss to the estate. Where A settles shares on trust there may also be incidental costs, and even CGT. Sections 164 and 165 direct that where these costs are borne by A they are not grossed up; where they are borne by the trust, they reduce the value transferred.

45.4 Special Cases

45.4.1 Disposition of Excluded Property

A's estate is the aggregate of all the property to which A is beneficially entitled, except that the estate of a person immediately before death does not include excluded property (section 5(1)). It follows from this that excluded property forms part of a person's estate at other times. From this it follows that there is no charge to tax if a person sells non-excluded property and invests the proceeds in excluded property—or vice versa.

It is further provided that no account is to be taken of the value of excluded property which ceases to form part of a person's estate as a result of a disposition (section 3(2)). It follows from this that while a transfer of excluded property will not give rise to liability in respect of the property transferred, liability will accrue if the transfer of non-excluded property causes a loss to the excluded property.

Example

A, a person domiciled outside the UK, owns 40% of the shares in X Ltd, an English company. Another 30% of the shares are held by Y Ltd, a foreign company. A owns 75% of the shares in Y Ltd. So A has control of X Ltd by virtue of the two holdings of 40% and 30%. If A makes a transfer of his 40% holding in X Ltd, there will be a transfer of value, whether immediately chargeable or potentially exempt. There is a transfer of value since those shares are not excluded property. The value transferred is the loss to A's estate, and this will therefore take account of the loss of control notwithstanding that control is achieved only by the inclusion of excluded property.

Liability may also arise if the transfer of excluded property causes a loss to other property forming part of the estate. Thus, if A had transferred the holding in Y Ltd first, there would again have been a loss to his estate, perhaps a loss of control. It might be argued that since no account is taken of the value of the excluded property transferred and since that property gave A control, it ought to follow that the loss of control will escape tax. However, it may be that the 'value of the excluded property' is to be valued on its own and so without reference to the power it gave A over X Ltd, so that the difference between the loss of control and the value of the excluded property on its own is taxable; the position is not completely clear but, on balance, liability seems to arise. A more absurd situation is where A has control of a company through shares which are all excluded property, eg a 55% holding, and he then gives a 10% holding to B. It seems unlikely that a charge to tax arises here, and yet the gift of the 10% causes a loss to A's estate reflecting the loss of control.

45.4.2 *Free or Subsidised Use of Property*

If A agrees to lend B an asset for a period of, say, five years without charge, it would be possible to calculate the loss to A's estate by reference to income forgone and other matters under general principles. Where the loan is for a period which is not fixed, there were, in the days of CTT, special provisions to calculate the loss based on the idea of an annual value;[33] these were scrapped in 1981, presumably leaving the matter to general principles and so giving rise, perhaps, to immediately chargeable transfers or PETs. Where the property can be recalled at will the loss appears to be negligible.

45.4.3 *Mutual Transfers*

In the days of CTT, special rules provided relief where A made a transfer of value to B and B later made a transfer of value to A. These were repealed in 1986.[34] These are no longer generally

---

[33] FA 1976, ss 115–117.
[34] FA 1986, Sch 19, para 25.

needed since the only dispositions by A and B that will qualify for relief are now PETs rather than chargeable transfers. However, the Board is empowered to make regulations to avoid a double charge where a PET by A to B proves to be a chargeable transfer and, immediately before A's death, A's estate includes property acquired by A from B otherwise than for full consideration. These regulations are considered below at §46.7. One reason behind the repeal may have been to prevent the undoing of previous chargeable transfers to enable PETs to be made instead.

45.4.4 Voidable Transfers

Section 150 provides that where, by virtue of any enactment or rule of law, the whole or any part of a transfer has been set aside as voidable or otherwise defeasible, a claim may be made and:

(1) any tax[35] due shall cease to be due;
(2) any tax[36] already paid in respect of that or any other chargeable transfer[37] made before the claim that would not have been payable if the transfer had been void ab initio may be reclaimed;
(3) where the transferor has subsequently made other transfers, the rates of tax are determined as if the first transfer had been void (section 150(1)).

Examples include bankruptcy[38] and gifts made under undue influence.
 The provision, although well-intentioned, is not without its difficulties:

(1) It applies not just where the transfer is voidable, but also where it is 'otherwise defeasible'. Hence, perhaps, a condition subsequent which defeats the grant of an interest may come within this rule. However, a transfer subject to a condition precedent which has not yet occurred would appear to be ineffective and so not to fall within this rule, even though the condition should never occur.
(2) It applies only where the transfer has been set aside, and so not where the parties elect or the court directs that the transferor shall receive damages in lieu of the setting-aside. Such matters ought technically to be treated as mutual transfers.
(3) It assumes that a voidable transfer is an effective transfer, yet in theory, the reduction in the value of the estate should be exactly offset by the value of the right to recover the property—until such time as the right to set aside is lost by limitation or some other rule of law (which alters the timing of the transfer of value).

45.5 Matters Which are not Transfers of Value

45.5.1 Transactions with no Intent to Give

45.5.1.1 The Rule

IHT is intended to be a tax on gratuitous transfers of value. Section 10 therefore provides that a transfer is not a transfer of value if the transferor shows:

---

[35] And any interest due (IHTA 1984, s 150(2)); interest paid to the taxpayer is tax free: s 236(3).
[36] *Ibid.*
[37] As when the voidable transfer was exempt under s 19 and the second would have been if the first had not been made.
[38] Insolvency Act 1986, ss 339, 340, 423.

(1)   (a)   that the transfer was made in a transaction at arm's length between persons not
            connected with each other;[39] or
      (b)   if they are so connected, that the transfer was such as might be expected to be
            made in a transaction at arm's length; and
(2)   that the transfer was not intended and was not made in a transaction intended to
      confer a gratuitous benefit on any person.

Intention is judged according to the normal legal rule that people are taken to intend the
natural and probable consequences of their acts[40] (or omissions); moreover, the onus is
placed on the transferor to show that this intention was not present. It is perfectly possible
for a taxpayer to discharge this burden even though the sale is at a figure less than that
ultimately determined to be the fair market value of the property, eg where the taxpayer is
acting under a mistake.[41]

The 'person' whose intention is in issue is the transferor. In *Re Postlethwaite*,[42] Dr P had
set up a company, P Co, of which he was the sole employee and sole shareholder. Dr P was
a brilliant car designer and engineer, and was one of the best of his era in Formula One
motor racing. P Co received fees from the Ferrari motor company and transferred them to
a pension fund for Dr P. The money was transferred to trustees on 31 August and Dr P was
admitted on 1 September. This one-day gap caused a resulting trust, and so the payment
did not come within section 13 (below §45.5.3.5). The Special Commissioners held that
the payment came within section 10 and that the person who was the transferor was P Co.
P Co did not intend to confer any gratuitous benefit on Dr P. The employment contract had
provided for setting up a pension fund. Moreover—and this was crucial—the payment was
not excessive when compared with what Dr P had earned for P Co from Ferrari. The person
he intended to benefit was himself, and that was not gratuitous.

Examples

(1)   G, a grandfather, pays £20,000 to a school fees scheme for his grandson. This does not
      escape tax since, although the purchase is an arm's-length transaction, G intends to
      confer a gratuitous benefit on his grandson. Moreover, it may well be an immediate
      chargeable transfer rather than a potentially exempt one (see above at §45.1.2).
(2)   G sells a picture for £10,000; unknown to him, the picture is worth £100,000. Assum-
      ing that these facts are established, section 10 prevents there being a transfer of value
      despite the loss to G's estate.
(3)   M grants her son, S, the protected tenancy of a dwelling house. Although S pays the
      maximum fair rent, the Revenue may treat the grant of the lease as subject to tax, as
      it is clearly a disposal causing loss to M's estate, and deny the availability of section 10
      on the ground that persons dealing at arm's length do not usually grant protected
      tenancies. A similar argument arose out of the grant of tenancies of agricultural land,

---

[39]   An example would be employers making ex gratia payments to their employees.
[40]   See, eg *Cunliffe v Goodman* [1950] 2 KB 237, 253.
[41]   *IRC v Spencer-Nairn* [1991] STC 60, Ct of Sess, dismissing Crown's appeal against the decision of the Special
Commissioners.
[42]   [2007] STC SCD 83 Sp C 571.

but there special legislation now applies (see below at §45.5.3.6). Returning to the grant of a protected tenancy, one may perhaps distinguish the mother who grants a tenancy of the only property she has other than her own home, from one who regularly lets property to protected tenants and who treats her son in the same way as any other tenant. As always, the question is one of fact. Since the lease is an asset of S's estate, the grant would seem to be capable of being a PET rather than an immediately chargeable one.

(4)   F takes his two children into partnership with him on terms which provide that the children must devote such time as the business may require, that F need only devote such time as he sees fit and that F's share will accrue to the children on F's death without further payment.[43] This should come within section 10.

45.5.1.2 Exclusions

Section 10 does not apply to:

(1)   the sale of unquoted shares or debentures,[44] unless it is shown that the sale was at a price freely negotiated at the time of the sale (so that, for example, a sale at a price fixed under the provisions of the company's articles of association may be liable to IHT); even then, the requirements of section 10(1) must presumably also be met;[45]
(2)   certain reversionary interests under section 55 (see below at §49.9).

45.5.1.3 Associated Operations

Section 10 applies to transactions, which term includes a series of transactions and any associated operations.

45.5.2 Dispositions for Maintenance of Family

Certain dispositions for the maintenance of a family are not transfers of value (section 11). One consequence of this is that a transfer to a trust coming within section 11 cannot take advantage of the CGT holdover rule in TCGA 1992, section 260. The question whether a disposition was for the maintenance of the other person was considered by a Special Commissioner in *Phizackerly v HMRC*.[46] Having been referred by both counsel to *Re Coventry*[47] on the meaning of 'maintenance' in the family provision legislation, he held that maintenance

---

[43] The inspiration for this example is *A-G v Boden* [1912] 1 KB 539, but it must be stressed that each case will turn on its own facts.

[44] On the meaning of quoted and unquoted shares, see IHTA 1984, s 272, as amended by FA 1987, Sch 8, para 1. Shares or securities listed on a recognised stock exchange or dealt in on the old Unlisted Securities Market (USM, which ran from 1986 to 1996) are quoted. Unquoted means shares neither so listed nor so dealt in. A list of recognised stock exchanges is available on the HMRC website at https://www.gov.uk/government/publications/designated-recognised-stock-exchanges-section-1005-income-tax-act-2007. The AIM is not a recognised stock exchange for this purpose.

[45] However, the Revenue may argue that when the vendor has a 75% holding, the sale of a 33% holding is freely negotiated only if the purchaser pays a price equal to 33/75ths of the value of the 75% holding.

[46] [2007] Sp C 591, [2007] STC (SCD) 328.

[47] [1980] Ch 461.

had a flavour of meeting recurring expenses. In this case a husband had put the house into the joint names of himself and his wife not for the maintenance of the wife but to give her security—and so not within section 11. For fuller facts, see below at §55.5.2.

45.5.2.1 Spouses and Civil Partners, and Ex-such

A disposition made by one party to a marriage or civil partnership in favour of the other party is not a transfer of value if it is for the maintenance of the other party. Further, 'marriage' is defined in relation to a disposition made on the occasion of the dissolution or annulment of a marriage, and in relation to a disposition varying a disposition so made, as including a former marriage; the definition also makes provision for civil partnerships on an analogous basis (section 11(6)). The exemption is necessary because the general exemption for transfers between such people (see below at §53.1) does not apply to former spouses; moreover it is limited to the nil rate band amount where the transferor is, but the transferee is not, domiciled in the UK (section 51(2)). However, the Revenue have indicated that transfers of money or property pursuant to an order of the court in consequence of a decree of divorce or nullity, etc will in general be regarded as exempt as being arm's-length transactions.[48]

The scope of this relief is uncertain in a number of respects. First, there is the problem of the precise meaning of the word 'disposition'. This is apt to cover a transfer within section 2 and is expressly stated to cover the termination of an interest in possession in settled property under section 51(1).[49] This leaves open those matters which are treated as transfers of value. Thus, a deemed transfer by participators in a close company under section 98(1) is treated as being a disposition by them; although a person is treated as having made a transfer of value on death (see below at §46.1), this is not expressly stated to be by way of disposition, although other provisions assume that he does make a disposition.[50] The Revenue view is that a transfer on death is not capable of coming within section 11. The correct view is probably that section 11 applies only where the transfer is by disposition or in circumstances in which the legislation in its charging provisions treats the transfer as made by disposition. On this view transfers under section 98 would fall within section 11, but those on death or under section 94 and payments ceasing to be relevant property under section 65 would not. This is hard to justify and in need of reform. It should also be recalled that a deemed transfer of value otherwise than by disposition cannot be a PET.

The second difficulty is that the transfer must be 'in favour of' the other party. This is sufficient to cover payments direct to the other person or to trustees for that person absolutely, and probably also a transfer to a trust to hold on trust for the spouse for life,[51] but may not extend to the creation of a discretionary trust of which that person is to be one of the objects. If a transfer to a trust under which the spouse or civil partner takes a life interest is completely exempt, it may follow that a transfer to a trust under which the spouse takes a reversionary interest is taxable in full. The question whether a gift is 'in favour of the other' person must presumably be decided according to such general legal broad principles. So where a person has an interest in possession but the trust is treated for IHT purposes as

---

[48] Statement of Practice SP E12.
[49] IHTA 1984, s 18(1).
[50] IHTA 1984, ss 18(1), 147; see also Administration of Estates Act 1925, s 1.
[51] See Revenue Consultative Document, [1980] *Simon's Tax Intelligence* 581.

falling not under the regime in section 49 but under the rules previously applying only to discretionary trusts, it is still 'in favour of' the other.

Problems may arise over the implementation of agreements or court orders on divorce or annulment. If the carrying-out of the agreement or order is deferred until after decree absolute, the transfer is presumably made 'on the occasion of' the dissolution or annulment and so qualifies for relief; moreover, a transfer is defined in terms of the date of the loss to the transferor's estate, and so presumably the date of the transfer is that on which the agreement or order was made. Such transfers ought therefore to be safe from IHT, whether carried out before or after decree absolute. Subsequent transfers in favour of the ex-spouse will, however, be exempt only if they vary the disposition made on the divorce or annulment; such transfers should therefore be expressed to be by way of such variation. Whether a completely new agreement can be by way of variation of the old is unclear.[52] It is unclear whether transfers which simply implement orders made by the court can ever have any tax consequences. It may be argued either that these are not 'dispositions' at all, provided there is no consensual element in them, or that they are protected from tax by section 10.

45.5.2.2 A Child of Either Party

A disposition by one party to a marriage or civil partnership in favour of a child of either party for the maintenance, education or training of the child for a period ending in the year in which the child attains the age of 18 or, if later, ceases to undergo full-time education or training, is not a transfer of value. 'Child' includes a stepchild and an adopted child. The word 'training' is undefined; presumably, solicitors' articles provide training, especially now they are called 'training contracts'. Section 11 enables a parent, but not a grandparent, to make transfers free of tax. There is no need for the transfer to be on the occasion of a divorce and the provision is presumably designed to exempt a parent from liability to tax in respect of private school fees. Where a child ceases and then resumes full-time education or training after attaining 18, a literal reading suggests that later transfers may not come within the provision.

Another problem is that where a husband covenants to pay his wife annual sums for a child until that child reaches 21, the payments will presumably be treated as made year by year, each year being a period. If, however, he hands over a lump sum for the maintenance of the child until the child reaches 21, regardless of whether or not the child receives full-time education after reaching the age of 18, the transfer would appear to fall outside the relief.

45.5.2.3 A Child not in Care of Parent

Where the child is not in the care of a parent, a disposition—by anyone—for maintenance, education or training is not a transfer of value if (a) it is for a period ending not later than the year in which the child attains the age of 18, or (b) if the child has, for substantial periods, been in the custody of the transferor, the year in which the full-time education or training ceases.

---

[52] *Cf* the cases in Variation of Trusts Act 1958, especially *Re Ball's Settlement* [1968] 2 All ER 438.

45.5.2.4 Illegitimate Child of the Transferor

A disposition in favour of an illegitimate child of the transferor is not a transfer of value. The disposition must be for the maintenance, education or benefit of the child and for the same period as for other children. The reference to illegitimacy is way out of date.

45.5.2.5 Dependent Relative

A disposition in favour of a dependent relative is not a transfer of value, provided it is a reasonable provision for that person's care or maintenance. The notion of a dependent relative is narrowly defined as (a) any relative of the transferor or his spouse who is incapacitated by old age or infirmity from maintaining himself, the term 'relative' not being further defined, and (b) the mother of the transferor or his spouse, if widowed or living apart from her husband or, in consequence of dissolution or annulment of the marriage, a single woman.[53] By concession this extends to a gift by a child to his unmarried mother, but only if the mother is genuinely financially dependent on the child making the disposition. This restriction forms no part of the statutory provision which applies if the mother does get married (and for which marriage to anyone will do) (section 11(6)(b)). The legislation now applies also—in analogous manner—to civil partnerships.

45.5.3 *Other Transfers Which are not Transfers of Value*

45.5.3.1 Trading

A disposition which is allowable in computing the transferor's profits or gains for income tax or corporation tax is not a transfer of value. The same applies where the sum would be so allowable if the profits or gains were sufficient and fell to be so computed.[54]

45.5.3.2 Pension

A disposition which is a contribution to a registered pension plan is not a transfer of value.[55] Two omissions to obtain an increased pension are treated as not being a transfer of value. The first arises where a person deferred a pension when in good health but his life expectancy later deteriorates. The deferral does not normally give rise to a charge. The charge will arise if at the time of the original deferral the person had reason to believe that he would be dead within two years. The second omission applies to death benefits and excludes a charge where omitting to exercise pension rights results in the payment of these benefits to a charity or to dependants.

45.5.3.3 Remuneration Waiver

A waiver or repayment of remuneration is not a transfer of value if: (a) it would have been chargeable to income tax under ITEPA 2003; and (b) the sum, if not waived, would have

---

[53] The same test was used in the now repealed TA 1988, s 263 and the obsolescent TCGA 1992, s 226.
[54] IHTA 1984, s 12. The wording is wide enough to cover a trade which, in fact, makes a loss, or which is not within the charge to UK tax, eg a foreign trade.
[55] IHTA 1984, s 12(2). FA 2004, s 203 amended s 12(2) and repealed s 12(3) and (4) as from 6 August 2006.

been deductible in computing the profits of the payer and, by reason of repayment or the waiver, is not allowed or is brought back into charge.[56]

45.5.3.4 Dividend Waiver

A waiver of any dividend on shares of a company within 12 months before—but not after—any right to dividend has accrued is not a transfer of value (section 15); the right accrues when the dividend is declared, not when it becomes enforceable.[57] It will be noted that there is no provision dealing with the waiver of interest or rent.

45.5.3.5 Employee Trust

A disposition by a close company to trustees for its employees is not a transfer of value;[58] this must be distinguished from a transfer of shares by an individual to certain employee trusts, which is capable of being an exempt transfer if the trust has control (section 28).

45.5.3.6 Agricultural Tenancy

The grant of an agricultural tenancy is declared not to be a transfer of value if it is made for full consideration in money or money's worth (section 16). The reason for this is that the grant of such a lease inevitably reduces the value of an estate because of the different values of freehold and tenanted land, and the system of control of agricultural rents. But for such a provision, a landlord might find himself liable to tax on granting a lease to his son even though the terms were the best he could obtain from any third party.[59] This provision does not address the quite separate problem of the lifetime transfer of a Scottish agricultural tenancy.[60]

45.5.3.7 Variations and Disclaimers

Special treatment applies to certain variations and disclaimers following a person's death; these are not treated as transfers of value. The precise status of disclaimers outside these rules is uncertain.[61]

45.6   Exempt Lifetime Transfers

45.6.1 *Transfers not Exceeding £3,000*

Each tax year a person may make transfers of value up to £3,000 without incurring any liability to tax. Such transfers are exempt under IHTA 1984—and so not potentially exempt.

---

[56] IHTA 1984, s 14. 'Remuneration' is not defined—quaere whether it extends to any payment falling within employment income under ITEPA 2003.

[57] Long-term waiver may cause liability to tax under section 98 (see below at §52.2) and to CGT under TCGA 1992, s 29.

[58] IHTA 1984, s 13 (note restriction of rights of participators to income only and inclusion of new share ownership plans in FA 2000, Sch 8, FA 2000, s 134(2)); see also Statement of Practice SP E11. This was the provision relevant to *Re Postlethwaite*, above §45.5.1.1.

[59] IHTA 1984, s 10 would not apply as, in the Revenue view, no one in their right mind would grant a lease of such land anyway and therefore there must have been an intention to confer a gratuitous benefit.

[60] See *Baird's Executors v IRC* [1991] 1 EGLR 201; Ede [1991] BTR 181.

[61] Potter and Monroe, *op cit*, §10-09.

Where several transfers are made in one year, the exemption is given according to the date of the transfer, the earlier transfers enjoying the exemption. Where two transfers are made on the same day, the exemption is apportioned between them in proportion to the values transferred; this is so even though the order in which the transfers were made is known (section 19(3)). To the extent that transfers in one year fall short of £3,000, the amount by which they fall short may be rolled forward to the next year and used to exempt gifts in that year (section 19(2)). Any shortfall still unused at the end of the second year is lost. This exemption applies to all lifetime dispositions, to the termination of a life interest in possession (section 19(5)) and to sums apportioned under section 94 (close companies) (section 94(5)). However, it does not apply on death or to a gift with reservation.[62]

Example

On 10 June in Year 1, A transfers £2,826 to B. He makes no other transfers in that year. In Year 2, A makes the following transfers:

10 May £1,400 (C)

11 May £1,000 (D) and £1,500 (E)

12 May £3,000 (F)

A can roll forward £174 of the £3,000 exemption from Year 1 to Year 2.

In Year 2, transfer C is exempt. Transfers D and E are partly exempt, the remaining exemption (£1,600 + £174) being apportioned two-fifths to D (£710) and three-fifths to E (£1,064), ie £290 of transfer D and £436 of transfer E are chargeable. The whole of transfer F is chargeable.

Where there is a PET in the year, the annual exemption is set first against any immediately chargeable transfers even if made after the PET (section 19(3A)(a)). If the PET later becomes a chargeable transfer, the better view is that it is treated, for this purpose only, as made after the other transfers in that year.[63] The result is different if they are in separate years.

Example

In Year 1, A makes a PET of £3,000. In Year 2, A makes an immediately chargeable transfer of £6,000. The whole of the transfer in Year 2 is exempt. However, if A dies in Year 3, the Year 1 exemption will be switched from year 2 to year 1.[64]

45.6.2 *Small Gifts to the Same Person*

Transfers of value made by a transferor in any one year by outright gifts to any one person are exempt under section 20 to the extent that the values transferred, without grossing up, do not exceed £250. There is no rollover of any unused portion of £250. This is intended as a

---

[62] FA 1986, s 102(5).
[63] IHTA 1984, s 19(3A)(b). For debate, see *Simon's Direct Tax Service*, Pt 13.322; Foster, *Inheritance Tax* (Butterworths, 1991) C3.22.
[64] IHTA 1984, s 19(3A) allows the PET to be left out of account only for the year in which it was made.

de minimis exception and so cannot be used to exempt the first £250 of a larger transfer. The restriction to 'outright gifts' bars, inter alia, a transfer to trustees to hold on trusts, unless perhaps to hold on bare trusts for one or more of full age and capacity.[65] The phrase would appear to exclude a transfer at an undervalue, and sums apportioned under section 94[66] (close companies). A loan is treated as an outright gift (section 29(3)). A gift with reservation cannot qualify for this exemption.[67]

45.6.3 Normal Expenditure Out of Income

45.6.3.1 The Rule

A transfer is exempt under section 21 to the extent that it is shown that:

(1)   it was made as part of the normal expenditure of the transferor; and
(2)   taking one year with another, it was made out of income; and
(3)   after allowing for all transfers forming part of his normal expenditure, the transferor was left with sufficient income (after tax) to maintain his usual standard of living.

Where the transfer exceeds this limit, only the excess is chargeable. In recent years this exception has become very important. Individuals with very high incomes, and for whom the annual £3,000 allowance is little more than an irritant, have been allowed to take advantage of section 21 and transfer large sums of money without incurring IHT. It says much for the disinterest of the HMRC in some IHT matters that they have not capped the amount.

45.6.3.2 Scope

The exemption is not confined to outright gifts but applies to any disposition inter vivos, including payments to a settlement. The exemption does not apply to events which are treated as transfers of value by section 3(4), such as a change in the share structure of a close company. Since the exemption does not apply on death, it is not surprising that it is expressly excluded from applying to gifts with reservation.[68]

45.6.3.3 Life Policies

This exemption is of the greatest practical importance in its application to the payment of premiums on a life policy. In deciding the level of a person's income, it is provided that the capital repayment element in a purchased life annuity is not to form part of the transferor's income—unless purchased before 13 November 1974, the date on which CTT was announced.[69]

---

[65] In practice, the reservation of an interest is ignored.
[66] Compare IHTA 1984, s 20(3) with s 79(5).
[67] FA 1986, s 102(5).
[68] *Ibid.*
[69] IHTA 1984, s 21(3), (4). For a definition of a purchased life annuity, see ex TA 1988, s 657.

45.6.3.4 Application: The Test

Whether a gift forms part of the deceased's normal expenditure is a question of fact.[70] According to Lightman J in *Bennett v IRC*,[71] there is no standard of reasonableness and a tax planning motive is no obstacle. What is needed is evidence to show the substantial conformity of each payment with an established pattern of expenditure by the individual concerned. Such a pattern may be established by proof of the existence of a prior commitment or resolution, or by reference only to a sequence of payments. On this basis a single transfer is unlikely to qualify unless the pattern of giving can be established. A single payment under a continuing obligation to pay may qualify, but all depends on the circumstances—a payment under a deed of covenant may not qualify if death was imminent at the time of that first payment. Payments of varying sums may qualify if made under a quantifiable formula, eg the costs of a sick or elderly dependant's residence at a nursing home. Whether it is possible to establish a normal pattern of expenditure by making isolated gifts to different people is uncertain; however, the exemption may apply to gifts to different people if their general character or the qualification for benefit is established, eg members of the family or needy friends.

In the *Bennett* case, a testator had left property on trust to pay the income to his widow, B, for her life and then to his three sons. Trust shares in the family company were sold in return for shares in another company and cash, a sale which meant a substantial increase in trust income. B felt adequately provided for even before the sale. The clear evidence was that she had a modest lifestyle, which was unlikely to, and in the event did not, change during the remainder of her life. B decided that surplus income should go to the sons, and authorised the trustees to distribute equally between them 'all or any of the income arising in each accounting year as is surplus to my financial requirements of which you are already aware'. In February 1989 and 1990, payments of £9,300 and £60,000 were made to each of the sons. This did not, in fact, exhaust the income in the relevant accounting years, as a conservative approach had been adopted in the administration of the trust which had resulted in delays in determining the surplus available for distribution. Mrs B died unexpectedly on 20 February 1990. Lightman J held that the payments in 1989 and 1990 were exempt.

45.6.4 *Gifts Made in Consideration of Marriage or Civil Partnership*

Transfers of value made by gift and made in consideration of marriage or civil partnership are exempt under section 22 up to certain limits. These gifts may be an outright gift or settled by the gift (section 22(2)). The following conditions apply:

(1) *Parent of either party*—the first £5,000 given to a child is exempt tax (section 22(1)(a)). The term 'child' includes an illegitimate child, an adopted child and a stepchild (section 22(2)). The net effect is that the four parents can between them make exempt transfers of £20,000 to the couple—but not to each of them.

(2) *Remoter ancestors*—the first £2,500 is exempt (section 22(2)).

---

[70] *Bennett v IRC* [1995] STC 54; and *A-G for Northern Ireland v Heron* [1959] TR 1. Principles in *Bennett* applied to deny relief in *Nadin v IRC* [1997] (SCD) 107.
[71] [1995] STC 54, 59d.

(3) *Parties*—the first £2,500 is exempt (section 22(2)).

(4) *Others*—the first £1,000 of a marriage gift made by a person other than a party to the marriage/civil partnership or his or her parent or remoter ancestor is also exempt.

If a single donor makes more than one gift in consideration of the same event, the exemption is applied to the gifts rateably according to their respective values (section 22(1)).

45.6.4.1 Scope

The exemption extends to a number of situations which receive special treatment under IHT. A gift with reservation is eligible.[72] An event causing a charge on settled property when there is a beneficial interest in possession within section 49, as where a power of appointment or advancement is exercised, may come within these rules provided notice is given to the trustees of the availability of this exemption.[73] Property which ceases to be settled property is treated as an outright gift; property remaining settled is treated as property becoming settled.

There is no qualification to these exemptions where the gift is an outright gift to one or other of the parties to the marriage (section 22(4)). Loans are treated as outright gifts (section 29(3)).

45.6.4.2 In Consideration of Marriage or Civil Partnership

Section 22 grants exemption only for gifts made in consideration of the new status. An outright gift made to a person other than a party to the marriage/civil partnership, eg a gift to a grandchild when the grandchild's parent remarries, is not treated as a gift made in consideration of marriage (section 22(3)).

Neither a gift made on the occasion of the event, nor one made conditional upon the change of status taking place, is necessarily made 'in consideration' of the new status. The question is one of fact, and where the gift is in settlement, the solution may lie in the terms of the settlement in the light of the surrounding circumstances.[74] If, therefore, the settler's prime motive was to save IHT and so benefit his family as a whole rather than the individual who was getting married, the gift is not 'in consideration of' marriage; the marriage was the occasion for the gift, not the consideration for it. However, it appears that an absolute disposition in favour of a party to their marriage cannot be attacked on this ground.[75] Subject to this, it is irrelevant to the question whether a gift is made for such consideration that there are beneficiaries outside the relevant consideration; however, the presence of such beneficiaries may be fatal under section 22(4) (see below).

45.6.4.3 Settled Gifts: Non-qualifying Beneficiaries

The legislation provides that where the gift is by way of settlement, exemption will be given only if the settlement is primarily for the benefit of the parties to the marriage or civil

---

[72] FA 1986, s 102(5).
[73] IHTA 1984, ss 22(6) (excluding s 3(4)) and 57(2).
[74] *Rennell v IRC* [1964] AC 173, 209, [1963] 1 All ER 803, 817, per Lord Guest.
[75] *Re Park (No 2)* [1972] 1 All ER 394.

partnership, their issue (including legitimated and adopted issue) and the spouses/civil partners of their issue. The list of those eligible is contained in section 22(4). By this provision, a disposition other than an outright gift is not a gift made 'in consideration' of the new status if those who are or may become entitled to any benefit under the disposition include any person other than:

(1) the parties to the marriage or civil partnership, any child of the family (ie the child of one or both of them) of the parties to the marriage or civil partnership, or a spouse or civil partner of any such issue;

(2) persons becoming entitled on the failure of trusts for any such child under which trust property would (subject only to any power of appointment to a person falling within (1) or (3)) vest indefeasibly on the attainment of a specified age or either on the attainment of such an age or on some earlier event, or persons becoming entitled (subject as aforesaid) on the failure of any limitation in tail;

(3) a subsequent spouse or civil partner of a party to the marriage or civil partnership, or any child of the family of the parties to any subsequent marriage or civil partnership or a spouse or civil partner of any such child;

(4) persons becoming entitled under protective trusts under the Trustee Act 1925, section 33, the Trustee Act (Northern Ireland) 1958, section 34(1) or corresponding provisions under Scots law, the principal beneficiary being a person falling within (1) or (3); potential beneficiaries within the enlarged class set out in sections 33(1)(ii) and 34(b) are also permitted;

(5) as respects a reasonable amount of remuneration, the trustees of the settlement.

The term 'child' is expressly stated to include any person legitimated by a marriage, or adopted by the husband and wife jointly, among the issue of that marriage (section 22(5)).

45.6.5 Transfers to Miscellaneous Favoured Trusts, Bodies and Persons

A transfer by an individual to an employee trust[76] is an exempt transfer if it meets the full requirements of section 28, in particular that the trustees have then, or within one year, control of the company.[77] A transfer to a maintenance fund for heritage property is an exempt transfer (section 27, Schedule 4). These receive special treatment because of their public character. There is therefore no such exemption for other favoured trust such as newspaper trusts, protective trusts, a trust for disabled persons or an accumulation and maintenance trust.

Other exemptions extend to gifts to a spouse, charity, political party, housing association or a body listed in Schedule 3, eg Scottish Natural Heritage.[78] These may apply to transfers on death just as much as to lifetime transfers and so are discussed in chapter fifty-three below.

---

[76] As defined by IHTA 1984, s 86.
[77] IHTA 1984, s 28(2); contrast s 13.
[78] IHTA 1984, ss 18, 23, 24, 24A, 25.

45.7 Disposition by Associated Operations: Section 268 and *Ramsay*

45.7.1 The Rule

A disposition is stated to include one made by associated operations (section 272). Further, section 10 provides that a transaction includes a series of transactions and any associated operations.[79] By section 268(3), such operations are telescoped; all are treated as made at the time of the last. Broadly, such operations are either two or more affecting one piece of property, or one paving the way for another. The word 'operation' is not defined save that it is to include 'omission'.[80]

More precisely, 'associated operations' are defined in section 268(1) as any two or more operations of any kind whether effected by the same person or by different persons and whether or not simultaneous being—

(a)   '(a)operations which affect the same property, or one of which affects some property and the other or others of which affect property which represents, whether directly or indirectly, that property, or income arising from that property, or any property representing accumulations of any such income, or

(b)   any two operations of which one is effected with reference to the other, or with a view to enabling the other to be effected or facilitating its being effected, and any further operation having a like relation to any of those two, and so on'.

It will be seen that it is not enough simply to show that two dispositions affect the same property; there must be one disposition effected by associated operations. Thus, the Special Commissioners have held that where shares were transferred to a discretionary trust and the company then repurchased the shares, there were two separate dispositions.[81] This meant that the Revenue could not push back the time of the disposition to that of the purchase of the shares, which would have disqualified a claim for business relief. The court also held that the Revenue could not achieve the same end by the *Ramsay*[82] doctrine.

An example of (a) would be the grant of a lease followed by the gift of the reversion to the lessee. However, where a lease is granted for full consideration in money or money's worth, the lease is not taken as associated with any operation effected more than three years after its grant pursuant to section 268(2).[83]

Example

Suppose that Alf has a house worth £250,000, and on 1 January 2008 he grants Ben, his son, a lease at full rent. The effect is to reduce the value of Alf's interest to £200,000. On 1 January 2010, when the house would have been worth £350,000 with vacant possession, Alf gives Ben the reversion then worth £275,000.

---

[79]   *Macpherson v IRC* [1988] STC 362, [1988] 2 All ER 753, HL.
[80]   A statutory reversal of *Nichols v IRC* [1975] STC 278, [1975] 2 All ER 120.
[81]   *Reynaud and others v IRC* [1999] STC (SCD) 185.
[82]   *WT Ramsay Ltd v IRC* [1982] AC 300; [1981] STC 174; 54 TC 101, discussed at §5.6.4 above.
[83]   The Revenue might argue that IHTA 1984, s 10 does not apply as no one would deliberately create the possibility of a protected tenancy unless he wished to confer a gratuitous benefit on the lessee.

The grant of the lease is not a transfer of value since it comes within section 10, but the gift of the reversion is such a transfer so that there would be a transfer of £275,000. However, the operations affect the same property and are associated; they are therefore treated as one transfer of property worth £350,000 taking place on 1 January 2010. This will almost certainly be a PET, but the point is that it is a PET of property worth £350,000, not £275,000. If the gift of the reversion had taken place on 1 January 2012, more than three years would have elapsed since the grant of the lease. The grant and the reversion would therefore not have been associated operations.

Another example of (a) would be the transfer of the fee simple followed by a lease back.

Situation (b) is directed particularly at persons trying to use exemptions, as where, in the above example, Alf, faced with a serious illness and so the real possibility that a PET will become chargeable, transfers £3,000 to his son and the same sum to his wife, so that she may pass that same sum to his son, in an attempt to knit together the exemption of the first £3,000 of otherwise chargeable transfers and that of transfers between spouses. These are sometimes called channelling operations. The Revenue regard such operations as safe from section 268, provided the gift to the spouse is, as a matter of substance, genuine.[84] It has been suggested[85] that in order for operations to be associated, the prime reasons for each of them taking place must be that the other will take place or has already done so. On this basis, channelling operations would not necessarily be associated. However, where T holds 51% of the shares in a company, transfers 2% to X, a stranger, for value and then transfers 20% to each of his two sons, the transfers to X and his sons might be associated operations; equally, the transfer of all a person's UK assets to a non-resident company in return for shares in the company, followed by the acquisition of a foreign domicile, might also be associated operations.

45.7.2 Consequences

The consequences of operations being associated are complex but fall into three distinct parts.

45.7.2.1 Timing

Where a transfer of value is carried out by associated operations at different times, it is treated as made at the time of the last operation (section 268(3)). This may increase the rate of tax payable on earlier transfers not only because there may have been other transfers in the interval raising the rate of tax, but also because the last transfer occurs within three years of the transferor's death, thus triggering the higher rates of tax. Thus, the grant of the lease and the gift of the reversion may be treated as a transfer of the fee simple made at the time of the gift of the reversion. Similarly, where A gives £250 to X and another £250 to Y for transmission to X, the scheme will be treated as being a disposal by A to X of £500 and so chargeable in full (see above at §45.6.2). It also affects the date for valuing the property involved.

---

[84] See below §45.7.3 and safe from *Ramsay* [1985] *Simon's Tax Intelligence* 571.
[85] *Law Society's Gazette*, April 1976, 350.

45.7.2.2 Earlier Transfers

Secondly, there is a rule requiring that earlier transfers of value be taken into account. Where two transactions are carried out by the same person, the value transferred by the earlier operation is treated as reducing the value transferred by all the operations taken together. This is to prevent a double charge to tax. Presumably, however, this could lead to a repayment of tax if the effect of the first rule is to bring the earlier transfer into a period of lower (or even nil) rates. Thus, if in the example above, Alf had granted the lease at a nominal rent so that there was a reduction in the value of Alf's estate of, say £50,000, and a consequent charge in 2008, this, in turn, would have reduced the later transfer from £350,000 to £300,000. This affects not only the value of the property transferred, but also the rate at which any grossing up is carried out. It also seems to follow that where there have been intermediate transfers, the tax on those transfers may have to be reopened since the first transfer is now treated as taking place at the time of the last of the associated transfers by section 268(1)(b) and section 272.

The rule requiring that earlier transfers of value be taken into account is subject to one important exception. The reduction does not apply to the extent that the transfer constituted by the earlier operations, but not that made by the operations taken together, is exempt as a transfer between spouses. Thus, where A transfers £3,000 to his son and another £2,500 to his wife for transmission to the son, the transfer will be treated as one of £5,500 to the son.

There is no prohibition on the reduction where the earlier transfer is exempt by reason of some other provision. Thus, if C gives his daughter, D, shares worth £10,000 in five equal instalments and makes no other transfers each year, the transfers will be associated operations and so will be treated as being of £10,000 in year 5, but reduced by the aggregate of the annual exemptions for each of years 1–4. Lest potential Cs should get carried away, it should be remembered that if, in year 5, the value of the shares rises sharply to £20,000, that increase will determine the value transferred.

45.7.2.3 Practice

The practical effect of this provision depends on Revenue practice, which has been fairly limited. Some channelling operations are caught. Thus, if H gives W property on condition that she passes it on to the real object of H's benevolence, such transactions will be treated as associated. Similarly, the subject matter of the transaction may invite the attention of the Revenue, as where H, having a 60% holding, transfers 35% to his son, having previously transferred 25%, to his wife who later transfers that holding to the son. The Revenue in such an instance might wish to ensure that the value of a controlling holding was taxed.[86]

Another consequence of the transactions being associated is that section 10 must be applied to the single transaction. Thus, if A grants B a lease at full rent and then sells him the reversion for full market value, there may still be a chargeable transfer if the grant of the lease caused a drop in market value.[87]

---

[86] See Hansard, vol 888, col 55, 10 March 1975, reproduced in Foster, *op cit*, X6.01. The loss of control will be taxed, thanks to the related property rules (see below at §55.2.1); however, the later transfer by the wife will not be caught by those rules.

[87] But, on agricultural land, see IHTA 1984, s 16.

One matter which section 268 does not resolve is just who is to be treated as making the reconstructed transfer. Thus, if A uses the spouse exemption to channel a controlling interest to his son, is the whole transfer to be treated as made by A, or is the value to be allocated between A and Mrs A? The latter will, at first sight, avoid problems if A has died before the associated transfer is made by Mrs A, but this will not avoid the problem of reopening the transfer by A to give it a different value. Where parents sell property to children but leave the purchase price outstanding to be released year by year using the annual exemption, the Revenue regard the operations as associated. However, the gift of an asset to a child, the child to pay the IHT, followed by gifts within the annual exemption limit to fund the IHT, is not so regarded.[88]

45.7.3 Section 268 and the Ramsay Principle—General

Although the effect of the decisions of the House of Lords on the *Ramsay* approach has been at times bewildering, since *Barclays Mercantile Business Finance*[89] it is now established that *Ramsay* did not introduce a new judicial anti-avoidance doctrine in tax law (see above at §5.6.4 *et seq*). Instead the approach taken in the *Ramsay* line of decisions is based on a principle of purposive statutory construction combined with a realistic view of the transaction. Thus, there is no reason why this approach should not apply in the IHT context where this is appropriate, a view confirmed by the case law.[90] Equally, the Revenue presumably may invoke the new approach to present the facts one way while arguing in the alternative that section 268 applies if the operations are associated. What is not clear is whether a firm conclusion in favour of the Revenue on one basis precludes a similar finding on the other (as opposed to making it possibly unnecessary).

  Where the new approach is invoked in such cases, it is important for the Revenue to make it clear what fiscal consequences they attach to what is said to be a single composite transaction, and under which provision of the taxing statutes a charge to tax arises or a claim for exemption or relief fails.[91] It thus follows that the courts will have to explore the relationship between a general anti-avoidance rule of construction (if that is what the new approach now is) and a specific, but wide-ranging anti-avoidance provision. The answer ought to be that the new approach helps the court to apply correctly the particular legislative provision invoked in the case.

45.7.3.1 Does Section 286 Exclude *Ramsay*?

If the operations are associated under section 268, will the courts allow the Revenue to use the new approach too? This issue is still open,[92] but *McGuckian* (see below at §45.7.4)

---

[88] *Law Society's Gazette*, 1 March 1978; Foster, *op cit*, X6.09.
[89] *Barclays Mercantile Business Finance Ltd v Mawson* [2005] STC 1(HL).
[90] *Fitzwilliam v IRC* [1993] STC 502, HL; and *Hatton v IRC* [1992] STC 140.
[91] *Fitzwilliam v IRC* [1990] STC 65, 120, approved by Nourse LJ at [1992] STC 185, 189, in the Court of Appeal. Here, Vinelott J concluded, as has since the House of Lords, that the transaction could not be treated as a single composite transaction and so it was unnecessary for him to consider how the single transaction could be treated for IHT purposes; but he did not think the Crown had been able to show how it should have been treated. In the Court of Appeal the Revenue submitted an amended notice of determination. Of this, Nourse LJ said simply, '[i]t has to my mind clarified both the essentials of the Crown's claim and its inability to sustain them' ([1992] STC 185, 189).
[92] *Fitzwilliam v IRC* [1993] STC 502, 536g, per Lord Browne-Wilkinson, HL.

suggests that they may do so. Logically, the new approach should be applied to assemble the facts to which section 268 will apply in so far as the Revenue rely on section 268. This will have the advantage that the courts can then allow the detailed provisions in section 268(3) as to the effects of operations being associated to apply. This is of particular importance where section 268(3) determines the timing of a transaction, the more so since it has been said that under the new approach a taxable transaction taken in steps is to be treated as taking place when the first step is taken.[93]

45.7.3.2 Role of Section 268(2)

If the only reason the operations are not associated is the applicability of the exclusion in section 268(2), will the courts allow the Revenue to use the new approach? The exclusion from section 268 is an implied direction that the matters must be treated as separate transactions for tax purposes.

45.7.3.3 Where Section 268 Does not Apply

If section 268 does not apply because the operations do not fall within the definition in section 268(1), will the courts allow the Revenue to use the new approach? The answer is now a clear 'Yes'. Since the answer to the previous question is affirmative, will the courts require the Revenue to proceed by analogy with section 268(3) in reconstructing the transaction? There would seem to be good sense in such a requirement, but the Revenue may find the timing rule in particular to be unnecessarily constraining, and again, it would appear that there is nothing in the reasoning in the cases to limit the applicability of the new approach in this way.

45.7.4 *The* Fitzwilliam *Case*

Fitzwilliam v IRC[94] was a House of Lords decision on the application of the *Ramsay* principle to a CTT saving scheme. Nothing was said about this case in the subsequent House of Lords decisions in *MacNiven*[95] or in *Barclays* although it was cited in argument. Writing extra-judicially, Lord Templeman, who had dissented in the case, said this about the majority decision:

> The majority in Fitzwilliam succeeded in upholding an elaborately planned scheme on the grounds that, in considering a tax savings plan whereby the taxpayer received £3.8 m without liability to tax, the correct approach to the consideration of the transactions included in the plan was to ask whether realistically they constituted a single and indivisible whole in which one or more transactions was simply an element without independent effect and whether it was intellectually possible for them to be so treated. The scheme was designed to avoid capital transfer tax and the majority seemed to find some significance in the fact that the scheme might fail in the event of an unexpected death and in the meantime attracted a small amount of income tax. I find it intellectually impossible to treat these reasons seriously.[96]

---

[93] Vinelott J in *Shepherd v Lyntress Ltd* [1989] STC 617, 650.
[94] [1993] STC 502, HL; see Whitehouse [1994] *Private Client Business* 71.
[95] *MacNiven v Westmoreland Investments Limited* [2001] UKHL 6.
[96] Shipwright (ed), *Tax Avoidance and the Law*, 1 at 9.

The facts of the case (see below) are complicated, but the lessons are relatively simple:

(1)   the Revenue cannot alter the nature of a particular transaction in a series of transactions;
(2)   the Revenue cannot pick some bits and reject others;
(3)   the fact that a series of transactions is preordained is not of itself enough to enable the Revenue to undo a scheme; where the scheme involves the use of a particular exemption, the Revenue must also be able to show that the reconstruction of the transaction which they are able to substantiate is inconsistent with the application of that exemption. This last point can be made to fit nicely with both the 1997 decisions in *IRC v McGuckian*[97] and *IRC v Willoughby*.[98]

Points (1)–(3) are principally from the speech of Lord Keith, who drew them together in the proposition that in order to treat a series of transactions as one composite whole, the Revenue had to show that it was realistically and intellectually possible to do so.

45.7.4.1 Facts

Lord Fitzwilliam (LF) died unexpectedly in September 1979 at the age of 75, leaving no issue. He was survived by his widow, Lady Fitzwilliam (F) and her daughter by a previous marriage, soon to be Lady Hastings (H). Under the terms of his will, LF had created a 23-month discretionary trust at the end of which the property was to be held on trust for F for life; with an ultimate trust over in favour of H provided she survived LF by one month. If nothing had been done then, on the expiry of the 23-month period, the property would have passed to F. The exemption for property transferred to a spouse would have applied on that transfer and another provision would have prevented a charge on the death of LF. Unhappily there was some risk that F would not survive the 23-month period; she was in a state of shock at the death of her husband and of her sister two weeks later. If she had died then the whole estate of some £11 m would have been subject to CTT at 75%. The world being as it is, F did not die and was still living at the time of the hearing in 1993, when she was 95, but in 1979 the risk of her early death was sufficiently substantial for the trustees of the estate to seek advice.

The scheme involved five steps:

(1)   *20 December 1979*: the trustees appointed £4 m in favour of F; no tax was due under the spouse exemption.
(2)   *7 January 1980*: F gave H £2 m funded out of the £4 m. This was found by the Commissioners to be a genuine gift. The fiscal effect would be that there would be a charge to CTT on this lifetime gift, but this effect was to be undone at step (4).
(3)   *14 January 1980*: the trustees appointed £3.8 m in trust to pay the income to F until 15 February 1980 or her death if earlier; subject to this, one half (the vested half) was to go to H absolutely and the other half to her contingently on surviving until the ending of F's income interest. H thus had two interests in the trust, each worth £1.9 m,

---

[97]   [1997] STC 908.
[98]   [1997] STC 995.

but one vested and the other contingent. The appointment in favour of F was exempt as a transfer to a spouse.

(4)   *31 January 1980*: F sold the income interest created at step (3) in the contingent half to H for £2 m. The ending of F's interest would normally have given rise to CTT, but that was not so if the amount paid by H matched or exceeded the £1.9 m in the settlement; as H paid £2 m there was no charge. F was left with a potential charge to tax on the gift of £2 m at step (2); however, the mutual transfer provisions (which were repealed in 1986 and do not form part of IHT) meant that the F–H transfer at step (2) was cancelled and that the H–F payment at step (4) was not a transfer of value. It may be seen that the single H–F payment of £2 m operated to prevent two heads of charge.

(5)   *5 February 1980*: H established a nominal settlement to pay income to F until 15 March 1980 or her earlier death, and subject thereto for H absolutely; two days later H assigned to this trust her interest in the vested half of the trust created at step (3). The financial effect was to prolong F's income interest created at step (3) by a further month. There was a potential charge to CTT on the establishment of the nominal settlement, but it was hoped that there would be none on its termination by reason of the reverter to settlor exemption; this depended on H being regarded as the settlor.

45.7.4.2 The House of Lords[99]

The Revenue argued that while step (1) was not part of a preordained series of transactions, steps (2)–(5) were. The House of Lords divided 4:1; Lord Templeman, as we saw above, dissented.[100]

Lord Keith[101] said that the correct approach was to ask whether, realistically, steps (2)–(5) constituted a single and indivisible whole in which one or more of them were simply an element without independent effect, and whether it was intellectually possible so to treat them.[102] This test was drawn from words used by Lord Oliver in his speech in *Craven v White*,[103] but those words were used in a descriptive rather than a prescriptive mode. Taking this test as established, Lord Keith then pointed to certain real fiscal consequences of each step—eg whether F was liable to pay tax on the income during the short period of her entitlement. One reads this with some anxiety, since Lord Keith fails to address the question whether income tax would have been due if the *Ramsay* case were correctly applied; later he pointed to the risk that there would have been a charge to CTT if H or F had died while entitled to an interest in possession—again, this assumes the answer. After *Barclays* the question may well not arise.

He then said that the Revenue reconstruction would have charged CTT on the £3.8 m passing to H on the basis that there was a termination of F's interest in possession; however, in order to substantiate that basis the Revenue had to admit that step (3), creating the two income interests in F, and steps (4) and (5), making the assignments, were effective. This,

---

[99] For valuable analysis, see Watson and Ingham [1993] BTR 414.

[100] Those who admire Lord Templeman's approach to these matters will enjoy the six points of disagreement with Lord Keith, listed at [1993] STC 502, 532–34, HL.

[101] With whom Lord Ackner and Lord Mustill agreed.

[102] [1993] STC 502, 513.

[103] [1988] STC 476, HL.

said Lord Keith, was simply not possible either realistically or intellectually. The Revenue could not both accept that step (2) was a genuine unconditional gift and then seek to recast it as a conditional gift; neither could they pick bits out of steps (3), (4) and (5) and treat them as effective in order to say that they were not effective. The fact of preordainment did not negative the application of the exemption which the transactions were seeking to create unless the series was capable of being construed in a manner inconsistent with that exemption. There was no rational basis under which steps (2)–(4) could be treated as effective for the purpose of creating a charge to tax on the ending of F's interest in possession, but ineffective for the purpose of attracting the exemptions for the purchase of the interest or the reverter to the settlor. It is hard to disagree with the comment that Lord Keith's reasoning is less than wholly convincing and that the case was not so much won by the taxpayer as lost by the Revenue with their different and inconsistent analyses.[104]

Lord Browne-Wilkinson took a very different approach. For him, part of that real transaction was a transfer out of the estate of LF of £3.8 m to H, and he would have treated it in that way if the elements of the *Ramsay* test had been satisfied so as to treat steps (1)–(5) as one transaction. The Crown had not sought to argue that, and therefore could not have steps (2)–(5) treated as a 'mini-*Ramsay*'. Speeches in cases like these should be read as guides to future developments. In that sense Lord Browne-Wilkinson's speech operates as a warning against relying too heavily on Lord Keith's words.

---

[104] Watson and Ingham, *op cit*, 423.

46

Death

46.1 Effect of Death on Lifetime Transfers

Lifetime transfers, other than gifts with reservation, take place when they are made, not when the transferor dies. However, the subsequent death of the transferor may affect lifetime transfers, whether PETs or immediately chargeable, in the following ways.

46.1.1 Transfer Undone by Court Order

Where a transfer of value is undone by an order made under Inheritance (Provision for Family and Dependants) Act 1975, section 10, any tax paid is to be repaid or, if unpaid, to cease to be payable; the transfer on death is charged as if the previous transfer had not been made, but the money or property recovered does form part of the estate for the purpose of the transfer on death.[1]

---

[1] IHTA 1984, s 146.

46.1.2 *Death Within Seven Years: And Tapering Relief*

PETs become chargeable if A, the donor, dies within seven years (section 3A(4), (5)). As already seen, the amount of tax will be determined by using the death rates prevailing at the time of the death, although the transfer is, for most purposes, treated as having taken place when it actually occurred (section 7(2)). Where the donor dies more than three years after the transfer, the amount of tax, as distinct from the amount of value transferred, is reduced by 20% for each complete year survived (section 7(4)). Thus, if the donor died four-and-a-half years after the transfer, having made a PET of £50,000, the death rate of 40%, giving tax of £20,000, is reduced to 60% of that rate, ie 24% or £12,000. Naturally, if the donor's cumulative total does not pass the top of the nil rate bands these problems are of no practical importance. The tax due under this rule is due from the donee, and so there is no grossing up to be carried out (section 199(2)).

These rules apply also if A, the transferor, has made an immediately chargeable transfer of value, and dies within seven years (section (7(2)). Tax will have been paid at lifetime rates, but now must be paid at death rates as well, but with credit for tax already paid and with tapering relief. Where the rates of tax have changed between the date of the transfer and that of the death, the additional tax is calculated on the rates prevailing at the time of death but with full credit for the lifetime tax actually paid (Schedule 2, paragraph 2). When the death rate figure would be less than the lifetime rate tax already charged, the lifetime tax is left to stand—there is no repayment of the lifetime tax (section 7(5)). A may provide that the additional liability is to be met from A's estate, or B, the donee, may take out an insurance policy to cover the risk. Where the death was due to some tort, the additional tax may be recoverable by way of damages.[2]

Example

A, whose cumulative total stood at £325,000 in July 2013, then settled on discretionary trusts shares worth £80,000, A agreeing to pay the tax. This would require a gross up of 20% to make a gross chargeable transfer of £100,000 and tax of £20,000.

(a)   If A died one month later, the additional tax would be calculated using death rates on a transfer of £100,000, ie at 40%, giving tax of £40,000, making the additional tax payable £20,000 (ie after allowing for the £20,000 already payable).

(b)   If A died in May 2016, the additional tax would be calculated using the 2016–17 death rates, with credit for IHT already paid.

(c)   If A died in August 2016, ie more than 3 years after the transfer, the additional tax would be calculated using the 2016–17 death rates but also with a 20% reduction for the tax due on A's death; there is no reduction in the £20,000 credit for IHT already paid.

As tapering relief reduces the amount of tax payable on the death to 40% or even 20% of the tax otherwise due, and the lifetime rates, which will have been charged on the

---

[2] *Davies v Whiteways Cyder Co Ltd* [1975] QB 262.

chargeable transfer, are half the death rates, it may be wondered how the tax charged under such tapered rates can ever exceed the tax charged at the lifetime rate. One answer lies in the fact that the death tax may be charged on a different value.[3] This is most likely to occur where the property qualified for business or agricultural relief at the time of the lifetime transfer, but does not qualify at the time of the death transfer (see below at §§55.2 and 55.3). The situation may also arise if the donor made a PET before the chargeable transfer, and which was therefore ignored when that transfer was made.

46.1.3 Relief for Decline in Value Between Transfer and Death

46.1.3.1 General Rule

Where tax on PETs and additional tax on chargeable transfers become due because the transferor dies within seven years, that tax is generally calculated by reference to the value actually transferred, so that the extent of liability (potential or actual) crystallises at the date of the transfer and later changes in value are ignored. However, this will not necessarily be so if the property has:

(1) since the transfer been held continuously by the transferee or his spouse or civil partner; or
(2) been the subject of a qualifying sale.

In (1), if the market value at the time of death is less than the market value at the time of the transfer, the value transferred is reduced by the decline in value for the tax or additional tax.[4] For property attracting agricultural or business relief, the reduction is that remaining after applying these reliefs (section 131(2A)). There is no provision requiring a higher value to be taken when the asset has increased in value since the transfer. In (2), the same applies, save that the market value at the date of the qualifying sale is taken rather than that at the time of death.[5] For qualifying sale, see below at §55.2.2. This relief does not apply to tangible movable property, which is a wasting asset (section 132).

Example

If A's shares, originally worth £80,000 (see example above at §46.1.2), had declined in value to £60,000 when A died in May 2016, the *additional* tax is calculated as if the value transferred (£100,000) were reduced by £20,000 to £80,000. This would make the tax due only £32,000, so that additional tax would be £12,000.

It will be noted that there is no recalculation of the original value transferred by the lifetime transfer so as to gross-up from a figure of £60,000 rather than £80,000. This seems to follow from the form of the legislation.

[3] Another possibility is that the rates in force at the time of the death may be higher than those in force at the lifetime transfer.
[4] IHTA 1984, s 131. This does not affect the value for tax on the original transfer. Market value is defined by s 140(2).
[5] IHTA 1984, s 131(3); these restrictions are the same as s 176.

46.1.3.2 Qualifications—Changes in Property

Further rules are needed where the property changes between the transfer and the death or sale as the case may be (section 131):

(1) *Shares.* Capital payments to which B, the transferee, or B's spouse or civil partner becomes entitled in respect of the shares, for example bonus issues, have to be brought into account and are added to the market value at the date of the death or sale (section 133(1)). Conversely, a reduction is to be made if any calls have been made (section 134). Certain alterations, such as a reorganisation or amalgamation on takeover, are disregarded.[6]

Where there has been a transfer of value by a close company under section 94(1), or an alteration in the rights attached to any unquoted shares or unquoted debentures and so a deemed transfer by the company and a transfer of value by the participators under section 98(1), the market value at the relevant date is treated as increased;[7] the amount of the increase is the reduction in value attributable to the transfer under section 94(1) or section 98(1), assuming it had occurred before the transfer now subject to additional tax (section 136(2)). Thus, if A gave B shares and later value flows out of these shares to C, that decrease must be added back. This hypothetically timed increase is reduced by any increase in the value of the estate of the transferor or his spouse or civil partner (section 136(3)) and does not affect the value of the shares at the time of the chargeable transfer (section 136(4)).

(2) *Land.* If the interest in land is not, at both critical dates, the same in all respects and with the same incidents, and/or the land is not in the same state and with the same incidents, the market value is increased or reduced to take account of what its value would have been if it had remained unaltered (section 137). This is both to give relief and to prevent abuse of the relief. If the interest was worth £120,000, but then became subject to a restrictive covenant which reduced its value to £100,000, and at the relevant time the land freed from the covenant would have been worth £130,000 but £100,500 subject to it, the market value for this relief is £130,000; and since that exceeds the original market value of £120,000, the relief does not apply.

If compensation is received under some enactment for a reduction in the value of the interest, that sum is added to the market value at the relevant time, just as bonus issues are added in the case of shares (section 137(2)). Leases which, at the time of the chargeable transfer, had no more than 50 years to run are subject to a special rule to offset the inevitable reduction in value due to the passing of time. The market value is increased by the amount by which the value of the lease is treated as having wasted between the two dates, the percentage table from CGT being used.[8]

---

[6] IHTA 1984, s 135; see now TCGA 1992, s 127 and associated provisions (ch 41 above). Allowance is made where value is paid or received on the takeover.

[7] IHTA 1984, s 136; on meaning of quoted and unquoted, see s 272.

[8] IHTA 1984, s 138; TCGA 1992, Sch 8, para 1 (see above at §37.2).

(3) *Other property.* Where the property is not in all respects the same at the time of the chargeable transfer and the relevant date, the market value is ascertained as if the change had not occurred (section 139). Where benefits in money or money's worth have been derived from the property, and those benefits are in excess of a reasonable return on its value at the time of the chargeable transfer, the excess is added back and any effect of those benefits on the transferred property is ignored (section 139(4)).

46.2 Transfer of the Estate on Death

Under section 4, tax is charged on the death of any person (D)[9] as if, immediately before death, D had made a transfer of value and the value transferred by it had been equal to the value of D's estate[10] immediately before death; this will include any gifts with reservation when the reservation exists down to the donor's death.[11] The rates at which IHT is charged will be determined both by the value transferred and by D's cumulative total of chargeable transfers (including PETs which have become chargeable by reason of D's death within seven years) over the last seven years (section 7(1)). The value transferred is simply that of the estate; there is no need to gross up since there will be no estate left after distribution— the transfer on death is necessarily gross. The amount of tax, but not the chargeable value, may be reduced by the availability of quick succession relief (see below at §46.6). On liability to the Revenue for tax, see below at §56.1.2.

Where D anticipated leaving both a surviving spouse or civil partner and children, it was common to leave directly to the children such sums as will use up D's nil rate band, with the balance to the spouse or civil partner. However, such simple arrangements may not be appropriate where substantial amounts of property are involved.[12] A separate issue is whether property, such as the family home, should be owned as joint tenants or as tenants in common.[13] As the result of an overdue change enacted by FA 2008, these devices may no longer be necessary from an IHT view point, though they may seem desirable from the view point of the children. The FA 2008 rule, allowing a proportion of the nil rate band unused on the death of the first spouse or civil partner to be used on the death of the second, is considered below at §46.9.

46.2.1 Transfer Immediately Before Death

The rule that the transfer of value is treated as taking place immediately before the death gives rise to the problem that it is not clear to whom the transfer is then made, a matter of importance if the estate is left to a spouse or civil partner. In practice the Revenue treat the transfer on the death as if it were made immediately before the death, and so avoid the problem. The rule means that domicile may be ascertained immediately before the death,

---

[9] On events after 12 March 1975 but relating to estates of persons dying earlier, see IHTA 1984, Sch 6, para 1.
[10] On estate, see above at §44.7.1.
[11] FA 1986, s 102.
[12] Potter and Monroe, *Tax Planning* (Sweet & Maxwell, 1982), ch 11.
[13] *Ibid*, §12-02, preferring tenancy in common so that each can deal with the half share as each wishes.

thus avoiding the need to investigate problems of theology and uncertainty as to the degree of optimism to be applied. Despite this general rule, the valuation is usually made immediately after the death (see below at §46.4).

46.2.1.1 Posthumous Acquisition

The general rule in section 4 means that property accruing to the estate after the death will not be subject to tax. This is of importance where it cannot be known which of two or more deceased persons survived the other or others. For most succession purposes (though not for intestacy) they are presumed to have died in order of seniority.[14] For IHT purposes they are assumed to have died at the same instant (section 4(2)). For example, suppose A left his residuary estate to his daughter B and they are both killed outright in a road accident; tax will be chargeable on the transfers made on their deaths by A and B. Under Law of Property Act 1925, section 184, A's property passes to B, so the property will pass from A to B and then from B to whomever B has selected. However, for IHT purposes A and B are deemed to have died simultaneously, so the property passing from A to B will be taxed on A's death as property forming part of his estate immediately before his death, but not on B's since the property did not form part of her estate at that time but only later.

This well-meaning rule gives rise to a number of technical difficulties.[15] Thus, it is unclear whether there is an initial transfer of value from A to B, or whether there is simply a transfer from A direct to the eventual beneficiaries. This matters if B is A's spouse so that the A–B transfer is also exempt under section 18; the practical consequences turn on the ability or inability to use the nil rate band in A's estate in such a situation. Another problem is whether section 142 may be used to change the disposition, since a variation will simply cause the property to fall into A's residuary estate. Another technical issue concerns quick succession relief. This IHT rule applies only where it cannot be known which of A and B died first. Where the order of deaths is known, and B survives A, there will be a transfer by A to B and then one by B, although the latter may qualify for quick succession relief. Quick succession relief is, however, available only in so far as the first transfer was a chargeable transfer.

46.2.1.2 Exemption—Members of Armed Forces, Emergency Services Personnel etc

IHT is not chargeable on the death of a person (D) dying from a wound inflicted, an accident occurring or a disease contracted or aggravated while a member of the armed forces of the Crown, if D was on active service or on service of a war-like nature or involving the same risks (section 154(1)). Service in Northern Ireland is currently regarded as coming within this exemption,[16] as was active service in the Falkland Islands.[17] D dies 'from' a wound if death comes earlier than it otherwise would have done.[18] The exemption applies only on death, but covers all property transferred on death under section 4, such as settled property in which D had a life interest. Similar reliefs apply to emergency services personnel

---

[14] LPA 1925, s 184.
[15] See Harris [1995] BTR 390.
[16] See ex ESC F5, now obsolete due to IHTA 1984, s 154.
[17] [1982] *Simon's Tax Intelligence* 271.
[18] *Barty-King v Ministry of Defence* [1979] STC 218, [1979] 2 All ER 80 (died 23 years after being wounded).

who die from disease or injury sustained in responding to emergency circumstances,[19] and on the death of constables and service personnel targeted because of their status.[20]

46.3   Estate on Death: Exclusions

The general notion of an estate is modified on death in the following ways:

(1)   *Excluded property.* Excluded property does not form part of the estate immediately before the death.[21]

(2)   *Pension rights and annuities.* See below at §46.10.

(3)   *Cash options under approved annuity schemes.* The existence of the lump sum option is not enough to make it part of D's estate.[22] However, where the option is exercised and the sum is paid, it will form part of the estate. This exception is stated to apply only where the scheme is approved or is an approved personal pension plan;[23] where the scheme is not so approved, therefore, the sum of money will form part of the estate whether or not the option is exercised.

(4)   *Overseas pensions.* In valuing a person's estate there is to be left out of account any pensions payable under a fund falling within the Government of India Act 1935, section 273 or the Overseas Pensions Act 1973, section 2. Sums payable to a person's estate on his death are exempt from tax (section 153). Further, pensions payable under certain schemes, including sums payable on death and returned contributions, are to be treated as paid by the government of the country in which the colonial service was performed, even though the obligation to pay them has been assumed by a fund in the UK(section 153(2)). The effect is simply to alter the situs of the pensions and so, where the deceased was not domiciled in the UK, to bring them into the category of excluded property (section 6(1)).

(5)   *Conditional exemption.* Works of art, any other objects and land may enjoy conditional exemption on a transfer on death; if they qualify they are left out of account (see below at §54.4).

(6)   *Timber.* The value of timber may be left out of account until such time as the timber is sold; it is then restored to the estate unless there has been another transfer on death in the meantime (see below at §54.5).

(7)   *Settled property.* If A died entitled to an interest in possession in settled property, the settled property rules apply (see below at §49.4; for exclusions, see §49.6).

(8)   *Already earned surviving spouse relief.* Under estate duty law, if property was left by one spouse to the other and the other was not competent to dispose of the property,

---

[19] IHTA 1984, s 153A.

[20] IHTA 1984, s 155A.

[21] IHTA 1984, s 5(1); this is significant because the value of non-excluded property will not take account of the value of excluded property unless, presumably, the latter is related property. For an example, see *Melville v IRC* [2001] EWCA Civ 1247; [2001] STC 1271.

[22] IHTA 1984, s 152, as amended by F(No 2)A 1987, s 98(5); also amended as from 6 April 2006 by FA 2004, s 203.

[23] Approval was given under ex TA 1988, ss 619–621, or predecessors such as FA 1956, s 22. Personal pension plans were authorised by ex TA 1988, ss 630–655. As from 6 April 2006, approval is given under FA 2004, Pt 4.

as for example where she had only a life interest, the property is exempt from estate duty on the death of the surviving spouse. Where the first death occurred before 13 November 1974, the settled property is exempt from IHT on the death of the surviving spouse.[24]

(9)   *Exempt transfers.* Transfers to a surviving spouse or civil partner, certain heritage bodies, charities and political parties are exempt transfers on death (see chapter fifty-three below). Values which are the subject of exempt transfers do not form part of the estate on death. Other exempt transfers, most notably £3,000 of value transferred in one year, do not apply on death.

(10)   *Survivorship clauses.* Property left to B contingently upon surviving a period of time may be treated as not forming part of B's estate if B should fail to survive that period (see below at §49.6). This avoids the second charge that would arise on the death of the beneficiary, a form of complete quick succession relief built in by the testator.

46.4   Valuation of the Estate on Death

The rule that on death a person, D, is deemed to make a transfer of all the value of the estate immediately before the death[25] is substantially modified when it comes to valuation. Changes in the value of the estate which have occurred by reason of D's death are taken into account as if they had occurred before the death.[26] Such changes are (a) additions to the property comprised in the estate, such as lump sums payable to the estate under pension schemes, and (b) any increase or decrease of the value of the property in the estate. Thus, the death of a proprietor of or a partner in a business frequently causes loss of goodwill, and this factor is taken into account in valuing the business or partnership share. An example of an increase in value is life assurance; the proceeds of life assurance policies are higher than the surrender value immediately before the death. However, it is also provided that 'the termination on the death of any interest or the passing of any interest by survivorship' does not fall within this special valuation rule. On the death of D, a joint tenant, his interest passes to the surviving joint tenants; in valuing D's right, the fact of his death is to be ignored since otherwise the value would be nil.[27] This provision may also be meant to ensure that life interests in settled property are valued in full.

Although property is valued at the date of death, relief is available where the property is realised for a lower value within a certain period after the death, the lower value being substituted. This relief applies only to certain securities—one year (see below at §55.4.1); and interests in land—four years (see below at §55.4.2). Relief is also available where property is valued by reference to related property and is later sold; here the related property valuation may be undone if the sale is within three years (see below at §55.2).

---

[24] IHTA 1984, Sch 6, para 2. See ESC F13 when the first death was before 12 March 1952 and the estate was exempt as the property of a common seaman, marine or soldier who died in the service of the Crown.

[25] IHTA 1984, s 4. For the general valuation rules, see ch 55 below.

[26] IHTA 1984, s 171. Despite this it is still not absolutely clear whether the estate should be valued on the basis that D's death was imminent: see McCutcheon [1988] BTR 431.

[27] Problems arise if an option expires on the death of an option holder.

46.5   Events after Death

46.5.1 *Disclaimers and Rearrangements*[28]

Where, within two years of a death, the disposition on death is varied or a benefit is disclaimed, neither the variation nor the disclaimer is a transfer of value. A disclaimer may be made by instrument or by conduct.[29] The variation is treated as if made by the deceased, the disclaimer as though the benefit had never been conferred.[30] In *Russell v IRC*,[31] it was held that a further deed varying a prior deed was not entitled to this treatment even though expressed to be supplemental to the prior deed and fulfilling the other requirements of the section. Thus, a variation of a variation is not entitled to the protection of this rule. Knox J stressed that the second deed substantially altered the beneficiaries' rights under the first and did not merely increase them. The result would have been different if the *first* deed could have been construed in the way the parties hoped[32] or had contained an error which could be the subject of a claim for rectification, in which case there would have been no second deed.[33]

In *Soutter's Executry v IRC*,[34] a Special Commissioner held that since the section applies to vary a disposition, it can apply only where the person making the variation or disclaimer has the right which is alleged to be assigned or disclaimed and has it at the time of the assignment or disclaimer. He cited approvingly the words of Knox J in *Russell v IRC*, that one could not use the deeming words of section 142 to create a right. The case involved a life rent under Scots law; the decision was that the executors of the liferentrix had nothing to vary as that had not passed to them. In upholding the Revenue's position, he referred to articles which had appeared in professional journals as 'fundamentally flawed', no doubt due to the diversion of thought brought about by the use of such terms as 'in the real world'.

The formalities for making the instrument of variation have been relaxed. At one time there was a duty to notify the Revenue within six months of the election, but this was removed in 2002. The variation must be carried out by an instrument in writing made by the relevant persons, ie the persons making the instrument.[35] Personal representatives are relevant persons if the variation results in an obligation to pay more tax; they may refuse to sign only if there are insufficient assets to pay the extra tax. The Revenue now accept that the document does not have to be expressed to be by way of variation of the will, provided it identifies the disposition to be varied and varies it. There is an obligation to inform the

---

[28] See Owen [1999] *Private Client Business* 237; see also McCutcheon [1998] *Private Client Business* 45; and McCutcheon [1995] *Private Client Business* 48, discussing *Re Sinclair* [1985] 1 All ER 1066 on succession law effect of disclaimer on intestacy.

[29] *Cook v IRC* [2002] STC (SCD) 317.

[30] IHTA 1984, ss 17, 142. These deeming provisions are not affected by *Marshall v Kerr* [1994] STC 638, HL; see Revenue Interpretation RI 101.

[31] [1988] STC 195, [1988] 2 All ER 405.

[32] As in *Schnieder v Mills* [1993] STC 430.

[33] On rectification, see *Lake v Lake* [1989] STC 565; *Matthews v Martin* [1991] STC 418; and *Racal Group Services Ltd v Ashmore* [1994] STC 416.

[34] [2002] STC (SCD) 385.

[35] IHTA 1984, s 142 (2) and (2A); see Chamberlain [2002] BTR 275.

Revenue within six months if the variation results in extra tax.[36] Where a beneficiary dies, the Revenue view is that the legal PRs of that beneficiary may enter into a variation and sign the form. If the variation reduces the rights of any beneficiary of the second deceased, the Revenue will require written evidence of that beneficiary's consent.[37]

In *Bhatt v Bhatt*,[38] Martin Mann QC held that he could set aside documents executed by the taxpayer on a mistaken basis in a misguided attempt to mitigate the effect of inheritance tax which the taxpayer believed arose on her late husband's death and which could arise on her own death if she did not execute the documents. In fact, no IHT was due on the death of her husband, because the surviving spouse exemption applied. Moreover, the transactions she mistakenly entered into had no IHT advantages but would have divested her of control of her property and possibly conferred interests in possession on certain of her children that she did not desire to create and which had the potential to trigger an IHT charge. Mann QC held the mistake was sufficiently serious to be set aside, subject to HMRC having the right to contest. In Budget 2015 the Government announced it was reviewing the use of deeds of variation for tax purposes.

46.5.1.1 Property

The rule applies to all property in the deceased's estate immediately before the death, eg property in which the deceased had a joint interest, save that excluded property is included. However, settled property in which the deceased had an interest in possession and gifts subject to a reservation where the reservation still exists at the death are not included.[39]

46.5.1.2 Beneficiary's Consideration

A beneficiary may not claim the protection of this rule if consideration other than another right in the succession is provided.[40] Thus, a variation in return for £15,000 would not be within these rules, whereas a variation in return for an interest under the will worth £15,000 would be. A transfer to the deceased's widow in return for property already owned by her would not be within these rules, and it is at such an arrangement that this requirement is aimed. Where a variation results in property being held in trust for a person for a period ending within two years of the death, that person's interest is disregarded (section 142(4)). If property is held under the variation of D's will for A for life with remainder to B, and A dies or releases his interest within two years of D's death, the property is treated as if it had passed direct from D to B. This result applies only where the parties have elected to treat the variation as made by D.

46.5.1.3 Two-Year Trusts

A more important rule is contained in section 144, which applies where D has created a discretionary trust by will; any distribution made within two years of D's death is treated as made by D. This is useful if the beneficiaries are unlikely to agree, or where one or more are

---

[36] IHTA 1984, s 218A, added by FA 2002; on penalties see s 245A(1A).
[37] Revenue Interpretation RI 101.
[38] [2009] STC 1540, [2009] EWHC 734 (Ch), applying *Re Griffiths* [2008] STC 776.
[39] IHTA 1984, s 142(5); FA 1986, Sch 19, para 24.
[40] IHTA 1984, s 142(3). On dangers of this trap where a testamentary gift to children is routed back through a surviving spouse, see (1991) *Capital Taxes and Estate Planning Quarterly* 1.

under-age.[41] This treatment does not apply to a distribution within the first three months after the death.[42] A nice question arises if D creates the discretionary trust by will, property is appointed to A and B under section 144, and A and B then want to make a variation under section 142. The better view is that A and B are not prevented from making such a variation by the decision in *Russell v IRC*, since that only prevents two variations under section 142 and not one under section 144 and one under section 142 (see above §46.5.1).[43]

46.5.1.4 Other Provisions

A similar rule applies to CGT (see above at §39.4) but, curiously, there is no provision in relation to ITTOIA 2005, section 619 (chapter thirty-one above). Thus, if a parent varies the grandparent's will in favour of the parent's infant children, the variation will be effective for IHT and CGT but may not be for income tax. The effects of the CGT provisions were limited by the decision of the House of Lords in *Marshall v Kerr*;[44] however, the Capital Taxes Office does not regard its IHT practice as affected by that decision.[45] A late set of government amendments ensured that the relief under section 144 applies to distributions made within two years of death from discretionary will trusts where used to create one of the new types of trusts provided for in FA 2006.[46] The 1989 Finance Bill contained proposals to alter this relief drastically, but the proposals were dropped.

46.5.2 Election by Surviving Spouse or Civil Partner to Redeem Life Interest on Intestacy

Where a surviving spouse or civil partner elects to redeem the life interest given under the intestacy legislation and the election is under those rules, the consequent ending of that life interest is not treated as a transfer of value (sections 17, 145). The normal effect of the termination of the interest is that there would be a transfer of value equal to the value of the settled property (save and to the extent that the person entitled to the interest in possession now becomes entitled to the capital).[47] This exception ensures that there is no transfer of value even though the survivor does not become entitled to the whole of the settled property.

46.5.3 Carrying out Testator's Wishes

A testator may express a wish that the legatee should transfer the property to someone else. If that wish is legally binding, the transfer to that other is a transfer by the testator; if, however, it is not legally binding, there would be a transfer by the testator followed by a transfer by the legatee. To avoid a double charge to tax, the transfer is treated as made by the testator provided the transfer by the legatee is made within two years of the death (sections 17, 143).

---

[41] Potter and Monroe, *op cit*, §10-07.
[42] *Frankland v IRC* [1997] STC 1450, CA; this disappointing result is defended by Lee [1998] BTR 262.
[43] Potter and Monroe, *op cit*, §10-08.
[44] [1995] 1 AC 148, [1994] STC 638, (1994) 67 TC 56.
[45] Revenue Interpretation RI 101.
[46] IHTA 1984, s 144(3) and (4), added by FA 2006.
[47] IHTA 1984, s 53(2) (see below at §§49.5, 49.6).

46.5.4 Inheritance (Provision for Family and Dependants) Act 1975

Where an order is made by a court under this Act, IHT is charged as if the property had devolved on the death in accordance with the order.[48]

46.5.5 Legitim

Under Scots law, a child is entitled to certain fixed rights in his parent's estate even against the surviving spouse or civil partner, but cannot renounce those rights while still a minor. When the bequest to the surviving spouse or civil partner reduces the child's rights, the executors may assume either that full rights of legitim will be claimed, thus reducing the spouse's or civil partner's share (and increasing the IHT), or that the will be allowed to stand. Any adjustments due when the child reaches 18 must be made (section 147). If the person renounces his claim to legitim, tax is repaid to the estate with (non-taxable) interest (section 236(4)).

46.6   Quick Succession Relief

Where B's estate is increased by a chargeable transfer—the first transfer—and B then dies within five years, the tax chargeable on B's death—the second transfer—is reduced by a percentage of the tax paid in respect of the first (section 141). The percentage is 100% for death within the first year and then drops by 20% a year. The tax paid on the first transfer qualifies for use later only if, and to the extent that, it relates to the amount of increase in the estate. For example, suppose in year 1, A makes a chargeable transfer to B of an asset worth £24,000; suppose tax is payable by A at a rate of 20%, making a gross transfer of £30,000 including tax of £6,000. If B then dies two-and-a-half years later, the amount available by way of credit on B's death will be 60% of tax at 20% on £24,000 (the increase in B's estate), ie £2,880.[49]

This credit is available regardless of any change in the value of the asset given. It applies whenever there is an increase in B's estate, and so whether what is given is an identifiable asset or cash. In determining whether a person's estate has been increased, excluded property is to be left out of account. Thus, if D died, leaving property to A for life with remainder to B and then B predeceased A, no quick succession relief would be available on B's death for any IHT paid on D's death since B's reversion is excluded property.

46.7   Reliefs for Earlier Transfers of the Same Property by the Same Transferor

With IHT reaching back to catch events that happened before death, there was the risk of a dual charge to tax in certain circumstances. Revenue regulations cover three defined sit-

---

[48] IHTA 1984, s 146; see also s 236(2), (3).
[49] There is no case for relief on the tax on the grossed-up value of £30,000 since B's estate was only increased by £24,000 and that is what B is now paying tax on.

uations—and any similar ones.[50] The regulations differ from the old CTT rules for mutual transfers which had been part of that tax code from its early days.[51] These are still live issues; 2005 saw an order giving relief where an arrangement concerning the pre-owned assets charge is undone.[52] Where A made a gift of property to B and one month later B transferred the property back to A, under CTT there should have been a charge on the gift by A to B and another when B made the gift to A. It was provided, however, that assuming no change in the value of the property, B's transfer to A should be exempt, and that A should be allowed to undo the transfer to B and recover any tax paid.[53] The old CTT rules for mutual transfers were repealed for deaths and other transfers after 17 March 1986.[54] The current IHT rules apply only where the second of the two transfers comes about on the death of the transferor (A). The rules require two sets of calculations and a comparison of the outcome. One set disregards the lifetime transfer; the other disregards the death transfer. The calculation giving the higher overall liability is preferred. When the two calculations give the same figure, the first calculation is preferred.[55]

46.7.1 First Transfer a PET Followed by Death Transfer of Same Property: Reg 4 Mutual Gifts

46.7.1.1 The Transfers

A makes a PET to B[56] which proves to be a chargeable transfer by reason of A's death within seven years, and immediately before A's death, A's estate includes property acquired by A from B after the A–B transfer and otherwise than for full consideration in money or money's worth.[57] A's death within seven years makes the A–B transfer chargeable instead of potentially exempt, while the property returned forms part of A's estate and so is chargeable on A's death.

46.7.1.2 The Property

The property transferred by B may be the original property given, or property which directly or indirectly represents that property.[58] It is hard to know whether to insist on giving these words meaning;[59] if A gives B a painting, must B give the identical one back? If A gives B money, must B give A money or will any property do—and must B be able to show that the money could in some way have been channelled into the property given to A? What

---

[50] Inheritance Tax (Double Charges Relief) Regulations 1987 (SI 1987/1130), [1987] *Simon's Tax Intelligence* 506, 602. The Regulations will hereafter be referred to by their SI number only.

[51] FA 1976, ss 87, 88.

[52] Inheritance Tax (Double Charges Relief) Regulations 2005 (SI 2005/3441), [2006] *Simons Tax Intelligence* 100.

[53] The rules were complex—see *Butterworths UK Tax Guide 1985–1986*, §§38:11–38:15.

[54] The old rules were Capital Transfer Tax Act 1984, ss 148, 149; repeal was effected by FA 1986, Sch 23, Pt X; and the preservation of the old rules where the donee's transfer was before 18 March 1986 was effected by FA 1986, Sch 19, para 40.

[55] SI 1987/1130, reg 8.

[56] By definition, therefore, but also expressly, the transfer must be on or after 18 March 1986.

[57] FA 1986, s 104(1)(a); SI 1987/1130, reg 4.

[58] The term 'property' is defined as including part of any property (SI 1987/1130, reg 4).

[59] Contrast the care lying behind the formulation in FA 1986, s 103.

is clear is that once the relevant property restored to A has been identified, regulation 4 requires that very property to be in A's estate on A's death and that it should be chargeable property on that death (and so not, for example, excluded property).

46.7.1.3 The Calculations

The rules then demand that two calculations should be made of the total tax chargeable as a consequence of the death of A. The first requires that in calculating the tax on the PET, the value of the property given by A to B, and then restored, should be disregarded, so leaving it to be part of the death transfer. The second calculation requires that one should disregard the same value in calculating the tax on the transfer on death, so leaving it to be taxed as an originally potentially exempt but now chargeable transfer.[60] Put more simply, one calculates the tax assuming that the value restored forms part of one transfer only. Where this results in two different figures, the lower one is reduced to nil and the higher is taken; if the two figures are the same, the transfer is treated as being part of the death transfer and not a PET.[61]

Example

This example is based on that issued by the Revenue as part of the Regulations but the material is rearranged.

The facts:

July 1987   A makes a PET of £100,000 to B.

January 1988   A makes a chargeable transfer of £95,000 and pays IHT of £750.

February 1988   A makes a further chargeable transfer of £45,000 and pays tax of £6,750.

January 1990   B dies and the property transferred by the 1987 PET returns to A.

December 1992 A dies. His estate (value £300,000) includes the property restored to him in 1990 (still worth £100,000).

The first calculation assumes that the £100,000 forms part of A's death estate and is not chargeable as a PET. A therefore has an estate on death of £300,000, but a lifetime cumulative total of £140,000. Tax on the death estate (ignoring quick succession relief under section 141) will be £116,000 which, when added to the additional tax due on the two chargeable transfers (because A dies within seven years), becomes liable to tax at death rates for 1992–93 (nil and nil), making a total of £116,000.

The second calculation charges the £100,000 as a PET (but with taper relief)[62] and reduces the estate on death to £200,000. Tax on the PET will be nil. Tax at 1992–93 death rates on an estate of £200,000 with a lifetime cumulative total of £240,000 will give tax on the death of £80,000; but when the additional tax on the chargeable transfers is included, £10,050 and £4,050 (after taking account of the reduction in tax by reason of the number

---

[60] SI 1987/1130, reg 4(4).
[61] SI 1987/1130, reg 8.
[62] Although the PET qualifies for taper relief of 60%, this does not affect the calculation since (a) the tax is nil anyway and (b) the reduction would be a reduction in tax and not in value transferred.

of years since the transfers and the higher cumulative total to take account of the £100,000 potentially exempt but actually chargeable transfer) gives a total for tax on death of £94,100.

As the first calculation gives the greater amount of tax, it is preferred, and tax is calculated for all purposes as if the PET were reduced to nil. This has the curious consequence that no additional tax is due on the two chargeable lifetime transfers.

46.7.2 First Transfer Immediately Chargeable Followed by Death Transfer of Same Property: Reg 7

46.7.2.1 The Transfers

A makes a chargeable transfer to B but dies within seven years and the property forms part of A's estate on his death, having been returned by B.[63] The difference from the situation in §46.7.1 is that the A–B transfer is a chargeable transfer, not a PET. As the A–B transfer must be made after 17 March 1986,[64] the scope of this rule is not great. Today, its principal application will be where A sets up a discretionary trust, of which A is an object to whom the trustees later advance property; however, this situation also falls within the gift with reservation rules dealt with in regulation 5 (see §46.7.3 below), and one might conclude that regulation 5 would apply in priority. The principles are the same as outlined above at §46.7.1, with credit being given for the tax already paid in respect of the chargeable A–B transfer.

46.7.2.2 The Calculations

Here, the same principles are applied as above, with credit being given for the tax already paid in respect of the A–B transfer. First, the lifetime transfer is disregarded. The death transfer is then also disregarded and the results are compared. If the second calculation gives the higher figure, that is that. If the first calculation gives the higher figure, it is taken. If this leads to a reduction in the value transferred by the A–B chargeable transfer, there is nonetheless no change to A's cumulative total for the purpose of any discretionary trust charges under the rules outlined in chapter fifty below. In making these calculations credit is given for tax paid before the death.[65]

Example

Again, this uses the Revenue example which forms part of the Regulations, but sets the material out differently and follows, rather than reproduces, that example. The example assumes that the 1987–88 rates apply rather than any later actual ones, in order to facilitate checking against the Revenue text, which is not easy to understand.

---

[63] This is treated in the Regulations as the fourth situation, as it is not expressly listed in FA 1986, s 104 but relies on the similar situations power in s 104(1)(d).

[64] The position of A–B transfers made before 18 March 1986 is obscure. They are, by definition, chargeable rather than PETs. They are unable to use IHTA 1984, ss 147, 148 if the B–A transfer is on or after that date, and yet are not covered by the Regulations.

[65] The credit is authorised by SI 1987/1130, reg 7(5)(b); the example which follows assumes that the credit rules are relevant in determining the amounts under reg 7(4) since this is what the Revenue example also assumes. However, a case may be made for saying that the credit is not relevant to the calculations under reg 7(4) and comes into play only when applying reg 7(5).

The facts:

May 1986	S makes a gross transfer of £150,000 on discretionary trusts and pays tax at 1986–87 rates of £13,750.
October 1986	S settles shares worth £85,000 on T for life; under the rules then in force this is a chargeable transfer (it would have been a PET if made a year later); tax is payable under 1986–87 rates of £19,500.
January 1991	S makes a PET to R of £20,000.
December 1992	T dies; shares revert to S. There is no charge to tax (see below at §49.6).
August 1993	S dies. His estate includes the shares (now worth £75,000); his other property is worth £144,000.

The first calculation treats the shares as part of the death estate. The May 1986 transfer occurs after more than seven years have passed and so there is no additional tax. The October 1986 gift is ignored;[66] there is no adjustment to tax already paid. The January 1991 PET attracts tax of £8,000.[67] The death estate is worth £219,000.[68] The cumulative total of chargeable transfers in the last seven years is £20,000, so tax would be £56,500, but this is reduced for the purpose of this calculation by £19,350 to £37,150 to take account of the lifetime tax already paid in respect of the shares.[69] This makes the total tax on death £45,150.

The second calculation treats the shares as settled on T in October 1986 and not part of the estate on death. The May 1986 transfer is treated as in the first calculation. The October 1986 chargeable transfer is followed by death within seven years but there is no additional tax.[70] The January 1991 PET attracts tax of £10,000 (PET of £20,000 by person with pre-potentially exempt cumulative total of £235,000). The death estate is now worth £144,000 and the transfer is made by the person with the cumulative lifetime total over last seven years of £105,000 (£85,000 and £20,000); this makes tax payable of £57,000, and so total tax of £65,000 is due on death. In this instance no credit can be given for the inter vivos tax since it is restricted to the amount of tax paid on the death, and as that amount is nil, there is no credit.

The second calculation gives the higher figure and so is taken.

46.7.3 *Transfer and Gift with Reservation of Same Property: Reg 5*

The third situation covered by the Regulations[71] is where there is a transfer of value which is also a gift with reservation under FA 1986, section 102 (see below at §47.1), but the

---

[66] It will be noted that although A gave B shares worth £85,000 and the value of the property on return is only £75,000, the whole of the A–B transfer is ignored and £10,000 of it is not chargeable. Presumably this is because what was restored by B was the entire holding.

[67] Tax at 1987–88 rates on transfer of £20,000 by person with cumulative total of £150,000.

[68] That is, (£144,000 + £75,000).

[69] The figure of £19,350 is the amount of the death tax which is attributable to the shares, ie £75,000/£219,000 × £56,500. The amount of lifetime tax was £19,500, but as the proportion of death tax attributable to the shares is less, that lesser figure is taken by way of credit.

[70] Tax, after taper relief, would be £7,100, but as this is less than the tax already paid (£19,500), no additional tax is due.

[71] SI 1987/1130, reg 5, stemming from FA 1986, s 104(1)(b).

property also forms part of the estate of the donor on death; an example is where A makes a gift to a discretionary trust of which A is a potential beneficiary and dies within seven years.[72] Section 102 will apply because of A's rights (or hopes) under the trust and the property does not otherwise form part of A's estate immediately before death. The property was also the subject of a (chargeable) transfer when it was settled; the risk of a dual charge is therefore present. This situation is illustrated by the example in the Regulations. The Regulations also embrace the situation in which the gift with reservation ceases to be subject to a reservation in circumstances amounting to a PET but the donor dies within seven years.[73]

As in the two previous examples, calculations are made on the alternative assumptions that the section 102 charge applies or the charge on the original property applies, and whichever assumption gives the higher tax is taken as the basis of liability. Where this leads to a reduction of the original inter vivos transfer, the reduction does not affect any discretionary trust charges arising before A's death if the transfer was chargeable when made.[74] Provision is also made for credit to be given for tax already paid on the original transfer to be set against the tax now charged on the assumption that the earlier transfer is to be ignored (or reduced).[75]

46.7.4 *Transfer and Non-Deductible Debts (Loan Backs): Reg 6*

Lastly, the Regulations provide for the situation in which A's estate is subject to a liability in favour of B, but A's estate is unable to deduct that liability because of FA 1986, section 103 (see below at §55.5.2). Broadly, this rule applies where A makes a gift to B but B later lends the property (or equivalent wealth) back to A; the liability to repay is clearly for money's worth but section 102 bars the deduction.[76] This could lead to a double charge if the original gift is also chargeable, whether because it was a chargeable transfer all along or has become one because A has died within seven years. The usual alternative calculations are made—one on the basis of disallowing the debt and ignoring the transfer, and the other on the basis of charging the transfer but allowing the debt. Section 102 applies only where the loan is made after 17 March 1986;[77] the Regulations apply only where the original transfer occurs after the same date.[78]

---

[72] Eg, A gives a house to B but takes a life interest in it in circumstances which do not permit A to argue that A gave B only the reversion. This is not a situation in which a double charge can arise, since FA 1986, s 102 applies only if the property which is the subject of the gift with reservation would not otherwise be chargeable on death.
[73] Thus, a charge arises under FA 1986, s 102(4).
[74] SI 1987/1130, reg 5(4)(b).
[75] *Ibid*, reg 5(4)(a).
[76] *Ibid*, reg 6.
[77] FA 1986, s 103(6).
[78] SI 1987/1130, reg 6(2); this therefore leaves without any relief against dual charges any case where the loan is made after 17 March 1986 but the gift was a chargeable transfer made before 18 March 1986. There is also no relief in any case where the loan is repaid within seven years of death and there is a charge under FA 1986, s 103(5).

46.7.5 *Situations not Covered*

Situations not covered by the Regulations include the following:[79]

(1)   A gives property to B; B gives it back to A; A gives it back to B again; A dies within seven years of his original gift to B, so that both his gifts to B become chargeable transfers.

(2)   A makes a gift with reservation. The benefit reserved has a significant value, and he makes a disposition of this benefit within seven years before his death so as to cause the reservation to cease. This is both a chargeable transfer under the ordinary rules, and a deemed chargeable transfer under the gift with reservation rules.

(3)   A gives property to B. A then borrows money from B. A then repays the debt and dies within seven years of both the gift to B and the repayment of the debt. The original gift to B is a chargeable transfer, and the repayment of the debt is treated as a PET, which has become chargeable by virtue of FA 1986, section 103(5).

46.8   Abatement of Exemptions on Death

Abatement applies to the exemptions in sections 18 and 23–28, ie transfer to a spouse or civil partner, charity, political party or housing association, or a gift made for national purposes, or to a trust for a maintenance fund for an historic building or an employee trust. Where the exemption extends up to a certain figure, these rules apply only to the extent that the transfer is exempt (section 29A(6)). The abatement applies where a transfer of value would be exempt but the beneficiary under the exempt transfer, known as the exempt beneficiary, disposes of property not derived from the exempt transfer of value to settle the whole or part of a 'claim' against the estate (section 29A(1)). The reduction in the value of the exempt beneficiary's estate by the payment or, if less, the legacy to that beneficiary is treated as a chargeable specific gift (section 29A(2), (3)). The exemption is abated to this extent. Moreover, since it is treated as a specific gift, it may give rise to grossing up (see below at §53.3.1.2). The term 'claim' is not defined. The abatement does not apply if the claim being settled is a liability which would be deductible in computing the value of the estate (section 168(5)).

Example

D leaves an estate worth £2,000,000 to his widow and has made chargeable lifetime transfers equal to the nil rate bands. His son makes a claim under the Inheritance (Provision for

---

[79] Selected from *Simon's Direct Tax Service*, Pt I.3.502. *Simon's* adds that in the case of mutual transfers, no relief is given for IHT charges that may be incurred by the donee or transferee by returning the property to the transferor. Similarly, there is no relief under these provisions where the donee of a gift with reservation incurs an IHT charge on the property subject to a reservation, as well as the donor doing so, or a person who has received property from another incurs an IHT charge on that property, but by virtue of his receipt of that property a loan made by him to the donor is not deductible from the donor's death estate or is subject to an IHT charge on the donor on his repaying it.

Family and Dependants) Act 1975 which is settled at £250,000. Under the normal rules of administration of estates, a payment would be made out of the estate to the son in satisfaction of his claim; this sum would not be deductible in computing the value of D's estate for IHT. The property remaining in the estate after satisfying the son's claim and the tax in respect of it would pass to the widow and be exempt, but, as just seen, IHT would have been paid on the value needed to finance the payment to the son. The calculation is as follows:

Gross	IHT	Net
£283,333	£33,333	£250,000

The chargeable estate is thus £283,333 and the IHT £33,333, an effective rate of 11.76%. This result would, but for the abatement rule, be avoided if the widow were to pay the £250,000 out of her own money. Now the whole £2,000,000 would pass to her free of tax and her payment of £250,000 would be a PET. To counter this freedom to opt out of IHT, section 29A provides that the reduction in the value of the exempt beneficiary's estate by the payment or, if less, the legacy to her, is to be treated as a chargeable specific gift by D. The exemption is thus abated. It will be noticed that this provision does not apply when the widow pays the son out of property derived from D's estate, but the payment falls outside section 146. The rationale for this is obscure.

Valuation. In determining the value of the exempt beneficiary's estate for this purpose, no deduction is to be made for the claim (section 29A(4)(i)). Neither agricultural nor business reliefs are available for the property which the exempt transferee transfers. No deduction is made for any tax borne by the exempt transferee (section 29A(4)(ii).

46.9 Spouses and Civil Partners: Transfer of Proportion of Unused Nil Rate Band

Section 8A, added by FA 2008, section 10 and Schedule 4, allows the transfer by one spouse or civil partner to the other of a proportion of the nil rate band remaining on the death of the first to die. It applies where the second death occurs on or after 9 October 2007. So if S1 died in July 2006, when the nil rate band was £285,000, and made no use of the nil rate band at all, the proportion is 100%. If S2 dies in July 2009 when the nil rate band was £325,000, S2 will be entitled not only to the S2's own nil rate of £325,000 band but also to the unused proportion from S1's death—ie a further £325,000. It must be stressed that the answer is £325,000, not £285,000. Similarly, if one half of the nil rate band had been used on S1's death—£142,500—then the half available on S2's death is £162,500. This allows the rules to operate sensibly even though the nil rate band rises—or falls.

The purpose of this provision is to help a family, faced with a potential IHT liability, to avoid wasting the nil rate band and to avoid unnecessary legal expenses. If the estate was worth £1m, and H died leaving all the property to W, the transfer would be exempt and no IHT would have been paid. If W then died, leaving the estate to the children, tax would be due at 40% on the value of the estate (£1m) reduced by W's nil rate band (£325,000), making a taxable estate of £675,000 and IHT of £270,000. If H had left £325,000 of his estate to the children direct, leaving only £675,000 to W, the value of the estate passing on W's death would have been £675,000. This, when reduced by her nil rate band of £325,000, would make a taxable estate of £350,000 and so IHT of £140,000, a simple saving of £130,000 because the family had made use of the nil rate bands of both H and W. Such an obvious advantage might not be easy to use if the estate could not readily find £325,000 to give the children on H's death, eg because the estate consisted principally of the home. Prior to the introduction of section 8A, many planning devices were used to prevent unnecessary loss. These often involved the use of trusts and thus involved costly fees.[80]

In addition, under section 8A, the band that may be used by any one surviving spouse or civil partner is limited to the value of the nil rate band in force at the time of their death. This may be relevant where a person dies having survived more than one spouse or civil partner. This may also be relevant where a person dies having been married to, or the registered civil partner of, someone who had themselves survived one or more spouses or civil partners. The relief must be claimed, but this is done by the PR of the estate of the second spouse or civil partner to die when they make an IHT return.

Alternatively secured pensions (ASPs) attract a similar relief. When 'relevant dependant's pension benefits' cease, a charge arises on left-over ASP funds. The rates of tax are those applying at the date of that event rather than as at the date of death of the scheme member. The changes made in 2008 mean that if the nil rate band was not used in full when the original 'owner' of the ASP died, the same proportion that was unused will be applied to the amount of the nil rate band in force at the date of the later event and will be available against the ASP.

Finally, the additional residence nil rate band (see above §44.4.1) operates in a similar way. It is transferable where the second spouse or civil partner of a couple dies on or after 6 April 2017 irrespective of when the first of the couple died.

46.10   Inheritance and Pension Savings

The FA 2004 revolutionary shake up of pensions created a need for new IHT rules. In the pre-2004 days the pension would be taken in the form of an annuity. It was in the nature of an annuity that it would end on the death of the annuitant. While this might cause a charge under the settled property rules for the ending of an interest in possession or under the discretionary trust rules, such a charge was usually excluded. Thus it was left out of account—provided it did not result from the application of any benefit provided otherwise than by way of a pension or an annuity (eg a lump sum).[81] Another situation where an IHT charge might arise was where property accrued through rights such as one to repayment of contributions on death before retirement; since the purpose of the exemption from charge was to allow a person to enjoy retirement, this was sensible. FA 2004, section 203 simply ensured that these arrangements continued. On the death of a member (D), a pension may become payable to D's surviving spouse, civil partner or dependant. If the sum might,

---

[80] See Tiley, *Parson's Lecture 2007*, available on the University of Sydney website at https://www.law.usyd.edu.au/parsons/pdfs/johntileylecture_290307.pdf.
[81] Ex IHTA 1984, s 151(2), repealed by FA 2011, s 65 for deaths occurring on or after 6 April 2011.

at D's option, have been paid to D's PRs instead, a rule provides that this does not to cause D to be treated as having a power over the property such as to bring it within D's estate.[82]

From 2004, people no longer had to commute their pension fund into an annuity until they reached age 75. So, where a scheme member died aged under 75 without having exercised any of the rights under the scheme, legislation provided that no charge to IHT arose by reason of that omission; this was previously a concession.[83] This left the ASP, which is a separate fund meeting the conditions laid down in FA 2004, Schedule 28, paragraph 11. An ASP is exclusive to the particular person, so there is no sharing of risk with others. The challenge for the legislature was to devise rules which respected the wish not to share risk without giving the funds, which had already enjoyed great protection from income tax, etc, further unjustified protection from IHT. The balancing act was drawn in sections 151A–151E. The replacement of unsecured pension and ASP provision with a single drawdown provision in the pension reforms of 2011, however, meant that a number of rules imposing an IHT charge were no longer relevant. FA 2011 repealed sections 151A–151E, as well as the rules in sections 12(2A)–(2E), which levied an IHT charge where a scheme member omitted to take their entitlements. In addition, section 12(2ZA) was introduced to specifically disapply section 3(3) where a scheme member omits to exercise pension rights. These changes took effect for deaths and omissions occurring on or after 6 April 2011.

---

[82] IHTA 1984, s 152, stating that it is not a power with s 5(2).
[83] IHTA 1984, s 12(2A)–(2G), added FA 2006, s 160 and Sch 22. Sections 12(2A)–(2E) subsequently repealed by FA 2011, s 65.

47

Gifts with Reservation

47.1   Introduction

FA 1986, section 102 directs[1] that property which A, the transferor, gave away while alive is treated as forming part of A's estate immediately before death if A reserved a benefit out of the property given. This applies no matter how long ago the gift was made (subject to the proviso that the rule applies only to gifts on or after 18 March 1986). Presumably the term 'gift' includes a sale at an undervalue.[2] One effect of the rule is to make the gift chargeable when it might otherwise have escaped tax as a potentially exempt transfer (PET) which the donor survived by seven years. The rule also makes it chargeable by reference to its value at death and not at the time of the gift. Where the gift is subject to a reservation, but that reservation is removed before the death, the gift is treated as a PET as from the date the reservation is removed.[3]

The object of the provision is to counter avoidance devices that might otherwise escape the PET rules and, in particular, to charge inheritance trusts and similar devices which

---

[1] On Revenue practice under s 102, note material reproduced in Foster, *Inheritance Tax*, (Butterworths, 1991) X6.36, 6.37 and 6.40.

[2] The Revenue so views it; see discussion of 'gift' in Potter and Monroe, *Tax Planning* (Sweet & Maxwell, 1982), §3-30; and, on whether an interest-free loan repayable on demand is a gift, see *ibid*, §5-20.

[3] FA 1986, s 102(4).

had proliferated following the advent of CTT and which enabled a person to give property away while deriving benefit from it for the remainder of his lifetime.[4] However, according to Lord Hoffmann, the policy of section 102 requires something more. That something was the precise definition of the interest retained.[5] He found this in an Australian[6] case, where it had been said that the policy was to avoid the 'delay, expense and uncertainty' of requiring the Revenue to investigate whether a gift was genuine or pretended. So section 102 lays down a rule that if A, the donor, continued to derive any benefit from the property in which an interest had been given, it would be treated as a pretended gift unless the benefit could be shown to be referable to a specific proprietary interest which A had retained. While the section treats the property as forming part of the estate on death—and is therefore valued at that time—the initial gift may also have been a transfer of value, whether chargeable or potentially exempt. Regulations provide for any tax paid on a chargeable inter vivos transfer to be credited on death.[7]

FA 1986, section 102 applies where an individual disposes of property and either: (i) possession and enjoyment of the property is not bona fide assumed by the donee at or before the beginning of 'the relevant period'; or (ii) at any time in the relevant period, the property is not enjoyed to the entire exclusion, or virtually the entire exclusion, (a) of the donor and (b) of any benefit to him by contract or otherwise. This follows the old estate duty definition.[8] The 'relevant' period begins seven years before the donor's death or, if later, with the date of the gift.[9] Section 102 expressly contemplates the possibility that a gift may be made subject to a reservation and that the reservation itself may end at a later time but before the death.

It will be seen that these rules concentrate on the exclusion of the donor and not of the donor's spouse. However, the reservation of benefit to a spouse will be taken into account when arrangements are entered into under which a policy of insurance is involved, the policy is on the life of the donor or the donor's spouse and the benefits accruing to the donee are related to the policy.[10] It will also be taken into account if the gift is of an interest in land coming within section 102A (see below at §47.4.3).

47.2   FA 1986, Section 102: Rules (i) and (ii)

47.2.1 *Rule (i)*

If the gift is to escape IHT on the ground that it was made outside the statutory period, the first essential is that possession or enjoyment must have been assumed by B, the donee,

---

[4] Inland Revenue Press Release, 18 March 1986, [1986] *Simon's Tax Intelligence* 193.

[5] In *Ingram v IRC* [1999] STC 36, 45.

[6] *Lang v Webb* (1912) 13 CLR 503, 513, per Isaacs J.

[7] Inheritance Tax (Double Charges Relief) Regulations 1987 (SI 1987/1130), reg 5 (above §46.7.3).

[8] FA 1894, s 2(1)(c), incorporating Customs and Inland Revenue Act 1881, s 38(2) and Customs and Inland Revenue Act 1889, s 11. However, the old legislation required the 'entire' exclusion and not just 'virtually the entire' exclusion of the donor. For a practice favourable to tax approved pension schemes, see Statement of Practice SP 10/86.

[9] FA 1986, s 102(1).

[10] FA 1986, Sch 20, para 7; see Potter and Monroe, *op cit*, §5.19.

outside the relevant period. In turn, therefore, the gift must have effectively deprived A, the donor, of all rights in the property before that time, a problem to be resolved by looking at the rules relevant to the transfer of the particular type of property involved.

47.2.2 Rule (ii)

Possession and enjoyment must then satisfy rule (ii), which contains two distinct limbs. There must be both: (a) the entire, or virtually the entire, exclusion of A, the donor; and (b) the entire, or virtually the entire, exclusion of any benefit to A by contract or otherwise.

47.2.2.1 Limb (a) of Rule (ii)

This requires the total exclusion of the donor both in law and in fact. Two cases illustrate the severity of this rule and explain the need for the rules in §47.3 below. In *Stamp Duties Commr of New South Wales v Permanent Trustee Co of New South Wales*,[11] A, the donor, had settled property on B, his daughter, contingently on her attaining the age of 30; A retained no benefit and was entirely excluded. Fourteen years later, shortly before the daughter reached 30, he arranged with the daughter to borrow some of the income of the trust fund. He later died within the relevant period beginning with the date of the loan. The court held that he had not been entirely excluded from the property, which was therefore taxed as part of his estate. Thus, the rule may apply not only where B, the donee, is obliged to allow A, the donor, to continue to use the property, but also where there is an 'honourable understanding' to this effect, and even where there is no such understanding but simply an application of the property for the benefit of the donor at some later time.

Chick v Stamp Duties Commr[12] is similar. In 1934, a father made an absolute gift of grazing land to his son. A year later the son brought the land into a farming partnership with his father and another brother. The partnership was an arm's-length arrangement, and yet the Privy Council held that the son had not retained possession and enjoyment of the land to the entire exclusion of the donor, so the land was liable to estate duty when the father died some 18 years after the original gift.

47.2.2.2 Limb (b) of Rule (ii)

This requires the property to be enjoyed to the entire exclusion, or virtually the entire exclusion, of any benefit to A, the donor, by contract or otherwise. To fall foul of this rule, however, it is not necessary that the benefit should be reserved out of the property itself; it suffices that it 'trenches on' the possession and enjoyment of the property given. Examples include a covenant by B, the donee, to pay A, the donor, an annuity, even though not charged on the property given,[13] and a right to remuneration as a trustee.[14] Where an annuity was charged on the whole of the property given, the whole property given was held to be a gift with reservation; it was immaterial how small a percentage of the property's income was needed for the annuity.[15] However, a covenant for quiet enjoyment given by a lessor

---

[11] [1956] 2 All ER 512, PC.
[12] [1958] 2 All ER 623, PC.
[13] *A-G v Worrall* [1895] 1 QB 99, CA.
[14] *Oakes v Stamp Duties Commr of New South Wales* [1953] 2 All ER 1563, PC.
[15] *Earl Grey v A-G* [1900] AC 124, HL.

to a lessee would not amount to the reservation of a benefit where the lessee had given the freehold interest to the lessor in the first place, since this was, in reality, nothing more than contractual backing for a landlord's obligation not to derogate from her grant.[16] Another example concerns a family company. If A wishes to make a gift of shares to the next generation, eg by a PET, the gift will fail if A takes out a service contract or pension plan with the company as part of the deal. The pension plan will not have this effect if it is 'a prior independent transaction'.[17]

These points are reinforced by the rule that a benefit obtained by virtue of any associated operations, as defined in section 268, of which the disposal by way of gift is one shall be treated as property comprised in the gift.[18]

The meaning of 'or otherwise' in the expression 'by contract or otherwise' has not been definitively settled by the courts. In *A-G v Seccombe*,[19] the court construed the expression *eiusdem generis* with contract so as to require a legally-enforceable obligation. This is at best doubtful, and the Revenue have indicated that they do not regard it as correct. It follows that there is probably no need for there to be a legally-binding obligation—at least provided there is a moral obligation.[20]

In *Seccombe*, the donor made a gift of a farm to his great nephew who resided with him and who had taken over the management of the farm the previous year. Until his death the donor continued to reside in the farmhouse and was, from the date of the gift, maintained by the donee. The donor no longer sat at the head of the table but at the side. There was no enforceable agreement, nor any arrangement, that the donor should continue to reside there. It was held that the donee had assumed possession and enjoyment of the property to the entire exclusion of the donor and of any benefit to him by contract or otherwise. The court said that 'or otherwise' should be construed *eiusdem generis* with contract and so required an enforceable obligation. If it is correct to conclude that the presence or absence of a legal right is irrelevant to the first limb, ie in determining whether the donor has been entirely excluded from the property, why should a different rule apply for the second limb? Why did *Seccombe* not fall within the limb (a) of rule (ii) in any case? Today it can hardly be contended that the extensive privileges enjoyed by the donor were such as to amount to his virtual exclusion from the property.

47.3 Qualifications to Rule (ii)

These qualifications apply to both limbs of rule (ii).

47.3.1 De minimis: *Virtually the Entire Exclusion*

FA 1986, section 10 2 requires the entire or 'virtually' the entire exclusion of A, the donor; by contrast, entire exclusion was required for estate duty. While these words are obviously apt

---

[16] *Ingram v IRC* [1997] STC 1234, 1247, per Nourse LJ (the matter did not arise in the House of Lords).
[17] Potter and Monroe, *op cit*, §§9-06A, 9-06B.
[18] FA 1986, Sch 20, para 6(1)(c).
[19] [1911] 2 KB 688.
[20] Potter and Monroe, *op cit*, §3-33.

to cover such matters as social visits paid by A, the donor, to B, the donee, at the property, their precise ambit is inevitably obscure. It is puzzling that the legislation retains the words 'entire exclusion' if 'virtually entire exclusion' will do.

The Revenue view is that these words exclude very small benefits, as where a gift of a house is followed by a short visit by A to B.[21] Revenue Interpretation RI 55, having cited the *Shorter Oxford English Dictionary*, interprets the words as meaning a benefit to the donor which is insignificant in relation to the gifted property, adding that it is not possible to reduce the test to a single, crisp proposition and that each case is one of fact and degree. It states:

> Some examples of situations in which we consider that FA 1986 s 102(1)(b) permits limited benefit to the donor without bringing the GWR provisions into play are given below to illustrate how we apply the *de minimis* test—
>
> — a house which becomes the donee's residence but where the donor subsequently—
>   — stays, in the absence of the donee, for not more than two weeks each year, or
>   — stays with the donee for less than one month each year;
> — social visits, excluding overnight stays made by a donor as a guest of the donee, to a house which he had given away. The extent of the social visits should be no greater than the visits which the donor might be expected to make to the donee's house in the absence of any gift by the donor;
> — a temporary stay for some short term purpose in a house the donor had previously given away, for example—
>   — while the donor convalesces after medical treatment;
>   — while the donor looks after a donee convalescing after medical treatment;
>   — while the donor's own home is being redecorated;
> — visits to a house for domestic reasons, for example baby-sitting by the donor for the donee's children;
> — a house together with a library of books which the donor visits less than five times in any year to consult or borrow a book;
> — a motor car which the donee uses to give occasional (ie less than three times a month) lifts to the donor;
> — land which the donor uses to walk his dogs or for horse riding provided this does not restrict the donee's use of the land.
>
> It follows, of course, that if the benefit to the donor is, or becomes, more significant, the GWR provisions are likely to apply. Examples of this include gifts of—
>
> — a house in which the donor then stays most weekends, or for a month or more each year;
> — a second home or holiday home which the donor and the donee both then use on an occasional basis;
> — a house with a library in which the donor continues to keep his own books, or which the donor uses on a regular basis, for example because it is necessary for his work;
> — a motor car which the donee uses every day to take the donor to work.

The Revenue claim that they do not operate section 102(1)(b) in such a way that donors are unreasonably prevented from having limited access to property they have given away, and that a measure of flexibility is adopted in applying the test.

---

[21] Revenue Booklet *IHT 1*, para 3.4.

47.3.2 Land and Chattels: Exclusion for Full Consideration

This was introduced for estate duty as a result of the *Chick* case (see above at §47.2.2). In the case of property which is an interest in land or a chattel, retention or assumption by the donor of actual occupation of the land or actual enjoyment of an incorporeal right over the land, or actual possession of the chattel is disregarded if it is for full consideration in money or money's worth.[22] Thus, where a donor makes a gift of a house to a donee and continues to reside in it under a lease providing for payment of a full rent, presumably the maximum allowed by law, there is no gift with reservation (GWR). It must also be noted that this qualification applies only to land and chattels, and that the only types of enjoyment ignored are actual occupation and enjoyment. Thus, the rule has no mitigating effect in a situation such as the New South Wales case or trusts of insurance policies. The taxpayer will have to prove that full consideration was given, as where both sides have bargained at arm's length and have been separately advised, and the lease follows normal commercial criteria in force at the time it is negotiated.[23] This was the subject of elaboration in the following statement in the course of the debate on the 1986 Finance Bill:[24]

> Elderly parents make unconditional gifts of undivided shares in their house to their children and the parents and the children occupy the property as their family home, each owner bearing his or her share of the running costs. In these circumstances, the parents' occupation or enjoyment of the part of the house they have given away is in return for similar enjoyment of the children of the other part of the property. Thus the donor's occupation is for full consideration.

Revenue Interpretation RI 55 states that while the Revenue take the view that

> ... such full consideration is required throughout the relevant period—and therefore [we] consider that the rent paid should be reviewed at appropriate intervals to reflect market changes—we do recognise that there is no single value at which consideration can be fixed as 'full'. Rather, we accept that what constitutes full consideration in any case lies within a range of values reflecting normal valuation tolerances, and that any amount within that range can be accepted as satisfying the para 6(1)(a) test.

47.3.3 Land: Exclusion for Unforeseen Circumstances

Where the property is an interest in land, any occupation by the donor may be ignored if it was unforeseen, was not brought about by the donor to receive the benefit of the rule, occurs when the donor is unable to maintain himself through old age, infirmity or otherwise, and it represents a reasonable provision for the care and maintenance of the donor.[25] The donee must also be a relative of the donor or his spouse.

---

[22] FA 1986, Sch 20, para 6(1)(a). See also Revenue Interpretation RI 55.
[23] *IHT* 1, para 3.5; this is simply an illustration. See *IRC v Spencer-Nairn* [1991] STC 60, Court of Session.
[24] HC Official Report, Finance Act 1986, Standing Committee G, col 425, 10 June 1986. Emphasis was placed on the fullness of the consideration.
[25] FA 1986, Sch 20, para 6(1)(b).

47.4 Determining the Property Given

Rule (ii) (see §47.2.2) requires that the property be enjoyed to the exclusion of the donor. It follows that only enjoyment which affects the property actually given can cause the rule to apply. Thus, if A has a block of shares in a company and gives some of them to B, FA 1986, section 102 does not cause A to be treated as having retained an interest in the shares given to B simply because A continues to enjoy dividends from the shares which are retained. The same would be true if A decided to use some of his spare capital to buy an annuity for himself.[26] As Lord Hoffmann put it:

> The theme which runs through all the cases is that although the section does not allow a donor to have his cake and eat it, there is nothing to stop him from carefully dividing up the cake, eating part and having the rest. If the benefits which the donor continues to enjoy are by virtue of property which was never comprised in the gift, he has not reserved any benefit out of the property of which he disposed.

Problems have arisen when planners have applied this technique to land because of the fineness of some of the distinctions, and because it was unclear whether the thing that was being split into a part retained and a part given was the land itself or the complex of interests which English land law recognises. Eventually, in the *Ingram* case,[27] the House of Lords found in favour of the latter approach and so upheld a scheme; that decision was reversed by legislation the same year.

47.4.1 *Examples of Planning*

Chick and the *Permanent Trustee* cases (see above at §47.2.2) concerned situations in which A, the donor, first gave away the property and then received some benefit from it. However, suppose that in the *Chick* case the formation of the partnership and the transfer of the land to the son had occurred at the same time. It could be argued that the gift to the son was not a complete gift of the grazing land, but rather a gift of the land subject to the rights of the partnership, with the result that there would have been no GWR.

In *Munro v Stamp Duties Commr*,[28] a father, the donor, owned freehold land which was farmed by a partnership of himself and his six children. In 1913 he gave the land to the children, but continued as a partner in the business until his death in 1929. The Privy Council held that the property given was not the land but his interest in the land subject to the rights of the partnership. There seems little justification for the different result reached in *Chick*, and the distinction that in *Chick* the father's interest was taken back out of property which had already been given has been described as 'so fine as to be almost beyond perception'.[29]

In *Stamp Duties Commr of New South Wales v Perpetual Trustee Co Ltd*,[30] a father settled property on his infant son but failed to direct what should happen to the property in the

---

[26] Eg, Lord Hoffmann in *Ingram v IRC* [1999] STC 36, 45; citing Lord Simonds in *St Aubyn v A-G (No 2)* [1952] AC 15, 22–23.
[27] *Ibid.*
[28] [1934] AC 61.
[29] Beattie, *Elements of Estate Duty*, 8th edn (Butterworths, 1974) 101.
[30] [1943] 1 All ER 525, PC.

event that the son should not reach the age of 21. The Privy Council held that the property given was not the entire settled property but rather that property minus the settlor's remainder interest. In this way, the charge to estate duty was avoided.

47.4.2 Ingram

In *Ingram v IRC*,[31] the deceased, D, died in February 1989 within two years of making the disposition which was in issue. D was the absolute owner of certain property and wished to settle it for her family but to retain a sufficient interest to enable her to continue to enjoy the physical occupation of the property for the rest of her life:

Step 1 (day 1): D transferred the property to her solicitor, S.

Step 2 (day 1): S declared that he held the property as nominee for D and agreed to deal with it as she might direct.

Step 3 (day 2): at the direction of D, S granted D rent-free leases of the whole of the property for a term of 20 years from that day.

Step 4 (day 3): again at D's direction, S transferred the property, subject to the leases in favour of D, to trustees.

Step 5 (day 3): the trustees, also acting at D's direction, declared trusts of the property for the family. D could not benefit under the trusts but could under the leases.

The plan was that the disposition in favour of the beneficiaries (step 5) would be a PET so that if, as happened, D died within seven years, it would become a chargeable transfer only on the death. A further crucial factor was that the property transferred and so chargeable would be the reversionary interest expectant of the leases in favour of D's estate and this would affect the value. The Revenue issued a determination on the basis that the whole property was 'subject to a reservation' within FA 1986, section 102(2).

The House of Lords held that the scheme worked. As Lord Hoffmann put it:[32]

[The Revenue] had argued that for Lady Ingram to have made a potentially exempt transfer and retained the right to stay in the house was simply too good to be true. But this approach ignores the fact that 'property' in section 102 is not something which has physical existence like a house but a specific interest in that property, a legal construct, which can co-exist with other interests in the same physical object. Section 102 does not therefore prevent people from deriving benefit from the object in which they have given away an interest. It applies only when they derive the benefit from that interest. If Lady Ingram had been dealing with a fund of investments instead of a house, she would have had no difficulty in achieving the same result, in economic terms, as the transaction in this case. She could have used part of the fund to purchase an annuity which would have guaranteed her exactly the same income as she had been receiving from the fund and given away the rest. Unless she needed to resort to capital, her outward circumstances would have continued unchanged. Why should it make a difference that her asset happened to consist of land? The gift

---

[31] [1999] STC 36. On this and other pre-FA 1999 schemes and on planning to protect the CGT private residence exemption, see Potter and Monroe, *op cit*, ch 12; on post-1999 schemes, see *Tolley's Estate Planning 1999–2000*, 215–30.

[32] [1999] STC 36, 45.

was a real gift of the capital value in the land after deduction of her leasehold interest in the same way as a gift of the capital value of a fund after deduction of an annuity.

It followed that the House did not have to consider issues such as whether the lease was validly granted, or the application of the *Ramsay* principle (see §5.6.4 above).

47.4.3 FA 1986, Sections 102A and 102B—the FA 1999 Intervention

The purpose of FA 1986, sections 102A and 102B is to enact the Revenue argument in *Ingram* that the property to be considered is the land itself and not the property. However, these sections apply only where section 102 itself does not[33]—which means that all the learning on section 102 remains in place. Further, they apply only where the property is land. Moreover, these sections have had to enact their own exemptions for exempt transfers (ie by virtue of any of the provisions listed in section 102(5)) and for benefits which would be taken out of charge under section 102 itself under Schedule 20, paragraph 6(1).[34] The rest of Schedule 20 is made to apply.[35]

Section 102A applies where an individual disposes of an interest in land by way of gift on or after 9 March 1999 and D, the donor, or D's spouse, enjoys a significant right or interest in the land in the relevant period. This is extended to cover the situation in which D (or his spouse) is party to a 'significant arrangement'. Where these conditions are satisfied, the interest disposed of is property subject to a reservation and section 102 applies to it.[36] A right, interest or arrangement is 'significant' if (and only if) it entitles or enables the donor to occupy all or part of the land, or to enjoy some right in relation to all or part of the land, otherwise than for full consideration in money or money's worth.[37]

Buzzoni v HMRC[38] involved a reversionary lease scheme undertaken to reduce the value of the taxpayer's estate for IHT purposes. The scheme was a variation of the lease carve-out scheme that was successful in *Ingram*. The Court of Appeal in *Buzzoni* held that the scheme was not caught by the reservation of benefit rules. Although Moses J decided that the taxpayer had reserved a benefit (the other two judges expressing no opinion on this point), the judges were unanimous in concluding that the benefit in question did not encroach upon the donee's enjoyment of the gift. Such a scheme would now fall foul of the extended reservation of benefit rules post-1999.[39]

47.4.3.1 Exclusions from Section 102A

Various matters are insignificant, eg a right, etc, which does not and cannot prevent the enjoyment of the land to the entire exclusion, or virtually the entire exclusion, of the donor. Another is one which entitles the donor to enjoy some right only after the interest given away has come to an end,[40] such as the gift of a lease where the donor retains the reversion

---

[33] FA 1986, s 102C(5)–(7); s 102B applies only where s 102A does not.
[34] FA 1986, s 102C(2), (3).
[35] FA 1986, s 102C(4).
[36] More accurately, FA 1986, s 102(3), (4) apply to it (s 102A(2)(b)).
[37] FA 1986, s 102A(3).
[38] [2013] EWCA Civ 1684.
[39] For commentary see Ashley [2014] BTR 17.
[40] This phrase from the Finance Bill 1999 Notes seems greatly preferable to the formal wording of FA 1986.

(the opposite of *Ingram*). To tie matters in with the parallel structure of section 102, a right cannot be significant if it was granted or acquired before the period of seven years ending with the date of the gift. Where an individual disposes of more than one interest in land by way of gift, these rules apply separately in relation to each interest.[41]

47.4.3.2 Joint Ownership and Section 102B

In a statement dated 18 May 1987 the Revenue reiterated an assurance[42] that they would continue to observe an estate duty practice on the treatment of gifts involving a share in a house where the gifted property is occupied by all the joint owners including the donor for FA 1986, section 102. This is embodied in section 102B. An arrangement will not necessarily be jeopardised merely because it involves a gift of an unequal share in a house. Section 102B provides separate rules for equivalent gifts (ie disposals on or after 9 March 1999) of an undivided share of an interest in land. They are, however, presented as being in the nature of reliefs—the separate provisions are essentially to ensure that the donor's occupation of the land concerned jointly with the donee does not of itself count as the reservation of a benefit.[43] The gifted share will not prevent the donor from being treated for IHT purposes as still owning the entire interest from which the share was carved out unless one of three exceptions applies.[44] One is where the donor, A, does not occupy the land. The second is where A pays full consideration for occupying the land to the exclusion of the donee. The third is where A occupies the land jointly with the donee and receives no benefit—or virtually no benefit—at the donee's expense for any reason connected with the gift.[45] Under the Revenue 1987 statement, the payment by the donee of the donor's share of the running costs, for example, might be such a benefit; however—to formulate an example not in the 1987 statement—an agreement to enter into a sexual relationship would not.

47.4.4 *Gift Involving Family Business*

The 1987 Revenue statement (§47.4.3 above) stated that a donor may make a gift involving family business without falling foul of the rules on GWR

> merely because the donor remains in the business, perhaps as a director or a partner. For example, where the gift is of shares of a company, the continuation of reasonable commercial arrangements in the form of remuneration for the donor's ongoing services to the company entered into before the gift will not of itself amount to a reservation provided the remuneration is in no way linked to or beneficially affected by the gift. Similar considerations will apply in the case where the gift is into trust which empowered a trustee, who may be the donor, to retain director's fees etc for his own benefit.

---

[41] FA 1986, s 102A(6)—this is whether or not the disposals are at the same time or to the same donee.

[42] Given by the Minister of State in Hansard, Standing Committee G, col 425, 10 June 1986.

[43] Inland Revenue Notes to Finance Bill 1999, cl 92, para 22.

[44] FA 1986, s 102B(2); other exceptions mentioned above (ie s 102(5) and Sch 20, para 6(1)(b)) must not be overlooked.

[45] FA 1986, s 102B(3), (4).

47.5   Consequences

47.5.1 *Basic Rules*

Where a GWR is made and the reservation continues until the death of the donor, A, the property is to be treated as property to which A was still beneficially entitled immediately before his death and so as part of A's estate for IHT.[46] Where, at some time before the end of the relevant period (ie A's death), the property ceases to be subject to a reservation, A is treated as if having made a disposition of property at that time; the disposition is a PET.[47] It is necessary, therefore, to wait a further seven years to see whether it becomes an exempt transfer; the annual exemption is not available on this occasion.

However, it may be that the original GWR is itself an immediately chargeable transfer, as where it is a settlement on discretionary trusts. In such circumstances, regulations prevent a double charge to tax.[48] Where a settlor settles property but is not entirely excluded from it and later releases the offending rights, there will, it is assumed, be a chargeable transfer on the occasion of the settlement; it is hard to see why there should also be a PET on the occasion of the release.[49] Since the property does not form part of A's estate on death, section 142 (alteration of disposition within two years of the death to undo the gift with reservation)[50] cannot be used. B, the donee, is primarily liable for the tax.[51]

47.5.2 *Exemptions*

FA 1986, sections 102 *et seq* do not normally apply where the transfer would be an exempt transfer. Thus, section 102 is excluded where the gift is to a spouse and would be exempt under section 18. The same applies to a gift which is a small gift or in consideration of marriage—ie exempt under sections 20 or 22.[52] Gifts to charities are subject to their own reservation of benefit rules.[53] However, the annual exemption or exemption for normal expenditure out of income cannot be invoked if section 102 applies.[54] These rules do not apply to gifts made after 17 March 1986 under the terms of regular premium insurance policies made before 18 March 1986 and not since altered.[55] IHT is not charged on death benefits payable from tax-approved occupational pension and retirement annuity schemes under discretionary trusts; this practice also applies to any IHT due under these gifts with reservation rules.[56]

---

[46] FA 1986, s 102(3).
[47] FA 1986, s 102(4); this is also now the Revenue view—Inland Revenue Interpretation, [1993] *Simon's Tax Intelligence* 1409, repudiating *IHT* 1 (1991), para 3.4.
[48] FA 1986, s 102(1)(b).
[49] The calculation of the charge is then given by the Inheritance Tax (Double Charges Relief) Regulations 1987 (SI 1987/1130), reg 5. The Schedule, Pt III to the SI gives numerical examples.
[50] See IHTA 1984, s 142(5).
[51] IHTA 1984, s 204(9).
[52] FA 1986, s 102(5).
[53] See IHTA 1984, s 23(4). These therefore apply also to ss 24–28.
[54] FA 1986, s 102(5) makes no mention of ss 19 or 21.
[55] By FA 1986, s 102(6), (7). See also Statement of Practice SP 10/86 on certain pension and retirement annuity schemes under discretionary trusts.
[56] Statement of Practice SP 10/86.

Spouses and civil partners: further rule. The exemption in section 18 is restricted.[57] The conditions are: (a) the property becomes settled property by virtue of the gift; (b) the transfer is exempt because the donor's spouse becomes entitled to an interest in possession in the settled property; (c) the spouse's interest in possession ceases; (d) at that time the spouse does not become entitled to an interest in the settled property or to another interest in possession in it. The legislation achieves its goal by saying that where these conditions are satisfied the original disposal is treated as having been made immediately after the ending of the spouse's interest in possession; in this way the previous events are ignored in applying section 102. This was passed to reverse the taxpayer's success in *IRC v Eversden*.[58] In the usual way the rules apply only to disposals on or after a certain date (20 June 2003), leaving earlier disposals to be dealt with under the court's decision. However, the income tax charge in FA 2004, Schedule 15 (below §47.6) may apply even though the events occurred before that date.

47.5.3 Tracing

The rules are designed to bring into the estate the value of the property immediately before the death of A, the donor, and not its original value at the time of the gift. Where the reservation ceases at an earlier time, but still within the relevant period, it is the value at that time which is taken. Rules must therefore be provided to determine how far the property may be traced between the date of the gift and the subsequent ending of the reservation or death. These are less sweeping than the estate duty rules in FA 1957, section 38. The first set of rules is designed to trace the value of the gift made with reservation into property substituted for the gift and into all accretions to the property.[59] Where an accretion involves expenditure by B, the donee, eg rights issues, any consideration provided for the accretion is deductible.[60] Where B dies before A, B's PRs take over; tracing continues into their acts.[61] The tracing rules do not apply where the property is settled (for which there are separate rules), or where the property given is a sum of money in sterling or any other currency.[62] The value of this gift is fixed for all time in the case of sterling; for foreign currency it is unclear whether exchange rates appropriate to the date of the gift rather than the death are used.

Where B, the donee, gives the property away, other than back to A, or otherwise than for consideration in money or money's worth not less than the value of the property at that time, B is treated as continuing to have the possession or enjoyment of the property.[63] A compulsory acquisition by another person is not treated as voluntary, but a merger of an interest leading to its destruction is.[64] This is presumably because the basic rule is defined in terms of B assuming possession and enjoyment of the property to the exclusion of A, the donor.

---

[57] FA 2003 s 102(5A)–(5C) added by FA 2003, s 185; see Inland Revenue Press release 20 June 2003, [2003] *Simon's Tax Intelligence* 1104 and Chamberlain [2003] BTR 415–16.
[58] *IRC v Eversden* 2002 EWCA Civ 668; [2003] STC 822.
[59] FA 1986, Sch, 20, para 2.
[60] FA 1986, Sch 20, para 3.
[61] FA 1986, Sch 20, para 4.
[62] FA 1986, Sch 20, para 2(2).
[63] FA 1986, Sch 20, para 2(4).
[64] FA 1986, Sch 20, para 2(5).

The rules as to settled property require that the property in the settlement should be taken as representing the original property.[65] If the settlement comes to an end, in whole or in part, before the reservation ends, the property ceasing to be settled is treated as the given property, but with a deduction for property becoming property of the donor and with an addition of any money the donor pays at that time. Where the property is not originally settled but is settled subsequently by B, the donee, these rules apply. Although income which is accumulated becomes part of the settled property, this does not apply to income accumulated after the date of the ending of the reservation.

47.6 Pre-owned Assets: Income Tax Charge to Protect the Gift with Reservation Rules[66]

47.6.1 *Purpose*

FA 2004 used the device of an income tax charge on the annual value of the assets, much like the pre-1963 Schedule A (above at §1.6.2), to counteract a potential IHT advantage.[67] In order to let people undo these transactions, and so bring themselves back within the GWR rules, the charge did not come into force until 2005—further rules provided some degree of tax protection for undoing these transactions.[68] The section applies to transfers all the way back to the introduction of IHT in March 1986 but avoids the stigma of retrospective legislation by using the device of a current income tax charge. These changes, predictably, generated a lot of criticism and a lot of commentary.[69] One has to grasp that the 2005 rules will undo many schemes already put in place, some of which have been upheld by the courts. Traditionally, where Parliament has intervened to reverse those decisions, it has done so only for future transfers of value.[70] The Parliamentary Joint Committee on Human Rights did not regard this as a breach of the human rights legislation.[71]

The legislation is intended to support not replace the GWR rules in FA 1986. So there is no charge under these rules if the GWR rules apply, or if the GWR rules would apply but are prevented from applying by an exception in the GWR rules. The Schedule contains rules for land and[72] chattels;[73] it applies to intangible property only if held in a trust from which

---

[65] FA 1986, Sch 20, para 4.

[66] See generally Chamberlain and Whitehouse with McCutcheon, *Pre Owned Assets; Capital Tax Planning in the New Era* (Sweet & Maxwell, 2004) (hereafter 'C and W').

[67] FA 2004, s 84 and Sch 15. See further IR Budget Note 40 and the Inland Revenue Notes both to the original Bill and to the many amendments made at the Committee Stage; Charge to Income Tax by Reference to Enjoyment of Property Previously Owned Regulations 2005 (SI 2005/724).

[68] FA 2004, Sch 15, para 20; SI 2005/724, para 6.

[69] Apart from C and W above, see Tallon, *Taxation*, 24 June 2004, 319–21, McCutcheon, *Taxation*, 16 September 2004, 626–29 and 30 September 686–89 and Chamberlain [2004] BTR 486–93. Also well worth reading is Drysdale, *Simon's Tax Briefing*, 126 and 127 (with helpful examples). For planning suggestions see Hutton, *Taxation*, 7 October 2004, 1–4.

[70] Eg FA 1986, s 102A, added by FA 1999 to reverse *IRC v Ingram* [1997] STC 1234, and s 102(5A), added by FA 2003 to reverse *IRC v Eversden* [2004] STC 822.

[71] 12th Report 2003–04 Session, esp at paras 1.48 and 1.50; for criticism see C and W, 1.22.

[72] FA 2004, Sch 15, paras 3–5.

[73] FA 2004, Sch 15, paras 6–7.

the settlor is not entirely excluded.[74] Each type of property has its own charging rule[75] and set of valuation rules. The Schedule has no application to loans of money, nor to intangible property held in other circumstances. The charging rules are followed by excluded transactions, exemptions from charge, international rules and a *de minimis* rule where the annual value or, more precisely, the aggregate of annual values does not exceed £5,000.[76]

The decision to legislate in this way followed the Revenue victory in *Eversden* (above §47.5.2). Some thought that the (prospective only) 2003 legislation would have been enough to protect the Revenue, but schemes intended to circumvent the rules were quickly marketed. Whether they would have been effective is uncertain, but the Revenue took the prompt drastic pre-emptive steps which follow.[77]

47.6.2 Land: The Conditions

Land first comes within these rules if the 'disposal' condition is satisfied. This condition is nicely summarised in the Revenue Note as where P 'previously owned an interest in the land or owned an interest in other property which funded its acquisition'.[78]

The disposal condition has two limbs. The first limb is where an individual P, called 'the chargeable person', (a) occupies land, called 'the relevant land', either alone or with others, and (b) owned an interest in the land at any time after 17 March 1986, and (c) has disposed of that land otherwise than by an excluded transaction.[79] The transaction is excluded if it is for full market value or otherwise is not a problem for IHT purposes—see further below. The second limb applies if, in the words of the statute, P has an interest in *other property* and the proceeds of disposal of that property were applied by another person, T, in acquiring an interest in the relevant land, eg if P gives the land (Cambridge) to T who sells it and T buys another piece of land (London). Thus the application may have been direct or indirect. The question whether T has to have disposed of the whole of the property received from P or whether the second limb applies if he has disposed only of an interest in it is a disputed one.[80] Land also comes within these rules if the 'contribution' condition is satisfied, ie where P has, directly or indirectly, funded T's acquisition of the interest.[81] Again, acquisitions by excluded transactions are ignored.

Suppose that M gave a child a flat 15 years ago and now lives in it rent free. This is a straightforward gift with reservation which is caught by FA 1986 and so the pre-owned asset rules in FA 2004 do not apply. Suppose that M gave a child £30,000 15 years ago; 12 years ago the child bought a flat and M moved in, and has lived in it rent free since then. This is not caught by the GWR rules as the tracing rules in FA 1986, Schedule 20, paragraph 2 do not apply to gifts of money. M is nevertheless within the contribution condition, and so FA 2004 may apply. Perhaps oddly, it seems that if the child uses the money to improve

[74] FA 2004, Sch 15, paras 8–9.
[75] FA 2004, Sch 15, paras 3(5), 6(4) and 8(3).
[76] FA 2004, Sch 15, paras 9–13; on £5,000 exemption, see C and W, ch 9.
[77] See C and W 1.05; on most FA 2004 planning see *ibid*, chs 14–29.
[78] Note cl 84 to FA 2004, Sch 15, para 5.
[79] FA 2004, Sch 15, para 3(2).
[80] *Simon's Direct Tax Service Handbook*, note to FA 2004, Sch 15, para 3.
[81] FA 2004, Sch 15, para 3(3).

an existing property, eg by building a granny flat, this is not caught by the contribution condition.[82]

It will be noted that in the above example, M moves in only three years after the gift of the money. Where the gap is seven years or more, the charge under FA 2004, Schedule 15 is excluded—the exclusion applies a rule analogous to a PET.[83] The boundary between the contribution condition and the disposal condition may be a subtle one. Although either condition causes the rules to apply, the exclusion rules in paragraph 10 are different. The prevailing opinion is that the disposal condition will be the more common one.[84] A disposition creating a new interest in land is taken as a part disposal of the land in question.

47.6.3 Land: The Charge

The statute then imposes a charge to income tax on an amount equal to the amount to be determined under a later provision.[85] The statute does not state precisely how the charge is to arise. The provision did not take effect until 2005, by which time Schedule D, Case VI was no more. Meanwhile relations with ITEPA 2003 are governed by other rules.[86] The amount of charge is governed by the appropriate rental value—less any qualifying payments made by P.[87] Payments qualify only if made under a legally-binding obligation and made within the taxable period.[88] The appropriate rental value is $R \times DV/V$, where R is the rental value of the relevant land[89] for the taxable period and V is the value of the relevant land, taking account of paragraph 15, which states the normal IHT valuation rule in section 160. So if a house is worth £300,000 and we take an assumed return of 5% on the basis set out in the legislation, the assumed rental value will be £15,000 pa. Any actual payment less than this, even of a full commercial rent, brings about a potential charge.[90]

The definition of DV varies according to the precise part of paragraph 3(2) or 3(3) which is being applied. In the simplest case—where P has an interest in the land disposed of—one takes the value of P's interest in the land at the relevant valuation date. Where either the representative disposal condition or the contribution condition applies, one is directed to look for that part of the value which can reasonably be attributed to the property originally disposed of or the contribution; this task is likely to be more difficult than the legislation assumes.[91] Regulation 3 of the Charge to Income Tax by Reference to Enjoyment of Property Previously Owned Regulations 2005 prescribes that the 'valuation date' is 6 April of the relevant tax year.[92] Regulation 4 of the 2005 Regulations deals with the frequency of valuations; in general a value is good for five years. Transitional elective relief to remain under the gift with reservation rules is provided.[93] Where the property is disposed of at an

[82] Drysdale, *Simon's Tax Briefing 126*, 6 August 2004, example 1.2.
[83] FA 2004, Sch 15, para 10(2)(c).
[84] C and W, §3.07.
[85] FA 2004, Sch 15, para 3(5).
[86] FA 2004, Sch 15, para 19.
[87] FA 2004, Sch 15, para 4.
[88] FA 2004, Sch 15, para 4(1).
[89] Computed under FA 2004, Sch 15, para 5.
[90] However, McCutcheon, *op cit*, points to FA 1986, Sch 20, para 6(1)(a).
[91] C and W, §3.19.
[92] SI 2005/724, reg 4, made under FA 2004, Sch 15, para 4(6).
[93] FA 2004, Sch 15, para 21.

undervalue so that it is part gift and part sale, a situation which the legislation calls a 'non-exempt sale', the charge applies on only the appropriate fraction of the value.[94]

47.6.4 Chattels

Broadly similar rules are then provided for chattels. Transitional elective relief is provided.[95] McCutcheon suggests that the Revenue will have no difficulty in establishing their notional rent under the statutory formula, but taxpayers will have great difficulty in proving that any rent they pay represents full value.[96] Again regulation 4 of the 2005 Regulations provides that a valuation is good for five years. Examples include (a) where D gives money to a child who uses it to buy a yacht which D then sails for six weeks each year, this giving rise to a charge on the six weeks of use, and (b) where D gives a child a picture but it remains in D's house as the insurance company insists upon it.[97]

47.6.5 Certain Intangible Property

The rules on intangible property are much narrower and apply only where the property is comprised in a settlement where the settlor retains an interest. While the rules as to when a settlor has an 'interest' are taken from ITTOIA 2005, section 625(1), the definition of settled property is taken from IHTA 1984 and not ITTOIA 2005.[98] The intangible property must have been settled, in this IHTA 1984 sense, or added to the settlement by P since 17 March 1986. Transitional elective relief is provided.[99] Where the provision applies it does so more strictly; there are no 'excluded transactions',[100] and the value of the settlor's 'interest' is ignored. Regulation 4 of the 2005 Regulations does not apply to intellectual property so annual valuations are called for. The problem of property falling under more than one head of charge is addressed, but not as fully as some would like. The addressing provision states that where a person is charged on value x under paragraphs 3 or 6 and value y under paragraph 8, and the intangible property in paragraph 8 derives its value from the land or chattel in paragraphs 3 or 6, P is not charged on $x + y$ but only on whichever is the higher of x and y.[101]

47.6.6 Exclusions

FA 2004, Schedule 15, paragraph 10 applies to land and to chattels but not to intangible property. Transactions falling within the *disposal condition* are excluded by paragraph 10(1) in five situations, all of which show that there are no IHT issues.[102] The first is where

---

[94] FA 2004, Sch 15, para 4(4).
[95] FA 2004, Sch 15, para 21.
[96] *Taxation*, 16 September 2004, 627.
[97] Drysdale, *op cit*, examples 1.4 and 1.5.
[98] FA 2004, Sch 15, paras 8 and 9.
[99] FA 2004, Sch 15, para 22.
[100] FA 2004, Sch 15, para 11 applies but para 10 does not.
[101] FA 2004, Sch 15, para 18.
[102] FA 2004, Sch 15, para 10(1); McCutcheon, *op cit*, notes that the definition of connected person in Sch 15, para 2, which now refers to ITA 2007, ss 993 and 994, is wider than for IHTA 1984, s 10.

S disposes of the whole interest in the property to a person other than a connected person in an arm's-length transaction or on arm's-length terms.[103] The insistence of a transfer of the whole interest means that the disposal of a half share by a parent to a child on the basis that they share expenses 50:50 will not escape Schedule 15. Similarly anxieties have been expressed about farms where a parent and child farm the land together, the parent having given the child a half share in return for working on the farm.[104] Regulations provide some relief for equity release schemes and sales of part of a home.

The second exclusion in paragraph 10(1) is a transfer by S to S's spouse or civil partner or, under court order, former spouse or civil partner. The third is where the disposal is by way of gift (or under court order) by virtue of which the property becomes settled property and S or S's spouse or civil partner is the person with an interest in possession. This exclusion does not apply if the interest in possession has come to an end otherwise then on the death of the spouse or civil partner, or former spouse or civil partner.[105] The fourth is where the disposal falls within the family maintenance rule in section 11 and so is not a transfer of value. The fifth is where the disposal is an outright gift to an individual and comes within the annual or small gifts exemption (sections 19 or 20).

A separate rule, paragraph 10(2), deals with the *contribution condition*. Where the consideration for another person's acquisition comes within the following five categories, the transaction is excluded. The first is where the other person was S's spouse or civil partner or, under court order, former spouse or civil partner. The second is where on acquisition the property became settled property and S or S's spouse or civil partner is the person with an interest in possession. This exclusion does not apply if the interest in possession has come to an end otherwise then on the death of the spouse or civil partner, or former spouse or civil partner.[106] The third is where the consideration is an outright gift of money made more than seven years before the earliest date on which the chargeable person occupied the land or acquired possession of the chattel. The fourth is where the disposal falls within the family maintenance rule in section 11 and so is not a transfer of value. The fifth is where the disposal is an outright gift to an individual and comes within the annual or small gifts exemption (sections 19 or 20).

47.6.7 Exemptions

Paragraph 11 continues the idea of excluding situations which do not give rise to IHT issues, but applies to intangible property as well as to the other heads of charge and does so by giving an exemption from charge. Referring to the Revenue notes to the clause (Committee Stage Amendment 140), it applies where the property being enjoyed by the former owner is included in his estate for IHT purposes or where the estate includes other property the value of which reflects the value of the property being enjoyed. A separate provision deals with the situation in which the estate includes some but not all of the value previously enjoyed.[107] Revenue examples include situations where the property is given back, the

[103] On planning for equity release scheme, see Drysdale, *op cit*.
[104] However, McCutcheon, *op cit*, suggests that FA 2004 will not apply.
[105] FA 2004, Sch 15, para 10(3).
[106] *Ibid*.
[107] FA 2004, Sch 15, para 11(2).

owner creates or is later given an interest in possession in the property under trust, or the former owner owns it indirectly, eg by owning shares in a company which owns the property. Further exemptions from charge include the situation in which the property is still in S's estate thanks to the GWR rules. The same is true if the property escapes the GWR rules thanks to some of those rules' own exemptions.[108]

The exemption rules have been narrowed in one respect as from 5 December 2005. The narrowing concerns interest in possession trusts where the settled property forms part of that person's estate and that person is the 'donor'. Where the effect would be to remove the property from the pre-owned assets charge because it forms part of that person's estate, it is no longer to do so.[109]

Exemptions may be added by regulation.[110] So far the only exemption is where the original disposal was by a transaction made at arm's length before 6 April 2005 with a person who was not a connected person. The disposal must not have been for money or other readily convertible asset, and must be such as might be expected to be made at arm's length between persons not connected with each other.[111] An exchange is an obvious example.

47.6.8 *Miscellaneous Rules*

In an attempt to head off possible avoidance, certain liabilities—called 'excluded liabilities'—are to be ignored when valuing the property otherwise eligible for relief. These are liabilities associated with some of the previous transactions.[112] So if a family home is subjected to such a liability which reduces the value for IHT purposes from £500,000 to £150,000, the normal IHT rules will apply to the £150,000 value remaining in the estate and the FA 2004 rules to the £350,000 of excluded liability.[113] To fit in with the contribution condition, it is expressly provided that the GWR exclusions are to be available even though the original gift was of money.[114]

The rules in sections 142 to 147 on disclaimers and variations are to apply here too.[115] Where a disposition on the death is changed by these rules, and what would otherwise be a transfer of value by a chargeable person is no longer so treated, the same happens here.

International aspects are an interesting blend of income tax and IHT principles.[116] There is no charge if the person is not resident in the UK during the year. If P is resident but not domiciled, the rules apply only to property in the UK. If the person was at one time not domiciled in the UK, one is to ignore excluded property, eg property disposed of before becoming domiciled in the UK. Domicile is determined on IHT rules.

---

[108] FA 2004, Sch 15, para 11(3)–(5).
[109] FA 2004, Sch 15, paras 11–13, added by FA 2006, s 80. For explanation and examples, see *Finance Act 2006 Handbook* (LexisNexis), 85–87.
[110] FA 2004, Sch 15, para 14.
[111] SI 205724, para 5.
[112] FA 2004, Sch 15, para 11(6)–(9).
[113] McCutcheon, *op cit*, 628–29.
[114] FA 2004, Sch 15, para 11(10).
[115] FA 2004, Sch 15, para 16; C and W, ch 29.
[116] FA 2004, Sch 15, para 12; C and W chs 8 and 20.

There is a *de minimis* exemption where the aggregate of all relevant annual values does not exceed £5,000.[117] It will be seen that this is tied to the relevant annul values, ie without any reduction for offsetting payments under legal obligations.

There is an express provision to deal with guarantees; guaranteeing another person's borrowing is not taken as funding the purchase.[118] This becomes relevant only when the guarantor later enjoys the property. Paying up under the guarantee seems, however, to fall outside the protection of this rule.

The Treasury are given power to make regulations conferring further exemptions.[119]

47.6.9 Elections

The income tax charge applies as from 6 April 2005. However, P may elect that the property should fall under the GWR rules instead for so long as P continues to enjoy the relevant property, as where P occupies the land or possesses or uses the chattel; an analogous provision applies to intangible property.[120]

As seen at §47.6.7 above, FA 2006 narrows the exemptions where the 'donor' has an interest in possession in settled property. Where the 'donor' is brought back into the pre-owned assets charge by this change, an election may be made to go back into the IHT regime. Once there, the property may once again use the reverter to settlor exemption for IHT.[121] The Act also contains rules allowing the donor's PRs to make the election if the donor died before the Royal Asset to FA 2006. The election must be made by the relevant filing date. This will normally have been 31 January 2007, ie the date by which income for 2005–06 had to be reported and tax paid.[122] However, a later alternative, which is the first year in which it would otherwise give rise to charge, may be taken instead—with a consequent alternative filing date. There is provision for a reasonable excuse extension. Any election made before that date may be withdrawn by that date.[123] Opting back into the GWR regime and out of the FA 2004 rules means just that. It does not follow that the GWR rule will cause a charge to apply. So if the original donor opts back in, ceases all beneficial enjoyment and then survives seven years, there is no GWR charge and no FA 2004 charge.[124]

---

[117] FA 2004, Sch 15, para 13; see C and W, ch 9.
[118] FA 2004, Sch 15, para 16.
[119] FA 2004, Sch 15, paras 15 and 20.
[120] FA 2004, Sch 15, para 21 and 22.
[121] Amendments to FA 2004, Sch 15, paras 21 and 22 made by FA 2006, s 80.
[122] FA 2004, Sch 15, para 23.
[123] FA 2004, Sch 15, para 23.
[124] Drysdale, citing Hansard, 20 May 2004, col 305; on opting, see C and W, ch 11.

48

Settled Property: Introduction

48.1   Introduction

This chapter deals with the definition and scope of 'settled property' and the application of IHT when a settlement is created. Where property is comprised in a settlement, tax is chargeable in circumstances defined in IHTA 1984, Part III, ie sections 43–85. After certain preliminary provisions (which are dealt with in this chapter) (sections 43–48), Part III provides one regime for settlements in which there is a relevant interest in possession (sections 49–57A) (see chapter forty-nine below) and another, more complex regime for settlements in which there is no such interest (sections 58–85) (see chapter fifty below); this complex regime is relaxed for certain favoured types of trust (see chapter fifty-one below).

The change from CTT to IHT in 1986 initially made little difference to these rules. However, one year later, transfers of beneficial interests in possession were made potentially exempt transfers (PETs) as opposed to immediately chargeable transfers; this relaxation was largely reversed in 2006. Where it applies, the PET treatment is subject to a special anti-avoidance provision on the rate of tax (see below at §49.5). These rules assume that one know when one is making a transfer. Under modern trust law, rights in land may be created quite informally thanks to doctrines such as proprietary estoppel, or constructive or resulting trusts. Davis has argued, convincingly, that most of the problems may be solved by a flexible interpretation of the tax provisions.[1]

---

[1] Davis [2006] BTR 458.

48.2 Settlements: General Definition

IHTA 1984, section 43(1), which was not amended in 2006, defines a settlement as

'... any disposition or dispositions of property, whether effected by instrument, by parol or by operation of law, or partly in one way and partly in another, whereby the property is for the time being—

(a)   held in trust for persons in succession or for any person subject to a contingency, or

(b)   held by trustees on trust to accumulate the whole or any part of any income of the property or with power to make payments out of that income at the discretion of the trustees or some other person, with or without power to accumulate surplus income, or

(c)   charged or burdened (otherwise than for full consideration in money or money's worth paid for his own use or benefit to the person making the disposition) with the payment of an annuity or other periodical payment payable for a life or any other limited or terminable period,

or would be so held or charged or burdened if the disposition or dispositions were regulated by the law of any part of the United Kingdom; or whereby, under the law of any other country, the administration of the property is for the time being governed by provisions equivalent in effect to those which would apply if the property were so held, charged or burdened.'

It will be seen that, in deciding whether property is settled, it is generally immaterial whether or not the settlement was created for value, except for head (c). However, the presence of value may well be relevant to the question whether the creation of the settlement is a chargeable transfer.

Head (a) is sufficient to cover life interests and contingent interests, but not purely concurrent interests; (b) catches discretionary and accumulation trusts; head (c) catches annuities or other periodical payments only if charged on property—annuities payable under a personal obligation only do not create settlements. The obligation must be for life or any other limited or terminable period, so that while a rent charge for a limited period will give rise to a settlement unless for full consideration, a perpetual rent charge will not. When full consideration is in issue, it does not matter who provides it.[2]

The concluding words of section 43(1) are aimed at foreign devices such as *stiftungen*. They had no counterpart in the earlier estate duty legislation. The words are also needed because these rules extend to property outside the UK if the settlor was domiciled in the UK at the time the settlement was made (section 48(3)). The definition is adapted for Northern Ireland.[3] There is a separate definition for Scotland (section 48(4)). Concessionary relief is available for certain old partnership assurance schemes.[4]

---

[2] *A-G v Boden* [1912] 1 KB 539.
[3] IHTA 1984, s 48(5), excluding leases within the Renewable Leasehold Conversion Act 1849, ss 1 or 37.
[4] ESC F10.

48.3 Leases for Lives

A lease for lives receives special treatment in the IHT legislation. This is because a lease for lives, ie one which is to last until the death or marriage of the lessee, does not usually create a trust of land under the Trusts of Land and Appointment of Trustees Act 1996 or the Settled Land Act 1925. Instead, the Law of Property Act 1925, section 149(6) provides that the lease falls outside the Settled Land Act if it is in consideration of a fine or at a rent, and converts it into a 90-year lease; this is, however, primarily a matter of machinery, since the 90-year lease ends on the death or marriage of the lessee.

Section 43(3) provides that a lease of property will be treated as a settlement for IHT purposes if it is a lease which is (a) for life or lives, or (b) for a period ascertainable only by reference to a death, or (c) terminable on, or at a date ascertainable only by reference to, a death. An example of (c) is a lease to end 10 days after A's death. However, a lease for lives must be distinguished from a fixed-term lease. If the lessee is expected to live for 10 years, a lease for 10 years is a fixed-term lease and not a lease for lives. There is no settlement if the lease was granted for full consideration in money or money's worth. The question whether full value has been given depends upon the facts. Where a vendor retains a lease for life, the reduction in price because of the reservation of the leasehold interest is taken into account.[5] Section 43(3) also provides that where a lease was not granted as a lease at a rack rent, but is at any time to become a lease at an increased rent, it is treated as terminable at that time. It follows that if the time at which the rent is to increase is related to death, it will come within section 43(3).

Where a lease for lives is a settlement, it is not the lease which is the settled property but the interest out of which the lease was created. If the lease is for no or negligible rent, the whole property is treated as the lessee's for IHT purposes. However, where a more-than-nominal rent is due, the lessor is treated as retaining a beneficial interest in part of the leased property. One looks for the proportion that the value of the consideration at the time the lease was granted bears to the then value of a full consideration: the tenant is treated as having a beneficial interest in the rest.[6] Thus, if property is let to T for life at one-tenth of the then full market rent, the lessor is treated as owning one-tenth of the property and T is treated as owning nine-tenths of the property. When a vendor wishes to retain a lease for life at a full rent, it makes no difference whether the lease is reserved out of the interest conveyed or is the subject of a separate grant.[7]

As regards trustees allowing a beneficiary to occupy a dwelling house, Statement of Practice SP 10/79 states that if the trustees, in exercise of their powers, grant a lease for life for less than full consideration, this will also be regarded as creating an interest in possession in view of section 43(3).

---

[5] Statement of Practice SP E10.
[6] IHTA 1984, ss 50(6), 170.
[7] Statement of Practice SP E10.

48.4   One Settlement or Two?

As with CGT (above at §40.5), it is often important to know whether property is part of an existing settlement or subject to a separate settlement. However, one should note that the sub-fund election introduced by FA 2006 applies only for income tax and CGT—and not for IHT. Where two documents create one compound settlement, there is just one settlement; equally, however, one document may create two settlements, as where a will creates a trust of a specific legacy and separate trusts or residue. What is not so clear is whether the addition of property by someone other than the original settlor creates a new settlement or merely adds to an existing one. Section 44(2) simply states that they may be treated as separate settlements where the circumstances so require. Trust law draws a clear distinction between an accretion to a settlement and a new settlement incorporating terms from another settlement.[8]

Some help may be obtained from the definition of 'settlor' in section 44(1). The 'settlor' is not only the person who makes the settlement, but also any other person who has provided funds for the purpose of the settlement or who has made reciprocal arrangements for another to make the settlement. As with the similar test of income tax and settlements, this test is satisfied only if there is some conscious association of the provider of funds with the settlement in question. It is not enough that the settled funds happen historically to have come from a person; otherwise anyone who gave funds unconditionally to another person who then settled them would be treated as a settlor.[9]

48.4.1 *The* Hatton *Case*

The ramifications of this definition of 'settlor' were explored by Chadwick J in *Hatton v IRC*.[10] The judge applied the associated operations rule to hold that both A and B were to be treated as settlors in relation to a composite settlement. Where A and B have separately provided funds from their own independent resources to be held on the trust of the same settlement, proportionate or identifiable parts should be attributed to two separate settlements, each with its notionally separate settlor.

Where the settled property cannot sensibly be apportioned or partitioned amongst a series of notionally separate settlements, section 44(2) makes IHTA 1984 apply as if there were a number of separate settlements, each with its own single settlor and each comprising the whole of the settled property. Thus, suppose that A wishes to benefit Y, and B to benefit X. However, under a reciprocal arrangement, A settles property on X for a term, while B settles property on Y for a similar term; each trust has a reverter to A and B after the term. Each of A and B is a settlor in relation to each settlement; neither could be regarded as the dominant settlor to the exclusion of the other. This logic is carried further; the A settlement must be divided into two separate settlements, A1, of which A was settlor, and A2, of which

---

[8] Eg, *Re Rydon's Settlement* [1955] Ch 1; *Re Gooch* [1929] 1 Ch 740.
[9] *Fitzwilliam v IRC* [1993] STC 502, 516, (1993) 67 TC 673, 733, per Lord Keith, HL.
[10] [1992] STC 140, 67 TC 759.

B was settlor. This is not designed as logic for its own sake but rather to enable other IHT rules to be applied. Thus, when applying the reverter to settlor exemption in section 53(3), the exemption rules are satisfied for A1, but not for A2. Hence, the exemption will not apply at all and tax will be due under section 52(1). A and B are worse off than if they had each made their own separate settlements of their own property.

48.4.2 *The* Rysaffe Trustee *Case*

In *Rysaffe Trustee Co (CI) v IR Commrs*,[11] the Revenue tried to treat five settlements as one by invoking the reference to associated operations in sections 272 and 268 (see §45.7 above). The settlor executed five separate instruments, each in identical form, in the sums of £10 each, the transfer being affected by a single cheque for £50 sent to the settlor's solicitors. Shares were added to the trusts later. Reversing the Special Commissioner and allowing the taxpayer's appeal, Park J first held that the reference in section 43 to 'disposition' was not to be extended by section 272 to a disposition made by associated operations. He also held that the right approach in applying section 64 was not to invoke the associated operations rule but to ask what property was comprised in the settlement at the relevant time. He went on to hold that the transfer of the shares was indeed associated with the transfer of the initial money, but that did not mean that there was one settlement rather than five. Park J's decision was upheld by the Court of Appeal, but only by considering what property was comprised in the settlement. Mummery LJ said that the associated operations rule was intended for cases where there was no relevant disposition at all—he agreed with Park J's concise and clear reasoning, but refrained from looking at the wider aspects raised by Park J.[12]

48.4.3 *Exercising the Power of Appointment: Sub-settlement or New Settlement?*

In the absence of any express statutory rule, the effect of the exercise of a power of appointment or advancement over settled property may be to bring a settlement to an end; however, much difficulty has arisen where the property is declared to be subject to new trusts— are these a continuation of the old trust, or the start of a new trust? This is a question of construction; the CGT case law (above §40.5) is used for IHT. However, as noted above, it appears that the sub-fund election introduced for CGT (TCGA 1992, section 69A) does not have any effect for IHT. Special provisions treat certain British government securities as excluded property and deal with the movement of such property between settlements.[13] There are also special rules for trusts where there is no interest in possession; here, it is expressly provided that the property is treated as remaining subject to the first settlement (section 81).

---

[11] [2003] EWCA Civ 356, [2003] STC 536; upholding [2002] EWHC ChD 1114, 2002 STC 872.
[12] [2003] EWCA Civ 356 at [25]–[26].
[13] IHTA 1984, s 44(2) makes these rules subject to s 48(4)–(6).

48.4.4 Trustees

The trustees of a settlement will normally be easily ascertained, but in the rare cases where there would otherwise be no trustees, 'trustees' are defined as any persons in whom the settled property or its management is for the time being vested.[14]

48.5   IHT and the Creation of a Settlement

48.5.1 Immediately Chargeable and Potentially Exempt Transfers

The creation of a settlement, whether by will or during lifetime, will usually be a transfer of value and so a chargeable transfer of value giving rise to tax.[15] When the settlement is a discretionary trust or, as a result of the 2006 changes, is one of those interest in possession trusts which are now treated in the same way as discretionary trusts, the transfer of value is immediately chargeable. Whether this gives rise to IHT will depend on the settlor's circumstances at that time. If a lifetime gift created an interest in possession before 22 March 2006 so that the old rules apply, the holder of that interest had his estate increased and the transfer was potentially exempt.[16] It followed that when the settlor made a settlement with an interest in possession in favour of someone else and died more than seven years after the creation of that settlement, no IHT will arise since it will have become an exempt transfer. This PET treatment was very favourable to those with money, as may be seen from the evidence given to the House of Lords Committee on the Finance Bill by the head of Tax Policy at HMRC, Mr Dave Hartnett, and discussed below (§48.6).

The 2006 rules do expressly allow PET treatment in two situations. The first is if it is a gift into a disabled trust, and the second is if it is a gift into a bereaved minor's trust or on the coming to an end of an immediate post-death interest. It will be appreciated that as an immediate post-death interest can arise only on death, its creation can never be a PET. The making of a settlement will not be a transfer of value if there is no loss to the transferor's estate. Thus, if Simon, S, settles property on himself for life, there is no transfer of value since a person beneficially entitled to an interest in possession is treated as beneficially entitled to the property in which the interest subsists (section 49(1)).

48.5.2 Settlor as Trustee

Where the settlor declares himself trustee of property for others, there will be a transfer of value since there is a reduction in the value of his estate. It appears that the settlor must pay on the grossed-up value of the settlement and that he cannot, *qua* trustee, pay tax on

---

[14] IHTA 1984, s 45. This ensures that there will always be some trustee as an accounting party liable for payment of IHT in respect of settled property (ss 199(4), 200(4), 201(1), 204(2), 216(1)(b)). The residence (and so the identity) of the trustees may affect the settlor's liability to pay the tax under s 201(1)(d).

[15] Under IHTA 1984, s 2 (lifetime) or s 4 (death).

[16] IHTA 1984, s 3A(2), added by FA 1987, Sch 19, para 1 for transfers after 16 March 1987. Transfers to accumulation and maintenance settlements and trusts for disabled persons could be PETs as from 1986 (IHTA 1984, s 3A(1)(c)).

the net transfer; it would be open for him to specify that the beneficiaries should pay the tax. While the settlor's declaration of trust will be a disposition and so a transfer of value, a mere covenant to settle which has effect simply in contract will not cause a transfer of value. This follows from the rule that while liabilities are deductible in computing the value of a person's estate—and so in determining whether there has been a loss in value—no deduction may be made for a liability except to the extent that it was incurred for a consideration in money or money's worth (section 5(5)). If the covenant to settle is construed as a completely constituted trust of a chose in action, the same result will follow since it is a completely constituted trust of a non-deductible liability.

48.5.3 Interaction with Income Tax

Statement of Practice SP 1/82 deals with the problem that arises if the trustees have power to pay (or do in fact pay) tax due on assets which the settlor transfers into the settlement. At first the Revenue took the view that this gave the settlor an interest in the income or property of the settlement. However, Statement of Practice SP 1/82 makes it clear that they will not treat the income of the settlement as that of the settlor for income tax purposes under the settlement provisions in ITTOIA 2005, Part 5, Chapter 5, solely because the trustees have power to pay or do in fact pay IHT on assets put into settlements.

48.5.4 PETs—Special Rate of Charge

Although the creation of the settlement might give rise to no charge because it was a PET, the rate of charge on a later chargeable event, such as the termination of an interest in possession, may attract a special rate of charge (see below at §49.5).

48.6   The 2006 Changes[17]

The policy of the 2006 changes is that trusts are to be accepted grudgingly and with suspicion. For far too long, trusts have been allowed to exist and, by a combination of rules, have paid little IHT. The position is well illustrated by the evidence of Mr Dave Hartnett of HMRC to the House of Lords Committee. He explained that, in Revenue thinking, there was not much difference between a discretionary trust and the 'flexible interest in possession trust':

> [A person] leaves the whole of his wealth on trust for his widow for life (this is an exempt transfer since she is treated as owning the underlying property and gifts to spouses are exempt).

So far so good. Then Mr Hartnett complains that the terms of the trust allow the trustees to do all sorts of things:

> Maybe the husband has left instructions. The sort of thing we see is that, almost the moment after the funeral, the trustees terminate the widow's life interest in the trust, the assets go to the children

---

[17] Tiley, *Parson's Lecture 2007*, available on the University of Sydney website at https://www.law.usyd.edu.au/parsons/pdfs/johntileylecture_290307.pdf.

or grandchildren and, prior to Budget 2006, provided the widow survives seven years, they all move tax free.[18]

Mr Hartnett also referred to a practice by which people had interests under trusts in everything—which, he had been told, was called 'Trustifarianism'. One may wonder whether what has changed is not the technique so much as the numbers of people taking advantage of those techniques, and the numbers of people with wealth in the first place. Then let us take Mr Hartnett's example of the termination of the widow's life interest and the absence of charge if she survives seven years. If I change two words—from 'husband' to 'grandfather' and from 'widow' to 'granny'—I can change the perception of risk of dying within seven years. There is little new about powers—there are all those wonderful 19th-century books on them. A power of appointment gave its holder extensive, even flexible, powers,[19] and the case law has explored the distinction between a dispositive power and an administrative power.[20] Whether more thought would have brought about a better balanced set of rules—and especially transitional rules—must await the unsealing of the records in 25 years' time.[21]

Whatever the reasoning, the effects are clear: a breach of neutrality. Today, if one wishes to give money to one's children, it is more advantageous—in fiscal terms—to make them entitled absolutely, since here PET treatment is still available. While one may wish to use the limited options of the immediate post-death interest, these are very limited.

[18] 22 May, p 110.
[19] *Pearson v IRC* [1981] AC 753 had drawn a distinction between a duty to accumulate, which prevented there being an interest in possession, and a power, which did not.
[20] And see Kessler, *Drafting Trusts and Will Trusts: A Modern Approach*, 8th edn (Thomson, 2007) ch 16.
[21] On lately discovered schemes, see 22 May, p 111; on difficulties with grandfathering, see 22 May, p 115.

49

Trusts with Interests in Possession

49.1 General Structure

The IHT legislation imposes a charge in a number of situations in which there is an interest in possession. In this chapter we look at those situations in which the person with such an interest is treated as having an interest in the settled property underlying that interest (section 49(1)). The principle was introduced into UK law with the advent of estate duty in 1894; its scope was greatly reduced in 2006, and we begin with that scope (§49.1.1). The amount of tax usually relates to the circumstances of the person with the interest in possession; however, the tax may be determined by reference to the circumstances of the settlor, ie where the settlement was created by a settlor who is still alive and the transfer creating the settlement was potentially exempt (see below §49.5).

49.1.1 The Post-2006 Regime[1]

Where a person becomes beneficially entitled to an interest in possession on or after 22 March 2006, the 1894 principle will apply only if and so long as: (a) it is an immediate post-death interest within section 49A; (b) it is a disabled person's interest as defined in section 89B; or (c) it comes within certain transitional rules compendiously referred to as transitional serial interests (TSIs).

49.1.1.1 An Immediate Post-death Interest (section 49A)

An immediate post-death interest arises where the settlement arises on a death, ie through a will or intestacy, and takes effect on the death of the testator or intestate. If the facts also fall—and continue to fall—within other specified provisions covered in chapter fifty-one below—IHTA 1984, sections 71A, 89A and 89B, as amended by FA 2006—those other provisions apply. So, if property is left to A for life and then to C, A's interest is an immediate post-death interest and the section 49 rules will apply. If A dies, the property then passing to C will be treated as part of A's estate. If property is left to A for life, then to B for life and then to C, A's interest may be an immediate post-death interest but B's is not. It follows that on A's death the rules in chapter fifty below will begin to apply to property in the trust unless B's interest qualifies under some other head, eg a disabled person's interest.

49.1.1.2 A Disabled Person's Interest

A disabled person's interest is defined by section 89 (below §51.4.4) and supplemented by section 89A, which allows a person with a condition expected to lead to disability to make a settlement in advance. The disabled person has an interest in possession which comes within section 49; moreover, the creation of such an interest may be a PET.

49.1.2 Transitional Rules

(1) Where a person became beneficially entitled to an interest in possession before 22 March 2006, section 49 treatment continues to apply. However, the rules in chapter fifty below apply as from the ending of that interest. Suppose that property was settled on trust in 1990 and X became entitled to a life interest in possession in 2004, the remainder being in favour of Y. Section 49 treatment will apply so long as X remain in possession. If X dies, the settled property forms part of his estate and will be taxed on passing to Y. If the property settled in 1990 was to be held for X for life, then passes to Y for life and then Z, and X dies in 2009, section 49 treatment will apply when X dies but the rules in chapter fifty apply as from then.

(2) Surviving spouse/civil partner rule (section 49D). Where P became beneficially entitled to an interest in possession before 22 March 2006 and on P's death Q, P's spouse or civil partner, takes over the successor interest, eg for life, section 49 treatment continues to apply under (1) for P but under section 49D for Q.

---

[1] IHTA 1984, ss 3A(1A), 49(1A), 89(2), 89A(4) and 89B.

A TSI may also arise under section 49D if the settlement itself began before 22 March 2006, if a person (E) becomes entitled to a beneficial interest in possession after 5 April 2008 and if the person with the beneficial interest in possession immediately before E was F, E's spouse or civil partner. So, if F became entitled in 2004 and E succeeds in 2009, E's interest is a TSI thanks to section 49D. If D was entitled in 2004 and F became entitled in 2007 and E in 2009, E will, however, not be able to take advantage of this if the marriage or partnership ends in 2008.

(3)   The years 2006–08 (section 49C). Where L became beneficially entitled to an interest in possession before 22 March 2006, and that interest came to an end before 6 October 2008 and the property then passed to M, section 49 treatment continues to apply to M's interest. This special provision gave people just over two years to adapt to the new rules, but only where the settlement had begun before 22 March 2006. The period was extended from 6 April to 6 October by FA 2008, section 141.

The legislation uses the characters 'B' and 'E', and so shall we. The first TSI arises (section 49C) if a person (B) becomes entitled to them between 22 March 2006 and 5 October 2008 (inclusive). The settlement itself must have begun before 22 March 2006, and at that time B or someone else must have been entitled to an interest in possession and B must have become beneficially entitled to that interest. Put shortly, B has a TSI if entitled immediately before 22 March 2006 or between then and 5 October 2008. The TSI remains a TSI as long as B holds it.

(4)   A TSI may also arise in connection with trusts of life insurance policies taken out— and settled—before 22 March 2006. Here, too, there is a two-and-a-half-year period of adjustment, so that C becomes entitled to it after 6 October 2008 on the coming to an end of another interest on the death of the person beneficially entitled to it (section 49E). It will be seen that both the taking out of the policy and the settlement of the policy must have taken place before 22 March 2006. It is common for life polices to allow variations, eg escalation of the premiums, during the life of the policy. Rules in sections 46A and 46 apply to allow these variations to continue after 21 March for life policies in which there is a permissible interest in possession or section 71 applied.

49.2   Interest in Possession

49.2.1   What Constitutes an Interest in Possession?

The existence of an interest in possession determines whether the trust is taxed under the rules in this chapter or those in chapter fifty below. It is therefore surprising that while there is a definition of such an interest for Scotland,[2] there is none for the rest of the United Kingdom. In ordinary property law, the term is used to distinguish present interests from

---

[2]   IHTA 1984, s 46 refers to an interest of any kind under a settlement actually being enjoyed by the person in right of that interest.

future interests, such as remainders or reversions. In ordinary property law, therefore, a gift to A for life but with power to pay the income over to someone else is an interest in possession notwithstanding its defeasibility;[3] different rules apply for IHT. A Scottish case has considered the nature of the rights of a beneficiary entitled to the free annual income of the trust fund but for her alimentary liferent use only. The Special Commissioner's analysis of those rights led him to conclude that she had an interest in possession.[4]

49.2.1.1 Power to Accumulate Prevents Possession

In *Pearson v IRC*,[5] property was held on trust for specified beneficiaries, subject to a power in the trustees to accumulate income for 21 years. In ordinary property law the interests of the beneficiaries would have been classified as being interests in possession. However, the House of Lords held that this power to accumulate prevented them from having such interests in possession. The basis for the view of the (bare) majority was that an interest in possession was one which gave a present right to present enjoyment. The beneficiaries had agreed that if there had been a duty to accumulate they would not have had a right to present enjoyment. The Revenue argued—successfully—that there was no difference between a duty to accumulate and a power, since the exercise of that power by the trustees would prevent the beneficiaries from having anything to enjoy.

49.2.1.2 Power to Advance Capital Does Not Prevent Possession

The House of Lords in *Pearson* also held that a power to advance capital to a remainderman would not have prevented the beneficiaries from having an interest in possession. This turns not, as it might be thought, on the need for the life tenant to give his consent to the exercise of the power to advance, but on the distinction between a power to terminate a present right to present enjoyment (eg advancement) and a power to prevent a present right of present enjoyment from arising (eg to accumulate).

49.2.1.3 Administrative (as Opposed to Dispositive) Power Does Not Prevent Possession

The decision in *Pearson* further holds that a power in the trustees to apply income to meet trust expenses, etc, does not prevent the life tenant from having an interest in possession. Although that power might be said to prevent a present right to present enjoyment, it does not have that effect since it is an administrative power as distinct from a dispositive power. This distinction is stated rather than explored in the speeches. Slightly more recently,[6] the Court of Session, in holding that a power to make a payment out of income in order to meet the depreciation of capital value was an administrative power, said that this was because it was not a power to increase the capital value of the estate by diverting the income to those in right of capital. A power to postpone sale was held to be dispositive in two cases but administrative in a third; clearly, all depends on the particular facts.[7]

---

[3] A has a right to the income once the period for the trustees to exercise their discretion has expired (*Re Allen-Meyrick's Will Trust* [1966] 1 All ER 740).

[4] *Trustees of Fairburn or Douglas Trust v HMRC* [2007] SpC 593, [2007] STC 328.

[5] [1980] STC 318, [1980] 2 All ER 479; see Murphy 43 *MLR* 712.

[6] *Miller v IRC* [1987] STC 108.

[7] *IRC v Lloyds Private Banking* [1998] STC 559 (dispositive) *Woodhall v IRC* [2000] STC (SCD) 558 (administrative) and *Faulkner v IRC* [2001] STC (SCD) 112 (administrative).

49.2.1.4 A Right to Income Under the Trustee Act 1925, Section 31(1)(ii)

This right creates an interest in possession.[8] If A has a life interest and there is no power to withhold income from him short of depriving him of capital, he has an interest in possession, notwithstanding that no income may in fact arise. Where there is a duty to distribute the income among a class and, at the relevant time, there is only one person in the class, but there is a chance that others may be added to it as the class is not closed, that one person does not have an interest in possession.[9] When trustees appoint property to a beneficiary but resolve to make the payment only after receiving an indemnity from the appointee, it is a question of construction whether the interest in possession arises at the time of the resolution or on receipt of the indemnity.[10]

49.2.1.5 Statement of Practice SP 10/79—Allowing a Beneficiary to Occupy a Dwelling House

Under Statement of Practice SP 10/79, where trustees have power to allow a beneficiary to occupy a house forming part of trust property simply as they think fit, the existence of the power prevents there being an interest in possession in the property. Statement of Practice SP 10/79 goes on to state the Revenue view that no interest in possession in the property in question arises if the effect of the exercise of the power is merely to allow non-exclusive occupation or to create a contractual tenancy for full consideration. Similarly, no interest in possession arises on the creation of a lease for a term or a periodic tenancy for less than full consideration, though this will normally give rise to a charge for tax under section 65(1)(b). However, an interest in possession is normally treated as arising if the power is drawn in terms wide enough to cover the creation of an exclusive or joint residence, albeit revocable, for a definite or indefinite period, and is exercised with the intention of providing a particular beneficiary with a permanent home. If the trustees, in exercise of their powers, grant a lease for life for less than full consideration, this will also be regarded as creating an interest in possession in view of section 43(3). A similar view is taken where the power is exercised over property in which another beneficiary had an interest in possession up to the time.

49.2.1.6 Purchased Interest in Possession

FA 2010 made changes to prevent unfair advantage being taken of the interaction of the rules on PETs and section 52. Under section 3A(6A), a transfer of value under section 52 will no longer be potentially exempt if the interest is part of the person's estate through section 5(1B), also added by FA 2010. Section 5(1B) brings into the estate an interest to which a UK domiciled person is entitled and that person acquired that interest in an arm's-length transaction (as defined in section 10). In these circumstances, the rule in section 49(1A) applies and the person is treated as owning the underlying property. There are related change to a number of other provisions, including sections 51, 52, 57A, 101 and 102(ZA).

---

[8] *Swales v IRC* [1984] STC 413.
[9] *Moore and Osborne v IRC* [1984] STC 236.
[10] *Stenhouse's Trustees v Lord Advocate* [1984] STC 195.

49.2.2 *Estates in Administration*

Under general property rules, a person having an interest in possession in the residuary estate of a testator which is still being administered does not have an interest in the property but only a right of action against the executor to ensure due administration.[11] However, for the purposes of IHT, the residuary estate is to be treated as if it had been administered. The interest is deemed to exist from the date when the beneficiary became entitled to income from the residue, which will usually be the date of death (section 91). Where the person who dies before the administration is complete would have become entitled to an interest in possession in the settled property, the extent of that person's interest in the income of the estate must be ascertained. This can raise complex calculation issues.[12]

The position of one entitled to an interest in a specific or pecuniary legacy is unclear in theory;[13] there is no special IHT provision.

Where property is held for a person conditional upon surviving the testator for a certain period, a settlement would normally be created by reason of the condition. Section 91(2) therefore provides that if the period does not exceed six months, the resulting disposition which takes effect, whether on surviving the six months or prior to death, is treated as having had effect from the beginning of the period. However, section 92 does not affect the application of tax to any distribution or application of property before the disposition takes effect.

49.3   Extent of Entitlement

A person beneficially entitled to an interest in possession in settled property is treated as beneficially entitled to the property in which the interest subsists (section 49(1)). It follows that if A dies leaving a free estate of £250,000, and was also life tenant of a fund the value of which was £130,000, he is treated as beneficially entitled to the whole of the property comprised in the settlement at his death, making a total transfer of property worth £380,000. Normally the rate of tax is related to the circumstances of the person entitled to the interest in possession; a special rule sometimes directs that the rate is taxed by reference to the circumstances of the settlor (see below §49.5). More than one person may be entitled to the interest. If property is settled on X for life, remainder to Y, and X declares himself trustee of his interest for P and Q, P and Q are together beneficially entitled to the interest in the settled property.

---

[11] *Stamp Duties Commr (Queensland) v Livingston* [1965] AC 694, [1964] 3 All ER 692.

[12] IHTA 1984, s 91(2) requires the exclusion not only of property devolving on the beneficiary otherwise than as assets for the payment of debts, but also property that is the subject of a 'specific' disposition. 'Due allowance' must also be made for outstanding charges on residue, and for any adjustments between capital and income remaining to be made in due course of administration. Following income tax rules, as required by IHTA 1984, s 91(2)(c), this would require an allowance to be made for specific dispositions, for annuities, for general and demonstrative legacies, statutory legacies on an intestacy, for funeral, testamentary and administration expenses, debts and liabilities, and any apportionment required between capital and income, eg under *Allhusen v Whittell* (1867) LR 4 Eq 295.

[13] See *Re Leigh's Will Trusts* [1969] 3 All ER 432; 86 *LQR* 20.

Where a person is entitled to part only of the income, his interest is treated as subsisting in that part of the property comprised in the settlement which corresponds with his share of the income (section 50(1)). Thus, a half share in the income gives rise to half shares in the capital. Where the part of the income is a specified amount, for example an annuity of £100, or the whole income less a specified amount, for example to B for life subject to the payment of an annuity of £100 to A, the interest corresponds with that part of the property which produces that income (section 50(2)). Where the annuity is fixed and the income of the fund is constant, no difficulty will be encountered in discovering the shares of capital. However, where the income fluctuates, the shares of A and B will vary from time to time. If A were old or critically ill, it would be in the interests of the trust to increase the income of the trust substantially so as to reduce the proportion of trust income needed to pay A's annuity; the opposite would arise if B were old or critically ill. In order to counter such arrangements, the Treasury prescribe higher and lower rates by statutory instrument (section 50(3)). The higher or maximum rate is applied in relation to A and IHT is charged as if the rate of return were that maximum rate.

Example 1

Under a settlement worth £200,000, A receives an annuity of £2,000 pa whilst B receives the balance of income. Out of the £40,000 income, A receives £2,000 and B £38,000. If A's interest terminates when the higher rate is 15%, A's share will not be taken as 2,000/40,000 of £200,000 = £10,000. The higher rate of 15% allows only a notional income of £30,000 instead of the actual £40,000 income. Thus, A's share is taken as 2,000/30,000 of £200,000 = £13,333.

It is expressly provided that the value taken as a result of this rule is not to exceed 100% of the settled property.

Example 2

Under a settlement worth £200,000, A receives an annuity of £32,000 pa whilst B receives the balance of income. Out of the £40,000 income, A receives his £32,000 and B £8,000. If A's interest terminates when the higher rate is 15%, A's share will not be taken as 32,000/40,000 of £200,000 = £160,000. On applying the higher rate of 15% as the maximum allowable yield a notional £30,000 income only is allowed, but 32,000/30,000 of £200,000 would result in a chargeable value of £213,333, which is £13,333 more than the whole capital value. Accordingly, A's share is treated as no greater than the whole capital value of £200,000. The lower or minimum rate is applied in relation to B.

Example 3

Under a settlement worth £200,000, A receives an annuity of £2,000 pa and B receives the balance of income. Out of the £6,000 income, B thus receives £4,000. If B's interest terminates when the lower rate is 5%, B's share will not be taken as 4,000/6,000 of £200,000 = £133,333. The lower rate of 5% treats a notional income of £10,000 to have arisen instead of the actual £6,000 income. Thus B's share is taken as 8,000/10,000 of £200,000 = £160,000.

However, neither of these rates applies where the chargeable transfers are made simultaneously and the tax is chargeable by reference to the interests of both A and B, as where both interests end on the death of X and the property then vests in C. In such circumstances the Revenue will collect tax on 100% anyway.

The higher rate is the yield on the FT Actuaries Share Index for irredeemable gilts; the lower rate is the gross dividend yield of the All-Share Index. The relevant rates are those for the date of the transfer.[14] These rules are similar to those evolved by the courts (see below §57.3.2). Although the legislation does not define how income is to be computed, presumably the income of the trust is taken after the deduction of trust expenses, but ignoring income tax, and this is compared with the rights of A and B, again before income tax. However, there are other possibilities. Concessionary relief is available when the annuitant dies or disposes of his interest and the annuity is charged in whole or in part on land. Where the capital valuation reflects an anticipated increase in rents available for use after the date of the transfer, 'appropriate' relief is given in calculating the proportion of the property on which tax is chargeable.[15]

Where the person entitled to the interest in possession is not entitled to any income but is entitled jointly or in common with one or more others to the use and enjoyment of the property, his interest is that proportion which the annual value of his interest bears to the aggregate of all their interests (section 50(5)). This applies only where the person is not entitled to the income, presumably because if he could turn his enjoyment into income, as by selling the asset and taking income from the proceeds of sale or by leasing it (eg by virtue of the powers conferred on the tenant for life under a strict settlement within the Settled Land Act 1925), the matter would fall within the previous rules. For the same reason, someone solely entitled to the use of property is not within this rule. Where the rule applies, annual value is presumably to be determined by reference to actual enjoyment of the property, but this is unclear. If A and B are entitled to a picture and B allows A to have the whole use of it, it is unclear whether A has all the interest or whether A and B each have 50%.

For extent of charge on a lease for lives, see above at §48.3.

49.4 Transfers of Settled Property with Interest in Possession

49.4.1 General

On the death of a person beneficially entitled to an interest in possession, the settled property, or, where appropriate, the relevant portion of that property, is treated as forming part of his estate under section 4; on aggregation, see §44.4.3. Such a transfer is not a PET and normal death rates will apply.

Certain events are treated as lifetime transfers of value by the person (A) beneficially entitled to the interest in possession (sections 51 and 52). From 17 March 1987 to 21 March 2006, most of these could be PETs and so no tax was due at that time (section 3A(6)). If A died within seven years, A's circumstances usually determine the rate of tax payable and whether any exemptions or reliefs apply. (For an exception where a trust is created by a PET and the settlor is still alive, see below at §49.5.) If the lifetime transfer is immediately chargeable and the principle in section 49 applies, the total transferred is added to A's lifetime total of chargeable transfers for the purpose of determining liability on any subsequent transfer. However, there is no grossing up.

---

[14] CTT (Settled Property Income Yield) Order 1980 (SI 1980/1000) (modified by SI 2000/174).
[15] ESC F11.

49.4.2 *Lifetime Termination of Beneficial Entitlement*

Where, at any time during the life of a person (A) beneficially entitled to an interest in possession, the interest comes to an end, eg A's interest ends on marriage, IHT is charged under section 52 as if A had then made a transfer of an amount corresponding to the value of the property in which his interest subsisted. In practice the settled property is valued in isolation without reference to any similar property.[16]

Where the interest mentioned is one to which A became beneficially entitled after 21 March 2006, a charge arises in relation to the coming to an end of the interest only if the interest comes within section 49, ie it is an immediate post-death interest, a disabled person's interest or a TSI. If the interest is not in this list there will be no charge on the underlying settled property under section 52—though there may be an exit charge under the rules examined in chapter fifty. The transfer will be a PET if it ceases to be settled property and so passes to an individual absolutely; this is because it counts as a gift. It is also a PET if it is a gift into a bereaved minor's trust on the coming to an end of an immediate post-death interest.

Planners often prefer A to terminate his interest during lifetime rather than on death. This is partly because of the PET status and partly because of the exemptions (such as the annual and marriage exemptions), which apply to lifetime endings but not on death. Another reason is that, as just seen, under section 52 only the trust property is valued. Thus, suppose that A held shares in a company, and that of the 100 issued shares, 33 were held by A's trust and 33 by A directly. On A's death the trust would be liable to pay IHT on one half of the value of a 66% holding, whereas under section 52 tax is due only on a 33% holding.[17]

Examples

(1) Property falling within section 49 is held on trust for C for the life of X, with remainder to B. C dies in 2009; X dies in 2011. On C's death there is a transfer by C under section 4. However, as a result of the 2006 changes, the trust will normally pass beyond the scope of section 49 on C's death and so fall under the rules set out in chapter fifty. On X's death the rules in chapter fifty will cease to apply and there will be an exit charge, as the property goes into the estate of B.

(2) Property falling within section 49 is held on trust for A for life, with remainder to B for life, with remainder to C. B dies; A dies. On B's death there is no charge on the settled property since B was not entitled in possession; on A's death there is a charge as in (1) under section 4.

(3) Property settled in 1980 is held on trust for A for life or until remarriage, with remainder on discretionary trusts. A remarries in 2004. There is a charge under section 52 and it cannot be a PET as a discretionary trust is created. If the remainder had not been on discretionary trusts but had passed in 2004 to N for life, there would have been a charge under section 52 and it would have been a PET.

---

[16] Inland Revenue Press Release, May 1990, [1990] *Simon's Tax Intelligence* 446.
[17] Potter and Monroe, *Tax Planning* (Sweet & Maxwell, 1982), §6.03/04; on CGT, see *ibid*, §6-13.

49.4.3 Disposal of Interest by Person Beneficially Entitled: Deemed Termination of Interest

49.4.3.1 The Disposal

Where the person beneficially entitled to an interest in possession does not wait for it to end but disposes of it, there is a charge under section 51 on the value of the settled property underlying his interest. It follows that the disposal is not treated as a transfer of value equal to the actuarial value of his actual interest. Before 22 March 2006 the transfer could be a PET (section 3A(2)). Where the interest mentioned is one to which A became beneficially entitled after 21 March 2006, a charge arises under section 51 in relation to the coming to an end of the interest only if the interest comes within section 49, ie it is an immediate post-death interest, a disabled person's interest or a TSI.[18] There is no transfer of value under section 51 if the person became beneficially entitled to the interest before 22 March 2006 and, immediately before the disposal, the property fell within section 71A (trust for bereaved minors) or section 71D (age 18 to 25 trust).[19] The disposal of the interest may be by assignment or, perhaps, by surrender; it may be voluntary or involuntary. If it results in the destruction of the interest, as on surrender, it is probably also an actual termination of the interest and comes within section 52.[20]

49.4.3.2 Consideration Provided in Return for Value Transferred

Where the disposal is for a consideration in money or money's worth, tax is charged as if the value transferred were reduced by the amount of the consideration (section 52(2)). However, in determining the value of that consideration, the value of any reversionary interest in the property or of any interest in any other property comprised in the same settlement is left out of account. Presumably the reference to any interest in any other property covers not just reversionary interests, but also, say, a life interest in another part of the settlement.

49.4.3.3 Partition

If property is settled on A for life, A's interest being one within section 49, with remainder to B, and there is a partition of the property, the value of B's interest is not treated as consideration for the disposal of the life interest; hence there is a deemed transfer of value of the property allotted to B but not that allotted to A (section 53(2)) (see below at §49.6.1). If B provides A not with an interest under the settlement but with full market value in cash, there will inevitably be a charge since the market value of A's life interest must be less than the full value of the settled property. However, B is also treated as making a transfer of value if he pays a sum equal to the value of the underlying settled property (section 49(2)). Such partitions or purchases made before 22 March 2006 would have been PETs (section 49(3)).

49.4.4 Depreciatory Transactions Reducing Value of Settled Property

A charge arises under section 52(3) where a depreciatory transaction is entered into between (a) the trustees, and (b) any beneficiary or potential beneficiary, or any person connected

---

[18] IHTA 1984, s 51(1A), added by FA 2006.
[19] IHTA 1984, s 51(1B), added by FA 2006.
[20] This is of importance in connection with the exemption in IHTA 1984, s 51(2), referring to s 11.

therewith. For example, under an express authorisation in the trust instrument, trustees might sell property at an undervalue or lease at a low rent, eg by allowing a beneficiary to occupy a house under a lease at less than the rack rent (see §49.2 above), or lend money for a fixed period at well below market rates without being in breach of trust. To the extent that such a transaction reduces the value of the settled property which will be chargeable to tax at some future date, section 52(3) deems a partial termination of the interest in possession in the property. The beneficiary with the interest is deemed to be the transferor in respect of this transfer of value (section 3(4)).

The transaction will not constitute a notional termination, however, if it would not be a transfer of value if the trustees had been beneficially entitled themselves, eg where the transaction was not intended to confer any gratuitous benefit and was such as might be expected to be made in a transaction at arm's length between persons not connected with each other (sections 52(3) and 10). It is thought (by the Revenue) that a payment out of capital to augment the income of a beneficiary other than one with an interest in possession falls within section 52(1) rather than section 52(3).[21] Once more it is assumed that the beneficiary has an interest falling within section 49. So, where the interest is one to which the person became beneficially entitled after 21 March 2006, that subsection applies in relation to the transaction only if the interest is (a) an immediate post-death interest, (b) a disabled person's interest, or (c) a TSI. If the interest is not in this list, the settlement falls within the rules in chapter fifty below, which have their own depreciatory transaction rule.

49.4.5 *Close Companies*

Transfers of value by close companies may be apportioned to the participators. Where the participator is a settlement, the transfer may be apportioned to the person with the beneficial interest in possession. Such a transfer has never been a PET (see below §52.3.2). Where there is a variation in the rights attached to securities in a close company and this is treated as a deemed disposal by the participators, the loss in value will be treated, where there is an interest in possession, as though that interest had come to an end to the extent of that loss (section 101). Again, such a transfer has never been a PET (see below §52.3.2).

49.5 Alternative Charge Using Settlor's Circumstances Where Transfer Creating Settlement a PET

49.5.1 *Background*

As a consequence of the introduction of the PET rule into the area of settled property in 1987, a special rate of charge may apply where a chargeable transfer of settled property follows a PET creating the settlement (section 54A). This charge is an alternative to the general rule; it applies only if it would give rise to a greater amount of tax. Today PET treatment is restricted; statute therefore provides that where the person became entitled to the interest

---

[21] See letter on the exercise of a power to augment income from capital; *Law Society's Gazette*, 5 November 1975; see also Statement of Practice SP E6.

after 21 March 2006, this charge applies only if the relevant interest was a disabled person's interest or a TSI (section 54A(1)).

The reason behind the rule is apparently to prevent a settlor, S, from gaining an advantage by creating a discretionary trust subject to an initial life interest in favour, say, of A, as distinct from creating one immediately. The advantage would be that S could avoid his personal cumulative total being used to calculate the tax on the chargeable (not potentially exempt) transfer arising on the creation of the discretionary trusts. This could be achieved by settling the property on trusts such that, before the discretionary trusts arise, there is a short interest in possession in favour of A, a person who, it is hoped, will have a cumulative total of zero by the time the interest in possession terminates and the discretionary trusts arise.

49.5.2 Five Conditions

The five conditions which trigger this charge are cumulative (section 54A(2)):

(1)   The creation of the settlement must have been a PET. If only part of the transfer was potentially exempt, the legislation uses the concept of 'special rate property' (section 54B(3)). The burden of the tax falls exclusively on this part of the settled property (section 265).

(2)   The ending of the interest in possession or death of the life tenant must occur within seven years of the PET by which the settlement was made.

(3)   The settlor must be alive at the time of the ending of the interest or the death of the life tenant.

(4)   On that termination or death, the property must become settled property in which no qualifying interest in possession subsists (other than an accumulation and maintenance settlement). Thus, the charge applies where property is settled by S on A for life with remainder over on discretionary trusts, and A dies within seven years or releases the life interest. There will be a chargeable transfer in either of these events; it cannot be a PET by A since the property does not become part of the estate of any other person.

(5)   The property must not have become settled property in which an interest in possession subsists or which is an accumulation and maintenance settlement, or become property to which an individual is beneficially entitled within six months of the termination. This rule, added late in the legislative process, gives the trust six months to escape from the special rate.

49.5.3 The Charge

The alternative charge assumes a hypothetical transfer by a person with a cumulative total of chargeable transfers equal to that of S's cumulative total at the time the settlement was created; this total includes any sums already caught by these rules (section 54B(4)–(6)). Lifetime rates are applied (section 54A(6)). The amount of tax is calculated that would have been due if the original transfer in trust had been chargeable and not potentially exempt, although using the current and not the original value of the settled property. If this tax would be greater, the greater amount is due now (section 54A(5)). The tax is due primarily from the trustees of the settlement (section 54B(3)). The charge applies only where S is still alive. If S should die later, but within seven years of the settlement, extra tax may be due from the settlement (section 54B(1)). Conversely, if A's interest ends but A dies within seven years, additional tax may also be due (section 54B(2)). These deaths are ignored in determining the sum initially due under these rules.

49.6 Exceptions to Charge Under Sections 52 and 51

49.6.1 *Beneficiary Entitled to Property or, Rarely, to Another Interest in Possession in Property*

This exception is dictated by the logic of the charge on interests in possession. Under section 53(2), if property is held on trust for A for life and the interest falls within section 49, A is treated as beneficially entitled to the whole property. It is not necessary that the new interest should arise under the terms of the settlement, so no charge arises whether the property is appointed to A under a power in the settlement or A partitions the property with the remainder man and becomes entitled to a capital sum absolutely. Equally, the exercise of a power to augment the tenant for life's income from capital causes no charge under these heads.[22] At one time section 53(2) also applied where the person with the interest in possession became entitled not absolutely but to another interest in possession in the settled property. A restriction applied, in that if the value of the property to which he became entitled was less than the value on which tax would otherwise be chargeable, tax was chargeable on the difference (section 52(4)(b)). Thus, if A was entitled to a life interest in the whole of the property until marriage, but that interest was to be reduced to two-thirds on marriage, there would, in the event of marriage, be a transfer of one-third of the settled property.

Where A became beneficially entitled after 21 March 2006 to an interest in possession in settled property, there is no charge if the new interest in possession is a disabled person's interest.[23] There is also no transfer of value under these sections if the person became beneficially entitled to the interest before 22 March 2006 and, immediately before the disposal, the property fell within section 71A (trust for bereaved minors) or section 71D (age 18 to 25 trust).[24] There is also no transfer of value under these provisions if an interest in possession comes to an end and the beneficiary under that interest becomes entitled to a new interest in possession, and the new interest in possession is either a disabled person's interest under section 89B or a TSI under sections 49C–49E.[25]

Example (assuming all events occurred before 22 March 2006)

S, who has made chargeable transfers of £350,000, settled £100,000 on A for life with remainder to B, and directed the trustees to pay the tax on the transfer. Five years later the

---

[22] Statement of Practice SP E6.
[23] IHTA 1984, s 53(2A), added by FA 2006.
[24] IHTA 1984, s 51(1B), added by FA 2006.
[25] IHTA 1984, s 53(2A), as amended FA 2008, s 140.

fund was still worth £100,000. A and B agreed to divide it equally. A had made previous transfers of £20,000, B of £1m. When S created the settlement he made a PET of £100,000; his total then rose to £450,000. When A and B divided the fund there was a termination of A's interest in £100,000 (section 52) but tax was not chargeable under section 52 on the half which A took. Since A's transfer to B of the other half, ie £50,000, was a PET, A's total remained at £20,000. IHT may become due if A dies within seven years.

49.6.2 Reversion to Settler

IHT is not chargeable if the interest falling within section 49 comes to an end during the settlor's life and on the same occasion reverts to the settlor. The purpose of this relief is to enable persons to provide life interests for relatives without charge to tax; however, this relief is not confined to such transfers and does not preclude a charge on the creation of the settlement. This exception applies only where the reversion is during the life of the settlor.

The exception is lost if the settlor acquired a reversionary interest in the property for money or money's worth (section 53(5)(a)). Thus, if the property was settled on B for life with remainder to C absolutely, the exception would not apply on the ending of B's interest in possession if S, the settlor, had bought C's remainder. However, if S had acquired the remainder by way of gift from C, the exception would apply. It appears that the purchase of any reversionary interest is fatal. If B's life interest had been preceded by a life interest to A, and S had then bought B's interest and been given C's interest, the exception would have been lost even though B predeceased A without his interest ever vesting in possession.

The exception is also lost if the reversionary interest has itself been settled (section 53(5)(b)). Property might be settled on A for life, remainder to B; B would then settle the remainder on C for life with remainder to B. While there would be a charge when A died, there would not be when B created the settlement since the subject matter was excluded property; neither would there be a charge when C died, thus leaving B free to enjoy the income after A's death without risk of IHT after the creation of the settlement. The effect is that there is a charge on C's death.

49.6.3 Transfer on Termination to the Settlor's Spouse or Civil Partner

Since a reversion to the settlor is the subject of the exception just considered and a transfer between spouses or civil partners is exempt, section 53(4) is logical in providing that tax is not chargeable under sections 52 or 51 if, on the occasion when the interest comes to an end, the settlor's spouse or civil partner becomes beneficially entitled to the settled property. However, the exception applies for a limited period after the death of the settlor, in that spouse or civil partner for this purpose includes widow or widower or surviving civil partner if the settlor has died less than two years before the interest ends.

The exception is lost if the settlor or the spouse/civil partner acquired a reversionary interest for consideration in money or money's worth (section 53(5)(a)). Moreover, this exception is also lost if the spouse/civil partner was not, at the relevant time, domiciled in the UK (section 53(4), since the general spouse/civil partner exemption applies only if the transferee is domiciled here), or lost if the reversionary interest has itself been settled (section 53(5)(b)).

49.6.4 Miscellaneous Exceptions

49.6.4.1 Disposition to Provide Family Maintenance

Where a disposition for the maintenance of a family satisfied the conditions of section 11 but amounts to the disposal of an interest in possession, and so would be treated as a termination, the interest is not treated as coming to an end (section 51(2)). This applies to partial terminations as well as to total terminations, as where a father tenant for life consents to an advance of capital to enable the outright purchase of an annuity to cover his son's future public school fees.

49.6.4.2 Disclaimer

On a disclaimer made otherwise than for consideration in money or money's worth, the person disclaiming is treated as never having become entitled to the interest.[26] A disclaimer cannot be made once the gift has been accepted; surrender is not a disclaimer. A variation relating to settled property cannot take advantage of section 142 (section 142(5)).

49.6.4.3 Trustees' Annuities

Under section 90, where a person is entitled to an interest in settled property as remuneration for his services as trustee, tax is not charged on the termination of that interest to the extent that it represents a reasonable amount of remuneration. This exclusion does not apply if the trustee disposes of the right. In valuing the interest of the trustee as opposed to the beneficiary, it is presumably possible to make allowance for that proportion of the trust income needed for the trustee's annuity.

49.6.4.4 Order Under the Inheritance (Provision for Family and Dependants) Act 1975

An order under this Act terminating an interest in possession gives rise to no charge (section 146(6)).

49.6.4.5 Redemption of Life Interest on Intestacy

Where A, the surviving spouse or civil partner of an intestate, has a life interest in possession and exercises her statutory right to redeem her life interest for a capital sum, she is to be treated as always having been entitled to the capital sum and so not as having been entitled to the interest in possession (section 145). Presumably this exemption applies only if the redemption takes place under Administration of Estates Act 1925, section 47A; hence, a simple partition, as opposed to redemption, will not be exempt under this rule.

49.6.4.6 Excluded Property

Tax is not charged under section 52 if the settled property is excluded property (section 53(1)).[27]

---

[26] IHTA 1984, s 93; *Re Sharman's Will Trusts* [1942] Ch 311, [1942] 2 All ER 74.
[27] On excluded property, see IHTA 1984, s 48.

49.7   Interaction of Settled Property Rules and Exempt Transfer Rules

Exempt transferees. While sections 18 and 23–27 may apply to transfers of settled property, there are a certain number of restrictions (see further below at §53.2). However, these restrictions do not apply to a transfer of value consisting of the use of money or other property being allowed by one person to another (section 56(6)).

Transfer to spouse. The exemption in section 18 may apply when the settled property passes from a beneficiary with an interest in possession to that beneficiary's spouse or civil partner.

Example

Property falling within section 49 is held on trust for H for life, with remainder to J. H transfers his life interest to Mrs H. Later, Mrs H consents to the power of advancement being exercised in favour of J. H's disposal of his life interest in possession to his spouse is an exempt transfer.[28] When Mrs H consents to the advancement there is a termination of her interest and so a charge under section 52 to the extent of the property advanced, assuming that her interest comes within section 49.

However, the exemption does not apply to property which is given in consideration of the transfer of a reversionary interest which, thanks to section 55(1), does not form part of the estate of the person acquiring it (section 56(1); see below at §49.9.3). Similarly, section 18 does not apply where a person acquires a reversionary interest in any settled property for a consideration in money or money's worth if and when it becomes the property of that person on the termination of the interest on which the reversionary interest is expectant (see below at §§49.9.4 and 53.2.1).[29]

Other favoured transfers: sections 23–27. The exemptions for transfers to charities, political parties, housing associations, or for national purposes and maintenance fund for historic buildings, etc, do not apply to property which is given in consideration of the transfer of a reversionary interest which, under section 55(1), does not form part of the estate of the person acquiring it (section 56(1)). See further §53.2.2.

Annual exemption: section 19. The beneficiary with an interest in possession may use the £3,000 annual exemption in relation to trust property, provided notice is given by the transferor to the trustees who, in turn, give notice to the Revenue within six months of the transfer.[30]

Marriage or civil partnership: section 57. The marriage or civil partnership exemption is adapted (section 57(2)). References to transfers of value made by gifts in consideration of marriage or civil partnership are read as references to the termination of such interests in consideration of marriage or civil partnership. References to outright gifts are read as references to cases where the property ceases on the termination to be settled property.

---

[28] Because of IHTA 1984, s 18.

[29] IHTA 1984, s 56(2). The exclusion of the exemption by s 56(2) does not apply if the reversionary interest was acquired before 16 April 1976; there is also a modification if the acquisition was before 12 April 1978 (s 56(7)).

[30] IHTA 1984, s 57(1), (3), (4).

References to cases where the property is settled by the gift are read as references to cases where it remains settled property after the termination.

Heritage. Other rules concern maintenance funds for heritage buildings (sections 57(5), 57A).

Reliefs not available. There is no relief under section 20 (small gifts), nor under section 11, except as allowed by section 51(2).

Transitional: earned surviving spouse relief. Where a person died before 13 November 1974 and left property to his spouse for life in circumstances qualifying for the old estate duty exemption, and the surviving spouse's interest terminates, no tax is chargeable. This applies whether the termination is on death or otherwise (Schedule 6, paragraph 2). It is understood that there are still some estates where this is a live issue.

49.8 Quick Succession Relief

Where section 49 interests are in issue—and so transfers may be related to particular individuals—quick succession relief is given under IHTA 1984, on the same basis as at §46.6 above. However, it applies whether or not the transfer is on death, provided it is settled property in which the transferor had an interest in possession and provided the first transfer was either the creation of the settlement or some subsequent event. This may still be of practical importance for some years.

Example

Property is inherited by S in year 1; in year 2 he settled it on P for life with remainder to Q; in year 3 P surrendered the life interest; in year 4 Q gives to the property to R.

No credit is available on the transfer in year 2 as it was an inter vivos transfer. In year 3 credit was available, but only for the tax from year 2—not that from year 1 since that was prior to the creation of the settlement. No credit was available in year 4 since the transfer was not then of settled property in which Q had an interest in possession.

If some of the credit remains unused after the first subsequent transfer, it may be rolled on to the next and so on, in sequence. The credit is used to the extent to which it is covered by the relief given. If £10,000 credit is available and £4,000 relief is given on tax of £5,000 in year 2 (ie 80% of £5,000), only £5,000 remains to be rolled forward—and to be subject to further percentage reductions.

49.9 Reversionary Interests in Settled Property

49.9.1 *Definition*

A reversionary interest is defined as a future interest under a settlement, whether vested or contingent. It therefore includes an interest expectant on the termination of a lease treated as a settlement under section 43(3), eg a lease for life at a nominal rent.

A future interest must be distinguished from a mere hope of succeeding. Thus, where property is settled on A for life with remainder to Y, but with overriding power for the trustees to appoint capital to such of B to X as they see fit, B merely has a hope, whilst Y has the reversionary interest.

49.9.2 *Reversionary Interest as Excluded Property*

Subject to exceptions, section 48(1) makes a reversionary interest excluded property. The purpose of this rule is to prevent double charging to IHT. Thus, if property was settled on A for life with remainder to B, and B died before A, the effect of section 48(1) is that there would be no transfer on B's death of B's reversionary interest in the settled property, the Revenue being content to wait to tax the transfer of the property on the termination of A's interest.

Since the general immunity of reversionary interests is open to exploitation, section 48(1) provides that a reversionary interest in settled property in the UK is not excluded property: (a) if it has at any time been acquired (whether by the person entitled to it or by a person previously entitled to it) for a consideration in money or money's worth; or (b) it is one to which either the settlor or his spouse or civil partner is or has been entitled under a settlement; or (c) if it is the interest expectant on the termination of a lease treated as a settlement, ie a lease for life at a nominal rent.

49.9.3 *Anti-avoidance: Purchase of Reversionary Interest*

49.9.3.1 The Rule

Section 55(1) provides that where a person entitled to an interest (whether or not in possession) in any settled property acquires a reversionary interest expectant (whether or not immediately) on that interest, the reversionary interest is not treated as part of that person's estate.

49.9.3.2 Simple Case—The Scheme

The purpose behind this rule is to prevent the avoidance of tax. If property worth £130,000 is held on trust for A for life, with remainder to B, and A has free estate worth £150,000, there will be a transfer of £280,000 on A's death. If A buys B's remainder for £70,000, the property will cease to be settled, but there will be no transfer of value in that event because, although A's life interest in the property terminates, he becomes on the same occasion absolutely entitled to it. When A dies, the formerly settled property will pass as his free estate. The avoidance consists in the fact that A purchases B's remainder for full consideration of £70,000. This has the effect of reducing the value of A's free estate by £70,000 to £80,000 so that on A's death the total value of the property transferred will be only £210,000 and not £280,000. Thus, A has depleted his free estate by a payment which is not a transfer of value and has replaced it with property which would have been chargeable in any event.

The legislative solution is to treat A's purchase of B's remainder as a transfer of value by A of the amount of the purchase price notwithstanding that full value has been given for the remainder. This is achieved by section 55(1), which directs that A's estate is not increased by the reversion, with the result that the money passing to B is pure loss to A's estate and so chargeable. Section 55(2) specifically excludes section 10, so that the fact the full value is given for the interest is irrelevant. The purchase was a PET if effected after 16 March 1987 but before 22 March 2006.

49.9.3.3 More Complex Case

Section 55(1) is also useful where A has both a life interest and a purchased remainder. Thus, suppose that property is settled on A for life, remainder to X for life, remainder to Y absolutely. On a purchase by A of Y's remainder, A will be deemed to make a gift to Y of the consideration he gives Y. However, owing to the purchase, the reversionary interest no longer ranks as excluded property and so forms part of A's estate in which the value of the settled property is already represented due to A's life interest in possession. Since A has already been charged with IHT in respect of the value of the reversionary interest, section 55(1) excludes the reversion from A's estate. A is thus deemed to have acquired nothing, so on a subsequent transfer of the reversion by A, eg on A's death, no transfer of value can arise since there can be no loss in the value of A's estate.

49.9.4 *Not Excluded Property if Settlor or Spouse/Civil Partner Entitled*

Exception (b), at §49.9.2 above, has the effect of treating a reversion falling within it as non-excluded property. If the settlor, S, settles property, say £100,000, on X for life with remainder to himself, the transfer by S is not of £100,000 but only of that sum less the (then) actuarial value of the reversion. It follows that if S then gives away the reversion there may be a charge to IHT; equally, it follows that if S sells it for full market value there will not.

This exception applies whenever S, or his spouse/civil partner, had at any time been entitled to the reversionary interest. Under the previous rule the interest would, as now, not be excluded property while S was alive; he could then leave the interest to his spouse/civil partner free of CTT. However, since a widow/surviving civil partner is not a spouse/civil partner, the interest becomes excluded property on reaching her. This rule makes sure that the reversion remains chargeable.

49.9.5 *Miscellaneous Rules for Reversionary Interests*

49.9.5.1 Quick Succession Relief

A reversionary interest which is excluded property does not increase the value of a person's estate for quick succession relief (section 141(6)).

49.9.5.2 Transitional (Pre-1974) Protection for Purchasers

Special provision was made to prevent purchasers or mortgagees of reversionary interests before 27 March 1974 being caught out by the then new CTT provisions. Their liability was not to exceed the amount of estate duty that would have been payable.[31] This also applies to IHT.

---

[31] IHTA 1984, Sch 6, para 3.

49.9.5.3 Foreign Element

On reversionary interests belonging to a person domiciled abroad, see chapter fifty-eight below.

49.9.5.4 Purchased Settlement Powers

As part of the fallout from the *Melville* litigation (§44.7.1 above), FA 2002 added IHTA 1984, section 55A. This applies where a person makes a disposition by which he acquires a 'settlement power' for consideration in money or money's worth.[32] The phrase 'acquires a settlement power' is widely defined (section 55A(2)). The person acquiring the power for consideration is treated as making a transfer of value, and the value transferred is determined without bringing into account the value of anything acquired on the disposition. Section 10(1) is excluded, as are various reliefs (to be found in sections 18 and 23–27). The purpose of this rule is to stop people buying settlement powers—and so depleting their estates—in return for something which is not property; the parallel with the provision on purchased reversions in underlined by the fact that they are now adjacent provisions. These amendments apply to transfers of value on or after 17 April 2002.

---

[32] Defined in IHTA 1984, s 47A.

50

Relevant Property Trusts with No Qualifying Interest in Possession

50.1   Introduction

The rules in IHTA 1984, sections 58–85 apply where property is settled but no qualifying interest in possession subsists in it, such as in the case of a discretionary trust. These rules apply only to 'relevant property', a term used to exclude certain situations which would otherwise come within the scope of the rules. Certain favoured trusts in which there are no interests in possession receive special and different treatment under sections 70–79 (see chapter fifty-one below). These rules apply whether the trust was created before or after 27 March 1974. The original CTT legislation contained severe rules for these trusts, which were drastically mitigated in 1982. The current rules apply to events after 8 March 1982, although changes have been made by FA 1986 as from 18 March 1986 to take account of the reduction of the basic cumulation period for transfers by individuals from 10 years to seven.[1] Importantly, the FA 2006 reforms to the IHT treatment of trusts shifted many trusts with interests in possession from the regime in section 49 (first established in 1894 and discussed in the previous chapter) and into the relevant trust regime discussed in this chapter. These reforms caused much outrage at the time. However, the relevant trust rules are in some ways quite arbitrary and therefore may be turned to advantage.[2]

---

[1] FA 1986, s 101 and Sch 19.
[2] See generally Venables, *Taxation of Trusts* (Key Haven, 2007) and Kessler, *Drafting Trusts and Will Trusts: A Modern Approach*, 8th edn (Thomson, 2007).

A discretionary trust may be ideal if the asset to be settled is cash or a non-chargeable asset (eg an insurance policy or a reversionary interest under another settlement) and the initial value is low. This ideal state is achieved by taking advantage of the complicated computation rules and IHT features such as the seven-year cumulation period. Such low-value discretionary trusts attract very little tax. Although the maximum rate of the 10-year charge is 6% this is the maximum rate; for modest trusts the rate can be easily reduced to zero. As will be seen, the calculation of the 10-year charge, and the charge when property is transferred out of trust, can become quite complicated. Some changes were made in 2014 and 2015 following a prolonged period of consultation, but the rules remain complicated.

50.2   Definitions

50.2.1 Relevant Property

Relevant property is settled property in which there is no qualifying interest in possession and which is not specifically excluded (section 58(1)). For the meaning of the term 'interest in possession', see above at §49.2. An interest in possession is a qualifying interest if it is one where the person entitled is either an individual or a special type of company (section 59). Such a company is one whose business consists wholly or mainly in the acquisition of interests in settled property; it is also necessary that the company should have acquired it for consideration in money or money's worth from an individual who was beneficially entitled to it (section 59(2)). The effect is that a trust does not shift from the interest in possession rules just because a beneficiary sells the interest to such a company.

50.2.2 Related Settlements

Although discretionary trusts are usually taxed separately from each other, the rate of tax may be directly affected by the presence of a related settlement (section 66(4)(c)). Settlements are related if they are made by the same settlor on the same day (section 62(1)). A settlement is not related if immediately after the settlement commenced the property was held for charitable purposes only and without limit of time.[3]

50.2.3 Time of Commencement of Settlement

In deciding when a settlement begins, it is necessary to consider the time when property first becomes comprised in it. However, section 60 applies if the settlement begins with an interest in possession in the settlor, or the settlor's spouse or civil partner (see below at §50.6).

---

[3] IHTA 1984, s 62(2); when part of the income is to be applied to such purposes, a corresponding part is treated as held for charitable purposes (*ibid*, s 84).

50.2.4 Relevant Property: Exclusions

Under section 58, property is not relevant property—and so these rules do not apply—if, although no qualifying interest in possession subsists in the settled property, the property is held on certain special trusts. These are:

(1) property held for charitable purposes only, whether for a limited time or otherwise;
(2) property held as maintenance funds for historic buildings, etc;
(3) property held on accumulation and maintenance settlements;
(4) property held on approved superannuation schemes (registered pension schemes as from 6 April 2006);
(5) property held on trusts for employees or the special newspaper trusts;
(6) property held on the discretionary trusts arising under a protective trust and before 12 April 1978;
(7) property held on trusts for disabled persons and settled before 10 March 1981;
(8) property held on a trade or professional compensation fund;
(9) excluded property;
(10) sums received by trustees and any assets representing them (but not any income or gains arising from them) if held by trustees as a result of the reduction in pool betting duty intended for football ground improvements or to support games, etc;[4] and
(11) property forming part of a premium trusts fund or ancillary trust fund of a corporate member of Lloyds.[5]

A charge to tax may nonetheless arise in relation to these trusts (see chapter fifty-one below).

50.3 Principal Occasion of Charge: 10-Year Anniversary

50.3.1 Introduction

50.3.1.1 The Property

Where, immediately before a 10-year anniversary, all or any of the property comprised in a settlement is relevant property, tax is charged on the value of that relevant property at that time (section 64). The Revenue view was that the relevant property did not include undistributed income which had yet not been accumulated. Once the income had been accumulated it became a taxable asset of the trust.[6] Since the value of this relevant property is taken, there is no grossing up. Despite the 1986 changes the periodic charge continues to arise at 10-yearly intervals, notwithstanding the reduction in the general cumulation period from 10 years to seven years. However, the hypothetical cumulative total used in calculating the charge assumes a cumulative period of seven years. FA 2014, Schedule 25 introduced new IHTA 1984, section 64(1A), which was designed to provide

---

[4] FA 1990, s 126; FA 1991, s 121.
[5] FA 1994, s 248(2); for definitions, see *ibid*, ss 222, 223.
[6] Statement of Practice SP 8/86.

greater certainty than the previous treatment of undistributed income in accordance with Statement of Practice SP 8/86. The new rule treats income that has arisen and remained undistributed for more than five years at the date of the 10 year anniversary as if it was 'relevant property'. This rule applies to all undistributed income, whenever it arose.[7]

50.3.1.2 Determining the 10-Year Anniversary

Under section 61, generally this means the tenth anniversary of the date on which the settlement commenced and subsequent 10-year anniversaries.

Creation not relevance

It will be noted that the 10-year period runs from the date of the creation of the settlement. This is not necessarily the same as that on which the property became relevant property. Thus, if the settlement created on 1 May 1990 began with a life interest in possession, the first 10-year anniversary would still be 1 May 2000, although no charge would then arise unless the property had then become relevant property, ie no qualifying interest in possession then subsisted in it. Special rules apply if the settlement begins with an interest in possession in the settlor or the settlor's spouse or civil partner (see below at §50.6).

The charge is mitigated where the property, although relevant property on the anniversary, has not been so throughout the period (see below at §50.3.3). This may be because it was not 'relevant', or because it was not comprised in the settlement at all. The mitigation takes the form of a reduction in the rate at which the tax is to be charged (section 66(2)).

Special dating rules

No date falling before 1 April 1983 could be a 10-year anniversary (section 61(3)). If a settlement was created on 1 May 1976, the first occasion for this charge would have been 1 May 1986, while if the settlement had been created on 1 March 1973, the first occasion of charge would not have arisen until 1 March 1993.[8]

50.3.1.3 Special Types of Property

The value of the property will be reduced if the property is entitled to agricultural or business relief.

50.3.1.4 Credit for Pre-1982 Tax

If a part periodic charge has been paid under the original CTT rules introduced in 1975, section 85 permits that payment to be used as a credit against any liability arising under the present rules.

50.3.2 Rate of Tax on The Principal Occasion of Charge

50.3.2.1 Trusts Created After 26 March 1974

Under section 66, the rate at which tax is charged is 30% of 'the effective rate'. The effective rate is the tax chargeable, using lifetime rates, expressed as a percentage of the amount on

---

[7] For commentary see Lemos [2014] BTR 438.
[8] On effect of court proceedings in 1983–84, see IHTA 1984, s 61(4).

which it is charged. In making these calculations only the lifetime rates of tax are used. With the top applicable rate of tax reduced to 20% this makes the maximum rate on a 10-year charge $30\% \times 20\% = 6\%$.

The tax chargeable depends on a calculation of a hypothetical value to be taxed and a hypothetical point from which that value is to start. It is inherent in these rules that a particular figure should not enter both hypothetical parts. These rules give rise to the important planning points that where a settlor proposes to make a 'discretionary trust' and another 'fixed trust', (a) they should be created on different days, and (b) the discretionary trust should be created first. Point (a) avoids the related property rules, while (b) ensures a lower starting point by reducing element (2)(i) below.

50.3.2.2 Element (1): Hypothetical Value Transferred

The value deemed to be transferred for this purpose is the aggregate of:

(a) the value charged under section 66(4);
(b) the value, immediately after the settlement was created, of any part of the property then comprised in the settlement which has not then and has not since become relevant property (eg a life interest which still subsists); and
(c) the value immediately after a related settlement commenced of the property then comprised in it.

Example 1

On 1 February Year 0 A settled £50,000, having made no chargeable previous transfers; on 1 February Year 10 the property is worth £150,000. The value is (a) £150,000; (b) nil; (c) nil and thus £150,000.

50.3.2.3 Element (2): The Starting Point—Hypothetical Cumulative Total

Section 66(5) assumes a transferor who has in the preceding seven years made aggregate total transfers of:

(i) all chargeable transfers made by the settlor in the seven-year[9] period ending with the date the settlement was made, but disregarding transfers made on that day; and
(ii) the amounts on the appropriate fractions of which any charges to tax arose under section 65 within the previous 10 years in respect of the settlement, ie any amount which has been the subject of a fractional charge under the rules to be considered (see below at §50.3.3).

Example 1 (cont)

As A had made no previous transfers, element (i) is nil, and as there is no event within section 65, so is (ii). Hence the starting point of zero is applied to £150,000 and the

---

[9] Seven years was substituted for 10 in IHTA 1984, s 66(3) by FA 1986, Sch 19, para 16. This applies to anniversaries after 17 March 1986.

applicable rate of tax is zero. If A had made a second settlement of £50,000 on 2 February and a third on 3 February, exactly the same calculations would have been made for the other two settlements.

Example 2

On 1 March Year 0 S settled £500,000, having made previous chargeable transfers equal to the nil rate band for that year (say £250,000). On 1 March Year 10 the property is worth £1,500,000. The value is (a) £1,500,000; (b) nil; (c) nil and thus £1,500,000.

The hypothetical starting point is (i) £250,000; (ii) nil. If the nil rate band in Year 10 is £500,000 and the rate is still 20%, the tax is calculated by assuming a transfer of £1,500,000 in Year 10 by someone with a starting point of £250,000, ie £1,500,000 + £250,000 − £500,000 = £1,250,000 × 20% = £250,000 / £1,500,000 = 16.66% and then taking 30% of that rate—5%. Tax is 5% of £1,500,000, which equals £75,000.

Example 3

Previous editions of this book contained more complex examples with related settlements. The following example (3) is designed to illustrate the points while encouraging the reader to follow the working out of the figures. The key is to grasp which elements use value at the start of the settlement and which are at the relevant anniversary.

Facts. On 10 January 1991, S, whose cumulative total of transfers stood at £100,000, made two settlements (so causing them to be related settlements). No 1 was of £100,000 and was to be held on discretionary trusts subject to a life interest in half the income in favour of A. No 2 was of £70,000 and was to be held only on discretionary trusts.

On the 10-year anniversary in January 2001 the value of No 1 was £320,000 and that of No 2 was £90,000; A was still alive; £10,000 was advanced to a beneficiary from No 2 on 1 February 2001.

Hypothetical value in January 2001. In calculating the 2001 charge, the hypothetical value transferred is calculated. For No 1 that is: (a) £160,000, ie the half of the £320,000 that is relevant property; (b) £50,000, ie the initial value of the property in which A has a life interest, and (c) £70,000, ie the initial value of the related property settlement. The total is £280,000.

The hypothetical value transferred for No 2 is: (a) £90,000; (b) nil; and (c) £100,000. The total is £190,000.

It will be noted that the sum charged under section 64 on a previous 10-year anniversary is ignored.

Hypothetical value in January 2011. On the second 10-year anniversary in 2011 the hypothetical value of No 1 will, assuming the value of No 1 to be £500,000 and that A is still alive and entitled to the interest which will qualify as a pre 2006 interest, be the sum of (a) £250,000, (b) £50,000 and (c) £70,000. This totals £370,000.

Example 3 (cont)

Settlement No 1. On 10 January 2001 the hypothetical starting point is (i) £100,000 + (ii) nil = £100,000.

Thus, putting the figures determined above together one calculates the IHT at lifetime rates of a transfer of £280,000 by a person with a cumulative total of £100,000.

The tax will be:

Tax at lifetime rates for 2000–01 on £380,000 (100,000 + 280,000)	£29,200
less tax at lifetime rates for 2000–01 on £100,000	nil
Total (Note threshold for tax in 2000–01 was £234,000)	£29,200

Tax of £29,200 on £280,000 would give an effective rate of 10.42%, so the rate of charge is 30% of that, ie 3.13% and this is applied to £160,000 to give total tax of £5,005.71.

Settlement No 2. The hypothetical starting point is (i) £100,000 + (ii) £10,000 (the sum advanced to the beneficiary) = £110,000.
    Thus, IHT is calculated at lifetime rates of a transfer of £190,000 by a person with a cumulative total of £110,000.

Tax at lifetime rates for 2000–01 on £(110,000 + 190,000)	£13,200
less tax at lifetime rates for 2000–01 on £110,000	nil
	£13,200

Tax of £13,200 on £190,000 would give an effective rate of 6.94%, so the rate of charge is 30% of that, ie 2.08% and this is applied to £90,000, to give total tax of £1,875.78.
    One effect of section 66(4) and (5) is that any tax paid by the settlor on the creation of the settlement is ignored.
    If the settlor has made a PET and then settles this property on discretionary trusts, but dies within seven years of the PET, there may be additional tax to pay on the creation of the settlement. However, there is also an increase in the total of chargeable transfers in the seven years ending with the date of the settlement. The extra tax is due six months from the death of the settlor.[10]

50.3.2.4 Trusts Created Before 27 March 1974

For settlements created before 27 March 1974 a simpler regime applies under section 66(6). First, the hypothetical value transferred consists simply of the value charged under section 64, ie the value of the relevant property on the anniversary. Secondly, for second and subsequent anniversaries the hypothetical cumulative total consists simply of sums charged under section 65. The reason for this simplicity is that since a pre-1974 settlement is involved, there will be no chargeable transfer made by the settlor before the settlement.

---

[10] IHTA 1984, s 226(3B), added by FA 1986, Sch 19, para 30(2). Instalment relief may be available under s 236(1A), added by FA 1986, Sch 19, para 33(2).

50.3.3 *Adjustments*

50.3.3.1 Reduction where Property is Relevant Property for only Part of the Period

Where the property to be charged under section 66, although relevant property on the anniversary, has not been so throughout the period, a reduced rate applies. The reduction is 1/40th for each quarter in that period which expired before the property became or last became relevant property comprised in the settlement.

Example

On the tenth anniversary the fund is worth £200,000. X dies halfway through the 10-year period. For the first five years, one half of the income of the fund was paid to X by reason of a life interest. X's one half of the property was not relevant property throughout the 10-year period; the rate otherwise due on that part, £100,000, is therefore reduced by 20/40ths. There will have been an occasion of charge on the ending of A's life interest but under the rules discussed in the chapter forty-nine above.

While the principle behind the mitigation is clear, it is anything but clear how the rules should be applied where the property was not relevant property by reason of some annuity, since it is difficult to see exactly what part of the property is to be reduced by the fortieths formula.

50.3.3.2 Added Property, etc: Alternative Starting Point Under Section 67

Post-1974 settlement

Special rules apply where value is added to the settlement[11] but at a time during the 10 years before the anniversary on which the principal charge arises. The risk of an increase in the hypothetical cumulative total stemming from even the slightest addition to the settlement is a major point in tax planning for such trusts. The Revenue accept that where settled property is sold and the proceeds reinvested, there are no sums 'added to' the settlement;[12] it is hard to imagine a court coming to any other conclusion.

These rules apply whenever the settlor, S, makes a chargeable transfer in that time as a result of which the property in the settlement is increased in value. Thus, the addition of funds by S will usually be a chargeable transfer so that these rules apply; a *de minimis* exception is made when the transfer was not primarily intended to increase the value of the settled property and the increase in the value of the settled property was not more than 5%. However, it is not necessary that there should have been any increase in the property in the settlement (section 67(2)). Thus, these rules will apply when S makes an omission which results in an increase in the value of the settlement and so a chargeable transfer (section 67(2)).

Such added value causes an adjustment of the starting point, ie the hypothetical cumulative total from which to begin the calculation of the effective rate. The rule is that instead of the values transferred under immediately chargeable transfers by S in the period of seven years before the day on which the settlement was made, there shall, if greater, be taken the

---

[11] After 8 March 1982.
[12] Statement of Practice SP E9.

aggregate of values transferred under chargeable transfers by S in the seven years ending with the day on which the *addition* occurred, but disregarding the transfers made on that day (section 67(3)).

If S has made more than one addition the highest figure is taken. If, as is likely, the seven-year period brings in the sum originally settled, that sum is excluded since it will be brought into account in other parts of the section 66 calculation. For similar reasons property which has ceased to be settled and on that account is part of the hypothetical starting point is also excluded (section 67(5)).

Example 4 to illustrate section 67

In 1997, S made an immediately chargeable transfer of £60,000.

In 2002, S made two settlements on discretionary trusts on the same day; A of £110,000 and B of £90,000.

In 2003, S made an immediately chargeable transfer of £40,000.

In 2009, S added £50,000 to A and £20,000 to B.

In 2012, the first 10-year anniversary comes round. The cumulative total will be the greater of (a) £60,000 and (b) £100,000 (ie £60,000 + 40,000); so (b) will apply.

If the chargeable transfer of £40,000 had taken place in 2008, not 2003 (and so more than 10 years after 1997), the figures would have been (a) £60,000 and (b) £40,000 and so (a) would have been taken.

It will be noticed that for A the £20,000 added to B is ignored since it is a transfer made on the same day as the value added to A. The sum of £90,000 is ignored because it is taken in as the initial value of a related settlement in calculating the amount to be used in calculating the value used to find the effective rate. The £50,000 added to A is itself added.

Pre-1974 settlement

Where the settlement was made before 27 March 1974 but an addition is made after 8 March 1982, the hypothetical cumulative total (or starting point) is the aggregate of the settlor's chargeable transfers made in the seven years before the addition.[13]

50.3.3.3 Sums Ceasing to be Relevant Property During Period but Coming Back in

If property ceases to be relevant property through, say, being appointed to A for life, and is then subject to a charge under section 65, but the property later comes back into the category of relevant property (because, say, A dies) also within the 10-year period, the sum charged under section 65 would feature in both hypothetical parts. A reduction in the hypothetical cumulative total is therefore directed. The reduction is by the lesser of (a) the amount on which the tax was charged (ignoring the fractions and any grossing-up), and (b) the hypothetical value chargeable (section 67(6)). Where only part of the property is involved, apportionments are made. It will be noted that only sums subject to the exit charge are taken into account—not capital distributions under the pre-1982 rules (section 67(4)).

---

[13] IHTA 1984, s 67(4); seven years was substituted for 10 for the period after 17 March 1986 by FA 1986, Sch 19, para 17.

50.4 Other Occasions of Charge

50.4.1 Ceasing to Be Relevant Property: The Exit Charge

50.4.1.1 General

A charge to tax arises where the property ceases to be relevant property (section 65(1)
(a)), unless this occurs in a quarter beginning with the day on which the settlement commenced or with a 10-year anniversary.[14] This is a relatively mild regime compared with
that in force between 1975 and 1982. Compared with the 1975 rules three points stand out.
First, the rate of charge is reduced; secondly, a number of exceptions in the 1975 rules (eg
reverter to settlor) are not part of the 1982 scheme. The reason for these is the same—the
1982 exit charge is a proportionate 10-year anniversary charge designed to compensate the
Revenue for the fact that this property will not be relevant property when the next 10-year
anniversary comes round; whereas the 1975 charge assumed that a donor (the trust) was
making a chargeable transfer to the beneficiary. The third difference is the change to basing
liability on loss to the trust.

50.4.1.2 Examples of Property Ceasing to Be Relevant Property

Property ceasing to be comprised in the settlement ceases to be relevant property. In
this connection the rule treating property moving to a different settlement as remaining
comprised in the first settlement (see below at §50.7) must not be overlooked. Property
transferred to a beneficiary under a power of appointment or of advancement, or simply
distributed from the discretionary settlement, could give rise to a charge under this rule.
Where the property is transferred to an individual absolutely, it is to be presumed that the
transfer is chargeable and cannot be potentially exempt.

In addition, property remaining in the settlement ceases to be relevant property where
the beneficiary is given a life interest in a fund—provided the life interest is charged under
the section 49 regime for interest in possession trusts (see chapter forty-nine). Where, as a
result of the 2006 changes, the life interest does not fall within section 49, the rules in this
chapter continue to apply and there is no charge.

Lastly, under section 81A (added by FA 2010, section 52), there is a disposition for IHT
purposes when a reversionary interest (as defined in section 47) in relevant property comes
to an end and the person (P) takes that interest if either P bought the reversionary interest,
or P is the spouse or civil partner of the settler of the trust.

50.4.1.3 Exceptions

No charge arises where the property (a) is a payment of costs and expenses properly attributable to the relevant property, or (b) if the payment is income of any person for the purposes of UK income tax—or would be if he were resident in the UK (section 65(5)).

50.4.1.4 Amount Charged

The amount to be taxed under section 65 is the reduction in the value of the property in
the settlement. Thus, if the trust had a 60% shareholding in a company and the trustees

---

[14] IHTA 1984, s 65(4)—this is to avoid very small charges.

granted A a 15% holding, the loss of control would be taken into account. If the tax is paid out of other relevant property remaining comprised in the settlement, the sum otherwise chargeable must be grossed up. If a part periodic charge was paid under the 1975 rules, that payment may be used as a credit against any liability arising under the 1982 rules (section 125).

50.4.2 Disposition by the Trustees; Loss to the Trust

A charge under section 65 arises if the case does not fall within the previous rule but the trustees make a disposition as a result of which the value of the relevant property comprised in the settlement is less than it would be but for the disposition (section 65(1)(b)). As with the previous rule, no charge arises if it occurs within three months of the creation of the settlement or a 10-year anniversary (section 65(4)). Equally, there is no charge if the disposition is a payment by way of expenses or costs fairly attributable to the relevant property, or the payment would be income of the recipient (or would be if he were resident in the UK) (section 65(5)). This head of charge is similar in formulation to the general rule applying to dispositions by individuals under section 3(1), and so the rules relating to transfers by omissions in section 3(3) are therefore adapted, as is the defence in section 10 where no gratuitous benefit is intended (section 65(6)).

50.4.3 Exceptions

50.4.3.1 Foreign Element

Where the settlement was created by a settlor who was not then domiciled in the UK, there will be no charge where the property becomes excluded property (and so ceases to be relevant property—thus causing a drop in the value of the relevant property) or, if the beneficiaries are also foreign, where the trustees acquire gilt-edged securities (which qualify as excluded property).[15]

50.4.3.2 Other Exclusions, etc

Since the rules do not create chargeable transfers as such, the rules for exempt transferees are not automatically brought into operation. It is therefore expressly provided that no charge arises if the property becomes settled on certain favoured trusts or by certain bodies—these are permanent trusts for charitable purposes, a qualifying political party or a qualifying national body.[16] If the amount chargeable but for this exclusion exceeds the value of the property becoming subject to most of these favoured trusts or bodies, the excess is chargeable (section 76(3), Schedule 4). There are also exceptions where property becomes the property of maintenance funds for heritage property (section 77, Schedule 4), and for shares or securities of a company becoming held on employee trusts (section 75).

[15] IHTA 1984, s 65(7) and (8), s 267.
[16] IHTA 1984, s 76; for qualifying parties and bodies, see ss 24, 25.

50.4.4 Calculation of Exit Charge

50.4.4.1 Before the First 10-Year Anniversary

Where a charge arises under section 65 before the first 10-year anniversary, the tax is charged at a special rate, which is the 'appropriate fraction' of the effective rate on a hypothetical transfer (section 68(1)).

The 'appropriate fraction' is three-tenths multiplied by so many fortieths as there are complete successive quarters in the period beginning with the day on which the settlement commenced and ending with the day before the occasion of charge—so the greater the number of quarters, the higher the appropriate fraction (section 68(2)). Thus, in the example above at §50.2.2 when considering the £10,000 advanced on 1 February 1998 from settlement No 2, the number of completed quarters would be 28 and the fraction therefore $3/10 \times 28/40$.

Adjustments are made to the number of quarters for chargeable property which was either not comprised in the settlement at all throughout these quarters—as when it was added later—or was not relevant property throughout these quarters—as where there was a life interest in possession which ended before the charge under section 65 arose. Quarters expiring before the property became (or last became) relevant property are excluded; conversely, the quarter then in progress is included (section 68(3)).

The hypothetical value to be transferred is the sum of (a) the value immediately after the settlement commenced of the property then comprised in it, (b) the similar value of any related settlement, and (c) the initial value of any property later added to the settlement (whether or not it remained in the settlement) (section 68(5)). There is no grossing up at this point. The hypothetical starting point is the sum of any chargeable transfers made by this settlor in the period of seven years ending with the day on which the settlement commenced, disregarding transfers made on that day (section 68(4)).

Example 3 (see above at §50.3.2, cont)

Settlement No 2. When £10,000 left the settlement on 1 February 2001 the hypothetical starting point is £100,000 and the hypothetical value to be transferred is (a) £70,000 + (b) £100,000 + (c) nil = £170,000.

Tax at 2000–2001 lifetime rates on 170,000–100,000	£11,000
less tax at 2000–2001 lifetime rates on £100,000	nil
	£11,000

The charge is therefore $11,000/170,000 \times 3/10 \times 28/40 \times 10,000 = £135.88$. As £10,000 is the gross sum, the beneficiary got £9,864.12.

Planning. The gearing of the rate of tax charged to the initial value of the settled property has led to the creation of nil rate band discretionary trusts.[17] Provided the settlor's cumulative total means that the rate of tax charged on the initial value is nil, any distribution out

---

[17] See the useful account by Ray, *Taxation*, 18 September 2003, 664–65.

of the capital of the trust before the tenth anniversary will be free of IHT. It is, of course, necessary to take any related settlements into account.

50.4.4.2 Between the 10-Year Anniversaries

When the charge under section 65 arises between 10-year anniversaries, the rate is the appropriate fraction of the rate used for section 64 on the most recent anniversary. Where this rate was further reduced for certain property which was not relevant property throughout the previous 10 years, those further reductions are ignored (section 69(1)). The rate used on the most recent anniversary is recalculated if there has been a reduction in the rates of tax since the anniversary (Schedule 2, paragraph 3). The appropriate fraction is determined as for section 65, save that the quarters begin with the last 10-year anniversary (section 69(4)).

Example (cont)

From settlement No 1 the trustees advance £25,000 to a beneficiary, the beneficiary to pay the tax. The advance is made on 1 March 2006, five years and two months after the first 10-year anniversary.

The amount charged is £25,000 and the appropriate fraction is 20/40. However the tax used on the previous anniversary (£29,200) has to be recalculated using the 2005–06 threshold of £275,000 instead of the 2000–01 threshold of £234,000. So tax at lifetime rates (20%) on a new transfer of £280,000 by someone with a hypothetical starting point of £100,000 is £21,000. So one computes 20/40 × 3/10 × 21,000 and then applies that to the £25,000 advanced making tax of £281.25.

Adjustments are made to the rate to take account of property becoming relevant property since the last 10-year anniversary and so not taken into account in computing the last 10-year charge. Property which has become comprised in this settlement and which either (a) became relevant property immediately, or (b) was not and has not become relevant property, is taken at its value when joining the settlement, ie its starting value (section 69(2), (3)). The rate is that which would have been charged on the anniversary if the property had been relevant property at that time; it will be noted that this applies whether or not the property has ever become relevant property. Other added property is taken at the value when it became (or last became) relevant property.

Property which was comprised in the settlement at the anniversary but was not then relevant property is similarly taken into account if it has since become relevant property by being added to the sum to be charged at the last 10-year anniversary; for this purpose it is valued as at the date it became (or last became) relevant property (section 69(2)(b), (3)).

Example

Suppose that in settlement No 1 A had died one year after the 2001 anniversary and that the value of the fund at that time was £400,000. The effect of A's death would be that half the fund, £200,000, would become relevant property, but that figure of £200,000 would be reduced by the tax payable on A's death to, eg, £120,000. Suppose again that £25,000 is advanced two years and two months after the anniversary.

This leads to a recalculation of the rate charged under section 66. The hypothetical value is now (a) £160,000 + £120,000 + (b) £nil + (c) £70,000 = £350,000.

The hypothetical starting point is unchanged at £100,000. Assuming that 2000–01 rates still apply, the tax would be:

Tax at lifetime rates on £(100,000 + 350,000)	£43,200
less tax at lifetime rates on £100,000	nil
	£43,200

The effective rate is therefore 30% of 43,200/350,000 of which 30% is taken, ie 3.7%.

The £25,000 is advanced to a beneficiary one year and two months after A's death, ie two years and two months after the 10-year anniversary. The appropriate fraction is 8/40, so the tax is 8/40 × 3/10 × 43,200/350,000 × £25,000 = £92.57.

This applies unless the property to be charged under section 69 is the property coming in on A's death. In that event the rate of tax is further reduced and a fraction of 4/40 is used instead of 8/40. This may mean some difficulty in trust administration, since it may not be clear where B's money comes from.

HMRC consulted for some time on changes to the calculation of the exit charge for relevant property trusts. The consultation was aimed primarily at simplifying the calculation. The June 2014 consultation document, however, proposed more controversial changes to the treatment of the nil-rate band where the settlor makes a number of settlements. Whilst under the present rules, each of a settlor's trusts is entitled to a full nil-rate band of its own, the consultation proposed that the nil-rate band of both new and existing settlements would be shared between all trusts set up by the settlor. It was intended to counter the established tax planning practice of setting up multiple pilot trusts to maximise inheritance tax relief on the total assets settled over time–the so-called *Rysaffe* strategy.

The changes ultimately enacted were not as radical as those proposed, but should still remove the benefits of multiple nil rate band trusts. From 6 April 2015, although trusts are still permitted to claim their own nil rate band, the calculation of the tax rate now has to take into account the value of the assets added to other trusts on the same day. Trusts established before 10 December 2014 are grandfathered and are not caught by the new rules, provided the settlor has not made further 'same day' additions to them since that date, or if the additions are small (less than £5,000). Other transitional protection applies on transfers into multiple trusts on death, provided the wills were substantially drawn up before 10 December 2014; the new rules will not apply to the trusts where death occurs before 6 April 2017.[18]

---

[18] For details of these changes, along with changes to remove the requirement to include non-relevant property in the calculation of the rate of tax charge for both the section 66 ten year and section 68 and section 69 exit charges, see F(No 2)A 2015, Sch 1 adding IHTA 1984, ss 62A-62C.

50.5 Planning

Among the points to bear in mind are the following, some of which have been mentioned already:

(1)   If the settlor's (S's) cumulative total on the making of the trust is low enough, it may well be that no tax will be paid on a modest discretionary trust at all.

(2)   If S wishes also to make non-discretionary trusts, these should be done by a separate settlement.

(3)   If S wishes to make both a discretionary and a non-discretionary trust, the discretionary trust should be made first.

(4)   S should avoid making two settlements on the same day.

(5)   It is better to make several small discretionary trusts rather than one big one.

(6)   It is better to create a new discretionary trust than to add to an existing one.

(7)   If a discretionary trust has been set up since March 1974, it is usually better to make any distribution before rather, than after, the 10-year anniversary.

50.6 Initial Interest of Settlor or Spouse or Civil Partner[19]

A special provision applies where the settlor or the settlor's spouse or civil partner—terms which include widow, widower or surviving civil partner—is beneficially entitled to a qualifying interest in possession in the settled property immediately after the settlement is set up.[20] Contrary to the general rule, such property is not treated as having become comprised in a settlement at that time. Where the beneficial entitlement begins on or after 22 March 2006, this provision applies only where the interest is an immediate post-death interest or a disabled person's interest; the legislation uses the term 'postponing interest' to cover these two situations.

When such property later becomes held on trusts such that neither the settlor nor the settlor's spouse or civil partner is so entitled, the property is treated as becoming comprised in a separate settlement made at the time by the person ceasing or last ceasing to be beneficially entitled. The consequences of this rule are found in the rules for calculating the effective rate of tax. However, the 10-year anniversaries are determined by reference to the date of the original settlement (section 60).

Example

H settled property on trust for W for life with remainder on discretionary trusts. Under section 80, such property does not become comprised in a settlement until W dies (or for

---

[19] These rules apply whether the property became settled before or after March 1982—but not if before 27 March 1974 (IHTA 1984, s 80(3)).

[20] IHTA 1984, s 80; on conditions for status as excluded property, see s 82.

some other reason her interest ends); on such occasion the settlement is treated as made by W at that time, with consequent results in calculating the effective rate.

If W had been entitled to a life interest in one-third of the settled property, two-thirds is treated as subject to the rules set out above on the basis that H is the settlor, while the remaining one-third will become subject to those rules when W's interest ends, but as a settlement made by W.

50.7   Property Moving between Settlements Does Not Move

Where property ceases to be part of one settlement and becomes comprised in another, it is provided that the property is to be treated as remaining in the first settlement.[21] The purpose here is probably to prevent a charge from arising. This rule does not apply if, in the meantime, any person becomes beneficially entitled to the property (as distinct from becoming entitled to an interest in possession in the property).

In applying this rule excluded property can retain its status as excluded property, but not only must the settlor of the first settlement not be domiciled in the UK when the settlement was made (as required by section 65(8)) but also the person who is the settlor in relation to the second of the settlements must not be domiciled in the UK when that settlement was made (section 82).

The basic rule in section 81(1) is not to apply to events occurring after 14 March 1983 if the reversion was settled before 11 December 1981 and the reversion is expectant on the termination of a qualifying interest in possession. The purpose of the change is to restore the law to the position which was expected when the reversion was settled.

---

[21] IHTA 1984, s 81(1). This rule applies only if the property ceases to be subject to one settlement after 10 December 1981 but a similar rule applies where the cesser occurred after 26 March 1974 but before 11 December 1981 (*ibid*, s 81(2)).

51

Favoured Trusts

51.1   Introduction

Under section 70, certain types of trust in which there is no qualifying interest in possession are not subject to the 10-year and intermediate charges, and so the property comprised in the settlement is prevented from being 'relevant property'. These favoured trusts have their own rules, which are considered in this chapter. A special tapered charge applies in some circumstances. One of the principal changes made in 2006 was to remove all mention of special treatment for the accumulation and maintenance (or A and M) trust. This change applied even to trusts in existence before 22 March 2006. The legislation offered a very pale form of the protection previously offered by the A and M trust; this consists of the bereaved minors trust (section 71A) and the age 18 to 25 trusts (section 71D). Today there is no point in trying to create an A and M trust within the old rules, since the rules in chapter fifty above apply anyway and give much greater flexibility. Three other rules are mentioned in section 70 and so apply to favoured trusts, although these are similar to the rules on unfavoured discretionary and other trusts within chapter fifty:

(1)   IHT is not charged if the property involved is a payment of costs or expenses fairly attributable to the property concerned, or is a payment which is income of the recipient (or would be if he were resident in the UK) (sections 70(3) and 71B(3)).

(2)   Where the trustees make a disposition reducing the value of the settled property, they can invoke sections 10 or 16 as a defence (sections 70(4) and 71B(4)).

(3)   The trustees may be treated as making a disposition if they do so by omission, by analogy with section 3(3) (sections 70(10) and 71B(5)).

51.2   The Tapered Charge

The amount on which the tapered charge is levied is the amount of the reduction in the value of the settled property as a result of the event. If the tax is paid out of the settled property subject to the charge, the value has to be grossed up (section 70(5)(b)). The rate at which the tax is charged reflects the length of time the property has been in the favoured settlement, referred to as the relevant period. The rate for the first 40 successive quarters in the relevant period is 0.25% each, ie 10% after the first 10 years. The figures for subsequent decades are 0.20% (8%), 0.15% (6%), 0.10% (4%) and 0.05% (2%) (section 70(6)). The relevant period begins with the date on which the property first fulfilled the conditions entitling it to special treatment, subject to the important proviso that the start cannot be taken back beyond 13 March 1975 (section 70(8)). Quarters throughout which the property was excluded property are ignored (section 70(7)). The effect of these rules is that the maximum applicable rate is 30%, which cannot be applied until the year 2025. Thus, a charge arising in October 2008 under a trust which has been in existence since February 1992 will have the reduction in value taxed at 40 (the number of quarters) × 0.25%, ie 10% plus 26 at 0.20%, ie 5.2%, making a total of 15.2%.

51.3   Accumulation and Maintenance Trusts; Trusts for Bereaved Minors and Age 18 to 25 Trusts

Section 71 contains a favourable regime for property in certain trusts; the section is still entitled 'Accumulation and Maintenance Trusts'. A trust created on or after 22 March 2006 will qualify for this treatment if—and only if—it qualifies as a trust for a bereaved minor as defined in section 71A.[1] A bereaved minor is one who is under the age of 18, at least one of whose parents has died; a step-parent can be a parent, but in any event the person must have parental responsibility for the child immediately before dying (sections 71C and 71H). Trusts by grandparents cannot come within section 71A unless the grandparent has parental responsibility.[2] If a trust is to come within section 71A it must have been created under the will of a deceased parent, under an intestacy (as issue of the deceased) or under a trust established by the Criminal Injuries Compensation Scheme. Thus it can never be a PET.

In contrast with all established sensible estate planning practice, section 71A(3) directs that the trust must provide that the minor will become entitled to the capital—and not just the income—at age 18. Section 71A(4) lists various well-known trust powers which do not cause a breach of this condition, eg the power of advancement in the Trustee Act 1925, section 32. Well-established planning practice had a great deal of common sense in it and so, following much pressure, those sponsoring the legislation eventually relented and allowed the vesting in capital to be deferred to age 25, so giving rise to the 'age 18–25 trusts' (sections 71D–71G). The principal effect of this is to allow the trust to continue, with property vesting at age 25, at which point a charge equivalent to the periodic charge but starting at the 18th birthday will apply—a maximum of 4.2%, as opposed to one of 6% (section 71E(1), (2)). An earlier distribution will attract a lower charge. The trust must ensure that only the bereaved minor(s) can benefit. Other conditions ensure that while the bereaved minor is living and under the age of 18, property or income applied for the benefit of a beneficiary is applied for the benefit of the bereaved minor. The bereaved minor must, if he has not done

[1]   IHTA 1984, s 71A, but note esp s 71B(3), adapting ss 70 and 71B(1) and (2).
[2]   Though some point out that it might arise on the intestacy of a grandparent.

so before attaining 18, become entitled to the settled property, any income arising and any accumulated income (section 71G).

Where these various conditions are met, the 10-year periodic charge (see §50.3 above) is excluded save to the extent adapted for the age 18 to 25 trusts. There is an exclusion from section 52 (section 53(1A)). A charge, using this tapered basis, arises if the property ceases to satisfy the conditions entitling it to this special treatment, or if the trustees make a disposition reducing the value of the settled property (section 71B(1)). However, not even this tapered charge arises if the beneficiary, B, becomes beneficially entitled at or under the age of 18 or the property is applied for B's benefit. Similarly, there is to be no charge on the death of a beneficiary before attaining age 18 (section 71B(2)). There is also no charge under the age 18–25 trust rules if the property comes within a bereaved minor's trust (section 71E(2)(c). In the event of death between 18 and attaining the specified age, there is no charge under section 4. This is because statute directs that the property does not form part of B's estate whether the trust arises under section 71A or under section 71D (section 5(1)). There is no charge under sections 71A or 71D if the property passes from these trusts to be applied for charitable purposes (section 76). As from 6 April 2008, the rules in section 71 are superseded by those in section 71A. For those needing an account for the earlier years, see the equivalent paragraphs of the 5th edition of this book.

51.4   Other Favoured Trusts

51.4.1 *Temporary Charitable Trusts*

Where property is held for charitable purposes, and only for such purposes, but for a limited time or period, section 58 saves the property from being relevant property and so the normal charges on trusts with no interest in possession charges cannot arise. Where a part of the income is to be so used, a corresponding part is subject to these rules (section 84). When the settled property ceases to be property fulfilling this description (apart from being applied for charitable purposes), or if the trustees make a disposition reducing the value of the settled property, the tapered charge applies (section 70(1), (2); see §51.2); naturally, a disposition which is an application of property for charitable purposes does not cause the tapered charge to arise. Although a temporary charitable trust is favoured in this way, a gift to such a trust will not be an exempt transfer (see below at §53.2).

51.4.2 *Employee Trusts and Newspaper Trusts*

Section 58 again saves property in employee and newspaper trusts from being relevant property; hence, the normal charges on trusts with no interest in possession under section 64 or section 65 cannot arise. Broadly, employee trusts are trusts for the benefit of employees in a particular trade or profession, or employment by, or office with, a body carrying on a trade, profession or undertaking, and those who are married to or dependent on them (section 86(3)). The trust may be indefinite or until the end of a period (whether defined by a date or another way).[3]

---

[3]   IHTA 1984, s 86(1); on gifts for charitable purposes, see s 86(2).

The tapered charge may apply in three situations (section 72(2)(a)–(c)):

(1)   Where the property ceases to be held on such trusts—otherwise than by a payment out of the settled property.
(2)   Payment out of the settled property made for the benefit of a defined person, ie one who is a settlor (above a *de minimis* limit of £1,000 a year) or who has bought an interest in the settled property, or the company is a close company and the person has a 5% interest (section 72(3)(a)–(c)). The bar extends to persons connected with such a persons. The rules are relaxed for appropriations under an approved profit-sharing scheme (section 72(4), (4A)).
(3)   Any other depreciatory disposition by the trustees.

Section 76 provides for an exemption from any charge under section 65 when shares or securities cease to be relevant property because they become held on employee trusts as defined in section 86. Further rules treat separate settlements as one settlement, allow the transfer of funds from one to another without charge and direct that an interest in possession in part of the property is ignored if that part is less than 5% of the whole.[4] Newspaper trusts are trusts under which shares in a newspaper publishing company (as defined) or a newspaper holding company are the only or principal property comprised in the settlement.

51.4.3 Protective Trusts

Since the abolition of estate duty in 1975 there have been two regimes for protective trusts. The first, which applies to events before 12 April 1978, uses the tapered charge regime, under section 73; the second (section 88) does not. Although under the Trustee Act 1925, section 33, a discretionary trust will arise on the bankruptcy of the principal beneficiary (PB) and will endure for the remainder of PB's life, this trust is ignored and the original interest is treated as still subsisting. It follows that sums paid to other objects to the discretionary trust will be treated as transfers by PB, but that there will be no charge on the arising of the discretionary trust. Another consequence is that if, on PB's death, the property devolves on a surviving spouse or civil partner, the spouse/civil partner exemption may apply.[5]

Here, too, the 2006 legislation has had to provide rules. If the protective trust was established before the 22 March 2006 changes but the event triggering the discretionary trust arises on or after that date, the event is treated as if it had occurred before that date—and so the pre-2006 rules continue to apply. If the protective trust was established on or after that date, section 88 will apply only if the interest held by the PB is an immediate post-death interest, a disabled person's interest or a TSI. To achieve these results, section 88 states that 'the failure or determination' of the life interests is to be disregarded. This was given a restrictive interpretation in *Cholmondley v IRC*,[6] so that one could not disregard property which left the settlement under the exercise of an overriding power and which did not bring

---

[4] IHTA 1984, s 84(4), (5); the treatment of the under 5% rule does not apply to s 55.
[5] *Egerton v IRC* [1982] STC 520.
[6] [1986] STC 384. This case is also important as a scheme case. Property was appointed on protective trusts which were ended within 24 hours by the use of the overriding power. Scott J said that there had never been intention to hold the property on protective trusts.

about the forfeiture of the life interest. Under section 73, the trust was treated as arising but the normal charges under sections 64 and 65 were excluded. A tapered charge could arise if the property ceased to be held on qualifying trusts, or if there were a depreciatory transaction.

51.4.4 *Trusts for and by Disabled People*

Section 89 applies if the property was settled on trust for disabled persons after 9 March 1981. The definition of 'disabled person' in section 89 is the definition in Schedule 1A to FA 2005, reflecting the alignment of the definition for all tax purposes in FA 2013. The disabled person is treated as being beneficially entitled to an interest in possession in the settled property. This excludes any charge under sections 65 or 66. It also means that payment out of the trust to that person is free of tax. The trust must secure that, if any of the settled property or income arising from it is applied during the disabled person's life for the benefit of a beneficiary, it is applied for the benefit of the disabled person (section 89(1)). Although the presence of the statutory power of advancement in the Trustee Act 1925, section 32 does not cause the trust to fail, an express power may do so especially if it is in terms wider than those in section 32. Section 89 is not amended by FA 2006 but is often cited in the Act, since it is one of the very few categories of trust where the interest in possession treatment in section 49 continues to apply; the person with the interest in possession is treated as holding a disabled person's interest (sections 49(1A), 89B(1)). So application of the property for the disabled person's benefit cannot give rise to any IHT charge. However, a trust which created an immediate post-death interest under section 49A is governed by section 49 and is not a disabled person's interest.

Section 89 is supplemented by the creation of a second type of trust where the interest in possession treatment in section 49 applies. Section 89A is correctly entitled 'self settlement by person with condition expected to lead to a disability'. The person making the settlement is treated as beneficially entitled to an interest in possession in the property settled—so as a disabled person's interest, no charge can arise on the creation of the settlement (sections 89A(4), 89B(1)). If the disabled person is between the ages of 18 and 25—and so the trust would also come within section 71D—the section 89 treatment prevails. The conditions for this treatment include an interesting rule that if there is a power to end the trust during the settlor's life, the property must either pass to the settlor (or someone else) absolutely or go to another disabled person's trust. Section 74 deals with property settled before 10 March 1981, and provides its own definition of 'disabled person'. The normal charges under sections 64 and 65 were excluded. A tapered charge might arise if the property ceased to be held on qualifying trusts, or if there was a depreciatory transaction.

51.4.5 *Trusts for the Maintenance of Heritage Property*[7]

See below at §54.4.5. Here, too, the rules have been remodelled to take account of the 2006 changes.

---

[7] For court's approval of plan to spending money on establishing such a trust, see *Raikes v Lygon* [1988] 1 WLR 281, [1988] BTR 441.

52

Companies

52.1   Transfers by Close Company as Transfer by Participators

IHT is charged on transfers of value from dispositions by individuals. Transfers by companies do not generally give rise to IHT, but an exception is made by section 94(1) for a transfer by a close company; otherwise, property could be transferred to a tame company in return for shares, only for the company then to give the property to the intended donee. The value transferred is charged as if each participant had made a transfer of value, an expression which ensures that it cannot be a potentially exempt transfer (PET) (sections 3A(6), 94(1)). The value transferred is apportioned among the participators in the company by reference to their rights immediately before the transfer. The transfer is treated as made by each participator; where that amount is less than 5% of the total value transferred by the company, it is charged but not cumulated.[1] When the participator is itself a close company, sub-apportionments are made until the individual participators are discovered. The amount apportioned is reduced by the amount by which the value of the participator's estate is increased. In making this calculation the value of P's rights in the company is ignored (section 94(1)); thus, the Revenue cannot use any loss in the value of the shares to increase yet further the loss to P's estate.

For example, suppose X *Ltd* is valued at £150,000 and is owned equally by A and B. X *Ltd* gives A £18,000 and B's daughter £24,000. The values transferred are apportioned to A and B equally. Of the £18,000, £9,000 is attributed to B and none to A (as the increase in his estate is set off against it). The £24,000 is attributed equally to A and B, and must be grossed up at their respective rates.

For this purpose the corporation tax definition of a close company is adopted (CTA 2010, section 439), save that it is extended to cover non-resident companies. The definition of participator is also adopted (CTA 2010, section 454), save that loan creditors are ignored (section 102).

---

[1] IHTA 1984, s 94(4): and only the company is liable (*ibid*, s 202(2)).

52.1.1 Liability

The primary liability to pay IHT rests on the company, but those liable to apportionment or to whom the transfer is made are also liable (section 202(1)); this secondary liability is limited to the amount apportioned or the increase in value, as appropriate. An exception is made in that a person to whom not more than 5% of the value transferred is apportioned is not liable, leaving the company solely liable (section 202(2)).

52.1.2 General Exemptions

If there is a transfer of value to a participator's spouse or civil partner, the spouse/civil partner exemption in section 18 will apply. Other exemptions available are the participator's annual £3,000 exemption (section 19) and those for charities, political parties and other national purposes (see §53.2 below). The small gifts and marriage/civil partnership gifts rules (see §45.6 above) do not apply.

52.1.3 Exclusions from Section 94

There is a specific exception for payments which fall to be taken into account in computing the recipient's profits or gains or losses for income or corporation tax[2]—eg dividends. Another example is where the transfer is caught by TCGA 1992, section 29 as a transfer at an undervalue, so causing a reduction in the acquisition value of the shares for CGT (see above at §36.6). There is also an exception where the person to whom the transfer would be apportioned is domiciled outside the UK and the apportionment is attributable to property situated outside the UK (section 94(2)(b)). In order to prevent over-nice calculation, further rules apply where the transfer of value has only a small effect on the value of preference shares; provision is also made for transfers between members of a group or between close companies in both of which the participators have an interest, the purpose here being to get the right value (sections 95–97). Further exceptions exclude changes to the rights and interest of minority participators arising from a disposal within a group which is tax free because of falling within TCGA 1992, section 171—and to any deemed election under section 171A.[3]

52.2 Alteration in Share Rights

A deemed disposition occurs where there is an alteration to the close company's unquoted share or loan capital, or any alteration in the rights attached to the unquoted shares or unquoted debentures of the company; alteration includes extinguishment (section 98(1),(2)). The effect is to charge the participators on the value shifted even though nothing emerges from the company; without such a rule, wealth could be shifted by juggling share rights.

---

[2] IHTA 1984, s 94(2)(a); or would do so but for CTA 2009, s 1285, ex TA 1988, s 208.
[3] IHTA 1984, s 97, as amended by FA 2001, s 106. Note amendment by FA 2000, Sch 29 to reflect changes to non-resident companies.

Although IHTA 1984 treats this as a disposition, it also makes it clear that this cannot be a PET (section 98(3)). This provision does not apply to alterations in the rights of quoted securities.[4] The company is not liable for the tax; the participators are.

Example

Y *Ltd* has an issued share capital of 100 ordinary shares of £1 owned equally by C and D; the value of each holding is £40,000. If the company now issues 75 such shares, each at par, to C's son (CS) and D's daughter (DD), the parents' holdings will drop in value. Suppose the value of each parent's holding after the issue of the new shares is £13,000. Hence, after the new shares are issued, the position is as follows:

	Holding	Value
C	50	£13,000
D	50	£13,000
CS	75	£27,000
DD	75	£27,000
		£80,000

C and D have each made a transfer of value of £40,000–£13,000 = £27,000.

   In order to prevent schemes to reduce tax by removing rights from shares on death, it is provided that a decrease in value occurring on death and resulting from an alteration coming within section 98(1) will not affect the valuation of the shares for the purposes of the transfer on death (section 171(2)).

52.3   Settled Property

52.3.1 *Trustees as Participators*

A transfer under section 94 or section 98 may be apportioned to trustee participators. In such an event, there is a deemed cessation of a qualifying interest in possession: the value concerned is that apportioned to the participators, less any increase in the value of the settled property (other than the value of rights in the company). Any person who is beneficially entitled to an interest in possession falling within section 49 under the settlement is treated as the participator in place of the trustees (sections 99, 100). If there is no qualifying interest in possession, as with a discretionary trust or many post-21 March 2006 interests in possession, the trustees are treated as having made a disposition reducing the value of the settled property by a similar amount and so giving rise to an exit charge under section 65. Where a person becomes entitled to an interest in possession after 21 March 2006, it is

---

   [4] On meaning of unquoted, see IHTA 1984, s 272. Shares or securities listed on a recognised stock exchange or dealt in on the old Unlisted Securities Market (which ran from 1986 to 1996) are quoted. Unquoted means shares neither so listed nor so dealt in. A list of recognised stock exchanges is available on the HMRC website at https://www.gov.uk/government/publications/designated-recognised-stock-exchanges-section-1005-income-tax-act-2007. The AIM is not a recognised stock exchange for this purpose.

within s 49 only if it is an immediate post-death interest, a disabled person's interest or a transitional serial interest.

52.3.2 *Close Company as Beneficiary of Settled Property*

Where a close company is entitled to an interest in possession, those who are participators in relation to the company are treated as entitled to the interest for all purposes other than in relation to acquired reversions and section 10 (s 101(1)). This deeming provision must be carried right through. When the interest in possession ends there is a transfer of value by the participators (s 52(1)). The company is not treated as having an interest in the settled property; in consequence any rights the company may have to the income are disregarded.[5] Once again, where a person becomes entitled to an interest in possession after 21 March 2006, it is within these rules only if it is an immediate post-death interest, a disabled person's interest or a transitional serial interest.

---

[5] *Powell Cotton v IRC* [1992] STC 625.

53

Exempt Transfers: Conditions and Allocation Where Partly Exempt

53.1 Transfers of Value by Spouse or Civil Partner

53.1.1 Introduction

A transfer of value by one spouse or civil partner is an exempt transfer (a) to the extent that the value transferred is attributable to[1] property which becomes comprised in the estate of the other spouse or civil partner,[2] or (b) so far as the value transferred is not so attributable, to the extent that that estate is increased.[3] Point (a) makes it clear that the transfer is exempt in full even though the loss to the transferor is greater than the benefit to the transferee, as might happen if W gives H one of a set of chairs, so breaking up the set. Point (b) is designed to deal with situations in which there would otherwise be a chargeable transfer but no asset becomes the property of the other, eg where W pays H's debts, or H pays a premium on a life policy belonging to W. A gift within section 18 is safe from the gift with reservation rules.[4]

53.1.1.1 Spouse or Civil Partner

IHTA 1984 does not contain a special definition of 'spouse' or 'civil partner', so the general law meaning by reference to the relevant legal status applies. A person cohabiting with

---

[1] This means that the relief is not confined to the value received by the transferee.

[2] A technical problem arises on death since the transfer is treated as taking place immediately before the death and the property does not vest in the beneficiaries (and then retrospectively) until the death (see above at §46.2).

[3] IHTA 1984, s 18; this formula is also used in s 3A(1).

[4] FA 1986, s 102(5)(a); see discussion by Potter and Monroe, *Tax Planning* (Sweet & Maxwell, 1982), §§2–33 et seq.

another as husband and wife but not with the legal status of marriage failed in a claim to obtain a right to the exemption; the claim was on the basis that this was discriminatory and so contrary to the Human Rights Act 1998. The Special Commissioners held that marriage was objectively different from cohabitation,[5] and that brothers and sisters sharing a house can neither marry nor enter into a civil partnership; a complaint that this was contrary to the Convention on Human Rights was rejected by the Court in Strasbourg—just.[6] An American scholar has written of the inheritance system as one of the last bastions of the traditional American family; the UK might add that that bastion is reinforced for IHT.[7]

An ex-spouse is not a spouse. However, a decree of divorce does not become effective until it is made absolute; a decree of nullity in relation to a voidable marriage has the same effect as a decree of divorce.[8] A void marriage, however innocent the parties, is not a marriage. A polygamous marriage will presumably be recognised. Fiancés are not spouses; however, when a man wishes to buy a house before his marriage and to give his future wife a half share, he can achieve his object by making her a loan with which she buys her half share, and then release the debt after marriage. On spouses and human rights, see above §2.4.

Where in this chapter the term 'spouse' is used, it must be taken to cover a civil partner as well.

53.1.1.2 Planning

At one time much attention was given to equalising the estates of husband and wife so as to avoid the top rates of tax. Today this is 'positively bad advice', since it is better to use the nil rate band and potentially exempt transfers (PETs) with their seven-year cumulation period or as many such periods as can be exploited.[9] Today a surviving spouse may make use of a proportion of the nil rate band left unused by the first to die—but only on death (see §46.9 above).

53.1.2 Conditions

The disposition by which the transfer of value takes effect must not take effect on the termination after the transfer of any interest or period (section 18(3)(a)). The phrase 'takes effect' is not defined but presumably means takes effect in possession. Thus, if D left his property to W, his widow, for life with remainder to S, the transfer on D's death to W would be free of tax—as an immediate post-death interest if D dies after 21 March 2006. However, if he had left his property to S for life with the remainder to his (D's) widow, the transfer on D's death would not be exempt under this rule (unless S predeceased D).

53.1.2.1 12 Months

The disposition by which the property is given may only depend on a condition which is satisfied within 12 months after the transfer (section 18(3)(b)). A legacy by D to W, the surviving spouse, conditional on surviving nine months will be exempt under this

---

[5] *Holland v IRC* [2003] STC (SCD) 43, SpC 350.
[6] *Burden and Burden v UK* (Application No 133378/05) [2007] STC 252—by four votes to three.
[7] Glendon, *The Transformation of Family Law* (Harvard University Press, 1989) 289.
[8] Matrimonial Causes Act 1973, s 16.
[9] Potter and Monroe, *op cit*, §1.02.

rule if she survives; if, however, she does not survive, her estate will not be entitled to the survivorship clause exemption.

53.1.2.2 Reversionary Interests

The exemption may apply when, on the termination of an interest, the property passes to the previous life tenant's spouse; however, this is not the case if that spouse purchased the reversionary interest for a consideration in money or money's worth (section 56(2)). This is to prevent abuse of the relief. For example, if D wishes to benefit his son, B, he might settle property on himself for life with remainder to B. On D's death there would be a transfer of value under section 4; however, if, on D's death, the property passed to S, D's widow, the transfer would be exempt. If, therefore, S bought B's remainder, the exemption on D's death would apply. It is true that the sum paid might well be a chargeable transfer, but this would be a transfer by S and not by B, and the sum paid by S would reflect the fact that the transfer by D would become exempt. The mischief lies in the payment; the exemption will therefore apply if B *gives* the remainder to S.[10] A similar restriction applies in relation to property given in return for a purchased reversionary interest.[11]

53.1.3 *Separate Domiciles and Transferor Domiciled in UK*

The exemption is limited if, immediately before the transfer, T, the transferor, was domiciled in the UK but the spouse was not. Such a transfer is exempt to the extent only that it does not an exemption limit, which is the amount of the nil rate band amount (ie £325,000) less any amount previously taken into account for the purposes of the relief (and not just within the last seven years);[12] once the £325,000 total has been exceeded, the exemption is lost. An amount is taken into account for the purpose of the relief for spouses even though it later transpires that it would have been exempt on different grounds such as the death of the donor more than seven years after the gift, so achieving actual, as opposed to potential, exemption; exhausting the £325,000 limit may cause a gift within the seven-year period to be chargeable. Similarly, an amount is taken into account if it is a transfer between spouses who, at that time, were both domiciled in the UK and even, it would seem, if made to a previous spouse of the transferor. The reason for this restriction is that foreign property will be excluded property in the hands of the transferee (see below at §58.5). Previous transfers are included whenever made; there is no 10- or seven-year cut-off period. In 1995 the scope of this restriction was said to be under review, particularly in view of its discrimination against nationals of other EU Member States.[13] Important changes were eventually implemented in 2013. In addition to bumping the exemption limit from £55,000 (at that time unchanged from 1982) to the nil rate band amount, FA 2013 added sections 267ZA and 267ZB, which allow a non-domiciled spouse to elect to be treated as domiciled in the UK for IHT purposes only.[14]

---

[10] F(No 2)A 1987, Sch 7, para 2.
[11] IHTA 1984, s 56(1); a reversionary interest is purchased if it falls within s 55(1).
[12] IHTA 1984, s 18(2), ie for s 18(1) or (2).
[13] HC Official Report, Standing Committee D, 23rd Sitting, col 726, [1995] *Simon's Weekly Tax Intelligence* 501.
[14] For commentary see McKeever [2013] BTR 491.

Example

In 2014, H, who is domiciled in the UK, gives W, his wife, who is domiciled in the United States and who has not elected to be treated as UK domiciled for IHT purposes, a gift of £300,000. The gift is exempt. In 2016, H makes a further gift of £30,000. The cumulative total for this exemption is £330,000 and the exemption is £325,000, so that there is a PET of £5,000.

53.2 Gifts for Public Purposes

This group of exempt transfers covers gifts to charities, etc and political parties. A further exemption for transfers of property for the public benefit was repealed in 1998.[15] It should also be noted that an estate can pay IHT at a reduced rate of 36% if 10% or more of the 'net value' of their estate is left to charity.[16]

53.2.1 Conditions

Gifts for public purposes must all satisfy certain conditions designed to prevent abuse of the exemptions given (section 23(2)(a)). The first two are the same as for transfers to a spouse (see §53.1 above):

(1) The disposition must not take effect on the termination after the transfer of value of any interest or period. Unlike the transfer to spouse, but for self-evident reasons, there is no relaxation of this condition for a period of survivorship (section 23(2)(b)).

(2) The disposition by which the property is given may only depend on a condition which is satisfied within 12 months after the transfer (section 23(2)).

(3) The disposition must not be defeasible (section 23(2)(c)). Any disposition which has not been defeated 12 months after the transfer and is not defeasible thereafter is treated as indefeasible, even though it was defeasible when made or at some time during the 12-month period (section 23(2)).

(4) The transfer will not be exempt if the property or any part of it may become applicable for purposes other than charitable purposes or those of a body mentioned in the exemptions (section 23(5)); this is to prevent exemptions for transfers to finite charitable trusts.

(5) The transfer will not be exempt if the disposition is of an interest in property and that interest is less than the donor's, or if the property is given for a limited period (section 23(3)). This question is to be decided as at a time 12 months after the transfer of value. This rule is relaxed to allow the donor to give the benefit of an agreement restricting the use of land which he retains to bodies specified in IHTA 1984, Schedule 3.

---

[15] IHTA 1984, s 26, repealed by FA 1998, s 143.
[16] IHTA 1984, Sch 1A. See also https://www.gov.uk/inheritance-tax/giving-to-charity-to-reduce-an-inheritance-tax-bill.

Example

If D leaves property by will to A for life (an immediate post-death interest is taking effect if D dies after 21 March 2006) with remainder to charity, and A dies two years after D, the property will not be exempt from tax on D's death since it breaks both conditions (1) and (5) above. If A had died after six months, the gift would have broken condition (1) but not (5). Therefore, whether A died two years or six months after D's death, there is a chargeable transfer on D's death. However, there will be an exempt transfer on A's death.

Further rules apply to prevent the avoidance of tax through this relief. The transfer is not exempt if:

(1) the property is an interest in possession in settled property and the settlement does not come to an end in relation to that settled property on the making of the transfer (section 56(3)); or

(2) the property is land or a building subject to an interest reserved or created by D, the donor, which entitles D (or D's spouse or any person connected with D) to possession of, or to occupy, the whole or part of the land or building rent free, or at a rent less than might be expected to be obtained in a transaction at arm's length between persons not connected with each other;

(3) the property is not land or building and is given subject to an interest reserved or created by the donor other than:

    (a) an interest created by him for full consideration in money or money's worth, or

    (b) an interest which does not substantially affect the enjoyment of the property by the person or body by whom it is given.[17]

Further, a special rule applies to reversionary interests. Where a person or body acquires a reversionary interest in any settled property for a consideration in money or money's worth, this relief does not apply to the property when it becomes the property of that person or body on the termination of the interest to which the reversionary interest is expectant (section 56(2)).

The purpose of rule (1) above is to prevent avoidance through the gift of a life interest in possession. D would create a settlement on herself for life with remainder to her son B, and would then assign the life interest to a charity; the charity would then be used as an intermediary and the benefit would pass to B. Rule (1) prevents the transfer to charity from enjoying relief. However, if the settlement had been on D for life with remainder to charity, the transfer to charity occurring on the ending of D's interest would be exempt. Here, however, the special rule applies. If the settlement had originally been on D for life with remainder to B, and the charity had bought B's interest, the price naturally reflecting the immunity from IHT that would result on the termination of D's interest, then the exemption is not to apply on that termination.

Rules (2) and (3) above are designed to cover arrangements similar to that in rule (1), but which are not technically settlements.

---

[17] IHTA 1984, s 23(4). These apply to transfers of value made after 15 April 1976 but not to certain payments out of discretionary trusts.

53.2.2 The Bodies

53.2.2.1 Charities

Transfers to charities are exempt transfers (section 23). The Revenue view is that the transfer is exempt even if the loss to the transferor's estate is greater than the value of the property in the hands of the transferee.[18] A transfer is to charity if it becomes the property of charities or is held on trust for charitable purposes only.[19] For this purpose a gift of residue for charitable purposes only is a gift to charity even though it could not be said that the residue was capable of being applied for such purposes immediately after the death of the testator by reason of an application for cy-près.[20]

53.2.2.2 Political Parties

Gifts to political parties are wholly exempt from IHT (section 24). Political parties qualify only if, at the general election preceding the transfer, they secured two seats, or one seat and not less than 150,000 votes.[21] There are no equivalent reliefs for parties represented only in the Scottish Parliament, the Welsh Assembly or the European Parliament.

53.2.2.3 Specified Bodies

Gifts to certain bodies are exempt whether on death or inter vivos (sections 24A, 25, and Sch 3). The bodies listed include the National Gallery, the British Museum, the Historic Buildings and Monuments Commission for England, any local authority, any government department, and any university or university college in the UK (Schedule 3). Oxford and Cambridge colleges are regarded as being on the list. Gifts of land to a registered housing association are also exempt (section 24A).

53.3   Partly Exempt Transfers—Allocation of Relief[22]

Where a transfer includes a gift to a spouse and the transfer is exempt only as to part of the value, whether because the limit of £325,000 is exceeded, because the gifts do not meet the conditions at §§53.1.2 or 53.2.1 above in relation to all the property, or because the transfer also contains gifts to others, special rules apply. The purpose of these rules is to ensure that the benefit of the exemption accrues primarily to the gifts which are exempt. These rules are not needed if the transfer is wholly chargeable or wholly exempt. Problems usually arise on death, but may arise on transfers inter vivos. Moreover, the gifts may be made separately out of separate funds, as where D holds free estate, a substantial part of which D plans to leave

---

[18] Statement of Practice SP E13.

[19] IHTA 1984, s 23(1), (6). On the position of Roman Catholic religious communities when there is no trust, note former ESC F2.

[20] *Guild v IRC* [1991] STC 281, Court of Session; this point was not pursued in the House of Lords ([1992] STC 162).

[21] For list, see *Simon's Direct Tax Service*, Pt I4.216.

[22] This area of law was simplified by FA 1976; the earlier version was the subject of one of Wheatcroft's tours de force—[1975] BTR 331; the present rules were considered in an appendix at [1976] BTR 156; but see also [1976] BTR 268 and 333; and Ive [1986] BTR 24.

to a political party, and also holds a life interest in possession in settled property which, on D's death, is to pass at least in part to a political party. Where this occurs, the rules which follow are applied separately to the gifts taking effect out of each fund, with the necessary adjustments of values and amounts referred to in those provisions.[23] The practical (ie arithmetical) difficulties in this area have been greatly reduced by the advent of a single rate of IHT. However, problems still arise.

53.3.1 Definitions

53.3.1.1 Gift

'Gift' is widely defined and means the benefit of any disposition or any rule of law by which, on the making of a transfer, any property becomes the property of any person or applicable for any purpose, or would do so if it were not abated (section 42(1)). The benefit of a disposition inter vivos, by will or on intestacy, all qualify as a gift. A surviving joint tenant obtains the benefit of the rule of law known as the *ius accrescendi* whereby the interest of the deceased joint tenant is extinguished; however, the interest of the deceased joint tenant does not 'become' the property of the survivor, so it is doubtful whether such a transfer technically comes within this definition. Although these rules use the word 'gift', and require these gifts to be valued, they do not state how this valuation is to be carried out. Presumably, all must be valued as at the time of the transfer; since the transfer on death is treated as occurring immediately before death, any expenses of administration must be left out in valuing the estate, as must any gains or losses realised in the course of administration save, perhaps, in so far as they are the subject of later relief.[24]

53.3.1.2 Specific Gift

The rules distinguish gifts of residue, which must necessarily bear their own tax, from other gifts. Any gifts which are not of residue, or of a share in residue, are specific gifts.[25] A liability which is not deductible in computing the value of the estate is treated as a specific gift for this purpose (section 38(6)), including one not deductible by FA 1986, section 103. Legal rights in Scotland are also treated as specific gifts (section 42(4)).

53.3.1.3 Bearing its Own Tax

A gift bears its own tax if the tax attributable to it falls on the person who becomes entitled to the property given, or if the tax is payable out of property applicable for the purposes for which the property given becomes applicable (section 42(2)). The direction that the tax must fall on the person suggests that the mere presence of a Revenue charge will not be sufficient to make the gift bear its own tax. The same direction also suggests that if the tax is in fact paid by someone else, the gift does not bear its own tax; presumably the draftsman intended to indicate that the tax should fall on the beneficiary rather than on some other part of the estate, but this is not stated.

---

[23] IHTA 1984, s 40. On change in Revenue practice, see [1990] *Simon's Tax Intelligence* 446.
[24] See above at §46.4.
[25] IHTA 1984, s 42(1); see also *Russell v IRC* [1988] STC 195, [1988] 2 All ER 405.

53.3.2 The Calculations

53.3.2.1 Preliminary—Aggregate Gifts

Where the value transferred or part of it is attributable to property which is the subject of two or more gifts, and the aggregate value of the property so given is less than the value transferred, the value of each gift is the proportion of the value transferred or part of it which the value of the property given by it bears to the aggregate (section 42(3)). Thus, if a 90% shareholding is left to two people equally, each is treated as obtaining half the value of a 90% holding—not that of a 45% holding.

53.3.2.2 The Task

The values which are exempt are calculated to discover both the value of residue and the tax due on the transfer. The major problem is the calculation of the value of specific gifts (section 38). The residue is whatever is left after the valuation of the specific gifts (section 39).

Situation (1): where the only gifts are specific gifts which either bear their own tax or are wholly exempt. Here a simple rule applies—the face value is taken.

Example

D, who has made chargeable lifetime transfers of £305,000, dies on 1 December 2009 leaving an estate of £150,000, a legacy of £40,000 to his son on condition that he pays the tax, and the residue to his widow. The relevant nil rate band is £325,000, so £20,000 of the £40,000 will be charged at the nil rate and the other £20,000 at 40%. Tax due will be £8,000, being the tax due on a gross transfer on death of £40,000 by one who has already made transfers of £305,000; this tax will fall on the son. The residue of £110,000 passes to the widow as an exempt transfer.

Situation (2): where there are specific gifts bearing their own tax and only a part of the residue is exempt. This, again, is relatively simple; there is no grossing up.

Example

D, who has made chargeable lifetime transfers of £305,000, dies on 1 December 2009 leaving an estate of £150,000. He leaves a legacy of £40,000 to his son on condition that he pays the tax, and the residue to be divided between his widow and his sister.

The value attributable to the legacy to the son is £40,000, the residue is therefore £110,000 and the half share in the residue is worth £55,000. Tax is therefore due on £95,000 at death rates for one who has already transferred £305,000, ie £30,000. The son will therefore pay $40/95 \times £30,000 = £12,631.58$ and the sister will pay $55/95 \times £30,000 = £17,368.42$. The widow receives her half share, ie £55,000, free of tax, while the sister receives her £55,000 net of £17,368.42 tax, ie £37,631.58.

Situation (3): where the only gifts with respect to which the transfer might be chargeable are specific gifts which do not bear their own tax. Here, a grossing-up process is carried out. The amount to be attributed to the specific gifts is the aggregate of (a) the sum of the value of those gifts, and (b) the amount of tax chargeable if the value transferred equalled that aggregate (section 38(3)). The grossing-up process is thus geared to the tax applicable if the transfer consisted only of these free-of-tax gifts. This grossing-up process tends to induce numbing terror; however, it is really logical once it is remembered that gross-up on death is unnecessary. The purpose of this rule is to ensure that the tax should be the same whether the legacy is at the grossed-up figure bearing its own tax or at the net figure but not bearing its own tax.

Example

D, who has made chargeable lifetime transfers of £305,000, dies on 1 December 2009 leaving an estate of £150,000, bequeathing a legacy of £40,000 to his son and the residue to his widow. Unlike the first example above, the son's legacy does not bear its own tax; this tax therefore falls on the residue which has been left to the widow.

The calculation requires care, since it is necessary to gross up from a net figure, when all the previous calculations have involved gross figures. The cumulative total of £305,000 is turned into a net calculation, but as the nil rate band has not been exhausted the gross and net figures are the same. D is treated as having made a net transfer on death of £40,000 on top of a net cumulative total of £305,000. Of the £40,000, £20,000 is able to use the nil rate bands but the other half must be grossed at 40% to £33,333.

	Net £	Tax £	Gross £
Previous cumulative total	305,000	0	305,000
Legacy	40,000	13,333	53,333
	345,000	13,333	358,333

The grossed-up value of the legacy is £53,333 and the tax borne by the estate is £13,333. Thus, the son gets £40,000 and the widow £96,667, ie £13,333 less than in the first example above.

Situation (4): Where there are not only taxable specific gifts not bearing their own tax but also other potentially chargeable gifts. This is the most complex situation so far. It arises if there is a specific legacy not bearing its own tax and a division of residue between exempt and non-exempt transferees; there may also be other specific gifts, some exempt, others not. Here the non-exempt specific gifts are grossed up at 'the assumed rate' which is (section 38(4), (5)):

(a) the rate found by dividing the assumed amount of tax by that part of the value transferred with respect to which the transfer would be chargeable on the hypothesis that—

   i. the amount corresponding to the value of specific gifts not bearing their own tax [grossed-up as in situation (3) above], and

   ii. the parts of the value transferred attributable to specific gifts and to gifts of residue or shares in residue are determined accordingly; and

(b) the assumed amount of tax is the amount that would be charged on the value transferred on the hypothesis mentioned in (a).

Example

D, who has made chargeable lifetime transfers of £305,000, dies on 1 December 2009 leaving an estate of £150,000, bequeathing a legacy of £40,000 to his son, one half of the residue to his widow and the other half of the residue to his daughter. If there had been no other taxable gift, the grossed-up legacy to the son would be £53,333.

This is taken as the initial gross value of the legacy in order to determine the value of the non-exempt share of residue which will be ½ × (£150,000–£53,333) = £48,333. The total chargeable transfer based on these initial values would be:

Gross legacy	£ 53,333	((a)(i))
Non-exempt residue	48,333	((a)(ii))
Total	£101,666	

The tax which would be chargeable on a transfer of this amount is calculated to give the assumed rate for the purposes of the revised grossing up of the legacy.

	Gross £	Tax £
Previous cumulative total	305,000	0
Gross transfer on death	101,666	32,666
	406,666	32,666

The assumed rate is 32,666/101,666. The net legacy of £40,000 is now grossed-up at this assumed rate: £40,000 × 101,666/(101,666–32,666) = £58,936

It should be noted that the revised gross value of the legacy will be higher than the earlier gross value as it reflects the fact that one half of the residue is also chargeable to tax. The total chargeable transfer on death is re-calculated using the revised gross value of the legacy:

Gross legacy	£ 58,936
Non-exempt residue ½ × (£150,000—£58,936)	45,532
	£104,468

The actual tax borne by the estate is charged on this amount.

	Gross £	Tax £
Previous cumulative total	305,000	0
Gross transfer on death	104,468	33,787
	409,468	33,787

The tax on the estate is therefore £33,787: the actual division of the after tax sum is calculated below at §53.3.3.

53.3.2.3 Further Possibilities

It is possible to create more complex examples where there are: (a) exempt specific gifts, (b) non-exempt specific gifts bearing their own tax, (c) non-exempt specific gifts not bearing their own tax, (d) exempt shares in residue, and (e) non-exempt shares in residue. In such instances the gifts in (c) are first grossed up using the calculation in situation (3), and then all the non-exempt gifts in (b) at probate value, (c) at probate value but as just grossed up and (e) are aggregated to discover the assumed rate. This assumed rate is then again applied to (c) to give the revised grossed-up value. It will be seen that both in this example and the worked example the only gift requiring to be grossed up is the non-exempt gift not bearing its own duty, and this is done at the assumed rate, which, however, takes account of the previous grossing up. There are therefore two grossing-up steps to be taken. The purpose of the calculation is simply to put a value on the specific gift not bearing its own duty. The assumed rate is not the rate applied to the chargeable portion of the estate.

53.3.2.4 Two Limited Specific Gifts

Where two or more specific gifts are exempt, but only up to a limit, two rules apply: (a) the excess is attributed to gifts not bearing their own tax before gifts which do bear their own tax; and (b) subject to rule (a) the excess is attributed to the gifts in proportion to their value (section 38(2)). The removal of all but one of the pecuniary limits for exemptions makes the application of this rule a rarity.[26]

53.3.2.5 Abatement

Where a gift would be abated owing to an insufficiency of assets but ignoring tax, the gift must be abated before the rules for valuation of specific gifts are applied (section 37(1)). Those rules are then applied. A separate problem arises where the grossing-up process leads to the value exceeding the total value transferred. Here, the gift is to be treated as reduced to the extent necessary to reduce its value to that of the value transferred. The reduction is made in the order in which, under the terms of the relevant disposition or any rule of law, it would fall on a distribution of assets (section 37(2)).

53.3.3 *Burden of Tax*

The purpose of these rules in trying to ensure that the burden of tax and the benefit of the exemptions fall where they should and not where they should not, is well shown by the next rule. Section 41 lays down that:

Notwithstanding the terms of any disposition—

(a)   none of the tax on the value transferred shall fall on any specific gift if or to the extent that the transfer is exempt with regard to the gift; and

(b)   none of the tax attributable to the value of the property comprised in residue shall fall on any gift of a share of residue if or to the extent that the transfer is exempt with regard to the gift.

This significant restriction on the testator's freedom of testamentary disposition is clearly needed to prevent the subversion of the policy underlying the preceding rules, as well as to enable the calculations to be carried out. Where, therefore, there is a non-exempt specific legacy not bearing its own tax, the tax due will not fall on an exempt specific legacy but on residue, whether or not the residue is exempt. However, tax in respect of non-exempt shares in residue must fall on the non-exempt parts.

---

[26] The remaining pecuniary limit is the £55,000 ceiling on a transfer by a UK-domiciled spouse to a non UK-domiciled spouse (see above at §53.1.3).

Example

Resuming situation (4) in §53.3.2 above, the tax due on the estate was £33,787. The tax attributable to the legacy will be borne equally by the exempt and non-exempt shares of residue; but the tax attributable to the non-exempt share of residue must be borne entirely by that share. Suppose the administration costs of the estate were £2,213. The total residue is:

Estate		£ 150,000
Less:		
Legacy	£40,000	
Tax	33,787	
Costs	2,213	76,000
Total available for distribution divided		£ 74,000

The tax attributable to the legacy is considered to be £58,936/104,468 × £33,787 = £19,061. The shares of residue are calculated as follows:

Total for distribution	£ 74,000
Tax on non-exempt share (£33,787—£19,061)	14,726
	88,726
Widow's exempt share ½ × 88,726	£ 44,363
Daughter's non-exempt share ½ × 88,726 less tax 14,726	£ 29,637

Thus, the widow gets £44,363, the daughter gets £29,637, the son gets £40,000 and the Capital Taxes Office gets £33,787; £2,213 goes in costs.

These calculations assume that, since the tax was charged on the basis of the legacy grossed up at the assumed rate, the proportion of tax attributable to the legacy will also be calculated on that gross value. This problem is treated with complete disdain by the legislation.

The application of the rules in section 41 may depend on questions of construction. The courts have not found the problem easy.[27] In *Re Ratcliffe*,[28] Blackburne J said that he was not likely to use construction questions to overturn the basic policy of section 41 which was to make the burden of the tax fall on the non-exempt share of residue. T had divided her residuary estate between relatives, R, and charities, C. R argued for a net division approach of the net residue; the estate of just over £2.2 m would be taxed and the net sum would be divided between R and C. This would make for IHT of £500,000, with £870,000 accruing to

---

[27] On problems generally, see Ive [1986] BTR 24.

[28] [1999] STC 262; see critical comment by Campbell [1999] *Private Client Business* 134, and defence by Mitchell, *ibid*, 198. *Re Benham* [1995] STC 210 has attracted much discussion in *Private Client Business*, beginning with Stirling [1995] 319.

each of R and C. C argued that the net residue should be divided and only the half belonging to R should be taxed, the half belonging to C should be exempt. This would mean IHT of only £400,000, R receiving £720,000 and C £1.12 m. C won. Blackburne J made two points. First, although the testatrix's PRs were entitled to recover the payment of IHT as a 'testamentary expense', and the testatrix had directed a division of what was left after payment of her testamentary expenses, nonetheless the IHT attributable to R's half was a part of her gift to them and, as such, was a part of her disposable residue. Secondly, the judge held that it made no difference if T had been directing an equal division of her residuary estate after payment of all IHT. This was because the only explicit reference to any proportions in the will was to a division in equal (half) shares. It followed from this that it was at least as likely that T was impliedly directing an equal division of her residuary estate before payment of IHT (on the basis that the tax attributable to R's half would be first discharged as a testamentary expense under section 211) and the balance divided between the two classes of beneficiary, as it was that she was impliedly directing an unequal division of her residuary estate before payment of IHT. The inevitable consequence of the former direction would have been that, by virtue of section 41(b), the tax would have had to have been borne by R's half share. It therefore made no difference whether in directing an equal division of her residuary estate, T was referring to her residuary estate before or after payment of IHT. This involved overruling *Re Benham*,[29] Blackburne J saying, with more than a little irony, that he would have followed it if he had considered that it laid down some principle.[30]

It is still open to T to direct an equal division between R and C after all the IHT has been paid. However, very clear words will be needed.

53.3.4 *Other Reliefs and Planning*

Particular care is needed when part of the property is entitled to a relief such as business or agricultural relief. If such property is left to the exempt person, and other property to a chargeable person, the benefit of the relief is lost; if the gifts were reversed, the property going to the exempt person would attract no tax, while the other gift would be reduced in chargeable value.

Rules are provided for the interaction of the reliefs for agricultural and business property and the rules for PETs (section 39A). The purpose of these rules is to protect the Revenue. Before these rules, it was common to avoid CTT by leaving to the surviving spouse a pecuniary legacy of a value equal to the estate as reduced by these reliefs. This attributed the whole of the value transferred on the death to the spouse's legacy, the residue passing to the other beneficiaries free of tax—thanks to the reliefs. The first rule is that the values of specific gifts of business or agricultural property are to be taken to be their value as reduced by the relevant reliefs (section 39A(2)). The second rule is more complex and directs that the value of any other specific gifts shall be 'the appropriate fraction' of their value (section 39A(3)). The numerator of the appropriate fraction is the difference between the value transferred and the value of any specific gifts of business or agricultural property as reduced after the application of the first rule; and the denominator is the difference between the

---

[29] [1995] STC 210.
[30] [1999] STC 262, 269.

unreduced value transferred and the value, before the reduction, of property falling within the first rule (section 39A(4)).

Example

D dies, leaving a total estate of £600,000. Of this, £280,000 is attributable to agricultural property attracting the 50% relief, £120,000 to business property attracting the 50% relief and the rest to other property. D leaves the business property to his son, but on terms requiring him to pay the tax concerned, a pecuniary legacy of £100,000 to his widow and the residue to his daughter.

The total value of the estate is £600,000. Of this amount, £400,000 is attributable property which attracts the 50% reliefs. After applying these reliefs the value transferred is £400,000. The gift to the son falls within the first rule and so the value attributed to it is £60,000.

The gift to the widow is the 'appropriate fraction' of their value. The numerator is the value transferred (£400,000), less the property within the first rule (£60,000), giving a figure of £340,000. The denominator is the pre-relief value of the estate (£600,000), less the pre-relief value of the property within the first rule (£120,000), giving a figure of £480,000. The fraction is thus: 340,000/480,000.

This fraction is applied to the pecuniary legacy of £100,000 to give a figure of £70,833. The consequence is that the part entitled to the spouse exemption is £70,833 and the remainder of the value transferred (£400,000–£70,833 = £329,167) is chargeable.

In essence what the rule is trying to do is to provide a formula whereby a part of the benefit of the agricultural and business reliefs is attributed to the exempt transfer even though the effect is that the estate loses the value of part of the relief. It will thus no longer be possible to have the chargeable part of the estate reduced by the full amount of the reliefs even though the property goes, or is treated as going, in part, to an exempt beneficiary.

It is further provided that, in calculating the value of the specific gift of agricultural or business property, any pecuniary legacy which is charged on that property must be deducted before these rules are applied (section 39A(5)). The pecuniary legacy will then come within the second rule.

54

Particular Types of Property

54.1 Insurance Policies

54.1.1 Introduction

Insurance policies are a vital part of IHT planning. The presence of such a policy may ensure that there is enough liquid cash to pay any IHT due from an estate, while the reliefs for lifetime gifts may be used to fund insurance premiums.[1] On the death of the life assured, the proceeds of the policy will be payable to the person owning the policy. If that person is the life assured, A, the proceeds will be paid to A's PRs, form part of A's estate, and so be the subject of the transfer of value deemed to have been made under section 4 immediately before death. Since the value of the policy after death, ie the proceeds, will be greater than that immediately before death, ie its then surrender value, the higher value is taken. If that person is not the life assured, the proceeds do not form part of the estate of the life assured. On the death of a beneficial owner of the policy, O, being a person other than the life assured, the policy will form part of O's estate and must be valued at that time. On a lifetime transfer of the policy, the special valuation rule in section 167 (see below at §54.1.3) may apply.

---

[1] Potter and Monroe, *Tax Planning* (Sweet & Maxwell, 1982), ch 5.

A non-deduction rule is aimed at insurance-based IHT unification schemes. In determining the value of a person's estate immediately before death, no account is taken of any liability under or in connection with a life insurance policy made after 30 June 1986 unless the whole of the sum assured is part of the estate.[2] Thus, if D, the deceased, made a contract with the company that on death the company would pay out a sum to a named person in return for a premium to be paid out of D's estate on his death, the liability to the company is not deductible. It should also be noted that the gift with reservation rules are widened to take account of the right of the donor's spouse or civil partner where insurance arrangements are entered into.[3]

54.1.2 *Premiums as Transfers of Value*

Where a life policy has been taken out by A (the life assured who assigns the policy but still pays the premiums), each premium payment will be a transfer of value, being the amount paid in respect of the premiums, grossed up as necessary. There is no provision deeming A to have transferred a proportion of the policy proceeds as opposed to the amount of the premium. Where A pays a premium on a policy owned by another, that payment, although a transfer of value, may fall within one of the exemptions, in particular the exemption for normal and reasonable expenditure out of income (section 21, and see above at §45.5 et seq).

54.1.3 *Valuation*

Where there is a transfer otherwise than on the death of the life assured, the normal market valuation rule would be the surrender value of the policy. However, section 167 provides that there shall be taken instead, if greater than the market value, the total of premiums paid under the policy transferred (or earlier policy for which it has been substituted) less previous payments under, or in consideration for the surrender of rights conferred by, the policy (or any earlier policy for which it has been substituted). Examples of sums which may be deducted are payments under partial surrender and cash bonuses. Such sums will have formed part of the payee's estate and so be taken into account anyway. The purpose of the rule is to prevent avoidance by the payment of high premiums but on terms which give a low value when transferred during lifetime. Its effect is harsh, since the net cost is often higher than the surrender value. This rule applies to life policies and annuity contracts.

Example

A took out a policy on the life of D. Before D died A gave the policy to B, having paid £12,000 by way of premiums and received £1,500 as a cash bonus. The surrender value of the policy at the time of the gift is £7,500. The value under section 167 is £12,000–£1,500 = £10,500 (not £7,500).

---

[2] FA 1986, s 103(7).
[3] FA 1986, Sch 20, paras 7, 8; see Potter and Monroe, *op cit*, §5-19.

Certain exceptions and modifications apply:

(1) The valuation rule does not apply to term assurance policies where the indemnity period exceeds three years and the premiums are paid at normal intervals (section 167(3)).

(2) Where the benefit secured is expressed in units the value of which is published and subject to fluctuation, and the payment of each premium secures the allocation of a specified number of units to the policy, and the value of the units is less than when they were first allocated to the policy, the reduction is taken into account (section 167(4)). Thus, any investment loss on these unit-linked policies is deducted from the premiums paid in applying the market value or total premium rule of valuation.

(3) The rule does not apply to a transfer on death.

(4) The rule applies only where the transfer in value results in the policy ceasing to be part of A's estate (section 167(2)(b)). This was introduced to counter avoidance schemes centred on the high value imposed by section 167. A would pay a large single premium on a policy which would mature only if he reached, say, 100 years of age; he would also take out a policy in favour of B, which would mature on A's death before 100 years but which would carry only a small premium. The second policy would contain a clause allowing surrender in return for the premium within seven days—a device which prevented there being a substantial transfer to B. The right would not be exercised; this omission would not give rise to a charge under section 3(3) since the value of the policy was taken to be the premium; on A's death the charge would be limited to the value of the first policy. In addition, the second policy would often be exempt by reason of the smallness of the premium. To counter this, section 167 is excluded so that the drop in value of the policy is brought into charge when the right to surrender lapses.[4]

54.1.4 Associated Operations and Life Insurance Policies

Annuities on wealthy persons' lives coupled with life assurance policies on those lives in the hands of relatives may fall foul of section 263. Section 263 applies where: (a) a policy of life insurance has been issued (or varied or substituted) on or after 27 March 1974, or is on or after that date varied or substituted for an earlier policy; (b) an annuity on the life of the insured is purchased; and (c) the benefit of the policy is vested in a person other than the person who bought the annuity. The person buying the annuity is treated as having made a transfer of value by a disposition made at the time when the benefit of the policy vested under (c). This charge excludes any other transfer of value. The charge is excluded if it can be shown that the purchase of the annuity and the making (or substitution or variation) of the insurance were not associated operations. In practice, operations will be regarded as associated only if the life policy has been issued on terms different from those which would have applied if the annuity had not been taken out, or if there are exceptional circumstances, such as a very short life expectancy, whether due to bad health or advanced

---

[4] See McCutcheon [1980] BTR 161.

age, or the payer is very old and dies before the second payment is made. In essence the life policy must be issued on normal underwriting terms.

When the life policy and the annuity are regarded as associated operations, not only will the exemption for normal and reasonable gifts be lost, but the two transfers will be merged and treated as a transfer of the total sums spent by the person purchasing the annuity.

Example

M, an elderly millionaire on his deathbed, spends his £1m (without having a medical examination) with the L Assurance Co *Ltd* of The Bahamas on an annuity of £100,000 pa for the rest of his life. M could give this annuity to his only son, S, who could then assure M's life (without a medical examination) with the L Assurance Co *Ltd* for £960,000 with a first premium payable of £101,000, which could virtually be paid for out of the first annuity payment. If M then died, his estate shortly before his death will have been diminished by the value of the annuity given to S: but this diminution would have been small, since the value of the annuity lost by him would have been small in view of his terminal state of health. S would receive £960,000 under the life assurance policy.

M is regarded as making a transfer of value to S. The transfer is treated as taking place when the benefit is so vested, so that the rule cannot be avoided by vesting the benefit of the policy in M, who later assigns the policy. It will be seen that the rule does not require the benefit to be vested in that person beneficially.

The value thus transferred is whichever is the lesser of (a) the consideration given for the annuity and any premium paid or other consideration given for the policy on or before, but not after, the transfer (£1,101,000), and (b) the value of the greatest benefit capable of being conferred at any time by the policy, calculated as if that time were the date of the transfer (£960,000); by taking the lower figure the legislation recognises the cost to M.

The value of the benefit of the policy is that of the greatest benefit capable of being conferred at any time by the policy, so that if the benefit should vary under the terms of the policy, only the highest benefit will be taken. Great practical problems arise over the valuation of with-profits policies and unit-linked policies. There would appear to be no discounting of that value even though the sum is not payable until a future event—the death of the life assured.

54.2   Business Property Reliefs

The question of how to transfer a business from one generation to the next without incurring unnecessary taxes is an important part of tax practice. The taxes concerned will usually be CGT and IHT. As so often, it is important first to get the right business structure in place; tax considerations are of secondary importance.[5] With the current IHT reliefs in place, the main point is to ensure that full advantage is taken of those reliefs and, in the case of a PET,

---

[5] Potter and Monroe, *op cit*, §9-03; Price Waterhouse, *Tolley's Estate Planning 1999–2000* (Tolleys, 1999) 231–89; Collison, *Passing on the Family Business: Tax Digest No. 196* (Institute of Chartered Accountants Accountancy Books, 1999).

not subsequently lost. Other points are to ensure that there is no reservation of benefit and to determine exactly what is to be given away.[6] Since IHT depends on property being transferred, it may be possible to avoid IHT by allowing a new company to develop new lines of business, and even to set up a rival company to compete for existing business.[7] Relief[8] of either 100% or 50% is applied to the amount of value transferred by transfers of certain business property. There are four elements:

(1)   the asset must be relevant business property;
(2)   the business must be a qualifying business;
(3)   the asset must have been held for the minimum period of ownership; and
(4)   the asset must not be an excepted asset.

The relief is applied to the value transferred as distinct from the chargeable transfer and the property (sections 103–104); it must therefore be applied before other relief, eg for CGT borne by the donee. There are further rules for companies and for lifetime transfers made within seven years of death.

Where the property is the subject of a chargeable transfer but the donor dies within seven years (so that additional tax may be due), or where it is the subject of a PET (so that tax may become due), the benefit of the relief may be clawed back unless further conditions are satisfied at the time of the death. On interaction with agricultural property relief, see below at §54.3.2. The relief requires that the actual shares form part of the estate; it is not enough that the value which they represent forms part of the estate. For this reason, shares forming part of an unadministered estate in which D, the deceased, had a share or which are held by a partnership under which D has no rights to the specific assets, cannot qualify for this relief. However, a legacy that may be satisfied only by resort to an identified asset subject to business property relief is entitled to this relief.[9]

54.2.1 Element (1): Relevant Business Property: Rates and Categories

For transfers of value on or after 6 April 1996,[10] there are six categories of relevant business property. The first three attract 100% relief; the others attract 50% relief: category (1) deals with the unincorporated business, whether run by a sole trader or a partnership; categories (2) and (4) with a controlling interest in any company; category (3) with an interest in an unquoted company; category (5) with assets held other than by a sole trader; and category (6) with settled property (for definitions, see below). In looking at control one has regard simply to the statutory tests as to ownership and ignores the watering-down effects of any fiduciary duties towards the company.[11]

---

6   Potter and Monroe, *op cit*, §§9-05, 9-06.
7   *Ibid*, §§9-09 *et seq*.
8   For payment by instalments, see below at §56.5.1.
9   *Russell v IRC* [1988] STC 195, [1988] 2 All ER 405.
10 A different rule applied from 1992 to 1996.
11 *Walkers Exors v IRC* [2001] STC (SCD) 86.

54.2.1.1 100% Relief

Relief of 100% is available to the following business property (section 105(1)(a)–(bb)):

(1) Property consisting of a business or interest in a business.
(2) Securities of a company which are unquoted and which (either by themselves or together with other such securities owned by the transferor and any unquoted shares so owned) gave the transferor control of the company immediately before the transfer (on control, see below). These words cause some uncertainty in connection with estate freezes, as where a father freezes the value of his interest in a company at its present level leaving new growth to accrue to the next generation. This is often done by the father taking new non-voting shares and new voting shares being issued to the children. If the father still has some voting shares, he may be given 'control' and so relief; however, the Revenue do not give relief for the new non-voting shares since these are not relevant in determining control.[12]
(3) Any unquoted shares in a company.

54.2.1.2 50% Relief

Relief of 50% is available to the following business property:

(4) Quoted shares or securities which give the transferor control of the company either by themselves or with other shares or securities owned by the transferor.
(5) Land or building, machinery or plant which, immediately before the transfer, was used wholly or mainly for the purposes of a business carried on by a company of which the transferor then had control or by a partnership of which he was then a partner. Where an asset is concerned, it must be used in the business; an asset used to secure a guarantee or loan used in or for the business is not itself used in the business.[13] This category is restricted in that it will qualify only if the transferor's interest in the business, or shares or securities of the company carrying on the business fulfils the conditions of relevant business property under (1)–(4) above. On the meaning of machinery and plant, see above at §24.2.3.
(6) Land or buildings used for the purposes of a business carried on by the transferor, where the property is settled but the transferor had a beneficial interest in possession at the time of the transfer. The Act is strangely silent on the question whether 'interest in possession' means such an interest in its general property law sense or in its IHT meaning, in which case the scope of this rule is narrowed by the changes made by FA 2006. One might argue that FA 2006 has no such effect. The business property rules do not refer to an interest in possession 'as defined by section 49' and FA 2006, Schedule 20 does not refer to these rules at all. The definition section (section 272) does not define the term, though it does define concepts such as 'immediate post-death interest'. A person with an interest in possession may be taken to have a sufficient stake in the

---

[12] Potter and Monroe, *op cit*, 1, §9-08.
[13] *IRC v Mallender* [2001] STC 514 (bank guarantee provided as part of commitment of assets to Lloyd's; bank taking charge over land; land not business property just because charged to bank to enable Lloyd's business to operate).

business to qualify for relief from IHT, and before 2006 the question did not arise. However, it is understood that HMRC thinks that the IHT meaning is to be taken.

It will be seen that there is no restriction on the location of the business or the stock exchange on which the shares or securities are quoted.

Section 110 uses the net value of the business, ie the value of the assets used in the business (including goodwill), reduced by the aggregate amount of any liabilities incurred for the purposes of the business (section 110(2)). No regard is had to assets or liabilities other than those by reference to which the net value of the entire business would fall to be ascertained.[14] Encumbrances are taken to reduce the value of the property encumbered first (section 162(4)).

54.2.1.3 Control

'Control' is defined by reference to voting power; settled property in which the transferor has an interest in possession is included; once more, one has the question whether this is affected by the changes made by FA 2006 (section 269). The legislation does not refer to the point. On balance, it is thought that in this context at least it makes sense to follow the IHT meaning. In computing the voting power needed, any related property is also included.[15] Thus, if a wife has 40% of the shares, and her husband 11%, each has control. This does not apply if the related property valuation has been undone. There appears to be no provision allowing the withdrawal of a claim for relief under section 176 once made.

54.2.1.4 Quoted

Whether shares are quoted or unquoted for the purpose of this relief depends on whether they are quoted on a recognised stock exchange.[16] Shares dealt in on the London Stock Exchange's Alternative Investment Market (AIM) are not.[17] The stock exchange on which the shares or securities are quoted need not be in the UK.

54.2.1.5 Disqualifying Effect of Binding Contract for Sale, etc

The relief is designed to alleviate the tax consequences of the transfer of a business. For this reason, the transfer of property subject to a binding contract for sale is not relevant business property (section 113). It follows that property subject to certain 'buy and sell' agreements entered into by members of a partnership, under which a deceased partner's PRs are obliged to sell and the surviving partners obliged to buy the deceased's partnership interest, is not eligible for this relief; similarly, provisions requiring the automatic vesting of the property in the surviving partners subject to an obligation on them to pay for it is considered to be a binding

---

[14] IHTA 1984, s 110(3); on excepted assets, see below at §54.2.4.
[15] IHTA 1984, s 269(2), referring to s 161. It is expressed to apply to rule (4) but the problem also seems to arise under (2).
[16] IHTA 1984, s 105(1ZA), overriding the general definition in s 272.
[17] IHTA 1984, s 272; Inland Revenue Press Release, 20 February 1995, [1995] *Simon's Weekly Tax Intelligence* 343. A table of recognised stock exchanges is available on the HMRC website at https://www.gov.uk/government/publications/designated-recognised-stock-exchanges-section-1005-income-tax-act-2007.

contract and so excludes business relief.[18] Such rights and obligations must be distinguished from those arising where either or both parties merely have an option to buy or sell.

Consistent with the policy of the relief, the relief is available on the incorporation of a business or, more formally, where the property is a business or an interest in a business and the sale is to a company which is to carry on that business and is made in consideration wholly or mainly of shares or securities in that company. For similar reasons a sale of shares or securities for the purpose of reconstruction or amalgamation is ignored.

54.2.2 *Element (2): Qualifying Business*

Business 'includes' a business carried on in the exercise of a profession or vocation unless carried on otherwise than for gain.[19] The definition of a business as including a business carried on in the course of a profession or vocation may suggest that some professions or vocations are not businesses. Thus, where an author dies, the Revenue at one time said that business relief did not apply since the business ended on the death of the author and the beneficiary simply received copyrights by way of succession.[20]

Some businesses do not qualify. If the business consists wholly or mainly of dealing in securities, stocks, shares, land, buildings or the making or holding of investments, it does not qualify for relief.[21] In applying this rule of disqualification, a Special Commissioner has held that a business is disqualified whether the holding and making of investments is active or passive;[22] another has held that there is no relief where trading income is ancillary to the main business of receiving rents,[23] or where a business manages a caravan park and derives its income from pitch fees and caravans.[24] However, these matters have to be determined 'in the round' to see which activity is ancillary to which.[25] In a later case, land used as the place where a caravan park was managed was held to qualify for business relief, the earlier cases being distinguishable either on their facts or on the arguments put forward.[26] Relief was also held to be due where a person had sold a nightclub and died before buying another, so that at death there was a large cash balance.[27]

---

[18] Statement of Practice SP 12/80; on background, see ICAEW Memorandum TR 557, reproduced in Foster, *Inheritance Tax* (Butterworths, 1991), X6.27.

[19] IHTA 1984, s 103(3). The exclusion of a business which is not carried on for gain is simply phrased; there is no incorporation of the more elaborate wording in ex TA 1988, s 384. While an adventure in the nature of trade qualifies for relief, casual services taxed under Sch D, Case VI might not. If a strict approach is taken, a business whose income is taxed under Sch A might not qualify, although this is harder to sustain after the reshaping of Sch A. If a strict approach is maintained, a business which lets land (Sch A) and supplies services (Sch D, Case I) might find itself in an anomalous position: see [1985] *Simon's Tax Intelligence* 316 (anomaly No 23).

[20] There is some evidence of a softening of that stance, but it is still the case the Revenue will not grant business relief to a lifetime transfer (*Simon's Direct Tax Service*, Pt I7.171). Other problem areas concern certain types of property deposited at Lloyd's by underwriters and loans (*ibid*, Pt I7.172, 173). Trees and underwood may qualify for business relief on the deferred charge (IHTA 1984, s 127(3)).

[21] IHTA 1984, s 102(3); for exceptions see s 105(4), eg 'market maker' as defined in s 105(7). See also SI 1992/3181.

[22] *Martin v IRC* [1995] STC (SCD) 5; see also *Burkinyoung v IRC* [1995] STC (SCD) 29.

[23] *Hall v IRC* [1997] STC (SC) 126; *cf* [1985] *Simon's Tax Intelligence* 316 (anomaly No 23).

[24] *Weston v IRC* [2000] STC (SCD) 30; citing *Farmer v IRC* [1999] STC (SCD) 321; and distinguishing *Furness v IRC* [1999] STC (SCD) 232.

[25] *Farmer v IRC* [1999] STC (SCD) 321 approved in *IRC v George* [2004] STC 147 para 13; see Whitehouse [2004] *Private Client Business* 74.

[26] *IRC v George* [2004] STC 147, para 13.

[27] *Browns Executors v IRC* [1996] STC (SCD) 277.

The meaning of 'wholly or mainly' is not defined in the legislation and is beginning to be explored by the courts. One suggestion is that regard should be had to the ratio of trading profits to investment income but that 'intention' should also play a part; for example, a long-established genuinely trading company may well have significant holdings of investments. A building company with stocks of land held for development may qualify.[28] In *HMRC v Lockyer & Robertson (Mrs NV Pawson's Personal Representative),*[29] the Upper Tribunal held that a share in a holiday-let bungalow did not qualify for Business Property Relief because the taxpayer's business was 'mainly' that of holding the bungalow as an investment.[30] It appears that the meaning of 'business' for this IHT relief may be less generous for taxpayers than the meaning of 'business' for CGT relief (*cf* the *Elizabeth Ramsay* case discussed above at §42.3). If a business is disqualified under this rule, no relief is available at all; there is no room for apportionment.

The business must be carried on at the right time. In this connection it must be remembered that the effect of the associated operations provision (section 286, see §45.7 above) may be to change the time of the disposition.[31] In *Re Nelson Dance Family Sett,*[32] Sales J upheld the Special Commissioner and rejected the views expressed in three leading works (McCutcheon, Dymond and Foster). In that case a sole trader farmed agricultural land consisting of two farms and two cottages. He made a transfer of the farm and got agricultural relief on the agricultural value of the land. The land had development value and so was worth more. HMRC argued, as the books suggested, that for the relief to apply there had to be a transfer of value of the business and not just business assets. However, Sales J held that D's executor was entitled to business property relief on the balance of the value.

54.2.3 Element (3): Periods of Ownership

54.2.3.1 The Rule

The property must have been owned by the transferor throughout the two years immediately preceding the transfer (section 106). Ownership by a spouse or civil partner will not qualify—although an exception is made for property acquired on the death of such a person (see §54.2.3.3 below). This condition refers to ownership, not voting control. If a father has 40% of the shares and his daughter 15%, and she settles the 15% on him with an interest in possession in him, he will now have 55% and so the 100% relief will apply to his immediate transfer of the 40% holding.[33]

Gifts with Reservation

If the gift with reservation rules apply on the death of the donor (or the ending of the reservation within seven years of the death), the question whether the property qualifies for business

---

[28] See HC Official Report, cols 1268, 1269, 30 June 1976; *Simon's Direct Tax Service*, Pt I7.112.

[29] [2013] UKUT 50 (TCC).

[30] See note by Lewis in Taxation (13 March 2013). For a similar decision, this time concerning the letting of an office building, see *The Zetland Settlement v HMRC* [2013] UKFTT 284 (TC).

[31] See *Reynaud v IRC* [1999] STC SCD 185 for an unsuccessful Revenue attempt to invoke s 286.

[32] [2009] STC 802, [2009] EWHC 71 (Ch). See also *Brander (Representative of James (deceased), Fourth Earl of Balfour) v Revenue and Customs Commissioners* [2010] UKUT 300 (TCC), [2010] STC 2666, where the Upper Tribunal held that the deceased had operated an estate 'as one business' prior to November 2002 (the date when a particular piece of property had been replaced), and that the business was not disqualified for being one of 'holding investments'.

[33] Potter and Monroe, *op cit*, §9-05G.

relief is determined as if the transfer were one by the donee so far as it is attributable to property comprised in the gift. However, in determining whether the property qualifies for the 100% relief under elements (2) or (3), the transfer is treated as if it were by the donor— so enabling the donor's other holdings (including related and settled property) to be taken into account.[34]

54.2.3.2 Replacement Property

The property transferred will qualify if it replaced other property and that other property (and any property directly or indirectly replaced by the other property) was owned by the transferor for periods which together comprised at least two years within the five years immediately preceding the transfer of value (section 107(1)(a)). For this rule it is also necessary that any replaced property should have fulfilled all the conditions of relevant business property other than the minimum period of ownership (section 107(1)(b)). The number of replacements is not limited; neither is there any need for two businesses to be related in any way when one business replaces the other.

Where property has been replaced and the new property has not been owned for two years, the relief must not exceed what it would have been had the replacement not been made (section 107(2)). This is designed to prevent a person from obtaining relief through deathbed purchases of extra business property. It is achieved by comparing the values at the time the property is replaced, but this is difficult to reconcile with a literal interpretation. Changes resulting from the formation, alteration or dissolution of a partnership and from the incorporation of a business into a company controlled by the former owner of the business are ignored for this rule (section 107(3)). Changes in shares owned as a result of a reorganisation within TCGA 1992, sections 126–136 are also ignored when dealing with unquoted shares in element (3) (section 107(4)).

54.2.3.3 Succession: Death of Spouse or Civil Partner

Where T, the transferor, became entitled to the property on the death of another person, the period of T's ownership is taken right back to the date of the death, and if the deceased was T's spouse or civil partner, T may also use any of that person's periods of ownership (section 108). However, it is necessary to show that the asset has been a business asset throughout. If one carried on a profession and transferred an asset on death to the survivor, the successor may be treated a starting a new business—and so not entitled to relief. This relief must be distinguished from §54.2.3.4 below.

54.2.3.4 Successive Transfers: Section 109—The Relief

Where A transfers the property to B (T1) and within two years B transfers the property to C (T2), the minimum period of ownership cannot be complied with by B. However, relief may still be obtained if:

(i) either T1 or T2 was a transfer on death;
(ii) the property fulfilled the conditions for relief at T1—including the minimum period of ownership;

---

[34] FA 1986, Sch 20, para 8.

(iii) the property transferred under T1 had become the property of B, or B's spouse or civil partner; and

(iv) the property would have been relevant business property but for the minimum period of ownership rule (section 109(1)).

Where only a part of the property under T1 qualified for relief, whether because some of the assets were excepted assets or there was some replacement element in the T1 transfer only, that same part qualifies for relief on T2 (section 109(2)).

Example

In Year 5, A, who had owned the relevant business property for five years, sold it to B; the property was then worth £60,000 but the sale was for £20,000. In Year 6, B died, leaving the property to C, the property then being worth £75,000. Both A and B fulfilled all the conditions for relief apart from the period of B's ownership. The relief is available on B's death.

Under this rule, unlike that on succession to the property of a spouse or civil partner, the two-year ownership condition must be satisfied at the time of the first transfer.

54.2.4 Element (4): Excepted Assets—Two Years of Use

54.2.4.1 Exclusion

Any value attributable to an excepted asset is left out of account (section 112(1)). This is to prevent private assets from being disguised as business assets. An asset, unless relevant business property by virtue of category (4) only, is excepted if it was not either used wholly or mainly for the purposes of the business concerned throughout the whole or the last two years of the relevant period, or required at the time of the transfer for future use for those purposes (section 112(2)). The relevant period is that immediately preceding the transfer during which the asset was owned by T, the transferor or T's company (section 112(5)). Cash is often an excepted asset and so not eligible for relief.[35] An asset which is used wholly or mainly for the personal benefit of the transferor, or of any connected person, is deemed not to be used wholly or mainly for the purposes of the business and so is an excepted asset (section 112(6)).

54.2.4.2 Replacements

Where the asset is relevant business property by virtue of category (4) only, the rule is adjusted to take account of replacements. In order that the property be treated as relevant business property, it must be shown that (a) the asset was used wholly or mainly for the purposes of the business concerned throughout the two years immediately preceding the transfer, or (b) it replaced another asset so used and the periods of such use together with those of any other assets replaced comprised at least two of the last five years immediately preceding the transfer (section 112(3)). It will be seen that assets not so used are not technically 'excepted assets' but simply do not qualify as relevant business property.

---

[35] *Barclays Bank Trust Ltd v IRC* [1998] STC (SCD) 125.

54.2.4.3 Parts of Assets as Separate Assets

Where a part of any land or building is used exclusively for business purposes, but the land or building would be an excepted asset, the two parts may be treated as separate assets and the value of the part used exclusively for business will qualify for relief (section 112(4)). Thus, a surgery attached to a doctor's home will qualify for relief. The benefit of this rule does not extend beyond land and buildings, and so not to machinery or plant.

54.2.4.4 Group Companies

With regard to excepted assets, where the company is a member of a group, use by another company within the group is treated as use for the purposes of the business, provided the other company was a member of the group both at the time of the use and immediately before the transfer (section 112(2), (5) subject to section 111 discussed in §54.2.5 below).

54.2.5 Business Relief and Companies: Further Rules

Where the company is a member of a group and another company in the group has a non-qualifying business, the shares and securities in the company are valued as if the non-qualifying company was not a member of the group (section 111).[36] An exception is made where the business consists wholly or mainly in the holding of land or buildings wholly or mainly occupied by members of the group with qualifying businesses.

No relief can be given if the company is in liquidation (section 105(5)).

54.2.6 Transfers Within Seven Years Before Death of Transferor

54.2.6.1 Outline

Under the IHT regime, qualification of the property for business property relief is not determined exclusively by reference to facts known at the date of the transfer. Where A makes a PET and dies within seven years, tax will not have been due at the time of the transfer but may become due on the death. Business relief is available on that death only if further conditions are fulfilled as at the date of death (section 113A). If the transfer is chargeable, it will enter A's cumulative total for later transfers.

Where an immediately chargeable transfer has taken place, additional tax may become due by reason of A's death within seven years. The 'claw back' rule does not affect the tax due on the original transfer, but it does affect the additional tax now due, which is calculated as if the value transferred had not been reduced by the relief (and not as if the value itself is not reduced) (section 113A(2)). It follows that only the amount of the tax on the chargeable transfer itself is affected by such a loss of business relief; the value transferred by the transfer remains as reduced by the business relief for the purposes of aggregation with subsequent transfers, including A's estate immediately before his death. This loss of relief explains why the additional tax may be greater than the original tax, even though the original tax was calculated at lifetime rates whereas the additional tax is charged at 40% or 20% of the death rates in force at the time of the death. This claw back charge may be avoided if

---

[36] On valuation of business, see s 110.

certain conditions are satisfied (see below); in addition, the normal conditions for the relief must have been satisfied when the original lifetime transfer was made.

54.2.6.2 The Conditions

Under the first condition, the original property must have been owned by B, the transferee, from the time of the original transfer down to A's death or, if earlier, B's death (section 113A(3)(a), (4)). This condition is framed in terms of ownership rather than beneficial entitlement. As expressed, this condition is absolute, so that even a transfer by way of gift to a spouse or civil partner, something which in terms of the theory of IHT (and CTT before it) is meant to be a tax-free event, will bring about the potential loss of the relief. The legislation provides that where the property is settled on trusts with no interest in possession, the trustees are treated as the owners and transferees (section 113A(8)). This leaves open the situation where property is settled on trusts with an interest in possession, although it is thought that the person with the interest in possession will, under the general principles, be treated as the transferee. This, however, raises again the question whether this means general principles of property law or general principles of IHT. As the legislation is framed in terms of ownership and not of whether the property forms part of a person's estate, the former is preferred. Where the property is settled on discretionary trusts or, on the Revenue view, any trusts with interest in possession which fall to be taxed under the discretionary trust rules and the trustees then appoint that property to someone absolutely, the condition is, presumably, not satisfied. In determining what is the original property, a change of shares on a reorganisation of a company is ignored, as is a transfer of a business in exchange for shares.[37]

The second condition supposes a hypothetical transfer by the transferee on the death of A (or, if earlier, the death of B) and requires that the property should be 'relevant business property' at that time (section 113A(3)(b), (4)). It is not necessary that the property should be relevant business property of the same type. Where only a part of the property meets these conditions, relief is available only in part (section 113A(5)). This condition is severe. Thus, if the gift is of shares in a company which, at the date of the death of the transferor were unquoted but, since the date of the transfer, have been admitted to the full Stock Exchange, relief would not be available in calculating the tax or additional tax (section 113A(3A)). This condition is subject to some relaxation. Where the transfer is out of a controlling shareholding which was in a quoted company, it will suffice that B, the transferee, retains ownership of the property given until death; it will not be necessary that the property should still be relevant business property at that time. Where the transfer is out of an unquoted holding, it will suffice that B retained ownership and the shares remained unquoted.[38] This condition is relaxed in one other way: in determining whether the property is relevant business property at the time of the notional transfer on the death, the condition as to two years' ownership is ignored (section 113A(3)(b)). This presumably refers to the situation in which B dies within two years of the A–B transfer.

---

[37] IHTA 1984, s 113A(6); the reorganisation rules are defined by reference to TCGA 1992, ss 126–130, ss 132–136.

[38] FA 1987, Sch 8, para 8.

54.2.6.3 Replacement Property: Section 113B

Since B, the transferee, may legitimately (ie for business reasons) wish to replace the actual property given, provision is made for the wider problem of replacement property. In essence, the property given and the property replacing it must be the subject of arm's-length transactions, the whole of the proceeds must be applied in acquiring the replacement property and the replacement must occur within an allowed period after the disposal (section 113B(2)(a), (5)(b)). These rules are much stricter than for rollover relief under TCGA 1992, section 152; for example, no provision is made for the situation in which the replacement property is acquired before the disposal. The allowed period is now three years or such longer period as the Board may allow; for transfers of value made before 30 November 1993, that period was 12 months.

The conditions are then adapted for the replacement of two properties. Provision is also made for the situation in which A dies before B, but B has disposed of the property by that time; B may replace it within the allowed period, which begins with B's own disposal (section 113B(5)). The rules are also adapted for the situation in which B predeceases A (section 113B(4)), and apply where only part of the property is replaced. Shares acquired under any reorganisation within the rules contained in TCGA 1992, sections 126–136 are treated as the original property (section 113B(6)).

54.3 Agricultural Property

Special reductions apply to the agricultural value element in transfers of agricultural property in the UK, the Channel Islands or the Isle of Man (section 115(5)(a)). Relief was extended to land in the EEA in 2009 (section 115(5)(b)). The relief also applies to controlling interests in farming companies (section 122). It applies whether the transfer is inter vivos, on death or relates to settled property. Since the reduction applies only to the agricultural value of the land, there is no reduction for the value attributable to non-agricultural purposes, eg land with development value. Agricultural property is defined as meaning agricultural land or pasture, and as including the woodlands (as distinct from the timber) and buildings for intensive fish-farming or livestock-rearing, if occupied[39] with such land or pasture; land used for short rotational coppice qualifies.[40] Stud farms qualify (section 115(4)), but a meadow used for grazing horses does not, at least where the horses have no agricultural role.[41] Sport is not agriculture,[42] but land in wildlife habitat schemes qualifies.[43] Such property also includes cottages, farm buildings and farm houses of a character appropriate to that property. A substantial six-bedroom farmhouse and outbuildings were held not to be agricultural property since they were not agricultural land or pasture.[44]

---

[39] A building which is undergoing reconstruction and in which the farmer does not live is not occupied for agricultural purposes (*Harrold v IRC* [1996] STC (SCD) 195).

[40] FA 1995, s 154(2).

[41] Ie as livestock or for stud purposes (*Wheatley v IRC* [1998] STC (SCD) 60).

[42] Earl of *Normanton v Giles* [1980] 1 WLR 28, [1980]1 All ER 106.

[43] IHTA 1984, s 124C, added in 1997.

[44] *Starke v IRC* [1994] STC 295; there are also several Special Commissioner decisions, eg *Harrold v IRC* [1996] STC (SCD) 195; *Lloyds TSB v IRC* [2002] STC (SCD) 467; and *Rosser v IRC* [2003] (SCD) STC 311 Sp 368.

The relief is a reduction of the 'transfer of value' and not, as at one time, of the chargeable transfer. The relief is now very similar to that for business property, eg the relief is lost if the transferor has entered into a binding contract of sale at the time of the transfer (unless the property is being sold to a company which the transferor controls) (section 124). The Revenue have issued guidance on the interaction with business relief, as where agricultural property is sold and the proceeds reinvested in business property—and vice versa. The reduction applies to the value before the exemptions but before any grossing up (section 116(7)); it is excluded by business relief where that applies.

54.3.1 *100% and 50% Reliefs*

The rate of relief for transfers and other events on or after 10 March 1992 is 100% in three principal situations:

(1)   Where A, the transferor, has vacant possession of the property or the right to obtain it within 12 months.[45] Joint tenants and tenants in common satisfy this requirement if the aggregate of their interests carry the right to vacant possession (section 116(6)).

(2)   Where A does not have vacant possession but this is because the property is let on a tenancy beginning on or after 1 September 1995 (section 116(2)(c)). This rule is supplemented by other provisions dealing with cases where, after that date, a person succeeds to a tenancy (as opposed to being granted one) and where the tenant gives notice of retiring in favour of a new tenant but A dies before the notice takes effect. These supplementary rules are principally relevant to issues of timing in relation to 31 August 1995.[46]

(3)   Where A has been beneficially entitled to the interest since before 10 March 1981 and would have been entitled to the relief under the pre-1981 rules but has no right to vacant possession.[47] Relief at 100% is also available but, by concession only, where A's interest carries a right to vacant possession within 24 months (as distinct from the statutory 12 months) or the value of that interest was, despite the tenancy, broadly equivalent to vacant possession value.[48]

In most other instances, eg where the transferor is the landlord of tenanted land under a tenancy begun before September 1995, the reduction as from 10 March 1992 is 50%.[49]

A can claim the transitional relief not only by having held the interest since before 10 March 1981, but also by succeeding to the property on the death of A's spouse or civil partner after 9 March 1981—provided that person would have been entitled to the relief. A is treated as beneficially entitled to the other's interest. The condition barring the relief if the taxpayer could have obtained vacant possession is applied to both of them (section 120(2)).

---

[45]   IHTA 1984, s 116(2)(a), as amended by F(No 2)A 1992, Sch 14, paras 4, 8.
[46]   IHTA 1984, s 5A–5E, added by FA 1996, s 185; see discussion in *Finance Act Handbook* (Butterworths, 1996).
[47]   There is a restriction to £250,000, or 1,000 acres, for this transitional relief.
[48]   ESC F17.
[49]   IHTA 1984, s 116(2)(b), (4), as amended by F(No 2)A 1992, Sch 14, paras 4, 8.

54.3.2 Conditions

To qualify for the relief, whether 100% or 50%, the transferor must either (a) have occupied the property for agricultural purposes throughout the last two years, or (b) have owned the land throughout the last seven years, provided, in this instance, that the land has been occupied by him or another for agricultural purposes (section 117). The purpose behind (b) is to prevent short-term investment in land simply for tax purposes. The requirement of occupation has been relaxed for cases of representative occupation.[50]

54.3.2.1 Periods and Death

If A became entitled to the property on a death, ownership or occupation runs from the date of death (section 120(1). If the death was that of A's spouse or civil partner, that person's ownership or occupation may be used (section 120(2)). Occupation by a controlled company or by a Scottish partnership is attributed to the controller or partners (section 119). It is not necessary that the main business of the company should be farming in the UK.[51]

54.3.2.2 Periods and GWRs

Where there is an IHT charge under the GWR rules (see chapter forty-seven above), special provisions enable the donor's ownership and occupation to be taken into account.[52] The donor's ownership and occupation are included as if they were the donee's, to see whether this two-year minimum ownership rule is satisfied.

54.3.2.3 Replacement Farms

The period of occupation may be satisfied by including the occupation of a previous farm within the last five years, and that of ownership by seven of the last 10 years (section 118(1)). Where these farms differ in value, only the lowest agricultural value qualifies, although special rules apply to partnership changes.

54.3.2.4 Acquisition Under Qualifying Transfer

Provision is also made for relief where the conditions as to length of occupation or ownership are not satisfied but the farm was acquired on a previous transfer which did qualify for relief. It is further necessary that it should only be these conditions which prevent relief on this occasion, and that one of the transfers should be on death (section 121). Provision is made for the replacement of property between the two transfers; as with the general replacement rule, relief is restricted to the lower of the agricultural values of the replaced and present farms (section 121(2)). Where, on the previous transfer, only a part of the value qualified for relief, as where the earlier transfer was a part purchase, only a like part may be reduced on the present transfer (section 121(3)).

---

[50] ESC F16.
[51] On valuation, see IHTA 1984, s 122.
[52] FA 1986, Sch 20, para 8.

54.3.3 *Identifying Property Under a Lifetime Transfer*

Where A makes a PET and dies within seven years, tax may become due; similarly where an immediately chargeable transfer takes place, additional tax may become due. The problem— and the legislative solution—is the same as that for business relief (see above at §54.2.4).

As with business relief, the first condition is that the original property transferred must be owned by B, the transferee, from the time of the transfer down to the death of A or, if earlier, B (section 124A(3)(a), (4)). Where property is settled on a trust in which there is no interest in possession, the trustees are to be treated as the transferee (section 124A(8)). It must be presumed that where the property is settled on trusts which give a person a beneficial interest in possession, that person is the transferee. Once more this raises the question whether this means the transferee under general principles of property law or under general principles of IHT. As the legislation is framed in terms of ownership and not of whether the property forms part of a person's estate, the former is preferred. The condition means that a gift to a spouse or civil partner results in loss of relief.

The second condition is that the original property should be agricultural property immediately before the death (of A or, if earlier, of B) and should have been occupied by B (or another) for the purpose of agriculture throughout the relevant period (section 124A(3)(b)). This condition is obviously inapplicable where the original property consists of shares in a farming company, and so, in this instance, it will suffice that the company owned the land and the farm was occupied for the purposes of agriculture throughout the period (section 124A(3)(c)).The insistence on the property being the original property is relaxed where there has been a reorganisation of share capital, or where the property held at the date of the death consists of shares for which the original property was exchanged (section 124A(6)).

As with business relief, there is a further rule to cover the situation in which the agricultural property is replaced (section 124B). As with the other relief, the rule may apply only where both the disposal of the original property and the acquisition of the replacement are made in a bargain at arm's length or on such terms as would be contained in such a bargain (section 124B(2)). The current time limit, three years or such longer period as the Board may allow, is also the same.[53] The conditions for the relief are then applied to the original and replacement property, so that the transferee must have owned the original property down to the date of the disposal, and the replacement as from the date of the acquisition. The properties must have been occupied for purposes of agriculture during these times and the replacement property must be agricultural property immediately before the death (section 124B(3)). The rules are also adapted where the transferor dies before the transferee but the replacement process is not then complete as the new property has not yet been acquired by the transferee (section 124B(5)).

54.3.4 *Scottish Agricultural Tenancies*

Under Scots law, if neither party gives notice of termination to end the lease when it expires, the tenant can stay on by virtue of the doctrine of tacit relocation. It is expressly provided

---

[53] IHTA 1984, s 124B(2)(a), (5)(b), as amended by FA 1994, s 247 for transfers made on or after 30 November 1993.

that in valuing a person's estate immediately before death, this prospect of renewal by tacit relocation, which is, in effect, a right to extend a lease, is not taken into account when valuing a tenant's existing rights—whether those rights arise under a lease or already by tacit relocation (section 177(1)–(3)). This is subject to the condition that the deceased had been a tenant for at least two years before his death or had acquired the tenancy by succession. The value left out of account must not include any rights in respect of compensation for tenants' improvements (section 177(4)). However, this rule does not extend to lifetime transfers of such property.[54] This distinction between a lifetime transfer and one on death seems anomalous; amending legislation has not so far been introduced.

54.4 Heritage Property: Conditional Exemption[55]

IHT contains a number of rules for heritage property; these have been tightened up in recent years, some of these changes raising the possibility of human rights issues.[56] The rules include exemption for transfer of such property to certain listed bodies (section 25) and where a PET of such property is followed by a transfer to a special body (section 26A), and a Revenue power to accept land and other items in satisfaction of tax (section 230). Here we consider the rules for conditional exemption for such property where certain undertakings are given to the Treasury (sections 30–35) and trusts for the maintenance of such property. Where the taxpayer has a choice between 100% agricultural or business relief and the present exemption, the 100% reliefs should be taken; the present relief is conditional, in that a later event may cause the exemption to cease to apply.

54.4.1 Qualifying Transfers

A conditional exemption is given for transfers of value on death (section 30(3)(a)). The exemption is available in respect of lifetime transfers only if (a) A, the transferor, or A's spouse or civil partner, or A and A's spouse or civil partner between them, have been beneficially entitled to the property throughout the six years ending with the transfer, or (b) A, the transferor, acquired the property on death and the property was then the subject of a conditionally exempt transfer (section 30(3)(b)).

54.4.1.1 Potentially Exempt Transfers

No claim for conditional exemption may be made until the death of the transferor, and no claim at all may be made if the property has been sold before then (sections 3A–3C). The transfer becomes exempt if, between the transfer and the death, the property is given or sold by private treaty to an exempt public body (section 26A).

---

[54] See Eden [1991] BTR 181, comments by Scottish ICA, [1991] *Simon's Tax Intelligence* 1143; and *Baird's Executors v IRC* [1991] 1 EGLR 201.

[55] See Shepherd [1999] *Private Client Business* 264 and 321.

[56] See Lichten, *Taxation Practitioner* (October 1999); and see former ESC F7 for foreign-owned work of art temporarily in the UK, now codified in IHTA 1984, ss 5(1)(b), 64(2), and relevant definitions in section 272.

54.4.1.2 Trusts without a Relevant Interest in Possession

A similar exemption applies where there is an occasion giving rise to tax in relation to property held on discretionary trusts or any other trusts without a relevant interest in possession (section 78). Exemption may be claimed both in respect of the 10-year charge (see §50.3 above) and the exit charge (see §50.4 above) pursuant to section 79. Exemption from the 10-year charge is complete if there was a conditionally exempt transfer of the asset or a CGT rollover on or before the occasion on which it became settled. In other situations a subsequent chargeable event may give rise to the special rate of charge when privileged tax treatment of a favoured discretionary trust ceases (section 79(3)–(8)). If the trust buys a 'designated object' it enters the cumulative hypothetical total for the calculation of the tax.[57] F(No 2)A 2015 amended IHTA 1984, section 79 to remove the requirement that a claim in respect of heritage property must be made and the property designated before the 10-year charge. Instead, trustees will be allowed to make a claim for exemption within two years of the 10-year charge arising.

54.4.1.3 Trusts with a Relevant Interest In Possession

The person entitled to a relevant interest in possession is treated as beneficially entitled to the underlying property. As these rules are framed in terms of the different charges to IHT, it is thought clear that the general principles of section 49 apply.

54.4.2 The Property

The Treasury may designate the following categories of property:[58]

(1) pictures, prints, books, manuscripts, works of art, scientific collections or other things not yielding income which appear to the Treasury to be pre-eminent for their national, scientific, historic or artistic interest; this may also apply to groups of such objects taken as a whole;

(2) any land which, in the opinion of the Treasury, is of outstanding scenic, historic or scientific interest;

(3) any building for the preservation of which special steps should, in the opinion of the Treasury, be taken by reason of its outstanding historic or architectural interest;

(4) any area of land which, in the opinion of the Treasury, is essential for the protection of the character and amenities of a building within (3); and

(5) any object which, in the opinion of the Treasury, is historically associated with such a building within (3).

'National' interest includes interest within any part of the UK (section 31(5)). The 'pre-eminence' required for category (1) applies only as from 31 July 1998.[59] In the case of a PET, the question whether the asset meets these criteria is decided at the time of the death which

---

[57] Ie under IHTA 1984, s 66(5); see s 79(9), (10).

[58] IHTA 1984, s 31(1). On criteria, see Statements on Practice made in the House of Commons by relevant ministers and recorded in [1992] *Simon's Tax Intelligence* 699.

[59] FA 1998, Sch 25.

makes the PET chargeable, and not at the time of the PET (section 31(1A)). These matters may become even more important where owners of assets within category (1) realise that their assets are not of pre-eminent quality so that while their own pre-1998 acquisitions were conditionally exempt, any new disposal cannot be.[60]

54.4.3 Undertakings

Exemption is conditional on the giving of undertakings by such persons as the Treasury think appropriate in the circumstances. Undertakings must be given to keep the object permanently in the UK (save for a purpose and a period approved by the Treasury).[61] Undertakings must also be given (i) to take reasonable steps for the maintenance, repair and preservation of the asset, (ii) to provide reasonable access to the public, and facilities for the asset's examination to make sure that it is being preserved and (iii) to provide reasonable access for purposes of research by persons approved by the Treasury.[62] The access rules were made more demanding in 1998.[63] The rules provide for a number of situations. Amongst these are (a) where different persons are entitled (either beneficially or otherwise) to different properties (here, separate undertakings are to be given), and (b) where some other undertaking for maintenance, repair, preservation and access is already effective (here, undertakings may still be required). The Revenue keep a register of the relevant objects, which it publishes on a regularly updated basis and which is on the Internet.[64]

   Some of these conditions apply only as from 1998, but existing arrangements are being reviewed with a view to widening the conditions. There is no legal basis for the Revenue request, but no doubt cooperation now will bring its reward in due course. The exemption is conditional in that a charge will arise if the Treasury is satisfied that the undertakings are broken in a material respect (section 32). The rules with regard to land contain one significant difference from the rules for objects, in that where a chargeable event arises with regard to a part of the property, it is treated as a chargeable event relating to the whole and any associated property unless the Treasury otherwise directs. Where there is a part disposal of property which is conditionally exempt, the conditional exemption is reviewed.[65]

54.4.4 The Charge

54.4.4.1 Chargeable Events

Chargeable events are: (a) a breach of the undertakings (section 32(2)), (b) the death of the person beneficially entitled to the property (section 32(3)(a)), and (c) disposal of the

---

[60] See Lichten, *op cit*, 18.
[61] This undertaking is not needed for land!
[62] The Treasury may here allow some degree of protection for confidential or other information (IHTA 1984, s 31(2)–(4)).
[63] IHTA 1984, s 31(4FA)—it is no longer open to insist on a prior appointment.
[64] [1996] *Simon's Weekly Tax Intelligence* 2096; the address is http://www.cto.eds.co.uk.
[65] Current practice is that if the disposal does not materially affect the heritage entity, the designation remains in force and the charge is limited to the part disposal: Inland Revenue Press Release, 7 May 1993, [1993] *Simon's Tax Intelligence* 760. This statement also covers rights of leasehold enfranchisement under the Leasehold Reform, Housing and Urban Development Act 1993, or the Leasehold Reform Act 1967.

property by sale or gift or otherwise (section 32(3)(b)). A chargeable event with regard to one property may be a chargeable event with regard to associated properties.[66] Thus, a building falling within (3) in the list in §54.4.2 will be 'associated' with an area of land falling within (4) and objects falling within (5) if, in each case, they are connected to the building. Presumably, the word 'disposal' receives its ordinary meaning and does not extend to situations where there is a deemed disposal for CGT, as where the object is accidentally destroyed by fire and insurance proceeds are received (sections 22–24). Liability for the tax is governed by section 207 (see below at §56.1.2). A disposal will not cause a charge if the object is sold by private treaty to a specified public body,[67] or if it is disposed of otherwise than by sale, and fresh undertakings are accepted (section 32(5)). Acceptance of the object by way of payment of tax similarly causes no charge (sections 32(4), 230).

54.4.4.2 Amount of Charge

When a chargeable event occurs and the conditional exemption ceases, tax is charged on an amount equal to the value of the property at the time of the chargeable event.[68] The value will be measured by the sale proceeds or market value as appropriate.

54.4.4.3 Relevant Person

The tax is calculated by reference to the circumstances of the 'relevant person'. This will be the person who made the last conditionally exempt transfer, save that where there have been two or more such transfers within the last 30 years, the Revenue may select whichever of the transferors it chooses (section 33(5)); the object is to prevent the use of a man of straw to make the fateful transfer. For these purposes the Revenue may not go back beyond a chargeable event (section 33(6)).

Example

A made a conditionally exempt transfer to B in 1983.
B made a conditionally exempt transfer to Y (A's son) in 1988.
Y gives the property to Z, his son, in 2001. At the time of the transfer in 2001, A has a cumulative total of £180,000 and B has a cumulative total of £40,000. The Revenue are entitled to select A as the relevant person and charge tax at the rate appropriate to his cumulative total of chargeable transfers.

The rate of tax, if the relevant person is still alive, is the lifetime rate. The tax is calculated as on a transfer made by the relevant person at the time of the chargeable event (section 33(1)(b)(i)). If the relevant person has died, tax is charged as if it had been added to the value transferred on his death and had formed the highest part of that value (section 33(1)(b)(ii)). The lifetime rate is used even where the transfer was within three years of the death; the death rates are used if the transfer was on death (section 33(2)).

---

[66] IHTA 1984, s 32A. Properties are associated if they come within s 32A(1).
[67] Ie a body in IHTA 1984, Sch 3 (s 32(4)).
[68] IHTA 1984, s 33(1)(a); on calculation of estate duty clawback charge, see Statement of Practice SP11/84; Inland Revenue Press Release, 3 May 1984, [1984] *Simon's Tax Intelligence* 359 and [1987] *Simon's Tax Intelligence* 815.

Example

C makes conditionally exempt lifetime transfers to P and Q.

P makes a conditionally exempt lifetime transfer to V.

C dies; C's cumulative total of chargeable transfers (including the value of his estate immediately before his death) is £300,000.

On 22 April 2005 Q sells her property for £65,000 and this is a chargeable event (event 1). The rate of tax is 20% (the lifetime rate) on the top £65,000 slice of an estate of £365,000 (£300,000 + £65,000), ie £13,000.

On 3 December 2005 V sells his property for £30,000 and this is a chargeable event (event 2). C is nominated as the relevant person. The rate of tax is 20% (the lifetime rate) charged on the top £30,000 slice of an estate of £395,000, ie £6,000.

It should be emphasised that the only function of the relevant person is the calculation of tax. The relevant person is not liable for the tax.

Where the asset is transferred in circumstances which do not qualify for conditional exemption, it may be not only that tax will be due but also that the conditional exemption on the previous transfer will be lost, so that two lots of tax are due. In such cases the tax on the present transfer is available as a credit against the tax due in respect of the earlier transfer; this is a credit of tax against tax. If the chargeable transfer is not a chargeable event, the tax paid will be available as a credit against liability when the conditional exemption is lost (section 33(7)). Similar arrangements exist for crediting the tax on a chargeable event against the tax on a PET which becomes chargeable and which was made after the conditionally exempt transfer to which the chargeable event relates (section 33(8)).

54.4.4.4 Transferor's Cumulative Total

General rules

Where there has been a chargeable event so that the conditional exemption is lost, the cumulative total of the person (X) making that conditionally exempt disposal is adjusted, whether or not he is the relevant transferor. If X is still alive, the amount chargeable is added to the total as at the time of the chargeable event and so affects rates of tax on chargeable transfers made after that event (section 34(1)). If, however, X has died and is the relevant transferor in relation to more than one chargeable event, the amounts liable to IHT are added to the value of the estate in chronological order (section 34(2)).

Settled property

If, within the previous five years, the property was comprised in a settlement made within the previous 30 years, and the person who made the last conditionally exempt transfer is not the relevant transferor, the previous rules are applied to the estate of the settlor, S, if S has made a conditionally exempt transfer of the property within the 30 years (section 34(3)). Thus, suppose that in year 1, S settled property on A for life, remainder to B, and that the transfer was conditionally exempt, as was the transfer on A's death in year 21. If, in year 25, a chargeable event occurs, the Revenue may select S as the relevant transferor and may alter S's total. The total of the person who made the last conditionally exempt transfer is not affected where this rule applies. For this rule, any conditionally exempt transfer by the settlor prior to a chargeable event relating to the property is ignored, as are transfers prior to an event which is declared not to be a chargeable event because it is a disposal to an approved body or in payment of tax (section 34(4)).

If a chargeable event follows 'a conditionally exempt occasion', the relevant person is the settlor or, if more than one, whichever the Board selects (section 78(4)). The rule assumes a further transfer by that person. The sum is added to that person's cumulative total if still alive; otherwise it is added to the estate. Death rates are used only if the trust was established by will. The rate is then reduced to 30% of that death rate if there have been no 10-year anniversaries while the asset was comprised in the settlement, and to 60% if there had been only one. Other rules applied for conditional exemption on death before 7 April 1976[69] and under estate duty.[70] Some transitional rules therefore apply.

54.4.5 Maintenance Funds

Special rules apply to the taxation of maintenance funds of historic buildings, etc. These rules are distinct from those for the exemption of property given for the upkeep of property coming within the relief in section 25. These funds must meet various conditions,[71] as must the property, which must have been designated by the Treasury under section 32 or related provisions (and not have become chargeable since being so designated), or now meet those criteria (Schedule 4, paragraph 3). Transfers to such trusts are exempt.[72] Relief also applies to property which enters the settlement within two years of the death of a person who, at death, was beneficially entitled to an interest in possession.[73] There is also exemption from any exit charge on a trust with no qualifying interest in possession (Schedule 4, paragraphs 16–18). The settled property is not relevant property; this excludes the 10-year charge (see §50.3 above) (section 58(1)(c)). There are, however, charges if property leaves such trusts other than for its favoured purposes or the trustees make a depreciatory disposition, ie one reducing the value of the property.[74] Naturally, this charge does not apply where the property is being applied to its proper maintenance purposes.

After an initial six years the property may be applied for non-qualifying purposes or returned to the settlor, in which case there will be an income tax charge to put the settlor back into the position he would have been in if he had simply maintained the property out of post-tax income.[75] There may also be CGT and IHT charges.

54.5   Timber

54.5.1 Introduction

Relief is available in respect of growing timber if certain conditions are satisfied, the person liable so elects[76] and the value is transferred on death (section 125). IHT may be deferred until

---

[69] FA 1975, ss 31–34; IHTA 1984, Sch 5.

[70] FA 1930, s 40; see Inland Revenue Press Release, 3 May 1984; and *Simon's Direct Tax Service, op cit,* Pts I7.521–523, I4.521.

[71] IHTA 1984, Sch 4, Pt I, ie paras 1–7.

[72] IHTA 1984, s 27; there is a two-year time limit for claiming relief under s 27(1A), added by FA 1998, s 144.

[73] IHTA 1984, s 57A—subject to s 56.

[74] IHTA 1984, Sch 4, para 8 (subject to further exceptions in paras 9, 10).

[75] ITA 2007, ss 507–516, ex TA 1988, s 694.

[76] Presumably different elections may be made for different areas of woodland.

the timber is disposed of, or until the value is transferred on another death. In the former case the tax becomes due on the net proceeds or value. In the latter case no IHT will ever become due in respect of the first death. The relief does not apply to lifetime transfers, nor to land outside the UK. The relief was extended to land in the EEA by FA 2009, section 121. The relief applies to the timber and not to the land; the 1995 changes in the income tax treatment of short rotation coppice do not extend to IHT. The effect of the relief is to reduce the overall IHT due on the death; however, the relief is one of postponement, not exemption.

54.5.2 The Deceased

The deceased, D, must have been beneficially entitled to the land or to an interest in possession in the land (section 49(1)) throughout the five years immediately preceding death, or became beneficially entitled to it otherwise than for consideration in money or money's worth. Hence, a person who inherits timber land and dies after only three years of beneficial entitlement may use the relief, but a person who buys such land may not. This condition is aimed at deathbed purchases of timber. Beneficial ownership of shares in a company which is entitled to possession of the land does not suffice.[77] The refusal to extend this treatment to lifetime transfers or to discretionary trusts seems odd.

54.5.3 The Relief

The relief provided is that the value of the timber may be left out of account in determining the value transferred on death if the person liable so elects within two years of death or such longer period as the Board may allow (section 125(1)). The relief applies only to the trees or underwood; it does not apply to the value of the land itself which, however, may qualify for agricultural or business relief. Land used for short rotational coppice may qualify for agricultural relief.[78]

Where the person liable has elected to take the relief, the tax will nonetheless become payable if the timber is disposed of before the next death, whether or not by sale for full consideration. Since the tax has merely been deferred since death, the tax will become payable on a subsequent disposal whether or not that disposal is itself a chargeable transfer. The only exception is that an inter-spousal disposal will not cause the provisional exemption to be lost (section 126). Where the disposal is itself a chargeable transfer, so that two sets of liability to tax will arise—the first by reference to the previous death and the second by reference to the disposal—it is provided that in computing the value transferred on the second transfer a deduction is made for the tax chargeable on the first (section 127). The deduction is simply in valuing the transfer; it is not a credit of tax against tax. Where the second transfer is an occasion for business relief, the reduction under that relief is applied to the value as reduced by the tax paid in respect of the first death (section 114(2)).

---

[77] However, this may qualify for agricultural or business relief under IHTA 1984, ss 115(2), 103 (see also s 127(2)).

[78] FA 1995, s 154(2).

This regime for timber is still highly favourable, but not as favourable as that under estate duty, where the value of the timber was excluded from the estate and the proceeds of sale of the timber were taxed at the rate which had applied to the estate; this was the basis upon which the proceeds were charged until the next death when the process would be resumed using the new deceased person's estate rate. Where a person died under the estate duty regime this option was preserved notwithstanding the introduction of CTT; however, it was provided that the period during which this potential charge to tax was calculated on this basis should end not only on the death of that person but on any prior chargeable transfer.[79]

54.5.4 *Charge on Later Disposal*

If the timber is sold for full consideration in money or money's worth, IHT is due on the net proceeds of sale. The person exclusively liable is the person who is or would be entitled to the proceeds. In any case other than sale for full consideration in money or money's worth, tax is payable on the net value of the trees or underwood valued at the time of the chargeable event, not the date of death (section 130); however, plantings since the death are ignored (section 126(1)). The proceeds are therefore aggregated with the rest of the property transferred on the previous death. There is, however, no retrospective increase in the amount of tax payable in respect of all the other items in the estate, the whole burden of the marginal rate of tax thus falling on the timber. It will also be seen that the proceeds caught are the net proceeds of sale or the net value. In computing net proceeds of sale, certain expenses must be deducted from the proceeds, ie those incurred in the disposal, in replanting within three years or such longer time as the Board may allow,[80] and in replanting to replace earlier disposals so far as not allowable on those previous disposals (section 128). These deductions, however, are not permitted if they are allowable for income tax, a phrase which presumably means theoretically allowable and so excludes deduction for IHT whether or not there is sufficient income to absorb its expense. The net value is the value of the timber after allowing for these deductions. When rates of IHT change, the tax is charged at the death rates prevailing at the time of the sale (Schedule 2, paragraph 4); it may be inferred that this is because it is presumed that the increase in rates simply reflects the change in values due to inflation, a presumption that has often been false.

Example

D made lifetime chargeable transfers of £90,000 and left to E her entire estate which, after omitting the timber, came to £200,000. After D's death, E sold one parcel for £5,000 and another for £15,000, these being the net proceeds of sale.

IHT is due at 40% on the disposals, so that the tax will be £2,000 and £6,000 respectively.

If E had given the second parcel, still worth £15,000, to his son, F, this would again trigger IHT liability of £6,000 as regards D's death. However, the tax is deducted to leave £9,000 as the value of the property in calculating such tax as might arise on the PET to F if E should die within seven years.

---

[79] FA 1975, s 49(4). Such a transfer after 30 June 1986 is not treated as a PET so far as concerns that part of the value transferred which is attributable to the woodlands which are subject to a deferred estate duty charge (FA 1986, Sch 19, para 46, modified by ESC F15).

[80] This power is needed because planning permission can take substantially more than three years.

55

Valuation: Rules, Charges and Reliefs

55.1 General Principles of Valuation

55.1.1 Introduction

The value of property is the price it might reasonably be expected to fetch if sold on the open market[1] at the relevant time; the costs of such a sale are ignored. The price must not be reduced on the ground that the whole property is placed on the market at the same time; this means that a different value may be placed on the property than could be obtained if it were actually sold in the open market. The usual effect of the hypothesis, eg in the valuation of shareholdings, is to increase the value for IHT.[2] While this exercise presupposes a hypothetical value of hypothetical property between hypothetical parties, it does not follow that evidence of actual transactions is inadmissible, the question of what weight should be attached to those transactions is one of fact.[3]

---

[1] IHTA 1984, s 160; this rule is identical to TCGA 1992, s 272(2) and re-enacts the estate duty law, eg *Duke of Buccleuch v IRC* [1967] 1 AC 506, HL.

[2] For a major and critical review of practice in valuing controlling holdings, see Sutherland [1996] BTR 397.

[3] *IRC v Stenhouse's Trustees* [1992] STC 103, Court of Session; on *Stenhouse*, see Adams [1993] BTR 240. Although s 160 sets out the basis on which a valuation is to be made, it must yield to the real world. If in the real world the asset is worthless, the assumption in s 160 cannot make it valuable: see Lewison J in *Revenue & Customs Commissioners v Bower* [2009] STC 510, [2008] EWHC 3105 (Ch).

55.1.2 *Twelve Case Law Principles*[4]

(1)   It is accepted that the value to be determined is the statutory value; it is not a question of ascertaining the property's actual value, its true value, its intrinsic value or its value in some particular person's ownership.[5]

(2)   In judging the market value for statutory purposes, all restrictions must be assumed to be removed and any person who would have to give consent to a sale is assumed to have given that consent. In the real world there may be restrictions on a sale taking place. These restrictions may be legal, administrative or purely practical, but are to be disregarded for IHT purposes. Thus, where shares were held by an enemy in time of war, and so any sale would have been illegal, the court said that the illegality of a sale was to be ignored in judging the market value of the shares.[6] However, while the fact that the property cannot be sold, or may be sold only to certain persons, does not preclude the finding of an open market value, it does not follow that those restrictions on sale may be ignored when the property is valued. Where a person acquired a long leasehold interest in a flat at a large discount under the 'right to buy' legislation and later died, it was held that the value of the lease on death had to take account of the tenant's obligation to repay the discount if he sold within five years of his acquisition. However, this was to be done on the basis that the hypothetical purchaser's hypothetical acquisition did not of itself give rise to the obligation to repay.[7]

When valuing land, it must be assumed that the purchaser, buying freely in the market, will be subject, after becoming the purchaser, to the same restrictions on sale as those affecting the vendor.[8] Although this view has been widely held, it has been denied by the Revenue where the property concerned was a lease containing a covenant against assignment. The Revenue argued that the covenant should be disregarded and the asset treated as simply any other assignable leasehold; this seems wrong.[9]

On legislation to prevent artificial lowering of value by restrictions, see below at §55.1.3.

(3)   All possible purchasers must be considered and due consideration paid to any special purchasers. In *IRC v Clay*,[10] Cozens-Hardy J said:

> To say that a small farm in the middle of a wealthy landowner's estate is to be valued without reference to the fact that he will probably be willing to pay a large price, but solely with reference to its ordinary agricultural value, seems to me absurd. If the landowner does not at the moment buy, land brokers or speculators will give more than its purely agricultural value with a view to reselling it at a profit to the landowner.

---

[4]   See also the general description by Hoffmann LJ in *IRC v Gray* [1994] STC 360, 371–72.

[5]   Lord Russell in *IRC v Crossman* [1937] AC 26; see also Danckwerts J in *IRC v Holt* [1953] 2 All ER 1499.

[6]   *Re Aschrott* [1927] 1 Ch 313.

[7]   *Alexander v IRC* [1991] STC 112, (1991) 64 TC 59, CA.

[8]   Provided, of course, that those restrictions bind the purchaser (*IRC v Crossman* [1937] AC 26; *IRC v Mann* [1937] AC 26, [1936] 1 All ER 762; *Lynall v IRC* [1972] AC 680, [1971] 3 All ER 914, (1971) 47 TC 375).

[9]   There is no question of IHTA 1984, s 163 applying. The case relied on by the Revenue was *A-G (Ireland) v Jameson* [1905] 2 IR 218. See Park et al (eds), *Simon's Taxes* (LexisNexis, 2008) §18.204.

[10]   [1914] 3 KB 466 (an increment duty case); note Lord Pearson in *Lynall v IRC* [1971] 3 All ER 914, 920, that in the *Clay* case the fact enhancing the price was assumed to be a matter of local knowledge. See also *Glass v IRC* [1915] SC 449.

(4)   If a higher price is to be obtained by dividing up an asset, such as a shareholding, this higher price must be taken.[11]

(5)   The same appears to be true if a higher price would be obtained by amalgamating different assets, as where the purchase of two blocks of different classes of share would give control.[12] This approach was taken by the Court of Appeal in *IRC v Gray*,[13] where the value of the freehold of agricultural land encumbered by a lease was determined on the assumption that the sale of the land would take place along with the sale of the deceased's 98% interest in the partnership which was entitled to the tenancy under the lease.

(6)   The valuation must be as at the actual date. As Lord Morris put it: ' "At the time of the death" must not be paraphrased or altered so as to read "within a short time of the death." '[14] However, this does not prevent the court from taking account of imminent rights, as with building society shares where the society was about to be demutualised.[15]

(7)   Hindsight.   Events after the valuation date are ignored, except in so far as they could have been foreseen. It follows that the price actually realised on a later sale of the property in the open market after the transfer may provide some evidence of the value of that property at the time of the transfer. Of course, it is necessary to distinguish carefully those situations in which the law allows the later value to be substituted for the value at the date of transfer.[16] The general principle against hindsight means that the law assumes the prophetic vision of a prospective purchaser at the moment of the death of the deceased, and rejects the wisdom which might be provided by the knowledge of subsequent events.[17] Thus, there is no room for supposing that the owner would do as many prudent owners do—withdraw the property if he does not get a sufficient offer and wait until a time when he can get a better offer.[18]

(8)   In making a valuation, no regard is had to the expenses that would arise on an actual sale.[19]

(9)   Private and family companies. The valuation of shares in a private company calls for close attention to the presumptions used. The hypothetical purchaser is entered onto the company register, but is taken to have acquired shares subject to all the restrictions on any subsequent sale in the articles.[20] The courts have recognised that many family companies are run on the basis that only members of the family are allowed to hold

---

[11]   *Smyth v Revenue Comrs* [1931] IR 643.

[12]   *A-G of Ceylon v Mackie* [1952] 2 All ER 775, per Lord Reid; *IRC v Clay* [1914] 3 KB 466; *IRC v Buchanan* [1914] 3 KB 466 (an increment duty case); and note the comment of Lord Pearson in *Lynall v IRC* [1971] 3 All ER 914, 920, that in the *Clay* case the fact enhancing the price was assumed to be a matter of local knowledge. See also *Glass v IRC* [1915] SC 449.

[13]   [1994] STC 360.

[14]   *Duke of Buccleuch v IRC* [1967] 1 AC 506, 535.

[15]   *Ward v IRC* [1999] STC (SCD) 1.

[16]   Ie land sold within three years (IHTA 1984, s 191) and shares sold within one year (s 179).

[17]   *Holt v IRC* [1953] 2 All ER 1499, per Danckwerts J. See also *IRC v Marr's Trustees* (1906) 44 SLR 647; and *Lynall v IRC* [1972] AC 680, HL.

[18]   *Duke of Buccleuch v IRC* [1967] 1 AC 506, 525.

[19]   *Ibid.*

[20]   For example *A-G v Jameson* [1905] 2 IR 218.

shares and are, in reality, allowed to decide on the conduct of the company.[21] The problem of the special purchaser frequently arises in case of shares in a private company. The other shareholders may be particularly anxious to acquire the deceased's shares in order to prevent them going to the public or to strangers. Most of the case law has been concerned with valuing minority interests; it has, however, been shown that much care is needed when valuing a controlling interest since there is so much capacity for variation according to the different sets of articles and where the minority shareholdings are held by shareholders with different characteristics.[22]

(10) Special purchaser. The area of law relating to the role of the special purchaser is of some subtlety. In *IRC v Crossman*,[23] at least one of the Law Lords rejected an argument that a higher valuation should have been put on the shares because they were a kind of investment which was particularly attractive to a trust corporation. However, the decision cannot be treated as binding authority for the view that the existence of such a special purchaser should be disregarded, because in that particular case restrictions in the company's articles would have discouraged an acquisition by a trust corporation. In *Re Lynall*,[24] Harman LJ was asked whether directors must be excluded from amongst possible purchasers because they would be special purchasers:

> I do not accept this … In *Crossman's* case it was decided that the fact that a 'special' purchaser, namely a trust company, would have offered a special price must be ignored, but this was because that particular purchaser had a reason special to him for so doing. So here a director who would give an enhanced price because he would thus obtain control of the company would be left out of account. But that is not to say that directors as such are to be ignored. All likely purchasers are deemed to be in the market.

(11) A prospective purchaser is expected to be prudent,[25] ie not rush hurriedly into the transaction but seek to get the fullest possible information about the company and its future prospects.

(12) It is for the Tribunals to make the finding of fact. The role of the court on appeal is limited to considering points of law that arise. Valuation is an art, not a science; no valuation is merely an automatic numerical exercise.[26]

55.1.3 *Effect of Creating Gratuitous Restrictions*

Under section 163, where a restriction or exclusion has been placed upon the right to dispose then, on the occasion of the next relevant event, ie a chargeable transfer of the property, that

---

[21] *Re Thornley* (1928) 7 ATC 178, per Rowlatt J; see also *Salvesen's Trustees v IRC* (1930) 9 ATC 43, per Lord Fleming; and *Dean v Prince* [1953] Ch 590, per Sir Raymond Evershed MR.

[22] Sutherland [1996] BTR 397, esp 411 *et seq*.

[23] [1937] AC 26, [1936] 1 All ER 762.

[24] [1969] 3 All ER 984, 990; note that the decision of the Court of Appeal was reversed by the House of Lords at [1971] 3 All ER 914.

[25] Danckwerts J in *Holt v IRC* [1953] 2 All ER 1499.

[26] *Caton's Administrators v Couch* [1995] STC (SCD) 34, where the Commissioner valued the shares at 56p each, the taxpayer's expert witness suggested 88p per share on the basis that 'secret information' was available and the Revenue had proposed 35p per share. See also *Clark v Green* [1995] STC (SCD) 99, where the valuation dispute represented 3% of the company's issued share capital and the published information was more than a year out of date.

restriction or exclusion is to be taken into account only to the extent that consideration in money or money's worth was given for it. The purpose of this rule is to prevent restrictions on the right to dispose of the property from providing an easy way of saving tax. But for this rule, a restriction could be created by contract, the value of the property would fall and, on a subsequent transfer, only the reduced value would be transferred.

Example

A grants B an option to buy Blackacre at any time in the next three years for £400,000, its then market value. B pays £40,000 for the option, its then market value. After two years, when Blackacre's value, ignoring the option, is £700,000, A gives the land to B. A then dies, so making the transfers chargeable rather than potentially exempt.

In calculating the value transferred when A gives the land to B, the option is taken into account only to the value of the consideration given. Thus, £700,000 is reduced only by the £40,000 paid by B for the option; Blackacre enters B's estate at £700,000 but that estate will already have been depleted by the £40,000 already paid.

The option is ignored only on the next chargeable transfer. Thus, if A had given the land to C, the option would have been taken into account only to this limited extent. If C later gave the land to D, the option would now be taken into account in full.

If the next transfer by A is not a chargeable one, eg because it is an inter-spousal gift, the rule would still apply to the next chargeable transfer of the land by the transferee spouse or civil partner.

The rule applies even though the option is granted for full consideration. Its effect is that the issue of whether or not there is a chargeable transfer and, if so, its extent, is left in suspense until the next chargeable transfer.

If the grant of the option is itself a chargeable transfer of value, a rule is needed to prevent a double charge. An allowance is made on the next chargeable transfer for the value already transferred, ignoring any grossing up, or for so much of it as is attributable to the restriction.

Example

P grants Q an option to buy Whiteacre at any time in the next three years for £500,000, its current market value. If Q paid nothing for the option which had a value of £50,000, that sum, perhaps grossed up, would have been chargeable on that occasion. If P later gives the land to Q when it is worth £900,000, there must be a deduction for the £50,000, making the value of the property £850,000. This is so whether the original £50,000 was grossed up or was reduced by the annual exemption.

55.2 Related Property and Similar Property, the Charge in Section 161

55.2.1 *Basic Rule*

Where there is (a) a transfer of property, and (b) other property is related to it, and (c) the value of the property transferred is less than the value of the 'appropriate portion' of that plus the related property, the value of the property transferred is that portion. In determining the appropriate portion, the general rule is that the value of each property is taken as if it did not form part of the aggregate; however, this rule does not affect the calculation of the aggregate value.[27] Where shares of the same class are concerned, the appropriate proportion will be found simply by taking the number of shares (section 161(4)). Shares are treated as being of the same class unless they are not so treated by the practice of a recognised stock exchange, or would be so treated if dealt with on such a stock exchange (section 161(5)). Although shares in a family company are the most likely objects of these rules, other assets caught will be collections and sets of valuable objects, and property held jointly or by a partnership. It has been suggested that if a wife holds a lease and her husband holds the reversion, these rules do not apply. This seems doubtful.

Property is related if (a) it forms part of the estate of the transferor's spouse or civil partner, or (b) it is property which has, within the preceding five years, been the property of a charity or other exempt body under an exempt transfer made by the transferor or spouse/civil partner. Under (b), the property remains related property, despite being disposed of by the trust or body, for a period of five years after that disposal. The purpose of this rule is to prevent the avoidance of IHT through the use of exempt transfers.

Example

A holds 800 of the 1,000 shares of a family company and transfers 350 of them to his child. There will be a transfer of value which will take account of the loss of control of the company. However, if he transfers 350 shares to his wife instead, the transfer will be exempt and he is left with 450 shares. If after giving 350 shares to his wife he then gives a further 350 to his son, he will, but for section 161, be taken as reducing a 45% holding to a 10% holding and so there will be no loss of control. Section 161 therefore provides that where the value of the property transferred[28]—35%—is less than the appropriate portion of the aggregate of the holdings of A and Mrs A—35/80ths of an 80% holding—the higher value is taken. So the value of the property transferred by A to A's son will be 35/80 times the value of their combined holdings.

It will be seen that this rule applies whether it is A or Mrs A who makes the transfer to the son. However, a subsequent transfer of her 35% holding by Mrs A to make the child's total up to 70% will only be a transfer of 35/45ths of a 45% holding, so that IHT may be reduced by this procedure.

The purpose of group (b) is to prevent the loss of IHT arising on an exempt transfer which results in a loss of control. Thus, if A holds 51% of the shares in a company and gives 2% to charity, he will have lost control of the company and perhaps reduced the value of the holding substantially.

55.2.2 Section 176 Relief from Section 161—Undoing Related Property Valuation after Death

Where, within three years of the death, the executors or beneficiaries sell property which has been valued as related property, the value for IHT purposes may be recalculated as if the

---

[27] IHTA 1984, s 161(3); this is not crystal clear, but is (undoubtedly) the official view.
[28] The actual value transferred will depend on who bears the tax.

related property rules did not apply. This is needed to achieve fairness where, for example, shares are left to beneficiaries who are not related to the spouse or civil partner.[29]

Thus, varying the example above, if A, who had 80% of the shares in a company, then transferred 35% to his wife, the transfer would be exempt and no IHT would be payable notwithstanding that A had lost control of the company. If A died, his 45% holding would, as just seen, be valued as the appropriate portion (45/80ths) of the 80% holding by section 161. If, however, A's executors sold the 45% for the market value of a 45% holding, the related property rule would be excluded; this does not necessarily mean taking the sale proceeds instead, but rather recalculating the value at death.

To qualify for this relief the sale must be an arm's-length sale for a price freely negotiated and not in conjunction with a sale of any of the related or other property to which the relief applies; there must be no provision for reacquisition and no person concerned as vendor (or having an interest in the proceeds of sale) may be the same as or connected with any person concerned as purchaser (or having an interest in the purchase). Further, the vendors must be the deceased's PRs or those in whom the property vested immediately after the death.

An alteration in the company's share, loan capital, rights attached to shares or securities of a close company will disqualify the property from relief if the effect of the alteration is to reduce the value of the property by more than 5% (section 176(5)).

The relief in section 176 applies also whenever property falls to be valued in conjunction with property which was also comprised in the deceased's estate but has not, at any time since the death, been vested in the vendors. An example would be where D held a 60% holding in a company and died, leaving half to A and half to B. D's estate would be valued on the basis of a controlling interest. If A now sells his half for the value appropriate to a 30% holding, A may substitute the actual proceeds of sale.

55.3   Other Valuation Rules

55.3.1 Shares and Securities

In the case of quoted stocks and shares, the CGT quarter-up rule is used.[30] Stocks and shares which are not quoted or dealt in on a stock exchange must be valued on an estimate of market worth. This involves a consideration of the value of the company's assets as at the date of death, and its earning power and dividend record for recent years. The value of assets may become the dominating factor if liquidation was imminent at the date of death. Where unquoted shares and securities are valued, an important factor will be the amount of information which the hypothetical purchaser will have (on which, see above at §55.1.2, principle (1)).

---

[29] IHTA 1984, s 176(1)(a). There are risks in electing for relief, since agricultural or business relief may be lost if the farm or business is incorporated.

[30] TCGA 1992, s 272 (see above at §43.7).

55.3.2 *Debts Due to the Transferor*

In valuing the debt, it is assumed that the debt will be paid in full unless and to the extent that recovery of the sum is impossible or not reasonably practicable. Even then, recovery will be assumed if the non-recoverability is due to any act or omission on the transferor's part (section 166). Where a debt thought at the death of the creditor to be irrecoverable is subsequently paid, the debt will, on payment, become part of the deceased's estate and so will be added to it.

55.3.3 *Accrued Income to Date of Transfer*

Every estate presumably[31] includes all income upon the property included therein down to and outstanding at the relevant date, usually the death of the transferor. In the case of quoted securities, which are not ex-dividend, the accrued income is included in the valuation and does not have to be accounted for separately. In all other cases, such as land producing rents, income which is accruing due at the date of transfer must be apportioned, and the proportion (less income tax, if deductible) up to the relevant date included in the estate.

55.4   Reliefs for Realised Changes in Value

55.4.1 *Relief for Sales of Qualifying Investments: Shares, etc Sold at a Loss Following Transfer on Death*

Normally, shares are valued as they were immediately before the death. If, however, qualifying investments are sold at a lower value within 12 months of the death, the lower value may be used instead (section 179(1)). Where the sale is preceded by a contract, the date of sale is that of the contract (section 189). If the sale results from the exercise of an option, the critical date is that of the grant of the option.

Qualifying. The relief applies only to qualifying investments,[32] ie broadly, quoted shares and securities and units in authorised unit trusts. It applies to any shares forming part of the deceased's estate on death, whether free estate or settled property, save for shares held by a company in which the deceased had a controlling interest.

Cancelled or suspended. Since this relief, as originally drafted, applied only to sales of investments, it did not apply where shares became worthless or were cancelled. Qualifying investments which were in the estate immediately before the death, but which were cancelled within the next 12 months without being replaced, are now treated as sold for a

---

[31] There is no express provision similar to FA 1894, s 6(5) which applied for estate duty; however, if this income were not included there would have been no need for FA 1975, Sch 12, para 16(2), amending what became TA 1988, s 699, now ITTOIA 2005, s 669 (see above at §30.1).

[32] IHTA 1984, s 178; on meaning of quoted and unquoted, see *ibid*, s 272, as amended by FA 1987, Sch 8, para 17. Shares or securities listed on a recognised stock exchange or dealt in on the old Unlisted Securities Market (USM, which ran from 1986 to 1996) are quoted. Unquoted means shares neither so listed nor so dealt in. A list of recognised stock exchanges is available on the HMRC website at https://www.gov.uk/government/publications/designated-recognised-stock-exchanges-section-1005-income-tax-act-2007. The AIM is not a recognised stock exchange for this purpose.

nominal consideration of £1 immediately before the cancellation (section 186A), provided they were held by the appropriate person at the cancellation. When shares are suspended within 12 months of the death and are still suspended on the first anniversary of the death, their value on that anniversary is taken by a similar deemed sale, but this time for market value (section 186B).

Multiple sales. Where more than one sale of qualifying investments takes place within the 12-month period, all such sums received must be aggregated to determine the relief. If the sum is less than the principal value at the date of death, the difference, called the loss on sale, is deducted from the value at death.[33] Thus, if an estate includes eight blocks of shares, each worth £1,000 at the date of death, and in the next 12 months three blocks are sold at £700, £900 and £1,050 respectively, the loss on sale is £3,000—£2,650 = £350 and the value will be reduced to £7,650.

55.4.1.1 Price

In making these calculations the Revenue may substitute for the actual sale price the best consideration which could reasonably have been obtained.[34] Any commission or stamp duty (section 178(5)) and, in accordance with general principles,[35] any expenses of sale and any capital gains liability, are all ignored. There are rules for bringing into account both capital sums received (section 181) and calls made (section 182) in respect of the investments between the death and the sale. In no circumstances may any investment be treated as being sold at a loss greater than its basic value at the date of death (section 188), as might occur if calls were made and the shares were then sold for a low price.

55.4.1.2 The Sale—The Vendor

The sale must have been carried out by the appropriate person (section 179(1)), who is the person liable for the tax in respect of the investments (section 178), ie the executors, trustees or the beneficiary. If only one of them is paying the tax, that is the appropriate person. For this purpose, the PRs of the estate and the trustees of a settlement are each treated as a single and continuing body of persons (section 178(4)). The very fact that A holds property subject to a charge for the tax is sufficient to make A—as well as the property—liable, and so A is an appropriate person (section 200(1)(c)).

55.4.1.3 Restricting Effect of New Purchase

The primary reason for the relief was to provide for the case where securities, having been valued at death, were then sold at a loss in order to pay tax. The relief is not confined to such sales and may be claimed simply because of a change in investments. However, where new shares or securities are bought, the relief may be extinguished or reduced.[36] This will occur if the purchases take place within the period beginning at the date of death and ending two months after the last sale within the 12-month period. Where the purchase

---

[33] IHTA 1984, s 179; on effect of sale of part of a holding, see s 186.
[34] IHTA 1984, s 179(1): this rule is ignored for cancelled and suspended shares (ss 186A(2), 186B(3)).
[35] IHTA 1984, s 5(5) (see below at §55.3.1).
[36] IHTA 1984, s 180(1); distinguish subscribing for new shares: *Re VGM Holdings Ltd* [1942] Ch 235, [1942] 1 All ER 224.

is by a PR or trustee then all the purchases of qualifying investments are aggregated. This forms the numerator of a fraction the denominator of which is the total sales figure for the qualifying investments sold since the death, taking actual price obtained or the best consideration that could have been obtained, as above. This fraction is then applied to the loss on sale and only the proportion of that loss remaining after taking away the fraction is eligible for relief. Thus, suppose that the proceeds of sale come to £3,000 giving a loss on sale of £600, and that £1,000 is then reinvested. The fraction will be 1,000/3,000. The relief will therefore be reduced by one-third to £400.

Effect depending on who sells. If the reinvestment is carried out by someone other than a trustee or PR, the loss claim will be reduced only if the purchase is of the same description as the investments sold (section 180(3)). Investments are not of the same description if they are quoted separately on a recognised stock exchange or if they are different authorised unit trusts (section 180(3)). A beneficiary selling Bank of Scotland shares could therefore purchase Barclays Bank shares the next day without imperilling the claim for relief. Where shares or securities are exchanged for other property and the market value of the investments at the time of the exchange is greater than their value on death, that market value is taken into account (section 184).

Transactions ignored. Special rules apply to ignore certain transactions which relate more to the form than the substance of an investment, for example a reorganisation or reduction of the share capital, or the conversion of securities (section 183). These transactions are only partly ignored if the appropriate person has to give new consideration for the new holding. If the new holding is itself sold within 12 months of the death, the sale is treated in the normal way.

55.4.2 Land; Relief for Sales at a Loss Following Transfer on Death

Where an interest in land was included in D's estate immediately before death and was later sold within four years of the death, and the sale price was less than the value at the date of death, the sale price may be substituted if the 'appropriate person' so claims.[37] This recognition of a decline in value after the death applies only where the sale is by the appropriate person, and is not to a beneficiary of the estate or one of his near relatives, and the vendor has no right to repurchase the interest sold or any other interest in the same land (section 191). The sale price is not necessarily conclusive, since the Revenue will substitute the best consideration that could reasonably have been obtained for the land at the time of the sale if this would be greater. This relief will not apply if the change in the value of the interest is £1,000 or 5% of the value at death, whichever is the lower; however, a drop of £1,001 will be recognised in full (section 191(2)). Importantly, if the election is made, all sales within the period must be brought into account to determine the overall loss.

---

[37] IHTA 1984, ss 191, 197A, added by FA 1993, s 199. The costs of sale are ignored (IHTA 1984, s 190(4)). The period was originally three years but was extended to four by s 197A; this extension does not apply to compulsory purchase. The reason for the extension of the period in 1993 was probably to recognise the difficulties of the housing market, a reason which did not apply to compulsory acquisition. A notice of compulsory purchase delivered within the three-year period will bring the eventual conveyance within relief whatever the date of completion (s 197).

Example

A died in June. The estate included four pieces of land, two of which were sold in November of that year and two in January of the next year.

	Value at date of death £	Actual sales value £	Difference between value at date of death and sales value £
Property 1	10,500	6,750	(3,750)
Property 2	16,000	16,200	200
Property 3	18,000	17,850	(150)
Property 4	23,000	24,900	1,900
Total	67,500	65,700	(1,800)

Although the total decrease in value on all four properties since death is £1,800, the increase on property 2 (£200) and the decrease on property 3 (£150) are ignored because they are neither £1,000 nor 5% of the value of the properties at death. The overall decrease in value that can be taken into account if the election is made is therefore £1,850.

An interest in land is not defined. While an interest in the proceeds of sale is in practice treated as an interest in land, neither an interest in a company owning land nor an interest in unadministered residue appears to qualify.

In deciding whether the sale is within four years of the death, the critical date is that of the contract to sell; if the sale results from the exercise of an option to sell, the date will be the exercise of the option unless the exercise was within six months of the grant, in which case the date of grant is preferred (section 198).

In comparing the sale price with the value at date of death, a number of adjustments may have to be made:

(1) Any change in the interest in land arising between the death and the sale must be taken into account (section 193); similarly, if the interest is a lease with less than 50 years to run, the value is increased to take account of the inevitable loss due to the passage of time (section 194). This is to ensure that the two values are compared on the same basis.

(2) Where, on the death, other interests, whether in the same or other land, were taken into account, as occurs where the other interest is related property, the excess attributable to that other value must be brought into account again by being added to the sale price (section 195).

(3) Where other interests in land in the estate are sold by the claimant in the same capacity, that is as PR or as beneficiary, any gains on such sales must be set off against the loss. If the claim relates to more than one interest, the gains are apportioned between the interests. The same applies to a sale to a connected person (section 196).

(4) If the claimant reinvests in land, by buying other land within the period beginning with the death and ending four months after the last sale in respect of which relief is claimed, then, if the aggregate of the purchase prices (A) exceeds the aggregate of the

sales (B), no relief may be claimed. If A does not exceed B, the fraction A/B is applied to the sale price and the resulting sum is added to it (section 192). In applying this rule no account is to be taken of a sale in the fourth year; when a claim relates only to sales in the fourth year, rule (4) does not apply (section 197A(3)). If, in consequence of this rule the sale price is reduced or increased, that reduction or increase must be given effect (section 192(3), (4)).

55.5   Liabilities

Liabilities fall to be valued and taken into account either to determine the overall value of an estate, whether of D or someone else, or to determine the loss to that estate when a liability is incurred (section 5(3)). FA 2013, section 176 and Schedule 36 introduced new limits on the circumstances in which liabilities will be deductible for IHT purposes. The changes are aimed at various tax planning schemes involving the use of debts and liabilities to reduce the value of the estate, namely liabilities incurred to acquire assets that are eligible for business property relief or are excluded assets for IHT purposes or when the debt will not be repaid.[38] Further restrictions were introduced in FA 2014, Schedule 25 to close a loophole in respect of liabilities attributable to financing non-residents' foreign currency accounts.[39]

55.5.1 Liabilities Incurred by the Transferor

55.5.1.1 General—Only if for Money or Money's Worth

Liabilities are, in general, allowable deductions, provided that, and then only to the extent that, they were incurred for a consideration in money or money's worth (section 5(5)). This proviso does not apply to liabilities imposed by law. If there is no such consideration the liability will be non-deductible even though a binding legal obligation has been incurred. The subsequent discharge of the obligation will be the chargeable transfer. Payments by a husband to his wife under a valid deed of separation may continue during the life of the wife, whether or not the husband predeceases her. On the death of the husband, the wife being still alive, future covenanted payments are a debt of his estate. The payments are for full consideration in money or money's worth, since he would have had to pay larger amounts during his lifetime had he not entered into a covenant binding on his executors.

Where the liability is incurred for a consideration in money or money's worth, it is not necessary that that consideration should move to the transferor. Thus, if A agrees to sell a chair worth £500 for that sum on condition that the proceeds of sale are paid to B, but dies before making delivery, the liability to transfer the chair is an allowable deduction in valuing A's estate. Equally, of course, the direction to pay £500 to B would, if discharged before A's death, itself have been a separate transfer of value. In these instances, however, deduction is still only allowed to the extent of the consideration in money or money's worth. Suppose, therefore, that A has agreed to *buy* a chair worth £500 from B for £800. The liability to pay £800 is deductible only to the extent of £500 and so not allowable as to £300.

---

[38] For commentary see McKeever [2013] BTR 491.
[39] For commentary see Lemos [2014] BTR 438.

55.5.1.2 Incumbrances Created by the Transferor Over Particular Property

A liability which is an incumbrance (defined in section 272) on any property is, as far as possible, taken to reduce the value of that property (section 162(4)). If a husband leaves the matrimonial home to his widow subject to a mortgage, the transfer to the widow is exempt and the debt to the lender is taken as reducing the value of the property transferred to the widow, and so will be ignored in computing the value of the rest of the estate (unless the debt is greater than the value of the house). It will be seen that the rule refers to a liability which is an incumbrance. The husband, in our example, is liable to the building society for the sum owed, and this liability is personal as well as being an incumbrance on the house itself. It is not open to him to deduct his personal debt as distinct from the sum secured by the incumbrance since there is only one liability and that is an incumbrance on the property. The rule is also important in terms of liability for the tax. Property bearing its own tax may find the burden greatly reduced and the Revenue charge will be for a lower sum. It is to be assumed that where the debt is properly payable out of more than one item of property, the person liable to pay the debt must apportion the liability.

55.5.2 *Valuing the Estate Immediately Before Death—Disallowing Debts as Deductions Where Consideration Consists of Property, etc Derived from Deceased*

With the introduction of IHT it became necessary to revive certain estate duty rules for determining the value of a person's estate immediately before death. By FA 1986, section 103(1)(a), a debt is disallowed to the extent to which the consideration given for it is property derived from the deceased.[40] Section 103(1)(b) extends the disallowance to the situation in which the consideration is given not for the very property derived from the deceased, but from the economic value which that property represents. Thus, it disallows the deduction where there is consideration given by any person who was at any time entitled to property derived from the deceased or among whose resources such property was at any time to be found.[41] This rule is aimed at the simple device of a loan back.[42] A mother gives money to her son; some time later the son lends it back to his mother. When the mother dies the loan would, but for section 103, be an allowable deduction. The prohibition on the deduction of debts incurred otherwise than for full consideration (see above at §55.5.1) would not apply since there would be full consideration. Deduction of the debt is disallowed by this rule.

The expression 'property derived from the deceased' is defined widely to cover property which was the subject matter of a disposition by the deceased, whether alone or in concert with others and whether directly or indirectly, and including any property which repre-

---

[40] The provision re-enacts FA 1939, s 31. Pre-18 March 1986 debts are outside this rule (FA 1986, s 103(6)).

[41] It is unclear what is added by the idea of property 'found' among his resources.

[42] See McCutcheon, *Inheritance Tax*, 3rd edn (Sweet & Maxwell, 1990) §§13:56ff; the so-called 'inheritance trust' is a further example popular in the days of CTT. F would lend money to trustees of a trust for his children. The trustees would buy a single premium insurance bond; they would withdraw 5% pa as allowed as tax-free return of capital and pay this to the father. Thus the capital would enure to the children with no CTT other than that (if any) due on the creation of the trust and the father would enjoy a tax-free 5% return until the debt was paid off.

sented the subject matter of such a disposition.[43] The term 'disposition' includes disposition by associated operations (IHTA 1984, section 272; see §45.7 above). This wide definition of property derived from the deceased is not without its difficulties. Thus, if a mother gives her son a house which the son sells, and the son then uses the proceeds to buy shares,[44] it appears that there are three sets of property ready to trigger this rule should the mother buy the shares and not have paid the debt before she dies, ie the house, the price and the shares. There is nothing in the legislation to state that only the house is to be taken as the property derived from the mother, or that it is replaced by the shares. This very wide definition is then narrowed by a provision that it cannot apply to a disposition which is not a transfer of value.[45] Thus, if the mother gives the property to the son as in the previous example, the deduction will be disallowed, but if she sells the property for full value and later buys it back and the price is left outstanding, the debt will be an allowable deduction. It will be seen that if the initial sale by the mother is at an undervalue, the rule will apply.

The points made in these paragraphs are well illustrated by *Phizackerly v HMRC*.[46] Here W died in April 2000 and H in 2002. The issue concerns the deductibility of a debt when H died. She left a settled legacy on discretionary trusts and left the residue of her estate to H absolutely. Her half share in their house was valued at £150,000. In December 2000, D and others entered into a deed relating to the settled legacy. D assented to himself an undivided half share of the house and promised to pay £150,000, index-linked, to the trustees of the settled legacy. The sum was outstanding when he died—was it deductible? The Special Commissioner was satisfied that the property was derived from H. H and W had bought the house as joint tenants in 1992. H provided the money. In 1996, H severed the joint tenancy so that H and W held as beneficial tenants in common in equal shares. The only escape would be on the basis that the disposition was not a transfer of value because section 11 applied—but that too failed (above §45.5.2).

55.5.2.1 Partial Disallowance

Section 103 disallows the liability if the consideration for the debt was given by any person who was then entitled to any property derived from the deceased or among whose resources the property was at any time to be found. The formula for determining the disallowance involves an abatement of the liability otherwise deductible to an extent proportionate to the value of any consideration given which consists of the property derived directly or indirectly from the transferor.[47] This is necessary for situations in which the amount of the debt and that of the consideration do not correspond. Thus, if a mother gives her son a house and the son does not sell the house but lends the mother money, this rule applies to the extent that the mother's liability to repay falls within the value of the house.[48] If the house is worth £50,000 and the son lends her £40,000, there is no deduction for the liability to repay

---

[43] FA 1986, s 103(3); the term 'subject matter' is defined in s 103(6) to include annual or periodical payments due under the disposition.

[44] The problem was raised by Venables, *Inheritance Tax Planning* (Key Haven, 1988), §2.4.4.6.

[45] FA 1986, s 103(4); it is also necessary that the disposition should not be part of associated operations designed to circumvent this rule.

[46] [2007] Sp C 591, [2007] STC (SCD) 328.

[47] FA 1986, s 103(2).

[48] It will be noted that what is at issue is the value of the property derived by the son from the mother; this may be a different value from that of the loss of the mother's estate.

in calculating the value of the mother's estate; if the loan is for £60,000, there is a disallowance to the extent of £50,000.

55.5.2.2 Timing

Timing is not addressed in the legislation. Where the property in respect of which the liability arises is the same as that received under the original transfer of value, the change in the value of the property will have to be taken into account. What is not clear is how matters will be treated under section 103(1)(b). Thus, in the example just considered, what will happen if the house was worth £50,000 at the time of the transfer but is worth £60,000 when the son makes the loan back? In applying this rule, property is excluded which is not derived from the deceased (but only brought in under the wider formula), 'as to which it is shown that the disposition of which it, or the property which it represented, was the subject matter was not made with reference to, or with a view to enabling or facilitating, the giving of the consideration or the recoupment in any manner of the cost thereof'.[49]

To continue with the same generous mother, suppose that she gives her son a house and some shares, and the son later sells her the shares and some other property, and the sums due have not been paid at the time she dies. Section 103(1) will apply in relation to the debt due in respect of the shares,[50] but in relation to the other property the present exclusion rule will exclude the liability (ie permit its deduction after all) if it can be shown that the gift of the house was not made to enable the other property to be sold to the mother. If this cannot be shown then the liability in respect of the other property will be non-deductible subject to an upper limit equal to the value of the house.

This rule will also be relevant if the son sells the house to X, a stranger, and the mother subsequently buys property from X and dies with the liability still outstanding. However, it appears that this rule has no relevance if the mother buys the house from X and leaves the liability outstanding when she dies.[51]

55.5.2.3 Repayment Problems

To reinforce this legislative strategy it is provided that the repayment of a loan which is non-deductible by reason of the rules outlined above is treated as a transfer of value; the only relief is that the transfer is treated as potentially exempt and so will not cause a charge if the payment occurs more than seven years before the payer's death.[52] To continue the example of mother and son, suppose that the mother gives the property to her son and buys it back, leaving the purchase price outstanding, but later pays off the debt. The son is better off to the extent of the payment of the debt and the mother has reduced her estate by a similar amount. If she dies within seven years, IHT may become due.

This rule causes some surprises. Thus, if the mother gives a house to her son who sells it to X, a stranger, and she later buys it from X and dies without paying the debt, there will, as already seen, be no deduction for the liability. What this rule seems to provide is that if the

---

[49] FA 1986, s 103(2)(b).
[50] FA 1986, s 103(2)(a).
[51] Because of FA 1986, s 103(2)(a).
[52] FA 1986, s 103(5).

liability is paid off, there will be a chargeable transfer if the mother dies within seven years.[53] This rule is also difficult in that it fails to define when there is a liability, a matter of some importance since the rule applies only where there is a discharged liability. The intention is to reinforce the rule barring the deduction of a liability remaining unpaid at the date of death. If, therefore, no liability is created, the rule cannot apply. Thus, if the mother buys the property back from the son and does not leave the money outstanding but pays the price at the same time as—or before—the date of performance, it appears that this rule cannot apply. It is arguable whether a few days' delay in settling the debt will be enough to trigger the present rule, or whether some clear intention to allow time to pay will be required.

55.5.3 *Other Debts and Incumbrances—Not Made by Transferor*

In the case of debts which were not incurred, and incumbrances which were not created, by D, the transferor, but for which D or the property is liable, allowance is made whether or not the debts were incurred or the incumbrances were created for consideration. Thus, if D had acquired property subject to a mortgage, the mortgage money would be deductible even if the mortgagee received his mortgage as a gift from the previous owner of the property. No allowance is to be made for any debt in respect of which there is a right to reimbursement from any other estate or person, unless such reimbursement cannot reasonably be expected to be obtained (section 162(1)).

55.5.3.1 Valuing Debts Due from the Estate

There is no statutory provision stating how debts owing by D are to be valued. It is, therefore, a matter of calculating how much money really is owed at the date of transfer, or, in the case of liabilities of uncertain amounts and contingent liabilities, of estimating the value of the debt as at the date of transfer in the light of circumstances which then exist. In the case of a certain liability which is not to mature until a future date, the amount will have to be discounted according to the time which is to elapse before maturity (section 162(2)). Any payments in advance which fell due before the transfer but are unpaid at the transfer are proper deductions. The value obtained by advance payment is not taxable as an asset of the estate, unless it is capable of being turned into money. For example, if council tax on the house occupied by the deceased was payable in advance before the date of death, the amount (if not paid) would be a proper deduction from his estate. The value to the estate of the council tax paid in advance would not be included unless the executors were reasonably able to obtain a cash advantage therefrom by arrangements with an incoming occupier.

55.5.3.2 Unenforceable Debts

If neither the executor nor anyone else is liable to pay the debt, and it is not charged on any property, then no deduction is allowed. In *Re Barnes*,[54] the deceased had made gifts inter vivos amounting to £185,101 within the statutory period before death, thus rendering them liable to estate duty. He died, leaving assets worth £12 and debts and funeral expenses

---

[53] See Venables, *op cit*, §2.4.4.10.
[54] [1939] 1 KB 316, [1938] 4 All ER 870.

amounting to £90,390. It was held that estate duty was payable on the value of the gifts inter vivos without deduction of the debts and funeral expenses, because those liabilities were neither chargeable on the gifts nor payable by the donees. It was immaterial that the donees in fact paid the debts. For the same reason, debts which are unenforceable, such as gaming debts, debts under illegal contracts and debts of which evidence in writing required by statute is absent, are not allowable. Statute-barred debts, which an executor may pay if he chooses, are apparently allowable if actually paid.[55]

55.5.3.3 Executor's Debts

Debts incurred or incumbrances created by the executor, such as administration expenses, not being debts of the deceased, are not deductible, but exceptions are allowed for certain funeral expenses.

55.5.3.4 Funeral Expenses

In determining the value of the estate immediately before death, allowance is made for reasonable funeral expenses (section 172) and the cost of a tombstone or gravestone.[56]

55.5.4 Taxes and Incidental Expenses

55.5.4.1 Interaction of IHT and CGT and Incidental Expenses—Bearing the Burdens

Where A makes a chargeable transfer of property to B, both IHT and CGT may arise. The following rules should be borne in mind in deciding whether the IHT should be borne by A or by B; it should also be noted that IHT may be paid by instalments if B pays this tax (see below at §56.5).

(1) Where IHT is borne by A it may have to be grossed up. This is because the transferor's liability to tax resulting from the transfer is taken into account in determining the value of his estate immediately after the transfer.[57] Where the tax is borne by B there is no grossing up. In PETs there is no grossing up.

(2) Where CGT falls due and is borne by A, no deduction may be made on account of the CGT in calculating the value for IHT (section 165). Thus, where the transfer gives rise to a liability to CGT, the value transferred is the value of the asset grossed up as necessary to take account of the IHT only—no account is taken of the CGT. However, the amount payable by way of CGT is not deductible in computing the value transferred.

The reason for (1) above is self-evident; the reason for (2) is to prevent anomalies. If A transfers an asset worth £50,000 on which there is a capital gains liability of £10,000, A's liability to CGT and IHT should be the same as where the asset is sold for £50,000 and the proceeds of sale are then given to B.

---

[55] *Norton v Frecker* (1737) 1 Atk 524.
[56] Statement of Practice SP 7/87.
[57] IHTA 1984, s 5(4). On settled property, see *ibid*, s 165.

It should be noted that the liability to CGT is ignored only in determining the value of the estate immediately after the transfer. Thus, if A dies the day after making the transfer, his liability to CGT on the previous transfer is deductible in computing the value of the estate. Different rules apply when the CGT is borne by B; there, the tax paid by B is deductible in computing the value transferred. It should be noted that this is deductible whether it is A or B who actually pays the IHT. Similar rules apply to the payment of incidental expenses, which are deductible only if borne by B (section 164).

(3) For situations in which holdover relief may be claimed for CGT, see above at §§36.3 and 36.4.

(4) Where CGT arises but an election to defer the CGT liability was made under the now repealed FA 1980, section 79,[58] and IHT also arises, the IHT will be deductible in computing the chargeable gain on a subsequent disposal by B, but only to the extent of wiping out a chargeable gain; the IHT cannot be used to create a loss. This applies even though the IHT is borne by A; in this instance the IHT is that due after the grossing-up rules have been applied. If the IHT is subsequently increased through A dying within seven (in practice not more than five) years of the gift, adjustments are made to the CGT to give effect to the extra deduction now due. A similar rule applies where the transfer is potentially exempt but tax becomes due because the donor dies within seven years.

55.5.4.2 Other Taxes

Income and other taxes due from and repayments of such taxes due to the estate must be taken into account. An outstanding liability to pay tax on an earlier transfer tax (CTT or IHT) is deductible on death only if actually paid out of the estate (section 174(2)). Foreign taxes are generally allowed only as deductions from foreign property.[59]

---

[58] Repealed by FA 1989, Sch 17, Pt VII, but effect preserved for disposals before 14 March 1989.
[59] Because not generally enforceable in the UK.

56

Accountability and Administration

56.1 Introduction

Accountability means the liability of a person to account to the Revenue for the tax due; this liability is distinct from the questions of who should report the transfer (see below at §56.3) and how the burden of the tax is allocated (see chapter fifty-seven below). Accountability of persons is supplemented by the Revenue charge which enables the Revenue to obtain payment out of the property itself, whether or not the owner is accountable. Accountability gives rise to legal liability *vis à vis* the Revenue; those accountable may have rights to recover the tax from others.[1]

In the rules which follow, where two or more persons are liable for the tax, each is liable for the whole of the amount, unless some other provision expressly states otherwise (section 205). There are extensive penalties, the limits of which were reviewed in 1999 and again in 2004.[2] FA 2004 made further changes to penalties, usually to bring IHT penalties into line with those for income tax or CGT; for example, it fixed the charge at £100 a day for late delivery of an IHT account, unless the tax involved is less than £100 or there is reasonable excuse, and extended the reasonable excuse rules to all failures to provide information or to deliver accounts.[3] It removed the charge where a person liable to tax delivers incorrect material fraudulently or negligently but no additional IHT is payable.[4] A person who is not

---

[1] Eg, by virtue of IHTA 1984, ss 211(3), 212.
[2] FA 1999, s 108, FA 2004, s 295.
[3] FA 2004, s 295, amending IHTA 1984, ss 245 and 245A.
[4] IHTA 1984, s 247(1), as amended by FA 2004, s 295(2).

liable to tax but who furnishes such information fraudulently or negligently is subject to a penalty not exceeding £3,000; the same maximum penalty applies to a person assisting in the provision of such information which he knew to be incorrect (section 247(3)). Further changes were made by FA 2008, section 122 and Schedule 40, which apply from 1 April 2009 at the latest. These extended the FA 2007 changes to penalties for income tax, etc (above at §4.5.3) to IHT. These distinguish (a) failure to take reasonable care from (b) deliberate understatement and (c) deliberate understatement with concealment. Disclosure, especially if unprompted, reduces the penalties.

56.2   Accountability to the Revenue for Tax

56.2.1 *Lifetime Transfers*

56.2.1.1 General Rules

By section 199 those liable are:

(1)   the transferor;
(2)   the transferee;
(3)   any person in whom the property is vested, whether beneficially or not, or who is beneficially entitled to an interest in possession in the property; and
(4)   where the property has become settled property as a result of the transfer, any person for whose benefit the property or income is applied.

'Property' includes property directly or indirectly representing that property (section 199(5)). To this list may be added the transferor's PRs and spouse or civil partner (see further below).

Category (3) is further refined in three ways—one widening and two restrictive. First, the definition of 'vesting' is widened by section 199(4) to include anyone who takes possession of or intermeddles with, or otherwise acts in relation to, property so as to become liable as executor or trustee (or, in Scotland, any person who intromits with property or has become liable as a vitious intromitter). This covers not only the executor de son tort, but also many constructive trustees. In *IRC v Stype Investments (Jersey) Ltd*,[5] the Court of Appeal held that procuring the payment of proceeds of sale of trust property from PRs constituted in England to PRs constituted in Jersey, was an act of intermeddling sufficient to make the person procuring that payment liable. The same provision also extends the notion of vesting to cover anyone to whom the management of property is entrusted on behalf of a person not of full legal capacity. Secondly, it is restricted in the case of a purchaser (and anyone deriving title from such a purchaser) to property subject to a Revenue charge (section 199(3)). Thirdly, the liability of those in category (3) having possession of or a beneficial interest in property is limited to the extent of that property (section 204(3)). This limitation does not mean that they are liable only to the extent that the tax is attributable to that property; the value of the whole property may be taken.

---

[5] [1982] STC 625.

Liability for those in category (4) is limited, in that those liable as receiving benefits under a discretionary trust cannot be made liable beyond the amount received (less income tax) (section 204(5)). It is perhaps odd that while there is mention of an allowance for income tax under Chapter 2 of Part 13 of ITA 2007 (ex TA 1988, sections 739 and 740), there is no equivalent mention of the analogous CGT rules.

56.2.1.2 Liability of Personal Representatives of Transferor

The transferor's (A's) PRs are liable (but not primarily liable) for tax due in respect of: (a) PETs which become chargeable; (b) any additional tax due in respect of other chargeable transfers;[6] and (c) any tax due in respect of a gift with reservation.[7]

56.2.1.3 Liability of Spouse or Civil Partner of Transferor

A's spouse or civil partner may also be liable through having received a transfer of value from A and having been A's spouse or civil partner at the time of each transfer (section 203(1)). However, this liability is limited in two ways. First, liability cannot exceed the market value of the property at the time of the transfer to the spouse or civil partner (section 203(1)). Secondly, liability may be further limited for a decline in value judged by the market value at the relevant time or the proceeds of a prior qualifying sale (section 203(2)). This second limitation does not apply to tangible movable property (section 203(2)(d)); while this may make sense for household goods, it does not do so for works of art.

56.2.1.4 Primary Liability of Transferor for Immediately Chargeable Transfers

Under section 199(1), the transferor, A, is primarily liable for tax due in respect of chargeable transfers (section 204(6)); others listed in section 199(1) become liable only if the tax remains unpaid after the due date. Presumably the others are not liable to a greater extent than if the transfer had been gross rather than net, ie for no more than the tax due if the transfer had not been grossed up. Section 204(5) makes this express for category (4). If a transferee bears the tax in this way, it is presumably not open to the Revenue to collect the balance of tax due to the grossing up from A, the transferor; however, if A reimburses the transferee for the tax, this will be a further transfer of value.

56.2.1.5 Primary Liability for Additional Tax on Death Within Seven Years

Under section 199(2), additional tax may be due in respect of an immediately chargeable transfer where A, the transferor, dies within seven years, or on a PET where A dies within that period. Here, there is no point in making A primarily liable. Moreover, while section 199(2) makes A's PRs liable, it does not make them primarily liable.[8] In these two instances the primary liability remains that of B, the transferee, and the liability of the PRs is limited. For PETs, it appears that PRs are liable only after all other possible candidates, or if the tax

---

[6] IHTA 1984, s 199(2), subject to the limits in s 204(9).

[7] Capital Taxes Office practice is not to pursue PRs after they have obtained a certificate of discharge and distributed the estate, provided they have made the 'fullest enquiries that are reasonably practicable in the circumstances' to discover lifetime transfers. See [1991] *Simon's Tax Intelligence* 238. It must also be recalled that the 1991 CTO letter states that it is sent without prejudice to the application of s 199(2) in an appropriate case.

[8] IHTA 1984, s 204(6), excluded by s 204(7).

remains unpaid 12 months after the end of the month in which the death occurred, and then subject to the limit of the assets.[9]

56.2.1.6 Gift with Ceased Reservation

Where there is a gift with reservation and the reservation ceases to exist before the donor's death, the ending of the reservation is treated as a PET. The primary liability is that of the donee (sections 199(2), 204(8)).

56.2.2 Transfer on Death

56.2.2.1 General Rule

Section 200 provides that the people liable for the tax under a charge arising under section 4 are:

(1) the deceased's PRs—but with the exclusion of settled property unless it is settled land in the UK which devolves on them;
(2) the trustees—so far as concerns property settled immediately before death;
(3) the beneficiaries, or any other person in whom the property is vested after the death, eg the trustees of a settlement created by the will; and
(4) where property was settled at the time of the death, any person for whose benefit property or income is applied, eg a person benefiting under a trust which became discretionary on the death of the life tenant.

As with lifetime gifts, 'property' includes property directly or indirectly representing that property.[10] The definition of 'vesting' is also widened to include intermeddlers—those who manage the property on behalf of a person not of full legal capacity. There is a similar exception for a purchaser and any person deriving title from such a purchaser unless the property is subject to a Revenue charge.[11]

The rules limiting the liability of trustees and beneficiaries set out in §56.1.3 below apply here too.[12] Similarly, a person who succeeds to a part interest in income from settled property is treated as entitled to an interest in the whole of the settled property.[13] There is no immunity from liability simply because the person is not resident in the UK and that the liability is personal (not simply representative).[14]

Personal representatives are liable only to the extent of the assets they received or would have received but for their own neglect or default.[15] A similar rule applies to limit their liability to tax on UK land in a settlement and which devolves on them (section 204(1)(b)). Where PRs have distributed the estate and obtained a certificate of discharge but a lifetime transfer then comes to light, they are liable for any extra tax. However, as with lifetime transfers, the Revenue will not usually make any claim if the PRs have made the fullest

[9] The wording of IHTA 1984, s 204(7), (8) is extremely obscure—see Venables, *Inheritance Tax Planning* (Key Haven, 1988), 22.
[10] IHTA 1984, s 200(4) applies s 199(4), (5) to s 200.
[11] IHTA 1984, s 200(1). Quite why s 199(3) was not made to apply in the same way as s 199(4), (5) is unclear.
[12] IHTA 1984, s 204(2), (3), (5).
[13] IHTA 1984, s 200(3), excluding s 50.
[14] *IRC v Stannard* [1984] STC 245. Note concessionary relief for certain foreign assets in ESC F6.
[15] IHTA 1984, s 204(1)(a).

possible enquiries that were reasonably practicable in the circumstances and have done all in their power to make full disclosure.[16]

These rules are adapted for succession in Scotland where particular comparative interest focuses on the treatment of legitim (section 209).

56.2.2.2 Special Cases

(1) *Close companies.* Where a charge arises under section 94(1) (company's transfer attributed to participators) or section 99(2) (settled property trustees as participators), only three categories of persons are liable (section 202(1)). The company is primarily liable; if the tax remains unpaid after it ought to have been paid, liability may fall on those to whom any amounts have been apportioned under section 94. There is an exclusion for any person to whom the amount of the value apportioned is not more than 5% of the value transferred. Others to whom a part of the value is apportioned are liable only for a proportionate part of the tax. An individual the value of whose estate is increased by the transfer is also liable, but only up to the amount of the increase.

(2) *Works of art, etc: conditional exemption.* Where there is a loss of conditional exemption in respect of designated objects, those liable are (a) those who disposed of the object, and (b) those for whose benefit the object was disposed (section 207).

(3) *Woodlands.* Where this value is not taxed on death but deferred, and there is a later disposal giving rise to IHT, liability for the tax deferred from death falls on those entitled to the proceeds of sale or who would be if there were a sale (section 208).

(4) *Pension rights continuing after death of pensioner.* Where a pension continues for a guaranteed period after death, the trustees of the pension scheme are not liable for any IHT in respect of the continuing pension on his death.[17] Where a charge arises under section 151B (dependant dying having inherited pension fund from member over 75), the person liable is the scheme administrator (section 210(2)).

(5) For obligations when there is a transfer of unused nil rate band under section 8A, see section 8C and §46.9 above.

56.2.3 Settled Property

56.2.3.1 Liability

Under section 201, those liable for a chargeable transfer falling within Part III of IHTA 1984 (ie sections 43–85) are:

(1) the trustees;

(2) any person entitled to an interest in possession in the settled property whether beneficially or not, eg the trustees of a subsequent settlement; and

(3) any person for whose benefit the property or income is applied, eg a discretionary beneficiary.

---

[16] [1991] *Simon's Tax Intelligence* 238; this is without prejudice to any claim under IHTA 1984, s 199(2).
[17] IHTA 1984, s 210. The pensioner's PRs are primarily liable on the actuarial value of the balance of the pension or annuity; under s 200(1)(c) there may also be liability for a person in whom the pension is vested or who is entitled to any interest in possession in it. If the pension ceases on the death there is usually no charge (s 151).

There is also a potential liability for S, the settlor, if the settlement was made in S's lifetime and the trustees are not for the time being resident in the UK. As with other liability provisions, it is expressly provided that references to any property include references to any property directly or indirectly representing it (section 201(6)). The scope of this provision is not affected by the 2006 changes to trusts.

The primary liability rests with the trustees (section 204(6)). Those liable otherwise than as a trustee are liable only if the tax remains unpaid after it ought to have been paid.

56.2.3.2 Limits on Liability

The general rules limiting liability apply here too. Thus, trustees are liable only to the extent of the property available to them as trustees or which they have actually received or disposed of, or where they have become liable to account to the beneficiaries.[18] Other rules already mentioned also apply here. Those liable in category (2) above as having possession of or a beneficial interest in property have their liability limited to the extent of that property,[19] and those liable in category (3) above as receiving benefits under a discretionary trust, cannot be made liable beyond the amount received (section 204(5)).

56.2.3.3 Settlor of Lifetime Trust with Non-resident Trustees

Under section 201(1)(d), S, the settlor, is liable if the chargeable transfer arising under Part III is made during S's life and the trustees are not for the time being resident in the UK. The trustees will be not resident in the UK unless the general administration of the settlement is ordinarily carried on in the UK and the trustees or a majority of them (and, where there is more than one class of trustees, a majority of each class) are for the time being resident in the UK (section 201(5)). If there is more than one settlor in relation to the settlement, this rule has effect as if there were separate settlements (section 201(4)); as this rule is stated to apply where 'the circumstances so require', its scope is uncertain. Section 201(1)(d) does not apply to any additional tax that becomes due by reason of the settlor's death within seven years of the chargeable transfer setting up the trust (section 201(2)). There are also transitional rules for settlements before 11 December 1974 and 17 March 1987 (section 201(3), (3A)).

56.3   Revenue Certificates and Charge

56.3.1 *Two Revenue Certificates*

56.3.1.1 Certificate of Tax Paid

A person may be liable for the tax even though not having ultimately to bear the burden of it. To assist the recovery process, the Board may grant a certificate specifying the tax paid (including interest) (section 214). The certificate may also state the debts and encumbrances allowed in valuing the property. The application for such a certificate must be made

---

[18] IHTA 1984, s 204(2). The property here means the property in relation to which the charge arises.
[19] IHTA 1984, s 204(3). This limitation does not mean that they are liable only to the extent that the tax is attributable to that property; the value of the whole property may be taken.

by a person who is not ultimately liable for the tax but who has paid or borne the tax attributable to the value of that property. This is conclusive as between the person who must bear the burden of the tax and the person seeking to recover it. This conclusive quality does not extend to any repayment which may be or may become due from the Board. (See also below §57.1.)

56.3.1.2 Certificate of Discharge

A person liable for tax may apply for a certificate of discharge under section 239. The certificate discharges all persons from any further claim for tax on the transfer and extinguishes the Revenue charge. It may also be given to discharge specific property from the charge when it is being acquired by a purchaser, but the application must be by a person liable to pay the tax. The Board must give a certificate if the chargeable transfer was on death or the transferor has died, and may do so in other cases.[20] Section 256(1)(b) empowers the Board to make regulations to grant certificates of discharge in wider circumstances; this power was widened in 2004 but has not yet been exercised.

56.3.2 Revenue Charge

56.3.2.1 General

Where tax is charged in respect of a chargeable transfer and that tax is 'for the time being unpaid', a charge for the unpaid tax arises (section 237(1)). The charge extends to the property[21] to which the value transferred is attributable, but in the case of a charge arising in respect of settled property under IHTA 1984, Part III (sections 43–93) it extends to all the property comprised in the settlement. The meaning of 'for the time being unpaid' is uncertain. It probably refers to the time of the occasion giving rise to the charge rather than that when the tax becomes due for payment, but this is unclear.[22] Since the scope of the charge relates directly to the tax unpaid, it may not always be for the same sum. Thus, if the IHT is paid by the donor, it will be calculated on a grossed-up amount; if it is paid by a donee, it will be grossed up on the net amount. As from 1999 the Revenue's charge has extended to IHT arising because of the loss of conditional exemption.[23]

56.3.2.2 Restricted Charge on Death

Section 237(3) excludes from the charge such property as (a) is personal or movable property, (b) is situated in the UK, (c) was beneficially owned[24] by D, the deceased, immediately before death, and (d) vests in D's PRs. The charge does, however, apply to leaseholds, since 1999,[25] and, since 1996, to undivided shares in land held on trust for sale, whether or not statutory.[26] The underlying rationale of the provision is to treat the charge as unnecessary

---

[20] IHTA 1984, s 239(1); on time limits see s 239(2), (2A).
[21] Widened to include property directly or indirectly representing it (s 237(2)).
[22] See discussion in *Simon's Direct Tax Service*, Pt I11.601.
[23] IHTA 1984, s 237(3B), (3C), added by FA 1999, s 107.
[24] IHTA 1984, s 49(1), which treats a person with a beneficial interest in possession in settled property as entitled to the underlying property, does not apply here.
[25] FA 1999, s 95.
[26] By the Trusts of Land and Appointment of Trustees Act 1996, Sch 4.

where the property devolves on the PRs. The charge does not apply to heritable property in Scotland (section 237(4)).

Property subject to the charge on death consists of (a) property, moveable or immovable, outside the UK, (b) land (including traditional real property, leases and proceeds of sale of trust land), (c) joint personal property which has accrued to a surviving joint owner, and (d) personal property nominated under a general power to dispose (eg under a power to nominate benefits over funds in a registered pension scheme)[27] unless the general power is contained in a settlement (when the trustees are liable for the tax, although it is a charge on the settled property). If the PRs have transferred the property to B, the beneficiary, they may still recover from B the tax that they have paid, though there will be obvious practical difficulties in the case of property situated outside the UK if the foreign executors and the beneficiary are out of the jurisdiction. The charge takes effect subject to existing incumbrances.

56.3.2.3 Potentially Exempt Transfers

The charge applies to property subject to a PET when that property is still retained by the transferee at the transferor's death (section 237(3A)). However, when the property is sold before the transferor's death, the charge is placed instead on the property received in its place. Property which is disposed of by the donee otherwise than by sale remains subject to the charge.

56.3.2.4 Protection of Purchaser

If the property is land in England, Wales or Northern Ireland and the charge is not registered at the time of disposition, P, a purchaser, takes clear of the charge, which is transferred to the proceeds of sale.[28] In other cases P will take clear of the charge if having no notice of it at the time of disposition (section 238(1)(c)). P will also escape the charge if, at the time of disposition, the Revenue have issued a certificate of discharge and P is not aware of any grounds that would invalidate it. A charge may cease by the effluxion of time (section 238(2)). The certificate of discharge under section 239 may be particularly useful here.

56.3.2.5 Loss of Conditional Exemption

The charge covers unpaid IHT and interest arising under the relevant provisions. The property charged is that to which the exemption has ceased to apply but, in the case of a sale, extends to assets representing the asset sold.[29]

56.4   Reporting Transfers

56.4.1 General

The duty to report the transfer is set out in section 216. This duty is distinct from questions of accountability (or liability) for the tax and of the final incidence or burden of the tax.

---

[27] IHTA 1984, s 151(4); *O'Grady v Wilmot* [1916] 2 AC 231.
[28] IHTA 1984, s 238(1)(a), (b); on timing, see s 238(3).
[29] IHTA 1984, s 237(3B), (3C), added by FA 1999.

Having a duty to report does not necessarily entail either being accountable for the tax or having to bear its burden. If a person discovers that the account is defective in a material respect, there is a duty to correct it.[30] The obligation is to deliver an account specifying to the best of one's knowledge and belief all appropriate property and the value of that property (section 216(1)). 'Knowledge' means personal knowledge, including information contained in documents in that person's possession. There is, however, no obligation to seek information from others (even servants or agents).[31] There is an interesting obligation in relation to certain non-resident trusts. Where a person (other than a barrister) is concerned in making an inter vivos settlement with a UK-domiciled settlor but non-resident trustees, such a person must inform the Revenue of the names and addresses of the settlor and the trustees within three months of the settlement being made (section 218).

56.4.1.1 Chargeable Transfers

In the case of a chargeable transfer, A, the transferor, must give an account[32] of all such transfers unless some other person liable for the tax, eg B, the transferee, has already done so (section 216). An account is required of all chargeable transfers on which tax may fall due; hence, there is an obligation to report transfers within the nil rate band or which fall within one or other of the exemptions unless the matter comes within Revenue *de minimis* limits.[33] The account must be delivered within 12 months or, if later, three months from the date on which a person first becomes liable for the tax. Trustees are required to deliver the IHT account six months after the end of the month in which a chargeable event under IHTA 1984, Part 3, chapter 3 occurs.[34] There is no implied limitation based on territoriality. If a person such as a trustee is liable for the tax then such a person is also under a duty to comply with the administrative machinery preceding the payment of the tax.[35]

56.4.1.2 PETs and GWRs

Where the transfer is a PET, B, the transferee, has a duty to report it (section 216(1)(bb)). The same applies to GWRs (section 216(1)(bc)). In each case the account must be delivered not later than 12 months after the end of the month in which death occurred (section 216(6)(aa), (ab)). A similar rule applies when the termination of an interest in possession is a PET (section 216(1)(bd)).

56.4.2 Death

Personal representatives are obliged to deliver an account of the property forming the estate of D, the deceased (section 216(3)). Since 1999, that account must extend to all

---

[30] IHTA 1984, s 217. On penalties for failing to provide the information required by s 216 or s 217, for providing incorrect information and for failing to correct an error, see ss 245–248.
[31] *Re Clore (No 3), IRC v Stype Trustees (Jersey) Ltd* [1985] STC 394.
[32] On use of substitute forms, see Statement of Practice SP 2/93. On information likely to be required by the Capital Taxes Office, see Capital Taxes Office leaflet, [1994] *Simon's Tax Intelligence* 739.
[33] See [1984] *Simon's Tax Intelligence* 570.
[34] IHTA 1984, s 216(6)(ad), which apply to chargeable transfers made on or after 6 April 2014.
[35] *Re Clore (No 3), IRC v Stype Trustees (Jersey) Ltd* [1985] STC 394. However, see Avery Jones [1985] BTR 255, noting that dicta in *Whitney v IRC* (1925) 10 TC 88 were not cited.

chargeable transfers made by D within the last seven years (section 216(3)(b)); naturally, PETs which have become chargeable are caught. The Revenue have a direction-
making power.[36]

This account must be delivered before the grant of representation can be obtained;
sometimes the tax must also be paid (see below at §56.5.1). This creates a practical problem
in that the PRs must pay the tax but, not yet having the grant of probate, cannot prove title
to a purchaser. Payment of the IHT may therefore be funded by a loan from the beneficiaries, the sale of assets for which probate need not be produced, the appropriate use of a life
policy (ie one not belonging to the deceased's estate) or, if necessary, a loan from a bank.[37]
There is a further practical problem in that the PRs may not be able to find the exact value
of the property. The legislation explicitly allows them to make a provisional estimate once
they have made all reasonable enquiries.[38]

Where no UK grant of representation has been obtained within 12 months of the death,
those in whom the property is vested (at the time of death or since) or those beneficially
entitled to an interest in possession are under a duty to account; this extends to the actual
beneficiaries of a discretionary trust (section 216(2)).

From 6 July 2015, a new online service for inheritance tax filing came into effect.[39] The
online service, which will include electronic delivery of IHT returns, is being introduced in
stages, starting in Autumn 2015.

56.4.2.1 Excepted Estates

The Board now has power by regulation to dispense with the delivery of accounts; in such
situations further regulations may provide for the delivery of information or documents,
and in particular may provide that information given to the Probate Registry may be treated
as given to the Board.[40]

There is no duty to account for persons dying after 5 April 2000 where the estate is
'excepted'.[41] This term covers three situations and is backed up by information powers.[42]
The first has become more detailed over the years;[43] it arises when:

(1)   the gross value of the estate and certain other property is less than the IHT threshold,
       currently £325,000;
(2)   the estate comprises only property passing under D's will or intestacy, or by nomina-
       tion or under a single settlement in which he is entitled to an interest in possession
       or beneficially by survivorship or in Scotland by survivorship in a special destination;
(3)   not more than £150,000 is settled property;

---

[36] IHTA 1984, s 216(3B), added by FA 1999, s 105 and replacing old s 216(3)(b).
[37] For relief from income tax for interest paid, see below at §56.5.5.
[38] IHTA 1984, s 216(3A), added by FA 1999, and replacing old s 216(3); *Robertson v IRC* [2002] STC (SCD)
181.
[39] See The Inheritance Tax (Electronic Communications) Regulations, SI 2015/1378.
[40] IHTA 1984, s 256(1) as amended by FA 2004.
[41] Inheritance Tax (Delivery of Accounts) Regulations 2004 (SI 2004/2543) (as amended by SI 2006/2141),
para 4(2).
[42] *Ibid*, para 4(2), (3) and (5); on information powers, see paras 6 and 7.
[43] *Ibid*, para 4(2).

(4)   not more than £100,000 consists of property outside the UK;

(5)   chargeable lifetime transfers, including transfers of personal chattels and other corporeal movable property, do not exceed £150,000; and

(6)   D died domiciled in the UK.

The 'certain other property' referred to in (1) is the value of certain specified (or specified exempt) transfers made by D.[44] As a result of (2), an estate is not excepted if the deceased made a gift with reservation of benefit, unless it ceased to subsist more than seven years before the death.

The second situation,[45] which was quite new in 2004, contains some details similar to the first but then goes on to state that it applies where the gross value of the estate and certain specified lifetime transfers does not exceed £1 million; the aggregate is A. One then deducts (B + C) from A, where B is the amount of value transferred on death to a spouse or civil partner or charity[46] and C is the liabilities of the estate. If the resulting figure is below the IHT threshold the estate is an excepted estate.

The third situation involves a non UK-domiciled deceased person. D must not ever have been domiciled or deemed domiciled in the UK, and the UK estate must consist only of cash or quoted shares or securities with a gross value not exceeding £150,000.[47]

The effect of the estate being excepted is that there is no obligation to deliver an account, that all persons are discharged from any relevant liability for IHT and that any Revenue charge is extinguished.[48] A simplified and short account form (IHT 202/202N) is available if the applicant for a grant of representation is professionally represented, provided the total gross value of the estate (before deducting exemptions and relieves) does not exceed twice the threshold at death.[49]

56.4.2.2 Deferred Tax—Heritage, Timber, etc

A person liable for tax under sections 32, 32A, 79 or 126, or Schedule 5, must deliver an account before six months have expired from the end of the month in which the event by reason of which the tax is chargeable occurs.

56.5   Revenue Procedure and Appeals

56.5.1 *General*

56.5.1.1 Appeals from Determination

The account is delivered to the Capital Taxes Office, which determines the tax payable and then issues a notice of determination (section 221). Appeals from the Revenue determination

---

[44] Defined *ibid*, para 4(6).
[45] *Ibid*, para 4(3).
[46] Defined *ibid*, para 5.
[47] *Ibid*, para 4(5).
[48] *Ibid*, paras 3, 8 and 9.
[49] Inland Revenue Press Release, 24 February 1993, [1993] *Simon's Tax Intelligence* 319.

lie to the Tribunals (ex Special Commissioners) and from there to the Court of Appeal, Court of Session, etc, on points of law; this is now by simple appeal and no longer by way of case stated.[50] The Tribunals and courts must confirm the determination appealed against, unless they are satisfied that the determination ought to be varied or quashed; the burden of proof is thus on the taxpayer (section 224(5)).

56.5.1.1 Finality—Existing View of the Law

Section 255 applies where a payment has been made—and accepted—in satisfaction of any liability for tax and on a view of the law then generally received or adopted in practice. Any question of whether too little or too much has been paid, or what was the right amount of tax payable, is determined on that view and without regard to any subsequent legal decision. This protects the taxpayer—and the Revenue. In addition, the information and inspection powers introduced in FA 2008, Schedule 36 were extended to IHT by FA 2009, section 96.

56.5.2 *Administration of Tax*

IHT is administered by the Board of Revenue and Customs[51] through one of its branches, the Capital Taxes Office. The Board has an express power to remit or mitigate any penalty (section 253), but it has been pointed out that it has no express power to remit IHT. The Capital Taxes Office has various divisions and is located in Nottingham, Belfast and Edinburgh. The Valuation Office is separate agency. The Solicitor for HMRC is part of the Capital Taxes Office and has a counterpart in Scotland. In Northern Ireland tax litigation is handled by the Crown Solicitor. The Board may authorise any person to inspect property for the purpose of valuing it; this may permit entry but does not say so (section 220).

56.5.2.1 Accounts

Section 257 authorises the Board to insist on proper formalities for accounts. An account delivered to a Probate Registry may be treated as made to the Board.[52]

56.5.2.2 Time Limits For Claims and Underpayments

Under IHTA 1984, sections 240 and 240A, the Revenue generally have four years from the date of accepting payment in full satisfaction of IHT to pursue a claim for underpayment. This is extended to six years where there is a loss of tax brought about by the failure of a person to take reasonable care to avoid the loss, and to 20 years if the loss is brought about deliberately. In the case of an overpayment of tax, section 241 provides that a claim for repayment must be made within four years of the overpayment.

---

[50] IHTA 1984, ss 222–225, as amended by the General and Special Commissioners (Amendment of Enactments) Regulations 1994 (SI 1994/1813). The power to allocate jurisdiction and to change the title of Special Commissioner is contained in IHTA 1984, s 225A. On the role of the Lands Tribunal where land value is concerned, see s 222 and *Alexander v IRC* [1991] STC 112, CA. On penalties, see ss 245, 245A.

[51] IHTA 1984, s 215; for the Board, see s 272, which still refers to 'Commissioners of Inland Revenue' and Inland Revenue Regulation Act 1890, ss 1, 2. See also §4.2 above.

[52] IHTA 1984, s 257(3); the Revenue have indicated their willingness to accept facsimiles of the forms issued under s 257; on criteria for acceptance and on need for prior approval, see Statement of Practice SP 2/93.

56.6   Payment

56.6.1   *General*

56.6.1.1   Due Dates

The due date is the date from which interest runs, whether or not a notice of determination has been issued. Tax may therefore be paid on account. In general, IHT is due six months after the end of the month in which the transfer takes place; however, tax due on a chargeable lifetime transfer made between 6 April and 30 September is not due until the end of April in the following year (section 226(1)). Tax is due for PETs where the transferor dies within seven years, and additional tax arising for the same reason is due six months after the month in which death occurred (section 226(3), (3A)). Tax chargeable on transfers to relevant property trusts is due six months after the end of the month in which the chargeable transfer is made (section 226(3C)). The same six-month rule applies to any additional tax due under the rules in sections 58–85 because the settlor dies within seven years of making the settlement (section 226(3B)). Tax due from PRs as a prerequisite to obtaining probate must be paid on delivery of the account to the Probate Registry (section 226(2)). This does not apply to tax on instalment property or on property for tax on which the PRs are not primarily liable, eg PETs.

56.6.1.2   Deferred Tax

Tax chargeable on a chargeable event under section 32 or section 32A for associated properties, or on discretionary trusts falling within section 79 under the pre-1976 conditional exemption rule in Schedule 5, is due six months after the end of the month in which the event by reason of which it is chargeable occurs (section 226(4)). The same applies to tax on trees or underwood deferred under section 126.

56.6.1.3   Amount

The Board may, in the first instance, rely on the value stated in the account delivered under sections 216 or 217 (section 226(5)). The Board may not request sums which exceed the limits for which a particular person is liable under section 204 (section 226(6)).

56.6.1.4   Administration Actions

Where tax is attributable to a chargeable transfer of property and proceedings for the administration of that property are pending, the court must pay the tax (section 232).

56.6.1.5   Certificates of Tax Deposit

The tax may be paid by certificates of tax deposit.[53]

---

[53] National Loans Act 1968, s 12. See *Simon's Taxes*, A.3. 1328.

56.6.2 *Acceptance of Property in Satisfaction of Tax*

56.6.2.1 The Power

The Board may accept property in whole or part satisfaction of a liability to tax and interest (section 230). The value may be taken either at the day the property is offered, or that on which it is accepted. If the former is chosen, the terms may provide that no interest is due after the date of the offer (section 233(1A)). An application to the Board to accept property may be made by any person with a power to sell the property to raise IHT—and not just the person liable for the tax (section 231). At one time the Revenue had to be compensated for this loss of tax by the relevant cultural department, but this was ended in 1998.[54] Until the mid-1980s there was another problem which arose if the picture, etc was worth more than the tax due; the Treasury would not, until then, make up the difference. The policy change was to allow the Tate Gallery to acquire Picasso's 'Weeping Woman'.[55]

56.6.2.2 The Property

(1) *Land.* In practice, land and buildings of outstanding interest will be accepted only if an appropriate recipient for them can be found (eg the National Trust or national park authorities) and they are capable of being used for the public benefit (section 230(2)).

(2) *Objects and building.* This group comprises objects which are or have been in a building where the building itself is accepted. Alternatively, the building must either be in Crown ownership or guardianship, or belong to a body such as the National Trust.[56]

(3) *Works of art, etc.* The Board may accept any picture, print, book, manuscript, work of art, scientific object or other thing—or collections—meeting the pre-eminent test for conditional exemption (see §54.4 above).

56.6.2.3 Douceurs and Calculations

The market valuation of the property must be agreed and then the amount of tax (IHT and CGT) payable if that property had been sold on the open market. This gives the property's value net of IHT and CGT. The Office then adds a 'douceur' of 10% of the tax to the net value to ascertain the special price at which it is accepting the property. Since tax is not due in respect of the property accepted, the acceptance of the property is payment in kind for an amount of tax due on other property. Where objects are offered on terms that they pass to a particular body, the 'douceur' is higher—25% of the tax payable.

56.6.3 *Interest*

Unpaid tax carries interest on all transfers (section 233); the current rate applicable as at February 2012 is 3%.[57] This runs from the date the tax fell due and is not generally affected

---

[54] FA 1998, s 145.

[55] The picture was valued at £3.1m; £1.2m was to pay the tax due; the owners received £1m from the Tate and £900,000 from the National Heritage Memorial Fund (*The Economist*, 10 October 1987, 34).

[56] IHTA 1984, s 230(3)(a), (b) or (c); for a list of the bodies, see Sch 3.

[57] http://www.hmrc.gov.uk/rates/interest.htm.

by changes in rates of IHT. Interest can cease to run from the offer date where property is accepted in satisfaction of tax on the basis of an offer date valuation. If IHT is overpaid, interest is paid on the repayments and is calculated from the date of payment to the date of repayment. Such interest is not taxable as income of the recipient. The rate is the same as that for underpayment. The rates for unpaid and overpaid IHT are now the same as for other taxes.[58]

56.6.4 *Payment by Instalments*

The basic rule is that IHT may be paid by instalments if:

(1) it is attributable to certain types of property; and
(2) the transfer is either—
    (a) on death, or
    (b) is a lifetime transfer with the transferee paying the tax; or
(3) the charge relates to settled property and either the property remains settled (eg it passes to another life tenant) or the tax is borne by the beneficiary (section 227).

Taxpayers must elect to pay by instalments in writing. Taxpayers who have already paid in full may decide instead to pay by instalments, but are not given any interest in respect of repayments.[59]

56.6.4.1 PETs and Additional Tax on Chargeable Lifetime Transfers

Instalment relief is available here only to the extent that one of two conditions is met (section 227(1C)): (a) either the property must have been owned by the transferee throughout the period beginning with the date of the chargeable transfer and ending with the death of the transferor (or, if earlier, the death of the transferee); or (b) the property may be classified as replacement property for agricultural or business reliefs.[60]

56.6.4.2 Unquoted Shares or Securities[61]

'Unquoted' means not quoted on a recognised stock exchange, so appearance on the AIM will not make the shares quoted.[62]

56.6.4.3 Instalments

Tax is payable by 10 equal yearly instalments. The first instalment is due when the whole of the tax would otherwise have been payable, or, in the case of a transfer on death, six months

---

[58] FA 2009, ss 103 and 104.
[59] See McLeod and Adams [1986] BTR 2.
[60] IHTA 1984, s 113B or s 124B. The transferee is the person whose property the qualifying property became on the transfer; where the property became comprised in a settlement in which there was no qualifying interest in possession, the trustees of the settlement are taken instead (s 227(1B)).
[61] IHTA 1984, ss 227(1AA), 228(3A).
[62] The same was true of the old Unlisted Securities Market, which were generally treated as quoted shares but not for this purpose.

after the end of the month in which death occurred (section 227(3)). For woodlands, the first instalment is due six months after the end of the month in which the transfer is made (section 229).

56.6.4.4 End of Instalments

The taxpayer has the right to pay off the outstanding tax at any time (s 227(4)). However, the taxpayer must pay off the outstanding tax if the property is sold. A sum received in satisfaction of an interest in a partnership is treated as a sale at the date of payment; similarly, the sale of an interest in the business is treated as a sale of part of the business (s 227(6)). Where only a part of the property is sold or transferred only a proportionate part of the tax becomes due. In the case of a lifetime transfer on which the transferee pays the tax, the right to pay by instalments ends if there is a further lifetime chargeable transfer of the property (s 227(5)(a)). However, this is subject to an exception where the transferor dies before the transferee, causing tax to arise (s 227(1A)). The right to pay by instalments ends if the qualifying property ceases to be comprised in the settlement.

56.6.4.5 Qualifying Property

The property qualifying for this treatment is listed in section 227(2) as follows:

(1)   land and buildings situated in or out of the UK;
(2)   certain shares and securities, as further defined in section 228 (see further below);
(3)   the net value of a business or an interest in a business, provided it is carried on for gain (ie not as a hobby); and
(4)   a charge arising under section 129 in relation to woodlands.

The availability (since 1992) of 100% relief for certain property within (2) and (3) has reduced the importance of the present relief—for now.

56.6.4.6 Shares and Securities

Section 228 lists four situations—situations (2)–(4) apply only if (1) does not:

(1)   *Controlling interest.* The shares and securities qualify if, immediately before the chargeable transfer, they gave control of the company to the appropriate persons. In the case of a transfer on death, the appropriate person was the deceased; in the case of a transfer under the rules for trusts without a qualifying interest in possession, the control must rest with trustees and, in any other case, with the transferor. Under section 269, 'control' means having a majority of the votes on all issues affecting the company as a whole; at one time it sufficed to have a majority on any particular question affecting the company as a whole, but this gave rise to avoidance devices. Where husband and wife have shares or securities, each is deemed to have control if they have control together.
(2)   *Unquoted: death and 20%.* Shares also qualify if, although not giving control, they are unquoted and the transfer is on death. In addition, those liable for the tax must show that at least 20% of the tax for which they are liable is attributable

to unquoted shares or securities, or other property in respect of which instalment relief is available.[63]

(3) *Unquoted: undue hardship.* Shares and securities also qualify if they are unquoted and it is shown to the Board that undue hardship would otherwise result from having to pay the tax in one sum. This applies to all types of transfer. In making this assessment of hardship in transfers otherwise than on death, it is assumed that those liable for the tax will retain the shares or securities.

(4) *Shares only: £20,000 and 10% holding.* Lastly, shares (as opposed to securities) also qualify if the value transferred is more than £20,000 and the shares constitute at least 10% of the nominal value of all the shares then issued by the company, or they are ordinary shares and their nominal value is at least 10% of all the ordinary shares then issued.[64] Unquoted securities cannot qualify under this head. Ordinary shares are shares which carry either a right to dividends not restricted to dividends at a fixed rate, or a right to conversion into shares carrying such a right to dividends (section 228(4)).

56.6.4.7 Interest on Instalments

For qualifying property within categories (2)–(4) of 'Qualifying property' above, interest normally runs only as from the date the instalment falls due, so that tax on each instalment is interest-free if it is paid on time (section 234(1)). For land within category (1), interest runs from the date the first instalment falls due. The date the first instalment falls due is also taken for property within (2)–(4) if the business relates to certain types of investment company not qualifying for business property relief; these will qualify for instalment relief—but not for interest-free instalment relief.[65]

56.6.5 Two Further Tax Rules

56.6.5.1 Income Tax Relief for Interest Paid on a Loan to Pay

Subject to general restrictions,[66] income tax relief is available for interest paid on a loan to the deceased's PRs under section 364. The loan must be applied in paying IHT before the grant of representation; in addition, the IHT must be attributable to personal property to which the deceased was beneficially entitled immediately before his death and which vests in the PRs or would vest in them if it were situated in the UK. The relief extends to replacement loans. The relief is available only for one year from the making of the loan. Interest is set against the income of the estate for the year in which the interest was paid. If the income is insufficient the interest may be carried back one year (section 364(2). A certificate of the Board as to the amount of IHT paid is sufficient evidence for the purposes of claiming tax

---

[63] IHTA 1984, s 228(1)(b), (2).
[64] IHTA 1984, s 228(1)(d), 228(3).
[65] By virtue of IHTA 1984, s 234(2). Section 234(3) provides exceptions to this exception.
[66] Ie those in TA 1988, s 353.

relief. Interest in respect of unpaid CTT or IHT is not deductible in computing income of the estate.

56.6.5.2 Purchase of Own Shares by an Unquoted Trading Company to Facilitate Payment of IHT

Normally, payment by a company for the redemption, repayment or purchase of its own shares gives rise to a non-CD distribution (formerly a qualifying distribution) and so an income tax liability on a non-corporate recipient. However, CGT treatment is available if the whole or substantially the whole—a phrase taken by the Revenue to mean almost all— of the payment must be paid in respect of the liability to IHT falling on the shareholder as a result of a death; this rule is applied after taking out the funds needed to pay any CGT liability consequent upon the purchase. The IHT payment must be made within two years of death and it must be shown that the liability could not have been met without undue hardship otherwise than through the purchase.[67]

---

[67] See CTA 2010, s 1033, ex TA 1988, s 219(2) and Statement of Practice SP 2/82, esp para 6.

57

Incidence of Tax

57.1   Introduction and Indemnities

The law relating to incidence determines on which beneficial interests the ultimate burden of IHT will fall. The special rules for potentially exempt transfers (PETs) are considered above at §45.1.2. These rules are distinct from questions of accountability or liability. A person may be liable to the Revenue for the tax even though not having to bear the burden of it, eg as a trustee.

Two rights of indemnity are referred to in context below. The first is a right for the PRs to recover tax and interest paid on death where the tax is not recoverable as part of the general testamentary expense as the property falls outside that rule.[1] The second is a power, given to anyone liable for tax otherwise than as a transferor, to sell or charge the property; this power arises whether or not the property is vested in that person (section 212) and extends to payment of interest and any costs properly incurred in respect of the tax (section 212(4)). The bar on the transferor also extends to the transferor's spouse or civil partner accountable under section 203. The legislation further provides that where the tax could have been paid by instalments (see §56.5.4 above), the person liable to reimburse the payer under the indemnity may also insist on paying by instalments (section 213).

The Board has the power to grant a certificate specifying the tax attributable to the value of that property and which has been paid (including interest) (section 214); the certificate may also state the debts and encumbrances allowed in valuing the property. The application is made by a person who is not ultimately liable for the tax. The certificate is part of the indemnity process and is conclusive as between the person who has to bear the burden of the tax and the person seeking to recover it; it is not conclusive *vis à vis* the Revenue, eg when repayments are in issue.

---

[1] IHTA 1984, s 211(3); on such property see below, §57.3.

57.2 Position of Accounting Parties

57.2.1 *Transferors*

If A, the transferor, pays the tax, there is no right to raise the tax out of the property[2] or to recover it from B, the transferee, unless B has expressly agreed to pay it (section 162(3)).

57.2.2 *Transferees*

B, the beneficial transferee, who pays the tax as a liable person, has no statutory right of recovery from the transferor, A. There may, however, be a contractual or similar right if A has expressly agreed to pay it. This similar right may arise as a term of the original transfer or by some separate enforceable agreement. B will have paid tax on the net value of the transfer. If A later pays the amount of this tax to B, there will be a further transfer of value (section 5(5))—unless, of course, it is exempt or excluded by other rules, eg section 21 (normal expenditure out of income). Today, most transfers will be PETs, so making the transferee primarily liable (section 204(8)). The transferee may raise the tax by sale or mortgage (section 212(1)).

57.2.3 *Trustees*

Trustees who pay the tax may recover the amount out of any money in the settlement held on the same trusts as the property in respect of which the tax was payable. This is a general equitable right of indemnity for trust expenses properly incurred. Whether or not the property in respect of which the trustees have paid tax is vested in them (as will usually be the case), they have power to raise the amount of the tax by sale or mortgage of the property (section 212(2)).

57.2.4 *Limited Interest Owners*

A person having a limited interest in property (a term not defined in IHTA 1984 but covering, eg, a life tenant, an annuitant or a remainderman) who pays the tax in respect of the property is entitled to the same power to sell or charge the property under section 212(1) as any other person (section 212(2)). Presumably, the fact of reimbursing PRs tax paid by them should enable a person to fall within section 212(2) as a person who 'pays the tax attributable to' the property. This charge arises automatically.[3]

57.2.5 *Discretionary Beneficiaries*

A beneficiary under a discretionary trust (or the object of a power of appointment) who pays the tax may also use the power of sale or charge in section 212(1). The power may be used for the purpose of paying the tax in the first place.

---

[2] IHTA 1984, s 212(1) specifically excludes the transferor.
[3] *Lord Advocate v Countess of Moray* [1905] AC 531, 539.

57.2.6 *Personal Representatives*

Where the PRs have paid IHT in respect of a chargeable transfer on death, and the tax is not a testamentary expense (see below at §57.3.1), they have a right to repayment by the person in whom the property is vested; property includes any property directly or indirectly representing the original property (section 211(3)). They also have an indemnity where pre-1997 settled land or formerly settled land vests in them.[4] Similar rules exist for heritable property in Scotland.[5]

57.3 Beneficiaries

57.3.1 *Estates of Deceased Persons*

Where, under the rules outlined at §56.1.2, the PRs are liable for tax, the tax is treated as part of the general testamentary and administration expenses of the estate (section 211(1)). The effect is to cause the incidence of the tax to fall on the assets of the estate in the order set out in the Administration of Estates Act 1925, Schedule 1, Part II, or as varied by the testator.[6]

This broad rule does not apply to all types of property which are treated as disposed of on the death, but only to property in the UK which vests in the PRs and was not, immediately before the death, comprised in a settlement. The rule is further narrowed by the right of testators to express a contrary intention in the will (section 211(2)). The broad rule draws no distinction between real and personal property. This marks a change not only from the old law of estate duty, but also from the original CTT provision as it was thought it should be construed.[7] When property does not fall under this general rule, whether because the rule does not, in terms, apply, or because it is excluded by the testator, it bears its own tax. If, nonetheless, the PRs have paid the tax, as may have been necessary in order to obtain probate, the amount of tax is to be repaid by the person in whom the property is vested. The burden of deferred tax on works of art, etc, falls on those entitled to the proceeds of sale and not on the estate (section 207). For other special cases (timber and pension rights), see chapter fifty-six above.

57.3.2 *Apportionment of Tax*

57.3.2.1 General

Where tax is payable as a testamentary expense, the general rule is that the tax exhausts each category of property available for payment of testamentary expenses and, to the extent that

---

[4] See Administration of Estates Act 1925, s 22(1); Supreme Court Act 1981, s 116; *Re Bridgett and Hayes Contract* [1928] Ch 163; and IHTA 1984, ss 211(1), 237.

[5] IHTA 1984, ss 211(1)(b), 237(4).

[6] Administration of Estates Act 1925, s 34(3), Sch 1, para 8.

[7] However, in *Re Dougal* [1981] STC 514, what is now the broad rule was accepted by a Scottish court for CTT; the rule was made statutory in 1983.

a particular category of property is only partially reduced, the partial reduction is borne rateably by all those interested in that particular category of property.

Where PRs have a right to recover the tax under section 212, no problems arise if the beneficiaries are absolutely entitled between them to the property: the tax is simply divided between them according to their appropriate interests in the property. If property is left on trust for A for life, with remainder to B, the tax charged in respect of it under section 49 comes out of the capital of the settled property, though interest should come out of income (section 212). A receives less income through diminution of the capital. A pecuniary legacy will always bear the tax when it has to be paid out of property in respect of which PRs have a right of recovery, as where T bequeaths foreign property subject to payment of legacies thereout, or where legacies have to be paid thereout in due cause of administration. If there is no express direction for payment of legacies out of property but, in due course of administration, it is necessary to pay legacies out of, say, foreign property, then, to the extent that they are so paid, they must bear the tax.

57.3.2.2 Apportionment between Annuitant and Remainderman: Case Law

If real property is left on trust for A for life and, after A's death, on trust to pay an annuity to X for life, and subject thereto to hold the property on trust for B absolutely, the tax is payable out of the capital of the settled property (section 212). However, when A dies, thereby causing IHT to fall on the settled property, whether real or personal, X, the annuitant, and B, the residuary legatee, bear the tax on the property in respect of A's death rateably according to the value of their respective interests.[8] The burden on X's share will fall on X by way of a reduction in the amount of the annuity and not by a lump sum payment of a part of the tax. The tax will be paid out of the capital of the property, being raised by way of sale, mortgage or otherwise.

The difficulty lies in determining the amount by which the annuity is to be reduced. In simple cases it will no doubt be a sufficient approximation to reduce the annuity by the percentage equal to the overall effective rate of IHT. However, if greater accuracy is necessary, the method lay down in *Re Parker-Jervis*[9] may be followed. First, the 'slice' of capital supporting the annuity is calculated according to the income yield of the estate; secondly, the tax between this 'slice' of capital and the rest of the estate is notionally apportioned; and lastly, the annuitant, in reduction of the annuity, is charged with interest on the tax so apportioned to the 'slice' of capital. The interest should be charged at the rate at which interest is payable on tax until payment of the tax, and, thereafter, at the rate at which the amount of the tax can be raised by mortgage of the property.

This method is not satisfactory when the yield is abnormally high or low.[10] In such cases the 'slice' of capital should, perhaps, be found by reference to the mean between the gross dividend yield appearing in the Financial Times Actuaries Share Index and the yield obtained from irredeemable gilts as revealed by the same Index. Similar rules are now part of the IHT statutes (see above §49.3). These problems of valuation also arise on the death of the annuitant, as where property is settled on trust to pay an annuity of £2,000 a year to

---

[8] *Re McNeill* [1957] 3 All ER 508.
[9] [1898] 2 Ch 643.
[10] *Re Portman* [1924] 2 Ch 677.

X and, on X's death, a similar annuity to A and, subject to these, for B absolutely.[11] On X's death the burden must be shared between A and B on the basis of one of the methods just outlined.

57.3.2.3 Death of Life Tenant of Part

If a life tenant of part of settled property dies and a charge arises under section 4, the loss of income arising from the payment of the tax is borne solely by those who become entitled to the income of the deceased's share and the loss of capital by those who eventually take the deceased's share, and not by the other beneficiaries.[12] This will occur if T leaves property on trust to pay the income equally between X, Y and Z during their respective lives and, on the death of each of them, to pay his share of income to his children during their lives. X then dies. The distinctive feature of this kind of case is that what is charged to tax on the death of X is a proportionate share of the property to which X's children succeed. The reduction of income to be suffered by the children can be calculated at current mortgage interest rates on the amount of IHT payable, as in *Re Parker-Jervis* above, unless the fund is physically divided following the death.

57.3.2.4 Person Exercising Option

If T, by will, gives B an option to purchase foreign property at a price below its probate value, and B exercises the option, B must bear the proportion of tax attributable to the excess of the value of the property above the option price. Essentially, B is obtaining a pecuniary legacy of the excess value and, to the extent that it is paid out of property in respect of which the PRs have a right or recovery of tax, it will bear a proportion of that tax.[13] Thus, if foreign property worth £21,000 is purchased under an option for £14,000, B will have to bear one-third of the tax payable in respect of the foreign property. The position is otherwise if the option was to purchase some of T's property in the UK, since in such a case the PRs have no right of recovery: the tax in respect of such property is a testamentary expense, and such property subject to an option at an undervalue is the last category of property available for payment of testamentary expenses, debts and liabilities.[14]

57.4 Variation of Incidence by Will or Other Document

A clause in a will or settlement varying the ordinary rules of incidence must be interpreted in accordance with the precise words of the will or settlement. The only case law concerns estate duty. 'Free of estate duty' includes free of CTT or IHT; 'free of CTT' includes free of IHT:[15] the use of expressions like 'clear of all deductions' or 'net sum' will probably be regarded as importing freedom from CTT and IHT.[16]

---

[11] See *Re Palmer* [1916] 2 Ch 391; *Re Weigall's Will Trusts* [1956] 2 All ER 312.
[12] Cf *Betts Brown's Trustees v Whately Smith* [1941] SC 69.
[13] Cf *Re Lander* [1951] 1 All ER 622.
[14] *Re Eve* [1956] 2 All ER 321.
[15] IHTA 1984, Sch 6, para 1; and FA 1986, s 100(1)(b).
[16] *Re Sebright* [1944] 2 All ER 547; *Re Saunders* [1898] 1 Ch 17.

The general approach of the courts where there has been any ambiguity has been to presume that 'free of estate duty' clauses have altered the ordinary rules of incidence as little as possible. It seems that such a clause in a will should be interpreted as conferring only freedom from tax payable in respect of a testator's death.[17] Thus, if a testator gives foreign property free of tax to A for life, with remainder to B, it will be presumed that the clause refers only to IHT payable in respect of the testator's death and not A's death or on an earlier disposal of A's interest, so that B will bear the tax on A's death or on the earlier disposal of A's interest; being a presumption, this position may, of course, be rebutted.[18] This facilitates the administration of the testator's estate, since it is most inconvenient if the executors have to retain a significant part of the residuary estate to meet the tax claim that will arise if A disposes of his life interest or when A dies. It is likely that a similar approach will prevail in respect of 'free of inheritance tax' clauses in a settlement, though not quite so severely since the executor's convenience rationale is absent.

It would seem that a direction to pay 'testamentary expenses' out of residue would be construed as a direction to pay thereout only such IHT which ranks as a testamentary expense, and so not tax on foreign property.[19] Where a testator directs the payment of tax out of residue, this will usually be construed as freeing from tax any property in respect of which IHT does not rank as a testamentary expense.[20] However, if, in such a case, the will contains not only a general clause for payment of tax out of residue, but also clauses specially freeing certain devises and bequests from IHT, the general provisions for payment of tax out of residue will not necessarily be construed as referring to tax on gifts of foreign property which are not specially freed from IHT;[21] everything depends on the context of the particular will.[22] A bequest free of IHT of designated works of art, etc, on which tax is not payable until they are sold or until certain conditions are broken, will relieve only the beneficiary under the will. If the beneficiary gives the articles away, and the donee sells them, thereby attracting IHT, the donee will not be able to take advantage of the clause, and will have to bear the burden of the tax.[23]

---

[17] *Re Shepherd* [1948] 2 All ER 932; *Re Embleton's Will Trusts* [1965] 1 All ER 771.
[18] *Re Paterson* [1963] 1 All ER 114.
[19] *Re Owers* [1940] 4 All ER 225.
[20] *Re Pimm* [1904] 2 Ch 345.
[21] *Re King* [1942] 2 All ER 182.
[22] *Re Neeld* [1964] 2 All ER 952n, 953.
[23] *Re Oppenheimer* [1948] Ch 721.

58

International

58.1 Introduction and Practicalities

The provisions of IHTA 1984 relating to IHT operate as law in the UK, ie England, Wales, Scotland and Northern Ireland. They do not extend to the Channel Islands, nor to the Isle of Man. Broadly, where the transferor is domiciled, or deemed so, in the UK, a charge to IHT arises regardless of the location of the asset. If the transferor is neither domiciled nor deemed to be domiciled in the UK but the asset is located in the UK, an IHT charge will arise; however, if such property is located outside the UK, the property will be excluded property (section 6(1)). The rules are thus very different from those for CGT. The rules may be overridden by double tax agreement.[1]

---

[1] IHTA 1984, s 158; and see ESC F6. On enforcement of foreign revenue law, including those of other EU Member States, see chapter seventy below.

58.1.1 Practical Matters—Incidence and Liability

When a charge is imposed on foreign property, it does not follow that the Revenue will be able to collect the tax. The Revenue may find themselves unable to sue in the foreign court.[2] In such circumstances the liability of property or persons within the UK for tax on property outside the UK assumes great importance.

58.1.2 Foreign Debts and Foreign Property

A liability to a person resident outside the UK is allowable as a deduction in computing the value of the estate provided it satisfies the general rules at §55.3 above. However, where the liability falls to be discharged outside the UK and is not an encumbrance on property inside the UK, the liability is, so far as possible, taken to reduce the value of property outside the UK (section 162(5)). One reason for this rule is that a person not domiciled in the UK is liable to IHT only on property in the UK, and it would be giving such persons an undue advantage to allow the deduction of all their overseas liabilities, while taxing only some of their overseas property. Such people may avoid the problem by making their creditors reside in the UK or creating an encumbrance on their UK property. Another reason for the rule concerns persons domiciled in the UK. Such persons pay tax on their foreign property, but there may be double tax relief by way of allowing a credit for the foreign tax payable in respect of the property. Foreign liabilities must be set off against the value of overseas property so far as possible. If, therefore, the particular asset is exempt from tax under the double tax treaty, the benefit of that exemption may be cancelled by the disallowance of the liability.

58.1.3 Administration Expenses and Foreign Property

Additional expenses of administering foreign property, incurred by reason of its being situate abroad, may be allowed as a deduction from the value of the property for the purpose of IHT, but not exceeding 5% of the value of the property (section 173).

58.1.4 Liability and Incidence

F, a foreign resident, may become liable for tax, or liable to indemnify English executors or others who have paid tax which falls to be borne by F. If the property is outside the UK, section 211(1) does not apply, and section 211(3) preserves the personal liability of the holder of the property to indemnify the PRs. F's personal liability cannot be enforced by legal process in the UK unless F is personally present in, or having assets situate in, the UK—or the foreign courts permit enforcement. Moreover, a charge of duty on foreign property cannot be enforced in the UK, unless the property, or the proceeds of sale thereof, is brought to the UK or unless the foreign courts permit enforcement, which they are unlikely to do.

---

[2] See chapter seventy below on this point.

58.1.5 *Concessionary Relief for Foreign Restrictions on Transfer*

Where, because of restrictions imposed by the foreign government, executors cannot immediately transfer to the UK sufficient of the foreign assets to pay the IHT attributable to them, concessionary relief allows them to defer payment. If the amount brought in is less than the tax deferred, this balance is waived.[3]

58.2 Location of Assets

Location is determined by reference to English, Scots or Northern Ireland laws; foreign law rules are irrelevant save for double taxation relief. The Capital Taxes Office has published a leaflet detailing some of the information it may require.[4] The rules which follow are the general UK conflicts of laws rules.[5] These have evolved in case law over the centuries and care is needed in their application.

58.2.1 *Land*

Land is located in the country in which it is physically situated. The conflict of laws rules use the concept of immovable and immovable property rather than of real and personal property, so leases of land are located where the land is. The distinction between movables and immovables may also be relevant in applying double tax treaty provisions.

58.2.2 *Mortgages of Land*

Even if taking the English form of a lease for 3,000 years, mortgages of land are treated as debts, not land. This is due to the presence of the personal liability to repay. Where there is a charge on the land not accompanied by any personal obligation of the mortgagor to repay, as may occur in the Channel Islands, or a non-recourse mortgage, the mortgage is located where the land is. There is some authority that if the mortgage is not created by deed it will be the residence of the borrower (and not the situation of the mortgaged property) which will locate the property.[6] The equity of redemption is, of course, a proprietary interest in the property and so located where that property is. Exceptionally, a Scottish heritable bond is treated in the same way as land.

58.2.3 *Contracts to Buy and Sell Property*

Where there is a contract for sale of land, the buyer's interest is normally treated as a proprietary interest and so as located where the property is. Since the basis is the

---

[3] ESC F6, not yet codified.

[4] [1994] *Simon's Tax Intelligence* 736.

[5] See, generally, Collins *et al* (eds), *Dicey and Morris, Conflicts of Laws*, 13th edn (Sweet & Maxwell, 2000), ch 22.

[6] *Payne v R* [1902] AC 552, PC.

availability of specific performance, the same principles apply to other property if the contract is specifically enforceable. The situs of the interest of the vendor of land was discussed *IRC v Stype Investments (Jersey) Ltd*.[7] The deceased, C, was the sole beneficial owner of land held in trust for him by a nominee company, S. The land was in the UK but the company conducted its business in Jersey. S had made a contract to sell the land when C died. The Court of Appeal held that the interest of C was located in the UK; the land was situate in the UK and the rights to specific performance and damages were enforceable in the UK; it was also relevant that the purchaser was in the UK.

58.2.4 Options

If an option holder has a proprietary right in the subject of the option, the right is situated where the property is; normally, however, the right will be purely personal.[8] A right of pre-emption is contractual only and the right is situated where the obligor resides.[9]

58.2.5 Debts

A simple contract debt is, in general, situated in the country where the debtor resides, that being the country where the debt may be recovered. A specialty debt, eg one payable by virtue of a document under seal, is located in the country where the document evidencing the debt is physically situated. Different rules apply under Scots law, and the normal rule looking to the place where the debt may be recovered is applied. A judgment debt is located in the country where the judgment is recorded.

58.2.6 Life Policy

A life assurance policy (unless issued under seal) is simply another debt and so is located where primarily payable. Thus, if the policy stipulates payment at a particular place, the policy will be situated there provided the company is resident there (as opposed to having a mere agency or branch there) and the debt is solely or primarily payable there.[10] If a life policy is issued under seal it is regarded as a specialty debt and is located where the deed itself is located from time to time.

58.2.7 Stocks, Shares and Other Securities

A bearer security is located in the country where the document of title is physically situated. It is not always easy to determine whether a document is a bearer instrument, eg where securities are issued with a form of transfer endorsed, which has been executed by the

---

[7] [1982] STC 625, CA.
[8] *London and South Western Rly Co v Gomm* [1882] 20 Ch D 562, 581.
[9] *Pritchard v Briggs* [1980] 1 All ER 294, CA.
[10] *New York Life Insurance Co v Public Trustee* [1924] 2 Ch 101, CA.

registered proprietor. Registered or inscribed securities are located in the country in which the register ought to be kept. This rule extends to debenture stock, but not, apparently, to a debenture, which, if under seal, is to be regarded as a specialty debt. Stocks and shares in a company registered under the Companies Acts are therefore generally situated in the UK, even though the entire business of the company, and even its residence, may be abroad. Thus, while dividends may be treated as income from a foreign source, the shares themselves may be treated as located in the UK for IHT purposes. Rights under renouncable letters of allotment have been held to be situated where the company resides or is registered, since this is where the rights are enforceable. For an instrument to be treated as analogous to a chattel, more is required than mere transferability of title by delivery; what is required is a market for these rights.[11]

Companies incorporated abroad cause problems, especially when securities are entered on two principal registers, one in the UK and one abroad. The rational approach is to ask where the transferor dealt, or, for a transfer on death, would have dealt, with the shares in the ordinary course of affairs.[12] Physical presence of the share certificate in one country may be sufficient to tip the scales in favour of that country.[13]

It is unclear where the rights of a unit holder in a unit trust are located. The contenders are where the register is kept and where the underlying property is situated.[14]

58.2.8 Tangible Property

Tangible property, such as furniture, coins or banknotes, is located in the country of physical situation. Thus, a yacht berthed in an English harbour, ie within territorial waters, was situated in the UK even though it was registered in Jersey;[15] this case left open the question of situs if the yacht had been berthed in the UK port for a purely temporary purpose. There is, however, some doubt about the precise rule for goods or cargo on or over the high seas; if such goods are capable of being dealt with in the UK by a bill of lading, this may be enough to locate them in the UK. Ships and aircraft may be located at their port or country of registration.[16]

58.2.9 Intellectual Property

A trade mark or patent, and a licence to use a trade mark or patent, is located where the trade mark or patent is registered. Where, however, the use of the trade mark, etc is permitted in another country, the rights of the user may be located in that other country.[17] Copyright in relation to any particular work is probably located where it can be

---

[11] *Young v Phillips* [1984] STC 520.
[12] *Standard Chartered Bank Ltd v IRC* [1978] STC 272.
[13] *R v Williams* [1942] 2 All ER 95.
[14] The views are held by Shipwright and Ghosh, (1993) 4 *Personal Tax Planning Review* 1; and Venables (1998) 8 *Offshore Taxation Review* 221.
[15] *Trustees Executors and Agency Co Ltd v IRC* [1973] 1 All ER 562.
[16] Collins *et al* (eds), *op cit*, 936–38.
[17] *British Nylon Spinners Ltd v ICI Ltd* [1953] Ch 19.

protected. For CGT purposes, copyright and copyright licences are situated in the UK if exercisable here.[18]

58.2.10 Business Assets

Business assets, including goodwill, or a share in a partnership firm, are located in the country where the business is carried on.[19] This does not, however, determine the situs of the beneficiary's interest save where a beneficiary with a valid interest in possession is treated as having a right in rem in the trust assets. The underlying principle is that a partner does not have a share in the firm's assets as such, but simply a right to a share in the surplus on the dissolution of the partnership. Thus, where separate businesses are carried on in separate countries, each business and share is treated separately. Goodwill is situated where the business to which it is attached is situated[20]—generally the principal place of business creating the goodwill.

58.2.11 Equitable Interests in Property: Classification

If the interest is regarded as a proprietary right, it is located where the asset is situated; if, however, it is a personal right of action against the legal owner or trustee, it is located where the right of action is enforceable, ie generally where the legal owner or trustee resides. The question whether the right is in rem or in personam is determined by the law of the place of the underlying asset, at least for immovables.[21] In the case of movables, the nature of an equitable interest would appear to be governed by the proper law applying to the disposition under which the interest is acquired. In the case of a will, this is the law of the domicile of the testator; and in the case of a lifetime disposition, it is the system of law intended, or presumed to have been intended, to govern the disposition (though an arbitrary choice of law would, it is thought, not be effective).[22]

58.2.11.1 Trusts for Sale

A reversionary interest under a trust for sale has been treated as a chose in action and so as located where the trustees are resident.[23] The Trusts of Land and Appointment of Trustees Act 1996, converting all trusts for sale into trusts of land whenever the trust was created, may have some consequences and should be considered.[24]

58.2.11.2 Estates

A share in the unadministered estate of a deceased person giving rise to an interest in possession is located in the country where the assets are found and not, as one might generally expect, the place of the administration of the estate. This view is based on section 91, which

---

[18] TCGA 1992, s 275(1)(h).
[19] Collins *et al* (eds), *op cit*, 935–36.
[20] *IRC v Muller & Co's Margarine Ltd* [1901] AC 217, HL.
[21] *Philipson-Stow v IRC* [1961] AC 727.
[22] Recognition of Trusts Act 1987, s 1, and arts 6–10 of the Convention scheduled to it.
[23] *Re Smyth* [1898] 1 Ch 89.
[24] For an account of this Act see Gray and Gray, *Elements of Land Laws*, 4th edn (Butterworths, 2004) ch 11.

provides that where a person would be entitled to an interest in possession in the whole or part of the residue of an unadministered estate if the administration were complete, the same consequences follow for the purposes of IHT as if that person had an interest in possession in the whole or an appropriate part of the estate as from the death of the person whose estate it is.

However, section 91 applies only where the person would be entitled to an interest in possession if the administration were complete. Where the person's interest is less substantial, other principles apply. Such a person has no right to any specific asset in the estate but simply a personal right to have the property duly administered.[25] This will locate the right at the place of administration of the estate, ie the residence of the PRs. If there are no PRs, or the PRs reside in more than one country, a different rule applies and the domicile of the deceased is usually chosen.

58.2.11.3 Bare Trusts

The equitable interest in property held by a nominee or bare trustee is situated where the property is; this is because the beneficiary has the entire equitable interest in the property and his rights are not merely rights in contract against the trustee.[26] The location of property held in trust is found according to the rules applying to the particular property, without regard to the proper law of the trust or the residence of the trustees.

58.2.12 Currency

Currency is located in the country of physical situation, without regard to the country by which the currency was issued.

58.2.13 Bank Accounts

A bank account is located in the country in which the branch of the bank at which the money is payable is situated.[27] Sterling certificates of deposit issued (not under seal) by a bank in the UK apparently create a simple contract debt and so are located where the debtor bank resides. It appears that dollar certificates of deposit issued by a bank in the UK on which repayment is to be made abroad are located outside the UK.

58.2.14 Pensions

Certain pensions in respect of service overseas are treated as payable outside the UK even though the UK Government may have become liable to pay them. Normal life assurance policies are regarded simply as debts—but different rules may apply if a seal has been used.

---

[25] *Sudeley v A-G* [1897] AC 11, HL.

[26] *IRC v Stype Investments (Jersey) Ltd* [1982] STC 625.

[27] *R v Lovitt* [1912] AC 212, PC; subject to IHTA 1984, s 135 creating an exception on death for certain foreign currency accounts.

58.2.15 Cause of Action

A cause of action in tort is probably located where it arose, ie where the proceedings may be brought.[28] This view is adopted in most double taxation conventions.

58.3   Domicile and Deemed Domicile

The notion of domicile was extended for IHT in three ways, of which only two are of importance today (see below). These extensions may be overridden by a double tax treaty (section 267(2)); they are also excluded as regards two types of excluded property, ie (a) securities issued on terms that they are not subject to UK tax if held by a person neither domiciled nor ordinarily resident in the UK nor similar settled property (sections 6(2), 48(4)), and (b) holdings of certain certified savings schemes by person domiciled in the Channel Islands or Isle of Man (section 6(3)).

At the time of writing the UK government is planning major reform to the IHT treatment of non-UK domiciled individuals ('non-doms').[29] The changes would broadly align the existing IHT deemed domicile provisions for individuals with the proposed changes for income tax and CGT. As confirmed at Budget 2016, from April 2017 non-doms will be deemed UK domiciled for all tax purposes after they have been UK resident for 15 of the past 20 tax years (the 'long-term residence rule'). Further, individuals who were born in the UK and who have a UK domicile of origin (see §69.5.1) will be deemed domiciled for IHT purposes whilst they are resident in the UK, provided they were resident in at least one of the previous two tax years ('returning UK domiciles'). Detailed transitional rules will be required. The reforms are expected to be legislated in FA 2017.

58.3.1 First Three Years of New Foreign Domicile

A person is treated as domiciled in the UK and not elsewhere if so domiciled after 9 December 1974 and within three years immediately preceding the relevant time (section 267(1)(a)). The three-year period begins to run from the date on which the new domicile is acquired. Thus, where A, a person previously domiciled in the UK, establishes a domicile overseas, any transfer made within the succeeding three years will be caught regardless of the situs of the asset. This—highly questionable—rule appears to be based on the practice of the Revenue for income tax, under which a person is treated as remaining resident in this country for the following three years. However, there is an essential difference in that the income tax practice is simply a provisional matter and if residence is not resumed within three years, the taxpayer is reassessed for those three years as if he had not been resident. There is no such provisional character about the rule for IHT.

---

[28] *Sutherland v Administrator of German Property* [1934] 1 KB 423.
[29] See   https://www.gov.uk/government/publications/inheritance-tax-reforms-to-the-taxation-of-non-domiciles/inheritance-tax-reforms-to-the-taxation-of-non-domiciles.

58.3.2 Seventeen Years of Residence Out of Last 20

A person is treated as domiciled in the UK and not elsewhere if resident in the UK on or after 10 December 1974 and in not less than 17 of the 20 years of assessment ending with the year of assessment in which the relevant time falls (section 267(1)(b)). In deciding whether a person is resident, income tax rules are used (section 267(4)). This is far more justifiable than the first rule above, in that a person resident here for 17 of the previous 20 years might be said to have a substantial connection with this country, and it is only the very permanent tie required for the UK notion of domicile that prevents such a person being treated as domiciled here.

58.3.3 Eu Aspect

The question whether deemed domicile rules were in breach of EU law and, in particular, freedom of movement of capital, was settled in the Dutch case, Case C513/03 *Heirs of van Hilten v Inspecteur*.[30] The ECJ ruled that there was no breach of EU law; there, the Dutch deemed domicile persisted for 10 years.

58.4   The Property

58.4.1 General

Property in the UK, whether real or personal, which is the subject of a chargeable transfer, is liable to tax whatever foreign elements may be concerned in the passing. For example, if an Arab sheikh domiciled and resident in a Middle Eastern country owns a house in London and some shares on the register of a company incorporated in England, and gives these to his son, IHT is payable on the house and the shares (assuming these to be or to become chargeable transfers). The value of these gifts will be aggregated with previous chargeable transfers to ascertain the rate of tax, and will thus raise the rate of tax payable on subsequent transfers. On the other hand, transfers by the same person of property situated outside the UK will be transfers of 'excluded' property and so will not be aggregated. In order to convert the real interest into excluded property, it is common for the sheikh in our example above to establish a non-resident company which buys the house. In turn, however, the Revenue may try to charge the sheikh to income tax under employee benefit rules in respect of living accommodation provided to employees and directors (ITEPA 2003, section 97 *et seq*).[31] In addition, this common tax planning technique may need to be revisited in light of recent policy changes targeting non-natural persons, including companies. These changes include a 15 per cent rate of stamp duty on residential properties over £500,000 purchased by non-natural persons, the extension of the CGT regime to tax gains on the disposal of UK residential property by non-residents including non-natural persons and the introduction of the annual tax on enveloped dwellings (see above §33.2).

---

[30] [2008] STC 1245.
[31] See, generally, Kessler (1991) 1 *Offshore Tax Planning Review* 27–40; but see also *R v Allen* [1999] STC 846.

58.4.2 Uk Property: Special Rules

58.4.2.1 Double Tax Treaty

Property otherwise located in the UK may be deemed to be located abroad under a double tax treaty; such property is therefore foreign property (section 158).

58.4.2.2 Pensions

Certain pensions payable in respect of colonial service do not form part of a person's estate for the purposes of the transfer on death (section 153).

58.4.2.3 National Savings

National Savings and other 'small' savings held by persons actually (as opposed to deemed) domiciled in the Channel Islands or the Isle of Man are treated as excluded property.[32]

58.4.2.4 Armed Forces

Property of members of visiting forces or of staff of allied headquarters is also excluded property.[33]

58.4.2.5 International Securities

The effect of various particular provisions is that securities of certain international organisations will be excluded property in the same circumstances as those in which foreign property is excluded property, eg while in the ownership of an individual domiciled outside the UK. This is so whether or not the securities are actually located in the UK.[34]

58.4.2.6 Works of Art

Foreign-owned works of art which are chargeable to IHT solely by reason of their presence in the UK at the relevant date will be excluded from tax if their presence here was solely for public exhibition, cleaning or restoration.[35] This relief extends also to works of art held by discretionary trusts.

58.4.2.7 Bank Accounts

Money in a non-resident's bank account does not form part of a person's estate for the purpose of the transfer immediately before death (section 157(1)(a)). The person must not be domiciled in the UK or resident or ordinarily resident here at the time of death. The account must not be denominated in sterling. Similar rules apply to bank accounts held by trustees of settled property in which the deceased had a beneficial interest in possession, although the exclusion will be lost if the settlor was domiciled in the UK when he made the settlement, or if the trustees were domiciled resident or ordinarily resident in the UK immediately before the beneficiary's death (section 157(1)(b)).

---

[32] IHTA 1984, s 6(3); deemed domicile is excluded by s 267(2).
[33] See §44.8 above.
[34] See §44.7.3 above.
[35] Formerly ESC F7 and codified in 2009; see IHTA 1984, ss 5(1)(b), 64(2), and relevant definitions in section 272.

58.4.2.8 British Government Securities

Certain British government securities are excluded property if owned by persons neither domiciled nor ordinarily resident in the UK.[36] The power to issue securities on such terms was granted in 1915 because of the sharp increase in tax rates due to war, under F(No 2)A 1915, section 47; the power lapsed in 1922 but was revived by FA 1931, section 22. (See now FA 1996, section 154.)

58.4.3 *Foreign Property*

Property other than settled property situated outside the UK will be excluded property if the person beneficially entitled to it is an individual domiciled outside the UK.[37] The individual in question is the transferor, not the transferee, and generally the question must be answered by reference to the facts at the time of the transfer. It follows that a person who is not domiciled in the UK may avoid IHT by converting UK property into foreign property—even as a deathbed transaction.

Examples

(1) X dies domiciled in England, leaving land abroad and shares in companies whose registers of shareholders are abroad. The land abroad and the shares are liable to UK IHT.

(2) X dies domiciled abroad, leaving land abroad and shares in companies whose registers of shareholders are abroad. The land and shares are excluded property and so not liable to UK IHT.

(3) X, domiciled in Canada, gives Y, domiciled in the UK, £10,000 in Toronto; the gift is of excluded property.

(4) X, domiciled in Canada, wishes to give Y, domiciled in the UK, £10,000, and does so by sending Y a cheque drawn on X's account in London; the gift is not of excluded property.

58.5   Settled Property

58.5.1 *British Government Securities*

British government securities will be excluded property, provided the person beneficially entitled to an interest in possession in them is neither domiciled nor ordinarily resident in the UK (section 48(4)). There is some doubt as to the position where there are two or more persons entitled to interests in possession, for example joint life tenants, only some of whom are ordinarily resident and domiciled outside the UK. In such a situation it would

---

[36] IHTA 1984, s 6(2); for this purpose, deemed domicile is ignored (s 267(2)).
[37] IHTA 1984, s 6. For addition of s 6 (1A) by FA 2003 on unit trusts etc, see above §44.7.3.

appear that since there is a deemed transfer of only a part of the settled property and the legislation speaks only of 'an interest' as opposed to 'the interest' in possession, it will be sufficient that the conditions are fulfilled with regard to the person who is making the deemed transfer, and the property will not be excluded on the occasion of a deemed transfer by a person who did not fulfil those conditions.

Securities which are settled property but in which no qualifying interest in possession subsists are excluded property only if it can be shown that all known persons for whose benefit the settled property or the income from it has been or might be applied, or who might become beneficially entitled to an interest in possession in it, are persons neither domiciled nor ordinarily resident in the UK (section 48(4)(b)). This extraordinarily wide list was narrowed slightly by the decision of the Court of Appeal in *Von Ernst & Cie SA v IRC*,[38] in that an unincorporated association or company established only for charitable purposes cannot become beneficially entitled, nor have property or income applied for it. It followed that the relief applied where the beneficiaries comprised UK resident charities and non-resident non-domiciled individuals. This case also held that the test as to the list of beneficiaries and their residence must be answered on the facts as they are immediately before the relevant event. In *Minden Trust (Cayman) Ltd v IRC*,[39] government securities were bought by trustees of the A settlement; the trustees resolved to advance these to be held on trust for the B settlement. The trustees of the B settlement then appointed the property in favour of X, a non-resident. The court held that in applying section 48, the expression 'the settled property' referred to the property which had been in the A settlement and which was advanced to the B settlement; it followed that that property was excluded property.

Special rules apply to property which moved from one settlement to another between 19 April 1978 and 10 December 1981 (exclusive), or from the first settlement to the second after December 1981, without any person having, in the meantime, become beneficially entitled to the property (and not merely to an interest in possession in it). These conditions had to be satisfied by the beneficiaries of both settlements (section 48(5)). However, if a qualifying reversionary interest arising under the first settlement was settled on the trusts of the second before 10 December 1981, only the beneficiaries under the second settlement need to be considered in relation to that second settlement (section 48(6)).

58.5.2 Foreign Settled Property

The key elements of foreign settled property are the domicile (including deemed domicile) of the settlor at the time of the settlement and the situs of the asset. The status of the trustees and even of the beneficiaries is ignored. The rule, which applies whether or not there is an interest in possession, is that where property is situated outside the UK, the property (but not a reversionary interest in that property) is excluded property unless the settlor was domiciled in the UK at the time the settlement was made (section 48(3)). A similar rule also applies to holdings in unit trusts and open-ended investment companies (section 48(3A)). The rule is framed in terms of exclusion of the property comprised in the settlement; however, changes of investments by the trustees after the settlor has become

---

[38] [1980] STC 111.
[39] [1985] STC 758.

domiciled in the UK do not deprive the settled property of its status as excluded property.[40] The settlor's domicile at the time of the settlement fixes liability to the tax on the settlement, regardless of any subsequent changes of domicile.[41]

Planners found a way of exploiting the status of excluded property. X, an elderly or terminally-ill person, would buy his or her way into becoming a beneficiary of a settlement made by a non UK-domiciled settlor. The non-UK property in the trust would then become excluded property. In response, in 2006 IHTA section 48(3B) was added, which provides that property is not excluded property when the beneficial interest has been bought for consideration in money or money's worth.[42] Space precludes any further examination, but one critic has described the 2006 change as 'clumsy' and 'a trap for the unwary'.[43]

Excluded property held on discretionary trusts is not 'relevant' property and so is safe from the 10-year or intermediate charges (section 58(1)(f), and see §50.3 and §50.4 above). Where the property is situated in the UK it will not be excluded property and so may be relevant property; however, section 65 expressly provides that no charge arises under that section simply because the property ceases to be situate in the UK or is invested in government securities and so becomes, in either case, excluded property.[44] Where the excluded property is held on favoured discretionary trusts, section 48 is adapted (sections 82, 267(3)(c)).

Collection of the tax will be a separate matter, but it must not be forgotten that the settlor will be liable for the tax on a chargeable transfer, for example the death of a life tenant, which occurs during the settlor's life and where the trustees are not resident in the UK (section 201(1)(d)). A reversionary interest in settled property does not come under the settled property rule in section 48(3) but under the general rule in section 6(1): thus, it is excluded property if the person beneficially entitled to it is an individual domiciled outside the UK and it is situated outside the UK; the situs of the reversionary interest is not necessarily that of the settled property (section 6(1)). Where the settled property is itself a reversionary interest, the settled property rule applies to it.

Examples

(1)   In 1994, A, domiciled in the UK, settled English property on B for life with remainder to C, both of whom were domiciled in the UK. In 1997, B migrated to Canada and established domicile there. C remained in the UK and died in 2004. B died in 2005. On B's death there will be a charge by reason of the location of the property in the UK and A's domicile in 1994. There will be no charge on the reversionary interest on C's death in 2004.

(2)   In 1994, X, domiciled in Canada, settled Canadian property on Y for life with remainder to Z, both of whom were then domiciled in Canada. In 1997, Y and Z migrated

---

[40]   *Law Society's Gazette*, 3 December 1975.

[41]   If the property became comprised in a settlement before 10 December 1974, 'domicile' has its ordinary and not its extended meaning (IHTA 1984, s 267(3)(a)).

[42]   IHTA 1984, s 48(3B); see FA 2006, s 157.

[43]   Harper [2006] BTR 638, 642.

[44]   IHTA 1984, s 65(7), (8). In the case of government securities the deemed domicile rules do not apply (s 267(1)(b)).

to and established domicile in the UK. Z died in 2003. Y died in 2004. On Y's death there will be no charge since the property was situated outside the UK and the settlor was not domiciled here when the settlement was made. There will be a charge on the reversionary interest on Z's death.

(3)   A testator dies domiciled in England, leaving foreign land and shares on trust for X for life, which may be a pre-22 March 2006 interest within section 49(1A) or an immediate post-death interest in possession within section 49A. X dies domiciled abroad. The shares and the land are liable to IHT on the death of the testator and, in theory, on the later death of X, but the testator's estate is not liable for the IHT on X's death.

(4)   A testator dies domiciled abroad, leaving foreign property on trust for X for life, an immediate post-death interest in possession within section 49A. X dies domiciled in England, and at his death the trust fund consists of foreign land and shares. There is no charge to IHT on the death of the testator, nor on that of X.

58.6   Double Taxation Relief

58.6.1 General

Double taxation relief may be granted either by the terms of a treaty made under section 158 or unilaterally by section 159.[45] Where tax is payable in both countries, it is generally on the basis of the location of the property in one country and the domicile of the transferor in the other. The law of the UK (and of many foreign countries) makes provision for relief in respect of such double taxation in certain circumstances. What follows is concerned with relief granted by the law of the UK; for relief granted by the laws of a foreign country, reference must be made to those laws.

Double tax treaties were made in relation to estate duty between the UK and various overseas countries. These remain in force, but only for transfers of value on death. New conventions covering lifetime transfers were made after the introduction of CTT in 1975; these will now have to be adapted for IHT. A small number of treaties apply to IHT specifically. These are treaties made with Ireland, The Netherlands, South Africa, Sweden, Switzerland and the United States. FA 2000 provides powers for exchanging information with treaty partners.[46]

58.6.2 Situs and Credit Codes Under Estate Duty Arrangements

Estate duty arrangements were made under F(No 2)A 1945, section 54; their effect is preserved for IHT (section 158(6)). Such arrangements are relevant to France and Italy.[47]

---

[45] On avoiding multiple inheritance taxation within Europe, see Sonneveldt [2001–02] *EC Tax Law Rev* 81–97.
[46] IHTA 1984, s 220A, added by FA 2000, s 142; on which see Inland Revenue Press Release, 20 March 2000; [2000] *Simon's Weekly Tax Intelligence* 499.
[47] There are also such treaties with India and Pakistan, but these are of limited effect since those countries have abolished estate duties.

Estate duty arrangements contain codes for determining the situs of certain kinds of property, which may, in certain cases, lead to property which is situated in the UK being treated as situated in the other country and so as excluded property. These rules were sometimes not enough to prevent double taxation where both states claimed the transferor as a person domiciled there, and so some treaties (France and Italy) went on to provide further rules to determine the appropriate law.

Except for the pre-1995 Swiss Treaty, estate duty agreements provide that one tax may be used as a credit against the other; the effect is that the transfer will not bear tax in excess of the larger amount due to each country separately. The difference between the two reliefs is substantial. Not only will a transfer within the first relief escape UK tax completely and usually only partly under the latter, but the transfer under the former relief will be of excluded property and so exempt from aggregation, whereas under the latter the value transferred must be aggregated with any other value transferred and cumulated.

58.6.3 *IHT and Double Taxation Relief Under Treaties*

The OECD Model Treaty allows states the primary right to tax on the basis of situs if the property is immovable or is a business based there, and otherwise to grant the (primary) right to tax to the country of fiscal domicile, a concept loosely defined as almost any connecting factor on which a state may wish to tax, but with a tie-breaker clause. The small number of UK treaties designed for IHT (and previously CTT) follow this lead—in general. They do not use the situs approach, but instead seek to find the appropriate domicile and resolve dual domicile problems by a tie-breaker process.[48] Treaties of this sort have been made with Ireland, The Netherlands, South Africa, Sweden and the United States. The absence of treaties with Australia, New Zealand and Canada is because none of those countries levies estate taxes; unlike the UK they do, however, charge CGT on a deemed disposal on death. The Swiss Treaty applies to deaths on or after 6 March 1995.[49] The OECD Model Treaty follows the traditional model where the person concerned had only one fiscal domicile. However, a radically different approach is adopted in the UK–Swiss treaty where the person concerned had a dual domicile; here it is the state of situs rather than that of the treaty domicile which has the primary right to tax.[50]

58.6.4 *Unilateral Relief by Way of Credit*

Unilateral relief is available against any amount of tax chargeable by reason of any disposition or event, provided: (a) the tax is similar in character to IHT, or is chargeable on or by reference to death or gifts inter vivos; and (b) the IHT chargeable is attributable to the value of that property (section 159(1)). This relief is by way of credit so that the transfer remains nonetheless a chargeable transfer and must be cumulated in the usual way. The reference

---

[48] The Revenue do not currently charge IHT under FA 1986, s 102 (gift with reservation of benefit rules) so far as a settlement comprises excluded property (Davies [1995] *Private Client Business* 101); settled property situated within the UK is not excluded property. For a list of UK treaties applying to IHT see https://www.gov.uk/guidance/inheritance-tax-double-taxation-relief.

[49] Inland Revenue Press Release, 6 March 1995, [1995] *Simon's Weekly Tax Intelligence* 4031.

[50] See Note [1995]1 and Avery Jones [1997] *Private Client Business* 2.

to foreign tax is to the tax due under the law of the foreign country and paid by the person liable to pay it (section 159(6)). Unilateral relief may be claimed even if there is a double tax agreement, provided it exceeds the relief under the agreement (section 159(7)).

58.6.4.1 Single Situs

Where the asset is situated in the foreign country, the credit is for the full amount of the foreign tax on the property.[51] This credit concedes priority of taxation to the country of situs.

58.6.4.2 Dual Situs

Where the property is situate in both (or neither) of the UK and the foreign country, credit is determined by the formula $[A/(A + B)] = C$, where A is the IHT, B is the overseas tax and C is whichever is the smaller of A and B.[52] Presumably, situs is determined according to the law of each country and not just by the law of the UK; this is the official view—thus, if UK law says that the situs is X and X says that the situs is the UK, or vice versa, relief is available. However, there appears to be a gap if UK law says that the situs is X while X says that the situs is Y. This form of relief is used in some double tax agreements (the old US agreement, South Africa, India and Pakistan) and is often more advantageous than that in other agreements. The relief has the curious effect that the greater the foreign tax, the less credit is available; this is understandable where, as in a treaty, the other country uses the same formula, but is very odd in unilateral relief.

58.6.4.3 Third Country Taxes

Where three countries are involved, B becomes the aggregate of the foreign taxes and C the aggregate of A and B, minus the largest single charge.[53]

58.6.4.4 Effect of Foreign Credit

Where relief by credit is available, whether by convention or unilaterally, and more than one country is involved, any credit under the $[A/(A + B)] = C$ formula is calculated by treating A as the tax as reduced by any credit relief due in respect of tax in another country; equally, B is reduced by any credit available under the foreign law.[54]

Examples

(1) A dies domiciled in the UK but some of the assets are in another country, Q. Suppose that the charge to tax is £5,000 and Q charges tax of £3,000. Assuming that under UK rules the assets are in Q, the IHT liability will be £2,000.

(2) If, however, Q says that the assets are in Q, and the UK says that the assets are in the UK, the formula will be applied: $[5,000/(5,000 + 3,000)] \times 3,000 = £1,875$. So IHT liability would be £5,000–1,875 = £3,125. The same would result if both the UK and

---

[51] IHTA 1984, s 159(2).
[52] IHTA 1984, s 159(3).
[53] IHTA 1984, s 159(4).
[54] IHTA 1984, s 159(5).

Q regarded the property as located in a third country, R, assuming that R charged no tax. Assuming that Q uses the same formula the credit there will be 3,000/8,000 × 3,000 = £1,125, making a tax liability in Q of £1,875. The aggregate of the liabilities in the UK and Q will be £5,000. If, however, Q has no treaty, the total tax liability may be as much as £(3,000 + 3,125).

(3) If R also charged tax on the property, say, of £1,000, the credit against tax would, for the tax charged in Q and R, be [5,000/(5,000 + (3,000 + 1,000))] × (3,000 + 1,000) = £2,222.

(4) If, however, the UK and Q gave credit for the tax of £1,000 in R, the credit against IHT is adjusted and the formula gives the following credit for the tax levied in Q [(5,000–1,000)/((5,000–1,000) + (3,000 + 1,000–1,000))] × (3,000–1,000) = £1,143.

PART V

Corporation Tax

59

Corporation Tax—Introduction,
History and Policy

59.1   Structure of UK Corporation Tax

Companies resident in the United Kingdom (UK) are subject to corporation tax on their profits; the term 'profits' includes both income and capital gains.[1] The general rate of corporation tax has been steadily declining for years; it is now normally 20% but is set to decrease to 19% in 2017 and 17% in 2020.[2] Corporation tax is charged by reference to 'financial years' which begin on 1 April each year and end on 31 March the following year. Tax is charged on the company whether it distributes or retains its profits. Corporation tax was introduced in 1965. Before that time corporations were subject to income tax but not surtax on their income, with further taxes (profits taxes) also charged on their income to make up for the absence of surtax.

59.1.1   The Legislation and the Rewrite

Since 2009 nearly all of the corporation tax legislation has been rewritten. The rules formerly in the Taxes Act (TA) 1988 are now spread across, primarily but not entirely, the Corporation Tax Act (CTA) 2009, the Corporation Tax Act 2010 and the Taxation

---

[1] CTA 2009, ss 2 and 5, ex TA 1988, s 6; on non-residents, see below at §60.9; on gains, see TCGA 1992, s 8(3).
[2] FA 2012, s 5. The rate is to drop to 19% for the financial years 2017–19, and to 18% for 2020; see FA (No 2) 2015, s 7. A further reduction in the rate to 17% for 2010 was announced at Budget 2016.

(International and Other Provisions) Act (TIOPA) 2010. CTA 2009, Part 2 contains the basic charge to corporation tax in respect of both income and chargeable gains. It then follows the ITTOIA 2005 model dealing with Trading Income (Part 3) and Property Income (Part 4), before going on to Loan Relationships (Parts 5 and 6), Derivative Contracts (Part 7), Intangible Fixed Assets (Part 8), Intellectual Property (Part 9), Company Distributions (Part 9A) and Miscellaneous Income (Part 10). Parts 11–21 deal with other matters. The capital gains rules are still primarily found in the Taxation of Chargeable Gains Act (TCGA) 1992.

59.1.2 Shareholder Tax on UK Dividends

A company subject to UK corporation tax generally is not subject to corporation tax on dividends received from another company.[3] Individual shareholders are liable to income tax on dividends (and other distributions) received from the company and pay tax under ITTOIA 2005, Part 4, Chapter 3.[4] Prior to 6 April 2016, a dividend came with a tax credit attached to it of one-ninth of the dividend, so a dividend of £90 came with a credit of £10. Assuming that the shareholder was entitled to use the credit, the income of the shareholder was the sum of the dividend (£90) and the credit (£10), or £100. Basic-rate and savings-rate shareholders paid tax at the dividend ordinary rate of 10% so that there was no further income tax to pay; this had been the case for many years. Higher-rate taxpayers paid at the special dividend upper rate of 32.5%, which means that after the £10 credit the taxpayer had to pay another £22.50. The additional dividend rate of 37.5% plus credit applied to taxpayers in the 45% income tax bracket. It was a fundamental feature of this system that the shareholder could not, subject only to very limited exceptions, claim any repayment of the tax credit from the Revenue—and never from the company.

In 2016, a radical change was made to the taxation of dividends received by individuals. From 6 April 2016, the tax credit has been abolished and instead all individuals have a £5,000 tax free amount of dividends (the 'Dividend Allowance'). The Dividend Allowance applies to dividends received from UK resident and non-UK resident companies. Dividends within this allowance technically are taxed at the 'dividend nil rate' and still count in determining the taxpayer's tax band, however. In addition, new dividend tax rates apply: 7.5% on dividend income within the basic rate band, 32.5% on dividend income within the higher rate band and 38.1% on dividend income within the additional rate band. An individual's personal allowance can shield dividend income. As a result, in 2016–17 a taxpayer with no other income will be able to receive dividends of approximately £16,000 without a tax charge.

Example

In the 2016–17 tax year, T has non-dividend income of £40,000 and receives dividends of £12,000 outside of an ISA. Of the £40,000 non-dividend income, £11,000 is covered by T's personal allowance, leaving £29,000 to be taxed at the basic rate. This leaves £3,000 of

---

[3] CTA 2009, Pt 9A, ex TA 1988, s 208.
[4] Ex TA 1988, s 20.

income that can be earned within the basic rate limit before the higher rate threshold is crossed. T's Dividend Allowance covers this £3,000 first, leaving £2,000 of allowance to use in the higher rate band. All of the first £5,000 of T's dividend income is therefore covered by T's Dividend Allowance and is not subject to tax. The remaining £7,000 of dividends fall within the higher-rate band and are taxed at 32.5%.

59.2 A Brief History of UK Company Taxation

59.2.1 Before 1965

The UK corporate tax system has suffered major shifts of policy in its (relatively) recent past. In the 19th century the system charged companies, like other persons, to income tax;[5] this lasted until 1965. Until that year dividends were not subject to *income* tax but were grossed up to give a figure for *surtax*,[6] whether or not the company paid income tax on its profits. This system was subject to two major modifications. First, the fact that a company was subject to income tax, but not to surtax, meant that it was advantageous for a high-rate taxpayer to leave income behind the veil of a company where it would be taxed at lower rates and so multiply more rapidly. Legislation was therefore introduced in 1922 to deal with 'one-man' companies, which took the form of a surtax direction treating the income of the companies as if it were the income of its owners and so liable to surtax.[7] The legislation continued in substance, but in a new form, as part of the modern close company legislation from 1965–89.

The second modification was the introduction in 1937 of the National Defence Contribution, which in due course became profits tax.[8] This was an extra tax on the profits of the company, which, not being income tax, could not be recovered by the shareholder. This device could be used to levy tax at differential rates on distributed and retained profits, and was so used between 1947 and 1958.[9] The two-tax system was subject to a number of disadvantages separate from the issue of whether it should encourage the retention of profits. First, since the basic tax on the company was income tax, not only was it subject to all the complexities of matters such as the commencement and cessation provisions, but the rate would also alter whenever the Government thought it right to alter the rate in the personal sector. Secondly, profits under the two taxes were computed differently. Not only was profits tax levied on a current as opposed to a preceding year basis, but some items were deductible in computing profits for profits tax which were not deductible for income tax, thus necessitating two sets of calculations; consequently, until 1952 profits tax was itself deductible for income tax. Further, companies whose profits were less than £2,000 were exempt from profits tax.

---

[5] For an explanation, see Royal Commission on the Taxation of Profits and Income, *Final Report*, Cmnd 9474 (1955), ch 2.

[6] However, where dividends fitted in with the Schedular system was obscure but Sch D, Case VI was the prime candidate; see Heyworth Talbot [1962] BTR 394.

[7] See Royal Commission on the Income Tax, *Final Report*, Cmnd 615 (1920), para 1021(2).

[8] See Royal Commission (1955), *op cit*, ch 20. This tax was precedented not only in the excess profits duty of the First World War, but also in the general corporation profits tax introduced in 1920 and repealed in 1924.

[9] For figures, see Singh and Whittington, *Growth, Profitability and Valuation* (CUP, 1968), 4.

59.2.2 1965–73

This untidy system was ended in 1965 when corporation tax replaced the previous income and profits taxes; this was a classical system. Dividends were taxed under Schedule F, which was entirely separate from corporation tax on the profits. This system was based on a view that corporations should be encouraged to retain their profits rather than distribute them to their shareholders (see further §59.4).

59.2.3 1973–97

For these years the tax system emphasised the close relationship between the shareholder and the corporation by allowing the shareholders to use a part of the corporation tax paid by the company to offset their own liability to Schedule F income tax. This was known as the imputation system because of the way in which the corporation tax paid by the company was imputed to the shareholder. Technically it was a 'partial imputation' system, since only part of the corporation tax paid by the company was imputed to the shareholder. In order to ensure that the tax used as a credit by the shareholder represented tax actually paid by the company, the company, when paying the dividend (or any other qualifying distribution), had to pay advance corporation tax (ACT) to the Inland Revenue. Liability to pay ACT arose whether or not the company was itself liable to pay corporation tax, eg through lack of taxable profits. ACT could, within limits, be set against the company's liability to corporation tax.

In 1973 the choice lay between the imputation system and a two-rate system (also called a split-rate system), whereby corporation tax would be charged at one rate on retained profits and another on distributed profits, the difference between the two rates being that of the basic rate of income tax. In a closed economy there would be little practical difference between the two; it would not matter to resident shareholders whether the distributed profit of the company was taxed at 50%, but shareholders were allowed to take three-fifths of that tax as a credit against their own liability (the credit or imputation system), or the tax on the company was 20% and there was no credit.

The imputation system was preferred for international reasons.[10] Under a two-rate system the lower rate of tax on distributed profits could not distinguish between resident and non-resident shareholders without risking complaints of discrimination from tax treaty partners.[11] However, the imputation system could restrict the income tax credit to residents. Non-residents requesting the tax credit were turned away; when they requested double tax relief for the ACT paid by the company on the dividend, they were denied this on the basis that ACT was a tax on the company in respect of its profits and not a tax on their dividends. It followed that no UK tax was payable on the dividend, and so there was no such tax to be used as a foreign tax credit against the non-residents shareholders' liability to income tax in their own country. The UK could protect its own revenue without great risk

---

[10] See Green Paper, *Reform of Corporation Tax*, Cmnd 4630 (1970); *Report of the Select Committee on Corporation Tax*, HC 1970–1971, No 622; and Prest [1972] BTR 15. In 1973 the basic rates of income tax and corporation tax were 30% and 50%, respectively.
[11] TA 1988, s 231, ex FA 1972, s 86.

of discouraging foreign private investment. This was designed to lead to the renegotiation of double tax treaties and the second reason for the imputation system. The two-rate system would, for the reasons given above, give rise to a lower tax take by the UK Government. This could be adjusted by a double tax treaty with the other country. However, the United States was firmly wedded to the classical system and so saw no reason to grant a different rate of withholding tax to the other country just because that other had moved to a two-rate system; it was therefore unwilling to negotiate agreements other than those giving identical rates of withholding tax for both countries. Thus the attraction of the imputation system was that by being so nasty to US shareholders, the UK could encourage that government to come to the negotiating table.[12]

The imputation system as implemented in the UK was found to have a serious flaw, in that surplus ACT could arise (see below at §61.6). As implemented in the UK and in most other countries, it was also found, eventually, to be incompatible with EU law; the very discrimination which lay at the heart of the system was contrary to EU discrimination law (see below at §§59.3 and 77.3.1).[13]

59.2.4 1997—New Labour

The reforms which began in 1997 and which were completed in 1999 retained the shell of the imputation system. Shareholders receiving dividends still received a tax credit on account of some of the corporation tax paid by the company. However, two major changes were made. The first was the restriction of the use of the tax credit. Until 1997 a tax credit might be used by the shareholder not only as an offset against an actual UK tax liability on the dividend but also where the circumstances allowed (eg where there was little other income to use the personal relief) to be repaid, the claim being made to the Revenue and not to the company. After 1997 there was virtually no right to a repayment, whether the shareholder was a UK pensioner with low income, a charity, a pension fund or most types of non-resident (see §61.3.1). On this last point, the 1997 change had one thing in common with 1973—a wish to attack the foreign shareholder and so the foreign fisc. One effect was to reduce to a minimum a non-resident's right to recover, under the relevant double tax treaty, part of the UK tax withheld on the dividend. The second major change was the abolition of ACT. To make up for the Government's loss of cash flow from ACT, a new scheme of quarterly payments of corporation tax in advance was introduced. The overall effect was a system which for most individual shareholders was much the same as a two-rate system. Later the New Labour Government decided to offer a starting rate initially of 10% then of 0% if profits were below £10,000. Many thought this unwise as it over-encouraged incorporation. However, others thought it an important part of an overall scheme of tax for small businesses.[14]

The professed objective behind the 1997–99 changes was to encourage long-term investment. Companies had to be encouraged to make long-term investment decisions with confidence; hence, part of the money taken by ending the repayment of the credit

---

[12] For US retaliation, see Kaplan [1978] BTR 206.
[13] Case C-319/02 *Manninen v Finland* [2004] ECR I-07477.
[14] For a wide-ranging policy view, see Chittenden and Sloan [2007] BTR 58.

was returned as a cut in corporation tax rates. Companies were also expected to retain more earnings instead of paying them out by way of dividend, a point achieved by making dividends for investors, such as pension funds, more expensive. It was believed that many pension funds were in substantial surplus and that many companies were enjoying pension holidays, but that proved to be a very short-term view. What was true was that a pension fund had an incentive to ask for profits to be distributed, in that if the dividend came out of the company with a credit which could be reclaimed, there was more money to reinvest, perhaps in that very company, than if the money had been simply left in the company.

The attack on short termism was based on the hypothesis that fund managers, especially pension fund managers, take a short-term view of investments and that this is a bad thing for the economy as a whole.[15] It is thus a mixture of facts, and assessment of those facts. The facts asserted are that there is excess volatility in the investment behaviour of managers; this may, in turn, be due in part to the next fact which is the practice under which trustees regularly monitor their managers' handling of funds in their care against the performance of other managers and the various stock indices. Managers who feel threatened in this way will tend to favour opportunities for short-term gains. This leads to the undervaluation of firms with good earning prospects and a willingness by managers to sell shares in the event of a threatened takeover when there is no real business advantage to be gained from that takeover. In turn, this leads to a discouragement of long-term investment in research and development rather than paying dividends because the company wants the shortest pay-off period possible, and leads to fund managers wanting to sell out rather than help when a company hits bad times. It may also lead to pension funds being bad at investing in small and medium-sized enterprises. This last point may have other explanations; it may be because (a) the shares may not be marketable, (b) funds have difficulty in researching firms without track records and/or (c) there may be limits on the amount of equity which may be held. These objections may be met by the development of small share markets such as the Alternative Investment Market (AIM). It should also be said that some of the UK's entrepreneurs, such as Richard Branson and Alan Sugar, have not liked dealing with 'The City', regarding it as very expensive and unhelpful. The 'market discipline' exercised by the threat to sell out in the event of a hostile takeover must be balanced against the often negative effects of such takeovers.[16]

59.2.5 *2010—Coalition Politics*

The Conservative–Liberal Democrat Coalition, led by Prime Minister David Cameron, that formed the Government following the general election in May 2010 looked to business as the driver of future economic growth and innovation in the UK. To that end, the Government released a Roadmap for Corporate Tax Reform, which included plans to reduce the headline rate of corporation tax and create the most competitive tax system for business

---

[15] For critical discussion of the short-term hypothesis, see Walker (1985) 25 *Bank of England Quarterly Bulletin* 570–75; and Marsh, *Short Termism on Trial* (Ifma, 1993). For an examination of pension funds investment practices—and much else—see Davis, *Pension Funds* (OUP, 1995); and LSE Financial Markets Group, *Special Paper No 107* (LSE, 1999).

[16] Eg Deakin and Slinger (1997) 24 *Journal of Law and Society* 124. See also Singh, 'Corporate Takeovers' in *The New Palgrave Dictionary of Money and Finance* (Palgrave Macmillan, 1992).

in the G20.[17] The main rate of corporation tax dropped from 28% to 20% in this period. Even with tax rate cuts, however, research by the Oxford University Centre for Business Taxation made it clear that the UK remained a considerable way off its G20 competitiveness goal if effective average tax rate rather than the headline statutory rate was the measure.[18] In 2011 the Government also introduced a new levy on UK banks.[19] In 2015 the Oxford Tax Centre produced an interesting report describing and evaluating these measures and others taken by the Coalition government to reform the UK business tax regime.[20] Those other measures include reforms to the controlled foreign company regime, reductions in capital allowances, and the introduction of the patent box, diverted profits tax, a code of conduct for banks, and the GAAR.

Simplification was another key aim of the Coalition Government's tax reform agenda.[21] In 2010, the Government created the Office of Tax Simplification (OTS) to provide the Government with independent advice on simplifying the UK tax system. In its first report, the OTS recommended abolishing some 47 tax reliefs and simplifying others; many of those recommendations were implemented. The OTS has since released other influential reports on small business taxation, partnerships, employee share schemes, and alignment of income tax and national insurance.[22] The OTS became a permanent office of HM Treasury from April 2016.

59.2.6 2015—Present and Future

The Conservative government led by David Cameron that won a majority in the May 2015 election wasted little time before announcing further corporation tax rate cuts were on the way—down to 17% by 2020. Following the June 2016 advisory referendum on Brexit in which the UK public voted by a narrow margin to leave the EU, the then Chancellor George Osborne publicly floated the idea of reducing the corporate tax rate further, to below 15%, in order to encourage businesses to continue investing in the UK.[23] A few days later the new Prime Minister Theresa May installed Philip Hammond as Chancellor, and he refused to commit to further corporate tax cuts.

In a 2016 report, researchers at the Oxford University Centre for Business Tax concluded that the UK had improved its competitiveness internationally, with the lowest statutory tax rate amongst the G20 countries and 5th lowest effective average tax rate.[24] The government also introduced a fundamental reform to the taxation of dividends. From 6 April 2016, the

---

[17] See http://www.hm-treasury.gov.uk/corporate_tax_reform.htm. See also *The Coalition: our programme for government*, at http://www.direct.gov.uk/prod_consum_dg/groups/dg_digitalassets/@dg/@en/documents/digitalasset/dg_187876.pdf.

[18] See http://www.sbs.ox.ac.uk/newsandevents/news/Pages/UKcorporatetax.aspx. The UK is at the bottom of the G20 for allowances on capital expenditure, so the fairly competitive corporation tax rate applies to a broad base of profits.

[19] FA 2011, Sch 19, and commentary by Cummings and Gall [2011] BTR 454.

[20] See Maffini (ed), *Business Taxation under the Coalition Government* (2015) available at https://www.sbs.ox.ac.uk/sites/default/files/Business_Taxation/Docs/Publications/Reports/cbt-coalition-report-final.pdf.

[21] For a recent academic work on simplification see Evans, Krever and Mellor (eds), *Tax Simplification* (Kluwer Law, 2015).

[22] See the OTS's website at https://www.gov.uk/government/organisations/office-of-tax-simplification.

[23] BBC News, 'Brexit: George Osborne pledges to cut corporation tax' (4 July 2016).

[24] Devereux, Habu, Lepoev, and Maffini, *G20 Corporation Tax Ranking* (March 2016).

tax credit system was abolished and instead all individuals have a £5,000 tax free amount of dividends (the 'Dividend Allowance') and new dividend tax rates of up to 38.1%. A new Business Tax Road Map also was published in 2016. Further measures to clamp down on tax planning, avoidance and evasion were introduced, including a tax-geared GAAR penalty along with new anti-hybrid rules and restrictions on interest deductibility following on from the G20/OECD Base Erosion and Profit Shifting (BEPS) project (see below §69.11). Additional possible implications for UK corporate tax arising from Brexit are discussed in chapter seventy-seven.

59.2.7 Small is Beautiful

One other long term trend deserves mention. This is the granting of special reliefs for small and medium-sized enterprises. Although small companies no longer benefit from a lower rate of corporation tax—as had been the case until the main rate was reduced to the former small profits rate of 20% in 2015—other special reliefs for small companies are available in the form of:

(1)   exemption from payments of corporation tax by quarterly instalments;
(2)   a special tax credit for research and development; and
(3)   exemption from the transfer pricing rules.

The status as qualifying companies is determined for (1) on the basis of taxable profits, and for (2) and (3) on a more complex formula taking account also of assets and turnover. Other rules designed to benefit small companies include the generous rules for share options under the enterprise management incentive (EMI) scheme.

Some see these incentives as necessary assistance for a sector of the economy which suffers disproportionately from compliance costs while also providing substantial new employment opportunities. Others point out that statistics can show that small companies provide lower productivity, lower wages and less secure employment than large companies, or wonder why a large company should be entitled to some of these benefits just because it makes low profits.[25] A system might be preferred which distinguishes on the basis of newness and growth, or sees all done away with in the name of tax neutrality and the efficient allocation of resources by the market. The Institute for Fiscal Studies (IFS)-led Mirrlees Review recommended against blanket support for all small businesses on the basis that it is unlikely to be an efficient policy response, and concluded:

> There may be some justification for targeted forms of tax support that would tend to favour some kinds of smaller businesses—for example, those undertaking significant expenditures on investment or research and development—more than a typical large company. However, it seems difficult to rationalize the nature and scale of generalized tax advantages for all small businesses that we see in the UK and in many other developed countries.[26]

---

[25] See Chennells, Dilnot and Emmerson (eds), *Green Budget 2000* (Institute for Fiscal Studies, 2000) §8.1.
[26] Mirrlees *et al* (eds), *Tax by Design: The Mirrlees Review* (OUP, 2011) 455. The Review, chaired by Nobel Laureate Professor Sir James Mirrlees and drawing on the work of leading international experts in economics and tax law, undertook the most comprehensive study of the UK tax system since the 1978 Meade Committee: see https://www.ifs.org.uk/publications/mirrleesreview/.

For many years a related concern has been the effective tax burden on small business across various legal forms.[27] Historically it has been tax-advantageous for small businesses to adopt a company structure over an incorporated form, due to lower levels of taxation on distributed and undistributed corporate profits as compared to income tax on the profits of an unincorporated business. In turn, both of these business forms have been more lightly taxed than employees carrying on similar economic activity, principally due to higher NICs on earnings from employment. Both the Mirrlees Review and the OTS have concluded that a difference in the combined tax and NIC treatment of employees, self-employed and corporations is undesirable.[28] First, it is potentially distortionary as it may lead to a choice of business form that is not the most appropriate and efficient in the particular circumstances. Second, it penalises some activities that are unable to adopt the most advantageous form of organisation. Third, it creates incentives for taxpayers to convert earned income into unearned income where possible, such as by choosing to take remuneration in the form of dividends rather than highly-taxed salary. Lastly, the discrepancy in tax treatment may favour more economic activity being undertaken by small firms and less activity being undertaken by employees of larger firms.

The Mirrlees Review recommended aligning the personal and corporate tax rates to equalise the tax/NICs on income derived from employment, self-employment and running a small company.[29] The key ingredients of this rate alignment were (1) uniform application of NICs to income from employment and self-employment, and to distributed profits and capital gains, (2) lower personal tax rates for dividend income and capital gains on company shares to reflect corporate tax paid; and (3) abolition of the small profits corporation tax rate.[30] The OTS and Crawford & Freedman also have argued that such alignment could go some way towards reducing the present difficulties with the employee/self-employed classification and the application of IR35.[31] The 2016 introduction of higher taxes on dividends above the new tax-free Dividend Allowance were aimed specifically at addressing the 'imbalance' in favour of incorporating small businesses and unquestionably have gone a considerable distance towards aligning tax/NICs across legal forms on distributed profits at least. Finally, in 2016, the OTS undertook a special study of small company taxation. It its report, the OTS suggested a number of simplification measures including optional cash-flow accounting (currently available to small unincorporated traders) and also advocated examining the merits of 'look through' taxation of nano-businesses as well as whether a new trading vehicle (a 'sole enterprise with protected assets' or SEPA) would be useful.[32]

---

[27] See eg Mirrlees, *op cit*, ch 19 and Crawford & Freedman, *Dimensions of Tax Design: The Mirrlees Review* (OUP, 2010), ch 11. The discussion that follows is an excerpt from a larger article on this subject: see Loutzenhiser (2013) 72 *CLJ* 35.

[28] Mirrlees, *op cit*, ch 19; Crawford & Freedman, *op cit*, ch 11; OTS, *Small Business Tax Review*, (March 2011), para 6.3.

[29] Mirrlees, *op cit*, ch 19; Crawford & Freedman, *op cit*, ch 11.

[30] *Ibid.*

[31] Crawford & Freedman, *op cit*, ch 1044–46; OTS, *Small Business Tax Review*, (March 2011), para 5.10.

[32] OTS, *Small Company Taxation Review*, (March 2016).

59.3   The EU Dimension

The UK is, for now at least, a Member State of the European Union (EU). It is understandable that the EU should take an interest in tax matters with a view to harmonisation
either with regard to the structure of the corporate tax system, or at least with regard to
the tax base.[33] Tax systems and their differences represent significant obstacles to a free
market across the EU. The various proposals on corporate tax structure show how difficult
it is to reach agreement on any of the underlying economic or commercial principles.[34]
The Neumark Report, in 1962, recommended the two-rate system; the Van den Tempel
Report, in 1967, recommended the classical system; and the Simonet Report, in 1973, recommended the imputation system.[35] A White Paper was anticipated in 1987, but nothing
materialised.[36] Subsequently, there were proposals for harmonisation on particular aspects,
eg the draft directive of 1984 concerning the carry-over of losses and a report in 1980 on
the possibility of convergence, but nothing much was achieved until 1990 and the arrival of
Mme Scrivener. She abandoned the search for the holy grail of harmonisation in favour of
a series of highly specific proposals to attack specific problems of discrimination. However,
at the same time she set up the Ruding Committee to see how seriously tax problems led
to distortions affecting the functioning of the internal market. The report accepted that
distortions arose from the interaction of the different tax systems, but that other considerations argued not for heroic action on a broad front but for specific (ie piecemeal or
targeted, depending on the point of view) removal of the major distortions. These reasons
included the need to allow Member States much flexibility to collect revenue through direct
taxes and the principle of subsidiarity.[37] In the new millennium efforts have switched to
greater co-operation amongst Member States on tax administration, fighting tax avoidance
by multinationals in particular, and trying to achieve agreement on a common consolidated
corporate tax base (CCCTB).

As discussed below in chapter seventy-seven, the Court of Justice of the European Union
(CJEU, formerly ECJ) has proved to be an unpredictable body, especially when invoking
its non-discrimination jurisdiction. Until 2000 many of the corporation tax rules which
follow were confined to entities resident in the UK, and it was uncertain when those would
be found to be incompatible with EU law and when not. Thus, Lodin, writing in 1998,[38]
suggested (and as it happened suggested very correctly) that because imputation systems
imposed heavier burdens on foreign dividends than on domestic dividends, they must be

---

[33] Literature (with citations) includes Gammie [2001] BTR 233; Haufler (1999) 20 *Fiscal Studies* 133; and
Devereux (1999) 20 *Fiscal Studies* 155. For lessons to be learnt by EU Member States from explicitly federal
systems, see Daly and Weiner (1993) 46 *National Tax Jo* 441. See also chapter seventy-seven.
[34] See Easson (1992) 40 *Can Tax J* 600. There is a broader analysis in Radaelli, *The Politics of Corporate Taxation
in the European Union* (Routledge, 1997), esp chs 5 and 6.
[35] See [1975] BTR 422; and [1976] BTR 39.
[36] See [1987] *Simon's Tax Intelligence* 423.
[37] Ruding (chair), *Report of the Committee of Independent Experts* (EC Commission, 1992); for discussion, see
(1992) 13(2) *Fiscal Studies* 85. Dr Ruding's rather brief Tillinghast lecture for 1999 is printed in (2000) 54 *Tax
L Rev* 101 and is followed by a longer comment by Stewart at 111. See also comments by members reported in
(1993) 33(1) *European Taxation*; Daly (1992) 40 *Can Tax J* 1053 (Daly was Secretary to the Committee); and, more
generally, (1991) 1 *EC Tax Review* 12 and (1991) 2 *EC Tax Review* 116.
[38] (1998) 7 *EC Tax Review* 229.

incompatible with EU law. In the 2005 case of *Manninen*, the Court said that Member State A might use an imputation system only if it gave its resident shareholder taxpayers a credit for the tax paid in another Member State.[39] Similar problems emerged from cases involving the UK itself (see below at §77.3.1). Although this was not something Member States wanted to do, some have granted partial dividend relief with respect to foreign dividends. So Germany grants the same half exemption for foreign dividends as domestic dividends. The UK has followed suit, to a point, by, for example, exempting dividends received by a company from corporation tax irrespective of whether the payer is a UK or a foreign company. It is the hope of some that this very unpredictability may persuade the Member States to try to harmonise their tax rules in this area. The choice was well put by Vanistendael in 1996:[40]

> 1) Further unplanned destruction of national tax systems by successive decisions of the ECJ which has to fulfil its mandate and cannot refuse to do so. 2) Approximation of the basic structure of income tax thereby legitimising and defining the place of national tax systems in the EC legal order and giving guidance to the ECJ about what types of income tax are compatible with the treaty. 3) Full restoration of national sovereignty of income tax which means the beginning of the end of the EU because full national tax sovereignty is incompatible with EMU and a single currency.

Developments from 2000 to 2005 provided more examples of this 'unplanned destruction' of national systems, but there are signs of a more sophisticated and deferential approach by the CJEU more recently (see §77.2.2 below).

59.4   Theory and Practice[41]

59.4.1 Significance of Corporation Tax

In most OECD economies companies pay several forms of tax. In addition to a national tax on their profits, they may also pay a regional or local tax, one or more local property taxes (in the UK the business rate is charged on all businesses whether in corporate or unincorporated form), a payroll tax, an annual wealth tax and some minor forms of tax—as well as paying social security contributions as employers.[42] For the countries concerned, of these

---

[39] AG Kokott in Case C-319/02 *Manninen v Finland* [2004] ECR I-07477.

[40] (1996) 5 *EC Tax Review* 122.

[41] The literature on this topic is prodigious. Among many books and articles, see Gammie [1992] BTR 148 and Gammie [1992] BTR 243; McLure, *Must Profits be Taxed Twice?* (Brookings Institute, 1979); Cnossen, *Corporate Taxes in the European Community* (IBFD, 1992); Cnossen in Sandford (ed), *Key Issues in Tax Reform* (Fiscal Publications, 1993); King, *Public Policy and the Corporation* (Chapman and Hall, 1977), reviewed [1978] BTR 321; Ballantine, *Equity, Efficiency and the US Corporate Income Tax* (Brookings Institute, 1980); and McLure (1975) 88 *HLR* 532. For older material, see Whittington, *IFS Lecture Series No 1* (Institute for Fiscal Studies, 1974), a review of the then economic literature; Royal Commission (1955), *op cit*, ch 2; Carter (chair), Canada Royal Commission on Taxation, *Report*, vol 4 (Queen's Printer, 1966), ch 19; Reamonn, *The Philosophy of Corporate Taxation* (Institute of Public Administration, 1970); Chown, *The Reform of Corporation Tax* (Institute for Fiscal Studies, 1971); Coyle [1964] BTR 408, 417; Wheatcroft [1964] BTR 416. For a fascinating, fresh view see Snape, *The Political Economy of Corporation Tax* (Oxford, Hart Publishing, 2011).

[42] See annual guides by OECD—'OECD in figures'.

forms of tax the national tax on company profits is often much less important as a source of revenue than social security contributions.[43] It may therefore be that the tax on corporate profits is significant rather than critical.

59.4.2 Should Companies be Taxed?[44]

The first question is whether companies should be taxed at all. On a benefit theory approach, the company should be taxed because it has legal personality and receives benefits, such as the protection of its property and the privilege of limited liability. This is generally considered a weak argument since there is no systemic relationship between the tax on profits and the benefits received.[45] Other reasons may be that taxing companies is politically more acceptable than taxing individuals, being less personal, and that companies occupy so important a place in the economy that governments cannot afford not to tax them.[46] One suggestion is that companies should be taxed because they lock in capital which should reach the shareholders.[47]

If a tax system had a truly comprehensive income tax (CIT) at shareholder level it would not be necessary to tax companies, although a tax may be charged on a basis other than profits along the lines of one of those just listed in §59.4.1. Under a CIT, shareholders would be taxed each year on any dividends received and, importantly, on the change in the value of their interest in the company. Since profits of the company would be taken into account in valuing those interests, they would be taxed in the hands of the shareholders. Under a universal expenditure tax (ET) the return on savings is taxed only when consumed and, since profits retained by the company are not consumed, there is no tax charge on such profits. Under a CIT, there is therefore a tax charge on the shareholder in respect of the change in value due to the retained profits, while under a ET there is no charge at all.[48]

However, neither a CIT nor an ET is feasible. The main general issues with an ET are the potentially high tax rate and the problematic distinction between a business expense incurred in producing income (and so deductible) and a (chargeable) consumption expense: for more see §1.6.3.4 above. The obvious problems with a CIT include the difficulty of identifying the shareholder to which the retained profits may be attributed,[49] especially in a world of volatile stock markets and nominee companies, and the liquidity issues for a shareholder who has to pay the tax but has no money to do it with. Exempting corporate entities from tax opens up opportunities for tax avoidance by accumulating profits in the company and then selling the shares—opportunities which are not wholly

---

[43] For 2009, in the OECD countries corporation tax yielded an average of 8% of the tax take and social security yielded 27% (OECD, Tax Stuctures in the OECD-area, Table C); the UK percentages were 7% and 19% (HM Treasury, *Budget 2010*, Table C11: Current receipts).

[44] A good starting point is the Mirrlees Review, 408–12. See also the Green Paper, *Reform of Corporation Tax*, Cmnd 8456 (1982), Pts I and II.

[45] Messere, *Tax Policy of OECD Countries* (IBFD, 1993) 325.

[46] Eg Blough (1943) 10 *Law and Contemporary Problems* 108, 110.

[47] Bank (2004) 30 *Journal of Corporation Law* 1.

[48] See Gammie [1992] BTR 148, 149.

[49] On significance of accruals basis versus receipts basis, see *ibid*, 154.

corrected by having a capital gains tax.[50] Therefore a tax on companies may be needed to protect the individual income tax.

59.4.2.1 Profits or Turnover?

A related question is whether the tax should be on the profits of the company or on its turnover.[51] The argument in favour of the latter is that it can be shown that a tax on some companies enters into the company's pricing process and so is shifted forward to the consumers of the company's products rather than falling on the shareholders—or backwards on the employees of the company through lower wages or other suppliers. If this view is correct or, more accurately, partially correct, a tax on companies is in effect an indirect tax, and a tax on the profits of profit-making companies is simply an erratic and therefore inequitable tax which penalises the profitable companies and subsidises the inefficient. This argument has rarely found favour. First, the shifting of the tax by companies is a matter of great speculation and it is less than clear that taxes are shifted on to consumers. Secondly, a turnover tax would presumably have to apply to individual businesses as well as companies in order to avoid too great a gap between the incorporated and unincorporated business, thus, in turn, making a further division between the self-employed and others.

59.4.2.2 Profits and Shareholders

If the tax falls on the profits of the company rather than on its turnover, it is easy to begin to design an ideal tax system; however, it is less easy to complete the task. This is because there are major disagreements over how the corporation tax works, not only as to whether it is 'shifted', ie the burden falls not the company and its shareholders but on others, but also on the corporate finance implications and the role of equity finance in comparison with other sources. Moreover, the topic cannot be taken in isolation from decisions about taxation of savings in general. These problems multiply when other countries are considered, not as a source of ideas but as trading partners—if individual nations find it hard to settle on a coherent tax policy in a purely domestic setting, it is very unlikely that two or more nations will agree on their policy objectives. Under these conditions one nation's tax policy may be cancelled out by another's.[52]

59.4.3 *Various Models of Tax Treatment of Dividends under Personal and Corporate Income Tax*

If the tax falls on the profits of the company rather than on its turnover, the next question is whether that tax is to be regarded as separate from the taxation of the shareholder.[53] Taxing profits first at the corporate level and again at the shareholder level when distributed

---

[50] Bagchi (1990) *IBFD Bulletin* 243.

[51] See Richardson (chair), Committee on Turnover Taxation, *Final Report*, Cmnd 2300 (1964), which rejected the idea of a VAT on companies.

[52] See, generally, Gammie [1992] BTR 148, Gammie [1992] BTR 243 and *Taxing Profits in a Global Economy* (OECD, 1991), ch 2, part D.

[53] See, generally, Gammie [1992] BTR 148 and [1992] BTR 243; Cnossen in Sandford (ed), *op cit*, 40; and Cnossen (1996) 17(4) *Fiscal Studies* 67.

gives rise to economic double taxation. The polar starting points are that the corporate and shareholder tax should be treated as entirely distinct or as one integrated whole. A major report from the OECD in 1991 identified at least seven models of taxing companies and their shareholders that may be discerned.[54] All of these methods have been used at one time or the other in OECD countries. The further we move down this list of models, the more the two tax systems are viewed as an integrated whole, with a corresponding greater attention paid to reducing or eliminating economic double taxation, either at the corporate or at the shareholder level:

Model 1 – Classical system—tax paid by company on profits; tax paid by shareholders on dividends received

Model 2 – Split rate—tax paid by company on undistributed profits at one rate and on distributed profits at a lower rate; tax paid by shareholders on dividends received

Model 3 – Partial dividend deduction—tax paid by company on profits but with a partial deduction for dividends paid; tax paid by shareholder on dividends received

Model 4 – Partial imputation system—tax paid by company on profit; tax paid by shareholder on dividends received, but with a partial credit for corporate tax paid

Model 5 – Partial shareholder relief schemes—tax paid by company on profit, tax paid by shareholder on dividends received, but with a partial credit for domestic shareholders only

Model 6 – Zero rate system. Tax paid by company on profits; a zero rate of tax paid at shareholder level on distributed profits

Model 7 – Full imputation system or full shareholder relief system. Tax paid by company on profits; shareholders receive a full tax credit for corporate tax paid in computing their personal income tax liability.

Under *model 1*, usually called the 'classical system',[55] the corporate level and shareholder level taxes are viewed as separate and distinct. Profits distributed to shareholders are fully or almost fully liable to both corporation tax and personal income tax. Under this model there is little or no reduction in economic double taxation of distributed corporate profits. The total tax taken from distributed profits is greater than that from undistributed (or retained) profits. The classical system also discriminates between equity finance and debt finance, the latter being cheaper.[56] This model was part of the UK system from 1965–73, and has been in force in the US and other countries for much longer.[57]

The remaining models (*models 2–7*) provide some degree of relief from economic double taxation.[58] The opposite pole from model 1 (*models 6 and 7*) treats company and

---

[54] *Taxing Profits in a Global Economy*, Table 3.1.

[55] See Royal Commission (1955), *op cit*, 382 (Memorandum of Dissent). As Cnossen in Sandford (ed), *op cit*, points out, the classical system is actually more recent than some of the imputation systems.

[56] However, see Andrews (1984) 30 *Wayne LR* 1057–71, pointing out that shareholders gain by not having their income taxed until the profits are distributed by way of dividend.

[57] For a 2003 survey, see IFA Cahiers LXXXVIIIa (International Fiscal Association, 2003).

[58] Cnossen (1996) 17(4) *Fiscal Studies* 67, 81.

shareholder as effectively identical.[59] Double taxation is eliminated either by levying a zero rate of tax on dividends at the shareholder level (*model 6*), or by giving a full tax credit to the shareholder for the tax paid at the corporate level (*model 7*). The difference between the two is that it will be possible to apply progressive taxation to shareholders under model 7, but not under a pure model 6. Model 7 is likely to break down at international level.[60] The UK's regime after 6 April 2016 is a hybrid system, combining a model 1 classical system with elements of model 6 as the first £5,000 of dividends are subject to a nil-rate of tax.

Models 2–5 are intermediate positions seeking to reduce rather than eliminate economic double taxation. The difference between some of these models may seem insignificant but becomes critical when considering the position of foreign shareholders, and especially their rights under double tax treaties. The reduction in economic double taxation may be effected at the corporate level—by having a split-rate system in which the tax on corporate profits is charged at one rate on retained earnings and another (lower) rate on distributed earnings (*model 2*), or by allowing the company to claim a partial deduction for dividends paid (*model 3*). There are two ways to reduce economic double taxation at the shareholder level. One (*model 4*) gives the shareholder a partial credit for the corporate tax paid, eg the UK system prior to 6 April 2016; the other (*model 5*) gives a partial credit for domestic shareholders only.

59.4.3.1 Hybrids

Variations of these models start with the classical system but then apply a special (flat rate) tax on dividends separate from normal progressive rates. The 'dual income tax' has become fashionable in EU countries and examples of it may be found in Sweden, Denmark and Finland.[61]

59.4.3.2 The Role of Capital Gains Tax

One other point of comparison should be made—the burden of capital gains tax (CGT) on shares. In the UK we are used to having this charge, although it may, in practice, be softened by the annual exemption, or by the use of intermediaries such as individual savings accounts (ISAs). In the UK there is now a corporation tax exemption for substantial shareholdings held by companies (§62.3.3). A CGT is found in many other European countries as well as in the US, Canada and Australia; however, it is not found at the individual level in Greece, New Zealand and Switzerland.[62] The lesson to be drawn is that comparison is hazardous unless complete and detailed; the more so since local taxes, a wealth tax or other taxes on businesses, such as social security or payroll taxes, have not been considered. It is therefore appropriate to turn to the arguments used in the debates on the choice of model.

---

[59] Full integration was recommended by the Canadian Royal Commission in 1966, the US Treasury in 1979 and the Campbell Committee in Australia in 1981, but was rejected as impracticable by the US Treasury in 1992; on the United States see, generally, McLure, *Must Corporate Income be taxed Twice?* (Brookings Institute, 1979); and US Department of the Treasury, *Integration of the Individual and Corporate Tax Systems: Taxing Business Income Once* (1992); for US colloquium on 1992 proposals, see (1992) 47 *Tax L Rev*.

[60] *Ibid*, 248.

[61] OECD, *Taxation of SMEs in OECD and G20 Countries*, (2015), 35–36. See also Cnossen (1996) 17(4) *Fiscal Studies* 67, 87–89; and Gammie [1992] BTR 243, 252.

[62] Harding, 'Taxation of Dividend, Interest, and Capital Gain Income', *OECD Taxation Working Papers, No 19*, (2013), 32–33.

59.4.4 The Arguments

59.4.4.1 Classical Versus Imputation Systems

The debate over the two poles of the classical and imputation systems is long and unresolved, and has been governed by a mixture of rhetoric and business. Critics of the classical system regard the interests of shareholders and those of companies as being one and the same; its defenders point to the role of the equity market and claim that most investors take little interest in management, provided their dividends continue to be paid. In the 1970s fundamental problems arose over the virtues of the free market system; these problems are thought to be less important now, but memories are short.

The classical system is favoured by those who believe that the company is not the alter ego of the shareholders but is run instead by managers for their own interests[63] and by those who believe that the burden of the tax is not borne by the shareholders, ie that it is shifted to employees or customers. The classical system also has attracted support from those who believe in the 'new' view of dividends, ie that the form of corporate tax is completely irrelevant to a company's dividend decisions.[64]

Behind the rhetoric are debates over various 'distortions' or examples of discrimination. As with all these situations there are two reactions: one is to find a countervailing device to correct the distortion; the other is to try to remove the bias which underlies the distortion. The classical system means a higher burden of tax on incorporated business than on unincorporated business; in turn, this means that, assuming distribution, the rate of return required by a company to make a profit is higher than that for an unincorporated business.[65] The classical system discriminates in favour of retained, as opposed to distributed, profits. This is not necessarily efficient since it makes it more expensive for a company to maintain its net flow of dividends to its shareholders. This, in turn, makes it more expensive for the company to raise the money for its needs, and especially its growth, from the equity market; instead it must look to borrowing or its own income. On this view a shift away from a classical system and to integration will provide more funds for the corporate sector.[66]

Critics of the classical system assert that an investment financed from outside may be looked after more closely than one funded purely from within. They also suggest that a tax which discriminates against distributions means that companies are encouraged to retain money which could be used better by other companies and so encourages businesses which already have adequate reserves at the expense of those which wish to expand faster than their present profitability will allow. If a company is not expanding, managers should not be encouraged to keep liquid reserves for their own sake; reducing retentions would limit the financial discretion of—and so potential misuse by—management.

---

[63] See, generally, Bratton (1989) 1 *Stanford LR* 1471, reprinted in Wheeler, *A Reader on the Law of the Business Enterprise* (OUP, 1995), 117. For an historical account see Bank, *Anglo-American Corporate Taxation* (CUP, 2011).

[64] Bagchi (1990) *IBFD Bulletin* 244, considering the views of Bradford. For an explanation of Bradford's views by himself, see *Untangling the Income Tax* (Harvard University Press, 1986), ch 6.

[65] *Report of the Select Committee on Corporation Tax*, op cit, §259; see also Bittker and Lokken, *Federal Taxation of Income, Estates and Gifts* (Warren, Gorman & Lamont, 1989) §§95–96.

[66] Eg the Department of the US Treasury (1992), *op cit*, 138.

Supporters of the classical system approve of the use of borrowed money to expand a business;[67] the right to deduct interest but not dividends in computing profits encourages the practice of high gearing. This practice is beneficial because lenders have an incentive to monitor the activities of the managers.[68] Whether the double tax (on profits and dividends) makes investment more expensive for the corporate sector than for the unincorporated sector depends on whether the 'optimistic' view of corporate tax is accepted. This view argues that because companies rely on debt-finance at the margin, the tax is neutral or even mildly beneficial. This is highly controversial.[69] However, it remains true that since most countries not only allow a full deduction for interest payments but also allow inflation to erode the value of corporate debt, they give an artificial stimulus to debt.

These arguments were much debated in the UK in the 1970s at and around the time of the switch from the classical system to the imputation system.[70] The perceived view of dividends at that time (the 'old' or 'traditional' view) was that tax had a major influence on company pay out rates. A classical system, combined with preferential tax on capital gains,[71] made dividends more expensive than retentions. This led people to ask why companies continued to pay dividends when other devices were cheaper in tax terms, and why they preferred to try to raise new equity to finance new investment in order to prevent dividends being lowered even though the effect of this might be that the investment would not be made at all. The explanation seemed to be that a company paying a dividend saw itself as sending a signal that it was in a healthy state and its future earnings prospects were good; critics thought this an expensive way of making such an announcement.

The modern view of dividend taxation suggests that shareholders should, as rational people, prefer lightly taxed capital gains to heavily taxed dividends, and that corporations should therefore retain as much as possible. On this view retained earnings are a much more important source of investment than a new share issue. The new view also asserts that dividend taxes do not affect the profitability of investments funded from retained earnings and so do not distort investment choices; this is because a tax on the shareholder may reduce the value of the shareholding and so the value of the firm, but this will not affect the company's decision whether or not to invest. Since dividend taxes must eventually be paid, they are capitalised into the share values, reducing share prices to compensate for those taxes. In effect, a dividend tax is a lump-sum tax on equity existing when the tax is imposed or new equity is issued.[72] However, this view contains two assumptions and one caveat. First, it assumes that capital gains will be lightly taxed in the hands of the shareholders. Secondly, the non-distortion argument assumes that the tax on dividends remains unchanged. Thirdly, the new view applies only to mature businesses; new businesses will

---

[67] On the importance of non-tax aspects for preferring equity to debt, eg the costs of financial distress and bankruptcies, see Department of the US Treasury (1992), *op cit*, ch 1, 115.

[68] See Department of the US Treasury (1992), *op cit*, 115 *et seq*, where it is pointed out that this might be an ineffective way of improving performance, especially as it did not work where the variation in the firm's cash flow was the same as that of other firms.

[69] See Stiglitz (1973) 2 *Journal of Public Economics* 1.

[70] These paragraphs draw unashamedly from *Taxing Profits in a Global Economy*, ch 2, and Messere, *Tax Policy of OECD Countries* (IBFD, 1993), ch 12, section D, 365–66.

[71] UK CGT was charged at a maximum of 30% until 1988.

[72] Department of the US Treasury (1992), *op cit*, 116.

not have enough retained earnings and so will need external finance in the form either of loans or shares.

In 1991 the OECD Report reached the dull conclusion that there was some truth in both views, but highlighted the more interesting point that the differences in policy implications should not be exaggerated.[73] By contrast, Cnossen states that most empirical studies support the old or traditional view,[74] and the US Treasury 1992 Report states that the tax policy implications are different.[75] The US Report argues that, on the new view, reducing the tax on dividends would increase the value of the shares and so benefit existing shareholders, and that companies would not pay more dividends. The old view asserts that shares values would not go up just because of a change in the law, making dividends less disfavoured, and that making the tax system more neutral between retentions and distributions would increase distributions and so economic efficiency. These (Treasury) views thus deal with the effect of the transition, itself as well as the long term.

Three concluding points may be noted on the dividend debate. First, the attractiveness of shares is affected by many matters other than tax. Secondly, although the imputation system discriminates less strongly than the classical system in favour of retained profits, it may discriminate to some extent against them. Thirdly, it may be a mistake to tax all companies, other than close companies, in the same way, regardless of size and function. In fact, the present UK structure, by withholding capital allowances from buildings, does discriminate substantially against property companies, and by giving special reliefs to small companies, tries, however unsuccessfully, to distinguish large companies from small.

59.4.4.2 International Matters

The policy issues have so far been considered primarily in the domestic context. However, companies operate increasingly in the international economy, and the cosy fireside view is no longer appropriate. Cross-border investment brings its own problems; thus why is it that tax systems almost invariably make international investment more expensive than purely domestic investment[76]—and what can be done about it? What is to be done about those differences between tax systems which cause distortions and, in extreme cases, naked tax competition between countries,[77] or about those domestic souls who can make use of foreign entities, legally or illegally? We also have new problems of equity and neutrality— as between resident and non-resident shareholder and between resident and non-resident company. The G20/OECD Base Erosion and Profit Shifting (BEPS) project is already having an impact on the international tax sphere, even if critics argue it was a missed opportunity for more fundamental reform (see below §69.11).

---

[73] *Taxing Profits in a Global Economy*, 29.

[74] Cnossen (1996) 17(4) *Fiscal Studies* 67, 93, citing, eg, Zodrow (1991) 44 *National Tax Jo* 497.

[75] Department of the US Treasury (1992), *op cit*, 116.

[76] *Taxing Profits in a Global Economy*, ch 2, part D, and ch 5. See also the slightly more recent Chennells and Griffith, *Taxing Profit in a Changing World* (Institute for Fiscal Studies, 1997), 102.

[77] A good starting place is the Mirrlees Review, *op cit*, ch 18 and below at §75.1. For a view of the problem in the corporate as opposed to the tax field, see Charney (1991) 32 *Harvard Journal of International Law* 423; reprinted in Wheeler, *A Reader on the Law of the Business Enterprise* (OUP, 1994), 365.

59.4.5 Cash Flow Tax

In 1978 the Meade Committee developed ideas for taxing companies on cash flow rather than profits.[78] This might simply total receipts and deduct payments other than those made to banks and others for finance, including shareholders, and pay tax on the resulting figure. It would also universalise capital allowances, and abolish the difference between capital and income. It would have the advantage of taxing property companies, but would initially cause difficulties for highly geared companies. Special provision would have to be made for banks, which could be taxed under the then existing system. There are several variant forms.

59.4.6 Tackling the Bias Against Equity[79]—Widening the Deductions

59.4.6.1 The IFS and Mirrlees Review ACE Proposals[80]

In so far as the debate concerns the different treatments of debt and equity finance (ie the deductibility of debt and the non-deductibility of dividends), one solution is to allow the deduction of dividends at corporate level either completely (*model 6*) or in part (*model 3*). An alternative approach is to have an allowance for corporate equity (ACE). The essential idea is simple—a company would be entitled to deduct an allowance based on the value of the shareholder's equity employed in the business for the period. A set percentage representing the normal rate of return, as determined by the Government, is applied to the value of the shareholders' funds. Those funds would consist of the sums of: (a) funds from the previous period; plus (b) any new equity contributed; plus (c) the ACE allowance for the previous period; plus (d) taxable profits. From this total would be deducted: (a) the tax paid on those profits and dividends; and (b) distributions to shareholders and capital repaid. In order to avoid a double allowance, adjustments would have to be made when one company invested in another. The allowance would leave most of the UK system of corporation tax exactly as it was. The result is that tax is levied only on 'excess' returns above the normal rate of return.

Three advantages in taxing the company are seen to flow from the idea:

(1)   neutrality as between debt and equity finance—since a full allowance would be given for the costs of finance, whether debt or equity, and without regard to the level of dividends actually paid, the treatment of equity finance would be assimilated to that of debt finance;

(2)   neutrality as between realised and unrealised profit—realisation of profit will lead to more funds and so a higher rate of allowance; deferral of profit means deferral of tax but a lower rate of allowance; and

---

[78]   See Meade, *The Structure and Reform of Direct Taxation* (Allen & Unwin, 1978), ch 12. The idea is supported on administrative and economic grounds by McLure and Zodrow (1996) 3 *International Tax and Public Finance* 97.

[79]   For a good review of methods of tackling the debt-equity distinction, see Wood (1999) 47 *Can Tax Jo* 49.

[80]   See the Mirrlees Review, *op cit*, ch 17. Earlier work includes the influential Gammie (chair), Report of the IFS Capital Taxes Group, *Equity for Companies; A Corporation Tax for the 1990s* (Institute for Fiscal Studies, 1991). For a summary of the 1991 IFS report, see Gammie (1991) 31 *European Taxation* 238–42; there is another summary in Devereux and Freeman (1991) 12(3) *Fiscal Studies* 1.

(3) inflation—as shareholders' funds rise in response to inflation, so the value of the
     allowance would also rise.

In addition, the ACE proposal would be economically neutral in terms of its effect on decisions on scale of investment, since only excess returns are taxed.[81]

The system would have to face the familiar problems of interaction between corporate
and shareholder levels.[82] The favoured solution is to adopt a classical system for the taxation of dividends, since the effect of the ACE system is that the company's finance costs are
fully deductible and so there is no need for imputation. The system can, however, work
perfectly well in conjunction with an imputation system. More problems arise over the
taxation of capital gains, but these are seen as arising from the nature of the personal tax
system—if the corporate tax system is neutral but the personal tax system is not, an overall
neutral system cannot be created simply by dealing with the corporate side. The Mirrlees
Review recommended taxing capital gains on shares (and dividends) at a lower rate than
earned income to reflect in part tax paid at the corporate level.[83]

Although the ACE proposal has been generally admired rather than widely implemented,
it was the inspiration behind a reform in Croatia lasting from 1994 to 2001, and more
recent relief for equity finance offered in Belgium and Italy.[84] Like other reforms which
increase the amount that may be deducted, the change would mean that the same amount
of tax would have to be raised from a smaller amount of net profits—assuming that the
change is to be revenue neutral.[85] On this basis, ACE would mean both an increase in the
rate of corporation tax if the change were to be revenue neutral (Isaac suggested an increase
of 10% under an imputation system, say, from 35% to 45%[86] for the years 1973–91, with a
25% rate under a classical system) and a major increase in the burden of tax between different companies, with successful companies paying more tax and less successful companies
enjoying a tax reduction.

It is likely that the rate of ACE would be set at a level which would protect a certain
amount of real profit. There would be problems on the taxation of capital gains in the
hands of companies, in that these ought to be taxed at the same rate without indexation
relief; such a high rate would be vulnerable to weakening as a result of either political pressure or avoidance, or both. Furthermore, the ACE does not solve, and may exacerbate as
a consequence of its potentially high tax rate, economic distortions related to location of
discrete investment projects (especially for more profitable projects) and location of taxable

---

[81] See Auerbach, Devereux and Simpson, 'Taxing Corporate Income' in Mirrlees *et al* (eds), *Dimensions of Tax
Design: The Mirrlees Review* (OUP, 2010); the Mirrlees Review, *op cit*, chs 17–19; de Mooij and Devereux, 'An
applied analysis of ACE and CBIT reforms in the EU' (2011) *International Tax and Public Finance* 118, 93–120.

[82] See Report of the IFS Capital Taxes Group (1991), *op cit*, paras 2.4.12–2.4.16; and Cnossen (1996) 17(4)
Fiscal Studies 67, 85.

[83] The Mirrlees Review, *op cit*, 489. The RRA is discussed in detail *ibid* chs 13–14.

[84] Keen and King (2002) 23 *Fiscal Studies* 401–18 (on Croatia), and the Mirrlees Review, *op cit*, 449
(on Belgium).

[85] The Mirrlees Review did not support revenue neutrality, opting instead for lower corporation tax revenues,
principally on international competitiveness grounds: 'If a source-based tax on the normal return component of
corporate profits is undesirable, and the current UK corporate tax rate is considered more or less appropriate, the
implication is that less revenue should be raised from the corporate tax' (Mirrlees *Review, op cit*, 450).

[86] Isaac (1997) 18 *Fiscal Studies* 303, 305. Contrast Bond, Devereux and Gammie (1996) 12 *Oxford Review of
Economic Policy* 109–19.

profit (ie profit shifting to lower-tax jurisdictions).[87] There would be the further question whether the principle—that the opportunity cost of capital should not be taxed—should be extended to income tax. In fact, the Mirrlees Review recommended a rate of return allowance (RRA) for income tax as a 'natural counterpart' to the ACE for corporation tax.[88] As with all fundamental changes, there may also be international tax problems in implementing such a change unilaterally. Cnossen agrees that there are attractive neutrality aspects, but suggests that these are best achieved if capital markets are perfect.[89]

59.4.6.2 The American Law Institute Proposal[90]

The American Law Institute (ALI) had other ideas for reforming the US system so as to reduce the bias against distributed earnings in a classical system. One would be to allow a company to deduct dividends paid on new capital up to a certain percentage geared to the long-term interest rate plus 2%. It differs from the ACE, *inter alia*, in that it applies only to new equity.

59.4.7 *Tackling the Bias Against Equity—Narrowing the Deductions*[91]

A second way to reduce the bias against equity is to look at the company rather than the shareholder, and at the company's inability to deduct dividend payments. Why not reduce or remove the company's right to deduct interest? In fact, following on from the G20/OECD's Base Erosion and Profit Shifting recommendations the UK government is planning to introduce restrictions on corporate interest deductibility from April 2017: see below §63.2.9. In 1992 the US Treasury issued a report on integration which suggested a comprehensive business income tax (CBIT).[92] Under this scheme, all company earnings would be taxed at the company level, and there would be no deductions for either dividends or interest paid to shareholders and debt holders; these items would not be taxed as the recipient's income. This would make the debt/equity distinction irrelevant and reduce the retained/distributed distinction; whether the distinction is abolished would depend on what happened to capital gains rates. The attack on the debt/equity distinction means that many familiar problems would disappear, eg thin capitalisation. The idea has the further attraction of benefiting growing firms at the expense of existing ones—one person's benefit is another person's distortion. Another advantage of the CBIT is that it has a wider base than the ACE and thus lends itself to a lower tax rate than the ACE, all else being equal. This

---

[87] See Auerbach, Devereux and Simpson, *op cit*; Mirrlees Review, *op cit*, chs 17–19; de Mooij and Devereux, *op cit*, 93–120.

[88] Mirrlees Review, *op cit*, 496.

[89] Cnossen (1996) 17(4) *Fiscal Studies* 67, 85.

[90] Andrews, *Reporter's Study Draft for the ALI Federal Income Tax Project, Subchapter C* (American Law Institute, 1989). See also Department of the US Treasury (1992), *op cit*, 108–09; and American Law Institute, *Federal Income Tax Project, Tentative Draft No 2, Subchapter C—Corporate Distributions* (American Law Institute, 1979). The 1979 proposals were criticised as unworkable by Warren (1981) 94 *HLR* 719 and Warren, *ALI Federal Income Tax Project: Integration of the income and corporate income taxes, reporter's study of corporate tax integration* (American Law Institute, 1993).

[91] See Gammie [1992] BTR 244, esp 246. This paragraph is based on the summary by Cnossen (1996) 17(4) *Fiscal Studies* 67, 86–87.

[92] For comment, see Gammie [1992] BTR 244, esp 257–61; and, for a comparison with ACE, see *ibid*, 273–75. See also Goode (1992) *Tax Notes* 1667; and, for an economic viewpoint, Sunley (1992) 47 *Tax L Rev* 621.

would in turn mean a reduced level of economic distortions related to location of discrete investment projects and location of taxable profit compared to an ACE, but the CBIT would not be neutral in terms of decisions on scale of investment (unlike the ACE).[93] Research by Devereux and de Mooij also suggest potential economic benefits could be had from adopting a half-way house approach to reducing the debt/equity distortion with a combination of partial interest restictions and a partial ACE.[94] Finally, it should be emphasised that as corporate tax rates continue to fall generally in the UK and elsewhere, the benefits from a tax deduction for interest and the bias in favour of debt financing over equity fall as well.

---

[93] de Mooij and Devereux, *op cit*, 93–120.
[94] *Ibid*, 110–113.

60

Structure

60.1   The Charge to Corporation Tax

Corporation tax is chargeable on the profits of companies.[1] 'Profits' means income and chargeable capital gains, so, importantly, the same rate of tax is now charged on all company profits, whether income or capital gain.[2] Chargeable gains are computed in accordance with the CGT rules in TCGA 1992.[3] The charge to corporation tax excludes any charge to income tax and CGT.[4] Profits in the form of a distribution by another company generally are excluded from corporation tax.[5] There is no charge to corporation tax where profits accrue to a company in a representative or fiduciary capacity.[6] Where profits accrue in the course of winding up, corporation tax is payable notwithstanding the fact that various

---

[1] CTA 2009, s 2(1), ex TA 1988, s 6(1).
[2] CTA 2009, s 2(2), ex TA 1988, s 6(4). From 1973 to 1987 only a certain fraction (six-sevenths for the financial year 1986) of capital gains was included in the computation (see below at §60.3). This meant, in effect, a lower rate of tax on capital gains but avoided the inelegance of two rates.
[3] TCGA 1992, s 8(3).
[4] CTA 2009, ss 3 and 4, ex TA 1988, s 6(2), (3).
[5] CTA 2009, Pt 9A, ex TA 1988, s 208.
[6] CTA 2009, s 6, ex TA 1988, s 8(2).

fiduciary obligations are also owed to the shareholders. Where profits accrue to the company under a trust or partnership, the company is chargeable to corporation tax.[7]

For the financial year 2016, which began on 1 April 2016, the rate of tax is 20%; there is also a 30% rate applied to ring-fence companies that make profits from oil extraction or oil rights in the UK or UK continental shelf. As discussed in chapter five, since 2013 the UK now has a GAAR. The Revenue remain unwilling to provide a general clearance (or rulings) service. It is well worth noting the number of parts of the corporation tax system which have their own mini anti-avoidance rules in the form of rules forbidding deductions, etc where the transaction is entered into for a non-allowable purpose—and the list of non-allowable purposes will include avoidance. Such a list includes avoidance involving charges on income (§62.4), tax arbitrage (§62.7) and rules on the use of foreign tax credit relief (§75.6).

Nearly all of the corporation tax rules formerly in TA 1988 have been rewritten, and are now found primarily, but not exclusively, in a combination of the CTA 2009, CTA 2010 and TIOPA 2010. References to the old rules are included in the footnotes throughout this book to assist readers with the transition, and because the old rules are relevant for the discussion of the cases.

60.2   A Company

A company means[8] any body corporate or unincorporated association,[9] but does not include a partnership,[10] a local authority or a local authority association.[11] Individuals who invest in a joint account, eg as members of an investment club, are not treated as a company carrying on business together. For problems of identifying a company when considering a foreign entity, see below at §71.3.2. On the European Company, see below at §60.14.

In *Conservative and Unionist Central Office v Burrell*,[12] Lawton LJ said that an unincorporated association arose where:

(1)   two or more persons bound together for one or more common purposes, not being business purposes, by mutual undertakings;

(2)   each having mutual duties and obligations;

(3)   in an organisation which had rules which identified in whom control of it and its funds rested and on what terms; and

---

[7]   CTA 2009, ss 6 and 7, ex TA 1988, s 8(2).

[8]   CTA 2010, s 1121, ex TA 1988, s 832(1), (2). Contrast the more detailed definition in TCGA 1992, s 170. On charitable bazaars, see ITA 2007, s 529, CTA 2010, s 484 and ESC C4. On thrift funds and holiday funds, see former ESC C3.

[9]   *Blackpool Marton Rotary Club v Martin* [1988] STC 823, (1988) 62 TC 286. On liability of officers, see TMA 1970, s 108(2), (3).

[10]   On whether there is a partnership, see *Engineer v IRC* [1997] STC (SCD) 189.

[11]   There is an exemption from income tax (ITA 2007, s 838) and corporation tax (CTA 2010, s 984, ex TA 1988, s 519) for a local authority and local authority association, as defined in CTA 2010, ss 1130 and 1131, ex TA 1988, s 842A, as amended by FA 1995, s 144. TCGA 1992, s 271(3) provides an exemption from CGT.

[12]   [1982] STC 317, (1982) 55 TC 671, CA. See also *Re Koeppler's Will Trusts* [1985] 2 All ER 869, 874, where Slade LJ described an unincorporated association as an association of persons bound together by identifiable roles and having an identifiable membership.

(4)   which might be joined or left at will.

He went on to hold that the structure of the Conservative Party was such that it lacked elements (2) and (3); rather, it was, as it described itself, an amorphous combination of elements, with the result that the Party was not liable to corporation tax on its investment income. The Revenue had accepted that the Party's 'Central Office' was not an unincorporated association, but argued that 'the Party' was such an association, comprising all the individual members of the local constituency associations and the parliamentary party. The individual constituency associations can be unincorporated associations.[13]

Authorised unit trusts are treated as if they were companies.[14] Special rules apply for various special companies such as friendly societies[15] and trade unions.[16] Securitisation companies are also the subject of special rules; these are to take the form of statutory instruments rather than primary legislation.[17] The London Organising Committee for the 2012 Olympic Games was given exemption.[18] The Treasury was given a power to exempt the International Olympic Committee and any subsidiaries from any liability to income tax, CGT or corporation tax, and to treat the Committee as not having a permanent establishment in the UK. A similar power arises in connection with competitors and staff.

60.3   Associated Companies

Prior to 1 April 2015, the benefit of a lower rate of tax on small profits of company was restricted if there were 'associated companies'. Companies were associated if at any time one company had control of the other, or both were under the control of the same person or persons.[19] With the alignment of the main and small profits rate in 2015 these rules were repealed. Interested readers are directed to earlier editions of this book.

60.4   Financial Years—Accounting Periods and Periods of Account

60.4.1 Financial Years

Corporation tax is charged on the profits of the corporation during the financial year.[20] The 'financial year' is the year starting on 1 April.[21] Hence 'financial year 2016' is 1 April 2016 to

---

[13]   Hence, TCGA 1992, s 264 (change of constituency bodies).
[14]   CTA 2010, s 617, ex TA 1988, s 468. See below at §79.3.
[15]   TA 1988, s 463 (not rewritten).
[16]   CTA 2010, s 981, ex TA 1988, s 467.
[17]   CTA 2010, Pt 13, Ch 4, formerly regulations made under FA 2005, s 84.
[18]   FA 2006, ss 65 and 66.
[19]   CTA 2010, s 25, with further elaboration in ss 26–30 and referring to the meaning of 'control' in ss 450 and 451; ex TA 1988, s 416(1). On shareholdings by different trusts with common trustees, see *IRC v Lithgows* (1960) 39 TC 270; for small companies relief, see ESC C9; and, for close companies, see Statement of Practice SP C4.
[20]   CTA 2009, s 2(1), ex TA 1988, s 6(1).
[21]   Interpretation Act 1978, Sch 1.

31 March 2017.[22] The rates of corporation tax are set for the financial year but assessments are made by reference to accounting periods.[23] Where the accounting period does not correspond with the financial year, the profits of the period are apportioned to compute the tax liability.

Where the rate changes from one financial year to the next, each rate is applied to that portion of the accounting period falling within it. So suppose that the rate is 20% in financial Year 1 and 19% in financial Year 2. The company makes up its accounts to 30 June and the total profit for the accounting period ending on 30 June Year 2 amounts to £1,830,000. For Year 1 the share of the profits will be 274/365 × £1,830,000 or £1,373,753, and so corporation tax will be 20% of that, ie £274,751; for Year 2 the share will be 91/365 or £456,247, and so corporation tax at 19% will be £86,687, making a total of £361,438 or 19.75%.

The financial year is relevant only to the rate of tax. If the method of computing income or capital gains and so corporate profits changes from one year to the next, the accounting period is treated as if it were a year of assessment,[24] although various provisions (eg change of ownership) may require an accounting period to be split for specific purposes.

60.4.2 *Accounting Periods and Periods of Account*

Accounting periods are usually the successive periods for which the company makes up its accounts. An accounting period cannot exceed 12 months. A period of account is simply the period taken by the company in computing its accounts.[25] Where the period of account exceeds 12 months, the fiscal accounting period will end after 12 months and a new one will begin; so where a company's period of account is 16 months, there will be a fiscal accounting period of 12 months, followed by one of four months. Where, as here, one set of accounts covers more than one period, an apportionment is made on a time basis unless a more accurate method can be established.[26] This apportionment is carried out on the basis of days, not months.[27]

When a company draws up accounts, the accounting date to which the accounts are drawn determines the accounting periods for assessment of the company's profits. The Revenue have no power to substitute an accounting period they would prefer. Once an assessment is made for an accounting period, that assessment cannot be revised by virtue of the inspector wishing to use a different period as the accounting period.[28] Where, however, at the time of making an assessment, the date on which an accounting period begins or ends appears to the inspector to be uncertain, the inspector is empowered to make an assessment for such period 'as appears to him appropriate';[29] these tests are subjective. The inspector

[22] CTA 2010, s 1119, ex TA 1988, s 834(1).
[23] CTA 2009, s 8, ex TA 1988, s 8(3).
[24] CTA 2009, s 8, ex TA 1988, s 9(1).
[25] On the position where a company makes up its accounts both yearly and six-monthly, see *Jenkins Productions Ltd v IRC* [1943] 2 All ER 786, (1943) 29 TC 142. On accounts for an unauthorised period, see *BFP Holdings Ltd v IRC* (1942) 24 TC 483.
[26] CTA 2009, s 52, ex TA 1988, s 72; *Marshall Hus & Partners Ltd v Bolton* [1981] STC 18, (1981) 55 TC 539.
[27] CTA 2009, s 52(3), ex FA 1995, s 121.
[28] *Kelsall v Stipplechoice Ltd* [1995] STC 681, (1995) 67 TC 349, CA.
[29] TA 1988, s 12(8), not rewritten.

may be required to identify an 'appropriate' period only if the rules in TA 1988, section 12 fail to identify a period.[30]

60.4.2.1 Start

An accounting period begins because the previous accounting period has ended and the company remains subject to charge, or if the company, not then being within the charge to corporation tax, comes within it, whether by the company becoming resident or acquiring a source of income.[31] A UK resident company which has not yet commenced business may not yet be within the charge to corporation tax.[32]

60.4.2.2 End

An accounting period ends[33] on the expiration of 12 months from its beginning or, if earlier, any of the following:

(1) the end of the company's period of account;
(2) if there is a period during which no accounts have been taken, at the end of that period;
(3) the company begins or ceases to trade or to be within the charge to corporation tax in respect of the trade, as where a non-resident company continues to trade but no longer through a branch or agency in the UK; if the company carries on more than one trade, the charge to tax must cease in respect of all of them if the period is to end;
(4) the company begins or ceases to be resident; or
(5) the company ceases to be within the charge to corporation tax.

60.4.2.3 Two Trades

The scheme of tax is designed so that the period of account will usually coincide with the accounting period and is designed to interfere as little as possible with the freedom of the company to take whatever period of account it likes. If the company has two trades, each trade has a separate period of account and the company does not make up accounts for the company as a whole, an Officer of the Revenue may determine which accounting date to take for tax purposes, and the profits of the other trade will have to be apportioned.[34] This emphasises the point that the taxable person is the corporation and not the trade.

60.4.2.4 Winding up and Administration

An accounting period ends and a new one begins when the winding up of a company commences or the company goes into administration.[35] Thereafter, the accounting period

[30] *Kelsall v Stipplechoice Ltd* [1995] STC 681, 683, (1995) 67 TC 349, 374, *per* Peter Gibson LJ.
[31] CTA 2009, s 9(1), ex TA 1988, s 12(2).
[32] CTA 2009, s 9(2), ex TA 1988, s 12(4).
[33] CTA 2009, s 10, ex TA 1988, s 12(3).
[34] CTA 2009, s 11, ex TA 1988, s 12(5A) but only if the Officer, on reasonable grounds, thinks the company's own choice inappropriate.
[35] CTA 2009, ss 12 (winding up) and 10(1)(i) (entering administration), ex TA 1988, s 12(7) as amended by FA 2002.

will end every 12 months until the winding up is complete. A new period begins when the company comes out of administration.[36]

60.4.2.5 Gaps

It is possible for there to be gaps between accounting periods, eg when the company ceases to trade and subsequently starts again. This gives rise to a problem if a capital gain accrues during this period of quiescence. It is therefore provided that an accounting period commences when the chargeable gain or allowable loss accrues to the company.[37] Should the company subsequently begin to trade again, the deemed period will end and a new one will begin.

60.5 Rates

As already seen, the main rate of corporation tax[38] for the financial year 2016 is 20%;[39] it is set to drop to 19% in financial years 2017–19 and 17% in 2020. Until 1 April 2015 a 'small profits' rate of 20% applied where the company's profits did not exceed £300,000. Where the company's profits exceeded £300,000, the benefit of the small profits rate was steadily removed by having a higher marginal rate of tax. This regime gave lower rates of corporation tax to companies with low profits, but the benefits of these lower rates were withdrawn successively, resulting in a very odd looking overall marginal rate structure. The abolishment of the small profits rate in 2015 greatly simplified the rate structure—though one wonders how long it will be before a future Chancellor decides to support small companies by reintroducing a lower rate of tax.

At one time there was an even lower rate of 0% for profits below £10,000. This was controversial; it complicated the decision whether to incorporate a business; and, in so far as it purported to encourage people to do so, sat oddly with the legislation on personal service companies. When people responded by putting businesses into companies the Government reacted by withdrawing the benefit of the 0% rate for profits which were distributed to people other than companies; this was called the non-corporate distribution rate.

These days, the rates of corporation tax are usually known by the start of the financial year. This was not so in the early days and so there was formerly an express provision allowing the use of the previous year's rate if a company was fully wound up before the rate was known.[40] A similar provision (now repealed) was introduced for companies in administration in 2003.[41]

Finally, there is special rate of tax of 30% on 'ring-fenced' companies with certain profits from oil and gas activities in the UK and its related Continental Shelf.[42] The definition of

---

[36] CTA 2009, s 10(1)(j), ex TA 1988, s 12(3)(da).
[37] CTA 2009, s 9(3), ex TA 1988, s 12(6).
[38] CTA 2010, s 3, ex TA 1988, ss 13, 13AA. Capital gains accruing before 17 March 1987 did not qualify for small profits relief and were effectively taxed at 30%; however, the small profits rate was below 30% only for 1986. For pre-1973 rules, see Bolton (chair), *Report on Small Firms*, Cmnd 4811 (1971), ch 13.
[39] FA 2011, s 5(2)(a) modified by rate reduction announced at Budget 2012.
[40] Former TA 1988, s 342.
[41] Former TA 1988, s 342A.
[42] CTA 2010, Pt 8, Ch 6, s 330, ex TA 1988, s 501A added by FA 2002, s 91.

profits is taken from corporation tax but with exclusion for financing costs. Very carefully, the legislation states that this is a sum charged on the company as if it were corporation tax, and so is not corporation tax itself. The company may claim enhanced capital allowances and use them against profits for general corporation tax liability as well as the supplementary charge.[43]

60.6 Administration

60.6.1 *Quarterly Instalments in Advance*

The UK has a system of payment of corporation tax in instalments.[44] The regime applies to tax due in respect of profits of companies, including sums in respect of loans to participators (taxable under CTA 2010, section 455, ex TA 1988, section 419) and the controlled foreign companies legislation.[45] The system was phased in just as ACT payments ceased. Most companies which formerly paid ACT on a quarterly basis will now instead pay corporation tax by instalments, also on a quarterly basis. The key difference is that payments must be made under the new system regardless of whether there has been a distribution.

Instalment payments are due electronically and only from 'large' companies. A company is large if its profits exceed the upper limit for small profits relief (£1.5 million).[46] A *de minimis* exception applies if the total corporation tax liability for the accounting period does not exceed £10,000.[47] To protect growing companies, a company is not large if its profits did not exceed £1.5 million last year and do not exceed £10 million this year.[48] Groups of companies may pay on a group-wide basis.[49] The Regulations also contain rules on the surrender of excessive instalment payments within groups.[50]

Tax is due in four instalments, the first instalment being due six months and 13 days after the start of the accounting period, and the last three months and 13 days after the end of that period;[51] the gap between instalments must not exceed three months.[52] For a 12-month accounting period this makes the payments fall 13 days into months 7, 10, 13 and 16. In a nine-month period the sums would fall due 13 days into months 7, 10 and 13. The Regulations provide for the apportionment of profits to the different periods.[53] Underpayments attract an interest charge;[54] deliberate or reckless underpayments attract a

---

[43] FA 2002, s 63 and Sch 21.

[44] Corporation Tax (Instalment Payments) Regulations 1998 (SI 1998/3175), (hereafter 'IP Regs'), made under TMA 1970, s 59E, added by FA 1998, s 30. See also http://www.hmrc.gov.uk/ct/managing/pay-repay/instalment. htm.

[45] IP Regs, reg 2(3).

[46] IP Regs, reg 3(1); see also reg 3(4) and (5).

[47] IP Regs, reg 3(2).

[48] IP Regs, reg 3(3); on meaning of last year for new companies, see reg 3(6).

[49] Arrangements are made under FA 1998, s 36; for details, see *Inland Revenue Guide to Self Assessment* (1999), ch 13.

[50] IP Regs, reg 9.

[51] IP Regs, reg 5(3).

[52] IP Regs, reg 5(3).

[53] IP Regs, reg 5(5)–(9).

[54] IP Regs, reg 7.

penalty of twice the interest charge.[55] For accounting periods beginning on or after 1 April 2019, companies with annual taxable profits exceeding £20 million will be required to make payments four months earlier. For a 12-month accounting period, payments will be due in the third, sixth, ninth and 12th months of the period to which the liability relates.[56]

If a company has overestimated its potential liability to corporation tax, it may simply pay less in a later quarter, with consequent risks of an interest charge.[57] These rules are different from the general corporation tax interest provisions; they provide that interest in respect of an underpayment, called 'debit interest' by the Revenue, is to be paid at the 'reference rate' plus 1%,[58] which is lower than the normal interest rate of 2.5% over that rate.[59] If, however, the company has paid more than it should, and this is due to a change in the circumstances of the company since the payments were made, it may seek a repayment from the Revenue[60]—with interest.[61] The rules also differ from normal rules in allowing a company that has paid excessive instalments to make a repayment claim. This is known as 'credit interest' and is based on the reference rate minus 0.25%,[62] in contrast to the normal repayment supplement rate of the reference rate minus 1%.[63] Interest may also be paid if the company has not been a large company in the accounting period concerned.[64]

This inflexible obligation is grossly unjust to companies. Many factors can make an honest profit estimate completely wrong, eg a shift in the exchange rate. Moreover, it may cause distortions; thus, a company considering a major disposal of a capital asset in month 12 may be well advised to wait until month 1 of the next year. It seems odd that the company cannot rely on the previous year's figures, as the Revenue happily insist upon under the self-assessment regime for individuals.

For current and historical interest rates, see HMRC's website.[65]

60.6.2 *Self-assessment*

Corporation tax has had a full self-assessment system since 1998.[66] Responsibility for making the assessment rests on the company.[67] The figures in the return are conclusive[68] until amended, whether by the company[69] or by the Revenue.[70] The Revenue may determine the

---

[55] IP Regs, reg 13.

[56] Budget 2016. Originally the bringing forward of instalments was due to take place in 2017 but this was deferred to 2019.

[57] IP Regs, reg 7.

[58] Taxes (Interest Rates) Regulations 1989 (SI 1989/1297), reg 3ZA.

[59] *Ibid*, reg 3ZB.

[60] IP Regs, reg 6.

[61] IP Regs, reg 8.

[62] Taxes (Interest Rates) Regulations 1989, reg 3BA.

[63] *Ibid*, regs 3B and 3BB.

[64] IP Regs, reg 8(1)(b).

[65] Available at https://www.gov.uk/government/publications/rates-and-allowances-hmrc-interest-rates-for-late-and-early-payments/rates-and-allowances-hmrc-interest-rates.

[66] FA 1994, s 199; Finance Act 1999, Section 199 (Appointed Day) Order 1998 (SI 1998/3173), [1991] *Simon's Weekly Tax Intelligence* 97. The Revenue have published a useful *Guide to Corporation Tax Self-Assessment* (hereafter 'CTSA Guide').

[67] FA 1998, Sch 18, para 7.

[68] FA 1998, Sch 18, para 88.

[69] For example under FA 1998, Sch 18, para 15 or 30.

[70] For example under FA 1998, Sch 18, paras 16 (correction of obvious errors) or 34.

amount of tax payable if the company fails to file a return at all.[71] Where claims are made they must be quantified.[72] Only since 2004 has there been an obligation on a company coming within the scope of corporation tax, whether for the first time or after a dormant period, to notify the Revenue.[73] The company must include any sums due under CTA 2010, section 455 (loans to participators: see below at §67.4) and the controlled foreign company legislation (see chapter seventy-three below).[74] The company must also take account of various anti-avoidance rules; other rules require a Revenue notice before the assessed company must take account of them.[75]

Interest paid in respect of late tax is not deductible;[76] the system also provides for credit interest in respect of corporation tax paid early (such interest received by the company being taxable).[77] Like the income tax self-assessment regime, the corporation tax system is based on 'process now—check later'; once the enquiry window of 12 months has passed, the corporation tax return becomes final.[78]

Corporation tax self-assessment is not the same as income tax self-assessment in several ways. Most noticeably, at least for authors and advisers, the legislation on corporation tax self-assessment is laid out in coherent form and modern language (in FA 1998, Schedule 18) and not scattered around that jigsaw known as TMA 1970 (as amended *ad infinitum*).

60.6.3 Liability for Another Company's Tax

A company is usually liable only for its own corporation tax.[79] In 1993 schemes appeared under which companies were sold in circumstances intended to ensure that their corporation tax liabilities arising prior to the date of sale could not be collected.[80] Dicta had already suggested a distinction between tax avoidance and a scheme to prevent the recovery of tax,[81] making the latter a situation for possible penalties. In any event, new rules were introduced by FA 1994 and strengthened in 1997.[82] There are also rules for collecting tax from other group companies.[83]

---

[71] FA 1998, Sch 18, para 36; on which see *CTSA Guide*, ch 9.
[72] FA 1998, Sch 18, paras 54 *et seq*.
[73] FA 2004, s 55.
[74] FA 1998, Sch 18, para 1.
[75] Eg FA 2005, s 88.
[76] TMA 1970, s 90, as amended by FA 1998, s 33.
[77] TA 1988, s 826, as amended by FA 1998, s 34.
[78] On which, see *CTSA Guide*, ch 6.
[79] There are certain exceptions, eg where someone other than the company realising the gain may be accountable: see TCGA 1992, ss 189 (shareholder following capital distribution of gain), 190 (recovery from another group member), 139(7), (8) (tax on transfer of assets following reconstruction or amalgamation), 179(11), (13) (crystallisation of deferred tax on intra-group transfer of assets, and 137(4) (share-for-share exchange outside protection of bona fide commercial reasons zone); and FA 1990, s 86(8) (unpaid tax from company to which loss transferred by group relief).
[80] See Inland Revenue Press Release, 30 November 1993, [1993] *Simon's Tax Intelligence* 1533.
[81] *Roome v Edwards* [1979] STC 546, 561–65.
[82] CTA 2010, Pt 14, Ch 6 and particularly s 710, ex TA 1988, s 767A, 767B, added by FA 1994, s 135; see also TA 1988, ss 767AA, 767C, added by FA 1998, ss 114–116. For Revenue practice on 1993 rules, see Revenue Interpretation RI 90.
[83] CTA 2010, Pt 22, Ch 7, ex FA 2000, Sch 28 (non-resident group members).

60.6.4 *Senior Accounting Officer Responsibilities and Tax Strategy*

FA 2009, section 93 and Schedule 46 imposed duties on senior accounting officers (SAOs) of qualifying companies to take reasonable steps to ensure that the company establishes and maintains appropriate tax and accounting arrangements in relation to relevant tax liabilities.[84] The SAO must also take reasonable steps to monitor the accounting arrangements and identify any in respect of which the arrangements are not appropriate tax accounting arrangements.[85] A company qualifies if its balance sheet exceeds £2 billion or its turnover exceeds £200 million.[86] FA 2009, section 94 authorises HMRC to publish details of deliberate tax defaulters where the potential lost revenue and penalties exceed £25,000. In addition, at Budget 2016, the Government confirmed it will introduce a new requirement that large businesses publish their tax strategies. As outlined in HMRC's draft guidance on the FA 2016, Schedule 19 provisions, this obligation will apply to companies or partnerships subject to the same turnover/balance sheet test as for SAO obligations. The tax strategy must include details on how the business manages tax risk, internal governance arrangements relevant to tax risks, what those tax risks are, the business's attitude to tax planning including an outline of 'tax motives', and the business's approach to working with HMRC.[87]

60.7   Considerations in Incorporation of a Business

The consequences of incorporation are varied.[88] The first and obvious difference from being taxed as an unincorporated business is that the profits of the business or other income source, including capital gains, will now be subject to corporation tax instead of income tax, National Insurance Contributions (NICs) and CGT. In this connection, the widening differences between the tax bases are significant. The rate of corporation tax will depend on the level of profits. Directors' remuneration is deductible,[89] so that although the company is not entitled to personal allowances, enough may be paid out to ensure that the personal allowances of the incorporators and their bands of income liable to basic rate income tax are all used up, or to pay out the much smaller sum needed to ensure that the employee had a full year of contributions for National Insurance.

Assuming that the company's profit was substantial and that the director's marginal rate of income tax exceeds the corporation tax rate of 20%, the company appears to be a tax shelter. This seems to be a significant advantage over an unincorporated business if the business is looking to internal sources of finance for growth, and the advantage become more marked as the general rate of corporation tax has dropped from its 1982 rate of 52%. However, taxpayers will, presumably, eventually wish to get their capital out of the

---

[84] FA 2009, Sch 46, paras 1–15.
[85] For details on the information that must be provided by certificate by the SAO, see FA 2009, Sch 46, para 2.
[86] FA 2009, Sch 46, para 15.
[87] See https://www.gov.uk/guidance/large-businesses-publish-your-tax-strategy.
[88] A good starting points is Rayney in *Tolley's Tax Planning*, ch 28.
[89] Subject to ITTOIA 2005, s 34/CTA 2009, s 54, which may prevent the deduction of such part of it as is unreasonable.

company, which means selling shares and so incurring CGT, or taking dividends, which means paying income tax though not NICs. Today the use of the rules relating to demergers or to the purchase by the company of its own shares for its own trading purposes is a way of avoiding dividend treatment.

From the directors' point of view there are advantages and disadvantages to incorporating a business. First, directors become liable to tax under ITEPA 2003 and so to the PAYE system and, of ever greater importance, to NICs payable by both the directors and the company. Secondly, they become liable to the stringent rules surrounding benefits derived from the company (see chapter sixteen above). Against this, they may find that the benefit rules are not as strict as might appear at first sight. Further, they will be substantially better off as far as pensions are concerned. As directors, they may have either a defined benefit plan or a defined contribution scheme; as self-employed persons, they fund their own pension and only under a defined contribution scheme. Unless the taxpayers start young and have taken maximum advantage of this entitlement throughout their working lives, they cannot hope to build up so large a fund. Income distributed as salary to the employee/director is fully deductible by the company; income distributed as dividend is not deductible.

Since the company is a separate legal person, its trading or capital losses cannot be set off against the shareholder's income or gains—or vice versa. Other relevant issues are that:

(1)   gains made by the company are, in effect, subject to double taxation (see below at §62.3);
(2)   a company may need Treasury consent for some of its international transactions (see below at §69.7); and
(3)   ITA 2007, section 684 (ex TA 1988, section 703—below §68.5) hangs over the problem of extracting reserves from the company otherwise than by dividend or straightforward liquidation.

Once a company is established, it is possible to use the annual £3,000 exemption for inheritance tax (IHT) to make gifts of shares to trusts for children or others. More generally, it is easier to pass a share in an incorporated business to a child than a portion of an unincorporated business.[90] The present exemption of many business assets and shareholdings from IHT mitigates this difference to some extent (see above §54.2). On the other hand, individuals exporting a business to a non-resident may run into ITA 2007, section 720 (ex TA 1988, section 739—see below at §71.6) and, as self-employed persons, they must pay the applicable NICs.

When the business is incorporated, the shift from ITTOIA 2005, Part 2 income tax to corporation tax is made by discontinuing the trade for income tax with an assessment for a long period, perhaps with only a little overlap profit relief. However, loss relief may be preserved and rollover relief is granted for CGT provided all the business assets are transferred to the company in return for shares. All these issues apply whether the business being incorporated is run by a sole person or by a partnership.[91]

---

[90]   On passing on the family business, see Maas, in *Tolley's Tax Planning*, ch 45.
[91]   On LLPs see below §60.13.

The above list has concentrated on the tax aspects of incorporation. However, the non-tax aspects are of great importance and include:

(1)   the costs of running the paperwork of a company;
(2)   the fact of limited liability, although this is likely to be qualified by the bank's insistence on collateral personal liability at least in the early stages; and
(3)   the significant change in status (where more than one person is involved) when moving from equal partner to minority shareholder.

Further, company law requirements seem to be becoming more stringent, and some professions discourage incorporation.

This list has concentrated on problems—because they need to be considered. However, there are also advantages in being able to raise finance through equity as well as debt, and through devices such as a floating charge which an individual cannot create.[92]

60.8   Disincorporation

In 1987 the Inland Revenue and the Department of Trade and Industry produced a discussion document on the problems of removing tax obstacles to disincorporation. They decided that any new legislation would have to be aimed at small, private trading companies, because it was essentially these companies (small, owner-managed, essentially incorporated sole traders or partnerships, with a relatively narrow range of secured and unsecured creditors) that would be interested. Investment companies, groups of companies and non-resident companies would all be excluded. The legislation would have to contain protections to ensure that there was continuity of ownership, trade and management in the new unincorporated form.

Among the problems to be resolved was the treatment of trading losses. To refuse to allow these to be carried forward would be to leave an obstacle, yet to give a rollover on analogy with TCGA 1992, section 162 would ignore the fact that the losses would be reflected in the value of the shares in the company and would make the legislation complicated. To provide relief would be all the more complex when, as in 1987, there were substantial differences in tax rates between the incorporated and the unincorporated sectors. Some elements in determining the loss might have to be removed (eg directors' remuneration). There would also be problems identifying the particular entities to which the losses should be attributed after disincorporation, ie whether they should be set against the business itself and, if the business was run by a partnership, whether losses should be apportioned by reference to profit-sharing ratios or equity interests. Following the analogy of section 162, the document suggested that losses should be allocated to the shareholders in the company, to be set against later income derived from the business.

Other relatively minor difficulties highlighted in the 1987 report included the correct treatment of post-cessation trading income and expenditure of the company, the valuation

---

[92]   On tax considerations in raising finance generally, see Ball, *Tolley's Tax Planning*, ch 9. For a comparison of companies with partnerships, see *Simon's Direct Tax Service*, para D2.114.

of trading stock, provision for the continuation of capital allowances and the treatment of bad debts that had been allowed as deductions by the company but which were subsequently paid to the new owners. The report concluded it might be necessary to remove the application of the golden handshake provisions but to retain the relief for interest paid on loans to acquire shares in the enterprise while it was incorporated, provided the shareholder retained an interest in the business. There would also have to be legislation to prevent taxpayers disincorporating and then reincorporating simply for the tax advantages. Special rules would be needed for IHT, eg to treat the old and new ownership as one for the purpose of business relief.

Another significant problem raised in the 1987 report was the correct treatment of capital gains. This stems from the double charge to tax on gains in the corporate sector as contrasted with the single layer for the unincorporated sector. One instance in which the dual charge arises is on liquidation. A disposal occurs at corporate level and a deemed disposal to the shareholders under TCGA 1992, section 122. Parity of reasoning suggests a similar dual charge on disincorporation, and yet this would deter the process. To provide relief, the document discusses, but finds fault with, the idea of eliminating one of the two tiers of charge.

This area raises deep questions about the nature of capital gains taxation, particularly in the corporate sector:

(1)   The value of the shares will not generally equate with that of the company's assets but will take into account the general prospects of the company, whether good or bad. Moreover, to the extent that the shares are related to the company's assets, it must be remembered that not all those assets are relevant to capital gains taxation. Thus, cash, whether from trading profits, a new issue of share capital or the disposal of a capital asset, is not relevant to CGT and, in the case of the first or the third sources, will already have been taxed.

(2)   To grant exemption would make disincorporation more advantageous than other forms of corporate reorganisation which simply granted deferrals.

(3)   The situation in which the disincorporated company is treated more favourably than the continuing company must be avoided.

These considerations led to the idea that the correct solution would be deferral at both shareholder and asset level, and various practical solutions were suggested. Thus, the assets would be transferred on a no gain, no loss basis—but only for trade assets. Problems on the deferral of the share tier charge are concerned principally with the question of what events should trigger the charge. An alternative idea, put forward by the Institute of Taxation, is that the share tier should be exempt, but that shareholders who receive a share of undistributed income accruing with the previous six years should pay income tax on those receipts. The assimilation of tax rates on income and capital gains has done much to reduce the importance of the applicable tax rate, but not the figure to which the rate is to be applied. The Institute also suggested that investors not participating in the business after disincorporation should be taxed under the present system.

In February 2012, the OTS sought to revive interest in this issue, releasing a report recommending the introduction of disincorporation relief for 'micro' companies, which would allow the business of a trading company (including goodwill and possibly property, plant and machinery used wholly in the trade) to pass to an unincorporated business without attracting an immediate tax charge.[93] FA 2013, sections 58–61 introduced a limited form of disincorporation relief from 1 April 2013. The new rules are loosely based on the recommendations made by the OTS. The temporary new relief allows a company to transfer its business together with all the assets of the business (cash can be excluded) to its individual shareholders who continue to operate the business in an unincorporated form as a going concern, without the company incurring a corporation tax charge on the disposal of the assets. The qualifying transfer must occur between 1 April 2013 and 31 March 2018 for the relief to apply. Although the relief is available to a wide range of businesses, a number of conditions must be satisfied. Most notably, pursuant to section 59, Condition C the total market value of the qualifying assets of the business (including land and goodwill) included in the transfer must not exceed £100,000.[94] The claim for disincorporation relief must be made jointly by the company and all of the shareholders to whom the business is transferred. The claim is irrevocable and must be made within two years of the business transfer date (section 60).

60.9   Non-resident Companies

The rules on the taxation of non-resident companies were modernised in 2003. Under the present rules, such companies are subject to corporation tax only if they are carrying on a trade through a permanent establishment (PE) in the UK and are taxable on all the chargeable profits attributable to the PE.[95] Chargeable profits are then defined[96] as:

(1)   trading income arising directly or indirectly through or from the PE;
(2)   income from property or rights held by the PE, eg royalties on a patent held by the branch and profits on the realisation of assets held on a short-term basis and funded by an insurance company's surpluses;[97] and
(3)   chargeable gains arising—
       (a)   as a result of assets being used in or for the purposes of the trade carried on by the company through the PE, or
       (b)   as a result of assets being used or held for the purpose of the PE, or
       (c)   as a result of assets being acquired for use by or for the purposes of the PE.

Gains under head (3) must also come with TCGA 1992, section 10B, another new provision unique to non-resident companies with a PE. That makes it clear that it applies only to companies carrying on a trade in the UK at the relevant time through the PE.[98]

---

[93]   OTS, *Small business tax review: Final report—Disincorporation relief* (Feb 2012).
[94]   For commentary see Gotch [2013] BTR 446 and for detailed guidance on the new regime see HMRC CGT manual para CG65800 et seq.
[95]   CTA 2009, s 5, ex TA 1988, ss 11 and 11AA; on mode of assessment, see TMA 1970, ss 85, 78, 79. On place of trade, see below at §72.2; for an example, see *IRC v Brackett* [1986] STC 521, (1986) 60 TC 134.
[96]   CTA 2009, s 19(3), ex TA 1988, s 11(2).
[97]   *General Reinsurance Co Ltd v Tomlinson* (1970) 48 TC 81.
[98]   TCGA 1992, s 10B(3) (see below at §74.1).

Example

X Ltd, a non-resident company, carries on a trade in the UK through a PE. The PE has UK trading income of £1,750,000 and sells UK property from its trade, realising a capital gain of £60,000; it also sells overseas property realising a gain of £75,000. UK corporation tax is due on the first two items, but not on the third. This makes chargeable profits of £1,810,000, on which corporation tax is due at 20% (£362,000).

The purpose behind the 2003 changes was to treat the UK branch of a foreign company as if it were a subsidiary with its own capital and to talk in terms of 'permanent establishment', not 'branch or agency' as is still done for income tax.[99] The concept of the PE is well known in double tax treaties and is considered below at §76.6.2.[100] The main assumption on which the income arising under these rules is to be calculated is that the PE is a distinct and separate enterprise engaged in the same or similar activities under the same or similar conditions and dealing wholly independently with the non-resident company.[101] The PE is assumed to have the same credit rating as the non-resident company. It is also assumed to have the amount of equity or loan capital that might reasonably be expected under the basic assumption. There is an express provision on allowable expenses, ie expenses of a kind which would be allowable under UK corporation tax. These are deductible if incurred for the purpose of the PE, including executive and general administration expenses incurred for that purpose, whether incurred in the UK or elsewhere.[102]

Further rules include an assumption of arm's length dealing for transactions between the PE and any other part of the non-resident company, and prohibitions on deductions for payments in respect of intangible assets and for interest and other financing costs.[103] Where goods or services are provided by the non-resident company to the PE, an arm's length rules applies if the goods or services are of the kind which the company provides to third parties as part of its business; otherwise the matter is dealt with as an expense incurred by the non-resident company for the purposes of the PE.[104] There are also rules for banks.[105]

Income outside CTA 2009, section 19 and accruing to a non-resident company is charged not to corporation tax but to income tax. There is a limit to liability in respect of certain types of investment and other income; this mirrors the income tax provision discussed in §72.6.3. Lastly, there is a general regulation-making power in section 156 to enable the Treasury to adapt these various changes to overseas life insurance companies.

---

[99] Inland Revenue Budget Note 25/02, [2002] *Simon's Tax Intelligence* 586. The change was expected to increase the profits taxed in the UK, and to affect foreign banks and insurance companies in particular.
[100] See Arnold, de Sasseville and Zolt (2002) 50 *Canadian Tax J* 1979–2024.
[101] CTA 2009, s 21, ex TA 1988, s 11AA(2).
[102] CTA 2009, s 29, ex TA 1988, s 11AA(4), Sch A1, para 3.
[103] CTA 2009, ss 22, 31, 32, ex TA 1988, Sch A1, added by FA 2003, Sch 25, paras 2–5.
[104] CTA 2009, s 23, ex TA 1988, Sch A1, para 6.
[105] CTA 2009, ss 25–28, ex TA 1988, Sch A1, paras 7–10.

60.9.1 Change of Status

If a resident company ceases to be resident or ceases to be liable to UK tax, there is a deemed disposal of its capital assets.[106] However, there is no deemed disposal of assets which remain in a PE in the UK and so within the charge to corporation tax.[107] If the company fails to pay the tax within six months from its becoming payable, the tax may be collected from others.[108] Those 'others' are any other group company and the controlling director of that or any other group company at the relevant time.[109] Schemes to avoid this charge by leaving the assets within a branch in the UK at the time of migration but then leasing them to another UK resident company were stopped by the creation of another deemed disposal.[110] Where the change of residence arises from the 1994 statutory rule for companies treated as not resident for Treaty purposes, there is no immediate charge.[111] Where the change of residence is to another EU Member State, the provision may violate the fundamental freedoms.[112]

60.9.2 FA 2000: From Residence to Chargeability

Many UK tax rules used to apply only to companies resident in the UK.[113] These rules came under review following the decisions of the ECJ, particularly *ICI v Colmer*.[114] As a result, FA 2000 made major changes to the status of non-resident companies which are subject to UK tax by reason of the rules set out above. These changes are mentioned at various parts of the book, but some may be noted now:

(1)   A non-resident may claim capital allowances (FA 2000, section 74).
(2)   A non-resident company can be a member of a group of companies for purposes of group relief and chargeable gains deferrals (FA 2000, sections 96 and 101; see chapters sixty-four and sixty-five below).
(3)   The UK branch of a non-resident company may claim double tax relief (see §75.4.1 below).

In all these instances the non-resident company is relevant because it is chargeable to UK tax and the rules are recast in those terms. Yet the list is not comprehensive; among provisions remaining unaffected is CTA 2010, section 1049 (stock dividends).

---

[106] TCGA 1992, s 185; see also below at §69.6.
[107] TCGA 1992, s 185(4).
[108] TCGA 1992, s 191(1).
[109] TCGA 1992, s 191(4)–(7). On special capital gains rules for dual resident investment companies, see below at §69.6.5.
[110] Now in TCGA 1992, s 25(3); see below at §74.1.
[111] FA 1994, s 250(3)–(6); see below at §69.6.
[112] See eg Case C-371/10 *National Grid Indus BV v Inspecteur van de Belastingdienst Rijnmond/kantoor Rotterdam* [2012] STC 114 and Case C-9/02 *Lasteyrie du Saillant v Ministere de l'Economie* [2005] STC 1722.
[113] See eg the list in Shipwright and Keeling [1995] *EL Rev* 580, 596–97.
[114] Case C-264/96 [1998] All ER (EC) 585; [1998] STC 874.

60.10   Beneficial Ownership[115]

Many corporation tax rules refer to shares being in a person's beneficial ownership.[116] These rules may contain further detailed rules of their own, but there is a background of general case law concerning two issues:

(1)   what rights A must have to qualify to be beneficial owner; and
(2)   the effect on those rights of an impending or possible transfer of those shares by A to someone else.

On (1), A is taken as owning shares beneficially if entitled to the dividends. The fact that A is entitled only to the dividends—and not entitled to any share of the assets on a winding up—is irrelevant. On (2), the general approach of the courts has been that a company owns shares beneficially if it is free to dispose of them as it wishes; it is irrelevant that the shares may not be owned for a long period.[117] If a contract for sale has been made, beneficial ownership may at some point shift to the purchaser, but this depends on the contract.[118] It is possible that the ownership may leave the vendor before it reaches the purchaser, ie be in suspense, but this is not favoured these days. So A was treated as still being the beneficial owner of the shares even though B had an option to acquire them, and the terms of the option were such that B was likely to exercise it.[119]

In *BUPA*,[120] the Upper Tribunal considered the cases on beneficial ownership at some length and helpfully digested them into the following propositions:

(1)   Beneficial entitlement is the same as beneficial ownership, albeit entitlement refers to future and ownership to present
(2)   Beneficial entitlement/beneficial ownership is a wider concept than the private law concept of 'equitable entitlement'. The group relief provisions expressly contemplate that beneficial entitlement/ ownership can be achieved indirectly (through ownership of another company).
(3)   The test is applied to the person claiming beneficial entitlement/ownership, so that when considering whether the seller of an asset has beneficial ownership, the question is not whether ownership has passed to the purchaser (citing the *Wood Preservation* case).
(4)   Although beneficial ownership may be 'in suspense' (again from *Wood Preservation*), a commercial contract for the sale of an asset will 'not normally' result in such a suspension. Assets held in a discretionary trust are the classic case of an asset of which no person has beneficial ownership.

---

[115]   See Rowland [1997] BTR 178.
[116]   Eg CTA 2010, s 1154(6), ex TA 1988, s 838(3), to which TCGA 1992, s 170 refers.
[117]   *Burman v Hedges and Butler* [1979] STC 136, (1979) 52 TC 501.
[118]   *Wood Preservation Ltd v Prior* (1969) 45 TC 112.
[119]   *J Sainsbury plc v O'Connor* [1991] STC 318, (1991) 64 TC 208 CA.
[120]   *BUPA Insurance Ltd v HMRC [2014] UKUT 262 (TCC).*

(5)   Although equitable ownership may be sufficient to confer beneficial ownership/
      entitlement, this will not necessarily be the case. A person can have equitable enti-
      tlement without beneficial entitlement, such as when the owner of an asset is
      contractually bound to on-sell that asset to another party.
(6)   Any incident of ownership which amounts to 'more than a mere legal shell' will give
      beneficial ownership for group/consortium relief purposes; for example, the right to
      dispose of the asset OR enjoy its fruits (citing the *J Sainsbury* case).

The postponement rules in TCGA 1992, section 171 do not apply to transfers between
subsidiary and a parent in liquidation since, once liquidation of the parent has begun, the
shares in the subsidiary are not held by the parent beneficially but on trust for its own
members.[121] The effect of a voluntary winding up is less clear.[122]
    The meaning of the term 'beneficial ownership' also arises in the international context,
where it may carry a different sense.[123] There is no reason why the trustee, whether of a
pension fund or of a private trust, should not be treated as having beneficial ownership in
the international context.

60.11   Subsidiaries, Control, etc

Subsidiary status is a matter of frequent concern in tax law. Section 1154 of CTA 2010
(ex TA 1988, section 838) defines subsidiaries in terms of ownership of ordinary share
capital,[124] and refers to 51%, 75% and 90% subsidiaries. The rules allow for direct and
indirect holdings to be taken into account and provide calculation rules. If A owns shares
in C, A's holding is direct; if A holds share in B which holds shares in C, A's holding in B
is direct, but A's holding in C is indirect.
    The tax legislation has several tests for determining whether one company has control
over another and whether both are under the control of a third party.
    The simplest test is that set out in CTA 2010, section 1124 (ex TA 1988, section 840),
which refers to the power of a person (P) (ie whether or not a company)

> to secure (a) by means of the holding of shares or the possession of voting power in relation to that
> or any other body corporate; or (b) as a result of any powers conferred by the articles of association
> or other document regulating that or any other body corporate, that the affairs of [the] company
> … are conducted in accordance with P's wishes.

In relation to a partnership, it means the right to a share of more than one half of the assets,
or of more than one half of the income, of the partnership. Thus, CTA 2010, section 1124
is satisfied by 51% control. On whether control means (a) the power to carry a resolution

---

[121]   *Ayerst v C & K (Construction) Ltd* [1975] STC 345, [1975] 2 All ER 537, (1975) 50 TC 651. The House of
Lords decided only that the company ceased to be beneficial owner of its assets The Court of Appeal had held that
the ownership was in suspense; [1975] STC 1, [1975] 1 All ER 162.
[122]   *Wadsworth Morton Ltd v Jenkinson* [1966] 3 All ER 702, (1966) 43 TC 479.
[123]   See OECD discussion draft 'Clarification of the Meaning of "Beneficial Owner" in the OECD Model Tax
Convention' (2011) at http://www.oecd.org/dataoecd/49/35/47643872.pdf and also Collier [2011] BTR 684.
[124]   Defined in CTA 2010, s 1118, ex TA 1988, s 832(1); founder members' deposits with a mutual society were
not such capital in *South Shore Mutual Insurance v Blair* [1999] STC (SCD) 296.

at a general meeting, including the power to elect the board of directors; or (b) more nar-rowly, the power to run the company's affairs, that is power at the director level, the point being that the general meeting cannot usually tell its directors how to manage the day-to-day affairs of the company, see *Steele v EVC International NV*[125] (above at §60.3). A second test is that used in CTA 2010, section 450 (ex TA 1988, section 416) to determine whether a company is a close company. This is a wider test, in that it looks at more factors than CTA 2010, section 1124, but still requires a 51% result (see further below at §67.2.2).

Individual rules may impose further tests and different percentages for their own pur-poses, especially where groups are concerned. Thus, group relief for losses[126] uses the concept of a 75% subsidiary and imposes further tests by asking whether: (a) the parent company is beneficially entitled to not less than 75% of any profits available for distribu-tion to equity holders of the subsidiary company; and (b) the parent company would be beneficially entitled to not less than 75% of any assets of the subsidiary company available for distribution to its equity holders on a winding up. The question whether these percent-ages are satisfied by equity holders is then subject to further conditions set out in CTA 2010, sections 158 *et seq* (ex TA 1988, Schedule 18).

60.12   Reorganisations and Acquisitions[127]

60.12.1 Introduction

In this short section we touch on some practical issues, the details of which will arise later in these chapters, especially those on groups. The purpose of this section is to alert the reader to the significance of some of the things which follow and so to make them more interesting—or, at least, less intimidating; this section provides cross-references to the text rather than repeating what will be said later on.

The tax effects of the incorporation—and disincorporation—of a business have been outlined above at §§60.7 and 60.8, but many of the same issues arise when one is looking at one company buying a business. Thus, how does one decide upon ownership of the new business; what does one do about claims for trading losses, capital allowances, unsold trad-ing stock, capital gains and losses in respect of the business being taken over? In so far as the new business is going to be fitted into a group structure alongside the existing businesses, how will the rules discussed in this and the preceding chapter affect things? In so far as the tax system likes to avoid unnecessary dislocation, how might one take advantage of the various reliefs, especially the CGT rules about shareholdings and corporate reorganisations in TCGA 1992, sections 127 *et seq*? How far are the interests of the seller of the business compatible with what the buyer wants? A good but still daunting starting point is pro-vided by the chapters in the annual *Tolley's Tax Planning*. The best account of the technical

---

[125] [1996] STC 785, (1996) 69 TC 88.

[126] CTA 2010, s 151, ex TA 1988, s 413(7).

[127] For some assessments of the worth of mergers and takeovers, see papers collected in Fairburn and Kay (eds), *Mergers and Merger Policy* (OUP, 1989), Hughes and Singh (1987) 6 *Contributions to Political Economy* 73 and Singh, 'Corporate Takeovers' in *The New Palgrave Dictionary of Money and Finance* (Palgrave Macmillan, 1992).

legal material is to be found in the latest edition of *Bramwell's Taxation of Companies and Company Reconstructions*.

Naturally the reconstruction of some types of company receives special attention. One important example is provided by companies with a business of leasing plant and machinery, such as that in the famous *BMBF* case.[128] The problem for the Revenue was that these contracts usually generate losses in the early years and profits later on. On a solution by CTA 2010, Part 9 (ex FA 2006, Schedule 10), see further §62.5.6 below.

60.12.2 *Scenario: Questions*

H Ltd, a holding company, owns a business currently held in a subsidiary, G Ltd, and X Ltd, an unconnected company, wants to buy it.

A list of some common questions:

(1)   What is to be sold; assets or shares in G?
(2)   When is the sale to take place? Effect on time limits for loss relief/CGT loss carry-back rules, etc.
(3)   Who should make the sale? Should the business be 'hived down' by G to a separate subsidiary company (GS)?
(4)   What should be the form of the consideration provided by X?
(5)   How much of the consideration should be left outstanding?
(6)   Should there be a pre-sale dividend by G to H to extract cash from the company?
(7)   A further set of problems arises if, as is not the case here, the seller wants to have some interest in the company after the sale.

60.12.3 *Hive Down*

If X wants to buy an incorporated business, X may wish either to buy G Ltd or to buy a separate company (GS) to which G transfers the business. The latter is known as a hive down, ie hiving down the business to a subsidiary, which is a more precise expression than 'hiving off'.

When G transfers the business and its assets to GS, there is a change of ownership but also a 100% parent-subsidiary group relationship. Trading losses will pass to GS on the basis that there is no discontinuance and commencement assuming that the requirements of CTA 2010, sections 940A–953 (ex TA 1988, section 343) (see below at §62.5.2) are met. The trade carried on by GS must be the same as that carried on by G. The transfer does not count as a release of debt so no charge arises under CTA 2009, section 94 (ex TA 1988, section 94). Capital allowances are treated the same as trading losses—CTA 2010, section 948 (ex TA 1988, section 343(2)); this excludes any CAA 2001 rules. Assets subject to capital gains taxation pass on a 'no gain, no loss' basis, thanks to TCGA 1992, section 171 (see below at §65.2.1). However, there is now a potential extra tier of CGT.

<hr/>

[128] *Barclays Mercantile Business Finance Ltd v Mawson* [2005] STC 1 (HL); and see above §5.6.

60.12.4 Pros and Cons of Assets Versus Shares in the Trading Company

The key difference lies in the differing tax treatments of assets and shares. If X takes assets there is no risk of accidentally inheriting some liability incurred by G. However, it is usual for X to buy the business and make G provide all sorts of warranties as to the tax history of the company being sold. GS will now be ignored.

60.12.4.1 Capital Allowances

There are no capital allowances for shares in G bought by X from H; however, G will, subject to conditions, continue to be able to claim the allowances for assets used in the business. If X buys the assets and not the shares, capital allowances may be available to X as a purchaser of machinery or plant. There may also be balancing allowances or charges for G.

60.12.4.2 Trading Losses

If X buys the assets, any trading loss will cease to be available to G (unless terminal loss relief applies). X cannot use the losses. If X buys the shares in G, G may also continue to claim the benefit of loss relief—subject to the usual conditions about changes in the conduct of the trade. There may also be problems with surplus property business losses[129] (see below at §62.5.2).

60.12.4.3 Capital Gains

If shares in G are sold by H to X, there is a disposal of those shares by H. As H is a company, we are concerned with indexation and the availability of the substantial shareholding exemption (see below at §62.3.3). If the assets are sold by G, after leaving H and joining X, there will be a CGT liability on G; the (net of tax) gain will be reflected in the value of the shares to be taxed again should the shares be sold—the dual CGT liability providing the rationale for the substantial shareholding exemption. If the exemption is not available X may wish to reduce the value of shares before the sale by getting cash out of the company; hence hive downs, pre-transfer distributions, etc.

60.12.4.4 Trading Stock

Proceeds are taxable if G sells these assets pursuant to CTA 2009, section 162 (ex TA 1988, section 100(1)(a)). There is also the very important question of liability for the existing contracts made by G. If X buys only the assets, the contracts remain with G; if X buys the shares in G, X also buys the continuing contracting party. If X buys shares, G will be joining a group with X. Pre-entry capital losses are governed by TCGA 1992, section 177A and Schedule 7A (reversing *Shepherd v Lyntress*)[130] and pre-entry capital gains by TCGA 1992, section 184A *et seq* (especially section 184B), added by FA 2006 and repealing Schedule 7AA (see below at §65.2). If the company forms part of X's group, it will leave H's group so that there may be an exit charge under TCGA 1992, section 179.

---

[129] CTA 2010, ss 683–684 (ex Schedule A loss, TA 1988, s 768D).
[130] [1989] STC 617.

60.12.5 *Warranties*

If X buys the shares it will want to know all the tax risk inherent in G. For this reason it is customary for the buyer to ask for—and the seller to give—warranties as to the tax history of the company. The list of warranties in the standard books, eg *Tolley's Tax Planning*, provides a checklist for a revision course in corporation tax law.

60.12.6 *How Will X, the Buyer, Pay for It?*

If X is paying cash, it may need to borrow money; it will therefore have to observe all the loan relationship rules to ensure that interest is deductible. If X is going to issue H with shares, it may need to observe TCGA 1992, section 135. If X issues H with loan stock, H may be able to choose when to realise them and so determine its CGT liability.

60.12.6.1 Deferred Consideration

Consideration may be tied to profitability of business in the hands of new owners. Depending on the form of the consideration, there may be problems in so far as interest may be treated as a distribution under CTA 2010, sections 1000(1)F and 1015(4) (ex TA 1988, section 209(2)(e)(iii))—and so not be deductible by B—or it may be a separate asset with its own potential CGT liability thanks to *Marren v Ingles* (see above §43.1.1).

60.12.6.2 Annuity—the Other *Ramsay*[131]

X may choose to pay H an annuity. The annuity is deductible as a charge on income. The downside is that X must pay tax on the whole amount received as income under ITTOIA 2005, Part 5, Chapter 7, ex Schedule D, Case III. A stream of payments may have to be analysed to see whether it is an annuity or a loan relationship (see above §27.4.5).

60.12.7 *International*

All these problems become more interesting when one or more of the parties is resident outside the UK. Where the other country involved is a Member State of the EU, the EU dimension (see chapter seventy-seven below) must be noted, especially the EU's Mergers Directive and its consequent UK legislation (see §62.3.6 below).

60.13 Limited Liability Partnerships

Limited liability partnerships (LLPs) established under the Limited Liability Partnership Act 2000 (LLPA 2000) are a relatively new form of legal entity. An LLP is a body corporate with legal personality separate from that of its members and has unlimited capacity (as distinct from liability).[132] The new LLP form was aimed in particular at large professional

[131] *Ramsay v IRC* (1935) 20 TC 97.
[132] LLPA 2000, ss 1–4.

partnerships, such as lawyers and accountants, as a response to concerns over the potential risks associated with large legal claims against such firms set up as general partnerships.[133] LLPs offer the same advantage of limited liability for members as is enjoyed by shareholders of a company but with the organisational flexibility of a general partnerships. There are no requirements for board meetings or annual meetings, and LLPs do not have memorandum or articles of association. LLPs are required to keep accounting records, submit audited annual accounts and annual returns to Companies House just the same as companies, however, but are also eligible for the abbreviated accounts and exemption from audit rules available to companies. LLPs are much more flexible than limited partnerships (LPs), which were introduced in the UK in 1907 and also offer limited liability for some members of the partnerships but only so long as they are not involved in the management of the partnership's business. The numbers of LLPs are quite small in comparison to other legal forms. The effective number of registered LLPs in the UK according to the Companies House register at the end of 2015 was a mere 55,260.

From a tax perspective, the policy aim was for equivalence of treatment of LLPs and general partnerships for tax purposes.[134] The tax rules provide that, despite having independent legal personality, the LLP is taxed on the basis that its partnership activities are carried on by the members and not by the LLP itself; so gains and profits are taxed as accruing to the partner and will be subject to income tax and CGT, and will attract corporation tax only in the case of a corporate partner.[135]

There are also anti-avoidance rules. These were introduced at a late stage in the passage of the FB 2001, and apply to prevent pension funds and similar bodies and friendly societies, etc from claiming their normal exemptions from tax where they have interests in a property investment LLP.[136] Interest relief under ITA 2007, sections 398–399 (ex TA 1988, section 362(2)) is not available for a loan to buy an interest in an investment LLP.

More recently, advisors began to appreciate the flexibility and tax possibilities offered by an LLP. In turn, HMRC began to pay closer attention to tax avoidance involving LLPs and also so-called 'mixed partnerships'—partnerships with a mix of individual and corporate members. At Budget 2013 the Government announced a consultation on (1) the use of LLPs to avoid employment tax and (2) artificial profit allocations involving LLPs and also mixed partnerships. On (1), an interesting tax feature of LLPs dating back to 2000 was that all members of the LLP were deemed by the tax legislation to be partners for all the activities of the LLP and thus taxed under the sole proprietor rules.[137] This rule applied even where a member would have been treated as an employee if the LLP had been a traditional or general partnership.[138] Perhaps unsurprisingly, this deeming feature was abused to minimise employment tax liability on persons who were in substance employees of the LLP but who were made members in order to take advantage of the more generous NIC regime applicable to the self-employed. Testimony before the House of Lords Finance Bill

---

[133] House of Lords Finance Bill Sub Committee 2014 report, para 44.

[134] House of Lords Finance Bill Sub Committee 2014 report, paras 44–45.

[135] CTA 2009, s 1273 (ex TA 1988, s 118ZA) and TCGA 1992, s 59A added by FA 2001, s 75.

[136] ITA 2007, s 399(6), 1004(1), (2), and CTA 2010, s 1135(1), (2), ex TA 1988, s 842B. The restrictions were contained in TA 1988, s 659D. These rules were introduced by FA 2001, Sch 25.

[137] ITTOIA 2005, s 863.

[138] House of Lords Finance Bill Sub Committee 2014 report, abstract.

Sub Committee in 2014 revealed examples including 'one so-called LLP partnership that had 20,000 partners in it' and 'occasional fruit pickers being officially partners in an LLP.'[139] FA 2014, Schedule 17, Part 1 introduced new ITTOIA 2005, sections 863A-G, which seek to counter this abuse by setting out conditions that if met results in the LLP member being treated for tax purposes as an employee of the LLP. Condition A in section 863B is met if, at the relevant time, it is reasonable to expect that at least 80% of the total amount payable by the LLP in respect of the member's performance during the relevant period of services for the LLP is disguised salary.

Turning to (2), a common practice apparently had developed whereby a disproportionate share of profits of LLPs and also general partnerships was allocated to corporate members in order to minimise or defer the total amount of tax borne by the individual partners.[140] In particular, such an arrangement could be used to reduce the tax charge on profits intended for reinvestment in the partnership's business—a form of self-help remedy to address one of the significant tax disadvantages of adopting the partnership form instead of a company. HMRC was also concerned with schemes attributing losses of mixed partnerships to members subject to high rates of tax, and with arrangements where partnership members reduced their profit entitlement in return for payment made by other members who were taxed more favourably on those profits.[141]

In the forward to HMRC's May 2013 consultation document on this issue, the Exchequer Secretary to the Treasurer stated that the Government's objective in legislating in this area was 'to prevent unfairness and market distortion within the tax system by ensuring that inappropriate partnership allocations to a company or similar vehicle cannot create tax advantages.'[142] The rules ultimately legislated in FA 2014, Schedule 17, Part 2, which added new ITTOIA 2005, sections 850C-E, seek to prevent excess profit allocation to non-individual partners and other inappropriate allocations. Under Section 850C, for example, a member A's profit share can be increased by so much of the amount of another member B's profit share as, it is reasonable to suppose, is attributable to either (a) A's deferred profit, or (b) A's power to enjoy B's profit share, as determined on a just and reasonable basis.

60.14 European Company

The *Societas Europeae* (SE) or European Company was created by EC Council Regulation in 2001. It receives special tax treatment as part of the revised EU Mergers Directive, and as a result UK tax rules are modified so that a UK company's decision to merge with an SE in another Member State obtains tax neutral treatment in the same way that a company merging with a company in another Member State gets such treatment under the existing Mergers Directive-based rules. They are rules of last resort and so apply only when the ordinary rules do not.

---

[139] House of Lords Finance Bill Sub Committee 2014 report, testimony of John Whiting, OTS, para 47.
[140] House of Lords Finance Bill Sub Committee 2014 report, paras 62–63.
[141] HMRC, *Partnerships: A review of two aspects of the tax rules* (20 May 2013), 15.
[142] HMRC, *Partnerships: A review of two aspects of the tax rules* (20 May 2013), 4.

The first set of rules concern capital gains treatment of assets transferred on the merger. TCGA 1992, section 140E applies to the assets remaining within UK tax charge, while section 140F applies if they do not. Section 140G applies to securities issued on merger. None of these rules applies if section 139 does (see below §§62.3.4–62.3.5). Similar rules are provided for the separate code applicable to intangible fixed assets.[143] Similar treatment for loan relationships is provided in CTA 2009, Part 5, Chapter 14, and for derivatives in CTA 2009, section 683. Capital allowance treatment is provided by CAA 2001, section 561A. Continuity of group identity is provided by TCGA 1992, section 171(10A) and, for intangible fixed assets, by CTA 2009, section 770. Further rules provide for held-over gains on such a merger.[144] Lastly, there are special rules on corporate residence (see §69.6). Where the SE transfers its registered office to the UK, CTA 2009, section 16 makes it resident in the UK, and a later move of its registered office out of the UK will not alter that resident status. The rule in CTA 2009, section 18, which says that a company treated as not resident in the UK for tax treaty purposes is non-resident for all UK tax purposes, applies to an SE.

---

[143] CTA 2009, s 821, ex FA 2002, Sch 29, paras 85A and 87A: see §5.3.
[144] Including TCGA 1992, ss 179(1B) and (1C) (see §8.6) and 154(2A) and (2B). F(No 2)A 2005, s 65 dealt with whether the merger is a relevant event for calculating losses on pre-entry assets for Sch 7A (see §65.2.3).

61

Distributions

61.1 Introduction

Income tax is charged on dividends and other distributions of a UK resident company.[1] Prior to fundamental reform of the taxation of dividends in 2016, distributions were classified either as 'qualifying' or 'non-qualifying' distributions. Qualifying distributions carried tax credits, non-qualifying did not.[2] In 2016 the dividend tax credit was abolished, thus rendering the qualifying/non-qualifying distinction irrelevant. In its place we have the new (and much less elegant) concept of a 'CD distribution', which means a distribution that is only a distribution because of section 1000(1) paragraphs C or D of the CTA 2010.

---

[1] ITTOIA 2005, Pt 4, Ch 3, s 383. Under the schedular system set out in TA 1988, where a distribution is made by a company resident in the UK, the recipient was assessable to income tax under Sch F: TA 1988, s 20. On 'Unit Trusts and Open-ended Investment Companies', see §79.3 below. On shares in SIPs, see ITTOIA 2005, ss 392–396.

[2] For the meaning of 'qualifying distribution', see ex CTA 2010, s 1136(1), (2), referring to distributions within s 1000(1)C or D; ex TA 1988, s 14(2).

From April 2016, in many provisions the phrase 'CD distribution' replaces 'non-qualifying distribution', and 'non-CD distribution' replaces the term 'qualifying distribution'. The new terms are defined in ITTOIA 2005, section 401 and discussed in more detail below. Distributions, whether qualifying/non-qualifying, CD or non-CD, are not deductible in computing the profits of the company.[3]

While TA 1988 formerly used the expression 'Schedule F income', the rewritten rules in ITTOIA 2005, Part 4, Chapter 3 instead simply refer to 'dividend income'. In addition, while TA 1988 dealt with payments by companies not resident in the UK under Schedule D, Case V, such 'foreign dividend income' is now taxed under ITTOIA 2005, Part 4, Chapter 4.[4] With the abolition of the dividend tax credit in 2016, the income tax treatment of foreign dividend income is no longer different from that of UK dividend income in terms of what receipts are taxable and how they are taxed.[5] Similarly, for corporation tax purposes, most dividends received by a UK resident company will be exempt from corporation tax whether paid by a UK or a non-UK resident company.[6]

Under UK company law, money may be returned to shareholders in three main ways:

(1)   dividend;
(2)   return of capital on liquidation; and
(3)   authorised reduction in capital.

Tax law mirrors company law by treating the first as giving rise to income, but the second and third as matters of capital gains. Special tax rules apply to stock dividends, where the tax system imposes tax even though no cash comes out of the company (see below at §61.4). Special rules also apply to purchases by a company of its own shares (see below at §61.5) and demergers (see chapter sixty-six below), where the tax system grants capital gains treatment rather than income treatment on the assumption that this will be advantageous. Distributions in respect of share capital in a winding up,[7] including surplus assets distributed, are not distributions within ITTOIA 2005, Part 4, Chapter 3, or within any other Schedule.[8] They are simply treated as the return of capital, and perhaps as giving rise to chargeable capital gains or allowable losses.[9] This is so even if the payments represent arrears of undeclared cumulative preference dividends.[10] However, where a payment is treated as a distribution for income tax, it does not matter that it is treated as capital for other purposes, eg trust law.[11]

---

[3]   CTA 2009, s 1305, ex TA 1988, ss 6(4) and 337A(1).
[4]   In this book foreign dividend income is considered in chapter seventy-one.
[5]   On the taxation of shareholders, see below at §61.3.
[6]   CTA 2009, Pt 9A, applicable on or after 1 July 2009.
[7]   This includes dissolution under the Companies Act 2006, s 1000 or s 1003 (ex Companies Act 1985, s 652 or s 652A), where the Registrar strikes off a defunct company—provided certain assurances are given to the inspector in time (ESC C16).
[8]   TA 1988, s 209(1); *IRC v Burrell* [1924] 2 KB 52, (1924) 9 TC 27. This exclusion applies, by concession, to the winding up of social or recreational unincorporated associations, provided the distributions are not large (ESC C15).
[9]   TCGA 1992, s 122; see above at §41.3.
[10]   *Re Dominion Tar and Chemical Co Ltd* [1929] 2 Ch 387.
[11]   ITTOIA 2005, s 383(3).

61.1.1 ITTOIA 2005, Part 4, Chapter 3

If the distribution fell within former Schedule F it was taxed under that Schedule and was not, subject to exceptions, chargeable under any other provision of the Income Tax Acts.[12] ITTOIA 2005 has similar priority rules.[13] Where the income accrues to a person dealing in securities, the trading income rules in Part 2 apply instead. The dealer is not entitled to the tax credit and the sum received is not grossed up.[14]

Income charged under ITTOIA 2005, Part 4, Chapter 3 cannot be relevant income—and so cannot be used to calculate pensionable earnings.[15]

61.1.2 Definitions: Non-CD and CD Distributions

Non-CD distributions are defined by exclusion—all distributions but two are non-CD distributions. The two exceptions are:

(1) the issue of bonus redeemable shares and bonus securities; and
(2) the issue of any share capital or security which the company making the distribution has directly or indirectly received from another company in the form of bonus redeemable shares or securities (see below at §61.2.3).[16]

Broadly, distributions resulting in immediate distribution of reserves are non-CD distributions, whereas those causing only a potential claim on profits are CD distributions.

61.2 Distributions

61.2.1 Meaning of 'Distribution'

The definition of 'distribution' for corporation tax purposes formerly in TA 1988, sections 209 *et seq* was rewritten into CTA 2010, sections 1000 *et seq*. According to section 1000(1)A, a distribution, in relation to any company, includes any dividend paid by the company, including a capital dividend. A dividend is regarded as paid when it becomes due and payable,[17] ie when it becomes an enforceable debt, not necessarily at the date of the resolution. A final dividend is, in the absence of any other date in the resolution, prima facie due when declared and so creates an immediate debt; directors have power to stipulate the date and, if this power is exercised, the debt arises only when that date is reached. An interim dividend resolved upon by the directors may be reviewed by them and so does not

---

[12] Ex TA 1988, s 20(2).
[13] ITTOIA 2005, s 366.
[14] ITTOIA 2005, s 366, ex TA 1988, s 95, as amended by F(No 2)A 1997, s 24.
[15] See above at §7.8.
[16] CTA 2010, s 1136(1), (2), referring to distributions within s 1000(1)C or D; ex TA 1988, s 14(2).
[17] CTA 2010, s 1168, ex TA 1988, s 834(3).

create an immediate debt.[18] The waiver of a dividend in advance of payment is effective to prevent the income from accruing to the shareholder.[19]

The reference to a 'capital dividend' has caused some confusion. In the 6th edition of *Revenue Law*, it was noted that a dividend paid out of capital is still a dividend, but the matter had given rise to problems before 1965.[20] This issue re-emerged with the introduction of Part 9A of CTA 2009, which extended the scope of exemption for corporation tax purposes for distributions received by UK companies, but specifically excluded from the exemption distributions 'of a capital nature'.[21] In an apparently successful attempt to clarify the situation, section 1027A was introduced in F(No 3)A 2010, to provide that a dividend arising from a reduction of share capital is to be treated as if it were made out of profits available for distribution. In addition, the exclusion for capital dividends from the exemption in CTA 2009, section 931A(2) was removed. As a result, it should no longer be necessary to consider whether a dividend is income or capital for purposes of the exemption.[22]

61.2.2 *Other Distribution out of Assets but in Respect of Shares*

CTA 2010, section 1000(1)B covers any other distribution out of the assets of the company, in cash or otherwise, made in respect of shares,[23] eg a distribution by A Ltd to its shareholders of shares held by A Ltd in X Ltd.

A payment is excluded from section 1000(1)B if it represents a repayment of capital on the share or if, and to the extent that, new consideration is received by the company for the distribution.[24] Consideration is new if it is external to the company, ie it is not provided directly or indirectly by the company itself.[25] Thus, a bonus issue is not a distribution since there is no cost to the company; neither is a rights issue, since the consideration is new. The issue of a bonus issue of redeemable shares may give rise to other consequences.

The purchase by a company of its own shares from its shareholders will give rise to distribution treatment under section 1000(1)B unless special rules direct otherwise (see below at §61.5). The amount of the distribution must allow for the deduction of the consideration originally paid for them; since this is an income tax charge, there is neither indexation nor tapering relief. The section applies only to a distribution out of the assets in respect of the shares; a purchase by the company from the shareholder direct is such a purchase, but a purchase in the open market is not. A market purchase is how many large companies buy back shares today; they thus avoid section 1000(1)B problems.

---

[18] *Potel v IRC* [1971] 2 All ER 504, (1971) 46 TC 658.

[19] For IHT consequences, see above at §45.5.3.4.

[20] Wilson, *Tax-efficient Extraction of Cash from Companies* (Key Haven, 1989), §2.31.

[21] CTA 2009, s 931A(2). See Tank, Weston and Melia [2011] BTR 47. As the authors note in this and a previous article ([2010] BTR 119), HMRC added to the confusion by apparently altering their longstanding position on this issue in arguments made in *First Nationwide v HMRC* [2010] UKFTT 24 (TC).

[22] Tank, Weston and Melia [2011] BTR 47, 48.

[23] Ex TA 1988, s 209(2)(b). On timing, see *John Paterson (Motors) Ltd v IRC* [1978] STC 59, (1978) 52 TC 39 (decision of Special Commissioners that date of approval of balance sheet was correct date upheld).

[24] Ex TA 1988, s 209(2)(b), but note s 1002(1) (ex s 209(6)) excluding transfers between independent companies.

[25] CTA 2010, Pt 23, Ch 8 and especially s 1113 'in respect of shares' and s 1115 'new consideration'; ex TA 1988, s 254(1).

61.2.3 Issue of Redeemable Share Capital or Securities

Under CTA 2010, section 1000(1)C and D, the issue of any redeemable share capital or any security in respect of shares or securities of the issuing company is a distribution unless it is wholly or in part for new consideration.[26] Where part of the amount issued is referable to the old consideration, the excess is treated as a distribution.[27] Thus, the issue of bonus redeemable preference shares, or debentures or loan stock in A Ltd by A Ltd are all treated as distributions. This definition does not cover non-redeemable bonus shares. The mere prospect of an eventual return of capital on a winding up or, since 1981, repurchase probably does not make an ordinary share redeemable, but this is unclear. Bonus securities, on the other hand, are in their nature redeemable and can therefore fall within the term 'distribution'.

Importantly, the issue of bonus securities or bonus redeemable share capital is a 'CD distribution' (and, prior to April 2016, a qualifying distribution). It is provided elsewhere that the redemption of such securities is a 'non-CD distribution'.[28]

61.2.4 Excessive Interest Payments

Under CTA 2010, section 1000(1)E, interest above a certain threshold may be treated as a distribution.[29] More specifically, any interest (or other distribution out of the assets of the company in respect of its securities) will be a distribution if the consideration given by the company represents more than a reasonable commercial return. This rule applies only to the amount of interest which exceeds that reasonable commercial return. CTA 2010 refers to such securities as 'non-commercial securities', which are defined in section 1005.

61.2.5 Thin Capitalisation

TA 1988, section 209(2)(da) formerly treated interest as a distribution to the extent that it was attributable to the tax planning device known as 'thin capitalisation'.[30] This device is now countered by the transfer pricing rules (see below §62.6).

61.2.6 Other Interest Payments

Under CTA 2010, section 1000(1)F, other interest payments are treated as distributions *in full* and not just in part.[31] Although interest payments on debentures are not within the term 'distribution', and therefore are deductible in computing profits, there are rules designed to equate debenture interest payments with dividends where the debenture is more like a share than a genuine debenture. CTA 2010 refers to such securities as 'special securities', which are defined in section 1015. Thus, if the debentures had themselves been

---

[26] Ex TA 1988, s 209(2)(c).
[27] CTA 2010, s 1003 and s 1004, plus definition of 'new consideration' in CTA 2010, s 1115, ex TA 1988, s 254(1).
[28] TA 1988, ss 210, 211; see below at §§61.2.8 and 61.2.9.
[29] Ex TA 1988, s 209(2)(d).
[30] Introduced by FA 1995; see Oliver [1995] BTR 224.
[31] Ex TA 1988, s 209(2)(e).

distributions, any interest payments or other distribution of assets in respect of those securities are treated as distributions. In addition, payments of interest on securities which are convertible directly or indirectly into shares of the company are distributions, unless the securities are quoted on a recognised stock exchange or are on terms comparable with those of quoted securities.[32]

CTA 2010 also treats certain payments of interest by a company as distributions if the consideration given by the company for the use of the money is to any extent dependent on the results of the company's business.[33] This was exploited by certain company borrowers whose tax position was such that they would receive no immediate benefit from being able to deduct the interest for corporation tax purposes, but for whom the credit attached to a dividend was, under the prevailing law, most useful. A small part of the consideration for the loan was made dependent on the results of the company's business (so coming within then TA 1988, section 209(2)(e)(iii)); the interest would become a distribution and the lender received the interest as franked investment income instead of as profits liable to corporation tax: the benefit of this was then shared with the borrower by charging a lower rate of interest.

To counter such schemes, CTA 2010, section 1032 directs that the interest paid on such a loan which is paid to a company within the charge to corporation tax is no longer treated as a distribution, save where the recipient would in any case be exempt from tax thereon.[34] Since 1996 the interest (non-distribution) element of the payment enters into the loan relationship calculations. Where the consideration for the loan exceeds a reasonable commercial return for the use of the principal sum, the interest is treated as a distribution to the extent only of the excess.[35] Interest payments on ratchet loans are removed from distribution treatment. Ratchet loans are those where the interest rate falls as business results improve or vice versa, ie are inversely related to the results of the business. Such interest will also therefore fall within the loan relationship rules (see below at §63.1) and will be deductible.[36] Lastly, interest on certain securities 'connected with' shares of the company is caught.[37]

61.2.7 Transfer of Asset at Undervalue

Where a company transfers an asset (or liability) to a member[38] for less than market value, the difference between any new consideration given and that market value is a distribution.[39] Consideration is new if it is external to the company, ie it is not provided directly or indirectly by the company.[40] Exemptions apply to transfers by subsidiary companies to parents or between truly independent companies.[41]

---

[32] CTA 2010, s 1015(3).
[33] CTA 2010, s 1015(4) and s 1017, ex TA 1988, s 209(2)(e)(iii).
[34] Ex TA 1988, s 212. Note that s 212(4), added by FA 1995, s 87(4) and dealing with charity, was repealed by FA 2004.
[35] CTA 2010, s 1000(1)F(b), ex TA 1988, s 209(2)(d).
[36] CTA 2010, s 1017(1). FA 2000, s 86 added ex TA 1988, s 209(3B) for the purpose of s 209(e)(iii).
[37] CTA 2010, s 1015(5) and s 1017(2); ex TA 1988, s 209(2)(e)(vi).
[38] On the definition of 'member of company', see Companies Act 2006, s 112 (ex Companies Act 1985, s 22).
[39] CTA 2010, s 1020, ex TA 1988, s 209(4).
[40] CTA 2010, s 1115, ex TA 1988, s 254(1).
[41] CTA 2010, ss 1002(2), (3) and 1021(1), ex TA 1988, s 209(5).

61.2.8 Perpetual Debt/Equity Notes

The boundary between distribution and debt has been further highlighted by the phenomenon of the perpetual debt instrument under which a loan is not repaid, commonly known as equity notes.[42] A decision of the Special Commissioners held that payments of interest under such instruments were interest rather than dividends for the purpose of the relevant double tax treaty, and that they were not distributions under the present definition. This led to a tax asymmetry between the US and the UK. Money would be borrowed in the US where interest would be deductible; the money would then be transferred to an associated company in the UK as a debt; the repatriation of that money to the US as interest meant that no tax was charged or withheld by the UK tax authorities.[43] In consequence, payments will be distributions if the equity notes are issued by one company and held by a company which is associated with the issuing company or is a funded company.[44] An equity note is elaborately defined, but broadly means a security which is not redeemable within 50 years from the date of issue; redeemability is defined in terms of the real world.[45]

61.2.9 CD Distribution Followed by non-CD Distribution in Respect of Capital Issued

The rule that a distribution out of the assets of the company in respect of shares is a non-CD distribution expressly excludes a repayment of capital (see above at §61.2.2). CTA 2010 goes on to provide two important qualifications of this rule. The first is section 1026, which applies where a company has issued (or paid up) any share capital otherwise than for new consideration, and the amount so paid up was not a non-CD distribution at that time. In such circumstances a subsequent distribution in respect of the capital is not treated as a repayment of capital; it will therefore be treated as a non-CD distribution, with the usual consequences for the dividend status of the receipt.

Since neither a bonus issue of paid-up irredeemable shares nor the repayment of share capital is a distribution, avoidance would be rife but for this rule. If a company had £10,000 to distribute, it would be unwise for the Revenue—from their point of view—to allow the company to capitalise the reserve and distribute it by way of bonus shares and then repay the bonus capital without at any stage falling foul of ITTOIA 2005, Part 4, Chapter 3. The effect of section 1026 is that if a company has made a bonus issue which was not treated as a non-CD distribution, repayments of such share capital are so treated to the extent to which those repayments of capital exceed the amount paid up on the share.[46] Thus, if the company had an issued share capital of 20,000 £1 shares, and distributed by way of bonus 10,000 fully paid-up £1 shares, subsequently making a reduction of capital of 50p per share on all 30,000 issued shares, the payments to shareholders would amount to £15,000, of

---

[42] For examples of devices exploiting the debt-equity distinction, see Wood (1999) 47 *Can Tax Jo* 49; see also Harlton (1994) 49 *Tax Law Review* 499.

[43] HC Official Report, Standing Committee B, cols 439, 440, 30 June 1992.

[44] CTA 2010, s 2015(6), ex TA 1988, s 209(2)(e)(vii) added by F(No 2)A 1992, s 31; see also Inland Revenue Press Release, 15 May 1992, [1992] *Simon's Tax Intelligence* 519. For history from the Revenue standpoint, see Inland Revenue, *International Tax Manual*, para 1249. On double taxation provision, see below at §76.6.

[45] CTA 2010, s 1016, ex TA 1988, s 209(9) added by F(No 2)A 1992, s 31; on scope, see also ICAEW, Guidance Note Tax 5/93, 19 March 1993.

[46] CTA 2010, ss 1024–1127, ex TA 1988, s 211.

which £10,000 would be treated as distribution and £5,000 as repayment of capital. To the extent that money has been distributed by way of non-distributions, subsequent repayments of capital will be treated as distributions. In applying this rule any previous repayments are brought into account.[47]

Special rules apply to premiums. A premium paid on redemption is not treated as a return of capital.[48] If the share was issued at a premium which represented new consideration, the amount of the premium is treated as part of the share capital and so the repayment of the premium will fall outside section 1026.[49] This exception does not apply where the premium has been applied in paying up share capital.[50] Importantly, section 1026 is subject to a time limit. A distribution in respect of a share originally issued as a bonus which is made more than 10 years after the issue will escape section 1026 provided the company is not closely controlled.[51]

Where a reduction in capital is followed by or concurrent with the distribution of bonus shares, it is provided that although the reduction in capital will not be treated as a distribution, the issue of the bonus shares will be so treated to the extent of the earlier payments.[52]

61.2.10 Bonus Issue Following Repayment of Capital

Where the repayment of share capital is followed by a bonus issue, CTA 2010, section 1022 treats as a distribution the amount paid up on the new shares or the amount repaid on the old shares, whichever is the lower.[53]

Example

A Ltd repaid 50p per £ on its £20,000 ordinary stock; the nominal value of the stock is reduced to £10,000. This stock was originally issued wholly for new consideration, so no distribution arose on the repayment. Two years later A Ltd capitalises its reserves and makes a distribution of stock on the basis of 1 for every £5 stock held. The amount paid up is £2,000. As this is less than the amount repaid (£10,000), the whole £2,000 will be a distribution.

This rule is modified in two important ways. First, as with section 1026, there is a time limit. Where the new shares are irredeemable bonus shares issued more than 10 years after the reduction in share capital, section 1022 applies only where the company is closely controlled.[54] Secondly, there is an exception for preference shares issued before 6 April 1965, or issued after that time but for new consideration not derived from ordinary shares.[55]

---

[47] CTA 2010, s 1027(3), ex TA 1988, s 211(3).
[48] CTA 2010, s 1024, ex TA 1988, s 211(7).
[49] CTA 2010, s 1025(1), (2), ex TA 1988, s 211(5).
[50] CTA 2010, s 1025(3), ex TA 1988, s 211(6); the share capital may have been paid up under Companies Act 2006, s 610 (ex Companies Act 1985, s 130).
[51] CTA 2010, s 1026(3), referring to a 'relevant company' for purposes of s 739, which includes a company under the control of not more than 5 persons; ex TA 1988, s 211(2). Control is defined by reference to CTA 2010, s 450, ex TA 1988, s 416 (see below at §65.1.1).
[52] CTA 2010, ss 1022–1023, ex TA 1988, s 210.
[53] *Ibid.*
[54] CTA 2010, s 1023(1), (2), ex TA 1988, s 210(3).
[55] CTA 2010, s 1023(3), ex TA 1988, s 210(2).

61.3   Taxation of Shareholders—ITTOIA 2005, Part 4, Chapter 3

61.3.1 UK Resident Individuals

61.3.1.1 Overview

From 6 April 2016, the amount charged to tax under ITTOIA 2005, Part 4, Chapter 3 is the amount of the distribution.[56] The first £5,000 of dividends are subject to a nil rate of tax, with the remainder taxed at 7.5%, 32.5% or 38.1%. This income is treated as the highest part of the person's income. Repayments to pension funds, authorised unit trusts and open-ended investment companies were stopped for distributions on or after 2 July 1997.[57]

61.3.1.2 History

From 1999–2016, the tax of 10% payable by an individual on corporate dividends received was cancelled out by a credit for lower and basic rate taxpayers and non-taxpayers. The dividend tax credit was equal to one-ninth of the qualifying distribution and was not refundable even if the recipient was a non-taxpayer. Higher rate taxpayers paid an additional amount of tax, equal to 25% of the cash dividend after taking into account the tax credit (31.1% for additional rate taxpayers). From 1996–99, dividends were taxed either at the lower rate (20%) or the higher rate (40%). This meant that a basic rate taxpayer paid at 20% not at the then basic rate (always more than 20%), but as the credit was restricted to 20% this did not make much practical difference. From 1973–96, dividends were taxed at whatever might be the individual's appropriate rate as the lower rate had not been introduced; a zero-rate individual taxpayer could recover the tax represented by the credit—but from the Revenue, not the company.

61.3.2 Non-residents

It is in connection with the treatment of non-residents that the purpose of some features of the 1999 scheme becomes clearer. Where the non-resident was a resident in another country which had a treaty with the UK, the first relevant article was the dividend article.[58] This usually begins by saying that the UK may tax the dividend but subject to a cap. That cap is usually first described as 15% of the gross amount of the dividend; the cap on the UK's taxing right is reduced to only 5% if the beneficial owner was a company controlling at least 25% of the company paying the dividend.

There will then usually be a further provision, which applied instead of the one just described, so long as individuals resident in the UK were entitled to tax credits, ie as was the case until the dividend tax credit was abolished from 6 April 2016. This will say that the UK 15% applies not to 'the gross amount of the dividend' but to the sum of the dividend and the credit. It will also say that the 5% cap begins with a holding of only 10%, not 25%.

---

[56] ITTOIA 2005, ss 384 and 394(3), ex TA 1988, ss 20(2), 231(3A).

[57] Ex TA 1988, s 231A, added by F(No 2)A 1997, s 19; the list of funds is contained in s 231A(5).

[58] Eg the UK–US Treaty, Art 10(2)(a)(ii). The withholding of this credit in certain circumstances is authorised by TA 1988, s 812 (not rewritten). On settlement with California, see Treasury Press Release 13 May 1993 and [1993] *Simon's Tax Intelligence* 858, 1250.

The treaty will then say that T is entitled to a tax credit under UK tax law and that the amount of credit is, unless the beneficial owner is a company controlling at least 10% of the company paying the dividend, one half that to which the UK resident would have been entitled. Moreover, T is entitled to repayment of any excess of that tax credit over his liability to UK tax. Thus, where T receives a dividend of £9,000, T will also be entitled to the UK tax credit of £500, but the UK will be entitled to levy tax at 15% on £9,500, ie £1,425; this is charged at source as a withholding tax. Since the withholding tax (£1,425) exceeds the credit (£500), T's repayment claim to the UK Revenue will fail. T may, of course, use the credit of £500 against tax in T's own country of residence. The UK legislation makes it clear that where, as here, the withholding tax exceeds the credit, the effect is to reduce the amount to which T is entitled by way of repayment of the credit to nil.[59]

Where T is a company with a large enough stake in the company paying the dividend, the UK tax is reduced to 5% of the sum of the dividend and half the credit. If the dividend is £90,000 and the credit is £5,000, the UK will be entitled to withhold 5% of £95,000, ie £4,750, so leaving T with a repayment claim for £250 against the UK Revenue.

These examples explain the 1997 selection of the general credit rate of 10% as opposed to the previous 20%. The rate of 10% was designed to reduce to a minimum the rights of non-residents to reclaim tax from the UK. This minimum was preferred to outright abolition, since abolition would have invited retaliatory action by treaty partners.[60] The ECJ has held that the 5% withholding tax is not in breach of the Parent–Subsidiary Directive.[61]

When a UK resident company made a distribution to a non-resident, Z, who was not entitled to a tax credit, eg because there was no applicable treaty, Z was liable to income tax on the distribution on the same basis as non-qualifying distributions.[62]

Where no credit was available, there was no liability to income tax at the 10% ordinary rate but only at the higher rate. Z was assessed on the amount of the distribution of £90 grossed up to take account of the credit. Thus, if Z received a dividend of £90 but was liable to tax at the upper dividend rate, there was a liability to tax at 32.5% on £100 (£32.50), but since Z was treated as having already paid £10, the final liability was £22.50. Whether Z actually had to pay the tax was another matter since other rules restricted the UK's right to tax to situations in which Z had a UK representative, eg a permanent establishment here (see §72.6.3).[63]

The post-6 April 2016 taxation of dividends paid to non-residents is discussed below at §72.6.3.

61.3.3 Companies

Where the recipient is another company resident in the UK, the non-CD distribution is income of the recipient, but it is not liable to corporation tax.[64] A CD distribution also is

---

[59] F(No 2)A 1997, s 30(10).
[60] Eg UK–US Treaty, Art 10; abolition of the credit would mean that the scheme in Art 10(2) would not apply and the much less advantageous (to the UK) rules in Art 10(1) would apply instead.
[61] *IRC v Océ Van Der Grinten NV* [2003] STC 1248.
[62] ITTOIA 2005, s 399.
[63] FA 1995, s 128.
[64] CTA 2009, s 931A *et seq*, ex CTA 2009, s 1285, ex TA 1988, s 208.

not liable to corporation tax. The concept of franked investment income for the category of income which carries a credit was abolished in 2016 and replaced by the new phrase 'exempt ABGH Distributions'. The related concept of 'franked payment' also is obsolete and has been abolished.[65] The position of non-resident companies is that they are entitled to the benefit of the exemption from corporation tax if the dividend accrues to a permanent establishment in the UK. The position under treaties was explored at §61.3.3.[66]

61.4 Stock Dividend Income

Where a person has an option to receive either a dividend or additional share capital, special rules treat the share capital so issued as giving rise to a charge to tax on the recipient under ITTOIA 2005, section 410.[67] The payment, however, is not a distribution as such. Prior to 6 April 2016 there was no liability to rates of tax below the dividend upper rate; if there was such a liability, credit was given for the dividend ordinary rate even though not actually paid. From 6 April 2016, and in line with the broader 2016 reforms to the taxation of dividends, the credit at the dividend ordinary rate in ITTOIA 2005, section 411 was abolished. Payments to other companies are not income of the recipient.[68]

These rules also apply where: (a) the shareholder has shares which carry the right to receive bonus share capital;[69] and (b) that right is conferred by the terms on which the shares were issued (or later varied if bonus share capital is then issued).[70] It is inherent in every share that it carries the right to any scrip issue, the right arising from the articles of association, but the provision has not been given so wide a scope.[71] These rules apply only to stock dividends paid by companies resident in the UK.

Under ITTOIA 2005, liability is based on 'the cash equivalent of the share capital'.[72] The market value of the shares is substituted where the dividend is substantially greater or smaller than that, or the number of shares issued is not related to any cash dividend. ITTOIA 2005 enacts the Revenue statement of practice that 'substantial' means 15% or more.[73]

The incentive for the company to grant a stock dividend rather than a simple cash dividend is that the company's cash position is not affected. Before 1999, ie during the days of

---

[65] TA 1988, s 238, repealed by FA 1998, Sch 3, para 11.

[66] For example the UK-US Treaty, Art 10(2)(a)(i). On interpretation, see FA 1989, s 115, comprehensively and retrospectively, reversing *Union Texas International Corpn v Critchley* [1990] STC 305, (1990) 63 TC 224, CA; see Inland Revenue Press Release, 25 October 1988, [1988] *Simon's Tax Intelligence* 784; see also *Getty Oil Co v Steele* [1990] STC 434. (1990) 63 TC 376.

[67] ITTOIA 2005, s 410, defined in CTA 2010, s 1051(3), ex TA 1988, s 251(l)(c). The failure to exercise a right is taken to be the exercise of the option: s 1051(4).

[68] CTA 2010, ss 1049–1051, ex TA 1988, ss 249–251.

[69] Ie share capital issued otherwise than wholly for new consideration: CTA 2010, s 1051(1), ex TA 1988, s 251(l)(a).

[70] CTA 2010, s 1049(2), ex TA 1988, s 249(2).

[71] Nor, it seems, was it meant to be: see HC Official Report, vol 895, col 1881, 18 July 1975.

[72] Ex TA 1988, s 251(2). On trusts and estates, see ex s 249(5), (6).

[73] ITTOIA 2005, s 412(2) and Statement of Practice A8. On tax treatment where an enhanced stock dividend is received by a trust, see Statement of Practice SP 4/94; *Simon's Direct Tax Service*, Division 113, now ITTOIA 2005, s 414(1).

ACT, there were also tax advantages for the company in that ACT was not due on a stock dividend but was due on an ordinary dividend; such issues have now been removed.[74] The tax position of the shareholder was also changed in 1999, in that a non-taxable shareholder lost the right to repayment of the tax credit. The credit had been repayable on an ordinary dividend but not on a stock dividend.

61.5 Purchase by Company of Own Shares[75]

61.5.1 *Orthodox Distribution and CGT Treatment*

These rules are not directly affected by ITTOIA 2005. Company law[76] allows a company to issue redeemable equity shares and to purchase its own shares, subject to authorisation in the company's memorandum and articles of association and to various conditions imposed by the Companies Act. For tax purposes, any amount by which the redemption proceeds or purchase consideration exceeds the amount subscribed for the shares is a distribution within CTA 2010, section 1000(1)B and so is treated as dividend income. There is also a disposal of the shares for capital gains purposes. At one time a company had actually to cancel shares bought in this way, but this was changed in 2003[77] when it was allowed to keep them in its treasury—hence the term 'treasury shares'. The tax rules were amended to treat the shares bought in as if they had been cancelled and then issued as brand new shares when actually reissued.[78] They are treated as not being acquired by the company or as existing in any other way while resting in the treasury.[79] There are further rules to govern the interaction with the reorganisation rules in TCGA 1992, section 126 where the company holding the shares in its treasury makes a bonus issue.[80] There is also a rule excluding all these rules on the tax treatment of the price paid by the company if the price would be relevant in computing trading income.[81] Reissued treasury shares do not qualify for venture capital trusts (below §78.4).

61.5.2 *Pure CGT Treatment for Unquoted Trading Companies*

The orthodox treatment was thought to be an obstacle to the new power of companies to buy back their own shares; special legislation was therefore passed directing that there should be no distribution but only CGT.[82] Either the purchaser must have the purpose of benefiting the trade, or the proceeds must be used to meet certain IHT liabilities.[83] There are elaborate anti-avoidance rules.

---

[74] Hutton, *Tolley's Tax Planning*, ch 58.
[75] For history of and critical comment on the legislation, see Tiley [1992] BTR 21.
[76] Companies Act 2006, ss 684–708 (ex Companies Act 1985, ss 159–162).
[77] Companies (Acquisition of Own Shares) Regulations 2003 (SI 2003/1116).
[78] FA 2003, s 195(4) and (8); these rules also apply for IHT; see Hardwick [2003] BTR 417–19.
[79] FA 2003, s 195(2) and (3).
[80] FA 2003, s 195(5) and (6).
[81] FA 2003, s 195(9).
[82] FA 1982, s 53.
[83] CTA 2010, s 1033(2), (3), ex TA 1988, s 219(1)(a), (b).

61.5.2.1 Conditions

(1) *Unquoted.* A company buying its own shares must be an unquoted company; this is because there is a ready market for shares in quoted companies, ie companies quoted on an official stock exchange, or the 51% subsidiary of such a company.[84]

(2) *Trading.* The company must be a trading company or a holding company of a trading group. For these purposes a holding company is one whose main business (apart from any trading activities of its own) is to hold shares in one or more 75% subsidiaries.[85] Trades of dealing in shares, securities, land or futures do not qualify.[86]

(3) *Purpose—benefit to trade.* The purchase, etc of shares must be made wholly or mainly to benefit the trade of the company concerned or of any of its 75% subsidiaries.[87] A benefit to the selling shareholder is not the same as a benefit to the trade. It is necessary also to distinguish a benefit to the trade from both (a) some wider commercial purpose to which the seller may put the payment received, and (b) a business purpose of the company which is not itself a trade, eg an investment activity it may carry on.[88] One reason which might qualify as benefiting the trade would be resolving a disagreement at boardroom level. However, in the Revenue view, disagreements as to whether or not to cease trading and become an investment company, where the shareholder being bought out wants the trade to continue, would not qualify. Other qualifying reasons might be allowing an outside shareholder who has provided equity finance to withdraw, enabling a proprietor to retire to make way for new management, or on the death of a shareholder, allowing beneficiaries of the estate to sell the shares. There must not be an avoidance purpose.

(4) *Residence.* The vendor must meet certain residence requirements.[89]

(5) *Minimum holding periods.* The vendor must have owned the shares for at least five years at the time they are purchased by the company.[90] Special rules allow the aggregation of periods when the shares were held by a spouse or civil partner, provided the transferor was then living with the vendor and was then the vendor's spouse or civil partner.[91] Further rules apply where shares were acquired on death, whether as PR or as successor, in which case the overall period is reduced from five years to three.[92] A rule directs a first in, first out system where shares are bought and sold,[93] while another treats bonus shares and other shares acquired on a company reconstruction,

---

[84] CTA 2010, s 1048(1), ex TA 1988, s 229.

[85] *Ibid.* A trading group will consist of a holding company or one or more 75% subsidiaries where the main business of the members taken together is the carrying on of the trade or trades.

[86] CTA 2010, s 1048(1), ex TA 1988, s 229.

[87] CTA 2010, s 1033(2), ex TA 1988, s 219(1)(a). The purpose of benefiting the trade will not, of itself, make legal and other expenses associated with the purchase deductible (Revenue Interpretation RI 4).

[88] See Statement of Practice SP 2/82, para 2.

[89] CTA 2010, s 1034, ex TA 1988, s 220. The residence status of a PR is taken to be that of the deceased immediately before his death. The residence and ordinary residence of trustees is determined as for CGT (TCGA 1992, s 69).

[90] CTA 2010, s 1035(1), ex TA 1988, s 220(5).

[91] CTA 2010, s 1036(1), (2), ex TA 1988, s 220(6). It follows that the period may not be added if they are separated, or no longer married or civil partners at the date of the purchase.

[92] CTA 2010, s 1036(3), ex TA 1988, s 220(7).

[93] CTA 2010, s 1035(2), ex TA 1988, s 220(8).

reorganisation or amalgamation as acquired at the same time as the original holding in respect of which they are issued—a treatment which is not extended to rights issues or stock dividends.[94]

(6) *Extent of disposal—severing or substantially reducing the link.* The vendor's interest in the company must either be completely eliminated or substantially reduced as a result of the purchase of the shares by the company.[95] A reduction is substantial only if it is 25% or more.[96] For these purposes, the holdings of associates may be taken into account,[97] and the combined holdings of vendor and associate must be reduced by at least 25%.[98] It is also necessary that there should be a corresponding reduction in shareholders' entitlement to profits.[99] These rules are of great importance where the vendor retains shares of another class.

Where the vendor's holding is not eliminated, there may be difficulty in meeting requirement (3) above—that the purchase is for the sole or main purpose of benefiting the company's trade. Where the vendor's continuing presence is regarded as a danger to the trade the interest ought to be eliminated completely.[100] It is unclear whether a series of purchases by the company can be linked together so as to achieve the 25% reduction where no individual purchase meets that condition; such a linkage is allowed in the US under the step transaction doctrine, but the doctrine has also had this effect where the taxpayer sells some shares and gives others away, provided it is all part of the one plan; at this stage it is thought unlikely that the UK courts would accede to such an argument, but the Revenue seem prepared to accept it.[101]

(7) *No avoidance.* The purchase must not be part of a scheme or an arrangement which is designed or likely to result in the vendor or any associate having an interest in the company such that if he had that interest immediately after the purchase, any of the previous conditions would not be satisfied.[102] Transactions within one year of each other are presumed to be part of such a scheme.[103]

(8) *No continuing connection.* The vendor must not, immediately after the purchase, be connected with the company or any other member of the group.[104]

---

[94] CTA 2010, s 1035(3), ex TA 1988, s 220(9).

[95] CTA 2010, s 1037(1), ex TA 1988, s 221.

[96] CTA 2010, s 1037(3)–(5), ex TA 1988, s 221(4). If the company is a member of a 51% group, it is the shareholder's interest in the group that must be reduced by at least 25% (CTA 2010, s 1038(1), (2), ex TA 1988, s 221(6)).

[97] CTA 2010, s 1037(2), ex TA 1988, s 221(2); for the definition of 'associate', see ss 1059–1061, ex s 227.

[98] CTA 2010, s 1039(1), (4), (5), ex TA 1988, s 222(3), which extend the rule in s 1040(3) (ex s 222(2)) to the situation in which groups are involved, and s 1043(1), (2) (ex s 224), which provide that where the conditions are satisfied as to the combined holdings of the vendor and the associate and the vendor joined in to help the associate meet those conditions, all the conditions in ss 1037–1042 (ex ss 221–223) are to be treated as satisfied for both of them.

[99] CTA 2010, s 1038, ex TA 1988, s 221(5)–(8).

[100] There is some evidence that a more lenient attitude is adopted where the shares were acquired under a tax-advantaged share option scheme, since here the Revenue do not insist that the vendor should cease to be an employee (*Simon's Direct Tax Service*, D2.508).

[101] Statement of Practice SP 2/82, para 5.

[102] CTA 2010, s 1042(2), (3), (5), ex TA 1988, s 223(2).

[103] CTA 2010, s 1042(4). However, succession to property on death is not regarded as a 'transaction' for this purpose (see Statement of Practice SP 2/82, para 8).

[104] CTA 2010, s 1042(1), (5), ex TA 1988, s 223(1); on the definition of 'connected', see ss 1062–1063, ex s 228.

61.5.3 Sales to Pay IHT

Special treatment is also available if the purchase is not for the benefit of the trade but the vendor needs the funds to discharge a liability to IHT arising on death. In these circumstances it is only necessary for conditions (1) and (2) above to be met; as such, (3)–(8) do not apply. The whole or substantially the whole—a phrase taken by the Revenue to mean almost all[105]—of the payment must be paid in respect of the liability to IHT falling on the shareholder as a result of a death; this rule is applied after taking out the funds needed to pay any CGT liability consequent upon the purchase. The IHT payment must be made within two years of death and it must be shown that the liability could not have been met without undue hardship otherwise than through the purchase.[106]

61.5.4 Consequences: Choices

If the conditions outlined above are complied with, the transaction will be treated as a disposal by the shareholder for CGT purposes and not as a distribution. If the shareholder is a dealer in securities, the transaction will be treated as a trading transaction and not as a distribution.[107] The company may apply to the Revenue for advance clearance as to the treatment of any payment made by it for the purchase of shares.[108]

The story of this area of law illustrates the way in which the policy of the law may be affected by changes elsewhere in the system. The policy was to remove a fiscal obstacle to a corporate practice. The rule was absolute rather than a matter of election; the assumption behind the policy was that CGT treatment would be advantageous and therefore available only for virtuous cases. This assumption was undermined by the 1988 changes assimilating the rates of tax on income and capital gains. For many shareholders thinking of selling shares back to their companies, the 1988 change did not make matters neutral but actually made income treatment preferable. This was because of the availability of the tax credit alongside the qualifying distribution. Thus, an individual receiving £80 purchase price and paying income tax at 40% only had to find at that time an extra £20, ie 40% of (£80 + £20) less £20 already paid, as opposed to £32 (40% of £80) if CGT treatment were directed. For corporate shareholders there were further advantages, in that the company was treated as receiving 'franked investment income' which was not only exempt from corporation tax but could also be used to frank its own distributions, or sometimes to secure a repayment of the tax credit.

There were still further issues concerning the calculation of the consideration received for the shares and whether or not it included the qualifying distribution received. On one view the sum should not have been included since it was a qualifying distribution; the other view was that it should have been included because it was not subject to corporation tax under TA 1988, section 208. If the former view was right, not only could the company have used the tax credit in the various ways indicated, but it could also have

---

[105] Statement of Practice SP 2/82, para 6.
[106] CTA 2010, s 1033(4), ex TA 1988, s 219(2).
[107] CTA 2009, s 130, ex TA 1988, s 95.
[108] CTA 2010, s 1044–1045, ex TA 1988, s 225.

ended up with a capital loss.[109] The Revenue rejected this view and their position was eventually upheld.[110]

Today the question whether it is advantageous to use these rules so as to receive capital gains treatment is a complex one depending upon individual circumstances.

61.6   The ACT System: Historical Outline

61.6.1   Overview of ACT

ACT is not payable in respect of distributions on or after 6 April 1999. Previously, ACT was paid by a company when it made a qualifying distribution.[111] The ACT could be set off against its liability to corporation tax; at first this was restricted to tax on income, but after 1987 it was set off against corporation tax payable in respect of all profits including, therefore, capital gains.[112] If the company had no liability to corporation tax that year it could carry the ACT back a number of years (originally two years, but eventually six), and could carry it forward indefinitely.

A restriction on ACT set off was that it could not exceed a sum equal to the ACT which would have been paid if the company had made the maximum possible distribution out of the profits of that year.[113] Suppose that a company had £2 million profits and that the ACT rate was one-quarter of the dividend.[114] If the company distributed £1.6 million, it would have to pay £400,000 of ACT. This would be the maximum set off allowed for that year. The company would have a corporation tax liability of £2 million charged at the relevant rate for that year, eg £700,000 at 35%. The company could set off a maximum of £400,000 against that £700,000. The company would have to find the money to pay the ACT and the £300,000 mainstream corporation tax, as well as the dividend, no doubt using past profits to do so.

ACT was a tax due from the company and so had to be paid whenever the company made a qualifying distribution payment. It made no difference whether the company had any liability to corporation tax that year (eg because it made a loss), or whether the recipient shareholders were rich individuals taxable at the top rate of income tax (which varied between 98% and 40%) or charities or pension funds and so exempt from tax.

A common way in which surplus ACT arose was from the credit system of double taxation relief. A UK multinational company would receive income from foreign subsidiaries and branches. The foreign tax paid would often completely offset any UK corporation tax liability. However, this did not prevent the company from being liable to pay ACT to the Inland Revenue whenever it made a qualifying distribution. To solve the surplus ACT problem the Government did two things. The first was to reduce the rate of ACT and so the rate

---

[109] Especially when, after FA 1985, the indexation rules could have been used to create a loss.
[110] *Strand Option and Futures Ltd v Vojak* [2003] EWCA Civ 1457; [2004] STC 64 (CA), upholding Statement of Practice SP 4/89. This outcome has now been legislated—see CTA 2009, s 931A.
[111] Ex TA 1988, s 14(1).
[112] Ex TA 1988, s 239.
[113] Ex TA 1988, s 239(2).
[114] As was the case in 1998–99.

of tax credit, with consequent reductions in the repayment claims of zero-rate or exempt taxpayers. The second was to introduce the foreign income dividend (FID) scheme.[115] If the company could show that it paid no UK tax on a foreign income stream because of the foreign tax credit, it could recover the ACT it had paid. It will be noted that the ACT had to be paid in the first place and then recovered, although there was an exception for certain headquarters companies. This was often burdensome in administrative terms; it was also unpopular with exempt funds, because the corollary of the absence of ACT was that there was no tax credit and so, in those days, no tax repayment. During the two-year period from 1997–99 when the foreign dividend scheme was in place, but the pension funds had lost their right to repayment, there was a sharp increase in FID payments.

61.6.2 *Franked Investment Income and Franked Payments*

Under TA 1988, section 208, qualifying distributions received by a company resident in the UK were not subject to corporation tax. One purpose of this rule was to secure tax neutrality between distributions to individual shareholders and distributions to corporate shareholders. It also meant that, provided money stayed within the UK resident corporate sector, only one charge to ACT was made. The recipient company received franked investment income; when it made qualifying distribution payments of its own, it could use the credit element on what it had received to 'frank', ie remove its own liability to pay, ACT.

61.6.3 *Pre-1999 Surplus ACT and Post-1999 Shadow ACT: The 1999 Rules*

ACT is not payable in respect of qualifying distributions on or after 6 April 1999. Regulations govern the treatment of any remaining unrelieved surplus ACT which had not, by then, been set off against a company's corporation tax liability.[116] This is not of exclusively historical interest—for details see *Revenue Law*, 4th edition.

---

[115] Ex TA 1988, ss 246A *et seq*. See Harris [1997] BTR 82.
[116] Corporation Tax (Treatment of Unrelieved Surplus ACT) Regulations 1999 (SI 1999/573), [1999] *Simon's Weekly Tax Intelligence* 573.

62

Computation (1): General Rules

62.1   Introduction

The 'profits' of a company subject to corporation tax means both income and chargeable gains, and profits are computed according to the principles used for income tax and CGT.[1] Profits accruing for the benefit of the company arising by virtue of its being a partner in a partnership are chargeable to corporation tax as if they had accrued directly to the company.[2] Profits accruing for the benefit of the company arising under a trust are also chargeable to corporation tax as if they had accrued directly to the company.[3] The company is also

---

[1] CTA 2009, s 2(2), ex TA 1988, ss 8, 6(1)–(3).
[2] CTA 2009, s 6, ex TA 1988, s 8(2).
[3] CTA 2009, s 7, ex TA 1988, s 8(2).

chargeable on profits accruing during winding up.[4] This could be made to suggest that both corporation tax and income tax could be chargeable on income arising to the company as trustee during the winding up. Income arising to a company as trustee is chargeable to income tax even though the beneficiary is a company.

A consultation document issued in 2002 suggested that tax profits and accounting profit should be aligned more closely.[5] The consultation would have permitted, at least as a starting point, full depreciation in place of capital allowances, but would have required, under fair value accounting, that accrued but unrealised gains on capital assets would have been brought into the tax net. This proposal eventually petered out. However, the common consolidated corporate tax base (CCCTB) towards which the European Commission is working is very much alive, even if it is unlikely that the UK will be involved as a partner in the outcome.

62.2   Profits of a Company—Income

62.2.1 Income

The amount of income is computed according to income tax principles, except where statute otherwise provides.[6] Where those principles change from one fiscal year to the next and the accounting period spans the two fiscal years, it is the principles in force for the second fiscal year that are applied.[7] It follows that income should be computed under the applicable, rewritten Schedules and Cases. It also follows that a company whose business is to let real property or to make investments is not regarded as trading for tax purposes,[8] and so its income will be assessed under the rules in CTA 2009, Part 4 (ex Schedule A), and Parts 5–10 (depending on the type of investment), rather than CTA 2009, Part 3 (ex Schedule D, Case I). The Capital Allowances Act (CAA) 2001 and ITEPA 2003 have effect for both — corporation tax and income tax.

62.2.2 Distinguishing Corporation Tax from Income Tax and CGT

There has been a trend, beginning in the 1990s, to define income and capital gains separately for corporation tax. It was even proposed that a general anti-avoidance rule (GAAR) be applied for corporation tax only, though more recent GAAR proposals—and the UK

---

[4] CTA 2009, s 6(1), (2), ex TA 1988, s 8(2); on the liability of the liquidator, see *Re Mesco Properties Ltd* [1979] STC 788, (1979) 54 TC 238.

[5] HM Treasury, *Reform of Corporation Tax*, August 2002. Later documents include *Corporation Tax Reform*, 2003, which should be read with the background notes, and *Corporation Tax Reform: The Next Steps*, December 2003 and November 2004.

[6] CTA 2009, s 2, and see the charging sections of each specific forms of income, eg s 35 for trading income; ex TA 1988, s 9(1); any exemption from income tax applies to corporation tax (CTA 2009, ss 2(4), 969(4), 979(2), ex TA 1988, s 9(4)).

[7] Broadly incorporated in the charging sections of each specific forms of income, eg s 35 for trading income; ex TA 1988, s 9(2).

[8] *Webb v Conelee Properties Ltd* [1982] STC 913, (1982) 56 TC 149.

GAAR eventually legislated in FA 2013—do not do so.[9] Such a limitation is objectionable in theory and causes much difficulty when, for example, there are mixed partnerships with corporate and non-corporate members. Thus, there have been separate rules for Schedule A (1994–98), and still are for, say, interest from a UK or non-UK source. Among the present differences between corporation tax and income tax are the following:

(1)   A company cannot use any relief (eg personal reliefs) or be subject to any burden (eg higher rate tax) which is expressed to apply to individuals as opposed to persons.[10]
(2)   The special basis of period rules in ITTOIA 2005, sections 196 *et seq* do not apply for corporation tax.[11]
(3)   The special rules for loan relationships and derivatives (discussed in chapter sixty-three below) do not apply for income tax.
(4)   The remittance basis of taxation does not apply for corporation tax.[12]
(5)   Dividend income generally is not subject to corporation tax.[13]
(6)   The controlled foreign company legislation which attributes the gains of foreign companies to UK participators applies only to those participators subject to UK corporation tax.
(7)   The limit on offsetting carryforwarded losses to a maximum of 50% of profits and the flexibility to carryforward trading losses against profits other than from the same trade (see below §62.5.1.1) applies only to companies.

62.2.3 Debts

As part of the changing world of accounting standards, FA 2005, Schedule 4 rewrote the UK tax rules on debts for corporation tax. The very long-standing TA 1988, section 74(1)(j) was repealed and replaced by TA 1988, section 88D, now CTA 2009, sections 55 and 970. Other changes refer to 'statutory insolvency arrangements' instead of arrangement or compromises. The rules on the release of debts, formerly TA 1988, section 89 and now CTA 2009, section 55, were widened to cover impairment losses and debts to be settled otherwise than in money. The corporation tax rules on impairment losses and debt are discussed in more detail below beginning at §63.1.1.2. Similar changes were made for income tax by ITTOIA 2005.

62.2.4 Transactions Between a Dealing and an Associated Non-dealing Company

The rule that an expense may be a revenue expense of the payer but a capital receipt of the payee, with consequent leakage of tax, was modified where one company was a dealing

---

[9] No such limitation was suggested in the 2011 Aaronson GAAR study, available at http://webarchive.nationalarchives.gov.uk/20130321041222/http:/www.hm-treasury.gov.uk/d/gaar_final_report_111111.pdf.
[10] Broadly incorporated in the charging sections of each specific forms of income, eg s 35 for trading income, and made clear in the specific reliefs, eg in ITA 2007, Pt 3; ex TA 1988, s 9(2).
[11] Ex TA 1988, s 9(6).
[12] CTA 2009, s 180(1), ex TA 1988, s 70; and see below at §71.4. Neither did the reduced income basis (TA 1988, s 65(3)), a matter relevant to losses.
[13] CTA 2009, Pt 9A, ex TA 1988, s 208.

company and the other was an associated non-dealing company.[14] Section 774 of Taxes Act 1988 (repealed in 2013) applied if the dealing company became entitled to a deduction on account of the depreciation of any right against the other company or made any deductible payment to the other, and the depreciation or payment was not brought into account in computing the profits or gains of the other; section 774 made the latter company chargeable to corporation tax on an amount equal to the deduction.[15]

62.2.5 Enhanced Expenditure

62.2.5.1 Research Expenditure

FA 2000 introduced enhanced tax relief for expenditure on research and development (R&D)[16] which is incurred by companies;[17] this was widened by FA 2002 and rewritten as CTA 2009, Part 13. Rules are designed to prevent relief if the payments have been artificially inflated.[18]

The relief was at first confined to small or medium-sized enterprises (SMEs),[19] the EU definition being used rather than that in the UK companies legislation. It was extended to larger companies, but in a slightly modified form, in 2002.[20] That year also saw a separate credit for vaccine research.[21] As from 2008, claims by SMEs for R&D relief and by a company of any size for vaccine research relief are barred if the company is not a going concern (and see also the Government announcement on vaccine research relief, below).[22] In order to satisfy the EU state aid rules, the same Act required large companies to declare that the availability of the relief had resulted in an increase in the amount of research and work, or increased the amount of R&D expenditure.[23] For similar reasons, FA 2008 introduced a cap on the total amount of R&D aid that may be claimed—the limit is €7.5 million.[24] If the SME relief limit is passed, the company may still claim relief at the rate for large companies.[25]

---

[14] See *IRC v Lithgows Ltd* (1960) 39 TC 270.
[15] Section 774(3) excludes s 774 if the non-dealing company has incurred a non-allowable capital loss as a result of the loan or payment being used as abortive expenditure.
[16] For policy see Dilnot, Emmerson and Simpson (eds), *Green Budget 2002* (Institute for Fiscal Studies, 2002), §6.1; and Chote, Emmerson and Simpson (eds), *Green Budget 2003* (Institute for Fiscal Studies, 2003), §6.5 and symposium (2001) 22 *Fiscal Studies* 271–399 (before changes of 2002 and later years). On 2002 and 2003 changes, see Inland Revenue Budget Note BN 16/02, [2002] *Simon's Tax Intelligence* 577. See Christian [2002] BTR 277–81 and Inland Revenue Budget Note Rev BN 17, [2003] *Simon's Tax Intelligence* 722.
[17] CTA 2009, Pt 13, ss 1039–1142, ex FA 2000, Sch 20.
[18] CTA 2009, s 1084, ex FA 2000, Sch 20, para 21.
[19] FA 2000, Sch 20, para 2; ie Commission Recommendation 96/280/EC of 3 April 1996; for detail see §4.6. The rules for SMEs are now in CTA 2009, Pt 13, Chs 2–4.
[20] FA 2002, Sch 12, Pt 1. The rules for large companies are now in CTA 2009, Pt 13, Ch 5.
[21] The FA 2002, Sch 13 rules for vaccine research are now in CTA 2009, Pt 13, Ch 5. For history, see Inland Revenue Budget Note 14/02, [2002] *Simon's Tax Intelligence* 575; widened by FA 2006, s 28 and Sch 2 to include payments to clinical trial volunteers.
[22] CTA 2009, ss 1046, 1057, 1094, ex FA 2000, Sch 20, para 18A and FA 2002, Sch 13, added by FA 2008, s 28 and Sch 9.
[23] FA 2008, s 30 adding F(No 2)A 2002, Sch 13, para 3A.
[24] CTA 2009, s 1113, ex FA 2008, s 29 and Sch 10, adding, for SMEs, FA 2000, Sch 20, para 1(5) and, for vaccine research, FA 2002, Sch 13, para 1(3).
[25] CTA 2009, ss 1068 and 1073, ex FA 2002, Sch 12, para 10C.

For R&D expenditure to qualify it must be:[26]

(1) not of a capital nature;
(2) attributable to 'relevant research and development'[27] directly undertaken by the company or on its behalf;
(3) incurred on staffing costs or on software or other consumable stores, or be 'qualifying expenditure' on externally-provided workers or payments to the subjects of a clinical trial;
(4) not incurred by the company in carrying on activities the carrying on of which is contracted out to the company by any person; and
(5) not subsidised.[28]

Subcontractors. Special rules[29] apply if the company uses a subcontractor which is a connected person. The subcontractor payment must have been brought into account in determining the subcontractor's profit or loss for a relevant period along with all of the subcontractor's expenditure, and this must have been in accordance with normal accounting practice. In such circumstances the payment is qualifying expenditure on subcontracted R&D—up to the amount of the subcontractor's relevant expenditure. This treatment is compulsory for connected parties and may be opted into by others. It provides a form of 'see through'. If these rules do not apply, the company may take 65% of the subcontractor payment as its qualifying expenditure.

Tax treatment. For SMEs the payment is to be increased by 130% and taken as a deductible expense[30] or by 230% as a pre-trading expenditure (without having to wait for the trade to begin).[31] It may also be used as a tax credit and used to generate a cash payment by being set against a 'surrenderable' loss, in which case there are consequential restrictions on the carry forward of the loss.[32] The cash payment, which is expressly declared not to be income, works out at 14.5% of the loss;[33] there are caps on the amount of loss that may be surrendered in this way.[34]

Large companies. For large companies there is simply an additional relief of 30%.[35] Large companies may also claim relief for work subcontracted to SMEs.[36] In turn SMEs may claim the relief—but only at the larger company 30% rate—for subsidised work which would meet the conditions for relief but for being subsidised. The expenditure is known as

---

[26] CTA 2009, ss 1052–1053, ex FA 2000, Sch 20, para 3; the various terms are defined in ss 1123–1140, ex paras 4–9.
[27] See CTA 2009, ss 1041–1042.
[28] CTA 2009, s 1138, ex FA 2000, Sch 20, para 8, is framed in terms of 'notified state aids' but adds that R&D tax credits themselves are not 'notified state aids'; on the effect of the subsidy rule, note also FA 2002, Sch 12, paras 10A and 10B below.
[29] CTA 2009, s 1133–1136, ex FA 2000, Sch 20, paras 10, 11, 12 (as amended).
[30] CTA 2009, s 1044, ex FA 2000, Sch 20, para 13.
[31] CTA 2009, s 1045, ex FA 2000, Sch 20, para 14.
[32] CTA 2009, ss 1054–1062, ex FA 2000, Sch 20, paras 15, 19.
[33] CTA 2009, s 1058. The previous rate was 11% after FA 2011 reduced the rate from 14%; prior to 1 April 2008 the rate had been 16%.
[34] CTA 2009, ss 1058–1061, ex FA 2000, Sch 20, paras 16–18, 20.
[35] CTA 2009, s 1074, ex FA 2002, Sch 12, para 11. The large companies rate was increased from 25% to 30% from 1 April 2008.
[36] CTA 2009, ss 1063–1067, ex FA 2002, Sch 12, paras 7–10.

'qualifying additional SME expenditure'. The reason for this formula is that the tax credit is a state aid for the purposes of EU law. Where the SME receives a subsidy, this reduces the amount of the qualifying expenditure, something which would not happen if the company were a large company; these rules allow the SME to claim the credit (but only at the large companies rate of 30%).[37] At Budget 2016 the Government announced it will amend legislation for the SME R&D tax credit scheme to ensure that it continues to work as intended after the previous large company scheme ends on 31 March 2016.

Vaccine research. This relief is modelled on the general regime. SME relief was abolished in FA 2012. Formerly, the SME rate at which relief was given was 20% of qualifying expenditure as a deductible expense[38] or a pre-trading expenditure.[39] A tax credit option was available at 16%.[40] The relief for large companies remains, for now, and is 40%.[41] At Budget 2016 the Government announced it will end Vaccine Research Relief when its State aid approval runs out on 31 March 2017.

RDEC credit. In 2013 the Government introduced a new 'above the line' credit with the aim of replacing the relief for large company R&D expenditure given in the form of a 'superdeduction', which closed for new expenditure on 31 March 2016 (as described above). The Research and Development expenditure credit (RDEC) is calculated instead as a percentage of a company's spending on R&D, with the credit recorded in companies' accounts as a trading receipt (ie above the tax line in the accounts).[42] The current minimum rate for the credit is 11% before tax,[43] and the credit is payable to loss-making companies. A company cannot claim both the RDEC and relief under CTA 2009, Part 13.[44] Although directed primarily at large companies, the regime is also applicable to funded or subsidised R&D expenditure incurred by SMEs in the same way the existing large company super-deduction regime can be claimed for such costs.[45]

62.2.5.2 Contaminated or Derelict Land

Under CTA 2009, Part 14, enhanced relief is available for company expenditure (including capital expenditure) on remediation of contaminated land.[46] The scope of relief was widened by FA 2009 to provide incentives to bring long-term derelict land—commonly known as brownfield land—into use and to include costs of removing Japanese Knotweed.[47] The company may not claim the relief if it or anyone connected with the company is

---

[37] CTA 2009, ss 1068–1072, ex FA 2002, Sch 12, paras 10A and 10B, added FA 2003.
[38] Formerly CTA 2009, Pt 13, Ch 7. The rate was in s 1089. It was reduced from 50% to 40% by FA 2008, s 26 and Sch 8, para 3, and from 40% to 20% by FA 2011, before being abolished by FA 2012, ss 16–32.
[39] Formerly CTA 2009, s 1092, ex FA 2002, Sch 13, paras 15 and 15A. If the company was not entitled to a deduction for the qualifying expenditure in computing its trading profits for corporation tax purposes the rate was 140%.
[40] Formerly CTA 2009, ss 1103–1112, ex FA 2002, Sch 13, paras 16–24.
[41] CTA 2009, s 1091, ex FA 2002, Sch 13, para 21(1)–(4). If the company is not entitled to relief under Ch 2 the rate is 120%.
[42] CTA 2009, ss 104A–104Y.
[43] CTA 2009, ss 104M.
[44] CTA 2009, ss 104B.
[45] CTA 2009, ss 104A(3). For more see: http://www.taxadvisermagazine.com/article/taking-credit.
[46] CTA 2009, Pt 14, ss 1143–1179, ex FA 2001, Sch 22, para 1; on contamination see s 1145 (ex para 3).
[47] FA 2009, s 26 and Sch 7. See especially CTA 2009, ss 1145A and 1146A.

responsible for the contamination or dereliction, or if the polluter has an interest in the land.[48] The company may not claim the relief if the expenditure qualified for an allowance under CAA 2001.[49]

The relief may be claimed if the land is acquired for the purposes of the company's trade or property business.[50] The conditions for the relief are that the land was in a contaminated or derelict state when the major interest[51] in it was acquired, that the expenditure was incurred on relevant land remediation, that the expenditure was incurred on employees, materials or allowable subcontracting costs, that the expenditure would not have been incurred but for the land being contaminated and that the costs are not subsidised.[52] The relief does not extend to the acquisition costs of the land.

If the conditions of the relief are satisfied and the company makes the appropriate election, it may take a deduction for the qualifying capital expenditure and an additional 50% of the qualifying non-capital remediation expenditure (on top of the deduction already allowed in computing profits for corporation tax purposes).[53] If this creates or increases a loss, the loss may be treated as a loss for group relief purposes. A second option, modelled on the R&D tax credit (§62.2.5.1), is to give the company a tax credit equal to 16% of the expenditure.[54] The credit is not taxable income and there are consequential provisions to deal with matters such as loss relief and capital gains computations, so preventing double relief.[55]

62.2.5.3 Capital Allowance First Year Credits for Green Technologies

This applies where a company has incurred expenditure qualifying for first year capital allowance for certain 'green' technologies (below at §64.2.5.2) but is unable to use the allowance because of having a surrenderable loss, ie having a loss arising from the activity which is the qualifying activity for the green capital first year allowance.[56] The company must not be an excluded company.[57] The amount is the lesser of (a) the relevant first year allowance and (b) the unrelieved loss.[58] The credit is 19% of the loss, but this must not exceed an upper limit or cap. The cap is the greater of (a) £250,0000 and (b) the amount of the company's total PAYE and NICs liabilities for the period.[59] Artificially inflated claims are disregarded.[60]

---

[48] CTA 2009, ss 1150 and 1163, ex FA 2001, Sch 22, paras 2(5) and 7; on relevant connection, see s 1178 (ex para 31(3)).
[49] CTA 2009, ss 1147(8) and 1149(8), ex FA 2001, Sch 22, para 1(4).
[50] CTA 2009, ss 1147(2) and 1149(2), ex FA 2001, Sch 22, para 1(1) and Sch 23, para 1.
[51] Defined in CTA 2009, s 1178A. For derelict land, the relevant time is the earlier of 1 April 2008 and date of acquisition.
[52] CTA 2009, ss 1147 (capital expenditure) and 1149 (remediation expenditure), ex FA 2001, Sch 22, para 2; the terms are elaborated on in ex paras 3–11.
[53] CTA 2009, ss 1147(6) (capital expenditure) and 1149(7), (8), ex FA 2001, Sch 22, Pts 2 and 3 (paras 12–19).
[54] CTA 2009, ss 1154, ex FA 2001, Sch 22, para 14.
[55] CTA 2009, ss 1155–1158, ex FA 2001, Sch 22, paras 15–19.
[56] CAA 2001, s 262A and Sch A1, added by FA 2008, s 79 and Sch 25; the first-year allowance s are listed in Sch A1, para 3. The procedure is set out in para 18.
[57] Listed in CAA 2001, Sch A1, para 1(4).
[58] first-year allowance s are listed in CAA 2001, Sch A1, para 3, losses in paras 4–9 and unrelieved losses in para 10–16.
[59] CAA 2001, Sch A1, para 2; for (b) see para 17.
[60] CAA 2001, Sch A1, para 28.

The payment is not income but may carry interest.[61] Where the company surrenders the loss in this way, there are restrictions on other ways in which it may carry the loss forward.[62]

If the item on which the expenditure was incurred is disposed of within four years after the end of the chargeable period for which the credit is paid, there may be a clawback.[63] If this happens the amount of the original loss is restored.[64]

62.2.5.4 Relief for Film Production Companies

CTA 2009, Part 15 (sections 1180–1216) contains the rules formerly in FA 2006, Part 2, Chapter 3, providing a new form of relief for film production companies[65] and withdrawing older reliefs.[66] As with the similarly-structured R&D and remediation regimes just discussed, this scheme provides for additional deductions in calculating profits[67] or a payment in the form of a tax credit,[68] if the relevant conditions are satisfied.[69] This regime was developed after much discussion.[70]

62.2.5.5 Relief for Television, Video Game and Theatre Production

At Budget 2012, the Government finally announced its long-debated plans to introduce corporation tax reliefs, of some description, for the production of video games, television animation programmes and high–end television productions, with a view to making the UK 'the technology hub of Europe'. The rules governing the reliefs are CTA 2009, Part 15A, ss 1216A-1216EC (television) and Part 15B, sections 1217A to 1217EC (video games). Rules providing relief for theatre production are in CTA 2009, Part 15C, sections 1217F-OB.

62.2.6 Purchasing Annual Payments and 'Settlement' Income

FA 2007, Schedule 5, paragraphs 1 and 2 introduced new rules designed to stop schemes involving purchasing annual payments and settlement income. HMRC do not admit that these schemes work but have produced pre-emptive legislation anyway. TA 1988, section 347A(1)(b) directed that certain types of annual payment were not within the charge to corporation tax. Companies have purchased such rights and argued that as financial traders they are entitled to deduct their expenses, eg the price, while not being liable to tax on the proceeds. Similarly, companies have tried to enter into arrangements which are settlements in ITTOIA 2005, Part 5, Chapter 5 (ex TA 1988, sections 660A–660G); the company then uses the settlor's (lower) tax rate rather than ordinary corporation tax rate. To prevent such schemes, the words in TA 1988, sections 347A and 660C removing any liability to corporation tax were repealed.

---

[61] CAA 2001, Sch A1, para 23; see amendments to TA 1988, s 826 (not rewritten).
[62] CAA 2001, Sch A1, paras 19–22.
[63] CAA 2001, Sch A1, paras 24 and 25(10); on administration, see para 27.
[64] CAA 2001, Sch A1, para 26.
[65] Defined in CTA 2009, s 1182, ex FA 2006, s 32.
[66] See §6.2.14 below.
[67] CTA 2009, ss 1199–1200, ex FA 2006, Sch 5, paras 1–5.
[68] CTA 2009, ss 1201–1203, ex FA 2006, Sch 5, paras 6–14.
[69] CTA 2009, ss 1196–1198, ex FA 2006, Sch 5, paras 39–41.
[70] See FA 2006 note by Shipwright [2006] BTR 517.

62.3   Capital Gains

Corporation tax is levied on the 'profits' of companies, and 'profits' include chargeable gains.[71] Corporations are not subject to CGT but only to corporation tax. The acts of a liquidator are treated as the acts of the company so as to bring them on to the corporation tax side of the line and to ignore disposals between company and liquidator. Although shareholders are taxed separately from the company, they may be made liable for corporation tax on gains accruing to the company if they are connected with the company and receive a capital distribution arising from a reduction in the capital of the company.[72]

62.3.1 Distinctions

Gains are treated differently from income. Since 1987, the importance of the distinction between capital gains and ordinary income for companies has been reduced since the same rate of tax is charged on both types of profit.

Despite these changes, the distinction from CGT still remains of importance:

(1)   Indexation relief still applies in full for corporation tax.
(2)   If a company ceases to be resident or subject to tax in the UK, there is a deemed disposal of assets. A similar rule applies to trustees but not to individuals; the corporation tax rule arguably violates EU principles.[73]
(3)   The share identification rules are different for the two taxes.

There are also some important distinctions between income and capital gains in the corporation tax area:

(1)   Where a trading loss is carried forward to a later accounting period under CTA 2010, section 45, it may only be set off against trading income—and not capital gains—of that trade of that period.
(2)   A capital loss cannot be set off against ordinary income—even income of the same accounting period.

62.3.2 The Company and the Shareholder—General

A double charge to tax may arise if the company realises a gain but for some reason does not distribute those profits to the shareholders. In such circumstances there will have been a full charge to tax on the gain in the hands of the company and a further charge on the shareholder when the shares are sold. This leads to double taxation where there is a profit,

---

[71] CTA 2009, s 2(2), ex TA 1988, s 8.
[72] TCGA 1992, s 189.
[73] See eg Case C-371/10 *National Grid Indus BV v Inspecteur van de Belastingdienst Rijnmond/kantoor Rotterdam* [2012] STC 114 and Case C-9/02 *Lasteyrie du Saillant v Ministere de l'Economie* [2005] STC 1722. Whether the trust rule breaks such principles depends on finding the appropriate freedom for it to break.

and to double relief where there is a loss. In principle double relief for losses should follow the double charge on gains.

Two major avoidance techniques have been used, particularly when small companies are concerned. The first is to ensure that any appreciating assets are held by the individual shareholder rather than the company.[74] The second is to transfer the asset at full value to a wholly-owned subsidiary which makes the disposal. This transfer will not give rise to a chargeable gain,[75] provided the disposal of the shares in the subsidiary occurs more than six years after the section 171 disposal;[76] the liability in respect of the gain accruing before the transfer to the subsidiary will have been avoided.

62.3.3 Substantial Shareholding Exemption

TCGA 1992, Schedule 7AC exempts gains arising from the disposal of substantial share-holdings.[77] Whether deferral or exemption is the better policy option is a matter for debate, but unquestionably the exemption is highly valued by UK corporate groups and multina-tionals. The practical effect of the exemption is very great and removes a major obstacle to corporate restructuring. The effect of the exemption is also to disallow any losses. The exemption applies only where certain conditions are met. At Budget 2016 the Government announced a consultation on the 'extent to which the SSE is still delivering on its origi-nal policy objective and whether there could be changes to its detailed design in order to increase its simplicity, coherence and international competitiveness'.[78] In particular, there are concerns that the regime has become overly-complicated especially in comparison to foreign counterparts, relies too heavily on factors outside the company's control, and has not kept up with the general movement towards a more territorial UK tax system.[79] The consultation has outlined a number of possible changes, ranging from tinkering with the 10% shareholding threshold to making the exemption much more 'comprehensive'.[80]

62.3.3.1 Terms

Using the terminology of Schedule 7AC, the regime includes one 'main exemption' and two 'subsidiary exemptions'. The company realising the gain, V (vendor), is called the invest-ing company and the company whose shares are being disposed of is called the 'company invested in', here T (target). The company acquiring the shares will be referred to as P (pur-chaser). V must have a sufficient shareholding in T to be 'substantial'.[81] The period for which this condition must be satisfied is a continuous 12 months in the two years before the disposal. The calculations involved where a fluctuating holding is concerned may be complex. V's holding must be not less than 10% of the ordinary share capital of T. The shareholding must entitle V to the appropriate rights with regard to profits available for

---

[74] This may, however, risk the loss of rollover relief under TCGA 1992, s 152; on the obsolete retirement relief see *Plumbly v Spencer* [1999] STC 677.

[75] TCGA 1992, s 171; see below at §66.2.

[76] The transfer must be later than six years after the acquisition to avoid TCGA 1992, s 179; see below at §66.6.

[77] TCGA 1992, Sch 7AC, added by FA 2002, Sch 8; among much writing, see Haskew [2003] *Private Client Business* 11, comparing this relief with the (then available) taper relief for CGT.

[78] HM Treasury, *Business Tax Road Map* (March 2016), para 2.65.

[79] Armstrong, *Tax Journal* (10 June 2016).

[80] See https://www.gov.uk/government/consultations/reform-of-the-substantial-shareholdings-exemption.

[81] TCGA 1992, Sch 7AC, paras 7–9.

distribution or assets on a winding up; for this purpose the rules in CTA 2010, Part 5, Chapter 6 (group relief) are adopted with slight modifications. Shares held by other group companies are taken into account to reach the 10%.

In ascertaining the two-year period one can look past any earlier no gain/no loss transfers, and conversely not look past any deemed disposals and reacquisition.[82] The period also ceases to run if there has been a sale and repurchase agreement and the shares have come back to the original owner (or other group company); a similar rule applies to stock lending arrangements. The legislation directs one to look through any earlier company reconstructions or demergers.[83] A company is not treated as ceasing to be the beneficial owner just because it is put into liquidation; there are separate rules for insurance companies.[84]

62.3.3.2 Conditions

Various conditions must be satisfied by both V and T.[85] In broad terms, V must be a sole trading company or member of a qualifying group, which is defined as a trading group with an extension for certain not-for-profit activities. Express provision is made to cover the situation in which V is a sole trading company for part of the period and a member of a group for the other. Broadly similar but simpler conditions have to be satisfied by T. The legislation goes on to define the key concepts of 'trading company', 'member of a trading group' and 'member of a trading subgroup', and to make provision for joint ventures, for demergers and reconstructions, etc for T. Various other definitions follow.[86]

62.3.3.3 The Exemptions[87]

There are three exemptions:

(1)   Under the main exemption, where these various conditions are met, capital gains and losses arising on the disposal of the shares in T will be disregarded for corporation tax.

(2)   The second (or first subsidiary) exemption applies where the disposal is not of shares but of rights related to the shares, such as options, convertible securities and options to acquire convertible securities.

(3)   The third (or second subsidiary) exemption extends relief under the main or the first subsidiary exemption to situations in which the conditions were met previously but are not met at the time of the disposal; in very broad terms, this relatively complicated provision allows V and T to look back a further two years.

These exemptions are regarded as so important that they override three rules which would otherwise apply.[88] The three are all deferral rules which maintain the old cost base for the assets, so the effect of excluding them is that P acquires the assets at the current market value rather than at some out-of-date and usually lower figure. These are the reconstruction

---

[82]   TCGA 1992, Sch 7AC, paras 10–13.
[83]   TCGA 1992, Sch 7AC, paras 14–17.
[84]   TCGA 1992, Sch 7AC, para 18.
[85]   TCGA 1992, Sch 7AC, paras 18–26.
[86]   TCGA 1992, Sch 7AC, paras 27–31.
[87]   TCGA 1992, Sch 7AC, paras 1–3.
[88]   TCGA 1992, Sch 7AC, para 4.

provisions in TCGA 1992, sections 127, 135 and 136,[89] the exchange of shares for qualifying corporate bonds under section 116(10) and a demerger section 192(2)(a).

There is a detailed anti-avoidance rule.[90] The exemptions are excluded if, as a result of relevant arrangements:

(1) an untaxed gain arises, ie profits which have not been brought into account for UK tax purposes;
(2) the disposal takes place either—
     (a) after the company has acquired control, or
     (b) after a significant change in trading activities.

Arrangements are relevant if having as their sole or main benefit the realisation of a gain which would have been exempt under these rules.

The exemptions do not apply if the relevant disposal is a no gain/no loss disposal.[91] So an intra-group transfer of a substantial shareholding is given its normal effect.

62.3.3.4 Special Rules

Just to underline the complexities of the capital gains regime, there are a number of consequential rules. So it is expressly provided that the exempt shares remain 'chargeable' for the purposes of the corporate venturing scheme.[92] Further, if the new rules would prevent the loss from being an allowable loss, the taxpayer cannot use the negligible value relief in TCGA 1992, section 24(2) to back-date the disposal and so create an allowable loss after all.[93] This rule is followed by other rules designed to ensure that other special gains or losses are dealt with appropriately. So if a substantial shareholding is appropriated as trading stock and now held as trading stock, and this would give rise to an exemption under Schedule 7AC, the shares are still treated for general capital gains purposes as having been acquired for their market value at the time of the appropriation.[94] This rule is beneficial to the taxpayer, but the next protects the Revenue. Where CGT has been deferred under a claim for gift relief, a later disposal of the asset triggers the deferred charge even though it meets the terms of Schedule 7AC.[95] Other rules referred to are reorganisations under section 116(10), the deferred charge under section 140(4), the degrouping charge under TCGA 1992, section 179 and the Forex matching rules.[96]

62.3.4 Transfer of Business on Company Reconstruction

Under TCGA 1992, section 139, where a company's business is transferred to another company,[97] the transfer will normally involve the transfer, and so the disposal, of chargeable

[89] On which there is an interesting Revenue Guidance Note of 21 June 2002.
[90] TCGA 1992, Sch 7AC, para 5.
[91] TCGA 1992, Sch 7AC, para 6.
[92] TCGA 1992, Sch 7AC, para 32.
[93] TCGA 1992, Sch 7AC, para 33.
[94] TCGA 1992, Sch 7AC, para 36.
[95] TCGA 1992, Sch 7AC, paras 37.
[96] TCGA 1992, Sch 7AC, paras 34, 35, 38 and 39.
[97] But not to a unit trust or an investment trust (TCGA 1992, s 139(4)).

assets. This result will be mitigated for assets other than trading stock[98] in that neither gain nor loss accrues to the company making the disposal, provided:

(1)   the scheme involves the transfer of the business in whole or in part, as opposed simply to the transfer of assets;[99]
(2)   both companies are UK resident or, for disposals after 31 March 2000, the assets are chargeable assets, ie liable to tax under TCGA 1992, section 10(3);[100] and
(3)   the transferor receives no consideration other than the transferee taking over any liabilities from the transferor.

This provision is mandatory, not a matter of election. It is similar in intent to those which apply on the incorporation or takeover of a business; where the rule applies, the disponee takes over the base cost of the disponor.

If the main purpose, or one of the main purposes, is the avoidance of liability to corporation tax, CGT or income tax, TCGA 1992, section 139 does not apply and the normal rules applicable to a disposal will apply;[101] any corporation tax due may be recovered from the disponee if the disponor has not paid within six months of the tax becoming payable.[102]

The term 'reconstruction' has been construed by the courts to require a degree of continuity of common ownership.[103] On this view, section 139 would not apply where a business is split between two different groups of shareholders, but the Revenue take a more generous position.[104]

62.3.5 Transfer of Overseas Business to Non-resident Company

Under TCGA 1992, section 140, the charge arising on the disposal of an overseas trade plus its assets[105] to a non-resident company in return for shares may be deferred, provided the transferor company ends up with at least 25% of the ordinary share capital of the transferee company.[106] The charge is postponed until:

(1)   the transferor company disposes of all or any of the shares; or
(2)   the transferee company disposes of all or some of the assets.

---

[98]   TCGA 1992, s 139(2). Trading stock of the transferor will be valued under CTA 2009, ss 162–170 (ex TA 1988, s 100) for computing income, and so is excluded.

[99]   *Cf McGregor v Adcock* [1977] STC 206, (1977) 51 TC 692 and similar cases (see above at §42.5.1).

[100]   Section 140(1A) added by FA 2000, Sch 21, para 9. On transfer to a non-resident, TCTA 1992, s 140 may apply; there are also rules for EU transfers (s 140A) and the risk of challenge under the non-discrimination rules in the TFEU.

[101]   TCGA 1992, s 139(5).

[102]   TCGA 1992, s 139(7); tax may also be recovered from certain subsequent holders. On clearance procedure, see s 139(5) referring to s 138 (see above at §41.5.3).

[103]   *Brooklands Selangor Holdings Ltd v IRC* [1970] 2 All ER 76.

[104]   Statement of Practice SP 5/85.

[105]   But not if the assets consist wholly of cash.

[106]   TCGA 1992, s 140; a claim under s 140C excludes a claim under s 140, and vice versa (see ss 140(6A), 140C(4)). Ordinary share capital is defined in CTA 2010, s 1118 (ex TA 1988, s 832(1)).

However, the charge under (2) arises only if the disposal is within six years.[107] Where only part of the consideration received is in the form of shares or loan stock, then only a proportionate part of the charge is postponed. The purpose of the rule is to acknowledge that the gain is primarily a paper gain, and to give the company time to find the cash; the technique used is a form of rollover. This is a matter of taxpayer election; it has the effect of deferring losses as well as gains, and so the alternative of electing for TCGA 1992, section 152 rollover should be considered. The fact that foreign tax may have been paid and so is available for credit relief may make these elections superfluous or inadvisable. FA 2010 altered the mechanics of section 140(4) with the effect that UK tax is not lost where the consideration received consists of qualifying corporate bonds (QCBs). As QCBs are exempt from tax, the postponed gains previously escaped tax.[108]

62.3.6 *The European Union—Tax-free Transfers and the Mergers Directive*

The Mergers Directive, which took effect on 1 January 1992[109] and was revised and consolidated in 2009,[110] is concerned with allowing companies to merge or demerge their business operations[111] without triggering immediate charges on capital gains.[112] The normal corporation tax rules are modified in a number of situations involving a qualifying company,[113] company A, making a transfer to another qualifying company, company B, resident in another Member State. A company is resident in a Member State if it is subject to a charge to tax under the law of that state because it is regarded as resident there for the purposes of the charge; this is subject to any overrule by a double taxation agreement giving a different residence for treaty purposes.[114]

62.3.6.1 Transfers of a UK Trade by A to B

First, where there is a transfer of the whole or part of a trade carried on by A in the UK to B, that transfer is wholly in exchange for shares or debentures and, where both A and B so elect,[115] the two companies, subject to further conditions, are treated so that the assets are transferred at such figure that neither gain nor loss accrues.[116] Although the transfer must be 'wholly' in exchange for shares or debentures, the fact that the buyer takes over

---

[107] Other than by a group transfer within TCGA 1992, s 171; the non-residence bars in s 170 are ignored for (2). The definitions are modified by FA 2000 to take account of the changed definition of 'groups' to include non-resident companies.

[108] See Ministerial Statement of 6 January 2010 and Notes to Finance Act.

[109] Council Directive 90/434/EEC, [1990] OJ L225/1, on the common system of taxation applicable to mergers, divisions, transfers of assets and exchanges of shares concerning companies of different Member States, as amended by Council Directive 2005/19/EC of 17 February 2005.

[110] Council Directive 2009/133/EC, OJ L 310, 25.11.2009, on the common system of taxation applicable to mergers, divisions, partial divisions, transfers of assets and exchanges of shares concerning companies of different Member States and to the transfer of the registered office of an SE or SCE between Member States, as amended by Council Directive 2013/13/EU of 13 May 2013 (hereafter 'Mergers Directive').

[111] For an explanation of why the UK legislation speaks in terms of 'trade' and the Directive in terms of 'business', see HC Official Report, Standing Committee B, col 296, 24 June 1992.

[112] Inland Revenue, EC Direct Measures—a consultative document (1991), para 2.1.

[113] Defined as a body incorporated under the law of a Member State; see TCGA 1992, ss 140A(7), 140C(9).

[114] TCGA 1992, ss 140A(5), (6), 140C(6), (7).

[115] TCGA 1992, s 140A, added by F(No 2)A 1992, s 44.

[116] TCGA 1992, s 140A(4); the legislation excludes the deemed disposal otherwise arising under *ibid*, s 25(3) where the owner of an asset ceases to carry on a trade in the UK through a branch or agency here (s 140A(4)(b)).

liabilities does not disqualify it.[117] It is not necessary that A should be resident in the UK; it is sufficient that A is carrying on the trade in the UK. However, as seen above, if A and B are resident in the same EU country, this provision does not apply.

A condition relates to B's residence. If immediately after the transfer B is not resident in the UK, the condition is that any disposal of the asset would give rise to a charge to corporation tax.[118] If B is resident in the UK, the condition is that the company is not able to escape a charge to UK corporation tax in relation to any of the assets by reference to a double taxation agreement.[119] The effect is to allow deferral only when B will be fully exposed to UK tax in due course.

There is also an anti-avoidance rule. Section 140A does not apply unless the transfer of the business is effected for bona fide commercial reasons and does not form part of a scheme or arrangements of which the main purpose, or one of the main purposes, is the avoidance of liability to income tax, corporation tax or CGT.[120] There is a clearance procedure on an application by A and B.[121] In *Leur-Bloem v Inspecteur der Belastingsdienst*,[122] the European Court considered the application of the Directive to the creation of a holding company and an exchange of shares of the holding company for shares in two trading companies. It held that although the Directive allowed a Member State to prevent its use by taxpayers for avoidance purposes, this did not permit the Member State to prohibit whole categories of transactions whether or not there was actual tax avoidance or evasion. The court also held that the Directive could apply even if:

(1) the acquiring company did not carry on a business itself;
(2) there was no merger of two companies into a single unit from the financial or economic viewpoint; or
(3) the same person was sole shareholder and director of both companies.

62.3.6.2 A, Resident in the UK, Transfers a Non-UK Trade to B[123]

Here, A, resident in the UK, makes a transfer of a business in whole or in part to B and, immediately before the transfer, the business is carried on by A in a Member State other than the UK through a permanent establishment. No gain, no loss treatment of the aggregate of gains and losses arising is directed, provided:

(1) the transfer includes the whole of the assets of company A used for the purposes of the business (although cash, a term which is not defined, may be excluded);
(2) the transfer is wholly or partly in exchange for shares or debentures issued by B to A; and
(3) the aggregate of the chargeable gains exceeds the aggregate of allowable losses.[124]

---

[117] HMRC *Capital Gains Manual*, para CG 45709.
[118] Ie under TCGA 1992, s 10B (s 140A(2)).
[119] TCGA 1992, s 140A(3).
[120] TCGA 1992, s 140B.
[121] TCGA 1992, s 140B(2); s 138(2)–(5) also apply (s 140B(3)).
[122] Case C-28/59 [1997] STC 1205. See also Case C-436/00 *XY v Rikskatteverkel* [2004] STC 1271.
[123] TCGA 1992, s 140C; and TA 1988, s 815A, added by F(No 2)A 1992, s 50.
[124] TCGA 1992, s 140C(1), (3), added by F(No 2)A 1992, s 45; in relation to insurance companies, see TCGA 1992, s 140C(8).

A claim need be made only by A (not A and B).[125] A special double taxation relief rule (see above at §62.3.4) applies.[126]

There is an anti-avoidance provision similar to that for TCGA 1992, section 140A, although here only A applies for clearance.[127] Relief under this rule is excluded if the more general deferral for the transfer by a UK company of a trade to a non-UK resident company (section 140) applies.[128]

This leads to the double taxation relief rule.[129] Double taxation relief, whether unilateral or under a treaty, applies as if the amount of the tax that would have been payable in the other Member State had actually been paid as tax—and so is available on a subsequent disposal of the asset. The effect of this is that the UK gives relief for the tax not paid in the state where the permanent establishment is situated, but is not required to give relief for any other foreign tax.

62.3.6.3 Capital Allowances

Where there is a no gain, no loss rollover on the transfer of a UK trade in circumstances satisfying TCGA 1992, section 140A, the transfer is not to be treated as giving rise to any allowances or charges, and everything done by company A is treated as done by company B.[130] Whether this was required by the Directive is uncertain.[131] There is no provision requiring capital allowance rollover on a transfer within section 140C—presumably because this is now a matter for the law of the other Member State. However, this means that a balancing charge or allowance may have to be calculated.

62.3.6.4 Other Mergers Directive Matters

Under TCGA 1992, section 135, taxes on an exchange of shares may be deferred.[132] The conditions in section 135(1)(c) were relaxed both to meet the terms of the Directive and for purely domestic matters. It is unclear whether the relief is available for shares obtained in excess of an existing majority, or how a majority is determined where the target company has different classes of shares.[133]

62.3.7 *Capital Losses; Restrictions on Allowable Capital Losses*[134]

FA 2006 introduced major changes to limit tax avoidance through the creation of capital losses. One provision was a wide-ranging anti-avoidance rule, but this was confined to corporation tax. This has been superseded by TCGA 1992, section 16A, which applies both to corporation tax and to CGT. The 2006 rules on groups are considered below at §65.2.5.

---

[125] TCGA 1992, s 140C(1)(e).
[126] Ie TA 1988, s 815A; TCGA 1992, s 140C(5).
[127] TCGA 1992, s 140D(2); again s 138(2)–(5) apply.
[128] TCGA 1992, s 140C(4).
[129] TIOPA 2010, ss 122–123, ex TA 1988, s 815A.
[130] CAA 2001, s 561, originally added by F(No 2)A 1992, s 67; on just and reasonable apportionment of expenditure between assets included in the transfer and other assets, see s 561(3).
[131] Inland Revenue, Guidance Note, 21 June 2002, para 2.5.
[132] Mergers Directive, Art 8; on definition, see Art 2(d) and Inland Revenue, *op cit*, para 2.9.
[133] See Lurie, *Tolley's International Tax Planning*, 4th edn (Tolley, 1999), ch 9.
[134] See Williams [2006] BTR 23 and 550.

Two further 2006 rules on capital losses are considered here. First, TCGA 1992, section 184G involves schemes for converting income into capital. Broadly, the relevant company must have a receipt arising from the disposal of an asset, there are relevant 'arrangements' and the company has a gain arising from that disposal but it also has losses arising from the disposal of another asset.

The next condition is that, but for the arrangements, an amount would have fallen to be taken into account wholly or partly instead of the receipt in calculating the income chargeable to corporation tax of either the relevant company or a group member as set out in section 170. The final condition is that the main purpose, or one of the main purposes, of the arrangements is to secure a tax advantage involving the deduction of any of the losses from the relevant gain.

The Board may then give the relevant company a notice covering the matter set out in the legislation in the form specified. The effect is to forbid the deduction of the loss from the relevant gain. Section 184I contains rules as to notices.

The other rule, section 184H, is aimed at schemes securing deductions. The structure of the provision is similar to that in section 184G, but aimed at any expenditure which is allowable as a deduction in calculating a company's total profits chargeable to corporation tax but which is not allowable as a deduction in computing its gains under section 38.

62.4 Charities and Charges on Profits (Income and Capital)

62.4.1 Charges

For many years charges on profits (ie income and capital) formed a distinct category of deductible items; the origins of the system go back to the 1803 legislation introducing deduction at source for many types of income (see above chapter six). Before FA 1996 the list of charges included many types of interest, annuities, and annual payments and royalties; it also included certain gifts to charity, manufactured overseas dividends, the income element of a deep discount security and the discount on a bill of exchange.[135] By March 2005 the list of charges had been reduced to (a) annuities and annual payments payable otherwise than in respect of any of the company's loan relationships, and (b) qualifying donations to charities.[136]

In November 2004 the review of corporation tax had proposed the abolition of the charges on income, for reasons of simplification. After November 2004 the Revenue discovered that tax avoidance schemes had been devised using annuities and annual payments; these schemes relied on the fact that, unlike almost all other deduction rules, there was no unallowable purpose test. FA 2005 therefore removed the category of annual payments leaving just the charitable donation.[137] Annuities and other annual payments for trading purposes are treated as deductible expenses, while others are moved to the category of allowable management expenses of a company with investment business (§79.2 below). The charitable donation relief rules were rewritten as CTA 2010, Part 6. The discussion

---

[135] Ex TA 1988, s 338.
[136] Ex TA 1988, s 339, amended by FA 2000, s 40.
[137] FA 2005, s 132.

below is a brief summary and mostly historical. Interested readers are directed to previous editions of this book.

62.4.2 Deduction of Charges from Profits

The company may deduct charges on income (now restricted to qualifying charitable donations) against its total profits for the period.[138] This applies only to payments actually made—not payments due.

Example

In financial year 2012, X Ltd has trading profit of £165,000, chargeable gains of £166,667 and received rent of £25,000, a total of £356,667. Assume that X Ltd makes annual payments to charity of £75,000 (gross).

X Ltd has overall profits of £356,667. This figure is then reduced by the £75,000 to leave the profits subject to corporation tax at £281,667.

62.4.3 Special Rules for Payments to Charities

Until April 2000 the UK legislation provided two sets of rules for payments by companies to charities. The first, the covenanted donation to charity, relaxed some of conditions (1)–(8) above if a payment to charity was to qualify as a charge. The second, the qualifying donation to charity, was a separate category of charge as gift aid. These rules were recast in 2000[139] and rewritten as CTA 2010, Part 6, sections 189–217. All references to covenanted donation to charities were removed in 2000.

The general rule in CTA 2010, section 189 is that qualifying charitable donations made by a company are allowed as deductions from the company's total profits chargeable to corporation tax. The donation may be treated as made in an earlier accounting period than that in which it is actually paid, but the company cannot carry it back more than nine months.[140] Dividends and other distributions cannot be a qualifying donation (unless the payment falls within CTA 2010, section 1020 (transfer of assets or liabilities)).[141] A payment by a company which is itself a charity cannot be a qualifying donation.[142] The rules extending charitable relief to gifts of shares and land apply to gifts by companies.[143]

As with the rules for individuals:

(1) there is no obligation to deduct tax from the payment;
(2) there is no need for a gift aid certificate;

---

[138] CTA 2010, s 189, ex TA 1988, s 338(1), as reduced by any relief other than group relief; on use of excess charges as trading losses, see below at §62.5.1. Double tax treaty relief by way of credit is not available since it does not 'reduce profits' (*Shaw v Commercial Union* [1999] STC 109).

[139] FA 2000, s 40; see further at chapter eighty-one.

[140] CTA 2010, s 199, ex TA 1988, s 339(7AA). This provision was originally enacted following a submission by the DTI Deregulation Unit and is deemed to avoid the necessity to estimate profits on insufficient information and then deliberately to overpay the covenanted sum, creating a loan of the excess.

[141] CTA 2010, s 194, ex TA 1988, s 339(1)(a).

[142] CTA 2010, s 191(4), ex TA 1988, s 339(3G).

[143] CTA 2010, ss 203–216, ex TA 1988, s 587B, added FA 2000, land added FA 2002, s 97.

(3)   the rules as to permissible benefits where the gift is by a close company were rewritten;

(4)   any gift of money is treated as a net sum, so enabling the charity to claim repayment.

62.4.4 *Payer's Duty to Deduct Income Tax*

The obligation to deduct income tax at source arises in a number of contexts. These were set out in TA 1988, section 349(1) and (2),[144] rewritten primarily into ITA 2007, sections 874 *et seq*, and cover annuities and other annual payments, royalties and certain type of interest.

For many years companies had to deduct income tax at the 'applicable rate', ie currently the lower rate of 20%,[145] when making the payment, and account to the Revenue on a quarterly basis for the sums deducted.[146] The scope of the obligations was reduced in 2001, in line with Government policy in its negotiations with other EU Member States that the right way to make sure that tax is paid is by exchange of information rather than a general withholding tax.[147]

Under the 2001 rules there is no obligation to deduct—and so no right to deduct either— if the payment is made by a company,[148] and at that time the company reasonably believes that either of two conditions specified in ITA 2007, sections 933–937 (ex TA 1988, section 349B) is satisfied. The first condition is that the person beneficially entitled to the income in respect of which the payment is made is (a) a company resident in the UK, or (b) a partnership each member of which is a company resident in the UK. The second condition is similar but international: (a) that the person beneficially entitled to the income in respect of which the payment is made is a company not resident in the UK ('the non-resident company'), (b) the non-resident company carries on a trade in the UK through a branch or agency, and (c) the payment falls to be brought into account in computing the chargeable profits of the non-resident company. The effect of this condition is that the payee must be within the UK corporation tax net, and so the Revenue will get their money anyway. Where the payment is made gross, the payer may deduct the payment in computing profits.

Penalties may be charged where the belief is non-existent or unreasonable.[149] Where the belief is reasonable but incorrect, the Revenue may still collect tax,[150] leaving the company to such restitution or other claims as it may have. This point apart, it will be recognised that the reason for making the test one of reasonable belief rather than the actual state of the payee company is that the question whether the payee company meets one or other condition is often not easy for the paying company to determine, and may be much more easily answered by the payee. The Board may issue a notice directing that tax is to be withheld after all if the Board has reasonable grounds for believing, as respects each payment to which the direction relates, that it is likely that neither of the specified conditions will be satisfied in relation to the payment at the time the payment is made.[151]

---

[144] See above at §27.5; on changes in 2001 and 2002 see Hardwick [2001] BTR 339–43 and [2002] BTR 321–25.

[145] TA 1988, s 4(1), (1A).

[146] For details, see TA 1988, Sch 16, paras 2, 9.

[147] See §64.4.2 on the EU's Interest and Royalties Directive of 2003, which exempts payments of interest, etc where the source is a UK company and the recipient is an associate company in another Member State.

[148] ITA 2007, s 930, ex TA 1988, s 349A(5), (6).

[149] TMA 1970, s 98 (4A)–(4C).

[150] ITA 2007, s 932 and 938, ex TA 1988, s 349D.

[151] ITA 2007, s 931, ex TA 1988, s 349C.

The duty to withhold was removed from payments by local authorities in 2002. At the time the duty was removed from payment by companies to various specified tax-exempt bodies, or to partnerships consisting of companies or such tax-exempt bodies.[152]

In 2002 the right to make royalty payments without withholding tax was extended to royalties paid by a company in the UK where it reasonably believes that the recipient company is entitled to relief under a double tax arrangement.[153] This was extended by FA 2004 to payments of royalties between associated companies under the Interest and Royalties Directive (see §65.4.1). At Budget 2016, however, the Government announced it will change the deduction of tax at source regime to bring all international royalty payments arising in the UK within the charge to income tax, unless those taxing rights have been given up under a double taxation agreement or the EU Interest and Royalties Directive.

Where the duty to account survives, it applies quarterly and extends to all payments within ex TA 1988, section 349, now ITA 2007,[154] including yearly interest. This obligation is therefore not affected by the introduction of the FA 1996 rules for loan relationships (see below at §63.1).

62.5 Losses[155]

62.5.1 *Trading Loss*

The rules for calculating losses generally are the same under income tax and corporation tax, but there are different rules for loss relief. Unlike individuals, companies can continue forever and companies with losses can be bought and sold. These features raise difficult tax design issues. According to Donnelly and Young, a tax system that offers a full and immediate refund of losses is the 'most conceptually and philosophically "pure" model of loss relief'.[156] However, as the authors note, 'the fact that governments around the world have uniformly rejected a full refund system suggests that the conceptual advantage of such a policy is not enough to overcome the more pragmatic need to preserve the business tax base and survive the practical realities of revenue considerations'.[157]

In designing loss relief regimes, Donnelly and Young contend that tax jurisdictions are faced with two fundamental tax issues: time-averaging and loss ownership.[158] Under the first, a decision must be made on the extent to which a company is allowed to average its income by offsetting loss years against years of profit. Undoubtedly, there is an inherent

---

[152] FA 2002 s 94.

[153] ITA 2007, ss 911–913, ex TA 1988, s 349E, added by FA 2002 s 96.

[154] ITA 2007, ss 946 and 961(1), (6), ex TA 1988, s 350(4); on payment of interest to the UK branch of a non-resident company, see Revenue Interpretation RI 49.

[155] For some dated comparative material, see *Taxing Profits in a Global Economy* (OECD, 1991), ch 3, Table 3.8; for an invaluable analysis of tax losses from a primarily Canadian policy perspective, see Donnelly and Young (2002) 50 *Canadian Tax J* 429 and [2005] BTR 432. See also the Tucker Committee Report, Cmnd 8189 (1951), paras 77–83 and Royal Commission on the Taxation of Profits and Income, *Final Report*, Cmnd 9474 (1955), paras 480–88.

[156] Donnelly and Young [2005] BTR 432 at 434. The authors cite as authority for this proposition Campisano and Romano, 'Recouping Losses: The Case for Full Loss Offsets' (1981) 76 Northwestern Univ L Rev 709 at 715.

[157] Donnelly and Young, *ibid.*

[158] Donnelly and Young, *ibid*, 435.

artificiality in requiring taxable profits of a business to be computed in and allocated to twelve-month slices. This suggests some degree of income averaging should be permitted (see above §12.3), but the difficult question then becomes how much? The second fundamental design issue is identifying the 'owner' of the loss. Donnelly and Young list several possibilities:[159]

(1) the loss belongs to the business that incurs it;
(2) the loss belongs to the company that carries on the business; or
(3) the loss belongs to the shareholders of the company that carries on the business.

If the loss is considered to belong to the business, the tax jurisdiction may insist that the taxpayer continue to operate either the business or a business similar to it in order to make use of losses of the business. If such a position is adopted, there is a risk that this restrictive tax policy will distort the efficiency of the taxpayer's choices, eg where non-tax factors suggest that the business making a loss should be abandonded,[160] or where management wish to introduce changes to improve profitability but risk the tax authority deciding the changed business is no longer 'similar enough' to the loss-making business to permit use of the losses. Alternatively, if the loss belongs to the company that carries on the business, can the company sell the business and its losses to another company? Similarly, what happens to the losses if the company is sold to new shareholders? If the new owners of the business or company are permitted to make use of the losses, this could be avoidance or abuse of the tax system, on one view, although on another this is simply sensible, commercial use of the losses.

Clearly, there is a lack of an international consensus on loss-relief regimes, including how far back business or trading losses can be carried to get a refund of previous tax paid (Australia none; UK 1 year; US 2 years; Canada 3 years), how long unused losses can be carried forward to future years to offset against future profits (Canada 20 years; US 20 years; UK and Australia indefinitely), and when losses can be shared with other taxpayers, eg parent/subsidiary/sister companies. The UK loss relief rules for companies are described next, and the application of these rules in the context of a group of companies is considered below in chapter sixty-four.

62.5.1.1 Set-off Against Future Trading Income from the Trade

Where a company incurs a trading loss, it may roll the loss forward and set it off against the trading income of *the* trade of succeeding accounting periods under CTA 2010, section 45 (ex TA 1988, section 393(1)), provided the company remains within the charge to corporation tax, the loss being set off against the earliest available profits.[161] Note the emphasis on *the* trade—if the company carries on multiple trades the carryforwarded loss is streamed and can be applied against future profits only from the same trade that had generated the loss.

However, at Budget 2016 the Government announced the current rules would be made more flexible, so that losses arising on or after 1 April 2017 will be useable, when carried forward, against profits from other income streams or other companies within a group.

---

[159] Donnelly and Young, *ibid*.
[160] Donnelly and Young, *ibid*, 436.
[161] CTA 2010, ss 45 and 36(3), ex TA 1988, s 393(1), (10). The general rules for claim under self-assessment are in FA 1998, Sch 18, Pt VII, ie paras 54–77.

This new flexibility comes at a price for larger companies—also from 1 April 2017, companies will only be able to use losses carried forward against up to 50% of their profits above £5 million. For groups, the £5 million allowance will apply to the group. These changes will not apply to the North Sea ring-fenced corporation tax regime.

Further, more restrictive limits on carried forward losses apply to banks. The banks built up considerable losses during the financial crisis of 2007–08, so much so that under the usual rules for carryforward losses it would have been many years before the banks paid any corporation tax at all on subsequent trading profits. This was thought to be unsatisfactory, particularly in light of the government intervention and support provided to that sector during the crisis. As a result, FA 2015 introduced limits restricting the proportion of banks' annual taxable profit that can be offset by carried forward losses to 50%;[162] this was subsequently lowered to 25% from 1 April 2016. This restriction is subject to a £25 million allowance for building societies and an exemption for losses incurred by new-entrant banks.

62.5.1.2 Interest or Dividends as Trading Income

Alternatively, where there are not enough trading profits for a period to absorb all or even some of the loss, the loss may be set against 'any interest or dividends' which would have been taken into account as trading receipts in computing that income but for the fact that they have been subjected to tax under other provisions.[163] In applying this test the courts look to the nature of the business and the purpose for which the fund is held, and ask whether the investment is in some way integral to the trade.[164] A bank or an insurance business would meet this test, but it is not clear how many others will. In *Nuclear Energy plc v Bradley*,[165] the House of Lords held that in the particular circumstances of that case, interest received on long loans taken out to fund expenses on the eventual decommissioning of nuclear power stations could not be regarded as trading income against which brought forward losses could be put. The case concerned large sums of money over long periods; short-term deposits by a trader to meet current or short-term liabilities would be treated differently.[166]

The other element is 'interest or dividends'. Profits from loan relationships arising out of trading transactions now enter into the trading profit calculation. Profits from non-trading relationships will usually fail to satisfy the first element anyway. It will be noted that the test used is 'dividends' and not 'distributions'. The effect of these rules is to break down the boundaries of the schedular system, but only where the investment income would have been trading income but for that system.

62.5.1.3 Set-off Against General Profits of the Same Accounting Period and the Preceding Year (Three Years for Terminal Losses)

The rules on carrying across and back losses in TA 1988, section 393A and now in CTA 2010, section 37 were recast in 1991 to allow greater carry-back of losses[167]—felt to be

---

[162] CTA 2010 Part 7A s 269CA.
[163] CTA 2010, s 46, ex TA 1988, s 393(8).
[164] *Nuclear Electric plc v Bradley* [1996] STC 405, 68 TC 670, HL.
[165] *Ibid*; see also *Bank Line Ltd v IRC* [1974] STC 342, 49 TC 307 (fund to pay for replacement of company's fixed assets—interest not available for loss relief).
[166] [1996] STC 405, 412, 68 TC 670, 717, *per* Lord Jauncey.
[167] FA 1991, s 73.

necessary in time of recession. The flexibility was largely withdrawn in 1997.[168] The whole loss eligible for relief must be used; partial claims are not allowed.[169] Whether a company should cut short an accounting period straddling the year end in order to accelerate the loss relief is a matter of judgement. Any unused capital allowances which have not been given effect as deductions in computing profits, and so in calculating the loss, are to be treated similarly.[170]

(1) The company may set the loss against its profits of whatever description, ie covering both non-trading income and capital gains, of the same accounting period.[171]

(2) The company may carry the loss back and set it against its profits of whatever description of preceding accounting periods falling wholly or partly within the period of one year immediately preceding the period in which the loss occurs; to qualify for this carry-back the company must have been carrying on the trade and been within the charge to corporation tax in that prior accounting period.[172] Where there is an accounting period straddling the anniversary, the loss may be set only against that part of the profits attributable to the period falling within the year.

(3) The period of one year is extended to three years in the case of a terminal loss, ie any loss incurred in the trade in the last 12 months of trading, apportioning the profits of any period straddling that anniversary.[173] This preserves one effect of the 1991 change, in that the loss may be set against profits of whatever description and not just trading income.

The general rule is that losses must be set against profits of later periods first.[174] Any repayment supplement due in respect of a repayment of tax already paid will be calculated by reference to the year in which the loss arises.[175] Relief under (2) above must not interfere with any relief given for a charge on income.[176]

62.5.1.4 Non-allowable Trading Losses

The privilege of loss relief under CTA 2010, section 37 does not apply to trades carried on wholly outside the UK,[177] nor to dealings in commodity futures.[178] The income tax restrictions on loss relief applied to persons in respect of farming and market gardening also apply here.[179] Further, as with income tax, the trade, whether or not connected with farming, must either have been carried on (a) under some enactment, or (b) on a commercial basis and with a view to the realisation of gain, whether in itself or as part of a larger undertaking

---

[168] F(No 2)A 1997, s 39; on transition, note *Camcrown Ltd v Mcdonald* [1999] STC (SCD) 255.
[169] CTA 2010, s 37(1)–(8), ex TA 1988, s 393A(1) refers to 'the amount of the loss'.
[170] Ex TA 1988, s 393A(5), repealed.
[171] CTA 2010, s 37, ex TA 1988, s 393A(1).
[172] CTA 2010, ss 35–37, ex TA 1988, s 393A(1)(b), (2), (9).
[173] CTA 2010, s 39, ex TA 1988, s 393A(7A).
[174] CTA 2010, s 37(8), ex TA 1988, s 393A(1).
[175] This was by analogy to the rules for the carry-back of surplus ACT (HC Official Report, Standing Committee B, col 358, 18 June 1991).
[176] Ex TA 1988, s 393A(8).
[177] CTA 2010, s 37(5), ex TA 1988, s 393A(3).
[178] CTA 2010, s 52, ex TA 1988, s 399(2)–(4).
[179] CTA 2010, ss 48–51, ex TA 1988, s 397; see above at §20.10.5.

of which the trade formed part.[180] A reasonable expectation of gain at the end of the period will satisfy this test.[181]

62.5.1.5 Charges Incurred for Trading Purposes as Losses

The scope of this rule was greatly reduced by F(No 2)A 2005, which removed annual payments from the scope of charges (see above §62.4.1). However, the rule remains in place. Annual payments paid before 16 March 2005 remain 'charges'.

Where charges on income consisting of payments made wholly and exclusively for the purposes of a trade carried on by the company, and those and other charges on income, exceed the profits of that period against which they are deductible then, whichever is the smaller of those payments or the excess, is treated as a trading expense[182] and so becomes entitled to loss relief. If the company has charges of £500 and profits of £600, the profits will be reduced to £100; if, however, the profits are only £410, the excess charges of £90 will available as loss relief. Where the company carries on two trades, the excess charge which falls to be treated as an allowable loss may only be set off against future income of the trade for which the charge was raised; the fact that there are individual (beneficial) side-effects for the other trade is irrelevant.[183]

62.5.2 Carry Forward for Use by Another Company—Company Reconstruction Without Change of Ownership

Where a company:

(1)   transfers a trade or part of a trade to another company; and
(2)   there is no change of ownership,

the change is ignored so as to allow any trading loss to be rolled forward to be set off against the subsequent trading income under CTA 2010, section 45, subject only to the first company's right to set the loss against other profits under section 37.[184] This treatment is given only where the conditions in CTA 2010, Part 22, Chapter 1, sections 940A–953 (ex TA 1988, section 343) are satisfied. Where a company ceases to trade or to carry on a part of a trade, restrictions apply if the transferring company is insolvent;[185] in these circumstances, the amount of the loss that may be taken over is reduced by the amount by which the transferor company's 'relevant liabilities' exceed its 'relevant assets'.

These are the only purposes for which the change is ignored. Therefore the successor company cannot use any miscellaneous losses under CTA 2010, section 91 (ex Schedule D,

---

[180] CTA 2010, ss 37(5),(6) and 44(1),(2),(4), ex TA 1988, s 393A(3).
[181] CTA 2010, s 44(1), (3), ex TA 1988, s 393A(4).
[182] Ex TA 1988, s 393(9); on management expenses of an investment company, see CTA 2010, ss 1219(3) and 1221(1), ex TA 1988, s 75(3).
[183] *Olin Energy Systems Ltd v Scorer* [1982] STC 800, (1982) 58 TC 592.
[184] CTA 2010, s 944(3), (4), ex TA 1988, s 343(3). The change is also ignored for capital allowances in so far as they have not been given relief as trading expenses. Assets qualifying for capital allowances will be transferred at the written-down value (CAA 2001, ss 557 and 559 (general) and 265 *et seq* (machinery and plant)); there will therefore be no balancing charges (or allowances), or any first-year allowance.
[185] CTA 2010, s 945(1), (4), (5), ex TA 1988, s 343(4); on relevant assets and liabilities, see ex TA 1988, ss 344(5) *et seq*. A liability assumed by the transferee company cannot be a relevant liability (s 344(6)).

Case VI) or capital losses of its predecessor.[186] This is scarcely unreasonable since, for this rule to apply, it is only necessary that the predecessor company cease to trade. It is not necessary that the company should cease to exist; such losses will be relieved by being set against subsequent miscellaneous gains or capital gains of the predecessor company.

62.5.2.1 Conditions

There must be no change of ownership. This will be satisfied if on, or at any time within two years of, the ending of the trade by the predecessor, the trade or an interest amounting to not less than a three-quarter share in it should belong to the same persons as the trade or such interest belonged to within one year before the event.[187] It is also necessary that the trade should be carried on by companies which are within the charge to corporation tax.[188]

Provision is also made for the situation in which the successor company transfers its trade to a new owner,[189] and for that in which the successor company treats the trade as part of its trade.[190] Where the first successor company does not satisfy the common control test, but the second one does (in comparison with the original transferor), the losses may be used by the second successor—provided this is within the three-year period.

In *Leekes Ltd v R & C Comrs*,[191] at issue was whether carryforward losses are available under TA 1988, section 343 only against future profits arising from the old trade (ie 'streamed'). The First-tier Tribunal allowed the taxpayer's appeal, holding that such streaming was too difficult to do where the old trade is carried on as part of a larger trading operation by the successor. This is a controversial conclusion and at the time of writing the decision was under appeal to the Upper Tribunal.

62.5.2.2 Hive-downs

If a company wishes to separate a particular business and place it in a subsidiary (often called a hive-down), CTA 2010, section 944 on accrued trading losses will often be invoked (see further above at §60.12.3). TCGA 1992, section 171 (see below at §65.2.1) will be used for assets with potential capital gains liability. Capital assets qualifying for capital allowances which take effect in taxing the trade will be transferred to the new owner but will usually be transferred at the written-down value;[192] there will therefore be no balancing charges (or allowances), nor any first year allowance. The Revenue have indicated that where a receiver intending to sell off a company, trade or part of it affects a hive-down, the *Ramsay*[193] composite-transactions doctrine under which intermediate steps inserted into a transaction entirely for tax purposes could be ignored,will not normally be considered relevant, provided the entire trade (or part) and its assets are transferred with a view to its being carried on in other hands.[194]

---

[186] See below at §62.5.7.

[187] CTA 2010, s 944(1), ex TA 1988, s 343(1)(a).

[188] CTA 2010, s 944(1), ex TA 1988, s 343(1)(b).

[189] CTA 2010, s 953, ex TA 1988, s 343(7).

[190] CTA 2010, ss 951(1)–(4), 952(1), ex TA 1988, s 343(8), (9); as to whether enough trading activities have been taken over, see *Falmer Jeans Ltd v Rodin* [1990] STC 270, (1990) 63 TC 65; and above at §20.8.3.

[191] [2015] UKFTT 93 (TC).

[192] Under CAA 2001, ss 265 *et seq* (machinery and plant), 557 and 559.

[193] *WT Ramsay Ltd v IRC* [1982] AC 300 and, see in particular, *Furniss v Dawson* [1984] AC 474. The evolution of the *Ramsay* doctrine is discussed in detail above §5.6.4.

[194] See HMRC manual CTM06210, referring to a letter sent by the Revenue to the ICAEW, [1985] *Simon's Tax Intelligence* 568; but the Revenue would not give an assurance that the new approach would never be relevant.

62.5.2.3 Beneficial Ownership[195]

In determining whether the trade belongs to the same persons, the law pierces not only the veil of any company but also any trust, identifying shareholders and beneficiaries as the people with the interest in each case.[196] Persons who are relatives or who are entitled to the income of the trust are treated as one person.[197] If shares in company A Ltd are held on trust for L, M, N and P, and the company transfers the trade to a company whose shares are held on trust for L, M, N, P and Q, it would appear that there has been a change in ownership since, although less than 75% of the interest has been changed, each body of beneficiaries is treated as a single person. In determining the extent of a person's interest in a trade, it is necessary to look to the extent of his entitlement to share in the profits.[198]

62.5.2.4 Companies Leasing Plant and Machinery

CTA 2010, section 950 (ex TA 1988, section 343A) applies in place of section 944 where there is what the legislation calls a qualifying change of ownership of such a company (or partner company).[199]

62.5.2.5 Historical Note

Section 343 read (and CTA 2010, Part 22, Chapter 1 still does read) oddly and more like an anti-avoidance provision than a permissive one—hence its restrictions as to time and the fact that it is not an election. This is probably precisely because the structure was originally used as an anti-avoidance provision.[200]

62.5.3 *Restriction on Carryforward—Change of Ownership of Company and Change in Trade*

The converse case arises where the control of the trade passes to other people but the identity of the person trading remains the same. The right to roll losses forward under CTA 2010, section 45 is excluded under sections 673–675 (ex TA 1988, section 768) if either:

(1) within any period of three years there is both a change in the ownership of the company *and* (either earlier, or later or simultaneously) a major change in the nature or conduct of a trade carried on by the company; or
(2) there is a change in the ownership of the company at any time—and not just within a three-year period—after the scale of the activities in a trade carried on by a company has become small or negligible, and before any considerable revival of the trade.

Where these conditions are satisfied, losses accruing up to the date of the change in ownership are not carried forward. These provisions were introduced in 1969 to stop the sale of companies simply for their tax losses. The going rate was then the equivalent of 10p for £1

---

[195] CTA 2010, s 942(2), (3), (6), (8), ex TA 1988, s 344(3)(a); on beneficial ownership, see above at §60.10.
[196] CTA 2010, s 941(6), ex TA 1988, s 344(1).
[197] CTA 2010, s 941(7), (8), ex TA 1988, s 344(4).
[198] CTA 2010, s 941(5), ex TA 1988, s 344(1).
[199] Added FA 2007, s 31.
[200] FA 1954, s 17.

of loss. Some companies were kept in existence only for their losses—hence (2) above. This provision does not apply to capital losses, which have their own rules.

A similar rule applies to prevent the carry back of losses to accounting periods beginning before the change in ownership.[201] There are also further rules about investment companies[202] for surplus UK property business losses,[203] and a category added by F(No 2)A 2005 for non-trading loan relationship deficits.[204]

62.5.3.1 Change of Ownership[205]

Two rules apply to changes of ownership. First, a change of ownership is to be disregarded if, before and after the change, the company is a 75% subsidiary of another company. This provision is aimed at the situation in which the company ceases to be the directly-owned 75% subsidiary of another company but remains within the same ultimate ownership.[206] Secondly, and conversely, where a company, P, owns a 75% subsidiary, S, directly or indirectly, a change of ownership of P also brings about a change in the ownership of S (save where the first rule applies). There may also be a deemed change of ownership where a subsidiary is a 60% subsidiary of one company within a group and the 40% subsidiary of another such company (or the 50% subsidiary of each); the sale of the 60% holding and of the 40% holding to the same purchaser brings about a change in the ownership of the subsidiary for this purpose.[207]

62.5.3.2 Major Change in Trade

The concept of a major change in the trade is amplified by 'including' a major change in the property dealt in, services or facilities provided, or in the customers, outlets or markets.[208] Moreover, where the change has been a gradual process, it may be treated as a change even though it took more than three years. In *Purchase v Tesco Stores Ltd*,[209] it was said that the word 'major' imported something more than significant but less than fundamental; the effects of the change should be considered. In *Willis v Peeters Picture Frames Ltd*,[210] it was emphasised that these are essentially matters of fact. There, the taxpayer company was taken over by a group, and its sales to its former customers were divided among distribution companies in the same group; this reorganisation was held by the Commissioners not to be a major change and the court declined to interfere with that decision. Since it is almost inevitable that a person taking over a loss-making business will want to make some changes, the courts may have some nice questions to decide; Revenue practice is not to treat a change as major if a company rationalises its product range by withdrawing unprofitable items

---

[201] CTA 2010, s 673–674, ex TA 1988, s 768A; s 768(2)–(4), (8)–(9) were applied by s 768A(2).

[202] CTA 2010, ss 677–682 and 692–702, ex TA 1988, ss 768B, 768C.

[203] CTA 2010, ss 677–705, ex TA 1988, s 768D.

[204] CTA 2010, ss 680(2), (3) and 697(3), (4), ex TA 1988, Sch 28A paras 9A and 10A, added by F(No 2)A 2005, Sch 7, para 3.

[205] CTA 2010, ss 677–682 and 692–702, ex TA 1988, ss 768B, 768C.

[206] CTA 2010, s 724. On wide test of ownership, see CTA 2010, ss 719–726, ex TA 1988, s 769(6C).

[207] CTA 2010, s 723, ex TA 1988, s 769 as amended by FA 1989, s 100.

[208] CTA 2010, 673(4), ex TA 1988, s 768(4). Of course, if the change in trade was sufficiently great, losses could not be carried forward, whether the trader was an individual or a company, by virtue of the rules as to discontinuance of a trade (see above at §20.7).

[209] [1984] STC 304 (1984) 58 TC 46; see also *Pobjoy Mint Ltd v Lane* [1985] STC 314, (1985) 58 TC 421, CA (both cases on stock relief under FA 1976, Sch 5, para 23).

[210] [1983] STC 453, (1983) 56 TC 436.

and, possibly, replacing them with new items of a kind already being produced, or if the company makes changes to increase its efficiency or to keep pace with changing technology or management techniques.[211]

Technical provisions treat a company reconstruction without a change in ownership as concerning only one company[212] and for allowing for intra-group transfers to take place without triggering CTA 2010, section 674.[213] Where the loss is due to an unused capital allowance, provisions ensure that no balancing charge applies to the extent that the charge reflects the unallowable loss.[214]

62.5.3.3 Further Restriction on Loss Carryovers

Two minor rules require mention. First, CTA 2010, section 53 (ex TA 1988, section 395) excludes sections 45 and 37 where a company has incurred expenditure on machinery and plant which it leases to another person, and there are arrangements[215] whereby a successor company will be able to carry on any part of that company's trade which includes that lease. But for this special provision, the first company would be able to create a loss to set off against its profits while giving the successor company profits to set off against its losses, thus, in effect, permitting the assignment of the generous capital allowances provided for machinery and plant.

Another rule bars the transfer of relief where the company is a member of a partnership and arrangements exist for adjusting the company's share of profits or losses in return for consideration in money or money's worth.[216]

62.5.4 *Other Income Losses*

UK property business (ex Schedule A) losses may be set against total profits for the period of the loss[217] and then rolled forward to be set against total profits of a later period, provided the UK property business is carried on.[218] It will be noted that the word used is 'profits'— not 'income'—and it is indeed true that UK property business losses, like trading losses, may be set off against capital gains from that business realised in later years. Losses from an overseas property business (ex Schedule D, Case V losses) may only be set against profits of that business for later years.[219] Miscellaneous losses (ex Schedule D, Case VI losses) may be set off against other miscellaneous losses for that or any subsequent accounting period.[220]

In the unusual case of *English Holdings v HMRC*,[221] a non-resident company carrying on a trade in UK land through a permanent establishment (PE) in the UK incurred a loss for corporation tax purposes. The same company carried on a letting business in the UK but

---

[211] Statement of Practice SP 10/91, amended 1996.
[212] CTA 2010, s 676, ex TA 1988, s 768(5).
[213] CTA 2010, ss 675(1)–(3) and 687(4), (5), ex TA 1988, s 768(6).
[214] CTA 2010, ss 675(4) and 687(6), ex TA 1988, s 768(7).
[215] Arrangements may be of any kind, whether or not in writing (CTA 2010, s 53(5), ex TA 1988, s 395(5)); see also *Pilkington Bros Ltd v IRC* [1982] STC 103, (1982) 55 TC 705.
[216] CTA 2010, ss 958–962, ex TA 1988, s 116.
[217] CTA 2010, s 62(1),(3), ex TA 1988, s 392A(1).
[218] CTA 2010, s 62(4), (5), ex TA 1988, s 392A(2).
[219] CTA 2010, ss 66(1)–(3) and 67, ex TA 1988, s 392B.
[220] CTA 2010, s 91, ex TA 1988, s 396.
[221] [2016] UKFTT 436.

not through a PE, with the result that the profits from the lettings were subject to income tax (and not corporation tax). The First-tier Tribunal agreed with the taxpayer that the corporation tax loss from trading could be set off against the income tax profit from the lettings under ITA 2007, section 64.

A problem arises with post-trading expenses where a company has ceased trading and, in the process of selling up its assets, receives investment income on its funds. Reliefs for the incidental expenses will not be available since it is no longer a trading company and was not set up as an investment company. Unrelieved trading losses from its trading days cannot be used since the company is no longer trading.

62.5.5 *Loss Relief and Partnership Schemes*

FA 2004 includes rules countering schemes where a company is in a partnership and receives capital from the partnership.[222] Where the company receives an amount greater than the amounts the company has put into the partnership, a charge on the excess may be charged under miscellaneous losses (ex Schedule D, Case VI). The charge does not arise if the excess results from a sharing of profits in accordance with the partnership capital shares.

62.5.6 *Leasing Plant and Machinery*

Companies with a business of leasing plant and machinery, such as that in the famous *Barclays BMBF* case,[223] caused problems for the Revenue. The main problem was that these contracts usually generate losses in the early years and profits later on. Hence these companies were often sold as they moved into profit, to buyers who then used the losses against their own profits. This practice is countered by the rules in FA 2006, Schedule 10. These were widened in 2008 to counter sales to a single company.[224] The rules in FA 2006, Schedule 10 were amended by FA 2009, section 63 and Schedule 31, to make changes to help industry during the recession. FA 2010, section 29 amends the rules on when a company is owned by a consortium. An indirect 75% subsidiary of a company owned by a consortium will now be treated as a company owned by a consortium, so that any change in the consortium member's interest will now generate a proportionate charge.

62.5.7 *Capital Losses*

Allowable capital losses may be set off against chargeable gains of that or any later accounting period,[225] but not against income. Such losses are not affected by CTA 2010, sections 673–675. Group relief does not extend to capital losses. These rules are not affected by the changes made by FA 2005. It should be noted that while CTA 2010, section 37 allows relief for trading losses against capital gains of the relevant accounting periods, section 45 does not provide the same relief.

---

[222] FA 2004, ss 131 and 132; s 133 deals with the interaction with capital gains taxation; see Shipwright [2004] BTR 510–19.

[223] *Barclays Mercantile Business Finance Ltd v Mawson* [2005] STC 1 (HL) and see above §5.6.

[224] Changes made by FA 2008, s 56.

[225] TCGA 1992, s 8(1).

62.6   Transfer Pricing and Thin Capitalisation

The current rules on transfer pricing and thin capitalisation were introduced by FA 2004 and applied as from 1 April 2004, with the consequent splitting of many accounting periods that did not end on 31 March 2004. The 2004 changes took the form of (a) a substantial rewriting of the rules on transfer pricing,[226] and (b) making the rule on thin capitalisation part of the transfer pricing rules.[227]

Transfer pricing refers to the problem of how the tax system should deal with transfers of assets or services between companies or other traders who are not at arm's length. Unfettered taxpayer freedom here would allow the taxpayers to allocate profits or losses to different parts of their enterprise. In the international context this would allow the profits to appear in low tax areas and the losses in high tax areas. In the purely domestic context, the profits and losses might find their way to tax-advantageous areas. For many years the UK tax system worried about only the international problem. However, ECJ case law declared such rules to be discriminatory. In reaction (or, more likely, overreaction) the UK rules were extended to purely domestic situations. The rules contained in TIOPA 2010, Parts 4 and 5 (ex TA 1988, section 770A and Schedule 28AA), as amended, substitute an arm's length price for any price agreed between the parties.

Thin capitalisation refers to a technique whereby one company (P) set up another company (S) on terms which provide a thin amount of share capital and a thick amount of debt. In this way P can in due course make S pass profits back to it as tax-deductible interest rather than non-deductible dividends. While it is perfectly normal for companies to set up subsidiaries with a mixture of equity and debt, the tax issue arises when the balance is not such as could be obtained in a normal commercial transaction. Before 2004 this was addressed by a rule in TA 1988, section 209 treating the excess interest element as a dividend. Since 2004 the loan is treated as a provision of services (money) and so within the transfer pricing regime.[228]

Although it was thought that the 2004 rules applied to corporation tax and not to income tax—and so they are discussed in this book in their corporation tax setting—TIOPA 2010, section 146 now clearly states that the transfer pricing regime applies for income tax purposes as well. The (now somewhat moot) argument that the transfer pricing regime applied only to corporation tax was that the rules can apply only where there is the relevant degree of control, and that the test for control seemed to apply where companies were involved but not where individuals or trusts were parties.[229]

Control is defined in a particular way for the transfer pricing rules; a 40% interest can be treated as giving control.[230] Under the control test, one of the affected persons must be

---

[226] FA 2004, ss 30–33, see Van der Wolk [2004] BTR 465–68.

[227] Ex TA 1988, Sch 28AA, paras 1A, 1B, 6C–6E, added by FA 2004, ss 34–36.

[228] TIOPA 2010, ss 152–154, ex TA 1988, Sch 28AA, para 1A. On claims, see TIOPA 2010, ss 181–184, 191 (ex TA 1988, Sch 28AA, para 6C); on guarantees see ss 153–154 (ex para 1B) and ss 201–204 (ex para 7D). See also the EU law aspects discussed in ch 21 below.

[229] See *Simon's Direct Tax Service*, B.3.1815; also the FA 2004 rules appear in the statute under the heading 'Corporation tax'. Despite this, competent figures in the Revenue had been heard to say that the rules could apply to income tax.

[230] TIOPA 2010, ss 157–163, ex TA 1988, Sch 28AA, para 4.

directly or indirectly involved in the management, control or capital of the other; or the same person must be directly or indirectly involved in the management, control or capital of each of the affected persons. FA 2005 adds a further twist by applying the transfer pricing rules if persons have been 'acting together' in relation to financing arrangements.[231]

The rules do not apply to dormant companies. More importantly, they do not usually apply to SMEs,[232] though such enterprises may elect irrevocably to be subject to these rules and the Revenue may direct that a medium-sized enterprise apply them.[233] Unusually, the meaning of 'small' and 'medium' are determined by reference to an EU law definition.[234] To be small an enterprise must have fewer than 50 employees, and either its turnover or its assets (or both) must be no more than €10 million. The enterprise is not just the individual company but any other companies with certain joint consolidated accounts and any 'linked' enterprises.[235] To be medium-sized an enterprise must have fewer than 250 employees, its turnover must be less than €50 million and its assets must be less than €43 million. It is clear that decisions to increase or reduce staff, or turnover or assets may have significant effects—as may the exchange rate.

The exemption does not apply if the other affected person or some other party is a resident of a non-qualifying territory. 'Qualifying'—and so 'non-qualifying'—territories are defined. A territory qualifies if it is one with which the UK has a double tax treaty containing a non-discrimination clause. A dual-resident company with residence in a qualifying territory and a non-qualifying territory is excluded from the exemption.[236]

The transfer pricing rules apply to each transaction (or 'provision') separately rather than having the broad sweep of the US code (IRC §482). They compare the actual provision with the provision that would have been made between independent enterprises (the arm's-length provision) and then ask whether the actual provision confers a potential advantage in relation to UK taxation on one of the affected persons or (whether or not the same advantage) on each of them. The legislation will apply only if the arm's-length principle means a potential tax advantage for UK taxpayers, ie it will apply only to reduce a loss or increase a profit.[237] The legislation enables the parties to make tax-free balancing payments to each other to bring their cash position into line with the tax result.[238]

Further rules in TIOPA 2010, Part 4 eliminate double counting, make provision for trading stock on closing the business, allow a compensating adjustment where the advantaged person is a controlled foreign company, for guarantees, for double taxation relief, for securities, for foreign exchange transactions and derivatives—and for oil. The rules are not to affect the computation of capital allowances or charges or capital gains.[239]

These rules are considered further in their international context—see below §72.4.

---

[231] TIOPA 2010, ss 148, 149, 158, 161, 162, ex TA 1988, Sch 28AA, para 4A, added by F(No2) A 2005, s 40 and Sch 8; see Green Taxation, 28 April 2005 106–108. On transition, see F(No 2)A 205, Sch 8, para 4.

[232] TIOPA 2010, s 166, ex TA 1988, Sch 28AA, paras 5B–5E; referring to the European Commission recommendation 263/2003/EC, 6 May 2003.

[233] TIOPA 2010, s 167(2), ex TA 1988, Sch 28AA, paras 5B and 5C.

[234] Annex to European Commission recommendation 263/2003/EC, 6 May 2003.

[235] TIOPA 2010, s 172, ex TA 1988, Sch 28AA, para 5D.

[236] TIOPA 2010, ss 166, 167 and 173, ex TA 1988, Sch 28AA, para 5B esp (4) and 5E.

[237] The expression 'tax advantage' is defined in TIOPA 2010, s 155, ex TA 1988, Sch 28AA, para 5.

[238] TIOPA 2010, ss 195–204, ex TA 1988, Sch 28AA, paras 6–7.

[239] TIOPA 2010, s 213, 214, ex TA 1988, Sch 28AA, para 13.

62.7   Avoidance Involving Tax Arbitrage

Tax arbitrage refers to transactions or arrangements which exploit differences in tax rules; the differences may arise in a purely domestic situation or between the tax codes of different countries. Part 6 of TIOPA 2010 provides rules, which apply only to companies, to enable the Revenue to issue notices counteracting the effects of such arbitrage; this may be seen as part of a worldwide movement by tax authorities.[240] Examples of such rules include the double dip—under which a company obtains a deduction of the same expense in two countries (the deduction problem), or has obtained a deduction but the equivalent receipt has escaped tax (the receipts problem). The UK legislation has a rule for each problem. However, they apply only where the Revenue issue a notice, and Revenue guidance notes show that they are not overly concerned with simple schemes such as the double dip. Thus, although the Revenue have gone for wide words in the legislation, they apply them narrowly. This does not raise quite the same issue as the legality of extra statutory concessions because of the requirement of a notice. Practitioner reaction suggests that HMRC is applying the rules sensibly.[241]

The arbitrage rules apply to certain types of hybrid entity and instruments having hybrid effect. The rules apply to deny or reduce a deduction (sections 232–48), or to impose a chargeable receipt (sections 249–54). Sections 255–57 deal with administrative matters and interpretation.

The deduction rule applies where there is a qualifying scheme, there will be a tax deduction or other set off, and the purpose or one of the main purposes of the scheme is to obtain a UK tax advantage, unless it is minimal.[242] The deduction is disallowed if the same expense is allowed for the purpose of any other tax, which means UK or foreign tax.[243] The effect may be to disallow the expense in both countries, so the lesson is not to claim it twice. A second rule applies where a transaction or series of transactions involves a payment which creates a deduction or an allowance for the payer but the recipient is not subject to tax unless because of specified exemptions.[244] The receipts rule applies when five conditions are satisfied:

(1)   there must be a scheme, a company on whom the notice is served and a person making the payment to the company;
(2)   there is a qualifying payment—one which increases the capital of the company;
(3)   the person making the payment is entitled to certain types of deduction, whether in the UK or elsewhere;
(4)   the amount received has not been taken into account for its own tax assessment; and
(5)   a benefit arises from (4).[245]

---

[240] TIOPA 2010, Pt 6, ss 232–259, ex F(No 2)A 2005, ss 24–31 and Sch 3; detailed Revenue guidance on the rule is available on their website. On policy, see Edgar (2003) 51 *Canadian Tax Jo* 1082–1158.

[241] Luder, *Tax Journal* (24 October 2005), 9; Collins and Bird, *Tax Journal* (22 May 2006), 13, though the unannounced withdrawal of HMRC's FAQs in relation to the anti-arbitrage rules came under some criticism in 2011—see Mehta, *Tax Journal* (7 October 2011), 9.

[242] 'Scheme' or 'arrangement' and 'UK tax advantage' are defined in TIOPA 2010, ss 258(1)–(5) and 234(1)–(3), ex F(No 2)A 2005, s 30.

[243] TIOPA 2010, ss 244(1)–(5), ex F(No 2)A 2005, s 25(3)–(5).

[244] TIOPA 2010, ss 239–242, 259, ex F(No 2)A 2005, Sch 3, paras (7)–(11).

[245] TIOPA 2010, ss 249–252, ex F(No 2)A 2005, s 26.

The correct amount treated as arising under this rule must be brought into the company's self-assessment, whether by making or amending its self-assessment.[246]

The G20/OECD Base Erosion and Profit Shifting (BEPS) project (see §69.11) identified international arbitrage using hybrids as an area requiring action. Action 2, 'Neutralizing the effect of hybrid mismatch arrangements' attempts to target the use of hybrid securities and entities to achieve double non-taxation, including long-term deferral.[247] According to the OECD, 'these types of arrangements are widespread and result in a substantial erosion of the taxable bases of the countries concerned. They have an overall negative impact on competition, efficiency, transparency and fairness.' At the beginning of the BEPS project, this area was thought to be 'low hanging fruit' but in fact it proved to be very difficult.[248] The final report on Action 2 is one of the longest (over 450 pages) and most detailed of all the BEPS action reports.

Action 2 targets hybrid mismatch arrangements producing three types of outcomes in particular:[249]

(1) payments that give rise to a deduction/no inclusion outcome (D/NI outcome), ie payments that are deductible under the rules of the payer jurisdiction and are not included in the ordinary income of the payee;
(2) payments that give rise to a double deduction outcome (DD outcome), ie payments that give rise to two deductions in respect of the same payment; and
(3) payments that give rise to an indirect D/NI outcome, ie payments that are deductible under the rules of the payer jurisdiction and that are set-off by the payee against a deduction under a hybrid mismatch arrangement.

The Action 2 final report provides recommendations for both domestic legislative responses (in Part 1) and changes to the OECD Model Treaty (in Part 2). In terms of domestic response, the OECD recommends 'linking rules' that align the tax treatment of an instrument or entity with the tax treatment in the counterparty jurisdiction but otherwise do not disturb the commercial outcomes.[250] The recommended primary rule is 'that countries deny the taxpayer's deduction for a payment to the extent that it is not included in the taxable income of the recipient in the counterparty jurisdiction or it is also deductible in the counterparty jurisdiction.'[251] Furthermore, if the primary rule is not applied, then 'the counterparty jurisdiction can generally apply a defensive rule, requiring the deductible payment to be included in income or denying the duplicate deduction depending on the nature of the mismatch.'[252] Following a period of consultation, the UK introduced new domestic anti-hybrid rules in FA 2016 to implement the Action 2 recommendations.[253] The main recommended changes to the OECD Model Treaty are a new provision and new detailed Commentary 'that will ensure that benefits of tax treaties are granted in appropriate cases

---

[246] TIOPA 2010, ss 254(1)–(3) and 250(4), ex F(No 2)A 2005, s 27.

[247] OECD, *BEPS Action 2 'Neutralizing the effect of hybrid mismatch arrangements' Final Report* (Oct 2015).

[248] Vella, Oxford tax lecture (February 2016).

[249] OECD, *BEPS Action 2 'Neutralizing the effect of hybrid mismatch arrangements' Final Report* (Oct 2015), 16–17.

[250] *Ibid*, 11.

[251] *Ibid*, 12.

[252] *Ibid*.

[253] See FA 2016, s 66 and Sch 10 and also HMRC, 'Policy Paper: Anti-Hybrid Rules', (December 2015).

to the income of [hybrid] entities but also that these benefits are not granted where neither State treats, under its domestic law, the income of such an entity as the income of one of its residents.'[254] Additional recomendations are intended to ensure the Model Treaty and Commentary are compatible with the recommended domestic legislative responses.[255]

62.8   The Patent Box

As part of its move towards a more competitive, territorial-focused and business-friendly UK corporate tax regime, the Government announced in its November 2010 Corporate Tax Roadmap plans to attract and encourage innovation in the UK by introducing a preferential rate of corporation tax of 10% for profits attributable to patents and other similar types of intellectual property (IP). The so-called 'patent box' regime was introduced by FA 2012, Schedule 2 as CTA 2010, Part 8A. The patent box was initially to be phased in over five years from 1 April 2013, and applies to existing IP as well as newly-commercialised IP. The regime is intended to apply to a proportion of profits derived from the sale or licensing of patent rights, or from the sale of patented inventions or products incorporating the patented invention.[256]

The main operative provision is section 357A of CTA 2010, which provides that a company may elect that any 'relevant IP profits' of a trade of the company for an accounting period for which it is a 'qualifying company' are chargeable at a special IP rate of corporation tax of 10%. Part 8A, Chapter 2 sets out the conditions for a 'qualifying company'. Pursuant to section 357B, the company must satisfy either condition A or B: condition A is that the company holds qualifying IP rights, or an exclusive licence in respect of qualifying IP rights; condition B is that the company held such rights in the past and has received income in respect of those rights. Section 357BB defines qualifying IP rights as, principally, UK or European Patent Office patents. A company that is a member of a group must satisfy an additional condition C, requiring active ownership and management of the IP rights. All companies must satisfy a further 'development condition' in section 357BC, which basically requires that they:

(1)   create or significantly contribute to the creation of items protected by the patent; or
(2)   perform a significant amount of activity for the purposes of developing items protected by the patent or any item incorporating protected items.

A company's 'relevant IP profits' are determined in accordance with a complex formulaic approach set out in Part 8A, Chapter 3. There are five broad types of profits that may qualify:

(1)   profits from the sale of the patented item, or an item incorporating it;
(2)   licence fees and royalties from rights the company grants others;
(3)   income from the sale or disposal of the patent;

---

[254] OECD, *BEPS Action 2 'Neutralizing the effect of hybrid mismatch arrangements' Final Report* (Oct 2015), 12.
[255] *Ibid.*
[256] As described in the HMRC Technical Note and Guide to the Draft Legislation, dated 6 December 2011.

(4) infringement receipts; and

(5) a notional arm's-length royalty for the use of the patent in other parts of the company.[257]

Section 357CJ provides a simpler 'small claims treatment' for qualifying profits of a company (and any associated companies) below £1 million—the company is able to allocate 75% of its qualifying profits to the patent box.

Chapter 4 provides an alternative method of determining relevant IP profits, known as 'streaming': see sections 357D *et seq*. Chapter 5 outlines rules in respect of relevant IP losses of a trade. Basically, patent box losses must be offset against current year patent box profits of other companies in the group, or be carried forward against the company's own future patent box profits. The obligatory anti-avoidance rules are found in Chapter 6 and attempt to prevent companies from seeking to obtain an artificial tax advantage by inflating their patent box profits.

In November 2014, in the midst of the G20/OECD BEPS project (see §69.11), the UK entered into what might be described as side-discussions with Germany about the UK's patent box regime. Germany had a general concern with such regimes, and with the UK's in particular, especially in light of the work being undertaken by the OECD in the Forum on Harmful Tax Practices and in BEPS, and a review of patent box regimes in the EU by the European Commission. The UK ultimately agreed to modify its patent box regime in line with the modified nexus approach proposed by the OECD, which requires tax benefits to be connected directly to research and development expenditures.[258] As part of the compromise reached with Germany, it was agreed that related party outsourcing or acquisition costs incurred that is not qualifying expenditure will give rise to a maximum of a 30% uplift in qualifying expenditure included within the formula, subject to a cap. The changes will be phased in from June 2016. At Budget 2016, the Government announced it would legislate to make the lower tax rate dependant on, and proportional to, the extent of research and development expenditure incurred by the company claiming the relief.[259] This is consistent with BEPS Action 5 (see below §69.10). The UK plans to close the existing regime to new entrants from June 2016, and abolish its patent box completely by 30 June 2021. The expectation is that a new beneficial tax incentive for IP agreed on by all EU member states will be implemented well before then; the 2021 expiry date is meant to provide ample time for transition to the new regime.

---

[257] *Ibid.*

[258] See joint UK-Germany statement on proposals for new rules for preferential IP regimes, available at https://www.gov.uk/government/uploads/system/uploads/attachment_data/file/373135/GERMANY_UK_STATEMENT.pdf.

[259] See https://www.gov.uk/government/publications/corporation-tax-patent-box-compliance-with-new-international-rules.

63

Computation (2): Accounting-based Rules for Specific Transactions

63.1 Introduction

In this chapter we look at four sets of tax rules which draw heavily on accounting concepts: loan relationships (including foreign exchange transactions, §63.2), derivatives (previously called financial instruments, §63.3), fixed asset intangibles or intellectual property (§63.4) and certain rules about the currency to be used in calculating profits (§63.5). They are treated together because they raise similar problems and because they were for a time the leading edge area of tax law as the UK moved from the ideas of 1803 towards the world of accounting principles—but only for corporation tax.

The modern financial world offers products which fragment a transaction into different elements and then reconstitute them in a different way with different tax results; other products enable the risk inherent in a transaction to be removed and sold (shifted) to someone else. Matters began to get out of hand (from a tax point of view) when corporate finance theory developed in the 1960s. A typical example was the put-call parity theorem.[1] Using the language of options, where 'put' means sell and 'call' means buy, this theorem stated that if one holds shares but takes out an option to sell shares (a put option), one is in exactly the same economic position as having debt and an option to buy shares (a call option). Thus one is able to turn any pure equity position into a pure debt position (or vice versa) by taking out the appropriate option. An option is one example of a category called derivative instruments, so called because they derive their values from something else.

Faced with this fragmented world, the tax system could do any one or more of five things:[2]

(1)   move away from its traditional basis of taxing income when realised and a capital gain only when the asset was disposed of, in favour of a new accounting basis such as mark-to-market or fair value, or whatever other practices the accountants manage to devise;

(2)   integrate the financial products by treating them as one and taxing the unit according to its economic substance;

(3)   bifurcate products into separate parts and tax each according to economic substance;

(4)   develop specific formulae for specific products; or

(5)   limit the deduction of expenses associated with the product unless the income is taxed currently.

UK corporation tax has opted for (1) in the areas considered in this chapter, but has developed as accounting practice has developed. Income tax and CGT, by contrast, have been left to struggle with the traditional concepts, subject only to ITTOIA 2005, section 25 for income tax.

The topics discussed in this chapter involve very technical and detailed legislation. What follows is an examination of the key elements of the various regimes.

63.2   Loan Relationships

63.2.1   Introduction

63.2.1.1   Structure and Development

Since 1 April 1996, corporate and government debt have been subject to a single regime called 'loan relationships'.[3] The scheme brings together rules governing (1) income and

---

[1]   See, generally, Warren (1993) 107 *HLR* 460; and Colloquium on Financial Instruments (1995) 50 *Tax L Rev* 487.

[2]   Schenk (1995) 50 *Tax L Rev* 571, summarising Warren, *op cit*.

[3]   CTA 2009, Pts 5–7, ex FA 1996, ss 80–105, Schs 8–11, all as much amended. The ideas are explained in Revenue Consultative Document, *Taxation of Gilts and Bonds* (May 1995). See Hole [1995] BTR 511 and [1996] BTR 347. For the likely source of inspiration, see New Zealand Treasury Consultative Document (October 1986); for a review of New Zealand legislation, see Smith (1998) 46 *Can Tax Jo* 819 and Glazebrook *et al*, *The New Zealand Accruals Regime: A practical guide* (CCH New Zealand, 1999). There is very useful guidance in the HMRC *Corporate Finance Manual* at http://www.hmrc.gov.uk/manuals/cfmmanual/cfm30000.htm.

expenses arising on debt and (2) gains or losses arising from the holding of a financial instrument.

The modern loan relationships legislation has developed in five principal stages—1996, 2002, 2004, 2009 and 2015. The first stage was the introduction of the loan relationship rules in FA 1996. The second and third stages both took the form of amending the original 1996 legislation. FA 2002 made two major sets of changes with different timescales. The first consisted of a series of changes designed to prevent avoidance and was generally dated back to their announcement to the House of Commons.[4] The second was a major rewriting of the loan relationships rules to take account of experience since 1996,[5] and to incorporate into the loan relationships rules most of the provisions relating to FOREX transactions.[6] FA 2004 introduced changes to incorporate the general move to generally-accepted accounting practice (GAAP), whether UK or under International Accounting Standards (IASs).

In the fourth stage, FA 2009 rewrote the existing legislation into CTA 2009, Parts 5–7. FA 2009 also added two main sets of rules. Firstly, sections 486A–486E were introduced to deal with disguised interest payments. The detail of those rules is way beyond a book such as this; interested readers are directed to the HMRC manual.[7] Secondly, sections 521A–521F were added to deal with shares accounted as liabilities. Further anti-avoidance provisions were added with some regularity in successive years' Finance Acts.

The fifth stage is the product of an important HMRC consultation in 2013 to 'modernise' the taxation of corporate debt and derivative contracts.[8] According to the consultation document, the Government's aim was 'providing simpler and fairer tax treatment, minimising the scope for abuse, reducing uncertainty and improving structural and legislative clarity as well as reducing administrative burdens.' It is noteworthy that the consultation document emphasised that '[t]he Government is also conscious of the history of tax avoidance associated with these financial instruments.' Following on from the consultation, F(No 2)A 2015 made significant structural changes to the loan relationships regime and also introduced a powerful new regime TAAR.[9] The primary structural change was to clarify how the loan relationships regime rely on accounting rules. The need for clarity arose partly out of changes to the accounting rules themselves over time—including the eventual introduction of a new UK GAAP in 2015 in the form of FRS 102 (see above §21.1.2.2)—and also partly to respond to a growing body of cases in which amounts recognised in taxpayers' accounts differed from what HMRC thought should be recognised.[10]

The loan relationships regime as amended over the years represents a significant rationalisation of the scope of the tax charge on debt, with more coherent rules for both receipts and expenditure. The intricacies flowing from having one set of rules for capital gains and another (but chaotic) set for income were swept away. In addition, many special statutory provisions introduced over a number of years to deal with special situations were abolished

---

[4] FA 2002, ss 71–78.

[5] FA 2002, Sch 25.

[6] CTA 2009, s 328, ex FA 1996, s 84A, added by FA 2002, s 79; see Lindsay [2002] BTR 292–96.

[7] See http://www.hmrc.gov.uk/manuals/cfmmanual/CFM42010.htm.

[8] See https://www.gov.uk/government/consultations/modernising-the-taxation-of-corporate-debt-and-derivative-contracts.

[9] F(No 2)A 2015, s 32 and Sch 7. For commentary see Challen [2015] BTR 624.

[10] *Greene King plc v HMRC* [2014] UKUT 178 (TCC) and *GDF Suez Teesside Ltd (Formerly Teesside Power Ltd) v HMRC* [2015] UKFTT 413 (TC). See also Challen, ibid, 625.

for corporation tax.[11] However, this is not to say that everything has moved to a Haig-Simons world of comprehensive income taxation. While the distinction between capital and income is abandoned, that between trading and non-trading is not. Relief for trade interest expense is obtained by bringing the expense into the calculation of the company's trading profit subject to tax under CTA 2009, Part 3;[12] tax relief for non-trade interest is dealt with in a separate provision in the loan relationships regime, CTA 2009, section 301.[13] Although the rules do not usually turn on the actual time when payments are made, that issue remains important for other reasons.[14]

63.2.1.2 Practical Issues[15]

Borrowers and their advisers want to know the answers to the following questions:

— Are the sums paid in respect of loans deductible and, if so, when?
— Will the interest payment be subject to withholding tax?
— Is the benefit received from a premium or a discount taxable—whether on redemption or earlier?
— How is the lender/investor taxed, and does he get any tax benefit which could be shared with the other party?

The lenders/investors want to know the answers to the equivalent questions in reverse:

— Are the sums paid in respect of loans taxable and, if so, when?
— Will the sums paid be subject to withholding tax?
— Will the premium or discount on redemption be taxable and, if so, when?
— Will any special tax benefit be obtained which could be shared with the other party?

63.2.2 *Loan Relationship—Definition*

A loan relationship[16] occurs whenever:

(1) a company is a debtor or a creditor in respect of a money debt which arose as a result of a transaction for the lending of money; or
(2) an instrument is issued for the purpose of representing security for, or the rights of a creditor in respect of, a money debt.[17]

---

[11] These are the accrued income scheme and the statutory provisions for deep discounted securities.
[12] CTA 2009, s 297, ex FA 1996, s 82(2).
[13] Ex FA 1996, s 82(3).
[14] Eg CTA 2009, s 464 and 465, ex FA 1996, Sch 9, para 2 (interest due between connected parties).
[15] This list adapted gratefully from Murphy, 'Interest and Currency Management', in *Tolley's Tax Planning 1999–2000*, 865.
[16] CTA 2009, ss 302 and 303, ex FA 1996, s 81(1).
[17] CTA 2009, s 303(3), ex FA 1996, s 81; a money debt is one which falls to be settled by the payment of money or the transfer of a right to settlement, such as by the issue of a security or 'by the issue or transfer of any share in any company' (s 303(1)(a), ex s 81(2), the words quoted added by FA 2008, Sch 4, para 10—to prevent avoidance).

The HMRC Corporate Finance Manual provides a useful list of examples of loan relationships;[18]

— overdrafts, mortgages, bank loans and other borrowings
— bank deposits and building society shares and deposits
— inter-company and directors' loan accounts where there is lending of money (but not where these accounts simply reflect the supply of goods and services)
— company bonds, loan notes and debentures
— eurobonds
— bills of exchange
— commercial paper
— certificates of deposit
— gilts and government stock
— funding bonds

Examples that are not loan relationships are:

— distributions, including interest recharacterised as a distribution by the operation of the rules in CTA 2010, section 1000 *et seq* eg interest above a commercial rate of return[19]
— ordinary and preference shares
— debts for the supply of goods and services, or arising from leasing or hire purchase arrangements
— rents
— payments made as a result of guaranteeing another person's liabilities

A guarantee is not within (1) because, in order for a loan relationship to exist, the company must be a creditor or a debtor, and a guarantor is not, itself, in that relationship.[20] This does not stop relief as a trading expense for a loss on a guarantee being given if the company carries on a trade of providing guarantees. In (2) the critical words are 'instrument' and 'security'. The issue of an insurance policy is not the issue of a security, neither is the issue of a share.[21] Loan notes and promissory notes are instruments; if no instrument is issued, the debt cannot come within (2).[22]

Gains and losses on annual valuations of debts, or on other events such as the purchase or sale of securities, which are called 'related transactions', are brought into the CTA 2009, Part 5 scheme only if there is a loan relationship.[23] However, interest on money debts is brought within the rules whether or not there is a loan relationship due to the rules in CTA 2009, Part 6 concerning 'relationships treated as loan relationships'. Thus, interest arising from a

---

[18] HMRC Corporate Finance Manual, CFM30150.
[19] CTA 2009, s 465.
[20] HMRC Corporate Finance Manual, CFM31100.
[21] CTA 2009, s 303(4), ex FA 1996, s 81(4). See also HMRC *Corporate Finance Manual*, CFM31070.
[22] Statement by the Economic Secretary to the Treasury, HC Official Report, col 613, 28 February 1996. See also HMRC *Corporate Finance Manual*, CFM31060.
[23] CTA 2009, ss 479–481, ex FA 1996, s 100(1), (2).

trade creditor is aggregated with other interest even though it does not arise as a result of a money-lending transaction and thus is not a loan relationship, as is interest computed under judgment debts and under the transfer pricing legislation.[24] Profits from the disposal of interest and from all discounts are also included.[25] Other examples of deemed loan relationships involve collective investment schemes, shares with guaranteed returns, returns from partnerships, manufactured interest, repos, and certain life insurance contracts.[26]

63.2.3 Debits, Credits and Timing

63.2.3.1 The General Rule: Follow GAAP

The all-important general rule is that the amounts brought into account as credits (eg interest income) or debits (eg interest expense) under the loan relationships rules are those that are recognised in determining the company's profit or loss in the period in accordance with GAAP.[27] Matters in respect of which amounts are to be brought into account are (a) the profits and losses of the company arising from its loan relationships and related transactions, (b) interest under those relationships and (c) expenses incurred by the company under or for the purposes of those relationships.[28] The key concept of 'related transaction' is defined in CTA 2009, section 304 as any disposal or acquisition (in whole or in part) of rights and liabilities under a loan relationship, including where rights or liabilities under the loan relationship are transferred or extinguished by any sale, gift, exchange, surrender, redemption or release. Where interest paid is capitalised by the payer, the interest is, nevertheless, brought into the calculation for tax purposes and relief is obtained; the relief is granted on an accruals basis.[29]

63.2.3.2 Expenses

Section 306A also specifies the expenses for which relief is available. They are restricted to expenses incurred directly:

(1)　in bringing the loan relationship into existence;
(2)　in entering into or giving effect to any of the related transactions;
(3)　in making payments under those relationships or as a result of those transactions; or
(4)　in taking steps to ensure the receipt of payments under any of those relationships or in accordance with any of those transactions.

Abortive expenditure is specifically allowed, provided it falls within the categories of expenditure that are permitted where a project is taken to its anticipated conclusion.[30]

---

[24] CTA 2009, s 477 et seq. See also HMRC *Corporate Finance Manual*, CFM30200 and CFM41000.

[25] CTA 2009, s 480, ex FA 1996, s 100(1A) and related changes made by F(No 2)A 2005, Sch 7, para 12 and by FA 2006, Sch 6, para 17—to prevent avoidance; see relevant HMRC Notes on Clauses.

[26] See HMRC *Corporate Finance Manual*, CFM41000.

[27] CTA 2009, s 307(2), ex FA 1996, ss 85A and 85B. F(No 2) 2015, Sch 7 simplified the scope of section 307, which formerly required that credits and debts should 'fairly represent' the profits and losses and also referred to particular accounting statements: see Challen [2015] BTR 625–26.

[28] CTA 2009, s 306A.

[29] CTA 2009, s 320, ex FA 1996, Sch 9, para 14. Relief is also given for the capitalised costs of obtaining loan finance written off over the life of the loan, as required by FRS 4.

[30] CTA 2009, s 329(1), (2), ex FA 1996, s 84(4).

63.2.3.3 Sums

Sums included are interest payable, interest receivable, any discount, premiums, gains and losses arising from the disposal of the instrument, any reimbursement required to a lender, the costs of obtaining loan finance such as bank fees, abortive expenditure in respect of loan finance which is not drawn down, early redemption penalties and any costs in pursuing debtors.[31]

63.2.4 *GAAP and Basis of Accounting*

CTA 2009, section 307(2) directs that the amounts to be brought into account are those which, in accordance with GAAP, are recognised in determining the profit or loss for the period. Where the company's accounts do not confirm to GAAP, the correct GAAP principles are to be applied.[32] If the company uses correct accounts for the period but has used incorrect accounts for an earlier period, the correct treatment is applied to that earlier period if this is relevant.[33]

Section 308 provides more guidance on the amounts recognised in determining a company's profit or loss, and was comprehensively revised by F(No 2)A 2015. It refers not only to amounts recognised in the company's accounts as an item of profit or loss, but also amounts previously recognised as an item of 'other comprehensive income' that is transferred to become an item of profit or loss in determining the company's profit or loss for the period. The meaning of both types of item are the meaning they have for accounting purposes.

Section 303 provides another important general rule—that the amounts to be brought into account by a company as credits and debits for any period of account may be determined on any basis of accounting that is in accordance with GAAP, except as otherwise specified. The section then sets out a list of exceptions where the use of one of two bases is required—the 'amortised cost' basis and the 'fair value' basis.[34] In essence, fair value accounting recognises as items of profit or loss not only interest payments but also changes in the value of the underlying rights and liabilities. It must be used for eg index-linked gilt-edged securities and company partners. 'Amortised cost basis' means a basis under which an asset or a liability representing the loan is shown in the company's accounts at cost, adjusted for cumulative amortisation. It must be used eg where the parties have a connection.

At one time there was a separate rule giving relief for bad debts.[35] As the concept of amortisation includes relief for 'impairment', there was no need for this separate rule and the term 'bad debt' was replaced by 'impairment losses'. There is still a need for a rule governing releases, and this removes the taxable credit that would otherwise arise in the circumstances stated.[36] There are also rules on the relationship between consortium group relief and impairment losses,[37] impairment losses where the parties are connected,[38] and

---

[31] HMRC Corporate Finance Manual, CFM31040.
[32] CTA 2009, s 309, ex FA 1996, s 85A(2).
[33] CTA 2009, s 309(2), ex FA 1996, s 85A(3).
[34] CTA 2009, s 313(4), (4A), (5) and s 476.
[35] FA 1996, Sch 9, para 5 (original version).
[36] CTA 2009, ss 322(1), (2), 358(1), (2) and 359(1), (2), ex FA 1996, Sch 9, para 5(3).
[37] CTA 2009, ss 364–371, ex FA 1996, Sch 9, para 5A.
[38] CTA 2009, ss 353–360, ex FA 1996, Sch 9, para 6.

insolvency.[39] Where there is a release of a liability concerning the writing off a government investment, the sum is credited in the period of the release.[40]

63.2.5 Tax Consequences of Loan Relationships

The legislation distinguishes 'trade' purposes from 'non-trade' purposes in determining the tax consequences of debits (eg interest expense) and credits (eg interest income) under the loan relationships rules.

63.2.5.1 Trading debits and credits

Where the company is a party to a loan relationship for the purposes of a trade carried on by it—[41] including, therefore, interest payable on a loan to purchase a trading asset—the debits (eg interest expense of the debtor on the loan as determined under GAAP) in respect of the relationship for the period are treated as expenses of the trade which are deductible in calculating its trading profits under CTA 2009, Part 3.[42] A stricter test applies where the company is the creditor rather than the debtor; here, the loan must be an integral part of the trade, eg interest income earned by a bank.[43] If the test is satisfied, the credits (eg interest income as determined under GAAP) in respect of the relationship for the period are treated as receipts of the trade which are to be brought into account in calculating the company's trading profits for that period under CTA 2009, Part 3.

63.2.5.2 Non-trading debits and credits

Non-trading debits and credits are aggregated each accounting period and brought into the calculation of the sum subject to income tax under CTA 2009, section 301.[44] A company with a non-trading deficit on its loan relationships (ie where debits exceed credits) may claim for the whole or part of the deficit to be set against any of its profits of the deficit period unless it has been surrendered for group relief,[45] to be carried back against profits of earlier accounting periods;[46] or, if not surrendered for group relief, to be carried forward as a deficit to be set against non-trading profits of the next accounting period.[47] It is convenient to follow the statute and use 'deficit' rather than 'loss' to describe an excess of debits over credits to avoid confusion with other types of loss.

63.2.5.3 Carry-back of Deficits

Priority is given for relief against profits of the current accounting period.[48] The carry-back of a non-trading deficit is against any profits of the preceding 12 months, with relief

---

[39] CTA 2009, s 357, ex FA 1996, Sch 9, paras 6B and 6C.

[40] CTA 2009, s 326, ex FA 1996, Sch 9, para 7.

[41] CTA 2009, s 297, ex FA 1996, s 82(2).

[42] CTA 2009, s 297, ex FA 1996, s 82(2).

[43] CTA 2009, s 298, ex FA 1996, s 103(2); and HMRC *Corporate Finance Manual*, CFM32020; see also *Nuclear Electricity plc Ltd v Bradley* [1996] STC 405, 68 TC 670, HL, above at §4.5.1.2.

[44] CTA 2009, s 301(2), (4), (6), ex FA 1996, s 82(3). Interest incurred on pre-trading loans is the subject of a special provision (TA 1988, s 401(1AC)).

[45] CTA 2009, s 459(1)(a), ex FA 1996, s 83(2)(a). On making the claim, see also s 461.

[46] CTA 2009, s 459(1)(b), ex FA 1996, s 83(2)(c). On making the claim, see also s 462.

[47] CTA 2009, s 457, ex FA 1996, s 83(3A)(a). On making the claim, see also s 458.

[48] CTA 2009, ss 461(5), (6) and 462(5), ex FA 1996, Sch 8, para 3(2).

being applied in a later year before an earlier year.[49] Certain other current year reliefs must be used before carry-back relief is allowed.[50] These include CTA 2010, section 37 trading losses, CTA 2009, section 459(1)(a) deficit set-offs, and charitable donations relief under CTA 2010, Part 6.

63.2.9 Miscellaneous Rules

The loan relationships scheme contains many more rules, including special rules for transactions between connected parties[51] and for special types of securities such as gilt strips.[52] A rule directs tax-neutral continuity of treatment of related transactions between the members of the same group.[53] There are also rules on manufactured interest.[54] Separate regimes deal with collective investment schemes and insurers.[55] Where a loan giving rise to a charge under CTA 2010, section 455 is written off in favour of a participator (see further §10.4.5), no debit arises under the loan relationship rules.[56] A detailed discussion of these rules is beyond the scope of this book.

63.2.7 Anti-avoidance

There are a number of specific anti-avoidance rules, and a powerful regime TAAR. One of the specific rules deals with the importing of a loan relationship where a loss arose at a time when the relationship was not subject to UK tax, and excludes such losses unless fair value accounting is used.[57] Another imposes special valuation rules where the transaction is not made at arm's length.[58]

A more wide-ranging rule bars relief for debits where or to the extent that the loan relationship was incurred for an 'unallowable purpose';[59] this bar extends not just to the loan relationship rules but for any other rule of corporation tax.[60] This tainting purpose may arise from the loan relationship itself, or from a related transaction. Although a business or commercial purpose is normally an allowable purpose, this will not be so if the purpose relates to an activity not within the charge to corporation tax, eg the purposes of an overseas subsidiary. A tax avoidance purpose is not a business purpose unless it is not the main or one of the main purposes—the concept of tax avoidance takes its familiar meaning in terms of a tax advantage under CTA 2010, section 732. The Revenue will not give advice on the

---

[49] CTA 2009, s 459(1)(b), ex FA 1996, s 83(2)(c), Sch 8, para 3.
[50] CTA 2009, s 463(5), ex FA 1996, Sch 8, para 3(6).
[51] CTA 2009, Pt 5, Ch 5, and note that the 2013 consultation proposed abolishing the special rules for connected party debt and intra-group transfers of loan relationships.
[52] CTA 2009, ss 401–403, ex FA 1996, s 95.
[53] CTA 2009, Pt 5, Ch 4, ex FA 1996, Sch 9, para 12, amended by F(No 2)A 2005, Sch 7, paras 17 and 18.
[54] CTA 2009, ss 539–541, ex FA 1996, s 97 and F(No 2)A 2005, Sch 7, para 11.
[55] CTA 2009, Pt 5, Chs 10–11, ex FA 1996, Schs 10 and 11.
[56] CTA 2009, s 321A, added by FA 2010, s 43, for releases, etc on or after 24 March 2010.
[57] CTA 2009, s 327, ex FA 1996, Sch 9, para 10.
[58] CTA 2009, ss 444–452, ex FA 1996, Sch 9, paras 11 and 11A (exchange transactions).
[59] CTA 2009, s 441–442, ex FA 1996, Sch 9, para 13; note [1997] *Simon's Weekly Tax Intelligence* 544. F(No 2)A 2015 made a number of clarificatory changes to the 'unallowable purpose' rules in CTA 2009, sections 441–442.
[60] CTA 2009, s 441(4),(5), ex FA 1996, Sch 9, para 13(1A) added by FA 2002.

meaning of the term beyond the recitation of a ministerial mantra.[61] Other rules give tax-neutral continuity of treatment for loan relationship transactions on a group basis, with intra-group transactions generally ignored.[62] These rules were refined by FA 2003, 2005 and 2006 to prevent avoidance.[63]

F(No 2)A 2015 introduced a detailed set of rules that apply where a company recognises profits or losses at a time when it is not yet, or is no longer, party to the relevant loan relationship, or where the company is economically exposed to the loan relationship without technically being a party to it.[64] In these circumstances, the company is required to bring into account loan relationship credits or debits accordingly.

Most importantly, F(No 2)A 2015 also introduced a powerful new anti-avoidance provision known as the 'regime TAAR' in CTA 2009, sections 455B to 455D.[65] An indication of HMRC's faith in the regime TAAR is that its introduction coincided with the repeal of a number of specific anti-avoidance rules. By the combination of sections 455B and 455C, the regime TAAR counteracts the effect of 'relevant avoidance arrangements', which are arrangements that have a main purpose of enabling a company to obtain a 'loan-related tax advantage'. A company obtains a loan-related tax advantage if it brings into account a greater debit than it would otherwise have been entitled to, the amount of any credit it brings into account is lower than it would otherwise have been, or it brings a debit or credit into account earlier or later than it otherwise would.[66] Section 455C(4) provides an important carve-out: arrangements are not 'relevant avoidance arrangements if the obtaining of any loan-related tax advantages that would arise from them can reasonably be regarded as consistent with any principles on which the provisions of CTA 2009, Part 5 that are relevant to the arrangements are based (whether expressed or implied) and the policy objectives of those provisions.

Section 455D sets out a number of features which might indicate that the arrangements are not consistent with the principles of the legislation. These include where economic profits arising to the company from a loan relationship are reduced or eliminated for corporation tax purposes; the creation of deductible expenses where for economic purposes no loss or expense, or a smaller loss or expense, arises from the relationship; preventing or delaying the recognition as an item of profit or loss of an amount in the company's accounts; and ensuring that a loan relationship is treated for accounting purposes in a way in which it would not otherwise have been treated in the absence of some other transaction forming part of the arrangements.

If the regime TAAR applies, section 455B provides that the counteraction takes the form of such adjustments as are just and reasonable to the credits and debits to be brought into account for the purposes of Part 5.

---

[61] For terms of mantra, see Hansard, Finance Bill Report Stage, cols 1192–93, 28 March 1996; reprinted in HMRC *Corporate Finance Manual*, CFM38170. The section is not to be applied without reference to CD(SIS 1); see *Corporation Tax Manual*, para 12681.

[62] CTA 2009, Pt 5, Ch 4, ex FA 1996, Sch 9, para 12.

[63] Eg CTA 2009, ss 340(8), 341(1)–(4), ex FA 1996, Sch 9, para 12(2A), added by FA 2006, Sch 6, para 19.

[64] CTA 2009, ss 330A to 330C.

[65] For commentary see Challen [2015] BTR 624.

[66] CTA 2009, s 455C(5).

63.2.8 Foreign Exchange

As has been indicated in the text above, the rule on FOREX is now part of the loan relationships regime. The operative provision is CTA 2009, section 328, and in particular subsection (1), which states that the reference in section 306A(1) to the profits and losses arising
to a company from its loan relationships and related transactions includes a reference to
exchange gains and losses so arising. The area is of historic interest as it was the first one to
be modernised—by FA 1993—which was brought into force in 1996 at the same time as the
loan relationship and financial instrument (now derivative) rules. The exchange gains may
arise from an asset or a liability, or where a branch profit is translated. The Treasury may, by
regulation, prescribe gains which are to be disregarded.

63.2.9 BEPS and Restrictions on Interest Deductibility

The G20/OECD Base Erosion and Profit Shifting (BEPS) project (see §69.11) advocated
domestic law restrictions on interest deductibility as an important anti-BEPS response.
In the final report on Action 4, 'Limiting Base Erosion Involving Interest Deductions and
Other Financial Payments', the OECD identified three basic BEPS scenarios involving interest and financing expenses:[67]

(1)   groups placing higher levels of third party debt in high tax countries;
(2)   groups using intragroup loans to generate interest deductions in excess of the group's
      actual third party interest expense; and
(3)   groups using third party or intragroup financing to fund the generation of tax exempt
      income.

The Action 4 final report analyses several best practices to target these practices. The main
recommendation is that countries adopt a 'fixed ratio rule which limits an entity's net
deductions for interest and payments economically equivalent to interest to a percentage of
its earnings before interest, taxes, depreciation and amortisation (EBITDA).'[68] As a minimum the OECD recommends that this fixed ratio rule should apply to entities in multinational groups though it could be extended more broadly. The report suggested the fixed
ratio be set between 10% and 30%, and included factors which countries should take into
account in setting their fixed ratio within this range.[69] For example, a country may apply a
ratio towards the higher end of the range if it also has other targeted rules to address BEPS
risks or if interest rates are comparatively high in that country.[70]
    The problem with a 'one-size fits all' fixed-ratio approach is that it fails to take into
account that some groups are highly leveraged with third party debt for non-tax reasons.
To address this concern, the Action 4 final report proposes a 'group ratio rule' alongside the fixed ratio rule, which 'would allow an entity with net interest expense above a

---

[67] OECD, BEPS Action 4 'Limiting Base Erosion Involving Interest Deductions and Other Financial Payments'
Final Report (Oct 2015), 11.
    [68] *Ibid.*
    [69] *Ibid.*
    [70] *Ibid.*

country's fixed ratio to deduct interest up to the level of the net interest/EBITDA ratio of its worldwide group'.[71] If a country does not introduce a group ratio rule, the report recommends that the country apply the fixed ratio rule 'to entities in multinational and domestic groups without improper discrimination'.[72] Other suggestions include an uplift of up to 10% to the group's net third party interest expense to prevent double taxation, a carryforward of disallowed deductions/unused capacity under the formula for use in future years, a *de minimas* threshold and so-called 'equity escape' rules—which compares an entity's level of equity and assets to those held by its group—as an alternative to a group ratio rule.[73]

In 2015 the UK government consulted on introducing restrictions on interest deductibility in line with the OECD's recommendations in Action 4.[74] In the 2016 Business Tax Road Map, the Government confirmed that it plans to introduce a restriction on the tax deductibility of corporate interest expense consistent with the OECD recommendations.[75] At the time of writing a further consultation on the details of the new rules was underway.[76] The new interest limitation rules, which will apply from 1 April 2017, look set to include a fixed ratio rule limiting corporation tax deductions for net interest expense to 30% of a group's UK EBITDA. In recognition that some groups may have high external gearing for genuine commercial purposes, the UK will also be implementing a group ratio rule based on the net interest /EBITDA ratio for the worldwide group as recommended in the OECD Action 4 final report. The new rules will include a *de minimis* group threshold of £2 million net of UK interest expense, which is expected to exclude 95% of groups from the rules. Rules will also be introduced to protect the provision of private finance for certain public infrastructure in the UK where there are no material risks of BEPS. Further rules will address volatility in earnings and interest. Finally, the existing worldwide debt cap will be repealed and incorporated into the new rules (see also §64.9).

Although a 30% of EBITDA cap on interest expense is at the generous end of the Action 4 recommendation, this nevertheless represents a seismic change in UK tax policy. For many years politicians have trumpeted the UK's comparatively generous rules on interest deductibility as an important feature of the UK's competitiveness on tax internationally. This was clearly evident in the Government's 2010 Corporate Tax Road Map, which stated 'The UK's current interest rules, which do not significantly restrict relief for interest, are considered by businesses as a competitive advantage and it is the Government's view that this advantage outweighs potential benefits from moving towards a more territorial system for interest.'[77]

---

[71] *Ibid*, 50.

[72] *Ibid*, 12.

[73] *Ibid*.

[74] HM Treasury, 'Consultation on Tax Deductibility of Corporate Interest Expense', (October 2015). See also HMRC, 'Policy Paper: Anti-Hybrid Rules', (as updated December 2015) and Collier, Devereux and Maffini, *Response to the Consultation on the Tax Deductibility of Corporate Interest Expense* (OUCBT, 2016).

[75] HM Treasury, *Business Tax Road Map*, (March 2016), paras 2.30–2.37.

[76] HM Treasury, 'Consultation on Tax Deductibility of Corporate Interest Expense', (as updated 26 May 2016), available at https://www.gov.uk/government/consultations/tax-deductibility-of-corporate-interest-expense/tax-deductibility-of-corporate-interest-expense-consultation.

[77] Vella, Oxford tax lecture (February 2016) citing UK Government, *The Corporate Tax Road Map* (2010), [3.8], available at https://www.gov.uk/government/uploads/system/uploads/attachment_data/file/193239/Corporation_tax_road_map.pdf.

63.3 Derivatives

63.3.1 Introduction

As with loan relationships, so here FA 2004 made major changes to the derivative legislation for accounting periods beginning on or after 1 January 2005.[78] F(No 2)A 2015 made further major structural changes. Like the loan relationship changes, these build on the IP rule precedents (§63.4) and give GAAP direct, as opposed to indirect, effect. For accounting periods not under FA 2004 but beginning on or after 1 October 2002, the rules were to be found in FA 2002, section 83 and Schedules 26–28; these were a complete rewrite of the 'financial instruments' regime enacted by FA 1994 and not, as with loans relationships, a change to the original rules. The 2002 changes made the rules for derivatives closer to those for loan relationships. The 2004 rules prepare the way for the use of GAAP, whether UK or IAS. The 2015 changes now require all UK companies to use either International Financial Reporting Standards (IFRS) or UK GAAP (FRS 102) for their entity level accounts.[79]

The current rules, now rewritten as CTA 2009, Part 7, apply to all profits arising to a company from its derivative contracts and treat the profits as income.[80] There is no deduction at source.

63.3.2 Derivative Contracts: Definitions

The model for many of these definitions is the Regulated Activities Order 2001 (SI 2001/544), articles 83–85. A derivative contract is (a) an option, (b) a future, or (c) a contract for differences (CfD).[81] These terms are defined in CTA 2009, sections 580–582. An option includes a warrant.[82] A future is a contract to sell property with delivery at a later date but agreed at the time of the contract and at a price agreed then, too. A contract which includes a term not for the delivery of property but for the payment of a cash sum is not within (a) or (b)[83] but may come within (c). The term 'contract for differences' is defined at some length.[84] It is a contract the purpose or pretended purpose of which is to make a profit or avoid a loss by reference to fluctuations in (a) the value or price of property described in the contract, or (b) an index or other factor designated in the contract.[85] For the purposes of sub-paragraph (b), an index or other factor may be determined by reference to any matter and, for those purposes, a numerical value may be attributed to any variation in a matter.

Certain matters are excluded from being a CfD.[86] These are: (a) an option; (b) a future; (c) a contract of insurance; (d) a capital redemption policy; (e) a contract of indemnity; (f) a guarantee; (g) a warranty; (h) a loan relationship. As already noted, a 'future' is a contract

---

[78] Lindsay [2004] BTR 468.
[79] For commentary see Challen [2015] BTR 627–28.
[80] CTA 2009, s 571(1), ex FA 2002, Sch 26, para 1—based on FA 1996, s 80(1); see Ball [2002] BTR 296.
[81] CTA 2009, s 576 and 577, ex FA 2002, Sch 26, para 2.
[82] CTA 2009, s 580(1), ex FA 2002, Sch 26, para 12(8).
[83] CTA 2009, s 581, ex FA 2002, Sch 26, para 12(10).
[84] For an example of when it matters whether a contract is a CfD or some other type of derivative, see ex FA 2002, Sch 26, para 46, allowing apportionment for futures and options but not for CfDs.
[85] CTA 2009, s 582(1), ex FA 2002, Sch 26, para 12(3) and (4).
[86] CTA 2009, s 582(2), ex FA 2002, Sch 26, para 12(5).

for the sale of property under which delivery is to be made at a future date agreed when the contract is made, and at a price so agreed; but this is followed by further language glossing the notion of a price being agreed when the contract is made where the price relates to a market or can be adjusted by reference to a certain level of quality or quantity. An 'option' is stated to include a warrant, which is then defined as an instrument which entitles the holder to subscribe for shares in a company or assets representing a loan relationship of a company; for these purposes it is immaterial whether the shares or assets to which the warrant relates exist or are identifiable.

A contract cannot be a future or option for these purposes if the contract does not provide for the delivery of property but for a settlement by cash payments—such a contract is treated as a CfD and so may still be a derivative but of a different sort.[87] However, a future or option the underlying subject matter of which is currency is included as a future or option.

63.3.3 Subject Matter Narrowed

The contract must meet one of three tests to be a relevant contract for these rules:

(1) The contract must be treated as a derivative financial instrument for accounting purposes.[88]
(2) It must be treated as a financial asset for accounting purposes, though this applies only to certain types of such contract.[89]
(3) The third test is satisfied where the underlying subject matter[90] of the contract is either commodities, or a CfD where the underlying subject matter is intangible fixed assets, weather conditions or creditworthiness.[91]

The presence of certain underlying subject matters, in whole or in part, will often prevent Part 7 from applying; the list includes real assets such as land, shares and loan relationships, as well as tangible movable property, intangible fixed assets and rights as unit holder in a unit trust scheme.[92] There is also a *de minimis* rule.[93] The Treasury may amend any of these rules by order.[94] Further rules were added in 2006, designed to treat contracts like derivatives as derivatives.[95]

63.3.4 Tax Treatment

The new rules are close to those in force for loan relationships. To the extent that the contract is one to which the company is party for the purposes of a trade, the relevant credits

---

[87] This may matter from time to time, eg ex FA 2002, Sch 26, para 46 applied only to futures and options.
[88] CTA 2009, s 579(1)(a), ex FA 2002, Sch 26, para 3(1)(a).
[89] CTA 2009, s 579(1)(b), ex FA 2002, Sch 26, para 3(1)(b).
[90] Defined in CTA 2009, s 583, ex FA 2002, Sch 26, para 11.
[91] CTA 2009, s 579(2), ex FA 2002, Sch 26, para 3(2).
[92] CTA 2009, s 589(2), ex FA 2002, Sch 26, para 4.
[93] CTA 2009, s 590, ex FA 2002, Sch 26, para 9.
[94] CTA 2009, s 701, ex FA 2002, Sch 26, para 13.
[95] Ex FA 2002, Sch 26, para 16.

and debits are treated as receipts or expenses of the trade.[96] Non-trading credits and debits are treated as if they arise under the loan relationship rules.[97] Which debits and credits are to be brought into account when and at what value is determined by reference to GAAP.[98] As with loan relationships, the amounts to be brought into account are those recognised in the company's accounts in determining the company's profit or loss for the period.[99] This general rule may be altered under extensive regulation-making powers.[100] Section 594A also specifies the expenses for which relief is available, which mirrors the rule for loan relationships. The discharge of the contract by performance is a related transaction.[101] The profits and losses arising to a company from its derivative contracts include an exchange gains and losses so arising.[102]

63.3.5 Other Rules

(1) *Release of liability.* The rules on releases of debts are the same as for loan relationships.[103]
(2) *Migration.* The company is treated as assigning its rights for fair value and immediately reacquiring them.[104]
(3) *Groups.* When one group company replaces another as party to the contract, the matter is treated as simply that and so as giving rise to no relevant event.[105] There are also rules on leaving groups.[106] Other rules deal with groups and transactions under which fair value accounting gives an inappropriate result.[107]
(4) *Capitalisation.* Where debits and credits are capitalised as allowed under a GAAP, they are treated as giving rise to debits and credits at the time of capitalisation.[108]

63.3.6 Anti-avoidance

CTA 2009, Part 7, Chapter 11, entitled 'Tax Avoidance', begins with rules about derivative contracts which have an unallowable purpose.[109] These rules operate in a similar way as those for loan relationships. Most importantly, F(No 2)A 2015 also introduced a powerful new anti-avoidance provision in CTA 2009, sections 698B to 698D, which is analogous to the loan relationships 'regime TAAR'.

---

[96] CTA 2009, s 573, ex FA 2002, Sch 26, para 14(2) and (4).
[97] CTA 2009, s 574, ex FA 2002, Sch 26, para 14(3).
[98] CTA 2009, ss 594A and 595, ex FA 2002, Sch 26, para 15.
[99] CTA 2009, ss 597.
[100] CTA 2009, ss 598.
[101] CTA 2009, s 596, ex FA 2002, Sch 26, para 15(7) and (8).
[102] CTA 2009, ss 606, ex FA 2002, Sch 26, para 16.
[103] CTA 2009, s 611, ex FA 2002, Sch 26, para 22 derived from FA 1996, Sch 9, para 5. There is, however, no rule analogous to Sch 9, para 6 concerning connected parties—IR Notes to Finance Bill 2002, para 111.
[104] CTA 2009, s 609, ex FA 2002, Sch 26, para 22A; added by FA 2004—based on FA 2002, para 108.
[105] CTA 2009, s 625, ex FA 2002, Sch 26, para 28; however, note refinements by FA 2003, s 179 dealing with novation and by F(No 2)A 2005, Sch 7, para 22 to prevent avoidance.
[106] CTA 2009, ss 630–632, ex FA 2002, Sch 26, para 30A, added by F(No 2)A 2005, Sch 7, para 24.
[107] CTA 2009, s 628, ex FA 2002, Sch 26, para 28 as amended by FA 2006, Sch 6, paras 22 and 23.
[108] CTA 2009, ss 604–605, ex FA 2002, Sch 26, para 25.
[109] CTA 2009, ss 690–692, ex FA 2002, Sch 26, paras 23 and 24.

63.3.7 Special Situations

63.3.7.1 Special Savings Vehicles

The Part 7 rules make special provision for various savings vehicles. For example, contracts relating to holdings in unit trusts, open-ended investment companies (OEICs) and offshore funds start by not being derivative contracts, but the rules treat them as if they were and require them to use an authorised mark-to-market.[110] Further provisions set out how the transition to the derivative regime applies to an existing contract which changes its character so as to become subject to the rules.[111] Other rules apply to VCTs and investment trusts; for example, carrying debts and credits to reserve does not give rise to a debit or credit.[112] Yet further rules apply to insurance and mutual trading companies.[113]

63.3.7.2 Apportionments

The next rules apply only to contract and futures and not to CfD. Where the contract would be excluded as relating to a prohibited underlying subject matter of an excluded type, an apportionment can be made between the part qualifying for derivative treatment, eg debt, and the non-qualifying part.[114] The apportionment is on a just and reasonable basis.

63.3.7.3 Partnerships Involving Companies

Following the loan relationship rules, each partner's share is calculated separately, including the share of the corporate partner.[115] A normal GAAP basis must be used, save where the company does not account for the partnership assets separately, in which case a fair value accounting basis must be used.[116]

63.3.7.4 Hedged Index-linked Gilt-edged Securities

Where a company holds indexed-linked gilts (ILGs) the normal rule is that gains are exempt. Where the company is not exposed to the inflationary aspect of holding the ILG because of a hedging arrangement, the exemption is reduced.[117]

63.4 Intangible Fixed Assets (Capital Intellectual Property)

63.4.1 Introduction

The rules governing intangibles introduced by FA 2002 and rewritten as CTA 2009, Part 8 are important for a number of reasons. First, they have provided a coherent and relatively satisfactory way of dealing with the tax problems presented by the ever-growing field of IP.

---

[110] CTA 2009, s 587, ex FA 2002, Sch 26, para 36.
[111] CTA 2009, s 602, ex FA 2002, Sch 26, para 37.
[112] CTA 2009, ss 637–638, ex FA 2002, Sch 26, para 38.
[113] CTA 2009, ss 633 and 634, ex FA 2002, Sch 26, paras 41–43.
[114] CTA 2009, s 593, ex FA 2002, Sch 26, para 46.
[115] CTA 2009, s 619–620, ex FA 2002, Sch 26, para 49 following FA 1996, Sch 9, para 19.
[116] CTA 2009, s 621, ex FA 2002, Sch 26, para 50.
[117] CTA 2009, ss 400A–400C, introduced by FA 2010, s 41 and Sch 14.

Those problems arose, as had those for loan relationships and derivatives, from the unsatisfactory nature of the traditional income tax and capital gains tax rules. The success of the 2002 rules paved the way for the 2004 adoption of GAAP elsewhere.

Secondly, these rules attempt to solve these problems by bringing the tax treatment closer to the treatment in the accounts by reference to accounting principles and practice. Accounting concepts are deeply embedded. These will determine not only the measure of a liability, but also the occasion on which a liability may arise. In contrast to the loan relationships and derivative rules, F(No 2)A 2015 did not substantially alter the operation of the intangible fixed asset rules in this respect. F(No 2)A 2015 made one very important change, however; it abolished tax relief under these rules in respect of the purchase of goodwill and other closely-related intangibles (eg customer information) on or after 8 July 2015. The restriction in section 816A does not apply to goodwill and other 'relevant assets' acquired before 8 July 2015, and it does not affect tax relief on other acquired intangibles including patents and know-how. According to the Explanatory Notes, the aim of this change was to restrict the ability of companies to reduce their corporation tax profits following a merger or acquisition and to remove what was described as an artificial incentive to buy assets rather than shares.[118]

Thirdly, they provide a self-standing code for rules dealing with the income and capital gains consequences of holding IP as a fixed asset. They therefore present an alternative model for a possible future general corporation tax code.

63.4.2 *Outline*

FA 2002, Schedule 29 introduced radically new rules for expenditure on and receipts from fixed intangible assets on or after 1 April 2002.[119] The scope of the new rules—now in CTA 2009, Part 8 (sections 711–906)—is wide since they apply to all IP, goodwill (subject to what was just said about the abolition of relief on purchased goodwill and other relevant assets from 8 July 2015)[120] and other intangible assets held as fixed assets or, as the statute puts it, acquired or created by the company for use on a continuing basis in the course of the company's activities.[121] The paradigm case of fixedness is found where the asset has been capitalised in the balance sheet of the company. The rules are confined to companies subject to corporation tax.

Where assets were acquired before 1 April 2002 they remain subject to the old rules until there is a disposal and acquisition, the disposal being treated under the old rules and the acquisition under the new rules. This rather broad statement needs to be taken in conjunction with the detailed interpretation rules in Chapter 16 (ex Part 14). Rules were found to be needed where assets were derived from pre-2002 assets to prevent unintended relief.[122]

---

[118] CTA 2009, s 816A, introduced by F(No 2) Act 2015, s 33; see Explanatory Notes to Finance Bill 2015, clause 32. For commentary see Miller, *Tax Journal* (31 July 2015) and Miles and Price, *Tax Journal* (23 Oct 2015).

[119] See Shipwright [2002] BTR 301.

[120] CTA 2009, s 715, ex FA 2002, Sch 29, para 4. FA 2009, s 70 enacted the view held widely, but not apparently universally, that goodwill created in the course of carrying on the business is subject to these rules. CTA 2009, s 712(2) was amended to confirm that an intangible asset includes an internally-generated asset.

[121] CTA 2009, s 713, ex FA 2002, Sch 29, para 3.

[122] CTA 2009, Ch 16, ss 880–900, ex FA 2002, Sch 29, paras 14A, 127A and 127B, added by FA 2006, s 77.

To paraphrase the Revenue's explanation,[123] the tax treatment is to follow the accounting treatment, and so will in most cases be based on the amortisation reflected in their accounts. 'Amortisation' is a term used by accountants in relation to writing-off the capitalised value of intangible assets over time (with 'depreciation' used for tangibles). The fall-back allowance is at a fixed rate of 4% per annum, but accounting principles will normally provide a more rapid rate of write off so that the 4% rate is for indefinite or longer-life assets.[124]

The regime applies to all expenditure, whether capital or revenue, incurred on the creation, acquisition and enhancement of intangible assets (including abortive expenditure), as well as expenditure on their preservation and maintenance. Relief under the new regime will therefore be available for the cost of internal development, as well as acquisition, of intangible assets. As already noted, however, no relief is given for acquired goodwill and closely-related intangibles from 8 July 2015.

Payments made for the use of intangibles, eg royalties, also come within the new regime and so are treated in line with accounting principles, as do royalty receipts. Disposals of intangible assets are taxed on an income basis; however, a roll-over relief applies where disposal proceeds are reinvested in new intangible assets within the regime.

There is a wide-ranging anti-avoidance rule, which directs that certain tax avoidance arrangements are to be disregarded in determining whether a debit or credit is to be brought into account under Part 8, or the amount of such debit or credit.[125] The term 'arrangements' is widely defined; arrangements are tax avoidance arrangements if their main object or one of their main objects is to enable a company to obtain debits or increased debit, or to avoid having to bring any credit into account at all or only a reduced amount.

Another major provision excludes an intangible fixed asset from Part 8 to the extent that it is held (a) for a purpose that is not a business or other commercial purpose of the company, or (b) for the purpose of activities in respect of which the company is not within the charge to corporation tax.[126] Although section 803 contains the words 'to the extent that', section 802 indicates that an apportionment may be made in the case of dual purposes, with the apportioned part treated as a separate asset.

Lastly, CTA 2009, Part 9 provides special rules in respect of dispositions of know-how (sections 908–910), sales of patent rights (sections 911–923) and relief from corporation tax on patent income (sections 924–925), as well as supplementary provisions (sections 926–931).

63.4.3 Basic Rules: Credits and Debits Generally

The new rules are concerned with IP and any other intangible fixed assets[127]—so not with tangible fixed assets, nor with intangible assets held as trading stock. Thus, they cover patents, copyrights, trademarks and know-how, as well as design rights. Not just ownership but also the rights to use these types of property will be subject to Part 8 if they are fixed assets.

---

[123] See HMRC manual CIRD10000 *et seq* and in particular CIRD10115. See also Inland Revenue Press Release BN10 23 April 2002, [2002] *Simon's Tax Intelligence* 571.

[124] CTA 2009, s 731, ex FA 2002, Sch 29, para 10.

[125] CTA 2009, s 864, ex FA 2002, Sch 29, para 111—words were added by FA 2003 to make sure that debits and credits arising under all parts of Sch 29 were caught.

[126] CTA 2009, s 803, ex FA 2002, Sch 29, para 77.

[127] CTA 2009, ss 712–713, ex FA 2002, Sch 29, para 2.

Also covered is any information or technique not protected by a right but having industrial, commercial or other economic value. There are also many exclusions in Chapter 10; there are many definitions and boundaries too. There are express rules governing the adjustments to be made on a change of accounting policy.[128]

The assets must be acquired or created by the company for use on a continuing basis in the course of the company's activities.[129] The paradigm case of fixedness is found where the asset has been capitalised in the balance sheet of the company—which means that rules have to be provided for assets which have not yet been capitalised, or which having lost all value are no longer so capitalised or which cease to be capitalised. Special rules apply if the company uses incorrect accounts—the bedrock rule being to make them use accounting rules anyway.[130] Another special rule applies if the consolidated group accounting rule is different from this company's.[131]

The rules are framed in terms of gains and losses in respect of intangible fixed assets.[132] The rules have to be described in terms of the schedular system and so cover assets held for trades, for property business, for businesses which the tax legislation treats as trades and then non-trading situations.

We start with trades and assume that the asset is held for the purposes of the trade. To determine gains and losses one has to have regard to debits (or accounting losses), which are sums which may be deducted as trading expenses, and credits (or accounting gains), which are to be brought in as trading receipts.[133]

63.4.3.1 Debits (Expenditures)

Sums recognised in the company's profit and loss account are debits and are recognised as incurred, eg a royalty for using the fixed asset.[134] So the rules recognise all expenditure of an income nature but leave the treatment entirely in the hands of the accountants. The accounting treatment determines both its deductibility and the timing, and so, in the absence of any other rule, the value of that deductibility.

A debit may also arise as a result of writing down. This may be either for amortisation, or for a loss recognised following an impairment review if it is recognised in the profit and loss account.[135] As already noted, amortisation is a term used in place of depreciation when talking of intangibles. The general rule recognising debits when and if they are recognised in the accounts leaves everything to accounting principles—whether there can be a claim at all and the extent of the claim. As an alternative, the legislation grants amortisation at the fixed rate of 4% of the written-down value on a straight-line basis.[136]

Thus, the deduction will be an appropriate portion, whether as recognised in the accounts or 4%, of the written-down value. The statute refers to the amount of loss recognised for accounting purposes applied to a fraction the numerator of which is the tax written-down

---

[128] CTA 2009, Ch 15, ss 871–879, ex FA 2002, Sch 29, para 116A added by FA 2004.
[129] CTA 2009, s 713, ex FA 2002, Sch 29, para 3.
[130] CTA 2009, ss 716–717, ex FA 2002, Sch 29, para 5.
[131] CTA 2009, s 718, ex FA 2002, Sch 29, para 6.
[132] CTA 2009, s 711, ex FA 2002, Sch 29, para 1.
[133] CTA 2009, s 747, ex FA 2002, Sch 29, para 31.
[134] CTA 2009, s 728, ex FA 2002, Sch 29, para 8. Pursuant to ITA 2007, s 903 royalties remain subject to deduction of tax at source, but this is subject to double tax treaties.
[135] CTA 2009, s 729, ex FA 2002, Sch 29, para 9.
[136] CTA 2009, ss 730–731, ex FA 2002, Sch 29, paras 10 and 11.

value of the expenditure and the denominator the value of the asset recognised for accounting purposes.[137] Where the company elects for the 4% fixed rate basis, this is applied to the cost of the asset or, if less, the tax written-down value.[138] So if the asset costs £100,000, the fixed rate allowance is £4,000 pa. If the company elects for the 4% rule, the company will avoid any revaluation charge.[139]

A loss also arises if there is a reversal of a previous accounting gain and this is recognised in the profit and loss account.[140]

63.4.3.2 Credits (Receipts)

Mirroring the rule for expenses, the first rule for credits is that sums recognised in the company's profit and loss account as receipts in respect of intangible fixed asset are credits; again, this accounting treatment determines both its liability to tax in this way and its timing, and so, in the absence of any other rule, the extent of that liability.[141] The principal example of such receipts will be the royalty, but the rule applies to any receipt recognised in the account as being in respect of the intangible fixed asset.

A credit will also arise on a revaluation in the very limited circumstances envisaged by FRS 102, section 18.18B (formerly FRS 10).[142] The credit arising on the sale or other disposal of an asset is not within this part of the Act but within Chapter 4—the key difference being that only sums falling within Chapter 4 qualify for reinvestment relief. A credit may also arise if a gain is recognised in the profit and loss account in respect of negative goodwill.[143] A credit may further arise if a previous accounting loss is reversed and, again, is recognised in the profit and loss account.[144]

63.4.4 *Realisations, Tax Written-down Values, Taxing the Net Sums*

CTA 2009, Part 8, Chapter 4 (sections 733–741) concerns the treatment of debits and credits arising when an intangible fixed assets is realised.[145] Realisation means an event as a result of which the asset is no longer recognised in the balance sheet, eg a sale. It also means an event which gives rise to a reduction in accounting value.[146] If the asset has no balance sheet value, it is treated as if it had one.[147]

The net debit or credit is calculated by reference to the difference between the proceeds of realisation and the tax written-down value.[148] If the net sum is positive, it is treated as a credit (like the old balancing charge); if it is negative, it is treated as a debit (like the old balancing allowance). If the asset has not yet been written down when it is sold, eg sold soon

[137] CTA 2009, s 729(5), ex FA 2002, Sch 29, para 9.
[138] CTA 2009, s 731, ex FA 2002, Sch 29, para 11(1); 'tax written-down value' is explained in ss 742–743 (ex para 28).
[139] This arises under CTA 2009, s 723, ex FA 2002, Sch 29, para 15; the exclusion is in 723(6), ex para 15(6).
[140] CTA 2009, s 732, ex FA 2002, Sch 29, para 12.
[141] CTA 2009, ss 720–722, ex FA 2002, Sch 29, paras 13–14A, but subject to any rules in Ch 4 and TIOPA 2010, Pt 4 (transfer pricing).
[142] CTA 2009, s 723, ex FA 2002, Sch 29, para 15.
[143] CTA 2009, s 724, ex FA 2002, Sch 29, para 16. The relevant GAAP is FRS 102, section 19.24, formerly FRS 7.
[144] CTA 2009, s 725, ex FA 2002, Sch 29, para 17.
[145] CTA 2009, s 733, ex FA 2002, Sch 29, para 18(1).
[146] Defined in CTA 2009, s 734, ex FA 2002, Sch 29, para 19; on part realisation, see s 734(4), ex para 19(3).
[147] CTA 2009, s 734(3), ex FA 2002, Sch 29, para 19(2).
[148] CTA 2009, s 735, ex FA 2002, Sch 29, para 20.

after acquisition, the relevant cost is the capital expenditure as adjusted.[149] This is all very much like the old CAA rules, not the capital gains rules—there is no indexation relief. There is a part realisation provision, the apportionment rules of which resemble TCGA 1992, section 42, but it uses accounting values.[150] If the assets are not shown in the balance sheet and so have no balance sheet value, the proceeds of realisation are brought in in full.[151]

The meaning of 'proceeds of realisation' is, once more, defined by reference to accounting principles. There is also a deduction for incidental cost—if recognised for accounting purposes.[152] Where expenditure is incurred on a transaction that would have been a realisation but which is not completed, the abortive expenditure is recognised as a debit.[153]

Further rules govern the calculation of any tax written-down value. Normally this will be the tax cost less the debits recognised under section 729, but plus any credits recognised under the revaluation rules.[154] The situation is simpler if the company has opted for the rate of 4% in section 731, as there are no revaluation complications[155] and one looks simply at the tax cost less any debits made under section 731. There is a separate rule for part realisation.[156]

The way in which these debits and credits are recognised is set out in Chapter 6. Debits and credits arising from an asset held for trade purposes are treated as expenses or receipts of the trade.[157] Assets held for the purposes of a property business are treated as credits and debits of that business.[158] Mines and transport undertakings also have their own basis.[159] Other gains and losses, called non-trading gains and losses, are netted out. Net non-trading gains are chargeable to corporation tax,[160] while non-trading losses may be offset against total profits on a claim being made.[161] This offset may be surrendered to other group companies; any non-trading loss balance may be carried forward as a non-trading debit.[162]

63.4.5 Rollover Relief

Part 8, Chapter 7 provides relief if a company realises an intangible fixed asset and incurs expenditure on other intangible fixed assets. The asset being disposed of must fall within the requirements necessary for a realisation to have taken place.[163] The intention of the statute here is to differentiate between those intangibles that are basically of a revenue nature, and thus dealt with by the credits and debits outlined above, and those that are really capital by nature for which rollover relief is available.

---

[149] CTA 2009, s 736, ex FA 2002, Sch 29, paras 21 and 135.
[150] CTA 2009, s 737, ex FA 2002, Sch 29, para 22.
[151] CTA 2009, s 738, ex FA 2002, Sch 29, para 23.
[152] CTA 2009, s 739, ex FA 2002, Sch 29, para 25.
[153] CTA 2009, s 740, ex FA 2002, Sch 29, para 26.
[154] CTA 2009, s 742, ex FA 2002, Sch 29, para 27.
[155] CTA 2009, s 743, ex FA 2002, Sch 29, para 28.
[156] CTA 2009, s 744, ex FA 2002, Sch 29, para 29.
[157] CTA 2009, s 747, ex FA 2002, Sch 29, para 31.
[158] CTA 2009, s 748, ex FA 2002, Sch 29, para 32.
[159] CTA 2009, s 749, ex FA 2002, Sch 29, para 33 and TA 1988, s 55.
[160] CTA 2009, s 751–52, ex FA 2002, Sch 29, para 34.
[161] CTA 2009, s 753, ex FA 2002, Sch 29, para 35.
[162] CTA 2009, s 753(3), ex FA 2002, Sch 29, para 35(3).
[163] CTA 2009, s 734, ex FA 2002, Sch 29, para 19.

Rollover relief may be claimed[164] where the proceeds from a chargeable intangible asset,[165] including those from a partial realisation,[166] are reinvested in chargeable intangible assets. These assets must be capitalised in the accounts and the reinvestment must take place within 12 months before or three years after the date of realisation.[167] The effect of the claim is to reduce the realisation proceeds of the old asset and the cost of the new asset by the same amount.[168] It is possible to make a declaration of provisional entitlement to relief before formally making the claim.[169] Partial relief is available where part only of the proceeds is reinvested.[170] Generally, deemed acquisition and disposals are disregarded for this rollover relief, with the exception of the charge arising on degrouping (see §63.4.6 below).[171] Capital gains arising on the disposal of IP acquired or created before 1 April 2002, and so under the old regime, are also eligible for this rollover relief.[172] This also includes circumstances when there is a degrouping charge on an old-regime intangible asset.[173] It should be noted that this rollover relief may not be particularly beneficial, because the amortisation subsequently allowed each year will be based on a lower cost figure.

63.4.6 Groups

Part 8, Chapter 8 defines groups and is modelled on the definition in TCGA 1992, section 170, expanded by the approach adopted by the Tax Law Rewrite project. Chapter 9 contains the group rules for transfers of chargeable intangible assets. So these may be transferred at book value on a tax-neutral basis in a similar way to chargeable assets covered by the capital gains rules.[174] The rollover relief has its own rules which, if satisfied, allow two group companies to be treated as one;[175] while another rule extends the reinvestment relief to the acquisition of shares in certain companies, with the acquisition of the group companies being treated as equivalent to the acquisition of the underlying assets.[176]

Part 8 also has to have its own degrouping charge for use when a company leaves the group within six years of a transfer.[177] Special rules apply if the degrouping comes about by reason of an exempt distribution or a merger carried out for bona fide commercial reasons.[178]

There is a rollover relief for the degrouping charge, while other rules allow the companies to reallocate the charge within the group, and so there is a rule governing reinvestment

---

[164] CTA 2009, s 757, ex FA 2002, Sch 29, para 40.
[165] CTA 2009, s 755, ex FA 2002, Sch 29, paras 38 and 136.
[166] CTA 2009, s 755(2)(b), ex FA 2002, Sch 29, para 38.
[167] CTA 2009, s 756, ex FA 2002, Sch 29, paras 38, 39 and 40.
[168] CTA 2009, s 758, ex FA 2002, Sch 29, para 41.
[169] CTA 2009, s 761, ex FA 2002, Sch 29, para 43.
[170] CTA 2009, s 759, ex FA 2002, Sch 29, paras 41 and 42.
[171] CTA 2009, s 763, ex FA 2002, Sch 29, para 35 referring to paras 65, 67 and 45.
[172] CTA 2009, s 898, ex FA 2002, Sch 29, para 129.
[173] CTA 2009, s 899, ex FA 2002, Sch 29, paras 130–136, as amended by F(No 2)A, s 41(4).
[174] CTA 2009, ss 775–776, ex FA 2002, Sch 29, para 55—a rule which overrides the more general rules.
[175] CTA 2009, s 777, ex FA 2002, Sch 29, para 56.
[176] CTA 2009, ss 778–779, ex FA 2002, Sch 29, para 57.
[177] CTA 2009, ss 780–788, ex FA 2002, Sch 29, paras 58–60.
[178] CTA 2009, ss 789–790, ex FA 2002, Sch 29, paras 61 (referring to TA 1988, s 213(2)) and 62.

relief where the charge is reallocated.[179] The charge, whether as originally arising or real-located, may be recovered from a director or a controlling director.[180]

Lastly, payments between group members for reinvestment relief or the reallocation of a degrouping charge may be tax free.[181]

63.4.7 Excluded Assets

Some assets are excluded for all purposes of Part 8 by the rules in Chapter 10; others are brought into Part 8 so far as royalties are concerned but excluded for all other purposes, while there is also a third miscellaneous category of intermediate exclusion.[182]

The first group of complete exclusions is for rights over assets which are not intangi-bles. So there is a complete exclusion for rights over land or tangible movable property, oil licences, film production, financial assets and shares/rights/interests in companies, trusts and partnerships.[183] FA 2004 added to this list an asset in respect of which capital allow-ances were previously made as plant and machinery because it was a tangible asset, but which is now an intangible asset.[184] Section 803 is rather different—it excludes assets held for non-business purposes or for purposes outside the scope of UK corporation tax. More formally, it excludes an intangible fixed assets held (a) for a purpose that is not a busi-ness or other commercial purpose of the company, or (b) for the purpose of activities in respect of which the company is not within the charge to corporation tax. Although these are described as entirely excluded, this is only half true. The exclusions apply to the extent that there are such rights or purposes, and section 802 makes it clear that there is to be an apportionment where the exclusion relates to part of an asset; here the untainted part of the asset is treated as a separate asset.

The second group of exclusions in sections 810–813 allows Part 8 to apply so far as royal-ties are concerned. The new accounting-based rules, especially for timing, are thought to be so superior to the old that they must apply even though it is not appropriate to apply rules like reinvestment relief. There are exclusions for mutual trade or business, film and sound recordings, and for computer software to the extent that it is treated as part of the related hardware.[185]

The third group in sections 814–815 concerns two situations. First, Chapters 2 and 3 of Part 8 do not apply to expenditure on R&D; here, presumably, the R&D tax credit (see §62.2.5 above) is more appropriate. However, Chapter 4, realisations, does apply—on the basis that any expense on R&D is excluded.[186] The other rule concerns computer software and allows that company to elect (irrevocably) for first-year allowances.[187] Again, Chapter 4 may apply on a realisation of the software.

---

[179] CTA 2009, ss 791–794, ex FA 2002, Sch 29, para 65–67.
[180] CTA 2009, ss 795–798, ex FA 2002, Sch 29, paras 68–70.
[181] CTA 2009, s 799, ex FA 2002, Sch 29, para 71.
[182] CTA 2009, s 800, ex FA 2002, Sch 29, para 72.
[183] CTA 2009, ss 805–809, ex FA 2002, Sch 29, paras 73–26.
[184] CTA 2009, s 804, ex FA 2002, Sch 29, para 73A.
[185] CTA 2009, ss 810–813, ex FA 2002, Sch 29, paras 79 and 80.
[186] CTA 2009, s 814, ex FA 2002, Sch 29, paras 81 and 82.
[187] CTA 2009, s 815, ex FA 2002, Sch 29, para 83.

63.4.8 Remaining Rules

63.4.8.1 Chapter 11—Transfer of Business or Trade

Since Part 8 is free-standing, it has to have its own version of a number of CGT rules. So where one has a scheme of reconstruction or amalgamation involving the transfer of the whole or part of a business from one company to another, a special rule provides a deferral.[188] This is subject to the intra-group transfer rules. Other rules concern:

(1) the transfer of a UK trade between companies resident in different EU Member States;
(2) the transfer of intangible fixed assets to certain non-resident companies; and
(3) the transfer of a non-UK trade from a EU company resident in another EU state or when a company makes a qualifying merger with the new European Company.[189]

There is a statutory clearance procedure.[190]

Other deferrals concern transfers from a building society to a company and amalgamation of certain societies, eg building or provident societies (or the transfer of engagements from one society to another).[191]

63.4.8.2 Chapters 12–13—Related Parties

Transfers of chargeable intangible assets between related parties are treated as taking place at market value;[192] however, this is subject to TIOPA 2010, Part 4—the transfer pricing rules—and other exceptions. There is also a rule denying rollover relief under Chapter 7 for part realisations involving related parties;[193] while another rule deals with the delayed payment of royalties, denying any deduction until the sum is paid.[194] Further provisions define related parties in terms of control and, in the case of a close company, participators and their associates.[195] Curiously, the original definition of a 'related party' in section 95 did not cover the situation in which the two companies were simply companies in the same group, but that this was remedied by FA 2003. Another change was needed to ensure that a person (other than an individual) remained a related party even though going into insolvency or similar arrangements.[196]

63.4.8.3 Chapters 14–18—Supplementary

Chapter 14 contains a number of rules of varying degrees of interest which show further the need to legislate carefully when creating a self-contained area of law. Thus, there are rules dealing with grants and contributions which require them to be taken into account unless

---

[188] CTA 2009, s 818, ex FA 2002, Sch 29, para 84 echoing TCGA 1992, s 139.
[189] CTA 2009, ss 819–823 and 827, ex FA 2002, Sch 29, paras 85A–87A.
[190] CTA 2009, ss 831–833, ex FA 2002, Sch 29, para 88.
[191] CTA 2009, ss 824–830, ex FA 2002, Sch 29, paras 89–91.
[192] CTA 2009, ss 845–849A, ex FA 2002, Sch 29, para 92, exception added by F(No 2)A 2005, s 41(2).
[193] CTA 2009, s 850, ex FA 2002, Sch 29, para 93.
[194] CTA 2009, s 851, ex FA 2002, Sch 29, para 94.
[195] CTA 2009, ss 834–843, ex FA 2002, Sch 29, paras 95–101 as amended by F(No 2)A 2005, s 41(3).
[196] CTA 2009, s 835(7)–(9), ex FA 2002, Sch 29, para 95A, added by FA 2008, s 65.

exempt,[197] and a rule that empowers the Treasury to bring finance lessors within the scope of Part 8 by statutory instrument.[198]

There are apportioning powers for situations in which assets are acquired or realised together,[199] while another rule deals with the situation in which the legislation directs a disposal at market value but the assets have no accounting value in the hands of the transferee; the assets are treated as acquired at market value anyway.[200] Fungible assets, ie those of a nature to be dealt in without identifying the particular assets involved, are taken as forming one single asset.[201]

There are deemed realisations at market value when an intangible ceases to be a 'chargeable intangible asset'.[202] This occurs where:

(1)   the company ceases to be resident in the UK;
(2)   the asset is held by a company not resident in the UK and the company stops using it for the UK permanent establishment's trade; or
(3)   the asset begins to be used for the purposes of a mutual business.

It may be possible to postpone the gain arising. The question whether (1) and (2) will be acceptable under EU law may need to be considered in light of ECJ rulings on exit charges.[203] There is a converse deemed acquisition at market value when the asset becomes a chargeable intangible asset.[204]

Chapter 15 contains express rules governing the adjustments to be made on a change of accounting policy.[205]

Since Part 8 operates outside the normal structure, there are rules about deductibility of payments.[206] Thus, debits may not be brought into account if in respect of expenditure that is generally not deductible for tax purposes. This leads to a reference to a number of rules elsewhere in CTA 2009, including sections 1298 (business entertainment or gifts), 1304 (crime-related expenditure) and 56 (expensive hired cars), and FA 2004, section 246(2) (benefits under employer-financed retirement benefits schemes). Sections 866–867 apply if there is a delayed payment of employees' remuneration where such employees are associated with the intangible asset. An example might be staff employed in promoting the company's brand names. Section 869 governs the treatment of bad debts.

Lastly, Chapter 17 deals with insurance companies, and Chapter 18 sets out priority rules for corporation tax purposes.

---

[197]   CTA 2009, ss 852–853, ex FA 2002, Sch 29, paras 102 and 103.
[198]   CTA 2009, ss 854–855, ex FA 2002, Sch 29, para 104.
[199]   CTA 2009, s 856, ex FA 2002, Sch 29, para 105.
[200]   CTA 2009, s 857, ex FA 2002, Sch 29, para 106.
[201]   CTA 2009, s 858, ex FA 2002, Sch 29, para 107.
[202]   CTA 2009, ss 859–862, ex FA 2002, Sch 29, paras 108 and 109.
[203]   See eg Case C-371/10 *National Grid Indus BV v Inspecteur van de Belastingdienst Rijnmond/kantoor Rotterdam* [2012] STC 114 and Case C-9/02 *Lasteyrie du Saillant v Ministère de l'Economie* [2005] STC 1722.
[204]   CTA 2009, s 863, ex FA 2002, Sch 29, para 110.
[205]   CTA 2009, ss 871–879, ex FA 2002, Sch 29, para 116A added by FA 2004.
[206]   CTA 2009, s 865, ex FA 2002, Sch 29, paras 112–114.

63.5   International Trade—Trading Currency

63.5.1 Introduction

One must distinguish the currency in which the company's profits are computed for fiscal purposes and expressed from that used to determine the profits and losses of the business which are to be 'computed' and 'expressed'. The first task must be carried out in sterling;[207] for the second one usually looks to use either the currency in which the company reports its earnings (also called the 'accounts currency') or its functional currency.[208] The company's functional currency is defined as the currency of the primary economic environment in which the company operates.[209]

The original rules were introduced by FA 1993, and they were rewritten by FA 2000 in an attempt to make them more friendly to business. They were rewritten again in 2004 as a result of the use of GAAP. The 2004 rules, rewritten once more and now found in CTA 2010, Part 1, Chapter 4, apply to periods of account beginning on or after 1 January 2005.[210] Part of their interest is as one more historical example of tax law moving closer to accounting practice. Before FA 2000 the use of the foreign currency was a matter of taxpayer election.[211] The rules still apply only for corporation tax and not for income tax.

63.5.2 Detail

The premise is that for corporation tax, the income and chargeable gains of a company for an accounting period should be calculated and expressed in sterling. However, the determination of the profits or losses to be reported is a separate matter, and the choice of currency depends on the situation to be covered. Profits and losses are not defined further; before FA 2004 capital gains and allowable losses were excluded, but this is no longer needed.[212] A number of short rules are set out. These rules apply only where profits and losses fall to be computed in accordance with GAAP.[213] They are, therefore, irrelevant both to capital gains and to capital allowances. Under CTA 2009, section 46 they are relevant to trading profits and, under section 210(2) referring to section 46, to profits from land. They are also relevant to matters dealt with elsewhere in this chapter—loan relationships, derivatives, intangible fixed assets—and also to management expenses. These are the principal GAAP-related tax rules—but not the only ones.

The first rule, which, it is thought, will be rare, arises where the functional currency is sterling but the accounts are prepared in a foreign currency. Here the sterling figures are used.[214]

---

[207] CTA 2010, s 5(1), ex FA 1993, s 92(1); previous version introduced by FA 2004, Sch 10, Pt 4.
[208] CTA 2010, s 5(2), ex FA 1993, s 93(1).
[209] CTA 2010, s 17(4), ex FA 1993, s 92E(3).
[210] FA 2004, s 52(3); the original Bill was oddly arranged and a revised version was introduced at the Report stage—Report Stage Amendment 84.
[211] Ex FA 1993, s 93(1)(b) original version. The original rules were in FA 1993 and SI 1994/3230; see Inland Revenue *Corporation Tax Manual*, paras 13620 *et seq*.
[212] Ex FA 1993, s 93(5).
[213] CTA 2010, s 5(2), ex FA 1993, s 93(2).
[214] CTA 2010, s 6, ex FA 1993, s 92A; the view on rarity is in Revenue Notes to the Report Stage Amendment 84, para 6; the other currency is likely to be used only in the consolidated accounts which are not relevant to UK tax.

The second rule[215] applies where the company is resident in the UK but, in order to fit in with a GAAP such as IAS (IAS 21), the company prepares the accounts in one currency but in those accounts identifies another currency as being the currency of the primary economic environment and that currency is not sterling. The company is to calculate its profits using the functional currency and then taking the sterling equivalent of those profits or losses.[216] IAS 21, paragraph 53 requires a company to disclose its functional currency if this is not the accounts currency.

The third rule[217] has two strands. The first is where the company prepares its accounts not in sterling but in some other currency and neither of the first two rules applies.[218] Here the accounts currency is taken and that figure is translated into sterling. The second strand of the third rule arises where the company is not resident in the UK but prepares its accounts in a non-sterling currency.[219] Here too, the accounts currency is taken and that figure is translated into sterling.

The legislation contains its own rules for translating results from one currency to another. This may be needed to translate an amount in a foreign currency into sterling, or an amount into its foreign currency equivalent or the accounts currency.[220] In either event, one uses either the average exchange rate of the current accounting period or the spot rate for the transaction in question.[221] A special proviso overrides one of the self-assessment rules which would otherwise upset this scheme.[222]

FA 2009 amended CTA 2010, section 11 and inserted sections 12–17 in reaction to uncertainty in the currency markets. The old rules required unused losses to remain converted into sterling when they accrued. Sections 12–13 allows them to be computed in the currency in which they were originally computed; so, as the Notes on Clauses explain, losses incurred in a foreign currency will be set against the same measure of profits. Sections 14–15 deal with losses computed in sterling which are used in a different period and the profits are computed in that other period in a currency other than sterling. Sections 16–17 contain definitions.

63.6 Repos

The rules applicable to the sale and repurchase of securities (repos), formerly in FA 2007, Schedule 13, have been (mostly) rewritten as CTA 2009, Part 6, Chapter 10. The Chapter 10 repo rules reflect the influence of the Australian draft legislation by starting in section 542 with a purpose clause—the purpose being that arrangements involving the sale and subsequent purchase of securities which equate in substance to the lending of money by or to a company (with securities in substance acting as collateral) are to be subject to a charge for corporation tax that reflects that substance.

---

[215] CTA 2010, s 7, ex FA 1993, s 92B; and see Revenue Notes to the Report Stage Amendment 84, paras 10 *et seq.*
[216] CTA 2010, s 7(2), ex FA 1993, s 92B(2).
[217] CTA 2010, s 8, ex FA 1993, s 92C; Revenue Notes to the Report Stage Amendment 84, paras 16 *et seq.*
[218] CTA 2010, s 8(1)(b), ex FA 1993, s 92C(1).
[219] CTA 2010, s 9, ex FA 1993, s 92C(2).
[220] CTA 2010, s 11(1), ex FA 1993, s 92D(1).
[221] CTA 2010, s 11(2), ex FA 1993, s 92D(2).
[222] CTA 2010, s 9(4), ex FA 1993, s 92E(2) overrides FA 1988, Sch 18, para 88.

The legislation distinguishes 'debtor repos', which are usually executed under normal market documentation,[223] from 'debtor quasi repos', which are economically similar but on non-standard terms.[224] The elements of debtor repos are similar to the structured finance arrangements rules introduced in 2006 (see §63.7 below). One condition is that the subsequent buying of the securities extinguishes the financial liability recorded in the accounts. Section 550[225] introduces an anti-avoidance rule for 'relevant arrangements'. FA 2010 added section 550(5A) and Schedule 13, paragraph 4(aa) to ensure that where manufactured payments are received by companies in the course of a repo transaction, they are to be brought into account whether or not they are recognised on the companies' balance sheets. As the HMRC notes have it, the GAAP result is respected even if the accounts take in manufactured payments instead of real income. Interestingly, this change is treated as 'always having had effect', ie back to 1 October 2007.

Subject to that, section 551 then directs that the borrower is to obtain relief for any finance charge shown in the accounts and which represents the cost of borrowing. FA 2007, Schedule 13, paragraph 6 (not rewritten) replaces TCGA 1992, section 263A for corporation tax purposes—but not for CGT. Section 543 introduces 'creditor repos', which are the reverse of debtor repos, and section 544 creditor quasi-repos. Section 545 is the anti-avoidance analogue of section 550. Section 546 contains the basic rule analogous to section 551.

Finally, for a useful explanation of repos, an attack on the form of the legislation and a decision not to HMRC's liking, see the High Court decision in *DCC Holdings v Revenue & Customs Commissioners*.[226] HMRC's appeal in *DCC Holdings* was successful before the Court of Appeal[227] and, for slightly different reasons, the Supreme Court, where Lord Walker invoked a principle of symmetry.[228] Readers are also directed to relevant aspects of the G20/OECD Base Erosion and Profit Shifting (BEPS) project (see §69.11), and particularly Action 2.[229]

63.7 Structured Finance Arrangements; Factoring of Income Receipts; Abusing Finance Transaction Treatment

The structured finance arrangements (SFA) rules in CTA 2010, Part 16, Chapter 2 apply to corporation tax; the counterparts for income tax are in ITA 2007, Part 13, Chapters 5B and 5C (not discussed here).[230] The Part 16, Chapter 2 rules supersede the rent factoring rules, as the rules on rent factoring now apply to a wider range of assets and not just land. It cannot be pretended that this material is at all easy either to understand or to digest;

---

[223] CTA 2009, s 548, ex FA 2007, Sch 13, para 2.
[224] CTA 2009, s 549, ex FA 2007, Sch 13, para 3.
[225] Ex FA 2007, Sch 13, para 4, only partially repealed.
[226] [2009] STC 77, [2008] EWHC 2429 (Civ), *per* Norris J, [1] and [22], and generally.
[227] [2009] EWCA Civ 1165.
[228] [2010] UKSC 58, [2011] STC 326.
[229] OECD, BEPS Action 2 'Neutralizing the effect of hybrid mismatch arrangements' Final Report (Oct 2015).
[230] The corporation tax rules were formerly TA 1988, ss 774A–774G, introduced by FA 2006. The income tax rules in ss 809BZA *et seq* were introduced by TIOPA 2010, Sch 5.

Fraser and Gething's Finance Act Note devotes 26 pages to it.[231] The discussion that follows focuses on the key elements.

HMRC's *Corporate Finance Manual* has useful material at paragraphs 6752 *et seq*, and it provides the following example at paragraph 6758. Suppose a company obtains a loan of £100 million at interest from a finance provider. It would typically have to give security for the loan. Over the five-year period it might pay, say, £2.5 million interest pa, giving total repayments of £112.5 million. For tax purposes, relief would be available for each annual payment of £2.5 million interest, but not for repayment of the £100 million principal. No one in their right mind would think this treatment in any way inappropriate.

However, consider this alternative, which uses a structured finance-income alienation scheme. Company A holds an asset on which income of £22.5 million a year will arise. It transfers this asset to the finance provider, a bank, for a lump sum of £100 million for a period of five years, at the end of which it can reacquire the asset for nothing. During the five years, income of total £112.5 million is paid to the bank. The income stream acquired by the bank will be enough to repay both the lump sum and the interest. There are likely to be arrangements such as options under which the asset and income reverts to the company at the end of five years. The transfer of the asset is in substance by way of security only. As the company has retained substantially all the risks and rewards of ownership of that asset, and is in effect simply applying the income that arises from it to repaying the loan, under GAAP it will continue to recognise the asset and will record the lump sum as a financial liability, that is, as a loan. Income from the asset will continue to be shown in the accounts, and over five years a finance charge equal to the difference between the gross receipts and the lump sum will be debited to profit and loss account.

The substance of the second example is exactly the same as the first example. In both cases the lender has had the benefit of the income that is paid to the lender, but in the second has applied it directly in repaying the lump sum. However, under the second method the company claims in effect to escape tax on the £112.5 million of income which would arise to it during the period of the arrangement.

CTA 2010, sections 758–762 (ex TA 1988, sections 774A and 774B) counter the income alienation scheme, referred to in the legislation as a 'type 1 finance arrangement'. Section 758 begins by describing the scheme as one where, first, a borrower (B) sells a right to income (or an income-bearing asset) to a third party, the lender (L), and B either avoids being assessed to tax on such income or becomes entitled to a deduction. Secondly, the transaction is treated (correctly) under GAAP as a financing transaction in the relevant accounts. Thirdly, the arrangement is structured so that either (a) the asset or right to income ceases to exist after a given period, or (b) the asset or income right is transferred back to B, so that in either event it disappears from the books of L. The legislation counteracts the scheme by directing (sections 759–762) that B is taxable after all or cannot obtain the deduction. The transaction is still treated as a financing transaction but for B and not L—any finance charges are treated as payments of interest to L only.[232] There are some exceptions in sections 771–773—these are usually because the income is brought into account for tax purposes by some other mechanism.

[231] [2006] BTR 560.
[232] On interaction with capital gains rules, see TCGA 1992, s 263E.

Sections 763–769 concern more complex schemes involving partnerships, referred to in the legislation as 'type 2' and 'type 3' finance arrangements. HMRC's *Corporate Finance Manual* has an example at paragraph 6796. Once more, the company wishes to borrow £100 million and has an asset on which income of £112.5 million will arise over the next five years. But instead of selling the asset to the lender, the borrower transfers it to a partnership of which it is a member. The lender then joins the partnership for a capital contribution of, say, £100 million, in return for the right to receive partnership profits amounting to £112.5 million over the next five years. The partnership will then lend the £100 million to the company. After five years, all of the rights to receive partnership profits will revert to the borrower (who may be able to buy out the lender's interest for a nominal consideration or have the right to expel the lender). In substance, the lender has made a loan of £100 million for the benefit of the borrower which is repaid with interest by the borrower.

Again, it is claimed that the borrower is not taxable on the income of £112.5 million, which flows to the partnership and is allocated to the lender. In these types of arrangements, the lender's 'loan' is made in the form of a contribution to the partnership, and its profit share is such that payments are made to it which repay that contribution together with interest. Once the repayment with interest has been made, the lender will cease to be a member of the partnership or to share in its profits.

These arrangements would not be caught by section 758; that provision deals with cases where it is the partnership itself that borrows by transferring to the lender an income-producing asset of the partnership. However, in this case the borrower is a member of a partnership who transfers to that partnership an income-producing asset, with the bulk of that income then appropriated to another partner who supplies the amount that equates to a loan. The schemes are now caught by sections 765–766 and 768–769.

The rules as enacted were found not to be completely fireproof. As a result, FA 2007 added three further sets of rules. The first brought into the scheme arrangements under which existing liabilities are refinanced using an structured finance arrangement. The second brought into the scheme assets which are not income-producing at the time of transfer but later produce income which equates in substance to a repayment. The third dealt with assets which have been used as collateral, and makes the charge continue to apply even though the assets have been changed.

Readers are also directed to relevant aspects of the G20/OECD Base Erosion and Profit Shifting (BEPS) project (see §69.11), and particularly Action 2.[233]

63.8   Risk Transfer Schemes

FA 2010, section 46 and Schedule 16 added CTA 2010, sections 937A to 937O on risk transfer schemes. These rules deal with over- and under-hedging arrangements. The effect is that any losses are ring-fenced and may be relieved only against profits from the same risk transfer scheme. The details of the risk transfer scheme rules are beyond the scope of this book.

---

[233] OECD, BEPS Action 2 'Neutralizing the effect of hybrid mismatch arrangements' Final Report (Oct 2015).

64

Groups and Consortium Companies: General

64.1 Overview of Groups and Consortia

The UK tax system starts from the premise that each company is a separate taxpayer.[1] The effects of this premise are then modified by a number of special rules which apply either to groups or to consortia.

64.1.1 Groups

A group consists of a parent company and its subsidiaries which may, in turn, have their own subsidiaries. Broadly, a company is a subsidiary if the other company owns the relevant percentage of its ordinary share capital[2]—more than 50% (commonly called a 51%

---

[1] For an example of the basic principle of UK tax law that the tax system respects the separate existence of members of a corporate group, see *Gripple Ltd v Revenue and Customs Commissioners* [2010] EWHC 1609 (Ch), [2010] STC 2283, where staffing costs incurred in one company could not be used in another company for purposes of the R&D credit.

[2] CTA 2010, s 1154, ex TA 1988, s 838(1). On the meaning of ordinary share capital, see HMRC Brief 54/2007, 6 August 2007.

subsidiary), 75% or more, 90% or more and even 100%. A parent must be a company and not an individual. A group can exist only if there is more than one company; thus, if all but one of the members of a group leaves that group, the group ceases to exist and the survivor is no longer a member of a group.[3]

64.1.1.1 Ordinary Share Capital

Ordinary share capital is defined by excluding share capital the holders of which have a right to a dividend at a fixed rate and no other right to share in the profits of the company.[4] Thus, loan stock and non-participating preference shares are not treated as ordinary share capital unless convertible into, or giving an option to acquire, shares or securities carrying a right greater than that of a dividend at a fixed rate. Conversely, however, shares may be ordinary share capital even if they carry no voting rights. Shares with no dividend entitlement may or may not qualify as ordinary share capital—the First-tier Tribunal has issued conflicting decisions as to whether shares with no right to a dividend could be viewed as shares which carried a right to a dividend at a 'fixed rate' of zero.[5]

Ownership of such capital must be beneficial,[6] but may be direct or indirect.[7] Indirect ownership is determined by multiplication. If A Ltd owns 80% of the ordinary share capital of B Ltd and B Ltd owns 70% of such share capital of C Ltd, A Ltd is taken to own 56% of C and so C has '51% subsidiary' status vis-à-vis A. If B Ltd had owned only 60% of C Ltd, A Ltd would have had a 48% share in C, and C would not have been a 51% subsidiary. If P Ltd owns 70% of Q Ltd and Q Ltd owns 30% of M Ltd, but P Ltd also owns 35% of M Ltd, P Ltd's ownership of M Ltd is a mixture of direct (35%) and indirect (21%), making M Ltd a 51% subsidiary of P Ltd.

In particular instances[8] the statute may provide that only share capital held as an investment and not as a trading asset may be included.[9] It may also be necessary to satisfy[10] these percentages not just in terms of the beneficial ownership of share capital, but also in terms of the economic reality, ie an entitlement to similar percentages of profits available for distribution and the division of assets available on winding up.

It is unclear how companies without share capital, eg a company incorporated by Royal Charter or limited by guarantee, can fit some of these rules.[11]

---

[3] *Dunlop International AG v Pardoe* [1999] STC 909 CA.

[4] CTA 2010, s 1118, ex TA 1988, s 832(1); a preference share with a fixed rate of dividend but a right to share in surplus assets on a winding up is ordinary share capital since the surplus assets are from profits of the company (*Tilcon Ltd v Holland* [1981] STC 365, (1981) 54 TC 464).

[5] In *McQuillan v HMRC* [2016] UKFTT 305, the tribunal held that such shares were not ordinary share capital by equating no right to dividends to a right to receive zero based on a purposive interpretation of the legislation. In *Castledine v HMRC* [2016] UKFTT 145 305, the Tribunal took the opposite view. See commentary by Lom, *Tax Journal* (24 June 2016) who (sensibly) prefers the *Castledine* approach and suggests a practical solution to avoid ordinary share capital treatment where desired would be to offer a fixed right to a very small dividend.

[6] See above §60.10 and CTA 1154(6), ex TA 1988, s 838(3). See also Statement of Practice SP 3/93.

[7] CTA 2010, s 1154(5), ex TA 1988, s 838(2).

[8] Eg CTA 151(3), ex TA 1988, s 413(5)(a).

[9] On which, see *Cooper v C & J Clark Ltd* [1982] STC 335, (1982) 54 TC 670.

[10] Other rules involving groups include CTA 2010, s 271(1), ex TA 1988, s 502(3), and see also TCGA 1992, s 140, Sch 2 (assets held on 6 April 1965).

[11] *Simon's Direct Tax Service*, para D2.621 and *Southshore Mutual Insurance Co v Blair* [1999] SRC (SCD) 296, where a company limited by guarantee was held not to have ordinary share capital for the purpose of being a 75% subsidiary. Some later statutes have attempted to address this issue—eg FA 2002, rewriting TCGA 1992, s 135(5).

64.1.1.2 Residence

Statute might provide that a company must be resident in the UK, eg in the old rule that a company was to be regarded as a holding company of a trading group only if the majority of the subsidiaries were UK-resident trading companies.[12] In *ICI v Colmer*,[13] the taxpayer company claimed consortium relief by reference to an investment company which had 23 trading subsidiaries. Both sides agreed that the claim would fail if only UK-resident companies could be counted for this purpose. The ECJ held that the restriction to UK-resident companies was in breach of EC Treaty law on freedom of establishment, and that companies with seats in other Member States should also be taken into account.[14]

In response to the decision in *Colmer*, FA 2000 changed radically the treatment of non-resident companies. So group relief (below at §64.6) may be claimed by a non-resident company which is a member of a group whether the company is resident or is carrying on a trade in the UK through a permanent establishment (PE).[15] In addition, two UK companies with a common non-resident parent may now form a group, whether or not the non-resident company has a branch trading in the UK. In consequence, any rules using the group relief definition of 'group' will also extend to take account of non-resident companies. There are also many changes to the rules for capital gains (see chapter sixty-five below). There are also rules for recovering tax payable by a non-resident company from other group companies. The company paying the tax may not claim any relief in computing profits; however, it is given a right of indemnity against the defaulting company. These changes are noted in the text, and apply whether the non-resident is resident in the EU or elsewhere. The treatment of losses was not addressed in FA 2000; for new rules introduced in 2006, see below at §64.6.7.

However, it is also worth recalling now those rules which have not been widened to assist the non-resident PE. See also §60.9.2 above.

64.1.2 *Consortia*

Some—but not all[16]—of the group rules also apply to consortia of companies. These are to encourage and facilitate the ad hoc merger of a number of different corporate interests in a single common enterprise.[17] The different corporate interests (the consortium members) come together to finance a project which is developed through a company (the consortium company). Allowing the consortium company to pay interest or charges gross, or to pass the benefit of losses through to the members, is designed to help the

---

[12] Ex TA 1988, s 413(5).

[13] Case C-264/96 [1998] All ER (EC) 585; [1998] STC 874; restriction ruled unlawful in so far as it did not take account of companies with seats in other Member States (answers implemented by the House of Lords at [1999] STC 1089).

[14] It is probably not enough simply to show that a majority of the companies had seats in the Member States—the courts may have regard to matters such as turnover (see Lord Nolan at *ICI v Colmer* [1996] STC 352, 361h) or some other measure to be determined.

[15] CTA 2010, ss 130–134, ex TA 1988, s 402(3A) and (3B), added by FA 2000, Sch 27, para 1.

[16] Eg the CGT rules discussed in chapter sixty-five do not apply to consortia.

[17] *ICI v Colmer* [1996] STC 352, 358e, *per* Lord Nolan.

members to pool resources and risks. The definition of a consortium varies, as will be seen in §64.6.4 below.

64.2   Choice of Structure—One Company or a Group?

If a company's trading activities are divided up between different companies, the premise of UK tax law is that each company is a separate entity with separate profits and therefore separate corporation tax liability. There is no simple charging of the group as a whole on its group profits—as there is in other countries which allow 'group reporting'. However, this premise is relaxed by the following rules. Special rules apply, say, to continuity treatment of loan relationships within groups, the ability of groups to pay corporation tax under self-assessment and the quarterly instalments on a group basis.

The decision whether to run a business through one company or through a group of companies depends upon many factors, not all concerned with taxation. It appears that, in practice, the activities of a single company will be regarded as one trade unless they are widely different. This has tax advantages, in that expenditure incurred for dual purposes is non-deductible unless those purposes are regarded as one trade;[18] the problem of the non-deductibility of pre-commencement and post-cessation expenses may also be avoided. Further, trade sales within the group will give rise to immediate profits, whereas in a single company profits will not accrue until the sale is made to an outsider. By concession the existence of separate companies is ignored for certain rules concerning directors.[19]

64.3   Intra-group Dividends—Group Income

A subsidiary, S, may wish to pass profit to its parent, P, by way of dividend. In the ACT era, ACT would be due unless the companies made a 'group income' election.[20] Today, intra-group dividends are treated in the same way as other dividends and so are not subject to corporation tax in the hands of the recipient.[21] Even the term 'group income' has disappeared from the tax lexicon.[22]

64.3.1   The Parent–Subsidiary Directive

If S is resident in one country and P in another, S's state may require a withholding tax[23] to be charged on the dividend. The Parent–Subsidiary Directive of 1990 (revised in 2011)

---

[18] See above at §22.2.
[19] See ESC A4.
[20] TA 1988, s 247.
[21] CTA 2009, ss 931A *et seq*, ex TA 1988, s 208.
[22] TA 1988, s 13(7) was amended by FA 1998 to read 'franked investment income'. However, there are echoes in the shadow ACT regulations—Corporation Tax (Treatment of Unrelieved Surplus ACT) Regulations 1999 (SI 1999/358), reg 11(2)–(4).
[23] ACT was not—in UK eyes—a withholding tax on the dividend since it was a tax on the company. The reduction in the value of the tax credit to 10% as from 1999 weakened but did not destroy the UK argument: Gammie (1997) 25 *Intertax* 333, 339.

was designed to enable dividends to flow free of such taxes within groups where the groups straddle national boundaries within the European Community (now European Union or EU).[24] The Directive bars a withholding tax where S, resident in one Member State, pays a dividend to P, a company resident in another Member State, provided P has the relevant minimum holding. The 2011 version of the Directive also applies to distribution of profits to/from permanent establishments, and includes an anti-avoidance provision.

While normal UK tax law (prior to 2009) did not allow a non-resident to have a tax credit on a dividend, many treaties allow a partial credit subject to abatement (or withholding). A question arises whether this abatement is a withholding tax, and therefore prohibited by the Directive if paid between subsidiary and parent. The UK view that this practice is permitted under another part of the Directive[25] has been upheld by the ECJ.[26]

Under the Directive, P must have a minimum percentage of the capital of 10% from 1 January 2009.[27] Member States may withhold this treatment unless the company maintains that holding for an uninterrupted period of at least two years. The ECJ has held that this allows the Member State to refuse P the benefit of the Directive during those two years, but that it is not permissible to refuse to repay the tax in respect of those two years once the period has expired.[28]

64.3.2 *The Parent–Subsidiary Directive—Specific Issues*

The Directive raises many other issues, including the following:[29]

(1) *Company residence*—the conditions for applicability include a requirement that each company should be a resident and subject to corporation tax in that State. Certain Luxembourg holding companies are not subject to (Luxembourg) corporation tax and therefore cannot use the Directive. Certain dual resident companies similarly fail to qualify if the country of second residence is outside the EU.

(2) *Percentage condition*—the percentage condition raises a further issue, ie whether the shares must be owned beneficially. Is the percentage condition simply a reference to 10% of issued share capital—in which case the issue of abnormal share capital might enable a company to use the Directive?[30] From 2011 the anti-avoidance rule must also be considered.

---

[24] Council Directive 90/435/EEC of 23 July 1990, replaced by Council Directive 2011/96/E, OJ L 345, 29.12.2011, on the common system of taxation applicable in the case of parent companies and subsidiaries of different Member States, as amended by Directive 2013/13/EU of 13 May 2013, Directive 2014/86/EU of 8 July 2014, Directive (EU) 2015/121 of 27 January 2015 (hereinafter the Parent-Subsidiary Directive). See [1990] *Simon's Tax Intelligence* 749 and de Hosson (1990) 10 *Intertax* 414. The original 1990 Parent-Subsidiary Directive was implemented in the UK by F(No 2)A 1992; on which, see McGregor [1992] BTR 131.

[25] Art 7(2); see also Inland Revenue, *EC Direct Tax Measures: a Consultative Document* (December 1991), 21.

[26] *IRC v Océ Van Der Grinten NV* [2003] STC 1248. The court separated the tax on the dividend from the treaty credit arrangement and held that the credit was not affected by Art 5(1) of the Directive at all as it was a fiscal instrument to prevent double taxation. The tax on the dividend *was* covered by Art 5(1) but was saved by Art 7(2).

[27] Parent-Subsidiary Directive, Art 3(1).

[28] *Denkavit International BV v Bundesamt für Finanzen* [1996] STC 1445 (see ch 77 below).

[29] See Lurie, *Tolley's International Tax Planning*, 4th edn (Tolleys, 1999), ch 9.

[30] See also the invaluable IBFD survey by Wijnen, *op cit.*

64.4 Transfer Payments—Interest Payments and Other Charges on Income

At one time TA 1988, sections 247 and 248 gave group companies the right to opt out of the normal rules requiring companies to withhold income tax (at 20%) when making payments of interest or other charges on income to another group company. As these rules were framed in terms of companies resident in the UK they were contrary to EU law.[31] The general rules requiring withholding were repealed in 2001 for payment where both companies were resident in the UK,[32] and so these special group rules were repealed from the same date.[33]

64.4.1 *Interest and Royalties Directive—25% Associates*

In accordance with the Interest and Royalties Directive of 2003,[34] ITTOIA 2005 exempts from UK tax certain payments arising in the UK but made to a company of another Member State.[35] The company must be beneficially entitled to the income, and the payer and the payee must be 25% associates.[36] The person beneficially entitled must be an EU company, or its PE (other than a UK PE or PE outside the EU).[37] Where the payment is one of interest, as opposed to royalties, HMRC must have issued an exemption notice.[38] Where the payment is of royalties, the payer may make the payment without deducting tax so long as the payer has a reasonable belief that the recipient is entitled to the exemption. There are restrictions on the exemptions where there are special relationships, and there is a purpose-based anti-avoidance rule.[39]

The rule just discussed affects payments going from the UK to another EU Member State. Although the broad effect of the Interest and Royalties Directive is to exempt these types of income from tax—and so remove any duty or right to withhold tax—some Member States were given a transitional period during which they could continue to levy withholding tax. A second set of rules provides relief against UK tax by way of credit for the tax charged in the other Member States.[40]

64.5 Special Rules for Distributions: Assets at Undervalue

The transfer of an asset at undervalue is normally to be treated as a distribution. However, this does not apply when both transferor and recipient are resident in the UK and one is a

---

[31] By extension from *ICI v Colmer* [1998] STC 874.
[32] Ex TA 1988, s 349B(1).
[33] FA 2001, s 85(5).
[34] Council Directive 2003/49/EC, OJ L 157, 26.6.2003, on a common system of taxation applicable to interest and royalty payments made between associated companies of different Member States, implemented by FA 2004, ss 97–106, and amended by Directive 2004/66/EC of 26 April 2004, Directive 2004/76/EC of 29 April 2004, Directive 2006/98/EC of 20 November 2006 and Directive 2013/13/EU of 13 May 2013 (hereinafter the Interest and Royalties Directive). Terms defined FA 2004, ss 98(3), (4) and 103
[35] For terms see Arts 1.2 and 3(a) of the Interest and Royalties Directive.
[36] ITTOIA 2005, s 758(1)–(4), ex FA 2004, ss 98(3), 98(4) and 103.
[37] ITTOIA 2005, s 758(3), ex FA 2004, s 98(3).
[38] ITTOIA 2005, s 758(5), ex FA 2004, ss 98(4) and 95.
[39] ITTOIA 2005, ss 764 and 765, ex FA 2004, ss 103 and 104.
[40] TIOPA 2010, Pt 3, ex FA 2004, ss 107–115.

51% subsidiary of the other, or both are 51% subsidiaries of another resident company.[41] In determining whether one company is a 51% subsidiary of the other, holdings, whether direct or indirect, do not qualify if a profit on the sale would be a trading receipt or if the company is non-resident.[42]

In other respects the definition of distribution is unchanged, save that a distribution made by one company out of its assets but in respect of shares or securities of another company in the same 90% group is treated as a distribution if all other conditions are satisfied.[43] This is primarily concerned to extend to groups another provision dealing with distribution by two or more companies to each other's members under an arrangement made between them.[44]

64.6   Group and Consortium Relief for Losses, etc

64.6.1 Basics

Group relief enables current trading losses, capital allowances, non-trading deficit on loan relationships, excess management expenses of investment companies and excess charges on income to be surrendered by one company (the surrendering company) to another (the claimant company), enabling the latter to put the other company's loss, etc, against its total profits.[45] Both companies must satisfy the group or consortium tests throughout their respective accounting period; however, they need not be members of the same group or consortium when the claim is made.[46] Relief is not available to a company which is a 'dual resident investing company'.[47] The self-assessment legislation contains rules for claiming this relief.[48] It often comes as a surprise to those from civil law backgrounds that a company can assign a loss to another group member in this way without the assignee company becoming liable for the debts of the assignor—but it is so. Under UK company law, groups of companies have the right to arrange affairs so as to isolate risk in subsidiaries.[49]

If company A makes a loss and surrenders that relief to company B, company A may insist upon receiving some payment. This will be particularly so if it is not a wholly-owned subsidiary so that there will be different minority interests as well as different creditors. If the amount paid is due under a legally enforceable agreement[50] and does not exceed the amount surrendered, the payment is ignored in computing the profits and losses of either company, and is treated neither as a distribution nor as a charge on income. This device is of particular use when, for example, a company with foreign income is already relieved from corporation tax by the foreign tax credit.

---

[41] CTA 2010, s 1021(1), ex TA 1988, s 209(5).
[42] CTA 2010, s 1021(1)–(3), ex TA 1988, s 209(7).
[43] CTA 2010, s 1072(1), (2), ex TA 1988, s 254(3).
[44] CTA 2010, s 1112(1)–(3), ex TA 1988, s 254(8).
[45] CTA 2010, Pt 5, esp ss 99–109, ex TA 1988, s 402.
[46] *AW Chapman Ltd v Hennessey* [1982] STC 214, (1982) 55 TC 516.
[47] CTA 2010, s 109, ex TA 1988, s 404(1).
[48] FA 1998, Sch 18, paras 67–77. For modification to take account of non-resident companies, see FA 2000, Sch 27, para 11.
[49] *Adams v Cape Industries plc* [1990] Ch 433.
[50] *Haddock v Wilmot Breeden Ltd* [1975] STC 255, (1975) 50 TC 132.

64.6.2 The Group[51]

64.6.2.1 Basic Rule: Residence

Two companies are members of the same group for group relief purposes if one is a 75% subsidiary of the other or both are 75% subsidiaries of a third company. Today group relief may now be claimed or surrendered by a company which is a member of a group and either resident in the UK or carrying on a trade in the UK through a PE.[52] For periods not affected by FA 2000 the rules on group membership stated that only a body corporate resident in the UK qualified;[53] the status of this rule in the light of the EU's non-discrimination principles was not directly in issue in *ICI v Colmer*,[54] which was concerned with consortium relief, but it was clearly vulnerable. If *Colmer* applies, two UK-resident companies with a French parent should be able to pass losses to each other; whether they could pass losses to the French parent to set against some of the parent's UK income is a separate question.

The rules restricting group relief where a member of the group is a resident of a non-EU state were challenged in *FCE Bank plc v Revenue and Customs Commissioners*.[55] In this case, a loss-making UK-resident subsidiary (FL) of a US company (FM) sought to surrender losses to a profitable sister company (FC) also resident in the UK. HMRC rejected FC's claim for group relief on the grounds that the parent company was resident in the US. The First-Tier Tribunal allowed the appeal on the basis that the effect of the non-discrimination article in the 1975 UK/US double taxation agreement was that group relief should be available between two UK-resident directly-held 75% subsidiaries of a US parent company in circumstances where it would be available if the parent company were UK-resident.

Trading. Any share capital owned directly or indirectly in a non-resident company and any share capital owned directly or indirectly must be ignored if a profit on sale would be a trading receipt of the direct owners.[56]

64.6.2.2 Anti-avoidance—Unreal Holdings, Arrangements and Options

Three sets of rules apply here:

(1)   *Real holdings.* The parent must be entitled to not less than 75% of any profits available for distribution to equity holders of the subsidiary company, and to not less than 75% of any of its assets available for distribution to its equity holders on a winding up.[57] In determining this percentage, certain loans of a non-commercial nature are treated as equity,[58] and the court must have regard to any 'arrangements' which might affect

---

[51] CTA 2010, ss 150–153, ex TA 1988, s 413 and Sch 18.

[52] CTA 2010, s 112 and 136, ex TA 1988, s 402(3A) and (3B) added by FA 2000, Sch 27.

[53] Ex TA 1988, s 413(5).

[54] Case C-264/96 [1998] All ER (EC) 585; [1998] STC 874.

[55] [2010] UKFTT 136 (TC).

[56] CTA 2010, s 151(3), ex TA 1988, s 413(5)(a)–(c).

[57] CTA 2010, s 151(4), ex TA 1988, s 413(7).

[58] CTA 2010, ss 157 and 158, ex TA 1988, Sch 18, para 1. Sections 162 *et seq*, ex paras 1(5) *et seq*, define 'normal commercial loan' and treat certain non-recourse loans as commercial loans and not as equity. Interest payments on ratchet loans are treated as normal commercial loans; these are loans where the interest rate falls as business results improve or vice versa, ie are inversely related to the results of the business: CTA 2010, s 163(1), (2), ex TA 1988, Sch 18, para 1(5E) amended by FA 2000.

those rights.[59] Rules determine the notional profit distribution and the assets available on a winding up.[60] Any limitation on the rights of equity holders is to be given effect if this would yield a lower percentage.[61] These provisions have received a narrow but purposive construction.[62] The purpose of these rules is to confine the passing of the reliefs, especially capital allowance, to parents which were such in commercial as well as legal terms at some time during the accounting period in which the loss arises.

(2)   *Transfer arrangements—no temporary holdings.* It is also necessary, for similar reasons, to show that there are no arrangements in existence for transfer of control of the surrendering company without also transferring control of the claimant company.[63] Here, the term 'arrangements' is broadly construed.[64] However, the arrangement must be one by which control is or might be obtained. An arrangement subject to the consent of X is not in existence until X consents.[65] Without such a rule an outside company could buy participation preference shares to establish 75% control, and later the shares would be redeemed or sold back to the parent; in this way the loss might be sold to an outsider. Where arrangements are in force, the effect of these provisions is to bar relief for those losses attributable to the period during which the arrangements subsisted.[66] The Revenue do not view the offer of 'first refusal' as sufficient to trigger these rules.[67]

(3)   *Options.* As originally enacted, these provisions were held not to reach the alteration of rights which might follow from the exercise of an option to acquire or dispose of shares, since the option did not affect the nature of the rights attached to the shares but only the ownership of those shares.[68] This decision is now reversed by statute. The essence of the new rules is that in order to calculate the extent of the equity holder's entitlement to profits or assets, the entitlements must be recalculated on the basis that the option has been exercised. The equity holder is then treated as being entitled only to the lowest percentage.[69]

The legislation makes it clear that each of the tests is to be applied to the original sets of rights (ie percentage of profits or assets on winding up) independently and cumulatively, with only the lowest percentages used.[70] This is then applied to situations in which there

---

[59]   CTA 2010, s 169–72, ex TA 1988, Sch 18, para 5.

[60]   CTA 2010, ss 165, 166, ex TA 1988, Sch 18, paras 2, 3.

[61]   CTA 2010, ss 169–170, ex TA 1988, Sch 18, para 4.

[62]   *J Sainsbury plc v O'Connor* [1991] STC 318, (1991) 64 TC 208 CA.

[63]   CTA 2010, ss 154–156, ex TA 1988, s 410(1)–(6). For this purpose, members of a consortium are not held to be 'acting together' to control a company (s 410(5) as amended by FA 1997, s 68); and see Revenue Interpretation RI 160).

[64]   *Pilkington Bros Ltd v IRC* [1982] STC 103; see notes by Wyatt [1982] BTR 244 and [1981] BTR 241. See also *Irving v Tesco Stores (Holdings) Ltd* [1982] STC 881.

[65]   *Scottish and Universal Newspapers Ltd v Fisher* [1996] STC (SCD) 311.

[66]   *Shepherd v Law Land plc* [1990] STC 795, (1990) 63 TC 692, rejecting the Revenue view that relief was barred for all the losses arising in the accounting period during part of which the arrangements subsisted.

[67]   On scope of arrangements, see Statement of Practice SP 3/93.

[68]   *J Sainsbury plc v O'Connor* [1991] STC 318, (1991) 64 TC 208 CA.

[69]   CTA 2010, ss 173, 174, ex TA 1988, Sch 18, para 5B, added by F(No 2)A 1992; Inland Revenue Press Release, 29 January 1992, [1992] *Simon's Tax Intelligence* 90, and Inland Revenue Press Release, 15 November 1991, [1991] *Simon's Tax Intelligence* 1042.

[70]   CTA 2010, s 174(1), ex TA 1988, Sch 18, para 5B(9), added by F(No 2)A 1992, Sch 6, para 6.

are both fixed-element rights and variable rights.[71] All 'relevant preference shares' will be ignored. If the relevant shares carry a right to a dividend they must meet various conditions, including one relating to a reasonable commercial return.

64.6.2.3 Overlapping Accounting Periods

The relief allows one company to use the losses sustained by the other in the overlapping accounting period.[72] If both companies have the same accounting period, the whole loss is available for offset, assuming, of course, that they fulfil all the other conditions for group membership at that time.[73] Conversely, when the company joins or leaves the group, the profits of the relevant accounting periods must be apportioned to ensure that only losses of post-entry or pre-departure periods are used. To carry out this process the legislation creates the concepts of the 'surrenderable amount' of the loss and the 'unrelieved part of the profits'. The amount of the loss which may be set off against the profits of the claimant is the lesser of two sums—one is the unused part of the surrenderable amount for the overlapping period, and the other is the unrelieved part of the claimant's profits for the period. The balance of the loss may either be set off against profits of other group companies, or be rolled forward under the rule set out below.[74] In computing the first of these sums, account must be taken of any previous surrenders which have already been made during that period; in computing the second sum, account must be taken of any previous group relief claims.

A time basis is used to allocate these amounts to different parts of an accounting period unless that would be unjust or unreasonable in relation to any person, in which case a just and reasonable basis is used, but only to the extent necessary to avoid injustice and unreasonableness.[75] This last formulation is a considerable tightening in comparison with the old law and creates its own problems, eg if what would be required to be just to one party would create injustice for another; presumably the time apportionment applies.

64.6.3 *Groups and Consortia: Link Companies*

Where a consortium member is itself a member of a group, it is known as a 'link' company.[76] The consortium relief may flow through the link company to the member's own group.[77] The usual rules on group membership for the appropriate accounting periods apply:[78] the link may not increase the amount of relief.[79] It is also possible to surrender part of the available relief to a group company and part to a consortium company, subject to restrictions on the amount available for relief.[80]

[71] CTA 2010, s 175, ex TA 1988, Sch 18, para 5A, replacing the old para 5(5).
[72] CTA 2010, ss 138–42, ex TA 1988, s 403A, added by F(No 2)A 1997, Sch 7 and replacing older rules; see Inland Revenue Press Release, 2 July 1997, para 6, [1997] *Simon's Tax Intelligence* 912.
[73] CTA 2010, s 99–106, 137, ex TA 1988, s 403(1), (8)–(10).
[74] CTA 2010, ss 99–105, 147, ex TA 1988, s 403(2), 403ZA–403ZE.
[75] CTA 2010, ss 139–141, ex TA 1988, s 403B, replacing s 408.
[76] CTA 2010, s 133(1), (2), ex TA 1988, s 406(1).
[77] CTA 2010, ss 133, 142, 145–49, ex TA 1988, s 406.
[78] CTA 2010, ss 133(1), (3), (4), 145(2), 147(2), 148(2), 149(2), ex TA 1988, s 406(2), (9).
[79] CTA 2010, ss 146(2), (3), (8) and 146(5)–(8), ex TA 1988, s 406(4), (8).
[80] CTA 2010, ss 148, 149, ex TA 1988, ss 405, 411(9).

64.6.4 *Consortium Relief*

Relief may also be claimed by members of a consortium for losses incurred by companies owned by the consortium.[81] However, a member's right to use the loss sustained by the consortium company is limited to that proportion of the loss which corresponds to the member's interest.[82] This was expanded in the new form of the relief introduced in 2000. The maximum amount available for consortium relief depends on the 'relevant fraction'. This relates to the interest which the member has in the consortium, and is the lowest of ordinary share capital, profits available for distribution and on any distribution of assets. Fluctuating percentages are dealt with by averaging. Where the claimant company is a member of the consortium this fraction is applied to the company's surrenderable amount for the overlapping period.[83] A similar fraction is applied where the surrendering company is a member of the consortium.[84]

A consortium owns a company if 75% of the ordinary share capital of that company is directly and beneficially owned between the consortium members, each owning at least 5%.[85] FA 2000 amended the definition of 'consortium' so that a non-resident company with a UK PE can be a member.[86] For periods unaffected by FA 2000 and subject to the requirements of EU law as stated in *ICI v Colmer*,[87] all the companies had to be resident in the UK.[88] Like group relief, consortium relief is strictly controlled in the case of overlapping accounting periods.[89]

Group relief may be claimed by members of a consortium in three situations:[90]

(1) the surrendering company is owned by the consortium and is not a 75% subsidiary of any company but is a trading company;
(2) the surrendering company is a 90% subsidiary of a holding company which is owned by the consortium and is not a 75% subsidiary of any other company but is a trading company; and
(3) the surrendering company is a holding company which is owned by the consortium and is not a 75% subsidiary of any company.

The relief is claimed by the member of the consortium, not by the holding company. At one time the claim was barred if the member company's share in the consortium company in that company's accounting period was nil.[91] Since a company is only a consortium

---

[81] CTA 2010, ss 132, 133, 153, ex TA 1988, s 402(3).
[82] CTA 2010, s 144, ex TA 1988, s 403C(3) replacing s 403(9).
[83] CTA 2010, ss 143, 144, ex TA 1988, s 403C(2) added by FA 2000, s 100 which also repeals s 413(8), (9).
[84] CTA 2010, s 144, ex TA 1988, s 403C(3) added by FA 2000, s 100.
[85] CTA 2010, s 153(1)–(3), ex TA 1988, s 413(6).
[86] FA 2000, Sch 27, para 32, repealing TA 1988, s 413(5).
[87] Case C-264/96 [1998] All ER (EC) 585; [1998] STC 874.
[88] Thus, before FA 2000 the membership of one non-resident company was fatal to group relief for the other members. In such circumstances assets are commonly owned by the non-resident company and leased by the company owned by the consortium—of which, of course, the non-resident was not a member. Whereas a group of resident companies within a larger group may form a group on its own, this is not open to a consortium.
[89] CTA 2010, ss 143–144, ex TA 1988, s 403C.
[90] CTA 2010, s 153, ex TA 1988, s 402(3); the terms are defined in s 185 (ex s 413(3)(b), (c)).
[91] CTA 2010, ss 132(4), (5) and 133(3), (4), ex TA 1988, s 402(4) and FA 2000, s 100(3)(a).

company if the members have at least a 5% holding, it was not clear how this provision was meant to operate, and it was repealed with retroactive effect by FA 2000.[92]

Relief within a consortium may pass in either direction,[93] but not between the members of the consortium themselves. As already seen, each member may claim only that part of the loss which is proportionate to its share in the consortium.[94] Where a member surrenders downwards to a trading company, that amount may be set only against a similar proportion of the trading company's profits. There is no surrender to the intermediate holding company, but that company may claim group relief proper. There is no objection to finding a group within a group or a group within a consortium.

In response to *Philips Electronics UK Ltd v HMRC,*[95] F(No 3)A 2010, Schedule 6 replaced the requirement to be UK resident for consortium relief with the requirement that the link company be UK resident or established in the EEA. In 2015, this requirement was abandoned and the rules extended so that claims are possible under the conditions of CTA 2010, section 133 regardless of the location of the link company.

64.6.5 The Sums Qualifying for Relief[96]

The following may be surrendered to the claimant company and set against total profits of the claimant company for its overlapping accounting period:

(1) trading losses[97]—the trading losses of a consortium-owned company must, as far as possible, be set off against the company's other profits of the same accounting period, and only the balance is available for set off against the profits of consortium member companies;[98]

(2) minor capital allowances[99]—these allowances attract relief through the discharge of tax rather than being treated as a trading expense (see above at §63.1);

(3) any non-trading deficit on loan relationships;[100]

(4) non-trading losses on intangible fixed assets;[101]

(5) UK property business (ex Schedule A) losses;[102]

(6) excess management expenses;[103]

(7) qualifying charitable donations.[104]

---

[92] CTA 2010, s 153(1), ex TA 1988, s 413(6)(a); presumably the remaining member companies can meet the consortium conditions on their own, but this still leaves the problem of a company with, say, a 3% stake.

[93] CTA 2010, ss 132(2), (3), 133(1), (2), 153(1), (3), ex TA 1988, s 402(3); a surrender downwards may affect that company's ability to surrender further losses within its group.

[94] CTA 2010, s 144(2)–(4), ex TA 1988, s 403C(3).

[95] [2009] UKFTT 226 (TC).

[96] This formulation is used because of the words of Lord Hoffmann in *Taylor v MEPC Holdings* [2004] STC 123, para 19.

[97] CTA 2010, s 100, ex TA 1988, s 403(1), as amended by FA 1988, Sch 5, para 29.

[98] CTA 2010, ss 143–144, ex TA 1988, s 403C.

[99] CTA 2010, s 101, ex TA 1988, s 403(1)(a), 403ZB.

[100] CTA 2010, s 99, ex TA 1988, ss 83(2), 403ZC.

[101] CTA 2010, s 104.

[102] CTA 2010, s 102, ex TA 1988, s 403(1)(b).

[103] CTA 2010, s 103. See below at §79.2.

[104] CTA 2010, Pt 6.

Reliefs (1)–(3) may be surrendered even if the surrendering company has other profits for that period against which it might set them.[105] Items (4)–(6) may be surrendered only to the extent that they exceed the surrendering company's gross profits for the period, and are to be taken in the order (4), (5) and (6).[106] This means, for example, that if charges are carried forward from a previous period, they cannot be used to free current reliefs for grouping; such charges may therefore become locked into the company. A problem has arisen over these charges, since the Revenue sometimes argue that excess charges may be surrendered only if incurred wholly and exclusively for the purpose of the trade of the surrendering company. On this reasoning, no relief could be given where a loan is raised to finance the acquisition of a subsidiary; there seems to be nothing in the group relief rules to justify this approach. Relief for items (4)–(6) may be permanently lost if the company's income bears only foreign, as opposed to UK, tax since none may be rolled forward.

The relief, if claimed, is taken as first exhausting profits of the accounting period in which it is claimed in priority to other reliefs that may be brought back into that period from future periods.[107]

64.6.6 *International Aspects*

Further rules govern the group relief rules applicable to the UK PE of a non-resident company and the overseas PE of a UK company. These apply to accounting periods ending on or after 1 April 2000.[108]

The non-resident company with the UK PE may only surrender amounts which:

(1)   are attributable to activities within the charge to the UK corporation tax;
(2)   are not exempt from corporation tax by virtue of any double taxation arrangement; and
(3)   are not relievable, in any period, against non-UK profits of any person for the purposes of any foreign tax.[109]

'Non-UK profits' are amounts on which a person is charged to foreign tax but which are not chargeable to UK corporation tax. The purpose behind rule (3), which is supplemented by a number of detailed rules,[110] is to make losses relievable against profits arising in the place where the company is resident rather than in the UK.

In the converse case of the foreign branch of the UK-resident company, restrictive rules apply to the amounts available for surrender by a UK-resident company where the loss is attributable to an overseas PE and any part of it is relievable, in any period, against non-UK profits of another person for the purposes of any foreign tax.[111] A loss attributable to an

---

[105] CTA 2010, s 99(3), ex TA 1988, s 403(2).
[106] CTA 2010, s 99(4), 105(1)–(4), ex TA 1988, s 403(3).
[107] CTA 2010, s 137(4)–(6), ex TA 1988, s 407. Terminal loss relief may be given only against trading income, whereas group relief may be given against total profits—hence, group relief should be claimed against non-trading income and chargeable gains if terminal loss relief is foreseen.
[108] For more precise transitional rules, see FA 2000, Sch 27, para 6.
[109] CTA 2010, ss 108(1)–(3), 140(8), ex TA 1988, s 403D(2), (3).
[110] CTA 2010, ss 107(7)–(9), 108(3), ex TA 1988, s 403D(4)–(6).
[111] CTA 2010, s 106(1), (2), (5), ex TA 1988, s 403E(1), (2).

overseas PE is the amount which would be available for surrender by the company if that amount were computed only by reference to the overseas PE.[112]

Where deductibility under the foreign law depends on deductibility in the UK, it is treated as deductible if and only if the company resident in the UK is also treated as resident in the relevant foreign territory.[113] The result of this is that the country of residence (the UK) has the primary responsibility for relieving the loss except in the case of dual residence.

64.6.7 Legislation on EEA Losses Post-Marks & Spencer

In response to the decision of the ECJ in *Marks & Spencer*[114] (see §77.3.4 below), FA 2006 inserted new rules for relief where the surrendering company is not resident in the UK.[115] The conditions to be satisfied by such losses are contained in CTA 2010, sections 112 and 113 (ex TA 1988, section 403F and Schedule 18A). These rules have effect as from 1 April 2006 and allow a claim if the company is resident in an EEA territory, or not so resident but carries on a trade there through a PE. Claims are made under the new FA 1998, Schedule 18, paragraph 77A. This is backed up by an anti-avoidance rule in CTA 2010, section 127 (ex TA 1988, section 403G), which has effect from 20 February 2006 and bans losses claimed as a result of relevant arrangements, ie arrangements where the main purpose—or one of the main purposes—was to secure that the amount would qualify for group relief. On commencement, see also FA 2006, Schedule 1, paragraph 9.

The loss must meet four conditions:

(1)   an equivalence condition—the loss must be equivalent to one for which relief is given to companies resident in the UK (CTA 2010, section 114);
(2)   an EEA tax loss condition—where the company is resident in an EEA territory, section 115 provides that there must be a loss in the overseas territory which must not be attributable to a UK PE of the company. Where the company is not so resident, section 116 applies; the loss must arise in the overseas territory and the loss must not relate to activities outside the UK tax net by reason of a double tax treaty;
(3)   qualifying loss condition—under section 117, the loss is limited to an amount which cannot be given relief in the EEA and for which relief has not been given in any territory outside the UK; these rules are amplified in sections 11–120;
(4)   lastly, there is a precedence condition—relief may be given under these rules only if it cannot be given in a qualifying territory (section 121).

CTA 2010, sections 122–126 contain rules on the assumptions to be made when the UK rules are applied to the non-resident company and how the 'EEA amount' of the loss is determined.

Cussons has pointed out that this legislation concentrates on the fact situation in *Marks & Spencer* and does not go as far as it might. Thus it does not deal with 'sideways' cross-border

---

[112]   CTA 2010, s 106(3), (4); this is determined using the same rules as those in ss 107–108 (ex 403D) when finding the loss of a UK branch of a non-resident company, ex s 403E(4), (5).

[113]   CTA 2010, s 106(6), (7), ex TA 1988, s 403E(8).

[114]   Case C-446/03 *Marks & Spencer v Halsey* [2006] STC 237.

[115]   CTA 2010, ss 112, 113,127, and Sch 2, ex TA 1988, ss 403F, 403G and Sch 18A, inserted by FA 2006, s 27 and Sch 1; for analysis, see Cussons [2006] BTR 497.

relief claimed by a profitable subsidiary of an EU non-UK parent with a loss-making EU (non-UK) sister subsidiary of a non-UK parent.[116] The European Commission considered that the UK's group relief legislation still infringed the freedom of establishment, and referred the matter to the CJEU. The CJEU eventually decided in the UK's favour, primarily on the grounds that the Commission did not satisfy the evidential burden required to make its case.[117]

64.7   Transfer of Company Tax Refund under Self-assessment

The rate of interest charged on unpaid tax is distinct from that used for repayment supplement. Where one company in a group, A, has a duty to pay unpaid tax and another, B, has a right to a tax repayment, the companies may merge the duty and the right, and so avoid letting the Revenue get the benefit of the difference in interest rates.[118] A and B must share the same accounting period for the period in respect of which the repayment claim is being surrendered, and must be members of the same group from the start of the accounting period for which the claim is made until the date of the surrender notice.[119] Any sums paid in exchange for the surrender are ignored, provided they do not exceed the amount of the refund in question—they are neither taxable receipts of the surrendering company nor deductible items for the claimant company.[120] The definition of 'group' is the same as 'group' relief (see above at §64.6.2).[121] The rules apply not only to normal corporation tax liabilities but also to over—and under—payments under the quarterly instalment payments regime. A company entitled to a refund[122] may prefer to transfer the benefit of that overpayment to another group company.[123]

64.8   Transfer of Loans

Where a loan is transferred between companies in a 75% group, the basic provision is that the transfer is not treated as giving rise to any charge or allowance on either the transferor or the transferee.[124] The transferee company, following the transfer, becomes entitled to any debits and credits arising thereafter which are not related to the transfer. This treatment extends to a 'related transaction'[125] between two group companies and to any series of

---

[116] Cussons [2006] BTR 497.

[117] Case C-172/13 *European Commission v UK* [2015] STC 1055.

[118] CTA 2010, ss 963–966, ex FA 1989, s 102.

[119] CTA 2010, ss 963(1)–(5), ex FA 1989, s 102(1)–(2), (4). Provisions ensure that the interest rules apply equally to companies in the group as they apply to single companies (ex s 102(4A), added by FA 1993, Sch 14, para 11).

[120] CTA 2010, s 966(1), (2), ex FA 1989, s 102(7); this is similar to payments for group relief under CTA 2010, s 183(1), (2), ex TA 1988, s 402(6).

[121] CTA 2010, s 963(5), ex FA 1989, s 102(8).

[122] Corporation Tax (Instalment Payments) Regulations 1998 (SI 1998/3175), reg 6.

[123] *Ibid*, reg 9.

[124] CTA 2009, ss 335–347, ex FA 1996, Sch 9, para 12, as much amended.

[125] CTA 2009, ss 293, 304, 307, 329, ex FA 1996, s 84.

transactions, where two companies were members of the same group at some time during the course of the series of transactions. The treatment applies where there is an effective transfer by novation. Thus, the release of the former borrower does not cause a taxable receipt in the hands of that company.

64.9 Group Financing Costs—The Worldwide Debt Cap

The worldwide debt cap applies to accounting periods beginning on or after 1 January 2010, and the rules are found in TIOPA 2010, Part 7, sections 260 *et seq*. The legislation introducing the cap—FA 2009, section 35 and Schedule 15—was altered considerably during the passage of the Finance Bill; the changes are explained in HMRC Technical Note, 8 April 2009.[126]

The purpose of the worldwide debt cap is to restrict the tax deduction in the UK of finance expenses of groups of companies. TIOPA 2010, section 261 directs that the rules apply if the UK net debt (see sections 262–263) exceeds 75% of the worldwide gross debt (section 264); the figure of 75% may be changed by statutory instrument. Subject to this 75% threshold, the system limits the aggregate UK tax deduction for the UK members of a group of companies that have net finance expenses to the consolidated group's finance expense. The disallowance is laid down by section 274. The restriction is calculated by comparing the UK measure of net finance expenses with the worldwide measure of the groups finance expense. More technically, section 274 asks whether (a) the tested expense amount, defined in Chapter 8 (sections 329–331), exceeds (b) the available amount, defined in Chapter 9 (sections 332–336). If so, the excess is disallowed. Sections 275–285 set out the procedure for making a report detailing the allocation of the disallowed amount to one or more UK group companies.

Chapter 4 deals with the group's financing income amounts. These give rise to exemption from corporation tax if the group has had finance expenses which have been disallowed; further rules deal with the allocation of the exemptions among the companies. Chapter 5 deals with various EEA matters where financing income is received from certain EEA countries. Chapter 6 contains various anti-avoidance rules. Chapter 7 contains the key definitions of the financing expenses of a company, the financing income amounts of a company, and Group Treasury companies. There follow special rules granting conditional exclusions for Real Estate Investment Trusts, companies with oil extraction activities, intra-group short-term finance, short-term loan relationships, stranded deficits and stranded management expenses; there are exemptions for amounts paid to charities and other bodies. The exclusion for financial services is in Chapter 2.

Regular changes have been made to the operation of the worldwide debt cap since its introduction.[127] In the 2016 Business Tax Road Map, the UK Government announced it

---

[126] The detail of the rules are beyond the scope of this book; interested readers are referred to Richards [2009] BTR 541.

[127] See Sch 5 to F(No 3)A 2010 for the details, and analysis by Ball [2011] BTR 51. See also FA 2012, Sch 5.

intends to repeal the worldwide debt cap and integrate rules with similar effect into the new interest restriction rules to take effect from 1 April 2017 (see above §63.2.9).[128] The aim will be to ensure that a group's net UK interest deductions cannot exceed the global net third party expense of the group.

---

[128] HM Treasury, *Business Tax Road Map*, (March 2016), para 2.37.

65

Control, Groups and Consortium Companies: Capital Gains

65.1 Introduction

65.1.1 General: 75% Test

TCGA 1992 contains a number of provisions for groups. A group comprises a principal company and all its 75% subsidiaries, including 75% subsidiaries of those subsidiaries and so on.[1] The 75% test is applied simply to the beneficial ownership[2] of shares; unlike group income reliefs, this test ignores the presence of shares held as trading stock.

This is one more of those areas in which, in response to the decision in *Colmer* (see above §64.1.1.2), FA 2000 changed radically the treatment of non-resident companies. For disposals before 1 April 2000, the definition of a 'group' meant that the group could consist only of companies resident in the UK.[3] For disposals on or after that date the definition of group is changed,[4] so that a non-resident company may be a group member; in addition, a number of detailed rule changes mean that transfer by or to a non-resident company may qualify

---

[1] TCGA 1992, s 170(2).
[2] See above at §60.10.
[3] TCGA 1992, s 170(2).
[4] TCGA 1992, s 170, as amended by FA 2000, Sch 29, para 1; for transitional provision, see Sch 29, para 46.

for special tax-neutral treatment, provided the transfer concerns a UK PE. The key to tax-neutral treatment is no longer residence but chargeability to UK tax. Merger with one of the SEs resident in another Member State may get similar treatment.[5]

It is expressly provided that the winding up of a company in the group does not result in either that company or any other company in the group being treated as ceasing to be a member of the group.[6] The mere passing of a winding-up resolution or order is not sufficient to end group membership.[7] Further, the group remains the same group provided the same company remains the principal company. If the principal company becomes a 75% subsidiary of another company, the group is regarded as expanded rather than ended and refounded.

65.1.2 Bridge Companies and the 51% Effective Subsidiary Test

A subsidiary which is a 75% subsidiary on the first test may be a member of a group only if it is also an 'effective' 51% subsidiary.[8] A company is an effective 51% subsidiary only if the parent is beneficially entitled to more than 50% of any profits available for distribution or of any assets on a winding up.[9] Further, a company is a 'principal company' only if it is at the head of the corporate chain. Thus, a company cannot be a principal company if it is a 75% subsidiary of another company;[10] however, a company prevented from being part of a group because it is not an effective 51% subsidiary (but is a 75% subsidiary) may be a principal company.[11]

To reinforce this policy it is provided that a company may not be a member of more than one group. To carry this policy through, the legislation contains a descending order of tests.[12] To prevent a charge from arising unexpectedly as a result of this change where a principal company subsequently becomes a 75% subsidiary of another company, thereby bringing two groups together, the two are regarded as being the same group for the purposes of determining whether there has been a transfer of an asset within the group (TCGA 1992, section 171) and whether a company has ceased to be a member of another group (section 179).[13] Thus, a charge under section 179 is not triggered simply by such an event.

The 51% test was designed to counter the use of 'bridge' companies.[14] These were companies with special classes of share which enabled the commercial control of companies to pass to a company outside the group, while allowing the company to remain within the group structure for TCGA 1992 purposes and so avoiding the triggering of charges that would otherwise arise on the company ceasing to be a member of the group.[15]

---

[5] TCGA 1992, s 170(10A) added by F(No 2)A 2005, s 61.
[6] TCGA 1992, s 170(12).
[7] TCGA 1992, s 170(11).
[8] TCGA 1992, s 170(3).
[9] TCGA 1992, s 170(7); CTA 2010, Pt 5, Ch 6 (ex TA 1988, Sch 18, etc) applies here (s 170(8)).
[10] TCGA 1992, s 170(4).
[11] TCGA 1992, s 170(5).
[12] TCGA 1992, s 170(6).
[13] TCGA 1992, s 170(11).
[14] There is also a consequential change for IHT under IHTA 1984, s 97. These rules are further backed up by a cross-reference to CTA 2010, Pt 5, Ch 6 (ex TA 1988, Sch 18).
[15] [1989] *Simon's Tax Intelligence* 222; HC Official Report, Standing Committee G (1989), col 597.

65.1.3 *Control*

It has become common for rules, sometimes of an anti-avoidance character, to be enacted which apply (a) when a company joins a group of companies, (b) when it ceases to be a member of the group, or (c) when the company becomes subject to different control. Rules introduced in 2006 are typical.[16] A company becomes subject to different control in three situations. The first is where a person (P) has control of the company (C) at that time (whether alone or together with one or more others) and P did not previously have control of C. The second is where P has control of the company at that time together with one or more others and P previously had control of the company alone. The third is where P ceases to have control of the company at that time (whether having control alone or together with one or more others).

The general rule is subject to the following exceptions:

(1)   A company does not become subject to different control in any case where it joins a group of companies and the case is the excepted case mentioned at §65.1.2 above.
(2)   A company ('the subsidiary') does not become subject to different control at any time in any case where:
    (a)   immediately before that time the subsidiary is the 75% subsidiary of another company; and
    (b)   (although there is a change in the direct ownership of the subsidiary) that other company continues immediately after that time to own it as a 75% subsidiary.

65.2   Intra-group Transfers of Capital Assets

65.2.1 *Tax Neutrality: TCGA 1992, Section 171*

The transfer of a chargeable asset between two members of a group takes place at such figure as ensures that there is neither a chargeable gain nor an allowable loss.[17] The effect is to postpone any capital gains liability until the asset is disposed of outside the group. This is a matter of law, not of election, and overrides the normal rule that bargains otherwise than at arm's length are to be treated as taking place at market value.[18] A nice question arises if one company surrenders a lease of land to another group member, since it may be argued that the lease ends and the landlord company acquires no asset at all.[19]

The companies must be members of the same group, and either both must be resident in the UK or, if either or both are non-resident, the asset must be subject to charge to corporation tax, ie within TCGA 1992, section 10.[20]

---

[16]   TCGA 1992, s 184C(6)–(9), added by FA 2006, s 70.
[17]   TCGA 1992, s 171.
[18]   TCGA 1992, s 17; s 171 applies 'notwithstanding any provision in CGTA fixing the amount of the consideration deemed to be received'. It might be argued that if a sale takes place at market value, s 171 should not apply as there is nothing 'deemed' about the consideration; however, this seems unlikely to succeed.
[19]   See Law Society, *Revenue Law Reform Proposals* (1991) *Simon's Tax Intelligence* 1069.
[20]   TCGA 1992, s 171(1A), added by FA 2000, Sch 29, para 2; on commencement, see Sch 29, para 6.

65.2.1.1 Exceptions

The general rule in TCGA 1992, section 171(1) is excluded in certain situations by further rules in section 171; what these have in common is that value is being received by one company but the capital gains system, for reasons of its own, treats the receipt as being in exchange for an asset. The first situation is where a debt is disposed of by one group member to another and the debt is disposed of by being satisfied in whole or in part.

The second is where redeemable shares are disposed of on redemption. Thus, a gain on redemption will be taxable notwithstanding that there is a disposal of the shares in exchange for the consideration received on redemption.

The third is a disposal by or to an investment trust, venture capital trust, qualifying friendly society, dual resident investing company, a company which is, or is a member of, a UK REIT,[21] or to a group company which is or will become exempt from tax on its gains, such as an investment trust or venture capital trust.[22]

The fourth is the deemed disposal of shares in a company on receipt of a capital distribution within TCGA 1992, section 122; there will still be a disposal by the company making the capital distribution and this may fall within section 171.[23]

Where the asset is disposed of by destruction and compensation is payable, the disposal is deemed to be to the person who ultimately bears the burden of paying the compensation money, eg an insurance company.[24]

Fifthly, tax-neutral treatment does not apply to a disposal by a company in fulfillment of its obligations under an option granted to another company at a time when the two companies were not members of the same group.[25]

65.2.1.2 Deemed Disposals and No Disposals

Section 171 applies whether there is an actual disposal or a deemed disposal and acquisition. However, it is now provided that the principle does not apply where the statute directs that there is neither a disposal nor an acquisition, as on a corporate reorganisation.[26]

65.2.1.3 Liquidation, etc

Section 171's postponement rules do not apply to transfers between a subsidiary and a parent in liquidation since, once liquidation of the parent has begun, the shares in the subsidiary are not held by the parent beneficially but on trust for its own members.[27] The effect of a voluntary winding up is less clear.[28] Distributions by a subsidiary in liquidation are

---

[21] TCGA 1992, s 171(2)(c)-(d)(a).

[22] TCGA 1992, s 101A-101C, inserted by FA 1998, ss 131-133.

[23] *Innocent v Whaddon Estates Ltd* [1982] STC 115, (1982) 55 TC 476, discussed in the Revenue CGT manual CGT45320.

[24] TCGA 1992, s 171(4).

[25] TCGA 1992, s 171(2)(db), added by FA 2007, Sch 5, para 10.

[26] TCGA 1992, s 171(3): the corporate reorganisation provisions are ss 127, 135 (see above at §41.5). This provision reverses *Westcott v Woolcombers Ltd* [1986] STC 182, 60 TC 575; on which, see London [1986] BTR 117; see also *NAP Holdings UK Ltd v Whittles* [1994] STC 979, 67 TC 166, HL.

[27] *Ayerst v C & K (Construction) Ltd* [1975] STC 345, [1975] 2 All ER 537, 50 TC 651. The House of Lords decided only that the company ceased to be beneficial owner of its assets. The Court of Appeal had held that the ownership was in suspense ([1975] STC 1, [1975] 1 All ER 162).

[28] *Wadsworth Morton Ltd v Jenkinson* [1966] 3 All ER 702, (1966) 43 TC 479.

similarly taxed immediately. These problems may be overcome by arranging for transfers and distributions by or to the parent before liquidation.

65.2.2 Sink Companies and Capital Losses

Since there was no group relief for capital losses until 2000, it was common to use one company, known as a 'sink' company because of the number of assets put into it, to make all disposals of all chargeable assets outside the group. This ensured that allowable losses and chargeable gains arose in the same company and so were available for set off. Legislation was passed to counter bringing pre-entry losses into the group, ie by acquiring companies which had assets with unrealised losses (TCGA 1992, Schedule 7A; see below at §65.2.3) and a related scheme concerning post-entry gains (Schedule 7AA, now superseded by other provisions; see below at §65.2.4). The Revenue view was that it was unlikely that the new approach in *Ramsay*[29] could have been used to counter this use of sink companies 'where losses were a relatively insubstantial element in the acquisition, as evidenced by the circumstances in which they were utilised and the commerciality of the circumstances surrounding the acquisition'.[30] This cautious view of the applicability of the new approach to intra-group transfers was confirmed by the decision of Vinelott J in *Shepherd v Lyntress Ltd*.[31]

The legislature finally realised the futility of its refusal to allow relief for capital losses in 2000, when TCGA 1992, section 171A was introduced. Under this rule, whenever A, one company in a group, disposes of an asset to C, a person who is not a member of the group, the disposal may be treated as made by another group member, B.[32] C may use the incidental costs incurred by A.[33] Under the sink practice, A would have transferred the asset to B, which would have transferred it to C. The same result is achieved by a simple election instead of an actual transfer; the election may be made if an actual transfer between A and B would have been within section 171.[34]

The election must be made by notice in writing to an officer of the Board, and must be made jointly by A and B; it must also be made before the second anniversary of the end of the accounting period of A in which the disposal to C was made.[35]

TCGA 1992, section 171A was further simplified and completely rewritten by FA 2009, section 31 and Schedule 12; it is now sections 171A–171C. Where a gain or loss would arise on a transfer to another group member, the companies may simply elect that the gain or loss be transferred—in whole or in part—from the disposing company to any other member of the group. This allows full and immediate matching of gains and losses within the group without having to wait for there to be a disposal outside the group. The effects of the election are spelt out in section 171B; there is a special rule for insurance companies

---

[29] *WT Ramsay Ltd v IRC* [1982] AC 300, giving rise to the composite transactions doctrine under which intermediate steps inserted into a transaction entirely for tax purposes could be ignored; for a detailed discussion of the evolution of the *Ramsay* doctrine see above at §5.6.4.
[30] [1985] *Simon's Tax Intelligence* 568, 570.
[31] [1989] STC 617, (1989) 62 TC 495.
[32] TCGA 1992, s 171A, added by FA 2000, s 101.
[33] TCGA 1992, s 171A(2)(d), added by FA 2001.
[34] TCGA 1992, s 171A(3).
[35] TCGA 1992, s 171A(2), (4).

in section 171C. An amendment ensures that the new rule applies where the group wishes to reallocate a gain or loss to a non-resident group member carrying on a trade in the UK through a PE.

65.2.3 *Statutory Restriction on Use of Pre-entry Losses*[36]

Whatever the vulnerability under the new approach of schemes to use losses incurred before the company entered the group, matters are now governed by legislation restricting the use of such losses. TCGA 1992, Schedule 7A ring-fences the capital losses available to a company at the time it joins the group. Such losses will, in future, enjoy unrestricted rights of set off only against gains arising in respect of assets held by the company at the date of its entry into the group, or acquired by that company from outside the new group and used in a trade carried on by the company before it joined the new group.[37] Although FA 2006 added many new rules to restrict the rights of companies to buy losses and gains, Schedule 7A remains in place.[38] These rules were simplified and eased by FA 2011. In particular, the use of losses that arise after a company joins a group are no longer restricted under the amended regime.

The key concept of pre-entry loss is defined as covering any allowable loss that accrued to that company at a time before it became a member of the relevant group.[39] Pre-entry losses may be set against certain specified gains only.[40] These are later defined as those accruing from:

(1) disposals made before the company joined the group;
(2) assets held at the time of joining; and
(3) assets acquired from persons outside the group after joining and which have been used only for the purposes of a trade which had been carried on before the company joined the group.[41]

FA 2011 expanded the scope for the use of restricted pre-entry losses by allowing them to be used against gains arising on assets used in the same *business* that the company conducted before joining the group; previously this was restricted to assets used in the same *trade*.[42] Further rules apply if the initial company was a member of another group when it joined the group and other companies joined at the same time.[43]

These rules were adapted by FA 2000 to meet the new worldwide definition of groups. New events, called 'relevant events', can trigger Schedule 7A. Thus losses are restricted by Schedule 7A whenever a company joins the worldwide group and it is either resident in the UK, or brings assets within the UK tax net. Schedule 7A also applies if the non-resident

---

[36] TCGA 1992, s 177A and Sch 7A, added by FA 1993; on timing, see TCGA 1992, Sch 7A, para 6(2)(a); FA 1993, s 88(3)(b)(i). On effect of change of law on contract for sale of such losses, see *Bromarin v IMD Investments* [1999] STC 301; and Virgo [1999] *CLJ* 273.

[37] Inland Revenue Press Release, 16 March 1993, [1993] *Simon's Tax Intelligence* 474.

[38] On overlap see Williams [2006] BTR 27.

[39] TCGA 1992, Sch 7A, para 1(2).

[40] TCGA 1992, Sch 7A, para 6.

[41] TCGA 1992, Sch 7A, para 7(1).

[42] HMRC Explanatory Notes to cl 46 and Sch 11.

[43] TCGA 1992, Sch 7A, para 7(3).

company being already a member of the worldwide group transfers assets so that they become chargeable to UK corporation tax, either because they are transferred to a UK PE or because the company itself becomes UK resident. Schedule 7A excludes that part of the loss referable to the period prior to these events.[44] Naturally, the legislation contains rules for the order in which the reliefs are to be given. Broadly, where pre-entry losses can be set against a gain, those of the current or a previous accounting period are offset before other losses of such periods,[45] and pre-entry losses of the current period are used before those brought forward from an earlier period. Where there is more than one pre-entry loss, the company may elect the order in which they are to be set off, but must do so within two years of the end of the accounting period in which the gain offset accrues; in the absence of an election, older losses are used first.

Further restrictions apply where, within a three-year period, there is both a major change in the nature of the company's trade or business and the company joins the group.[46] Rules also cover the situation in which the company belongs to more than one group, and to determine which the relevant group is and how the loss should be apportioned.[47] Rules apply to appropriations of trading stock[48] and various changes of company form.[49]

65.2.4 Statutory Restriction on Use of Pre-entry Gains (Superseded 2006)

While TCGA 1992, Schedule 7A prevented the import of companies with accrued capital losses into groups with gains, it failed to deal with the opposite case—where a company with realised gains, G, was imported into a group with unrealised losses. Once in the new group, G would transfer the assets to the company with the potential loss, L; this transfer would be tax free under section 171, and L would then realise those losses and set them off against the gains. This was first dealt with by Schedule 7AA, introduced by FA 1998.[50] Where two companies left one group and joined a second group together, the two companies were treated as one so that pre-entry gains of one might be set against pre-entry losses of the other. FA 2006 added many new rules to restrict the rights of companies to buy losses and gains, and Schedule 7AA is superseded.

65.2.5 Pre-change Assets and Losses (FA 2006)

TCGA 1992, section 184A imposes restrictions on buying losses where there has been at any time a 'qualifying change of ownership'.[51] It restricts losses arising to a 'relevant company' (RC) on the disposal of a pre-change asset. A pre-change asset is, in broad terms, an asset held by the RC before the relevant change of ownership. The restriction applies if the change of ownership is tainted with a tax advantage purpose.[52] All these terms are

---

[44] TCGA 1992, Sch 7A, para 1(3A), added by FA 2000, Sch 29, para 7. For example, see Inland Revenue Notes to Finance Bill 2000, paras 79–82.
[45] TCGA 1992, Sch 7A, para 6(1).
[46] TCGA 1992, Sch 7A, para 8.
[47] TCGA 1992, Sch 7A, para 9; strengthened by FA 1998.
[48] TCGA 1992, Sch 7A, para 10.
[49] TCGA 1992, Sch 7A, paras 11, 12.
[50] FA 1998, s 135(5) and TCGA 1992, Sch 7AA, para 1 (removing companies joining a group before that date).
[51] Defined in TCGA 1992, s 184C.
[52] Defined in TCGA 1992, s 184D.

elaborately defined. The effect of the restriction is that the loss may be set off only against gains arising to the company on a disposal of pre-change assets. This is so whether the loss precedes or follows the change of ownership, and whether the advantage accrues to the company or any other company.[53]

Various events do not trigger the restriction. These include the insertion of a new holding company.[54] Similarly, if a company, Y, is the 75% subsidiary of X—and remains so—then Y does not undergo a change of ownership even though there is a change in the ownership of X.[55] Further provisions deal with the interaction of the identification of pre-change assets with the various deferral rules.[56]

Another problem arises where the asset has been disposed of under these rules but then goes outside the group on a disposal which is normal disposal and not one within the no-gain, no-loss rule in section 171. If the asset loses its pre-change status, does it resume it if comes back in? The answer seems to be that it does not.

The technicalities of these rules is emphasised by the fact that the contributor to the *British Tax Review* takes many pages to discuss the original proposals, and still more to discuss the Act.[57]

Even this provision proved vulnerable to the planners and was amended a year later. As just seen, there was a limited set of reliefs for losses accruing on the disposal of assets held before the change of ownership. HMRC became aware of schemes which involved arranging for the company incurring a qualifying loss or gain to be sold with one or more subsidiary companies (S) whose shares would be pre-change assets. Once under the new ownership, S would acquire other assets on which a gain—or loss—might be expected to arise. When these assets come to be sold, the sale would be carried out by a sale of the shares of S. Under the FA 2007 changes this offset is no longer available. However, an exception is still made.[58] As the HMRC notes put it:

> Qualifying losses can be set against gains on pre-change assets held by a company that was a member of the group that the relevant company left so long as the company seeking to use the loss is still controlled by the parent company of the group.

65.3   Intra-group Transfers and Trading Stock

Where one company transfers a capital asset to another company in the group, and the recipient company appropriates the asset to trading stock, the rule that the disposal should be at such a figure that neither gain nor loss accrues collides with the principle that the asset should enter the trading stock at market value. The legislation therefore provides that the recipient company should receive the asset as a capital asset and then transfer the asset to trading stock at market value.[59] This gives the recipient the right to

---

[53] TCGA 1992, s 184A(5).
[54] TCGA 1992, s 184C.
[55] TCGA 1992, s 184C(7).
[56] TCGA 1992, s 184E(9).
[57] DF Williams [2006] BTR 26 and 550.
[58] FA 2006, s 70(12), added by FA 2007.
[59] TCGA 1992, s 173, referring to s 161; see above at §42.3.

choose between an immediate chargeable gain and a later trading profit. Where the asset transferred was trading stock of the transferring company, but is received as a capital asset by the recipient, it is treated as having ceased to be trading stock before the transfer; the consequence is that for capital gains purposes the transferor is treated as having disposed of the asset to itself at whatever figure is entered in the books of the trade in respect of the asset.[60] For a company to appropriate an asset as trading stock there must be a genuine intention to trade and not simply a wish to gain a tax advantage.[61] The asset must not only be of a kind sold in the ordinary course of the trade, it must have been acquired with a view to resale at a profit.[62]

This provision was rewritten by FA 2000 to extend its rules to transfers between companies within the new worldwide group.[63]

65.4 Disposal Outside the Group

Once the asset is disposed of to a person outside the group, the normal liability to corporation tax in respect of the capital gain will follow.[64] If an asset has been acquired under an intra-group transfer or on the transfer of an asset from the PE of a non-resident company to a UK company, and is later disposed of outside the group, provision must be made to reflect the group's ownership of the asset. Thus, the disposing company is treated as having acquired the asset when it was originally acquired by a group member.[65] Provision is made for recognising the previous ownership by another group member both for pre-1965 acquisitions[66] and for capital allowances, so account must be taken of any capital allowances made to previous group owners.[67] The tax may be recovered from the principal member at the time the gain accrues and from any previous owner.[68]

65.5 Replacement Asset Rollover Relief

Another way in which the group is recognised as the relevant owner concerns the replacement asset rollover provisions for business assets.

---

[60] TCGA 1992, s 173(2), referring to s 161 which treats the disposal as being at such figure as is entered in the computation of trading profit; this will usually be current market value following *Sharkey v Wernher* [1956] AC 58.

[61] *Coates v Arndale Properties Ltd* [1984] STC 637, (1984) 59 TC 516, HL; *Reed v Nova Securities Ltd* [1985] STC 124, (1985) 59 TC 516 HL. See also *Re Loquitur* [2003] STC 1394 and *New Angel Court v Adam* [2004] STC 779; and above at §42.3.

[62] *Reed v Nova Securities Ltd* [1985] STC 124, 130, (1985) 59 TC 516, 563 HL, *per* Lord Templeman.

[63] FA 2000, Sch 29, para 11.

[64] TCGA 1992, s 8.

[65] TCGA 1992, s 174(1)–(3), referring to ss 171, 172; however, this does not apply to a disposal to or by an investment trust (see s 174(5)).

[66] TCGA 1992, s 174(4).

[67] TCGA 1992, s 174(1), applying s 41.

[68] TCGA 1992, s 190.

65.5.1 *All One Trade*

First, all the trades of the member companies are treated as being one trade, so that if X Co sells an asset and buys another for use by Y Co (its subsidiary), rollover relief may be claimed.[69] As a result of FA 2000, the trade may be carried on either by a company resident in the UK or by a company resident elsewhere but trading in the UK through a PE. However, the relief is still not available if the investment in the new asset is made by a dual resident investment company.[70] It is also excluded where the company acquiring the asset does so on an occasion which is a no gain, no loss disposal;[71] here, the no gain, no loss rule prevails, and the gain made cannot be rolled into the acquisition.[72]

65.5.2 *Timing of Group Status*

Rollover relief also applies where the disposal is by a company which, at the time of the disposal, is a member of a group of companies and the acquisition is by another company which, at the time of the acquisition by the first company, is a member of the same group. It is not necessary for the acquiring company to satisfy the group requirements when the other company made the disposal.[73]

65.5.3 *Non-trading Member*

Rollover relief applies where a non-trading member of the group disposes of assets (or an interest in assets) used, and used only, for the purposes of the trade deemed to be carried on by the other trading members of the group.[74] The same applies to acquisitions by the non-trading member.

For the purposes of the rule restricting rollover relief where the replacement asset is a depreciating asset, not only are all the trades treated as one, but that trade is deemed to be carried on by one person.[75] Where an event occurs giving rise to a chargeable gain, that gain accrues to the member holding the replacement asset at that time.

65.6 Company Leaving Group After Section 171 Acquisition: Degrouping Charge

The privilege given by TCGA 1992, section 171 of postponing tax liability on transfers within the group was in addition to the basic rule that there could be no charge without a

---

[69] TCGA 1992, s 175(1).
[70] TCGA 1992, s 175(2), as amended by FA 1994, s 251(8) (unless the asset was acquired before 29 November 1994). On dual resident investment companies, see below at §69.6.5.
[71] TCGA 1992, s 175(2C), added by FA 1995.
[72] TCGA 1992, s 175(2C), inserted by FA 1995, s 48(1).
[73] TCGA 1992, s 175(2A), enacting Revenue view set out in Statement of Practice SP 8/81 and so deemed always to have had effect (FA 1995, s 48(3)). The claim must be made by both companies.
[74] TCGA 1992, s 175(2B), enacting ex ESC D30 and added by FA 1995, s 48. On the position of a non-trading member, see [1971] BTR 268.
[75] TCGA 1992, s 175(3).

disposal of the asset. An asset would therefore be transferred to another company within the group in exchange for shares, which would then be sold to a stranger company without giving rise to a chargeable gain.

This situation is regulated by section 179. Perhaps surprisingly, this does not prescribe a deemed disposal when the company ceases to be a member of the group, but instead directs that if a company (the departing company) leaves a group[76] and it then holds a chargeable asset which it has acquired from another member of the group within the previous six years, the departing member is treated as having disposed of the asset and reacquired it at its market value at the time of that intra-group *acquisition*.[77]

FA 2011, section 45 and Schedule 10 significantly changed the operation of the degrouping provisions. The amended section 179 is now extremely long and detailed, but essentially where a transferee company ceases to be a member of the group as a consequence of one or more disposals of shares made by another group member, the chargeable gain or allowable loss that would arise under the degrouping provisions may be treated as increasing or reducing the gain on the disposal of those shares and not as accruing to the transferee company: section 179(3D). The substantial shareholding exemption then may apply to exempt the gain (or disallow the loss). If the specified conditions are not satisfied, the original provisions under which the gain is treated as accruing to the transferee company will apply. FA 2011, section 31 also amended TCGA 1992, section 179(2A) by adding an additional circumstance in which the degrouping charge arises—where there ceases to be a connection between the first group of companies and the second group of companies, before the transferee company has ceased to be a member of the second group of companies. Also, for section 179(2A) to apply, the new rules make it clear that the transferee company must become a member of the second group of companies on leaving the first group.[78]

65.7   Losses Attributable to Depreciatory Transactions Within a Group and Dividend Stripping

65.7.1   Depreciatory Transactions Within a Group

If there is a disposal[79] by one group member to another of an asset at a nominal figure, neither gain nor loss arises (section 171). This may cause a decline in the value of the former company. Losses resulting from such depreciatory transactions[80] which are realised on a subsequent disposal of the shares or securities within six years of the depreciatory transaction are disallowed by section 176. The disallowance is limited to the undervalue of the

---

[76] TCGA 1992, s 170(10).

[77] TCGA 1992, s 179(1), (3). On extension of time limit for election in respect of pre-1965 assets, see Statement of Practice SP D21. Where a company becomes non-resident as a result of the new rule for companies which are non-resident for treaty purposes, no charge arises under s 179 (FA 1994, s 250(2)).

[78] See Ball [2011] BTR 395 and 406 for an analysis of the detail, including the new rules applicable to subgroups addressing the issues raised in *Johnston Publishing (North) Limited v HMRC* [2008] EWCA Civ 858; [2008] STC 3116 and *Dunlop International AG v Pardoe (Inspector of Taxes)* [1999] STC 909 (CA).

[79] TCGA 1992, s 176(8) includes a claim under s 24(2) that the value of shares or securities has become negligible. However, s 29 (value shifting) (see above at §36.6), does not apply to intra-group transfers.

[80] Defined by TCGA 1992, s 176(3) as including the cancellation of securities under Companies Act 2006, s 641 (ex Companies Act 1985, s 135).

transaction.[81] If there is a later disposal of the shares in the acquiring company, the previously disallowed loss may reduce the gain.[82] Section 176 restricts losses; it does not create
or increase gains.[83]

65.7.2 Dividend Stripping

Under TCGA 1992, section 177, payment of accumulated profits by means of an intra-
group dividend may be treated as giving rise to a depreciatory transaction, and any resulting capital loss is therefore disallowed by section 176. This was introduced in 1969 as a
companion to ex TA 1988, section 736 (see below at §68.4), which deals with share-dealing
companies.

Example

X buys the share capital of Y for £100,000. A dividend of £60,000 is then declared by Y
which is then liquidated. The distribution to X on the liquidation of Y is £40,000. Although
X has a capital loss of £60,000 on its investment in Y, section 177 enables the inspector to
disallow that loss to the extent of the dividend received (£60,000).

Section 177 deals only with the disallowance of losses; it does not apply to the reduction
of gains. It follows that the common practice of a subsidiary making a distribution shortly
before it is sold—so reducing the gain on the sale of those shares—is not caught by this
provision. TCGA 1992, sections 178 and 180, which also applied to depreciating transactions, have been repealed.[84]

65.8   Value-shifting Transactions

By 1989 the practice of reducing the value of subsidiary companies prior to disposal of
those companies outside the group had become a standard feature of UK tax practice. The
purpose was to reduce the capital gains liability of the owners, and to reduce the exposure to double taxation. The Revenue distinguished two situations: in the first the value
was reduced by extracting profits from a subsidiary before sale by an ordinary intra-group
dividend payment where the profits supporting that dividend had borne tax; in the second
the gains were extracted by the payment of a dividend from artificially-created profits that
had not borne tax.[85] The Revenue were not concerned about the first situation, but became
very concerned about the second. TCGA 1992, section 30 (see above §35.5) was not able to
prevent this since, in its original version, it specifically excluded the shifting of value arising from the payment of dividends between members of a group of companies within the
meaning of section 170 and the disposal of assets between them.

---

[81] On effect of indexation allowance, see *X plc v Roe* [1996] STC (SCD) 139 and *Whitehall Electric Investments v
Owen* [2002] STC (SCD) 228.
[82] TCGA 1992, s 176(6).
[83] Defined by TCGA 1992, s 176(7).
[84] Repealed by FA 2000, Sch 29, paras 26, 27 (spent); TCGA 1992, s 177 is amended by para 25.
[85] HC Official Report, Standing Committee G, col 598 (Mr Lamont). One example was where a group lent
money to one subsidiary to buy an asset from another.

FA 2011, section 44 and Schedule 9 replaced the long, complex value-shifting rules in TCGA 1992, sections 30–33, which allowed the Revenue to adjust the consideration received on certain disposals to take account of material reductions in value, thereby reducing a loss realised on the disposal, increasing a gain realised on the disposal, or converting a loss into a gain.[86] The amended section 30 provides that it does not have effect for the purposes of corporation tax if the disposal of the asset is a disposal by a company of shares in, or securities of, another company. This is subject to a targeted anti-avoidance rule in new section 31, which sets out three conditions:

(1) arrangements have been made whereby the value of those shares or securities, or of a relevant asset, is materially reduced;
(2) the main purpose, or one of the main purposes, of the arrangements is to obtain a tax advantage; and
(3) the arrangements do not consist solely of making an exempt distribution.

If these three conditions are satisfied, any allowable loss or chargeable gain accruing on the disposal is to be calculated as if the consideration were to be increased by such amount as is just and reasonable, having regard to the arrangements and any charge to, or relief from, corporation tax that, in the absence of section 31, would arise in consequence of the disposal or the arrangements.

---

[86] See Ball [2011] BTR 403 for background and more detail.

66

Exempt Distributions: Demergers

66.1 Introduction

Until 1980 it was difficult—but not impossible—to split a group. The difficulty was that the transfer of the piece being split off would cause the value received by the shareholder to be treated as a qualifying distribution and so give rise to dividend income (see above at §61.2.1). In addition, capital gains, development land tax (DLT, now long repealed) and stamp duty problems arose when a company or assets left the group. As part of a campaign to free British industry from unnecessary constraints, Parliament included certain provisions—now CTA 2010, sections 1073–1099 (ex TA 1988, sections 213–218)—to encourage the process of 'demerging' by removing some of the obstacles.[1]

The three types of demerger allowed are explained below at §66.3. These rules do not apply where the company has a trade which it wishes to transfer to its shareholders directly, ie by transferring ownership of the trade itself (section 1076). It should also be noted that the scheme is not designed to assist intra-group demergers; when dealing with a chain of companies, the group must be demerged from the bottom up. If these rules apply, the distribution is an 'exempt distribution' (section 1075).

To assist the process in some respects, it is possible to apply to the Revenue for clearance and thus obtain their binding agreement that the proposed distribution is indeed within these rules.

66.2 Conditions

(1) There must be a transaction which would otherwise be a distribution of income under CTA 2010, sections 1000 *et seq* (ex TA 1988, section 209). This means, *inter alia*, that these reliefs cannot apply to a demerger in the course of liquidation. In addition,

---

[1] See [1980] *Simon's Tax Intelligence* 171, 418; and Statement of Practice SP 13/80.

a distribution other than a dividend, eg a distribution of shares, is not a distribution if it represents a repayment of capital.[2]

(2) The company making the distribution must, at the time of the distribution, be a trading company[3] (or a member of a trading group—a phrase which will not be repeated); certain trades, notably those dealing in shares, land and commodity futures, are excluded.[4]

(3) The transaction must be wholly or mainly to benefit some or all of the trading activities involved in the demerger.[5] This test is narrow. A demerger will not qualify simply because there are bona fide commercial reasons for it. It is probably sufficient that the benefit should be either to the retained or to the transferred trade and not to both, but this is not absolutely clear. The combination of conditions (2) and (3) means that relief is available only where trade is being demerged from trade and so not, for example, to the demerger of trade from investment. In many instances the exact status of the secondary business of an unlisted company may be in doubt; such doubts need to be resolved before a demerger is embarked upon.

(4) The newly-demerged trade should be left free to operate under its new independent management—separate from the former parent. To this end it is provided that where the company distributes shares in its subsidiary to its members (see below at §66.3.1), those shares must not be redeemable and must represent the whole or substantially the whole of the distributing company's interest.[6] If the transfer is of a trade to another company (see below at §66.3.2), the distributing company must not retain anything more than a minor interest in the trade;[7] while if the transfer is of shares in a subsidiary (see below at §66.3.3), the shares must not be redeemable and must represent the whole or substantially the whole of the distributing company's interest.[8]

(5) All the companies involved must be resident in an EU Member State at the time of the distribution.[9]

(6) The transfer must not fall foul of the elaborate anti-avoidance provisions. Thus, the demerger must not be part of a scheme or an arrangement for the avoidance of tax, for the making of a chargeable payment,[10] for the acquisition of control of any company involved by a third person, or for the cessation of a trade or its sale after demerger. The purpose of the demerger provisions is to encourage the hiving-off of active businesses so that they may thrive on their own. As such, the provisions are designed to ensure that assets remain within the corporate sector and are not used to obtain tax advantages on what is really the sale of a business. Hence, a passing of control to another company in return for shares which flow back to the shareholders in the previous owners is essential. Intra-group transfers cannot qualify for this treatment.

---

[2] See above at §61.1.
[3] CTA 2010, s 1081(2), ex TA 1988, s 213(5); the terms are defined in s 1099 (ex s 218).
[4] CTA 2010, s 1099, ex TA 1988, s 218(1)—'trading'.
[5] CTA 2010, s 1081(3), ex TA 1988, s 213(10).
[6] CTA 2010, s 1082(1)–(2), ex TA 1988, s 213(6).
[7] CTA 2010, s 1083(1), ex TA 1988, s 213(8)(a).
[8] CTA 2010, s 1083(2), ex TA 1988, s 213(8)(b).
[9] CTA 2010, s 1081(1), ex TA 1988, s 213(4), which formerly required UK residence.
[10] CTA 2010, s 1081(4)–(7), ex TA 1988, s 213(11).

66.3   The Three Situations

66.3.1 *Demerger of Existing Subsidiaries*

Demerger of an existing subsidiary occurs where one company, C, transfers to all or any of its members, ie ordinary shareholders,[11] shares in a directly-owned 75% subsidiary, S.[12] This allows a simple spinning-off of the distinct business run by S which is already a separate entity, and takes the form of a simple distribution in specie. The insistence on a 75% holding in S is to be noted. The transfer must be to C's shareholders and not simply to another conglomerate.

A transfer of shares by C of this sort would normally cause a number of tax consequences; some of these are modified. First, the distribution is to be exempt;[13] it follows that there will be no dividend income tax, neither will there be a capital distribution to the shareholders which might otherwise cause capital gains consequences under TCGA 1992, section 122[14] (capital gains liability is thus deferred until the shares are disposed of). Further, as S is leaving the group, there may be a deferred charge under TCGA 1992, section 179 on assets acquired from other members of the group within the last six years.[15] However, the receipt of a chargeable payment within five years will revive such a charge (below §66.4).[16]

Some tax consequences, however, remain. First, since S ceases to be a member of the group it will not in future be entitled to group privileges such as, for example, group loss relief. Secondly, the change in control of S will mean that the restrictions on loss relief in TA 1988, section 768 and the potential liability for unpaid corporation tax under section 767AA may have to be noted should a change in S's trade be contemplated. However the Revenue have indicated sympathetic treatment in such circumstances by treating the underlying ownership as remaining unchanged. Thirdly, where close companies are involved there may be IHT implications.

Another very important tax consequence is that C will be disposing of its holding in S, a disposal that may give rise to substantial liability on the gains involved, save where the substantial shareholding exemption applies. This cost may be reduced either if the gains are minimal or if C has unrelieved capital losses. Where this is not so, it may be possible to reduce the value of the shares in S by paying a dividend. However, the more unusual the steps taken, the greater the risk that the scheme will fall into the anti-avoidance provisions on the ground that it forms part of a scheme one of the main purposes of which is the avoidance of tax. This very high tax cost used to inhibit many schemes of demerger under these rules.

---

[11] CTA 2010, s 1099, ex TA 1988, s 218(1).
[12] CTA 2010, s 1076, ex TA 1988, s 213(3)(a).
[13] CTA 2010, ss 1075–1077, ex TA 1988, s 213(2).
[14] TCGA 1992, s 192.
[15] TCGA 1992, s 192(3).
[16] TCGA 1992, s 192(4).

66.3.2 Three-Part Demergers

Here C disposes of a trade to Y and, in exchange, Y issues shares not to C but to the ordinary shareholders of C. In this way the trade is hived-off from the rest of C's activities and thus demerged, and C's ordinary shareholders receive shares in Y.[17]

Normally, such a distribution by C of its assets would be treated as a distribution, but as with the first type of demerger, it is provided that the distribution is exempt and so does not give rise to dividend income.[18] In addition, TCGA 1992, section 179 is excluded.[19] The legislature has not thought it necessary to exclude any charge as a capital distribution under TCGA 1992, section 122 in these circumstances, presumably because Y rather than C is making the distribution to C's shareholders. However, the rules make no provision for other consequences. Thus, C is disposing of the trade, one of its capital assets, and its shareholders are receiving an amount with capital gains implications; these consequences may be avoided by ensuring that the scheme is a company reconstruction and so making use of the deferral provisions such as TCGA 1992, sections 136 and 139. In addition, the fact that C ceases to carry on this trade and Y carries it on will give rise to all the usual problems of discontinuance and commencement, with restrictions on losses, unused capital allowances and possible changes of accounting date.

66.3.3 Indirect Demerger to Shareholders

This is a mixture of the first two types of demerger. Here, C transfers shares in its 75% subsidiary, S, to Y, and Y, in turn, issues shares in S to the ordinary shareholders of C.

The tax consequences are a similar mixture of the first and the second type of demerger. As with the first type, the distribution of the shares in Y is to be an exempt distribution,[20] with the result that there is no dividend income tax liability. S leaves the group controlled by C and there is exemption from TCGA 1992, section 179.[21] C's disposal of the shares in S may give rise to chargeable gains, but those may be avoided by using a reconstruction; the same device will save the shareholders in C from liability. Since the control of S passes from C, matters of losses and loss of group benefits will be raised as already set out under the first type. Where this type of demerger scores over the first is in the matter of the tax cost arising from the realisation of any gains on the disposal of the shares in S; that tax cost is avoided.

---

[17] CTA 2010, s 1077, ex TA 1988, s 213(3)(b). On consequences where trusts are involved, see Law Society Press Release, 22 July 1992, [1992] *Simon's Tax Intelligence* 762.

[18] CTA 2010, ss 1075–1077, ex TA 1988, s 213(2).

[19] TCGA 1992, s 192(3); however, the receipt of a chargeable payment within five years will revive the liability under these rules (s 192(4)).

[20] CTA 2010, ss 1075–1077, ex TA 1988, s 213(2).

[21] TCGA 1992, s 192(3); this is subject to the receipt of a chargeable payment in the next five years (s 192(4)).

66.4   Anti-avoidance: Subsequent Chargeable
Payments as Income, etc

Although a demerger under these rules may have been successfully carried through, a subsequent 'chargeable payment'[22] during any of the next five years may have serious consequences. A chargeable payment is any payment which is not itself a distribution (or an exempt distribution) made otherwise than for a bona fide commercial reason, or forming part of a scheme or an arrangement for the avoidance of tax and made between companies or between a company and a shareholder in a company involved in the demerger. The payment must have been made in connection with the shares of the company.[23] Only intragroup payments are saved from the ambit of this definition,[24] which is widened yet further when in relation to unquoted companies.[25] Such a payment within the five-year period is treated as income of the recipient and chargeable to tax.[26] No deduction for the payment can be made in computing profits chargeable to corporation tax.[27]

An example of a situation in which this will arise is where a company demerges a subsidiary by transferring shares to its members and then buys them back. The repurchase price would normally be a capital receipt, but is instead taxed as income of the shareholder. Parliament has preferred this device to the alternative of retrospectively withdrawing exemption from the distribution.

---

[22] Defined in CTA 2010, s 1088, ex TA 1988, s 214(2), (3).

[23] CTA 2010, s 1088(3), ex TA 1988, s 214(2).

[24] CTA 2010, s 1088(5), ex TA 1988, s 214(2)(c).

[25] CTA 2010, s 1089, ex TA 1988, s 214(3).

[26] CTA 2010, s 1086, ex TA 1988, s 214(1)(a); the reference to s 349(1) is removed by ITA 2007.

[27] CTA 2010, s 1087, ex TA 1988, s 214(1)(c); neither is it a repayment of capital within ss 210, 211; see TA 1988, s 214(1)(d).

67

Close Companies

67.1 Introduction

67.1.1 Overview

This chapter deals with certain rules which apply only to close companies or to a subset called 'close investment holding companies'. However, the definition of a 'close company' is of importance in many other areas of the tax system, including not only corporation tax, but also income tax and IHT.[1]

The present taxation of close companies differs from that of other companies in two major respects. First, the law takes a wider view of what amounts to a distribution, with the result that not only are such payments not deductible in computing profits of the close company, but they are also taxable as ITTOIA 2005, Part 4, Chapter 6 income in the hands of the recipients. Secondly, a payment equivalent to corporation tax at a special rate of 32.5% must be made to the Revenue where the company makes a loan to a participator. The close companies rules formerly in TA 1988, sections 414–422 were rewritten as CTA 2010, sections 438–465 and 1064–1069.

In so far as the shareholders envisage an eventual sale of the company, they may find that their expected CGT liability is turned into an income tax liability by ITA 2007, Part 13, Chapter 1,[2] a provision which applies particularly to small companies, although it is not so confined. The 1988 assimilation of CGT and income tax rates undermined this point in part, but the exemption of pre-1982 gains remained. The 1998 introduction of tapering relief restored the point that income tax treatment may be different from that

---

[1] For further examples, see above at §44.3.1.5 on IHT on transfer of value by a close company, and see §65.2.2 above.
[2] Ex TA 1988, s 703. See also ITA 2007, s 689, ex TA 1988, s 704D; see below at §68.6.

under CGT, as does the present situation where CGT rates are lower than the rates of income tax.

67.1.2 History[3]

For earlier accounting periods, some very different principles have applied. From 1965–89, the law specified a certain amount of profit which might be distributed.[4] The sum by which actual distributions fell short of that amount was notionally apportioned among the participators; the income tax due on these notional distributions was collected from the company. The purpose of this rule was to prevent the use of companies as incorporated piggy-banks in which profits might be taxed at company rates instead of individual rates, the latter sometimes reaching 98%; the retained profits might then be realised as capital gains and so, before 1965, free of further tax. With the reduction in 1979 in top rates of tax on earned income to 60%, there was no tax advantage in retaining profits in the company, and so the power to apportion trading income of trading companies was abolished; however, it remained for non-trading income of such companies and for all income of non-trading companies. This power to apportion undistributed profit was repealed in 1989 following the further reduction of the top rate of income tax to 40%.

Between 1965 and 1973 the classical system of taxation meant that the participator could not claim credit for basic rate income tax paid by the company. Hence, participators were liable to basic rate tax as well as excess liability when an apportionment was made. The same fact led to special rules for restrictive covenants;[5] these rules were repealed on the introduction of the imputation system in 1973.

Before the introduction of corporation tax in 1965, companies paid income tax and other taxes on their profits. Even then, rules treated the income of the company as income of the participators; these rules empowered the Revenue to make 'surtax directions' on companies which were known, however inaccurately, as 'one-man companies'.

Today, a deduction for excessive remuneration paid by the company to a director, whether or not the company is close, may be disallowed under the rules for computing trading profits or CTA 2009, Part 16, ex TA 1988, section 75 (companies with investment business). The payment is, however, valid in that the director is perfectly entitled to retain the excess. For tax purposes the excess is treated as a distribution—unless it is refunded.[6] Between 1965 and 1969 there were special restrictions on the level of director's remuneration for close companies;[7] however, these were abolished because they were too complicated. Retention might have pre-empted *Jones v Garnett (Inspector of Taxes).*[8]

---

[3] For older history, see Royal Commission on the Income Tax, *Final Report*, Cmnd 615 (1920), §575; Royal Commission on the Taxation of Profits and Income, *Final Report*, Cmnd 9474 (1955), paras 1021, 1036; for 1965 regime, see Talbot, *Corporation Tax and Income Tax upon Company Distributions* (Sweet & Maxwell, 1968), chs 15–17.

[4] For detail, see *Butterworths UK Tax Guide 1989–1990* (Butterworths, 1989), §27:13.

[5] TA 1970, s 288.

[6] On which, see Statement of Practice SP C4. On policy, see Oliver and Harris in Avery Jones, Harris & Oliver (eds), *Comparative Perspectives on Revenue Law* (CUP, 2008), ch 11.

[7] FA 1965, s 74.

[8] [2007] UKHL 35, [2007] STC 1536.

67.2 Definition of a Close Company

67.2.1 *The Tests*

A company will be designated a close company if it satisfies any of three tests. There are exceptions discussed below. The tests are:

(1) that it is controlled by five or fewer participators;[9] or
(2) that it is controlled by its directors; or
(3) if there are five or fewer participators, or participators who are directors, together they possess or are entitled to acquire such rights as would, in the event of the winding up of the company, entitle them to receive the greater part of the assets of the relevant company which would then be available for distribution among the participators.[10]

For test (3) above, the company will also be a close company if these persons could obtain such rights as would in that event entitle them to that greater part if the rights of all loan creditors were disregarded.[11] Elaborate rules set out the basis upon which the hypothetical winding up is to be carried out.[12] Rules also provide for the possible winding up of any other company which is a participator in the close company.[13] In the application of this rule to the notional winding up of the other company and to any further notional winding up required by CTA 2010, section 439(3)(b) (or by any further application of that paragraph), references to 'the relevant company' have effect as references to the company concerned. In applying these rules the rights of a participator which is a company are not taken into account unless it holds the rights in a fiduciary or representative capacity.[14]

Examples

(1) The share capital of X Ltd (a private company) is owned as to 25% by three directors and the 75% balance by 10 individuals, no five of which own over 50%. X Ltd is not a close company.
(2) The directors of X Ltd, numbering 12, own 51% of the ordinary share capital. X Ltd is a close company.
(3) The directors of Z Ltd, numbering three, own 45% of the ordinary share capital. Two other unconnected individuals own 8%. Since five persons own 53% of the share capital of Z Ltd, it is a close company.

The Revenue have extensive information-gathering powers.[15]

---

[9] CTA 2010, s 439(2), ex TA 1988, s 414(1).
[10] CTA 2010, s 439(3)(a), ex TA 1988, s 414(2)(a).
[11] CTA 2010, s 439(3)(b), ex TA 1988, s 414(2)(b), as amended by FA 1989, s 104.
[12] CTA 2010, s 440, ex TA 1988, s 414(2A), added by FA 1989, s 104.
[13] CTA 2010, s 440, ex TA 1988, s 414(2B), added by FA 1989, s 104. Section 441(2) (ex 414(2C)) provides that a person is to be treated as a participator in or as a director of the relevant company if he is a participator in or director of any other company which would be entitled to receive assets in the notional winding up of the relevant company on the basis set out in s 440 (ex s 414(2A), (2B)). CTA 2009, s 451 (ex TA 1988, s 416(4)–(6)) also applies, by the operation of s 439(5), ex s 414(2D).
[14] CTA 2010, s 441(3), ex TA 1988, s 414(2C); however, s 439(3) (ex s 414(2)(a)) is an exception to this.
[15] CTA 2010, s 465, ex FA 1989, Sch 12, paras 1–4.

67.2.2 Control

67.2.2.1 What Is It?

This element is central to the first two tests set out in §67.2.1 above, but it may be satisfied in many, sometimes overlapping, ways. A person is taken to control a company if he exercises or is able to exercise now or as of right in the future, or is entitled to acquire (now or as of right in the future) control over the company's affairs.[16] 'Control over the company's affairs' is not defined and may mean control at a general meeting or control of those matters which are within the discretion of the directors. Precise analysis is unnecessary since the statute gives the following instances, which are additional to and therefore do not detract from the generality of the principle.[17] A person will have control where he holds:

(1)   the greater part of the share capital or of the issued share capital; or
(2)   the greater part of the voting power of the company; or
(3)   so much of the issued share capital as would entitle him to receive the greater part of the income of the company if, ignoring the rights of loan creditors, it was all distributed among the participators; or
(4)   such rights as would enable him to receive the greater part of the assets of the company in the event of a winding up or in any other circumstances.

67.2.2.2 Who Has It?

If two or more persons together satisfy the test of control they are taken together to have control.[18] In assessing the extent of a person's control, all rights and powers held by him or by nominees are, of course, included.[19]

Less obviously, but equally crucial in establishing the extent of a person's control, is the attribution to a person of all the rights and powers held by an associate.[20] An associate means[21] any relative—which means spouse or civil partner, direct ancestor or issue, or brother or sister[22]—or partner, and any trustee of a settlement of which he, or any relative, as previously defined, is the settlor.[23] If the Revenue form the view that those other persons are indeed associates, they have a duty to attribute those rights to the other

---

[16]   CTA 2010, s 450–451, ex TA 1988, s 416(2); see also above at §60.11.
[17]   *R v IRC, ex parte Newfield Developments Ltd* [2001] STC 901 (HL); case concerns TA 1988, s 13, but is applicable here too. Dicta by Lord Hoffmann cited by Lightman J in *Gascoine's Group Ltd v Inspector of Taxes* [2004] EWHC ChD 640; [2004] STC 844.
[18]   CTA 2010, s 451(5), ex TA 1988, s 416(3).
[19]   CTA 2010, s 451(3), ex TA 1988, s 416(5). The Revenue have no really effective means of discovering whether a shareholder is a nominee. TMA 1970, s 26 is, in practice, insufficient.
[20]   CTA 2010, s 451(4)–(6), ex TA 1988, s 416(6). On the (non) relationship between TA 1988, s 416(6) and the definition of control in TA 1988, s 13(4), see *R v IRC, ex parte Newfield Developments Ltd* (HL), *op cit*, at para 32.
[21]   CTA 2010, s 448, ex TA 1988, s 417(3). For a nice example of section 417(3)(a) operating see Revenue Note to Finance Bill 2004, cl 48, para 15.
[22]   CTA 2010, s 448(2), ex TA 1988, s 417(4). But in practice relatives other than spouse or civil partner and minor children are usually ignored; see Statement of Practice SP C4, para 2.
[23]   The definition of 'settlor' is now by reference to ITA 2007, ss 467 *et seq* for both income tax and corporation tax. A will is not a settlement (*Willingale v Islington Green Investment Co* [1972] 1 All ER 199, (1972) 48 TC 547); see Goldberg [1971] BTR 380.

persons; they have no discretion in the matter.[24] Where the participator is interested in any shares or obligations of a company which are subject to any trust, the trustees of the settlement concerned are associates.[25] Similarly, if the participator is a company and is interested in shares held on trust, any other company interested in those shares or obligations is an associate.[26] These rules also apply where shares are held as part of the estate of a deceased person. The effect is to make the trustees associates rather than the beneficiaries, save where the beneficiary is another company.[27] The term 'interested' is not defined; it is unclear whether being an object of a discretion is sufficient to make one 'interested'.

If a participator has control of another company, the powers of that company and of any other he may control are attributed to him, as are powers of companies controlled by him and his associates.[28] While the powers of nominees of associates are attributed to the participator, those of associates of associates are not, so the rights of a sister-in-law would be ignored.

67.2.2.3 Control by Directors[29]

A company controlled by its directors is a close company no matter how many directors there are. Persons listed as directors are any persons occupying the position of director by whatever name called, and any person in accordance with whose wishes the directors are accustomed to act. Also qualifying as a director is any person who is a manager or otherwise concerned with the management of the company's trade or business, and who controls (or is able to control) 20% of the ordinary share capital of the company. There is the customary attribution of the control of associates and intermediate companies even if the manager himself has no shares at all.

67.2.2.4 Control by Participators

If control does not rest in the directors, the company will still be close if control rests in five or fewer participators.[30] A participator is defined as any person with a share or interest in the capital or income of the company and, in particular:

(1) one with—or who is entitled to acquire—share capital or voting rights; or

(2) one who is entitled to secure that income or assets (present or future) will be applied directly or indirectly for his benefit; or

(3) one who is entitled to receive or participate in distributions of the company, or entitled to any amounts payable by the company in cash or in kind by way of premium on redemption; or

---

[24] Lord Hoffmann in *R v IRC, ex parte Newfield Developments Ltd* [2001] STC 901 at para 18.

[25] CTA 2010, s 448(1)(d), ex TA 1988, s 417(3)(c)(i), modified by FA 2006.

[26] CTA 2010, s 448(1)(e), ex TA 1988, s 417(3)(c)(ii).

[27] For previous law, see TA 1970, s 303(3)(c); it was then held that an executor was interested in shares held as part of an incompletely administered estate (*Willingale v Islington Green Investment Co* [1972] 1 All ER 199, (1972) 48 TC 547).

[28] CTA 2010, s 451(4)–(6), ex TA 1988, s 416(6).

[29] CTA 2010, s 452, ex TA 1988, s 417(5).

[30] CTA 2010, s 454, ex TA 1988, s 417(1).

(4)   certain loan creditors,[31] a term defined to include one who has a beneficial interest in
       the debt. A creditor of a nearly insolvent company may be entitled to the greater part
       of the company's assets and thus could be a participator, with the result that the com-
       pany would be a close company. To avoid such complications, bona fide commercial
       loans, salvage operations and business loans made by a person carrying on a banking
       business are ignored.

A person may be a director even though not a participator.

67.2.2.5 Exceptions

Certain companies cannot be close companies even though they satisfy one or other of
the above tests, eg non-resident companies[32] or those controlled by the Crown.[33] Further,
a company is not a close company if it is controlled by one or more open companies and
it cannot be treated as close except by taking an open company as one of its five or fewer
participators.[34] Thus the subsidiary of a non-close company is not close any more than a
company set up by two or three such companies. However, if another test of control would
result in its being a close company, the company would be close.

   Also excluded is a company which is close only because it has one or more open companies as loan creditors with control,[35] under the rule which gives control to one entitled to
the greater share of the assets on a winding up.

   In looking at these cases of control by non-close companies, a non-resident company
which would be a close company if it were resident is treated as if it were close.[36]

67.2.2.6 Quoted Companies—the 35% Rule

A quoted company is not a close company if shares carrying 35% or more of the voting
power[37] of the company have been allotted unconditionally to, or acquired unconditionally
by, and are at the time beneficially held by, members of the public.[38] Shares entitled to a
fixed rate of dividend do not count towards the 35%, but they do count towards the 100%,
even though they carry voting rights and participate in profits.

   Shares are not treated as held by the public if they are owned by:

(1)   a principal member (ie the top five[39] of those with more than 5% of the voting power,
       other than an approved pension scheme or a non-close company);
(2)   any director or his associate;

---

[31] Defined in CTA 2010, s 453, ex TA 1988, s 417(7)–(9). This is omitted for IHT. Recognised money brokers
lending to stock jobbers formerly were excluded by concession (ex ESC C8).
   [32] CTA 2010, s 442, ex TA 1988, s 414(1).
   [33] CTA 2010, s 443, ex TA 1988, s 414(4).
   [34] CTA 2010, s 444(2), ex TA 1988, s 414(5)(a).
   [35] CTA 2010, s 444(3), ex TA 1988, ss 414(5)(b), 416(2)(c).
   [36] CTA 2010, s 444(4), ex TA 1988, s 416(2)(c).
   [37] Thus, the surrender of voting shares for non-voting shares may enable a company to come within this rule.
Where the public own less than 35% only for a short period, which unhappily straddles the end of the accounting
period, the Revenue promise 'sympathetic treatment' (Statement of Practice SP C4, para 9).
   [38] CTA 2010, s 446(1), ex TA 1988, s 415.
   [39] CTA 2010, s 446(4), ex TA 1988, s 415(6)(a): if there are two or more with equal percentages, five may be
increased to six or more.

(3) any company controlled by (2);

(4) any associated company; and

(5) any fund (eg a pension fund) for the benefit of any employee or director of the company or of a company within (3) or (4).

This exception does not apply if the voting power possessed by all the principal members is more than 85%. At first sight, since shares held in a principal member's holding cannot be held by the public, it is hard to see how a company with 35% of its shares held by the public could have 85% of its shares held by principal members. However, shares held by open companies or approved superannuation funds are treated as owned by the public even if the company or fund is a principal member. Therefore, where one of the principal members is an open company with, say, 25% of the voting power, and together the principal members control 80% of the voting power, the company so controlled is an open company under the 35% rule. If, however, the principal members controlled 86%, it would be a close company.

67.3 Wider Definition of Distribution: Incurring Expense on Participators or Their Associates

The definition of 'distribution' is widened in the case of a close company to cover expenses incurred by the company for the benefit of a participator. When a company has incurred expense in providing a participator, including one who is a participator in a controlling company or who is an associate of a participator,[40] with the provision of living or other accommodation, entertainment, domestic or other services, or other benefits or facilities of whatsoever nature, CTA 2010, section 1064 (ex TA 1988, section 418) directs that expense so incurred is to be treated as a distribution.[41] The analogy is with ITEPA 2003, Part 3, Chapter 10; section 1064 is excluded if the participator comes within that head of charge.[42] The rules laid down for valuation in Chapter 10 are incorporated into section 1064.[43] There is no grossing-up of the expense and there is a deduction for sums made good by the participator. The very wide meaning given by the House of Lords to the concept of the 'shadow director' means that the scope of these rules is not as wide as at once thought.[44]

Section 1064 does not apply to expenses incurred in the provision of living accommodation provided by reason of the employment, or of benefits on death or retirement for the participator or his dependants.[45] It is also excluded if the participator is another close company and one is the subsidiary of the other, or both are subsidiaries of a third company, and the benefit arises on the transfer of assets or liabilities by or to the company.[46]

Attempts could be made to avoid section 1064 where there is a participator in one close company but not in another close company, and the companies agree that the other pays or

---

[40] CTA 2010, s 1069, ex TA 1988, s 418(8).
[41] CTA 2010, s 1064, ex TA 1988, s 418(2).
[42] See above chapter sixteen.
[43] CTA 2010, s 1064(3), ex TA 1988, s 418(4).
[44] Mullan [2002] BTR 156 commenting on *R v Allen* [2001] UKHL 45, [2001] STC 1537.
[45] CTA 2010, s 1065, ex TA 1988, s 418(3).
[46] CTA 2010, s 1066, ex TA 1988, s 418(5); 'subsidiary' is defined in s 1066(2), ex s 418(6).

should provide the facilities for that person. In such circumstances the payment is treated as coming from the company in which the person is a participator.[47]

The payment is a distribution; income tax under ITTOIA 2005, Part 4, Chapter 3 is therefore due.

67.4 Quasi-distributions: Loans or Advances to Participators or Their Associates

67.4.1 The Charge

Where a close company makes a loan or advances money to a participator or an associate of a participator, CTA 2010, section 455 (ex TA 1988, section 419) directs that a sum equal to corporation tax at a special rate of 32.5% is payable by the company. The rate for many years was 25% but it was increased to 32.5% from 6 April 2016 to match the higher rate of dividend tax. From 2013, the charge also extends to loans or advances through intermediaries, including to trustees and partnerships where one or more of the trustees, beneficiaries or partners is a participator or associate of a participator. This payment cannot be set off against the company's own liability to corporation tax on its profits; it is a payment 'equal to' corporation tax, not corporation tax itself. It is, however, part of the company's self-assessment liability and may therefore form part of the liability of a large company to be paid on instalments.[48] One reason for this non-deduction is that when (or if) the loan is repaid, the tax is refunded to the company,[49] so the rule operates as requiring the company to pay a special refundable deposit. Without some rule governing loans to participators and their associates, it would be easy for the company to avoid the widened definition of 'distribution' and still enable the participators to enjoy the untaxed capital reserves of the company.[50] Section 455 does not apply if the loan is made in the ordinary course of a business carried on by the company, which includes the lending of money;[51] a company which made eight loans over 14 years was held not to come within this exception.[52] However, section 455 does apply whenever a 'debt' has been incurred (see below at §67.4.3). If the loan is at a low rate of interest, the borrower may also incur liability under ITEPA 2003 (see above §16.4.3). Before 1999 the sum paid was a sum equal to ACT.[53]

Further rules in CTA 2010, sections 464A–464D were introduced in FA 2013 to block schemes exploiting weaknesses in the close company regime.[54] Section 464A imposes a tax charge if a close company is party to tax avoidance arrangements under which a benefit is conferred (directly or indirectly) on an individual who is a participator in the close company or an associate of such a participator. The aim is to broaden the close company regime

---

[47] CTA 2010, s 1067, ex TA 1988, s 418(7).
[48] On self-assessment, see FA 1998, Sch 18, para 8. On payment by instalments, see above at §60.6.1.
[49] CTA 2010, s 458, ex TA 1988, s 419(4).
[50] See *Jacobs v IRC* (1925) 10 TC 1.
[51] CTA 2010, s 456(1), ex TA 1988, s 419(1); and see Revenue Interpretation RI 16.
[52] *Brennan v Deanby Investments Ltd* [2001] STC 536 (CA, NI) reversing Special Commissioner.
[53] TA 1988, s 419(1) (original version).
[54] See commentary by Shipwright [2013] BTR 476.

beyond the section 455 charge on loans or advances of money by levying a charge on other forms of untaxed extractions of value from close companies which end up in the hands of their participators or their associates.[55] Section 464B provides relief if the extracted value is repaid. Sections 464C–464D target 'bed and breakfasting' arrangements in which a loan from the close company to the participator is repaid prior to the point in time when the section 455 charge would have arisen, only for the close company to make a new loan to the participator shortly afterwards.[56] Under these provisons, the relief ordinary given on repayment is denied where arrangements had been made for new payments to be made to replace some or all of the amount repaid.

67.4.2 Extension

Section 460 applies when the loan is made neither by the close company, A, nor by another close company which A controls, but by a non-close company which A controls.[57] To catch obvious avoidance devices, loans existing when A acquires control are treated as being made after that control was acquired, thus falling within section 460.

   Section 460 is aimed at schemes to avoid section 455, and therefore section 461 provides an exception when it is shown that no person has made any arrangements (otherwise than in the ordinary course of a business carried on by the person) as a result of which there is a connection:

(1)   between—
      (a)   the making of the loan or advance, and
      (b)   the acquisition of control; or
(2)   between—
      (a)   the making of the loan or advance, and
      (b)   the provision by the close company of funds for the company making the loan.

Section 461(2) further provides that the close company shall be regarded as providing funds as aforesaid if it directly or indirectly makes any payment or transfers any property to, or realises or satisfies (in whole or in part) a liability of, the company making the loan. The onus of establishing that the loan was in the ordinary course of business or that there was no arrangement is thus placed on the taxpayer.

   Interest runs against the company if the payment is not made by the due date. In the case of a company outside the obligation to pay by quarterly instalments, interest runs nine months after the end of the accounting period. A consequence of this provision is that no corporation tax is payable and no interest charge arises if the participator has repaid the loan by that date.[58] If the loan is repaid after this date, relief by way of refund of the tax may not be given until nine months after the end of the accounting period in which the repayment is made.[59]

[55] HMRC, Technical Note, *Close Company Loans to Participators (Loophole Closures)* (20 March 2013) and Shipwright, *op cit*, 477.
[56] *Ibid.*
[57] CTA 2010, s 458, ex TA 1988, s 419(4); when two or more companies control the lender, the company is treated as controlled by each but the loan is apportioned between them: s 459 (ex s 419(5)).
[58] TA 1988, s 826(4)—not rewritten—amended by FA 1996, s 173(5).
[59] CTA 2010, s 458(5), ex TA 1988, s 419(4A), added by FA 1996, s 173(3).

67.4.3 Loans

The statute gives a wide definition of 'loan'.[60] It has been held that there must be some consensual element, so that money due to a company by way of restitution of sums misappropriated by a director was not within ex TA 1988, section 419 (now CTA 2010, section 456).[61] However, it is also provided that a company is regarded as making a loan when a person 'incurs a debt' to the close company, and this liability to make good the misappropriation was held to be a loan for this purpose.[62] In *Andrew Grant Services Ltd v Watton*,[63] it was held that a debt was incurred for this purpose when the fact of liability was established, even though the payment became due at some future time and was for an indefinite amount. In that case an estate agent ran his business as an unincorporated business but formed a personal service company of which he was a participator; the sums unpaid and due from the business to the company were held to fall within the former TA 1988, section 419.

67.4.4 Exceptions from Charge

67.4.4.1 Full-time Worker

If the borrower is a full-time worker for, and does not have a material interest in, the company or an associated company, section 455 is excluded if the total loan outstanding does not exceed £15,000.[64] In computing the amount of the loan, included are loans made to the spouse or civil partner of the director or employee, but not to other associates. Provision is made for the possibility of acquiring a material interest after the date of the loan by deeming a new loan on that occasion. A participator who is neither a director nor an employee is not entitled to these exceptions.

67.4.4.2 Others

Exceptions are also made for ordinary trade credit (subject to a six-month maximum period) and for certain loans made to certain directors or employees of that or an associated company.[65]

67.4.4.3 Non-resident Company

At one time, TA 1988, section 419 applied to loans made by a non-resident company which was a participator. However, non-resident companies were removed in 1996, at least in part, for fear of challenge under the EU free movement of capital provisions.[66]

---

[60] CTA 2010, s 455(4), ex TA 1988, s 419(2).

[61] *Stephens v T Pittas Ltd* [1983] STC 576, (1983) 56 TC 722.

[62] This was held by the Special Commissioners in *Stephens v T Pittas Ltd*, but was not the subject of an appeal to the High Court. The issue raises interesting questions about the meaning of the word 'debt'. CTA 2010, s 455(4), ex TA 1988, s 419(2) also covers the assignment of a debt due from the participator to another person by that person to the close company.

[63] [1999] STC 330.

[64] CTA 2010, s 456. A special rule applied for pre-1971 housing loans under TA 1988, s 420(2).

[65] CTA 2010, s 456, ex TA 1988, s 420(2).

[66] See Brannan [1996] BTR 378, commenting on FA 1996, s 173.

67.4.5 *Release of Loan Treated as Distribution*

Where a loan, falling within CTA 2010, section 455, is later released or written off in whole or in part, the person to whom it was made is treated as receiving a distribution and taxed at the appropriate dividend tax rate. This part of TA 1988 was rewritten by ITTOIA 2005, Part 4, Chapter 6. Unfortunately, and rather confusingly given the numbering of the close company provisions of CTA 2010, the relevant sections of Chapter 6 comprise sections 415–421A. The income cannot form part of modified net income for the purposes of ITA 2007, Part 8, Chapter 4 (deduction of tax from annual payments, etc), ex TA 1988, sections 348 and 349.[67]

The term 'release' is not defined, and is therefore given its plain and ordinary meaning. It is not necessary that the release should be voluntary or for inadequate consideration; the substitution of a new debtor for the original borrower is therefore a release.[68] The only question is whether the taxpayer has been released from his obligation to pay otherwise than by performance or satisfaction. A covenant not to sue will, on this broad interpretation, be treated as a release.

If the loan is repaid, so causing a repayment of tax, that repayment is calculated by reference to the amount of corporation tax paid when the loan was made.[69] For repayment supplement purposes, the repayment is treated as being corporation tax paid in the repayment period[70]—ie the supplement, if any, is not calculated by reference to the date of the original payment to the Revenue under CTA 2010, section 455.

ITTOIA 2005 breaks open TA 1988, section 421 (and part of section 422). It has four general provisions (sections 416–418 and section 421) plus the separate rules on loans to persons who die (section 419) and loans to trusts that have ended (section 420). Under ITTOIA 2005, section 420, tax is due from the person from whom the debt is due when released or written off. The same rule applies under ITTOIA 2005, section 419, unless the debt is due for the borrower's PRs.

67.5 Close Investment-holding Companies

Following FA 1989, profits of close investment-holding companies could not take advantage of the former small profits rate ($60.5 above) and must instead have borne the full corporation tax rate.[71] The Act also contained provisions restricting the repayment of credits if the actual pattern of distributions by the company was unusual;[72] however, the virtual abolition of the right of repayment of such credits made these provisions redundant and they were repealed as from 6 April 1999. The 1989 Finance Bill had originally proposed that such companies should be subjected to corporation tax at the top rate of income tax (then 40%). With the alignment of the small profits and main corporation tax rates, the

---

[67] ITTOIA 2005, s 421, TA 1988, s 421(1).
[68] *Collins v Addies* [1991] STC 445.
[69] CTA 2010, s 458, ex TA 1988, s 419(4).
[70] TA 1988, s 825.
[71] TA 1988, s 13A, added by FA 1989, s 105.
[72] TA 1988, s 231(3A).

significance of this category has waned from 1 April 2015. The discussion that follows is primarily of historical interest.

A company is a close investment-holding company if it is a close company and fails to satisfy the statutory test[73] which allows the company to escape designation. It should be noted that the rewritten definition formerly in CTA 2010, section 34 was moved to ITA 2007, section 393A by FA 2014. The company will escape such designation if, throughout the relevant accounting period, it exists wholly or mainly for any one or more of six purposes, of which the first two are the most important. In practice, the Revenue accept that a company exists *mainly* for one of these purposes if more than 50% of its business is for that purpose. The effect of the list is to exclude trading companies and property investment companies that are part of a group the main purpose of which is to support the trading or property investment activities of the group.[74]

The first qualifying purpose is carrying on a trade or trades on a commercial basis.[75] This definition does not extend to professions. The second purpose is the making of investments in land where the land is, or is intended to be, let to unconnected persons.[76]

The remaining qualifying purposes embroider the first two. Thus, a company will escape close investment-holding company status if its purpose is to hold shares in and securities of, or making loans to, a qualifying company[77] or to co-ordinate the administration of two or more qualifying companies.[78] A company may also exist for the purposes either:

(1)   of a trade carried on, on a commercial basis, by a company which controls it or by a qualifying company; or
(2)   of making investments by a company which controls it or by another qualifying company.

There is a special provision for companies in the course of a winding up.[79]

---

[73] CTA 2010, ss 439–441. FA 1989, s 104, replaced TA 1988, s 414(2) and inserted the now rewritten rules at s 414(2)–(2D).

[74] HC Official Report, Standing Committee G, col 587, 22 June 1989.

[75] ITA 2007, s 393A(2)(a), ex CTA 2010, s 34(2)(a), ex TA 1988, s 13A(2)(a), added by FA 1989, s 105(2).

[76] ITA 2007, s 393A(2)(b), ex CTA 2010, s 34(2)(b), ex TA 1988, s 13A(2)(b), added by FA 1989, s 105(2).

[77] ITA 2007, s 393A(2)(c), ex CTA 2010, s 34(2)(c), ex TA 1988, s 13A(2)(c), added by FA 1989, s 105(2); on definition of 'qualifying company', see CTA 2010, s 34(2)(6), ex TA 1988, s 13A(3).

[78] ITA 2007, s 393A(2)(d), ex CTA 2010, s 34(2)(d), ex TA 1988, s 13A(2)(d), added by FA 1989, s 105(2).

[79] ITA 2007, s 393A(5), ex CTA 2010, s 34(5), ex TA 1988, s 13A(4), added by FA 1989, s 105(2); on application to companies in liquidation, see Revenue Interpretation RI 21; *Simon's Direct Tax Service*, Div 115.4.

68

Anti-avoidance: Special Provisions

68.1   Introduction

68.2.1 Overview

This chapter deals with a number of anti-avoidance provisions mostly relating to companies,[1] shares and bonds. More general issues relating to the control of avoidance are considered in chapter five. The provisions were designed in and for an age of Revenue assessment; the advent of self-assessment and surcharges for incorrect returns make these particularly sharp weapons where they apply. The provisions were also devised for the most part against a background of very high rates of income tax for individuals[2] and low, or non-existent, rates of CGT. These anti-avoidance rules are detailed and complex; what follows is a discussion of the key elements.

68.2.2 Dividend Stripping—The Idea

When a taxpayer transfers shares in a company, the tax system is normally content to accept that income payments made by the company after a sale of shares must be taxed according

---

[1] Or, in the case of ITA 2007, ss 773–785 and 752–766 (ex TA 1988, ss 775, 776), other persons; however, companies are usually used.

[2] Eg 91.25%; see below at §68.6.

to the tax circumstances of the new owner of the shares; the fact that the previous owner had a higher marginal tax rate does not entitle the Revenue to tax the new owner at his predecessor's rates. However, if the new owner is able to extract all the surplus cash in the company without incurring any liability to tax, ie to strip the company of its cash tax free, the Revenue have cause to worry and the legislature to come to their aid.

68.2.3 The Strip

This stripping may be achieved in the following way. A has a controlling interest in company X. A sells those shares to B. B uses the voting power to compel the company to pay a large dividend to B. B then sells the shares back to A or to someone else. At first sight there is nothing inequitable about this. If B's marginal rate is simply lower than that of A, there is a loss of tax. However, this lower rate may be achieved not only if B is simply less well-off than A, but also if B is an exempt person, such as a charity or pension fund. Moreover, if B is a dealer in securities, the dividend paid out may be offset by the trading loss incurred on the sale of shares back to A, even though the loss is due to the payment of the dividend out of the cash reserve of the company. The effect is that the payment will have been drawn out free of tax while A has received a sum which reflects the value of those cash reserves, and that sum will be treated as a capital payment only.

68.2.4 Legislative Reaction

Attempts to obstruct these schemes have proved ineffective unless drastic. Thus, it was not clear whether the courts would hold that the transaction of buying in order to resell at a loss was a trading transaction.[3] If it was not a trading transaction, no relief could be given in respect of the loss and the scheme would fail. The UK courts at first accepted the arguments on behalf of B that it was a trading transaction and so allowed the whole dividend-stripping industry to get underway.

   Some legislation was designed to prevent the accumulations from arising in the first place, this being the purpose of much of the early close company legislation (repealed in 1989). In the 1950s the Revenue tried, by a separate avenue, to undo the tax advantages of stripping. Such devices, however, have always been subject to exceptions which exemplify the ambivalent attitudes of government to small, and therefore largely unregulated, businesses. At first, legislation was designed to interfere with the sales to security dealers and exempt persons, but in 1960 the legislature aimed at transactions in securities generally. See below at §68.5.

---

[3] This is not a happy area for believers in precedents. Although the final 1970s' view seems to be that this is not a trading transaction—see *FA and AB Ltd v Lupton* [1971] 3 All ER 948, (1971) 47 TC 580—earlier cases, especially *Griffiths v J P Harrison (Watford) Ltd* [1962] 1 All ER 909, (1962) 40 TC 281, were distinguished not overruled (see [1970] BTR 77 and 153) and the issues were still live in cases like *Barclays Mercantile Business Finance Ltd v Mawson* [2005] STC 1 (HL). See above §§5.6 and 19.3.2.

68.2   Bond Washing

68.2.1   General

Securities, ie stocks and shares, generate income in the form of dividends and interest. These become taxable income only when they are due and payable, or sometimes when paid;[4] for tax purposes the income is not apportioned over the period in respect of which it is declared.[5] Time usually elapses between the announcement of a proposed dividend by the company and its becoming payable. If, during this time, high-rate taxpayers sell securities to others paying tax at a lower rate, the purchase price received, although reflecting the value of the impending payment, cannot be segregated into an amount on account of capital and another amount on account of the dividend so as to tax the latter.[6]

This is still the premise of the law. However, that premise has been reversed by legislative schemes such as the accrued income scheme (above §26.4), which splits the payment received, the rules for deeply-discounted securities (above §26.6) and the loan relationship rules for companies (see chapter sixty-three above), which, more radically, abolish the distinction between income and capital. However, none of these changes affects shares.

Legislation to counter bond-washing schemes is not complete and so 'abuses' remain. One abuse is where a vendor, V, sells shares to a purchaser, P, who collects the dividend taxed at P's lower rate and then sells the shares back to V, all this being planned under the original agreement.[7] In this way the bond or shares[8] are said to be 'washed' of their dividend. It cannot be argued that P, the temporary purchaser, was not beneficially entitled to the dividend, since it is of the essence of the scheme that P is so entitled. It is also hard to apply ITTOIA 2005, Part 5, Chapter 5 (ex TA 1988, section 660A *et seq*) since there is no element of bounty about the scheme.

68.2.2   Legislative Counteraction

In 1937,[9] a more serious attempt was made to counteract one type of tax avoidance involving the sale and repurchase of securities. This applied where a high-rate taxpayer agreed to transfer securities,[10] and either in the same or in a collateral[11] agreement there was an agreement, or an option, to buy back those or similar securities.[12] If the result of such a transaction was that any interest (a term defined to include a dividend) became payable in respect of the securities and was receivable by someone other than the vendor, it was deemed to be the vendor's income. Thus, the legislation was primarily intended to nullify

---

[4] See above at §26.1.2, and §61.1.
[5] *Wigmore v Thomas Summerson & Sons Ltd* [1926] 1 KB 131, (1926) 9 TC 577; it may be apportioned for other purposes.
[6] *Thompson v Trust and Loan Co of Canada* [1932] 1 KB 517, (1932) 16 TC 394.
[7] TA 1988, s 231B, added by F(No 2)A 1997, s 28, concerns schemes to claim repayment of credits and does not address the situation of different tax rates.
[8] On the treatment of certificates of deposit and of rights to have such certificates issued, see above at §26.7.
[9] FA 1937, s 12.
[10] TA 1988, s 729.
[11] See *Re Athill; Athill v Athill* (1880) 16 Ch D 211, 222.
[12] Defined in TA 1988, s 729(2)(c).

any advantage to the vendor. Section 729 was first reduced in scope and finally repealed in 1996.[13] Its scope has been taken over by the accrued income scheme (above §26.4) and by the repo rules in ITA 2007, sections 601–606 (ex TA 1988, section 737A—see §68.3 below).

Section 730 was passed in 1938[14] to cover the situation where the vendor sold not the shares but simply the right to the dividend. In *Paget v IRC*,[15] the taxpayer held Hungarian bonds which carried the right to interest payable in sterling in London; the right to interest was attached to coupons. She was held not to be taxable on the purchase price received by her when she sold the coupons to a coupon dealer. Section 730 deems the interest to belong to the coupon vendor. It should be noted that in *IRC v McGuckian*[16] the House of Lords treated the payment of a price for the right to dividends as income for the purposes of section 730. While an Australian case suggested that *Paget* may be ripe for re-examination, it is unlikely that UK courts would think so.[17] As the coupon is almost certainly going to arise from a foreign asset, the income tax charge now arises under ITTOIA 2005, Part 4, Chapter 13. Section 730 was repealed in 2009 as part of a streamlining of the statue book.

The rules on the distinction between interest and other payments are refined by section 730A, added in 1995, dealing with price differentials arising from the sale and repurchase of securities (known as 'repo' transactions). This was rewritten into ITA 2007, sections 607–611.[18] Section 730C, added in 1996 and now rewritten as ITTOIA 2005, sections 151–154, deals with the stripping and reconstitution of gilts, which includes a regulation-making power.[19]

Sales of the right to interest payment have now been brought within the deeply-discounted securities rules in ITTOIA 2005, Part 4, Chapter 8. Sales of the right to non-excluded annual payments now have their own rule.

FA 2009 replaced section 730 and two other provisions with a new general rule on the transfer of income streams affecting both income tax (ITA 2007, sections 809AZA–809AZG) and corporation tax (CTA 2009, sections 486F–486G and CTA 2010, sections 752–757).[20] It is an important and welcome essay in a new style of drafting. The new general rule, in its income tax form ITA 2007, section 809AZA, applies where a person makes a transfer of a right to 'relevant receipts'. *McGuckian*[21] would be a classic example. Receipts are 'relevant' if they would, but for the transfer, be income in the hands of the transferor or brought into

---

[13] Except for certain transactions entered into before 6 November 1996.

[14] FA 1938, s 24.

[15] [1938] 2 KB 25, (1938) 21 TC 677; on deduction of tax from interest, see Inland Revenue Tax Bulletin, Issue 20 (December 1995).

[16] [1997] STC 908, (1997) 69 TC 1; see above at §5.6.4.

[17] *IRC v John Lewis Properties plc* [2003] STC 117 (CA); the Australian case is *FCT v Myer Emporium Ltd* (1987) 18 ATR 693. At one time s 730 extended to shares, interest and annual payments, but F(No 2)A 2005 restricted it to distributions in respect of shares.

[18] On history, see Henderson J in *Revenue and Customs Commissioners v Bank of Ireland Britain Holdings Ltd* [2008] STC 253, [2007] EWHC 941 (Ch). See also above at §5.5. Ex TA 1988, ss 731–734 were repealed by FA 2008, s 66, along with ss 735 and 736. The reason why these are no longer needed is that CTA 2009, Pt 3, Ch 9 (ex TA 1988, s 95) makes dealers in securities, etc taxable under the trading rules.

[19] See HMRC Notes to Finance Bill 2008, cl 63, para 10. However, some rule is needed for insurance companies with non-life business as s 95 does not apply to them; the new rule is 95ZA, added by FA 2008, Sch 17, and not rewritten. Care is needed on the commencement provisions.

[20] The additional provisions repealed were TA 1988, ss 775A and 785A, the latter concerning rent factoring of leases of plant and machinery. Among the fascinating points in the Notes on Clauses are the 2006 American case of *Lattera v Lattera* (see para 9) and an explanation of a change to TA 1988 s 785A made by FA 2008 (see para 19).

[21] *IRC v McGuckian* [1997] STC 908, HL.

account in computing profits of the transferor. So the rules catch both a transfer of a right to pure income and the sale of a right to income which forms part of trading profits. Section 809AZA does not apply if the transfer also applies to the asset from which the receipts arose, though there is an express exclusion if the asset is a right to annual payments.[22]

Section 809AZB charges the amount of the consideration or, if that is too low, the market value of the right. These rules do not apply if the receipt is already taxed as income in some other way (section 809AZC). There are also exceptions for life annuities and pension income, and for transfers by way of security (section 809AZE).

Sections 809AAZA-809AAZB apply to disposals of income streams through partnerships.

68.3 Manufactured Dividends and Repos

These rules are an updated version of a provision first introduced in 1960, when the scheme was described as something 'which the ordinary layman could fairly describe as a swindle at the expense of the honest taxpayer—not a criminal conspiracy but a racket'.[23] The essence of the scheme is that individuals make 'manufactured' payments but do not suffer any overall economic loss.[24]

Manufactured payments are payments due under a contract or other arrangements for the transfer of shares, and represent dividend or interest. Tax is charged in various sets of circumstances on the amount representing the dividend or interest; the definition of that amount is made according to precise rules in each set of circumstances. The charge arises only if the manufacturer is not itself entitled to the dividend or interest payment. The legislation has been frequently amended and now includes a non-allowable purpose test.[25]

The rules are now mostly to be found in CTA 2010, Part 17 (ex TA 1988, Schedule 23A) for corporation tax and ITA 2007, Part 11 (for income tax). The rules apply to manufactured dividends on UK equities and interest on UK securities.[26] There are further rules for manufactured overseas dividends[27] and irregular manufactured payments.[28] All try to apply to the manufactured payments at least some of the rules which would apply to actual payments of dividend or interest.

The rules in ex TA 1988, section 737A and Schedule 23A, rewritten as CTA 2010, Part 17, Chapter 5 and ITA 2007, sections 596–607, also apply to certain deemed manufactured payments arising from the sale and repurchase of securities, and deemed manufactured payments in the case of stock lending. In all instances there are duties on the person making the payment to supply the appropriate information for tax purposes. A charge under these rules excludes any charge under the accrued income scheme.[29] The detail is way beyond a book such as this, but the topic is interesting.

[22] ITA 2007, s 809AZA(1)(b) and (3).
[23] HC Official Report 1960, Vol 624, col 451 (Sir Edward Boyle).
[24] See further Tiley and Collison, *UK Tax Guide* (LexisNexis, 2012)§§4.18 *et seq.*
[25] CTA 2010, ss 799–801, ex TA 1988, Sch 23A, para 7A added by FA 2004.
[26] CTA 2010, ss 782–789 (on manufactured dividends) and ITA 2007, ss 573–578 (manufactured dividends and interest), ex TA 1988, Sch 23A, paras 2–3.
[27] CTA 2010, ss 790–795 and ITA 2007, s 581, ex TA 1988, Sch 23A, para 4.
[28] CTA 2010, ss 796–798 and ITA 2007, s 583, ex TA 1988, Sch 23A, para 7.
[29] TA 1988, s 715(6), rewritten to ITA 2007, ss 638(2), (3), 647(2)–(4), (6), 663(1)–(3).

68.4   Dividend Stripping

TA 1988, section 736 was one of a number of provisions introduced because of dividend stripping. Many of these provisions were repealed following the 1999 changes to corporation tax abolishing the right of an exempt person to reclaim tax on a dividend. However, section 736 survived until 2008.[30] It applied where a company dealing in securities obtained a holding of more than 10% in another company and there was one or more distributions by that other company, the net effect of which was materially to reduce the value of the holding. Section 736 directed that the reduction in the value of the holding was added to the value of the security.[31] The purpose of this was to counteract the tax advantage obtained in a typical dividend strip by simply wiping out the loss on the shares which the dealing company would hope to put against the distribution. When section 736 applied, the rules for accounting for tax on manufactured dividends and interest were modelled on those for real dividends and interest (ie quarterly accounting).[32] Leading up to its repeal in 2008, the Revenue used ex TA 1988, section 703 (discussed in §68.5.1 below) in preference to section 736, a course which is scarcely surprising. The Revenue also used the (now drastically reduced) CGT value-shifting rules (TCGA 1992, sections 30 *et seq*).

68.5   Cancellation of Tax Advantages: Transactions in Securities

68.5.1   General

ITA 2007, Part 13, Chapter 1, sections 682–713 contain rules originally introduced in 1960; the corporation tax rules are contained in CTA 2010, Part 15, sections 731–751 (ex TA 1988, sections 703–709). The technique used is to allow the Revenue to issue a notice counteracting tax advantages gained in certain circumstances prescribed in language of broad and so often uncertain scope.[33] The effect of the notice is to undo the transaction but only for tax purposes. Briefly, (a) the tax advantage must have been obtained as a result of a transaction in securities, and (b) it must fall within one of three (formerly five) sets of circumstances (described at §68.5.3 below). It is, however, open to the taxpayer to show that the transaction was carried out either for bona fide commercial reasons, or in the ordinary course of making or managing investments and, in either event, not with the obtaining of a tax advantage as its main or one of its main objects.[34] The modern approach of the court is not to restrict the section to contrived transactions carried on away from the open market, but simply to ask whether the particular transaction comes within its scope.[35]

The rewritten income tax legislation in ITA 2007 was rewritten again in 2010, to simplify the rules and limit their scope. The definition of 'tax advantage' in ITA 2007, section 687 was

---

[30] Repealed by FA 2008 s 66(1) with effect in relation to distributions made on or after 1 April 2008.
[31] *Cf* TCGA 1992, s 177; see above at §65.7.
[32] See ex TA 1988, Sch 23A.
[33] However, the Revenue are under a duty to exercise their power fairly (*R v IRC, ex parte Preston* [1983] STC 257, 59 TC 1).
[34] ITA 2007, s 685 and CTA 2010, s 734, ex TA 1988, s 703(1).
[35] *IRC v Trustees of the Sema Group Pensions Scheme* [2002] EWCA Civ 1857, [2003] STC 95.

narrowed, and the references to a 'relevant company' were replaced by 'close company'. The sets of circumstances triggering the application of the transaction in securities counteraction were condensed into one section (section 685) with two conditions corresponding to circumstances (D) and (E) that apply for corporation tax (discussed below). In addition, a new exemption was introduced for transactions immediately following a fundamental change in the ownership of the close company (new ITA 2007, section 686). The discussion below focuses on the corporation tax formulation in CTA 2010, Part 15.

The original section 703 was introduced before the new approach in *Ramsay*,[36] and judicial views on the relationship between the two have wavered. However, a sensible way forward, consistent with the *Barclays Mercantile Business Finance* case,[37] is to say that the new approach is simply a way of interpreting the facts to which the legislation applies. In *Bird v IRC*,[38] Lord Keith said that it was open to the Revenue to choose whether to use section 703 or the new approach as a means of applying section 419. Similarly, in *McGuckian v IRC*,[39] some judges felt able to bring the facts within section 703 without having to rely on the new approach at all; this now seems correct. These provisions are among the most difficult in the UK tax law. Thirty years ago they were denounced as being, generally speaking, the most obscure, while the penalties for infringing them were the most severe, and they were barely touched upon by published statements of Revenue practice.[40] Since then we have got used to other wide provisions, and the language of the ITA 2007 and CTA 2010 versions is undoubtedly somewhat easier to disentangle (as opposed to understand), but the other criticisms are still correct. A further difficulty is the absence of any provision governing the interaction with CGT. Where the proceeds of sale of shares fall within these rules, Revenue practice is to allow the tax so charged as a credit against CGT; the concessionary status of this way of avoiding double taxation has been condemned.[41] A clearance procedure applies.[42]

A good example of the operation of these rules is *IRC v Wiggins*.[43] A company restored and sold picture frames. One frame was found to contain a valuable painting, *The Holy Family*, by Poussin.[44] Rather than simply sell the painting and distribute the profits as dividend, the company first sold all its other stock to one company, after which another company bought the shares of the first company for £45,000. The courts held that the £45,000 represented the value of trading stock, so that section 704, paragraph D (now CTA 2010,

---

[36] *WT Ramsay Ltd v IRC* [1982] AC 300; see above §5.6.4.

[37] *Barclays Mercantile Business Finance Ltd v Mawson* [2005] STC 1 (HL), and see above §5.6.

[38] [1985] STC 584, (1985) 61 TC 238. At first instance Vinelott J said that it was not open to the Revenue to rely on *Furniss v Dawson* [1984] AC 474 and TA 1988, s 704 in the same transaction, while in the same case the Court of Appeal held that the taxpayer could not use the new approach to disregard a step which s 703 said had to be taken into account.

[39] [1997] STC 908, 69 TC 1, HL. See also the interesting but now outdated dicta of Vinelott J in *Bird v IRC* [1985] STC 584, 647; 61 TC 238, 312.

[40] Nolan, IFS Conference (28 June 1974) 25, para 3.

[41] See Lord Wilberforce in *IRC v Garvin* [1981] STC 344, and Lord Bridge, *ibid* at 349, 353; 55 TC 24, 86, 90.

[42] ITA 2007, s 701 and CTA 2010, s 748, ex TA 1988, s 707; see *Balen v IRC* [1978] STC 420, 52 TC 406; and Statement of Practice SP 3/80. Prior to 2009 there was also a special tribunal to hear appeals from the Tribunals, appeal from which was on a point of law only and was still by way of case stated. ITA 2007, ss 706–711, TA 1988, ss 705, 706. On jurisdiction, see *Marwood Homes Ltd v IRC* [1998] STC (SCD) 53.

[43] [1979] STC 244, [1979] 2 All ER 245; see Walters [1979] BTR 183.

[44] The frame was bought in 1955 for £50; the picture was found to be by Poussin 10 years later, valued at £130,000.

section 737) applied, and the £45,000 could be treated as income of those who had sold their shares. More recently, in *Grogan v Revenue & Customs Commissioners*, Warren J held that a scheme involving a qualifying employee share trust (QUEST) was caught by these anti-avoidance rules.[45]

At Budget 2016, the Government confirmed a previous announcement that it intends to amend the transactions in securities rules and introduce a new targeted anti-avoidance rule to prevent opportunities for income to be converted to capital in order to gain a tax advantage.

68.5.2 The Three Elements

68.5.2.1 Tax Advantage

'Tax advantage' is defined for corporation tax as:

(1) a relief or increased relief from corporation tax;
(2) a repayment or increased repayment of corporation tax;
(3) the avoidance or reduction of a charge to or an assessment to corporation tax; or
(4) the avoidance of a possible assessment to corporation tax.[46]

It does not matter whether the avoidance or reduction is effected by receipts accruing in such a way that the recipient does not pay or bear corporation tax on them, or by a deduction in calculating profits or gains. A similar definition used to apply for income tax, but the definition was narrowed in 2010. ITA 2007, section 687 now provides that a person obtains an income tax advantage if:

(1) the amount of any income tax which would be payable by the person in respect of the relevant consideration if it constituted a distribution, exceeds the amount of any CGT payable in respect of it; or
(2) income tax would be payable by the person in respect of the relevant consideration if it constituted a distribution and no CGT is payable in respect of it.

Exemption and relief. At one time a relief was distinguished from an exemption. A relief indicated an alleviation of an obligation, whereas an exemption indicated a removal of the obligation altogether. It followed that a person with no obligation to pay tax did not obtain a tax advantage if income accrued to him rather than to someone else in whose hands it would not be exempt from tax. This over-nice distinction, which placed far too much weight on a particular view of the tax structure not always appreciated by a draftsman, has quite rightly been rejected. It follows that where a company issued shares in favour of charitable trustees and other shareholders waived their rights to a dividend, so that all the dividends accrued to the trustees, the trustees were not entitled to a tax repayment and were stopped by section 703.[47]

---

[45] [2011] STC 1, [2010] UKUT 416 (TTC).
[46] CTA 2010, s 732, ex TA 1988, s 709.
[47] *Universities Superannuation Scheme Ltd v IRC* [1997] STC 1; overruling *Sheppard v IRC (No 2)* [1993] STC 240.

Advantage. The definition of 'tax advantage' for corporation tax suggests that there must be a contrast of the actual case where there is an accrual in a non-taxable way with a possible accrual in a taxable way.[48] Thus, where a company had issued and later redeemed bonus debentures, there was an avoidance of tax in that, had the money been distributed as dividends, it would have been taxable.[49] However, whether the issue or the redemption constitutes the tax advantage is still unclear.[50]

In *Cleary v IRC*[51] it was argued that the words 'avoidance of a possible assessment thereto' indicated that Parliament had in mind the reduction of profits available for dividends and not the reduction of physical assets for that purpose, so that there would be no tax advantage if a company simply used its cash resources to buy shares in another company. However, this view was rejected by the House of Lords. In the case, two sisters owned the shares of two companies and extracted the cash from one company by allowing that company to buy their shares in the other. They thus avoided the possible assessment that would have arisen if the cash had been paid out by way of dividend.[52] The fact that this would have been the worst possible procedure, and so unlikely to happen, did not matter. This case is disturbing since, when the purchasing company in turn made its distribution, no credit could have been claimed for the tax already exacted.[53]

In *Emery v IRC*,[54] where a company had made a large trading profit, the taxpayer was held to have derived a tax advantage when he sold his shares because he could have got the company to declare a dividend or go into liquidation. In *Bird v IRC*,[55] Lord Keith said that the quantum of the advantage was ascertained by contrasting the non-taxable receipt with a similar receipt that might have accrued in some other, taxable way. Further, the House of Lords held that in determining what should be done to counter such an advantage there was an obligation to make an accurate measure of the tax advantage obtained. When the taxpayer has to make good the liability of another person, that should reduce the tax advantage obtained.

In the earlier case of *IRC v Brebner*,[56] Lord Upjohn said that one choice of a method which carried less tax than another did not necessarily mean that one of its main objects was to obtain a tax advantage. In another early case it was said that a charity does not have a tax advantage as one of its main objects simply because, in reaching a decision, it is influenced by its privileged tax status.[57]

---

[48] *IRC v Parker* [1966] AC 141, 178–79, (1966) 43 TC 396, 441, *per* Lord Wilberforce.
[49] *IRC v Parker*, *ibid*; cf *Anysz v IRC* [1978] STC 296.
[50] See *IRC v Parker*, *op cit.*
[51] [1967] 2 All ER 48, (1967) 44 TC 399.
[52] See *Hague v IRC* [1968] 2 All ER 1252, 44 TC 619. In a judgment not easy to reconcile with *IRC v Parker* or *Cleary v IRC*, the Court of Appeal refused to accept as a 'possible' assessment one which would arise if spouses at that time had opted for separate assessments, a possibility scarcely more fanciful than that envisaged by the House of Lords in *Cleary v IRC*. This was later reversed by TA 1988, s 703(7)—now repealed (FA 1988, Sch 14, Pt VIII).
[53] In the Court of Appeal Lord Denning said that 'the courts are well able to take care of that contingency'. However, there is no legislation analogous to TA 1988, s 419(4) or the now long-repealed TA 1988, s 427(4). It is therefore hard to see what his Lordship had in mind.
[54] [1981] STC 150, 54 TC 607.
[55] [1988] STC 312, 316–17; 61 TC 238, 341–43.
[56] (1968) 43 TC 705, 718.
[57] *IRC v Kleinwort Benson Ltd* [1969] 2 All ER 737, 743; 45 TC 369, 382, *per* Cross J.

68.5.2.2 Transaction in Securities

'Transaction' is defined for both income tax and corporation tax as including transactions of whatever description relating to securities and, in particular:

(1)   the purchase, sale or exchange of securities;
(2)   issuing or securing the issue of new securities;
(3)   applying for or subscribing for new securities; and
(4)   altering or securing the alteration of the rights attached to securities.[58]

This wide definition is not qualified in any way.[59] Hence, repayment of share capital as a reduction is a transaction,[60] as is the payment of the purchase price for shares by instalments, at least when the instalments were related to dividends,[61] and perhaps even if not so related.[62] The definition is based on the premise that the liquidation of a company is not a transaction in securities.[63] This has now been decided by the House of Lords, their Lordships saying that there was no sound reason to distinguish a payment in the course of a liquidation from the payment of a dividend;[64] however, the combination of a transaction with a liquidation may give rise to a charge.[65] In reliance on various statements in the House of Lords, the rewritten income tax rule makes it clear that the definition is exhaustive.[66]

68.5.2.3 Securities

'Securities' is defined to include shares and stock, and, in relation to a company not limited by shares (whether or not it has a share capital), includes a reference to the interest of a member of the company as such.[67] Thus, debentures and securities are included, and their redemption is a transaction in securities. A loan note, even though unsecured, is a security;[68] similarly, the receipt of a loan from—and repayable to—a controlled company is a transaction in securities.[69]

68.5.3 The Sets of Circumstances

68.5.3.1 Abnormally High Dividends to Exploit Relief—Repealed

The first circumstance, formerly TA 1988, section 704 paragraph A and repealed in 2010, concerned abnormally high dividends where, in connection with the distribution of profits

---

[58] ITA 2007, s 684(2) and CTA 2010, s 751, ex TA 1988, s 709(2).
[59] *IRC v Parker* [1966] AC 141, 172–3, 43 TC 396, 437, per Lord Guest.
[60] *IRC v Brebner* [1967] 1 All ER 779, 43 TC 705.
[61] *Greenberg v IRC* [1972] AC 109, 47 TC 240; see [1971] BTR 319.
[62] See a reluctant Lord Reid in *Greenberg v IRC* (*ibid*), 137, 272.
[63] This view was accepted by Lord Dilhorne and Lord Diplock in *IRC v Joiner* [1975] 3 All ER 1050, 1057, 1060, 50 TC 449, 483, 488.
[64] *Laird Group plc v IRC* [2003] UKHL 54; [2003] STC 722.
[65] *IRC v Joiner, op cit.*
[66] See explanatory notes to ex ITA 2007, s 713.
[67] ITA 2007, s 713 and CTA 2010, s 751, ex TA 1988, s 703(2).
[68] *IRC v Joiner* [1975] 3 All ER 1050, 1056, per Lord Wilberforce. What if, in *Cleary v IRC* [1967] 2 All ER 48, 44 TC 399, the assets sold had been personal property, such as a picture, and not shares?
[69] *Williams v IRC* [1980] STC 535, [1980] 3 All ER 321, 54 TC 247, HL.

of a company or in connection with the sale or purchase of securities followed by the purchase or sale of the same or other securities, the person in question received an abnormal amount by way of dividend, being entitled by reason of:

(1) any exemption from tax;
(2) the setting off of losses against profits or income;
(3) the deduction for interest under ITA 2007, section 383.

The rules for corporation tax also referred to:

(4) the giving of group relief, to recover tax in respect of dividends received by that person;
(5) the application of franked investment income for the purpose of the shadow ACT regulations;[70]
(6) the computation of profits or gains out of which are made payments within TA 1988, sections 348 and 349.

There were further rules in the days of ACT.

A dividend is regarded as abnormal—the present tense is used here as this definition continues to be relevant for other, non-repealed provisions—if:[71]

(1) it substantially exceeds a normal return on the consideration provided for securities (the 'excessive return condition'); or
(2) it is a dividend at a fixed rate and substantially exceeds the amount which the recipient would have received if the dividend had accrued from day to day and he had been entitled only to so much of the dividend as accrued while he held the securities (the 'excessive accrual condition').

Rule (2) applies only if the recipient sells or acquires a right to sell those or similar securities within six months. The word 'profits' is defined to include income, reserves or other assets. This is unfortunate when compared with standard accountancy definitions, but indicated the wide scope of the section.[72] The burden of proof lies with the Revenue to establish that the distribution was of an abnormal amount.[73]

This test of abnormality is exhaustive. In *IRC v Sema Group Pensions Scheme*,[74] dividends were paid to pension fund trustees as part of a buy-back scheme; at that time pension fund trustees were entitled to a tax credit repayment. The Court of Appeal held that the trustees had not received an abnormal amount by way of dividend since it was not abnormal when one looked at the length of time the trustees had held the shares and the total amount of dividends and other distributions made during that time, this being the test set out in the

---

[70] Corporation Tax (Treatment of Unrelieved Surplus Advance Corporation Tax) Regulations 1999 (SI 1999/358), reg 23.
[71] ITA 2007, ss 692–694, and CTA 2010, 740–742, ex TA 1988, s 709(4). For example, see Inland Revenue Tax Bulletin, Issue 5 (November 1992).
[72] See comments by Lord Upjohn in *Cleary v IRC* [1967] 2 All ER 48, 56; 44 TC 396, 428.
[73] *Universities Superannuation Scheme Ltd v IRC* [1997] STC 1.
[74] [2002] EWCA Civ 1857, [2003] STC 95.

statute.[75] It was not right simply to look at the particular payment and decide that it was large—and so abnormal—when viewed on its own. The Court agreed that the trustees had obtained a tax advantage and had, as one of their objects, the avoidance of tax, but section 703 would apply only if the facts came within paragraph A—and they did not.

68.5.3.2 No Abnormal Dividend: Deduction for Loss Arising from Distributions or Dealings—Repealed

This circumstance, formerly TA 1988, section 704 paragraph B and also now repealed, concerned the drop in the value of securities as a result of the dividend. It was of relevance when the person involved was tax exempt or a share dealer. Since a dealer in shares is no longer exempt from tax on dividends and since exempt bodies can no longer claim back any tax or tax credits on dividends, this provision was found to be superfluous and was repealed by FA 2008, section 66. The purpose here was to catch the dividend stripper who did not receive an abnormal dividend but who simply claimed a loss, as in *IRC v Kleinwort Benson Ltd*.[76]

68.5.3.3 Receipt of Consideration Representing Company's Assets, Future Receipts or Trading Stock

CTA 2010, section 736 (ex TA 1988, section 704, paragraph C) applies if a company receives consideration which:

(1)   is or represents the value of assets which are available for distribution by a company by way of dividend (or which would have been so available apart from anything done by the company in question);
(2)   is received in respect of future receipts of a company; or
(3)   is or represents the value of trading stock of a company,

and the receipt is 'in consequence of' a transaction whereby another person subsequently receives or has received an abnormal amount by way of dividend and, further, the company receiving the consideration does not pay or bear corporation tax on income in respect of the receipt.

This deals with the opposite side of the transaction from that covered by the circumstances set out in §§68.5.3.1 and 68.5.3.2 above. The definition of 'abnormal dividend' just described in (now repealed) TA 1988, section 704, paragraph A (above §68.5.3.1) continues to apply for this purpose. 'Available for distribution by way of dividend' means legally available, not commercially available.[77]

In the ordinary dividend strip or bond-washing operation, it was not to be supposed that all the economic advantage would be confined to the purchaser. Thus, in one instance[78] a company had 15,000 unclassified £1 shares. These were converted into 300,000 1s ordinary shares and a once-for-all dividend of 47s 6d was declared. These shares were sold to

---

[75] TA 1988, s 709(4)(b) and (6)(b).
[76] [1969] 2 All ER 737, (1969) 45 TC 369.
[77] Ex TA 1988, s 704(3); *IRC v Brown* [1971] 3 All ER 502, even though current liabilities exceed current assets. See now Companies Act 2006, ss 830 and 841.
[78] HC Official Report 1960, vol 624, col 626 (Sir Edward Boyle).

superannuation funds and to charities at 67s 6d, which then reclaimed the tax paid on the dividend. After the dividend the shares were worth about 1s 6d each. The funds and charities had paid 67s 6d in effect for a net dividend of 47s 6d, an operation that made sense only on the basis that they collected tax of about 30s per share thanks to their exempt status. Thus the vendor made £1 and the funds 10s per share—free of tax. Hence this circumstance.

Scissors and forward strip. This rule catches two other devices, known as forward stripping and 'scissors', or stock stripping. Forward stripping occurred when a company was about to make a large profit.[79] Special shares were created carrying a high rate of dividend, and these would be sold to a dealing company for a capital sum. The dealer would then set off the loss on resale against the predicted dividend which had subsequently accrued.

Stock stripping occurs where a company has stock on its books at the correct conservative figure of cost or market value, whichever is the lower. If the stock were realised there would be a considerable income receipt. Enter the finance company which also deals in stock. The company buys both stock and shares at book value. The increased price obtained by sale at market value is offset by the drop in the value of the shares. Thanks to CTA 2010, section 736 the original company, if it is allowed its loss, will be subject to tax as having obtained a tax advantage.

The Revenue must not only establish each element but also show that the transaction and the abnormal dividend (or whatever it may be) are causally linked; this flows from the word 'whereby'.[80] In deciding the scope of the transaction the court may take a broad view and is not limited to the immediate cause of the dividend, but still the causal connection must be shown.[81] Where, as is usually the case, more than one step is involved, this causal connection may be established even though the taxpayer does not take part in each one.[82] It has also been decided that the causal link may be found in the purpose and design of those who, for a fee and instructed by the taxpayers, controlled the operation of the schemes.[83]

68.5.3.4 Relevant Company Distribution and Receipt of Consideration

This circumstance has given the courts the most difficulty. *IRC v Wiggins* (see above at §68.5.1) is an example of this rule. In its TA 1988 version in section 704, paragraph D it contained an outstandingly unhelpful example of legislation by reference.[84] The CTA 2010 version is much improved, and the ITA 2007 version was simplified.

CTA 2010, section 737 refers to a 'relevant company', which is defined in section 739 as under the control[85] of five or fewer persons and all unquoted companies, unless under the control of a quoted company. Like the previous circumstance (§68.5.3.3), this circumstance applies to the vendor rather than the purchaser, but unlike the situation described in §68.5.3.3, there is no requirement that there should be an abnormal payment. These

---

[79] See *Greenberg v IRC* [1972] AC 109, [1971] 3 All ER 136, 47 TC 240, HL.
[80] *Bird v IRC* [1985] STC 584.
[81] *IRC v Garvin* [1981] STC 344.
[82] *Emery v IRC* [1981] STC 150.
[83] *Bird v IRC* [1985] STC 584.
[84] TA 1988, s 704 para D stated 'in connection with the distribution of profits of a company to which this paragraph applies, the person in question so receives as is mentioned in paragraph C (i), (ii) or (iii) such a consideration as is therein mentioned'. When the Finance Bill 1960 was first presented, para D was part of para C; hence, perhaps, the reference.
[85] Defined this by reference to the close company test in CTA 2010, s 450, ex TA 1988, s 416(2)–(6); see above at §67.2.

matters give this circumstance its wide ambit. Section 737 refers to assets of the relevant company; assets are ignored if they represent a return of sums paid to subscribers on the issue of such securities.[86]

Under section 737, the company must have received consideration in connection with the distribution, transfer or realisation of assets of a relevant company, or the application of such assets in discharge of liabilities. The consideration will be caught if it:

(1)   is or represents the value of assets which are available for distribution by way of dividend by the company, or assets which would have been available but for anything done by the company;

(2)   is or is received in respect of future receipts of the company; or

(3)   is or represents the value of trading stock by the company.

Thus, the capitalisation of undistributed profits, followed by a reduction in capital, is a distribution for this purpose,[87] as are a reduction in capital followed by capitalisation,[88] an issue and redemption of debentures,[89] and even the purchase of one company's shares by another.[90] There may be a distribution of profits without diminution of assets.[91] Control must be shown to exist. This will trigger liability whether it exists at the time the asset is realised or at the time of the subsequent distribution, but it is not enough for the Revenue simply to prove control when the sum is received.[92]

This rule requires that the sum be received 'in connection with' the distribution of profits. This imposes a less definite causal link than the word 'whereby' in the circumstance described in §68.5.3.3.[93] Returning to *IRC v Wiggins* (see above at §68.5.1), we find that the purchase price paid for the shares in the company owning the picture represented the value of that company's trading stock, so that the taxpayer received consideration of the proscribed type; the company was controlled, a tax advantage was obtained and there was a transaction in securities. As the sum was not otherwise chargeable to income tax, these rules made it so.

68.5.3.5 Twin Trouble; Receipt of Assets of Relevant Company

Here again we are concerned with a relevant company as just defined above. This circumstance, formerly TA 1988, section 704 paragraph E now CTA 2010, section 738, was originally added in 1966. It applies where there are two or more relevant companies and where the taxpayer receives non-taxable consideration in the form of share capital or a security issued by a relevant company in connection with the transfer, directly or indirectly, of assets of one such company to another, and the consideration is or represents the value of assets available for distribution by such a company. If the consideration is non-redeemable share

[86]   CTA 2010, s 737(5), ex TA 1988, s 704(C2).
[87]   *Hague v IRC* [1968] 2 All ER 1252, 44 TC 619.
[88]   *IRC v Horrocks* [1968] 3 All ER 296, 44 TC 645.
[89]   *IRC v Parker* [1966] 1 All ER 399, 43 TC 396.
[90]   *Cleary v IRC* [1967] 2 All ER 48, 44 TC 399.
[91]   *Ibid.*
[92]   *IRC v Garvin* [1981] STC 344, 55 TC 24.
[93]   *Emery v IRC* [1981] STC 150, 54 TC 607, referring to TA 1988, s 704 para C.

capital, the liability arises when the share capital is repaid.[94] If it takes any other form, liability arises upon receipt. It is very unclear whether this adds anything to the other paragraphs. In *Williams v IRC*,[95] the Court of Appeal held that where a transaction falls within both TA 1988, section 704, paragraph D and paragraph E then paragraph E should apply. This point was not considered in the House of Lords.

68.5.4 Defences

For corporation tax, these rules do not apply if the taxpayer shows that the transaction was carried out for genuine commercial reasons,[96] or in the ordinary course of making or managing investments, and that no transaction had as its main object or one of its main objects to enable tax advantages to be obtained.[97] It is perhaps interesting, in view of the decision of the House of Lords in *FA and AB Ltd v Lupton*,[98] to note that this defence presupposes that a transaction the main object of which was the obtaining of a tax advantage could be in the ordinary course of making investments or have bona fide commercial reasons. This is an area in which appellate courts will not interfere if the Tribunals (previously the Commissioners) have asked the right questions and considered all the evidence.[99] For income tax purposes, the purpose condition is no longer a defence but has been incorporated into the main charging provision; thus the rules apply only if the main purpose, or one of the main purposes, is to obtain an income tax advantage.[100]

Perhaps correctly, this is the only part of the legislation in which the courts have shown any sympathy for the taxpayer. In determining what are bona fide commercial reasons, the word 'commercial' includes non-financial reasons. Hence, a view that to retain family control of a company is important for the future prosperity of the company, whether in the context of company–customer or employer–employee relationships, can be good commercial reasons, so that steps taken to preserve that control will escape these rules.[101] Similarly trustees of a pension fund required by the Occupational Pensions Board to reduce a particular holding were given the protection of this defence when the route they took (purchase of share by the company) was cheaper and simpler and was what any prudent investor would have done.[102]

In *Marwood Homes v IRC*,[103] a Special Commissioner held that the main object of an intra-group transfer of shares followed by the payment of dividends totalling £1,040,000

---

[94] CTA 2010, s 738(5), ex TA 1988, s 704 para E(2).

[95] [1979] STC 598, 54 TC 257.

[96] TA 1988, s 703(1) used the older form 'bona fide'. On the importance of onus of proof, note *Hasloch v IRC* (1971) 47 TC 50, where the transaction was instituted by a board of directors of which the taxpayer was not a member. The transaction was the redemption of certain preference shares, a move which would improve the capital structure of the company but also confer a tax advantage on the taxpayer, who failed to persuade the Commissioners that the latter was not an object. The case also shows that the transactions in securities provisions apply even though the intention to save tax exists only for some of the time.

[97] CTA 2010, s 734, ex TA 1988, s 703(1).

[98] [1971] 3 All ER 948; see above at §19.3.2.

[99] Eg *IRC v Sema Group Pensions Scheme* [2002] EWCA Civ 1857; [2003] STC 95, esp para 117.

[100] ITA 2007, s 684(1)(c), ex s 685.

[101] *IRC v Goodwin* [1976] STC 28, HL.

[102] *Lewis v IRC* [1999] STC (SCD) 349.

[103] [1997] STC (SCD) 37.

from subsidiary companies, the payment being outside a group income election, was to enable the reserves in the subsidiaries to be passed through to the taxpayer company in order to strengthen the financial position of the taxpayer company. However, this decision was reversed by the special appeal tribunal, which held that the obtaining of a tax advantage was a main reason, even if it was not *the* main reason for the transaction.[104]

In deciding whether there are commercial reasons it is not necessary for the taxpayer to show that those reasons are connected with the company concerned. Thus, in *Clark v IRC*,[105] the taxpayer, a farmer, decided to sell shares in a controlled company in order to raise money with which to buy another farm; his claim to use this defence was upheld. Most litigants have argued that the obtaining of a tax advantage was not one of the main objects. The test is subjective and the question is one of fact.[106] If a business operation is carried out in two distinct phases, one of which is purely commercial and the other having tax advantages as its main objects, it is a question of fact for the Tribunals (previously the Commissioners) whether there was one transaction or two. The House of Lords has commended a 'broad commonsense view' to the Commissioners.[107]

In *IRC v Brebner*,[108] the respondent and his colleagues were resisting a takeover bid and so made a counter-offer for the shares. This was financed by a loan from a bank on terms requiring early repayment. After two unsuccessful attempts to persuade the minority interests to sell out, the original counter-offer was accepted by a majority of the shareholders. The company then resolved first to increase its capital by £75,000 by capitalising its reserves, and then to reduce them by the same amount, thus causing £75,000 to come out of the company to the new shareholders who used the sum to pay off the loans from the bank. The Commissioners held that the whole was one transaction and that it did not have as one of its main objects the obtaining of a tax advantage. A notice to counteract the advantage therefore failed. The House of Lords held that there was ample evidence to support the findings. Lord Upjohn said that a choice of a method which carried less tax than another did not necessarily mean that one of its main objects was to obtain a tax advantage.[109]

Another defence is that the Revenue notice counteracting the advantage is made out of time (ie more than six years after the chargeable period to which the tax advantage relates).[110]

68.6 Sale of Income Derived from Individual's Personal Activities

ITA 2007, Part 13, Chapter 4 provides a special regime for certain income derived from personal activities. It was introduced in 1969 to prevent taxpayers from converting future

---

[104] [1999] *Simon's Weekly Tax Intelligence* 55.

[105] [1978] STC 614, [1979] 1 All ER 385.

[106] *IRC v Brebner* [1967] 2 AC 18, 30 *per* Lord Upjohn; *ibid*, 26, *per* Lord Pearce. In the first five reported cases the Commissioners' decision on fact has (eventually) been upheld (*IRC v Brebner* (*ibid*); *IRC v Hague* [1968] 2 All ER 1252; *Hasloch v IRC* (1971) 47 TC 50; *IRC v Goodwin* [1976] STC 28, HL; and *Clark v IRC* [1978] STC 614, [1979] 1 All ER 385). The sixth is *Marwood Homes v IRC* [1999] *Simon's Weekly Tax Intelligence*, 55, in which the Special Commissioner was reversed by the s 703 tribunal.

[107] Lord Pearce in *IRC v Brebner* [1967] 2 AC 18, 26.

[108] *Ibid*.

[109] *Ibid*, 30, *per* Lord Upjohn.

[110] ITA 2007, s 698(5) and CTA 2010, s 746(5), ex TA 1988, s 703(12); this may be what the taxpayer's adviser was trying to achieve in *IRC v McGuckian* [1997] STC 908, HL with his tactics of non co-operation.

taxable income into capital; the income tax escaped would have been 91.25%.[111] The practice was particularly prevalent in the entertainment industry, the members of which were,
of course, more likely than others to suffer from the absence of any proper averaging clause
in the UK tax system at a time of very high marginal rates of tax. This provision is quite
distinct for that applying a duty to deduct tax from certain payments to non-resident entertainers and sportsmen (see below at §72.6.4).

Suppose that a film was about to be made and that £1 million was available for the
star's services. A company would acquire the star's services in return for an option to take
shares in the company. It would pay £50,000 by way of living allowance to cover expenses,
these being taxable to the individual under what is now ITEPA 2003, but deductible by
the company. The company would sell the star's services to the film company in return for
£1 million, would receive that sum and would suffer corporation tax, so that some tax
would be paid but significantly less than the 91.5% which might (then) apply for income
tax.

The scope of these rules as drafted is much wider than the covering of these devices in the
entertainment industry. It applies where:

(1)   arrangements are made to exploit the earning capacity of an individual by putting
      some other person (eg the company) into a position to receive the income from his
      activities; and
(2)   as part of the arrangement the individual or any other receives a capital amount;
      provided
(3)   that the main object or one of the main objects was the avoidance of tax.[112]

Since the purpose of the provision appears to be to stop rather than to regulate this kind of
contract, the whole capital sum is taxable under Part 13 of ITA 2007; there is no provision
for top-slicing or any other form of relief, and it does not appear to be treated as relevant
earnings for pension purposes since the capital sum is charged under ITA 2007, Part 13 and
not ITTOIA 2005, Part 2.[113] Further, the section applies to all persons regardless of their
residence, provided the occupation is carried on in whole or in part in the UK,[114] and to any
indirect methods of enhancing the value of property.[115]

The section does not apply to a capital amount obtained in respect of the disposal of
assets (including any goodwill) of a profession or vocation, or shares in a company so far
as the value is attributable to the value of the business as a going concern.[116] However, an
exception is made where the value of the business as a going concern is derived to a material
extent from the individual's activities and for which he does not get full consideration. A
capital amount means any amount in money or money's worth which would not otherwise
fall to be included in any computation of income for the purpose of the Tax Acts.[117]

---

[111] The provision began life as FA 1969, s 31, Sch 16.
[112] Presumably, this has a subjective meaning; *cf* the transaction in securities rules above at §12.5.1.
[113] On 'relevant earnings', see FA 2004, s 189 (not rewritten).
[114] ITA 2007, s 777, ex TA 1988, s 775(9).
[115] ITA 2007, s 780 and CTA 2010, s 823(1), ex TA 1988, s 777(2).
[116] ITA 2007, s 784, ex TA 1988, s 775(4).
[117] ITA 2007, s 777(7) and CTA 2010, ss 829–830, ex TA 1988, s 777(13). Consider unremitted partnership
profits when the remittance basis applies. Is there a charge at once under this rule and again when the profits are
remitted? Presumably not, as the remittance basis has to be claimed (ITTOIA 2005, s 833).

The position with regard to losses is the same as for §68.7 below—loss relief is available under ITA 2007, section 152 because this head of charge is listed in section 1016(2) of Part 2 of that Act.

68.7   Transactions in Land[118]

TA 1988, section 776 for corporation tax was also introduced in 1969 to charge to income tax certain gains of a capital nature arising from the disposal of land. The purpose was to charge profits that escaped being trading income and to charge the prime mover in schemes such as *Ransom v Higgs*[119] rather than the person making the trading profit.[120] The section is not confined to 'artificial transactions' in land, ie to transactions entered into for the purpose of tax avoidance.[121] It is no wonder that some regard the section as being concerned not with artificial transactions in land so much as with artificial taxation of natural transactions in land. They were no doubt pleased that the word 'artificial' does not appear in the title in the rewritten income tax version in ITA 2007, Part 13, Chapter 3, or the rewritten corporation tax version in CTA 2010, Part 18.

CTA 2010, section 819(1) (ex TA 1988, section 776(2)) states that the section applies to a gain if any of the conditions in section 819(2) is met in respect of land, the gain is a capital gain from the disposal of all or part of the land, the land is situated in the UK and a person within section 820(1)(a), (b) or (c) obtains the gain. The conditions are:

(1)   that the land, or any property deriving its value from the land, is acquired with the sole or main object of realising a gain from disposing of the land; or

(2)   the land is held as trading stock; or

(3)   the land is developed with the sole or main object of realising a gain from disposing of the land when developed, and any gain of a capital nature is obtained from the disposal of all or part of the land when developed.

The person described in section 820(1) is:

(a)   the person acquiring, holding or developing the land, or

(b)   a connected person, or

(c)   a person who is a party to, or concerned in, the arrangement or scheme that is effected as respects the land which enables a gain to be realised by any indirect method, or by any series of transactions.

---

[118] The heading in TA 1988 was 'Artificial transactions in land', but the word 'artificial' is not in ITA 2007 or CTA 2010.

[119] [1974] 3 All ER 949 and see above at §19.1.2.

[120] FA 1969, s 32. On validity of alternative assessments, see *Lord Advocate v McKenna* [1989] STC 485; and on whether assessments are cumulative or alternative, see *IRC v Wilkinson* [1992] STC 454, CA. On these provisions see also Holroyd Pearce [1980] BTR 382 and Avery Jones [1980] BTR 465.

[121] *Page v Lowther* [1983] STC 799 (CA). The taxpayer argued unsuccessfully that the heading of TA 1988, Pt XVII (in which s 776 occurs) 'Tax avoidance', and the side heading of s 776, 'Artificial transactions in land', restricted the scope of the section.

The same words are to be found in ITA 2007, sections 756 and 757.

Thus, the section applies only to the gain arising on an actual disposal of the land which had been so acquired, held or developed. The rule that the gain must be derived from the disposal of land is taken more widely where (c) is involved. In *Page v Lowther*,[122] X granted a lease of land to Y and, in accordance with an arrangement between X and Y, Y arranged for payments due on the grants of sub-leases to be made to X by the sub-lessee. Y having developed the land, the court held that X was liable under section 776(2)(c), as X had arranged for a gain to be realised by X by an indirect method, getting Y to make the sub-lessee make the payments to X.

The charge arises under CTA 2010, section 818 for corporation tax and under ITA 2007, section 755 for income tax, and is generally made on the person realising the gain.[123] However, when A provides B with an opportunity of realising a gain, the gain which B makes may be taxed as the income of A: A is given an indemnity against B.[124] The charge is on the whole of the gain and is made for the year in which the gain is obtained, but an amount in money or money's worth will not be regarded as receivable by some person until that person is able effectively to enjoy or dispose of it.[125] Thus, A's liability does not arise until B effectively enjoys or disposes of the gain. The income is investment income, not earned income.

The charge arises regardless of the residence of the taxpayer if all or any part of the land is situated in the UK.[126] This is of crucial importance since until recently CGT generally did not apply to non-residents; from 2015 the reach of CGT has extended to encompass non-residents disposing of UK residential property (see §33.2). The extent to which taxpayers can get round this charge by invoking double tax treaties is a matter of great interest—and difficulty.

68.7.1 Disposal of Land with the Object of Realising a Gain

68.7.1.1 Land or Property

'Land' includes references to all or any part of the land, and includes buildings and any estate or interest in land or buildings.[127] A disposal of the benefit of a contract to buy land or the grant of a lease is covered. The interest may be legal or equitable.[128] Property deriving its value from land includes a shareholding in a company deriving its value directly or indirectly from land. A right to insist that a sale should take place only with A's consent may give A the necessary property deriving its value from the land.

---

[122] [1983] STC 799 (CA).

[123] See ITA 2007, s 759 and CTA 2010, s 820–821, ex TA 1988, s 776(3)(b).

[124] ITA 2007, s 768 and CTA 2010, s 821, ex TA 1988, s 776(8). The indemnity is in ITA 2007, s 768–769 and CTA 2010, s 821, 829, ex TA 1988, s 777(8). B is treated as having paid income tax for the purposes of CGT.

[125] ITA 2007, s 768(2) and CTA 2010, s 829(2), ex TA 1988, s 777(13).

[126] ITA 2007, ss 756(1), 759(8) and CTA 2010, s 819(1)(c), ex TA 1988, s 776(14); in the case of a non-resident the Board may direct the deduction of income tax at basic rate under ITA 2007, s 944.

[127] ITA 2007, s 756, and CTA 2010, s 819, and explicitly so defined in ex TA 1988, ss 776(13), 777(5).

[128] *Winterton v Edwards* [1980] STC 206, [1980] 2 All ER 56, 52 TC 655.

68.7.1.2 Disposal

The property is disposed of if the property in the land or the property deriving its value from the land, or control over the land is effectually disposed of.[129] The words are widened still further[130] by taking account of any method, however indirect, by which any property or right is transferred or transmitted, or the value of any property or right is enhanced or diminished. A number of transactions may be treated as one disposal.[131]

68.7.1.3 Object

The sole or main object must be the realising of a gain from disposing of the land; this should be the object at the time of acquisition.[132] The object of gain must relate to the property acquired and not some other land. If two objects are equal, it would appear to follow that the charge cannot apply. If land is acquired with this object, a subsequent change of mind is irrelevant. On similar Australian legislation the section applies to property acquired under a testamentary gift;[133] however, buying the land from executors in satisfaction of a pecuniary legacy is clearly distinguishable.

Objects other than making a gain include deriving income from land, the preservation of visual or other amenity value of existing land, the provision of accommodation for a relative and in the case of company retention of family control.

68.7.2 Trading Stock

When land held as a trading stock is disposed of, the profits would normally enter a computation under ITTOIA 2005, Part 2 and, as such, would be outside this charge. The purpose of ITA 2007, section 756(3)(c) and CTA 2010, section 819(2)(c) is to catch the indirect disposals which might otherwise give rise to income accruing to others. This charge does not extend to property deriving its value from land.

68.7.3 Later Development

If land is acquired without the object of realising a gain from disposing of the land, the first situation (§68.7.1) is not established. Where, however, land is later developed with that object, a charge arises. 'Development' is not defined. The object of realising a gain on disposal must presumably exist at the moment of development, but it is unclear whether it is necessary that the object should be to dispose of the land immediately the land is developed. The fact that it is envisaged that the land should be used as a source of, say, rental income for a few years before its final effectual disposal, should be only one factor in deciding whether the sole or main object of the development is to realise the gain.

Conversely, if the object is to use the property developed as a source of rental income but, after development, a change of mind occurs, no charge under these rules can arise. What

---

[129] ITA 2007, s 757 and CTA 2010, s 820, ex TA 1988, s 776(4).
[130] By ITA 2007, s 761(1) and CTA 2010, s 823(1), ex TA 1988, s 777(2).
[131] ITA 2007, s 757(3) and CTA 2010, s 820(3), ex TA 1988, s 776(5).
[132] For example *Sugarwhite v Budd* [1988] STC 533, CA.
[133] *McCelland v Taxation Comr of Australian Commonwealth* [1971] 1 All ER 969.

happens when the change of mind occurs during the development is less clear, since the rule states simply that the land is to be developed with the object of realising a gain. Such words would appear apt to cover any development in the course of which there was at any time such a sole or main object.

The rule does not catch a gain attributable to the period before the intention to develop is formed.[134] ITA 2007 expressly notes that the reader must not overlook the ITTOIA 2005, Part 2 rules on appropriation of property as trading stock.

HMRC has an information-gathering power specific to these rules.[135]

68.7.4 *Exceptions*

68.7.4.1 Residence

The charge does not apply to a gain accruing on the disposal of the taxpayer's principal private residence, as defined for CGT purposes. However, such a residence which was bought partly with a view to gain, while not exempt from CGT, is not liable to a charge under ITA 2007, section 755.[136]

68.7.4.2 Companies

The charge does not apply where there is a disposal of shares in a company which holds land as trading stock, or in a company which is a dealing company, not an investment company, and which owns directly or indirectly 90% or more of the ordinary share capital of another company which holds land as trading stock, provided all the land so held is disposed of in the normal course of trade, and so that all opportunity of profit accrues to the company.[137] This exclusion applies to the straightforward disposition of the shares, but does not apply to a scheme or an arrangement enabling a gain to be achieved by indirect means.

When the land is held by a company, it may be in the company's interest to escape this charge since, as well as tax being paid at a lower rate, the company may also be able to use rollover relief. Apparently some companies avoid the charge by revaluing the property and then distributing a capital profit dividend.

68.7.5 *Computation, Clearance and Losses*

The computation of the gain is defined in very broad terms, the statute merely directing that there shall be used such method as is just and reasonable in the circumstances, taking into account the value obtained for the land, but allowing only such expenses as are attributable to the land disposed of.[138] This broadness may assist the taxpayer. If T submits a computation based on ITTOIA 2005, Part 2 principles, it appears that in practice it will be for the Revenue to show that the computation is not just and reasonable—it is not enough for the Revenue to show that another method is also just and reasonable.

---

[134] ITA 2007, s 765 and CTA 2010, s 827, ex TA 1988, s 776(7). This slice is chargeable to CGT. Presumably the existing use value is taken as the figure at which the change for capital gain to taxable income occurs.

[135] ITA 2007, s 771 and CTA 2010, s 832, ex TA 1988, s 778.

[136] ITA 2007, s 767, ex TA 1988, s 776(9) (repealed because no application to corporation tax).

[137] ITA 2007, s 766 and CTA 2010, s 828, ex TA 1988, s 776(10); in practice, the Revenue confine this provision to companies already dealing.

[138] ITA 2007, s 760 and CTA 2010, s 822, ex TA 1988, s 776(6).

Because of the vague and broad nature of the charge there is one of those rare examples of a statutory clearance procedure.[139] However, taxpayers seldom apply for clearance and, when they do, are usually refused. Income arising under ITA 2007, Chapter 13, Part 3 is expressly listed in section 1016(2) of Part 2, so is available for the set-off of losses under ITA 2007, section 152. So losses under Chapter 3 may be set against profits in that list—and vice versa. There is no such clear-cut provision for corporation tax, but the result is the same under the miscellaneous losses (ex Schedule D, Case VI loss) rules.[140]

The Revenue may direct that the payer is to deduct basic income tax if it appears to them that a person who is entitled to any consideration or other amount taxable under these rules was not resident in the UK.[141] This does not allow the Revenue to issue a notice before the person becomes entitled to any consideration.[142]

Example—*Yuill v Wilson*[143]

The taxpayer, T, and connected settlements controlled company X which owned two pieces of land. T set up a non-resident trust which controlled two other non-resident companies, C and M, which each bought a property from X for full market value. The trust then disposed of its shares in C and M to an overseas company in which neither the taxpayer nor his family had any interest; the consideration due to C and M was to be paid in instalments on the happening of certain contingencies.

The House of Lords held that TA 1988, section 776(2) (now ITA 2007, section 756) applied to the gains realised by C and M. The gains had been obtained for the companies either directly or through T's companies, with the aid of the trustees, and T remained liable notwithstanding the subsequent sale of his shares in C and M to the overseas company. However, the House of Lords also held that a right to money which could not be said to be effectively enjoyed was not yet taxable; it followed that as yet there was no liability in respect of the unpaid conditional instalments.[144]

68.8 Transfer of Right to Receive Annual Payments

The sale of the right to receive certain annuities or interest payments was at one time dealt with under provisions considered above at §68.2. Following a redrawing of boundaries in 2005, TA 1988, section 775A was inserted by F(No 2)A 2005.[145] This section applied both for income tax and for corporation tax, but was not rewritten for income tax and was repealed by FA 2009.

---

[139] ITA 2007, s 770 and CTA 2010, s 831, ex TA 1988, s 776(11).

[140] CTA 2010, s 91. TA 1988, s 396 was *sub silentio* authority for this: there was an express bar on losses arising under TA 1988, ss 34–36 but there was no mention of s 776.

[141] ITA 2007, s 944, ex TA 1988, s 777(9).

[142] *Pardoe v Energy Power Development Corp* [2000] STC 286.

[143] [1980] STC 460, [1980] 3 All ER 7, 52 TC 674; for another example, see *Chilcott v IRC* [1982] STC 1, (1982) 55 TC 446.

[144] In *Yuill v Fletcher* [1984] STC 401, the taxpayer appealed again on the grounds that the contingent rights of the companies to the instalments were 'money's worth', capable of being valued and sold within a year of the contract. The appeal failed; the gains were realised only when the instalments were received and ceased to be subject to restriction.

[145] F(No 2)A 2005, Sch 7, para 4.

PART VI

International and European Union Tax

69

International Tax: Introduction
and Connecting Factors

69.1 Introduction

International tax is concerned with the tax system as soon as it moves beyond the purely domestic scene.[1] It is concerned with the taxation of non-UK source income accruing to residents (see chapter seventy-one below) and with UK source income accruing to

---

[1] For a general critique and call to action, see Graetz, (2001) 54 *Tax L Rev* 261 (the Tillinghast lecture). Other possible starting points are Vogel (1988) 16 *Intertax* 216, 310, 393; Kingson (1981) 81 *Columbia L Rev* 1151; Avi-Yonah (1996) 74 *Texas L Rev* 1301; and Easson, in Krever (ed), *Tax Conversations* (Kluwer, 1999) 419. For a good practical introduction, see Arnold, *International Tax Primer*, 3rd edn (Kluwer, 2015) and Avi-Yonah, *Advanced Introduction to International Tax Law* (Edward Elgar, 2015). For further study, see Harris and Oliver, *International Commercial Tax* (CUP, 2010) and Panayi, *Advanced Issues in International and European Tax Law* (Bloomsbury, 2015). Elliffe, *International and Cross-Border Taxation in New Zealand* (Thomson Reuters, 2015) is also recommended for its broader discussion, as well as the interesting New Zealand approach to these issues.

non-residents (chapter seventy-two below). The problems posed by controlled foreign companies are considered in chapter seventy-three. International aspects of capital gains tax are discussed in chapter seventy-four. These issues often raise questions of double taxation, by which is usually meant the provision of relief when two (or more) countries try to tax the same income (see chapters seventy-five and seventy-six below). By way of preface, this chapter is concerned with the connecting factors used in the UK system, while chapter seventy deals with the question of the enforcement of foreign revenue laws. Tax lawyers usually treat these rules as giving rise to points of domestic law in an international context rather than as part of international law proper; such an attitude is incomprehensible to international lawyers.[2] Thus tax lawyers debate whether the International Court of Justice is a suitable way of resolving tax disputes and usually conclude that it is not.[3] The UK tax system, with its pragmatic approach to things, treats these issues as esoteric.

National tax systems are truly national and are one of the ultimate expressions of national sovereignty. They are usually drawn up in the interests of the nation and not of the nation's neighbours, which indifference is, at least in common law systems, returned by the neighbours. Continental European systems find themselves able to consider their neighbours with politeness. National tax systems resemble the continental plates of the plate tectonic systems—they are massive, they collide, and the impact usually causes one to go under and the other to rise up. Those caught at the point of collision may be able to take advantage of opportunities,[4] but equally they may be trying to avoid injustices such as double taxation or non-relief.

National sovereignty is no longer enough. It is one cliché that the world is getting smaller, and another that business is getting more integrated; research work by the OECD and EC (2001) shows how tax still gets in the way.[5] As trade gets more integrated, yesterday's concepts may need to be revised or scrapped. A system based on determining business profits of a multinational on the basis of source alone becomes unreal—especially as world trade becomes ever more involved in terms of intangible services and intellectual property—and it becomes tempting to move to other measures for dividing up the total profits of the multinational, such as the number of employees or the amount of capital investment in each State. This 'unitary' approach has its problems, but it is a symptom of an underlying fact which cannot be wished away. Another solution is to tax internationally by creating a supranational tax authority, such as the European Union may well have to create one day. The OECD's much less radical response to these challenges in the context of the G20/OECD Base Erosion and Profit Shifting (BEPS) project is considered below at §69.11.

Tax law does not form part of that branch of study known as private international law; one of the most constant UK rules directs that the UK courts will not enforce a claim by another state which is of a revenue nature. However, international co-operation on

---

[2] See Avi Yonah (2004) 57 *Tax L Rev* 483.

[3] See Van der Bruggen (2001) 29 *Intertax* 250.

[4] Rosenbloom (2000) 53 *Tax L Rev* 137.

[5] See *Taxing Profits in a Global Economy* (OECD, 1991) and *Tax Effects on Foreign Direct Investment* (OECD, 2007). For the EU, see the EC Commission Working Paper, *Company Taxation in the Internal Market*, COM(2001)582 and the ongoing work on the CCCTB (http://ec.europa.eu/taxation_customs/taxation/company_tax/common_tax_base/index_en.htm). The impact of tax on business investment is also the subject of ongoing research by the Oxford University Centre for Business Taxation (http://www.sbs.ox.ac.uk/faculty-research/tax).

tax administration and enforcement has developed considerably through international institutions such as the OECD, the United Nations, the EU and various intergovernmental bodies in different parts of the world. These institutions develop appropriate tax policy for governments, but they generally fail to create beneficial tax rights for individual taxpayers. Tax plays an important role in world trade law, and the World Trade Organisation (WTO) has had to adjudicate on matters of permissible and impermissible discrimination.[6] However tax policy issues arise quite outside the remit of the WTO. For example, it has been suggested that integrating shareholder and company taxation presents a major challenge to the international tax structure.[7] Another example is the challenge to traditional concepts by the development of electronic commerce.[8]

International tax has developed its own criteria, sometimes building on but always distinct from the general tax policy and design criteria outlined in chapter one of this book.[9] When a national government examines its international tax rules it wants to achieve three things:

(1)   to get a reasonable share of tax from international, ie transnational, business;
(2)   to maintain horizontal equity for its people, whether they have foreign or domestic income; and
(3)   to encourage its own businesses, or at least see that they are not unfairly discriminated against.

As usual in tax policy, it is not possible to do all these things. In the international tax context this is prevented by the absence of a universal flat rate tax on a uniform base with uniform (high) levels of administration.

Tax theorists talking about objective (1) use the term 'inter-nation equity'. The objective for the UK is to devise rules which collect enough tax on profits earned by foreigners in the UK, while enabling the UK to gather enough tax on profits earned by its own people abroad. This may be seen as an area either for crude international bargaining or, more rationally, for trying to develop principles within which the bargaining process may take place. The view that the role of inter-nation equity in international taxation is just about politics did not go without challenge.[10] A growing band of scholars, arguing from varying combinations of normative and empirical work, have argued that the concept must be understood more broadly and take account of poverty and international

---

[6] Warren (2001) 54 *Tax L Rev* 131; for a comparison of EU and WTO approaches, see Gaines, Olson and Sørenson, *Liberalising Trade in the EU and the WTO: A Legal Comparison* (CUP, 2012) and Ortino, *Basic Legal Instruments for the Liberalisation of Trade* (Hart Publishing, 2004).

[7] Warren, *op cit*, 139.

[8] OECD, *BEPS Action 1 'Addressing the Tax Challenges of the Digital Economy' Final Report* (Oct 2015), and see the various OECD Reports gathered together in the annual van Raad, *Materials on International and EU Tax Law*, vol 1 (International Tax Centre Leiden) and the Symposium (1997) 52 *Tax L Rev* 557. See Shalhav (2003) 31 *Intertax* 131.

[9] See Arnold and McIntyre, *op cit*, ch 1; Graetz, *op cit*; and Warren, *op cit*, 158–68.

[10] Musgrave and Musgrave suggested a redistributive mechanism for relations between developed and developing countries: see (1972) 'Inter-nation Equity' in Bird and Head (eds), *Essays in Honor of Carl S Shoup* (University of Toronto Press, 1973), 63, 70.

justice.[11] Some writers suggest that at present international income tax policy is irrespon-
sive to inequalities between States[12] and so more weight—or at least more effectiveness—
should be given to source-based taxation of, at least corporate, income.[13]

Objective (2) suggests that the state will want to ensure that the total tax burden on X's
income will be the same whether X earns that income at home or abroad. Carried to its
conclusion this has some surprising results. Thus, it will cover income whether or not it is
remitted to the UK and whatever the cause of non-remittance; it may also apply whether
the non-remittance is because a capital gain has not been realised or the wealth is in an
insurance policy or bond, but only if the same principles had been enacted as part of the
domestic system. The same journey to a conclusion suggests that, where the foreign tax
charged on income is higher than the UK tax, the UK should refund the difference; it does
not, and is not likely to.

The tensions within (3) are clear from the way it is formulated; the UK wants to ensure
that its people are not discriminated against by other governments when they carry out
transactions abroad. However, at home it may be torn between wanting to protect its
own residents and ensuring a competitive economy, whether the competition comes
from residents or non-residents. As the global economy becomes ever more closely integrated, the distinction between the home trader and the foreigner becomes unreal. As
Nation States become increasingly desperate to attract investment, they compete with their
neighbours and rivals. Within the European Union much of this competition is now controlled by rules on state aids, but this may simply switch the area of competition to that
of tax. Agreements between Member States to control harmful tax competition have been
reached but are based on international agreement rather than binding EU law (see below
§75.1.2).

In resolving these problems, tax systems use different concepts and techniques. Thus, the
connecting factors for the taxpayer may be citizenship, or residence or domicile; the connecting factor for the particular receipt will be that of source (however determined). The
foreign income may be relieved from tax by allowing the foreign tax to be used as a deduction in computing the UK income, as a credit, or by simply exempting the foreign income
(such as dividends) from UK tax. These solutions are discussed in the context of phrases
about capital neutrality.[14]

---

[11] Other writing emphasises that inter-nation equity requires allocation of fiscal jurisdiction in accordance
with prevailing views of justice internationally: see Kaufman, 'Fairness and International Income Taxation' (1998)
29 *Law and Policy in International Business* 145, 194. For a lead into theories of inter-nation equity, see Vogel,
'Worldwide versus Source Taxation on Income: A Review and Re-evaluation of Arguments (part III)' (1988)
10 *Intertax* 394, and Peggy Brewer Richman (later Musgrave) *Taxation of Foreign Investment Income* (Johns
Hopkins Press, 1963). Connections between international taxation and philosophical ideas of international justice
are made by Cappellan (2001) 15 *Ethics and International Affairs* 97.

[12] On adjusting US international tax policy to the needs of developing countries, Brown (2002) 23 *U PA J Intl
Econ L* 45.

[13] Vogel, *op cit* (1988). The source of income is a difficult concept, so a simpler mechanism to allow developing
countries take a greater share of MNE (multinational enterprise) revenue has interested some writers: see Avi-
Yonah (2000) 113 *H L Rev* 1573, esp 1648–49.

[14] For inadequacies of these and other concepts, see Graetz, *op cit*. See also Devereux and Pearson, *Corporate
Tax Harmonisation and Economic Efficiency*, IFS Report Series No 35 (Institute for Fiscal Studies, 1989), 16–24,
suggesting that achieving CEN may be more important than achieving CIN.

Capital import neutrality (CIN) focuses on investment in the particular market and demands that non-residents investing in the market (those by whom the capital is imported) should be treated the same as those who are also resident. CIN thus stresses the importance of neutrality in the country of source. An international system based on source only and not on residence would satisfy CIN; so a system which simply exempted foreign income of UK residents from UK tax would meet this test. Continental European thinking finds CIN attractive for the respect it pays to the sovereignty of the other State.[15]

Capital export neutrality (CEN) focuses on investment by the particular individual and demands that residents investing in a foreign market (those by whom the capital is exported) should be treated the same as those who invest at home.[16] CEN thus stresses the importance of neutrality in the country of residence. An international system based on residence and not on source would satisfy CEN.

Early in the 21st century, economists have demonstrated that CIN and CEN do not exhaust the forms which neutrality might take.[17] So one comes across capital ownership neutrality (CON) and national ownership neutrality (NON). CON suggests that the tax system should strive for the same result whether assets are owned at home or abroad, ie tax rules do not distort the ownership of assets. This system too emphasises source. An international regime paying attention to world welfare in which all countries exempt foreign income satisfies CON, but so also may a credit system.[18] NON is satisfied when all activities within the national area are taxed alike, whether investment is by domestic or by foreign firms. Here too one finds a call for the exemption of foreign income no matter what other countries do. Additional outbound investment does not reduce domestic tax revenue, since the reduction in domestic investment is offset by an increase in foreign investment.

69.2   UK Connecting Factors: General

In general, UK residents are taxable in respect of all income no matter where it arises; non-residents are taxable on income arising from sources within the UK.[19] UK residents are taxed because, whether or not British subjects, they enjoy the benefit of our laws for the protection of their property; non-residents because, in respect of property in the UK, they enjoy the benefit of our law for the protection of that property.[20] The burden of proof is on the Revenue to establish that a taxpayer is resident in the UK.[21] The UK used to regard citizenship[22] as a suitable test of the jurisdiction for executing people, but not for taxing

---

[15] Schön, *Tax Notes International*, 4 February 2008, 423; *in memoriam* Klaus Vogel.

[16] For critique, see Graetz, *op cit*.

[17] Desai and Hines (2003) 56 *National Tax Jo* 487.

[18] *Ibid*, 494.

[19] On definition of 'United Kingdom', see above at §2.1; for an example of this fundamental principle, see discussion of *Becker v Wright*, above at §31.4.2.3.

[20] *Whitney v IRC* [1926] AC 37, 54, (1926) 10 TC 88, 112, *per* Lord Wrenbury.

[21] *Untelrab v McGregor* [1996] STC (SCD) 1; see Oliver [1996] BTR 505.

[22] A company incorporated abroad is a subject of that country (*Janson v Driefontein Consolidated Mines* [1902] AC 484). See also Vaughan Williams and Crussach (1933) 49 *LQR* 334; and Farnsworth, *The Residence and Domicile of Corporations* (Butterworths, 1939) 302–09.

them. Citizenship does, however, have some tax consequences for the UK.[23] The United States uses citizenship as one of its bases of tax.[24] Every so often proposals are made to reform and tighten the UK rules on the taxation of residents with a foreign domicile; these usually fail for fear of upsetting the large expatriate community in London, especially the Greek shipping community, which might otherwise sail away from the UK.[25] In recent years, the preferred approach to 'non-doms' has been to avoid major reform and instead impose an annual charge on those wishing to take advantage of the special non-dom rules; however, more fundamental changes are currently under consultation and likely to be legislated in 2017.

69.3   UK Connecting Factors: Individual's Residence[26]

For an individual, from 6 April 2013 'residence' is defined by statute.[27] Previously, residence was determined under a combination of case law and Revenue guidance, formerly in leaflet IR 20 and, from 2009, in guide HMRC6.[28] The basis for the Revenue's position was uncertain since the cases on which it rested were, for the most part, illustrations of the principle that since residence is a question of fact, the courts cannot reverse a finding by the Tribunals (formerly Commissioners) simply because they would not reach the same conclusion. The Revenue practice also relied heavily on decisions in favour of the Revenue and conveniently ignored those in favour of the taxpayer.

Gaines-Cooper[29] was an important Supreme Court decision on the proper construction of the Revenue's guidance in IR 20. By the time the case reached the Supreme Court, the Revenue had accepted that their guidance was binding on them and could found a case based on legitimate expectation. The taxpayers in the joined cases argued that an alleged benevolent interpretation of the law on ceasing to be resident and ordinarily resident in IR 20 and/or benevolent HMRC practice gave rise to legitimate expectations of benevolent treatment. These arguments were rejected by the Supreme Court (4:1). Lord Wilson, giving the lead judgment for the majority, concluded that the evidence adduced was too thin to support the taxpayers' assertions (at 49). The *Gaines-Cooper* case provided further impetus for rethinking the approach to residence, leading ultimately to the introduction of the statutory residence test (SRT) in FA 2013, section 218 and Schedule 45 with effect from 6 April 2013. The rules are now more clear, detailed and mechanical, and extensive guidance on their application including examples is provided in HMRC guidance note RDR3. The

---

[23] Eg ITTOIA 2005, ss 831–839, ex TA 1988, s 65(4) remittance basis if not ordinarily resident; citizenship is also relevant to tax treaties.

[24] The effects of this base are often reduced by double tax treaties; see Gann (1982) 38 *Tax L Rev* 1, 58–69.

[25] On 1988 Inland Revenue Consultative Document, see Hauser [1989] BTR 29.

[26] See Sumption, *Taxation of Overseas Income* (Butterworths, 1977), ch 1; Farnsworth, *op cit*, ch 1; Olowofoyeku [2003] BTR 306.

[27] HM Treasury, *Budget 2012*, HC 1853 (21 March 2012), para 2.51. For the latest see http://www.hm-treasury.gov.uk/consult_statutory_residence_test.htm.

[28] Inland Revenue leaflet IR 20 was first published in 1973.

[29] *R (on the application of Davies and another) v Revenue and Customs Commissioners and R (on the application of Gaines-Cooper) v Revenue and Customs Commissioners* [2011] UKSC 47. See also case note by Welsh and Eden [2011] BTR 643.

discussion that follows focuses on just the key elements of the SRT. Readers interested in the pre-6 April 2013 situation are directed to earlier editions of this book.

It should be emphasised that residence is distinct from domicile in its legal nature and purpose. The tax system usually asks whether X is resident in the UK or not resident in the UK, and not whether X is resident in the UK or in another country; the conflict of laws asks where a person has his domicile. Hence, X may have two residences, but not two domiciles;[30] equally, X may have no residence—but must have a domicile.[31] In the rare contexts where it is important to determine whether a person is resident in a particular country, such as that of double tax treaties, special rules determine residence; these treaty rules have nothing to do with common law residence.[32]

69.3.1 Basic Test for Residence

Under the SRT, an individual 'P' (the reference used in the statute) will be resident in the UK for a tax year X for income tax and capital gains tax purposes,[33] and at all times in that tax year (subject to some relaxation for split-year treatment), if:

— P does not meet any of the automatic overseas tests and:
— P meets at least one of the automatic UK tests or the sufficient ties test.[34]

The Revenue guidance note RDR3 provide a helpful flowchart on the steps to be taken to ascertain an individual's residence status under the SRT:

— **Step 1**: Consider whether P spent 183 days in the UK in the tax year. If so, he or she will be resident in the UK. If not:
— **Step 2**: Consider the three automatic overseas tests. If P meets one of these he or she is not UK resident. If not:
— **Step 3**: Consider if P meets the second and third UK tests. If he or she meets one of these, he or she is UK resident. If not:
— **Step 4**: Consider the sufficient ties test. If P meets this he or she is UK resident. If not, he or she is not UK resident.

For SRT purposes, if P is present in the UK at the end of a day, that day usually counts as a day spent in the UK.[35]

69.3.2 Automatic Overseas Tests

If P meets one of these three automatic overseas tests then P is not UK resident. The first test is met if P was resident in the UK for one or more of the 3 tax years preceding year

[30] *A-G v Coote* (1817) 4 Price 183, (1817) 2 TC 385; *Lloyd v Sulley* (1885) 2 TC 37.
[31] *Bell v Kennedy* (1868) LR 1 Sc & Div 307, 320.
[32] On double tax treaties, see below at §76.6.1; see also CFC legislation, below ch 73.
[33] FA 2013, Sch 45, para 1(4). The SRT also applies, so far as the residence status of individuals is relevant to them, inheritance tax and corporation tax.
[34] FA 2013, Sch 45, paras 3–5.
[35] FA 2013, Sch 45, paras 22–24. This is subject to some exceptions eg for days in transit.

X and P spends less than 16 days in the UK in year X.[36] The second automatic overseas test is satisfied if P was resident in the UK for none of the 3 tax years preceding year X and P spends less than 46 days in the UK in year X.[37] The third automatic overseas test is met if:[38]

(1)   P works full time (ie on average 35 hours per week or more) overseas in year X,
(2)   There are no significant breaks[39] from overseas work during year X,
(3)   P works less than 31 days in the UK in year X in which he works more than 3 hours, and
(4)   P spends less than 91 days in the UK in year X.

P is considered to be working if P is doing something in the performance of P's duties of employment or in the course of a trade carried on by P.[40] A special fourth and fifth automatic test apply where P dies during year X.[41]

69.3.3 *Automatic UK Tests*

Under the first automatic UK test, P will be resident in the UK if he or she spends at least 183 days in the UK in the tax year.[42] Further, if P satisfies either the second or third automatic UK test, then P will be UK resident. According to the second test, P will be UK resident in year X if:[43]

(1)   P has a home in the UK during all or part of the year,
(2)   P is present in the UK home for a 'sufficient time', meaning on at least 30 days (can be non-consecutive), and
(3)   There is at least one period of 91 consecutive days while P has the UK home when P either (a) has no overseas home or (b) has one or more overseas homes but spends fewer than 30 days in total in them. In addition, of the 91 days at least 30 days must fall in year X.

An individual's 'home' is broadly defined to include a vessel, vehicle or structure of any kind which has a sufficient degree of permanence or stability for the individual whether or not the individual owns it or has any legal interest in it.[44]

Under the third automatic UK test, P will be UK resident in year X if:[45]

(1)   P works full-time in the UK over a period of at least 365 days,

---

[36]   FA 2013, Sch 45, para 12.
[37]   FA 2013, Sch 45, para 13.
[38]   FA 2013, Sch 45, para 14.
[39]   FA 2013, Sch 45, para 29. A significant break is a period of at 31 days without working more than 3 hours or being on sick leave or annual leave from such work days.
[40]   FA 2013, Sch 45, para 26.
[41]   FA 2013, Sch 45, paras 15–16.
[42]   FA 2013, Sch 45, para 7.
[43]   FA 2013, Sch 45, para 8.
[44]   FA 2013, Sch 45, para 25.
[45]   FA 2013, Sch 45, para 9.

(2) during that period there are no significant breaks from UK work,

(3) all or part of the period falls within year X,

(4) more than 75% of the total number of days in the period on which P works more than 3 hours are days on which P works for more than 3 hours in the UK, and

(5) at least one day which falls in both year X and that period is a day on which P works more than three hours in the UK.

A special fourth automatic test applies where P dies during year X.[46]

69.3.4 *Sufficient Ties Test*

If P meets none of the automatic UK or overseas tests, P will be UK resident if he or she satisfies the sufficient ties test in year X. This requires P to have 'sufficient UK ties' for that year. The 'sufficient UK ties' are defined in FA 2013, Schedule 45, Part 2, and comprise a family tie, an accommodation tie, a work tie, a 90-day tie and (if P is resident in the UK in the 3 tax years preceding year X) a country tie. The required number of sufficient ties to meet the test depends on whether P was resident in the UK in the 3 tax years preceding year X and also the number of days that P spends in the UK in year X.[47] For example, assuming P was resident in the UK in the 3 preceding tax years, then if P spends more than 120 days in the UK in year X only 1 sufficient tie is required to meet the test. If P spends more than 15 but not more than 45 days in the UK in year X, however, at least 4 sufficient ties are required.

Briefly, a family tie includes having a spouse/civil partner, unmarried partner or minor child who is resident in the UK.[48] P has an accommodation tie if P has a place to live in the UK available in year X for a continuous period of at least 91 days and P spends at least one night there in year X.[49] P has a work tie if P works more than 3 hours per day in the UK for at least 40 days in year X.[50] The 90-day tie is met where P has spent more than 90 days in the UK in the tax year preceding year X or the tax year preceding that year.[51] Finally, the country tie is satisfied for year X if P spends the greatest number of days at the end of the day in the UK relative to other countries.[52] There are further complications and exceptions to all these ties; readers interested in the finer details are directed to the legislation and RDR3.

69.3.5 *Split-Year Treatment*

Under the SRT, split-year treatment is available in limited 'cases' as set out in FA 2013, Schedule 45, Part 3. The consequences of a tax year being a split year is to relax the effect of Schedule 45, paragraph 2(3), which treats individuals who are UK resident 'for' a tax

---

[46] FA 2013, Sch 45, para 10.
[47] FA 2013, Sch 45, para 18.
[48] FA 2013, Sch 45, paras 32–33.
[49] FA 2013, Sch 45, para 34.
[50] FA 2013, Sch 45, paras 35–36.
[51] FA 2013, Sch 45, para 37.
[52] FA 2013, Sch 45, para 38.

year as being UK resident *at all times* in that year.[53] Thus, a tax year can be split between a resident and a non-resident period. Cases 1-3 involve actual or deemed departure from the UK in the year, and include situations where an individual starts full-time work overseas, accompanies a spouse leaving the UK or leaves the UK to live abroad.[54] Cases 4–8 cover actual or deemed arrivals in the UK, including where persons come to live or work full-time in the UK, cease to work full-time overseas, accompany a spouse arriving in the UK or start to have a home in the UK.[55]

69.3.6 Anti-Avoidance and Miscellaneous

FA 2013, Schedule 45, Part 4 provides the obligatory anti-avoidance provisions, focusing on periods of temporary non-residence. Essentially, where an individual having been UK resident in at least 4 out of the 7 years prior to departure is then non-resident for five years or less, these rules permit certain income arising during the period of non-residence to be taxed in the year of return. Part 5 provides miscellaneous details including interpretation.

69.4   Ordinary Residence

Previously, the Tax Acts also talked of 'ordinary residence'.[56] Following a period of consultation, however, the Government abolished ordinary residence for tax purposes from 6 April 2013 when the new statutory test for individual residence was introduced. Readers interested in the meaning of ordinary residence are directed to previous editions of this book.

69.5   Domicile[57]

Persons are domiciled[58] where they have or are deemed by law to have their permanent home. Everyone must have a domicile, but cannot have more than one domicile. Subject to two qualifications, the test of domicile is that developed by the general rules of the conflict of laws.

---

[53] FA 2013, Sch 45, para 40.
[54] FA 2013, Sch 45, paras 44–46.
[55] FA 2013, Sch 45, para 47–51.
[56] For example ITTOIA 2005, s 857 (4) and TA 1988, s 334. For reviews of case law, see Smart (1989) 38 *ICLQ* 1715; and Wosner [1983] BTR 347.
[57] For a discussion of possible reform and of some of the case law, see Fentiman, (1986) 6 *OJLS* 353 and [1999] *CLJ* 445; and, in a tax context, see Sheridan [1989] BTR 230; Green [1991] BTR 21; and Lyons [1993] BTR 42. See also Revenue guidance in HMRC6, ch 4.
[58] For an example, see *Anderson (Anderson's Executors) v IRC* [1998] STC (SCD) 43; see also *Re Clore (No 2), Official Solicitor v Clore* [1984] STC 609. On the importance of domicile in tax matters, see the Law Commission, Joint Report on Domicile, Cm 200 (1987), but note subsequent changes, especially in relation to ITEPA 2003.

The first qualification is that for tax purposes the question is whether or not a person is domiciled in the UK.[59] For general conflict of law purposes the question will be whether a person is domiciled in England and Wales, or Scotland or some other separate jurisdiction. Although, generally, a person domiciled in the UK will be domiciled in one of its constituent parts, this is not necessarily so, since a person with a domicile of origin in France who decides to live in the UK, but who is undecided as between Scotland and England, may have a UK domicile for UK tax purposes and a French domicile for conflict of laws purposes. However, it is understood that the Revenue do not take this point and would treat the person as still domiciled in France. The second qualification is that for tax purposes an individual's registration on the UK electoral roll as an overseas voter is disregarded in determining domicile.[60] This rule may be disregarded if the individual so wishes.

At the time of writing the UK government is planning major reform to the income, capital gains and inheritance tax treatment of non-UK domiciled individuals ('non-doms'). As noted in the policy paper accompanying the proposals, the UK currently provides tax advantages for non-doms that mean that foreign individuals can live and work in the UK without being subject to UK tax on income and gains earned outside the UK and not brought into the UK.[61] For many years this has led to concerns that the preferential non-dom tax rules can give rise to unfair outcomes. According to the policy paper, the government is still committed to special tax treatment for non-doms 'so that the UK can continue to benefit from the presence of talented foreigners', but in a way that also undresses unfair tax outcomes.[62] According to the most recent plans as outlined at Budget 2016, from April 2017 non-doms will be deemed UK domiciled for all tax purposes after they have been UK resident for 15 of the past 20 tax years. Further, individuals who were born in the UK and who have a UK domicile of origin (see §69.5.1) will revert to their UK domiciled status for tax purposes whilst resident in the UK. Detailed transitional rules will be required, eg it is expected that non-doms who become deemed-domiciled in April 2017 will be permitted to treat the cost base of their non-UK based assets as being the market value on 6 April 2017. The reforms are expected to be legislated in FA 2017.

69.5.1 *Meaning of Domicile*

People are domiciled where they have or are deemed by law to have their permanent home.[63] They must have a domicile, but may not have more than one. 'Domicile of origin' is the domicile which the law attributes to every individual at birth. If a child is legitimate, this is the domicile of the father at the date of the child's birth; if the child is illegitimate, this is the domicile of the mother.[64] 'Domicile of choice' is the domicile which people may acquire by leaving the country of their domicile of origin and taking up residence in another country with the intention of making their permanent home there. However, until there is both

---

[59] Eg ITEPA 2003, s 21, ITTOIA 2005, s 87 and ITA 2007, s 726 (ex TA 1988, s 739).
[60] FA 1996, s 200.
[61] See https://www.gov.uk/government/publications/domicile-income-tax-and-capital-gains-tax/domicile-income-tax-and-capital-gains-tax.
[62] *Ibid.*
[63] *Whisker v Hume* [1858] 7 HL Cas 124, 160, *per* Lord Cranworth.
[64] *Udny v Udny* [1869] LR 1 Sc & Div 441, 457.

the intention to change the domicile and also the establishment of residence in the new territory, the domicile of origin remains. Mere length of stay in a country is not sufficient to establish a domicile of choice in that country. A domicile of choice is acquired by the combination of residence and intention of permanent or indefinite residence.[65] Thus, civil servants, missionaries and other persons whose domicile of origin was in one of the constituent countries of the UK and who reside abroad for vocational or business reasons, even for the greater part of their lives, retain that domicile unless they have abandoned the intention of ultimately returning to live in the country of their domicile of origin and have formed the definite settled intention of taking up permanent residence in the particular country in which they reside. The illegality of that presence is normally irrelevant.[66]

69.5.2 Change of Domicile

The domicile of origin continues until a domicile of choice is acquired. On the other hand, a domicile of choice is lost by departure from the country of such domicile without the intention of returning there to live; in that event, the domicile of origin revives unless and until a new domicile of choice is acquired.[67] The onus of proof of abandonment of the domicile of origin is upon those who seek to establish the acquisition of a domicile of choice, and very strong evidence is required for this purpose.[68]

69.5.3 Married Women, Civil Partners and Domicile

The law relating to the domicile of married women is governed by the Domicile and Matrimonial Proceedings Act 1973, which came into force on 1 January 1974. The domicile of a married woman is no longer the same as her husband's by virtue only of marriage but is ascertained by reference to the same factors as in the case of any other individual capable of having an independent domicile. This is necessarily true for civil partners, whose status did not exist in 1974.

Where, immediately before 1 January 1974, a married woman had her husband's domicile by dependence, she is treated as retaining that domicile (as a domicile of choice if not also her domicile of origin) unless and until it is changed by acquisition or revival of another domicile either on or after the coming into force of the Act. Prior to 1 January 1974 a woman, of whatever age, acquired at marriage the domicile of her husband, and her domicile followed his throughout their married life notwithstanding separation (even judicial separation). On termination of the marriage, by death of the husband or divorce, the woman reacquired the capacity to have an independent domicile. She did not, however, then revert automatically to her domicile of origin. The domicile which a woman acquired on marriage (where it was not her domicile of origin) ranked as a domicile of choice and, like any other domicile of choice, could be lost only by permanent departure from the country of domicile.

---

[65] On nationality as a factor, see *Bheekhun v Williams* [1999] 2 FLR 229; noted by Stibbard (1999) *Private Client Business* 360.
[66] *Mark v Mark* [2005] UKHL 42 *per* Baroness Hale, paras 49–50 and *per* Lord Hope, para 13.
[67] See *Bell v Kennedy* [1868] LR 1 Sc & Div 307.
[68] Eg *F and F v IRC* [2000] STC (SCD) 1.

69.5.4 Domicile of Child

Normally, the domicile of a child changes automatically with that of the father, although the position may be different where the parents are deceased, separated or divorced. An individual is capable of having an independent domicile when he or she attains the age of 16, or marries under that age.

69.6 Residence of Corporations[69]

UK tax law imposes UK residence on (a) any company the central management and control (CMC) of which is located in the UK; and (b) a company incorporated in the UK or, being a *Societas Europaea* (SE), registered in the UK.[70] Test (a) is a common law test; (b) is a statutory test introduced in 1988. A company which is both incorporated and managed in the UK will be treated as resident in the UK. If a company is incorporated in the UK but managed abroad, it will be treated as resident in the UK under test (b).[71] Tests (a) and (b) are subject to a third test, (c), introduced in 1994, under which a company which is resident in the UK on one of these tests, but which is treated as resident in another country and not resident in the UK for treaty purposes, will not be treated as resident for general purposes either. Double tax treaties frequently specify another test—the place of effective management (POEM)—as a tie-breaker for resolving cases where a company is treated under domestic law as a resident of both contracting states. These tests are discussed next.

69.6.1 Rule (a): The Common Law Test of Central Management and Control (CMC)

69.6.1.1 The General Rule

Since income tax originally applied both to individuals and to companies, it was perhaps inevitable that residence would be taken as the basis of taxation of companies. The long-established case-law test of residence was laid down by Lord Loreburn (the other Lords concurring) in *De Beers Consolidated Mines Ltd v Howe*.[72] Lord Loreburn began with the proposition that '[i]n applying the conception of residence to a company, we ought, I think, to proceed as nearly as we can upon the analogy of an individual.'[73] Further, whilst clearly a company cannot 'eat or sleep', Lord Loreburn said that one should look to where the company 'keeps house and does business'.[74] This reasoning led to his famous and oft-cited

---

[69] See Farnsworth, *The Residence and Domicile of Corporations* (Butterworth & Co, 1939); Pyrez (1973) 21 *Can Tax Jo* 374; Owen [2005] BTR 186 and 390; Fraser [2006] BTR 692; Harris and Oliver, *op cit*, 59–68.

[70] CTA 2009, s 14, ex FA 1988, s 66A, added by F(No 2)A 2005, s 60.

[71] CTA 2009, s 14, ex FA 1988, s 66(1), and note minor transitional exceptions to statutory incorporation test in CTA 2009, Sch 2 para 13 et seq, ex FA 1988, Sch 7.

[72] [1906] AC 455. See also the excellent analysis and commentary by Loomer (2015) *Can Tax J* 91, 103 *et seq.*

[73] [1906] AC 455, 458.

[74] *Ibid.*

articulation of the CMC test: '...a company resides, for the purpose of income tax, where its real business is carried on ... and the real business is carried on where central management and control actually abides.'[75] As Lord Radcliffe has remarked, 'this judgment must be treated today as if the test which it laid down was as precise and unequivocal as a positive statutory injunction.[76] However, while the test is treated as if it were statute, the issue is one of fact; it follows that if the Commissioners or Tribunals have understood the law, there is very little hope of getting a decision reversed by the courts.[77] For problems in applying this test, see §69.6.4 below.

In the *De Beers* case, South Africa provided the place of registration, the mines where the diamonds were extracted and which were marketed by the company, its head office and its shareholders' meetings. The diamonds were sold through a London syndicate. Directors' meetings were held both in South Africa and London, but it was in London that the majority of the directors resided. The Commissioners held that London was the place from which the directors controlled and managed the chief operations of the company. In challenging this conclusion, the company took as a point of law the proposition that, being incorporated and registered in South Africa, it must be resident in South Africa. That proposition was rejected by the House of Lords.

It did not automatically follow that, in the converse case, a company incorporated in the UK but managed and controlled from abroad was resident abroad. There was authority before *De Beers* for this view, but these cases were overruled in *Todd v Egyptian Delta Land and Investments Company Ltd* in 1929.[78]

69.6.1.2 Rule (c) Modifying Rule (a): Double Tax Treaty

Where a company would be treated as resident in the UK under rule (a), but as non-resident under the terms of an applicable double taxation agreement, it is to be treated as non-resident for all UK tax purposes.[79] Clearly, this rule has no effect if the company would be treated as resident in the UK for treaty purposes. Less obviously, the rule has no effect if the treaty, because it has no tie-breaker clause, concludes that the company is resident in both countries for treaty purposes; treaties without a tie-breaker clause include those with Greece, the Isle of Man and the Channel Islands. The 2001 UK–US Treaty has a half-hearted tie-breaker clause under which the tie may be broken, but only by mutual agreement procedure; if they do not reach agreement only very limited benefits may be taken from the treaty, and so presumably the tie is not broken.[80]

Normally, the change of residence occurs as soon as the facts are satisfied; however, if the treaty applies the tie-breaker clause only when the two taxing authorities have reached agreement on the point, the change of residence is deferred until that agreement is reached.[81] Where rule (c) applies, the treaty provision prevents dual residence. The reason

---

[75] *Ibid.*
[76] In *Unit Construction Co Ltd v Bullock* [1960] AC 351, 366; (1960) 38 TC 712, 738. The test was present, in the 1975 UK–US Double Tax Treaty, Art 4(1)(a)(ii), but is not part of the 2001 treaty.
[77] Inland Revenue, *International Tax Handbook*, para 315.
[78] [1929] AC 1, (1929) 14 TC 119.
[79] CTA 2009, s 18, ex FA 1994, s 249; on the SE, see also CTA 2009, s 16.
[80] Art 4(5). The previous (1975) treaty had no such clause.
[81] Eg, UK–Canada Treaty, Art 4(3).

for this change was partly to relieve companies of unwanted burdens and partly to protect the exchequer. The principal burden of which companies were relieved was the liability to ACT when making a qualifying distribution. The protection of the exchequer arises mostly in connection with a company which is a member of a group. Such a company may be exempt from UK tax on its profits but, as a UK-resident company, may pass any loss to other UK-resident group companies; rule (c) prevents group relief from arising (subject to EU law considerations).[82] The Revenue have announced that they do not intend to invoke rule (c) in marginal cases where there is no mischief—unless the company invokes the treaty.[83]

The effect of the rule was to cause the company to cease to be resident as from 30 November 1993. Certain specific consequences of this change were addressed in FA 2004, section 250; these rules were repealed in 2010.

69.6.2 Rule (b): The Statutory Test of Incorporation in the UK

69.6.2.1 The General Rule

FA 1988, section 66 introduced the second test, now in CTA 2009, section 14, that a company which is incorporated in the UK is resident here for tax purposes. If such a company has its central management and control elsewhere, it is still treated for domestic law purposes as resident in the UK only.[84] This major change brings the UK tax system into line with many others. It applies as from 1988, generally regardless of when the company had been incorporated. As from 1 April 2005 a similar rule applies to an SE.[85] A subsequent transfer of the SE's registered office out of the UK does not of itself end the UK residence.[86] A company which ceases to carry on any business, or which is being wound up, is treated as retaining its prior residence.[87]

69.6.2.2 Rule (c) Modifying Rule (b)

Like the common law rule of residence, rule (b) is modified from 30 November 1993. Where a company would be treated as resident in the UK under this rule, but as non-resident under the terms of an applicable double taxation agreement, it is now to be treated as non-resident for all UK tax purposes.[88]

---

[82] See CTA 2010, ss 130–134, which allow the non-resident company to use group relief if it is within the charge to UK tax; above §7.1.1.

[83] Thus, Inland Revenue, *International Tax Handbook*, para 453: 'For instance, the location of effective management of the holding company for the UK subgroup of an overseas group may be unclear in a case where a company is mainly managed here but some management decisions are taken abroad. We would not regard as objectionable the fact that the company exists to allow losses to flow as group relief between members of the UK subgroup and the benefit of any doubt on the location of effective management may be given to the company.'

[84] CTA 2009, s 14(2), ex FA 1988, s 66(1).

[85] CTA 2009, s 16(2), ex FA 1988, s 66A, added by F(No 2)A 2005, s 60.

[86] CTA 2009, s 16(4), ex FA 1988, s 66A, added by F(No 2)A 2005, s 60.

[87] CTA 2009, s 15, ex FA 1988, s 66(2).

[88] CTA 2009, s 18, ex FA 1994, s 249.

In looking at rule (b) it must be remembered that a company which is incorporated in the UK cannot change either its place of incorporation or its registered office; this is because it is domiciled in the UK. It may, of course, be struck off the Register of Companies and begin a new life as a new company in a new country, but under UK company law that is exactly what has happened—the UK company has not changed its residence; it has ceased to exist.

69.6.2.3 Reasons for Introducing Rule (b)

There were broadly three reasons for the introduction of the incorporation test.[89] The first was the possible threat posed by EC law to the provision in what became TA 1988, section 765 that UK resident companies could not lawfully cease to be resident without Treasury consent. This provision was repealed when the incorporation rule became law. The second was the realisation that the UK rules were out of line with those of other countries. The third reason is the most interesting and shows the world in which the Revenue have to work; this third was the growing use of what the Revenue called 'nowhere companies'. As the Revenue Handbook sadly puts it (at para 445), these were

> [c]ompanies incorporated in the UK by non-residents but non-resident under UK tax rules. Such a company was not subject to tax on worldwide income anywhere and was unlikely to suffer tax at all. In the 1970s, foreign operators began to realise that the UK provided an ideal opportunity for such companies. Traditional tax-haven countries such as the Channel Islands and Isle of Man have provided tax shelters for companies incorporated but not having real activity there on payment of a fee. In the UK there was no fee—only the cost of setting up and keeping the company on the register. All the operators had to do was to make sure that there was nothing like management and control or trading activity or income here. There was the added advantage of the respectability of UK incorporation. Before other countries got wise to the ploy they might even have assumed the company to be taxable here. Until 1979, exchange control was something of a hindrance because these companies had to get Bank of England permission to be treated as non-resident for exchange control—they obviously did not want their money in blocked sterling. The Bank of England would have given permission but might have asked awkward questions about the background which the operators would have been reluctant to disclose, even though bank officials would not have divulged anything to the Revenue or to anybody else.

> Our own attempts at getting information met with little success. Not only would this information identify the exceptional case of UK resident ownership, it could be passed on to the countries of the beneficial owners where this exchange of information is authorised by a Double Taxation Agreement. But some companies operating in low tax areas such as the Middle East used the UK for the benefit of recourse to its law and had no reason to hide anything. Representations on behalf of these companies were partly responsible for stifling the proposal for an incorporation rule in 1981. By 1988 the number of dubious companies had increased enormously, the Revenue authorities of some countries were complaining at our acquiescence and it was suspected that a number of companies were being used for criminal activities.

---

[89] See Inland Revenue, *International Tax Handbook*, paras 357, 445; see also Edwardes Ker, *International Tax Strategy* (In-depth Publishing, 1974) 2, describing a UK incorporated but non-resident company as one of the best 'no-tax companies'.

69.6.3 Place of Effective Management (POEM)

Tax treaties will often refer to a company's 'place of effective management' (POEM) as a tie-breaker where a company is considered to be a resident of both contracting states under their domestic laws. This can happen, for example, if one state applies a place of incorporation test for company residence whilst the other state applies the central management and control test. 'Effective management' is usually found where the managers of the actual business are, as opposed to the central management and control exercised by directors.[90] According to the OECD Commentary to Article 4(3) of the Model Treaty, the place of effective management is the place 'where key management and commercial decisions that are necessary for the conduct of the entity's business as a whole are in substance made. All relevant facts and circumstances must be examined to determine the place of effective management.' The Commentary also makes the important point that a company can only have one place of effective management at one time.

Notwithstanding the traditional distinction, others have argued that there is no practical difference between CMC and POEM.[91] In *Wood v Holden*, Park J analysed CMC and POEM as separate tests, but came up with the same result under both.[92] The Court of Appeal did not decide the question but Chadwick LJ suggested, *in obiter*, that the two tests were equivalent: 'It is not clear at least, not clear to me whether the article 4(3) test differs in substance from the *De Beers* test ...'[93]

Finally, it should be noted that in Action 6 of the G20/OECD Base Erosion and Profit Shifting (BEPS) Project (see §69.11), the OECD highlights BEPS concerns related to the use of dual-resident entities and recommends addressing them in part by changing the OECD Model Treaty to provide that cases of dual residence under a treaty be resolved on 'a case-by-case basis' rather than on the basis of the POEM tie-breaker rule.[94]

69.6.4 Issues in Determining CMC and POEM

Two issues in determining CMC and POEM have been addressed by the courts:

(1) What sort of control/level of management is needed?
(2) Can control be split so that there is dual residence?

69.6.4.1 What Sort of Control/Level of Management is Needed?

Relevant control. The control which is important, at least for a company under an English type of company law, is that of the directors rather than the shareholders.[95] The shareholders

---

[90] See Statement of Practice SP 1/90; and Inland Revenue, *International Tax Handbook*, paras 347 *et seq.*

[91] Owen, 'Can Effective Management be Distinguished from Central Management and Control?' [2003] BTR 296.

[92] *Wood v Holden* [2005] EWHC 547 (Ch), at paras 64–81.

[93] *Wood v Holden* [2006] EWCA Civ 26, at para 6.

[94] OECD, *BEPS Action 6, 'Preventing the Granting of Treaty Benefits in Inappropriate Circumstances', Final Report,* (Oct 2015), 72. For more see below §76.6.1.

[95] *American Thread Co v Joyce* (1911) 6 TC 1, 32–33; cf *John Hood & Co Ltd v Magee* (1918) 7 TC 327, 351, 353, 358.

may, by virtue of their votes, control the corporation; they may compel the directors to do their will, but it does not follow that the shareholders are managing the corporation.[96] The control which the test requires is often equated with the place where the directors meet; however, this is subject to a test of genuineness. The Revenue adopt the following approach:[97] (i) they first try to ascertain whether the directors of the company in fact exercise central management and control; (ii) if so, they seek to determine where the directors exercise this central management and control (which is not necessarily where they meet);[98] (iii) in cases where the directors apparently do not exercise central management and control of the company, the Revenue then look to establish where and by whom it is exercised.

However, the mere fact that English company law takes this view is not conclusive. The question is one of the control of the business and, under a foreign system of company law, a different conclusion might be justified.

In such circumstances, the Revenue divide management up into (i) the pinnacle, (ii) the head office where the executives who make the company tick work and (iii) the shop floor itself. The CMC test looks for level (i)—central management and control refers to the axis or pinnacle of a corporation's activities.[99] The Revenue add that the distinction between (i) and (ii) may sometimes be hard to draw. They note that it is much easier for (i) to move than (ii). It is clear from the Revenue *Handbook* that the Revenue would really like to move the CMC test from level (i) to (ii),[100] and that their failure to achieve this has probably been one of the reasons for the introduction of the incorporation test.

Where the power to control is exercised—or ought to be exercised? The place of control and management means that of actual control and not merely the place where control should properly be exercised. In the rather extraordinary case of *Unit Construction Co Ltd v Bullock*,[101] three subsidiary companies had been incorporated and registered in Kenya. Their articles of association placed the management and control of the business in the hands of directors and provided that meetings might be held anywhere outside the UK. The purpose of this scheme was to use the profits for development in Africa without becoming liable to UK taxation, and to forestall possible difficulties in the event of African nationalisation. Two years later the Kenya companies had incurred substantial losses, and the parent

---

[96] *Automatic Self Cleansing Filter Syndicate Co Ltd v Cunninghame* [1906] 2 Ch 34, confirming that directors' mandate was the mandate of the whole body of shareholders, not of the majority only.

[97] Statement of Practice SP 1/90, para 15, but note para 18 on need for genuine commercial reasons.

[98] On this point see the Revenue win in *Laerstate BV v HMRC* [2009] UKFTT 209, when control was held to have been exercised in the UK by a sole Dutch director making decisions in the UK, despite board meetings taking place elsewhere. For commentary, see Loomer [2009] BTR 378.

[99] For a recent and detailed examination of CMC and corporate residence generally, and the implications for the taxation of companies under the international tax regime, readers are directed to Loomer (2015) *Can Tax J* 91, and especially 111 on the 'pinnacle' point.

[100] Eg the 1981 proposals for redefining residence, on which they say, at para 348 of the *Handbook*: 'At one time the view of the UK was that our domestic concept of central management and control meant the same thing as place of effective management and there was a note to this effect in the Commentary on the 1977 OECD Model Double Taxation Convention. We no longer believe that necessarily to be so and the note does not appear in the 1992 edition of the OECD Model. The place of effective management is generally understood to be the place where the Head Office is: the Head Office in the sense of—not the registered office—but the central directing source.'

[101] [1960] AC 351, (1960) 38 TC 712.

company took over the management and control of the subsidiaries in an attempt to save its investment. All decisions of major importance and many of minor importance were thereafter taken by the parent company; the Kenyan directors had stood aside. The House of Lords held that despite the admission by the Kenya companies that they were resident in Kenya, they were in fact resident in the UK. As Viscount Simonds put it: 'The business is not the less managed in London because it ought to be managed in Kenya.'[102]

A vigorous use of *Unit Construction* might[103] have enabled the Revenue to achieve their wish to move from the pinnacle level of control to that of effective management, but this did not happen and eventually was answered, in the negative, by the Court of Appeal in *Wood v Holden*.[104] In this important case the Court of Appeal treated *Unit Construction* as a rare case in which the parent had *usurped* the powers of the subsidiary company.[105] The difficult practical question was just when the subsidiary company, by following a parent's advice, had surrendered control to that parent. In *Unit Construction*, Lord Cohen suggested that the facts were most unusual;[106] parent companies do not usually usurp control but operate through the boards of the subsidiary companies.

In *Wood v Holden*, an elaborately choreographed series of transactions was given the effect wished for by its designers, but that was because each participant was a free agent simply doing what they had all agreed to do. The Revenue practice[107] is to invoke the *Unit Construction* case where the parent usurps the functions of the board of the subsidiary, or where that board merely rubber-stamps the parent company's decisions without giving it any independent consideration of its own; the Revenue treat the subsidiary as having the same residence as its parent. In applying the test to an international group, they place emphasis on the degree of autonomy which those directors have in conducting the company's business and ask about the extent to which the directors of the subsidiary take decisions on their own authority as to investment, production, marketing and procurement, without reference to the parent. So in *Wood v Holden* the Revenue did not believe the steps were independent, but, it must be emphasised Park J and the judges of the Court of Appeal disagreed. As Chadwick LJ put it in *Wood v Holden*:[108]

'...a management decision does not cease to be a management decision because it might have been taken on fuller information; or even, as it seems to me, because it was taken in circumstances which might put the director at risk of an allegation of breach of duty. Ill-informed or ill-advised decisions taken in the management of a company remain management decisions'.

Thus, there remains an important difference between actually exercising management and control and being able to 'influence' those who exercise management and control—the first is CMC and the second is not.[109]

---

[102] [1960] AC 351, 363; (1960) 38 TC 712, 736.
[103] But might not: see *Untelrab v McGregor* [1996] STC (SCD) 1; for discussion of the case, see Oliver [1996] BTR 505.
[104] [2006] EWCA Civ 26, [2006] STC 443; for comment see Fraser [2006] BTR 692, note also comment on Chancery Division in Owen [2005] BTR 390.
[105] Eg para 27, Chadwick LJ agreeing with Park J at first instance.
[106] [1960] AC 351, 374, (1960) 38 TC 712, 744.
[107] Statement of Practice SP 1/90, paras 16, 17; but note para 18 on the need for genuine commercial reasons.
[108] *Wood v Holden, op cit*, para 43.
[109] See also Loomer (2015) *Can Tax J* 91,115–121.

Finally, the constitution of the company remains an important factor in determining where control is exercised, and the courts have not had any opportunity to show us how far they might delve back in the decision-making process. If major decisions are taken by a company only after consultations with a principal shareholder who lives in another jurisdiction, it may be that the company is resident where the shareholder is resident.

69.6.4.2 Can Control be Split so that there is Dual Residence?

As already noted, a company can only have one POEM at one time. It was not clear, however, whether Lord Loreburn's CMC test meant that a company could have only one residence.[110] The matter came up in the difficult and unfortunate decision of *Swedish Central Rly Co Ltd v Thompson*.[111] The decision of the House of Lords four years later in *Todd v Egyptian Delta Land and Investment Co Ltd*[112] is not easy to reconcile with *Swedish Central*.[113] However the cases are reconciled,[114] they may be taken as authority for three propositions:

(1)   that the test of residence laid down in the *De Beers* case applies to all corporations regardless of the place of registration or incorporation;
(2)   that a company may be resident in two places; and
(3)   that a finding of dual residence is not to be made unless the control of the general affairs of the company is not centrally placed in one country but is divided among two or more.[115]

It is also clear that residence may be in one country and the company's sole trade carried on in another,[116] and, conversely, that the mere carrying on of trade in the UK is not sufficient to establish residence here.[117]

Where rule (b) applies and a company is resident in the UK through incorporation, a dual residence problem cannot arise since incorporation is the only test.[118] The same is true where rule (c) applies. The scope for dual residence problems has therefore been reduced.

69.6.5 Double or Dual Resident Investing Companies

Certain reliefs are restricted where a company is resident in two countries under the domestic tax systems of each—ie the UK and the other country.[119] The problem may be illustrated

---

[110] It is now clear that the test is the same for all companies; see below. However, in practice the Revenue tend to rely on ITA 2007, s 720, ex TA 1988, s 739 to tax individuals who clearly are resident, rather than make direct assessments on companies incorporated abroad.

[111] [1925] AC 495, (1925) 9 TC 342.

[112] [1929] AC 1, (1929) 14 TC 119.

[113] See, among others, Farnsworth, *op cit*, 107–20; and Dixon J in *Koitaki Para Rubber Estates Ltd v Federal Commr of Taxation* (1940) 64 CLR 15.

[114] See *Revenue Law*, 1st edn (Butterworths, 1976), 779–81.

[115] See Farnsworth, *op cit*, 311.

[116] Eg *Saõ Paulo (Brazilian) Rly Co v Carter* [1896] AC 31, (1896) 3 TC 407; *New Zealand Shipping Co Ltd v Thew* (1922) 8 TC 208, HL.

[117] *A-G v Alexander* (1874) LR 10 Exch 20.

[118] CTA 2009, s 14(2), ex FA 1988, s 66(1).

[119] The proposal to restrict these reliefs goes back to a consultative document issued by the Revenue in November 1984.

simply. When a company is incorporated in the US but has its central management and control in the UK, it will be treated as resident in the US under US rules and in the UK under UK rules. Before 2002, the company was not treated as not resident in the UK despite rule (c) above, since the UK–US treaty did not then contain a 'tie-breaker' clause.[120] The company is able to use many UK reliefs, such as loss relief and capital allowances, on the basis that it is a UK-resident company and will be able to pass the benefit of those reliefs to other companies within its group, notwithstanding that it is also resident in the US and so able to claim reliefs under that tax system as well. Particular problems arise from the payment of interest. The dual resident company may pass the benefit of such a payment to other companies in the US and UK groups, and so get relief twice. Where the borrowing is from another company within the multinational's structure, the recipient of the interest will perhaps pay tax once, but this will be more than offset by the double relief. The 2005 rules on tax arbitrage (above §62.7) address similar issues but are not confined to dual resident companies.

Restrictions now apply where the company is a 'dual resident investing company'.[121] The process of defining an investing company begins by saying that an investing company is one which is not a trading company; however, the term 'trading company' is itself defined so as to exclude a company the main function of which is to carry on all or any of various activities, such as acquiring and holding shares in dual resident companies or raising finance. This is backed up by the exclusion of other companies carrying on such activities to an extent which does not appear to be justified by any trade it does carry on, or for a purpose which does not appear to be appropriate to any such trade.[122] There is also a special definition of 'residence' in the other territory, so as to cover being subject to charge to tax in the other county by reason of almost anything other than source.[123]

The reliefs restricted are those relevant to group relief, ie losses, excess capital allowances, expenses of management and charges on income.[124] These rules should be seen as complementary to US rules.[125] The effect is to ban relief under the rules of both systems where a dual resident company makes the payment, and so to encourage the group to ensure that deductible payments are in future made only by companies which are resident in only one jurisdiction.

69.6.6 Ordinary Residence

No point seems to turn on the distinction between residence and ordinary residence of corporations, and ordinary residence was abolished for Taxes Act purposes from 6 April 2013. It was apparently admitted in *Union Corpn v IRC*[126] that residence and ordinary

---

[120] On rule (c), see above at §69.6.1.
[121] CTA 2010, s 109, ex TA 1988, s 404(1), adapted for the 1996 loan relationship rules by FA 1996, Sch 14, para 21.
[122] CTA 2010, s 109(4), (5), ex TA 1988, s 404(6).
[123] CTA 2010, s 109(1), ex TA 1988, s 404(4); the wording is, however, different from that in s 749(1) (CFC legislation).
[124] CTA 2010, s 109(1), (2), ex TA 1988, s 404(2).
[125] IRC §1503(d), introduced by Tax Reform Act 1986, s 1249; for a comparison of the two sets of rules, see *Law Society's Gazette*, 11 March 1987, 713, 714.
[126] [1952] 1 All ER 646.

residence of companies were co-extensive, but it has been suggested that in cases of dual residence, ordinary residence is linked with the registered office.[127]

69.6.7 Domicile

The law of domicile can be applied to corporations only 'with a certain sense of strain'.[128] This connecting factor is used only occasionally.[129] A corporation is domiciled in its place of incorporation.[130] It would appear to follow that its domicile cannot change,[131] save for some exceptional circumstance such as a private Act of Parliament.

69.6.8 Tax Presence

In *Clark v Oceanic Contractors Inc*[132] the House of Lords invented a new connecting factor—tax presence. This is a presence sufficient to make the PAYE system applicable (see above at §69.4).

69.6.9 Seat

In certain European countries the legislation refers to the legal 'seat' of the company, and so this concept is also found in various EU legislative acts.[133] Under German law a dual resident company was a conceptual impossibility, but the ECJ has compelled the German tax system to accept the legal personality of a foreign company that transferred its place of management, and so its residence, to Germany.[134]

The following extract comes from a Consultation Paper by the 'High Level Group of Company Law Experts' which was commissioned by the European Commission to develop ideas for EU-wide company law.[135] The experts acknowledged the difficulty of defining the 'real seat doctrine':

> 5. Other Member States adopt the real seat doctrine—the validity of incorporation and legal status of a company are recognised by reference to the law of claimed formation only if it maintains its 'real seat' or siege réel, siege effectif, etc within that jurisdiction. The meaning of 'real seat' varies; generally, if there is no substantial connection between the 'central', or 'controlling' operations (particularly the place where the governing organs meet) and the jurisdiction of formation, then recognition by reference to that law is denied. Thus if a company is formed under the law of one Member State and moves its undertaking or central functions to another, which applies the real seat doctrine, without re-incorporation within that other, its legal security will be undermined.

---

[127] Hannan and Farnsworth, *The Principles of Income Taxation* (Sweet & Maxwell, 1952), 306.
[128] Morris, *Conflict of Laws*, 5th edn (Sweet & Maxwell, 2000) 29.
[129] See, eg F(No 2)A 1931, s 22(1)(b); and TA 1988, ss 739, 740, 761, 762.
[130] *Gasque v IRC* [1940] 2 KB 80, (1940) 23 TC 210.
[131] Farnsworth, *The Principles of Income Taxation*, 4th edn (Sweet & Maxwell, 1964) 273–74.
[132] [1983] STC 35; see Norfolk [1983] BTR 172.
[133] Ault *et al*, *Comparative Income Taxation*, 2nd edn (Kluwer, 2004), 349–56, ie Pt 4 A Residence Taxation, esp §§1.2, 2.2 and 2.3.
[134] *Ibid*, 356.
[135] Available at http://europa.eu.int/comm/internal_market/en/company/company/modern/consult/.

Similarly, if a company, which has been formed in a real seat doctrine state, makes a similar move to a second state but needs to maintain legal relations in the state of formation, then even if the new host state would apply the incorporation doctrine, its position will still be unsatisfactory, since its status in the formation state will be impugned. This will apparently be so even if the new host state would recognise the company's status and validity subject to the law of its original state of origin, thus applying the policy of the latter state (which is presumably what the real seat doctrine is designed to protect). Finally, even if both a state of origin and a host state apply the incorporation doctrine, the corporation's status may be nullified in a third state, if that third state applies the real seat doctrine.

69.7 Movement of Corporate Capital: Reporting and Penalties

Until 1988 it was a criminal offence for a company to change its residence without Treasury consent.[136] The same applied if a trade or business was transferred to a non-resident company by setting up a non-resident subsidiary company to run the trade in a foreign country.[137] These offences were part of an era which believed in exchange control and restriction on the free movement of capital. Exchange control was abolished in the UK in 1979; freedom of movement of capital within the European Community (now the EU) was established in 1992. The validity of these pre-1988 provisions as a restriction on freedom of establishment and freedom to provide services was challenged in *R v HM Treasury, ex parte Daily Mail Trust*,[138] and while the ECJ found in favour of the Crown, this was largely because of the undeveloped state of (then) EC company law.

The 1988 introduction of the incorporation rule of residence meant that it was no longer possible for a company incorporated in the UK to change its residence simply by changing the place of its central management and control. A company incorporated here but resident abroad under previous rules ceased to be so resident on 15 March 1993. Two of four criminal offences could be—and were—repealed. However, special rules were still needed to prevent companies moving too much out of the reach of the tax authorities. The Revenue's view of former TA 1988, section 765 is salutary:[139]

These provisions go very deep and they really mean that a United Kingdom company must seek consent for almost any change in the structure of the overseas interests which it controls. One can only surmise the reason for this very sweeping approach. It is likely that our predecessors either realised or suspected that tax planning arrangements had been made or conceived which might have been very costly to the Revenue. The most effective course seen was a very fine net that would

---

[136] TA 1988, s 765(1)(a). A prosecution could be brought only with the consent of the Attorney-General; apparently no prosecution was ever brought. On history of s 765, see Dewhurst [1984] BTR 282; the subsection was repealed by FA 1988, s 105.

[137] TA 1988, s 765(1)(b); subsection repealed by FA 1988, s 105.

[138] [1988] STC 787—the freedom of establishment in Art 52 EEC Treaty (now Art 49 TFEU) was not breached. For more on EU law and exit taxes, see chapter seventy-seven below.

[139] Inland Revenue, *International Tax Handbook* (2003), para 1303, text superseded by new corporation tax and income tax manuals but still very relevant.

allow the Treasury, with Revenue advice, to inspect everything that was proposed and to have the opportunity of stopping transactions which it saw as objectionable before they were carried out.

Prior to 2009, if a body corporate which was resident in the UK wished to cause or permit its non-resident subsidiary to create or issue any shares or debentures, it was required to obtain the consent of the UK Treasury.[140] If this matter related to movements of capital within the European Community, there was simply a duty to report.[141] The Revenue views on the boundary between the duty to report and the need to obtain consent were explained in a Revenue document.[142] A similar consent or duty to report was needed if the resident body corporate wished to transfer shares or debentures of its non-resident subsidiary; this consent was needed only if the resident body owned or had an interest in the shares or debentures, and was not needed if the transfer was for the purpose of enabling a person to be qualified to act as a director.[143] On deemed disposals for capital gains, see below at §74.4. In addition, there was an obligation on a company to settle its tax matters before ceasing to be resident. A failure to do so gave rise to penalties.[144]

As part of the reform of the UK tax system to help international businesses, TA 1988, sections 765–767 and associated provisions were repealed altogether in 2009.[145] In their place, FA 2009, Schedule 17 imposes a duty to notify HMRC of reportable events or transactions of a value exceeding £100 million.[146]

69.8 Partnerships and European Economic Interest Groupings

69.8.1 *Partnerships*

Trading partnerships are resident where the control and management of the trade is situate, regardless of the residence of the partners.[147] Non-trading partnerships are presumably not treated as entities separate from their partners, and so each partner is liable according to his own residence or non-residence. There is no reported case on other unincorporated bodies.

69.8.2 *European Economic Interest Groupings*

A European Economic Interest Grouping (EEIG) is a form of business entity set up by enterprises of two or more Member States.[148] It is intended to be an attractive vehicle for

---

[140] TA 1988, s 765(1)(c). On history, see Inland Revenue, *International Tax Handbook*, ch 13.
[141] TA 1988, s 765A, added by FA 1990, s 68(2), (4). See also the Movements of Capital (Required Information) Regulations 1990 (SI 1990/1671).
[142] Statement of Practice SP 2/92; note the Revenue view that the investment must be made 'with a view to establishing or maintaining economic links'.
[143] TA 1988, s 765(1)(d).
[144] FA 1988, ss 130–131; other companies may be liable for unpaid tax, s 132.
[145] FA 2009, Sch 17, paras 1–3.
[146] FA 2009, Sch 17, paras 4–8. The list of events is in para 8(2) and the exclusions are in para 9. A group with more than one UK corporate parent must nominate a single reporting body (para 6).
[147] Inference from ITTOIA 2005, ss 6, 856(2) and 878(3). Much clearer in the superseded TA 1988, s 112; *Padmore v IRC* [1989] STC 493, (1989) 62 TC 352, CA.
[148] ITA 2007, s 842 and CTA 2010, s 990, ex TA 1988, s 510A, introduced by FA 1990, s 69, Sch 11, para 1; see Council Regulation (EEC) No 2137/85 of 25 July 1985; for information-gathering powers, see TMA 1970, s 12A.

international co-operation within the European Union among enterprises, which may include companies and other bodies subject to corporation tax, or partnerships or sole traders subject to income tax. The purposes for which an EEIG may be formed include such activities as packaging, processing, marketing or research which are ancillary to the business of and which are for the common benefit of members of the EEIG. An EEIG may not be formed in order to make profits for itself.[149] The scope for using EEIGs is therefore very limited.

The principle to be applied in charging an EEIG to tax is fiscal transparency; the grouping is simply an agent for its members.[150] Profits of the EEIG are taxed in the hands of the members only and not at the level of the EEIG. Where it carries on a trade or profession, an EEIG is treated as a partnership.[151] Subject to any contractual arrangements, shares are governed by the share of profits to which the members are entitled under the contract.[152] Where, however, no trade or profession is carried on, a member joining a EEIG is treated as acquiring a proportionate share in the assets of the EEIG; similarly, on disposal there is a disposal of a share in the assets then held. A disposal of the assets by the EEIG is treated as a disposal by the members of their shares in the assets.[153] Contributions towards running expenses and capital allowances for contributions towards capital expenditure are determined according to the normal rules.[154] However, this principle of fiscal transparency does not apply to machinery provisions. Thus, where the EEIG is a UK-registered company, it may have to deduct tax at source of making a payment of interest or other charge on income.[155] This simple outline of the legislation masks many conceptual and practical problems.[156] These entities are the subject of their own Revenue manual.

69.9   Trustees and Personal Representatives

The position with regard to trustees is now governed in part by legislation. By TCGA 1992, section 69, as amended as part of the trusts modernisation package in 2006, trustees are treated as a single body of persons. They are treated as resident in the UK if:

(1)   all of them are so resident; or
(2)   if at least one is resident and one is not resident, so long as the settlor fulfils the necessary condition. That condition is that the settlor (S) was resident or domiciled in the

---

[149] Inland Revenue Press Release, 19 April 1990, [1990] *Simon's Tax Intelligence* 382, citing Art 3.1 of the Council Regulation 2137/85.

[150] ITA 2007, s 842(1), r 1 and CTA 2010, s 990(1), r 1, ex TA 1988, s 510A(2).

[151] ITA 2007, s 842(1), r 4 and CTA 2010, s 990(1), r 4, ex TA 1988, s 510A(6).

[152] ITA 2007, s 842(2) and CTA 2010, s 990(2), ex TA 1988, s 510A(4), (5).

[153] ITA 2007, s 842(1), r 3 and (4), and CTA 2010, s 990(1), r 3 and (4), ex TA 1988, s 510A(3)(b).

[154] Inland Revenue Press Release, 19 April 1990, [1990] *Simon's Tax Intelligence* 382, para 2.

[155] Under ITA 2007, ss 874–964, ex TA 1988, s 349 or 350; Inland Revenue Press Release, 19 April 1990, [1990] *Simon's Tax Intelligence* 382, paras 3–5.

[156] See Dixon and Morgan, *Tolley's International Tax Planning*, 4th edn (Tolley, 1999), ch 11; Anderson, *European Economic Interest Groupings* (Butterworths, 1990), chs 4 and 8; and Wales [1990] BTR 335.

UK; this is answered at the time the trust is made or, if made on death, immediately before S's death.

In applying these rules, a trustee who would otherwise be treated as non-resident will be treated as resident in the UK if he acts as a trustee in the course of a business carried on in the UK through a branch, agency or PE.[157] In addition, an individual trustee resident in the UK is treated as non-resident if he or she becomes or ceases to be a trustee of the settlement during the tax year, it is a split year for the individual, and in that year the only period when the individual is a trustee of the settlement is during the overseas part of the year.[158] Section 62(3) of TCGA 1992 directs that PRs should take the residence and domicile of the deceased.

The income tax rules are the same. However, they have been rewritten as ITA 2007, sections 474–476, which means they say the same but in more words. Provocatively, these provisions are also to apply for corporation tax while still not applying for CGT.

The effect of these rules is that a settlement with a UK settlor will be taxed on its foreign income provided there is at least one UK resident trustee. Conversely, a foreign settlor will be able to appoint UK trustees and preserve non-resident status for the trust by retaining at least one non-resident trustee.[159] As a non-resident body, the provisions of ITA 2007, section 720 (Part 13, Chapter 2) may fall to be considered.[160]

At one time there was no direct provision for income tax. The Revenue view was that the residence of one trustee within the UK was enough to make the whole trust liable to UK income tax on the basis of residence. However, this view was rejected by the House of Lords in *Dawson v IRC*.[161] Parliament responded by passing FA 1989, sections 110 and 111, which are the basis for the rules just described.

Finally, as Loomer notes and in contrast to cases on company residence including *Wood v Holden* (see above §69.6.4), recent decisions including *Smallwood Trust v HMRC*[162] have demonstrated some judicial willingness, at least in the case of tax avoidance arrangements involving foreign trusts, to look beyond the formalities of trustee administration to ascertain where the 'realistic, positive management' of the trust was exercised.[163]

---

[157] TCGA 1992, s 69(2D). For a decision on the different question of where a trust is effectively managed, a question which arises in the context of double taxation treaties, see *Wensleydale's Settlement Trustees v IRC* [1996] STC (SCD) 241.

[158] TCGA 1992, s 69(2DA).

[159] Hansard, Standing Committee G, cols 609, 610, 22 June 1989. If the non-resident trustee were to become a UK resident, eg by staying in the UK for more than six months in a year of assessment, would any action lie at the suit of the beneficiaries?

[160] Ex TA 1988, ss 739–746. For transitional rules, see FA 1989, s 110(6)–(9); on 1989 changes, see Avery Jones [1989] BTR 249.

[161] [1989] STC 473; on the Court of Appeal decision, see Francis [1988] BTR 46.

[162] *Smallwood Trust v HMRC*, [2008] STC (SCD) 629, reversedd [2009] STC 1222 (Ch.), reversed [2010] STC 2045 (CA).

[163] See Loomer [2010] BTR 468 and Loomer (2015) *Can Tax J* 91,128–129.

69.10   Harmful Tax Competition and Tax Havens

A tax haven is simply a place with a favourable tax climate.[164] Among the favourites are the Channel Islands, the Isle of Man or, with greater tax advantages, Barbados, the Bahamas, the Turks and Caicos Islands, the Cayman Islands and Liechtenstein. All depend on the local rules with regard to tax, trust and company law. Even the UK has tax advantages for foreigners, as the continuing row over non-domiciles as well as the chequered history of the UK's patent box regime aptly demonstrate. Such fiscal prostitution is widespread. One country's tax incentive causes another country to brand it as a tax haven. Some countries need overseas earnings, and may accept it in fees for financial services rather than the profits of polluting plant and machinery. If other countries tax so highly as to encourage the flight of fiscal refugees, they have to take the consequences. UK tax legislation has a number of rules directed against the use of controlled foreign companies resident in low tax countries, but the breadth and scope of these rules have narrowed in recent years to comply with the fundamental freedoms of EU law and to reflect the UK's general move to a more territorial system of taxing income of its residents (see chapter seventy-three below).

While much effort has been expended over the last few decades to try to remove discrimination against non-residents (see chapter seventy-five below), beginning in the late 20th Century the attention of the OECD turned to the opposite problem—tax discrimination in favour of non-residents. This practice has developed as states scramble for inward investment. Where this goes too far it is referred to as 'fiscal dumping'; the use of the term 'dumping', which is also used for practices banned under GATT and now the World Trade Organisation, is deliberate. The OECD has developed rules which would prevent, or at least limit, harmful tax competition; the European Commission has set up a code of practice.[165] The OECD has set up a Forum on Harmful Tax Practices, with a soft approach to compliance based on periods of self-review followed by peer review; its powers are limited to financial services and similar mobile service activities.[166] It is not concerned about a state's right to charge lower rates of tax than other states, provided that rate is applied generally; so, a 12.5% corporation tax rate would not be objectionable, but a general rate of 20% and a 3% rate on mobile activities is likely to be, especially if such companies are allowed to provide these services only to people outside the state and, almost conclusively, if the state has refused to supply details of these transactions to other states.

In its important and influential 1998 report on harmful tax competition, the Forum highlighted four key factors in identifying a tax haven:[167]

(1)   no or only nominal taxation;
(2)   lack of effective exchange of information;

---

[164] For a focused inquiry see Zucman, *The Hidden Wealth of Nations: The Scourge of Tax Havens* (University of Chicago Press, 2015). See also Orlov (2004) 32 *Intertax* 95.

[165] See introductory article by Weiner and Ault (1998) 51 *National Tax Jo* 601. See OECD Reports for 1998, 2000, 2001 and 2004, van Raad, *Materials on International and EC Tax Law, 2004–05*, vol 1 (International Tax Centre Leiden, 2004) 811–1002, and see, generally, Schön (ed), *Tax Competition in Europe* (IBFD, 2003).

[166] See OECD website for progress reports at www.oecd.org.

[167] OECD, *Harmful Tax Competition: An Emerging Global Issue* (1998), 23. The report is available at http://www.oecd.org/tax/transparency/44430243.pdf.

(3) lack of transparency in the operation of the legislative, legal or administrative provisions; and

(4) absence of a requirement that the activity undertaken be substantial.

The report also listed four key factors, plus a number of additional factors, in identifying preferential tax regimes in OECD member and non-member countries. The key factors were:[168]

(1) low or no taxation on the relevant income, either because of a low rate or because of how the tax base is defined;

(2) 'ring-fencing' of regimes, such that the preferential tax regimes are partly or fully insulated from the domestic markets of the country providing the regime;

(3) lack of transparency in the operation of the regime; and

(4) lack of effective exchange of information in relation to taxpayers benefitting from the regime.

The 1998 OECD harmful tax competition report remains well worth reading, for one because it clearly demonstrates that political concerns over base erosion and profit shifting have been around for quite some time.[169] The report also begins with an interesting and robust defence of tax competition generally before attempting to draw the line between healthy tax competition and harmful tax competition. Progress reports were published in 2001 and 2004; by 2004 countries previously described as 'tax havens' had become 'participating partners', but this was because they had joined the project—up to a point. The OECD also turned its attention to exchange of information on tax matters. In the OECD's Global Forum on Transparency and Exchange of Information for Tax Purposes 2011 progress report, all jurisdictions surveyed committed to implementing the OECD's international standard on exchange of information.[170]

Of course, the focus on these issues has shifted and intensified in recent years with the G20/OECD Base Erosion and Profit Shifting (BEPS) project, discussed next in §69.11, and in particular with the work on BEPS Action 5 'Countering Harmful Tax Practices More Effectively, Taking into Account Transparency and Substance'.[171] Action 5 builds upon the early and more recent work of the Forum in reviewing preferential tax regimes and contains two important developments. First, in order to enhance transparency, a framework covering all rulings that could give rise to BEPS concerns in the absence of compulsory spontaneous exchange was agreed.[172] Second, it was agreed that the 'substantial activity' requirement used in the Forum's previous work—as a key factor in identifying a tax haven and an additional factor in identifying preferential tax regimes generally—should

---

[168] OECD, *Harmful Tax Competition: An Emerging Global Issue* (1998), 27. The report is available at http://www.oecd.org/tax/transparency/44430243.pdf.

[169] *Ibid*, 9.

[170] The 2011 report is available at http://www.oecd.org/site/0,3407,en_21571361_43854757_1_1_1_1_1,00.html.

[171] OECD, *Action 5: Countering Harmful Tax Practices More Effectively, Taking into Account Transparency and Substance* (October 2015).

[172] *Ibid*, 10.

be elevated in importance in the assessment of preferential tax regimes 'in order to realign taxation of profits with the substantial activities that generate them'.[173] Several approaches were considered on how best to pursue this aim, and consensus was reached on the 'nexus approach', which was developed in the context of IP regimes.[174] As described in the Action 5 final report, '[t]he nexus approach uses expenditure as a proxy for activity and builds on the principle that… a substantial activity requirement should ensure that taxpayers benefiting from these regimes did in fact engage in such activities and did incur actual expenditures on such activities'.[175] The report also states that the nexus principle can be applied to non-IP preferential tax regimes 'so that such regimes would be found to require substantial activities where they grant benefits to a taxpayer to the extent that the taxpayer undertook the core income-generating activities required to produce the type of income covered by the preferential regime'.[176]

The EU harmful tax competition scheme is wider in that it concentrates on any type of activity and not just mobile services. However, it is concerned with competition within the EU, and so would find nothing wrong with a low rate of tax on some services if other Member States charged similarly low rates. A Code of Conduct for business taxation was adopted by the Council of Economics and Finance Ministers (ECOFIN) on 1 December 1997. By adopting this Code, the Member States undertook to (a) roll back existing tax measures that constitute harmful tax competition, and (b) refrain from introducing any such measures in the future.[177] A survey of Member State practices was completed in 1999.[178] The Code is not legally binding but has political force. It is monitored by a Code of Conduct Group that reports regularly to the Council. The EU scheme also makes allowances for state aid factors in favour of outermost regions and small islands. As with the OECD, the European Commission's attention has recently turned to dealing with the base erosion and profit shifting activities of multinationals (see §77.4.2).

69.11   Base Erosion and Profit Shifting (BEPS)

According to the OECD, base erosion and profit shifting (BEPS) refers to tax planning strategies that exploit gaps and mismatches in tax rules 'to artificially shift profits to low or no-tax locations where there is little or no economic activity, resulting in little or no overall corporate tax being paid.'[179] Research undertaken on the potential magnitude of the BEPS

[173] *Ibid*, 10.

[174] *Ibid*, 10.

[175] *Ibid*, 10.

[176] *Ibid*, 10.

[177] For recent developments, see the Commission's website on harmful tax competition at http://ec.europa.eu/taxation_customs/taxation/company_tax/harmful_tax_practices/index_en.htm.

[178] Inland Revenue Press Release; for (earlier) reservations, see House of Lords Select Committee on European Union Legislation, HL-92, 15th Report, 1998–1999 session, paras 119–46.

[179] OECD website on BEPS: http://www.oecd.org/ctp/beps-about.htm. For literature see eg Devereux and Vella, 'Are we heading towards a corporate tax system fit for the 21st century?' (2014) *Fiscal Studies*, Vol 35. No. 4, 449, available at http://papers.ssrn.com/sol3/papers.cfm?abstract_id=2532933; British Tax Review, special editions on BEPS, volume 5 of 2013 and volume 3 of 2015; Brauner, 'What the BEPS?' (2014) 16 *Florida Tax Rev* 55; Panayi, *Advanced Issues in International and European Tax Law* (Bloomsbury 2015).

problem estimates that it results in annual losses of anywhere from 4–10% of global corporate income tax revenues, ie USD 100 to 240 billion annually.[180]

As just noted, towards the end of the 20th Century the OECD and the G7 (now G8) began to take some steps aimed at preventing harmful tax competition amongst states, with a particular focus on tax havens. In the early 21st Century, however, it was becoming increasingly clear to those involved with international tax that a framework designed in the 1920s to reduce double taxation on cross-border trade had failed to keep up with changes in business methods, technology and communications. Worryingly for governments, well advised multinationals (MNEs) that were vocal about abolishing measures giving rise to double taxation were also very busy creating elaborate structures that pushed the limits of key elements of the international framework such as residency, the arm's length principle and permanent establishment in a bid to reduce the MNE's worldwide corporate tax burden. Technological developments also made it increasingly possible for MNEs to be heavily involved in the economic life of a country without the need to establish a traditional taxable presence in that country—eg by selling digital products over the internet directly to consumers.[181] These developments in turn led to rising public concern over the equity and efficacy of the international tax framework, and particularly whether MNEs were gaining an unfair competitive advantage over domestic businesses by 'dodging' taxes, and depriving both developed and developing countries from much needed revenue in the process.

Following a series of high-profile media campaigns, the BEPS issue became a political issue. At the G20 leaders conference in Mexico in June 2012 the final declaration referred to 'the need to prevent base erosion and profit shifting.' At the meeting of the G20 finance ministers in November 2012, the ministers—and especially those from the UK, Germany and France—encouraged the OECD to report on the progress of its work on BEPS at their next meeting.[182]

Spurred on by the backing of the G20 countries, and perhaps concerned to protect its leading role in international tax matters, the OECD set an ambitious working agenda with an equally ambitious timeframe aimed at finding solutions to the BEPS problem.[183] Developing countries were also invited to participate to some degree in the OECD's work, and eventually over 80 non-OECD, non-G20 jurisdictions had at least some input in the process. BEPS was described by the OECD Secretary-General in 2014 as 'the most prominent step towards modernization of the international tax system in a hundred years'.[184]

The G20/OECD BEPS project eventually was divided into 15 distinct areas of 'action':

Action 1: Addressing the Tax Challenges of the Digital Economy
Action 2: Neutralising the Effects of Hybrid Mismatch Arrangements
Action 3: Designing Effective Controlled Foreign Company Rules
Action 4: Limiting Base Erosion Involving Interest Deductions and Other Financial Payments

---

[180] *Ibid*, and see OECD, *BEPS Action 11 'Measuring and Monitoring BEPS' Final Report* (Oct 2015).
[181] OECD, *Addressing Base Erosion and Profit Shifting* (2013), 7.
[182] OECD, *Addressing Base Erosion and Profit Shifting* (2013), 14.
[183] OECD, *Action Plan on Base Erosion and Profit Shifting* (July 2013).
[184] Remarks by Angel Gurría, OECD Secretary-General, delivered at the Joint Press Conference on the G20 Tax Agenda, with Treasurer Joe Hockey MP, and Tax Commissioner Chris Jordan at Cairns, Australia (20 September 2014).

Action 5: Countering Harmful Tax Practices More Effectively, Taking into Account Transparency and Substance

Action 6: Preventing the Granting of Treaty Benefits in Inappropriate Circumstances

Action 7: Preventing the Artificial Avoidance of Permanent Establishment Status

Actions 8–10: Aligning Transfer Pricing Outcomes with Value Creation

Action 11: Measuring and Monitoring BEPS

Action 12: Mandatory Disclosure Rules

Action 13: Guidance on Transfer Pricing Documentation and Country-by-Country Reporting

Action 14: Making Dispute Resolution Mechanisms More Effective

Action 15: Developing a Multilateral Instrument to Modify Bilateral Tax Treaties

In October 2015, the OECD issued the final reports on the above actions. The final reports run in total to many thousands of pages and run the risk of overwhelming readers in voluminous minutia, but fortunately each report begins with a helpful and concise executive summary. The contents of the various actions are discussed in this book in the relevant chapters, eg Action 5 on harmful tax competition is considered in the immediately preceding section and Action 3 on CFCs is considered in chapter seventy-three. But for now some general overarching observations can be made.

First, for those readers new to the BEPS project it is well worth beginning with the lucid and relatively short (90 pages) first paper issued in 2013 entitled 'Addressing BEPS'. This paper provides valuable historical and political context for the project, identifies the key pressure areas (eg tax arbitrage and hybrid mismatch arrangements, related party debt financing arrangements, transfer pricing) and outlines some preliminary data on the scale of BEPS (pursued further in Action 14).

Second, it is important to bear in mind that the action plans take a variety of forms, ranging from (1) primarily reports on topics such as Action 1 on the digital economy to (2) suggestions for domestic legislation that can be introduced unilaterally by states to (3) proposals for changes to the OECD's Transfer Pricing Guidelines, Model Tax Treaty and Commentary to the Model. The recommendations in Action 7, for example, involve relatively minor changes to the definition of permanent establishment in Article 5 of the OECD Model Tax Treaty as well as to the related Commentary. In the ordinary course, those changes would gradually filter into new bilateral treaties based on the Model and in amendments to existing treaties. Hence Action 15, which seeks to speed up the usual implementation timeframe through the novel idea of a multilateral treaty. Action 3, on the other hand, sets out options and recommendations for individual states to consider in implementing and modifying domestic CFC rules. The timeframe for implementation is potentially much shorter, depending of course on the tax legislative process and political willpower in individual states. Enhanced transparency and co-operation amongst domestic tax administrations is another key component of BEPS, and include recommendations for MNEs to file transfer pricing documentation and reports on economic activity plus taxes paid on a country-by-country basis with tax administrations (Action 13).

Thirdly, readers should ask themselves whether the BEPS actions likely will lead to significant changes to the international tax regime or if this is all just tinkering at the edges, with some important changes to transfer pricing rules and restrictions on interest deductibility plus a few extra bits tacked on?[185] Was an opportunity for more substantial reform lost? Early indications were that the OECD was open to considering major structural changes to the international tax framework, possibly even the source/residence allocation of taxing rights. In the first BEPS paper, the OECD said 'it is also important to revisit some of the fundamentals of the existing standards. Indeed, incremental approaches may help curb the current trends but will not respond to several of the challenges government face.'[186] But ultimately the cornerstones of the old framework were accepted as given, including the source/residence distinction and the decision to view subsidiaries of MNEs as separate entities capable of being treated as interacting with other members of the group on an arm's length basis for tax purposes. On the other hand, the action plans show a willingness to depart from the traditional framework in favour of focusing on 'economic activity', 'substance' and 'value creation' in cases of perceived abuse.[187] It should also be noted that BEPS says nothing about other 'competitive' features of domestic tax systems, including tax rates. If the available options for tax competition become more and more limited, further falls in corporate tax rates internationally seem inevitable.[188] Other yet-undiscovered oversights as well as newly-created problems no doubt lie ahead.

Finally, the response of individual countries including the UK to the BEPS actions is crucial.[189] At the time of writing the UK has decided to introduce restrictions on interest deductibility in line with the recommendations in Action 4.[190] This is a seismic change in UK tax policy; for many years politicians have trumpeted the UK's comparatively generous rules on interest deductibility as an important feature of the UK's competitiveness on tax internationally. For example, the UK Government's 2010 Corporate Tax Road Map states: 'The UK's current interest rules, which do not significantly restrict relief for interest, are considered by businesses as a competitive advantage and it is the Government's view that this advantage outweighs potential benefits from moving towards a more territorial system for interest.'[191] On the other hand the UK introduced its own limited anti-BEPS measure in the form of the diverted profits tax (see below §72.7) in the midst of the ongoing BEPS work without waiting for, and seemingly with little regard to, the OECD's final action reports.[192] Was this purely a politically-motivated response to media and public attention on the low amount of UK tax being paid by primarily US-based MNEs, or the introduction of a bargaining chip that could be surrendered in return for garnering the grudging acceptance by the MNEs of other anti-BEPs reforms?

Most importantly, how will the US respond to BEPS? It can be argued that many of the problems with the operation of the existing international tax rules are directly related to particular features of the US tax regime—including the 'check-the-box rules' and the

---

[185] Devereux and Vella, *op cit.*

[186] OECD, *Addressing Base Erosion and Profit Shifting* (2013), 8. See also Devereux and Vella, *op cit*, text at fn 12.

[187] Devereux and Vella, *op cit.*

[188] Collier, Oxford lecture on Transfer Pricing and BEPS (24 Feb 2016).

[189] To begin, see HMT and HMRC, 'Tackling aggressive tax planning in the global economy, UK Priorities for the G20-OECD project for countering Base Erosion and Profit Shifting' (March 2014).

[190] HMT, 'Consultation on Tax Deductibility of corporate interest expense', (latest update January 2016). See also HMRC, 'Policy Paper: Anti-Hybrid Rules', (latest update December 2015).

[191] UK Government, *The Corporate Tax Road Map* (2010), [3.8], available at https://www.gov.uk/government/uploads/system/uploads/attachment_data/file/193239/Corporation_tax_road_map.pdf.

[192] Self, 'Diverted profits tax: give BEPS a chance' *Tax Journal* (15 December 2014).

comparatively high US federal and state corporate tax rates—features that incentivise US-based MNEs to leave foreign profits offshore in tax havens and not repatriate them to the US.[193] If US policymakers are content with the level of US taxes being paid by US-based MNEs (competitiveness again?), will there be any appetite for substantial US tax reform eg on CFCs/Subpart F? Moreover, whilst much public and political attention has been focused on the transfer pricing arrangements between UK members of US-based MNEs, others point out that for many MNEs the real value underlying their world-wide profits arises from their IP. What difference does it make to the UK tax take whether the US tax regime makes it conducive for US-based MNEs to hold their valuable IP offshore in tax havens or onshore in the US?[194] How much 'value' lies in making sales to UK customers, if those sales are primarily driven by that IP? If sales/market access should be considered a more important contributor to the MNEs' profit, perhaps this suggests an entirely different approach to taxing MNEs is required, such as formulary apportionment[195] or a destination-based corporate tax.[196]

[193] Collier, Oxford lecture on Transfer Pricing and BEPS (24 Feb 2016).

[194] Collier, Oxford lecture on Transfer Pricing and BEPS (24 Feb 2016).

[195] See eg Picciotto, 'Towards Unitary Taxation of Transnational Corporations', Tax Justice Network, available at http://www.taxjustice.net/cms/upload/pdf/Towards_Unitary_Taxation_1–1.pdf.

[196] Devereux and de la Feria, 'Designing and implementing a destination-based corporate tax' (2014), available at http://eureka.sbs.ox.ac.uk/5081/1/WP1407.pdf.

70

Enforcement of Foreign Revenue Laws

70.1 General Rule: No Enforcement

In *Government of India v Taylor*,[1] the House of Lords held that the UK courts would decline to exercise jurisdiction to entertain a suit for the enforcement of the revenue law of another country, whether by direct or indirect means.[2] A foreign judgment for a sum payable in respect of taxes cannot be registered under the Foreign Judgments (Reciprocal Enforcement) Act 1933.[3] Following the same approach, it has been held that such a judgment is not a civil matter within Article 1 of the Brussels Convention.[4] Where a foreign government had successfully sued in its own courts for tax due to it and recovered the tax but not the costs, it was not able to sue for the costs in the UK since no separate claim lies for costs under English or Scots law.[5] The UK approach is adopted in other countries too, eg the US.[6] It is becoming more common, however, for UK tax treaties to include an article based on Article 27 of the OECD Model Tax Convention on assistance in the collection of taxes. In any event, the general rule is now subject to a major exception for taxation charged under the law of another Member State under EU law (see §70.3.1 below).

What is a revenue law is a matter for the *lex fori*. It has extended to compulsory contributions to a state insurance scheme, since a compulsory contribution levied by a state organisation is a revenue matter.[7] A payment for services supplied by the state[8] would seem

---

[1] [1955] AC 491, [1955] 1 All ER 292; noted in 3 *ICLQ* 161, 465; 4 *ICLQ* 564. See, generally, Carter (1989) 48 *CLJ* 417; Smart, *Cross-Border Insolvencies*, 2nd edn (Butterworths, 1998), 197–211; Baker [1993] BTR 313; and Baker, in *Tolley's International Tax Planning*, 5th edn (2002), ch 33.

[2] [1955] AC 491, 510; on indirect enforcement, see Smart (1986) 35 *ICLQ* 704.

[3] Section 1(2)(b).

[4] Ie the Convention on Jurisdiction and Enforcement of Judgment in Civil and Commercial Matters; see QRS 1 *Aps and others v Fransden* [1999] STC 616.

[5] *A-G for Canada v William Schulze & Co* (1901) 9 SLT 4.

[6] Baker (2002) 30 *Intertax* 216.

[7] *Metal Industries (Salvage) Ltd v ST Harle (Owners)* 1962 SLT 114 (employer's contribution); issues which have been held not to be revenue matters include exchange control (*Kahler v Midland Bank Ltd* [1950] AC 24, [1949] 2 All ER 621) and a legal aid contribution (*Connor v Connor* [1974] 1 NZLR 632).

[8] See above chapter one.

to fall outside this definition, however, at least where there is some choice over whether to accept the services.

In the *Taylor* case the House of Lords also held that the foreign tax liability was not an allowable liability under the companies legislation. UK insolvency legislation provides for assistance between courts in territories designated by the Secretary of State. The matter arises where X is insolvent in one state, owing tax there, but has assets in another state. The legislation, as interpreted by the courts in other countries, allows the trustee in bankruptcy or the receiver to get at the assets in the other country; however, it should be noted that none of these cases concerns the situation in which the only creditor is the tax authority.[9] UK case law establishes that an assignee acting as nominee for a foreign tax-gathering authority may obtain the assistance of the English court in gathering evidence, but may not sue in England or otherwise recover assets in England.[10] The now lapsed European Convention on Insolvency Proceedings, Article 39 would have abolished the common law approach and allowed the enforcement of a claim by a foreign Revenue authority.[11] In one common law jurisdiction a judge declined to apply the basic principle in bankruptcy proceedings.[12]

The principle probably originates in a dictum of Lord Mansfield in 1775 where, upholding a vendor's claim for the purchase money due on goods sold in France and which the purchaser intended, to the vendor's knowledge, to smuggle into England, he said that 'no country ever takes notice of the revenue laws of another'.[13] The proper law of the contract being French, English law was irrelevant.

An attempt to enforce a foreign revenue law indirectly was made in the Irish case of *Peter Buchanan Ltd and MacHarg v McVey*.[14] The taxpayer, a director of a Scottish company, had disposed of his shares in two other companies and, after full disclosure to the UK Inland Revenue, was assured that the deal did not involve excess profits levy. Subsequently, the levy was retrospectively applied to the taxpayer. He therefore arranged to transfer his stock of whisky and his private assets to safe hands in Ireland, followed his wealth to Ireland and thought that 'he might safely snap his hands in the face of the disgruntled Scottish Revenue'. The liquidator of Peter Buchanan Ltd, a man chosen by the Revenue because of his potentialities as a financial Sherlock Holmes, then sued in the Irish courts on the ground that the stripping of the company's assets was ultra vires the company and a breach of his duty as director. The action was dismissed on the ground that it was in substance an indirect attempt to enforce the revenue laws of another country. At first instance, Kingsmill Moore J placed some weight on the fact that the Inland Revenue was the only unpaid creditor, but this point was not touched on by the Supreme Court of Eire.

---

[9] See Smart, *op cit*, 197–211; see also Baker, in *Tolley's International Tax Planning*, 33.4; and note Avery Jones [1991] BTR 109 on an unsatisfactory case from Florida.

[10] Smart, *op cit*, 200–01, referring to *Re State of Norway's Application* [1990] 1 AC 723, [1989] 1 All ER 745, HL; and the curious case of *Re Tucker* [1990] 1 Ch 148, CA, on which Smart refers to Fidler (1997) 5 *Journal of International Banking and Finance Law* 19.

[11] Smart, *op cit*, 209.

[12] Forsyth J in the Alberta, Canada case of *Re Sefel Geophysical Ltd* [1989] 1 WWR 251, 260.

[13] *Holman v Johnson* (1775) 1 Cowp 341.

[14] [1954] IR 89.

70.2   Recognising Without Enforcing

70.2.1 Contract

The rule is that UK courts will not enforce a foreign revenue law, not that they must not recognise it. Thus, in *Regazzoni v KC Sethia (1944) Ltd*,[15] Viscount Simonds said that '[i]t does not follow from the fact that today the court will not enforce a revenue law at the suit of a foreign state that today it will enforce a contract which requires the doing of an act in a foreign country which violates the revenue laws of that country', a statement which may limit the initial decision of Lord Mansfield.

70.2.2 Evidence

In *Re State of Norway's Application*,[16] the House of Lords held that Norway could seek the assistance of the UK courts in obtaining evidence in relation to a tax case in Norway under the Evidence (Proceedings in Other Jurisdictions) Act 1975. The case did not concern a tax liability arising under a third country which had begun proceedings in Norway, neither did it deal with the recovery of assets as distinct from information.

70.2.3 Title to Goods

In *Brokaw v Seatrain UK Ltd*,[17] household goods were on the high seas on a US ship sailing from Baltimore to England when the US Treasury served a notice of levy on the shipowner and demanded the surrender of all property in its possession. When the ship reached England the US Government claimed possession; the consignees of the goods sued the shipowner in detinue. It was held that the service of the notice of levy was insufficient to reduce the goods into the possession of the US Government, and therefore that the Government had to rely upon its revenue law to support its claim to possession. If, however, the notice of the levy had been sufficient, under English conflict of law rules, to reduce goods into the possession of the US Government, that claim would have been enforced because the English courts would then be enforcing an actual possessory title and not a revenue law.[18] How this can be reconciled with those cases in which courts have refused indirectly to enforce a revenue law is a difficult matter.[19] Perhaps a proprietary claim cannot be an indirect enforcement, whereas a personal claim may be.[20]

---

[15] [1957] 3 All ER 286, 292.
[16] [1990] AC 723; for comment, see Lipstein (1990) 39 *ICLQ* 120.
[17] [1971] 2 QB 476, [1971] 2 All ER 98.
[18] *Ibid*, 482, 100. *Cf Singh v Ali* [1960] AC 167, [1960] 1 All ER 269.
[19] *Buchanan Ltd v McVey* (above at §14.1); see also *Jones v Boriand* (1969) 4 SA 29; and *Rossano v Manufacturer's Life Insurance Co Ltd* [1963] 2 QB 352, [1962] 2 All ER 214. If a foreign court made a person bankrupt for non-payment of tax, how far would the UK courts go in deciding the consequences of that status?
[20] Thus, if a foreign country holds X liable for Y's tax (*cf* TMA 1970, s 78), can X bring an action on an indemnity against Y in the UK courts? Such a claim succeeded in *Re Reid* (1970) 17 DLR (3d) 199.

70.2.4 Extradition

The English courts have held that a person may be extradited for an offence of fraud falling within the relevant treaty, even though the fraud relates to a tax matter.[21]

70.2.5 Trustee's Obligation to Pay

Since a foreign tax law cannot be enforced in the UK courts, it follows that it cannot give rise to a legal obligation enforceable here; it might, in turn, follow that for a trustee to pay such a tax would be a breach of trust. However, in deciding such issues the court must pay attention to the consequences for the trust of non-payment. These points emerge from *Re Lord Cable's Will Trusts*.[22] The issue was whether the court should grant an injunction to prevent the passing of money from the UK to trustees in India, given that the primary purpose of the payment was to enable the trustees to make payments due under the Indian exchange control legislation. If the payment was not made, the trustees were liable to imprisonment and to a penalty of up to five times the sum involved. Slade J refused to grant an injunction.

This leaves various questions open. First, would the position be the same for a tax as for exchange control? The answer appears to be 'Yes', since Slade J went on to consider obiter the position of payments of Indian estate duty.[23] Secondly, would it be a breach of trust for the trustees to pay? The refusal of an injunction to prevent the trustees from paying is not conclusive of this issue; however, Slade J said that the reimbursement of the trustees from the trust funds in respect of estate duty so paid would be a proper payment.[24] Thirdly, would it be a breach of trust not to pay? The effects for the trust fund would be so drastic that it would appear that the trustees' general duty to preserve the trust fund would require them to pay and so would make it a breach of trust not to pay. However, both in relation to this and the second point it must be remembered that this was a case of an Indian trust with funds and trustees in India; had there been no such connection with the country asserting a claim against the trust funds, a different result might have followed as, indeed, might have been the case if the consequences of non-payment had been minimal. Other problems arise when a foreign country will regard payment of UK tax as a breach of trust and the present UK trustees are trying to export the trust to that other country. There is considerable variation between different countries on these issues.[25]

---

[21] *R v Chief Metropolitan Stipendiary Magistrate, ex parte Secretary of State for the Home Department* [1988] 1 WLR 1204, [1989] 1 All ER 151, DC.

[22] [1976] 3 All ER 417.

[23] *Ibid*, 417, 435, 436.

[24] *Ibid*; citing *Re Reid* (1970) 17 DLR (3d) 199 (Canada) and explaining dicta of Lord Robertson in *Scottish National Orchestra Society Ltd v Thomson's Executors* 1969 SLT 325, 330. This would distinguish the payment of a foreign tax from the payment of a statute-barred debt.

[25] Baker, *Tolley's International Tax Planning, op cit*, para 33.6.

70.3 Exceptions

70.3.1 EU Law

For now, at least, the UK is a member of the EU. Under EU law, various levies are now charged by the authorities of the Union rather than by the Member States.[26] There have long been extensive obligations with regard to the provision of information with regard to certain taxes. The ECJ gives full scope to these obligations; so there is no need for the Member State to have made an assessment to tax before a duty arises on other States to supply information.[27]

Since 2002 UK courts may enforce a claim to listed taxes arising in another Member State, and the list includes taxes on income and capital.[28] The UK revenue department litigates on behalf of the foreign tax authority. Recovery may be enforced even though the claim is contested, though at the risk of having to pay compensation, under human rights jurisprudence, to the extent that the claim proves to be unfounded.[29] The ECJ has held that the Directive is retroactive and affects claims arising before it was introduced. The Court reasoned that the change was procedural and not substantive; it did not set out rules about the accrual or scope of claims, and there was nothing in it to indicate that it was not to apply to pre-existing debts.[30]

Other UK legislation authorises the transfer of *information* to the competent authorities of another Member State, provided the officer is satisfied that the other State's confidentiality rules are at least as strict as the UK's.[31] Similarly, the Treasury is authorised to make regulations for obtaining information about various types of savings income for matters arising out of any Union obligation to ensure the effective taxation of savings under the law of the UK; this power applies also to non-Member States.[32] Further, there is an express provision imposing a duty on the relevant UK tax authorities to notify a person when the competent authority in another Member State requests the UK to inform that person of an 'instrument or decision' emanating from the other Member State and concerning taxes covered by the mutual assistance directive;[33] no doubt there are similar rules in other Member States.

In 2011 the ECOFIN Council adopted an amended directive on mutual administrative assistance that pointed towards new directions for exchange of information. The directive requires automatic exchange, permits spontaneous exchange, and allows information in certain circumstances to be passed on to non-tax authorities and to third States.[34] In 2014 the directive was extended to include automatic exchange of financial

---

[26] See Decision 70/243/EEC (OJ 1970 L94/19).
[27] Case C-420/98 *W N v Staatssecretaris van Financien* [2001] STC 974.
[28] Directive 76/308/EEC as amended.
[29] Baker, *op cit*, citing App No 349895/97 *Janosevic v Sweden*, para 106.
[30] Case C- 361/02, 362/02 *Greece v Tsaplois* [2004] STC 1220.
[31] FA 2003, s 197 (not rewritten), ex FA 1978, s 77 and FA 1990, s 125.
[32] TMA 1970 ss 18B–18E, inserted by TIOPA 2010, Sch 7, para 103, ex FA 2003, s 199.
[33] F(No 2)A 2005, s 68 (not rewritten).
[34] Council Directive 2011/16/EU of 15 February 2011 on administrative co-operation in the field of taxation, repealing Directive 77/799/EEC. For commentary, see Baker [2011] BTR 125, 126.

account information,[35] in 2015, to include information on cross-border tax rulings and advance pricing arrangements,[36] and in 2016, to include country-by-country reporting information.[37] Looking ahead, one can see much more radical ideas. One is for multilateral tax auditing.[38]

70.3.2 Tax Treaties

The rules at §70.3.1 are matters of EU law and therefore relevant only where EU principles apply. Most double tax treaties to be found around the world, including most of those made by the UK, attempt to counter some evasion techniques by providing for the exchange of information.[39] Some treaties, and recently some UK treaties, actually make provision for providing assistance to treaty partners in the collection of tax, as in Article 27 of the OECD Model Treaty.[40] The 2011 UK–South Africa treaty protocol added such an article and, interestingly, included a provision to the effect that there is no obligation to assist where the requested state considers that the taxes at issue are imposed 'contrary to generally accepted taxation principles'.[41] On whether the treaty requires the UK tax authorities to provide information to a foreign tax authority if there is no UK tax in issue, see below at §76.5.[42] Some treaties require mutual assistance in recovering tax due, to ensure that treaty benefits are not given to people who are not entitled to them.[43]

In 2006 the UK took a decisive, further step down this road. By FA 2006, section 173, the Crown was given powers to bring into effect the 1988 OECD Convention on Mutual Administrative Assistance. The Convention aims to help governments enforce their tax laws and provides an international legal framework for co-operation among countries in countering international tax avoidance and evasion. In 2010, the Convention was amended by protocol, which updated it to reflect developments internationally in this area (and particularly in the EU) and opened it up to all countries. At the time of writing 94 jurisdictions participate in the Convention. Furthermore, Competent Authorities from 80 jurisdictions have signed a multilateral agreement under Article 6 of the Convention, which provides for the automatic exchange of information. Moreover, FA 2006, section 175 allows the Treasury to make regulations for the recovery in the UK of debts relating to a foreign tax under the arrangements in section 173.[44]

Further developments in this area include the UK's 2009 tax information exchange agreement with Liechtenstein, which was accompanied by a somewhat controversial disclosure

---

[35] Council Directive 2014/107/EU of 9 December 2014.
[36] Council Directive 2015/2376/EU of 8 December 2015.
[37] Council Directive (EU) 2016/881 of 25 May 2016.
[38] Van der Hel-van Dijk and Kaerling (2003) 31 *Intertax* 4.
[39] OECD Model, Art 26; see generally McCracken (2002) 50 *Canadian Tax Jo* 1869–1912.
[40] See now OECD Model, Art 27, added 2003. On unhappy if dated US experience, see 50 *Columbia L Rev* 490. The US entered a reservation in relation to the OECD treaty of 1988, so far as it related to enforcement.
[41] See Baker [2011] BTR 125 for analysis. Baker notes that no assistance provisions were included in 2011 treaties with Bahrain or Hong Kong, which suggests to him that the UK policy on such articles is to include them only if the other negotiating state wishes to do so.
[42] *US v AL Burbank* 96 Sup Ct 2647; cited by Baker, in *Tolley's International Tax Planning*, para 34.67.
[43] OECD Model, Commentary on Art 27, para 2.
[44] See Recovery of Foreign Taxes Regulations 2007 (SI 2007/3507) and Recovery of Foreign Taxes (Amendment) Regulations 2010 (SI 2010/794).

facility to allow UK taxpayers with undeclared investments in Liechtenstein to come for-ward and get their tax affairs in order.[45] While this arrangement is believed to have generated over £3 billion in tax receipts for the UK until it closed in 2015, the favourable terms pro-vided (eg maximum penalty of 10% rather than 100%, and restricting the inquiry period to the past 10 years rather than the usual 20 years) could be viewed as overly-generous treat-ment of tax evaders, including ones who moved investments from other jurisdictions into Liechtenstein purely to make use of this facility. In addition, in 2011 the UK entered into a tax co-operation agreement with Switzerland, aimed at raising revenue from UK taxpayers on undeclared income and gains in Swiss banks.[46] As noted above (at §4.2.2), the amounts raised did not meet expectations.

70.4   Criminal Law

Despite these rules, one very difficult and important issue remains unresolved—whether a breach of a foreign revenue law giving rise to criminal liability under that foreign law can give rise to criminal liability in the UK under the 1993 amendments to the Criminal Justice Act 1988, which are concerned with money laundering.[47]

70.5   Final Thoughts

For many years the result of the general rule considered in this chapter was to permit people to avoid tax due to a foreign country by bringing themselves and their wealth within the UK. Reasons for this rule are not completely convincing.[48] Sometimes the rule has been justified on the notion that tax, as an expression of the sovereign power of a state, should not be allowed to encroach on the sovereign power of another state,[49] a problem the logical solution of which is to allow the forum state a choice. Similarly, a state should be able to waive the argument that its presence in court is inconsistent with its sovereignty. Another argument equate taxes with fines and penalties,[50] which the UK courts will also enforce; however, this ignores the fact that for some offences a fugitive criminal may, unlike a pru-dent tax traveller, be extradited. Other, more practical explanations are the wish to avoid entanglements on questions of proof of foreign tax laws[51] and the real risk that there might be much litigation. Further, there are real political and economic risks when the courts are asked to decide which tax laws they will enforce and which not.[52] Clearly, some territorial

---

[45] For details see https://www.gov.uk/government/publications/offshore-disclosure-facilites-liechtenstein.
[46] Available at https://www.gov.uk/government/publications/uk-swiss-confederation-taxation-co-operation-agreement.
[47] See Bennett [1999] *Private Client Business* 159. On money laundering more generally, see Rider [1996] *Private Client Business* 134, 201, 265.
[48] For discussions, see Castel, 42 *Can BR* 277; Leflar (1932) 46 *HLR* 193, 215.
[49] Lord Keith in *Government of India v Taylor* [1955] AC 491, 511.
[50] *Ibid*, 506, *per* Viscount Simonds; Leflar, *op cit*, 193.
[51] Read, *Enforcement of Foreign Judgments* (Harvard University Press, 1938), 290.
[52] Eg Kingsmill Moore J in [1954] *IR* 89, 105–06.

limitations would have to be worked out if the present rule were to be abandoned; there is no real reason why English courts should uphold a claim by a foreign government to levy a poll tax on inhabitants in England. The solution of such problems has been the function of the conflict of laws. Even when territorial problems have been settled, there must remain the possibility of refusing to enforce a foreign revenue law on grounds of public policy;[53] the 1970s Russian tax on emigrating Jews might prove one such.[54]

Improvements in international co-operation have long been sought—by revenue departments and so by the OECD and the Council of Europe. An important development on this front was the 1988 OECD Multilateral Convention on Mutual Administrative Assistance in Tax Matters, which was amended in 2010 to modernise it and open it up to all countries. Since the Convention was designed by revenue departments, however, little thought is given to protection for taxpayers. There is no requirement under the Convention that the external revenue department should display competence in its affairs, no requirement that the departments should devote earmarked resources to treating taxpayers as efficiently and courteously as they would in their countries of residence, and no obligation to open an office in its embassy so as to handle matters. The EU directive on mutual administrative assistance was another important development, and it continues to expand the boundaries of cooperation amongst Member States' tax authorities. The US federal Foreign Account Tax Compliance Act (FATCA) requiring non-US financial institutions to report the assets and identities of US persons to the US Department of the Treasury—and the intergovernmental agreements implementing FATCA, including one with the UK—is another example of the more general trend towards greater information sharing amongst jurisdictions.[55] Looking towards the future, the G20/OECD Base Erosion and Profit Shifting (BEPS) project (see above §69.11) promises yet further tax co-operation amongst jurisdictions. It can now be said with some confidence that the general rule against enforcing foreign revenue laws is looking less and less like a general rule and more and more like an anachronistic exception.

---

[53] Perhaps retrospective legislation would not be enforced.

[54] However, emigration taxes were once a lively issue: see Bhagwati and Partington, *Taxing the Brain Drain* (North-Holland, 1976).

[55] For details see https://www.gov.uk/government/publications/uk-us-automatic-exchange-of-information-agreement/uk-us-automatic-exchange-of-information-agreement.

71

UK Residents and Foreign Income

71.1   Introduction

Residents of the UK may find themselves taxable on overseas income under the following provisions, but the extent of liability may be affected by other connecting factors. A recent example is the treatment of 'non-doms', ie people who are resident but not domiciled in the UK and who benefit from certain tax advantages, most importantly the remittance basis of income taxation. The efforts of government to change the rules on the taxation of non-doms provide an interesting exercise in government advance and retreat; see §71.4 below. However, these are not the only rules which require discussion.

71.1.1 Income Tax

Under the income tax provisions, UK residents with foreign income will probably find themselves facing potential double taxation. While the UK wishes to tax the foreign income, the country of source, ie where the income arises, may also wish to do so. The basic principle that UK residents are taxable on their overseas income is to be found in the terms of ITEPA 2003, ITTOIA 2005 and ITA 2007. The charge on foreign source income in ITEPA 2003 arises under Part 2, Chapter 5.[1] ITTOIA 2005, Part 2, Chapter 2 contains the rules for

---

[1] See above §69.3.

trades carried on within and without the UK. ITTOIA 2005, Part 3, Chapter 2 deals with both UK property businesses and overseas property business. The tax treatment of UK dividends received by individuals from UK companies is treated in ITTOIA 2005, Part 4, Chapter 3, while the rules for dividend income from non-UK resident companies are dealt with in Chapter 4. The point is that the UK legislation deals with domestic and foreign matters side by side.[2]

A major feature of international tax systems is the obligation to deduct at source when income crosses a border. In the UK there have also been obligations on persons within the UK financial system to deduct tax on certain payments received from overseas and passing through their hands. These withholding rules have 19th-century origins, and have been rewritten several times in more recent years. These rules were reformed in 1996, 2000 and 2001, but were then reduced in a dramatic way in 2004 when the EC Savings Directive was implemented (since repealed); they have been rewritten for income tax by ITA 2007, Part 15.[3] There are also special withholding tax rules, eg on payments to entertainers. Lastly, a charge may arise under an anti-avoidance rule. Under these withholding rules, UK residents may be liable to tax on certain foreign income accruing to non-residents.

71.1.2 Capital Gains Tax

Capital gains tax, as discussed in more detail in chapter seventy-four, is levied on all gains accruing to a person resident in the UK regardless of the location of the asset, with a remittance basis for those not domiciled in UK. For charge on temporary non-residents arising when they resume UK residence, see below at §74.1.2.

71.1.3 Corporation Tax

Corporation tax was formerly levied on the income of the corporation as computed under the schedular system, eg Schedules A and D, Cases I–VI, on all income arising within the period. The corporation tax legislation, whilst still scheduler in design terms, has been rewritten and the rules are now spread across, primarily but not entirely, the Corporation Tax Act 2009, Corporation Tax Act 2010 and Taxation (International and Other Provisions) Act 2010. Neither the remittance basis nor the now obsolete percentage reductions (see below §71.4.1) apply to corporation tax. For rules on the taxation of the UK permanent establishment of a foreign company (introduced in 2003), see §60.9 above.

---

[2] For the list of foreign income heads under ITEPA 2003 and ITTOIA 2005 (in the remittance context), see below §71.4.3. The older heads of charge, now superseded for income tax by ITTOIA 2005, segregated foreign source income into (a) Sch D, Case IV—securities outside the UK; (b) Sch D, Case V—possessions outside the UK (TA 1988, s 18); and (c) Sch D, Case VI (see above chapter twenty-eight). In addition, statute imposes liability in respect of offshore income gains. Sch D, Case V (but not Case IV) survived for corporation tax until the 2010 rewrite (see below).

[3] See TA 1988, ss 118A–118K, introduced by FA 1996 but superseded by FA 2000, s 111, which came into force in 2001; FA 2000, s 111. See further below at §72.6.4.

71.1.4 Foreign Dividends

The taxation of foreign dividends accruing to a company subject to UK corporation tax was reviewed by the ECJ in the cases discussed in more detail below in chapter seventy-seven. Prior to 2009, where a UK-resident company had dividend income from a UK-resident company, the dividend was not subject to UK corporation tax by virtue of TA 1988, section 208. Now, CTA 2009, Part 9A exempts most dividends received by a UK company, whether from another UK company or from a company overseas. If the distribution is not exempt it is subject to corporation tax; if it is exempt the company may elect to treat it as taxable. In determining eligibility for the exemption, different rules apply depending on whether the company is 'small' or 'not small'; these rules are discussed below at §75.3.

In general, the UK tax system respects the legal form in which investments overseas are made and allows deferral of tax until income arises from the investment or, in some situations, is actually received in the UK (the remittance basis). However, deferral is overridden in the case of the controlled foreign company (CFC) legislation; these are rules designed to prevent the use of foreign companies to defer liability to UK corporation tax (see chapter seventy-three below). From 1956 until 1965 the UK tax system had a special category of 'overseas trade corporation'. These were UK-resident companies with foreign trading income, and were exempt from UK tax on that foreign income provided it was not distributed.[4]

71.2   Issues in Foreign Income

71.2.1 Place of Trade

71.2.1.1 General

For income tax, the profits of a trade carried on by a UK resident are chargeable to tax under ITTOIA 2005, Part 2, Chapter 2 wherever the trade is carried on.[5] A non-resident, on the other hand, is taxable under ITTOIA 2005, Part 2, Chapter 2 on profits of a trade only if they arise from a trade wholly or partly carried on in the UK. Thus, a non-resident is not taxable on profits accruing from a trade carried on wholly outside the UK. An old example of the distinction in the law between former Schedule D, Case I and Case V is *Sulley v A-G*.[6] Here, the taxpayer bought goods in the UK for export to America, where they were resold by his partners; the trade was carried on wholly overseas, and so was within Case V (now relevant foreign income within ITTOIA 2005, sections 7(5) and 830), not Case I (now ITTOIA 2005, section 6(1)).

It will be more difficult for a sole trader to establish that the trade is carried on wholly overseas. In *Ogilvie v Kitton*,[7] the taxpayer, who was resident in Aberdeen, was the sole owner of a business of woollen warehousing carried on by his employees in Toronto.

---

[4] See Royal Commission on Taxation of Profits and Income, *Final Report*, Cmnd 9474 (1955), ch 24; and Ilersic [1957] BTR 7.

[5] ITTOIA 2005, s 6. Transfer pricing rules (see above at §62.6) may also apply here.

[6] (1860) 5 H & N 711, (1860) 2 TC 149.

[7] (1908) 5 TC 338.

He had the sole right to manage and control his business, and although that right was not exercised, it could have been. The trade was therefore not wholly overseas.

Where a company wishes to trade overseas, it may do so by direct exporting, by a licensing system, by establishing a branch in the foreign country or by establishing a foreign subsidiary company.[8] In such instances, the profits will flow back to the UK in the form of dividends, interest, royalty payments and other forms, such as payments for services. The flow may be reversed by loans. The company may thus become an overseas incorporated pocket book—subject to any possible application of the CFC rules (see chapter seventy-three below). Loans to overseas subsidiaries often have advantages over direct equity investment in that interest, unlike a dividend, is generally deductible in computing profits, and it is in general easier to reduce investment by repaying capital than by re-exporting it; hence the thin capitalisation problem—above §62.6.

71.2.1.2 Subsidiary Company not Necessarily a Stooge

Where the resident company sets up a wholly-owned subsidiary in the foreign country to carry on a trade there, it is a question of fact whether that subsidiary is carrying on its own trade or is simply acting as agent for its parent's trade.[9] The question is not concluded, however, by saying that the overseas company is a wholly-owned subsidiary.[10] The question depends on who manages the trade and not on who owns the shares.[11]

71.2.1.3 Resident Company can Trade Wholly Overseas

A corporation may be resident in the UK because its central management and control abides in the UK. It might appear to follow that it cannot trade wholly overseas.[12] Despite this, the House of Lords held in *Mitchell v Egyptian Hotels Ltd*[13] that a company resident in the UK could be trading wholly abroad. The company was resident in England and carried on the business of hotel proprietors. It so amended its articles of association as to provide for the carrying on of the Egyptian business by a local board[14] in that country, which was to be wholly independent of the London board or any other part of the company. The only way in which the London board might have influenced its activities was by controlling the remuneration of the directors in Egypt. The Court of Appeal held that the company was carrying on a trade wholly outside the UK, and an evenly divided House of Lords could not reverse that decision.[15] Other cases[16] have shown that regular oversight of the foreign trade

---

[8] At one time conversion of a branch into a subsidiary fell within TA 1988, s 765 (see above at §69.7); today, it may cause a chargeable gain to arise (but see TCGA 1992, s 140; above at §62.3.3.4).

[9] *Apthorpe v Peter Schoenhofen Brewing Co Ltd* (1899) 4 TC 41.

[10] *Gramophone and Typewriter Ltd v Stanley* [1908] 2 KB 89, (1908) 5 TC 358; and see *Watson v Sandie and Hull* [1898] 1 QB 326, (1898) 3 TC 611.

[11] *Kodak Ltd v Clark* [1903] 1 KB 505, (1903) 4 TC 549.

[12] Eg *American Thread Co v Joyce* (1911) 6 TC 1, 18, *per* Hamilton J; see also Lord Halsbury in *Saõ Paulo (Brazilian) Railway Co v Carter* [1896] AC 38, (1895) 3 TC 410.

[13] [1915] AC 1022, (1915) 6 TC 542. For a similar result in relation to a trust, see *Ferguson v Donovan* [1929] IR 489. Inland Revenue, *International Tax Handbook*, para 343 suggests that the Revenue would now view the company as non-resident.

[14] The Egyptian Board controlled only the Egyptian business: *Swedish Central Rly Co Ltd v Thompson* [1925] AC 495, 523, 524, *per* Viscount Cave LC.

[15] Mere oversight regularly exercised is sufficient control, but merely to have the right to intervene and not to exercise that right is not (*Mitchell v Egyptian Hotels Ltd* [1915] AC 1022, 1040; 6 TC 542, 551, *per* Lord Sumner).

[16] *Saõ Paulo (Brazilian) Railway Co v Carter* [1896] AC 31, (1895) 3 TC 407.

will prevent it from being one carried on wholly overseas, so it is important that on the facts of the case there was no power directly to control the Egyptian trade.

In *Mitchell v BW Noble Ltd*,[17] control was shared between London and Paris, and it was held that the trade did not fall within Schedule D, Case V. Where the trade was carried on partly in the UK and partly overseas, so that Schedule D, Case I applied, concessionary relief formerly was available for certain unremittable debts.[18] Where a trade or business is carried on by a partnership and the control and management is abroad, it is deemed to be carried on by a person resident outside the UK.[19] If the partnership trades in, as opposed to with, the UK, tax will become due in respect of the profits of that trade as with any other non-resident person, and an assessment may be made on the partnership in the name of any partner resident here.

71.2.2 Basis of Assessment: ITTOIA 2005—Trading, Savings and Property Income[20]

71.2.2.1 Trading

Under ITTOIA 2005, the foreign aspects of income are treated as part of the general charging rules which apply to domestic income too. It follows that the normal charging rules, including the basis period rules for opening and closing years, also apply here. Likewise, the charge under Part 2, Chapter 17 (adjustment income and expenses on a change of accounting basis) applies just as easily to the purely foreign trade as to a purely domestic one. Under the schedular system an individual enjoying income arising from an overseas trade, profession or vocation was assessed to tax under Schedule D, Case V; however, the basis period was determined by the rules applicable to Schedule D, Cases I and II.[21] The opening and closing year provisions apply to overseas trades, etc, as they apply to UK trades, etc. Overlap profit charge and overlap profit relief are still relevant today under ITTOIA 2005.

71.2.2.2 Other

All other income assessable under ITTOIA 2005 (ex Schedule D, Case IV or V) is assessed on a strict fiscal year basis, unless it arises to a partnership. Thus, the basis period for 2016–17 is income arising from 6 April 2016 to 5 April 2017.[22]

71.2.2.3 Remittance

Where this basis applies (see below §71.4) the charge is on income remitted to the UK during the fiscal year.[23] This applies irrespective of the nature of the overseas income; so for a non-domiciled individual (and so taxable on the remittance basis) carrying on trade, the

---

[17] [1927] 1 KB 719, (1927)11 TC 372.

[18] Ex ESC B37.

[19] ITTOIA 2005, s 872(3), ex TA 1988, s 112 (but not for mixed partnership—see CTA 2009, s 1266 and Sch 1, para 364(3), ex TA 1988, s 115(5)).

[20] Before 1996–97 tax was charged on a preceding year basis; before 1926, Sch D, Case IV was charged on a current year basis and Case V on a three-year average—see Royal Commission on the Taxation of Profits and Income, *Final Report*, Cmnd 9474 (1955), para 785.

[21] TA 1988, s 65(3), as amended by FA 1994, s 207 (repealed by ITTOIA 2005).

[22] TA 1988, s 65(1) (repealed by ITTOIA 2005).

[23] ITTOIA 2005, Pt 8, Ch 2, s 831, ex TA 1988, s 65(4).

taxable profits from an overseas trade are the amount remitted to the UK in the fiscal year and not the accounting period.

71.2.2.4 Overseas Income of a UK Partnership

Where an individual is a member of a UK partnership which has profits assessable under ITTOIA 2005, the basis period which applies to that partnership income is applied to all other income arising to the partnership, eg overseas investment income. The income of that basis period is then allocated to the individual partners.[24] This overrides other basis period rules.

71.2.2.5 History: Schedule D, Case IV—Scope

Schedule D, Case IV charged income from securities. 'Securities' meant a debt or claim the payment of which was in some way secured, eg a debenture;[25] the term has been held to extend to a personal guarantee,[26] but not to stocks and shares. Case IV no longer applies for corporation tax and so is repealed by ITTOIA 2005. The location of the source of interest income has arisen only in cases where all the facts pointed one way.[27]

71.2.2.6 History: Schedule D, Case V—Scope of Possessions

Schedule D, Case V charged income from possessions, a phrase which it has been held includes any source of income,[28] presumably other than securities. A payment under a discretionary trust becomes a possession at least once the trustees have exercised their discretion.[29] A foreign trade is also a possession.[30]

Maintenance payments which have a foreign source are not income under UK tax law.[31] This is regardless of the treatment of the payment under the foreign tax system, ie whether or not the payment is taxable to the payee or deductible by the payer. An alimony order by a foreign court was held to be a foreign possession.[32]

A foreign pension fell within Schedule D, Case V, but a foreign employment within Schedule E;[33] both now come under ITEPA 2003.[34] Income from a pension was held to be income from a foreign possession and not income from employment, even though the pension arose from contributions made to a fund as a result of a foreign employment.[35]

---

[24] ITTOIA 2005, s 852, ex TA 1988, s 111(4) and (8).

[25] Viscount Cave LC in *Singer v Williams* [1921] 1 AC 41, 49; (1921) 7 TC 419, 431.

[26] *Westminster Bank Executor and Trustee Co (Channel Islands) Ltd v National Bank of Greece* [1971] 1 All ER 233, (1971) 46 TC 491, [1969] BTR 415. On location of source of interest, see Inland Revenue Interpretation RI58.

[27] See the exchange of views in *Offshore Taxation Review*, vol 8, 65 (Thornton), 115 (Simpson) and 235 (Venables); and Inland Revenue Interpretation RI 58.

[28] *Colquhoun v Brooks* (1889) 14 App Cas 493, 508, *per* Lord Herschel, and 514, *per* Lord MacNaghten. In *IRC v Reid's Trustees* [1949] AC 361, 371, Lord Simmonds suggested that 'income' for Sch D, Case V might be wider than income for the rest of the Taxes Acts.

[29] *Drummond v Collins* [1913] 3 KB 583, 594; (1913) 6 TC 525 at 532, *per* Horridge J.

[30] *Colquhoun v Brooks* (1889) 14 App Cas 493.

[31] ITTOIA 2005, s 730, ex TA 1988, s 347A(4).

[32] *IRC v Anderstrom* (1928) 13 TC 452; on concessionary double taxation relief, see ESC A12.

[33] TA 1988, s 19.

[34] ITEPA 2003, Pt 9, Ch 4, and Pt 2, Ch 5 respectively.

[35] *Apin v Estill* [1987] STC 723; followed in *Albon v IRC* [1998] STC 1181.

Certain borrowings on life policies were treated as falling within Case V but are swept into the general rules in ITTOIA 2005, Part 4, Chapter 10.[36]

71.2.2.7 Income from Overseas Land

Today ITTOIA 2005, Part 3 applies to both UK and overseas property businesses.[37] From 1998 until 2005 income from overseas land was the subject of a statutory regime similar to that which prevailed for land in the UK.[38] Capital allowances are available.[39] ITTOIA 2005, Part 3 excludes some Part 2 computational rules from applying to all property businesses, whether domestic or foreign. The rules in ITTOIA 2005, Part 3, Chapter 6 on furnished holiday accommodation applies to UK and property in other EEA states.[40]

71.2.2.8 Foreign Savings Income: Dividends and Distributions

By ITA 2007, section 8, domestic dividends and distributions chargeable under Part 4, Chapter 3 now attract rates of 0% on the first £5,000, then 7.5% (dividend ordinary rate), 32.5% (dividend upper rate), or 38.1% (dividend additional rate and dividend trust rate). These rates also apply to equivalent distributions by foreign companies, called 'relevant foreign distributions', chargeable under Part 4, Chapter 4, ie if the distribution would be income chargeable under Part 4, Chapter 3 if the company were resident in the UK.[41] Whether such income is domestic or foreign, it is treated as the highest part of the person's income.[42] There may be credit relief under other provisions for foreign tax paid.

It must not be overlooked that the definition of what is income under Part 4, Chapter 4 is very different from that for Chapter 3 (see below at §71.3). Section 13(1), when defining which foreign dividend income is subject to these rates of tax as opposed to the normal income tax rates, uses the Chapter 3 definition for domestic income. The dividend rates of 7.5%, 32.5% and 38.1% are also excluded if the income is taxable on a remittance basis (see below at §71.4).[43] On domestic rules, see above §64.7.

The taxation of foreign dividends accruing to a company subject to UK corporation tax is normally exempt from UK tax (see further §75.3 below).

71.2.2.9 Other Foreign Savings Income

ITA 2007, as amended for 2008 and later years, applies the 0% starting rate to domestic interest within ITTOIA 2005, Part 4, Chapter 2; the same applies to equivalent income from foreign sources.[44] There are the same exceptions for income which is charged under the remittance basis.

While the definition of 'savings income' in ITA 2007, section 18 covers many types of income from savings and investments (including purchased life annuities), it is expressly

---

[36] ITTOIA 2005, s 501, ex TA 1988, s 554(1).
[37] On definition of 'overseas land', see s 356.
[38] Formerly TA 1988, s 65A, as amended by FA 1998. See also Inland Revenue, *Inspectors' Manual*, paras 1595 *et seq.*
[39] CAA 2001, s 15 as amended by ITTOIA 2005; before ITTOIA 2005 an ordinary Sch A business and an overseas property business were specified as separate qualifying activities.
[40] Ex TA 1988, s 65A(6), (7). See above §25.3.
[41] ITA 2007, s 19(3).
[42] ITA 2007, s 16.
[43] ITA 2007, s 16(7).
[44] ITA 2007, ss 10,12 and 18.

excluded from annuities and other annual payments which are not interest, and fails to mention various payments falling within ITTOIA 2005, Part 3, Chapter 8 (ex TA 1988, section 119); these exclusions presumably apply to analogous foreign income.

71.2.2.10 Deduction for Business Travel Expenses

An individual who carries on a trade, profession or vocation wholly outside the UK but who is not taxable on a remittance basis may claim the deduction of certain travel costs.[45] The allowable expenses are those for travel by the businessman from any place in the UK to any place where the business is carried on, or from any such place to any place in the UK, and for board and lodging.[46]

These rules are similar to those introduced for ITEPA 2003.[47] The similarity is taken further in that the ITTOIA 2005 rules allow also for the deduction of the costs of travel for a spouse, civil partner and child aged under 18.[48] In these cases the taxpayer's absence from the UK must be wholly and exclusively for the purpose of performing the functions of the trade, profession or vocation or those of some other business, with apportionment between the different businesses.

Where there are two or more overseas locations, the taxpayer may deduct the cost of travel from one to the other; of the two, at least one must satisfy the rules, ie be that of a business carried on wholly outside the UK.[49] The absence from the UK must still be wholly and exclusively for the purpose of performing the functions of both activities, and the taxpayer must actually perform those functions at each location. The deduction is put against the trade carried on at the destination unless it is outside these rules, in which case the place of departure is taken instead. Where there are two businesses at the place of destination or departure, an apportionment is carried out.[50]

71.3 Characterisation of Receipts and Entities: The Role of Foreign Law

Two questions arise: (a) is a receipt income (or capital gain) for UK tax purposes; and (b) whose income is it? Both issues involve taking the legal rights and relations arising under a legal system different from that of the UK and classifying them in accordance with concepts used by UK tax law. In this process, the way in which the foreign country's tax system would treat the facts is at best of marginal relevance, although that treatment will be highly relevant to the very different question of double tax relief subsequently. The process considered here is the same as that known as 'characterisation' in the conflict of laws. The problems presented by different tax classifications of the same entity by different tax systems gave rise to planning opportunities—hence the tax arbitrage rules—above §62.7.

---

[45] ITTOIA 2005, s 92, ex TA 1988, s 80.
[46] ITTOIA 2005, s 92(3), ex TA 1988, s 80(2).
[47] See above at §13.3, but not identical, eg there is no need for separate reimbursement (because there is no one to do the reimbursing).
[48] ITTOIA 2005, ss 92(3) and 94, ex TA 1988, s 80(5)–(8).
[49] ITTOIA 2005, s 92(3)(d) and (4), ex TA 1988, s 81.
[50] ITTOIA 2005, s 93.

71.3.1 Receipts

The question whether a particular payment is income arising from a source within ITTOIA 2005 is a question for UK tax law, but that question must be determined according to the legal nature of the rights arising from the security or possession under the foreign law. In *Archer-Shee v Garland*,[51] a tenant for life was entitled under a New York trust, and the issue was whether money to which the taxpayer was entitled was income 'from stock and securities',[52] the alternative view being that a tenant for life had only a right to see that the property was correctly administered by the trustees. Under English law the former had already been held to be correct,[53] but on evidence being presented that under New York law the latter was correct, the House of Lords held that the rights of this beneficiary could not be said to be income arising 'from stocks and shares'. Since the UK tax liability turned on the nature of that foreign right, foreign trust law was relevant in determining that right.

These matters have arisen also in connection with payments by companies to shareholders. Under UK company law, the rights of shareholders are to participate in profits, to participate in assets on liquidation and to have a reduction of capital. Of these the first is income for tax purposes, but the other two are capital;[54] this treatment is mirrored in UK tax law and provides the procrustean UK categories by reference to which foreign rights will be assessed. In *Reid's Trustees v IRC*,[55] the House of Lords held that a dividend from a foreign company might be classified as income even though the equivalent payment by a UK resident company would have been taxed quite differently—as a payment of capital and so, at that time,[56] not taxed at all. Lord Reid said that this was due to a peculiarity of the system for taxing domestic dividends at that time.[57] He noted the formal point that the payment did not alter the nature of the capital asset, ie the shareholding, but added that it clearly altered its value. On the other hand, there were other ways, such as the payment of a large dividend before sale, which also lowered that value and were clearly income. He therefore concluded that if a foreign company chose to pay a dividend it was taxable income, even though paid out of capital profits.

In *Reid's Trustees* the South African company declared what was fairly obviously a dividend, and in the absence of evidence of South African law, the foreign rights were assumed to be the same as under English company law. Other cases have concerned different ways of paying shareholders. In *Rae v Lazard Investment Co Ltd*,[58] a Maryland company carried out what we now know as a demerger; it transferred a business to a subsidiary company and then transferred shares in that subsidiary to the shareholders. Under Maryland corporate law the process was called a 'distribution in partial liquidation' and was regarded as a capital

---

[51] [1931] AC 212, (1931) 15 TC 693.

[52] See Income Tax Act 1918, Sch D, Case IV, r 1.

[53] *Baker v Archer-Shee* [1927] AC 844, (1927) 11 TC 749.

[54] Buckley J in *Courtaulds Investments Ltd v Fleming* [1969] 3 All ER 1281, (1969) 46 TC 111, 124.

[55] (1949) 30 TC 431; Reid was applied by the Privy Council in *Bicber v IT Commrs* [1962] 3 All ER 294.

[56] Today it would come within CTA 2010, s 1000(1), ex TA 1988, s 209(2)(a).

[57] (1949) 30 TC 431, esp 449; a shareholder was not at that time directly assessable on a dividend paid out of profits which were not taxable in the hands of the company. Lord Reid could have added that the (pre-1965) system by which the shareholder was taxable on a dividend paid out of profits which were taxable in the hands of the company was unusual and not to be extended to foreign companies, which paid no UK tax on their profits.

[58] (1963) 41 TC 1; noted at [1963] BTR 121.

transaction. The Court of Appeal held that it was also a payment of capital for UK tax purposes. Again, in *Courtaulds Investments Ltd v Fleming*[59] the court held that a payment by way of repayment of a share premium was capital, even though under the relevant foreign law it could only be repaid out of profits accumulated in a special account. By contrast, in *Inchyra v Jennings*,[60] a direction in an American trust that a beneficiary should receive 1% of the trust capital each year was held to create annual payments[61] and so income for UK tax law.

Four lessons may be drawn:

(1)   the court rejects a purely formal approach which would simply ask whether the foreign possession was intact;[62]
(2)   the source of the payment is irrelevant;
(3)   the question 'What is the nature of the rights?' is answered using the UK three-part test where appropriate, and otherwise seeking the relevant foreign law analogy; and
(4)   the analogy of fruit and tree is unhelpful.[63]

71.3.2 Entities

The same approach is found when looking at the question whether a payment, which is clearly income for UK tax purposes, is income of A or B. The problem usually arises in connection with the distinction between companies and partnerships—income of the company being income of the company, while income of the partnership flows through to the individual partners. Of course there is the initial fact that a foreign company is not a legal entity under UK law, and so it was only by the comity of nations that it can be recognised.[64]

The issue whether a foreign entity is to be treated as a company or as a partnership for UK tax law is often described, these days, as one of 'transparency', but that simply reformulates the issue. The transparent taxation of UK partnerships is directed by ITTOIA 2005, section 849; there are special provisions on the remittance basis (section 858) and on double tax agreements (section 859). In this connection (as discussed above §20.10.7), to counteract various schemes Parliament has enacted that the members of a firm include any person entitled to a share of income of the partnership. This rule applies for income tax, corporation tax and CGT; unusually the provisions are declared always to have had effect.[65]

However, this leaves the question, what is a partnership? The problem arises in connection with foreign associations or entities which are not clearly one or the other, and the court has to determine the characteristics which make a UK association one rather than

---

[59]   [1969] 3 All ER 1281, (1969) 46 TC 111.
[60]   [1965] 2 All ER 714, (1965) 42 TC 388.
[61]   See above at §29.2. *Cf Lawson v Rolfe* [1970] 1 All ER 761, (1970) 46 TC 199; see [1970] BTR 142.
[62]   *Courtaulds v Fleming* (1969) 46 TC 111, 126.
[63]   *Ibid*, 125H; see also Lord MacDermott in *Reid Trustees v IRC* (1949) 30 TC 431, 448.
[64]   Eg Lord Hanworth in *Ryall v Du Bois* (1933) 18 TC 431, 440.
[65]   ITTOIA 2005, s 858 (4), TA 1988, s 115(5C) and TCGA 1992, s 59(4), all added by FA 2008, s [55].

the other.[66] The matter was considered in *Memec plc v IRC*.[67] Those characteristics of an English partnership, and so of transparency, are:

— no separate legal personality
— carrying on business together
— the ability of every partner to bind the firm and the other partners
— joint liability of every partner for all debts and obligations of the firm
— the fact that partners own the firm and are entitled to an undivided share of each partnership assets.

Although these characteristics have to be modified when discussing limited partnerships and Scottish partnerships, the overall idea of a partnership is reasonably clear. What is very clear is that the matter is treated as one of substance, and that the parties cannot determine the issue of transparency by the use of labels. In earlier case law the UK court held that a French *société en nom collectif* was a legal person separate from its members,[68] but this has been disavowed by the Revenue.[69] In France itself an EEIG has been characterised as a partnership and not a company.[70] The area will become one of fine distinction, and there is much to be said for the US approach which allows taxpayers to select the characterisation of their choice in borderline cases.[71]

There is no reason why a classification reached for UK domestic rules has to be applied for treaty purposes too. This may be desirable from the point of view of symmetry and elegance but is not necessary. The Revenue's long-standing view is that a US limited liability corporation (LLC) is a corporate entity and not a partnership (following US rules), but it does not accept that an LLC is a US corporation as defined in the UK–US Tax Treaty.[72] In *Anson v HMRC*,[73] the Supreme Court was asked to consider the question of whether Mr Anson was entitled to relief for US tax against his UK tax on income received from a Delaware LLC of which he was a member. Mr Anson was resident but not domiciled in the UK for UK tax purposes, and was liable to UK income tax on foreign income remitted to the UK. In accordance with its long standing practice, HMRC contended that what Mr Anson received was a distribution from the LLC, an entity, and no relief was due because the US tax was charged *on the LLC on a share of the profit* rather than *on a distribution of it*. The Supreme Court, however, agreed with Mr Anson that on the facts as found by the First-tier Tribunal the profits belonged to members as they arose. Hence Mr Anson was taxed on

---

[66] See Avery Jones *et al* [2002] BTR 375–436.
[67] [1998] STC 754, esp 764–66, *per* Peter Gibson LJ. For comment, see [1999] BTR 153; and Venables (1998) 8 *The Offshore Taxation Review* 189. In the case, M had been receiving dividends from a German subsidiary (GS) and got credit relief for the tax paid by GS's German subsidiaries. Under a new arrangement they got a better or more secure deal under German tax, but eventually lost out at the UK end because they lost the right to credits for tax paid by the subsidiaries. See also *Newstead v Frost* [1980] STC 123, (1980) 53 TC 525, HL.
[68] (1929) 14 TC 560; see esp 577–78, *per* Lord Hanworth MR.
[69] Inland Revenue, *International Tax Handbook*, para 1673. For effects of Revenue advice on borderline cases, see *R v IRC, ex parte Bishopp and ex parte Allan* [1999] STC 531.
[70] *Société Kingroup*, Conseil d'état, 4 April 1997; on treatment of Swiss general partnerships, see *Oxnard Financing SA v Rahn* [1968] 1 WLR 1465; and Kent [1999] BTR 125.
[71] Ault *et al*, 278.
[72] Fraser [2001] BTR 153; see also *Engineer v IRC* [1997] STC (SCD) 189. On such companies, see Freedman 63 *MLR* 317.
[73] [2015] UKSC 44.

the same profits in the UK as had been taxed in the US and was therefore entitled to relief under the UK–US Tax Treaty. On one view the Supreme Court decision seemed to suggest that the LLC was transparent, at least for UK income tax purposes; however, the Supreme Court did not address this question head-on, and distinguished *Memec* on the facts. HMRC quickly responded to the uncertainty raised by the decision by announcing that it planned to continue to adhere to its long-standing position on LLCs in general, but would consider claims based on *Anson* on a case-specific basis:[74]

> HMRC has after careful consideration concluded that the decision is specific to the facts found in the case. This means that where US LLCs have been treated as companies within a group struc-ture HMRC will continue to treat the US LLCs as companies, and where a US LLC has itself been treated as carrying on a trade or business, HMRC will continue to treat the US LLC as carrying on a trade or business. HMRC also proposes to continue its existing approach to determining whether a US LLC should be regarded as issuing share capital. Individuals claiming double tax relief and relying on the *Anson v HMRC* decision will be considered on a case by case basis.

For the OECD's position on the use of hybrid entities in BEPS Action 2: see above §62.7.

71.4   Remittance Basis for Relevant Foreign Income and Chargeable Gains

71.4.1 The Concept and the Basics

FA 2008 inserted Part 14, Chapter A1 into ITA 2007; this runs from section 809A to section 809Z10 and revolutionised the UK rules for the remittance basis of taxation. Chapter A1 provides one coherent and modern scheme for taxation on a remittance basis; it aligns the administrative arrangements for—and applies similar rules as to what is a remittance to—the various different types of foreign income and to capital gains (hence FIGs). It removes the rules under which Irish income could not benefit from the remittance basis.[75] It also introduced a special charge for long-term residents (LTRs), called the remittance basis charge (RBC) (see below at §71.4.7). Section 809Z10 contains interpretations. It cannot be pretended that these rules are always easy to grasp, but that is because they are a compro-mise designed to improve the remittance basis. Others may well feel that it should either have been abolished altogether or left alone. One might also note the perils for a govern-ment being bounced into a change because of a wish to trump a proposal from an opposi-tion party. For the meaning of 'domicile' and on yet more planned reforms to the income tax, CGT and IHT treatment of 'non-doms' see above §69.5.

An individual (T) is not obliged to use the remittance basis, but the consequence of not doing so is that the FIGs are taxed on an arising basis, ie whether or not remitted to the UK. If the arising basis does apply, however, T becomes entitled to the personal allow-ances set out in ITA 2007, Part 3, Chapter 2 (personal and blind person's allowances), tax

---

[74] HMRC, *Revenue and Customs Brief 15 (2015): HMRC response to the Supreme Court decision in George Anson v HMRC (2015) UKSC 44* (15 September 2015).
[75] HMRC Notes to Finance Bill, paras 99 *et seq.*

reduction as per Chapters 3 and 3A (married persons and civil partners, including partially transferrable tax allowance) or life assurance (sections 457–458) that are disallowed for those subject to the remittance basis by section 809G. Further, the annual exempt amount for CGT is not available if the remittance basis is chosen.[76]

The Revenue practice of entering into forward agreements with individual taxpayers, under which their liability to tax was agreed as a fixed sum for a certain number of years, was held to be ultra vires.[77]

FA 2009 Schedule 24 made a few changes in the light of one year's experience of the new rules, including amendments to the relevant person test in section 809M. The value of a remittance where property forming part of a larger set is remitted was redefined in the Revenue's favour (paragraph 8). There were some procedural changes to do with self-assessment (paragraphs 3 and 4). Property is now 'remitted to the UK' if used to pay interest on a debt—and not just the debt itself (paragraph 6)—and the scope of the exemption in section 809X was widened slightly (paragraph 10).

71.4.1.1 Categories of Income—or Capital Gains—Eligible for Remittance Basis Treatment

The categories of remittances which are charged to tax are set out in the legislation (see below §71.4.3).

Statute also provides rules to determine the order in which sums are to be taken to be remitted from a mixed fund (ITA 2007, section 809Q). If sums are not mixed but kept isolated and distinct, the actual source will give the answer. Usually the issue will be whether the sum remitted is or capital gain. The order is as follows:

(1) employment income (other than income within (2), (3) and (7));
(2) relevant foreign earnings (ITEPA 2003, sections 22 and 26);[78]
(3) foreign specific employment income (ITEPA 2003, section 41A);
(4) relevant foreign income (ITTOIA 2005, section 830);
(5) foreign chargeable gains (TCGA 1992, section 12);
(6) employment income subject to a foreign tax;
(7) relevant foreign income subject to a foreign tax;
(8) foreign chargeable gains subject to a foreign tax;
(9) other income or capital.

This order for remittances from a mixed fund is mandatory (see also, in relation to CGT, §74.2 below). This gives rise to a need, not so much for planning opportunities, but for caution in arranging one's affairs to avoid unnecessary charges. The (extensive) use of separate accounts may become the norm. A mixed fund may arise either because it contains different sorts of FIGs chargeable on a remittance basis, or because it contains both chargeable FIGs and non-chargeable sums.

---

[76] TCGA 1992, s 3(1A).
[77] *Al Fayed v Advocate General for Scotland* [2004] STC 1703; the judgment of the Lord Justice Clerk [2002] STC 910 contains a fascinating account of the way in which the Revenue exercised the power.
[78] Section 809Z(3).

71.4.1.2 Remittances

Where income is eligible to be taxed on a remittance basis, it is taxed only when remitted to the UK and not when it arises. The question whether the foreign income, etc has been remitted to the UK is the subject of further rules: see §71.4.6.

71.4.1.3 Exempt Remittances

In certain situations the arrival of the money or property in the UK does not cause the remittance basis to apply: see §71.4.6.3.

71.4.1.4 Migrant Exemption

ITA 2007, sections 828A–828D are designed to exempt from UK tax altogether people not wanting to use the remittance basis. The person in mind is the migrant worker employed seasonally in agriculture in the UK and other countries in the same tax year, and whose non-UK income is subject to tax where it is earned. By granting the exemption these rules remove the duty to file a self-assessment return. Relevant foreign income for the year must not exceed £10,000, and relevant foreign investment income must not exceed £100. The worker must have been liable only to basic or starting-rate income tax.

71.4.2 Using the Remittance Basis: Categories of Taxpayers

71.4.2.1 Long-term Residents

Only long-term residents (LTRs) are liable to the RBC charge. An individual is an LTR if he or she is age 18 or over and has been a UK resident for at least 7 of the last 9 tax years. So a person continuously resident in the UK since attaining the age of 10 will become an LTR on his or her 18th birthday and will be an LTR for the whole of that tax year. Such a person is required to nominate income or gains for the application of the charge: see further below at §71.4.7.

71.4.2.2 *De Minimis* (Section 809D)

A *de minimis* rule applies where C, an individual, is entitled to the remittance basis. C comes within this rule if the total of unremitted FIGs does not exceed £2,000. The *de minimis* person *is* entitled to the various allowances normally forbidden by section 809G (see §71.4.1 above). C may simply apply this basis in making the self-assessment—there is no need for a claim under section 809B.

71.4.2.3 Neither *De Minimis* Nor LTR

Such an individual (C) is entitled to use the remittance basis. If money is actually remitted, a claim must be made under section 809. C is not entitled to the various allowances forbidden by section 809G and set out at §71.4.1 above.

71.4.2.4 Claims According to the Finance Bill Notes

Section 809E is designed to ensure that an individual does not have to complete a self-assessment form if entitled to the remittance basis but no tax liability will result. So it applies where T has neither remitted foreign income nor taxable UK income—assuming that T is not an LTR.

71.4.3 FIGs

The categories of FIGs with charging provisions are set out in section 809Z7:

— relevant foreign earnings—the individual's chargeable overseas earnings as determined under ITEPA 2003, section 22 if the individual does not meet the requirements of section 26A; otherwise the individual's general earnings within section 26
— foreign specific employment income—ITEPA 2003, sections 41A, 554Z9(2), 554Z10(2) and 554Z4
— relevant foreign income—ITTOIA 2005, sections 830 and 832
— foreign chargeable gains—TCGA 1992, section 12(4).

'Relevant foreign income' categories, as set out in ITTOIA 2005, section 830, ie income accruing from a source outside the UK, are:

Part 2: Trading Profits

Part 3: Profits of Property Business

Part 4: Interest and Savings

— Chapter 2 Interest
— Chapter 4 Dividends from Non-UK Resident Company
— Chapter 7 Purchased Life Annuity Payments
— Chapter 8 Deep Gain Securities
— Chapter 13 Sales of Foreign Dividend Coupons

Part 5: Miscellaneous

— ITTOIA 2005, section 579 Royalty Payments etc from Intellectual Property
— Chapter 3 Films and Sound Recordings
— Chapter 4 Telecommunication Rights
— ITTOIA 2005, section 649 Estate Income
— Chapter 7 Annual Payments
— Chapter 8 Income Not Otherwise Charged

ITTOIA 2005, section 830(4) adds, inter alia, a list of other income treated as relevant foreign income, including a partner's share of a firm's trading income (ITA 2007, section 857(3)), a distribution by the Commonwealth Development Corporation, certain foreign pensions within ITEPA 2003, sections 575(3), 613(4), 631(3) and 635(4), and foreign social security income (ITEPA 2003, section 679(2)).

ITTOIA 2005, like TCGA 1992 (below §74.1.2), is backed up by a rule to catch temporary non-residents.[79] The purpose is to prevent avoidance. A person with unremitted foreign ITTOIA 2005 income might decide to become non-resident for a year and during that year remit all that income to the UK. Neither the arising basis nor the remittance basis

---

[79] ITTOIA 2005, s 832A, added by FA 2008.

would apply. Section 832A applies the statutory resident test (SRT) anti-avoidance rule in FA 2013, Schedule 45, Part 4 to determine when an individual is regarded as 'temporarily non-resident'. Essentially it applies where an individual having been UK resident in at least 4 out of the 7 years prior to departure is then non-resident for five years or less.

71.4.4 History of the Remittance Basis[80]

A remittance received in the UK may be exempt from UK tax under a double tax treaty.[81] Before 1914[82] all income accruing to a resident from a foreign source, ie one wholly outside the UK, was taxed on a remittance basis. In 1914 the remittance basis was replaced by the arising basis for income from stocks, shares and rents—hence the *Archer–Shee* litigation (see §71.3.1 above); this was extended in 1940[83] to a few remaining categories of investment income, such as income on foreign bank deposits and income arising to beneficiaries under foreign trusts.[84] In 1974 the remittance basis was effectively abolished for residents, although it remains of importance to those who are not domiciled in the UK or who are not ordinarily resident here.[85] When the UK abolished the Schedule E remittance basis for residents, special percentage reductions in the amount falling to be taxed (100%, 50%, 25% or 10%) were introduced; since then, reductions have in turn been removed as a result of the general lowering of tax rates. At one time a 25% percentage reduction applied to income from trades and professions.[86] The pre-2008 remittance basis was full of holes and anomalies—many are discussed in the notes to the Finance Bill 2008.

71.4.5 What must be Remitted; Pre-2008 Law—The Need for Reform

The rules in ITA 2007, Part 14, Chapter A1, added by FA 2008, determine whether there has been a remittance—and so a charge to tax—and how it is to be valued. In order to appreciate the scope of these rules it is worth just noting the pre-2008 situation first.

71.4.5.1 Alienation before Remittance

Where the remittance basis applied, the sum received had to be received as the income of the recipient in the UK; that is, it must not only have been income according to UK tax law, but must have been received in the UK by the taxpayer in whose hands it was subject to UK tax. So the remittance basis could be avoided by making sure that what was remitted was not income of the taxpayer but money belonging to another person, eg another family member to whom the one-time income was passed by way of gift. The leading case illustrating this was *Carter v Sharon*.[87] Here the taxpayer arranged for a banker's draft to be sent to

---

[80] Avery Jones, in Tiley (ed), *Studies in the History of Tax Law* (Hart Publishing, 2004), 15.

[81] *Lord Strathalmond v IRC* [1972] 3 All ER 715, (1972) 45 TC 537.

[82] FA 1914, s 5; FA 1940, s 19—as recommended by Royal Commission (1920), §27.

[83] FA 1940, s 19.

[84] Thus, undoing *Archer-Shee v Garland* (see above at §71.3.1).

[85] The restriction to Commonwealth citizens or citizens of the Republic of Ireland was removed by ITTOIA 2005 as from 6 April 2005.

[86] FA 1978, s 27, Sch 4; repealed by FA 1984, s 30. For transitional effects, see TA 1988, Schs 29, 30.

[87] [1936] 1 All ER 720, (1936) 20 TC 22; *cf Thomson v Bensted* (1918) 7 TC 137. Accepted by the CA as good law in the professional negligence case of *Grimm v Newman* [2002] EWCA Civ 1621, [2002] STC 1388. The

her daughter from California. It was shown that by Californian law the gift was complete not later than when the draft was posted; the money therefore was not a remittance of income to the taxpayer. Had the mother simply sent her daughter a cheque drawn on her California bank account, the money, when it arrived in England, would still have been taxable since it belonged to the taxpayer as she could have revoked the cheque.[88] The question of the effectiveness of the gift is judged according to the foreign law. Today this is stopped by the 'relevant person' rules, which treat a remittance by the individual or by someone in a detailed list in section 809M as a taxable remittance.

71.4.5.2 Conversion

Another line of reasoning accepted by the Revenue was that unless there was an express provision directing otherwise, the conversion of the foreign unremitted income into something else, eg an object, meant that the remittance of the object to the UK did not amount to a remittance of the original income. It followed that if foreign income was converted into a car which was then brought into the UK, no liability would arise under the remittance basis. If, however, the car were then sold, the proceeds might be taxable.[89] If, by that time, the car had been given to someone else, the proceeds might not be taxable under ITTOIA 2005.[90] Such distinctions and traps brought no credit on the system.

For income falling within ITEPA 2003, ex Schedule E, Case III, it was expressly provided[91] that emoluments shall be treated as received in the UK if—and when—they are paid, used or enjoyed in the UK, or in any manner or form transmitted or brought to the UK. The wording of this ITEPA 2003 rule was much wider, and clearly contemplates the possibility of transmission in kind, while the ITTOIA 2005 rule did not. The rule was confined to emoluments received in kind but which had not altered their form. The point remained untested by litigation.

71.4.5.3 Exporting Debt

Then there was the device under which a taxpayer, with funds overseas taxable on a remittance basis, borrowed money in the UK and the loan was then repaid from the fund overseas. The problem is whether the economic value accruing to the taxpayer results from the receipt of income in the UK or from the export of a debt from the UK. Statute intervened to widen or render certain the scope of remittance when the taxpayer is ordinarily resident in the UK.[92] However, taxpayers who were not ordinarily resident had to rely on the old case law.

Court considered the possible impact of *Harmel v Wright* [1974] STC 88 on *Carter v Sharon* but distinguished that case (paras 51–62); it also discounted any application of the *Ramsay* principle in the light of *MacNiven* (para 60).

[88] As in *Timpson's Executors v Yerbury* [1936] 1 All ER 186, (1936) 20 TC 155.

[89] In the year in which the car was sold (*Scottish Provident Institution v Farmer* (1912) 6 TC 34). On tracing, see Coles [1979] BTR 238. Other relevant cases include *Patuck v Lloyd* (1944) 26 TC 284.

[90] *Bray v Best* [1989] 1 All ER 969, [1989] STC 159, (1989) 61 TC 705, HL. This was a decision under Sch E, Case I and involved no international element; it has since been reversed by legislation (FA 1989, s 36(3)); see above at §14.1.1. The 1989 change affected what is now ITEPA 2003 but not ITTOIA 2005.

[91] ITEPA 2003, s 33(2), ex TA 1988, s 132(5).

[92] ITTOIA 2005, ss 833 and 834, ex TA 1988, s 65(6)–(9), as amended by FA 2008, Sch 7.

71.4.5.4 Source

There was the further rule that the original source had still to exist in the year in which the income was remitted. This was reversed in 1989 for what became ITEPA 2003, but not, until 2008, for ITTOIA 2005.[93]

71.4.6 *What is a Remittance? The Current Rules*

71.4.6.1 Remittances

In a turgid and hard-to-read style, the 2008 rules consign all these situations in which FIGs escaped, or have at some time escaped, liability to history. The purpose is clear: it is to keep FIGs safe from being taxed as a remittance only where they remain genuinely outside the UK.

Section 809L is a long and complicated provision, and deals with the various problems of alienation, conversion and exporting debts set out in §71.4.5 above. In form it has four conditions, (A)–(D). The receipt is taxable as a remittance if it comes within (A) and (B) and either (C) or (D) considered below. As from 6 April 2008, FIG is remitted first if money or property is brought into the UK, or received or used in the UK by or for a 'relevant person'; this is condition (A). Condition (A) then goes further and reaches a benefit consisting not of money or property but a service provided in the UK by or for a relevant person. Condition (A) specifies—and widens—the type of receipt.

Under section 809M, a person is 'relevant' if being the person with the income or gain (E), or a close relative of that person. Close relatives include spouses and civil partners (and people living together as husband and wife or civil partners). They also include children and grandchildren under 18,[94] and extend to entities related to E, such as a company in which E is a participator (whether or not a close company), or a settlement in which E is a settlor or beneficiary or a body connected with a settlement.[95] The definition of 'close company' now includes subsidiaries, and there is a new definition of 'participator'.[96] FA 2010 extended this to include certain subsidiaries of a non-resident company. It will be noted that the list of 'relevant' persons does not include children over 17. Attempts to take advantage of this situation may be vulnerable under the associated operations rule. The same is true of schemes involving parents, who are not relevant persons either. It seems that a child under 18 who marries does not cease to be a relevant person. It should also be noted that, as the result of a late change, trustees of a settlement are relevant persons only if their beneficiaries include persons relevant under other paragraphs of section 809M(2).

Condition (B) provides the link to the FIG. It is satisfied if the property—or consideration for the service—is wholly, or in part, the FIG. Condition (B) then goes on to deal with 'relevant debts'. It is also satisfied if the FIG—or anything derived from the FIG—is used outside the UK (directly or indirectly in respect of a relevant debt). Looking at what we have covered so far, a debt is relevant if it is a debt relating to the property or service mentioned above under condition (A).

---

[93] ITEPA 2003, s 30, ex FA 1989, s 36(3). The reversal seems to be by ITA 2007, ss 832 *et seq.*
[94] Child or grandchild may be of any person within ITA 2007, s 809M(2)(a)–(c).
[95] ITA 2007, s 809M(1)–(3).
[96] ITA 2007, s 809M(3)(ca).

Gift recipients.[97] Condition (C) deals with gifts (alienation). It is satisfied if qualifying property of a gift recipient is brought into the UK and enjoyed by a relevant person. The various terms are defined.[98] So a gift recipient is someone, other than a relevant person, to whom E gave the property, and it is, or represents, the FIGs. Qualifying property is the property given or derived from it.[99]

Needless to say, the rules are framed to cover not only property brought into the UK, but also property used as consideration for a service in the UK or to pay a relevant debt outside the UK.

Connected operation.[100] The final condition (D) is an alternative to (C). If the sum, etc is to be taxable as remitted FIG, it must have met conditions (A) and (B). Condition (D) applies where the property is not a qualifying property of a gift recipient (so (C) cannot apply anyway) but the property is brought into the UK and enjoyed by a relevant person in circumstances where there is a connected operation (CO). There are exceptions for full consideration or enjoyment on the same terms as the general public. There is also an exception if the property or service is enjoyed virtually to the entire exclusion of the relevant person.[101]

Connected operations are defined by section 809O. An operation is connected if effected with reference to a qualifying disposition (QD), or with a view to enabling or facilitating a QD; a QD is one made by a relevant person.[102]

71.4.6.2 Timing and Valuation

The amount remitted is governed by section 809P. Where the property or consideration caught is the foreign income or gain itself, the amount of the FIG remitted is taken. If it derives from that FIG, the value of the underlying FIG is taken, not the value of the derived property. When used to pay a relevant debt, the amount remitted is that used to pay the debt, not the value of the liability.

Further, but similar, rules apply where the remittance comes within conditions (C) and (D).[103]

The statutory list in section 809Q(4) setting out order in which sums remitted to the UK are taxed was discussed above in §71.4.1.

One curious timing provision deserves mention. Under section 809U, if the normal remittance rules give one timing outcome but a deeming provision would make it earlier, the normal timing rule prevails.

71.4.6.3 Exempt Property

Having widened the net so comprehensively, Chapter A1 then has to narrow it (sections 809V–809Z10). Section 809V excludes certain payments to HMRC where the taxpayer is a long-term UK resident. The idea is, presumably, to allow the taxpayer to pay the RBC

---

[97] ITA 2007, s 809L(4).
[98] ITA 2007, s 809N.
[99] ITA 2007, s 809N(7) and (8).
[100] ITA 2007, s 809L(5).
[101] ITA 2007, s 809O(6).
[102] ITA 2007, s 809O(3).
[103] ITA 2007, s 809(6).

charge from untaxed foreign income or gains to HMRC without incurring further liability. The HMRC notes to the Bill are very restrictive—thus the money must come direct from the overseas account to HMRC, whether by cheque or electronic transfer, and not via UK bank account.

Sections 809VA-809VO provide an exemption for money or other property used to make qualifying business investments. Another exemption, section 809W, a late addition to the Bill, deals with sum used to pay for certain services relating to property outside the UK, eg legal fees. The sums must be paid to a bank account outside the UK.

Property, defined so as to exclude money (section 809Z6), will be exempt even though brought into the UK or used in the UK if it satisfies one of three tests. The link provision in section 809X provides the exemption, which sets out the categories of exempt property and gives references to the detailed rules. Property ceasing to satisfy these tests—whether because it breaches the conditions or is sold—is treated as remitted (section 809U). The categories are:

(1) *Property consisting of works of art or collector's pieces.* Such property will be exempt if meeting a public access test (section 809Z). Normally the property must be in a museum or gallery, in storage at such a place or in transit from such a place between there and outside the UK. Normally the work must be on public display, but this is softened to being available on request for works which are too fragile. Works on public display in connection with their sale also qualify for this rule. However, a charge will arise if the property is actually sold in the UK (section 809U(3)).

(2) *Personal use items.* Clothing, footwear, jewellery and watches derived from relevant foreign income will be exempt if they meet a personal use rule (section 809Z2).

(3) *Temporary presence.* Property of any kind will be exempt if it meets a rule for repairs (section 809Z3) or more generally the temporary importation rule (section 809Z4); the latter uses the concept of 275 'countable days'. Days on which the property meets the rules for personal use or repair are not countable days; further conditions apply where public access is in issue (section 809Z4).

Finally, sections 809Z8 and 809Z9 provide further guidance on the meaning of disposal proceeds and when something is taken offshore.

71.4.6.4 Exception Interest on Grandfathered Loans

It has been common for a person, T, wanting to buy property in the UK to borrow money from abroad. If the loan were made in the UK, T would need to pay interest and, in due course, pay off the capital, eg out of FIGs. Before FA 2008 the UK tax treatment of a payment to the bank by T would depend on whether it was to pay interest or repay capital. A repayment of capital was treated as being remitted income or gain, while a payment of interest was not.

The FA 2008 changes abolished this distinction, and so a transitional clause (119) was added. No charge arises where the loan was made before 12 March 2008 with the sole purpose of enabling the individual to buy a residential property in the UK. The money lent has to be received in the UK and used to acquire the property before 6 April 2008. Repayment of the debt must be secured on the property. In the circumstances, interest payment will not be treated as remittance—for the period of the loan or until 2028 if sooner. Any variation of the terms of the loan or any further loan will cause the exception to end forthwith—unless the new terms would satisfy these rules.

71.4.7 Special Rules for Long-term Residents

The remittance basis charge—or RBC—applies if T (a) is an individual resident in the UK and is 18 or over in that year, and (b) has been resident for:[104]

(1)   at least 7 of the last 9 tax years (the '7 year residence test),
(2)   at least 12 of the last 14 tax years (the '12 year residence test), or
(3)   at least 17 of the last 20 tax years (the '17 year residence test).

Section 809C directs that T must nominate an amount of unremitted offshore income or gains which will be subject to the charge. The amount of the charge depends on which residence test applies, so is:[105]

(1)   £30,000 for a 7 year resident,
(2)   £60,000 for a 12 year resident, and
(3)   £90,000 for a 17 year resident.

The point of nominating—or identifying—these FIGs is that when in a later year those identified income or gains are actually remitted to the UK, they will not be taxed again. However, it is not quite as simple as that. If in the later year there are FIGS which have *not* been nominated (and so not taxed in the UK by the RBC), any sums received in the UK will be attributed first to untaxed—and so now taxable—FIGs; only when the untaxed FIGs are exhausted will the sums be attributed to the nominated FIGs.[106] In view of these rules, it is not surprising that section 809C(4) directs that the nominated income or gains must not be such that tax on the relevant FIGs exceeds £30,000/£60,000/£90,000.

When the nomination is made, the effect of this is laid out by section 809H(2) and (3)—the technicalities make the sum due (on the nominated income or gains) taxable on an arising basis. So for a 7 year resident, where the amount of tax due would be £30,000 or more, the £30,000 ceiling applies.[107] If the income tax due on the nominated income or gains is less than £30,000, the tax system increases the liability to £30,000 anyway.[108] The only way to avoid the charge is not to be taxed on the remittance basis for that year—ie to be taxed on all income or gains, whether or not remitted.

The £30,000/£60,000/£90,000 payment is a payment of income tax or, if the nominated profits are capital gains, CGT. It follows that it may be used for gift aid purposes under UK tax law.[109] It should also be recognised by a foreign tax system as such a payment, and so be

---

[104] ITA 2007, s 809C.
[105] ITA 2007, s 809C(4) and (5).
[106] ITA 2007, s 809H—the full order is in s 809I.
[107] ITA 2007, s 809G(2) and (3)
[108] ITA 2007, s 809G(4) and (5).
[109] ITA 2007, s 809H(2).

available for credit or other double taxation relief purposes; this is, initially at least, a question for the foreign tax system.

71.5 Reliefs for Unremittable (Stranded) Foreign Income

UK income and corporation tax may be postponed where income taxed on an arising basis, whether in full or on a reduced sum, cannot be remitted, whether because of laws, executive action or the impossibility of obtaining foreign currency, and the taxpayer has not realised the income outside the territory for a consideration either in sterling or in a currency which might be converted into sterling.[110] Impossible means that it is impossible to obtain currency which may be transferred to the UK.[111] In view of this redefinition of impossibility, it is not clear whether the export to the UK of an object paid for with the foreign currency will end the relief before it is sold. The consequences of spending the income within the foreign country are also unclear. Taxpayers must show that they were not able to remit it. When this can no longer be shown, they, or their estates, become liable to income tax or corporation tax,[112] which will be assessed by reference to the year in which it first arose. There are specific rules for valuing the unremittable income.[113]

71.6 Anti-avoidance: Transfers of Assets Abroad— Attribution of Income for Income Tax

71.6.1 Introduction

71.6.1.1 Overview

This is a difficult area, not least because, as has been said, no argument has been too esoteric for the Revenue to pursue in administering these rules.[114] The taxation of residents, coupled with the non-taxation of non-residents, might encourage residents to arrange for income which would otherwise come to them to be held by non-residents, and especially by such artificial entities as trusts.[115] Legislation was introduced in 1936[116]—now found in ITA 2007, Part 13, Chapter 2, sections 714 to 751—to counter devices whereby assets would be transferred to persons abroad, ie resident or domiciled outside the UK, in whose hands the income would not be subject to UK tax, and where some benefit of that income

---

[110] ITTOIA 2005, Pt 8, Ch 4 and CTA 2009, Pt 3, Ch 12 (trading income) and Pt 18, ex TA 1988, s 584, originally FA 1953, s 21; on which see Royal Commission on the Taxation of Profits and Income, First Report, Cmnd 8761 (1952). Distinguish the situation where the income, although due, has not been paid.

[111] ITTOIA 2005, s 841(3)(c); Explanatory Notes Change.

[112] For corporation tax a slightly different rule applies and it is treated as income when the conditions no longer apply: CTA 2009, s 175 (for trading income) and s 1276 (ex TA 1988, s 585(2A)).

[113] ITTOIA 2005, s 845, based on TA 1988, s 585(8).

[114] Ashton [1990] BTR 251 at 252; see also Boyd [1980] BTR 442 on history of early cases.

[115] Eg *Astor v Perry* [1935] AC 398, (1935) 19 TC 255.

[116] FA 1936, s 18; for debates on clause, see *Whiteman on Income Tax*, 3rd edn (Sweet & Maxwell, 2008), §§23.03 *et seq.*

would or might accrue to the original resident. In this legislation references to individuals include references to their spouse or civil partner, but not to cohabitees.[117] The term 'person abroad' (to whom the property is transferred) is defined in ITA 2007, section 718 as meaning a person either resident or domiciled outside the UK.[118] The legislation applies only for income tax; corporation tax has more far-reaching rules for CFCs, considered in chapter seventy-three below. However, the presence of a CFC may reduce the charge under the first head of charge.[119]

In 2011, the European Commission formally requested the UK to amend these rules, which it viewed as contrary to EU Treaty fundamental freedoms, namely the freedom of establishment and free movement of capital. This led to the enactment of a uniquely-tailored exemption in ITA 2007, section 742A for 'genuine transactions' effected on or after 6 April 2012 where liability to tax would 'constitute an unjustified and disproportionate restriction' on those freedoms.

There are three heads of charge, of which the first two go back to 1936. These two impose a charge on the transferor and are:

(1)   the receipt of a benefit derived from a power to enjoy the income;[120] or
(2)   the receipt of a capital sum.[121]

The third head of charge was added in 1981 and applies to:

(3)   certain non-transferors who receive a benefit as a result of 'relevant transactions'.[122]

FA 2008, in its revolution of the remittance basis, made changes to the remittance rules in relation to each head of charge. The purpose is to ensure that the taxpayer may claim the benefit of the remittance basis in the same circumstances as if the payment had been received direct, while taking full account of the new remittance rules which allow the payments to remain untaxed only so long as they remain genuinely offshore.[123]

Each head will cause the UK tax system to attribute the income accruing to the person abroad to the UK resident. It is not necessary for the transferor to receive the income.[124] These rules have given rise to major issues of statutory construction.[125] In particular, they were given a very wide construction on one aspect by the House of Lords in *Congreve v IRC* in 1945.[126] This was reversed in 1979 by the House of Lords in *Vestey v IRC*.[127] Many cases between 1945 and 1979, giving a wide construction to other parts of these rules, have cited

---

[117]   ITA 2007, s 714(4).
[118]   ITA 2007, s 718; for trusts and estates, see s 718(2).
[119]   But see ITA 2007, s 725, ex TA 1988, 474(4).
[120]   ITA 2007, s 720, ex TA 1988, s 739(2).
[121]   ITA 2007, s 727, ex TA 1988, s 739(3).
[122]   ITA 2007, s 731, ex TA 1988, s 740).
[123]   HMRC Notes to Sch 7, para 88; the provisions changed and strengthened are ss 726, 730 and 735, backed up by s 735A.
[124]   See Carswell LJ in *IRC v McGuckian* [1994] STC 888, 916; (1994) 69 TC 1, 41, CA (NI).
[125]   See also *Revenue Bulletin*, Issue 40, [1999] *Simon's Weekly Tax Intelligence* 829.
[126]   [1945] 1 All ER 945, 30 TC 163.
[127]   [1980] AC 1145, [1980] STC 10, 54 TC 503; see Sumption [1980] BTR 4, reversing the earlier House of Lords decision in *Congreve v IRC* [1945] 1 All ER 945, 30 TC 163. On the scope of the *Vestey* decision, see Venables (1991) 1 *The Offshore Tax Planning Review* 19.

Congreve as part of their background reasoning. *Vestey* has not stopped the Revenue from taking strong positions in such litigation on section 739, eg in *IRC v Willoughby* in 1997.[128] The *Vestey* case held that the first two heads of charge applied only where the person with the power to enjoy the income or who had received the capital sum was the transferor (or spouse or civil partner).[129] The primary reason for this decision was the absence of any provision in the section whereby the income of the foreign entity could appropriately be attributed to the beneficiaries, and reluctance on the part of the court to allow that attribution to be carried out simply by Revenue discretion. Similarly, in *IRC v Pratt*,[130] the court held that these rules did not apply to multiple transfers if the respective interests of the assets transferred could not be separated and clearly identified. The rules in ITA 2007, sections 731–733 are designed to fill the resulting gap by making persons other than the transferor liable when—and to the extent that—they receive a benefit which is not otherwise chargeable to income tax. To meet the objections of the judges, further rules allow HMRC to allocate the charges.[131]

71.6.1.2 The First Head of Charge—Power to Enjoy Income

ITA 2007, section 720 applies where there has been a transfer of assets, and charges: (a) any individual[132] who (b) has, by virtue of the transfer or any associated operations, (c) the power to enjoy income which (d) in consequence of the transfer (e) becomes that of a person abroad. Such income is deemed to be that of the person with the power to enjoy and is taxed under the relevant parts of ITTOIA 2005—previously under Schedule D, Case VI.[133] It is in this context that the decision of the House of Lords in *IRC v McGuckian*,[134] characterising as income a sum received for the sale of a right to a dividend, assumes its importance. In *IRC v Brackett*,[135] the concept of income becoming payable to a non-resident was held to include the profits of a non-resident trader. This decision involved a tax haven company employing an individual resident in the UK but not domiciled in the UK, and so potentially able to use the remittance basis.

Under the first head there is a special rule where the benefits are provided out of the income of a person abroad; here there will be a charge on the value of the benefit received, except to the extent that the individual has been taxed already.[136]

The elements of this head of charge are considered further below at §71.6.2.

71.6.1.3 The Second Head of Charge—Capital Sum

ITA 2007, section 727 applies where there is a transfer of assets and, whether before or after the transfer, a UK-resident individual receives a capital sum. This sum must be connected

---

[128] [1997] STC 995.
[129] ITA 2007, s 714(4).
[130] [1982] STC 756, 57 TC 1.
[131] ITA 2007, s 743, ex TA 1988, s 744.
[132] Ie the transferor or spouse or civil partner, but not a widow (*Vestey's Executors v IRC* [1949] 1 All ER 1108, (1949) 31 TC 1).
[133] ITA 2007, s 735(3)(4), ex TA 1988, s 743(1)–(1B).
[134] [1997] STC 908, (1997) 69 TC 1; see above at §5.6.4. For comment, see Venables (1997) 7 *The Offshore Taxation Review* 69.
[135] [1986] STC 521, 60 TC 134.
[136] See Ashton [1990] BTR 251.

with the transfer and be either (a) a sum paid or payable by way of loan,[137] or (b) any other sum paid or payable otherwise than as income and which is not paid or payable for full consideration in money or money's worth. Thus, this does not apply where a resident simply sells assets for full market value to a non-resident.

'Capital sum' is widened by section 729(4) to cover sums paid to third parties at the direction of the individual or by assignment from him, and sums received jointly. Where there is a capital sum as defined, the income accruing from the assets to the person abroad is treated by section 727 as that of the individual who received the capital sum. It will be noticed that tax under this section is not limited to the capital sum[138] but goes on forever— or at least for the duration of the life of the individual, or so long as income accrues to the person abroad. All that is required is a capital sum connected with the transfer.

71.6.1.4 The Third Head of Charge: Benefit Received by Non-Transferor

Where a non-transferor receives a benefit as a result of a relevant transaction, tax cannot be charged under the first two heads but is charged instead under ITA 2007, section 731. There must be a relevant transfer and the receipt of a benefit by a UK-resident individual. The charge arises to the extent that the receipt falls within 'relevant income'.[139] 'Relevant income' is income accruing to a person abroad and which may, by virtue or in consequence of the transfer or associated operations, be used directly or indirectly for providing a benefit for the individual.[140] The benefit must be provided out of assets available for the purpose as a result of the transfer or one or more associated operations. The allocation system in section 733 requires a comparison of (a) the total untaxed benefits, and (b) the available relevant income. The income arising which is to be charged under section 733 is the smaller of (a) and (b).[141] ITA 2007, section 735 provides a limited role for the remittance basis if the individual receiving the benefit is not domiciled in the UK; this was amended by FA 2008.[142]

Thus, as with section 720, there must be an initial transfer of assets, either alone or in conjunction with associated operations, and, as a result, income must become payable to a person abroad. Further, the person chargeable must be an individual resident in the UK. Also like section 720, various supporting provisions, including ITA 2007, sections 748–749 on information powers, are made expressly applicable (discussed below at §71.6.2). In addition, the general defences such as an innocent purpose apply to section 731. The payment may also include a capital gains element; on interaction, see below at §74.5.4.

71.6.1.5 No Tax Avoidance Purpose Tests

Under a test inserted by FA 2006, and applying to transactions on or after 5 December 2005, none of the above provisions will apply if the individual meets an interesting test based on objective factors, viz that it would not be reasonable to draw the conclusion, from all the circumstances of the case, that the purpose of avoiding liability to taxation was the purpose

---

[137] Unless wholly repaid before the beginning of the year (ITA 2007, s 729(2), ex TA 1988, s 739(6)). Leaving money outstanding on a purchase is not a loan (*Ramsden v IRC* (1957) 37 TC 619).

[138] *Vestey v IRC* [1980] AC 1145, [1980] STC 10, (1980) 54 TC 503.

[139] ITA 2007, ss 731–733, ex TA 1988, s 740(2).

[140] ITA 2007, s 718(1) and 733(1), ex TA 1988, s 740(3).

[141] ITA 2007, s 724, ex TA 1988, s 743(5).

[142] ITA 2007, s 735, replaced by FA 2008 as ss 735 and 735A.

or one of the purposes for which the relevant transaction or any of them was effected.[143] There is an alternative test under which all the relevant transactions were genuine commercial transactions, ie effected in the course of trade or business and for its purposes (the test also applied to a transaction with a view to setting up a trade or business). There is also an arm's-length test. 'Tax' means any revenue within the ambit of HMRC's responsibilities and 'revenue' means taxes, duties and NICs.[144] Foreign taxes are therefore not within the definition.

An older test still applies where transactions were carried out before 5 December 2005.[145] Here the person must show[146] to the satisfaction of an officer of HMRC that: (a) the purpose of avoiding tax liability was not the purpose or one of the purposes[147] for which the transfer or associated operations were made; or (b) that the transfer was a bona fide commercial transaction and not designed for the purpose of avoiding liability to taxation.[148] This was one of the first legislative attempts at an anti-avoidance clause; later clauses prefer references to objects over those to purposes.[149] The test of purpose is subjective.[150] Although the purpose test provides a defence to a charge under these rules, one cannot turn that round and say that the presence of a tax avoidance motive is a condition precedent to their applying.[151]

In *IRC v Willoughby*,[152] Lord Nolan said that it would be absurd to describe as tax avoidance the acceptance of an offer of freedom from tax which Parliament had deliberately made. A UK resident might opt not to own investments directly but to profit from the investments through the medium of the personal portfolio bond. The former would be liable to income tax at both basic and higher rates on the income from the investments, and also to CGT on chargeable gains realised on disposal. The latter, under the tax regime applicable to overseas life policies, would pay no tax on the income or capital gains until the maturity of the bond or the occurrence of one of the other specified chargeable events. Taking the option so offered was not tax avoidance.[153]

This pre-5 December 2005 test of purpose is applied only to the transfer in question, ie the one which conferred on the taxpayer the power to enjoy the income of the person abroad or the capital sum. It is not clear whether a subsequent tax-induced associated operation may infect the initial transfer.[154] Taxation includes taxes other than income tax, eg death duties,[155] but, it appears, not foreign taxes.[156] The burden is on the taxpayer to bring

[143] ITA 2007, s 738, ex TA 1988, s 741A(5)–(7).
[144] ITA 2007, s 737(7).
[145] ITA 2007, ss 739 (all relevant transactions before 5 December 2005) and 740 (some transactions before that date), ex TA 1988, ss 741A–741C, added by FA 2006.
[146] On importance of burden of proof on the taxpayer, see *Philippi v IRC* [1971] 3 All ER 61, 47 TC 75.
[147] The 1936 test was one of the 'main purposes', but this was amended in 1938; contrast, eg ITA 2007, s 685, ex TA 1988, s 703 and TCGA 1992, s 30.
[148] ITA 2007, ss 739(2)–(4), and 751, ex TA 1988, s 741.
[149] See Avery Jones [1983] BTR 9, esp 18–30, arguing that they are the same; see also [1983] BTR 113.
[150] *A Beneficiary v IRC* [1999] STC (SCD) 134.
[151] *Carvill v IRC* [2002] EWHC 1488; [2002] STC 1167.
[152] [1997] STC 995.
[153] *IRC v Willoughby* [1997] STC 995, 1001–02, per Lord Nolan; the question whether the transaction came within (b) as a bona fide commercial transaction was deliberately left open.
[154] See *IRC v Herdman* [1969] 1 All ER 495, 45 TC 394.
[155] *Sassoon v IRC* (1943) 25 TC 154.
[156] *IRC v Herdman* [1969] 1 All ER 495, (1969) 45 TC 394.

the facts within the defence. There is no formal clearance procedure. Under self-assessment the taxpayer must disclose any income or benefit assessable under these rules and whether reliance is placed on the purpose defence.[157] A court looking for a person's purpose is entitled to look at what he did subsequently.[158]

71.6.2 Elements

71.6.2.1 Transfer of Assets

For all three heads of charge there must be a transfer of assets or operations associated with the transfer.[159] Further, the income accruing to the person abroad must accrue by virtue of, or in consequence of, that transfer or those operations.[160] It is not necessary that the income should come from the transferred assets. The situs of the assets is unimportant. The term 'asset' is defined to include property or rights of any kind.[161] It has been construed in a way similar to that for CGT, and so includes rights under a contract of employment.[162] The term 'transfer' is defined to include the creation of rights or property.[163]

71.6.2.2 Connecting Factors

The transferee must be either not resident or not domiciled in the UK when the income accrues, so disregarding questions of residence when the transfer is made.[164] Whether ITA 2007, section 718 applies if the transferor becomes resident in the UK only after the transfer is not completely clear, but it is unlikely that it does.[165] They clearly do apply whether or not the particular individual, ie the one with the power to enjoy or in receipt of a capital sum, was resident in the UK at the time of the transfer.[166]

71.6.2.3 Associated Operations

The associated operations may be by the transferor, or the transferee or any other person.[167] The scope of an 'associated operation' is widely defined in ITA 2007, section 719 as operations of any kind affected by any person in relation to any of the assets, or income or assets representing those assets or that income. Thus, the transfer of shares or a partnership to a company,[168] taking up residence or domicile overseas,[169] an exchange of debentures[170]

---

[157] Revenue Interpretation (April 1999).

[158] Salmon LJ in *Philippi v IRC* (1971) 47 TC 75, 113–14.

[159] Now defined by ITA 2007, ss 715–719.

[160] See *Vestey's Executors v IRC* [1949] 1 All ER 1108, 31 TC 1; and see below §71.6.4.

[161] ITA 2007, s 717, ex TA 1988, s 742(9)(b).

[162] *IRC v Brackett* [1986] STC 521, 60 TC 134.

[163] ITA 2007, s 716(2), ex TA 1988, s 742(9)(b).

[164] *Congreve v IRC* [1946] 2 All ER 170, 30 TC 163.

[165] But in pre-(1980) *Vestey* days a person within s 739(2) who acquired UK ordinary residence after the transfer was caught (*IRC v Herdman* [1969] 1 All ER 495, 45 TC 394). For discussion, see Venables (1991) 1 *The Offshore Tax Planning Review* 19.

[166] ITA 2007, s 718, ex TA 1988, s 739(1A)(a); added 1997 to reverse, in part, *IRC v Willoughby* [1997] STC 995.

[167] Eg *Lord Chetwode v IRC* [1977] STC 64, [1977] 1 All ER 638.

[168] *Latilla v IRC* [1943] 1 All ER 265, (1943) 25 TC 107.

[169] *Congreve v IRC* [1946] 2 All ER 170, (1946) 30 TC 163.

[170] *Earl Beatty's Executors v IRC* (1940) 23 TC 574.

and the making of a will,[171] have all been held to be associated operations; mere inactivity resulting in intestate succession is not.[172] The issue of debentures may be associated with an acquisition of rights.[173]

71.6.2.4 Power to Enjoy (First Head Only)

Under the first head—and only under that head—there has to be a power to enjoy income. This requirement is satisfied if any of the following sets of circumstances exists:[174]

(1) The income is in fact so dealt with by any person as to be calculated, at some point of time and whether or not in the form of income, to enure for the benefit of the individual (whom we will call A). 'So dealt with' denotes some element of dealing;[175] something passive, such as retention and investment of income for future use, may qualify.[176]

(2) The receipt or accrual of the income operates to increase the value to A of assets held by A or for A's benefit. The income need not be received by the transferor, but it must increase the value of the transferor's assets, as where assets were transferred to a non-resident company in return for promissory notes; income subsequently accruing to the company increased the value of the notes.[177] Similarly, where a vendor transferred shares to a company but left the purchase money outstanding, it was held that he had the power to enjoy the income accruing to the company in the form of dividends, since the income of the company increased by the value of the right to recover the debt.[178] This seems open to question, at least where the company could always meet its obligations—but the legislation directs attention to substance not form (see below).

(3) A receives or is entitled to receive, at any time, any benefit provided or to be provided out of that income, or out of moneys that are or will be available for the purpose by reason of the effect or successive effects of the associated operations on that income and on any assets which directly or indirectly represent that income. This turns on actual receipt or entitlement to receipt by the transferor. The possession of shares in a company gives a right to any dividends that may be declared.[179] There is some doubt whether loans fall within this rule.[180] In *IRC v Brackett*,[181] the benefits provided included the provision of liquidity through the purchase of assets the taxpayer could not otherwise dispose of easily, the provision of money for repairs he could not otherwise afford and the payment of money in discharge of his moral obligations. These were held sufficient. Where liability arises under this head, the extent of liability is

---

[171] *Bambridge v IRC* [1955] 3 All ER 812, 36 TC 313.
[172] *Bambridge v IRC* (1955) 36 TC 313, 328, *per* Jenkins LJ.
[173] *Corbett's Executrices v IRC* [1943] 2 All ER 218, 25 TC 305.
[174] ITA 2007, s 723, ex TA 1988, s 742(2).
[175] Lord Simonds in *Lord Vestey's Executors v IRC* [1949] 1 All ER 1108, 31 TC 1.
[176] *IRC v Botnar* [1999] STC 711, 727 (para. 33).
[177] See *Lord Howard de Walden v IRC* [1942] 1 KB 389, (1942) 25 TC 121.
[178] *Ramsden v IRC* (1957) 37 TC 619; *Earl Beatty's Executors v IRC* (1940) 23 TC 574.
[179] *Lee v IRC* (1941) 24 TC 207.
[180] See Lord Normand in *Lord Vestey's Executors v IRC* [1949] 31 TC 1, 90.
[181] [1986] STC 521.

probably limited to the value of the benefit received and does not extend to the whole of the income accruing to the transferee.[182]

(4)	A may, in the event of the exercise or successive exercise of one or more powers by whomsoever exercisable and whether with or without the consent of any other persons, become entitled to the beneficial enjoyment of the income. This is designed to apply where foreign trustees of a discretionary trust own shares in an overseas company controlled by persons other than the trustees. The term 'power' is undefined and therefore unlimited, save that it means something other than rights that come from pure dominion over the property.[183] The income which accrued to B will almost certainly have ceased to have that character before it reaches A; there is no rule of law which requires it still to have the character at that time.[184]

(5)	A is able in any manner whatsoever, and whether directly or indirectly, to control the application of the income. For this, it will be noted, there is no need for the control to be for A's own benefit. It has, however, been held that a right to control investments is not a right to control the application of the income. Control of a company gives control over income through control over the directors.[185] However, the donee of a special power of appointment among a defined and ascertainable group of persons does not have the power required for this head,[186] a decision since extended to the donee of an intermediate power, that is a power to appoint among the whole world subject to the exclusion of a defined class of persons which included the donee.[187] Where a settlor has a power to appoint and remove trustees, it should not be assumed that the trustees will disregard their fiduciary duties and simply act as the settlor directs.[188]

As if (1)–(5) were not wide enough, it is further provided that when these tests are applied, regard is to be had to the substantial results and effects of the transfer or the operations, and all benefits accruing as a result of the transfer are to be taken into account regardless of the nature or form of the benefits and whether or not the individual had any rights.[189] This clause was intended to counteract the Cayman Islands legislation[190] reducing the legal character of interests of beneficiaries under trusts subject to Cayman Island law to that of *mere spes* or chance.

In determining whether a person has this power, the terms of any relevant instrument must be construed to ascertain their true legal effect; thus, if a person apparently able to exercise a power in his own favour would find such an appointment barred by the doctrine of fraud on a power, there is no power to enjoy under this head. The fact that the resident has no power to enjoy the income of the transferee is not conclusive. One must ask whether

---

[182]	*IRC v Botnar* [1999] STC 711, 731 (paras 52–53).
[183]	*Ibid*, 729 (para. 40).
[184]	*Ibid*, 730 (para 45).
[185]	*Lee v IRC* (1941) 24 TC 207.
[186]	*Vestey's Executors v IRC* [1949] 1 All ER 1108.
[187]	*IRC v Schroder* [1983] STC 450, 57 TC 94.
[188]	*Ibid*.
[189]	ITA 2007, s 722, ex TA 1988, s 742(3).
[190]	*IRC v Botnar* [1998] STC 38, 41; this was reversed on appeal but on a different construction of the terms of the trust ([1999] STC 711).

A has the power to enjoy any income of any person; thus, control over the transferee is sufficient.[191]

HMRC officers have the most extensive power to demand information in applying this section, both from the transferor and from any other person.[192] There is some protection for lawyers[193] and bankers.[194]

71.6.3 The Charge

Under the first head the whole of the income of the person abroad may be treated as that of the transferor, even though the 'power to enjoy' does not extend so far.[195] Logically, this should extend to all income, whether or not from the assets transferred; but in practice the Revenue appear to take a less exacting line. Under the second head the Revenue treat as taxable only the income of the person abroad derived from the transfer or associated operations.[196] As already seen, where the individual is not domiciled in the UK a remittance basis is used—where the third head applies.[197]

ITA 2007, section 731 charges on a different basis—by reference to the benefit received to the extent that it falls within relevant income.[198] 'Relevant income' is income accruing to a person abroad and which may, by virtue or in consequence of the transfer or associated operations, be used directly or indirectly for providing a benefit for the individual.[199] The section then proceeds along lines similar to ITTOIA 2005, section 641 (see above at §31.6). To the extent that the benefit falls within the amount of relevant income up to and including that year, it is taxable as income of the individual. If the benefit should exceed that income, it is carried forward and may be made liable to tax in later years by reason of the existence of relevant income in those later years.[200] Where the person is not domiciled in the UK, a remittance basis is applied.[201] There is no charge if the benefit is not received in the UK. On a literal interpretation, a benefit received abroad and later brought to the UK escapes charge as it is not received in the UK.

These rules are deeming provisions and the courts will not allow one to deem too far, especially if this would mean that a person they deem fraudulent would otherwise escape prison. In *R v Dimsey* and *R v Allen*,[202] the accused had been found guilty of cheating the public revenue by committing certain offences in relation to the profits of companies liable to, but not declared for, corporation tax. Under these rules the profits of the companies

---

[191] *Earl Beatty's Executors v IRC* (1940) 23 TC 574, 590.

[192] ITA 2007, s 748(1), (2), ex TA 1988, s 745(1); eg *Clinch v IRC* [1973] 1 All ER 977, 49 TC 52.

[193] ITA 2007, ss 748(4) and 749(1)–(5), ex TA 1988, s 745(3).

[194] ITA 2007, s 750, ex TA 1988, s 745(4); strictly construed in *Royal Bank of Canada v IRC* [1972] 1 All ER 225, 47 TC 565.

[195] The Revenue view derives some support from the now overruled decision in *Congreve v IRC* [1945] 1 All ER 945, 954; (1945) 30 TC 163, 199, *per* Cohen LJ.

[196] *Whiteman and Wheatcroft on Income Tax*, 2nd edn (Sweet & Maxwell, 1976) §§19.57–19.59.

[197] ITA 2007, ss 726 and 730, ex TA 1988, s 743(3).

[198] ITA 2007, s 731, ex TA 1988, s 740(2).

[199] ITA 2007, s 733(1), ex TA 1988, s 740(3).

[200] ITA 2007, s 732, ex TA 1988, s 740(2).

[201] ITA 2007, s 735, ex TA 1988, s 740(5).

[202] [2001] UK HL 46, [2001] STC 1520 and also [2001] UK HL 45, [2001] STC 1537. On the Court of Appeal's consideration, see Morgan [2001] BTR 13 regarding the problem of double taxation.

could have been taxed to another person, and so the accused argued that there was no tax liability on the companies and so no criminal liability on their part. The judges reasoned that, although these rules deemed the income of the foreign entity to be that of someone else, it did not follow that it ceased to be the income of the foreign entity. The risk of double taxation was thought to be too unrealistic to worry about.[203]

The income caught is that 'which becomes payable' to the non-resident, and the House of Lords has held that no deduction may be made for the non-resident's management charges.[204] Expenses of collection are allowable, as are deductions and reliefs that would be allowed if the individual had received the amount.[205]

To prevent double charges, section 743 provides that no amount of income may be charged more than once under these rules. The problem arises, for example, if the transferor who has a power to enjoy then receives a benefit. In such circumstances, the Revenue attribute the income as appears to them just and reasonable. This is one of several Revenue decisions under this Chapter specifically made reviewable by the Tribunal (section 751).

There is also a provision (section 747) governing the interaction of these rules with those on accrued income profits under ITA 2007, Part 12, Chapter 2 (see above §26.4).

71.6.4 Limitations

ITA 2007, section 718 is not completely unlimited:

(1)   The provision applies only where the power to enjoy income or the receipt of a capital sum or of a benefit rests in or accrues to an individual. Intermediaries, such as UK trusts and companies, are not individuals, although, of course, transfers by such bodies may be associated with earlier or later transfers by individuals.

(2)   The income must accrue to the person abroad in consequence of the transfer or the associated operations. In *Fynn v IRC*,[206] an individual had a right to demand repayment of a loan from a foreign company which he had set up. He also had a charge on the company's assets. It was held that he had no power to enjoy the income accruing to the company in consequence of the charging of the assets of the company.

(3)   The section applies only where the individual is UK resident for the tax year.

(4)   All three heads are limited to situations where income accrues to the person abroad. Investment of assets transferred abroad so that no income is produced therefore avoids these provisions.[207] The question whether a particular receipt is income is presumably to be decided by UK tax law in the light of the rights and duties arising under the foreign law.[208]

---

[203] See Lord Scott in *R v Allen* [2001] STC 1520, [57].

[204] *Lord Chetwode v IRC* [1977] STC 64, [1977] 1 All ER 638; on the meaning of 'payable', see also *Latilla v IRC* [1943] 1 All ER 265, 25 TC 107.

[205] ITA 2007, s 746, TA 1988, s 743(2).

[206] [1958] 1 All ER 270, 37 TC 629.

[207] For CGT anti-avoidance provisions, see below at §74.3.

[208] See above at §71.3. On 'disguised interest' see ITTOIA 2005, Part 4, Chapter 2A. On inclusion of guaranteed returns on transactions in futures and options, see ex ITTOIA 2005, s 569, ex TA 1988, Sch 5AA, para 8, inserted by FA 1997, Sch 11, extended to options by FA 1998, s 97.

72

Source: The Non-resident and the
UK Tax System

72.1 Introduction

The taxation of the non-resident on income[1] arising in the UK is governed by three sets of rules:

(1) rules embodying the doctrine of the source: these limit but do not deny the non-UK resident's liability to income arising in the UK;
(2) rules providing for 'default' tax rates (basic, higher and additional) on most forms of income of non-UK residents; and
(3) rules requiring a person paying the income to the non-UK resident to withhold tax.

The effect of these rules may be modified by applicable double tax treaty rules (see chapter seventy-six below). There are other administrative rules defining the ways in which the non-resident may be made liable for the tax, and especially when the tax may be collected from the non-resident's UK agent (see below at §72.6).

The changes to the tax treatment of non-resident companies made by FA 2000 were designed to go some way to equating the treatment of the UK branch or agency of a non-resident company with that of a resident company by recasting rules in terms of liability to UK corporation tax rather than simple residence (see above §§60.9 and 64.1, and below §75.4.1). Thus, the corporation tax references to 'branch' or 'agency' were replaced

---

[1] For capital gains, see below at chapter seventy-four.

by references to 'permanent establishments' (PEs) by 2003. Income tax retains the terms 'branch' and 'agency'. The overall effect does not disturb the three principal rules just outlined. See also chapter sixty-one above.

72.2   Source—General

It is a basic principle of UK income tax that tax is charged on income arising to non-residents from sources within the UK.[2] This is so stated for ITTOIA 2005, Part 2 (section 6), Part 4 (section 361) and Part 5 (section 621). Unfortunately ITTOIA 2005 does not use the simple technique for Part 3. In Part 3 (property income), section 260 tells us that this Part will tax income from a UK property business and from an overseas property business. Then section 269 tells us that both the UK resident and the non-UK resident may carry on a UK property business but—and here at last is the point—that only a UK resident may carry on an overseas property business. Budget 2016 announced new rules to make it clear that profits from trading in UK land are always taxable, whether made by UK residents or overseas property developers. ITEPA 2003 has its own rules—Part 2, Chapters 4 and 5.

Previously these principles were expressed in the following provisions:

(1) Schedule A—land in the UK (TA 1988, section 15);
(2) Schedule D, Cases I and II—profit from any trade or profession carried on within the UK to the extent of the profits there arising (TA 1988, section 18(1)(a)(iii);
(3) Case III—from any property (as defined) within the UK (TA 1988, section 18(1)(a) (iii)); however, certain types of interest are exempt (TA 1988, sections 47 and 48);
(4) Case VI—any annual profits or gains not falling under any other Case or Schedule;
(5) distributions by companies resident in the UK (TA 1988, section 20). However, the view of the ECJ is that, correctly analysed, the UK rules do not attempt to charge these dividends to UK tax at all (see above at §§61.3.3 *et seq*).

Corporation tax is charged on non-resident companies trading through a PE in the UK on the profits attributable to the PE.[3] The profits of a trade carried on in the UK but without a PE are chargeable to income tax, but this is subject to override by an applicable double tax treaty that would very likely bar the UK, as source country, from imposing tax in this situation.

CGT is charged on the trade assets situated in the UK of non-residents trading through a PE,[4] and on dispositions of UK residential property (see §74.1.1). Otherwise, a non-resident is not subject to UK CGT. The UK's refusal to use the source basis of taxation for CGT

---

[2] A UK patent is a UK source (CTA 2009, ss 914–915, ex TA 1988, s 524(2)); but see ESC B8. For another concession see ESC A12 (alimony paid by a person no longer resident under UK court order). For criticisms of source concept in multinational context, see Green (1993) 79 *Cornell LR* 18.

[3] CTA 2009, s 5, ex TA 1988, ss 6 and 11.

[4] CTA 2009, s 19(3)(c) and TCGA 1992, s 10(B).

more generally means that the boundary between income and capital gain acquires greater importance, and that when the legislature moves a receipt from capital gain to income, eg for premiums on leases[5] or transactions in land,[6] there are substantial implications for non-residents.[7]

Example

John Smith is not resident in the UK, neither does he have a UK domicile. His five UK sources of income are as follows:

(1)	Rent from UK property	£3,000
(2)	Dividends from UK companies	£10,000
(3)	Duties performed outside UK with non-resident employer	£10,000
(4)	Duties performed in UK under employment with a non UK-resident employer	£2,500
(5)	Interest in the following UK government stocks:	£4,700
	3% War Loan (interest £3,500)	
	6% Funding Loan (interest £1,200)	

John Smith's items of assessable income would be (1), (2) and (4) (total £15,500). Item (3) is not subject to UK tax and (5) is exempt because of the non-resident status.

Importantly, FA 2016 establishes a new framework for taxing non-UK residents (and Scottish residents). As outlined in ITA 2007, section 9A, a non-UK resident individual will be subject to a new category of 'default' tax rates (basic, higher and additional) on most forms of income, but the same rates as UK resident individuals on savings and dividend income. Thus, to finish John Smith's example:

(a) *personal reliefs*—on whether he is entitled to these, see ITA 2007, section 56 (above at §11.1.1);

(b) *dividends*—prior to 6 April 2016, assuming there is no double taxation treaty and that Smith is not entitled to personal reliefs, he is not entitled to claim any credit on UK company dividends; there is no grossing up but there is no liability to dividend ordinary or upper rates. From 6 April 2016, however, the dividend tax credit is abolished and new ITA 2007, section 11C provides that a non-UK resident individual will be subject to the same rate of tax on dividends as a resident individual under ITA 2007, section 13; however, importantly, he is treated as having paid tax at the dividend ordinary rate on the dividend (see §72.6.3 below).

---

[5] ITTOIA 2005, Pt 3, Ch 4 and CTA 2009, ss 243 and 244, ex TA 1988, s 34.

[6] ITA 2007, s 755 and CTA 2010, s 819, ex TA 1988, s 776.

[7] On whether such re-designations are effective for treaty purposes, see Avery Jones in Vogel, Raad, Van Raad and Kirchhof (eds), *Essays in Honour of Klaus Vogel* (Kluwer, 2002).

72.3 Place of Trade

A non-resident is taxable under ITTOIA 2005, Part 2 on profits from a trade within, as opposed to one with, the UK.[8] So, if the non-resident establishes a branch in the UK from which the trade is carried on, he is trading in the UK; by contrast, the presence of a mere administrative office, or perhaps a representative office supplying information in London, will not give rise to tax—provided the office does not trade. Although corporation tax has moved to the concept of a PE, it still asks whether the trade is being carried on in the UK through the PE.

In asking where the trade is carried on, the UK has used two tests: the first, which is particularly appropriate to the sale of goods, asks where the contract was made; the second, and broader, test asks where, in substance, the operations take place from which the profits in substance arise. Both tests place the source in one, and only one, place. This all-or-nothing approach applies to determine the source of the income for the purposes of the UK's schedular system; however, this is quite separate from the question where the income arises. Although the trade is the source and therefore must have only one place, its income may arise in more than one place, as is shown by a 1991 decision on a double tax treaty point relying in part on a 1990 Privy Council decision.[9]

The mere purchase of goods in this country for export and resale abroad is not enough to amount to trading here.[10] What is enough was defined by Brett LJ in *Erichsen v Last:*[11]

> I should say that wherever profitable contracts are habitually made in England, by or for foreigners, with persons in England, because they are in England, to do something for or to supply something to those persons, such foreigners are exercising a profitable trade in England, even though everything to be done by them in order to fulfil the contract is done abroad.

72.3.1 Sale of Goods: Where is the Contract Made?

Most of the cases have concerned the sale of goods by a non-resident to someone in the UK, and the basic test has been that the trade is carried on where the contracts of sale are made.[12] The place of a contract is determined according to English domestic law—the place at which the acceptance of an offer is communicated. It follows that an acceptance by post completes the contract at the place of posting, whereas an acceptance by telex completes the contract at the place of receipt. This principle is comparatively simple to apply when a

---

[8] ITTOIA 2005, s 6(2), ex TA 1988, s 18(l)(a)(iii); see, generally, Norfolk [1980] BTR 72. This is subject to the application of a double tax treaty, which would likely deny the UK the right as source country to tax such trading profits.

[9] *CIR v Hang Seng Bank Ltd* [1990] STC 733; *Yates v CGA* [1991] STC 157, 64 TC 37.

[10] *Sulley v A-G* (1860) 5 H&N 711, (1860) 2 TC 149n; *cf Greenwood v FL Smidth & Co* [1922] 1 AC 417, (1922) 8 TC 205 where the goods were sold in England; and *Taxation Commrs v Kirk* [1900] AC 588, PC, where the goods were manufactured here for export and not simply bought. The danger in the rule in *Sulley v A-G* is that a foreigner may employ an agent here to buy goods and yet the agent may have an undisclosed interest in the business. This may lead to evasion, especially when the agent is a relative of the principal.

[11] (1881) 8 QBD 414, 418; 4 TC 422, 425; see also *Neilsen, Andersen & Co v Collins* [1928] AC 34, 13 TC 91.

[12] Eg *Maclaine & Co v Eccott* [1926] AC 424, (1926) 10 TC 481. On importance of place of delivery, see Wills J in *Thomas Turner (Leicester) Ltd v Rickman* (1898) 4 TC 25, 34; but *cf* Lord Cave in *Maclaine & Co v Eccott*, 432, 575.

foreigner deals directly with the customer, but difficult questions of fact arise when an intermediary is employed. The fact that the foreigner uses an agent or stations an employee[13] in England is not sufficient to create a trade within, as distinct from with, the UK. Here, too, great attention is paid to the place of the contract.[14] The arrival of e-commerce might seem to put these simple concepts under strain, since the physical process by which the contract is created may take place through servers in many different parts of the globe. However, it is best to approach these problems simply and regard the Internet as just one more step in a process which began with telex machines—or even the telephone. Websites are little more than passive agents and should therefore be disregarded.

Where a contract is made through an agent, the normal principles of offer and acceptance must be applied to determine where the contract is made. Where an agent merely has to consult his foreign principal before accepting contracts, the trade is carried on here. If, however, his sole function is to pass the offer to head office, which communicates directly with the customer, the foreigner is trading with, and not within, the UK.

In *Grainger & Son v Gough*,[15] Louis Roederer canvassed orders for champagne in the UK through the firm of Grainger and Son, which would pass on all orders and money received from the customers in the UK to Rheims, from where Roederer would despatch the champagne. The contracts for the sale of wine being made in France and both the property and the risk passing to the purchasers in France, the House of Lords held, reversing the Commissioners, that Roederer was not trading in, but with, the UK. There being no liability on Roederer, Grainger and Son was not accountable for tax as agents of Roederer.

The place of the contract distinguished *Grainger v Gough* from the earlier cases in which the courts had that a trade was carried on in the UK. In *Pommery and Greno v Apthorpe*,[16] the London agents of Pommery held stocks of wine in London which were used for all save orders for 'considerable quantities', and paid monies received into Pommery's London bank account. The court had little difficulty upholding the Commissioners' finding that the trade was carried on in England. The fact that Pommery had a principal establishment outside the UK, and that its sales in the UK amounted to only a small part of its total trade, was irrelevant.

72.3.2 Operations from which Profits Arise

The notion that the place of the contract determines the place of the trade is a very English notion since it combines the obsession with sale as the paradigm contract with the doctrine of the source. As Esher MR put it in *Werle & Co v Colquhoun*: '[T]he contract is the very foundation of the trade. It is the trade really.'[17] There has to be some practical limit saying how far the courts will go back in locating profits. The question is where the profits are made, and not why. So the courts do not go beyond the business operations from which the profits derive. Once again, the arrival of e-commerce does not change the nature of the issue to be resolved, although it may make the factual background against which the decision has to be made more fragmented.

---

[13] As in *Greenwood v FL Smith & Co* [1922] 1 AC 417, (1922) 8 TC 205.
[14] Eg *Thomas Turner (Leicester) Ltd v Rickman* (1898) 4 TC 25, 34, *per* Will J.
[15] [1896] AC 325, (1896) 3 TC 462.
[16] (1886) 2 TC 182; *cf Werle & Co v Colquhoun* (1888) 20 QBD 753, (1888) 2 TC 402.
[17] (1908) 2 TC 402, 410, PC. See also Rowlatt J in *FL Smidth & Co v Greenwood* (1920) 8 TC 193, 199.

The cases also show that the place of the contract is not a touchstone. In *Maclaine & Co v Eccott*,[18] while describing the place of the contract as the most important and, indeed, the crucial question, Lord Cave listed other factors, such as the place where payment is to be made for the goods sold and the place where the goods are to be delivered, and disclaimed any exhaustive test. The place of contract was further downgraded by Lord Radcliffe,[19] who described it as capable of being somewhat ingenuous in modern (1950s) business conditions.

The place of contract, although useful as a test in the area of simple sale, is less appropriate in the manufacturing sphere.[20] In *FL Smidth v Greenwood*, Atkin LJ said[21] that it was perfectly possible for a manufacturing business to be carried on here even though the contracts for the sale of goods are made abroad:

> The contracts in this case were made abroad. But I am not prepared to hold that this test is decisive. I can imagine cases where the contract of resale is made abroad and yet the manufacture of the goods, some negotiation of the terms and complete execution of the contract take place here under such circumstances that the trade was in truth exercised here. I think the question is where the operations take place from which the profits in substance arise.

In *Firestone Tyre and Rubber Co Ltd v Lewellin*,[22] the UK subsidiary (Brentford) of a US parent (Akron) made tyres in the UK and supplied them to foreign subsidiaries at cost plus 5%. The court held that the US parent was trading in the UK, as was the UK subsidiary, and that the location of the master agreement governing the trade between the parent and its subsidiaries was not conclusive. The operations, the supply of the tyres and delivery alongside ship in a UK port, took place in England, constituted the carrying on of a trade in England, and that trade, the Commissioners had correctly held, was the trade of Akron, not Brentford.[23] The obligation on Brentford to account to Akron for any profit in excess of 5% was of crucial importance here. It followed that Brentford, as the regular agents of Akron, could be assessed to the tax due from Akron.

72.4   Computation of Profits—Transfer Pricing

72.4.1 The Problem

Profits of a trade carried on within the UK will be computed according to the normal principles applicable to ITTOIA 2005.[24] TIOPA 2010, Part 4 (ex TA 1988, section 770A and

---

[18] [1926] AC 424, 432. To the same effect, see Scrutton LJ in *Balfour v Mace* (1928) 13 TC 539, 558.
[19] *Firestone Tyre and Rubber Co v Lewellin* (1957) 37 TC 111, 142.
[20] *Cf* Lord Salvesen in *Crookston Bros v Furtado* (1910) 5 TC 602, 623.
[21] [1921] 3 KB 583, 593; (1921) 8 TC 193, 209. *Cf* Lord Esher in *Grainger & Son v Gough* (1896) 3 TC 311, 317. For an example, see *IRC v Brackett* [1986] STC 521, 60 TC 134; B was a property consultant working for a Jersey company created by a settlement of which he was the settlor. B was held assessable under TA 1988, s 739 (see above at §71.5) on his own account and on behalf of the company under the now superseded TMA 1970, s 79 (see below at §72.6).
[22] (1957) 37 TC 111.
[23] (1957) 37 TC 111, 143, *per* Lord Radcliffe.
[24] For example of problem, see *Taxation Commissioner (NSW) v Hillsdon Watts Ltd* (1937) 57 CLR 36, esp 51–52, *per* Dixon J. On application in purely domestic UK transactions, see above at §21.10 and chapter sixty-two.

Schedule 28AA) enables both the Revenue and the taxpayer to allocate profits arising from a business with concerns in several countries between those different concerns. The transfer pricing regime in TIOPA 2010, Part 4 also enables the Revenue to counteract traders who seek to prevent profits arising in this country through the manipulation of prices; in such circumstances the price that would have been paid if the parties had been at arm's length will be taken.[25] Other ways of reducing profits are to establish in the UK other aspects of business of an inherently loss-making character, such as administration or research. These are not necessarily harmful to the UK even though induced by considerations of tax saving. One must remember, however, that transfer pricing is not just, or even primarily, a tax issue. It is a vital part of business planning and management in any international concern. The scope of the UK transfer pricing regime was radically altered by FA 2004, not only by being extended to domestic transactions but also by excluding many SMEs (see §62.6).

Before plunging into the current rules on transfer pricing, a different method of taxation should be noted, ie taxation of a group on a unitary basis by means of formulary apportionment. This abandons the present attempt to attribute particular profits to particular sources and takes a global (or unitary) view. Once the profit of the group as a whole has been ascertained, this method allocates the profits among the different entities by reference to a formula using criteria such as payroll, property and receipts.[26] This method has caused much anguish between the United States and the rest of the world, partly because it means that the worldwide profits of a group as taxed in each state are likely to exceed 100% in total, and partly because of the substantial compliance costs involved in negotiating the basis of taxation.[27]

72.4.1.1 Methods[28]

The international standard used in determining transfer prices for tax purposes is the arm's-length principle as stated in Article 9 of the OECD Model Tax Convention, which allows enterprise profits to be adjusted and taxed accordingly where conditions are made or imposed between associated enterprises that differ from those which would be made between independent enterprises. The OECD has published a list of its approved transfer

For material on the position in EU countries, see *Company Taxation in the Internal Market*, COM (2001) 582, Part II, Chapter 5.

[25] TIOPA 2010, s 147, ex TA 1988, Sch 28AA, para 1. On treaty practice, see Vogel, *Klaus Vogel on Double Tax Conventions*, 3rd edn (Kluwer, 1997), Art 9, paras 18–45. On Revenue practice, see the Revenue's *International Tax Handbook*, ch 15. On whether the Revenue's powers under the now superseded TA 1988, s 770 could be widened by a double tax treaty, see Oliver [1970] BTR 388, 396. For important OECD guidance, see the latest version of the OECD *Transfer Pricing Guidelines for Multinational Enterprises and Tax Administrations* (22 July 2010, referred to in this chapter as the 'OECD Guidelines'). In 2012, the UN released a *Practical Manual on Transfer Pricing for Developing Countries*—see http://www.un.org/esa/ffd/tax/documents/bgrd_tp.htm.

[26] See Kaplan [1983] BTR 203; and McLure (ed), *The State Corporation Income Tax* (Hoover Foundation, 1984); reviewed in [1984] BTR 191.

[27] See above at §61.3.3.

[28] See generally Hamaekers, *Rivista di Diritto Tributario Internazionale* 3/1999, Staaten and Steuern, *Festschrift for Klaus Vogel* (Muller, Heidleberg 2001) 1043–65 and the *International Transfer Pricing Journal* published by IBFD Amsterdam. Many of the issues were discussed in OECD publications *Transfer Pricing and Multinational Enterprises* (OECD, 1979), and *Transfer Pricing and Multinational Enterprises: Three Taxation Issues* (OECD, 1984) 73–91. These have now been superseded by the ongoing OECD Guidelines, the current version of which are reprinted in the annual edition of van Raad, *Materials on International and EU Tax Law* (International Tax Centre Leiden).

pricing methods for implementing the arm's-length principle in its Transfer Pricing Guidelines.[29] The issue of transfer pricing has become highly topical, not least because of extreme US legislative reaction to a small-scale problem. The problem arises in various contexts. In connection with the sale of goods, the problems generally concern the method by which the goods are priced. In some situations there will be an actual market in which identical goods are dealt in at arm's length. Where this is not so, another method must be sought. A figure may give a profit similar to that of the other companies in the same sector (the comparable uncontrolled price or 'CUP'),[30] or the yield on the capital involved may be employed. CUP, though attractive, requires great attention to detail in order to ensure that true comparability exists.

However, both these methods make a series of assumptions which may be misplaced, and the more usual methods are either cost plus or resale price, the latter being more correctly described as 'price minus'. Cost plus involves taking the cost of production and adding an appropriate percentage. This involves many problems in determining cost and the appropriate mark-up.[31] It may, however, be useful where semi-finished goods are sold, or when the subsidiary is, in essence, a subcontractor. It may also be useful for services. The resale price method begins with the price at which the goods are sold on to an independent purchaser and then reduces that price by a percentage to reflect the vendor's costs, expenses and a reasonable profit.[32] Here, problems arise over the appropriate mark-up, save where the goods are sold on very quickly with little risk to the person reselling and without having been subjected to any intermediate process.

Problems also arise in connection with royalty and trademark licence payments,[33] with the allocation of R&D,[34] head office and other central administration costs.[35] There are also many problems in connection with banking enterprises.[36] However, one of the principal current problems is the effect of a loan by one company to another within the same group but usually, although not necessarily, in different jurisdictions. This is known as the thin capitalisation problem (see above at §62.6). The UK now deals with the thin capitalisation through its transfer pricing rules.

72.4.1.2 Administration: The Taxpayer as Shuttlecock

Where problems of this nature arise, there will be obvious difficulties in negotiating with the Revenue to see whether TIOPA 2010, Part 4 should apply and, if so, how it should be applied. There are, however, even more substantial problems where the income tax folk may take one view but the revenue authorities in another jurisdiction—or even indirect tax folk in the same country—may take a different view. Where double tax treaties apply, it may be

---

[29] OECD Guidelines, Ch I discusses the arm's-length principle and Ch II discusses transfer pricing methods.
[30] Comparability must extend to many things, eg market conditions (comparable levels of demand), the market level (ie wholesale or retail), comparable goods, comparable volume (a large order attracts a discount) and contract terms (ie are there warranties, is delivery cif or fob, etc?): OECD Guidelines, Ch II, Pt II, B.
[31] OECD Guidelines, Ch II, Pt II, D.
[32] OECD Guidelines, Ch II, Pt II, C.
[33] OECD Guidelines, Ch VI.
[34] OECD Guidelines, Ch VIII.
[35] *Transfer Pricing and Multinational Enterprises: Three Taxation Issues* (OECD, 1984), 73–91; OECD Guidelines, Ch VII.
[36] *Transfer Pricing and Multinational Enterprises: Three Taxation Issues* (OECD, 1984), 45–70.

possible to use the mutual agreement and competent authority provisions to resolve these problems to avoid double taxation, but the time taken may be substantial.[37] Since 1995 a multilateral Arbitration Convention has been in force within the European Union (see below at §72.4.3).

72.4.1.3 Information Powers; Taxpayer Costs

The Revenue have extensive information-gathering powers. These are potentially extremely expensive for taxpayers in view of the compliance costs involved. It has been held that the court has jurisdiction to allow a taxpayer to challenge a demand for information, not least because the taxpayer, under the statutory code, has no way of appealing against the demand for information, and a failure to comply with the demand entails a penalty.[38]

72.4.1.4 US Attitudes

Reference has been made to the US rules as reformed in 1986 and subsequently. There are two main problems for the rest of the world. The first is that the United States has decided to reject the OECD approach and provide that taxpayers should adopt a 'best method' approach. If the taxpayer has not adopted what the Internal Revenue Service (IRS) (eventually) regards as the best method, it is open to the taxpayer to use a comparable profits method (CPM). This may involve looking at a number of average-operating profits earned by uncontrolled distributors and seeing how their profits ratios compare. The taxpayer will be safe if the operating profit-to-sale ratio comes within the middle 50% of the range of figures established, ie between 25% and 75%. As so often with the United States, there are further incentives to compliance (ie overpayment to the United States) in the shape of semi-automatic penalties. The OECD approach rejects the idea of a 'best' method and prefers CUP, cost plus and resale price to profit adjustments. It also, very sensibly, states that administrators should refrain from making minor adjustments.[39]

Another problem concerns the transfer of intangible property. Here the US Internal Revenue Code (IRC) §482 requires the Internal Revenue Service (IRS) to make periodic adjustments to the sums received, ie to use hindsight. This is also completely contrary to OECD principles. Apparently, it arose because US rules allowed US companies to transfer intangibles to Puerto Rica at cost, so ensuring that all future income arose outside the mainland United States. The simple solution of stopping the transfer of such assets at such a low cost was not pursued as Congress got excited by the prospect of making multinationals pay a 'fair share' of US tax.

72.4.2 UK Transfer Pricing Rules[40]

Dissatisfaction with the existing transfer pricing rules, when combined with the realisation that the change to corporate self-assessment in 1999 required changes, led to a

---

[37] *Ibid*, 21, ch 42. See more generally OECD Guidelines, Ch IV.
[38] *Beecham Group plc v IRC* [1992] STC 935, (1992) 65 TC 219.
[39] On non-OECD approved methods, see OECD Guidelines, Ch III.
[40] FA 1988, s 108 and Sch 16. The Inland Revenue Consultative Document was announced on 9 October 1997, [1997] *Simon's Weekly Tax Intelligence* 911. For comment, see Hadari (1998) *Can Tax Jo* 29. For similar proposals for change in Canada, see Vincent and Freedman (1998) 46 *Can Tax Jo* 1213.

detailed consultation exercise followed by proposals for reform which were implemented as part of FA 1998. The rules took effect for the first accounting period ending on or after 1 July 1999;[41] the new rules avoid some of the defects of the old. These rules, now rewritten as TIOPA 2010, Part 4, were amended in three directions by FA 2004. First, in response to ECJ rulings in discrimination cases, it was decided to extend the rules to purely UK-domestic transactions. Secondly, the rules were narrowed by excluding most SMEs; this change applies both transnationally and domestically. Thirdly, these rules were extended to cover all cases of thin capitalisation; these had previously been dealt with, at least in part, by TA 1988, section 209(2)(da), which treated excessive interest as a distribution.

TIOPA 2010, Part 4 (ex TA 1988, Schedule 28AA) uses the arm's-length rule for transfer pricing events. Under the self-assessment system, taxpayers must use this rule in making their returns and not, as previously, sit back and wait to see if the inspector raised questions on the accounts, and then ask the Board to make a direction. This change makes matters more equitable between taxpayers of different degrees of conscientiousness, as well as making the UK system more like those in other countries. The legislation applies to each transaction (or 'provision') separately[42] rather than having the broad sweep of the US Code (IRC §482). Payments of excessive interest by a thinly-capitalised UK taxpayer company under finance arrangements guaranteed by affiliates come within these rules. However, control is defined in a different way from the usual definition in CTA 2010, section 450; not only is a 40% interest treated as giving control, but also, as from 2005, persons acting together in relation to financing arrangements.[43]

The legislation applies only if the arm's-length principle means a potential tax advantage for UK taxpayers, ie it applies only to reduce a loss or increase a profit.[44] The legislation does not include provision for *secondary* adjustments to other taxpayers, but does enable the parties to make tax-free payments to each other to bring their cash position into line with the tax result.[45] An HMRC central monitoring system is intended to ensure uniformity of application of these rules. Board involvement is still needed in that adjustments to profits under these rules requires a Board determination unless there is a written agreement between the Revenue and the taxpayer.[46]

Before 2004, TA 1988, Schedule 28AA was excluded for all transfers between UK taxpayers.[47] This was achieved by saying that the actual provision was not treated as conferring a potential advantage in relation to UK tax if various conditions were met, ie the person was chargeable to UK tax and not exempt. However, FA 2004 changed this by removing that exemption. TIOPA 2010, Part 4 does not apply to foreign exchange and financial

---

[41] Transitional rules allowed existing joint venture arrangements to remain outside the scope of the new rules for a maximum period of three years from 17 March 1997 (FA 1998, s 108(5), (6)).

[42] TIOPA 2010, s 147, ex TA 1988, Sch 28AA, para 1.

[43] TIOPA 2010, ss 148 and 160, ex TA 1988, Sch 28AA, paras 4 and 4A. added by F(No 2)A 2005, Sch 8, para 1.

[44] Potential advantage is defined in TIOPA 2010, s 155, ex TA 1988, Sch 28AA, para 5.

[45] TIOPA 2010, ss 195–196, ex TA 1988, Sch 28AA, paras 6 and 7.

[46] FA 1998, s 108, esp sub-ss (5), (6) (not rewritten); for procedures to inform disadvantaged persons of rights of appeal, etc, where both are UK persons but the exemption in ex TA 1988, Sch 28AA, para 5(3) does not apply, see FA 1998, s 11. This also applies for persons within ex TA 1988, Sch 28AA, para 12(4): see now TIOPA 2010, s 212.

[47] Ex TA 1988, Sch 28AA, para 5(2)–(6).

instrument legislation since these have their own rules,[48] neither does it apply for the purposes of calculating capital allowances, balancing charges or capital gains and losses.[49]

72.4.2.1 Adjustments

Where a company, A, resident in X, sells goods to B, a company resident in Y, the price may be increased by the X revenue authorities under TIOPA 2010, section 147. A 'corresponding' adjustment ought then to be made by state Y when dealing with the same company. Where both A and B are resident in the UK, the transfer-pricing rules give a right to the corresponding adjustment.[50] This may, in turn, lead to an adjustment to a right to treaty relief, for example where B is a foreign branch of a UK company.[51]

Corresponding adjustments, which are relatively straightforward, are to be distinguished from 'secondary' adjustments. These arise where A, a UK resident, buys goods from B, a foreign company, and the price paid by A to B is later reduced; there is no machinery for making B repay A and many good commercial reasons why B should not do so, but how should that part of the sum which has ceased to be a price for goods be treated for tax purposes? Under the 'secondary' adjustment the sum could be treated as a payment by A to B by way of dividend if B is shareholder in A, and as a loan in other circumstances. If the sum is a dividend, withholding tax may be due under a tax treaty; if it is a loan, A may be deemed to receive interest. These secondary adjustments are much loved by countries where theory prevails over pragmatism, ie not the UK.

72.4.2.2 Interpretation

The UK transfer pricing rules contain express reference to the OECD Guidelines for construction purposes.[52] FA 2016 updates this link to the OECD Guidelines to incorporate the revisions to the Guidelines which were agreed as part of the G20/OECD BEPS Actions 8–10. Some see this link as a dubious delegation of a rule-making power to an intergovernmental quango; others express more practical objections to having to refer to a document published in an ever-changing loose-leaf format.[53] The UK precedent was followed by The Netherlands.

72.4.2.3 Administration

Transfer pricing may be financially important to government and fascinating to academics but is, potentially, hugely expensive and time-consuming to business. In response to a consultation exercise in 2007 following HMRC's Review of Links with Large Business, a team of transfer-pricing specialists was assembled at HMRC, charged with the goal of resolving transfer pricing enquiries within 18–36 months.[54]

---

[48] CTA 2009, ss 447 and 694, ex TA 1988, Sch 28AA, para 8.
[49] TIOPA 2010, ss 213–214, ex TA 1988, Sch 28AA, para 13; on oil companies, see ss 205–206 and 217, ex paras 9–11.
[50] TIOPA 2010, s 174, ex TA 1988, Sch 28AA, para 6.
[51] TIOPA 2010, ss 188–189, ex TA 1988, Sch 28AA, para 7.
[52] TIOPA 2010, s 164, ex TA 1988, Sch 28AA, para 2; see also IR Notes to Finance Bill 1998, paras 49–54, esp para 49, which states that the Schedule cannot be interpreted in a way which goes beyond Art 9 of the OECD Model Treaty. On story of OECD Guidelines, see articles by Elliott, Self and Morton [1995] BTR 348–77.
[53] Ault (1994) 22 *Intertax* 144.
[54] HMRC website, 'transfer pricing'.

72.4.3 The EU Arbitration Convention

The EU Arbitration Convention was to last for five years in the first instance, was extended to 2005 and is now renewed every five years unless a Contracting State objects in writing.[55] A compulsory arbitration procedure does not usually feature in the mutual agreement procedures article in double tax treaties, but it has become more common in recent times. The US–German Treaty contains an arbitration process—but only where both States agree. Article 25(5) of the OECD Model Tax Convention now provides for arbitration if the competent authorities are unable to resolve disputes within two years. Some recent UK double tax treaties also include an arbitration provision in Article 25.[56] The G20/OECD BEPS Action 14 final report also sets out measures aimed at strengthening the effectiveness and efficiency of the treaty dispute resolution process, which promise to aid in resolving transfer pricing disputes in particular more quickly (see §76.5.2).

The EU Arbitration Convention is concerned only with transfer pricing and builds on the mutual agreement procedures in double tax treaties. It does not mention 'transfer pricing' as such, but concerns 'the elimination of double taxation in connection with the adjustment of profits of associated enterprises'. The enterprise must be an enterprise of a Contracting State. Interestingly, the Convention is based on the former Article 220 of the EC Treaty. Interpretation is to be done by the national court. The enterprise may not use the Convention if it is liable to serious penalties.[57] Despite its name, the Convention does not provide for binding arbitration, as the April 1990 draft directive had proposed, but instead for the appointment of an independent advisory commission which is to advise the competent authorities in the Member States. The taxpayer may require the authorities to establish a commission if they fail to agree within two years of the matter being put before them. The authorities will make their decision in the light of that advice; they may ignore that advice only if they are agreed on an alternative outcome. The Convention is backed up by a Joint Transfer Pricing Forum, comprising Member State and business representatives with an independent chairperson, and a detailed Code of Conduct; the Code is not part of the Convention and is a political document.

The UK legislation implementing the Convention goes further than is required and compels the Commissioners to give effect to the agreement or decision made under the Convention by HMRC and any other competent authority or any opinion of the advisory commission.[58] This is to override any other rule of law.[59] Normal time limits for claiming

---

[55] 90/436/EEC of 23 July 1990 and Code of Conduct 2695/5/04, with materials and related documents on the EU website at <http://ec.europa.eu/taxation_customs/taxation/company_tax/transfer_pricing/arbitration_convention/index_en.htm>. See also van Raad, *Materials on International and EC Tax Law, 2007–08*, vol 1 (International Tax Centre Leiden, 2007), 1809 *et seq*; Oliver [1998] BTR 389; Oliver (1990) 18 *Intertax*, 437. For critical EU Commission comments, see COM (2001) 582, Pt III, esp at 5.5. For detailed analysis, see Hinnekens [1996] BTR 154 and 272; and, on interpretation issues, see (1998) 8 *EC Tax Law Review* 247.

[56] Recent UK DTAs with such an arbitration provision include treaties with Germany, Bahrain, Iceland, Norway and Armenia, the 2013 protocol with Japan and the 2014 protocol to the Canada/UK Treaty (in that case where the dispute is unresolved after three years, not two). Other recent UK DTAs do not, including Hungary and China. For more see Baker [2011] BTR 125 at 130. Baker draws the inference that the inclusion of an arbitration provision is now part of UK treaty policy, at least if the other negotiating party is willing to agree to it.

[57] Art 8.

[58] TIOPA 2010, s 126–128, ex TA 1988, s 815B, added by F(No 2)A 1992, s 51; on need to implement, see Inland Revenue, *EC Direct Measures: A Consultative Document* (1991).

[59] TIOPA 2010, s 127(3), ex TA 1988, s 815B(2).

relies are overruled.[60] The Revenue are given statutory authority to provide the advisory commission with information required under a request from the commission.[61] Any member of the advisory commission who discloses information acquired by him in this capacity is guilty of an offence unless it has already been made public or the disclosure is with the consent of the party supplying; it is a defence for that person to prove that he believed that the information had already been made public and that he had no reasonable cause to believe otherwise.[62] A prosecution requires the consent of the Commissioners or the appropriate DPP.[63]

72.4.4 BEPS and Transfer Pricing

From the outset of the G20/OECD Base Erosion and Profit Shifting (BEPS) project (see §69.11), transfer pricing was identified as a key area of focus. The 2013 Action Plan highlighted concerns that the existing international standards for transfer pricing rules can be misapplied so that they result in outcomes in which the allocation of profits is not aligned with the economic activity that produced the profits.[64] Nevertheless, the report defended the 'cornerstone' arm's length principle overall, and specifically rejected moving to a system of formulary apportionment of profits as 'not a viable way forward'.[65] In the final report on Actions 8–10, the OECD again robustly defended the usefulness of the arm's length principle 'as a practical and balanced standard for tax administrations and taxpayers to evaluate transfer prices between associated enterprises, and to prevent double taxation.'[66] The OECD went on to acknowledge, however, that 'with its perceived emphasis on contractual allocations of functions, assets and risks, the existing guidance on the application of the principle has also proven vulnerable to manipulation.'[67]

The OECD's work on transfer pricing under the BEPS Action Plan centred on three main areas. Action 8 focused on transfer pricing issues relating to transactions involving valuable intangibles, which was identified as a significant contributor to BEPS.[68] Action 9 examined the contractual allocation of risks, and the resulting allocation of profits to those risks. Action 9 also considered the level of returns to funding provided by MNE group members.[69] Action 10 centred on other high-risk areas, including (1) the potential for recharacterisation of transactions which are not commercially rational for the individual enterprises concerned, (2) addressing the use of transfer pricing methods in a way which results in diverting profits from the most economically important activities of the MNE group, and (3) neutralising the use of intra-group payments such as management fees and head office expenses to erode the tax base.[70]

---

[60] TIOPA 2010, s 127(5), ex TA 1988, s 815B(3).
[61] TIOPA 2010, ss 128(1), ex TA 1988, s 816(2A), added by F(No 2)A 1992, s 51.
[62] FA 1989, s 182A (not rewritten), added by F(No 2)A 1992, s 51(3); such provisions are authorised by Art 9(6) of the OECD Model Treaty.
[63] FA 1989, s 182A(5).
[64] OECD, *Action Plan on Base Erosion and Profit Shifting* (July 2013), 19.
[65] *Ibid.*
[66] OECD, *BEPS Actions 8–10 'Aligning Transfer Pricing Outcomes with Value Creation' Final Report* (Oct 2015), 9.
[67] *Ibid.*
[68] *Ibid.*
[69] *Ibid,* 9–10.
[70] *Ibid,* 10.

The primary method of implementing the OECD's response in all three action areas was by changes to the OECD's Transfer Pricing Guidelines. The recommendations are quite technical in places and what follows is a summary of the key reforms. Beginning first with Action 8, the revised Guidelines will clarify that 'legal ownership alone does not necessarily generate a right to all (or indeed any) of the return that is generated by the exploitation of the intangible'.[71] Further, any return should reflect the value of the contributions made:

> The group companies performing important functions, controlling economically significant risks and contributing assets, as determined through the accurate delineation of the actual transaction, will be entitled to an appropriate return reflecting the value of their contributions. Specific guidance will ensure that the analysis is not weakened by information asymmetries between the tax administration and the taxpayer in relation to hard-to-value intangibles, or by using special contractual relationships, such as a cost contribution arrangement.[72]

Under Action 9, risks contractually assumed by a party that 'cannot in fact exercise meaningful and specifically defined control over the risks, or does not have the financial capacity to assume the risks, will be allocated to the party that does exercise such control and does have the financial capacity to assume the risk'.[73] The guidance on Action 10 ensures that pricing methods will allocate profits to the most important economic activities: '[i]t will no longer be possible to allocate the synergistic benefits of operating as a group to members other than the ones contributing to such synergistic benefits'.[74] Further work will be undertaken on the transactional profit split method, leading to detailed guidance 'on the ways in which this method can usefully and appropriately be applied to align transfer pricing outcomes with value creation, including in the circumstances of integrated global value chains'.[75]

The OECD's guidance in Actions 8–10 is linked with other Actions, the combination of which are intended to ensure in particular 'that capital-rich entities without any other relevant economic activities ("cash boxes") will not be entitled to any excess profits'.[76] Thus, if the level of profit in the cash box as determined in accordance with the revised Transfer Pricing Guidelines qualifies as interest then those profits will also be targeted by rules restricting interest deductibility (Action 4), will be potentially subject to withholding taxes when paid to the cash box under the guidance on preventing treaty abuse (Action 6), and a cash box with limited or no economic activities is likely to be the target of CFC rules (Action 3).[77] These substantive approaches are supported by the transparency requirements agreed under Action 13. So, in the OECD's view, access to the transfer pricing documentation provided by Action 13 will enable the guidance provided in the final report on Actions 8–10 to be applied in practice, in accordance with relevant information on global and local operations in the master file and local file.[78] Finally, the Country-by-Country Report 'will

---

[71] *Ibid.*
[72] *Ibid.*
[73] *Ibid.*
[74] *Ibid,* 11.
[75] *Ibid.*
[76] *Ibid.*
[77] *Ibid.*
[78] *Ibid.*

enable better risk assessment practices by providing information about the global allocation of the MNE group's revenues, profits, taxes, and economic activity'.[79]

Clearly a great deal of time and effort have gone into the guidance in Actions 8–10. It
remains to be seen, however, how effective the OECD's attempts to better align transfer
pricing outcomes with value creation will prove to be in practice. The great advantage of
the OECD's work in Actions 8–10 compared to other Actions is that the recommendations
can be implemented quickly simply by changing the OECD's Transfer Pricing Guidelines,
rather than requiring new domestic legislation or treaty modifications. This is particularly important for the UK, where the domestic transfer pricing rules expressly provide
that the legislation is to be construed in a manner that best secures consistency with the
Guidelines.[80]

72.5 Advance Pricing Arrangements

TIOPA 2010, Part 5 contains statutory authority for advance pricing arrangements between
the Revenue and the taxpayers[81]—as is practised elsewhere, most frequently in the United
States.[82] The Revenue will make these agreements only if there is significant doubt about
how the arm's-length principle should be applied;[83] the agreement must be bilateral but
there may be multiple bilateral agreements.[84] The procedure is important because it goes
wider than TIOPA 2010, Part 4. The agreement must be in writing and made as a consequence of an application by the taxpayer, T, to the Commissioners.[85] The matters which
may be covered are: (a) the attribution of income (actual or prospective) to an individual's
branch or agency or (b) a company's permanent establishment in the UK; (c) the attribution of income (actual or prospective) to T's permanent establishment in the UK (if T is
foreign) or elsewhere (and T is resident in the UK); and (d) the extent to which T's income
is to be taken to be income arising in a country or territory outside the UK (this last is
expected to be important where credit relief for foreign tax may be in issue).[86] The Revenue
notes seem to assume that the presence of a double tax treaty will prevent the need for
such agreements; however, T may wish to secure his position under unilateral credit relief.
The list extends to (e) the treatment for transfer-pricing tax purposes of any provision
made or imposed between T and any associated person.[87] This last category also applies to
(f) any provision between T's North Sea ring-fenced trade and other activities.[88] If a mutual
agreement is reached with the tax authorities of another country, the legislation imposes a

---

[79] *Ibid.*
[80] TIOPA 2010, s 164.
[81] TIOPA 2010, ss 218-230, ex FA 1999, ss 85–87; for practice, see Statement of Practice SP 3/99. See also Inland
Revenue Press Release, 31 March 1999; [1999] *Simon's Weekly Tax Intelligence* 722.
[82] See also OECD Transfer Pricing Guidelines, Ch IV, Pt F.
[83] See Statement of Practice SP 3/99, para 19.
[84] *Ibid*, paras 11–14.
[85] TIOPA 2010, s 218(1), ex FA 1999, s 85(1).
[86] TIOPA 2010, s 218(2), ex FA 1999, s 85(2)(a)–(c).
[87] TIOPA 2010, s 218(2)(e), ex FA 1999, s 85(2)(d); on associated persons, see s 219, ex s 85(6); the limitation
to transfer-pricing rules is in s 220, ex s 85(4).
[88] TIOPA 2010, s 218(2)(f), ex FA 1999, s 85(2)(e).

duty on the Commissioners to make consequential adjustments to its agreement with the taxpayer.[89] Where a provision made between T and another party is the subject of an agreement, the equivalent consequential transfer-pricing rules are made to apply.[90] These enable the other party to use the price established in accordance with the agreement.

The advantages of such arrangements are that they remove late confrontation with one or other tax authority, they are binding on the Revenue and mean that there can be no penalties provided they are adhered to. They provide certainty and avoid double taxation, assuming that the other country also accepts them. The disadvantages are the amount of time, effort and costs incurred in assembling the information and making disclosure, the fact that the arrangements may be cancelled by the Revenue and the fact that some countries, eg France and Germany, will not participate. The French dislike is based partly on a dislike of other parts of the US system, notably the CPM which is designed to increase the US take at the expense of other countries.[91] The UK Revenue see a very limited role for such agreements.[92]

72.6 Administration: Assessing and Collecting the Tax

72.6.1 General

The rules for collecting tax from non-residents, introduced in 1995 and rewritten into ITA 2007, Part 14, Chapters 2B and 2C, have two limbs.[93] The first defines rules for taxing a trade carried on through a branch or agency here (see below at §72.6.2), and defines the circumstances in which the UK representative of a non-resident cannot be made liable for UK tax due from that non-resident.[94] Similar rules (see below at §72.6.3) apply for CGT. Further rules (see below at §72.6.4) outline the liability of the non-resident for income and corporation tax; other rules apply to paying and collecting agents.[95]

Many general UK rules impose an obligation on a person paying income to another to withhold income tax; some apply only to transnational transactions (see below at §72.6.4). In addition to these rules, a special rule applies to entertainers and sportsmen (see below at §72.6.5).

72.6.2 Trade Carried on Through a Branch or Agency: Income Tax

Where a non-resident carries on a trade, profession or vocation in the UK through a branch or agency, that branch or agency is treated as the UK representative of the non-resident and

---

[89] TIOPA 2010, s 229, ex FA 1999, s 86(3); for penalties, see TIOPA 2010, s 227, ex FA 1999, s 86(4)–(9) and Statement of Practice SP 3/99, paras 55, 56.

[90] TIOPA 2010, s 222, ex FA 1999, s 87, applying TA 1988. Sch 28AA, paras 6, 7. FA 1998, s 11 (notice to the other party) also applies (s 223, ex s 85(5)).

[91] See, generally, Bertram and Lymer, Tax Research Network Conference.

[92] SP3/99 and Inland Revenue Bulletin, October 1999, 697.

[93] Smith [1995] BTR 241.

[94] On transitional relief preserving ESC B40 up to 2005, see Inland Revenue Press Release, 17 February 1995, paras 5–10, [1995] *Simon's Weekly Tax Intelligence* 283.

[95] Ex TA 1988, ss 118A *et seq*; see Southern [1996] BTR 375.

as a person distinct from the non-resident.[96] Liability for sums received continues even after the end of the agency.[97] If the branch or agency is a partnership, the partnership is the agent.[98] The income of the branch or agency comprises the amount arising directly or indirectly through or from the branch or agency, and the amount of any income from property or rights used or held by or for the branch or agency;[99] these expressions echo the words of the OECD Model Double Tax Treaty, Article 7. There are further rules for capital gains and insurance companies.

It is possible for a non-resident to carry on a trade in the UK without having a branch or agency. Such a non-resident is liable to UK tax under the self-assessment rules.

Three principal categories of agents are excluded. The first is the occasional agent, ie not in the course of carrying on a regular agency for the non-resident. This repeats words found in earlier legislation, where they were described by one judge as 'apparently very vague'.[100] The second category is the defined broker.[101] A broker, unlike an agent, acts for both sides.[102] If the conditions are satisfied, the broker is not liable even though he acts regularly for the non-resident. There is no definition of the term 'broker'.[103]

The third category is the investment manager carrying out investment transactions for the non-resident.[104] The manager must be carrying on a business of providing investment management services, have carried out the transaction in the ordinary course of business and have received not less than the customary charge for the service. Further, the manager must have acted in an independent capacity.[105] Other rules may disqualify the manager from protection if he and any connected persons are beneficially entitled to more than 20% of the taxable income of the non-resident from transactions carried out through brokers and investment managers.[106] The 20% rule is softened to exclude situations where this percentage is exceeded owing to matters outside the manager's control (assuming the manager takes reasonable mitigating steps); this is primarily to prevent the agent from becoming liable just because of a sudden swing in the market. These rules are modified for collective investment schemes.[107] The reasons for allowing even 20% participation are concerned with managers wanting to put 'seed money' into investment schemes.

---

[96] ITA 2007, s 835E, ex FA 1995, s 126(2), (4); for definition, see s 126(8).
[97] ITA 2007, s 835E, r 1, ex FA 1995, s 126(3).
[98] ITA 2007, s 835E, r 3, ex FA 1995, s 126(5)–(7).
[99] ITA 2007, s 835(2), ex FA 1995, s 126(2). See also Inland Revenue Tax Bulletin (August 1995), 237.
[100] ITA 2007, s 835G, ex FA 1995, s 127(1)(a); *TL Boyd & Sons Ltd v Stephen* (1926) 10 TC 698, 747, *per* Rowlatt J. For another example, see *Willson v Hooker* [1995] STC 1142, 67 TC 585.
[101] ITA 2007, s 835H, ex FA 1995, s 127(1)(b), (2).
[102] *Wilcock v Pinto & Co* [1925] 1 KB 30, 42; 9 TC 111, 130, *per* Bankes LJ.
[103] In general, the words of ITA 2007, s 835J, ex FA 1995, s 127 re-enact TMA 1970, s 82(1); however, s 82 defined a broker as including a 'general commission agent'. In *Fleming v London Produce Co Ltd* [1968] 2 All ER 975, 985–86, Megarry J said that 'general commission agent' must be construed eiusdem generis with broker, and that such an agent held himself out as willing to act for others. Rowlatt J once said that a general commission agent generally negotiates for commission; in that case the agent was held not to be a general commission agent when he paid for the goods as soon as he received them instead of waiting to pay the principal out of the proceeds of the sale (*TL Boyd & Sons Ltd v Stephen* (1926) 10 TC 698, 746).
[104] ITA 2007, s 835I, ex FA 1995, s 127(1)(c), (3); such transactions are defined in s 127(12).
[105] On which, see ITA 2007, s 835M, ex FA 1995, s 127(18).
[106] ITA 2007, s 835N, ex FA 1995, s 127(4)–(8); see Smith [1995] BTR 241, 244.
[107] ITA 2007, s 835Q, ex FA 1995, s 127(9)–(11).

72.6.3 Tax on Investment Income

In principle a non-resident is liable to UK income tax in full on profits arising from a trade, profession or vocation carried on in the UK and from land in the UK. The same is true of other sources of income, provided the non-resident has a UK representative under the rules in ITA 2007.

However, if there is no chargeable UK representative, ITA 2007, Part 14, Chapter 1 (ex FA 1995, section 128) directs that the non-resident's tax liability to income tax on these other sources is limited to the tax deducted at source. It also directs that the income subject to such deduction is not to be aggregated with the non-resident's other income to calculate the tax due in respect of that other income.[108] As was seen above, not all UK intermediaries are representatives; the purpose of the rule is to prevent exposure to extra UK tax just because the non-resident uses a UK investment manager.[109] FA 2008 brought a welcome flexibility by giving HMRC the power to make an order designating transactions as investment transactions for the purpose of these rules.[110] The list is published on the HMRC website.[111]

As noted earlier in this chapter, however, FA 2016 establishes a new framework for taxing non-UK residents (and Scottish residents). As outlined in ITA 2007, section 9A, a non-UK resident individual will be subject to a new category of 'default' tax rates (basic, higher and additional) on most forms of income, but the same rates as UK resident individuals on savings and dividend income. Importantly, the rule in ITTOIA 2005, section 399, whereby a non-UK resident is treated as having paid tax at the dividend ordinary rate on the amount or value of the dividend has been retained, but without the previous grossing up of the dividend by reference to the dividend ordinary rate. Other non-UK residents (ie companies) will be subject to the default basic rate on savings income, the dividend ordinary rate on dividend income, and the default tax rates on other forms of income. It is not immediately clear to what extent non-residents will be subject to higher taxes than before under this new regime and, if so, how the tax will be collected. At the time of writing HMRC had not yet issued guidance on how the new regime is to operate in practice.

72.6.4 Deduction at Source

Various provisions require deduction by the person making the payment where the payee is non-resident, eg rent (ITA 2007, sections 971–972, ex TA 1988, section 42A), yearly interest (ITA 2007, section 874(1)(d), ex TA 1988, section 349(2)(c)), sale of patent rights (ITA 2007, section 910, ex TA 1988, section 349ZA), and copyright royalties and public lending rights (ITA 2007, sections 906–909, ex TA 1988, sections 536 and 537). These are a vital part of the system of taxing non-residents.

In this connection one must note the major changes made in the last decade reducing the scope of deduction at source for payments of interest and public revenue dividends. These

---

[108] ITA 2007, s 811, ex FA 1995, s 128(1).

[109] ITA 2007, ss 813 and 814, ex FA 1995, s 128(2), (3); for earlier years, see ESC B13.

[110] ITA 2007, ss 827(2) and 835S, ex FA 1995, s 127(12), introduced by FA 2008, s 35 and Sch 12. Investment Manager (Specified Transactions) Regulations 2009 specifiy such transactions, including any transaction in stocks or shares, units in a collective investment scheme, securities or foreign currency. The regulation does not carry the usual SI number, but is nevertheless secondary legislation with full statutory force.

[111] HMRC international manual INTM269070.

should be seen in conjunction with other provisions on the exchange of information and as part of the UK view that tax on interest accruing to non-residents is better protected by the exchange of information than by a withholding tax. This view is consistent with UK attitudes but not with Continental ones, where bank secrecy has been treasured not so much as a way of evading tax as a way of protecting oneself against the power of the State, a problem which has of course been much more acute on the Continent than in the UK.

Again, at the time of writing HMRC had not yet issued guidance on how the new regime for taxing UK investment and other income of non-UK residents is to operate in practice.

72.6.5 Entertainers, etc

This part of the law does not show the rewrite in a good light; the provisions which used to be TA 1988, sections 555–558 are now spread between ITTOIA 2005, ITA 2007 and CTA 2009. A charge is imposed on the profits arising where a non UK-resident performer, as defined, performs a relevant activity in the UK in the tax year.[112] The need for such a provision and its history are well explained by Lord Scott in *Agassi v Robinson*.[113] ITA 2007, Part 15, Chapter 18, sections 965–970 (ex TA 1988, section 555) provide for the deduction of tax from any payment or transfer made which is connected with the relevant activity.[114] Performers caught include entertainers and sportsmen. The task of prescribing and refining is carried out by regulations.[115] The Revenue accept that the obligation to deduct is subject to the provisions of the relevant double taxation agreement; thus, the UK–US Treaty grants an exemption where the gross receipts of the person do not exceed $20,000 in the tax year concerned.[116]

The regulations contain considerable scope for problems of interpretation and timing, but their main thrust is clear and they are widely drawn. Among matters to be noted is the rule that while the maximum amount to be withheld is the basic rate of tax, now 20%, the amount paid may be treated by the Revenue as a net sum, thus causing the sums to be grossed up,[117] a process which makes the effective rate of tax on the net sum 28%.

The scope of these rules was considered in *Agassi v Robinson*.[118] A, the well-known tennis player not resident in the UK, set up a controlled company to handle endorsements, etc. Sums were paid to the company by other non-resident companies, Nike and Head, under such contracts. A came to the UK to play in tournaments such as Wimbledon. It was not disputed that these payments could properly be attributed to his time playing tennis in the UK. However, A argued that what is now ITA 2007, section 966 had a territorial limitation; since it imposed a duty to withhold tax, it could apply only where the payer could be made to deduct tax, ie if the payer had a tax presence in the UK. Head and Nike had no such presence. Agreeing with Lightman J and reversing the Court of Appeal, the House of Lords held that it would be absurd to attribute to the legislature the intention that liability

---

[112] ITTOIA 2005, s 13 and CTA 2009, s 1309, ex TA 1988, s 555.

[113] [2006] UKHL 23, [2006] STC 1056 at paras 8 *et seq.*

[114] See comparative study by Sandler (1995), research sponsored by the Chartered Institute of Taxation (Kluwer, 1995).

[115] Income Tax (Entertainers and Sportsmen) Regulations 1987 (SI 1987/530).

[116] Art 16 of the UK–US Treaty (2001).

[117] SI 1987/530, reg 17.

[118] [2006] UKHL 23, 2006 STC 1056.

could in any and all cases be avoided by the simple expedient of channelling the payment through a foreign company with no tax presence here. If this were the case, the tax would effectively become voluntary.[119] Lord Walker dissented. The case concerns the liability of A; no attempt was made to use these rules to recover the tax from Nike or Head, a view which seems consistent with principle.

Then there is the European law issue. A similar provision of the German tax code imposing a flat rate tax on visiting entertainers and sportsmen was held to break Article 43 EC (now Article 49 TFEU) unless it gave rise to a lower tax burden.[120] As an American national, Mr Agassi was not able to use this line of argument.

72.7   Diverted Profits Tax

At Autumn Statement 2014, in the midst of the G20/OECD Base Erosion and Profit Shifting (BEPS) project (see §69.11), the UK Government announced that it was moving unilaterally and introducing a new anti-profit shifting tax—the Diverted Profits Tax (DPT). The DPT was intended to counter the use of contrived tax planning arrangements by MNEs to circumvent rules on permanent establishment and transfer pricing in order to divert profits from the UK. Legislation (30 pages of it!) was introduced in FA 2015, Part 3 to establish the new charge and related administration, with effect from 1 April 2015. HMRC issued over 100 pages of detailed guidance on the operation of the DPT.[121] This entirely new type of tax—popularly referred to as the 'Google Tax'—is at a rate of 25 per cent of diverted profits relating to UK activity. The rate is deliberately higher than the usual corporate tax rate 'to encourage those businesses with arrangements within the scope of DPT to change those arrangements and pay corporation tax on profits in line with economic activity'.[122]

The DPTs rules are very detailed, but briefly, pursuant to FA 2015 sections 77–116, the DPT charge arises if either of two rules applies. The first rule is designed to address arrangements which avoid a UK permanent establishment (PE) and comes into effect if a person is carrying on activity in the UK in connection with supplies of goods and services by a non-UK resident company to customers in the UK, provided that the detailed conditions are met. This is the rule that prompted the tax to be called the 'Google Tax', as Google has been accused of painstakingly avoiding having a UK PE, with sales to UK-based customers finally agreed and profits booked in Ireland. It should be noted that even if Google had a UK PE, under the general rules it is taxable only on profits attributable to the PE as determined under transfer pricing rules. Such profits may not be substantial given the important role played by Google's non-UK developed IP and technology products in those sales to UK-based customers.

---

[119]   Eg Lord Mance, *ibid*, at [32].

[120]   Case C-234/01 *Arnoud Gerritse v FinanzAmt NeuKoln-Nord Gerritse* [2003] ECR I-5933; see Hinnekens [2003] 12 *EC Tax Rev* 207.

[121]   HMRC, *Diverted Profits Tax: guidance* (Nov 2015), available at https://www.gov.uk/government/publications/diverted-profits-tax. For commentary see Neidle [2015] BTR 147 and Baker [2015] BTR 167.

[122]   HMRC, *Diverted Profits Tax: guidance* (Nov 2015), DPT1000.

The second rule will apply to certain arrangements which lack economic substance involving entities with an existing UK taxable presence. The primary function is to counteract arrangements that exploit tax differentials and will apply where the detailed conditions, including those on an 'effective tax mismatch outcome' are met. Typically the rule is directed at non-residents with a UK PE, but it is drafted broadly enough to encompass a UK company using entities or transactions that lack economic substance to exploit tax mismatches.[123]

Neither rule applies to small or medium-sized enterprises and the first rule is subject to an exemption based on the level of the foreign company's (or a connected company's) total sales revenues from all supplies of goods and services to UK customers not exceeding £10 million for a twelve month accounting period.

The expected tax take from the DPT is not large—around £360 million per annum. Readers may well ask whether the introduction of this new tax was really necessary, given the BEPS work and now that the UK has a GAAR. The answer is most likely because it made for good politics at a time when MNEs were being portrayed in the media as running circles around HMRC. The decision to introduce the DPT before waiting for the results of the BEPS project is highly questionable.[124]

---

[123] HMRC, *Diverted Profits Tax: guidance* (Nov 2015), DPT1010.
[124] Self, 'Diverted profits tax: give BEPS a chance', *Tax Journal* (15 Dec 2014).

73

Controlled Foreign Companies

73.1 Introduction

73.1.1 Overview

The 'Controlled Foreign Company' (CFC) rules formerly in TA 1988, Part XVIII, Chapter IV and now in TIOPA 2010, Part 9A can be traced back to FA 1984. These rules look at particular non-resident companies and treat the income arising in those companies as subject to UK corporation tax in the hands of those with the right level of interest in the company. This is done whether or not the income has been passed to the shareholders, and in particular shareholders resident in the UK, by way of dividend. It will be seen that the rules look at income and not capital gains; moreover, the regime applies to companies and not to individuals (or trusts or partnerships). As we shall see, the CFC regime has a number of other limiting features.

Since 1984 the rules have been changed both in detail and in substance on a number of occasions. The UK Government's 2007 discussion document on the taxation of foreign profits proposed a general move away from taxing UK resident companies on worldwide income to a more territorial approach, including an exemption system for foreign dividends (since implemented, see below §75.3). The discussion document also contained proposals for major changes in the CFC area. The original proposal was to move from the 'entity' method—which looks at particular companies or entities—to a 'tainted income' method. This proposal was ultimately rejected as unworkable, and replaced with one focusing again on entities but with a much narrower scope than the previous regime, in keeping with the territorial approach.

The current rules in TIOPA 2010, Part 9A are effective for CFCs with accounting periods beginning on or after 1 January 2013. As Richards notes,[1] much of the architecture of the

---

[1] Richards [2012] BTR 3.

present regime is similar to that of the former TA 1988 regime. The rules, it is fair to say, remain exceedingly complicated. Very briefly, a charge is levied on UK resident companies holding a significant interest in certain non UK-resident companies with some form of UK-related profits and controlled by one or more UK persons. Companies not subject to a lower level of taxation still will not be CFCs; under the old rules this was a condition for the CFC regime to apply but under the new rules this is by the operation of an exemption. Similarly, there are some mechanical exemptions, which, like the old regime, include a form of low profit exemption and an exemption for excluded countries. One important and obvious difference from the old regime is that companies carrying on financial trades may qualify for a partial finance company exemption, with only one-quarter of the company's relevant profits eligible for apportionment (an effective tax rate of 5% assuming a 20% corporation tax rate).

73.1.2 The Rationale for CFC Regimes

A fundamental element of many tax regimes, including the UK's, is the recognition of a company as an entity separate from its shareholders—even a 100% owned subsidiary is viewed as separate from its parent. This feature, combined with an international tax framework dividing tax jurisdiction according to residence and source, can give rise to opportunities to avoid or defer the payment of UK tax on foreign profits earned by a foreign subsidiary of a UK resident where those profits are subject to tax at a lower tax rate than the UK's. This could be viewed as a breach of capital export neutrality (CEN) if UK resident companies through the simple expedient of setting up a foreign subsidiary are able to pay less tax on foreign earnings than on domestic earnings. The 2009 move to an exemption system for most foreign dividends received by a UK company provides an even greater incentive for UK resident companies to earn profits abroad through foreign subsidiaries as those earnings can now generally be repatriated to the UK without incurring any further UK corporate tax charge. It should be noted that exempting foreign dividends from further UK corporate tax advances the competing goal of capital import neutrality (CIN), in that all investors in a particular foreign economy (residents and non-residents) face the same after-tax rate of return on similar investments.

CFC legislation has a second objective, which has become more important to the UK since 2009—to counter harmful tax competition. Of particular concern to the UK Government and to many other countries is the diversion or shifting of profits that properly 'belong' (on some measure of value creation) to companies resident in their country into other companies of the group that are resident in other jurisdictions including tax havens. The G20/OECD Base Erosion and Profit Shifting (BEPS) project (see §69.11) has endorsed domestic CFC regimes as an important tool in combatting BEPS in Action 3:[2]

> Controlled foreign company (CFC) rules respond to the risk that taxpayers with a controlling interest in a foreign subsidiary can strip the base of their country of residence and, in some cases, other countries by shifting income into a CFC. Without such rules, CFCs provide opportunities for profit shifting and long-term deferral of taxation.

---

[2] OECD, *BEPS Action 3 'Designing Effective Controlled Foreign Company Rules' Final Report* (Oct 2015), 9.

The BEPS Action 3 final report sets out the following six building blocks for the design of effective domestic CFC rules:[3]

(1) *Definition of a CFC.* The report sets out recommendations on how to determine when shareholders have sufficient influence over a foreign company for that company to be a CFC.

(2) *CFC exemptions and threshold requirements.* The report recommends that CFC rules only apply to controlled foreign companies that are subject to effective tax rates that are meaningfully lower than those applied in the parent jurisdiction.

(3) *Definition of income.* The report recommends that CFC rules include a definition of CFC income, and provides a list of example approaches.

(4) *Computation of income.* The report recommends that CFC rules use the rules of the parent jurisdiction to compute the CFC income to be attributed to shareholders.

(5) *Attribution of income.* The report recommends that, when possible, the attribution threshold should be tied to the control threshold and that the amount of income to be attributed should be calculated by reference to the proportionate ownership or influence.

(6) *Prevention and elimination of double taxation.* The report emphasises the importance of both preventing and eliminating double taxation, and it recommends, for example, that jurisdictions with CFC rules allow a credit for foreign taxes actually paid, including any tax assessed on intermediate parent companies under a CFC regime. It also recommends that countries consider relief from double taxation on dividends on, and gains arising from the disposal of, CFC shares where the income of the CFC has previously been subject to taxation under a CFC regime.

73.2 CFC Regime in Outline

The UK's current CFC regime is very much in line with the OECD's recommendations in BEPS Action 3—and in fact had a significant influence on them. The rules apply if, in any accounting period, a company is 'resident' outside the UK but is controlled by persons resident in the UK, and a significant mismatch exists between key business activities undertaken in the UK and the profits arising from those activities which are allocated outside the UK.[4] Unless an exemption applies, the CFC rules apportion chargeable profits of the foreign company computed as for UK corporation tax and any creditable tax, among all the persons who had an interest in the company during the accounting period.

The rules are quite detailed, and what follows is an outline of the key elements. The issue of compatibility of the UK's CFC regime with EU law in light of the *Cadbury Schweppes* case[5] is considered below at §77.3.5.

---

[3] *Ibid*, 9–10.

[4] The original rules were introduced by FA 1984, ss 82–108. See, generally, Arnold, *The Taxation of Foreign Controlled Companies: An International Comparison* (Canadian Tax Foundation, 1986); and Arnold [1985] BTR 286, 362. The 2012 reforms are examined in a series of FA notes by Richards: see [2012] BTR 3 and 454. For an interesting critique of the very different US rules known as sub part F as they were, see US Treasury Policy Study December 2000 (available in electronic format from the US Treasury website).

[5] Case C-196/04 [2006] ECR I-07995.

73.2.1 *The Gateway*

TIOPA 2010, Part 9A, Chapter 2 sets out the basic details of the CFC charge. The center-piece of the UK's CFC regime is the 'Gateway' that is used to identify situations with a significant mismatch between key business activities undertaken in the UK and the profits arising from those activities which are allocated outside the UK. The design thus reflects the central concern of combatting base erosion and profit shifting. The Gateway, found in Chapters 3–8, effectively replaces the old motive test, and limits the CFC's chargeable profits to only so much of its profits as pass through the Gateway (section 371BA). Therefore, from a taxpayer's perspective, it is better to be outside the Gateway than in.

Chapter 3 operates as an initial filter and begins by laying down rules for determin-ing which, if any, of Chapters 4–8 apply for an accounting period (section 371BB). Non-financial profits that meet any one of the four conditions in section 371CA will be outside the CFC charge:

Condition A (Tax purpose)—at no time during the accounting period does the CFC hold assets or bear risks under an arrangement (a) the main purpose, or one of the main purposes, of which is to reduce or eliminate UK tax, and (b) in consequence of the arrangement the CFC expects its business to be more profitable. In addition, there must not be an expectation that, as a consequence of the arrangement, a person's tax liabilities in any territory will be reduced and it is reasonable to suppose that, but for that expectation, the arrangement would not have been made.
Condition B (UK activities)—at no time during the accounting period does the CFC have any UK-managed assets or bear any UK-managed risks. Assets or risks are 'UK-managed' if (a) the acquisition, creation, development or exploitation of the asset, or (b) the taking on, or bearing of, the risk, is managed or controlled to any significant extent by way of activities carried on in the UK by the CFC (otherwise than through a UK PE) or by companies connected with the CFC operating on a non-arm's-length basis.
Condition C (Capability and commercial effectiveness)—throughout the accounting period the CFC has itself the capability to ensure that its business would be commer-cially effective were its UK-managed assets or risks no longer UK-managed.
Condition D—the CFC's assumed profits consist only of one or both of non-trading finance profits or property business profits.

If none of these four conditions is satisfied then the remaining chapters of the Gateway or, alternatively, the exemptions which apply to the CFC as a whole, will need to be consid-ered. Chapter 4, the primary remaining Gateway chapter, seeks first to identify the share of the CFC's assets and risks that would be attributed to a UK PE of the CFC, assuming that all the significant people functions (SPFs) relevant to those assets and risks were under-taken by a single enterprise. If there are no relevant UK SPFs then there are no Chapter 4 Gateway profits. If there are relevant UK SPFs, the Chapter 4 Gateway profits are those which the CFC would not earn if its ownership of the assets and its bearing of the risks were correspondingly reduced.[6] Various exclusions may also apply. Chapter 5 applies for a

---

[6] As described in HM Treasury and HMRC, 'Controlled Foreign Companies (CFC) reform: a Gateway update' (February 2012) 10.

CFC's accounting period if the CFC has non-trading finance profits. Chapter 6 concerns trading finance profits of the CFC where the CFC has funds or other assets which derive from UK-connected capital contributions. Chapter 7 relates to captive insurance businesses and Chapter 8 deals with solo consolidation waivers under section BIPRU 2.1 of the FSA Handbook.

73.2.2 Minimum 25% Interest and CFC Charge

A CFC charge may be made only on a company resident in the UK which has a minimum 25% interest in the CFC.[7] The CFC charge is the sum equal to the UK corporation tax rate multiplied by the appropriate percentage of the CFC's chargeable profits reflecting the company's interest in the CFC as pass through the Gateway less any applicable creditable tax.[8] Where the CFC keeps its accounts in a currency other than sterling, the chargeable profits are calculated in that foreign currency for the purpose of these rules.[9]

Chapter 17 sets out the rules on how to apportion a CFC's chargeable profits and creditable tax among the persons who have relevant interests in the CFC. The minimum 25% interest rule might seem to encourage schemes under which holdings are divided among other companies. However, the legislation used to have a 10% minimum, so showing that the Revenue saw no threat from such schemes. The answer is likely to be that commercial considerations prevented such schemes from getting off the ground unless they were very artificial, in which case other doctrines would apply.

In order to prevent the avoidance of the 25% minimum by fragmentation of share ownership, it is provided that shares held by connected or associated persons are to be taken into account in calculating the extent of the interest.[10] This does not mean that the connected or associated persons are liable to tax under these rules, or that the amounts apportioned to them are taxable in the hands of the UK-resident taxpayer.

73.2.3 Control

The CFC rules apply only if the CFC is controlled by persons (not just companies) resident in the UK.[11] This slightly confusing position means that not only companies but also individuals and trusts are taken into account when deciding whether the company is controlled by persons resident in the UK, but it is still the case that the actual charge is on a company. Thus, if a company is resident outside the UK but has 30% non-UK shareholders, 40% UK corporate shareholders and 30% UK individual shareholders, the company is controlled by persons resident in the UK and the CFC rules can apply; however, they apply only to the 40% UK corporate shareholders. In general, pursuant to section 371RB, a person ('P') controls a company ('C') if—

---

[7] TIOPA 2010, s 371BD, ex TA 1988, s 747(5), as amended by FA 1998, Sch 17, para 3.
[8] TIOPA 2010, s 371BC, ex TA 1988, s 747(4)(a) and FA 1998, Sch 18, para 8, third step.
[9] TIOPA 2010, s 371SI, ex FA 1993, ss 92–92E as added by FA 2004 (see above §5.4); the addition of these rules meant that s 747A was superfluous and it was repealed by FA 2005, Sch 7, para 24.
[10] TIOPA 2010, s 371OD, ex TA 1988, s 747(5)(b).
[11] TIOPA 2010, Pt 9A, Ch 18, ss 371RA–371RF.

(a)   by means of the holding of shares or the possession of voting power in or in relation to C or any other company, or

(b)   by virtue of any powers conferred by the articles of association or other document regulating C or any other company,

P has the power to secure that the affairs of C are conducted in accordance with P's wishes.

In addition, P will control C if it is reasonable to assume that P would receive more than 50% of the proceeds of the sale of all of C's share capital, of the income if all of C's income was distributed, or of the assets on the winding up of C. Importantly if two or more persons, taken together, meet the requirement for controlling a company, those persons are taken to control the company. Future powers and rights are taken into account for purposes of these tests.[12]

73.2.4 Exemptions

Turning now to the exemptions, Chapter 9 begins by providing both partial and full exemption for qualifying loan relationships. Chapter 10 contains an exempt period exemption; basically, if a company comes within the CFC rules for a short time (generally less than 12 months) and in a subsequent period none of its profits are chargeable then the first period is exempted. Chapter 11 contains the excluded territories exemption for CFCs resident in a territory with a headline tax rate of >75% of the UK main corporation tax rate that satisfy a number of further conditions. The low profits exemption in Chapter 12 applies if the CFC's accounting profits (a) are not more than £50,000, or (b) are not more than £500,000 and the amount of those profits representing non-trading income is not more than £50,000. Chapter 13 is an entirely novel exemption for low profit margins, where the CFC's accounting profits basically represent 10% or less of relevant operating expenditure. Lastly, Chapter 14 sets out the 'tax exemption', which replaces the former lower level of tax test and applies if the CFC is subject to local tax of at least 75% of the corresponding UK tax. These exemptions are discussed below at §73.4.

73.3   Definitions

73.3.1 Residence

The legislation applies only where the CFC is not resident in the UK. This is one of the unusual situations in which the UK tax system, having decided that a company is not resident in the UK, must determine exactly where the company is resident; the rules are therefore artificial. Chapter 20 contains the rules for determining the territory in which a CFC is resident for the purposes of Part 9A. The basic rule is that a company is regarded as resident in any territory in which, throughout the relevant accounting period, it is liable to tax (whether or not it actually pays any) by reason of its domicile, residence or place of management.[13] These phrases are designed to distinguish tax on the basis of residence from tax on the

---

[12] TIOPA 2010, s 371RD.
[13] TIOPA 2010, s 371TB, ex TA 1988, s 749(1); these words are familiar to international tax specialists in other contexts: see OECD Model Treaty, Art 4(1).

basis of source. Presumably, this question is determined by reference to the UK tax system's assessment of the foreign tax law; the question whether the entity is a company is, again, presumably to be decided by UK tax law.

Where the company is liable to tax in more than one country, officers of the company or companies with more than 50% of the interests which are chargeable may select the territory.[14] Failing such an election one looks first to the place of effective management, followed by the situs of the majority of the assets; as a last resort a Revenue officer may designate the country.[15] These elections and designations are irrevocable.[16]

73.3.2 Other Definitions

73.3.2.1 Accounting Periods

These are defined as for corporation tax; however, a period begins when a company becomes a CFC and ends when it ceases to be so.[17]

73.3.2.2 Creditable Tax

This is defined to comprise:[18]

(1)   any double taxation relief which would be available if the foreign company's chargeable profits were liable to corporation tax, in respect of any foreign tax attributable to income comprised in those chargeable profits;

(2)   income tax deducted at source from income received by the company which could be set off against such corporation tax;

(3)   income or corporation tax actually charged on the chargeable profits and not repayable; and

(4)   any amount of foreign CFC charge paid in respect of income included or represented in the CFC's chargeable profits for the accounting period.

73.3.2.3 Assumed Taxable Total Profits and Corporation Tax Assumptions

A CFC's 'assumed taxable total profits' for an accounting period are what, applying the 'corporation tax assumptions', would be the CFC's taxable total profits of the accounting period for corporation tax purposes.[19] The corporation tax assumptions are set out in sections 371SD–371SR. The principal assumption is that the CFC has claimed or is to be given the maximum amount available of those reliefs which have to be claimed and allowances which are given automatically but which may be disclaimed in whole or part, unless any UK company or companies holding a majority interest disclaims any such relief or claims a smaller amount.[20]

---

[14]   TIOPA 2010, s 371TC, ex TA 1988, ss 749(4), 749A(1).
[15]   TIOPA 2010, s 371TB(5)-(9), ex TA 1988, s 749(2), (3), (6).
[16]   TIOPA 2010, s 371TC, ex TA 1988, s 749A(1)(b).
[17]   TIOPA 2010, s 371VB, ex TA 1988, s 751(1)–(5A).
[18]   TIOPA 2010, s 371PA, ex TA 1988, s 751(6).
[19]   TIOPA 2010, s 371SB.
[20]   TIOPA 2010, ss 371SF–371SG.

Group relief and related provisions are excluded for the purposes of computing charge-able profits. Accordingly, the foreign company is not treated as a member of a UK group or consortium.[21] The full range of capital allowances, including scientific research allowances, is treated as available.[22]

73.4 Exemptions

73.4.1 Summary of Exemptions and Structural Exclusions

The CFC charge is subject to some important exemptions and structural exclusions. Thus, the rules apply only:

(1) to income, and not to capital gains nor to qualifying loan relationships;
(2) to bodies subject to corporation tax, and not to income tax;
(3) to non-exempt periods;
(4) where the minimum of 25% of the chargeable profits may be attributed to this com-pany (and to persons connected or associated with it);
(5) where the local tax burden in the territory of residence is less than 75% of the cor-responding UK tax;
(6) if the territory in which the CFC resident is not on a list of excluded territories;
(7) if the CFC's accounting profits (a) are not more than £50,000, or (b) are not more than £500,000 and the amount of those profits representing non-trading income is not more than £50,000; or
(8) CFC's accounting profits basically represent 10% or less of relevant operating expenditure.

The exemptions in (5) and (6) are discussed in further detail next.

73.4.2 The Tax Exemption–Where Local Tax Burden Less Than 75% of the Corresponding UK Tax

The 'tax exemption' in Chapter 14 applies where the local tax paid by the CFC in the CFC's territory of residence is less than three-quarters of 'the corresponding UK tax'.[23] Before 1993 the fraction was one-half. The change was a delayed reaction to the general reduction in UK corporation tax rates since 1984. Some foreign tax systems responded to this rule by creating so-called designer tax rates, eg making a company pay just enough tax to reach the 75% limit, either by letting the company choose its rate of tax or by setting two rates of tax for two types of income and then allowing the company to allocate its income between the two categories.[24] Such devices were stopped by FA 2000 with effect from 6 September

---

[21] TIOPA 2010, s 371SL.
[22] TIOPA 2010, s 371SM, ex TA 1988, Sch 24, para 10.
[23] TIOPA 2010, s 371NB, ex TA 1988, s 750, as amended by FA 1993, s 119(1), (2).
[24] Inland Revenue Press Release, 6 September 1999.

1999.[25] The friendly countries indulging in this behaviour were Guernsey, Jersey, the Isle of Man, Gibraltar and Ireland.

The 'corresponding UK' tax is the hypothetical corporation tax on the chargeable profits of the foreign company computed on the assumptions described above at §73.3.2.3.[26] UK income or corporation tax actually charged on chargeable profits is deducted from the corresponding UK tax. Double taxation relief attributable to the local tax is not taken into account.

73.4.3 The Excluded Territories Exemption

If the CFC is resident in an 'excluded territory' for the accounting period and certain other conditions are met, an exemption applies. HMRC publishes a list of territories which are regarded as either wholly or completely outside these rules; with the introduction of self-assessment the list has taken the form of a statutory instrument.[27] A company which is resident in a territory in Part I of the list is outside these rules, but Part II provides a further condition in respect of insurance businesses any part of which are carried on in Luxembourg.[28] A modified excluded territories exemption applies in other specified cases.[29] In addition, various tests of sources and forms of income apply very generally to require 90% of the CFC's commercially quantified income (or £50,000 if higher) to be local source income.[30]

The list of excluded territories is not a list of countries which are regarded as not having a low level of taxation. The basis for the exclusion of the rules must be sought in the old motive test. The point is explained by Arnold thus:

> [T]he reason ... appears to be that low taxation is determined only for the country in which the company is resident. By adding the requirement that a company derive at least 90% of its income from the country, the list permits inclusion of high tax countries (such as France) that exempt foreign income.[31]

The excluded territories exemption was found to be subject to abuse, and so amendments were made by FA 2005, withdrawing the exemption where the company had been involved in a scheme or an arrangement to reduce UK tax.[32]

---

[25] TIOPA 2010, s 371ND, ex TA 1988, s 750A, added by FA 2000, Sch 31, para 3.
[26] TIOPA 2010, s 371NE, ex TA 1988, s 750(3).
[27] Controlled Foreign Companies (Excluded Territories) Regulations, SI 2012/3024.
[28] Controlled Foreign Companies (Excluded Territories) Regulations, SI 2012/3024, regs 3 and 5.
[29] Controlled Foreign Companies (Excluded Territories) Regulations, SI 2012/3024, reg 4.
[30] TIOPA 2010, ss 371KD-KJ.
[31] [1985] BTR 302; see also Arnold, *Taxation of Controlled Foreign Corporations: an International Comparison* (Canadian Tax Foundation, 1986) 321.
[32] FA 2005, s 87; see now TIOPA 2010, s 371KB(1)(d).

74

Capital Gains

74.1 General Rules

74.1.1 Residence and Non-residence

In general, a person is chargeable to CGT if resident in the UK for at least part of the year of assessment.[1] If the person is not so resident, a charge arises only if:

(1) a trade or profession is being carried on in the UK through a branch or agency; and

(2) the asset was both situated in the UK and either used in or for the trade when or before the gain accrued, or used by or for the branch or agency when or before the gain accrued;[2] or

(3) the non-resident disposes of a UK residential property interest on or after 6 April 2015.[3]

With respect to category (1), the corporation tax principles are similar, though the legislation refers to a 'permanent establishment' rather than a 'branch or agency'.[4]

These rules preserve the basic premise that a person is taxable either because of residence or source, but curiously restricts the source primarily to two types—UK assets of a branch/

---

[1] TCGA 1992, s 2(1) and (1A).
[2] TCGA 1992, s 10; he may also be exempt by treaty (*ibid*), and see below at §76.6. On post-cessation disposals, see *ibid*, s 10(2).
[3] TCGA 1992, ss 14B–14H.
[4] TCGA 1992, s 10B.

agency or for UK residential property interests. Thus a non-resident without such a trade or profession bears no CGT even though the asset is in the UK unless it is residential property. Equally, T, a resident individual with a substantial liability to CGT could, until 1998, go overseas, cease to be resident and ordinarily resident, and then dispose of the assets free of all UK tax—at least if the disposal was in the next year of assessment.[5] This reluctance to tax the non-resident is the norm in other countries.[6]

Today, this approach is subject to a growing list of qualifications:

(1) Special rules apply to individuals who cease to be resident but then resume their UK residence (TCGA 1992, sections 10A and 10AA; see below §74.1.2).
(2) There is a general deemed disposal rule for companies ceasing to be resident (section 185).
(3) There is a similar rule for trusts (section 80).
(4) Certain non-residents with chargeable assets in the UK will be deemed to dispose of them when the assets cease to be chargeable (section 25).
(5) Certain gains of non-resident companies and collective investment vehicles owning high-value UK residential property subject to the Annual Tax on Enveloped Dwellings (ATED), referred to as 'ATED-related gains' (section 2B).
(6) Certain gains of non-resident companies may be attributed to UK members (below §74.3).
(7) Certain gains of non-resident trusts may be attributed to relevant UK persons (below §74.5).

Residence for CGT purposes has the same meaning as for income tax (see above §69.3).[7] If the year is a split year as respects an individual under the income tax rules, the individual is not chargeable to capital gains tax in respect of any chargeable gains accruing to the individual in the overseas part of that year.[8]

Where an asset is acquired and disposed of in foreign currency, acquisition cost and disposal proceeds are calculated at the exchange rates prevailing at the acquisition and disposal (above at §43.1.2).[9] On foreign currency as a chargeable or exempt asset, see above §33.7.

74.1.2 Temporary Non-residence and Capital Gains

The relative ease with which properly-advised taxpayers with mobile lifestyles could achieve non-resident status[10] gave rise to Revenue worries. The resulting legislation[11] in TCGA 1992, sections 10A and 10AA is specific; it is not concerned with migrants so much as with temporary non-residents. The meaning of temporary residence for income tax purposes is

---

[5] On dangers of relying on ESC D2 when carrying out an avoidance scheme, see *R v IRC, ex parte Fulford-Dobson* [1987] STC 344; discussed by Williams [1987] BTR 271.
[6] Exceptions include India and Japan. The reluctance is based on the difficulty in collecting the tax, but has not stopped the UK expanding income tax to catch certain receipts.
[7] On residence of partners, see TCGA 1992, s 59 and TA 1988, s 112.
[8] TCGA 1992, s 2(1B) and see above §69.3.5.
[9] *Capcount Trading v Evans* [1993] STC 11, CA; reaffirming *Bentley v Pike* [1981] STC 360, (1991) 53 TC 590.
[10] Eg *Reed v Clark* [1985] STC 323, (1985) 58 TC 528.
[11] Introduced by FA 1998, s 127.

used here as well.[12] Section 10A applies if B, an individual having been UK resident in at least 4 out of the 7 years prior to departure is then non-resident for five years or less. When B reacquires UK-resident status, a CGT charge can arise in the year of return.[13]

Section 10A charges gains realised during the period of non-residence, including any liability in respect of section 13 (see below at §74.3) and section 86 (see below at §74.4) which would have arisen if B had been resident.[14] Relief is given for any losses.[15] Gains and losses on assets acquired after becoming non-resident are, in general, excluded. Further rules deny relief where the new asset exploits a deferral of or exemption from UK tax, eg the acquisition was one on which neither gain nor loss accrued to the disposer or rollover relief reduced the cost of the asset, or the asset was acquired from a spouse or civil partner or was an interest in the settlement.[16] If the remittance basis applies to the taxpayer for the year of return (see below §74.2), foreign chargeable gains that were remitted to the UK during the temporary period of non-residence are to be treated as remitted to the UK in the period of return.[17]

Some of the problems presented by double tax treaties were addressed in FA 2005. The original version of section 10A expressly preserved the effect of double tax treaties. This meant that where the treaty contained a capital gains clause, B was usually protected from section 10A, so giving rise to avoidance.[18] Section 10AA now provides that nothing in any double tax treaty is to prevent the UK from charging tax in the year of return.[19] Where the relevant treaty does not have a capital gains article in the appropriate form, the foreign state may not give credit for the UK tax charged later and the UK may not give relief for the foreign tax charged earlier.[20] This shows the haphazard nature of treaty relief and the unsatisfactory nature of CGT, with its insistence on asset and disposal.

74.1.3 Delayed Remittances

Where a gain arises from the disposal of an asset situated overseas, but the gain cannot be remitted to the UK, the taxpayer may make a claim for deferral of CGT on conditions analogous to income tax relief (see above at §71.5).[21] The inability to remit gains to the UK must arise from the laws of the territory where the asset was situated, from the executive action of its government or from the impossibility of obtaining foreign currency there.

---

[12] TCGA 1992, s 10A(1), referring to FA 2013, Sch 45, Pt 4.

[13] On period during which assessment may be made, see TCGA 1992, s 10A(7); the rules apply to individuals becoming non-resident on or after 17 March 1998 (FA 1998, s 127(4)).

[14] TCGA 1992, s 10A(2).

[15] TCGA 1992, s 10A(2).

[16] TCGA 1992, s 10AA. The no gain, no loss disposals are those in ss 58 (husband and wife), 73 (death) and 258(4) (works of art); the reductions are those under ss 23 (reinvestment of compensation money), 152 (acquisition of business asset), 162 (transfer of business) and 247 (compulsory acquisition). There are further rules for reorganisation of bonds and gilts (s 116), acquisition of compensation stock (s 134) and rollover relief where the new assets are depreciating assets (s 154).

[17] TCGA 1992, s 10A(9).

[18] Such clauses usually gave the States of treaty residence exclusive right to tax, so that the UK could not tax someone who was resident under normal UK rules but non-resident for treaty purposes.

[19] TCGA 1992, s 10A(9C), inserted by FA 2005, s 32.

[20] Avery Jones [1999] BTR 325.

[21] TCGA 1992, s 279.

Since tax is levied as soon as the conditions cease, gains accruing over several years may come into charge at one time. In such circumstances, unlike income tax, there is no charge by reference to the years in which the gain accrued. This may mean the loss of the annual exemption for the years in which the gains actually arose. Similar Revenue reasoning means that this relief does not apply where the taxpayer is chargeable on a remittance basis.

74.2   Remittance Basis

As already seen (above §71.4), the FA 2008 remittance rules apply both to income and to chargeable gains (FIGs). The remittance basis applies to foreign chargeable gains real-ised by an individual resident, but not domiciled, in the UK; however, this applies only to gains from the disposal of an asset outside the UK.[22] For the meaning of 'domicile' and on planned reforms to the income tax, CGT and IHT treatment of 'non-doms' see above §69.5. In computing the amount of the gain, any liability to foreign tax is deductible in full.[23] The scope of remittance is widened in the same way as for income tax.[24] If split-year treatment applies (see above §69.3.5), the chargeable gains are treated as accruing to the individual in the part of the year (the overseas part or the UK part) in which the foreign chargeable gains are so remitted.[25] The availability of the remittance basis is thus governed by the status of the person rather than simply by the location of the asset.

TCGA 1992, section 16(4), now repealed, actually barred loss relief where the remit-tance basis was available. After FA 2008 the situation is more complex. An individual who is resident but not domiciled in the UK may simply decide to use the arising basis and not the remittance basis. Such a person is entitled to loss relief under the normal CGT rules. If, however, he elects to use the remittance basis, more complex rules (TCGA 1992, sections 16ZA–16ZD) apply. Section 16ZA directs that they apply once the individual has elected, irrevocably, to be taxed on the remittance basis under ITA 2007, section 809B; any year during which this election is in force is called a 'relevant tax year'. So sections 16ZA–16ZD apply for all later years, save only for those in which the individual is domiciled in the UK.

If the gains are remitted in the year in which they accrue, they are charged (under section 12) in the normal way. However, if losses arise in Year 1 but gains are remitted in Year 3 so that they become chargeable in Year 3 under TCGA 1992, section 12, the normal remittance basis rule, section 16ZB, applies to determine the amount that will be taxable. Section 16ZC deals with the order in which losses are set off against gains, and does so on a two-step basis familiar in modern UK tax legislation. Section 16ZC also sets out what is to happen when the gain and loss arise in the same year.

The essence of the scheme in section 16ZB is that the loss may be set off against the gain which is remitted and so becomes taxable in the UK under section 12. However, if the taxpayer still has unremitted gains from any previous year or that year, the loss is set off against those other still unremitted gains. This result is not unlike the old rule in section 16(4) (now repealed).

---

[22] TCGA 1992, s 12.
[23] TIOPA 2010, ss 2 or 18 (tax credit) or s 113 (deduction), ex TCGA 1992, s 277–78.
[24] TCGA 1992, s 12(2).
[25] TCGA 1992, s 12(1A), (2A).

74.2.1 Remittance from Mixed Fund

Also as seen above (§71.4), where the fund from which money consideration or service has been funded is mixed, FA 2008, section 809Q(4) lists the order in which remittance is taken to come. The order is as follows:

(1) employment income (other than income within (2), (3) and (7));
(2) relevant foreign earnings (ITEPA 2003, sections 22 and 26);
(3) foreign specific employment income (ITEPA 2003, section 41A);
(4) relevant foreign income (ITTOIA 2005, section 830);
(5) foreign chargeable gains (TCGA 1992, section 12);
(6) employment income subject to a foreign tax;
(7) relevant foreign income subject to a foreign tax;
(8) foreign chargeable gains subject to a foreign tax;
(9) other income or capital.

The list is intended to benefit the Revenue. Taking sums which have not borne tax (paragraphs (1)–(5)) before those which have (paragraphs (6)–(8)) takes into account the fact that the UK may have to give relief for the foreign tax, whether by credit of deduction. Placing income or capital in (9) and so last is a major change. Previous HMRC practice was to treat it as comprising capital and capital gain in proportion to their presence in the account.[26] This is now enacted as treating the fund as containing income or capital if and to the extent that it is just and reasonable to do so.[27]

Separate problems arise where the fund includes receipts from the sale of two assets. Thus, if one asset is sold with a gain of £500 and another asset for a loss of £500, it is presumably open to argue that the loss should be set off against the gain. Further issues arise might have arisen if the gains were treated differently, eg if one is exempt and the other not, but this will usually be anticipated by noting that the legislation in framed in terms of chargeable gains.

74.2.2 Location of Assets—CGT Rules

The situs of assets is important, as the remittance basis applies only to foreign assets. TCGA 1992, section 275, widened in 2005,[28] contains 14 rules, including the following:

(1) Most rights over immovable property follow the location of the immovable property. Similarly, most rights in or over tangible movable property follow that of that property. However, debts, secured or unsecured, are generally situated in the UK if and only if the creditor is resident in the UK.[29]
(2) Registered shares or debentures are generally situated where they are registered; and if registered in more than one register, where the principal register is situated. If the

---

[26] Inland Revenue, *Capital Gains Manual*, paras CG 25380, 25400–401.
[27] FA 2008, s 809Q(3).
[28] F(No 2)A 2005, s 34 and Sch 4.
[29] See Oliver [1991] BTR 189, n 1.

company does not have share capital, the rule looks to the interests of the members of the company.

(3)   Intangible assets subject to UK law are always treated as located in the UK for CGT.[30] Futures and options have their own rules which relate to the location of the underlying subject matter.[31]

(4)   Co-owners have their own provision.[32] Their interests are located where the asset in which their interests subsist is located.

74.3   Gains Realised by Certain Closely-held Non-resident Companies

It will be remembered that the CFC legislation discussed in chapter seventy-three does not apply to capital gains. Gains accruing to a company are not usually attributable to those with interests in the company, but an exception is made by TCGA 1992, section 13 (as much amended) where the company would be a close company but for being non-resident.[33] The gain will be attributed to participators as defined for the close company legislation (see above §68.2);]. As a *de minimis* rule the gain will be attributed only if it is more than one-quarter of the relevant gain.[34] The participator must be resident in the UK. Special rules apply to determine the place of this gain in the hierarchy of the participator's total income.[35] Before 1996 the test was based not on being a participator but on being a shareholder, which gave rise to much planning.[36] Until 2008, section 13 did not apply to a participator who did not have a UK domicile. As from 6 April 2008, the part of the gain treated as accruing to the individual is deemed to be a foreign chargeable gain.[37] If a gain arises when the individual disposes of the interest in the company, relief may be claimed for any tax paid under section 13.[38]

Section 13 applies also to trustee participators.[39] Where a participator is a beneficiary of the trust, and the intermediate trustee participators do not make any payment to the participator, only the trustees are vulnerable under section 13. However, there are many problems where the trustee or the settlor is already at risk under one of the other attribution rules.[40]

The charge cannot be avoided by placing another company (or several companies) between the participator and the company to which the gain accrues, since the Revenue are

---

[30]   TCGA 1992, s 275A(1)–(3) and 275B, added by FA 2005, Sch 10, para 5.
[31]   TCGA 1992, s 275A(4)–(9) and 275B added by FA 2005, Sch 10, para 5.
[32]   TCGA 1992, s 275C added by FA 2005, Sch 10, para 6.
[33]   See generally, McCutcheon [1996] BTR 379. On original version, see Bennion [1983] BTR 74.
[34]   TCGA 1992, s 13(4) amended by FA 2013, s 62 (raising the threshold from one-tenth) and FA 2001, s 80; see also TCGA 1992, s 13(10B), added by FA 2001 s 80.
[35]   TCGA 1992, s 13(7A).
[36]   McCutcheon, *op cit.*
[37]   TCGA, s 14A, added by FA 2008, Sch 7, para 104.
[38]   HMRC Notes to Finance Bill.
[39]   TCGA 1992, s 13(10).
[40]   TCGA 1992, ss 86, 87.

given power to attribute the gain down through any number of intervening companies to the real shareholders.[41] ATED-related gains and gains on UK residential property interests are excluded.[42]

The participator can use the tax paid under section 13 as a credit against any tax due on a later disposal of the shares or other asset giving rise to participator status.[43] If not already so used, it may be used as a credit against any tax due on a later distribution by the company, whether a distribution of income or capital, or on a winding up.[44] These rules are well-intentioned but incomplete; the substitution of participator status for shareholder status, and the fact that attribution does not follow the precise legal chain of ownership, means that the person liable to tax under section 13 and the persons receiving the distribution may be different.[45]

It was found that section 13 could be circumvented where offshore assets were held by an offshore company owned by a trust and a double tax treaty gave an exemption for such gains, even though the offshore company would have been a close company (and the UK resident trustees would have been participators) if it were resident in the UK. So where gains of non-resident companies arise, section 13 is now to be applied without regard to such a treaty.[46]

The amount of gain or loss accruing to the company is calculated on the basis that the company was within the charge to corporation tax on capital gains.[47] Presumably, this assumption may be extended to other companies so that a no gain, no loss rule applies, for example, on an intra-group transfer even though both companies are non-resident.[48]

The section does not apply to gains accruing on the disposal of an asset used only in a foreign or partly foreign and partly UK trade.[49] Losses may be attributed to attributable gains, provided the loss would have been taxable under these rules if it had been a gain instead, ie in the same accounting period.[50]

The section carries the very real risk of taxpayers having to pay CGT without being able to secure any payment from the company. If the tax is reimbursed by the company, it will reduce any credit available to be set against other tax. Relief for unremittable gains[51] does not extend to gains which cannot be got at simply because of minority shareholder status.[52] Further provisions adapt these rules for non-resident groups.[53]

In 2011, the European Commission formerly requested the UK to amend these rules, which it viewed as contrary to EU treaty fundamental freedoms, namely, the freedom of

---

[41] TCGA 1992, s 13(9).

[42] TCGA 1992, s 13(1A).

[43] TCGA 1992, s 13(7); on time limits see TCGA 1992, s(5A) and (5B), added FA 2001 s 80.

[44] TCGA 1992, s 13(5A). Before 1996 the s 13 assessment was undone if the company distributed the gain to the shareholder; this is inappropriate in a world of self-assessment.

[45] *Simon's Direct Tax Service Handbook to FA 1996*, s 174.

[46] TCGA 1992, s 79B, added by FA 2000, s 94.

[47] TCGA 1992, s 13(11A).

[48] Revenue Interpretation RI 43.

[49] TCGA 1992, s 13(5), as amended FA 2001 s 80.

[50] TCGA 1992, s 13(8).

[51] TCGA 1992, s 279; see above at §74.1.3.

[52] One solution may be to sell the shares in the non-resident company before the company disposes.

[53] TCGA 1992, s 14.

establishment and free movement of capital. FA 2013 introduced two new exceptions in section 13(5) to address the Commission's concerns. The first applies to chargeable gains accruing on the disposal of assets used for the purposes of 'economically significant activities' carried on by the company wholly or mainly outside the UK. The second applies to chargeable gains accruing to the company where neither the disposal, acquisition or holding of the asset by the company formed part of a tax avoidance scheme.

74.4   Trading Non-residents

74.4.1 Overview

Non-residents are subject to CGT if they carry on a trade, etc, in the UK through a branch or an agency.[54] Gains or losses are within the scope of CGT if they arise in respect of UK assets:

(1)   used for the purposes of the branch trade, etc; or
(2)   held for the purposes of the branch.

The allowable costs of such assets are established in the normal way.[55] If the branch assets are transferred to a UK-resident company controlled by the non-resident, they are deemed to have been disposed of at their open market value and a charge to tax may therefore arise.[56] However, the disposal is treated as made for a consideration giving rise neither to gain nor loss if the whole or part of the branch trade is transferred and the disposal falls within TCGA 1992, section 171.[57] No gain, no loss treatment may also be claimed for transfers of a UK trade between companies resident in other EU Member States, where the consideration is satisfied by the issue of securities in the transferee company (see further above at §62.3.5).[58]

   A number of anti-avoidance provisions counter the transfer of such assets outside the CGT net. These are the transfer of assets abroad prior to disposal;[59] a disposal after cessation of UK trade (unless the trade is transferred in circumstances falling within TCGA 1992, section 139);[60] a rollover of gains against non-UK assets;[61] and the use of tax treaty relief by persons resident both in the UK and in another country.[62]

---

[54] TCGA 1992, s 10.
[55] Even if acquired from another non-resident, but subject to TCGA 1992, s 17 if the non-residents are connected persons.
[56] By TCGA 1992, ss 17(1), 286 or, alternatively, 25(3).
[57] TCGA 1992, s 172 was repealed for disposals after 31 March 2000; this had confined the no gain, no loss treatment to situations in which both companies were resident in the UK; see FA 2000, Sch 29, para 3.
[58] TCGA 1992, s 140A(4)(a).
[59] TCGA 1992, s 25(1).
[60] TCGA 1992, s 25(3), modified by s 28(3A) for disposals after 31 March 2000.
[61] TCGA 1992, s 159(1).
[62] TCGA 1992, s 159(3).

As just seen, rollover relief under section 152 is restricted for non-residents;[63] if the old assets are 'chargeable assets in relation to a person' at the time of the disposal, the new assets must be similarly related. This exclusion of rollover relief is not needed—and does not apply—if the person acquiring the new asset is within the UK tax net by reason of personal status, ie by becoming resident in the UK, when the asset was acquired.[64] However, this (logical) generosity is withheld (logically) from dual residents in whose hands the assets are safe from the UK tax charge by reason of a double tax agreement.[65]

As for income tax, the UK branch or agency of a non-UK resident is treated as the non-UK resident's UK representative under Part 7A of the TCGA 1992 (sections 271A–271J). These rules are a rewritten and updated version of the former rules in FA 1995, sections 126–127. The scheme in Part 7A parallels and refers to the analogous income tax rules in ITA 2007, Part 14, Chapter 2B. Part 7A Chapter 2 imposes various obligations and liabilities in respect of the assessment, collection and recovery of CGT, etc on the UK representative branch or agency. Under section 271F, the obligations and liabilities of the non-UK resident are to be treated as if they were also the obligations and liabilities of the UK representative. Section 271G provides certain exceptions to the rule in section 271F in respect of notices and information requests to the non-UK resident unless the branch or agency has itself been given notice, and does not require an independent agent acting as UK representative to do anything except 'as it is practicable for the representative to do so.' Section 271H provides further exceptions to section 271F in the case of criminal offences and civil penalties.

74.4.2 Deemed Disposals

A non-resident, N, is liable to CGT only if holding chargeable assets in the UK, ie the assets are connected with a trade or profession being run through a branch or an agency here. By TCGA 1992, section 25(1), N is treated as making a disposal of any chargeable assets when the assets are removed from the UK and so cease to be chargeable.[66] If N is also ceasing, contemporaneously, to carry on the trade or profession through a branch or an agency in the UK, section 25(1) does not apply[67] but section 25(3) does. Section 25(3) directs a deemed disposal when the trade ends or the asset ceases to be a chargeable asset; hence there is no deemed disposal if the asset remains a chargeable asset. The transfer of a branch or an agency to a UK-resident company under the same control can now give rise to a deferral of liability.[68]

---

[63] TCGA 1992, s 159.
[64] TCGA 1992, s 159(2).
[65] TCGA 1992, s 159(3).
[66] TCGA 1992, s 25(1), (7).
[67] TCGA 1992, s 25(2), or, if the asset is an exploration or exploitation asset, as defined by s 25(6).
[68] TCGA 1992, s 171, as widened by FA 2000; for disposals before 1 April 2000, s 172 applied.

74.5   Settlements and Trusts

74.5.1 Introduction and Residence

74.5.1.1 Introduction

There are four sets of special rules affecting settlements:

(1)   the first set applies on the migration of settlements (§74.5.2);
(2)   the second set applies on the disposal of a beneficial interest (§74.5.3);
(3)   the third set attributes all trust gains to a settlor who retains an interest (§74.5.4); and
(4)   the fourth set attributes gains realised by foreign trustees to UK beneficiaries (in contravention of the normal principle that only the trustees are liable for CGT) (§74.5.6).

The normal CGT definition of 'settlement' applies for (1) and (2); the wider income tax definition in ITTOIA 2005, section 620 applies for (3) and (4). The third set of rules is backed up by rules for transfers of value linked with borrowing (see §74.5.5). These scope of these rules is not affected by the FA 2008 repeal of the general settlor-interested provisions formerly in TCGA 1992, sections 77–79.

These rules represent a growing awareness on the part of the UK tax system that trusts are not just for the support of aged relatives and young children but avoidance devices of a very sophisticated type.[69] The rules offer sophisticated responses to sophisticated schemes, and so reinforce a climate in which sophistication may be attempted. These rules were first introduced in 1991 but have since been amended.[70] This was one of those areas in which the rate of CGT might be higher than the income tax charge. Before 2008 these rates might reach 64% or, in unlucky combination, 104%.[71]

74.5.1.2 Residence

In 2006 the capital gains rules on residence of trustees were aligned with those for income tax (under TCGA 1992, section 69; above §69.9). A trustee who is not resident will be treated as being so if acting as a trustee in the course of a business carried on in the UK through a branch, an agency or a PE here (section 69(2D)). It can be appreciated that there will be major fiscal consequences from a quite small change in the way such trustees run their businesses. The trustees are a single body of persons (under section 69(1)).

In *Roome v Edwards*,[72] an assessment on UK trustees of part of the fund was upheld even though the gain accrued to the trustees of another part—all those trustees being non-resident. FA 2006 introduced an election by which a sub-fund may elect to be taxed as a separate settlement; such an election may preclude such an assessment, but it will mean that there may be a disposal and consequent CGT charge where a transfer is made to a sub-settlement.

---

[69] For the Australian response to these problems, see Burns and Krever, *Interest in Non-Resident Trusts* (Australian Tax Research Foundation Study No 28).

[70] FA 1991, ss 83 *et seq*; see Inland Revenue Press Release, 19 March 1991, [1991] *Simon's Tax Intelligence* 290. On 1998 changes, see McCutcheon [1998] BTR 476.

[71] McCutcheon (1998) *Taxation* 617.

[72] [1981] STC 96, [1981] 1 All ER 736, (1981) 54 TC 349.

Trustees may cease to be resident in the UK. This might happen because of a change in the residence status of a trustee, or by a transfer of the property from one set of trustees to a new set. The concession allowing individuals to be treated as non-resident for the remainder of the year in which they migrate does not apply to trustees in their capacity as trustees.[73] A migration within six years of the creation of the settlement may cause the tax held over on the creation of the settlement to fall due.[74] TCGA 1992, section 10A, which applies to temporary non-residents, applies only to individuals and so not to trusts; this is because there is an exit charge when a trust migrates, but not where an individual does, and this was thought to be sufficient. Section 10A may become relevant where a settlor is charged under section 86.

It was found that the deemed disposal rule was not sufficient where a double tax treaty was involved. A rule added in 2005 tries to address this problem.[75] Where a chargeable gain accrues to trustees during a year of assessment for which they are 'within the charge to CGT' but at a time when they are 'non UK resident', nothing in a double tax treaty is to prevent the normal CGT tax charge from arising. Trustee are 'within the charge' for a year if for any part of that year they are resident and, in a glorious double negative, 'not Treaty non-resident'. A person is treated as a Treaty non-resident if he or she is non-resident for the purpose of that tax treaty (see below §76.6.1).

74.5.2 Deemed Disposal on Trustees Becoming Non-resident: Section 80

Where trustees cease to be resident in the UK there is a deemed disposal of all 'defined assets';[76] assets are defined assets unless they stay within the UK CGT net, or if they were already outside that net by reason of a double tax treaty.[77] Rollover relief will be excluded in analogous circumstances.[78]

Death is not regarded as a tax avoidance device, and so special rules apply where the migration is caused by the death of a trustee. If the trust resumes its UK residence within six months from the death of the trustee, the deemed disposal is excluded, save for assets which have been the subject of an actual disposal in the meantime[79] or which would have been protected by a double tax treaty in any case.[80] Conversely, a trust which has become UK resident by reason of such a death will not be the subject of a deemed disposal (save for assets which have been the subject of holdover relief) if it resumes its non-resident status within six months.[81]

Tax due under a deemed disposal may be collected from any person who ceased to be a trustee within the period of 12 months ending with the migration; the ex-trustee has a right of indemnity in such circumstances.[82] This potential liability does not apply to trustees who

---

[73] ESC A11.
[74] TCGA 1992, s 168. The holdover will have been under ss 165 or 260, on which see above at §§36.3–36.5.
[75] TCGA 1992, s 83A, added by F(No 2)A 2005, s 33, with effect from 16 March 2005.
[76] TCGA 1992, s 80(1), (2). For definitions, see TCGA 1992, ss 169E–169G, added by FA 2004; cross-references from s 80 added by FA 2008. On practice under ss 80–85, see Statement of Practice SP 5/92, paras 4–6.
[77] TCGA 1992, s 80(3), (4), referring to assets remaining in a UK branch or agency.
[78] TCGA 1992, s 81.
[79] TCGA 1992, s 81(6), (7).
[80] TCGA 1992, s 81(1), (3).
[81] TCGA 1992, ss 81(5)–(7), 84.
[82] TCGA 1992, s 82.

establish that they ceased to be trustees before the end of the relevant period and that, at that time, there was no proposal that the trustees might become non-resident.[83]

There is a similar deemed disposal if the trust, while remaining resident under UK ordinary tax rules, ceases to be so thanks to the application of a double tax treaty.[84] There is also a restriction on rollover relief where the new asset is acquired by such trustees.[85]

74.5.3 Disposal of Beneficial Interests in Non-resident Settlement: Section 85

The disposal of a beneficial interest does not usually give rise to a charge to CGT,[86] the charge on disposals by the trustees being thought sufficient. However, the disposal of a beneficial interest by a UK-resident beneficiary under a non-resident trust is expressly made chargeable[87] since, in such cases, there will be no charge at the trustee level.

With effect from 6 March 1998, the disposal of a beneficial interest became chargeable where the trust is treated as resident in the UK but has been an offshore trust at any time during its history.[88] Where there is a charge on the migration of the trust under section 80 and that migration was after the beneficiary had acquired the interest, whether by purchase or having the interest conferred, the gain accruing on a subsequent disposal of that interest is calculated on the assumption that it was acquired for market value at the time of the migration, the so-called uplift.[89] The effect will be to give relief for those gains charged at the trustee level when the trust migrates, assuming that there are gains; where there are losses the same rules apply, so that the real function of the rule is simply to mark the boundary between trustee taxation and beneficiary taxation. There is no provision allowing the beneficiary to use losses sustained by the trust.

This approach must be modified where the trust continues to be resident under normal CGT rules but is treated as non-resident by a double tax treaty. Where this occurred before the beneficial interest was acquired by the beneficiary, no relief applies; otherwise, there is a deemed acquisition when the treaty migration occurs.[90]

There is no uplift for 'relevant offshore gains', a phrase preferred by the legislation to the more common 'stockpiled gains'.[91] The relevant gains are those which would have been available to become chargeable if there had been capital payments to UK-resident beneficiaries.[92] The avoidance scheme at which the charge is aimed arose where a non-resident trust had such gains but had not made any chargeable payments; the gains remained 'stockpiled'. The trust would become resident in the UK before being taken offshore again, allowing the trust to take advantage of the uplift as it left the UK. This change applies to trusts becoming non-resident on or after 21 March 2000.[93]

---

[83] TCGA 1992, s 82(3).
[84] TCGA 1992, s 83.
[85] TCGA 1992, s 84.
[86] TCGA 1992, s 76.
[87] TCGA 1992, s 85(1); and see above at §40.6. On practice, see Statement of Practice SP 5/92, paras 4–6.
[88] TCGA 1992, s 76, (1A) and (1B), added by FA 1998, s 128.
[89] TCGA 1992, s 85(3).
[90] TCGA 1992, s 85 (4)–(8).
[91] TCGA 1992, s 85(10), added by FA 2000, s 95.
[92] Ie those within TCGA 1992, s 89(2) and Sch 4C, para 8(3) (s 85(11)).
[93] FA 2000, s 95(5).

74.5.4 Attribution of Gains under Non-resident Trust to Settlor with Interest in Non-resident or Dual Resident Settlements: Section 86

Under section 86, gains of a non-resident trust are attributed to the settlor who is domiciled in the UK at some time in the year and is resident in the UK during the year in which the gain arises.[94] The term 'settlement' is defined in the same way as for income tax legislation and so covers a whole variety of situations in which property originates from the settlor.[95] These rules have been progressively widened. In 2008, thought was given to widening this provision to cover a settlor who was not domiciled in the UK but was resident and possibly a remittance basis user, but this did not happen. Other widenings did occur to take account of the new remittance basis. The rules are quite detailed; what follows is a summary of the key provisions.

74.5.4.1 Qualifying Settlement

The charge applies if the settlement is a 'qualifying settlement', ie (a) created on or after 17 March 1998, or (b) created before that date but in relation to which various 'triggering events' occur on or after that date.[96] The first event is that property is provided for the settlement otherwise than by way of bargain at arm's length.[97] The second event is the migration of the trust, or the trust acquiring non-resident status under a double tax treaty.[98] The third event is a variation of the terms of the trust so that any one of a list of people becomes for the first time a person who will or might become entitled to a benefit from the settlement.[99] The fourth event is where a person falling within that list enjoys a benefit from the settlement for the first time and that person is not one who (looking at the matter before that date) might be expected to enjoy a benefit on or after that date.[100]

74.5.4.2 Interest

The settlor is taken to have an interest in a very wide variety of circumstances. The definition covers circumstances in which income or property is, or will or may become applicable, in any circumstances whatsoever, for the benefit of or payable to defined persons. The list of defined persons includes the settlor and a long list of others—the settlor's spouse or civil partner, children and grandchildren,[101] the spouse or civil partner of any such child or grandchild, any company controlled by such persons and any company associated with such a company.[102] There are exclusions for certain types of interest.[103] The charge is avoided if

---

[94] TCGA 1992, s 86(1), (3); details of the charge are set out in s 86(4), (5). On practice, see Statement of Practice, SP 5/92, paras 7–10.

[95] TCGA 1992, ss 169E–169G and Sch 5, paras 7, 8.

[96] TCGA 1992, Sch 5, para 2A.

[97] TCGA 1992, Sch 5, para 9(3); the section is not in terms confined to property being provided by the settlor, but the definition of 'settlement' is confined to property originating from the settlor. On practice, see Statement of Practice SP 5/92, paras 11–37.

[98] TCGA 1992, Sch 5, para 9(4).

[99] TCGA 1992, Sch 5, para 9(5).

[100] TCGA 1992, Sch 5, para 9(6).

[101] TCGA 1992, Sch 5, para 2(3)(da), (db), added in 1998.

[102] TCGA 1992, Sch 5, para 2(1)–(3).

[103] TCGA 1992, Sch 5, para 2(4)–(6).

the settlor dies during the year, or if the only listed person giving rise to such an interest dies (or all such persons die) in the year.[104]

The settlor has a statutory indemnity against the trustees,[105] but this may not be worth very much. Of course, it is not likely to be less successful than a claim by the Revenue, but the point of this provision is that because the trustees are non-resident, there is no charge on them in respect of the gains.

74.5.4.3 Trusts Created before 17 March 1998

These are subject to different rules, in that the class of disqualifying beneficiaries included children but not grandchildren. The existence of grandchildren will therefore not cause section 86 to apply unless a triggering event occurs on or after 16 March 1998.

74.5.4.4 Trusts Created before 9 March 1991

The attribution to settlor rules were introduced in 1991 and did not apply to trusts created before 19 March 1991 unless one of the triggering events happened on or after that date. However, these trusts were brought within section 86 with effect from 6 April 1999.[106] Such trusts might be saved from the change if they were 'protected settlements'.[107] In order to avoid capital gains being charged on a UK-resident settlor, it became necessary for the children of the settlor, children of the settlor's spouse or civil partner and any spouses or civil partners of such children to exclude themselves as beneficiaries (or, alternatively, for the trust to be wound up or to become resident in the UK). A child under the age of 18 does not have the legal capacity to exclude himself as a beneficiary without consent of the court. Hence, the charge on the settlor does not apply where the only members of the settlor's immediate family who can benefit are children who are under the age of 18 as at 5 April 1999.[108] Unborn children and future spouses or civil partners of the settlor or of his children being within the class of potential beneficiaries are also ignored in applying this test.[109] The presence of the settlor's grandchildren among the beneficiaries is not fatal to the trust's claim to be a protected settlement and so outside these rules.[110] Anti-avoidance provisions covered the period from the Budget Day announcement on 17 March 1998 to 5 April 1999.[111]

74.5.4.5 Section 86 and the Returning Settlor: Section 86A

Section 86 treats the gains realised by a non-resident trust as attributable to the resident settlor. If the settlor is non-resident, section 86 has no application, though section 87 may. If a settlor has become non-resident but then becomes resident again in circumstances falling within TCGA 1992, section 10A, rules are needed to settle the status of gains which have been realised by the trust during the period of non-residence. These gains will have been 'trust gains' for the purposes of section 87 when realised, but now should cease to

---

[104] TCGA 1992, Sch 5, paras 3–5.
[105] TCGA 1992, Sch 5, para 6.
[106] TCGA 1992, Sch 5, para 9(1A), added by FA 1998, s 132.
[107] TCGA 1992, Sch 5, para 9(1B).
[108] TCGA 1992, Sch 5, para 9(10A)(a).
[109] TCGA 1992, Sch 5, para 9(10A)(b)–(d).
[110] Revenue Interpretation RI 198 (December 1998)
[111] FA 1998, Sch 23.

be so because of being attributed to the settlor under section 10A. The trust gains when the settlor ceases to be resident are calculated first; this sum should be nil since section 86 excludes section 87.[112] Where distributions have been charged to beneficiaries under section 87 they are not also taxed to the settlor; where they are taxed to the settlor on resuming residence, they cease to be trust gains under section 87.[113]

74.5.5 Transfer of Value Linked with Borrowing; Attribution of Gains to Beneficiary: Schedules 4B/4C

Trennery v West,[114] decided by the House of Lords in 2005, held that flip-flop schemes did not work. Under these schemes, taxpayers attempted to mitigate CGT liability on sales of unquoted trading company shares by first transferring the shares to interest in possession trusts, which at that time were liable to CGT at a rate of only 25% (compared to the then 40% top rate of CGT for individuals). Since Parliament could not be absolutely sure that the Revenue would win, special legislation—TCGA 1992, Schedule 4B—was added by FA 2000. This imposes a charge where transfers of value by trustees are linked with borrowing by trustees. Among the trusts caught by Schedule 4B are those within TCGA 1992, sections 87 or 88, ie offshore trusts with one or more UK beneficiaries.[115] Schedule 4B is backed up by Schedule 4C; this ensures that the rules in Schedule 4B apply in these circumstances rather than the rules in TCGA 1992, sections 86–98. These rules were supplemented by FA 2003, which added a new section 85A and made many revisions to Schedule 4C;[116] taxpayers had decided to use the stringent new rules to create a suspension of the operation of sections 87–89. In view of the decision of the House of Lords, it is thought unnecessary to go into this special legislation further.

74.5.6 Attribution of Gains Arising under Trusts and Other Arrangements to Beneficiaries Receiving Capital Payment: Section 87

Section 87 was the subject of much discussion in connection with the reform of the remittance basis; eventually many of the wilder ideas were discarded.[117] The rules are quite detailed; what follows is a summary of the key provisions.

74.5.6.1 Which Settlements?

Gains realised by overseas trustees of a settlement are attributed to beneficiaries.[118] For this purpose, the term 'settlement' receives not its narrow, CGT meaning but its wide, income tax meaning of arrangement.[119] These provisions also apply to trusts which are resident in the UK for domestic purposes, but which are treated as non-resident by a double tax treaty;

---

[112] TCGA 1992, s 87(3).
[113] TCGA 1992, s 86A, applying where year of departure is 1997–98 or later (FA 1998, s 129(1)).
[114] [2005] UKHL 5. See above at §40.2.2.
[115] TCGA 1992, Sch 4C, para 1; Schedule added by FA 2000, s 92, Sch 25.
[116] See Revenue BN33, [2003] *Simon's Tax Intelligence* 752, and Chamberlain [2003] BTR 396.
[117] See HMRC Finance Bill Notes, Sch 7, paras 50 *et seq.*
[118] TCGA 1992 s 87(2).
[119] TCGA 1992, s 97(7), ie ITTOIA 2005, s 620.

in such circumstances the trust gains giving rise to potential attribution to the settlor will be the lesser of (a) the actual gains, and (b) gains protected by the treaty; these are called dual resident settlements.[120]

74.5.6.2 The Statutory Scheme

Chargeable gains are treated as accruing in the relevant tax year to the beneficiary of a settlement who has received a capital payment from the trustees in the relevant year.[121] This applies to all beneficiaries, whether domiciled in the UK at some time during the year or not, but the remittance basis may apply in certain situations, ie when the non-UK domiciled beneficiary comes within sections 809B, 809C or 809D (see above at §71.4).[122] When a capital payment is made to a beneficiary in one year and a trust gain arises in a later year, a charge may arise in that later year under 'matching' rules. Relief may be claimed for trust losses.[123] Under the pre-2008 rules all such trust gains were placed in one big pool. The 2008 rules make a welcome change to a year-by-year basis; matching rules are provided on a last in, first out basis (see below).[124] The location of the asset from which the trust gains arise does not matter.[125]

The gains are attributed to beneficiaries in proportion to the capital payment received by them, but are not to exceed those payments.[126] This obscure provision seems to mean that if the only payments made to the beneficiaries are made to A, then A can be assessed for all the gains accruing to the non-resident trustees up to the amount A has received.

74.5.6.3 Capital Payment: Section 97(1), (2)

A capital payment is defined as one which is not chargeable to income tax. The term covers the transfer of an asset, a loan and various indirect payments. It does not cover a payment by way of bargain at arm's length.[127] An interest-free loan repayable on demand has been held to be a payment—and so a capital payment—for the purposes of this rule.[128] The court should prefer a bold interpretation to a narrow one if the latter would reduce the legislation to futility; the value of the payment could be determined retrospectively.[129]

74.5.6.4 Transition: Non UK-domiciled Beneficiaries and 6 April 2008

There are several important transitional rules. No charge arises where such beneficiaries receive capital payments before 6 April 2008 which are matched to trust gains accruing after 5 April 2008. Similarly no charge arises in the converse case—where payments received after 5 April are matched with trust gains accruing before 6 April 2008.[130]

---

[120] TCGA 1992, s 88.
[121] TCGA 1992, s 87(2).
[122] TCGA 1992, s 87B, added by FA 2008.
[123] TCGA 1992, s 97(6).
[124] TCGA 1992, s 87A, added by FA 2008, para 108; ss 92–95 are all repealed by para 113.
[125] HMRC Notes, para 51.
[126] TCGA 1992, s 87A.
[127] TCGA 1992, s 97(1), (2); on valuation, see s 97(4).
[128] *Billingham v Cooper* [2001] STC 1177 (CA).
[129] *Ibid, per* Robert Walker LJ at para 35, quoting a passage from Lord Simon LC in *Nokes v Doncaster Amalgamated Collieries* [1940] AC 1014, 1022.
[130] FA 2008, Sch 7, paras 119 *et seq.*

74.5.6.5 Rebasing Option

FA 2008 included an option under which trustees on non UK-resident trusts might rebase their assets as at 6 April 2008. This would make compliance with the UK rules much easier. It will be seen that the election was given to the trustees, not the beneficiaries.[131] Rebasing was to be effective for capital gains but not for income tax. During the passage of the Finance Bill 2008 a number of changes were made to soften this approach.[132]

74.5.6.6 'Interest' Charge on Matched Payments to Beat Deferral: Section 91

In an effort to discourage the use of settlements as devices to retain gains rather than distribute them, the charge under section 87 is supplemented.[133] Increased tax is due if a capital payment is made and the payment can be matched to trust gains from an earlier period (referred to as the qualifying amount).[134] Now that the general matching approach is 'last in, first out', it follows that payments matched with gains of the same year are not subject to this rule. The exclusion applies to the trusts gains of the previous year as well.

The increased tax is equal to the amount of interest that would be chargeable on a sum equal to the tax in respect of the chargeable amount for a period beginning on 1 December in the year of assessment following that for which it is the chargeable amount, and ending on 30 November in the year of assessment following that in which the capital payment is made. The rate of interest is currently set at 10%, but may be varied by Treasury order.[135] Thus, if a capital payment was made in 2015–16 and the payment is matched with trust gains accruing in 2010–11, there would have been 50% supplementary charge for the five-year period 1 December 2011 to 30 November 2016. This charge will now be related to the top rate of CGT, and runs regardless of when in 2015–16 the capital payments are made. The extra tax is not to exceed the amount of the capital payment.[136] In reckoning the period for the calculation of interest, it is not possible to go back before 1 December falling six years before 1 December in the year of assessment following that in which the payment is made (making a maximum of four chargeable years).[137]

Matching etc, section 87A. As already seen, rules matching capital payments with trust gains generally adopt a last in, first out approach.[138] HMRC has produced worked examples for their Notes to the Finance Bill.

74.5.6.7 Payment by Controlled Company

The idea of a chargeable payment includes a payment by a company controlled by the trustees; a payment received from a qualifying company controlled by the trustees is treated as if it had been received direct from the trustees. A company is a qualifying company if it is a close company, or if it would be close if it were resident in the UK.[139] In consequence,

---

[131] FA 2008, Sch 7, para 126.
[132] See Public Bill Committee, 19 June 2008, col 873 (Jane Kennedy, MP).
[133] TCGA 1992, s 91.
[134] TCGA 1992, s 91(2).
[135] TCGA 1992, s 91(3), (6); the charge cannot affect payments made before 6 April 1992.
[136] TCGA 1992, s 91(2).
[137] TCGA 1992, s 91(4), (5).
[138] TCGA 1992, s 87A; reversing the previous rule in TCGA 1992, s 92(4).
[139] TCGA 1992, s 96(10).

the definition of 'beneficiary' is amended to include people who receive capital payments from the settlement. However, the trustees of a settlement are not treated as beneficiaries, a rule which prevents appointments or advances to sub-trusts being capital payments.[140] It was found that the definition of 'control' was too loose, and so the requirement that persons with control had to be resident or ordinarily resident in the UK was removed.[141] This change in determining control does not affect the rules about the extent of the interest which the UK resident is treated as having and so the extent to which the capital payment would be chargeable.

74.5.6.8 Interaction with ITA 2007, Section 731 (ex TA 1988, Section 740)

ITA 2007, section 731 treats a capital payment as income to the extent that there is relevant income. Where a payment falling within section 731 exceeds the then relevant income, the excess may be taxed in future years under section 731 should relevant income arise; however, it may also be taxed immediately under these rules (including the rules for migration of settlements).[142] When this occurs, the excess reduces the amount liable to be taxed under section 731 in later years, ie the charge under these rules excludes the subsequent charge under section 731.[143]

Section 731 does not apply if there is no tax avoidance motive. Moreover, since the top income tax rate is higher than the top capital gains tax rate, there is no longer any point in a beneficiary arguing that he should come within section 731 rather than the TCGA 1992 provision.[144]

74.5.6.9 Migration: Section 89

The charge under these rules must take account of the migration of the trust from the UK complete with trust gains. Capital payments subsequent to the distribution are treated as chargeable gains of the beneficiaries.[145] Payments made before it ceases to be resident are treated only as capital payments (thus causing a liability in respect of subsequent gains) if made in anticipation of a disposal by the trustees in the non-resident period.[146]

74.5.6.10 Transfer between Settlements: Section 90

Where property is transferred to other trusts, whether or not the latter were made by the original settlor, the infection of 'trust gains' will be transferred with the property so far as not already attributed to the beneficiaries and so far as not made for a consideration in money or money's worth.[147]

On transfer of value linked with borrowing, see §74.5.5.

---

[140] TCGA 1992, s 97(8)–(10).

[141] TCGA 1992, s 86(5), as amended by FA 2000, s 96.

[142] TCGA 1992, ss 87 or 89.

[143] ITA 2007, s 734, ex TA 1988, s 740(6).

[144] Butterworth's Finance Act 1998, Commentary to FA 1998, s 130, points out two other differences: (a) that a distribution to a non-resident will wash out the gain for s 87 but not for s 731; and (b) that s 87 does not apply if the beneficiary is resident but not domiciled, whereas s 731 is excluded for such people only if the relevant income is foreign and the capital distributed is kept abroad.

[145] TCGA 1992, s 89(2). This appears to be in addition to any liability that may arise under the deemed disposal rule in s 71.

[146] TCGA 1992, s 89(1).

[147] TCGA 1992, s 90.

75

Unilateral Relief Against Double Taxation

75.1 Introduction

The UK taxes income if it arises here, or if the person entitled to it is resident here. This leaves untaxed only foreign income[1] arising to a non-resident. If other countries adopt a similarly generous view of their own taxing powers—as they often do—it is inevitable that some income will be taxed twice. Double taxation may also arise in connection with capital gains, but this is reduced because the UK taxes gain primarily on the basis of residence only; as discussed in chapter seventy-four a non-resident does not pay CGT in respect of assets sited in the UK, with the exception of UK residential property and assets used in a trade carried on through a UK permanent establishment, branch or agency. UK rules have for many years allowed the UK resident a credit for the foreign tax paid. The rules for credit relief were based on the idea of the individual source and individual country rather than pooling, and so could be quite restrictive. FA 2000 allowed pooling for certain dividends (§75.5.4)

---

[1] See above §72.1.

and FA 2005 allows it for royalty income from the same source but different countries. However, FA 2005 also introduced several new rules to restrict relief in ways which marked the end of the idea of the credit system as something which needed little justification.

With the credit system having been brought into disrepute, voices were raised in support of a system which exempted foreign source dividends from UK tax altogether. A discussion document was issued in 2007, and a new regime was introduced by FA 2009. The relevant legislation on the exemption for foreign (and domestic) dividends received by a UK-resident company is found in CTA 2009, Part 9A. This was followed in 2011 by the introduction of an election to exempt profits of foreign permanent establishments of UK residents. Foreign tax credit and other relief, formerly in TA 1988 and written into TIOPA 2010, are still available, but are less important than they once were now that the vast majority of foreign dividends are exempt from UK tax.

75.1.1 The Problems of Double Taxation

75.1.1.1 Background

Double taxation of cross-border income is thought to be objectionable since, by making overseas profits accruing to UK residents more expensive than domestic profits, it discourages a person from trading overseas and so interferes with international trade, a breach of capital export neutrality (CEN). It will also cause extra costs to persons resident in other countries but with UK source income. The extra costs to business were examined by the OECD in 1991[2] (the OECD report) and formed the focus for much of the work of the Ruding Committee's report on EC countries in 1992 (the Ruding report) and the later EC Commission Staff Working Paper on Company Taxation in the Internal Market (2001).[3] The reports of 1991 and 1992 showed first that in order to achieve a 5% return on an investment after tax, the domestic tax system produces its own costs—requiring an average pre-tax return of 5.8%. However, they showed that the required pre-tax rate of return rose to 7.5% once international factors were considered; the UK figures were 5.9%, 6.7% for investment from the UK into all other OECD countries and 7.0% for investment from other countries into the UK. These UK figures were reached after taking account of tax treaties; without such treaties the figures were 8.2% and 9.0%.[4] Tables 23 and 24 of the 2001 report, based on figures from 1999, showed it was still the case that neither CEN nor capital import neutrality (CIN) was respected in the EU; outbound and inbound investments were still taxed more heavily than domestic investment.[5] In the absence of a will to have one tax system common to all countries (though slow progress is being made on a common consolidated corporate tax base), steps may be taken towards the less glamorous goal of reducing these costs by domestic and bilateral action. It is worth noting that for a multinational, compliance costs came to 1.9% of tax payments, while for a medium-sized enterprise with international business they came to 30.9%.

---

[2] *Taxing Profits in a Global Economy* (OECD, 1991).
[3] Ruding (chair), *Report of the Committee of Independent Experts* (EC Commission, 1992) and EC COM(2001) 582.
[4] OECD report, table 5.9; see *ibid*, ch 2, Pt D, ch 5, ch 6, Pt C; and Ruding report, chs 2, 5.
[5] For much useful technical background, see Loretz (2007) 28 *Fiscal Studies* 227.

On the role of the European Union (EU) in making of treaties and on the relation between EU law and treaties, see below at §76.1.

75.1.1.2 The FA 2000 Modernisation of the Credit System

FA 2000 contained many changes to the rules for double taxation relief (DTR) as a result of the consultation process begun in 1999.[6] It has to be said that this process was very unprofessional and the resulting legislative wrangle one of the least edifying of recent memory. The most public problems revolved around the proposal to stop the use of mixer companies, ie foreign companies with UK parents, which were used to mix receipts from various parts of the world before they were transmitted to the UK as dividends. This enabled companies to get round one of the then universal principles of the system—that foreign tax should be set against UK tax on the same source, ie no pooling.

The problems were two-fold. First, the proposal had not been part of the consultation process. Secondly, it ran into such heavy opposition that it had to be scrapped. However, the form in which it was scrapped was not a simple abandonment of the proposal, or even a brand new provision allowing pooling. Instead the section which was going to outlaw mixing was amended so as to become one which allowed pooling in prescribed circumstances.

This wrangling meant that other important changes have tended to get overlooked. Many of the changes made by FA 2000 were beneficial to the taxpayer, either enacting existing practice or making significant changes, such as the excess credit loss rules for dividends. Of the 21 paragraphs, 15 could be seen as beneficial. One such was the revision of time limits for claiming relief; this had been made necessary by the 1996 loan relationship and similar rules which would mean that with the UK accounting-base rule, the UK would have taxed interest long before the foreign tax system did.[7] More controversial are the relationship between treaty relief and unilateral relief, and the rule requiring taxpayers to take reasonable steps to minimise their foreign tax in TIOPA 2010, section 33.

75.2 Methods for Reducing or Eliminating Double Taxation[8]

75.2.1 Exemption[9]

A tax system could achieve the avoidance of double taxation in a number of ways. One is not to tax overseas income, either generally or particularly. Such was, in effect, the case when the remittance basis was at its height, before 1914,[10] and until 1974 when the remittance basis was available to UK residents in respect of income earned overseas. The special

---

[6] See Inland Revenue, *Double Taxation Relief for Companies—a discussion paper*, March 1999 and *Double Taxation Relief for Companies: Outcome of Review*, March 2000. See also the articles in [1999] BTR by Waters at 448, Oliver at 459 and Harris 469.

[7] On time limits see TIOPA 2010, ss 19, 79 and 80, ex TA 1988, s 806, amended by FA 2000, Sch 30, para 13.

[8] On history, see Harris [1999] BTR 469.

[9] The merits of credit and exemption are considered in Inland Revenue, *Double Taxation for Companies—a discussion paper* (March 1999), chs 3, 4; here, the Inland Revenue came down in favour of the status quo, ie credit not exemption (see para 4.18).

[10] FA 1914, s 5; for history, see Royal Commission on the Taxation of Profits and Income, *1st Report*, Cmnd 8761 (1953), §§15–20 and Inland Revenue discussion paper (1999), *op cit*, Annex 5.

status afforded to overseas trade corporations, whereby they were exempt on trading income reinvested overseas, was another example.[11] Many countries give substantial exemptions for overseas trade in an attempt to assist their own balance of trade and general level of economic activity.[12] Today, France practices an extensive but not universal exemption system for foreign income. Some countries operate an exemption system for income from a country which is a tax treaty country (Canada, Germany and in part Australia).[13] The Netherlands is closer to France on this matter but applies a principle of exemption with progression. Under this approach the foreign income is not itself taxed but, because it is in effect treated as the bottom slice of overall income, it will, assuming a progressive rate structure, increase the rate of tax charged on that part which is chargeable.[14] For the UK's 2009 move to exempt participation dividends and profits of foreign PEs, see §75.3 below.

Short of abandoning the taxation of overseas income, the Government has three other options, examined in §§75.2.2–75.2.4 below.

75.2.2 Credits: Direct and Indirect

The first option for the Government is unilaterally to allow the foreign tax paid as a credit against the UK tax liability. This is permitted by TIOPA 2010, section 18 (ex TA 1988, section 790). Similar provisions apply to CGT[15] and to corporation tax on capital gains.[16] The rules which the foreign tax must satisfy in order to qualify as a tax credit are generally, but not always, the same whether the credit arises under treaty or unilaterally.[17] It is customary to talk about 'direct' and 'indirect' credits. Direct credits are credits for tax charged directly on the income, eg rent from land or a dividend on shares. Indirect credits are credits for tax paid on the profits out of which the direct income has emerged. Thus, while a tax on the dividend paid by a company carries a direct credit, the tax paid by the company on the profits out of which the dividend is paid is available for indirect credit against the tax on the dividend itself. The same point is made by saying that the indirect credit is credit for the tax on the underlying profits. The UK refers to this by the formula 'relief for the underlying tax', rather than 'indirect tax credit'; the UK formula may be long-winded, but it is precise and avoids problems of confusion with relief for indirect taxes. In order to qualify for the relief for the underlying tax it is usually necessary to have a significant—or 'investment' or 'participating'—shareholding; holdings falling short of this are often referred to as 'portfolio' holdings. The boundary between the two is often 10%.

---

[11] See above at §71.1.

[12] See Royal Commission (1953), *op cit*; and Royal Commission on the Taxation of Profits and Income, *Final Report*, Cmnd (1955), app III.

[13] See Arnold, Li and Sandler, *Working Paper 96-1 for the Technical Committee on Business Taxation* (Canada Department of Finance, 1996). Australia has moved from a listed country approach to a general exemption for branch income and non-portfolio dividends (otherwise a foreign tax credit). This is used in conjunction with the CFC rules under which the credit system is used.

[14] There is much valuable material on the rules in 10 foreign countries in Inland Revenue discussion paper (1999), *op cit*, Annex 6.

[15] TIOPA 2010, ss 31–33, ex TCGA 1992, ss 277, 278; on which, see Statement of Practice SP 6/88; and [1989] BTR 105. A treaty may be useful in providing its own rules for the situs of assets.

[16] TIOPA 2010, s 18, ex TA 1988, ss 788(1), 790(1).

[17] Eg the rules in TIOPA 2010, ss 2–9 (treaty) versus 8–17 (unilateral), both giving rise to the credit in s 18; ex TA 1988, ss 794–806.

If the foreign tax is available as a credit at a rate which wipes out any UK tax liability, it might appear that there is very little difference between a credit system and an exemption system. However, under a credit system the foreign income will still be relevant in calculating the person's total income and so the marginal rate of tax. However, this distinction is itself blurred if the country still takes account of the foreign income in computing taxable income—exemption with progression.

75.2.3 Deduction

The second option for the Government is to specify that the foreign tax shall be deductible in computing the profits of the business, thus treating the foreign tax like any other business expense. A foreign tax may be deductible under the principles applicable to ITTOIA 2005, Part 2/CTA 2009, Part 3, but case law establishes that this cannot be true of an income tax (above §22.3.2). Deduction for income tax and corporation tax purposes in respect of non-UK tax paid on overseas income and profits is permitted in the UK by TIOPA 2010, section 112 (ex TA 1988, section 811). Section 113 provides a deduction from a capital gain for foreign tax on the disposal of an asset. Such foreign tax may not be deducted in respect of income charged on a remittance basis.

75.2.4 Treaty

The third option for the Government is to enter into a double taxation agreement with the other country, a process authorised by TIOPA 2010, section 2 (ex TA 1988, section 788). Treaty relief may exempt some income from tax in one country and give credit for foreign taxes on other income (see further below at §76.3).

75.2.5 Electing Against Credit

Under UK tax law, a person may elect not to take the credit relief.[18] There are circumstances in which this may be advantageous. Thus, if the foreign tax arises on part of a source of income but there is an overall loss in respect of that source, credit relief will be useless; a deduction will, however, increase the loss and the loss, unlike unused credits, may be set off against other income or rolled forward to later years. Taxpayers may not elect to treat a part of the foreign tax as a credit and the balance as a deduction.[19] However, they may treat one foreign tax as a credit and another as a deduction. For new rules on unused credits, see below §75.6.

75.2.6 UK as Source

As country of source, the UK may wish to levy income tax on income accruing to a non-resident. Here it may decide not to tax at all (eg certain government securities held

---

[18] TIOPA 2010, s 27, ex TA 1988, s 805.
[19] TIOPA 2010, s 31(2), ex TA 1988, s 795(2).

by non-residents), give credit for tax paid in the country of residence (not a feature of the UK tax system) or, under a treaty, levy a reduced rate of tax, often called a withholding tax, leaving the other country to give credit if it wishes.

75.2.7 Further Issues

It should not be thought that the selection of the appropriate method of avoiding double taxation completes these issues. Enough has been said in this book about different ways of taxing income to warn one that many complexities remain. If one country taxes a particular receipt and the other does not, there is no problem of double taxation; however, if one country allows a particular deduction in computing income and the other does not, the two systems will achieve different levels of income and so another but different reason for variable amounts of tax. Again the two systems may disagree about when the income arises. More fundamentally, they may disagree about where the taxpayer resides, where the income arises, what sort of income it is (eg business income or royalties) or even whose income it is. At this point the plate tectonics analogy for the collision of tax systems (above §69.1) becomes ever more apt, and the analogy of three-dimensional chess to provide solutions may have to add the fourth dimension of time.

75.3   Foreign Dividend and Foreign PE Profits Exemptions

75.3.1 Introduction

Prior to the FA 2009 reforms, the UK double tax relief system for foreign-sourced income was based on the concept of granting a credit under a treaty for foreign taxes, although the UK also offered a comprehensive form of unilateral tax credit and a deduction. In June 2007 a discussion document raised the possibility of replacing the credit system with an exemption system for shareholdings of 10% or more.[20] The first argument was that the credit system had become too complicated for multinationals and other large businesses, especially in relation to calculating the indirect credit, so compliance costs would be reduced. One might add that there was still the risk of uncredited foreign taxes. The second was that with an exemption system, these businesses would be encouraged to repatriate foreign profits without having to worry about UK taxes instead of leaving the profits offshore awaiting reinvestment, so life would be simpler. To simplicity and reduced compliance costs the supporters added the politically essential argument that it would enhance UK competitiveness, and that the cost in terms of lost tax revenue would not be substantial.

For such a major reform, the time between discussion proposals and legislative enactment was relatively short.[21] From July 2009, most dividends received by a UK-resident company from foreign companies (and other UK companies) are exempt from UK tax.

---

[20] See chapter sixty-one above.
[21] The regime was inserted by FA 2009, s 34 and Sch 14: see Voisey's FA 2009 note in [2009] BTR 533 for more details.

Non-exempt foreign dividends may be eligible for relief from double tax under the existing tax credit system, along with various forms of foreign income other than dividends. As part of the package of reforms, including the move to exemption, the UK introduced a world-wide debt cap to limit group interest expense deducted in the UK and reformed its CFC rules. The Government also studied the case for a reduced rate of corporation tax applied to income from patents, which led to the introduction of the so-called 'patent box', discussed above at §62.8.

The detailed rules governing the dividend exemption system (sometimes called the 'dividend participation system') are in CTA 2009, Part 9A. Companies have the option to elect out of the exemption regime, such as where a relevant double tax treaty provides for a lower rate of withholding tax on dividends if the dividends are 'subject to tax' in the UK.[22] The regime begins by prescribing that all dividends and other distributions are chargeable to corporation tax unless they qualify for at least one specified category of exemption (CTA 2009, section 931A(1)).[23] The legislation provides different regimes for 'small companies' (defined in section 931S by reference to a European test) and for 'non-small' companies. The discussion that follows begins with non-small companies, before moving on to consider the rules applicable to small companies.

75.3.2 *Non-small Companies*

The exemption regime as it applies to 'non-small companies' is in CTA 2009, Part 9A, Chapter 3. There are five 'exempt classes' of distribution, which should cover most distributions received by UK-resident companies, whether from other UK companies or from non-UK companies. It is necessary to fall into only one of these classes in order to qualify for exemption.

The exempt classes are:

— section 931E—distributions from controlled companies (ie subsidiaries);
— section 931F—distributions in respect of non-redeemable ordinary shares (ie most ordinary dividends);[24]
— section 931G—distributions from portfolio shareholdings (no more than 10%);
— section 931H—distributions that are not designed to reduce UK tax; and
— section 931I—distributions in respect of shares accounted for as liabilities for loan relationships (there is a cross-reference to section 521C).

Excluded from these exemptions are any amounts of interest which are deemed to be distributions under CTA 2010, section 1000(1)E or F.[25] Also excluded are distributions where the paying company is able to claim a tax deduction in the country of origin (section 931D(c)).

Lastly, dividends are excluded from exemption if they are made 'as part of a scheme the main purpose, or one of the main purposes, of which is to obtain a tax advantage', or if the

---

[22] Voisey [2009] BTR 533, 540.
[23] F(No 3)A 2010 removed a somewhat confusing exemption for dividends 'of a capital nature' (ex s 931A(2)); see Tank, Weston and Melia [2011] BTR 47.
[24] CTA 2009, s 931U sets out the meaning of 'ordinary share' and 'redeemable' for this purpose.
[25] Ex TA 1988, s 209(2)(d) or s 209(2)(e)). The exclusion is in CTA 2009, s 931D(b).

scheme is one of the specific prescribed schemes in the legislation.[26] Sections 931J to 931Q contain eight categories of schemes which will prevent an exemption from applying. These are schemes involving:

(1) the manipulation of the controlled company rules;
(2) quasi-preference or quasi-redeemable shares;
(3) manipulation of portfolio holdings;
(4) arrangements in the nature of loan relationships;
(5) distributions for which deductions are given;
(6) payments for distributions;
(7) payments not on arm's length terms; and
(8) the diversion of trade income.

In summary, from 2009, the vast majority of distributions received by large (more precisely 'non-small') UK companies should be covered by at least one of these exemptions. As a result, the UK rules should comply with the requirements of EU law, and also provide analogous treatment where a non-Member State is involved.

75.3.3 Small Companies

The rules applying to dividends received by 'small' companies are in CTA 2009, Part 9A, Chapter 2. A small company for this purpose is defined in section 931S as one with fewer than 50 full-time employee equivalents and turnover or a balance sheet total of €10 million or less.[27] Certain investment companies, eg an authorised unit trust, cannot be small. Under section 931B, dividends received by a small company will be exempt if:

(1) the payer is a resident of (and only of) the UK or a qualifying territory at the time that the distribution is received;
(2) the distribution is not a deemed distribution in respect of interest under CTA 2010, section 1000(1)E or F;
(3) no deduction is allowed to a resident of any territory outside the UK under the law of that territory in respect of the distribution; and
(4) the distribution is not made as part of a tax advantage scheme.

The vast majority of dividends received by a small company will satisfy these conditions for exemption. A list of qualifying territories for the purposes of requirement (3) above is available on the HMRC website. These are countries with which the UK has double tax treaties that contain a non-discrimination clause, ie normally countries which levy tax on corporate profits as opposed to tax havens.

---

[26] CTA 2009, s 931V sets out the meaning of 'scheme' and 'tax advantage scheme'; 'tax advantage' is defined in TA 1988, s 840ZA (not rewritten).

[27] Adopting by reference the definition in the Annex to Commission Recommendation 2003/361/EC of 6 May 2003.

75.3.4 Exemption for Foreign PE Profits

FA 2011 introduced a new optional exemption from corporation tax on profits arising from foreign PEs of UK-resident companies (CTA 2009, sections 18A *et seq*).[28] The introduction of the new exemption is consistent with the UK's move towards a territorial approach to taxation of foreign dividends, as just discussed. Absent an election into the new regime, a UK-resident company with a foreign PE is taxed in the UK on its worldwide income, including income attributable to the activities of the PE. Consequently, the UK-resident company gets immediate relief in the UK on any losses attributable to the activities of the PE.[29] Any profits of the PE, on the other hand, are likely to be subject to tax in the foreign jurisdiction. To address the risk of double taxation of the foreign PE profits, the UK allows relief for foreign tax by way of credit against the UK tax on those profits, either under a tax treaty or under the UK's unilateral relief rules in TIOPA 2010, Part 2, Chapter 1 (discussed in §75.4 below).

Should the UK resident company elect (irrevocably) into the new exemption regime, any profits attributable to its foreign PEs are exempt from UK corporation tax. The downside is that no relief is given in the UK for losses attributable to foreign PEs either (CTA 2009, sections 18A and 18F). The decision whether to elect for exemption treatment rather than tax credit relief will depend on the particular circumstances of the UK-resident company and its foreign PEs.

75.4 Credit Relief: The Framework

75.4.1 Introduction

Although FA 2009 introduced an wide-ranging exemption system for dividends (see §75.3), there will be many circumstances in which that system does not apply and the existing credit system does. The unilateral tax credit is a generous relief; indeed, its generosity can weaken the UK Government's bargaining power when negotiating treaties. The main rules on unilateral relief were written into TIOPA 2010, Part 2, Chapter 1, and, subject to some caveats discussed next, generally apply even though treaty relief may also be available.

Situations in which unilateral relief will be particularly important are where:

(1) there is no double tax treaty with the country of source;[30] or
(2) there is such a treaty, but it does not cover this particular tax;[31] or
(3) taxes have been levied by municipalities or other constituent parts of the state and the relevant treaty applies only to the national state;[32] or
(4) treaty relief applies only to certain classes of income.[33]

---

[28] For more detail, see Ball [2011] BTR 424. Note also the implementing no gain/no loss rule in TCGA 1992, 276A, where an exemption election has been made under CTA 2009, s 18A.

[29] The details of the exemption are discussed in Ball, *op cit*.

[30] On interaction with treaties, see TIOPA 2010, s 11. On application to dividend income, see Statement of Practice SP 12/93.

[31] TIOPA 2010, s 6(1)–(4), ex TA 1988, s 788(3).

[32] TIOPA 2010, s 8(3), ex TA 1988, s 790(12), refers to 'territory' not 'State'.

[33] See ex TA 1988, s 800, repealed by FA 2000, Sch 30, para 9.

Treaty relief of course remains vital when considering a non-resident with UK-source income.

75.4.1.1 Treaty Relief Excluding Unilateral Relief

The interaction of unilateral and treaty relief was changed fundamentally but not completely in 2000. TA 1988, section 793A provided that treaty rules will exclude unilateral relief in two situations.[34] These rules may provide an interesting example of a treaty imposing a charge to tax which would not otherwise arise. The situations are:

(1) where the treaty (or the law of the foreign country implementing the treaty) expressly grants a credit for foreign tax paid; and
(2) where the treaty expressly denies a credit.

In each case unilateral relief will not be available. This new relationship applies only to future treaties. It is not clear that this change is justified in principle. The section 793A rules are now found in TIOPA 2010, sections 10 and 25.

In *Bayfine UK v Revenue & Customs Commissioners*,[35] the Court of Appeal considered the relationship between unilateral credit relief under TA 1988, section 790 and relief under the US–UK Treaty, Article 23. Arden LJ held that since the purpose of the treaty was to eliminate double taxation and prevent evasion, a construction under which both States had to give relief was wrong. In the present case this was avoided by paying proper attention to Article 1(4).[36] The overall result was that the UK was not obliged to give credit relief for the US tax, but the US authorities were. She also held that HMRC was not obliged to allow unilateral relief as treaty relief was available.[37]

75.4.1.2 History

Unilateral relief was introduced into the UK in 1950, although relief for tax charged in a dominion had been known since 1916.[38] In 1950 the credit was to be for three-quarters of Commonwealth taxes and for one-half of foreign taxes. This may have been because of the notion of imperial preference, or because to give full credit unilaterally would weaken the hand of the UK negotiators as they worked towards a full set of bilateral arrangements. The pace of negotiation was slow, and in 1953 these limits on credit were abolished.[39]

There is something profoundly unhistorical in treating unilateral relief before treaty relief. The 1950 unilateral relief rules built on the rules which had been introduced for treaties in 1945. The present legislative framework governing relief by way of credit in TIOPA 2010, Part 2 applies both to unilateral credit[40] and to treaty relief.[41]

---

[34] Added by FA 2000, Sch 30, para. 5.
[35] [2011] STC 717, [2011] EWCA Civ 304.
[36] *Ibid*, [57].
[37] *Ibid*, [67]. There are many further issue lurking here, including some involving TA 1988, s 793A (now TIOPA 2010, s 25). In view of Arden LJ's decision on these points it was not necessary for her to decide whether the taxpayer was bound to take steps to reclaim UK tax under then TA 1988, s 795A, but she considered these at [68–77].
[38] For an account of the History of DTR, see Inland Revenue discussion document (1999), *op cit*, Annex 5.
[39] As recommended by Royal Commission (1953), *op cit*, §§40–42.
[40] TIOPA 2010, Pt 2, s 18(1)(b), ex TA 1988, s 788(3).
[41] TIOPA 2010, Pt 2, s 18(1)(a), ex TA 1988, s 788(4).

75.4.2 Residence

The taxpayer generally must have been resident in the UK—whether or not also resident in another country—for the chargeable period.[42] One effect of this was that until FA 2000, the UK branch of a non-resident company was not entitled to credit relief. Moreover, the branch was unlikely to be able to invoke the treaty's non-discrimination clause, since this statutory provision overrides anything the treaty might say.[43] A foreign branch of a company resident in the EU might, however, be able to rely on EU Treaty non-discrimination rules, such as Article 49 TFEU (ex Article 43 TEC) and Article 56 TFEU (ex Article 49 TEC).

The residence rule is relaxed for certain banks with a branch or agency in the UK for foreign tax paid on certain types of interest accruing to the branch. It is also relaxed for tax paid in the Channel Islands or Isle of Man, to a person resident in the UK or the Isle of Man or the Channel Islands, and for tax due under ITEPA 2003 in respect of foreign tax where the duties are performed wholly or mainly in the foreign country and the person is resident here or in that country.[44]

The denial of relief to the UK branch of a person resident in another EU Member State was likely to be challenged successfully under EU law. FA 2000 therefore provides that for accounting periods ending after 20 March 2000 the restriction ceases to apply. The branch may claim credit relief for foreign tax paid, but not for tax paid in the home state. The total relief is not to exceed what could have been claimed if the branch had been a person resident in the UK.[45] This legislation is still framed in terms of branches.

75.4.3 Foreign Tax

Four principal rules apply, to which FA 2005 added a fifth which is relevant only when tax is withheld at source and the business is that of a financial trader: see §75.4.3.5 below.

75.4.3.1 Payable

First, the tax payable must have been chargeable under the laws of the foreign territory.[46] The foreign tax is that chargeable rather than that paid; credit is given only to the extent of the tax properly payable to the foreign country. Thus, if a relief had to be claimed in due time under the foreign tax system and is not so made, the UK will grant relief only on the basis that the claim had been made in time. A curious exception arises when there is a transfer of a non-UK trade by a person resident in the UK to a person resident in another EU Member State; here, double tax relief may be given for tax which has not been actually paid.[47] Another such exception, known as 'tax sparing', arises only in the treaty context (see below at §76.2.3.1).

---

[42] TIOPA 2010, s 26, ex TA 1988, s 794.
[43] *Sun Life of Canada v Pearson* (1986) 59 TC 250; this point was not considered beyond the High Court.
[44] TIOPA 2010, ss 28–30, ex TA 1988, s 792(2).
[45] TIOPA 2010, s 30(5), ex TA 1988, s 794(2)(bb), added by FA 2000, Sch 30, para 4.
[46] TIOPA 2010, s 8(2), ex TA 1988, s 792(1). On interpretation of chargeable or payable, see *Sportsman v IRC* [1998] STC (SCD) 289.
[47] TIOPA 2010, ss 122–123, ex TA 1988, s 815A, added by F(No 2)A 1992, s 50 (see above at §60.9).

There is now a statutory obligation to take all reasonable steps to minimise the foreign tax payable.[48] This applies to claims made after 20 March 2000 and has been the cause of much unhappiness among practitioners, who have good cause to wonder what it means. The Revenue think that people should claim reliefs such as capital allowances but would not be expected to carry a loss forward rather than back.[49] The rational basis for this distinction is not clear. Where relief is claimed for foreign tax by the taxpayer but a payment is made by a tax authority to the taxpayer or to a person connected to the taxpayer by reference to the foreign tax, the credit is reduced by the amount of the payment.[50]

75.4.3.2 Correspond to UK Income Tax

Secondly, the tax must be a tax on income which corresponds to UK income tax.[51] In *Yates v GCA International Ltd*,[52] a Venezuelan tax charging 90% of the gross receipts was held to be a tax corresponding to income tax. At first sight a tax on 90% of the receipts would, as the Revenue argued, seem to be a tax on turnover rather than on income, but in the particular case Scott J said that there was no evidence that the 10% reduction was unrealistic for the majority of businesses falling to be taxed under the Venezuelan rule; he accepted that it was unrealistic for this taxpayer, but that was not the point.[53] The Revenue's apparent aversion to treating a gross profits tax as a tax on income is presumably to be taken only in the context of business profits, since the UK's domestic income tax system allows no deduction for expenses in connection with interest income under ITTOIA 2005, Part 4, Chapter 2, or dividend income under Chapter 3. The Revenue publish a list of admissible and inadmissible taxes.[54]

Accepting *Yates*, the Revenue announced that they would solve this issue by examining the foreign tax in its legislative context in the foreign territory and deciding whether it served the same function as income and corporation tax serve in the UK in relation to the profit of a business. Turnover taxes as such are still excluded, but taxes on gross receipts or on a percentage of gross receipts are not necessarily excluded.[55]

75.4.3.3 In Respect of Income Arising There

Thirdly, the tax must be payable in respect of income arising in that territory.[56] *Yates* establishes that this is determined as a matter of UK law using UK concepts, and is not determined by the local law.[57] The test is that profits arise where the operations take place from which those profits in substance arise.[58] Further, it must be accepted that profits may arise in more than one place, so that an apportionment may be necessary.[59]

---

[48] TIOPA 2010, s 33, ex TA 1988, s 795A, added by FA 2000, Sch 30, para 6.
[49] Outcome of Inland Revenue Review, March 2000, paras 1.40–1.41.
[50] TIOPA 2010, s 34, ex TA 1988, s 804G, introduced by FA 2009, s 59(2).
[51] TIOPA 2010, s 8(2), (3), ex TA 1988, s 790(12).
[52] [1991] STC 157, (1991) 64 TC 37; on the *Yates* case generally, see Oliver [1993] BTR 201.
[53] [1991] STC 157, 168j; (1991) 64 TC 387, 53A.
[54] See HMRC website, formerly Inland Revenue booklet IR 146; see Inland Revenue Press Release, 27 March 1995, [1995] *Simon's Weekly Tax Intelligence* 518.
[55] Statement of Practice SP 7/91.
[56] TIOPA 2010, s 9(1)–(3), ex TA 1988, s 790(4).
[57] [1991] STC 157, at 170d; (1991) 64 TC 37, 54H.
[58] *Smidth v Greenwood* [1922] 1 AC 417, 8 TC 193; and *IRC v Hang Seng Bank Ltd* [1990] STC 733.
[59] [1991] STC 157, 172; 64 TC 37, 570, Scott J said that if he had not been allowed to apportion he would have said that the profits arose in the UK (*ibid*, 173; 571).

The *Yates* case raises another issue—the correct measure of the foreign income. Where the foreign income is investment income, it is not too difficult to measure it; the gross amount of the dividend or interest will usually be accurate. Problems arise when consideration turns from free-standing income, to income which is taxed on the gross amount in the foreign country but on a net amount in the UK. Baker[60] puts forward the following scenario: A UK-resident company has total receipts of £1,000, which includes foreign royalties of £100 on which foreign tax of £25 has been paid. The company has deductible expenses of £600 and profits of £400, and so UK corporation tax of £120. How much of the £25 foreign tax is available for credit? Is it (a) £25 (the tax paid on the receipt of £100), or (b) £12 (100/1,000 × 120) or (c) £10 (this takes 100/1,000 of the net profit of £400 and infers that only £40 of the business profit is doubly taxed; £10 is the foreign tax at 25% on £40). The current state of UK law is uncertain. In *Yates*, the Special Commissioner decided that £12 would be the right answer. Although this is likely to be particularly striking in cash terms where one is dealing with income taxed on the gross amount in the foreign country, but only as part of a net amount in the UK, it is likely to arise whenever the two systems adopt different measures of the income.

75.4.3.4 By Claimant

Fourthly, where underlying tax is concerned, the tax must have been paid by the person claiming the credit. While this might seem to be obvious, it actually raises a number of problems. Thus, in the area of relief for underlying tax, no claim may be made for tax paid by a company which has been merged into the group if it ceases to exist as a result of the merger, a metaphysical concept depending on the precise analysis of the effects of the merger under the foreign company law system.[61] Similarly, there are issues if one person, often a company, is made liable for the tax due from another, but related, person.

The situation was addressed in 2000. If company A has paid the tax on the underlying profits and the profits have become the profits of company B otherwise than by a dividend payment, any dividend payment by B to company C will carry a right to the tax paid by A.[62] There is a cap on the amount of relief; this is set at the amount B would have been able to claim if A had paid the sums by way of dividend.

The axiom that the foreign tax must have been paid by the taxpayer was also softened by FA 2000 at some other points, eg where foreign groups or certain foreign entities are concerned.[63] Here the group may be treated as a single entity if it is so treated by the foreign tax system.

75.4.3.5 Tax Withheld at Source

Further rules apply where tax is withheld at source from income taxed as a receipt of a trade, ie interest and dividends received by financial traders and certain royalties. These were the results of a Revenue consultation which started from the premise that certain expenses were relevant, eg changes in the value of the underlying asset (if that was a revenue

---

[60] (1998) 52 *Bulletin for IBFD*, 445.
[61] See also Inland Revenue, *Outcome of Review* (2000), para 1.20. In practice relief was often given.
[62] TIOPA 2010, s 69(1)–(3), ex TA 1988, s 801B, added by FA 2000.
[63] TIOPA 2010, s 71, ex TA 1988, s 803A, added by FA 2000, Sch 30, para 15.

asset), borrowings and overheads. However, determining the amount of those costs refer-
rable to a particular piece of income was not straightforward.

75.4.3.6 Minor Points

The exchange rate to be used to calculate the amount of foreign tax paid is that in force at
the time of payment.[64] Later fluctuations, which may go either way, are ignored. The problem of calculating the correct amount of tax in California has been the subject of Revenue
guidance.[65] If the amount of the foreign tax liability changes, so that relief given becomes
excessive, there is now an explicit obligation on the taxpayer to inform the Revenue.[66]

One UK statutory rule added in 2005 was at first applied only to companies but was
extended to income tax in 2008.[67] The changes conform to HMRC practice, but were necessary to remove doubts arising from the case law.[68] The 'doubts' arose because the court did
not agree with the HMRC view of the law. The case arose in connection with portfolio dividends received as part of a financial company's trade. The Special Commissioners held that
the general rule in TA 1988, section 787 meant that one should look at the UK corporation
tax on the financial trade as a whole. The HMRC view, now enacted as statute, was that one
should just look at the dividend income, less any expenses attributable to that dividend. The
purpose was to ensure that credit relief was not given against tax due on other trade profits
unrelated to the payment of the foreign tax. The 2008 change also extended to income tax
the rule that the credit must be computed by reference to the UK tax on the profit, and that
in doing so account must be taken of any deductions or expenses that would be allowable
in computing the taxpayer's liability.[69]

Although the provisions added in 2005 are headed 'trade income', this is slightly misleading.
In income tax terms the rules cover not only ITTOIA 2005, Part 2, Chapter 2, but also Chapter
18 (post-cessation receipts) and property business income taxable under Part 3, Chapters 3,
10 and 11.[70] For corporation tax they cover profits chargeable under CTA 2009, Part 3 and
also Part 4 post-cessation receipts and any other income computed in accordance with trading
principles.[71] The key point is that all these sources use trading principles to compute income.
However, they become relevant only if the receipt from which the tax is withheld is a trading
receipt. Most dividends and most interest payments will not be trading receipts. All the Revenue literature in 2005 suggested that they were focusing on withholding tax and that the rules
do not go wider—which is why this section of the text has the heading it does. So withholding
tax must be deducted in computing the foreign tax available for credit, and the credit is limited
to the UK tax on those profits. Royalties paid in respect of asset in more than one jurisdiction
are treated as a single asset.[72] Any disallowed credit may be taken as a deduction.[73]

---

[64] *Greig v Ashton* (1956) 36 TC 581.
[65] Revenue Interpretation RI 102.
[66] TIOPA 2010, ss 45–46, ex TA 1988, s 798B, introduced by FA 1998, s 105; see Inland Revenue Press Release,
17 March 1998, [1998] *Simon's Weekly Tax Intelligence* 466 on timing.
[67] TIOPA 2010, ss 37(2)–(4) and 44(1)–(5), ex TA 1988, s 798(1A) for income tax and s 798A(2) for corporation tax.
[68] *Legal and General Assurance v Thomas* [2005] Sp 461; see generally Cussons [2005] BTR 371.
[69] TIOPA 2010, ss 37–38, ex TA 1988, s 798.
[70] TIOPA 2010, s 37(7), ex TA 1988, s 798(5).
[71] TIOPA 2010, s 44(6), ex TA 1988, s 798A(4).
[72] TIOPA 2010, s 47, ex TA 1988, s 798(4).
[73] TIOPA 2010, s 35, ex TA 1988, s 798C.

Four further special rules apply for corporation tax. Three are asset identification rules:

(1)   Where the asset is a hedging relationship with a derivative contract, this may be treated as one asset.[74]
(2)   As with income tax, royalties paid in respect of assets in more than one jurisdiction are treated as a single asset.[75]
(3)   A portfolio of investments is treated as a single asset where it is not reasonably practical to treat the investments separately.[76]

The fourth special rule acts as an anti-avoidance rule, undoing any scheme of arrangement between A, a trader, and B, a main purpose of which is to alter the effect of the tax credit rules; the income is to be treated as B's not A's.[77] There is an anti-fragmentation rule for banks designed to clarify the existing rules and ensure that such schemes do not work.[78]

The FA 2005 corporation tax rules apply to any payment of a foreign tax on or after 16 March 2005, or to income received on or after that date but under deduction of tax at source; the income tax rules use 6 April instead.

75.4.4   UK Taxable Income

The credit is allowed against the UK tax on that income; this requires first the calculation of the UK income on which the UK tax would be due.[79] This being the purpose of the exercise, the income is calculated according to UK tax rules.[80] Foreign income taxed on an arising basis is taken gross, ie without any deduction for the foreign tax.[81] It follows that any withholding tax must be added back. Where the income is a dividend and credit relief is due for the corporation tax underlying it, the sum must be grossed up to take account of the underlying tax. Income which is taxed on a remittance basis is grossed up to include the foreign tax payable.[82] One cannot remit a sum net of tax and ask to have the foreign credit set against the UK tax on the net sum.

75.4.5   UK Tax

The UK tax payable in respect of that income is now calculated; the expression *in respect of that income* articulates the UK's source doctrine for DTR. Naturally, the calculation of UK tax is done in accordance with UK tax rules. The Revenue view is that relief for foreign income tax may not be set against Class 4 NICs.[83]

---

[74] TIOPA 2010, s 46, ex TA 1988, s 798B(1) and (2).
[75] TIOPA 2010, s 47, ex TA 1988, s 798B(3).
[76] TIOPA 2010, s 48, ex TA 1988, s 798B(5).
[77] TIOPA 2010, s 45, ex TA 1988, s 798B(4).
[78] TIOPA 2010, s 45, ex TA 1988 ss 798A(3A)–(3C) and B(4A)–(4C), introduced by FA 2009, s 60.
[79] TIOPA 2010, ss 31–32, ex TA 1988, s 795; on loan relationships, see TIOPA 2010, s 31(5), ex TA 1988, s 795(4), overriding FA 1996, s 80(5).
[80] The *Bowater* case (see below at §76.5.2) has no application here.
[81] TIOPA 2010, s 31(2), ex TA 1988, s 795(2); s 795(1) contained the treaty rule. On tax sparing, see TIOPA 2010, ss 31(4) and 32(5), ex TA 1988, ss 788(5), 795(3).
[82] TIOPA 2010, s 32(2), ex TA 1988, s 795(2).
[83] Inland Revenue, *Double Taxation Relief Manual*, para 601.

75.4.6 *The Credit*

Where credit is to be allowed against any of the UK taxes chargeable in respect of any income, the amount of the UK taxes so chargeable shall be reduced by the amount of the credit.[84] This simple rule masks many problems.

75.4.6.1 Different Basis Periods

Problems arise where profits accrue over a period (eg business profits) and the foreign tax system and the UK have different basis periods, as where the UK operates on its year of assessment financial year while the foreign system operates on a calendar-year basis. Here an apportionment of the foreign tax must be made. Thus, if X has foreign income for the year 2009–10, relief will be given against UK tax for three-quarters of the foreign tax paid in the calendar year 2009 and one-quarter of that paid for 2010; the fact that X may not know the amount of foreign tax paid in 2010 when making the return for 2009–10 is immaterial save at the practical level.[85] This problem should not arise where a withholding tax is levied at source, since here the withholding tax will be the tax on the income.

75.4.6.2 Business Income—Overlap Profits

The purpose of the current-year rules (above §20.1) is broadly to ensure that all relief available for foreign tax is given over the life of the business. Under this system, relief is given against the UK tax on the overlap profits even though it has been given effect as a credit once already. It will be seen that the concept of the overlap profit is central to the new solution. Therefore, the credit may be used in respect of the overlap profit, notwithstanding that it has been allowed as a credit against income taxed in a previous year of assessment.[86]

Where such double relief has been given, a compensating reduction must be made if the original income of the overlap period becomes deductible under ITTOIA 2005, section 205 or section 220. The first step is to ascertain the total amount of credit that was set off over the two years of assessment when the original income was taxed twice, and deduct from it the amount that would have been set off if that income had been taxed only once.[87] This original excess is now used to reduce any double tax credit which would have been allowed in respect of that source in the final period under section 220, and only the balance, if any, is available for set off as a foreign tax credit.[88] If the original excess exceeds the credit for the final period a special charge to income tax is made—the person chargeable is treated as having received in that year a payment of an amount such that income tax on it at the basic rate is equal to that excess.[89] Where there is an overlap period and a deduction under section 220, ie not on the discontinuance of the trade, the double tax credit in relation to each element of the overlap is treated in the proportion which the overlap profit bears to that aggregate of taxable profits.[90]

---

[84] TIOPA 2010, s 18, ex TA 1988, s 793(1), on credit for banks, sees s 30 (ex s 794).

[85] For Revenue practice, see Inland Revenue, *op cit*, para 651.

[86] TIOPA 2010, s 22, ex TA 1988, s 804(1), amended by FA 1994, s 217; on overlap profile, see ITTOIA 2005, Pt 2, Ch 15.

[87] TIOPA 2010, s 24(1)–(3), ex TA 1988, s 804(5A), added by FA 1994, s 217.

[88] TIOPA 2010, s 24(5), ex TA 1988, s 804(5B)(b), added by FA 1994, s 217

[89] TIOPA 2010, s 24(4), ex TA 1988, s 804(5B)(a), added by FA 1994, s 217.

[90] TIOPA 2010, s 24(7), ex TA 1988, s 804(5C), amended by FA 1994, s 217.

75.4.6.3 (Old) Preceding Year

Further problems used to arise owing to the preceding-year basis of assessment. Where, under that system, income earned in the foreign country in Year 5 was used as the basis of UK tax in Year 6, unilateral credit was given for the Year 5 foreign tax in calculating UK tax for Year 6.[91]

75.4.7 The Relief

75.4.7.1 Income Tax and Capital Gains Tax

Once the amount of the credit has been ascertained, it is set against the UK tax chargeable, which is reduced by the amount of the credit. This means that foreign income taxes on the income from the foreign source are allowed against the UK tax charged on the income from that source. Care may have to be taken in identifying the source.

75.4.7.2 The Source

In *George Wimpey International Ltd v Rolfe*,[92] a company (GW) tried, unsuccessfully, to widen this rule. GW had paid foreign tax in respect of foreign profits from foreign branches of its trade, but made an overall trading loss when all its operations, including the UK operations, were taken into account. It argued that it should be entitled to set off the foreign tax against the UK corporation tax in respect of its non-trading income. Hoffmann J, upholding the decision of the Special Commissioner, held that the taxpayer company was not entitled to DTR. He referred to the scheme of the legislation and said that that led to the need to identify exactly the fund charged to overseas tax with a fund also chargeable to UK tax. He said:[93]

> The reference in [TA 1988, section 790(4), now TIOPA 2010, section 9(1)(b)] to United Kingdom tax being computed by reference to income on which the foreign tax had been computed was … intended to ensure that the identity was not between funds which might notionally be regarded as taxable income in that foreign territory and the UK but between the actual funds by reference to which the computation of tax was made … [I]t seems to me the income in respect of which the taxpayer company became liable to corporation tax was its non-trading income notwithstanding that the computation of that income was made subject to deduction for losses which took into account the company's trading in the three territories. The company was not chargeable to any tax in respect of the income which had been subject to foreign tax and accordingly no credit can be allowed.

---

[91] On old form of treaty, see *Duckering v Gollan* [1965] 2 All ER 115, 42 TC 333; the effect of this case was undone for treaties by a change in treaty practice, and for unilateral relief by substituting 'by reference to' the foreign income for 'in respect of'.

[92] [1989] STC 609, 62 TC 597.

[93] *Ibid*, 616, 606.

75.4.7.3 Restriction on Credit

The amount of the credit must not exceed the difference between:

(1)   the amount of income tax which would be borne by the taxpayer if he were charged to income tax on his total income from all sources, including the foreign income grossed up as necessary; and
(2)   the tax borne by him on his total income but minus the foreign income as computed.[94]

The effect of this rather inelegant, but taxpayer-friendly formula is to treat the income as the top slice of income; this means that the UK tax against which the foreign tax is credited is that taxed at top slice rate and not an overall average rate.

   Although the foreign tax must be paid in respect of the same source, it does not have to be paid by the same taxpayer. Thus, if state A taxes the income of a child as income of the child, and the UK taxes it as income of the parent, the parent may use the foreign tax paid.

   Where more than one foreign source is involved, each is treated separately but in order— the order being at the taxpayer's option.[95] In such circumstances it obviously pays to take the income taxed at the highest foreign rates first. In any event, the total tax credit must not exceed the total income tax payable.[96]

75.4.7.4 Capital Gains Tax

Equivalent relief is given[97] for foreign tax charged on the same disposal. Where credit relief is not available, or not available in full, the unused foreign tax may be treated as an allowable deduction. Owing to the variety of systems of taxing gains around the world, this relief may be lost. Thus, different events may give rise to a tax liability in respect of what is, in substance, the same gain. For example, a capital asset in a foreign branch may incur a tax charge in that country if, without being sold, it is written up in the books and the foreign country charges tax on the unrealised gain. If, in a later year, the asset is sold and UK CGT liability arises, it seems that, strictly, DTR should not be available in respect of the earlier foreign disposal. However, a Statement of Practice provides that the foreign tax credit will be given on the occasion of the subsequent disposal which gives rise to UK CGT.[98] The Statement does not cover the converse situation where the UK tax becomes due before the foreign tax.

75.4.7.5 Corporation Tax

Equivalent relief is also given for income and capital gains subject to corporation tax; the amount of credit must not exceed the corporation tax attributable to that income.[99] Since all the income chargeable is charged at one rate, companies with high overseas income from countries with high rates of tax may decide to expand their UK operations.

---

[94] TIOPA 2010, s 36, ex TA 1988, s 796(1).
[95] TIOPA 2010, s 36(3), ex TA 1988, s 796(2).
[96] TIOPA 2010, s 41, ex TA 1988, s 796(3).
[97] TIOPA 2010, s 40, ex TCGA 1992, s 277.
[98] Statement of Practice SP 6/88.
[99] TIOPA 2010, s 42, ex TA 1988, s 797(1), (2).

75.4.7.6 Allocation of Charges, etc

Where a company has overseas income and domestic income, it is necessary to allocate such items as expenses of management and charges on income among the different sources, so as to calculate the amount of UK corporation tax attributable to that foreign income. The general approach is to allow the company to allocate these as it sees fit.[100]

These rules are adapted for non-trading deficits on loans relationships.[101] TIOPA 2010, section 50 provides first that non-trading credits are calculated on their own, ie without any deduction for non-trading debits. The non-trading debits must be calculated by taking the debits for the period and then deducting any which have been relieved in other ways or which have been carried forward from an earlier period. In accordance with the general scheme for loan relationships in CTA 2009, Part 5 (see above §63.1), those carried forward may be set only against non-trading profits. Provision is made to exclude deficits which have been set off against general profits of the same or the preceding period. The purpose of section 50 is to permit the operation of section 42 even though the foreign interest is no longer separately distinguished. Where section 50 does not apply, TIOPA 2010 still allows the company to allocate these deficits as it thinks fit, subject to three qualifications. First, any decision by the company to set off a non-trading deficit against trading profits of the same period must be respected here too.[102] Secondly, if the deficit is carried forward from an earlier period, it may be set only against non-trading profits.[103] Thirdly, it is not open to a company to allocate excess charges to UK income greater than the amount of that income so as to set up a loss which might be carried forward.[104] This treatment applies to all non-trading credits and not just interest.[105]

It remains the case that when loss relief is available it will be applied first, thus cancelling the tax credit for any double tax relief. As unused double tax relief may not be carried forward as double tax relief but only, when relevant, as a deduction, and so perhaps a trading loss, the point is of some importance.

There was much legislation dealing with ACT; here, the rule eventually established was that the foreign tax credit was deductible before the ACT.[106] As a result, it has ceased to be necessary to set ACT against domestic source income rather than foreign source income.

75.4.7.7 International Companies; Getting the Source Right

Since, subject to the rules in §76.4, each source is taken separately and credit is given only on a yearly basis with no carry forward of unused credit reliefs, the problem of unused foreign tax credits is a very real one in the UK system. The use of an overseas company through which the foreign income may be channelled has two potential advantages. First, the source is the foreign company, so enabling the income from the different sources and possibly different rates to be pooled; pooling leads to the averaging of the foreign taxes and prevents a loss of tax credit where the foreign tax on some of the sources is higher than the

---

[100] TIOPA 2010, s 52, ex TA 1988, s 797(3).
[101] TIOPA 2010, s 50, ex TA 1988, ss 797, amended by FA 1996, and 797A, added by FA 1996.
[102] TIOPA 2010, s 55, ex TA 1988, s 797(3A), added by FA 1996.
[103] TIOPA 2010, s 53, ex TA 1988, s 797(3B), added by FA 1996.
[104] *Commercial Union Assurance Co plc v Shaw* [1998] STC 386.
[105] TIOPA 2010, s 50, ex TA 1988, s 797A, as amended by FA 2000, Sch 30, para 7.
[106] Ex TA 1988, s 797(4), (5); see also *Collard v Mining and Industrial Holdings Ltd* [1989] STC 384, 62 TC 448, HL.

UK rate. Secondly, the foreign income may, subject to the CFC legislation, be accumulated in the foreign company and then remitted back into the UK when there is enough UK tax to make use of the credits. The first advantage is particularly useful where dividends from a number of overseas countries are involved and the company is known as a 'dividend mixer company'; the second leads to the description of a 'Case V trap company'.[107]

75.5   Indirect Credit: Dividends and Underlying Tax

Where a UK-resident company receives a dividend from a non-resident company, liability to corporation tax will arise under CTA 2009, Part 9A (ex Schedule D, Case V), which then provides an exemption from UK tax where specified conditions are met; the vast majority of dividends will qualify for exemption.[108]

For the small minority of foreign dividends received by UK companies that will not be exempt, and for foreign dividends received by individuals, a tax credit under TIOPA 2010 may be available instead. The tax deducted in the country of source will have been a withholding tax, probably at the rate of 5% or 15% where a treaty exists and at the full domestic withholding rate if there is no applicable treaty. These taxes may be taken as credits against the UK tax due, whether income tax or corporation tax. Where the foreign tax system has charged a separate tax on the profits of the company, it would be equitable to allow credit not only for the income tax charged on the dividend but also for at least a proportion of the tax levied on the profits of the company which underlie the dividend—hence the UK expression 'relief for underlying tax'. Relief for underlying tax is governed by TIOPA 2010, sections 14–16 (unilateral relief) and 63–66 (tax treaty relief).

Example

In 2011 Y Ltd, a UK-resident company, has trading profits of £400,000 and receives a dividend of £864,000 net (£960,000 gross) from one of its overseas subsidiaries. Foreign tax on the profits and local withholding tax on dividends paid are 40% and 10% respectively. Y Ltd pays dividends (net) of £750,000 to its shareholders.

UK source income is £400,000, making tax liability of £100,000 @ 25%.

The foreign dividend of £864,000 must first be grossed up at 10% to give the gross dividend (taking account of the withholding tax) and then at 40% to take account of the foreign tax on the profits out of which the dividend has been paid. This gives a gross figure of £1.6 million, on which the UK tax at 25% will be £400,000. The foreign tax available for credit relief is £640,000 (40% of £1.6m) plus £96,000 (10% of £960,000), making a total of £736,000. Since this exceeds the UK tax of £400,000, there will be no more UK tax to pay on the foreign income; the tax liability of £100,000 on UK-source income remains unaffected.

---

[107] On which see Collier, Hughes and Payne, *Tolley's International Tax Planning*, 4th edn (Tolley, 1999), paras 27.38–27.57 and Inland Revenue discussion paper (1999), *op cit*, ch 6. Revenue Interpretation RI 149 assumes that these schemes work.

[108] See §19.3 above. Under the former rules, the payment was not exempt from corporation tax through TA 1988, s 208 as the payer was a non-resident.

Since Y Ltd is not a financial trader there is no room for the restrictions on credit relief where there is withholding tax to apply.

No underlying relief may be claimed if a tax deduction is given in another country by reference to the dividend.[109] This change was made in 2005 to counter schemes which used payments characterised as interest for tax purposes in another jurisdiction but as dividend for UK tax purposes. If, as normally happens, the interest is deductible in full in the foreign system, it cannot give rise to underlying relief. The thinking behind this is similar to that behind the tax arbitrage rules above at §62.7, but the rule is quite distinct.

75.5.1 Related Company

Indirect relief applies only to companies.[110] The foreign company (FR) must be a 'related' company of the UK parent company (UKP), ie UKP must control at least 10% of the voting power of FR.[111] The figure of 10% is historically low; it was originally 50% in 1930, and reduced to 25% in 1965. An alternative test by reference to ordinary share capital applies to dividends paid on or after 1 January 2005; this is to satisfy the revised EU Parent and Subsidiary Directive but is not confined to EU States.[112]

UKP may hold that 10% either directly or indirectly through an intermediate subsidiary company (SUB). SUB will be a subsidiary of UKP if UKP controls at least 50% of the voting power of SUB.[113]

Thus, if UKP has a 9% direct stake in FR it is not entitled to relief. If, however, SUB has a 1% stake in FR, UKP will become entitled to indirect relief if it controls 50% or more of the voting power of SUB. It must be noted that this is a simple test for UKP. If UKP controls 50% of the voting power of SUB, this will entitle UK to the underlying relief. The legislation does not say, as it does in many other tax contexts, that because UKP has only 50% of the shares in SUB it may therefore include only 50% of the 1% holding in FR (and so fall short of the magic 10%).

Although the 10% threshold is a magic figure, provision is made for the preservation of this relief where a 10% holding is reduced by dilution.[114] Where treaty relief applies only to certain classes of dividend, eg ordinary shares, unilateral relief for the underlying tax may be claimed for other classes, eg preference dividends.[115]

75.5.2 Relevant Underlying Profits: Source of Dividends

Where relief for the underlying tax is given, the next step is to ascertain the profits underlying the dividend, the rate of tax available for credit depending on a comparison of the tax paid with the profits.

---

[109] TIOPA 2010, s 57(3), ex TA 1988, s 799(2A), added by FA 2005, s 85 as from 16 March 2005.
[110] TIOPA 2010, ss 14(3) and 57(2), ex TA 1988, ss 790(6)(a), 801.
[111] TIOPA 2010, ss 14(4) and 63(2), ex TA 1988, s 801(5); on control, see CTA 2010, s 1124, ex s 840.
[112] TIOPA 2010, s 64(6), ex TA 1988, s 801(5A) added by F(No 2)A 2005 s 43.
[113] TIOPA 2010, ss 14(5) and 63(6), ex TA 1988, s 792(2).
[114] TIOPA 2010, s 15(6), ex TA 1988, s 790(6)(b)–(10); eg nationalisation.
[115] TIOPA 2010, s 14, ex TA 1988, s 800.

The relevant profits are:

(1)   if the dividend is paid for a specified period, the profits of that period;
(2)   if the dividend is not specified for a period but is stated to come out of specified profits, those profits; and
(3)   if the dividend is neither for a specified period nor from a specified source, the last complete internal accounting period of the company before the payment.

If under rules (1)–(3) the dividend exceeds the profits, profits from previous years may underlay the dividend unless they have already done so.[116] Case law established that the profits are those appearing in the company's accounts, and not those which are the basis upon which the foreign tax is assessed; a statutory basis for this was supplied by FA 2000.[117] If distributable profits are restricted, the average rate of foreign tax payable will be increased.

75.5.3 Subsidiaries as Related Companies

In the example at §75.5.1 above, UKP, the first company, resident in the UK, had a 10% stake in FR, and so FR became a related company of UKP. However, FR may have a subsidiary of its own (FRS1). If FR controls at least 10% of the voting power of FRS1, FR and FRS1 will be related; more importantly, UKP will be able to claim the indirect credit relief for the tax paid by FRS1. It does not matter that UKP does not control 10% of the voting power of FRS1; what matters is that FR has such control over FRS1 and that UKP has such control over FR. A company may, in turn, be related to another company, the third company, and so on, down a chain.[118]

The UK permits an indefinite number of links in the chain, and requiring only a 10% stake at each link; this is most unusual (and generous) in comparative terms. Since 1971 the first company has been able to claim credit relief in respect of the tax borne by the third company on its profits when those profits are passed back up the chain in the form of dividends. It is necessary that the general UK conditions for tax relief would have been satisfied at each stage up the chain.[119] It is also necessary that the appropriate degree of relationship exists at each link stage. The relationship requires that either the second company controls, directly or indirectly, not less than 10% of the voting power of the third company, or that it is a subsidiary of a company which controls 10% of that voting power.

FRS1, the third company, may be resident in some third country or even in the UK. Where any company in the chain is resident in the UK, the tax on its profits for which relief is claimed is not to include income tax paid in respect of dividends received by that company from other companies resident in the UK.[120]

---

[116] TIOPA 2010, s 59, ex TA 1988, s 799. Where, under the tax law in a foreign country, a dividend is increased for tax purposes by an amount which may be set against T's own tax liability (or, if in excess thereof, paid to him) then any such increase is to be subtracted from the underlying tax (TIOPA 2010, s 58, ex TA 1988, ss 788, 799, 808). It is thus clear that foreign imputation credit is excluded from the calculation of credit relief for underlying tax.

[117] *Bowater Paper Corpn Ltd v Murgatroyd* [1969] 3 All ER 111, 46 TC 3, and FA 2000, Sch 30, para 8, adding ex TA 1988, s 799(5)–(7), now ITOPA 2010, s 59.

[118] TIOPA 2010, s 64, ex TA 1988, s 801(1) and s 802 for insurance business.

[119] TIOPA 2010, s 65, ex TA 1988, s 801(2).

[120] TIOPA 2010, s 66, ex TA 1988, s 801(4).

75.5.4 Mixer Companies and Onshore Pooling

75.5.4.1 Introduction

As just seen, the principal use of the dividend mixer company was to allow the foreign profits which would have been taxed at various rates to be mixed together in one pot out of which the dividend would come. Since the UK tax system regarded the dividends as coming from the immediate source, ie the mixer company, relief could be given for the underlying tax at whatever rate that tax had actually been paid. This practice allowed companies to circumvent the basic principle of UK credit relief, which was that where the foreign tax exceeded the UK tax, credit relief was restricted to the amount of the UK tax. As a result of the review of DTR for companies, the Government decided to try to end this circumvention. The rules eventually enacted apply to claims on or after 31 March 2001, unless the dividend was paid by the mixer company to the UK company before that date.

What the rules do, as finally enacted, is explicitly to allow mixing in defined circumstances; to move from implicit tolerance of offshore pooling through foreign mixer companies to explicit acceptance of on-shore pooling in restricted circumstances. There are three principal forms of restriction. The first is that the extent to which dividends may be pooled is restricted by the use of a cap on the amount of credit that may be used. The second is that while onshore pooling is available to companies resident in the UK through and to certain UK branches or agencies of persons resident elsewhere,[121] it is not available to individuals or trusts. The third, and now no longer operative following CFC reform, was that onshore pooling was not open to dividends which escaped the CFC legislation because they satisfied the acceptable distribution test (now repealed); these dividends must always have been streamed separately. There is a suspicion that it was these CFC dividends which caused the real problems for the Revenue, and that much anxiety would have been avoided if that problem, and only that problem, had been addressed directly at the beginning. However, by then, too much political capital had been invested for the simple solution to be acceptable to the Government.

75.5.4.2 Three Rules (Two Now Repealed)

The first rule: Normal UK corporation tax rate cap. Where there is a chain of companies including a UK company, any dividends paid by companies in the chain below the UK company will have the foreign tax credit capped by reference to M, the maximum relievable rate, which is the normal corporation tax rate (currently 20%).[122] A very great deal depends on the way in which the tax is calculated. Where underlying tax is involved, the formula in TIOPA 2010, section 58 is:

$$(D + PA) \times M$$

where D is the amount of the dividend, PA the underlying tax properly attributable to the proportion of the relevant profits represented by the dividend and M the corporation tax rate of the recipient for the accounting period in which the dividend is received.[123]

---

[121] Through ex ss 806A and 806K respectively.
[122] TIOPA 2010, s 58, ex TA 1988, s 799(1A) as added by FA 2001, Sch 27, para 2 and superseding the version originally added by FA 2000, Sch 30, para 8. On the old 28% rate and HMRC error, see HMRC Note, 4 July 2008.
[123] For examples, see *Simon's Finance Act Handbook 2001* (Butterworths, 2001) 176–78.

The company may make a claim to exclude a certain amount of the underlying tax (U) if it wishes;[124] it might wish to do so if this will bring the amount of tax down below the cap level and so avoid 'tainting' the dividend.[125] The foreign tax cannot be used as a deduction.[126]

At one time a further deduction could be made where the amount given by the formula exceeded U. In calculating U it was at one time possible, before 2005, to bring UK tax into account. This would happen if the foreign company had shares in a UK company and the UK company paid a dividend out of profits charged to UK tax; here the underlying UK was treated as if it were foreign underlying tax.[127] This was used as the basis for avoidance and therefore abolished in 2005.

The second rule: pooling with 45% maximum (now repealed). The effect of the first rule is to deprive the UK company of the benefit of any foreign tax above the normal UK corporation tax rate. The second rule, prior to its repeal in 2009 with the introduction of the dividend exemption system, was therefore all-important. Despite the normal UK corporation tax rate restriction, relief might have been available under the second rule for foreign tax, whether underlying or on the dividend itself, which was above the cap but below a maximum of 45%.[128] This foreign tax might have been credited against the UK tax payable on certain other foreign dividends and so gave us the official pooling—at the expense of additional complexity.

The third rule: not from CFC, now also repealed. For the purposes of these pooling rules, the dividends must have met various criteria but, in particular, must not have been a dividend paid by a CFC which escaped the CFC legislation because, and only because, of the acceptable distribution test, or which represented such a dividend.[129] Such dividends were required to be separately streamed.[130] This rule no longer applies following the repeal of the acceptable distribution test in the 2013 CFC reforms. For further detail on the operation of the onshore pooling system, and the calculation of eligible unrelieved foreign tax (EUFT), see *Revenue Law*, 6th edition.

75.5.5 Restriction of Relief for Underlying Tax

Rules apply to dividends paid to a company resident in the UK to counter devices which artificially increased the underlying tax. These rules[131] apply where a UK company (UKA) makes a claim for this relief in respect of a dividend paid by the overseas company (FB), that dividend includes tax paid by FB or one of the other companies further

---

[124] TIOPA 2010, s 60, ex TA 1988, s 799(1B), added by FA 2001.

[125] See Inland Revenue Press Release 8 November 2000, [2000] *Simon's Weekly Tax Intelligence* 1593 and Budget Note 24/01, [2001] *Simon's Weekly Tax Intelligence* 460.

[126] TIOPA 2010, ss 60(3) and 57(3), ex TA 1988, s 811, as amended by FA 2001, Sch 26, para 6.

[127] Ex TA 1988, s 801(4B)–(4D), added by FA 2001, Sch 27, para 3, but repealed by FA 2005; for Revenue explanation of original rule, see Revenue Briefing Note BN 24 (7 March 2001) 2.

[128] Ex TA 1988, s 806B; on upper percentage, see ex s 806J. On the repeal of these rules by FA 2009, see Voisey [2009] BTR 533, 540.

[129] Ex TA 1988, s 806C(1).

[130] Ex TA 1988, s 801C.

[131] TIOPA 2010, ss 67–68, ex TA 1988, s 801A, added by FA 1997, s 90(2) as from 26 November 1996; see Oliver [1997] BTR 250.

down the chain and is paid 'at a high rate'.[132] A rate is high if it exceeds the 'relievable rate', ie the rate of UK corporation tax in force when the dividend is paid.[133] So far these rules would have a dramatic effect of reducing the availability of relief for underlying tax. It is therefore essential to appreciate that these rules apply only if there is an avoidance scheme.[134]

An avoidance scheme is defined as one where there is a specified relationship between the companies and there is a scheme or an arrangement the parties to which include those companies, and the purpose, or one of the main purposes, of the scheme or arrangement is an amount of underlying tax taken into account in a claim for a tax credit.[135] Further rules cover the relationship between the companies, and provide that the term 'arrangement' covers an arrangement of any kind and need not be in writing.[136]

Where these conditions are met, the amount of credit is restricted to the amount of tax that would be paid at the relievable rate on 'the relevant profits'.[137] An example of the sort of scheme at which these rules are aimed is where A receives a dividend from B at a normal rate, but A then arranges for B to acquire from some unconnected person a stake in another company (C) which is proposing to pay out a dividend from an income taxed at a high rate. A will, in these circumstances, claim DTR in respect not only of the direct tax on the dividend from B but also the indirect tax paid by B and C on the profits out of which B's dividend to A is paid.[138] These rules restrict the relief for the underlying tax to what it would have been at normal UK corporate rates on the profits used to pay the dividend. The rules do not go further and restrict the credit to the amount of tax that would have been paid if the only profits had been those of company B ignoring the acquisition of the stake in company C.

In 1997 the Minister stated, long before FA 2000, that the section was not intended to catch the acquisition of a dividend mixer company, or to interfere with reorganisation—unless there was a scheme of the sort under attack.[139]

75.5.6 Banks and Underlying Tax

The purpose of TIOPA 2010, section 70 (ex TA 1988, section 803) is to bolster sections 37–38 where the claim is for indirect tax credit. Without this rule companies would circumvent the rules by the simple device of inserting an overseas subsidiary between them and the source of the interest or dividends. Unlike the old rule, it covers both interest and dividends, and also covers associates of financial traders. Its scope was greatly reduced in 2005.

---

[132] TIOPA 2010, s 67, ex TA 1988, s 801A(1).
[133] TIOPA 2010, s 67(7), ex TA 1988, s 801A(5).
[134] TIOPA 2010, s 67(4),(5), ex TA 1988, s 801A(1)(c).
[135] TIOPA 2010, s 68, ex TA 1988, s 801A(6), (7).
[136] TIOPA 2010, s 68(9), ex TA 1988, s 801A(8)–(11)
[137] TIOPA 2010, s 67(6), ex TA 1988, s 801A(3), (4).
[138] *Simon's Finance Act Handbook 1997* (Butterworths, 1997), 121.
[139] Hansard, 13th Sitting, cols 458–460; [1997] *Simon's Weekly Tax Intelligence* 278. See also Revenue Interpretation RI 171.

75.6   Schemes and Arrangements to Increase Credit Relief

TIOPA 2010, sections 81 *et seq* (ex TA 1988, section 804ZA) empower HMRC to issue a notice counteracting schemes and arrangements to increase foreign tax credit relief in connection with schemes set out in section 83.[140] The legislation prescribes various things that must be included in the notice, and may include HMRC's view about the adjustments required.[141]

Section 81 applies where an officer of HMRC considers, on reasonable grounds, that the conditions in section 82 are or may be met, namely: (a) a credit is allowable for the period, (b) there is a scheme or an arrangement of which the (or a) main purpose is to cause an amount of foreign tax to be taken into account, and (c) the scheme is in the list prescribed in section 83. The legislation does not apply to schemes the purpose of which is to cause an amount of underlying tax to be taken into account.[142] The provisions are excluded if the amount of tax claimed by the taxpayer—and any connected persons with corresponding chargeable periods—is minimal.[143]

The section applies whether the tax credit claimed is the normal direct tax credit, or the indirect or underlying tax credit where a foreign dividend is paid out of profits which have borne tax. The legislation expressly authorises an adjustment to the foreign tax which the specified foreign company is treated as having paid; the foreign company is treated as having paid only so much as would qualify for relief if it were UK resident.[144]

Section 83 refers to situations described in sections 84–88, which may be described broadly as follows:[145]

(1)   where the foreign tax is properly attributable to another source of income or chargeable gain which is really unrelated to the foreign tax;

(2)   where a foreign tax payment is less than the amount allowable as a credit (usually this is where the payment of the tax does not increase the overall tax liability of the scheme participants, eg because the tax payment is matched by a tax-saving elsewhere);

(3)   where a claim, election or other arrangement under the foreign law increases the claim to the foreign tax credit (the claim may arise under the domestic law of the foreign territory or some treaty);

(4)   where under the scheme the amount of UK tax is less than if the scheme were disregarded (eg where the credit not only covers the tax on the scheme income but is also set against other income, thereby reducing total UK tax liabilities); and

(5)   there are tax deductible payments by A in return for which A or a person connected with A receives income for which credit relief is available.

---

[140]   Added by FA 2005, s 87; formerly in TA 1988, Sch 28AB.

[141]   TIOPA 2010, ss 81(2) and 89(2), ex TA 1988, s 804ZA(8), (9).

[142]   TIOPA 2010, s 83(2), ex TA 1988, Sch 28AB, para 1(3); on (staggered) commencement, see FA 2005, s 87(3)–(5).

[143]   TIOPA 2010, s 82(5)–(7), ex TA 1988, s 804ZA(5)–(7); periods correspond if they have at least one day in common.

[144]   TIOPA 2010, s 89(3), ex TA 1988, s 804ZA(10).

[145]   The explanatory instances are taken from the Inland Revenue Notes to the Finance Bill.

The way in which the scheme applies to the underlying tax relief has to be spelt out. Here the scheme is prescribed if it would be prescribed if the foreign company were resident in the UK but making no different assumptions about where its activities are carried on.[146]

The rules in TIOPA 2010, sections 81 *et seq* were widened and strengthened in 2010. Manufactured overseas dividends are now subject to section 85A—where deemed overseas tax deducted is not to be treated more favourably than tax credits on real dividends. There were also revenue-protecting changes to section 86 and also to section 112 (ex TA 1988, section 811), which provides for a deduction from income for foreign tax instead of a credit.

75.7 Miscellaneous Matters: Accrued Income Scheme

The accrued income scheme for income tax (above §26.4) contained its own DTR rules. Thus, credit relief was given if the sums treated as received under that scheme would have fallen under ex Schedule D, Case IV or V. When a payment which had been received was reduced for tax purposes by these rules, the foreign tax available for relief was also reduced.[147] With the introduction of the 1996 rules for loan relationships for corporation tax (now in CTA 2009, Part 5), the accrued income scheme no longer applies to companies falling within that tax.[148] Separate (but similar) provision was made for accrued income credits in such situations, but it was found to be abused and so was repealed by FA 2008.[149]

---

[146] TIOPA 2010, s 83(3)–(7), ex TA 1988, Sch 28AB, para 1(2)–(5).
[147] TIOPA 2010, ss 10, 39 and 112, referring to the relevant ITA 2007 provisions; ex TA 1988, s 807.
[148] Ex TA 1988, s 807(6), added by FA 1996, Sch 14.
[149] Ex TA 1988, s 807A(3), added by FA 1996, Sch 14, but repealed by FA 2008, s 59 and Sch 22, para 2.

76

Double Taxation: UK Treaty Relief

76.1   Introduction

76.1.1 The UK Tax Treaty Network[1]

The UK today has treaties with over 115 countries,[2] including (separately) the Isle of Man, Jersey and Guernsey (including Alderney). In 1997 the UK was the first country to reach this century. At that time there were over 1,300 treaties worldwide;[3] by 2015 that number had become more than 3000.[4] The UK has treaties with nearly all Western European countries, with most members of the Commonwealth and with all other OECD countries, such

---

[1] Discussions of tax treaty problems require the reader to consult Baker, *Double Taxation Conventions* (Sweet & Maxwell, 2001); Vogel, *Klaus Vogel on Double Tax Conventions*, 3rd edn (Kluwer, 1997). One must also consult the invaluable if now slightly dated Edwardes Ker, *Tax Treaty Service* (In-depth Publishing, 1994) and the accompanying book, Edwardes Ker, *Tax Treaty Interpretation* (In-depth Publishing, 1995). HMRC has their own *Double Taxation Manual*, available on the HMRC website. See also Harris and Oliver, *International Commercial Tax* (CUP, 2010).

[2] More correctly, the agreements are with 'territories' (TIOPA 2010, s 2, ex TA 1988, s 788).

[3] Inland Revenue Press Release, 10 April 1996, [1996] *Simon's Weekly Tax Intelligence* 701.

[4] OECD, *BEPS Action 15 'Developing a Multilateral Instrument to Modify Bilateral Tax Treaties' Final Report* (Oct 2015), 15. For a list of UK treaties see HMRC website at https://www.gov.uk/government/collections/tax-treaties.

as Japan. There are no treaties with many of the Arab countries such as Yemen.[5] but treaties have been signed with some tax havens including Liechtenstein (in 2012) and the Cayman Islands (in 2009). Arrangements with some countries are limited to transport profits and employees, eg Brazil and Iran. Countries which exempt foreign income from tax often have treaties with the UK, finding this useful for matters such as rules on the location of sources and administrative arrangements.

Bilateral treaties are a palliative for an understandable failure to reach international agreement on the principles of tax law. They have been well-described as a bolt-on exercise in damage limitation.[6] They do not solve all problems of the interaction of tax systems, and give rise to particularly acute problems when payments from or to third countries become involved.[7] How well they work may be assessed more generally by asking how far they reduce the distortions otherwise imposed on business.[8]

Although the UK has prided itself on its network of treaties and has often proclaimed *pacta sunt servanda* ('treaties are to be observed'), FA 2005 marked a determined effort to introduce a significant number of 'treaty overrides' or provisions designed to overrule the normal effect of tax treaty provisions. When considered along with some of the FA 2005 changes to credit relief considered in chapter seventy-five above (and which apply to UK treaty credit relief), it is as though tax treaties are now seen as another part of the tax avoider's armoury rather than as a necessary way of helping UK-based international business or even as a civilised way of dividing taxing power with treaty partner States.

76.1.2 EU Aspects and the Role of the OECD

The EU does not, as yet, have a multilateral convention for Member States. Article 293 TEC formerly imposed an obligation on Member States to eliminate double taxation within the Community, but this was too broad to give rise to direct effect and so could not be invoked by an individual taxpayer.[9] In any event, Article 293 TEC was not reproduced in the TEU or TFEU post-Lisbon Treaty. At one time the EU expressed an interest in co-ordinating the work of individual governments in treaty matters by looking at major issues, and especially at limitation of benefit clauses, but nothing was done at institution level.[10] Since the launch of the G20/OECD Base Erosion and Profit Shifting (BEPS) project (see §69.11), the European Commission has released its own 'Anti Tax Avoidance Package' (see §77.4.2).

The Court of Justice of the European Union (CJEU) has indicated that it will not regard the division of taxing rights between Member States as automatically giving rise to unjustified discrimination. However, this does not mean that the Court will simply waive its non-discrimination jurisprudence in the face of a tax treaty. Thus, where a state invokes the need

---

[5] The Agreement with Saudi Arabia covers air transport profit and dependent personal services.

[6] This does not mean that one should not think about better concepts, eg Verdoner (2003) 31 *Intertax* 147.

[7] See Harris and Oliver, *op cit*, ch 5 (on 'beyond the bilateral').

[8] For an outline of areas in which parts of the OECD Model Treaty do not fit well together, see Avery Jones (1999) 53 *Tax Law Review* 1, 25–37.

[9] Case C-336/96 *Gilly v Directeur des Services Fiscaux du Bas-Rhin* [1998] STC 1014, [1998] All ER (EC) 826. On other aspects of *Gilly*, see ch 21 below.

[10] Institute of Taxation TR6/93, [1993] *Simon's Tax Intelligence* 350.

to protect the cohesion of its tax system, it may find that the effect of the treaty between it and the other Member State is to deprive its cohesion argument of any force.[11]

In addition there is the big question whether a treaty made by state A, which gives its resident entities certain rights *vis-à-vis* another state, whether or not a member of the EU, is bound to give the same benefits to an entity resident in another Member State, B, but which has a branch in A.[12] In the *St Gobain* case,[13] state A was Germany and state B was France. A French company with a German branch was held entitled to the protection of a clause in a German treaty with a non-Member State. However, this was not because the relief arose directly from the treaty but because German domestic law incorporated that treaty relief into its own domestic law. The ECJ allowed the French company to claim the relief. The UK Government accepted the wide approach in FA 2000 by allowing non-resident companies to claim DTR if they had a branch, now a PE, in the UK (see above at §75.4.1). The ECJ has now ruled on the 'most favoured nation' issue and held that there is no obligation on the Member State to extend treaty rights to someone resident in a state which is not a party to the treaty.[14]

Today the dominant influence in UK tax treaty design is the OECD Model Treaty, which is revised periodically, most recently in 2010.[15] The OECD is an intergovernmental organisation with some 35 Member States (as of 2016). Since the OECD consists of States with 'advanced' economies, its Treaty was not as suitable for developing countries; the United Nations came to the assistance with its own model. The UN Model Treaty, however, is based heavily on the OECD version. Today, the OECD Model Treaty is used by many non-OECD Member States, and the views of non-Member States may sometimes now be found in the commentaries to the OECD Model Treaty. Developing countries were also invited to participate to some degree in the OECD's work on BEPS, and eventually over 80 non-OECD, non-G20 jurisdictions had at least some input in the process. The OECD Model Treaty consists of clauses to which commentaries are attached. The status of these commentaries in the interpretation of tax treaties is a matter of great importance. It must, however, be remembered that those at the OECD who approve changes to the treaty or its commentaries are government representatives and not disinterested experts. The OECD Model Treaty does not purport to be comprehensive; thus, there is no article dealing with trust income as such.[16]

The UN Model Treaty for the benefit of developing countries was first published in 1988 and revised in 2011.[17] The United States and The Netherlands have published their own

---

[11] See Case C-80/94 *Wielockx* [1995] STC 876, discussing the effect of Case C-204/90 *Bachmann v Belgium State* [1994] STC 855.

[12] See discussion by Kessermann (1997) 6 *EC Tax Review* 146 (before *Gilly*); and de Graaf (1998) 7 *EC Tax Review* 258.

[13] Case C-307/97 [2000] STC 854; and see Oliver [2000] BTR 174 and Kostense [2000] 9 *EC Tax Review* 220.

[14] Case C-376/03 *D v Inspecteur van de Belastingdienst/Particulieren/Ondernemingen Buitenland te Heerlen* [2005] STC 1211.

[15] See http://www.oecd.org. See also discussion in Avery Jones (1999) 53 *Tax Law Review* 1, 2. The Treaty is the subject of an excellent book by Baker, *Double Taxation Agreements and International Tax Law*, 2nd edn (Sweet & Maxwell, 2001).

[16] For an attempt to fit income from trusts into the existing treaty framework, see Avery Jones *et al* [1989] BTR 41 and 65; on accumulation trust and tax treaties, see Prebble [2001] BTR 69.

[17] For a comparison of the treaties, see van Raad, *Materials on International and EC Tax Law 2007–08*, vol 1 (International Tax Centre Leiden, 2007), 391. On the 2001 version, see Bruggen [2002] BTR 119; on 1978 version, see Surrey (1979) 19 *Harvard Intl L J* 1, 4.

model treaties. Multilateral treaties are relatively rare.[18] An important and evolving aspect of BEPS is Action 15 involving the development of a multilateral instrument to streamline the implementation of the BEPS recommendations.[19]

Having got through all this activity one is faced with another instance of the question raised earlier about the roles of principle and equity as opposed to brute negotiating strength.[20]

76.2 The Nature of UK Treaty Relief

76.2.1 *Treaty-Making Power*

Under UK law treaties do not have direct effect. Tax treaties, or more correctly 'arrangements', are made in relation to a territory (so avoiding problems over states the UK did not recognise)[21] and take effect under statutory authority,[22] being incorporated into domestic law by statutory instrument.[23] In accordance with general UK constitutional principles, these treaties may only include the matters permitted by the legislation.[24] TIOPA 2010, section 6(2) and (3) (ex TA 1988, section 787(3)) state that double taxation arrangements have effect so far as they provide, inter alia:

— for relief from income tax or corporation tax;
— for taxing income of non UK-resident persons that arises from sources in the UK;
— for taxing chargeable gains accruing to non UK-resident persons on the disposal of assets in the UK;
— for relief from CGT; and
— for taxing capital gains accruing to non UK-resident persons on the disposal of assets in the UK.

On the relationship between unilateral relief and treaty relief, see §75.4.1 above.

TIOPA 2010, section 7 allows the Revenue to propose Orders in Council only if they are consistent with the purposes spelt out in sections 2 to 6. Since sections 2 to 4 refer to granting relief for foreign taxes, it is thought that the UK treaties may only relieve from tax and not increase it.[25] However, the former version of these rules in TA 1988, section 788 had less

---

[18] They are to be found in Africa and in the Nordic countries: see Vogel, *op cit*, 11; see also Lang *et al*, *Multilateral Tax Treaties: New Developments in International Tax Law* (Kluwer, 1998).

[19] OECD, *BEPS Action 15 'Developing a Multilateral Instrument to Modify Bilateral Tax Treaties' Final Report* (Oct 2015).

[20] Eg Bird and Mintz in Cnossen and Sinn (eds), *Public Finance and Public Policy in the New Century* (MIT Press, 2003) 405–47.

[21] TIOPA 2010, s 2(1)(a), ex TA 1988, s 788(1), as amended by FA 2002 s 88 to reach an agreement with Taiwan. Similar problems have arisen over the precise area to be covered, eg the Israeli-occupied West Bank of the Jordan, or where the two governments both claim *de jure* sovereignty over the same territory (eg Northern Ireland).

[22] TIOPA 2010, s 2, ex TA 1988, s 788; IHTA 1984, s 155.

[23] Explained in TIOPA 2010, s 2(1), ex TA 1988, s 788(2).

[24] TIOPA 2010, s 6, ex TA 1988, s 788(3).

[25] The Revenue were known to be interested in the question whether use of the Article 9 in the OECD Model Treaty on associated enterprises could increase the burden of tax on companies as compared with the application

happy aspects for taxpayers; its limited nature was used, before FA 2000, to deny credit relief for foreign taxes to the UK PE of a non-resident company and repayment supplement.[26]

A double taxation treaty provision being made under statutory authority[27] becomes part of municipal law; it follows that where the text of the Order in Council does not agree with that of the treaty, the former prevails.[28] The Order may override the normal rules of UK tax law, but whether it does so or not is a matter of construction.[29] Where a treaty assigns a tax exclusively to the UK, this is not a direction that the UK *shall* tax but rather the recognition of a *power* to tax.

The treaty-making power in TIOPA 2010, section 2 is limited to relief for income tax, corporation tax, CGT, petroleum revenue tax and any taxes of a similar character imposed by the laws of that territory. It is usual for the treaty to state precisely the taxes which may be claimed for credit, so avoiding the problem of having to convince the Revenue some time later that the particular tax is of such a character. A hypothetical question is how the court would view an attempt by the Revenue to argue that a tax which had been mentioned in the treaty was not eligible for credit relief because it was not of the right character and that the Revenue had been in error in agreeing with the other state that it was. The Revenue argument would have to be that section 2 did not authorise it to make such a treaty.

A problem arose over development land tax (DLT). The Revenue took the view that this was not a tax of a similar character. As the DLT legislation had no enabling clause, it followed that no treaty relief was available for DLT.[30] If the UK had tried to incorporate DLT into one of its treaties, a person not resident in the UK but resident in the other state would have been without remedy. Then TA 1988, section 788 prevented any claim under domestic law, and the individual could not claim any relief in international law since states, not individuals, are parties to treaties in international law.

Another example concerns the days of the advance corporation tax (ACT) regime (now repealed)—*Boake Allen and other test claimants v IRC*[31] (at the lower level of appeal this case was known as the *NEC Semi-Conductors* case). Here, a majority of the House of Lords held that TA 1988, section 788 did not apply to ACT. Section 788(3) spelt out the parts of the Treaty which would be incorporated into domestic UK tax law. Section 788(3)(a) referred to a 'corporation tax in respect of income or chargeable gains', and the ACT did not fit that description.[32] Naturally this depends on the finding that ACT was not a corporation tax. The case makes a nice contrast with non-discrimination under EU law.

---

of the former UK statutory transfer-pricing rules in TA 1988, s 770; the switch to the OECD Model in s 770A, now TIOPA 2010, Pt 4, should mean that this particular issue has now gone away. Contrast IHT, where the Revenue view is that the treaty cannot enlarge the tax—see *Manual on Inheritance Tax Double Tax Conventions*, para 7.

[26] Avery Jones [1991] BTR 407; citing *Sun Life Assurance of Canada v Pearson* [1984] STC 461, 516b (on which see also Oliver [1986] BTR 195) and *R v IRC, ex parte Commerzbank* [1991] STC 271.

[27] On process of implementation, see Bartlett [1991] BTR 76. For criticism of some of Bartlett's views, see Edwardes Ker *Tax Treaty Interpretation*, §44.03, who argues that the treaties are made under the Crown's prerogative power and given effect by Order in Council. Moreover, since the Crown has no prerogative power to tax, this provides another reason why a treaty cannot widen the charge to tax.

[28] See Oliver [1970] BTR 388, 398–400.

[29] *IRC v Collco Dealings Ltd* [1961] 1 All ER 762, 39 TC 509; and see *Ostime v Australian Mutual Provident Society* [1960] 1 AC 459, 38 TC 492 (TA 1988, s 445 excluded by treaty).

[30] Oliver [1984] BTR 193.

[31] [2007] UKHL 25, [2007] STC 1265.

[32] [2007] UKHL 25, [45] *et seq.*

UBS AG v HMRC[33] is a case that involved another part of the pre-1999 UK corporation tax system, viz a claim to release a credit from surplus franked investment income under the now repealed TA 1988, section 243. UBS was a bank resident in Switzerland but with a branch in London. Moses LJ said that the claim for relief under section 243 of the 1988 Act did not fall within TA 1988, section 788(3)(a), as a claim for the release of the credit under section 243 was not a relief from corporation tax. UBS had no liability; it sought payment of a tax credit in an amount calculated by reference to the distributions it had received. UBS was not seeking 'relief … from corporation tax' because there was no liability to an amount of tax which would otherwise be payable.[34] Neither was it within section 788(3)(d) as it was not a right to a tax credit.[35] The judges disagreed on the scope of the non-discrimination clause, but the decision on section 788 was enough to make the Revenue win.

76.2.2 Who can Invoke a Treaty?[36]

While under general UK law individuals cannot claim the benefit of a treaty, the fact that the tax treaty has become part of domestic law by reason of the Order in Council does give rise to such rights, but only so far as that incorporation allows. A treaty based on the OECD Model will usually say that it applies to persons who are resident. 'Person' is then defined to 'include' an individual, a company or any other body of persons, and a 'company' as including any body corporate or other entity treated as a body corporate for tax purposes, a process which requires a reference back to the internal law of the state concerned.[37]

The question whether rights arising under a bilateral treaty may be used by a person who is resident only in a third country depends on the construction of the agreement. Thus, in *IRC v Commerzbank AG*,[38] dividends paid by a US corporation to the UK branch of a German bank were not subject to UK corporation tax because of the terms of the 1975 US–UK Treaty. Today, a different decision would be reached.[39]

76.2.3 The Credit

Where a treaty provides for relief by way of credit for the foreign tax paid, the way of giving relief is a matter for UK law, and the rules are stated in TIOPA 2010, sections 2–7 and 18.[40] The UK Treasury has power to deny tax credit refund under a treaty to companies which have, or are associated with companies which have, a qualifying presence in a state which

---

[33] [2007] EWCA Civ 119, [2007] STC 588.

[34] [2007] EWCA Civ 119, [42] *et seq*; Arden and Sedley LJJ agreed, [51 and 87].

[35] *Ibid*, [49–50]; Arden and Sedley LJJ agreed, [51 and 87].

[36] See Edwardes Ker, *Tax Treaty Interpretation*, chs 50–52, 56.

[37] See *Padmore v IRC (No 1)* [1989] STC 493 (CA), dismissing appeal from [1987] STC 36; Avery Jones [1987] BTR 88. See also Harris [2011] BTR 188.

[38] [1990] STC 285, decided under the 1945 Treaty. On interpretation techniques in this case, see Avery Jones [1990] BTR 388; and White and Avery Jones [1991] BTR 35.

[39] See US–UK Treaty 1975, Art 1(1), confining the 1975 Treaty to persons resident in one or other country; there was no such clause in the 1945 Treaty and the 1975 Treaty did not come into force until 1980. The 1977 Treaty excludes not only branches of companies resident in third countries but also branches of a company resident in the other Contracting State.

[40] Ex TA 1988, ss 788(2) and 792–806; see above at §75.4.

practises unitary taxation (called a 'unitary state').[41] This power would have been exercised in relation to California, but happily that dispute was resolved.[42]

76.2.3.1 Credit for Tax not Paid: Pioneer Relief or Tax Sparing[43]

The logic of the tax credit scheme of relief means that concessions, whereby the country of source lowers its tax rates, are cancelled out since it results simply in a lower credit to set against the tax liability in the country of residence. Since 1961,[44] provisions allow the taxpayer to treat the amount in respect of which the relief was given by the foreign country as if that tax had been paid.[45]

FA 2000 made changes for certain overseas dividends paid to a UK company. Relief may be claimed for the underlying tax on the profits out of which the dividends are paid in only two situations, the second of which has two limbs. The first is where the treaty specifically provides such relief. The second is where the relief sought is unilateral and either both the overseas company and the subsidiary are resident in the same country, or the sparing relief is provided by the treaty between the UK and the territory from which the profits arose.[46]

The device of tax sparing has been heavily criticised in—and scarcely used by—the US. The main objection is that by giving a positive advantage to the citizen trading overseas, it breaks the fundamental principle underlying the notion of the tax credit, which is neutrality between citizens trading abroad and those trading at home.[47] Other objections are that it gives the largest tax benefits to the countries with the highest nominal tax rates[48] without any necessary relationship to the fundamental economic needs of the country. It should not, however, be inferred that the United States ignores the problem; it gives relief in a different way by, in effect, granting capital allowances in respect of expenditure outside the United States, something permitted under the UK capital allowance system only if the trade is carried on at least partly in the UK. A more substantial objection is that tax sparing is a very inefficient way of achieving its goals unless carefully targeted.[49]

---

[41] TA 1988, ss 812–814 (not rewritten).

[42] Treasury Press Releases, 13 May 1993 and 15 September 1993, [1993] *Simon's Tax Intelligence* 858 and 1250.

[43] See OECD, *Tax Sparing: A Reconsideration* (OECD, 1998); summarised by Gosselin (1999) 47 *Can Tax Jo* 405. The statutory basis for tax sparing in TA 1988, s 788(5) was amended by FA 2000, Sch 30, para 1; see rewritten version in TIOPA 2010, ss 4 and 20.

[44] FA 1961, s 17; then TA 1988, s 788(3), now TIOPA 2010, s 6(1)–(4). Section 17 was amended in 1976; TIOPA 2010, s 32(1), (2) (ex TA 1988, s 795(1)) contains the treaty rule. On tax sparing, see TIOPA 2010, ss 4 and 20 (ex TA 1988, ss 788(5), 795(3)).

[45] Treaties containing such clauses include ones with Barbados, Israel, Jamaica, Malaysia, Malta, Pakistan, Portugal, Singapore, and Trinidad and Tobago.

[46] FA 2000, Sch 30, para 2, amending s 788(5) (treaty relief), and para 3, adding TA 1988, s 790(10A)–(10C) (unilateral relief); see rewritten version of s 790(10A)–(10C) in TIOPA 2010, s 17(1)–(5).

[47] See Surrey (1956) 56 *Col LR* 815; and (1958) 11 *National Tax Jo* 156.

[48] Counter-measures taken by developing countries include conditional withholding tax (Jamaica) and the raising of the tax level (Panama).

[49] See OECD, *op cit*, 31.

76.3 Interpretation of Treaties[50]

76.3.1 *Approaches to Interpretation*

The correct approach to the interpretation of a treaty is controversial.[51] There are several distinct issues—thus, should treaties be interpreted in the same way as domestic tax legislation, and what materials should the court look at when interpreting a treaty? Some would like the courts simply to resolve the immediate dispute in a pragmatic fashion; others would like the courts of all countries to develop a supranational interpretation, if necessary with a supranational court.[52]

What is clear is that interpretation issues can be complex. A treaty regulates the interaction of two tax systems which are complex in themselves, and the answer has to make sense in terms of the tax systems involved. There is no reason why a term should be interpreted in the same way in each system. The OECD reports on financial instruments and on software showed how divergent these views could be.[53] Even if the system can agree on how a particular receipt should be classified for treaty purposes, there will still be more fundamental characterisation problems, such as whether income can be attributed to this person or to someone else, how anti-abuse doctrines should apply or how the entity receiving the income should be classified (as a partnership or a company), as well as issues as to the source of the income or the problem of quantifying branch income.[54]

The Vienna Convention on the Law of Treaties 1969[55] requires that a treaty be interpreted in good faith in accordance with the ordinary meaning to be given to the terms of the treaty in their context, and in the light of their object and purpose.[56] It then defines 'context' as including any associated agreements and instruments, and goes on to permit reference to subsequent agreements and practices between the parties directed to interpretation and to *travaux préparatoires*. Where the treaty is authenticated in two languages, each is of equal weight unless the agreement states otherwise.[57] The English courts have authorised reference to *travaux préparatoires* and to the commentaries to the OECD Model Treaty.[58] *Travaux préparatoires* may extend to an interpretative document prepared by state

---

[50] See the works cited above in n 1.

[51] See, generally, Avery Jones [1984] BTR 14 and 90, and the long list cited by Sandler and Li (1997) 45 *Can Tax Jo* 893, 898. For an interesting Australian example, see *Lamesa Holdings Ltd BV v FCT* [1997] FCA 785, see also [1999] FCA 612, dealing with the capital gains article in the Australia–Netherlands Double Tax Treaty and whether the term 'real property' could extend to shares in a company owning real property.

[52] On history of such ideas see Edwardes Ker, *Tax Treaty Interpretation, op cit*, ch 2; and Avery Jones [2001] BTR 382–84.

[53] *Issues in International Taxation No 4* (Software) (1992); and *Taxation of New Financial Instruments* (1994).

[54] See Avery Jones *et al* [1996] BTR 212.

[55] The leading work on the Treaty is Sinclair, *The Vienna Convention of the Law of Treaties*, 2nd edn (Manchester University Press, 1984).

[56] Article 31; on good faith and treaty interpretation see Bruggen [2003] BTR 25–68.

[57] Articles 31–33.

[58] *Sun Life Assurance Co of Canada v Pearson* [1986] STC 335, CA. In *The Queen v Crown Forest Industries Ltd* [1995] 2 CTC 64, (1995) 95 DTC 5389 the Canadian Supreme Court gave the OECD Model Treaty (and commentaries) high persuasive authority; for critical discussion, see Ward *et al* (1996) 44 *Can Tax Jo* 408; but see also Vincent (1996) 44 *Can Tax Jo* 38.

A which is part of the negotiating process, or which is shown to the representatives of state B before the treaty is promulgated.[59]

Authorising reference to the commentaries is a long way from being bound by them.[60] However, the question arises whether the court should look at such materials to resolve an ambiguity, or more permissively whether or not there is an ambiguity.[61] The Vienna Convention suggests the less permissive approach is likely; US practice prefers the more permissive approach, but then the United States has not ratified the Vienna Convention. It is not clear how the OECD Model Treaty can be fitted in with the words of the Vienna Convention.[62]

UK tax treaties are not necessarily to be interpreted as though they have been drafted in Lincoln's Inn.[63] However, it does not follow that a purposive approach is to be preferred to a textual one, and it should be noted that the Vienna Convention prefers a textual approach.[64] Moreover, the OECD commentaries do not claim too much for themselves[65] and are all too often self-serving.[66] The actual results reached are consistent with the traditional English approach of strict interpretation. Looking at the result reached in *Commerzbank* (see §76.2.2), one commentator concluded that while the article was meant to mean something else, there was no admissible evidence to contradict the plain words interpretation, which all goes to show that it is what one says, rather than what one means, that matters.[67]

On the broader question of the role of public international law, Edwardes Ker concludes, depressingly:[68]

> Unfortunately even those judges who have recently focused on the applicability of the [Vienna] Convention have done little more than just cite it. Just as unfortunately some of those judges who have focused on principles of public international law have applied them with insensitivity as inappropriate as their colleagues' lack of focus.

The English approach was summarised by Mummery J as follows:[69]

(1)   It is necessary to look first for a clear meaning of the words used in the relevant article of the convention, bearing in mind that 'consideration of the purpose of an enactment is always a legitimate part of the process of interpretation': a strictly literal approach to interpretation is not appropriate in construing legislation which gives effect to

---

[59] See Arnold, Edgar, Li and Sandler, *Material on Canadian Income Tax*, 11th edn (Carswell, 1996), 207.

[60] However, for an example of UK tax law expressly incorporating OECD principles, see the transfer pricing rules in TIOPA 2010, s 164.

[61] The Canadian Supreme Court took the more permissive approach in the *Crown Forest* case [1995] 2 CTC 64, 77.

[62] Arnold *et al, op cit*, 206.

[63] Peter Gibson LJ in *Memec plc v IRC* [1998] STC 754, 766; approving Mummery J in *IRC v Commerzbank* [1990] STC 285, 297–8, (1990) 63 TC 218, 235–6.

[64] See Smith (1996) 49 *The Tax Lawyer* 845.

[65] See Avery Jones (1999) 53 *Tax Law Review* 1, 19.

[66] Sandler and Li (1997) 45 *Can Tax Jo* 893.

[67] Avery Jones [1990] BTR 388, 392.

[68] Edwardes Ker, *Tax Treaty Interpretation, op cit*, §1.03.

[69] In *IRC v Commerzbank* [1990] STC 285, 297–98; (1990) 63 TC 218, 235–36; approved by Peter Gibson LJ in *Memec plc v IRC* [1998] STC 754, 766. Mummery J's starting point was the decision of the House of Lords in *Fothergill v Monarch Airlines Ltd* [1981] AC 251; the cross-references to that case have been removed here. On *Commerzbank*, see Avery Jones [1990] BTR 388; and White and Avery Jones [1991] BTR 35.

or incorporates an international treaty. [Such an] interpretation may be obviously inconsistent with the purposes of the particular article or of the treaty as a whole. If the provisions of a particular article are ambiguous, it may be possible to resolve that ambiguity by giving a purposive construction to the convention looking at it as a whole by reference to its language as set out in the relevant United Kingdom legislative instrument.

(2)   The process of interpretation should take account of the fact that the language of an international convention has not been chosen by an English parliamentary draftsman. It is neither couched in the conventional English legislative idiom nor designed to be construed exclusively by English judges ...

(3)   Among those principles is the general principle of international law, now embodied in art 31(1) of the Vienna Convention on the Law of Treaties ...

(4)   If the adoption of this approach to the article leaves the meaning of the relevant provision unclear or ambiguous or leads to a result which is manifestly absurd or unreasonable recourse may be had to 'supplementary means of interpretation' including *travaux préparatoires*.

(5)   Subsequent commentaries on a convention or treaty have persuasive value only, depending on the cogency of their reasoning. Similarly, decisions of foreign courts on the interpretation of a convention or treaty text depend for their authority on the reputation and status of the court in question.

(6)   Aids to the interpretation of a treaty such as *travaux préparatoires*, international case law and the writings of jurists are not a substitute for study of the terms of the convention. Their use is discretionary, not mandatory, depending, for example, on the relevance of such material and the weight to be attached to it.

76.3.2 Whose Meaning?

Some of the problems thrown up are familiar to students of private international law. Thus, Article 3(2) of the OECD Model Treaty provides that any term which is not defined shall, unless the context otherwise requires, have the meaning that it has at that time under the law of the relevant state for the purposes of the taxes to which the convention applies, the tax meaning being preferred to that under other laws of the state.[70] It is anything but clear what is meant by 'context' or what meaning is to be assigned to the term if the context excludes the domestic meaning.

However, Article 3(2) is seen as one of the 'really clever' things about the OECD Model Treaty, since it enables the two systems to work together even though each has a different set of rules defining 'income'. It does not require that the words should have the same meaning in each system; instead it enables the treaty relieving provisions to correspond to the tax system in force in each.[71] It is generally assumed that the sort of problem addressed by Article 3(2) arises where the state of residence (R) is trying to give credit for tax in the state of source (S). Article 3(2) encourages R to give its own meaning to the tax paid in S. It has,

---

[70] See discussion by Avery Jones *et al* [1996] BTR 212 (also in (1996) 36 *European Taxation* 118); see also Avery Jones (1993) 33 *European Taxation* 252; and Edwardes Ker, *Tax Treaty Interpretation, op cit*, ch 8.

[71] Avery Jones (1999) 53 *Tax Law Review* 1, 18.

however, been used to suggest that R should apply its own rules where it is giving relief as the state of residence. Thus, if R says that if it had been S it would not have taxed this item, it may follow that it is not obliged to give relief for the tax paid by S.[72]

Problems will arise when the two domestic systems give different meanings; in the absence of a common meaning, double taxation may ensue. If countries A and B agree on a meaning, it would seem to follow that B will want to use the same meaning when dealing with country C; this means that the accidents of litigation, rather than systematic and thorough analysis, may shape the answer. One solution lies in the development of autonomous interpretations, perhaps developed by a body attached to the OECD. It is hard to fit such ideas into traditional common law notions of procedure, but it certainly is easier following the Woolf reforms of 1999.

A word used in more than one article in a treaty does not necessarily mean the same in each article—even though the courts of the other party have so held; arguments framed in terms of trying to achieve symmetry or harmonisation are not conclusive.[73]

76.3.3 Ambulatory?

Another problem is that of choosing the right interpretation if the domestic meaning is A when the treaty is signed, but B by the time the relevant year is reached. Canadian courts have favoured the static approach over the ambulatory, but have been almost instantly reversed by the legislature.[74] If OECD commentaries are looked at, it may be inferred that this may extend only to those commentaries existing at the time of ratification of the particular convention.[75] The UK position is undecided.[76] The ambulatory position is to be preferred as a matter of theory, and has been part of the OECD commentary on Article 3(2) since 1995.[77]

76.4   Relief by Exemption

Clauses may simply provide that income of the type stated shall be exempt from tax in one country.[78] Whether and to what extent it will be taxable in the other country is a

---

[72] For criticisms of such an approach, see Avery Jones *et al* [1996] BTR 212.

[73] See divergence of view in *Memec plc v IRC* [1998] STC 754 between Sir Peter Gibson LJ (at 768) and Sir Christopher Staughton (at 771).

[74] Tax Conventions Interpretation Act (Canada) 1984, reversing *R v Melford Developments Inc* (1982) 82 DTC 6281.

[75] See Ward *et al* (1996) 44 *Can Tax Jo* 408, discussing the decision of the Canadian Supreme Court in *The Queen v Crown Forest Industries Ltd* (1995) 95 DTC 5389, giving the OECD Model (and commentaries) high persuasive authority.

[76] However Baker, *Double Taxation Agreements and International Tax Law*, op cit, 27, points out that the Canadian Supreme Court in the *Melford* case placed some reliance on dicta in *IRC v Collco Dealings Ltd* [1962] AC 1 and *Woodend (KV Ceylon) Rubber and Tea Co Ltd v Commr of Inland Revenue* [1971] AC 321, PC.

[77] See Baker, *Double Taxation Agreements and International Tax Law, op cit*, 29–31.

[78] Receipts by a non-resident carrying on a banking, insurance or share-dealing business in the UK, although exempt from UK tax, are not excluded in computing the profits of that business so as to give rise to a loss for corporation tax purposes. This ends a 'fascinating anomaly' by which UK branches of US banks and insurance

matter for the revenue law of that other country. For example, income earned overseas by a visiting teacher there for temporary purposes may be exempt from tax in the country of service but is taxed in the country of residence.[79] Until 1998, that income might also escape UK tax.[80]

A more common form of exemption will exempt a person from tax in the country where the income arises if he is subject to tax in respect of the income in the other country. It appears to be the generous practice of some foreign countries to regard income taxed in the UK on preferential reduced or remittance bases as being 'subject to tax' in the UK and so not liable to the foreign tax. Examples of income which is often given exemption in either of these forms include trading profits arising otherwise than through a PE, and pensions and salaries paid by governments.

The effect of the exemption is that these receipts are not included in the receipts of the taxpayer's business. This might, in turn, mean that the business had a loss rather than a profit. A further rule applies, therefore, where the person is not resident in the UK but is carrying on a business in the UK. Receipts accruing to such persons would not be excluded where they consisted of interest, dividends or royalties.[81]

76.5 General Matters

Treaties are based on the twin poles of residence and source. This was because when treaties began, some countries, like the UK, taxed income on a worldwide basis, while others appeared to have collection of taxes levied on sources within their territory.[82] The meaning of 'residence' for treaty purposes is explored below. The equally fundamental concept of 'source' contains an ambiguity: does it mean the origin or actual source from which the income arises (as the term has been used throughout this book), or simply the territory in which it originates, ie from what or just from where? This may be tested by asking whether the UK gives credit for tax paid by a PE abroad.[83] The matter is addressed in modern treaties by express provision, and so 'source' means taxable in the other state in accordance with the treaty. Older treaties had no such clause; however, Article 3(2) of the OECD Model Treaty may be used to infer that the context required the rejection of the normal tax concept of tax origin in favour of the broader territory meaning, so giving relief.

---

companies could claim treaty exemption on US-source interest without restriction on the right to offset interest paid on the corresponding borrowing against their other UK income.

[79] For example UK–US Treaty 1975, Art 20. See *IRC v Vas* [1990] STC 137, (1990) 63 TC 430; and the more straightforward case of *Devai v IRC* [1997] STC (SCD) 31.

[80] Ex TA 1988, s 193, Sch 12, para 3; on 1998 repeal of the 100% reduction with immediate effect, see above at §69.3.

[81] CTA 2010, s 54, ex TA 1988, s 808, as amended by FA 1994, s 140.

[82] See Avery Jones [2001] BTR 382.

[83] Avery Jones [1994] BTR 191.

76.5.1 Discrimination

The OECD Model Treaty[84] prohibits the government from discriminating against citizens of other countries with sources in the first country.[85] This does not prevent the first country raising or lowering its own tax rates, but only from discriminating against non-residents. The purpose of this clause is to prevent discriminatory legislation, not to prevent unfairness.[86] The UK Revenue allow taxpayers to invoke such a provision only sparingly.[87] The clause has an odd history[88] and is very narrow; by being confined to tax, it does not apply to a rule barring repayment supplement to a taxpayer resident in the other signatory territory,[89] a point which makes a nice contrast with the vigorous jurisprudence of the ECJ (now CJEU).[90] Many UK treaties with former colonies do not include a non-discrimination clause. Where enterprises of a Contracting State are concerned, a comparison is made with the treatment of other similar enterprises, a phrase which enables comparison of the treatment of one enterprise with that of enterprises controlled by persons in the other state or in some third state altogether.[91]

Whether there is a breach of the non-discrimination article will depend not only on a close examination of the different situations covered by the article, but also on finding the right comparator. In *Boake Allen (previously NEC Semi-Conductors Ltd) and other test claimants v IRC*,[92] the taxpayer companies were UK subsidiaries of a parent based in Japan. Under TA 1988, section 247 (since repealed), UK-resident companies could make a group income election, as a result of which there was no liability to pay the now-repealed ACT. This election was not available where the payment was made to a parent resident outside the UK; such restrictions had been held to be in breach of EC non-discrimination law principles in the *Metalgesellschaft* case,[93] but did they breach the treaty? The House of Lords held that there was no breach.

Following on the intervening decision of the House in *Pirelli Cable Holding NV v IRC*,[94] their Lordships held that what the group income election was concerned with was deciding how to allocate the liability to ACT between the two companies. It followed that the section

---

[84] Art 24. For comments on earlier version, see [1981] BTR 47; and Avery Jones *et al* (1990) 30 *European Taxation* 309; and Avery Jones [1991] BTR 359 and 421. For 1993 survey of country practices, see International Fiscal Association, *Cahiers* 78b. On (dismal) performance by US authorities, see Goldberg and Glicklich (1992) 1 *Florida Tax Review* 51.

[85] See, generally, Avery Jones *et al* [1991] BTR 359 and 421. For earlier comment, see Oliver [1977] BTR 148; and van Raad [1981] BTR 43.

[86] *Sun Life Assurance Co of Canada v Pearson* [1984] STC 461.

[87] There is much valuable comparative material in Arnold, *Canadian Tax Foundation Paper No 90* (1991); see also Friedlander [2002] BTR 71.

[88] Van Raad, *Non-Discrimination in International Tax Law* (Kluwer, 1986); this book is a slightly dated but still very useful analysis of the US and Netherlands laws.

[89] Arnold *et al, op cit*, 220.

[90] On German courts' move towards bringing EC principles into tax treaties, see (2004) 32 *Intertax* 134.

[91] On meaning of 'other similar enterprises', see Oliver [1989] BTR 141, pointing out that the OECD report on transfer pricing takes a much broader view.

[92] [2007] UKHL 25.

[93] Joined Cases C-397/98 and C-410/98 *Metalgesellschaft Ltd v IRC and AG; Hoechst AG v IRC and A-G* [2001] STC 452.

[94] [2006] UKHL 4, [2006] STC 548.

had no meaning where the parent was not subject to ACT. This was why the election, with its cash-flow advantages, was rightly denied. This reason had nothing to do with the control being in foreign hands, and so there was no breach of the non-discrimination article.

The House of Lords decision in *Pirelli* left open the question—one of fact—whether the Pirelli company would have made a group income election. Despite the clarity of the House of Lords decision, the taxpayers returned to court to argue the question whether they were entitled to tax credits and so should not have to bring them into account. The taxpayers' argument was rejected at first instance and by the Court of Appeal.[95]

UBS AG v HMRC[96] involved another part of the pre-1999 UK corporation tax system, viz a claim to release a credit from surplus franked investment income under the now repealed TA 1988, section 243. UBS was a bank resident in Switzerland but with a branch in London. As seen in §76.2.1 above, the Court unanimously rejected the claim since it did not come within TA 1988, section 788(3)(a) or (d). Moses LJ held that the matter had to be dealt with under the dividend article (Article 10) and that the non-discrimination article (Article 23) could not intervene. Arden LJ thought that Article 23 could still apply. Moses LJ agreed with the Special Commissioners, but they had reached their decision with great reluctance and had been scathing of the failure of the Government properly to implement a treaty (see paragraph 41 of their decision). They invited HMRC to revisit section 788; the FA 2006 changes, below, did not address these issues.

In 2008 the OECD, as part of the ongoing review project, included major changes to the OECD commentary on non-discrimination. One may read this in part as an effort to make sure that the OECD approach to non-discrimination remains very different from that prevailing under EU rules.

76.5.2 Administration; Mutual Agreement, Exchange of Information and Mutual Assistance in Collecting Tax

There will be a mutual agreement procedure (MAP) article enabling the competent authorities in the Contracting States to resolve issues by agreement.[97] The competent authorities are usually the tax departments—often acting under an authorisation from the relevant Ministry of Finance. Such a clause authorises them to act without having to go through diplomatic channels or international court process. Such an article usually covers not only procedures for specific cases involving specific individuals, but also more general interpretative problems, and even allows the competent authorities to consult together for the elimination of double taxation in cases not provided for in the convention (a legislative role). Unfortunately, the individual taxpayer does not usually have any rights in this process, and often ends up as a pawn in a battle between two revenue machines.[98] Interestingly, the US–Germany Treaty contains an arbitration provision,[99] while the Austrian–German

---

[95] *Pirelli Cable Holding v HMRC* [2008] EWCA Civ 70.

[96] [2007] EWCA Civ 119, [2007] STC 588.

[97] OECD Model, Art 25. On old law on nature of legal rights under the mutual agreement procedure, see Avery Jones *et al* [1979] BTR 329; [1980] BTR 13; and [2001] BTR 9.

[98] On the nature of legal rights under such articles, see Avery Jones *et al*, *ibid*.

[99] On arbitration generally in tax treaties, see Groen (2002) 30 *Intertax* 3.

treaty provides for matters to be put before the ECJ, though whether that Court can take jurisdiction is another matter.[100]

Interpretative agreements are general rather than specific. In *IRC v Commerzbank*,[101] Mummery J held that a joint statement by the two signatory states on a point of interpretation did not make that interpretation binding on the courts. However, the wording of the treaty in that case was not based on the OECD Model Treaty.

The Revenue have statutory authority to give effect to the solutions and agreements reached under this procedure; statute also provides for claim for reliefs and various time limits.[102] The normal time limit for claiming the relief as determined by the agreement is 12 months after being notified of it. The claim itself, which may give rise to the mutual agreement, must at present be made six years from the end of the period to which it relates. The agreement is not binding on the taxpayer, who may then use the normal appeals procedure. The OECD reviewed the effectiveness of the mutual agreement procedure and produced a draft manual in 2006 and proposals on arbitration in 2007; the changes finally agreed in 2008 include a change to the treaty itself for arbitration (new clause 5). Under Article 25(5), where the competent authorities of the Contracting States have been unable to reach agreement to resolve a taxpayer's case within two years from the presentation of the case to one of the competent authorities, the taxpayer may request any unresolved issues to be submitted to binding arbitration. Furthermore, in a major change of practice, the commentaries suggest a mechanism for arranging for arbitration under *existing* treaties.[103] For the EU Arbitration Convention for transfer pricing, see above at §72.4.3. Of seven UK tax treaties or amending protocols signed in 2010 and 2011, three contain such an arbitration provision—Germany, Bahrain and Armenia—but four others do not.[104]

The treaty will likely include a clause providing for the exchange of information.[105] Some, but not all, recent UK treaties also include a provision based on Article 27 of the OECD Model Treaty, providing for mutual assistance in the collection of tax.[106] The 2011 UK–South Africa Treaty protocol added such an article and, interestingly, included a provision to the effect that there is no obligation to assist where the requested state considers that the taxes at issue are imposed 'contrary to generally accepted taxation principles'.[107] It is not yet clear whether the treaty requires the UK tax authorities to provide information to a

---

[100] On Germany–US Treaty, see Fogarasi, Gordon and Venuti (1989) 18 *Tax Management Intl J* 317.On German–Austrian Treaty, see van der Bruggen [2002] 11 *EC Tax* 52–64.

[101] [1980] STC 285, 392.

[102] TIOPA 2010, ss 124–125, ex TA 1988, s 815AA, added by FA 2000, Sch 30, para 20; changes to TCGA 1992, s 278 are made by para 21.

[103] In van Raad, *Materials on International and EC Tax Law, 2007–08*, vol 1 (International Tax Centre Leiden, 2007) 796–835, also available from OECD website along with country profiles.

[104] Baker [2011] BTR 125, 129–30 and Baker [2011] BTR 626, 627. This suggests to Baker (at 627) that the inclusion in UK tax treaties of the provision for arbitration 'depends upon the position taken by the other Contracting State, and some states (China is an example) do not appear to be very enthusiastic about arbitration'.

[105] OECD Model Art 26. See McCracken (2002) 50 *Canadian Tax Jo* 1869.

[106] See now OECD Model, Art 27, added 2003. On unhappy if dated US experience, see 50 *Columbia L Rev* 490. The US entered a reservation in relation to the OECD Treaty of 1988, so far as it related to enforcement.

[107] See Baker [2011] BTR 125 for analysis. Baker notes that no assistance provisions were included in 2011 treaties with Bahrain or Hong Kong, which suggests to him that the UK policy on such articles is to include them only if the other negotiating state wishes to do so.

foreign tax authority if there is no UK tax in issue[108] (see above at §70.3.2). On obligations to exchange information with other EU Member States, see above at §70.3.1.

The powers to make treaties including such matters are now to be found in FA 2006 (not rewritten). This Act not only provides the basic authority in this area but widens the Revenue powers to obtain information (in TMA 1970) needed for 'a relevant foreign tax', ie one imposed in the foreign territory and covered by the treaty. The Treasury is allowed to make regulations allowing the recovery in the UK of debts arising from these relevant foreign taxes. In negotiating treaties covering these matters, the Revenue officer must be satisfied that the confidentiality rules in that state are no less strict than those in the UK.[109]

The G20/OECD BEPS Action 14 final report outlined an agreed minimum standard with respect to the resolution of treaty-related disputes.[110] The minimum standard will:[111]

(1) Ensure that treaty obligations related to the mutual agreement procedure are fully implemented in good faith and that MAP cases are resolved in a timely manner;
(2) Ensure the implementation of administrative processes that promote the prevention and timely resolution of treaty-related disputes; and
(3) Ensure that taxpayers can access the MAP when eligible.

The minimum standard is complemented by a set of best practices. The UK and 19 other countries—a group involved in over 90% of outstanding MAP disputes—committed to adopt and implement mandatory binding arbitration in their treaty network as a mechanism to guarantee that treaty-related disputes will be resolved within a specified timeframe.[112] As noted in the 2016 Business Tax Road Map, the UK also committed to developing a mandatory binding arbitration provision and implementing other dispute resolution changes as part of the negotiation of the multilateral instrument in Action 15 (discussed next).[113]

76.5.3 Changes to Treaties

Double tax treaties are not immutable. The usual method of change adopted is renegotiation, a process which may be accelerated by announcing that a particular country will no longer be bound by its present treaties after a certain date.[114] Changes in the domestic tax law are not inhibited by the presence of a treaty,[115] and some changes may have the effect of altering completely the basis of a treaty, eg the adoption of the imputation system of

---

[108] In *State of Norway's Application* [1990] AC 723, the English courts exercised their discretion under the Evidence (Proceedings in Other Jurisdictions) Act 1975.

[109] FA 2006, ss 173 and 175; s 173 supersedes the separate provision in TA 1988, s 815C and IHTA 1984, ss 158 and 220A.

[110] OECD, *BEPS Action 14 'Making Dispute Resolution Mechanisms More Effective' Final Report* (Oct 2015).

[111] *Ibid*, 9.

[112] *Ibid*, 10

[113] HM Treasury, *Business Tax Road Map*, (March 2016), 23.

[114] Eg Dominica in 1986, or the UK ending the agreement with the Netherlands Antilles in 1989; on new Antilles regimes, see Arts (2002) 30 *Intertax* 153.

[115] Whether the new domestic law is excluded by the treaty is a question of construction (*IRC v Collco Dealings Ltd* [1961] 1 All ER 762, (1961) 39 TC 509). See, generally, Edwardes Ker, *Tax Treaty Interpretation, op cit*, ch 9.

corporate taxation in 1973.[116] These are, of course, only UK rules; other countries, especially those which incorporate treaties into domestic law directly, may well take a different view. It may also be noted that the 1998 changes which extended the CGT charge to temporary non-residents originally contained express provision to ensure that it did not override treaties; seven years of experience convinced the Revenue of the need for change and so a treaty override provision was introduced in 2005.[117]

An interesting example of this process is TA 1988, section 112(4) and (5) (now ITTOIA 2005, section 852), originally passed in 1989, which was designed to reverse the decision in *Padmore v IRC*.[118] That case had held that where a partnership was resident in Jersey, the effect of the UK–Jersey Treaty was that not only was the Jersey partnership as such exempt from UK tax on its profits, but, more surprisingly, that a UK-resident individual partner was exempt from UK income tax on his share of the profits. The rules were amended to reverse this decision (with retroactive effect)[119] and now provide that the treaty is not to affect any liability to tax in respect of the resident partner's share of any income or capital gains of the partnership.[120] An argument that the 1989 change was ineffective failed.[121]

One of the most important innovations of the G20/OECD BEPS project has been the work done on Action 15 involving the development of a multilateral instrument to streamline the implementation of the BEPS recommendations;[122] relying on implementation through the traditional method of renegotiating changes to bilateral treaties would have taken decades.

76.5.4 Beneficial Ownership

Several treaty articles require that the person claiming the benefit of the treaty provision should be beneficially entitled to the particular receipt. This may be partly intended to prevent treaty shopping ($76.7.1 below), but it is capable of having a meaning for the tax avoidance situation outside. The meaning of the expression beneficial ownership came before the English Court of Appeal in *Indofoods International Finance v JP Morgan Chase Bank*.[123] The Court held that on the facts a company was not the beneficial owner. Bizarrely, the case concerned a contract dispute between two non-UK companies as to what the Indonesian view of beneficial ownership might be—and whether it was reasonable to expect a company to indulge in a restructuring which would succeed only on one answer to

---

[116] Taylor [1973] BTR 174; on 'erosion' of US treaties by domestic changes made by congress and the courts, see Kaplan [1986] BTR 211.

[117] TCGA 1992, s 10A(1). On s 10A, see above at §74.1.

[118] [1989] STC 493, CA, dismissing appeal from [1987] STC 36. For comment on first-instance decision, see Avery Jones [1987] BTR 88.

[119] The provision is deemed always to have been made, save that it is not to affect any court decision before 25 October 1988 or the law to be applied by an appellate court where the judgment of the High Court or Court of Session was given before that date (from which it can be inferred that no litigation was concluded in Northern Ireland).

[120] Such a formula had already been employed in other treaties, eg Art 11(3) of the UK–Switzerland Treaty 1955.

[121] *Padmore v IRC (No 2)* [2001] STC 280.

[122] OECD, *BEPS Action 15 'Developing a Multilateral Instrument to Modify Bilateral Tax Treaties' Final Report* (Oct 2015).

[123] [2006] EWCA (Civ) 158, [2006] STC 1195 CA, reversing Evans Lombe J [2005] EWHC 103 (Ch), [2006] STC 192; see generally Fraser and Oliver [2006] BTR 424 and, on HMRC draft guidance, [2007] BTR 39.

the beneficial ownership question. The Court held that the expression had an established meaning in international tax law, and produced an interpretation which gave great pleasure to the taxing authorities.

The case law on the meaning of beneficial ownership continues to develop, see eg the Canadian case *Prevost Car Inc v R*, where the court took a narrow view of beneficial ownership, holding that a company that receives dividends is the beneficial owner unless the company is a conduit with absolutely no discretion over the use or application of the income.[124] This narrow interpretation in *Prevost Car* was applied in the taxpayer's favour in a 2012 case involving IP royalties, *Velcro Canada Inc v The Queen*.[125] In 2011 the OECD issued a discussion document proposing changes to the commentary on the meaning of 'beneficial ownership' in Articles 10, 11 and 12 of the OECD Model Treaty.[126] With respect to Article 10, the OECD Commentary now states that the recipient of a dividend is the beneficial owner of that dividend where he has the full right to use and enjoy the dividend unconstrained by a contractual or legal obligation to pass the payment received to another person. For the related G20/OECD BEPS recommendations on combatting treaty shopping see below §76.7.1. Finally, 2015 saw the launch of several initiatives aimed at greater disclosure of the beneficial ownership of companies and other entities to aid in addressing corruption and combatting illicit financial flows. The UK has legislated a new public statutory register—the PSC or 'persons with significant control' register—which requires most UK companies and LLPs to identify the individuals who are their ultimate beneficial owners and controllers along with their holdings.[127] The EU introduced similar measures in the Fourth Money Laundering Directive, which came into force on 25 June 2015.[128] The release of the Panama Papers has provided yet further public and political support for such developments worldwide, and at the time of writing the EU is pursuing further amendments to the Fourth Money Laundering Directive, including full public access of registers interconnected across Member States.[129]

76.6 Specific Clauses

The treaty will usually begin by specifying the taxes covered and its personal scope (eg whether it is confined to persons resident in each state).[130] Other definitions of terms used in the treaty follow. UK treaties often state that the party to the treaty is the UK, and go on to define what the UK means, ie to determine its territorial scope. Sometimes the

---

[124] 2008 TCC 231.

[125] 2012 TCC 57.

[126] Available on the OECD website. See also Collier [2011] BTR 684.

[127] See https://www.gov.uk/government/uploads/system/uploads/attachment_data/file/512333/bis-16-161-beneficial-ownership-transparency.pdf.

[128] Directive (EU) 2015/849 of the European Parliament and of the Council of 20 May 2015 on the prevention of the use of the financial system for the purposes of money laundering or terrorist financing.

[129] See http://europa.eu/rapid/press-release_IP-16-2380_en.htm?locale=en.

[130] As the current US–UK Treaty does; however, the old treaty as interpreted in *IRC v Commerzbank* [1990] STC 285 did not.

definition changes, as with the UK deciding to extend its view of itself for treaty and other fiscal purposes by including the Continental Shelf.[131]

However, these questions raise a more fundamental question,[132] which is whether a tax treaty can have any territorial scope or whether it is universal. If a treaty is universal it will protect against all attempts by the state of source to tax the person resident in the other state, ie it applies to the same geographical area as that to which the state's tax laws are applied, unless the treaty provides otherwise. Thus, if the tax jurisdiction changes, the scope of the treaty changes too. On a territorial view, a change in the tax jurisdiction does not automatically change the scope of the treaty's application.

76.6.1 Residence

The interpretative section of the treaty establishes the meaning of the term 'resident' for the purposes of the treaty rules which follow. A person must be a resident of one Contracting State—and not of the other—to make the treaty work. To this end there is often a tie-breaker clause in Article 4. The terms used are much more familiar to civil lawyers than to common lawyers.[133] The civil law test of residence outside the tax area was probably closer to the UK's concept of domicile than to our concept of residence. Unlike the civil law systems, the OECD Model Treaty provides an order in which the tests are to be applied, and has made the outcome less abstract and more fact-based than in civil law systems.[134] Naturally, these definitions are quite distinct from the normal rules of residence.[135] There are definitions of 'residence' for both individuals and other entities such as companies. Article 4(3) of the treaty will often refer to a company's 'place of effective management' (POEM) as the tie-breaker if a company is considered resident in both treaty countries under those countries' domestic law. As discussed above at §69.6.3, effective management is usually found where the managers of the actual business are, as opposed to the central management and control exercised by directors.[136]

The 2008 Update to the OECD Model Tax Treaty introduced an alternative version of Article 4(3), which provided that the competent authorities of the Contracting States shall, having regard to a number of relevant factors, endeavour to determine by mutual agreement the state of which the company is a resident for treaty purposes.[137] Settlement of a dual-residence issue by mutual agreement rather than purely on a tie-breaker such as POEM has since become more common in UK treaties, as evident in treaties with the Netherlands (2008) and Norway (2013), but a POEM tie-breaker is still found in others, eg Crotia (2015). In the absence of agreement to resolve dual residency, the treaty usually provides a restriction of treaty benefits—though with the possibility of arbitration under

---

[131] On differences between UK and Norway, see Oliver [1990] BTR 303.
[132] Skaar [1993] BTR 189.
[133] Avery Jones et al [1981] BTR 14 and 104; see discussion by Venables (1998) 8 *Offshore Taxation Review* 189.
[134] *Ibid*, 119.
[135] *IRC v Exxon Corpn* [1982] STC 356. For an example of the importance of such definitions, see *Lord Strathalmond v IRC* [1972] 3 All ER 715, (1972) 48 TC 537; and compare *Avery Jones v IRC* [1976] STC 290, [1976] 2 All ER 898. See, generally, Avery Jones et al [1981] BTR 15 and 104. On ordinary rules, see c 13 above.
[136] See Statement of Practice SP 1/90; and Inland Revenue, *International Tax Handbook*, paras 347 *et seq*.
[137] OECD, *Commentary to the Model Tax Convention*, Art 4, paras 24 and 24.1.

Article 25. Although treaty provisions are usually intended to be effective only for treaty purposes, the treaty may have an effect in domestic law, as where a company which is non-resident for treaty purposes is treated as not resident for other purposes as well.[138]

The final report on the G20/OECD BEPS Action 6 goes a step further by recommending removing the POEM tie-breaker in Article 4(3) of the OECD Model Treaty and replacing it instead with a 'case-by-case' approach, whereby the competent authorities of the Contracting States by mutual agreement endeavour to decide the company's state of residence, 'having regard to its place of effective management, the place where it is incorporated or otherwise constituted and any other relevant factors'.[139] In the absence of such agreement, the company would not be entitled to any treaty relief or exemption from tax, 'except to the extent and in such manner as may be agreed upon by the competent authorities of the Contracting States'.[140]

76.6.2 Trader and Professional: Permanent Establishment

Traders resident in the UK and carrying on a trade partly inside and partly outside the UK are taxable under ITTOIA 2005, Part 2 or CTA 2009, Part 3 on the profits as they arise. Whether they are taxable in the foreign country depends first on that country's tax law. If no foreign tax is payable, no double tax problem arises. If, however, foreign tax is payable, the next step is to look at the treaty, which will probably permit the foreign country to tax the industrial and commercial profits allocable to the enterprise's 'permanent establishment' (PE) in that state.[141] This last term is separately defined in each treaty, but generally includes[142] a branch, place of management,[143] factory or other fixed place of business, but not an agency (unless the agent has and habitually exercises a general power to negotiate and conclude contracts on behalf of his principal), a bona fide broker or a general commission agent.[144] It has been suggested, convincingly, that these clauses are an inaccurate translation from a French original.[145] Often, treaties will also state that certain non-core activities, such as the display of goods, do not amount to having a PE.[146]

In the final report of October 2015, the G20/OECD BEPS Action 7 made several recommendations for changes to the definition of PE in Article 5 of the Model Treaty, and also to

---

[138] FA 1994, s 249; treaties usually have a tie-breaker clause, but this practice has not been invariable: eg the US–UK Treaty 1975, Art 4 had no tie-breaker clause for companies. Above, §69.6.5.

[139] OECD, *BEPS Action 6, 'Preventing the Granting of Treaty Benefits in Inappropriate Circumstances, Final Report'* (Oct 2015), 72.

[140] Ibid.

[141] For case law down to 1997, see Edwardes Ker, *International Tax Treaties Service, op cit.*

[142] See OECD Model Treaty, Art 5. A PE in the foreign country will also give rise to tax on capital gains and may result in a heavier tax on dividends from that country if the business is incorporated there. On some divergent definitions in European countries, see Skaaar [1997] BTR 494; on history, see Huston and Williams, *Permanent Establishments: A Planning Primer* (Kluwer, 1993).

[143] This derives from the UK test of residence. A person may have a PE in the UK and yet not be resident here (*Greenwood v FL Smidth & Co Ltd* [1922] 1 AC 417, (1922) 8 TC 193. See also *OECD Discussion Draft on Place of Effective Management* (OECD, 2003); van Raad, *Materials on International and EC Tax Law, 2007–08*, vol 1 (International Tax Centre Leiden, 2007) 580–84; and Hinnekens (2003) 31 *Intertax* 314.

[144] OECD Model Treaty, Art 5(5), (6); on agency, see Pleijsier (2001) 29 *Intertax* 167 and 218.

[145] See discussion by Avery Jones *et al* [1993] BTR 341.

[146] OECD Model Treaty, Art 5(4).

the related Commentary, in order to target attempts to artificially avoid PE status.[147] The two main focuses of Action 7 were commissionaire arrangements and abuse of the 'preparatory or auxiliary' activity exceptions in Article 5(4). A commissionnaire arrangement is an arrangement through which a person sells products in a state in its own name but on behalf of a foreign enterprise that is the owner of these products. The OECD was concerned with a foreign enterprise using a commissionnaire arrangement and claiming that the dependent agent PE rule in Article 5(5) did not apply because the contracts concluded by the person acting as a commissionnaire were not binding on the foreign enterprise. This was thought to be abusive where the arrangement was intended to result in the regular conclusion of contracts to be performed by the foreign enterprise; in such a case, the OECD was of the view that the foreign enterprise should be considered to have a PE. The main change to Article 5(5) involved adding to the requirement that the person habitually conclude contracts to also include situations where the person 'habitually plays the principal role leading to the conclusion of contracts that are routinely concluded without material modification by the enterprise.'

Second, when the exceptions to the definition of PE found in Article 5(4) of the OECD Model Treaty were first introduced, the activities covered by these exceptions were generally considered to be of a preparatory or auxiliary nature. As the OECD states in Action 7, activities previously considered to be merely preparatory or auxiliary in nature have become core business activities for many businesses. Thus, Article 5(4) was modified to ensure that *each* of the exceptions included therein is restricted to activities that are otherwise of a preparatory or auxiliary character. New Article 5(4.1) was also added to clarify that it is not possible to avoid PE status by fragmenting a cohesive operating business into several small operations in order to argue that each part is merely engaged in preparatory or auxiliary activities. Action 7 provided further recommendations for preventing abuse related to splitting up contracts. Finally, with a view to speeding up the implementation of these changes in the existing bilateral treaty network, the recommended changes to the definition of PE in the Action 7 report are among the changes to be included in the multilateral instrument proposed in Action 15.

Assuming a PE does exist in the foreign state, that state will usually be allowed to tax only so much of the investment income and profits as are attributable to the PE,[148] and the treaty may say how the profits are to be allocated to that establishment. There have been serious problems about applying this important concept to the world of electronic commerce. Formerly, the rules emphasised the making of contracts, but this focus began to look inadequate when applied in a world where, increasingly, the only physical manifestations

---

[147] OECD, *BEPS Action 7, 'Preventing the Artificial Avoidance of Permanent Establishment Status, Final Report'* (Oct 2015).

[148] Eg see OECD Model Treaty, Art 7. For an interesting Canadian example of the problems of application, see *Cudd Pressure Control Inc v The Queen* [1995] 2 CTC 2382: the case draws attention to tensions in the OECD commentary shown by the different approaches adopted in Art 7 on permanent establishment and Art 9 on associated enterprises; both articles create a fictional independence for the establishment and company. The court disallowed notional deductions apparently permitted by Art 7 on the basis that they would not have been allowed under Canadian domestic law. On *Cudd Pressure*, see van Raad (2000) 28 *Intertax* 162 and 253; and Ward (2000) 48 *Can Tax Jo* 559.

of business were servers, websites, Internet service providers and telecommunications infrastructure.[149]

The OECD undertook a detailed study into the attribution of profits to PEs[150] that led to amendments to Article 7(2) in the 2010 version of the OECD Model Treaty. The changes to the Article 7 commentary and treaty provision represented major and profound changes to the way in which profits are to be attributed to a PE. The concept of the related business activity was replaced by that of the functionally separate enterprise. Article 7(2) now provides that profits are to be attributed 'taking into account the functions performed, assets used and risks assumed by the enterprise through the permanent establishment and through other parts of the enterprise'. As only some of the OECD member countries so far have accepted the new wording, it is likely that it will only be new UK treaties and protocols with those states which will have this wording for some time to come.[151]

76.6.3 *Business Profits*

Where a business is carried on through a PE in a foreign country, business profits earned by that PE are taxable in the country of source.[152] Profits earned otherwise than by the establishment are taxable in the country of residence. If the trader decides to set up a subsidiary company in the country of source, OECD Model Treaty, Article 9 will apply. The words of the business profits article mask an important difference between civil law and common law countries: in civil law countries all income of the PE is treated as business income; whereas in common law countries this is not necessarily so.[153]

Some UK residents had tried to use foreign trusts and partnerships to avoid tax (above §20.10.7 and §71.3.2), relying on treaty provisions that provided that the trading profits of a non-resident enterprise are taxable in the UK only to the extent that they are attributable to a business carried on by or through a PE in the UK. TIOPA 2010, section 130 ensures that this treaty provision does not prevent persons resident in the UK from being liable to tax in the UK. This rule, which applies to income arising on or after 12 March 2008, is to prevent avoidance where partnerships are not involved.[154]

Shipping and similar sources of profits have their own article.[155] At one time there was a separate article dealing with independent personal services—Article 14—but this was removed from the OECD model in 2000, largely on the ground that Article 7 was

---

[149] See, *inter alia*, Doernberg and Hinnekens, *Electronic Commerce and International Taxation* (Kluwer, 1999); Bourgeois and Blanchette (1997) 45 *Can Tax Jo* 1127 and 1378; Thorpe Emory (1997) 11 *International Law Review* 633. For official UK revenue views, see Customs and Excise Press Release 6 October 1998, [1998] *Simon's Tax Intelligence* 1436. The OECD Commentary to Art 5 states that the mere presence of a server in a state does not give rise a PE in that state. The Revenue have indicated that in their view neither websites nor servers are PEs: Inland Revenue Press Release, 11 April March 2000, [2000] *Simon's Weekly Tax Intelligence* 625.

[150] The OECD's *Report on the Attribution of Profits to Permanent Establishments* (OECD, 2008) was reissued with minor revisions in 2010.

[151] Baker [2011] BTR 625, 626. Baker notes that none of the seven most recent UK treaties signed in 2010 and 2011 used the new wording.

[152] OECD Model Treaty, Art 7(1); for an interesting discussion of the problems which arise, see the report on the International Seminar held at Harvard in late 2002; the report is by Arnold, de Sasseville and Zolt and is published in (2002) 50 *Can Tax Jo* 1979–2024. On relationship between Art 7(2) and (3), see commentary added 1994.

[153] Avery Jones *et al* [2003] BTR 224.

[154] TIOPA 2010, s 130, ex TA 1988, s 815AZA, added by FA 2008, s 56.

[155] Art 8. On history, see Maisto (2003) 31 *Intertax* 232.

sufficient.[156] However the article remains in force in many, as yet unrenegotiated, treaties.[157] Under such treaties the country of residence has the exclusive right to tax unless there is a 'fixed base' in the other Contracting State; so much of the profit as was attributable to that fixed base is taxed there.[158] The article was modified for artistes and sportsmen.[159] The change to Article 7 also meant rewriting of the concept of the PE.

In considering these matters it is important to remember the role of the PE concept to allocate profit to the operations of a person resident in one country to activities carried on in the other. It does not give the PE legal personality.

76.6.4 Associated Enterprises

Article 9 of the OECD Model Treaty imposes an arm's-length principle and is the basis of the UK's rules for transfer-pricing legislation. Like Article 7 dealing with the profits of a PE, this creates a fictional independence for the entities involved. Article 9 deals with enterprises under common control, and allows an adjustment of profits by one state and then directs the other state to make a corresponding adjustment if, and only if, it agrees. Double tax problems may arise when interest payments are made to the parent company and when the profits earned by the subsidiary leave that country in the form of dividends.

76.6.5 Dividends, Interest and Royalties

The OECD Model Treaty provides for a withholding tax of a maximum of 10% on payments of interest[160] and of 15% on dividends, except where the recipient is a company holding at least 25% of the shares in the paying company when the rate is 5%.[161] Royalty payments are taxable only in the country of residence, except where there is an effective connection between the PE in the source country and the property giving rise to royalties.[162] By contrast, the old Mexico model gave the taxation of dividends to the place where the capital was invested,[163] of interest to the place of indebtedness[164] and of royalties to the place of exploitation[165]—that is the country of source. Many of these provisions in the OECD Model Treaty, particularly those relating to dividends, were simply unacceptable to less 'developed' countries.

The definition of 'interest'[166] is a matter for the UK courts, but statute now provides special rules.[167] Treaties often provide that where, owing to a special relationship, the amount

---

[156] De Kort (2001) 29 *Intertax* 72.
[157] Oliver (2001) 29 *Intertax* 204.
[158] OECD Model Treaty, Art 14.
[159] OECD Model Treaty, Art 17, Nitikman (2001) 29 *Intertax* 268. There are also many domestic law problems; see generally, Sandler, *Taxation of International Entertainers and Athletes* (CIOT and Kluwer, 1995).
[160] OECD Model Treaty, Art 11. Some treaties exempt interest on normal intra-group loans.
[161] OECD Model Treaty, Art 10; on OECD history, see Harris in (2000) 15 *Australian Tax Forum* 1–72 and 75–224.
[162] OECD Model Treaty, Art 12.
[163] Mexico Model, Art IX.
[164] Mexico Model, Art II.
[165] Mexico Model, Art X (copyright royalties were excluded).
[166] On problems of the source of interest, see Avery Jones (1999) 53 *Tax Law Review* 1, 31.
[167] TIOPA 2010, s 131, ex TA 1988, s 808A, added by F(No 2)A 1992, s 52. For the correspondence between The Law Society and the Inland Revenue, see [1993] *Simon's Tax Intelligence* 307.

of the interest paid exceeds the amount that would have been paid in the absence of the relationship, only that hypothetical amount is treated as interest. Where such a clause is relevant, under TIOPA 2010, section 131 the special relationship is to take account of all factors, but express mention is made of whether the loan would have been made at all, the amount of the loan, the rate of interest and other terms that would have been made. The burden is then on the taxpayer to establish that there is no such special relationship. Section 131 further provides that where the company making the loan does not have a business of making loans generally, that fact is to be disregarded.[168] It also provides that the direction to regard all the factors does not apply where the relationship expressly requires regard to be had to the amount of the debt on which the interest is paid and it limits the factors to be taken into account.[169]

Where relief from UK tax in respect of interest is in issue, it is essential that a claim is made as soon as possible in order that tax is not deducted at source. Notice of exemption from such deduction may have retroactive effect, but only to the date that the certified treaty claim is received by the proper officer of the Revenue.[170]

76.6.6 Royalties

References to 'special relationships' are found not only in articles on interest but also in those on royalties. The factors to be taken into account are equivalent to those for interest.[171]

The definition of 'royalty' gave rise to a famous US case involving Pierre Boulez, the composer and conductor. Boulez was resident in Germany and received payments for fees for making recordings in the United States with US orchestras. The US Tax Court[172] held that these were payments for personal services, even though the German tax authorities viewed them as royalty payments. The German view became part of a revised treaty.

A company making a payment of a royalty to a non-resident is now allowed to deduct tax at the treaty rate and not the normal 20%.[173] The risk that the treaty does not in fact apply falls on the paying company.

76.6.7 Employees

UK residents going to work for a foreign company overseas will usually be taxable under the UK tax rules on foreign earnings. Under the treaty they may well be declared to be taxable only in the country of their residence and not in the country of the employment if the employment is exercised there. Some treaties tax in the country of source only if the taxpayer spends a certain number of days in that country.[174] The 2008 Commentary changes clarify the way the days are counted.

---

[168] TIOPA 2010, s 131 (5), ex TA 1988, s 808A(4).
[169] TIOPA 2010, s 131(4), ex TA 1988, s 808A(5). See also Inland Revenue Press Release, 15 May 1992, [1992] *Simon's Tax Intelligence* 519.
[170] Revenue Interpretation RI 79; that officer is now the Financial Intermediaries and Claims Office (FICO) (International), formerly the Inspector of Foreign Dividends.
[171] TIOPA 2010, s 132, ex TA 1988, s 808B, added by FA 2000, Sch 30, para 17.
[172] (1984) 83 TC 584.
[173] ITA 2007, ss 911–913, ex TA 1988, s 349E, added by FA 2002, s 96.
[174] For example US–Belgium Treaty (90 days).

76.6.8 Capital Gains

Subject to three exceptions, Article 13 of the OECD Model Treaty gives the right to charge capital gains exclusively to the country of residence. The three exceptions which allow the country of source to tax are: (a) gains from immovable property; (b) gains from assets held as part of the business property of a PE; and (c) gains from certain ships and aircraft. The scope of the capital gains article can be uncertain. As this book shows, the distinction between capital and income is deeply ingrained in the UK tax system, but some capital receipts are regarded as income for income tax purposes. It is a nice question whether for treaty purposes such receipts should be governed by the article to which they belong as income, the present article or the 'other income' article. A pragmatic approach would suggest that when the UK redefines a receipt for domestic purposes in a way which is more precise, eg as part of employment income under ITEPA 2003 or trading income under ITTOIA 2005, Part 2, that redesignation should apply for treaty purposes too. Where the item is simply lobbed into miscellaneous rules (eg ex Schedule D, Case VI), the other income article may be relevant but ought to yield place to the more precise capital gains article.[175] Of course, UK rules also include situations in which what had been income was moved to capital gain, eg where a company buys its own shares in circumstances coming within CTA 2010, section 1033. The decision by ITTOIA 2005 no longer to use the miscellaneous provisions (ex Schedule D, Case VI) as a dumping-ground reformulates the issues—but does not solve them.

76.6.9 Other Income

Not every treaty contains another income article, which means that gaps can sometimes occur.[176] This may be because the treaty fails to mention certain categories of income, or because the income mentioned arises in the other state and in a third country. The presence of such an article does not solve all problems; thus the article does not cover payments to or by transparent entities such as partnerships.[177]

76.7   Other Problems and Issues

76.7.1 Treaty Shopping

No chapter on treaties would be complete without a reference to the practice of treaty shopping.[178] This practice consists in a resident of a state, which is not a party to the treaty, establishing an entity within a state which is party to the treaty in order to take advantage of

[175] See conclusion to Avery Jones [2001] BTR 382.
[176] See Ward *et al* [1990] BTR 352; also in (1990) 38 *Can Tax Jo* 233.
[177] On tax treaties and partnerships, see the commentary to Art 1 of the OECD Model Treaty.
[178] For an early survey, see Becker and Wurm (eds), *Treaty Shopping* (Kluwer, 1988).

its provisions.[179] An OECD report concluded that the practice is consistent with treaty law but should be countered by express provisions in the treaties themselves, or by the extension of domestic anti-avoidance legislation.[180] The general attitude of the UK has been to avoid over-hasty provisions of wide ambit.[181] The United States, by contrast, has been active in seeking to limit the benefits of its treaties to persons genuinely resident in the other state; the famous article dealing with this matter in the Netherlands–US Treaty covers nine pages.[182]

The final report of 2015 on the G20/OECD BEPS Action 6 *Preventing the Granting of Treaty Benefits in Inappropriate Circumstances* described treaty abuse, and in particular treaty shopping, as 'one of the most important sources of BEPS concerns'.[183] Action 6 thus mandates an agreed minimum level of protection against treaty shopping (the 'minimum standard') involving a three-prong approach to thwart treaty shopping, and accepting that some states might prefer one or the other of (2) and (3) below, which would still satisfy the required minimum standard of protection:

(1)   A clear statement to be included in tax treaties that the states that enter into the treaty intend to avoid creating opportunities for non-taxation or reduced taxation through tax evasion or avoidance, including through treaty shopping arrangements;

(2)   A US-style limitation-on-benefits (LOB) rule, that limits the availability of treaty benefits to entities that meet certain conditions, is to be included in the OECD Model Treaty. The conditions are based on the legal nature, ownership in, and general activities of the entity, and seek to ensure that there is a sufficient link between the entity and its state of residence.

(3)   A new general anti-abuse rule known as the Principal Purpose Test (PPT) is to be included in the OECD Model Treaty. Under the PPT test, if one of the principal purposes of a transaction or arrangement is to obtain treaty benefits those benefits can be denied unless they are in accordance with the objects and purposes of the treaty provisions.

76.7.2 Domestic Anti-Avoidance Rules

There are two distinct issues in relation to the application of anti-avoidance rules.[184] One is whether, when the domestic system reclassifies a particular receipt, that reclassification is also accepted for treaty purposes. Thus, CTA 2010, Part 18 redesignates certain capital

---

[179] Baker, *Double Taxation Agreements and International Tax Law, op cit*, 52; see also Edwardes Ker, *Tax Treaty Interpretation, op cit*, chs 58–60.

[180] OECD, *International Tax Avoidance and Evasion—Four Related Studies* (1987). For literature and discussion, see Baker, *op cit*, 52–63.

[181] Beighton (1994) *FT World Tax Report* 2.

[182] US–Netherlands Double Tax Treaty, Art 26; on which see Troup [1993] BTR 97; and, on compatibility with EC (now EU) law, see Hinnekens (1995) 4 *EC Tax Review* 282, and Jimenez (1996) 5 *EC Tax Review* 76.

[183] OECD, *BEPS Action 6 'Preventing the Granting of Treaty Benefits in Inappropriate Circumstances' Final Report* (Oct 2015).

[184] See Edwardes Ker, *Tax Treaty Interpretation, op cit*, chs 57–60.

receipts as income; does this shift matters from the capital gains article to the income from land (or some other income) article?

The second issue is whether doctrines such as the composite transaction doctrine have effect for treaty purposes. After the *Barclays Mercantile Business Finance* case,[185] there is no reason why they should not.

To these two issues a third may be added—now that the UK has adopted a GAAR, how will it apply in the treaty context?

---

[185] *Barclays Mercantile Business Finance Ltd v Mawson* [2005] STC 1 (HL), and see above §5.6.

European Union Tax Law

77.1 EU Law Restraints on Member States Fiscal Sovereignty: The Basic Position

The operation of EU law has important implications for the domestic direct tax regimes of the Member States, including, for now at least, the UK. It is no longer possible to consider domestic tax rules, like those of the UK corporation tax regime, without turning one's mind to the effect EU law might have on those rules. Since the beginning of the 21st century, EU law has taken on an ever-increasing role in the direct tax sphere, and the law in this area continues to evolve, sometimes rapidly, occasionally fundamentally. This chapter aims to give the reader a background to important EU law principles of relevance to direct tax, and a framework for analysing the key cases in direct tax matters of the Court of Justice of the European Union (CJEU, formerly ECJ). It also seeks to provide a snapshot of the present (but constantly developing) state of the case law on the application to selected corporation tax topics of the fundamental freedoms under the Treaty on the Functioning of the European Union (TFEU). Readers should note that for convenience the court is referred to as the CJEU throughout this chapter, even when discussing earlier ECJ decisions.

To begin, EU law[1] limits the rights of the UK government to levy taxes by taking precedence over Acts of Parliament.[2] This supremacy does not apply to those areas in which sovereignty has not been ceded. Supremacy issues first arise in connection with UK legislation. The UK Parliament may find that its legislation conflicts with principles of the EU law,[3] or that it has not followed the proper procedure, for example by not consulting the Commission,[4] so that in either case its legislation is of no effect. However, issues also arise when an individual taxpayer is accorded rights under EU law through the doctrine of direct effect.[5] A provision giving rise to direct effect must be clear and concise; it must be unconditional and unqualified, and not subject to the taking of any further measures on the part of a Union or national authority; and must leave no substantial discretion in its implementation to a Union or national authority.[6] Several Treaty provisions have been given direct effect in taxation. The CJEU has asserted a pre-emptive jurisdiction to forestall divergent interpretations of a directive by allowing a reference by a national court on what is actually a domestic tax issue but which arises from legislation based on an EU law.[7]

A failure to implement directives properly and in time will enable a taxpayer to assert the rights set out in the directive against the Member State,[8] if the conditions for direct effect apply. In addition, the citizen may be able to recover damages from the state under the principle in *Francovitch*[9] for failure to implement the directive—this right may arise even though the principle required for direct effect is not satisfied.[10]

At the time of writing the status of the UK's membership in the EU is up-in-the-air following the result of the June 2016 advisory referendum in which a slim majority of the public voted in favour of the UK leaving the EU. The implications of Brexit for UK tax law are uncertain but for now at least the UK remains an EU member and EU law continues to apply in the UK. It is likely that in the short term little in the way of substantial tax law

---

[1] The literature on EU tax law has become vast. Reference material includes Lang et al, *Introduction to European Tax Law on Direct Taxation*, 4th ed (Linde, 2016); Panayi, *European Union Corporate Tax Law* (CUP, 2013); Panayi, *Advanced Issues in International and European Tax Law* (Bloomsbury, 2015); and Cerioni, *The European Union and Direct Taxation: A Solution for a Difficult Relationship* (Routledge, 2015). Other recommend reading includes Schön, 'Free Movement of Capital and Freedom of Establishment' Max Planck Institute for Tax Law and Public Finance Working Paper 2015—03; Schön, 'Taxing Multinationals in Europe' (2012) 11 Max Planck Institute for Tax Law and Public Finance 2; Wattel, 'Non-Discrimination à la Cour: The ECJ's (Lack of) Comparability Analysis in Direct Tax Cases' [2015] 12 *European Taxation*; van Thiel, 'The Direct Income Tax Case Law of the European Court of Justice: Past Trends and Future Developments' (2008) 62 *Tax Law Rev* 143; and Cordewener et al, 'The Clash between European Freedoms and National Direct Tax Law: Public Interest Defences Available to the Member States' (2009) 46 CMLR 1951. For a broad, technical, overall account of EU tax harmonisation policy, see Terra and Wattel, *European Tax Law*, 6th edn (Kluwer, 2012). For an overview of EU law and the Union institutions, see Dashwood *et al*, *Wyatt & Dashwood's European Union Law* (Hart Publishing, 2011), and on tax set in a wider context see chs 17 and 20. Other interesting, but dated, sources include Williams, *EC Tax Law* (Longman, 1998); Farmer and Lyal, *EC Tax Law* (OUP, 1994); and Radaelli, *The Politics of Corporate Taxation in the European Union* (Routledge, 1997), esp chs 5 and 6.

[2] *Stoke-on-Trent City Council v B&Q plc* [1991] 4 All ER 221, 223.

[3] As in the famous *Factortame* case: *R v Secretary of State for Transport, ex parte Factortame* [1991] 1 AC 603.

[4] As in *R v Customs and Excise Commrs, ex parte Lunn Poly Ltd* [1999] STC 350.

[5] Case 26/62 *Van Gend en Loos v Nederlandse Tariefcomissie* [1963] ECR 1.

[6] Edward and Lane, *European Community Law* (Butterworths, 1995), para 133.

[7] Case C-28/95 *Leur Bloem* [1997] STC 1205; see Betten (1999) 36 *CML Rev* 165.

[8] The so-called 'vertical' direct effect of directives allows the enforcement of rights against the Member State but not against other citizens: Edward and Lane, *op cit*, para 148.

[9] *Ibid*, para 141.

[10] Case C-91/9 *Faccinni Dori v Recreb* [1994] ECR I-3325.

changes will be made during what could be a prolonged period leading up to exit—should it happen at all. The taxes most likely to be affected by Brexit are customs and excise duties, and the UK would have greater flexibility to modify its VAT should it wish to do so. On direct taxes including corporation tax, if the UK opts for membership of the European Economic Area (EEA) in order to retain the benefits of trading in the internal market, the UK may well still be required to comply with the fundamental freedoms as discussed below at §77.2.2. These fundamental freedoms have had the greatest impact on the UK's otherwise purely domestic corporation tax.

77.1.1 State Aid

Article 107 TFEU (ex Art 87 TEC) concerns the prohibition on state aid.[11] Pursuant to Article 107 TFEU, save as otherwise provided in the EU Treaties, any aid granted by a Member State or through State resources in any form whatsoever which distorts or threatens to distort competition by favouring certain undertakings or the production of certain goods shall, in so far as it affects trade between Member States, be incompatible with the internal market. Case law establishes clearly that tax provisions which are in substance state aid fall foul of these provisions unless clearance has been obtained for them from the Commission under Article 108 TFEU (ex Art 88 TEC).[12] So, when the UK Parliament increased the rate of insurance premium tax for certain types of insurance sold through travel agents without obtaining clearance from the Commission, the English court held that this differential taxation would distort competition and intra-Community trade and so breached (now) Article 107 TFEU.[13] The Court of Appeal has held that the detriment imposed on personal service companies by the IR35 legislation in ITEPA 2003, Part 2, Chapter 8 could be found to be an unlawful state aid only if it favoured other competing businesses; the applicants had not established this.[14] These rules may apply where a state's legislation deliberately favours a non-resident over a resident. The distinctions are subtle. The FA 2008 changed the limits for reliefs for venture capital trusts (VCTs) via the Corporate Venturing Scheme and for Enterprise Investment Schemes (EISs). The EISs required state aid approval but the others did not.[15]

In an important development with potentially far-reaching implications, in 2014 the European Commission launched in-depth investigations to examine whether decisions by tax authorities in Ireland, the Netherlands and Luxembourg in relation to some

---

[11] Recent works on this topic include Quigley, *European State Aid Law and Policy,* 3rd ed (Bloomsbury, 2015), Rust and Micheau, *State Aid and Tax Law* (Kluwer, 2012) and Micheau, *State Aid, Subsidy and Tax Incentives under EU and WTO Law* (Kluwer, 2014). Other recommended readings include Panayi, *Advanced Issues in International and European Tax Law* (Bloomsbury, 2015) ch 7, Hare et al, '20 Questions on State Aid and Tax' *Tax Journal* (25 February 2016); Lebovitz, 'State Aid and Tax: the US View' *Tax Journal* (24 February 2016); Schön, 'Tax Legislation and the Notion of Fiscal Aid: A Review of Five Years of European Jurisprudence' Max Planck Institute for Tax Law and Public Finance Working Paper 2015—14 and Rossi-Maccanico, 'Fiscal State Aids, Tax Base Erosion and Profit Shifting' [2015] 2 *EC Tax Review* 63. Earlier works are Evans, *State Aid* (OUP, 1998) and Schon (1999) 36 *CML Rev* 911.

[12] There is a helpful notice on tax and state aid by the Commission, Notice of 11 November 1998, 98/C384/03 and an EC Commission Report C (2004) 434.

[13] *R v Customs and Excise Commrs, ex parte Lunn Poly Ltd* [1999] STC 350.

[14] *R (Professional Contractors Group) v IRC* [2001] EWCA Civ 1945; [2002] STC 165.

[15] FA 2008, s 31 and HMRC Budget Technical Note BN16 (12 March 2008).

very well-known multinationals complied with the EU rules on state aid. Although this development came as a surprise to many in the international tax field, in 1988 the Commission had highlighted the potential application of State aid in the field of direct business taxation.[16] At the time of writing the investigations were still ongoing. If the Commission finds that selective benefits were given to these taxpayers eg in the form of favourable tax rulings on the companies' transfer pricing arrangements—as is the early indication—the taxpayers in question may have to repay the benefit they are deemed to have received, which could amount to billions of euros.[17] The inevitable litigation that will ensue given the principles and amounts involved will undoubtedly run for years. In the meantime, the Commission has issued a new draft Communication on the application of the State aid rules, which specifically addresses tax rulings, settlements, amnesties, depreciation, collective investment vehicles and excise duties.[18]

Finally, it is noteworthy that at Budget 2016, the Government announced it will allow HMRC to collect additional data from businesses on certain tax reliefs and allowances in order to help the UK improve the monitoring of tax State aids and compliance with State aid guidelines.

77.1.2 Indirect Taxes and Similar Charges

Article 110 TFEU (ex Art 90 TEC) prohibits discrimination against imports from other Member States by the levying of charges higher than those imposed on domestic products. Article 111 TFEU (ex Art 91 TEC) prohibits refunds on exports exceeding the actual taxation imposed on the goods. Article 113 TFEU (ex Art 93 TEC) addresses how the legislation of turnover taxes may be harmonised, a process which has given us the famous Sixth Directive imposing a common tax base to VAT throughout the Union, enacted in the UK as the VATA 1984, now consolidated as the VATA 1994. This surrender of sovereignty in relation to turnover taxes does not extend to taxes which are not turnover taxes, eg insurance premium tax.

77.1.3 Direct Taxes—No Compensation for Effects on Trade

Article 112 TFEU (ex Art 92 TEC) extends the principle of Article 111 TFEU (ex Art 91 TEC) to direct taxation and prohibits Member States from operating systems of compensation for the effects of direct taxation on trade within the EU. However, this is subject to a right of derogation, provided the Government obtains authorisation from the Commission.

---

[16] Commission Notice on the application of the State aid rules to measures relating to direct business taxation [1988] OJ C384 (10 December 1988).

[17] Self, *Tax Journal* (17 April 2015) and Lyons [2014] BTR 113. For an examination of the circumstances under which tax rulings could violate EU state aid law see Lang [2015] BTR 391, and for a consideration of whether the EU's state aid regime will survive the G20/OECD Base Erosion and Profit Shifting (BEPS) project see Luja [2015] BTR 379.

[18] See http://ec.europa.eu/competition/state_aid/modernisation/notice_of_aid_en.pdf. See also Stricklin-Coutinho, *Tax Journal* (10 June 2016).

77.2   Positive and Negative Harmonisation

77.2.1 Positive Harmonisation

Article 115 TFEU (ex Art 94 TEC) provides for the approximation of laws by directives, and it is on this basis that the Commission has tried to achieve harmonisation of company taxes. No article *requires* harmonisation of direct taxes in the way that Article 113 TFEU does for indirect taxes. Directives under Article 115 TFEU require unanimity in the Council. There has been regular UK legislation to implement directives, as in 1990 when the Revenue were placed under a duty to provide information about liabilities to tax in another Member State.[19] The Single Market programme provided its own impetus, leading to the Ruding Committee's 1992 report on the distortions caused by different corporation tax systems, the extent to which those could be removed by market forces and the desirability of legislation towards harmonisation should those forces not be enough.

Two important Directives were enacted in 1990, the Parent-Subsidiary Directive[20] and the Mergers Directive, designed to grant to cross-border transactions the same favourable treatment as is provided for equivalent purely domestic transactions.[21] The UK introduced the appropriate implementing legislation, but the Revenue conceded that the directives would probably have had direct effect anyway.[22] Should the UK ultimately exit the EU, multinational groups relying on these directives could see an increase in their UK tax bill, eg due to withholding taxes on dividends and interest paid to a UK holding company from related companies resident in EU countries. In addition, a multilateral convention on transfer pricing is now in force, along with a Council regulation on administrative co-operation in the field of indirect taxation.[23] A proposed directive on losses was withdrawn.[24] The new millennium saw Directives on Interest and Royalties[25] and (temporarily) on Savings Income,[26] along with administratively important Directives on Administrative Cooperation[27] and Mutual Assistance in Recovery of Taxes.[28]

---

[19] FA 1990, s 125.

[20] Council Directive 90/435/EEC of 23 July 1990, replaced by Council Directive 2011/96/E, OJ L 345, 29.12.2011, on the common system of taxation applicable in the case of parent companies and subsidiaries of different Member States, as amended by Directive 2013/13/EU of 13 May 2013, Directive 2014/86/EU of 8 July 2014, Directive (EU) 2015/121 of 27 January 2015.

[21] Council Directive 90/434/EEC [1990] OJ L225/1, replaced by Council Directive 2009/133/EC, OJ L 310, 25.11.2009, on the common system of taxation applicable to mergers, divisions, partial divisions, transfers of assets and exchanges of shares concerning companies of different Member States and to the transfer of the registered office of an SE or SCE between Member States, and amended by Directive 2013/13/EU of 13 May 2013.

[22] *EC Direct Tax Measures: A Consultative Document* (December 1991), para 2.13.

[23] [1992] *Simon's Tax Intelligence* 161.

[24] Com (90) 505.

[25] Council Directive 2003/49/EC, OJ L 157, 26.6.2003, on a common system of taxation applicable to interest and royalty payments made between associated companies of different Member States, implemented by FA 2004, ss 97–106, and amended by Directive 2004/66/EC of 26 April 2004, Directive 2004/76/EC of 29 April 2004, Directive 2006/98/EC of 20 November 2006 and Directive 2013/13/EU of 13 May 2013.

[26] Council Directive 2004/76/EC of 29 April 2004 [2004] OJ L157/106 and EC 2003/48/EC, operational until the end of 2015 and replaced by Council Directive 2014/107/EU on administrative cooperation in the field of direct taxation.

[27] Council Directive 2011/16/EU, OJ L 064, 11.3.2011, on administrative cooperation in the field of taxation and repealing Directive 77/799/EEC, and amended by Directive 2014/107/EU of 9 December 2014.

[28] Council Directive 2010/24/EU of 16 March 2010 [2010] OJ L84/1.

It is work on the Common Consolidated Corporate Tax Base (CCCTB) which has perhaps been the most tantalisingly slow. After substantial policy work in 2001 and 2003, progress ground to a halt; however, subsequent work led to a 2011 Commission proposal for a Council Directive.[29] Progress stalled again, but the proposal was relaunched by the Commission in 2015 with an emphasis on first securing a common corporate tax base (CCTB) before working on the consolidation aspects.[30] It is quite possible that a CCTB will be agreed and operated by a number of the Member States under the enhanced co-operation rules in Article 20 of the Treaty on European Union (TEU), with the UK remaining resolutely outside (and perhaps completely outside after Brexit). Finally, the EU has also begun to flex its muscles on base erosion and profit shifting by releasing a series of proposals aimed at tackling corporate tax avoidance (discussed below §77.4.2).[31]

77.2.2 Negative Harmonisation

77.2.2.1 Background

The starting point has to be that the EU treaties leave direct taxes as matters for the Member States. As a result, the Court cannot offer to citizens of the Union transferring their activities to another Member State any guarantee that this will be neutral as regards taxation.[32] However, the CJEU has said again and again that those powers must be exercised in a manner consistent with EU law. The CJEU has gone on to make what some see as erratic, narrow and often destructive contributions to Member States' tax law on the basis of the non-discrimination principle. This important principle is embodied for tax purposes in the Treaty fundamental freedoms, including the free cross-border movement of employees (Article 45 TFEU; ex Art 39 TEC); freedom of establishment for businesses (Article 49 TFEU; ex Art 43 TEC); freedom to provide services (Article 56 TFEU; ex Art 49 TEC); and free movement of capital (Article 63 TFEU; ex Art 56 TEC).

One of the points most often made was that national legislation should not have one set of rules for a purely domestic situation and another for cross-border operations. Related to this is the series of cases stemming from the famous *Avoir Fiscal* or *French Tax Credits* case,[33] which rather routinely said that a Member State should not have one rule for a branch and another for a subsidiary. These simple mantras opened Pandora's Box, and case after case was decided against the revenue authorities of the Member States.[34] Supporters of the CJEU argue that it has been consistent in its approach and that Member States have

---

[29] COM(2011) 121/4. For the latest status, see http://ec.europa.eu/taxation_customs/taxation/company_tax/common_tax_base/index_en.htm. Background work includes COM (2001) 582 and supporting study SEC (2001) 582, COM (2003) 726 European Tax Survey SEC 2004, 1128/2 and Report of CEPS Task Force Brussels, November 2005. See also Mitroyanni [2011] BTR 246.

[30] EC, 'A Fair and Efficient Corporate Tax System in the European Union: 5 Key Areas for Action' EC COM (2015) 302 final.

[31] See http://europa.eu/rapid/press-release_IP-16-159_en.htm.

[32] Eg, A-G Geelhoed in Case C-403/03 *Schempp v Finanzamt Munchen* [2005] ECR I-06421, para 33 (January 2005).

[33] *Commission v French Republic (Avoir Fiscal)*, Case 270/83 [1986] ECR 273.

[34] Until 2005 the decisions in favour of the Member States were *R v HM Treasury ex p. Daily Mail*, Case 81/87, [1988] ECR 5483, *Bachmann v Belgium*, Case C-204/90, [1992] ECR I-249, *Futura Participations SA*, Case C-250/953, [1997] ECR I-2471 and *Gilly v Directeur des Services Fiscaux du Bas-Rhin*, Case C-336/96, [1998] ECR I-2793.

to pay through court cases for their failure to adjust their legal systems to take account of the thinking of the CJEU. Critics of the CJEU say that it has not been consistent, that it has widened the basis on which it has acted, and that it has created and then abandoned a number of limitations on its jurisdiction.[35] What has encouraged critics of the CJEU is the way in which the language used falls short of what one might expect from such an important body. An interesting report for the European Parliament, published in March 2008, not only assessed the CJEU's judgments in this area, but also tried to assess how far the Members States have amended their laws in response to the CJEU's decisions.[36]

Acting under this power (or duty), the CJEU has considered a number of standard tax rules. These include:

(1)   the taxation of dividends and the UK's imputation system of corporation tax;
(2)   the deemed disposal charge for CGT when a taxpayer moves to another Member State ('exit charge');
(3)   thin capitalisation rules;
(4)   relief for certain cross-border losses;
(5)   controlled foreign company (CFC) rules; and
(6)   the most-favoured-nation clauses in tax treaties.

There was already a duty on Member States to take the most-favoured principles into account when negotiating with third parties in the field of aviation, but this was not applied in the tax case in (6).[37] These and other CJEU tax cases are explained and considered further below. What matters for present purposes is that such defeats presented problems for Member States. The loss of revenue could be addressed by increasing tax rates or providing new taxes. The rules regarding non-discrimination might be addressed by removing the discrimination; so when thin capitalisation rules were declared unlawful by the CJEU—and so possibly transfer pricing rules too—Member States such as Germany and the UK reacted by making the restrictive rules apply to arrangements between domestic companies as well as to foreign ones. The result of all these pressures might, however, be less good domestic tax systems.

77.2.2.2 Non-discrimination Principles and the Fundamental Freedoms[38]

When the CJEU is asked to provide an opinion on whether some aspect of a Member State's domestic tax law violates the EU principle of non-discrimination, the CJEU applies a two-stage test: (a) has the threshold test of discrimination been met, and (b) if there is discrimination, can it be justified by the Member State?

---

[35] For criticism of the Revenue for not taking steps earlier, see Martin, *The Tax Journal*, 10 January 2005, p 7. See also Vanistedael (ed), *EATLP International Tax Series, Vol 2, EU Freedoms and Taxation* (IBFD, 2006); Schoen (ed), *Tax Competition in Europe* (EATLP IBFD, 2003); A Park, [2006] BTR 322; and Ghosh, *Principles of the Internal Market and Direct Taxation* (Key Haven, 2007).
[36] Malherbe *et al*, 'The Impact of the Rulings of European Court of Justice in the Area of Direct Taxation', (2008) European Parliament Policy Department: Economic and Scientific Policy PE404.888.
[37] Cases C–466/98–476/98 *Commission v UK* ('the *Open Skies* case') [2002] ECR I-09427. The remarks of AG Tizzano are particularly wide-ranging. See Panayi [2003] BTR 189.
[38] Good starting points are Terra and Wattel, *op cit*; Kingston (2007) 44 *CML Rev* 1321; and Sir Andrew Park [2006] BTR 322–44. See also Vanistedael (ed), *op cit*; Schoen (ed), *op cit*; Ghosh, *op cit*. Others, though written before the ECJ's change of approach, are Lyons [2003] BTR 98; Gammie, *IBFD Bulletin* 2003, 86–98.

Tax provisions which breach, or may breach, these provisions can be challenged in court actions brought by taxpayers in the national courts and referred to the CJEU for advice under the reference procedure in Article 267 TFEU (ex Art 234 TEC). After the CJEU has opined on the EU law questions referred to it by the national court, the matter is then thrown back to the national court to apply to the specific facts. What appeared initially to be taxpayer wins in the CJEU have appeared less so as national tax authorities including HMRC battle to mitigate the damage done by the CJEU to the public finances. The result has often been prolonged litigation in the courts with a succession of very long and detailed lower court judgments on eg the application of domestic limitation periods and other procedural hurdles. This has been followed by seemingly endless rounds of appeals and yet further submissions to the CJEU asking for clarification. Even with all its faults, an EU-wide CCCTB is starting to look more and more appealing.

Discriminatory national laws are also often the subject of investigation by the European Commission, which may bring its own court proceedings against a Member State under Articles 258 and 260 TFEU. The Commission also exercises its right to make submissions to the Court in cases brought by taxpayers.[39] It is thought that these specific powers prevent the Court from relying on the more general anti-discrimination rule in Article 18 TFEU (ex Art 12 TEC).[40]

77.2.2.3 The General Approach[41]

The CJEU has usually taken a broad approach to the non-discrimination principle and a narrow approach to any attempted justification. In the *French Tax Credits* case,[42] an Italian insurance company had set up a branch in France. The branch received dividend income from French sources. Under French tax law, companies could reclaim the tax credit accompanying the dividend from the French Revenue; however, repayment was refused if the company was not resident in France. The refusal was held to breach the freedom of establishment. Even if the disadvantage to the Italian company under the present rule was compensated for by other advantages, the French Government could not justify this breach of the duty under (now) Article 49 TFEU, which was to accord foreign companies the same treatment as was accorded to French companies. The extent of the disadvantage could not be in issue since the treaty prohibits all discrimination, even if only of a limited nature. Moreover, the fact that the Italian company could have got the benefit of the credit if it had established a French subsidiary (rather than a branch) was irrelevant, since this interfered with the freedom to trade in another Member State in a vehicle of its own choice—whether branch or subsidiary. The idea that a branch and a subsidiary are somehow interchangeable has been seen as economically illiterate, but it has not stopped the CJEU from developing a stream of case law in which distinctions between the two have been struck down.

---

[39] Usually these are in support of the taxpayers, but in Case C-168/01 *Bosal Holding BV v Staatssecretaris van Financien* [2003] STC 1483 the Commission made some submissions in support of the Member State—to no effect.

[40] See Richardson [1998] BTR 281, 291, citing Case C-112/91 *Werner v FZA Aachen-Innenstadt* [1993] ECR I-429, para 20. While the case law has been concerned to make sure that a non-national is treated at least as favourably as a national, attention is now being paid (but not yet by the Court) to the opposite problem—where the non-resident is treated more favourably, and the Member States compete unfairly for business. The EU has an (unenforceable) code of conduct for Member States in such matters: see generally Schön (ed), *op cit*.

[41] See Lyons [1994] BTR 554; Stanley (1997) 34 *CML Rev* 713.

[42] Case 270/83 *Commission v French Republic* [1986] ECR 273.

What was wrong with the mantras above was that the CJEU too readily accepted that the domestic and cross-border situations had to be treated alike, instead of addressing the more subtle question of how to achieve equality of treatment of the two situations after allowing for the fact that domestic and cross-border situations are not alike.[43] The first hints of new thinking may be found in the *Manninen* case.[44] The need for a more nuanced approach was recognised by the Court,[45] especially following a major change in personnel, as in the case of *D*.[46] The story is well told by Kingston, who was legal secretary to Advocate General Geelohoed.[47] All these uncertainties create difficulties for the self-assessment system.[48]

The principal direct tax cases involving the UK decided since the change are *Marks & Spencer*[49] on group losses, *Cadbury Schweppes*[50] on CFC legislation, and three group litigation cases—*Group Litigation Class IV ACT*,[51] *Group Litigation Franked Investment Income*[52] and *Group Litigation Thin Capitalisation*.[53] What these cases have in common is an approach by the CJEU which avoids a blanket condemnation of a Member State's tax rules just because of the possible restrictions. It accepts that the Member States have an interest in limiting the avoidance of tax, provided that appropriate objective tests are in place or can be designed to determine when the anti-avoidance provisions should apply and when not. Equal treatment of the two situations after allowing for the fact that domestic and cross-border situations are not alike was achieved by a new mantra, by which the CJEU accepts the need for a balanced allocation of taxing power between the Member States and that the CJEU is not there to destroy them one by one.

77.2.2.4 Freedom of Establishment

Article 49 TFEU (ex Art 43 TEC) guarantees freedom of establishment and expressly bans restrictions on the setting-up of agencies, branches or subsidiaries by nationals of any Member State in the territory of any other Member State. This is extended to companies and firms by Article 54 TFEU (ex Art 48 TEC). It has been interpreted broadly so as to ban not only overt discrimination by reason of nationality or, in the case of a company, its seat, but, for a time at least, all covert forms of discrimination which, by the application of other criteria of differentiation, lead to the same result.[54] Here too, joint assessment issues have arisen.[55] The wide scope of protection offered the freedom of establishment has already been seen in the *French Tax Credits* case.

---

[43] CEPS Task Force Report (November 2005) 7.

[44] Case C 319/02 *Manninen v Finland* [2004] ECR-I-07477.

[45] Se eg Case C-141/99 *AMID v Belgium* [2000] ECR I-11619 and Case C-374/04 *Test Claimants in Class IV of the ACT Group Litigation* [2006] ECR I-11673.

[46] Case C-376/03 [2005] ECR I-05821.

[47] Kingston (2007) 44 *CML Rev* 1321

[48] On which see *HMRC v Vodafone 2* [2006] EWCA Civ 1132 [2006] STC 1530.

[49] Case C-446/03 *Marks & Spencer plc v Halsey (Inspector of Taxes)* [2006] STC 237.

[50] Case C-196/04 [2006] ECR I-07995.

[51] Case C-374/04 [2006] ECR I-11673.

[52] Case C-446/04 [2006] ECR I-11753.

[53] Case C-524/04 [2007] ECR I-02107.

[54] Judgment of the ECJ in *Commerzbank* (below, para 4, citing Case 152/73 *Sotgiu v Deutsche Bundespost* [1974] ECR 153, para 11; *R v IRC, ex parte Commerzbank AG* [1993] STC 605, 621, para 14 (ECJ)).

[55] Case C-329/05 *Finanzamt Dinslaken v Meindl (Meindl-Berger, third party)* [2007] STC 314.

The taxpayer also won in *R v IRC, ex parte Commerzbank AG*.[56] Here, a German bank with a UK branch had successfully argued that it was entitled to exemption from UK tax on interest received from US corporations;[57] its claim to repayment supplement was successful, even though the UK domestic legislation clearly did not allow repayment supplement to a non-resident. The UK had argued that it was entitled to withhold the repayment supplement since Commerzbank, unlike resident companies, was exempt on the income originally in issue. This was swept aside: 'The argument cannot be upheld. The fact that the exemption in question was available only to non-resident companies cannot justify a rule of a general nature withholding the benefit. That rule is therefore discriminatory.'[58] This seems to leave it open to the UK to introduce a rule barring repayment supplement where the repayment claim arises in respect of income which is exempt from tax only by reason of non-residence; however, the UK statute was amended more generously, by removing the restriction altogether.[59] Meanwhile, it should be noted that the ban on repayment supplement remains effective for individuals, etc, not entitled to invoke EU rules, eg persons not resident in a Member State.

In the *St Gobain*[60] case, the German branch of a French company sought to take advantage of certain clauses in treaties made by Germany with other states (ie, not France). The Court held that the French branch was entitled to do so. The UK legislature, perhaps wisely, took it as its cue to extend various double taxation reliefs to UK branches of foreign companies; see §76.1.1 above.

77.2.2.5 Free Movement of Capital[61]

Free movement of capital is protected under Article 63 TFEU (ex Art 56 TEC). A straightforward case on free movement of capital is provided by *Ministre des Finances v Weidert*.[62] The taxpayers, a married couple resident in Luxembourg, had subscribed for 200 shares in a Belgian company. If they had acquired shares for cash in fully taxable capital companies while resident in Luxembourg, they would have been entitled to a relief from Luxembourg income tax. The Court held that the relief was discriminatory and so the taxpayers were entitled to the benefit of the relief. The effect of the Luxembourg rules was to discourage Luxembourg nationals from investing their capital in companies established in another Member State; the provision also constituted an obstacle to a Belgian company seeking to raise capital in another Member State.

This article has given the Court problems. First, there is the inconvenient fact that Article 63 TFEU, unlike its neighbours, protects free movement of capital not only between Member States but also, subject to a condition, between Member States and

---

[56] [1993] STC 605 (ECJ). For subsequent action, see [1993] *Simon's Tax Intelligence* 1091, 1264. For speculation about ambit, see Sandler [1993] BTR 517.

[57] *IRC v Commerzbank AG* [1990] STC 285; unusually the applicable treaty was not confined to residents.

[58] [1993] STC 605, 622 (ECJ).

[59] FA 1994, Sch 19, amending TA 1988, s 824 (income tax) and TA 1988, s 826, superseding s 825 for corporation tax as from start of pay and file (1993).

[60] Case C-307/97 *Compagnie de Saint-Gobain v Finanzamt Aachen-Innenstadt*; see [1999] *Simons Weekly Tax Intelligence* 1856. See also Oliver [2000] BTR 174.

[61] For a general discussion, see the chapter by Peers in Barnard and Scott (eds), *The Law of the Single Market: Unpacking The Premises* (Hart Publishing, 2002); Peers criticises (at 348) Case C-35/98 *Verkooijen* [2002] STC 654.

[62] Case C-242/03 [2005] STC 1241; see also Case C-334/02 *EC Commission v French Republic* [2007] STC 54.

third countries. The condition relates to restrictions existing on 31 December 1993 (Article 64 TFEU, ex Art 57 TEC). Secondly, Article 65 TFEU (ex Art 58 TEC) directs that the freedom of movement of capital is without prejudice to the rights of Member States to apply provisions of their tax law which distinguish between taxpayers who are not in the same situation with regard to their place of residence or with regard to where their capital is invested. Thirdly, Article 63 TFEU is without prejudice to the rights of Member States to take all requisite measures to prevent infringement of national law with regard to various specific areas, including taxation.

These points might have made the courts wary in applying Article 63 TFEU, but instead they have treated the scope of discrimination just as widely as in the other articles. However, this has raised the question of the relationship between Article 63 TFEU and the others. Faced with a case which could have been decided under what are now Articles 49, 56 or 63 TFEU, the CJEU could simply have declined to rule on the application under Article 63 on the ground that its decision was already covered by the other Articles. However, the Court sometimes went further and tried to develop boundary rules, such as that where the case concerned a shareholding which gave a significant amount of control—not necessarily 50%—then the case belonged under (now) Article 49 and not Article 63 TFEU.[63] Fortunately this appears no longer to be so.[64] However, in the *FII* case, the CJEU started another line of reasoning to the effect that the justification that a court might accept might be different where the transfer was to a third country.[65]

The first case to be decided solely on the basis of freedom of movement of capital was Case C-35/98 *Secretaris van Financien v Verkooijen*.[66] This freedom was then set out in Article 73(1)(d) of the Treaty (now Article 63(1)(a) TFEU) and was implemented by Directive 88/361/EEC of 24 June 1988. In this case V, a Dutch resident, received dividend income from a Belgian company, which was subject to 25% withholding in Belgium in the usual way. If the dividends had been from a company with its seat in The Netherlands, V would have been entitled to an exemption on the first NLG 1,000 of dividend income. V appealed on the basis that (then) EC law did not allow Dutch tax law to restrict the exemption to companies resident in The Netherlands but should apply it to companies resident in all Member States. On a reference from the Hoge Raad under ex Article 177, the CJEU agreed with V. The first purpose of the exemption was partly to increase interest in equity shareholdings—and so the amount of capital subscribed to Dutch companies—and the second was to compensate in some small way for the effect of the Dutch classical system of corporate taxation, which meant that no part of the corporate tax was imputed through to the shareholder.[67] This was treated by the Court as a clear breach of EC law, since it constituted an obstacle to a Belgian company raising capital in The Netherlands.

In *EC Commission v Belgium*,[68] the Belgian Government had issued a public loan on the Eurobond market. Under the terms of the issue, withholding tax on interest payable on loan

---

[63] Case C 251/98 *Baars* and Case C-436/00 *X and Y*.

[64] See eg Case 446/04, AG Geelhoed, para 34 and the full court at 58 *et seq*.

[65] Case C-446/04, para 121.

[66] Case C-35/98 *Verkooijen* [2002] STC 654. For the Directive, see [1988] OJ L178/5. Art 56 was raised in *Bachmann*, Case C-204/90 [1994] STC 855 at para 34—see also §77.2.2.6 below.

[67] Case C-35/98 *Verkooijen* [2002] STC 654, para 11.

[68] Case C-478/98 [2000] STC 830.

was waived but residents of Belgium were prohibited from subscribing for the loan. Not surprisingly, this restriction was held to breach (now) Article 63 TFEU. This free movement article was originally quite rudimentary and took effect in its present expansive form only in 1992. At that time a clause was added to the effect that the provision on free movement of capital was to be without prejudice to the rights of Member States to apply the relevant provisions of their tax law which distinguish between taxpayers who are not in the same situation with regard to their place of residence or with regard to where their capital is invested.

77.2.2.6 Application of the Non-Discrimination Principles[69]

Proceeding analytically, one might say that taxpayers face a two-stage test:

(1)   Has the threshold test of discrimination been met?
(2)   If there is discrimination, can it be justified by the Member State?

If a measure is justified, an additional question (or perhaps a third-stage test) then needs to be asked:

(3)   Is the measure proportionate?

In the tax context discrimination is usually on grounds of nationality. Moreover, while Treaty articles concern nationals and non-nationals, case law often concerns non-residents, and sometimes requires Member States to treat non-residents either as if they were residents or at least not worse than residents. This is because the most frequent example of the non-national is the non-resident. It should be understood that when passages in cases talk about 'non-residents', they are actually concerned only with nationals of the EU.

As already seen, the concept of discrimination is not straightforward. The case law of the CJEU began by distinguishing direct discrimination from indirect or covert discrimination. The language used by the CJEU is not always precise, but the distinction seems to be between those measures which break the non-discrimination principle on their face, eg rules applying only to nationals of a certain state, and those which simply have that effect. The importance of the difference is that if a measure falls within the direct category then justification must be sought within the words of the Treaty itself.[70] Not only are there few such justifications,[71] but the CJEU also has interpreted them strictly. In *Danner*, the Advocate General invited the CJEU to revisit this distinction and allow direct discrimination to be justified by reference to matters of overriding general interest, but this invitation was not accepted.[72] However, most tax discrimination problems arose in the context of residence rather than nationality, and so normally belonged in the covert or indirect discrimination category. Indirect or covert discrimination may be justified provided (a) the discriminatory measure pursues a legitimate objective compatible with the Treaty, and (b) the national rules are proportionate, in that the rules are appropriate to attain that objective and go no

---

[69] Good starting points are Terra and Wattel, *op cit*; Kingston, *op cit*; and Park, *op cit*. See also Vanistedael (ed), *op cit*; Schön (ed), *op cit*; and Ghosh, *op cit*.

[70] *Bond van Adverteerders v Netherlands* [1988] ECR 2805, para 34.

[71] Eg, Art 52 TFEU (ex Art 46 TEC) lists public policy, public security and public health.

[72] *Danner*, Case C–136/00, [2002] STC 1283, AG Jacobs, paras 32–42. See Lyons [2003] BTR 98–101.

further than what is necessary for that purpose.[73] It has to be said that in many of the cases the Member States have failed test (b). Article 54 TFEU (ex Art 48 TEC) makes it clear that when one is dealing with the right of establishment of enterprises, ie companies or firms as opposed to individuals, those with a registered office or central administration within a Member State of the EU are to be treated the same way as natural persons who are nationals of Member States. This means that what may be covert discrimination for an individual may be overt discrimination for an enterprise.

The CJEU then decided to apply a more expansive test of discrimination. This new test meant that the CJEU could review national measures which, although not actually discriminatory, were liable to hinder or make less attractive the exercise of the fundamental freedoms guaranteed by the Treaty.[74] The 'making less attractive' threshold was significantly lower; it came close to saying that any difference between tax systems was a source of discrimination.[75] Eventually the obstacles/restriction itself came under attack by Advocate General Tizzano.[76] Such a broad approach to the 'restrictions' allowed economic operators, both national and foreign, to abuse the Treaty to oppose any national measure that, solely because it regulated the conditions for pursuing an economic activity, could in the final analysis narrow profit margins and hence reduce the attractiveness of pursuing that particular economic activity. He therefore advocated a return to a 'non-discrimination plus market access' approach: where the principle of non-discrimination is respected, a national measure cannot be described as a restriction on the freedom of movement of persons *unless* the measure 'directly affects market access'. He added that this approach makes it possible to reconcile the objective of merging the different national markets into a single common market with the continuation of Member States' general powers to regulate economic activities. Such a completely articulated approach has appealed to Advocates General rather than the CJEU, but the overall effect has been substantial, at least in language.

77.2.2.7 Justifications

The cases cited in the preceding paragraphs assert that it is open to any Member State to justify its discriminatory provision either in accordance with Article 65 TFEU or, if the discrimination is covert rather than overt, on more general grounds.[77] The general grounds are more important in tax cases than those listed in Article 65, ie public policy, public security and public health. We now turn to the justifications which have succeeded—justifications (1)–(4) and (6)–(8) below—and an important but problematic limitation (at (5) below). It will be seen that some of these limiting principles created by the CJEU did not live long, a fact which does little for the CJEU's reputation. These taxpayer defeats—or Member State victories—are of different sorts. Some, eg (4) and (5), are inherent in the nature of EU law; (1) is temporary. In *Marks & Spencer v Halsey*,[78] the CJEU

---

[73] Case C–19/92 *Kraus v Land Baden-Wurtemburg* [1993] ECR I-1663, para 32.
[74] Case C–55/94 *Gebhard* [1996] ECR I-1416, para 37; discussed by Richardson [1998] BTR 302, who also cites the opinion of the AG in Case C–80/94 *Wielockx* [1995] ECR I-2493, para 17.
[75] See *Marks & Spencer v Halsey* [2003] STC (SCD) 70, paras 59 *et seq.*
[76] AG Tizzano, Case C–442/02 *Caixa-Bank v Ministère de l'Économie, des Finances and de l'Industrie* [2004] ECR I-8961.
[77] On the evolving law of these 'mandatory' requirements see the chapter by Scott, in Barnard and Scott, (eds), *op cit*, 269–93.
[78] [2003] STC (SCD) 70.

considered several justifications together (balanced allocation of taxing rights, preventing double deduction of losses, and tax avoidance). In later cases the Court held that it was not necessary for all of those justifications to be present; one or more would be sufficient.[79]

The CJEU has also spelt out reasons which are *not* sufficient to justify discrimination. The most important for tax lawyers is that, as the CJEU has consistently said, the need to protect tax revenues of a Member State does not justify discrimination. While the judges have also said that protecting the tax base against avoidance is a sufficient justification, they have gone to insist that the provision relied on by the Member State must then meet the test of proportionality; the rules have usually failed.[80] Other clearly unacceptable grounds of justification have included arguments that tax rates are lower in other Member States, compensating advantages exist taking into account other rules, administration would be difficult, and other avenues are available to avoid the discrimination.

(1) *Community law insufficiently developed.* In the *Daily Mail* case,[81] a UK-resident company failed to circumvent the then UK rule requiring the company to obtain Treasury consent before emigrating because the UK consents could insist on the settlement of tax liabilities prior to departure. However, this was partly because of the undeveloped nature of European company law rules on freedom of movement, eg the diversity of rules in different Member States on matters such as whether the company's personality could continue in the new country.[82] It is unlikely that this justification would be of much assistance now, given that EU law has developed considerably since the early days of *Daily Mail*.

(2) *The need to protect cohesion of B's tax system: Bachmann.* This is one of the principles which, although formulated by the CJEU, lay undeveloped and despised for many years. In *Bachmann v Belgian State*,[83] the CJEU allowed Belgium to maintain rules necessary to the 'cohesion' of its system. Here Belgium allowed X to deduct sickness and invalidity insurance contributions only if paid to a company recognised by the authorities in Belgium. Belgium established an objective reason for the refusal; under Belgian law, any income eventually paid out under the policies would be taxed in Belgium,[84] and this could be monitored by restricting the deduction to contributions made to a Belgian company. Moreover, where contributions had not been deducted, the sums paid out were not subject to tax. The restriction of the right to deduct to payments made in Belgium was therefore justified in the interests of the cohesion of its tax system. No less crucially, Belgium had established that there was no other way of protecting that cohesion, and that the provisions met the principle of proportionality.

---

[79] Case C-414/06 *Lidl Belgium* [2008] ECR I-6373. See also Case C-231/05 *OyAA* [2007] ECR I-6373 and Case C-337/08 *X Holding*.

[80] Eg Case C-330/91 *R v IRC, ex parte Commerzbank AG* [1993] STC 605. In *R (on application of Professional Contractors Group Ltd) v IRC* [2001] STC 629, the UK legislation countering the use of personal service companies (text at p 205) was held not to break EC law; not only was it non-discriminatory, but it was also proportionate to the legitimate objective of countering tax avoidance.

[81] *R v HM Treasury and IRC, ex parte Daily Mail and General Trust plc* [1988] STC 787.

[82] *Ibid*, 807, para 21.

[83] Case C-204/90 [1994] STC 855.

[84] The Court assumed that tax was paid by the company; this was not correct: see Lyons [1995/96] *EC Tax J* 27, 47.

Where, in a later case, double tax treaty provisions were in place, the CJEU said that those provisions were sufficient to protect the cohesion of Belgium's system.[85]

The *Bachmann* case was distinguished in the *Verkooijen* case.[86] The CJEU said that in *Bachmann* there had been a direct link in the case of one and the same taxpayer between the grant of the tax advantage and the offsetting of that tax advantage by a fiscal levy, both of which related to the same tax. Some see the approach of the CJEU in cases like *Marks & Spencer v Halsey*,[87] where it talks of the balanced allocation of taxing powers, as a reassertion of the cohesion justification. It will also be remembered that in that case the Advocate General suggested that *Verkooijen* was too strict.[88]

(3) *Need to provide effective fiscal supervision.* This was recognised, but then not applied for reasons of proportionality, in *Futura Participations SA and Singer v Luxembourg*.[89] The taxpayer was the Luxembourg branch of a French company. In such circumstances Luxembourg taxed only the profits attributable to the branch (or PE) and did not insist that accounts be kept in Luxembourg. Stricter rules applied, however, when the branch sought to use trading losses from a previous year. Here Luxembourg insisted that accounts had to be kept in Luxembourg. The CJEU held that this requirement did breach (now) Article 49 TFEU as it went further than necessary to achieve the legitimate purpose advanced by the tax authorities. It did not follow, however, that Luxembourg had to accept a simple apportionment basis.

Although the need to provide effective fiscal supervision looks promising from the Member State's point of view, it must be remembered that the CJEU takes the view that the exchange of information powers in double tax treaties or under EU law, along with mutual assistance by Member States in the collection of tax, may well suffice.[90]

(4) *Territoriality.* The decision in *Futura Participations* (see (3) above) had another point. Luxembourg insisted that the loss had to be economically related to the income. The CJEU held that this did not breach (now) Article 49 TFEU as the Luxembourg position was completely reasonable. However, this potentially sensible doctrine was not applied by the court in *Bosal*.[91] In *Marks & Spencer* (above), the Advocate General said that the purpose of the territoriality principle was to prevent conflicts in tax jurisdiction between Member States, and suggested that territoriality could be seen as an aspect of the cohesion principle.[92] In the CJEU's decision this becomes the famous phrase about the need for the Court to protect 'a balanced allocation of the taxing powers between the Member States'.[93]

---

[85] Case C-80/94 *Wielockx* [1995] STC 876; however, it has been pointed out that the particular article of the OECD Model Treaty on which the Court relied did not apply to pensions from self-employment: see Richardson [1998] BTR 283, 284. On use of treaty to avoid cohesion problems, see *Danner* Case C-136/00 [2002] STC 1283, para 41. On coherence/cohesion generally, see also Case C-418/07 *Papilion* [2008] ECR I-08947 and Case C-157/07 *Krankenheim* [2008] ECR I-08061.

[86] Case C-35/98 *Verkooijen* [2002] STC 654.

[87] Case C-446/03, paras 43 *et seq.*

[88] AG Maduro's suggestions are at para 71 of his Opinion. See also Case C-397/98 *Metallgesellscahft/Hoechst* [2001] ECR-1727 and Case C-324/00 *Lankhorst-Hohorst GmbH* [2002] ECR I-11779.

[89] Case C-250/95 [1997] STC 1301.

[90] As in eg Case C-371/10 *National Grid Indus BV v Inspecteur van de Belastingdienst Rijnmond/kantoor Rotterdam* [2012] STC 114.

[91] Case C-168/01 *Bosal Holding BV v Staatssecretaris van Financien* [2003] STC 1483, paras 37 *et seq.*

[92] *Marks & Spencer v Halsey*, Case C-446/03, paras 62 and 64.

[93] *Ibid*, para 43.

(5) *Treaty-making powers.* The CJEU has said that these freedom articles do not prevent states from making tax treaties which allocate tax jurisdiction on the basis of national-ity, at least where they are in accordance with international norms. This was reasserted by the Court in its ground-breaking decision in *Re D*,[94] where it recognised the need for a balanced allocation of taxing powers between the states. Moreover, it recognised that a treaty gave rise to reciprocal rights and obligations for residents of the two states concerned; the rights could not be invoked by someone resident in a third country. The case involved the Dutch wealth tax; the taxpayer was resident in Germany and was trying, unsuccessfully, to invoke the benefit of the treaty made between The Nether-lands and Belgium. Ghosh sees the reasoning as articulated in this case as inconsistent with other decisions of the Court.[95]

This approach may be seen as justification for the older case of *Gilly v Directeur des Services Fiscaux Bas Rhin*.[96] Unfortunately, the boundary between *Gilly*, on the one hand, and *Schumacker*[97] and *Wielockx*,[98] on the other, was not easy to determine.[99] The view taken here is that the Court quite deliberately—and, some might say, wisely—backed off from a decision which could have been used to unpick the tax treaty network. *Re D* follows that approach.

(6) *Interpretation of national law still a matter for national court.* In *ICI plc v Colmer*,[100] the House of Lords was faced with two ways of interpreting UK tax law. The first would have prevented a breach of EU law; the second would not. The CJEU ruled that there was no EU law obligation on a national court to prefer the first construction to the second. A controversial example of consistent interpretation is *Vodafone 2*.[101] The UK Court of Appeal concluded that the UK's CFC legislation could be interpreted so as to be compatible with EU law by 'reading in' a new exception applying retrospectively to companies actually established in another EEA state which carry on genuine eco-nomic activities there. Such 'reading in' strikes many as more judicial rule-making than interpretation, but it should be noted that stretching the boundaries of interpre-tation in order to find compatibility between national and EU law is not unheard of in other areas of law, subject only the general rule against *contra legem* interpretation.[102]

(7) *Nationals of Member State only.* In general, the purpose of the treaty and so of this case law is to protect nationals of other Member States; residence has been equated with nationality, because most non-residents will be nationals of other Member States,

---

[94] Case C-376/03 *D v Inspecteur van de Belastingdienst/Particulieren/Ondernemingen Buitenland te Heerlen* [2005] STC 1211.

[95] Ghosh, *op cit*, 73.

[96] Case C-336/96 [1998] ECR I-2793; [1998] STC 1014; see comments in [1998] *IBFD Journal* 328.

[97] Case C-279/93 *Finanzamt Koln-Alstadt v Schumacker* [1995] ECR I-225.

[98] Case C-80/94 *Wielockx v Inspecteur der Directe Belastingen* [1995] STC 876.

[99] See, generally, Hedemann-Robinson [1999] BTR 128, 135–38; see also Avery Jones [1999] BTR 11, suggesting that if *Gilly* is right, and the Schumackers had been resident in France, the *Schumacker* decision would have been different for the year in which Mrs Schumacker had some earned income, but the same for the year in which she had none.

[100] Case C-264/96 [1998] All ER (EC) 585; [1998] STC 874; on treatment of outstanding cases, see Inland Revenue Press Release, 26 February [1999] *Simons Weekly Tax Intelligence* 312.

[101] *Vodafone v Revenue & Customs Commissioners (No 2)* [2009] STC 1480, [2009] EWCA Civ 446.

[102] See eg Cases C-397/01 to C-403/01 *Pfeiffer etc.* [2004] ECR I-8835. On the rule against *contra legem* interpretation see eg C-268/06 *Impact* [2008] ECR I-2483, paras 100–10.

so that covert discrimination is revealed. Nationals of states outside the EU are not entitled to protection under these rules, as shown by the UK litigation involving NEC, a Japanese company.[103] Therefore, a US company with a branch in the UK cannot complain about being discriminated under, say, French law. However, some care is needed where subsidiaries are involved. If a US company establishes a UK subsidiary, it will be open to the subsidiary to complain of discrimination under French law since, as a company established under UK law, it has UK nationality. The reason why this paragraph begins with the words 'In general' is to remind one that the free movement of capital can affect non-EU countries.

(8)   *Targeting tax avoidance.* While the CJEU has held that a 'blanket' tax avoidance provision cannot be justified,[104] other forms of tax avoidance rules may be. In *Marks & Spencer* and *Cadbury Schweppes*, the Court accepted that group relief restrictions and controlled foreign company rules, respectively, aimed at 'wholly artificial arrangements' could be justified, subject to proportionality. These cases are discussed in more detail in §77.3 below.

77.2.2.8   Conclusion on the EU Law Qualification

Few disputes could better illustrate the problems that arise from the nature of the European venture. Without genuine agreement about the goals and fundamental principles of the venture itself, it is not surprising that the effect of EU law on the UK tax system is bit of a mess. The uncertainty arising from the UK's possible exit from the EU and the impact Brexit would have on the UK corporation tax system only increases uncertainty in the short term. The Commission's view[105] that the CJEU will rein itself in when a common base for corporate tax has been achieved, has been overtaken by the modern nuanced-approach to discrimination. More kindly perhaps, one might say that what the Commission is trying to do is not to enjoy itself at the expense of Member States but to remove obstacles to the doing of business in the Single Market, and that of the remaining obstacles it is the tax ones which are among the most urgent. Moreover, one does not want to see the restoration of a Member State's right to discriminate through direct taxation.

77.3   The CJEU Case Law on Selected Cross-Border Corporation Tax Topics

Acting under its power (or duty), the CJEU has considered a number of standard elements of corporation tax that have cross-border implications. Some of these cases have already been mentioned in the discussion of their particular topics, but are brought together here as an aid to understanding the broader context of the development of the CJEU's growing body of non-discrimination case law. The discussion that follows focuses on a select number of cases in a few key areas to illustrate the broader principles.

---

[103]   Now called *Boake Allen and others v HMRC* [2007] UKHL 25, [2007] STC 1265, above at §20.2.1; compare Case C-446/04 *Test Claimants of the FII Group* [2006] ECJ 326.

[104]   Case C-324/00 *Lankhorst-Hohorst GmbH* [2002] ECR I-11779

[105]   Eg, in *Bosal Holding BV* [2003] ECR I-9409.

77.3.1 Taxation of Dividends and Imputation

The first issue is the imputation system of corporation tax itself. In *Manninen*,[106] the CJEU suggested that a Member State may use an imputation system only if it gives its resident shareholder taxpayers credit for tax paid in another Member State. In *Hoechst AG v IRC* and *Metallgesellschaft Ltd v IRC*,[107] the UK's then imputation system's group income election was held to discriminate against groups in other (then) EC states, since it conferred a tax cash-flow advantage which was available only if the parent was resident in the UK. In turn, this led to actions based in restitution to recover the costs, principally financial costs, of having had to pay money earlier than was right.

On dividends, *Amurta SGPS v Inspecteur van den elastingdienst/Amsterdam*[108] concerned the Dutch tax system's 25% withholding tax on dividends. Company A receiving a dividend from Company B could claim exemption if Company A's seat or PE was in The Netherlands and it had at least 5% of the shares of Company B. In other situations, a higher percentage (25%) was required. The CJEU had little difficulty in finding that there was a breach of (then) Article 56 TEC where the percentage was less than 25% and the seat was not in The Netherlands. In a case concerning (then) Articles 56 and 57 TEC, *Holböck v Finanzamt Salzburg-Land*,[109] the taxpayer, H, was an Austrian who was the sole shareholder in a Swiss company. Under Austrian tax law, dividends from an Austrian company were taxed at half rate, while dividends from companies in non-Member States were taxed at the ordinary rate. The relevant years were from 1992 to 1996. The Court held that it was a pre-existing restriction within Article 57 TEC. The Court also held that the Austrian legislation was not intended to apply only to those shareholdings which enabled the holder to have a definite influence on a company's decisions and to determine its activities—this meant that (then) Article 43 TEC did not apply but Article 56 TEC did, and Article 56 TEC was excluded by Article 57 TEC.

77.3.1.1 Outbound Dividends

In Case 374/04 *Test Claimants in Class IV of the ACT Group Litigation*,[110] the Court considered the compatibility of the UK rules on the taxation of outbound dividends with EU principles under (then) Articles 43 and 56 TEC. It upheld the right of the UK to refuse credits on such dividends. The essence of the case was an argument by the companies that there was a difference between the treatment accorded to dividend payments to other UK-resident companies (TA 1988, section 208 made them exempt) and that accorded to non-resident companies (where section 208 did not apply). The Court examined TA 1988, section 233 and concluded that the effect of that provision was that the UK did not attempt to tax the outbound dividend. This was acceptable to the Court and the companies' argument was rejected. The conclusion that the UK did not even attempt to tax the outbound dividend is what distinguishes the UK case from the *Denkavit* case on dividends outbound from France. In *Denkavit*,[111] the French system taxation of dividends differed depending on

---

[106] Case C 319/02 *Manninen v Finland* [2004] ECR I-07477.
[107] [2001] STC 452; for comment, see Richardson [2001] BTR 273 and Dourado (2002) 11 *EC Tax Rev* 147.
[108] Case C-379/05 [2008] STC 2851.
[109] Case C-157/05 [2008] STC 92.
[110] Case C-374/04 *Test Claimants in Class IV of the ACT Group Litigation* [2006] ECR I-11673.
[111] On Case C-170/05 *Denkavit International BV* [2006] ECR I-11949, see Cussons, *The Tax Journal* (15 January 2007), 10–12.

whether the dividends were going to domestic parent companies or foreign parent companies; this was held contrary to (then) Article 43 TEC.

Other aspects of the ACT system were considered in the important case *Test Claimants of the FII Group*.[112] Under the ACT rules then in force but repealed in 1999, when a UK company was making a qualifying distribution, eg a dividend, to a shareholder, the company had to pay ACT. The company could use the ACT against its own liability to mainstream corporation tax on its profits for the period in respect of which the dividend had been paid. A problem arose if the company had foreign income which benefited from foreign tax credit relief—the effect of the credit, especially if the taxpayer had a holding of at least 10% and so benefited from the credit relief for tax on the underlying profits, would be that there would be no mainstream corporation tax against which to set the ACT. This was the surplus ACT problem.

There was also the franking problem. If the shareholder was a company resident in the UK and made a distribution of its own, it could, for example, set the credit accompanying the dividend (called franked investment income) against its own liability to pay ACT when it made its own dividend payment, so 'franking' the dividend; there were other ways of using the credit, eg in relation to losses, but what the company could not generally do was to reclaim the tax from the Revenue. The franking problem was a timing problem.

One argument in the case was that the Court should reject the whole UK two-track approach which distinguished so sharply between purely domestic dividends and foreign dividends. The Court upheld the two-track approach, but with conditions which could be, as far as the UK Revenue were concerned, expensive. The Court held that having an exemption system for domestic distributions (then TA 1988, section 208) while subjecting incoming dividends to the UK's imputation system, might breach EC principles in (then) Articles 43 and 56 TEC. The question was to be answered by looking at the tax burden. The UK rules would satisfy Articles 43 and 56 TEC if the rate on inbound dividends was not greater than that on domestic dividends *and* that the credit was at least equal to the amount paid in the Member State of the company making the distribution up to the limit of the tax charged in the Member State on the company receiving the dividends. The UK courts struggled in understanding and applying the CJEU's decision and sought further clarification in a second referral.[113] In *FII GLO 2*, the CJEU said that by exempting domestic dividends the UK was effectively giving a credit for UK tax at the nominal (statutory) rate irrespective of the actual effective rate of tax paid by the UK subsidiary, and that on the evidence provided by the UK courts the effective level of tax on profits of resident companies generally was lower than the nominal rate. In taxing foreign dividends, however, the credit given was only for the effective foreign tax. Thus, the CJEU decided that the imputation method and exemption method were not equivalent and the difference in treatment between the taxation of domestic and foreign dividends was in breach of both the freedom of establishment and the free movement of capital. Further, although the difference in treatment could be justified by the need to protect the cohesion of the tax system, the operation of the rules was not proportionate. The *FII* case and the EU law issues it raised were a key driver behind the UK's move in 2009 to an exemption system for most domestic and foreign dividends received by a UK company.

---

[112] Case C-446/04 *Test Claimants of the FII Group* [2006] ECJ 326.
[113] Case C-35/11 *FII GLO 2* [2013] STC 612.

The case also involved the foreign income dividend (FID) scheme. This was introduced in 1994 (FA 1994, Schedule 16) to help companies with surplus ACT problems. A company was allowed to match the FID with foreign profits. However, the company had first to pay the ACT in the usual way; when it then matched the foreign dividend, it could get the ACT repaid by the Revenue—but not until the mainstream corporation tax became due, usually nine months after the end of the period. The vulnerability of this scheme to an argument based on the cash-flow advantage which succeeded in *Metalgesellchaft* is obvious. However, the companies went further and argued that some companies should be compensated for the enhanced dividend they had to pay to those shareholders, eg pension funds, who lost out on the tax credits normally accompanying the dividends (and which were not available to FIDs). The Court also held that the FID scheme breached (then) Articles 43 and 56 TEC because of the denial of the tax credit.

77.3.2 Exit Charges

A deemed disposal charge for CGT when a taxpayer moves to another Member State may violate EU law. In *Lasteyrie du Saillant v Ministère de l'Economie*,[114] the Court ruled that the capital gains exit charge levied by France on a business person emigrating from France to another Member State breached the freedom of establishment. The Court expressly approved the UK rule in TCGA 1992, section 10A (see above §74.1.2), which imposes a charge on a temporary non-resident when the non-residence ends; but of course while that applies for CGT itself, it does not apply for corporation tax, where TCGA 1992, section 185 directs a deemed disposal.

In an important 2011 case directly concerning the application of exit taxes to companies, *National Grid Indus BV*,[115] the CJEU held that The Netherlands' attempt to tax an unrealised exchange gain when the company moved its place of management from The Netherlands to the UK was a restriction on the company's freedom of establishment. While the Court accepted that the restriction might be justified on the ground of balanced allocation of taxing powers, which gave The Netherlands the right to tax the amount of the gain (as ascertained at time of exit), it held that requiring immediate payment of the tax on that amount was disproportionate. The CJEU suggested that it would be less harmful to the freedom of establishment if the company had the option to pay the tax immediately or defer payment of tax (possibly with interest) until the gain was realised, if the company was prepared to accept the administrative burden of tracing that that would entail. In the *DMC* case,[116] the CJEU opined that national legislation which provides for the immediate taxation of unrealised capital gains generated in its territory is justified and proportionate, provided that, where the taxable person elects for deferred payment, the requirement to provide a bank guarantee is imposed on the basis of the actual risk of non-recovery of the tax.

---

[114] Case C-9/02 *Lasteyrie du Saillant v Ministère de l'Economie* [2005] STC 1722.
[115] Case C-371/10 *National Grid Indus BV v Inspecteur van de Belastingdienst Rijnmond/kantoor Rotterdam* [2012] STC 114. For commentary see Panayi [2012] BTR 41.
[116] Case C-164/12 *DMC*, ECLI:EU:C:2014:20.

77.3.3 *Thin Capitalisation*

Rules which apply differently according to the residence of taxpayer or its companies attract frequent attention. In *Lankhorst-Hohorst GMBH v Finanzamt Steinfurt*,[117] a German rule treated the waiver of a debt repayment due from a subsidiary to its parent as a constructive dividend; however, while this rule applied to non-resident subsidiaries and some domestic ones, it did not apply to most domestic ones. Thin capitalisation/transfer-pricing rules were extended by Germany to domestic transitions—as in the UK.[118] In *Bosal*,[119] a Dutch rule said that finance costs, such as interest, incurred by the parent company to finance subsidiaries in other Member States could be deducted only if they contributed to profits which were taxable in The Netherlands. This rule was held to be discriminatory and so the parent was entitled to deduct the cost. The result was that UK's transfer-pricing and thin capitalisation rules appeared at risk.

The CJEU also ruled on the UK thin capitalisation rules in its group litigation. In Case C-524/04 *Thin Capitalisation GLO Test Case*,[120] the Court used its customary approach, asking whether the rules were a restriction, whether they might be justified and whether they were proportionate. There were three sets of UK rules. The original rule in TA 1988 directed that where the thin capitalisation rules applied, the whole payment was treated as dividend and not as interest. This bizarre all-or-nothing rule was held to break EC law. The original rule was amended by FA 1995, which concentrated on the amount of interest as opposed to the rate and directed that only the excess over the amount that would have been paid if there had been no connection between the parties was to be treated as interest. These rules were in turn amended by FA 2004 following the decision of the CJEU rejecting the German thin capitalisation rules in Case 324/00 *Lankhorst Hohorst* (above). The 2004 changes use the transfer-pricing rules instead of a separate provision, and apply to certain domestic situations as well.

Importantly, the Court did not reject the 1995 rules as necessarily contrary to EC law principles. Rather, it used the abuse approach developed in *Cadbury Schweppes* (see below §77.3.5). The taxpayers had a right to arrange intra-group finance as they wished, but the states had interests in preventing artificial transfers of profit across borders. Ultimately the Court held that taxpayers must be allowed to show that non arm's-length prices may be justified commercially. So, as in *Cadbury Schweppes*, the rule must be applied on a case-by-case basis. When the CJEU's decision was sent back to the UK courts for implementation, the Court of Appeal interpreted the CJEU's 'commercial reasons' test simply to mean that intra-group finance had to be on arm's-length terms. As the UK rules allowed a deduction for arm's-length financing costs, the Court of Appeal concluded that there could be no further remedy for amounts in excess of that.[121] The CJEU has not yet considered the 2004 rules. Some commentators dared to hope for the repeal of the 2004 rules extending the UK's

---

[117] Case C-324/00 [2003] STC 607; Korner (2003) 31 *Intertax* 162; and Gutman and Hinnekens (2003) 12 *EC Tax Rev* 90.

[118] German transfer pricing reaction, Endres (2004) 32 *Intertax* 137 and de la Feria and Fuest, 'Closer to an Internal Market? The Economic Effects of EU Tax Jurisprudence', Oxford University Centre for Business Taxation WP 11/12 (July 2011).

[119] Case C-168/01 [2003] STC 1483.

[120] Case C-524/04 *Thin Capitalisation GLO Test Case* [2007] ECR I-2107.

[121] [2011] EWCA Civ 127.

transfer pricing regime to purely domestic transactions in the light of this decision—so far in vain.[122]

The case contains other important—and controversial—comments on the scope of (then) Article 56 TEC as opposed to Article 43 TEC, and on the role of the justification of cohesion.[123]

77.3.4 Cross-Border Loss Relief

The UK legislation in response to the CJEU decision in *Marks & Spencer*[124] was considered briefly above (§64.6.7). In *Marks & Spencer*, the UK taxpayer sought to deduct from UK profits a loss sustained in France. If the loss had been sustained by a French branch, the loss would have been allowable. In fact, it had been sustained by a French subsidiary and so could not be used under UK tax rules. It is axiomatic in tax planning that foreign ventures begin as branches, so that full relief may be obtained against the parent's income for the almost inevitable start-up losses, and then switch to subsidiaries to shield the foreign income from UK tax until actual distribution. Here the foreign subsidiary's venture had ended badly and the loss was a liquidation loss.

It became conventional to say the CJEU's ruling was, in football parlance, a 'score draw'. The CJEU held:[125]

> As Community law now stands, arts 43 EC and 48 EC do not preclude provisions of a Member State which generally prevent a resident parent company from deducting from its taxable profits losses incurred in another Member State by a subsidiary established in that Member State although they allow it to deduct losses incurred by a resident subsidiary. However, it is contrary to arts 43 EC and 48 EC to prevent the resident parent company from doing so where the non-resident subsidiary has exhausted the possibilities available in its state of residence of having the losses taken into account for the accounting period concerned by the claim for relief and also for previous accounting periods and where there are no possibilities for those losses to be taken into account in its state of residence for future periods either by the subsidiary itself or by a third party, in particular where the subsidiary has been sold to that third party.

The UK Court of Appeal remitted the question whether there was 'no possibility' of the loss being used in another way to the First-tier Tribunal.[126] Litigation continued in the UK courts for nearly a decade, and included two Supreme Court rulings.[127] Meanwhile, the European Commission considered that the UK's group relief legislation, as narrowly amended following the CJEU decision in *Marks & Spencer*, still infringed the freedom of establishment, and referred the matter to the CJEU. The CJEU eventually decided in the UK's favour.[128]

The foreign loss case of *AMID*[129] added little to *Marks & Spencer*. In *Lidl Belgium*,[130] the Court agreed with Advocate General Sharpston on the general principle but disagreed

---

[122] See eg Mahalingham [2012] BTR 134.
[123] See Morgan and Bridges, *The Tax Journal* (19 March 2007), 7 *et seq.*
[124] Case C-446/03 *Marks & Spencer v Halsey* [2006] STC 237.
[125] *Ibid*, 268.
[126] *Marks & Spencer v Halsey* [2007] EWCA Civ 117, [43] *et seq.*
[127] *Marks & Spencer v HMRC* [2013] UKSC 30 and [2014] UKSC 11.
[128] Case C-172/13 *European Commission v UK* [2015] STC 1055.
[129] Case C-141/99 [2003] STC 357.
[130] Case C-414/06 *Lidl Belgium GmbH v Finanzamt Heilbronn* [2008] ECR I-3601.

with her on the question of proportionality. The Court upheld the Member State rule in question.[131]

77.3.5 Controlled Foreign Company Rules

The UK's CFC rules (discussed in chapter seventy-three above) attribute the profits of certain overseas companies to UK corporate shareholders. In *Cadbury Schweppes v IRC*,[132] the taxpayer was such a shareholder and the overseas subsidiaries were such companies. The subsidiaries had been set up in Ireland under the terms of the relevant Irish legislation and paid tax at 10%, being within the International Financial Services Centre in Dublin. A previous structure had involved a Jersey company. The question referred to Luxembourg was whether the application of the CFC legislation interfered with the taxpayer's rights under the free movement provisions in (then) Articles 43, 49 and 56 TEC.

The Court's first principle was that measures to counter potential abuse were legitimate if aimed at 'wholly artificial arrangements'. Such conduct undermined the right of the Member States to exercise their tax jurisdiction in relation to the activities carried out in their territory and thus jeopardised a balanced allocation between Member States of the power to impose taxes (referring to *Marks & Spencer*, at [46]). However, in deciding whether the arrangements were wholly artificial, the Member State could not say just that the burden of tax was lower in the other state. So the CFC rules would not be compatible with EU law if they applied where, despite the existence of tax motives, the incorporation of a CFC reflected economic reality and the incorporation corresponded with an actual establishment intended to carry on genuine economic activities in the host Member State. Any finding of artificiality had to be based on objective factors ascertainable by third parties with regard, in particular, to the extent to which the CFC physically exists in terms of premises, staff and equipment, such as a 'letterbox' or 'front' subsidiary.[133] As noted in §77.2.2.6(6) above, in *Vodafone 2*, the UK Court of Appeal concluded that the UK's CFC legislation could be interpreted so as to be compatible with EU law by 'reading in' a new exception applying retrospectively to companies actually established in another EEA state which carry on genuine economic activities there.[134]

When the UK revised and narrowed its CFC regime in 2012, the new Gateway-based regime was thought to be EU compliant without the need for a specific EEA carve-out. Moreover, this is one area of corporation tax that is unlikely to be greatly affected by Brexit because EU compliance overlapped with the Government's general policy aims. The UK's position, which is based on the CJEU's approach in the *Thin Cap GLO* case, is that a CFC

---

[131] For criticism of AG Sharpston's opinion, see Airs, *The Tax Journal* (21 April 2008), 9–11. Other notable CJEU decisions on losses include Case C-418/07 *Papillon* [2008] ECR I-08947, Case C-157/07 *Krankenheim* [2008] ECR I-8061, Case C-337/08 *X Holding* [2010] ECR I-1215, Case C-18/11 *Philips Electronics UK*, ECLI:EU:C:2012:532, C-123/11 *A Oy*, ECLI:EU:C:2013:84, Case C-48/13 *Nordea Bank Danmark* ECLI:EU:C:2014:2087 and Case C-388/14 *Timac Agro Deutschland* ECLI:EU:C:2015:829. For commentary see Lang, 'Has the Case Law of the ECJ on Final Losses Reached the End of the Line?' (2014) 12 *European Taxation* 530.
[132] Case C-196/04 [2004] STC (SCD) 342.
[133] See Case C-341/04 *Re Eurofood IFSC Ltd* [2006] All ER (EC) 1078, paras 34 and 35. For a more detailed analysis, see Simpson [2006] BTR 677 and practical comments by Dodwell, Williams and Pleasant, *Tax Journal* (13 November 2006), 7. See further ch 73 above.
[134] *Vodafone v Revenue & Customs Commissioners (No 2)* [2009] STC 1480, [2009] EWCA Civ 446.

rule in an EU Member State that targets income earned by a CFC that is not itself wholly artificial may be justified so long as the transaction giving rise to the income is at least partly artificial. The G20/OECD BEPS Action 3 final report also considers the controversial issue of domestic CFC rules and compatibility with EU law. The OECD presents several options for Member States to consider in EU-proofing CFC regimes, including the UK approach. The OECD suggests another option would be to include domestic as well as cross-border subsidiaries in the CFC regime to avoid discrimination as well as designing CFC rules that rely on the justification of balanced allocation of taxing power.[135]

77.3.6 Tax Avoidance

In the seminal 1986 *French Tax Credits* case,[136] the CJEU stated that tax avoidance was not a permitted derogation from the freedom of establishment. More recently, however, in *Marks & Spencer* and *Cadbury Schweppes*, the Court accepted that group relief restrictions and CFC rules, respectively, aimed at 'wholly artificial arrangements' could be justified on the ground of prevention of abusive practices, subject to proportionality. The 'wholly artificial' requirement is very problematic for CFC regimes in particular. In the *Thin Cap GLO* case, the CJEU stated that, in determining whether thin capitalisation legislation was justified by the need to prevent abusive practices, it should be determined 'whether the transaction in question represents, in whole *or in part*, a purely artificial arrangement, the essential purpose of which is to circumvent the tax legislation of that Member State'.[137] As just noted in §77.3.5, this case provides some authority for the position that a CFC rule in an EU Member State that targets income earned by a CFC that is not itself wholly artificial *may* be justified so long as the transaction giving rise to the income is at least partly artificial.[138]

Of further interest is the EU doctrine of abuse of rights,[139] which was considered in the VAT case *Halifax*. The Court concluded that although Community (now Union) law must not be used for abusive ends, it must also value the principle of certainty.[140] Further, where the taxable person chooses one of two transactions, the Sixth (VAT) Directive does not require him to choose the one which involves paying the highest amount of VAT. If the doctrine of abuse of rights is to apply, it must be on the basis that there are sufficient objective factors. In *Cadbury Schweppes*, the CJEU considered and rejected the idea that the taxpayer was abusing the freedom of establishment by choosing to locate subsidiaries in Ireland solely due to its low corporate tax rate.

---

[135] OECD, *BEPS Action 3 'Designing Effective Controlled Foreign Company Rules' Final Report* (Oct 2015), paras 19–22.

[136] Case 270/83 *Commission v French Republic* ('Avoir Fiscal') [1986] ECR 273.

[137] Case C-524/04, *Test Claimants in the Thin Cap Group Litigation v Commissioners of Inland Revenue*, para 81.

[138] OECD, *BEPS Action 3 'Designing Effective Controlled Foreign Company Rules' Final Report* (Oct 2015), 17–18.

[139] On abuse of rights and European tax law, see Schön in *Comparative Perspectives on Revenue Law* (CUP, 2008) ch 4. See also de la Feria and Vogenauer, *Prohibition of Abuse of Law: A New General Principle of EU Law?* (Hart, 2011) and especially ch 25 (Freedman).

[140] Case C-255/02 *Halifax PLC and others* [2006] STC 919 at para 72.

77.3.7 *The Relationship Between EU Law and Bilateral Tax Treaties*

There was already a duty on Member States to take the most-favoured-nation principles into account when negotiating with third parties in the field of aviation.[141] In the direct tax context, *Bouanich v Skatterverket*[142] concerned a rule which allowed resident shareholders to deduct certain items from dividends. A non-resident shareholder was not allowed to do so. The Court held that this was a breach of (then) Article 56 TEC. The Court also considered national legislation derived from a double tax treaty between France and Sweden, and held that it too could breach EC non-discrimination principles in appropriate circumstances. Similarly, *Meilicke v Finanzamt Bonn-Innerstedt*[143] concerned a rule under which a resident was allowed a tax credit for dividends from a resident company but not from a non-resident company. The Court held that this was a breach of (then) Article 56 TEC.

77.4   Other Aspects of EU Law

77.4.1 *Interpretation*

In EU law the courts adopt a purposive interpretation and treat VAT law, in particular, as a matter of principle and purpose.[144] The courts state the principle and then work down to the facts. Moreover, literal interpretations are rejected in favour of the purpose of the directive;[145] only if all else fails do the courts proceed to a literal approach.[146] This approach comes naturally when UK courts face problems of interpreting EU law as such, or UK rules based on EU directives: see, for example, the Court of Appeal reading in a new exemption to the CFC rules in *Vodafone 2* as just discussed in §77.3.5 above. However, the schizophrenic state under which tax matters are tested on a literal basis in a domestic context and on a purposive basis in a European context may become unstable, especially as the volume of EU material expands. The idea of English courts finding they are championing a minority tradition in a sea of other ideas is particularly piquant for Scots lawyers, who have had to suffer this since the Act of Union. A related phenomenon is the practice, already seen in UK legislation implementing the Mergers Directive, of ensuring that cross-border transactions are not favoured at the expense of purely domestic ones.[147]

---

[141] Cases C-466/98–476/98 *Commission v UK* ('the *Open Skies* case') [2002] ECR I-09427. The remarks of AG Tizzano are particularly wide-ranging. See Panayi [2003] BTR 189.

[142] Case C-256/04 [2008] STC 2020.

[143] Case C-292/04 [2008] STC 2267.

[144] See Avery Jones (1996) 17(3) *Fiscal Studies* 63; see further above §3.1.2.

[145] For example, Case 154/80 *Staatssecretaris van Financiën v Coöperatieve Vereniging Coöperatieve Aardappelenbe-waarplaats GA* [1981] 3 CMLR 337 (the *Dutch Potato* case), and Case 89/91 *Staatssecretaris van Financiën v Hong Kong Trade Development Council* [1983] 1 CMLR 73 (ECJ).

[146] Case 139/84 *Van Dijk's Boekhuis BV v Staatssecretaris van Financiën* [1986] 2 CMLR 575 (ECJ), distinguishing the creation of a new article from the thorough repair of an old article.

[147] Inland Revenue, *EC Direct Measures—A Consultative Document* (1991), paras 2.4, 2.5, 2.10.

77.4.2 *The Role of the Commission—and its Views*

Since the Commission has enforcement powers under the EU Treaty, one must pay particular attention to its views. However, the Commission was largely instrumental in pressing the *French Tax Credits* case (see §77.2.2.2 above) and the refusal to allow the Court to weigh the advantages and disadvantages of doing business as a branch rather than as a subsidiary; many see this as the false start of the Court's adventures into this area.

Most recently, the Commission has also weighed in on base erosion and profit shifting by releasing a series of proposals aimed at tackling corporate tax avoidance.[148] The 'Anti Tax Avoidance Package' calls on Member States 'to take a stronger and more coordinated stance against companies that seek to avoid paying their fair share of tax and to implement the international standards against base erosion and profit shifting.' The main features of the new proposals include:

(1)   legally-binding measures to block the most common methods used by companies to avoid paying tax;
(2)   a recommendation to Member States on how to prevent tax treaty abuse;
(3)   a proposal for Member States to share tax-related information on multinationals operating in the EU;
(4)   actions to promote tax good governance internationally; and
(5)   a new EU process for listing third countries that refuse to play fair.

The Commission put forward other initiatives in 2015 to boost tax transparency and reform corporate taxation, including the re-launch of the CCCTB now CCTB project and a proposal (later agreed by the Member States) for transparency on tax rulings. In 2016, the Council adopted an amended Administrative Cooperation Directive to implement country-by-country reporting by multinationals as well as automatic exchange of the information in the CbC reports between Member States. Also in 2016 the Council adopted the Anti-Tax Avoidance Directive.[149] The Directive has five main components, most of which are consistent with the actions of the G20/OECD BEPS project but in some respects go further than the BEPS recommendations; the Directive also goes further than simply providing a framework for Member State action.[150] The Directive will require Member States to enact measures on: (1) CFCs, (2) exit taxes, (3) interest limitation, (4) hybrids and (5) a GAAR.[151] The Member States will have until 31 December 2018 to transpose it into their national laws and regulations, except for the exit taxation rules, for which they will have until 31 December 2019.

---

[148] See http://europa.eu/rapid/press-release_IP-16-159_en.htm.
[149] See http://europa.eu/rapid/press-release_MEMO-16-2265_en.htm.
[150] See commentary by Wesel and Wyatt, *Tax Journal* (15 July 2016).
[151] For commentary see Moreno, 'A pan-European GAAR? Some (un)expected consequences of the proposed EU Tax Avoidance Directive combined with the Dzodzi line of cases' [2016] BTR 143.

PART VII

Tax-preferred Savings and Charities

78

Favoured Methods

78.1 Introduction

The UK has a number of tax rules designed to encourage saving. These rules are considered in this chapter and in chapters seventy-nine and eighty below. One interesting side-effect of this encouragement to save has been that people often end up with a larger estate when they die. The tax rules are designed to give relief from income tax and/or CGT, not IHT. So the Chancellor may take three times as much in IHT as he gives away in the other taxes.[1]

This chapter covers the UK tax treatment of certain favoured forms of saving. The treatment of—and of income from—investment intermediaries is discussed in chapter seventy-nine below. The division between chapters seventy-eight and seventy-nine is not precise. The extent of these rules, and in particular the extent of the exemptions and reliefs, is made very clear by the gathering together of the material in ITTOIA 2005, Part 4 (savings and investment income) and Part 6 (exempt income). However, the boundary between a rule prescribing the limits of a section, and so to be found in Part 4, and an exemption, to be found in Part 6, is not precise, and so the arrangement adopted in previous editions has largely been followed here. The treatment of the biggest tax privileges of all, those for pension arrangements, was completely rewritten by FA 2004 and took effect in April 2005; this treatment is outlined in chapter eighty below.

The correct tax treatment of income from savings is a highly contentious issue, marking, as it does, the divide between comprehensive income tax (CIT) and expenditure tax (ET). Thus the debate is a reflection of that larger debate: partly a belief that income from saving is doubly taxed, since savings are usually made out of taxed income; and partly a belief that saving is a good thing and so should be encouraged. The 1995 OECD report *Taxation*

---

[1] *Sunday Times*, 4 February 2007, Money Section.

and Household Savings showed that most countries' systems penalise savings.[2] However, if tax-efficient ways of saving are introduced, it must be expected, as US and UK experience shows, that there will be long transitional phase during which money is simply moved from existing savings into the new accounts. The OECD report also showed that countries with the most generous interest deductions, then the United States and Scandinavia, had the lowest rate of savings (2%); the least generous group (most other large industrial economies) had a savings rate of 11.5%. Perhaps the most dramatic experiment concerned New Zealand where, in the late 1980s, pension contributions ceased to receive any privileged treatment; deductions to pension funds ceased to be deductible and tax was charged on the income of the funds, although not on the eventual pension. The effect was a sharp fall in pension savings, small firms winding up their pension schemes and large firms reducing promised benefits. Household saving dropped from 1.3% of GDP in 1987 to −1.9% in 1989–90.[3]

In the UK there is a strong government wish to encourage saving for retirement, and one strand of the debate is whether such savings should be compulsory. The strongest objection to compulsion comes from the very people whom the Government sees as most in need of having such savings, ie those at the lower end of the income scale. These people not only understand that their disposable income would be reduced while working, they also realise that any benefit from their saving is likely to be swallowed up by the pension credit mechanism (below). This leaves those who would save anyway as the people who object much less to compulsion. Thus government policy confounds itself.

Tax encouragement to save may take many forms:

(1) the annual return received by the investor may be free, in whole or in part, from income tax;
(2) there may be an income tax deduction, in whole or in part, for the sum invested;[4]
(3) the sum received on disposal may be exempt, in whole or in part, from CGT.

In addition:

(4) the entity with which the money is invested may be free of tax on its income and or capital gains; and
(5) the CGT liability normally arising on a disposal may be deferred on a reinvestment.

78.2   Current UK Savings Incentives

With the introduction of the Personal Savings Allowance (PSA) from 6 April 2016, basic-rate taxpayers do not pay tax on the first £1,000 of savings income such as interest earned on bank current and savings accounts. Higher-rate taxpayers can earn up to £500 of savings

---

[2] See comment by Robson (1995) 16(1) *Fiscal Studies* 38. For a broad economics-based survey of theories on saving, see Boadway and Wildasin (1994) 15(3) *Fiscal Studies* 19.
[3] Davis, *Pension Funds*, (OUP, 1998), 87–88; citing Fitzgerald and Harper (1992) 9 *Australian Tax Forum* 194.
[4] There is no CGT deduction until the disposal—unless, perhaps, rollovers are treated as a form of deduction since the investment is greater by the amount of the tax not charged.

income tax-free but additional-rate taxpayers have no tax-free allowance. As a result, the vast majority of taxpayers pay no tax on their ordinary savings income. In addition, income and capital gains from particular forms of savings are exempt from tax, as follows (the ITTOIA provisions apply for income tax, while TA 1988 and later legislation still apply for corporation tax where relevant):

(1) Interest and bonuses on National Savings Certificates; maturity bonuses on defence bonds, British savings bonds and national development bonds; and, for persons resident and ordinarily resident in Northern Ireland, Ulster Savings Certificates.[5]

(2) SAYE interest and bonuses under certain certified contractual savings schemes; for schemes certified on or after 1 December 1994,[6] exemption is limited to savings-related arrangements linked to share option schemes within ITEPA 2003.[7]

(3) Capital gains from government stocks and qualifying corporate bonds.[8]

(4) Income and capital gains of authorised pension and retirement benefit schemes.

(5) Income and capital gains on investments held under an individual investment plans, ie ISAs and formerly personal equity plans (PEP) and TESSAs[9] (see §78.3 below).

(6) Income and capital gains from funds invested with a venture capital trust,[10] enterprise investment scheme, seed enterprise investment scheme, corporate venturing scheme, social investment or real estate investment trust (REIT) (see §§78.4–78.8 and §79.10 below).

(7) Pension funds (chapter eighty below).

(8) Unit trusts, etc (see §79.3 below).

(9) Securities which are free of tax to residents abroad (FOTRA) securities.[11]

Other tax privileges include the following:

(10) Tax deductions for investments by an individual in shares in certain qualifying trading companies under the venture capital trusts, enterprise investment scheme, and seed enterprise investment scheme, below §78.4–78.6.

(11) An individual's contribution to a pension scheme is deductible from income, for income tax purposes, within limits: see chapter eighty below.

(12) CGT exemptions and deferrals of gain if reinvested (see CGT chapters above and especially chapter thirty-two).

---

[5] ITTOIA 2005, Pt 6, Ch 2, ss 692 and 693, ex TA 1988, s 46 (still in force for corporation tax). See Explanatory Notes Draft Bill, changes 122 and 123. ITTOIA 2005, s 693 makes statutory the former concessionary relief for accumulated interest on Ulster Savings Certificates following the death of the holder (ex ESC A34). An exemption for National Savings Bank interest up to £70 on ordinary accounts (formerly ITTOIA 2005, s 691, ex TA 1988, s 325) was repealed by FA 2011.

[6] ITTOIA 2005, Pt 6, Ch 4, ss 702–708, ex TA 1988, s 326 and Sch 15A (not relevant for corporation tax).

[7] ITTOIA 2005, s 703 refers to ITEPA 2003, s 516(4).

[8] TCGA 1992, s 115.

[9] ITTOIA 2005 generalised the PEP regulation-making powers in TA 1988, ss 333 *et seq* and repealed the TESSA regulation-making powers in TA 1988, ss 326A *et seq* (added by FA 1990, s 28)—not relevant for corporation tax.

[10] ITTOIA 2005, Pt 6, Ch 5, ss 709–712.

[11] ITTOIA 2005, Pt 6, Ch 6, ss 713–716, FA 1996, s 154 (still in force for corporation tax).

(13) The first £5,000 of dividends earned by an individual are tax-free by virtue of the Dividend Allowance, with excess dividends taxed at more favourable rates than other forms of income—eg 7.5% on dividend income falling within the basic rate band—and no NICs.

78.3   Individual Savings Accounts[12]

As from 6 April 1999 the former favoured savings devices of tax exempt special savings accounts (TESSAs) and personal equity plans (PEPs) ceased to be available for new investment. They were succeeded by individual savings accounts (ISAs). On 1 July 2014 ISAs were reformed and rebadged as 'New ISAs' (NISAs); since most financial institutions and the public still use the term ISA that term is retained in this book. Unlike the predecessor schemes, the ISA includes a number of voluntary standards designed to make some schemes attractive to savers as distinct from fund managers; these are the 'CAT standards', which set levels for charges, access and terms.[13] There was much delight in certain circles when ISAs had a slow start; since investors had just rushed to save with TESSAs and PEPs for the last time, some savings fatigue was not surprising. Later figures suggested that ISAs became quite popular.[14] For many taxpayers, however, the combination of the Dividend Allowance and the PSA from 6 April 2016 has greatly reduced the benefits of ISAs—especially in a low interest rate environment.

An ISA is a scheme of investment which may be used by a qualifying individual[15] aged 18 or over and resident in the UK.[16] For many years ISAs had maxi accounts and mini accounts. Currently ISAs are divided into two types: (1) stocks and shares ISAs, and (2) cash ISAs. Savers can make contributions into one of each type of ISA per tax year. The overall maximum ISA subscription level per tax year is £15,240 (for 2016–17), and savers can invest this entire amount in cash ISAs or stocks and shares ISAs or a combination. The limit is to rise to £20,000 from 6 April 2017. From 2011, Junior ISAs are available for children aged under 18, with a maximum subscription limit of £4,080 (for 2016–17). Junior ISAs replaced an earlier investment product called Child Trust Funds. From April 2015 existing Child Trust Funds can be transferred into Junior ISAs. Junior ISAs remain tax-free until the child turns 18, at which point it is converted into a normal ISA.

Like TESSAs and PEPs, ISAs allows individuals to hold various investments free of income tax and CGT.[17] Unlike those schemes, ISAs allow investors to use an insurance policy. An ISA, by abolishing the PEP distinction between qualifying and non-qualifying funds, has a slightly wider geographical spread than a PEP, and permits investments in gilts.

---

[12]   Regulations were made under FA 1998, s 75, which refers to TA 1988, ss 333 and 333B, TCGA 1992, s 151. The principal regulations are the Individual Savings Account Regulations 1998 (SI 1998/1870) (hereafter 'ISA Regs'), [1998] *Simon's Weekly Tax Intelligence* 1200; and the Individual Savings Account (Amendment) Regulations 1999 (SI 1998/3174), [1999] *Simon's Weekly Tax Intelligence* 97. See also Inland Revenue Press Release, 1 April 1999, [1999] *Simon's Weekly Tax Intelligence* 730.

[13]   See Treasury Press Release, 22 December 1998, [1999] *Simon's Weekly Tax Intelligence* 32.

[14]   Chennells, Dilnot and Emmerson (eds), *Green Budget 2000* (Institute for Fiscal Studies, 2000), 78.

[15]   ISA Regs 1998, reg 4(1).

[16]   ISA Regs 1998, reg 10; Crown employees within TA 1988, s 132(4)(a) also qualify.

[17]   ISA Regs 1998, reg 22.

Like a PEP, but unlike a TESSA, an ISA has no lock-in period to qualify for tax relief. An ISA may be opened by someone on behalf of the qualifying individual and does not have to be opened in writing.

A 'help-to-buy' ISA was introduced in 2015 to assist first-time homebuyers.[18] The government provides a cash bonus of 25% of amounts saved. The maximum government bonus is £3,000 per person (£6,000 if a couple). From April 2017, a new more flexible Lifetime ISA will allow individuals aged 18–40 to save up to £4,000 per annum plus receive a government bonus of 25% of the amount saved. The Lifetime ISA can be used to buy a first home or withdrawn after the age of 60. Earlier withdrawals can be made but with a penalty. Those with help-to-buy ISAs will be able to transfer them into the Lifetime ISA. Amounts saved in Lifetime ISAs will count towards the £20,000 annual ISA limit.

78.4 Venture Capital Trusts[19]

Rules for venture capital trusts (VCTs) were first introduced in 1995, but were extensively revised by FA 2004 and have been occasionally modified since then. The income tax legislation gives relief from income tax for qualifying investments by individuals in approved VCTs; as from 6 April 2007 these are to be found in ITA 2007, Part 6 (previously TA 1988, section 332A and Schedule 15B). The legislation is quite lengthy, and the discussion below focuses on the key elements. Exemption from CGT is given both to the VCT itself in respect of its gains (TCGA 1992, section 100) and to the individual on a disposal of the qualifying shareholding (TCGA 1992, section 151A); these remain part of TCGA 1992. There is no charge to income tax on distributions by the VCT to the shareholders. The conditions to be satisfied by a VCT seeking approval and as to the holding it may acquire are now set out in ITA 2007, Part 6, Chapter 3 (previously TA 1988, section 842AA and Schedule 28B). The VCT is liable to tax on its income as distinct from its realised capital gains; the practice of using borrowings to fund acquisitions means that there may well be no taxable income. The following account relates to the year 2016–17. The VCT must be approved by the Commissioners; loss of approval has tax consequences.[20] The 2004 changes followed a review of VCTs and enterprise investment schemes (EISs) (see §78.5 below).

The individual investor may claim relief from income tax; as at 6 April 2016 an individual could claim at the maximum of 30% (earlier years allowed relief at 20% or even 40%) for sums up to £200,000 invested in the VCT;[21] relief for investors applies only in relation to shares for which the individual has subscribed. For CGT reliefs, see above at §41.7. Many, but not all, of these changes bring the VCT relief closer to that for EISs (§78.5 below). Immediately before 2004 there was a reinvestment relief for gains otherwise chargeable

---

[18] See https://www.helptobuy.gov.uk/help-to-buy-isa/how-does-it-work/.

[19] See Shirley (1994) 15(2) *Fiscal Studies* 98, arguing that the legislation should have subsidised debt, not equity. On practice, see Stratton, *Tolleys Tax Planning 2003–04*, ch 64, 1841. For instructive information on US and Canada, see Sandler, *Venture Capital and Tax Incentives: A Comparative Study of Canada and the United States*, Tax Paper No 108 (Canadian Tax Foundation, 2004).

[20] ITA 2007, ss 259, 274–275, 283, ex TA 1988, s 842AA(1)–(4); the rules on withdrawal of approval and its consequences begin in s 281, ex s 842AA(6).

[21] ITA 2007, ss 261 *et seq*, ex TA 1988, Sch 15B, para 1, as amended by FA 2008, s 32.

to CGT if the gains could be matched with an investment in the VCT (the serial investor relief), but this was repealed since the 40% income tax relief was then made available.[22]

Income tax relief[23] is given for the cost of eligible shares issued by a VCT. The maximum amount qualifying for relief in one year is now £200,000; shares are eligible if they carry no preferential rights to dividends or assets, nor any right to be redeemed.[24] The shares must not be loan-linked; a loan is linked if it is one made to the individual (or an associate) which would not have been made if the individual had not subscribed for the shares.[25]

The relief must be claimed and takes effect at step 6 of the process set out in above §12.2.5.[26] For shares issued after 5 April 2006 the relief is lost if there is a disposal within five years of the issue or certain other events occur; the benefit of the relief may be recovered by an assessment to income tax.[27] (For shares issued after 5 April 2000 and before 6 April 2006 the period was three years.)[28] A disposal is ignored if between spouses or civil partners living together.[29]

FA 2001 also provided that VCT relief was not lost when the VCT went into liquidation or merged; rules to facilitate mergers were added in 2002.[30] The funds raised must be put to work within 24 months.[31] The rule that the trade had to be carried on by the same company throughout the period was softened in 2004 to allow the trade to be carried on by another qualifying group company.[32] There are restrictions on the type of business which the company may carry on; FA 2008 added shipbuilding, coal production and steel production.[33] The relief is also lost if the VCT approval is withdrawn.[34]

Extensive rules define the qualifying holdings rules for the trust.[35] Since 17 March 2004 these rules have allowed more subsidiaries to qualify, in particular:

(1)   a 51% subsidiary rather than a 75% subsidiary; and
(2)   in certain circumstances a 90% property management subsidiary; the 90% test also applies if the subsidiary carries on the trade R&D which benefits the VCT investment.[36]

These and other changes mirror those made to the EIS scheme.[37] The trust is obliged to distribute income and capital gains regularly to its investors.[38] There is no charge to income tax on a dividend from the trust;[39] this extends to dividends paid to assignees, provided they

---

[22]   TCGA 1992, Sch 5C, repealed by FA 2004, Sch 19.
[23]   ITA 2007, s 261, ex TA 1988, s 332A, added by FA 1995 and enacting TA 1988, Sch 15B.
[24]   Definition of 'eligible share' ITA 2007, s 273, ex TA 1988, Sch 15B, para 6.
[25]   ITA 2007, s 264, ex TA 1988 Sch 15B, para 2.
[26]   ITA 2007, ss 263 and 271–273.
[27]   ITA 2007, ss 266–270, ex TA 1988, Sch 15B, paras 3, 4; on information, see s 271, ex Sch 15B, para 5.
[28]   See also changes made by FA 2000, Sch 18 for shares issued on or after 6 April 2000.
[29]   ITA 2007, s 267, ex TA 1988, Sch 15B, para 3.
[30]   ITA 2007, ss 314–325; the merger rules (ss 321 *et seq*) were added by FA 2002, Sch 33.
[31]   ITA 2007, ss 293–294, ex TA 1988, Sch 28B, para 6(1)–(2A).
[32]   ITA 2007, ss 290–292, ex TA 1988, Sch 28B, para 3, as amended by FA 2004.
[33]   ITA 2007, s 303 (VCT) or s 192 (EIS).
[34]   ITA 2007, s 268; on assessment, see s 270.
[35]   ITA 2007, Pt 6, Ch 4 (ss 286–313), ex TA 1988, s 842AA, Sch 28AB.
[36]   ITA 2007, ss 301 and 299, ex TA 1988, Sch 28B, paras 5A and 10ZA.
[37]   Revenue Notes to Finance Bill 2004, cls 88 and 89.
[38]   ITA 2007, s 275(2).
[39]   ITTOIA 2005, Pt 6, Ch 5, ex TA 1988, Sch 15B, para 7.

were acquired for bona fide commercial purposes and not as part of an avoidance scheme. The exemption from income tax should not be given too much weight; there is no exemption from corporation tax for the companies in which the trust invests.

The VCT income must derive wholly or mainly from shares or securities;[40] it is thought that this test will be satisfied at 70%. The same test applies to the value of qualifying holdings as a proportion of the trust investments. At least 30% of the trust's holdings must be in eligible shares.[41] The VCT's ordinary shares must be listed on a regulated market, but the relevant company in which the qualifying activity is carried on must be unquoted.[42] No one holding by the VCT must exceed 15% of its total investments.[43] There are also rules limiting the amount of money raised which is not invested (it must not exceed £1 million) and on the maximum value of the assets of the company invested in.[44] Various trades do not qualify.[45] There are rules to ensure the independence of the company invested in.[46] Finally, F(No 2)A 2015 introduced a new £12 million lifetime limit on the amounts a company or group can raise under any combination of the VCT, EIS, SEIS or other State aid; the limit is £20 million for 'knowledge intensive' companies.[47]

The VCT offers better tax incentives than PEPs and, unlike the EIS, allows the investor to spread the risk over a number of companies. It was thought that a typical trust would invest in between 20 and 40 companies, including those on the AIM.

78.5 Enterprise Investment Scheme

The EIS, introduced by FA 1995, is a version of a device which began in 1983; it too was revised by FA 2004, but changes over the years have been frequent, with particularly major revision in 2001. The income tax legislation has been rewritten and is now ITA 2007, Part 5 (sections 156–257). The legislation is quite lengthy, and the discussion below focuses on the key elements. In this chapter the older references are retained but preceded by the term 'ex'. However, TA 1988, Part VII, Chapter II (sections 289–312) still applies to shares issued before 6 April 2007 and 'ex' must be understood in this sense. None of the rules has been affected by ITTOIA 2005. Although the relief shares many rules with VCT, it is quite distinct. EIS is a relief from income tax for sums invested in shares issued by a qualifying company carrying on a qualifying business. Any gain made by the investor is exempt from CGT, provided the shares are held for at least three years; if the shares are sold below cost, the cost for capital loss purposes is reduced by any EIS relief given.[48] There is no relief from income tax for distributions by the company. Increases in EIS investment limits have to go through the EU Commission system to check for compliance with state aid rules.

---

[40] ITA 2007, s 276. There are also rules on the receipt of royalties or licence fees as a qualifying trade; ITA 2007, s 306, ex TA 1988, Sch 28B, para 4(5), (6), amended by FA 2000, Sch 18, para 5.

[41] ITA 2007, ss 275 and 277–279.

[42] ITA 2007, s 295, TA 1988, Sch 28B, para 2. For problems, see Stratton, *op cit*.

[43] ITA 2007, ss 275 and 277.

[44] ITA 2007, ss 287 and 297, ex Sch 28B, paras 7 and 8. These limits are £15 million before the issue of the relevant holding and £16 million afterwards.

[45] ITA 2007, ss 303 *et seq*, added to by FA 2008, s 33.

[46] ITA 2007, ss 296 and 310.

[47] F(No 2)A 2015, Sch 6, cl 8 adding ITA 2007, s 292AA et seq.

[48] On relevant CGT rules, see TCGA 1992, s 150A; and on taper relief, s 150D applying Sch 5BA.

Income tax relief is given for the cost of eligible shares in and issued by a qualifying company.[49] The maximum amount which may be subscribed in one year is £1,000,000; it was set at £400,000 in 2006, having been £200,000 in 2004.[50] Relief is given at the EIS rate of 30%, but may not create any right to repayment.[51] Shares must be ordinary shares and carry neither preferential rights to dividends or assets, nor any right to be redeemed.[52] The share must be subscribed for wholly in cash and be fully paid-up when issued.[53] There are rules for allocating the relief to the different shares.[54] The relief must be claimed and takes effect at step 6 of the process set out above §12.2.5.[55]

On the part of both the investor and the company, the shares must be subscribed for genuine commercial reasons and not for tax-avoidance purposes;[56] the shares must be issued by the company for the purpose of a qualifying business activity.[57] Individuals must not be connected with the company; a director is not necessarily connected, provided no unreasonable payments are received from the company.[58]

The company must be a qualifying company, ie unquoted and carrying on one or more qualifying trades.[59] Qualifying trades are elaborately defined by excluding many trades;[60] the exclusions include not only share dealing but also running a nursing home.[61] The company must have a UK permanent establishment.[62] It must also be independent.[63] The courts have held that a company providing accounting services to a firm of accountants was not providing independent accountancy services and so did not qualify; in a similar vein they have held that the payment of a dividend was not a qualifying business activity.[64]

The money raised must be put to work in the qualifying activity within two years.[65] As with VCTs, there is a gross assets limit—the company's assets must not exceed £15 million before the issue or £16 million afterwards.[66] The annual investment limit for qualifying

---

[49] ITA 2007, ss 156 *et seq*, the share requirements are in Pt 5, Ch 3 and the issuing company conditions are in Ch 4, ex TA 1988, ss 289, 289A, 293 and 297. See Way, *Tolley's Tax Planning 2007–08*, ch 19.

[50] ITA 2007, s 158, ex TA 1988, s 290(2); there is also a minimum subscription of £500 (s 157(2), ex s 290(1)).

[51] ITA 2007, s 158(2), ex TA 1988, s 289A(2); renamed by FA 2008, Sch 3.

[52] ITA 2007, s 173 (2), ex TA 1988, s 289(7).

[53] ITA 2007, s 173, ex TA 1988, s 289(1).

[54] ITA 2007, ss 201 *et seq*.

[55] ITA 2007, ss 158(3) and 201–207.

[56] ITA 2007, ss 165 and 178.

[57] ITA 2007, s 175.

[58] ITA 2007, ss 163 and 166–171, ex TA 1988, ss 291, 291A, 291B; the permitted payments are listed in s 168(2), ex s 291A(3). *Taylor v Revenue & Customs Commissioners* [2010] UKUT 417, [2011] STC 126 concerned the question whether the investor was connected with the company, viz whether the investor had to have (a) 30% of the share capital and 30% of the loan capital, or (b) 30% of the amalgamated capital. Roth J preferred (b).

[59] ITA 2007, ss 181–184, s 293; on effect of land holding, but note s 188 on property managing subsidiaries. The parent company of a trading group qualifies.

[60] ITA 2007, ss 192 *et seq*, ex TA 1988, ss 297, 298. On effect of IP rights, see s 195 continuing changes made by FA 2000.

[61] ITA 2007, s 198, ex TA 1988, s 297(fe).

[62] ITA 2007, s 180A.

[63] ITA 2007, s 185, ex TA 1988, s 293(8).

[64] The cases are *Castleton Management Service Ltd v Kirkwood* [2001] STC (SCD) 95; and *Forthright (Wales) Ltd v Davis* [2004] EWHC Civ 524; [2004] STC 875.

[65] ITA 2007, s 175, ex TA 1988, s 289(1)(c). *Blackburn v Revenue & Customs Commissioners* [2009] STC 188, [2008] EWCA Civ 1454 is an interesting case on proving that money had been subscribed for shares when it had been left with the company and allowed to build up.

[66] ITA 2007, s 186.

companies is £5 million. The company may have subsidiaries, but these must meet various conditions; some rules refer to 51% subsidiaries and others to 90% subsidiaries.[67] As with VCTs, shares must not be loan-linked.[68] There must be no prearranged exit.[69] Further rules are provided for corporate reorganisations, the acquisition of the share capital by a new company and its application to subsidiaries, and where there are nominees, etc.[70] Finally, F(No 2)A 2015 introduced a new £12 million lifetime limit on the amounts a company or group can raise under any combination of the VCT, EIS, SEIS or other State aid; the limit is £20 million for 'knowledge intensive' companies.[71]

Enterprise investment schemes are also of importance because of the rules allowing CGT to be deferred when gains have been realised and the proceeds are reinvested in an EIS.[72] These rules date from 1998 and replace the old CGT general reinvestment relief; they also broaden an earlier relief which allowed deferrals on an investment in an EIS. CGT deferral relief is useful as it is available in cases where the CGT exemption is not available, eg when the investor is connected or the subscription limit is exceeded.

The rules reflect much experience with the business expansion scheme (BES) (1984–93). About one-quarter of BES projects failed in the first two or three years, and more than £196 million was sunk into assured tenancy companies just before the worst slump to hit the property market since 1945. Making money only came from offers in the early 1990s, especially when accompanied by loan-back schemes (now blocked as loan-linked transactions). Original investments were farmland, hotels and even wine. In 1988 the assured tenancy companies had attracted £100 million; other investments £5 million.[73]

78.6   Seed Enterprise Investment Scheme

FA 2012 introduced another favourable investment scheme—the Seed Enterprise Investment Scheme (SEIS).[74] The legislation is quite lengthy, and mirrors many of the EIS provisions; the discussion that follows is a brief summary of the key elements. Individuals who invest up to £100,000 in shares in qualifying seed companies issued on or after 6 April 2012 are eligible for income tax relief of 50%[75] as well as CGT relief on disposal of the shares.[76] The relief must be claimed and takes effect at step 6 of the process set out above §12.2.5.[77] In addition to meeting the EIS qualifying conditions, an SEIS qualifying company must have fewer than 25 employees at the date of the share issue, and its gross assets must not exceed £200,000 before the share issue.[78] The maximum amount a company can raise under

---

[67] ITA 2007, ss 189–191, ex TA 1988, s 308 and ss 293(6ZA), 300(2)(b) as added by FA 2004.
[68] ITA 2007, s 164, ex TA 1988, s 299A.
[69] ITA 2007, s 177, ex TA 1988, s 299B.
[70] ITA 2007, ss 247–249, 191 and 250, ex TA 1988, ss 304A, 305, 308, 311.
[71] F(No 2)A 2015, Sch 5, cl 8 adding ITA 2007, s 173AA et seq.
[72] TCGA 1992, Sch 5B, added by FA 1998. On 1998 changes, see Hutton [1998] *PCB* 285; and McKie [1998] *PCB* 174.
[73] See *The Economist*, 3 December 1988.
[74] ITA 2007, Part 5A, ss 257A *et seq*; TCGA 1992, ss 150E-G and Sch 5BB.
[75] ITA 2007, s 257AB.
[76] TCGA 1992, ss 150E–150G.
[77] ITA 2007, ss 257AB(4).
[78] ITA 2007, ss 257DJ and 257DI.

this scheme is £150,000.[79] From 2013–14, gains realised on the disposal of assets that are reinvested through SEISs qualify for a 50% CGT exemption.[80]

78.7   Corporate Venturing Scheme

It is something of a relief, after wading through the statutory provisions on VCTs and EIS, to come across the more modern rules on the corporate venturing scheme (CVS) which took effect on 1 April 2000 and are contained in FA 2000, Schedule 15 (not rewritten). Unlike the previous reliefs in this chapter, it is aimed at investment by companies and so applies only for corporation tax. However, many of the rules have been changed along with those for VCTs and EIS, eg as to the gross capital, the number of employees and the limits on the amount invested in the issuing company in any 12-month period.[81] The investing company gets relief at 20% of the amount it subscribes for new ordinary shares which are held throughout the qualification period, which is usually three years.[82] There are also reliefs against income for losses on these shares, net of any investment relief remaining after the disposal,[83] and provision for deferring any capital gains liability on reinvesting in another such scheme.[84] There are further rules about the application of corporate reorganisation provisions; these are to be applied to these shares separately from other shares.[85]

The investing company[86] must not at any time during the qualification period (three years) have a material interest in the issuing company, nor may it control it. The issuing company must carry on only non-financial trades. The investment must be subscribed for commercial reasons and not for tax-avoidance purposes.

The rules on the company issuing the shares[87] are similar to those for EIS and VCTs. Such a company must be small, independent, unquoted and trading. It must not carry on certain prohibited activities, eg nursing homes.[88] It must not derive a substantial part of its income from licence fees and royalties, save where these have been generated by its own R&D.[89] The relief is not lost if the company becomes quoted within the three-year period, provided this was not imminent when the shares were issued. The relief is lost if the shares are disposed of within the qualification period.[90] Further restrictions apply if value is received from the company by the investing company or other persons.[91] Loss of relief is tempered in certain circumstances.[92] The relief is not lost if the company goes into liquidation or receivership

---

[79] ITA 2007, ss 257DL.
[80] TCGA 1992, Sch 5BB.
[81] FA 2000, Sch 15, paras 22 (amended 2006), 22A (added 2007) and 35A (added 2007). For further examples, see paras 23A and 29(3).
[82] FA 2000, Sch 15, para 39.
[83] FA 2000, Sch 15, para 67.
[84] FA 2000, Sch 15, para 73.
[85] FA 2000, Sch 15, para 80.
[86] FA 2000, Sch 15, paras 4–14.
[87] FA 2000, Sch 15, paras 15–33.
[88] FA 2000, Sch 15, para 32.
[89] FA 2000, Sch 15, para 29.
[90] FA 2000, Sch 15, paras 3 and 46.
[91] FA 2000, Sch 15, paras 47 and 56.
[92] FA 2000, Sch 15, para 60.

within the three-year period. The relaxations which we have seen for VCTs and EIS apply here too. So FA 2004 allows a subsidiary to be a qualifying subsidiary if it is a 51% subsidiary of the CVS company, although the 90% test applies to a property management subsidiary and to subsidiaries whose activities benefit most from the money raised through the CVS.[93] Some of the 2001 changes to VCTs and EIS, eg rules on ignoring insignificant repayments,[94] had been part of the CVS as first enacted in 2000, but some changes were made to CVS in 2001, eg: (a) the change to the period within which the money raises had to be put to use;[95] and (b) the amendment of the rule on ignoring replacement value when considering whether the benefit of the relief should be withdrawn where the investing company received value from the issuing company.[96]

78.8 Social Investment Tax Relief

FA 2014 introduced a different type of favourable investment scheme aimed at helping charities and other social enterprises—the Social Investment Tax Relief (SITR).[97] The discussion that follows is a brief summary of the key elements. Individuals who invest up to £1,000,000 per year in qualifying social enterprises between 6 April 2015 and 5 April 2019 are eligible for income tax relief of 30%[98] as well as CGT relief on disposal of their investment in shares or qualifying debt of the enterprise. The investment must be held for a minimum period of 3 years for the relief to be retained. The relief must be claimed and takes effect at step 6 of the process set out above §12.2.5.[99] Gains realised on the disposal of assets that are reinvested through SITRs qualify for hold over relief. At Budget 2015, the government announced plans to introduce a new Social Venture Capital Trust (Social VCT) scheme. The scheme will encourage investment in companies that invest in social organisations, and will be similar to the Venture Capital Trust Scheme. Investors in a Social VCT will be eligible for income tax relief at 30% of the value of their investment.

78.9 Purchased Annuities

There are several types of purchased life annuity, which may be immediate or deferred and may be for life or for a period of years (or a mixture with life but a guaranteed five-year period). Their attraction is that they are an insurance against outliving capital. Their weakness, apart from the risk that the annuitant dies the day after the purchase without any minimum period of payment, is that they will either be eroded by inflation or, if proofed against inflation, will be lower than the purchaser may expect.

---

[93] FA 2004 does this principally by adding FA 2000, Sch 15, para 21A, and amending paras 5 and 23.
[94] FA 2000, Sch 15, para 57.
[95] Amendment to FA 2000, Sch 15, para 15.
[96] FA 2000, Sch 15, para 54.
[97] ITA 2007, Part 5B.
[98] ITA 2007, s 257JA.
[99] ITA 2007, ss 257JA(3).

78.9.1 Theory and Avoidance

The investment of one's capital in the purchase of an annuity meant that one was buying income with capital and that income tax was therefore due on the whole of each payment received, even though, in commercial reality, one was receiving back each year a part of one's capital together with interest. A number of ways around this all-income treatment were devised. The first, which lasted until 1949, provided for an advance by way of interest-free loan each month, which was to be extinguished by set-off against a capital sum due under the contract on death. The Revenue's argument that these were in substance annual payments was rejected.[100] Such loans are now treated as income. A second way, which still survives, applies to an annuity certain, ie an annuity payable for a stated number of years, not depending on the survival of the annuitant. The Court of Appeal held that tax was chargeable only on so much of the payment as represented interest and not on the whole sum.[101] This split treatment was not accorded to normal annuities, which terminated on the death of the annuitant, and so companies would issue 'split annuities', meaning an annuity certain for a stated number of years, to be followed by a deferred annuity. The payments under the former annuity would be divided into capital and interest. While the latter would be taxable in full, it was arranged that the sum payable under the contract would be higher and, in any case, the cost of it would be lower in view of the more advanced age of the annuitant.

78.9.2 Current Law—Splitting

The premise that a purchased life annuity is taxed in full is maintained by the charging rule in ITTOIA 2005, Part 4, Chapter 7. This is, however, subject to the partial exemption in Part 6, Chapter 7, which allows splitting and has been part of the law since 1956. Only those who love the Rewrite can understand why these two batches of provisions, consisting of five and eight sections, are separated in this way. The statute includes procedural rules, eg on claims and appeals, and a regulation-making power.[102] The rules in TA 1988, sections 657 *et seq* that formerly applied for corporation tax were repealed by FA 2008 when life insurance contracts were brought into the loan relationship rules. The relevant legislation is now in CTA 2009, Part 6, Chapter 11, sections 560–569. The discussion below focuses on the income tax treatment.

Under the splitting procedure, that part which represents the estimated capital content is exempt from tax and only the balance is income. This approach does not apply where the annuity is already given some relief or is not purchased by the annuitant. An annuity is not split if, apart from Part 6, Chapter 6, it is treated as having a capital element, or if the premiums have qualified for life insurance premium tax relief.[103] Also taxable in full are annuities purchased or provided for under a will or settlement, out of income of property disposed of by the will or settlement (whether with or without resort to capital).[104]

---

[100] *IRC v Wesleyan and General Assurance Society* (1946) 30 TC 11; see above at §27.3.

[101] *Perrin v Dickson* [1930] 1 KB 107, (1930) 14 TC 608; but doubted in *Southern-Smith v Clancey* [1941] 1 All ER 111, (1941) 24 TC 1.

[102] ITTOIA 2005, ss 717, 723 and 724.

[103] ITTOIA 2005, s 718 (2)(a), ex TA 1988, s 657(2).

[104] ITTOIA 2005, ss 718 (2)(b) and (c).

Annuities provided under schemes such as those for retirement benefits or personal pensions—under which the contributors have already received tax reliefs—are also outside the apportionment rules, but this is because of the provisions in ITEPA 2003, Part 9 (pension income) which have priority.[105] Apportionments are made if the sums paid are partly for the annuity and partly for other reasons.[106]

The method of apportionment between income and capital—or, as ITTOIA 2005, now puts it, between income and the exempt amount—is carried out by dividing the sum spent by the normal expectation of life according to government mortality tables, regardless of the individual.[107] The rules contain two variables, thus creating four situations. The first variable is whether or not the amount of the annuity depends solely on the duration of a human life or lives;[108] the second variable is whether the term of the annuity depends solely on the duration of a human life or lives.[109] The four situations are:

— Situation 1: where the amount of the annuity payments depends solely on the duration of a human life or lives. Here the statutes direct how one calculates the exempt proportion.[110]

— Situation 2: where the amount also depends on another contingency. Here each payment is exempt only in so far as it does not exceed a fixed sum; shortfalls in payments may be carried over to other years.[111]

— Situation 3; where the term depends solely on the duration of human life or lives. Here the exempt proportion and the exempt sums are calculated under rules in sections 720 and 721.[112]

— Situation 4: where the term of the annuity depends on other factors too. Here the rules in sections 720 and 721 are applied, and a just and reasonable apportionment is made.[113]

If one spouse, H, transfers an annuity to the other spouse, W, with whom H is living, the transfer will be ineffective for tax purposes since the transfer is of a right to income and so the settlement rules discussed above in chapter thirty-one will apply.[114]

If the annuitant cashes in the policy, the same charge to tax may arise as under the chargeable event rules (below §79.5.3).

The calculation of the taxable income element and the tax-free capital element used to be done by HMRC. This is not really appropriate in the days of self-assessment, and so FA 2007, section 46 amended TA 1988, sections 656 and 658, and ITTOIA 2005, sections 717 and 623 remove this HMRC role.

---

[105] ITTOIA 2005, Pt 4, Ch 1, s 366 and explanatory notes. The same goes for a sum taxable in full under Pt 2 or Pt 10.

[106] ITTOIA 2005, s 722.

[107] The tables are authorised under ITTOIA 2005, s 724, ex TA 1988, s 658; the manner of computing them was put under statutory authority only in 1991 (with retroactive effect) (FA 1991, s 76). The tables must be obeyed (*Rose v Trigg* (1963) 41 TC 365). This is hard, since a person with lower-than-average life expectancy may get special terms from a company.

[108] ITTOIA 2005, s 719(2)–(5).

[109] ITTOIA 2005, ss 719(2) and (6)–(8).

[110] ITTOIA 2005, s 719(3).

[111] ITTOIA 2005, ss 719(4) and (5).

[112] ITTOIA 2005, ss 719(6) and (7).

[113] ITTOIA 2005, s 719(8).

[114] ITTOIA 2005, s 625(3), ex TA 1988, s 660A(6).

79

Investment Intermediaries

79.1 Introduction

At first sight there should be no need for special legislation to deal with investment companies, and also almost no need for anyone to create such a company. An individual who wishes to hold investments is usually much better advised to hold them directly rather than through a company. Although the corporation tax rate may be lower than the income tax rate (and is set to fall further still), money extracted as dividends in excess of £5,000 annually will be subject to a further layer of tax of up to 38.1%, and the close company rules designed to penalise loans may apply. In the unlikely event that money is extracted by way of capital gain, as by the sale of shares, there will be the further problem of a double charge on capital gains already realised by the company. Without special reliefs, the addition of investment intermediaries could mean triple or quadruple taxation of capital gains.

However, this is to see things simply in terms of the individual wealth holder. Investment companies are important parts of the investment market. Some, such as approved investment trusts, open-ended investment companies and approved unit trusts (which are taxed as if they were companies), receive special reliefs from some or all of these consequences. They will not be close companies, and are usually exempt from corporation tax on their profits and gains. This chapter begins with special expenses rule for all investment companies and then considers the specially-approved intermediaries.

79.2 Management Companies with Investment Business— Deduction of Management Expenses

CTA 2009, Part 16 (ex TA 1988, section 75) allows companies with investment business to deduct certain expenses of management from their profits in addition to those already deductible, eg under CTA 2009, Parts 3 or 4. Pursuant to section 1218B, a 'company with investment business' means a company whose business consists wholly or partly of making investments (and is not a credit union).[1] The reason why Part 16 is needed lies in the schedular system. Most revenue expenses incurred in earning trading profits or income from property are deductible from gross receipts in arriving at the net income assessable, under the rules now in CTA 2009, Parts 3 and 4. However, relief was not normally given for expenses incurred in earning investment income, such as company dividends and interest. TA 1988, section 75 was first introduced in 1915 in response to increased taxation during the First World War; it was substantially amended by FA 2004 which added section 75A and a new section 75.[2] The new rules widened the situations in which expenses may be claimed, and made the timing of the deduction depend on accounting principles and not when the payment is made.

The relief to a 'company with investment business' applies not only to companies whose business consists wholly of making investments, but also to those whose business partly so consists, eg companies which have a trade of their own but also hold shares in subsidiaries. The definition of 'investment company' in TA 1988, section 130 is still there after the Rewrite, as it has a role to play in other rules.[3] In *IRC v Tyre Investment Trust Ltd*,[4] the phrase 'the making of investments' was held to mean 'investing'. It was not necessary for an investment company to buy and sell investments regularly, provided it takes some active interest in the investments which it has made. The asset must be held in order to produce a profitable return and not be merely incidental to some other activity; for this reason a property management company might well not be an investment company.[5] A holding company formed to hold shares in subsidiary companies can be an investment company and can be a company with investment business.[6] The effect of the 2004 change may be seen when considering a trading company deriving income from the investment of large amounts of surplus cash. It will not be an 'investment company' unless it can establish that the main part of its business consists in the making of investments, and the principal part of its income is derived from it. It will, however, be a company with an investment business, and so come within this regime as from 2004.

---

[1] CTA 2009, s 1218B, ex TA 1988, s 130.

[2] FA 1915, s 14; later ITA 1918, s 33. On FA 2004, ss 38–46, see Inland Revenue Notes to Clauses 38 *et seq*.

[3] The Revenue Notes, para 26, suggests TA 1988, s 573 (now in CTA 2010, ss 69–73) and the transitional rules in ss 42 and 43.

[4] (1924) 12 TC 646—where the effect of the decision was to bring the company within the charge to Excess Profits Duty.

[5] *100 Palace Gardens Terrace v Winter* [1995] STC (SCD) 126, 129f; distinguished on the facts in *Cook v Medway Housing Society Ltd* [1997] STC 90.

[6] In *IRC v Tyre Investment Trust Ltd* (1924) 12 TC 646, the company was formed to acquire shares in two companies and sell them on. More recently, in *Dawson Group plc v Revenue & Customs Commissioners* [2010] STC 1906, [2010] EWHC 1061 (Ch), Mann J held that a company was an investment company and that certain expenses were not deductible as they were not expenses of management.

79.2.1 Qualifying Expenses of Management

The term 'expenses of management' was not defined by TA 1988, section 75 and has been said to be 'insusceptible of precise definition'.[7] Nevertheless, CTA 2009, section 1219 makes an attempt, describing such expenses as in respect of so much of the company's investment business as consists of making investments that are not held for an unallowable purpose. Capital expenditure is not deductible.[8] These will include staff costs, indirect costs, including repairs to equipment, legal and other professional fees,[9] and property maintenance costs, including rents, rates, maintenance and repairs of premises occupied for business purposes. Sums paid to purchase investments are not management expenses since they are part of the costs of buying investments, not managing them. However, it does not follow that only expenses incurred in the function and process of management may qualify. Relief is available for expenditure incurred in evaluating an investment, such as the legal costs of investigating title, as well as for expenditure on an abortive investment. Judges have indicated that a broad view may be taken of what is an (allowable) expense of investigation as opposed to a (non-allowable) expense of acquisition.[10] In an ideal world one might think that an expense was either an expense of management allowable under this rule, or an expense allowable for capital gains under TCGA 1992 rules. The pre-2004 version of section 75 expressly included commissions;[11] today the matter is left to general principles.

Among the items that will not qualify are capital expenditure, entertainment expenditure, other specifically barred payments, such as bribes and losses on the disposal of investments.[12] In addition, the expense must not be in respect of an investment held for an unallowable purpose, a phrase defined as a purpose which is not a business or commercial purpose of the company, or for the purpose of activities which are outside the charge to corporation tax.[13] Following Revenue guidance, one may say that 'unallowable purposes' therefore covers social or recreational purposes. The insistence that the investment be within the charge to corporation tax means that an investment held by a non-resident company with a UK PE will qualify if the management is part of the activities of the PE of a company, but not otherwise. Expenses of a members' club will not qualify since the club is outside the charge to tax by reason of mutuality.[14]

These rules now have their own anti-avoidance provision. Expenses are excluded if the main purpose (or one of the main purposes) of incurring the expense or of surrounding

---

[7] *Sun Life Assurance Society v Davidson* [1958] AC 184, 196; 37 TC 330, 354, *per* Viscount Simonds.

[8] CTA 2009, s 1219(3), ex TA 1988, s 75(3) added to reverse the Court of Appeal decision in *Camas v Atkinson* [2004] STC 860. Draft Guidance on these changes, and in particular the exclusion of capital expenditure, is discussed in a Revenue Guidance Note, 15 June 2004, [2004] *Simon's Tax Intelligence* 1472.

[9] *Holdings Ltd v IRC* [1997] STC (SCD) 144.

[10] Carnwath LJ in *Camas v Atkinson*, above, para 32.

[11] TA 1988, s 75, but not everything called a commission qualifies (see *Hoechst Finance Ltd v Gumbrell* [1983] STC 150, (1983) 56 TC 594).

[12] Unless CTA 2010, ss 68–71, ex TA 1988, s 573 applies—certain losses on the disposal of shares in unquoted trading companies.

[13] CTA 2009, s 1220, ex TA 1988, s 75(3) and (5). These words are becoming common, see eg the loan relationships legislation in chapter 5, above.

[14] Revenue Notes to Clauses 39 *et seq*, paras 14–16.

arrangements is to obtain a tax advantage.[15] Where both this rule and that on manufactured payments apply, this rule has precedence.[16]

79.2.1.1 Dual Purpose

There is no requirement that expenses must be 'wholly and exclusively' incurred for the purposes of the company's business. Apportionment of expenditure is therefore possible. In particular, if expenditure is excessive, only amounts reasonably incurred will qualify as expenses of management.[17]

79.2.1.2 Relief

Relief is given by deducting expenses of management first from income not otherwise charged to tax as held in the course of the company's investment activities.[18] The balance of expenses remaining is then deducted from other income and chargeable gains of the company. Expenditure still unrelieved may be carried forward, without time limit, against future income, from whatever source, of the company,[19] or it may be relieved by way of group relief.[20] Excess management expenses, unlike trading losses, cannot be carried back to previous accounting periods.

Since 2004 the expense must be 'referable to an accounting period' as opposed to the earlier 'disbursed'. The rules for this are set out in sections 1224–1227, the basic one being when an expense is debited in the company's accounts in accordance with GAAP.[21] Because this means that an expense may be allowed before it is paid, the rules provide for a charge to tax to arise where sums have been credited in the accounts to reverse a previous deduction, eg section 1228.

Restrictions are imposed on the carry-forward of unused expenses where there has been a change in the ownership of a company with an investment business. In addition to the usual references to increases in the scale of the company's activities or revival from quiescence, the rules refer to a 'significant increase' in the amount of the company's capital. There is a 'significant increase' in the amount of an investment company's capital if, in the three years after the change of ownership, the company's capital is either at least double, or greater by £1 million than, the amount of capital before the change.[22] The rules also aim to prevent avoidance by the manipulation of capital at or around the time of the change of ownership.

79.2.2 Investment Dealing Companies

If the company crosses the line to become an investment dealing company, its profits will be computed under the trading rules in CTA 2009, Part 3. Dividends received are treated as arising under its trade.

---

[15] CTA 2009, s 1220(2)–(5), ex TA 1988, s 75, as amended by FA 2007, s 28, for accounting periods beginning after 19 June 2007.
[16] Ie CTA 2010, s 799, ex TA 1988, Sch 23A, para 7A.
[17] *LG Berry Investment Ltd v Attwooll* [1964] 2 All ER 126, (1964) 41 TC 547; see also *Fragmap Developments Ltd v Cooper* (1967) 44 TC 366.
[18] CTA 2009, s 1219–1222, ex TA 1988, s 75(6).
[19] CTA 2009, s 1223, ex TA 1988, ss 75(8) and (9).
[20] CTA 2010, ss 99(1)(f), (4), 103 and 105(1)–(4), ex TA 1988, s 403(4), (5).
[21] CTA 2009, s 1225, ex TA 1988, s 75A(2).
[22] CTA 2010, s 677 *et seq*, and in particular s 682, ex TA 1988, s 768B and Sch 28A, Pt I, added in 1995 and updated by FA 2004, Sch 6.

79.3   Unit Trusts and Open-ended Investment Companies

Unit trusts and open-ended investment companies (OEICs) operate in the same sector of the market; both provide a form of pooled investment. Unit trusts have been established for many years; OEICs are a relatively recent invention. Some unit trust managers are changing from unit trust status to OEICs, presumably in the hope of attracting more clients through greater clarity and lower costs. For investors, the biggest difference concerns pricing. Unit trusts offer a dual pricing system, with an offer price and a bid price—'offer' for sale to the client and 'bid' to buy from the client. Shares in an OEIC will have only one price, with the costs of buying and selling appearing as separate items on the transaction. There are, however, other differences, for example one is a trust and the other is a company.

79.3.1 Unit Trusts[23]

Unit trusts are trusts in the strict legal sense of the word, and operate in accordance with the terms of their trust deed. The trustee is usually a bank or an insurance company, but the management of the trust is carried on by a separate management company. The unit holders are simply beneficiaries under the trust whose rights are regulated by the trust deed. Unit holders dispose of their units by selling them to the trust manager at a price equal to asset value, less a small discount. The manager may either hold the units for sale to an investor, or it may sell them back to the trustee, when they are cancelled. It follows that there is no 'discount' as there is for shares in an investment trust; equally, because the trust is not allowed to borrow, there is no 'gearing'.

79.3.1.1   Authorised Unit Trust[24]

An authorised unit trust is treated, in relation to income received by the trustees, as though it were a UK-resident company, and as if the units were shares in the company.[25] Profits consist of income less expenses of management. Capital gains are not chargeable to tax.[26] Corporation tax is charged at a rate equal to the basic rate of income tax, ie 20%.[27] CTA 2009, section 1218, allowing the deduction of management expenses, applies whether or not the trust would be accompanied by investment business within section 1219. Some unit trusts operate under an umbrella scheme, under which unit holders may switch from one type of unit to another. Although the different funds are treated as one for the purposes of the Financial Services Act 1986, each must be taken separately for tax purposes.[28]

HMRC v Smallwood[29] shed light on the intricacies of TCGA 1992, sections 38, 39, 41 and 99 in the context of unit trusts. The taxpayer, T, subscribed £10,000 for units in an

---

[23] See Leslie, *Tolley's Tax Planning 2007–08*, ch 6.

[24] Financial Services Act 1986, s 78. The relevant tax rules are in CTA 2010, Pt 13, Ch 2, ss 612–619, ex TA 1988, s 468(6). ITTOIA 2005, ss 389–391.

[25] CTA 2010, s 617, ex TA 1988, s 468.

[26] TCGA 1992, s 100(1).

[27] CTA 2010, s 618, ex TA 1988, s 468(1A), added in 1996; immediately before 1996 it had been the basic rate, the change marking the introduction of the lower rate for basic- and lower-rate taxpayers.

[28] CTA 2010, s 619(3), ex TA 1988, s 468(7)–(9), added in 1994 and TCGA 1992, s 99A added by FA 2004, s 118.

[29] [2007] EWCA Civ 462, [2007] STC 1237.

enterprise zone property unit trust. Capital allowances of 100% were available for money invested in buildings (£9,678), which T claimed as a deduction against his general income for 1988–89. Ten years later T received distributions of £5,000 and £125, which were treated as part disposals of his holding and generated a capital loss of £4,865. The Court of Appeal held that because section 99 deemed the relevant asset to be the shares in the unit trust, the capital allowances given in respect of the buildings were not relevant to the calculation of the loss under sections 38 and 39. As a result, the Revenue's challenge failed. Sedley LJ remarked that he had an uncomfortable sense that the taxpayer was doing better than he should out of the tax system.

79.3.1.2 Income Distributions

The tax treatment of income distributed or available for distribution by an authorised unit trust to its unit holders depends on what the trustees want to do. The trust may treat the distribution as:

(1) a franked payment under ITTOIA 2005, Part 4, Chapter 3, referred to as a 'dividend distribution';[30] or
(2) an interest distribution under ITTOIA 2005, Part 4, Chapter 2, ie yearly interest subject to deduction of basic rate income tax at source (referred to as an 'interest distribution').[31]

The purpose of (2), introduced in 1994, is to enable the UK-based bond and money funds to compete on roughly equal terms with Continental counterparts.

79.3.2 *Open-ended Investment Companies*[32]

FA 1995 made provision for the taxation of OEICs;[33] the rules have been rewritten in CTA 2010, sections 612–615. These companies are open-ended in that their shares may be continuously created or redeemed depending on the net demand by investors. As with existing authorised unit trusts (and unlike investment trusts), the transactions will be undertaken at a price derived from the net asset value of the OEIC's underlying investments.[34] These companies are common elsewhere in the EU, where they are used for a variety of purposes; in the UK, however, it seems that they will be permitted only as collective investment vehicles. Broadly, the investor buys redeemable share capital in the company, and realises the value either by selling the shares to another person or by requiring the company to redeem them.

An OEIC is taxed in broadly the same way as unit trusts.[35] There is no charge on the OEIC in respect of capital gains, and income is subject to tax at the basic rate.[36] The shareholders

---

[30] ITTOIA 2005, s 389.
[31] ITTOIA 2005, s 376.
[32] See Leslie, *op cit*, 1323. Also, more generally, Grimmett in Wright, *Zurich Investment and Savings Handbook 2004–05* (Zurich, 2004), ch 8.
[33] FA 1995, s 152.
[34] [1994] *Simon's Tax Intelligence* 1492.
[35] CTA 2010, ss 614–615, ex FA 1995, s 152(1), ITTOIA 2005, ss 373–375 (interest payments) and 386–389 (dividend distributions).
[36] CTA 2010, s 614 and TCGA 1992, s 99. Ex TA 1988, s 468A1 added by F(No 2)A 2005, s 17.

are taxed each year on the full net income earned for them (whether or not distributed).[37] A unit trust may convert itself into an OEIC without incurring a tax charge on the transfer.[38] FA 2005 authorises the Revenue to rationalise the provisions on OEICs by regulation.[39]

79.4   Investment Trusts

An investment trust is a company, not a trust.[40] It has share capital and wide powers of investment, although these are usually narrowed to achieve 'approved investment trust' status in the eyes of the Revenue. The company will usually be prohibited from trading in securities. The form is very flexible, and investment trusts therefore range from conservative to the exotic. Some trusts issue only ordinary shares, but others offer split capital trusts which may be repaid at different dates. Some trusts offer income, others only a capital sum on redemption. ISAs may invest in investment trusts only if the trusts meet certain conditions, eg that at least one half of the shares are ordinary shares in EU-resident companies.

The ordinary shares in the investment trust company may be bought and sold on the stock exchange. Because of the way companies are structured, the price paid for the shares is at a discount to the value of the underlying securities; this discount applies equally when the shares come to be sold. This means that in a declining stock market the discount may get greater; such discount will be exacerbated if the investment trust has borrowed money (through debentures) to finance purchases. If the company has borrowed a relatively large sum of money it is said to be highly geared (in US terminology, 'highly leveraged'). In the conventional part of the UK investment trust industry, gearing of 10–15% is moderate, and 30% or more is high.[41] Investors wishing to avoid the risks of discounting and gearing may prefer unit trusts.

If an investment company is an approved investment trust, it is allowed to switch its investments without worrying about capital gains liability; the company is exempt.[42] All other income of the company is taxed in the usual way. The shareholders will pay tax on any income they receive from the company in the usual way. If the company has 'approved' status, its memorandum and articles of association must prohibit the distribution by way of dividend of surpluses arising on the realisation of investments. The exemption from CGT for the company does not extend to the shareholders.

An approved investment trust must meet various conditions: it must be UK resident; it must not be a 'close' company; every class of its ordinary share capital must be quoted on a recognised stock exchange; and its income must be derived wholly or mainly from shares or securities. The Revenue regard this final condition as satisfied if 70% of gross income, before expenses, is so derived.[43] Further, the company must not retain, for any accounting

---

[37] ITTOIA 2005, ss 386 *et seq*; Open-ended Investment Companies (Tax) Regulations 1997 (SI 1997/1154).
[38] Open-ended Investment Companies (Tax) Regulations 1997 (SI 1997/1154), reg 25.
[39] F(No 2)A 2005, ss 17–19.
[40] Macleod [1994] BTR 111; Watson and Bullock, *Tolley's Tax Planning 2007–08*, ch 33.
[41] Wright, *Zurich Investment and Savings Handbook 2004–05, op cit*, para 7.6.5.
[42] TCGA 1992, ss 100, 288.
[43] By agreement with the Association of Investment Trust Companies.

period, more than 15% of the income it derives[44] from shares and securities (or, if greater, £10,000).[45] In general, no holding of shares and securities in a company must represent more than 15% by value of the investing company's investments.[46]

FA 2009, section 45 granted the Treasury regulation-making power, duly exercised,[47] to give these companies the option to treat dividends as distributions of interest instead. This treatment shifts the tax point from the company to the shareholder and makes investment by such companies in interest-bearing assets more efficient.

79.5 Insurance Policies

79.5.1 Introduction

Life assurance presents the UK tax system with various problems. First, the funds held by insurance companies are huge. Secondly, those funds are held for a variety of purposes—of which some are long-term, known as 'life business', eg pensions, annuities and life assurance, while others are short-term, known as 'general business', eg motor, accident and property. Thirdly, some of the companies are 'mutual', ie all the profits accrue to the members of the company (ie the policyholders), as opposed to 'proprietary' where profits are shared between the policyholder members and the owners of the company (the shareholders). It is noteworthy that in the last two decades a number of companies have moved from mutual to proprietary status. While some of the arguments are controversial, it is beyond doubt that among the effects of the change have often been large pay increases for those who previously ran the companies but continue to do so. Members were bribed with their own money to enable other people to make more—a very odd result, but typical of its time. The subsequent need to divide the profits of the company between shareholders and policyholders has exacerbated the decline in returns on investments in this sector.

Lastly, while the principles of taxation of these companies were originally worked out on the basis of established principles, recent years have seen ever more precise tranches of legislation to secure for the UK a proper share of the profits of an increasingly international business.

Much of the language of insurance—and so of insurance taxation—is unique or, if one prefers, obscure.[48] However, certain basic distinctions need to be borne in mind. First, there is the distinction between assurance and insurance. Under an *assurance* contract, a sum of money will definitely become payable, the only question is when, eg at age 60 or on prior death; under an *insurance* contract, the sum will become payable only if the event occurs, eg if rain forces the cancellation of a cricket match. This is close to, but not identical with, the distinction between life business and general business.

---

[44] This rule does not apply to income, which cannot be distributed because of a legal restriction.

[45] CTA 2010, s 1161 and ITA 2007, s 276; ex TA 1988, s 842(2A)–(2C) inserted by FA 1990, s 55.

[46] This condition does not apply where the holding, when it was acquired, was worth no more than 15% of the then value of the investing company's investments; the 15% condition does not apply if the company is itself an investment trust—or would be if its ordinary share capital were quoted. On unit trusts, see Statement of Practice SP 5/91.

[47] Investment Trusts (Dividends) (Optional Treatment as Interest Distributions) Regulations, SI 2009/2034.

[48] For a glossary, see a general work such as Wright, *Zurich Investment and Savings Handbook 2004–05, op cit.*

In connection with life policies of assurance it is customary to talk of 'endowment policies' (with a strong savings element), under which the sum will be payable at a certain age or on prior death, of 'whole life policies' (payable only on death) and of 'term' or 'temporary' policies of insurance, under which the sum is paid only if the person dies within the term of years specified. These three categories reflect the different ways of achieving the basic goals of life assurance, which are the provision of capital for later years and protection of the family against premature loss of the contribution (whether financial or in kind) of the life assured. Endowment policies are often 'with profits'. Here the policyholder receives not only the sum assured, but also a share of the profits earned by the company in the intervening years. Profits may be attached to the policy each year, called 'reversionary' or 'annual' bonuses, in which case they become guaranteed to be paid when the assured is paid. They may also be declared on the termination of the policy, when they are called 'terminal' bonuses. Because of the success of the stock market in the 1980s and 1990s, these profits could be very substantial and might be three or four times the sum originally assured. These were often linked with mortgages, in which the building society lent the borrower the sum originally assured. Because house prices rose very fast, endowment policies became an expensive way of borrowing; as a cost-cutting expedient, people would borrow a sum and take out a policy on which the sum assured would be less than the sum borrowed, in the hope that the profits would bridge the gap. These 'lean' or low-cost endowment options came unstuck when the bonuses declined along with the stock market.

A second form is the 'without-profit' policy—naturally, the premiums on these were lower than for with-profits policies. A third form began as an alternative to with-profits policies; companies began to offer unit-linked polices, which would still offer sums assured, but the money not needed to cover that risk was put directly into units instead of being placed in a large pot. The policyholder could see the value of the units each day of the week. The choice between these was matter of temperament and need. What the story shows is the flexibility of the life assurance policy as an element of prudent financial management. What the story, as told so far, does not show is the lack of flexibility which stems from the essence of these as long-term arrangements; they suit the investment patterns of civil servants or academics rather than entrepreneurs in that they reward regular saving. While the policy could be cancelled by surrendering to the assurance company, there were major financial disadvantages—not only would those terminal bonuses be missed out on, but the sum received back from the company would, in the early years, be much less than the sums already contributed. This reduction would occur because of the sums paid by way of commission to an agent, eg £4,000 out of £75,000 paid for a single premium policy.

From the point of view of the tax system, life assurance began as a good thing and attracted a special relief for premiums. By 1984, the industry was competing in the investment and savings market with its products, and the Chancellor saw it as competing unfairly because of the tax relief.[49] The relief was stopped for new policies. Already, however, the tax system had felt it necessary to counter certain dealings in the first 10 years of a life policy—these rules remain in place and concern policies which do not meet certain criteria (non-qualifying policies); these rules were rewritten by ITTOIA 2005.

---

[49] See Lawson, *The View from No 11: Memoirs of a Tory Radical* (Bantam Press, 1992) 355–56.

Today, the question whether an individual investor should use these products depends, so far as tax is concerned, on whether the investor pays tax at or above the higher rate, and whether the policy is a qualifying policy.[50] The advantage of the qualifying policy is that there is no income tax or CGT charge on the policy itself and the company pays tax at a rate below 40%; income tax will be charged on most transactions involving non-qualifying policies, however, and on some transactions involving qualifying policies. Premium relief for pre-1984 policies applied only to qualifying policies.

The UK tax system accords special treatment to the life insurance industry. The pre-1984 income tax relief on premiums remains in force for existing policies. A special system of taxing income and gains applies to insurance companies. Other companies may find a life policy useful as way of investing surplus funds.[51]

The legislation talks a great deal of qualifying and non-qualifying policies. The advantages of qualifying policies are that there may be some tax relief on the premiums (if the policy was taken out before 1984) and that the proceeds are tax-free if maintained for at least 10 years (or three-quarters of its term) and the policy has not been paid up within that period. Non-qualifying policies do not attract premium relief and are subject to charges on the occurrence of various chargeable events whenever they may be. Whether the policy is qualifying or non-qualifying, there is no charge to income tax on the policyholder while the policy continues intact. There is also an exemption from CGT on a disposal by the original beneficial owner or an assignee otherwise than for value. The 10-year rule has become relevant recently where people have under-invested in 'lean' endowment policies in connection with mortgages and are invited to increase their premiums in the last 10 years of the policy.

Lastly, it should be noted that the special income tax and CGT rules applicable to life insurance policies have been targeted by tax avoidance schemes (see also above §43.2). In *Drummond v Revenue & Customs Commissioners*,[52] the taxpayer (D) carried out a CGT loss avoidance scheme. D had bought a second-hand life policy in 2001 for £1.962 million. He then surrendered the policy and obtained its surrender value of £1.75 million (based on the premiums paid); the surrender cost him £210,000. He claimed, invoking TCGA 1992, section 37 that in calculating his gain he could exclude the £1.75 million of surrender value from the proceeds of sale because this was liable to the special rules for income tax in TA 1988, section 541. This would leave him with the large loss now claimed. Today this would be countered by TGCA 1992, section 16A, added in 2007. The Court of Appeal held that this was not a correct application of section 37. Rimer LJ was not going to be party to any 'black letter literalism' (paragraph 23); the purpose of these rules was to avoid double taxation and not to avoid tax altogether.

79.5.2 Income Tax Relief for Premiums on Pre-14 March 1984 Policies

79.5.2.1 The Relief

For pre-14 March 1984 polices, the claimant, T, is entitled to deduct from the premium a sum equal to 12.5% of the premium;[53] thus, if the premium is £100, the actual payment is

---

[50] Potter and Monroe, *Tax Planning* (Sweet & Maxwell, 1982) §5-01.
[51] Wright, *Zurich Investment and Savings Handbook 2004–05, op cit*, para 14.3.7.
[52] [2009] EWCA Civ 608, [2009] STC 2206.
[53] TA 1988, s 266, not rewritten.

£87.50. There is a ceiling of £1,500, or one-sixth of total income, whichever is the greater.[54] When T receives the commission in respect of the policy, the 12.5% deduction must be applied to the net sum paid.[55] A premium is paid even if the payer borrows the money to pay it, and even if the lender is the insurer.[56]

The policy must be on the life of T or T's spouse, or on their joint lives;[57] it must secure a capital sum payable on death, whether or not in connection with other benefits, so that a temporary term policy is not eligible.[58]

79.5.2.2 'Qualifying' Policy[59]

The purpose of these conditions is to ensure that premiums are paid each year and with a reasonably even spread. Although aimed at the single premium policy, the rules go much wider. For endowment assurances the term must be at least 10 years. The premiums must be payable at yearly or shorter intervals for at least 10 years or until the event specified, whether death or disability. The total premiums payable under the policy in any period of 12 months must not exceed twice the amount payable in any other 12-month period, or one-eighth of the total premiums payable if the policy were to run for the specified term.

The policy must guarantee that the sum payable on death will be at least 75%[60] of the total premiums payable if the policy were to run its term. Broadly similar principles apply to whole life and term assurances.[61] A temporary assurance for a period of not more than 10 years may be a qualifying policy, but only if the surrender value is not to exceed the total premiums previously paid. A term policy of less than 12 months cannot be a qualifying policy.[62]

The legislation also contains a number of special rules. Any exceptional mortality risk is disregarded.[63] A policy issued in connection with another policy cannot qualify if either policy provides unreasonable benefits.[64] Certain policies issued outside the UK are treated as non-qualifying; they may become 'qualifying' policies subsequently.[65] At one time the issuing life assurance company had to certify that a policy was a qualifying policy, but this was changed with effect from 5 May 1996. Today, under the self-assessment regime, taxpayers must report gains from non-qualifying policies on their tax returns.[66] Special rules

---

[54] TA 1988, s 274.
[55] CCAB Press Release, 26 April 1977, [1977] *Simon's Tax Intelligence* 97.
[56] Certain borrowings may be treated as income (TA 1988, s 554).
[57] TA 1988, s 266(2)(b); on year of marriage, see s 280.
[58] TA 1988, s 266(3)(a), but note exceptions in *ibid*.
[59] The rules were relaxed for certain industrial insurance policies (TA 1988, Sch 15, para 7), but these policies have fallen into disfavour. ITTOIA 2005 rewrites para 20 on replacement of qualifying policies (see ITTOIA 2005, s 542), but only for income tax.
[60] There is a 2% reduction for every year by which the person exceeds 55 years of age (TA 1988, Sch 15, para 2(1)(d)(i)). The conditions imposed by FA 1975 apply to policies issued after the appointed day, 1 April 1976.
[61] There is no relaxation for those over 55, including the 75% rule, unless the policy makes no provision for payment on surrender and the term does not run beyond age 75. Where the capital sum may be taken as a single sum or a series of sums, the 75% rule is applied to the smallest sum that may be taken—an obvious anti-avoidance measure (TA 1988, Sch 15, para 1(9)).
[62] TA 1988, Sch 15, para 10.
[63] TA 1988, Sch 15, para 12.
[64] TA 1988, Sch 15, para 14.
[65] TA 1988, Sch 15, para 24.
[66] FA 1995, s 55; replacing old certification system in paras 21 and 22.

apply to determine whether a policy is a qualifying policy where one policy is substituted for another or the terms of a policy are varied.[67] Some variations of terms are prevented from having this effect.[68]

79.5.2.3 Clawback of Relief

These rules apply only to qualifying life policies issued after 26 March 1974 but before 14 March 1984. Some, applied only to the first four years of existence, are not of current interest;[69] their purpose was to prevent the taxpayer from realising a quick profit due simply to the tax relief obtained. Events more than four years after the issue of the policy give rise to clawback only if two conditions are satisfied:[70]

(1) that the event is either—
(a) the surrender of the whole or part of the rights conferred by the policy, or
(b) the falling due (other than on death or maturity) of a sum payable in pursuance of a right conferred by the policy to participants in profits; and
(2) that either of these events has already happened, whether more or less than four years after the issue of the policy.

The effect of (2) is one may make a single such arrangement—but not two. Its purpose is to prevent the payment of premiums out of the proceeds of periodic partial surrenders.[71]

The sum clawed back is the lesser of 12.5% of (a) the total premiums payable during the year of assessment, and (b) the sums payable on surrender or otherwise falling due.[72]

79.5.3 *Sums Payable on Chargeable Events: Liability to Tax in Excess of Basic Rate—Non-qualifying Policies*

The investments caught by these rules are not only life insurance policies, but also contracts for life annuities and capital redemption policies.[73] However, many areas of life insurance are excluded from these rules. These are certain older policies, mortgage repayment policies, pension policies, exempt group life policies and credit union life policies.[74] Some reliefs apply only for qualifying policies, while further rules apply to portfolio bonds (see §23.6) and foreign policies and contracts.[75] It is here that ITTOIA 2005 has rewritten the rules—but only for income tax. TA1988, sections 539–554 have been replaced by ITTOIA 2005, Part 4, Chapter 9, sections 461–566. The rules as they formerly applied for

---

[67] TA 1988, Sch 15, para 25.
[68] FA 2006, s 87, amending TA 1988, Sch 15, para 18(3)—the change in the method of calculating returns on qualifying policy does not cause a charge.
[69] TA 1988, s 268.
[70] TA 1988, s 269.
[71] Inland Revenue Press Release, 10 December 1974, [1974] *Simon's Tax Intelligence* 518.
[72] TA 1988, s 269(2); if there is more than one event, s 269(3) applies.
[73] ITTOIA 2005, s 473(1).
[74] ITTOIA 2005, ss 477–483.
[75] ITTOIA 2005, ss 474–476.

corporation tax were repealed by FA 2008 when life insurance contracts were brought into the loan relationship rules.[76] The relevant legislation is now in CTA 2009, Part 6, Chapter 11, sections 560–569. The brief account which follows focuses on income tax and is intended very much as an introductory outline.

The purpose here is to charge the policyholder on profits made by the insurance company for the policyholder and passed to the holder in some form (including a loan), notwithstanding that the company will already have paid tax on the profits;[77] there is no indexation relief. However, in broad terms, the charge applies to non-qualifying policies at any time and to qualifying policies only within a certain period. There is usually a charge only to the extent that a rate higher than basic rate is due from the holder; top-slicing relief may reduce that burden further.

Examples of such policies are single premium property bonds and policies; the rules do not apply to mortgage protection policies, retirement annuity policies or to policies forming part of pension schemes. At present these are charged to tax at $(40 - 20)\% = 20\%$. Chargeable events are death, maturity, surrender, assignment for money or money's worth and the drawing-down of money by way of payment or loan in excess of permitted limits.[78]

The rules are softened for qualifying policies. In the case of death and maturity, the charge arises only if the policy is converted into a paid-up policy before the expiry of 10 years from the making of the insurance or, if earlier, three-quarters of the term for which the policy was to run if not ended by death or disability (no charges arises on the surrender of a 12-year policy after nine years). In the case of the other events, the question is simply whether those events have occurred within that same 10-year or three-quarter time-frame.[79] No charge arises for a qualifying policy simply because the death occurred within 10 years—dealing is also needed.

Tax at higher rates may be applied if the company's profits will not have been charged to UK tax.[80] Where a non-resident individual who owns a non-resident policy becomes resident in the UK, any tax charge arising, subsequently, on the non-resident policy will be limited, proportionally, to the period of UK residence.

When a charge arises, ITTOIA 2005, section 530 treats basic rate income tax as paid. ITA 2007, sections 152 and 153 deal with losses arising (ex Schedule D Case VI). According to the HMRC Notes on Clauses, schemes tried to 'create loss relief from offshore life insurance policies against offshore income gains'. This was stopped by FA 2009, section 69 amending ITA 2007, section 125(8), which directs that gains from polices, etc, whether foreign or not, will not be eligible for claiming income tax loss relief. Some parts apply from 2008–09 (section 69(3)).

---

[76] See HMRC Explanatory Notes to Finance Bill 2008, cl 33 and Schs 13 and 14.

[77] However, companies are able to defer realisations of assets over a long period—as their many investments in office buildings and shopping centres show.

[78] ITTOIA 2005, s 484, ex TA 1988, s 540(1)(a).

[79] ITTOIA 2005, s 485, ex TA 1988, s 540(1)(b).

[80] ITTOIA 2005, s 530, ex TA 1988, s 547(6) as amended; sometimes only the 20% charge applies (s 547(6A), added in 1995).

79.5.3.1 Chargeable Events[81]

The chargeable events are:

(1)   death giving rise to benefits under a life policy;[82]
(2)   maturity of the policy;[83]
(3)   total surrender[84] of the rights under the policy including bonus;[85] and
(4)   assignment of the rights for money or money's worth.[86] However, an assignment between spouses living together is ignored, as is an assignment by way of security for a debt or the discharge of a debt secured by the rights under the policy.[87]

Rules have been added to deal with rebated or reinvested commissions.[88]

79.5.3.2   Calculating the Charge by Calculating the Gain[89]

On death, the gain is the amount by which the surrender value immediately before the death,[90] plus what TA 1988 called the 'relevant capital payments' and ITTOIA 2005 calls 'compendiously total benefit value', such as bonuses, exceeds the total amount paid by way of premiums, plus any sums already treated as gains on some previous partial surrender or assignment.[91] These provisions are backed up by five further sections containing rules on valuing the policy, calculating the deductions, disregarding certain amounts, a special rule on qualifying endowment policies held as securities for a company's debts and—an ITTOIA 2005 innovation—a rule expressly disregarding trivial inducement benefits.[92] These basic rules also apply on maturity or surrender in whole, and on an outright assignment.[93]

Partial surrenders[94] and partial assignments are also chargeable events. Many modern policies allow partial surrenders at frequent intervals, and such surrenders gave rise to complex calculations. In an attempt to reduce the work involved, both for life offices and the

---

[81]   ITTOIA 2005, s 462 and 484, ex TA 1988, s 540(1); s 540(3), preserved by ITTOIA 2005, Sch 2, para 53, had a transitional exception for certain second-hand bonds issued before 1982. Liability in respect of such bonds may still arise (see s 544 and ITTOIA 2005, Sch 2, para 53).

[82]   ITTOIA 2005, s 484(1)(b).

[83]   Ex TA 1988, s 540(2) allowed a deferral of liability if a replacement policy was taken out, but this was repealed by FA 2003, s 173 and Sch 34, Pt 4. No chargeable event arises where a qualifying policy is substituted for a new non-resident policy (*ibid*, Sch 15, para 26).

[84]   On when events are treated as part surrender, see ITTOIA 2005, s 500, ex TA 1988, ss 539(4), 542(2) and 548(1). See Explanatory Note Change 100.

[85]   Payment of a bonus may be treated as a surrender (ITTOIA 2005, s 500, ex TA 1988, s 539(4)), as may loans (see below).

[86]   ITTOIA 2005, s 484(1)(a)(ii), ex TA 1988, s 540(1).

[87]   ITTOIA 2005, s 487, ex TA 1988, s 540(4).

[88]   ITTOIA 2005, ss 541A and 541B, ex TA 1988, ss 548A and 548B, added by FA 2007, s 29. Changes affect policies only where the premiums paid exceed £100,000 a year (there is a nice anti-fragmentation rule) and the policy is not held for at least three complete years. The rules are aimed at schemes described in the Revenue Notes.

[89]   See also ITTOIA 2005, s 476, ex TA 1988, s 553(3) for certain foreign policies.

[90]   ITTOIA 2005, s 493(7).

[91]   ITTOIA 2005, ss 491(1), 493(1), ex TA 1988, s 541(1)(a).

[92]   ITTOIA 2005, ss 492–497.

[93]   ITTOIA 2005, s 491(1)(a) refers to events within s 484(1)(a)(i)–(iii) and (b)–(e), so omitting only (a)(iv)–(vi), ie ITTOIA 2005, ss 509, 514 and 525(2).

[94]   Payment of a bonus may be treated as a surrender (ITTOIA 2005, s 539(4)); as may loans (see below).

Revenue, a different system of determining both whether there has been a gain and its extent applies.[95] At one time partial assignments were chargeable events only if for money or money's worth, but this was changed in 2001.[96]

The chargeable amount under TA 1988 was the excess of 'reckonable aggregate value', ie the sum of all the values of surrender and assignments not brought into account,[97] over 'allowable aggregate amount',[98] ie the sum of all appropriate portions of premiums paid.[99] The effect of these rules was to allow withdrawals of up to 5% of premiums paid without attracting any charge. This 5% drawdown was of great practical importance. In ITTOIA 2005 these rules are greatly spread out. They start with rules for events requiring periodic calculations, such as part surrender and assignments (including certain loans),[100] and then provide the relevant calculation rules.[101] These are followed by further rules for 'transaction-related' calculations; these calculations are required only if the first set of calculations produces a particular situation.[102]

79.5.3.3 Relief by Top-slicing

Individuals may claim top-slicing relief, a process which first requires the calculation of the slice of the gain, which is now called the 'annual equivalent' of the gain.[103] To do this the gain is spread back over a number of years by multiplying it by one over the number of complete years (a) on the first chargeable event—back to the start of the policy, (b) on any later chargeable event other than final termination—back to the previous chargeable event, (c) on final termination—the number of whole years from the start of the policy.[104]

The slice of the gain is then added to T's other income to discover the amount of extra tax payable by reason of its addition.[105] If the addition of that sum does not give rise to anything but tax at the basic rate, no tax is, usually, payable.[106] If, however, extra tax is payable, the amount of that tax is then calculated. The average of that tax rate is then ascertained, the basic rate deducted and the resulting rate applied to the whole gain.[107] Although a policy gain is not liable to basic rate income tax, the amount is part of total income and so may restrict the amount of age relief.

When a chargeable event occurs through death or maturity and there is a loss or, as the statute has it, a deficiency, an individual may deduct that loss from total income so far as it does not exceed gains taxed in earlier partial surrenders or assignments;[108] this allows

---

[95] Inland Revenue Press Release, 10 December 1974, [1974] *Simon's Tax Intelligence* 518.

[96] ITTOIA 2005, s 507(4), Step 1(b), ex TA 1988, s 546(1)(a)(ii).

[97] Ex TA 1988, s 546(2).

[98] Ex TA 1988, s 540(1)(a)(v).

[99] Ex TA 1988, s 546(3).

[100] ITTOIA 2005, ss 498–506.

[101] ITTOIA 2005, ss 507–509.

[102] ITTOIA 2005, ss 510–514; the situation is defined in s 510(1).

[103] ITTOIA 2005, ss 535–537, ex TA 1988, s 550. This relief is not affected by the abolition of the general top-slicing relief in *ibid*, Sch 2 by FA 1988, s 75.

[104] ITTOIA 2005, s 463(1) (Step 1).

[105] *Ibid*, Steps 2 and 3.

[106] ITTOIA 2005, s 530. However, if the effect is to increase total income and so cause the withdrawal of age relief, some liability may arise.

[107] Ex TA 1988, s 541(1).

[108] ITTOIA 2005, ss 539–541, ex TA 1988, s 549.

the tax on gains made earlier to be recovered. The relief does not apply to losses on assignments, neither does it make any allowance for inflation. It applies only to the extent of any 'excess' or 'extra' liability.

Basic rate tax is payable in certain situations to do with certain foreign policies or policies issued by friendly societies in connection with tax-exempt business.[109] The foreign policy rules are subject to special reliefs for EEA insurers where a comparable EEA tax charge has been levied, and to another rule for a more general foreign tax relief.[110] Further rules apply to multiple interests.[111]

Example

It will be seen that T's liability is tied to that of the year of the chargeable event. Thus, if T is able to delay the surrender until a period of low income, such as retirement, the charge may be avoided altogether. Suppose T has a non-qualifying policy which has run for 12 years and a gain of £12,000; the slicing rule will take one-twelfth as the right slice (£1,000). If T is more than £1,000 below the higher rate threshold, there will be no charge under these rules. If T is already paying tax at 40%, then 20% of the £1,000 will be taxed and the same proportion applied to the remaining £11,000, making a total of £2,160. If T is just £500 below the higher rate threshold, so that £500 will be taxed at 20%, the tax on the £1,000 slice will be £100 and the total tax £1,200.

79.5.3.4 Trusts, Estates and Companies

Where a chargeable event happens in relation to an individual but the policy is held by trustees, the trustees may be liable for the tax in certain prescribed situations,[112] although there is an indemnity against the trustees.[113] These rules are supplemented by others where the trustees are not resident.[114]

Where X, the individual, dies, X's personal representatives will not usually be liable to tax since they do not pay tax at the higher rates.[115] Special rules therefore apply where the gain would have been liable to basic rate tax.[116]

There were also rules for gains accruing to companies, which were repealed in 2008 when life insurance contracts were brought into the loan relationship rules.[117] For policies issued to a company, close or otherwise, after 13 March 1989, or existing policies which were varied or extended after that date, the entire gain, ie the excess of the surrender value of the policy over premiums paid, was treated as taxable under Schedule D, Case VI.[118] A company was similarly liable in respect of a policy which secured a debt owed by the company, as

---

[109] ITTOIA 2005, s 531.
[110] ITTOIA 2005, ss 533 and 534.
[111] ITTOIA 2005, ss 469–472, ex TA 1988, s 547A, added in 1998.
[112] ITTOIA 2005, s 467, ex TA 1988, s 547(1)(a).
[113] ITTOIA 2005, s 530 (indemnity), ex TA 1988, s 551 (indemnity).
[114] ITTOIA 2005, s 468.
[115] ITTOIA 2005, s 467(4).
[116] ITTOIA 2005, s 467.
[117] Ex TA 1988, s 547(1)(b).
[118] Ex TA 1988, s 541(4A)–(4B) added in 1989 and repealed by FA 2008.

well as a policy settled by the company on trust. Special rules applied to the calculation of a policy gain where the policy secures a debt.

79.5.3.5 Loans as Surrenders

If money were able to be withdrawn in the form of loans instead of by the normal surrender of policy rights, these rules might be frustrated. It is therefore provided that loans are in general equivalent to a surrender of rights.[119] There are exceptions, eg for interest payable at a commercial rate or when the loan is for a qualifying purpose such as to provide a life annuity and the interest qualifies for relief under TA 1988, section 365 (not yet rewritten).[120] Any repayment of the loan is treated as a premium.[121] This counters the common, borrow-all arrangement under which T, the policyholder, paid the first few premiums out of his own resources and then borrowed from the insurance company—at interest—to pay subsequent premiums.

79.5.3.6 Life Annuity Contracts and Guaranteed Income Bonds

The rules prescribing excess liability on chargeable events in relation to endowment policies are adapted to the surrender of life annuity contracts.[122] Unfortunately, ITTOIA 2005 no longer deals with them in discrete sections but scatters them through the single code.[123] Sometimes a charge to basic rate income tax is made.[124]

Payments under a guaranteed income bond are treated as partial surrenders, except for the final one, which is treated as a total surrender.[125]

79.6   Personal Portfolio Bonds

Rules[126] were introduced to reverse the decision of the House of Lords in *IRC v Willoughby*.[127] In that case, the House of Lords held that a UK resident who had purchased a single premium personal portfolio bond at a time when he was a non-resident of the UK was not taxable on the income arising on the bond until its maturity. The rules reversing that result apply to the gain deemed to accrue on such bonds on an annual basis, save for the final year when the actual proceeds are used.[128] The rules adapt the life policy chargeable event rules described above.[129] These have been rewritten as primary legislation for income tax by ITTOIA 2005.[130]

---

[119] ITTOIA 2005, s 501.
[120] ITTOIA 2005, ss 502 and 503(2), ex TA 1988, s 548.
[121] ITTOIA 2005, 494(1)(c), ex TA 1988, s 548(1).
[122] By ITTOIA 2005, ss 484 *et seq*, TA 1988, ss 542–544.
[123] Eg ITTOA 2005, s 484(1)(d) and (e).
[124] ITTOIA 2005, s 531, ex TA 1988, s 547(6).
[125] ITTOIA 2005, ss 593 and 490, ex FA 1997, s 79(3).
[126] SI 1999/1029, made under ex TA 1988, s 553C. For useful guidance, see Redston (1999) 143 *Taxation* 114.
[127] [1997] STC 995.
[128] SI 1999/1029, reg 5.
[129] *Ibid*, reg 6.
[130] ITTOIA 2005, Pt 4, Ch 9, ss 475 and 515–526.

79.7   Friendly Societies

The products offered by friendly societies are broadly similar to those offered by other life assurance companies. However, friendly societies are usually exempt from corporation tax on the profits of certain life and annuity business, a fact which enables them to offer better rates of return. This advantage was reduced by an obligation to hold 50% of their assets in narrow-range securities as defined by the now superseded Trustee Investment Act 1961.

The conditions under which policies and contracts constitute exempt business of friendly societies have been the subject of frequent changes in recent years. Life policies and contracts issued after 30 April 1995 are exempt policies if the premiums or premiums payable in any 12-month period do not exceed £270.[131] Annuity contracts are exempt if the annual sum payable does not exceed £156. Surrenders of policies may be chargeable events.[132] A friendly society is taxed as a mutual life assurance company in respect of its taxable insurance business, ie insurance business which is not tax-exempt under TA 1988, section 461.[133] A change to the definition of life or endowment business made by FA 2007 was found to have unintended effects for friendly societies and was therefore reversed retrospectively by FA 2008. FA 2008 also modified the rules on transfer between friendly societies.[134]

79.8   Insurance Companies

Although the taxation of insurance companies is far too detailed a topic for this book, three points are of general interest. The first is that for many years the fundamental principles underlying the liability to tax of insurance companies were unsettled and uncertain. The second point is that the life assurance business must be separate from other (general) business. The third point is that there were broadly two ways in which insurance companies were taxed—under the Schedule D, Case I trading principles,[135] or on the basis of income as computed under the various Schedules plus capital gains,[136] minus allowed expenses[137] (the I–E). Until 2007 the choice between the two lay with the Revenue, which generally preferred I–E. The Schedule D, Case I rules included provisions for the deduction of reserves and matching receipts when the reserves were drawn down.[138] The investment income and capital gains must have been allocated between two classes of business: (a) basic life and general annuity business; and (b) pension business. There were further rules for foreign

---

[131] FA 1995, s 54, Sch 10. Lower figures applied to earlier years; see also TA 1988, s 460(2) (not rewritten).

[132] Ex TA 1988, s 539(3), now dealt with under the loan relationship rules.

[133] TA 1988, s 463(1). Regulations modify the way in which the legislation on life assurance taxation, in TA 1988, Pt XII, is applied: Friendly Societies (Modification of the Corporation Tax Acts) Regulations 1992 (SI 1992/1655).

[134] FA 2008, s 44.

[135] *Sun Life Assurance Company of Canada (UK) Ltd v Revenue & Customs Commissioners* [2010] STC 1173, [2010] EWCA Civ 394 is a case on the application of trading loss rules in TA 1988 s 393 to insurance companies—and on FA 1989, s 89.

[136] See TCGA 1992, ss 212 (as amended in 1993) and 213.

[137] TA 1988, s 76 (not rewritten); FA 1989, s 86.

[138] See TA 1988, ss 82, 83, 83AA, 83AB, added in 1996. See also *Prudential Assurance Co v Bibby* (1999) STC 952.

business.[139] The rules on management expenses were modernised by FA 2004. A company with insurance business and other investment management business may find itself using TA 1988, section 76 for its insurance business and CTA 2009, section 1218 (ex TA 1988, section 75) for its other business. Nearly every year we now have statutes continuing the ongoing process of revising insurance company taxation in consultation with the industry.

79.9   Offshore Income Gains

As with insurance, the taxation of offshore funds is a difficult, technical subject and what follows is merely a brief introduction. Various entities or funds may be formed offshore (ie outside the UK) with which an investor, T, may place money. Since these are not resident in the UK they are not subject to UK tax. Since they are not controlled from the UK they cannot be swept into the CFC legislation (and in any case often take the form of a trust rather than a company). Since T not only provides the funds but also expects to realise all the profits and gains in due course, there is no scope for those settlement provisions aimed at diversion of income or gains. So why is the tax system bothered?

The system is concerned, first, because the offshore entity, being outside the UK, will not be subject to UK tax and will often be located in a territory where it pays no tax at all; this will enable the funds to grow faster than if placed an equivalent UK-based entity.[140] The second concern is that the fund will 'roll up' the income it receives every year, leaving T with a single payment at the end. Although T will suffer from being kept out of the money because of its time value, T will usually gain, because what is eventually received will be capital and not income. Since 1984, when the offshore fund rules were first introduced, the consequence of this has been greatly reduced—but not eliminated. Investors are subject to tax under ITTOIA 2005, Part 5, Chapter 8 (income tax) or CTA 2009, Part 10, Chapter 8 (corporation tax). The relevant rules for determining the tax on returns to UK-resident investors holding interests in offshore funds are now found principally in the Offshore Funds (Tax) Regulations 2009.[141] Interested readers are also directed to the relevant HMRC manual.[142]

79.10   Real Estate Investment Trusts

CTA 2010, Part 12, sections 518–609[143] allow qualifying companies or groups of companies to give notice under sections 523 and 524 that they wish to be treated under the real estate

---

[139] TA 1988, s 442.

[140] If it takes the form of an insurance policy the gain may be taxed under TA 1988, s 540 as a non-qualifying policy.

[141] SI 2009/3001 as amended by SI 2011/1211, ex TA 1988, ss 757–764, Schs 27, 28, originally FA 1984, ss 92–100.

[142] HMRC Offshore Funds Manual, available at http://www.hmrc.gov.uk/manuals/ofmanual/Index.htm.

[143] Ex FA 2006, Pt 4, ss 103–145.

investment trust (REIT) regime. The legislation results from a long period of consultation; what follows is a brief overview of the key elements.

The REIT regime seeks to avoid problems of economic double taxation for companies which invest in properties as sources of rental income as opposed to development. The company is exempt from corporation tax on its property rental business profits (section 534). A separate rule (section 535) exempts some or all of the gain arising from the disposal of an asset used, which has been used for the purpose of the property rental business. The assets within the REIT are ring-fenced and rules apply to assets moving over the fence, whether moving outwards (sections 555–556), inwards (section 557) or on a demerger (section 558). When the profits are distributed to the shareholders, the burden of tax falls on them under CTA 2009, Part 4 or ITTOIA 2005, Part 3 (sections 548–549). The dividends are paid under deduction of basic rate income tax of 20% (ITA 2007, sections 973 and 974 is now the regulation-making power).

There are many conditions; the main ones are described next. First, the company must carry on a property rental business (sections 518–519); the property may be in the UK or abroad. Certain businesses, eg lettings incidental to a development business, and certain types of income, eg rent from siting a wind turbine, are excluded. Further conditions apply (sections 527–531) to make sure the company has the right balance of business. Thus, the property rental business must involve at least three properties, and no single property may represent more than 40% of the total value of properties involved (section 529). There is also a distribution requirement; normally at least 90% of the profits must be distributed by the normal tax filing date of the company (usually 12 months from the end of the accounting period, section 530). Profits of the property rental business must be at least 75% of the aggregate profits of the group or company (section 531). It will be clear from this that a company may qualify for the REITs regime even though only a part of its income is tax exempt; profits arising from the residual business are subject to corporation tax in the usual way (section 534). The company—in the case of a group, the parent company—must be UK-resident for tax purposes, it must not be an OEIC, its shares must be listed on a recognised stock exchange, it must not be a close company and it must have a relatively simple share structure (section 528).

Section 541 ring-fences the tax-exempt business so that all its profits, losses and gains are separate from those of the other parts of its activities. Section 542 provides that the REIT is subject to the transfer-pricing rules in TIOPA 2010, Part 4, even though it is technically a small or medium-sized company. Two further restrictions should be borne in mind. First, no one investor may be beneficially entitled to 10% or more of distributions, or control directly or indirectly 10% or more of the share capital or voting rights (section 553). Secondly, the ratio of interest on loans to fund the tax-exempt business to rental income of that business must be less than 1.25:1 (section 543). This is to stop the company borrowing money which effectively gives the lender a share of the profits.

Section 545 contains a mini GAAR and gives HMRC the power to cancel a tax advantage, collecting tax to counteract that advantage. Section 546 outlines the appeal process against such counteraction. There is also an interesting anti-avoidance rule (section 582), designed to stop a company engineering its own departure from the regime, eg because it is facing a significant loss in the tax-exempt business which is only tax-effective if the company leaves the group. Section 582 enables HMRC to trap the loss by changing the normal cessation date.

The company may elect to end the treatment under this regime (section 571); section 570 also lists other terminating events, eg automatically for breach of the conditions (section 578) or notice by HMRC (sections 573–577); on effects of termination, see sections 579–582. There is a very interesting HMRC power (sections 561–569) to overlook minor or inadvertent breaches; this may involve some payment of tax as opposed to termination.

The rules for groups of companies are set out in sections 601 and 606.

79.11   Authorised Investment Funds

The Financial Services Authority introduced a regime for Regulations made in 2008 which apply where authorised investment funds (AIFs) invest in REITs and related securities. Building on the REIT model, these may elect to have a property AIF regime, under which the tax point is moved from the fund to the investor.[144]

Although Property Authorised Investment Funds (PAIFs) are subject to tax treatment in some ways similar to REITs, the tax treatment in other ways is quite different. Readers are referred to the relevant HMRC manual (CTM48811) for more information on PAIFs.

---

[144] HMRC BN 34, March 2008.

80

Pensions

80.1   Introduction

80.1.1   General[1]

A key government choice, made in 1980 and only recently reversed, was to increase the basic state retirement pension in line with inflation and not, as previously, in line with average earnings. This provided a major saving to the Treasury, and even more encouragement for people (and their employers) to take out private (and expensive) arrangements, eg with insurance companies. The result was a bonanza for pension advisers, who received commission income, and, for those running the schemes, huge bonuses paid in real money out of paper gains. The stock market declines of 2000 combined with drops in the interest rates

---

[1] There is much background literature on this topic, eg the papers from the British Association Economics Section printed in (2005) 26 *Fiscal Studies* 1–134, Pensions Commission, *Pensions: Challenges and Choices. The First Report of the Pensions Commission* (2004), an independent body established by the Government following the Pensions Green Paper of December 2002, the practical Reardon, *Zurich Pensions Handbook,* 9th edn (Pearson, 2004), and a major study for the World Bank—Mitchell, *Trends in Retirement Systems and Lessons for Reform* (World Bank, 1993). The Report of the Committee on the Taxation Treatment of Provisions for Retirement, Cmnd 9063 (1954) tells the story to 1954 and contains many proposals for reform, most of which were later implemented. Among broader books there is much of value and interest in Davis, *Pension Funds* (OUP, 1995) and Dilnot, Disney, Johnson and Whitehouse, *Pension Policy in the UK* (Institute for Fiscal Studies, 1994).

and so in annuity values coincided with the start of tougher accounting valuations, which for the first time made some companies fully realise what they had undertaken to provide for their employees in the shape of terminal salary schemes.

Companies decided to close their terminal salary schemes to new employees and, in some cases, even for existing employees for future years of employment. This led to a pensions crisis which was as much as anything a crisis of confidence; this in turn led to very cautious investment policies, which in turn missed out on the subsequent rise in stock market values. Subsequent legislation to provide some degree of protection through the Pension Protection Fund is controversial since it is unclear whether the protection will be sufficient.[2] What was bad enough for those companies which had not made full and proper provision for their liabilities was writ large for government, which ultimately ran away from trying to change the public sector schemes from a final salary scheme to a lifetime average salary scheme. The balance sheets of many governments around the world will look very bad if properly-valued pension liabilities are taken into account; fools' paradises are rarely comfortable places in which to live. When healthcare costs are also taken into account, the figures can look even worse.[3]

Behind this lies the problem of the dependency ratio, ie the ratio between those in work and those in retirement. It has been calculated that, as a result of changes in the birth rate and the increased life expectancy of those now coming up to pensionable age, by the year 2035 each pensioner will be supported by only 1.6 persons in employment as against 2.3 persons in 1985.[4] The practical solution to this problem is seen as extending the working life or by increasing contributions. It actually involves more fundamental matters, such as inter-generational equity and what one might in quasi-socialist periods have called a 'duty to work'. Those who regard the obligation to work as fundamental to a social welfare system, such as the UK tax credits system described in chapter nine, will presumably accept that entitlement to pensions may also be tied to an obligation to work longer—and to have a proper reduction in pension benefits for those who retire early. The different pattern of pension entitlement is regarded as the main reason why by the age of 69 virtually no men are working in Belgium, whereas in Japan almost 50% of men are still in the labour force.[5] There is, however, also an even more basic economic point here. As argued by Eatwell, there have to be enough people to whom the generation in retirement can sell the financial rights and assets (stocks and shares) in return for the annuities on which they need to live.[6] This takes us back to the question whether the tax system should do more to encourage the relevant generation to have more children.

Few areas provide better examples of the problems of tax policy than pensions. Having decided that pension provision was a good thing and that tax advantages should be provided to encourage it, the UK legislature proceed to pile rule upon rule—and to widen existing rules. Change had to come, and so FA 2004 introduced new rules, which replaced all the old rules with one basic set and came into force on 1 April 2006 (below §80.9).

---

[2] Besely and Prat (2005) 26 *Fiscal Studies* 119, 130.
[3] Wise (2005) 26 *Fiscal Studies* 5.
[4] The same applies to the basic retirement pension.
[5] Wise (2005) 26 *Fiscal Studies* 5, 21; the different pattern in Denmark is attributed by Sefton, Van de ven and Weale (2005) 26 *Fiscal Studies* 83 *et seq* to strong government policies in favour of work.
[6] See http://www.cerf.cam.ac.uk/publications.

Amendments have been made each year since, with particularly significant changes made in FA 2011.

The legislation governing the tax treatment of pension income is found primarily in ITEPA 2003, Part 9. ITEPA 2003 provides one single chapter, Chapter 5A, on the taxation of benefits (below §80.2). Chapter 15A exempts certain lump sums. Other exemptions are to be found in Chapters 17 (any taxpayer) and 18 (non-residents).

80.1.2 Privileges and Patterns

Employees, with or without financial assistance from their employer, are encouraged to set money aside for retirement. Sums set aside under a scheme approved by HMRC will not be treated as income for the year in which they are so set aside, and the fund in which the money is saved will usually be allowed to accumulate free of tax. In return for these privileges,[7] savers are taxed on their eventual pensions; income is spread forward to retirement years. This pattern of exemption for the sums saved and exemption for the income in the fund in return for eventual taxability of the pension (often reduced to 'EET'), may also be seen in some other countries. However, the UK has not had a pure EET since 1997, when pension funds lost the right to claim repayment of the tax credit on dividends.

A pension is a provision for old age, and therefore its provision is one of the prime functions of life assurance. Indeed, until 1916 there were no special rules concerning pensions as distinct from life assurance, and premiums under life assurance policies were deductible. However, in 1916[8] the relief for life assurance policies was restricted, even for policies already in force, to a deduction for income tax only (and not what shortly after became surtax) and to those premiums that secured the payment of a capital sum on death. The full relief was, however, still made available to certain superannuation and bona fide pension schemes for employees and the self-employed, even though commenced after 1916. Superannuation funds were made exempt in 1921.[9] Following the Report of the Committee on the Taxation Treatment of Provisions for Retirement (Cmnd 9063 (1954)—the Tucker Report) further changes were made; in particular, provision was made for the self-employed, who were allowed complete deduction for premiums paid to secure a retirement annuity (see below at §80.6).[10] The more limited life assurance relief was abolished, but not for existing policies, in 1984. Life assurances had the attraction that one might buy an annuity with the proceeds and take advantage of ITTOIA 2005, Part 6, Chapter 7 (ex TA 1988, section 656); however, the attractions of this were reduced in a time of high inflation. For the self-employed an alternative is a life consultancy, although here not only do the payments have to be justified in order to be deductible for tax by the payer, but no protection is provided for dependants.

As seen above, reform has continued through to the new millennium and beyond.[11] Responsibility for providing for the cost of living in old age is a major political and

---

[7] On whether these incentives actually cost the government money, see Ruggeri and Fougere (1997) 18 *Fiscal Studies* 143.

[8] FA 1916, s 36; the special rules for pre-1916 policies were repealed in 1976.

[9] FA 1921, s 32.

[10] FA 1956, s 22; TA 1970, s 226.

[11] See also Disney and Emmerson (2005) 26 *Fiscal Studies* 55, 63 listing a number of apparently minor changes.

economic issue in our society.[12] Long ago it could be regarded as a private matter (not least because life expectancy was so low). Those wanting to make that provision might take out a life assurance policy. An entrepreneur would build up a business and then sell it to provide the necessary funds. A partner in a firm of solicitors would not retire but carried on (and on), worked as a consultant or sold his (almost invariably his) share of the firm to an incoming partner. For those fortunate enough to have family wealth behind them there was the possibility of having an annuity from the family settlement. War, inflation, taxation, social change and market forces have swept away some of these ways of providing for old age, but the need is still there. The cost of meeting that need is exacerbated by greater life expectancy and by a reluctance to index-link the retirement age to that expectancy. As the state realises the cost of providing for people in old age, it is very anxious to encourage thrift—and then to penalise the rewards of thrift by taking money away for residential care in old age. The role of taxation in this has been twofold. First, very high rates of tax, especially income tax and estate duty, made some of these sources of support unreliable; the chances of saving much from earned income (with rates up to 83%) were remote, while the destruction of the family trust may be attributed to a combination of income tax and estate duty. Secondly, the granting of reliefs from tax for certain types of support, beginning with life assurance relief in 1799, meant that funds were channelled into tax-favoured forms of provision rather than other forms. The story of these reliefs has been one of change—and not always in one direction. In recent years the changes have been in the direction of choice, flexibility and, most recently, restricting tax relief. Despite this, the non-approved pension scheme (which attracts no special tax subsidies) is still a standard part of the remuneration package for very important people in the private sector.

For the majority of the people in the UK these options were not at first available. The state was looked to, to provide support through the system of National Insurance. In the UK the state provides a basic retirement pension. Employees qualify through payments of Class I NICs charged on employer and employee, although the pension is related to the number of years of contribution; the self-employed qualify by paying Class 2 NICs at present, and from paying the contributory element of Class 4 contributory NICS from April 2018. The basic state pension is below the poverty line. Those who retire and have no other source of income rely on the state for supplementary, income-related (ie means-tested) benefits.

It is in the interests of both the individuals and the state that people should save for retirement. Employees were at one time covered by the State Earnings Related Pension Scheme (SERPS) unless an approved employment-related pension scheme or private pension plan was taken out.[13] SERPS was regarded as still the scheme of last resort, and the state not only provided subsidies to persuade people to take out private cover instead but also reduced the value of the benefits to be provided.[14] An additional state pension, or state second pension (S2P),[15] superseded SERPS in 2002, but only for future years, so that anyone retiring between 2002 and 2050 may well have rights under both schemes. These were aimed primarily at low and moderate earners. Like SERPS, the S2P was not available

---

[12] On pensioners' (financial) behaviour, see Symposium (1998) 19 *Fiscal Studies* 141.
[13] Introduced by Social Security Act 1975; from 1961 to 1975 there was also a graduated pension scheme.
[14] Reardon, *op cit*, §11.5.
[15] Introduced by Child Support, Pensions and Social Security Act 2002; see Disney and Emmerson, (2005) 26 *Fiscal Studies* 55.

to the self-employed. The state charged a rebate or lower (contracted-out) rate of NICs when the employee had contracted out of S2P.[16] As company schemes began to fold or close, some experts even advised their people to return to the state system, but without offering to reimburse all the commissions they had earned in the meantime. Both the S2P and contracting out ended when the new flat-rate, single-tier state pension came into force after 6 April 2016.

80.1.3 Types of Provision

There are two major types of pension provision—the terminal salary scheme (TSS) sometimes called 'defined benefit' (DB), and the money purchase scheme (MPS), sometimes called 'defined contribution' (DC).[17] These govern the size of the pot available for deployment on retirement, but in different ways. The TSS is tied to the value of the final salary (measured in various ways over various periods) and the maximum contributions are geared to the sums needed to meet this target. The MPS provides no limit on the pot available on retirement but has a ceiling on the amount which may be contributed each year. In the UK, until relatively recently, many occupational pension schemes were examples of the TSS, while personal pensions schemes and retirement annuities are examples of the MPS.

From a labour economist's point of view, there may be important differences between these two schemes. TSS (or DB) may

> sort stayers from quitters and help match stayers to long-tenure firms ... strengthen worker-attachment firms, enabling investments of firm-specific skills ... reward, through pay-back loading, high achievers at zero cost to the firm.[18]

The disadvantages include the need to provide long-term contracts and the requirement of a normal retirement age. There are also advantages and disadvantages for the employee, and general economic issues. Thus, does the investment policy of a defined benefit scheme become unnecessarily conservative? Given the great weight of money in these funds, what are the effects of rules which favour investment in equities rather than bonds, or vice versa, and what would be the consequences for capital markets of changing them?[19]

80.1.4 Types of Benefit

80.1.4.1 Annuities and Lump Sums Versus Annuities

The typical benefit payable is an annuity, which is to last for the life of the assured but may be for the life of that person and another (eg a surviving spouse). Under a TSS, the amount of the annuity is fixed by reference to the terminal salary retirement age; under a MPS, the annuity is fixed by the annuity rates prevailing at the relevant time. The present low interest rate environment has greatly reduced the payout levels and attractiveness of annuities, spurring recent moves to give retirees more flexibility over their pension pots.

---

[16] Set by the Government Actuary.
[17] FA 2004, s 164 *et seq* and Sch 28.
[18] See Davis, *op cit*, ch 10.
[19] See, generally, Davis, *op cit*, ch 10.

80.1.4.2 Flexible Annuities

An additional type of personal pension scheme was introduced in FA 1995, which gave members the right to elect to defer the purchase of an annuity and to take income withdrawals from their pension fund in the meantime. This was achieved by means of the alternatively secured pension (or 'ASP'), or withdrawal from the 'alternatively secured fund.[20] Under the general 'pension freedom' rule changes from 6 April 2015, it is now possible for those aged 55 or over to withdraw up to their entire pension fund in cash rather than as an annuity. The first 25% is tax-free, with the rest added to the taxpayer's income and thus taxed at his or her highest marginal tax rate. As a result, it will often be more tax efficient (and also more prudent) to spread the withdrawal over a number of years.

80.2 Approved Retirement Benefit Schemes

The major influence on the development of approved retirement benefit schemes has been the Civil Service model; basically, no one should get a better deal than civil servants.[21] This, perhaps cynical, view ignores the major influence the Civil Service model has had in improving levels of pension provision, especially since railway companies and other large commercial concerns of the 19th century used that model for their own schemes.

80.2.1 Types of Scheme

Today schemes are governed by the rules in FA 2004, sections 149–284 (not rewritten) and secondary legislation. For earlier schemes, see the 5th edition of *Revenue Law*.

80.2.2 Taxation of Pensions

ITEPA 2003, section 570 states that the word 'pension' includes a pension which is paid voluntarily or is capable of being discontinued. The charge is on the full amount accruing during the year; the liability is on the person receiving or entitled to the pension.[22] FA 2004 does not rewrite this part of ITEPA 2003. The rules in Chapter 3 and 4 apply only if one of the more specific sets of rules later in the chapter do not. As from 2006, payments under all registered pension schemes are governed by ITEPA 2003, Part 9, Chapter 5A.

The term 'pension' has not been defined by statute or judicially; indeed, judges have refused to attempt such a definition. In *McMann v Shaw*,[23] a series of payments was held to be compensation for loss of office as opposed to a pension, the deciding factor being that they were not payments for services past or present—they were in fact payments to the former Borough Treasurer of Southall whose position was abolished under the London

---

[20] FA 2004, s 165, rr 6–7 and Sch 28, paras 5, 7, 11 and 12.

[21] When the 'old code' of approval was brought in by FA 1921, the Revenue, in exercising their discretionary power to approve schemes, looked to the rules of the state schemes in deciding what might be accepted: hence, such rules as the maximum pension payable being 40/60ths of final salary became part of the code.

[22] ITEPA 2003, ss 571 and 572.

[23] [1972] 3 All ER 732, (1972) 48 TC 330.

Government reorganisation in 1963, and the payments were made from the time the employee became redundant until he became entitled to a pension in respect of his previous service. In *Johnson v Holleran*,[24] it was held that retirement was not an essential condition for certain payments to be a pension, but that the former employment must have ceased. In *HMRC v Barclays Bank*,[25] the Bank had provided various services tax free to some of its pensioners. The Bank withdrew the concession and compensated the pensioners for their loss; the compensation payments were held to be relevant benefits and so chargeable under TA 1988, section 596A(1).

If the pension is payable under the rules of an approved scheme, whether or not an exempt approved scheme, it is charged to tax under ITEPA 2003, Part 9, Chapter 3 and so under PAYE.[26] Foreign pensions are chargeable under ITEPA 2003, Part 9, Chapter 4;[27] today, the chargeable amount is reduced by 10%; at one time the remittance basis applied.

80.2.2.1 Tax—Free Lump Sums

Under the Civil Service superannuation arrangements introduced in 1973, the lump sum gratuity which had previously been discretionary was made payable as of right, and it was thought desirable to declare that lump sums payable on retirement were not taxable, whether or not payable as of right.[28] In this way the lump sum was assimilated to the proceeds of a life assurance policy.

80.2.2.2 Restrictions

Tax-free status does not apply to an unjustified payment of compensation for early retirement unless due to ill-health; such a payment falls within ITEPA 2003, section 401.[29] Neither does it apply to unauthorised payments from a fund, or to payments after the cessation of tax exemptions.[30] The scheme in question must be an approved scheme, a statutory scheme or a foreign government scheme; or a funded, unapproved retirement benefits scheme where the lump sum is attributable to employer contributions to the scheme on which the employee has been charged to tax.[31] The sum may not exceed 3/80ths of final salary for each year of service up to 40.

80.2.2.3 Other Lump Sum Tax Rules

If consideration is received for a restrictive covenant given in connection with an office or employment, past, present or future, there may be liability under ITEPA 2003, section 225. Sums payable for termination of the office may be chargeable under section 401 to the extent that they exceed £30,000. An ex-gratia lump sum payment given on retirement will now be regarded as a benefit provided by an unfunded, unapproved pension scheme and

---

[24] [1989] STC 1, (1989) 61 TC 428.

[25] [2006] EWHC 2118 (Ch), [2007] STC 74, considering the meaning of a relevant benefit for the purposes of TA 1988, ss 596A and 612.

[26] ITEPA 2003, s 683(3), ex TA 1988, s 597(1).

[27] ITEPA 2003, s 575(2), as amended by ITTOIA 2005, ex TA 1988, s 65(2).

[28] Ex TA 1988, s 189, rewritten as ITEPA 2003, Pt 9, Ch 16 and superseded by Ch 15A.

[29] Ex TA 1988, s 189(2) and Sch 11, para 4. A payment is justified if it is properly regarded as a benefit earned by past service.

[30] Ex TA 1988, s 600.

[31] Ex TA 1988, ss 189, 595, 596A(8).

so be taxable in full.[32] Concessionary relief is given for lump sums paid by overseas pension schemes.[33]

80.2.3 *Correction of Surpluses*

In his review of pensions, Nigel Lawson decided to act against those funds which had sums of money beyond what was needed to meet future obligations. The precise position depended on the method of actuarial valuation, which was consistently followed. TA 1988, sections 601–603 and Schedule 22 addressed pension scheme surpluses. They applied only to exempt approved schemes. Many of the substantive rules were contained in supporting regulations dealing with valuation and administration respectively.[34] It is arguable that these rules were almost as damaging to pension schemes as former Chancellor Gordon Brown's decision to remove the repayment of tax credits on dividends in 1997. They do not survive FA 2004; for further details, see the 5th edition of *Revenue Law*.

80.3   Additional Voluntary Contributions

Before 2006 many employees used the additional voluntary contributions (AVCs) scheme.[35] Although the maximum contribution to an exempt approved scheme for which an employee may make and obtain deduction is normally limited to 15% of annual remuneration, very few schemes have this level of funding. Moreover, although qualifying remuneration has been capped since 1989–90, most employees are still below this cap. This is now absorbed into the general scheme in FA 2004, which came into force in 2006. For further details, see the 5th edition of *Revenue Law*.

80.4   Simplified Occupational Schemes

Simplified occupational schemes have now been absorbed into the general scheme in FA 2004, which came into force in 2006. For details, see the 5th edition of *Revenue Law*.

80.5   Approved Personal Pensions

Approved personal pensions have now been absorbed into the general scheme in FA 2004, which came into force in 2006. For details, see the 5th edition of *Revenue Law*.

---

[32] Exceptions are made for redundancy and compensation for loss of office, including the case of forced voluntary resignation, unless the employee does not belong to an approved scheme (see Statement of Practice SP 13/91); in such a case a lump sum ex-gratia payment may be made on retirement, but subject to normal Revenue limits and subject to a *de minimis* limit for which prior approval is not required.

[33] ESC A10.

[34] Pension Scheme Surpluses (Valuation) Regulations 1987 (SI 1987/412); and Pension Scheme Surpluses (Administration) Regulations 1987 (SI 1987/352).

[35] Social Security Act 1986, s 12 made it mandatory for members of exempt approved schemes to be given this opportunity as of right.

80.6 Retirement Annuity Contracts

As from 2006, these ceased to exist as a separate category.[36] For details see the 5th edition of *Revenue Law*. This scheme was frozen in 1988;[37] no new schemes were permitted. Originally proposed by the Millard Tucker Committee Report.[38]

80.7 Flexible Annuities—Income Drawdown

The idea of income drawdown is important in retirement planning; the individual may draw down some of the income while leaving the capital in the fund untouched and not having to turn that sum into an annuity. For pre-FA 2004 rules, see the 5th edition of *Revenue Law*.

80.8 Stakeholder Pensions

Another important part of the story of pensions is the stakeholder pension scheme; this cut the link between pension provision and relevant earnings. As paragraph 4 of the Revenue Notes to the Finance Bill 2000 proudly states: 'The changes mean that for the first time non-earners can contribute to a pension. This opens up pension savings to groups such as carers and parents taking career breaks to bring up children.' This is built on the importance of saving regularly and over a long period to build up a really significant fund. Indeed one wonders whether these people were really the object of the Chancellor's concern rather than the lower-paid. It was also intended that stakeholder pensions should have low administration costs and be open to a wider range of pension provider.

During the passage of the Finance Bill 2000, a late amendment allowed stakeholder pensions to be used by most but not all employees who were already in an occupational pension scheme, ie to contribute to the stakeholder scheme in addition to their existing scheme.[39] For details, see the 5th edition of *Revenue Law*.

80.9 FA 2004, Part 4 Rules

From 6 April 2006 (known as 'A day'), the general tax rules on pensions changed dramatically. As from that date, there has been one set of, at times necessarily complex, rules instead of the eight or nine previously in force. What follows is an outline of the key features of the legislation. FA 2011 made some important changes to the FA 2004 rules, as discussed below.

---

[36] FA 2004, Sch 24, Pt 3.
[37] For transitional rules, see TA 1988, s 618. On interaction, see *ibid*, s 655(1) and Revenue Interpretation RI 76, ss 4.10–4.13; see also Tiley and Collison, *UK Tax Guide 1998–1999* (Butterworths, 1998) paras 30.33 *et seq*.
[38] Report of the Committee on the Taxation Treatment of Provisions for Retirement, Cmnd 9063 (1954), ch 6.
[39] TA 1988, s 632B.

80.9.1 Introduction

As can now be seen, the pension scheme rules had become so numerous and expansive that the whole structure was about to collapse under its own weight. Another report, a set of proposals and finally legislation—FA 2004—followed. One of the main attractions for the FA 2004 regime was that once it was in force, on 6 April 2006, all rights under existing schemes could be transferred across. This regime, as initially drafted, was generous, but it represented a new beginning. FA 2004 has been much amended by later Acts. These rules are not affected by the Rewrite and provide one example of income tax charges arising outside the three main income tax Acts.[40]

The objective was simplification. The FA 2004 rules apply uniformly to all personal pension arrangements. All schemes must be registered (Part 4, Chapter 2).

80.9.1.1 Benefits

There is flexibility of benefits (Part 4, Chapter 3). So all pensioners are entitled to take up to 25% of their fund as a tax-free lump sum. Personal pension schemes have always allowed pensioners to take up to 25% of the value of the fund as a lump sum (retirement annuities were more generous still at 33.3%). However, the maximum lump sum for members of occupational schemes was a multiple of their pension—this is what changed. As just noted, under the 'pension freedom' rule changes from 6 April 2015, it is now possible for those aged 55 or over to withdraw up to their entire defined contribution pension fund in cash rather than as an annuity. The first 25% is tax-free, with the rest added to the taxpayer's income and thus taxed at his or her highest marginal tax rate.

There is also a greater flexibility of benefits then there once was when one considers the transition from work to retirement. Under FA 2004, one may draw a pension and still work. Again, this change is primarily of benefit to the members of occupational schemes. It was a condition of retiring from an occupational schemes that one retired—ie did not work—hence all the litigation in *Venables v Hornby*.[41] The self-employed were under no such restriction, as they could draw down their personal pension scheme benefits as required.

80.9.1.2 Contributions—Limit 1 (Total Value)

Tax reliefs and rules about maximum contributions are contained in Part 4, Chapter 4. Employers may deduct contributions to a registered pension scheme. There is, however, flexibility regarding contributions: the 2004 rules restrict tax relief for contributions in just two ways (see also §80.9.1.3 below). First, there is a maximum lifetime contributions allowance: set initially at £1.5 million, it rose to £1.8 million in 2010, before it was cut back to £1.5 million again from 6 April 2012, £1.25 million from 6 April 2014 and £1 million from 6 April 2016 (for other years, see below at §80.9.6.3). This has caused some anguish for some people who would see themselves as moderately, rather than immoderately, well-off. It has to be said that the drop in interest rates and so the annuity rate means that £1 million generates a lower pension now than it would have done in 2000; this was one of the main reasons behind the 'pensions freedom' move in 2015, which allowed the over-55s to withdraw up to their entire pension fund as cash rather than purchase an annuity.

---

[40] See ITA 2007, s 3(2), referring to FA 2004, Pt 4, Ch 7.
[41] [2003] UKHL 65, [2004] STC 84.

The calculation of the lifetime limit for those on defined benefit salary-linked schemes uses a different formula, generally multiplying the first-year pension by 20; so a pension of £50,000 gives a value of £1 million (and is safe), while one of £80,000 gives a value of £1.6 million (and becomes overfunded). It is also the case that sums generated in private pension schemes, where the old limitations were on the annual percentages of relevant earnings contribution not the value of the fund, could have grown above this figure. One solution was to retire before the new rules came in—as many of Her Majesty's judges felt compelled to do but for special treatment—or take advantage of the limited transitional rules, see §80.9.10.

80.9.1.3 Contributions—Limit 2 (Annual)

Secondly, there is an annual restriction on amounts added to the fund—this used to be a percentage (the basis allowance being 25%) of annual earnings but is now a simple annual sum. Originally £215,000, the annual allowance rose to £255,000 for 2010–11 before being cut back to £50,000 from 6 April 2011 and then £40,000 from 6 April 2014. From 6 April 2016 if income excluding any pension contributions exceeds £110,000 the allowance is reduced by £1 for each £2 of 'adjusted' income (income plus pension contributions) between £150,000 and £210,000. The minimum allowance (for those earning £210,000 or more) is £10,000. Unused annual allowance from the previous three years may be carried forward if pension savings were made in those years. In considering whether this limit might be exceeded, it must be remembered that one can now put into the fund not only cash but also shares or land, the values of which may be matters of dispute.

80.9.1.4 Investments

The ability to put property into the fund was welcome news for wealthier savers with big pension funds and other sources of income, but it may prove dangerous for others. It must be appreciated that once the property is in the scheme, it must be treated as an investment asset like any other. So if a person puts a holiday home into the fund, there would have to be a charge at full market rent if it is occupied by the would-be pensioner and family. If a buy-to-let house is transferred, there will be CGT and stamp duty to pay, and then, as there is no taxable income, there will be no deduction for any interest either. Eventually rules were added restricting the powers of an investment-regulated pension scheme (defined in FA 2004, Schedule 29A, paragraphs 1–3) to acquire certain types of property, including residential property. A scheme acquiring such property is treated as making an unauthorised payment—and so is liable to a charge.[42] An occupational pension scheme is outside this embargo, whereas an individual member may not be.[43]

80.9.1.5 Charge

A tax charge arises (FA 2004, Part 4, Chapter 5) once the value of the fund (not of the contributions) passes the lifetime allowance. A tax charge of 25% is imposed (to remove the benefit of the tax exemption on the lifetime allowance). If money is taken out of the fund in an unauthorised way—paid back to the member to bring the value of the fund down—a

---

[42] FA 2004, s 174A and Sch 29A, added by FA 2006.
[43] See amendment by FA 2008, Sch 29, para 3.

55% charge is imposed to claw back the allowance. This may look severe, but there is nothing to stop the person adding further sums if the value of the fund drops below the lifetime allowance—and there will be further relief in that year.

80.9.2 Basic Concepts and Overview

FA 2004, Part 4, Chapter 1 (sections 149–152) defines basic concepts; Chapter 2 (sections 153–159D) covers the registration and de-registration of pension schemes; Chapter 3 (sections 160–185J) provides for the payments that may be made by registered pension schemes and related matters; Chapter 4 (sections 186–203) deals with tax reliefs and exemptions in connection with registered pension schemes; Chapter 5 (sections 204–242) imposes tax charges in connection with registered pension schemes; Chapter 6 (sections 243–249) covers certain schemes that are not registered pension schemes; Chapter 7 (sections 250–274A) makes provisions regarding compliance; and Chapter 8 (sections 275–284) contains interpretation and other supplementary provisions.

All references in this section of the chapter are to FA 2004, Part 4 unless otherwise stated.

80.9.3 Pension Schemes and Their Registration

A pension scheme is one which provides specified benefits to or in respect of persons on retirement, on death, on having reached a particular age, on the onset of serious ill-health or incapacity, or in similar circumstances.[44] Any scheme properly registered is a 'registered pension scheme'.[45] Other terms used are 'public service pension scheme',[46] 'occupational pension scheme'[47] and 'overseas pension scheme', this last having a subset of 'recognised overseas pension scheme' which means recognised by the UK tax authorities.[48]

There are several categories of member, viz active member, pensioner member, deferred member or pension credit member of the pension scheme.[49] A pension credit member is someone whose rights under the scheme are attributable (directly or indirectly) to pension credits.

Lastly, FA 2004 refers to 'arrangements', ie arrangements between the scheme and the person. Here we find not only defined benefits and money purchase but also cash balance benefits.[50] Hybrid arrangements consist of a mixture of these three benefits.

The registration of pension schemes is governed by Chapter 2.

80.9.4 Permitted Payments

Chapter 3 (sections 160–185J) defines various categories of payments and has two functions, one being to list the payments which properly may be made, and the other being

---

[44] FA 2004, s 150.
[45] FA 2004, s 150(2).
[46] FA 2004, s 150(3), (4).
[47] FA 2004, s 150(5), (6).
[48] FA 2004, s 150(7), (8).
[49] FA 2004, s 151.
[50] FA 2004, s 152.

to identify those which may not be made and so attract penalties. The only payments which a registered pension scheme is authorised to make to or in respect of a member of the pension scheme are those specified in section 164 (section 160); it follows that all other payments are unauthorised. Each permitted payment is subject to detailed statutory amplification; the list comprises pensions (sections 165 and 167), lump sums (sections 166 and 168), recognised transfers (section 169), scheme administration member payments (section 171) and payments pursuant to a pension-sharing order or provision. Also expressly permitted are payments of a description to be prescribed by regulations made by the Board. Sections 161–163 contain definitions and cover payments, loans and borrowing. The definition of 'payments' covers rules not only about what amounts to payment but also about the person to whom or for whose benefit the payment is treated as being made. 'Loans' are defined, as they may be or become unauthorised payments (sections 171, 178 and 179) and so attract penalties. 'Borrowings' are defined because section 182 limits the number of borrowings that a scheme may make.

80.9.5 Chapter 4, Sections 186–205 Registered Pension Schemes: Tax Reliefs and Exemptions

80.9.5.1 Exemption for Fund

Exemption from income tax is given to the scheme by section 186. The exempt income is that derived from investments or deposits held for the purposes of a registered pension scheme, or underwriting commissions applied for the purposes of a registered pension scheme, which would otherwise be chargeable to tax under ITTOIA 2005, Part 5, Chapter 8/ the miscellaneous loss rules in CTA 2010, section 91. Other parts of section 186 ensure that investments are widely defined and that the exemption covers relevant stock lending fees. The exemption does not apply where the investment or deposit is held as a member of a property investment LLP. The exemption from CGT is given by section 187, which amends TCGA 1992, section 271 and exempts gains accruing to a person on a disposal of investments held for the purposes of a registered pension scheme.

80.9.5.2 Relief for Members' Contributions

Relief for members' contributions is provided by section 188. The payments must be 'relievable pension contributions', ie anything not excluded by section 188(3) or (3A), such as payments after a person has reached the age of 75. Also excluded are contributions paid by an employer of the individual. A pension credit which increases the rights of the individual under the pension scheme is treated as a contribution on behalf of the individual only if it derives from a pension scheme that is not a registered pension scheme.[51]

Since the level of contributions is important, other rules go on to provide that certain sums are not treated as contributions for the purpose of FA 2004, Part 4. So one ignores transfers of sums representing accrued rights under a pension schemes.[52] Although the contributions will usually be in the form of money, section 195 allows the transfer of

---

[51] FA 2004, s 188(4).
[52] FA 2004, s 188(5).

shares acquired under SAYE option schemes or under tax-advantaged share incentive schemes.

Other conditions for relief. The individual must be a relevant UK individual for the tax year, which means satisfying any one of four tests in FA 2004, section 189. The first is having 'relevant UK earnings' chargeable to income tax for that year. The second is being resident in the UK at some time during the year. The third is being resident in the UK both at some time during the five tax years immediately before that year and when the individual became a member of the pension scheme. The fourth is having general earnings from overseas Crown employment subject to UK tax. Section 189(2) then defines 'relevant UK earnings'; for discussion, see the related earned income concepts above at §7.8. Section 189(2) lists employment income, income which is chargeable under ITTOIA 2005, Part 2 derived immediately from the carrying on or exercise of a trade, profession or vocation (whether individually, or as a partner acting personally in a partnership), ITTOIA 2005, Part 3 income from furnished holiday letting businesses, and patent income of an individual in respect of inventions. Any income that is exempt from UK tax under double taxation agreements is not 'taxable in the UK'.

Section 190 annual limits. Carrying over from the stakeholder pension system, there is a basic amount of £3,600 which may be contributed. Otherwise the limit is the amount of the individual's relevant UK earnings chargeable to income tax for the tax year. Relief is given either by deduction at source (section 192), or under a net pay agreement, ie by deduction from the relevant employment income (section 193). There is also provision for making a claim for deduction from total income (section 194).

Other rules provide relief for employer's contributions (section 196) and for the spreading of the relief in appropriate cases (sections 197–198); so section 197 directs, subject to exceptions, spreading over four years. The deductions are from profits taxed under ITTOIA 2005, Part 2 or, in the case of a company with investment business, as expenses of management under TA 1988, section 75 or under section 76, step 1 for an insurance company (sections 196 and 200). There is a separate rule allowing the deduction of sums required to be added to make good any deficiency in the scheme (section 199). Section 199A, added in 2008, allows certain indirect contributions, ie a payment of a contribution by someone other than the employer, to be spread in the same way.[53] Any minimum contributions made by the Revenue under the Pensions Schemes Act 1993, section 43 are grossed up (section 202).

80.9.5.3 Relevant Earnings

The definition of 'relevant earnings' uses many of the terms and expressions originally used in making the distinction between earned income and investment income, and still important for retirement annuity and personal pension relief calculations. Even though some of the rules were relaxed by FA 2004, the 'relevant earnings' used to calculate such entitlements still use broadly the same categories.[54] It is still important for identifying certain income of husband and wife and civil partners.[55] The distinction is not the same as that discussed in

[53] Added by FA 2008, s 90.
[54] FA 2004, s 189(2), ex TA 1988, ss 623(2), 644.
[55] TA 1988, s 282A(4A): earned income cannot fall within s 282A.

§7.7 above, ie between savings and other income for tax rate purposes; thus, income from land will be investment income, but is not savings income.

Relevant earnings are defined in three main categories, with one addition:[56]

(1)   *Category I* is any employment income charged to tax under ITEPA 2003.[57] In *Dale v IRC*,[58] annuity payments to a trustee 'so long as he acts as trustee' were held by the House of Lords to be earned income. In that case the trustee was to receive the payments; the amount and value of the work actually done was irrelevant.[59] The Revenue argued that since a trustee was not at that time entitled to remuneration for his services as distinct from the reimbursement of expenses, the annuity was a conditional gift. However, the House of Lords held that the income was earned, since the condition of the annuity was compliance with the testator's condition of serving as a trustee.

In *White v Franklin*,[60] dividends were held to be income earned from employment, provided they were a reward for services. However, this case was decided before the introduction of Schedule F in 1965, now ITTOIA 2005, Part 4, Chapter 3. The priority rules in ITTOIA 2005 make it clear that, in general, income taxed under ITEPA 2003 is not taxed under ITTOIA 2005, Part 4 (income from savings and investment); however, they go on to say that this does not apply to Chapter 3 (dividend income from UK-resident companies). It will be interesting to see how the courts get round this nonsense—if it ever comes to court.[61] In *White v Franklin*, the taxpayer (T) was assistant managing director of a company. T's mother and brother settled 50% of the issued share capital on trust to pay the income to the taxpayer, 'so long as he shall be engaged in the management of the company', with remainder to the mother and others. It was held that his income from the trust was earned income. The Commissioners had found that the settlement had been made as an inducement to T to remain with the company, and so the income accrued to him because, and not simply while, he was an active director.[62] It was also important that the trust held a large block of shares in the employing company, so that T's work would produce direct results. These, however, were matters of fact to support the inference that the purpose of the settlement was to keep T interested in the company, and was not simply an arrangement in a family settlement distributing income arising from family property to persons with certain qualifications.[63] This appears to be a borderline case.[64]

If a payment of income is not only in return for services but also for some other consideration, there can be no apportionment of the income so as to treat even a part of it as earned;[65] the question is one of the construction of the arrangement.

The TA 1988 definition of 'earned income' included any income from any property which is attached to or forms part of the employment of any office or employment of

[56] FA 2004, s 189(2), TA 1988, s 833(4); the list is supplemented in s 833(5), (6).
[57] FA 2004, s 189(2)(a).
[58] [1953] 2 All ER 671, 34 TC 468.
[59] 34 TC 468, 493 (*per* Lord Normand).
[60] [1965] 1 All ER 692, 42 TC 283, [1965] BTR 152.
[61] ITTOIA 2005, s 366(3); the rule may be dated back to 1965 and the start of Sch F.
[62] 42 TC 283, 284.
[63] [1965] 1 All ER 692, 699, 42 TC 283, 297.
[64] See Vinelott J in *O'Leary v McKinlay* [1991] STC 42, 53.
[65] *Hale v Shea* [1965] 1 All ER 155, 42 TC 260.

profit held by the individual. However, these words are not part of FA 2004, section 189(2). We may therefore exclude them for present purposes. Nevertheless, some see that *White v Franklin* may be justified on this basis. For details, see *Revenue Law*, 5th edition, at §7.8.2.

(2) *Category II* consists of any income which is charged under ITTOIA 2005, Part 2 (ex Schedule D) and immediately derived by the individual from a trade, profession or vocation carried on by him as an individual or as a partner personally acting in the partnership.[66] This has given rise to some 'nice' distinctions. The earnings will be relevant only if the trade was carried on by the individual. In *Fry v Shiels Trustees*,[67] trustees legally owned and managed a business, the income of which was held for infant beneficiaries. It was held that the income was not earned since the profits were earned by the trustees, and so by individuals who certainly did not own them. A trustee-beneficiary would, in such circumstances, presumably be allowed to treat the income as earned and would be allowed to keep the benefit. In a similar vein, it has been held that income received as a name at Lloyds, ie as a member of a syndicate, was not 'relevant earnings' for pension purposes; the taxpayer's activities, which mostly involved deciding with which syndicate he would place his money, were preparatory to a trade which was, in fact, carried on by others on his behalf.[68]

Further difficulties have arisen from the requirement that the profit must be derived immediately from the business. An example is *Northend v White, Leonard and Corbin Greener*,[69] where interest accruing to a solicitor on money deposited at a bank on general deposit account was held to be investment income. The source was not the carrying-on of the profession but rather the loan deposit with the bank. This conclusion has been criticised.[70]

Today, income in the form of dividends may be earned income for ITTOIA 2005. This is because ITTOIA 2005, section 366 makes it clear that the Part 2 classification is to take priority over Part 4, Chapter 3. This is because statute contains a statutory provision that where shares are held as trading assets, the dividends arising from those shares are now treated as part of the trading profits of the business[71] and so may be earned income.

(3) *Category III* is income under ITTOIA 2005, Part 3 from carrying on a UK or EEA furnished holiday letting business.

(4) *Category IV* is patents. FA 2004, as amended, adds patent income, provided the individual, alone or jointly, devised the invention for which the patent was granted. At one time these payments were relevant earnings only if paid to the person who alone devised the invention; this test has been softened.[72]

---

[66] See the comments of Lindsay J in *Koenigsberger v Mellor* [1993] STC 408, 414.

[67] [1915] SC 159; 6 TC 583.

[68] *Koenigsberger v Mellor* [1993] STC 408.

[69] [1975] STC 317; 50 TC 121, the interest belonged to the solicitor thanks to Solicitors Act 1965, s 8(2).

[70] The decision in *Northend* rests on a statement by Pennycuick J in *Bucks v Bowers* [1970] 2 All ER 202, 46 TC 267, which may only be a dictum; the decision in that case was later reversed by statute.

[71] ITTOIA 2005, s 366, ex F(No 2)A 1997, s 24, which applied as from 2 July 1997.

[72] FA 2004, s 189(2A); the test was softened by the removal of TA 1988, s 833(5C) and (5E), ITA 2007, explanatory notes change 125.

80.9.6 *FA 2004 Part 4, Chapter 5, Registered Pension Schemes: Tax Charges*

Chapter 5 (sections 204–242) is the longest and contains details of the tax charges. There are six heads of charge:

— Charges on authorised payments—sections 204–207
— Unauthorised payments charge—sections 208–213
— Lifetime allowance charge—sections 214–226
— Annual allowance charge—sections 227–238
— Scheme sanction charge—sections 239–241
— De-registration charge—section 242.

Many of these provisions contain rates and financial limits. The legislation usually enables the Treasury to vary these rates and limits by order. FA 2006 made many detailed changes to ensure that members and former members are treated alike. Thus, an exemption from charge for payments to members extends to payments to former members too—and to payments of wages to former members for work done for the pension scheme itself. Similarly, the charge on unauthorised payments to members also extends to unauthorised payments to former members.[73]

80.9.7 *Schemes That are not Registered Pension Schemes*

Chapter 6 provides rules for schemes that are not registered pension schemes. It begins with section 243, which simply enacts Schedule 33 containing the detailed rules applicable to 'migrant member relief' in respect of contributions under overseas pension schemes; section 244 then enacts Schedule 34 on how certain UK charges apply to non-UK schemes.

Schedule 35 rewrites a number of other tax rules which refer to pension schemes. So FA 2003, Schedule 24, which attacks certain fringe benefit schemes by denying a deduction to the employer for payments made, did not disallow deductions for pension schemes; this is now achieved (section 245) by making an exception for 'employer financed retirement scheme', a phrase which is defined not in the general definition section to Chapter 4 but in ITEPA 2003, Part 6, Chapter 2. The introduction in FA 2011 of the new 'disguised remuneration' rules means that it is now tax-inefficient to provide employee-financed retirement benefit schemes. Section 246 contains a self-standing deferral rule for certain other contributions.

There are further amendments to ITEPA 2003, Chapter 6, including the outright repeal of the charge under Chapter 1[74] and changes to Chapter 2 (taxation of non-pension benefits).[75]

Section 248 amends ITEPA 2003, section 307 by imposing a tax charge on the employee where the employer takes out insurance against the risk of non-payment of a pension by reason of the employer's insolvency. The cost of the insurance is a taxable benefit in kind.

---

[73] FA 2006, Sch 17, paras 1–19.
[74] FA 2004, s 247.
[75] FA 2004, s 249.

80.9.8 Scheme Administrator

With Chapter 7 we come to a number of compliance rules, most of which focus on the scheme administrator.[76] Under section 250, the Revenue may issue a notice requiring the scheme administrator to make a return. The return must contain any information reasonably required by the notice and the administrator must deliver any accounts or other documents relating to information contained in the return, which may reasonably be required by the notice. This is followed by a statutory list of matters that can be required, ending with (*k*) 'any other matter relating to the administration of the pension scheme'. The Revenue are then given a power to make regulations requiring persons 'of a prescribed description' to provide further information.[77]

Further rules explain how scheme administrators who find themselves liable to income tax under FA 2004 Part 4 must account for that tax (sections 254–269). Lastly, the statute address the question of who is treated as a scheme administrator for these rules. Section 270 defines a scheme administrator and lists the required qualifications, eg must be resident in the EU or EEA, and must make a declaration to the Revenue. Section 271 directs what is to happen when there is a change in the scheme administrator. In general, a replacement scheme administrator inherits the existing liabilities of the outgoing one. A person cannot simply escape liability by resigning as a scheme administrator without a replacement (and any replacement must meet the terms of section 270). The Revenue have power to release the scheme administrator in such situations.

If the scheme administrator defaults, there are further rules making trustees of the funds liable as scheme administrator[78] or even, as a last resort and in the case certain liabilities, the members themselves.[79]

80.9.9 Miscellaneous

The legislation concludes with definitions and certain rules as to valuations.[80]

80.9.10 Transitional

FA 2004, Schedule 36 contains various transitional rules. For example, on 6 April 2006, all schemes approved under the existing legislation were deemed to become registered schemes under the FA 2004 regime.[81] Scheme administrators could opt out of the deemed registration on payment of income tax at 40% on the value of the fund at that date.[82] The Revenue were given the power to modify the rules of existing schemes.[83] Existing scheme administrators became administrators under the FA 2004 regime[84]—with continuing liabilities for

---

[76] Defined in FA 2004, ss 270–274.
[77] FA 2004, s 251.
[78] FA 2004, ss 272–272C.
[79] FA 2004, s 273.
[80] FA 2004, ss 276–278.
[81] FA 2004, Sch 36, para 1.
[82] FA 2004, Sch 36, para 2.
[83] FA 2004, Sch 36, para 3.
[84] FA 2004, Sch 36, para 4.

any pre-commencement liabilities.[85] The old rules on withdrawal of approval of schemes, eg TA 1988, section 650(1), continue to operate after 6 April 2006.[86]

The protection of pre-commencement rights from the lifetime allowance charge is governed by FA 2004, Schedule 36, paragraphs 7–20. The protection of pre-commencement benefits rights is governed by FA 2004, Schedule 36, paragraphs 21–36. Other provisions follow dealing with a variety of matters, including pensions taxed pre-commencement but accruing post-commencement[87] and the IHT treatment of a fund which was not a registered pension scheme or superannuation fund but which came within IHTA 1984, section 153 immediately before 6 April 2006 (it may remain within section 151 as long as no contributions are made on or after that date). There is a separate rule on IHT and discretionary trusts; this protects a certain proportion of the assets of the fund.[88]

---

[85] FA 2004, Sch 36, para 6.
[86] FA 2004, Sch 36, para 5.
[87] FA 2004, Sch 36, para 45.
[88] FA 2004, Sch 36, paras 57 and 58.

81

Charities

81.1 Introduction

Charities receive generous treatment under many tax codes;[1] such treatments therefore qualify as tax expenditures.[2] The provisional HMRC figures for 2014–15 show that covenants and gift aid by individuals caused tax repayments of £1,210 million; the payroll giving scheme cost £40 million.[3] Payments by companies are made gross and so do not cause repayments. Other figures available for 2014–15 are the tax relief for charities on national non-domestic rates (£1,690 million) and VAT (£300 million). The total cost of tax relief for charities was £3.39 billion, and total relief for individual giving including IHT and higher rate relief on gift aid was £1.18 billion. A reason behind the major changes made to the Charities Act 1993 by the Charities Act 2006 was the need to see whether these benefits were justified.

---

[1] Among many background tax policy sources, see Inland Revenue, *Discussion Document* (1999); Banks and Tanner, *Taxing Charitable Giving*, IFS Commentary 75 (Institute for Fiscal Studies, 1999); Chesterman (1999) 62 *MLR* 333; Chesterman, *Charities Trusts and Social Welfare* (Weidenfeld & Nicolson, 1979), esp ch 10; Krever and Kewley (eds), *Charities and Philanthropic Organisations: Reforming the Tax Subsidy and Regulatory Regimes* (Australian Tax Research Foundation, 1991); Scharf, Cherniavsky and Hogg, *Canadian Policy Research Network Working Paper* (1996); Surrey (1976) 84 *HLR* 352; Surrey, *Pathways to Tax Reform* (Harvard University Press, 1973); Andrews (1972) 86 *HLR* 309, esp 344–75; Bittker (1969) 78 *Yale LJ* 1285; Bittker (1972) *Tax Law Review* 37; McDaniel (1972) 27 *Tax Law Review* 377; and McNulty (1984) 3 *Virginia Tax Review* 229.

[2] See Surrey, *Pathways to Tax Reform*, esp 20, 223–32; and Feldstein, in Aaron and Boskin (eds), *The Economics of Taxation* (Brookings Institute, 1980). For vigorous criticism of one application of this approach, see Bittker (1969) 78 *Yale LJ* 1285. On US rules for deduction, see Bittker and Lokken, *Federal Taxation of Income, Estates and Gifts* (Warren, Gorman & Lamont, 1989), ch 35; see also Griffith (1989) *Hastings LJ* 343.

[3] HMRC Statistics 2015, Cost of Reliefs, available at https://www.gov.uk/government/statistics/cost-of-tax-relief.

The income tax provisions have been rewritten by ITA 2007, and the TA 1988 rules, much amended and rephrased in 2006, were rewritten by CTA 2010 for companies. The 2006 changes were heavily criticised as giving a general impression of attempts to stifle charitable giving and limiting charitable tax relief.[4] The rules on transactions between charities and tainted donations have, it is said, enormous potential for damaging relations between charities and donors, and for increasing administration costs. So much will depend on how the sometimes vague rules are applied by HMRC.

81.1.1 Tax Policy Considerations

Turning briefly to the general tax policy considerations, it is noteworthy that Simon says nothing about the charitable deduction in his *Personal Income Taxation*. The Canadian Royal Commission recommended the continuation of the deduction for charitable contributions and the exemption of the income of charities, but also recommended that the beneficiary should be taxed on any benefits received.[5] The 1955 Report of the UK Royal Commission made some suggestions, but its most telling point was that a more restrictive definition of 'charity' was needed.[6] The Meade Committee Report and the Mirrlees Review say virtually nothing about charities.

81.1.2 Definition of Charity

FA 2010, Schedule 6, paragraph 1 defines a 'charity' for tax purposes as a body of persons or trust that—

(1) is established for charitable purposes only,
(2) meets the jurisdiction condition,
(3) meets the registration condition, and
(4) meets the management condition.

Two other definitions are also set out in paragraph 1: a 'charitable company' means a charity that is a body of persons and 'charitable trust' means a charity that is a trust. 'Charitable purposes' are defined by reference to the Charities Act 2011, section 2, as purposes that fall within section 3(1) of that Act and are for the public benefit (as defined in section 4). The list of charitable purposes in section 3 includes the prevention or relief of poverty and the advancement of such matters as education, religion, health, human rights or animal welfare plus a general 'sweeper up' head for purposes analogous to or within the spirit of the listed purposes. In *The Independent Schools Council v The Charity Commission for England and Wales (and others)*,[7] the Upper Tribunal shed some light on the meaning of the 'public

---

[4] Evans [2006] BTR 531; see also Parry-Wingfield, *The Tax Journal* (14 August 2006) 9, and (21 August 2006) 5.
[5] Carter (chair), Canada Royal Commission on Taxation, *Report*, vol 3 (Ottawa, 1966) 222–27 and *ibid*, vol 4, 131–36.
[6] Royal Commission on the Taxation of Profits and Income, *Final Report*, Cmnd 9474 (1955) para 175.
[7] [2011] UKUT 421 (TCC). For a case in which the taxpayer company failed to show that it was established for charitable purposes only, see *Helena Housing Ltd v Revenue & Customs Commissioners* [2011] STC 1307 (UT).

benefits' requirement in the Charities Act 2006—which is substantially the same as that now in the 2011 Act—as it related to fee-charging schools. The decision is also relevant to other charities that charge for services. According to the Tribunal, the provision of education by independent schools is not in itself a public benefit, and charitable schools must ensure that children of families who cannot afford the fees are able to benefit from what the schools do in a way that is neither minimal nor token. The Tribunal also decided that it was for the charitable trustees to decide how best to do this in each charity's particular circumstances. Following the decision the Charity Commission issued revised guidance on the public benefit requirement.[8]

Returning to the other elements of the definition of charity in FA 2010, Schedule 6, the jurisdiction condition in paragraph 2 requires that the charity must be subject to the jurisdiction of the High Court, Court of Session, High Court in Northern Ireland or any other court in the exercise of a corresponding jurisdiction under the law of a relevant territory. Relevant territory for this purpose is a Member State of the EU or a territory recognised by statutory instrument. Further, the charity must be registered with a regulator in its own country analogous to the Charity Commission (paragraph 3), and those in control and management must be fit and proper persons (paragraph 4).

Leaving aside the possibility of registration elsewhere, in the UK a charity must be registered with the Charity Commission unless it is an exempt charity. Registration with the Charity Commission is conclusive evidence that the body is a charity. For this reason the Revenue may object to a registration, as in *IRC v McMullen*,[9] or may ask the Charity Commission to take steps to deregister a charity; they may also refuse relief on the ground that income is not applied for charitable purposes. In addition, charities must be 'recognised' by HMRC in order to qualify for tax relief. Recognition is an administrative process, which involves providing HMRC with the charity's details including bank account information and registration number along with the creation of a digital account with HMRC.

Political parties are not charities, and while there are specific reliefs from CGT and IHT for gifts to them, there is no specific income tax relief. Special but restricted reliefs have been made available to those community amateur sports clubs which do not qualify as charities.[10]

81.1.3 *Tax Relief for Charities*

In general, the most important tax reliefs available to a recognised charity are:

(1) charities do not pay tax on most income and gains used for charitable purpose ('charitable expenditure). This includes donations received, profits from trading and fund-raising events, bank interest and other investment income, rental income, and gains from the disposition of capital property;

(2) charities are eligible for an 80% discount on business rates on non-domestic buildings;

---

[8] See https://www.gov.uk/government/collections/charitable-purposes-and-public-benefit.

[9] [1981] AC 1, (1981) 54 TC 413.

[10] CTA 2010, ss 658–671, ex FA 2002, s 58 and Sch 18, as amended, eg by FA 2004, s 56. Such clubs that register with HMRC are allowed gift aid repayments, with retroactive effect from 1 April 2010 in relation to gift aid and 6 April 2010 in relation to gift aid claims.

(3) charities can reclaim tax that has been deducted on donations (ie gift aid);
(4) charities are exempt from stamp duty land tax on property not purchased for re-sale;
(5) charities are entitled to pay a reduced rate of 5% VAT on fuel and power and a zero rate on some goods and services, including advertising and items for collecting donations as well as medicine and medical equipment.

Charities are required to pay tax on other forms of income, including profits from developing land and money not used for charitable purposes ('non-charitable expenditure').

81.2 Tax Treatment of Gifts to Charity

In UK tax law, gifts to charity have been deductible for income tax purposes if they were made in the form of (a) charitable covenants, (b) gift aid, (c) payments under a payroll deduction scheme ((a) is now merged into (b), on which see above §10.6).[11] Today the starting point for gifts of money is ITA 2007, sections 520–523 (charitable trusts) and CTA 2010, sections 475–477A (charitable companies). If the gift qualifies for gift aid, it is grossed up at the basic rate and treated as the charity's income of the grossed up amount.[12] If the charity becomes liable to income tax later on, the charge is made under section 521, as envisaged by ITA 2007, section 3(2). Payment by HMRC to the charity is authorised as from the passing of FA 2008; it is not technically a repayment of tax but an authorised payment from public funds. Since 2013 there is a small donations scheme which provides a top-up payment of 25p for every £1 of eligible donations of £20 or less up to an annual maximum payment of £1,250, without the paperwork normally required for gift aid.[13]

There are deductions in computing trading income of costs incurred in sending employees to work for charities.[14] For gifts of trading stock to charities, special rules override the usual deemed market value receipt for disposals other than in the course of the trade.[15] Other rules have removed the application of the non-deduction rule for business gifts, etc[16] from gifts to charities.[17] For CGT purposes, a taxpayer who makes a gift of an asset to a charity is treated as if the asset were sold for a sum such that no gain, no loss arises on the disposal.[18] The relief exempts a donor from liability to CGT on the gain. It is far less generous than the US rules, which not only exempt the donor from any liability on the gain but also permit the donor to treat the full market value as a contribution to charity for income tax purposes and so as available for deduction against other income.[19] These US rules were

---

[11] On payroll schemes, see above at §18.3.4.

[12] ITA 2007, s 520 and CTA 2010, s 475, ex FA 1990, s 25(10) and (12).

[13] Small Charitable Donations Act 2012 and see https://www.gov.uk/government/publications/charities-detailed-guidance-notes/chapter-8-the-gift-aid-small-donations-scheme.

[14] ITTOIA 2005, ss 70–71 and CTA 2009, ss 70–71, ex TA 1988, s 86

[15] ITTOIA 2005, s 108–110 and CTA 2009, 105–108, ex TA 1988, s 83A (gift in kinds to charity) and 84 (gifts to educational establishments).

[16] Ie ITTOIA 2005, s 45, ITEPA 2003, ss 356–358, CTA 2009, ss 1298–1300, ex TA 1988, s 577 (but not other rules such as ITTOIA 2005, s 34, CTA 2009, s 54, ex TA 1988, s 74(1)(a)).

[17] ITTOIA 2005, s 47(5) and CTA 2009, s 1300(1),(5), ex TA 1988, s 577(9).

[18] TCGA 1992, s 257.

[19] See eg Speiller (1980) 80 *Columbia L Rev* 214.

wide open to abuse: for example, T would give a car to his church and claim—and get a deduction of—the value of the car ($10,000) even if the church eventually sold it for only $3,000. Restrictions eventually followed.

Gift rules introduced by FA 2000 were at first confined to shares and other securities; they gave rise to abuse which was countered by legislation in 2004.[20] Relief for gifts of land was introduced by FA 2002.[21] Gifts of other assets, eg pictures or books, do not yet qualify.

The favourable CGT treatment extends also to settled property. Thus, where property has been held in a non-charitable trust and then, under the terms of the trust, a charity becomes absolutely entitled to that property, there is no charge to CGT. This is achieved by the charge on the deemed disposal specified by TCGA 1992, section 71 being treated as if it were a no gain, no loss disposal.[22]

Under the IHT rules, a transfer of value to charity may be an exempt transfer (see above §53.2).[23] Also, an estate can pay IHT at a reduced rate of 36% if 10% or more of the net value of the estate is left to charity.[24]

81.3   Reliefs Accruing to the Charity: Income

Income accruing to charities receives privileged treatment. Trading income is dealt with separately, along with miscellaneous income (ex Schedule D, Case VI); see §81.4.1 below. ITA 2007 and CTA 2010 follow the ITTOIA 2005 precedent of considering the trading rules before other types of income. However, as the exemptions are more restricted, we follow the former order in TA 1988. After (a) exemptions for certain types of income of the charity (§81.3.1), we turn to (b) gifts received by the charity (§81.3.2) and then (c) trading and miscellaneous income received by the charity (§81.4).

81.3.1 Exemptions for Certain Types of Income

Various types of income are exempt from income tax and corporation tax.[25] In each case the exemption applies only so far as the income is applied for charitable purposes only:

(1)   Property income. ITA 2007 exempts income under ITTOIA 2005, Part 3 and certain property income taken across to ITTOIA 2005, Part 2 by section 261. Distributions

---

[20] TA 1988, s 587B, added by FA 2000, s 43 and amended by FA 2004, s 139. These rules are now in ITA 2007, ss 431–440 and CTA 2010, ss 206–212. The schemes attracting the Revenue's attention are described in Press Release 2 July 2004, [2004] *Simon's Tax Intelligence* 1573.

[21] ITA 2007, ss 441–442 and CTA 2010, ss 213 and 216, ex TA 1988, s 587C, added by FA 2002, s 97.

[22] TCGA 1992, s 257(3).

[23] IHTA 1984, ss 23–25.

[24] IHTA 1984, Sch 1A. See also https://www.gov.uk/inheritance-tax/giving-to-charity-to-reduce-an-inheritance-tax-bill.

[25] ITA 2007, ss 531–537 and CTA 2010, ss 475–491, ex TA 1988, s 505(1) and s 9(4)). On CGT, see below at §§25.3, 25.6, 25.7. There are also reliefs from VAT under VATA 1994, Sch 8, Group 15 and from stamp duty and NICs (FA 1977, s 57).

from a REIT is also exempt.[26] The equivalent corporation tax provision is in CTA 2010, section 485.[27]

(2) ITA 2007 and CTA 2010 exempt most income from savings and investment,[28] public revenue dividends,[29] transaction in deposits,[30] certain miscellaneous income,[31] and income for estates in administration.[32]

(3) Certain profits from fund-raising events[33] and lotteries.[34]

(4) Offshore income gains.[35]

This list does not exhaust the range of taxable income, so that the charity is chargeable on any other income it may receive, for example such as falls within ITEPA 2003, or which falls within ITTOIA 2005 and is not yearly interest or other annual payments.

The exemptions are permitted only where the income is actually applied for charitable purposes; this gives the Revenue a policing role. In considering whether money is applied for charitable purposes, the court looks to see how the money has been applied. If it has been applied to charitable purposes, it does not matter that the charity was obliged to apply it that way; neither, probably, is it relevant what reason or motive the trustees may have had, nor that they may confer some incidental benefit upon some third person.[36] However, this requirement was not met where a charity established for the public benefit gave all its income to the children of employees of a particular firm which was connected with the managers of the charity.[37]

If charity A gives the money to charity B, the money has been applied for charitable purposes.[38] At one time this entitled charity A to claim any exemptions or repayments whether or not B used the money properly, and even though charities A and B were under common control; this is now restricted (see below §81.6).[39]

---

[26] ITA 2007, s 531(2A), referring to FA 2006, s 121.

[27] On application for charitable purposes, see *IRC v Helen Slater Charitable Trust Ltd* [1981] STC 471, CA; the scope of that decision is, however, greatly restricted by the rules outlined below at §81.6.

[28] ITA 2007, s 532(2) and CTA 2010, s 486. CTA 2010 excludes non-trading profits from loan relationships as well.

[29] ITA 2007, s 533 and CTA 2010, s 487.

[30] ITA 2007, s 534.

[31] ITA 2007, s 536 and CTA 2010, s 488.

[32] ITA 2007, s 538 and CTA 2010, s 489.

[33] ITA 2007, s 529, CTA 2010, s 484 and ESC C4.

[34] ITA 2007, s 530 and CTA 2010, s 484, ex TA 1988, s 505(1)(f), added by FA 1995, s 138.

[35] ITA 2007, s 535, TA 1988, s 761.

[36] *Campbell v IRC* (1966) 45 TC 427, 443, 444, *per* Buckley J.

[37] *IRC v Educational Grants Association* [1967] 2 All ER 893, (1967) 44 TC 93.

[38] *IRC v Helen Slater Charitable Trust* [1981] STC 471, CA; see Gillard, *In the Name of Charity* (Chatto & Windus, 1987), 20; on recovery of tax, see ITA 2007, s 523 and CTA 2010, s 474, ex TA 1988, s 505(2).

[39] ITA 2007, ss 540, 562, and CTA 2010, ss 492, 393, 515, ex TA 1988, s 505(3).

81.3.2 Income from Gifts

81.3.2.1 Gift Aid

An individual[40] donor (D) making a qualifying donation is treated as making a payment to charity equal to the amount of the gift grossed up at basic rate (20%).[41] Payment is authorised as from the passing of FA 2008; it is not technically a repayment of tax but an authorised payment from public funds. Thus, a payment of £800 is treated as a gift of £1,000 and the charity recovers £200 tax from the Revenue.[42] If D is a higher-rate taxpayer, D is entitled to total relief of £400, of which £200 is treated as having already been withheld by D; the remaining £200 of relief is given in the self-assessment as a deduction in computing total income. The form allows the taxpayer to direct the Revenue to make this repayment to the charity; the form also allows the taxpayer to direct that any repayment of tax due overall be paid to charity (ITA 2007, section 429).

Where the basic rate tax treated as deducted exceeds the amount of income tax (and CGT) with which D is charged for the year, D is assessable to pay tax at basic rate to make good the shortfall.[43] This rule refers to D's total liability for the year, not to the amount of tax charged on the £1,000 given. So provided D has a taxable income sufficient to generate £200 of tax, it does not matter that part of that is at 10% and the rest at 20%. The tax rules for different types of income mean that the tax cost to D of making a gift will vary according to its source.[44]

81.3.2.2 History

For most of the last century the normal form was the charitable covenant. This was a covenant giving rise to income for the charity under Schedule D, Case III as an annuity. The covenantor obtained a deduction for the gross value of the covenant through the basic rate mechanism in the now repealed TA 1988, section 348, and a deduction for surtax. In order to escape from the settlement rules in what became TA 1988, section 660A (now ITTOIA 2005, Part 5, Chapter 5), the covenant had to be for a period which was capable of exceeding six years, later reduced to three years. Basic arithmetic tells one that if a covenant is to be capable of exceeding six or three years there must be seven or four payments, and so these became known as seven-year covenants or four-year covenants.[45]

When Schedule D, Case III was reformed by FA 1988, a new category of payment was invented, the covenanted payment to charity. This was similar to the old annual payment but relied on specific rules rather than general Schedule D, Case III principles as they then

---

[40] On the boundary between making a gift as an individual and as PR, see *St Dunstans v Major* [1997] STC (SCD) 212.

[41] ITA 2007, ss 414 and 423(1)–(5), ex FA 1990, s 25(6); the grossing-up rate is tied to the date the payment is made (ITA 2007, s 909 (2)) and no longer when it was due. The 2008 reduction in the basic rate from 22% to 20% would have had the effect of reducing the overall value of a gift aid payment. FA 2008 s 53 and Sch 19 temporarily allowed charities to use a 'notional basic rate' of 22% for payments between 6 April 2008 and 5 April 2011.

[42] FA 1990, s 25(10).

[43] ITA 2007, ss 424(3) and 425, ex FA 1990, s 25(8).

[44] For an example using out-of-date rates but making the essential point, see Lathwood (2000) 145 *Taxation* 118.

[45] For details see *Revenue Law*, 3rd edn, §§17:42 *et seq* and Tiley and Collison's *UK Tax Guide 1999–2000* (Butterworths, 1999), §§13.28 *et seq*.

were, eg as to permissible benefits. Still, however, the covenantor deducted basic rate tax at source (and got a deduction for higher-rate purposes) and the charity reclaimed the basic rate tax from the Revenue.

The 'covenanted payment to charity' was at first supplemented and later superseded by gift aid in FA 1990, section 25. These were single payments, and at first had to be not less than £250 and had to be accompanied by a certificate. Relief for single donations by individuals to charities may be traced back to the payroll deduction scheme originally introduced by FA 1986, section 27 and now in ITEPA 2003, Part 12. As these payments were made gross, there was no question of any tax repayment to the charity; moreover, they were not income of the charity. Relief for single donations by companies was also introduced in 1986 by FA 1986, section 29, which made amendments to TA 1988, section 339; these were supplemented by changes made by FA 1990, section 26. As a result of FA 2000 there is now no minimum sum.[46]

FA 2004 allowed a person entitled to a repayment of tax under the self-assessment regime to elect that the repayment be given to a charity on a list maintained by the Revenue.[47] As with other gift aid payments, the amount is grossed up at basic rate but is then entitled to higher-rate relief. The payment is treated as made in the year in which the repayment arises, not the year to which that repayment relates.

81.3.2.3 Gifts of Shares, Securities and Real Property

A donor making a gift of a qualifying investment or qualifying interest in land (as defined) is entitled to an income tax deduction in computing net income[48] equal to 'the relievable amount', ie the market value of the investments, defined as for CGT and any associated costs of disposal.[49] When the value of the net benefit to the charity is less than the market value, the net benefit is taken instead.[50] Investments qualify if they are quoted shares or securities, units in an authorised unit trust, shares in an OEIC or an interest in an offshore fund.[51] The idea is to give relief where the assets are easy to value and easy to realise.[52] There are equivalent rules for corporation tax.[53]

The relevant amount also takes account of any consideration or benefit received, as where the benefactor sells the shares to the charity at a low price.[54] This relief is distinct from and in addition to the CGT rules exempting the donor from CGT liability. The charity's base cost of the asset is reduced by the relevant amount (or to nil if the base cost is less than the relevant amount).[55] Where the charity becomes subject to a disposal-related

---

[46] FA 1990, s 25 amended by FA 2000, s 39. In 1992–93 the minimum was £600. On millennium aid, see FA 1998, s 47; the list of countries is derived from the World Bank designation of 'low income countries': Inland Revenue Press Release, 14 March 1998, [1998] *Simon's Weekly Tax Intelligence* 393.

[47] FA 2004, s 83.

[48] Step 2, ITA 2007, s 23; see ex TA 1988, s 587B(2)(a)(ii); s 83B added by FA 2000, s 43; on timing, see s 43(3).

[49] ITA 2007, ss 434–436, ex TA 1988, s 587B(10).

[50] ITA 2007, s 434, ex TA 1988, s 587B(4), as amended by FA 2004.

[51] ITA 2007, s 432, ex TA 1988, s 587B(9).

[52] Revenue Notes on Clause 43, para 18.

[53] CTA 2010, ss 203 *et seq*, ex TA 1988, s 587B(a)(ii).

[54] ITA 2007, s 434, ex TA 1988, s 587B.

[55] ITA 2007, s 434, ex TA 1988, s 587B; among the consequential rules are references to total income for s 550 (s 587B(2)(b)).

obligation, the effect of that obligation must be taken into account in determining the net value to the charity.[56]

The taxpayer may claim a deduction for qualifying gifts of land.[57] Pedants and exasperated legal historians will note that while the legislation applies to qualifying interests in land, including leasehold interests, the section is incorrectly headed 'gifts of real property'. The gift aid treatment applies to a lease carved out of an existing freehold or leasehold interest subsection.[58] Special rules require the individual to provide a certificate. Further rules apply where the land is held jointly or, the opposite case, where there is a joint disposal.[59]

81.3.2.4 Disqualifying Benefits

The gift aid rules require that neither the donor nor any person connected with him may receive a benefit in consequence of making the donation.[60] A saving of IHT has been held to be a benefit.[61] These rules were revised by FA 2007 to provide that the benefit must not exceed 5% of the amount of the gift, subject to a maximum of £500 (which is 5% of £10,000).[62] FA 2011, section 41 further extended the thresholds for the value of benefits from £500 to £2,500. There are also rules which annualise the value of certain benefits and donations, eg where the right to receive benefits extends over a period of less than 12 months.[63]

Like the 1988 rules before them, certain admission rights are disregarded, viz the right to free admission to view property or wildlife where the preservation of property or conservation of wildlife is the sole or main purpose of the charity.[64] As from 6 April 2006 the free admission exclusion is amended, partly to counter the practice of people making a gift aid donation equal to the normal admission price in lieu of simply paying that price, and partly to widen the charities for which the right of admission is not a disqualifying benefit. The right to make a donation must be open to any member of the public; the right must be to enter or view specified types of property preserved, maintained, kept or created by the charity in pursuance of its charitable objects (no longer just heritage preservation and wildlife conservation). In addition, either the right of admission must be for at least one year at times when the public can come in, or the gift must be for at least 10% more than the normal admission price.[65]

---

[56] ITA 2007, ss 437–40, ex TA 1988, ss 587B(8B) *et seq.*
[57] ITA 2007, s 431, ex TA 1988, s 587B(9A)–(9E) and s 587C, both added by FA 2002, s 97.
[58] ITA 2007, s 433, ex TA 1988, s 587B(9C).
[59] ITA 2007, ss 441–443.
[60] ITA 2007, s 418, ex FA 1990, s 25(2)(e); on mechanics, see above at §10.6.
[61] FA 1990, s 25(5E)–(5G) so as to safeguard benefits such as free admission to National Trust properties, etc. *St Dunstans v Major* [1997] STC (SCD) 212.
[62] FA 1990, s 25(5) and (5A).
[63] ITA 2007, s 419, FA 1990, s 25(5B)–(5D).
[64] ITA 2007, s 420, FA 1990, s 25(5E)–(5G); on earlier law, see FA 1989, s 53.
[65] ITA 2007, s 420(8), FA 1990, s 25(5F)–(5H) added by F(No 2)A 2005, s 11.

81.4 Trading and Miscellaneous Income

81.4.1 Specific Exemption for Certain Types of Trading Income

ITA 2007, section 524 and CTA 2010, section 478 grant exemption from income tax and corporation tax for 'profits etc' of charitable trades. The exempt profits are, as we shall see, circumscribed. However, they extend to a number of receipts—hence the 'etc'.

If a charity carries on a trade, it will be exempt from the tax on the profits of that trade if the profits are applied solely for the purposes of the charity and the trade is for the relevant period 'a charitable trade'. A trade is a 'charitable trade' if either (a) the trade is exercised in the course of the actual carrying out of a primary purpose of the charity, or (b) the work in connection with the trade is mainly carried out by beneficiaries of the charitable trust.[66] Trading profits now expressly include post-cessation receipts and adjustment income.[67]

An example of requirement (a) is where a charity runs a law surgery and one of its objects is the provision of lectures and general legal education; the profits of conferences for solicitors escape tax. Similarly, if a school or college carries on the trade of education and charges fees, the trade is exercised in the course of the actual carrying-out of a primary purpose of the charity.

Requirement (b) above contemplates 'the basket factory of a blind asylum, the blind inmates being the beneficiaries by whose work the trade of manufacturing baskets for sale is mainly carried on'.[68] However, it has been extended to a charitable association which organised a competitive music festival, the competitors being treated as the beneficiaries.[69] More obviously, the profits of a school run by nuns have been held exempt, the nuns, and not just the pupils, being regarded as the beneficiaries.[70] However, it does not follow that ordinary school teachers are beneficiaries.[71]

It will be seen that commercially-orientated trading, such as the sale of Christmas cards or the organisation of the sales of gifts, gives rise to taxable, not exempt, profits, such sales not being integral parts of the charity's purposes. However, profits from bazaars or jumble sales run by voluntary organisations are not generally charged to tax.[72] A result similar to complete exemption of trading income from income tax may be achieved by letting the trade be carried on by a company whose shares are held by the charity and which then covenants to make the payments to the charity equal to its profits; such payments are charges on income of the company[73] and so, in effect, deductible (see above at §62.4). The Revenue have for many years taken the view that such schemes would not usually be challenged provided no circularity is involved; circularity would be involved if the charity provided an

---

[66] ITA 2007, ss 524 and 525, and CTA 2010, ss 478 and 479; requirement (b) was introduced by FA 1920, s 30(1)(c) to reverse *Coman v Governors of the Rotunda Hospital* [1921] 1 AC 1.

[67] ITA 2007, s 524(2) and CTA 2010, s 478(2).

[68] *IRC v Glasgow Musical Festival Association* (1926) 11 TC 154, 163, *per* Lord Clyde.

[69] *Ibid.*

[70] *Brighton Convent of the Blessed Sacrament v IRC* (1933) 18 TC 76.

[71] *Brighton College v Marriott* [1926] AC 192, 203; (1926) 10 TC 213, 234, *per* Lord Buckmaster.

[72] ITA 2007 s 529, CTA 2010, s 483 and ESC C4.

[73] As annual payments; see *R v IT Special Commrs, ex parte Shaftesbury Home and Arethusa Training Ship* [1923] 1 KB 393, (1923) 8 TC 367; distinguishing *Trustees of Psalms and Hymns v Whitwell* (1890) 3 TC 7.

interest-free loan to the trading entity, or the trader effectively controlled the charity using it as a tax-free money box.[74] Today the company is able to use gift aid; a qualifying donation is still effective.

Where a charity incurs expense and so a loss on its charitable but non-trading activities, it cannot set off that loss against its profits from a taxable trade.[75] However, if a charity carries on two trades, one exempt, on whom it makes a loss, and the other taxable, on which it makes a profit, the loss may be relieved.[76] This view seems doubtful but has not been tested in the courts. The charity would, in any case, have to surmount ITA 2007, section 66 first.[77] On the other hand, it is perfectly permissible for a loss on a taxable trade to be set off against the profit of another taxable trade. In broad terms, these reliefs apply only if the trade is a charitable trade, ie one qualifying under section 525. If the trade is not within that section, a loss will usually be treated as non-charitable expenditure, so giving rise to a loss of reliefs under the rules at §81.6.

81.4.2 Exemption for Small-scale Trades

To avoid putting charities to the cost of using companies as just described, ITA 2007, section 526 for income tax and CTA 2010, section 480 for corporation tax provide a simpler but limited regime. Income under ITTOIA 2005, Part 2 for income tax and CTA 2009, Part 3 for corporation tax is exempt up to a certain level, called, for corporation tax, the 'requisite limit'.[78] That limit has remained unchanged since 2000–01 and is the greater of (a) £5,000, and (b) whichever is the lesser of (i) £50,000 and (ii) 25% of the charitable trust's (or company's) trading incoming resources for the tax year (or accounting period). So if the income from all sources is £10,000, the limit will be set at £5,000 by rule (a); if the income is £100,000, the limit will be set at £25,000 by rule (b)(ii); while if the income is £1 million, the limit will be set at £50,000 by rule (b)(i). In order to avoid problems of retrospection, the legislation allows the charity to use the exemption if it had a reasonable expectation, at the beginning of the chargeable period, that it would be within the limit.[79] Where a chargeable period is less than 12 months, the limits of £5,000 and £50,000 are reduced proportionately.[80] The equivalent rules for income tax are in ITA 2007, section 528. As with other charity exemption rules, the income must be applied solely for the purposes of the charity.[81]

Where a charity has a trade which consists of one activity which is wholly exempt under (for income tax) section 525 and another which must seek exemption under section 526, the statute as amended in 2006 deems there to be separate trades.[82] Thanks to

---

[74] [1985] *Simon's Tax Intelligence* 572; of course, the company must comply with the requirements of TA 1988, Sch 16.

[75] *Religious Tract and Book Society of Scotland v Forbes* (1896) 3 TC 415.

[76] Under ITA 2007, s 64, ex TA 1988, s 380 (see above at §20.10), or CTA 2010, ss 45 and 37, ex TA 1988, ss 393, 393A (see above at §62.5).

[77] Ex TA 1988, s 384. See above at §20.10.

[78] CTA 2010, s 482(1).

[79] CTA 2010, s 482(1)(b).

[80] CTA 2010, s 482(7).

[81] ITA 2007, s 527(5) and CTA 2010, s 480(5).

[82] ITA 2007, s 525(4) ex TA 1988, s 505(1B).

section 527, the limited exemption in section 528 applies also to 'miscellaneous income' of the charitable trust. The heads of miscellaneous income are listed in section 1016, but subject to exclusions in section 527. The figures setting out the limit are applied to the sum of the trading and miscellaneous income (there is one relief, not two). The equivalent rules for corporation tax are in CTA 2010, section 479.

81.5 Capital Gains Realised by a Charity

A gain made by a charity is not a chargeable gain 'if it accrues to a charity and is applicable and applied for charitable purposes'.[83] Thus, where a charity sells an asset for cash and applies the proceeds to its charitable endeavours, no charge to tax arises.[84]

81.5.1 Problems

81.5.1.1 Gifts

Technical problems arise if no actual consideration is received by the charity, since there is nothing to be 'applied'. Thus, if a charity, in the course of carrying out charitable work, gives an asset to a beneficiary, any chargeable gain arising may be assessable on the charity. The Revenue are likely to adopt a generous approach where the gift of the asset was clearly made in the pursuance of the charity's objects.

81.5.1.2 Deemed Disposals

Similar problems arise on a deemed disposal since, again, there is no actual consideration and no gain is 'applied for charitable purposes'. In such cases, the charity is subject to CGT on the gain that arises. Suppose that charity A owns a freehold which it lets for a commercial rent to B, another charity. In order to help B, A reduces the rent from a commercial rent to a peppercorn rent. This alteration of the lease causes a deemed disposal.[85] The charity exemption is not available on this deemed disposal.

81.5.1.3 TCGA 1992, Section 171

If C, a charity, sets up S in the form of a wholly-owned subsidiary, and passes assets to S, TCGA 1992, section 171 should operate to treat the transfer as at no gain, no loss. However, this is specified in statute as applying only where one company is a subsidiary of another, and it is not clear whether S can be a subsidiary of C since a charity does not have an equitable interest in its assets as such; instead, it holds those assets on trust for the ultimate beneficiaries.[86] If S cannot be a subsidiary, section 171 cannot apply to defer the charge. Moreover, section 256 cannot exempt the gain since, as in the A–B lease problem in §81.5.1.2

---

[83] TCGA 1992, s 256(1); there is no requirement that the gain be applied for charitable purposes only.

[84] The exemption is also available where the charity retains the proceeds in its general fund; see *IRC v Helen Slater Charitable Trust* [1981] STC 471 (CA).

[85] Under TCGA 1992, Sch 8, para 3(7).

[86] *Von Ernst v IRC* [1980] STC 111.

above, the gain cannot be said to have been 'applied for charitable purposes' as there is no consideration. In practice, the Revenue allow the use of section 171.

The Revenue view is that a capital payment from an offshore trust which has been realised as 'trust gains' cannot come within section 256 as 'being applied for' charitable purposes. This is because section 87(3) deems a chargeable gain to accrue.[87]

81.6 Restriction of Exemptions: Charitable and Non-charitable Expenditure

There are two groups of rules which may cause a charity to lose the benefit of any exemption to which it is otherwise entitled. One was added in 1986 and was designed to discourage a charity from hoarding its income (§81.6.1). The second was added in 2006 and reworked in 2011; it was designed to counter benefits connected to donations (§81.6.2). In 2006 the original rule was totally recast. One effect is to make the rules applying in the first situation significantly more severe; thus the disregard of the first £10,000 of non-charitable expenditure has been abolished. In both situations the effect of the rules applying is that the charity loses the benefit of the exception it had hoped to enjoy. The burden thus falls on the charity, which must be ever alert. Where the rules apply there are provisions which allow the charity to decide which parts of its otherwise exempt income, etc should lose the protection.[88] It is these rules which have been criticised as having enormous potential for damaging relations between charities and donors, and for increasing administration costs.

If it appears to the Board that two or more charities are acting in concert, with the avoidance of tax (whether by the charities or by another person) as one of their main aims, the Board must serve notice in writing on the charities, which have the right to appeal against its decision.[89]

81.6.1 Non-charitable Expenditure

This rule is aimed at the charity which makes the wrong sort of expenditures (treating certain investments and loans as expenditures), or which fails to spend enough on the right things. So if a charity incurs (or is treated as incurring) non-charitable expenditure in a relevant period, relief is withdrawn or disallowed for so much of the 'relievable income and gains' as equals the 'non-charitable expenditure'. ITA 2007, sections 540 and 541, and CTA 2010, sections 493 and 494 refer to the 'exempt' and 'non-exempt' amounts. The rules include a special but common-sense timing rule to deal with the situation in which expenditure actually incurred in one period properly belongs in another.[90]

---

[87] Potter and Monroe, *Tax Planning* (Sweet & Maxwell, 1982) §7–10A.

[88] ITA 2007, ss 541 and 542, and CTA 2010, ss 494 and 495, ex TA 1988, s 505(7). Similar rules apply for CGT—see TCGA 1992, ss 256A–256D.

[89] ITA 2007, s 542 and CTA 2010, s 495, ex TA 1988, s 505(7).

[90] ITA 2007, s 546 and CTA 2010, s 499, ex TA 1988, s 506(2).

A payment made (or to be made) to a body situated outside the UK is not charitable expenditure unless the charity concerned takes such steps as may be reasonable in the circumstances to ensure that the payment will be applied for charitable purposes.[91]

The list of non-qualifying expenditure in former TA 1988, section 505 was relatively easy to understand. Study of the rewritten rules in ITA 2007, sections 543–545, and CTA 2010, sections 496–498 shows a number of changes. Some are based on Revenue practice, but the more interesting is the frequent use of the word 'loss' rather than 'expenditure'. Paraphrasing the explanatory notes, two principal points emerge. The first is that it is the losses which may count, rather than expenses taken into account in calculating the losses concerned. The second is that the rules are designed to ensure that losses are not disqualified as a non-charitable expenditure if corresponding profits would have been exempt under the rules in ITA 2007, sections 526 and 529–531, and CTA 2010, sections 480 and 483–485. Any lingering thought that a loss on a charitable trade is necessarily non-charitable expenditure is quashed by the opening part of section 543/section 496. While one may admire the rewrite team for their courage, it is a sad comment that the explanatory notes are much more helpful than the text.

Loans and investments are also treated as non-qualifying expenditure unless they fall within the categories of qualifying loans and qualifying investments. Loans qualify for exemption—in the rewritten language they are 'approved charitable loans'—if:

(1) they are made to another charity for charitable purposes only;
(2) they are made to a beneficiary of the charity in the course of its charitable activities; or
(3) money is placed in a current account with a bank (unless this forms part of an arrangement under which the bank makes a loan to another person).[92]

Investment in non-qualifying investments is non-charitable expenditure; qualifying investments are also elaborately defined.[93] The list of approved investments begins with various types set out in section 558/section 511. Section 559/section 512, which is type 1, lists approved securities, but section 560/section 513 imposes further conditions designed to make sure that the securities are sound. Type 12 of section 558/section 511 allows an officer of HMRC to designate any loan or investment as 'qualifying investment' where, on a claim being made, the officer is satisfied that the loan or investment is made for the benefit of the charity and not for the avoidance of tax.[94]

A further rule ensures that if a non-qualifying investment is made and realised, or loan is made and repaid, during the same chargeable period, the reinvestment of the proceeds during that chargeable period is left out of account when calculating the amount of 'non-charitable expenditure' incurred by the charity.[95]

---

[91] ITA 2007, s 547 and CTA 2010, s 500, ex TA 1988, s 506(3).
[92] ITA 2007, s 561 and CTA 2010, s 514, ex TA 1988, Sch 20, Pt II.
[93] ITA 2007, ss 558–560 and CTA 2010, ss 511–513, ex TA 1988, Sch, 20, Pt I.
[94] ITA 2007, s 558 and CTA 2010, s 511, ex TA 1988, Sch 20, para 9.
[95] ITA 2007, s 548 and CTA 2010, s 501, ex TA 1988, s 506(5).

81.6.2 Tainted Donations

A targeted anti-avoidance rule in ITA 2007, Part 13, Chapter 8 and CTA 2010, Part 21C removes the tax exemption and counteracts income tax advantages on donations to charity in circumstances in which benefits received from the charity are connected to the donations. Section 257A of TCGA 1992 similarly disapplies the no gain/no loss treatment provided under section 257 if the gifted property is a tainted donation under the ITA 2007 or CTA 2010 rules. Under these rules, tax relief is denied if Conditions A and B are met, unless an exemption applies:

— Condition A is that is reasonable to assume that the donation would not have been made and the arrangements would not have been entered into independently of one another.
— Condition B requires that the main purpose, or one of the main purposes, for entering into the arrangements is to obtain a financial advantage.

A number of exemptions are set out in ITA 2007, section 809ZL and CTA 2010, section 939E, such as where the financial advantage is within the threshold limits allowed for gift aid relief, or is applied for charitable purposes only by the person for whom the advantage was obtained. A further exemption (Condition C) provides that the rules will not apply if a donor is a wholly-owned trading subsidiary of the charity or a housing provider which is linked with the charity.

81.7 CGT Charge if Property Ceases to be held on Charitable Trusts

There is a deemed disposal of property when it ceases to be held on charitable trust and the gain arising on that deemed disposal is chargeable.[96] There is, therefore, no immunity for unrealised capital gains built up behind the screen of charity.[97]

---

[96] TCGA 1992, s 256(2).

[97] On one view, a temporary charitable trust is not really a qualifying charity at all; see Whiteman, *Capital Gains Tax*, 4th edn (Sweet & Maxwell, 2002) 27; there was a concession for a temporary loss of charitable status due to the reverter of a site such as a school and the reversioner cannot be found (ex ESC D47). For problems where gift aid was paid out of dividend income, see Hiddleston, 144 *Taxation* 62 (21 October 1999).

Index